PETERSON'S

SCHOLARSHIPS, GRANTS & PRIZES

2006

Australia • Canada • Mexico • Singapore • Spain • United Kingdom • United States

About Thomson Peterson's

Thomson Peterson's (www.petersons.com) is a leading provider of education information and advice, with books and online resources focusing on education search, test preparation, and financial aid. Its Web site offers searchable databases and interactive tools for contacting educational institutions, online practice tests and instruction, and planning tools for securing financial aid. Thomson Peterson's serves 110 million education consumers annually.

For more information, contact Thomson Peterson's, 2000 Lenox Drive, Lawrenceville, NJ 08648; 800-338-3282; or find us on the World Wide Web at www.petersons.com/about.

Editor: Joe Krasowski; Production Editor: Bret Bollmann; Copy Editor: Jill C. Schwartz; Research Project Manager: Jennifer Fishberg; Research Associate: Helen L. Hannan; Programmer: Alex Lin; Manufacturing Manager: Ivona Skibicki; Composition Manager: Michele Able

ISBN 0-7689-1888-X

Printed in the United States of America

10 9 8 7 6 5 4 3 07 06 05

Tenth Edition

OTHER RECOMMENDED TITLES

Peterson's College Money Handbook
Peterson's Financial Aid Answer Book: Your Quick Reference Guide to Paying for College
Peterson's Sports Scholarships & College Athletic Programs

CONTENTS

A NOTE FROM THE PETERSON'S EDITORS

Billions of dollars are given to students and their families every year to help pay for college. Last year, private donors gave more than $7 billion in financial aid to help undergraduate students pay for college. Yet, to the average person, the task of finding financial aid awards in this huge network of scholarships, grants, and prizes appears to be nearly impossible.

For more than thirty-five years, Thomson Peterson's has given students and parents the most comprehensive, up-to-date information on how to get their fair share of the financial aid pie. *Peterson's Scholarships, Grants & Prizes* was created to help students and their families pinpoint those specific private financial aid programs that best match students' backgrounds, interests, talents, or abilities.

In *Peterson's Scholarships, Grants & Prizes,* you will find more than 3,950 scholarship/grant programs and prize sources that provide financial awards to undergraduates in the 2005–06 academic year. Foundations, fraternal and ethnic organizations, community service clubs, churches and religious groups, philanthropies, companies and industry groups, labor unions and public employees' associations, veterans' groups, and trusts and bequests are all possible sources.

For those seeking to enter college, *Peterson's Scholarships, Grants & Prizes* includes information needed to make financing a college education as seamless as possible.

Features include:

- More than 1.8 million awards, totaling nearly $8 billion
- Up-to-date eligibility requirements, award amounts, and application deadlines
- Proven tips to identify and avoid scholarship scams
- Information about online financial aid resources

The **Find an Award That's Right for You** section paints a complete picture of the financial aid landscape, discusses the connection between honors students and scholarship eligibility, provides important tips on how to avoid scholarship scams, and offers insight into how to make scholarship management organizations work for you.

Also found in **Find an Award That's Right for You** is the "How To Use This Guide" article, which describes the more than 3,950 awards included in the guide, along with information on how to search for an award in one of ten categories.

If you would like to compare awards quickly, refer to the **Quick-Reference Chart.** Here you can search through "Scholarships, Grants & Prizes At-a-Glance" and select awards by highest dollar amount.

In the **Profiles of Scholarships, Grants & Prizes** section you'll find updated award programs, along with information about the award sponsor. The profile section is divided into three categories: *Academic Fields/Career Goals, Nonacademic/Noncareer Criteria,* and *Miscellaneous Criteria.* Each profile provides all of the need-to-know information about available scholarships, grants & prizes.

Finally, the back of the book features thirteen **Indexes** listing scholarships, grants & prizes based on award name; sponsor; academic fields/career goals; civic, professional, social, or union affiliation; corporate affiliation; employment experience; impairment; military service; nationality or ethnic heritage; religious affiliation; state of residence; state of study; and talent.

Thomson Peterson's publishes a full line of resources to help guide you through the pitfalls of the financial aid process. Thomson Peterson's publications can be found at your local bookstore, library, and high school guidance office or you can access our comprehensive information online at www.petersons.com/finaid. Be sure to take full advantage of the many real opportunities that have been opened up to students and their families by the many organizations, foundations, and businesses that can help you with the burden of college expenses.

The editors at Thomson Peterson's wish you the best of luck in your scholarship search efforts!

FIND AN AWARD THAT'S RIGHT FOR YOU

HONORS STUDENTS AND SCHOLARSHIPS

Dr. Gary M. Bell
Dean, University Honors College, Texas Tech University

Let's begin with some really good news: Students who are considering an honors program are the very people most likely to be eligible for scholarship assistance. Let's face it, college is expensive! Scholarships provide part of the solution for how to finance an undergraduate career. Honors students are precisely the ones whom colleges recruit most eagerly. Good high school students add to the prestige of an institution, and schools typically advertise a student's decision to attend their institution. Thus, there is an excellent chance that the school of your choice may provide scholarship assistance in order to encourage you to enroll and to enhance the school's "bragging rights."

During the next four (or more) years you will spend earning your college baccalaureate degree, think of the learning task as your primary employment. It is helpful to think of a scholarship as part of the salary for undertaking your job of learning. From this perspective, you have the right, again as a potential honors student, to seek the best pay, or scholarship, possible. One of your first inquiries as you examine a potential college setting is about the type of assistance it might provide given your interests, academic record, and personal history. Talk to a financial aid officer or a scholarship coordinator at the school. At most schools, these are special officers—people specifically employed to assist you in your quest for financial assistance. Virtually all schools also have brochures or publications that list scholarship opportunities at their institution. Get this literature and read it carefully.

Also, visit either your local bookstore or your local public library and get books that have several hundred scholarships listed in different categories. These books are inexpensive and can be found in the reference section. Excellent information is also available on the Web at http://www.petersons.com/finaid.

Last, high school counselors often have keen insight into resources available at colleges, especially the schools in your area. These people are the key points of contact between institutions of higher education and you.

In general, it is not a particularly good practice to use a private company that promises to provide you with a list of scholarships for which you might be eligible. Such lists are often very broad, and you can secure the same results by using available high school, university, and published information. The scholarship search you perform online will probably be more fruitful than what any private company can do for you.

What do we mean by the word "scholarship" anyway? In the very broadest sense, scholarships consist of outright grants of monetary assistance to eligible students to help them attend college. The money is applied to tuition or the cost of living while in school. Scholarships do not need to be repaid. They do, however, often carry stringent criteria for maintaining them, such as the achievement of a certain grade point average, the carrying of a given number of class hours, matriculation in a specific program, or membership in a designated group. Scholarships at many schools may be combined with college work-study programs—where some work is also required. You should also be sensitive to the fact that many scholarships can be bundled, that is, put together with other scholarships so that collectively they provide you with a truly attractive financial aid package. Of equal importance is that scholarships can also be bundled with low-interest loan programs to make the school of your choice financially feasible.

Scholarships generally fall into three major categories: *need-based scholarships*, predicated on income; *merit-based scholarships*, based on your academic and sometimes extracurricular achievements; and *association-based scholarships*, which are dependent on as many different associations as you can imagine (for instance, your home county, your identification with a particular group, fraternal and religious organizations, or the company for which a parent may work). The range of reasons for which scholarships are given is almost infinite.

Many schools accommodate students who have financial need. The largest and best grant programs are the U.S. government-sponsored Federal Pell Grants and the Federal Supplemental Educational Opportunity Grants, which you might want to explore with your financial aid counselor. Also inquire about state-sponsored grant programs.

Merit-based scholarships can come from a variety of sources—the university, individual departments or colleges within the university, state scholarship programs, or special donors who want to assist worthy students. This fact should be remembered as you meet with your financial aid officer, because he or she knows that different opportunities may be available for you as a petroleum engineering, agriculture, accounting, pre–veterinary, or performing arts major. Merit-based scholarships are typically designed to reward the highest performers on such precollege measures as standardized tests (the SAT or ACT) and high school grades. Since repeated performance on standardized tests often leads to higher scores, it may be financially advantageous for you to take these college admissions tests several times.

Frequently, schools have endowed scholarships (scholarships based on a fund, the principal of which can never be used) given by alumni or others with a particular interest in supporting honors students. Thus, your acceptance to an honors program can carry with it not only enhanced educational benefits but also substantial monetary assistance. A warning needs to be interjected here, however. If you are joining an honors program only for the financial advantage, you are joining for the wrong reason. Honors education is about broadening your educational experiences, opening an array of academic opportunities, and challenging yourself to become a better person. If money is your only incentive for becoming associated with an honors program, you probably need to look elsewhere for financial assistance.

Inquire about each of these three categories of scholarships. The association-based scholarships can sometimes be particularly helpful and quite surprising. Employers of parents, people from specific geographic locations, or organizations (churches, civic groups, unions, special interest clubs, and even family name associations) may provide assistance for college students. Campus scholarship literature is the key to unlocking the mysteries of association-based financial assistance (and the other two categories as well), but personal interviews with financial officers are also crucial.

There are several issues to which you must attend as you seek scholarship assistance. Probably the most important is to determine deadlines that apply to a scholarship for which you may be eligible. It's always wise to begin your search early, so that your eligibility is not nullified by having applied too late. Most scholarship opportunities require an application form, and it is time well spent to make sure the application is neat, grammatically correct, and logical. Correct spelling is essential. Have someone proofread your application (these are not bad guidelines to follow with your honors application as well if the honors program of your choice requires an application). Keep in mind that if applications require essays, fewer students typically take the time to complete these essays, giving those students who do a better chance of winning that particular scholarship. Always be truthful in these applications but, at the same time, provide the most positive self-portrayal to enhance your chances of being considered. Be sensitive to the fact that most merit-based and association-based scholarships are awarded competitively.

Finally, let the people who offer you assistance know whether or not you will accept their offer. Too many students simply assume that a scholarship offer means automatic acceptance. This is not the case! In most instances, you must send a letter of acknowledgement and acceptance. Virtually all schools have agreed that students must make up their minds about scholarship acceptance no later than May 1. But earlier deadlines may apply.

How do you make the choice of which school to attend? There are many elements to consider, such as reputation, programs offered, courses provided, and the school's success in placing graduates. Visit the prospective school and see if the student profile, the campus amenities, and the atmosphere of the campus fit your needs and aspirations. But above all, pay attention to cost. Where can you realistically afford to go without incurring the very large debts that could plague you after graduation? In the end, you must choose the college or university that seems best for you and that fits your budget. Scholarships should play a very big role in your decision-making process.

As you undoubtedly know, tuition at private schools is typically higher than tuition at state colleges and universities. Scholarships can narrow this gap. Many private institutions have a great deal of money to spend on scholarship assistance, so you may find that going to a private college will cost no more than attending a state-supported college or university. Take note, a substantial scholarship from a private school may still leave you with a very large annual bill to cover the difference between the scholarship amount and the actual cost of tuition, fees, and living expenses. When you evaluate a scholarship, factor in your final out-of-pocket costs. Also consider the length of time for which the school extends scholarship support. Be cautious about schools that promise substantial assistance for the first year in order to get you there, but then provide little or nothing in subsequent years. The most attractive and meaningful scholarships are offered for four to five years.

The scholarship search should not be abandoned once you are enrolled at the school of your choice. There are often a number of additional scholarship opportunities for you once enrolled, especially as you prove your ability and interest in a given field. Also, honors students have been particularly successful in national scholarship competitions, such as the Rhodes, Fulbright, Goldwater, Truman, and Udall. Finally, your earned scholarship may well be applied to study-abroad or the National Collegiate Honors Council (NCHC) Honors Semester programs, so begin to consider early in your college career the benefits that an off-campus experience can bestow upon you.

When searching for college funding, low-interest or even interest-free, government-provided educational loans should be considered depending on your personal circumstances. Many states also have similar loan programs available for their residents. Loans are to be sought only after scholarship possibilities are exhausted. But, in the final analysis, your education is probably the best investment you will ever make. So borrowing for your college expenses is both a justifiable and sometimes necessary element in securing the most precious and enduring of all personal assets—a quality education. Always check with the financial aid office for more information on the various loan programs that will work best for you and your family.

SCHOLARSHIP SCAMS: WHAT THEY ARE AND WHAT TO WATCH OUT FOR

Several hundred thousand students seek and find scholarships every year. Most students' families require some outside help to pay for tuition costs. Although most of this outside help, in the form of grants, scholarships, low-interest loans, and work-study programs, comes either from the state and federal government or the colleges themselves, scholarships from private sources are an extremely important component of this network. An award from a private source can tilt the scales with respect to a student's ability to attend a specific college during a particular year. Unfortunately, for prospective scholarship seekers, the private aid sector is virtually without patterns or rules. It has, over many years, become a combination of individual programs, each with its own award criteria, timetables, application procedures, and decision-making processes. Considerable effort is required to understand and effectively benefit from private scholarships. One of the principal reasons that *Peterson's Scholarships, Grants & Prizes* has been developed is to facilitate this task of grabbing the applicable prize from this complex web of scholarships.

Regrettably, the combination of an urgency to locate money, limited time, and this complex and bewildering system has created opportunities for fraud. It has been estimated that for every 10 students who receive a legitimate scholarship, one is victimized by a fraudulent scheme or scam that poses as a legitimate foundation, scholarship sponsor, or scholarship search service. Every year, an estimated 350,000 families are cheated in various scholarship scams, totalling more than $5 million.

These fraudulent businesses advertise in campus newspapers, distribute flyers, mail letters and postcards, provide toll-free phone numbers, and have Web sites. The most obvious frauds operate as scholarship search services or scholarship clearinghouses. Another segment sets up as a scholarship sponsor, pockets the money from the fees that are paid by thousands of hopeful scholarship seekers, and returns little, if anything, in proportion to the amount it collects. A few of these scams inflict great harm by gaining access to individuals' credit or checking accounts with the intent to extort funds.

A typical mode of operation is for a fraudulent firm to send out a huge mailing to college and high school students, claiming that the company has either a scholarship or a scholarship list for the students. These companies often provide toll-free numbers. When recipients call, they are told by high-pressure telemarketers that the company has unclaimed scholarships and that for fees ranging from $10 to $400 the callers get back at least $1000 in scholarship money or the fee will be refunded. Customers who pay, if they receive anything at all, are mailed a list of sources of financial aid that are no better than, and are in many cases inferior to, what can be found in *Peterson's Scholarships, Grants & Prizes* or any of the other major scholarship guides available in bookstores or libraries. The "lucky" recipients have to apply on their own for the scholarships. Many of the programs are contests, loans, or work-study programs rather than gift aid. Some are no longer in existence, have expired deadlines, or set eligibility requirements that students cannot meet. Customers who seek refunds have to demonstrate that they have applied in writing to each source on the list and received a rejection letter from each of them. Frequently, even when customers can provide this almost-impossible-to-obtain proof, refunds are not given. In the worst cases, the companies ask for consumers' checking account or credit card numbers and take funds without authorization.

The Federal Trade Commission (FTC) warns students and their parents to be wary of fraudulent search services that promise to do all the work for you. "Bogus scholarship search services are just a variation of the 'you have won' prize-promotion scam, targeted to a particular audience—students and parents who are anxious about paying for college," said Jodie Bernstein, former director of the FTC's Bureau of Consumer Protection. "They guarantee students and their families free scholarship money . . . all they have to do to claim it is pay an up-front fee."

There are legitimate scholarship search services. However, a scholarship search service cannot truthfully guarantee that a student will receive a scholarship, and students almost always will fare as well or better by doing their own homework using a reliable scholarship information source, such as *Peterson's Scholarships, Grants & Prizes*, than by wasting money and more importantly time with a search service that promises a scholarship.

The FTC warns scholarship seekers to be alert for these seven warning signs of a scam:

- "This scholarship is guaranteed or your money back."

  No service can guarantee that it will get you a grant or scholarship. Refund guarantees often have impossible conditions attached. Review a service's refund policies in writing before you pay a fee. Typically, fraudulent scholarship search services require that applicants show rejection letters from each of the sponsors on the list they provide. If a sponsor no longer exists, if it really does not provide scholarships, or if it has a rolling application deadline, letters of rejection are almost impossible to obtain.

- "The scholarship service will do all the work."

  Unfortunately, nobody else can fill out the personal information forms, write the essays, and supply the references that many scholarships may require.

- "The scholarship will cost some money."

  Be wary of any charges related to scholarship information services or individual scholarship applications, especially in significant amounts. Some legitimate scholarship sponsors charge fees to defray their processing expenses. True scholarship sponsors, however, should distribute money, not make it from application fees. Before you send money to apply for a scholarship, investigate the sponsor.

- "You can't get this information anywhere else."

  In addition to Peterson's, scholarship directories from other publishers are available in any large bookstore, public library, or high school guidance office. Additional information on private scholarship programs can be found at www.petersons.com/finaid.

- "You are a finalist"—in a contest you never entered, or "You have been selected by a national foundation to receive a scholarship."

  Most legitimate scholarship programs almost never seek out particular applicants. Most scholarship sponsors will only contact you in response to an inquiry. Most lack the budget and mandate to do anything more than this. If you think that there is any real possibility that you may have been selected to receive a scholarship, before you send any money investigate to make sure the sponsor or program is legitimate.

- "The scholarship service needs your credit card or checking account number in advance."

  Never provide your credit card or bank account number over the telephone to the representative of an organization that you do not know. A legitimate need-based scholarship program will not ask for your checking account number. Get information in writing first. **Note:** An unscrupulous operation does not need your signature on a check. It schemes to set up situations that allow it to drain a victim's account with unauthorized withdrawals.

- "You are invited to a free seminar (or interview) with a trained financial aid consultant who will unlock the secrets of how to make yourself eligible for more financial aid."

  Sometimes these consultants offer some good tips on preparing for college, but often they are trying to get you to sign up for a long-term contract for services you don't need. Often these "consultants" are trying to sell you other financial products, such as annuities, life insurance, or other financial services that have little to do with financial aid. By doing your own research with books from Thomson

Peterson's or other respected organizations, using the Web, and working with your high school guidance office and the college financial aid office, you will get all the help you need to ensure you have done a thorough job of preparing for the financing of your college education.

In addition to the FTC's seven signs, here are some other points to keep in mind when considering a scholarship program:

- Fraudulent scholarship operations often use official-sounding names containing words such as federal, national, administration, division, federation, and foundation. Their names often are a slight variation of the name of a legitimate government or private organization. Do not be fooled by a name that seems reputable or official, an official-looking seal, or a Washington, D.C., address.

- If you win a scholarship, you will receive official written notification by mail, not over the telephone. If the sponsor calls to inform you, it will follow up with a letter in the mail. If a request for money is made over the phone, the operation is probably fraudulent.

- Be wary if an organization's address is a post office box number or a residential address. If a bona fide scholarship program uses a post office box number, it usually will include a street address and telephone number on its stationery.

- Beware of telephone numbers with a 900 area code. These may charge you a fee of several dollars a minute for a call that could be a long recording that provides only a list of addresses or names.

- A dishonest operation may put pressure on an applicant by claiming that awards are on a first-come, first-served basis. Some scholarship programs give preference to early applicants. However, if you are told, especially over the telephone, that you must respond quickly, but you will not hear about the results for several months, there may be a problem.

- Be wary of endorsements. Fraudulent operations claim endorsements by groups with names similar to well-known private or government organizations. The Better Business Bureau (BBB) and other government agencies do not endorse businesses.

If an organization requires that you pay something for a scholarship and you have never heard of it before and cannot verify that it is a legitimate operation, the best advice is to pay nothing. If you have already paid money to such an organization and find reason to doubt its legitimacy, call your bank to stop payment on your check, if possible, or call your credit card company and tell it that you think you were the victim of consumer fraud.

To find out how to recognize, report, and stop a scholarship scam, contact:

The Federal Trade Commission
600 Pennsylvania Avenue, N.W.
Washington, D.C. 20580
Web site: www.ftc.gov

The National Fraud Information Center can be contacted by phone at 800-876-7060 (toll-free) or online at www.fraud.org The Better Business Bureau (BBB) maintains files of businesses about which it has received complaints. You should call both your local BBB office and the BBB office where the organization in question is located; each local BBB has different records. Call 703-276-0100 to get the telephone number of your local BBB or log on to www.bbb.org for a directory of local BBBs and downloadable BBB complaint forms. The national address is:

The Council of Better Business Bureaus
4200 Wilson Boulevard, Suite 800
Arlington, VA 22203-1838

There are many wonderful scholarships available to qualified students who spend the time and effort to locate and apply for them. However, we advise you to exercise caution in using scholarship search services and, when you must pay money, always use careful judgment when considering a scholarship program's sponsor.

SCHOLARSHIP MANAGEMENT ORGANIZATIONS

Richard Woodland
Director of Financial Aid, Rutgers University, Camden

The search for private scholarships can be confusing and frustrating for parents and students. Many families feel they just don't know how to go about the process, so they either hire a private scholarship search company or simply give up. The success rate of many scholarship search firms is not good, and college financial aid professionals always warn parents to be skeptical of exaggerated claims.

The process also confuses many donors. A corporation may want to help its employees or the children of its employees or may want to offer a national scholarship program to its customers or the general public. Unfortunately, the corporation may not want to devote valuable administrative time managing a scholarship program. Similarly, there are many donors who want to target their funds to a particular group of students but simply do not know how.

Stepping in to help are scholarship management organizations. Although many have been around for a long time, the majority of the general public knows very little about them. The reason for this is that scholarship management organizations often do not administer scholarship funds directly to students. Rather, they serve as a clearinghouse for their member donor organizations. Today, savvy parents and students can go online to find these organizations and the scholarship programs they administer.

Two of the largest scholarship management programs are the National Merit Scholarship Corporation™ and Scholarship America™ (formerly Citizen's Scholarship Foundation of America). The National Merit Scholarship Corporation sponsors a competitive scholarship program that seeks to identify and reward the top students in the nation. High school students who meet published entry/participation requirements enter these competitions by taking the Preliminary SAT/National Merit Scholarship Qualifying Test (PSAT/NMSQT®), usually as juniors. A particular year's test is the entry vehicle to a specific annual competition. For example, the 2004 PSAT/NMSQT was the qualifying test for entry into competitions for scholarships to be awarded in 2006. For more information, visit http://www.nationalmerit.org.

Another major player is Scholarship America™, which has distributed more than $1 billion dollars to more than one million students over the past forty-five years, making it the nation's largest private-sector scholarship and educational support organization. By involving communities, corporations, organizations, and individuals in the support of students through its three major programs, Dollars for Scholars®, Scholarship Management Services™, and ScholarShop®, Scholarship America distributed more than $130.5 million in 2004. Whether it is working with national leaders in response to the September 11th tragedy through the Families of Freedom Scholarship Fund, or with corporations such as Target, Kohl's Department Stores, and Tylenol (McNeil Consumer and Specialty Pharmaceuticals), Scholarship America is an important organization that helps thousands of students every year. For more information, go to www.scholarshipamerica.org.

In addition to the National Merit Scholarship Fund and Scholarship America, there are other organizations that raise funds and administer scholarships for specific groups of students. Some of these organizations include:

- American Indian College Fund
  www.collegefund.org
- Hispanic Scholarship Fund Institute
  www.hsfi.org

- United Negro College Fund
  www.uncf.org
- Organization of Chinese Americans
  www.ocanatl.org
- Future Farmers of America
  www.ffa.org
- Gates Millennium Scholarship Fund
  www.gmsp.org

These are just a few of the many scholarship sources available on the Web. In addition to using scholarship search engines, think broadly about yourself, your background, your interests, your family connections (work, religious, fraternal organizations), and your future career plans. Then spend some time browsing the Web. We hope that some of the sources mentioned here will help. Remember, the key is to start early (junior year in high school is best) and be persistent.

A STRATEGY FOR FINDING AWARDS

Private scholarships and awards can be characterized by unpredictable, sometimes seemingly bizarre, criteria. Before you begin your award search, write a personal profile of yourself that will help establish as many criteria as possible that might form a basis for your scholarship award. Here is a basic checklist of what you should consider:

1. **What are your career goals?** Be both narrow and broad in your designations. If, for example, you have a career aim to be a TV news reporter, you will find many awards specific to this field in the *TV/Radio Broadcasting* section. However, collegiate broadcasting courses can be offered in departments or schools of communication. So, be sure to also consider *Communications* as a relevant section for your search. Consider *Journalism,* too, for the same reasons. Then look under some more broadly inclusive but possibly relevant areas, such as *Trade/Technical Specialties.* Or check a related but different field, such as *Performing Arts.* Finally, look under marginally related basic academic fields, such as *Humanities, Social Sciences, or Political Science.* We make every attempt to provide the best cross-reference aids, but the nuances of specific awards can be difficult to capture with even the most flexible cross-referencing systems. So you will need to be broadly associative in your thinking in order to get the most out of this wealth of information.

   If you have no clear career goal, browsing through the huge variety of academic/career awards may well spark new interest in a career path. Be open to imagining yourself filling different career roles that you previously may not have considered.

2. **In what academic fields might you major?** Your educational experiences to this point or your sense about your personal talents or interests may have given you a good idea of what academic discipline you wish to pursue. Again, use both broad and narrow focuses in designing your search and look at related subject fields. For example, if you want to major in history, there is a *History* section. Also, be sure to check out *Social Sciences* and *Humanities* and, maybe, *Area/Ethnic Studies. Education,* for example, could have the perfect scholarship for a future historian.

3. **In which jobs, industries, or occupations have your parents or other members of your immediate family been employed? What employment experiences might you have?** Individual companies, employee organizations, trade unions, government agencies, and industry associations frequently set up scholarships for workers or children or other relatives of workers from specific companies or industries. These awards might require that you study to stay in the same career field, but most are offered regardless of the field of study you wish to undertake. Also, if one of your parents worked as a public service employee, especially as a firefighter or police officer, and most especially if he or she was killed or disabled in the line of duty, there are many relevant awards available.

4. **Do you have any hobbies or special interests? Have you ever been an officer or leader of a group? Do you possess special skills or talents? Have you won any competitions? Are you a good writer?** From bowling to clarinet playing, from caddying to ham radio operating, from winning a beauty contest to simply "being interested in leadership," there are a host of special interests that can win awards for you from groups that wish to promote and/or reward these pursuits.

5. **Where do you live? Where have you lived? Where will you go to college?** Residence criteria are among the most common qualifications for scholarship aid. Local clubs and companies provide millions of dollars in scholarship aid to students who live in a particular state, province, region, or section of a state. This means that your residential identity puts you at the head of the line for these grants. State of

residence can—depending on the sponsor's criteria—include the place of your official residence, the place you attend college, the place you were born, or any place you have lived for more than a year.

6. **What is your family's ethnic heritage?** Hundreds of scholarships have been endowed for students who can claim a particular nationality or racial or ethnic descent. Partial ethnic descent frequently qualifies, so don't be put off if you do not think of your identity as fully tagged as a specific "ethnic" entity. There are awards for Colonial American, English, Welsh, Scottish, European, and other backgrounds that students may not consider to be especially "ethnic." There is even one for descendants of signers of the Declaration of Independence, whatever ethnicity that might have turned out to be some ten generations later.

7. **Do you have a physical disability?** There are many awards given to individuals with physical disabilities. Of course, commonly recognized impairments of mobility, sight, communication, and hearing are recognized, but, also, learning disabilities and chronic diseases, such as asthma and epilepsy, are criteria for some awards.

8. **Do you currently or have you ever served in a branch of the armed forces? Or, did one of your parents serve? In a war? Was one of your parents lost or disabled in the armed forces?** There are hundreds of awards that use one of these qualifications. There are even awards for descendants of Confederate soldiers.

9. **Do you belong to a civic association, union, or religious organization? Do your parents?** Hundreds of clubs and religious groups provide scholarship assistance to members or children of members.

10. **Are you male or female?**

11. **What is your age?**

12. **Do you qualify for need-based aid?**

13. **Did you graduate in the upper half, upper third, or upper quarter of your class?**

14. **Do you plan to attend a two-year college, a four-year college, or a trade/technical school?**

15. **In what academic year will you be entering?**

Be expansive when considering your possible qualifications. Although some awards may be small, you may qualify for more than one award, and these can add up to significant amounts in the end.

SEARCHING FOR SCHOLARSHIPS, GRANTS, & PRIZES ONLINE

Today's students need all the help they can get when looking for ways to pay for their college education. Skyrocketing tuition costs, state budget cuts, and diminished personal savings have combined to make financing a college education perhaps the number one concern for parents. College sticker shock is driving many families away from college. No wonder. The "purchasing power" of all aid programs from federal, state, and institutional sources has declined over the past two decades. State education budgets have been slashed. Tuition at public institutions is increasing at an average annual rate of 14 percent; private tuition, by 6 percent. And it's not only lower-income families who are affected. Some fear they make *too much* money to qualify for financial aid. Regardless of their situation, most families struggle to make sense of the college financial aid process and to decide which aid package is the right one for them.

Despite the confusion, students and parents can and should continue to research as many sources as they can to find the money they need. The Internet can be a great source of information. There are many worthwhile sites that are ready to help you search and apply for your fair share of awards, including Thomson Peterson's comprehensive financial aid site at www.petersons.com/finaid.

THOMSON PETERSON'S SCHOLARSHIP SEARCH

Get access to one of the largest undergraduate scholarship databases available! Thomson Peterson's free Scholarship Search will connect you to more than 1.8 million scholarships, grants, and prizes totaling nearly $8 billion.

In addition to the abundant award opportunities available, www.petersons.com/finaid provides information on the basics of financial aid, including:

- Estimated Expected Family Contribution (EFC) calculator
- Financial Aid Overview
- Financial Aid: Terms Defined
- Financial Aid: Discover Your Financial Aid Literacy
- Family Financial Situations
- Federal Student Aid
- Savings Calculator
- Tuition Finder

Thomson Peterson's has also partnered with many of today's leading providers of federal and private student aid. You can access these providers through Peterson's Education Loan Finder and apply for loans immediately by logging on to www.petersons.com/finaid. Providers include:

- Army ROTC
- Citibank
- Fox College Funding
- Loan to Learn
- SallieMae College Answer
- Your Tuition Solution

Thomson Peterson's financial aid site is also the home of the Internet's first online financial aid resource to provide truly personalized assistance, Peterson's BestCollegeDeals® (www.BestCollegeDeals.com) provides information on more than 2,000 scholarships, grants, and other awards (both need- and non-need-based) that are generally not well publicized.

USE THE TOOLS TO YOUR ADVANTAGE

Searching and applying for financial aid is an involved and complicated process. The tools available to you on www.petersons.com/finaid can help you get your fair share of the financial aid pie. So, what are you waiting for? Fire up the computer; free money for college is just a mouse click away.

HOW TO USE THIS GUIDE

The more than 3,950 award programs described in this book are organized into ten broad categories that represent the major factors used to determine eligibility for scholarships, awards, and prizes. To build a basic list of awards available to you, look under the broad category or categories that fit your particular academic goals, skills, personal characteristics, or background. The ten categories are:

- Academic Fields/Career Goals
- Civic, Professional, Social, or Union Affiliation
- Corporate Affiliation
- Employment Experience
- Impairment
- Military Service
- Nationality or Ethnic Heritage
- Religious Affiliation
- State of Residence/State of Study
- Talent

The *Academic Fields/Career Goals* category is subdivided into 115 individual subject areas that are organized alphabetically by the award sponsor. The *Military Service* category is subdivided alphabetically by branch of service. All other categories are simply organized A to Z by the name of the award sponsor.

Full descriptive profiles appear in only one location in the book. Cross-references to the name and page number of the full descriptive profile are made from other locations under the other relevant categories for the award. The full description appears in the first relevant location in the book; cross-references at later locations. You will always be referred toward the front of the book.

Your major field of study and career goal have central importance in college planning. As a result, we have combined these into a single category and have given this category precedence over the others. The *Academic Fields/Career Goals* section appears first in the book. If an academic major or career area is a criterion for a scholarship, the description of this award will appear in this section.

Within the *Academic Fields/Career Goals* section, cross-references are made only from and to other academic fields or career areas. Cross-references are not provided to this section from the other ten categories. You will be able to locate relevant awards from nonacademic or noncareer criteria through the indexes in the back of this book.

For example, the full descriptive profile of a scholarship for any type of engineering student who resides in Ohio, Pennsylvania, or West Virginia might appear under *Aviation/Aerospace,* which happens to be the alphabetically first engineering category heading in the *Academic Fields/Career Goals* section. Cross-references to this first listing may occur from any other relevant engineering or technological academic field subject areas, such as *Chemical Engineering, Civil Engineering, Electrical Engineering/Electronics, Engineering-Related Technologies, Engineering/Technology, Mechanical Engineering,* or *Nuclear Science.* There would not be a cross-reference from the *State of Residence* category. However, the name of the award will appear in the *State of Residence Index* under Ohio, Pennsylvania, and West Virginia. You will always want to check the indexes relevant to your search to get the most out of the guide's listings.

Within the major category sections, descriptive profiles are organized alphabetically by the name of the sponsoring organization. If more than one award from the same organization appears in a particular section, the awards are listed alphabetically under the sponsor name, which appears only once, by the name of the first award.

HOW THE PROFILES ARE ORGANIZED

Here are the elements of a full profile:

I. **Name of Sponsoring Organization**

These appear alphabetically under the appropriate category. In most instances acronyms are given as full names. However, occasionally a sponsor will refer to itself by an acronym. Thus, we present the sponsor's name as an acronym.

II. **World Wide Web Address**

III. **Award Name**

IV. **Brief Textual Description of the Award**

V. **Academic/Career Areas (only in the Academic Fields/Career Goals section of the book)**

This is a list of all academic or career subject terms that are assigned to this award.

VI. **Award**

Is it a scholarship? A prize for winning a competition? A forgivable loan? An internship?

For what type and for what years of college can it be used? Is it renewable or is it for only one year?

VII. **Eligibility Requirements**

VIII. **Application Requirements**

What do you need to supply in order to be considered? What are the deadlines?

IX. **Contact**

If provided by the sponsor, this element includes the name, mailing address, telephone and fax numbers, and e-mail address of the person to contact for information about a specific award.

USING THE INDEXES

The alphabetical indexes in the back of the book are designed to aid your search. Two indexes are name indexes. One lists scholarships alphabetically by academic fields and career goals. The other nine indexes supply access by eligibility criteria. The criteria indexes give you the page number of the descriptions of relevant awards regardless of the part of the book in which they appear.

These are the indexes:

Award Name
Sponsor
Academic Fields/Career Goals
[115 subject areas, from Accounting to Women's Studies]
Civic, Professional, Social, or Union Affiliation
Corporate Affiliation
Employment Experience
Impairment
Military Service
Nationality or Ethnic Heritage
Religious Affiliation
State of Residence
State of Study
Talent

In general, when using the indexes, writing down the names and page numbers of the awards that you are interested in is an effective technique.

DATA COLLECTION PROCEDURES

Thomson Peterson's takes its responsibility as a provider of trustworthy information to its readers very seriously. The data on the award programs in this guide were collected between January and April 2005 through survey mailings and phone interviews with the sponsoring organizations. Every entry is completely up-to-date when this survey is completed. However, changes in particular program information may occur after the book is published. To be sure that you have the most current information about a program, always contact the sponsors directly.

CRITERIA FOR INCLUSION IN THIS BOOK

The programs listed in this book have the primary characteristics of legitimate scholarships: verifiable sponsor addresses and telephone numbers, appropriate descriptive materials, and fees that, if required, are not exorbitant. Approximately 100 of the more than 3,950 awards programs in this volume require application fees, and Thomson Peterson's assumes that these fees are used to defray administrative expenses and are not major sources of income. Although it is impossible for us to investigate every sponsoring organization, we will investigate programs that our readers suspect may be fraudulent. Should our investigations provide convincing evidence that a scholarship sponsor relies upon fees, accessory marketing schemes, or other types of payments from scholarship applicants for its income, Thomson Peterson's will exercise its editorial prerogative to exclude that sponsor's programs from its publications. Concerned readers should address their queries to: Editor, *Peterson's Scholarships, Grants & Prizes,* Thomson Peterson's, 2000 Lenox Drive, P.O. Box 67005, Lawrenceville, NJ 08648

QUICK-REFERENCE CHART

SCHOLARSHIPS, GRANTS & PRIZES AT-A-GLANCE

This chart lists 608 award programs that indicate that their largest award provides $2000 or more. The awards are ranked in descending order on the basis of the dollar amount of the largest award. Because the award criteria in the "Academic/Career Areas and Eligibility Requirements" column may represent only some of the criteria or limitations that affect eligibility for the award, you should refer to the full description in the award profiles to ascertain all relevant details.

Award Name	Page Number	Highest Dollar Amount	Lowest Dollar Amount	Number of Awards	Academic/Career Areas and Eligibility Requirements
National Health Service Corps Scholarship Program	295	$135,000	$67,500	200–300	Health and Medical Sciences, Nursing.
Boettcher Foundation Scholarships	646	$120,000	$40,000	40	State: Colorado; Studying in Colorado.
Intel Science Talent Search	764	$100,000	$ 5000	40	Talent: designated field specified by sponsor.
Careers Through Culinary Arts Program Cooking Competition for Scholarships	180	$ 78,000	$ 1000	88–95	Culinary Arts; State: Arizona, California, District of Columbia, Illinois, Massachusetts, New York, Pennsylvania, Virginia.
DeVry Grant for Surviving Dependents of Rescue Workers, Civil Servants and Military Personnel	664	$ 60,515	$26,600	varies	Studying in Arizona, California, Colorado, Florida, Georgia, Illinois, Missouri, New Jersey, New York, Ohio, Pennsylvania, Tennessee, Texas, Virginia, Washington.
DeVry University First Scholar Award	780	$ 60,465	$42,610	1	Must be in high school.
Elks Most Valuable Student Contest	782	$ 60,000	$ 4000	500	Must be in high school.
Health Professional Loan Repayment and Scholarship Programs	188	$ 60,000	$ 6500	55	Dental Health/Services, Health and Medical Sciences, Nursing, Public Health.
DeVry Presidential Scholarships	664	$ 55,755	$26,600	48	Studying in Alberta, Arizona, California, Colorado, Florida, Georgia, Illinois, Missouri, New Jersey, New York, Ohio, Pennsylvania, Texas, Virginia, Washington.
Micron Science and Technology Scholars Program	144	$ 55,000	$16,500	10–13	Chemical Engineering, Computer Science/Data Processing, Electrical Engineering/ Electronics, Engineering-Related Technologies, Engineering/Technology, Materials Science, Engineering, and Metallurgy, Mechanical Engineering, Physical Sciences and Math, Science, Technology, and Society; State: Colorado, Idaho, Texas, Utah, Virginia; Talent: leadership.
DeVry University Regional First Scholar Awards	664	$ 53,370	$21,280	10	Studying in Arizona, California, Colorado, Florida, Georgia, Illinois, New York, Pennsylvania, Texas.
Intel International Science and Engineering Fair	763	$ 50,000	$ 500		Talent: designated field specified by sponsor.
Miss America Organization Competition Scholarships	757	$ 50,000	$ 1000	69	Talent: beauty pageant.

Scholarships, Grants & Prizes At-a-Glance

Award Name	Page Number	Highest Dollar Amount	Lowest Dollar Amount	Number of Awards	Academic/Career Areas and Eligibility Requirements
Gates Millennium Scholars Program	576	$40,000	$ 500	150	Limited to American Indian/Alaska Native students.
Ron Brown Scholar Program	580	$40,000	$10,000	10–20	Talent: leadership. Limited to Black (non-Hispanic) students.
Pratt and Whitney Maintenance Scholarships	109	$36,000	$ 2400	6	Aviation/Aerospace; Civic Affiliation: Women in Aviation, International.
DeVry Skills USA VICA Scholarships	780	$30,232	$ 9000	18	
Best Teen Chef Culinary Scholarship Competition	179	$30,000	$ 2000	10–18	Culinary Arts.
Florida Space Research and Education Grant Program	697	$30,000	$10,000	9–12	Studying in Florida.
Gina Bachauer International Artists Piano Competition Award	400	$30,000	$ 600	6	Performing Arts; Talent: music/singing.
South Carolina Police Corps Scholarship	801	$30,000	$ 7500	20	
W. Eugene Smith Grant in Humanistic Photography	766	$30,000	$ 2500	varies	Talent: photography/photogrammetry/filmmaking.
AAA High School Travel Challenge	769	$25,000	$ 500	8	Must be in high school.
Discover Card Tribute Award Scholarship Program	770	$25,000	$ 2500	478	Must be in high school.
Hugh Fulton Byas Memorial Grant	311	$25,000	$ 1000	3–10	History, International Migration, Journalism, Peace and Conflict Studies.
Lilly Endowment Community Scholarship, Tippecanoe County	673	$25,000	$ 6250	6	State: Indiana; Studying in Indiana.
National Art Honor Society Scholarship	85	$25,000	$ 2500	5	Arts.
National Poster Design Contest	285	$25,000	$ 2000	10	Graphics/Graphic Arts/Printing.
Primary Care Resource Initiative for Missouri Loan Program	186	$25,000	$ 3000	varies	Dental Health/Services, Health and Medical Sciences, Nursing; State: Missouri; Studying in Missouri.
Princess Grace Scholarships in Dance, Theater, and Film	268	$25,000	$ 5000	15–20	Filmmaking/Video, Performing Arts.
Sons of Italy National Leadership Grants Competition General Scholarships	602	$25,000	$ 4000	10–13	Nationality: Italian.
University and Community College System of Nevada NASA Space Grant and Fellowship Program	101	$25,000	$ 2500	1–20	Aviation/Aerospace, Chemical Engineering, Computer Science/Data Processing, Electrical Engineering/Electronics, Engineering/Technology, Meteorology/Atmospheric Science, Physical Sciences and Math; State: Nevada; Studying in Nevada.
Voice of Democracy Program	808	$25,000	$ 1000	59	Must be in high school.
Youth for Adolescent Pregnancy Prevention Leadership Recognition Program	297	$25,000	$ 5000	8	Health and Medical Sciences, Nursing; State: California; Studying in California.
American Institute for Foreign Study Minority Scholarships	577	$24,000	$ 2000	1–4	Talent: leadership. Limited to ethnic minority students.
Tuition Exchange Scholarships	521	$20,800	$10,000	3400–4000	Employment Experience: designated career field.
Chairscholars Foundation, Inc. Scholarships	506	$20,000	$ 5000	10–12	Employment Experience: community service; Disability: Hearing Impaired, Physically Disabled, Visually Impaired.

Award Name	Page Number	Highest Dollar Amount	Lowest Dollar Amount	Number of Awards	Academic/Career Areas and Eligibility Requirements
Coca-Cola Scholars Program	752	$20,000	$ 4000	250	Talent: leadership.
Duke Energy Scholars Program	496	$20,000	$ 1000	20	Corporate Affiliation.
Four-Year and Three-Year Advance Designees Scholarship	539	$20,000	$ 5000	700–3000	Military Service: Army, Army National Guard.
Fulbright Program	198	$20,000	$ 1000	80–100	Education; Employment Experience: teaching.
Glaxo Smith Kline Opportunities Scholarship	733	$20,000	$ 1000	1–5	State: North Carolina; Studying in North Carolina.
Jonathan R. Lax Scholarship Fund	773	$20,000	$ 5000	8–10	
Junior Achievement Joe Francomano Scholarship	466	$20,000	$ 5000	1	Civic Affiliation: Junior Achievement; Talent: leadership.
National Security Education Program David L. Boren Undergraduate Scholarships	786	$20,000	$ 2500	150–200	
Scholastic Art and Writing Awards-Art Section	85	$20,000	$ 100	600	Arts, Literature/English/Writing; Talent: art.
SME Family Scholarship	254	$20,000	$ 5000	3	Engineering/Technology.
Washington Crossing Foundation Scholarship	766	$20,000	$ 1000	5–10	Talent: designated field specified by sponsor.
William Kapell International Piano Competition and Festival	399	$20,000	$ 1000	12	Performing Arts; Talent: music.
Maryland Association of Private Colleges and Career Schools Scholarship	127	$19,950	$ 500	58	Business/Consumer Services, Computer Science/Data Processing, Dental Health/Services, Engineering/Technology, Food Science/Nutrition, Home Economics, TV/Radio Broadcasting, Trade/Technical Specialties; State: Maryland; Studying in Maryland.
Assumption Programs of Loans for Education	647	$19,000	$11,000	7700	State: California; Studying in California.
Rotary Foundation Cultural Ambassadorial Scholarship	283	$19,000	$12,000	150–200	Foreign Language; Talent: leadership.
American Legion National Headquarters National High School Oratorical Contest	746	$18,000	$ 1500	54	Talent: public speaking.
Army ROTC Historically Black Colleges and Universities Program	539	$16,000	$ 5000	180–250	Military Service: Army, Army National Guard.
Army ROTC Two-Year, Three-Year and Four-Year Scholarships for Active Duty Army Enlisted Personnel	539	$16,000	$ 5000	150–350	Military Service: Army, Army National Guard.
Two- and Three-Year Campus-Based Scholarships	539	$16,000	$ 5000	250–1500	Military Service: Army, Army National Guard.
Two-Year Reserve Forces Duty Scholarships	542	$16,000	$ 5000	140–300	Military Service: Army National Guard.
Armenian Relief Society Undergraduate Scholarship	577	$15,000	$13,000	varies	Nationality: Armenian.
Bross Prize	413	$15,000	$ 4000	1	Religion/Theology.
Discovery Channel Young Scientist Challenge	763	$15,000	$ 500	40	Talent: designated field specified by sponsor.
First in Family Scholarship	679	$15,000	$12,500	10	State: Alabama; Studying in Alabama.
HCR Manor Care Nursing Scholarship Program	384	$15,000	$ 2000	40–50	Nursing.

Scholarships, Grants & Prizes At-a-Glance

Award Name	Page Number	Highest Dollar Amount	Lowest Dollar Amount	Number of Awards	Academic/Career Areas and Eligibility Requirements
Illinois Department of Public Health Center for Rural Health Allied Health Care Professional Scholarship Program	297	$15,000	$7500	20	Health and Medical Sciences; State: Illinois.
Illinois Future Teachers Corps Program	203	$15,000	$5000	1150	Education; State: Illinois; Studying in Illinois.
Jesse Brown Memorial Youth Scholarship Program	508	$15,000	$5000	12	Employment Experience: helping handicapped.
Knight Ridder Minority Scholarship Program	126	$15,000	$5000	5	Business/Consumer Services, Graphics/Graphic Arts/Printing, Journalism. Limited to ethnic minority students.
McFarland Charitable Nursing Scholarship	384	$15,000	$1000	3–5	Nursing.
National FFA College and Vocational/Technical School Scholarship Program	792	$15,000	$1000	1700	
San Antonio International Piano Competition	763	$15,000	$ 500	8	Talent: music/singing.
Texas 4-H Opportunity Scholarship	729	$15,000	$1500	150	State: Texas; Studying in Texas.
Utah Police Corps Scholarship Program	343	$15,000	$7500	30	Law Enforcement/Police Administration.
Sharon Christa McAuliffe Teacher Education-Critical Shortage Grant Program	206	$14,775	$ 200	137	Education; State: Maryland; Studying in Maryland.
Arkansas Health Education Grant Program (ARHEG)	62	$14,600	$5000	258–288	Animal/Veterinary Sciences, Dental Health/Services, Health and Medical Sciences; State: Arkansas.
DeVry Dean's Scholarships	663	$13,550	$7550	varies	Studying in Alberta, Arizona, California, Colorado, Florida, Georgia, Illinois, Missouri, New Jersey, New York, Ohio, Pennsylvania, Texas, Virginia, Washington.
Legislative Scholarship	709	$13,448	$2600	80	State: Ohio; Studying in Ohio.
Amarillo Area Foundation Scholarships	632	$12,000	$ 400	varies	State: Texas.
California Masonic Foundation Scholarship Awards	647	$12,000	$1000		State: California.
Central Valley Nursing Scholarship	384	$12,000	$8000	90–140	Nursing; State: California; Studying in California.
Fond du Lac Scholarship Program	584	$12,000	$ 500	75–125	Limited to American Indian/Alaska Native students.
Mable and Lawrence S. Cooke Scholarship	455	$12,000	$5000	5	Civic Affiliation: Boy Scouts.
Math and Science Scholarship Program for Alabama Teachers	111	$12,000	$2000		Biology, Earth Science, Meteorology/Atmospheric Science, Natural Sciences, Physical Sciences and Math; Studying in Alabama.
Nursing Scholarship Program	383	$12,000	$8000	15–30	Nursing; State: Florida; Studying in Florida.
Guaranteed Access Grant-Maryland	689	$11,600	$ 400	1000	State: Maryland; Studying in Maryland.
Competitive Cal Grant B	648	$11,259	$ 700	22,500	State: California; Studying in California.
Entitlement Cal Grant B	648	$11,259	$ 700	varies	State: California; Studying in California.
Law Enforcement Personnel Development Scholarship	506	$11,259	$ 100	varies	Employment Experience: police/firefighting; State: California; Studying in California.

Award Name	Page Number	Highest Dollar Amount	Lowest Dollar Amount	Number of Awards	Academic/Career Areas and Eligibility Requirements
Alberta Heritage Scholarship Fund Aboriginal Health Careers Bursary	111	$10,557	$ 811	20–40	Biology, Dental Health/Services, Health Administration, Health and Medical Sciences, Nursing, Therapy/Rehabilitation; State: Alberta. Limited to American Indian/ Alaska Native students.
Tupperware U.S., Inc. Scholarship	494	$10,500	$1000	varies	Corporate Affiliation.
A Legacy of Hope Scholarships for Survivors of Childhood Cancer	727	$10,000	$1000	1–6	State: Arizona, California, Colorado, Montana.
Alton and Dorothy Higgins, MD Scholarship	304	$10,000	$5000		Health and Medical Sciences. Limited to Black (non-Hispanic) students.
America's Highschool Idol	770	$10,000	$ 500	1–50	Must be in high school.
American Legion National Headquarters Eagle Scout of the Year	450	$10,000	$2500	4	Civic Affiliation: American Legion or Auxiliary, Boy Scouts; Employment Experience: community service.
Angelus Awards Student Film Festival	748	$10,000	$1500	5–7	Talent: photography/photogrammetry/filmmaking.
Boys & Girls Clubs of America National Youth of the Year Award	456	$10,000	$5000	5	Civic Affiliation: Boys or Girls Club; Talent: leadership.
California Junior Miss Scholarship Program	647	$10,000	$ 500	25	State: California; Talent: leadership.
CAPPS Scholarship Program	646	$10,000	$1000	200–250	State: California.
CollegeNET Scholarship	777	$10,000	$1000	1–3	
DC Tuition Assistance Grant Program	664	$10,000	$2500	4000	State: District of Columbia.
Executive Women International Scholarship Program	754	$10,000	$1000	80–100	Talent: designated field specified by sponsor.
Federation of American Consumers and Travelers Current Student Scholarship	460	$10,000	$2500	2	Civic Affiliation: Federation of American Consumers and Travelers.
Federation of American Consumers and Travelers Graduating High School Senior Scholarship	460	$10,000	$2500	2	Civic Affiliation: Federation of American Consumers and Travelers.
Federation of American Consumers and Travelers Returning Student Scholarship	461	$10,000	$2500	2	Civic Affiliation: Federation of American Consumers and Travelers.
Film and Fiction Scholarship	87	$10,000	$3000	varies	Arts, Filmmaking/Video, Literature/English/Writing.
Fisher Broadcasting, Inc., Scholarship for Minorities	159	$10,000	$1000	2–4	Communications, Engineering/Technology, Journalism, Photojournalism/Photography, TV/Radio Broadcasting. Limited to ethnic minority students.
Fountainhead College Scholarship Essay Contest	751	$10,000	$ 50	251	Talent: writing.
Girls Going Places Scholarship Program	784	$10,000	$1000	15	Must be in high school.
Governor's Scholars-Arkansas	644	$10,000	$4000	75–250	State: Arkansas; Studying in Arkansas.
GUIDEPOSTS Young Writer's Contest	347	$10,000	$ 250	20	Literature/English/Writing.
Health Professions Education Scholarship Program	184	$10,000	$5000	10–15	Dental Health/Services, Health and Medical Sciences, Nursing; State: California; Studying in California.
Hellenic Times Scholarship Fund	585	$10,000	$ 500	30–40	Nationality: Greek.

Scholarships, Grants & Prizes At-a-Glance

Award Name	Page Number	Highest Dollar Amount	Lowest Dollar Amount	Number of Awards	Academic/Career Areas and Eligibility Requirements
Herschel C. Price Educational Foundation Scholarships	785	$10,000	$ 500	200–300	
Horatio Alger Association Scholarship Program	786	$10,000	$1000	1400	Must be in high school.
Illinois Restaurant Association Educational Foundation Scholarships	180	$10,000	$ 500	50–70	Culinary Arts, Food Science/Nutrition, Food Service/Hospitality, Hospitality Management; Employment Experience: food service, hospitality; State: Illinois.
Intellectual Capital Partnership Program, ICAPP	431	$10,000	$7000	328	Trade/Technical Specialties; State: Georgia; Studying in Georgia.
International Music Competition of the ARD Munich	364	$10,000	$5000	12	Music.
Junior Girls Scholarship Program	468	$10,000	$5000	2	Civic Affiliation: Veterans of Foreign Wars or Auxiliary; Talent: leadership.
Kappa Alpha Theta Foundation Merit Based Scholarship Program	466	$10,000	$1000	120–150	Civic Affiliation: Greek Organization.
Louis C. and Amy E. Nuernberger Memorial Scholarship	513	$10,000	$5000	1	Employment Experience: designated career field; State: Nebraska.
Mas Family Scholarships	123	$10,000	$1000	10–15	Business/Consumer Services, Chemical Engineering, Communications, Economics, Electrical Engineering/Electronics, Engineering-Related Technologies, Engineering/Technology, Journalism, Mechanical Engineering, Political Science; Nationality: Latin American/Caribbean; Talent: leadership.
Medicus Student Exchange	603	$10,000	$2000	1–5	Nationality: Swiss; Talent: foreign language.
Miller Electric IYSC Scholarship	238	$10,000	$1000	1	Engineering/Technology, Trade/Technical Specialties.
NAAS-USA Awards	790	$10,000	$ 200	10–14	Must be in high school.
National Association of Pastoral Musicians Members' Scholarship	365	$10,000	$2000	1	Music, Religion/Theology; Talent: music/singing.
National Italian American Foundation Category I Scholarship	594	$10,000	$2500	varies	Nationality: Italian.
National Italian American Foundation Category II Scholarship	82	$10,000	$2500	varies	Area/Ethnic Studies; Talent: Italian language.
National Merit Scholarship Program	792	$10,000	$ 500	9600	Must be in high school.
National Network for Environmental Management Studies Fellowship	371	$10,000	$6000	35–40	Natural Resources.
National Peace Essay Contest	398	$10,000	$1000	50	Peace and Conflict Studies.
National Teen-Ager Scholarship Foundation	792	$10,000	$1000	250–1510	
NRA Youth Educational Summit (YES) Scholarships	792	$10,000	$1000	1–6	Must be in high school.
Olive W. Garvey Fellowship Competition	786	$10,000	$1000	6	
Phillips Foundation Ronald Reagan Future Leaders Scholarship Program	796	$10,000	$2500	10–20	

Award Name	Page Number	Highest Dollar Amount	Lowest Dollar Amount	Number of Awards	Academic/Career Areas and Eligibility Requirements
Promotion of Excellence Grants Program	203	$10,000	$2000	varies	Education; Civic Affiliation: Phi Kappa Phi.
R.O.S.E. Fund Scholarship Program	718	$10,000	$1000	10–15	Studying in Connecticut, Maine, Massachusetts, New Hampshire, Rhode Island, Vermont.
Regional and Restricted Scholarship Award Program	740	$10,000	$ 250	175–220	State: Connecticut.
Scholastic Art and Writing Awards-Writing Section Scholarship	85	$10,000	$ 100	300	Arts, Literature/English/Writing; Talent: writing.
Short-term Student Exchange Promotion Program Scholarship	773	$10,000	$5650	1950	
Soroptimist Women's Opportunity Award	800	$10,000	$ 500	varies	
Spencer Risk Management and Insurance Scholarship	327	$10,000	$5000	10–20	Insurance and Actuarial Science.
Stephen Phillips Memorial Scholarship Fund	801	$10,000	$3000	150–200	
Stonehouse Golf Youth Scholarship	765	$10,000	$ 500	20	Talent: golf.
Talbots Women's Scholarship Fund	802	$10,000	$1000	5–50	
Teacher of the Visually Impaired Loan Program	422	$10,000	$ 250	varies	Special Education; State: Wisconsin; Studying in Illinois, Iowa, Michigan, Minnesota, Wisconsin.
Toshiba/NSTA ExploraVision Awards Program	792	$10,000	$5000	16–32	
Veteran's Tribute Scholarship	566	$10,000	$3000	3	Military Service: General.
Worldfest Student Film Award	269	$10,000	$1000	10	Filmmaking/Video.
Young American Creative Patriotic Art Awards Program	758	$10,000	$2500	3	Talent: designated field specified by sponsor.
Competitive Cal Grant A	648	$ 9708	$2046	22,500	State: California; Studying in California.
Entitlement Cal Grant A	648	$ 9708	$2046	varies	State: California; Studying in California.
Washington Award for Vocational Excellence	740	$ 9498	$4284	147	State: Washington; Studying in Washington.
Vermont Incentive Grants	737	$ 9100	$ 500	varies	State: Vermont.
DeVry High School Community Scholars Award	664	$ 9050	$5050	4753	Studying in Alberta, Arizona, California, Colorado, Florida, Georgia, Illinois, Missouri, New Jersey, New York, Ohio, Pennsylvania, Texas, Virginia, Washington.
Pennsylvania Institute of Certified Public Accountants Sophomore Scholarship	46	$ 9000	$1000	18	Accounting; Studying in Pennsylvania.
Visby Program: Higher Education and Research	603	$ 9000	$7500	varies	Nationality: Latvian, Lithuanian, Polish, Russian, Ukrainian.
New Jersey Society of Certified Public Accountants High School Scholarship Program	45	$ 8500	$6500	15–20	Accounting; State: New Jersey.
Associate Degree Nursing Scholarship Program	384	$ 8000	$4000	15–30	Nursing; State: California; Studying in California.
Johnson Controls Foundation Scholarship Program	497	$ 8000	$2000	45	Corporate Affiliation.

Scholarships, Grants & Prizes At-a-Glance

Award Name	Page Number	Highest Dollar Amount	Lowest Dollar Amount	Number of Awards	Academic/Career Areas and Eligibility Requirements
Kentucky Transportation Cabinet Civil Engineering Scholarship Program	153	$8000	$7200	10–20	Civil Engineering; State: Kentucky; Studying in Kentucky.
Lee-Jackson Educational Foundation Scholarship Competition	684	$8000	$1000	27	State: Virginia; Talent: writing.
New Jersey War Orphans Tuition Assistance	560	$8000	$2000	varies	Military Service: General; State: New Jersey.
North Carolina Student Loan Program for Health, Science, and Mathematics	187	$8000	$3000		Dental Health/Services, Health Administration, Health and Medical Sciences, Nursing, Physical Sciences and Math, Therapy/Rehabilitation; State: North Carolina.
Portuguese Heritage Scholarship	599	$8000	$1000	8–10	Nationality: Portuguese.
Registered Nurse Education Loan Repayment Program	385	$8000	$4000	50–70	Nursing; State: California; Studying in California.
RN Education Scholarship Program	385	$8000	$6000	50–70	Nursing; State: California; Studying in California.
Seneca Nation Higher Education Program	601	$8000	$3000	varies	Limited to American Indian/Alaska Native students.
SPIE Educational Scholarships in Optical Science and Engineering	70	$8000	$1000	30–80	Applied Sciences, Aviation/Aerospace, Chemical Engineering, Electrical Engineering/Electronics, Engineering-Related Technologies, Engineering/Technology, Materials Science, Engineering, and Metallurgy, Mechanical Engineering; Civic Affiliation: International Society for Optical Engineering (SPIE).
William Winter Teacher Scholar Loan Program	207	$8000	$ 500	varies	Education; State: Mississippi; Studying in Mississippi.
Minnesota State Grant Program	693	$7662	$ 100	71,000–75,000	State: Minnesota; Studying in Minnesota.
Eleanor Allwork Scholarship Grants	74	$7500	$2500	4	Architecture; State: New York; Studying in New York.
Harold F. Wilkins Scholarship Program	119	$7500	$1000	1–3	Business/Consumer Services, Horticulture/Floriculture.
Leveraged Incentive Grant Program	702	$7500	$ 200	varies	State: New Hampshire; Studying in New Hampshire.
Outstanding Scholar Recruitment Program	703	$7500	$2500	varies	State: New Jersey; Studying in New Jersey.
Phelan Art Award in Filmmaking	269	$7500	$2500	1	Filmmaking/Video.
Phelan Art Award in Video	269	$7500	$2500	1–2	Filmmaking/Video.
William Faulkner-William Wisdom Creative Writing Competition	761	$7500	$ 750	7	Talent: English language, writing.
Tuition Aid Grant	704	$7272	$ 868	varies	State: New Jersey; Studying in New Jersey.
Delegate Scholarship Program-Maryland	688	$7200	$ 200	3500	State: Maryland; Studying in Maryland.
Freeman-Asia Award Program	765	$7000	$3000	varies	Talent: Asian language, foreign language.
Higher Education Supplemental Scholarship	600	$7000	$ 500	150	Limited to American Indian/Alaska Native students.
J. Wood Platt Caddie Scholarship Trust	512	$7000	$ 200	250–300	Employment Experience: private club/caddying; Talent: golf.
National Federation of the Blind Scholarships	515	$7000	$3000	18	Employment Experience: community service; Disability: Visually Impaired.

Award Name	Page Number	Highest Dollar Amount	Lowest Dollar Amount	Number of Awards	Academic/Career Areas and Eligibility Requirements
National Solo Competition	747	$7000	$ 500	26	Talent: music.
Sid Richardson Memorial Fund	520	$7000	$ 500	50–60	Employment Experience: designated career field.
Society of Hispanic Professional Engineers Foundation	146	$7000	$ 500	varies	Chemical Engineering, Civil Engineering, Electrical Engineering/Electronics, Engineering-Related Technologies, Engineering/Technology, Materials Science, Engineering, and Metallurgy, Mechanical Engineering, Natural Sciences, Nuclear Science, Science, Technology, and Society. Limited to Hispanic students.
Vermont Part-time Student Grants	737	$6830	$ 250	varies	State: Vermont.
North Carolina Police Corps Scholarship	179	$6667	$5000	15–30	Criminal Justice/Criminology, Law Enforcement/Police Administration.
Indiana National Guard Supplemental Grant	538	$6516	$ 200	503–925	Military Service: Air Force National Guard, Army National Guard; State: Indiana; Studying in Indiana.
Twenty-first Century Scholars Award	727	$6516	$1000	2800–8100	State: Indiana; Studying in Indiana.
Liquitex Excellence in Art Purchase Award Program	88	$6500	$1500	5	Arts.
NBFAA/Security Dealer Youth Scholarship Program	514	$6500	$ 500	32	Employment Experience: fire service, police/firefighting; State: California, Connecticut, Georgia, Indiana, Kentucky, Louisiana, Maryland, Minnesota, New Jersey, New York, North Carolina, Pennsylvania, Tennessee, Virginia, Washington.
Paraprofessional Teacher Preparation Grant	206	$6500	$ 750	varies	Education; State: Massachusetts.
Pennsylvania Burglar and Fire Alarm Association Youth Scholarship Program	518	$6500	$ 500	6–8	Employment Experience: police/firefighting; State: Pennsylvania.
Halton Scholars	496	$6499	$1260	1–5	Corporate Affiliation; Employment Experience: designated career field; State: Oregon, Washington.
Adeline Rosenberg Memorial Prize	754	$6000	$4000	2	Talent: music/singing.
Adult Vocational Training Education Scholarships	582	$6000	$3000	3	Limited to American Indian/Alaska Native students.
AMBUCS Scholars-Scholarships for Therapists	299	$6000	$ 500	300	Health and Medical Sciences, Therapy/Rehabilitation.
American Legion Department of New York State High School Oratorical Contest	639	$6000	$ 75	65	State: New York; Talent: public speaking.
Archbold Scholarship Program	298	$6000	$ 600	50	Health and Medical Sciences, Nursing; State: Florida, Georgia.
Davis-Putter Scholarship Fund	779	$6000	$1000	25–30	
Department of Education Scholarship for Programs in China	199	$6000	$ 500	10–20	Education; Talent: foreign language.
GCSAA Scholars Competition	320	$6000	$ 500	varies	Horticulture/Floriculture; Civic Affiliation: Golf Course Superintendents Association of America.
Georgia PROMISE Teacher Scholarship Program	201	$6000	$3000	700–1400	Education; Studying in Georgia.
Higher Education Scholarship Program	596	$6000	$ 50	72	Limited to American Indian/Alaska Native students.

Scholarships, Grants & Prizes At-a-Glance

Award Name	Page Number	Highest Dollar Amount	Lowest Dollar Amount	Number of Awards	Academic/Career Areas and Eligibility Requirements
IFMA Foundation Scholarships	77	$6000	$1000	10–15	Architecture, Engineering-Related Technologies.
JVS Jewish Community Scholarship	627	$6000	$ 500	varies	State: California; Religion: Jewish.
Marion Huber Learning Through Listening Awards	478	$6000	$2000	6	Civic Affiliation: Recording for the Blind and Dyslexic; Employment Experience: community service; Disability: Learning Disabled; Talent: leadership.
Mary P. Oenslager Scholastic Achievement Awards	479	$6000	$1000	9	Civic Affiliation: Recording for the Blind and Dyslexic; Employment Experience: community service; Disability: Visually Impaired; Talent: leadership.
Mississippi Health Care Professions Loan/Scholarship Program	299	$6000	$1500	varies	Health and Medical Sciences, Psychology, Therapy/Rehabilitation; State: Mississippi; Studying in Mississippi.
National Association of Black Accountants National Scholarship Program	43	$6000	$ 500	40	Accounting, Business/Consumer Services, Economics; Civic Affiliation: National Association of Black Accountants. Limited to ethnic minority students.
National Minority Junior Golf Scholarship	595	$6000	$1000	varies	Talent: golf. Limited to ethnic minority students.
North Dakota Department of Transportation Engineering Grant	154	$6000	$1000	varies	Civil Engineering, Engineering/Technology; Studying in North Dakota.
OFA 2002 National Scholarship/ Casey Family Scholars	795	$6000	$2000	350	
St. Petersburg Golf Classic Scholarship	619	$6000	$2000	4	State: Florida. Limited to Black (non-Hispanic) students.
Undergraduate Education Scholarships	582	$6000	$3000	12	Limited to American Indian/Alaska Native students.
Victor and Margaret Ball Program	119	$6000	$1500	20	Business/Consumer Services, Horticulture/Floriculture.
Zisovich Jewish Studies Scholarship Fund to teach the Holocaust	204	$6000	$3000	varies	Education, History; State: California.
Indiana Freedom of Choice Grant	727	$5915	$ 200	10,000–11,830	State: Indiana; Studying in Indiana.
Academic Scholars Program	711	$5500	$3500	varies	Studying in Oklahoma.
Contemporary Record Society National Festival for the Performing Arts Scholarship	753	$5500	$1900	1	Talent: music/singing.
Heartland Scholarship Fund	794	$5500	$3500	varies	
Legislative Essay Scholarship	662	$5500	$ 500	62	State: Delaware.
South Carolina Press Association Foundation Newspaper Scholarships	339	$5500	$4000	3	Journalism; Studying in South Carolina.
Ohio Instructional Grant	710	$5466	$ 78	varies	State: Ohio; Studying in Ohio, Pennsylvania.
Young Artist Competition	402	$5250	$ 500	9–14	Performing Arts; State: Illinois, Indiana, Iowa, Kansas, Manitoba, Michigan, Minnesota, Missouri, Nebraska, North Dakota, Ontario, South Dakota, Wisconsin; Talent: music.
"My Turn" Essay Competition	788	$5000	$1000	10	Must be in high school.
7-Eleven Scholarship Program	126	$5000	$ 500	varies	Business/Consumer Services, Computer Science/Data Processing, Engineering/ Technology; State: California. Limited to Hispanic students.

Award Name	Page Number	Highest Dollar Amount	Lowest Dollar Amount	Number of Awards	Academic/Career Areas and Eligibility Requirements
Academy of Motion Pictures Student Academy Awards	267	$5000	$2000	3–12	Filmmaking/Video.
Actuarial Scholarships for Minority Students	326	$5000	$ 500	varies	Insurance and Actuarial Science. Limited to ethnic minority students.
American Council of the Blind Scholarships	522	$5000	$ 500	28	Disability: Visually Impaired.
American Dietetic Association Foundation Scholarship Program	270	$5000	$ 500	200	Food Science/Nutrition; Civic Affiliation: American Dietetic Association.
American Legion Department of Alabama State Oratorical Scholarship	635	$5000	$1000	3	State: Alabama; Talent: public speaking.
Arby's-Big Brothers Big Sisters Scholarship Award	454	$5000	$1000	2–10	Civic Affiliation: Big Brothers/Big Sisters; Employment Experience: community service.
Arkansas Service Memorial Fund	643	$5000	$ 500		State: Arkansas; Studying in Arkansas.
Ashby B. Carter Memorial Scholarship Fund Founders Award	469	$5000	$3500	3	Civic Affiliation: National Alliance of Postal and Federal Employees.
Asian-American Journalists Association Scholarship	157	$5000	$1000	10–15	Communications, Journalism, Photojournalism/Photography, TV/Radio Broadcasting; Employment Experience: journalism; Talent: photography/photogrammetry/filmmaking, writing.
ASSE-United Parcel Service Scholarship	396	$5000	$3000		Occupational Safety and Health; Civic Affiliation: American Society of Safety Engineers.
Association of State Dam Safety Officials Undergraduate Scholarship	152	$5000	$2500	3	Civil Engineering, Engineering/Technology.
Atlas Shrugged Essay Competition	751	$5000	$ 50	49	Talent: writing.
AXA Foundation Fund Achievement Scholarship	130	$5000	$2000		Business/Consumer Services; State: New York; Talent: leadership. Limited to Black (non-Hispanic) students.
BEEM Foundation Scholarship	363	$5000	$1000	3	Music; State: California.
Bigwood Memorial Fund	304	$5000	$1000	varies	Health and Medical Sciences, Nursing. Limited to Black (non-Hispanic) students.
BMI Student Composer Awards	751	$5000	$ 500	5–10	Talent: music/singing.
Boys and Girls Clubs of Chicago Scholarships	456	$5000	$3000	varies	Civic Affiliation: Boys or Girls Club; State: Illinois.
Bushrod Campbell and Adah Hall Scholarship	607	$5000	$1000	varies	State: Massachusetts. Limited to Black (non-Hispanic) students.
Calgon, Take Me Away to College Scholarship Competition	802	$5000	$ 500	9	
California Congress of Parents and Teachers, Inc. Scholarship	647	$5000	$ 500	varies	State: California.
Carpe Diem Foundation of Illinois Scholarship Competition	774	$5000	$2500	10–15	
Children, Adult, and Family Services Scholarship	712	$5000	$ 500	varies	State: Oregon; Studying in Oregon.
Christa McAuliffe Teacher Scholarship Loan-Delaware	200	$5000	$1000	1–60	Education; State: Delaware; Studying in Delaware.
Chrysler Corporation Scholarship	175	$5000	$1000	varies	Computer Science/Data Processing, Engineering/Technology. Limited to Black (non-Hispanic) students.

Scholarships, Grants & Prizes At-a-Glance

Award Name	Page Number	Highest Dollar Amount	Lowest Dollar Amount	Number of Awards	Academic/Career Areas and Eligibility Requirements
College Scholarship Assistance Program	725	$5000	$ 400	varies	State: Virginia; Studying in Virginia.
Colorado Student Grant	654	$5000	$ 500	varies	State: Colorado; Studying in Colorado.
Connecticut Special Education Teacher Incentive Grant	421	$5000	$2000	varies	Special Education.
Constant Memorial Scholarship for Aquidneck Island Residents	90	$5000	$2000	1–2	Arts, Music; State: Rhode Island; Talent: art, music.
Contemporary Record Society National Competition for Performing Artists	399	$5000	$1500	1	Performing Arts; Talent: music/singing.
Culinary Trust Scholarship Program for Culinary Study and Research	271	$5000	$1000	21	Food Science/Nutrition, Food Service/ Hospitality; Employment Experience: food service.
Delaware Nursing Incentive Scholarship Loan	382	$5000	$1000	1–40	Nursing; State: Delaware.
Department of Energy Scholarship Program	125	$5000	$ 500	15	Business/Consumer Services, Chemical Engineering, Electrical Engineering/ Electronics, Energy and Power Engineering, Engineering-Related Technologies, Engineering/Technology, Environmental Science, Materials Science, Engineering, and Metallurgy, Mechanical Engineering, Natural Resources, Natural Sciences, Nuclear Science.
Doris and John Carpenter Scholarship	610	$5000	$2000		Limited to Black (non-Hispanic) students.
Dough for Brains Essay Contests	781	$5000	$ 250	50–200	
Edward M. Nagel Foundation Scholarship	49	$5000	$2000	varies	Accounting, Business/Consumer Services, Economics; State: California. Limited to Black (non-Hispanic) students.
Edwards Scholarship	666	$5000	$ 250	varies	State: Massachusetts.
El Nuevo Constructor Scholarship Program	76	$5000	$ 500	varies	Architecture, Drafting, Heating, Air-Conditioning, and Refrigeration Mechanics, Industrial Design. Limited to Hispanic students.
Elie Wiesel Prize in Ethics Essay Contest	754	$5000	$ 500	5	Talent: writing.
Elmer O. and Ida Preston Educational Trust Grants and Loans	666	$5000	$ 250	varies	State: Iowa; Studying in Iowa.
Engineering Scholarship	136	$5000	$2000	varies	Chemical Engineering, Civil Engineering, Electrical Engineering/Electronics, Engineering-Related Technologies, Engineering/Technology, Materials Science, Engineering, and Metallurgy, Mechanical Engineering.
Environmental Protection Scholarships	142	$5000	$4000	3–5	Chemical Engineering, Civil Engineering, Earth Science, Materials Science, Engineering, and Metallurgy; Studying in Kentucky.
Ernst and Young Scholarship Program	42	$5000	$ 500	varies	Accounting, Business/Consumer Services, Economics. Limited to Hispanic students.
Eunice Walker Johnson Endowed Scholarship	806	$5000	$2000	varies	
First in My Family Scholarship Program	585	$5000	$1000	100–200	Limited to Hispanic students.

Award Name	Page Number	Highest Dollar Amount	Lowest Dollar Amount	Number of Awards	Academic/Career Areas and Eligibility Requirements
Florida Bankers Educational Foundation Scholarship/Loan	124	$5000	$ 750	10–50	Business/Consumer Services; Employment Experience: banking; State: Florida; Studying in Florida; Talent: leadership.
Foundation of Research and Education Undergraduate Merit Scholarships	305	$5000	$1000	40–60	Health Information Management/Technology; Civic Affiliation: American Health Information Management Association.
Foundation of the National Student Nurses' Association General Scholarships	383	$5000	$1000	50–100	Nursing.
Francis Sylvia Zverina Scholarship	320	$5000	$2000	1–3	Horticulture/Floriculture, Landscape Architecture.
Fred Scheigert Scholarship Program	524	$5000	$ 500	1	Disability: Visually Impaired.
Future Teachers Conditional Scholarship and Loan Repayment Program	215	$5000	$ 600	50	Education; State: Washington; Studying in Washington.
George A. Nielsen Public Investor Scholarship	124	$5000	$2500	1–2	Business/Consumer Services; Employment Experience: designated career field.
Geraldo Rivera Scholarship	333	$5000	$1000		Journalism, TV/Radio Broadcasting.
Graduate and Professional Scholarship Program-Maryland	186	$5000	$1000	40–200	Dental Health/Services, Health and Medical Sciences, Law/Legal Services, Nursing, Social Services; State: Maryland; Studying in Maryland.
H.H. Harris Foundation Annual Scholarship	351	$5000	$ 500		Materials Science, Engineering, and Metallurgy.
Harry C. Jaecker Scholarship	304	$5000	$2000		Health and Medical Sciences. Limited to Black (non-Hispanic) students.
Herbert Hoover Uncommon Student Award	675	$5000	$ 750	18	State: Iowa.
HHAF Chase and Mastercard Academic Excellence Youth Award	586	$5000	$2000	25	Nationality: Hispanic. Limited to Hispanic students.
HHAF Dr. Pepper Leadership and Community Service Youth Award	586	$5000	$2000	25	Nationality: Hispanic. Limited to Hispanic students.
HHAF Exxon Mobil Mathematics Youth Award	586	$5000	$2000	25	Nationality: Hispanic. Limited to Hispanic students.
HHAF Glaxo Smith Kline Health and Science Youth Award	586	$5000	$2000	25	Nationality: Hispanic. Limited to Hispanic students.
HHAF NBC Journalism Youth Award	586	$5000	$2000	25	Nationality: Hispanic. Limited to Hispanic students.
HHAF Sports Youth Award	586	$5000	$2000	25	Nationality: Hispanic. Limited to Hispanic students.
HHAF/Warner Bros. Entertainment, Inc. Arts and Entertainment Youth Award	587	$5000	$2000	25	Nationality: Hispanic. Limited to Hispanic students.
Hispanic College Fund Scholarship Program	585	$5000	$1000	500–750	Limited to Hispanic students.
Hispanic College Fund/INROADS/ Sprint Scholarship Program	125	$5000	$1000	10–20	Business/Consumer Services, Communications, Computer Science/Data Processing, Economics, Electrical Engineering/ Electronics, Engineering-Related Technologies, Engineering/Technology, Mechanical Engineering. Limited to Hispanic students.

Scholarships, Grants & Prizes At-a-Glance

Award Name	Page Number	Highest Dollar Amount	Lowest Dollar Amount	Number of Awards	Academic/Career Areas and Eligibility Requirements
Hispanic Engineer National Achievement Awards Corporation Scholarship Program	99	$5000	$2000	12–20	Aviation/Aerospace, Biology, Chemical Engineering, Civil Engineering, Computer Science/Data Processing, Electrical Engineering/Electronics, Engineering/ Technology, Materials Science, Engineering, and Metallurgy, Mechanical Engineering, Nuclear Science; Nationality: Hispanic. Limited to Hispanic students.
Houston Symphony Ima Hogg Young Artist Competition	757	$5000	$1000	3	Talent: music.
Howard Rock Foundation Scholarship Program	650	$5000	$2500	3	State: Alaska.
HSF-ALPFA Scholarships	38	$5000	$1000	varies	Accounting, Business/Consumer Services. Limited to Hispanic students.
HSF/Camino al éxito Scholarship Program	588	$5000	$2500	varies	Limited to Hispanic students.
ICI Educational Foundation Scholarship Program	42	$5000	$ 500	varies	Accounting, Business/Consumer Services, Computer Science/Data Processing, Engineering/Technology. Limited to Hispanic students.
Indiana Nursing Scholarship Fund	394	$5000	$ 200	490–690	Nursing; State: Indiana; Studying in Indiana.
Instrumentation, Systems, and Automation Society (ISA) Scholarship Program	99	$5000	$ 500	5–15	Aviation/Aerospace, Chemical Engineering, Electrical Engineering/Electronics, Engineering-Related Technologies, Engineering/Technology, Heating, Air-Conditioning, and Refrigeration Mechanics, Mechanical Engineering.
Irish Research Funds	82	$5000	$1000	1–10	Area/Ethnic Studies, Humanities, Social Sciences.
James L. and Genevieve H. Goodwin Memorial Scholarship	661	$5000	$1000	10	State: Connecticut.
Jaycee War Memorial Fund Scholarship	807	$5000	$1000	25–30	
Jesse Jones, Jr. Scholarship	132	$5000	$2000		Business/Consumer Services. Limited to Black (non-Hispanic) students.
Jimi Hendrix Endowment Fund Scholarship	401	$5000	$2000		Performing Arts. Limited to Black (non-Hispanic) students.
John F. and Anna Lee Stacey Scholarship Fund	88	$5000	$1000	3–5	Arts; Talent: art.
John Kimball, Jr. Memorial Trust Scholarship Program for the Study of History	312	$5000	$ 250	5–20	History.
Kansas City Initiative Scholarship	735	$5000	$2500	varies	State: Kansas, Missouri.
Kapadia Scholarships	262	$5000	$1500	varies	Engineering/Technology; Religion: a member of the specified denomination.
Kappa Alpha Theta Foundation Named Endowment Grant Program	466	$5000	$ 100	50	Civic Affiliation: Greek Organization.
Keck Foundation Scholarship	806	$5000	$2000	varies	
Kentucky Minority Educator Recruitment and Retention (KMERR) Scholarship	204	$5000	$2500	300	Education; State: Kentucky; Studying in Kentucky. Limited to ethnic minority students.
Kentucky Teacher Scholarship Program	204	$5000	$ 250	600–700	Education; State: Kentucky; Studying in Kentucky.

Award Name	Page Number	Highest Dollar Amount	Lowest Dollar Amount	Number of Awards	Academic/Career Areas and Eligibility Requirements
Kosciuszko Foundation Chopin Piano Competition	400	$5000	$1500	3	Performing Arts; Talent: music/singing.
L.A. Darling Company Scholarship Fund	643	$5000	$ 500		State: Arkansas.
Legislative Incentives for Future Excellence Program	722	$5000	$2000	varies	State: South Carolina; Studying in South Carolina.
Leveraging Educational Assistance State Partnership Program (LEAP)	676	$5000	$ 400	varies	State: Idaho; Studying in Idaho.
Liederkranz Foundation Scholarship Award for Voice	758	$5000	$1000	14–18	Talent: music/singing.
Lockheed Martin Scholarship Program	141	$5000	$ 500	varies	Chemical Engineering, Computer Science/Data Processing, Electrical Engineering/ Electronics, Energy and Power Engineering, Engineering-Related Technologies, Engineering/Technology, Materials Science, Engineering, and Metallurgy, Military and Defense Studies, Physical Sciences and Math. Limited to Hispanic students.
Lois McMillen Memorial Scholarship Fund	91	$5000	$ 500	varies	Arts; State: Connecticut.
M & T Bank/ Hispanic College Fund Scholarship Program	42	$5000	$1000	5–10	Accounting, Business/Consumer Services, Computer Science/Data Processing, Economics, Engineering-Related Technologies, Engineering/Technology; State: Maryland, New York, Pennsylvania, Virginia. Limited to Hispanic students.
Mae Maxey Memorial Scholarship	615	$5000	$1000		Limited to Black (non-Hispanic) students.
Maine Community Foundation Scholarship Programs	688	$5000	$ 500	150–700	State: Maine.
Mary E. Scott Memorial Scholarship	615	$5000	$1500		Limited to Black (non-Hispanic) students.
Mary Oenslager Scholarship	615	$5000	$2000		Limited to Black (non-Hispanic) students.
Math, Engineering, Science, Business, Education, Computers Scholarships	121	$5000	$ 500	180	Business/Consumer Services, Computer Science/Data Processing, Education, Engineering/Technology, Humanities, Physical Sciences and Math, Science, Technology, and Society, Social Sciences. Limited to American Indian/Alaska Native students.
Maverick Scholarship Fund	491	$5000	$ 500		Corporate Affiliation; State: Arkansas.
Michael P. Metcalf Memorial Scholarship	719	$5000	$2000	2–4	State: Rhode Island.
Miss Outstanding Teenager and Leadership Training Program	694	$5000	$1000	8–12	State: Hawaii, Montana; Studying in Hawaii, Montana.
Morris K. Udall Scholars	59	$5000	$ 350	110	Agriculture, Biology, Earth Science, Geography, History, Natural Resources, Nuclear Science, Political Science.
National Association of Minority Engineering Program Administrators National Scholarship Fund	101	$5000	$1000	10–50	Aviation/Aerospace, Chemical Engineering, Civil Engineering, Computer Science/Data Processing, Electrical Engineering/ Electronics, Engineering-Related Technologies, Engineering/Technology, Materials Science, Engineering, and Metallurgy, Mechanical Engineering. Limited to American Indian/Alaska Native, Black (non-Hispanic), Hispanic students.

Scholarships, Grants & Prizes At-a-Glance

Award Name	Page Number	Highest Dollar Amount	Lowest Dollar Amount	Number of Awards	Academic/Career Areas and Eligibility Requirements
National Competition for Composers' Recordings	753	$5000	$1500	1	Talent: music/singing.
National High School Journalist of the Year/Sister Rita Jeanne Scholarships	160	$5000	$2000	5	Communications, Journalism.
National Hispanic Explorers Scholarship Program	69	$5000	$ 500	125–200	Applied Sciences, Aviation/Aerospace, Biology, Chemical Engineering, Civil Engineering, Communications, Computer Science/Data Processing, Earth Science, Electrical Engineering/Electronics, Engineering-Related Technologies, Engineering/Technology, Food Science/Nutrition.
National Leadership Development Grants	584	$5000	$ 500	75	Religion: Methodist. Limited to ethnic minority students.
National Senior High Communication Contest	267	$5000	$ 100	30–40	Filmmaking/Video, Graphics/Graphic Arts/Printing, Literature/English/Writing.
Native American Leadership in Education (NALE)	122	$5000	$ 500	30	Business/Consumer Services, Education, Humanities, Physical Sciences and Math, Science, Technology, and Society. Limited to American Indian/Alaska Native students.
Network of Executive Women in Hospitality, Inc. Scholarship	78	$5000	$ 500	varies	Architecture, Food Service/Hospitality, Hospitality Management, Interior Design, Landscape Architecture, Travel/Tourism.
Nevada Student Incentive Grant	701	$5000	$ 100	400–800	State: Nevada; Studying in Nevada.
Nevada Women's Fund Scholarships	701	$5000	$ 500	50–80	State: Nevada.
New England Film and Video Festival Awards	267	$5000	$ 250	9–15	Filmmaking/Video; State: Connecticut, Maine, Massachusetts, New Hampshire, New York, Rhode Island, Vermont.
New York Council Navy League Scholarship Fund	544	$5000	$3000	15	Military Service: Coast Guard, Marine Corp, Navy; State: Connecticut, New Jersey, New York.
New York State Tuition Assistance Program	706	$5000	$ 500	350,000–360,000	State: New York; Studying in New York.
North Carolina CPA Foundation Accounting Scholarship Program	45	$5000	$1000	20–30	Accounting, Business/Consumer Services; State: North Carolina; Studying in North Carolina.
North Dakota Board of Nursing Education Loan Program	390	$5000	$2000	30–35	Nursing; State: North Dakota.
Nurse Education Scholarship Loan Program (NESLP)	390	$5000	$3000	varies	Nursing; State: North Carolina; Studying in North Carolina.
Nurse Scholars Program—Undergraduate (North Carolina)	390	$5000	$3000	600	Nursing; State: North Carolina; Studying in North Carolina.
Optimist International Essay Contest	794	$5000	$ 650	53–56	
Police Officers and Firefighters Survivors Education Assistance Program-Alabama	503	$5000	$2000	15–30	Employment Experience: police/firefighting; State: Alabama; Studying in Alabama.
Pride Foundation/Greater Seattle Business Association Scholarship	718	$5000	$ 500	60–65	State: Alaska, Idaho, Montana, Oregon, Washington.
Quaker Chemical Foundation Scholarships	502	$5000	$2000	1	Corporate Affiliation; Employment Experience: designated career field.

Award Name	Page Number	Highest Dollar Amount	Lowest Dollar Amount	Number of Awards	Academic/Career Areas and Eligibility Requirements
Raymond W. Cannon Memorial Scholarship Program	304	$5000	$2000		Health and Medical Sciences, Law/Legal Services. Limited to Black (non-Hispanic) students.
Regents Professional Opportunity Scholarship	45	$5000	$1000	220	Accounting, Architecture, Dental Health/Services, Engineering/Technology, Health and Medical Sciences, Interior Design, Landscape Architecture, Law/Legal Services, Nursing, Pharmacy, Psychology, Social Services; State: New York; Studying in New York.
Regents Professional Opportunity Scholarships	706	$5000	$1000	220	State: New York; Studying in New York.
Robert Guthrie PKU Scholarship and Awards	529	$5000	$ 500	6–12	Disability: Physically Disabled.
Roseburg Forest Products Sons and Daughters Scholarship	500	$5000	$2000	varies	Corporate Affiliation; Employment Experience: designated career field; State: Oregon.
Sallie Mae Fund American Dream Scholarship	618	$5000	$ 500	varies	Limited to Black (non-Hispanic) students.
Scholarship Grants for Prospective Educators	210	$5000	$1000	30	Education.
Scholarship Program	495	$5000	$ 500	4000	Corporate Affiliation; Employment Experience: designated career field.
Screen Actors Guild Foundation/John L. Dales Scholarship (Transitional)	479	$5000	$3000	varies	Civic Affiliation: Screen Actors' Guild; Employment Experience: designated career field.
Scroll Technologies Scholarship Fund	491	$5000	$ 500		Corporate Affiliation; State: Arkansas.
Silvestre Reyes Scholarship Program	586	$5000	$ 500	varies	State: Texas. Limited to Hispanic students.
SME Corporate Scholars	254	$5000	$1000	varies	Engineering/Technology, Trade/Technical Specialties.
Society of Plastics Engineers Scholarship Program	147	$5000	$1000	19	Chemical Engineering, Civil Engineering, Electrical Engineering/Electronics, Engineering/Technology, Industrial Design, Materials Science, Engineering, and Metallurgy, Mechanical Engineering, Trade/Technical Specialties.
South Carolina Teacher Loan Program	211	$5000	$2500	1121	Education, Special Education; State: South Carolina; Studying in South Carolina.
Southwestern Bell Bates Scholarship Fund	577	$5000	$ 500		State: Arkansas. Limited to ethnic minority students.
Sun Student College Scholarship Program	519	$5000	$1000	1–11	Employment Experience: community service; State: Arizona.
TCU Texas Youth Entrepreneur of the Year	729	$5000	$1000	6	State: Texas.
TELACU Engineering Award	141	$5000	$2500	1–2	Chemical Engineering, Computer Science/Data Processing, Electrical Engineering/Electronics, Engineering-Related Technologies, Engineering/Technology, Mechanical Engineering; Nationality: Hispanic; State: California. Limited to Hispanic students.

Scholarships, Grants & Prizes At-a-Glance

Award Name	Page Number	Highest Dollar Amount	Lowest Dollar Amount	Number of Awards	Academic/Career Areas and Eligibility Requirements
Tribal Business Management Program (TBM)	38	$5000	$ 500	35	Accounting, Business/Consumer Services, Computer Science/Data Processing, Economics, Electrical Engineering/Electronics, Engineering-Related Technologies, Engineering/Technology, Travel/Tourism. Limited to American Indian/Alaska Native students.
Underwood-Smith Teacher Scholarship Program	216	$5000	$1620	53	Education; State: West Virginia; Studying in West Virginia.
United Agribusiness League Scholarship Program	56	$5000	$1000	10–15	Agribusiness, Agriculture, Animal/Veterinary Sciences, Economics, Food Science/Nutrition, Horticulture/Floriculture, Landscape Architecture.
United Agricultural Benefit Trust Scholarship	56	$5000	$1000	7	Agribusiness, Agriculture, Animal/Veterinary Sciences, Economics, Food Science/Nutrition, Horticulture/Floriculture, Landscape Architecture; Civic Affiliation: United Agribusiness League.
University Film and Video Association Carole Fielding Student Grants	269	$5000	$1000	5	Filmmaking/Video.
Utah Centennial Opportunity Program for Education	736	$5000	$ 300	3500	State: Utah; Studying in Utah.
Vincent Abate Memorial Scholarship	511	$5000	$1000	1–3	Employment Experience: harness racing.
Warner Norcross and Judd LLP Scholarship for Minority Students	344	$5000	$1000	3	Law/Legal Services. Limited to ethnic minority students.
William Randolph Hearst Endowed Scholarship for Minority Students	324	$5000	$2500	1	Humanities, Social Sciences. Limited to ethnic minority students.
Willits Foundation Scholarship Program	503	$5000	$1000	10	Corporate Affiliation.
Women in New Media Young Women's College Scholarship Program	176	$5000	$1000	3–5	Computer Science/Data Processing; State: New York; Studying in New York; Talent: designated field specified by sponsor.
Women's Independence Scholarship Program	802	$5000	$ 250	500–600	
Women's Jewelry Association Scholarship Program	431	$5000	$ 500	5–15	Trade/Technical Specialties; Talent: designated field specified by sponsor.
Worldstudio Foundation Scholarship Program	80	$5000	$1000	30–50	Architecture, Arts, Fashion Design, Filmmaking/Video, Graphics/Graphic Arts/Printing, Industrial Design, Interior Design, Landscape Architecture.
Missouri College Guarantee Program	695	$4900	$ 100	varies	State: Missouri; Studying in Missouri.
Chaffer Scholarship Trust	363	$4800	$ 700	22–25	Music; Talent: music.
Teacher Assistant Scholarship Program	208	$4800	$1600	varies	Education; State: North Carolina; Studying in North Carolina.
Indiana Higher Education Award	727	$4700	$ 200	38,000–43,660	State: Indiana; Studying in Indiana.
Washington State Work Study Program	739	$4650	$2212	8000	State: Washington; Studying in Washington.

Award Name	Page Number	Highest Dollar Amount	Lowest Dollar Amount	Number of Awards	Academic/Career Areas and Eligibility Requirements
ASCSA Summer Sessions	65	$4500	$ 500	10	Anthropology, Archaeology, Architecture, Art History, Arts, Historic Preservation and Conservation, History, Humanities, Museum Studies, Near and Middle East Studies, Philosophy, Religion/Theology; Talent: designated field specified by sponsor.
Big 33 Scholarship Foundation, Inc. Scholarships	645	$4500	$ 500	150–200	State: Ohio, Pennsylvania.
Community Foundation for Greater Buffalo Scholarships	655	$4500	$ 200	600–900	State: New York.
Florida College Student of the Year Award	668	$4500	$1500	20	Studying in Florida; Talent: leadership.
Northeast Georgia Pilot Nurse Service Cancelable Loan	393	$4500	$2500	100	Nursing; State: Georgia; Studying in Georgia.
Registered Nurse Service Cancelable Loan Program	393	$4500	$ 200	varies	Nursing; State: Georgia; Studying in Georgia.
Service-Cancelable Stafford Loan-Georgia	187	$4500	$2000	500–1200	Dental Health/Services, Health and Medical Sciences, Nursing, Therapy/Rehabilitation; State: Georgia; Studying in Georgia.
Terry Fox Humanitarian Award	604	$4457	$2600	20	
State Need Grant	739	$4300	$2200	55,000	State: Washington; Studying in Washington.
Iowa Foster Child Grants	678	$4200	$2000	varies	State: Iowa; Studying in Iowa.
Tennessee Teaching Scholars Program	214	$4200	$1000	30–250	Education; State: Tennessee; Studying in Tennessee.
Canada Millennium Excellence Award Program	579	$4084	$3267	2100	Nationality: Canadian.
Persons Case Scholarships	575	$4055	$ 811	5–20	State: Alberta; Studying in Alberta.
American Legion Department of Tennessee Oratorical Contest	641	$4000	$1000	1–3	State: Tennessee; Talent: public speaking.
American Society for Enology and Viticulture Scholarships	56	$4000	$ 500	varies	Agriculture, Chemical Engineering, Food Science/Nutrition, Horticulture/Floriculture.
Biller/Jewish Foundation for Education of Women	626	$4000	$2000	varies	State: New York; Religion: Jewish; Studying in New York.
Bridging Scholarships	282	$4000	$2500	40–80	Foreign Language.
California Wine Grape Growers Foundation Scholarship	649	$4000	$1000	5	State: California; Studying in California.
Church's Chicken Opportunity Scholarship	488	$4000	$2000		Civic Affiliation: National Academic Advising Association, Corporate Affiliation. Limited to Black (non-Hispanic) students.
Community Banker Association of Illinois Annual Scholarship Program	655	$4000	$1000	13	State: Illinois.
Community Banker Association of Illinois Children of Community Banking Scholarship	458	$4000	$1000	1	Civic Affiliation: Community Banker Association of Illinois; Employment Experience: banking; State: Illinois.
Congressional Black Caucus Spouses Education Scholarship Fund	778	$4000	$ 500	200	
Congressional Black Caucus Spouses Health Initiative	288	$4000	$ 500	200	Health Administration, Health Information Management/Technology, Health and Medical Sciences.
Donna Reed Performing Arts Scholarships	400	$4000	$ 500	9	Performing Arts.

Scholarships, Grants & Prizes At-a-Glance

Award Name	Page Number	Highest Dollar Amount	Lowest Dollar Amount	Number of Awards	Academic/Career Areas and Eligibility Requirements
E. Urner Goodman Scholarship	456	$4000	$1000	3–6	Civic Affiliation: Boy Scouts, Order of the Arrow.
Federal Junior Duck Stamp Conservation and Design Competition	91	$4000	$1000	3	Arts.
Firefighter, Ambulance, and Rescue Squad Member Tuition Reimbursement Program-Maryland	270	$4000	$ 200	100–300	Fire Sciences, Health and Medical Sciences, Trade/Technical Specialties; Employment Experience: police/firefighting; State: Maryland; Studying in Maryland.
Gerald W. and Jean Purmal Endowed Scholarship	612	$4000	$1000	varies	Limited to Black (non-Hispanic) students.
Grant Program for Dependents of Police, Fire, or Correctional Officers	511	$4000	$3000	50–55	Employment Experience: police/firefighting; State: Illinois; Studying in Illinois.
Indiana Minority Teacher and Special Education Services Scholarship Program	213	$4000	$1000	280–370	Education, Special Education, Therapy/ Rehabilitation; State: Indiana; Studying in Indiana. Limited to Black (non-Hispanic), Hispanic students.
International Association of Fire Chiefs Foundation Scholarship Award	511	$4000	$ 350	10–30	Employment Experience: fire service.
Iowa Tuition Grant Program	679	$4000	$ 100	varies	State: Iowa; Studying in Iowa.
Iowa Vocational Rehabilitation	527	$4000	$ 500	5000	Disability: Hearing Impaired, Learning Disabled, Physically Disabled, Visually Impaired; State: Iowa.
Judith McManus Price Scholarship	438	$4000	$2000	1	Urban and Regional Planning. Limited to American Indian/Alaska Native, Black (non-Hispanic), Hispanic students.
Knights of Lithuania National Scholarships	467	$4000	$1000	3–6	Civic Affiliation: Knights of Lithuania; Nationality: Lithuanian; Religion: Roman Catholic.
L. Ron Hubbard's Illustrators of the Future Contest	750	$4000	$ 500	13	Talent: art.
L. Ron Hubbard's Writers of the Future Contest	750	$4000	$ 500	13	Talent: writing.
Malcolm Baldrige Scholarship	134	$4000	$1000	1–2	Business/Consumer Services, International Studies; State: Connecticut; Studying in Connecticut.
Marion D. and Eva S. Peeples Scholarships	205	$4000	$ 500	15–30	Education, Engineering/Technology, Food Science/Nutrition, Nursing, Trade/Technical Specialties; State: Indiana; Studying in Indiana.
Minnesota Nurses Loan Forgiveness Program	299	$4000	$3000	25–35	Health and Medical Sciences, Nursing.
NAIW College Scholarship	326	$4000	$1000	varies	Insurance and Actuarial Science.
NASA Delaware Space Grant Undergraduate Tuition Scholarship	70	$4000	$1400	6–12	Applied Sciences, Aviation/Aerospace, Chemical Engineering, Civil Engineering, Earth Science, Electrical Engineering/Electronics, Engineering-Related Technologies, Engineering/Technology, Mechanical Engineering, Meteorology/Atmospheric Science, Physical Sciences and Math, Science, Technology, and Society; Studying in Delaware, Pennsylvania.
National Scholarship Contest	771	$4000	$1000	7	Must be in high school.
Part-time Grant Program	727	$4000	$ 50	4680–6700	State: Indiana; Studying in Indiana.

Award Name	Page Number	Highest Dollar Amount	Lowest Dollar Amount	Number of Awards	Academic/Career Areas and Eligibility Requirements
Red River Valley Association Scholarship Grant Program	564	$4000	$ 500	10–40	Military Service: General.
Richard and Ethel Koff Memorial Scholarship Fund	363	$4000	$1000	1	Music; State: Massachusetts.
Screen Actors Guild Foundation/ John L. Dales Scholarship Fund (Standard)	479	$4000	$3000	varies	Civic Affiliation: Screen Actors' Guild; Employment Experience: designated career field.
Sigma Delta Chi Scholarships	721	$4000	$3000	4–7	Studying in District of Columbia, Maryland, Virginia; Talent: designated field specified by sponsor, leadership, writing.
Society of Physics Students Scholarships	481	$4000	$1000	17–22	Civic Affiliation: Society of Physics Students.
Travel and Training Fund	767	$4000	$ 500	25–100	Talent: athletics/sports.
Union Plus Scholarship Program	484	$4000	$ 500	110–130	Civic Affiliation: AFL-CIO.
Union Plus Credit Card Scholarship Program	441	$4000	$ 500	varies	Civic Affiliation: American Federation of State, County, and Municipal Employees.
United Parcel Service Diversity Scholarship Program	263	$4000	$3000	2	Environmental Science, Health and Medical Sciences, Occupational Safety and Health; Civic Affiliation: American Society of Safety Engineers. Limited to ethnic minority students.
United Way/YWCA Scholarship Fund for Women	660	$4000	$3000	1	State: Massachusetts.
Verizon Foundation Scholarship	621	$4000	$2000		State: New Jersey, New York, Pennsylvania. Limited to Black (non-Hispanic) students.
Vertical Flight Foundation Scholarship	108	$4000	$2000	10–12	Aviation/Aerospace, Electrical Engineering/ Electronics, Mechanical Engineering.
Washington National Guard Scholarship Program	538	$4000	$ 200	varies	Military Service: Air Force National Guard, Army National Guard; State: Washington.
Weyerhaeuser Company Foundation Scholarships	503	$4000	$1000	65	Corporate Affiliation.
HOPE—Helping Outstanding Pupils Educationally	671	$3900	$ 300	140,000–170,000	State: Georgia; Studying in Georgia.
TOPS Honors Award	686	$3894	$1541	varies	State: Louisiana; Studying in Louisiana.
Sallie Mae Fund Unmet Need Scholarship Program	799	$3800	$1000	varies	
National Beta Club Scholarship	470	$3750	$1000	208	Civic Affiliation: National Beta Club.
United States Naval Academy Class of 1963 Foundation Grant	570	$3750	$1000		Military Service: Navy.
Osler, Hoskin and Harcourt National Essay Competition	700	$3714	$ 743	3	Studying in Alberta, British Columbia, Manitoba, New Brunswick, Newfoundland, North West Territories, Nova Scotia, Ontario, Prince Edward Island, Quebec, Saskatchewan, Yukon.
Teletoon Animation Scholarship Award Competition	90	$3714	$1486	12	Arts, Filmmaking/Video; State: Alberta, British Columbia, Manitoba, New Brunswick, Newfoundland, North West Territories, Nova Scotia, Ontario, Prince Edward Island, Quebec, Saskatchewan.

Scholarships, Grants & Prizes At-a-Glance

Award Name	Page Number	Highest Dollar Amount	Lowest Dollar Amount	Number of Awards	Academic/Career Areas and Eligibility Requirements
American Society of Naval Engineers Scholarship	66	$3500	$2500	18–22	Applied Sciences, Aviation/Aerospace, Civil Engineering, Electrical Engineering/ Electronics, Energy and Power Engineering, Engineering/Technology, Marine/Ocean Engineering, Materials Science, Engineering, and Metallurgy, Mechanical Engineering, Nuclear Science, Physical Sciences and Math.
Angus Foundation Scholarships	471	$3500	$1000	20	Civic Affiliation: American Angus Association.
Armenian Students Association of America, Inc. Scholarships	577	$3500	$1000	30	Nationality: Armenian.
Corporate Sponsored Scholarship Program	678	$3500	$ 400	20–70	Studying in Washington.
Edmund F. Maxwell Foundation Scholarship	665	$3500	$1000	110	State: Washington.
Foundation Scholarships	721	$3500	$1500	20–30	State: New York.
Graco Inc. Scholarship Program	496	$3500	$1500	varies	Corporate Affiliation; Employment Experience: designated career field.
Kansas National Guard Educational Assistance Award Program	536	$3500	$ 250	400	Military Service: Air Force National Guard, Army National Guard; State: Kansas; Studying in Kansas.
National Federation of Paralegal Associates, Inc. West Scholarship	344	$3500	$1500	2	Law/Legal Services.
Outdoor Writers Association of America Bodie McDowell Scholarship Award	163	$3500	$2500	3–6	Communications, Filmmaking/Video, Journalism, Literature/English/Writing, Photojournalism/Photography, TV/Radio Broadcasting; Talent: amateur radio, photography/photogrammetry/filmmaking, writing.
Paul and Edith Babson Scholarship	617	$3500	$1000	varies	State: Massachusetts. Limited to Black (non-Hispanic) students.
Twin Cities Chapter Undergraduate Scholarship	44	$3500	$ 500	varies	Accounting, Business/Consumer Services. Limited to Black (non-Hispanic) students.
TOPS Performance Award	687	$3494	$1141	varies	State: Louisiana; Studying in Louisiana.
American Society of Landscape Architects/NSSGA Student Competition	340	$3400	$1000	3	Landscape Architecture.
New Century Scholarship	737	$3400	$1060	145	State: Utah; Studying in Utah.
Pennsylvania State Grants	717	$3300	$ 300	151,000	State: Pennsylvania.
Veterans Grant-Pennsylvania	563	$3300	$ 800	varies	Military Service: General; State: Pennsylvania.
South Carolina Tuition Grants Program	723	$3240	$ 100	11,000	State: South Carolina; Studying in South Carolina.
Ashby B. Carter Memorial Scholarship Fund Scholarship Achievement Award	469	$3200	$1900	3	Civic Affiliation: National Alliance of Postal and Federal Employees.
Cal Grant C	647	$3168	$ 576	7761	State: California; Studying in California.
UPS Scholarship	742	$3150	$1050	21–63	Studying in Wisconsin.
TOPS Opportunity Award	687	$3094	$ 741	varies	State: Louisiana; Studying in Louisiana.
1040 K Race Scholarships	41	$3000	$1000	1–3	Accounting; State: Florida; Studying in Florida. Limited to Black (non-Hispanic) students.
A.T. Cross Scholarship	502	$3000	$1000	varies	Corporate Affiliation; State: Rhode Island.

Award Name	Page Number	Highest Dollar Amount	Lowest Dollar Amount	Number of Awards	Academic/Career Areas and Eligibility Requirements
AACE International Competitive Scholarship	73	$3000	$ 750	15–25	Architecture, Aviation/Aerospace, Chemical Engineering, Civil Engineering, Computer Science/Data Processing, Electrical Engineering/Electronics, Engineering-Related Technologies, Engineering/Technology, Mechanical Engineering.
Actuarial Scholarships for Minority Students	121	$3000	$ 500	20–40	Business/Consumer Services. Limited to American Indian/Alaska Native, Black (non-Hispanic), Hispanic students.
African-American Achievement Scholarship	581	$3000	$2500	9	Nationality: African; State: Massachusetts. Limited to Black (non-Hispanic) students.
Airports Council International-North America Commissioners Committee Scholarship	95	$3000	$2000	3	Aviation/Aerospace.
Al-Ameen Scholarship	790	$3000	$1000	1–2	Must be in high school.
Alice M. and Samuel Yarnold Scholarship	289	$3000	$1000	20–30	Health and Medical Sciences, Nursing, Therapy/Rehabilitation; State: New Hampshire.
American Chemical Society Scholars Program	136	$3000	$2500	100–200	Chemical Engineering, Materials Science, Engineering, and Metallurgy, Natural Sciences. Limited to American Indian/Alaska Native, Black (non-Hispanic), Hispanic students.
American Foreign Service Association (AFSA) Financial Aid Award Program	441	$3000	$ 500	50–60	Civic Affiliation: American Foreign Service Association; Employment Experience: U.S. Foreign Service.
American Indian Education Foundation Scholarship	576	$3000	$1500	100–150	Limited to American Indian/Alaska Native students.
American Legion Scholarship—Ohio	449	$3000	$2000	15–20	Civic Affiliation: American Legion or Auxiliary.
American Nuclear Society James R. Vogt Scholarship	235	$3000	$2000	1	Engineering/Technology, Nuclear Science.
American Physical Society Scholarship for Minority Undergraduate Physics Majors	406	$3000	$2000	20–25	Physical Sciences and Math. Limited to American Indian/Alaska Native, Black (non-Hispanic), Hispanic students.
Arizona Nursery Association Foundation Scholarship	314	$3000	$ 500	12–15	Horticulture/Floriculture.
Arkansas Academic Challenge Scholarship Program	643	$3000	$2000		State: Arkansas; Studying in Arkansas.
Arthur Ross Foundation Scholarship	734	$3000	$1000	varies	State: Alabama, Florida, Georgia, Kentucky, Louisiana, Mississippi, New York, North Carolina, South Carolina.
Arts Recognition and Talent Search (ARTS)	89	$3000	$ 100	varies	Arts, Filmmaking/Video, Literature/English/Writing, Performing Arts, Photojournalism/Photography.
Associated General Contractors of America-New York State Chapter Scholarship Program	151	$3000	$2500	10–15	Civil Engineering, Surveying; Surveying Technology, Cartography, or Geographic Information Science, Transportation; State: New York.
Charles C. Ely Educational Fund	691	$3000	$1000	varies	State: Massachusetts.
College Scholarship Program	587	$3000	$1000	2900–3500	Nationality: Latin American/Caribbean, Mexican, Spanish. Limited to Hispanic students.
CollegeBound Last-Dollar Grant	651	$3000	$ 400	90–250	State: Maryland.
Curt Greene Memorial Scholarship	756	$3000	$2500	1–2	Talent: animal/agricultural competition.

Scholarships, Grants & Prizes At-a-Glance

Award Name	Page Number	Highest Dollar Amount	Lowest Dollar Amount	Number of Awards	Academic/Career Areas and Eligibility Requirements
Daughters of the Cincinnati Scholarship	534	$3000	$1000	10	Military Service: Air Force, Army, Coast Guard, Marine Corp, Navy.
Deerfield Plastics/Barker Family Scholarship	495	$3000	$1000	12	Corporate Affiliation; Employment Experience: designated career field; State: Kentucky, Massachusetts.
Developmental Disabilities, Mental Health, Child Welfare and Juvenile Justice Workforce Tuition Assistance Program	298	$3000	$ 500	300–400	Health and Medical Sciences, Nursing, Social Services, Special Education, Therapy/Rehabilitation; Employment Experience: designated career field; State: Maryland; Studying in Maryland.
Donaldson Company, Inc. Scholarship Program	495	$3000	$1000		Corporate Affiliation.
Eaton Corporation Henry R. Towne Trust Scholarship	496	$3000	$1000	12	Corporate Affiliation.
Edna F. Blum Foundation	610	$3000	$1000		State: New York. Limited to Black (non-Hispanic) students.
Educators for Maine Program	200	$3000	$2000	varies	Education; State: Maine.
Edward and Hazel Stephenson Scholarship	611	$3000	$1000		Limited to Black (non-Hispanic) students.
Elks Emergency Educational Grants	460	$3000	$1000	varies	Civic Affiliation: Elks Club.
Federated Garden Clubs of Connecticut, Inc.	113	$3000	$2000	2–5	Biology, Horticulture/Floriculture, Landscape Architecture; State: Connecticut.
Financial Support for Marine or Maritime Studies	809	$3000	$ 500	varies	
Firefighters National Trust FDNY September 11th Scholarship Fund	509	$3000	$1000	varies	Employment Experience: police/firefighting.
Francis D. Lyon Scholarships	268	$3000	$2000	2	Filmmaking/Video.
Golden Gate Restaurant Association Scholarship Foundation	277	$3000	$1000	1–15	Food Service/Hospitality, Hospitality Management; State: California.
Hispanic Association of Colleges and Universities Scholarship Programs	785	$3000	$ 500	varies	
Hope Pierce Tartt Scholarship Fund	675	$3000	$1000	varies	State: Texas; Studying in Texas.
Hormel Foods Scholarship	497	$3000	$1000	10	Corporate Affiliation.
Hubertus W.V. Willems Scholarship for Male Students	144	$3000	$2000	varies	Chemical Engineering, Engineering-Related Technologies, Physical Sciences and Math; Civic Affiliation: National Association for the Advancement of Colored People. Limited to ethnic minority students.
Incentive Scholarship for Certain Constituent Institutions	708	$3000	$2000	varies	State: North Carolina; Studying in North Carolina.
Institute of Management Accountants Memorial Education Fund Diversity Scholarships	42	$3000	$1000	varies	Accounting.
International Order Of The Golden Rule Award of Excellence	284	$3000	$ 500	1–3	Funeral Services/Mortuary Science.
Joseph H. Bearns Prize in Music	752	$3000	$2000	2	Talent: music.
Joseph Shinoda Memorial Scholarship	320	$3000	$ 250	10–20	Horticulture/Floriculture; Talent: designated field specified by sponsor.

Award Name	Page Number	Highest Dollar Amount	Lowest Dollar Amount	Number of Awards	Academic/Career Areas and Eligibility Requirements
Kentucky Department of Agriculture Agribusiness/ Governor's Scholars Program Scholarship	54	$3000	$ 300	10–20	Agribusiness, Agriculture; State: Kentucky.
Kildee Scholarships	59	$3000	$2000	3	Agriculture.
King Olav V Norwegian-American Heritage Fund	83	$3000	$ 250	12–15	Area/Ethnic Studies; Employment Experience: community service, designated career field.
Logistics Education Foundation Scholarship	234	$3000	$1000	5–10	Engineering-Related Technologies.
Maryland State Nursing Scholarship and Living Expenses Grant	386	$3000	$ 200	600	Nursing; State: Maryland; Studying in Maryland.
Memorial Foundation for Jewish Culture International Scholarship Program for Community Service	82	$3000	$1000	varies	Area/Ethnic Studies, Education, Religion/ Theology, Social Services; Religion: Jewish.
Montana University System Honor Scholarship	696	$3000	$2000	300–400	State: Montana; Studying in Montana.
NAAS II National Scholarship Awards	790	$3000	$1000	1	
National Asphalt Pavement Association Scholarship Program	154	$3000	$ 500	50–150	Civil Engineering.
Native American Journalists Association Scholarships	334	$3000	$ 500	10–14	Journalism; Talent: writing. Limited to American Indian/Alaska Native students.
New Jersey Society of Certified Public Accountants College Scholarship Program	44	$3000	$2500	4–45	Accounting; State: New Jersey; Studying in New Jersey.
New Jersey State Golf Association Caddie Scholarship	516	$3000	$1500	200	Employment Experience: private club/caddying; State: New Jersey.
NJSA Scholarship Program	74	$3000	$1500	5–8	Architecture; State: New Jersey.
Nursing Student Loan Program	395	$3000	$ 250	150–1800	Nursing; State: Wisconsin; Studying in Wisconsin.
Ohio American Legion Scholarships	474	$3000	$2000	15–18	Civic Affiliation: American Legion or Auxiliary; Military Service: General.
Ordean Loan Program	45	$3000	$1500	40–50	Accounting, Education, Health Administration, Health Information Management/ Technology, Nursing, Social Services; State: Minnesota; Studying in Minnesota.
Oregon Collectors Association Bob Hasson Memorial Scholarship	714	$3000	$1500	3	State: Oregon; Studying in Oregon.
Oregon Collectors Association Bob Hasson Memorial Scholarship Fund	711	$3000	$1500	3	State: Oregon; Studying in Oregon.
OSCPA Educational Foundation Scholarship Program	46	$3000	$ 500	50–100	Accounting; State: Oregon; Studying in Oregon.
Pennsylvania Youth Foundation Scholarship	477	$3000	$1000	varies	Civic Affiliation: Freemasons; State: Pennsylvania.
Pepsi-Cola Youth Bowling Championships	490	$3000	$ 500	292	Civic Affiliation: Young American Bowling Alliance; Talent: bowling.
PFLAG Scholarship Awards Program	795	$3000	$1500	5–10	

Scholarships, Grants & Prizes At-a-Glance

Award Name	Page Number	Highest Dollar Amount	Lowest Dollar Amount	Number of Awards	Academic/Career Areas and Eligibility Requirements
PHCC Educational Foundation Scholarship Program	79	$3000	$1500	5	Architecture, Business/Consumer Services, Civil Engineering, Engineering-Related Technologies, Engineering/Technology, Heating, Air-Conditioning, and Refrigeration Mechanics, Mechanical Engineering, Trade/Technical Specialties.
Polish Heritage Scholarship	599	$3000	$1500	varies	Nationality: Polish; State: Maryland.
Print and Graphics Scholarships	286	$3000	$ 500	200–300	Graphics/Graphic Arts/Printing; Talent: designated field specified by sponsor.
Profile in Courage Essay Contest	788	$3000	$ 500	7	Must be in high school.
Sara Lee Branded Apparel Scholarships	493	$3000	$1000	varies	Corporate Affiliation.
SARA Student Design Competition	79	$3000	$1000	3	Architecture.
Scholarship for Young Women	805	$3000	$1000	15	
Scholarship Program for the Blind and Visually Impaired	523	$3000	$1000	15	Disability: Visually Impaired.
Scholarships for Education, Business and Religion	125	$3000	$ 500	varies	Business/Consumer Services, Education, Religion/Theology; State: California.
Seaspace Scholarship Program	417	$3000	$ 500	10–15	Science, Technology, and Society.
Society of Louisiana CPAs Scholarships	46	$3000	$ 500	8–12	Accounting; State: Louisiana; Studying in Louisiana.
SURFLANT Scholarship	570	$3000	$ 500	varies	Military Service: Navy.
Sussman-Miller Educational Assistance Fund	631	$3000	$ 500	30–40	State: New Mexico.
TELACU Scholarship Program	665	$3000	$ 500	150	State: California; Studying in California.
Tennessee Education Lottery Scholarship Program Tennessee HOPE Scholarship	729	$3000	$1500	varies	State: Tennessee; Studying in Tennessee.
Truckload Carriers Association Scholarship Fund	130	$3000	$1500	18	Business/Consumer Services, Transportation; Employment Experience: designated career field.
Two/Ten International Footwear Foundation Scholarship	521	$3000	$ 200	200–250	Employment Experience: leather/footwear.
United Methodist Church Hispanic, Asian, and Native American Scholarship	605	$3000	$1000	200–250	Religion: Methodist. Limited to American Indian/Alaska Native, Asian/Pacific Islander, Hispanic students.
Video Contest for College Students	775	$3000	$ 100	8	
Vincent J. Maiocco Scholarship	661	$3000	$1000	1–4	State: Connecticut.
William P. Willis Scholarship	711	$3000	$2000	32	State: Oklahoma; Studying in Oklahoma.
Women's Partnership Scholarship Fund for Women	660	$3000	$1000	4	State: Massachusetts; Studying in Massachusetts.
Writer's Digest Self-Published Book Awards	768	$3000	$ 500	10	Talent: writing.
WSTLA American Justice Essay Scholarship Contest	740	$3000	$1000	3	Studying in Washington.
West Virginia Higher Education Grant Program	741	$2846	$ 350	10,755–11,000	State: West Virginia; Studying in Pennsylvania, West Virginia.
California Farm Bureau Scholarship	52	$2750	$2000	23	Agribusiness, Agriculture; State: California; Studying in California.
Michigan Tuition Grants	692	$2750	$ 100	varies	State: Michigan; Studying in Michigan.

Award Name	Page Number	Highest Dollar Amount	Lowest Dollar Amount	Number of Awards	Academic/Career Areas and Eligibility Requirements
Educational Assistance Grants-Maryland	689	$2700	$ 400	11,000–20,000	State: Maryland; Studying in Maryland.
Aero Club of New England Aviation Scholarship Program	92	$2500	$ 500	13	Aviation/Aerospace; State: Connecticut, Maine, Massachusetts, New Hampshire, Rhode Island, Vermont; Studying in Connecticut, Maine, Massachusetts, New Hampshire, Rhode Island, Vermont; Talent: designated field specified by sponsor.
Agnes Jones Jackson Scholarship	469	$2500	$1500	varies	Civic Affiliation: National Association for the Advancement of Colored People. Limited to ethnic minority students.
Air Traffic Control Association Scholarship	92	$2500	$ 600	7–12	Aviation/Aerospace, Engineering/Technology; Employment Experience: air traffic controller field.
Albert and Florence Newton Nurse Scholarship Newton Fund	390	$2500	$ 250	5–20	Nursing; Studying in Rhode Island.
Albert E. and Florence W. Newton Nurse Scholarship	393	$2500	$ 500	varies	Nursing; Employment Experience: designated career field; State: Rhode Island; Studying in Rhode Island.
All-Ink.com College Scholarship Program	769	$2500	$1000	5–10	
American Association of University Women - Aviaetric Fund	770	$2500	$ 100	varies	
American Association of University Women - Blackwell Fund	771	$2500	$ 100	varies	
American Institute of Architects Minority/Disadvantaged Scholarship	74	$2500	$ 500	20	Architecture.
American Institute of Architects/ American Architectural Foundation Minority/ Disadvantaged Scholarships	74	$2500	$ 500	20	Architecture.
American Legion Auxiliary Department of Florida National President's Scholarship	545	$2500	$1000	1	Military Service: General; State: Florida.
American Legion Auxiliary National President's Scholarship	546	$2500	$1000	3	Military Service: General; State: Michigan.
American Legion Auxiliary National President's Scholarships	550	$2500	$2000	10	Military Service: General.
American Legion Auxiliary, National President's Scholarship	504	$2500	$1000	3	Employment Experience: community service; Military Service: General.
American Legion Department of Pennsylvania State Oratorical Contest	640	$2500	$1000	3	State: Pennsylvania; Talent: public speaking.
American Legion Department of Washington Children and Youth Scholarships	450	$2500	$1500	2	Civic Affiliation: American Legion or Auxiliary; Military Service: General; State: Washington; Studying in Washington.
American Legion High School Oratorical Contest	641	$2500	$ 100	15	State: Texas.

Scholarships, Grants & Prizes At-a-Glance

Award Name	Page Number	Highest Dollar Amount	Lowest Dollar Amount	Number of Awards	Academic/Career Areas and Eligibility Requirements
ARTBA-TDF Highway Workers Memorial Scholarship Program	772	$2500	$1000	varies	
Artist's Magazine's Annual Art Competition	750	$2500	$ 50	45	Talent: art.
ASCAP Foundation Morton Gould Young Composer Awards	362	$2500	$ 250	20–25	Music; Talent: music.
Association for Women in Architecture Scholarship	75	$2500	$1000	3	Architecture, Interior Design, Landscape Architecture.
Bank of America Minority Scholarship	122	$2500	$ 750	1	Business/Consumer Services; State: Florida. Limited to ethnic minority students.
Bat Conservation International Student Scholarship Program	112	$2500	$ 500	15	Biology, Natural Resources, Natural Sciences.
BIA Higher Education Grant	588	$2500	$ 50	1–130	Limited to American Indian/Alaska Native students.
Bildner Family Scholarship	607	$2500	$1000		State: New Jersey. Limited to Black (non-Hispanic) students.
Bowfin Memorial Scholarship	520	$2500	$ 250	8–40	Employment Experience: designated career field; Military Service: Navy; State: Hawaii.
Bronislaw Kaper Awards for Young Artists	686	$2500	$ 500	4	State: California; Talent: music.
Burlington Northern Santa Fe Foundation/Hispanic College Fund Scholarship Program	41	$2500	$ 500	10	Accounting, Business/Consumer Services, Computer Science/Data Processing, Economics, Engineering-Related Technologies, Engineering/Technology; State: Arizona, California, Colorado, Illinois, Missouri, New Mexico, Texas. Limited to Hispanic students.
California Council of the Blind Scholarships	524	$2500	$ 375	varies	Disability: Visually Impaired; State: California; Studying in California.
Career Aid to Technology Students Program	702	$2500	$ 100	300	State: New Hampshire.
Charles and Lucille King Family Foundation Scholarships	159	$2500	$1250	10–20	Communications, Filmmaking/Video, TV/Radio Broadcasting.
Claire B. Schultz Memorial Scholarship	655	$2500	$ 750	1–3	State: Florida.
Colonial Bank Scholarship	581	$2500	$ 750		State: Florida. Limited to ethnic minority students.
Common Knowledge Scholarship	778	$2500	$ 250	5–30	
Community College Transfer Programs	587	$2500	$1500	varies	Nationality: Hispanic. Limited to Hispanic students.
COMTO Boston/Garrett A. Morgan Scholarship	75	$2500	$1000	7	Architecture, Civil Engineering, Drafting, Education, Electrical Engineering/Electronics, Engineering-Related Technologies, Engineering/Technology, Mechanical Engineering, Surveying; Surveying Technology, Cartography, or Geographic Information Science, Transportation; State: Massachusetts. Limited to ethnic minority students.
Congressional Hispanic Caucus Institute Scholarship Awards	582	$2500	$1000	111	Limited to Hispanic students.
Connecticut SPJ Bob Eddy Scholarship Program	330	$2500	$ 500	4	Journalism, Photojournalism/Photography; Talent: writing.
Denise Lynn Padgett Scholarship Fund	656	$2500	$ 750	1	State: Florida.

Award Name	Page Number	Highest Dollar Amount	Lowest Dollar Amount	Number of Awards	Academic/Career Areas and Eligibility Requirements
Duck Brand Duct Tape "Stuck at Prom" Scholarship Contest	785	$2500	$ 500	3	Must be in high school.
Edna Aimes Scholarship	299	$2500	$2000	1–3	Health and Medical Sciences, Pharmacy, Psychology, Public Health; State: New York; Studying in New York.
Emerging Texas Artist Scholarship	90	$2500	$ 500	8–15	Arts; Studying in Texas.
Engineers Foundation of Ohio Engineering Scholarships	243	$2500	$ 500	10–14	Engineering/Technology; State: Ohio; Studying in Ohio.
Felix Morley Journalism Competition	757	$2500	$ 250	6	Talent: writing.
Foundation for Surgical Technology Scholarship Fund	296	$2500	$ 500	5–10	Health and Medical Sciences.
Fulfilling Our Dreams Scholarship Fund	601	$2500	$ 500	40–60	Nationality: Hispanic, Latin American/Caribbean. Limited to Hispanic students.
George M. Brooker Collegiate Scholarship for Minorities	412	$2500	$1000	3	Real Estate. Limited to ethnic minority students.
Gubelmann Family Foundation Scholarship Fund	656	$2500	$ 750		State: Florida.
Harry and Bertha Bronstein Memorial Scholarship	656	$2500	$ 750		State: Florida.
Harry and Rose Howell Scholarship	807	$2500	$2000	1	
HBCU-Central.com Minority Scholarship Program	585	$2500	$1000	3–10	Limited to ethnic minority students.
Hemophilia Resources of America	526	$2500	$1000	22	Disability: Physically Disabled.
Henry Belknapp Memorial Scholarship	691	$2500	$1000	14	State: Massachusetts.
High School Program	587	$2500	$1000	varies	Nationality: Hispanic. Limited to Hispanic students.
Hilton Head Jazz Society Scholarship Award	400	$2500	$1500	1–3	Performing Arts; Talent: music/singing.
Horticulture Research Institute Timothy Bigelow Scholarship	314	$2500	$1500	varies	Horticulture/Floriculture, Landscape Architecture; State: Connecticut, Maine, Massachusetts, New Hampshire, Rhode Island, Vermont.
HSF/Association of Latino Professionals in Finance and Accounting Scholarship	42	$2500	$1250	varies	Accounting. Limited to Hispanic students.
Humana Foundation Scholarship Program	497	$2500	$1250	75	Corporate Affiliation.
Hydro Power Contest	224	$2500	$ 500	6–10	Energy and Power Engineering, Hydrology.
Indian American Scholarship Fund	589	$2500	$ 500	varies	Nationality: Indian; State: Georgia. Limited to Asian/Pacific Islander students.
Inez Peppers Lovett Scholarship Fund	198	$2500	$ 750	1	Education; State: Florida. Limited to Black (non-Hispanic) students.
International Airlines Travel Agent Network Ronald A. Santana Memorial Foundation	322	$2500	$ 500	2–14	Hospitality Management, Travel/Tourism.

Scholarships, Grants & Prizes At-a-Glance

Award Name	Page Number	Highest Dollar Amount	Lowest Dollar Amount	Number of Awards	Academic/Career Areas and Eligibility Requirements
International Foodservice Editorial Council Communications Scholarship	160	$2500	$1000	1–6	Communications, Food Science/Nutrition, Food Service/Hospitality, Graphics/Graphic Arts/Printing, Hospitality Management, Journalism, Literature/English/Writing, Photojournalism/Photography, Travel/ Tourism; Talent: photography/ photogrammetry/filmmaking, writing.
James F. Lincoln Arc Welding Foundation Awards Program	787	$2500	$ 50	200–400	
Jennifer Curtis Byler Scholarship for the Study of Public Affairs	162	$2500	$1000	1	Communications, Journalism, Political Science; Employment Experience: designated career field.
John F. Duffy Scholarship	506	$2500	$1200	varies	Employment Experience: police/firefighting.
Jos L. Muscarelle Foundation Scholarship	614	$2500	$1000		Limited to Black (non-Hispanic) students.
Kaiser Permanente Allied Healthcare Scholarship	297	$2500	$2000	20–40	Health and Medical Sciences, Social Services, Therapy/Rehabilitation; State: California; Studying in California.
Kentucky Educational Excellence Scholarship (KEES)	682	$2500	$ 125	55,000–60,000	State: Kentucky; Studying in Kentucky.
Kim Love Satory Scholarship	39	$2500	$ 750	1	Accounting; State: Florida; Talent: English language, leadership.
Koniag Education Foundation Scholarship	591	$2500	$ 500	130–170	Limited to American Indian/Alaska Native students.
Korean-American Scholarship Foundation Northeastern Region Scholarships	591	$2500	$1000	60	Nationality: Korean; Studying in Connecticut, Maine, Massachusetts, New Hampshire, New Jersey, New York, Rhode Island, Vermont. Limited to Asian/Pacific Islander students.
Larry Fullerton Photojournalism Scholarship	403	$2500	$ 500	1–2	Photojournalism/Photography; State: Ohio; Studying in Ohio; Talent: photography/photogrammetry/filmmaking.
Law Enforcement Officers' Dependents Scholarship-Arkansas	505	$2500	$2000	27–32	Employment Experience: police/firefighting; State: Arkansas; Studying in Arkansas.
Legislative Endowment Scholarships	705	$2500	$1000		State: New Mexico; Studying in New Mexico.
Leveraging Educational Assistance Partnership	643	$2500	$ 100	varies	State: Arizona; Studying in Arizona.
Leveraging Educational Assistance Partnership (LEAP)	736	$2500	$ 300	3000	State: Utah; Studying in Utah.
Library Research Grants	84	$2500	$ 500	varies	Art History, Arts; Studying in California; Talent: art.
Lilly Lorenzen Scholarship	747	$2500	$1500	1	Talent: Scandinavian language.
Loblolly Scholarship Fund	656	$2500	$ 750		State: Florida.
Mabry M. Noxon Scholarship Fund	75	$2500	$ 750		Architecture, Business/Consumer Services; State: Florida.
Maine State Society Foundation Scholarship	688	$2500	$1000	5–10	State: Maine; Studying in Maine.
Major General James Ursano Scholarship Fund	538	$2500	$ 800	varies	Military Service: Army.
Marine Corps Scholarship Foundation	568	$2500	$ 500	1000	Military Service: Marine Corp.
Marshall E. McCullough- National Dairy Shrine Scholarships	59	$2500	$1000	2	Agriculture, Animal/Veterinary Sciences.

Award Name	Page Number	Highest Dollar Amount	Lowest Dollar Amount	Number of Awards	Academic/Career Areas and Eligibility Requirements
Mary Rubin and Benjamin M. Rubin Scholarship Fund	650	$2500	$ 500	30–35	State: Maryland.
Massachusetts Gilbert Matching Student Grant Program	386	$2500	$ 200	varies	Nursing; State: Massachusetts; Studying in Massachusetts.
Matthew "Bump" Mitchell /Sun-Sentinel Scholarship	656	$2500	$ 750	1	State: Florida.
Michael and Donna Griffith Scholarship	616	$2500	$1000		Limited to Black (non-Hispanic) students.
Michelin North America Dependent Scholarship	493	$2500	$1000	15	Corporate Affiliation.
Michelin/TIA Scholarships	457	$2500	$1250	3	Civic Affiliation: Tire Industry Association.
Michigan Merit Award	692	$2500	$1000	varies	State: Michigan.
Millie Belafonte Wright Scholarship and Grant Evaluation	110	$2500	$1000	varies	Behavioral Science, Women's Studies.
Minnesota Gay/Lesbian/Bisexual/ Transgender Scholarship Fund	790	$2500	$ 500	20–30	
Minority Retention Grant-Wisconsin	623	$2500	$ 250	varies	State: Wisconsin; Studying in Wisconsin. Limited to ethnic minority students.
National Achievement Scholarship Program	594	$2500	$ 500	800	Must be in high school. Limited to Black (non-Hispanic) students.
National Beef Ambassador Program	772	$2500	$ 800	1–3	Must be in high school.
New Jersey Society of Architects Scholarship	78	$2500	$1500	varies	Architecture; State: New Jersey.
New Mexico Student Incentive Grant	705	$2500	$ 200		State: New Mexico; Studying in New Mexico.
NHCF Statewide Student Aid Program	702	$2500	$ 100	300–400	State: New Hampshire.
NPM Koinonia/Board of Directors Scholarship	365	$2500	$2000	2	Music, Religion/Theology; Talent: music/singing.
OEEF Scholarship	265	$2500	$1250	18	Environmental Science; State: Ohio; Studying in Ohio.
Page Education Foundation Grant	598	$2500	$ 900	500–600	State: Minnesota; Studying in Minnesota. Limited to ethnic minority students.
Pellegrini Scholarship Grants	604	$2500	$ 500	50	Nationality: Swiss; State: Connecticut, Delaware, New Jersey, New York, Pennsylvania.
Promise of Nursing Scholarship	383	$2500	$1000	varies	Nursing; Studying in California, Florida, Georgia, Illinois, Massachusetts, Michigan, New Jersey, Tennessee, Texas.
Rhode Island Masonic Grand Lodge Scholarship	789	$2500	$ 750	200–250	
Sacramento Bee Journalism Scholarship Program	337	$2500	$1500	16	Journalism; State: California.
Sacramento Bee Scholar Athlete Scholarship	720	$2500	$1500	1–10	State: California.
Scholarship-Leadership Awards Program	466	$2500	$ 500	275–280	Civic Affiliation: Greek Organization.
Scotts Company Scholars Program	320	$2500	$ 500	7	Horticulture/Floriculture.
Society of Physics Students Outstanding Student in Research	480	$2500	$1500	1–2	Civic Affiliation: Society of Physics Students.

Scholarships, Grants & Prizes At-a-Glance

Award Name	Page Number	Highest Dollar Amount	Lowest Dollar Amount	Number of Awards	Academic/Career Areas and Eligibility Requirements
Stephen Madry Peck, Jr. Memorial Scholarship	282	$2500	$ 750	1	Foreign Language; State: Florida. Limited to Black (non-Hispanic) students.
Stockholm Scholarship Program	807	$2500	$2000	1	
Student Design Competition	325	$2500	$1000	3–7	Industrial Design.
SuperCollege.com Scholarship	802	$2500	$ 500	1–2	
Surgical Technology Scholarships	295	$2500	$ 500	5–10	Health and Medical Sciences.
Swiss Benevolent Society of Chicago Scholarships	603	$2500	$ 750	30	Nationality: Swiss; State: Illinois, Wisconsin.
Terrill H. Bell Teaching Incentive Loan	215	$2500	$ 900	365	Education; State: Utah; Studying in Utah.
Virginia Tuition Assistance Grant Program (Private Institutions)	726	$2500	$1900	18,600	State: Virginia; Studying in Virginia.
Washington State Trial Lawyers Association Presidents' Scholarship	740	$2500	$2000	1	State: Washington.
Wisconsin Higher Education Grants (WHEG)	743	$2500	$ 250	varies	State: Wisconsin; Studying in Wisconsin.
Angelfire Scholarship	555	$2400	$1000	15	Military Service: General.
Datatel Scholars Foundation Scholarship	779	$2400	$1000	varies	
Glenn Miller Instrumental Scholarship	755	$2400	$1200	2	Talent: music/singing.
Kentucky Tuition Grant (KTG)	682	$2400	$ 200	10,000–12,000	State: Kentucky; Studying in Kentucky.
American Cancer Society, Florida Division College Scholarship Program	632	$2300	$1850	150–175	State: Florida; Studying in Florida.
American Legion Department of Virginia High School Oratorical Contest Award	641	$2300	$ 500	3	State: Virginia.
DC Department High School Oratorical Contest	636	$2300	$ 100	4	State: District of Columbia, Maryland, Virginia.
Massachusetts Assistance for Student Success Program	690	$2300	$ 300	25,000–30,000	State: Massachusetts; Studying in Connecticut, District of Columbia, Maine, Massachusetts, New Hampshire, Pennsylvania, Rhode Island, Vermont.
Institute of Food Technologists Food Engineering Division Junior/Senior Scholarship	271	$2250	$1000	61	Food Science/Nutrition.
Peter and Alice Koomruian Armenian Education Fund	598	$2250	$1000	5–20	Nationality: Armenian.
Phi Kappa Tau Foundation Scholarships	477	$2250	$1000	20–25	Civic Affiliation: Greek Organization.
Postsecondary Child Care Grant Program-Minnesota	693	$2200	$ 100	varies	State: Minnesota; Studying in Minnesota.
Scholarship Incentive Program-Delaware	663	$2200	$ 700	1000–1300	State: Delaware; Studying in Delaware, Pennsylvania.
Tennessee Student Assistance Award Program	729	$2130	$ 100	26,000	State: Tennessee; Studying in Tennessee.
Prairie Baseball Academy Scholarships	631	$2049	$ 405	16–80	Studying in Alberta; Talent: athletics/sports.

PROFILES OF SCHOLARSHIPS, GRANTS & PRIZES

ACADEMIC FIELDS/CAREER GOALS

ACCOUNTING

ACCOUNTANCY BOARD OF OHIO http://acc.ohio.gov/

ACCOUNTANCY BOARD OF OHIO EDUCATIONAL ASSISTANCE PROGRAM

Program intended for minority students or students with financial need. Applicant must be enrolled as accounting major at an accredited Ohio college or university in a five-year degree program. Applicant must be an Ohio resident. Please refer to Web site for further details: http://acc.ohio.gov/educasst.html.

Academic Fields/Career Goals: Accounting.

Award: Scholarship for use in sophomore, junior, or senior years; not renewable. *Number:* varies. *Amount:* $7700.

Eligibility Requirements: Applicant must be enrolled or expecting to enroll at a four-year institution or university; resident of Ohio and studying in Ohio. Available to U.S. citizens.

Application Requirements: Application, financial need analysis, transcript, FAFSA. *Deadline:* varies.

Contact: Kay Sedgmer, Scholarship Secretary, Accountancy Board of Ohio
Accountancy Board of Ohio
77 South High Street, 18th Floor
Columbus, OH 43266-0301
Phone: 614-466-4135
Fax: 614-466-2628
E-mail: kay.sedgmer@acc.state.oh.us

AMERICAN INSTITUTE OF CERTIFIED PUBLIC ACCOUNTANTS http://www.aicpa.org

ACCOUNTEMPS/AMERICAN INSTITUTE OF CERTIFIED PUBLIC ACCOUNTANTS STUDENT SCHOLARSHIP

Scholarships are given to students who are declared accounting, finance, or information systems major with an overall and major GPA of at least 3.0. Eligible applicants will have completed at least 30 semester hours. Must be enrolled as a full-time undergraduate student at an accredited college or university in the United States. Must be an AICPA student affiliate member.

Academic Fields/Career Goals: Accounting.

Award: Scholarship for use in sophomore, junior, senior, or graduate years; not renewable. *Number:* 2. *Amount:* $2500.

Eligibility Requirements: Applicant must be enrolled or expecting to enroll full-time at a two-year or four-year institution or university. Applicant must have 3.0 GPA or higher. Available to U.S. citizens.

Application Requirements: Application, references, test scores, transcript. *Deadline:* April 1.

Contact: Scholarship Coordinator
American Institute of Certified Public Accountants
1211 Avenue of the Americas
New York, NY 10036-8775
Phone: 212-596-6270
E-mail: educat@aicpa.org

SCHOLARSHIPS FOR MINORITY ACCOUNTING STUDENTS

Scholarships are given to minority students who are declared accounting majors with an overall and major GPA of 3.3. Must be a minority student who has satisfactorily completed at least 30 semester hours (or equivalent) including at least six semester hours in accounting. Must be enrolled as a full-time undergraduate or graduate student at an accredited college or university.

Academic Fields/Career Goals: Accounting.

Award: Scholarship for use in junior, senior, or graduate years; not renewable. *Number:* varies. *Amount:* up to $5000.

Eligibility Requirements: Applicant must be American Indian/Alaska Native, Asian/Pacific Islander, Black (non-Hispanic), or Hispanic and enrolled or expecting to enroll full-time at a four-year institution or university. Available to U.S. citizens.

Application Requirements: Application, essay, financial need analysis, references, transcript. *Deadline:* June 1.

Contact: Scholarship Coordinator
American Institute of Certified Public Accountants
1211 Avenue of the Americas
New York, NY 10036-8775
Phone: 212-596-6270
E-mail: educat@aicpa.org

AMERICAN SOCIETY OF WOMEN ACCOUNTANTS http://www.aswa.org

AMERICAN SOCIETY OF WOMEN ACCOUNTANTS SCHOLARSHIP

Recipients of The American Society of Women Accountants Scholarship will be chosen from applicants that have completed a minimum of 60 semester hours or 90 quarter hours with a declared major in accounting. Applicants shall be attending an accredited college, university, or professional school of accounting. Please contact local chapter for further details; Chapter Directory is located at http://www.aswa.org

Academic Fields/Career Goals: Accounting.

Award: Scholarship for use in junior, senior, graduate, or postgraduate years; not renewable. *Number:* varies. *Amount:* varies.

Eligibility Requirements: Applicant must be enrolled or expecting to enroll full or part-time at a two-year or four-year or technical institution or university. Available to U.S. and non-U.S. citizens.

Application Requirements: Application, essay, financial need analysis, references, transcript. *Deadline:* varies.

Contact: Local Chapter directory at http://www.aswa.org
American Society of Women Accountants
8405 Greensboro Drive, Suite 800
McLean, VA 22102

AMERICAN WOMAN'S SOCIETY OF CERTIFIED PUBLIC ACCOUNTANTS–GEORGIA AFFILIATE http://www.awscpa.org

AMERICAN WOMAN'S SOCIETY OF CERTIFIED PUBLIC ACCOUNTANTS-GEORGIA AFFILIATE SCHOLARSHIP

Scholarship available for undergraduate and graduate students enrolled in a Georgia college or university in the field of accounting. Must have either completed or be currently enrolled in Intermediate Accounting II. Must submit essay with application on why you are interested in receiving this scholarship. Deadline for applications is April 30. For information and application contact Scholarship Committee Chair.

Academic Fields/Career Goals: Accounting.

Award: Scholarship for use in sophomore, junior, senior, or graduate years; not renewable. *Number:* 2. *Amount:* $750.

Eligibility Requirements: Applicant must be enrolled or expecting to enroll at a four-year institution or university and studying in Georgia. Available to U.S. citizens.

American Woman's Society of Certified Public Accountants–Georgia Affiliate (continued)

Application Requirements: Application, essay, references, transcript. *Deadline:* April 30.

Contact: Amy Knowles-Jones, Scholarship Committee Chair
American Woman's Society of Certified Public Accountants–Georgia Affiliate
Oxford Industries, Inc.
222 Piedmont Avenue, NE
Atlanta, GA 30308
Phone: 404-653-1242
Fax: 404-653-1575

AMERICAN WOMAN'S SOCIETY OF CERTIFIED PUBLIC ACCOUNTANTS–NEW YORK CITY AFFILIATE http://www.awscpa-nyc.org

AMERICAN WOMAN'S SOCIETY OF CERTIFIED PUBLIC ACCOUNTANTS–NEW YORK CITY AFFILIATE SCHOLARSHIP

Scholarships offered to encourage students to enter, and excel in, the field of accounting. May qualify in two ways: Attend a school within 50 miles of New York City with no restrictions on location of permanent residence, or, have permanent residence within 50 miles of New York City with no restrictions on location of institution you attend.

Academic Fields/Career Goals: Accounting.

Award: Scholarship for use in sophomore, junior, or senior years; not renewable. *Number:* 1–2. *Amount:* $1000–$1500.

Eligibility Requirements: Applicant must be enrolled or expecting to enroll full or part-time at a two-year or four-year institution or university. Applicant must have 3.0 GPA or higher. Available to U.S. and non-U.S. citizens.

Application Requirements: Application. *Deadline:* April 15.

Contact: Director of Scholarships
American Woman's Society of Certified Public Accountants–New York City Affiliate
PO Box 7643 FDR Station
New York, NY 10150-1913
E-mail: info@awscpa-nyc.org

ASSOCIATION OF CERTIFIED FRAUD EXAMINERS http://www.cfenet.com

RITCHIE-JENNINGS MEMORIAL SCHOLARSHIP

Available to full-time criminal justice and accounting majors only. Please provide transcripts, original essay, and three letters of recommendation, including one from a certified fraud examiner (CFE).

Academic Fields/Career Goals: Accounting; Criminal Justice/Criminology.

Award: Scholarship for use in freshman, sophomore, junior, senior, graduate, or postgraduate years; not renewable. *Number:* 15. *Amount:* $1000.

Eligibility Requirements: Applicant must be enrolled or expecting to enroll full-time at a four-year institution or university. Available to U.S. and non-U.S. citizens.

Application Requirements: Application, essay, interview, references, transcript. *Deadline:* April 30.

Contact: Tony Rolston, Research Editor
Association of Certified Fraud Examiners
The Gregor Building, 716 West Avenue
Austin, TX 78701
Phone: 800-245-3321
Fax: 512-478-9297
E-mail: scholarships@cfenet.com

ASSOCIATION OF LATINO PROFESSIONALS IN FINANCE AND ACCOUNTING http://www.alpfa.org

HSF-ALPFA SCHOLARSHIPS

One-time award to undergraduate and graduate Latino students pursuing degrees in accounting, finance, and related majors based on financial need and academic performance. Must be enrolled full-time at a U.S. college or university. Minimum 3.0 GPA required. Must be U.S. citizen or legal permanent resident.

Academic Fields/Career Goals: Accounting; Business/Consumer Services.

Award: Scholarship for use in freshman, sophomore, junior, senior, or graduate years; not renewable. *Number:* varies. *Amount:* $1000–$5000.

Eligibility Requirements: Applicant must be Hispanic and enrolled or expecting to enroll full-time at a two-year or four-year institution or university. Applicant must have 3.0 GPA or higher. Available to U.S. citizens.

Application Requirements: Application, essay, financial need analysis, references, transcript. *Deadline:* April 15.

Contact: Shanina Rivera, Executive Director
Association of Latino Professionals in Finance and Accounting
510 West Sixth Street
Suite 400
Los Angeles, CA 90014
Phone: 213-243-0004
Fax: 213-243-0006
E-mail: scholarships@national.alpfa.org

CATCHING THE DREAM

TRIBAL BUSINESS MANAGEMENT PROGRAM (TBM)

Renewable scholarships available for Native-American and Alaska Native students to study business administration, economic development, and related subjects, with the goal to provide experts in business management to Native-American tribes in the U.S. Must be at least one-quarter Native-American from a federally recognized, state recognized, or terminated tribe. Must demonstrate high academic achievement, depth of character, leadership, seriousness of purpose, and service orientation. Application deadlines are March 15, April 15, and September 15.

Academic Fields/Career Goals: Accounting; Business/Consumer Services; Computer Science/Data Processing; Economics; Electrical Engineering/Electronics; Engineering/Technology; Engineering-Related Technologies; Travel/Tourism.

Award: Scholarship for use in freshman, sophomore, junior, senior, or graduate years; renewable. *Number:* up to 35. *Amount:* $500–$5000.

Eligibility Requirements: Applicant must be American Indian/Alaska Native and enrolled or expecting to enroll full-time at a four-year institution or university. Available to U.S. citizens.

Application Requirements: Resume, transcript. *Deadline:* varies.

Contact: Recruitment Office
Catching the Dream
8200 Mountain Road, NE, Suite 203
Albuquerque, NM 87110
Phone: 505-262-2351
Fax: 505-262-0534
E-mail: nscholarsh@aol.com

CENTER FOR SCHOLARSHIP ADMINISTRATION http://www.scholarshipprograms.org

BANK OF AMERICA ADA ABILITIES SCHOLARSHIP

Renewable scholarships are available to students who meet the definition of disabled as defined by the American with Disabilities Act and who reside in states where Bank of America has retail operations. For more details and an application see Web site.

Academic Fields/Career Goals: Accounting; Business/Consumer Services; Computer Science/Data Processing.

Award: Scholarship for use in freshman, sophomore, or junior years; renewable. *Number:* varies. *Amount:* up to $5000.

Eligibility Requirements: Applicant must be age 39 or under and enrolled or expecting to enroll at a two-year or four-year or technical institution or university. Applicant must be hearing impaired, physically disabled, or visually impaired. Applicant must have 3.0 GPA or higher. Available to U.S. citizens.

Application Requirements: Application, essay, financial need analysis, references, transcript. *Deadline:* February 15.

Contact: Application available at Web site.

CENTRAL INTELLIGENCE AGENCY http://www.cia.gov

CENTRAL INTELLIGENCE AGENCY UNDERGRADUATE SCHOLARSHIP PROGRAM

Highly competitive, need and merit-based award for students with minimum 3.0 GPA, who are interested in working for the Central Intelligence Agency upon graduation. Renewable for four years of undergraduate study. After graduation, must work 3 to 6 years, based on years of sponsorship. Deadlines are August 2 and November 1. Information at Web site: http://www.cia.gov. Must apply in senior year of high school or sophomore year in college.

Academic Fields/Career Goals: Accounting; Business/Consumer Services; Computer Science/Data Processing; Economics; Electrical Engineering/Electronics; Foreign Language; Geography; Graphics/Graphic Arts/Printing; International Studies; Political Science; Surveying; Surveying Technology, Cartography, or Geographic Information Science.

Award: Scholarship for use in freshman, sophomore, junior, or senior years; renewable. *Number:* varies. *Amount:* up to $18,000.

Eligibility Requirements: Applicant must be enrolled or expecting to enroll full-time at a four-year institution or university. Applicant must have 3.0 GPA or higher. Available to U.S. citizens.

Application Requirements: Application, financial need analysis, resume, references, test scores, transcript. *Deadline:* varies.

Contact: Scholarship Information
Central Intelligence Agency
Recruitment Center
L 100 LF7
Washington, DC 20505

CIRI FOUNDATION http://www.ciri.com/tcf

CARL H. MARRS SCHOLARSHIP FUND

To encourage students seeking an undergraduate degree or graduate degree in business administration, economics, finance, organizational management, accounting, or similar field. Applicant must be Alaska Native student. For more details see Web site: http://www.ciri.com/tcf.

Academic Fields/Career Goals: Accounting; Business/Consumer Services; Economics.

Award: Scholarship for use in freshman, sophomore, junior, senior, or graduate years; not renewable. *Number:* varies. *Amount:* varies.

Eligibility Requirements: Applicant must be enrolled or expecting to enroll full-time at a two-year or four-year institution or university.

Application Requirements: Application, essay, references, transcript, proof of eligibility, birth certificate or adoption decree. *Deadline:* June 1.

Contact: CIRI Foundation
2600 Cordova Street, Suite 206
Anchorage, AK 99503
Phone: 907-263-5582
Fax: 907-263-5588
E-mail: tcf@ciri.com

COLORADO SOCIETY OF CERTIFIED PUBLIC ACCOUNTANTS EDUCATIONAL FOUNDATION http://www.cocpa.org

COLORADO COLLEGE AND UNIVERSITY SCHOLARSHIPS

Award of $1000 available to declared accounting majors at Colorado colleges and universities with accredited accounting programs. Must have completed at least 8 semester hours of accounting courses. Overall GPA and accounting GPA must each be at least 3.0. Must be Colorado resident.

Academic Fields/Career Goals: Accounting.

Award: Scholarship for use in sophomore, junior, senior, graduate, or postgraduate years; not renewable. *Number:* 15–20. *Amount:* $1000.

Eligibility Requirements: Applicant must be enrolled or expecting to enroll full or part-time at a four-year institution or university; resident of Colorado and studying in Colorado. Applicant must have 3.0 GPA or higher. Available to U.S. citizens.

Application Requirements: Application, references, transcript. *Deadline:* March 1.

Contact: Gena Mantz, Membership Coordinator
Colorado Society of Certified Public Accountants Educational Foundation
7979 East Tufts Avenue, Suite 500
Denver, CO 80237-2845
Phone: 303-741-8613
Fax: 303-773-2877
E-mail: gmantz@cocpa.org

ETHNIC DIVERSITY COLLEGE AND UNIVERSITY SCHOLARSHIPS

Award of $1000 for declared accounting major at a Colorado college or university. Must be African-American, Hispanic, Asian-American, American-Indian, or Pacific Islander and have completed at least 8 semester hours of accounting courses. Scholarship is awarded for the fall semester. Must be Colorado resident. Minimum 3.0 GPA required.

Academic Fields/Career Goals: Accounting.

Award: Scholarship for use in sophomore, junior, senior, graduate, or postgraduate years; not renewable. *Number:* 2. *Amount:* $1000.

Eligibility Requirements: Applicant must be American Indian/Alaska Native, Asian/Pacific Islander, Black (non-Hispanic), or Hispanic; enrolled or expecting to enroll full or part-time at a four-year institution or university; resident of Colorado and studying in Colorado. Applicant must have 3.0 GPA or higher. Available to U.S. citizens.

Application Requirements: Application, transcript. *Deadline:* June 30.

Contact: Gena Mantz, Membership Coordinator
Colorado Society of Certified Public Accountants Educational Foundation
7979 East Tufts Avenue, Suite 500
Denver, CO 80237-2845
Phone: 303-741-8613
Fax: 303-773-2877
E-mail: gmantz@cocpa.org

GORDON SCHEER SCHOLARSHIP

Award of $1250 for a declared accounting major attending a college or university in Colorado. Must have completed intermediate accounting. Minimum 3.5 GPA required. Submit application, official transcript, and three references. May reapply. Must be Colorado resident.

Academic Fields/Career Goals: Accounting.

Award: Scholarship for use in sophomore, junior, senior, graduate, or postgraduate years; not renewable. *Number:* 1. *Amount:* $1250.

Eligibility Requirements: Applicant must be enrolled or expecting to enroll full or part-time at a four-year institution or university; resident of Colorado and studying in Colorado. Applicant must have 3.5 GPA or higher. Available to U.S. citizens.

Application Requirements: Application, references, transcript. *Deadline:* June 30.

Contact: Gena Mantz, Membership Coordinator
Colorado Society of Certified Public Accountants Educational Foundation
7979 East Tufts Avenue, Suite 500
Denver, CO 80237-2845
Phone: 303-741-8613
Fax: 303-773-2877
E-mail: gmantz@cocpa.org

COMMUNITY FOUNDATION FOR PALM BEACH AND MARTIN COUNTIES, INC. http://www.yourcommunityfoundation.org

KIM LOVE SATORY SCHOLARSHIP

For female graduating senior from a Palm Beach or Martin County public or private high school interested in banking and finance. Must provide evidence of strong commitment to community service and involvement. Must demonstrate financial need.

Academic Fields/Career Goals: Accounting.

Community Foundation for Palm Beach and Martin Counties, Inc. (continued)

Award: Scholarship for use in freshman year; not renewable. *Number:* 1. *Amount:* $750–$2500.

Eligibility Requirements: Applicant must be high school student; planning to enroll or expecting to enroll full-time at a four-year institution or university; female; resident of Florida and must have an interest in English language or leadership. Available to U.S. citizens.

Application Requirements: Application, financial need analysis. *Deadline:* March 1.

Contact: Carolyn Jenco, Grants Manager/Scholarship Coordinator
Community Foundation for Palm Beach and Martin Counties, Inc.
700 South Dixie Highway
Suite 200
West Palm Beach, FL 33401

EDUCATIONAL FOUNDATION OF THE MASSACHUSETTS SOCIETY OF CERTIFIED PUBLIC ACCOUNTANT'S

http://www.cpatrack.com

F. GRANT WAITE, CPA, MEMORIAL SCHOLARSHIP

Scholarship available to undergraduate accounting major who has completed sophomore year. Must demonstrate financial need and superior academic standing. Preference given to married students with children. Information available on Web site at http://www.cpatrack.com.

Academic Fields/Career Goals: Accounting.

Award: Scholarship for use in junior or senior years. *Number:* 1. *Amount:* $1000.

Eligibility Requirements: Applicant must be enrolled or expecting to enroll full-time at a four-year institution or university. Available to U.S. citizens.

Application Requirements: Application, financial need analysis, references, transcript. *Deadline:* March 26.

Contact: Barbara Iannoni
Educational Foundation of the Massachusetts Society of Certified Public Accountant's
105 Chauncy Street
Boston, MA 02111
Phone: 800-392-6145
E-mail: biannoni@MSCPAonline.org

KATHLEEN M. PEABODY, CPA, MEMORIAL SCHOLARSHIP

Scholarship available for Massachusetts resident who has completed sophomore year. Must be accounting major with plans to seek an accounting career in Massachusetts. Must demonstrate academic excellence and financial need. Information on Web site at http://www.cpatrack.com.

Academic Fields/Career Goals: Accounting.

Award: Scholarship for use in junior or senior years. *Number:* 1. *Amount:* $2500.

Eligibility Requirements: Applicant must be enrolled or expecting to enroll full-time at a four-year institution or university and resident of Massachusetts. Available to U.S. citizens.

Application Requirements: Application, financial need analysis, references, transcript. *Deadline:* March 26.

Contact: Barbara Iannoni
Educational Foundation of the Massachusetts Society of Certified Public Accountant's
105 Chauncy Street
Boston, MA 02111
Phone: 800-392-6145
E-mail: biannoni@MSCPAonline.org

PAYCHEX, INC. ENTREPRENEUR SCHOLARSHIP

Scholarships available to students who are residents of Massachusetts and attending a Massachusetts college or university. Must be an accounting major entering their junior year, have a minimum 3.0 GPA, and demonstrate financial need. Deadline is March 26. Application and information on Web site at http://www.cpatrack.com.

Academic Fields/Career Goals: Accounting.

Award: Scholarship for use in junior year; not renewable. *Number:* 1. *Amount:* $1000.

Eligibility Requirements: Applicant must be enrolled or expecting to enroll at a four-year institution or university; resident of Massachusetts and studying in Massachusetts. Applicant must have 3.0 GPA or higher. Available to U.S. citizens.

Application Requirements: Application, financial need analysis, transcript. *Deadline:* March 26.

Contact: Barbara Iannoni
Educational Foundation of the Massachusetts Society of Certified Public Accountant's
105 Chauncy Street
Boston, MA 02111
Phone: 800-392-6145
E-mail: biannoni@MSCPAonline.org

STUDENT MANUSCRIPT CONTEST

Prizes available for students enrolled in an undergraduate accounting course at a Massachusetts college or university. Visit Web site for specific details: http://www.cpatrack.com.

Academic Fields/Career Goals: Accounting.

Award: Prize for use in freshman, sophomore, junior, or senior years. *Number:* 3. *Amount:* $500–$1500.

Eligibility Requirements: Applicant must be enrolled or expecting to enroll at a four-year institution or university and studying in Massachusetts. Available to U.S. citizens.

Application Requirements: Applicant must enter a contest, manuscript, entry form. *Deadline:* June 1.

Contact: Barbara Iannoni
Educational Foundation of the Massachusetts Society of Certified Public Accountant's
105 Chauncy Street
Boston, MA 02111
Phone: 800-392-6145
E-mail: biannoni@MSCPAonline.org

FLORIDA INSTITUTE OF CPAS EDUCATIONAL FOUNDATION

http://www.ficpa.org

EDUCATIONAL FOUNDATION SCHOLARSHIPS

Scholarships are for accounting majors who are Florida residents attending Florida college/universities. Applicants must be planning to sit for CPA exam and indicate desire to practice accounting in Florida. Scholarships are granted based on educational achievement, financial need, and demonstrated professional, social, and charitable activities. Citizens of other countries may apply, if planning to work in Florida. Minimum 3.0 GPA required.

Academic Fields/Career Goals: Accounting.

Award: Scholarship for use in senior, or graduate years; not renewable. *Number:* up to 54. *Amount:* $1250.

Eligibility Requirements: Applicant must be enrolled or expecting to enroll full-time at a four-year institution or university; resident of Florida and studying in Florida. Applicant must have 3.0 GPA or higher. Available to U.S. and non-U.S. citizens.

Application Requirements: Application, financial need analysis, references, transcript. *Deadline:* March 15.

Contact: Betsy Wilson, Educational Foundation Assistant
Florida Institute of CPAs Educational Foundation
325 West College Avenue
PO Box 5437
Tallahassee, FL 32314
Phone: 850-224-2727 Ext. 200
Fax: 850-222-8190
E-mail: wilsonb@ficpa.org

FICPA CHAPTER SCHOLARSHIP PROGRAM

Scholarships are for accounting majors who are Florida residents attending Florida college/universities. Applicants must be planning to sit for CPA exam and indicate desire to practice accounting in Florida. Scholarships are granted based on educational achievement, financial need and demonstrated professional, social, and charitable activities. Citizens of other countries may apply, if planning to work in Florida. Minimum 3.0 GPA required.

Academic Fields/Career Goals: Accounting.

Award: Scholarship for use in senior, or graduate years; not renewable. *Number:* varies. *Amount:* $1000–$1250.

Eligibility Requirements: Applicant must be enrolled or expecting to enroll full or part-time at a four-year institution or university; resident of Florida and studying in Florida. Applicant must have 3.0 GPA or higher. Available to U.S. and non-U.S. citizens.

Application Requirements: Application, financial need analysis, references, transcript. *Deadline:* Continuous.

Contact: Betsy Wilson, Educational Foundation Assistant
Florida Institute of CPAs Educational Foundation
325 West College Avenue
PO Box 5437
Tallahassee, FL 32314
Phone: 850-224-2727 Ext. 200
Fax: 850-222-8190
E-mail: wilsonb@ficpa.org

1040 K RACE SCHOLARSHIPS

Scholarships are for African-American accounting majors who are Florida residents attending Florida colleges/universities. Applicants must be planning to sit for CPA exam and indicate desire to practice accounting in Florida. Scholarships are granted based on educational achievement, financial need and demonstrated professional, social, and charitable activities. Citizens of other countries may apply, if planning to work in Florida. Must be a permanent Dade County resident.

Academic Fields/Career Goals: Accounting.

Award: Scholarship for use in senior, or graduate years; not renewable. *Number:* 1–3. *Amount:* $1000–$3000.

Eligibility Requirements: Applicant must be Black (non-Hispanic); enrolled or expecting to enroll full-time at a four-year institution or university; resident of Florida and studying in Florida. Available to U.S. and non-U.S. citizens.

Application Requirements: Application, financial need analysis, references, transcript. *Deadline:* January 31.

Contact: Betsy Wilson, Educational Foundation Assistant
Florida Institute of CPAs Educational Foundation
325 West College Avenue
PO Box 5437
Tallahassee, FL 32314
Phone: 850-224-2727 Ext. 200
Fax: 850-222-8190
E-mail: wilsonb@ficpa.org

GOVERNMENT FINANCE OFFICERS ASSOCIATION

http://www.GFOA.org

MINORITIES IN GOVERNMENT FINANCE SCHOLARSHIP

Award given to upper-division undergraduate or graduate student of public administration, governmental accounting, finance, political science, economics, or business administration to recognize outstanding performance by minority student preparing for career in state and local government finance.

Academic Fields/Career Goals: Accounting; Business/Consumer Services; Economics; Political Science.

Award: Scholarship for use in junior, senior, or graduate years; not renewable. *Number:* 1. *Amount:* $5000.

Eligibility Requirements: Applicant must be American Indian/Alaska Native, Asian/Pacific Islander, Black (non-Hispanic), or Hispanic and enrolled or expecting to enroll full or part-time at a four-year institution or university. Available to U.S. and Canadian citizens.

Application Requirements: Application, essay, resume, references, transcript. *Deadline:* varies.

Contact: Jake Lorentz, Assistant Director
Government Finance Officers Association
Scholarship Committee
203 North LaSalle Street, Suite 2700
Chicago, IL 60601
Phone: 312-977-9700 Ext. 267
Fax: 312-977-4806
E-mail: jlorentz@gfoa.org

GRAND RAPIDS COMMUNITY FOUNDATION

http://www.grfoundation.org

ECONOMIC CLUB OF GRAND RAPIDS BUSINESS STUDY ABROAD SCHOLARSHIP

Financial assistance to students studying business abroad. Individual must be interested in contributing to the growing economic health of the Grand Rapids, Michigan metropolitan area. Refer to Web site for details and application: http://www.grfoundation.org

Academic Fields/Career Goals: Accounting; Business/Consumer Services; Computer Science/Data Processing; Economics; Engineering/Technology; Engineering-Related Technologies; Physical Sciences and Math.

Award: Scholarship for use in sophomore, junior, senior, or graduate years. *Number:* 1. *Amount:* up to $2500.

Eligibility Requirements: Applicant must be enrolled or expecting to enroll at a four-year institution or university and resident of Michigan. Applicant must have 3.0 GPA or higher.

Application Requirements: Application, essay, references, transcript. *Deadline:* April 1.

Contact: See Web site.

HISPANIC COLLEGE FUND, INC.

http://www.hispanicfund.org

BURLINGTON NORTHERN SANTA FE FOUNDATION/HISPANIC COLLEGE FUND SCHOLARSHIP PROGRAM

Scholarships ranging from $500 to $2500 are available for full-time undergraduate students of Hispanic origin who reside in any of the following Burlington Northern Santa Fe-served states: Arizona, Colorado, Illinois, Missouri, New Mexico, California and Texas. Must be pursuing a bachelor's degree in accounting, economics, engineering, finance, information systems, marketing or a related major. Minimum GPA of 3.0.

Academic Fields/Career Goals: Accounting; Business/Consumer Services; Computer Science/Data Processing; Economics; Engineering/Technology; Engineering-Related Technologies.

Award: Scholarship for use in freshman, sophomore, junior, or senior years; not renewable. *Number:* 10. *Amount:* $500–$2500.

Eligibility Requirements: Applicant must be Hispanic; enrolled or expecting to enroll full-time at a two-year or four-year institution or university and resident of Arizona, California, Colorado, Illinois, Missouri, New Mexico, or Texas. Applicant must have 3.0 GPA or higher. Available to U.S. citizens.

Application Requirements: Application, essay, financial need analysis, resume, references, transcript. *Deadline:* April 15.

Contact: Stina Augustsson, Program Manager
Hispanic College Fund, Inc.
1717 Pennsylvania Avenue, NW, Suite 460
Washington, DC 20006
Phone: 202-296-5400
Fax: 202-296-3774
E-mail: hcf-info@hispanicfund.org

DENNY'S/HISPANIC COLLEGE FUND SCHOLARSHIP

One-time scholarship award open to full-time undergraduates of Hispanic descent pursuing a degree in business or a business-related major with a GPA of 3.0 or better. Eligible students who have applied to the Hispanic College Fund need not re-apply.

Academic Fields/Career Goals: Accounting; Architecture; Business/Consumer Services; Chemical Engineering; Communications; Computer

Hispanic College Fund, Inc. (continued)

Science/Data Processing; Economics; Electrical Engineering/Electronics; Engineering/Technology; Engineering-Related Technologies; Graphics/Graphic Arts/Printing; Hospitality Management.

Award: Scholarship for use in freshman, sophomore, junior, or senior years; not renewable. *Number:* 80–100. *Amount:* $1000.

Eligibility Requirements: Applicant must be Hispanic and enrolled or expecting to enroll full-time at a two-year or four-year institution or university. Applicant must have 3.0 GPA or higher. Available to U.S. citizens.

Application Requirements: Application, essay, financial need analysis, resume, references, test scores, transcript, college acceptance letter, copy of taxes, copy of SAR. *Deadline:* April 15.

Contact: Stina Augustsson, Program Manager
Hispanic College Fund, Inc.
1717 Pennsylvania Avenue, NW, Suite 460
Washington, DC 20006
Phone: 202-296-5400
Fax: 202-296-3774
E-mail: hcf-info@hispanicfund.org

ERNST AND YOUNG SCHOLARSHIP PROGRAM

Program intended for undergraduate student pursuing his or her bachelor's degree in accounting or related field. Applicant must be a U.S. citizen of Hispanic background; may reside in the U.S. or Puerto Rico. Must attend college or university in U.S. or Puerto Rico. Online application only: http://www.hispanicfund.org.

Academic Fields/Career Goals: Accounting; Business/Consumer Services; Economics.

Award: Scholarship for use in sophomore or junior years; not renewable. *Number:* varies. *Amount:* $500–$5000.

Eligibility Requirements: Applicant must be Hispanic and enrolled or expecting to enroll full-time at a four-year institution or university. Available to U.S. citizens.

Application Requirements: Application. *Deadline:* April 15.

Contact: Stina Augustsson, Program Manager
Hispanic College Fund, Inc.
1717 Pennsylvania Avenue, NW, Suite 460
Washington, DC 20006
Phone: 202-296-5400
Fax: 202-296-3774
E-mail: hcf-info@hispanicfund.org

ICI EDUCATIONAL FOUNDATION SCHOLARSHIP PROGRAM

Program intended for undergraduate student pursuing his or her associate's or bachelor's degree in business, computer science, or engineering. Applicant must be U.S. citizen of Hispanic background; may reside in U.S. or Puerto Rico. Must attend college in U.S. or Puerto Rico. Online application only: http://www.hispanicfund.org.

Academic Fields/Career Goals: Accounting; Business/Consumer Services; Computer Science/Data Processing; Engineering/Technology.

Award: Scholarship for use in freshman, sophomore, junior, or senior years; not renewable. *Number:* varies. *Amount:* $500–$5000.

Eligibility Requirements: Applicant must be Hispanic and enrolled or expecting to enroll full-time at a two-year or four-year institution or university. Applicant must have 3.0 GPA or higher. Available to U.S. citizens.

Application Requirements: Application. *Deadline:* April 15.

Contact: Stina Augustsson, Program Manager
Hispanic College Fund, Inc.
1717 Pennsylvania Avenue, NW, Suite 460
Washington, DC 20006
Phone: 202-296-5400
Fax: 202-296-3774
E-mail: hcf-info@hispanicfund.org

M & T BANK/ HISPANIC COLLEGE FUND SCHOLARSHIP PROGRAM

One-time scholarship open to full-time undergraduates of Hispanic descent pursuing a degree in business, accounting, economics, or finance. Must be a U.S. citizen residing in Maryland, Pennsylvania, Virginia or New York and have a minimum 3.0 GPA. Eligible students who have applied to the Hispanic College Fund need not re-apply.

Academic Fields/Career Goals: Accounting; Business/Consumer Services; Computer Science/Data Processing; Economics; Engineering/Technology; Engineering-Related Technologies.

Award: Scholarship for use in freshman, sophomore, junior, or senior years; not renewable. *Number:* 5–10. *Amount:* $1000–$5000.

Eligibility Requirements: Applicant must be Hispanic; enrolled or expecting to enroll full-time at a two-year or four-year institution or university and resident of Maryland, New York, Pennsylvania, or Virginia. Applicant must have 3.0 GPA or higher. Available to U.S. citizens.

Application Requirements: Application, essay, financial need analysis, resume, references, transcript, college acceptance letter, copy of taxes, copy of SAR. *Deadline:* April 15.

Contact: Stina Augustsson, Program Manager
Hispanic College Fund, Inc.
1717 Pennsylvania Avenue, NW, Suite 460
Washington, DC 20006
Phone: 202-296-5400
Fax: 202-296-3774
E-mail: hcf-info@hispanicfund.org

HISPANIC SCHOLARSHIP FUND **http://www.hsf.net**

HSF/ASSOCIATION OF LATINO PROFESSIONALS IN FINANCE AND ACCOUNTING SCHOLARSHIP

Scholarship for undergraduate and graduate college students of Hispanic heritage who are pursuing degrees in accounting or finance related fields.

Academic Fields/Career Goals: Accounting.

Award: Scholarship for use in freshman, sophomore, junior, senior, or graduate years. *Number:* varies. *Amount:* $1250–$2500.

Eligibility Requirements: Applicant must be Hispanic and enrolled or expecting to enroll at an institution or university.

Application Requirements: Application. *Deadline:* April 15.

Contact: HSF Scholarship Department
Hispanic Scholarship Fund
55 Second Street, Suite 1500
San Francisco, CA 94105
Phone: 877-HSF-INFO
Fax: 415-808-2302
E-mail: info@hsf.net

INSTITUTE OF MANAGEMENT ACCOUNTANTS **http://www.imanet.org**

INSTITUTE OF MANAGEMENT ACCOUNTANTS MEMORIAL EDUCATION FUND DIVERSITY SCHOLARSHIPS

One-time award for IMA student member pursuing a career in management accounting, financial management, and information technology. Must be U.S. or Canadian citizen. Preference given to minority students, and students with physical disabilities. Application deadline is February 15.

Academic Fields/Career Goals: Accounting.

Award: Scholarship for use in junior, senior, graduate, or postgraduate years; not renewable. *Number:* varies. *Amount:* $1000–$3000.

Eligibility Requirements: Applicant must be enrolled or expecting to enroll full or part-time at a four-year institution or university. Applicant must have 3.0 GPA or higher. Available to U.S. and Canadian citizens.

Application Requirements: Application, essay, resume, references, transcript. *Deadline:* February 15.

Contact: Susan Bender, Chapter and Council Services
Institute of Management Accountants
10 Paragon Drive
Montvale, NJ 07645-1760
Phone: 800-638-4427 Ext. 1543
Fax: 201-474-1602
E-mail: sbender@imanet.org

INSTITUTE OF MANAGEMENT ACCOUNTANTS MEMORIAL EDUCATION FUND SCHOLARSHIPS

One-time award for IMA student members pursuing a career in management accounting, financial management, and information technology. Open to upper-level undergraduates and graduate students. Minimum 3.0 GPA required. Must be U.S. or Canadian citizen. Application deadline is February 15.

Academic Fields/Career Goals: Accounting.

Award: Scholarship for use in junior, senior, graduate, or postgraduate years; not renewable. *Number:* varies. *Amount:* $3000.

Eligibility Requirements: Applicant must be enrolled or expecting to enroll full or part-time at a four-year institution or university. Applicant must have 3.0 GPA or higher. Available to U.S. and Canadian citizens.

Application Requirements: Application, essay, resume, references, transcript. *Deadline:* February 15.

Contact: Susan Bender, Chapter and Council Services
Institute of Management Accountants
10 Paragon Drive
Montvale, NJ 07645-1760
Phone: 800-638-4427 Ext. 1543
Fax: 201-474-1602
E-mail: sbender@imanet.org

KENTUCKY SOCIETY OF CERTIFIED PUBLIC ACCOUNTANTS http://www.kycpa.org

KENTUCKY SOCIETY OF CERTIFIED PUBLIC ACCOUNTANTS COLLEGE SCHOLARSHIP

Non-renewable award for accounting majors at a Kentucky college or university. Must rank in upper third of class or have a minimum 3.0 GPA. Must be a Kentucky resident.

Academic Fields/Career Goals: Accounting.

Award: Scholarship for use in junior year; not renewable. *Number:* up to 3. *Amount:* $1000.

Eligibility Requirements: Applicant must be enrolled or expecting to enroll full-time at a four-year institution or university; resident of Kentucky and studying in Kentucky. Applicant must have 3.0 GPA or higher. Available to U.S. citizens.

Application Requirements: Application, essay, references, transcript. *Deadline:* January 30.

Contact: Chad Sleczkowski, Public Relations Manager
Kentucky Society of Certified Public Accountants
1735 Alliant Avenue
Louisville, KY 40299
Phone: 502-266-5272
Fax: 502-261-9512
E-mail: chads@kycpa.org

KENTUCKY SOCIETY OF CERTIFIED PUBLIC ACCOUNTANTS HIGH SCHOOL SCHOLARSHIPS

One-time award for Kentucky high school seniors interested in becoming a certified public accountant. For use full time at a Kentucky four-year institution only. Financial need may be considered when judging equally qualified candidates. Application deadline March 1.

Academic Fields/Career Goals: Accounting.

Award: Scholarship for use in freshman year; not renewable. *Number:* 10. *Amount:* $500.

Eligibility Requirements: Applicant must be high school student; planning to enroll or expecting to enroll full-time at a four-year institution or university; resident of Kentucky and studying in Kentucky. Available to U.S. citizens.

Application Requirements: Application, transcript, list of potential colleges. *Deadline:* March 1.

Contact: Chad Sleczkowski, Public Relations Manager
Kentucky Society of Certified Public Accountants
1735 Alliant Avenue
Louisville, KY 40299
Phone: 502-266-5272
Fax: 502-261-9512
E-mail: chads@kycpa.org

LAWRENCE P. DOSS SCHOLARSHIP FOUNDATION

LAWRENCE P. DOSS SCHOLARSHIP FOUNDATION

Renewable scholarships are available to residents of Michigan who are seniors graduating from a high school in the greater Detroit area. Must be pursuing a degree in accounting, finance, management or business. Financial need considered. For more details see Web site: http://www.lawrencepdossfnd.org.

Academic Fields/Career Goals: Accounting; Business/Consumer Services.

Award: Scholarship for use in freshman, sophomore, junior, or senior years; renewable. *Number:* 5. *Amount:* $5000.

Eligibility Requirements: Applicant must be high school student; planning to enroll or expecting to enroll full-time at a four-year institution or university; single and resident of Michigan. Applicant must have 2.5 GPA or higher. Available to U.S. citizens.

Application Requirements: Application, essay, financial need analysis, interview, references, test scores, transcript. *Deadline:* March 15.

Contact: Lawrence P. Doss Scholarship Foundation
7 Oak Station
PO Box 351037
Detroit, MI 48325

MARYLAND ASSOCIATION OF CERTIFIED PUBLIC ACCOUNTANTS EDUCATIONAL FOUNDATION http://www.tomorrowscpa.org

STUDENT SCHOLARSHIP IN ACCOUNTING MD ASSOCIATION OF CPAS

Award for Maryland residents who will have completed at least 60 credit hours at a Maryland college or university by the time of the award. Must have 3.0 GPA, demonstrate commitment to 150 semester hours of education, and intend to pursue a career as a certified public accountant. Number of awards varies. Must submit accounting department chairman's signature on required statement. Must be a member of the tomorrowscpa program. U.S. citizenship required. See Web site at http://www.tomorrowscpa.org for further details.

Academic Fields/Career Goals: Accounting.

Award: Scholarship for use in junior, senior, or graduate years; renewable. *Number:* up to 20. *Amount:* $1000.

Eligibility Requirements: Applicant must be enrolled or expecting to enroll full-time at a two-year or four-year institution or university; resident of Maryland and studying in Maryland. Applicant must have 3.0 GPA or higher. Available to U.S. citizens.

Application Requirements: Application, financial need analysis, transcript. *Deadline:* April 15.

Contact: Richard Rabicoff, Director of Communications and Marketing
Maryland Association of Certified Public Accountants Educational Foundation
PO Box 4417
Lutherville, MD 21094-4417
Phone: 800-782-2036

NATIONAL ASSOCIATION OF BLACK ACCOUNTANTS, INC. http://www.nabainc.org

NATIONAL ASSOCIATION OF BLACK ACCOUNTANTS NATIONAL SCHOLARSHIP PROGRAM

One-time award for minority college students to study, full-time, any business-related discipline at an accredited institution. Candidate must be a member of the National Association of Black Accountants with a minimum GPA of 2.5. Must submit a copy of visa, if a non-U.S. citizen.

Academic Fields/Career Goals: Accounting; Business/Consumer Services; Economics.

Award: Scholarship for use in freshman, sophomore, junior, senior, or postgraduate years; not renewable. *Number:* 40. *Amount:* $500–$6000.

Eligibility Requirements: Applicant must be American Indian/Alaska Native, Asian/Pacific Islander, Black (non-Hispanic), or Hispanic and enrolled or expecting to enroll full-time at a four-year institution or university. Applicant or parent of applicant must be member of National Association of Black Accountants. Applicant must have 2.5 GPA or higher. Available to U.S. and non-U.S. citizens.

National Association of Black Accountants, Inc. (continued)

Application Requirements: Application, autobiography, essay, financial need analysis, resume, transcript, visa, if non-U.S. citizen. *Deadline:* December 31.

Contact: Challenge Okiwe, Director, Center for Advancement of Minority Accountants
National Association of Black Accountants, Inc.
7249-A Hanover Parkway
Greenbelt, MD 20770
Phone: 301-474-6222 Ext. 114
Fax: 301-474-3114
E-mail: cokiwe@nabainc.org

NATIONAL BLACK MBA ASSOCIATION-TWIN CITIES CHAPTER

http://www.nbmbaatc.org/scholarships.html

TWIN CITIES CHAPTER UNDERGRADUATE SCHOLARSHIP

Award for minority students in first, second, third, or fourth year full-time in an accredited undergraduate business or management program during the fall semester working toward a bachelors degree. Get application from Web site at http://www.nbmbaatc.org.

Academic Fields/Career Goals: Accounting; Business/Consumer Services.

Award: Scholarship for use in freshman, sophomore, junior, or senior years. *Number:* varies. *Amount:* $500–$3500.

Eligibility Requirements: Applicant must be Black (non-Hispanic) and enrolled or expecting to enroll full-time at a four-year institution or university. Available to U.S. citizens.

Application Requirements: Application, essay, transcript. *Deadline:* March 31.

Contact: Andre Thomas, President
National Black MBA Association-Twin Cities Chapter
PO Box 2709
Minneapolis, MN 55402
Phone: 651-233-7373
E-mail: scholarship@postebox.com

NATIONAL SOCIETY OF ACCOUNTANTS

http://www.nsacct.org

NATIONAL SOCIETY OF ACCOUNTANTS SCHOLARSHIP

Awards available to undergraduate students. Applicants must maintain a 3.0 GPA and have declared a major in accounting. Must submit an appraisal form and transcripts in addition to application. Must be U.S. or Canadian citizen attending an accredited U.S. school. One-time award of $500-$1000.

Academic Fields/Career Goals: Accounting.

Award: Scholarship for use in sophomore, junior, or senior years; not renewable. *Number:* 36. *Amount:* $500–$1000.

Eligibility Requirements: Applicant must be enrolled or expecting to enroll full or part-time at a two-year or four-year institution or university. Applicant must have 3.0 GPA or higher. Available to U.S. and Canadian citizens.

Application Requirements: Application, transcript, appraisal form. *Deadline:* March 10.

Contact: Susan Noell, Director of Education Programs
National Society of Accountants
1010 North Fairfax Street
Alexandria, VA 22314-1574
Phone: 703-549-6400
Fax: 703-549-2984
E-mail: giving@nsacct.org

NSA LOUIS AND FANNIE SAGER MEMORIAL SCHOLARSHIP AWARD

Up to $1000 will be awarded annually to a graduate of a Virginia public high school who is enrolled as an undergraduate at a Virginia college or university. Applicant must major in accounting. Must submit proof of graduation from a Virginia public school.

Academic Fields/Career Goals: Accounting.

Award: Scholarship for use in sophomore, junior, or senior years; not renewable. *Number:* 1. *Amount:* up to $1000.

Eligibility Requirements: Applicant must be high school student; planning to enroll or expecting to enroll full or part-time at a two-year or four-year institution or university; resident of Virginia and studying in Virginia. Applicant must have 3.0 GPA or higher. Available to U.S. and Canadian citizens.

Application Requirements: Application, transcript, appraisal form. *Deadline:* March 10.

Contact: Susan Noell, Director of Education Programs
National Society of Accountants
1010 North Fairfax Street
Alexandria, VA 22314-1574
Phone: 703-549-6400
Fax: 703-549-2984

STANLEY H. STEARMAN SCHOLARSHIP

One award for accounting major who is a relative of an active, retired, or deceased member of National Society of Accountants. Must be citizen of U.S. or Canada and attend school in the U.S. Minimum GPA of 3.0. Not available for freshman year. Submit application, appraisal form, and letter of intent.

Academic Fields/Career Goals: Accounting.

Award: Scholarship for use in sophomore, junior, senior, or graduate years; renewable. *Number:* 1. *Amount:* $2000.

Eligibility Requirements: Applicant must be enrolled or expecting to enroll full or part-time at a two-year or four-year institution or university. Applicant or parent of applicant must be member of National Society of Accountants. Applicant must have 3.0 GPA or higher. Available to U.S. and Canadian citizens.

Application Requirements: Application, essay, transcript, appraisal form. *Deadline:* March 10.

Contact: Susan Noell, Director of Education Programs
National Society of Accountants
1010 North Fairfax Street
Alexandria, VA 22314-1574
Phone: 703-549-6400
Fax: 703-549-2984
E-mail: giving@nsacct.org

NEW HAMPSHIRE SOCIETY OF CERTIFIED PUBLIC ACCOUNTANTS

http://www.nhscpa.org

NEW HAMPSHIRE SOCIETY OF CERTIFIED PUBLIC ACCOUNTANTS SCHOLARSHIP FUND

One-time award for New Hampshire resident majoring full-time in accounting. Must be entering junior or senior year at a four-year college or university or pursuing a master's degree. Transcript and recommendation required. Must apply online at Web site: http://www.nhscpa.org.

Academic Fields/Career Goals: Accounting.

Award: Scholarship for use in junior, senior, or graduate years; not renewable. *Number:* varies. *Amount:* varies.

Eligibility Requirements: Applicant must be enrolled or expecting to enroll full-time at a four-year institution or university and resident of New Hampshire.

Application Requirements: Application, references, transcript. *Deadline:* October 24.

Contact: New Hampshire Society of Certified Public Accountants
1750 Elm Street, Suite 403
Manchester, NH 03104

NEW JERSEY SOCIETY OF CERTIFIED PUBLIC ACCOUNTANTS

http://www.njscpa.org

NEW JERSEY SOCIETY OF CERTIFIED PUBLIC ACCOUNTANTS COLLEGE SCHOLARSHIP PROGRAM

Award for college juniors or those entering an accounting-related graduate program. Based upon academic merit. Must be a New Jersey resident attending a four-year New Jersey institution. Must be nominated by accounting department chair or submit application directly. Minimum 3.0 GPA required. Interview required. One-time award of up to $3000.

Academic Fields/Career Goals: Accounting.

Award: Scholarship for use in junior, or graduate years; not renewable. *Number:* 4–45. *Amount:* $2500–$3000.

Eligibility Requirements: Applicant must be enrolled or expecting to enroll full or part-time at a four-year institution or university; resident of New Jersey and studying in New Jersey. Applicant must have 3.0 GPA or higher. Available to U.S. citizens.

Application Requirements: Interview, resume, references, transcript. *Deadline:* January 21.

Contact: Ms. Janice Amatucci, Student Programs Coordinator
New Jersey Society of Certified Public Accountants
425 Eagle Rock Avenue, Suite 100
Roseland, NJ 07068-1723
Phone: 973-226-4494
Fax: 973-226-7425
E-mail: jamatucci@njscpa.org

NEW JERSEY SOCIETY OF CERTIFIED PUBLIC ACCOUNTANTS HIGH SCHOOL SCHOLARSHIP PROGRAM

This program is open to all NJ high school seniors. Selection is based on a one-hour aptitude exam and the highest scorers on this exam are invited for an interview. The winners receive accounting scholarships to the college of their choice. Five-year awards range in value from $6500-$8500.

Academic Fields/Career Goals: Accounting.

Award: Scholarship for use in freshman, sophomore, junior, senior, or graduate years; renewable. *Number:* 15–20. *Amount:* $6500–$8500.

Eligibility Requirements: Applicant must be high school student; planning to enroll or expecting to enroll full-time at a four-year institution or university and resident of New Jersey. Available to U.S. citizens.

Application Requirements: Interview, test scores. *Deadline:* October 31.

Contact: Janice Amatucci, Student Programs Coordinator
New Jersey Society of Certified Public Accountants
425 Eagle Rock Avenue, Suite 100
Roseland, NJ 07068-1723
Phone: 973-226-4494
Fax: 973-226-7425
E-mail: jamatucci@njscpa.org

NEW YORK STATE EDUCATION DEPARTMENT http://www.highered.nysed.gov

REGENTS PROFESSIONAL OPPORTUNITY SCHOLARSHIP

Scholarship for New York residents beginning or already enrolled in an approved degree-bearing program of study in New York that leads to licensure in a particular profession. See the Web site for the list of eligible professions. Must be U.S. citizen or permanent resident. Award recipients must agree to practice upon licensure in their profession in New York for 12 months for each annual payment received. Priority given to economically disadvantaged members of minority groups underrepresented in the professions.

Academic Fields/Career Goals: Accounting; Architecture; Dental Health/Services; Engineering/Technology; Health and Medical Sciences; Interior Design; Landscape Architecture; Law/Legal Services; Nursing; Pharmacy; Psychology; Social Services.

Award: Scholarship for use in freshman, sophomore, junior, senior, or graduate years. *Number:* 220. *Amount:* $1000–$5000.

Eligibility Requirements: Applicant must be enrolled or expecting to enroll full-time at a two-year or four-year institution or university; resident of New York and studying in New York. Available to U.S. citizens.

Application Requirements: *Deadline:* May 3.

Contact: Lewis J. Hall, Coordinator
New York State Education Department
Room 1078 EBA
Albany, NY 12234
Phone: 518-486-1319
Fax: 518-486-5346

NEW YORK STATE SOCIETY OF CERTIFIED PUBLIC ACCOUNTANTS FOUNDATION FOR ACCOUNTING EDUCATION http://www.nysscpa.org

FOUNDATION FOR ACCOUNTING EDUCATION SCHOLARSHIP

Up to 200 $1500 scholarships will be given to college students to encourage them to pursue a career in accounting. Must be a New York resident studying in New York and maintaining a 3.0 GPA.

Academic Fields/Career Goals: Accounting.

Award: Scholarship for use in junior or senior years; renewable. *Number:* 1–200. *Amount:* $1500.

Eligibility Requirements: Applicant must be enrolled or expecting to enroll full or part-time at a four-year institution or university; resident of New York and studying in New York. Applicant must have 3.0 GPA or higher. Available to U.S. citizens.

Application Requirements: Application, financial need analysis, transcript. *Deadline:* April 1.

Contact: Bill Pape, Associate Director Member Relations
New York State Society of Certified Public Accountants Foundation for Accounting Education
530 Fifth Avenue, Fifth Floor
New York, NY 10036-5101
Phone: 212-719-8420
E-mail: wpape@nysscpa.org

NORTH CAROLINA CPA FOUNDATION, INC. http://www.ncacpa.org

NORTH CAROLINA CPA FOUNDATION ACCOUNTING SCHOLARSHIP PROGRAM

Awards are made to juniors, seniors and fifth-year students pursuing undergraduate and graduate degrees in accounting. Applicants must be a North Carolina resident attending a North Carolina four-year college or university. Must submit essay. Details available on Web site: http://www.ncacpa.org

Academic Fields/Career Goals: Accounting; Business/Consumer Services.

Award: Scholarship for use in junior, senior, or graduate years; not renewable. *Number:* 20–30. *Amount:* $1000–$5000.

Eligibility Requirements: Applicant must be enrolled or expecting to enroll full-time at a four-year institution or university; resident of North Carolina and studying in North Carolina. Applicant must have 3.0 GPA or higher. Available to U.S. citizens.

Application Requirements: Application, applicant must enter a contest, essay, transcript. *Deadline:* February 9.

Contact: Fran Wilson, Executive Director
North Carolina CPA Foundation, Inc.
PO Box 80188
Raleigh, NC 27623-0188
Phone: 919-469-1040
Fax: 919-469-3959
E-mail: jtahler@ncacpa.org

ORDEAN FOUNDATION

ORDEAN LOAN PROGRAM

Renewable award for low-income students who are from Hermantown, Proctor, or Duluth. Students must be fully admitted into social work, management, education, accounting or nursing. Students must work in their designated field in the Duluth area for up to 3 years after graduation. Open to full-time junior or senior undergraduates. Must be U.S. citizens. Minimum 2.5 GPA required.

Academic Fields/Career Goals: Accounting; Education; Health Administration; Health Information Management/Technology; Nursing; Social Services.

Award: Forgivable loan for use in junior or senior years; renewable. *Number:* 40–50. *Amount:* $1500–$3000.

Eligibility Requirements: Applicant must be enrolled or expecting to enroll full-time at a four-year institution; resident of Minnesota and studying in Minnesota. Applicant must have 2.5 GPA or higher. Available to U.S. citizens.

Ordean Foundation (continued)

Application Requirements: Application, financial need analysis, transcript. *Deadline:* Continuous.

Contact: Trish Johnson, Financial Aid Counselor
Ordean Foundation
College of Saint Scholastica
1200 Kenwood Avenue
Duluth, MN 55811
Phone: 218-723-7027
Fax: 218-733-2229
E-mail: tjohnson@css.edu

OREGON STUDENT ASSISTANCE COMMISSION http://www.osac.state.or.us

HOMESTEAD CAPITAL HOUSING SCHOLARSHIP

Applicant must have graduated from an Oregon high school, be entering at least junior year, have a 2.75 minimum cumulative GPA, and be majoring in one of the following at a 4-year Oregon or Washington college: accounting, architecture, community development, construction management, finance, real estate, or engineering (structural, civil, or environmental). Essay required. See Web site. (http://www.osac.state.or.us).

Academic Fields/Career Goals: Accounting; Architecture; Business/Consumer Services; Civil Engineering; Engineering/Technology; Real Estate.

Award: Scholarship for use in junior or senior years; not renewable. *Number:* varies. *Amount:* $500.

Eligibility Requirements: Applicant must be enrolled or expecting to enroll at a four-year institution; resident of Oregon and studying in Oregon or Washington. Available to U.S. citizens.

Application Requirements: Application, essay, financial need analysis, transcript, activity chart. *Deadline:* March 1.

Contact: Director of Grant Programs
Oregon Student Assistance Commission
1500 Valley River Drive, Suite 100
Eugene, OR 97401-7020
Phone: 800-452-8807 Ext. 7395
E-mail: awardinfo@mercury.osac.state.or.us

OSCPA EDUCATIONAL FOUNDATION http://www.orcpa.org

OSCPA EDUCATIONAL FOUNDATION SCHOLARSHIP PROGRAM

One-time award for students majoring in accounting. Must attend an accredited Oregon college/university or community college on full-time basis. High school seniors must have a minimum 3.5 GPA. College students must have a minimum 3.2 GPA. Must be a U.S. citizen and Oregon resident. Deadline is February 7.

Academic Fields/Career Goals: Accounting.

Award: Scholarship for use in freshman, sophomore, junior, senior, graduate, or postgraduate years; not renewable. *Number:* 50–100. *Amount:* $500–$3000.

Eligibility Requirements: Applicant must be enrolled or expecting to enroll full-time at a two-year or four-year institution or university; resident of Oregon and studying in Oregon. Applicant must have 3.5 GPA or higher. Available to U.S. citizens.

Application Requirements: Application, resume, references, test scores, transcript. *Deadline:* February 7.

Contact: Tonna Hollis, Member Services/Manager
OSCPA Educational Foundation
PO Box 4555
Beaverton, OR 97076-4555
Phone: 503-641-7200 Ext. 29
Fax: 503-626-2942
E-mail: tonna@orcpa.org

PENNSYLVANIA INSTITUTE OF CERTIFIED PUBLIC ACCOUNTANTS http://www.picpa.org

JOSEPH F. TARICANI MEMORIAL SCHOLARSHIP

To promote the accounting profession and CPA credential, the PICPA awards a one-time award of $1000 to an eligible sophomore in the name of Joseph F. Taricani. Must be enrolled in a postsecondary institution in Pennsylvania.

Academic Fields/Career Goals: Accounting.

Award: Scholarship for use in sophomore year; not renewable. *Number:* 1. *Amount:* $1000.

Eligibility Requirements: Applicant must be enrolled or expecting to enroll full-time at a two-year or four-year institution or university and studying in Pennsylvania. Applicant must have 3.0 GPA or higher. Available to U.S. and non-U.S. citizens.

Application Requirements: Application, essay, resume, references, test scores, transcript. *Deadline:* March 15.

Contact: Meghan Reday, Careers in Accounting Administrator
Pennsylvania Institute of Certified Public Accountants
1650 Arch Street
17th Floor
Philadelphia, PA 19103-2099
Phone: 215-496-9272

PENNSYLVANIA INSTITUTE OF CERTIFIED PUBLIC ACCOUNTANTS SOPHOMORE SCHOLARSHIP

To promote the accounting profession and CPA credential as an exciting and rewarding career path, the PICPA awards $34,000 annually in new scholarships to full-time sophomore undergraduate students enrolled at Pennsylvania colleges and universities. Minimum 3.0 GPA required.

Academic Fields/Career Goals: Accounting.

Award: Scholarship for use in sophomore year; renewable. *Number:* 18. *Amount:* $1000–$9000.

Eligibility Requirements: Applicant must be enrolled or expecting to enroll full-time at a two-year or four-year institution or university and studying in Pennsylvania. Applicant must have 3.0 GPA or higher. Available to U.S. and non-U.S. citizens.

Application Requirements: Application, essay, resume, references, test scores. *Deadline:* March 15.

Contact: Meghan Reday, Careers in Accounting Administrator
Pennsylvania Institute of Certified Public Accountants
1650 Arch Street
17th Floor
Philadelphia, PA 19103-2099
Phone: 215-496-9272

RHODE ISLAND FOUNDATION http://www.rifoundation.org

CARL W. CHRISTIANSEN SCHOLARSHIP

Award for Rhode Island residents pursuing study in accounting or related fields.

Academic Fields/Career Goals: Accounting.

Award: Scholarship for use in senior, or graduate years. *Number:* 1–9. *Amount:* $1000.

Eligibility Requirements: Applicant must be enrolled or expecting to enroll at a two-year or four-year institution or university and resident of Rhode Island.

Application Requirements: Application.

Contact: Raymond Church, Executive Director, RI Society of Public Accountants
Phone: 401-331-5720
E-mail: rchurch@riscpa.org

SOCIETY OF LOUISIANA CERTIFIED PUBLIC ACCOUNTANTS http://www.lcpa.org

SOCIETY OF LOUISIANA CPAS SCHOLARSHIPS

One-time award for accounting majors. Applicant must be a Louisiana resident attending a four-year college or university in Louisiana. For full-time undergraduates entering their junior or senior year, or full-time graduate students. Minimum 2.5 GPA required. Deadline: January 3. Must be U.S. citizen.

Academic Fields/Career Goals: Accounting.

Award: Scholarship for use in junior, senior, or graduate years; not renewable. *Number:* 8–12. *Amount:* $500–$3000.

Eligibility Requirements: Applicant must be enrolled or expecting to enroll full-time at a four-year institution or university; resident of Louisiana and studying in Louisiana. Applicant must have 2.5 GPA or higher. Available to U.S. citizens.

Application Requirements: Application, essay, references, transcript. *Deadline:* January 3.

Contact: Lisa Richardson, Member Services Manager
Society of Louisiana Certified Public Accountants
2400 Veterans Boulevard, Suite 500
Kenner, LA 70062-4739
Phone: 504-904-1139
Fax: 504-469-7930
E-mail: lrichardson@lcpa.org

SOUTH DAKOTA CPA SOCIETY http://www.sdcpa.org/

EXCELLENCE IN ACCOUNTING SCHOLARSHIP

Scholarships available for senior undergraduate and graduate students majoring in accounting. Must have completed 90 credit hours, demonstrated excellence in academics and leadership potential. Application available online at http://www.sdcpa.org. Deadline is April 15.

Academic Fields/Career Goals: Accounting.

Award: Scholarship for use in senior, or graduate years; renewable. *Number:* 4–10. *Amount:* $500–$1500.

Eligibility Requirements: Applicant must be enrolled or expecting to enroll full-time at a four-year institution or university. Available to U.S. citizens.

Application Requirements: Application, transcript. *Deadline:* April 15.

Contact: Laura Coome, Executive Director
South Dakota CPA Society
PO Box 1798
Sioux Falls, SD 57101-1798
Phone: 605-334-3848
E-mail: lcoome@iw.net

SOUTH DAKOTA RETAILERS ASSOCIATION http://www.sdra.org

SOUTH DAKOTA RETAILERS ASSOCIATION SCHOLARSHIP PROGRAM

One-time award to assist full-time students studying for a career in retailing. Applicants must have graduated from a South Dakota High School or be enrolled in postsecondary school in South Dakota. One or more awards are given out each year. Deadline is April 2.

Academic Fields/Career Goals: Accounting; Business/Consumer Services; Computer Science/Data Processing; Electrical Engineering/Electronics; Food Service/Hospitality; Graphics/Graphic Arts/Printing; Heating, Air-Conditioning, and Refrigeration Mechanics; Hospitality Management; Interior Design; Law Enforcement/Police Administration; Trade/Technical Specialties; Travel/Tourism.

Award: Scholarship for use in freshman, sophomore, junior, senior, graduate, or postgraduate years; not renewable. *Number:* 1–10. *Amount:* $200–$1000.

Eligibility Requirements: Applicant must be enrolled or expecting to enroll full-time at a two-year or four-year or technical institution or university. Available to U.S. citizens.

Application Requirements: Application, essay, resume, references, transcript. *Deadline:* April 2.

Contact: Donna Leslie, Communications Director
South Dakota Retailers Association
PO Box 638
Pierre, SD 57501
Phone: 800-658-5545
Fax: 605-224-2059
E-mail: dleslie@sdra.org

SUNSHINE LADY FOUNDATION, INC. http://www.sunshineladyfdn.org

COUNSELOR, ADVOCATE, AND SUPPORT STAFF SCHOLARSHIP PROGRAM

Scholarship for workers in the field of domestic violence. Minimum one year working in the field of DV; employer recommendation required. For further information view Web site: http://www.sunshineladyfdn.org.

Academic Fields/Career Goals: Accounting; Business/Consumer Services; Child and Family Studies; Psychology; Social Sciences; Social Services; Therapy/Rehabilitation; Women's Studies.

Award: Scholarship for use in freshman, sophomore, junior, senior, or graduate years; renewable. *Number:* 50. *Amount:* up to $4000.

Eligibility Requirements: Applicant must be enrolled or expecting to enroll full or part-time at a two-year or four-year or technical institution or university. Applicant or parent of applicant must have employment or volunteer experience in human services. Available to U.S. citizens.

Application Requirements: Application, essay, references. *Deadline:* Continuous.

Contact: Nancy Soward, Program Director
Sunshine Lady Foundation, Inc.
4900 Randall Parkway
Suite H
Wilmington, NC 28403
Phone: 910-397-7742
Fax: 910-397-0023
E-mail: nancy@sunshineladyfdn.org

TEXAS HIGHER EDUCATION COORDINATING BOARD http://www.collegefortexans.com

FIFTH-YEAR ACCOUNTING STUDENT SCHOLARSHIP PROGRAM

One-time award for students enrolled as fifth-year accounting students at a Texas institution. Must sign statement confirming intent to take the written exam for the purpose of being granted a certificate of CPA to practice in Texas. Contact college/university financial aid office for application information.

Academic Fields/Career Goals: Accounting.

Award: Scholarship for use in senior, or graduate years; not renewable. *Number:* varies. *Amount:* up to $3000.

Eligibility Requirements: Applicant must be enrolled or expecting to enroll full or part-time at a four-year institution or university and studying in Texas. Available to U.S. and non-U.S. citizens.

Application Requirements: Application, financial need analysis, transcript, letter of intent. *Deadline:* Continuous.

Contact: Financial Aid Office at college
Texas Higher Education Coordinating Board
PO Box 12788
Austin, TX 78711-2788
Phone: 512-427-6101
Fax: 512-427-6127
E-mail: grantinfo@thecb.state.tx.us

TKE EDUCATIONAL FOUNDATION http://www.tkefoundation.org

HARRY J. DONNELLY MEMORIAL SCHOLARSHIP

One-time award of $250 given to a member of Tau Kappa Epsilon pursuing an undergraduate degree in accounting or a graduate degree in law. Applicant should have demonstrated leadership ability within his chapter, campus, or community. Should have 3.0 GPA and plan to be a full-time student the following academic year. Recent head and shoulders photograph must be submitted with application.

Academic Fields/Career Goals: Accounting; Law/Legal Services.

Award: Scholarship for use in freshman, sophomore, junior, senior, or graduate years; not renewable. *Number:* 1. *Amount:* $250.

Eligibility Requirements: Applicant must be enrolled or expecting to enroll full-time at a four-year institution or university; male and must have an interest in leadership. Applicant must have 3.0 GPA or higher. Available to U.S. and non-U.S. citizens.

TKE Educational Foundation (continued)

Application Requirements: Application, essay, photo, transcript. *Deadline:* May 15.

Contact: Tim Taschwer, President/CEO
TKE Educational Foundation
8645 Founders Road
Indianapolis, IN 46268-1393
Phone: 317-872-6533
Fax: 317-875-8353
E-mail: tef@tkehq.org

W. ALLAN HERZOG SCHOLARSHIP

One $3000 award for an undergraduate member of TKE who is a full-time student pursuing a finance or accounting degree. Minimum 2.75 GPA required. Preference given to members of Nu Chapter. Applicant should have record of leadership within chapter and campus organizations. Application deadline is May 15.

Academic Fields/Career Goals: Accounting; Business/Consumer Services.

Award: Scholarship for use in freshman, sophomore, junior, or senior years; not renewable. *Number:* 1. *Amount:* $3000.

Eligibility Requirements: Applicant must be enrolled or expecting to enroll full-time at a four-year institution or university; male and must have an interest in leadership. Available to U.S. and non-U.S. citizens.

Application Requirements: Application, essay, photo, transcript. *Deadline:* May 15.

Contact: Tim Taschwer, President/CEO
TKE Educational Foundation
8645 Founders Road
Indianapolis, IN 46268-1393
Phone: 317-872-6533
Fax: 317-875-8353
E-mail: tef@tkehq.org

UNITED NEGRO COLLEGE FUND http://www.uncf.org

ALLIANT TECHSYSTEMS INTERNSHIP/SCHOLARSHIP

Scholarship is available to undergraduates in their sophomore or junior year. Applicant must be an accounting major enrolled in a UNCF member college or university. Scholarship awardees must participate in a paid summer internship in order to receive the $5000 for the following academic year. Please visit Web site for more information: http://www.uncf.org.

Academic Fields/Career Goals: Accounting.

Award: Scholarship for use in sophomore or junior years. *Number:* varies. *Amount:* $5000.

Eligibility Requirements: Applicant must be Black (non-Hispanic) and enrolled or expecting to enroll at a four-year institution or university. Applicant must have 3.0 GPA or higher. Available to U.S. citizens.

Application Requirements: Application, financial need analysis, FAFSA, SAR. *Deadline:* varies.

Contact: Program Services Department
United Negro College Fund
8260 Willow Oaks Corporate Drive
Fairfax, VA 22031

AVON WOMEN IN SEARCH OF EXCELLENCE SCHOLARSHIPS

Scholarships for female UNCF students majoring in business or economics. At least half of the awards go to women slightly over the traditional college age. Prospective applicants should complete the Student Profile found at Web site: http://www.uncf.org.

Academic Fields/Career Goals: Accounting; Business/Consumer Services; Economics.

Award: Scholarship for use in freshman, sophomore, junior, or senior years; not renewable. *Amount:* $2500.

Eligibility Requirements: Applicant must be Black (non-Hispanic); enrolled or expecting to enroll at a four-year institution or university and female. Applicant must have 2.5 GPA or higher. Available to U.S. citizens.

Application Requirements: Application. *Deadline:* October 28.

Contact: Program Services Department
United Negro College Fund
8260 Willow Oaks Corporate Drive
Fairfax, VA 22031

BANK ONE / UNCF CORPORATE SCHOLARS PROGRAM

Prospective applicants should complete the Student Profile found at Web site: http://www.uncf.org. Program consists of an 8-10 week internship. All majors are welcome, but business, finance, accounting, and retail are preferred. Each student must submit an official transcript, a letter of recommendation from a faculty member, and a statement of financial need certified by the financial aid office.

Academic Fields/Career Goals: Accounting; Business/Consumer Services.

Award: Scholarship for use in sophomore or junior years; not renewable. *Amount:* up to $10,000.

Eligibility Requirements: Applicant must be Black (non-Hispanic); enrolled or expecting to enroll full-time at a four-year institution or university; resident of Arizona, Delaware, Illinois, Indiana, Louisiana, Michigan, Ohio, or Texas and studying in Arizona, Delaware, Illinois, Indiana, Louisiana, Michigan, Ohio, or Texas. Applicant must have 3.0 GPA or higher. Available to U.S. citizens.

Application Requirements: Application, financial need analysis, references, transcript. *Deadline:* January 31.

Contact: UNCF/Bank One Corporate Scholars Program
United Negro College Fund
PO Box 1435
Alexandria, VA 22313-9998

BEST BUY ENTERPRISE EMPLOYEE SCHOLARSHIP

UNCF is partnered with Best Buy to offer this program to UNCF students majoring in business, finance, marketing, or sales. Selected students will receive a $2500 scholarship and an opportunity for an internship at a Best Buy retail store or at a corporate facility. Minimum 3.0 GPA required. Prospective applicants should complete the Student Profile found at Web site: http://www.uncf.org.

Academic Fields/Career Goals: Accounting; Business/Consumer Services; Communications; Journalism.

Award: Scholarship for use in freshman, sophomore, junior, or senior years; not renewable. *Amount:* $2500.

Eligibility Requirements: Applicant must be Black (non-Hispanic) and enrolled or expecting to enroll full-time at a four-year institution or university. Applicant must have 3.0 GPA or higher. Available to U.S. citizens.

Application Requirements: Application. *Deadline:* varies.

Contact: Program Services Department
United Negro College Fund
8260 Willow Oaks Corporate Drive
Fairfax, VA 22031

CARDINAL HEALTH SCHOLARSHIP

Scholarship awarded to African-American undergraduate freshmen, sophomores, or juniors attending any four-year accredited college or university. Must be majoring in accounting/finance, information systems, computer science, engineering or chemistry, marketing, purchasing/operations, or pharmacy. Please visit Web site for more information: http://www.uncf.org.

Academic Fields/Career Goals: Accounting; Business/Consumer Services; Computer Science/Data Processing; Engineering/Technology; Pharmacy.

Award: Scholarship for use in freshman, sophomore, or junior years; renewable. *Number:* varies. *Amount:* $5000.

Eligibility Requirements: Applicant must be Black (non-Hispanic); enrolled or expecting to enroll at a four-year institution or university and must have an interest in leadership. Applicant must have 3.0 GPA or higher.

Application Requirements: Application, financial need analysis, FAFSA, SAR. *Deadline:* November 30.

Contact: Program Services Department
United Negro College Fund
8260 Willow Oaks Corporate Drive
Fairfax, VA 22031

CARGILL SCHOLARSHIP PROGRAM

Scholarship awarded to undergraduate freshman, sophomore, or junior enrolled in a UNCF member college or university or one of the following institutions: University of Minnesota, Iowa State University, North Carolina A&T State University, and University of Wisconsin-Madison. Please visit Web site for more information: http://www.uncf.org.

Academic Fields/Career Goals: Accounting; Agriculture; Animal/Veterinary Sciences; Biology; Chemical Engineering; Computer Science/Data Processing; Food Science/Nutrition; Mechanical Engineering.

Award: Scholarship for use in freshman, sophomore, or junior years. *Number:* varies. *Amount:* $5000.

Eligibility Requirements: Applicant must be enrolled or expecting to enroll at a four-year institution or university. Applicant must have 3.0 GPA or higher. Available to U.S. citizens.

Application Requirements: Application, financial need analysis, FAFSA, SAR. *Deadline:* March 15.

Contact: Program Services Department
United Negro College Fund
8260 Willow Oaks Corporate Drive
Fairfax, VA 22031

CON EDISON SCHOLARSHIP

Scholarship available to students majoring in: accounting, computer science, and electrical, mechanical, or nuclear engineering. Applicant must be a resident of New York State. Please visit Web site for more information: http://www.uncf.org.

Academic Fields/Career Goals: Accounting; Computer Science/Data Processing; Energy and Power Engineering; Engineering/Technology; Mechanical Engineering.

Award: Scholarship for use in sophomore, junior, or senior years. *Number:* varies. *Amount:* varies.

Eligibility Requirements: Applicant must be Black (non-Hispanic); enrolled or expecting to enroll at a four-year institution or university and resident of New York. Applicant must have 3.0 GPA or higher.

Application Requirements: Application, financial need analysis, FAFSA, SAR. *Deadline:* varies.

Contact: Program Services Department
United Negro College Fund
8260 Willow Oaks Corporate Drive
Fairfax, VA 22031

CREDIT SUISSE FIRST BOSTON SCHOLARSHIP

The program provides internships and renewable scholarship support for students for three years, totaling $24,000. Applicants must be second semester freshmen attending a UNCF member college or university majoring in business, finance, economics, math, accounting, or computer science/MIS. Minimum 3.4 GPA required. Prospective applicants should complete the Student Profile found at Web site: http://www.uncf.org.

Academic Fields/Career Goals: Accounting; Business/Consumer Services; Computer Science/Data Processing; Economics.

Award: Scholarship for use in freshman year; renewable. *Amount:* $8000.

Eligibility Requirements: Applicant must be Black (non-Hispanic) and enrolled or expecting to enroll full-time at a four-year institution or university. Available to U.S. citizens.

Application Requirements: Application, financial need analysis. *Deadline:* March 15.

Contact: Program Services Department
United Negro College Fund
8260 Willow Oaks Corporate Drive
Fairfax, VA 22031

EDWARD M. NAGEL FOUNDATION SCHOLARSHIP

Scholarships available for African American students in the top 25% of their high school graduating class. Must be a California resident. Must be enrolled in a UNCF member college or university and pursue a degree in business, economics, or accounting. Visit Web site for details: http://www.uncf.org.

Academic Fields/Career Goals: Accounting; Business/Consumer Services; Economics.

Award: Scholarship for use in freshman, sophomore, junior, senior, or graduate years; not renewable. *Number:* varies. *Amount:* $2000–$5000.

Eligibility Requirements: Applicant must be Black (non-Hispanic); enrolled or expecting to enroll at a four-year institution or university and resident of California. Applicant must have 3.5 GPA or higher.

Application Requirements: Application, financial need analysis, FAFSA, SAR. *Deadline:* varies.

Contact: Program Services Department
United Negro College Fund
8260 Willow Oaks Corporate Drive
Fairfax, VA 22031

EMERSON ELECTRIC COMPANY SCHOLARSHIP

Scholarship awards students majoring in: accounting, computer science, engineering or human resources. Applicant must attend a UNCF member college or university and be a resident of St. Louis, Missouri. Please visit Web site for more information: http://www.uncf.org.

Academic Fields/Career Goals: Accounting; Computer Science/Data Processing; Engineering/Technology; Hospitality Management.

Award: Scholarship for use in freshman, sophomore, junior, senior, or graduate years. *Number:* varies. *Amount:* $6000.

Eligibility Requirements: Applicant must be Black (non-Hispanic); enrolled or expecting to enroll at a four-year institution or university and resident of Missouri. Applicant must have 3.0 GPA or higher.

Application Requirements: Application, financial need analysis, FAFSA, SAR. *Deadline:* varies.

Contact: Program Services Department
United Negro College Fund
8260 Willow Oaks Corporate Drive
Fairfax, VA 22031

FINANCIAL SERVICES INSTITUTION SCHOLARSHIP

Scholarship intended to provide exciting opportunities for students to learn about and be exposed directly to the financial services industry. Applicant must attend a UNCF member college or university. Please visit Web site for more information: http://www.uncf.org.

Academic Fields/Career Goals: Accounting; Business/Consumer Services.

Award: Scholarship for use in freshman, sophomore, junior, senior, or graduate years; renewable. *Number:* varies. *Amount:* varies.

Eligibility Requirements: Applicant must be Black (non-Hispanic) and enrolled or expecting to enroll at a four-year institution or university. Applicant must have 2.5 GPA or higher.

Application Requirements: Application, financial need analysis, FAFSA, SAR. *Deadline:* varies.

Contact: Program Services Department
United Negro College Fund
8260 Willow Oaks Corporate Drive
Fairfax, VA 22031

FORD/UNCF CORPORATE SCHOLARS PROGRAM

Program is designed to provide selected African-American college students with a unique educational opportunity through annual scholarships and a possible paid summer internship with Ford Motor Company offices. Students must be undergraduate sophomores majoring in engineering, finance, accounting, information systems, marketing, computer science, operations management, or electrical engineering at a UNCF member college or university or at a selected historically black college or university. Minimum 3.0 GPA required. Prospective applicants should complete the Student Profile found at Web site: http://www.uncf.org.

United Negro College Fund (continued)

Academic Fields/Career Goals: Accounting; Computer Science/Data Processing; Engineering/Technology.

Award: Scholarship for use in sophomore year; not renewable. *Amount:* up to $15,000.

Eligibility Requirements: Applicant must be Black (non-Hispanic); enrolled or expecting to enroll at a four-year institution or university and resident of Michigan. Applicant must have 3.0 GPA or higher.

Application Requirements: Application, financial need analysis. *Deadline:* February 28.

Contact: Program Services Department
United Negro College Fund
8260 Willow Oaks Corporate Drive
Fairfax, VA 22031

GENERAL MILLS SCHOLARS PROGRAM/INTERNSHIP

Scholarships and paid summer internships awarded to college sophomores and juniors majoring in accounting, business (sales interest), computer science, engineering, finance, human resources, information systems, information technology, or marketing at a UNCF member college or university. Minimum 3.5 GPA required. Prospective applicants should complete the Student Profile found at Web site: http://www.uncf.org.

Academic Fields/Career Goals: Accounting; Business/Consumer Services; Computer Science/Data Processing; Engineering/Technology.

Award: Scholarship for use in sophomore or junior years; not renewable. *Amount:* $5000.

Eligibility Requirements: Applicant must be Black (non-Hispanic) and enrolled or expecting to enroll full-time at a four-year institution or university. Applicant must have 3.5 GPA or higher. Available to U.S. citizens.

Application Requirements: Application, financial need analysis, test scores. *Deadline:* January 2.

Contact: Program Services Department
United Negro College Fund
8260 Willow Oaks Corporate Drive
Fairfax, VA 22031

PECO ENERGY SCHOLARSHIP

Scholarships available to African American students who reside in the Philadelphia metropolitan community. Must attend a UNCF institution, Cheyney University, or Lincoln University. Must be pursuing a degree in business, accounting, engineering, chemistry, biology, computer science, or physics. See Web site for details. http://www.uncf.org.

Academic Fields/Career Goals: Accounting; Biology; Business/Consumer Services; Computer Science/Data Processing; Engineering/Technology; Physical Sciences and Math.

Award: Scholarship for use in freshman, sophomore, junior, or senior years; renewable. *Number:* varies. *Amount:* up to $3000.

Eligibility Requirements: Applicant must be Black (non-Hispanic); enrolled or expecting to enroll at a four-year institution or university and resident of Pennsylvania. Applicant must have 2.5 GPA or higher.

Application Requirements: Application, financial need analysis, FAFSA, SAR. *Deadline:* October 15.

Contact: Program Services Department
United Negro College Fund
8260 Willow Oaks Corporate Drive
Fairfax, VA 22031

ROBERT HALF INTERNATIONAL SCHOLARSHIP

Scholarship available to students attending a UNCF member college or university and pursuing a college degree in accounting or business. Minimum 2.5 GPA required. Prospective applicants should complete the Student Profile found at Web site: http://www.uncf.org.

Academic Fields/Career Goals: Accounting; Business/Consumer Services.

Award: Scholarship for use in freshman, sophomore, junior, or senior years; not renewable. *Amount:* up to $1750.

Eligibility Requirements: Applicant must be Black (non-Hispanic) and enrolled or expecting to enroll at a four-year institution or university. Applicant must have 2.5 GPA or higher.

Application Requirements: Application, financial need analysis. *Deadline:* Continuous.

Contact: Program Services Department
United Negro College Fund
8260 Willow Oaks Corporate Drive
Fairfax, VA 22031

SPRINT SCHOLARSHIP/INTERNSHIP

Award includes a summer internship and a need-based scholarship to cover educational expenses for junior or senior year. Must major in engineering, business, economics, accounting, math, information systems, computer science/MIS, computer science, electrical engineering, information technology, computer engineering, engineering management, industrial engineering, or statistics. Must have 3.0 GPA. Please visit Web site for more information: http://www.uncf.org

Academic Fields/Career Goals: Accounting; Business/Consumer Services; Computer Science/Data Processing; Economics; Electrical Engineering/Electronics; Engineering/Technology; Physical Sciences and Math.

Award: Scholarship for use in junior or senior years; renewable. *Number:* varies. *Amount:* up to $7500.

Eligibility Requirements: Applicant must be Black (non-Hispanic) and enrolled or expecting to enroll at an institution or university. Applicant must have 3.0 GPA or higher.

Application Requirements: Application, financial need analysis, references, transcript, FAFSA, SAR. *Deadline:* October 5.

Contact: Sprint Scholars Program
United Negro College Fund
PO Box 1435
Alexandria, VA 22313-9998

UNCF/ORACLE SCHOLARS/INTERNS PROGRAM

Juniors and seniors enrolled in UNCF schools and other HBCU's are eligible. Must major in business, marketing, finance, computer engineering, computer science, or human resources. Minimum 3.0 GPA required. Scholarship awarded upon successful completion of internship. Prospective applicants should complete the Student Profile found at Web site: http://www.uncf.org.

Academic Fields/Career Goals: Accounting; Business/Consumer Services; Computer Science/Data Processing; Engineering/Technology.

Award: Scholarship for use in junior or senior years; not renewable. *Amount:* up to $10,000.

Eligibility Requirements: Applicant must be Black (non-Hispanic); enrolled or expecting to enroll full-time at a four-year institution or university and resident of California or Virginia. Applicant must have 3.0 GPA or higher.

Application Requirements: Application, financial need analysis, references, transcript. *Deadline:* March 15.

Contact: Program Services Department
United Negro College Fund
8260 Willow Oaks Corporate Drive
Fairfax, VA 22031

UNCF/SPRINT SCHOLARS PROGRAM

Award available to undergraduate sophomores and juniors majoring in accounting, communications, computer engineering, computer science, economics, electrical engineering, finance, information systems, journalism, logistics, marketing, management information systems, public relations, industrial engineering, or statistics. Students must attend a UNCF member college or university or a historically black college or university. Minimum 3.0 GPA required. Prospective applicants should complete the Student Profile found at Web site: http://www.uncf.org.

Academic Fields/Career Goals: Accounting; Business/Consumer Services; Communications; Computer Science/Data Processing;

Economics; Electrical Engineering/Electronics; Engineering/Technology; Engineering-Related Technologies; Journalism.

Award: Scholarship for use in sophomore or junior years; not renewable. *Amount:* up to $7500.

Eligibility Requirements: Applicant must be Black (non-Hispanic) and enrolled or expecting to enroll full-time at a four-year institution or university. Applicant must have 3.0 GPA or higher.

Application Requirements: Application, financial need analysis, resume, references, transcript. *Deadline:* October 5.

Contact: Program Services Department
United Negro College Fund
8260 Willow Oaks Corporate Drive
Fairfax, VA 22031

VIRGINIA SOCIETY OF CERTIFIED PUBLIC ACCOUNTANTS EDUCATION FOUNDATION

http://www.vscpa.com

VIRGINIA SOCIETY OF CPAS EDUCATIONAL FOUNDATION MINORITY UNDERGRADUATE SCHOLARSHIP

One-time award for a student currently enrolled in a Virginia college or university undergraduate program with the intent to pursue accounting or a business related field of study. Applicant must have at least six hours of accounting and be currently registered for at least 3 more accounting credit hours. Applicant must be a member of one of the VSCPA-defined minority groups (African-American, Hispanic-American, Native-American or Asian Pacific American). Minimum overall and accounting GPA of 3.0 is required.

Academic Fields/Career Goals: Accounting; Business/Consumer Services.

Award: Scholarship for use in sophomore, junior, or senior years; not renewable. *Number:* 3. *Amount:* $15,000.

Eligibility Requirements: Applicant must be American Indian/Alaska Native, Asian/Pacific Islander, Black (non-Hispanic), or Hispanic; enrolled or expecting to enroll at a two-year or four-year institution or university and studying in Virginia. Applicant must have 3.0 GPA or higher. Available to U.S. citizens.

Application Requirements: Application, essay, resume, references, transcript. *Deadline:* April 15.

Contact: Tracey Zink, Public Relations Coordinator
Virginia Society of Certified Public Accountants Education Foundation
PO Box 4620
Glen Allen, VA 23058-4620
Phone: 800-733-8272
Fax: 804-273-1741
E-mail: tzink@vscpa.com

VIRGINIA SOCIETY OF CPAS EDUCATIONAL FOUNDATION UNDERGRADUATE SCHOLARSHIP

One-time award for a student currently enrolled in a Virginia college or university undergraduate program with the intent to pursue accounting or a business related field of study. Applicant must have at least six hours of accounting and be currently registered for at least 3 more accounting credit hours. Minimum overall and accounting GPA of 3.0 is required.

Academic Fields/Career Goals: Accounting; Business/Consumer Services.

Award: Scholarship for use in sophomore, junior, or senior years; not renewable. *Number:* 5. *Amount:* $1500.

Eligibility Requirements: Applicant must be enrolled or expecting to enroll at a two-year or four-year institution or university and studying in Virginia. Applicant must have 3.0 GPA or higher. Available to U.S. citizens.

Application Requirements: Application, essay, resume, references, transcript. *Deadline:* April 15.

Contact: Tracey Zink, Public Relations Coordinator
Virginia Society of Certified Public Accountants Education Foundation
PO Box 4620
Glen Allen, VA 23058-4620
Phone: 800-733-8272
Fax: 804-273-1741
E-mail: tzink@vscpa.com

WASHINGTON SOCIETY OF CERTIFIED PUBLIC ACCOUNTANTS

http://www.wscpa.org

WSCPA ACCOUNTING SCHOLARSHIPS

These merit based scholarships are open to any community college, vocational and transfer accounting students who have completed 2 quarters of accounting at the time of application, and who plan to complete their education in Washington state. Minimum 3.0 GPA required. Deadline is April 15.

Academic Fields/Career Goals: Accounting.

Award: Scholarship for use in junior or senior years; not renewable. *Number:* 8. *Amount:* $500–$1000.

Eligibility Requirements: Applicant must be enrolled or expecting to enroll full or part-time at a two-year or technical institution and studying in Washington. Applicant must have 3.0 GPA or higher. Available to U.S. citizens.

Application Requirements: Application, essay, resume, references, transcript. *Deadline:* April 15.

Contact: Mark Peterson, Academic and Student Relations Administrator
Washington Society of Certified Public Accountants
902 140th Avenue, NE
Bellevue, WA 98005-3480
Phone: 425-644-4800
Fax: 425-586-1119
E-mail: mpeterson@wscpa.org

WSCPA SCHOLARSHIPS FOR ACCOUNTING MAJORS

These $3,000 need-based scholarships are available to college juniors and seniors majoring in accounting. The one time award is intended for those studying at a four-year college or university in the state of Washington and may be used for full- or part-time study. Must maintain a 3.0 GPA. Deadline is April 15.

Academic Fields/Career Goals: Accounting.

Award: Scholarship for use in junior or senior years; not renewable. *Number:* up to 11. *Amount:* up to $3000.

Eligibility Requirements: Applicant must be enrolled or expecting to enroll full or part-time at a four-year institution or university and studying in Washington. Applicant must have 3.0 GPA or higher. Available to U.S. citizens.

Application Requirements: Application, essay, resume, references, transcript. *Deadline:* April 15.

Contact: Mark Peterson, Academic and Student Relations Administrator
Washington Society of Certified Public Accountants
902 140th Avenue, NE
Bellevue, WA 98005-3480
Phone: 425-644-4800
Fax: 425-586-1119
E-mail: mpeterson@wscpa.org

WSCPA SCHOLARSHIPS FOR MINORITY ACCOUNTING MAJORS

Scholarship for $3000 is available to a minority accounting student who will have completed his/her sophomore year by fall of application year at an accredited four-year institution in Washington state. Deadline is April 15. Minimum 3.0 GPA required.

Academic Fields/Career Goals: Accounting.

Award: Scholarship for use in junior or senior years; not renewable. *Number:* 1. *Amount:* up to $3000.

Eligibility Requirements: Applicant must be American Indian/Alaska Native, Asian/Pacific Islander, Black (non-Hispanic), or Hispanic; enrolled or expecting to enroll full or part-time at a four-year institution or university and studying in Washington. Applicant must have 3.0 GPA or higher. Available to U.S. citizens.

Washington Society of Certified Public Accountants (continued)

Application Requirements: Application, essay, resume, references, transcript. *Deadline:* April 15.

Contact: Mark Peterson, Academic and Student Relations Administrator
Washington Society of Certified Public Accountants
902 140th Avenue, NE
Bellevue, WA 98005-3480
Phone: 425-644-4800
Fax: 425-586-1119
E-mail: mpeterson@wscpa.org

WISCONSIN FOUNDATION FOR INDEPENDENT COLLEGES, INC. http://www.wficweb.org

WE ENERGIES SCHOLARSHIP

Scholarships for minority, nontraditional students (older than 25) and or women. Must attend a WFIC member institution. Must show financial need. See Web site for details. http://www.wficweb.org.

Academic Fields/Career Goals: Accounting; Business/Consumer Services; Communications; Economics; Political Science.

Award: Scholarship for use in freshman, sophomore, junior, or senior years. *Number:* varies. *Amount:* $2000.

Eligibility Requirements: Applicant must be American Indian/Alaska Native, Asian/Pacific Islander, Black (non-Hispanic), or Hispanic; enrolled or expecting to enroll full-time at a four-year institution or university and studying in Wisconsin. Available to U.S. citizens.

Application Requirements: Application, financial need analysis, references, transcript. *Deadline:* March 15.

Contact: Christy Miller, Marketing Program Manager
Wisconsin Foundation for Independent Colleges, Inc.
735 North Water Street, Suite 600
Milwaukee, WI 53202
Phone: 414-273-5980
Fax: 414-273-5995
E-mail: wfic@execpc.com

AFRICAN STUDIES

AMERICAN HISTORICAL ASSOCIATION http://www.theaha.org

WESLEY-LOGAN PRIZE

Prize offered for book on some aspect of the history of dispersion, settlement, adjustment, and return of peoples originally from Africa. Only books of high scholarly and literary merit considered. Copies of book must be sent to each committee member. Refer to Web site (http://www.theaha.org) for names and mailing addresses.

Academic Fields/Career Goals: African Studies; Area/Ethnic Studies; History; Humanities.

Award: Prize for use in freshman, sophomore, junior, senior, graduate, or postgraduate years; not renewable. *Number:* 1. *Amount:* varies.

Eligibility Requirements: Applicant must be enrolled or expecting to enroll at an institution or university and must have an interest in writing. Available to U.S. citizens.

Application Requirements: Applicant must enter a contest, copies of book. *Deadline:* May 17.

Contact: Book Prize Administrator
American Historical Association
400 A Street, SE
Washington, DC 20003
E-mail: aha@theaha.org

CULTURE CONNECTION http://www.theculturеconnection.com

CULTURE CONNECTION FOUNDATION SCHOLARSHIP

Scholarships available for students in single parent families. May be used for undergraduate or graduate study. Those interested in foreign languages, culture, and ethnic studies are encouraged to apply. Application deadline is August 1.

Academic Fields/Career Goals: African Studies; Anthropology; Area/Ethnic Studies; Art History; Asian Studies; Education; European Studies; Foreign Language; International Studies; Law/Legal Services.

Award: Scholarship for use in freshman, sophomore, junior, senior, or graduate years; renewable. *Number:* 1000. *Amount:* $4700.

Eligibility Requirements: Applicant must be enrolled or expecting to enroll full or part-time at a two-year or four-year or technical institution or university and single. Applicant must have 2.5 GPA or higher. Available to U.S. and non-U.S. citizens.

Application Requirements: Application, essay, financial need analysis, interview, references, self-addressed stamped envelope, test scores, transcript, birth certificate, divorce decree. *Deadline:* August 1.

Contact: Anna Leis, National Program Director
Culture Connection
8888 Keystone Crossing
Suite 1300
Indianapolis, IN 46240
Phone: 317-547-7055
Fax: 317-547-7083
E-mail: annaleis@theculturеconnection.com

AGRIBUSINESS

ALASKA COMMISSION ON POSTSECONDARY EDUCATION http://www.state.ak.us/acpe/

A.W. "WINN" BRINDLE MEMORIAL EDUCATION LOANS

Renewable loan for study of approved curriculum in fisheries, seafood processing, food technology or related fields for Alaska residents. Must maintain good standing at institution. Eligible for up to 50% forgiveness if recipient returns to Alaska for employment in fisheries-related field.

Academic Fields/Career Goals: Agribusiness; Animal/Veterinary Sciences; Biology; Food Science/Nutrition; Natural Resources.

Award: Forgivable loan for use in freshman, sophomore, junior, senior, or graduate years; renewable.

Eligibility Requirements: Applicant must be enrolled or expecting to enroll full-time at a two-year or four-year or technical institution or university and resident of Alaska. Available to U.S. citizens.

Application Requirements: Application, essay. *Deadline:* May 15.

Contact: Lori Stedman, Administrative Assistant, Special Programs
Alaska Commission on Postsecondary Education
3030 Vintage Boulevard
Juneau, AK 99801-7100
Phone: 907-465-6741
Fax: 907-465-5316

CALIFORNIA FARM BUREAU SCHOLARSHIP FOUNDATION http://www.cfbf.com/programs/scholar/

CALIFORNIA FARM BUREAU SCHOLARSHIP

Renewable award given to students attending a four-year college or university in California. Applicants must be California residents preparing for a career in the agricultural industry.

Academic Fields/Career Goals: Agribusiness; Agriculture.

Award: Scholarship for use in freshman, sophomore, junior, or senior years; renewable. *Number:* 23. *Amount:* $2000–$2750.

Eligibility Requirements: Applicant must be enrolled or expecting to enroll full or part-time at a four-year institution or university; resident of California and studying in California.

Application Requirements: Application, essay, interview, references, transcript. *Deadline:* March 1.

Contact: Darlene Licciardo, Scholarship Coordinator
California Farm Bureau Scholarship Foundation
2300 River Plaza Drive
Sacramento, CA 95833
Phone: 800-698-3276

CHS FOUNDATION http://www.chsfoundation.org

AGRICULTURE SCHOLARSHIPS

Merit-based awards for students enrolled in agricultural programs at participating vocational or technical and community colleges. Application must be submitted through participating school. School submits ten applications to the CHS Foundation. Recipients are selected in the spring. One-time award of $600. Application must be submitted to the school by the students before February 15.

Academic Fields/Career Goals: Agribusiness; Agriculture.

Award: Scholarship for use in freshman or sophomore years; not renewable. *Number:* up to 81. *Amount:* $600.

Eligibility Requirements: Applicant must be enrolled or expecting to enroll full-time at a two-year or technical institution; resident of Colorado, Idaho, Iowa, Kansas, Minnesota, Montana, Nebraska, North Dakota, Oklahoma, Oregon, South Dakota, Utah, Washington, Wisconsin, or Wyoming and studying in Colorado, Idaho, Iowa, Kansas, Minnesota, Montana, Nebraska, North Dakota, Oregon, South Dakota, Utah, or Washington. Available to U.S. and non-U.S. citizens.

Application Requirements: Application, transcript. *Deadline:* February 14.

Contact: Mary Kaste, Scholarship Director
CHS Foundation
5500 Cenex Drive
Inver Grove Heights, MN 55077
Phone: 651-355-5129
Fax: 651-355-5073
E-mail: mary.kaste@chsinc.com

COOPERATIVE STUDIES SCHOLARSHIPS

Renewable awards for college juniors and seniors attending agricultural colleges of participating universities. Must be enrolled in courses on cooperative principles and business practices. Each university selects a recipient in the spring. If the award is given in the junior year, the student is eligible for an additional $750 in their senior year without reapplying provided that eligibility requirements are met. A maximum of $1500 will be awarded to any one student in the cooperative studies program.

Academic Fields/Career Goals: Agribusiness; Agriculture.

Award: Scholarship for use in junior or senior years; renewable. *Number:* 82. *Amount:* $750–$1500.

Eligibility Requirements: Applicant must be enrolled or expecting to enroll full-time at a four-year institution or university; resident of Colorado, Idaho, Iowa, Kansas, Minnesota, Montana, Nebraska, North Dakota, Oklahoma, Oregon, South Dakota, Utah, Washington, Wisconsin, or Wyoming and studying in Colorado, Idaho, Iowa, Kansas, Minnesota, Montana, Nebraska, North Dakota, Oregon, South Dakota, Utah, or Washington. Available to U.S. and non-U.S. citizens.

Application Requirements: Application, transcript. *Deadline:* April 15.

Contact: Mary Kaste, Scholarship Director
CHS Foundation
5500 Cenex Drive
Inver Grove Heights, MN 55077
Phone: 651-355-5129
Fax: 651-355-5073
E-mail: mary.kaste@chsinc.com

FIRST–FLORICULTURE INDUSTRY RESEARCH AND SCHOLARSHIP TRUST http://www.firstinfloriculture.org

HAROLD BETTINGER MEMORIAL SCHOLARSHIP

One-time scholarship available to undergraduate or graduate student majoring in horticulture with a business or marketing emphasis, or majoring in business or marketing with a horticulture emphasis. Must have completed one year of study at a four-year institution in the U.S. or Canada. Minimum GPA of 3.0 required. To apply you must register with lunch-money.com, which is partnering with FIRST to make the application process easier. You only need to fill out one application online, and there is a link to lunch-money.com from the FIRST Web site: http://www.firstinfloriculture.org/schl_req_app.htm In addition to the application, you must submit two letters of recommendation and transcripts via email to: scholarships@firstinfloriculture.org. Application deadline is May 1.

Academic Fields/Career Goals: Agribusiness; Agriculture; Business/Consumer Services; Horticulture/Floriculture.

Award: Scholarship for use in sophomore, junior, senior, or graduate years; not renewable. *Number:* 1. *Amount:* $1000.

Eligibility Requirements: Applicant must be enrolled or expecting to enroll at a four-year institution or university. Applicant must have 3.0 GPA or higher. Available to U.S. and non-U.S. citizens.

Application Requirements: Application, references, transcript. *Deadline:* May 1.

Contact: Scholarship Information
FIRST–Floriculture Industry Research and Scholarship Trust
PO Box 280
East Lansing, MI 48826-0280
E-mail: scholarship@firstinfloriculture.org

JACOB VAN NAMEN/VANS MARKETING SCHOLARSHIP

Award open to undergraduates at a four-year college or university in the U.S. or Canada. Must be studying horticulture or a related major and be involved in agribusiness marketing and distribution of floral products. Minimum GPA of 3.0 required. To apply you must register with lunch-money.com, which is partnering with FIRST to make the application process easier. You only need to fill out one application online, and there is a link to lunch-money.com from the FIRST Web site: http://www.firstinfloriculture.org/schl_req_app.htm In addition to the application, you must submit two letters of recommendation and transcripts via email to: scholarships@firstinfloriculture.org. Application deadline is May 1.

Academic Fields/Career Goals: Agribusiness; Horticulture/Floriculture.

Award: Scholarship for use in sophomore, junior, or senior years; not renewable. *Number:* 1. *Amount:* $1250.

Eligibility Requirements: Applicant must be enrolled or expecting to enroll at a four-year institution or university. Applicant must have 3.0 GPA or higher. Available to U.S. and non-U.S. citizens.

Application Requirements: Application, references, transcript. *Deadline:* May 1.

Contact: Scholarship Information
FIRST–Floriculture Industry Research and Scholarship Trust
PO Box 280
East Lansing, MI 48826-0280
E-mail: scholarship@firstinfloriculture.org

FUHRMANN ORCHARDS

KARL "PETE" FUHRMANN IV MEMORIAL SCHOLARSHIP

One-time award for Ohio residents studying horticulture or agribusiness at any two- or four-year postsecondary institution in the U.S. Must be a U.S. citizen. Must be a graduate of an Ohio high school. Write for more information.

Academic Fields/Career Goals: Agribusiness; Horticulture/Floriculture.

Award: Scholarship for use in freshman, sophomore, junior, or senior years; not renewable. *Number:* up to 2. *Amount:* $600–$1000.

Eligibility Requirements: Applicant must be enrolled or expecting to enroll full-time at a two-year or four-year institution and resident of Ohio. Available to U.S. citizens.

Application Requirements: Application, essay, transcript. *Deadline:* May 15.

Contact: Paul W. Fuhrmann, Partner
Fuhrmann Orchards
510 Hansgen-Morgan Road
Wheelersburg, OH 45694

GOLF COURSE SUPERINTENDENTS ASSOCIATION OF AMERICA http://www.gcsaa.org

GOLF COURSE SUPERINTENDENTS ASSOCIATION OF AMERICA STUDENT ESSAY CONTEST

Up to three awards for essays focusing on the golf course management profession. Undergraduates and graduate students pursuing turfgrass science, agronomy, or any field related to golf course management may apply. In addition to cash prizes, winning entries may be published or excerpted in Newsline or Golf Course Management magazine. Must be member of GCSAA.

Academic Fields/Career Goals: Agribusiness; Horticulture/Floriculture.

Award: Prize for use in freshman, sophomore, junior, senior, or graduate years; not renewable. *Number:* up to 3. *Amount:* $1000–$2000.

Golf Course Superintendents Association of America (continued)

Eligibility Requirements: Applicant must be enrolled or expecting to enroll full-time at a two-year or four-year institution or university. Applicant or parent of applicant must be member of Golf Course Superintendents Association of America. Available to U.S. and non-U.S. citizens.

Application Requirements: Applicant must enter a contest, essay. *Deadline:* March 31.

Contact: Pam Smith, Scholarship/Student Programs Manager
Golf Course Superintendents Association of America
1421 Research Park Drive
Lawrence, KS 66049-3859
Phone: 800-472-7878 Ext. 678
Fax: 785-832-4449
E-mail: psmith@gcsaa.org

INTERTRIBAL TIMBER COUNCIL http://www.itcnet.org

TRUMAN D. PICARD SCHOLARSHIP

This program is dedicated to assisting Native-American/Native-Alaskan youth seeking careers in natural resources. Graduating senior high school students and those currently attending institutions of higher education are encouraged to apply. A valid Tribal/Alaska Native corporations enrollment card is required. Contact for deadline.

Academic Fields/Career Goals: Agribusiness; Agriculture; Natural Resources.

Award: Scholarship for use in freshman, sophomore, junior, senior, or graduate years; not renewable. *Number:* 10–14. *Amount:* $1200–$1800.

Eligibility Requirements: Applicant must be American Indian/Alaska Native and enrolled or expecting to enroll full-time at a two-year or four-year institution or university. Available to U.S. citizens.

Application Requirements: Application, essay, resume, references, transcript, enrollment card. *Deadline:* varies.

Contact: Education Committee
Intertribal Timber Council
1112 Northeast 21st Avenue
Portland, OR 97232-2114
Phone: 503-282-4296
Fax: 503-282-1274
E-mail: itc1@teleport.com

KENTUCKY HIGHER EDUCATION ASSISTANCE AUTHORITY (KHEAA) http://www.kheaa.com

KENTUCKY DEPARTMENT OF AGRICULTURE AGRIBUSINESS/ GOVERNOR'S SCHOLARS PROGRAM SCHOLARSHIP

Scholarships available for alumni of the Governor's Scholars Program. Must agree to pursue an education and career in agriculture or agribusiness. Must be resident of Kentucky.

Academic Fields/Career Goals: Agribusiness; Agriculture.

Award: Scholarship for use in freshman, sophomore, junior, or senior years. *Number:* 10–20. *Amount:* $300–$3000.

Eligibility Requirements: Applicant must be enrolled or expecting to enroll at a two-year or four-year institution or university and resident of Kentucky. Available to U.S. citizens.

Application Requirements: Application. *Deadline:* March 29.

Contact: Sherleen Sisney, Executive Director, Governor's Scholars Program
Kentucky Higher Education Assistance Authority (KHEAA)
1024 Capital Center Drive, Suite 210
Frankfort, KY 40601-8204
E-mail: kim.sisk@mail.state.ky.us

MAINE DEPARTMENT OF AGRICULTURE, FOOD AND RURAL RESOURCES http://www.maine.gov/agriculture

MAINE RURAL REHABILITATION FUND SCHOLARSHIP PROGRAM

One-time scholarship open to Maine residents enrolled in or accepted by any school, college, or university. Must be full time and demonstrate financial need. Those opting for a Maine institution given preference. Major must lead to an agricultural career. Minimum 2.7 cumulative GPA required; or minimum 3.0 GPA for most recent semester or quarter.

Academic Fields/Career Goals: Agribusiness; Agriculture; Animal/ Veterinary Sciences.

Award: Scholarship for use in freshman, sophomore, junior, senior, graduate, or postgraduate years; not renewable. *Number:* 10–20. *Amount:* $800–$2000.

Eligibility Requirements: Applicant must be enrolled or expecting to enroll full-time at a two-year or four-year or technical institution or university and resident of Maine. Available to U.S. citizens.

Application Requirements: Application, autobiography, financial need analysis, transcript. *Deadline:* June 15.

Contact: Rod McCormick, Research Associate
Maine Department of Agriculture, Food and Rural Resources
28 State House Station
Augusta, ME 04333-0028
Phone: 207-287-7628
Fax: 207-287-7548
E-mail: rod.mccormick@maine.gov

MINNESOTA SOYBEAN RESEARCH AND PROMOTION COUNCIL http://mnsoybean.org

MINNESOTA SOYBEAN RESEARCH AND PROMOTION COUNCIL YOUTH SOYBEAN SCHOLARSHIP

Up to eight $1000 scholarships are available to graduating high school seniors who are residents of Minnesota. Must demonstrate activity in agriculture with plans to study in an agricultural related program. For more details see Web site: http://www.mnsoybean.org.

Academic Fields/Career Goals: Agribusiness; Agriculture; Food Science/Nutrition.

Award: Scholarship for use in freshman year; not renewable. *Number:* up to 8. *Amount:* $1000.

Eligibility Requirements: Applicant must be high school student; planning to enroll or expecting to enroll full or part-time at a two-year or four-year or technical institution or university and resident of Minnesota. Applicant or parent of applicant must have employment or volunteer experience in agriculture or farming.

Application Requirements: Application, references, self-addressed stamped envelope, transcript. *Deadline:* March 29.

Contact: J J. Morgan, Scholarship Coordinator
Minnesota Soybean Research and Promotion Council
360 Pierce Avenue, Suite 110
North Mankato, MN 56003
Phone: 888-896-9678
Fax: 507-388-6751
E-mail: jj@mnsoybean.com

NATIONAL DAIRY SHRINE http://www.dairyshrine.org

NDS STUDENT RECOGNITION CONTEST

Awards available to college seniors enrolled in dairy science courses. Applicants must be nominated by their college or university professor and must intend to continue in the dairy field. A college or university may nominate up to two applicants.

Academic Fields/Career Goals: Agribusiness; Agriculture; Animal/ Veterinary Sciences; Food Science/Nutrition.

Award: Prize for use in senior year; not renewable. *Number:* 5–10. *Amount:* $500–$1500.

Eligibility Requirements: Applicant must be enrolled or expecting to enroll at a four-year institution. Available to U.S. citizens.

Application Requirements: Application, references, transcript, nomination. *Deadline:* March 15.

Contact: Mr. Maurice E. Core, Executive Director
National Dairy Shrine
1224 Alton Darby Creek Road
Columbus, OH 43228-4792
Phone: 614-878-5333
Fax: 614-870-2622
E-mail: shrine@cobaselect.com

NATIONAL POTATO COUNCIL WOMEN'S AUXILIARY http://www.nationalpotatocouncil.org

POTATO INDUSTRY SCHOLARSHIP

The Auxiliary scholarship is for full-time students studying in a potato-related field who desire to work in the potato industry after graduation. Minimum 3.0 GPA required.

Academic Fields/Career Goals: Agribusiness; Agriculture; Food Science/Nutrition.

Award: Scholarship for use in senior, graduate, or postgraduate years; not renewable. *Number:* 2. *Amount:* $2000.

Eligibility Requirements: Applicant must be enrolled or expecting to enroll full-time at a four-year institution or university. Applicant must have 3.0 GPA or higher. Available to U.S. citizens.

Application Requirements: Application, resume, references. *Deadline:* April 1.

Contact: John Keeling, Executive Vice President and CEO
National Potato Council Women's Auxiliary
1300 L Street, NW, Suite 910
Washington, DC 20005
Phone: 202-682-9456 Ext. 203
Fax: 202-682-0333
E-mail: johnkeeling@nationalpotatocouncil.org

NATIONAL POULTRY AND FOOD DISTRIBUTORS ASSOCIATION http://www.npfda.org

NATIONAL POULTRY AND FOOD DISTRIBUTORS ASSOCIATION SCHOLARSHIP FOUNDATION

The scholarships are awarded to full-time students in their junior or senior years at a U.S. college pursuing degrees in poultry science, food science, dietetics or other related areas of study pertaining to the poultry and food industries.

Academic Fields/Career Goals: Agribusiness; Agriculture; Animal/Veterinary Sciences; Food Science/Nutrition; Food Service/Hospitality; Home Economics.

Award: Scholarship for use in junior or senior years; not renewable. *Number:* 4. *Amount:* $1500–$2000.

Eligibility Requirements: Applicant must be enrolled or expecting to enroll full-time at a four-year institution or university. Available to U.S. and non-U.S. citizens.

Application Requirements: Application, essay, references, transcript. *Deadline:* May 31.

Contact: Kristin McWhorter, Executive Director
National Poultry and Food Distributors Association
Scholarship Committee
958 McEver Road Ext., Unit B-8
Gainesville, GA 30504
Phone: 877-845-1545
Fax: 770-535-7385
E-mail: info@npfda.org

PENNSYLVANIA ASSOCIATION OF CONSERVATION DISTRICTS AUXILIARY http://www.blairconservationdistrict.org

PACD AUXILIARY SCHOLARSHIPS

Award for residents of Pennsylvania who are upperclassmen pursuing a degree program in agricultural and/or environmental science, and/or environmental education. Must be studying at a two- or four-year Pennsylvania institution. Must be a U.S. citizen. Submit resume. One-time award of $500.

Academic Fields/Career Goals: Agribusiness; Agriculture; Biology; Environmental Science; Horticulture/Floriculture; Natural Resources.

Award: Scholarship for use in junior or senior years; not renewable. *Number:* 1. *Amount:* $500.

Eligibility Requirements: Applicant must be enrolled or expecting to enroll full or part-time at a two-year or four-year institution or university; resident of Pennsylvania and studying in Pennsylvania. Available to U.S. citizens.

Application Requirements: Application, autobiography, financial need analysis, resume, transcript. *Deadline:* June 13.

Contact: Margaret Angle, District Clerk
Pennsylvania Association of Conservation Districts Auxiliary
1407 Blair Street
Hollidaysburg, PA 16648-2468
Phone: 814-696-0877 Ext. 5
Fax: 814-696-9981
E-mail: blairconsdist@lazerlink.com

SOCIETY FOR RANGE MANAGEMENT http://www.rangelands.org

MASONIC RANGE SCIENCE SCHOLARSHIP

One award available to applicant pursuing degree in agribusiness, agriculture, animal/veterinary sciences, earth science, natural resources, and range science (or range management). Recipient receives $2000 a year for four years at college or university.

Academic Fields/Career Goals: Agribusiness; Agriculture; Animal/Veterinary Sciences; Earth Science; Natural Resources.

Award: Scholarship for use in freshman or sophomore years; renewable. *Number:* 1. *Amount:* varies.

Eligibility Requirements: Applicant must be enrolled or expecting to enroll full-time at a four-year institution or university. Available to U.S. and non-U.S. citizens.

Application Requirements: Application, autobiography, essay, references, test scores, transcript. *Deadline:* January 15.

Contact: Scholarship Office
Society for Range Management
445 Union Boulevard, Suite 230
Lakewood, CO 80228
Phone: 303-986-3309
Fax: 303-986-3892

SOIL AND WATER CONSERVATION SOCIETY-NEW JERSEY CHAPTER http://www.geocities.com/njswcs

EDWARD R. HALL SCHOLARSHIP

Two $500 scholarships awarded annually to students attending a New Jersey accredited college or New Jersey residents attending any out-of-state college. Undergraduate students-with the exception of freshmen-are eligible. Must be enrolled in a curriculum related to natural resources. Other areas related to conservation may qualify. Deadline: April 15.

Academic Fields/Career Goals: Agribusiness; Agriculture; Animal/Veterinary Sciences; Biology; Earth Science; Horticulture/Floriculture; Journalism; Materials Science, Engineering, and Metallurgy; Natural Resources; Natural Sciences; Surveying; Surveying Technology, Cartography, or Geographic Information Science.

Award: Scholarship for use in sophomore, junior, or senior years; not renewable. *Number:* 2. *Amount:* $500.

Eligibility Requirements: Applicant must be enrolled or expecting to enroll full-time at a two-year or four-year institution or university. Available to U.S. and non-U.S. citizens.

Application Requirements: Application, essay, financial need analysis, references, transcript. *Deadline:* April 15.

Contact: Chapter President
Soil and Water Conservation Society-New Jersey Chapter
Firman East Bear Chapter, SWCS
220 Davidson Avenue, 4th Floor
Somerset, NJ 08873
Phone: 732-932-9295
E-mail: njswcs@yahoo.com

SOUTH DAKOTA BOARD OF REGENTS http://www.ris.sdbor.edu

SOUTH DAKOTA BOARD OF REGENTS BJUGSTAD SCHOLARSHIP

Scholarship for graduating North or South Dakota high school senior who is a Native-American. Must demonstrate academic achievement, character and leadership abilities. Submit proof of tribal enrollment. One-time award of $500. Must rank in upper half of class or have a minimum 2.5 GPA. Must be pursuing studies in agriculture, agribusiness, or natural resources.

South Dakota Board of Regents (continued)

Academic Fields/Career Goals: Agribusiness; Agriculture; Natural Resources.

Award: Scholarship for use in freshman year; not renewable. *Number:* 1. *Amount:* $500.

Eligibility Requirements: Applicant must be American Indian/Alaska Native; high school student; planning to enroll or expecting to enroll at a two-year or four-year or technical institution or university; resident of North Dakota or South Dakota and must have an interest in leadership. Applicant must have 2.5 GPA or higher.

Application Requirements: Application, references, transcript, proof of tribal enrollment. *Deadline:* February 25.

Contact: South Dakota Board of Regents
306 East Capitol Avenue, Suite 200
Pierre, SD 57501-3159

UNITED AGRIBUSINESS LEAGUE http://www.ual.org

UNITED AGRIBUSINESS LEAGUE SCHOLARSHIP PROGRAM

Award of $1000-$5000 available to students enrolled or planning to enroll in a full-time degree program in agribusiness at a two- or four-year institution. Award is only for students who are studying or residing in the U.S., Canada or Mexico. Minimum 2.5 GPA required. Application deadline varies.

Academic Fields/Career Goals: Agribusiness; Agriculture; Animal/Veterinary Sciences; Economics; Food Science/Nutrition; Horticulture/Floriculture; Landscape Architecture.

Award: Scholarship for use in freshman, sophomore, junior, senior, or graduate years; renewable. *Number:* 10–15. *Amount:* $1000–$5000.

Eligibility Requirements: Applicant must be enrolled or expecting to enroll full-time at a two-year or four-year institution or university. Applicant must have 2.5 GPA or higher. Available to U.S. and non-U.S. citizens.

Application Requirements: Application, essay, financial need analysis, resume, references, test scores, transcript. *Deadline:* varies.

Contact: Christiane Steele, Scholarship Coordinator
United Agribusiness League
54 Corporate Park
Irvine, CA 92606-5105
Phone: 949-975-1424
Fax: 949-975-1671
E-mail: csteele@ual.org

UNITED AGRICULTURAL BENEFIT TRUST SCHOLARSHIP

Award for an employee, spouse, or child participating in the United Agricultural Benefit Trust health care program. Submit essay that reflects chosen agricultural career path. Submit resume of any educational, work, community, or extracurricular activities that are relevant. Applicant should be a member or affiliated with United Agriculture Benefit Trust.

Academic Fields/Career Goals: Agribusiness; Agriculture; Animal/Veterinary Sciences; Economics; Food Science/Nutrition; Horticulture/Floriculture; Landscape Architecture.

Award: Scholarship for use in freshman, sophomore, junior, or senior years; renewable. *Number:* 7. *Amount:* $1000–$5000.

Eligibility Requirements: Applicant must be enrolled or expecting to enroll full-time at a two-year or four-year institution or university. Applicant or parent of applicant must be member of United Agribusiness League. Applicant must have 2.5 GPA or higher. Available to U.S. and non-Canadian citizens.

Application Requirements: Application, essay, resume, references, test scores, transcript. *Deadline:* varies.

Contact: Christiane Steele, Scholarship Coordinator
United Agribusiness League
54 Corporate Park
Irvine, CA 92606-5105
Phone: 949-975-1424
Fax: 949-975-1671
E-mail: csteele@ual.org

AGRICULTURE

ALBERTA HERITAGE SCHOLARSHIP FUND/ ALBERTA SCHOLARSHIP PROGRAMS http://www.alis.gov.ab.ca/scholarships

ALBERTA BARLEY COMMISSION EUGENE BOYKO MEMORIAL SCHOLARSHIP

A CAN$500 scholarship is available for students enrolled in the second or subsequent year of postsecondary study and taking courses with an emphasis on crop production and/or crop processing technology. Must be a Canadian citizen and Alberta resident. For more details see Web site: http://www.alis.gov.ab.ca.

Academic Fields/Career Goals: Agriculture.

Award: Scholarship for use in sophomore, junior, or senior years; not renewable. *Number:* 1. *Amount:* $405.

Eligibility Requirements: Applicant must be enrolled or expecting to enroll full-time at a four-year institution or university and resident of Alberta. Available to Canadian citizens.

Application Requirements: Application. *Deadline:* August 1.

Contact: Director
Alberta Heritage Scholarship Fund/Alberta Scholarship Programs
9940 106th Street, 9th Floor
Box 28000, Station Main
Edmonton, AB T5J 4R4
Canada
Phone: 780-427-8640
Fax: 780-422-4516
E-mail: heritage@gov.ab.ca

AMERICAN SOCIETY FOR ENOLOGY AND VITICULTURE http://www.asev.org

AMERICAN SOCIETY FOR ENOLOGY AND VITICULTURE SCHOLARSHIPS

One-time award for college juniors, seniors, and graduate students residing in North America and enrolled in a program studying viticulture, enology, or any field related to the wine and grape industry. Minimum 3.0 GPA for undergraduates; minimum 3.2 GPA for graduate students. Must be a resident of the U.S., Canada, or Mexico.

Academic Fields/Career Goals: Agriculture; Chemical Engineering; Food Science/Nutrition; Horticulture/Floriculture.

Award: Scholarship for use in junior, senior, or graduate years; not renewable. *Number:* varies. *Amount:* $500–$4000.

Eligibility Requirements: Applicant must be enrolled or expecting to enroll full-time at a four-year institution or university. Applicant must have 3.0 GPA or higher. Available to U.S. and non-U.S. citizens.

Application Requirements: Application, essay, financial need analysis, references, transcript. *Deadline:* March 1.

Contact: Scholarship Committee Chair
American Society for Enology and Viticulture
PO Box 1855
Davis, CA 95617-1855
Phone: 530-753-3142
Fax: 530-753-3318
E-mail: society@asev.org

AMERICAN SOCIETY OF AGRICULTURAL ENGINEERS http://www.asae.org

AMERICAN SOCIETY OF AGRICULTURAL ENGINEERS FOUNDATION SCHOLARSHIP

One scholarship will be awarded to an undergraduate student member of ASAE who has completed at least one year of undergraduate study and has at least one year of undergraduate study remaining. Must be majoring in agriculture or biological engineering. For more details see Web site: http://www.asae.org.

Academic Fields/Career Goals: Agriculture.

Award: Scholarship for use in sophomore or junior years; not renewable. *Number:* 1. *Amount:* $1000.

Eligibility Requirements: Applicant must be enrolled or expecting to enroll full-time at a four-year institution or university. Applicant must have 2.5 GPA or higher. Available to U.S. and Canadian citizens.

Application Requirements: Application. *Deadline:* April 15.

Contact: Carol Flautt, Scholarship Program
American Society of Agricultural Engineers
2950 Niles Road
St. Joseph, MI 49085
Phone: 269-428-6336
Fax: 269-429-3852
E-mail: flautt@asae.org

JOHN L. AND SARAH G. MERRIAM SCHOLARSHIP

One scholarship will be awarded to an undergraduate student member of ASAE who has completed at least one year of undergraduate study and has at least one year of undergraduate study remaining. Must be majoring in agriculture or biological engineering with an emphasis on the study of soil and water. For more details see Web site: http://www.asae.org.

Academic Fields/Career Goals: Agriculture.

Award: Scholarship for use in sophomore or junior years; not renewable. *Number:* 1. *Amount:* $1000.

Eligibility Requirements: Applicant must be enrolled or expecting to enroll full-time at a four-year institution or university. Applicant must have 2.5 GPA or higher. Available to U.S. and Canadian citizens.

Application Requirements: Application. *Deadline:* April 15.

Contact: Carol Flautt, Scholarship Program
American Society of Agricultural Engineers
2950 Niles Road
St. Joseph, MI 49085
Phone: 269-428-6336
Fax: 269-429-3852
E-mail: flautt@asae.org

WILLIAM J. AND MARIJANE E. ADAMS, JR. SCHOLARSHIP

One-time award for a full-time U.S. or Canadian undergraduate who is a student member of the American Society of Agricultural Engineers and a declared major in biological or agricultural engineering. Must be at least a sophomore and have minimum 2.5 GPA. Must be interested in agricultural machinery product design or development. Write for application procedures.

Academic Fields/Career Goals: Agriculture; Biology.

Award: Scholarship for use in sophomore or junior years; not renewable. *Number:* 1. *Amount:* $1000.

Eligibility Requirements: Applicant must be enrolled or expecting to enroll full-time at a four-year institution or university. Applicant must have 2.5 GPA or higher. Available to U.S. and Canadian citizens.

Application Requirements: Application, financial need analysis. *Deadline:* April 15.

Contact: Carol Flautt, Scholarship Program
American Society of Agricultural Engineers
2950 Niles Road
St. Joseph, MI 49085
Phone: 269-428-6336
Fax: 269-429-3852
E-mail: flautt@asae.org

CALIFORNIA FARM BUREAU SCHOLARSHIP FOUNDATION http://www.cfbf.com/programs/scholar/

CALIFORNIA FARM BUREAU SCHOLARSHIP

• *See page 52*

CALIFORNIA WATER AWARENESS CAMPAIGN http://www.wateraware.org

CALIFORNIA WATER AWARENESS CAMPAIGN WATER SCHOLAR

To provide economic support to graduating high school and/or junior college students who exhibit an interest or are actively pursuing a career in the water industry.

Academic Fields/Career Goals: Agriculture; Environmental Science; Hydrology; Landscape Architecture; Natural Resources.

Award: Scholarship for use in freshman, sophomore, junior, or senior years; not renewable. *Number:* up to 2. *Amount:* $2500.

Eligibility Requirements: Applicant must be enrolled or expecting to enroll full-time at a four-year institution or university; resident of California and studying in California. Available to U.S. citizens.

Application Requirements: Application, essay, references, transcript. *Deadline:* March 31.

Contact: Lynne Wichmann, Campaign Coordinator
California Water Awareness Campaign
910 K Street
Sacramento, CA 95814
Phone: 916-325-2596
Fax: 916-325-4849
E-mail: cwac@acwanet.com

CANADIAN RECREATIONAL CANOEING ASSOCIATION http://www.paddlingcanada.com

BILL MASON MEMORIAL SCHOLARSHIP FUND

One-time award for Canadian citizens attending a Canadian college or university. Applicant must at least be a sophomore majoring in an outdoor recreation or environmental studies program. An academic standing of B+ (75%) is required. Applicant must be planning a career in this field. Must also provide history of past involvement and leadership as it pertains to major and career goals. Background in canoeing and kayaking is considered an asset. Application deadline is September 30.

Academic Fields/Career Goals: Agriculture; Anthropology; Earth Science; Environmental Science; Geography; Marine Biology; Natural Resources; Natural Sciences; Oceanography; Recreation, Parks, Leisure Studies; Travel/Tourism.

Award: Scholarship for use in sophomore, junior, or senior years; not renewable. *Number:* 1–2. *Amount:* $743.

Eligibility Requirements: Applicant must be Canadian citizen; enrolled or expecting to enroll full-time at a two-year or four-year institution or university; resident of Alberta, British Columbia, Manitoba, New Brunswick, Newfoundland, North West Territories, Nova Scotia, Ontario, Prince Edward Island, Quebec, Saskatchewan, or Yukon and studying in Alberta, British Columbia, Manitoba, New Brunswick, Newfoundland, North West Territories, Nova Scotia, Ontario, Prince Edward Island, Quebec, Saskatchewan, or Yukon.

Application Requirements: Application, essay, financial need analysis, transcript, birth certificate, cover letter. *Deadline:* September 30.

Contact: Sue Hopson, Administrative Assistant
Canadian Recreational Canoeing Association
446 Main Street West, PO Box 398
Merrickville, ON K0G 1N0
Canada
Phone: 613-269-2910
Fax: 613-269-2908
E-mail: info@paddlingcanada.com

CHS FOUNDATION http://www.chsfoundation.org

AGRICULTURE SCHOLARSHIPS

• *See page 52*

COOPERATIVE STUDIES SCHOLARSHIPS

• *See page 53*

FAMILY, CAREER AND COMMUNITY LEADERS OF AMERICA-TEXAS ASSOCIATION http://www.texasfccla.org

FCCLA SAN ANTONIO LIVESTOCK EXPOSITION, INC. SCHOOL TOURS GUIDE SCHOLARSHIP

Scholarships to Texas residents who are graduates of Texas high schools, to attend Texas colleges or universities to pursue fields of study consistent with agriculture. Applicants must have participated as a School Tours Guide during a sale show. Applicants should visit the Web site (http://www.texasfccla.org) or write to Texas FCCLA for complete information, submission guidelines, and restrictions.

Academic Fields/Career Goals: Agriculture.

Award: Scholarship for use in freshman year; not renewable. *Number:* 4. *Amount:* $1000.

Family, Career and Community Leaders of America-Texas Association (continued)

Eligibility Requirements: Applicant must be high school student; planning to enroll or expecting to enroll full-time at a four-year institution or university; resident of Texas and studying in Texas. Available to U.S. citizens.

Application Requirements: Application, essay, references, test scores, transcript. *Deadline:* March 1.

Contact: FCCLA Staff
Family, Career and Community Leaders of America-Texas Association
3530 Bee Caves Road, #101
Austin, TX 78746-9616
Phone: 512-306-0099
Fax: 512-306-0041
E-mail: fccla@texasfccla.org

FIRST–FLORICULTURE INDUSTRY RESEARCH AND SCHOLARSHIP TRUST http://www.firstinfloriculture.org

HAROLD BETTINGER MEMORIAL SCHOLARSHIP

• *See page 53*

GARDEN CLUB OF AMERICA http://www.gcamerica.org

GARDEN CLUB OF AMERICA AWARDS FOR SUMMER ENVIRONMENTAL STUDIES

One-time award available to students following their first, second, or third year of college who are majoring in environmental studies, ecology, or related field for credit in a summer course at a U.S. college or university. Submit course plan. For use in summer only. Funds two or more students annually. Application on GCA Web site: http://www.gcamerica.org.

Academic Fields/Career Goals: Agriculture; Earth Science; Meteorology/Atmospheric Science; Natural Resources; Physical Sciences and Math.

Award: Scholarship for use in freshman, sophomore, or junior years; not renewable. *Number:* 2. *Amount:* $1500.

Eligibility Requirements: Applicant must be enrolled or expecting to enroll at a four-year institution. Available to U.S. and non-U.S. citizens.

Application Requirements: Application, essay, references, self-addressed stamped envelope, transcript. *Deadline:* February 10.

Contact: Connie Sutton, Scholarship Committee
Garden Club of America
14 East 60th Street
New York, NY 10022
Phone: 212-753-8287
Fax: 212-753-0134

HEART OF AMERICA RESTAURANTS AND INNS/ MACHINE SHED SCHOLARSHIPS http://www.hoari.com

HEART OF AMERICA RESTAURANTS AND INNS/MACHINE SHED AGRICULTURE SCHOLARSHIP

One-time scholarship for college and university students who major in agriculture or a related field. Applicant must be enrolled in a postsecondary educational institution in Iowa, Illinois, Kansas, Minnesota or Wisconsin. Contact institution's financial aid office for application deadline.

Academic Fields/Career Goals: Agriculture.

Award: Scholarship for use in freshman year; not renewable. *Number:* 19. *Amount:* $1000.

Eligibility Requirements: Applicant must be enrolled or expecting to enroll full-time at a two-year or four-year institution or university and studying in Illinois, Iowa, Kansas, Minnesota, or Wisconsin. Available to U.S. citizens.

Application Requirements: Application. *Deadline:* varies.

Contact: Heart of America Restaurants and Inns/Machine Shed Scholarships
1501 River Drive
Moline, IL 61265

ILLINOIS STATE TREASURER'S OFFICE http://www.state.il.us/treas

ILLINOIS STATE TREASURER'S OFFICE EXCELLENCE IN AGRICULTURE SCHOLARSHIP PROGRAM

Scholarships awarded annually to Illinois high school seniors who plan to enroll as full-time students in agriculture or agriculture-related studies in an Illinois institution and be committed to pursuing a career in agriculture or an agriculture-related field.

Academic Fields/Career Goals: Agriculture; Animal/Veterinary Sciences.

Award: Scholarship for use in freshman year; not renewable. *Number:* 5. *Amount:* $2500.

Eligibility Requirements: Applicant must be high school student; planning to enroll or expecting to enroll full-time at a two-year or four-year or technical institution or university; resident of Illinois and studying in Illinois. Applicant must have 2.5 GPA or higher. Available to U.S. citizens.

Application Requirements: Application, essay, references, test scores, transcript, goal statement, list of activities. *Deadline:* April 15.

Contact: Mindy Varley, Scholarships
Illinois State Treasurer's Office
One West Old State Capitol Plaza, Suite 814
Springfield, IL 62701
Phone: 217-558-6215
Fax: 217-557-6439
E-mail: mvarley@treasurer.state.il.us

INTERTRIBAL TIMBER COUNCIL http://www.itcnet.org

TRUMAN D. PICARD SCHOLARSHIP

• *See page 54*

KENTUCKY HIGHER EDUCATION ASSISTANCE AUTHORITY (KHEAA) http://www.kheaa.com

KENTUCKY DEPARTMENT OF AGRICULTURE AGRIBUSINESS/ GOVERNOR'S SCHOLARS PROGRAM SCHOLARSHIP

• *See page 54*

KENTUCKY NATURAL RESOURCES AND ENVIRONMENTAL PROTECTION CABINET http://www.uky.edu/waterresources

CONSERVATION OF NATURAL RESOURCES SCHOLARSHIP

Scholarship available for a student currently enrolled in college in a Kentucky public institution who has declared a major in the field of agriculture or conservation of natural resources. Must be Kentucky resident.

Academic Fields/Career Goals: Agriculture; Environmental Science; Natural Resources.

Award: Scholarship for use in sophomore, junior, or senior years; not renewable. *Number:* 1. *Amount:* $1000.

Eligibility Requirements: Applicant must be enrolled or expecting to enroll at a four-year institution or university; resident of Kentucky and studying in Kentucky. Available to U.S. citizens.

Application Requirements: Application. *Deadline:* April 2.

Contact: Kentucky Association of Conservation Districts Auxiliary
Kentucky Natural Resources and Environmental Protection Cabinet
663 Teton Trail
Frankfort, KY 40601
Phone: 502-564-3080
E-mail: steve.coleman@mail.state.ky.us

CONSERVATION OF NATURAL RESOURCES SCHOLARSHIP FOR NONTRADITIONAL STUDENTS

Scholarship available for student at least age 25 pursuing an undergraduate degree in agriculture or a related natural resources field. Must be enrolled in a Kentucky public institution and be a resident of Kentucky.

Academic Fields/Career Goals: Agriculture; Environmental Science; Natural Resources.

Award: Scholarship for use in freshman, sophomore, junior, or senior years; not renewable. *Number:* 1. *Amount:* $1000.

Eligibility Requirements: Applicant must be age 25; enrolled or expecting to enroll at a two-year or four-year institution or university; resident of Kentucky and studying in Kentucky. Available to U.S. citizens.

Application Requirements: Application. *Deadline:* April 2.

Contact: Kentucky Association of Conservation Districts Auxiliary
Kentucky Natural Resources and Environmental Protection Cabinet
663 Teton Trail
Frankfort, KY 40601
Phone: 502-564-3080
E-mail: steve.coleman@mail.state.ky.us

GEORGE R. CRAFTON SCHOLARSHIP

Scholarship available for a high school student applying for enrollment in a Kentucky public institution in the forthcoming year in an area related to agriculture and conservation of natural resources. Must be a Kentucky resident.

Academic Fields/Career Goals: Agriculture; Environmental Science; Natural Resources.

Award: Scholarship for use in freshman year; not renewable. *Number:* 1. *Amount:* $1000.

Eligibility Requirements: Applicant must be high school student; planning to enroll or expecting to enroll at a two-year or four-year institution or university; resident of Kentucky and studying in Kentucky. Available to U.S. citizens.

Application Requirements: Application. *Deadline:* April 2.

Contact: Kentucky Association of Conservation Districts Auxiliary
Kentucky Natural Resources and Environmental Protection Cabinet
663 Teton Trail
Frankfort, KY 40601
Phone: 502-564-3080
E-mail: steve.coleman@mail.state.ky.us

MAINE DEPARTMENT OF AGRICULTURE, FOOD AND RURAL RESOURCES http://www.maine.gov/agriculture

MAINE RURAL REHABILITATION FUND SCHOLARSHIP PROGRAM

• *See page 54*

MASTER BREWERS ASSOCIATION OF THE AMERICAS http://www.mbaa.com

MASTER BREWERS ASSOCIATION OF THE AMERICAS

Renewable award to college students entering their third year of study in a science related to the technical areas of malting and brewing. Must be a child of an MBAA member or person employed at least 5 years in the brewing industry. Minimum 3.0 GPA required.

Academic Fields/Career Goals: Agriculture; Biology; Chemical Engineering; Food Science/Nutrition.

Award: Scholarship for use in junior year; renewable. *Number:* 2. *Amount:* $4000.

Eligibility Requirements: Applicant must be enrolled or expecting to enroll full-time at a four-year institution. Applicant or parent of applicant must have employment or volunteer experience in brewing industry. Applicant must have 3.0 GPA or higher. Available to U.S. and non-U.S. citizens.

Application Requirements: Application, references. *Deadline:* February 28.

Contact: Linda Schmitt, Scholarship Coordinator
Master Brewers Association of the Americas
3340 Pilot Knob Road
St. Paul, MN 55121-2097
Phone: 651-994-3828
Fax: 651-454-0766
E-mail: lschmitt@scisoc.org

MINNESOTA SOYBEAN RESEARCH AND PROMOTION COUNCIL http://mnsoybean.org

MINNESOTA SOYBEAN RESEARCH AND PROMOTION COUNCIL YOUTH SOYBEAN SCHOLARSHIP

• *See page 54*

MORRIS K. UDALL FOUNDATION http://www.udall.gov

MORRIS K. UDALL SCHOLARS

One-time award to full-time college sophomores or juniors for study of the environment and related fields. Must be nominated by college. Minimum GPA of at least "B" or the equivalent. Must be U.S. citizen, a permanent resident alien or U.S. national.

Academic Fields/Career Goals: Agriculture; Biology; Earth Science; Geography; History; Natural Resources; Nuclear Science; Political Science.

Award: Scholarship for use in sophomore or junior years; not renewable. *Number:* up to 110. *Amount:* $350–$5000.

Eligibility Requirements: Applicant must be enrolled or expecting to enroll full-time at a two-year or four-year institution. Available to U.S. citizens.

Application Requirements: Application, essay, references, transcript, nomination. *Deadline:* March 3.

Contact: Morris K. Udall Foundation
130 South Scott Avenue, Suite 3350
Tucson, AZ 85701-1922

NATIONAL DAIRY SHRINE http://www.dairyshrine.org

KILDEE SCHOLARSHIPS

Top twenty-five contestants in the three most recent national intercollegiate Dairy Cattle Judging contests are eligible to apply for two $3000 one-time scholarships for graduate study in the field related to dairy cattle production at university of choice. Also the top 25 contestants in the most recent National 4-H & National FFA Dairy Judging Contests are eligible to apply for one $2000 Scholarship for undergraduate study in the field related to dairy cattle production at university of choice.

Academic Fields/Career Goals: Agriculture.

Award: Scholarship for use in freshman, or graduate years; not renewable. *Number:* 3. *Amount:* $2000–$3000.

Eligibility Requirements: Applicant must be enrolled or expecting to enroll full-time at an institution or university. Available to U.S. and non-U.S. citizens.

Application Requirements: Application, applicant must enter a contest. *Deadline:* March 15.

Contact: Mr. Maurice E. Core, Executive Director
National Dairy Shrine
1224 Alton Darby Creek Road
Columbus, OH 43228-9792
Phone: 614-878-5333
Fax: 614-870-2622
E-mail: shrine@cobaselect.com

MARSHALL E. MCCULLOUGH- NATIONAL DAIRY SHRINE SCHOLARSHIPS

Applicant must be a high school senior planning to enter a four-year college or university with intent to major in dairy/animal science with a communications emphasis or agricultural journalism with a dairy/animal science emphasis.

Academic Fields/Career Goals: Agriculture; Animal/Veterinary Sciences.

Award: Scholarship for use in freshman or junior years; not renewable. *Number:* 2. *Amount:* $1000–$2500.

Eligibility Requirements: Applicant must be high school student and planning to enroll or expecting to enroll full-time at a four-year institution or university. Available to U.S. and non-U.S. citizens.

National Dairy Shrine (continued)

Application Requirements: Application, transcript. *Deadline:* March 15.

Contact: Mr. Maurice E. Core, Executive Director
National Dairy Shrine
1224 Alton Darby Creek Road
Columbus, OH 43228-9792
E-mail: shrine@cobaselect.com

NATIONAL DAIRY SHRINE/DAIRY MARKETING, INC. MILK MARKETING SCHOLARSHIPS

One-time awards for undergraduate students pursuing careers in marketing of dairy products. Major areas can include: dairy science, animal science, agricultural economics, agricultural communications, agricultural education, general education, and food and nutrition.

Academic Fields/Career Goals: Agriculture; Animal/Veterinary Sciences; Food Science/Nutrition.

Award: Scholarship for use in sophomore, junior, or senior years; not renewable. *Number:* 7–10. *Amount:* $1000–$1500.

Eligibility Requirements: Applicant must be enrolled or expecting to enroll full-time at a four-year institution or university. Applicant must have 2.5 GPA or higher. Available to U.S. citizens.

Application Requirements: Application, references, transcript. *Deadline:* March 15.

Contact: Mr. Maurice E. Core, Executive Director
National Dairy Shrine
1224 Alton Darby Creek Road
Columbus, OH 43228-9792
Phone: 614-878-5333
Fax: 614-870-2622
E-mail: shrine@cobaselect.com

NATIONAL DAIRY SHRINE/KLUSSENDORF SCHOLARSHIP

A $1,000 NDS/Klussendorf Scholarship will be granted to a student successfully completing their first, second or third years at a 2-year or 4-year college or university. To be eligible, students must major in a Dairy Science (Animal Science) curriculum with plans to enter the dairy cattle field as a breeder, owner, herdsperson or fitter.

Academic Fields/Career Goals: Agriculture.

Award: Scholarship for use in freshman, sophomore, or junior years; not renewable. *Number:* 1. *Amount:* $1000.

Eligibility Requirements: Applicant must be enrolled or expecting to enroll full-time at a two-year or four-year institution or university. Available to U.S. and non-U.S. citizens.

Application Requirements: Application, applicant must enter a contest. *Deadline:* March 15.

Contact: Mr. Maurice E. Core, Executive Director
National Dairy Shrine
1224 Alton Darby Creek Road
Columbus, OH 43228-9792
Phone: 614-878-5333
Fax: 614-870-2622
E-mail: shrine@cobaselect.com

NDS STUDENT RECOGNITION CONTEST

• *See page 54*

PROGRESSIVE DAIRY PRODUCER AWARD

Two $2000 educational/travel awards for outstanding young dairy producers 21-45 years of age. Must be U.S. citizen.

Academic Fields/Career Goals: Agriculture.

Award: Prize for use in freshman, sophomore, junior, senior, or graduate years; not renewable. *Number:* 2. *Amount:* $2000.

Eligibility Requirements: Applicant must be age 21-45 and enrolled or expecting to enroll at an institution or university. Available to U.S. citizens.

Application Requirements: Application, applicant must enter a contest. *Deadline:* March 15.

Contact: Mr. Maurice E. Core, Executive Director
National Dairy Shrine
1224 Alton Darby Creek Road
Columbus, OH 43228-9792
Phone: 614-878-5333
Fax: 614-870-2622
E-mail: shrine@cobaselect.com

NATIONAL GARDEN CLUBS, INC.

http://www.gardenclub.org

NATIONAL GARDEN CLUBS, INC. SCHOLARSHIP PROGRAM

One-time award for full-time students in plant sciences, agriculture and related or allied subjects. Contact Garden Club chairperson in state of residence or write for brochure.

Academic Fields/Career Goals: Agriculture; Biology; Earth Science; Economics; Environmental Science; Horticulture/Floriculture; Landscape Architecture.

Award: Scholarship for use in junior, senior, or graduate years; not renewable. *Number:* 31–34. *Amount:* $3500.

Eligibility Requirements: Applicant must be enrolled or expecting to enroll full-time at a four-year institution or university. Available to U.S. citizens.

Application Requirements: Application, financial need analysis, photo, resume, references, transcript. *Deadline:* March 2.

Contact: National Garden Clubs, Inc.
W161 N5711 Bette Drive
Menomonee Falls, WI 53051-5647

NATIONAL POTATO COUNCIL WOMEN'S AUXILIARY

http://www.nationalpotatocouncil.org

POTATO INDUSTRY SCHOLARSHIP

• *See page 55*

NATIONAL POULTRY AND FOOD DISTRIBUTORS ASSOCIATION

http://www.npfda.org

NATIONAL POULTRY AND FOOD DISTRIBUTORS ASSOCIATION SCHOLARSHIP FOUNDATION

• *See page 55*

NEW YORK STATE GRANGE

HOWARD F. DENISE SCHOLARSHIP

Awards for undergraduates under 21 years old to pursue studies in agriculture. Must be a New York resident with a minimum 3.0 GPA. One-time award of $1000.

Academic Fields/Career Goals: Agriculture.

Award: Scholarship for use in freshman, sophomore, junior, or senior years; not renewable. *Number:* 6. *Amount:* $1000.

Eligibility Requirements: Applicant must be age 20 or under; enrolled or expecting to enroll at a two-year or four-year institution and resident of New York. Applicant must have 3.0 GPA or higher. Available to U.S. citizens.

Application Requirements: Application, financial need analysis, references, transcript. *Deadline:* April 15.

Contact: Ann Hall, Scholarship Chairperson
New York State Grange
100 Grange Place
Cortland, NY 13045
Phone: 607-756-7553
Fax: 607-756-7757
E-mail: nysgrange@nysgrange.com

OREGON SHEEP GROWERS ASSOCIATION

http://www.oregonsheep.com

OREGON SHEEP GROWERS ASSOCIATION MEMORIAL SCHOLARSHIP

One-time award for college students majoring in agricultural science or veterinary medicine pursuing careers in the sheep industry. Must be U.S. citizen and Oregon resident studying at a four-year institution or university. Freshmen are not eligible.

Academic Fields/Career Goals: Agriculture; Animal/Veterinary Sciences.

Award: Scholarship for use in sophomore, junior, senior, or graduate years; not renewable. *Number:* 1–2. *Amount:* $500–$1000.

Eligibility Requirements: Applicant must be enrolled or expecting to enroll full-time at a four-year institution or university and resident of Oregon. Available to U.S. citizens.

Application Requirements: Application, essay, references, transcript. *Deadline:* July 1.

Contact: Scholarship Committee
Oregon Sheep Growers Association
1270 Chemeketa Street, NE
Salem, OR 97301
Phone: 503-364-5462
Fax: 503-585-1921
E-mail: contact@oregonsheep.com

OREGON STUDENT ASSISTANCE COMMISSION http://www.osac.state.or.us

AGRICULTURAL-WOMEN-IN-NETWORK SCHOLARSHIP

One scholarship for Oregon residents who are, agricultural majors with junior or senior undergraduate standing. Must attend a four-year college in Washington, Oregon, or Idaho. See Web site at http://www.osac.state.or.us for more information. Preference for female students.

Academic Fields/Career Goals: Agriculture.

Award: Scholarship for use in junior or senior years; not renewable. *Number:* 1. *Amount:* $1000.

Eligibility Requirements: Applicant must be enrolled or expecting to enroll at a four-year institution; resident of Oregon and studying in Idaho, Oregon, or Washington. Available to U.S. citizens.

Application Requirements: Application, essay, financial need analysis, test scores, transcript, activity chart. *Deadline:* March 1.

Contact: Director of Grant Programs
Oregon Student Assistance Commission
1500 Valley River Drive, Suite 100
Eugene, OR 97401-7020
Phone: 800-452-8807 Ext. 7395
E-mail: awardinfo@mercury.osac.state.or.us

PENNSYLVANIA ASSOCIATION OF CONSERVATION DISTRICTS AUXILIARY http://www.blairconservationdistrict.org

PACD AUXILIARY SCHOLARSHIPS

• *See page 55*

PROFESSIONAL GROUNDS MANAGEMENT SOCIETY http://www.pgms.org

ANNE SEAMAN PROFESSIONAL GROUNDS MANAGEMENT SOCIETY MEMORIAL SCHOLARSHIP

One-time award for citizens of the U.S. and Canada who are studying to enter the field of grounds management or a closely related field such as agronomy, horticulture, landscape contracting, and irrigation on a full-time basis. Write for further information. Must be sponsored by a PGMS member. The member must write a letter of recommendation for the applicant.

Academic Fields/Career Goals: Agriculture; Civil Engineering; Horticulture/Floriculture; Landscape Architecture.

Award: Scholarship for use in freshman, sophomore, junior, or senior years; not renewable. *Number:* 3. *Amount:* $250–$1500.

Eligibility Requirements: Applicant must be enrolled or expecting to enroll full-time at a two-year or four-year institution. Available to U.S. and Canadian citizens.

Application Requirements: Application, autobiography, financial need analysis, resume, references, transcript. *Deadline:* July 1.

Contact: Heather Waldschmiat, Association Coordinator
Professional Grounds Management Society
720 Light Street
Baltimore, MD 21230
Phone: 410-223-2861
Fax: 410-752-8295
E-mail: pgms@assnhqtrs.com

SOCIETY FOR RANGE MANAGEMENT http://www.rangelands.org

MASONIC RANGE SCIENCE SCHOLARSHIP

• *See page 55*

SOIL AND WATER CONSERVATION SOCIETY http://www.swcs.org

SWCS MELVILLE H. COHEE STUDENT LEADER CONSERVATION SCHOLARSHIP

Provides financial assistance to members of the SWCS who are in their junior or senior year of full-time undergraduate study or are pursuing graduate level studies with a natural resource conservation orientation at properly accredited colleges or universities. Download the application form from the SWCS homepage at http://www.swcs.org.

Academic Fields/Career Goals: Agriculture; Economics; Natural Resources; Natural Sciences.

Award: Scholarship for use in junior, senior, or graduate years; not renewable. *Number:* 2. *Amount:* $1000.

Eligibility Requirements: Applicant must be enrolled or expecting to enroll full-time at a four-year institution or university. Applicant must have 3.0 GPA or higher. Available to U.S. and non-U.S. citizens.

Application Requirements: Application, financial need analysis. *Deadline:* February 12.

Contact: Nancy Herselius, Member Services Coordinator
Soil and Water Conservation Society
7515 NE Ankeny Road
Ankeny, IA 50021-9764
Phone: 515-289-2331 Ext. 17
Fax: 515-289-1227
E-mail: nancyh@swcs.org

SOIL AND WATER CONSERVATION SOCIETY-NEW JERSEY CHAPTER http://www.geocities.com/njswcs

EDWARD R. HALL SCHOLARSHIP

• *See page 55*

SOUTH DAKOTA BOARD OF REGENTS http://www.ris.sdbor.edu

SOUTH DAKOTA BOARD OF REGENTS BJUGSTAD SCHOLARSHIP

• *See page 55*

UNITED AGRIBUSINESS LEAGUE http://www.ual.org

UNITED AGRIBUSINESS LEAGUE SCHOLARSHIP PROGRAM

• *See page 56*

UNITED AGRICULTURAL BENEFIT TRUST SCHOLARSHIP

• *See page 56*

UNITED NEGRO COLLEGE FUND http://www.uncf.org

CARGILL SCHOLARSHIP PROGRAM

• *See page 49*

WOMEN GROCERS OF AMERICA http://www.nationalgrocers.org

MARY MACEY SCHOLARSHIP

Award for students intending to pursue a career in the independent sector of the grocery industry. One-time award for students who have completed freshman year. Submit statement and recommendation from sponsor in the grocery industry.

Academic Fields/Career Goals: Agriculture; Business/Consumer Services; Communications; Economics; Food Service/Hospitality.

Award: Scholarship for use in sophomore, junior, senior, graduate, or postgraduate years; not renewable. *Number:* 2. *Amount:* $1000.

Eligibility Requirements: Applicant must be enrolled or expecting to enroll full-time at a two-year or four-year institution or university. Available to U.S. citizens.

Women Grocers of America (continued)

Application Requirements: Application, transcript, personal statement. *Deadline:* June 1.

Contact: Ms. Anne Wintersteen, Director of Administration
Women Grocers of America
1005 North Glebe Road, Suite 250
Arlington, VA 22201-5758
Phone: 703-516-0700
Fax: 703-516-0115
E-mail: wga@nationalgrocers.org

AMERICAN STUDIES

ORGANIZATION OF AMERICAN HISTORIANS http://www.oah.org

BINKLEY-STEPHENSON AWARD

One-time award of $500 for the best scholarly article published in the Journal of American History during the preceding calendar year.

Academic Fields/Career Goals: American Studies; History.

Award: Prize for use in freshman, sophomore, junior, senior, graduate, or postgraduate years; not renewable. *Number:* 1. *Amount:* $500.

Eligibility Requirements: Applicant must be enrolled or expecting to enroll at a two-year or four-year or technical institution or university. Available to U.S. and non-U.S. citizens.

Application Requirements: Applicant must enter a contest. *Deadline:* Continuous.

Contact: Kara Hamm, Award and Prize Committee Coordinator
Organization of American Historians
112 North Bryan Avenue
Bloomington, IN 47408-4199
Phone: 812-855-9852
Fax: 812-855-0696
E-mail: awards@oah.org

ANIMAL/VETERINARY SCIENCES

ALASKA COMMISSION ON POSTSECONDARY EDUCATION http://www.state.ak.us/acpe/

A.W. "WINN" BRINDLE MEMORIAL EDUCATION LOANS

• *See page 52*

AMERICAN ORNITHOLOGISTS' UNION http://www.aou.org

AMERICAN ORNITHOLOGISTS' UNION RESEARCH AWARDS

One-time award for students without recourse to regular funding for research on any aspect of avian biology. Must be members of the American Ornithologists' Union. For more details see Web site: http://www.aou.org.

Academic Fields/Career Goals: Animal/Veterinary Sciences; Biology; Natural Sciences.

Award: Grant for use in freshman, sophomore, junior, or senior years; not renewable. *Number:* 28–30. *Amount:* up to $1800.

Eligibility Requirements: Applicant must be enrolled or expecting to enroll full or part-time at a four-year institution or university. Applicant or parent of applicant must be member of American Ornithologist's Union. Available to U.S. and non-U.S. citizens.

Application Requirements: Application, references, self-addressed stamped envelope. *Deadline:* February 1.

Contact: Application available at Web site.

AMERICAN QUARTER HORSE FOUNDATION (AQHF) http://www.aqha.org/aqhya

AQHF RACING SCHOLARSHIPS

Must be member of AQHA or AQHYA and intend to pursue a career in the American Quarter Horse racing industry or related field. Recipients receive $2000 per year for four years. Minimum 2.5 GPA required.

Academic Fields/Career Goals: Animal/Veterinary Sciences.

Award: Scholarship for use in freshman, sophomore, junior, or senior years; renewable. *Number:* 1–5. *Amount:* $8000.

Eligibility Requirements: Applicant must be enrolled or expecting to enroll full-time at a two-year or four-year or technical institution or university. Applicant or parent of applicant must be member of American Quarter Horse Association. Applicant must have 2.5 GPA or higher. Available to U.S. and Canadian citizens.

Application Requirements: Application, essay, financial need analysis, photo, references, transcript. *Deadline:* February 1.

Contact: Laura Owens, Scholarship Coordinator
American Quarter Horse Foundation (AQHF)
2601 I-40 East
Amarillo, TX 79104
Phone: 806-376-5181
Fax: 806-376-1005
E-mail: lowens@aqha.org

APPALOOSA HORSE CLUB-APPALOOSA YOUTH PROGRAM http://www.appaloosa.com

LEW AND JOANN EKLUND EDUCATIONAL SCHOLARSHIP

One-time award for college juniors and seniors and graduate students studying a field related to the equine industry. Must be member or dependent of member of the Appaloosa Horse Club. Submit picture and three recommendations. Award based on merit.

Academic Fields/Career Goals: Animal/Veterinary Sciences.

Award: Scholarship for use in junior, senior, or graduate years; not renewable. *Number:* 1. *Amount:* $2000.

Eligibility Requirements: Applicant must be enrolled or expecting to enroll full-time at a four-year institution or university. Applicant or parent of applicant must be member of Appaloosa Horse Club/ Appaloosa Youth Association. Applicant must have 3.5 GPA or higher. Available to U.S. and non-U.S. citizens.

Application Requirements: Application, essay, photo, references, transcript. *Deadline:* June 10.

Contact: Keeley Gant, AYF Coordinator
Appaloosa Horse Club-Appaloosa Youth Program
2720 Pullman Road
Moscow, ID 83843
Phone: 208-882-5578 Ext. 264
Fax: 208-882-8150
E-mail: aphc@appaloosa.com

ARKANSAS DEPARTMENT OF HIGHER EDUCATION http://www.arscholarships.com

ARKANSAS HEALTH EDUCATION GRANT PROGRAM (ARHEG)

Award provides assistance to Arkansas residents pursuing professional degrees in dentistry, optometry, veterinary medicine, podiatry, chiropractic medicine, or osteopathic medicine at out-of-state, accredited institutions (programs that are unavailable in Arkansas).

Academic Fields/Career Goals: Animal/Veterinary Sciences; Dental Health/Services; Health and Medical Sciences.

Award: Grant for use in sophomore, junior, senior, or graduate years; renewable. *Number:* 258–288. *Amount:* $5000–$14,600.

Eligibility Requirements: Applicant must be enrolled or expecting to enroll full-time at a four-year institution or university and resident of Arkansas. Available to U.S. citizens.

Application Requirements: Application, affidavit of Arkansas residency. *Deadline:* Continuous.

Contact: Ms. Judy McAinsh, Coordinator, Arkansas Health Education Grant Program
Arkansas Department of Higher Education
114 East Capitol
Little Rock, AR 72201-3818
Phone: 501-371-2013
Fax: 501-371-2002
E-mail: judym@adhe.arknet.edu

ASSOCIATION FOR WOMEN IN SCIENCE EDUCATIONAL FOUNDATION

http://www.awis.org/ed_foundation.html

ASSOCIATION FOR WOMEN IN SCIENCE COLLEGE SCHOLARSHIP

The College Scholarship is for women who plan a career in science as a researcher and/or teacher. Applicants must be high school seniors with a GPA of 3.75 or higher and SAT scores of at least 1200. Open to U.S. citizens only.

Academic Fields/Career Goals: Animal/Veterinary Sciences; Biology; Chemical Engineering; Computer Science/Data Processing; Earth Science; Engineering/Technology; Materials Science, Engineering, and Metallurgy; Mechanical Engineering; Meteorology/Atmospheric Science; Natural Sciences; Nuclear Science; Physical Sciences and Math.

Award: Scholarship for use in freshman year; not renewable. *Number:* 2–15. *Amount:* $100–$1000.

Eligibility Requirements: Applicant must be high school student; planning to enroll or expecting to enroll full-time at a four-year institution or university and female. Available to U.S. citizens.

Application Requirements: Application, essay, references, test scores, transcript. *Deadline:* January 20.

Contact: Barbara Filner, President
Association for Women in Science Educational Foundation
7008 Richard Drive
Bethesda, MD 20817-4838
E-mail: awisedfd@awis.org

ILLINOIS STATE TREASURER'S OFFICE

http://www.state.il.us/treas

ILLINOIS STATE TREASURER'S OFFICE EXCELLENCE IN AGRICULTURE SCHOLARSHIP PROGRAM

• *See page 58*

LOUISIANA OFFICE OF STUDENT FINANCIAL ASSISTANCE

http://www.osfa.state.la.us

ROCKEFELLER STATE WILDLIFE SCHOLARSHIP

For Louisiana residents attending a public college within the state studying wildlife, forestry, or marine sciences full-time. Renewable up to five years as an undergraduate and two years as a graduate. Must have at least a 2.5 GPA and have taken the ACT or SAT.

Academic Fields/Career Goals: Animal/Veterinary Sciences; Applied Sciences; Marine Biology; Natural Resources.

Award: Scholarship for use in freshman, sophomore, junior, senior, or graduate years; renewable. *Number:* 60. *Amount:* $1000.

Eligibility Requirements: Applicant must be enrolled or expecting to enroll full-time at a four-year institution or university; resident of Louisiana and studying in Louisiana. Applicant must have 2.5 GPA or higher. Available to U.S. citizens.

Application Requirements: Application, test scores, transcript. *Deadline:* July 1.

Contact: Public Information
Louisiana Office of Student Financial Assistance
PO Box 91202
Baton Rouge, LA 70821-9202
Phone: 800-259-5626 Ext. 1012
Fax: 225-922-0790
E-mail: custserv@osfa.state.la.us

MAINE DEPARTMENT OF AGRICULTURE, FOOD AND RURAL RESOURCES

http://www.maine.gov/agriculture

MAINE RURAL REHABILITATION FUND SCHOLARSHIP PROGRAM

• *See page 54*

MANOMET CENTER FOR CONSERVATION SCIENCES

http://www.manomet.org

KATHLEEN S. ANDERSON AWARD

One-time award for research projects in the Western Hemisphere involving the ecological and behavioral activities of birds, and especially for projects relevant to bird conservation. Must submit two copies of proposal with budget and references. This award is not a scholarship. This is a grant for research only.

Academic Fields/Career Goals: Animal/Veterinary Sciences; Biology.

Award: Grant for use in junior, senior, graduate, or postgraduate years; not renewable. *Number:* 1–2. *Amount:* $500–$1000.

Eligibility Requirements: Applicant must be enrolled or expecting to enroll full or part-time at a four-year institution or university. Available to U.S. and non-U.S. citizens.

Application Requirements: Application, essay, references, proposal, budget. *Deadline:* December 1.

Contact: Jennie Robbins, Administrative Coordinator
Manomet Center for Conservation Sciences
PO Box 1770
Manomet, MA 02345-1770
Phone: 508-224-6521
Fax: 508-224-9220
E-mail: jrobbins@manomet.org

MID-COAST AUDUBON SOCIETY

http://www.midcoastaudubon.org

JEAN BOYER HAMLIN SCHOLARSHIP IN ORNITHOLOGY

One-time award for tuition/coursework in ornithology studies. Available to residents of Mid-coast Maine. Must be at least 18 years of age.

Academic Fields/Career Goals: Animal/Veterinary Sciences; Biology; Earth Science; Education; Natural Sciences.

Award: Scholarship for use in freshman, sophomore, junior, senior, or graduate years; not renewable. *Number:* varies. *Amount:* varies.

Eligibility Requirements: Applicant must be age 18; enrolled or expecting to enroll full or part-time at a four-year institution or university and resident of Maine. Available to U.S. citizens.

Application Requirements: Application, autobiography, references, self-addressed stamped envelope. *Deadline:* Continuous.

Contact: Jo Haney, Scholarship Chair
Mid-Coast Audubon Society
PO Box 862
Rockland, ME 04841
Phone: 207-633-6610

NATIONAL DAIRY SHRINE

http://www.dairyshrine.org

MARSHALL E. MCCULLOUGH- NATIONAL DAIRY SHRINE SCHOLARSHIPS

• *See page 59*

NATIONAL DAIRY SHRINE/DAIRY MARKETING, INC. MILK MARKETING SCHOLARSHIPS

• *See page 60*

NDS STUDENT RECOGNITION CONTEST

• *See page 54*

NATIONAL POULTRY AND FOOD DISTRIBUTORS ASSOCIATION

http://www.npfda.org

NATIONAL POULTRY AND FOOD DISTRIBUTORS ASSOCIATION SCHOLARSHIP FOUNDATION

• *See page 55*

OREGON SHEEP GROWERS ASSOCIATION

http://www.oregonsheep.com

OREGON SHEEP GROWERS ASSOCIATION MEMORIAL SCHOLARSHIP

• *See page 60*

OREGON STUDENT ASSISTANCE COMMISSION

http://www.osac.state.or.us

ROYDEN M. BODLEY SCHOLARSHIP

One-time award open to high school graduates who earned their Eagle rank in Boy Scouts of America Cascade Pacific Council. Must major in forestry, wildlife, environment, or related field. Must attend an Oregon college.

Academic Fields/Career Goals: Animal/Veterinary Sciences; Natural Resources; Natural Sciences.

Oregon Student Assistance Commission (continued)

Award: Scholarship for use in freshman year; not renewable. *Number:* 5. *Amount:* $1400.

Eligibility Requirements: Applicant must be enrolled or expecting to enroll at an institution or university; male; resident of Oregon and studying in Oregon. Applicant or parent of applicant must be member of Boy Scouts. Available to U.S. citizens.

Application Requirements: Application, essay, financial need analysis, transcript, activity chart. *Deadline:* March 1.

Contact: Director of Grant Programs
Oregon Student Assistance Commission
1500 Valley River Drive, Suite 100
Eugene, OR 97401-7020
Phone: 800-452-8807 Ext. 7395
E-mail: awardinfo@mercury.osac.state.or.us

RESOURCE CENTER
http://www.resourcecenterscholarshipinfo.com

MARIE BLAHA MEDICAL GRANT

One-time award of up to $1000 given to students pursuing any medical related field (e.g. nursing, therapy, dental, psychiatry, veterinary science). In honor of Marie Blaha who lost her life in an auto accident. Deadlines are January 1 and July 1. Recipient selection will be based on a 250-word original essay and referral letters. Applications are available via the Web site only: http://www.resourcecenterscholarshipinfo.com.

Academic Fields/Career Goals: Animal/Veterinary Sciences; Child and Family Studies; Cosmetology; Dental Health/Services; Food Science/ Nutrition; Health Administration; Health and Medical Sciences; Nursing; Pharmacy; Social Services; Therapy/Rehabilitation.

Award: Grant for use in freshman, sophomore, junior, senior, graduate, or postgraduate years; not renewable. *Number:* 1–10. *Amount:* up to $1000.

Eligibility Requirements: Applicant must be enrolled or expecting to enroll full or part-time at a two-year or four-year or technical institution or university. Available to U.S. and non-U.S. citizens.

Application Requirements: Application, essay, references, self-addressed stamped envelope, transcript. *Fee:* $5. *Deadline:* varies.

Contact: Dee Blaha, Owner
Resource Center
16362 Wilson Boulevard
Masaryktown, FL 34604-7335
E-mail: blaha@dialfla.com

SOCIETY FOR RANGE MANAGEMENT
http://www.rangelands.org

MASONIC RANGE SCIENCE SCHOLARSHIP
• *See page 55*

SOIL AND WATER CONSERVATION SOCIETY-NEW JERSEY CHAPTER
http://www.geocities.com/njswcs

EDWARD R. HALL SCHOLARSHIP
• *See page 55*

UNITED AGRIBUSINESS LEAGUE
http://www.ual.org

UNITED AGRIBUSINESS LEAGUE SCHOLARSHIP PROGRAM
• *See page 56*

UNITED AGRICULTURAL BENEFIT TRUST SCHOLARSHIP
• *See page 56*

UNITED NEGRO COLLEGE FUND
http://www.uncf.org

CARGILL SCHOLARSHIP PROGRAM
• *See page 49*

UNCF/PFIZER CORPORATE SCHOLARS PROGRAM

Open to minority students enrolled in UNCF schools and other HBCU's. Minimum 3.0 GPA required and major in business, finance, chemistry, microbiology, human resources, law, pre-veterinary medicine, animal science, supply chain management, or organizational development. Must be rising college junior, senior, graduate student, or first-year law student. Must complete internship at Pfizer location. Prospective applicants should complete the Student Profile found at Web site: http://www.uncf.org.

Academic Fields/Career Goals: Animal/Veterinary Sciences; Biology; Business/Consumer Services; Chemical Engineering; Law/Legal Services.

Award: Scholarship for use in sophomore, junior, or graduate years; not renewable. *Amount:* up to $15,000.

Eligibility Requirements: Applicant must be American Indian/Alaska Native, Asian/Pacific Islander, Black (non-Hispanic), or Hispanic; enrolled or expecting to enroll full-time at a four-year institution or university and resident of Connecticut, Michigan, New Jersey, or New York. Applicant must have 3.0 GPA or higher.

Application Requirements: Application, financial need analysis. *Deadline:* January 31.

Contact: Program Services Department
United Negro College Fund
8260 Willow Oaks Corporate Drive
Fairfax, VA 22031

WASHINGTON THOROUGHBRED FOUNDATION
http://www.washingtonthoroughbred.com

THOROUGHBRED HORSE RACING'S UNITED SCHOLARSHIP TRUST

Awards for those majoring in an equine industry-related field of study, or journalism. One renewable scholarship and three one-time grants. Must describe in writing, on video, audiotape, or film how the expansion of gaming in Washington state has affected the thoroughbred industry. See Web site at http://www.washingtonthoroughbred.com for application and further information. Deadline is February 1.

Academic Fields/Career Goals: Animal/Veterinary Sciences; Journalism.

Award: Scholarship for use in freshman, sophomore, junior, or senior years; not renewable. *Number:* up to 4. *Amount:* up to $2500.

Eligibility Requirements: Applicant must be enrolled or expecting to enroll full-time at a four-year institution or university and resident of Washington.

Application Requirements: Application, essay, interview. *Deadline:* February 1.

Contact: Washington Thoroughbred Breeders Association
Washington Thoroughbred Foundation
PO Box 1499
Auburn, WA 98071-1499

WILSON ORNITHOLOGICAL SOCIETY
http://www.ummz.lsa.umich.edu/birds/wosawards.html

GEORGE A. HALL / HAROLD F. MAYFIELD AWARD

One-time award for scientific research on birds. Available to independent researchers without access to funds or facilities at a college or university. Must be a nonprofessional to apply. Submit research proposal.

Academic Fields/Career Goals: Animal/Veterinary Sciences; Biology; Natural Resources.

Award: Grant for use in freshman, sophomore, junior, senior, graduate, or postgraduate years; not renewable. *Number:* 1. *Amount:* $1000.

Eligibility Requirements: Applicant must be enrolled or expecting to enroll at an institution or university. Available to U.S. and non-U.S. citizens.

Application Requirements: Application, references, proposal. *Deadline:* January 15.

Contact: Leann B. Blem, Scholarship Committee
Wilson Ornithological Society
Virginia Commonwealth University, Department of Biology,
1000 West Cary Street
Richmond, VA 23284-2012
Phone: 804-828-0474
E-mail: lblem@saturn.vcu.edu

PAUL A. STEWART AWARDS

One-time award for studies of bird movements based on banding, analysis of recoveries, and returns of banded birds, or research with an emphasis on economic ornithology. Submit research proposal.

Academic Fields/Career Goals: Animal/Veterinary Sciences; Biology; Natural Resources.

Award: Grant for use in freshman, sophomore, junior, senior, graduate, or postgraduate years; not renewable. *Number:* 1–4. *Amount:* up to $500.

Eligibility Requirements: Applicant must be enrolled or expecting to enroll full or part-time at an institution or university. Available to U.S. and non-U.S. citizens.

Application Requirements: Application, references, proposal. *Deadline:* January 15.

Contact: Leann B. Blem, Scholarship Committee
Wilson Ornithological Society
Virginia Commonwealth University, Department of Biology, 1000 West Cary Street
Richmond, VA 23284-2012
Phone: 804-828-0474
E-mail: lblem@saturn.vcu.edu

ANTHROPOLOGY

AMERICAN SCHOOL OF CLASSICAL STUDIES AT ATHENS http://www.ascsa.edu.gr

ASCSA SUMMER SESSIONS

Award for graduate and undergraduate students and to middle school, high school, and college teachers. Six-week sessions to travel within Turkey to study sites, monuments, and museums. Deadline: January 15.

Academic Fields/Career Goals: Anthropology; Archaeology; Architecture; Art History; Arts; Historic Preservation and Conservation; History; Humanities; Museum Studies; Near and Middle East Studies; Philosophy; Religion/Theology.

Award: Scholarship for use in senior, graduate, or postgraduate years; not renewable. *Number:* 10. *Amount:* $500–$4500.

Eligibility Requirements: Applicant must be enrolled or expecting to enroll full or part-time at a four-year institution or university and must have an interest in designated field specified by sponsor. Available to U.S. and non-U.S. citizens.

Application Requirements: Application, references, transcript. *Deadline:* January 15.

Contact: Timothy Winters, Chair, Committee of Summer Sessions
American School of Classical Studies at Athens
6-8 Charlton Street
Princeton, NJ 08540
Phone: 609-683-0800
Fax: 609-924-0578
E-mail: ascsa@ascsa.org

CANADIAN RECREATIONAL CANOEING ASSOCIATION http://www.paddlingcanada.com

BILL MASON MEMORIAL SCHOLARSHIP FUND

• *See page 57*

CULTURE CONNECTION http://www.thecultureconnection.com

CULTURE CONNECTION FOUNDATION SCHOLARSHIP

• *See page 52*

LAMBDA ALPHA NATIONAL COLLEGIATE HONORS SOCIETY FOR ANTHROPOLOGY http://www.lambdaalpha.com

LAMBDA ALPHA NATIONAL COLLEGIATE HONOR SOCIETY FOR ANTHROPOLOGY NATIONAL DEAN'S LIST AWARD

Award for juniors majoring in anthropology to encourage them to continue their studies in the field. One award of $1000. Deadline: March 1. Must rank in upper half of class or have a minimum 2.5 GPA. For further information applicant should contact the Lambda Alpha faculty sponsor at their own department.

Academic Fields/Career Goals: Anthropology.

Award: Scholarship for use in senior year; not renewable. *Number:* 1. *Amount:* $1000.

Eligibility Requirements: Applicant must be enrolled or expecting to enroll full or part-time at a four-year institution or university. Applicant or parent of applicant must be member of Lambda Alpha National Collegiate Honor Society for Anthropology. Applicant must have 2.5 GPA or higher. Available to U.S. and non-U.S. citizens.

Application Requirements: Application, autobiography, resume, references, transcript. *Deadline:* March 1.

Contact: Lambda Alpha Faculty Sponsor
Lambda Alpha National Collegiate Honors Society for Anthropology
Department of Anthropology, Ball State University
Muncie, IN 47306-0435

APPLIED SCIENCES

AMERICAN INDIAN SCIENCE AND ENGINEERING SOCIETY http://www.aises.org

A.T. ANDERSON MEMORIAL SCHOLARSHIP

Award for full-time students majoring in math or science secondary education, engineering, science, business, medicine, or natural resources. Must be at least one-quarter American-Indian or Alaska Native or have tribal recognition, and be member of AISES. Deadline: June 15. Must have minimum 2.0 GPA.

Academic Fields/Career Goals: Applied Sciences; Biology; Business/Consumer Services; Earth Science; Health and Medical Sciences; Meteorology/Atmospheric Science; Natural Resources; Natural Sciences; Nuclear Science; Physical Sciences and Math.

Award: Scholarship for use in freshman, sophomore, junior, senior, or graduate years; not renewable. *Number:* varies. *Amount:* $1000–$2000.

Eligibility Requirements: Applicant must be American Indian/Alaska Native and enrolled or expecting to enroll full-time at a two-year or four-year institution or university. Available to U.S. citizens.

Application Requirements: Application, essay, financial need analysis, references, transcript. *Deadline:* June 15.

Contact: Scholarship Information
American Indian Science and Engineering Society
PO Box 9828
Albuquerque, NM 87119-9828
Phone: 505-765-1052
Fax: 505-765-5608
E-mail: info@aises.org

BURLINGTON NORTHERN SANTA FE FOUNDATION SCHOLARSHIP

Award for high school senior for study of science, business, education, and health administration. Must reside in Arizona, Colorado, Kansas, Minnesota, Montana, North Dakota, New Mexico, Oklahoma, Oregon, South Dakota, Washington, or San Bernadino County, California. Must be at least one quarter American-Indian or Alaska Native and/or member of federally recognized tribe. Minimum 2.0 GPA required. Must be a current AISES member.

Academic Fields/Career Goals: Applied Sciences; Biology; Business/Consumer Services; Health Administration; Meteorology/Atmospheric Science; Natural Sciences; Nuclear Science; Physical Sciences and Math.

Award: Scholarship for use in freshman, sophomore, junior, or senior years; renewable. *Number:* varies. *Amount:* $2500.

Eligibility Requirements: Applicant must be American Indian/Alaska Native; high school student; planning to enroll or expecting to enroll at an institution or university and resident of Arizona, California, Colorado, Kansas, Minnesota, Montana, New Mexico, North Dakota, Oklahoma, Oregon, South Dakota, or Washington. Available to U.S. citizens.

American Indian Science and Engineering Society (continued)

Application Requirements: Application, essay, references, transcript. *Deadline:* April 15.

Contact: Scholarship Information
American Indian Science and Engineering Society
PO Box 9828
Albuquerque, NM 87119-9828
Phone: 505-765-1052
Fax: 505-765-5608
E-mail: info@aises.org

AMERICAN INSTITUTE OF AERONAUTICS AND ASTRONAUTICS http://www.aiaa.org

AIAA UNDERGRADUATE SCHOLARSHIP

Renewable award available to college sophomores, juniors and seniors enrolled full-time in an accredited college/university. Must be AIAA student member or become one prior to receiving award. Course of study must provide entry into some field of science or engineering encompassed by AIAA. Minimum 3.0 GPA required.

Academic Fields/Career Goals: Applied Sciences; Aviation/Aerospace; Electrical Engineering/Electronics; Engineering/Technology; Materials Science, Engineering, and Metallurgy; Mechanical Engineering; Physical Sciences and Math; Science, Technology, and Society.

Award: Scholarship for use in sophomore, junior, or senior years; renewable. *Number:* 30. *Amount:* $2000.

Eligibility Requirements: Applicant must be enrolled or expecting to enroll full-time at a two-year or four-year or technical institution or university. Applicant must have 3.0 GPA or higher. Available to U.S. and non-U.S. citizens.

Application Requirements: Application, essay, references, transcript. *Deadline:* January 31.

Contact: Stephen Brock, Student Programs Director
American Institute of Aeronautics and Astronautics
1801 Alexander Bell Drive, Suite 500
Reston, VA 20191
Phone: 703-264-7536
Fax: 703-264-7551
E-mail: stephenb@aiaa.org

AMERICAN METEOROLOGICAL SOCIETY http://www.ametsoc.org/AMS

AMERICAN METEOROLOGICAL SOCIETY INDUSTRY UNDERGRADUATE SCHOLARSHIPS

Renewable scholarship for students entering their junior year of study in the fall, pursuing a degree in atmospheric sciences, oceanography, hydrology, chemistry, computer sciences, mathematics, engineering or physics. For further information or application, visit Web site: http://www.ametsoc.org/AMS

Academic Fields/Career Goals: Applied Sciences; Computer Science/Data Processing; Earth Science; Engineering/Technology; Meteorology/Atmospheric Science; Physical Sciences and Math.

Award: Scholarship for use in junior year; renewable. *Number:* varies. *Amount:* $2000.

Eligibility Requirements: Applicant must be enrolled or expecting to enroll full-time at a four-year institution or university. Available to U.S. citizens.

Application Requirements: Application, essay, references, self-addressed stamped envelope, transcript. *Deadline:* February 13.

Contact: Donna Fernandez, Fellowship/Scholarship Coordinator
American Meteorological Society
45 Beacon Street
Boston, MA 02108-3693
Phone: 617-227-2426 Ext. 246
Fax: 617-742-8718
E-mail: dfernand@ametsoc.org

AMERICAN SOCIETY OF HEATING, REFRIGERATING, AND AIR CONDITIONING ENGINEERS, INC. http://www.ashrae.org

AMERICAN SOCIETY OF HEATING, REFRIGERATION, AND AIR CONDITIONING ENGINEERING TECHNOLOGY SCHOLARSHIP

Applicants must have at least one full year of remaining study and must attend full-time. One award to student in engineering technology program leading to associate degree and one award to student in ABET-accredited program leading to bachelor's degree in engineering technology.

Academic Fields/Career Goals: Applied Sciences; Engineering/Technology; Heating, Air-Conditioning, and Refrigeration Mechanics; Trade/Technical Specialties.

Award: Scholarship for use in sophomore, junior, or senior years; not renewable. *Number:* 2. *Amount:* $3000.

Eligibility Requirements: Applicant must be enrolled or expecting to enroll full-time at a two-year or four-year institution and must have an interest in leadership. Applicant must have 3.0 GPA or higher.

Application Requirements: Application, financial need analysis, references, transcript. *Deadline:* May 1.

Contact: Scholarship Administrator
American Society of Heating, Refrigerating, and Air Conditioning Engineers, Inc.
1791 Tullie Circle, NE
Atlanta, GA 30329
Phone: 404-636-8400
Fax: 404-321-5478

AMERICAN SOCIETY OF NAVAL ENGINEERS http://www.navalengineers.org

AMERICAN SOCIETY OF NAVAL ENGINEERS SCHOLARSHIP

Award for naval engineering students in the final year of an undergraduate program or after one year of graduate study at an accredited institution. Must be full-time student and a U.S. citizen. Must study in specified fields. Minimum 2.5 GPA required. One-time award of $2500 for undergraduates and $3500 for graduate students. No doctoral candidates or candidates who already have an advanced degree. Graduate student applicants are required to be member of the American Society of Naval Engineers.

Academic Fields/Career Goals: Applied Sciences; Aviation/Aerospace; Civil Engineering; Electrical Engineering/Electronics; Energy and Power Engineering; Engineering/Technology; Marine/Ocean Engineering; Materials Science, Engineering, and Metallurgy; Mechanical Engineering; Nuclear Science; Physical Sciences and Math.

Award: Scholarship for use in senior, or graduate years; not renewable. *Number:* 18–22. *Amount:* $2500–$3500.

Eligibility Requirements: Applicant must be enrolled or expecting to enroll full-time at a four-year institution or university. Applicant must have 2.5 GPA or higher. Available to U.S. citizens.

Application Requirements: Application, references, test scores, transcript. *Deadline:* February 15.

Contact: Dennis Pignotti, Operations Manager
American Society of Naval Engineers
1452 Duke Street
Alexandria, VA 22314
Phone: 703-836-6727
Fax: 703-836-7491
E-mail: scholarships@navalengineers.org

ARRL FOUNDATION, INC. http://www.arrl.org/arrlf/scholgen.html

CHARLES N. FISHER MEMORIAL SCHOLARSHIP

One-time award available to students licensed in any class of amateur radio operators who are majoring in electronics, communications, or a related field. Must be resident of Arizona or California. Must attend regionally accredited institution.

Academic Fields/Career Goals: Applied Sciences; Communications; Electrical Engineering/Electronics; Engineering/Technology; Trade/Technical Specialties.

Award: Scholarship for use in freshman, sophomore, junior, or senior years; not renewable. *Number:* 1. *Amount:* $1000.

Eligibility Requirements: Applicant must be enrolled or expecting to enroll at an institution or university; resident of Arizona or California; studying in Arizona or California and must have an interest in amateur radio.

Application Requirements: Application, transcript. *Deadline:* February 1.

Contact: Mary Lau, Scholarship Director
ARRL Foundation, Inc.
225 Main Street
Newington, CT 06111-4845

HENRY BROUGHTON, K2AE MEMORIAL SCHOLARSHIP

One award per year (multiple as income permits) to students who are licensed amateur radio operators with a minimum general class license. Must be pursuing baccalaureate course of study in engineering, sciences, or related field at an accredited four-year college or university. Must reside within 70 miles of Schenectady, New York.

Academic Fields/Career Goals: Applied Sciences; Engineering-Related Technologies.

Award: Scholarship for use in freshman, sophomore, junior, or senior years; not renewable. *Amount:* $1000.

Eligibility Requirements: Applicant must be enrolled or expecting to enroll at a four-year institution or university; resident of Massachusetts, New York, or Vermont and must have an interest in amateur radio.

Application Requirements: Application, transcript. *Deadline:* February 1.

Contact: Mary Lau, Scholarship Director
ARRL Foundation, Inc.
225 Main Street
Newington, CT 06111-4845

IRVING W. COOK, WA0CGS, SCHOLARSHIP

One-time award to students pursuing a degree in communications, electronics, or related fields who are amateur radio operators. Must be a Kansas resident but may attend school in any state.

Academic Fields/Career Goals: Applied Sciences; Communications; Electrical Engineering/Electronics; Engineering/Technology; Trade/ Technical Specialties.

Award: Scholarship for use in freshman, sophomore, junior, or senior years; not renewable. *Number:* 1. *Amount:* $1000.

Eligibility Requirements: Applicant must be enrolled or expecting to enroll at an institution or university; resident of Kansas and must have an interest in amateur radio.

Application Requirements: Application, transcript. *Deadline:* February 1.

Contact: Mary Lau, Scholarship Director
ARRL Foundation, Inc.
225 Main Street
Newington, CT 06111-4845

MISSISSIPPI SCHOLARSHIP

Available to students pursuing a degree in electronics, communications, or related fields who are licensed in any class of amateur radio operators. Must reside in Mississippi, attend school in Mississippi, and be age 30 or under. Must be a member of the Amateur Radio Relay League.

Academic Fields/Career Goals: Applied Sciences; Communications; Electrical Engineering/Electronics; Engineering/Technology; Trade/ Technical Specialties.

Award: Scholarship for use in freshman, sophomore, junior, or senior years; not renewable. *Number:* 1. *Amount:* $500.

Eligibility Requirements: Applicant must be age 30 or under; enrolled or expecting to enroll at an institution or university; resident of Mississippi; studying in Mississippi and must have an interest in amateur radio. Applicant or parent of applicant must be member of American Radio Relay League.

Application Requirements: Application, transcript. *Deadline:* February 1.

Contact: Mary Lau, Scholarship Director
ARRL Foundation, Inc.
225 Main Street
Newington, CT 06111-4845

PAUL AND HELEN L. GRAUER SCHOLARSHIP

Available to students licensed as novice amateur radio operators who are majoring in electronics, communications, or a related field. Preference given to residents of Iowa, Kansas, Missouri, and Nebraska. Pursuit of a baccalaureate or higher degree preferred at an institution in ARRL Midwest Division.

Academic Fields/Career Goals: Applied Sciences; Communications; Electrical Engineering/Electronics; Engineering/Technology; Trade/ Technical Specialties.

Award: Scholarship for use in freshman, sophomore, junior, senior, or graduate years; not renewable. *Number:* 1. *Amount:* $1000.

Eligibility Requirements: Applicant must be enrolled or expecting to enroll at a four-year institution or university and must have an interest in amateur radio.

Application Requirements: Application, transcript. *Deadline:* February 1.

Contact: Mary Lau, Scholarship Director
ARRL Foundation, Inc.
225 Main Street
Newington, CT 06111-4845

ASPRS, THE IMAGING AND GEOSPATIAL INFORMATION SOCIETY http://www.asprs.org

ROBERT E. ALTENHOFEN MEMORIAL SCHOLARSHIP

One-time award is available for undergraduate or graduate study in theoretical photogrammetry. Applicant must supply a sample of work in photogrammetry and a statement of plans for future study in the field. Must be a member of ASPRS. One scholarship of $2000.

Academic Fields/Career Goals: Applied Sciences; Engineering/Technology.

Award: Scholarship for use in freshman, sophomore, junior, senior, or graduate years; not renewable. *Number:* 1. *Amount:* $2000.

Eligibility Requirements: Applicant must be enrolled or expecting to enroll full-time at a two-year or four-year institution or university and must have an interest in photography/photogrammetry/filmmaking. Applicant or parent of applicant must be member of American Society for Photogrammetry and Remote Sensing. Available to U.S. and non-U.S. citizens.

Application Requirements: Application, essay, references, transcript, work sample. *Deadline:* December 1.

Contact: Jesse Winch, Program Manager
ASPRS, The Imaging and Geospatial Information Society
5410 Grosvenor Lane, Suite 210
Bethesda, MD 20814-2160
Phone: 301-493-0290 Ext. 101
Fax: 301-493-0208
E-mail: scholarships@asprs.org

SPACE IMAGING AWARD FOR APPLICATION OF HIGH RESOLUTION DIGITAL SATELLITE IMAGERY

Award for undergraduate or graduate students to stimulate development of applications of digital data through the granting of data for applied research. This is not a cash award. The award consists of data valued at up to $2,000, and a plaque inscribed with the recipient's name and his/her institution. Must be ASPRS member.

Academic Fields/Career Goals: Applied Sciences; Engineering/ Technology; Physical Sciences and Math.

Award: Scholarship for use in freshman, sophomore, junior, senior, or graduate years; not renewable. *Number:* 1. *Amount:* $2000.

Eligibility Requirements: Applicant must be enrolled or expecting to enroll full-time at a four-year institution or university and must have

ASPRS, The Imaging and Geospatial Information Society (continued)

an interest in photography/photogrammetry/filmmaking. Applicant or parent of applicant must be member of American Society for Photogrammetry and Remote Sensing. Available to U.S. citizens.

Application Requirements: Application, autobiography, references, transcript, proposal. *Deadline:* December 1.

Contact: Jesse Winch, Program Manager
ASPRS, The Imaging and Geospatial Information Society
5410 Grosvenor Lane, Suite 210
Bethesda, MD 20814-2160
Phone: 301-493-0290 Ext. 101
Fax: 301-493-0208
E-mail: scholarships@asprs.org

Z/I IMAGING SCHOLARSHIP

A $2000 scholarship will be awarded to current or prospective graduate students who have graduate-level studies and career goals adjudged to address new and innovative uses of signal processing, image processing techniques and the application of photogrammetry to real-world techniques within the earth imaging industry. Must be a member of ASPRS.

Academic Fields/Career Goals: Applied Sciences; Engineering/Technology; Physical Sciences and Math.

Award: Scholarship for use in senior, or graduate years; not renewable. *Number:* 1. *Amount:* $2000.

Eligibility Requirements: Applicant must be enrolled or expecting to enroll at an institution or university. Available to U.S. citizens.

Application Requirements: Application, essay, references, transcript. *Deadline:* December 1.

Contact: Jesse Winch, Program Manager
ASPRS, The Imaging and Geospatial Information Society
5410 Grosvenor Lane, Suite 210
Bethesda, MD 20814-2160
Phone: 301-493-0290 Ext. 101
Fax: 301-493-0208
E-mail: scholarships@asprs.org

ASSOCIATION OF CALIFORNIA WATER AGENCIES
http://www.acwanet.com

ASSOCIATION OF CALIFORNIA WATER AGENCIES SCHOLARSHIPS

There are 6-8 $1500 awards available to juniors and seniors that are California residents attending California universities. Must be in a water-related field of study. Students applying can be transferring to a university from a junior college as long as they will be a junior in the fall. Applications available on the Web at http://www.acwanet.com/news_info/scholarships/index1.asp.

Academic Fields/Career Goals: Applied Sciences; Biology; Civil Engineering; Environmental Science; Hydrology; Natural Resources; Natural Sciences; Surveying; Surveying Technology, Cartography, or Geographic Information Science.

Award: Scholarship for use in junior or senior years; not renewable. *Number:* 6–8. *Amount:* $1500.

Eligibility Requirements: Applicant must be enrolled or expecting to enroll full-time at a four-year institution or university; resident of California and studying in California. Available to U.S. citizens.

Application Requirements: Application, essay, references, transcript. *Deadline:* April 1.

Contact: La Vonne Watson, Communications Coordinator
Association of California Water Agencies
910 K Street, Suite 100
Sacramento, CA 95814
Phone: 916-441-4545
Fax: 916-325-2316
E-mail: lavonnew@acwanet.com

CLAIR A. HILL SCHOLARSHIP

The Clair A. Hill award scholarship is administered by a different member agency each year. The guidelines vary by administering agency and therefore it is best to contact ACWA for information. Generally, winner is in a water-related field of study. Must be a resident of California enrolled in a California four-year college or university.

Academic Fields/Career Goals: Applied Sciences; Biology; Civil Engineering; Environmental Science; Hydrology; Natural Resources; Natural Sciences; Surveying; Surveying Technology, Cartography, or Geographic Information Science.

Award: Scholarship for use in junior, senior, or graduate years; not renewable. *Amount:* $3000.

Eligibility Requirements: Applicant must be enrolled or expecting to enroll full-time at a four-year institution or university; resident of California and studying in California. Available to U.S. citizens.

Application Requirements: Application, essay, references, transcript. *Deadline:* April 1.

Contact: Mark Norton, Santa Ana Watershed Project Authority
Association of California Water Agencies
910 K Street, Suite 100
Sacramento, CA 95814
Phone: 909-354-4220
Fax: 909-352-3422
E-mail: mnorton@SAWPA.org

ASTRONAUT SCHOLARSHIP FOUNDATION
http://www.astronautscholarship.org

ASTRONAUT SCHOLARSHIP FOUNDATION

Provides scholarships for deserving college science and engineering students.

Academic Fields/Career Goals: Applied Sciences; Aviation/Aerospace; Biology; Chemical Engineering; Computer Science/Data Processing; Earth Science; Electrical Engineering/Electronics; Engineering-Related Technologies; Materials Science, Engineering, and Metallurgy; Mechanical Engineering; Meteorology/Atmospheric Science.

Award: Scholarship for use in junior, senior, graduate, or postgraduate years; renewable. *Number:* 17. *Amount:* $10,000.

Eligibility Requirements: Applicant must be enrolled or expecting to enroll full-time at an institution or university. Available to U.S. citizens.

Application Requirements: Financial need analysis, references, transcript. *Deadline:* April 15.

Contact: Mr. Howard Benedict, Executive Director
Astronaut Scholarship Foundation
6225 Vectorspace Boulevard
Titusville, FL 32780
Phone: 321-269-6119
Fax: 321-267-3970
E-mail: mercurysvn@aol.com

BARRY M. GOLDWATER SCHOLARSHIP AND EXCELLENCE IN EDUCATION FOUNDATION
http://www.act.org/goldwater

BARRY M. GOLDWATER SCHOLARSHIP AND EXCELLENCE IN EDUCATION PROGRAM

One-time award to college juniors and seniors who will pursue advanced degrees in mathematics, natural sciences, or engineering. Students planning to study medicine are eligible if they plan a career in research. Candidates must be nominated by their college or university. Must be U.S. citizen or resident alien demonstrating intent to obtain U.S. citizenship. Minimum 3.0 GPA required. Nomination deadline: February 1. Please visit Web site for further updates. (http://www.act.org/goldwater)

Academic Fields/Career Goals: Applied Sciences; Biology; Chemical Engineering; Civil Engineering; Computer Science/Data Processing; Earth Science; Engineering/Technology; Materials Science, Engineering, and Metallurgy; Mechanical Engineering; Natural Sciences; Nuclear Science; Physical Sciences and Math.

Award: Scholarship for use in junior or senior years; renewable. *Number:* up to 300. *Amount:* up to $7500.

Eligibility Requirements: Applicant must be enrolled or expecting to enroll full-time at a two-year or four-year institution or university. Applicant must have 3.0 GPA or higher. Available to U.S. citizens.

Application Requirements: Application, autobiography, essay, references, transcript, school nomination. *Deadline:* February 1.

Contact: On-Campus Faculty Representative
Barry M. Goldwater Scholarship and Excellence in Education Foundation
6225 Brandon Avenue, Suite 315
Springfield, VA 22150-2519

CHEMICAL INSTITUTE OF CANADA

http://www.cheminst.ca

ALFRED BADER SCHOLARSHIP

Up to three scholarships available to undergraduate seniors who are members of the Canadian Society for Chemistry and who have achieved excellence in organic chemistry or biochemistry. Students must be nominated and submit a project report. U.S. citizens must be enrolled in a Canadian university.

Academic Fields/Career Goals: Applied Sciences.

Award: Scholarship for use in senior year; not renewable. *Number:* up to 3. *Amount:* $743.

Eligibility Requirements: Applicant must be enrolled or expecting to enroll full-time at an institution or university. Applicant or parent of applicant must be member of Canadian Society for Chemistry. Available to U.S. and Canadian citizens.

Application Requirements: Application, references, transcript. *Deadline:* May 15.

Contact: Gale Thirlwall-Wilbee, Manager of Outreach and Career Services
Chemical Institute of Canada
130 Slater Street, Suite 550
Ottawa, ON K1P 6E2
Canada
Phone: 613-232-6252 Ext. 223
Fax: 613-232-5862
E-mail: gwilbee@cheminst.ca

DESK AND DERRICK EDUCATIONAL TRUST

http://www.addc.org

DESK AND DERRICK EDUCATIONAL TRUST

Must be a U.S. or Canadian citizen; minimum 3.0 GPA required. Must have financial need, must be enrolled in an energy related major such as oil, gas, allied industries, and alternative energy. Open to full- or part-time junior and senior undergraduates. Applicant must be Desk and Derrick member.

Academic Fields/Career Goals: Applied Sciences; Chemical Engineering; Earth Science; Engineering-Related Technologies; Natural Resources; Natural Sciences; Nuclear Science.

Award: Scholarship for use in junior or senior years; not renewable. *Number:* 7. *Amount:* $750–$1500.

Eligibility Requirements: Applicant must be enrolled or expecting to enroll full or part-time at a four-year institution or university. Applicant must have 3.0 GPA or higher. Available to U.S. and Canadian citizens.

Application Requirements: Application, financial need analysis, transcript. *Deadline:* April 1.

Contact: See Web site.

HERB SOCIETY OF AMERICA

http://www.herbsociety.org

HERB SOCIETY RESEARCH GRANTS

One to five awards of up to $5000. Awards for persons with a proposed program of scientific, academic, or artistic investigation of herbal plants. Must submit proposal and budget with application by January 31.

Academic Fields/Career Goals: Applied Sciences; Art History; Arts; Biology; Earth Science; Food Science/Nutrition; Health and Medical Sciences; Horticulture/Floriculture; Landscape Architecture; Literature/English/Writing.

Award: Grant for use in freshman, sophomore, junior, senior, graduate, or postgraduate years; not renewable. *Number:* 1–5. *Amount:* up to $5000.

Eligibility Requirements: Applicant must be enrolled or expecting to enroll full or part-time at a two-year or four-year or technical institution or university. Available to U.S. and non-U.S. citizens.

Application Requirements: Application, references, proposal. *Deadline:* January 31.

Contact: Research Grant Chairperson
Herb Society of America
9019 Kirtland-Chardon Road
Kirtland, OH 44094
Phone: 440-256-0514
Fax: 440-256-0541
E-mail: herbs@herbsociety.org

HISPANIC COLLEGE FUND, INC.

http://www.hispanicfund.org

NATIONAL HISPANIC EXPLORERS SCHOLARSHIP PROGRAM

One-time scholarship award open to full-time undergraduates pursuing a degree in science, math, engineering, or NASA-related major. Must be a U.S. citizen and have a minimum of a 3.0 GPA.

Academic Fields/Career Goals: Applied Sciences; Aviation/Aerospace; Biology; Chemical Engineering; Civil Engineering; Communications; Computer Science/Data Processing; Earth Science; Electrical Engineering/Electronics; Engineering/Technology; Engineering-Related Technologies; Food Science/Nutrition.

Award: Scholarship for use in freshman, sophomore, junior, or senior years; not renewable. *Number:* 125–200. *Amount:* $500–$5000.

Eligibility Requirements: Applicant must be enrolled or expecting to enroll full-time at a two-year or four-year institution or university. Applicant must have 3.0 GPA or higher. Available to U.S. citizens.

Application Requirements: Application, essay, financial need analysis, resume, references, transcript, college acceptance letter, copy of taxes, proof of U.S. citizenship. *Deadline:* April 15.

Contact: Stina Augustsson, Program Manager
Hispanic College Fund, Inc.
1717 Pennsylvania Avenue, NW, Suite 460
Washington, DC 20006
Phone: 202-296-5400
Fax: 202-296-3774
E-mail: hcf-info@hispanicfund.org

INDEPENDENT LABORATORIES INSTITUTE SCHOLARSHIP ALLIANCE

http://www.acil.org

INDEPENDENT LABORATORIES INSTITUTE SCHOLARSHIP ALLIANCE

Scholarships are given to full-time undergraduate juniors or seniors, or graduate students majoring in the physical sciences: physics, chemistry, geology, engineering, biology or environmental science. Application deadline is April 11.

Academic Fields/Career Goals: Applied Sciences; Biology; Chemical Engineering; Civil Engineering; Earth Science; Electrical Engineering/Electronics; Engineering/Technology; Engineering-Related Technologies; Fire Sciences; Materials Science, Engineering, and Metallurgy; Mechanical Engineering; Physical Sciences and Math.

Award: Scholarship for use in junior, senior, or graduate years; not renewable. *Number:* 1–2. *Amount:* $1000–$2000.

Eligibility Requirements: Applicant must be enrolled or expecting to enroll full-time at a four-year institution or university. Available to U.S. and non-U.S. citizens.

Application Requirements: Application, autobiography, essay, references, self-addressed stamped envelope, transcript. *Deadline:* April 11.

Contact: Janet Allen, Senior Administrator
Independent Laboratories Institute Scholarship Alliance
1629 K Street, NW, Suite 400
Washington, DC 20006
Phone: 202-887-5872 Ext. 204
Fax: 202-887-0021
E-mail: jallen@acil.org

INNOVATION AND SCIENCE COUNCIL OF BRITISH COLUMBIA

http://www.scbc.org

PAUL AND HELEN TRUSSEL SCIENCE AND TECHNOLOGY SCHOLARSHIP

CAN$20,000 award to a new recipient each year. Student must be enrolled in the sciences and have graduated high school in the Kootenay/Boundary region

Innovation and Science Council of British Columbia (continued)

of British Columbia. Student must be entering 3rd year of studies at a BC or AB postsecondary institution. Available to Canadian citizens and landed immigrants.

Academic Fields/Career Goals: Applied Sciences; Biology; Chemical Engineering; Computer Science/Data Processing; Earth Science; Geography; Meteorology/Atmospheric Science; Natural Resources; Natural Sciences; Nuclear Science; Physical Sciences and Math; Science, Technology, and Society.

Award: Scholarship for use in junior, senior, or graduate years; renewable. *Number:* 1. *Amount:* $14,856.

Eligibility Requirements: Applicant must be Canadian citizen; enrolled or expecting to enroll full-time at a four-year institution or university; resident of British Columbia and studying in Alberta or British Columbia. Applicant must have 3.0 GPA or higher. Available to U.S. and non-U.S. citizens.

Application Requirements: Application, autobiography, references, transcript, proof of citizenship. *Deadline:* May 31.

Contact: Ms. Dawn Wood, Assistant Programs Coordinator
Innovation and Science Council of British Columbia
1048-4720 Kingsway
Burnaby, BC VSH 4N2
Canada
Phone: 604-438-2752 Ext. 269
Fax: 604-438-6564
E-mail: dwood@scbc.org

INTERNATIONAL SOCIETY FOR OPTICAL ENGINEERING-SPIE http://www.spie.org/info/scholarships

SPIE EDUCATIONAL SCHOLARSHIPS IN OPTICAL SCIENCE AND ENGINEERING

Application forms must show demonstrated personal commitment to and involvement of the applicant in the fields of optics, optical science and engineering, and indicate how the granting of the award will contribute to these fields. Applications will be judged by the SPIE Scholarship Committee on the basis of the long range contribution which the granting of the award will make to these fields. Must be member of SPIE.

Academic Fields/Career Goals: Applied Sciences; Aviation/Aerospace; Chemical Engineering; Electrical Engineering/Electronics; Engineering/Technology; Engineering-Related Technologies; Materials Science, Engineering, and Metallurgy; Mechanical Engineering.

Award: Scholarship for use in freshman, sophomore, junior, or senior years; not renewable. *Number:* 30–80. *Amount:* $1000–$8000.

Eligibility Requirements: Applicant must be enrolled or expecting to enroll full-time at a two-year or four-year or technical institution or university. Applicant or parent of applicant must be member of International Society for Optical Engineering (SPIE). Available to U.S. and non-U.S. citizens.

Application Requirements: Application, references, self-addressed stamped envelope. *Deadline:* January 31.

Contact: Scholarship Committee
International Society for Optical Engineering-SPIE
PO Box 10
Bellingham, WA 98227
Phone: 360-676-3290
Fax: 360-647-1445
E-mail: scholarships@spie.org

LOUISIANA OFFICE OF STUDENT FINANCIAL ASSISTANCE http://www.osfa.state.la.us

ROCKEFELLER STATE WILDLIFE SCHOLARSHIP

• *See page 63*

LUCENT TECHNOLOGIES FOUNDATION http://www.iie.org/programs/lucent

LUCENT GLOBAL SCIENCE SCHOLARS PROGRAM

Award competition is open to graduating U.S. high school seniors who meet the eligibility criteria detailed on http://www.iie.org/programs/lucent, including: outstanding academics and interests in IT-related careers. Females and minorities are encouraged to apply. The competition is open to international undergraduates in participating countries. See Web site for further information.

Academic Fields/Career Goals: Applied Sciences; Aviation/Aerospace; Chemical Engineering; Computer Science/Data Processing; Electrical Engineering/Electronics; Engineering/Technology; Engineering-Related Technologies; Physical Sciences and Math.

Award: Grant for use in freshman year; not renewable. *Number:* 24. *Amount:* $5000.

Eligibility Requirements: Applicant must be high school student; planning to enroll or expecting to enroll full-time at a four-year institution or university and must have an interest in designated field specified by sponsor. Applicant must have 3.5 GPA or higher. Available to U.S. citizens.

Application Requirements: Application, essay, interview, references, test scores, transcript. *Deadline:* February 25.

Contact: Program Administrator
Lucent Technologies Foundation
809 United Nations Plaza
New York, NY 10017
Phone: 212-984-5419
E-mail: sciencescholars@iie.org

MIDWEST ROOFING CONTRACTORS ASSOCIATION http://www.mrca.org

MRCA FOUNDATION SCHOLARSHIP PROGRAM

All candidates for the MRCA Foundation Scholarship must be current, enrolled or intending to enroll in an accredited university, college, community college, or trade school. Applicant must be pursuing a curriculum leading to a career in the construction industry.

Academic Fields/Career Goals: Applied Sciences; Architecture; Business/Consumer Services; Engineering/Technology; Heating, Air-Conditioning, and Refrigeration Mechanics; Materials Science, Engineering, and Metallurgy; Mechanical Engineering; Natural Sciences; Science, Technology, and Society; Surveying; Surveying Technology, Cartography, or Geographic Information Science; Trade/Technical Specialties.

Award: Scholarship for use in freshman, sophomore, junior, or senior years; renewable. *Number:* 1–5. *Amount:* $500–$1000.

Eligibility Requirements: Applicant must be enrolled or expecting to enroll full or part-time at a two-year or four-year or technical institution or university. Available to U.S. and non-U.S. citizens.

Application Requirements: Application, essay, photo, references, test scores, transcript. *Deadline:* June 20.

Contact: Shannon Meier, Membership Coordinator
Midwest Roofing Contractors Association
4840 West 15th Street, Suite 1000
Lawrence, KS 66049-3876
Phone: 800-497-6722
Fax: 785-843-7555
E-mail: membership@mrca.org

NASA DELAWARE SPACE GRANT CONSORTIUM http://www.delspace.org

NASA DELAWARE SPACE GRANT UNDERGRADUATE TUITION SCHOLARSHIP

The NASA/DESGC Undergraduate Summer and Undergraduate Tuition Scholarships are awarded annually to encourage and recognize highly qualified undergraduate students interested in careers related to aerospace engineering and space science related fields. All must be enrolled in a DESGC affiliate member college or university. Must be a U.S. citizen.

Academic Fields/Career Goals: Applied Sciences; Aviation/Aerospace; Chemical Engineering; Civil Engineering; Earth Science; Electrical Engineering/Electronics; Engineering/Technology; Engineering-Related Technologies; Mechanical Engineering; Meteorology/Atmospheric Science; Physical Sciences and Math; Science, Technology, and Society.

Award: Scholarship for use in sophomore, junior, or senior years; not renewable. *Number:* 6–12. *Amount:* $1400–$4000.

Eligibility Requirements: Applicant must be enrolled or expecting to enroll full-time at a two-year or four-year institution or university and studying in Delaware or Pennsylvania. Available to U.S. citizens.

Application Requirements: Application, essay, references, transcript, proof of U.S. citizenship. *Deadline:* March 1.

Contact: Ms. Sherry L. Rowland-Perry, Program Coordinator
NASA Delaware Space Grant Consortium
217 Sharp Lab, University of Delaware
Newark, DE 19716-4793
Phone: 302-831-1094
Fax: 302-831-1843
E-mail: desgc@bartol.udel.edu

NASA IDAHO SPACE GRANT CONSORTIUM http://www.uidaho.edu/nasa_isgc

NASA IDAHO SPACE GRANT CONSORTIUM SCHOLARSHIP PROGRAM

Program awards a $1000 scholarship renewable for four years based on GPA (above a 3.0), area of study (science/math/engineering or math/science education), full-time status, and attending an Idaho institution. $1000 is per academic year ($500 each semester).

Academic Fields/Career Goals: Applied Sciences; Aviation/Aerospace; Biology; Chemical Engineering; Computer Science/Data Processing; Earth Science; Education; Electrical Engineering/Electronics; Engineering/Technology; Health and Medical Sciences; Physical Sciences and Math; Science, Technology, and Society.

Award: Scholarship for use in freshman, sophomore, junior, or senior years; renewable. *Number:* 1–22. *Amount:* $1000.

Eligibility Requirements: Applicant must be enrolled or expecting to enroll full-time at a two-year or four-year institution or university and studying in Idaho. Applicant must have 3.0 GPA or higher. Available to U.S. citizens.

Application Requirements: Application, essay, resume, references, test scores, transcript. *Deadline:* March 1.

Contact: Dr. Jean Teasdale, Director
NASA Idaho Space Grant Consortium
University of Idaho, PO Box 441011
Moscow, ID 83844-1011
Phone: 208-885-6438
Fax: 208-885-1399
E-mail: isgc@uidaho.edu

NASA VERMONT SPACE GRANT CONSORTIUM http://www.emba.uvm.edu/vsgc

VERMONT SPACE GRANT CONSORTIUM SCHOLARSHIP PROGRAM

Career goals must be in area related to NASA's interest. Applicant must be resident of Vermont, U.S. citizen, and attend or plan to attend an institution within Vermont. Three scholarships are designated to Native-American recipients. Awards subject to availability of NASA funding. Deadline: March 1.

Academic Fields/Career Goals: Applied Sciences; Aviation/Aerospace; Biology; Earth Science; Engineering/Technology; Engineering-Related Technologies; Health and Medical Sciences; Materials Science, Engineering, and Metallurgy; Meteorology/Atmospheric Science; Natural Sciences; Physical Sciences and Math; Transportation.

Award: Scholarship for use in freshman, sophomore, junior, or senior years; renewable. *Number:* 10. *Amount:* $1500.

Eligibility Requirements: Applicant must be enrolled or expecting to enroll full-time at a two-year or four-year or technical institution or university; resident of Vermont and studying in Vermont. Applicant must have 3.0 GPA or higher. Available to U.S. citizens.

Application Requirements: Application, essay, references, test scores, transcript. *Deadline:* March 1.

Contact: Laurel Zeno, VSGC Grant Administrator/Program Coordinator
NASA Vermont Space Grant Consortium
Votey Building, University of Vermont, College of Engineering and Math
Burlington, VT 05405-0156
Phone: 802-656-1429
Fax: 802-656-1102
E-mail: zeno@emba.uvm.edu

NATIONAL INVENTORS HALL OF FAME http://www.invent.org/collegiate

COLLEGIATE INVENTORS COMPETITION - GRAND PRIZE

The Collegiate Inventors Competition is a national competition designed to encourage college students to be active in science, engineering, mathematics, technology and creative invention, while stimulating their problem-solving abilities. This prestigious challenge recognizes the working relationship between a student and his or her advisor who are involved in projects leading to inventions that can be patented. The grand prize-winning student - or student team - receives a $50,000 cash prize. Advisors each receive a $10,000 cash prize.

Academic Fields/Career Goals: Applied Sciences; Biology; Chemical Engineering; Computer Science/Data Processing; Engineering/Technology; Engineering-Related Technologies; Environmental Science; Health and Medical Sciences; Materials Science, Engineering, and Metallurgy; Physical Sciences and Math.

Award: Prize for use in freshman, sophomore, junior, senior, graduate, or postgraduate years; not renewable. *Number:* 1. *Amount:* up to $50,000.

Eligibility Requirements: Applicant must be enrolled or expecting to enroll full or part-time at a two-year or four-year institution or university. Available to U.S. and non-U.S. citizens.

Application Requirements: Application, applicant must enter a contest, form on Web site. *Deadline:* June 1.

Contact: Ray DePuy, Program Coordinator
National Inventors Hall of Fame
221 South Broadway Street
Akron, OH 44308-1505
Phone: 330-849-6887
Fax: 330-762-6313
E-mail: rdepuy@invent.org

COLLEGIATE INVENTORS COMPETITION FOR UNDERGRADUATE STUDENTS

The Collegiate Inventors Competition is a national competition designed to encourage college students to be active in science, engineering, mathematics, technology, and creative invention, while stimulating their problem solving abilities. This prestigious challenge recognizes the working relationship between a student and their advisor who are involved in projects that can be patented. The prize winning undergraduate student or student-team receives a $15000 cash prize. Advisors each receive a $5000 cash prize.

Academic Fields/Career Goals: Applied Sciences; Biology; Chemical Engineering; Computer Science/Data Processing; Engineering/Technology; Engineering-Related Technologies; Environmental Science; Health and Medical Sciences; Materials Science, Engineering, and Metallurgy; Physical Sciences and Math.

Award: Prize for use in sophomore, junior, or senior years; not renewable. *Number:* up to 1. *Amount:* up to $15,000.

Eligibility Requirements: Applicant must be enrolled or expecting to enroll full or part-time at a four-year institution or university. Available to U.S. and non-U.S. citizens.

Application Requirements: Application, form on Web site. *Deadline:* June 1.

Contact: Ray DePuy, Program Coordinator
National Inventors Hall of Fame
221 South Broadway Street
Akron, OH 44308-1505
Phone: 330-849-6887
Fax: 330-762-6313
E-mail: rdepuy@invent.org

SOCIETY FOR MINING, METALLURGY AND EXPLORATION - CENTRAL WYOMING SECTION

COATES, WOLFF, RUSSELL MINING INDUSTRY SCHOLARSHIP

One-time award for Wyoming residents studying mining related fields. Must be full-time undergraduate at sophomore level or above. Minimum 2.5 GPA required. Open to U.S. citizens. Application deadline is November 30.

Society for Mining, Metallurgy and Exploration - Central Wyoming Section (continued)

Academic Fields/Career Goals: Applied Sciences; Chemical Engineering; Civil Engineering; Earth Science; Materials Science, Engineering, and Metallurgy; Mechanical Engineering; Natural Resources; Natural Sciences.

Award: Scholarship for use in sophomore, junior, or senior years; not renewable. *Number:* 3. *Amount:* $1000.

Eligibility Requirements: Applicant must be enrolled or expecting to enroll full-time at a two-year or four-year or technical institution or university and resident of Wyoming. Applicant must have 2.5 GPA or higher. Available to U.S. citizens.

Application Requirements: Application, essay, transcript. *Deadline:* November 30.

Contact: Wayne Heili, Scholarship Committee Chairman
Society for Mining, Metallurgy and Exploration - Central Wyoming Section
4210 Deer Run
Casper, WY 82601
Phone: 307-234-5019

SOCIETY OF MEXICAN AMERICAN ENGINEERS AND SCIENTISTS

http://www.maes-natl.org

GRE AND GRADUATE APPLICATIONS WAIVER

Grant serves as a fee waiver for the cost of testing for and applying to graduate school. Must be Mexican-American and a member of the Society of Mexican-American Engineers and Scientists, Inc. (MAES). Minimum GPA of 2.75 required. For more details and an application go to Web site: http://www.maes-natl.org.

Academic Fields/Career Goals: Applied Sciences; Aviation/Aerospace; Biology; Chemical Engineering; Civil Engineering; Earth Science; Electrical Engineering/Electronics; Engineering/Technology; Engineering-Related Technologies; Environmental Science; Science, Technology, and Society.

Award: Grant for use in senior year; not renewable. *Number:* 12. *Amount:* $135–$235.

Eligibility Requirements: Applicant must be of Mexican heritage; Hispanic and enrolled or expecting to enroll full or part-time at an institution or university. Available to U.S. citizens.

Application Requirements: Application, essay, resume, test scores, application for graduate school. *Deadline:* varies.

Contact: Gary Cruz, Pagess Director
Society of Mexican American Engineers and Scientists
711 West Bay Area Boulevard, Suite 206
Webster, TX 77598-4051
Phone: 281-557-3677
Fax: 281-557-3757
E-mail: pagess@maes-natl.org

TEXAS HIGHER EDUCATION COORDINATING BOARD

http://www.collegefortexans.com

FIREFIGHTER EXEMPTION PROGRAM-TEXAS

One-time award assists firemen enrolled in fire science courses as part of a fire science curriculum. Award is exemption from tuition and laboratory fees at publicly supported Texas colleges. Contact the admissions/registrar's office for information on how to apply.

Academic Fields/Career Goals: Applied Sciences; Physical Sciences and Math; Trade/Technical Specialties.

Award: Scholarship for use in freshman, sophomore, junior, or senior years; not renewable. *Number:* varies. *Amount:* varies.

Eligibility Requirements: Applicant must be enrolled or expecting to enroll full or part-time at a two-year or four-year or technical institution; resident of Texas and studying in Texas. Applicant or parent of applicant must have employment or volunteer experience in fire service or police/firefighting. Available to U.S. citizens.

Application Requirements: Application. *Deadline:* Continuous.

Contact: Financial Aid Office at college
Texas Higher Education Coordinating Board
PO Box 12788
Austin, TX 78711-2788
Phone: 512-427-6101
Fax: 512-427-6127
E-mail: grantinfo@thecb.state.tx.us

TKE EDUCATIONAL FOUNDATION

http://www.tkefoundation.org

CARROL C. HALL MEMORIAL SCHOLARSHIP

One-time award of $350 given to a full-time undergraduate member of Tau Kappa Epsilon who has demonstrated leadership within chapter, campus, and community. Must be earning a degree in education or science and planning to become a teacher or pursue a profession in science. Recent head and shoulders photograph must be submitted with application. Minimum 3.0 GPA required.

Academic Fields/Career Goals: Applied Sciences; Biology; Earth Science; Education; Meteorology/Atmospheric Science; Physical Sciences and Math.

Award: Scholarship for use in freshman, sophomore, junior, or senior years; not renewable. *Number:* 1. *Amount:* $350.

Eligibility Requirements: Applicant must be enrolled or expecting to enroll full-time at a four-year institution or university; male and must have an interest in leadership. Applicant must have 3.0 GPA or higher. Available to U.S. and non-U.S. citizens.

Application Requirements: Application, essay, photo, transcript. *Deadline:* May 15.

Contact: Tim Taschwer, President/CEO
TKE Educational Foundation
8645 Founders Road
Indianapolis, IN 46268-1393
Phone: 317-872-6533
Fax: 317-875-8353
E-mail: tef@tkehq.org

UNIVERSITIES SPACE RESEARCH ASSOCIATION

http://www.usra.edu/hq/scholarships/overview.shtml

UNIVERSITIES SPACE RESEARCH ASSOCIATION SCHOLARSHIP PROGRAM

Award for full-time undergraduate students attending a 4-year accredited college or university that offers courses leading to a degree in physical sciences or engineering. Applicants must have completed at least two (2) years of college credits by the time the award is received. Must be U.S. citizens. Applicants must be majoring in the physical sciences or engineering. This would include, but is not limited to, aerospace engineering, astronomy, biophysics, chemistry, chemical engineering, computer science, electrical engineering, geophysics, geology, mathematics, mechanical engineering, physics, and space science education. Minimum 3.5 GPA required. Visit Web site at http://www.usra.edu /hq/scholarships/overview.shtml for more information and to download application. No forms will be mailed out.

Academic Fields/Career Goals: Applied Sciences; Aviation/Aerospace; Chemical Engineering; Civil Engineering; Earth Science; Electrical Engineering/Electronics; Engineering/Technology; Materials Science, Engineering, and Metallurgy; Mechanical Engineering; Nuclear Science; Physical Sciences and Math; Science, Technology, and Society.

Award: Scholarship for use in junior or senior years; not renewable. *Number:* 1–3. *Amount:* $500.

Eligibility Requirements: Applicant must be enrolled or expecting to enroll full-time at a four-year institution or university. Applicant must have 3.5 GPA or higher. Available to U.S. citizens.

Application Requirements: Application, essay, references, transcript. *Deadline:* May 1.

Contact: Application forms available at Web site only.

ARCHAEOLOGY

AMERICAN SCHOOL OF CLASSICAL STUDIES AT ATHENS http://www.ascsa.edu.gr

ASCSA SUMMER SESSIONS

• *See page 65*

AMERICAN SCHOOLS OF ORIENTAL RESEARCH (ASOR) http://www.asor.org

CYPRUS AMERICAN ARCHAEOLOGICAL RESEARCH INSTITUTE HELENA WYLDE AND STUART SWINY FELLOWSHIP

One $750 grant for an upper-level undergraduate student in a U.S. college or university to pursue a research project relevant to an ongoing field project in Cyprus. Residence at CAARI is mandatory. Submit project statement, work schedule, budget, curriculum vitae, and 2 letters of recommendation. Application deadline: February 2.

Academic Fields/Career Goals: Archaeology; European Studies; Near and Middle East Studies.

Award: Grant for use in junior or senior years; not renewable. *Number:* 1. *Amount:* $750.

Eligibility Requirements: Applicant must be enrolled or expecting to enroll at a four-year institution or university. Available to U.S. citizens.

Application Requirements: Application, references, project statement, work schedule, budget, curriculum vitae. *Deadline:* February 2.

Contact: CAARI at Boston University
American Schools of Oriental Research (ASOR)
656 Beacon Street, 5th Floor
Boston, MA 02215
Fax: 617-353-6575
E-mail: caari@bu.edu

HARVARD TRAVELLERS CLUB

HARVARD TRAVELLERS CLUB GRANTS

Approximately three grants made each year to persons with projects that involve intelligent travel and exploration. The travel must be intimately involved with research and/or exploration. Prefer applications from persons working on advanced degrees.

Academic Fields/Career Goals: Archaeology; Area/Ethnic Studies; Geography; History; Humanities; Natural Sciences.

Award: Grant for use in freshman, sophomore, junior, senior, graduate, or postgraduate years; not renewable. *Number:* 3–4. *Amount:* $500–$1000.

Eligibility Requirements: Applicant must be enrolled or expecting to enroll full or part-time at a four-year institution or university. Available to U.S. and non-U.S. citizens.

Application Requirements: Application, financial need analysis, resume. *Deadline:* February 28.

Contact: Mr. Jesse R. Page, Trustee
Harvard Travellers Club
PO Box 162
Lincoln, MA 01773
Phone: 781-259-8865
E-mail: jessepage@comcast.net

ARCHITECTURE

AACE INTERNATIONAL http://www.aacei.org

AACE INTERNATIONAL COMPETITIVE SCHOLARSHIP

One-time awards to full-time students pursuing a degree in engineering, construction management, quantity surveying and related fields. Application deadline is October 15.

Academic Fields/Career Goals: Architecture; Aviation/Aerospace; Chemical Engineering; Civil Engineering; Computer Science/Data Processing; Electrical Engineering/Electronics; Engineering/Technology; Engineering-Related Technologies; Mechanical Engineering.

Award: Scholarship for use in sophomore, junior, senior, or graduate years; not renewable. *Number:* 15–25. *Amount:* $750–$3000.

Eligibility Requirements: Applicant must be enrolled or expecting to enroll full-time at a two-year or four-year or technical institution or university. Available to U.S. and non-U.S. citizens.

Application Requirements: Application, essay, transcript. *Deadline:* October 15.

Contact: Ms. Charla Miller, Staff Director-Education and Administration
AACE International
209 Prairie Avenue, Suite 100
Morgantown, WV 26501
Phone: 304-296-8444 Ext. 113
Fax: 304-291-5728
E-mail: cmiller@aacei.org

ACI INTERNATIONAL/CONCRETE RESEARCH AND EDUCATION FOUNDATION (CONREF) http://www.concrete.org

PETER D. COURTOIS CONCRETE CONSTRUCTION SCHOLARSHIP

Two $1000 awards are available for the pursuit of study in a concrete-related field. The student must have senior status in a four-year or longer undergraduate program in engineering, construction, or technology and demonstrate interest and ability to work in the field of concrete construction. See Web site for more details (http://www.concrete.org).

Academic Fields/Career Goals: Architecture; Civil Engineering; Engineering/Technology; Materials Science, Engineering, and Metallurgy.

Award: Scholarship for use in senior year; not renewable. *Number:* 2. *Amount:* $1000.

Eligibility Requirements: Applicant must be enrolled or expecting to enroll at a four-year institution or university. Available to U.S. and Canadian citizens.

Application Requirements: Application, references. *Deadline:* December 15.

Contact: Ms. Jessie Bournay, Fundraising and Scholarship Assistant
ACI International/Concrete Research and Education Foundation (CONREF)
38800 Country Club Drive
Farmington Hills, MI 48331
Phone: 248-848-3832
Fax: 248-848-3740
E-mail: scholarships@concrete.org

ADELANTE! U.S. EDUCATION LEADERSHIP FUND

ADELANTE U.S. EDUCATION LEADERSHIP FUND

Renewable award for college juniors or seniors of Hispanic descent. Award primarily created to enhance the leadership qualities of the recipients for transition into postgraduate education, business and/or corporate America. Financial need is a factor for this award. Minimum 3.0 GPA required. Awards available for study at only a limited number of colleges. All of these colleges are located in the states of California, New Mexico, Arizona, Texas, Florida, Illinois, and New York. Applicants should contact the scholarship aid office of their university to find out if the award is available at their school.

Academic Fields/Career Goals: Architecture.

Award: Scholarship for use in junior or senior years; renewable. *Number:* varies. *Amount:* $3000.

Eligibility Requirements: Applicant must be Hispanic; enrolled or expecting to enroll full-time at a four-year institution or university and studying in Arizona, California, Florida, Illinois, New Mexico, New York, or Texas. Applicant must have 3.0 GPA or higher. Available to U.S. citizens.

Application Requirements: Application, essay, financial need analysis, references, transcript. *Deadline:* Continuous.

Contact: scholarship aid office at your college

AIA NEW JERSEY SCHOLARSHIP FOUNDATION, INC.

NJSA SCHOLARSHIP PROGRAM

One-time award for legal residents of New Jersey enrolled in an accredited architecture program. Minimum 2.5 GPA required. Must show evidence of financial need, scholarship, and promise in architecture. Submit portfolio and $5 application fee.

Academic Fields/Career Goals: Architecture.

Award: Scholarship for use in sophomore, junior, senior, or graduate years; not renewable. *Number:* 5–8. *Amount:* $1500–$3000.

Eligibility Requirements: Applicant must be enrolled or expecting to enroll full-time at a four-year or technical institution or university and resident of New Jersey. Applicant must have 2.5 GPA or higher. Available to U.S. citizens.

Application Requirements: Application, essay, financial need analysis, portfolio, references, transcript. *Fee:* $5. *Deadline:* April 25.

Contact: Robert Zaccone, President
AIA New Jersey Scholarship Foundation, Inc.
212 White Avenue
Old Tappan, NJ 07675-7411
Fax: 201-767-5541

AMERICAN ARCHITECTURAL FOUNDATION http://www.archfoundation.org

AMERICAN INSTITUTE OF ARCHITECTS MINORITY/DISADVANTAGED SCHOLARSHIP

Renewable award for high school seniors and college freshmen who are entering an architecture degree program. Must be nominated by architect firm, teacher, dean, civic organization director by December. Must include drawing. Deadline for nominations: December 6. Deadline for applications: January 15. Co-sponsored by AIA and AAF.

Academic Fields/Career Goals: Architecture.

Award: Scholarship for use in freshman year; renewable. *Number:* 20. *Amount:* $500–$2500.

Eligibility Requirements: Applicant must be enrolled or expecting to enroll full-time at a four-year institution or university. Available to U.S. citizens.

Application Requirements: Application, financial need analysis, references, test scores, transcript, drawing. *Deadline:* January 15.

Contact: Mary Felber, Director of Scholarship Programs
American Architectural Foundation
1735 New York Avenue, NW
Washington, DC 20006-5292
Phone: 202-626-7511
Fax: 202-626-7509
E-mail: mfelber@archfoundation.org

AMERICAN INSTITUTE OF ARCHITECTS http://www.aia.org

AMERICAN INSTITUTE OF ARCHITECTS/AMERICAN ARCHITECTURAL FOUNDATION MINORITY/DISADVANTAGED SCHOLARSHIPS

Award to aid high school seniors and college freshmen from minority or disadvantaged backgrounds who are planning to study architecture in an NAAB accredited program. Twenty awards per year, renewable for two additional years. Amounts based on financial need. Must be nominated by either a high school guidance counselor, AIA component, architect, or other individual who is aware of the student's interest and aptitude. Nomination deadline is early December; applications will be mailed to eligible students. Application deadline is mid-January.

Academic Fields/Career Goals: Architecture.

Award: Scholarship for use in freshman, sophomore, junior, or senior years; renewable. *Number:* up to 20. *Amount:* $500–$2500.

Eligibility Requirements: Applicant must be enrolled or expecting to enroll at a four-year institution or university. Available to U.S. citizens.

Application Requirements: Application, essay, references, transcript, statement of disadvantaged circumstances, a drawing. *Deadline:* January 15.

Contact: Mary Felber, Scholarship Chair
American Institute of Architects
1735 New York Avenue, NW
Washington, DC 20006-5292
Phone: 202-626-7511
Fax: 202-626-7509
E-mail: mfelber@aia.org

AMERICAN INSTITUTE OF ARCHITECTS, HAMPTON ROADS CHAPTER http://www.aiahr.com

AIA HAMPTON ROADS CHAPTER SCHOLARSHIP FOR ARCHITECTURAL STUDIES

Scholarship for an architectural student in third undergraduate year or above at accredited U.S. school of architecture. Must demonstrate high level of achievement in academics, community, and civic activity, and be a resident of AIA Hampton Roads geographic service area (southeastern Virginia). Contact Executive Director for application format. Apply through letter of recommendation from Dean of applicant's school.

Academic Fields/Career Goals: Architecture.

Award: Scholarship for use in junior, senior, or graduate years; not renewable. *Number:* 1. *Amount:* $1500–$2000.

Eligibility Requirements: Applicant must be enrolled or expecting to enroll full-time at a four-year institution or university and resident of Virginia. Available to U.S. citizens.

Application Requirements: Application, autobiography, financial need analysis, photo, references, transcript. *Deadline:* May 1.

Contact: Karenlee Oreo, Executive Director
American Institute of Architects, Hampton Roads Chapter
6282 Wailes Avenue
Norfolk, VA 23502
Phone: 757-455-5571
Fax: 757-455-9618
E-mail: aiahr@cox.net

AMERICAN INSTITUTE OF ARCHITECTS, NEW YORK CHAPTER http://www.aiany.org

ELEANOR ALLWORK SCHOLARSHIP GRANTS

Award available to students seeking first professional degree in architecture from an accredited New York school. Must demonstrate financial need. Must be a resident of New York metropolitan area. Must be nominated by Dean of architectural school.

Academic Fields/Career Goals: Architecture.

Award: Scholarship for use in freshman, sophomore, junior, senior, or graduate years; not renewable. *Number:* 4. *Amount:* $2500–$7500.

Eligibility Requirements: Applicant must be enrolled or expecting to enroll full-time at an institution or university; resident of New York and studying in New York.

Application Requirements: References, student project. *Deadline:* April 5.

Contact: Patty West, Manager of Special Programs and Communications
American Institute of Architects, New York Chapter
536 LaGuardia Place
New York, NY 10012
Phone: 212-683-0023
Fax: 212-696-5022

HASKELL AWARDS FOR STUDENTS IN ARCHITECTURAL JOURNALISM

One-time award for architectural students. The Douglas Haskell awards were founded to encourage excellence in writing on architecture and related design fields. Submit published article, essay, or journal with 100-word statement of purpose. Minimum $1000 prize.

Academic Fields/Career Goals: Architecture; Art History; Engineering/Technology; Landscape Architecture.

Award: Prize for use in freshman, sophomore, junior, or senior years; not renewable. *Number:* 1–3. *Amount:* $1000–$2000.

Eligibility Requirements: Applicant must be enrolled or expecting to enroll full or part-time at a two-year or four-year or technical institution or university. Available to U.S. citizens.

Application Requirements: Application, essay. *Deadline:* April 12.

Contact: Patty West, Manager of Special Programs and Communications
American Institute of Architects, New York Chapter
536 LaGuardia Place
New York, NY 10012
Phone: 212-683-0023
Fax: 212-696-5022

AMERICAN INSTITUTE OF ARCHITECTS, WEST VIRGINIA CHAPTER http://www.aiawv.org

AIA WEST VIRGINIA SCHOLARSHIP PROGRAM

Applicant must have completed junior year of an accredited undergraduate architectural program or enrolled in an accredited Masters of Architecture program. Select applicants must present a portfolio of work to judging committee. Please refer to Web site for further details: http://www.aiawv.org

Academic Fields/Career Goals: Architecture.

Award: Scholarship for use in senior, or graduate years. *Number:* varies. *Amount:* up to $7000.

Eligibility Requirements: Applicant must be enrolled or expecting to enroll at a four-year institution or university and resident of West Virginia. Available to U.S. citizens.

Application Requirements: Application, resume, references, transcript, personal letter. *Deadline:* May 30.

Contact: Roberta Guffey, Executive Director
American Institute of Architects, West Virginia Chapter
223 Hale Street
Charleston, WV 25301-2207
Phone: 304-344-9872
Fax: 304-343-0205
E-mail: roberta.guffey@aiawv.org

AMERICAN SCHOOL OF CLASSICAL STUDIES AT ATHENS http://www.ascsa.edu.gr

ASCSA SUMMER SESSIONS

• *See page 65*

ASSOCIATION FOR WOMEN IN ARCHITECTURE FOUNDATION http://www.awa-la.org

ASSOCIATION FOR WOMEN IN ARCHITECTURE SCHOLARSHIP

Must be a California resident or nonresident attending school in California. Must major in architecture or a related field and have completed 1 year (18 units) of schooling. Recipients may reapply. Open to women only. Interview in Los Angeles required. Application deadline is April 28. Applications available the beginning of February.

Academic Fields/Career Goals: Architecture; Interior Design; Landscape Architecture.

Award: Scholarship for use in sophomore, junior, senior, or graduate years; not renewable. *Number:* 3. *Amount:* $1000–$2500.

Eligibility Requirements: Applicant must be enrolled or expecting to enroll full-time at a two-year or four-year or technical institution or university and female. Available to U.S. and non-U.S. citizens.

Application Requirements: Application, essay, financial need analysis, interview, references, self-addressed stamped envelope, transcript. *Deadline:* April 28.

Contact: Nina Briggs, Scholarship Chair
Association for Women in Architecture Foundation
386 Beech Avenue Unit B4
Torrance, CA 90501-6203
Phone: 310-533-4042
E-mail: ninabriggs@earthlink.net

COMMUNITY FOUNDATION FOR PALM BEACH AND MARTIN COUNTIES, INC. http://www.yourcommunityfoundation.org

MABRY M. NOXON SCHOLARSHIP FUND

Graduating female high school senior attending public or private school in Palm Beach or Martin Counties. Must pursue a degree in business. Based on financial need.

Academic Fields/Career Goals: Architecture; Business/Consumer Services.

Award: Scholarship for use in freshman year; not renewable. *Amount:* $750–$2500.

Eligibility Requirements: Applicant must be high school student; planning to enroll or expecting to enroll full-time at a two-year or four-year or technical institution or university; female and resident of Florida. Available to U.S. citizens.

Application Requirements: Application, financial need analysis. *Deadline:* March 1.

Contact: Carolyn Jenco, Grants Manager/Scholarship Coordinator
Community Foundation for Palm Beach and Martin Counties, Inc.
700 South Dixie Highway
Suite 200
West Palm Beach, FL 33401

COMTO-BOSTON CHAPTER http://www.bostoncomto.org

COMTO BOSTON/GARRETT A. MORGAN SCHOLARSHIP

The COMTO-Boston scholarship program is designed to help minority youth maximize their educational potential in the transportation industry. We offer three corporate-sponsored scholarships specifically for engineering students and four chapter scholarships for graduating high school seniors pursuing careers in both transportation and non-transportation related fields.

Academic Fields/Career Goals: Architecture; Civil Engineering; Drafting; Education; Electrical Engineering/Electronics; Engineering/Technology; Engineering-Related Technologies; Mechanical Engineering; Surveying; Surveying Technology, Cartography, or Geographic Information Science; Transportation.

Award: Scholarship for use in freshman or sophomore years; not renewable. *Number:* up to 7. *Amount:* $1000–$2500.

Eligibility Requirements: Applicant must be American Indian/Alaska Native, Asian/Pacific Islander, Black (non-Hispanic), or Hispanic; enrolled or expecting to enroll full-time at a four-year or technical institution or university and resident of Massachusetts. Applicant must have 2.5 GPA or higher. Available to U.S. citizens.

Application Requirements: Application, essay, references, transcript. *Deadline:* March 31.

Contact: Virginia Turner, Scholarship Chairperson
COMTO-Boston Chapter
Scholarship Program
PO Box 1173
Boston, MA 02117-1173
Phone: 617-248-2878
Fax: 617-248-2904
E-mail: virginia.turner@state.ma.us

CONNECTICUT BUILDING CONGRESS http://www.cbc-ct.org

CONNECTICUT BUILDING CONGRESS SCHOLARSHIP FUND

Renewable award for Connecticut residents pursuing postsecondary studies in a construction-related field. Must be a U.S. citizen. Write for more information.

Academic Fields/Career Goals: Architecture; Civil Engineering; Drafting; Electrical Engineering/Electronics; Engineering/Technology; Engineering-Related Technologies; Heating, Air-Conditioning, and Refrigeration Mechanics; Landscape Architecture; Mechanical Engineering; Trade/Technical Specialties.

Award: Scholarship for use in freshman, sophomore, junior, or senior years; renewable. *Number:* 2–4. *Amount:* $500–$2000.

Connecticut Building Congress (continued)

Eligibility Requirements: Applicant must be enrolled or expecting to enroll full-time at a two-year or four-year institution or university and resident of Connecticut. Available to U.S. citizens.

Application Requirements: Application, essay, financial need analysis, interview, references, test scores, transcript. *Deadline:* March 1.

Contact: Jane Cox, Scholarship Director
Connecticut Building Congress
2600 Dixwell Avenue
Hamden, CT 06514-1833
Phone: 203-281-3183
Fax: 203-248-8932
E-mail: info@cbc-ct.org

DESIGN FIRM MANAGEMENT EDUCATION FOUNDATION, INC.

A/E PRONET SCHOLARSHIP

Award for full-time students who are sophomores, juniors, seniors, or first year graduate students whose studies include courses related to development of a higher level of design firm management skills. Working students who have completed at least 18 units of college level courses may also apply.

Academic Fields/Career Goals: Architecture; Business/Consumer Services.

Award: Scholarship for use in sophomore, junior, senior, graduate, or postgraduate years; not renewable. *Number:* 2–3. *Amount:* $500–$1500.

Eligibility Requirements: Applicant must be enrolled or expecting to enroll full or part-time at a two-year or four-year institution or university. Available to U.S. and non-U.S. citizens.

Application Requirements: Application, essay, transcript. *Deadline:* March 1.

Contact: Francine LaRose, SDA/C
Design Firm Management Education Foundation, Inc.
Hornberger & Worstell
170 Maiden Lane, Sixth Floor
San Francisco, CA 94108
Phone: 415-391-1080
E-mail: larose@hwiarchitects.com

FLORIDA EDUCATIONAL FACILITIES PLANNERS' ASSOCIATION

http://www.fefpa.org

FEFPA ASSISTANTSHIP

Scholarship supports full-time juniors, seniors and graduate students enrolled in an accredited four-year Florida university. Must be a resident of Florida with a 3.0 GPA. For more information go to Web site: http://www.fefpa.org.

Academic Fields/Career Goals: Architecture; Civil Engineering; Electrical Engineering/Electronics; Engineering/Technology; Engineering-Related Technologies; Landscape Architecture; Mechanical Engineering.

Award: Scholarship for use in junior, senior, or graduate years; renewable. *Number:* 2. *Amount:* $3000.

Eligibility Requirements: Applicant must be enrolled or expecting to enroll full-time at a four-year institution or university; resident of Florida and studying in Florida. Applicant must have 3.0 GPA or higher. Available to U.S. and non-U.S. citizens.

Application Requirements: Application, essay, financial need analysis, references, transcript. *Deadline:* April 3.

Contact: Florida Educational Facilities Planners' Association
Florida International University
University Park CSC 236
Miami, FL 33199

FOUNDATION OF THE WALL AND CEILING INDUSTRY

http://www.awci.org/thefoundation.shtml

FOUNDATION OF THE WALL AND CEILING INDUSTRY SCHOLARSHIP PROGRAM

This scholarship provides financial assistance to an Association of the Wall and Ceiling Industries (AWCI) member or the dependent of an AWCI member who will be pursuing a degree in architecture, engineering or construction management. Funds can be used at any accredited college or university or a trade/technical institution. Eligible applicants must have a 3.0 GPA.

Academic Fields/Career Goals: Architecture; Civil Engineering; Engineering/Technology; Engineering-Related Technologies; Materials Science, Engineering, and Metallurgy.

Award: Scholarship for use in freshman, sophomore, junior, senior, graduate, or postgraduate years; not renewable. *Number:* 1. *Amount:* $10,000.

Eligibility Requirements: Applicant must be enrolled or expecting to enroll full-time at a two-year or four-year or technical institution or university. Applicant or parent of applicant must be member of Association of the Wall and Ceiling Industry International. Applicant must have 3.0 GPA or higher. Available to U.S. and non-U.S. citizens.

Application Requirements: Application, essay, references, test scores, transcript. *Deadline:* August 1.

Contact: Jane Northern, Director of Membership Marketing and Programs
Foundation of the Wall and Ceiling Industry
803 West Broad Street, Suite 600
Falls Church, VA 22046
Phone: 703-538-1615
Fax: 703-534-8307
E-mail: northern@awci.org

HAWAIIAN LODGE, F.& A. M.

http://www.hawaiianlodge.org/

HAWAIIAN LODGE SCHOLARSHIPS

Dedicated to worthy students in the areas of engineering, sciences, Hawaiian studies, and education who would otherwise not be able to attend college.

Academic Fields/Career Goals: Architecture; Biology; Chemical Engineering; Civil Engineering; Computer Science/Data Processing; Dental Health/Services; Electrical Engineering/Electronics; Energy and Power Engineering; Engineering/Technology; Engineering-Related Technologies; Health and Medical Sciences.

Award: Scholarship for use in freshman, sophomore, junior, or senior years; renewable. *Number:* 4–16. *Amount:* $1000.

Eligibility Requirements: Applicant must be high school student; planning to enroll or expecting to enroll full-time at a four-year institution or university and resident of Hawaii. Applicant must have 3.0 GPA or higher. Available to U.S. citizens.

Application Requirements: Application, autobiography, essay, financial need analysis, interview, references, test scores, transcript. *Deadline:* May 1.

Contact: Chairman, Scholarship Committee
Hawaiian Lodge, F.& A. M.
1227 Makiki Street
Honolulu, HI 96814
Phone: 808-979-7809
E-mail: secretary@hawaiianlodge.org

HISPANIC COLLEGE FUND, INC.

http://www.hispanicfund.org

DENNY'S/HISPANIC COLLEGE FUND SCHOLARSHIP

• *See page 41*

EL NUEVO CONSTRUCTOR SCHOLARSHIP PROGRAM

Program intended for undergraduate student pursuing his or her associate's or bachelor's degree in a construction related field. Applicant must be a U.S. citizen with Hispanic background. Must attend college or university in U.S. or Puerto Rico. Online application only: http://www.hispanicfund.org.

Academic Fields/Career Goals: Architecture; Drafting; Heating, Air-Conditioning, and Refrigeration Mechanics; Industrial Design.

Award: Scholarship for use in freshman, sophomore, junior, or senior years; not renewable. *Number:* varies. *Amount:* $500–$5000.

Eligibility Requirements: Applicant must be Hispanic and enrolled or expecting to enroll full-time at a two-year or four-year institution or university. Applicant must have 3.0 GPA or higher. Available to U.S. citizens.

Application Requirements: Application. *Deadline:* April 15.

Contact: Stina Augustsson, Program Manager
Hispanic College Fund, Inc.
1717 Pennsylvania Avenue, NW, Suite 460
Washington, DC 20006
Phone: 202-296-5400
Fax: 202-296-3774
E-mail: hcf-info@hispanicfund.org

ILLUMINATING ENGINEERING SOCIETY OF NORTH AMERICA http://www.iesna.org

ROBERT W. THUNEN MEMORIAL SCHOLARSHIPS

One-time award for juniors, seniors, or graduate students enrolled at four-year colleges and universities in northern California, Nevada, Oregon, or Washington pursuing lighting career. Submit statement describing proposed lighting course work or project and three recommendations, at least one from someone involved professionally or academically with lighting. Curriculum must be accredited by ABET, ACSA, or FIDER.

Academic Fields/Career Goals: Architecture; Engineering/Technology; Engineering-Related Technologies; Interior Design; Performing Arts; TV/Radio Broadcasting.

Award: Scholarship for use in junior, senior, or graduate years; not renewable. *Number:* 2. *Amount:* $2500.

Eligibility Requirements: Applicant must be enrolled or expecting to enroll full-time at a four-year institution or university and studying in California, Nevada, Oregon, or Washington. Available to U.S. and non-U.S. citizens.

Application Requirements: Application, references, transcript. *Deadline:* March 1.

Contact: William Hanley, Executive Department
Illuminating Engineering Society of North America
120 Wall Street
New York, NY 10005-4001
Phone: 212-248-5000
Fax: 212-248-5017
E-mail: whanley@iesna.org

ILLUMINATING ENGINEERING SOCIETY OF NORTH AMERICA–GOLDEN GATE SECTION http://www.iesgg.org

ALAN LUCAS MEMORIAL EDUCATIONAL SCHOLARSHIP

Scholarship available to full time student for pursuit of lighting education or research as part of undergraduate, graduate, or doctoral studies. Must attend a four year college or university located in Northern California (including San Luis Obispo, Fresno, and north). Must submit application, statement of purpose, description of work in progress, transcripts, and three recommendations by April 3.

Academic Fields/Career Goals: Architecture; Electrical Engineering/Electronics; Filmmaking/Video; Interior Design.

Award: Scholarship for use in junior, senior, or graduate years; not renewable. *Number:* 1. *Amount:* $1500.

Eligibility Requirements: Applicant must be enrolled or expecting to enroll full-time at a four-year institution or university and studying in California. Available to U.S. citizens.

Application Requirements: Application, references, transcript, statement of purpose, Scholar Agreement. *Deadline:* April 3.

Contact: Phil Hall, Coordinator
Illuminating Engineering Society of North America–Golden Gate Section
1514 Gibbons Drive
Alameda, CA 94501
Phone: 510-208-5005 Ext. 3030
E-mail: information@iesgg.org

ROBERT W. THUNEN MEMORIAL SCHOLARSHIPS

Scholarships for full-time undergraduate, or graduate study in the lighting field. Must be a junior, senior, or graduate student in a 4-year college or university in Northern Nevada, Northern California, Oregon, or Washington. Must submit a least three letters of recommendation, statement of purpose, transcripts. Applications and complete information can be obtained from Web site: http://www.iesgg.org. Applications must be received by April 1.

Academic Fields/Career Goals: Architecture; Electrical Engineering/Electronics; Filmmaking/Video; Interior Design.

Award: Scholarship for use in junior, senior, or graduate years; not renewable. *Number:* up to 2. *Amount:* $2500.

Eligibility Requirements: Applicant must be enrolled or expecting to enroll full-time at a four-year institution or university and studying in California, Nevada, Oregon, or Washington. Available to U.S. citizens.

Application Requirements: Application, references, transcript, statement of purpose, Scholar Agreement. *Deadline:* April 1.

Contact: Phil Hall, Coordinator
Illuminating Engineering Society of North America–Golden Gate Section
1514 Gibbons Drive
Alameda, CA 94501
Phone: 510-208-5005 Ext. 3030
E-mail: information@iesgg.org

INTERNATIONAL FACILITY MANAGEMENT ASSOCIATION FOUNDATION http://www.ifma.org

IFMA FOUNDATION SCHOLARSHIPS

One-time scholarship of up to $6000 awarded to students currently enrolled in full-time facility management programs. Minimum 3.0 GPA required for undergraduates and 3.5 for graduate students. Application deadline is May 31.

Academic Fields/Career Goals: Architecture; Engineering-Related Technologies.

Award: Scholarship for use in freshman, sophomore, junior, senior, graduate, or postgraduate years; not renewable. *Number:* 10–15. *Amount:* $1000–$6000.

Eligibility Requirements: Applicant must be enrolled or expecting to enroll full-time at a four-year institution or university. Available to U.S. and non-U.S. citizens.

Application Requirements: Application, resume, references, transcript, letter of intent. *Deadline:* May 31.

Contact: Kim Coffey, Foundation Manager
International Facility Management Association Foundation
One East Greenway Plaza, Suite 1100
Houston, TX 77046-0194
Phone: 713-623-4362
Fax: 713-623-6124
E-mail: kim.coffey@ifma.org

MIDWEST ROOFING CONTRACTORS ASSOCIATION http://www.mrca.org

MRCA FOUNDATION SCHOLARSHIP PROGRAM

• *See page 70*

NATIONAL ASSOCIATION OF WOMEN IN CONSTRUCTION http://nawic.org

NAWIC UNDERGRADUATE SCHOLARSHIPS

One-time award for any student having at least one year of study remaining in a construction-related program leading to an associate or higher degree. Awards range from $500-$2000. Submit application and transcript of grades.

Academic Fields/Career Goals: Architecture; Civil Engineering; Drafting; Electrical Engineering/Electronics; Engineering/Technology; Engineering-Related Technologies; Interior Design; Landscape Architecture; Mechanical Engineering; Trade/Technical Specialties.

Award: Scholarship for use in sophomore, junior, or senior years; not renewable. *Number:* 40–50. *Amount:* $500–$2000.

Eligibility Requirements: Applicant must be enrolled or expecting to enroll full-time at a two-year or four-year or technical institution or university. Applicant must have 3.0 GPA or higher. Available to U.S. and non-U.S. citizens.

Application Requirements: Application, essay, financial need analysis, interview, transcript. *Deadline:* February 1.

Contact: Scholarship Administrator
National Association of Women in Construction
327 South Adams Street
Fort Worth, TX 76104

NATIONAL FEDERATION OF THE BLIND

http://www.nfb.org

HOWARD BROWN RICKARD SCHOLARSHIP

For legally blind full-time students planning to study architecture, engineering, law, medicine, or natural science. Must submit a letter from National Foundation of the Blind state officer with whom they have discussed their application. May reapply. Based on academic excellence, service to the community, and financial need. One-time award of $3000. Must attend school in the U.S.

Academic Fields/Career Goals: Architecture; Biology; Engineering/Technology; Health and Medical Sciences; Law/Legal Services; Natural Resources; Physical Sciences and Math.

Award: Scholarship for use in freshman, sophomore, junior, or senior years; not renewable. *Number:* 1. *Amount:* $3000.

Eligibility Requirements: Applicant must be enrolled or expecting to enroll full-time at an institution or university. Applicant or parent of applicant must have employment or volunteer experience in community service. Applicant must be visually impaired. Applicant must have 3.5 GPA or higher. Available to U.S. and non-U.S. citizens.

Application Requirements: Application, autobiography, essay, financial need analysis, references, transcript. *Deadline:* March 31.

Contact: Peggy Elliot, Chairman, Scholarship Committee
National Federation of the Blind
805 Fifth Avenue
Grinnell, IA 50112
Phone: 641-236-3366

NATIONAL INSTITUTE OF BUILDING SCIENCES, MULTIHAZARD MITIGATION COUNCIL

http://www.nibs.org

ARCHITECTURE, CONSTRUCTION, AND ENGINEERING MENTOR PROGRAM SCHOLARSHIPS

Scholarships intended to assist students in starting or completing an undergraduate degree program in a field directly related to architecture, construction, and/or engineering. Accompanying mentor activities will ensure that the students receive instruction in principles and practice of risk management. Three of the scholarships will be awarded to registered members of Federally-recognized Indian tribes.

Academic Fields/Career Goals: Architecture; Civil Engineering; Construction Engineering/Management; Engineering/Technology.

Award: Scholarship for use in freshman, sophomore, junior, or senior years. *Number:* 6. *Amount:* varies.

Eligibility Requirements: Applicant must be enrolled or expecting to enroll full-time at a four-year institution or university. Available to U.S. citizens.

Application Requirements: Application.

Contact: Pamela Mullender, Acting Executive Director, ACE Mentor Program
National Institute of Building Sciences, Multihazard Mitigation Council
National Institute of Building Sciences, 1090 Vermont Avenue, NW, Suite 700
Washington, DC 20005
Phone: 202-898-6396
Fax: 202-289-1092

NETWORK OF EXECUTIVE WOMEN IN HOSPITALITY

http://www.newh.org

NETWORK OF EXECUTIVE WOMEN IN HOSPITALITY, INC. SCHOLARSHIP

Each NEWH chapter provides scholarships for those wishing to enter the hospitality industry and related fields. Awards vary in number and dollar amount for each chapter. Must have completed half the requirements for a degree or certification program in which enrolled. Visit Web site or contact your local chapter for deadlines and further details.

Academic Fields/Career Goals: Architecture; Food Service/Hospitality; Hospitality Management; Interior Design; Landscape Architecture; Travel/Tourism.

Award: Scholarship for use in freshman, sophomore, junior, senior, or graduate years; not renewable. *Number:* varies. *Amount:* $500–$5000.

Eligibility Requirements: Applicant must be enrolled or expecting to enroll full or part-time at a two-year or four-year or technical institution or university. Applicant must have 3.0 GPA or higher. Available to U.S. and non-U.S. citizens.

Application Requirements: Application, financial need analysis, references, transcript. *Deadline:* varies.

Contact: Rebecca Folkerts, local NEWH Chapter
Phone: 800-593-6394

NEW JERSEY SOCIETY OF ARCHITECTS/AIA NEW JERSEY SCHOLARSHIP FOUNDATION

NEW JERSEY SOCIETY OF ARCHITECTS SCHOLARSHIP

Award for students with a career interest in architecture who are studying full time at an accredited four-year institution. Must be a resident of New Jersey. Scholarship is for sophomore, junior, or senior year, or master's-level study. Must demonstrate financial need or academic achievement. Application deadline is April 30.

Academic Fields/Career Goals: Architecture.

Award: Scholarship for use in sophomore, junior, senior, or graduate years; not renewable. *Number:* varies. *Amount:* $1500–$2500.

Eligibility Requirements: Applicant must be enrolled or expecting to enroll full-time at a four-year institution or university and resident of New Jersey.

Application Requirements: Application, essay, financial need analysis, references, transcript, photos of projects, FAFSA. *Fee:* $5. *Deadline:* April 30.

Contact: Robert Zaccone, President
New Jersey Society of Architects/AIA New Jersey Scholarship Foundation
212 White Avenue
Old Tappan, NJ 07675
Phone: 201-767-9575
Fax: 201-767-5541

NEW YORK STATE EDUCATION DEPARTMENT

http://www.highered.nysed.gov

REGENTS PROFESSIONAL OPPORTUNITY SCHOLARSHIP

• *See page 45*

OREGON STUDENT ASSISTANCE COMMISSION

http://www.osac.state.or.us

GLENN R. AND JUANITA B. STRUBLE SCHOLARSHIP II

One-time award for residents of Benton, Douglas, Jackson, Josephine, Lane, Linn, or Marion counties who are studying arts, engineering, or business management. Minimum 2.75 GPA for graduating high school seniors. Graduate students may be enrolled full or part time in the same majors.

Academic Fields/Career Goals: Architecture; Arts; Business/Consumer Services.

Award: Scholarship for use in freshman, sophomore, junior, senior, or graduate years; not renewable. *Number:* 1. *Amount:* $2800.

Eligibility Requirements: Applicant must be enrolled or expecting to enroll full or part-time at an institution or university and resident of Oregon.

Application Requirements: Application, essay, financial need analysis, transcript. *Deadline:* March 1.

Contact: Director of Grant Programs
Oregon Student Assistance Commission
1500 Valley River Drive, Suite 100
Eugene, OR 97401-7020
Phone: 800-452-8807 Ext. 7395
E-mail: awardinfo@mercury.osac.state.or.us

HOMESTEAD CAPITAL HOUSING SCHOLARSHIP

• *See page 46*

PLUMBING-HEATING-COOLING CONTRACTORS ASSOCIATION EDUCATION FOUNDATION

http://www.phccweb.org

BRADFORD WHITE CORPORATION SCHOLARSHIP

Scholarship for students enrolled in either an approved four-year PHCC apprenticeship program or an accredited two-year community college, technical college or trade school.

Academic Fields/Career Goals: Architecture; Business/Consumer Services; Civil Engineering; Engineering/Technology; Engineering-Related Technologies; Heating, Air-Conditioning, and Refrigeration Mechanics; Mechanical Engineering; Trade/Technical Specialties.

Award: Scholarship for use in freshman, sophomore, junior, or senior years. *Number:* 3. *Amount:* $2500.

Eligibility Requirements: Applicant must be enrolled or expecting to enroll at a two-year or four-year or technical institution.

Application Requirements: Application. *Deadline:* June 1.

Contact: Scholarship Administrator
Plumbing-Heating-Cooling Contractors Association Education Foundation
PO Box 6808
Falls Church, VA 22040
Phone: 800-533-7694
Fax: 703-237-7442
E-mail: naphcc@naphcc.org

DELTA FAUCET COMPANY SCHOLARSHIP PROGRAM

Applicants must be sponsored by a member of the National Association of Plumbing-Heating-Cooling Contractors. Applicants must pursue studies in a major related to the plumbing-heating-cooling industry. Visit Web site for additional information.

Academic Fields/Career Goals: Architecture; Business/Consumer Services; Civil Engineering; Engineering/Technology; Engineering-Related Technologies; Heating, Air-Conditioning, and Refrigeration Mechanics; Mechanical Engineering; Trade/Technical Specialties.

Award: Scholarship for use in freshman, sophomore, junior, or senior years; not renewable. *Number:* 6. *Amount:* $2500.

Eligibility Requirements: Applicant must be enrolled or expecting to enroll full or part-time at a four-year institution or university. Applicant must have 2.5 GPA or higher. Available to U.S. and non-U.S. citizens.

Application Requirements: Application, interview, references, test scores, transcript. *Deadline:* June 1.

Contact: Scholarship Administrator
Plumbing-Heating-Cooling Contractors Association Education Foundation
PO Box 6808
Falls Church, VA 22040
Phone: 800-533-7694
Fax: 703-237-7442
E-mail: naphcc@naphcc.org

PHCC EDUCATIONAL FOUNDATION NEED-BASED SCHOLARSHIP

Need-based scholarship worth a maximum of $2500 to a student enrolled in an approved four-year PHCC apprenticeship program, an accredited two-year technical college, community college or trade school or an accredited four-year college or university.

Academic Fields/Career Goals: Architecture; Business/Consumer Services; Civil Engineering; Engineering/Technology; Engineering-Related Technologies; Heating, Air-Conditioning, and Refrigeration Mechanics; Mechanical Engineering; Trade/Technical Specialties.

Award: Scholarship for use in freshman, sophomore, junior, or senior years; not renewable. *Number:* 1. *Amount:* $2500.

Eligibility Requirements: Applicant must be enrolled or expecting to enroll at a two-year or four-year or technical institution or university.

Application Requirements: Application. *Deadline:* May 1.

Contact: Scholarship Administrator
Plumbing-Heating-Cooling Contractors Association Education Foundation
PO Box 6808
Falls Church, VA 22040
Phone: 800-533-7694
Fax: 703-237-7442
E-mail: naphcc@naphcc.org

PHCC EDUCATIONAL FOUNDATION SCHOLARSHIP PROGRAM

Applicants must be sponsored by a member of the National Association of Plumbing-Heating-Cooling Contractors. Applicants must pursue studies in a major related to the plumbing-heating-cooling industry. Visit Web site for additional information.

Academic Fields/Career Goals: Architecture; Business/Consumer Services; Civil Engineering; Engineering/Technology; Engineering-Related Technologies; Heating, Air-Conditioning, and Refrigeration Mechanics; Mechanical Engineering; Trade/Technical Specialties.

Award: Scholarship for use in freshman, sophomore, junior, or senior years; renewable. *Number:* 5. *Amount:* $1500–$3000.

Eligibility Requirements: Applicant must be enrolled or expecting to enroll full or part-time at a two-year or four-year institution or university. Applicant must have 2.5 GPA or higher. Available to U.S. and non-U.S. citizens.

Application Requirements: Application, interview, references, test scores, transcript. *Deadline:* May 1.

Contact: Scholarship Administrator
Plumbing-Heating-Cooling Contractors Association Education Foundation
PO Box 6808
Falls Church, VA 22040
Phone: 800-533-7694
Fax: 703-237-7442
E-mail: naphcc@naphcc.org

SOCIETY OF AMERICAN REGISTERED ARCHITECTS

http://www.sara-national.org

SARA STUDENT DESIGN COMPETITION

One-time award for undergraduate or graduate students attending accredited architectural schools and enrolled in a B.A. or B.S. Architecture or M.Arch. program. Must submit five to ten slides of architectural project. Application deadline varies.

Academic Fields/Career Goals: Architecture.

Award: Prize for use in freshman, sophomore, junior, senior, or graduate years; not renewable. *Number:* up to 3. *Amount:* $1000–$3000.

Eligibility Requirements: Applicant must be enrolled or expecting to enroll full or part-time at a four-year institution or university. Available to U.S. and non-U.S. citizens.

Application Requirements: Applicant must enter a contest, essay, 5 to 10 slides, project. *Fee:* $15. *Deadline:* varies.

Contact: Cathie Moscato, Program Administrator
Society of American Registered Architects
PO Box 280
Cosby, TN 37822
Phone: 423-487-0365
Fax: 423-487-0365
E-mail: cathiemoscato@hotmail.com

UNICO NATIONAL, INC

http://www.unico.org

THEODORE MAZZA SCHOLARSHIP

Scholarship available to graduating high school senior. Must reside and attend high school within the corporate limits or adjoining suburbs of a city wherein an active chapter of UNICO National is located. Application must be signed by student's principal and properly certified by sponsoring Chapter President and Chapter Secretary. Must have letter of endorsement from President or Scholarship Chairperson of sponsoring Chapter.

Academic Fields/Career Goals: Architecture; Art History; Arts; Music.

UNICO National, Inc (continued)

Award: Scholarship for use in freshman, sophomore, junior, or senior years; renewable. *Number:* 1. *Amount:* $1500.

Eligibility Requirements: Applicant must be high school student and planning to enroll or expecting to enroll at a four-year institution. Available to U.S. citizens.

Application Requirements: Application, financial need analysis, references, transcript. *Deadline:* varies.

Contact: local UNICO chapter

WAVERLY COMMUNITY HOUSE, INC.

http://waverlycomm.com

F. LAMMOT BELIN ARTS SCHOLARSHIP

One-time award to current or former Northeastern Pennsylvania resident artists of outstanding aptitude and promise in the fine arts to further their development into professional artists. "Fine arts" is understood to mean creative, performing, or composing activities in such fields as painting, sculpture, photography, music, drama, dance, literature, and architecture. Application fee: $15. Application deadline: December 15. This grant is not intended for academic tuition.

Academic Fields/Career Goals: Architecture; Arts; Literature/English/Writing; Music; Performing Arts.

Award: Grant for use in freshman, sophomore, junior, senior, graduate, or postgraduate years; not renewable. *Number:* 1. *Amount:* $10,000.

Eligibility Requirements: Applicant must be enrolled or expecting to enroll at an institution or university and resident of Pennsylvania. Available to U.S. citizens.

Application Requirements: Application, references, tapes (VHS or cassette), compact disc, or slides. *Fee:* $15. *Deadline:* December 15.

Contact: Chairperson
Waverly Community House, Inc.
PO Box 142
1115 North Abington Road
Waverly, PA 18471
Phone: 570-586-8191
Fax: 570-586-0185
E-mail: info@waverlycomm.com

WEST VIRGINIA SOCIETY OF ARCHITECTS/AIA

WEST VIRGINIA SOCIETY OF ARCHITECTS/AIA SCHOLARSHIP

Award for West Virginia resident who has completed at least sixth semester of NAAB-accredited architectural program by May 30. Must submit resume and letter stating need, qualifications, and desire. Deadline: May 30.

Academic Fields/Career Goals: Architecture.

Award: Scholarship for use in junior, senior, graduate, or postgraduate years; not renewable. *Number:* varies. *Amount:* up to $7000.

Eligibility Requirements: Applicant must be enrolled or expecting to enroll at an institution or university and resident of West Virginia. Available to U.S. citizens.

Application Requirements: Application, resume, references, transcript. *Deadline:* May 30.

Contact: Ms. Roberta Guffey, Executive Director
West Virginia Society of Architects/AIA
223 Hale Street
Charleston, WV 25323
Phone: 304-344-9872
Fax: 304-343-0205

WORLDSTUDIO FOUNDATION

http://www.worldstudio.org

WORLDSTUDIO FOUNDATION SCHOLARSHIP PROGRAM

Worldstudio Foundation provides scholarships to minority and economically disadvantaged students who are studying the design/architecture/arts disciplines in American colleges and universities. Among the foundation's primary aims are to increase diversity in the creative professions and to foster social and environmental responsibility in the artists, designers, and studios of tomorrow. To this end, scholarship recipients are selected not only for their ability and their need, but also for their demonstrated commitment to giving back to the larger community through their work.

Academic Fields/Career Goals: Architecture; Arts; Fashion Design; Filmmaking/Video; Graphics/Graphic Arts/Printing; Industrial Design; Interior Design; Landscape Architecture.

Award: Scholarship for use in freshman, sophomore, junior, senior, graduate, or postgraduate years; not renewable. *Number:* 30–50. *Amount:* $1000–$5000.

Eligibility Requirements: Applicant must be enrolled or expecting to enroll full-time at a two-year or four-year or technical institution or university. Applicant must have 2.5 GPA or higher. Available to U.S. and non-U.S. citizens.

Application Requirements: Application, essay, financial need analysis, photo, portfolio, references, self-addressed stamped envelope, transcript. *Deadline:* March 19.

Contact: Scholarship Coordinator
Worldstudio Foundation
200 Varick Street, Suite 507
New York, NY 10014
Phone: 212-366-1317 Ext. 18
Fax: 212-807-0024
E-mail: scholarships@worldstudio.org

AREA/ETHNIC STUDIES

AMERICAN HISTORICAL ASSOCIATION

http://www.theaha.org

JOHN K. FAIRBANK PRIZE FOR EAST ASIAN HISTORY

Annual prize for best recent book on history of China proper, Vietnam, Chinese Central Asia, Mongolia, Manchuria, Korea, or Japan, since 1800. Only books of high scholarly and literary merit will be accepted. Copies must be sent to each committee member. Refer to Web site (http://www.theaha.org) for names and mailing addresses.

Academic Fields/Career Goals: Area/Ethnic Studies; Foreign Language; History; Humanities.

Award: Prize for use in freshman, sophomore, junior, senior, graduate, or postgraduate years; not renewable. *Number:* 1. *Amount:* varies.

Eligibility Requirements: Applicant must be enrolled or expecting to enroll at an institution or university and must have an interest in writing. Available to U.S. citizens.

Application Requirements: Applicant must enter a contest, copies of book. *Deadline:* May 17.

Contact: Book Prize Administrator
American Historical Association
400 A Street, SE
Washington, DC 20003
E-mail: aha@theaha.org

WESLEY-LOGAN PRIZE

• *See page 52*

CANADIAN INSTITUTE OF UKRAINIAN STUDIES

http://www.ualberta.ca/cius/

LEO J. KRYSA UNDERGRADUATE SCHOLARSHIP

One-time award for Canadian citizen or landed immigrant to enter their final year of undergraduate study in pursuit of a degree with emphasis on Ukrainian and/or Ukrainian-Canadian studies in the disciplines of education, history, humanities, or social sciences. To be used at any Canadian university for an eight-month period of study. Award is in Canadian dollars.

Academic Fields/Career Goals: Area/Ethnic Studies; Education; History; Humanities; Social Sciences.

Award: Scholarship for use in senior year; not renewable. *Number:* 1. *Amount:* up to $2600.

Eligibility Requirements: Applicant must be Canadian citizen; enrolled or expecting to enroll full-time at an institution or university; resident of Alberta, British Columbia, Manitoba, New Brunswick, Newfoundland, North West Territories, Nova Scotia, Ontario, Prince Edward Island, Quebec, Saskatchewan, or Yukon and studying in

Alberta, British Columbia, Manitoba, New Brunswick, Newfoundland, Nova Scotia, Ontario, Prince Edward Island, Quebec, or Saskatchewan.

Application Requirements: Application, references, transcript. *Deadline:* March 1.

Contact: Administrator
Canadian Institute of Ukrainian Studies
University of Alberta
Edmonton, AB T6G 2E8
Canada
Phone: 780-492-2972
Fax: 780-492-4967

CIRI FOUNDATION http://www.ciri.com/tcf

PETER KALIFORNSKY MEMORIAL ENDOWMENT SCHOLARSHIP FUND

Preference given to students enrolled in Alaska Native studies. Applicant must be Alaska Native student. For details see Web site: http://www.ciri.com/tcf.

Academic Fields/Career Goals: Area/Ethnic Studies.

Award: Scholarship for use in freshman, sophomore, junior, senior, or graduate years; not renewable. *Number:* varies. *Amount:* varies.

Eligibility Requirements: Applicant must be enrolled or expecting to enroll full-time at a two-year or four-year institution or university.

Application Requirements: Application, essay, references, transcript, proof of eligibility, birth certificate or adoption decree. *Deadline:* June 1.

Contact: CIRI Foundation
2600 Cordova Street, Suite 206
Anchorage, AK 99503
Phone: 907-263-5582
Fax: 907-263-5588
E-mail: tcf@ciri.com

CLAN MACBEAN FOUNDATION http://www.clanmacbean.net

CLAN MACBEAN FOUNDATION GRANT PROGRAM

Open to men and women of any race, color, creed or nationality. Grant is for course of study or project which reflects direct involvement in the preservation or enhancement of Scottish culture, or an effort that would contribute directly to the improvement of the human family. Applications may be obtained from the foundation. Deadline: May 1.

Academic Fields/Career Goals: Area/Ethnic Studies; Child and Family Studies.

Award: Grant for use in freshman, sophomore, junior, senior, or graduate years; not renewable. *Number:* 3–5. *Amount:* up to $3000.

Eligibility Requirements: Applicant must be enrolled or expecting to enroll full-time at a two-year or four-year institution or university. Available to U.S. and non-U.S. citizens.

Application Requirements: Application, references, transcript. *Deadline:* May 1.

Contact: Raymond Heckethorn, Treasurer
Clan MacBean Foundation
441 Wadsworth Boulevard, Suite 213
Denver, CO 80226
Phone: 303-233-6002
Fax: 303-233-6002
E-mail: macbean@ecentral.com

COSTUME SOCIETY OF AMERICA http://www.costumesocietyamerica.com

ADELE FILENE TRAVEL AWARD

One-time award for Costume Society of America members currently enrolled as students to assist their travel to Costume Society of America national symposium to present either a juried paper or a poster.

Academic Fields/Career Goals: Area/Ethnic Studies; Art History; Arts; Historic Preservation and Conservation; History; Home Economics; Museum Studies; Performing Arts.

Award: Prize for use in freshman, sophomore, junior, senior, or graduate years; not renewable. *Number:* 1–4. *Amount:* $150–$500.

Eligibility Requirements: Applicant must be enrolled or expecting to enroll full or part-time at a two-year or four-year or technical institution or university. Applicant or parent of applicant must be member of Costume Society of America. Available to U.S. and non-U.S. citizens.

Application Requirements: Application, references. *Deadline:* March 1.

Contact: Ms. Kaye Boyer, Manager
Costume Society of America
PO Box 73
Earleville, MD 21919-0073
Phone: 410-275-1619
Fax: 410-275-8936
E-mail: national.office@costumesocietyamerica.com

STELLA BLUM RESEARCH GRANT

One-time award for members of Costume Society of America with research projects in the field of North American costume which are part of the degree requirement. Must be enrolled at an accredited institution. Submit faculty recommendation. Merit-based award of up to $3000.

Academic Fields/Career Goals: Area/Ethnic Studies; Art History; Arts; Historic Preservation and Conservation; History; Home Economics; Museum Studies; Performing Arts.

Award: Grant for use in freshman, sophomore, junior, senior, or graduate years; not renewable. *Number:* 1. *Amount:* up to $3000.

Eligibility Requirements: Applicant must be enrolled or expecting to enroll full or part-time at a two-year or four-year or technical institution or university. Applicant or parent of applicant must be member of Costume Society of America. Available to U.S. and non-U.S. citizens.

Application Requirements: Application, essay, references, transcript, proposal, if necessary: permission letter from research site, budget. *Deadline:* May 1.

Contact: Ms. Kaye Boyer, Manager
Costume Society of America
PO Box 73
Earleville, MD 21919-0073
Phone: 410-275-1619
Fax: 410-275-8936
E-mail: national.office@costumesocietyamerica.com

CULTURE CONNECTION http://www.thecultureconnection.com

CULTURE CONNECTION FOUNDATION SCHOLARSHIP

• *See page 52*

HARVARD TRAVELLERS CLUB

HARVARD TRAVELLERS CLUB GRANTS

• *See page 73*

INSTITUTE OF CHINA STUDIES

INSTITUTE OF CHINESE STUDIES AWARDS

Renewable award for minority students already in college. Must major in China studies including Mandarin, history or other related studies. Minimum 3.0 GPA required. Students who have completed 30 hours and 15 hours of studies are eligible for $1000 award and $500 award, respectively.

Academic Fields/Career Goals: Area/Ethnic Studies.

Award: Scholarship for use in freshman, sophomore, junior, or senior years; renewable. *Number:* 10. *Amount:* up to $1000.

Eligibility Requirements: Applicant must be American Indian/Alaska Native, Asian/Pacific Islander, Black (non-Hispanic), or Hispanic and enrolled or expecting to enroll full-time at a four-year institution or university. Applicant must have 3.0 GPA or higher. Available to U.S. citizens.

Application Requirements: Photo, transcript, birth certificate. *Deadline:* Continuous.

Contact: Harry Kiang, President
Institute of China Studies
2549 West Golf Road #185
Hoffman Estates, IL 60194-1165
Phone: 847-756-4098

IRISH-AMERICAN CULTURAL INSTITUTE

http://www.iaci-usa.org

IRISH RESEARCH FUNDS

One-time award for research which has an Irish-American theme in any discipline of humanities and social science. Primary research preferred, but will fund such projects as museum exhibits, curriculum development, and the compilation of bibliographies. Submit proposal.

Academic Fields/Career Goals: Area/Ethnic Studies; Humanities; Social Sciences.

Award: Grant for use in freshman, sophomore, junior, senior, or graduate years; not renewable. *Number:* 1–10. *Amount:* $1000–$5000.

Eligibility Requirements: Applicant must be enrolled or expecting to enroll at an institution or university. Available to U.S. and non-U.S. citizens.

Application Requirements: Application, resume, references. *Deadline:* October 1.

Contact: Irish Research Funds Coordinator
Irish-American Cultural Institute
1 Lackawanna Place
Morristown, NJ 07960
Phone: 973-605-1991
Fax: 973-605-8875
E-mail: info@iaci-usa.org

JAPANESE GOVERNMENT/THE MONBUSHO SCHOLARSHIP PROGRAM

http://www.pk.emb-japan.go.jp/EDUCATION/Undergrad.htm

JAPANESE STUDIES SCHOLARSHIP

One-time award open to university-enrolled students ages 18 through 29. (university must be outside Japan). One-year course designed to develop Japanese language aptitude and knowledge of the country's culture, areas which the applicant must currently be studying. Scholarship comprises transportation, accommodations, medical expenses, and monthly and arrival allowances. Contact for more information.

Academic Fields/Career Goals: Area/Ethnic Studies.

Award: Scholarship for use in freshman, sophomore, junior, or senior years; not renewable. *Number:* varies. *Amount:* varies.

Eligibility Requirements: Applicant must be age 18-29; enrolled or expecting to enroll full-time at an institution or university and must have an interest in Japanese language. Available to U.S. and non-U.S. citizens.

Application Requirements: Application, autobiography, essay, interview, photo, references, test scores, transcript, medical certificate, certificate of enrollment. *Deadline:* Continuous.

Contact: See Web site for information.

KOSCIUSZKO FOUNDATION

http://www.kosciuszkofoundation.org

YEAR ABROAD PROGRAM IN POLAND

Grants for upper-division and graduate students who wish to study in Poland. Must have letters of recommendation, personal statement, and a physical exam. Covers tuition and provides stipend for housing. Application fee: $50. Minimum 3.0 GPA required. Restricted to U.S. citizens and permanent residents. See Web site http://www.kosciuszkofoundation.org for complete details. Application is available for download from September through December.

Academic Fields/Career Goals: Area/Ethnic Studies; Foreign Language.

Award: Scholarship for use in junior, senior, or graduate years; not renewable. *Number:* 10. *Amount:* $675–$1350.

Eligibility Requirements: Applicant must be enrolled or expecting to enroll at a four-year institution and must have an interest in Polish language. Applicant must have 3.0 GPA or higher. Available to U.S. citizens.

Application Requirements: Application, interview, photo, references, transcript, personal statement. *Fee:* $50. *Deadline:* December 15.

Contact: Ms. Addy Tymczyszyn, Grants Department
Kosciuszko Foundation
15 East 65th Street
New York, NY 10021-6595
Phone: 212-734-2130 Ext. 210

MEMORIAL FOUNDATION FOR JEWISH CULTURE

http://www.mfjc.org

MEMORIAL FOUNDATION FOR JEWISH CULTURE INTERNATIONAL SCHOLARSHIP PROGRAM FOR COMMUNITY SERVICE

Scholarships for students preparing for careers as educators, rabbis, or religious functionaries in social services. Must be planning a career of service to small Jewish communities outside of the United States, Israel, or Canada.

Academic Fields/Career Goals: Area/Ethnic Studies; Education; Religion/Theology; Social Services.

Award: Scholarship for use in freshman, sophomore, junior, or senior years; renewable. *Number:* varies. *Amount:* $1000–$3000.

Eligibility Requirements: Applicant must be Jewish and enrolled or expecting to enroll at an institution or university.

Application Requirements: Application, interview, references. *Deadline:* November 30.

Contact: Dr. Jerry Hochbaum, Executive Vice President
Memorial Foundation for Jewish Culture
50 Broadway, 34th Floor
New York, NY 10004
Phone: 212-425-6606
Fax: 212-425-6602
E-mail: office@mfjc.org

NATIONAL ITALIAN AMERICAN FOUNDATION

http://www.niaf.org/scholarships

NATIONAL ITALIAN AMERICAN FOUNDATION CATEGORY II SCHOLARSHIP

Award available to students majoring or minoring in Italian language, Italian Studies, Italian-American Studies or a related field who have outstanding potential and high academic achievements. Minimum 3.25 GPA required. Must be a U.S. citizen and be enrolled in an accredited institution of higher education. Application can only be submitted online. For further information, deadlines, and online application visit Web site: http://www.niaf.org/scholarships/index.asp.

Academic Fields/Career Goals: Area/Ethnic Studies.

Award: Scholarship for use in freshman, sophomore, junior, or senior years; not renewable. *Number:* varies. *Amount:* $2500–$10,000.

Eligibility Requirements: Applicant must be enrolled or expecting to enroll full or part-time at a four-year institution or university and must have an interest in Italian language. Available to U.S. citizens.

Application Requirements: Application, essay, references, transcript.

Contact: Application available at Web site.

PRINCE KUHIO HAWAIIAN CIVIC CLUB

PRINCE KUHIO HAWAIIAN CIVIC CLUB SCHOLARSHIP

Renewable award for full-time students of Hawaiian ancestry. Must be enrolled in accredited degree-seeking program and have a minimum 2.5 GPA. Must have academic and leadership potential.

Academic Fields/Career Goals: Area/Ethnic Studies.

Award: Scholarship for use in freshman, sophomore, junior, senior, or graduate years; renewable. *Number:* 10–20. *Amount:* $500–$1000.

Eligibility Requirements: Applicant must be Asian/Pacific Islander and enrolled or expecting to enroll full-time at a two-year or four-year or technical institution or university. Applicant must have 2.5 GPA or higher. Available to U.S. and non-U.S. citizens.

Application Requirements: Application, autobiography, essay, references, transcript. *Deadline:* April 1.

Contact: Cyr Pakele, Scholarship Chair
Prince Kuhio Hawaiian Civic Club
PO Box 4728
Honolulu, HI 96812
Phone: 808-842-8934
Fax: 808-847-6209
E-mail: cypakele@ksbe.edu

SONOMA CHAMBOLLE-MUSIGNY SISTER CITIES

HENRI CARDINAUX MEMORIAL SCHOLARSHIP

This cash award is for travel to France. Must have a 3.5 GPA. Must be a resident of California. Must have a permanent address in Sonoma County or attend school in Sonoma County.

Academic Fields/Career Goals: Area/Ethnic Studies; Foreign Language.

Award: Scholarship for use in freshman, sophomore, junior, senior, graduate, or postgraduate years; not renewable. *Number:* 1. *Amount:* $1500.

Eligibility Requirements: Applicant must be enrolled or expecting to enroll full or part-time at a two-year or four-year or technical institution or university; resident of California and studying in California. Applicant must have 3.5 GPA or higher. Available to U.S. citizens.

Application Requirements: Application, transcript. *Deadline:* varies.

Contact: Ivy Cardinaux, Scholarship
Sonoma Chambolle-Musigny Sister Cities
Chamson Scholarship Committee
PO Box 1633
Sonoma, CA 95476-1633
Phone: 707-938-9081
E-mail: icardin@aol.com

SONS OF NORWAY FOUNDATION http://www.sofn.com

KING OLAV V NORWEGIAN-AMERICAN HERITAGE FUND

Available to American students 18 or older interested in studying Norwegian heritage, or any Norwegian students interested in studying American heritage. Selection of applicants is based on a 500-word essay, educational and career goals, community service, work experience, and GPA. Must have minimum 3.0 GPA.

Academic Fields/Career Goals: Area/Ethnic Studies.

Award: Scholarship for use in freshman, sophomore, junior, or senior years; not renewable. *Number:* 12–15. *Amount:* $250–$3000.

Eligibility Requirements: Applicant must be age 18 and enrolled or expecting to enroll full or part-time at a four-year institution or university. Applicant or parent of applicant must have employment or volunteer experience in community service or designated career field. Applicant must have 3.0 GPA or higher. Available to U.S. and non-U.S. citizens.

Application Requirements: Application, essay, references, self-addressed stamped envelope, transcript. *Deadline:* March 1.

Contact: Administrative Director
Sons of Norway Foundation
1455 West Lake Street
Minneapolis, MN 55408
Phone: 612-827-3611
Fax: 612-827-0658
E-mail: colson@sofn.com

WATERBURY FOUNDATION http://www.waterburyfoundation.org

TADEUSZ SENDZIMIR SCHOLARSHIPS-ACADEMIC YEAR SCHOLARSHIPS

Academic year scholarships of $7500 available for graduate and undergraduate students, preferably of Polish descent, residing in Connecticut, who are studying Polish language, history or culture during the academic year at a college or university in the United States or Poland. Scholarship for exchange study in the United States or Poland.

Academic Fields/Career Goals: Area/Ethnic Studies.

Award: Scholarship for use in freshman, sophomore, junior, senior, or graduate years; not renewable. *Number:* varies. *Amount:* up to $7500.

Eligibility Requirements: Applicant must be enrolled or expecting to enroll at a four-year institution or university and resident of Connecticut.

Application Requirements: Application, essay, references, transcript. *Deadline:* April 1.

Contact: Elizabeth Moore, Program Officer
Waterbury Foundation
81 West Main Street
Waterbury, CT 06702-1216
Phone: 203-753-1315
Fax: 203-756-3054
E-mail: emoore@waterburyfoundation.org

TADEUSZ SENDZIMIR SCHOLARSHIPS-SUMMER SCHOOL PROGRAMS

Summer scholarships of $3000 available for graduate and undergraduate students, preferably of Polish descent, residing in Connecticut, who are studying Polish language, history or culture during the academic year at a college or university in the United States or Poland. Scholarship for exchange study in the United States or Poland.

Academic Fields/Career Goals: Area/Ethnic Studies.

Award: Scholarship for use in freshman, sophomore, junior, senior, or graduate years; not renewable. *Number:* varies. *Amount:* up to $3000.

Eligibility Requirements: Applicant must be age 18; enrolled or expecting to enroll at a four-year institution or university and resident of Connecticut.

Application Requirements: Application, financial need analysis, references, transcript, physician's certificate. *Fee:* $50. *Deadline:* April 15.

Contact: Elizabeth Moore, Program Officer
Waterbury Foundation
81 West Main Street
Waterbury, CT 06702-1216
Phone: 203-753-1315
Fax: 203-756-3054
E-mail: emoore@waterburyfoundation.org

WELSH NATIONAL GYMANFA GANU ASSOCIATION, INC. http://www.wngga.org

WNGGA SCHOLARSHIP PROGRAM

One-time award program from which scholarships may be granted to applicants or organization who are enrolled in courses or projects which preserve, develop, and promote the Welsh religious and cultural heritage. Applicant must be U.S. or Canadian citizen. Deadline: March 1.

Academic Fields/Career Goals: Area/Ethnic Studies.

Award: Grant for use in freshman, sophomore, junior, senior, graduate, or postgraduate years; not renewable. *Number:* 5–10. *Amount:* $200–$2000.

Eligibility Requirements: Applicant must be of Welsh heritage and enrolled or expecting to enroll full or part-time at an institution or university. Applicant or parent of applicant must have employment or volunteer experience in designated career field. Available to U.S. and Canadian citizens.

Application Requirements: Application, autobiography, financial need analysis, references, project description, budget. *Deadline:* March 1.

Contact: Myfanwy S. Davies, Chairperson, Scholarship Committee
Welsh National Gymanfa Ganu Association, Inc.
3205 Uplands Drive, Unit 2
Ottawa, ON K1V 9T3
Canada
Phone: 613-526-3019

ART HISTORY

AMERICAN INSTITUTE OF ARCHITECTS, NEW YORK CHAPTER http://www.aiany.org

HASKELL AWARDS FOR STUDENTS IN ARCHITECTURAL JOURNALISM

• *See page 74*

AMERICAN LEGION AUXILIARY, DEPARTMENT OF WASHINGTON http://www.walegion-aux.org

FLORENCE LEMCKE MEMORIAL SCHOLARSHIP IN FINE ARTS

One-time award for the son, daughter, or grandchild of a veteran. Must be senior in high school in Washington and planning to pursue an education in the fine arts. Submit statement of veteran's military service. Contact Washington Auxiliary for application. Must be a resident of Washington state.

Academic Fields/Career Goals: Art History; Arts; Humanities; Literature/English/Writing.

Award: Scholarship for use in freshman year; not renewable. *Number:* 1. *Amount:* $500.

Eligibility Requirements: Applicant must be high school student; age 20 or under; planning to enroll or expecting to enroll at an institution or university; resident of Washington and must have an interest in art or writing. Available to U.S. citizens. Applicant or parent must meet one or more of the following requirements: general military experience; retired from active duty; disabled or killed as a result of military service; prisoner of war; or missing in action.

Application Requirements: Application, essay, references, transcript. *Deadline:* April 1.

Contact: Lois Boyle, Education Chairman
American Legion Auxiliary, Department of Washington
PO Box 5867
Lacey, WA 98509-5867
Phone: 360-456-5995
Fax: 360-491-7442
E-mail: alawash@qwest.net

AMERICAN SCHOOL OF CLASSICAL STUDIES AT ATHENS http://www.ascsa.edu.gr

ASCSA SUMMER SESSIONS

• *See page 65*

COSTUME SOCIETY OF AMERICA http://www.costumesocietyamerica.com

ADELE FILENE TRAVEL AWARD

• *See page 81*

STELLA BLUM RESEARCH GRANT

• *See page 81*

CULTURE CONNECTION http://www.thecultureconnection.com

CULTURE CONNECTION FOUNDATION SCHOLARSHIP

• *See page 52*

GETTY GRANT PROGRAM http://www.getty.edu/grants

LIBRARY RESEARCH GRANTS

Grant intended for scholars at any level who demonstrate compelling need to use materials in Getty Research Library. Applicant's place of residence must be at least 80 or more miles away from Getty Center. Research period may last several days to maximum three months. Grant only supports one research trip to Getty Center. Grantee may reapply after two years; if project is different, grantee may reapply the next year. See Web site at http://www.getty.edu/grants for details.

Academic Fields/Career Goals: Art History; Arts.

Award: Grant for use in freshman, sophomore, junior, senior, graduate, or postgraduate years; not renewable. *Number:* varies. *Amount:* $500–$2500.

Eligibility Requirements: Applicant must be enrolled or expecting to enroll at an institution or university; studying in California and must have an interest in art.

Application Requirements: *Deadline:* November 1.

Contact: Kathleen Johnson, Program Associate
Getty Grant Program
1200 Getty Center Drive, Suite 800
Los Angeles, CA 90049-1685
Phone: 310-440-7320
Fax: 310-440-7703
E-mail: researchgrants@getty.edu

HERB SOCIETY OF AMERICA http://www.herbsociety.org

HERB SOCIETY RESEARCH GRANTS

• *See page 69*

POLISH ARTS CLUB OF BUFFALO SCHOLARSHIP FOUNDATION

POLISH ARTS CLUB OF BUFFALO SCHOLARSHIP FOUNDATION TRUST

Provides educational scholarships to students of Polish background who are legal residents of New York. Must be enrolled at the junior level or above in an accredited college or university in NY. Must be a U.S. citizen. Send SASE for more information.

Academic Fields/Career Goals: Art History; Arts; Filmmaking/Video; Humanities; Journalism; Performing Arts.

Award: Scholarship for use in junior, senior, graduate, or postgraduate years; not renewable. *Number:* 1–3. *Amount:* $1000.

Eligibility Requirements: Applicant must be of Polish heritage; enrolled or expecting to enroll full or part-time at a four-year institution or university; resident of New York and studying in New York. Available to U.S. citizens.

Application Requirements: Application, essay, interview, portfolio, resume, references, self-addressed stamped envelope, transcript. *Deadline:* May 15.

Contact: Ann Flansburg, Selection Chair
Polish Arts Club of Buffalo Scholarship Foundation
PO Box 1362
Williamsville, NY 14231-1362
Phone: 716-626-9083
E-mail: donflans123@aol.com

ROBERT H. MOLLOHAN FAMILY CHARITABLE FOUNDATION, INC. http://www.mollohanfoundation.org

MARY OLIVE EDDY JONES ART SCHOLARSHIP

Scholarship awarded to a rising sophomore or junior seriously interested in pursuing an art-related degree. Applicant must be a West Virginia resident attending a West Virginia college or university.

Academic Fields/Career Goals: Art History; Arts; Graphics/Graphic Arts/Printing.

Award: Scholarship for use in sophomore or junior years; not renewable. *Number:* 1–3. *Amount:* $1000.

Eligibility Requirements: Applicant must be enrolled or expecting to enroll full or part-time at a four-year institution or university; resident of West Virginia and studying in West Virginia. Available to U.S. citizens.

Application Requirements: Application, essay, portfolio, resume, references, transcript. *Deadline:* February 7.

Contact: Teah Bayless, Program Manager
Robert H. Mollohan Family Charitable Foundation, Inc.
1000 Technology Drive, Suite 2000
Fairmont, WV 26554
Phone: 304-333-2251
Fax: 304-333-3900
E-mail: tmbayless@wvhtf.org

UNICO NATIONAL, INC http://www.unico.org

THEODORE MAZZA SCHOLARSHIP

• *See page 79*

ARTS

ACADEMY OF TELEVISION ARTS AND SCIENCES FOUNDATION http://www.emmys.tv/foundation

ACADEMY OF TELEVISION ARTS AND SCIENCES COLLEGE TELEVISION AWARDS

The College Television Awards competition recognizes excellence in college student film or video productions by honoring student producers of films or videos produced for college course credit. The academy gives 1st, 2nd, and 3rd place awards in the following categories: comedy, drama, music programs, documentary, newscasts, children's programs, traditional animation, and non-traditional animation. Submit film or video on 1/2 inch VHS or Beta SP tape. Entry forms available September-December.

Academic Fields/Career Goals: Arts; Communications; Filmmaking/Video; Journalism; Performing Arts; Photojournalism/Photography; TV/Radio Broadcasting.

Award: Prize for use in freshman, sophomore, junior, senior, or graduate years; not renewable. *Number:* 25. *Amount:* $500–$2000.

Eligibility Requirements: Applicant must be enrolled or expecting to enroll full-time at a two-year or four-year or technical institution or university. Available to U.S. citizens.

Application Requirements: Application, applicant must enter a contest. *Deadline:* December 15.

Contact: Hap Lovejoy, Educational Programs and Services Administrator
Academy of Television Arts and Sciences Foundation
5220 Lankershim Boulevard
North Hollywood, CA 91601
Phone: 818-754-2839
Fax: 818-761-8524
E-mail: collegeawards@emmys.org

ALLIANCE FOR YOUNG ARTISTS AND WRITERS, INC. http://www.artandwriting.org

SCHOLASTIC ART AND WRITING AWARDS-ART SECTION

Award for students in grades 7-12. Winners of preliminary judging advance to national level. For further details visit Web site: http://www.artandwriting.org.

Academic Fields/Career Goals: Arts; Literature/English/Writing.

Award: Scholarship for use in freshman, sophomore, junior, or senior years; not renewable. *Number:* 600. *Amount:* $100–$20,000.

Eligibility Requirements: Applicant must be high school student; planning to enroll or expecting to enroll at an institution or university and must have an interest in art. Available to U.S. and Canadian citizens.

Application Requirements: Application, applicant must enter a contest, essay, portfolio, references. *Deadline:* varies.

Contact: Alliance for Young Artists and Writers, Inc.
557 Broadway
New York, NY 10012-1396
Phone: 212-343-6493
E-mail: a&wgeneralinfo@scholastic.com

SCHOLASTIC ART AND WRITING AWARDS-WRITING SECTION SCHOLARSHIP

Award for students in grades 7-12. Winners of preliminary judging advance to national level. For further details visit Web site: http://www.artandwriting.org.

Academic Fields/Career Goals: Arts; Literature/English/Writing.

Award: Scholarship for use in freshman, sophomore, junior, or senior years; not renewable. *Number:* 300. *Amount:* $100–$10,000.

Eligibility Requirements: Applicant must be high school student; planning to enroll or expecting to enroll at an institution or university and must have an interest in writing. Available to U.S. and Canadian citizens.

Application Requirements: Application, applicant must enter a contest, essay, manuscript. *Deadline:* varies.

Contact: Alliance for Young Artists and Writers, Inc.
557 Broadway
New York, NY 10012-1396
Phone: 212-343-6493
E-mail: a&wgeneralinfo@scholastic.com

AMERICAN LEGION AUXILIARY, DEPARTMENT OF WASHINGTON http://www.walegion-aux.org

FLORENCE LEMCKE MEMORIAL SCHOLARSHIP IN FINE ARTS

• *See page 84*

AMERICAN PHILOLOGICAL ASSOCIATION http://www.apaclassics.org

MINORITY STUDENT SUMMER SCHOLARSHIP

The award supports summer study in the United States, or in Europe, intended to better prepare the recipient for graduate work in classical studies. Please refer to Web site for ethnic heritage specifications and further details: http://www.apaclassics.org

Academic Fields/Career Goals: Arts; Foreign Language; History; Humanities.

Award: Scholarship for use in junior or senior years; not renewable. *Number:* 1. *Amount:* $3000.

Eligibility Requirements: Applicant must be of African, Chinese, Latin American/Caribbean, Mexican, or Vietnamese heritage; American Indian/Alaska Native, Asian/Pacific Islander, Black (non-Hispanic), or Hispanic and enrolled or expecting to enroll full-time at an institution or university. Available to U.S. and non-U.S. citizens.

Application Requirements: Application, essay, financial need analysis, references, transcript. *Deadline:* February 15.

Contact: Adam Blistein, Executive Director
American Philological Association
Department of Classical Studies, Loyola University
Box 113 6363 Saint Charles Avenue
New Orleans, LA 70118
Phone: 215-898-4975
Fax: 215-573-7874
E-mail: blistein@sas.upenn.edu

AMERICAN SCHOOL OF CLASSICAL STUDIES AT ATHENS http://www.ascsa.edu.gr

ASCSA SUMMER SESSIONS

• *See page 65*

ART INSTITUTES http://www.artinstitutes.edu

NATIONAL ART HONOR SOCIETY SCHOLARSHIP

Senior class members of National Art Honor Society are eligible to compete for these tuition scholarships: 1st Place-$25,000, 2nd Place-$15,000, 3rd Place-$10,000, 4th Place: $5,000, 5th Place-$2,500.

Academic Fields/Career Goals: Arts.

Award: Scholarship for use in freshman, sophomore, junior, or senior years; renewable. *Number:* 5. *Amount:* $2500–$25,000.

Eligibility Requirements: Applicant must be high school student and planning to enroll or expecting to enroll full-time at a technical institution.

Application Requirements: Application, applicant must enter a contest, six slides of artwork. *Deadline:* March 4.

Contact: National Art Honor Society Scholarship
Art Institutes
c/o The Art Institute of Pittsburgh, 420 Boulevard of the Allies
Pittsburgh, PA 15219-1328

ARTIST-BLACKSMITH'S ASSOCIATION OF NORTH AMERICA, INC. http://www.abana.org

ARTIST'S- BLACKSMITH'S ASSOCIATION OF NORTH AMERICA, INC. SCHOLARSHIP PROGRAM

The award is designed to provide financial assistance to ABANA members at all skill levels to assist with the development of their blacksmithing skills and abilities. Applications selected throughout the year. Award money may be used for blacksmith workshops, demonstrations, lectures, etc. Awards granted are not for tuition.

Academic Fields/Career Goals: Arts.

Award: Scholarship for use in freshman year; not renewable. *Number:* 8–10. *Amount:* $400–$1500.

Eligibility Requirements: Applicant must be enrolled or expecting to enroll part-time at a technical institution. Available to U.S. and non-U.S. citizens.

Artist-Blacksmith's Association of North America, Inc. (continued)

Application Requirements: Application, financial need analysis, photo, resume, references, self-addressed stamped envelope. *Deadline:* Continuous.

Contact: Lee Ann Mitchell, Central Office Administrator
Artist-Blacksmith's Association of North America, Inc.
PO Box 816
Farmington, GA 30638-0816
Phone: 706-310-1030
Fax: 706-769-7147
E-mail: abana@abana.org

ARTIST'S-BLACKSMITH'S ASSOCIATION OF NORTH AMERICA, INC. AFFILIATE VISITING ARTIST GRANT PROGRAM

Grant is for ABANA Affiliates wishing to bring in demonstrators or other educational opportunities for their membership.

Academic Fields/Career Goals: Arts.

Award: Grant for use in freshman, sophomore, junior, senior, graduate, or postgraduate years; not renewable. *Number:* 8. *Amount:* $600.

Eligibility Requirements: Applicant must be enrolled or expecting to enroll part-time at an institution or university. Available to U.S. and non-U.S. citizens.

Application Requirements: Essay, financial need analysis, photo, resume. *Deadline:* Continuous.

Contact: Lee Ann Mitchell, Central Office Administrator
Artist-Blacksmith's Association of North America, Inc.
PO Box 816
Farmington, GA 30638-0816
Phone: 706-310-1030
Fax: 706-769-7147
E-mail: abana@abana.org

CALIFORNIA ALLIANCE FOR ARTS EDUCATION (CAAE)

http://www.artsed411.org

EMERGING YOUNG ARTIST AWARDS

Renewable award for California high school seniors studying dance, music, theater, or visual arts. For use at a four-year institution or accredited training program. Must demonstrate financial need. Application fee of $10. Application deadline is February 2.

Academic Fields/Career Goals: Arts; Music; Performing Arts.

Award: Scholarship for use in freshman, sophomore, junior, or senior years; renewable. *Number:* up to 12. *Amount:* up to $5000.

Eligibility Requirements: Applicant must be high school student; age 16-19; planning to enroll or expecting to enroll full-time at a four-year institution or university and resident of California. Applicant must have 2.5 GPA or higher. Available to U.S. citizens.

Application Requirements: Application, applicant must enter a contest, essay, financial need analysis, references, performance, work sample. *Fee:* $10. *Deadline:* February 2.

Contact: Peggy Burt, Project Manager
California Alliance for Arts Education (CAAE)
495 East Colorado Boulevard
Pasadena, CA 91101
Phone: 626-578-9315 Ext. 102
Fax: 626-578-9894
E-mail: peggy@artsed411.org

CIRI FOUNDATION

http://www.ciri.com/tcf

CIRI FOUNDATION SUSIE QIMMIQSAK BEVINS ENDOWMENT SCHOLARSHIP FUND

$2,000 per semester is offered to Alaska Native Student original enrollees/descendants of Cook Inlet Region, Inc., who are studying the literary, performing, and visual arts. Recipients can reapply every semester. Must be accepted or enrolled in a two- or four-year undergraduate degree or graduate degree program. Deadlines are June 1 and December 1.

Academic Fields/Career Goals: Arts; Literature/English/Writing; Performing Arts.

Award: Scholarship for use in freshman, sophomore, junior, senior, or graduate years; not renewable. *Number:* varies. *Amount:* $2000.

Eligibility Requirements: Applicant must be enrolled or expecting to enroll full-time at a two-year or four-year institution or university. Applicant must have 2.5 GPA or higher. Available to U.S. citizens.

Application Requirements: Application, essay, references, transcript, proof of eligibility, birth certificate or adoption decree. *Deadline:* varies.

Contact: CIRI Foundation
2600 Cordova Street, Suite 206
Anchorage, AK 99503
Phone: 907-263-5582
Fax: 907-263-5588
E-mail: tcf@ciri.com

LAWRENCE MATSON MEMORIAL ENDOWMENT SCHOLARSHIP FUND

Scholarships available for studies in language, education, social sciences, arts, communications, and law. Applicant must be Alaska Native student. For more details see Web site: http://www.ciri.com/tcf.

Academic Fields/Career Goals: Arts; Communications; Education; Law/Legal Services; Social Sciences.

Award: Scholarship for use in freshman, sophomore, junior, senior, or graduate years; not renewable. *Number:* varies. *Amount:* varies.

Eligibility Requirements: Applicant must be enrolled or expecting to enroll full-time at a two-year or four-year institution or university.

Application Requirements: Application, essay, references, transcript, proof of eligibility, birth certificate or adoption decree. *Deadline:* June 1.

Contact: CIRI Foundation
2600 Cordova Street, Suite 206
Anchorage, AK 99503
Phone: 907-263-5582
Fax: 907-263-5588
E-mail: tcf@ciri.com

COLLEGEBOUND FOUNDATION

http://www.collegeboundfoundation.org

JOE SANDUSKY FOUNDATION-RUTH SANDUSKY ARTS SCHOLARSHIP

Award for Baltimore City public high school graduates. Please see Web site: http://www.collegeboundfoundation.org for complete information on application process. Must have financial need. Must submit essay of 500 words or less on how pursuing an education and career in the arts will enable you to live a more fulfilling life and make a greater contribution to your community. Must submit CollegeBound Competitive Scholarship/Last-Dollar Grant Application.

Academic Fields/Career Goals: Arts.

Award: Scholarship for use in freshman, sophomore, junior, or senior years; renewable. *Number:* 1. *Amount:* $500–$2000.

Eligibility Requirements: Applicant must be enrolled or expecting to enroll full-time at a two-year or four-year institution or university and resident of Maryland. Available to U.S. citizens.

Application Requirements: Application, essay, financial need analysis, references, transcript, financial aid award letters, Student Aid Report. *Deadline:* March 19.

Contact: April Bell, Associate Program Director
CollegeBound Foundation
300 Water Street, Suite 300
Baltimore, MD 21202
Phone: 410-783-2905 Ext. 208
Fax: 410-727-5786
E-mail: abell@collegeboundfoundation.org

COSTUME SOCIETY OF AMERICA

http://www.costumesocietyamerica.com

ADELE FILENE TRAVEL AWARD

• *See page 81*

STELLA BLUM RESEARCH GRANT
• *See page 81*

ELIZABETH GREENSHIELDS FOUNDATION

ELIZABETH GREENSHIELDS AWARD/GRANT

Award of CAN$12,500 available to candidates working in painting, drawing, printmaking, or sculpture. Work must be representational or figurative. Must submit at least one color slide of each of six works. Must reapply to renew. Applications from self-taught individuals are also accepted.

Academic Fields/Career Goals: Arts.

Award: Grant for use in freshman, sophomore, junior, senior, or graduate years; not renewable. *Number:* 40–60. *Amount:* $9285.

Eligibility Requirements: Applicant must be enrolled or expecting to enroll full or part-time at a two-year or four-year or technical institution or university and must have an interest in art. Available to U.S. and non-U.S. citizens.

Application Requirements: Application, slides. *Deadline:* Continuous.

Contact: Diane Pitcher, Applications Coordinator
Elizabeth Greenshields Foundation
1814 Sherbrooke Street West, Suite 1
Montreal, QC H3H IE4
Canada
Phone: 514-937-9225
Fax: 514-937-0141
E-mail: greenshields@bellnet.ca

GENERAL FEDERATION OF WOMEN'S CLUBS OF MASSACHUSETTS

GENERAL FEDERATION OF WOMEN'S CLUBS OF MASSACHUSETTS PENNIES FOR ART

Scholarship in art for graduating high school seniors. Must submit letter of endorsement from president of sponsoring General Federation of Women's Clubs of Massachusetts and three examples of original work. Must be resident of Massachusetts.

Academic Fields/Career Goals: Arts.

Award: Scholarship for use in freshman year; not renewable. *Number:* varies. *Amount:* up to $800.

Eligibility Requirements: Applicant must be high school student; planning to enroll or expecting to enroll full-time at a four-year institution or university; resident of Massachusetts and must have an interest in art.

Application Requirements: Application, autobiography, essay, portfolio, references, self-addressed stamped envelope. *Deadline:* February 1.

Contact: Mary Barnes, Art Scholarship Coordinator
General Federation of Women's Clubs of Massachusetts
PO Box 679
Sudbury, MA 01776-0679
Phone: 978-443-4569
E-mail: gfwcma@aol.com

GETTY GRANT PROGRAM http://www.getty.edu/grants

LIBRARY RESEARCH GRANTS
• *See page 84*

GOLDEN KEY INTERNATIONAL HONOUR SOCIETY http://www.goldenkey.org

ART INTERNATIONAL AWARD

$1000 will be awarded to winners in each of the following eight categories: painting, drawing, mixed media, sculpture, photography, applied art, printmaking, computer-generated art/illustration/graphic design/set design. See Web site for more information: http://goldenkey.gsu.edu.

Academic Fields/Career Goals: Arts; Graphics/Graphic Arts/Printing.

Award: Prize for use in junior, senior, graduate, or postgraduate years; not renewable. *Number:* 8. *Amount:* $1000.

Eligibility Requirements: Applicant must be enrolled or expecting to enroll full or part-time at a four-year institution or university and must have an interest in art. Available to U.S. and non-U.S. citizens.

Application Requirements: Application, artwork. *Deadline:* April 1.

Contact: Member Services
Golden Key International Honour Society
621 North Avenue, NE
Suite C-100
Atlanta, GA 30308
Phone: 404-377-2400
Fax: 678-420-6757
E-mail: scholarships@goldenkey.org

HERB SOCIETY OF AMERICA http://www.herbsociety.org

HERB SOCIETY RESEARCH GRANTS
• *See page 69*

INSTITUTE FOR HUMANE STUDIES http://www.theihs.org

FILM AND FICTION SCHOLARSHIP

Scholarship program to support students pursuing degrees in filmmaking or creative writing. First stage deadline is January 15; second stage deadline is March 15.

Academic Fields/Career Goals: Arts; Filmmaking/Video; Literature/English/Writing.

Award: Scholarship for use in senior, or graduate years; not renewable. *Number:* varies. *Amount:* $3000–$10,000.

Eligibility Requirements: Applicant must be enrolled or expecting to enroll full-time at a four-year institution or university. Available to U.S. and non-U.S. citizens.

Application Requirements: Application, essay. *Deadline:* January 15.

Contact: Institute for Humane Studies
3301 North Fairfax Drive, Suite 440
Arlington, VA 22201-4432
Phone: 703-993-4880
Fax: 703-993-4890
E-mail: ihs@gmu.edu

INTERNATIONAL FURNISHINGS AND DESIGN ASSOCIATION http://www.ifdaef.org/scholarships.html

RUTH CLARK SCHOLARSHIP

Scholarship available to students studying design at an accredited college or design school with a focus on residential furniture design. Applicant must submit 5 examples of original designs, 3 of which must be residential furniture examples. May be CD-ROM (pdf format only), slides, photographs, or copies of drawings no larger than 8 1/2"x11". Include 5 sets of each design example with a short description of each illustration.

Academic Fields/Career Goals: Arts; Industrial Design.

Award: Scholarship for use in sophomore, junior, or senior years; not renewable. *Number:* 1. *Amount:* $1500.

Eligibility Requirements: Applicant must be enrolled or expecting to enroll full-time at a four-year institution or university. Available to U.S. and non-U.S. citizens.

Application Requirements: Application, essay, references, transcript. *Deadline:* March 31.

Contact: Dr. Nancy Wolford, Director of Grants and Scholarships
International Furnishings and Design Association
16171 Jasmine Way
Los Gatos, CA 95032-3630
Phone: 408-356-2465
E-mail: nlwolford@earthlink.net

JACK J. ISGUR FOUNDATION

JACK J. ISGUR FOUNDATION SCHOLARSHIP

Awards scholarships to juniors, seniors, and graduate students with intentions of teaching the humanities in Missouri schools. Applicants interested in teaching in rural schools will take precedence. The deadline is May 1.

Academic Fields/Career Goals: Arts; Education; Humanities; Literature/English/Writing; Music; Performing Arts.

Award: Scholarship for use in junior, senior, graduate, or postgraduate years; not renewable. *Number:* 5–10. *Amount:* $500–$1000.

Jack J. Isgur Foundation (continued)

Eligibility Requirements: Applicant must be enrolled or expecting to enroll full-time at a four-year institution or university. Available to U.S. and non-U.S. citizens.

Application Requirements: Application, references, transcript. *Deadline:* May 1.

Contact: Charles Jensen, Attorney at Law
Jack J. Isgur Foundation
c/o Charles F. Jensen, Stinson, Morrison, Hecker LLP
1201 Walnut Street, 28th Floor
Kansas City, MO 64106
Phone: 816-691-2760
Fax: 816-691-3495
E-mail: cjensen@stinsonmoheck.com

JOHN F. AND ANNA LEE STACEY SCHOLARSHIP FUND http://www.nationalcowboymuseum.org

JOHN F. AND ANNA LEE STACEY SCHOLARSHIP FUND

Scholarships for artists who are high school graduates between the ages of 18 and 35, who are U.S. citizens, and whose work is devoted to the classical or conservative tradition of western culture. Awards are for drawing or painting only. Must submit no more than 10 35mm color slides of work. Applications accepted between October 1 and February 1. Contact for further details and application.

Academic Fields/Career Goals: Arts.

Award: Scholarship for use in freshman, sophomore, junior, senior, graduate, or postgraduate years; not renewable. *Number:* 3–5. *Amount:* $1000–$5000.

Eligibility Requirements: Applicant must be age 18-35; enrolled or expecting to enroll full or part-time at a four-year institution or university and must have an interest in art. Available to U.S. citizens.

Application Requirements: Application, applicant must enter a contest, photo, references, 35mm slides. *Deadline:* February 1.

Contact: Ed Muno, Art Curator
John F. and Anna Lee Stacey Scholarship Fund
1700 Northeast 63rd Street
Oklahoma City, OK 73111
Phone: 405-478-2250
Fax: 405-478-4714

JUNIOR ACHIEVEMENT http://www.ja.org

WALT DISNEY COMPANY FOUNDATION SCHOLARSHIP

Must be a high school senior who completed JA Company Program or JA Economics. Tuition-only scholarship renewable annually for up to four years leading to a bachelor degree in either business administration or fine arts at an accredited college or university. $200 cash accompanies the scholarship each year for incidental fees.

Academic Fields/Career Goals: Arts; Business/Consumer Services.

Award: Scholarship for use in freshman, sophomore, junior, or senior years; renewable. *Number:* 1.

Eligibility Requirements: Applicant must be high school student and planning to enroll or expecting to enroll full-time at a four-year institution or university. Applicant or parent of applicant must be member of Junior Achievement. Available to U.S. and Canadian citizens.

Application Requirements: Application, references, test scores, transcript. *Deadline:* February 1.

Contact: Steven Carruth, Scholarship and Curriculum Specialist
Junior Achievement
One Education Way
Colorado Springs, CO 80906-4477
Phone: 719-535-2954
Fax: 719-540-6175
E-mail: scarruth@ja.org

LIBERTY GRAPHICS, INC. http://www.libertygraphicstshirts.com

ANNUAL LIBERTY GRAPHICS OUTDOOR ACTIVITIES ART CONTEST

One-time scholarship goes to the successful student who submits the winning design for depicting human powered outdoor activities, not wind or motor powered. Liberty Graphics reserves the right not to award. Applicants must be residents of Maine and be high school student.

Academic Fields/Career Goals: Arts.

Award: Scholarship for use in freshman year; not renewable. *Number:* 2. *Amount:* $1000.

Eligibility Requirements: Applicant must be high school student; planning to enroll or expecting to enroll full-time at a two-year or four-year institution or university and resident of Maine. Available to U.S. citizens.

Application Requirements: Application, applicant must enter a contest, autobiography, self-addressed stamped envelope, art contest submission. *Deadline:* April 24.

Contact: Jay Sproul, Art Director
Liberty Graphics, Inc.
PO Box 5
Liberty, ME 04949
Phone: 207-589-4596
Fax: 207-589-4415
E-mail: jay@lgtees.com

LINCOLN COMMUNITY FOUNDATION http://www.lcf.org

HAYMARKET GALLERY EMERGING ARTISTS SCHOLARSHIP

Scholarship for current graduating seniors or current college students enrolled in a qualified accredited college or university in Lancaster County in Nebraska who are pursuing art degrees. Must be residents of Lancaster County, Nebraska and show extraordinary artistic promise.

Academic Fields/Career Goals: Arts.

Award: Scholarship for use in freshman year; not renewable. *Number:* 1. *Amount:* $500.

Eligibility Requirements: Applicant must be enrolled or expecting to enroll full-time at a two-year or four-year institution or university; resident of Nebraska; studying in Nebraska and must have an interest in art. Available to U.S. citizens.

Application Requirements: Application, portfolio, references. *Deadline:* April 15.

Contact: Application available at Web site.

LIQUITEX ARTIST MATERIALS PURCHASE AWARD PROGRAM http://www.liquitex.com

LIQUITEX EXCELLENCE IN ART PURCHASE AWARD PROGRAM

Prizes up to $5000 in cash plus $1,500 in Liquitex products will be awarded to the best art submissions. Submission should be made on 35mm color slides. Void in Quebec or where prohibited by law. For more details see Web site: http://www.liquitex.com.

Academic Fields/Career Goals: Arts.

Award: Prize for use in freshman, sophomore, junior, senior, graduate, or postgraduate years; not renewable. *Number:* 5. *Amount:* $1500–$6500.

Eligibility Requirements: Applicant must be enrolled or expecting to enroll full or part-time at a two-year or four-year or technical institution or university. Available to U.S. and Canadian citizens.

Application Requirements: Application, applicant must enter a contest, 35mm color slides of artwork. *Deadline:* January 15.

Contact: Application available at Web site.

MAINE MEDIA WOMEN SCHOLARSHIPS COMMITTEE http://www.mainemediawomen.org/scholarships.html

MAINE MEDIA WOMEN'S SCHOLARSHIP

Recipient is selected by an independent panel. Award is based on talent, need, and past involvement in media-related activities in school. Available only to women who are residents of Maine and interested in pursuing a career in journalism, writing, photography, graphic design, arts, marketing, communications, and broadcasting.

Academic Fields/Career Goals: Arts; Communications; Graphics/Graphic Arts/Printing; Journalism; Literature/English/Writing; Photojournalism/Photography; TV/Radio Broadcasting.

Award: Scholarship for use in freshman, sophomore, junior, or senior years; not renewable. *Number:* 1. *Amount:* $700.

Eligibility Requirements: Applicant must be enrolled or expecting to enroll full-time at a four-year institution or university; female and resident of Maine. Available to U.S. citizens.

Application Requirements: Application, applicant must enter a contest, essay, financial need analysis, references, transcript. *Deadline:* April 1.

Contact: Jude Stone, Scholarship Committee Chairperson
Maine Media Women Scholarships Committee
9 Sanborns' Grove Road
Bridgton, ME 04009
Phone: 207-647-5960

MEDIA ACTION NETWORK FOR ASIAN AMERICANS http://www.manaa.org

MANAA MEDIA SCHOLARSHIPS FOR ASIAN AMERICAN STUDENTS

One-time award to students pursuing careers in film and television production as writers, directors, producers, and studio executives. Students must have a strong desire to advance a positive and enlightened understanding of the Asian-American experience in mainstream media. See Web site (http://www.manaa.org) for application deadline and additional information.

Academic Fields/Career Goals: Arts; Filmmaking/Video; TV/Radio Broadcasting.

Award: Scholarship for use in freshman, sophomore, junior, senior, or graduate years; not renewable. *Number:* 1. *Amount:* $1000.

Eligibility Requirements: Applicant must be enrolled or expecting to enroll full-time at a two-year or four-year or technical institution or university. Available to U.S. citizens.

Application Requirements: Essay, financial need analysis, references, transcript, work sample. *Deadline:* June 1.

Contact: Ken Kwok, Board Member
Media Action Network for Asian Americans
PO Box 11105
Burbank, CA 91510
Phone: 213-486-4433
E-mail: manaaletters@yahoo.com

NATIONAL ART MATERIALS TRADE ASSOCIATION http://www.namta.org

NATIONAL ART MATERIALS TRADE ASSOCIATION ART MAJOR SCHOLARSHIP

One-time award for students majoring or planning to major in, the field of art or art education. A NAMTA member must sponsor candidates. Application deadline is April 1. For further details, see Web site at http://www.namta.org or email inquiries to scholarship@namta.org.

Academic Fields/Career Goals: Arts.

Award: Scholarship for use in freshman, sophomore, junior, senior, graduate, or postgraduate years; not renewable. *Number:* 2. *Amount:* $2500.

Eligibility Requirements: Applicant must be enrolled or expecting to enroll full-time at a two-year or four-year or technical institution or university. Available to U.S. and non-U.S. citizens.

Application Requirements: Application, essay, test scores, transcript. *Deadline:* April 1.

Contact: Katharine Coffey, Scholarship Coordinator
National Art Materials Trade Association
15806 Brookway Drive, Suite 300
Huntersville, NC 28078
Phone: 704-892-6244
Fax: 704-892-6247
E-mail: kcoffey@namta.org

NATIONAL FOUNDATION FOR ADVANCEMENT IN THE ARTS http://www.artsawards.org

ARTS RECOGNITION AND TALENT SEARCH (ARTS)

One-time award for high school seniors or others that are 17-18 years old who show talent in dance, film and video, jazz, music, photography, theater, visual arts, voice, and/or writing. Must submit portfolio, videotape or audiotape, along with application fee. Must be citizens or permanent residents of the U.S., except applicants for the music/jazz discipline.

Academic Fields/Career Goals: Arts; Filmmaking/Video; Literature/English/Writing; Performing Arts; Photojournalism/Photography.

Award: Grant for use in freshman year; not renewable. *Number:* varies. *Amount:* $100–$3000.

Eligibility Requirements: Applicant must be high school student; age 17-18 and planning to enroll or expecting to enroll full or part-time at a two-year or four-year or technical institution or university. Available to U.S. and non-U.S. citizens.

Application Requirements: Application, applicant must enter a contest, portfolio. *Fee:* $30. *Deadline:* varies.

Contact: Programs Department
National Foundation for Advancement in the Arts
444 Brickell Avenue, Suite R14
Miami, FL 33133
Phone: 800-970-ARTS
Fax: 305-377-1149
E-mail: nfaa@nfaa.org

NATIONAL LEAGUE OF AMERICAN PEN WOMEN, INC. http://www.americanpenwomen.org

NLAPW VIRGINIA LIEBELER BIENNIAL GRANTS FOR MATURE WOMEN (ARTS)

One-time award given in even-numbered years to female artists ages 35 and older who are U.S. citizens to be used to further creative purpose of applicant. Submit three 4x6 or bigger color prints (no slides) of work in any media. For photography, submit three 4x6 prints in color or black and white. All applicants submit statements of background, purpose of grant, and how applicant learned of grant. Application fee of $8. Send self-addressed stamped envelope for further requirements. Deadline for entry is October 1 of odd-numbered year.

Academic Fields/Career Goals: Arts.

Award: Grant for use in freshman, sophomore, junior, senior, graduate, or postgraduate years; not renewable. *Number:* 1. *Amount:* $1000.

Eligibility Requirements: Applicant must be age 35; enrolled or expecting to enroll at an institution or university; female and must have an interest in art or photography/photogrammetry/filmmaking. Available to U.S. citizens.

Application Requirements: Applicant must enter a contest, self-addressed stamped envelope, proof of U.S. citizenship. *Fee:* $8. *Deadline:* October 1.

Contact: NLAPW Virginia Liebeler Biennial Grants for Women
National League of American Pen Women, Inc.
1300 17th Street, NW
Washington, DC 20036-1973

NATIONAL OPERA ASSOCIATION http://www.noa.org

NOA VOCAL COMPETITION/ LEGACY AWARD PROGRAM

Awards granted based on competitive audition to support study and career development. Singers compete in Scholarship and Artist Division. Legacy Awards are granted for study and career development in any opera-related career to those who further NOA's goal of increased minority participation in the profession.

Academic Fields/Career Goals: Arts; Performing Arts.

Award: Prize for use in freshman, sophomore, junior, senior, graduate, or postgraduate years; not renewable. *Number:* 3–8. *Amount:* $250–$1000.

Eligibility Requirements: Applicant must be age 18-24; enrolled or expecting to enroll full or part-time at a two-year or four-year or technical institution or university and must have an interest in music or music/singing. Available to U.S. and non-U.S. citizens.

National Opera Association (continued)

Application Requirements: Application, applicant must enter a contest, autobiography, photo, references, audition tape/proposal. *Fee:* $20. *Deadline:* November 1.

Contact: Robert Hansen, Executive Secretary
National Opera Association
PO Box 60869
Canyon, TX 79016-0869
Phone: 806-651-2857
Fax: 806-651-2958
E-mail: hansen@mail.wtamu.edu

NATIONAL SCULPTURE SOCIETY

http://www.nationalsculpture.org

NATIONAL SCULPTURE COMPETITION FOR YOUNG SCULPTORS

For any sculptors age 18-35. Must submit slides of five to ten works with biography. Slides will be returned if self-addressed stamped envelope is included. One medal award and six monetary awards. Deadline in early April. See Web site for details (http://www.nationalsculpture.org).

Academic Fields/Career Goals: Arts.

Award: Prize for use in freshman, sophomore, junior, senior, or graduate years; not renewable. *Number:* 7. *Amount:* $200–$1000.

Eligibility Requirements: Applicant must be age 18-35; enrolled or expecting to enroll full or part-time at an institution or university and must have an interest in art. Available to U.S. citizens.

Application Requirements: Application, applicant must enter a contest, autobiography, self-addressed stamped envelope, slides of work. *Deadline:* varies.

Contact: Gwen Pier, Executive Director
National Sculpture Society
237 Park Avenue
New York, NY 10017
Phone: 212-764-5645 Ext. 15
Fax: 212-764-5651
E-mail: gwen@nationalsculpture.org

NATIONAL SCULPTURE SOCIETY SCHOLARSHIPS

Scholarships available for students of figurative or representational sculpture. Scholarships are paid directly to the academic institution through which the student applies. Applicant must submit 8-10 photographs of at least three different works. Application deadline is April 30.

Academic Fields/Career Goals: Arts.

Award: Scholarship for use in freshman, sophomore, junior, senior, or graduate years; not renewable. *Number:* 1–6. *Amount:* $1000.

Eligibility Requirements: Applicant must be enrolled or expecting to enroll full or part-time at a two-year or four-year or technical institution or university and must have an interest in art. Available to U.S. and non-U.S. citizens.

Application Requirements: Application, financial need analysis, references, self-addressed stamped envelope, transcript, photographs of work. *Deadline:* April 30.

Contact: Gwen Pier, Executive Director
National Sculpture Society
237 Park Avenue
New York, NY 10017
Phone: 212-764-5645
Fax: 212-764-5651
E-mail: gwen@nationalsculpture.org

OREGON STUDENT ASSISTANCE COMMISSION

http://www.osac.state.or.us

GLENN R. AND JUANITA B. STRUBLE SCHOLARSHIP II

• *See page 78*

POLISH ARTS CLUB OF BUFFALO SCHOLARSHIP FOUNDATION

POLISH ARTS CLUB OF BUFFALO SCHOLARSHIP FOUNDATION TRUST

• *See page 84*

RHODE ISLAND FOUNDATION

http://www.rifoundation.org

CONSTANT MEMORIAL SCHOLARSHIP FOR AQUIDNECK ISLAND RESIDENTS

One-time scholarships between $2000 and $5000 are awarded to benefit visual art and/or music major entering his/her sophomore year in college. Applicants must be able to demonstrate financial need and a three year residency in Portsmouth, Middletown, or Newport, RI.

Academic Fields/Career Goals: Arts; Music.

Award: Scholarship for use in sophomore year; not renewable. *Number:* 1–2. *Amount:* $2000–$5000.

Eligibility Requirements: Applicant must be enrolled or expecting to enroll at a four-year institution; resident of Rhode Island and must have an interest in art or music. Available to U.S. citizens.

Application Requirements: Application. *Deadline:* June 4.

Contact: Libby Monahan, Scholarship Coordinator
Rhode Island Foundation
One Union Station
Providence, RI 02903
Phone: 401-274-4564
Fax: 401-272-1359
E-mail: libbym@rifoundation.org

ROBERT H. MOLLOHAN FAMILY CHARITABLE FOUNDATION, INC.

http://www.mollohanfoundation.org

MARY OLIVE EDDY JONES ART SCHOLARSHIP

• *See page 84*

TELETOON

http://www.teletoon.com

TELETOON ANIMATION SCHOLARSHIP AWARD COMPETITION

Scholarship competition created by TELETOON to encourage creative, original, and imaginative animation by supporting Canadians studying in the animation field or intending to pursue studies in animation. One-time award. Must submit portfolio. Award of CAN$2000-5000. Deadline is May 21.

Academic Fields/Career Goals: Arts; Filmmaking/Video.

Award: Scholarship for use in freshman, sophomore, junior, senior, graduate, or postgraduate years; not renewable. *Number:* 12. *Amount:* $1486–$3714.

Eligibility Requirements: Applicant must be enrolled or expecting to enroll full-time at a two-year or four-year or technical institution or university and resident of Alberta, British Columbia, Manitoba, New Brunswick, Newfoundland, North West Territories, Nova Scotia, Ontario, Prince Edward Island, Quebec, or Saskatchewan. Available to Canadian citizens.

Application Requirements: Application, applicant must enter a contest, essay, portfolio, transcript. *Deadline:* May 21.

Contact: Denise Vaughan, Senior Coordinator, Public Relations
Teletoon
BCE Place
181 Bay Street, PO Box 787
Toronto, ON M5J 2T3
Canada
Phone: 416-956-2060
Fax: 416-956-2070
E-mail: scholarship@teletoon.com

TEXAS ARTS AND CRAFTS EDUCATIONAL FOUNDATION

http://www.tacef.org

EMERGING TEXAS ARTIST SCHOLARSHIP

Scholarships are awarded as prizes in a juried art exhibit at the Texas State Arts and Crafts Fair. The students are chosen by their art department and attend under their school's banner. The students exhibit and sell their works at the fair. See Web site for details http://www.tacef.org. Must be enrolled in a Texas school.

Academic Fields/Career Goals: Arts.

Award: Scholarship for use in freshman, sophomore, junior, senior, graduate, or postgraduate years; not renewable. *Number:* 8–15. *Amount:* $500–$2500.

Eligibility Requirements: Applicant must be enrolled or expecting to enroll full or part-time at a two-year or four-year institution or university and studying in Texas. Available to U.S. citizens.

Application Requirements: Application, applicant must enter a contest, references, chosen by art department of their art school. *Deadline:* March 15.

Contact: Texas Arts and Crafts Educational Foundation
PO Box 291527
Kerrville, TX 78029-1527
Phone: 830-896-5711

U.S. FISH AND WILDLIFE SERVICE

http://duckstamps.fws.gov

FEDERAL JUNIOR DUCK STAMP CONSERVATION AND DESIGN COMPETITION

Any student in grades K-12, public, private, or home schooled, may enter this competition in all 50 states, the District of Columbia, and U.S. Territories. Teachers will use the curriculum guide which we provide to teach conservation issues to students. Student then does an artistic rendering of one of the North American Migratory Waterfowl and enters it into their state's Junior Duck Stamp Contest. Each state picks one Best of Show to be sent to the National Office in Arlington, VA. A national competition is held in D.C. and one winner is picked. Deadlines: South Carolina January 30, Florida February 21, all other states and territories March 15. Further information is available at: http://duckstamps.fws.gov.

Academic Fields/Career Goals: Arts.

Award: Prize for use in freshman year; not renewable. *Number:* 3. *Amount:* $1000–$4000.

Eligibility Requirements: Applicant must be enrolled or expecting to enroll full or part-time at an institution or university. Available to U.S. citizens.

Application Requirements: Applicant must enter a contest, artistic rendering. *Deadline:* March 15.

Contact: Submit entry to State Coordinator, see Web site for contact information.

UNICO NATIONAL, INC

http://www.unico.org

THEODORE MAZZA SCHOLARSHIP

• *See page 79*

UNITED NEGRO COLLEGE FUND

http://www.uncf.org

CATHERINE W. PIERCE SCHOLARSHIP

Award available to students enrolled in a UNCF member college or university. Must major in art or history. Minimum 3.0 GPA required. Prospective applicants should complete the Student Profile found at Web site: http://www.uncf.org.

Academic Fields/Career Goals: Arts; History.

Award: Scholarship for use in freshman, sophomore, junior, or senior years; not renewable. *Amount:* up to $5000.

Eligibility Requirements: Applicant must be Black (non-Hispanic) and enrolled or expecting to enroll at a four-year institution or university. Applicant must have 3.0 GPA or higher.

Application Requirements: Application, financial need analysis. *Deadline:* Continuous.

Contact: Program Services Department
United Negro College Fund
8260 Willow Oaks Corporate Drive
Fairfax, VA 22031

CHARLES STROSACKER FOUNDATION SCHOLARSHIP

Award restricted to Detroit, MI students who are art majors. Please visit Web site for more information: http://www.uncf.org.

Academic Fields/Career Goals: Arts.

Award: Scholarship for use in freshman, sophomore, junior, or senior years; renewable. *Number:* varies. *Amount:* varies.

Eligibility Requirements: Applicant must be Black (non-Hispanic); enrolled or expecting to enroll at an institution or university and resident of Michigan. Applicant must have 2.5 GPA or higher.

Application Requirements: Application, financial need analysis, FAFSA, SAR. *Deadline:* varies.

Contact: Program Services Department
United Negro College Fund
8260 Willow Oaks Corporate Drive
Fairfax, VA 22031

HOUSTON SYMPHONY/ TOP LADIES SCHOLARSHIP

Scholarship awarded to Iowa residents attending a UNCF member college or university and majoring in art. Minimum 2.5 GPA required. Prospective applicants should complete the Student Profile found at Web site: http://www.uncf.org.

Academic Fields/Career Goals: Arts.

Award: Scholarship for use in junior or senior years; not renewable.

Eligibility Requirements: Applicant must be Black (non-Hispanic); enrolled or expecting to enroll at a four-year institution or university and resident of Iowa. Applicant must have 2.5 GPA or higher.

Application Requirements: Application, financial need analysis. *Deadline:* Continuous.

Contact: Program Services Department
United Negro College Fund
8260 Willow Oaks Corporate Drive
Fairfax, VA 22031

JACQUELINE FEIGENSON SCHOLARSHIP

Scholarship awards students majoring in arts or humanities and attending a UNCF member college or university. Applicant must be a resident of the Detroit area in Michigan. Please visit Web site for more information: http://www.uncf.org.

Academic Fields/Career Goals: Arts; Humanities.

Award: Scholarship for use in freshman, sophomore, junior, senior, or graduate years. *Number:* varies. *Amount:* varies.

Eligibility Requirements: Applicant must be Black (non-Hispanic); enrolled or expecting to enroll at a four-year institution or university and resident of Michigan. Applicant must have 2.5 GPA or higher.

Application Requirements: Application, financial need analysis, FAFSA, SAR. *Deadline:* varies.

Contact: Program Services Department
United Negro College Fund
8260 Willow Oaks Corporate Drive
Fairfax, VA 22031

JANET JACKSON/RHYTHM NATION SCHOLARSHIP

Awards made annually to students majoring in communications, art, music, the performing arts, and English. Must attend a UNCF member college or university. Minimum 3.0 GPA required. Prospective applicants should complete the Student Profile found at Web site: http://www.uncf.org.

Academic Fields/Career Goals: Arts; Communications; Literature/English/Writing; Performing Arts.

Award: Scholarship for use in freshman, sophomore, junior, or senior years; not renewable. *Amount:* $2000.

Eligibility Requirements: Applicant must be Black (non-Hispanic) and enrolled or expecting to enroll at a four-year institution or university. Applicant must have 3.0 GPA or higher. Available to U.S. citizens.

Application Requirements: Application. *Deadline:* varies.

Contact: Program Services Department
United Negro College Fund
8260 Willow Oaks Corporate Drive
Fairfax, VA 22031

WATERBURY FOUNDATION

http://www.waterburyfoundation.org

LOIS MCMILLEN MEMORIAL SCHOLARSHIP FUND

Scholarships to women who are actively pursuing or who would like to pursue an artistic career. Must reside in the Foundation's service area, which is the greater Waterbury area of Connecticut. Awarded for the purpose of

Waterbury Foundation (continued)

attending an accredited college or university or a qualified artists-in-residence program in a chosen artistic field. Preference will be given to artists in the visual arts of painting and design.

Academic Fields/Career Goals: Arts.

Award: Scholarship for use in freshman, sophomore, junior, senior, or graduate years; not renewable. *Number:* varies. *Amount:* $500–$5000.

Eligibility Requirements: Applicant must be enrolled or expecting to enroll at a four-year institution or university; female and resident of Connecticut.

Application Requirements: Application, essay, references. *Deadline:* April 1.

Contact: Elizabeth Moore, Program Officer
Waterbury Foundation
81 West Main Street
Waterbury, CT 06702-1216
Phone: 203-753-1315
Fax: 203-756-3054
E-mail: emoore@waterburyfoundation.org

WAVERLY COMMUNITY HOUSE, INC.

http://waverlycomm.com

F. LAMMOT BELIN ARTS SCHOLARSHIP

• *See page 80*

WORLDSTUDIO FOUNDATION

http://www.worldstudio.org

WORLDSTUDIO FOUNDATION SCHOLARSHIP PROGRAM

• *See page 80*

ASIAN STUDIES

CULTURE CONNECTION

http://www.thecultureconnection.com

CULTURE CONNECTION FOUNDATION SCHOLARSHIP

• *See page 52*

AVIATION/AEROSPACE

AACE INTERNATIONAL

http://www.aacei.org

AACE INTERNATIONAL COMPETITIVE SCHOLARSHIP

• *See page 73*

AERO CLUB OF NEW ENGLAND

http://www.acone.org

AERO CLUB OF NEW ENGLAND AVIATION SCHOLARSHIP PROGRAM

One-time awards for study of aviation aeronautics and aircraft maintenance. Must be a U.S. citizen residing in New England and enrolled in an educational institution in New England.

Academic Fields/Career Goals: Aviation/Aerospace.

Award: Scholarship for use in freshman, sophomore, junior, senior, graduate, or postgraduate years; not renewable. *Number:* 13. *Amount:* $500–$2500.

Eligibility Requirements: Applicant must be enrolled or expecting to enroll full or part-time at a two-year or four-year or technical institution or university; resident of Connecticut, Maine, Massachusetts, New Hampshire, Rhode Island, or Vermont; studying in Connecticut, Maine, Massachusetts, New Hampshire, Rhode Island, or Vermont and must have an interest in designated field specified by sponsor. Available to U.S. citizens.

Application Requirements: Application, essay, financial need analysis, interview, references, transcript, flight time record. *Deadline:* March 30.

Contact: Kevin Currie, Chair, Education Committee
Aero Club of New England
25 Forest Circle
Waltham, MA 02452
Phone: 781-894-4330
Fax: 978-649-2145
E-mail: krcurrie@aopa.net

AIR TRAFFIC CONTROL ASSOCIATION, INC.

http://www.atca.org

AIR TRAFFIC CONTROL ASSOCIATION SCHOLARSHIP

Scholarships for students in programs leading to a bachelor's degree or higher in aviation-related courses of study and for full-time employees engaged in advanced study to improve their skills in air traffic control or aviation. Visit Web site for additional information: http://www.atca.org.

Academic Fields/Career Goals: Aviation/Aerospace; Engineering/Technology.

Award: Scholarship for use in freshman, sophomore, junior, senior, or graduate years; not renewable. *Number:* 7–12. *Amount:* $600–$2500.

Eligibility Requirements: Applicant must be enrolled or expecting to enroll full or part-time at a four-year institution or university. Applicant or parent of applicant must have employment or volunteer experience in air traffic controller field. Available to U.S. citizens.

Application Requirements: Application, autobiography, essay, financial need analysis, references, transcript. *Deadline:* May 1.

Contact: James Crook, Vice President of Operations
Air Traffic Control Association, Inc.
2300 Clarendon Boulevard, Suite 711
Arlington, VA 22201-2302
Phone: 703-522-5717
Fax: 703-527-7251
E-mail: jim.crook@atca.org

AIRCRAFT ELECTRONICS ASSOCIATION EDUCATIONAL FOUNDATION

http://www.aea.net

BENDIX/KING AVIONICS SCHOLARSHIP

Award for anyone who plans to attend or is attending an accredited school in an avionics or aircraft repair program. Must have minimum 2.5 GPA. One-time award of $1000.

Academic Fields/Career Goals: Aviation/Aerospace.

Award: Scholarship for use in freshman, sophomore, junior, or senior years; not renewable. *Number:* 1. *Amount:* $1000.

Eligibility Requirements: Applicant must be enrolled or expecting to enroll full or part-time at a two-year or four-year or technical institution or university. Applicant must have 2.5 GPA or higher. Available to U.S. and non-U.S. citizens.

Application Requirements: Application, essay, transcript. *Deadline:* February 15.

Contact: Mr. Mike Adamson, Educational Foundation Executive Director
Aircraft Electronics Association Educational Foundation
4217 South Hocker Drive
Independence, MO 64055-0963
Phone: 816-373-6565
Fax: 816-478-3100
E-mail: info@aea.net

BUD GLOVER MEMORIAL SCHOLARSHIP

Award for anyone who plans to or is attending an accredited school in an avionics or aircraft repair program. Minimum 2.5 GPA required. One-time award of $1000.

Academic Fields/Career Goals: Aviation/Aerospace; Trade/Technical Specialties.

Award: Scholarship for use in freshman, sophomore, junior, or senior years; not renewable. *Number:* 1. *Amount:* $1000.

Eligibility Requirements: Applicant must be enrolled or expecting to enroll full-time at a two-year or four-year or technical institution or university. Applicant must have 2.5 GPA or higher. Available to U.S. and non-U.S. citizens.

Application Requirements: Application, essay, references, test scores, transcript. *Deadline:* February 15.

Contact: Mr. Mike Adamson, Educational Foundation Executive Director
Aircraft Electronics Association Educational Foundation
4217 South Hocker Drive
Independence, MO 64055-0963
Phone: 816-373-6565
Fax: 816-478-3100
E-mail: info@aea.net

CHUCK PEACOCK MEMORIAL SCHOLARSHIP

Award for high school seniors or college students who plan to attend or are attending an accredited school in an aviation management program. Must have minimum 2.5 GPA. One time award of $1000.

Academic Fields/Career Goals: Aviation/Aerospace.

Award: Scholarship for use in freshman, sophomore, junior, or senior years; not renewable. *Number:* 1. *Amount:* $1000.

Eligibility Requirements: Applicant must be enrolled or expecting to enroll at a two-year or four-year or technical institution or university. Applicant must have 2.5 GPA or higher. Available to U.S. and non-U.S. citizens.

Application Requirements: Application, essay, transcript. *Deadline:* February 15.

Contact: Mr. Mike Adamson, Educational Foundation Executive Director
Aircraft Electronics Association Educational Foundation
4217 South Hocker
Independence, MO 64055-0963
Phone: 816-373-6565
Fax: 816-478-3100
E-mail: info@aea.net

DAVID ARVER MEMORIAL SCHOLARSHIP

One-time award for any student who plans to attend an accredited vocational or technical school in Illinois, Indiana, Iowa, Kansas, Michigan, Minnesota, Missouri, Nebraska, North Dakota, South Dakota, or Wisconsin. Must plan to study aviation electronics and have a minimum 2.5 GPA.

Academic Fields/Career Goals: Aviation/Aerospace.

Award: Scholarship for use in freshman, sophomore, junior, or senior years; not renewable. *Number:* 1. *Amount:* $1000.

Eligibility Requirements: Applicant must be enrolled or expecting to enroll full-time at a two-year or four-year or technical institution or university and studying in Illinois, Indiana, Iowa, Kansas, Michigan, Minnesota, Missouri, Nebraska, North Dakota, South Dakota, or Wisconsin. Applicant must have 2.5 GPA or higher. Available to U.S. and non-U.S. citizens.

Application Requirements: Application, essay, references, test scores, transcript. *Deadline:* February 15.

Contact: Mr. Mike Adamson, Educational Foundation Executive Director
Aircraft Electronics Association Educational Foundation
4217 South Hocker
Independence, MO 64055-0963
Phone: 816-373-6565
Fax: 816-478-3100
E-mail: info@aea.net

DUTCH AND GINGER ARVER SCHOLARSHIP

Award for anyone who plans to attend or is attending an accredited school in an avionics or aircraft repair program. Must have minimum 2.5 GPA. One-time award of $1000.

Academic Fields/Career Goals: Aviation/Aerospace.

Award: Scholarship for use in freshman, sophomore, junior, or senior years; not renewable. *Number:* 1. *Amount:* $1000.

Eligibility Requirements: Applicant must be enrolled or expecting to enroll full-time at a two-year or four-year or technical institution or university. Applicant must have 2.5 GPA or higher. Available to U.S. and non-U.S. citizens.

Application Requirements: Application, essay, references, test scores, transcript. *Deadline:* February 15.

Contact: Mr. Mike Adamson, Educational Foundation Executive Director
Aircraft Electronics Association Educational Foundation
4217 South Hocker Drive
Independence, MO 64055-0963
Phone: 816-373-6565
Fax: 816-478-3100
E-mail: info@aea.net

FIELD AVIATION CO., INC., SCHOLARSHIP

Award for high school seniors and/or college students who plan to or are attending an accredited college/university in an avionics or aircraft repair program. The educational institution must be located in Canada.

Academic Fields/Career Goals: Aviation/Aerospace; Trade/Technical Specialties.

Award: Scholarship for use in freshman, sophomore, junior, or senior years; not renewable. *Number:* 1. *Amount:* $1000.

Eligibility Requirements: Applicant must be enrolled or expecting to enroll full-time at a two-year or four-year or technical institution or university and studying in Alberta, British Columbia, Manitoba, New Brunswick, Newfoundland, North West Territories, Nova Scotia, Ontario, Prince Edward Island, Quebec, Saskatchewan, or Yukon. Applicant must have 2.5 GPA or higher. Available to U.S. and non-U.S. citizens.

Application Requirements: Application, essay, references, test scores, transcript. *Deadline:* February 15.

Contact: Mr. Mike Adamson, Educational Foundation Executive Director
Aircraft Electronics Association Educational Foundation
4217 South Hocker Drive
Independence, MO 64055-0963
Phone: 816-373-6565
Fax: 816-478-3100
E-mail: info@aea.net

GARMIN SCHOLARSHIP

Award for students of avionics or aircraft repair at a college or technical school. One-time award of $2000. Must have minimum 2.5 GPA.

Academic Fields/Career Goals: Aviation/Aerospace.

Award: Scholarship for use in freshman, sophomore, junior, or senior years; not renewable. *Number:* 1. *Amount:* $2000.

Eligibility Requirements: Applicant must be enrolled or expecting to enroll full-time at a two-year or four-year or technical institution or university. Applicant must have 2.5 GPA or higher. Available to U.S. and non-U.S. citizens.

Application Requirements: Application, essay, references, test scores, transcript. *Deadline:* February 15.

Contact: Mr. Mike Adamson, Educational Foundation Executive Director
Aircraft Electronics Association Educational Foundation
4217 South Hocker Drive
Independence, MO 64055-0963
Phone: 816-373-6565
Fax: 816-478-3100
E-mail: info@aea.net

JOHNNY DAVIS MEMORIAL SCHOLARSHIP

One-time award for anyone who plans to or is attending school in an avionics or aircraft repair program. Must have minimum 2.5 GPA. One time award of $1000.

Aircraft Electronics Association Educational Foundation (continued)

Academic Fields/Career Goals: Aviation/Aerospace.

Award: Scholarship for use in freshman, sophomore, junior, or senior years; not renewable. *Number:* 1. *Amount:* $1000.

Eligibility Requirements: Applicant must be enrolled or expecting to enroll full or part-time at a two-year or four-year or technical institution or university. Applicant must have 2.5 GPA or higher. Available to U.S. and non-U.S. citizens.

Application Requirements: Application, essay, transcript. *Deadline:* February 15.

Contact: Mr. Mike Adamson, Educational Foundation Executive Director
Aircraft Electronics Association Educational Foundation
4217 South Hocker Drive
Independence, MO 64055-0963
Phone: 816-373-6565
Fax: 816-478-3100
E-mail: info@aea.net

L-3 AVIONICS SYSTEMS SCHOLARSHIP

Award for high school seniors or college students who plan on or are attending an accredited school in an avionics or aircraft repair program. Must have minimum 2.5 GPA. One-time award of $2500.

Academic Fields/Career Goals: Aviation/Aerospace.

Award: Scholarship for use in freshman, sophomore, junior, or senior years; not renewable. *Number:* 1. *Amount:* $2500.

Eligibility Requirements: Applicant must be enrolled or expecting to enroll at a two-year or four-year or technical institution or university. Applicant must have 2.5 GPA or higher. Available to U.S. and non-U.S. citizens.

Application Requirements: Application, essay, transcript. *Deadline:* February 15.

Contact: Mr. Mike Adamson, Educational Foundation Executive Director
Aircraft Electronics Association Educational Foundation
4217 South Hocker
Independence, MO 64055-0963
Phone: 816-373-6565
Fax: 816-478-3100
E-mail: info@aea.net

LEE TARBOX MEMORIAL SCHOLARSHIP

Award for students of avionics or aircraft repair at any college or technical school. Minimum 2.5 GPA required. One-time $2500 award.

Academic Fields/Career Goals: Aviation/Aerospace.

Award: Scholarship for use in freshman, sophomore, junior, or senior years; not renewable. *Number:* 1. *Amount:* $2500.

Eligibility Requirements: Applicant must be enrolled or expecting to enroll full-time at a two-year or four-year or technical institution or university. Applicant must have 2.5 GPA or higher. Available to U.S. and non-U.S. citizens.

Application Requirements: Application, essay, references, test scores, transcript. *Deadline:* February 15.

Contact: Mr. Mike Adamson, Educational Foundation Executive Director
Aircraft Electronics Association Educational Foundation
4217 South Hocker Drive
Independence, MO 64055-0963
Phone: 816-373-6565
Fax: 816-478-3100
E-mail: info@aea.net

LOWELL GAYLOR MEMORIAL SCHOLARSHIP

Award for anyone who plans to or is attending an accredited school in avionics or aircraft repair program. Minimum 2.5 GPA required. One-time award of $1000.

Academic Fields/Career Goals: Aviation/Aerospace; Trade/Technical Specialties.

Award: Scholarship for use in freshman, sophomore, junior, or senior years; not renewable. *Number:* 1. *Amount:* $1000.

Eligibility Requirements: Applicant must be enrolled or expecting to enroll full-time at a two-year or four-year or technical institution or university. Applicant must have 2.5 GPA or higher. Available to U.S. and non-U.S. citizens.

Application Requirements: Application, essay, references, test scores, transcript. *Deadline:* February 15.

Contact: Mr. Mike Adamson, Educational Foundation Executive Director
Aircraft Electronics Association Educational Foundation
4217 South Hocker Drive
Independence, MO 64055-0963
Phone: 816-373-6565
Fax: 816-478-3100
E-mail: info@aea.net

MID-CONTINENT INSTRUMENT SCHOLARSHIP

Award for anyone who plans to attend or is attending an accredited school in an avionics or aircraft repair program. Minimum 2.5 GPA required. One-time award of $1000.

Academic Fields/Career Goals: Aviation/Aerospace.

Award: Scholarship for use in freshman, sophomore, junior, or senior years; not renewable. *Number:* 1. *Amount:* $1000.

Eligibility Requirements: Applicant must be enrolled or expecting to enroll full-time at a two-year or four-year or technical institution or university. Applicant must have 2.5 GPA or higher. Available to U.S. and non-U.S. citizens.

Application Requirements: Application, essay, references, test scores, transcript. *Deadline:* February 15.

Contact: Mr. Mike Adamson, Educational Foundation Executive Director
Aircraft Electronics Association Educational Foundation
4217 South Hocker Drive
Independence, MO 64055-0963
Phone: 816-373-6565
Fax: 816-478-3100
E-mail: info@aea.net

MONTE MITCHELL GLOBAL SCHOLARSHIP

Scholarship is available to a student from Europe, Australia, New Zealand, and surrounding Southern Pacific regions pursuing a degree in aviation maintenance technology, avionics, or aircraft repair at an accredited school located in Europe or the U.S. Minimum 2.5 GPA required.

Academic Fields/Career Goals: Aviation/Aerospace; Trade/Technical Specialties.

Award: Scholarship for use in freshman, sophomore, junior, or senior years; not renewable. *Number:* 1. *Amount:* $1000.

Eligibility Requirements: Applicant must be enrolled or expecting to enroll full-time at a two-year or four-year or technical institution or university. Applicant must have 2.5 GPA or higher. Available to citizens of countries other than the U.S. or Canada.

Application Requirements: Application, essay, references, transcript. *Deadline:* February 15.

Contact: Mr. Mike Adamson, Educational Foundation Executive Director
Aircraft Electronics Association Educational Foundation
4217 South Hocker Drive
Independence, MO 64055-0963
Phone: 816-373-6565
Fax: 816-478-3100
E-mail: info@aea.net

PLANE AND PILOT MAGAZINE/GARMIN SCHOLARSHIP

Award for high school, college, or vocational or technical school students who plan to or are attending an accredited vocational or technical school in an avionics or aircraft repair program. Minimum 2.5 GPA required. One-time award of $2000.

Academic Fields/Career Goals: Aviation/Aerospace; Trade/Technical Specialties.

Award: Scholarship for use in freshman or sophomore years; not renewable. *Number:* 1. *Amount:* $2000.

Eligibility Requirements: Applicant must be enrolled or expecting to enroll full-time at a two-year or four-year or technical institution or university. Applicant must have 2.5 GPA or higher. Available to U.S. and non-U.S. citizens.

Application Requirements: Application, essay, references, test scores, transcript. *Deadline:* February 15.

Contact: Mr. Mike Adamson, Educational Foundation Executive Director
Aircraft Electronics Association Educational Foundation
4217 South Hocker Drive
Independence, MO 64055-0963
Phone: 816-373-6565
Fax: 816-478-3100
E-mail: info@aea.net

PRIVATE PILOT MAGAZINE SCHOLARSHIP

Award for high school seniors or college students who plan to attend or are attending an accredited school in avionics or aircraft repair program. Must have minimum 2.5 GPA. One time award of $1000.

Academic Fields/Career Goals: Aviation/Aerospace.

Award: Scholarship for use in freshman, sophomore, junior, or senior years; not renewable. *Number:* 1. *Amount:* $1000.

Eligibility Requirements: Applicant must be enrolled or expecting to enroll at a two-year or four-year or technical institution or university. Applicant must have 2.5 GPA or higher. Available to U.S. and non-U.S. citizens.

Application Requirements: Application, essay, transcript. *Deadline:* February 15.

Contact: Mr. Mike Adamson, Educational Foundation Executive Director
Aircraft Electronics Association Educational Foundation
4217 South Hocker
Independence, MO 64055-0963
Phone: 816-373-6565
Fax: 816-478-3100
E-mail: info@aea.net

SPORTY'S PILOT SHOP/CINCINNATI AVIONICS

One-time award available to high school seniors or college students who plan to or are attending an accredited school in avionics or aircraft repair program. Minimum 2.5 GPA required.

Academic Fields/Career Goals: Aviation/Aerospace.

Award: Scholarship for use in freshman, sophomore, junior, or senior years; not renewable. *Number:* 1. *Amount:* $2000.

Eligibility Requirements: Applicant must be enrolled or expecting to enroll full or part-time at a two-year or four-year or technical institution or university. Applicant must have 2.5 GPA or higher. Available to U.S. and non-U.S. citizens.

Application Requirements: Application, essay, references, test scores, transcript. *Deadline:* February 15.

Contact: Mr. Mike Adamson, Educational Foundation Executive Director
Aircraft Electronics Association Educational Foundation
4217 South Hocker
Independence, MO 64055-0963
Phone: 816-373-6565
Fax: 816-478-3100
E-mail: info@aea.net

AIRPORTS COUNCIL INTERNATIONAL - NORTH AMERICA http://www.aci-na.org

AIRPORTS COUNCIL INTERNATIONAL- NORTH AMERICA COMMISSIONERS COMMITTEE SCHOLARSHIP

Up to three annual scholarships will be awarded in amounts up to $3000 per recipient. Previous scholarship recipients may reapply. Must reside and attend school in U.S., Guam, Saipan, U.S. VI, or Canada. Must possess minimum 3.0 GPA. Must be used in program focused on career in airport management.

Academic Fields/Career Goals: Aviation/Aerospace.

Award: Scholarship for use in junior, senior, or graduate years; not renewable. *Number:* up to 3. *Amount:* $2000–$3000.

Eligibility Requirements: Applicant must be enrolled or expecting to enroll full-time at a two-year or four-year or technical institution or university. Applicant must have 3.0 GPA or higher. Available to U.S. citizens.

Application Requirements: Application, essay, financial need analysis, references, transcript. *Deadline:* December 15.

Contact: Patricia Ornst, Director, Legislative Affairs
Airports Council International - North America
1775 K Street, Suite 500
Washington, DC 20006
Phone: 202-293-8500
Fax: 202-887-5365
E-mail: pdornst@aci-na.org

ALASKAN AVIATION SAFETY FOUNDATION http://www.alaska.net/~etc/aasf/

ALASKAN AVIATION SAFETY FOUNDATION MEMORIAL SCHOLARSHIP FUND

Scholarships for undergraduate or graduate study in aviation. Must be a resident of Alaska and a U.S. citizen. Write for deadlines and details.

Academic Fields/Career Goals: Aviation/Aerospace.

Award: Scholarship for use in freshman, sophomore, junior, senior, or graduate years; not renewable. *Number:* 1–3. *Amount:* $500–$750.

Eligibility Requirements: Applicant must be enrolled or expecting to enroll full or part-time at a two-year or four-year or technical institution or university and resident of Alaska. Available to U.S. citizens.

Application Requirements: Application, autobiography, driver's license, financial need analysis, references, test scores, transcript. *Deadline:* varies.

Contact: Y.R. Hyatt, Secretary, Board of Directors
Alaskan Aviation Safety Foundation
4340 Postmark Drive
Anchorage, AK 99502-1066
Phone: 907-243-7237
Fax: 907-243-7237
E-mail: aasfanc@attglobal.net

AMERICAN ASSOCIATION OF AIRPORT EXECUTIVES http://www.airportnet.org

AMERICAN ASSOCIATION OF AIRPORT EXECUTIVES FOUNDATION SCHOLARSHIP

$1000 granted each year to juniors or higher who are enrolled in an aviation program and have a minimum 3.0 GPA. Awards based on academic records, financial need, school participation, community activities, work experience, and a personal statement. Must be recommended by school. One student per institution. Multiple recommendations from the same institution will be returned.

Academic Fields/Career Goals: Aviation/Aerospace.

Award: Scholarship for use in junior or senior years; not renewable. *Number:* up to 10. *Amount:* $1000.

Eligibility Requirements: Applicant must be enrolled or expecting to enroll full-time at a four-year institution or university. Applicant must have 3.0 GPA or higher. Available to U.S. citizens.

Application Requirements: Financial need analysis, references, self-addressed stamped envelope, transcript. *Deadline:* May 31.

Contact: Scholarship Coordinator
American Association of Airport Executives
601 Madison Street, Suite 400
Alexandria, VA 22314
Phone: 703-824-0504
Fax: 703-820-1395
E-mail: member.services@airportnet.org

AMERICAN ASSOCIATION OF AIRPORT EXECUTIVES FOUNDATION SCHOLARSHIP-NATIVE AMERICAN

Yearly $1000 grant to a number of Native-American students who are juniors or higher and who are enrolled in an aviation program. Must have a minimum 3.0 GPA. Award based on academic records, financial need, school participation, community activities, work experience, race, and a personal statement. Must be recommended by a school (one student per institution). Multiple recommendations from the same institution will be returned.

Academic Fields/Career Goals: Aviation/Aerospace.

Award: Scholarship for use in junior or senior years; not renewable. *Amount:* $1000.

Eligibility Requirements: Applicant must be American Indian/Alaska Native and enrolled or expecting to enroll full-time at a four-year institution or university. Applicant must have 3.0 GPA or higher. Available to U.S. citizens.

Application Requirements: Financial need analysis, references, self-addressed stamped envelope, transcript. *Deadline:* May 31.

Contact: Scholarship Coordinator
American Association of Airport Executives
601 Madison Street, Suite 400
Alexandria, VA 22314-1756
Phone: 703-824-0504
Fax: 703-820-1395
E-mail: member.services@airportnet.org

AMERICAN INSTITUTE OF AERONAUTICS AND ASTRONAUTICS http://www.aiaa.org

AIAA UNDERGRADUATE SCHOLARSHIP

• *See page 66*

AMERICAN SOCIETY OF NAVAL ENGINEERS http://www.navalengineers.org

AMERICAN SOCIETY OF NAVAL ENGINEERS SCHOLARSHIP

• *See page 66*

AOPA AIR SAFETY FOUNDATION http://www.asf.org

AOPA AIR SAFETY FOUNDATION/DONALD BURNSIDE MEMORIAL SCHOLARSHIP

One-time scholarship of $1000 will be given to a United States citizen who, without assistance, would find it difficult to obtain a college education. The recipient must be enrolled in and plan to continue a college curriculum leading to a degree in the field of aviation. Must maintain a 3.25 GPA. Visit http://www.aopa.org/asf/scholarship for more information and an application.

Academic Fields/Career Goals: Aviation/Aerospace.

Award: Scholarship for use in junior or senior years; not renewable. *Number:* 1. *Amount:* $1000.

Eligibility Requirements: Applicant must be enrolled or expecting to enroll at a four-year institution. Available to U.S. citizens.

Application Requirements: Application, essay, transcript. *Deadline:* March 31.

Contact: Scholarship Coordinator
AOPA Air Safety Foundation
421 Aviation Way
Frederick, MD 21701

AOPA AIR SAFETY FOUNDATION/KOCH CORPORATION SCHOLARSHIP

A $1500 scholarship will be awarded to a deserving United States citizen. Recipients will be enrolled in an accredited college or university pursuing a course of study focusing on aviation. Must maintain a 3.25 GPA. Visit http://www.aopa.org/asf/scholarship for more information and an application.

Academic Fields/Career Goals: Aviation/Aerospace.

Award: Scholarship for use in freshman, sophomore, junior, or senior years; renewable. *Number:* 1. *Amount:* $1500.

Eligibility Requirements: Applicant must be enrolled or expecting to enroll at a four-year institution or university. Available to U.S. citizens.

Application Requirements: Application, essay, transcript. *Deadline:* July 31.

Contact: Scholarship Coordinator
AOPA Air Safety Foundation
421 Aviation Way
Frederick, MD 21701

AOPA AIR SAFETY FOUNDATION/MCALLISTER MEMORIAL SCHOLARSHIP

One-time scholarship of $1000 will be given to a United States citizen who, without assistance, would find it difficult to obtain a college education. The recipient must be enrolled in and plan to continue a college curriculum leading to a degree in the field of aviation. Must maintain a 3.25 GPA. Visit http://www.aopa.org/asf/scholarship for more information and an application.

Academic Fields/Career Goals: Aviation/Aerospace.

Award: Scholarship for use in junior or senior years; not renewable. *Number:* 1. *Amount:* $1000.

Eligibility Requirements: Applicant must be enrolled or expecting to enroll at a four-year institution. Available to U.S. citizens.

Application Requirements: Application, essay, self-addressed stamped envelope, transcript. *Deadline:* March 31.

Contact: Scholarship Coordinator
AOPA Air Safety Foundation
421 Aviation Way
Frederick, MD 21701

ARMED FORCES COMMUNICATIONS AND ELECTRONICS ASSOCIATION, EDUCATIONAL FOUNDATION http://www.afcea.org

AFCEA SCHOLARSHIP FOR WORKING PROFESSIONALS

Must be a U.S. citizen currently enrolled as a sophomore, junior or senior in an accredited U.S. school. Part time status is defined as enrollment in at least two classes per semester at any two- or four-year accredited U.S. college or university with a declared major in a science or technology degree program. Eligible majors include electrical, aerospace, or computer engineering, computer science, computer information systems, physics or mathematics. An overall GPA of 3.5 is required.

Academic Fields/Career Goals: Aviation/Aerospace; Computer Science/Data Processing; Electrical Engineering/Electronics; Engineering/Technology; Physical Sciences and Math.

Award: Scholarship for use in sophomore, junior, or senior years; not renewable. *Number:* varies. *Amount:* $1500.

Eligibility Requirements: Applicant must be enrolled or expecting to enroll part-time at a two-year or four-year institution or university. Applicant must have 3.5 GPA or higher. Available to U.S. citizens.

Application Requirements: Application, references, transcript. *Deadline:* September 15.

Contact: Norma Corrales, Director, Scholarships and Award Programs
Armed Forces Communications and Electronics Association, Educational Foundation
4400 Fair Lakes Court
Fairfax, VA 22033-3899
Phone: 703-631-6149
Fax: 703-631-4693
E-mail: scholarship@afcea.org

ARMED FORCES COMMUNICATIONS AND ELECTRONICS ASSOCIATION ROTC SCHOLARSHIP PROGRAM

Award for ROTC students enrolled in four-year accredited colleges or universities in the U.S. At the time of application students must be sophomore or junior studying electronics or electrical, communications, or aerospace engineering; physics; mathematics; or computer science. Must exhibit academic excellence and potential to serve as officer in the Armed Forces of the U.S. Nominations are submitted by professors of military science, naval science, or aerospace studies by April 1.

Academic Fields/Career Goals: Aviation/Aerospace; Computer Science/Data Processing; Electrical Engineering/Electronics; Engineering/Technology; Physical Sciences and Math.

Award: Scholarship for use in sophomore or junior years; not renewable. *Number:* varies. *Amount:* $2000.

Eligibility Requirements: Applicant must be enrolled or expecting to enroll full-time at a four-year institution or university. Available to U.S. citizens.

Application Requirements: Application, references, transcript. *Deadline:* April 1.

Contact: Armed Forces Communications and Electronics Association, Educational Foundation
4400 Fair Lakes Court
Fairfax, VA 22033-3899
E-mail: scholarship@afcea.org

ASSOCIATION FOR FACILITIES ENGINEERING (AFE)

ASSOCIATION FOR FACILITIES ENGINEERING CEDAR VALLEY CHAPTER # 132 SCHOLARSHIP

Applicant must be a high school graduate, have a 2.5 or higher GPA, be U.S. citizen, and an Iowa resident. Applicant may be enrolled in any engineering program leading to an AA, BA, or BS degree. Awards are paid directly to the institution in the student's name.

Academic Fields/Career Goals: Aviation/Aerospace; Chemical Engineering; Civil Engineering; Electrical Engineering/Electronics; Engineering/Technology; Engineering-Related Technologies; Materials Science, Engineering, and Metallurgy; Mechanical Engineering; Trade/Technical Specialties.

Award: Scholarship for use in freshman, sophomore, junior, or senior years; not renewable. *Number:* 2. *Amount:* $500.

Eligibility Requirements: Applicant must be enrolled or expecting to enroll full-time at a two-year or four-year or technical institution or university; resident of Iowa and studying in Iowa. Applicant must have 2.5 GPA or higher. Available to U.S. citizens.

Application Requirements: Application, autobiography, transcript, copy of birth certificate, high school diploma. *Deadline:* May 1.

Contact: Joe Zachar, Special Events Chair
Association for Facilities Engineering (AFE)
1203 Forest Glen Court, SE
Cedar Rapids, IA 52403

ASTRONAUT SCHOLARSHIP FOUNDATION http://www.astronautscholarship.org

ASTRONAUT SCHOLARSHIP FOUNDATION

• *See page 68*

AVIATION COUNCIL OF PENNSYLVANIA http://www.acpfly.com

AVIATION COUNCIL OF PENNSYLVANIA SCHOLARSHIP PROGRAM

Awards for Pennsylvania residents to pursue studies at Pennsylvania institutions leading to career as professional pilot or in the fields of aviation technology or aviation management. Awards at discretion of Aviation Council of Pennsylvania. Three to four scholarships ranging from $500 to $1000. Applicants for the aviation management scholarship may attend institutions outside of Pennsylvania.

Academic Fields/Career Goals: Aviation/Aerospace.

Award: Scholarship for use in freshman, sophomore, junior, or senior years; not renewable. *Number:* 3–4. *Amount:* $500–$1000.

Eligibility Requirements: Applicant must be enrolled or expecting to enroll full or part-time at a two-year or four-year or technical institution or university; resident of Pennsylvania and studying in Pennsylvania. Available to U.S. citizens.

Application Requirements: Application, financial need analysis, references, transcript. *Deadline:* August 1.

Contact: Robert Rockmaker, Executive Secretary
Aviation Council of Pennsylvania
3111 Arcadia Avenue
Allentown, PA 18103-6903
Phone: 610-797-6911
Fax: 610-797-8238
E-mail: info@acpfly.com

CIVIL AIR PATROL, USAF AUXILIARY http://www.capnhq.gov

MAJOR GENERAL LUCAS V. BEAU FLIGHT SCHOLARSHIPS SPONSORED BY THE ORDER OF DAEDALIANS

One-time scholarships of $2100 for active cadets of the Civil Air Patrol who desire a career in military aviation. Award is to be used toward flight training for a private pilot license. Must be 15 1/2-18 1/2 years of age on April 1st of the year for which applying. Must be an active CAP cadet officer. Not open to the general public.

Academic Fields/Career Goals: Aviation/Aerospace.

Award: Scholarship for use in freshman year; not renewable. *Number:* 5. *Amount:* $2100.

Eligibility Requirements: Applicant must be age 16-19; enrolled or expecting to enroll at an institution or university and single. Applicant or parent of applicant must be member of Civil Air Patrol.

Application Requirements: Application, essay, photo, references, test scores, transcript. *Deadline:* March 1.

Contact: Tanjula Sankey, Assistant Program Manager
Civil Air Patrol, USAF Auxiliary
105 South Hansell Street, Building 714
Maxwell Air Force Base, AL 36112-6332
Phone: 334-953-8640
Fax: 334-953-6699
E-mail: cpr@capnhq.gov

COMMUNITY FOUNDATION OF CAPE COD http://www.capecodfoundation.org

GEORGE E. PARMENTER AERONAUTICAL SCHOLARSHIP FUND

George E. Parmenter Aeronautical Scholarship Fund awards $1,000 annually to a high school senior who has demonstrated a commitment to pursue a career directly related to aeronautics. For more details see Web site: http://www.capecodfoundation.org.

Academic Fields/Career Goals: Aviation/Aerospace.

Award: Scholarship for use in freshman, sophomore, junior, or senior years; not renewable. *Number:* 1. *Amount:* $1000.

Eligibility Requirements: Applicant must be high school student; planning to enroll or expecting to enroll full-time at a four-year institution or university and resident of Massachusetts. Available to U.S. citizens.

Application Requirements: Application, essay, financial need analysis, references, test scores, transcript. *Deadline:* April 1.

Contact: Pauline Greenberg, Scholarship Associate
Community Foundation of Cape Cod
PO Box 406
259 Willow Street
Yarmouthport, MA 02675
Phone: 508-790-3040
Fax: 508-790-4069
E-mail: pgreenberg@capecodfoundation.org

DAEDALIAN FOUNDATION http://www.daedalians.org

DAEDALIEAN FOUNDATION MATCHING SCHOLARSHIP PROGRAM

One-time award to students interested in pursuing a career in military aviation. Matching scholars program matches the dollars given by chapters throughout the U.S. Must submit flight/ROTC/CAP recommendation.

Academic Fields/Career Goals: Aviation/Aerospace.

Award: Scholarship for use in freshman, sophomore, junior, or senior years; not renewable. *Number:* varies. *Amount:* up to $2000.

Eligibility Requirements: Applicant must be enrolled or expecting to enroll full-time at a two-year or four-year institution or university. Available to U.S. citizens.

Application Requirements: Application, photo, references, test scores, flight/ROTC/CAP recommendation. *Deadline:* Continuous.

Contact: Robert Karre, Colonel, United States Air Force (Retired)
Daedalian Foundation
55 Main Circle (Building 676)
PO Box 249
Randolph AFB, TX 78148-0249
Phone: 210-945-2113

EAA AVIATION FOUNDATION, INC. http://www.eaa.org

DAVID ALAN QUICK SCHOLARSHIP

Renewable scholarship awarded to an undergraduate junior or senior in good standing. Applicant must be pursuing degree in aerospace or aeronautical engineering at an accredited college or university. Applications may be downloaded from the Web site http://www.eaa.org. Deadline is March 30. Must be an EAA member.

Academic Fields/Career Goals: Aviation/Aerospace.

Award: Scholarship for use in junior or senior years; renewable. *Number:* 1. *Amount:* $1000.

Eligibility Requirements: Applicant must be enrolled or expecting to enroll at a four-year institution or university. Applicant or parent of applicant must be member of Experimental Aircraft Association. Available to U.S. citizens.

Application Requirements: Application, essay, references, transcript. *Fee:* $5. *Deadline:* March 30.

Contact: See Web site for application.

EAA AVIATION ACHIEVEMENT SCHOLARSHIPS

Award for individuals active in recreational aviation endeavors to further their aviation education or training. Two awards in the amount of $500 each. Must submit two or more recommendations. $5 application fee. Please check Web site at http://www.eaa.org for criteria and to download official application. Must be an EAA member.

Academic Fields/Career Goals: Aviation/Aerospace.

Award: Scholarship for use in freshman, sophomore, junior, senior, graduate, or postgraduate years; not renewable. *Number:* 2. *Amount:* $500.

Eligibility Requirements: Applicant must be enrolled or expecting to enroll full or part-time at a two-year or four-year or technical institution or university. Applicant or parent of applicant must be member of Experimental Aircraft Association. Available to U.S. citizens.

Application Requirements: Application, essay, financial need analysis, references, test scores, transcript. *Fee:* $5. *Deadline:* March 30.

Contact: See Web site for application.

H. P. "BUD" MILLIGAN AVIATION SCHOLARSHIP

Renewable scholarship for applicants enrolled in accredited aviation program. Financial need is not a requirement. Applications may be downloaded from the Web site at http://www.eaa.org. Must be an EAA member.

Academic Fields/Career Goals: Aviation/Aerospace.

Award: Scholarship for use in freshman, sophomore, junior, or senior years; renewable. *Number:* 1. *Amount:* $1000.

Eligibility Requirements: Applicant must be enrolled or expecting to enroll at a two-year or four-year or technical institution or university. Applicant or parent of applicant must be member of Experimental Aircraft Association. Available to U.S. citizens.

Application Requirements: Application, essay, references, transcript. *Fee:* $5. *Deadline:* March 30.

Contact: See Web site for application.

HANSEN SCHOLARSHIP

Renewable scholarship of $1000 for student enrolled in accredited institution pursuing a degree in aerospace engineering or aeronautical engineering. Student must be in good standing; financial need not a requirement. Applications may be downloaded from the Web site at http://www.eaa.org. Deadline is March 30. Must be an EAA member.

Academic Fields/Career Goals: Aviation/Aerospace.

Award: Scholarship for use in freshman, sophomore, junior, or senior years; renewable. *Number:* 1. *Amount:* $1000.

Eligibility Requirements: Applicant must be enrolled or expecting to enroll at a two-year or four-year or technical institution or university. Applicant or parent of applicant must be member of Experimental Aircraft Association. Available to U.S. citizens.

Application Requirements: Application, essay, references, transcript. *Fee:* $5. *Deadline:* March 30.

Contact: See Web site for application.

HERBERT L. COX MEMORIAL SCHOLARSHIP

Award for students accepted by or attending an accredited college or university in pursuit of a degree leading to an aviation profession. Must show financial need. Self-supporting students encouraged to apply; recipients encouraged to reapply annually. One award, expected to exceed $500 annually. Must submit two or more recommendations. Deadline is March 30. $5 application fee. Please check Web site http://www.eaa.org for criteria and to download official application. Must be an EAA member.

Academic Fields/Career Goals: Aviation/Aerospace.

Award: Scholarship for use in freshman, sophomore, junior, or senior years; not renewable. *Number:* 1. *Amount:* $500.

Eligibility Requirements: Applicant must be enrolled or expecting to enroll full or part-time at a four-year institution or university. Applicant or parent of applicant must be member of Experimental Aircraft Association. Available to U.S. citizens.

Application Requirements: Application, essay, financial need analysis, references, test scores, transcript. *Fee:* $5. *Deadline:* March 30.

Contact: See Web site for application.

PAYZER SCHOLARSHIP

Must be accepted or enrolled in an accredited college, university, or postsecondary school with an emphasis on technical information. Awarded to an individual who is seeking a major and declares an intention to pursue a professional career in engineering, mathematics, or the physical/biological sciences. Deadline is March 30. $5 application fee. Please check Web site http://www.eaa.org for criteria and to download official application. Must be an EAA member.

Academic Fields/Career Goals: Aviation/Aerospace; Biology; Engineering/Technology; Physical Sciences and Math.

Award: Scholarship for use in freshman, sophomore, junior, or senior years; not renewable. *Number:* 1. *Amount:* $5000.

Eligibility Requirements: Applicant must be enrolled or expecting to enroll full-time at a four-year institution or university. Applicant or parent of applicant must be member of Experimental Aircraft Association. Available to U.S. citizens.

Application Requirements: Application, essay, references, test scores, transcript. *Fee:* $5. *Deadline:* March 30.

Contact: See Web site for application.

GENERAL AVIATION MANUFACTURERS ASSOCIATION http://www.gama.aero

EDWARD W. STIMPSON "AVIATION EXCELLENCE" AWARD

One-time scholarship award for students who are graduating from high school and have been accepted to attend aviation college or university in upcoming year. See Web site at http://www.gama.aero for additional details.

Academic Fields/Career Goals: Aviation/Aerospace.

Award: Scholarship for use in freshman year; not renewable. *Number:* 1. *Amount:* $500.

Eligibility Requirements: Applicant must be high school student and planning to enroll or expecting to enroll at an institution or university. Applicant must have 3.0 GPA or higher. Available to U.S. citizens.

Application Requirements: Application, essay, references, transcript. *Deadline:* April 19.

Contact: Bridgette Bailey, Director of Administration
General Aviation Manufacturers Association
1400 K Street, NW, Suite 801
Washington, DC 20005-2485
Phone: 202-393-1500
Fax: 202-842-4063
E-mail: bbailey@gama.aero

HAROLD S. WOOD AWARD FOR EXCELLENCE

One-time scholarship award for a university student who is attending a National Intercollegiate Flying Association (NIFA) school. Must have completed at least one semester of coursework. See Web site at http://www.gama.aero for additional details.

Academic Fields/Career Goals: Aviation/Aerospace.

Award: Scholarship for use in freshman, sophomore, junior, or senior years; not renewable. *Number:* 1. *Amount:* $1000.

Eligibility Requirements: Applicant must be enrolled or expecting to enroll at a four-year institution or university. Applicant must have 3.0 GPA or higher. Available to U.S. citizens.

Application Requirements: Application, references, transcript, nomination. *Deadline:* February 15.

Contact: Bridgette Bailey, Director of Administration
General Aviation Manufacturers Association
1400 K Street, NW, Suite 801
Washington, DC 20005-2485
Phone: 202-393-1500
Fax: 202-842-4063
E-mail: bbailey@gama.aero

HISPANIC COLLEGE FUND, INC.

http://www.hispanicfund.org

NATIONAL HISPANIC EXPLORERS SCHOLARSHIP PROGRAM

• *See page 69*

HISPANIC ENGINEER NATIONAL ACHIEVEMENT AWARDS CORPORATION (HENAAC)

http://www.henaac.org

HISPANIC ENGINEER NATIONAL ACHIEVEMENT AWARDS CORPORATION SCHOLARSHIP PROGRAM

Scholarships available to Hispanic students maintaining a 3.0 GPA. Must be studying an engineering or science related field. For more details and an application go to Web site: http://www.henaac.org

Academic Fields/Career Goals: Aviation/Aerospace; Biology; Chemical Engineering; Civil Engineering; Computer Science/Data Processing; Electrical Engineering/Electronics; Engineering/Technology; Materials Science, Engineering, and Metallurgy; Mechanical Engineering; Nuclear Science.

Award: Scholarship for use in freshman, sophomore, junior, senior, or graduate years; not renewable. *Number:* 12–20. *Amount:* $2000–$5000.

Eligibility Requirements: Applicant must be of Hispanic heritage and enrolled or expecting to enroll full-time at a four-year institution or university. Applicant must have 3.0 GPA or higher. Available to U.S. and non-U.S. citizens.

Application Requirements: Application, essay, resume, references, transcript. *Deadline:* April 23.

Contact: Application available at Web site.

ILLINOIS PILOTS ASSOCIATION

http://www.illinoispilots.com

ILLINOIS PILOTS ASSOCIATION MEMORIAL SCHOLARSHIP

Recipient must be a resident of Illinois established in an Illinois postsecondary institution in a full-time aviation-related program. The applicants will be judged by the scholarship committee and the award (usually $500 annually) will be sent directly to the recipient's school. For further details visit Web site: http://www.illinoispilots.com.

Academic Fields/Career Goals: Aviation/Aerospace.

Award: Scholarship for use in sophomore, junior, or senior years; not renewable. *Number:* 1. *Amount:* $500.

Eligibility Requirements: Applicant must be enrolled or expecting to enroll full-time at a two-year or four-year or technical institution or university; resident of Illinois and studying in Illinois. Available to U.S. citizens.

Application Requirements: Application, essay, photo, references, transcript. *Deadline:* April 1.

Contact: Ruth Frantz, Scholarship Committee Chairman
Illinois Pilots Association
40W297 Apache Lane
Huntley, IL 60142
Phone: 847-669-3821
Fax: 847-669-3822
E-mail: landings8e@aol.com

INSTRUMENTATION, SYSTEMS, AND AUTOMATION SOCIETY (ISA)

http://www.isa.org

INSTRUMENTATION, SYSTEMS, AND AUTOMATION SOCIETY (ISA) SCHOLARSHIP PROGRAM

The ISA grants scholarships worldwide to full-time students studying in technical fields related to instrumentation systems and automation. Minimum 3.0 GPA required. Applications available at http://www.isa.org

Academic Fields/Career Goals: Aviation/Aerospace; Chemical Engineering; Electrical Engineering/Electronics; Engineering/Technology; Engineering-Related Technologies; Heating, Air-Conditioning, and Refrigeration Mechanics; Mechanical Engineering.

Award: Scholarship for use in junior, senior, or graduate years; not renewable. *Number:* 5–15. *Amount:* $500–$5000.

Eligibility Requirements: Applicant must be enrolled or expecting to enroll full-time at a two-year or four-year or technical institution or university. Applicant must have 3.0 GPA or higher. Available to U.S. and non-U.S. citizens.

Application Requirements: Application, references, self-addressed stamped envelope, transcript. *Deadline:* varies.

Contact: Michaela Johnson-Tena, Coordinator, Education Services
Instrumentation, Systems, and Automation Society (ISA)
67 Alexander Drive
Research Triangle Park, NC 27709
Phone: 919-990-9400
Fax: 919-549-8288
E-mail: mtena@isa.org

INTERNATIONAL SOCIETY FOR OPTICAL ENGINEERING-SPIE

http://www.spie.org/info/scholarships

SPIE EDUCATIONAL SCHOLARSHIPS IN OPTICAL SCIENCE AND ENGINEERING

• *See page 70*

INTERNATIONAL SOCIETY OF WOMEN AIRLINE PILOTS (ISA+21)

http://www.iswap.org

INTERNATIONAL SOCIETY OF WOMEN AIRLINE PILOTS AIRLINE SCHOLARSHIPS

Scholarship available to ISA members and nonmembers. Program disburses cash awards toward pilot certificates, ratings, and type ratings to qualifying women. Each year the number and type of these awards vary. All applicants must meet FAA medical requirements for a CLASS I Medical certificate. Visit Web site at http://www.iswap.org for additional information and deadlines.

Academic Fields/Career Goals: Aviation/Aerospace.

Award: Scholarship for use in freshman, sophomore, junior, or senior years; not renewable. *Number:* up to 5. *Amount:* varies.

Eligibility Requirements: Applicant must be age 21; enrolled or expecting to enroll at an institution or university and female. Applicant must have 3.5 GPA or higher. Available to U.S. and non-U.S. citizens.

Application Requirements: Application, autobiography, financial need analysis, interview, resume, references, transcript. *Deadline:* April 15.

Contact: Application available at Web site.

INTERNATIONAL SOCIETY OF WOMEN AIRLINE PILOTS FINANCIAL SCHOLARSHIP

Scholarship available to ISA members and nonmembers. Program disburses cash awards towards pilot certificates, ratings, and type ratings to qualifying women. This award is used solely for advanced pilot ratings. All applicants must meet FAA Medical requirements for CLASS I Medical certificate. Visit Web site at http://www.iswap.org for additional information and deadlines.

International Society of Women Airline Pilots (ISA+21) (continued)

Academic Fields/Career Goals: Aviation/Aerospace.

Award: Scholarship for use in freshman, sophomore, junior, or senior years; not renewable. *Number:* varies. *Amount:* varies.

Eligibility Requirements: Applicant must be age 21; enrolled or expecting to enroll at an institution or university and female. Applicant must have 3.5 GPA or higher. Available to U.S. and non-U.S. citizens.

Application Requirements: Application, autobiography, financial need analysis, interview, resume, references, transcript. *Deadline:* April 15.

Contact: Application available at Web site.

INTERNATIONAL SOCIETY OF WOMEN AIRLINE PILOTS FIORENZA DE BERNARDI MERIT SCHOLARSHIP

Scholarship available to ISA members and nonmembers. Program disburses cash awards towards pilot certificates, ratings, and type ratings to qualifying women. Award for applicants that do not meet the requirements for the Career Scholarship. All applicants must meet FAA Medical requirements for CLASS I Medical certificate. Visit Web site at http://www.iswap.org for additional information and deadlines.

Academic Fields/Career Goals: Aviation/Aerospace.

Award: Scholarship for use in freshman, sophomore, junior, or senior years; not renewable. *Number:* varies. *Amount:* varies.

Eligibility Requirements: Applicant must be age 21; enrolled or expecting to enroll at an institution or university and female. Applicant must have 3.5 GPA or higher. Available to U.S. and non-U.S. citizens.

Application Requirements: Application, autobiography, financial need analysis, interview, resume, references, transcript. *Deadline:* April 15.

Contact: Application available at Web site.

INTERNATIONAL SOCIETY OF WOMEN AIRLINE PILOTS GRACE MCADAMS HARRIS SCHOLARSHIP

Scholarship available to ISA members. Program disburses cash awards towards pilot certificates, ratings, and type ratings to qualifying women. This award may fund any ISA scholarship if the applicant has demonstrated exceptional spirit and attitude under difficult circumstances as it pertains to the field of aviation. All applicants must meet FAA Medical requirements for CLASS I Medical certificate. Visit Web site at http://www.iswap.org for additional information and deadlines.

Academic Fields/Career Goals: Aviation/Aerospace.

Award: Scholarship for use in freshman, sophomore, junior, or senior years; not renewable. *Number:* varies. *Amount:* varies.

Eligibility Requirements: Applicant must be age 21; enrolled or expecting to enroll at an institution or university and female. Applicant must have 3.5 GPA or higher. Available to U.S. and non-U.S. citizens.

Application Requirements: Application, autobiography, financial need analysis, interview, references, transcript. *Deadline:* April 15.

Contact: Application available at Web site.

INTERNATIONAL SOCIETY OF WOMEN AIRLINE PILOTS HOLLY MULLENS MEMORIAL SCHOLARSHIP

Scholarship available to ISA members and nonmembers. Program disburses cash awards towards pilot certificates, ratings, and type ratings to qualifying women. Award for single mother applicants. All applicants must meet FAA Medical requirements for CLASS I Medical certificate. Visit Web site at http://www.iswap.org for additional information and deadlines.

Academic Fields/Career Goals: Aviation/Aerospace.

Award: Scholarship for use in freshman, sophomore, junior, or senior years; not renewable. *Number:* varies. *Amount:* varies.

Eligibility Requirements: Applicant must be age 21; enrolled or expecting to enroll at an institution or university and single female. Applicant must have 3.5 GPA or higher. Available to U.S. and non-U.S. citizens.

Application Requirements: Application, autobiography, financial need analysis, interview, references, transcript. *Deadline:* April 15.

Contact: Application available at Web site.

INTERNATIONAL SOCIETY OF WOMEN AIRLINE PILOTS NORTH CAROLINA FINANCIAL SCHOLARSHIP

Scholarship available to ISA members and nonmembers. Program disburses cash awards towards pilot certificates, ratings, and type ratings to qualifying women. Must be a North Carolina resident interested in a career with the airline industry. All applicants must meet FAA Medical requirements for CLASS I Medical certificate. Visit Web site at http://www.iswap.org for additional information and deadlines.

Academic Fields/Career Goals: Aviation/Aerospace.

Award: Scholarship for use in freshman, sophomore, junior, or senior years; not renewable.

Eligibility Requirements: Applicant must be age 21; enrolled or expecting to enroll at an institution or university; female and resident of North Carolina. Applicant must have 3.5 GPA or higher. Available to U.S. and non-U.S. citizens.

Application Requirements: Application, autobiography, financial need analysis, interview, resume, references, transcript. *Deadline:* April 15.

Contact: Application available at Web site.

LINCOLN COMMUNITY FOUNDATION http://www.lcf.org

LAWRENCE "LARRY" FRAZIER MEMORIAL SCHOLARSHIP

Scholarship for graduating seniors and former graduates of a high school in Nebraska who, upon graduation, intend to pursue a career in the field of aviation, insurance, or law. Applicants must attend a two- or four-year college or university in Nebraska. Preferred applicants will have experience in debate and participated in Girl Scouts or Boy Scouts during her/his youth.

Academic Fields/Career Goals: Aviation/Aerospace; Business/Consumer Services; Law/Legal Services.

Award: Scholarship for use in freshman, sophomore, junior, or senior years; not renewable. *Number:* 1. *Amount:* $500.

Eligibility Requirements: Applicant must be enrolled or expecting to enroll full-time at a two-year or four-year institution or university; resident of Nebraska and studying in Nebraska. Applicant must have 2.5 GPA or higher. Available to U.S. citizens.

Application Requirements: Application, essay, financial need analysis, test scores, transcript. *Deadline:* April 15.

Contact: Application available at Web site.

LUCENT TECHNOLOGIES FOUNDATION http://www.iie.org/programs/lucent

LUCENT GLOBAL SCIENCE SCHOLARS PROGRAM

• *See page 70*

MOONEY AIRCRAFT PILOTS ASSOCIATION (MAPA) SAFETY FOUNDATION, INC. http://mooneypilots.com

AL AND ART MOONEY SCHOLARSHIPS

One-time award for students interested in flying or aviation as a career. Must be college freshman to apply and demonstrate strong academic performance. Essay and letters of recommendation are required. Essay topic "How I Would Like to be Able to Promote and Improve Aviation." Minimum 3.0 GPA required.

Academic Fields/Career Goals: Aviation/Aerospace.

Award: Scholarship for use in freshman, sophomore, junior, or senior years; not renewable. *Number:* 1. *Amount:* $2500.

Eligibility Requirements: Applicant must be enrolled or expecting to enroll full-time at a two-year or four-year or technical institution or university. Applicant must have 3.0 GPA or higher. Available to U.S. citizens.

Application Requirements: Application, essay, references, transcript. *Deadline:* July 15.

Contact: Lela Hughes, Assistant Executive Director
Mooney Aircraft Pilots Association (MAPA) Safety Foundation, Inc.
PO Box 460607
San Antonio, TX 78246
Phone: 210-525-8008
Fax: 210-525-8085

NAMEPA NATIONAL SCHOLARSHIP FOUNDATION
http://www.namepa.org

NATIONAL ASSOCIATION OF MINORITY ENGINEERING PROGRAM ADMINISTRATORS NATIONAL SCHOLARSHIP FUND

NAMEPA offers one-time scholarships for African-American, Hispanic, and American-Indian students who have demonstrated potential and interest in pursuing an undergraduate degree in engineering. Must have a minimum 3.0 GPA. Must have a score above 25 on ACT, or above 1000 on SAT. Visit Web site at http://www.namepa.org for application materials and further details.

Academic Fields/Career Goals: Aviation/Aerospace; Chemical Engineering; Civil Engineering; Computer Science/Data Processing; Electrical Engineering/Electronics; Engineering/Technology; Engineering-Related Technologies; Materials Science, Engineering, and Metallurgy; Mechanical Engineering.

Award: Scholarship for use in freshman year; not renewable. *Number:* 10–50. *Amount:* $1000–$5000.

Eligibility Requirements: Applicant must be American Indian/Alaska Native, Black (non-Hispanic), or Hispanic and enrolled or expecting to enroll full-time at a two-year or four-year institution or university. Applicant must have 3.0 GPA or higher. Available to U.S. and non-U.S. citizens.

Application Requirements: Application, essay, resume, references, test scores, transcript. *Deadline:* March 30.

Contact: Latisha Moore, Administrative Assistant
NAMEPA National Scholarship Foundation
1133 West Morse Boulevard, Suite 201
Winter Park, FL 32789
Phone: 407-647-8839
Fax: 407-629-2502
E-mail: namepa@namepa.org

NASA DELAWARE SPACE GRANT CONSORTIUM
http://www.delspace.org

NASA DELAWARE SPACE GRANT UNDERGRADUATE TUITION SCHOLARSHIP

• *See page 70*

NASA IDAHO SPACE GRANT CONSORTIUM
http://www.uidaho.edu/nasa_isgc

NASA IDAHO SPACE GRANT CONSORTIUM SCHOLARSHIP PROGRAM

• *See page 71*

NASA MINNESOTA SPACE GRANT CONSORTIUM
http://www.aem.umn.edu/msgc

MINNESOTA SPACE GRANT CONSORTIUM

Between twenty-five and fifty $1000 scholarships are awarded to students registered with MN colleges and universities who belong to the MNSGC consortium. Preference is given to students currently involved in aerospace science or engineering. Minimum 3.0 GPA required. Must be U.S. citizen. For more details see Web site: http://www.aem.umn.edu/msgc or http://calspace.ucsd.edu/spacegrant/

Academic Fields/Career Goals: Aviation/Aerospace; Computer Science/Data Processing; Engineering/Technology; Physical Sciences and Math.

Award: Scholarship for use in sophomore, junior, senior, graduate, or postgraduate years; renewable. *Number:* 25–50. *Amount:* $1000.

Eligibility Requirements: Applicant must be enrolled or expecting to enroll full-time at a two-year or four-year institution or university and studying in Minnesota. Applicant must have 3.0 GPA or higher. Available to U.S. citizens.

Application Requirements: Application, essay, references, transcript. *Deadline:* Continuous.

Contact: Randi Quanbeck-Lundell, Program Coordinator
NASA Minnesota Space Grant Consortium
University of Minnesota, Department of Aerospace Engineering and Mechanics
107 Akerman Hall, 110 Union Street, SE
Minneapolis, MN 55455
Phone: 612-626-9295
Fax: 612-626-1558
E-mail: quanbeck@aem.umn.edu

NASA MONTANA SPACE GRANT CONSORTIUM
http://www.spacegrant.montana.edu

MONTANA SPACE GRANT SCHOLARSHIP PROGRAM

Awards are made on a competitive basis to students enrolled in fields of study relevant to the aerospace sciences and engineering. Must be U.S. citizen enrolled as full-time student at a Montana Consortium campus.

Academic Fields/Career Goals: Aviation/Aerospace; Engineering/Technology.

Award: Scholarship for use in freshman, sophomore, junior, or senior years; not renewable. *Number:* 15–20. *Amount:* $1000.

Eligibility Requirements: Applicant must be enrolled or expecting to enroll full-time at a two-year or four-year institution or university and studying in Montana. Available to U.S. citizens.

Application Requirements: Application, applicant must enter a contest, essay, references, transcript. *Deadline:* April 1.

Contact: Clarice Koby, Program Coordinator
NASA Montana Space Grant Consortium
261 EPS Building, Montana State University
Bozeman, MT 59717-3835
Phone: 406-994-4223
Fax: 406-994-4452
E-mail: koby@spacegrant.montana.edu

NASA NEBRASKA SPACE GRANT CONSORTIUM
http://nasa.unomaha.edu

NASA NEBRASKA SPACE GRANT

Undergraduate and graduate students attending any of the academic affiliates in Nebraska of the NASA Nebraska Space Grant are eligible for financial assistance in the form of scholarships and fellowships. These funds assist students pursuing research with faculty or coursework in the aerospace and aeronautics fields. Must be U.S. citizen.

Academic Fields/Career Goals: Aviation/Aerospace; Biology; Communications; Computer Science/Data Processing; Earth Science; Electrical Engineering/Electronics; Engineering/Technology; Engineering-Related Technologies; Natural Sciences; Physical Sciences and Math; Science, Technology, and Society; Transportation.

Award: Scholarship for use in freshman, sophomore, junior, senior, or graduate years; not renewable. *Number:* 5. *Amount:* $250–$750.

Eligibility Requirements: Applicant must be enrolled or expecting to enroll full or part-time at a four-year institution or university and studying in Nebraska. Available to U.S. citizens.

Application Requirements: Application, transcript, proof of citizenship. *Deadline:* April 30.

Contact: Mary Fink, Coordinator
NASA Nebraska Space Grant Consortium
Aviation Institute, Allwine Hall 22
6001 Dodge Street
Omaha, NE 68182-0589
Phone: 402-554-3772
Fax: 402-554-3781
E-mail: nasa@unomaha.edu

NASA NEVADA SPACE GRANT CONSORTIUM
http://www.unr.edu/spacegrant

UNIVERSITY AND COMMUNITY COLLEGE SYSTEM OF NEVADA NASA SPACE GRANT AND FELLOWSHIP PROGRAM

Nevada Space Grant provides graduate fellowships and undergraduate scholarship to qualified student majoring in aerospace science, technology

NASA Nevada Space Grant Consortium (continued)

and related fields. Must be Nevada resident studying at a Nevada college/university. Minimum 2.5 GPA required.

Academic Fields/Career Goals: Aviation/Aerospace; Chemical Engineering; Computer Science/Data Processing; Electrical Engineering/Electronics; Engineering/Technology; Meteorology/Atmospheric Science; Physical Sciences and Math.

Award: Scholarship for use in freshman, sophomore, junior, senior, or graduate years; renewable. *Number:* 1–20. *Amount:* $2500–$25,000.

Eligibility Requirements: Applicant must be enrolled or expecting to enroll full-time at a two-year or four-year institution or university; resident of Nevada and studying in Nevada. Applicant must have 2.5 GPA or higher. Available to U.S. citizens.

Application Requirements: Application, autobiography, essay, resume, references, transcript. *Deadline:* April 1.

Contact: Lori Rountree, Program Coordinator
NASA Nevada Space Grant Consortium
University of Nevada, Reno
MS 172
Reno, NV 89557-0138
Phone: 775-784-6261
Fax: 775-327-2235
E-mail: lori@mines.unr.edu

NASA VERMONT SPACE GRANT CONSORTIUM

http://www.emba.uvm.edu/vsgc

VERMONT SPACE GRANT CONSORTIUM SCHOLARSHIP PROGRAM

• *See page 71*

NASA VIRGINIA SPACE GRANT CONSORTIUM

http://www.vsgc.odu.edu

AEROSPACE UNDERGRADUATE RESEARCH SCHOLARSHIPS

Scholarships designated for undergraduate students pursuing any field of study with aerospace relevance. Must attend one of the five Virginia Space Grant colleges and universities, with at least two years of undergraduate degree completed. Applicant must have minimum 3.0 GPA. Please refer to Web site for further details: http://www.vsgc.odu.edu.

Academic Fields/Career Goals: Aviation/Aerospace.

Award: Scholarship for use in junior or senior years; not renewable. *Number:* varies. *Amount:* $8500.

Eligibility Requirements: Applicant must be enrolled or expecting to enroll full-time at a four-year institution or university and studying in Virginia. Applicant must have 3.0 GPA or higher. Available to U.S. citizens.

Application Requirements: Application, essay, resume, references, transcript. *Deadline:* February 2.

Contact: Coordinator
NASA Virginia Space Grant Consortium
Old Dominion University Peninsula Center
600 Butler Farm Road
Hampton, VA 23666
Phone: 757-766-5210
E-mail: vsgc@odu.edu

VIRGINIA SPACE GRANT CONSORTIUM COMMUNITY COLLEGE SCHOLARSHIPS

Scholarships designated for Virginia community college students studying technological fields involving aerospace. Applicant must be U.S. citizen with a minimum GPA of 3.0. Please refer to Web site for further details: http://www.vsgc.odu.edu.

Academic Fields/Career Goals: Aviation/Aerospace; Engineering/Technology.

Award: Scholarship for use in freshman or sophomore years; not renewable. *Number:* varies. *Amount:* $1500.

Eligibility Requirements: Applicant must be enrolled or expecting to enroll full-time at a two-year institution and studying in Virginia. Applicant must have 3.0 GPA or higher. Available to U.S. citizens.

Application Requirements: Application, essay, resume, references, transcript. *Deadline:* February 2.

Contact: Coordinator
NASA Virginia Space Grant Consortium
Old Dominion University Peninsula Center
600 Butler Farm Road
Hampton, VA 23666
Phone: 757-766-5210
E-mail: vsgc@odu.edu

VIRGINIA SPACE GRANT CONSORTIUM TEACHER EDUCATION SCHOLARSHIPS

Scholarships designated for students enrolled at a Virginia Space Grant college or university in a program that will lead to teacher certification in a pre-college setting. Students may apply as graduating high school seniors, sophomore community college students or any undergraduate year. Please refer to Web site for further details: http://www.vsgc.odu.edu.

Academic Fields/Career Goals: Aviation/Aerospace; Earth Science; Education; Engineering/Technology; Environmental Science; Physical Sciences and Math.

Award: Scholarship for use in freshman, sophomore, junior, or senior years; not renewable. *Number:* varies. *Amount:* $1000.

Eligibility Requirements: Applicant must be enrolled or expecting to enroll full-time at a two-year or four-year institution or university and studying in Virginia. Applicant must have 3.0 GPA or higher. Available to U.S. citizens.

Application Requirements: Application, essay, resume, references, transcript. *Deadline:* February 2.

Contact: Coordinator
NASA Virginia Space Grant Consortium
Old Dominion University Peninsula Center
600 Butler Farm Road
Hampton, VA 23666
Phone: 757-766-5210
E-mail: vsgc@odu.edu

NASA WEST VIRGINIA SPACE GRANT CONSORTIUM

http://www.nasa.wvu.edu

WEST VIRGINIA SPACE GRANT CONSORTIUM UNDERGRADUATE SCHOLARSHIP PROGRAM

Scholarships intended to support undergraduate students pursuing an aerospace related degree. Students are given opportunities to work with faculty members within their major department on research projects, or students may participate in the Consortium Challenge Program. Please refer to Web site for further details: http://www.nasa.wvu.edu.

Academic Fields/Career Goals: Aviation/Aerospace; Computer Science/Data Processing; Earth Science; Energy and Power Engineering; Engineering/Technology; Engineering-Related Technologies; Environmental Science; Meteorology/Atmospheric Science; Natural Sciences; Nuclear Science; Physical Sciences and Math.

Award: Scholarship for use in freshman, sophomore, junior, or senior years; not renewable. *Number:* varies. *Amount:* $1000–$2000.

Eligibility Requirements: Applicant must be enrolled or expecting to enroll at a four-year institution or university; resident of West Virginia and studying in West Virginia. Available to U.S. citizens.

Application Requirements: Application. *Deadline:* varies.

Contact: Candy Ramsey, Program Director
NASA West Virginia Space Grant Consortium
PO Box 6070
Morgantown, WV 26506-6070
Phone: 304-293-4099
Fax: 304-293-4970
E-mail: candy.ramsey@mail.wvu.edu

NASA WISCONSIN SPACE GRANT CONSORTIUM

http://www.uwgb.edu/WSGC

WISCONSIN SPACE GRANT CONSORTIUM UNDERGRADUATE RESEARCH PROGRAM

One-time award of up to $3500 for a U.S. citizen enrolled full-time, admitted to, or applying to any undergraduate program at a Wisconsin Space Grant

Consortium (WSGC) college or university. Award goes to a student to create and implement their own small research study. Minimum 3.0 GPA required. Submit proposal with budget. Application deadline is February 14. Please refer to Web site for more information: http://www.uwgb.edu/wsgc.

Academic Fields/Career Goals: Aviation/Aerospace.

Award: Grant for use in freshman, sophomore, junior, or senior years; not renewable. *Number:* varies. *Amount:* up to $3500.

Eligibility Requirements: Applicant must be enrolled or expecting to enroll full-time at a four-year institution or university; resident of Wisconsin and studying in Wisconsin. Applicant must have 3.0 GPA or higher. Available to U.S. citizens.

Application Requirements: References, transcript, proposal with budget. *Deadline:* February 14.

Contact: Thomas Bray, Associate Director of Fellowships
NASA Wisconsin Space Grant Consortium
2420 Nicolet Drive
Green Bay, WI 54311-7001
Phone: 920-465-2108
Fax: 920-465-2376
E-mail: wsgc@uwgb.edu

WISCONSIN SPACE GRANT CONSORTIUM UNDERGRADUATE SCHOLARSHIP PROGRAM

Scholarship of up to $1500 for a U.S. citizen enrolled full-time in, admitted to, or applying to any undergraduate program at a Wisconsin Space Grant Consortium (WSGC) college or university. Awards will be given to students with outstanding potential in programs of aerospace, space science, or other interdisciplinary space-related studies. Minimum 3.0 GPA required. Deadline is February 14. Please refer to Web site for more information: http://www.uwgb.edu/wsgc.

Academic Fields/Career Goals: Aviation/Aerospace.

Award: Scholarship for use in freshman, sophomore, junior, or senior years; not renewable. *Number:* varies. *Amount:* up to $1500.

Eligibility Requirements: Applicant must be enrolled or expecting to enroll full-time at a four-year institution or university; resident of Wisconsin and studying in Wisconsin. Applicant must have 3.0 GPA or higher. Available to U.S. citizens.

Application Requirements: Application, essay, references, transcript. *Deadline:* February 14.

Contact: Thomas Bray, Associate Director of Fellowships
NASA Wisconsin Space Grant Consortium
2420 Nicolet Drive
Green Bay, WI 54311-7001
Phone: 920-465-2108
Fax: 920-465-2376
E-mail: wsgc@uwgb.edu

NATIONAL AIR TRANSPORTATION ASSOCIATION FOUNDATION

DAN L. MEISINGER, SR. MEMORIAL LEARN TO FLY SCHOLARSHIP

A $2500 scholarship is available to students currently enrolled in an aviation program. Must be a high academic achiever. Application must be postmarked by the last Friday in November. For more details see Web site: http://www.nata-online.org.

Academic Fields/Career Goals: Aviation/Aerospace.

Award: Scholarship for use in freshman, sophomore, junior, or senior years; not renewable. *Number:* 1. *Amount:* $2500.

Eligibility Requirements: Applicant must be age 18; enrolled or expecting to enroll full-time at a four-year institution or university and resident of Illinois, Kansas, or Missouri. Available to U.S. and non-U.S. citizens.

Application Requirements: Application, interview, references, test scores, transcript. *Fee:* $5. *Deadline:* varies.

Contact: Lisa Copella, Receptionist
National Air Transportation Association Foundation
4226 King Street
Alexandria, VA 22302
Phone: 703-845-9000
Fax: 703-845-8176
E-mail: lcopella@nata-online.org

JOHN E. GODWIN, JR. MEMORIAL SCHOLARSHIP AWARD

A $2500 scholarship is available to students currently enrolled in an aviation program. Must be a high academic achiever. Application must be postmarked by the last Friday in November. For more details see Web site: http://www.nata-online.org.

Academic Fields/Career Goals: Aviation/Aerospace.

Award: Scholarship for use in freshman, sophomore, junior, or senior years; not renewable. *Number:* 1. *Amount:* $2500.

Eligibility Requirements: Applicant must be age 18 and enrolled or expecting to enroll full-time at a four-year institution or university. Available to U.S. and non-U.S. citizens.

Application Requirements: Application, interview, references, test scores, transcript. *Fee:* $5. *Deadline:* varies.

Contact: Lisa Copella, Receptionist
National Air Transportation Association Foundation
4226 King Street
Alexandria, VA 22302
Phone: 703-845-9000
Fax: 703-845-8176
E-mail: lcopella@nata-online.org

PIONEERS OF FLIGHT SCHOLARSHIP PROGRAM

Two $1000 scholarships are available to college students currently enrolled in an aviation program. Must be a high academic achiever. Application must be postmarked by the last Friday in December. For more details see Web site: http://www.nata-online.org.

Academic Fields/Career Goals: Aviation/Aerospace.

Award: Scholarship for use in junior or senior years; not renewable. *Number:* 2. *Amount:* $1000.

Eligibility Requirements: Applicant must be age 18 and enrolled or expecting to enroll full-time at a four-year institution or university. Available to U.S. and non-U.S. citizens.

Application Requirements: Application, interview, references, test scores, transcript. *Fee:* $5. *Deadline:* varies.

Contact: Lisa Copella, Receptionist
National Air Transportation Association Foundation
4226 King Street
Alexandria, VA 22302
Phone: 703-845-9000
Fax: 703-845-8176
E-mail: lcopella@nata-online.org

NATIONAL BUSINESS AVIATION ASSOCIATION, INC. http://www.nbaa.org/scholarships

NBAA INTERNATIONAL OPERATORS SCHOLARSHIP

NBAA International Operators Committee is dedicated to promoting education and training for individuals to increase safety and professionalism. One-time $5000 scholarship offered to one or more recipients for this purpose. Scholarship will be awarded at the Annual International Operators Conference. Include with application: 500 word essay explaining how this scholarship will help the applicant achieve their international aviation career goals, statement of the funds required to achieve these goals, and at least one professional letter of recommendation, preferably from an NBAA Member Company employee. For further information see Web site: http://www.nbaa.org.

Academic Fields/Career Goals: Aviation/Aerospace.

Award: Scholarship for use in freshman, sophomore, junior, or senior years; not renewable. *Number:* 1. *Amount:* $5000.

Eligibility Requirements: Applicant must be enrolled or expecting to enroll full-time at a two-year or four-year or technical institution or university. Available to U.S. citizens.

National Business Aviation Association, Inc. (continued)

Application Requirements: Application, essay, references. *Deadline:* January 30.

Contact: Jay Evans, Director, Operations
National Business Aviation Association, Inc.
1200 18th Street, NW, Suite 400
Washington, DC 20036-2527
Phone: 202-783-9000
Fax: 202-331-8364
E-mail: info@nbaa.org

NBAA JANICE K. BARDEN SCHOLARSHIP

One-time $1000 scholarship for students officially enrolled in NBAA/UAA (National Business Aviation Association/University Aviation Association) programs. Must be U.S. citizen, officially enrolled in an aviation-related program with 3.0 minimum GPA. Include with application: 250-word essay describing the applicant's interest and goals for a career in the business aviation industry; letter of recommendation from member of aviation department faculty at institution where applicant is enrolled. For further information, and to see a list of NBAA/UAA Member Colleges and Universities, visit Web site: http://www.nbaa.org.

Academic Fields/Career Goals: Aviation/Aerospace.

Award: Scholarship for use in sophomore, junior, senior, graduate, or postgraduate years; not renewable. *Number:* 5. *Amount:* $1000.

Eligibility Requirements: Applicant must be enrolled or expecting to enroll at a two-year or four-year institution or university. Applicant must have 3.0 GPA or higher. Available to U.S. citizens.

Application Requirements: Application, essay, resume, references, transcript. *Deadline:* November 3.

Contact: Jay Evans, Director, Operations
National Business Aviation Association, Inc.
1200 18th Street, NW, Suite 400
Washington, DC 20036-2527
Phone: 202-783-9000
Fax: 202-331-8364
E-mail: info@nbaa.org

NBAA LAWRENCE GINOCCHIO AVIATION SCHOLARSHIP

One-time $5000 scholarship for students officially enrolled in NBAA/UAA (National Business Aviation Association/University Aviation Association) programs. Must be officially enrolled in aviation-related program with 3.0 minimum GPA. Include with application: a 500 to 1,000 word essay describing interest in and goals for a career in the business aviation industry while demonstrating strength of character. Must also have 2 letters of recommendation, including one from member of aviation department faculty at institution where applicant is enrolled. A letter of recommendation from an NBAA Member Company representative is encouraged. For further information, and to see a list of NBAA/UAA Member Colleges and Universities, visit Web site: http://www.nbaa.org.

Academic Fields/Career Goals: Aviation/Aerospace.

Award: Scholarship for use in sophomore, junior, senior, or graduate years; not renewable. *Number:* 5. *Amount:* $5000.

Eligibility Requirements: Applicant must be enrolled or expecting to enroll at a two-year or four-year institution or university. Applicant must have 3.0 GPA or higher. Available to U.S. citizens.

Application Requirements: Application, essay, resume, references, transcript, proof of enrollment. *Deadline:* August 9.

Contact: Jay Evans, Director, Operations
National Business Aviation Association, Inc.
1200 18th Street, NW, Suite 400
Washington, DC 20036-2527
Phone: 202-783-9000
Fax: 202-331-8364
E-mail: info@nbaa.org

NBAA WILLIAM M. FANNING MAINTENANCE SCHOLARSHIP

One-time award given to two students pursuing careers as maintenance technicians. One award will benefit a student who is currently enrolled in an accredited airframe and powerplant (A&P) program at an approved FAR Part 147 school. The second award will benefit an individual who is not currently enrolled but has been accepted into an A&P program. Include with application: a 250-word essay describing applicant's interest in and goals for a career in the aviation maintenance field. A letter of recommendation from an NBAA Member Company representative is encouraged.

Academic Fields/Career Goals: Aviation/Aerospace.

Award: Scholarship for use in freshman, sophomore, junior, senior, or graduate years; not renewable. *Number:* 2. *Amount:* $2500.

Eligibility Requirements: Applicant must be enrolled or expecting to enroll full-time at a two-year or four-year or technical institution or university. Available to U.S. citizens.

Application Requirements: Application, essay, resume, references, transcript. *Deadline:* August 9.

Contact: Jay Evans, Director, Operations
National Business Aviation Association, Inc.
1200 18th Street, NW, Suite 400
Washington, DC 20036-2527
Phone: 202-783-9000
Fax: 202-331-8364
E-mail: info@nbaa.org

U.S. AIRCRAFT INSURANCE GROUP PDP SCHOLARSHIP

One-time $1,000 scholarship for applicants enrolled full-time in a college or university offering the NBAA (National Business Aviation Association) Professional Development Program (PDP). Must be U.S. citizen, officially enrolled in aviation-related program with 3.0 minimum GPA. Include with application: 250 word essay describing goals for a career in the business aviation flight department. A letter of recommendation from an NBAAA Member Company representative is encouraged. For further information, and to see a list of NBAA/UAA Member Colleges and Universities offering PDP curricula, visit Web site: http://www.nbaa.org.

Academic Fields/Career Goals: Aviation/Aerospace.

Award: Scholarship for use in sophomore, junior, senior, graduate, or postgraduate years; not renewable. *Number:* 3. *Amount:* $1000.

Eligibility Requirements: Applicant must be enrolled or expecting to enroll full-time at a two-year or four-year institution or university and studying in Arizona, Florida, Indiana, Michigan, Missouri, New Jersey, North Dakota, or Oklahoma. Applicant must have 3.0 GPA or higher. Available to U.S. citizens.

Application Requirements: Application, essay, resume, references, transcript, proof of enrollment. *Deadline:* August 9.

Contact: Jay Evans, Director, Operations
National Business Aviation Association, Inc.
1200 18th Street, NW, Suite 400
Washington, DC 20036-2527
Phone: 202-783-9000
Fax: 202-331-8364
E-mail: info@nbaa.org

NINETY-NINES, SAN FERNANDO VALLEY CHAPTER/VAN NUYS AIRPORT http://sfv99s.org

SAN FERNANDO VALLEY CHAPTER OF THE NINETY-NINES CAREER SCHOLARSHIP

Men and women pursuing a career in the aviation field are eligible for a $3,000 scholarship. Must reside in the Greater Los Angeles area and be over 21. Must be a U.S. citizen. Must attend a California school. Deadline is April 2.

Academic Fields/Career Goals: Aviation/Aerospace; Transportation.

Award: Scholarship for use in freshman, sophomore, junior, senior, graduate, or postgraduate years; not renewable. *Number:* 3. *Amount:* $3000.

Eligibility Requirements: Applicant must be age 22; enrolled or expecting to enroll full or part-time at a two-year or four-year or technical institution or university; resident of California and studying in California. Applicant or parent of applicant must have employment or volunteer experience in air traffic controller field or aviation maintenance. Available to U.S. citizens.

Application Requirements: Application, essay, financial need analysis, interview, references, self-addressed stamped envelope, transcript. *Deadline:* April 2.

Contact: Jeanne Fenimore, Co-Chair
Ninety-Nines, San Fernando Valley Chapter/Van Nuys Airport
PO Box 8160
Van Nuys, CA 91409
Phone: 818-989-0081
Fax: 818-787-0743

OREGON STUDENT ASSISTANCE COMMISSION http://www.osac.state.or.us

BRIAN L. MOODY MEMORIAL AVIATION SCHOLARSHIP

One-time award for aviation-related studies. Preference is for graduates of high schools in Baker, Grant, Morrow, Umatilla, Union, or Wallowa counties enrolled at least half time. Application deadline is March 1.

Academic Fields/Career Goals: Aviation/Aerospace.

Award: Scholarship for use in freshman, sophomore, junior, or senior years; not renewable. *Number:* 2. *Amount:* $1000.

Eligibility Requirements: Applicant must be enrolled or expecting to enroll full or part-time at an institution or university and resident of Oregon.

Application Requirements: Application, essay, financial need analysis, transcript. *Deadline:* March 1.

Contact: Director of Grant Programs
Oregon Student Assistance Commission
1500 Valley River Drive, Suite 100
Eugene, OR 97401-7020
Phone: 800-452-8807 Ext. 7395
E-mail: awardinfo@mercury.osac.state.or.us

PALWAUKEE AIRPORT PILOTS ASSOCIATION http://www.pwkpilots.org

PALWAUKEE AIRPORT PILOTS ASSOCIATION SCHOLARSHIP PROGRAM

Scholarship offered to Illinois individuals who are attending accredited programs in Illinois institutions pursuing a course of study in an aviation-related program. Applications on Web site: http://www.pwkpilots.org.

Academic Fields/Career Goals: Aviation/Aerospace.

Award: Scholarship for use in sophomore, junior, or senior years; not renewable. *Number:* 1. *Amount:* $1000.

Eligibility Requirements: Applicant must be age 18; enrolled or expecting to enroll full or part-time at a two-year or four-year or technical institution or university; resident of Illinois and studying in Illinois. Applicant must have 2.5 GPA or higher. Available to U.S. citizens.

Application Requirements: Application, autobiography, references, transcript. *Deadline:* June 30.

Contact: Chairman, Scholarship Committee
Palwaukee Airport Pilots Association
1005 South Wolf Road, Suite 106
Wheeling, IL 60090
E-mail: papa@pwkpilots.org

RHODE ISLAND PILOTS ASSOCIATION http://www.ripilots.com

RHODE ISLAND PILOTS ASSOCIATION SCHOLARSHIP

A scholarship open to Rhode Island residents to begin or advance a career in aviation.

Academic Fields/Career Goals: Aviation/Aerospace.

Award: Scholarship for use in freshman, sophomore, junior, or senior years; not renewable. *Number:* 2–4. *Amount:* $500–$1000.

Eligibility Requirements: Applicant must be enrolled or expecting to enroll full or part-time at a two-year or four-year or technical institution and resident of Rhode Island. Available to U.S. citizens.

Application Requirements: Application, essay, financial need analysis, references, test scores, transcript. *Deadline:* varies.

Contact: Marilyn Biagetti, Scholarship Chair
Rhode Island Pilots Association
644 Airport Road
Warwick, RI 02886
Phone: 401-568-3497
Fax: 401-568-5392
E-mail: ripaemail@aol.com

SOCIETY OF AUTOMOTIVE ENGINEERS http://www.sae.org/students/stuschol.htm

BMW/SAE ENGINEERING SCHOLARSHIP

Renewable award for high school seniors with a minimum 3.75 GPA. Must be a U.S. citizen pursuing an engineering degree at an accredited four-year institution. Test scores must be in the 90th percentile in both math and verbal. Application should be retrieved from the SAE Web site at http://www.sae.org/students/stuschol.htm.

Academic Fields/Career Goals: Aviation/Aerospace; Chemical Engineering; Electrical Engineering/Electronics; Engineering/Technology; Engineering-Related Technologies; Materials Science, Engineering, and Metallurgy; Mechanical Engineering.

Award: Scholarship for use in freshman year; renewable. *Number:* 1. *Amount:* $1500.

Eligibility Requirements: Applicant must be high school student and planning to enroll or expecting to enroll full-time at a four-year institution. Available to U.S. citizens.

Application Requirements: Application, essay, test scores, transcript. *Fee:* $6. *Deadline:* December 1.

Contact: Connie Harnish, SAE Customer Service
Society of Automotive Engineers
400 Commonwealth Drive
Warrendale, PA 15096-0001
Phone: 724-776-4970
E-mail: customerservice@sae.org

EDWARD D. HENDRICKSON/SAE ENGINEERING SCHOLARSHIP

Renewable $1000 award for a high school senior who is a U.S. citizen pursuing an undergraduate degree in engineering at a four-year institution. Must rank in the 90th percentile in both math and verbal on ACT or SAT. Minimum 3.75 GPA required. Application should be retrieved from the SAE Web site at http://www.sae.org/students/stuschol.htm.

Academic Fields/Career Goals: Aviation/Aerospace; Chemical Engineering; Electrical Engineering/Electronics; Engineering/Technology; Engineering-Related Technologies; Materials Science, Engineering, and Metallurgy; Mechanical Engineering.

Award: Scholarship for use in freshman year; renewable. *Number:* 1. *Amount:* $1000.

Eligibility Requirements: Applicant must be high school student and planning to enroll or expecting to enroll full-time at a four-year institution or university. Available to U.S. citizens.

Application Requirements: Application, essay, test scores, transcript. *Fee:* $6. *Deadline:* December 1.

Contact: Connie Harnish, SAE Customer Service
Society of Automotive Engineers
400 Commonwealth Drive
Warrendale, PA 15096-0001
Phone: 724-776-4970
E-mail: customerservice@sae.org

TMC/SAE DONALD D. DAWSON TECHNICAL SCHOLARSHIP

Renewable scholarship for high school seniors with a minimum 3.25 GPA. Transfer students from four-year colleges with a minimum 3.0 GPA or students from a post-secondary technical/vocational school with a minimum 3.5 GPA may also apply. Must be pursuing an engineering program at a post secondary institution. Application should be retrieved from SAE Web site http://www.sae.org/students/stuschol.htm

Academic Fields/Career Goals: Aviation/Aerospace; Chemical Engineering; Electrical Engineering/Electronics; Engineering/

Society of Automotive Engineers (continued)

Technology; Engineering-Related Technologies; Materials Science, Engineering, and Metallurgy; Mechanical Engineering.

Award: Scholarship for use in freshman year; renewable. *Number:* 1. *Amount:* $1500.

Eligibility Requirements: Applicant must be enrolled or expecting to enroll full-time at a four-year institution or university. Available to U.S. citizens.

Application Requirements: Application, essay, test scores, transcript. *Fee:* $6. *Deadline:* December 1.

Contact: Connie Harnish, SAE Customer Service
Society of Automotive Engineers
400 Commonwealth Drive
Warrendale, PA 15096-0001
Phone: 724-776-4970
E-mail: customerservice@sae.org

SOCIETY OF MEXICAN AMERICAN ENGINEERS AND SCIENTISTS http://www.maes-natl.org

GRE AND GRADUATE APPLICATIONS WAIVER

• *See page 72*

SOCIETY OF WOMEN ENGINEERS http://www.swe.org/scholarships

JUDITH RESNIK MEMORIAL SCHOLARSHIP

One-time award available to aerospace or astronautical engineering major at the sophomore, junior, or senior level. Must be a member of the Society of Women Engineers. Minimum 3.0 GPA required. Deadline: February 1.

Academic Fields/Career Goals: Aviation/Aerospace; Engineering/Technology.

Award: Scholarship for use in sophomore, junior, or senior years; not renewable. *Number:* 1. *Amount:* $2500.

Eligibility Requirements: Applicant must be enrolled or expecting to enroll at a four-year institution or university and female. Applicant or parent of applicant must be member of Society of Women Engineers. Applicant must have 3.0 GPA or higher. Available to U.S. citizens.

Application Requirements: Application, references, self-addressed stamped envelope, transcript. *Deadline:* February 1.

Contact: Program Coordinator
Society of Women Engineers
230 East Ohio Street, Suite 400
Chicago, IL 60611-3265
Phone: 312-596-5223
Fax: 312-644-8557
E-mail: hq@swe.org

NORTHROP GRUMMAN CORPORATION SCHOLARSHIPS

Scholarships awarded to female undergraduate students majoring in computer engineering, computer science, aeronautical/aerospace engineering, electrical engineering, industrial engineering, mechanical engineering or manufacturing engineering.

Academic Fields/Career Goals: Aviation/Aerospace; Computer Science/Data Processing; Electrical Engineering/Electronics; Engineering/Technology; Materials Science, Engineering, and Metallurgy; Mechanical Engineering.

Award: Scholarship for use in freshman, junior, or senior years; not renewable. *Number:* 5. *Amount:* $5000.

Eligibility Requirements: Applicant must be enrolled or expecting to enroll full-time at a four-year institution or university and female. Applicant must have 3.0 GPA or higher. Available to U.S. citizens.

Application Requirements: Application. *Deadline:* varies.

Contact: Program Coordinator
E-mail: hq@swe.org

STUDENT PILOT NETWORK http://www.studentpilot.net

STUDENT PILOT NETWORK-FLIGHT DREAMS AWARD

Award is for General Aviation Pilot Flight Training. Open to all persons actively engaged in flight training at a registered SPN flight school. Must be a U.S. or Canadian citizen.

Academic Fields/Career Goals: Aviation/Aerospace.

Award: Grant for use in freshman, sophomore, junior, senior, graduate, or postgraduate years; not renewable. *Number:* 1–3. *Amount:* $250–$1000.

Eligibility Requirements: Applicant must be enrolled or expecting to enroll full or part-time at an institution or university. Available to U.S. and Canadian citizens.

Application Requirements: Application, essay. *Deadline:* November 15.

Contact: W. Terry, Secretary
Student Pilot Network
PO Box 854
West Chicago, IL 60186-0854
E-mail: info@studentpilot.net

TRANSPORTATION CLUBS INTERNATIONAL http://www.transportationclubsinternational.com

ALICE GLAISYER WARFIELD MEMORIAL SCHOLARSHIP

Award is available to currently enrolled students majoring in transportation, logistics, traffic management, or related fields. Available to citizens of the U.S., Canada, and Mexico.

Academic Fields/Career Goals: Aviation/Aerospace; Transportation.

Award: Scholarship for use in sophomore, junior, senior, graduate, or postgraduate years; not renewable. *Number:* 1. *Amount:* $1000.

Eligibility Requirements: Applicant must be enrolled or expecting to enroll full or part-time at a two-year or four-year or technical institution or university. Available to U.S. and Canadian citizens.

Application Requirements: Application, essay, photo, references, transcript. *Deadline:* April 30.

Contact: Gay Fielding, Traffic Manager
Transportation Clubs International
7031 Manchester Street
New Orleans, LA 70126
Phone: 504-243-9825
E-mail: gcfielding@cs.com

DENNY LYDIC SCHOLARSHIP

Award is available to currently enrolled college students majoring in transportation, logistics, traffic management, or related fields. Available to citizens of the U.S., Canada, and Mexico.

Academic Fields/Career Goals: Aviation/Aerospace; Transportation.

Award: Scholarship for use in sophomore, junior, senior, graduate, or postgraduate years; not renewable. *Number:* 1. *Amount:* $500.

Eligibility Requirements: Applicant must be enrolled or expecting to enroll full or part-time at a two-year or four-year or technical institution or university. Available to U.S. and non-U.S. citizens.

Application Requirements: Application, essay, photo, references, transcript. *Deadline:* April 30.

Contact: Gay Fielding, Traffic Manager
Transportation Clubs International
7031 Manchester Street
New Orleans, LA 70126-1751
Phone: 504-243-9825
E-mail: gcfieldin@cs.com

TEXAS TRANSPORTATION SCHOLARSHIP

Merit-based award for student who is at least a sophomore studying transportation, traffic management, and related fields. Must have been enrolled in a school in Texas during some phase of education (elementary, secondary, high school). Include photo. One-time scholarship of $1000. Submit three references. Available to citizens of the U.S., Canada, and Mexico.

Academic Fields/Career Goals: Aviation/Aerospace; Transportation.

Award: Scholarship for use in sophomore, junior, senior, graduate, or postgraduate years; not renewable. *Number:* up to 1. *Amount:* $1000.

Eligibility Requirements: Applicant must be enrolled or expecting to enroll full or part-time at a two-year or four-year or technical institution or university. Available to U.S. and non-U.S. citizens.

Application Requirements: Application, essay, photo, references, transcript. *Deadline:* April 30.

Contact: Gay Fielding, Traffic Manager
Transportation Clubs International
7031 Manchester Street
New Orleans, LA 70126-1751
Phone: 504-243-9825

TRANSPORTATION CLUBS INTERNATIONAL CHARLOTTE WOODS SCHOLARSHIP

Award available to enrolled college student majoring in transportation or traffic management. Must be member or dependent of a member of a Transportation Club which is a member of Transportation Clubs International. Must have completed at least one year of post-high school education. One-time award of $1000. Submit three references.

Academic Fields/Career Goals: Aviation/Aerospace; Transportation.

Award: Scholarship for use in sophomore, junior, senior, graduate, or postgraduate years; not renewable. *Number:* 1. *Amount:* $1000.

Eligibility Requirements: Applicant must be enrolled or expecting to enroll full or part-time at a two-year or four-year or technical institution or university. Applicant or parent of applicant must be member of Transportation Club International. Available to U.S. and non-U.S. citizens.

Application Requirements: Application, essay, photo, references, transcript. *Deadline:* April 30.

Contact: Gay Fielding, Traffic Manager
Transportation Clubs International
7031 Manchester Street
New Orleans, LA 70126-1751
Phone: 504-243-9825

TRANSPORTATION CLUBS INTERNATIONAL FRED A. HOOPER MEMORIAL SCHOLARSHIP

Merit-based award is available to currently enrolled college students majoring in traffic management, transportation, physical distribution, logistics, or a related field. Must have completed at least one year of post-high school education. One-time award of $1500. Submit three references. Available to citizens of the U.S., Canada, and Mexico.

Academic Fields/Career Goals: Aviation/Aerospace; Transportation.

Award: Scholarship for use in sophomore, junior, senior, graduate, or postgraduate years; not renewable. *Number:* 1. *Amount:* $1500.

Eligibility Requirements: Applicant must be enrolled or expecting to enroll full or part-time at a two-year or four-year or technical institution or university. Available to U.S. and non-U.S. citizens.

Application Requirements: Application, essay, photo, references, transcript. *Deadline:* April 30.

Contact: Gay Fielding, Traffic Manager
Transportation Clubs International
7031 Manchester Street
New Orleans, LA 70126-1751
Phone: 504-243-9825

TRANSPORTATION CLUBS INTERNATIONAL GINGER AND FRED DEINES CANADA SCHOLARSHIP

One-time award for student of Canadian heritage attending a four-year college or university in Canada or the U.S. and majoring in transportation, traffic management, logistics, or a related field. Academic merit is considered. Submit three references.

Academic Fields/Career Goals: Aviation/Aerospace; Transportation.

Award: Scholarship for use in sophomore, junior, senior, graduate, or postgraduate years; not renewable. *Number:* 1.

Eligibility Requirements: Applicant must be of Canadian heritage and enrolled or expecting to enroll full or part-time at a two-year or four-year or technical institution or university. Available to Canadian citizens.

Application Requirements: Application, essay, photo, references, transcript. *Deadline:* April 30.

Contact: Gay Fielding, Traffic Manager
Transportation Clubs International
7031 Manchester Street
New Orleans, LA 70126-1751
Phone: 504-243-9825

TRANSPORTATION CLUBS INTERNATIONAL GINGER AND FRED DEINES MEXICO SCHOLARSHIP

Scholarship for a student of Mexican nationality/residency who is enrolled at an institution in Mexico or the U.S. Must be preparing for a career in transportation. Must have completed at least one year of study. Submit photo and three references.

Academic Fields/Career Goals: Aviation/Aerospace; Transportation.

Award: Scholarship for use in sophomore, junior, senior, graduate, or postgraduate years; not renewable. *Number:* 1. *Amount:* $1500.

Eligibility Requirements: Applicant must be of Mexican heritage; Hispanic and enrolled or expecting to enroll full or part-time at a two-year or four-year or technical institution or university.

Application Requirements: Application, essay, photo, references, transcript. *Deadline:* April 30.

Contact: Gay Fielding, Traffic Manager
Transportation Clubs International
7031 Manchester Street
New Orleans, LA 70126-1751
Phone: 504-243-9825

UNIVERSITIES SPACE RESEARCH ASSOCIATION http://www.usra.edu/hq/scholarships/overview.shtml

UNIVERSITIES SPACE RESEARCH ASSOCIATION SCHOLARSHIP PROGRAM

• *See page 72*

UNIVERSITY AVIATION ASSOCIATION http://www.aviation.siu.edu

JOSEPH FRASCA EXCELLENCE IN AVIATION SCHOLARSHIP

Established to encourage those who demonstrate the highest level of commitment to and achievement in aviation studies. Applicant must be a junior or senior currently enrolled in a UAA member institution. Must be FAA certified/qualified in either aviation maintenance or flight, have membership in at least one aviation organization, and be involved in aviation activities, projects, and events. Minimum 3.0 GPA required. Deadline is June 1.

Academic Fields/Career Goals: Aviation/Aerospace.

Award: Scholarship for use in junior or senior years; not renewable. *Number:* 2. *Amount:* $1000.

Eligibility Requirements: Applicant must be enrolled or expecting to enroll full or part-time at a four-year institution or university and must have an interest in designated field specified by sponsor. Applicant must have 3.0 GPA or higher. Available to U.S. citizens.

Application Requirements: Application, essay, financial need analysis, references, transcript, FAA certificates. *Deadline:* June 1.

Contact: Dr. David New Myer, Dept. Chair, Aviation Management and Flight
University Aviation Association
Southern Illinois University at Carbondale
College of Applied Sciences and Arts
Carbondale, IL 62901-6623
E-mail: newmyer@siu.edu

VERTICAL FLIGHT FOUNDATION http://www.vtol.org

VERTICAL FLIGHT FOUNDATION SCHOLARSHIP

This award is available for undergraduate, graduate, or doctoral study in aerospace, electrical, or mechanical engineering. Undergraduates must be in junior or senior year. Applicants must have an interest in vertical flight technology.

Academic Fields/Career Goals: Aviation/Aerospace; Electrical Engineering/Electronics; Mechanical Engineering.

Award: Scholarship for use in junior, senior, graduate, or postgraduate years; not renewable. *Number:* 10–12. *Amount:* $2000–$4000.

Eligibility Requirements: Applicant must be enrolled or expecting to enroll full-time at a four-year institution or university. Available to U.S. and non-U.S. citizens.

Application Requirements: Application, essay, references, transcript. *Deadline:* February 1.

Contact: Debbie Cochran, Deputy Director
Vertical Flight Foundation
217 North Washington Street
Alexandria, VA 22314
Phone: 703-684-6777
Fax: 703-739-9279
E-mail: debbie@vtol.org

WOMEN IN AVIATION, INTERNATIONAL http://www.wai.org

AIRBUS LEADERSHIP GRANT

Scholarship available to a woman pursuing a degree in an aviation-related field. Applicant must be in sophomore year or above. Must have minimum GPA of 3.0. Must be a member of Women in Aviation, International. Please refer to Web site for further details: http://www.wai.org.

Academic Fields/Career Goals: Aviation/Aerospace.

Award: Scholarship for use in sophomore, junior, senior, graduate, or postgraduate years; not renewable. *Number:* 1. *Amount:* $1000.

Eligibility Requirements: Applicant must be enrolled or expecting to enroll at a two-year or four-year or technical institution or university; female and must have an interest in leadership. Applicant or parent of applicant must be member of Women in Aviation, International. Applicant must have 3.0 GPA or higher. Available to U.S. citizens.

Application Requirements: Application, essay. *Deadline:* varies.

Contact: Kim Wheeler, Scholarship Co-Chair
Women in Aviation, International
Scholarship
101 Corsair Drive, Suite 101
Daytona Beach, FL 32114
E-mail: wiaischolarship@yahoo.com

CINCINNATI HEART OF IT ALL CHAPTER WOMEN IN AVIATION, INTERNATIONAL ELISHA HALL MEMORIAL SCHOLARSHIP

Scholarship offered to a woman seeking to further her aviation career in flight training, aircraft scheduling or dispatch, aviation management, aviation maintenance, or avionics. Preference will be given to applicants from Cincinnati area. Must be a member of Women in Aviation, International, but does not have to be member of Cincinnati Chapter. Please refer to Web site for further details: http://www.wai.org.

Academic Fields/Career Goals: Aviation/Aerospace.

Award: Scholarship for use in freshman, sophomore, junior, senior, or graduate years; not renewable. *Number:* 1. *Amount:* $1000.

Eligibility Requirements: Applicant must be enrolled or expecting to enroll at a two-year or four-year or technical institution or university and female. Applicant or parent of applicant must be member of Women in Aviation, International. Available to U.S. citizens.

Application Requirements: Application. *Deadline:* varies.

Contact: Kim Wheeler, Scholarship Co-Chair
Women in Aviation, International
Scholarship
101 Corsair Drive, Suite 101
Daytona Beach, FL 32114
E-mail: wiaischolarship@yahoo.com

DASSAULT FALCON JET CORPORATION SCHOLARSHIP

Scholarship available for a woman pursuing an undergraduate or graduate degree in an aviation-related field. Applicant must be a U.S. citizen with minimum 3.0 GPA. Must be a member of Women in Aviation, International. Please refer to Web site for further details: http://www.wai.org.

Academic Fields/Career Goals: Aviation/Aerospace.

Award: Scholarship for use in freshman, sophomore, junior, senior, or graduate years; not renewable. *Number:* 1. *Amount:* $1000.

Eligibility Requirements: Applicant must be enrolled or expecting to enroll at a two-year or four-year or technical institution or university and female. Applicant or parent of applicant must be member of Women in Aviation, International. Applicant must have 3.0 GPA or higher. Available to U.S. citizens.

Application Requirements: Application, essay. *Deadline:* varies.

Contact: Kim Wheeler, Scholarship Co-Chair
Women in Aviation, International
Scholarship
101 Corsair Drive, Suite 101
Daytona Beach, FL 32114
E-mail: wiaischolarship@yahoo.com

DELTA AIR LINES AIRCRAFT MAINTENANCE TECHNOLOGY SCHOLARSHIP

Scholarship available to a student currently enrolled in an aviation maintenance technology program, or a degree in aviation maintenance technology. Applicant must be a full-time student with a minimum of two semesters left in program/degree. Must have minimum GPA of 3.0. Must be a member of Women in Aviation, International. Please refer to Web site for further details: http://www.wai.org.

Academic Fields/Career Goals: Aviation/Aerospace.

Award: Scholarship for use in senior year; not renewable. *Number:* 1. *Amount:* $5000.

Eligibility Requirements: Applicant must be enrolled or expecting to enroll full-time at a two-year or four-year or technical institution or university. Applicant or parent of applicant must be member of Women in Aviation, International. Applicant must have 3.0 GPA or higher. Available to U.S. citizens.

Application Requirements: Application, essay. *Deadline:* varies.

Contact: Kim Wheeler, Scholarship Co-Chair
Women in Aviation, International
Scholarship
101 Corsair Drive, Suite 101
Daytona Beach, FL 32114
E-mail: wiaischolarship@yahoo.com

DELTA AIR LINES ENGINEERING SCHOLARSHIP

Scholarship available for an undergraduate junior or senior enrolled in a BA degree program in aerospace/aeronautical, electrical, or mechanical engineering. Applicant must have minimum GPA of 3.0. Must be a member of Women in Aviation, International. Please refer to Web site for further details: http://www.wai.org.

Academic Fields/Career Goals: Aviation/Aerospace; Electrical Engineering/Electronics; Mechanical Engineering.

Award: Scholarship for use in junior or senior years; not renewable. *Number:* 1. *Amount:* $5000.

Eligibility Requirements: Applicant must be enrolled or expecting to enroll full-time at a two-year or four-year or technical institution or university. Applicant or parent of applicant must be member of Women in Aviation, International. Applicant must have 3.0 GPA or higher. Available to U.S. and non-U.S. citizens.

Application Requirements: Application, essay. *Deadline:* varies.

Contact: Kim Wheeler, Scholarship Co-Chair
Women in Aviation, International
Scholarship
101 Corsair Drive, Suite 101
Daytona Beach, FL 32114
E-mail: wiaischolarship@yahoo.com

DELTA AIR LINES MAINTENANCE MANAGEMENT/AVIATION BUSINESS MANAGEMENT SCHOLARSHIP

Scholarship available to a full-time student pursuing an associate's degree or BA in aviation maintenance management or aviation business management. Applicant must be within two semesters of degree completion, and have a minimum 3.0 GPA. Must be a member of Women in Aviation, International. Please refer to Web site for further details: http://www.wai.org.

Academic Fields/Career Goals: Aviation/Aerospace.

Award: Scholarship for use in senior year; not renewable. *Number:* 1. *Amount:* $5000.

Eligibility Requirements: Applicant must be enrolled or expecting to enroll full-time at a two-year or four-year or technical institution or university. Applicant or parent of applicant must be member of Women in Aviation, International. Applicant must have 3.0 GPA or higher. Available to U.S. citizens.

Application Requirements: Application, essay. *Deadline:* varies.

Contact: Kim Wheeler, Scholarship Co-Chair
Women in Aviation, International
Scholarship
101 Corsair Drive, Suite 101
Daytona Beach, FL 32114
E-mail: wiaischolarship@yahoo.com

DR. MANNY HOROWITZ SCHOLARSHIP

Scholarship available to student pursuing degree in navigation, aircraft scheduling or dispatch, aviation management, aviation maintenance, or avionics. Must be a member of Women in Aviation, International. Please refer to Web site for further details: http://www.wai.org.

Academic Fields/Career Goals: Aviation/Aerospace.

Award: Scholarship for use in freshman, sophomore, junior, senior, or graduate years; not renewable. *Number:* 1. *Amount:* $1000.

Eligibility Requirements: Applicant must be enrolled or expecting to enroll at a two-year or four-year or technical institution or university. Applicant or parent of applicant must be member of Women in Aviation, International. Available to U.S. citizens.

Application Requirements: Application, essay. *Deadline:* varies.

Contact: Kim Wheeler, Scholarship Co-Chair
Women in Aviation, International
Scholarship
101 Corsair Drive, Suite 101
Daytona Beach, FL 32114
E-mail: wiaischolarship@yahoo.com

GAT WINGS TO THE FUTURE MANAGEMENT SCHOLARSHIP

Scholarship offered to a female student pursuing a degree in an aviation management or business program at an accredited college or university. Applicant must be full-time student with a minimum 3.0 GPA. Must be a member of Women in Aviation, International. Please refer to Web site for further details: http://www.wai.org.

Academic Fields/Career Goals: Aviation/Aerospace.

Award: Scholarship for use in freshman, sophomore, junior, or senior years; not renewable. *Number:* 1. *Amount:* $2500.

Eligibility Requirements: Applicant must be enrolled or expecting to enroll full-time at a two-year or four-year or technical institution or university and female. Applicant or parent of applicant must be member of Women in Aviation, International. Applicant must have 3.0 GPA or higher. Available to U.S. citizens.

Application Requirements: Application. *Deadline:* varies.

Contact: Kim Wheeler, Scholarship Co-Chair
Women in Aviation, International
Scholarship
101 Corsair Drive, Suite 101
Daytona Beach, FL 32114
E-mail: wiaischolarship@yahoo.com

KEEP FLYING SCHOLARSHIP

Scholarship of up to $3000 available for one or more applicants working on an instrument or multi-engine rating, commercial or initial CFI certificate. Applicant must have private pilot certificate, 100 hours of flight time, and a copy of 70+ applicable written test. Flight training must be completed within one year. Must be a member of Women in Aviation, International. Please refer to Web site for further details: http://www.wai.org.

Academic Fields/Career Goals: Aviation/Aerospace.

Award: Scholarship for use in freshman, sophomore, junior, senior, or graduate years; not renewable. *Number:* varies. *Amount:* varies.

Eligibility Requirements: Applicant must be enrolled or expecting to enroll at a two-year or four-year or technical institution or university. Applicant or parent of applicant must be member of Women in Aviation, International. Available to U.S. citizens.

Application Requirements: Application, essay, references. *Deadline:* varies.

Contact: Kim Wheeler, Scholarship Co-Chair
Women in Aviation, International
Scholarship
101 Corsair Drive, Suite 101
Daytona Beach, FL 32114
E-mail: wiaischolarship@yahoo.com

PRATT AND WHITNEY MAINTENANCE SCHOLARSHIPS

Six scholarships available to individuals pursuing careers in aviation maintenance. Scholarship includes the option to attend any maintenance course offered by Pratt and Whitney. Must be a member of Women in Aviation, International. Please refer to Web site for further details: http://www.wai.org.

Academic Fields/Career Goals: Aviation/Aerospace.

Award: Scholarship for use in freshman, sophomore, junior, senior, or graduate years; not renewable. *Number:* 6. *Amount:* $2400–$36,000.

Eligibility Requirements: Applicant must be enrolled or expecting to enroll at a two-year or four-year or technical institution or university. Applicant or parent of applicant must be member of Women in Aviation, International. Available to U.S. citizens.

Application Requirements: Application. *Deadline:* varies.

Contact: Kim Wheeler, Scholarship Co-Chair
Women in Aviation, International
Scholarship
101 Corsair Drive, Suite 101
Daytona Beach, FL 32114
E-mail: wiaischolarship@yahoo.com

PROFESSIONAL PUBLICATIONS SERVICES, INC. CORPORATE AVIATION SCHOLARSHIP

Scholarship available for student pursuing a career in corporate aviation, such as: corporate pilot, scheduler or dispatch, or management of corporate aviation department. Must maintain minimum GPA of 2.0. Must be a member of Women in Aviation, International. Please refer to Web site for further details: http://www.wai.org.

Academic Fields/Career Goals: Aviation/Aerospace.

Award: Scholarship for use in freshman, sophomore, junior, senior, or graduate years; not renewable. *Number:* 1. *Amount:* $1000.

Eligibility Requirements: Applicant must be enrolled or expecting to enroll at a two-year or four-year or technical institution or university. Applicant or parent of applicant must be member of Women in Aviation, International. Available to U.S. citizens.

Application Requirements: Application. *Deadline:* varies.

Contact: Kim Wheeler, Scholarship Co-Chair
Women in Aviation, International
Scholarship
101 Corsair Drive, Suite 101
Daytona Beach, FL 32114
E-mail: wiaischolarship@yahoo.com

ROCKWELL COLLINS ENGINEERING/TECHNICAL SCHOLARSHIP

Scholarship available for full-time student pursuing an engineering or technical degree in an aviation-related career field. Applicant must have minimum GPA of 3.0. Must be a member of Women in Aviation, International. Please refer to Web site for further details: http://www.wai.org.

Women in Aviation, International (continued)

Academic Fields/Career Goals: Aviation/Aerospace.

Award: Scholarship for use in freshman, sophomore, junior, senior, or graduate years; not renewable. *Number:* 1. *Amount:* $2500.

Eligibility Requirements: Applicant must be enrolled or expecting to enroll full-time at a two-year or four-year or technical institution or university. Applicant or parent of applicant must be member of Women in Aviation, International. Applicant must have 3.0 GPA or higher. Available to U.S. and non-U.S. citizens.

Application Requirements: Application. *Deadline:* varies.

Contact: Kim Wheeler, Scholarship Co-Chair
Women in Aviation, International
Scholarship
101 Corsair Drive, Suite 101
Daytona Beach, FL 32114
E-mail: wiaischolarship@yahoo.com

WOMEN IN AVIATION, INTERNATIONAL ACHIEVEMENT AWARDS

Two scholarships available at $500 each for full-time college or university student, and an individual, not necessarily a student, pursuing an aviation career. Must be a member of Women in Aviation, International. Please refer to Web site for further details: http://www.wai.org.

Academic Fields/Career Goals: Aviation/Aerospace.

Award: Scholarship for use in freshman, sophomore, junior, senior, or graduate years; not renewable. *Number:* 2. *Amount:* $500.

Eligibility Requirements: Applicant must be enrolled or expecting to enroll full-time at a two-year or four-year or technical institution or university. Applicant or parent of applicant must be member of Women in Aviation, International. Available to U.S. citizens.

Application Requirements: Application. *Deadline:* varies.

Contact: Kim Wheeler, Scholarship Co-Chair
Women in Aviation, International
Scholarship
101 Corsair Drive, Suite 101
Daytona Beach, FL 32114
E-mail: wiaischolarship@yahoo.com

WOMEN IN AVIATION, INTERNATIONAL MANAGEMENT SCHOLARSHIPS

Scholarship available to a female in an aviation management field who has demonstrated traits of leadership, community spirit, and volunteerism. Must be a member of Women in Aviation, International. Please refer to Web site for further details: http://www.wai.org.

Academic Fields/Career Goals: Aviation/Aerospace.

Award: Scholarship for use in freshman, sophomore, junior, senior, or graduate years; not renewable. *Number:* 1. *Amount:* $750.

Eligibility Requirements: Applicant must be enrolled or expecting to enroll at a two-year or four-year or technical institution or university; female and must have an interest in leadership. Applicant or parent of applicant must be member of Women in Aviation, International. Available to U.S. citizens.

Application Requirements: Application. *Deadline:* varies.

Contact: Kim Wheeler, Scholarship Co-Chair
Women in Aviation, International
Scholarship
101 Corsair Drive, Suite 101
Daytona Beach, FL 32114
E-mail: wiaischolarship@yahoo.com

WOMEN IN CORPORATE AVIATION CAREER SCHOLARSHIPS

Scholarships available to women pursuing a career in corporate aviation. Scholarship may be used toward NBAA Professional Development Program courses, flight training, dispatcher training, or upgrades in aviation education, but cannot be used for general business coursework. Must be a member of Women in Aviation, International. Please refer to Web site for further details: http://www.wai.org.

Academic Fields/Career Goals: Aviation/Aerospace.

Award: Scholarship for use in freshman, sophomore, junior, senior, or graduate years; not renewable. *Number:* 2. *Amount:* $1000.

Eligibility Requirements: Applicant must be enrolled or expecting to enroll at a two-year or four-year or technical institution or university and female. Applicant or parent of applicant must be member of Women in Aviation, International. Available to U.S. citizens.

Application Requirements: Application, financial need analysis. *Deadline:* varies.

Contact: Kim Wheeler, Scholarship Co-Chair
Women in Aviation, International
Scholarship
101 Corsair Drive, Suite 101
Daytona Beach, FL 32114
E-mail: wiaischolarship@yahoo.com

WOMEN MILITARY AVIATORS, INC. MEMORIAL SCHOLARSHIP

Scholarship available for tuition or flight training for an FAA private pilot rating, or advanced rating at an FAA accredited institution or flight school. Must complete flight training within one year of receiving scholarship funds. Must be a member of Women in Aviation, International. Please refer to Web site for further details: http://www.wai.org.

Academic Fields/Career Goals: Aviation/Aerospace.

Award: Scholarship for use in freshman, sophomore, junior, senior, or graduate years; not renewable. *Number:* 1. *Amount:* $2500.

Eligibility Requirements: Applicant must be enrolled or expecting to enroll at a two-year or four-year or technical institution or university. Applicant or parent of applicant must be member of Women in Aviation, International. Available to U.S. citizens.

Application Requirements: Application, financial need analysis. *Deadline:* varies.

Contact: Kim Wheeler, Scholarship Co-Chair
Women in Aviation, International
Scholarship
101 Corsair Drive, Suite 101
Daytona Beach, FL 32114
E-mail: wiaischolarship@yahoo.com

BEHAVIORAL SCIENCE

NATIONAL CHAMBER OF COMMERCE FOR WOMEN

http://fair-advantage.org

MILLIE BELAFONTE WRIGHT SCHOLARSHIP AND GRANT EVALUATION

Submit a publishable paper related to workplace behavioral psychology, preferably providing practical insights for women, helping women reach their performance-evaluation goal, pay-comparison goal, or business-plan goal.

Academic Fields/Career Goals: Behavioral Science; Women's Studies.

Award: Grant for use in freshman, sophomore, junior, senior, graduate, or postgraduate years; not renewable. *Number:* varies. *Amount:* $1000–$2500.

Eligibility Requirements: Applicant must be enrolled or expecting to enroll full or part-time at a two-year or four-year or technical institution or university. Available to U.S. and non-U.S. citizens.

Application Requirements: Essay, resume. *Deadline:* Continuous.

Contact: Ms. Caroline Westbrook, Coordinator
National Chamber of Commerce for Women
10 Waterside Plaza/Suite 6H
New York, NY 10010
Phone: 212-685-3454
Fax: 212-685-4547
E-mail: commerce-for-women@juno.com

BIOLOGY

AIR AND WASTE MANAGEMENT ASSOCIATION-CONNECTICUT CHAPTER http://www.awma-nes.org/

AIR AND WASTE MANAGEMENT ASSOCIATION-CONNECTICUT CHAPTER SCHOLARSHIP

Scholarship for Connecticut residents accepted to and enrolled in full-time courses of study in science and engineering leading to careers in the environmental field.

Academic Fields/Career Goals: Biology; Earth Science; Engineering/ Technology; Natural Resources; Natural Sciences; Physical Sciences and Math.

Award: Scholarship for use in freshman, sophomore, junior, senior, graduate, or postgraduate years; not renewable. *Number:* 1–2. *Amount:* $1000.

Eligibility Requirements: Applicant must be enrolled or expecting to enroll full-time at a four-year institution or university and resident of Connecticut. Available to U.S. and non-U.S. citizens.

Application Requirements: Application, essay, references, transcript. *Deadline:* April 15.

Contact: Ray Yarmac, Secretary, Connecticut Chapter
Air and Waste Management Association-Connecticut Chapter
c/o Sci-Tech Inc.
185 Silas Deane Highway
Wethersfield, CT 06109
E-mail: ryarmac@sci-techinc.com

ALABAMA STATE DEPARTMENT OF EDUCATION http://www.alsde.edu

MATH AND SCIENCE SCHOLARSHIP PROGRAM FOR ALABAMA TEACHERS

For students pursuing teaching certificates in mathematics, general science, biology, or physics. Applicants must agree to teach for five years (if a position is offered) in a targeted system with critical needs. Renewable if recipient continues to meet the requirements. Minimum 2.5 GPA required. Must attend school in Alabama.

Academic Fields/Career Goals: Biology; Earth Science; Meteorology/ Atmospheric Science; Natural Sciences; Physical Sciences and Math.

Award: Forgivable loan for use in junior, senior, or graduate years; renewable. *Amount:* $2000–$12,000.

Eligibility Requirements: Applicant must be enrolled or expecting to enroll full or part-time at a four-year institution or university and studying in Alabama. Applicant must have 2.5 GPA or higher. Available to U.S. citizens.

Application Requirements: Application. *Deadline:* varies.

Contact: Alabama State Department of Education
PO Box 302101
Montgomery, AL 36130-2101
Phone: 334-242-9935

ALASKA COMMISSION ON POSTSECONDARY EDUCATION http://www.state.ak.us/acpe/

A.W. "WINN" BRINDLE MEMORIAL EDUCATION LOANS

• *See page 52*

ALBERTA HERITAGE SCHOLARSHIP FUND/ ALBERTA SCHOLARSHIP PROGRAMS http://www.alis.gov.ab.ca/scholarships

ALBERTA HERITAGE SCHOLARSHIP FUND ABORIGINAL HEALTH CAREERS BURSARY

Award for aboriginal students in Alberta entering their second or subsequent year of postsecondary education in a health field. Must be Indian, Inuit, or Métis and a resident of Alberta for a minimum of three years prior to applying. Awards are valued up to CAN$13,000. Deadline: May 15. Must be ranked in upper half of class or have a minimum 2.5 GPA.

Academic Fields/Career Goals: Biology; Dental Health/Services; Health Administration; Health and Medical Sciences; Nursing; Therapy/Rehabilitation.

Award: Scholarship for use in sophomore, junior, senior, or graduate years; not renewable. *Number:* 20–40. *Amount:* $811–$10,557.

Eligibility Requirements: Applicant must be Canadian citizen; American Indian/Alaska Native; enrolled or expecting to enroll full-time at a two-year or four-year or technical institution or university and resident of Alberta. Applicant must have 2.5 GPA or higher.

Application Requirements: Application, essay, financial need analysis, references, transcript. *Deadline:* May 15.

Contact: Alberta Heritage Scholarship Fund/Alberta Scholarship Programs
9940 106th Street, 9th Floor, Box 28000 Station Main
Edmonton, AB T5J 4R4
Canada
Phone: 780-427-8640
Fax: 780-422-4516
E-mail: heritage@gov.ab.ca

AMERICAN INDIAN SCIENCE AND ENGINEERING SOCIETY http://www.aises.org

A.T. ANDERSON MEMORIAL SCHOLARSHIP

• *See page 65*

BURLINGTON NORTHERN SANTA FE FOUNDATION SCHOLARSHIP

• *See page 65*

ENVIRONMENTAL PROTECTION AGENCY TRIBAL LANDS ENVIRONMENTAL SCIENCE SCHOLARSHIP

Award for Native-American college juniors, seniors, or graduate students attending an accredited institution and studying full time in biochemistry, biology, chemical engineering, chemistry, entomology, environmental science, hydrology, or environmentally related disciplines. Deadline: June 15. Minimum 2.7 GPA required. Must be a current AISES member.

Academic Fields/Career Goals: Biology; Chemical Engineering; Earth Science; Meteorology/Atmospheric Science; Natural Sciences; Physical Sciences and Math.

Award: Scholarship for use in junior, senior, or graduate years; not renewable. *Number:* varies. *Amount:* $4000.

Eligibility Requirements: Applicant must be American Indian/Alaska Native and enrolled or expecting to enroll full-time at a four-year institution or university. Available to U.S. citizens.

Application Requirements: Application, references, transcript. *Deadline:* June 15.

Contact: Scholarship Information
American Indian Science and Engineering Society
PO Box 9828
Albuquerque, NM 87119-9828
Phone: 505-765-1052
Fax: 505-765-5608
E-mail: info@aises.org

AMERICAN ORNITHOLOGISTS' UNION http://www.aou.org

AMERICAN ORNITHOLOGISTS' UNION RESEARCH AWARDS

• *See page 62*

AMERICAN SOCIETY OF AGRICULTURAL ENGINEERS http://www.asae.org

WILLIAM J. AND MARIJANE E. ADAMS, JR. SCHOLARSHIP

• *See page 57*

ARKANSAS DEPARTMENT OF HIGHER EDUCATION http://www.arscholarships.com

EMERGENCY SECONDARY EDUCATION LOAN PROGRAM

Must be Arkansas resident enrolled full-time in approved Arkansas institution. Renewable award for students majoring in secondary math, chemistry, physics, biology, physical science, general science, special education, or foreign language. Must teach in Arkansas at least five years. Must rank in upper half of class or have a minimum 2.5 GPA.

Arkansas Department of Higher Education (continued)

Academic Fields/Career Goals: Biology; Education; Foreign Language; Physical Sciences and Math; Special Education.

Award: Forgivable loan for use in sophomore, junior, senior, or graduate years; renewable. *Number:* up to 50. *Amount:* up to $2500.

Eligibility Requirements: Applicant must be enrolled or expecting to enroll full-time at a two-year or four-year institution or university; resident of Arkansas and studying in Arkansas. Applicant must have 2.5 GPA or higher. Available to U.S. citizens.

Application Requirements: Application, transcript. *Deadline:* April 1.

Contact: Lillian K. Williams, Assistant Coordinator
Arkansas Department of Higher Education
114 East Capitol
Little Rock, AR 72201
Phone: 501-371-2050
Fax: 501-371-2001

ASSOCIATION FOR IRON AND STEEL TECHNOLOGY http://www.aist.org/foundation/scholarships.htm

ASSOCIATION FOR IRON AND STEEL TECHNOLOGY OHIO VALLEY CHAPTER SCHOLARSHIP

Scholarship of $1000 per year for up to four years provided that applicant continues to meet requirements and reapplies for scholarship. Applicant must be a dependent of Ohio Valley Chapter member, or Student or Young Professional member. Applicant also must attend or plan to attend an accredited school full-time and pursue a degree in any of a number of technological fields such as engineering, physics, computer sciences, chemistry or other fields approved by the scholarship committee . Application deadline is January 31 of high school senior year, or of freshman year.

Academic Fields/Career Goals: Biology; Computer Science/Data Processing; Earth Science; Electrical Engineering/Electronics; Engineering/Technology; Engineering-Related Technologies; Environmental Science; Geography; Materials Science, Engineering, and Metallurgy; Physical Sciences and Math.

Award: Scholarship for use in freshman, sophomore, junior, or senior years; not renewable. *Number:* 2. *Amount:* $4000.

Eligibility Requirements: Applicant must be enrolled or expecting to enroll full-time at a four-year institution or university and must have an interest in leadership. Applicant must have 3.0 GPA or higher. Available to U.S. citizens.

Application Requirements: Application, essay, resume, references, transcript, personal statement. *Deadline:* January 31.

Contact: Jeff McKain, Scholarship Chairman
Association for Iron and Steel Technology
11451 Reading Road
Cincinnati, OH 45241
E-mail: jeff.mckain@xtek.com

ASSOCIATION FOR WOMEN IN SCIENCE EDUCATIONAL FOUNDATION http://www.awis.org/ed_foundation.html

ASSOCIATION FOR WOMEN IN SCIENCE COLLEGE SCHOLARSHIP

• *See page 63*

ASSOCIATION OF CALIFORNIA WATER AGENCIES http://www.acwanet.com

ASSOCIATION OF CALIFORNIA WATER AGENCIES SCHOLARSHIPS

• *See page 68*

CLAIR A. HILL SCHOLARSHIP

• *See page 68*

ASTRONAUT SCHOLARSHIP FOUNDATION http://www.astronautscholarship.org

ASTRONAUT SCHOLARSHIP FOUNDATION

• *See page 68*

BARRY M. GOLDWATER SCHOLARSHIP AND EXCELLENCE IN EDUCATION FOUNDATION http://www.act.org/goldwater

BARRY M. GOLDWATER SCHOLARSHIP AND EXCELLENCE IN EDUCATION PROGRAM

• *See page 68*

BAT CONSERVATION INTERNATIONAL http://www.batcon.org

BAT CONSERVATION INTERNATIONAL STUDENT SCHOLARSHIP PROGRAM

The goal of this program is to support student research that will answer ecological or behavioral questions essential to bat conservation or management; document key ecological or economic roles of bats; or educate people who are directly relevant to conservation success. Submission of research proposal and budget required. Only senior level biology students and graduate students in biological disciplines are eligible. Application and instructions available on BCI's Web site at http://www.batcon.org/schol/schol.html. Applications are to be submitted electronically.

Academic Fields/Career Goals: Biology; Natural Resources; Natural Sciences.

Award: Grant for use in senior, or graduate years; not renewable. *Number:* 15. *Amount:* $500–$2500.

Eligibility Requirements: Applicant must be enrolled or expecting to enroll full-time at a four-year institution or university. Available to U.S. and non-U.S. citizens.

Application Requirements: Application, references, research proposal, budget. *Deadline:* December 15.

Contact: Sarah Keeton, Administrative Assistant
Bat Conservation International
PO Box 162603
Austin, TX 78716-2603
Phone: 512-327-9721
Fax: 512-327-9724
E-mail: skeeton@batcon.org

BUSINESS AND PROFESSIONAL WOMEN'S FOUNDATION http://www.bpwusa.org

BPW CAREER ADVANCEMENT SCHOLARSHIP PROGRAM FOR WOMEN

Scholarships of $1000 each are awarded for full or part-time study. Applicant must be studying in one of the following fields: biological sciences, teacher education certification, engineering, social science, paralegal studies, humanities, business studies, mathematics, computer science, physical sciences, or for a professional degree (JD, MD, DDS). The Career Advancement Scholarship Program was established to assist women seeking the education necessary for entry or re-entry into the work force, or advancement within a career field. Must be 25 or over. Send self-addressed double-stamped envelope between January 1 and April 1 for application.

Academic Fields/Career Goals: Biology; Computer Science/Data Processing; Dental Health/Services; Education; Engineering/Technology; Engineering-Related Technologies; Health and Medical Sciences; Humanities; Law/Legal Services; Physical Sciences and Math; Social Sciences.

Award: Scholarship for use in freshman, sophomore, junior, senior, or graduate years; not renewable. *Number:* 100–200. *Amount:* $1000.

Eligibility Requirements: Applicant must be age 25; enrolled or expecting to enroll full or part-time at a two-year or four-year or technical institution or university and female. Available to U.S. citizens.

Application Requirements: Application, essay, financial need analysis, references, self-addressed stamped envelope, transcript. *Deadline:* April 15.

Contact: Diane Thurston Frye, Development and Scholarship Manager
Business and Professional Women's Foundation
1900 M Street, NW, Suite 310
Washington, DC 20036
Phone: 202-293-1100 Ext. 183
Fax: 202-861-0298
E-mail: dthurston@bpwusa.org

CALIFORNIA SEA GRANT COLLEGE PROGRAM http://www-csgc.ucsd.edu

JOHN D. ISSACS SCHOLARSHIP

The scholarship provides $3000 for each of four years and is open to any high school junior or senior in California who is considering a career in marine science. Applicant must enter a marine science project in a regional or county science fair in their junior or senior year and in their senior year must have applied to (and by the following fall have enrolled in) a four-year college or university in California.

Academic Fields/Career Goals: Biology; Earth Science; Engineering/Technology; Marine Biology; Natural Resources; Natural Sciences.

Award: Scholarship for use in freshman year; renewable. *Number:* 1. *Amount:* $12,000.

Eligibility Requirements: Applicant must be high school student; age 16-18; planning to enroll or expecting to enroll full-time at a four-year institution or university; resident of California and studying in California. Available to U.S. citizens.

Application Requirements: Application, applicant must enter a contest, essay, photo. *Deadline:* April 2.

Contact: California Sea Grant
California Sea Grant College Program
9500 Gilman Drive, Department 0232
La Jolla, CA 92093-0232
Phone: 858-534-4440
Fax: 858-534-2231

COLLEGEBOUND FOUNDATION http://www.collegeboundfoundation.org

NATIONAL AQUARIUM IN BALTIMORE HENRY HALL SCHOLARSHIP

Award for Baltimore City public high school graduates 21 years of age or younger. Please see Web site: http://www.collegeboundfoundation.org for complete information on application process. Must have completed at least one year of high school biology, physical science, and algebra and have maintained an 85 average or better in science classes. Must major in biology, engineering, or environmental science and submit a typed one-page essay on why you are pursuing this field of study. Must submit CollegeBound Competitive Scholarship/Last-Dollar Grant Application.

Academic Fields/Career Goals: Biology; Engineering/Technology; Environmental Science.

Award: Scholarship for use in freshman year; not renewable. *Number:* 1–4. *Amount:* $1000.

Eligibility Requirements: Applicant must be age 21 or under; enrolled or expecting to enroll full-time at a two-year or four-year institution or university and resident of Maryland. Available to U.S. citizens.

Application Requirements: Application, essay, financial need analysis, references, transcript, financial aid award letters, Student Aid Report. *Deadline:* March 19.

Contact: April Bell, Associate Program Director
CollegeBound Foundation
300 Water Street, Suite 300
Baltimore, MD 21202
Phone: 410-783-2905 Ext. 208
Fax: 410-727-5786
E-mail: abell@collegeboundfoundation.org

CONNECTICUT STUDENT LOAN FOUNDATION http://www.cslf.com

CONNECTICUT INNOVATIONS TECHNOLOGY SCHOLAR PROGRAM

An earned scholarship program available to Connecticut high school seniors who plan on studying within the fields of science or technology at an accredited Connecticut college or university. Must work within the State of Connecticut for two years following graduation.

Academic Fields/Career Goals: Biology; Chemical Engineering; Computer Science/Data Processing; Earth Science; Electrical Engineering/Electronics; Engineering/Technology; Materials Science, Engineering, and Metallurgy; Mechanical Engineering; Natural Sciences; Physical Sciences and Math.

Award: Forgivable loan for use in freshman, sophomore, junior, or senior years; not renewable. *Number:* 30–70. *Amount:* up to $12,000.

Eligibility Requirements: Applicant must be high school student; planning to enroll or expecting to enroll full-time at a two-year or four-year institution or university; resident of Connecticut and studying in Connecticut. Applicant must have 3.0 GPA or higher. Available to U.S. citizens.

Application Requirements: Application, references, transcript. *Deadline:* February 15.

Contact: Laura Valenti, Manager, Scholarship Program
Connecticut Student Loan Foundation
525 Brook Street, PO Box 1009
Rocky Hill, CT 06067
Phone: 860-257-4001 Ext. 446
E-mail: lvalent@mail.cslf.org

CONSERVATION FEDERATION OF MISSOURI http://www.confedmo.com

CHARLES P. BELL CONSERVATION SCHOLARSHIP

Eight scholarships of $250-$600 for Missouri students and/or teachers whose studies or projects are related to natural science, resource conservation, earth resources, or environmental protection. Must be used for study in Missouri. See application for eligibility details.

Academic Fields/Career Goals: Biology; Natural Resources.

Award: Scholarship for use in junior, senior, or graduate years; not renewable. *Number:* 8. *Amount:* $250–$600.

Eligibility Requirements: Applicant must be enrolled or expecting to enroll full-time at a four-year institution or university; resident of Missouri and studying in Missouri. Available to U.S. citizens.

Application Requirements: Application, references, transcript. *Deadline:* January 15.

Contact: Administrative Associate
Conservation Federation of Missouri
728 West Main Street
Jefferson City, MO 65101
Phone: 573-634-2322
Fax: 573-634-8205
E-mail: confedmo@sockets.net

DELAWARE SOLID WASTE AUTHORITY http://www.dswa.com

DELAWARE SOLID WASTE AUTHORITY SCHOLARSHIP

One scholarship worth $2000 per year will be awarded to a Delaware resident studying at a Delaware college or university. The scholarship is renewable for up to four years. Must be pursuing a degree in engineering, biology, or natural resources related field. For more information about this scholarship speak with your scholarship advisor.

Academic Fields/Career Goals: Biology; Chemical Engineering; Civil Engineering; Engineering-Related Technologies; Natural Resources.

Award: Scholarship for use in freshman, sophomore, junior, or senior years; renewable. *Number:* 1. *Amount:* $2000.

Eligibility Requirements: Applicant must be enrolled or expecting to enroll full-time at a four-year institution or university; resident of Delaware; studying in Delaware and must have an interest in designated field specified by sponsor. Applicant must have 3.0 GPA or higher. Available to U.S. citizens.

Application Requirements: Application, essay, financial need analysis, references. *Deadline:* Continuous.

Contact: See your scholarship adviser.

EAA AVIATION FOUNDATION, INC. http://www.eaa.org

PAYZER SCHOLARSHIP

• *See page 98*

FEDERATED GARDEN CLUBS OF CONNECTICUT

FEDERATED GARDEN CLUBS OF CONNECTICUT, INC.

One-time award for Connecticut residents pursuing studies in gardening, landscaping, or biology. Minimum 3.5 GPA. Application deadline is July 1.

Academic Fields/Career Goals: Biology; Horticulture/Floriculture; Landscape Architecture.

Federated Garden Clubs of Connecticut (continued)

Award: Scholarship for use in junior, senior, or graduate years; not renewable. *Number:* 2–5. *Amount:* $2000–$3000.

Eligibility Requirements: Applicant must be enrolled or expecting to enroll full-time at a four-year institution or university and resident of Connecticut. Applicant must have 3.5 GPA or higher. Available to U.S. and non-U.S. citizens.

Application Requirements: Application, autobiography, financial need analysis, references, self-addressed stamped envelope, test scores, transcript. *Deadline:* July 1.

Contact: Mary Gray, Scholarship Chairman
Federated Garden Clubs of Connecticut
14 Business Park Drive
PO Box 854
Branford, CT 06405-0854
Phone: 203-458-2784

GARDEN CLUB OF AMERICA http://www.gcamerica.org

LOY MCCANDLESS MARKS SCHOLARSHIP IN TROPICAL ORNAMENTAL HORTICULTURE

Award affords a graduate student or advanced undergraduate opportunity to study tropical ornamental horticulture at an appropriate foreign institution specializing in the study of tropical plants. Application on the GCA Web site: http://www.gcamerica.org.

Academic Fields/Career Goals: Biology; Horticulture/Floriculture.

Award: Scholarship for use in senior, or graduate years; not renewable. *Number:* 1. *Amount:* $2000.

Eligibility Requirements: Applicant must be enrolled or expecting to enroll at an institution or university. Available to U.S. citizens.

Application Requirements: Application, interview, references, self-addressed stamped envelope, transcript. *Deadline:* January 10.

Contact: Connie Sutton, Scholarship Administrator
Garden Club of America
14 East 60th Street
New York, NY 10022
Phone: 212-753-8287
Fax: 212-753-0134

HAWAIIAN LODGE, F.& A. M. http://www.hawaiianlodge.org/

HAWAIIAN LODGE SCHOLARSHIPS
• *See page 76*

HERB SOCIETY OF AMERICA http://www.herbsociety.org

HERB SOCIETY RESEARCH GRANTS
• *See page 69*

HISPANIC COLLEGE FUND, INC. http://www.hispanicfund.org

NATIONAL HISPANIC EXPLORERS SCHOLARSHIP PROGRAM
• *See page 69*

HISPANIC ENGINEER NATIONAL ACHIEVEMENT AWARDS CORPORATION (HENAAC) http://www.henaac.org

HISPANIC ENGINEER NATIONAL ACHIEVEMENT AWARDS CORPORATION SCHOLARSHIP PROGRAM
• *See page 99*

INDEPENDENT LABORATORIES INSTITUTE SCHOLARSHIP ALLIANCE http://www.acil.org

INDEPENDENT LABORATORIES INSTITUTE SCHOLARSHIP ALLIANCE
• *See page 69*

INNOVATION AND SCIENCE COUNCIL OF BRITISH COLUMBIA http://www.scbc.org

PAUL AND HELEN TRUSSEL SCIENCE AND TECHNOLOGY SCHOLARSHIP
• *See page 69*

MANOMET CENTER FOR CONSERVATION SCIENCES http://www.manomet.org

KATHLEEN S. ANDERSON AWARD
• *See page 63*

MASTER BREWERS ASSOCIATION OF THE AMERICAS http://www.mbaa.com

MASTER BREWERS ASSOCIATION OF THE AMERICAS
• *See page 59*

MID-COAST AUDUBON SOCIETY http://www.midcoastaudubon.org

JEAN BOYER HAMLIN SCHOLARSHIP IN ORNITHOLOGY
• *See page 63*

MONTANA FEDERATION OF GARDEN CLUBS

LIFE MEMBER MONTANA FEDERATION OF GARDEN CLUBS SCHOLARSHIP

Applicant must be at least a sophomore, majoring in conservation, horticulture, park or forestry, floriculture, greenhouse management, land management, or related subjects. Must be in need of assistance. Must have a potential for a successful future. Must be ranked in upper half of class or have a minimum 2.8 GPA. Must be a Montana resident and all study must be done in Montana. Deadline: May 1.

Academic Fields/Career Goals: Biology; Earth Science; Horticulture/Floriculture; Landscape Architecture.

Award: Scholarship for use in sophomore, junior, or senior years; not renewable. *Number:* 1. *Amount:* $1000.

Eligibility Requirements: Applicant must be enrolled or expecting to enroll full-time at a four-year institution or university; resident of Montana and studying in Montana. Available to U.S. citizens.

Application Requirements: Autobiography, financial need analysis, photo, references, transcript. *Deadline:* May 1.

Contact: Elizabeth Kehmeier, Life Members Scholarship Chairman
Montana Federation of Garden Clubs
214 Wyant Lane
Hamilton, MT 59840
Phone: 406-363-5693
E-mail: elizabethhammt@aol.com

MORRIS K. UDALL FOUNDATION http://www.udall.gov

MORRIS K. UDALL SCHOLARS
• *See page 59*

NASA IDAHO SPACE GRANT CONSORTIUM http://www.uidaho.edu/nasa_isgc

NASA IDAHO SPACE GRANT CONSORTIUM SCHOLARSHIP PROGRAM
• *See page 71*

NASA NEBRASKA SPACE GRANT CONSORTIUM http://nasa.unomaha.edu

NASA NEBRASKA SPACE GRANT
• *See page 101*

NASA VERMONT SPACE GRANT CONSORTIUM http://www.emba.uvm.edu/vsgc

VERMONT SPACE GRANT CONSORTIUM SCHOLARSHIP PROGRAM
• *See page 71*

NATIONAL ASSOCIATION FOR THE ADVANCEMENT OF COLORED PEOPLE http://www.naacp.org

LOUIS STOKES SCIENCE AND TECHNOLOGY AWARD

Must be an incoming freshman at an Historically Black college or university and major in one of the following: engineering, physics, chemistry, biology, computer science or mathematical science. Freshman must be full-time student and have 2.5 minimum GPA. Award requires financial need. NAACP membership and participation is preferable. Application deadline is the last Friday in March.

Academic Fields/Career Goals: Biology; Chemical Engineering; Computer Science/Data Processing; Engineering-Related Technologies; Physical Sciences and Math.

Award: Scholarship for use in freshman year; not renewable. *Number:* varies. *Amount:* $2000.

Eligibility Requirements: Applicant must be American Indian/Alaska Native, Asian/Pacific Islander, Black (non-Hispanic), or Hispanic and enrolled or expecting to enroll full-time at a four-year institution or university. Applicant or parent of applicant must be member of National Association for the Advancement of Colored People. Applicant must have 2.5 GPA or higher. Available to U.S. citizens.

Application Requirements: Application, financial need analysis, references, transcript. *Deadline:* varies.

Contact: Donna Lakins, Education Department, Scholarship Request
National Association for the Advancement of Colored People
4805 Mt. Hope Drive
Baltimore, MD 21215-3297
Phone: 410-580-5760
Fax: 410-585-1329

NATIONAL ASSOCIATION OF WATER COMPANIES http://www.nawc.org

J .J. BARR SCHOLARSHIP

Award for a graduating undergraduate senior or graduate student pursuing studies which may lead to a career in the investor owned public water supply business. Must be a U.S. citizen. Write for information and restrictions. One-time award of $5000. Must study in one of the following states: WA, RI, CA, VT, PA, NH, NY, NJ, NC, SC, MA, FL, ME, IL, CT, MO, DE, IN or OH.

Academic Fields/Career Goals: Biology; Business/Consumer Services; Earth Science; Engineering-Related Technologies; Law/Legal Services; Natural Resources.

Award: Scholarship for use in senior, or graduate years; not renewable. *Number:* 1. *Amount:* $5000.

Eligibility Requirements: Applicant must be enrolled or expecting to enroll full or part-time at an institution or university. Available to U.S. citizens.

Application Requirements: Application, essay, references, transcript. *Deadline:* April 1.

Contact: Carlos Villanueva, Scholarship Coordinator
National Association of Water Companies
1725 K Street, NW, Suite 1212
Washington, DC 20006
Phone: 202-833-8383 Ext. 11
Fax: 202-331-7442
E-mail: carlos@nawc.com

NATIONAL ASSOCIATION OF WATER COMPANIES-NEW JERSEY CHAPTER

NATIONAL ASSOCIATION OF WATER COMPANIES-NEW JERSEY CHAPTER SCHOLARSHIP

For college students interested in a career in the investor-owned water utility industry. Must be U.S. citizen, five-year resident of New Jersey, high school senior or enrolled in a New Jersey college or university. Must maintain a 3.0 GPA.

Academic Fields/Career Goals: Biology; Business/Consumer Services; Communications; Computer Science/Data Processing; Earth Science; Economics; Engineering/Technology; Law/Legal Services; Natural Resources; Physical Sciences and Math; Trade/Technical Specialties.

Award: Scholarship for use in freshman, sophomore, junior, senior, or graduate years; not renewable. *Number:* 1–2. *Amount:* $2500.

Eligibility Requirements: Applicant must be enrolled or expecting to enroll full or part-time at a two-year or four-year institution or university; resident of New Jersey and studying in New Jersey. Applicant must have 3.0 GPA or higher. Available to U.S. citizens.

Application Requirements: Application, essay, references, transcript. *Deadline:* April 1.

Contact: Gail Brady, Scholarship Committee Chairperson
National Association of Water Companies-New Jersey Chapter
c/o Gail Brady, GB Consulting Services
49 Howell Drive
Verona, NJ 07044
Phone: 973-669-5807
Fax: 973-669-8327
E-mail: gbradygbconsult@comcast.net

NATIONAL FEDERATION OF THE BLIND http://www.nfb.org

HOWARD BROWN RICKARD SCHOLARSHIP

• *See page 78*

NATIONAL FISH AND WILDLIFE FOUNDATION http://www.nfwf.org

BUDWEISER CONSERVATION SCHOLARSHIP PROGRAM

One-time award supports and promotes innovative research or study that seeks to respond to today's most pressing conservation issues. This competitive scholarship program is designed to respond to many of the most significant challenges in fish, wildlife, and plant conservation in the United States by providing scholarships to eligible graduate and undergraduate students who are poised to make a significant contribution to the field of conservation.

Academic Fields/Career Goals: Biology; Geography; Natural Resources; Natural Sciences; Political Science; Surveying; Surveying Technology, Cartography, or Geographic Information Science.

Award: Scholarship for use in sophomore, junior, senior, or graduate years; not renewable. *Number:* 10–20. *Amount:* $10,000.

Eligibility Requirements: Applicant must be age 21 and enrolled or expecting to enroll full-time at a four-year institution or university. Available to U.S. citizens.

Application Requirements: Application, essay, references, transcript, title of proposed research and a short abstract. *Deadline:* January 18.

Contact: Tom Kelsch, Director, Conservation Education
National Fish and Wildlife Foundation
1120 Connecticut Avenue, NW
Suite 900
Washington, DC 20036
Phone: 202-857-0166
Fax: 202-857-0162
E-mail: tom.kelsch@nfwf.org

NATIONAL GARDEN CLUBS, INC. http://www.gardenclub.org

NATIONAL GARDEN CLUBS, INC. SCHOLARSHIP PROGRAM

• *See page 60*

NATIONAL INSTITUTE OF GENERAL MEDICAL SCIENCES, NATIONAL INSTITUTE OF HEALTH http://www.nigms.nih.gov

MARC UNDERGRADUATE STUDENT TRAINING IN ACADEMIC RESEARCH U*STAR AWARDS

Scholarships available for minority honors students enrolled in their junior and senior years at participating U*Star universities. Must major in science with the intent to pursue their PhD or MD degrees. Specific details and application are available on Web site: http://www.nigms.nih.gov

Academic Fields/Career Goals: Biology; Computer Science/Data Processing; Natural Sciences.

Award: Scholarship for use in junior or senior years; renewable. *Number:* varies. *Amount:* varies.

Eligibility Requirements: Applicant must be American Indian/Alaska Native, Asian/Pacific Islander, Black (non-Hispanic), or Hispanic; enrolled or expecting to enroll full-time at a four-year institution or university and studying in Alabama, Arizona, California, Colorado, Delaware, Florida, Georgia, Hawaii, Louisiana, Maryland, Minnesota, or Mississippi. Available to U.S. citizens.

National Institute of General Medical Sciences, National Institute of Health (continued)

Application Requirements: Application. *Deadline:* varies.

Contact: Susan Athey, Public Affairs
National Institute of General Medical Sciences, National Institute of Health
45 Center Drive MSC 6200
Bethesda, MD 20892-6200
Phone: 301-496-7301
Fax: 301-402-0224
E-mail: atheys@nigms.nih.gov

NATIONAL INSTITUTES OF HEALTH http://ugsp.info.nih.gov

NIH UNDERGRADUATE SCHOLARSHIP PROGRAM FOR STUDENTS FROM DISADVANTAGED BACKGROUNDS

The NIH Undergraduate Scholarship Program offers competitive scholarships to exceptional students from disadvantaged backgrounds who are committed to biomedical, behavioral and social science research careers at the NIH. Applicants must be U.S. citizens, nationals, or qualified permanent residents and have a minimum 3.5 GPA.

Academic Fields/Career Goals: Biology; Health and Medical Sciences; Social Sciences.

Award: Scholarship for use in freshman, sophomore, junior, or senior years; renewable. *Number:* 10–20. *Amount:* up to $20,000.

Eligibility Requirements: Applicant must be enrolled or expecting to enroll full-time at a four-year institution or university. Applicant must have 3.5 GPA or higher. Available to U.S. citizens.

Application Requirements: Application, essay, financial need analysis, references, transcript. *Deadline:* February 28.

Contact: NIH Undergraduate Scholarship Program Director
National Institutes of Health
2 Center Drive, Room 2E30, MSC 0230
Bethesda, MD 20892-0230
Phone: 800-528-7689
Fax: 301-480-3123
E-mail: ugsp@nih.gov

NATIONAL INVENTORS HALL OF FAME http://www.invent.org/collegiate

COLLEGIATE INVENTORS COMPETITION - GRAND PRIZE

• *See page 71*

COLLEGIATE INVENTORS COMPETITION FOR UNDERGRADUATE STUDENTS

• *See page 71*

NEW JERSEY ACADEMY OF SCIENCE http://www.njas.org

NEW JERSEY ACADEMY OF SCIENCE RESEARCH GRANTS-IN-AID TO HIGH SCHOOL STUDENTS

Selected New Jersey high school student research proposals will be funded up to $100 for materials. Scientific proposal must describe an originally designed experiment that will be conducted. These students must orally present the results of their research at the State Junior Academy Annual Meeting.

Academic Fields/Career Goals: Biology; Chemical Engineering; Computer Science/Data Processing; Earth Science; Engineering/Technology; Health and Medical Sciences; Mechanical Engineering; Meteorology/Atmospheric Science; Natural Sciences; Physical Sciences and Math; Science, Technology, and Society; Social Sciences.

Award: Grant for use in freshman year; not renewable. *Number:* 15–30. *Amount:* $30–$100.

Eligibility Requirements: Applicant must be high school student; planning to enroll or expecting to enroll full-time at an institution or university; resident of New Jersey and studying in New Jersey. Available to U.S. citizens.

Application Requirements: Application, applicant must enter a contest, references, proposal of scientific work to be completed. *Deadline:* November 1.

Contact: Dr. Laura Lorentzen, Chairperson, Grants-in-Aid Program of NJAS
New Jersey Academy of Science
Kean University, 1000 Morris Avenue, Biology C-13
Union, NJ 07083
Phone: 908-737-3668
Fax: 908-737-3666
E-mail: llorentz@kean.edu

NEW JERSEY DIVISION OF FISH AND WILDLIFE/NJ CHAPTER OF THE WILDLIFE SOCIETY http://www.njfishandwildlife.com

RUSSELL A. COOKINGHAM SCHOLARSHIP

Scholarship to assist qualified students majoring in wildlife/fisheries or conservation education/communications. Conservation education/communications majors must have at least 15 credits in biological sciences. Applicants must have completed at least one-half of the degree requirements for their major. Must be a permanent resident of New Jersey, attending an institution in-state or out-of-state. To apply, send official transcript, 2 letters of recommendation, resume, and cover letter explaining why you should be considered for this scholarship. Deadline is April 1.

Academic Fields/Career Goals: Biology; Communications; Environmental Science; Natural Resources.

Award: Scholarship for use in junior or senior years; not renewable. *Number:* 1. *Amount:* $1000.

Eligibility Requirements: Applicant must be enrolled or expecting to enroll full-time at a four-year institution or university and resident of New Jersey. Available to U.S. citizens.

Application Requirements: Resume, references, transcript, cover letter. *Deadline:* April 1.

Contact: P. Jim Sciascia
New Jersey Division of Fish and Wildlife/NJ Chapter of the Wildlife Society
605 Pequest Road
Oxford, NJ 07863
E-mail: jim.sciascia@dep.state.nj.us

OREGON STUDENT ASSISTANCE COMMISSION http://www.osac.state.or.us

OREGON FOUNDATION FOR BLACKTAIL DEER OUTDOOR AND WILDLIFE SCHOLARSHIP

One-time award for students majoring in forestry, biology, wildlife science or related fields indicating a serious commitment to careers in wildlife management. Must submit essay on, "Challenges of Wildlife management in coming 10 years." Submit copy of previous year's hunting license. Must be an Oregon resident attending an Oregon institution.

Academic Fields/Career Goals: Biology; Natural Resources; Natural Sciences.

Award: Scholarship for use in freshman, sophomore, junior, or senior years; not renewable. *Number:* 4. *Amount:* $500.

Eligibility Requirements: Applicant must be enrolled or expecting to enroll at a four-year institution; resident of Oregon and studying in Oregon. Available to U.S. citizens.

Application Requirements: Application, essay, financial need analysis, references, transcript, hunting license. *Deadline:* March 1.

Contact: Director of Grant Programs
Oregon Student Assistance Commission
1500 Valley River Drive, Suite 100
Eugene, OR 97401-7020
Phone: 800-452-8807 Ext. 7395
E-mail: awardinfo@mercury.osac.state.or.us

PENNSYLVANIA ASSOCIATION OF CONSERVATION DISTRICTS AUXILIARY http://www.blairconservationdistrict.org

PACD AUXILIARY SCHOLARSHIPS

• *See page 55*

RECREATIONAL BOATING INDUSTRIES EDUCATIONAL FOUNDATION http://mbia.org

RECREATIONAL BOATING INDUSTRIES EDUCATIONAL FOUNDATION SCHOLARSHIPS

Scholarships are awarded to students pursuing a degree that will eventually lead to a career in the recreational boating industry. Applicants must be residents of Michigan. Selection will be based on transcript, recommendations, an essay and financial need.

Academic Fields/Career Goals: Biology; Natural Resources; Travel/Tourism.

Award: Scholarship for use in freshman, sophomore, junior, or senior years; not renewable. *Number:* 10–30. *Amount:* $250–$1000.

Eligibility Requirements: Applicant must be enrolled or expecting to enroll full or part-time at a two-year or four-year institution or university and resident of Michigan. Available to U.S. citizens.

Application Requirements: Application, essay, financial need analysis, references, transcript. *Deadline:* March 15.

Contact: Mary Sherman, Administrator
Recreational Boating Industries Educational Foundation
32398 Five Mile Road
Livonia, MI 48154-6109
Phone: 734-261-0123
Fax: 734-261-0880
E-mail: msherm@mbia.org

ROBERT H. MOLLOHAN FAMILY CHARITABLE FOUNDATION, INC. http://www.mollohanfoundation.org

HIGH TECHNOLOGY SCHOLARS PROGRAM

Scholarship for West Virginia students pursuing a technology-related career and residing in one of the following counties: Barbour, Brooke, Calhoun, Doddridge, Gilmer, Grant, Hancock, Harrison, Marion, Marshall, Mineral, Monongalia, Ohio, Pleasants, Preston, Ritchie, Taylor, Tucker, Tyler, Wetzel, Wood. Scholarship recipients become eligible for a paid internship with a West Virginia business. Students may also apply for debt-forgiveness loans up to $2000 per year.

Academic Fields/Career Goals: Biology; Chemical Engineering; Computer Science/Data Processing; Electrical Engineering/Electronics; Energy and Power Engineering; Engineering/Technology; Engineering-Related Technologies; Mechanical Engineering; Physical Sciences and Math.

Award: Scholarship for use in freshman year; not renewable. *Number:* 1–60. *Amount:* $500.

Eligibility Requirements: Applicant must be high school student; planning to enroll or expecting to enroll full or part-time at a four-year institution or university and resident of West Virginia. Applicant must have 3.0 GPA or higher. Available to U.S. citizens.

Application Requirements: Application, essay, resume, references, test scores. *Deadline:* February 7.

Contact: Teah Bayless, Program Manager
Robert H. Mollohan Family Charitable Foundation, Inc.
1000 Technology Drive, Suite 2000
Fairmont, WV 26554
Phone: 304-333-2251
Fax: 304-333-3900
E-mail: tmbayless@wvhtf.org

ROCKY MOUNTAIN ELK FOUNDATION http://www.rmef.org

WILDLIFE LEADERSHIP AWARDS

The Rocky Mountain Elk Foundation's (RMEF) Wildlife Leadership Awards program was established in 1990 to "recognize, encourage and promote leadership among future wildlife management professionals." RMEF Wildlife Leadership Awards will be presented to up to 10 undergraduate wildlife students. Each award carries a $2000 scholarship, and a one-year membership to the RMEF.

Academic Fields/Career Goals: Biology; Natural Resources.

Award: Scholarship for use in junior or senior years; not renewable. *Number:* 1–10. *Amount:* $2000.

Eligibility Requirements: Applicant must be enrolled or expecting to enroll full-time at a four-year institution or university and must have an interest in designated field specified by sponsor. Available to U.S. and Canadian citizens.

Application Requirements: Application, essay, references. *Deadline:* March 1.

Contact: Denise Wagner
Rocky Mountain Elk Foundation
PO Box 8249
Missoula, MT 59807-8249
Phone: 800-225-5355
Fax: 406-523-4581
E-mail: dwagner@rmef.org

SOCIETY FOR INTEGRATIVE AND COMPARATIVE BIOLOGY http://sicb.org/grants/hyman/

LIBBIE H. HYMAN MEMORIAL SCHOLARSHIP

Scholarship provides assistance to students to take courses or to carry on research on invertebrates at a maritime, freshwater, or terrestrial field station. For more information and/or an application to go Web site: http://www.sicb.org.

Academic Fields/Career Goals: Biology.

Award: Scholarship for use in senior, or graduate years; not renewable. *Number:* 1. *Amount:* $750.

Eligibility Requirements: Applicant must be enrolled or expecting to enroll full or part-time at a four-year institution or university. Available to U.S. and non-U.S. citizens.

Application Requirements: Application, essay, financial need analysis, references, transcript. *Deadline:* March 3.

Contact: Application available at Web site.

SOCIETY OF MEXICAN AMERICAN ENGINEERS AND SCIENTISTS http://www.maes-natl.org

GRE AND GRADUATE APPLICATIONS WAIVER

• *See page 72*

SOCIETY OF TOXICOLOGY http://www.toxicology.org

MINORITY UNDERGRADUATE STUDENT AWARDS

Travel funds are provided for members of groups underrepresented in the sciences to attend a special program at the Society of Toxicology Annual Meeting. Must have a 3.0 GPA. The deadline is October 9.

Academic Fields/Career Goals: Biology; Health and Medical Sciences.

Award: Grant for use in freshman, sophomore, junior, or senior years; not renewable. *Number:* 20–50. *Amount:* $1000–$1500.

Eligibility Requirements: Applicant must be American Indian/Alaska Native, Black (non-Hispanic), or Hispanic and enrolled or expecting to enroll full-time at a two-year or four-year institution or university. Applicant must have 3.0 GPA or higher. Available to U.S. citizens.

Application Requirements: Application, essay, references, transcript. *Deadline:* October 9.

Contact: Nichelle Sankey, Program Coordinator
Society of Toxicology
1821 Michael Faraday Drive, Suite 300
Reston, VA 20190
Phone: 703-438-3115
Fax: 703-438-3113
E-mail: nichelle@toxicology.org

SOIL AND WATER CONSERVATION SOCIETY-NEW JERSEY CHAPTER http://www.geocities.com/njswcs

EDWARD R. HALL SCHOLARSHIP

• *See page 55*

SOUTHWEST STUDENT SERVICES CORPORATION http://www.sssc.com

ANNE LINDEMAN MEMORIAL SCHOLARSHIP

Three $1,000 scholarships are awarded annually to undergraduate students of junior or senior standing who are pursuing a program of study in Education, Social Sciences, or the Health Sciences, at designated Arizona institutions.

Southwest Student Services Corporation (continued)

Academic Fields/Career Goals: Biology; Dental Health/Services; Education; Food Science/Nutrition; Health and Medical Sciences; Nursing; Social Sciences; Social Services; Special Education; Therapy/Rehabilitation.

Award: Scholarship for use in junior or senior years; not renewable. *Number:* 3. *Amount:* $1000.

Eligibility Requirements: Applicant must be enrolled or expecting to enroll full-time at a four-year institution or university and studying in Arizona. Applicant must have 2.5 GPA or higher. Available to U.S. and non-U.S. citizens.

Application Requirements: Application, essay, resume, references, transcript. *Deadline:* April 1.

Contact: Linda Walker, Community Outreach Representative
Southwest Student Services Corporation
PO Box 41595
Mesa, AZ 85274
Phone: 480-461-6566
Fax: 480-461-6595
E-mail: scholarships@sssc.com

TKE EDUCATIONAL FOUNDATION http://www.tkefoundation.org

CARROL C. HALL MEMORIAL SCHOLARSHIP

• *See page 72*

TURF AND ORNAMENTAL COMMUNICATION ASSOCIATION http://www.toca.org

TURF AND ORNAMENTAL COMMUNICATORS ASSOCIATION SCHOLARSHIP PROGRAM

One-time award for undergraduate students majoring or minoring in technical communications or a green industry field such as horticulture, plant sciences, botany, or agronomy. The applicant must demonstrate an interest in using this course of study in the field of communications. Minimum 3.0 GPA required in major area of study.

Academic Fields/Career Goals: Biology; Horticulture/Floriculture.

Award: Scholarship for use in sophomore, junior, or senior years; not renewable. *Number:* 2. *Amount:* $1000.

Eligibility Requirements: Applicant must be enrolled or expecting to enroll full-time at a two-year or four-year institution or university. Applicant must have 3.0 GPA or higher. Available to U.S. and non-U.S. citizens.

Application Requirements: Application, essay, portfolio, resume, references, transcript. *Deadline:* March 1.

Contact: Den Gardner, Executive Director
Turf and Ornamental Communication Association
120 West Main Street, Suite 200
PO Box 156
New Prague, MN 56071
Phone: 952-758-6340
Fax: 952-758-5813
E-mail: gard2@aol.com

UNITED NEGRO COLLEGE FUND http://www.uncf.org

CARGILL SCHOLARSHIP PROGRAM

• *See page 49*

EARL AND PATRICIA ARMSTRONG SCHOLARSHIP

Scholarship available for students majoring in pre-medicine, biology, or health at a UNCF member college or university. Minimum 3.0 GPA required. Prospective applicants should complete the Student Profile found at Web site: http://www.uncf.org.

Academic Fields/Career Goals: Biology; Health and Medical Sciences.

Award: Scholarship for use in freshman, sophomore, junior, or senior years; not renewable. *Amount:* up to $3000.

Eligibility Requirements: Applicant must be Black (non-Hispanic) and enrolled or expecting to enroll full-time at a four-year institution or university. Applicant must have 3.0 GPA or higher.

Application Requirements: Application. *Deadline:* Continuous.

Contact: Program Services Department
United Negro College Fund
8260 Willow Oaks Corporate Drive
Fairfax, VA 22031

HEINZ ENVIRONMENTAL FELLOWS PROGRAM

Scholarships for UNCF students from Pennsylvania interested in environmental careers. A paid summer internship is included in this award. Minimum 2.5 GPA required. Prospective applicants should complete the Student Profile found at Web site: http://www.uncf.org.

Academic Fields/Career Goals: Biology; Physical Sciences and Math.

Award: Scholarship for use in sophomore year; not renewable. *Amount:* $7500.

Eligibility Requirements: Applicant must be Black (non-Hispanic); enrolled or expecting to enroll at a four-year institution or university and resident of Pennsylvania. Applicant must have 2.5 GPA or higher. Available to U.S. citizens.

Application Requirements: Application, financial need analysis. *Deadline:* Continuous.

Contact: Program Services Department
United Negro College Fund
8260 Willow Oaks Corporate Drive
Fairfax, VA 22031

MERCK SCIENCE INITIATIVE

Scholarship for undergraduate juniors, graduate students, or postdoctoral fellows majoring in the life or physical sciences. 3.3 GPA required. Visit Web site at http://www.uncf.org/merck for details. Prospective applicants should complete the Student Profile found at Web site: http://www.uncf.org.

Academic Fields/Career Goals: Biology; Health and Medical Sciences; Physical Sciences and Math.

Award: Scholarship for use in junior, graduate, or postgraduate years; not renewable. *Number:* 37. *Amount:* up to $7000.

Eligibility Requirements: Applicant must be Black (non-Hispanic) and enrolled or expecting to enroll at a four-year institution or university. Available to U.S. citizens.

Application Requirements: Application, financial need analysis. *Deadline:* varies.

Contact: Program Services Department
United Negro College Fund
8260 Willow Oaks Corporate Drive
Fairfax, VA 22031

OSTINA AND HERMAN HARTFIELD SCHOLARSHIP

Award for a student with strong interest in the Biological Science field. Those enrolled in Nursing and Pharmacy may also apply. Please visit Web site for more information: http://www.uncf.org.

Academic Fields/Career Goals: Biology; Chemical Engineering; Nursing; Pharmacy.

Award: Scholarship for use in freshman, sophomore, junior, senior, or graduate years. *Number:* up to 1. *Amount:* up to $2500.

Eligibility Requirements: Applicant must be Black (non-Hispanic) and enrolled or expecting to enroll at a four-year institution or university. Applicant must have 3.0 GPA or higher.

Application Requirements: Application, financial need analysis, FAFSA, SAR. *Deadline:* varies.

Contact: Program Services Department
United Negro College Fund
8260 Willow Oaks Corporate Drive
Fairfax, VA 22031

PECO ENERGY SCHOLARSHIP

• *See page 50*

UNCF/PFIZER CORPORATE SCHOLARS PROGRAM

• *See page 64*

WYETH SCHOLARSHIP

Must be nominated by financial aid director at the UNCF college. Scholarships for students with 3.0 GPA pursuing science-based or health-related careers. Must be New Jersey resident. Please visit Web site for more information: http://www.uncf.org.

Academic Fields/Career Goals: Biology; Business/Consumer Services; Health and Medical Sciences; Pharmacy; Physical Sciences and Math.

Award: Scholarship for use in freshman, sophomore, junior, or senior years; not renewable. *Amount:* $5000.

Eligibility Requirements: Applicant must be Black (non-Hispanic); enrolled or expecting to enroll at a four-year institution or university and resident of New Jersey. Applicant must have 3.0 GPA or higher. Available to U.S. citizens.

Application Requirements: Application, financial need analysis. *Deadline:* February 6.

Contact: Program Services Department
United Negro College Fund
8260 Willow Oaks Corporate Drive
Fairfax, VA 22031

VIRGINIA BUSINESS AND PROFESSIONAL WOMEN'S FOUNDATION http://www.bpwva.advocate.net/foundation.htm

WOMEN IN SCIENCE AND TECHNOLOGY SCHOLARSHIP

One-time award offered to women completing a bachelor's, master's or doctoral degree within two years who are majoring in actuarial science, biology, bio-engineering, chemistry, computer science, dentistry, engineering, mathematics, medicine, physics or similar field. The award may be used for tuition, fees, books, transportation, living expenses, or dependent care. Must be a Virginia resident studying in Virginia.

Academic Fields/Career Goals: Biology; Computer Science/Data Processing; Dental Health/Services; Engineering/Technology; Health and Medical Sciences; Physical Sciences and Math; Science, Technology, and Society.

Award: Scholarship for use in junior, senior, graduate, or postgraduate years; not renewable. *Number:* 1–5. *Amount:* $500–$1000.

Eligibility Requirements: Applicant must be age 18; enrolled or expecting to enroll full or part-time at a four-year institution or university; female; resident of Virginia and studying in Virginia. Available to U.S. citizens.

Application Requirements: Application, essay, financial need analysis, references, transcript. *Deadline:* April 1.

Contact: Scholarship Chair
Virginia Business and Professional Women's Foundation
PO Box 4842
McLean, VA 22103-4842
E-mail: bpwva@advocate.net

WILSON ORNITHOLOGICAL SOCIETY http://www.ummz.lsa.umich.edu/birds/wosawards.html

GEORGE A. HALL / HAROLD F. MAYFIELD AWARD

• *See page 64*

PAUL A. STEWART AWARDS

• *See page 64*

BUSINESS/CONSUMER SERVICES

AMERICAN CONGRESS ON SURVEYING AND MAPPING http://www.acsm.net

TRI-STATE SURVEYING AND PHOTOGRAMMETRY KRIS M. KUNZE MEMORIAL SCHOLARSHIP

One-time award for students pursuing college-level courses in business administration or business management. Candidates, in order of priority, include professional land surveyors and certified photogrammetrists, land survey interns, and students enrolled in a two- or four-year program in surveying and mapping. Must be ACSM member.

Academic Fields/Career Goals: Business/Consumer Services.

Award: Scholarship for use in freshman, sophomore, junior, or senior years; not renewable. *Amount:* $1000.

Eligibility Requirements: Applicant must be enrolled or expecting to enroll full or part-time at a two-year or four-year institution. Applicant or parent of applicant must be member of American Congress on Surveying and Mapping.

Application Requirements: Application, essay, references, transcript. *Deadline:* December 1.

Contact: Scholarship Information
American Congress on Surveying and Mapping
6 Montgomery Village Avenue
Suite 403
Gaithersburg, MD 20879

AMERICAN FLORAL ENDOWMENT http://www.endowment.org

HAROLD F. WILKINS SCHOLARSHIP PROGRAM

One-time award to aid and encourage students majoring in business, floriculture and ornamental horticulture, to have a floriculture internship outside the U.S. and to aid students who wish to travel to a foreign country to study the floriculture industry (convention, symposium, independent travel programs).

Academic Fields/Career Goals: Business/Consumer Services; Horticulture/Floriculture.

Award: Scholarship for use in freshman, sophomore, junior, senior, graduate, or postgraduate years; not renewable. *Number:* 1–3. *Amount:* $1000–$7500.

Eligibility Requirements: Applicant must be enrolled or expecting to enroll full-time at a two-year or four-year institution or university. Applicant must have 2.5 GPA or higher. Available to U.S. citizens.

Application Requirements: Application, photo, references, transcript. *Deadline:* varies.

Contact: Steven F. Martinez, Executive Vice President
American Floral Endowment
11 Glen Ed Professional Park
Glen Carbon, IL 62034
Phone: 618-692-0045
Fax: 618-692-4045
E-mail: afe@endowment.org

MOSMILLER SCHOLAR PROGRAM

Award for undergraduate students majoring in business, floriculture, and ornamental horticulture. Ten to sixteen weeks of paid training with floral retailers, wholesalers, and allied trades, in addition to a $2000 grant upon satisfactory completion. Deadlines: March 1st for fall and winter training; November 1 for spring and summer training.

Academic Fields/Career Goals: Business/Consumer Services; Horticulture/Floriculture.

Award: Scholarship for use in freshman, sophomore, junior, or senior years; not renewable. *Number:* 7. *Amount:* $2000.

Eligibility Requirements: Applicant must be enrolled or expecting to enroll full-time at a two-year or four-year institution or university. Applicant must have 2.5 GPA or higher. Available to U.S. citizens.

Application Requirements: Application, photo, references, transcript. *Deadline:* varies.

Contact: Steve F. Martinez, Executive Vice President
American Floral Endowment
11 Glen-Ed Professional Park
Glen Carbon, IL 62034
Phone: 618-692-0045
Fax: 618-692-4045
E-mail: afe@endowment.org

VICTOR AND MARGARET BALL PROGRAM

Award for undergraduate students majoring in business, floriculture, and ornamental horticulture. A paid training experience for students who are

American Floral Endowment (continued)

interested in a "production related" career (growing), and up to a $6000 grant upon satisfactory completion of six months of training. Deadlines: March 1 for fall/winter training; November 1 for spring/summer training.

Academic Fields/Career Goals: Business/Consumer Services; Horticulture/Floriculture.

Award: Scholarship for use in freshman, sophomore, junior, or senior years; not renewable. *Number:* 20. *Amount:* $1500–$6000.

Eligibility Requirements: Applicant must be enrolled or expecting to enroll full-time at a two-year or four-year institution or university. Applicant must have 2.5 GPA or higher. Available to U.S. citizens.

Application Requirements: Application, photo, references, transcript.

Contact: Steve F. Martinez, Executive Vice President
American Floral Endowment
11 Glen-Ed Professional Park
Glen Carbon, IL 62034
Phone: 618-692-0045
Fax: 618-692-4045
E-mail: afe@endowment.org

AMERICAN INDIAN SCIENCE AND ENGINEERING SOCIETY http://www.aises.org

A.T. ANDERSON MEMORIAL SCHOLARSHIP

• *See page 65*

BURLINGTON NORTHERN SANTA FE FOUNDATION SCHOLARSHIP

• *See page 65*

AMERICAN LEGION, DEPARTMENT OF KANSAS

CHARLES W. AND ANNETTE HILL SCHOLARSHIP

Available to high school seniors, college level freshmen, or sophomores who are in need of educational assistance, and are enrolled or intend to enroll in an approved school located in the state of Kansas. The applicant must be descendant of a member of the Kansas American Legion and/or Legion Auxiliary. Minimum 3.0 GPA required. Consideration given to those majoring in science, engineering, or business administration.

Academic Fields/Career Goals: Business/Consumer Services; Engineering/Technology; Physical Sciences and Math.

Award: Scholarship for use in freshman or sophomore years; not renewable. *Number:* 1. *Amount:* $1000.

Eligibility Requirements: Applicant must be enrolled or expecting to enroll at a two-year or four-year or technical institution or university and studying in Kansas. Applicant or parent of applicant must be member of American Legion or Auxiliary. Applicant must have 3.0 GPA or higher. Available to U.S. citizens. Applicant or parent must meet one or more of the following requirements: general military experience; retired from active duty; disabled or killed as a result of military service; prisoner of war; or missing in action.

Application Requirements: Application, financial need analysis, photo, references, transcript. *Deadline:* February 15.

Contact: Scholarship Administrator
American Legion, Department of Kansas
1314 Southwest Topeka Boulevard
Topeka, KS 66612-1886

AMERICAN PUBLIC TRANSPORTATION FOUNDATION http://www.apta.com

DAN REICHARD SCHOLARSHIP

Scholarship for study towards a career in the business administration/management area of the transit industry. Must be sponsored by APTA member organization and complete internship with APTA member organization. Minimum GPA of 3.0 required.

Academic Fields/Career Goals: Business/Consumer Services; Transportation.

Award: Scholarship for use in junior, senior, graduate, or postgraduate years; renewable. *Number:* 1. *Amount:* $2500.

Eligibility Requirements: Applicant must be enrolled or expecting to enroll full-time at a four-year institution or university. Applicant must have 3.0 GPA or higher. Available to U.S. and Canadian citizens.

Application Requirements: Application, essay, financial need analysis, references, transcript. *Deadline:* June 12.

Contact: Pamela Boswell, Vice President of Program Management
American Public Transportation Foundation
1666 K Street, NW
Washington, DC 20006-1215
Phone: 202-496-4803
Fax: 202-496-2323
E-mail: pboswell@apta.com

AMERICAN WELDING SOCIETY http://www.aws.org/foundation

JAMES A. TURNER, JR. MEMORIAL SCHOLARSHIP

Award for a full-time student pursuing minimum four-year bachelor's degree in business that will lead to a management career in welding store operations or a welding distributorship. Applicant must be working in this field at least 10 hours per week. Submit verification of employment, a copy of proposed curriculum, and acceptance letter.

Academic Fields/Career Goals: Business/Consumer Services.

Award: Scholarship for use in sophomore, junior, or senior years; not renewable. *Number:* 1. *Amount:* $3000.

Eligibility Requirements: Applicant must be enrolled or expecting to enroll full-time at a four-year institution. Available to U.S. citizens.

Application Requirements: Application, autobiography, financial need analysis, references, transcript. *Deadline:* January 15.

Contact: Ms. Neida Herrera, Development Coordinator
American Welding Society
550 Northwest Le Jeune Road
Miami, FL 33126
Phone: 800-443-9353 Ext. 461
Fax: 305-443-7559
E-mail: neida@aws.org

AMERICAN WHOLESALE MARKETERS ASSOCIATION http://www.awmanet.org

RAY FOLEY MEMORIAL YOUTH EDUCATION FOUNDATION SCHOLARSHIP

Scholarships available to an employee of an AWMA wholesaler member company or the immediate family member of an employee of an AWMA wholesaler member company (spouse, son, or daughter only). Applicant must be enrolled full time in an undergraduate or graduate business program and demonstrate sufficient interest in a career in the candy/tobacco/convenience products wholesale distribution industry. For more information, visit the Web site: http://www.awmanet.org/edu/edu-schol.html

Academic Fields/Career Goals: Business/Consumer Services.

Award: Scholarship for use in freshman, sophomore, junior, senior, or graduate years; not renewable. *Number:* 2. *Amount:* $5000.

Eligibility Requirements: Applicant must be enrolled or expecting to enroll full-time at a two-year or four-year institution or university. Available to U.S. citizens.

Application Requirements: Application. *Deadline:* May 7.

Contact: Application available at Web site.

APICS EDUCATIONAL AND RESEARCH FOUNDATION, INC. http://www.apics.org

DONALD W. FOGARTY INTERNATIONAL STUDENT PAPER COMPETITION

Annual competition on topics pertaining to resource management only. Must be original work of one or more authors. May submit one paper only. Must be in English. Open to full- and part-time undergraduate and graduate students. High school students ineligible. All queries are directed to Web site. Other queries must submit e-mail address and SASE.

Academic Fields/Career Goals: Business/Consumer Services; Natural Resources.

Award: Prize for use in freshman, sophomore, junior, senior, or graduate years; not renewable. *Number:* 58. *Amount:* $150–$1000.

Eligibility Requirements: Applicant must be enrolled or expecting to enroll full or part-time at a four-year institution or university. Available to U.S. and non-U.S. citizens.

Application Requirements: Application, applicant must enter a contest, essay, self-addressed stamped envelope. *Deadline:* May 15.

Contact: J . Chisholm, Board of Directors
APICS Educational and Research Foundation, Inc.
5301 Shawnee Road
Alexandria, VA 22312-2317
E-mail: cjames938@aol.com

ARRL FOUNDATION, INC.

http://www.arrl.org/arrlf/scholgen.html

WILLIAM R. GOLDFARB MEMORIAL SCHOLARSHIP

Award for baccalaureate or post-graduate study in business, computers, medical or nursing, engineering, or sciences. Must be a licensed amateur radio operator.

Academic Fields/Career Goals: Business/Consumer Services; Computer Science/Data Processing; Engineering/Technology; Health and Medical Sciences; Natural Sciences; Nursing.

Award: Scholarship for use in freshman, sophomore, junior, senior, or graduate years; not renewable. *Number:* 1. *Amount:* up to $10,000.

Eligibility Requirements: Applicant must be enrolled or expecting to enroll full-time at a four-year institution or university and must have an interest in amateur radio.

Application Requirements: Application, financial need analysis, transcript. *Deadline:* February 1.

Contact: Mary Hobart, Foundation Secretary
ARRL Foundation, Inc.
225 Main Street
Newington, CT 06111-4845
Phone: 860-594-0397
E-mail: mhobart@arrl.org

ASIAN PACIFIC AMERICAN HERITAGE COUNCIL

http://www.apahc.org

ASIAN PACIFIC AMERICAN HERITAGE COUNCIL SCHOLARSHIP

Scholarships for students studying in the fields of business, education, finance, law, public service/administration, or science/engineering. Open to all children of Asian-Pacific Americans who are seniors in high school and for students matriculating at a college or university.

Academic Fields/Career Goals: Business/Consumer Services; Education; Engineering/Technology; Law/Legal Services; Public Health.

Award: Scholarship for use in freshman, sophomore, junior, or senior years; not renewable. *Number:* 10–20. *Amount:* $1000.

Eligibility Requirements: Applicant must be Asian/Pacific Islander and enrolled or expecting to enroll full-time at a four-year institution or university. Available to U.S. citizens.

Application Requirements: Application, essay, references, test scores, transcript. *Deadline:* March 15.

Contact: Mr. Mark Au, Chairman, APAHC Scholarship Program
Asian Pacific American Heritage Council
8800 Fox Hills Trail
Potomac, MD 20854-4211
E-mail: mlau2@aol.com

ASSOCIATION FOR FINANCIAL PROFESSIONALS

http://www.AFPonline.org

ASSOCIATION FOR FINANCIAL PROFESSIONALS SCHOLAR'S AWARD

The AFP Scholar's Award is a merit competition based on an original paper written by a candidate (student) and submitted by a sponsor (faculty member of student's choosing). Papers submitted must have been written by the candidate between September and June on a subject related to treasury or financial management. Seven copies must be submitted with a single cover sheet. Only open to AFP student members or students enrolled in a corporate treasury management (CTM) program. Membership information is found on Web site: http://www.afponline.org. Deadline is June 30.

Academic Fields/Career Goals: Business/Consumer Services.

Award: Scholarship for use in senior, or graduate years; not renewable. *Number:* 1. *Amount:* $5000.

Eligibility Requirements: Applicant must be enrolled or expecting to enroll full or part-time at a four-year institution or university. Available to U.S. citizens.

Application Requirements: Transcript, seven copies of paper. *Deadline:* June 30.

Contact: Robin Kite, Manager of Student Membership and Regional Service
Association for Financial Professionals
7315 Wisconsin Avenue, Suite 600 West
Bethesda, MD 20814-3211
Phone: 301-907-2862
Fax: 301-907-2864
E-mail: student@afponline.org

ASSOCIATION OF LATINO PROFESSIONALS IN FINANCE AND ACCOUNTING

http://www.alpfa.org

HSF-ALPFA SCHOLARSHIPS

• *See page 38*

CASUALTY ACTUARIAL SOCIETY/SOCIETY OF ACTUARIES JOINT COMMITTEE ON MINORITY RECRUITING

http://www.BeAnActuary.org/minority/scholarship.cfm

ACTUARIAL SCHOLARSHIPS FOR MINORITY STUDENTS

Award for underrepresented minority students planning careers in actuarial science or mathematics. Applicants should have taken the ACT Assessment or the SAT. Number and amount of awards vary with merit and financial need. Must be a U.S. citizen or permanent resident. All scholarship information including application is available online. Do not send award inquiries to address.

Academic Fields/Career Goals: Business/Consumer Services.

Award: Scholarship for use in freshman, sophomore, junior, senior, or graduate years; not renewable. *Number:* 20–40. *Amount:* $500–$3000.

Eligibility Requirements: Applicant must be American Indian/Alaska Native, Black (non-Hispanic), or Hispanic and enrolled or expecting to enroll full or part-time at a two-year or four-year institution or university. Available to U.S. citizens.

Application Requirements: Application, financial need analysis, references, test scores, transcript. *Deadline:* May 1.

Contact: Minority Scholarship Coordinator
Casualty Actuarial Society/Society of Actuaries Joint Committee on Minority Recruiting
Society of Actuaries, 475 North Martingale Road, Suite 800
Schaumburg, IL 60173-2226
Phone: 847-706-3500

CATCHING THE DREAM

MATH, ENGINEERING, SCIENCE, BUSINESS, EDUCATION, COMPUTERS SCHOLARSHIPS

Renewable scholarships for Native-American students planning to study math, engineering, science, business, education, and computers, or presently studying in these fields. Study of social science, humanities and liberal arts also funded. Scholarships are awarded on merit and on the basis of likelihood of recipient improving the lives of Native American people. Deadlines are March 15, April 15, and September 15. Scholarships are available nationwide.

Academic Fields/Career Goals: Business/Consumer Services; Computer Science/Data Processing; Education; Engineering/Technology; Humanities; Physical Sciences and Math; Science, Technology, and Society; Social Sciences.

Award: Scholarship for use in freshman, sophomore, junior, senior, graduate, or postgraduate years; renewable. *Number:* 180. *Amount:* $500–$5000.

Eligibility Requirements: Applicant must be American Indian/Alaska Native and enrolled or expecting to enroll full-time at a two-year or four-year institution or university. Applicant must have 3.0 GPA or higher. Available to U.S. citizens.

Catching the Dream (continued)

Application Requirements: Application, essay, financial need analysis, photo, references, test scores, transcript, certificate of Indian blood. *Deadline:* varies.

Contact: Mary Foster, Recruiter
Catching the Dream
8200 Mountain Road, NE
Suite 203
Albuquerque, NM 87110
Phone: 505-262-2351
Fax: 505-262-0534
E-mail: nscholarsh@aol.com

NATIVE AMERICAN LEADERSHIP IN EDUCATION (NALE)

Renewable scholarships available for Native-American and Alaska Native students. Must be at least one-quarter Native-American from a federally recognized, state recognized, or terminated tribe. Must be U.S. citizen. Must demonstrate high academic achievement, depth of character, leadership, seriousness of purpose, and service orientation. Application deadlines are March 15, April 15, and September 15.

Academic Fields/Career Goals: Business/Consumer Services; Education; Humanities; Physical Sciences and Math; Science, Technology, and Society.

Award: Scholarship for use in freshman, sophomore, junior, or senior years; renewable. *Number:* up to 30. *Amount:* $500–$5000.

Eligibility Requirements: Applicant must be American Indian/Alaska Native and enrolled or expecting to enroll full-time at a four-year institution or university. Available to U.S. citizens.

Application Requirements: Application, essay, references, transcript. *Deadline:* varies.

Contact: Recruitment Office
Catching the Dream
8200 Mountain Road, NE, Suite 203
Albuquerque, NM 87110
Phone: 505-262-2351
Fax: 505-262-0534
E-mail: nscholarsh@aol.com

TRIBAL BUSINESS MANAGEMENT PROGRAM (TBM)

• *See page 38*

CENTER FOR SCHOLARSHIP ADMINISTRATION http://www.scholarshipprograms.org

BANK OF AMERICA ADA ABILITIES SCHOLARSHIP

• *See page 38*

CENTRAL INTELLIGENCE AGENCY http://www.cia.gov

CENTRAL INTELLIGENCE AGENCY UNDERGRADUATE SCHOLARSHIP PROGRAM

• *See page 39*

CHARLOTTE OBSERVER

CHARLOTTE OBSERVER MINORITY SCHOLARSHIPS

Scholarship is available for minority high school students who are interested in the newspaper business, either in the newsroom or business operations. Applicants must send in samples of their work along with the application. Deadline for submitting application is in December. Must be resident of North Carolina or South Carolina.

Academic Fields/Career Goals: Business/Consumer Services; Journalism.

Award: Scholarship for use in freshman year; not renewable. *Number:* 2. *Amount:* $1000.

Eligibility Requirements: Applicant must be American Indian/Alaska Native, Asian/Pacific Islander, Black (non-Hispanic), or Hispanic; high school student; planning to enroll or expecting to enroll full-time at a four-year institution or university and resident of North Carolina or South Carolina. Available to U.S. citizens.

Application Requirements: Application, essay, interview, resume, references, transcript. *Deadline:* December 27.

Contact: Zaira Goodman, Human Resources Manager
Charlotte Observer
600 South Tryon Street
Charlotte, NC 28202
Phone: 704-358-5715
E-mail: zgoodman@charlotteobserver.com

CIRI FOUNDATION http://www.ciri.com/tcf

CARL H. MARRS SCHOLARSHIP FUND

• *See page 39*

KIRBY MCDONALD EDUCATION ENDOWMENT SCHOLARSHIP FUND

To encourage achievement and general scholarships in culinary arts (preferred), business administration, and engineering. Applicant must be Alaska Native student. For more details see Web site: http://www.ciri.com/tcf.

Academic Fields/Career Goals: Business/Consumer Services; Culinary Arts; Engineering/Technology.

Award: Scholarship for use in freshman, sophomore, junior, senior, or graduate years; not renewable. *Number:* varies. *Amount:* varies.

Eligibility Requirements: Applicant must be enrolled or expecting to enroll full-time at a two-year or four-year or technical institution or university.

Application Requirements: Application, essay, references, transcript, proof of eligibility, birth certificate or adoption decree. *Deadline:* June 1.

Contact: CIRI Foundation
2600 Cordova Street, Suite 206
Anchorage, AK 99503
Phone: 907-263-5582
Fax: 907-263-5588
E-mail: tcf@ciri.com

COMMUNITY FOUNDATION FOR PALM BEACH AND MARTIN COUNTIES, INC. http://www.yourcommunityfoundation.org

BANK OF AMERICA MINORITY SCHOLARSHIP

Student member of minority community attending Palm Beach County public or private high school intending to major in business. Must have "C" average or better, financial need, be enrolled in an accredited four year college or university.

Academic Fields/Career Goals: Business/Consumer Services.

Award: Scholarship for use in freshman year; not renewable. *Number:* 1. *Amount:* $750–$2500.

Eligibility Requirements: Applicant must be American Indian/Alaska Native, Asian/Pacific Islander, Black (non-Hispanic), or Hispanic; high school student; planning to enroll or expecting to enroll full-time at a two-year or four-year institution or university and resident of Florida. Available to U.S. citizens.

Application Requirements: Application, financial need analysis, test scores, transcript. *Deadline:* March 1.

Contact: Carolyn Jenco, Grants Manager/Scholarship Coordinator
Community Foundation for Palm Beach and Martin Counties, Inc.
700 South Dixie Highway
Suite 200
West Palm Beach, FL 33401

MABRY M. NOXON SCHOLARSHIP FUND

• *See page 75*

THEODORE SATTER MEMORIAL SCHOLARSHIP

Scholarship awarded to Palm Beach or Martin County graduating high school senior, public or private, who plans on continuing his or her education. Applicant must be majoring in business, banking, or finance. Deadline is March 1. Applications are available online http://www.yourcommunityfoundation.org.

Academic Fields/Career Goals: Business/Consumer Services.

Award: Scholarship for use in freshman year; not renewable. *Number:* varies. *Amount:* varies.

Eligibility Requirements: Applicant must be high school student; planning to enroll or expecting to enroll at a four-year institution or university and resident of Florida. Available to U.S. citizens.

Application Requirements: Application, financial need analysis. *Deadline:* March 1.

Contact: Carolyn Jenco, Grants Manager/Scholarship Coordinator
Community Foundation for Palm Beach and Martin Counties, Inc.
700 South Dixie Highway
Suite 200
West Palm Beach, FL 33401

CUBAN AMERICAN NATIONAL FOUNDATION

MAS FAMILY SCHOLARSHIPS

Graduate and undergraduate scholarships in the fields of engineering, business, international relations, economics, communications, and journalism. Applicants must be Cuban-American and have graduated in the top 10% of high school class or have minimum 3.5 college GPA. Selection based on need, academic performance, leadership. Those who have already received awards and maintained high level of performance are given preference over new applicants.

Academic Fields/Career Goals: Business/Consumer Services; Chemical Engineering; Communications; Economics; Electrical Engineering/Electronics; Engineering/Technology; Engineering-Related Technologies; Journalism; Mechanical Engineering; Political Science.

Award: Scholarship for use in freshman, sophomore, junior, or senior years; renewable. *Number:* 10–15. *Amount:* $1000–$10,000.

Eligibility Requirements: Applicant must be of Latin American/Caribbean heritage; enrolled or expecting to enroll full-time at a two-year or four-year institution or university and must have an interest in leadership. Applicant must have 3.5 GPA or higher. Available to U.S. citizens.

Application Requirements: Application, autobiography, essay, financial need analysis, references, test scores, transcript. *Deadline:* March 31.

Contact: Director
Cuban American National Foundation
1312 Southwest 27th Avenue, 3rd Floor
Miami, FL 33145
Phone: 305-592-7768
Fax: 305-592-7889

DECA (DISTRIBUTIVE EDUCATION CLUBS OF AMERICA) http://www.deca.org

HARRY A. APPLEGATE SCHOLARSHIP

Available to current DECA members for undergraduate or graduate study. Must major in marketing education, merchandising, and/or management. Nonrenewable award for high school students based on DECA activities, grades, and need. Submit application to state office by state application deadline. National office must receive applications by the second Monday in March.

Academic Fields/Career Goals: Business/Consumer Services; Education; Food Service/Hospitality.

Award: Scholarship for use in freshman, sophomore, junior, senior, or graduate years; not renewable. *Number:* 30–100. *Amount:* $1000–$1500.

Eligibility Requirements: Applicant must be high school student; planning to enroll or expecting to enroll full or part-time at a two-year or four-year institution or university and must have an interest in leadership. Applicant or parent of applicant must be member of Distribution Ed Club or Future Business Leaders of America. Applicant must have 2.5 GPA or higher. Available to U.S. and Canadian citizens.

Application Requirements: Application, references, test scores, transcript. *Deadline:* varies.

Contact: Kathy Onion, Marketing Specialist
DECA (Distributive Education Clubs of America)
1908 Association Drive
Reston, VA 20191-4013
Phone: 703-860-5000 Ext. 248
Fax: 703-860-4013
E-mail: kathy_onion@deca.org

DESIGN FIRM MANAGEMENT EDUCATION FOUNDATION, INC.

A/E PRONET SCHOLARSHIP

• *See page 76*

FAMILY, CAREER AND COMMUNITY LEADERS OF AMERICA-TEXAS ASSOCIATION http://www.texasfccla.org

FCCLA REGIONAL SCHOLARSHIPS

Five scholarships will be awarded annually to applicants who have been members of the Texas FCCLA. Theme is required on how involvement in FCCLA or family and consumer sciences has prepared you for your future. Applicants should visit the Web site (http://www.texasfccla.org) or write to Texas FCCLA for complete information, submission guidelines, and restrictions.

Academic Fields/Career Goals: Business/Consumer Services; Home Economics.

Award: Scholarship for use in freshman year; not renewable. *Number:* 10. *Amount:* $1000.

Eligibility Requirements: Applicant must be high school student; planning to enroll or expecting to enroll full-time at a four-year institution or university; resident of Texas and studying in Texas. Applicant or parent of applicant must be member of Family, Career and Community Leaders of America. Available to U.S. citizens.

Application Requirements: Application, essay, references, test scores, transcript. *Deadline:* March 1.

Contact: FCCLA Staff
Family, Career and Community Leaders of America-Texas Association
3530 Bee Caves Road, #101
Austin, TX 78746-9616
Phone: 512-306-0099
Fax: 512-306-0041
E-mail: fccla@texasfccla.org

FCCLA TEXAS FARM BUREAU SCHOLARSHIP

Applicant must have been a regional or state FCCLA officer and must be planning to teach home economics/family and consumer sciences. Applicants should visit the Web site (http://www.texasfccla.org) or write to Texas FCCLA for complete information, submission guidelines, and restrictions. Must be a Texas resident and enroll in a Texas institution.

Academic Fields/Career Goals: Business/Consumer Services; Education; Home Economics.

Award: Scholarship for use in freshman year; not renewable. *Number:* 1. *Amount:* $1000.

Eligibility Requirements: Applicant must be high school student; planning to enroll or expecting to enroll full-time at a four-year institution or university; resident of Texas and studying in Texas. Applicant or parent of applicant must be member of Family, Career and Community Leaders of America. Available to U.S. citizens.

Application Requirements: Application, autobiography, essay, references, test scores, transcript. *Deadline:* March 1.

Contact: FCCLA Staff
Family, Career and Community Leaders of America-Texas Association
3530 Bee Caves Road, #101
Austin, TX 78746-9616
Phone: 512-306-0099
Fax: 512-306-0041
E-mail: fccla@texasfccla.org

FIRST–FLORICULTURE INDUSTRY RESEARCH AND SCHOLARSHIP TRUST http://www.firstinfloriculture.org

HAROLD BETTINGER MEMORIAL SCHOLARSHIP

• *See page 53*

FLORIDA BANKERS EDUCATIONAL FOUNDATION http://www.floridabankers.com

FLORIDA BANKERS EDUCATIONAL FOUNDATION SCHOLARSHIP/LOAN

Program has assisted over 2000 students since 1956 and is designed to support the education of future and/or current Florida bankers. Must be enrolled for at least 12 credit hours per year at FBEF participating Florida university. Loan to be paid back if degree is not obtained. Must also work for one year in a Florida bank upon graduation for loan to be forgiven. Award is up to $4000 for undergraduates and up to $5000 for graduate study.

Academic Fields/Career Goals: Business/Consumer Services.

Award: Forgivable loan for use in junior, senior, or graduate years; not renewable. *Number:* 10–50. *Amount:* $750–$5000.

Eligibility Requirements: Applicant must be enrolled or expecting to enroll full or part-time at a four-year institution; resident of Florida; studying in Florida and must have an interest in leadership. Applicant or parent of applicant must have employment or volunteer experience in banking. Applicant must have 2.5 GPA or higher. Available to U.S. citizens.

Application Requirements: Application, driver's license, essay, interview, resume, references, transcript, credit check (for loan). *Deadline:* varies.

Contact: Ms. Letty Newton, Director
Florida Bankers Educational Foundation
PO Box 1360
Tallahassee, FL 32302-1360
Phone: 850-224-2265
Fax: 850-224-2423
E-mail: lnewton@flbankers.net

FUKUNAGA SCHOLARSHIP FOUNDATION http://www.servco.com

FUKUNAGA SCHOLARSHIP FOUNDATION

Renewable scholarships available only to Hawaii residents pursuing a business degree at the undergraduate level at an accredited institution. Minimum 3.0 GPA required.

Academic Fields/Career Goals: Business/Consumer Services.

Award: Scholarship for use in freshman, sophomore, junior, or senior years; renewable. *Number:* 12–15. *Amount:* $2500.

Eligibility Requirements: Applicant must be enrolled or expecting to enroll full-time at a four-year institution or university and resident of Hawaii. Applicant must have 3.0 GPA or higher. Available to U.S. citizens.

Application Requirements: Application, financial need analysis, references, test scores, transcript. *Deadline:* February 15.

Contact: Sandy Wong, Administrator
Fukunaga Scholarship Foundation
PO Box 2788
Honolulu, HI 96803-2788
Phone: 808-564-1386
Fax: 808-523-3937
E-mail: sandyw@servco.com

GOLDEN KEY INTERNATIONAL HONOUR SOCIETY http://www.goldenkey.org

BUSINESS ACHIEVEMENT AWARD

Applicants will be asked to respond to a problem posed by an honorary member within the discipline. The response will be in the form of a professional business report. One winner will receive a $1000 award. The second place applicant will receive $750 and the third place applicant will receive $500. See Web site for more information: http://goldenkey.gsu.edu.

Academic Fields/Career Goals: Business/Consumer Services.

Award: Prize for use in junior, senior, graduate, or postgraduate years; not renewable. *Number:* 3. *Amount:* $500–$1000.

Eligibility Requirements: Applicant must be enrolled or expecting to enroll full or part-time at an institution or university.

Application Requirements: Application, applicant must enter a contest, essay, references, transcript, business-related report. *Deadline:* March 1.

Contact: Member Services
Golden Key International Honour Society
621 North Avenue, NE
Suite C-100
Atlanta, GA 30308
Phone: 404-377-2400
Fax: 678-420-6757
E-mail: scholarships@goldenkey.org

GOVERNMENT FINANCE OFFICERS ASSOCIATION http://www.GFOA.org

FRANK L. GREATHOUSE GOVERNMENT ACCOUNTING SCHOLARSHIP

One to two scholarships awarded to senior undergraduate students enrolled full-time preparing for a career in state or local government finance. Submit resume. One-time award of $3500.

Academic Fields/Career Goals: Business/Consumer Services.

Award: Scholarship for use in senior year; not renewable. *Number:* 1–2. *Amount:* $3500.

Eligibility Requirements: Applicant must be enrolled or expecting to enroll full-time at a two-year or four-year or technical institution or university and must have an interest in designated field specified by sponsor. Available to U.S. and Canadian citizens.

Application Requirements: Application, essay, resume, references, transcript. *Deadline:* varies.

Contact: Jake Lorentz, Assistant Director
Government Finance Officers Association
Scholarship Committee
203 North LaSalle Street, Suite 2700
Chicago, IL 60601
Phone: 312-977-9700 Ext. 267
Fax: 312-977-4806
E-mail: jlorentz@gfoa.org

GEORGE A. NIELSEN PUBLIC INVESTOR SCHOLARSHIP

Award for employee of local government or other public entity who is enrolled or plans to enroll in an undergraduate or graduate program in public administration, finance, business administration, or a related field.

Academic Fields/Career Goals: Business/Consumer Services.

Award: Scholarship for use in freshman, sophomore, junior, senior, or graduate years; not renewable. *Number:* 1–2. *Amount:* $2500–$5000.

Eligibility Requirements: Applicant must be enrolled or expecting to enroll full or part-time at a four-year institution or university. Applicant or parent of applicant must have employment or volunteer experience in designated career field. Available to U.S. and Canadian citizens.

Application Requirements: Application, essay, resume, references, transcript. *Deadline:* varies.

Contact: Jake Lorentz, Assistant Director
Government Finance Officers Association
Scholarship Committee
203 North LaSalle Street, Suite 2700
Chicago, IL 60601
Phone: 312-977-9700 Ext. 267
Fax: 312-977-4806
E-mail: jlorentz@gfoa.org

MINORITIES IN GOVERNMENT FINANCE SCHOLARSHIP

• *See page 41*

GOVERNOR'S OFFICE

GOVERNOR'S OPPORTUNITY SCHOLARSHIP

A $5,000 scholarship will be awarded in each of the following categories: business, education, nursing, health care, law enforcement/public service, and science. Must be applied and will be mailed directly to a related academic or work program in an accredited California institution. Scholarship winners must attend the Governor's conference for Women to receive the award. Minimum 3.3 GPA. Contact for further information and application deadline.

Academic Fields/Career Goals: Business/Consumer Services; Education; Health and Medical Sciences; Law Enforcement/Police Administration; Nursing; Political Science; Science, Technology, and Society.

Award: Scholarship for use in junior, senior, graduate, or postgraduate years; not renewable. *Number:* 6. *Amount:* $5000.

Eligibility Requirements: Applicant must be enrolled or expecting to enroll full or part-time at a two-year or four-year or technical institution or university; female; resident of California and studying in California. Available to U.S. citizens.

Application Requirements: Application, applicant must enter a contest, autobiography, essay, references, self-addressed stamped envelope, transcript.

Contact: Ms. Crystal Clark, Scholarship Coordinator
Governor's Office
State Capitol Building
Sacramento, CA 95814
Phone: 916-445-7097

GRAND CHAPTER OF CALIFORNIA-ORDER OF THE EASTERN STAR

http://www.oescal.org

SCHOLARSHIPS FOR EDUCATION, BUSINESS AND RELIGION

$500 to $3000 scholarships are awarded to students residing in California for postsecondary study. These scholarships are awarded for the study of business, education or religion.

Academic Fields/Career Goals: Business/Consumer Services; Education; Religion/Theology.

Award: Scholarship for use in freshman, sophomore, junior, senior, graduate, or postgraduate years; renewable. *Number:* varies. *Amount:* $500–$3000.

Eligibility Requirements: Applicant must be enrolled or expecting to enroll full-time at a two-year or four-year or technical institution or university and resident of California. Applicant must have 3.0 GPA or higher. Available to U.S. citizens.

Application Requirements: Application, financial need analysis, photo, references, self-addressed stamped envelope, test scores, transcript, proof of acceptance to college/university. *Deadline:* March 15.

Contact: Marie Louise Radford, Scholarship Chair, OES California
Grand Chapter of California-Order of the Eastern Star
16960 Bastanchury Road, Suite E
Yorba Linda, CA 92886-1711
Phone: 530-889-2429

GRAND RAPIDS COMMUNITY FOUNDATION

http://www.grfoundation.org

ECONOMIC CLUB OF GRAND RAPIDS BUSINESS STUDY ABROAD SCHOLARSHIP

• *See page 41*

GREATER KANAWHA VALLEY FOUNDATION

http://www.tgkvf.org

WILLARD H. ERWIN, JR. MEMORIAL SCHOLARSHIP FUND

Award for West Virginia residents who are starting their junior or senior year of undergraduate or graduate studies in a business or health-care finance degree program. Must be enrolled at a college in West Virginia. May apply for two Foundation scholarships but will only be chosen for one. Scholarships are awarded on the basis of financial need and scholastic ability.

Academic Fields/Career Goals: Business/Consumer Services; Health Administration.

Award: Scholarship for use in junior, senior, or graduate years; renewable. *Number:* 1. *Amount:* $1000.

Eligibility Requirements: Applicant must be enrolled or expecting to enroll full or part-time at a four-year institution or university; resident of West Virginia and studying in West Virginia. Applicant must have 2.5 GPA or higher. Available to U.S. citizens.

Application Requirements: Application, essay, financial need analysis, references, self-addressed stamped envelope, test scores, transcript. *Deadline:* February 17.

Contact: Susan Hoover, Scholarship Coordinator
Greater Kanawha Valley Foundation
PO Box 3041
Charleston, WV 25331
Phone: 304-346-3620
Fax: 304-346-3640

HISPANIC COLLEGE FUND, INC.

http://www.hispanicfund.org

BURLINGTON NORTHERN SANTA FE FOUNDATION/HISPANIC COLLEGE FUND SCHOLARSHIP PROGRAM

• *See page 41*

DENNY'S/HISPANIC COLLEGE FUND SCHOLARSHIP

• *See page 41*

DEPARTMENT OF ENERGY SCHOLARSHIP PROGRAM

Scholarship available to full-time undergraduate students in their sophomore or junior year who are pursuing a degree in business science, engineering or DOE-related major. Must be a U.S. citizen, have a minimum 3.0 GPA, and be available to participate in a paid internship in the summer of 2005.

Academic Fields/Career Goals: Business/Consumer Services; Chemical Engineering; Electrical Engineering/Electronics; Energy and Power Engineering; Engineering/Technology; Engineering-Related Technologies; Environmental Science; Materials Science, Engineering, and Metallurgy; Mechanical Engineering; Natural Resources; Natural Sciences; Nuclear Science.

Award: Scholarship for use in sophomore or junior years; not renewable. *Number:* 15. *Amount:* $500–$5000.

Eligibility Requirements: Applicant must be enrolled or expecting to enroll full-time at a four-year institution or university. Applicant must have 3.0 GPA or higher. Available to U.S. citizens.

Application Requirements: Application, essay, financial need analysis. *Deadline:* April 15.

Contact: Stina Augustsson, Program Manager
Hispanic College Fund, Inc.
1717 Pennsylvania Avenue, NW, Suite 460
Washington, DC 20006
Phone: 202-296-5400
Fax: 202-296-3774
E-mail: hcf-info@hispanicfund.org

ERNST AND YOUNG SCHOLARSHIP PROGRAM

• *See page 42*

HISPANIC COLLEGE FUND/INROADS/SPRINT SCHOLARSHIP PROGRAM

One-time award open to undergraduates of Hispanic descent pursuing a degree in a business- or technology-related major. Must be a U.S. citizen and have a minimum 3.0 GPA. Recipients will participate in INROADS Leadership Development Training while interning at Sprint during the summer.

Academic Fields/Career Goals: Business/Consumer Services; Communications; Computer Science/Data Processing; Economics; Electrical Engineering/Electronics; Engineering/Technology; Engineering-Related Technologies; Mechanical Engineering.

Award: Scholarship for use in freshman, sophomore, junior, or senior years; not renewable. *Number:* 10–20. *Amount:* $1000–$5000.

Eligibility Requirements: Applicant must be Hispanic and enrolled or expecting to enroll full-time at a two-year or four-year institution or university. Applicant must have 3.0 GPA or higher. Available to U.S. citizens.

Hispanic College Fund, Inc. (continued)

Application Requirements: Application, essay, financial need analysis, resume, references, transcript, college acceptance letter, copy of taxes, copy of SAR. *Deadline:* April 15.

Contact: Stina Augustsson, Program Manager
Hispanic College Fund, Inc.
1717 Pennsylvania Avenue, NW, Suite 460
Washington, DC 20006
Phone: 202-296-5400
Fax: 202-296-3774
E-mail: hcf-info@hispanicfund.org

ICI EDUCATIONAL FOUNDATION SCHOLARSHIP PROGRAM

• *See page 42*

M & T BANK/ HISPANIC COLLEGE FUND SCHOLARSHIP PROGRAM

• *See page 42*

7-ELEVEN SCHOLARSHIP PROGRAM

Program intended to provide financial assistance to full-time undergraduate student studying business, computer science, or engineering. Applicant must be a Mexican-American resident of the Los Angeles area. Must be a U.S. citizen attending a college or university in the U.S. or Puerto Rico. Online application only: http://www.hispanicfund.org.

Academic Fields/Career Goals: Business/Consumer Services; Computer Science/Data Processing; Engineering/Technology.

Award: Scholarship for use in freshman, sophomore, junior, or senior years; not renewable. *Number:* varies. *Amount:* $500–$5000.

Eligibility Requirements: Applicant must be Hispanic; enrolled or expecting to enroll full-time at a two-year or four-year institution or university and resident of California. Applicant must have 3.0 GPA or higher. Available to U.S. citizens.

Application Requirements: Application. *Deadline:* April 15.

Contact: Stina Augustsson, Program Manager
Hispanic College Fund, Inc.
1717 Pennsylvania Avenue, NW, Suite 460
Washington, DC 20006
Phone: 202-296-5400
Fax: 202-296-3774
E-mail: hcf-info@hispanicfund.org

HISPANIC SCHOLARSHIP FUND http://www.hsf.net

HSF/GENERAL MOTORS SCHOLARSHIP

Scholarships are available to Hispanic students pursuing a degree in business or engineering at an accredited U.S. four-year college. For more details, deadlines and an application see Web site: http://www.hsf.net.

Academic Fields/Career Goals: Business/Consumer Services; Chemical Engineering; Civil Engineering; Electrical Engineering/Electronics; Engineering/Technology; Engineering-Related Technologies; Mechanical Engineering.

Award: Scholarship for use in freshman, sophomore, junior, or senior years; not renewable. *Number:* 83. *Amount:* $2500.

Eligibility Requirements: Applicant must be Hispanic and enrolled or expecting to enroll full-time at a four-year institution or university. Applicant must have 3.0 GPA or higher. Available to U.S. citizens.

Application Requirements: Application. *Deadline:* June 16.

Contact: Application available at Web site.

HSF/LITTLE VILLAGE CHAMBER OF COMMERCE AMBASSADORS SCHOLARSHIP PROGRAM

Scholarship for undergraduate and graduate students from the Little Village Community on Chicago's West Side, who are pursuing a degree in business, finance, marketing, and related fields.

Academic Fields/Career Goals: Business/Consumer Services.

Award: Scholarship for use in freshman, sophomore, junior, senior, or graduate years. *Number:* varies. *Amount:* $2000.

Eligibility Requirements: Applicant must be Hispanic; enrolled or expecting to enroll full-time at an institution or university and resident of Illinois.

Application Requirements: Application, transcript. *Deadline:* June 23.

Contact: HSF Scholarship Department
Hispanic Scholarship Fund
55 Second Street, Suite 1500
San Francisco, CA 94105
Phone: 877-HSF-INFO
Fax: 415-808-2302
E-mail: info@hsf.net

JOHN M. AZARIAN MEMORIAL ARMENIAN YOUTH SCHOLARSHIP FUND

JOHN M. AZARIAN MEMORIAL ARMENIAN YOUTH SCHOLARSHIP FUND

Grants awarded to undergraduate students of Armenian descent, attending 4 year college or university within the United States full time. Compelling financial need is the main criteria. Minimum 2.5 GPA required. Preference to business majors given. Must be a member of the Armenian church.

Academic Fields/Career Goals: Business/Consumer Services.

Award: Grant for use in freshman, sophomore, junior, or senior years; renewable. *Number:* 3–10. *Amount:* $500–$2000.

Eligibility Requirements: Applicant must be of Armenian heritage and enrolled or expecting to enroll full-time at a four-year institution or university. Applicant must have 2.5 GPA or higher. Available to U.S. citizens.

Application Requirements: Application, autobiography, essay, financial need analysis, references, test scores, transcript. *Deadline:* May 31.

Contact: John Azarian, Jr., President
John M. Azarian Memorial Armenian Youth Scholarship Fund
Azarian Management and Development Company
6 Prospect Street, Suite 1B
Midland Park, NJ 07432
Phone: 201-444-7111
Fax: 201-444-6655
E-mail: azariangrp@aol.com

JORGE MAS CANOSA FREEDOM FOUNDATION

MAS FAMILY SCHOLARSHIP AWARD

Scholarship up to $10,000 per year to any financially needy, Cuban American student who is direct descendant of those who left Cuba or was born in Cuba. Minimum 3.5 GPA in college. Scholarships available only in the fields of engineering, business, international relations, economics, communications and journalism. Deadline is March 31. Write for application.

Academic Fields/Career Goals: Business/Consumer Services; Chemical Engineering; Civil Engineering; Communications; Economics; Electrical Engineering/Electronics; Engineering-Related Technologies; Journalism; Materials Science, Engineering, and Metallurgy; Mechanical Engineering.

Award: Scholarship for use in freshman, sophomore, junior, or senior years; renewable. *Number:* 10. *Amount:* up to $10,000.

Eligibility Requirements: Applicant must be of Latin American/ Caribbean heritage; Hispanic and enrolled or expecting to enroll at an institution or university. Applicant must have 3.5 GPA or higher. Available to U.S. citizens.

Application Requirements: Application, autobiography, essay, financial need analysis, test scores, transcript, proof of Cuban descent. *Deadline:* March 31.

Contact: Jorge Mas Canosa Freedom Foundation
Cuban American National Foundation, 1312 Southwest 27th Avenue
Miami, FL 33145

JUNIOR ACHIEVEMENT http://www.ja.org

WALT DISNEY COMPANY FOUNDATION SCHOLARSHIP

• *See page 88*

KNIGHT RIDDER http://www.kri.com

KNIGHT RIDDER MINORITY SCHOLARSHIP PROGRAM

Five $40,000 scholarships are given to graduating minority high school seniors who have plans of pursuing business or journalism as a college major and eventually as a career. Funds are given out over a four year period: $5,000 is given the first and second years, $15,000 is given out the third and fourth years. Recipients must work as an intern for a Knight-Ridder Company and maintain a 3.0 GPA. Must be sponsored by local Knight Ridder newspaper. Contact local Knight-Ridder Company for further information and deadlines.

Academic Fields/Career Goals: Business/Consumer Services; Graphics/Graphic Arts/Printing; Journalism.

Award: Scholarship for use in freshman, sophomore, junior, or senior years; renewable. *Number:* 5. *Amount:* $5000–$15,000.

Eligibility Requirements: Applicant must be American Indian/Alaska Native, Asian/Pacific Islander, Black (non-Hispanic), or Hispanic; high school student and planning to enroll or expecting to enroll full-time at a two-year or four-year institution or university. Applicant must have 3.0 GPA or higher. Available to U.S. citizens.

Application Requirements: Autobiography, essay, interview, references, test scores, transcript. *Deadline:* varies.

Contact: Larry Olmstead, Vice President, HR/Diversity and Development
Knight Ridder
50 West San Fernando Street, Suite 1200
San Jose, CA 95113-2413
Phone: 408-938-0335
Fax: 408-938-0205
E-mail: lolmstead@knightridder.com

LAGRANT FOUNDATION http://www.lagrantfoundation.org

LAGRANT FOUNDATION SCHOLARSHIP

Awards for undergraduate minority students who are attending accredited four-year institutions and are pursuing careers in the fields of advertising, marketing, and public relations.

Academic Fields/Career Goals: Business/Consumer Services; Communications.

Award: Scholarship for use in freshman, sophomore, junior, or senior years; renewable. *Number:* up to 10. *Amount:* up to $5000.

Eligibility Requirements: Applicant must be American Indian/Alaska Native, Asian/Pacific Islander, Black (non-Hispanic), or Hispanic and enrolled or expecting to enroll full-time at a four-year institution or university. Applicant must have 2.5 GPA or higher. Available to U.S. citizens.

Application Requirements: Application, essay, resume, references, transcript. *Deadline:* March 31.

Contact: Angie Ludena, Office Manager
Lagrant Foundation
555 South Flower Street, Suite 700
Los Angeles, CA 90071-2300
Phone: 323-469-8680

LAWRENCE P. DOSS SCHOLARSHIP FOUNDATION

LAWRENCE P. DOSS SCHOLARSHIP FOUNDATION

• *See page 43*

LEAGUE OF UNITED LATIN AMERICAN CITIZENS NATIONAL EDUCATIONAL SERVICE CENTERS, INC. http://www.lnesc.org

GE/LULAC SCHOLARSHIP

Renewable award for minority students who are enrolled as business or engineering majors at accredited colleges or universities in the United States and who will be entering their sophomore year. Must maintain a minimum 3.0 GPA. Selection is based in part on the likelihood of pursuing a career in business or engineering. Application deadline is July 15.

Academic Fields/Career Goals: Business/Consumer Services; Engineering/Technology.

Award: Scholarship for use in sophomore year; renewable. *Number:* 2. *Amount:* $5000.

Eligibility Requirements: Applicant must be Hispanic and enrolled or expecting to enroll full-time at a four-year institution or university. Applicant must have 3.0 GPA or higher. Available to U.S. citizens.

Application Requirements: Application, references, transcript. *Deadline:* July 15.

Contact: Scholarship Administrator
League of United Latin American Citizens National Educational Service Centers, Inc.
2000 L Street, NW
Suite 610
Washington, DC 20036

LEXINGTON HERALD-LEADER http://www.kentucky.com

LEXINGTON HERALD-LEADER/KNIGHT RIDDER MINORITY SCHOLARSHIPS

One-time award for any minority senior attending high school in specific Kentucky counties. Must plan to attend a four-year college and major in journalism or business-related field. May qualify for the national Knight Ridder Minority Scholarship. Application deadline is January 6.

Academic Fields/Career Goals: Business/Consumer Services; Journalism.

Award: Scholarship for use in freshman year; not renewable. *Number:* 2. *Amount:* $1000.

Eligibility Requirements: Applicant must be American Indian/Alaska Native, Asian/Pacific Islander, Black (non-Hispanic), or Hispanic; high school student; planning to enroll or expecting to enroll full-time at a four-year institution or university and resident of Kentucky. Applicant must have 2.5 GPA or higher. Available to U.S. citizens.

Application Requirements: Application, autobiography, essay, interview, references, test scores, transcript. *Deadline:* January 6.

Contact: Kathy Aldridge, Executive Assistant
Lexington Herald-Leader
100 Midland Avenue
Lexington, KY 40508
Phone: 859-231-3104
Fax: 859-231-3584
E-mail: kaldridge@herald-leader.com

LINCOLN COMMUNITY FOUNDATION http://www.lcf.org

LAWRENCE "LARRY" FRAZIER MEMORIAL SCHOLARSHIP

• *See page 100*

LOWE RMP http://www.dmscholarship.com

CANADIAN DIRECT MARKETING SCHOLARSHIP FOR BUSINESS STUDENTS

Award for students enrolled in a Canadian business school. Award consists of a four-month, paid summer internship, and a $2500 scholarship. Refer to Web site for details: http://www.dmscholarship.com.

Academic Fields/Career Goals: Business/Consumer Services.

Award: Scholarship for use in freshman, sophomore, junior, or senior years; not renewable. *Number:* up to 1. *Amount:* up to $1857.

Eligibility Requirements: Applicant must be enrolled or expecting to enroll full or part-time at a four-year institution or university. Available to Canadian citizens.

Application Requirements: Application, applicant must enter a contest, essay, resume, transcript. *Deadline:* March 24.

Contact: Allison Hill, Assistant Client Associate
Lowe RMP
200 Wellington Street West, Suite 200
Toronto, ON M5V 1E3
Canada
Phone: 416-260-4772
E-mail: scholarship@lowermp.com

MARYLAND ASSOCIATION OF PRIVATE COLLEGES AND CAREER SCHOOLS http://www.mapccs.org

MARYLAND ASSOCIATION OF PRIVATE COLLEGES AND CAREER SCHOOLS SCHOLARSHIP

Awards for study at trade schools only. Must enter school same year high school is completed. For use only in Maryland and by Maryland residents. Write for further information.

Maryland Association of Private Colleges and Career Schools (continued)

Academic Fields/Career Goals: Business/Consumer Services; Computer Science/Data Processing; Dental Health/Services; Engineering/Technology; Food Science/Nutrition; Home Economics; Trade/Technical Specialties; TV/Radio Broadcasting.

Award: Scholarship for use in freshman year; not renewable. *Number:* 58. *Amount:* $500–$19,950.

Eligibility Requirements: Applicant must be high school student; planning to enroll or expecting to enroll full-time at a technical institution; resident of Maryland and studying in Maryland. Available to U.S. citizens.

Application Requirements: Application, references, transcript. *Deadline:* April 18.

Contact: Diane MacDougall, Office Manager
Maryland Association of Private Colleges and Career Schools
3100 Dunglow Road
Baltimore, MD 21222
Phone: 410-282-4012
Fax: 410-282-4133
E-mail: mdapcs@yahoo.com

MIDWEST ROOFING CONTRACTORS ASSOCIATION http://www.mrca.org

MRCA FOUNDATION SCHOLARSHIP PROGRAM

• *See page 70*

MRA-THE MANAGEMENT ASSOCIATION http://www.mranet.org/

MRA INSTITUTE OF MANAGEMENT ENDOWMENT FUND SCHOLARSHIP

Non-renewable scholarship for students preparing for careers in the field of human resources management.

Academic Fields/Career Goals: Business/Consumer Services.

Award: Scholarship for use in junior or senior years; not renewable. *Number:* 1–2. *Amount:* $1000.

Eligibility Requirements: Applicant must be enrolled or expecting to enroll at a four-year institution or university; resident of Illinois, Iowa, or Wisconsin and studying in Illinois, Iowa, or Wisconsin. Applicant must have 3.0 GPA or higher. Available to U.S. citizens.

Application Requirements: Application, essay, interview, references, transcript, letter from university confirming human resources as major. *Deadline:* March 22.

Contact: Application available at Web site.

NATIONAL ASSOCIATION FOR THE ADVANCEMENT OF COLORED PEOPLE http://www.naacp.org

EARL G. GRAVES NAACP SCHOLARSHIP

One-time award of $5,000 to a full-time minority student. Must be an enrolled junior or senior at an accredited college or university in the United States as a declared business major, or a graduate student enrolled or accepted in a masters or doctoral program within a business school at an accredited university. Must demonstrate financial need. Application deadline is the last Friday in March.

Academic Fields/Career Goals: Business/Consumer Services.

Award: Scholarship for use in junior, senior, or graduate years; not renewable. *Number:* varies. *Amount:* $5000.

Eligibility Requirements: Applicant must be American Indian/Alaska Native, Asian/Pacific Islander, Black (non-Hispanic), or Hispanic and enrolled or expecting to enroll full-time at a four-year institution or university. Applicant must have 2.5 GPA or higher. Available to U.S. citizens.

Application Requirements: Application, financial need analysis, references, transcript. *Deadline:* varies.

Contact: Donna Lakins, Education Department, Scholarship Request
National Association for the Advancement of Colored People
4805 Mt. Hope Drive
Baltimore, MD 21215-3297
Phone: 410-580-5760
Fax: 410-585-1329

NATIONAL ASSOCIATION OF BLACK ACCOUNTANTS, INC. http://www.nabainc.org

NATIONAL ASSOCIATION OF BLACK ACCOUNTANTS NATIONAL SCHOLARSHIP PROGRAM

• *See page 43*

NATIONAL ASSOCIATION OF INSURANCE WOMEN EDUCATION FOUNDATION http://www.naiw-foundation.org

NAIW EDUCATION FOUNDATION PROFESSIONAL SCHOLARSHIP

Professional scholarships are given to applicants with a minimum of two years of experience in the insurance industry. They do not currently need to be employed in the industry. Recipients need to be engaged in a course of study designed to improve their knowledge and skills in performing their employment responsibilities. Scholarships are given three times a year. Application deadlines are March 1, September 1, December 1.

Academic Fields/Career Goals: Business/Consumer Services; Insurance and Actuarial Science.

Award: Scholarship for use in freshman, sophomore, junior, senior, graduate, or postgraduate years; not renewable. *Number:* 10–20. *Amount:* $100–$2000.

Eligibility Requirements: Applicant must be enrolled or expecting to enroll full or part-time at a two-year or four-year or technical institution or university. Available to U.S. and non-U.S. citizens.

Application Requirements: Application, essay, references, transcript. *Deadline:* varies.

Contact: Billie Sleet, Executive Director
National Association of Insurance Women Education Foundation
5310 East 31st Street, #302
Tulsa, OK 74135
Phone: 918-622-1816
Fax: 918-622-1821
E-mail: foundation@naiwfoundation.org

NATIONAL ASSOCIATION OF WATER COMPANIES http://www.nawc.org

J.J. BARR SCHOLARSHIP

• *See page 115*

NATIONAL ASSOCIATION OF WATER COMPANIES-NEW JERSEY CHAPTER

NATIONAL ASSOCIATION OF WATER COMPANIES-NEW JERSEY CHAPTER SCHOLARSHIP

• *See page 115*

NATIONAL BLACK MBA ASSOCIATION-TWIN CITIES CHAPTER http://www.nbmbaatc.org/scholarships.html

TWIN CITIES CHAPTER UNDERGRADUATE SCHOLARSHIP

• *See page 44*

NATIONAL URBAN LEAGUE http://www.nul.org

BLACK EXECUTIVE EXCHANGE PROGRAM JERRY BARTOW SCHOLARSHIP FUND

Scholarships for undergraduate students at participating Historically Black Colleges and Universities classified as sophomore, junior, or senior, majoring in business, management, technology or education. Must be available to receive award at BEEP's annual conference. All expenses will be provided by BEEP.

Academic Fields/Career Goals: Business/Consumer Services; Education; Engineering/Technology.

Award: Scholarship for use in sophomore, junior, or senior years; not renewable. *Number:* 2. *Amount:* $1500.

Eligibility Requirements: Applicant must be Black (non-Hispanic) and enrolled or expecting to enroll at a four-year institution or university.

Application Requirements: Application. *Deadline:* January 15.

Contact: William Dawson, Associate
National Urban League
120 Wall Street
New York, NY 10005
Phone: 212-558-5441
Fax: 212-344-5332
E-mail: wdawson@nul.org

NEW ENGLAND EMPLOYEE BENEFITS COUNCIL http://www.neebc.org

NEW ENGLAND EMPLOYEE BENEFITS COUNCIL SCHOLARSHIP PROGRAM

Renewable award designed to encourage undergraduate or graduate students to pursue a course of study leading to a bachelor's degree or higher in the employee benefits field. Must be a resident of/or studying in Maine, Massachusetts, New Hampshire, Rhode Island, Connecticut or Vermont.

Academic Fields/Career Goals: Business/Consumer Services.

Award: Scholarship for use in freshman, sophomore, junior, senior, or graduate years; renewable. *Number:* 1–3. *Amount:* up to $5000.

Eligibility Requirements: Applicant must be enrolled or expecting to enroll full-time at a four-year institution or university; resident of Connecticut, Maine, Massachusetts, New Hampshire, Rhode Island, or Vermont and studying in Connecticut, Maine, Massachusetts, New Hampshire, Rhode Island, or Vermont. Available to U.S. citizens.

Application Requirements: Application, essay, references, transcript. *Deadline:* April 1.

Contact: Linda Viens, Office Manager
New England Employee Benefits Council
440 Totten Pond Road
Waltham, MA 02451
Phone: 781-684-8700
Fax: 781-684-9200
E-mail: linda@neebc.org

NORTH CAROLINA CPA FOUNDATION, INC. http://www.ncacpa.org

NORTH CAROLINA CPA FOUNDATION ACCOUNTING SCHOLARSHIP PROGRAM

• *See page 45*

OREGON STUDENT ASSISTANCE COMMISSION http://www.osac.state.or.us

GLENN R. AND JUANITA B. STRUBLE SCHOLARSHIP II

• *See page 78*

HOMESTEAD CAPITAL HOUSING SCHOLARSHIP

• *See page 46*

PLUMBING-HEATING-COOLING CONTRACTORS ASSOCIATION EDUCATION FOUNDATION http://www.phccweb.org

BRADFORD WHITE CORPORATION SCHOLARSHIP

• *See page 79*

DELTA FAUCET COMPANY SCHOLARSHIP PROGRAM

• *See page 79*

PHCC EDUCATIONAL FOUNDATION NEED-BASED SCHOLARSHIP

• *See page 79*

PHCC EDUCATIONAL FOUNDATION SCHOLARSHIP PROGRAM

• *See page 79*

ROBERT H. MOLLOHAN FAMILY CHARITABLE FOUNDATION, INC. http://www.mollohanfoundation.org

TEAMING TO WIN BUSINESS SCHOLARSHIP

Scholarship for a rising sophomore or junior pursuing a degree in business administration at a West Virginia college or university.

Academic Fields/Career Goals: Business/Consumer Services.

Award: Scholarship for use in sophomore or junior years; not renewable. *Number:* 2. *Amount:* $1000.

Eligibility Requirements: Applicant must be enrolled or expecting to enroll full or part-time at a four-year institution or university; resident of West Virginia and studying in West Virginia. Applicant must have 3.0 GPA or higher. Available to U.S. citizens.

Application Requirements: Application, essay, interview, resume, references, test scores, transcript. *Deadline:* February 7.

Contact: Teah Bayless, Program Manager
Robert H. Mollohan Family Charitable Foundation, Inc.
1000 Technology Drive, Suite 2000
Fairmont, WV 26554
Phone: 304-333-2251
Fax: 304-333-3900
E-mail: tmbayless@wvhtf.org

ROYAL BANK NATIVE STUDENTS AWARDS PROGRAM http://www.rbc.com/community/rbc_community/articles/story_17.html

ROYAL BANK ABORIGINAL STUDENT AWARDS

Award for Canadian Aboriginal student who is status Indian, non-status Indian, Inuit or Métis, accepted or attending college or university in the Directory of Canadian Universities. Must be studying in a financial services discipline (e.g. business, economics, computer science). Award maximum of four years at university or two years at college. Must be permanent resident/citizen of Canada.

Academic Fields/Career Goals: Business/Consumer Services; Computer Science/Data Processing; Economics.

Award: Scholarship for use in freshman, sophomore, junior, or senior years; renewable. *Number:* 5. *Amount:* up to $2971.

Eligibility Requirements: Applicant must be Canadian citizen; American Indian/Alaska Native and enrolled or expecting to enroll full-time at a two-year or four-year institution or university.

Application Requirements: Application, essay, financial need analysis, references, transcript. *Deadline:* January 31.

Contact: Natasha Kassim, Coordinator
Royal Bank Native Students Awards Program
330 Front Street West
10th floor
Toronto, ON M5V 3B7
Canada
Phone: 416-348-6947
Fax: 416-348-6455
E-mail: natasha.kassim@rbc.com

SALES PROFESSIONALS-USA

SALES PROFESSIONALS- USA SCHOLARSHIP

Scholarships are awarded to students furthering their degree or obtaining a degree in business or marketing. The scholarships are initiated and awarded by the individual Sales Pros Clubs (located in Colorado, Kansas and Missouri) and are not nationally awarded. A listing of local clubs can be found at http://www.salesprofessionals-usa.com.

Academic Fields/Career Goals: Business/Consumer Services.

Award: Scholarship for use in freshman, sophomore, junior, or senior years; not renewable. *Number:* 3–5. *Amount:* $600–$1000.

Eligibility Requirements: Applicant must be enrolled or expecting to enroll full or part-time at a two-year or four-year institution or university; resident of Colorado, Kansas, or Missouri and studying in Colorado, Kansas, or Missouri. Applicant must have 3.0 GPA or higher. Available to U.S. citizens.

Application Requirements: Application, essay. *Deadline:* varies.

Contact: Mary Anne McCubbin, National President
Sales Professionals-USA
PO Box 149
Arvada, CO 80001
Phone: 800-763-7767

SOUTH DAKOTA RETAILERS ASSOCIATION http://www.sdra.org

SOUTH DAKOTA RETAILERS ASSOCIATION SCHOLARSHIP PROGRAM

• *See page 47*

SUNSHINE LADY FOUNDATION, INC.
http://www.sunshineladyfdn.org

COUNSELOR, ADVOCATE, AND SUPPORT STAFF SCHOLARSHIP PROGRAM
• *See page 47*

TKE EDUCATIONAL FOUNDATION
http://www.tkefoundation.org

W. ALLAN HERZOG SCHOLARSHIP
• *See page 48*

TRUCKLOAD CARRIERS ASSOCIATION
http://www.truckload.org

TRUCKLOAD CARRIERS ASSOCIATION SCHOLARSHIP FUND

This scholarship fund is for persons affiliated with the trucking industry and their families to pursue higher education. Special consideration will be given to applicants pursuing transportation or business degrees. Minimum 3.3 GPA required. For junior and senior undergraduate students at four-year college or university. Further information and application deadlines available at Web site http://www.truckload.org.

Academic Fields/Career Goals: Business/Consumer Services; Transportation.

Award: Scholarship for use in junior or senior years; not renewable. *Number:* 18. *Amount:* $1500–$3000.

Eligibility Requirements: Applicant must be enrolled or expecting to enroll full-time at a four-year institution or university. Applicant or parent of applicant must have employment or volunteer experience in designated career field. Available to U.S. citizens.

Application Requirements: Application, essay, financial need analysis, photo, transcript, course schedule including tuition and fees. *Deadline:* May 21.

Contact: Nancy O'Liddy, Scholarship Fund Administrator
Truckload Carriers Association
2200 Mill Road
Alexandria, VA 22314
Phone: 703-838-1950
Fax: 703-836-6610
E-mail: tca@truckload.org

UNITED DAUGHTERS OF THE CONFEDERACY
http://www.hqudc.org

WALTER REED SMITH SCHOLARSHIP

Award for full-time female undergraduate student who is a descendant of a Confederate soldier, studying nutrition, home economics, nursing, business administration, or computer science. Must carry a minimum of 12 credit hours each semester and have a minimum 3.0 GPA. Submit letter of endorsement from sponsoring chapter of the United Daughters of the Confederacy. Please refer to Web site for further details: http://www.hqudc.org

Academic Fields/Career Goals: Business/Consumer Services; Computer Science/Data Processing; Food Science/Nutrition; Home Economics; Nursing.

Award: Scholarship for use in freshman, sophomore, junior, or senior years; renewable. *Number:* 1–2. *Amount:* $800–$1000.

Eligibility Requirements: Applicant must be enrolled or expecting to enroll full-time at a four-year institution or university and female. Applicant or parent of applicant must be member of United Daughters of the Confederacy. Applicant must have 3.0 GPA or higher. Available to U.S. citizens.

Application Requirements: Application, essay, financial need analysis, photo, references, self-addressed stamped envelope, transcript. *Deadline:* February 15.

Contact: Second Vice President General
United Daughters of the Confederacy
328 North Boulevard
Richmond, VA 23220-4057
Phone: 804-355-1636

UNITED NEGRO COLLEGE FUND
http://www.uncf.org

AVON WOMEN IN SEARCH OF EXCELLENCE SCHOLARSHIPS
• *See page 48*

AXA FOUNDATION FUND ACHIEVEMENT SCHOLARSHIP

Scholarship for New York residents attending a UNCF member college or university. Must declare business-related major. Minimum 3.0 GPA required. Applicants must exemplify high academic achievement, leadership ability, and community service. Prospective applicants should complete the Student Profile found at Web site: http://www.uncf.org.

Academic Fields/Career Goals: Business/Consumer Services.

Award: Scholarship for use in freshman, sophomore, junior, or senior years; not renewable. *Amount:* $2000–$5000.

Eligibility Requirements: Applicant must be Black (non-Hispanic); enrolled or expecting to enroll at a four-year institution or university; resident of New York and must have an interest in leadership. Applicant must have 3.0 GPA or higher.

Application Requirements: Application, financial need analysis. *Deadline:* varies.

Contact: Program Services Department
United Negro College Fund
8260 Willow Oaks Corporate Drive
Fairfax, VA 22031

BANK ONE / UNCF CORPORATE SCHOLARS PROGRAM
• *See page 48*

BEST BUY ENTERPRISE EMPLOYEE SCHOLARSHIP
• *See page 48*

BOOZ, ALLEN & HAMILTON/WILLIAM F. STASIOR INTERNSHIP

Program available to college juniors majoring in engineering, business, finance, economics, math, science, information systems, or computer science at any of the following UNCF member colleges and universities: Florida A&M, Morehouse, Spelman, Morgan State, Hampton, Howard, Baruch, or Southern University. Minimum 3.3 GPA required. Prospective applicants should complete the Student Profile found at Web site: http://www.uncf.org.

Academic Fields/Career Goals: Business/Consumer Services; Computer Science/Data Processing; Earth Science; Engineering/Technology; Physical Sciences and Math.

Award: Scholarship for use in sophomore or junior years; not renewable. *Number:* varies. *Amount:* $10,000.

Eligibility Requirements: Applicant must be Black (non-Hispanic) and enrolled or expecting to enroll full-time at a four-year institution or university. Available to U.S. citizens.

Application Requirements: Application, financial need analysis. *Deadline:* February 29.

Contact: Program Services Department
United Negro College Fund
8260 Willow Oaks Corporate Drive
Fairfax, VA 22031

C.R. BARD SCHOLARSHIP AND INTERNSHIP PROGRAM

Scholarship awards $4000 to undergraduate sophomore majoring in business at a UNCF member college or university. Program provides paid internship during summer at the C. R. Bard headquarters in Murray Hill, New Jersey. Please visit Web site for more information: http://www.uncf.org.

Academic Fields/Career Goals: Business/Consumer Services.

Award: Scholarship for use in sophomore year. *Number:* varies. *Amount:* $4000.

Eligibility Requirements: Applicant must be Black (non-Hispanic) and enrolled or expecting to enroll at a four-year institution or university. Applicant must have 3.0 GPA or higher.

Application Requirements: Application, financial need analysis, FAFSA, SAR. *Deadline:* February 28.

Contact: Program Services Department
United Negro College Fund
8260 Willow Oaks Corporate Drive
Fairfax, VA 22031

CARDINAL HEALTH SCHOLARSHIP

• *See page 48*

CASTLE ROCK FOUNDATION SCHOLARSHIP

Scholarship awarded to students majoring in business or engineering and who attend the following institutions: Bethune-Cookman College, LeMoyne-Owen College, Morehouse College, Shaw University, Spelman College, Tuskegee University, or Xavier University. Please visit Web site for more information: http://www.uncf.org.

Academic Fields/Career Goals: Business/Consumer Services; Engineering/Technology.

Award: Scholarship for use in freshman, sophomore, junior, senior, or graduate years. *Number:* 10. *Amount:* $3600.

Eligibility Requirements: Applicant must be Black (non-Hispanic) and enrolled or expecting to enroll at a four-year institution or university. Applicant must have 2.5 GPA or higher.

Application Requirements: Application, financial need analysis, FAFSA, SAR. *Deadline:* varies.

Contact: Program Services Department
United Negro College Fund
8260 Willow Oaks Corporate Drive
Fairfax, VA 22031

COY G. EKLUND SCHOLARSHIP

Scholarship for business majors attending a UNCF member college or university. Minimum 2.5 GPA required. Prospective applicants should complete the Student Profile found at Web site: http://www.uncf.org.

Academic Fields/Career Goals: Business/Consumer Services.

Award: Scholarship for use in freshman, sophomore, junior, or senior years; not renewable.

Eligibility Requirements: Applicant must be Black (non-Hispanic) and enrolled or expecting to enroll at a four-year institution or university. Applicant must have 2.5 GPA or higher.

Application Requirements: Application, financial need analysis. *Deadline:* Continuous.

Contact: Program Services Department
United Negro College Fund
8260 Willow Oaks Corporate Drive
Fairfax, VA 22031

CREDIT SUISSE FIRST BOSTON SCHOLARSHIP

• *See page 49*

DELL/UNCF CORPORATE SCHOLARS PROGRAM

Program provides rising Texas juniors and seniors with an opportunity to gain valuable internship experience and earn a $10,000 scholarship. Students must attend a UNCF member college or university or an HBCU and major in engineering, business, finance, marketing, computer science/MIS, logistics, human resources, supply chain management, operations management, or electrical engineering. Minimum 3.0 GPA required. Prospective applicants should complete the Student Profile found at Web site: http://www.uncf.org.

Academic Fields/Career Goals: Business/Consumer Services; Computer Science/Data Processing; Electrical Engineering/Electronics; Engineering/Technology.

Award: Scholarship for use in sophomore, or graduate years; not renewable. *Amount:* up to $10,000.

Eligibility Requirements: Applicant must be Black (non-Hispanic); enrolled or expecting to enroll full-time at a four-year institution or university and resident of Texas. Applicant must have 3.0 GPA or higher. Available to U.S. citizens.

Application Requirements: Application, financial need analysis. *Deadline:* January 31.

Contact: Program Services Department
United Negro College Fund
8260 Willow Oaks Corporate Drive
Fairfax, VA 22031

DR. WILLIAM R. GILES MEMORIAL SCHOLARSHIP

Renewable scholarship for New Jersey residents attending a UNCF member college and university majoring in business. Minimum 3.0 GPA required. Prospective applicants should complete the Student Profile found at Web site: http://www.uncf.org.

Academic Fields/Career Goals: Business/Consumer Services.

Award: Scholarship for use in freshman, sophomore, junior, or senior years; renewable. *Amount:* varies.

Eligibility Requirements: Applicant must be Black (non-Hispanic); enrolled or expecting to enroll full-time at a four-year institution or university and resident of New Jersey. Applicant must have 3.0 GPA or higher. Available to U.S. citizens.

Application Requirements: Application, financial need analysis.

Contact: Program Services Department
United Negro College Fund
8260 Willow Oaks Corporate Drive
Fairfax, VA 22031

EDWARD M. NAGEL FOUNDATION SCHOLARSHIP

• *See page 49*

FINANCIAL SERVICES INSTITUTION SCHOLARSHIP

• *See page 49*

FLOWERS INDUSTRIES SCHOLARSHIP

Awards given to students majoring in business, marketing, computer science, or food service at one of the following colleges or universities: Bethune-Cookman, Clark Atlanta, Stillman, Virginia Union. Minimum 2.5 GPA required. Prospective applicants should complete the Student Profile found at Web site: http://www.uncf.org.

Academic Fields/Career Goals: Business/Consumer Services; Computer Science/Data Processing; Food Service/Hospitality.

Award: Scholarship for use in junior or senior years; not renewable. *Amount:* $2500.

Eligibility Requirements: Applicant must be Black (non-Hispanic) and enrolled or expecting to enroll at a four-year institution or university. Applicant must have 2.5 GPA or higher.

Application Requirements: Application, financial need analysis. *Deadline:* Continuous.

Contact: Program Services Department
United Negro College Fund
8260 Willow Oaks Corporate Drive
Fairfax, VA 22031

GENERAL MILLS SCHOLARS PROGRAM/INTERNSHIP

• *See page 50*

HOUSEHOLD INTERNATIONAL CORPORATE SCHOLARS

Scholarship provides opportunities for minority sophomores and juniors majoring in business, finance, accounting, marketing, computer science or human resources. Must attend a UNCF member college or university or a selected historically black college or university. Minimum 3.0 GPA required. Prospective applicants should complete the Student Profile found at Web site: http://www.uncf.org.

Academic Fields/Career Goals: Business/Consumer Services; Computer Science/Data Processing; Physical Sciences and Math.

Award: Scholarship for use in sophomore year; not renewable. *Number:* up to 30. *Amount:* up to $10,000.

Eligibility Requirements: Applicant must be American Indian/Alaska Native, Asian/Pacific Islander, Black (non-Hispanic), or Hispanic; enrolled or expecting to enroll at a four-year institution or university and studying in California, Delaware, Florida, Illinois, Indiana, New Jersey, North Carolina, Texas, or Virginia. Applicant must have 3.0 GPA or higher.

Application Requirements: Application, financial need analysis. *Deadline:* March 1.

Contact: Program Services Department
United Negro College Fund
8260 Willow Oaks Corporate Drive
Fairfax, VA 22031

JESSE JONES, JR. SCHOLARSHIP

Need-based scholarship for business students attending a UNCF member college or university. Minimum 2.5 GPA required. Prospective applicants should complete the Student Profile found at Web site: http://www.uncf.org.

Academic Fields/Career Goals: Business/Consumer Services.

Award: Scholarship for use in freshman, sophomore, junior, or senior years; not renewable. *Amount:* $2000–$5000.

Eligibility Requirements: Applicant must be Black (non-Hispanic) and enrolled or expecting to enroll at a four-year institution or university. Applicant must have 2.5 GPA or higher. Available to U.S. citizens.

Application Requirements: Application, financial need analysis. *Deadline:* Continuous.

Contact: Program Services Department
United Negro College Fund
8260 Willow Oaks Corporate Drive
Fairfax, VA 22031

KEYCORP SCHOLARS PROGRAM/INTERNSHIP

Scholarship, internship, and mentorship award for college sophomores, juniors, and first year graduate students at a UNCF member college or university who are majoring in finance, marketing, banking, or other business-related subjects. Minimum 3.0 GPA required. Prospective applicants should complete the Student Profile found at Web site: http://www.uncf.org.

Academic Fields/Career Goals: Business/Consumer Services.

Award: Scholarship for use in sophomore, junior, or graduate years; not renewable. *Amount:* up to $7000.

Eligibility Requirements: Applicant must be Black (non-Hispanic) and enrolled or expecting to enroll full-time at a four-year institution or university. Applicant must have 3.0 GPA or higher.

Application Requirements: Application, financial need analysis, resume, references, transcript. *Deadline:* February 1.

Contact: Program Services Department
United Negro College Fund
8260 Willow Oaks Corporate Drive
Fairfax, VA 22031

MASTERCARD SCHOLARS PROGRAM

Scholarship awarded covers the cost of tuition, fees, and room and board for students from New York, New Jersey, and Connecticut attending a UNCF member college or university. Students must major in business, finance, accounting, information systems, or marketing. Prospective applicants should complete the Student Profile found at Web site: http://www.uncf.org. Minimum 3.0 GPA required.

Academic Fields/Career Goals: Business/Consumer Services.

Award: Scholarship for use in sophomore or junior years; not renewable. *Amount:* $4500.

Eligibility Requirements: Applicant must be Black (non-Hispanic); enrolled or expecting to enroll at a four-year institution or university and resident of Connecticut, New Jersey, or New York. Applicant must have 3.0 GPA or higher.

Application Requirements: Application, financial need analysis. *Deadline:* varies.

Contact: Program Services Department
United Negro College Fund
8260 Willow Oaks Corporate Drive
Fairfax, VA 22031

MAYTAG COMPANY SCHOLARSHIP

Scholarship for students majoring in engineering, business, computer science, or information technology at one of the following colleges or universities: Benedict, Claflin, Lane, LeMoyne-Owen, Morris, Paine, Voorhees, Wilberforce, or a historically black college or university. Minimum 2.5 GPA required. Prospective applicants should complete the Student Profile found at Web site: http://www.uncf.org.

Academic Fields/Career Goals: Business/Consumer Services; Computer Science/Data Processing; Engineering/Technology.

Award: Scholarship for use in freshman, sophomore, junior, or senior years; not renewable. *Amount:* $1250.

Eligibility Requirements: Applicant must be Black (non-Hispanic) and enrolled or expecting to enroll at a four-year institution or university. Applicant must have 2.5 GPA or higher.

Application Requirements: Application, financial need analysis. *Deadline:* Continuous.

Contact: Program Services Department
United Negro College Fund
8260 Willow Oaks Corporate Drive
Fairfax, VA 22031

MBIA/WILLIAM O. BAILEY SCHOLARS PROGRAM

Two full-tuition awards given to qualified juniors from New York, New Jersey, or Connecticut with at least a 3.0 GPA and majoring in business or finance who attend a UNCF member college or university. Prospective applicants should complete the Student Profile found at Web site: http://www.uncf.org.

Academic Fields/Career Goals: Business/Consumer Services.

Award: Scholarship for use in junior year; not renewable. *Number:* 2.

Eligibility Requirements: Applicant must be Black (non-Hispanic); enrolled or expecting to enroll full-time at a four-year institution or university and resident of Connecticut, New Jersey, or New York. Applicant must have 3.0 GPA or higher. Available to U.S. citizens.

Application Requirements: Application, financial need analysis. *Deadline:* Continuous.

Contact: Program Services Department
United Negro College Fund
8260 Willow Oaks Corporate Drive
Fairfax, VA 22031

NORTHEAST UTILITIES SYSTEM SCHOLARSHIP PROGRAM

Scholarships available for African American students enrolled as a sophomore or junior at a participating UNCF college or university. Must be pursuing a degree in engineering, business, information systems, or computer science/MIS. Must complete an internship. Visit Web site for details. http://www.uncf.org.

Academic Fields/Career Goals: Business/Consumer Services; Computer Science/Data Processing; Energy and Power Engineering; Engineering/Technology; Engineering-Related Technologies.

Award: Scholarship for use in sophomore or junior years; not renewable. *Number:* varies. *Amount:* $10,000.

Eligibility Requirements: Applicant must be Black (non-Hispanic); enrolled or expecting to enroll at a four-year institution or university and resident of Connecticut. Applicant must have 3.0 GPA or higher.

Application Requirements: Application. *Deadline:* varies.

Contact: Program Services Department
United Negro College Fund
8260 Willow Oaks Corporate Drive
Fairfax, VA 22031

PECO ENERGY SCHOLARSHIP

• *See page 50*

PRINCIPAL FINANCIAL GROUP SCHOLARSHIPS

Scholarships available to students majoring in business, finance, information systems, or banking who are attending a UNCF member college or university. Minimum 2.8 GPA required. Selected students participate in a paid internship in Des Moines, Iowa. Prospective applicants should complete the Student Profile found at Web site: http://www.uncf.org.

Academic Fields/Career Goals: Business/Consumer Services; Computer Science/Data Processing.

Award: Scholarship for use in junior year; not renewable. *Amount:* up to $12,000.

Eligibility Requirements: Applicant must be Black (non-Hispanic) and enrolled or expecting to enroll at a four-year institution or university.

Application Requirements: Application, financial need analysis. *Deadline:* March 1.

Contact: Program Services Department
United Negro College Fund
8260 Willow Oaks Corporate Drive
Fairfax, VA 22031

ROBERT HALF INTERNATIONAL SCHOLARSHIP

• *See page 50*

ROCKWELL/UNCF CORPORATE SCHOLARS PROGRAM

Scholarships available for African-American students entering their sophomore year. Must have a minimum 3.0 GPA. Must pursue specified areas of study as well as attend specific universities. See Web site for more information. http://www.uncf.org.

Academic Fields/Career Goals: Business/Consumer Services; Earth Science; Electrical Engineering/Electronics; Psychology.

Award: Scholarship for use in sophomore year. *Number:* varies. *Amount:* up to $10,000.

Eligibility Requirements: Applicant must be Black (non-Hispanic); enrolled or expecting to enroll at a four-year institution or university and must have an interest in leadership. Applicant must have 3.0 GPA or higher.

Application Requirements: Application, essay, references. *Deadline:* March 1.

Contact: Program Services Department
United Negro College Fund
8260 Willow Oaks Corporate Drive
Fairfax, VA 22031

SBC FOUNDATION SCHOLARSHIP

Award for deserving minority students from Illinois, Indiana, Michigan, Ohio, and Wisconsin. Must be a junior at one of the 39 UNCF member institutions. Must major in business, economics, finance, engineering (IE/EE/ME), or computer science/information technology. Must have 3.0 GPA. Please visit Web site for more information: http://www.uncf.org.

Academic Fields/Career Goals: Business/Consumer Services; Computer Science/Data Processing; Economics; Electrical Engineering/Electronics; Engineering/Technology; Mechanical Engineering.

Award: Scholarship for use in junior or senior years; renewable. *Number:* varies. *Amount:* $5000.

Eligibility Requirements: Applicant must be Black (non-Hispanic); enrolled or expecting to enroll at an institution or university and resident of Illinois, Indiana, Michigan, Ohio, or Wisconsin. Applicant must have 3.0 GPA or higher.

Application Requirements: Application, financial need analysis, photo, resume, references, transcript, FAFSA, SAR. *Deadline:* October 30.

Contact: William Dunham, SBC Foundation Scholarship
United Negro College Fund
8260 Willow Oaks Corporate Drive, PO Box 10444
Fairfax, VA 22031

SBC PACIFIC BELL FOUNDATION SCHOLARSHIP

Scholarships for qualified business-related majors in junior year attending UNCF colleges and universities. Minimum 3.0 GPA required. Prospective applicants should complete the Student Profile found at Web site: http://www.uncf.org. Must be a California resident.

Academic Fields/Career Goals: Business/Consumer Services; Computer Science/Data Processing; Economics; Engineering/Technology.

Award: Scholarship for use in junior year; not renewable. *Amount:* $5000.

Eligibility Requirements: Applicant must be Black (non-Hispanic); enrolled or expecting to enroll at a four-year institution or university and resident of California. Applicant must have 3.0 GPA or higher. Available to U.S. citizens.

Application Requirements: Application, financial need analysis. *Deadline:* Continuous.

Contact: Program Services Department
United Negro College Fund
8260 Willow Oaks Corporate Drive
Fairfax, VA 22031

SOUTHTRUST SCHOLARSHIP

Need-based scholarship available to sophomores and juniors majoring in business who attend a UNCF member college or university. Minimum 3.0 GPA required. Prospective applicants should complete the Student Profile found at Web site: http://www.uncf.org.

Academic Fields/Career Goals: Business/Consumer Services.

Award: Scholarship for use in sophomore or junior years; not renewable. *Amount:* $6250.

Eligibility Requirements: Applicant must be Black (non-Hispanic) and enrolled or expecting to enroll at a four-year institution or university. Applicant must have 3.0 GPA or higher. Available to U.S. citizens.

Application Requirements: Application, essay, financial need analysis, references, transcript. *Deadline:* March 30.

Contact: Program Services Department
United Negro College Fund
8260 Willow Oaks Corporate Drive
Fairfax, VA 22031

SOUTHWESTERN BELL CORPORATION SCHOLARSHIP

Scholarship for residents of Michigan, Texas, Kansas, Arkansas, and Oklahoma attending a UNCF member college or university with a major in business, finance, economics, accounting, math, or computer science/MIS. Minimum 3.0 GPA required. Must be undergraduate junior and have financial need. Prospective applicants should complete the Student Profile found at Web site: http://www.uncf.org.

Academic Fields/Career Goals: Business/Consumer Services; Computer Science/Data Processing; Economics; Engineering/Technology; Physical Sciences and Math.

Award: Scholarship for use in junior year; not renewable. *Amount:* $5000.

Eligibility Requirements: Applicant must be Black (non-Hispanic); enrolled or expecting to enroll at a four-year institution or university and resident of Alaska, Kansas, Michigan, Oklahoma, or Texas. Applicant must have 3.0 GPA or higher.

Application Requirements: Application, essay, financial need analysis, references, transcript. *Deadline:* October 30.

Contact: Program Services Department
United Negro College Fund
8260 Willow Oaks Corporate Drive
Fairfax, VA 22031

SPRINT SCHOLARSHIP/INTERNSHIP

• *See page 50*

TOYOTA SCHOLARSHIP

Scholarship awarded to students with at least a 3.0 GPA majoring in business, information systems, English, or communications. Students must attend one of the following UNCF member colleges or universities: Clark Atlanta, Morehouse, Morris Brown, Spelman, Tuskegee, or Xavier. Prospective applicants should complete the Student Profile found at Web site: http://www.uncf.org.

Academic Fields/Career Goals: Business/Consumer Services; Communications; Literature/English/Writing.

Award: Scholarship for use in freshman year; not renewable. *Amount:* $7500.

Eligibility Requirements: Applicant must be Black (non-Hispanic) and enrolled or expecting to enroll at a four-year institution or university. Applicant must have 3.0 GPA or higher.

United Negro College Fund (continued)

Application Requirements: Application, financial need analysis. *Deadline:* varies.

Contact: Program Services Department
United Negro College Fund
8260 Willow Oaks Corporate Drive
Fairfax, VA 22031

UBS/PAINEWEBBER SCHOLARSHIPS

Scholarships for UNCF students with at least a 3.0 GPA interested in business-related fields. Must be a sophomore or junior level undergraduate. Prospective applicants should complete the Student Profile found at Web site: http://www.uncf.org.

Academic Fields/Career Goals: Business/Consumer Services.

Award: Scholarship for use in sophomore or junior years; not renewable. *Amount:* $8000.

Eligibility Requirements: Applicant must be Black (non-Hispanic) and enrolled or expecting to enroll at a four-year institution or university. Applicant must have 3.0 GPA or higher.

Application Requirements: Application, financial need analysis. *Deadline:* varies.

Contact: Program Services Department
United Negro College Fund
8260 Willow Oaks Corporate Drive
Fairfax, VA 22031

UNCF/ORACLE SCHOLARS/INTERNS PROGRAM

• *See page 50*

UNCF/PFIZER CORPORATE SCHOLARS PROGRAM

• *See page 64*

UNCF/SPRINT SCHOLARS PROGRAM

• *See page 50*

UPS CORPORATE SCHOLARS PROGRAM/INTERNSHIP

Award consists of both a scholarship and internship. Applicant must be a sophomore or junior undergraduate majoring in marketing, computer science, information technology, or mechanical engineering. Must have 3.0 GPA. Please visit Web site for more information: http://www.uncf.org.

Academic Fields/Career Goals: Business/Consumer Services; Computer Science/Data Processing; Mechanical Engineering.

Award: Scholarship for use in sophomore, junior, or senior years; renewable. *Number:* varies. *Amount:* up to $10,000.

Eligibility Requirements: Applicant must be Black (non-Hispanic) and enrolled or expecting to enroll at an institution or university. Applicant must have 3.0 GPA or higher.

Application Requirements: Application, financial need analysis, FAFSA, SAR. *Deadline:* March 15.

Contact: Program Services Department
United Negro College Fund
8260 Willow Oaks Corporate Drive
Fairfax, VA 22031

WEYERHAEUSER/UNCF CORPORATE SCHOLARS

Award for sophomores and juniors majoring in forestry, marketing, operations management, electrical engineering, or industrial engineering. Includes paid summer internship. Must have 3.0 GPA. Please visit Web site for more information: http://www.uncf.org.

Academic Fields/Career Goals: Business/Consumer Services; Electrical Engineering/Electronics; Engineering/Technology; Environmental Science; Natural Resources.

Award: Scholarship for use in sophomore, junior, or senior years; renewable. *Number:* varies. *Amount:* $10,000.

Eligibility Requirements: Applicant must be Black (non-Hispanic) and enrolled or expecting to enroll full-time at an institution or university. Applicant must have 3.0 GPA or higher.

Application Requirements: Application, essay, financial need analysis, resume, references, transcript, FAFSA, SAR. *Deadline:* March 15.

Contact: Weyerhaeuser/UNCF Corporate Scholars Program
United Negro College Fund
PO Box 1435
Alexandria, VA 22313-9998

WM. WRIGLEY, JR. COMPANY SCHOLARS PROGRAM

Must be rising junior or senior at a UNCF member college. Need-based scholarships offered to business, engineering, and chemistry majors with at least a 3.0 GPA. Prospective applicants should complete the Student Profile found at Web site: http://www.uncf.org.

Academic Fields/Career Goals: Business/Consumer Services; Chemical Engineering; Engineering/Technology.

Award: Scholarship for use in sophomore or junior years; not renewable. *Amount:* up to $3000.

Eligibility Requirements: Applicant must be Black (non-Hispanic) and enrolled or expecting to enroll at a four-year institution or university. Applicant must have 3.0 GPA or higher.

Application Requirements: Application, financial need analysis. *Deadline:* varies.

Contact: Program Services Department
United Negro College Fund
8260 Willow Oaks Corporate Drive
Fairfax, VA 22031

WYETH SCHOLARSHIP

• *See page 119*

URBAN FINANCIAL SERVICES COALITION-DELAWARE

URBAN BANKERS OF DELAWARE SCHOLARSHIP

Scholarship for high school seniors who are Delaware residents. Applicants must be planning on majoring in business at accredited college or university. Must demonstrate financial need. Minimum "C" grade point average required. Visit Web for additional information. Application deadline is March 30.

Academic Fields/Career Goals: Business/Consumer Services.

Award: Scholarship for use in freshman year; not renewable.

Eligibility Requirements: Applicant must be high school student; planning to enroll or expecting to enroll at a four-year institution or university and resident of Delaware. Available to U.S. citizens.

Application Requirements: Application, financial need analysis. *Deadline:* March 30.

Contact: Urban Financial Services Coalition-Delaware
PO Box 580
Wilmington, DE 19899-0580

VIRGINIA SOCIETY OF CERTIFIED PUBLIC ACCOUNTANTS EDUCATION FOUNDATION

http://www.vscpa.com

VIRGINIA SOCIETY OF CPAS EDUCATIONAL FOUNDATION MINORITY UNDERGRADUATE SCHOLARSHIP

• *See page 51*

VIRGINIA SOCIETY OF CPAS EDUCATIONAL FOUNDATION UNDERGRADUATE SCHOLARSHIP

• *See page 51*

WATERBURY FOUNDATION

http://www.waterburyfoundation.org

MALCOLM BALDRIGE SCHOLARSHIP

One-time award open to undergraduates studying international business or trade. Must be a Connecticut resident enrolled in a Connecticut college. Must be a U.S. citizen.

Academic Fields/Career Goals: Business/Consumer Services; International Studies.

Award: Scholarship for use in freshman, sophomore, junior, or senior years; not renewable. *Number:* 1–2. *Amount:* $1000–$4000.

Eligibility Requirements: Applicant must be enrolled or expecting to enroll at a two-year or four-year institution or university; resident of Connecticut and studying in Connecticut. Available to U.S. citizens.

Application Requirements: Application, essay, financial need analysis, references, transcript. *Deadline:* April 15.

Contact: Elizabeth Moore, Program Officer
Waterbury Foundation
81 West Main Street
Waterbury, CT 06702-1216
Phone: 203-753-1315
Fax: 203-756-3054
E-mail: emoore@waterburyfoundation.org

WISCONSIN FOUNDATION FOR INDEPENDENT COLLEGES, INC. http://www.wficweb.org

LAND'S END SCHOLARSHIP

Scholarships are awarded to students majoring in business, communications, economics or computer science. One scholarship awarded at each of Wisconsin's private colleges and universities. Minimum 3.0 GPA required.

Academic Fields/Career Goals: Business/Consumer Services; Communications; Computer Science/Data Processing; Economics.

Award: Scholarship for use in freshman, sophomore, junior, or senior years; renewable. *Number:* 20. *Amount:* $1000.

Eligibility Requirements: Applicant must be enrolled or expecting to enroll full-time at a four-year institution or university and studying in Wisconsin. Applicant must have 3.0 GPA or higher. Available to U.S. citizens.

Application Requirements: Application, autobiography, references. *Deadline:* March 12.

Contact: Christy Miller, Marketing Program Manager
Wisconsin Foundation for Independent Colleges, Inc.
735 North Water Street, Suite 600
Milwaukee, WI 53202
Phone: 414-273-5980
Fax: 414-273-5995
E-mail: wfic@execpc.com

SENTRY 21 CLUB SCHOLARSHIP

Scholarships are awarded to incoming freshmen majoring in business, economics, mathematics, management information systems, industrial design, communication design or interior architecture and design. One scholarship awarded at each of Wisconsin's private colleges and universities. Minimum 3.3 GPA required.

Academic Fields/Career Goals: Business/Consumer Services; Computer Science/Data Processing; Economics; Physical Sciences and Math.

Award: Scholarship for use in freshman, sophomore, junior, or senior years; renewable. *Number:* 20. *Amount:* $1000.

Eligibility Requirements: Applicant must be enrolled or expecting to enroll full-time at a four-year institution or university and studying in Wisconsin. Available to U.S. citizens.

Application Requirements: Application, autobiography, references. *Deadline:* April 18.

Contact: Christy Miller, Marketing Program Manager
Wisconsin Foundation for Independent Colleges, Inc.
735 North Water Street, Suite 600
Milwaukee, WI 53202
Phone: 414-273-5980
Fax: 414-273-5995
E-mail: wfic@execpc.com

WE ENERGIES SCHOLARSHIP

• *See page 52*

WOMEN GROCERS OF AMERICA http://www.nationalgrocers.org

MARY MACEY SCHOLARSHIP

• *See page 61*

WOMEN IN LOGISTICS, NORTHERN CALIFORNIA http://www.womeninlogistics.org

WOMEN IN LOGISTICS SCHOLARSHIP

Award for students who plan to study and eventually pursue a career in a logistics and supply chain management. Must enroll in a California institution. Must be a member of Women in Logistics.

Academic Fields/Career Goals: Business/Consumer Services; Trade/Technical Specialties; Transportation.

Award: Scholarship for use in freshman, sophomore, junior, senior, or graduate years; not renewable. *Number:* 1–3. *Amount:* $500–$1000.

Eligibility Requirements: Applicant must be enrolled or expecting to enroll full or part-time at a two-year or four-year or technical institution or university; studying in California and must have an interest in designated field specified by sponsor. Applicant or parent of applicant must be member of Women in Logistics. Available to U.S. and non-U.S. citizens.

Application Requirements: Application, essay, resume, references, transcript. *Deadline:* varies.

Contact: Dr. Susan Cholette, Scholarship Director
Women in Logistics, Northern California
PO Box 194681
San Francisco, CA 94119-4681
Phone: 415-405-2173
Fax: 415-405-0364
E-mail: cholette@sfsu.edu

WYOMING TRUCKING ASSOCIATION

WYOMING TRUCKING ASSOCIATION TRUST FUND SCHOLARSHIP

One-time award for Wyoming high school seniors who will enroll at a Wyoming college. Must plan a career in the transportation industry in Wyoming. Course of study includes business and sales management, computer skills, accounting, office procedures and management, communications, mechanics, truck driver training and safety.

Academic Fields/Career Goals: Business/Consumer Services; Communications; Computer Science/Data Processing; Mechanical Engineering; Trade/Technical Specialties; Transportation.

Award: Scholarship for use in freshman, sophomore, junior, or senior years; not renewable. *Number:* 1–10. *Amount:* $250–$960.

Eligibility Requirements: Applicant must be high school student; planning to enroll or expecting to enroll full-time at a two-year or four-year or technical institution or university; resident of Wyoming and studying in Wyoming. Available to U.S. citizens.

Application Requirements: Application, essay, financial need analysis, references, test scores, transcript. *Deadline:* varies.

Contact: Kathy Cundall, Administrative Assistant
Wyoming Trucking Association
Box 1909
Casper, WY 82602-1909
Phone: 307-234-1579
Fax: 307-234-7082
E-mail: wytruck@aol.com

ZONTA INTERNATIONAL FOUNDATION http://www.zonta.org

JANE M. KLAUSMAN WOMEN IN BUSINESS SCHOLARSHIPS

Awards for female students entering their third or fourth year in an undergraduate business degree. Application available at Web site http://www.zonta.org

Academic Fields/Career Goals: Business/Consumer Services.

Award: Scholarship for use in junior or senior years; not renewable. *Number:* 5. *Amount:* $4000.

Eligibility Requirements: Applicant must be enrolled or expecting to enroll at a four-year institution or university and female. Available to U.S. and non-U.S. citizens.

Zonta International Foundation (continued)

Application Requirements: Application, essay, references. *Deadline:* varies.

Contact: Ms. Ana Ubides, Foundation Assistant
Zonta International Foundation
557 West Randolph Street
Chicago, IL 60661-2206
Phone: 312-930-5848
Fax: 312-930-0951
E-mail: zontafdtn@zonta.org

CHEMICAL ENGINEERING

AACE INTERNATIONAL http://www.aacei.org

AACE INTERNATIONAL COMPETITIVE SCHOLARSHIP

• *See page 73*

AEA-OREGON COUNCIL http://www.ous.edu/ecs/scholarships

AEA- OREGON COUNCIL TECHNOLOGY SCHOLARSHIP PROGRAM

Over 30 scholarships given annually to Oregon high school seniors who plan to major in engineering, computer science or a closely related field and attend one of seven Oregon University system campuses. Must be U.S. citizen. Deadline is March 1. Must complete application on Web site: http://www.ous.edu/ecs/scholarships

Academic Fields/Career Goals: Chemical Engineering; Civil Engineering; Computer Science/Data Processing; Electrical Engineering/Electronics; Engineering/Technology; Engineering-Related Technologies; Materials Science, Engineering, and Metallurgy; Mechanical Engineering.

Award: Scholarship for use in freshman, sophomore, junior, or senior years; renewable. *Number:* 30–35. *Amount:* $2500.

Eligibility Requirements: Applicant must be high school student; planning to enroll or expecting to enroll full-time at an institution or university; resident of Oregon and studying in Oregon. Available to U.S. citizens.

Application Requirements: Application, essay, references, test scores, transcript. *Deadline:* March 1.

Contact: Gary Lietke, AeA Scholarship Program Manager
AeA-Oregon Council
18640 Northwest Walker Road, #1027
Beaverton, OR 97006-8927
Phone: 503-725-2920
Fax: 503-725-2921
E-mail: aeaschol@capital.ous.edu

AMERICAN CHEMICAL SOCIETY http://www.chemistry.org/scholars

AMERICAN CHEMICAL SOCIETY SCHOLARS PROGRAM

Renewable award for minority students pursuing studies in chemistry, biochemistry, chemical technology, chemical engineering, or any chemical sciences. Must be U.S. citizen or permanent resident and have minimum 3.0 GPA. Must be Native-American, African-American, or Hispanic. Scholarship amount for freshmen is up to $2500, and up to $3000 for sophomores, juniors and seniors.

Academic Fields/Career Goals: Chemical Engineering; Materials Science, Engineering, and Metallurgy; Natural Sciences.

Award: Scholarship for use in freshman, sophomore, junior, or senior years; renewable. *Number:* 100–200. *Amount:* $2500–$3000.

Eligibility Requirements: Applicant must be American Indian/Alaska Native, Black (non-Hispanic), or Hispanic and enrolled or expecting to enroll full-time at a two-year or four-year or technical institution or university. Applicant must have 3.0 GPA or higher. Available to U.S. citizens.

Application Requirements: Application, financial need analysis, references, test scores, transcript. *Deadline:* February 15.

Contact: Robert Hughes, Manager
American Chemical Society
1155 16th Street, NW
Washington, DC 20036
Phone: 202-872-6048
Fax: 202-776-8003
E-mail: scholars@acs.org

AMERICAN CHEMICAL SOCIETY, RUBBER DIVISION http://www.rubber.org/awards/scholarships.htm

AMERICAN CHEMICAL SOCIETY, RUBBER DIVISION-UNDERGRADUATE SCHOLARSHIP

Candidate must be majoring in a technical discipline relevant to the rubber industry with a "B" or better overall academic average. Two scholarships are awarded to juniors and seniors enrolled in an accredited college or university in the U.S., Canada, Mexico, or Columbia.

Academic Fields/Career Goals: Chemical Engineering; Engineering/Technology; Materials Science, Engineering, and Metallurgy; Mechanical Engineering; Science, Technology, and Society.

Award: Scholarship for use in junior or senior years; not renewable. *Number:* 2. *Amount:* $5000.

Eligibility Requirements: Applicant must be enrolled or expecting to enroll full-time at a four-year institution or university. Applicant must have 3.0 GPA or higher. Available to U.S. and non-U.S. citizens.

Application Requirements: Application, essay, interview, references, test scores, transcript. *Deadline:* March 15.

Contact: Ms. Victoria George, Education Manager
American Chemical Society, Rubber Division
250 South Forge Road, PO Box 499
Akron, OH 44325
Phone: 330-972-6938
Fax: 330-920-5269
E-mail: vgeorge@rubber.org

AMERICAN COUNCIL OF ENGINEERING COMPANIES OF PENNSYLVANIA (ACEC/PA) http://www.acecpa.org

ENGINEERING SCHOLARSHIP

Scholarship is available to a fourth-or fifth-year full-time engineering student. Must be U.S. citizen. Application deadline is January 15.

Academic Fields/Career Goals: Chemical Engineering; Civil Engineering; Electrical Engineering/Electronics; Engineering/Technology; Engineering-Related Technologies; Materials Science, Engineering, and Metallurgy; Mechanical Engineering.

Award: Scholarship for use in senior, or graduate years; not renewable. *Number:* varies. *Amount:* $2000–$5000.

Eligibility Requirements: Applicant must be enrolled or expecting to enroll full-time at a four-year institution or university. Available to U.S. citizens.

Application Requirements: Application, essay, resume, references, transcript. *Deadline:* January 15.

Contact: ACEC/PA
American Council of Engineering Companies of Pennsylvania (ACEC/PA)
2040 Linglestown Road, Suite 200
Harrisburg, PA 17110
Phone: 717-540-6811

AMERICAN ELECTROPLATERS AND SURFACE FINISHERS SOCIETY http://www.aesf.org

AMERICAN ELECTROPLATERS AND SURFACE FINISHERS SCHOLARSHIPS

One-time award to students majoring in materials science, chemical engineering, or environmental engineering. Applicant must be a junior or senior undergraduate studying full time. Also open to graduate students.

Academic Fields/Career Goals: Chemical Engineering; Engineering/Technology; Materials Science, Engineering, and Metallurgy.

Award: Scholarship for use in junior, senior, or graduate years; not renewable. *Number:* 5–10. *Amount:* $1500.

Eligibility Requirements: Applicant must be enrolled or expecting to enroll full-time at a four-year institution or university. Available to U.S. and non-U.S. citizens.

Application Requirements: Application, essay, resume, references, transcript. *Deadline:* April 15.

Contact: Janice Williams, Purchasing Manager
American Electroplaters and Surface Finishers Society
Central Florida Research Park
12644 Research Parkway
Orlando, FL 32826-3298
Phone: 407-281-6441
Fax: 407-281-6446
E-mail: janice@aesf.org

AMERICAN INDIAN SCIENCE AND ENGINEERING SOCIETY http://www.aises.org

ENVIRONMENTAL PROTECTION AGENCY TRIBAL LANDS ENVIRONMENTAL SCIENCE SCHOLARSHIP

• *See page 111*

AMERICAN INSTITUTE OF CHEMICAL ENGINEERS http://www.aiche.org

DONALD F. AND MILDRED TOPP OTHMER FOUNDATION-NATIONAL SCHOLARSHIP AWARDS

Each year, fifteen national AICHE student members are awarded a scholarship of $1000. Awards are presented on the basis of academic achievement and involvement in student chapter activities. The Student Chapter Advisor must make nominations. Only one nomination will be accepted from each AICHE Student Chapter or Chemical Engineering Club.

Academic Fields/Career Goals: Chemical Engineering.

Award: Scholarship for use in freshman, sophomore, junior, senior, or graduate years; not renewable. *Number:* 15. *Amount:* $1000.

Eligibility Requirements: Applicant must be enrolled or expecting to enroll at a four-year institution or university. Available to U.S. citizens.

Application Requirements: Application, nomination. *Deadline:* May 7.

Contact: Awards Administrator
American Institute of Chemical Engineers
Three Park Avenue
New York, NY 10016-5991
Phone: 212-591-7478
Fax: 212-591-8882
E-mail: awards@aiche.org

ENVIRONMENTAL DIVISION UNDERGRADUATE STUDENT PAPER AWARD

Cash prizes awarded to full-time undergraduate students who prepare the best original papers based on the results of research or an investigation related to the environment. The work must be performed during the student's undergraduate enrollment, and the paper must be submitted prior to or within six months of graduation. Student must be the sole author of the paper, but faculty guidance is encouraged. Student must be a member of the American Institute of Chemical Engineers Student Chapter. Student's college or university must have an accredited program in chemical engineering. Must be nominated.

Academic Fields/Career Goals: Chemical Engineering.

Award: Prize for use in freshman, sophomore, junior, or senior years; not renewable. *Number:* 3. *Amount:* $100–$300.

Eligibility Requirements: Applicant must be enrolled or expecting to enroll full-time at a four-year institution or university.

Application Requirements: Applicant must enter a contest, student paper. *Deadline:* September 2.

Contact: Awards Administrator
American Institute of Chemical Engineers
Three Park Avenue
New York, NY 10016-5991
Phone: 212-591-7478
Fax: 212-591-8882
E-mail: awards@aiche.org

JOHN J. MCKETTA UNDERGRADUATE SCHOLARSHIP

A $5000 scholarship will be awarded to a junior or senior student member of AICHE who is planning a career in the chemical engineering process industries. Must maintain a 3.0 GPA. Applicant should show leadership or activity in either the school's AICHE Student Chapter or other university sponsored campus activities.

Academic Fields/Career Goals: Chemical Engineering.

Award: Scholarship for use in junior or senior years; not renewable. *Number:* 1. *Amount:* $5000.

Eligibility Requirements: Applicant must be enrolled or expecting to enroll at a four-year institution or university. Applicant must have 3.0 GPA or higher. Available to U.S. citizens.

Application Requirements: Application, essay, references. *Deadline:* April 15.

Contact: Awards Administrator
American Institute of Chemical Engineers
Three Park Avenue
New York, NY 10016-5991
Phone: 212-591-7478
Fax: 212-591-8882
E-mail: awards@aiche.org

MINORITY AFFAIRS COMMITTEE AWARD FOR OUTSTANDING SCHOLASTIC ACHIEVEMENT

Award recognizing the outstanding achievements of a chemical engineering student who serves as a role model for minority students. $1000 award plus $500 travel allowance to attend AICHE meeting. Must be nominated.

Academic Fields/Career Goals: Chemical Engineering.

Award: Scholarship for use in freshman, sophomore, junior, senior, or graduate years; not renewable. *Number:* 1. *Amount:* $1500.

Eligibility Requirements: Applicant must be American Indian/Alaska Native, Asian/Pacific Islander, Black (non-Hispanic), or Hispanic and enrolled or expecting to enroll at an institution or university.

Application Requirements: Application. *Deadline:* April 15.

Contact: Awards Administrator
American Institute of Chemical Engineers
Three Park Avenue
New York, NY 10016-5991
Phone: 212-591-7478
Fax: 212-591-8882
E-mail: awards@aiche.org

MINORITY SCHOLARSHIP AWARDS FOR COLLEGE STUDENTS

One-time award for college undergraduates who are studying chemical engineering. Must be a member of a minority group that is underrepresented in chemical engineering. Must be nominated. Must be an AICHE national student member at the time of application.

Academic Fields/Career Goals: Chemical Engineering.

Award: Scholarship for use in freshman, sophomore, junior, or senior years; not renewable. *Number:* up to 10. *Amount:* $1000.

Eligibility Requirements: Applicant must be American Indian/Alaska Native, Asian/Pacific Islander, Black (non-Hispanic), or Hispanic and enrolled or expecting to enroll at a four-year institution or university.

Application Requirements: Application, financial need analysis. *Deadline:* April 15.

Contact: Awards Administrator
American Institute of Chemical Engineers
Three Park Avenue
New York, NY 10016-5991
Phone: 212-591-7478
Fax: 212-591-8882
E-mail: awards@aiche.org

MINORITY SCHOLARSHIP AWARDS FOR INCOMING COLLEGE FRESHMEN

Up to ten awards of $1000 for high school graduates who are members of a minority group that is underrepresented in chemical engineering. Must plan to study courses leading to a chemical engineering degree. Must be nominated.

American Institute of Chemical Engineers (continued)

Academic Fields/Career Goals: Chemical Engineering.

Award: Scholarship for use in freshman year; not renewable. *Number:* up to 10. *Amount:* $1000.

Eligibility Requirements: Applicant must be American Indian/Alaska Native, Asian/Pacific Islander, Black (non-Hispanic), or Hispanic; high school student and planning to enroll or expecting to enroll at an institution or university.

Application Requirements: Application, financial need analysis. *Deadline:* April 15.

Contact: Awards Administrator
American Institute of Chemical Engineers
Three Park Avenue
New York, NY 10016-5991
Phone: 212-591-7478
Fax: 212-591-8882
E-mail: awards@aiche.org

NATIONAL STUDENT DESIGN COMPETITION-INDIVIDUAL

Three cash prizes for student contest problem that typifies a real, working, chemical engineering design situation. Competition booklets are available from Student Chapter advisors. Must be nominated.

Academic Fields/Career Goals: Chemical Engineering.

Award: Prize for use in freshman, sophomore, junior, senior, or graduate years; not renewable. *Number:* 3. *Amount:* $200–$500.

Eligibility Requirements: Applicant must be enrolled or expecting to enroll at a four-year institution or university.

Application Requirements: Applicant must enter a contest, contest problem. *Deadline:* June 4.

Contact: Awards Administrator
American Institute of Chemical Engineers
Three Park Avenue
New York, NY 10016-5991
Phone: 212-591-7478
Fax: 212-591-8882
E-mail: awards@aiche.org

NATIONAL STUDENT PAPER COMPETITION

First-place winners from each of the ten Regional Student Paper Competitions present their prize-winning papers during the American Institute of Chemical Engineers meeting in November. First prize is $500, second prize is $300, and third prize is $200.

Academic Fields/Career Goals: Chemical Engineering.

Award: Prize for use in freshman, sophomore, junior, senior, or graduate years; not renewable. *Number:* 3. *Amount:* $200–$500.

Eligibility Requirements: Applicant must be enrolled or expecting to enroll at a four-year institution or university.

Application Requirements: Applicant must enter a contest, student paper. *Deadline:* varies.

Contact: Awards Administrator
American Institute of Chemical Engineers
Three Park Avenue
New York, NY 10016-5991
Phone: 212-591-7478
Fax: 212-591-8882
E-mail: awards@aiche.org

PROCESS DEVELOPMENT DIVISION STUDENT PAPER AWARD

Presented to a full-time graduate or undergraduate student who prepares the best technical paper to describe the results of process development related studies within chemical engineering. Must be carried out while the student is enrolled at a university with an accredited chemical engineering program. Student must be the primary author (faculty advisors may be co-authors). Paper must be suitable for publication in a refereed journal. Student must be a member of AIChE.

Academic Fields/Career Goals: Chemical Engineering.

Award: Prize for use in freshman, sophomore, junior, senior, or graduate years; not renewable. *Number:* 1. *Amount:* $200.

Eligibility Requirements: Applicant must be enrolled or expecting to enroll full-time at a four-year institution or university. Available to U.S. citizens.

Application Requirements: References. *Deadline:* June 15.

Contact: Glen Wheeler, Process Development Division Awards Committee, Alkermes, Inc.
American Institute of Chemical Engineers
265 Olinger Circle
Wilmington, OH 45177
Phone: 937-655-4411
Fax: 937-382-5949
E-mail: Glen.Wheeler@Alkermes.com

REGIONAL STUDENT PAPER COMPETITION

Students present technical papers at the student regional conferences which are held in the spring. Deadlines for regional conferences vary; contact regional host schools for details or look for schedules on Web site (http://www.aiche.org). First prize is $200, second prize is $100, and third prize is $50. First place winner from each region presents the paper at the National Student Paper Competition.

Academic Fields/Career Goals: Chemical Engineering.

Award: Prize for use in freshman, sophomore, junior, senior, or graduate years; not renewable. *Number:* 3. *Amount:* $50–$200.

Eligibility Requirements: Applicant must be enrolled or expecting to enroll at a four-year institution or university.

Application Requirements: Applicant must enter a contest, student paper. *Deadline:* varies.

Contact: Awards Administrator
American Institute of Chemical Engineers
Three Park Avenue
New York, NY 10016-5991
Phone: 212-591-7478
Fax: 212-591-8882
E-mail: awards@aiche.org

SAFETY AND CHEMICAL ENGINEERING EDUCATION (SACHE) STUDENT ESSAY AWARD

Two $500 dollar awards will be presented to the individuals submitting the best essays on the topic of chemical process safety. Essays may focus on process safety in education, relevance of safety in undergraduate education, or integrating safety principles into the undergraduate chemical engineering curriculum. The essay must be no more than 1500 words. The student must be an undergraduate student. The student's school must be a member of SACHE.

Academic Fields/Career Goals: Chemical Engineering.

Award: Prize for use in freshman, sophomore, junior, or senior years; not renewable. *Number:* 2. *Amount:* $500.

Eligibility Requirements: Applicant must be enrolled or expecting to enroll at a four-year institution or university. Available to U.S. citizens.

Application Requirements: Applicant must enter a contest, essay. *Deadline:* June 2.

Contact: Awards Administrator
American Institute of Chemical Engineers
Three Park Avenue
New York, NY 10016-5991
Phone: 212-591-7478
Fax: 212-591-8882
E-mail: awards@aiche.org

SAFETY AND HEALTH NATIONAL STUDENT DESIGN COMPETITION AWARD FOR SAFETY

Four $500 awards available for each of the teams or individuals who apply one or more of the following concepts of inherent safety in their designs: a) Design the plant for easier and effective maintainability; b) design the plant with less waste; c) Design the plant with special features that demonstrate inherent safety; d) Include design concepts regarding the entire life cycle. The school must have a student chapter of AIChE.

Academic Fields/Career Goals: Chemical Engineering.

Award: Prize for use in freshman, sophomore, junior, senior, or graduate years; not renewable. *Number:* 4. *Amount:* $500.

Eligibility Requirements: Applicant must be enrolled or expecting to enroll full or part-time at a four-year institution or university. Available to U.S. citizens.

Application Requirements: Design. *Deadline:* June 4.

Contact: AIChE Awards Administrator
American Institute of Chemical Engineers
3 Park Avenue
New York, NY 10016
Phone: 212-591-7478
Fax: 212-591-8882

W. DAVID SMITH, JR. GRADUATE STUDENT PAPER AWARD

$1500 and a plaque is awarded to an individual for published work on the application of computing and systems technology to chemical engineering. The work must have been done by the individual while pursuing graduate or undergraduate studies in chemical engineering.

Academic Fields/Career Goals: Chemical Engineering.

Award: Prize for use in freshman, sophomore, junior, senior, or graduate years; not renewable. *Number:* 1. *Amount:* $1500.

Eligibility Requirements: Applicant must be enrolled or expecting to enroll at a two-year or four-year institution or university. Available to U.S. citizens.

Application Requirements: Applicant must enter a contest. *Deadline:* April 15.

Contact: Awards Administrator
American Institute of Chemical Engineers
Three Park Avenue
New York, NY 10016-5991
Phone: 212-591-7478
Fax: 212-591-8882
E-mail: awards@aiche.org

AMERICAN SOCIETY FOR CLINICAL LABORATORY SCIENCE http://www.ascls.org

ASCLS FORUM FOR CONCERNS OF MINORITIES SCHOLARSHIP

Two scholarships will be awarded to a CLS/MT and a CLS/MLT student, if eligible applicants from both groups apply. Applicant must be minority student accepted in an NAACLS accredited clinical laboratory science/medical technology or medical laboratory technician program. Applicant must demonstrate financial need. Please refer to Web site for further details: http://www.ascls.org.

Academic Fields/Career Goals: Chemical Engineering; Health and Medical Sciences.

Award: Scholarship for use in freshman, sophomore, junior, or senior years; not renewable. *Number:* 2. *Amount:* varies.

Eligibility Requirements: Applicant must be American Indian/Alaska Native, Asian/Pacific Islander, Black (non-Hispanic), or Hispanic and enrolled or expecting to enroll full or part-time at a two-year or four-year or technical institution or university. Available to U.S. citizens.

Application Requirements: Application, financial need analysis. *Deadline:* April 1.

Contact: A. Casey Ceasor, Scholarship Chair, Forum for Concerns of Minorities
American Society for Clinical Laboratory Science
c/o ASCLS, 6701 Democracy Boulevard, Suite 300
Bethesda, MD 20817
E-mail: acaseyc@msn.com

ASCLS REGION IX CLINICAL LABORATORY SCIENTISTS OF ALASKA SHARON O'MEARA CONTINUING EDUCATION SCHOLARSHIP FUND

Scholarships awarded to students pursuing continuing education in clinical laboratory science or related fields. Students must be a member in good standing of the CLSA and have been a member for at least one year at time of application. Please refer to Web site for further details and application: http://www.clsaonline.org.

Academic Fields/Career Goals: Chemical Engineering; Health and Medical Sciences.

Award: Scholarship for use in freshman, sophomore, junior, senior, or graduate years; not renewable. *Number:* 1. *Amount:* varies.

Eligibility Requirements: Applicant must be enrolled or expecting to enroll full or part-time at a two-year or four-year or technical institution or university. Applicant or parent of applicant must be member of American Society for Clinical Laboratory Science. Available to U.S. citizens.

Application Requirements: Application. *Deadline:* varies.

Contact: Karen Martin, CLSA Webmaster
American Society for Clinical Laboratory Science
4382 Reka Drive
Anchorage, AK 99508-3679
E-mail: webmaster@clsaonline.org

ASCLS REGION VI MISSOURI ORGANIZATION FOR CLINICAL LABORATORY SCIENCE EDUCATION SCHOLARSHIP

Scholarship provides financial assistance to clinical laboratory science or medical laboratory technology students who are beginning or continuing their formal education, or conducting research that directly relates to laboratory science. Applicant must be a member of MOCLS for a minimum of two years. Please refer to Web site for further information and applications: http://www.mocls.org.

Academic Fields/Career Goals: Chemical Engineering; Health and Medical Sciences.

Award: Scholarship for use in freshman, sophomore, junior, or graduate years; not renewable. *Number:* varies. *Amount:* varies.

Eligibility Requirements: Applicant must be enrolled or expecting to enroll full or part-time at a two-year or four-year or technical institution or university. Applicant or parent of applicant must be member of American Society for Clinical Laboratory Science. Available to U.S. citizens.

Application Requirements: Application, references, transcript, proof of enrollment, personal letter. *Deadline:* varies.

Contact: Tom Reddig, Missouri Scholarship Fund Chair
American Society for Clinical Laboratory Science
31 West 59th Street
Kansas City, MO 64113
Phone: 816-931-8686

AMERICAN SOCIETY FOR ENOLOGY AND VITICULTURE http://www.asev.org

AMERICAN SOCIETY FOR ENOLOGY AND VITICULTURE SCHOLARSHIPS

• *See page 56*

ASSOCIATION FOR FACILITIES ENGINEERING (AFE)

ASSOCIATION FOR FACILITIES ENGINEERING CEDAR VALLEY CHAPTER # 132 SCHOLARSHIP

• *See page 97*

ASSOCIATION FOR IRON AND STEEL TECHNOLOGY http://www.aist.org/foundation/scholarships.htm

ASSOCIATION FOR IRON AND STEEL TECHNOLOGY DAVID H. SAMSON SCHOLARSHIP

Scholarship available for children of AIST members who are Canadian citizens. Scholarship is renewable for up to four years, student must be studying engineering at a Canadian institution or, in the absence of engineering applicants, the award may be made to an eligible student studying chemistry, geology, mathematics, or physics. Application forms and rules may be obtained by writing to scholarship contact.

Academic Fields/Career Goals: Chemical Engineering; Civil Engineering; Electrical Engineering/Electronics; Energy and Power Engineering; Engineering/Technology; Marine/Ocean Engineering; Materials Science, Engineering, and Metallurgy.

Association for Iron and Steel Technology (continued)

Award: Scholarship for use in freshman, sophomore, junior, or senior years; renewable. *Number:* 1. *Amount:* $2000.

Eligibility Requirements: Applicant must be enrolled or expecting to enroll full-time at a four-year institution or university. Available to Canadian citizens.

Application Requirements: Application, references, transcript. *Deadline:* June 30.

Contact: Robert Kneale, AIST Northern Member Chapter Scholarship Chair
Association for Iron and Steel Technology
PO Box 1734
Cambridge, ON N1R 7G8
CAN

ASSOCIATION FOR WOMEN IN SCIENCE EDUCATIONAL FOUNDATION http://www.awis.org/ed_foundation.html

ASSOCIATION FOR WOMEN IN SCIENCE COLLEGE SCHOLARSHIP

• *See page 63*

ASTRONAUT SCHOLARSHIP FOUNDATION http://www.astronautscholarship.org

ASTRONAUT SCHOLARSHIP FOUNDATION

• *See page 68*

AUTOMOTIVE HALL OF FAME http://www.automotivehalloffame.org

AUTOMOTIVE HALL OF FAME EDUCATIONAL FUNDS

Over a dozen available awards. Applicant must have a sincere interest in an automotive career. Candidate should maintain a satisfactory academic standing and be enrolled full-time. Financial need is considered but not necessary. Renewable award of varying amounts. Applicants in a four-year program must have completed at least one year of study. Must already be accepted at an accredited college, university, or trade school within the United States at the time of application. High school seniors must submit letter of acceptance. Applicant must send a self-addressed envelope.

Academic Fields/Career Goals: Chemical Engineering; Electrical Engineering/Electronics; Engineering/Technology; Engineering-Related Technologies; Mechanical Engineering; Trade/Technical Specialties.

Award: Scholarship for use in freshman, sophomore, junior, senior, or graduate years; renewable. *Number:* 12. *Amount:* $250–$2000.

Eligibility Requirements: Applicant must be enrolled or expecting to enroll full-time at a two-year or four-year or technical institution or university and must have an interest in automotive. Applicant must have 3.0 GPA or higher. Available to U.S. and non-U.S. citizens.

Application Requirements: Application, financial need analysis, references, self-addressed stamped envelope, transcript. *Deadline:* May 30.

Contact: Lynne Hall, Scholarship Coordinator
Automotive Hall of Fame
21400 Oakwood Boulevard
Dearborn, MI 48124-4078

BARRY M. GOLDWATER SCHOLARSHIP AND EXCELLENCE IN EDUCATION FOUNDATION http://www.act.org/goldwater

BARRY M. GOLDWATER SCHOLARSHIP AND EXCELLENCE IN EDUCATION PROGRAM

• *See page 68*

CHEMICAL INSTITUTE OF CANADA http://www.cheminst.ca

EDMONTON CHEMICAL ENGINEERING SCHOLARSHIP

One scholarship available to an undergraduate student in chemical engineering entering the second, third, fourth, or fifth year of studies at a Canadian university. Applicants must be members of the Canadian Society for Chemical Engineering. One-time award of CAN$1000 and up to CAN$750 in travel expenses.

Academic Fields/Career Goals: Chemical Engineering.

Award: Scholarship for use in sophomore, junior, or senior years; not renewable. *Number:* 1. *Amount:* $743.

Eligibility Requirements: Applicant must be enrolled or expecting to enroll full-time at an institution or university. Applicant or parent of applicant must be member of Canadian Society for Chemical Engineering. Available to U.S. and Canadian citizens.

Application Requirements: Application, essay, references, transcript. *Deadline:* April 30.

Contact: Gale Thirlwall-Wilbee, Manager of Outreach and Career Services
Chemical Institute of Canada
130 Slater Street, Suite 550
Ottawa, ON K1P 6E2
Canada
Phone: 613-232-6252 Ext. 223
Fax: 613-232-5862
E-mail: gwilbee@cheminst.ca

SARNIA CHEMICAL ENGINEERING COMMUNITY SCHOLARSHIP

One scholarship available to undergraduate students in chemical engineering about to enter their final year of studies at a Canadian university. Applicants must be members of the Canadian Society for Chemical Engineering. Applications should include evidence of contributions to the Society. One-time award of CAN$1000.

Academic Fields/Career Goals: Chemical Engineering.

Award: Scholarship for use in senior year; not renewable. *Number:* 1. *Amount:* $743.

Eligibility Requirements: Applicant must be enrolled or expecting to enroll full-time at an institution or university. Applicant or parent of applicant must be member of Canadian Society for Chemical Engineering. Available to U.S. and Canadian citizens.

Application Requirements: Application, references, transcript. *Deadline:* April 30.

Contact: Gale Thirlwall-Wilbee, Manager of Outreach and Career Services
Chemical Institute of Canada
130 Slater Street, Suite 550
Ottawa, ON K1P 6E2
Canada
Phone: 613-232-6252 Ext. 223
Fax: 613-232-5862
E-mail: gwilbee@cheminst.ca

SNC LAVALIN PLANT DESIGN COMPETITION

One prize available for students enrolled in an undergraduate chemical engineering program at a Canadian university. Entries should include a flowsheet and summary, a final report, list of students involved, and the name of any collaborating organization. A letter authorizing the release of information in "Canadian Chemical News" is also required. Projects will be presented at the Canadian Chemical Engineering Conference by the Canadian Society for Chemical Engineering. One-time prize of CAN$1000.

Academic Fields/Career Goals: Chemical Engineering.

Award: Prize for use in freshman, sophomore, junior, or senior years; not renewable. *Number:* 1. *Amount:* $743.

Eligibility Requirements: Applicant must be enrolled or expecting to enroll full-time at an institution or university. Available to U.S. and Canadian citizens.

Application Requirements: Application, essay. *Deadline:* May 15.

Contact: Gale Thirlwall-Wilbee, Manager of Outreach and Career Services
Chemical Institute of Canada
130 Slater Street, Suite 550
Ottawa, ON K1P 6E2
Canada
Phone: 613-232-6252 Ext. 223
Fax: 613-232-5862
E-mail: gwilbee@cheminst.ca

CONNECTICUT STUDENT LOAN FOUNDATION http://www.cslf.com

CONNECTICUT INNOVATIONS TECHNOLOGY SCHOLAR PROGRAM

• *See page 113*

CUBAN AMERICAN NATIONAL FOUNDATION

MAS FAMILY SCHOLARSHIPS

• *See page 123*

DELAWARE SOLID WASTE AUTHORITY http://www.dswa.com

DELAWARE SOLID WASTE AUTHORITY SCHOLARSHIP

• *See page 113*

DESK AND DERRICK EDUCATIONAL TRUST http://www.addc.org

DESK AND DERRICK EDUCATIONAL TRUST

• *See page 69*

EAST LOS ANGELES COMMUNITY UNION (TELACU) EDUCATION FOUNDATION

TELACU ENGINEERING AWARD

Scholarships available to low-income applicants from the Greater East Side of Los Angeles. Must be U.S. citizen or permanent resident with Hispanic heritage. Must be a resident of one of the following communities: East Los Angeles, Bell Gardens, Commerce, Huntington Park, Montebello, Monterey Park, Pico Rivera, Santa Ana, South Gate, and the City of Los Angeles. Must be the first generation in their family to achieve a college degree. Must have a record of community service. For sophomores, juniors and seniors only who have completed 12 credits or more of engineering course work at the time of application.

Academic Fields/Career Goals: Chemical Engineering; Computer Science/Data Processing; Electrical Engineering/Electronics; Engineering/Technology; Engineering-Related Technologies; Mechanical Engineering.

Award: Scholarship for use in sophomore, junior, or senior years; not renewable. *Number:* 1–2. *Amount:* $2500–$5000.

Eligibility Requirements: Applicant must be of Hispanic heritage; enrolled or expecting to enroll full-time at a four-year institution or university and resident of California. Applicant must have 3.0 GPA or higher. Available to U.S. citizens.

Application Requirements: Application, autobiography, essay, financial need analysis, interview, references, self-addressed stamped envelope, transcript. *Deadline:* April 3.

Contact: Mr. Michael A. Alvarado, Director
East Los Angeles Community Union (TELACU) Education Foundation
5400 East Olympic Boulevard, Suite 300
Los Angeles, CA 90022
Phone: 323-721-1655 Ext. 403
Fax: 323-724-3372
E-mail: malvarado@telacu.com

GEORGE BIRD GRINNELL AMERICAN INDIAN FUND

AL QOYAWAYMA AWARD

Up to $1000 scholarship for American-Indian/Alaska Native students majoring in either science or engineering in either an undergraduate or graduate program. Must demonstrate an outstanding interest and skill in any one of the arts (visual, performing or written). Applicants must demonstrate financial need, submit personal statement, proof of school enrollment or acceptance, and proof of tribal enrollment. Award of scholarship is totally contingent upon raising the needed funds. Application deadline June 1. Please include self-addressed stamped envelope.

Academic Fields/Career Goals: Chemical Engineering; Civil Engineering; Earth Science; Electrical Engineering/Electronics; Engineering/Technology; Engineering-Related Technologies; Materials Science, Engineering, and Metallurgy; Mechanical Engineering; Science, Technology, and Society.

Award: Scholarship for use in freshman, sophomore, junior, senior, graduate, or postgraduate years; renewable. *Number:* 1. *Amount:* up to $1000.

Eligibility Requirements: Applicant must be American Indian/Alaska Native; enrolled or expecting to enroll full or part-time at a two-year or four-year institution or university and must have an interest in art, music, music/singing, or writing. Available to U.S. citizens.

Application Requirements: Application, essay, financial need analysis, references, self-addressed stamped envelope, transcript, proof of tribal enrollment. *Deadline:* June 1.

Contact: Dr. Paula Mintzies, President
George Bird Grinnell American Indian Fund
PO Box 59033
Potomac, MD 20859
Phone: 301-424-2440
Fax: 301-424-8281

HAROLD B. & DOROTHY A. SNYDER FOUNDATION, INC.

HAROLD B. AND DOROTHY A. SNYDER FOUNDATION, INC., PROGRAM

Renewable scholarships for students studying for degrees in nursing (BSN), pastoral ministry (MDiv), or some aspect of building industry/engineering. Must be a U.S. citizen. Deadline: March 15.

Academic Fields/Career Goals: Chemical Engineering; Civil Engineering; Computer Science/Data Processing; Drafting; Electrical Engineering/Electronics; Engineering/Technology; Engineering-Related Technologies; Mechanical Engineering; Nursing; Religion/Theology.

Award: Scholarship for use in freshman, sophomore, junior, senior, or graduate years; renewable.

Eligibility Requirements: Applicant must be Presbyterian or Protestant and enrolled or expecting to enroll full-time at a four-year institution or university. Available to U.S. citizens.

Application Requirements: Application, essay, financial need analysis, interview, photo, references, test scores, transcript. *Deadline:* March 15.

Contact: Audrey Snyder, Executive Director
Harold B. & Dorothy A. Snyder Foundation, Inc.
525 Eaglebrook Drive
Moorestown, NJ 08057

HAWAIIAN LODGE, F.& A. M. http://www.hawaiianlodge.org/

HAWAIIAN LODGE SCHOLARSHIPS

• *See page 76*

HISPANIC COLLEGE FUND, INC. http://www.hispanicfund.org

DENNY'S/HISPANIC COLLEGE FUND SCHOLARSHIP

• *See page 41*

DEPARTMENT OF ENERGY SCHOLARSHIP PROGRAM

• *See page 125*

LOCKHEED MARTIN SCHOLARSHIP PROGRAM

Program intended for undergraduate student pursuing his or her bachelor's degree in computer science, engineering, or similar major. Applicant must be U.S. citizen with Hispanic background; may reside in U.S. or Puerto Rico. Must attend college or university in U.S. or Puerto Rico. Online application only: http://www.hispanicfund.org.

Hispanic College Fund, Inc. (continued)

Academic Fields/Career Goals: Chemical Engineering; Computer Science/Data Processing; Electrical Engineering/Electronics; Energy and Power Engineering; Engineering/Technology; Engineering-Related Technologies; Materials Science, Engineering, and Metallurgy; Military and Defense Studies; Physical Sciences and Math.

Award: Scholarship for use in freshman, sophomore, junior, or senior years; not renewable. *Number:* varies. *Amount:* $500–$5000.

Eligibility Requirements: Applicant must be Hispanic and enrolled or expecting to enroll full-time at a four-year institution or university. Applicant must have 3.0 GPA or higher. Available to U.S. citizens.

Application Requirements: Application. *Deadline:* April 15.

Contact: Stina Augustsson, Program Manager
Hispanic College Fund, Inc.
1717 Pennsylvania Avenue, NW, Suite 460
Washington, DC 20006
Phone: 202-296-5400
Fax: 202-296-3774
E-mail: hcf-info@hispanicfund.org

NATIONAL HISPANIC EXPLORERS SCHOLARSHIP PROGRAM
• *See page 69*

HISPANIC ENGINEER NATIONAL ACHIEVEMENT AWARDS CORPORATION (HENAAC)

http://www.henaac.org

HISPANIC ENGINEER NATIONAL ACHIEVEMENT AWARDS CORPORATION SCHOLARSHIP PROGRAM
• *See page 99*

HISPANIC SCHOLARSHIP FUND

http://www.hsf.net

HSF/GENERAL MOTORS SCHOLARSHIP
• *See page 126*

INDEPENDENT LABORATORIES INSTITUTE SCHOLARSHIP ALLIANCE

http://www.acil.org

INDEPENDENT LABORATORIES INSTITUTE SCHOLARSHIP ALLIANCE
• *See page 69*

INNOVATION AND SCIENCE COUNCIL OF BRITISH COLUMBIA

http://www.scbc.org

PAUL AND HELEN TRUSSEL SCIENCE AND TECHNOLOGY SCHOLARSHIP
• *See page 69*

INSTRUMENTATION, SYSTEMS, AND AUTOMATION SOCIETY (ISA)

http://www.isa.org

INSTRUMENTATION, SYSTEMS, AND AUTOMATION SOCIETY (ISA) SCHOLARSHIP PROGRAM
• *See page 99*

INTERNATIONAL SOCIETY FOR OPTICAL ENGINEERING-SPIE

http://www.spie.org/info/scholarships

SPIE EDUCATIONAL SCHOLARSHIPS IN OPTICAL SCIENCE AND ENGINEERING
• *See page 70*

JORGE MAS CANOSA FREEDOM FOUNDATION

MAS FAMILY SCHOLARSHIP AWARD
• *See page 126*

KENTUCKY NATURAL RESOURCES AND ENVIRONMENTAL PROTECTION CABINET

http://www.uky.edu/waterresources

ENVIRONMENTAL PROTECTION SCHOLARSHIPS

Renewable awards for college juniors, seniors, and graduate students for tuition, fees, and room and board at a Kentucky state university. Awards of $4000 to $5000 per semester for up to four semesters. Minimum 2.5 GPA required. Must agree to work full-time for the Kentucky Natural Resources and Environmental Protection Cabinet upon graduation. Interview is required.

Academic Fields/Career Goals: Chemical Engineering; Civil Engineering; Earth Science; Materials Science, Engineering, and Metallurgy.

Award: Forgivable loan for use in junior, senior, or graduate years; renewable. *Number:* 3–5. *Amount:* $4000–$5000.

Eligibility Requirements: Applicant must be enrolled or expecting to enroll full-time at a four-year institution or university and studying in Kentucky. Applicant must have 2.5 GPA or higher. Available to U.S. and non-U.S. citizens.

Application Requirements: Application, essay, interview, references, transcript, non-U.S. citizens must have valid work permit. *Deadline:* February 15.

Contact: James Kipp, Scholarship Program Coordinator
Kentucky Natural Resources and Environmental Protection Cabinet
233 Mining/Mineral Resources Building
Lexington, KY 40506-0107
Phone: 859-257-1299
Fax: 859-323-1049
E-mail: kipp@uky.edu

LOS ANGELES COUNCIL OF BLACK PROFESSIONAL ENGINEERS

http://www.lablackengineers.org/scholarships.html

AL-BEN SCHOLARSHIP FOR ACADEMIC INCENTIVE

Scholarships will be granted for notable academic achievements, interests in engineering, math, or science, and demonstrated desire and commitment to succeed in technical fields. Must be from a minority group that has traditionally been underrepresented in these areas. For more details or an application see Web site: http://www.lablackengineers.org.

Academic Fields/Career Goals: Chemical Engineering; Civil Engineering; Computer Science/Data Processing; Electrical Engineering/Electronics; Engineering/Technology; Engineering-Related Technologies; Materials Science, Engineering, and Metallurgy; Mechanical Engineering; Physical Sciences and Math.

Award: Scholarship for use in freshman, sophomore, junior, or senior years; not renewable. *Number:* 2. *Amount:* $500–$1000.

Eligibility Requirements: Applicant must be American Indian/Alaska Native, Asian/Pacific Islander, Black (non-Hispanic), or Hispanic and enrolled or expecting to enroll at an institution or university. Available to U.S. citizens.

Application Requirements: Application, essay, references, transcript. *Deadline:* April 5.

Contact: Application available at Web site.

AL-BEN SCHOLARSHIP FOR PROFESSIONAL MERIT

Scholarships will be granted for exemplary actions in campus organizations or community activities while maintaining an excellent GPA. Must be from a minority group. For more details or an application see Web site: http://www.lablackengineers.org.

Academic Fields/Career Goals: Chemical Engineering; Civil Engineering; Computer Science/Data Processing; Electrical Engineering/Electronics; Engineering/Technology; Engineering-Related Technologies; Materials Science, Engineering, and Metallurgy; Mechanical Engineering; Physical Sciences and Math.

Award: Scholarship for use in freshman, sophomore, junior, or senior years; not renewable. *Number:* 2. *Amount:* $500–$1000.

Eligibility Requirements: Applicant must be American Indian/Alaska Native, Asian/Pacific Islander, Black (non-Hispanic), or Hispanic and enrolled or expecting to enroll at an institution or university. Available to U.S. citizens.

Application Requirements: Application, essay, references, transcript. *Deadline:* April 5.

Contact: Application available at Web site.

AL-BEN SCHOLARSHIP FOR SCHOLASTIC ACHIEVEMENT

Scholarships will be granted for superlative scholastic achievements in the academic pursuits of engineering, math, computer or scientific studies. Must be from a minority group that has traditionally been underrepresented in these areas. For more details or an application see Web site: http://www.lablackengineers.org.

Academic Fields/Career Goals: Chemical Engineering; Civil Engineering; Computer Science/Data Processing; Electrical Engineering/Electronics; Engineering/Technology; Engineering-Related Technologies; Materials Science, Engineering, and Metallurgy; Mechanical Engineering; Physical Sciences and Math.

Award: Scholarship for use in freshman, sophomore, junior, or senior years; not renewable. *Number:* 2. *Amount:* $500–$1000.

Eligibility Requirements: Applicant must be American Indian/Alaska Native, Asian/Pacific Islander, Black (non-Hispanic), or Hispanic and enrolled or expecting to enroll at a four-year institution or university. Available to U.S. citizens.

Application Requirements: Application, essay, references, transcript. *Deadline:* April 5.

Contact: Application available at Web site.

LUCENT TECHNOLOGIES FOUNDATION http://www.iie.org/programs/lucent

LUCENT GLOBAL SCIENCE SCHOLARS PROGRAM

• *See page 70*

MASTER BREWERS ASSOCIATION OF THE AMERICAS http://www.mbaa.com

MASTER BREWERS ASSOCIATION OF THE AMERICAS

• *See page 59*

MICHIGAN SOCIETY OF PROFESSIONAL ENGINEERS http://www.michiganspe.org

ANTHONY C. FORTUNSKI, P.E. MEMORIAL GRANT

Grant of $2000 for engineering student demonstrating an interest in the fields of manufacturing and industry. Preference given to a student attending Lawrence Technical University and majoring in manufacturing engineering. Must be a member of MSPE Student Chapter or a state member-at-large. Minimum 3.0 GPA required. Restricted to Michigan residents attending Michigan schools.

Academic Fields/Career Goals: Chemical Engineering; Civil Engineering; Engineering/Technology; Mechanical Engineering.

Award: Grant for use in freshman, sophomore, junior, or senior years; not renewable. *Number:* 1. *Amount:* $2000.

Eligibility Requirements: Applicant must be enrolled or expecting to enroll full-time at an institution or university; resident of Michigan and studying in Michigan. Applicant or parent of applicant must be member of Michigan Society of Professional Engineers. Applicant must have 3.0 GPA or higher. Available to U.S. citizens.

Application Requirements: Application, essay, references, transcript. *Deadline:* varies.

Contact: Scholarship Coordinator
Michigan Society of Professional Engineers
PO Box 15276
Lansing, MI 48901-5276
Phone: 517-487-9388
Fax: 517-487-0635
E-mail: mspe@voyager.net

MICHIGAN SOCIETY OF PROFESSIONAL ENGINEERS UNDESIGNATED GRANT

Grant of $2000 for a top-ranking student enrolled in an ABET-accredited engineering program at a Michigan college or university. Renewal based on academic performance and approval of both the MSPE Scholarship Trust and Dean of School. Must be a member of MSPE student chapter or state member-at-large. Minimum 3.0 GPA required. Must be a Michigan resident.

Academic Fields/Career Goals: Chemical Engineering; Civil Engineering; Electrical Engineering/Electronics; Engineering/Technology; Mechanical Engineering.

Award: Grant for use in freshman, sophomore, junior, or senior years; renewable. *Number:* 1. *Amount:* $2000.

Eligibility Requirements: Applicant must be enrolled or expecting to enroll at an institution or university; resident of Michigan and studying in Michigan. Applicant or parent of applicant must be member of Michigan Society of Professional Engineers. Applicant must have 3.0 GPA or higher. Available to U.S. citizens.

Application Requirements: Application, essay, references, test scores, transcript. *Deadline:* varies.

Contact: Scholarship Coordinator
Michigan Society of Professional Engineers
PO Box 15276
Lansing, MI 48901-5276
Phone: 517-487-9388
Fax: 517-487-0635
E-mail: mspe@voyager.net

MICHIGAN SOCIETY OF PROFESSIONAL ENGINEERS 1980 NATIONAL SOCIETY OF PROFESSIONAL ENGINEERS ANNUAL MEETING COMMITTEE GRANT

One $2000 grant for a Michigan high school senior to study engineering at an ABET-accredited college or university in Michigan. Minimum 3.0 GPA required for grades 11 and 12.

Academic Fields/Career Goals: Chemical Engineering; Civil Engineering; Electrical Engineering/Electronics; Engineering/Technology; Mechanical Engineering.

Award: Grant for use in freshman year; not renewable. *Number:* 1. *Amount:* $2000.

Eligibility Requirements: Applicant must be high school student; planning to enroll or expecting to enroll full-time at an institution or university; resident of Michigan and studying in Michigan. Applicant must have 3.0 GPA or higher. Available to U.S. citizens.

Application Requirements: Application, test scores, transcript. *Deadline:* varies.

Contact: Scholarship Coordinator
Michigan Society of Professional Engineers
PO Box 15276
Lansing, MI 48901-5276
Phone: 517-487-9388
Fax: 517-487-0635
E-mail: mspe@voyager.net

MICHIGAN SOCIETY OF PROFESSIONAL ENGINEERS AUXILIARY GRANT

One $1000 grant for high ranking Michigan high school seniors interested in pursuing a career in engineering and planning to attend an ABET-accredited college or university in Michigan. Preference given to a son or daughter of an MSPE member. Minimum 3.0 GPA required in grades 11 and 12.

Academic Fields/Career Goals: Chemical Engineering; Civil Engineering; Electrical Engineering/Electronics; Engineering/Technology; Mechanical Engineering.

Award: Grant for use in freshman year; not renewable. *Number:* 1. *Amount:* $1000.

Eligibility Requirements: Applicant must be high school student; planning to enroll or expecting to enroll full-time at a four-year institution or university; resident of Michigan and studying in Michigan. Applicant or parent of applicant must be member of Michigan Society of Professional Engineers. Applicant must have 3.0 GPA or higher. Available to U.S. citizens.

Application Requirements: Application, test scores, transcript. *Deadline:* varies.

Contact: Scholarship Coordinator
Michigan Society of Professional Engineers
PO Box 15276
Lansing, MI 48901-5276
Phone: 517-487-9388
Fax: 517-487-0635
E-mail: mspe@voyager.net

MICHIGAN SOCIETY OF PROFESSIONAL ENGINEERS HARRY R. BALL, P.E. GRANT

One $2000 grant for a Michigan high school student to study engineering at an ABET-accredited college or university in Michigan. Minimum 3.0 GPA required in grades 11 and 12. Submit application to local MSPE Chapter Chair.

Academic Fields/Career Goals: Chemical Engineering; Civil Engineering; Electrical Engineering/Electronics; Engineering/Technology; Mechanical Engineering.

Award: Grant for use in freshman year; not renewable. *Number:* 1. *Amount:* $2000.

Eligibility Requirements: Applicant must be high school student; planning to enroll or expecting to enroll full-time at an institution or university; resident of Michigan and studying in Michigan. Applicant must have 3.0 GPA or higher. Available to U.S. citizens.

Application Requirements: Application, test scores, transcript. *Deadline:* varies.

Contact: Scholarship Coordinator
Michigan Society of Professional Engineers
PO Box 15276
Lansing, MI 48901-5276
Phone: 517-487-9388
Fax: 517-487-0635
E-mail: mspe@voyager.net

MICHIGAN SOCIETY OF PROFESSIONAL ENGINEERS KENNETH B. FISHBECK, P.E. MEMORIAL GRANT

One $1000 grant for a Michigan high school student to study engineering at an ABET-accredited college or university in Michigan. Minimum 3.0 GPA required in grades 11 and 12. Submit application to local MSPE Chapter Chair. Applicants should demonstrate qualifications of high merit and professional ethics.

Academic Fields/Career Goals: Chemical Engineering; Civil Engineering; Electrical Engineering/Electronics; Engineering/Technology; Mechanical Engineering.

Award: Grant for use in freshman year; not renewable. *Number:* 1. *Amount:* $1000.

Eligibility Requirements: Applicant must be high school student; planning to enroll or expecting to enroll full-time at an institution or university; resident of Michigan and studying in Michigan. Applicant must have 3.0 GPA or higher. Available to U.S. citizens.

Application Requirements: Application, test scores, transcript. *Deadline:* varies.

Contact: Scholarship Coordinator
Michigan Society of Professional Engineers
PO Box 15276
Lansing, MI 48901-5276
Phone: 517-487-9388
Fax: 517-487-0635
E-mail: mspe@voyager.net

MICHIGAN SOCIETY OF PROFESSIONAL ENGINEERS SCHOLARSHIP TRUST GRANT

One $2000 grant for Michigan high school senior planning to pursue a career in engineering at a Michigan ABET-accredited college or university. Minimum 3.0 GPA for grades 11 and 12 required.

Academic Fields/Career Goals: Chemical Engineering; Civil Engineering; Electrical Engineering/Electronics; Engineering/Technology; Mechanical Engineering.

Award: Grant for use in freshman year; not renewable. *Number:* 1. *Amount:* $2000.

Eligibility Requirements: Applicant must be high school student; planning to enroll or expecting to enroll full-time at an institution or university; resident of Michigan and studying in Michigan. Applicant must have 3.0 GPA or higher. Available to U.S. citizens.

Application Requirements: Application, test scores, transcript. *Deadline:* varies.

Contact: Scholarship Coordinator
Michigan Society of Professional Engineers
PO Box 15276
Lansing, MI 48901-5276
Phone: 517-487-9388
Fax: 517-487-0635
E-mail: mspe@voyager.net

MICRON TECHNOLOGY FOUNDATION, INC.

http://www.micron.com/scholars

MICRON SCIENCE AND TECHNOLOGY SCHOLARS PROGRAM

Merit-based scholarship for high school seniors who reside in and attend public or private school in Idaho, Utah, Texas, Colorado, or Virginia. Recognizing excellence in academics and leadership. One top prize of $55,000 college scholarship and ten to twelve $16,500 scholarships available each year. Awards will be paid out over 4 years. Must plan to major in computer science; physics; chemistry; material sciences; or electrical, computer, chemical, or mechanical engineering. Combined SAT score of at least 1350 or composite ACT score of at least 30 required.

Academic Fields/Career Goals: Chemical Engineering; Computer Science/Data Processing; Electrical Engineering/Electronics; Engineering/Technology; Engineering-Related Technologies; Materials Science, Engineering, and Metallurgy; Mechanical Engineering; Physical Sciences and Math; Science, Technology, and Society.

Award: Scholarship for use in freshman, sophomore, junior, or senior years; renewable. *Number:* 10–13. *Amount:* $16,500–$55,000.

Eligibility Requirements: Applicant must be high school student; planning to enroll or expecting to enroll full-time at a four-year institution or university; resident of Colorado, Idaho, Texas, Utah, or Virginia and must have an interest in leadership. Applicant must have 3.5 GPA or higher. Available to U.S. citizens.

Application Requirements: Application, essay, interview, references, test scores, transcript. *Deadline:* January 20.

Contact: Lyn Dauffenbach, Scholarship America
Micron Technology Foundation, Inc.
One Scholarship Way, PO Box 297
Saint Peter, MN 56082
Phone: 800-537-4180

NAMEPA NATIONAL SCHOLARSHIP FOUNDATION

http://www.namepa.org

NATIONAL ASSOCIATION OF MINORITY ENGINEERING PROGRAM ADMINISTRATORS NATIONAL SCHOLARSHIP FUND

• *See page 101*

NASA DELAWARE SPACE GRANT CONSORTIUM

http://www.delspace.org

NASA DELAWARE SPACE GRANT UNDERGRADUATE TUITION SCHOLARSHIP

• *See page 70*

NASA IDAHO SPACE GRANT CONSORTIUM

http://www.uidaho.edu/nasa_isgc

NASA IDAHO SPACE GRANT CONSORTIUM SCHOLARSHIP PROGRAM

• *See page 71*

NASA NEVADA SPACE GRANT CONSORTIUM

http://www.unr.edu/spacegrant

UNIVERSITY AND COMMUNITY COLLEGE SYSTEM OF NEVADA NASA SPACE GRANT AND FELLOWSHIP PROGRAM

• *See page 101*

NATIONAL ASSOCIATION FOR THE ADVANCEMENT OF COLORED PEOPLE

http://www.naacp.org

HUBERTUS W.V. WILLEMS SCHOLARSHIP FOR MALE STUDENTS

Must be male, full-time student, U.S. citizen majoring in one of the following: engineering, chemistry, physics, or mathematical sciences. Graduate student may be full- or part-time and have 2.5 minimum GPA. Graduating high school seniors and undergraduates must have 3.0 minimum GPA. Must demonstrate financial need. Undergraduate scholarship awards $2,000; graduate scholarship awards $3,000. NAACP membership and participation is highly preferable. Application deadline is the last Friday in March.

Academic Fields/Career Goals: Chemical Engineering; Engineering-Related Technologies; Physical Sciences and Math.

Award: Scholarship for use in freshman, sophomore, junior, senior, or graduate years; not renewable. *Number:* varies. *Amount:* $2000–$3000.

Eligibility Requirements: Applicant must be American Indian/Alaska Native, Asian/Pacific Islander, Black (non-Hispanic), or Hispanic; enrolled or expecting to enroll full or part-time at a four-year institution or university and male. Applicant or parent of applicant must be member of National Association for the Advancement of Colored People. Available to U.S. citizens.

Application Requirements: Application, financial need analysis, references, transcript. *Deadline:* varies.

Contact: Donna Lakins, Education Department, Scholarship Request
National Association for the Advancement of Colored People
4805 Mt. Hope Drive
Baltimore, MD 21215-3297
Phone: 410-580-5760
Fax: 410-585-1329

LOUIS STOKES SCIENCE AND TECHNOLOGY AWARD

• *See page 114*

NATIONAL INVENTORS HALL OF FAME http://www.invent.org/collegiate

COLLEGIATE INVENTORS COMPETITION - GRAND PRIZE

• *See page 71*

COLLEGIATE INVENTORS COMPETITION FOR UNDERGRADUATE STUDENTS

• *See page 71*

NATIONAL SOCIETY OF PROFESSIONAL ENGINEERS http://www.nspe.org

MAUREEN L. AND HOWARD N. BLITMAN, PE SCHOLARSHIP TO PROMOTE DIVERSITY IN ENGINEERING

$5000 scholarship to a high school senior entering an ABET-accredited 4-year engineering program. Intended to encourage underrepresented minorities to pursue this challenging and rewarding career.

Academic Fields/Career Goals: Chemical Engineering; Civil Engineering; Electrical Engineering/Electronics; Engineering/Technology; Engineering-Related Technologies; Materials Science, Engineering, and Metallurgy; Mechanical Engineering.

Award: Scholarship for use in freshman or sophomore years; not renewable. *Number:* 1. *Amount:* $5000.

Eligibility Requirements: Applicant must be American Indian/Alaska Native, Black (non-Hispanic), or Hispanic; high school student and planning to enroll or expecting to enroll full-time at a four-year institution or university. Applicant must have 3.5 GPA or higher. Available to U.S. citizens.

Application Requirements: Application, essay, references, test scores, transcript. *Deadline:* March 1.

Contact: Mary K. Maul, Education Manager NSPE
National Society of Professional Engineers
1420 King Street
Alexandria, VA 22314
Phone: 703-684-2833
E-mail: mmaul@nspe.org

NATIONAL SOCIETY OF PROFESSIONAL ENGINEERS/AUXILIARY SCHOLARSHIP

Renewable scholarship for a female student in the amount of $1000 per year for four years. The recipient of this scholarship may attend the college or university of her choice (the program must be accredited by the Engineering Accreditation Commission of the Accreditation Board for Engineering and Technology). The scholarship is awarded strictly on the basis of achievement. Must be a U.S. citizen. Must rank in the upper third of class or have a minimum 3.6 GPA.

Academic Fields/Career Goals: Chemical Engineering; Civil Engineering; Electrical Engineering/Electronics; Engineering/Technology; Engineering-Related Technologies; Materials Science, Engineering, and Metallurgy; Mechanical Engineering.

Award: Scholarship for use in freshman, sophomore, junior, or senior years; renewable. *Number:* 2. *Amount:* $1000.

Eligibility Requirements: Applicant must be high school student; planning to enroll or expecting to enroll full-time at a four-year institution or university and female. Available to U.S. citizens.

Application Requirements: Application, essay, references, test scores, transcript. *Deadline:* December 1.

Contact: Mary Maul, Education Manager
National Society of Professional Engineers
1420 King Street
Alexandria, VA 22314
Phone: 703-684-2833
Fax: 703-836-4875
E-mail: mmaul@nspe.org

PAUL H. ROBBINS HONORARY SCHOLARSHIP

The recipient of this scholarship may attend the college or university of their choice (the program must be accredited by the Engineering Accreditation Commission of the Accreditation Board for Engineering and Technology). The scholarship is awarded strictly on the basis of achievement. Must have GPA of 3.6 or higher and be a member of NSPE. A scholarship renewal report will be required for second-year payment.

Academic Fields/Career Goals: Chemical Engineering; Civil Engineering; Electrical Engineering/Electronics; Engineering/Technology; Engineering-Related Technologies; Materials Science, Engineering, and Metallurgy; Mechanical Engineering.

Award: Scholarship for use in junior or senior years; renewable. *Number:* 1. *Amount:* $5000.

Eligibility Requirements: Applicant must be high school student and planning to enroll or expecting to enroll full-time at a four-year institution or university. Applicant or parent of applicant must be member of National Society of Professional Engineers. Available to U.S. citizens.

Application Requirements: Application, essay, references, test scores, transcript. *Deadline:* December 1.

Contact: Mary Maul, Education Manager
National Society of Professional Engineers
1420 King Street
Alexandria, VA 22314
Phone: 703-684-2833
Fax: 703-836-4875
E-mail: mmaul@nspe.org

PROFESSIONAL ENGINEERS IN INDUSTRY SCHOLARSHIP

Applicants must be sponsored by an NSPE/PEI member. Must have completed 2 semesters of an undergraduate engineering program that is accredited by ABET.

Academic Fields/Career Goals: Chemical Engineering; Civil Engineering; Electrical Engineering/Electronics; Engineering/Technology; Engineering-Related Technologies; Materials Science, Engineering, and Metallurgy; Mechanical Engineering.

Award: Scholarship for use in sophomore, junior, senior, or graduate years; not renewable. *Number:* 1. *Amount:* $2500.

Eligibility Requirements: Applicant must be enrolled or expecting to enroll full-time at a four-year institution or university. Applicant must have 2.5 GPA or higher. Available to U.S. citizens.

National Society of Professional Engineers (continued)

Application Requirements: Application, essay, resume, references, transcript, work experience. *Deadline:* June 1.

Contact: Erin Garcia Reyes, MGR-PEI NSPE
National Society of Professional Engineers
1420 King Street
Alexandria, VA 22314
Phone: 703-684-2884
E-mail: egarcia@nspe.org

VIRGINIA HENRY MEMORIAL SCHOLARSHIP

The recipient of this scholarship may attend the college or university of her choice (the program must be accredited by the Engineering Accreditation Commission of the Accreditation Board for Engineering and Technology). The scholarship is awarded strictly on the basis of achievement. Must be female and have 3.6 GPA.

Academic Fields/Career Goals: Chemical Engineering; Civil Engineering; Electrical Engineering/Electronics; Engineering/Technology; Engineering-Related Technologies; Materials Science, Engineering, and Metallurgy; Mechanical Engineering.

Award: Scholarship for use in freshman year; not renewable. *Number:* 1. *Amount:* $1000.

Eligibility Requirements: Applicant must be high school student; planning to enroll or expecting to enroll full-time at a four-year institution and female. Available to U.S. citizens.

Application Requirements: Application, essay, references, test scores, transcript. *Deadline:* December 1.

Contact: Mary Maul, Education Manager
National Society of Professional Engineers
1420 King Street
Alexandria, VA 22314
Phone: 703-684-2833
Fax: 703-836-4875
E-mail: mmaul@nspe.org

NEW JERSEY ACADEMY OF SCIENCE http://www.njas.org

NEW JERSEY ACADEMY OF SCIENCE RESEARCH GRANTS-IN-AID TO HIGH SCHOOL STUDENTS

• *See page 116*

OREGON STUDENT ASSISTANCE COMMISSION http://www.osac.state.or.us

AMERICAN COUNCIL OF ENGINEERING COMPANIES OF OREGON SCHOLARSHIP

Renewable award for students considering a career in the consulting engineering profession. For use at any Oregon four-year college that offers Accreditation Board for engineering and technology accredited programs in chemical, civil, electrical, industrial, or mechanical engineering.

Academic Fields/Career Goals: Chemical Engineering; Civil Engineering; Electrical Engineering/Electronics; Engineering-Related Technologies; Mechanical Engineering.

Award: Scholarship for use in freshman, sophomore, junior, or senior years; not renewable. *Number:* varies. *Amount:* $500.

Eligibility Requirements: Applicant must be enrolled or expecting to enroll at a four-year institution; resident of Oregon and studying in Oregon.

Application Requirements: Application, essay, financial need analysis, transcript. *Deadline:* March 1.

Contact: Director of Grant Programs
Oregon Student Assistance Commission
1500 Valley River Drive, Suite 100
Eugene, OR 97401-7020
Phone: 800-452-8807 Ext. 7395
E-mail: awardinfo@mercury.osac.state.or.us

ROBERT H. MOLLOHAN FAMILY CHARITABLE FOUNDATION, INC. http://www.mollohanfoundation.org

HIGH TECHNOLOGY SCHOLARS PROGRAM

• *See page 117*

ROCKY MOUNTAIN COAL MINING INSTITUTE http://www.rmcmi.org

ROCKY MOUNTAIN COAL MINING INSTITUTE SCHOLARSHIP

Must be full-time college sophomore or junior at time of application pursuing a degree in mining-related fields or engineering disciplines such as mining, geology, mineral processing, or metallurgy. For residents of Arizona, Colorado, Montana, New Mexico, North Dakota, Texas, Utah, and Wyoming.

Academic Fields/Career Goals: Chemical Engineering; Civil Engineering; Electrical Engineering/Electronics; Engineering/Technology; Mechanical Engineering.

Award: Scholarship for use in junior, senior, or graduate years; renewable. *Number:* 16. *Amount:* $2000.

Eligibility Requirements: Applicant must be enrolled or expecting to enroll full-time at a four-year institution or university and resident of Arizona, Colorado, Montana, New Mexico, North Dakota, Texas, Utah, or Wyoming. Available to U.S. citizens.

Application Requirements: Application, interview, references. *Deadline:* February 1.

Contact: Karen Inzano, Executive Director
Rocky Mountain Coal Mining Institute
8057 South Yukon Way
Littleton, CO 80128-5510
Phone: 303-948-3300
Fax: 303-948-1132
E-mail: mail@rmcmi.org

SOCIETY FOR MINING, METALLURGY AND EXPLORATION - CENTRAL WYOMING SECTION

COATES, WOLFF, RUSSELL MINING INDUSTRY SCHOLARSHIP

• *See page 71*

SOCIETY OF AUTOMOTIVE ENGINEERS http://www.sae.org/students/stuschol.htm

BMW/SAE ENGINEERING SCHOLARSHIP

• *See page 105*

EDWARD D. HENDRICKSON/SAE ENGINEERING SCHOLARSHIP

• *See page 105*

TMC/SAE DONALD D. DAWSON TECHNICAL SCHOLARSHIP

• *See page 105*

SOCIETY OF HISPANIC PROFESSIONAL ENGINEERS FOUNDATION http://www.shpefoundation.org

SOCIETY OF HISPANIC PROFESSIONAL ENGINEERS FOUNDATION

Scholarships awarded to Hispanic engineering and science students throughout the U.S. Scholarships are awarded at the beginning of every academic year based upon academic achievement, financial need, involvement in campus and community activities, career goals and counselor recommendations.

Academic Fields/Career Goals: Chemical Engineering; Civil Engineering; Electrical Engineering/Electronics; Engineering/Technology; Engineering-Related Technologies; Materials Science, Engineering, and Metallurgy; Mechanical Engineering; Natural Sciences; Nuclear Science; Science, Technology, and Society.

Award: Scholarship for use in freshman, sophomore, junior, senior, or graduate years; not renewable. *Number:* varies. *Amount:* $500–$7000.

Eligibility Requirements: Applicant must be Hispanic and enrolled or expecting to enroll full-time at an institution or university. Available to U.S. citizens.

Application Requirements: Application, financial need analysis, resume, references. *Deadline:* May 15.

Contact: Kathy Borunda, Director, Educational Programs
Society of Hispanic Professional Engineers Foundation
3900 Whiteside Street
Los Angeles, CA 90063
E-mail: kathy@shpefoundation.org

SOCIETY OF MEXICAN AMERICAN ENGINEERS AND SCIENTISTS http://www.maes-natl.org

GRE AND GRADUATE APPLICATIONS WAIVER

• *See page 72*

SOCIETY OF PLASTICS ENGINEERS (SPE) FOUNDATION http://www.4spe.org

FLEMING/BASZCAK SCHOLARSHIP

Award available for full-time undergraduate student, with a demonstrated interest in the plastics industry, who is a U.S. citizen and can provide documentation of Mexican heritage. Application deadline is January 15.

Academic Fields/Career Goals: Chemical Engineering; Civil Engineering; Electrical Engineering/Electronics; Engineering/Technology; Industrial Design; Materials Science, Engineering, and Metallurgy; Mechanical Engineering; Trade/Technical Specialties.

Award: Scholarship for use in freshman, sophomore, junior, or senior years; not renewable. *Number:* 1. *Amount:* $2000.

Eligibility Requirements: Applicant must be of Mexican heritage; Hispanic and enrolled or expecting to enroll full-time at a four-year institution or university. Available to U.S. citizens.

Application Requirements: Application, essay, financial need analysis, references, transcript. *Deadline:* January 15.

Contact: Gail R. Bristol, Managing Director
Society of Plastics Engineers (SPE) Foundation
14 Fairfield Drive
Brookfield, CT 06804
Phone: 203-740-5447
Fax: 203-775-1157
E-mail: foundation@4spe.org

SOCIETY OF PLASTICS ENGINEERS SCHOLARSHIP PROGRAM

The SPE Foundation offers scholarships to full-time students who have demonstrated or expressed an interest in the plastics industry. They must be majoring in or taking courses that would be beneficial to a career in the plastics industry.

Academic Fields/Career Goals: Chemical Engineering; Civil Engineering; Electrical Engineering/Electronics; Engineering/Technology; Industrial Design; Materials Science, Engineering, and Metallurgy; Mechanical Engineering; Trade/Technical Specialties.

Award: Scholarship for use in freshman, sophomore, junior, senior, or graduate years; not renewable. *Number:* 19. *Amount:* $1000–$5000.

Eligibility Requirements: Applicant must be enrolled or expecting to enroll full-time at a two-year or four-year or technical institution or university. Available to U.S. and non-U.S. citizens.

Application Requirements: Application, essay, financial need analysis, references, transcript. *Deadline:* January 15.

Contact: Gail R. Bristol, Managing Director
Society of Plastics Engineers (SPE) Foundation
14 Fairfield Drive
Brookfield, CT 06804
Phone: 203-740-5447
Fax: 203-775-1157
E-mail: foundation@4spe.org

SOCIETY OF WOMEN ENGINEERS http://www.swe.org/scholarships

CHEVRON TEXACO CORPORATION SCHOLARSHIPS

Eight awards open to women who are sophomores or juniors majoring in civil, chemical, mechanical, or petroleum engineering. One-time award of $2000. Must be active SWE student member. Deadline: February 1.

Academic Fields/Career Goals: Chemical Engineering; Civil Engineering; Engineering/Technology; Mechanical Engineering.

Award: Scholarship for use in sophomore or junior years; not renewable. *Number:* 7. *Amount:* $2000.

Eligibility Requirements: Applicant must be enrolled or expecting to enroll full-time at a four-year institution or university and female. Applicant or parent of applicant must be member of Society of Women Engineers. Applicant must have 3.5 GPA or higher. Available to U.S. and non-U.S. citizens.

Application Requirements: Application, essay, references, self-addressed stamped envelope, test scores, transcript. *Deadline:* February 1.

Contact: Program Coordinator
Society of Women Engineers
230 East Ohio Street, Suite 400
Chicago, IL 60611-3265
Phone: 312-596-5223
Fax: 312-644-8557
E-mail: hq@swe.org

DUPONT COMPANY SCHOLARSHIPS

Seven one-time award available to female sophomore, junior, or senior undergraduate students majoring in chemical or mechanical engineering: two are for incoming freshmen. Minimum 3.0 GPA required. Limited to schools in the eastern U.S. Deadline: May 15 for freshman award; February 1 for sophomore, junior, and senior awards.

Academic Fields/Career Goals: Chemical Engineering; Mechanical Engineering.

Award: Scholarship for use in freshman, sophomore, junior, or senior years; not renewable. *Number:* 9. *Amount:* $2000.

Eligibility Requirements: Applicant must be enrolled or expecting to enroll full-time at a four-year institution or university and female. Applicant must have 3.0 GPA or higher.

Application Requirements: Application, references, self-addressed stamped envelope, test scores, transcript. *Deadline:* varies.

Contact: Program Coordinator
Society of Women Engineers
230 East Ohio Street, Suite 400
Chicago, IL 60611-3265
Phone: 312-596-5223
Fax: 312-644-8557
E-mail: hq@swe.org

GENERAL MOTORS FOUNDATION UNDERGRADUATE SCHOLARSHIPS

Renewable award for female student entering junior year who is interested in automotive/manufacturing career. Must hold a leadership position in a student organization. Send self-addressed stamped envelope for application. Includes $500 travel grant for SWE National Conference. Must have a 3.5 GPA. Deadline: February 1.

Academic Fields/Career Goals: Chemical Engineering; Electrical Engineering/Electronics; Engineering/Technology; Engineering-Related Technologies; Mechanical Engineering.

Award: Scholarship for use in junior year; renewable. *Number:* 2. *Amount:* $1225.

Eligibility Requirements: Applicant must be enrolled or expecting to enroll full-time at a four-year institution or university; female and must have an interest in leadership. Applicant must have 3.5 GPA or higher.

Application Requirements: Application, essay, references, self-addressed stamped envelope, test scores, transcript. *Deadline:* February 1.

Contact: Program Coordinator
Society of Women Engineers
230 East Ohio Street, Suite 400
Chicago, IL 60611-3265
Phone: 312-596-5223
Fax: 312-644-8557
E-mail: hq@swe.org

TEXAS ENGINEERING FOUNDATION http://www.tspe.org

TEXAS SOCIETY OF PROFESSIONAL ENGINEERS (TSPE) REGIONAL SCHOLARSHIPS

One recipient is selected from each of TSPE's five regions. Applicants must be high school seniors maintaining a 3.0 GPA. The deadline is January 15. Must be a resident of Texas and attend a postsecondary institution in Texas, majoring in a field of engineering.

Academic Fields/Career Goals: Chemical Engineering; Civil Engineering; Electrical Engineering/Electronics; Engineering/Technology; Mechanical Engineering.

Award: Scholarship for use in freshman year; not renewable. *Number:* 5. *Amount:* $500.

Eligibility Requirements: Applicant must be high school student; planning to enroll or expecting to enroll full-time at an institution or university; resident of Texas and studying in Texas. Applicant must have 3.0 GPA or higher. Available to U.S. citizens.

Application Requirements: Application, essay, references, transcript. *Deadline:* January 15.

Contact: Krista Weirman, Director of Education Programs
Texas Engineering Foundation
Attn: Programs Director
3501 Manor Road, PO Box 2145
Austin, TX 78768
Phone: 512-472-9286
Fax: 512-472-2934
E-mail: kristaw@tspe.org

UNITED NEGRO COLLEGE FUND http://www.uncf.org

CARGILL SCHOLARSHIP PROGRAM

• *See page 49*

MALCOLM PIRNIE, INC. SCHOLARS PROGRAM

Scholarships for UNCF juniors with 3.0 or better GPA majoring in civil, chemical or environmental engineering or one of the environmental sciences. Summer internship is included in program. Prospective applicants should complete the Student Profile found at Web site: http://www.uncf.org.

Academic Fields/Career Goals: Chemical Engineering; Civil Engineering; Earth Science; Natural Resources.

Award: Scholarship for use in junior year; not renewable. *Amount:* $3000.

Eligibility Requirements: Applicant must be Black (non-Hispanic) and enrolled or expecting to enroll at a four-year institution or university. Applicant must have 3.0 GPA or higher. Available to U.S. citizens.

Application Requirements: Application. *Deadline:* February 15.

Contact: Program Services Department
United Negro College Fund
8260 Willow Oaks Corporate Drive
Fairfax, VA 22031

OSTINA AND HERMAN HARTFIELD SCHOLARSHIP

• *See page 118*

UNCF/PFIZER CORPORATE SCHOLARS PROGRAM

• *See page 64*

WM. WRIGLEY, JR. COMPANY SCHOLARS PROGRAM

• *See page 134*

UNIVERSITIES SPACE RESEARCH ASSOCIATION http://www.usra.edu/hq/scholarships/overview.shtml

UNIVERSITIES SPACE RESEARCH ASSOCIATION SCHOLARSHIP PROGRAM

• *See page 72*

UTAH SOCIETY OF PROFESSIONAL ENGINEERS http://www.uspeonline.com

UTAH SOCIETY OF PROFESSIONAL ENGINEERS SCHOLARSHIP

One-time award for entering freshman pursuing studies in the field of engineering (civil, chemical, electrical, or engineering related technologies.) Minimum 3.5 GPA required. Must be a U.S. citizen and Utah resident attending school in Utah. Application deadline is March 25.

Academic Fields/Career Goals: Chemical Engineering; Civil Engineering; Electrical Engineering/Electronics; Energy and Power Engineering; Engineering/Technology; Mechanical Engineering.

Award: Scholarship for use in freshman year; not renewable. *Number:* 1. *Amount:* $1000.

Eligibility Requirements: Applicant must be high school student; planning to enroll or expecting to enroll full-time at a four-year institution or university; resident of Utah and studying in Utah. Applicant must have 3.5 GPA or higher. Available to U.S. citizens.

Application Requirements: Application, essay, resume, references, test scores, transcript. *Deadline:* March 25.

Contact: Dan Church, Scholarship Coordinator
Utah Society of Professional Engineers
488 East Winchester Street, Suite 400
Murray, UT 84107
Phone: 801-232-2853
Fax: 801-262-4303
E-mail: churchd@pbworld.com

XEROX http://xerox.com

TECHNICAL MINORITY SCHOLARSHIP

One-time award for minority students enrolled full time in a technical science or engineering discipline. Must be studying at a four-year institution and have a GPA of 3.0 or higher. Available to U.S. citizens and individuals with permanent resident visas. Application deadline is September 15. Further information is available at Web site http://www.xerox.com.

Academic Fields/Career Goals: Chemical Engineering; Computer Science/Data Processing; Electrical Engineering/Electronics; Engineering/Technology; Engineering-Related Technologies; Materials Science, Engineering, and Metallurgy; Mechanical Engineering; Physical Sciences and Math.

Award: Scholarship for use in freshman, sophomore, junior, senior, graduate, or postgraduate years; not renewable. *Number:* 125–150. *Amount:* $1000.

Eligibility Requirements: Applicant must be American Indian/Alaska Native, Asian/Pacific Islander, Black (non-Hispanic), or Hispanic and enrolled or expecting to enroll full-time at a four-year institution or university. Applicant must have 3.0 GPA or higher. Available to U.S. citizens.

Application Requirements: Application, resume, transcript. *Deadline:* September 15.

Contact: Application available at Web site.

CHILD AND FAMILY STUDIES

CLAN MACBEAN FOUNDATION http://www.clanmacbean.net

CLAN MACBEAN FOUNDATION GRANT PROGRAM

• *See page 81*

KENTUCKY HIGHER EDUCATION ASSISTANCE AUTHORITY (KHEAA) http://www.kheaa.com

EARLY CHILDHOOD DEVELOPMENT SCHOLARSHIP

Scholarship with conditional service commitment for part-time students currently employed by participating ECD facility or providing training in ECD for an approved organization.

Academic Fields/Career Goals: Child and Family Studies; Education.

Award: Scholarship for use in freshman, sophomore, junior, or senior years; not renewable. *Number:* 900–1000. *Amount:* up to $1400.

Eligibility Requirements: Applicant must be enrolled or expecting to enroll part-time at a four-year institution or university; resident of Kentucky and studying in Kentucky. Available to U.S. citizens.

Application Requirements: Application, resume. *Deadline:* Continuous.

Contact: Early Childhood Development Authority
Kentucky Higher Education Assistance Authority (KHEAA)
275 East Main Street, 2W-E
Frankfort, KY 40621
Phone: 502-564-8099

RESOURCE CENTER http://www.resourcecenterscholarshipinfo.com

MARIE BLAHA MEDICAL GRANT

• *See page 64*

SUNSHINE LADY FOUNDATION, INC. http://www.sunshineladyfdn.org

COUNSELOR, ADVOCATE, AND SUPPORT STAFF SCHOLARSHIP PROGRAM

• *See page 47*

CIVIL ENGINEERING

AACE INTERNATIONAL http://www.aacei.org

AACE INTERNATIONAL COMPETITIVE SCHOLARSHIP

• *See page 73*

ACI INTERNATIONAL/CONCRETE RESEARCH AND EDUCATION FOUNDATION (CONREF) http://www.concrete.org

PETER D. COURTOIS CONCRETE CONSTRUCTION SCHOLARSHIP

• *See page 73*

AEA-OREGON COUNCIL http://www.ous.edu/ecs/scholarships

AEA- OREGON COUNCIL TECHNOLOGY SCHOLARSHIP PROGRAM

• *See page 136*

AMERICAN COUNCIL OF ENGINEERING COMPANIES OF PENNSYLVANIA (ACEC/PA) http://www.acecpa.org

ENGINEERING SCHOLARSHIP

• *See page 136*

AMERICAN GROUND WATER TRUST http://www.agwt.org

AMERICAN GROUND WATER TRUST-AMTROL, INC. SCHOLARSHIP

Award for college/university entry-level students intending to pursue a career in ground water-related field. Must either have completed a science/environmental project involving ground water resources or have had vacation work experience related to the environment and natural resources. Must be U.S. citizen or legal resident with minimum 3.0 GPA. Submit two letters of recommendation and transcript. Deadline: June 1.

Academic Fields/Career Goals: Civil Engineering; Natural Resources.

Award: Scholarship for use in freshman year; not renewable. *Number:* 2. *Amount:* $2000.

Eligibility Requirements: Applicant must be high school student and planning to enroll or expecting to enroll full-time at a two-year or four-year institution or university. Applicant must have 3.0 GPA or higher. Available to U.S. citizens.

Application Requirements: Application, essay, references, transcript. *Deadline:* June 1.

Contact: Andrew Stone, Executive Director
American Ground Water Trust
PO Box 1796
Concord, NH 03302-1796
Phone: 603-228-5444
Fax: 603-228-6557
E-mail: agwthq@aol.com

AMERICAN GROUND WATER TRUST-CLAUDE LAVAL CORPORATION THE BEN EVERSON SCHOLARSHIP

For college/university entry-level students intending to pursue a career in ground water-related field. Must be U.S. citizen or legal resident with 3.0 GPA or higher. For more information see Web site: http://www.agwt.org.

Academic Fields/Career Goals: Civil Engineering; Natural Resources.

Award: Scholarship for use in freshman year; not renewable. *Number:* 1. *Amount:* $2500.

Eligibility Requirements: Applicant must be high school student and planning to enroll or expecting to enroll full or part-time at a two-year or four-year institution or university. Applicant or parent of applicant must have employment or volunteer experience in designated career field. Applicant must have 3.0 GPA or higher. Available to U.S. citizens.

Application Requirements: Application, essay, references, transcript, parent employment verification. *Deadline:* June 1.

Contact: Andrew Stone, Executive Director
American Ground Water Trust
PO Box 1796
Concord, NH 03302-1796
Phone: 603-228-5444
Fax: 603-228-6557
E-mail: agwthq@aol.com

AMERICAN PUBLIC TRANSPORTATION FOUNDATION http://www.apta.com

DONALD C. HYDE ESSAY PROGRAM

Prize awarded for best essay on the subject: "What segment of the public transportation industry interests you and why?" Must be applying for APTF scholarship.

Academic Fields/Career Goals: Civil Engineering; Electrical Engineering/Electronics; Engineering/Technology; Engineering-Related Technologies; Mechanical Engineering; Transportation.

Award: Prize for use in junior, senior, graduate, or postgraduate years; not renewable. *Number:* 1. *Amount:* $500.

Eligibility Requirements: Applicant must be enrolled or expecting to enroll full-time at a four-year institution or university. Applicant must have 3.0 GPA or higher. Available to U.S. and Canadian citizens.

Application Requirements: Application, essay, financial need analysis, references, transcript. *Deadline:* June 12.

Contact: Pamela Boswell, Vice President of Program Management
American Public Transportation Foundation
1666 K Street, NW
Washington, DC 20006-1215
Phone: 202-496-4803
Fax: 202-496-2323
E-mail: pboswell@apta.com

JACK GILSTRAP SCHOLARSHIP

Awarded to the applicant to the APTF scholarship with the highest score. Must be in public transportation industry-related fields of study. Must be sponsored by AFTA member organization and complete an internship program with a member organization. Minimum 3.0 GPA required.

Academic Fields/Career Goals: Civil Engineering; Electrical Engineering/Electronics; Engineering/Technology; Engineering-Related Technologies; Mechanical Engineering; Transportation.

Award: Scholarship for use in junior, senior, graduate, or postgraduate years; renewable. *Number:* 1. *Amount:* $2500.

Eligibility Requirements: Applicant must be enrolled or expecting to enroll full-time at a four-year institution or university. Applicant must have 3.0 GPA or higher. Available to U.S. and Canadian citizens.

Application Requirements: Application, essay, financial need analysis, references, transcript. *Deadline:* June 12.

Contact: Pamela Boswell, Vice President of Program Management
American Public Transportation Foundation
1666 K Street, NW
Washington, DC 20006-1215
Phone: 202-496-4803
Fax: 202-496-2323
E-mail: pboswell@apta.com

LOUIS T. KLAUDER SCHOLARSHIP

Scholarships for study towards a career in the rail transit industry as an electrical or mechanical engineer. Must be sponsored by APTA member organization and complete internship with APTA member organization. Minimum GPA of 3.0 required.

Academic Fields/Career Goals: Civil Engineering; Electrical Engineering/Electronics; Engineering/Technology; Engineering-Related Technologies; Mechanical Engineering; Transportation.

Award: Scholarship for use in junior, senior, graduate, or postgraduate years; renewable. *Number:* 1. *Amount:* $2500.

Eligibility Requirements: Applicant must be enrolled or expecting to enroll full-time at a four-year institution or university. Applicant must have 3.0 GPA or higher. Available to U.S. and Canadian citizens.

Application Requirements: Application, essay, financial need analysis, references, transcript. *Deadline:* June 12.

Contact: Pamela Boswell, Vice President of Program Management
American Public Transportation Foundation
1666 K Street, NW
Washington, DC 20006-1215
Phone: 202-496-4803
Fax: 202-496-2323
E-mail: pboswell@apta.com

PARSONS BRINCKERHOFF-JIM LAMMIE SCHOLARSHIP

Scholarship for study in public transportation engineering field. Must be sponsored by APTA member organization and complete internship with APTA member organization. Minimum GPA of 3.0 required.

Academic Fields/Career Goals: Civil Engineering; Electrical Engineering/Electronics; Engineering/Technology; Engineering-Related Technologies; Mechanical Engineering; Transportation.

Award: Scholarship for use in junior, senior, graduate, or postgraduate years; renewable. *Number:* 1. *Amount:* $2500.

Eligibility Requirements: Applicant must be enrolled or expecting to enroll full-time at a four-year institution or university. Applicant must have 3.0 GPA or higher. Available to U.S. and Canadian citizens.

Application Requirements: Application, essay, financial need analysis, references, transcript. *Deadline:* June 12.

Contact: Pamela Boswell, Vice President of Program Management
American Public Transportation Foundation
1666 K Street, NW
Washington, DC 20006-1215
Phone: 202-496-4803
Fax: 202-496-2323
E-mail: pboswell@apta.com

TRANSIT HALL OF FAME SCHOLARSHIP AWARD PROGRAM

Renewable award for undergraduate or graduate students studying transportation or rail transit engineering. Must be sponsored by APTA member organization and complete an internship program with a member organization. Must have a minimum 3.0 GPA and be a U.S. or Canadian citizen. Freshmen and sophomores ineligible.

Academic Fields/Career Goals: Civil Engineering; Electrical Engineering/Electronics; Engineering/Technology; Engineering-Related Technologies; Mechanical Engineering; Transportation.

Award: Scholarship for use in junior, senior, graduate, or postgraduate years; renewable. *Number:* 2. *Amount:* $2500.

Eligibility Requirements: Applicant must be enrolled or expecting to enroll full-time at a four-year institution or university. Applicant must have 3.0 GPA or higher. Available to U.S. and Canadian citizens.

Application Requirements: Application, essay, financial need analysis, references, transcript, nomination by APTA member. *Deadline:* June 12.

Contact: Pamela Boswell, Vice President of Program Management
American Public Transportation Foundation
1666 K Street, NW
Washington, DC 20006-1215
Phone: 202-496-4803
Fax: 202-496-4323

AMERICAN SOCIETY OF CIVIL ENGINEERS-MAINE SECTION

AMERICAN SOCIETY OF CIVIL ENGINEERS-MAINE HIGH SCHOOL SCHOLARSHIP

One-time award available to high school student in senior year, pursuing a course of study in civil engineering. Must be resident of Maine. Essay, references and transcript required with application. Deadline is January 30.

Academic Fields/Career Goals: Civil Engineering.

Award: Scholarship for use in freshman year; not renewable. *Number:* 1. *Amount:* $2000.

Eligibility Requirements: Applicant must be high school student; planning to enroll or expecting to enroll full-time at a four-year institution or university and resident of Maine. Available to U.S. citizens.

Application Requirements: Application, essay, references, transcript. *Deadline:* January 30.

Contact: Leslie Corrow, Project Engineer Kleinschmidt Associates
American Society of Civil Engineers-Maine Section
75 Main Street
Pittsfield, ME 04967-0016
Phone: 207-487-3328
E-mail: leslie.corrow@kleinschmidtusa.com

AMERICAN SOCIETY OF NAVAL ENGINEERS http://www.navalengineers.org

AMERICAN SOCIETY OF NAVAL ENGINEERS SCHOLARSHIP

• *See page 66*

AMERICAN WELDING SOCIETY http://www.aws.org/foundation

ARSHAM AMIRIKIAN ENGINEERING SCHOLARSHIP

Awarded to an undergraduate pursuing a minimum four-year degree in civil engineering or welding-related program at an accredited university.

Academic Fields/Career Goals: Civil Engineering; Materials Science, Engineering, and Metallurgy; Trade/Technical Specialties.

Award: Scholarship for use in sophomore, junior, or senior years; not renewable. *Number:* 1. *Amount:* $2500.

Eligibility Requirements: Applicant must be age 18 and enrolled or expecting to enroll full or part-time at a four-year institution. Applicant must have 3.0 GPA or higher. Available to U.S. citizens.

Application Requirements: Application, autobiography, financial need analysis, references, transcript. *Deadline:* January 15.

Contact: Ms. Neida Herrera, Development Coordinator
American Welding Society
550 Northwest Le Jeune Road
Miami, FL 33126
Phone: 305-443-9353 Ext. 461
Fax: 305-443-7559
E-mail: neida@aws.org

DONALD AND JEAN CLEVELAND-WILLAMETTE VALLEY SECTION SCHOLARSHIP

Award for students pursuing a degree in welding or welding technology. Award granted on an annual basis. For more information, see Web site: http://www.aws.org/foundation.

Academic Fields/Career Goals: Civil Engineering; Engineering-Related Technologies; Materials Science, Engineering, and Metallurgy; Trade/Technical Specialties.

Award: Scholarship for use in freshman, sophomore, junior, senior, graduate, or postgraduate years; not renewable. *Number:* up to 1. *Amount:* $1250.

Eligibility Requirements: Applicant must be enrolled or expecting to enroll at a four-year institution. Available to U.S. citizens.

Application Requirements: *Deadline:* March 1.

Contact: Neida Herrera, Development Coordinator
American Welding Society
550 Northwest Le Jeune Road
Miami, FL 33126
Phone: 305-443-9353 Ext. 461
Fax: 305-443-7559
E-mail: neida@aws.org

MATSUO BRIDGE COMPANY, LTD., OF JAPAN SCHOLARSHIP

Awarded to a college junior or senior, or graduate student pursuing a minimum four-year degree in civil engineering, welding engineering, welding engineering technology, or related discipline. Applicant must have a minimum 3.0 overall GPA. Financial need is not required to apply. Must be U.S. citizen.

Academic Fields/Career Goals: Civil Engineering; Engineering/Technology; Engineering-Related Technologies; Trade/Technical Specialties.

Award: Scholarship for use in junior, senior, or graduate years; not renewable. *Number:* 1. *Amount:* $2500.

Eligibility Requirements: Applicant must be age 18 and enrolled or expecting to enroll full or part-time at a four-year institution. Applicant must have 3.0 GPA or higher. Available to U.S. citizens.

Application Requirements: Application, autobiography, financial need analysis, references, transcript. *Deadline:* January 15.

Contact: Ms. Neida Herrera, Development Coordinator
American Welding Society
550 Northwest Le Jeune Road
Miami, FL 33126
Phone: 305-443-9353 Ext. 461
Fax: 305-443-7559
E-mail: neida@aws.org

ASSOCIATED BUILDERS AND CONTRACTORS SCHOLARSHIP PROGRAM http://www.abc.org

TRIMMER EDUCATION FOUNDATION SCHOLARSHIPS FOR CONSTRUCTION MANAGEMENT

Scholarships are available to students in a major related to the construction industry. Applicants must be enrolled at an educational institution with an ABC student chapter. For further information, and an application visit Web site: http://www.abc.org.

Academic Fields/Career Goals: Civil Engineering; Electrical Engineering/Electronics; Engineering/Technology; Engineering-Related Technologies; Mechanical Engineering.

Award: Scholarship for use in sophomore, junior, senior, or graduate years; not renewable. *Number:* 50. *Amount:* up to $1000.

Eligibility Requirements: Applicant must be enrolled or expecting to enroll full-time at a two-year or four-year institution or university. Available to U.S. and non-U.S. citizens.

Application Requirements: Application, essay, financial need analysis, references, transcript. *Deadline:* May 31.

Contact: Christine Hess, Director of Careers in Construction
Associated Builders and Contractors Scholarship Program
4250 North Fairfax Drive, 9th Floor
Arlington, VA 22203
Phone: 703-812-2008
Fax: 703-812-8234
E-mail: hess@abc.org

ASSOCIATED GENERAL CONTRACTORS EDUCATION AND RESEARCH FOUNDATION http://www.agcfoundation.org

AGC EDUCATION AND RESEARCH FOUNDATION UNDERGRADUATE SCHOLARSHIPS

Sixty or more named scholarships are available to, first- or second-year students at a two-year school who plan to transfer to a four-year program for the fall term or college sophomores, juniors, or beginning seniors in a five-year program. Junior and senior level applicants must have one full academic year of coursework remaining at the beginning of the fall term. Applicant must pursue a BS degree in construction or construction/civil engineering. Must be a U.S. citizen or permanent resident. Maximum award of $2,000 per year is renewable for up to four years. Application and complete guidelines are available on the web.

Academic Fields/Career Goals: Civil Engineering; Engineering/Technology; Trade/Technical Specialties.

Award: Scholarship for use in sophomore, junior, or senior years; renewable. *Number:* up to 100. *Amount:* up to $2000.

Eligibility Requirements: Applicant must be enrolled or expecting to enroll full-time at a four-year institution. Available to U.S. citizens.

Application Requirements: Application, essay, references, transcript. *Deadline:* November 1.

Contact: Floretta Slade, Director of Programs
Associated General Contractors Education and Research Foundation
333 John Carlyle Street
Suite 200
Alexandria, VA 22314
Phone: 703-837-5342
Fax: 703-837-5402
E-mail: sladef@agc.org

ASSOCIATED GENERAL CONTRACTORS OF AMERICA-NEW YORK STATE CHAPTER http://www.agcnys.org

ASSOCIATED GENERAL CONTRACTORS OF AMERICA-NEW YORK STATE CHAPTER SCHOLARSHIP PROGRAM

Program designed to encourage and attract students to the heavy and highway construction industry. Preferred courses of study include civil engineering, construction management and construction technology. Must be a resident of New York. Minimum 2.5 GPA required.

Academic Fields/Career Goals: Civil Engineering; Surveying; Surveying Technology, Cartography, or Geographic Information Science; Transportation.

Award: Scholarship for use in sophomore, junior, senior, or graduate years; not renewable. *Number:* 10–15. *Amount:* $2500–$3000.

Eligibility Requirements: Applicant must be enrolled or expecting to enroll full-time at a two-year or four-year institution or university and resident of New York. Applicant must have 2.5 GPA or higher. Available to U.S. citizens.

Application Requirements: Application, references, transcript. *Deadline:* May 15.

Contact: Liz Elvin, Communications Director
Associated General Contractors of America-New York State Chapter
1900 Western Avenue
Albany, NY 12203-5097
Phone: 518-456-1134
Fax: 518-456-1198
E-mail: lelvin@agcnys.org

ASSOCIATION FOR FACILITIES ENGINEERING (AFE)

ASSOCIATION FOR FACILITIES ENGINEERING CEDAR VALLEY CHAPTER # 132 SCHOLARSHIP

• *See page 97*

ASSOCIATION FOR IRON AND STEEL TECHNOLOGY http://www.aist.org/foundation/scholarships.htm

ASSOCIATION FOR IRON AND STEEL TECHNOLOGY DAVID H. SAMSON SCHOLARSHIP

• *See page 139*

ASSOCIATION OF CALIFORNIA WATER AGENCIES http://www.acwanet.com

ASSOCIATION OF CALIFORNIA WATER AGENCIES SCHOLARSHIPS

• *See page 68*

CLAIR A. HILL SCHOLARSHIP

• *See page 68*

ASSOCIATION OF STATE DAM SAFETY OFFICIALS http://www.damsafety.org

ASSOCIATION OF STATE DAM SAFETY OFFICIALS UNDERGRADUATE SCHOLARSHIP

One-time award for college seniors in civil engineering or related field as determined by the Association of State Dam Safety Officials. Must be interested in a career in dam safety engineering, hydrology, hydraulics, geotechnical disciplines, or another discipline related to design, construction and operation of dams. Minimum 3.0 GPA required. Merit-based.

Academic Fields/Career Goals: Civil Engineering; Engineering/Technology.

Award: Scholarship for use in senior year; not renewable. *Number:* 3. *Amount:* $2500–$5000.

Eligibility Requirements: Applicant must be enrolled or expecting to enroll full-time at a four-year institution or university. Applicant must have 3.0 GPA or higher. Available to U.S. citizens.

Application Requirements: Application, essay, financial need analysis, references, transcript. *Deadline:* February 14.

Contact: Maureen Hogle, Administrative Support Specialist
Association of State Dam Safety Officials
450 Old Vine Street, 2nd Floor
Lexington, KY 40507-1544
Phone: 859-257-5140
Fax: 859-323-1958
E-mail: info@damsafety.org

BARRY M. GOLDWATER SCHOLARSHIP AND EXCELLENCE IN EDUCATION FOUNDATION http://www.act.org/goldwater

BARRY M. GOLDWATER SCHOLARSHIP AND EXCELLENCE IN EDUCATION PROGRAM

• *See page 68*

COMTO-BOSTON CHAPTER http://www.bostoncomto.org

COMTO BOSTON/GARRETT A. MORGAN SCHOLARSHIP

• *See page 75*

CONNECTICUT BUILDING CONGRESS http://www.cbc-ct.org

CONNECTICUT BUILDING CONGRESS SCHOLARSHIP FUND

• *See page 75*

DELAWARE SOLID WASTE AUTHORITY http://www.dswa.com

DELAWARE SOLID WASTE AUTHORITY SCHOLARSHIP

• *See page 113*

FLORIDA EDUCATIONAL FACILITIES PLANNERS' ASSOCIATION http://www.fefpa.org

FEFPA ASSISTANTSHIP

• *See page 76*

FOUNDATION OF THE WALL AND CEILING INDUSTRY http://www.awci.org/thefoundation.shtml

FOUNDATION OF THE WALL AND CEILING INDUSTRY SCHOLARSHIP PROGRAM

• *See page 76*

GEORGE BIRD GRINNELL AMERICAN INDIAN FUND

AL QOYAWAYMA AWARD

• *See page 141*

HAROLD B. & DOROTHY A. SNYDER FOUNDATION, INC.

HAROLD B. AND DOROTHY A. SNYDER FOUNDATION, INC., PROGRAM

• *See page 141*

HAWAIIAN LODGE, F.& A. M. http://www.hawaiianlodge.org/

HAWAIIAN LODGE SCHOLARSHIPS

• *See page 76*

HISPANIC COLLEGE FUND, INC. http://www.hispanicfund.org

NATIONAL HISPANIC EXPLORERS SCHOLARSHIP PROGRAM

• *See page 69*

HISPANIC ENGINEER NATIONAL ACHIEVEMENT AWARDS CORPORATION (HENAAC) http://www.henaac.org

HISPANIC ENGINEER NATIONAL ACHIEVEMENT AWARDS CORPORATION SCHOLARSHIP PROGRAM

• *See page 99*

HISPANIC SCHOLARSHIP FUND http://www.hsf.net

HSF/GENERAL MOTORS SCHOLARSHIP

• *See page 126*

HSF/SOCIETY OF HISPANIC PROFESSIONAL ENGINEERS, INC. SCHOLARSHIP PROGRAM

Scholarship for students of Hispanic heritage pursuing degrees in the engineering, mathematics, science, and computer science fields. All students must be enrolled full-time in a degree seeking program in the U.S. or Puerto Rico.

Academic Fields/Career Goals: Civil Engineering; Computer Science/ Data Processing; Electrical Engineering/Electronics; Engineering/ Technology; Engineering-Related Technologies; Mechanical Engineering; Physical Sciences and Math; Science, Technology, and Society.

Award: Scholarship for use in freshman, sophomore, junior, senior, or graduate years. *Number:* varies. *Amount:* varies.

Eligibility Requirements: Applicant must be Hispanic and enrolled or expecting to enroll full-time at an institution or university.

Application Requirements: Application, transcript. *Deadline:* June 2.

Contact: HSF Scholarship Department
Hispanic Scholarship Fund
55 Second Street, Suite 1500
San Francisco, CA 94105
Phone: 877-HSF-INFO
Fax: 415-808-2302
E-mail: info@hsf.net

INDEPENDENT LABORATORIES INSTITUTE SCHOLARSHIP ALLIANCE http://www.acil.org

INDEPENDENT LABORATORIES INSTITUTE SCHOLARSHIP ALLIANCE

• *See page 69*

JORGE MAS CANOSA FREEDOM FOUNDATION

MAS FAMILY SCHOLARSHIP AWARD

• *See page 126*

KENTUCKY NATURAL RESOURCES AND ENVIRONMENTAL PROTECTION CABINET http://www.uky.edu/waterresources

ENVIRONMENTAL PROTECTION SCHOLARSHIPS

• *See page 142*

KENTUCKY TRANSPORTATION CABINET http://www.transportation.ky.gov/

KENTUCKY TRANSPORTATION CABINET CIVIL ENGINEERING SCHOLARSHIP PROGRAM

Scholarships are available to eligible applicants at 4 universities in Kentucky. Our mission is to continually pursue statewide recruitment and retention of bright, motivated civil engineers in the Kentucky Transportation Cabinet.

Academic Fields/Career Goals: Civil Engineering.

Award: Scholarship for use in freshman, sophomore, junior, senior, or graduate years; renewable. *Number:* 10–20. *Amount:* $7200–$8000.

Eligibility Requirements: Applicant must be enrolled or expecting to enroll full-time at an institution or university; resident of Kentucky and studying in Kentucky. Available to U.S. and non-U.S. citizens.

Application Requirements: Application, essay, interview, references, test scores, transcript. *Deadline:* March 1.

Contact: Jo Anne Tingle, Scholarship Program Manager
Kentucky Transportation Cabinet
Attn: Scholarship Program Manager
SHE's Office, Suite E6-S1-00, 200 Metro Street
Frankfort, KY 40622
Phone: 502-564-3730
Fax: 502-564-2277
E-mail: jo.tingle@ky.gov

LOS ANGELES COUNCIL OF BLACK PROFESSIONAL ENGINEERS http://www.lablackengineers.org/scholarships.html

AL-BEN SCHOLARSHIP FOR ACADEMIC INCENTIVE

• *See page 142*

AL-BEN SCHOLARSHIP FOR PROFESSIONAL MERIT

• *See page 142*

AL-BEN SCHOLARSHIP FOR SCHOLASTIC ACHIEVEMENT

• *See page 143*

MICHIGAN SOCIETY OF PROFESSIONAL ENGINEERS http://www.michiganspe.org

ANTHONY C. FORTUNSKI, P.E. MEMORIAL GRANT

• *See page 143*

MICHIGAN SOCIETY OF PROFESSIONAL ENGINEERS UNDESIGNATED GRANT

• *See page 143*

MICHIGAN SOCIETY OF PROFESSIONAL ENGINEERS 1980 NATIONAL SOCIETY OF PROFESSIONAL ENGINEERS ANNUAL MEETING COMMITTEE GRANT

• *See page 143*

MICHIGAN SOCIETY OF PROFESSIONAL ENGINEERS ABRAMS GRANT

One $3000 grant for a top ranking student interested in pursuing a career in civil or surveying engineering. Must be a Michigan resident enrolled in an ABET-accredited program at a Michigan college or university. Minimum 3.0 GPA required. Applicant must be a member of MSPE student chapter or a state member-at-large.

Academic Fields/Career Goals: Civil Engineering.

Award: Grant for use in freshman, sophomore, junior, or senior years; not renewable. *Number:* 1. *Amount:* $3000.

Eligibility Requirements: Applicant must be enrolled or expecting to enroll full-time at an institution or university; resident of Michigan and studying in Michigan. Applicant or parent of applicant must be member of Michigan Society of Professional Engineers. Applicant must have 3.0 GPA or higher. Available to U.S. citizens.

Application Requirements: Application, essay, references, transcript. *Deadline:* varies.

Contact: Scholarship Coordinator
Michigan Society of Professional Engineers
PO Box 15276
Lansing, MI 48901-5276
Phone: 517-487-9388
Fax: 517-487-0635
E-mail: mspe@voyager.net

MICHIGAN SOCIETY OF PROFESSIONAL ENGINEERS AUXILIARY GRANT

• *See page 143*

MICHIGAN SOCIETY OF PROFESSIONAL ENGINEERS HARRY R. BALL, P.E. GRANT

• *See page 144*

MICHIGAN SOCIETY OF PROFESSIONAL ENGINEERS KENNETH B. FISHBECK, P.E. MEMORIAL GRANT

• *See page 144*

MICHIGAN SOCIETY OF PROFESSIONAL ENGINEERS SCHOLARSHIP TRUST GRANT

• *See page 144*

MSPE AUXILIARY GRANT FOR UNDERGRADUATE STUDY

One grant of $1000 will be awarded to a student interested in pursuing a career in engineering. Preference is given to a son/daughter of an MSPE member, but is not required to apply.

Academic Fields/Career Goals: Civil Engineering; Engineering/Technology.

Award: Grant for use in freshman, sophomore, junior, or senior years; not renewable. *Number:* 1. *Amount:* $1000.

Eligibility Requirements: Applicant must be enrolled or expecting to enroll full-time at an institution or university; resident of Michigan and studying in Michigan. Applicant must have 3.0 GPA or higher. Available to U.S. citizens.

Application Requirements: Application, essay, references, transcript. *Deadline:* varies.

Contact: Scholarship Coordinator
Michigan Society of Professional Engineers
PO Box 15276
Lansing, MI 48901-5276
Phone: 517-487-9388
Fax: 517-487-0635
E-mail: mspe@voyager.net

ROBERT E. FOLMSBEE, P.E. MEMORIAL GRANT

One $2000 grant for a top-ranking student interested in pursuing a career in construction engineering. Preference given to a construction engineering student interested in general fields of construction engineering. Restricted to Michigan students attending Michigan postsecondary institutions. Must be a member of MSPE student chapter or state member-at-large. Minimum 3.0 GPA required.

Academic Fields/Career Goals: Civil Engineering; Electrical Engineering/Electronics; Engineering/Technology.

Award: Grant for use in freshman, sophomore, junior, or senior years; not renewable. *Number:* 1. *Amount:* $2000.

Eligibility Requirements: Applicant must be enrolled or expecting to enroll full-time at an institution or university; resident of Michigan and studying in Michigan. Applicant or parent of applicant must be member of Michigan Society of Professional Engineers. Applicant must have 3.0 GPA or higher. Available to U.S. citizens.

Application Requirements: Application, essay, references, test scores, transcript. *Deadline:* varies.

Contact: Scholarship Coordinator
Michigan Society of Professional Engineers
PO Box 15276
Lansing, MI 48901-5276
Phone: 517-487-9388
Fax: 517-487-0635
E-mail: mspe@voyager.net

NAMEPA NATIONAL SCHOLARSHIP FOUNDATION http://www.namepa.org

NATIONAL ASSOCIATION OF MINORITY ENGINEERING PROGRAM ADMINISTRATORS NATIONAL SCHOLARSHIP FUND

• *See page 101*

NASA DELAWARE SPACE GRANT CONSORTIUM http://www.delspace.org

NASA DELAWARE SPACE GRANT UNDERGRADUATE TUITION SCHOLARSHIP
• *See page 70*

NATIONAL ASPHALT PAVEMENT ASSOCIATION http://www.hotmix.org/justforstudents.php

NATIONAL ASPHALT PAVEMENT ASSOCIATION SCHOLARSHIP PROGRAM

Scholarship provides funding for full-time students majoring in civil engineering, construction management, or construction engineering. Applicant must take at least one course on HMA technology. Please refer to Web site for more details: http://www.hotmix.org/main.htm. Some state restrictions.

Academic Fields/Career Goals: Civil Engineering.

Award: Scholarship for use in sophomore, junior, senior, or graduate years; renewable. *Number:* 50–150. *Amount:* $500–$3000.

Eligibility Requirements: Applicant must be enrolled or expecting to enroll full-time at a four-year or technical institution or university. Applicant must have 2.5 GPA or higher. Available to U.S. citizens.

Application Requirements: Application, resume. *Deadline:* varies.

Contact: Kalena Mollon, Accounting Assistant
National Asphalt Pavement Association
NAPA Building
5100 Forbes Boulevard
Lanham, MD 20706-4413
Phone: 888-468-6499
Fax: 301-731-4798
E-mail: kmollon@hotmix.org

NATIONAL ASSOCIATION OF WOMEN IN CONSTRUCTION http://nawic.org

NAWIC UNDERGRADUATE SCHOLARSHIPS
• *See page 77*

NATIONAL INSTITUTE OF BUILDING SCIENCES, MULTIHAZARD MITIGATION COUNCIL http://www.nibs.org

ARCHITECTURE, CONSTRUCTION, AND ENGINEERING MENTOR PROGRAM SCHOLARSHIPS
• *See page 78*

NATIONAL SOCIETY OF PROFESSIONAL ENGINEERS http://www.nspe.org

MAUREEN L. AND HOWARD N. BLITMAN, PE SCHOLARSHIP TO PROMOTE DIVERSITY IN ENGINEERING
• *See page 145*

NATIONAL SOCIETY OF PROFESSIONAL ENGINEERS/AUXILIARY SCHOLARSHIP
• *See page 145*

PAUL H. ROBBINS HONORARY SCHOLARSHIP
• *See page 145*

PROFESSIONAL ENGINEERS IN INDUSTRY SCHOLARSHIP
• *See page 145*

VIRGINIA HENRY MEMORIAL SCHOLARSHIP
• *See page 146*

NEW ENGLAND WATER WORKS ASSOCIATION http://www.newwa.org

NEW ENGLAND WATER WORKS SCHOLARSHIPS

Scholarships are awarded to eligible students on the basis of merit, character, and need. Preference given to those students' whose programs are considered by a committee as beneficial to water works practice in New England.

Academic Fields/Career Goals: Civil Engineering; Natural Resources.

Award: Scholarship for use in freshman, sophomore, junior, senior, graduate, or postgraduate years; not renewable. *Number:* up to 7. *Amount:* $500–$2000.

Eligibility Requirements: Applicant must be enrolled or expecting to enroll full or part-time at a two-year or four-year or technical institution or university. Available to U.S. and non-U.S. citizens.

Application Requirements: Application, transcript, membership in NEWWA. *Fee:* $30. *Deadline:* July 31.

Contact: Melissa Ruozzi, Events and Publications Coordinator
New England Water Works Association
125 Hopping Brook Road
Holliston, MA 01746
Phone: 508-893-7979
Fax: 508-893-9898
E-mail: melissa@newwa.org

NORTH DAKOTA DEPARTMENT OF TRANSPORTATION http://www.state.nd.us/dot/

NORTH DAKOTA DEPARTMENT OF TRANSPORTATION ENGINEERING GRANT

Educational grants for civil or construction engineering, or civil engineering technology, are awarded to students who have completed one year of course study at an institution of higher learning in North Dakota. Recipients must agree to work for the Department for a period of time at least equal to the grant period or repay the grant at 6% interest. Minimum 2.0 GPA required.

Academic Fields/Career Goals: Civil Engineering; Engineering/Technology.

Award: Grant for use in sophomore, junior, or senior years; renewable. *Number:* varies. *Amount:* $1000–$6000.

Eligibility Requirements: Applicant must be enrolled or expecting to enroll full-time at a four-year or technical institution and studying in North Dakota. Available to U.S. citizens.

Application Requirements: Application, financial need analysis, interview, transcript. *Deadline:* Continuous.

Contact: Lorrie Pavlicek, Human Resources Manager
North Dakota Department of Transportation
503 38th Street South
Fargo, ND 58103
Phone: 701-239-8934
Fax: 701-239-8939
E-mail: lpavlice@state.nd.us

OREGON STUDENT ASSISTANCE COMMISSION http://www.osac.state.or.us

AMERICAN COUNCIL OF ENGINEERING COMPANIES OF OREGON SCHOLARSHIP
• *See page 146*

HOMESTEAD CAPITAL HOUSING SCHOLARSHIP
• *See page 46*

PLUMBING-HEATING-COOLING CONTRACTORS ASSOCIATION EDUCATION FOUNDATION http://www.phccweb.org

BRADFORD WHITE CORPORATION SCHOLARSHIP
• *See page 79*

DELTA FAUCET COMPANY SCHOLARSHIP PROGRAM
• *See page 79*

PHCC EDUCATIONAL FOUNDATION NEED-BASED SCHOLARSHIP
• *See page 79*

PHCC EDUCATIONAL FOUNDATION SCHOLARSHIP PROGRAM
• *See page 79*

PROFESSIONAL GROUNDS MANAGEMENT SOCIETY http://www.pgms.org

ANNE SEAMAN PROFESSIONAL GROUNDS MANAGEMENT SOCIETY MEMORIAL SCHOLARSHIP
• *See page 61*

ROCKY MOUNTAIN COAL MINING INSTITUTE http://www.rmcmi.org

ROCKY MOUNTAIN COAL MINING INSTITUTE SCHOLARSHIP

• *See page 146*

SOCIETY FOR MINING, METALLURGY AND EXPLORATION - CENTRAL WYOMING SECTION

COATES, WOLFF, RUSSELL MINING INDUSTRY SCHOLARSHIP

• *See page 71*

SOCIETY OF HISPANIC PROFESSIONAL ENGINEERS FOUNDATION http://www.shpefoundation.org

SOCIETY OF HISPANIC PROFESSIONAL ENGINEERS FOUNDATION

• *See page 146*

SOCIETY OF MEXICAN AMERICAN ENGINEERS AND SCIENTISTS http://www.maes-natl.org

GRE AND GRADUATE APPLICATIONS WAIVER

• *See page 72*

SOCIETY OF PLASTICS ENGINEERS (SPE) FOUNDATION http://www.4spe.org

FLEMING/BASZCAK SCHOLARSHIP

• *See page 147*

SOCIETY OF PLASTICS ENGINEERS SCHOLARSHIP PROGRAM

• *See page 147*

SOCIETY OF WOMEN ENGINEERS http://www.swe.org/scholarships

BECHTEL CORPORATION SCHOLARSHIP

Must major in either architectural, civil, electrical, environmental, or mechanical engineering. Must be a member of the Society of Women Engineers. Minimum 3.0 GPA required. Open to sophomores, juniors, and seniors. Deadline: February 1.

Academic Fields/Career Goals: Civil Engineering; Electrical Engineering/Electronics; Engineering/Technology; Mechanical Engineering.

Award: Scholarship for use in sophomore, junior, or senior years; not renewable. *Number:* 2. *Amount:* $1400.

Eligibility Requirements: Applicant must be enrolled or expecting to enroll at a four-year institution or university and female. Applicant or parent of applicant must be member of Society of Women Engineers. Applicant must have 3.0 GPA or higher. Available to U.S. citizens.

Application Requirements: Application, references, self-addressed stamped envelope, transcript. *Deadline:* February 1.

Contact: Program Coordinator
Society of Women Engineers
230 East Ohio Street, Suite 400
Chicago, IL 60611-3265
Phone: 312-596-5223
Fax: 312-644-8557
E-mail: hq@swe.org

CHEVRON TEXACO CORPORATION SCHOLARSHIPS

• *See page 147*

TEXAS DEPARTMENT OF TRANSPORTATION http://www.dot.state.tx.us

CONDITIONAL GRANT PROGRAM

Grants available for up to $6,000. Students must be considered economically disadvantaged based on federal guidelines. Must be pursuing a degree in Civil Engineering or Computer Science. Must be a Texas resident and study in Texas.

Academic Fields/Career Goals: Civil Engineering; Computer Science/Data Processing.

Award: Grant for use in freshman, sophomore, junior, or senior years; renewable. *Number:* varies. *Amount:* up to $6000.

Eligibility Requirements: Applicant must be American Indian/Alaska Native, Asian/Pacific Islander, Black (non-Hispanic), or Hispanic; enrolled or expecting to enroll full-time at a four-year institution; female; resident of Texas and studying in Texas. Applicant must have 2.5 GPA or higher. Available to U.S. citizens.

Application Requirements: Application, essay, interview, references, test scores, transcript. *Deadline:* March 1.

Contact: Minnie Brown, Program Coordinator
Texas Department of Transportation
125 East 11th Street
Austin, TX 78701-2483
Phone: 512-416-4979
Fax: 512-416-4980
E-mail: mbrown2@dot.state.tx.us

TEXAS ENGINEERING FOUNDATION http://www.tspe.org

TEXAS SOCIETY OF PROFESSIONAL ENGINEERS (TSPE) REGIONAL SCHOLARSHIPS

• *See page 148*

UNITED NEGRO COLLEGE FUND http://www.uncf.org

CDM SCHOLARSHIP/INTERNSHIP

Scholarship open to students attending a UNCF member college or university and majoring in environmental, civil, or electrical engineering. 3.0 GPA required. Prospective applicants should complete the Student Profile found at Web site: http://www.uncf.org.

Academic Fields/Career Goals: Civil Engineering; Electrical Engineering/Electronics; Engineering/Technology.

Award: Scholarship for use in freshman, sophomore, junior, or senior years; not renewable. *Amount:* $5000.

Eligibility Requirements: Applicant must be Black (non-Hispanic) and enrolled or expecting to enroll at a four-year institution or university. Applicant must have 3.0 GPA or higher.

Application Requirements: Application. *Deadline:* February 25.

Contact: Program Services Department
United Negro College Fund
8260 Willow Oaks Corporate Drive
Fairfax, VA 22031

CHEVRON/TEXACO SCHOLARS PROGRAM

Scholarship awarded to college sophomores and juniors attending one of six UNCF member colleges and universities (Clark, Atlanta, Morehouse, Morris Brown, Spelman, Tuskegee, or Florida A&M). Applicants must major in civil, mechanical, or petroleum engineering. Minimum 2.5 GPA required. Prospective applicants should complete the Student Profile found at Web site: http://www.uncf.org.

Academic Fields/Career Goals: Civil Engineering; Engineering/Technology; Mechanical Engineering.

Award: Scholarship for use in sophomore or junior years; not renewable. *Amount:* up to $3000.

Eligibility Requirements: Applicant must be Black (non-Hispanic) and enrolled or expecting to enroll full-time at a four-year institution or university. Applicant must have 2.5 GPA or higher. Available to U.S. citizens.

Application Requirements: Application, financial need analysis. *Deadline:* December 8.

Contact: Program Services Department
United Negro College Fund
8260 Willow Oaks Corporate Drive
Fairfax, VA 22031

MALCOLM PIRNIE, INC. SCHOLARS PROGRAM

• *See page 148*

UNIVERSITIES SPACE RESEARCH ASSOCIATION http://www.usra.edu/hq/scholarships/overview.shtml

UNIVERSITIES SPACE RESEARCH ASSOCIATION SCHOLARSHIP PROGRAM

• See page 72

UTAH SOCIETY OF PROFESSIONAL ENGINEERS http://www.uspeonline.com

UTAH SOCIETY OF PROFESSIONAL ENGINEERS SCHOLARSHIP

• See page 148

COMMUNICATIONS

ACADEMY OF TELEVISION ARTS AND SCIENCES FOUNDATION http://www.emmys.tv/foundation

ACADEMY OF TELEVISION ARTS AND SCIENCES COLLEGE TELEVISION AWARDS

• See page 84

ADC RESEARCH INSTITUTE http://www.adc.org

JACK SHAHEEN MASS COMMUNICATIONS SCHOLARSHIP AWARD

Awarded to Arab-American students who excel in the communications field (journalism, radio, television, or film). Must be a junior or senior undergraduate or graduate student. Must be U.S. citizen. Must have 3.0 GPA. Application deadline is March 15.

Academic Fields/Career Goals: Communications; Filmmaking/Video; Journalism; TV/Radio Broadcasting.

Award: Prize for use in junior, senior, or graduate years; not renewable. *Number:* 1. *Amount:* $1000.

Eligibility Requirements: Applicant must be of Arab heritage and enrolled or expecting to enroll at a four-year institution or university. Applicant must have 3.0 GPA or higher. Available to U.S. citizens.

Application Requirements: Essay, references, transcript, copies of original articles, videos, films. *Deadline:* March 15.

Contact: Marvin Wingfield, Director of Education and Outreach
ADC Research Institute
4201 Connecticut Avenue, NW Suite 300
Washington, DC 20008
Phone: 202-244-2990
Fax: 202-244-3196
E-mail: marvinw@adc.org

ADVERTISING FEDERATION OF FORT WAYNE, INC. http://adfedfortwayne.org

ADVERTISING FEDERATION OF FORT WAYNE, INC., SCHOLARSHIP

Applicant must be a full-time college student registered in an advertising or marketing related field. Must be a resident of one of the following Indiana counties: Adams, Allen, Dekalb, Huntington, Kosciusko, LaGrange, Noble, Steuben, Wabash, Wells or Whitley.

Academic Fields/Career Goals: Communications; Filmmaking/Video; Graphics/Graphic Arts/Printing; TV/Radio Broadcasting.

Award: Scholarship for use in sophomore, junior, or senior years; not renewable. *Number:* 1–3. *Amount:* $1000.

Eligibility Requirements: Applicant must be enrolled or expecting to enroll full-time at a four-year institution and resident of Indiana. Available to U.S. citizens.

Application Requirements: Application. *Deadline:* varies.

Contact: W. L. Rennecker, Executive Secretary
Advertising Federation of Fort Wayne, Inc.
PO Box 10066
Ft. Wayne, IN 46850
Phone: 260-427-9106

AMERICAN INSTITUTE OF POLISH CULTURE, INC. http://www.ampolinstitute.org

HARRIET IRSAY SCHOLARSHIP GRANT

Merit-based $1,000 scholarships for students studying communications, public relations, and/or journalism. All U.S. citizens may apply, but preference will be given to United States citizens of Polish heritage. Must submit 3 letters of recommendation on appropriate letterhead with application mailed directly to AIPC. For study in U.S. only. Deadline: March 17. Application fee is $25, now refundable.

Academic Fields/Career Goals: Communications; Journalism.

Award: Scholarship for use in freshman, sophomore, junior, or senior years; not renewable. *Number:* 10–15. *Amount:* $1000.

Eligibility Requirements: Applicant must be enrolled or expecting to enroll full-time at a two-year or four-year institution or university. Available to U.S. citizens.

Application Requirements: Application, resume, references, self-addressed stamped envelope, transcript. *Fee:* $25. *Deadline:* March 17.

Contact: Frances Waxman, Administrative Assistant
American Institute of Polish Culture, Inc.
1440 79th Street Causeway, Suite 117
Miami, FL 33141-4135
Phone: 305-864-2349
Fax: 305-865-5150
E-mail: info@ampolinstitute.org

AMERICAN LEGION, DEPARTMENT OF NEW YORK http://www.ny.legion.org

AMERICAN LEGION, DEPARTMENT OF NEW YORK PRESS ASSOCIATION SCHOLARSHIP

A $1000 scholarship is available to children of NY American Legion or American Legion Auxiliary members, members of SAL or ALA Juniors or graduates of NY AL Boys State or Girls State. Must be entering or attending accredited four-year college pursuing communications degree.

Academic Fields/Career Goals: Communications.

Award: Scholarship for use in freshman year; not renewable. *Number:* 1. *Amount:* $1000.

Eligibility Requirements: Applicant must be enrolled or expecting to enroll at a four-year institution or university. Available to U.S. citizens. Applicant or parent must meet one or more of the following requirements: general military experience; retired from active duty; disabled or killed as a result of military service; prisoner of war; or missing in action.

Application Requirements: Application. *Deadline:* May 1.

Contact: Scholarship Chairman
American Legion, Department of New York
PO Box 1239
Syracuse, NY 13201

AMERICAN LEGION, PRESS CLUB OF NEW JERSEY

AMERICAN LEGION PRESS CLUB OF NEW JERSEY AND POST 170 ARTHUR DEHARDT MEMORIAL SCHOLARSHIP

A $500 scholarship will be awarded to two students (one male, one female) entering their freshman year in an accredited four-year college. Eligible applicants will be the son, daughter, grandson, or granddaughter of a current or deceased, card-holding member of the American Legion. Must intend to work toward a degree related to the field of communications.

Academic Fields/Career Goals: Communications; Journalism; Photojournalism/Photography; TV/Radio Broadcasting.

Award: Scholarship for use in freshman year; not renewable. *Number:* 2. *Amount:* $500.

Eligibility Requirements: Applicant must be high school student; planning to enroll or expecting to enroll full-time at a four-year institution; single and resident of New Jersey. Available to U.S. citizens. Applicant or parent must meet one or more of the following requirements: general military experience; retired from active duty; disabled or killed as a result of military service; prisoner of war; or missing in action.

Application Requirements: Application, essay. *Deadline:* July 1.

Contact: Jack W. Kuepfer, Chairman
American Legion, Press Club of New Jersey
68 Merrill Road
Clifton, NJ 07012-1622
Phone: 973-473-5176

AMERICAN QUARTER HORSE FOUNDATION (AQHF)

http://www.aqha.org/aqhya

AQHF JOURNALISM OR COMMUNICATIONS SCHOLARSHIP

Must be member of AQHA or AQHYA who is pursuing a degree in journalism, communications, or a related field. Recipient receives $2000 per year for a four-year degree plan. Minimum 2.5 GPA required.

Academic Fields/Career Goals: Communications; Journalism.

Award: Scholarship for use in freshman, sophomore, junior, or senior years; renewable. *Number:* 1. *Amount:* $8000.

Eligibility Requirements: Applicant must be enrolled or expecting to enroll full-time at a two-year or four-year or technical institution or university. Applicant or parent of applicant must be member of American Quarter Horse Association. Applicant must have 2.5 GPA or higher. Available to U.S. and Canadian citizens.

Application Requirements: Application, essay, financial need analysis, photo, references, transcript. *Deadline:* February 1.

Contact: Laura Owens, Scholarship Coordinator
American Quarter Horse Foundation (AQHF)
2601 I-40 East
Amarillo, TX 79104
Phone: 806-376-5181
Fax: 806-376-1005
E-mail: lowens@aqha.org

ARRL FOUNDATION, INC.

http://www.arrl.org/arrlf/scholgen.html

CHARLES N. FISHER MEMORIAL SCHOLARSHIP

• *See page 66*

DR. JAMES L. LAWSON MEMORIAL SCHOLARSHIP

One-time award available to students who are licensed as general amateur radio operators. Preference given to residents of Connecticut, Maine, Massachusetts, New Hampshire, Rhode Island, Vermont, and New York attending school in those states. Preference given to communications or electronics majors.

Academic Fields/Career Goals: Communications; Electrical Engineering/Electronics.

Award: Scholarship for use in freshman, sophomore, junior, or senior years; not renewable. *Number:* 1. *Amount:* $500.

Eligibility Requirements: Applicant must be enrolled or expecting to enroll at an institution or university and must have an interest in amateur radio.

Application Requirements: Application, transcript. *Deadline:* February 1.

Contact: Mary Lau, Scholarship Director
ARRL Foundation, Inc.
225 Main Street
Newington, CT 06111-4845

FRED R. MCDANIEL MEMORIAL SCHOLARSHIP

Preference given to students with a 3.0 GPA and both residing and attending school in Texas, Oklahoma, Louisiana, Michigan, New Mexico, or Arkansas. Preference is also given to students in the fields of electronics, communications, or a related field. Must be an amateur radio operator with a general license minimum. One-time award of $500.

Academic Fields/Career Goals: Communications; Electrical Engineering/Electronics.

Award: Scholarship for use in freshman, sophomore, junior, or senior years; not renewable. *Number:* 1. *Amount:* $500.

Eligibility Requirements: Applicant must be enrolled or expecting to enroll at an institution or university and must have an interest in amateur radio. Applicant must have 3.0 GPA or higher.

Application Requirements: Application, transcript. *Deadline:* February 1.

Contact: Mary Lau, Scholarship Coordinator
ARRL Foundation, Inc.
225 Main Street
Newington, CT 06111-4845

IRVING W. COOK, WA0CGS, SCHOLARSHIP

• *See page 67*

L. PHIL WICKER SCHOLARSHIP

One-time award available to electronics or communications students pursuing a baccalaureate or higher degree who are licensed as general amateur radio operators. Preference given to those residing in North Carolina, South Carolina, Virginia or West Virginia and attending school in that area.

Academic Fields/Career Goals: Communications; Electrical Engineering/Electronics.

Award: Scholarship for use in freshman, sophomore, junior, senior, or graduate years; not renewable. *Number:* 1. *Amount:* $1000.

Eligibility Requirements: Applicant must be enrolled or expecting to enroll at an institution or university and must have an interest in amateur radio.

Application Requirements: Application, transcript. *Deadline:* February 1.

Contact: Mary Lau, Scholarship Director
ARRL Foundation, Inc.
225 Main Street
Newington, CT 06111-4845

MISSISSIPPI SCHOLARSHIP

• *See page 67*

PAUL AND HELEN L. GRAUER SCHOLARSHIP

• *See page 67*

PHD ARA SCHOLARSHIP

Award for journalism, computer science, or electronic engineering students who are amateur radio operators. Preference given to students residing in Iowa, Kansas, Missouri, or Nebraska, and those who are children of deceased amateur radio operators.

Academic Fields/Career Goals: Communications; Computer Science/Data Processing; Electrical Engineering/Electronics; Engineering/Technology; Journalism.

Award: Scholarship for use in freshman, sophomore, junior, or senior years; not renewable. *Number:* 1. *Amount:* $1000.

Eligibility Requirements: Applicant must be enrolled or expecting to enroll at an institution or university and must have an interest in amateur radio.

Application Requirements: Application, transcript. *Deadline:* February 1.

Contact: Mary Lau, Scholarship Director
ARRL Foundation, Inc.
225 Main Street
Newington, CT 06111-4845

ASIAN AMERICAN JOURNALISTS ASSOCIATION

http://www.aaja.org

ASIAN-AMERICAN JOURNALISTS ASSOCIATION SCHOLARSHIP

Awards for high school seniors and college students pursuing careers in the news media. Asian heritage is not required. Minimum 2.5 GPA required. Based on scholarship, goals, journalistic ability, financial need, and commitment to the Asian-American community. One-time award of up to $5000. Visit Web site http://www.aaja.org for application and details.

Academic Fields/Career Goals: Communications; Journalism; Photojournalism/Photography; TV/Radio Broadcasting.

Award: Scholarship for use in freshman, sophomore, junior, senior, or graduate years; not renewable. *Number:* 10–15. *Amount:* $1000–$5000.

Eligibility Requirements: Applicant must be enrolled or expecting to enroll full-time at a two-year or four-year institution or university and must have an interest in photography/photogrammetry/filmmaking or

Asian American Journalists Association (continued)

writing. Applicant or parent of applicant must have employment or volunteer experience in journalism. Applicant must have 2.5 GPA or higher.

Application Requirements: Application, essay, financial need analysis, resume, references, transcript. *Deadline:* varies.

Contact: Lila Chwee, Student Programs Coordinator
Asian American Journalists Association
1182 Market Street, Suite 320
San Francisco, CA 94102
Phone: 415-346-2051 Ext. 102
Fax: 415-346-6343
E-mail: programs@aaja.org

ASSOCIATION OF FEDERAL COMMUNICATIONS CONSULTING ENGINEERS

ASSOCIATION OF FEDERAL COMMUNICATIONS CONSULTING ENGINEERS SCHOLARSHIP FUND

Grants to full-time students who are undertaking accredited studies related to the goals of the AFCCE (consulting engineering as applied to the FCC). Must be upper-level undergraduate. Must be U.S. citizen.

Academic Fields/Career Goals: Communications; Electrical Engineering/Electronics; Engineering/Technology.

Award: Grant for use in junior or senior years; not renewable. *Number:* 4. *Amount:* $2000.

Eligibility Requirements: Applicant must be enrolled or expecting to enroll full-time at a four-year institution. Available to U.S. citizens.

Application Requirements: Application, essay, references, transcript. *Deadline:* Continuous.

Contact: John Dettra, Jr., Chairman, AFCCE Scholarship Committee
Association of Federal Communications Consulting Engineers
Dettra Communications
7906 Foxhound Road
McLean, VA 22102-2403
Phone: 703-790-1427
Fax: 703-790-0497

ATLANTA PRESS CLUB, INC. http://www.atlpressclub.org

ATLANTA PRESS CLUB JOURNALISM SCHOLARSHIP PROGRAM

A one-time award only for students attending a Georgia college accredited by the Southern Association of Colleges and Schools. Must be journalism or communications majors. Based on need and potential for contribution to field. Must interview with selection committee. Must be a U.S. citizen.

Academic Fields/Career Goals: Communications; Journalism; Literature/English/Writing; TV/Radio Broadcasting.

Award: Scholarship for use in freshman, sophomore, or junior years; not renewable. *Number:* 4. *Amount:* $1500.

Eligibility Requirements: Applicant must be enrolled or expecting to enroll full or part-time at a four-year institution or university; studying in Georgia and must have an interest in writing. Available to U.S. citizens.

Application Requirements: Application, essay, financial need analysis, interview, portfolio, transcript. *Deadline:* February 1.

Contact: Sarah Douglas, Executive Director
Atlanta Press Club, Inc.
34 Broad Street, 18th Floor
Atlanta, GA 30303
Phone: 404-577-7377
Fax: 404-223-3706

BOWEN FOUNDATION http://www.emmabowenfoundation.com

EMMA L. BOWEN FOUNDATION FOR MINORITY INTERESTS IN MEDIA

The Foundation's program is unlike other intern programs in that students work for a partner company during summers and school breaks from the end of their junior year in high school until they graduate from college. During that five-year period, students learn many aspects of corporate operations and develop company-specific skills. Corporations guide and develop minority students with the option of permanent placement upon completion of their college degree. Students in the program receive an hourly wage, as well as matching compensation to help pay for college tuition and expenses. Mentoring from selected staff in the sponsoring company is also a key element of the program.

Academic Fields/Career Goals: Communications; Journalism; TV/Radio Broadcasting.

Award: Scholarship for use in freshman, sophomore, junior, or senior years; renewable. *Number:* varies. *Amount:* varies.

Eligibility Requirements: Applicant must be American Indian/Alaska Native, Asian/Pacific Islander, Black (non-Hispanic), or Hispanic; age 16-20 and enrolled or expecting to enroll full-time at a four-year institution or university. Applicant must have 3.0 GPA or higher. Available to U.S. citizens.

Application Requirements: Application, essay, interview, photo, resume, references, test scores, transcript. *Deadline:* December 31.

Contact: Sandra D. Rice, Vice President, Eastern Division
Bowen Foundation
524 West 57th Street
New York, NY 10019
Phone: 212-975-2545
Fax: 212-975-5884
E-mail: sdrice@cbs.com

CALIFORNIA CHICANO NEWS MEDIA ASSOCIATION (CCNMA) http://www.ccnma.org

JOEL GARCIA MEMORIAL SCHOLARSHIP

Scholarships for Latinos interested in pursuing a career in journalism. Awards based on scholastic achievement, financial need, and community awareness. Submit sample of work. Award for California residents or those attending school in California. Deadline is first Friday of April.

Academic Fields/Career Goals: Communications; Journalism; Photojournalism/Photography; TV/Radio Broadcasting.

Award: Scholarship for use in freshman, sophomore, junior, senior, or graduate years; not renewable. *Number:* 10–20. *Amount:* $500–$2000.

Eligibility Requirements: Applicant must be of Latin American/Caribbean heritage; Hispanic; enrolled or expecting to enroll full-time at a two-year or four-year institution or university; resident of California and studying in California. Available to U.S. and non-U.S. citizens.

Application Requirements: Application, autobiography, essay, financial need analysis, interview, references, transcript, work samples. *Deadline:* April 2.

Contact: Julio Moran, Executive Director
California Chicano News Media Association (CCNMA)
USC Annenberg School of Journalism
3800 South Figueroa Street
Los Angeles, CA 90037-1206
Phone: 213-743-4960
Fax: 213-743-4989
E-mail: ccnmainfo@ccnma.org

CANADIAN ASSOCIATION OF BROADCASTERS http://www.cab-acr.ca

RUTH HANCOCK MEMORIAL SCHOLARSHIP

This CAN$1,500 scholarship is awarded annually to 3 students enrolled in a communications course at a Canadian school, who possess strong leadership qualities, natural talent, and a willingness to assist others. Must be a Canadian citizen.

Academic Fields/Career Goals: Communications; TV/Radio Broadcasting.

Award: Scholarship for use in freshman, sophomore, junior, senior, or graduate years; not renewable. *Number:* 3. *Amount:* $1114.

Eligibility Requirements: Applicant must be Canadian citizen; enrolled or expecting to enroll full or part-time at a two-year or four-year institution or university; studying in Alberta, British Columbia, Manitoba, New Brunswick, Newfoundland, North West Territories, Nova Scotia, Ontario, Prince Edward Island, Quebec, Saskatchewan, or Yukon and must have an interest in leadership.

Application Requirements: Application, essay, references. *Deadline:* June 30.

Contact: Vanessa Dewson, Special Events and Projects Coordinator
Canadian Association of Broadcasters
PO Box 627, Station B
Ottawa, ON K1P 5S2
Canada
Phone: 613-233-4035 Ext. 309
Fax: 613-233-6961
E-mail: vdewson@cab-acr.ca

CHARLES & LUCILLE KING FAMILY FOUNDATION, INC. http://www.kingfoundation.org

CHARLES AND LUCILLE KING FAMILY FOUNDATION SCHOLARSHIPS

Renewable award for college undergraduates at junior or senior level pursuing television, film, or communication studies to further their education. Must attend a four-year undergraduate institution. Minimum 3.0 GPA required to renew scholarship. Must have completed at least two years of study and be currently enrolled in a U.S. college or university. Must submit personal statement with application materials by April 15.

Academic Fields/Career Goals: Communications; Filmmaking/Video; TV/Radio Broadcasting.

Award: Scholarship for use in junior or senior years; renewable. *Number:* 10–20. *Amount:* $1250–$2500.

Eligibility Requirements: Applicant must be enrolled or expecting to enroll full-time at a four-year institution or university. Applicant must have 3.0 GPA or higher. Available to U.S. and non-U.S. citizens.

Application Requirements: Application, essay, financial need analysis, references, transcript. *Deadline:* April 15.

Contact: Michael Donovan, Educational Director
Charles & Lucille King Family Foundation, Inc.
366 Madison Avenue, 10th Floor
New York, NY 10017
Phone: 212-682-2913
Fax: 212-949-0728
E-mail: info@kingfoundation.org

CIRI FOUNDATION http://www.ciri.com/tcf

LAWRENCE MATSON MEMORIAL ENDOWMENT SCHOLARSHIP FUND

• *See page 86*

CUBAN AMERICAN NATIONAL FOUNDATION

MAS FAMILY SCHOLARSHIPS

• *See page 123*

DALLAS-FORT WORTH ASSOCIATION OF BLACK COMMUNICATORS http://www.dfwabc.org

FUTURE JOURNALISTS SCHOLARSHIP PROGRAM

Scholarships are available to minority high school seniors and college students pursuing careers in broadcast or print journalism, advertising, public relations, photojournalism, and graphic arts and have permanent residence in Dallas, Tarrant, Denton, Hunt, Collin or Ellis county, TX. Please see Web site for application and more information: http://www.dfwabc.org.

Academic Fields/Career Goals: Communications; Graphics/Graphic Arts/Printing; Journalism; Photojournalism/Photography; TV/Radio Broadcasting.

Award: Scholarship for use in freshman, sophomore, junior, senior, or graduate years; not renewable. *Number:* 12–15. *Amount:* $500–$1500.

Eligibility Requirements: Applicant must be American Indian/Alaska Native, Asian/Pacific Islander, Black (non-Hispanic), or Hispanic; enrolled or expecting to enroll full-time at a four-year institution or university and resident of Texas. Available to U.S. citizens.

Application Requirements: Application, autobiography, essay, photo, portfolio, references. *Deadline:* February 1.

Contact: Dallas-Ft. Worth Association of Black Communicators
Dallas-Fort Worth Association of Black Communicators
A.H. Belo Building Lock Box 11
Dallas, TX 75265

ELECTRONIC DOCUMENT SYSTEMS FOUNDATION http://www.edsf.org

ELECTRONIC DOCUMENT SYSTEMS FOUNDATION SCHOLARSHIP AWARDS

EDSF Scholarships are awarded to full-time students with a "B" minimum average who are preparing for careers in document preparation; production or distribution; one-to-one marketing; graphic arts and communication; e-commerce; imaging science; printing; web authoring; electronic publishing; computer science; telecommunications or related fields. Application deadline is May 15.

Academic Fields/Career Goals: Communications; Computer Science/Data Processing; Engineering/Technology; Graphics/Graphic Arts/Printing.

Award: Scholarship for use in freshman, sophomore, junior, senior, or graduate years; not renewable. *Number:* 30–40. *Amount:* $1000–$2000.

Eligibility Requirements: Applicant must be enrolled or expecting to enroll full-time at a two-year or four-year or technical institution or university. Applicant must have 3.0 GPA or higher. Available to U.S. and non-U.S. citizens.

Application Requirements: Application, essay, references, transcript, description of activities and work experience. *Deadline:* May 15.

Contact: Jeanne Mowlds, Executive Director
Electronic Document Systems Foundation
24238 Hawthorne Boulevard
Torrance, CA 90505-6506
Phone: 310-541-1481
Fax: 310-541-4803
E-mail: jcmowlds@aol.com

FISHER BROADCASTING COMPANY http://www.fisherbroadcasting.com/

FISHER BROADCASTING, INC., SCHOLARSHIP FOR MINORITIES

Award for minority students enrolled in a broadcast, journalism, or marketing curriculum. For residents of Washington, Oregon, Montana, and Idaho. Attending schools in or out-of-state, or for out-of-state students attending institutions in Washington, Oregon, Montana, or Idaho. Deadline: April 30.

Academic Fields/Career Goals: Communications; Engineering/Technology; Journalism; Photojournalism/Photography; TV/Radio Broadcasting.

Award: Scholarship for use in sophomore, junior, or senior years; not renewable. *Number:* 2–4. *Amount:* $1000–$10,000.

Eligibility Requirements: Applicant must be American Indian/Alaska Native, Asian/Pacific Islander, Black (non-Hispanic), or Hispanic and enrolled or expecting to enroll full-time at a two-year or four-year or technical institution or university. Applicant must have 2.5 GPA or higher. Available to U.S. citizens.

Application Requirements: Application, essay, financial need analysis, interview, references, transcript. *Deadline:* April 30.

Contact: Laura Boyd, Vice President, Human Resources
Fisher Broadcasting Company
600 University Street
Suite 1525
Seattle, WA 98101-3185
Phone: 206-404-7000
Fax: 206-404-6811
E-mail: laurab@fsci.com

GREATER KANAWHA VALLEY FOUNDATION http://www.tgkvf.org

WEST VIRGINIA BROADCASTERS ASSOCIATION FUND

Renewable award for students seeking education at a college or university in the field of communications and related areas. Must be a West Virginia resident and maintain at least a 2.5 GPA. Open to employees and family members of station employees that are members of the West Virginia Broadcasters Association. May apply for two Foundation scholarships but will only be chosen for one.

Academic Fields/Career Goals: Communications; Foreign Language; Trade/Technical Specialties; TV/Radio Broadcasting.

Greater Kanawha Valley Foundation (continued)

Award: Scholarship for use in freshman, sophomore, junior, or senior years; renewable. *Number:* 7. *Amount:* $1000.

Eligibility Requirements: Applicant must be enrolled or expecting to enroll at a two-year or four-year institution or university and resident of West Virginia. Applicant or parent of applicant must be member of West Virginia Broadcasters Association. Applicant or parent of applicant must have employment or volunteer experience in designated career field. Applicant must have 2.5 GPA or higher. Available to U.S. citizens.

Application Requirements: Application, essay, financial need analysis, references, self-addressed stamped envelope, test scores, transcript. *Deadline:* February 17.

Contact: Susan Hoover, Scholarship Coordinator
Greater Kanawha Valley Foundation
PO Box 3041
Charleston, WV 25331
Phone: 304-346-3620
Fax: 304-346-3640

HISPANIC COLLEGE FUND, INC.

http://www.hispanicfund.org

DENNY'S/HISPANIC COLLEGE FUND SCHOLARSHIP

• *See page 41*

HISPANIC COLLEGE FUND/INROADS/SPRINT SCHOLARSHIP PROGRAM

• *See page 125*

NATIONAL HISPANIC EXPLORERS SCHOLARSHIP PROGRAM

• *See page 69*

INDIANAPOLIS ASSOCIATION OF BLACK JOURNALISTS

http://www.iabj.org

LYNN DEAN FORD IABJ SCHOLARSHIP AWARDS

Scholarship available to full time, African-American students who have been accepted to, or are already matriculated at a four-year college or university. Students must be enrolled in a course of study leading to a career in the media. Must attend college in Indiana or be a graduate of an Indiana high school studying out of state. Information may be obtained from Web site. Deadline May 30.

Academic Fields/Career Goals: Communications; Journalism; Photojournalism/Photography; TV/Radio Broadcasting.

Award: Scholarship for use in freshman, sophomore, junior, or senior years; not renewable. *Number:* 1–2. *Amount:* $1000.

Eligibility Requirements: Applicant must be Black (non-Hispanic); enrolled or expecting to enroll full-time at a four-year institution or university and must have an interest in writing. Applicant must have 2.5 GPA or higher. Available to U.S. and non-U.S. citizens.

Application Requirements: Application, essay, portfolio. *Deadline:* May 30.

Contact: Courtenay Edelhart, Scholarship Committee Chairwoman
Indianapolis Association of Black Journalists
PO Box 441795
Indianapolis, IN 46244-1795
Phone: 317-388-8163
E-mail: courtenay.edelhart@indystar.com

INTERNATIONAL FOODSERVICE EDITORIAL COUNCIL

http://www.ifec-is-us.com

INTERNATIONAL FOODSERVICE EDITORIAL COUNCIL COMMUNICATIONS SCHOLARSHIP

Applicant must be a full-time student enrolled in an accredited postsecondary educational institution working toward an associate's, bachelor's, or master's degree. Must rank in upper half of class or have a minimum 2.5 GPA. Must have background, education and interests indicating preparedness for entering careers in editorial or public relations in the food-service industry.

Academic Fields/Career Goals: Communications; Food Science/Nutrition; Food Service/Hospitality; Graphics/Graphic Arts/Printing; Hospitality Management; Journalism; Literature/English/Writing; Photojournalism/Photography; Travel/Tourism.

Award: Scholarship for use in freshman, sophomore, junior, senior, graduate, or postgraduate years; not renewable. *Number:* 1–6. *Amount:* $1000–$2500.

Eligibility Requirements: Applicant must be enrolled or expecting to enroll full-time at a two-year or four-year or technical institution or university and must have an interest in photography/photogrammetry/filmmaking or writing. Applicant must have 2.5 GPA or higher. Available to U.S. and non-U.S. citizens.

Application Requirements: Application, essay, references, transcript. *Deadline:* March 15.

Contact: Carol Lally, Executive Director
International Foodservice Editorial Council
PO Box 491
Hyde Park, NY 12538-0491
Phone: 845-229-6973
Fax: 845-229-6993
E-mail: ifec@aol.com

JOHN BAYLISS BROADCAST FOUNDATION

http://www.baylissfoundation.org

JOHN BAYLISS BROADCAST RADIO SCHOLARSHIP

One-time award for college juniors, seniors, or graduate students majoring in broadcast communications with a concentration in radio broadcasting. Must have history of radio-related activities and a GPA of at least 3.0. Essay outlining future broadcasting goals required. Request information by mail, including stamped, self-addressed envelope, or by e-mail rather than by telephone. Must be attending school in U.S. Application is available at Web site: http://www.baylissfoundation.org.

Academic Fields/Career Goals: Communications; Journalism; TV/Radio Broadcasting.

Award: Scholarship for use in junior, senior, or graduate years; not renewable. *Number:* 15. *Amount:* up to $5000.

Eligibility Requirements: Applicant must be enrolled or expecting to enroll full-time at a four-year institution or university. Applicant must have 3.0 GPA or higher. Available to U.S. and Canadian citizens.

Application Requirements: Application, essay, references, self-addressed stamped envelope, transcript. *Deadline:* April 30.

Contact: Kit Hunter Franke, Executive Director
John Bayliss Broadcast Foundation
PO Box 51126
Pacific Grove, CA 93950
E-mail: info@baylissfoundation.org

JORGE MAS CANOSA FREEDOM FOUNDATION

MAS FAMILY SCHOLARSHIP AWARD

• *See page 126*

JOURNALISM EDUCATION ASSOCIATION

http://www.jea.org

NATIONAL HIGH SCHOOL JOURNALIST OF THE YEAR/SISTER RITA JEANNE SCHOLARSHIPS

One-time award recognizes the nation's top high school journalists. Open to graduating high school seniors who are planning to study journalism and/or mass communications in college and pursue a career in the field. Applicants must have an advisor who is a JEA member. Minimum 3.0 GPA required. Submit portfolio to state contest coordinator by February 15.

Academic Fields/Career Goals: Communications; Journalism.

Award: Scholarship for use in freshman year; not renewable. *Number:* 5. *Amount:* $2000–$5000.

Eligibility Requirements: Applicant must be high school student; age 17-19 and planning to enroll or expecting to enroll full-time at a four-year institution or university. Applicant must have 3.0 GPA or higher. Available to U.S. citizens.

Application Requirements: Application, applicant must enter a contest, essay, photo, portfolio, references, self-addressed stamped envelope, transcript, samples of work. *Deadline:* February 15.

Contact: Connie Fulkerson, Administrative Assistant
Journalism Education Association
c/o Kansas State University
103 Kedzie Hall
Manhattan, KS 66506-1505
Phone: 785-532-5532
Fax: 785-532-5563
E-mail: cfulker@ksu.edu

KATU THOMAS R. DARGAN MINORITY SCHOLARSHIP http://www.katu.com

THOMAS R. DARGAN MINORITY SCHOLARSHIP

Up to four awards for minority students who are citizens of the U.S. pursuing broadcast or communications studies. Must be a resident of Oregon or Washington attending an out-of-state institution or be enrolled at a four-year college or university in Oregon or Washington. Minimum 3.0 GPA required. Deadline: April 30.

Academic Fields/Career Goals: Communications; TV/Radio Broadcasting.

Award: Scholarship for use in sophomore, junior, or senior years; not renewable. *Number:* 1–4. *Amount:* $4000.

Eligibility Requirements: Applicant must be American Indian/Alaska Native, Asian/Pacific Islander, Black (non-Hispanic), or Hispanic and enrolled or expecting to enroll full-time at a four-year institution or university. Applicant must have 3.0 GPA or higher. Available to U.S. citizens.

Application Requirements: Application, essay, financial need analysis, interview, references, transcript. *Deadline:* April 30.

Contact: Rolonda Stoudamire, Human Resources Coordinator
KATU Thomas R. Dargan Minority Scholarship
PO Box 2
Portland, OR 97207-0002
Phone: 503-231-4222
Fax: 503-231-4233
E-mail: rolandas@katu.com

KCNC-TV CHANNEL 4 NEWS http://www.news4colorado.com

NEWS 4 PETER ROGOT MEDIA SCHOLARSHIP

One-time award for high school seniors pursuing a broadcasting career. Must be a U.S. citizen and a resident of Colorado. Minimum 2.5 GPA required. Application deadline: March 5. See Web site at http://news4colorado.com for application and rules.

Academic Fields/Career Goals: Communications; Engineering/Technology; Engineering-Related Technologies; Filmmaking/Video; Journalism; Photojournalism/Photography; TV/Radio Broadcasting.

Award: Scholarship for use in freshman year; not renewable. *Number:* 1–2. *Amount:* $5000.

Eligibility Requirements: Applicant must be high school student; planning to enroll or expecting to enroll full or part-time at a four-year institution or university and resident of Colorado. Applicant must have 2.5 GPA or higher. Available to U.S. citizens.

Application Requirements: Application, essay, financial need analysis, interview, references, test scores, transcript, IRS 1040 form. *Deadline:* March 5.

Contact: Elaine Torres, Community Affairs Director
KCNC-TV Channel 4 News
1044 Lincoln Street
Denver, CO 80203
Phone: 303-861-4444
Fax: 303-830-6537
E-mail: edtorres@cbs.com

LAGRANT FOUNDATION http://www.lagrantfoundation.org

LAGRANT FOUNDATION SCHOLARSHIP

• *See page 127*

MAINE MEDIA WOMEN SCHOLARSHIPS COMMITTEE http://www.mainemediawomen.org/scholarships.html

MAINE MEDIA WOMEN'S SCHOLARSHIP

• *See page 88*

NASA NEBRASKA SPACE GRANT CONSORTIUM http://nasa.unomaha.edu

NASA NEBRASKA SPACE GRANT

• *See page 101*

NATIONAL ACADEMY OF TELEVISION ARTS AND SCIENCES http://www.emmyonline.org/emmy/scholr.html

NATIONAL ACADEMY OF TELEVISION ARTS AND SCIENCES JOHN CANNON MEMORIAL SCHOLARSHIP

Scholarships distributed over a four-year period with $10,000 awarded prior to the first year of study and three additional awards of $10,000 granted in subsequent years if the recipient demonstrates satisfactory progress towards a degree in a communications-oriented program. Must submit SAT or ACT scores. Must be child or grandchild of NATAS member. Application available on the Web at: http://www.emmyonline.org/emmy/scholr.html. Deadline is February 2.

Academic Fields/Career Goals: Communications; TV/Radio Broadcasting.

Award: Scholarship for use in freshman, sophomore, junior, or senior years; renewable. *Number:* 1. *Amount:* $40,000.

Eligibility Requirements: Applicant must be high school student and planning to enroll or expecting to enroll full-time at a four-year institution. Applicant must have 3.0 GPA or higher. Available to U.S. and non-U.S. citizens.

Application Requirements: Application, essay, references, test scores, transcript. *Deadline:* February 2.

Contact: Luke E T. Smith, Scholarship Committee
National Academy of Television Arts and Sciences
111 West 57th Street, Suite 600
New York, NY 10019
Phone: 212-586-8424
Fax: 212-246-8129
E-mail: scholarship@natasonline.com

TRUSTEE SCHOLARSHIP PROGRAM

Renewable award for exceptional high school seniors who plan to pursue a baccalaureate degree in communications with an emphasis on any aspect of the television industry. Must attend a four-year college or university. Scholarship is distributed over a four-year period, based on continued eligibility. Application and information available at Web site: http://www.emmyonline.org/emmy/scholr.htm. Application deadline is December 9.

Academic Fields/Career Goals: Communications; TV/Radio Broadcasting.

Award: Scholarship for use in freshman, sophomore, junior, or senior years; renewable. *Number:* 2. *Amount:* $40,000.

Eligibility Requirements: Applicant must be high school student and planning to enroll or expecting to enroll full-time at a four-year institution or university. Applicant must have 3.0 GPA or higher. Available to U.S. and non-U.S. citizens.

Application Requirements: Application, essay, references, test scores, transcript. *Deadline:* December 9.

Contact: Luke E T. Smith, Scholarship Committee
National Academy of Television Arts and Sciences
111 West 57th Street, Suite 600
New York, NY 10019
Phone: 212-586-8424
Fax: 212-246-8129
E-mail: scholarship@natasonline.com

NATIONAL ASSOCIATION OF HISPANIC JOURNALISTS (NAHJ) http://www.nahj.org

NATIONAL ASSOCIATION OF HISPANIC JOURNALISTS SCHOLARSHIP

One-time award for high school seniors, college undergraduates, and first-year graduate students who are pursuing careers in English- or

National Association of Hispanic Journalists (NAHJ) (continued)

Spanish-language print, photo, broadcast, or online journalism. Students may major or plan to major in any subject, but must demonstrate a sincere desire to pursue a career in journalism. Must submit resume and work samples. Applications must be postmarked on or before the final Friday in January of each year. Applications available only on Web site: http://www.nahj.org.

Academic Fields/Career Goals: Communications; Journalism; Photojournalism/Photography; TV/Radio Broadcasting.

Award: Scholarship for use in freshman, sophomore, junior, senior, or graduate years; not renewable. *Number:* 20–25. *Amount:* $1000–$2000.

Eligibility Requirements: Applicant must be enrolled or expecting to enroll full-time at a two-year or four-year institution or university and must have an interest in photography/photogrammetry/filmmaking or writing. Available to U.S. citizens.

Application Requirements: Application, essay, financial need analysis, resume, references, transcript, work samples. *Deadline:* January 28.

Contact: Nancy Tita, Educational Programs Manager
National Association of Hispanic Journalists (NAHJ)
1000 National Press Building
529 14th Street, NW, Suite 1000
Washington, DC 20045-2001
Phone: 202-662-7145
Fax: 202-662-7144
E-mail: ntita@nahj.org

NATIONAL ASSOCIATION OF WATER COMPANIES-NEW JERSEY CHAPTER

NATIONAL ASSOCIATION OF WATER COMPANIES-NEW JERSEY CHAPTER SCHOLARSHIP

• *See page 115*

NATIONAL GAY AND LESBIAN TASK FORCE http://www.ngltf.org/about/messenger.htm

NATIONAL GAY AND LESBIAN TASK FORCE MESSENGER-ANDERSON JOURNALISM SCHOLARSHIP

Scholarship with internship program for lesbian, gay, bisexual, and transgender (LGBT) students. Open to high school seniors and undergraduate college students who plan to pursue a degree in journalism or communications at an accredited four-year college or university. Must be a member of NGLTF with minimum GPA of 2.5. Application deadline is February 15.

Academic Fields/Career Goals: Communications; Journalism.

Award: Scholarship for use in freshman, sophomore, junior, or senior years; renewable. *Number:* up to 4. *Amount:* up to $10,000.

Eligibility Requirements: Applicant must be enrolled or expecting to enroll full-time at a four-year institution or university. Applicant must have 2.5 GPA or higher. Available to U.S. citizens.

Application Requirements: Application, essay, interview, portfolio, resume, references, transcript. *Deadline:* February 15.

Contact: National Gay and Lesbian Task Force
5455 Wilshire Boulevard, Suite 1505
Los Angeles, CA 90036

NATIONAL INSTITUTE FOR LABOR RELATIONS RESEARCH http://www.nilrr.org

NATIONAL INSTITUTE FOR LABOR RELATIONS RESEARCH WILLIAM B. RUGGLES JOURNALISM SCHOLARSHIP

One-time award for undergraduate or graduate study in journalism or mass communications. Submit 500-word essay on the right-to-work principle. High school seniors accepted into certified journalism school may apply. Deadline: December 31. When corresponding regarding scholarship, please specify "Journalism" or "Ruggles" scholarship.

Academic Fields/Career Goals: Communications; Journalism.

Award: Scholarship for use in freshman, sophomore, junior, senior, or graduate years; not renewable. *Number:* 1. *Amount:* $2000.

Eligibility Requirements: Applicant must be enrolled or expecting to enroll full-time at a four-year institution or university and must have an interest in writing. Available to U.S. and non-U.S. citizens.

Application Requirements: Application, essay, transcript. *Deadline:* December 31.

Contact: Cathy Jones, Scholarship Coordinator
National Institute for Labor Relations Research
5211 Port Royal Road, Suite 510
Springfield, VA 22151
Phone: 703-321-9606
Fax: 703-321-7342
E-mail: research@nilrr.org

NATIONAL SPEAKERS ASSOCIATION http://www.nsaspeaker.org

NATIONAL SPEAKERS ASSOCIATION SCHOLARSHIP

One-time award for junior, senior, or graduate student majoring or minoring in speech or a directly related field. Must be full-time student at accredited four-year institution with above average academic record. Submit 500-word essay on goals. Application available only on Web site.

Academic Fields/Career Goals: Communications.

Award: Scholarship for use in junior, senior, or graduate years; not renewable. *Number:* 4. *Amount:* $4000.

Eligibility Requirements: Applicant must be enrolled or expecting to enroll full-time at a four-year institution or university. Applicant must have 3.5 GPA or higher. Available to U.S. and non-U.S. citizens.

Application Requirements: Application, essay, references, transcript. *Deadline:* June 1.

Contact: Audrey O'Neal, Scholarship Coordinator
National Speakers Association
1500 South Priest Drive
Tempe, AZ 85281
Phone: 480-968-2552
Fax: 480-968-0911
E-mail: audrey@nsaspeaker.org

NATIONAL STONE, SAND AND GRAVEL ASSOCIATION (NSSGA) http://www.nssga.org

JENNIFER CURTIS BYLER SCHOLARSHIP FOR THE STUDY OF PUBLIC AFFAIRS

Restricted to students whose parent(s) are employees of an aggregate (crushed stone or sand and gravel) producer member of the National Stone, Sand and Gravel Association. One-time award. Must be full-time student attending four-year college or university. Must demonstrate a commitment to a career in public affairs.

Academic Fields/Career Goals: Communications; Journalism; Political Science.

Award: Scholarship for use in freshman, sophomore, junior, or senior years; not renewable. *Number:* 1. *Amount:* $1000–$2500.

Eligibility Requirements: Applicant must be enrolled or expecting to enroll full-time at a four-year institution or university. Applicant or parent of applicant must have employment or volunteer experience in designated career field. Available to U.S. and non-U.S. citizens.

Application Requirements: Application, essay, references, transcript. *Deadline:* December 31.

Contact: Jennifer Curtis Byler Scholarship c/o NSSGA
National Stone, Sand and Gravel Association (NSSGA)
2101 Wilson Boulevard, Suite 100
Arlington, VA 22201-3062
Phone: 703-525-8788
Fax: 703-525-7782
E-mail: info@nssga.org

NATIONAL WRITERS ASSOCIATION FOUNDATION http://www.nationalwriters.com

NATIONAL WRITERS ASSOCIATION FOUNDATION SCHOLARSHIPS

Scholarships to those with serious interest in any writing field.

Academic Fields/Career Goals: Communications; Filmmaking/Video; Journalism; Literature/English/Writing; Photojournalism/Photography.

Award: Scholarship for use in freshman, sophomore, junior, senior, graduate, or postgraduate years; not renewable. *Number:* 4. *Amount:* $200–$1000.

Eligibility Requirements: Applicant must be enrolled or expecting to enroll full or part-time at a two-year or four-year or technical institution or university and must have an interest in English language, photography/photogrammetry/filmmaking, or writing. Available to U.S. and non-U.S. citizens.

Application Requirements: Application, transcript, writing samples. *Deadline:* December 31.

Contact: Brian Keithline
National Writers Association Foundation
3140 South Peoria, #295 PMB
Aurora, CO 80014
Phone: 303-841-0246
Fax: 303-841-2607

NEW JERSEY DIVISION OF FISH AND WILDLIFE/NJ CHAPTER OF THE WILDLIFE SOCIETY http://www.njfishandwildlife.com

RUSSELL A. COOKINGHAM SCHOLARSHIP

• *See page 116*

NEW YORK WOMEN IN COMMUNICATIONS, INC., FOUNDATION http://www.nywici.org/foundation/index.html

NEW YORK WOMEN IN COMMUNICATIONS, INC. FOUNDATION SCHOLARSHIP PROGRAM

Scholarships awarded to students majoring in a communication-related field who are permanent residents of selected states. Minimum 3.5 GPA for undergraduates and graduate students in major, and 3.0 overall. Minimum 3.5 GPA for high school students.

Academic Fields/Career Goals: Communications; Journalism; TV/Radio Broadcasting.

Award: Scholarship for use in freshman, sophomore, junior, senior, or graduate years; renewable. *Number:* varies. *Amount:* up to $10,000.

Eligibility Requirements: Applicant must be enrolled or expecting to enroll full-time at a two-year or four-year institution or university and resident of Connecticut, New Jersey, New York, or Pennsylvania. Applicant must have 3.5 GPA or higher. Available to U.S. and non-U.S. citizens.

Application Requirements: Application, essay, interview, resume, references, transcript, list communication courses completed. *Deadline:* January 28.

Contact: Amy Sokoloff, Executive Director
New York Women in Communications, Inc., Foundation
355 Lexington Avenue
17th Floor
New York, NY 10017-6603
Phone: 212-297-2133
Fax: 212-370-9047
E-mail: info@nywici.org

OREGON ASSOCIATION OF BROADCASTERS http://www.theoab.org

OAB BROADCAST SCHOLARSHIP

One-time award for students to begin or continue their education in broadcast and related studies. Must have a 3.0 GPA. Must be a resident of Oregon studying in Oregon.

Academic Fields/Career Goals: Communications; Journalism; TV/Radio Broadcasting.

Award: Scholarship for use in freshman, sophomore, junior, or senior years; not renewable. *Number:* 6. *Amount:* $1000.

Eligibility Requirements: Applicant must be high school student; planning to enroll or expecting to enroll full-time at a two-year or four-year institution or university; resident of Oregon and studying in Oregon. Applicant must have 3.0 GPA or higher. Available to U.S. citizens.

Application Requirements: Application, autobiography, essay, financial need analysis, resume, references, transcript. *Deadline:* March 2.

Contact: Bill Johnstone, President and CEO
Oregon Association of Broadcasters
7150 Southwest Hampton Street, Suite 240
Portland, OR 97223-8366
Phone: 503-443-2299
Fax: 503-443-2488
E-mail: theoab@theoab.org

OUTDOOR WRITERS ASSOCIATION OF AMERICA http://www.owaa.org

OUTDOOR WRITERS ASSOCIATION OF AMERICA BODIE MCDOWELL SCHOLARSHIP AWARD

One-time award for college juniors, seniors, and graduate level candidates who demonstrate outdoor communication talent and intend to make a career in this field. Applicants are nominated by their institution; one applicant per school in both graduate and undergraduate designations. Must submit examples of outdoor communications work. Applications accepted from January 1 to March 1.

Academic Fields/Career Goals: Communications; Filmmaking/Video; Journalism; Literature/English/Writing; Photojournalism/Photography; TV/Radio Broadcasting.

Award: Scholarship for use in junior, senior, or graduate years; not renewable. *Number:* 3–6. *Amount:* $2500–$3500.

Eligibility Requirements: Applicant must be enrolled or expecting to enroll full or part-time at a four-year institution or university and must have an interest in amateur radio, art, photography/photogrammetry/filmmaking, or writing. Available to U.S. and non-U.S. citizens.

Application Requirements: Application, essay, references, transcript. *Deadline:* March 1.

Contact: Executive Director
Outdoor Writers Association of America
121 Hickory Street, Suite 1
Missoula, MT 59801
Phone: 406-728-7434
Fax: 406-728-7445
E-mail: owaa@montana.com

PRESS WOMEN OF TEXAS

PRESS WOMEN OF TEXAS ROVING SCHOLARSHIP

One award for $500 at a Texas university other than University of Texas-Austin. Communications majors at Texas schools are eligible. Freshmen are not eligible for this program. Write for more information. Deadline varies with date of state conference.

Academic Fields/Career Goals: Communications; Journalism.

Award: Scholarship for use in sophomore, junior, or senior years; not renewable. *Number:* 1. *Amount:* $500.

Eligibility Requirements: Applicant must be enrolled or expecting to enroll full-time at a four-year institution or university and studying in Texas. Available to U.S. and non-U.S. citizens.

Application Requirements: Application, photo, work samples-print or broadcast. *Deadline:* varies.

Contact: Louise Wood, Scholarship Director
Press Women of Texas
PO Box 10011
Beaumont, TX 77710
Phone: 409-880-8415
Fax: 409-880-1873
E-mail: woodll@hal.lamar.edu

PUBLIC RELATIONS STUDENT SOCIETY OF AMERICA http://www.prssa.org

PUBLIC RELATIONS SOCIETY OF AMERICA MULTICULTURAL AFFAIRS SCHOLARSHIP

One-time award for members of principal minority group who are in their junior or senior year at an accredited four-year college or university. Must have at least a 3.0 GPA and be preparing for career in public relations or communications. Two scholarships at $1500 each. Must be a full-time student and U.S. citizen. Application deadline is April 16.

Public Relations Student Society of America (continued)

Academic Fields/Career Goals: Communications.

Award: Scholarship for use in junior or senior years; not renewable. *Number:* 2. *Amount:* $1500.

Eligibility Requirements: Applicant must be American Indian/Alaska Native, Asian/Pacific Islander, Black (non-Hispanic), or Hispanic and enrolled or expecting to enroll full-time at a four-year institution or university. Applicant must have 3.0 GPA or higher. Available to U.S. citizens.

Application Requirements: Application, essay, financial need analysis, references, transcript. *Deadline:* April 16.

Contact: Jeneen Garcia, Program Coordinator
Public Relations Student Society of America
33 Irving Place
New York, NY 10003-2376
Phone: 212-460-1474
Fax: 212-995-0757
E-mail: prssa@prsa.org

RADIO-TELEVISION NEWS DIRECTORS ASSOCIATION AND FOUNDATION http://www.rtndf.org

CAROLE SIMPSON SCHOLARSHIP

Award for minority sophomore, junior, or senior undergraduate student enrolled in an electronic journalism program. Submit one to three examples of reporting or producing skills on audiocassette tape or videotape, totaling 15 minutes or less, with scripts. One-time award of $2000. Entries must be postmarked by May 10.

Academic Fields/Career Goals: Communications; Journalism; TV/ Radio Broadcasting.

Award: Scholarship for use in sophomore, junior, senior, or graduate years; not renewable. *Number:* 1. *Amount:* $2000.

Eligibility Requirements: Applicant must be American Indian/Alaska Native, Asian/Pacific Islander, Black (non-Hispanic), or Hispanic; enrolled or expecting to enroll full-time at a four-year institution or university and must have an interest in photography/photogrammetry/ filmmaking or writing. Available to U.S. and non-U.S. citizens.

Application Requirements: Application, essay, resume, references, video or audio tape of work. *Deadline:* May 10.

Contact: Karen Jackson-Buillitt, Project Coordinator
Radio-Television News Directors Association and Foundation
1600 K Street, NW, Suite 700
Washington, DC 20006
Phone: 202-467-5218
Fax: 202-223-4007
E-mail: karenb@rtndf.org

ED BRADLEY SCHOLARSHIP

One-time award for minority sophomore, junior, or senior undergraduate student enrolled in an electronic journalism program. Submit one to three examples of reporting or producing skills on audiocassette tape or videotape, totaling 15 minutes or less, with scripts. Entries must be postmarked by May 10.

Academic Fields/Career Goals: Communications; Journalism; TV/ Radio Broadcasting.

Award: Scholarship for use in sophomore, junior, senior, or graduate years; not renewable. *Number:* 1. *Amount:* $10,000.

Eligibility Requirements: Applicant must be American Indian/Alaska Native, Asian/Pacific Islander, Black (non-Hispanic), or Hispanic and enrolled or expecting to enroll full-time at a four-year institution or university. Available to U.S. and non-U.S. citizens.

Application Requirements: Application, essay, resume, references, video or audio tape of work. *Deadline:* May 10.

Contact: Manager, Education Programs
Radio-Television News Directors Association and Foundation
1600 K Street, NW, Suite 700
Washington, DC 20006
Phone: 202-467-5218
Fax: 202-223-4007

KEN KASHIWAHARA SCHOLARSHIP

One-time award of $2500 for minority sophomore, junior, or senior whose career objective is electronic journalism. Submit one to three examples showing reporting or producing skills on audiocassette or VHS, with scripts. Entries must be postmarked by May 10.

Academic Fields/Career Goals: Communications; Journalism; TV/ Radio Broadcasting.

Award: Scholarship for use in sophomore, junior, senior, or graduate years; not renewable. *Number:* 1. *Amount:* $2500.

Eligibility Requirements: Applicant must be American Indian/Alaska Native, Asian/Pacific Islander, Black (non-Hispanic), or Hispanic and enrolled or expecting to enroll full-time at a four-year institution or university. Available to U.S. and non-U.S. citizens.

Application Requirements: Application, essay, resume, references, video or audio tape of work. *Deadline:* May 10.

Contact: Manager, Education Programs
Radio-Television News Directors Association and Foundation
1600 K Street, NW, Suite 700
Washington, DC 20006
Phone: 202-467-5218
Fax: 202-223-4007

LOU AND CAROLE PRATO SPORTS REPORTING SCHOLARSHIP

One-time tuition grant awarded to a deserving student planning a career in sports broadcasting. Entries must be postmarked by May 10.

Academic Fields/Career Goals: Communications; Journalism; TV/ Radio Broadcasting.

Award: Grant for use in sophomore, junior, senior, or graduate years; not renewable. *Number:* 1. *Amount:* $1000.

Eligibility Requirements: Applicant must be enrolled or expecting to enroll full-time at a four-year institution or university. Available to U.S. and non-U.S. citizens.

Application Requirements: Application, essay, resume, references. *Deadline:* May 10.

Contact: Manager, Education Programs
Radio-Television News Directors Association and Foundation
1600 K Street, NW, Suite 700
Washington, DC 20006
Phone: 202-467-5218
Fax: 202-223-4007

MIKE REYNOLDS $1,000 SCHOLARSHIP

Preference given to minority undergraduate student demonstrating need for financial assistance. Must include on resume jobs held related to media. Applicant must explain contribution he or she has made toward funding own education. Applications must be postmarked by May 10.

Academic Fields/Career Goals: Communications; Journalism; TV/ Radio Broadcasting.

Award: Scholarship for use in sophomore, junior, senior, or graduate years; not renewable. *Number:* 1. *Amount:* $1000.

Eligibility Requirements: Applicant must be American Indian/Alaska Native, Asian/Pacific Islander, Black (non-Hispanic), or Hispanic and enrolled or expecting to enroll full-time at a four-year institution or university. Available to U.S. and non-U.S. citizens.

Application Requirements: Application, essay, financial need analysis, resume, references, video or audio tape of work. *Deadline:* May 10.

Contact: Manager, Education Programs
Radio-Television News Directors Association and Foundation
1600 K Street, NW, Suite 700
Washington, DC 20006
Phone: 202-467-5218
Fax: 202-223-4007

PRESIDENT'S $2500 SCHOLARSHIP

Awards given honor of former RTNDA Presidents. Entries must be postmarked by May 10.

Academic Fields/Career Goals: Communications; Journalism; TV/Radio Broadcasting.

Award: Scholarship for use in sophomore, junior, or senior years; not renewable. *Number:* 2. *Amount:* $2500.

Eligibility Requirements: Applicant must be enrolled or expecting to enroll full-time at a four-year institution or university. Available to U.S. and non-U.S. citizens.

Application Requirements: Application, essay, resume, references, video or audio tape of work. *Deadline:* May 10.

Contact: Manager, Education Programs
Radio-Television News Directors Association and Foundation
1600 K Street, NW, Suite 700
Washington, DC 20006
Phone: 202-467-5218
Fax: 202-223-4007

RHODE ISLAND FOUNDATION http://www.rifoundation.org

RDW GROUP, INC. MINORITY SCHOLARSHIP FOR COMMUNICATIONS

One-time award to provide support to minority students who wish to pursue a course of study in communications at the undergraduate or graduate level. Must be a Rhode Island resident.

Academic Fields/Career Goals: Communications.

Award: Scholarship for use in freshman, sophomore, junior, senior, or graduate years; not renewable. *Number:* 1. *Amount:* $2000.

Eligibility Requirements: Applicant must be American Indian/Alaska Native, Asian/Pacific Islander, Black (non-Hispanic), or Hispanic; enrolled or expecting to enroll at an institution or university and resident of Rhode Island.

Application Requirements: Application, essay, self-addressed stamped envelope, transcript. *Deadline:* April 30.

Contact: Libby Monahan, Scholarship Coordinator
Rhode Island Foundation
One Union Station
Providence, RI 02903
Phone: 401-274-4564
Fax: 401-272-1359
E-mail: libbym@rifoundation.org

SOCIETY FOR TECHNICAL COMMUNICATION http://www.stc.org

SOCIETY FOR TECHNICAL COMMUNICATION SCHOLARSHIP PROGRAM

Applicants must have completed at least one year of postsecondary education. Applicants must be full-time students. They may either be graduate students working toward a master's or doctorate degree, or undergraduate students working toward a bachelor's degree. Students should have at least one full year of academic work remaining. They should be studying communication of information about technical subjects. Two awards available for undergraduate students, two available for graduate students.

Academic Fields/Career Goals: Communications; Engineering-Related Technologies.

Award: Scholarship for use in sophomore, junior, senior, or graduate years; not renewable. *Number:* up to 4. *Amount:* up to $1000.

Eligibility Requirements: Applicant must be enrolled or expecting to enroll full-time at a four-year institution or university. Available to U.S. and non-U.S. citizens.

Application Requirements: Application, essay, references, transcript. *Deadline:* February 16.

Contact: Attention: Scholarships
Society for Technical Communication
901 North Stuart Street, Suite 904
Arlington, VA 22203-1822
Phone: 703-522-4114
Fax: 703-522-2075
E-mail: stc@stc.org

SOCIETY OF PROFESSIONAL JOURNALISTS-SOUTH FLORIDA CHAPTER

GARTH REEVES, JR. MEMORIAL SCHOLARSHIPS

Scholarships for senior high school students, undergraduate, and graduate minority students preparing for a news career. Must be a South Florida resident. Amount is determined by need; minimum award is $500. One-time award, renewable upon application. Application deadline April 1. Academic performance and quality of work for student or professional news media is considered. For additional information and application go to Web site.

Academic Fields/Career Goals: Communications; Journalism.

Award: Scholarship for use in freshman, sophomore, junior, senior, or graduate years; not renewable. *Number:* 1–3. *Amount:* $500–$1000.

Eligibility Requirements: Applicant must be American Indian/Alaska Native, Asian/Pacific Islander, Black (non-Hispanic), or Hispanic; enrolled or expecting to enroll full or part-time at a two-year or four-year institution or university; resident of Florida and must have an interest in designated field specified by sponsor. Applicant must have 3.0 GPA or higher. Available to U.S. citizens.

Application Requirements: Application, financial need analysis, references, self-addressed stamped envelope, transcript, examples of applicant's journalism. *Deadline:* April 1.

Contact: Oline Cogdill, Chair, Scholarship Committee
Society of Professional Journalists-South Florida Chapter
200 East Las Olas Boulevard
Ft. Lauderdale, FL 33301
Phone: 954-356-4886
E-mail: ocogdill@sun-sentinel.com

TEXAS GRIDIRON CLUB, INC. http://www.spjfw.org

TEXAS GRIDIRON CLUB SCHOLARSHIPS

Awards for college juniors, seniors, or graduate students majoring in newspaper, photojournalism, or broadcast fields. Must submit work samples. Minimum grant $500. Recipient must be a Texas resident or going to school in Texas.

Academic Fields/Career Goals: Communications; Journalism; Photojournalism/Photography; TV/Radio Broadcasting.

Award: Scholarship for use in junior, senior, or graduate years; not renewable. *Number:* 10–15. *Amount:* $500–$1500.

Eligibility Requirements: Applicant must be enrolled or expecting to enroll full or part-time at a four-year institution. Available to U.S. and non-U.S. citizens.

Application Requirements: Application, essay, financial need analysis, references, transcript, work samples. *Deadline:* April 1.

Contact: Scholarship Coordinator/Fort Worth SPJ
Texas Gridiron Club, Inc.
PO Box 3212
Fort Worth, TX 76113-3212

TEXAS OUTDOOR WRITERS ASSOCIATION http://www.towa.org

TEXAS OUTDOOR WRITERS ASSOCIATION SCHOLARSHIP

Annual merit award available to students attending an accredited Texas college or university preparing for a career which would incorporate communications skills about the outdoors, environmental conservation, or resource management. Minimum 2.5 GPA required. Submit writing/photo samples.

Academic Fields/Career Goals: Communications; Environmental Science; Natural Resources.

Award: Scholarship for use in junior, senior, graduate, or postgraduate years; not renewable. *Number:* 2. *Amount:* $1000–$1500.

Eligibility Requirements: Applicant must be enrolled or expecting to enroll full or part-time at a four-year institution or university; resident of Texas; studying in Texas and must have an interest in writing. Applicant must have 2.5 GPA or higher. Available to U.S. citizens.

Texas Outdoor Writers Association (continued)

Application Requirements: Application, references, transcript, writing/photo samples. *Deadline:* December 31.

Contact: Chester Moore Jr., Scholarship Chair
Texas Outdoor Writers Association
101 Broad Street
Orange, TX 77630
Phone: 409-882-0945
E-mail: cmoorehunt@gt.rr.com

TKE EDUCATIONAL FOUNDATION http://www.tkefoundation.org

GEORGE W. WOOLERY MEMORIAL SCHOLARSHIP

This scholarship is available to initiated undergraduate members of Tau Kappa Epsilon who are full-time students in good standing pursuing a degree in communications or marketing with a cumulative grade point average of 2.50 or higher and a record of leadership within the TKE chapter and on campus. Preference will first be given to members of Beta-Sigma Chapter, but if no qualified candidate applies, the award will be open to any member of TKE.

Academic Fields/Career Goals: Communications.

Award: Scholarship for use in freshman, sophomore, junior, or senior years; not renewable. *Number:* 1. *Amount:* $200.

Eligibility Requirements: Applicant must be enrolled or expecting to enroll full-time at a four-year institution or university; male and must have an interest in leadership. Applicant must have 2.5 GPA or higher. Available to U.S. and non-U.S. citizens.

Application Requirements: Application, essay, photo, transcript. *Deadline:* May 15.

Contact: Tim Taschwer, President/CEO
TKE Educational Foundation
8645 Founders Road
Indianapolis, IN 46268-1393
Phone: 317-872-6533
Fax: 317-875-8353
E-mail: tef@tkehq.org

UNITED METHODIST COMMUNICATIONS http://www.umcom.org/scholarships

LEONARD M. PERRYMAN COMMUNICATIONS SCHOLARSHIP FOR ETHNIC MINORITY STUDENTS

One-time award to assist United Methodist ethnic minority students who are college juniors or seniors intending to pursue careers in religious communications. Submit examples of work. Contact for complete information.

Academic Fields/Career Goals: Communications; Journalism; Photojournalism/Photography; Religion/Theology; TV/Radio Broadcasting.

Award: Scholarship for use in junior or senior years; not renewable. *Number:* 1. *Amount:* $2500.

Eligibility Requirements: Applicant must be Methodist; American Indian/Alaska Native, Asian/Pacific Islander, Black (non-Hispanic), or Hispanic and enrolled or expecting to enroll full-time at a four-year institution or university. Available to U.S. and non-U.S. citizens.

Application Requirements: Application, essay, photo, references, transcript. *Deadline:* March 17.

Contact: Mrs. Amelia Tucker-Shaw, Coordinator
United Methodist Communications
810 12th Avenue, South
Nashville, TN 37202-4744
Phone: 888-278-4862
E-mail: scholarships@umcom.org

UNITED NEGRO COLLEGE FUND http://www.uncf.org

BEST BUY ENTERPRISE EMPLOYEE SCHOLARSHIP

• *See page 48*

BRYANT GUMBEL/WALT DISNEY WORLD CELEBRITY GOLF TOURNAMENT SCHOLARSHIP PROGRAM

Scholarship available to undergraduate juniors attending UNCF member colleges and universities. Minimum 3.0 GPA required. Students must be communications or liberal arts majors. Prospective applicants should complete the Student Profile found at Web site: http://www.uncf.org.

Academic Fields/Career Goals: Communications; Literature/English/Writing.

Award: Scholarship for use in junior year; not renewable. *Amount:* $5000.

Eligibility Requirements: Applicant must be Black (non-Hispanic) and enrolled or expecting to enroll at a four-year institution or university. Applicant must have 3.0 GPA or higher.

Application Requirements: Application, financial need analysis. *Deadline:* varies.

Contact: Program Services Department
United Negro College Fund
8260 Willow Oaks Corporate Drive
Fairfax, VA 22031

C-SPAN SCHOLARSHIP PROGRAM

Scholarship for students majoring in: communications, journalism, political science, English, history, or radio/TV/film. Applicant must be undergraduate sophomore or junior attending a UNCF member college or university. Program offers a paid summer internship. Please visit Web site for more information: http://www.uncf.org.

Academic Fields/Career Goals: Communications; History; Journalism; Library and Information Sciences; Political Science; TV/Radio Broadcasting.

Award: Scholarship for use in sophomore or junior years. *Number:* varies. *Amount:* $2000.

Eligibility Requirements: Applicant must be Black (non-Hispanic) and enrolled or expecting to enroll at a four-year institution or university. Applicant must have 3.0 GPA or higher.

Application Requirements: Application, financial need analysis, FAFSA, SAR. *Deadline:* April 9.

Contact: Program Services Department
United Negro College Fund
8260 Willow Oaks Corporate Drive
Fairfax, VA 22031

CBS CAREER HORIZONS SCHOLARSHIP PROGRAM

Open to students enrolled at a historically black college or university majoring in communications or journalism. Minimum 3.0 GPA required. Prospective applicants should complete the Student Profile found at Web site: http://www.uncf.org.

Academic Fields/Career Goals: Communications; Journalism.

Award: Scholarship for use in sophomore year; not renewable. *Amount:* $8000.

Eligibility Requirements: Applicant must be Black (non-Hispanic); enrolled or expecting to enroll at a four-year institution or university and resident of California or New York. Applicant must have 3.0 GPA or higher. Available to U.S. citizens.

Application Requirements: Application, financial need analysis. *Deadline:* February 16.

Contact: Program Services Department
United Negro College Fund
8260 Willow Oaks Corporate Drive
Fairfax, VA 22031

11-ALIVE COMMUNITY SERVICE SCHOLARSHIP TEST

Two $3000 scholarships awarded to an African-American male and a female graduating high school senior who plans on attending Clark Atlanta University, Morehouse College, or Spelman College. Must major in communications or journalism.

Academic Fields/Career Goals: Communications; Journalism.

Award: Scholarship for use in freshman year. *Number:* 2. *Amount:* up to $3000.

Eligibility Requirements: Applicant must be Black (non-Hispanic); high school student; planning to enroll or expecting to enroll full-time at a four-year institution or university and resident of Georgia. Applicant must have 2.5 GPA or higher.

Application Requirements: Application, essay, financial need analysis, references, transcript, FAFSA, SAR. *Deadline:* March 15.

Contact: United Negro College Fund, Inc.
United Negro College Fund
229 Peachtree Street NE, Suite 2505
Atlanta, GA 30303

JANET JACKSON/RHYTHM NATION SCHOLARSHIP

• *See page 91*

JOHN LENNON SCHOLARSHIP FUND

Scholarships for UNCF students in the performing arts and communications who have at least a 3.0 GPA. Prospective applicants should complete the Student Profile found at Web site: http://www.uncf.org.

Academic Fields/Career Goals: Communications; Performing Arts.

Award: Scholarship for use in freshman, sophomore, junior, or senior years; not renewable. *Amount:* $5000.

Eligibility Requirements: Applicant must be Black (non-Hispanic) and enrolled or expecting to enroll at a four-year institution or university. Applicant must have 3.0 GPA or higher. Available to U.S. citizens.

Application Requirements: Application, essay, financial need analysis, photo, references, transcript. *Deadline:* varies.

Contact: Program Services Department
United Negro College Fund
8260 Willow Oaks Corporate Drive
Fairfax, VA 22031

MICHAEL JACKSON SCHOLARSHIP

Scholarship for deserving students majoring in the performing arts or communications at a UNCF member college or university. Minimum 3.0 GPA required. Prospective applicants should complete the Student Profile found at Web site: http://www.uncf.org.

Academic Fields/Career Goals: Communications; Literature/English/Writing; Performing Arts.

Award: Scholarship for use in freshman, sophomore, junior, or senior years; not renewable. *Amount:* $4000.

Eligibility Requirements: Applicant must be Black (non-Hispanic) and enrolled or expecting to enroll at a four-year institution or university. Applicant must have 3.0 GPA or higher.

Application Requirements: Application, financial need analysis. *Deadline:* varies.

Contact: Program Services Department
United Negro College Fund
8260 Willow Oaks Corporate Drive
Fairfax, VA 22031

READER'S DIGEST SCHOLARSHIP

Scholarships for UNCF students majoring in journalism, English or communications. Minimum 3.0 GPA required. Prospective applicants should complete the Student Profile found at Web site: http://www.uncf.org.

Academic Fields/Career Goals: Communications; Journalism; Literature/English/Writing.

Award: Scholarship for use in junior or senior years; not renewable. *Amount:* $5000.

Eligibility Requirements: Applicant must be Black (non-Hispanic) and enrolled or expecting to enroll at a four-year institution or university. Applicant must have 3.0 GPA or higher. Available to U.S. citizens.

Application Requirements: Application, financial need analysis, photo, references, transcript, published writing sample. *Deadline:* November 14.

Contact: Program Services Department
United Negro College Fund
8260 Willow Oaks Corporate Drive
Fairfax, VA 22031

TOYOTA SCHOLARSHIP

• *See page 133*

UNCF/SPRINT SCHOLARS PROGRAM

• *See page 50*

VALLEY PRESS CLUB

VALLEY PRESS CLUB SCHOLARSHIPS, THE REPUBLICAN SCHOLARSHIP; PHOTOJOURNALISM SCHOLARSHIP, CHANNEL 22 SCHOLARSHIP

Nonrenewable award for graduating high school seniors from northern Connecticut and western Massachusetts interested in television journalism, photojournalism, broadcast journalism, or print journalism. Based on scholarship and financial need Must submit an autobiographical news story, not an essay.

Academic Fields/Career Goals: Communications; Journalism; Photojournalism/Photography; TV/Radio Broadcasting.

Award: Scholarship for use in freshman year; not renewable. *Number:* up to 4. *Amount:* $1000.

Eligibility Requirements: Applicant must be high school student; planning to enroll or expecting to enroll full-time at a two-year or four-year institution or university; resident of Connecticut or Massachusetts and must have an interest in photography/photogrammetry/filmmaking or writing.

Application Requirements: Application, financial need analysis, interview, references, test scores, transcript, autobiographical news story. *Deadline:* April 1.

Contact: Bob N. McClellan, Chairman of Scholarship Committee
Valley Press Club
PO Box 5475
Springfield, MA 01101
Phone: 413-783-3355

VIRGINIA ASSOCIATION OF BROADCASTERS http://www.vabonline.com

VIRGINIA ASSOCIATION OF BROADCASTERS SCHOLARSHIP AWARD

Scholarships are available to entering juniors and seniors majoring in mass communications-related courses. Must either be a resident of Virginia or go to a Virginia college or university. Must be U.S. citizen and enrolled full-time.

Academic Fields/Career Goals: Communications.

Award: Scholarship for use in junior or senior years; renewable. *Number:* 4. *Amount:* $500–$1000.

Eligibility Requirements: Applicant must be age 20 and enrolled or expecting to enroll full-time at a four-year institution or university. Available to U.S. citizens.

Application Requirements: Application, essay, financial need analysis, transcript. *Deadline:* February 15.

Contact: Ruby Seal, Director of Administration
Virginia Association of Broadcasters
630 Country Green Lane
Charlottesville, VA 22902
Phone: 434-977-3716
Fax: 434-979-2439
E-mail: ruby@easterassociates.com

WASHINGTON NEWS COUNCIL http://www.wanewscouncil.org

DICK LARSEN SCHOLARSHIP PROGRAM

One-time award for a student at a Washington state four-year public or private college with a serious interest in a career in communications-journalism, public relations, politics or a related field. Must be resident of Washington state and U.S. citizen. See Web site for more information.

Washington News Council (continued)

Academic Fields/Career Goals: Communications; Journalism; Political Science.

Award: Scholarship for use in sophomore, junior, or senior years; not renewable. *Number:* 1. *Amount:* $1000.

Eligibility Requirements: Applicant must be enrolled or expecting to enroll full-time at a four-year institution; resident of Washington and studying in Washington. Available to U.S. citizens.

Application Requirements: Application, essay, financial need analysis, references, transcript, 3 samples of work. *Deadline:* May 15.

Contact: John Hamer, Executive Director
Washington News Council
PO Box 3672
Seattle, WA 98124-3672
Phone: 206-262-9793
Fax: 206-464-7902
E-mail: jhamer@wanewscouncil.org

HERB ROBINSON SCHOLARSHIP PROGRAM

One-time award to a graduating Washington state high school senior who is entering a four-year public or private college or university in Washington. Must have a serious interest in a career in communications-journalism, public relations, politics or a related field. Must be resident of Washington state and a U.S. citizen. See Web site for more information.

Academic Fields/Career Goals: Communications; Journalism; Political Science.

Award: Scholarship for use in freshman year. *Number:* 1. *Amount:* $1000.

Eligibility Requirements: Applicant must be high school student; planning to enroll or expecting to enroll at an institution or university; resident of Washington and studying in Washington. Available to U.S. citizens.

Application Requirements: Application, essay, financial need analysis, references, transcript. *Deadline:* May 15.

Contact: John Hamer, Executive Director
Washington News Council
PO Box 3672
Seattle, WA 98124-3672
Phone: 206-262-9793
Fax: 206-464-7902
E-mail: jhamer@wanewscouncil.org

WISCONSIN FOUNDATION FOR INDEPENDENT COLLEGES, INC. http://www.wficweb.org

LAND'S END SCHOLARSHIP
• *See page 135*

WE ENERGIES SCHOLARSHIP
• *See page 52*

WOMEN GROCERS OF AMERICA http://www.nationalgrocers.org

MARY MACEY SCHOLARSHIP
• *See page 61*

WYOMING TRUCKING ASSOCIATION

WYOMING TRUCKING ASSOCIATION TRUST FUND SCHOLARSHIP
• *See page 135*

COMPUTER SCIENCE/DATA PROCESSING

AACE INTERNATIONAL http://www.aacei.org

AACE INTERNATIONAL COMPETITIVE SCHOLARSHIP
• *See page 73*

AEA-OREGON COUNCIL http://www.ous.edu/ecs/scholarships

AEA- OREGON COUNCIL TECHNOLOGY SCHOLARSHIP PROGRAM
• *See page 136*

ALICE L. HALTOM EDUCATIONAL FUND http://www.alhef.org

ALICE L. HALTOM EDUCATIONAL FUND SCHOLARSHIP

Award for students pursuing a career in information and records management. Up to $1,000 for those in an associate degree program. Up to $2,000 for students in a baccalaureate or advanced degree program. Application deadline is May 1.

Academic Fields/Career Goals: Computer Science/Data Processing; Library and Information Sciences.

Award: Scholarship for use in freshman, sophomore, junior, senior, or graduate years. *Number:* varies. *Amount:* $1000–$2000.

Eligibility Requirements: Applicant must be enrolled or expecting to enroll at a two-year or four-year institution or university. Available to U.S. and non-U.S. citizens.

Application Requirements: Application, references, transcript. *Deadline:* May 1.

Contact: Alice L. Haltom Educational Fund
PO Box 1794
Houston, TX 77251
E-mail: info@alhef.org

AMERICAN METEOROLOGICAL SOCIETY http://www.ametsoc.org/AMS

AMERICAN METEOROLOGICAL SOCIETY INDUSTRY UNDERGRADUATE SCHOLARSHIPS
• *See page 66*

AMERICAN SOCIETY FOR INFORMATION SCIENCE AND TECHNOLOGY http://www.asis.org

JOHN WILEY & SONS BEST JASIST PAPER AWARD

Award of $1500 to recognize the best refereed paper published in the volume year of the JASIT preceding the ASIST annual meeting. John Wiley & Sons, Inc., shall contribute $500 towards travel expenses to attend the ASIST annual meeting. All papers published in the volume year of JASIST preceding the ASIST annual meeting are eligible for the award. No nomination procedure is used for this award. All eligible papers are considered.

Academic Fields/Career Goals: Computer Science/Data Processing; Library and Information Sciences.

Award: Prize for use in freshman, sophomore, junior, senior, graduate, or postgraduate years; not renewable. *Number:* 1. *Amount:* $1500.

Eligibility Requirements: Applicant must be enrolled or expecting to enroll at an institution or university.

Application Requirements: *Deadline:* varies.

Contact: Awards Coordinator
American Society for Information Science and Technology
1320 Fenwick Lane, Suite 510
Silver Spring, MD 20910-3602
Phone: 301-495-0900
Fax: 301-495-0810
E-mail: asis@asis.org

ARMED FORCES COMMUNICATIONS AND ELECTRONICS ASSOCIATION, EDUCATIONAL FOUNDATION http://www.afcea.org

AFCEA SCHOLARSHIP FOR WORKING PROFESSIONALS
• *See page 96*

AFCEA SGT. JEANNETTE L. WINTERS, USMC MEMORIAL SCHOLARSHIP

Applications are requested from men and women currently on active duty in the U.S. Marine Corps or U.S. Marine Corps men and women veterans who are honorably discharged and currently attending four-year colleges or universities in the U.S. Applications will be accepted from qualified sophomore, junior, and senior undergraduate students enrolled either part-time or full-time in an eligible degree program.

Academic Fields/Career Goals: Computer Science/Data Processing; Electrical Engineering/Electronics; Engineering/Technology; Physical Sciences and Math.

Award: Scholarship for use in sophomore, junior, or senior years; not renewable. *Number:* varies. *Amount:* $2000.

Eligibility Requirements: Applicant must be enrolled or expecting to enroll full or part-time at a four-year institution or university. Available to U.S. citizens. Applicant must have served in the Marine Corp.

Application Requirements: Application, references, transcript. *Deadline:* September 15.

Contact: Norma Corrales, Director, Scholarships and Award Programs
Armed Forces Communications and Electronics Association, Educational Foundation
4400 Fair Lakes Court
Fairfax, VA 22033-3899
Phone: 703-631-6149
Fax: 703-631-4693
E-mail: scholarship@afcea.org

AFCEA/LOCKHEED MARTIN ORINCON IT SCHOLARSHIP

One-time award for active duty military personnel or veterans, their spouses or dependents who meet the general criteria for the General Paige Scholarship or civilians who meet the general criteria for the General Wickham Scholarship are eligible, provided the school they are attending is an accredited four-year college or university in the greater San Diego, California geographical area. Must be a sophomore or junior at the time of application.

Academic Fields/Career Goals: Computer Science/Data Processing; Electrical Engineering/Electronics; Engineering/Technology; Physical Sciences and Math.

Award: Scholarship for use in sophomore or junior years; not renewable. *Number:* varies. *Amount:* $2750.

Eligibility Requirements: Applicant must be enrolled or expecting to enroll full-time at a four-year institution or university and studying in California. Available to U.S. citizens. Applicant must have general military experience.

Application Requirements: Application, references, transcript. *Deadline:* March 1.

Contact: Norma Corrales, Director, Scholarships and Award Programs
Armed Forces Communications and Electronics Association, Educational Foundation
4400 Fair Lakes Court
Fairfax, VA 22033-3899
Phone: 703-631-6149
Fax: 703-631-4693
E-mail: scholarship@afcea.org

ARMED FORCES COMMUNICATIONS AND ELECTRONICS ASSOCIATION EDUCATIONAL FOUNDATION DISTANCE-LEARNING SCHOLARSHIP

Candidates must be enrolled full time in an eligible undergraduate degree-granting online program that is affiliated with a major, accredited 4-year college or university in the U.S. GPA of 3.5 overall required.

Academic Fields/Career Goals: Computer Science/Data Processing; Electrical Engineering/Electronics; Engineering/Technology.

Award: Scholarship for use in sophomore or junior years; not renewable. *Number:* varies. *Amount:* $1000.

Eligibility Requirements: Applicant must be enrolled or expecting to enroll full-time at a four-year institution or university. Applicant must have 3.5 GPA or higher. Available to U.S. citizens.

Application Requirements: Application, references, transcript. *Deadline:* April 1.

Contact: Norma Corrales, Director, Scholarships and Award Programs
Armed Forces Communications and Electronics Association, Educational Foundation
4400 Fair Lakes Court
Fairfax, VA 22033-3899
Phone: 703-631-6149
Fax: 703-631-4693
E-mail: scholarship@afcea.org

ARMED FORCES COMMUNICATIONS AND ELECTRONICS ASSOCIATION GENERAL EMMETT PAIGE SCHOLARSHIP

Award for persons on active duty in the uniformed military services or veterans, and their spouses or dependents. Must be enrolled full-time in four-year, accredited U.S. college or university and studying electrical engineering, computer science, computer engineering, physics, or mathematics. Must have a GPA of at least 3.4. Graduating high school seniors not eligible to apply, but veterans attending college full-time as freshman are eligible. All other applicants must be sophomores or juniors when applying. Spouses or dependents must be a sophomore or junior at the time of application. Deadline: March 1.

Academic Fields/Career Goals: Computer Science/Data Processing; Electrical Engineering/Electronics; Engineering/Technology; Physical Sciences and Math.

Award: Scholarship for use in freshman, sophomore, junior, or senior years; not renewable. *Number:* varies. *Amount:* $2000.

Eligibility Requirements: Applicant must be enrolled or expecting to enroll full-time at a four-year institution or university. Available to U.S. citizens. Applicant must have general military experience.

Application Requirements: Application, references, transcript. *Deadline:* March 1.

Contact: Armed Forces Communications and Electronics Association, Educational Foundation
4400 Fair Lakes Court
Fairfax, VA 22033-3899
E-mail: scholarship@afcea.org

ARMED FORCES COMMUNICATIONS AND ELECTRONICS ASSOCIATION GENERAL JOHN A. WICKHAM SCHOLARSHIP

Award for U.S. citizens enrolled full-time in four-year, accredited colleges or universities in the U.S. and studying electrical engineering, computer science, computer engineering, physics, or mathematics. At time of application, must be a sophomore or junior with GPA of at least 3.5. Deadline: May 1.

Academic Fields/Career Goals: Computer Science/Data Processing; Electrical Engineering/Electronics; Engineering/Technology; Physical Sciences and Math.

Award: Scholarship for use in sophomore or junior years; not renewable. *Number:* varies. *Amount:* $2000.

Eligibility Requirements: Applicant must be enrolled or expecting to enroll full-time at a four-year institution or university. Applicant must have 3.5 GPA or higher. Available to U.S. citizens.

Application Requirements: Application, references, transcript. *Deadline:* May 1.

Contact: Armed Forces Communications and Electronics Association, Educational Foundation
4400 Fair Lakes Court
Fairfax, VA 22033-3899
E-mail: scholarship@afcea.org

ARMED FORCES COMMUNICATIONS AND ELECTRONICS ASSOCIATION ROTC SCHOLARSHIP PROGRAM

• *See page 96*

ARRL FOUNDATION, INC.

http://www.arrl.org/arrlf/scholgen.html

PHD ARA SCHOLARSHIP

• *See page 157*

WILLIAM R. GOLDFARB MEMORIAL SCHOLARSHIP
• *See page 121*

ASSOCIATION FOR IRON AND STEEL TECHNOLOGY http://www.aist.org/foundation/scholarships.htm

ASSOCIATION FOR IRON AND STEEL TECHNOLOGY OHIO VALLEY CHAPTER SCHOLARSHIP
• *See page 112*

ASSOCIATION FOR WOMEN IN SCIENCE EDUCATIONAL FOUNDATION http://www.awis.org/ed_foundation.html

ASSOCIATION FOR WOMEN IN SCIENCE COLLEGE SCHOLARSHIP
• *See page 63*

ASTRONAUT SCHOLARSHIP FOUNDATION http://www.astronautscholarship.org

ASTRONAUT SCHOLARSHIP FOUNDATION
• *See page 68*

BARRY M. GOLDWATER SCHOLARSHIP AND EXCELLENCE IN EDUCATION FOUNDATION http://www.act.org/goldwater

BARRY M. GOLDWATER SCHOLARSHIP AND EXCELLENCE IN EDUCATION PROGRAM
• *See page 68*

BUSINESS AND PROFESSIONAL WOMEN'S FOUNDATION http://www.bpwusa.org

BPW CAREER ADVANCEMENT SCHOLARSHIP PROGRAM FOR WOMEN
• *See page 112*

CATCHING THE DREAM

MATH, ENGINEERING, SCIENCE, BUSINESS, EDUCATION, COMPUTERS SCHOLARSHIPS
• *See page 121*

TRIBAL BUSINESS MANAGEMENT PROGRAM (TBM)
• *See page 38*

CENTER FOR SCHOLARSHIP ADMINISTRATION http://www.scholarshipprograms.org

BANK OF AMERICA ADA ABILITIES SCHOLARSHIP
• *See page 38*

CENTRAL INTELLIGENCE AGENCY http://www.cia.gov

CENTRAL INTELLIGENCE AGENCY UNDERGRADUATE SCHOLARSHIP PROGRAM
• *See page 39*

CONNECTICUT STUDENT LOAN FOUNDATION http://www.cslf.com

CONNECTICUT INNOVATIONS TECHNOLOGY SCHOLAR PROGRAM
• *See page 113*

EAST LOS ANGELES COMMUNITY UNION (TELACU) EDUCATION FOUNDATION

TELACU ENGINEERING AWARD
• *See page 141*

ELECTRONIC DOCUMENT SYSTEMS FOUNDATION http://www.edsf.org

ELECTRONIC DOCUMENT SYSTEMS FOUNDATION SCHOLARSHIP AWARDS
• *See page 159*

GOLDEN KEY INTERNATIONAL HONOUR SOCIETY http://www.goldenkey.org

INFORMATION SYSTEMS ACHIEVEMENT AWARD

Applicants will be asked to respond to a problem posed by an honorary member within the discipline. The response may be in the form of an essay or a design. One winner will receive a $1000 award. The second place applicant will receive a $750 award and the third place applicant will receive $500. See Web site for more information: http://goldenkey.gsu.edu.

Academic Fields/Career Goals: Computer Science/Data Processing.

Award: Prize for use in junior, senior, graduate, or postgraduate years; not renewable. *Number:* 3. *Amount:* $500–$1000.

Eligibility Requirements: Applicant must be enrolled or expecting to enroll at an institution or university.

Application Requirements: Application, applicant must enter a contest, essay, references, transcript. *Deadline:* March 1.

Contact: Member Services
Golden Key International Honour Society
621 North Avenue, NE
Suite C-100
Atlanta, GA 30308
Phone: 404-377-2400
Fax: 678-420-6757
E-mail: scholarships@goldenkey.org

GRAND RAPIDS COMMUNITY FOUNDATION http://www.grfoundation.org

ECONOMIC CLUB OF GRAND RAPIDS BUSINESS STUDY ABROAD SCHOLARSHIP
• *See page 41*

HAROLD B. & DOROTHY A. SNYDER FOUNDATION, INC.

HAROLD B. AND DOROTHY A. SNYDER FOUNDATION, INC., PROGRAM
• *See page 141*

HAWAIIAN LODGE, F.& A. M. http://www.hawaiianlodge.org/

HAWAIIAN LODGE SCHOLARSHIPS
• *See page 76*

HISPANIC COLLEGE FUND, INC. http://www.hispanicfund.org

BURLINGTON NORTHERN SANTA FE FOUNDATION/HISPANIC COLLEGE FUND SCHOLARSHIP PROGRAM
• *See page 41*

DENNY'S/HISPANIC COLLEGE FUND SCHOLARSHIP
• *See page 41*

HISPANIC COLLEGE FUND/INROADS/SPRINT SCHOLARSHIP PROGRAM
• *See page 125*

ICI EDUCATIONAL FOUNDATION SCHOLARSHIP PROGRAM
• *See page 42*

LOCKHEED MARTIN SCHOLARSHIP PROGRAM
• *See page 141*

M & T BANK/ HISPANIC COLLEGE FUND SCHOLARSHIP PROGRAM
• *See page 42*

NATIONAL HISPANIC EXPLORERS SCHOLARSHIP PROGRAM
• *See page 69*

7-ELEVEN SCHOLARSHIP PROGRAM
• *See page 126*

HISPANIC ENGINEER NATIONAL ACHIEVEMENT AWARDS CORPORATION (HENAAC) http://www.henaac.org

HISPANIC ENGINEER NATIONAL ACHIEVEMENT AWARDS CORPORATION SCHOLARSHIP PROGRAM
• *See page 99*

HISPANIC SCHOLARSHIP FUND http://www.hsf.net

HSF/SOCIETY OF HISPANIC PROFESSIONAL ENGINEERS, INC. SCHOLARSHIP PROGRAM
• *See page 152*

INNOVATION AND SCIENCE COUNCIL OF BRITISH COLUMBIA http://www.scbc.org

IBM SCHOLARSHIP

Award to encourage the growth of the information technology sector in British Columbia given to students enrolled in a British Columbia post-secondary institute. Areas of study may include computer science, computer engineering, management information systems, electrical engineering, or physics. Available to Canadian citizens and landed immigrants.

Academic Fields/Career Goals: Computer Science/Data Processing; Electrical Engineering/Electronics; Physical Sciences and Math; Science, Technology, and Society.

Award: Scholarship for use in freshman, sophomore, junior, senior, or graduate years; renewable. *Number:* up to 10. *Amount:* up to $7428.

Eligibility Requirements: Applicant must be high school student; planning to enroll or expecting to enroll full-time at a two-year or four-year institution or university; resident of British Columbia and studying in British Columbia. Available to U.S. and non-U.S. citizens.

Application Requirements: Application, essay, resume, references, transcript, proof of citizenship. *Deadline:* March 1.

Contact: Dawn Wood, Assistant Programs Coordinator
Innovation and Science Council of British Columbia
Suite 1048
4720 Kingsway
Burnaby, BC V5H 4N2
Canada
Phone: 604-438-2752 Ext. 269
Fax: 604-438-6564
E-mail: dwood@scbc.org

PAUL AND HELEN TRUSSEL SCIENCE AND TECHNOLOGY SCHOLARSHIP
• *See page 69*

LOS ANGELES COUNCIL OF BLACK PROFESSIONAL ENGINEERS http://www.lablackengineers.org/scholarships.html

AL-BEN SCHOLARSHIP FOR ACADEMIC INCENTIVE
• *See page 142*

AL-BEN SCHOLARSHIP FOR PROFESSIONAL MERIT
• *See page 142*

AL-BEN SCHOLARSHIP FOR SCHOLASTIC ACHIEVEMENT
• *See page 143*

LUCENT TECHNOLOGIES FOUNDATION http://www.iie.org/programs/lucent

LUCENT GLOBAL SCIENCE SCHOLARS PROGRAM
• *See page 70*

MARYLAND ASSOCIATION OF PRIVATE COLLEGES AND CAREER SCHOOLS http://www.mapccs.org

MARYLAND ASSOCIATION OF PRIVATE COLLEGES AND CAREER SCHOOLS SCHOLARSHIP
• *See page 127*

MICRON TECHNOLOGY FOUNDATION, INC. http://www.micron.com/scholars

MICRON SCIENCE AND TECHNOLOGY SCHOLARS PROGRAM
• *See page 144*

NAMEPA NATIONAL SCHOLARSHIP FOUNDATION http://www.namepa.org

NATIONAL ASSOCIATION OF MINORITY ENGINEERING PROGRAM ADMINISTRATORS NATIONAL SCHOLARSHIP FUND
• *See page 101*

NASA IDAHO SPACE GRANT CONSORTIUM http://www.uidaho.edu/nasa_isgc

NASA IDAHO SPACE GRANT CONSORTIUM SCHOLARSHIP PROGRAM
• *See page 71*

NASA MINNESOTA SPACE GRANT CONSORTIUM http://www.aem.umn.edu/msgc

MINNESOTA SPACE GRANT CONSORTIUM
• *See page 101*

NASA NEBRASKA SPACE GRANT CONSORTIUM http://nasa.unomaha.edu

NASA NEBRASKA SPACE GRANT
• *See page 101*

NASA NEVADA SPACE GRANT CONSORTIUM http://www.unr.edu/spacegrant

UNIVERSITY AND COMMUNITY COLLEGE SYSTEM OF NEVADA NASA SPACE GRANT AND FELLOWSHIP PROGRAM
• *See page 101*

NASA WEST VIRGINIA SPACE GRANT CONSORTIUM http://www.nasa.wvu.edu

WEST VIRGINIA SPACE GRANT CONSORTIUM UNDERGRADUATE SCHOLARSHIP PROGRAM
• *See page 102*

NATIONAL ASSOCIATION FOR THE ADVANCEMENT OF COLORED PEOPLE http://www.naacp.org

LOUIS STOKES SCIENCE AND TECHNOLOGY AWARD
• *See page 114*

NATIONAL ASSOCIATION OF WATER COMPANIES-NEW JERSEY CHAPTER

NATIONAL ASSOCIATION OF WATER COMPANIES-NEW JERSEY CHAPTER SCHOLARSHIP
• *See page 115*

NATIONAL FEDERATION OF THE BLIND http://www.nfb.org

NATIONAL FEDERATION OF THE BLIND COMPUTER SCIENCE SCHOLARSHIP

One-time award for students who are legally blind and studying computer science. Must submit recommendation from state officer of National Federation of the Blind. Award based on financial need, minimum 3.5 GPA, scholarship, and community service. Must attend school in U.S.

Academic Fields/Career Goals: Computer Science/Data Processing.

Award: Scholarship for use in freshman, sophomore, junior, or senior years; not renewable. *Number:* 1. *Amount:* $3000.

Eligibility Requirements: Applicant must be enrolled or expecting to enroll at an institution or university. Applicant or parent of applicant must have employment or volunteer experience in community service. Applicant must be visually impaired. Applicant must have 3.5 GPA or higher. Available to U.S. and non-U.S. citizens.

Application Requirements: Application, autobiography, essay, financial need analysis, references, transcript. *Deadline:* March 31.

Contact: Peggy Elliot, Chairman, Scholarship Committee
National Federation of the Blind
805 Fifth Avenue
Grinnell, IA 50112
Phone: 641-236-3366

NATIONAL INSTITUTE OF GENERAL MEDICAL SCIENCES, NATIONAL INSTITUTE OF HEALTH http://www.nigms.nih.gov

*MARC UNDERGRADUATE STUDENT TRAINING IN ACADEMIC RESEARCH U*STAR AWARDS*

• *See page 115*

NATIONAL INVENTORS HALL OF FAME http://www.invent.org/collegiate

COLLEGIATE INVENTORS COMPETITION - GRAND PRIZE

• *See page 71*

COLLEGIATE INVENTORS COMPETITION FOR UNDERGRADUATE STUDENTS

• *See page 71*

NATIONAL SECURITY AGENCY http://www.nsa.gov

NATIONAL SECURITY AGENCY STOKES EDUCATIONAL SCHOLARSHIP PROGRAM

Renewable awards for high school students planning to attend a four-year undergraduate institution to study foreign languages, computer science, math, electrical engineering, or computer engineering. Must be at least 16 to apply. Must be a U.S. citizen. Minimum 3.0 GPA required, and minimum SAT score of 1100. For application visit Web site: http://www.nsa.gov/programs/employ/index.html.

Academic Fields/Career Goals: Computer Science/Data Processing; Electrical Engineering/Electronics; Foreign Language; Physical Sciences and Math.

Award: Scholarship for use in freshman, sophomore, junior, or senior years; renewable. *Number:* 10–30. *Amount:* varies.

Eligibility Requirements: Applicant must be high school student; age 16 and planning to enroll or expecting to enroll full-time at a four-year institution. Applicant must have 3.0 GPA or higher. Available to U.S. citizens.

Application Requirements: Application, essay, interview, resume, references, test scores, transcript. *Deadline:* November 30.

Contact: Program Manager
National Security Agency
Attn: STOKES, 9800 Savage Road, Suite 6779
Ft. Meade, MD 20755-6779
Phone: 866-672-4473
Fax: 410-854-3002

NEW JERSEY ACADEMY OF SCIENCE http://www.njas.org

NEW JERSEY ACADEMY OF SCIENCE RESEARCH GRANTS-IN-AID TO HIGH SCHOOL STUDENTS

• *See page 116*

OREGON STUDENT ASSISTANCE COMMISSION http://www.osac.state.or.us

HOWARD VOLLUM AMERICAN INDIAN SCHOLARSHIP

Renewable award for American-Indian residents of Clackamas, Multnomah, or Washington County in Oregon, or of Clark County in Washington. For study of science, computer science, engineering or mathematics. Must submit certification of tribal enrollment or American-Indian ancestry. Preference for those who have demonstrated commitment to the American-Indian community.

Academic Fields/Career Goals: Computer Science/Data Processing; Engineering/Technology; Physical Sciences and Math.

Award: Scholarship for use in freshman, sophomore, junior, or senior years; renewable. *Number:* 5. *Amount:* $3000.

Eligibility Requirements: Applicant must be American Indian/Alaska Native; enrolled or expecting to enroll at an institution or university and resident of Oregon or Washington.

Application Requirements: Application, essay, financial need analysis, transcript. *Deadline:* March 1.

Contact: Director of Grant Programs
Oregon Student Assistance Commission
1500 Valley River Drive, Suite 100
Eugene, OR 97401-7020
Phone: 800-452-8807 Ext. 7395
E-mail: awardinfo@mercury.osac.state.or.us

MENTOR GRAPHICS SCHOLARSHIP

One-time award for computer science, computer engineering, or electrical engineering majors entering junior or senior year at a four-year institution. Preference for one award to female, African-American, Native-American, or Hispanic applicant.

Academic Fields/Career Goals: Computer Science/Data Processing; Electrical Engineering/Electronics.

Award: Scholarship for use in junior or senior years; not renewable. *Number:* 4. *Amount:* $2000.

Eligibility Requirements: Applicant must be enrolled or expecting to enroll at a four-year institution and resident of Oregon. Available to U.S. citizens.

Application Requirements: Application, essay, financial need analysis, references, transcript, activity chart. *Deadline:* March 1.

Contact: Director of Grant Programs
Oregon Student Assistance Commission
1500 Valley River Drive, Suite 100
Eugene, OR 97401-7020
Phone: 800-452-8807 Ext. 7395
E-mail: awardinfo@mercury.osac.state.or.us

ROBERT H. MOLLOHAN FAMILY CHARITABLE FOUNDATION, INC. http://www.mollohanfoundation.org

HIGH TECHNOLOGY SCHOLARS PROGRAM

• *See page 117*

ROYAL BANK NATIVE STUDENTS AWARDS PROGRAM http://www.rbc.com/community/rbc_community/articles/story_17.html

ROYAL BANK ABORIGINAL STUDENT AWARDS

• *See page 129*

SOCIETY OF WOMEN ENGINEERS http://www.swe.org/scholarships

AGILENT MENTORING SCHOLARSHIP

One $1000 scholarship for undergraduate sophomore or junior studying biological engineering, computer engineering, computer science, electrical engineering, or mechanical engineering.

Academic Fields/Career Goals: Computer Science/Data Processing; Electrical Engineering/Electronics; Engineering/Technology; Mechanical Engineering.

Award: Scholarship for use in sophomore or junior years; not renewable. *Number:* 1. *Amount:* $1000.

Eligibility Requirements: Applicant must be enrolled or expecting to enroll full-time at a four-year institution or university and female. Applicant must have 3.0 GPA or higher. Available to U.S. citizens.

Application Requirements: Application. *Deadline:* February 1.

Contact: Program Coordinator
Society of Women Engineers
230 East Ohio Street, Suite 400
Chicago, IL 60611-3265
Phone: 312-596-5223
Fax: 312-644-8557
E-mail: hq@swe.org

DAVID SARNOFF RESEARCH CENTER SCHOLARSHIP

One-time award for female engineering or computer science major. Must be in junior year and have a minimum 3.5 GPA. Deadline: February 1.

Academic Fields/Career Goals: Computer Science/Data Processing; Engineering/Technology.

Award: Scholarship for use in junior year; not renewable. *Number:* 1. *Amount:* $1500.

Eligibility Requirements: Applicant must be enrolled or expecting to enroll at a four-year institution or university and female. Applicant must have 3.5 GPA or higher. Available to U.S. citizens.

Application Requirements: Application, references, self-addressed stamped envelope, transcript. *Deadline:* February 1.

Contact: Program Coordinator
Society of Women Engineers
230 East Ohio Street, Suite 400
Chicago, IL 60611-3265
Phone: 312-596-5223
Fax: 312-644-8557
E-mail: hq@swe.org

DELL COMPUTER CORPORATION SCHOLARSHIPS

Awarded to entering female juniors and seniors majoring in computer science, computer engineering, electrical engineering or mechanical engineering who demonstrate financial need and maintain a minimum 3.0 GPA. Deadline: February 1.

Academic Fields/Career Goals: Computer Science/Data Processing; Electrical Engineering/Electronics; Engineering/Technology; Mechanical Engineering.

Award: Scholarship for use in junior or senior years; not renewable. *Number:* 2. *Amount:* $2250.

Eligibility Requirements: Applicant must be enrolled or expecting to enroll at a four-year institution or university and female. Applicant must have 3.0 GPA or higher. Available to U.S. and non-U.S. citizens.

Application Requirements: Application, essay, financial need analysis, references, self-addressed stamped envelope, test scores, transcript. *Deadline:* February 1.

Contact: Program Coordinator
Society of Women Engineers
230 East Ohio Street, Suite 400
Chicago, IL 60611-3265
Phone: 312-596-5223
Fax: 312-644-8557
E-mail: hq@swe.org

GUIDANT CORPORATION SCHOLARSHIP

Two $5000 scholarships available to undergraduate seniors majoring in chemical engineering, computer engineering, computer science, electrical engineering, industrial engineering, mechanical engineering, manufacturing engineering, and materials science and engineering.

Academic Fields/Career Goals: Computer Science/Data Processing; Electrical Engineering/Electronics; Engineering/Technology; Engineering-Related Technologies; Materials Science, Engineering, and Metallurgy; Mechanical Engineering.

Award: Scholarship for use in senior year; not renewable. *Number:* 2. *Amount:* $5000.

Eligibility Requirements: Applicant must be enrolled or expecting to enroll full-time at a four-year institution or university and female. Applicant must have 3.0 GPA or higher. Available to U.S. citizens.

Application Requirements: Application. *Deadline:* February 1.

Contact: Program Coordinator
Society of Women Engineers
230 East Ohio Street, Suite 400
Chicago, IL 60611-3265
Phone: 312-596-5223
Fax: 312-644-8557
E-mail: hq@swe.org

LYDIA I. PICKUP MEMORIAL SCHOLARSHIP

Available to female sophomore, junior, or senior undergraduate student or graduate student. For graduate education to advance applicant's career in engineering or computer science. Minimum 3.0 GPA required. Deadline: February 1.

Academic Fields/Career Goals: Computer Science/Data Processing; Engineering/Technology.

Award: Scholarship for use in sophomore, junior, senior, or graduate years; not renewable. *Number:* 1. *Amount:* $2000.

Eligibility Requirements: Applicant must be enrolled or expecting to enroll at an institution or university and female. Applicant must have 3.0 GPA or higher. Available to U.S. citizens.

Application Requirements: Application, references, self-addressed stamped envelope, transcript. *Deadline:* February 1.

Contact: Program Coordinator
Society of Women Engineers
230 East Ohio Street, Suite 400
Chicago, IL 60611-3265
Phone: 312-596-5223
Fax: 312-644-8557
E-mail: hq@swe.org

MICROSOFT CORPORATION SCHOLARSHIPS

Scholarships for female computer engineering or computer science students in sophomore, junior, senior year, or first year master's degree students. Must exhibit career interest in the field of computer software. Minimum 3.5 GPA required. Deadline: February 1.

Academic Fields/Career Goals: Computer Science/Data Processing.

Award: Scholarship for use in sophomore, junior, senior, or graduate years; renewable. *Number:* 2. *Amount:* $2500.

Eligibility Requirements: Applicant must be enrolled or expecting to enroll at a four-year institution or university and female. Applicant must have 3.5 GPA or higher.

Application Requirements: Application, essay, references, self-addressed stamped envelope, test scores, transcript. *Deadline:* February 1.

Contact: Program Coordinator
Society of Women Engineers
230 East Ohio Street, Suite 400
Chicago, IL 60611-3265
Phone: 312-596-5223
Fax: 312-644-8557
E-mail: hq@swe.org

NORTHROP GRUMMAN CORPORATION SCHOLARSHIPS

• *See page 106*

SWE BALTIMORE-WASHINGTON SECTION SCHOLARSHIPS

Must be enrolled as an undergraduate or graduate engineering student in an ABET-accredited engineering or computer science within the Baltimore-Washington region. Please see Web site for more details: http://www.swe-bws.org

Academic Fields/Career Goals: Computer Science/Data Processing; Engineering/Technology.

Award: Scholarship for use in freshman, sophomore, junior, senior, or graduate years; not renewable. *Number:* 5. *Amount:* varies.

Eligibility Requirements: Applicant must be enrolled or expecting to enroll at a four-year institution or university; female and studying in District of Columbia, Maryland, or Virginia. Applicant must have 3.0 GPA or higher. Available to U.S. citizens.

Application Requirements: Application, essay, references, transcript. *Deadline:* March 1.

Contact: Program Coordinator
Society of Women Engineers
230 East Ohio Street, Suite 400
Chicago, IL 60611-3265
Phone: 312-596-5223
Fax: 312-644-8557
E-mail: hq@swe.org

SWE BATON ROUGE SECTION SCHOLARSHIPS

Applicant must be planning to attend college in the following fall semester for engineering or computer science. Applications available from high school guidance counselor.

Academic Fields/Career Goals: Computer Science/Data Processing; Engineering/Technology.

Award: Scholarship for use in freshman year; not renewable. *Number:* 6. *Amount:* $1000.

Eligibility Requirements: Applicant must be enrolled or expecting to enroll at a four-year institution; female and resident of Louisiana. Available to U.S. citizens.

Application Requirements: Application, test scores, transcript. *Deadline:* varies.

Contact: Donna Scott, Scholarship Chair
Phone: 225-473-5801
E-mail: swebrouge@hotmail.com

SWE CALIFORNIA GOLDEN GATE SECTION SCHOLARSHIPS

Scholarships awarded to female entering freshmen pursuing degrees in engineering, computer science, physical science, or mathematics. Applicants must be attending high school, or living within the boundaries of the Golden Gate Section. Counties include: San Francisco, Marin, Napa, Sonoma, San Mateo counties and parts of Contra Costa and Alameda counties.

Academic Fields/Career Goals: Computer Science/Data Processing; Engineering/Technology; Physical Sciences and Math.

Award: Scholarship for use in freshman year; not renewable. *Number:* 10–15. *Amount:* $500–$1000.

Eligibility Requirements: Applicant must be high school student; planning to enroll or expecting to enroll at a four-year institution or university; female and resident of California. Available to U.S. citizens.

Application Requirements: Application, essay, references. *Deadline:* April 19.

Contact: Lisa M. Duncan, SWE-GGS Scholarship Chair
Phone: 510-242-2554

SWE CONNECTICUT SECTION JEAN R. BEERS SCHOLARSHIP

Scholarship awarded to undergraduate sophomore, junior, or senior pursuing Bachelor of Science degree in engineering, mathematics, computers, or science. Applicant must attend school or live within the boundaries of the Connecticut Section.

Academic Fields/Career Goals: Computer Science/Data Processing; Engineering/Technology; Physical Sciences and Math.

Award: Scholarship for use in sophomore, junior, or senior years; not renewable. *Number:* varies. *Amount:* $1500.

Eligibility Requirements: Applicant must be enrolled or expecting to enroll at an institution or university; female and resident of Connecticut. Available to U.S. citizens.

Application Requirements: Application, essay, financial need analysis. *Deadline:* January 15.

Contact: Society of Women Engineers Scholarship Committee
Society of Women Engineers
PO Box 2624
Westport, CT 06880-9991

SWE GREATER NEW ORLEANS SECTION SCHOLARSHIP

Scholarships available to entering freshman planning on attending ABET accredited or SWE approved schools for engineering, or CSAB/ABET accredited schools, or SWE approved schools for computer science. Available to students from the following parishes: Jefferson, Lafourche, Orleans, Plaqremines, St. Bernard, St. Charles, St. James, St. John, St. Tammany, Tangipahoa, or Terrebonne.

Academic Fields/Career Goals: Computer Science/Data Processing; Engineering/Technology.

Award: Scholarship for use in freshman year; not renewable. *Number:* varies. *Amount:* varies.

Eligibility Requirements: Applicant must be enrolled or expecting to enroll at a four-year institution or university; female and resident of Louisiana. Available to U.S. citizens.

Application Requirements: Application. *Deadline:* March 31.

Contact: Jaime Lewis
Phone: 504-465-6827

SOCIETY OF WOMEN ENGINEERS - TWIN TIERS SECTION http://www.swetwintiers.org

SOCIETY OF WOMEN ENGINEERS - TWIN TIERS SECTION SCHOLARSHIP

Applicants must reside or attend school in the Twin Tiers SWE section of New York. This is limited to zip codes that begin with 148, 149, 169 and residents of Bradford County, Pennsylvania. Applicant must be accepted or enrolled in an undergraduate degree program in engineering or computer science at an ABET-, CSAB- or SWE-accredited school. Please refer to Web site for specific details http://www.swetwintiers.org/

Academic Fields/Career Goals: Computer Science/Data Processing; Engineering/Technology.

Award: Scholarship for use in freshman, sophomore, or junior years; not renewable. *Number:* 5. *Amount:* $1500.

Eligibility Requirements: Applicant must be high school student; planning to enroll or expecting to enroll at a four-year institution or university and female. Available to U.S. citizens.

Application Requirements: Application, essay, references, self-addressed stamped envelope, transcript, letter of acceptance, resume, personal information, achievements. *Deadline:* March 22.

Contact: Valerie Mis, Scholarship Chair
Society of Women Engineers - Twin Tiers Section
PO Box 798
Corning, NY 14830
Phone: 607-974-8846
E-mail: misvr@corning.com

SOCIETY OF WOMEN ENGINEERS-ROCKY MOUNTAIN SECTION http://www.swe.org

SOCIETY OF WOMEN ENGINEERS-ROCKY MOUNTAIN SECTION SCHOLARSHIP PROGRAM

One-time award for female high school seniors in Colorado and Wyoming who intend to enroll in engineering or computer science at an ABET-accredited college or university in those states. Female college students who have already enrolled in those programs may also apply. For more information visit http://www.swe.org and look for local scholarships.

Academic Fields/Career Goals: Computer Science/Data Processing; Engineering/Technology.

Award: Scholarship for use in freshman, sophomore, junior, senior, or graduate years; not renewable. *Number:* 3–5. *Amount:* $500–$1000.

Eligibility Requirements: Applicant must be enrolled or expecting to enroll full-time at a four-year institution or university; female; resident of Colorado or Wyoming and studying in Colorado or Wyoming. Applicant must have 3.5 GPA or higher. Available to U.S. and non-U.S. citizens.

Application Requirements: Application, essay, resume, references, test scores, transcript. *Deadline:* February 1.

Contact: Barbara Kontogiannis, Scholarship Chair
Society of Women Engineers-Rocky Mountain Section
Attn: Scholarship Committee Chair
PO Box 260692
Lakewood, CO 80226-0692
Phone: 303-971-5213
E-mail: barbekon@stanfordalumni.org

SOUTH DAKOTA RETAILERS ASSOCIATION http://www.sdra.org

SOUTH DAKOTA RETAILERS ASSOCIATION SCHOLARSHIP PROGRAM

• *See page 47*

TEXAS DEPARTMENT OF TRANSPORTATION http://www.dot.state.tx.us

CONDITIONAL GRANT PROGRAM

• *See page 155*

UNITED DAUGHTERS OF THE CONFEDERACY http://www.hqudc.org

WALTER REED SMITH SCHOLARSHIP

• *See page 130*

UNITED NEGRO COLLEGE FUND http://www.uncf.org

ACCENTURE SCHOLARSHIP

Applicant must be enrolled at one of the following schools: Morehouse College, Spelman College, Howard University, Florida A&M, North Carolina A&T, and Prairie View A&M University. Please visit Web site for more information: http://www.uncf.org.

Academic Fields/Career Goals: Computer Science/Data Processing; Engineering/Technology.

Award: Scholarship for use in sophomore or junior years; not renewable. *Number:* 5. *Amount:* $2000.

Eligibility Requirements: Applicant must be enrolled or expecting to enroll at an institution or university. Applicant must have 3.0 GPA or higher. Available to U.S. citizens.

Application Requirements: Application, financial need analysis, FAFSA, SAR. *Deadline:* varies.

Contact: Program Services Department
United Negro College Fund
8260 Willow Oaks Corporate Drive
Fairfax, VA 22031

ALFRED L. CHISHOLM SCHOLARSHIP

Scholarship assists one student from New Jersey majoring in engineering, chemistry, math, or computer science attending a UNCF member college or university. 3.0 GPA required. Prospective applicants should complete the Student Profile found at Web site: http://www.uncf.org.

Academic Fields/Career Goals: Computer Science/Data Processing; Engineering/Technology; Physical Sciences and Math.

Award: Scholarship for use in freshman, sophomore, junior, or senior years; not renewable. *Number:* 1. *Amount:* up to $5000.

Eligibility Requirements: Applicant must be Black (non-Hispanic); enrolled or expecting to enroll at a four-year institution or university and resident of New Jersey. Applicant must have 3.0 GPA or higher.

Application Requirements: Application, financial need analysis. *Deadline:* November 16.

Contact: Program Services Department
United Negro College Fund
8260 Willow Oaks Corporate Drive
Fairfax, VA 22031

BOOZ, ALLEN & HAMILTON/WILLIAM F. STASIOR INTERNSHIP

• *See page 130*

CARDINAL HEALTH SCHOLARSHIP

• *See page 48*

CARGILL SCHOLARSHIP PROGRAM

• *See page 49*

CHRYSLER CORPORATION SCHOLARSHIP

Award for minority undergraduate women in the fields of engineering or computer science. Must attend an ABET-accredited college or university; selection is based on merit. Minimum 3.5 GPA is required. Prospective applicants should complete the Student Profile found at Web site: http://www.uncf.org.

Academic Fields/Career Goals: Computer Science/Data Processing; Engineering/Technology.

Award: Scholarship for use in sophomore, junior, or senior years; not renewable. *Number:* varies. *Amount:* $1000–$5000.

Eligibility Requirements: Applicant must be Black (non-Hispanic); enrolled or expecting to enroll full-time at a four-year institution or university and female. Applicant must have 3.5 GPA or higher. Available to U.S. citizens.

Application Requirements: Application. *Deadline:* Continuous.

Contact: Scholarship Committee, Society of Women Engineers
United Negro College Fund
120 Wall Street, 11th Floor
New York, NY 10005-3902
Phone: 212-596-5223

CISCO/UNCF SCHOLARS PROGRAM

Scholarship provides financial support for African-American electrical engineering or computer science majors attending specific UNCF member college or university. Minimum 3.2 GPA required. Prospective applicants should complete the Student Profile found at Web site: http://www.uncf.org.

Academic Fields/Career Goals: Computer Science/Data Processing; Electrical Engineering/Electronics.

Award: Scholarship for use in sophomore year; not renewable. *Amount:* $4000.

Eligibility Requirements: Applicant must be Black (non-Hispanic) and enrolled or expecting to enroll full-time at a four-year institution or university. Available to U.S. citizens.

Application Requirements: Application, financial need analysis. *Deadline:* February 27.

Contact: Program Services Department
United Negro College Fund
8260 Willow Oaks Corporate Drive
Fairfax, VA 22031

CON EDISON SCHOLARSHIP

• *See page 49*

CREDIT SUISSE FIRST BOSTON SCHOLARSHIP

• *See page 49*

DELL/UNCF CORPORATE SCHOLARS PROGRAM

• *See page 131*

EDS CORPORATE SCHOLARS PROGRAM

Ten scholarships for juniors majoring in computer science or information systems attending a UNCF member college or university. Minimum 3.0 GPA required. Prospective applicants should complete the Student Profile found at Web site: http://www.uncf.org.

Academic Fields/Career Goals: Computer Science/Data Processing.

Award: Scholarship for use in junior year; not renewable. *Number:* 10. *Amount:* up to $7500.

Eligibility Requirements: Applicant must be Black (non-Hispanic) and enrolled or expecting to enroll at a four-year institution or university. Applicant must have 3.0 GPA or higher.

Application Requirements: Application, financial need analysis.

Contact: Program Services Department
United Negro College Fund
8260 Willow Oaks Corporate Drive
Fairfax, VA 22031

EMERSON ELECTRIC COMPANY SCHOLARSHIP

• *See page 49*

FLOWERS INDUSTRIES SCHOLARSHIP

• *See page 131*

FORD/UNCF CORPORATE SCHOLARS PROGRAM

• *See page 49*

GENERAL MILLS SCHOLARS PROGRAM/INTERNSHIP

• *See page 50*

HOUSEHOLD INTERNATIONAL CORPORATE SCHOLARS

• *See page 131*

KODAK ENGINEERING EXCELLENCE PROGRAM SCHOLARSHIP

Scholarships for engineering or computer science majors attending a UNCF member college or university. Minimum 3.0 GPA required. Prospective applicants should complete the Student Profile found at Web site: http://www.uncf.org.

Academic Fields/Career Goals: Computer Science/Data Processing; Engineering/Technology.

Award: Scholarship for use in junior year; not renewable. *Amount:* $4800.

Eligibility Requirements: Applicant must be Black (non-Hispanic) and enrolled or expecting to enroll at a four-year institution or university. Applicant must have 3.0 GPA or higher. Available to U.S. citizens.

Application Requirements: Application, financial need analysis, photo, resume, references, transcript. *Deadline:* varies.

Contact: Program Services Department
United Negro College Fund
8260 Willow Oaks Corporate Drive
Fairfax, VA 22031

MAYTAG COMPANY SCHOLARSHIP

• *See page 132*

NORTHEAST UTILITIES SYSTEM SCHOLARSHIP PROGRAM

• *See page 132*

PECO ENERGY SCHOLARSHIP

• *See page 50*

PRINCIPAL FINANCIAL GROUP SCHOLARSHIPS

• *See page 132*

SBC FOUNDATION SCHOLARSHIP

• *See page 133*

SBC PACIFIC BELL FOUNDATION SCHOLARSHIP

• *See page 133*

SOUTHWESTERN BELL CORPORATION SCHOLARSHIP

• *See page 133*

SPRINT SCHOLARSHIP/INTERNSHIP

• *See page 50*

TRW INFORMATION TECHNOLOGY MINORITY SCHOLARSHIP

Award for sophomore and junior minority college students majoring in engineering, computer science, and other information sciences at Howard University, George Mason University, Morgan State, Virginia Polytechnic Institute, or Pennsylvania State. Must have 3.0 GPA. Please visit Web site for more information: http://www.uncf.org

Academic Fields/Career Goals: Computer Science/Data Processing; Engineering/Technology.

Award: Scholarship for use in sophomore, junior, or senior years; renewable. *Number:* varies. *Amount:* $3000.

Eligibility Requirements: Applicant must be Black (non-Hispanic) and enrolled or expecting to enroll at an institution or university. Applicant must have 3.0 GPA or higher.

Application Requirements: Application, financial need analysis, FAFSA, SAR. *Deadline:* varies.

Contact: Program Services Department
United Negro College Fund
8260 Willow Oaks Corporate Drive
Fairfax, VA 22031

UNCF/ORACLE SCHOLARS/INTERNS PROGRAM

• *See page 50*

UNCF/SPRINT SCHOLARS PROGRAM

• *See page 50*

UPS CORPORATE SCHOLARS PROGRAM/INTERNSHIP

• *See page 134*

USENIX ASSOCIATION SCHOLARSHIP

Applicants should be majors in computer science, or information systems. Students must have 3.5 GPA to qualify. Prospective applicants should complete the Student Profile found at Web site: http://www.uncf.org.

Academic Fields/Career Goals: Computer Science/Data Processing.

Award: Scholarship for use in freshman, sophomore, junior, or senior years; not renewable. *Amount:* up to $10,000.

Eligibility Requirements: Applicant must be Black (non-Hispanic) and enrolled or expecting to enroll at a four-year institution or university. Applicant must have 3.5 GPA or higher.

Application Requirements: Application, financial need analysis. *Deadline:* Continuous.

Contact: Program Services Department
United Negro College Fund
8260 Willow Oaks Corporate Drive
Fairfax, VA 22031

VIRGINIA BUSINESS AND PROFESSIONAL WOMEN'S FOUNDATION

http://www.bpwva.advocate.net/foundation.htm

WOMEN IN SCIENCE AND TECHNOLOGY SCHOLARSHIP

• *See page 119*

WISCONSIN FOUNDATION FOR INDEPENDENT COLLEGES, INC.

http://www.wficweb.org

LAND'S END SCHOLARSHIP

• *See page 135*

SENTRY 21 CLUB SCHOLARSHIP

• *See page 135*

WOMEN IN NEW MEDIA

http://www.winm.org

WOMEN IN NEW MEDIA YOUNG WOMEN'S COLLEGE SCHOLARSHIP PROGRAM

Scholarship for female high school seniors entering an accredited post-secondary institution. Must pursue studies in the computer sciences, information technology, and interactive/digital technologies-including programming, design, and marketing. Must be resident of New York City.

Academic Fields/Career Goals: Computer Science/Data Processing.

Award: Scholarship for use in freshman year; not renewable. *Number:* 3–5. *Amount:* $1000–$5000.

Eligibility Requirements: Applicant must be high school student; planning to enroll or expecting to enroll full-time at a two-year or four-year institution or university; single female; resident of New York; studying in New York and must have an interest in designated field specified by sponsor. Applicant must have 3.0 GPA or higher. Available to U.S. citizens.

Application Requirements: Application, essay, financial need analysis, references, test scores, transcript. *Deadline:* varies.

Contact: Camilla Colgrave, Chairman, Scholarship Committee
Women in New Media
Grand Central Station
PO Box 2805
New York, NY 10163-2805
Phone: 212-439-4774
E-mail: scholarship@winm.org

WYOMING TRUCKING ASSOCIATION

WYOMING TRUCKING ASSOCIATION TRUST FUND SCHOLARSHIP

• *See page 135*

XEROX

http://xerox.com

TECHNICAL MINORITY SCHOLARSHIP

• *See page 148*

CONSTRUCTION ENGINEERING/MANAGEMENT

NATIONAL INSTITUTE OF BUILDING SCIENCES, MULTIHAZARD MITIGATION COUNCIL http://www.nibs.org

ARCHITECTURE, CONSTRUCTION, AND ENGINEERING MENTOR PROGRAM SCHOLARSHIPS

• *See page 78*

COSMETOLOGY

JOE FRANCIS HAIRCARE SCHOLARSHIP FOUNDATION http://www.joefrancis.com

JOE FRANCIS HAIRCARE SCHOLARSHIP PROGRAM

Scholarships are awarded for $1,000 each, with a minimum of twelve scholarships awarded annually. Applicants are evaluated for their potential to successfully complete school, their financial need, and their commitment to a long-term career in cosmetology. The deadline is June 1. Must be U.S. citizen and enrolled in school by fall of award year.

Academic Fields/Career Goals: Cosmetology.

Award: Scholarship for use in freshman or sophomore years; not renewable. *Number:* 12. *Amount:* $1000.

Eligibility Requirements: Applicant must be enrolled or expecting to enroll full or part-time at a technical institution. Available to U.S. citizens.

Application Requirements: Application, essay, financial need analysis, references. *Deadline:* June 1.

Contact: Kim Larson, Secretary
Joe Francis Haircare Scholarship Foundation
PO Box 50625
Minneapolis, MN 55405
Phone: 651-769-1757
Fax: 651-459-8371
E-mail: mklarson@awest.net

RESOURCE CENTER http://www.resourcecenterscholarshipinfo.com

MARIE BLAHA MEDICAL GRANT

• *See page 64*

CRIMINAL JUSTICE/CRIMINOLOGY

ALASKA STATE TROOPERS http://www.dps.state.ak.us/ast

MICHAEL MURPHY MEMORIAL SCHOLARSHIP LOAN FUND

Assists full-time undergraduate or graduate students enrolled in a program relating to law enforcement. Recipient receives forgiveness of 20% of the full loan amount for each year employed in law enforcement. Must be Alaska resident.

Academic Fields/Career Goals: Criminal Justice/Criminology; Law Enforcement/Police Administration; Social Services.

Award: Forgivable loan for use in freshman, sophomore, junior, senior, or graduate years; renewable. *Number:* 3–6. *Amount:* up to $1000.

Eligibility Requirements: Applicant must be enrolled or expecting to enroll full-time at a two-year or four-year institution or university and resident of Alaska. Available to U.S. citizens.

Application Requirements: Application. *Deadline:* April 1.

Contact: Ralph Reyes, Lieutenant
Alaska State Troopers
5700 East Tudor Road
Anchorage, AK 99507
Phone: 907-269-5759
Fax: 907-269-5751
E-mail: ralph_reyes@dps.state.ak.us

ALBERTA HERITAGE SCHOLARSHIP FUND/ ALBERTA SCHOLARSHIP PROGRAMS http://www.alis.gov.ab.ca/scholarships

ROBERT C. CARSON MEMORIAL BURSARY

Award for aboriginal Albertans without sponsorship enrolled full time in their second year of law enforcement, criminal justice diploma, or faculty of law programs at eligible institutions. Students should contact financial aid office of their institution for nomination deadline. Must be a resident of Alberta. Must be ranked in upper half of class or have a minimum 2.5 GPA.

Academic Fields/Career Goals: Criminal Justice/Criminology; Law Enforcement/Police Administration; Law/Legal Services.

Award: Scholarship for use in sophomore year; not renewable. *Number:* 5. *Amount:* $405.

Eligibility Requirements: Applicant must be Canadian citizen; American Indian/Alaska Native; enrolled or expecting to enroll full-time at a two-year or four-year institution or university; resident of Alberta and studying in Alberta. Applicant must have 2.5 GPA or higher.

Application Requirements: Application. *Deadline:* October 1.

Contact: Alberta Heritage Scholarship Fund/Alberta Scholarship Programs
9940 106th Street, 9th Floor, Box 28000 Station Main
Edmonton, AB T5J 4R4
Canada
Phone: 780-427-8640
Fax: 780-422-4516
E-mail: heritage@gov.ab.ca

AMERICAN CORRECTIONAL ASSOCIATION http://www.aca.org

MARTIN LUTHER KING, JR. SCHOLARSHIP AWARD

One-time award given to a minority who is a full-time student pursuing a degree in criminal justice. Applicants must submit an essay along with their application and transcript.

Academic Fields/Career Goals: Criminal Justice/Criminology.

Award: Scholarship for use in freshman, sophomore, junior, senior, graduate, or postgraduate years; not renewable. *Number:* 1. *Amount:* $1000.

Eligibility Requirements: Applicant must be American Indian/Alaska Native, Asian/Pacific Islander, Black (non-Hispanic), or Hispanic and enrolled or expecting to enroll full-time at a four-year institution or university. Available to U.S. and non-U.S. citizens.

Application Requirements: Application, essay, financial need analysis, resume, transcript. *Deadline:* June 1.

Contact: Debbi Seeger, Administrative Manager
American Correctional Association
4380 Forbes Boulevard
Lanham, MD 20706-4322
Phone: 301-918-1800
Fax: 301-918-1900
E-mail: debbis@aca.org

AMERICAN CRIMINAL JUSTICE ASSOCIATION-LAMBDA ALPHA EPSILON http://www.acjalae.org

AMERICAN CRIMINAL JUSTICE ASSOCIATION-LAMBDA ALPHA EPSILON NATIONAL SCHOLARSHIP

Awarded only to members of the American Criminal Justice Association. One-time award of $100-$400. Members may reapply each year. Must have minimum 3.0 GPA. Must pursue studies in law/legal services, criminal justice/law, or the social sciences. Application deadline is December 31.

Academic Fields/Career Goals: Criminal Justice/Criminology; Law/Legal Services; Social Sciences.

Award: Scholarship for use in sophomore, junior, senior, or graduate years; not renewable. *Number:* 9. *Amount:* $100–$400.

Eligibility Requirements: Applicant must be enrolled or expecting to enroll full or part-time at a two-year or four-year institution or university. Applicant or parent of applicant must be member of American Criminal Justice Association. Applicant must have 3.0 GPA or higher. Available to U.S. citizens.

American Criminal Justice Association-Lambda Alpha Epsilon (continued)

Application Requirements: Application, references, transcript. *Deadline:* December 31.

Contact: Karen Campbell, Executive Secretary
American Criminal Justice Association-Lambda Alpha Epsilon
PO Box 601047
Sacramento, CA 95860-1047
Phone: 916-484-6553
Fax: 916-488-2227
E-mail: acjalae@aol.com

AMERICAN SOCIETY OF CRIMINOLOGY http://www.ASC41.com

AMERICAN SOCIETY OF CRIMINOLOGY GENE CARTE STUDENT PAPER COMPETITION

Award for full-time undergraduate or graduate students. Must submit a conceptual or empirical paper on a subject directly relating to criminology. Papers must be 7500 words or less. Visit Web site for additional information.

Academic Fields/Career Goals: Criminal Justice/Criminology; Law Enforcement/Police Administration; Law/Legal Services; Social Sciences.

Award: Prize for use in freshman, sophomore, junior, senior, or graduate years; not renewable. *Number:* 3. *Amount:* $200–$500.

Eligibility Requirements: Applicant must be enrolled or expecting to enroll full-time at a four-year institution or university and must have an interest in writing.

Application Requirements: Applicant must enter a contest, essay. *Deadline:* April 15.

Contact: Award Director
American Society of Criminology
1314 Kinnear Road, Suite 212
Columbus, OH 43212
Phone: 614-292-9207
Fax: 614-292-6767
E-mail: asc41@compuserve.com

ASSOCIATION OF CERTIFIED FRAUD EXAMINERS http://www.cfenet.com

RITCHIE-JENNINGS MEMORIAL SCHOLARSHIP

• *See page 38*

CONNECTICUT ASSOCIATION OF WOMEN POLICE http://www.cawp.net

CONNECTICUT ASSOCIATION OF WOMEN POLICE SCHOLARSHIP

Available to Connecticut residents graduating from an accredited high school, entering a college or university in CT as a criminal justice major. The deadline is April 30.

Academic Fields/Career Goals: Criminal Justice/Criminology; Law Enforcement/Police Administration.

Award: Scholarship for use in freshman year; not renewable. *Number:* 1–3. *Amount:* $200–$500.

Eligibility Requirements: Applicant must be high school student; planning to enroll or expecting to enroll full-time at a two-year or four-year institution or university; resident of Connecticut; studying in Connecticut and must have an interest in designated field specified by sponsor. Available to U.S. citizens.

Application Requirements: Application, essay, financial need analysis, references, transcript. *Deadline:* April 30.

Contact: Application available at Web site.

FLORIDA POLICE CORPS http://www.floridapolicecorps.com

FLORIDA POLICE CORPS SCHOLARSHIPS

One-time award that covers undergraduate or graduate expenses. Requires a four-year commitment to a Florida law enforcement agency. Candidate must meet the employment standards of the agency where he or she will serve. Twenty-four week training period at Jacksonville Policy Academy.

Academic Fields/Career Goals: Criminal Justice/Criminology; Law Enforcement/Police Administration.

Award: Scholarship for use in senior year; not renewable. *Number:* 10. *Amount:* up to $15,000.

Eligibility Requirements: Applicant must be enrolled or expecting to enroll full-time at a four-year institution or university. Available to U.S. citizens.

Application Requirements: Application, driver's license, interview, photo, references, transcript. *Deadline:* Continuous.

Contact: Denise Bolton, Office Manager
Florida Police Corps
4715 Capper Road
Jacksonville, FL 32218
Phone: 904-713-4826
Fax: 904-713-4820

INDIANA SHERIFFS' ASSOCIATION

INDIANA SHERIFFS' ASSOCIATION SCHOLARSHIP PROGRAM

Applicant must be an Indiana resident majoring in a criminal justice/law enforcement field at an Indiana college or university. Must be a member or dependent child or grandchild of a member of the Indiana Sheriffs' Association. Must be a full time student with at least 12 credit hours.

Academic Fields/Career Goals: Criminal Justice/Criminology; Law Enforcement/Police Administration.

Award: Scholarship for use in freshman, sophomore, junior, or senior years; not renewable. *Number:* 40. *Amount:* $500.

Eligibility Requirements: Applicant must be enrolled or expecting to enroll full-time at a two-year or four-year institution or university; resident of Indiana and studying in Indiana. Applicant or parent of applicant must be member of Indiana Sheriffs' Association. Available to U.S. citizens.

Application Requirements: Application, essay, test scores, transcript. *Deadline:* April 1.

Contact: Laura Vest, Administrative Assistant
Indiana Sheriffs' Association
PO Box 19127
Indianapolis, IN 46219
Phone: 317-356-3633
Fax: 317-356-3996
E-mail: laura_vest@hotmail.com

MISSISSIPPI POLICE CORPS http://www.mississippipolicecorps.org

MISSISSIPPI POLICE CORPS SCHOLARSHIP

Program designed to motivate highly qualified young people to serve as police officers and sheriffs' deputies in the municipalities and counties that need them the most. Federal scholarships offered on a competitive basis to college students who agree to serve where needed on community patrol for at least four years. Participants who seek baccalaureate degrees begin their work as officers shortly after graduation from college. Those who pursue graduate study complete their service in advance. Minimum 2.50 GPA required.

Academic Fields/Career Goals: Criminal Justice/Criminology; Law Enforcement/Police Administration.

Award: Scholarship for use in senior, graduate, or postgraduate years; not renewable. *Number:* 65. *Amount:* $15,000.

Eligibility Requirements: Applicant must be enrolled or expecting to enroll full-time at a four-year institution or university. Applicant must have 2.5 GPA or higher. Available to U.S. citizens.

Application Requirements: Application, driver's license, essay, interview, resume, references, test scores, transcript. *Deadline:* Continuous.

Contact: Connie Keene, Training Specialist
Mississippi Police Corps
c/o University of Southern Mississippi
Box 5084
Hattiesburg, MS 39406-5084
Phone: 601-266-6770
Fax: 601-266-6786
E-mail: connie.keene@usm.edu

MISSOURI POLICE CORPS http://www.mocorps.org

MISSOURI POLICE CORPS FUND

The Missouri Police Corps is a scholarship program that awards its graduates up to $30,000 which can be applied to past student debt or graduate school. Applicants must be willing to serve four years as a law enforcement officer with a Missouri police or sheriff's department.

Academic Fields/Career Goals: Criminal Justice/Criminology; Law Enforcement/Police Administration.

Award: Scholarship for use in sophomore, junior, senior, or postgraduate years; renewable. *Amount:* up to $30,000.

Eligibility Requirements: Applicant must be enrolled or expecting to enroll full-time at a four-year institution or university. Available to U.S. citizens.

Application Requirements: Application, autobiography, driver's license, essay, interview, photo, resume, references, test scores, transcript. *Deadline:* varies.

Contact: Cindy Hicks, Project Coordinator
Missouri Police Corps
c/o Mineral Area College, PO Box 1000
Park Hills, MO 63601
Phone: 573-518-2179
Fax: 573-518-2326
E-mail: hicks@mocorps.org

MISSOURI SHERIFFS' ASSOCIATION

JOHN DENNIS SCHOLARSHIP

For college freshmen attending a Missouri college or university majoring in criminal justice. Award is based on financial need. Students must be in upper one-third of their graduating class and participate in extracurricular activities. Must be a Missouri resident.

Academic Fields/Career Goals: Criminal Justice/Criminology.

Award: Scholarship for use in freshman year; not renewable. *Number:* 16. *Amount:* $500.

Eligibility Requirements: Applicant must be high school student; planning to enroll or expecting to enroll full-time at a four-year institution or university; resident of Missouri and studying in Missouri. Applicant must have 3.0 GPA or higher. Available to U.S. citizens.

Application Requirements: Application, essay, financial need analysis, test scores. *Deadline:* January 31.

Contact: Karen Logan, Administrative Assistant
Missouri Sheriffs' Association
229 Madison
Jefferson City, MO 65101
Phone: 573-635-5925 Ext. 10
Fax: 573-635-2128
E-mail: karenlogan@earthlink.net

NATIONAL BLACK POLICE ASSOCIATION http://www.blackpolice.org

ALPHONSO DEAL SCHOLARSHIP AWARD

One-time award available to students interested in law enforcement or related fields. Must be a graduating high school senior accepted into a college or university and have at least a 2.5 GPA.

Academic Fields/Career Goals: Criminal Justice/Criminology; Law Enforcement/Police Administration; Law/Legal Services; Social Sciences; Social Services.

Award: Scholarship for use in freshman year; not renewable. *Number:* 2. *Amount:* $500.

Eligibility Requirements: Applicant must be high school student and planning to enroll or expecting to enroll full-time at a four-year institution or university. Applicant must have 2.5 GPA or higher. Available to U.S. citizens.

Application Requirements: Application, autobiography, references, transcript. *Deadline:* June 1.

Contact: Ronald Hampton, Executive Director
National Black Police Association
3251 Mt. Pleasant Street, NW
Washington, DC 20010
Phone: 202-986-2070
Fax: 202-986-0410
E-mail: nbpanatofc@worldnet.att.net

NORTH CAROLINA POLICE CORPS http://www.ncpolicecorps.org

NORTH CAROLINA POLICE CORPS SCHOLARSHIP

Selected participants must attend a four-year institution full-time. May receive up to $6667 per year with a maximum of $30,000. Must complete 24-week training course receiving $450 per week while in residence and serve four years in selected law enforcement agency. Must have physical, background investigation, drug test, and psychological evaluation.

Academic Fields/Career Goals: Criminal Justice/Criminology; Law Enforcement/Police Administration.

Award: Scholarship for use in freshman, sophomore, junior, senior, or graduate years; renewable. *Number:* 15–30. *Amount:* $5000–$6667.

Eligibility Requirements: Applicant must be enrolled or expecting to enroll full-time at a four-year institution or university. Available to U.S. citizens.

Application Requirements: Application, autobiography, essay, interview, photo, references, test scores, transcript. *Deadline:* November 15.

Contact: Neil Woodcock, Director, NC Police Corps
North Carolina Police Corps
NC Department of Crime Control and Public Safety, 4710 Mail Service Center
Raleigh, NC 27699-4710
Phone: 919-773-2823
Fax: 919-773-2845
E-mail: nwoodcock@ncpolicecorps.org

NORTH CAROLINA STATE EDUCATION ASSISTANCE AUTHORITY http://www.cfnc.org

NORTH CAROLINA SHERIFFS' ASSOCIATION UNDERGRADUATE CRIMINAL JUSTICE SCHOLARSHIPS

One-time award for full-time North Carolina resident undergraduate students majoring in criminal justice at a University of North Carolina school. Priority given to child of any North Carolina law enforcement officer. Letter of recommendation from county sheriff required.

Academic Fields/Career Goals: Criminal Justice/Criminology; Law Enforcement/Police Administration.

Award: Scholarship for use in freshman, sophomore, junior, or senior years; not renewable. *Number:* up to 10. *Amount:* $1000–$2000.

Eligibility Requirements: Applicant must be enrolled or expecting to enroll full-time at a four-year institution; resident of North Carolina and studying in North Carolina. Applicant or parent of applicant must have employment or volunteer experience in police/firefighting. Available to U.S. citizens.

Application Requirements: Application, essay, financial need analysis, references, transcript. *Deadline:* Continuous.

Contact: Sharon Scott, Assistant, Scholarship and Grant Division
North Carolina State Education Assistance Authority
PO Box 13663
Research Triangle Park, NC 27709-3663

CULINARY ARTS

ART INSTITUTES http://www.artinstitutes.edu

BEST TEEN CHEF CULINARY SCHOLARSHIP COMPETITION

Competition for high school seniors planning to pursue a career in culinary arts at The Art Institutes of their choice. Minimum of 10 semi-finalists will be

Art Institutes (continued)

chosen from each participating Art Institute school to compete in regional cook-offs. Winners will advance to national cook-off competition. Full and partial scholarships awarded.

Academic Fields/Career Goals: Culinary Arts.

Award: Scholarship for use in freshman, sophomore, junior, or senior years; renewable. *Number:* 10–18. *Amount:* $2000–$30,000.

Eligibility Requirements: Applicant must be high school student and planning to enroll or expecting to enroll full-time at a technical institution.

Application Requirements: Application, applicant must enter a contest, essay, transcript, menu and recipes. *Deadline:* February 14.

Contact: Julie Walsh, Admissions Department
Art Institutes
210 6th Avenue
Suite 3300
Pittsburgh, PA 15222
Phone: 800-275-2440
Fax: 412-456-2305
E-mail: webadmin@aii.edu

CAREERS THROUGH CULINARY ARTS PROGRAM, INC. http://www.ccap.org

CAREERS THROUGH CULINARY ARTS PROGRAM COOKING COMPETITION FOR SCHOLARSHIPS

Cooking competition with finalists receiving a scholarship. Must be a senior in a C-CAP-designated partner high school in Arizona, Tidewater Virginia, or the cities of Boston, Chicago, Los Angeles, New York, Philadelphia or Washington, DC. Must demonstrate mastery of select culinary skills. 25 from each area are chosen as finalists and receive scholarships ranging from $1000 to $78,000.

Academic Fields/Career Goals: Culinary Arts.

Award: Scholarship for use in freshman, sophomore, junior, or senior years; not renewable. *Number:* 88–95. *Amount:* $1000–$78,000.

Eligibility Requirements: Applicant must be high school student; planning to enroll or expecting to enroll full or part-time at a two-year or four-year or technical institution or university and resident of Arizona, California, District of Columbia, Illinois, Massachusetts, New York, Pennsylvania, or Virginia. Available to U.S. and non-U.S. citizens.

Application Requirements: Application, applicant must enter a contest, essay, interview, references, test scores, transcript, cooking competition. *Deadline:* varies.

Contact: Mei Campanella, College Advisor
Careers Through Culinary Arts Program, Inc.
250 West 57th Street, Suite 2015
New York, NY 10107
Phone: 212-974-7111
Fax: 212-974-7117
E-mail: mcampanella@ccapinc.org

CIRI FOUNDATION http://www.ciri.com/tcf

KIRBY MCDONALD EDUCATION ENDOWMENT SCHOLARSHIP FUND

• *See page 122*

ILLINOIS RESTAURANT ASSOCIATION EDUCATIONAL FOUNDATION http://www.illinoisrestaurants.org

ILLINOIS RESTAURANT ASSOCIATION EDUCATIONAL FOUNDATION SCHOLARSHIPS

Scholarship available to Illinois residents enrolled in a food service management, culinary arts, or hospitality management concentration in an accredited program of a two- or four-year college or university. Must be a U.S. citizen. Deadline is May 15.

Academic Fields/Career Goals: Culinary Arts; Food Science/Nutrition; Food Service/Hospitality; Hospitality Management.

Award: Scholarship for use in freshman, sophomore, junior, senior, graduate, or postgraduate years; not renewable. *Number:* 50–70. *Amount:* $500–$10,000.

Eligibility Requirements: Applicant must be enrolled or expecting to enroll full or part-time at a two-year or four-year or technical institution or university and resident of Illinois. Applicant or parent of applicant must have employment or volunteer experience in food service or hospitality/hotel administration/operations. Available to U.S. citizens.

Application Requirements: Application, essay, photo, references, transcript. *Deadline:* May 15.

Contact: Roxanne Charles, Program and Operations Manager
Illinois Restaurant Association Educational Foundation
200 North LaSalle, Suite 880
Chicago, IL 60601-1014
Phone: 312-787-4000
Fax: 312-787-4792
E-mail: roxannec@illinoisrestaurants.org

OREGON STUDENT ASSISTANCE COMMISSION http://www.osac.state.or.us

OREGON WINE BROTHERHOOD SCHOLARSHIP

One-time award for students majoring in oenology, viticulture, or culinary arts with an emphasis on wine. Must attend Chemeketa Community College, Oregon State University, or University of California, Davis. Minimum 3.0 GPA. Application deadline is March 1.

Academic Fields/Career Goals: Culinary Arts; Food Science/Nutrition.

Award: Scholarship for use in freshman, sophomore, junior, or senior years; not renewable. *Number:* varies. *Amount:* $500.

Eligibility Requirements: Applicant must be enrolled or expecting to enroll at a two-year institution or university; resident of Oregon and studying in California or Oregon. Applicant must have 3.0 GPA or higher.

Application Requirements: Application, essay, financial need analysis, transcript. *Deadline:* March 1.

Contact: Director of Grant Programs
Oregon Student Assistance Commission
1500 Valley River Drive, Suite 100
Eugene, OR 97401-7020
Phone: 800-452-8807 Ext. 7395
E-mail: awardinfo@mercury.osac.state.or.us

DENTAL HEALTH/SERVICES

ALBERTA HERITAGE SCHOLARSHIP FUND/ ALBERTA SCHOLARSHIP PROGRAMS http://www.alis.gov.ab.ca/scholarships

ALBERTA HERITAGE SCHOLARSHIP FUND ABORIGINAL HEALTH CAREERS BURSARY

• *See page 111*

AMERICAN ACADEMY OF ORAL AND MAXILLOFACIAL RADIOLOGY http://www.aaomr.org

CHARLES R. MORRIS STUDENT RESEARCH AWARD

One-time award plus additional benefits for dental or dental hygiene students who present the results of research in oral and maxillofacial radiology conducted while a full-time student.

Academic Fields/Career Goals: Dental Health/Services.

Award: Grant for use in junior, senior, or graduate years; not renewable. *Number:* 1. *Amount:* $1000.

Eligibility Requirements: Applicant must be enrolled or expecting to enroll full-time at a four-year institution or university. Available to U.S. and non-U.S. citizens.

Application Requirements: Application, references, manuscript. *Deadline:* June 16.

Contact: Dr. J. Sean Hubar
American Academy of Oral and Maxillofacial Radiology
LSU School of Dentistry, 1100 Florida Avenue
New Orleans, LA 70119
Phone: 504-619-8623
Fax: 504-619-8741
E-mail: jhubar@lsumc.edu

AMERICAN DENTAL ASSISTANTS ASSOCIATION

JULIETTE A. SOUTHARD/ORAL B LABORATORIES SCHOLARSHIP

Leadership-based award available to students enrolled in an ADAA dental assistant's program. Proof of acceptance into ADAA program and two letters of reference are required. ADAA membership required.

Academic Fields/Career Goals: Dental Health/Services.

Award: Scholarship for use in freshman, sophomore, junior, or senior years; not renewable. *Number:* 10. *Amount:* $500.

Eligibility Requirements: Applicant must be enrolled or expecting to enroll full or part-time at an institution or university and must have an interest in leadership. Applicant or parent of applicant must be member of American Dental Assistants Association. Available to U.S. citizens.

Application Requirements: Application, essay, financial need analysis, references, transcript. *Deadline:* January 31.

Contact: Dennis Marrell, Staff Assistant
American Dental Assistants Association
35 East Wacker Drive, Suite 1730
Chicago, IL 60601
Phone: 312-541-1550 Ext. 200
Fax: 312-541-1496
E-mail: adaa1@aol.com

AMERICAN DENTAL ASSOCIATION (ADA) FOUNDATION http://www.adafoundation.org

AMERICAN DENTAL ASSOCIATION FOUNDATION DENTAL ASSISTING SCHOLARSHIP PROGRAM

Applicant must be enrolled full-time with a minimum of twelve hours as an entering student in an accredited dental assistant program. Submit autobiographical sketch. Must be a U.S. citizen and have at least a 3.0 GPA on a 4.0 scale. One-time award of $1000. Applicant may obtain application materials from financial aid officer of school where he or she is currently enrolled.

Academic Fields/Career Goals: Dental Health/Services.

Award: Scholarship for use in freshman year; not renewable. *Number:* varies. *Amount:* $1000.

Eligibility Requirements: Applicant must be enrolled or expecting to enroll full-time at a two-year or technical institution. Applicant must have 3.0 GPA or higher. Available to U.S. citizens.

Application Requirements: Application, autobiography, essay, financial need analysis, references. *Deadline:* September 15.

Contact: Rose L. Famularo
American Dental Association (ADA) Foundation
211 East Chicago Avenue, 12th Floor
Chicago, IL 60611

AMERICAN DENTAL ASSOCIATION FOUNDATION DENTAL HYGIENE SCHOLARSHIP PROGRAM

Must be enrolled full-time with a minimum of twelve hours as a final-year student at an accredited dental hygiene program. Must be U.S. citizen with minimum 3.0 GPA on a 4.0 scale. Submit autobiographical statement. Applicant may obtain application materials from financial aid officer of school he or she is currently enrolled.

Academic Fields/Career Goals: Dental Health/Services.

Award: Scholarship for use in senior year; not renewable. *Number:* varies. *Amount:* $1000.

Eligibility Requirements: Applicant must be enrolled or expecting to enroll full-time at a two-year or four-year institution or university. Applicant must have 3.0 GPA or higher. Available to U.S. citizens.

Application Requirements: Application, autobiography, essay, financial need analysis, references. *Deadline:* August 15.

Contact: Rose Famularo
American Dental Association (ADA) Foundation
211 East Chicago Avenue, 12th Floor
Chicago, IL 60611

AMERICAN DENTAL ASSOCIATION FOUNDATION DENTAL LAB TECHNOLOGY SCHOLARSHIP

Must be enrolled full-time with a minimum of twelve hours as a last-year student at an accredited dental laboratory technology program. Must be U.S. citizen with a minimum 3.0 GPA on a 4.0 scale. Submit autobiographical statement. Applicant may obtain application materials from financial aid officer of school he or she is currently enrolled.

Academic Fields/Career Goals: Dental Health/Services.

Award: Scholarship for use in senior year; not renewable. *Number:* varies. *Amount:* $1000.

Eligibility Requirements: Applicant must be enrolled or expecting to enroll full-time at a two-year or four-year or technical institution. Applicant must have 3.0 GPA or higher. Available to U.S. citizens.

Application Requirements: Application, autobiography, essay, financial need analysis, references. *Deadline:* August 15.

Contact: Rose Famularo
American Dental Association (ADA) Foundation
211 East Chicago Avenue, 12th Floor
Chicago, IL 60611

AMERICAN DENTAL HYGIENISTS' ASSOCIATION (ADHA) INSTITUTE http://www.adha.org

ADHA INSTITUTE GENERAL SCHOLARSHIPS

One-time award to students enrolled in an accredited dental hygiene program in the United States. Must be a full-time student with a minimum 3.0 GPA and completed one year in a dental hygiene curriculum. Submit a Career Goals statements. Must enclose a copy of SADHA or ADHA membership card with application. Merit scholarships also awarded. Please refer to Web site for further details http://www.adha.org

Academic Fields/Career Goals: Dental Health/Services.

Award: Scholarship for use in sophomore, junior, senior, or graduate years; not renewable. *Number:* up to 34. *Amount:* up to $2000.

Eligibility Requirements: Applicant must be enrolled or expecting to enroll full-time at a two-year or four-year institution or university. Applicant or parent of applicant must be member of American Dental Hygienist's Association. Applicant must have 3.0 GPA or higher. Available to U.S. citizens.

Application Requirements: Application, financial need analysis, references. *Deadline:* May 1.

Contact: Scholarship Information
American Dental Hygienists' Association (ADHA) Institute
444 North Michigan Avenue, Suite 3400
Chicago, IL 60611
Phone: 800-735-4916
Fax: 312-467-1806
E-mail: institute@adha.net

AMERICAN DENTAL HYGIENISTS' ASSOCIATION INSTITUTE MINORITY SCHOLARSHIP

Nonrenewable awards for member of minority groups currently underrepresented in dental hygiene, including males. Must have a minimum 3.0 GPA, have completed one year of a dental hygiene curriculum, and show financial need of at least $1500. ADHA of SADHA membership required. Must be a U.S. citizen. Please refer to Web site for details http://www.adha.org

Academic Fields/Career Goals: Dental Health/Services.

Award: Scholarship for use in sophomore, junior, senior, or graduate years; not renewable. *Number:* 2. *Amount:* $1500–$2000.

Eligibility Requirements: Applicant must be American Indian/Alaska Native, Asian/Pacific Islander, Black (non-Hispanic), or Hispanic and enrolled or expecting to enroll full-time at a two-year or four-year institution or university. Applicant or parent of applicant must be member of American Dental Hygienist's Association. Applicant must have 3.0 GPA or higher. Available to U.S. citizens.

Application Requirements: Application, financial need analysis, references. *Deadline:* May 1.

Contact: Scholarship Information
American Dental Hygienists' Association (ADHA) Institute
444 North Michigan Avenue, Suite 3400
Chicago, IL 60611

AMERICAN DENTAL HYGIENISTS' ASSOCIATION PART-TIME SCHOLARSHIP

Awarded to a dental student pursuing a certificate, associate, baccalaureate, or graduate degree on a part-time basis. Minimum 3.0 GPA required. Submit application and financial need analysis form. ADHA membership required. Eligible after freshman year. Must be a U.S. citizen. Please refer to Web site for further details http://www.adha.org

Academic Fields/Career Goals: Dental Health/Services.

Award: Scholarship for use in sophomore, junior, senior, or graduate years; not renewable. *Number:* 1. *Amount:* $1500.

Eligibility Requirements: Applicant must be enrolled or expecting to enroll part-time at a two-year or four-year institution or university. Applicant or parent of applicant must be member of American Dental Hygienist's Association. Applicant must have 3.0 GPA or higher. Available to U.S. citizens.

Application Requirements: Application, financial need analysis, references. *Deadline:* May 1.

Contact: Scholarship Information
American Dental Hygienists' Association (ADHA) Institute
444 North Michigan Avenue, Suite 3400
Chicago, IL 60611

COLGATE "BRIGHT SMILES, BRIGHT FUTURES" MINORITY SCHOLARSHIP

One-time award to a member of a minority group currently underrepresented in dental hygiene programs, including men. Minimum 3.0 GPA required. For use after first year of study. ADHA or SADHA membership required. Must be a U.S. citizen. Please refer to Web site for further details http://www.adha.org

Academic Fields/Career Goals: Dental Health/Services.

Award: Scholarship for use in sophomore, junior, or senior years; not renewable. *Number:* 2. *Amount:* $1500.

Eligibility Requirements: Applicant must be American Indian/Alaska Native, Asian/Pacific Islander, Black (non-Hispanic), or Hispanic and enrolled or expecting to enroll full-time at a two-year or four-year institution or university. Applicant or parent of applicant must be member of American Dental Hygienist's Association. Applicant must have 3.0 GPA or higher. Available to U.S. citizens.

Application Requirements: Application, financial need analysis, references. *Deadline:* May 1.

Contact: Scholarship Information
American Dental Hygienists' Association (ADHA) Institute
444 North Michigan Avenue, Suite 3400
Chicago, IL 60611

DR. HAROLD HILLENBRAND SCHOLARSHIP

Awarded to a candidate who demonstrates specific academic excellence and outstanding clinical performance, in addition to having a minimum dental hygiene cumulative GPA of 3.5. Must demonstrate financial need of at least $1500. One-time award. ADHA membership required. Must be a U.S. citizen. Please refer to Web site for further details http://www.adha.org

Academic Fields/Career Goals: Dental Health/Services.

Award: Scholarship for use in sophomore, junior, or senior years; not renewable. *Number:* 1. *Amount:* $1500.

Eligibility Requirements: Applicant must be enrolled or expecting to enroll full-time at a two-year or four-year institution or university. Applicant or parent of applicant must be member of American Dental Hygienist's Association. Applicant must have 3.5 GPA or higher. Available to U.S. citizens.

Application Requirements: Application, financial need analysis, references. *Deadline:* May 1.

Contact: Scholarship Information
American Dental Hygienists' Association (ADHA) Institute
444 North Michigan Avenue, Suite 3400
Chicago, IL 60611

IRENE E. NEWMAN SCHOLARSHIP

One-time award to a candidate who has three years of a bachelor's degree in dental hygiene completed or is currently enrolled in a graduate degree program, and demonstrates potential in public health or community dental health. 3.0 GPA required. ADHA membership required. Must be a U.S. citizen. Please refer to Web site for further details http://www.adha.org

Academic Fields/Career Goals: Dental Health/Services.

Award: Scholarship for use in senior, or graduate years; not renewable. *Number:* 1. *Amount:* $1500.

Eligibility Requirements: Applicant must be enrolled or expecting to enroll full-time at a four-year institution or university. Applicant or parent of applicant must be member of American Dental Hygienist's Association. Applicant must have 3.0 GPA or higher. Available to U.S. citizens.

Application Requirements: Application, financial need analysis, references. *Deadline:* May 1.

Contact: Scholarship Information
American Dental Hygienists' Association (ADHA) Institute
444 North Michigan Avenue, Suite 3400
Chicago, IL 60611

MARGARET E. SWANSON SCHOLARSHIP

Awarded to a candidate who is pursuing a dental career and who demonstrates exceptional organizational leadership potential. Award is merit-based. Freshmen are not eligible. One-time award of up to $1500. Minimum 3.0 GPA required. ADHA membership required. Must be a U.S. citizen. Please refer to Web site for further details http://www.adha.org

Academic Fields/Career Goals: Dental Health/Services.

Award: Scholarship for use in sophomore, junior, senior, or graduate years; not renewable. *Number:* 1. *Amount:* up to $1500.

Eligibility Requirements: Applicant must be enrolled or expecting to enroll full-time at a two-year or four-year institution or university and must have an interest in leadership. Applicant or parent of applicant must be member of American Dental Hygienist's Association. Applicant must have 3.0 GPA or higher. Available to U.S. citizens.

Application Requirements: Application, financial need analysis, references. *Deadline:* May 1.

Contact: Scholarship Information
American Dental Hygienists' Association (ADHA) Institute
444 North Michigan Avenue, Suite 3400
Chicago, IL 60611

MARSH AFFINITY GROUP SERVICES SCHOLARSHIP

One-time award to full-time student pursuing a baccalaureate degree in dental hygiene. Minimum 3.0 GPA required. Sponsored by Marsh Affinity Group Services, a service of Seabury and Smith. Must submit a copy of SADHA or ADHA membership card with application. Please refer to Web site for further details http://www.adha.org

Academic Fields/Career Goals: Dental Health/Services.

Award: Scholarship for use in sophomore, junior, or senior years; not renewable. *Amount:* up to $2000.

Eligibility Requirements: Applicant must be enrolled or expecting to enroll full-time at a four-year institution or university. Applicant or parent of applicant must be member of American Dental Hygienist's Association. Applicant must have 3.0 GPA or higher. Available to U.S. citizens.

Application Requirements: Application, essay, financial need analysis, references. *Deadline:* May 1.

Contact: Scholarship Information
American Dental Hygienists' Association (ADHA) Institute
444 North Michigan Avenue, Suite 3400
Chicago, IL 60611
Phone: 800-735-4916
Fax: 312-467-1806
E-mail: institute@adha.net

ORAL-B LABORATORIES DENTAL HYGIENE SCHOLARSHIP

One-time award to full-time student at the baccalaureate degree level who demonstrates an intent to encourage professional excellence and scholarship, promote quality research, and support dental hygiene through public and private education. Minimum 3.5 GPA required. Sponsored by Oral-B

Laboratories. Must submit a copy of SADHA or ADHA membership card with application. Please refer to Web site for further details http://www.adha.org

Academic Fields/Career Goals: Dental Health/Services.

Award: Scholarship for use in sophomore, junior, or senior years; not renewable. *Number:* 2. *Amount:* up to $2000.

Eligibility Requirements: Applicant must be enrolled or expecting to enroll full-time at a four-year institution or university. Applicant or parent of applicant must be member of American Dental Hygienist's Association. Applicant must have 3.5 GPA or higher. Available to U.S. citizens.

Application Requirements: Application, essay, financial need analysis, references. *Deadline:* May 1.

Contact: Scholarship Information
American Dental Hygienists' Association (ADHA) Institute
444 North Michigan Avenue, Suite 3400
Chicago, IL 60611
Phone: 800-735-4916
Fax: 312-467-1806
E-mail: institute@adha.net

SIGMA PHI ALPHA UNDERGRADUATE SCHOLARSHIP

Awarded to an outstanding candidate who is pursuing an associate certificate or baccalaureate degree in dental hygiene at an accredited dental hygiene school with an active chapter of Sigma Phi Alpha Dental Hygiene Honor Society. One-time award. Minimum 3.5 GPA required. ADHA membership required. Must be a U.S. citizen. Please refer to Web site for further details http://www.adha.org

Academic Fields/Career Goals: Dental Health/Services.

Award: Scholarship for use in sophomore, junior, or senior years; not renewable. *Number:* 1. *Amount:* $1000.

Eligibility Requirements: Applicant must be enrolled or expecting to enroll full-time at a two-year or four-year institution. Applicant or parent of applicant must be member of American Dental Hygienist's Association. Applicant must have 3.5 GPA or higher. Available to U.S. citizens.

Application Requirements: Application, financial need analysis, references, transcript. *Deadline:* May 1.

Contact: Scholarship Information
American Dental Hygienists' Association (ADHA) Institute
444 North Michigan Avenue, Suite 3400
Chicago, IL 60611

WILMA MOTLEY CALIFORNIA MERIT SCHOLARSHIP

One-time award to full-time students pursuing an associate/certificate or baccalaureate degree in an accredited dental hygiene program within the state of California. Must demonstrate leadership experience. Minimum 3.5 GPA required. Award is based on merit. Must submit a copy of SADHA or ADHA membership card with application. Please refer to Web site for further details http://www.adha.org

Academic Fields/Career Goals: Dental Health/Services.

Award: Scholarship for use in sophomore, junior, or senior years; not renewable. *Number:* 1. *Amount:* up to $2000.

Eligibility Requirements: Applicant must be enrolled or expecting to enroll full-time at a two-year or four-year institution or university and studying in California. Applicant or parent of applicant must be member of American Dental Hygienist's Association. Applicant must have 3.5 GPA or higher. Available to U.S. citizens.

Application Requirements: Application, references. *Deadline:* May 1.

Contact: Scholarship Information
American Dental Hygienists' Association (ADHA) Institute
444 North Michigan Avenue, Suite 3400
Chicago, IL 60611
Phone: 800-735-4916
Fax: 312-467-1806
E-mail: institute@adha.net

AMERICAN LEGION AUXILIARY, DEPARTMENT OF WYOMING

PAST PRESIDENTS PARLEY HEALTH CARE SCHOLARSHIP

Scholarship available for student in the human health care field. Must be a resident of Wyoming, a U.S. citizen, and attend a school in Wyoming. Minimum 3.5 GPA required. Deadline for application is June 1.

Academic Fields/Career Goals: Dental Health/Services; Health and Medical Sciences; Nursing; Therapy/Rehabilitation.

Award: Scholarship for use in sophomore year; not renewable. *Number:* 1–2. *Amount:* $300.

Eligibility Requirements: Applicant must be enrolled or expecting to enroll full-time at a two-year or four-year or technical institution or university; resident of Wyoming and studying in Wyoming. Applicant must have 3.5 GPA or higher. Available to U.S. citizens.

Application Requirements: Application, applicant must enter a contest, financial need analysis, transcript. *Deadline:* June 1.

Contact: Department Secretary
American Legion Auxiliary, Department of Wyoming
PO Box 2198
Gillette, WY 82717

AMERICAN MEDICAL TECHNOLOGISTS

http://www.amt1.com

AMERICAN MEDICAL TECHNOLOGISTS STUDENT SCHOLARSHIP

One-time award for the undergraduate study of medical technology, medical laboratory technician, office laboratory technician, phlebotomy, or medical, dental assisting. Must attend an accredited institution. Preference to those with financial need. To request application write to AMT stating educational interest/goal. Include SASE. Deadline: April 1.

Academic Fields/Career Goals: Dental Health/Services; Health and Medical Sciences.

Award: Scholarship for use in freshman, sophomore, junior, or senior years; not renewable. *Number:* 5. *Amount:* $500.

Eligibility Requirements: Applicant must be enrolled or expecting to enroll at a four-year institution or university. Available to U.S. citizens.

Application Requirements: Application, essay, financial need analysis, references, self-addressed stamped envelope, transcript. *Deadline:* April 1.

Contact: Linda Kujbida, Scholarship Coordinator
American Medical Technologists
710 Higgins Road
Park Ridge, IL 60068-5765

ARKANSAS DEPARTMENT OF HIGHER EDUCATION

http://www.arscholarships.com

ARKANSAS HEALTH EDUCATION GRANT PROGRAM (ARHEG)

• *See page 62*

BECA FOUNDATION, INC.

ALICE NEWELL JOSLYN MEDICAL FUND

Scholarships to full-time Latino students entering the medical/health care profession and living or attending college in San Diego County. Financial need, scholastic determination, and community/cultural awareness are considered. Awarded for four years annually contingent on scholastic progress.

Academic Fields/Career Goals: Dental Health/Services; Health and Medical Sciences; Nursing; Therapy/Rehabilitation.

Award: Scholarship for use in freshman, sophomore, junior, senior, or graduate years; renewable. *Number:* varies. *Amount:* $1000–$2000.

Eligibility Requirements: Applicant must be of Hispanic heritage and enrolled or expecting to enroll full-time at a four-year institution or university. Applicant must have 2.5 GPA or higher. Available to U.S. citizens.

BECA Foundation, Inc. (continued)

Application Requirements: Application, essay, financial need analysis, references, transcript. *Deadline:* March 1.

Contact: Ana Garcia, Operations Manager
BECA Foundation, Inc.
830 East Grand Avenue
Suite B
Escondido, CA 92025
Phone: 760-741-8246

BETHESDA LUTHERAN HOMES AND SERVICES, INC. http://www.blhs.org

DEVELOPMENTAL DISABILITIES SCHOLASTIC ACHIEVEMENT SCHOLARSHIP FOR LUTHERAN COLLEGE STUDENTS

One-time award for Lutheran college students who have completed sophomore year in studies related to developmental disabilities. Awards of up to $1500. 3.0 GPA required.

Academic Fields/Career Goals: Dental Health/Services; Education; Health Administration; Health and Medical Sciences; Health Information Management/Technology; Humanities; Social Services; Special Education; Therapy/Rehabilitation.

Award: Scholarship for use in junior or senior years; not renewable. *Number:* 1–3. *Amount:* up to $1500.

Eligibility Requirements: Applicant must be Lutheran and enrolled or expecting to enroll full-time at a four-year institution or university. Applicant must have 3.0 GPA or higher. Available to U.S. and Canadian citizens.

Application Requirements: Application, autobiography, essay, references, transcript. *Deadline:* March 15.

Contact: Thomas Heuer, Coordinator, Outreach Programs and Services
Bethesda Lutheran Homes and Services, Inc.
National Christian Resource Center, 600 Hoffmann Drive
Watertown, WI 53094-6294
Phone: 920-261-3050 Ext. 4449
Fax: 920-262-6513
E-mail: theuer@blhs.org

BUSINESS AND PROFESSIONAL WOMEN'S FOUNDATION http://www.bpwusa.org

BPW CAREER ADVANCEMENT SCHOLARSHIP PROGRAM FOR WOMEN

• *See page 112*

FLORIDA DENTAL HEALTH FOUNDATION http://www.floridadental.org

DENTAL ASSISTING SCHOLARSHIPS

One-time award for dental assistant study. Must be resident of Florida for at least three years. Must have minimum 2.5 GPA and references from an accredited dental assistant's school. Application available on Web site.

Academic Fields/Career Goals: Dental Health/Services.

Award: Scholarship for use in freshman, sophomore, junior, or senior years; not renewable. *Number:* 10–15. *Amount:* $100–$400.

Eligibility Requirements: Applicant must be enrolled or expecting to enroll full or part-time at a two-year or technical institution; resident of Florida and studying in Florida. Applicant must have 2.5 GPA or higher. Available to U.S. citizens.

Application Requirements: Application, references, transcript. *Deadline:* Continuous.

Contact: Cheri Sutherland, Secretary
Florida Dental Health Foundation
1111 East Tennessee Street
Tallahassee, FL 32308-6914
Phone: 850-681-3629 Ext. 119
Fax: 850-681-0116
E-mail: csutherland@floridadental.org

DENTAL HYGIENE SCHOLARSHIPS

Award for dental hygienist study. Must have minimum 2.5 GPA. Must be Florida resident for at least three years. Application deadlines are May 1 for fall awards, and November 1 for spring awards. May reapply. Application available on Web site. (http://www.floridadental.org)

Academic Fields/Career Goals: Dental Health/Services.

Award: Scholarship for use in freshman or sophomore years; not renewable. *Number:* 15–20. *Amount:* $200–$500.

Eligibility Requirements: Applicant must be enrolled or expecting to enroll full or part-time at a two-year or technical institution; resident of Florida and studying in Florida. Applicant must have 2.5 GPA or higher. Available to U.S. citizens.

Application Requirements: Application, references, transcript. *Deadline:* varies.

Contact: Cheri Sutherland, Secretary
Florida Dental Health Foundation
1111 East Tennessee Street
Tallahassee, FL 32308-6914
Phone: 850-681-3629 Ext. 119
Fax: 850-681-0116
E-mail: csutherland@floridadental.org

HAWAIIAN LODGE, F.& A. M. http://www.hawaiianlodge.org/

HAWAIIAN LODGE SCHOLARSHIPS

• *See page 76*

HEALTH PROFESSIONS EDUCATION FOUNDATION http://www.healthprofessions.ca.gov

HEALTH PROFESSIONS EDUCATION SCHOLARSHIP PROGRAM

The scholarship is awarded to students pursuing a career as a dentist, dental hygienist, nurse practitioner, certified nurse midwife, or physician assistant. Eligible scholarship applicants may receive $10,000 per year in financial assistance. Applicants must agree to practice in a medically underserved area of California for a minimum of two years. Deadline: March 24. Must be a resident of CA and U.S. citizen. Minimum 2.0 GPA.

Academic Fields/Career Goals: Dental Health/Services; Health and Medical Sciences; Nursing.

Award: Scholarship for use in senior, graduate, or postgraduate years; not renewable. *Number:* 10–15. *Amount:* $5000–$10,000.

Eligibility Requirements: Applicant must be enrolled or expecting to enroll full or part-time at an institution or university; resident of California and studying in California. Available to U.S. citizens.

Application Requirements: Application, driver's license, financial need analysis, references, transcript. *Deadline:* March 24.

Contact: Sondra Jacobs, Program Officer
Health Professions Education Foundation
818 K Street, Suite 210
Sacramento, CA 95814
Phone: 916-324-6500

HISPANIC DENTAL ASSOCIATION http://www.hdassoc.org

DR. JUAN D. VILLARREAL/ HISPANIC DENTAL ASSOCIATION FOUNDATION

Scholarship offered to Hispanic U.S. students who have been accepted into or are currently enrolled in an accredited dental or dental hygiene program in the state of Texas. The awarding of these scholarships will obligate the grantees to complete the current year of their dental or dental hygiene program. Scholastic achievement, leadership skills, community service, and commitment to improving the health of the Hispanic community will all be considered. Deadlines are July 1 for dental students and July 15 for dental hygiene students.

Academic Fields/Career Goals: Dental Health/Services.

Award: Scholarship for use in freshman, sophomore, junior, or senior years; not renewable. *Number:* varies. *Amount:* $500–$1000.

Eligibility Requirements: Applicant must be of Hispanic heritage; enrolled or expecting to enroll full-time at a two-year or four-year institution; resident of Texas and studying in Texas. Available to U.S. citizens.

Application Requirements: Application, transcript. *Deadline:* varies.

Contact: Liz Valdivia, Office Manager
Hispanic Dental Association
188 West Randolph Street, Suite 415
Chicago, IL 60601
Phone: 312-577-4013
Fax: 312-577-0052
E-mail: lizvaldivia-hda@qwest.net

PROCTOR AND GAMBLE ORAL CARE AND HDA FOUNDATION SCHOLARSHIP

Scholarships available to Hispanic students entering into their first year of an accredited dental, dental hygiene, dental assisting, or dental technician program. Scholastic achievement, community service, leadership, and commitment to improving health of the Hispanic community will all be considered. Deadlines July 1 for dental students, and July 15 for dental hygiene students.

Academic Fields/Career Goals: Dental Health/Services.

Award: Scholarship for use in freshman year; not renewable. *Number:* varies. *Amount:* $500–$1000.

Eligibility Requirements: Applicant must be Hispanic and enrolled or expecting to enroll full-time at a two-year or four-year or technical institution or university. Applicant must have 3.0 GPA or higher. Available to U.S. citizens.

Application Requirements: Application, transcript. *Deadline:* varies.

Contact: Liz Valdivia, Office Manager
Hispanic Dental Association
188 West Randolph Street
Suite 1811
Chicago, IL 60601-3001
Phone: 800-952-7921
Fax: 312-577-0052
E-mail: hdassoc1@qwest.net

TRIDENT/HDA FOUNDATION SCHOLARSHIP PROGRAM

Scholarships available to all Hispanic U.S. citizens who have been accepted or are presently enrolled in an accredited dental or dental hygiene program. Must have a 3.0 GPA. Commitment and dedication to improving health in the Hispanic community. Deadline is July 1 for dental students and July 15 for dental hygiene students.

Academic Fields/Career Goals: Dental Health/Services.

Award: Scholarship for use in freshman, sophomore, junior, senior, or graduate years; not renewable. *Number:* varies. *Amount:* $1500.

Eligibility Requirements: Applicant must be Hispanic and enrolled or expecting to enroll full-time at a two-year or four-year or technical institution or university. Applicant must have 3.0 GPA or higher. Available to U.S. citizens.

Application Requirements: Application, transcript. *Deadline:* varies.

Contact: Liz Valdivia, Office Manager
Hispanic Dental Association
188 West Randolph Street
Suite 1811
Chicago, IL 60601-3001
Phone: 800-952-7921
Fax: 312-577-0052
E-mail: hdassoc1@qwest.net

INDIAN HEALTH SERVICES, UNITED STATES DEPARTMENT OF HEALTH AND HUMAN SERVICES http://www.ihs.gov

INDIAN HEALTH SERVICE HEALTH PROFESSIONS PRE-GRADUATE SCHOLARSHIPS

Renewable scholarship available to Native-American students. Minimum 2.0 GPA required. Award averages $18,500. New applicants must first submit to Area Scholarship Coordinator. Must enroll in courses leading to a bachelor degree in the areas of pre-medicine or pre-dentistry, and intend to serve Indian people upon completion of professional healthcare education. Priority is given to students in their junior and senior years. Contact office for more information.

Academic Fields/Career Goals: Dental Health/Services; Health and Medical Sciences.

Award: Scholarship for use in freshman, sophomore, junior, or senior years; renewable. *Number:* varies. *Amount:* $18,500.

Eligibility Requirements: Applicant must be American Indian/Alaska Native and enrolled or expecting to enroll full or part-time at a two-year or four-year or technical institution or university. Available to U.S. citizens.

Application Requirements: Application, applicant must enter a contest, essay, references, transcript, proof of descent. *Deadline:* February 28.

Contact: Jeff Brien, Acting Chief, Scholarship Branch
Indian Health Services, United States Department of Health and Human Services
801 Thompson Avenue, Suite 120
Rockville, MD 20852
Phone: 301-443-6197
Fax: 301-443-6048

INTERNATIONAL ORDER OF THE KING'S DAUGHTERS AND SONS http://www.iokds.org

HEALTH CAREERS SCHOLARSHIP

Award for students preparing for careers in medicine, dentistry, pharmacy, physical or occupational therapy, and medical technologies. Student must be a U.S. or Canadian citizen, enrolled full-time in a school accredited in the field involved and located in the U.S. or Canada. For all students, except those preparing for an RN degree, application must be for at least the third year of college. RN students must have completed the first year of schooling. Pre-medicine students are not eligible to apply. For those students seeking degrees of MD or DDS application must be for at least the second year of medical or dental school. Each applicant must supply proof of acceptance in the school involved. There is no age limit.

Academic Fields/Career Goals: Dental Health/Services; Health and Medical Sciences; Nursing; Therapy/Rehabilitation.

Award: Scholarship for use in sophomore, junior, or senior years; not renewable. *Number:* 40–50. *Amount:* $500–$1000.

Eligibility Requirements: Applicant must be enrolled or expecting to enroll full-time at an institution or university. Available to U.S. and Canadian citizens.

Application Requirements: Application, photo, resume, references, self-addressed stamped envelope, transcript, itemized budget. *Deadline:* April 1.

Contact: Director, Health Careers Department
International Order of the King's Daughters and Sons
PO Box 1017
Chautauqua, NY 14722-1017
Phone: 716-357-4951

JEWISH FEDERATION OF METROPOLITAN CHICAGO (JFMC) http://www.jvschicago.org

JEWISH FEDERATION OF METROPOLITAN CHICAGO ACADEMIC SCHOLARSHIP PROGRAM

Available for Jewish students only in the Chicago metropolitan area. Award available for undergraduates who have entered their junior year in career-specific programs which require no postgraduate education for professional level employment, or students enrolled in graduate or professional school. Students in a vocational program with a specific educational goal in the helping professions also are eligible.

Academic Fields/Career Goals: Dental Health/Services; Education; Engineering/Technology; Health and Medical Sciences; Law/Legal Services; Physical Sciences and Math; Psychology; Religion/Theology; Social Services.

Award: Scholarship for use in junior, senior, or graduate years; renewable. *Number:* 75. *Amount:* $5000.

Eligibility Requirements: Applicant must be Jewish; enrolled or expecting to enroll full-time at a four-year institution or university and resident of Illinois. Available to U.S. and non-U.S. citizens.

Jewish Federation of Metropolitan Chicago (JFMC) (continued)

Application Requirements: Application, essay, financial need analysis, interview, references, transcript. *Deadline:* March 1.

Contact: Lea Gruhn, Scholarship Secretary
Jewish Federation of Metropolitan Chicago (JFMC)
216 West Jackson Boulevard, Suite 700
Chicago, IL 60606
Phone: 312-673-3457
Fax: 312-553-5544
E-mail: jvsscholarship@jvschicago.org

JEWISH FOUNDATION FOR EDUCATION OF WOMEN http://www.jfew.org

SCHOLARSHIP PROGRAM FOR FORMER SOVIET UNION EMIGRES TRAINING IN THE HEALTH SCIENCES

Scholarships for female émigrés from the former Soviet Union who are studying for careers in medicine, dentistry, dental hygiene, nursing, pharmacy, occupational therapy, physician assistant programs, and physical therapy. Must live within 50 miles of New York City. Must demonstrate financial need and a good academic record.

Academic Fields/Career Goals: Dental Health/Services; Health and Medical Sciences; Nursing; Therapy/Rehabilitation.

Award: Scholarship for use in freshman, sophomore, junior, senior, or graduate years; renewable. *Number:* varies. *Amount:* $5000.

Eligibility Requirements: Applicant must be of former Soviet Union heritage; enrolled or expecting to enroll full-time at a four-year institution or university; female and resident of Connecticut, New Jersey, or New York. Available to U.S. and non-Canadian citizens.

Application Requirements: Application, financial need analysis, transcript. *Deadline:* varies.

Contact: Marge Goldwater, Executive Director
Jewish Foundation for Education of Women
135 East 64th Street
New York, NY 10021
Phone: 212-288-3931
Fax: 212-288-5798
E-mail: fdnscholar@aol.com

MARIN EDUCATION FUND http://www.marineducationfund.org

GOLDMAN FAMILY FUND, NEW LEADER SCHOLARSHIP

Applicant for scholarship must attend one of the Bay Area public universities (California State University, Howard; San Francisco State University; San Jose State University; Sonoma State University; University of California at Berkeley). Must be studying social sciences, human services, health-related fields, or public service and have completed at least 30 hours at that university. Must be upper division student, demonstrate financial need and high academic achievement. Preference given to women, recent immigrants, and students of color. Minimum 3.2 GPA required.

Academic Fields/Career Goals: Dental Health/Services; Food Science/Nutrition; Health Administration; Health and Medical Sciences; Health Information Management/Technology; Nursing; Social Sciences; Social Services; Therapy/Rehabilitation.

Award: Scholarship for use in junior or senior years; renewable. *Amount:* $5000.

Eligibility Requirements: Applicant must be enrolled or expecting to enroll full or part-time at an institution or university and studying in California. Available to U.S. and non-U.S. citizens.

Application Requirements: Application, financial need analysis, interview, transcript, proof of enrollment. *Deadline:* March 15.

Contact: Marin Education Fund
1010 B Street, Suite 300
San Rafael, CA 94901
Phone: 415-459-4240
Fax: 415-459-0527
E-mail: info@marineducationfund.org

MARYLAND ASSOCIATION OF PRIVATE COLLEGES AND CAREER SCHOOLS http://www.mapccs.org

MARYLAND ASSOCIATION OF PRIVATE COLLEGES AND CAREER SCHOOLS SCHOLARSHIP

• *See page 127*

MARYLAND HIGHER EDUCATION COMMISSION http://www.mhec.state.md.us

GRADUATE AND PROFESSIONAL SCHOLARSHIP PROGRAM-MARYLAND

Graduate and professional scholarships provide need-based financial assistance to students attending a Maryland school of medicine, dentistry, law, pharmacy, social work, or nursing. Funds are provided to specific Maryland colleges and universities. Students must demonstrate financial need and be Maryland residents. Contact institution financial aid office for more information.

Academic Fields/Career Goals: Dental Health/Services; Health and Medical Sciences; Law/Legal Services; Nursing; Social Services.

Award: Scholarship for use in freshman, sophomore, junior, senior, graduate, or postgraduate years; renewable. *Number:* 40–200. *Amount:* $1000–$5000.

Eligibility Requirements: Applicant must be enrolled or expecting to enroll full or part-time at a four-year institution or university; resident of Maryland and studying in Maryland. Available to U.S. citizens.

Application Requirements: Application, financial need analysis. *Deadline:* March 1.

Contact: institution financial aid office

MISSOURI DEPARTMENT OF HEALTH AND SENIOR SERVICES http://www.dhss.state.mo.us

PRIMARY CARE RESOURCE INITIATIVE FOR MISSOURI LOAN PROGRAM

Forgivable loans for Missouri residents attending Missouri institutions pursuing a degree as a primary care physician or dentist, studying for a bachelors degree as a dental hygienist, or a master of science degree in nursing leading to certification as an Advanced Practice Nurse. To be forgiven participant must work in a Missouri health professional shortage area.

Academic Fields/Career Goals: Dental Health/Services; Health and Medical Sciences; Nursing.

Award: Forgivable loan for use in freshman, sophomore, junior, senior, graduate, or postgraduate years; not renewable. *Number:* varies. *Amount:* $3000–$25,000.

Eligibility Requirements: Applicant must be enrolled or expecting to enroll full or part-time at a four-year institution or university; resident of Missouri and studying in Missouri. Available to U.S. citizens.

Application Requirements: Application, driver's license. *Deadline:* July 1.

Contact: Kristie Frank, Health Program Representative
Missouri Department of Health and Senior Services
PO Box 570
Jefferson City, MO 65102-0570
Phone: 800-891-7415
Fax: 573-522-8146
E-mail: frank@dhss.mo.gov

NEW MEXICO COMMISSION ON HIGHER EDUCATION http://www.nmche.org

ALLIED HEALTH STUDENT LOAN PROGRAM-NEW MEXICO

Renewable loans for New Mexico residents enrolled in an undergraduate allied health program. Loans can be forgiven through service in a medically underserved area or can be repaid. Penalties apply for failure to provide service. May borrow up to $12,000 per year for four years.

Academic Fields/Career Goals: Dental Health/Services; Health and Medical Sciences; Nursing; Social Sciences; Therapy/Rehabilitation.

Award: Forgivable loan for use in freshman, sophomore, junior, or senior years; renewable. *Number:* 1–40. *Amount:* up to $12,000.

Eligibility Requirements: Applicant must be enrolled or expecting to enroll full or part-time at a two-year or four-year institution or university; resident of New Mexico and studying in New Mexico. Available to U.S. citizens.

Application Requirements: Application, financial need analysis, transcript, FAFSA. *Deadline:* July 1.

Contact: Maria Barele, Financial Specialist
New Mexico Commission on Higher Education
PO Box 15910
Santa Fe, NM 87506-5910
Phone: 505-827-4026
Fax: 505-827-7392

NEW YORK STATE EDUCATION DEPARTMENT http://www.highered.nysed.gov

REGENTS PROFESSIONAL OPPORTUNITY SCHOLARSHIP

• *See page 45*

NORTH CAROLINA STATE EDUCATION ASSISTANCE AUTHORITY http://www.cfnc.org

NORTH CAROLINA STUDENT LOAN PROGRAM FOR HEALTH, SCIENCE, AND MATHEMATICS

Renewable award for North Carolina residents studying health-related fields, or science or math education. Based on merit, need, and promise of service as a health professional or educator in an underserved area of North Carolina. Need two co-signers. Submit surety statement.

Academic Fields/Career Goals: Dental Health/Services; Health Administration; Health and Medical Sciences; Nursing; Physical Sciences and Math; Therapy/Rehabilitation.

Award: Forgivable loan for use in freshman, sophomore, junior, senior, or graduate years; renewable. *Amount:* $3000–$8000.

Eligibility Requirements: Applicant must be enrolled or expecting to enroll full-time at a two-year or four-year institution or university and resident of North Carolina. Available to U.S. citizens.

Application Requirements: Application, financial need analysis, transcript. *Deadline:* June 1.

Contact: Edna Williams, Manager, Selection and Origination, HSM Loan Program
North Carolina State Education Assistance Authority
PO Box 14223
Research Triangle Park, NC 27709-4223
Phone: 919-549-8614

PNC BANK TRUST DEPARTMENT

H. FLETCHER BROWN SCHOLARSHIP

Renewable award based on academic performance, test scores, financial need, and interview. Applicant's family income must be below $75,000. Awards are made in spring of senior year of high school or spring of senior year of college. Must be pursuing studies in engineering, chemistry, law, medicine (limited to those pursuing MD or DO degree), or dentistry. Must have been born in Delaware and be a Delaware resident. Birth certificate required for documentation. Class rank must be in the upper 20 percentile. Applicant must maintain a 2.5 GPA in order to keep scholarship.

Academic Fields/Career Goals: Dental Health/Services; Engineering/Technology; Health and Medical Sciences; Law/Legal Services; Physical Sciences and Math.

Award: Scholarship for use in freshman, or graduate years; renewable. *Number:* 1–2. *Amount:* varies.

Eligibility Requirements: Applicant must be enrolled or expecting to enroll full-time at a four-year institution and resident of Delaware. Applicant must have 2.5 GPA or higher.

Application Requirements: Application, financial need analysis, interview, photo, references, test scores, transcript. *Deadline:* March 22.

Contact: Donald W. Davis, Vice President
PNC Bank Trust Department
222/16 Delaware Avenue
Wilmington, DE 19801
Phone: 302-429-1186
Fax: 302-429-5658

RESOURCE CENTER http://www.resourcecenterscholarshipinfo.com

MARIE BLAHA MEDICAL GRANT

• *See page 64*

SOUTHWEST STUDENT SERVICES CORPORATION http://www.sssc.com

ANNE LINDEMAN MEMORIAL SCHOLARSHIP

• *See page 117*

STATE OF GEORGIA http://www.gsfc.org

SERVICE-CANCELABLE STAFFORD LOAN-GEORGIA

To assist Georgia students enrolled in critical fields of study in allied health (e.g., nursing, physical therapy). For use at GSFA-approved schools. $3500 forgivable loan for dentistry students only. Contact school financial aid officer for more details.

Academic Fields/Career Goals: Dental Health/Services; Health and Medical Sciences; Nursing; Therapy/Rehabilitation.

Award: Forgivable loan for use in freshman, sophomore, junior, senior, or graduate years; not renewable. *Number:* 500–1200. *Amount:* $2000–$4500.

Eligibility Requirements: Applicant must be enrolled or expecting to enroll full or part-time at a two-year or four-year or technical institution or university; resident of Georgia and studying in Georgia. Available to U.S. citizens.

Application Requirements: Application, financial need analysis. *Deadline:* Continuous.

Contact: Peggy Matthews, Manager/GSFA Originations
State of Georgia
2082 East Exchange Place, Suite 230
Tucker, GA 30084-5305
Phone: 770-724-9230
Fax: 770-724-9225
E-mail: peggy@gsfc.org

UNITED STATES PUBLIC HEALTH SERVICE - HEALTH RESOURCES AND SERVICES ADMINISTRATION, BUREAU OF HEALTH PROFESSIONS http://bhpr.hrsa.gov/dsa

HEALTH RESOURCES AND SERVICES ADMINISTRATION-BUREAU OF HEALTH PROFESSIONS SCHOLARSHIPS FOR DISADVANTAGED STUDENTS

Scholarships to full-time students from disadvantaged backgrounds enrolled in health professions and nursing programs. Institution must apply for funding. One-time award. Students must contact financial aid office to apply. School must be eligible to receive SDS funds.

Academic Fields/Career Goals: Dental Health/Services; Health and Medical Sciences; Nursing; Therapy/Rehabilitation.

Award: Scholarship for use in freshman, sophomore, junior, senior, or graduate years; not renewable. *Number:* up to 350. *Amount:* varies.

Eligibility Requirements: Applicant must be enrolled or expecting to enroll full-time at a two-year or four-year institution or university. Available to U.S. citizens.

Application Requirements: Application, financial need analysis. *Deadline:* Continuous.

Contact: Financial Aid Office at college or university

UNIVERSITY OF MEDICINE AND DENTISTRY OF NJ SCHOOL OF OSTEOPATHIC MEDICINE http://www.umdnj.edu/studentfinancialaid

NEW JERSEY EDUCATIONAL OPPORTUNITY FUND GRANTS

Grants up to $4150 per year. Must be a New Jersey resident for at least twelve consecutive months and attend a New Jersey institution. Must be from a disadvantaged background as defined by EOF guidelines. EOF grant applicants must also apply for financial aid. EOF recipients may qualify for the Martin Luther King Physician/Dentistry Scholarships for graduate study at a professional institution.

Academic Fields/Career Goals: Dental Health/Services; Health and Medical Sciences.

Award: Grant for use in freshman, sophomore, junior, senior, or graduate years; renewable. *Number:* varies. *Amount:* up to $4150.

University of Medicine and Dentistry of NJ School of Osteopathic Medicine (continued)

Eligibility Requirements: Applicant must be enrolled or expecting to enroll full-time at a four-year institution or university; resident of New Jersey and studying in New Jersey. Available to U.S. citizens.

Application Requirements: Application, financial need analysis. *Deadline:* Continuous.

Contact: Sandra Rollins, Associate Director of Financial Aid
University of Medicine and Dentistry of NJ School of Osteopathic Medicine
40 East Laurel Road, Primary Care Center 119
Stratford, NJ 08084
Phone: 856-566-6008
Fax: 856-566-6015
E-mail: rollins@umdnj.edu

VIRGINIA BUSINESS AND PROFESSIONAL WOMEN'S FOUNDATION http://www.bpwva.advocate.net/foundation.htm

WOMEN IN SCIENCE AND TECHNOLOGY SCHOLARSHIP

• *See page 119*

WASHINGTON HIGHER EDUCATION COORDINATING BOARD http://www.hecb.wa.gov

HEALTH PROFESSIONAL LOAN REPAYMENT AND SCHOLARSHIP PROGRAMS

Loan repayment to licensed primary care health professionals. Scholarships to students training to become primary care health professionals. Participants agree to provide primary health care services for three to five years in medically underserved areas in Washington state. Loan repayment applications due first week in September. Scholarship applications due in April.

Academic Fields/Career Goals: Dental Health/Services; Health and Medical Sciences; Nursing; Public Health.

Award: Forgivable loan for use in junior, senior, graduate, or postgraduate years; renewable. *Number:* 55. *Amount:* $6500–$60,000.

Eligibility Requirements: Applicant must be enrolled or expecting to enroll full or part-time at a two-year or four-year or technical institution or university. Available to U.S. citizens.

Application Requirements: Application, essay, references, transcript. *Deadline:* varies.

Contact: Kathy McVay, Program Associate
Washington Higher Education Coordinating Board
310 Israel Road
Tumwater, WA 98501
Phone: 360-236-2816
Fax: 360-664-9273
E-mail: kathy.mcvay@doh.wa.gov

DRAFTING

COMTO-BOSTON CHAPTER http://www.bostoncomto.org

COMTO BOSTON/GARRETT A. MORGAN SCHOLARSHIP

• *See page 75*

CONNECTICUT BUILDING CONGRESS http://www.cbc-ct.org

CONNECTICUT BUILDING CONGRESS SCHOLARSHIP FUND

• *See page 75*

HAROLD B. & DOROTHY A. SNYDER FOUNDATION, INC.

HAROLD B. AND DOROTHY A. SNYDER FOUNDATION, INC., PROGRAM

• *See page 141*

HISPANIC COLLEGE FUND, INC. http://www.hispanicfund.org

EL NUEVO CONSTRUCTOR SCHOLARSHIP PROGRAM

• *See page 76*

NATIONAL ASSOCIATION OF WOMEN IN CONSTRUCTION http://nawic.org

NAWIC UNDERGRADUATE SCHOLARSHIPS

• *See page 77*

PROFESSIONAL CONSTRUCTION ESTIMATORS ASSOCIATION http://www.pcea.org

TED WILSON MEMORIAL SCHOLARSHIP FOUNDATION

Scholarship available to students wishing to pursue a career in the construction industry. Currently available in the following states: NC, SC, VA, GA, and FL.

Academic Fields/Career Goals: Drafting; Electrical Engineering/Electronics; Engineering/Technology; Heating, Air-Conditioning, and Refrigeration Mechanics; Landscape Architecture; Mechanical Engineering; Surveying; Surveying Technology, Cartography, or Geographic Information Science.

Award: Scholarship for use in freshman, sophomore, junior, senior, or graduate years; not renewable. *Number:* 5. *Amount:* $1500.

Eligibility Requirements: Applicant must be enrolled or expecting to enroll full-time at a two-year or four-year or technical institution or university and studying in Florida, Georgia, North Carolina, South Carolina, or Virginia. Available to U.S. and non-U.S. citizens.

Application Requirements: Application, financial need analysis, references, transcript. *Deadline:* March 15.

Contact: Kim Ellis, Executive Manager
Professional Construction Estimators Association
PO Box 680336
Charlotte, NC 28216
Phone: 704-987-9978
Fax: 704-987-9979
E-mail: pcea@pcea.org

EARTH SCIENCE

AIR AND WASTE MANAGEMENT ASSOCIATION-CONNECTICUT CHAPTER http://www.awma-nes.org/

AIR AND WASTE MANAGEMENT ASSOCIATION-CONNECTICUT CHAPTER SCHOLARSHIP

• *See page 111*

ALABAMA STATE DEPARTMENT OF EDUCATION http://www.alsde.edu

MATH AND SCIENCE SCHOLARSHIP PROGRAM FOR ALABAMA TEACHERS

• *See page 111*

AMERICAN INDIAN SCIENCE AND ENGINEERING SOCIETY http://www.aises.org

A.T. ANDERSON MEMORIAL SCHOLARSHIP

• *See page 65*

ENVIRONMENTAL PROTECTION AGENCY TRIBAL LANDS ENVIRONMENTAL SCIENCE SCHOLARSHIP

• *See page 111*

AMERICAN METEOROLOGICAL SOCIETY http://www.ametsoc.org/AMS

AMERICAN METEOROLOGICAL SOCIETY INDUSTRY UNDERGRADUATE SCHOLARSHIPS

• *See page 66*

ARIZONA HYDROLOGICAL SOCIETY http://www.azhydrosoc.org

ARIZONA HYDROLOGICAL SURVEY STUDENT SCHOLARSHIP

One-time award to outstanding undergraduate or graduate students that have demonstrated academic excellence in water resources related fields as a means of encouraging them to continue to develop as water resources professionals. Must be a resident of Arizona and be enrolled in a postsecondary Arizona institution.

Academic Fields/Career Goals: Earth Science; Natural Resources; Nuclear Science; Physical Sciences and Math; Science, Technology, and Society; Surveying; Surveying Technology, Cartography, or Geographic Information Science.

Award: Scholarship for use in sophomore, junior, senior, or graduate years; not renewable. *Number:* 3. *Amount:* $1500.

Eligibility Requirements: Applicant must be enrolled or expecting to enroll full-time at a two-year or four-year or technical institution or university; resident of Arizona and studying in Arizona. Available to U.S. citizens.

Application Requirements: Application, essay, financial need analysis, references, transcript. *Deadline:* June 30.

Contact: Dr. Aregai Tecle, Professor
Arizona Hydrological Society
Northern Arizona University School of Forestry, PO Box 15018
Flagstaff, AZ 86011
Phone: 928-523-6642
E-mail: aregai.tecle@nau.edu

ASSOCIATION FOR IRON AND STEEL TECHNOLOGY http://www.aist.org/foundation/scholarships.htm

ASSOCIATION FOR IRON AND STEEL TECHNOLOGY OHIO VALLEY CHAPTER SCHOLARSHIP

• *See page 112*

ASSOCIATION FOR WOMEN GEOSCIENTISTS, PUGET SOUND CHAPTER http://www.awg.org/

PUGET SOUND CHAPTER SCHOLARSHIP

Scholarship for undergraduate women committed to completing a bachelor's degree and pursuing a career or graduate work in the geosciences, including geology, environmental/engineering geology, geochemistry, geophysics, and hydrology. Must be sophomore, junior, or senior woman enrolled in a university or 2-year college in western Washington State, west of the Columbia and Okanogan Rivers. Must have minimum 3.2 GPA. Must be a U.S. citizen or permanent resident. Please refer to Web site for further information: http://www.scn.org/psawg.

Academic Fields/Career Goals: Earth Science; Physical Sciences and Math.

Award: Scholarship for use in sophomore, junior, or senior years; not renewable. *Number:* 1. *Amount:* $1000.

Eligibility Requirements: Applicant must be enrolled or expecting to enroll full-time at a two-year or four-year institution or university; female and studying in Washington. Available to U.S. citizens.

Application Requirements: Essay, financial need analysis, references, transcript. *Deadline:* varies.

Contact: Lynn Hultgrien, Geologist, Scholarship Committee Chair
Association for Women Geoscientists, Puget Sound Chapter
PO Box 4229
Kent, WA 98089
Phone: 206-543-9024
E-mail: awg_ps@yahoo.com

ASSOCIATION FOR WOMEN IN SCIENCE EDUCATIONAL FOUNDATION http://www.awis.org/ed_foundation.html

ASSOCIATION FOR WOMEN IN SCIENCE COLLEGE SCHOLARSHIP

• *See page 63*

AWIS KIRSTEN R. LORENTZEN AWARD IN PHYSICS

Award for female undergraduate students, to be used in their junior or senior year of study. Must be studying toward a degree in physics or geoscience and excel in both academic and non-academic pursuits. Applicants must be U.S. citizens, studying in the United States.

Academic Fields/Career Goals: Earth Science; Physical Sciences and Math.

Award: Scholarship for use in junior or senior years; not renewable. *Number:* 1. *Amount:* $1000.

Eligibility Requirements: Applicant must be enrolled or expecting to enroll full-time at a four-year institution or university and female. Available to U.S. citizens.

Application Requirements: Application, essay, references, transcript. *Deadline:* February 3.

Contact: Barbara Filner, President
Association for Women in Science Educational Foundation
7008 Richard Drive
Bethesda, MD 20817-4838
E-mail: awisedfd@awis.org

ASSOCIATION OF ENGINEERING GEOLOGISTS http://www.aegweb.org

MARLIAVE FUND

Several scholarships to support graduate and undergraduate students studying engineering geology and geological engineering. One-time awards.

Academic Fields/Career Goals: Earth Science; Engineering/Technology; Engineering-Related Technologies.

Award: Scholarship for use in senior, or graduate years; not renewable. *Number:* varies. *Amount:* $1000.

Eligibility Requirements: Applicant must be enrolled or expecting to enroll full-time at a four-year institution or university. Available to U.S. citizens.

Application Requirements: Application. *Deadline:* Continuous.

Contact: Kim Samford, Executive Secretary
Association of Engineering Geologists
Texas A&M University, Department of Geology and Geophysics
College Station, TX 77843-3115
Phone: 979-845-0142
Fax: 979-862-7959

TILFORD FUND

For undergraduate students, the scholarship goes toward the cost of a geology field camp course or senior thesis field research. For graduate students, the scholarship would apply to field research. Must be a student member of AEG.

Academic Fields/Career Goals: Earth Science.

Award: Scholarship for use in senior, or graduate years; not renewable. *Number:* 2–4. *Amount:* $1000.

Eligibility Requirements: Applicant must be enrolled or expecting to enroll at a four-year institution or university. Applicant or parent of applicant must be member of Association of Engineering Geologists.

Application Requirements: Application, essay, references, transcript. *Deadline:* January 31.

Contact: Deb Green Tilford, Chairman
Association of Engineering Geologists
NRT Scholarship Committee, 79 Forest Lane
Placitas, NM 87043
E-mail: tilgreen@aol.com

ASTRONAUT SCHOLARSHIP FOUNDATION http://www.astronautscholarship.org

ASTRONAUT SCHOLARSHIP FOUNDATION

• *See page 68*

BARRY M. GOLDWATER SCHOLARSHIP AND EXCELLENCE IN EDUCATION FOUNDATION http://www.act.org/goldwater

BARRY M. GOLDWATER SCHOLARSHIP AND EXCELLENCE IN EDUCATION PROGRAM

• *See page 68*

CALIFORNIA GROUNDWATER ASSOCIATION http://www.groundh2o.org

CALIFORNIA GROUNDWATER ASSOCIATION SCHOLARSHIP

Award for California residents who demonstrate an interest in some facet of groundwater technology. One to two $1000 awards. Must use for study in California. Submit letter of recommendation. Deadline: April 1.

Academic Fields/Career Goals: Earth Science; Natural Resources.

Award: Scholarship for use in freshman, sophomore, junior, or senior years; not renewable. *Number:* 1–2. *Amount:* $1000.

Eligibility Requirements: Applicant must be enrolled or expecting to enroll full or part-time at a two-year or four-year or technical institution or university; resident of California and studying in California. Available to U.S. citizens.

Application Requirements: Application, essay, references, transcript. *Deadline:* April 1.

Contact: Mike Mortensson, Executive Director
California Groundwater Association
PO Box 14369
Santa Rosa, CA 95402
Phone: 707-578-4408
Fax: 707-546-4906
E-mail: wellguy@groundh2o.org

CALIFORNIA SEA GRANT COLLEGE PROGRAM http://www-csgc.ucsd.edu

JOHN D. ISSACS SCHOLARSHIP

• See page 113

CANADIAN RECREATIONAL CANOEING ASSOCIATION http://www.paddlingcanada.com

BILL MASON MEMORIAL SCHOLARSHIP FUND

• See page 57

CONNECTICUT STUDENT LOAN FOUNDATION http://www.cslf.com

CONNECTICUT INNOVATIONS TECHNOLOGY SCHOLAR PROGRAM

• See page 113

DESK AND DERRICK EDUCATIONAL TRUST http://www.addc.org

DESK AND DERRICK EDUCATIONAL TRUST

• See page 69

GARDEN CLUB OF AMERICA http://www.gcamerica.org

GARDEN CLUB OF AMERICA AWARDS FOR SUMMER ENVIRONMENTAL STUDIES

• See page 58

GEORGE BIRD GRINNELL AMERICAN INDIAN FUND

AL QOYAWAYMA AWARD

• See page 141

HERB SOCIETY OF AMERICA http://www.herbsociety.org

HERB SOCIETY RESEARCH GRANTS

• See page 69

HISPANIC COLLEGE FUND, INC. http://www.hispanicfund.org

NATIONAL HISPANIC EXPLORERS SCHOLARSHIP PROGRAM

• See page 69

INDEPENDENT LABORATORIES INSTITUTE SCHOLARSHIP ALLIANCE http://www.acil.org

INDEPENDENT LABORATORIES INSTITUTE SCHOLARSHIP ALLIANCE

• See page 69

INNOVATION AND SCIENCE COUNCIL OF BRITISH COLUMBIA http://www.scbc.org

PAUL AND HELEN TRUSSEL SCIENCE AND TECHNOLOGY SCHOLARSHIP

• See page 69

INTERNATIONAL ASSOCIATION OF GREAT LAKES RESEARCH http://www.iaglr.org

PAUL W. RODGERS SCHOLARSHIP

Award given to any senior undergraduate, masters, or doctoral student who wishes to pursue a future in research, conservation, education, communication, management, or other knowledge-based activity pertaining to the Great Lakes. Deadline is March15.

Academic Fields/Career Goals: Earth Science; Education; Environmental Science; Hydrology; Marine Biology; Natural Resources; Natural Sciences.

Award: Scholarship for use in senior, or graduate years; not renewable. *Number:* 1. *Amount:* $2000.

Eligibility Requirements: Applicant must be enrolled or expecting to enroll full-time at a four-year institution or university.

Application Requirements: Application, references, transcript. *Deadline:* March 15.

Contact: International Association of Great Lakes Research
Attn: Business Office
2205 Commonwealth Boulevard
Ann Arbor, MI 48105
Phone: 734-665-5503
Fax: 734-741-2055
E-mail: office@iaglr.org

KENTUCKY NATURAL RESOURCES AND ENVIRONMENTAL PROTECTION CABINET http://www.uky.edu/waterresources

ENVIRONMENTAL PROTECTION SCHOLARSHIPS

• See page 142

MID-COAST AUDUBON SOCIETY http://www.midcoastaudubon.org

JEAN BOYER HAMLIN SCHOLARSHIP IN ORNITHOLOGY

• See page 63

MINERALOGICAL SOCIETY OF AMERICA http://www.minsocam.org

MINERALOGICAL SOCIETY OF AMERICA-GRANT FOR STUDENT RESEARCH IN MINERALOGY AND PETROLOGY

A $5000 grant for research in mineralogy and petrology. Selection based on qualifications of applicant; quality, innovativeness, and scientific significance of the research; and likelihood of project success. Application available on Web site at http://www.minsocam.org.

Academic Fields/Career Goals: Earth Science; Gemology; Museum Studies; Natural Resources; Natural Sciences; Physical Sciences and Math.

Award: Grant for use in junior, senior, or graduate years; not renewable. *Number:* 2. *Amount:* $5000.

Eligibility Requirements: Applicant must be enrolled or expecting to enroll full-time at a four-year institution or university. Available to U.S. and non-U.S. citizens.

Application Requirements: Application. *Deadline:* June 1.

Contact: Dr. J. Alexander Speer
Mineralogical Society of America
1015 Eighteenth Street, NW, Suite 601
Washington, DC 20036-5212
Phone: 202-775-4344
Fax: 202-775-0015
E-mail: j_a_speer@minsocam.org

MINERALOGY SOCIETY OF AMERICA-GRANT FOR RESEARCH IN CRYSTALLOGRAPHY

A $5000 grant for research in crystallography. Award selection based on qualifications of applicant; quality, innovativeness, and scientific significance of proposed research; and likelihood of project success. Application available on Web site at http://www.minsocam.org. For applicants between the ages of 25-35.

Academic Fields/Career Goals: Earth Science; Gemology; Materials Science, Engineering, and Metallurgy; Museum Studies; Natural Resources; Natural Sciences; Physical Sciences and Math.

Award: Grant for use in junior, senior, or graduate years; not renewable. *Number:* 1. *Amount:* $5000.

Eligibility Requirements: Applicant must be age 25-35 and enrolled or expecting to enroll full-time at a four-year institution or university. Available to U.S. and non-U.S. citizens.

Application Requirements: Application. *Deadline:* June 1.

Contact: Dr. J. Alexander Speer
Mineralogical Society of America
1015 Eighteenth Street, NW, Suite 601
Washington, DC 20036-5212
Phone: 202-775-4344
Fax: 202-775-0015
E-mail: j_a_speer@minsocam.org

MONTANA FEDERATION OF GARDEN CLUBS

LIFE MEMBER MONTANA FEDERATION OF GARDEN CLUBS SCHOLARSHIP

• *See page 114*

MORRIS K. UDALL FOUNDATION http://www.udall.gov

MORRIS K. UDALL SCHOLARS

• *See page 59*

NASA DELAWARE SPACE GRANT CONSORTIUM http://www.delspace.org

NASA DELAWARE SPACE GRANT UNDERGRADUATE TUITION SCHOLARSHIP

• *See page 70*

NASA IDAHO SPACE GRANT CONSORTIUM http://www.uidaho.edu/nasa_isgc

NASA IDAHO SPACE GRANT CONSORTIUM SCHOLARSHIP PROGRAM

• *See page 71*

NASA NEBRASKA SPACE GRANT CONSORTIUM http://nasa.unomaha.edu

NASA NEBRASKA SPACE GRANT

• *See page 101*

NASA VERMONT SPACE GRANT CONSORTIUM http://www.emba.uvm.edu/vsgc

VERMONT SPACE GRANT CONSORTIUM SCHOLARSHIP PROGRAM

• *See page 71*

NASA VIRGINIA SPACE GRANT CONSORTIUM http://www.vsgc.odu.edu

VIRGINIA SPACE GRANT CONSORTIUM TEACHER EDUCATION SCHOLARSHIPS

• *See page 102*

NASA WEST VIRGINIA SPACE GRANT CONSORTIUM http://www.nasa.wvu.edu

WEST VIRGINIA SPACE GRANT CONSORTIUM UNDERGRADUATE SCHOLARSHIP PROGRAM

• *See page 102*

NATIONAL ASSOCIATION OF WATER COMPANIES http://www.nawc.org

J .J. BARR SCHOLARSHIP

• *See page 115*

NATIONAL ASSOCIATION OF WATER COMPANIES-NEW JERSEY CHAPTER

NATIONAL ASSOCIATION OF WATER COMPANIES-NEW JERSEY CHAPTER SCHOLARSHIP

• *See page 115*

NATIONAL GARDEN CLUBS, INC. http://www.gardenclub.org

NATIONAL GARDEN CLUBS, INC. SCHOLARSHIP PROGRAM

• *See page 60*

NEW JERSEY ACADEMY OF SCIENCE http://www.njas.org

NEW JERSEY ACADEMY OF SCIENCE RESEARCH GRANTS-IN-AID TO HIGH SCHOOL STUDENTS

• *See page 116*

SOCIETY FOR MINING, METALLURGY AND EXPLORATION - CENTRAL WYOMING SECTION

COATES, WOLFF, RUSSELL MINING INDUSTRY SCHOLARSHIP

• *See page 71*

SOCIETY FOR RANGE MANAGEMENT http://www.rangelands.org

MASONIC RANGE SCIENCE SCHOLARSHIP

• *See page 55*

SOCIETY OF MEXICAN AMERICAN ENGINEERS AND SCIENTISTS http://www.maes-natl.org

GRE AND GRADUATE APPLICATIONS WAIVER

• *See page 72*

SOIL AND WATER CONSERVATION SOCIETY http://www.swcs.org

DONALD A. WILLIAMS SCHOLARSHIP SOIL CONSERVATION SCHOLARSHIP

Provides financial assistance to members of SWCS who are currently employed but who wish to improve their technical or administrative competence in a conservation-related field through course work at an accredited college or through a program of special study. Download the application form from the SWCS homepage at http://www.swcs.org.

Academic Fields/Career Goals: Earth Science; Natural Resources; Natural Sciences.

Award: Scholarship for use in freshman, sophomore, junior, or senior years; not renewable. *Number:* up to 3. *Amount:* $1500.

Eligibility Requirements: Applicant must be enrolled or expecting to enroll at a four-year institution or university. Applicant or parent of applicant must be member of Soil and Water Conservation Society. Applicant or parent of applicant must have employment or volunteer experience in designated career field. Available to U.S. and non-U.S. citizens.

Application Requirements: Application, financial need analysis. *Deadline:* February 12.

Contact: Nancy Herselius, Member Services Coordinator
Soil and Water Conservation Society
7515 NE Ankeny Road
Ankeny, IA 50021-9764
Phone: 515-289-2331 Ext. 17
Fax: 515-289-1227
E-mail: nancyh@swcs.org

SOIL AND WATER CONSERVATION SOCIETY-NEW JERSEY CHAPTER http://www.geocities.com/njswcs

EDWARD R. HALL SCHOLARSHIP
• *See page 55*

TKE EDUCATIONAL FOUNDATION http://www.tkefoundation.org

CARROL C. HALL MEMORIAL SCHOLARSHIP
• *See page 72*

UNITED NEGRO COLLEGE FUND http://www.uncf.org

BOOZ, ALLEN & HAMILTON/WILLIAM F. STASIOR INTERNSHIP
• *See page 130*

MALCOLM PIRNIE, INC. SCHOLARS PROGRAM
• *See page 148*

ROCKWELL/UNCF CORPORATE SCHOLARS PROGRAM
• *See page 133*

UNIVERSITIES SPACE RESEARCH ASSOCIATION http://www.usra.edu/hq/scholarships/overview.shtml

UNIVERSITIES SPACE RESEARCH ASSOCIATION SCHOLARSHIP PROGRAM
• *See page 72*

ECONOMICS

CATCHING THE DREAM

TRIBAL BUSINESS MANAGEMENT PROGRAM (TBM)
• *See page 38*

CENTRAL INTELLIGENCE AGENCY http://www.cia.gov

CENTRAL INTELLIGENCE AGENCY UNDERGRADUATE SCHOLARSHIP PROGRAM
• *See page 39*

CIRI FOUNDATION http://www.ciri.com/tcf

CARL H. MARRS SCHOLARSHIP FUND
• *See page 39*

CUBAN AMERICAN NATIONAL FOUNDATION

MAS FAMILY SCHOLARSHIPS
• *See page 123*

FUND FOR AMERICAN STUDIES http://www.tfas.org

ECONOMIC JOURNALISM AWARD

One-time award for the magazine or newspaper writer (or team of writers) who has done the most to shape public opinion by giving the public a better understanding of economic theory and reality. Multiple entries may be submitted, but no more than 20 stories per entry should be included. Entry deadline is March 15. See Web site at http://www.tfas.org for further information.

Academic Fields/Career Goals: Economics; Journalism.

Award: Prize for use in freshman, sophomore, junior, senior, or graduate years; not renewable. *Number:* 1. *Amount:* $5000.

Eligibility Requirements: Applicant must be enrolled or expecting to enroll at an institution or university. Available to U.S. citizens.

Application Requirements: Application, portfolio. *Deadline:* March 15.

Contact: Steve Slattery, Vice President of Programs
Fund for American Studies
1706 New Hampshire Avenue, NW
Washington, DC 20009
Phone: 202-986-0384
Fax: 202-986-8930
E-mail: sslattery@tfas.org

GOVERNMENT FINANCE OFFICERS ASSOCIATION http://www.GFOA.org

MINORITIES IN GOVERNMENT FINANCE SCHOLARSHIP
• *See page 41*

GRAND RAPIDS COMMUNITY FOUNDATION http://www.grfoundation.org

ECONOMIC CLUB OF GRAND RAPIDS BUSINESS STUDY ABROAD SCHOLARSHIP
• *See page 41*

HARRY S. TRUMAN LIBRARY INSTITUTE http://www.trumanlibrary.org

HARRY S. TRUMAN LIBRARY INSTITUTE UNDERGRADUATE STUDENT GRANT

Award to support an undergraduate senior writing a thesis on a Truman-related topic to come to the Library and conduct research. Intended to offset expenses incurred for that purpose only. With application, student must include a description of, and rationale for, the project and indicate how the research experience will contribute to the student's future development as a scholar or in an applied field. Deadline: December 1. Project description and proposal not to exceed five pages in length. Letter of support from faculty adviser required.

Academic Fields/Career Goals: Economics; Historic Preservation and Conservation; History; Political Science.

Award: Grant for use in senior year; not renewable. *Number:* 1. *Amount:* up to $1000.

Eligibility Requirements: Applicant must be enrolled or expecting to enroll at a four-year institution or university and studying in Missouri. Available to U.S. and non-U.S. citizens.

Application Requirements: Application, references, project description and proposal, faculty letter of support. *Deadline:* December 1.

Contact: Lisa Sullivan, Office Manager
Harry S. Truman Library Institute
500 West U.S. Highway 24
Independence, MO 64050-1798
Phone: 816-268-8248
Fax: 816-268-8299
E-mail: lisa.sullivan@nara.gov

HISPANIC COLLEGE FUND, INC. http://www.hispanicfund.org

BURLINGTON NORTHERN SANTA FE FOUNDATION/HISPANIC COLLEGE FUND SCHOLARSHIP PROGRAM
• *See page 41*

DENNY'S/HISPANIC COLLEGE FUND SCHOLARSHIP
• *See page 41*

ERNST AND YOUNG SCHOLARSHIP PROGRAM
• *See page 42*

HISPANIC COLLEGE FUND/INROADS/SPRINT SCHOLARSHIP PROGRAM
• *See page 125*

M & T BANK/ HISPANIC COLLEGE FUND SCHOLARSHIP PROGRAM
• *See page 42*

JORGE MAS CANOSA FREEDOM FOUNDATION

MAS FAMILY SCHOLARSHIP AWARD
• *See page 126*

JUNIOR ACHIEVEMENT OF MAINE http://maine.ja.org

NATIONAL ASSOCIATION OF INSURANCE WOMEN/JUNIOR ACHIEVEMENT OF MAINE SCHOLARSHIP

One-time award for a Maine high school student enrolled in a Junior Achievement high school program or who has taught a JA class in a lower grade. Also available to a college student who has taught a JA class. Recommendations and a minimum 3.0 GPA necessary. Deadline: March 15.

Academic Fields/Career Goals: Economics.

Award: Scholarship for use in freshman, sophomore, junior, or senior years; not renewable. *Number:* 1. *Amount:* $1000.

Eligibility Requirements: Applicant must be enrolled or expecting to enroll full-time at a two-year or four-year or technical institution or university and resident of Maine. Applicant or parent of applicant must be member of Junior Achievement. Applicant or parent of applicant must have employment or volunteer experience in community service. Applicant must have 3.0 GPA or higher. Available to U.S. citizens.

Application Requirements: Application, essay, resume, references, transcript. *Deadline:* March 15.

Contact: Anne Washburne, Program and Council Operations Director
Junior Achievement of Maine
90 Bridge Street, Suite 120
Westbrook, ME 04092
Phone: 207-591-9005
Fax: 207-591-9007
E-mail: program@jamaine.org

NATIONAL ASSOCIATION OF BLACK ACCOUNTANTS, INC. http://www.nabainc.org

NATIONAL ASSOCIATION OF BLACK ACCOUNTANTS NATIONAL SCHOLARSHIP PROGRAM
• *See page 43*

NATIONAL ASSOCIATION OF WATER COMPANIES-NEW JERSEY CHAPTER

NATIONAL ASSOCIATION OF WATER COMPANIES-NEW JERSEY CHAPTER SCHOLARSHIP
• *See page 115*

NATIONAL GARDEN CLUBS, INC. http://www.gardenclub.org

NATIONAL GARDEN CLUBS, INC. SCHOLARSHIP PROGRAM
• *See page 60*

NATIONAL SOCIETY DAUGHTERS OF THE AMERICAN REVOLUTION http://www.dar.org

NATIONAL SOCIETY DAUGHTERS OF THE AMERICAN REVOLUTION ENID HALL GRISWOLD MEMORIAL SCHOLARSHIP

For college juniors and seniors majoring in political science, history, government, or economics. Applicants need not be DAR members but must submit letter of sponsorship from local chapter and financial need form from parents. Merit based. Must submit self-addressed stamped envelope to be considered. Deadline is February 15.

Academic Fields/Career Goals: Economics; History; Political Science.

Award: Scholarship for use in junior or senior years; not renewable. *Number:* 1–5. *Amount:* $1000.

Eligibility Requirements: Applicant must be enrolled or expecting to enroll at a four-year institution. Applicant must have 3.0 GPA or higher. Available to U.S. citizens.

Application Requirements: Application, essay, financial need analysis, references, self-addressed stamped envelope, test scores, transcript. *Deadline:* February 15.

Contact: Office of Committees, Scholarship
National Society Daughters of the American Revolution
1776 D Street, NW
Washington, DC 20006-5392

ROYAL BANK NATIVE STUDENTS AWARDS PROGRAM http://www.rbc.com/community

ROYAL BANK ABORIGINAL STUDENT AWARDS
• *See page 129*

SOIL AND WATER CONSERVATION SOCIETY http://www.swcs.org

SWCS MELVILLE H. COHEE STUDENT LEADER CONSERVATION SCHOLARSHIP
• *See page 61*

UNITED AGRIBUSINESS LEAGUE http://www.ual.org

UNITED AGRIBUSINESS LEAGUE SCHOLARSHIP PROGRAM
• *See page 56*

UNITED AGRICULTURAL BENEFIT TRUST SCHOLARSHIP
• *See page 56*

UNITED NEGRO COLLEGE FUND http://www.uncf.org

AVON WOMEN IN SEARCH OF EXCELLENCE SCHOLARSHIPS
• *See page 48*

CREDIT SUISSE FIRST BOSTON SCHOLARSHIP
• *See page 49*

EDWARD M. NAGEL FOUNDATION SCHOLARSHIP
• *See page 49*

SBC FOUNDATION SCHOLARSHIP
• *See page 133*

SBC PACIFIC BELL FOUNDATION SCHOLARSHIP
• *See page 133*

SOUTHWESTERN BELL CORPORATION SCHOLARSHIP
• *See page 133*

SPRINT SCHOLARSHIP/INTERNSHIP
• *See page 50*

UNCF/SPRINT SCHOLARS PROGRAM
• *See page 50*

WISCONSIN FOUNDATION FOR INDEPENDENT COLLEGES, INC. http://www.wficweb.org

LAND'S END SCHOLARSHIP
• *See page 135*

SENTRY 21 CLUB SCHOLARSHIP
• *See page 135*

WE ENERGIES SCHOLARSHIP
• *See page 52*

WOMEN GROCERS OF AMERICA http://www.nationalgrocers.org

MARY MACEY SCHOLARSHIP
• *See page 61*

EDUCATION

ALASKA COMMISSION ON POSTSECONDARY EDUCATION http://www.state.ak.us/acpe/

ALASKA COMMISSION ON POSTSECONDARY EDUCATION TEACHER EDUCATION LOAN

Renewable loans for graduates of an Alaskan high school pursuing teaching careers in rural elementary and secondary schools in Alaska. Must be nominated by rural school district. Eligible for 100% forgiveness if loan recipient teaches in rural Alaska upon graduation. Several awards of up to $7500 each. Must maintain good standing at institution.

Academic Fields/Career Goals: Education.

Award: Forgivable loan for use in freshman, sophomore, junior, or senior years; renewable. *Number:* varies. *Amount:* up to $7500.

Eligibility Requirements: Applicant must be enrolled or expecting to enroll full-time at a four-year institution or university. Available to U.S. citizens.

Alaska Commission on Postsecondary Education (continued)

Application Requirements: Application, transcript. *Deadline:* July 1.

Contact: Lori Stedman, Administrative Assistant, Special Programs
Alaska Commission on Postsecondary Education
3030 Vintage Boulevard
Juneau, AK 99801-7100
Phone: 907-465-6741
Fax: 907-465-5316

ALBERTA HERITAGE SCHOLARSHIP FUND/ ALBERTA SCHOLARSHIP PROGRAMS http://www.alis.gov.ab.ca/scholarships

ANNA AND JOHN KOLESAR MEMORIAL SCHOLARSHIPS

One scholarship valued at CAN$1200 will be awarded to the applicant with the highest academic average in three designated subjects as shown on an Alberta Education Transcript. Applicants must be Alberta residents, planning to enroll in a Faculty of Education, and from a family where neither parent has a university degree.

Academic Fields/Career Goals: Education; Special Education.

Award: Scholarship for use in freshman or sophomore years; not renewable. *Number:* 1. *Amount:* $972.

Eligibility Requirements: Applicant must be Canadian citizen; high school student; planning to enroll or expecting to enroll full-time at a two-year or four-year institution or university and resident of Alberta. Applicant must have 3.0 GPA or higher.

Application Requirements: Application, transcript. *Deadline:* July 1.

Contact: Alberta Heritage Scholarship Fund/Alberta Scholarship Programs
9940 106th Street, 9th Floor, Box 28000 Station Main
Edmonton, AB T5J 4R4
Canada
Phone: 780-427-8640
Fax: 780-422-4516
E-mail: heritage@gov.ab.ca

LANGUAGES IN TEACHER EDUCATION SCHOLARSHIPS

Scholarships of $2500 CAN for education students in Alberta institutions with a specialty in languages other than English. Students must be nominated by their Alberta post-secondary institution. Nomination deadline is March 1.

Academic Fields/Career Goals: Education; Foreign Language.

Award: Scholarship for use in freshman, sophomore, junior, or senior years. *Number:* 12. *Amount:* $2049.

Eligibility Requirements: Applicant must be enrolled or expecting to enroll at an institution or university and studying in Alberta.

Application Requirements: Nomination by institution.

Contact: Director
Alberta Heritage Scholarship Fund/Alberta Scholarship Programs
9940 106th Street, 9th Floor
Box 28000, Station Main
Edmonton, AB T5J 4R4
Canada
Phone: 780-427-8640
Fax: 780-422-4516
E-mail: heritage@gov.ab.ca

ALPHA DELTA KAPPA FOUNDATION http://www.alphadeltakappa.org

INTERNATIONAL TEACHER EDUCATION SCHOLARSHIP

Enables women from foreign countries to study for their master's degree in the United States. Applicants must be single with no dependents, age 20-35, non-U.S. citizens residing outside the U.S., have at least one year of college completed, and plan to enter the teaching profession.

Academic Fields/Career Goals: Education.

Award: Scholarship for use in sophomore, junior, senior, or graduate years; renewable. *Number:* up to 7. *Amount:* up to $10,000.

Eligibility Requirements: Applicant must be age 20-35; enrolled or expecting to enroll full-time at a four-year institution or university and single female. Applicant must have 3.5 GPA or higher. Available to Canadian and non-U.S. citizens.

Application Requirements: Application, autobiography, financial need analysis, photo, references, test scores, transcript, certificates of health from physician and dentist, TOEFL scores, college acceptance. *Deadline:* January 1.

Contact: Dee Frost, Scholarships and Grants Coordinator
Alpha Delta Kappa Foundation
1615 West 92nd Street
Kansas City, MO 64114-3296
Phone: 816-363-5525
Fax: 816-363-4010
E-mail: headquarters@alphadeltakappa.org

AMERICAN ASSOCIATION FOR HEALTH EDUCATION http://www.aahperd.org/aahe

AMERICAN ASSOCIATION FOR HEALTH EDUCATION SCHOLARSHIP

Award for undergraduate student enrolled in health education program. Must submit resume, essay, and three letters of recommendation. One-time award of $1000. Deadline: December 1. For study in U.S. and U.S. territories. Minimum 3.5 GPA required.

Academic Fields/Career Goals: Education; Health and Medical Sciences.

Award: Scholarship for use in freshman, sophomore, junior, or senior years; not renewable. *Number:* 1. *Amount:* $1000.

Eligibility Requirements: Applicant must be enrolled or expecting to enroll full or part-time at a four-year institution or university. Applicant must have 3.5 GPA or higher. Available to U.S. and non-U.S. citizens.

Application Requirements: Application, essay, resume, references, transcript. *Deadline:* December 1.

Contact: Linda M. Moore, Program Administrator
American Association for Health Education
1900 Association Drive
Reston, VA 20191-1599
Phone: 703-476-3437
Fax: 703-476-6638
E-mail: aahe@aahperd.org

AMERICAN FEDERATION OF TEACHERS http://www.aft.org

ROBERT G. PORTER SCHOLARS PROGRAM-AFT DEPENDENTS

$8,000 scholarship ($2,000 per year) for high school seniors who are dependents of AFT members. Submit transcript, test scores, essay, and recommendations with application. Deadline: March 31. Must be U.S. citizen. Applicant should preferably be pursuing a career in labor, education, healthcare, or government service.

Academic Fields/Career Goals: Education; Health and Medical Sciences.

Award: Scholarship for use in freshman year; renewable. *Number:* 4. *Amount:* $8000.

Eligibility Requirements: Applicant must be high school student and planning to enroll or expecting to enroll full or part-time at a four-year institution or university. Available to U.S. citizens.

Application Requirements: Application, essay, references, test scores, transcript. *Deadline:* March 31.

Contact: Bernadette Bailey, Scholarship Coordinator
American Federation of Teachers
555 New Jersey Avenue, NW
Washington, DC 20001-2079
Phone: 202-879-4481
Fax: 202-879-4406
E-mail: bbailey@aft.org

ROBERT G. PORTER SCHOLARS PROGRAM-AFT MEMBERS

Non-renewable grant provides continuing education for school teachers, paraprofessionals and school-related personnel, higher education faculty and professionals, employees of state and local governments, nurses and other health professionals. Must be member of the American Federation of Teachers.

Academic Fields/Career Goals: Education; Health and Medical Sciences; Special Education.

Award: Grant for use in freshman, sophomore, junior, senior, or graduate years; not renewable. *Number:* 4. *Amount:* $1000.

Eligibility Requirements: Applicant must be enrolled or expecting to enroll full or part-time at a four-year institution or university. Available to U.S. citizens.

Application Requirements: Application, essay. *Deadline:* March 31.

Contact: Bernadette Bailey, Scholarship Coordinator
American Federation of Teachers
555 New Jersey Avenue, NW
Washington, DC 20001-2079
Phone: 202-879-4481
Fax: 202-879-4406
E-mail: bbailey@aft.org

AMERICAN FOUNDATION FOR THE BLIND http://www.afb.org

DELTA GAMMA FOUNDATION FLORENCE MARGARET HARVEY MEMORIAL SCHOLARSHIP

Award for legally blind junior, senior or graduate student studying rehabilitation or education of people who are blind or visually impaired. For additional information, refer to Web site: http://www.afb.org.

Academic Fields/Career Goals: Education; Therapy/Rehabilitation.

Award: Scholarship for use in junior, senior, or graduate years; not renewable. *Number:* up to 1. *Amount:* up to $1000.

Eligibility Requirements: Applicant must be enrolled or expecting to enroll full or part-time at a two-year or four-year institution or university. Applicant must be visually impaired. Available to U.S. citizens.

Application Requirements: Application, essay, transcript, evidence of legal blindness, letter of acceptance. *Deadline:* April 30.

Contact: Information Center
American Foundation for the Blind
11 Penn Plaza, Suite 300
New York, NY 10001
Phone: 212-502-7661
Fax: 212-502-7771
E-mail: afbinfo@afb.net

RUDOLPH DILLMAN MEMORIAL SCHOLARSHIP

Awards for undergraduate or graduate students who are legally blind and are studying rehabilitation and/or education of people who are blind or visually impaired. For additional information, refer to Web site: http://www.afb.org.

Academic Fields/Career Goals: Education; Therapy/Rehabilitation.

Award: Scholarship for use in freshman, sophomore, junior, senior, or graduate years; not renewable. *Number:* up to 4. *Amount:* up to $2500.

Eligibility Requirements: Applicant must be enrolled or expecting to enroll full or part-time at a two-year or four-year institution or university. Applicant must be visually impaired. Available to U.S. citizens.

Application Requirements: Application, essay, financial need analysis, references, transcript, evidence of legal blindness, acceptance letter. *Deadline:* April 30.

Contact: Information Center
American Foundation for the Blind
11 Penn Plaza, Suite 300
New York, NY 10001
Phone: 212-502-7661
Fax: 212-502-7771
E-mail: afbinfo@afb.net

AMERICAN LEGION AUXILIARY, DEPARTMENT OF IOWA http://www.ialegion.org/ala

HARRIET HOFFMAN MEMORIAL SCHOLARSHIP FOR TEACHER TRAINING

One-time award for Iowa residents attending Iowa institutions who are the children, grandchildren, or great-grandchildren of veterans. Must be studying education. Preference given to descendants of deceased veterans.

Academic Fields/Career Goals: Education.

Award: Scholarship for use in freshman, sophomore, junior, or senior years; not renewable. *Number:* 1. *Amount:* $400.

Eligibility Requirements: Applicant must be enrolled or expecting to enroll full or part-time at a four-year institution; resident of Iowa and studying in Iowa. Available to U.S. citizens. Applicant or parent must meet one or more of the following requirements: general military experience; retired from active duty; disabled or killed as a result of military service; prisoner of war; or missing in action.

Application Requirements: Application, autobiography, essay, financial need analysis, photo, references, self-addressed stamped envelope, test scores, transcript. *Deadline:* June 1.

Contact: Marlene Valentine, Secretary/Treasurer
American Legion Auxiliary, Department of Iowa
720 Lyon Street
Des Moines, IA 50309
Phone: 515-282-7987
Fax: 515-282-7583

AMERICAN LEGION, DEPARTMENT OF NEW YORK http://www.ny.legion.org

AMERICAN LEGION DEPARTMENT OF NEW YORK JAMES F. MULHOLLAND SCHOLARSHIP

Two scholarships for New York students who are high school seniors. Parent must be a New York State American Legionnaire. Must have been accepted by recognized learning institution and must attend for one year to receive award. One-time awards of $500.

Academic Fields/Career Goals: Education.

Award: Scholarship for use in freshman year; not renewable. *Number:* 2. *Amount:* $500.

Eligibility Requirements: Applicant must be high school student; planning to enroll or expecting to enroll full-time at an institution or university and resident of New York. Applicant or parent of applicant must be member of American Legion or Auxiliary. Applicant or parent of applicant must have employment or volunteer experience in community service.

Application Requirements: Application, financial need analysis, references, test scores, transcript. *Deadline:* May 1.

Contact: Richard Pedro, Department Adjutant
American Legion, Department of New York
112 State Street, Suite 400
Albany, NY 12207
Phone: 518-463-2215
Fax: 518-427-8443
E-mail: newyork@legion.org

AMERICAN MONTESSORI SOCIETY http://www.amshq.org

AMERICAN MONTESSORI SOCIETY TEACHER EDUCATION SCHOLARSHIP FUND

One-time award for aspiring Montessori teacher candidates. Must study full time and be under age 20. Submit verification that applicant has been accepted into the AMS program.

Academic Fields/Career Goals: Education.

Award: Scholarship for use in freshman, sophomore, or junior years; not renewable. *Number:* 5–20. *Amount:* varies.

Eligibility Requirements: Applicant must be age 19 or under and enrolled or expecting to enroll full-time at a two-year or four-year institution or university. Available to U.S. and non-U.S. citizens.

American Montessori Society (continued)

Application Requirements: Application, autobiography, essay, financial need analysis, references. *Deadline:* April 28.

Contact: Dottie Sweet Feldman, Fund Administrator
American Montessori Society
2720 Sonata Drive
Columbus, OH 43209
Phone: 614-237-2975
E-mail: dssf@juno.com

AMERICAN QUARTER HORSE FOUNDATION (AQHF) http://www.aqha.org/aqhya

AQHF EDUCATION OR NURSING SCHOLARSHIP

Must be current member of AQHA or AQHYA and pursuing a career in education or nursing. Recipient receives $2500 per year for four years. Minimum 2.5 GPA required.

Academic Fields/Career Goals: Education; Nursing.

Award: Scholarship for use in freshman, sophomore, junior, or senior years; renewable. *Number:* 1. *Amount:* $10,000.

Eligibility Requirements: Applicant must be enrolled or expecting to enroll full-time at a two-year or four-year or technical institution or university. Applicant or parent of applicant must be member of American Quarter Horse Association. Applicant must have 2.5 GPA or higher. Available to U.S. and Canadian citizens.

Application Requirements: Application, financial need analysis, photo, references, transcript. *Deadline:* February 1.

Contact: Laura Owens, Scholarship Coordinator
American Quarter Horse Foundation (AQHF)
2601 I-40 East
Amarillo, TX 79104
Phone: 806-376-5181
Fax: 806-376-1005
E-mail: lowens@aqha.org

ARCTIC INSTITUTE OF NORTH AMERICA http://www.ucalgary.ca/aina

JIM BOURQUE SCHOLARSHIP

One-time award to Canadian Aboriginal student enrolled in postsecondary training in education, environmental studies, traditional knowledge or telecommunications. Must submit, in 500 words or less, a description of their intended program of study and reasons for their choice of program.

Academic Fields/Career Goals: Education; Natural Resources; Natural Sciences.

Award: Scholarship for use in freshman, sophomore, junior, or senior years; not renewable. *Number:* 1. *Amount:* $743.

Eligibility Requirements: Applicant must be Canadian citizen and enrolled or expecting to enroll full-time at an institution or university.

Application Requirements: Autobiography, financial need analysis, references, transcript, proof of enrollment. *Deadline:* July 15.

Contact: Executive Director
Arctic Institute of North America
University of Calgary
2500 University Drive, NW
Calgary, AB T2N 1N4
Canada
Phone: 403-220-7515
Fax: 403-282-4609
E-mail: wkjessen@ucalgary.ca

ARKANSAS DEPARTMENT OF HIGHER EDUCATION http://www.arscholarships.com

ARKANSAS MINORITY TEACHER SCHOLARS PROGRAM

Renewable award for Native-American, African-American, Hispanic and Asian-American students who have completed at least 60 semester hours and are enrolled full-time in a teacher education program in Arkansas. Award may be renewed for one year. Must be Arkansas resident with minimum 2.5 GPA. Must teach for three to five years in Arkansas to repay scholarship funds received. Must pass PPST exam.

Academic Fields/Career Goals: Education.

Award: Forgivable loan for use in junior or senior years; renewable. *Number:* up to 100. *Amount:* up to $5000.

Eligibility Requirements: Applicant must be American Indian/Alaska Native, Asian/Pacific Islander, Black (non-Hispanic), or Hispanic; enrolled or expecting to enroll full-time at a four-year institution or university; resident of Arkansas and studying in Arkansas. Applicant must have 2.5 GPA or higher. Available to U.S. citizens.

Application Requirements: Application, transcript. *Deadline:* June 1.

Contact: Lillian Williams, Assistant Coordinator
Arkansas Department of Higher Education
114 East Capitol
Little Rock, AR 72201
Phone: 501-371-2050
Fax: 501-371-2001

EMERGENCY SECONDARY EDUCATION LOAN PROGRAM

• *See page 111*

ASIAN PACIFIC AMERICAN HERITAGE COUNCIL http://www.apahc.org

ASIAN PACIFIC AMERICAN HERITAGE COUNCIL SCHOLARSHIP

• *See page 121*

ASSOCIATION ON AMERICAN INDIAN AFFAIRS (AAIA) http://www.indian-affairs.org

EMILIE HESSMEYER MEMORIAL SCHOLARSHIP

Scholarship to full-time American Indian and Alaska Native students, with a preference given to students pursuing a major in Education. This scholarship is renewable up to four years toward any single degree.

Academic Fields/Career Goals: Education.

Award: Scholarship for use in freshman, sophomore, junior, or senior years; renewable. *Number:* varies. *Amount:* $1500.

Eligibility Requirements: Applicant must be American Indian/Alaska Native and enrolled or expecting to enroll full-time at an institution or university.

Application Requirements: Application, essay, financial need analysis, references, transcript, certificate of Indian blood, class schedule. *Deadline:* July 20.

Contact: Scholarship Coordinator
Association on American Indian Affairs (AAIA)
966 Hungerford Drive
Suite 12-B
Rockville, MD 20850
Phone: 605-698-3998
Fax: 605-698-3316
E-mail: aaia@sbtc.net

BETHESDA LUTHERAN HOMES AND SERVICES, INC. http://www.blhs.org

DEVELOPMENTAL DISABILITIES SCHOLASTIC ACHIEVEMENT SCHOLARSHIP FOR LUTHERAN COLLEGE STUDENTS

• *See page 184*

BROWN FOUNDATION FOR EDUCATIONAL EQUITY, EXCELLENCE, AND RESEARCH http://www.brownvboard.org/foundatn/sclrbroc.htm

BROWN SCHOLAR

Renewable scholarship award to college student entering junior year who is admitted to teacher education program at a four-year college or university. Applicants must be minority student. Minimum 3.0 GPA required. Award paid at $500 per semester for up to four semesters.

Academic Fields/Career Goals: Education.

Award: Scholarship for use in junior or senior years; renewable. *Number:* varies. *Amount:* $1000.

Eligibility Requirements: Applicant must be American Indian/Alaska Native, Asian/Pacific Islander, Black (non-Hispanic), or Hispanic and enrolled or expecting to enroll full-time at a four-year institution or university. Applicant must have 3.0 GPA or higher. Available to U.S. citizens.

Application Requirements: Application, essay, references, transcript. *Deadline:* March 30.

Contact: Chelsey Smith, Staff/Administrative Assistant
Brown Foundation for Educational Equity, Excellence, and Research
PO Box 4862
Topeka, KS 66604
Phone: 785-235-3939
Fax: 785-235-1001
E-mail: brownfound@juno.com

LUCINDA TODD BOOK SCHOLARSHIP

Book award of $300 to graduating high school senior planning to pursue teacher education at four-year college or university. Award paid to institution for books. Applicants must be minority student. Minimum 3.0 GPA required.

Academic Fields/Career Goals: Education.

Award: Scholarship for use in freshman year; not renewable. *Number:* varies. *Amount:* $300.

Eligibility Requirements: Applicant must be American Indian/Alaska Native, Asian/Pacific Islander, Black (non-Hispanic), or Hispanic; high school student and planning to enroll or expecting to enroll full or part-time at a four-year institution or university. Applicant must have 3.0 GPA or higher. Available to U.S. citizens.

Application Requirements: Application, references, transcript. *Deadline:* March 30.

Contact: Chelsey Smith, Staff/Administrative Assistant
Brown Foundation for Educational Equity, Excellence, and Research
PO Box 4862
Topeka, KS 66604
Phone: 785-235-3939
Fax: 785-235-1001
E-mail: brownfound@juno.com

BUSINESS AND PROFESSIONAL WOMEN'S FOUNDATION http://www.bpwusa.org

BPW CAREER ADVANCEMENT SCHOLARSHIP PROGRAM FOR WOMEN

• *See page 112*

CALIFORNIA TEACHERS ASSOCIATION (CTA) http://www.cta.org

L. GORDON BITTLE MEMORIAL SCHOLARSHIP

Three $2000 awards annually to active Student California Teachers Association (SCTA) members for study in a teacher preparatory program. Students may reapply each year. Applications available in October and due February 16th. Not available to those who are currently working in public schools as members of CTA.

Academic Fields/Career Goals: Education.

Award: Scholarship for use in freshman, sophomore, junior, senior, or graduate years; not renewable. *Number:* 3. *Amount:* $2000.

Eligibility Requirements: Applicant must be enrolled or expecting to enroll full-time at a two-year or four-year institution or university; resident of California and studying in California. Available to U.S. and non-U.S. citizens.

Application Requirements: Application, essay, references, transcript. *Deadline:* February 16.

Contact: Human Rights Department
California Teachers Association (CTA)
PO Box 921
Burlingame, CA 94011-0921
Phone: 650-697-1400
E-mail: scholarships@cta.org

MARTIN LUTHER KING, JR. MEMORIAL SCHOLARSHIP

For ethnic minority members of the California Teachers Association, their dependent children, and ethnic minority members of Student California Teachers Association who want to pursue degrees or credentials in public education. Applications available in January and due March 15.

Academic Fields/Career Goals: Education.

Award: Scholarship for use in freshman, sophomore, junior, senior, or graduate years; not renewable. *Number:* varies. *Amount:* $1000–$2000.

Eligibility Requirements: Applicant must be American Indian/Alaska Native, Asian/Pacific Islander, Black (non-Hispanic), or Hispanic and enrolled or expecting to enroll full-time at a two-year or four-year institution or university. Applicant or parent of applicant must be member of California Teachers Association. Available to U.S. and non-U.S. citizens.

Application Requirements: Application, essay, financial need analysis, references. *Deadline:* March 15.

Contact: Human Rights Department
California Teachers Association (CTA)
PO Box 921
Burlingame, CA 94011-0921
Phone: 650-697-1400
E-mail: scholarships@cta.org

CANADIAN INSTITUTE OF UKRAINIAN STUDIES http://www.ualberta.ca/cius/

LEO J. KRYSA UNDERGRADUATE SCHOLARSHIP

• *See page 80*

CATCHING THE DREAM

MATH, ENGINEERING, SCIENCE, BUSINESS, EDUCATION, COMPUTERS SCHOLARSHIPS

• *See page 121*

NATIVE AMERICAN LEADERSHIP IN EDUCATION (NALE)

• *See page 122*

CIRI FOUNDATION http://www.ciri.com/tcf

LAWRENCE MATSON MEMORIAL ENDOWMENT SCHOLARSHIP FUND

• *See page 86*

COLLEGEBOUND FOUNDATION http://www.collegeboundfoundation.org

ALICE G. PINDERHUGHES SCHOLARSHIP

Award for Baltimore City public high school graduates. Please see Web site: http://www.collegeboundfoundation.org for complete information on application process. Must major in education and plan to teach in grades K-12. Minimum GPA of 3.0, must have financial need. Must submit one-page essay describing a teacher who has made an impact on you. Must submit CollegeBound Competitive Scholarship/Last-Dollar Grant Application.

Academic Fields/Career Goals: Education.

Award: Scholarship for use in freshman, sophomore, junior, or senior years; renewable. *Number:* 1. *Amount:* $500.

Eligibility Requirements: Applicant must be enrolled or expecting to enroll full-time at a two-year or four-year institution or university and resident of Maryland. Applicant must have 3.0 GPA or higher. Available to U.S. citizens.

Application Requirements: Application, essay, financial need analysis, references, transcript, financial aid award letters, Student Aid Report. *Deadline:* March 19.

Contact: April Bell, Associate Program Director
CollegeBound Foundation
300 Water Street, Suite 300
Baltimore, MD 21202
Phone: 410-783-2905 Ext. 208
Fax: 410-727-5786
E-mail: abell@collegeboundfoundation.org

SHEILA Z. KOLMAN MEMORIAL SCHOLARSHIP

Award for Baltimore City public high school graduates. Please see Web site: http://www.collegeboundfoundation.org for complete information on appli-

CollegeBound Foundation (continued)

cation process. Must submit CollegeBound Competitive Scholarship/Last-Dollar Grant Application. Minimum GPA of 2.5 required, demonstrable financial need. Submit 500-1000 word essay on how a teacher affected your life in a positive way. Must major or minor in education.

Academic Fields/Career Goals: Education.

Award: Scholarship for use in freshman year; not renewable. *Number:* 1. *Amount:* $1000.

Eligibility Requirements: Applicant must be enrolled or expecting to enroll full-time at a four-year institution or university and resident of Maryland. Applicant must have 2.5 GPA or higher. Available to U.S. citizens.

Application Requirements: Application, essay, financial need analysis, references, transcript, financial aid award letters, Student Aid Report. *Deadline:* March 19.

Contact: April Bell, Associate Program Director
CollegeBound Foundation
300 Water Street, Suite 300
Baltimore, MD 21202
Phone: 410-783-2905 Ext. 208
Fax: 410-727-5786
E-mail: abell@collegeboundfoundation.org

COMMISSION FRANCO-AMERICAINE D'ECHANGES UNIVERSITAIRES ET CULTURELS

http://www.fulbright-france.org

FULBRIGHT PROGRAM

Fulbright program offered to senior scholars, advanced students, professionals and exchange teachers to carry out research, and/or lecture, study or teach in the United States or France. Program provides grants to approximately 100 nationals from both countries. Applicants must submit proof of their affiliation with their host institution. Grant is only available to American and French citizens. For French citizens, photo must accompany application. Application deadlines: August 1 (for U.S. applicants) and December 15 (for French applicants). For more information, see Web site: http://www.fulbright-france.org.

Academic Fields/Career Goals: Education.

Award: Grant for use in senior, graduate, or postgraduate years; not renewable. *Number:* 80–100. *Amount:* $1000–$20,000.

Eligibility Requirements: Applicant must be enrolled or expecting to enroll full or part-time at a four-year institution or university. Applicant or parent of applicant must have employment or volunteer experience in teaching. Available to U.S. and non-Canadian citizens.

Application Requirements: Application, essay, interview, photo, references, test scores, transcript. *Deadline:* varies.

Contact: Dr. Amy Tondu, Program Officer
Commission Franco-Americaine d'Echanges Universitaires et Culturels
Fulbright Commission
9 Rue Chardin
Paris 75016
France
Phone: 33-1-44145364
Fax: 33-1-42880479
E-mail: atondu@fulbright-france.org

COMMUNITY FOUNDATION FOR PALM BEACH AND MARTIN COUNTIES, INC.

http://www.yourcommunityfoundation.org

INEZ PEPPERS LOVETT SCHOLARSHIP FUND

African-American Palm Beach County graduating senior interested in pursuing a career in elementary education. Must have 3.0 GPA or better and demonstrate financial need.

Academic Fields/Career Goals: Education.

Award: Scholarship for use in freshman year; not renewable. *Number:* 1. *Amount:* $750–$2500.

Eligibility Requirements: Applicant must be Black (non-Hispanic); high school student; planning to enroll or expecting to enroll full-time at a four-year institution or university; female and resident of Florida. Applicant must have 3.0 GPA or higher. Available to U.S. citizens.

Application Requirements: Application, financial need analysis, transcript. *Deadline:* March 1.

Contact: Carolyn Jenco, Grants Manager/Scholarship Coordinator
Community Foundation for Palm Beach and Martin Counties, Inc.
700 South Dixie Highway
Suite 200
West Palm Beach, FL 33401

THOMAS WILLIAM BENNETT MEMORIAL SCHOLARSHIP

Scholarship is awarded to a high school senior, in public or private school, planning on pursuing a career in education, preferably teaching reading skills. Must have 2.5 GPA or better. Must be a resident of Palm Beach or Martin County. Applications are available online: http://www.yourcommunityfoundation.org. Deadline is March 1.

Academic Fields/Career Goals: Education.

Award: Scholarship for use in freshman year; not renewable. *Number:* varies. *Amount:* varies.

Eligibility Requirements: Applicant must be high school student; planning to enroll or expecting to enroll at a four-year institution or university and resident of Florida. Applicant must have 2.5 GPA or higher. Available to U.S. citizens.

Application Requirements: Application. *Deadline:* March 1.

Contact: Carolyn Jenco, Grants Manager/Scholarship Coordinator
Community Foundation for Palm Beach and Martin Counties, Inc.
700 South Dixie Highway
Suite 200
West Palm Beach, FL 33401

COMMUNITY FOUNDATION OF WESTERN MASSACHUSETTS

http://www.communityfoundation.org

MARGARET E. AND AGNES K. O'DONNELL SCHOLARSHIP FUND

For graduating seniors of Northampton High School and Smith Vocational High School, and for students of the College of Our Lady of the Elms and Fitchburg State College majoring in education.

Academic Fields/Career Goals: Education.

Award: Scholarship for use in freshman year; not renewable. *Number:* 12. *Amount:* $1000–$1800.

Eligibility Requirements: Applicant must be enrolled or expecting to enroll at a four-year institution or university and resident of Massachusetts. Available to U.S. citizens.

Application Requirements: Application, financial need analysis, transcript. *Deadline:* March 31.

Contact: Community Foundation of Western Massachusetts
1500 Main Street
PO Box 15769
Springfield, MA 01115

COMTO-BOSTON CHAPTER

http://www.bostoncomto.org

COMTO BOSTON/GARRETT A. MORGAN SCHOLARSHIP

• *See page 75*

CONFEDERATED TRIBES OF GRAND RONDE

http://www.grandronde.org

EULA PETITE MEMORIAL EDUCATION SCHOLARSHIPS

Available to any enrolled member of the Confederated Tribes of Grand Ronde. Available to education majors only. Renewable for six terms/four semesters of continuous study. Intended for last two years of undergraduate study, or any two years of graduate study.

Academic Fields/Career Goals: Education.

Award: Scholarship for use in junior, senior, or graduate years; renewable. *Number:* 1. *Amount:* $7000.

Eligibility Requirements: Applicant must be American Indian/Alaska Native and enrolled or expecting to enroll full or part-time at a four-year institution or university. Available to U.S. and non-U.S. citizens.

Application Requirements: Application, essay, references, transcript, verification of Tribal enrollment. *Deadline:* April 30.

Contact: Tribal Scholarship Coordinator
Confederated Tribes of Grand Ronde
9615 Grand Ronde Road
Grand Ronde, OR 97347
Phone: 800-422-0232 Ext. 2275
Fax: 503-879-2286
E-mail: education@grandronde.org

CONNECTICUT ASSOCIATION FOR HEALTH, PHYSICAL EDUCATION, RECREATION AND DANCE http://www.ctahperd.org

GIBSON-LAEMEL CAHPERD SCHOLARSHIP

Awarded to a college junior or senior accepted into a program of professional studies of health, physical education, recreation or dance. Must be a Connecticut resident and attend a university or four-year college in Connecticut. Minimum 2.5 GPA required.

Academic Fields/Career Goals: Education; Sports-related.

Award: Scholarship for use in junior or senior years; not renewable. *Number:* 1–2. *Amount:* $1000.

Eligibility Requirements: Applicant must be enrolled or expecting to enroll full-time at a four-year institution or university; resident of Connecticut and studying in Connecticut. Applicant must have 2.5 GPA or higher. Available to U.S. citizens.

Application Requirements: Application, essay, references, transcript. *Deadline:* May 1.

Contact: Mrs. Constance Kapral, Executive Director
Connecticut Association for Health, Physical Education, Recreation and Dance
563 Miller Road
South Windsor, CT 06074
Phone: 860-644-9206
Fax: 860-644-9206
E-mail: ckapral@ctahperd.org

MARY BENEVENTO CAHPERD SCHOLARSHIP

Scholarship awarded to a graduating high school senior who plans to engage in the professional studies of health education, physical education, recreation, or dance. Must be resident of Connecticut and plan to attend a university or four-year college in Connecticut.

Academic Fields/Career Goals: Education; Sports-related.

Award: Scholarship for use in freshman year; not renewable. *Number:* 1–2. *Amount:* $1000.

Eligibility Requirements: Applicant must be high school student; planning to enroll or expecting to enroll full-time at a four-year institution or university; resident of Connecticut and studying in Connecticut. Available to U.S. citizens.

Application Requirements: Application, essay, references, test scores, transcript. *Deadline:* April 1.

Contact: Mrs. Constance Kapral, Executive Director
Connecticut Association for Health, Physical Education, Recreation and Dance
563 Miller Road
South Windsor, CT 06074
Phone: 860-644-9206
Fax: 860-644-9206
E-mail: ckapral@ctahperd.org

CONNECTICUT EDUCATION FOUNDATION, INC. http://www.cea.org

SCHOLARSHIP FOR MINORITY COLLEGE STUDENTS

An award for qualified minority candidates who have been accepted into a teacher preparation program at an accredited Connecticut college or university. Must have a 2.75 GPA.

Academic Fields/Career Goals: Education.

Award: Scholarship for use in freshman, sophomore, junior, or senior years. *Number:* varies. *Amount:* $750.

Eligibility Requirements: Applicant must be American Indian/Alaska Native, Asian/Pacific Islander, Black (non-Hispanic), or Hispanic; enrolled or expecting to enroll at a four-year institution or university and studying in Connecticut.

Application Requirements: Application, essay, references, transcript, income verification, letter of acceptance, copy of S.A.R.. *Deadline:* May 1.

Contact: Phil Apruzzese, President
Connecticut Education Foundation, Inc.
21 Oak Street #500
Hartford, CT 06106-8006
Phone: 860-525-5641
E-mail: phila@cea.org

SCHOLARSHIP FOR MINORITY HIGH SCHOOL STUDENTS

Award for qualified minority candidates who have been accepted into an accredited two or four-year Connecticut college or university and intend to enter the teaching profession. Must have 2.75 GPA.

Academic Fields/Career Goals: Education.

Award: Scholarship for use in freshman year. *Number:* varies. *Amount:* $500.

Eligibility Requirements: Applicant must be American Indian/Alaska Native, Asian/Pacific Islander, Black (non-Hispanic), or Hispanic; high school student; planning to enroll or expecting to enroll at a two-year or four-year institution or university and studying in Connecticut.

Application Requirements: Application, essay, references, transcript, letter of acceptance, income verification, copy of S.A.R.. *Deadline:* May 1.

Contact: Phil Apruzzese, President
Connecticut Education Foundation, Inc.
21 Oak Street #500
Hartford, CT 06106-8006
Phone: 860-525-5641
E-mail: phila@cea.org

CONTINENTAL SOCIETY, DAUGHTERS OF INDIAN WARS

CONTINENTAL SOCIETY, DAUGHTERS OF INDIAN WARS SCHOLARSHIP

Award for certified Indian tribal member enrolled in an undergraduate degree program in education or social service. Must maintain minimum 3.0 GPA and plan to work with Native-American after college; work must be on a reservation. Preference given to those in or entering junior year.

Academic Fields/Career Goals: Education; Social Services.

Award: Scholarship for use in freshman, sophomore, junior, senior, or graduate years; not renewable. *Number:* 1. *Amount:* $1000.

Eligibility Requirements: Applicant must be American Indian/Alaska Native and enrolled or expecting to enroll full-time at a two-year or four-year institution. Applicant must have 3.0 GPA or higher. Available to U.S. and Canadian citizens.

Application Requirements: Application, autobiography, essay, financial need analysis, references, transcript. *Deadline:* June 15.

Contact: Mrs. Donald Trolinger, Scholarship Chairperson
Continental Society, Daughters of Indian Wars
Ottawa Hill
61300 East 10010 Road
Miami, OK 74357-4726
Phone: 918-542-5772
Fax: 918-540-0664

COUNCIL FOR INTERNATIONAL EDUCATIONAL EXCHANGE http://www.ciee.org/study

DEPARTMENT OF EDUCATION SCHOLARSHIP FOR PROGRAMS IN CHINA

Scholarships offered to students who are pursuing Chinese language programs in China. Must be a U.S. citizen enrolled in a CIEE program. Students must

Council for International Educational Exchange (continued)

have the equivalent of two years study in Chinese language documented. Deadlines are April 15 and November 15. For more details see Web site: http://www.ciee.org.

Academic Fields/Career Goals: Education.

Award: Scholarship for use in junior, senior, or graduate years; not renewable. *Number:* 10–20. *Amount:* $500–$6000.

Eligibility Requirements: Applicant must be enrolled or expecting to enroll full-time at a four-year institution or university and must have an interest in foreign language. Applicant must have 3.0 GPA or higher. Available to U.S. citizens.

Application Requirements: Application, essay, financial need analysis, references, transcript. *Deadline:* varies.

Contact: Scholarship Committee
Council for International Educational Exchange
7 Custom House Street, 3rd Floor
Portland, ME 04101
E-mail: scholarships@ciee.org

CULTURE CONNECTION http://www.thecultureconnection.com

CULTURE CONNECTION FOUNDATION SCHOLARSHIP

• *See page 52*

DECA (DISTRIBUTIVE EDUCATION CLUBS OF AMERICA) http://www.deca.org

HARRY A. APPLEGATE SCHOLARSHIP

• *See page 123*

DELAWARE HIGHER EDUCATION COMMISSION http://www.doe.state.de.us/high-ed

CHRISTA MCAULIFFE TEACHER SCHOLARSHIP LOAN-DELAWARE

Award for Delaware residents who are pursuing teaching careers. Must agree to teach in Delaware public schools as repayment of loan. Minimum award is $1000 and is renewable for up to four years. Available only at Delaware colleges. Based on academic merit. Must be ranked in upper half of class, and have a score of 1050 on SAT or 25 on the ACT.

Academic Fields/Career Goals: Education.

Award: Forgivable loan for use in freshman, sophomore, junior, or senior years; renewable. *Number:* 1–60. *Amount:* $1000–$5000.

Eligibility Requirements: Applicant must be enrolled or expecting to enroll full-time at a four-year institution or university; resident of Delaware and studying in Delaware. Applicant must have 2.5 GPA or higher. Available to U.S. citizens.

Application Requirements: Application, essay, test scores, transcript. *Deadline:* March 31.

Contact: Donna Myers, Higher Education Analyst
Delaware Higher Education Commission
820 North French Street
5th Floor
Wilmington, DE 19711-3509
Phone: 302-577-3240
Fax: 302-577-6765
E-mail: dhec@doe.k12.de.us

FAMILY, CAREER AND COMMUNITY LEADERS OF AMERICA-TEXAS ASSOCIATION http://www.texasfccla.org

FCCLA TEXAS FARM BUREAU SCHOLARSHIP

• *See page 123*

FINANCE AUTHORITY OF MAINE http://www.famemaine.com

EDUCATORS FOR MAINE PROGRAM

Loans for residents of Maine who are high school seniors, college students, or college graduates with a minimum 3.0 GPA, studying or preparing to study teacher education. Loan is forgivable if student teaches in Maine upon graduation. Awards are based on merit.

Academic Fields/Career Goals: Education.

Award: Forgivable loan for use in freshman, sophomore, junior, senior, or graduate years; not renewable. *Number:* varies. *Amount:* $2000–$3000.

Eligibility Requirements: Applicant must be enrolled or expecting to enroll full-time at a two-year or four-year institution or university and resident of Maine. Applicant must have 3.0 GPA or higher. Available to U.S. citizens.

Application Requirements: Application, essay, test scores, transcript. *Deadline:* April 1.

Contact: Trisha Malloy, Program Officer
Finance Authority of Maine
5 Community Drive
Augusta, ME 04332-0949
Phone: 800-228-3734
Fax: 207-623-0095
E-mail: trisha@famemaine.com

QUALITY CHILD CARE PROGRAM EDUCATION SCHOLARSHIP PROGRAM

Open to residents of Maine who are taking a minimum of one childhood education course or are pursuing a child development associate certificate, associate's degree, baccalaureate degree, or post-baccalaureate teacher certification in child care-related fields. Scholarships of up to $500 per course or $2,000 per year available. See Web site for information (http://www.famemaine.com).

Academic Fields/Career Goals: Education.

Award: Scholarship for use in sophomore, junior, senior, or graduate years; not renewable. *Number:* varies. *Amount:* $500–$2000.

Eligibility Requirements: Applicant must be enrolled or expecting to enroll at a two-year or four-year institution or university and resident of Maine. Available to U.S. citizens.

Application Requirements: Application, financial need analysis. *Deadline:* Continuous.

Contact: Trisha Malloy, Program Officer
Finance Authority of Maine
5 Community Drive
Augusta, ME 04332-0949
Phone: 800-228-3734
Fax: 207-623-0095
E-mail: trisha@famemaine.com

FLORIDA DEPARTMENT OF EDUCATION http://www.floridastudentfinancialaid.org

CRITICAL TEACHER SHORTAGE TUITION REIMBURSEMENT-FLORIDA

One-time awards for full-time Florida public school employees who are certified to teach in Florida and are teaching, or preparing to teach, in critical teacher shortage subject areas. Must earn minimum grade of 3.0 in approved courses. May receive tuition reimbursement up to 9 semester hours or equivalent per academic year, not to exceed $78 per semester hour, for maximum 36 hours. Must be resident of Florida.

Academic Fields/Career Goals: Education.

Award: Scholarship for use in freshman, sophomore, junior, senior, or graduate years; not renewable. *Number:* 1000–1200. *Amount:* up to $234.

Eligibility Requirements: Applicant must be enrolled or expecting to enroll part-time at a two-year or four-year institution or university; resident of Florida and studying in Florida. Applicant or parent of applicant must have employment or volunteer experience in teaching. Applicant must have 3.0 GPA or higher. Available to U.S. citizens.

Application Requirements: Application, financial need analysis. *Deadline:* September 15.

Contact: Scholarship Information
Florida Department of Education
Office of Student Financial Assistance
1940 North Monroe, Suite 70
Tallahassee, FL 32303-4759
Phone: 888-827-2004
E-mail: osfa@fldoe.org

GENERAL FEDERATION OF WOMEN'S CLUBS OF MASSACHUSETTS

GENERAL FEDERATION OF WOMEN'S CLUBS OF MASSACHUSETTS MUSIC SCHOLARSHIP

Scholarship for study in music (including piano), music education, and music therapy. Must include letter of endorsement from president of the sponsoring General Federation of Women's Clubs of Massachusetts. Audition required. For high school seniors who are Massachusetts residents.

Academic Fields/Career Goals: Education; Music; Performing Arts; Therapy/Rehabilitation.

Award: Scholarship for use in freshman year; not renewable. *Number:* varies. *Amount:* up to $800.

Eligibility Requirements: Applicant must be high school student; planning to enroll or expecting to enroll full-time at an institution or university; resident of Massachusetts and must have an interest in music/singing.

Application Requirements: Application, essay, interview, references, self-addressed stamped envelope, transcript. *Deadline:* February 1.

Contact: June Alfano, Music Chairperson
General Federation of Women's Clubs of Massachusetts
PO Box 679
Sudbury, MA 01776-0679
Phone: 978-443-4569
E-mail: joaheart@attbi.com

NEWTONVILLE WOMAN'S CLUB SCHOLARSHIPS

Award for Massachusetts high school seniors enrolling in a four-year institution. Must be in a teacher training program and seeking certification to teach. Interview is required. One-time award of $600. Must also include a letter of endorsement from president of the sponsoring General Federation of Women's Clubs of Massachusetts in the community of applicant's legal residence.

Academic Fields/Career Goals: Education.

Award: Scholarship for use in freshman year; not renewable. *Number:* 1. *Amount:* $600.

Eligibility Requirements: Applicant must be high school student; planning to enroll or expecting to enroll full-time at a four-year institution or university and resident of Massachusetts.

Application Requirements: Application, autobiography, essay, interview, references, self-addressed stamped envelope, transcript. *Deadline:* March 1.

Contact: Jane Howard, Scholarship Chairperson
General Federation of Women's Clubs of Massachusetts
PO Box 679
Sudbury, MA 01776-0679
Phone: 978-444-9105

GEORGIA ASSOCIATION OF EDUCATORS

http://www.gae.org

GAE GFIE SCHOLARSHIP FOR ASPIRING TEACHERS

Up to ten $1000 scholarships will be awarded to graduating seniors who currently attend a fully accredited public Georgia high school and will attend a fully accredited Georgia college or university within the next 12 months. Must have a 3.0 GPA. Must submit three letters of recommendation. Must have plans to enter the teaching profession.

Academic Fields/Career Goals: Education.

Award: Scholarship for use in freshman year; not renewable. *Number:* up to 10. *Amount:* $1000.

Eligibility Requirements: Applicant must be high school student; planning to enroll or expecting to enroll at a two-year or four-year institution or university; resident of Georgia and studying in Georgia. Applicant must have 3.0 GPA or higher. Available to U.S. citizens.

Application Requirements: Application, transcript. *Deadline:* March 15.

Contact: Sally Bennett, Professional Development Specialist
Georgia Association of Educators
100 Crescent Centre Parkway
Suite 500
Tucker, GA 30084-7049
Phone: 678-837-1103
E-mail: sally.bennett@gae.org

GEORGIA STUDENT FINANCE COMMISSION

http://www.gsfc.org

GEORGIA PROMISE TEACHER SCHOLARSHIP PROGRAM

Renewable, forgivable loans for junior undergraduates at Georgia colleges who have been accepted for enrollment into a teacher education program leading to initial certification. Minimum cumulative 3.0 GPA required. Recipient must teach at a Georgia public school for one year for each $1500 awarded. Available to seniors for renewal only. Write for deadlines.

Academic Fields/Career Goals: Education.

Award: Forgivable loan for use in junior or senior years; renewable. *Number:* 700–1400. *Amount:* $3000–$6000.

Eligibility Requirements: Applicant must be enrolled or expecting to enroll full or part-time at a four-year institution or university and studying in Georgia. Applicant must have 3.0 GPA or higher. Available to U.S. citizens.

Application Requirements: Application, transcript. *Deadline:* Continuous.

Contact: Stan DeWitt, Manager of Teacher Scholarships
Georgia Student Finance Commission
2082 East Exchange Place, Suite 100
Tucker, GA 30084
Phone: 770-724-9060
Fax: 770-724-9031

GOLDEN APPLE FOUNDATION

http://www.goldenapple.org

GOLDEN APPLE SCHOLARS OF ILLINOIS

100 scholars are selected annually. Scholars receive $7,000 a year for 4 years. Applicants must be between 17 and 21 and maintain a GPA of 2.5. Eligible applicants must be residents of Illinois studying in Illinois. The deadline is December 1. Recipients must agree to teach in high-need Illinois schools.

Academic Fields/Career Goals: Education.

Award: Forgivable loan for use in freshman, sophomore, junior, or senior years; renewable. *Number:* up to 100. *Amount:* $7000.

Eligibility Requirements: Applicant must be age 17-21; enrolled or expecting to enroll full-time at a four-year institution or university; resident of Illinois and studying in Illinois. Applicant must have 2.5 GPA or higher. Available to U.S. and non-U.S. citizens.

Application Requirements: Application, autobiography, essay, interview, photo, references, test scores, transcript. *Deadline:* December 1.

Contact: Pat Kilduff, Director of Recruitment and Placement
Golden Apple Foundation
8 South Michigan Avenue, Suite 700
Chicago, IL 60603-3318
Phone: 312-407-0006 Ext. 105
Fax: 312-407-0344
E-mail: kilduff@goldenapple.org

GOLDEN KEY INTERNATIONAL HONOUR SOCIETY

http://www.goldenkey.org

EDUCATION ACHIEVEMENT AWARDS

Applicants will be asked to create an original thematic unit comprised of individual lesson plans. One winner will receive a $1000 award. The second place applicant will receive $750 and the third place applicant will receive $500. See Web site for more information: http://goldenkey.gsu.edu.

Academic Fields/Career Goals: Education.

Award: Prize for use in junior, senior, graduate, or postgraduate years; not renewable. *Number:* 3. *Amount:* $500–$1000.

Golden Key International Honour Society (continued)

Eligibility Requirements: Applicant must be enrolled or expecting to enroll at an institution or university.

Application Requirements: Application, applicant must enter a contest, essay, references, transcript. *Deadline:* March 1.

Contact: Member Services
Golden Key International Honour Society
621 North Avenue, NE
Suite C-100
Atlanta, GA 30308
Phone: 404-377-2400
Fax: 678-420-6757
E-mail: scholarships@goldenkey.org

GOVERNOR'S OFFICE

GOVERNOR'S OPPORTUNITY SCHOLARSHIP

• *See page 124*

GRAND CHAPTER OF CALIFORNIA-ORDER OF THE EASTERN STAR

http://www.oescal.org

SCHOLARSHIPS FOR EDUCATION, BUSINESS AND RELIGION

• *See page 125*

GREATER KANAWHA VALLEY FOUNDATION

http://www.tgkvf.org

JOSEPH C. BASILE, II, MEMORIAL SCHOLARSHIP FUND

Award for residents of West Virginia who are majoring in education. Must be an undergraduate at a college or university in West Virginia. Award based on financial need. May apply for only two Foundation scholarships but will only be chosen for one.

Academic Fields/Career Goals: Education.

Award: Scholarship for use in freshman, sophomore, junior, or senior years; not renewable. *Number:* 2. *Amount:* $1000.

Eligibility Requirements: Applicant must be enrolled or expecting to enroll at a two-year or four-year institution; resident of West Virginia and studying in West Virginia. Applicant must have 2.5 GPA or higher. Available to U.S. citizens.

Application Requirements: Application, essay, financial need analysis, references, self-addressed stamped envelope, test scores, transcript. *Deadline:* February 17.

Contact: Susan Hoover, Scholarship Coordinator
Greater Kanawha Valley Foundation
PO Box 3041
Charleston, WV 25331
Phone: 304-346-3620
Fax: 304-346-3640

HAWAII EDUCATION ASSOCIATION

http://www.heaed.com/

FAITH C. AI LAI HEA STUDENT TEACHER SCHOLARSHIP

$5000 scholarship established for student teachers who are enrolled in a full-time undergraduate or post-baccalaureate program in accredited institution of higher learning. Minimum 3.5 GPA required. Preference to students in or from Hawaii.

Academic Fields/Career Goals: Education.

Award: Scholarship for use in senior, graduate, or postgraduate years; not renewable. *Number:* 2. *Amount:* $5000.

Eligibility Requirements: Applicant must be enrolled or expecting to enroll full-time at a four-year institution or university. Applicant must have 3.5 GPA or higher. Available to U.S. citizens.

Application Requirements: Application, autobiography, financial need analysis, photo, references, transcript. *Deadline:* April 11.

Contact: Jane Pang, Chairperson
Hawaii Education Association
1649 Kalakaua Avenue
Honolulu, HI 96826-2494
Phone: 808-949-6657
Fax: 808-944-2032
E-mail: hea.office@heaed.com

FAITH C. AI LAI HEA UNDERGRADUATE SCHOLARSHIP

Scholarship has been established for education majors, students in or from state of Hawaii with GPA of 3.5 or better, full-time undergraduate students. $2000 a school year. $1000 will be sent at beginning of each semester.

Academic Fields/Career Goals: Education.

Award: Scholarship for use in junior or senior years; not renewable. *Number:* 4. *Amount:* $2000.

Eligibility Requirements: Applicant must be enrolled or expecting to enroll full-time at a four-year institution or university and resident of Hawaii. Applicant must have 3.5 GPA or higher. Available to U.S. citizens.

Application Requirements: Application, autobiography, financial need analysis, photo, references, transcript. *Deadline:* April 11.

Contact: Jane Pang, Chairperson
Hawaii Education Association
1649 Kalakaua Avenue
Honolulu, HI 96826-2494
Phone: 808-949-6657
Fax: 808-944-2032
E-mail: hea.office@heaed.com

HAWAII EDUCATION ASSOCIATION STUDENT TEACHER SCHOLARSHIP

Scholarship available to children of HEA members. Intent is to minimize the need for employment during student teaching semester. Must be enrolled full-time in an undergraduate or post-baccalaureate program in accredited institution of higher learning.

Academic Fields/Career Goals: Education.

Award: Scholarship for use in senior, graduate, or postgraduate years; not renewable. *Number:* 2. *Amount:* $3000.

Eligibility Requirements: Applicant must be enrolled or expecting to enroll full-time at a four-year institution or university and resident of Hawaii. Applicant or parent of applicant must be member of Hawaii Education Association. Applicant must have 3.0 GPA or higher. Available to U.S. citizens.

Application Requirements: Application, autobiography, financial need analysis, photo, references, transcript. *Deadline:* April 4.

Contact: George K. Kagehiro, Chairman
Hawaii Education Association
1649 Kalakaua Avenue
Honolulu, HI 96826-2494
Phone: 808-949-6657
Fax: 808-944-2032
E-mail: hea.office@heaed.com

MAY AND HUBERT EVERLY HEA SCHOLARSHIP

Scholarship for education majors who intend to teach in state of Hawaii at K-12 level. Undergraduate student in two- or four-year college/university. $1000 scholarship paid beginning of each semester.

Academic Fields/Career Goals: Education.

Award: Scholarship for use in junior or senior years; not renewable. *Number:* 1. *Amount:* $1000.

Eligibility Requirements: Applicant must be enrolled or expecting to enroll full-time at a two-year or four-year institution or university and studying in Hawaii. Applicant must have 3.0 GPA or higher. Available to U.S. citizens.

Application Requirements: Application, autobiography, financial need analysis, photo, references, transcript. *Deadline:* April 4.

Contact: Sarah S. Moriyama, Chairperson
Hawaii Education Association
1649 Kalakaua Avenue
Honolulu, HI 96826-2494
Phone: 808-949-6657
Fax: 808-944-2032
E-mail: hea.office@heaed.com

HONOR SOCIETY OF PHI KAPPA PHI

http://www.phikappaphi.org

PROMOTION OF EXCELLENCE GRANTS PROGRAM

Grants up to $10,000 will be awarded to Phi Kappa Phi member-led teams for projects designed to establish or implement programs that promote academic excellence in higher education or designed to achieve greater clarity and further scientific understanding about some aspect of the promotion of academic excellence. For more details see Web site: http://www.phikappaphi.org.

Academic Fields/Career Goals: Education.

Award: Grant for use in freshman, sophomore, junior, senior, graduate, or postgraduate years; not renewable. *Number:* varies. *Amount:* $2000–$10,000.

Eligibility Requirements: Applicant must be enrolled or expecting to enroll at an institution or university. Applicant or parent of applicant must be member of Phi Kappa Phi. Available to U.S. and non-U.S. citizens.

Application Requirements: Application. *Deadline:* January 23.

Contact: Theresa Bard, Programs Coordinator
Honor Society of Phi Kappa Phi
Louisiana State University
PO Box 16000
Baton Rouge, LA 70893-6000
Phone: 225-388-4917 Ext. 13
Fax: 225-388-4900
E-mail: awards@phikappaphi.org

HOSTESS COMMITTEE SCHOLARSHIPS/MISS AMERICA PAGEANT

http://www.missamerica.org

ALBERT A. MARKS EDUCATION SCHOLARSHIP FOR TEACHER EDUCATION

Scholarship for Miss America contestants pursuing degree in education. Award available to women who have competed within the Miss America system on the local, state, or national level from 1993 to the present, regardless of whether title was won. One or more scholarships will be awarded annually, depending on the qualifications of the applicants. A new application must be submitted each year, previous applicants may apply. Applications must be received by June 30. Late or incomplete applications are not accepted.

Academic Fields/Career Goals: Education.

Award: Grant for use in freshman, sophomore, junior, or senior years; not renewable. *Number:* up to 4. *Amount:* up to $4000.

Eligibility Requirements: Applicant must be enrolled or expecting to enroll at a four-year institution or university; female and must have an interest in beauty pageant. Available to U.S. citizens.

Application Requirements: Application, essay, financial need analysis, references, transcript. *Deadline:* June 30.

Contact: See Web site.

IDAHO STATE BOARD OF EDUCATION

http://www.idahoboardofed.org

EDUCATION INCENTIVE LOAN FORGIVENESS CONTRACT-IDAHO

Renewable award assists Idaho residents enrolling in teacher education or nursing programs within state. Must rank in top 15% of high school graduating class, have a 3.0 GPA or above, and agree to work in Idaho for two years. Deadlines vary. Contact financial aid office at institution of choice.

Academic Fields/Career Goals: Education; Nursing.

Award: Forgivable loan for use in freshman, sophomore, junior, or senior years; renewable. *Number:* 13–45. *Amount:* varies.

Eligibility Requirements: Applicant must be enrolled or expecting to enroll full-time at a two-year or four-year institution or university; resident of Idaho and studying in Idaho. Applicant must have 3.0 GPA or higher. Available to U.S. citizens.

Application Requirements: Application, test scores, transcript. *Deadline:* varies.

Contact: Financial Aid Office

ILLINOIS CONGRESS OF PARENTS AND TEACHERS

http://www.illinoispta.org

LILLIAN E. GLOVER ILLINOIS PTA SCHOLARSHIP PROGRAM

This scholarship is for a student studying in the field of education or an education-related degree program, which requires certification from Illinois State Board of Education. Must be an Illinois resident. Must rank in upper quarter of class. Award for high school seniors graduating from any Illinois public high school. Applications available at every public high school in the counseling office/career center starting in January, or see Web site: http://www.illinoispta.org.

Academic Fields/Career Goals: Education.

Award: Scholarship for use in freshman year; not renewable. *Number:* 44. *Amount:* $500–$1000.

Eligibility Requirements: Applicant must be high school student; planning to enroll or expecting to enroll full-time at a four-year institution or university and resident of Illinois. Available to U.S. citizens.

Application Requirements: Application, essay, photo, references, self-addressed stamped envelope, transcript. *Deadline:* March 1.

Contact: See high school counselor.

ILLINOIS STUDENT ASSISTANCE COMMISSION (ISAC)

http://www.collegezone.org

ILLINOIS FUTURE TEACHERS CORPS PROGRAM

Scholarships available for students planning to become teachers in Illinois. Students must be Illinois residents enrolled or accepted as a junior or above in a Teacher Education Program at an Illinois college or university. By receiving award, students agree to teach for 5 years at either a public, private, or parochial Illinois preschool, or at a public elementary or secondary school. For an application and further information, visit http://www.collegezone.com.

Academic Fields/Career Goals: Education.

Award: Forgivable loan for use in junior, senior, or graduate years; renewable. *Number:* 1150. *Amount:* $5000–$15,000.

Eligibility Requirements: Applicant must be enrolled or expecting to enroll full or part-time at a four-year institution or university; resident of Illinois and studying in Illinois. Available to U.S. citizens.

Application Requirements: Application, financial need analysis, FAFSA. *Deadline:* March 1.

Contact: College Zone Counselor
Illinois Student Assistance Commission (ISAC)
1755 Lake Cook Road
Deerfield, IL 60015-5209
Phone: 800-899-4722
E-mail: collegezone@isac.org

MINORITY TEACHERS OF ILLINOIS SCHOLARSHIP PROGRAM

Award for minority students planning to teach at an approved Illinois preschool, elementary, or secondary school. Deadline: March 1. Must be Illinois resident.

Academic Fields/Career Goals: Education; Special Education.

Award: Forgivable loan for use in freshman, sophomore, junior, senior, graduate, or postgraduate years; renewable. *Number:* 450–550. *Amount:* up to $5000.

Eligibility Requirements: Applicant must be American Indian/Alaska Native, Asian/Pacific Islander, Black (non-Hispanic), or Hispanic; enrolled or expecting to enroll full or part-time at a two-year or four-year institution or university; resident of Illinois and studying in Illinois. Applicant must have 2.5 GPA or higher. Available to U.S. citizens.

Application Requirements: Application. *Deadline:* March 1.

Contact: College Zone Counselor
Illinois Student Assistance Commission (ISAC)
1755 Lake Cook Road
Deerfield, IL 60015-5209
Phone: 800-899-4722
E-mail: collegezone@isac.org

INDIANA RETIRED TEACHER'S ASSOCIATION (IRTA)

http://www.retiredteachers.org

INDIANA RETIRED TEACHERS ASSOCIATION FOUNDATION SCHOLARSHIP

Scholarship available to college sophomores or juniors who are enrolled full-time in an education program at an Indiana college or university for a first baccalaureate degree. The applicant must be the child, grandchild, legal dependent or spouse of an active, retired or deceased member of the Indiana State Teachers' Retirement Fund.

Academic Fields/Career Goals: Education.

Award: Scholarship for use in junior or senior years; not renewable. *Number:* 8. *Amount:* $1200.

Eligibility Requirements: Applicant must be enrolled or expecting to enroll full-time at a four-year institution or university; resident of Indiana and studying in Indiana. Applicant or parent of applicant must be member of Indiana State Teachers Association. Applicant or parent of applicant must have employment or volunteer experience in teaching. Applicant must have 2.5 GPA or higher. Available to U.S. citizens.

Application Requirements: Application, essay, financial need analysis, references, transcript. *Deadline:* February 18.

Contact: Joan Grubbs, Executive Assistant
Indiana Retired Teacher's Association (IRTA)
150 West Market Street, Suite 610
Indianapolis, IN 46204-2812
Phone: 888-454-9333
Fax: 317-637-9671
E-mail: irta@iquest.net

INTERNATIONAL ASSOCIATION OF GREAT LAKES RESEARCH

http://www.iaglr.org

PAUL W. RODGERS SCHOLARSHIP

• *See page 190*

IOWA COLLEGE STUDENT AID COMMISSION

http://www.iowacollegeaid.org

IOWA TEACHER FORGIVABLE LOAN PROGRAM

Forgivable loan assists students who will teach in Iowa secondary schools. Must be an Iowa resident attending an Iowa postsecondary institution. Contact for additional information.

Academic Fields/Career Goals: Education.

Award: Forgivable loan for use in freshman, sophomore, junior, or senior years; not renewable. *Number:* varies. *Amount:* $2686.

Eligibility Requirements: Applicant must be enrolled or expecting to enroll full or part-time at a four-year institution or university; resident of Iowa and studying in Iowa. Applicant or parent of applicant must have employment or volunteer experience in teaching. Available to U.S. citizens.

Application Requirements: Application, financial need analysis. *Deadline:* Continuous.

Contact: Brenda Easter, Special Programs Administrator
Iowa College Student Aid Commission
200 10th Street, 4th Floor
Des Moines, IA 50309-3609
Phone: 515-242-3380
Fax: 515-242-3388
E-mail: icsac@max.state.ia.us

JACK J. ISGUR FOUNDATION

JACK J. ISGUR FOUNDATION SCHOLARSHIP

• *See page 87*

JEWISH FAMILY AND CHILDREN'S SERVICES

http://www.jfcs.org

ZISOVICH JEWISH STUDIES SCHOLARSHIP FUND TO TEACH THE HOLOCAUST

Must be resident of San Francisco, San Mateo, northern Santa Clara, Marin, or Sonoma county. Scholarships for Jewish or non-Jewish students hoping to pursue careers which will include teaching the Holocaust to future generations. Amount of award varies. For more details and an application see Web site: http://www.jfcs.org.

Academic Fields/Career Goals: Education; History.

Award: Scholarship for use in freshman, sophomore, junior, or graduate years; not renewable. *Number:* varies. *Amount:* $3000–$6000.

Eligibility Requirements: Applicant must be enrolled or expecting to enroll at an institution or university and resident of California.

Application Requirements: Application, financial need analysis, transcript. *Deadline:* Continuous.

Contact: Eric Singer, Director, Financial Aid Center
Jewish Family and Children's Services
2150 Post Street
San Francisco, CA 94115
Phone: 415-449-1226
E-mail: erics@jfcs.org

JEWISH FEDERATION OF METROPOLITAN CHICAGO (JFMC)

http://www.jvschicago.org

JEWISH FEDERATION OF METROPOLITAN CHICAGO ACADEMIC SCHOLARSHIP PROGRAM

• *See page 185*

KENTUCKY DEPARTMENT OF EDUCATION

http://www.kde.state.ky.us

KENTUCKY MINORITY EDUCATOR RECRUITMENT AND RETENTION (KMERR) SCHOLARSHIP

Scholarship for minority teacher candidates who rank in the upper half of their class or have a minimum 2.5 GPA. Must be a U.S. citizen and Kentucky resident enrolled in one of Kentucky's eight public institutions. Must teach one semester in Kentucky for each semester the scholarship is received.

Academic Fields/Career Goals: Education.

Award: Forgivable loan for use in freshman, sophomore, junior, or senior years; renewable. *Number:* 300. *Amount:* $2500–$5000.

Eligibility Requirements: Applicant must be American Indian/Alaska Native, Asian/Pacific Islander, Black (non-Hispanic), or Hispanic; enrolled or expecting to enroll full-time at a four-year institution or university; resident of Kentucky and studying in Kentucky. Applicant must have 2.5 GPA or higher. Available to U.S. citizens.

Application Requirements: Application, essay, references, test scores, transcript. *Deadline:* Continuous.

Contact: Robby Morton, Director
Kentucky Department of Education
500 Mero Street, 17th Floor
Frankfort, KY 40601
Phone: 502-564-1479
Fax: 502-564-6952
E-mail: rmorton@kde.state.ky.us

KENTUCKY HIGHER EDUCATION ASSISTANCE AUTHORITY (KHEAA)

http://www.kheaa.com

EARLY CHILDHOOD DEVELOPMENT SCHOLARSHIP

• *See page 148*

KENTUCKY TEACHER SCHOLARSHIP PROGRAM

Award for Kentucky resident attending Kentucky institutions and pursuing initial teacher certification. Must teach one semester for each semester of award received. In critical shortage areas, must teach one semester for every two semesters of award received. Repayment obligation if teaching requirement not met. Submit Free Application for Federal Student Aid and Teacher Scholarship Application by May 1.

Academic Fields/Career Goals: Education.

Award: Forgivable loan for use in freshman, sophomore, junior, senior, or graduate years; renewable. *Number:* 600–700. *Amount:* $250–$5000.

Eligibility Requirements: Applicant must be enrolled or expecting to enroll full-time at a two-year or four-year institution or university; resident of Kentucky and studying in Kentucky. Available to U.S. citizens.

Application Requirements: Application, financial need analysis. *Deadline:* May 1.

Contact: Tim Phelps, Student Aid Branch Manager
Kentucky Higher Education Assistance Authority (KHEAA)
PO Box 798
Frankfort, KY 40602-0798
Phone: 502-696-7393
Fax: 502-696-7373
E-mail: tphelps@kheaa.com

MINORITY EDUCATOR RECRUITMENT AND RETENTION SCHOLARSHIP

Conversion loan/scholarship providing up to $5,000 per academic year to minority students majoring in teacher education pursuing initial teacher certification. Must be repaid with interest if scholarship requirements not met.

Academic Fields/Career Goals: Education; Special Education.

Award: Forgivable loan for use in freshman, sophomore, junior, senior, or graduate years; not renewable. *Number:* 200–300. *Amount:* up to $5000.

Eligibility Requirements: Applicant must be American Indian/Alaska Native, Asian/Pacific Islander, Black (non-Hispanic), or Hispanic; enrolled or expecting to enroll full-time at a four-year institution or university; resident of Kentucky and studying in Kentucky. Applicant must have 2.5 GPA or higher. Available to U.S. citizens.

Application Requirements: Application. *Deadline:* Continuous.

Contact: Dr. Lucian Yates III, Director, MERR, KY Department of Education
Kentucky Higher Education Assistance Authority (KHEAA)
500 Metro Street
Frankfort, KY 40601
Phone: 502-564-1479

LINCOLN COMMUNITY FOUNDATION http://www.lcf.org

DALE E. SIEFKES SCHOLARSHIP

Scholarship for a junior or senior attending any college or university in Nebraska. Must be pursuing studies in education and demonstrate financial need. Minimum 3.80 GPA required. Application deadline: April 15.

Academic Fields/Career Goals: Education.

Award: Scholarship for use in junior or senior years; not renewable. *Number:* 1. *Amount:* $500–$1000.

Eligibility Requirements: Applicant must be enrolled or expecting to enroll full-time at a two-year or four-year or technical institution or university and studying in Nebraska. Available to U.S. citizens.

Application Requirements: Application, essay, financial need analysis, test scores, transcript. *Deadline:* April 15.

Contact: Application available at Web site.

NEBRASKA RURAL COMMUNITY SCHOOLS ASSOCIATION SCHOLARSHIP

Scholarships are for students attending schools in Nebraska holding current memberships in NRCSA. Must major in education and demonstrate financial need. Applicants should also demonstrate academic achievement, leadership, character, and initiative. Preferred students will be involved in extracurricular activities. Must be a resident of Nebraska.

Academic Fields/Career Goals: Education.

Award: Scholarship for use in freshman year; not renewable. *Number:* 6. *Amount:* $500–$1000.

Eligibility Requirements: Applicant must be high school student; planning to enroll or expecting to enroll full-time at a two-year or four-year institution or university; resident of Nebraska and studying in Nebraska. Applicant must have 3.5 GPA or higher. Available to U.S. citizens.

Application Requirements: Application, essay, financial need analysis, references. *Deadline:* February 9.

Contact: Application available at Web site.

MARION D. AND EVA S. PEEPLES FOUNDATION TRUST SCHOLARSHIP PROGRAM http://www.jccf.org

MARION D. AND EVA S. PEEPLES SCHOLARSHIPS

Award for study in nursing, dietetics, and teaching in industrial arts. Applicant must reapply each year for renewal. Recipient must maintain 2.5 GPA and take at least 12 credit hours per semester. Minimum 1100 on SAT if high school student. Must be Indiana resident and attending an Indiana school.

Academic Fields/Career Goals: Education; Engineering/Technology; Food Science/Nutrition; Nursing; Trade/Technical Specialties.

Award: Scholarship for use in freshman, sophomore, junior, or senior years; not renewable. *Number:* 15–30. *Amount:* $500–$4000.

Eligibility Requirements: Applicant must be enrolled or expecting to enroll full-time at a two-year or four-year or technical institution or university; resident of Indiana and studying in Indiana. Applicant must have 2.5 GPA or higher. Available to U.S. citizens.

Application Requirements: Application, autobiography, financial need analysis, interview, references, self-addressed stamped envelope, test scores, transcript. *Deadline:* March 1.

Contact: Sonya Baker-Hallett, Scholarship Director
Marion D. and Eva S. Peeples Foundation Trust Scholarship Program
398 South Main Street
Franklin, IN 46131
Phone: 317-738-2213
Fax: 317-738-9113
E-mail: sonyah@jccf.org

MARYLAND HIGHER EDUCATION COMMISSION http://www.mhec.state.md.us

CHILD CARE PROVIDER PROGRAM-MARYLAND

Forgivable loan provides assistance for Maryland undergraduates attending a Maryland institution and pursuing studies in a child development program or an early childhood education program. Must serve as a professional day care provider in Maryland for one year for each year award received. Must maintain minimum 2.0 GPA. Contact for further information.

Academic Fields/Career Goals: Education.

Award: Forgivable loan for use in freshman, sophomore, junior, or senior years; renewable. *Number:* 100–150. *Amount:* $500–$2000.

Eligibility Requirements: Applicant must be enrolled or expecting to enroll full or part-time at a two-year or four-year institution or university; resident of Maryland and studying in Maryland. Available to U.S. citizens.

Application Requirements: Application, transcript. *Deadline:* June 15.

Contact: Margaret Crutchley, Office of Student Financial Assistance
Maryland Higher Education Commission
839 Bestgate Road, Suite 400
Annapolis, MD 21401-3013
Phone: 410-260-4545
Fax: 410-260-3203
E-mail: ofsamail@mhec.state.md.us

DISTINGUISHED SCHOLAR-TEACHER EDUCATION AWARDS

Up to $3,000 award for Maryland high school seniors who have received the Distinguished Scholar Award. Recipient must enroll as a full-time undergraduate in a Maryland institution and pursue a program of study leading to a Maryland teaching certificate. Must maintain annual 3.0 GPA for renewal. Must teach in a Maryland public school one year for each year award is received.

Academic Fields/Career Goals: Education.

Award: Forgivable loan for use in freshman, sophomore, junior, or senior years; renewable. *Number:* 20–80. *Amount:* up to $3000.

Eligibility Requirements: Applicant must be high school student; planning to enroll or expecting to enroll full-time at a two-year or four-year institution or university; resident of Maryland and studying in Maryland. Applicant must have 3.0 GPA or higher. Available to U.S. citizens.

Maryland Higher Education Commission (continued)

Application Requirements: Application, test scores, transcript, must be recipient of the Distinguished Scholar Award. *Deadline:* Continuous.

Contact: Monica Tipton, Office of Student Financial Assistance
Maryland Higher Education Commission
839 Bestgate Road, Suite 400
Annapolis, MD 21401-3013
Phone: 410-260-4568
Fax: 410-260-3200
E-mail: ofsamail@mhec.state.md.us

JANET L. HOFFMANN LOAN ASSISTANCE REPAYMENT PROGRAM

Provides assistance for repayment of loan debt to Maryland residents working full-time in nonprofit organizations and state or local governments. Must submit Employment Verification Form and Lender Verification Form.

Academic Fields/Career Goals: Education; Law/Legal Services; Nursing; Social Services; Therapy/Rehabilitation.

Award: Grant for use in freshman, sophomore, junior, senior, or graduate years; not renewable. *Number:* up to 400. *Amount:* up to $7500.

Eligibility Requirements: Applicant must be enrolled or expecting to enroll at an institution or university; resident of Maryland and studying in Maryland. Available to U.S. citizens.

Application Requirements: Application, transcript, IRS 1040 form. *Deadline:* September 30.

Contact: Marie Janiszewski, Office of Student Financial Assistance
Maryland Higher Education Commission
839 Bestgate Road, Suite 400
Annapolis, MD 21401
Phone: 410-260-4569
Fax: 410-260-3203
E-mail: osfamail@mhec.state.md.us

SHARON CHRISTA MCAULIFFE TEACHER EDUCATION-CRITICAL SHORTAGE GRANT PROGRAM

Renewable awards for Maryland residents who are college juniors, seniors, or graduate students enrolled in a Maryland teacher education program. Must agree to enter profession in a subject designated as a critical shortage area. Must teach in Maryland for one year for each award year. Renewable for one year.

Academic Fields/Career Goals: Education.

Award: Forgivable loan for use in junior, senior, or graduate years; renewable. *Number:* up to 137. *Amount:* $200–$14,775.

Eligibility Requirements: Applicant must be enrolled or expecting to enroll full or part-time at a four-year institution or university; resident of Maryland and studying in Maryland. Applicant must have 3.0 GPA or higher. Available to U.S. citizens.

Application Requirements: Application, essay, resume, transcript. *Deadline:* December 31.

Contact: Margaret Crutchley, Office of Student Financial Assistance
Maryland Higher Education Commission
839 Bestgate Road, Suite 400
Annapolis, MD 21401-3013
Phone: 410-260-4545
Fax: 410-260-3203
E-mail: ofsamail@mhec.state.md.us

MASSACHUSETTS OFFICE OF STUDENT FINANCIAL ASSISTANCE http://www.osfa.mass.edu

PARAPROFESSIONAL TEACHER PREPARATION GRANT

Grant providing financial aid assistance to Massachusetts residents who are currently employed as paraprofessionals in Massachusetts public schools and wish to obtain higher education and become certified as full time teachers.

Academic Fields/Career Goals: Education.

Award: Grant for use in freshman, sophomore, junior, or senior years. *Number:* varies. *Amount:* $750–$6500.

Eligibility Requirements: Applicant must be enrolled or expecting to enroll full or part-time at a two-year or four-year institution or university and resident of Massachusetts. Available to U.S. citizens.

Application Requirements: Application. *Deadline:* varies.

Contact: Clantha McCurdy, Associate Vice Chancellor
Massachusetts Office of Student Financial Assistance
454 Broadway, Suite 200
Revere, MA 02151
Phone: 617-727-9420
Fax: 617-727-0667
E-mail: cmccurdy@osfa.mass.edu

TOMORROW'S TEACHERS SCHOLARSHIP PROGRAM

Tuition waver for graduating high school senior ranking in top 25% of class. Must be a resident of Massachusetts and pursue a bachelor's degree at a public college or university in the Commonwealth. Must commit to teach for four years in a Massachusetts public school.

Academic Fields/Career Goals: Education.

Award: Scholarship for use in freshman, sophomore, junior, or senior years; renewable. *Number:* varies. *Amount:* varies.

Eligibility Requirements: Applicant must be high school student; planning to enroll or expecting to enroll full-time at a four-year institution or university; resident of Massachusetts and studying in Massachusetts. Applicant must have 3.5 GPA or higher. Available to U.S. citizens.

Application Requirements: Application, essay, references, transcript. *Deadline:* February 15.

Contact: Alison Leary
Massachusetts Office of Student Financial Assistance
454 Broadway, Suite 200
Revere, MA 02151
Phone: 617-727-9420
Fax: 617-727-0667
E-mail: osfa@osfa.mass.edu

MELLON NEW ENGLAND

JOHN L. BATES SCHOLARSHIP

Award for residents of Massachusetts who are majoring in education. Application deadline is April 15.

Academic Fields/Career Goals: Education.

Award: Scholarship for use in freshman, sophomore, junior, or senior years; not renewable. *Number:* varies. *Amount:* $200–$300.

Eligibility Requirements: Applicant must be enrolled or expecting to enroll full-time at a two-year or four-year or technical institution or university and resident of Massachusetts. Available to U.S. citizens.

Application Requirements: Application, essay, transcript. *Deadline:* April 15.

Contact: Sandra Brown-McMullen, Vice President
Mellon New England
One Boston Place, 024-0084
Boston, MA 02108
Phone: 617-722-3891

MEMORIAL FOUNDATION FOR JEWISH CULTURE http://www.mfjc.org

MEMORIAL FOUNDATION FOR JEWISH CULTURE INTERNATIONAL SCHOLARSHIP PROGRAM FOR COMMUNITY SERVICE

• *See page 82*

MID-COAST AUDUBON SOCIETY http://www.midcoastaudubon.org

JEAN BOYER HAMLIN SCHOLARSHIP IN ORNITHOLOGY

• *See page 63*

MISSISSIPPI STATE STUDENT FINANCIAL AID http://www.mississippiuniversities.com

CRITICAL NEEDS TEACHER LOAN/SCHOLARSHIP

Eligible applicants will agree to employment immediately upon degree completion as a full-time classroom teacher in a public school located in a critical teacher shortage area in the state of Mississippi. Must verify the intention to pursue a first bachelor's degree in teacher education. Award covers tuition and required fees, average cost of room and meals plus a $500 allowance for books. Must be enrolled at a Mississippi college or university.

Academic Fields/Career Goals: Education; Psychology; Therapy/Rehabilitation.

Award: Forgivable loan for use in junior or senior years; not renewable. *Number:* varies.

Eligibility Requirements: Applicant must be enrolled or expecting to enroll full or part-time at a four-year institution or university and studying in Mississippi. Applicant must have 2.5 GPA or higher. Available to U.S. citizens.

Application Requirements: Application, test scores, transcript. *Deadline:* March 31.

Contact: Mississippi Student Financial Aid
Mississippi State Student Financial Aid
3825 Ridgewood Road
Jackson, MS 39211-6453
Phone: 800-327-2980
E-mail: sfa@ihl.state.ms.us

WILLIAM WINTER TEACHER SCHOLAR LOAN PROGRAM

Awarded to Mississippi residents pursuing a teaching career. Must be enrolled full-time in a program leading to a Class A certification and maintain a 2.5 GPA. Must agree to teach one year for each year award is received.

Academic Fields/Career Goals: Education.

Award: Forgivable loan for use in junior or senior years; renewable. *Number:* varies. *Amount:* $500–$8000.

Eligibility Requirements: Applicant must be enrolled or expecting to enroll full-time at a two-year or four-year institution or university; resident of Mississippi and studying in Mississippi. Applicant must have 2.5 GPA or higher. Available to U.S. citizens.

Application Requirements: Application, driver's license, references, transcript. *Deadline:* March 31.

Contact: Board of Trustees
Mississippi State Student Financial Aid
3825 Ridgewood Road
Jackson, MS 39211-6453

MISSOURI DEPARTMENT OF ELEMENTARY AND SECONDARY EDUCATION http://www.dese.state.mo.us

MISSOURI MINORITY TEACHING SCHOLARSHIP

Award may be used any year up to four years at an approved, participating Missouri institution. Scholarship is for minority Missouri residents in teaching programs. Recipients must commit to teach for five years in a Missouri public elementary or secondary school. Graduate students must teach math or science. Otherwise, award must be repaid.

Academic Fields/Career Goals: Education.

Award: Scholarship for use in freshman, sophomore, junior, senior, or graduate years; renewable. *Number:* 100. *Amount:* $3000.

Eligibility Requirements: Applicant must be American Indian/Alaska Native, Asian/Pacific Islander, Black (non-Hispanic), or Hispanic; enrolled or expecting to enroll full-time at a two-year or four-year institution or university; resident of Missouri and studying in Missouri. Applicant must have 3.0 GPA or higher. Available to U.S. citizens.

Application Requirements: Application, essay, financial need analysis, resume, references, test scores, transcript. *Deadline:* February 15.

Contact: Laura Harrison, Administrative Assistant II
Missouri Department of Elementary and Secondary Education
PO Box 480
Jefferson City, MO 65102-0480
Phone: 573-751-1668
Fax: 573-526-3580
E-mail: laura.harrison@dese.mo.gov

MISSOURI TEACHER EDUCATION SCHOLARSHIP (GENERAL)

Nonrenewable award for Missouri high school seniors or Missouri resident college students. Must attend approved teacher training program at a participating Missouri institution. Must rank in top 15 % of high school class on ACT/SAT. Merit-based award. Recipients must commit to teach in Missouri for five years at a public elementary or secondary school or award must be repaid.

Academic Fields/Career Goals: Education.

Award: Scholarship for use in freshman, sophomore, junior, or senior years; not renewable. *Number:* 200–240. *Amount:* $2000.

Eligibility Requirements: Applicant must be enrolled or expecting to enroll full-time at a two-year or four-year institution or university; resident of Missouri and studying in Missouri. Applicant must have 3.5 GPA or higher. Available to U.S. citizens.

Application Requirements: Application, essay, resume, references, test scores, transcript. *Deadline:* February 15.

Contact: Laura Harrison, Administrative Assistant II
Missouri Department of Elementary and Secondary Education
PO Box 480
Jefferson City, MO 65102-0480
Phone: 573-751-1668
Fax: 573-526-3580
E-mail: laura.harrison@dese.mo.gov

NASA IDAHO SPACE GRANT CONSORTIUM http://www.uidaho.edu/nasa_isgc

NASA IDAHO SPACE GRANT CONSORTIUM SCHOLARSHIP PROGRAM

• *See page 71*

NASA VIRGINIA SPACE GRANT CONSORTIUM http://www.vsgc.odu.edu

VIRGINIA SPACE GRANT CONSORTIUM TEACHER EDUCATION SCHOLARSHIPS

• *See page 102*

NATIONAL ASSOCIATION FOR THE ADVANCEMENT OF COLORED PEOPLE http://www.naacp.org

NAACP LILLIAN AND SAMUEL SUTTON EDUCATION SCHOLARSHIP

Must be an education major, full-time student, and be enrolled in accredited college in the United States. Graduating high school seniors and undergraduate students must have 2.5 minimum GPA. Graduate students must have 3.0 and can be full- or part-time. Undergraduate scholarship awards $1,000; graduate scholarship awards $2,000. NAACP membership and participation is preferable, copy of NAACP membership card or receipt of membership is needed. Application deadline is the last Friday in March.

Academic Fields/Career Goals: Education.

Award: Scholarship for use in freshman, sophomore, junior, senior, or graduate years; not renewable. *Number:* varies. *Amount:* $1000–$2000.

Eligibility Requirements: Applicant must be American Indian/Alaska Native, Asian/Pacific Islander, Black (non-Hispanic), or Hispanic and enrolled or expecting to enroll full or part-time at a four-year institution or university. Applicant or parent of applicant must be member of National Association for the Advancement of Colored People. Available to U.S. citizens.

Application Requirements: Application, financial need analysis, references, transcript. *Deadline:* varies.

Contact: Donna Lakins, Education Department, Scholarship Request
National Association for the Advancement of Colored People
4805 Mt. Hope Drive
Baltimore, MD 21215-3297
Phone: 410-580-5760
Fax: 410-585-1329

NATIONAL FEDERATION OF THE BLIND http://www.nfb.org

NATIONAL FEDERATION OF THE BLIND EDUCATOR OF TOMORROW AWARD

Award for students who are legally blind and pursuing teaching careers. Must submit recommendation from state officer of National Federation of the Blind. Awards based on academic excellence, service to the community, and financial need. May reapply. Must attend school in U.S.

National Federation of the Blind (continued)

Academic Fields/Career Goals: Education.

Award: Scholarship for use in freshman, sophomore, junior, or senior years; not renewable. *Number:* 1. *Amount:* $3000.

Eligibility Requirements: Applicant must be enrolled or expecting to enroll at an institution or university. Applicant or parent of applicant must have employment or volunteer experience in community service. Applicant must be visually impaired. Applicant must have 3.5 GPA or higher. Available to U.S. and non-U.S. citizens.

Application Requirements: Application, autobiography, essay, financial need analysis, references, transcript. *Deadline:* March 31.

Contact: Peggy Elliot, Chairman, Scholarship Committee
National Federation of the Blind
805 Fifth Avenue
Grinnell, IA 50112
Phone: 641-236-3366

NATIONAL INSTITUTE FOR LABOR RELATIONS RESEARCH http://www.nilrr.org

APPLEGATE/JACKSON/PARKS FUTURE TEACHER SCHOLARSHIP

Scholarship available to all education majors currently attending school. Award is based on an essay demonstrating knowledge of and interest in compulsory unionism in education. When corresponding regarding scholarship, please specify "Education" or "Future Teacher Scholarship". High school seniors accepted into a teacher education program may apply.

Academic Fields/Career Goals: Education; Special Education.

Award: Scholarship for use in freshman, sophomore, junior, or senior years; not renewable. *Number:* 1. *Amount:* $1000.

Eligibility Requirements: Applicant must be enrolled or expecting to enroll full or part-time at a two-year or four-year institution or university. Available to U.S. citizens.

Application Requirements: Application, applicant must enter a contest, essay, transcript. *Deadline:* December 31.

Contact: Cathy Jones, Scholarship Coordinator
National Institute for Labor Relations Research
5211 Port Royal Road
Springfield, VA 22151
Phone: 703-321-9606
Fax: 703-321-7342
E-mail: research@nilrr.org

NATIONAL URBAN LEAGUE http://www.nul.org

BLACK EXECUTIVE EXCHANGE PROGRAM JERRY BARTOW SCHOLARSHIP FUND

• *See page 128*

NEW HAMPSHIRE POSTSECONDARY EDUCATION COMMISSION http://www.state.nh.us/postsecondary

WORKFORCE INCENTIVE PROGRAM

The Workforce Incentive Program links higher education with critical workforce needs. There are two components to the program: an incentive for students to study in particular areas (forgivable loan) and assistance for employees in critical workforce shortage areas (loan repayment). Critical shortage areas are: nursing, special education, and foreign language education. Please refer to Web site for further details: http://www.state.nh.us/postsecondary.

Academic Fields/Career Goals: Education; Foreign Language; Nursing; Special Education.

Award: Forgivable loan for use in freshman, sophomore, junior, senior, graduate, or postgraduate years. *Number:* varies. *Amount:* varies.

Eligibility Requirements: Applicant must be enrolled or expecting to enroll at an institution or university and studying in New Hampshire. Available to U.S. citizens.

Application Requirements: Application. *Deadline:* varies.

Contact: Judith Knapp, Student Financial Assistant Coordinator
New Hampshire Postsecondary Education Commission
3 Barrell Court, Suite 300
Concord, NH 03301-8543
Phone: 603-271-2555
Fax: 603-271-2696
E-mail: jknapp@pec.state.nh.us

NORTH CAROLINA ASSOCIATION OF EDUCATORS http://www.ncae.org

MARY MORROW-EDNA RICHARDS SCHOLARSHIP

One-time award for senior year of study in four-year education degree program. Preference given to members of the student branch of the North Carolina Association of Educators. Must be North Carolina resident attending a North Carolina institution. Must agree to teach in North Carolina for two years after graduation. Must be a junior in college when application is filed. Deadline is second Monday in January.

Academic Fields/Career Goals: Education.

Award: Forgivable loan for use in senior year; not renewable. *Number:* 3. *Amount:* $1000.

Eligibility Requirements: Applicant must be enrolled or expecting to enroll full-time at a four-year institution; resident of North Carolina and studying in North Carolina. Available to U.S. citizens.

Application Requirements: Application, essay, references, transcript. *Deadline:* varies.

Contact: Jackie Vaughn, Morrow/Richards Scholarship Coordinator
North Carolina Association of Educators
700 South Salisbury Street
Raleigh, NC 27611
Phone: 919-832-3000 Ext. 216
Fax: 919-839-8229
E-mail: jvaughn@nea.org

NORTH CAROLINA STATE EDUCATION ASSISTANCE AUTHORITY http://www.cfnc.org

TEACHER ASSISTANT SCHOLARSHIP PROGRAM

Funding to attend a public or private four-year college or university in North Carolina with an approved teacher education program. Applicant must be employed full-time as a teacher assistant in an instructional area while pursuing licensure and maintain employment to remain eligible. Refer to Web site for further details: http://www.ncseaa.edu/tas.htm

Academic Fields/Career Goals: Education.

Award: Scholarship for use in freshman, sophomore, junior, or senior years. *Number:* varies. *Amount:* $1600–$4800.

Eligibility Requirements: Applicant must be enrolled or expecting to enroll at a four-year institution or university; resident of North Carolina and studying in North Carolina. Applicant must have 2.5 GPA or higher.

Application Requirements: *Deadline:* varies.

Contact: See Web site: http://www.ncseaa.edu/tas.htm

NORTH CAROLINA TEACHING FELLOWS COMMISSION http://www.teachingfellows.org

NORTH CAROLINA TEACHING FELLOWS SCHOLARSHIP PROGRAM

Renewable award for North Carolina high school seniors pursuing teaching careers. Must agree to teach in a North Carolina public or government school for four years or repay award. Must attend one of the 14 approved schools in North Carolina. Merit-based. Must interview at the local level and at the regional level as a finalist. Application available online only: http://www.teachingfellows.org.

Academic Fields/Career Goals: Education.

Award: Forgivable loan for use in freshman, sophomore, junior, or senior years; renewable. *Number:* up to 400. *Amount:* $6500.

Eligibility Requirements: Applicant must be high school student; planning to enroll or expecting to enroll full-time at a four-year institution; resident of North Carolina and studying in North Carolina. Applicant must have 3.5 GPA or higher. Available to U.S. citizens.

Application Requirements: Application, essay, interview, references, test scores, transcript. *Deadline:* varies.

Contact: Ms. Sherry Woodruff, Program Officer
North Carolina Teaching Fellows Commission
3739 National Drive, Suite 210
Raleigh, NC 27612
Phone: 919-781-6833 Ext. 103
Fax: 919-781-6527
E-mail: tfellows@ncforum.org

NORTH DAKOTA UNIVERSITY SYSTEM http://www.ndus.nodak.edu

NORTH DAKOTA TEACHER SHORTAGE LOAN FORGIVENESS PROGRAM

Forgivable loan for individuals who received their education degree from a North Dakota public institution and teach in North Dakota at grade levels and/or content areas identified by the Department of Public Instruction as having a teacher shortage. Funding recipients are eligible to have indebtedness reduced for up to $1000 per year for every consecutive year they teach in a teacher shortage area for up to three years. Applications are available on Web site: http://www.ndus.nodak.edu/students/financial-aid.

Academic Fields/Career Goals: Education.

Award: Forgivable loan for use in freshman, sophomore, junior, or senior years; renewable. *Number:* 100–175. *Amount:* up to $1000.

Eligibility Requirements: Applicant must be enrolled or expecting to enroll at a four-year institution or university; resident of North Dakota and studying in North Dakota. Applicant or parent of applicant must have employment or volunteer experience in teaching. Available to U.S. citizens.

Application Requirements: Application, financial need analysis.

Contact: Peggy Wipf, Director of Financial Aid
North Dakota University System
600 East Boulevard
Department 215
Bismarck, ND 58505-0230
Phone: 701-328-4114
Fax: 701-328-2961
E-mail: peggy.wipf@ndus.nodak.edu

OKLAHOMA STATE REGENTS FOR HIGHER EDUCATION http://www.okhighered.org

FUTURE TEACHER SCHOLARSHIP-OKLAHOMA

Open to outstanding Oklahoma high school graduates who agree to teach in shortage areas. Must rank in top 15% of graduating class or score above 85th percentile on ACT or similar test, or be accepted in an educational program. Students nominated by institution. Reapply to renew. Must attend college/university in Oklahoma. Contact institution's financial aid office for application deadline.

Academic Fields/Career Goals: Education.

Award: Scholarship for use in freshman, sophomore, junior, senior, or graduate years; not renewable. *Number:* varies. *Amount:* up to $1500.

Eligibility Requirements: Applicant must be enrolled or expecting to enroll full or part-time at a two-year or four-year institution or university; resident of Oklahoma and studying in Oklahoma. Available to U.S. and non-U.S. citizens.

Application Requirements: Application, essay, test scores, transcript. *Deadline:* Continuous.

Contact: Oklahoma State Regents for Higher Education
PO Box 108850
Oklahoma City, OK 73101-8850
Phone: 800-858-1840
Fax: 405-225-9230

ORDEAN FOUNDATION

ORDEAN LOAN PROGRAM

• *See page 45*

OREGON PTA http://oregonpta.org

TEACHER EDUCATION SCHOLARSHIP

One-time award for Oregon resident studying education at an Oregon institution. Application deadline March 1.

Academic Fields/Career Goals: Education.

Award: Scholarship for use in freshman, sophomore, junior, or senior years; not renewable. *Number:* 4–10. *Amount:* $500.

Eligibility Requirements: Applicant must be enrolled or expecting to enroll full or part-time at a two-year or four-year institution or university; resident of Oregon and studying in Oregon. Available to U.S. citizens.

Application Requirements: Application, autobiography, essay, references, self-addressed stamped envelope, test scores, transcript. *Deadline:* March 1.

Contact: Jeanine Sinnott, TES Chair
Oregon PTA
9431 North Trumbull
Portland, OR 97203
Phone: 503-286-5193

OREGON STUDENT ASSISTANCE COMMISSION http://www.osac.state.or.us

ALPHA DELTA KAPPA/HARRIET SIMMONS SCHOLARSHIP

One-time award for elementary and secondary education majors entering their senior year, or graduate students enrolled in a fifth-year program leading to a teaching certificate. Visit Web site http://www.osac.state.or.us for more information.

Academic Fields/Career Goals: Education.

Award: Scholarship for use in senior, or graduate years; not renewable. *Number:* 1. *Amount:* $690.

Eligibility Requirements: Applicant must be enrolled or expecting to enroll at a four-year institution or university and resident of Oregon. Available to U.S. citizens.

Application Requirements: Application, essay, financial need analysis, transcript, activity chart. *Deadline:* March 1.

Contact: Director of Grant Programs
Oregon Student Assistance Commission
1500 Valley River Drive, Suite 100
Eugene, OR 97401-7020
Phone: 800-452-8807 Ext. 7395
E-mail: awardinfo@mercury.osac.state.or.us

FRIENDS OF OREGON STUDENTS SCHOLARSHIP

One-time award for non-traditional students (older, returning, single parent) who are working and will continue to work 20+ hours per week while attending college at least three-quarters time. Must be pursuing careers in the helping professions (health, education, social work, environmental or public service areas).

Academic Fields/Career Goals: Education; Health and Medical Sciences; Social Services.

Award: Scholarship for use in freshman, sophomore, junior, or senior years; not renewable. *Number:* 28. *Amount:* $2426.

Eligibility Requirements: Applicant must be enrolled or expecting to enroll at a four-year institution and resident of Oregon. Applicant or parent of applicant must have employment or volunteer experience in designated career field. Applicant must have 2.5 GPA or higher. Available to U.S. citizens.

Application Requirements: Application, essay, financial need analysis, references, transcript, activity chart. *Deadline:* March 1.

Contact: Director of Grant Programs
Oregon Student Assistance Commission
1500 Valley River Drive, Suite 100
Eugene, OR 97401-7020
Phone: 800-452-8807 Ext. 7395
E-mail: awardinfo@mercury.osac.state.or.us

HARRIET A. SIMMONS SCHOLARSHIP

Scholarship available for elementary and secondary education majors entering senior, fifth year, or graduate students in fifth year. Must be a resident of Oregon. Deadline is March 1.

Academic Fields/Career Goals: Education.

Oregon Student Assistance Commission (continued)

Award: Scholarship for use in senior, or graduate years; not renewable. *Number:* varies. *Amount:* $500.

Eligibility Requirements: Applicant must be enrolled or expecting to enroll at a four-year institution or university and resident of Oregon. Available to U.S. citizens.

Application Requirements: Application. *Deadline:* March 1.

Contact: Director of Grant Programs
Oregon Student Assistance Commission
1500 Valley River Drive, Suite 100
Eugene, OR 97401-7020
Phone: 800-452-8807 Ext. 7395
E-mail: awardinfo@mercury.osac.state.or.us

JAMES CARLSON MEMORIAL SCHOLARSHIP

One-time award for elementary or secondary education majors entering senior or fifth year or graduate students in fifth year for elementary or secondary certificate. Priority given to African-American, Asian, Hispanic, Native-American ethnic groups; dependents of Oregon Education Association members, and others committed to teaching autistic children.

Academic Fields/Career Goals: Education; Special Education.

Award: Scholarship for use in senior, or graduate years; not renewable. *Number:* 3. *Amount:* $1300.

Eligibility Requirements: Applicant must be enrolled or expecting to enroll at a four-year institution and resident of Oregon. Available to U.S. citizens.

Application Requirements: Application, essay, financial need analysis, test scores, transcript, activity chart. *Deadline:* March 1.

Contact: Director of Grant Programs
Oregon Student Assistance Commission
1500 Valley River Drive, Suite 100
Eugene, OR 97401-7020
Phone: 800-452-8807 Ext. 7395
E-mail: awardinfo@mercury.osac.state.or.us

MARIAN DU PUY MEMORIAL SCHOLARSHIP

One-time award for students accepted in teacher education programs. Must be enrolled or planning to enroll in full-time undergraduate study as a college junior or above with the career goal of becoming a teacher. Minimum 3.0 GPA. For use at Oregon four-year colleges only. Must be graduate of high schools in Multnomah, Clackamas, or Washington counties.

Academic Fields/Career Goals: Education.

Award: Scholarship for use in junior or senior years; not renewable. *Number:* varies. *Amount:* $500.

Eligibility Requirements: Applicant must be enrolled or expecting to enroll full-time at a four-year institution; resident of Oregon and studying in Oregon. Applicant must have 3.0 GPA or higher.

Application Requirements: Application, essay, financial need analysis, transcript. *Deadline:* March 1.

Contact: Director of Grant Programs
Oregon Student Assistance Commission
1500 Valley River Drive, Suite 100
Eugene, OR 97401-7020
Phone: 800-452-8807 Ext. 7395
E-mail: awardinfo@mercury.osac.state.or.us

NETTIE HANSELMAN JAYNES SCHOLARSHIP

One-time award for elementary and secondary education majors entering their senior or fifth year. Graduate students in their fifth year for elementary or secondary certificate also may apply. Application deadline is March 1.

Academic Fields/Career Goals: Education.

Award: Scholarship for use in senior, or graduate years; not renewable. *Number:* 1. *Amount:* $890.

Eligibility Requirements: Applicant must be enrolled or expecting to enroll at a four-year institution or university and resident of Oregon.

Application Requirements: Application, essay, financial need analysis, transcript. *Deadline:* March 1.

Contact: Director of Grant Programs
Oregon Student Assistance Commission
1500 Valley River Drive, Suite 100
Eugene, OR 97401-7020
Phone: 800-452-8807 Ext. 7395
E-mail: awardinfo@mercury.osac.state.or.us

OREGON EDUCATION ASSOCIATION SCHOLARSHIP

Scholarship open to graduating seniors of any Oregon public high school. Must plan to complete baccalaureate degree and teaching certification at an Oregon college. Renewable with satisfactory academic progress.

Academic Fields/Career Goals: Education.

Award: Scholarship for use in freshman, sophomore, junior, or senior years; renewable. *Number:* 5. *Amount:* $800.

Eligibility Requirements: Applicant must be high school student; planning to enroll or expecting to enroll at an institution or university; resident of Oregon and studying in Oregon.

Application Requirements: Application, essay, financial need analysis, transcript, activity chart. *Deadline:* March 1.

Contact: Director of Grant Programs
Oregon Student Assistance Commission
1500 Valley River Drive, Suite 100
Eugene, OR 97401-7020
Phone: 800-452-8807 Ext. 7395
E-mail: awardinfo@mercury.osac.state.or.us

PAGE FOUNDATION, INC. http://www.pagefoundation.org

PROFESSIONAL ASSOCIATION OF GEORGIA EDUCATORS FOUNDATION SCHOLARSHIP PROGRAM

Each scholarship is a one-time cash award of $1,000, payable to the recipient's college or university. Eligible applicants will be residents of Georgia studying education-related courses at an accredited college or university. Scholarships are given to juniors, seniors, undergraduates and teachers returning for a graduate degree. For more information go to http://www.pagefoundation.org. Applicant must be a PAGE or SPAGE member. Application due April 30.

Academic Fields/Career Goals: Education.

Award: Scholarship for use in junior, senior, graduate, or postgraduate years; not renewable. *Number:* 8–15. *Amount:* $1000.

Eligibility Requirements: Applicant must be enrolled or expecting to enroll full or part-time at a two-year or four-year institution or university and resident of Georgia. Applicant must have 3.0 GPA or higher. Available to U.S. citizens.

Application Requirements: Application, essay, references, transcript. *Deadline:* April 30.

Contact: Michelle Crawford, Scholarships Coordinator
PAGE Foundation, Inc.
PO Box 942270
Atlanta, GA 31141-2270
Phone: 770-216-8555
Fax: 770-216-9672
E-mail: mcrawford@pagefoundation.org

PHI DELTA KAPPA INTERNATIONAL http://www.pdkintl.org

SCHOLARSHIP GRANTS FOR PROSPECTIVE EDUCATORS

One-time award available to high school seniors in the top 50% of their graduating class. Applicants must plan to major in education and pursue a teaching career. Contact local Phi Delta Kappa chapter for more information. Do not send application to headquarters. Must have minimum 2.5 GPA.

Academic Fields/Career Goals: Education.

Award: Grant for use in freshman year; not renewable. *Number:* 30. *Amount:* $1000–$5000.

Eligibility Requirements: Applicant must be high school student and planning to enroll or expecting to enroll full-time at a two-year or four-year institution or university. Applicant must have 2.5 GPA or higher. Available to U.S. and non-U.S. citizens.

Application Requirements: Application, essay, references, transcript. *Deadline:* January 15.

Contact: local chapter for information

PI LAMBDA THETA, INC. http://www.pilambda.org

DISTINGUISHED STUDENT SCHOLAR AWARD

The Distinguished Student Scholar Award is presented in recognition of an education major who has displayed leadership potential and a strong dedication to education. Award given out in odd years. Minimum 3.5 GPA required.

Academic Fields/Career Goals: Education.

Award: Prize for use in sophomore, junior, or senior years; not renewable. *Number:* 1. *Amount:* $500.

Eligibility Requirements: Applicant must be enrolled or expecting to enroll full or part-time at a four-year institution or university and must have an interest in leadership. Applicant or parent of applicant must have employment or volunteer experience in community service. Applicant must have 3.5 GPA or higher. Available to U.S. and non-U.S. citizens.

Application Requirements: Application, resume, references, transcript. *Deadline:* February 10.

Contact: Pam Todd, Manager, Member Services
Pi Lambda Theta, Inc.
4101 East 3rd Street, PO Box 6626
Bloomington, IN 47407-6626
Phone: 812-339-3411
Fax: 812-339-3462
E-mail: endowment@pilambda.org

STUDENT SUPPORT SCHOLARSHIP

This scholarship is available to current members of Pi Lambda Theta who will be a full-time or part-time student enrolled in a minimum of three semester hours at a regionally accredited institution during the year following the award. Minimum 3.5 GPA required.

Academic Fields/Career Goals: Education.

Award: Scholarship for use in sophomore, junior, senior, graduate, or postgraduate years; not renewable. *Number:* 1–5. *Amount:* $750.

Eligibility Requirements: Applicant must be enrolled or expecting to enroll full or part-time at a four-year institution or university. Applicant must have 3.5 GPA or higher. Available to U.S. and non-U.S. citizens.

Application Requirements: Application, essay, transcript. *Deadline:* April 1.

Contact: Pam Todd, Manager, Member Services
Pi Lambda Theta, Inc.
4101 East 3rd Street, PO Box 6626
Bloomington, IN 47407-6626
Phone: 812-339-3411
Fax: 812-339-3462
E-mail: root@pilambda.org

SIGMA ALPHA IOTA PHILANTHROPIES, INC. http://www.sai-national.org

SIGMA ALPHA IOTA PHILANTHROPIES UNDERGRADUATE SCHOLARSHIPS

One-time award to undergraduate members of SAI who are freshman, sophomores or juniors. For use in sophomore, junior, or senior year. Must be female over 18 years of age studying performing arts or performing arts education. Contact local chapter for further details. 15 scholarships of $1000 each.

Academic Fields/Career Goals: Education; Performing Arts.

Award: Scholarship for use in sophomore, junior, or senior years; not renewable. *Number:* 15. *Amount:* $1000.

Eligibility Requirements: Applicant must be age 19; enrolled or expecting to enroll full-time at a four-year institution or university; female and must have an interest in music/singing. Available to U.S. and non-U.S. citizens.

Application Requirements: Application, essay, financial need analysis, references, transcript. *Deadline:* March 15.

Contact: Ms. Ruth Sieber Johnson, Executive Director of SAI
Sigma Alpha Iota Philanthropies, Inc.
34 Wall Street, Suite 515
Asheville, NC 28801-2710
Phone: 828-251-0606
Fax: 828-251-0644
E-mail: nh@sai-national.org

SIGMA ALPHA IOTA VISUALLY IMPAIRED SCHOLARSHIP

One-time award offered yearly for member of SAI who is visually impaired, and a member of a college or alumnae chapter. Submit fifteen-minute tape or evidence of work in composition, musicology, or research. One scholarship of $1000. Application fee: $25.

Academic Fields/Career Goals: Education; Music; Performing Arts.

Award: Scholarship for use in freshman, sophomore, junior, senior, or graduate years; not renewable. *Number:* 1. *Amount:* $1000.

Eligibility Requirements: Applicant must be enrolled or expecting to enroll full or part-time at a four-year institution or university; female and must have an interest in music/singing. Applicant must be visually impaired. Available to U.S. and non-U.S. citizens.

Application Requirements: Application, essay, references, transcript, tape. *Fee:* $25. *Deadline:* March 15.

Contact: Ms. Ruth Sieber Johnson, Executive Director of SAI
Sigma Alpha Iota Philanthropies, Inc.
34 Wall Street, Suite 515
Asheville, NC 28801-2710
Phone: 828-251-0606
Fax: 828-251-0644
E-mail: nh@sai-national.org

SOUTH CAROLINA STUDENT LOAN CORPORATION http://www.slc.sc.edu

SOUTH CAROLINA TEACHER LOAN PROGRAM

One-time awards for South Carolina residents attending four-year postsecondary institutions in South Carolina. Recipients must teach in the South Carolina public school system in a critical-need area after graduation. 20% of loan forgiven for each year of service. Write for additional requirements.

Academic Fields/Career Goals: Education; Special Education.

Award: Forgivable loan for use in freshman, sophomore, junior, senior, or graduate years; not renewable. *Number:* up to 1121. *Amount:* $2500–$5000.

Eligibility Requirements: Applicant must be enrolled or expecting to enroll full or part-time at a four-year institution or university; resident of South Carolina and studying in South Carolina. Applicant must have 3.0 GPA or higher.

Application Requirements: Application, test scores. *Deadline:* June 1.

Contact: Jennifer Jones-Gaddy, Vice President
South Carolina Student Loan Corporation
PO Box 21487
Columbia, SC 29221
Phone: 803-798-0916
Fax: 803-772-9410
E-mail: jgaddy@slc.sc.edu

SOUTH DAKOTA BOARD OF REGENTS http://www.ris.sdbor.edu

HAINES MEMORIAL SCHOLARSHIP

One-time scholarship for South Dakota public university students who are sophomores, juniors, or seniors having at least a 2.5 GPA and majoring in a teacher education program. Include resume with application. Must be South Dakota resident.

Academic Fields/Career Goals: Education.

Award: Scholarship for use in sophomore, junior, or senior years; not renewable. *Number:* 1. *Amount:* $2150.

Eligibility Requirements: Applicant must be enrolled or expecting to enroll at an institution or university; resident of South Dakota and studying in South Dakota. Applicant must have 2.5 GPA or higher.

South Dakota Board of Regents (continued)

Application Requirements: Application, autobiography, essay, resume. *Deadline:* February 25.

Contact: South Dakota Board of Regents
306 East Capitol Avenue, Suite 200
Pierre, SD 57501-3159

SOUTH DAKOTA BOARD OF REGENTS ANNIS I. FOWLER/KADEN SCHOLARSHIP

Scholarship for graduating South Dakota high school seniors to pursue a career in elementary education at a South Dakota public university. University must be one of the following: BHSU, BSU, NSU or USD. Applicants must have a cumulative GPA of 3.0 after three years of high school. One-time award.

Academic Fields/Career Goals: Education.

Award: Scholarship for use in freshman year; not renewable. *Number:* 2. *Amount:* $1000.

Eligibility Requirements: Applicant must be high school student; planning to enroll or expecting to enroll at an institution or university; resident of South Dakota and studying in South Dakota. Applicant must have 3.0 GPA or higher.

Application Requirements: Application, essay, references, test scores, transcript. *Deadline:* February 25.

Contact: South Dakota Board of Regents
306 East Capitol Avenue, Suite 200
Pierre, SD 57501-3159

SOUTHWEST STUDENT SERVICES CORPORATION http://www.sssc.com

ANNE LINDEMAN MEMORIAL SCHOLARSHIP

• *See page 117*

STATE COUNCIL OF HIGHER EDUCATION FOR VIRGINIA http://www.schev.edu

HIGHER EDUCATION TEACHER ASSISTANCE PROGRAM

Need-based scholarship for Virginia residents enrolled in a K-12 teacher preparation program in a participating Virginia college or university. Must be nominated by a faculty member in the Education Department at the institution. Applications must be obtained from and returned to the financial aid office at the participating institution.

Academic Fields/Career Goals: Education; Special Education.

Award: Scholarship for use in sophomore, junior, or senior years; renewable. *Number:* varies. *Amount:* $1000–$2000.

Eligibility Requirements: Applicant must be enrolled or expecting to enroll full-time at a two-year or four-year institution or university; resident of Virginia and studying in Virginia. Applicant must have 2.5 GPA or higher. Available to U.S. citizens.

Application Requirements: Application, financial need analysis, references, FAFSA.

Contact: Fin. Aid Office at participating VA institution
State Council of Higher Education for Virginia
James Monroe Building, 10th Floor
101 North 14th Street
Richmond, VA 23219

SOUTHSIDE VIRGINIA TOBACCO TEACHER SCHOLARSHIP/LOAN

Need-based scholarship for Southside Virginia natives to pursue a degree in K-12 teacher education in any four-year U.S. institution and then return to the Southside region to live and work. Must teach in Southside Virginia public school for scholarship/loan forgiveness.

Academic Fields/Career Goals: Education.

Award: Forgivable loan for use in freshman, sophomore, junior, or senior years; renewable. *Number:* varies. *Amount:* up to $4000.

Eligibility Requirements: Applicant must be enrolled or expecting to enroll full or part-time at a two-year or four-year institution or university and resident of Virginia. Available to U.S. citizens.

Application Requirements: Application, financial need analysis, FAFSA.

Contact: Christine Fields
State Council of Higher Education for Virginia
PO Box 1987
Abingdon, VA 24212
Phone: 276-619-4376 Ext. 4002

VIRGINIA TEACHING SCHOLARSHIP LOAN PROGRAM

Forgivable loan for students enrolled full- or part-time in a Virginia institution pursuing a teaching degree. The loan is forgiven if the student teaches in any Virginia public school for four semesters in the critical shortage fields. Must be a Virginia resident and maintain a GPA of at least 2.7. Must be nominated by the Education Department of the eligible institution.

Academic Fields/Career Goals: Education.

Award: Forgivable loan for use in sophomore, junior, senior, or graduate years; not renewable. *Number:* varies. *Amount:* up to $3720.

Eligibility Requirements: Applicant must be enrolled or expecting to enroll full or part-time at a four-year institution or university; resident of Virginia and studying in Virginia. Available to U.S. citizens.

Application Requirements: Application, references.

Contact: Fin. Aid Office at participating VA institution
State Council of Higher Education for Virginia
James Monroe Building, 10th Floor
101 North 14th Street
Richmond, VA 23219

STATE OF GEORGIA http://www.gsfc.org

TEACHER PREPARATION RECRUITMENT INITIATIVE

One-time award targeted at preparing second career candidates to become teachers in high-need schools. Awards will be available up to $5000. Institutions participating in the pilot program include: Albany State University, Armstrong Atlantic State University, Georgia State University, Georgia Southern University, East Georgia College, Georgia Southwestern State University, Valdosta State University, Abraham Baldwin Agricultural College, Waycross College, and South Georgia College. Within six months upon completion of the program, the individual will become a teacher and repay the scholarship by working in a school district and school that faces a serious teacher shortage.

Academic Fields/Career Goals: Education.

Award: Forgivable loan for use in freshman, sophomore, junior, or senior years; not renewable. *Number:* 300–350. *Amount:* up to $5000.

Eligibility Requirements: Applicant must be enrolled or expecting to enroll full or part-time at a four-year institution or university; resident of Georgia and studying in Georgia. Available to U.S. citizens.

Application Requirements: Application. *Deadline:* June 3.

Contact: Peggy Matthews, Manager/GSFA Originations
State of Georgia
2082 East Exchange Place, Suite 230
Tucker, GA 30084-5305
Phone: 770-724-9230
Fax: 770-724-9225
E-mail: peggy@gsfc.org

STATE OF WYOMING, ADMINISTERED BY UNIVERSITY OF WYOMING http://www.uwyo.edu/scholarships

SUPERIOR STUDENT IN EDUCATION SCHOLARSHIP-WYOMING

Available to Wyoming high school graduates who have demonstrated high academic achievement and plan to teach in Wyoming public schools. Award is for tuition at Wyoming institutions. Must maintain 3.0 GPA.

Academic Fields/Career Goals: Education.

Award: Scholarship for use in freshman, sophomore, junior, or senior years; renewable. *Number:* 16–80. *Amount:* varies.

Eligibility Requirements: Applicant must be enrolled or expecting to enroll full-time at a two-year or four-year institution or university; resident of Wyoming and studying in Wyoming. Applicant must have 3.0 GPA or higher. Available to U.S. citizens.

Application Requirements: Application, references, test scores, transcript. *Deadline:* October 31.

Contact: Joel Anne Berrigan, Assistant Director, Scholarships
State of Wyoming, administered by University of Wyoming
Student Financial Aid, Department 3335, 1000 East University Avenue
Laramie, WY 82071-3335
Phone: 307-766-2117
Fax: 307-766-3800
E-mail: finaid@uwyo.edu

STATE STUDENT ASSISTANCE COMMISSION OF INDIANA (SSACI) http://www.ssaci.in.gov

INDIANA MINORITY TEACHER AND SPECIAL EDUCATION SERVICES SCHOLARSHIP PROGRAM

For Black or Hispanic students seeking teaching certification or for students seeking special education teaching certification or occupational or physical therapy certification. Must be a U.S. citizen and Indiana resident enrolled full-time in an eligible Indiana institution. Must teach in an Indiana-accredited elementary or secondary school after graduation. Contact institution for application and deadline. Minimum 2.0 GPA required.

Academic Fields/Career Goals: Education; Special Education; Therapy/Rehabilitation.

Award: Scholarship for use in freshman, sophomore, junior, or senior years; not renewable. *Number:* 280–370. *Amount:* $1000–$4000.

Eligibility Requirements: Applicant must be Black (non-Hispanic) or Hispanic; enrolled or expecting to enroll full-time at a four-year institution or university; resident of Indiana and studying in Indiana. Available to U.S. citizens.

Application Requirements: Application, financial need analysis. *Deadline:* Continuous.

Contact: Ms. Yvonne Heflin, Director, Special Programs
State Student Assistance Commission of Indiana (SSACI)
150 West Market Street, Suite 500
Indianapolis, IN 46204-2805
Phone: 317-232-2350
Fax: 317-232-3260
E-mail: grants@ssaci.state.in.us

TENNESSEE EDUCATION ASSOCIATION http://www.teateachers.org

TEA DON SAHLI-KATHY WOODALL FUTURE TEACHERS OF AMERICA SCHOLARSHIP

This scholarship is available to a high school senior planning to major in education, attending a high school which has an FTA Chapter affiliated with TEA, and planning to enroll in a Tennessee college.

Academic Fields/Career Goals: Education.

Award: Scholarship for use in freshman year; not renewable. *Number:* 1. *Amount:* $1000.

Eligibility Requirements: Applicant must be high school student; planning to enroll or expecting to enroll full-time at a four-year institution or university; resident of Tennessee and studying in Tennessee. Applicant must have 3.0 GPA or higher. Available to U.S. citizens.

Application Requirements: Application, essay, financial need analysis, references, transcript, statement of income. *Deadline:* March 1.

Contact: Jeanette DeMain, Administrative Assistant
Tennessee Education Association
801 Second Avenue North
Nashville, TN 37201-1099
Phone: 615-242-8392
Fax: 615-259-4581
E-mail: jdemain@tea.nea.org

TEA DON SAHLI-KATHY WOODALL MINORITY SCHOLARSHIP

This scholarship is available to a minority high school senior planning to major in education and planning to enroll in a Tennessee college. Application must be made by an FTA Chapter, or by the student with the recommendation of an active TEA member.

Academic Fields/Career Goals: Education.

Award: Scholarship for use in freshman year; not renewable. *Number:* 1. *Amount:* $1000.

Eligibility Requirements: Applicant must be American Indian/Alaska Native, Asian/Pacific Islander, Black (non-Hispanic), or Hispanic; high school student; planning to enroll or expecting to enroll full-time at a four-year institution or university; resident of Tennessee and studying in Tennessee. Applicant must have 3.0 GPA or higher. Available to U.S. citizens.

Application Requirements: Application, essay, financial need analysis, references, transcript, statement of income. *Deadline:* March 1.

Contact: Jeanette DeMain, Administrative Assistant
Tennessee Education Association
801 Second Avenue North
Nashville, TN 37201-1099
Phone: 615-242-8392
Fax: 615-259-4581
E-mail: jdemain@tea.nea.org

TEA DON SAHLI-KATHY WOODALL UNDERGRADUATE SCHOLARSHIP

This scholarship is available to undergraduate students who are student TEA members. Application must be made through the local STEA Chapter.

Academic Fields/Career Goals: Education.

Award: Scholarship for use in freshman, sophomore, junior, or senior years; not renewable. *Number:* 4. *Amount:* $500–$1000.

Eligibility Requirements: Applicant must be enrolled or expecting to enroll full or part-time at a four-year institution or university; resident of Tennessee and studying in Tennessee. Applicant or parent of applicant must be member of Tennessee Education Association. Applicant must have 3.0 GPA or higher. Available to U.S. citizens.

Application Requirements: Application, essay, financial need analysis, references, transcript, statement of income. *Deadline:* March 1.

Contact: Jeanette DeMain, Administrative Assistant
Tennessee Education Association
801 Second Avenue North
Nashville, TN 37201-1099
Phone: 615-242-8392
Fax: 615-259-4581
E-mail: jdemain@tea.nea.org

TENNESSEE STUDENT ASSISTANCE CORPORATION http://www.state.tn.us/tsac

MINORITY TEACHING FELLOWS PROGRAM/TENNESSEE

Forgivable loan for minority Tennessee residents pursuing teaching careers. High school applicant minimum 2.75 GPA. Must be in the top quarter of the class or score an 18 on ACT. College applicant minimum 2.50 GPA. Submit statement of intent, test scores, and transcripts with application and two letters of recommendation. Must teach one year per year of award or repay as a loan.

Academic Fields/Career Goals: Education; Special Education.

Award: Forgivable loan for use in freshman, sophomore, junior, or senior years; renewable. *Number:* 19–29. *Amount:* $5000.

Eligibility Requirements: Applicant must be American Indian/Alaska Native, Asian/Pacific Islander, Black (non-Hispanic), or Hispanic; enrolled or expecting to enroll full-time at a two-year or four-year institution or university; resident of Tennessee and studying in Tennessee. Available to U.S. citizens.

Application Requirements: Application, essay, references, test scores, transcript. *Deadline:* April 15.

Contact: Kathy Stripling, Scholarship Coordinator
Tennessee Student Assistance Corporation
404 James Robertson Parkway, Suite 1950, Parkway Towers
Nashville, TN 37243-0820
Phone: 615-741-1346
Fax: 615-741-6101
E-mail: kathy.stripling@state.tn.us

TENNESSEE TEACHING SCHOLARS PROGRAM

Forgivable loan for college juniors, seniors, and college graduates admitted to an education program in Tennessee with a minimum GPA of 2.5. Students must commit to teach in a Tennessee public school one year for each year of the award.

Academic Fields/Career Goals: Education.

Award: Forgivable loan for use in junior, senior, or graduate years; not renewable. *Number:* 30–250. *Amount:* $1000–$4200.

Eligibility Requirements: Applicant must be enrolled or expecting to enroll full or part-time at a four-year institution or university; resident of Tennessee and studying in Tennessee. Applicant must have 2.5 GPA or higher. Available to U.S. citizens.

Application Requirements: Application, references, test scores, transcript, letter of intent. *Deadline:* April 15.

Contact: Mike McCormack, Scholarship Administrator
Tennessee Student Assistance Corporation
Suite 1950, Parkway Towers
Nashville, TN 37243-0820
Phone: 615-741-1346
Fax: 615-741-6101
E-mail: mike.mccormack@state.tn.us

TEXAS HIGHER EDUCATION COORDINATING BOARD http://www.collegefortexans.com

EDUCATIONAL AIDES EXEMPTION

Assist certain educational aides by exempting them from payment of tuition and fees at public colleges or universities in Texas. Applicants must have worked as an educational aide in a Texas public school for at least one year and must be enrolled in courses required for teacher certification. Contact your college or university financial aid office for information on applying for this scholarship. Application cycles are as follows: Fall, June 1 through February 1; Spring, November 1 through July 1; and Summer, April 1 through October 1.

Academic Fields/Career Goals: Education.

Award: Scholarship for use in freshman, sophomore, junior, or senior years; not renewable. *Number:* varies. *Amount:* varies.

Eligibility Requirements: Applicant must be enrolled or expecting to enroll at a four-year institution or university; resident of Texas and studying in Texas.

Application Requirements: Application, financial need analysis. *Deadline:* varies.

Contact: Financial Aid Office at college
Texas Higher Education Coordinating Board
PO Box 12788
Austin, TX 78711-2788
Phone: 512-427-6101
Fax: 512-427-6127
E-mail: grantinfo@thecb.state.tx.us

THE EDUCATION PARTNERSHIP http://www.edpartnership.org

LOUIS FEINSTEIN MEMORIAL SCHOLARSHIPS

For students who are interested in a teaching career and best exemplify the qualities of brotherhood, compassion, integrity, leadership, and a determination to make a positive difference in the lives of others. Students will receive benefits including an $8000 scholarship for those attending Rhode Island colleges and universities, and $2000 to all scholars upon graduation. Only high school juniors may apply. Application deadline is June 30.

Academic Fields/Career Goals: Education.

Award: Scholarship for use in freshman, sophomore, junior, or senior years; renewable. *Number:* 10–20. *Amount:* $10,000.

Eligibility Requirements: Applicant must be high school student; age 16-17; planning to enroll or expecting to enroll full-time at a two-year or four-year institution or university and studying in Rhode Island. Applicant must have 2.5 GPA or higher. Available to U.S. citizens.

Application Requirements: Application, essay, interview, references, test scores, transcript. *Deadline:* June 30.

Contact: Keturah Johnson, Scholarships and Communications Coordinator
The Education Partnership
345 South Main Street
Providence, RI 02903
Phone: 401-331-5222 Ext. 112
Fax: 401-331-1659
E-mail: kjohnson@edpartnership.org

TKE EDUCATIONAL FOUNDATION http://www.tkefoundation.org

CARROL C. HALL MEMORIAL SCHOLARSHIP

• *See page 72*

FRANCIS J. FLYNN MEMORIAL SCHOLARSHIP

Award of $550 for an undergraduate member of TKE who is a full-time student pursuing a degree in mathematics or education. Minimum 2.75 GPA required. Leadership within chapter or campus organizations recognized. Preference will be given to members of Theta-Sigma Chapter. Application deadline: May 15.

Academic Fields/Career Goals: Education; Physical Sciences and Math.

Award: Scholarship for use in freshman, sophomore, junior, or senior years; not renewable. *Number:* 1. *Amount:* $550.

Eligibility Requirements: Applicant must be enrolled or expecting to enroll full-time at a four-year institution or university; male and must have an interest in leadership. Available to U.S. and non-U.S. citizens.

Application Requirements: Application, essay, photo, transcript. *Deadline:* May 15.

Contact: Tim Taschwer, President/CEO
TKE Educational Foundation
8645 Founders Road
Indianapolis, IN 46268-1393
Phone: 317-872-6533
Fax: 317-875-8353
E-mail: tef@tkehq.org

UNITED NEGRO COLLEGE FUND http://www.uncf.org

EARL C. SAMS FOUNDATION SCHOLARSHIP

Award for elementary or secondary education majors attending Jarvis Christian College, Paul Quinn College, or Wiley College in Texas. Please visit Web site for more information: http://www.uncf.org.

Academic Fields/Career Goals: Education.

Award: Scholarship for use in freshman, sophomore, junior, or senior years; renewable. *Number:* varies. *Amount:* up to $3000.

Eligibility Requirements: Applicant must be Black (non-Hispanic); enrolled or expecting to enroll at an institution or university and studying in Texas. Applicant must have 2.5 GPA or higher.

Application Requirements: Application, financial need analysis, FAFSA, SAR. *Deadline:* varies.

Contact: Program Services Department
United Negro College Fund
8260 Willow Oaks Corporate Drive
Fairfax, VA 22031

JEAN CHILDS YOUNG SCHOLARSHIP

Award for an Atlanta, GA public high school student who exhibits a strong desire to teach. Please visit Web site for more information: http://www.uncf.org.

Academic Fields/Career Goals: Education.

Award: Scholarship for use in freshman, sophomore, junior, or senior years; renewable. *Number:* 1. *Amount:* $5000.

Eligibility Requirements: Applicant must be Black (non-Hispanic); high school student; planning to enroll or expecting to enroll at an institution or university and resident of Georgia. Applicant must have 2.5 GPA or higher.

Application Requirements: Application, financial need analysis, FAFSA, SAR. *Deadline:* varies.

Contact: Program Services Department
United Negro College Fund
8260 Willow Oaks Corporate Drive
Fairfax, VA 22031

WINSTON-SALEM/FORSYTH COUNTY PUBLIC SCHOOLS SCHOLARSHIP

Award to a graduating high school senior in one of the eight regular high schools in the Winston-Salem/Forsyth County, NC area, who plans to pursue a career in education. Please visit Web site for more information: http://www.uncf.org.

Academic Fields/Career Goals: Education.

Award: Scholarship for use in freshman, sophomore, junior, or senior years; renewable. *Number:* 1. *Amount:* $5000.

Eligibility Requirements: Applicant must be Black (non-Hispanic); high school student; planning to enroll or expecting to enroll at an institution or university and resident of North Carolina. Applicant must have 2.5 GPA or higher.

Application Requirements: Application, financial need analysis, FAFSA, SAR. *Deadline:* varies.

Contact: Program Services Department
United Negro College Fund
8260 Willow Oaks Corporate Drive
Fairfax, VA 22031

UTAH STATE BOARD OF REGENTS http://www.utahsbr.edu

TERRILL H. BELL TEACHING INCENTIVE LOAN

Designed to provide financial assistance to outstanding Utah students pursuing a degree in education. The incentive loan funds full-time tuition and general fees for eight semesters. After graduation/certification the loan may be forgiven if the recipient teaches in a Utah public school or accredited private school (K-12). Loan forgiveness is done on a year-for-year basis. For more details see Web site: http://www.utahsbr.edu.

Academic Fields/Career Goals: Education.

Award: Forgivable loan for use in freshman, sophomore, junior, senior, or graduate years; renewable. *Number:* 365. *Amount:* $900–$2500.

Eligibility Requirements: Applicant must be enrolled or expecting to enroll full-time at a two-year or four-year institution or university; resident of Utah and studying in Utah. Available to U.S. citizens.

Application Requirements: Application, essay, references, test scores, transcript. *Deadline:* varies.

Contact: David Colvin, Program Manager
Utah State Board of Regents
Board of Regents Building, the Gateway
60 South 400 West
Salt Lake City, UT 84101-1284
Phone: 801-321-7107
Fax: 801-321-7199
E-mail: dcolvin@utahsbr.edu

UTAH STATE OFFICE OF EDUCATION http://www.usoe.k12.ut.us/cert/scholarships/scholars.htm

T.H. BELL TEACHING INCENTIVE LOAN-UTAH

Renewable awards for Utah residents who are high school seniors and wish to pursue teaching careers. Award pays for tuition and fees at a Utah institution. Must agree to teach in a Utah public school or pay back loan through monthly installments. Must be a U.S. citizen.

Academic Fields/Career Goals: Education; Special Education.

Award: Forgivable loan for use in freshman, sophomore, junior, or senior years; renewable. *Number:* 25. *Amount:* varies.

Eligibility Requirements: Applicant must be high school student; planning to enroll or expecting to enroll full-time at a two-year or four-year institution or university; resident of Utah and studying in Utah. Available to U.S. citizens.

Application Requirements: Application, essay, test scores, transcript. *Deadline:* March 29.

Contact: Diane DeMan, Executive Secretary
Utah State Office of Education
250 East 500 South
Salt Lake City, UT 84111
Phone: 801-538-7741
Fax: 801-538-7973

VERMONT TEACHER DIVERSITY SCHOLARSHIP PROGRAM http://templeton.vsc.edu/teacherdiversity/

VERMONT TEACHER DIVERSITY SCHOLARSHIP PROGRAM

Loan forgiveness program for students from diverse racial and ethnic backgrounds who attend college in Vermont with a goal of becoming public school teachers. After three years of teaching in the Vermont public school system, they may receive up to $12,000 in loan forgiveness. Preference will be given to residents of Vermont. Application and information available on Web site: http://templeton.vsc.edu/teacherdiversity. Applications are due in April or November.

Academic Fields/Career Goals: Education.

Award: Forgivable loan for use in freshman, sophomore, junior, senior, or graduate years; not renewable. *Number:* up to 4. *Amount:* up to $4000.

Eligibility Requirements: Applicant must be American Indian/Alaska Native, Asian/Pacific Islander, Black (non-Hispanic), or Hispanic; enrolled or expecting to enroll full or part-time at a four-year institution or university and studying in Vermont. Available to U.S. citizens.

Application Requirements: Application, resume, references, transcript. *Deadline:* varies.

Contact: Phyl Newbeck, Director
Vermont Teacher Diversity Scholarship Program
PO Box 359
Waterbury, VT 05676-0359
Phone: 802-241-3379
Fax: 802-241-3369
E-mail: phyl.newbeck@vsc.edu

WASHINGTON HIGHER EDUCATION COORDINATING BOARD http://www.hecb.wa.gov

FUTURE TEACHERS CONDITIONAL SCHOLARSHIP AND LOAN REPAYMENT PROGRAM

This program is designed to encourage outstanding students and paraprofessionals to become teachers. In return for conditional scholarships or loan repayments, participants agree to teach in Washington K-12 schools. Additional consideration is given to individuals seeking certification or additional endorsements in teacher subject shortage areas, as well as to individuals with demonstrated bilingual ability. Must be residents of Washington and attend an institution in Washington.

Academic Fields/Career Goals: Education.

Award: Forgivable loan for use in freshman, sophomore, junior, or senior years; renewable. *Number:* 50. *Amount:* $600–$5000.

Eligibility Requirements: Applicant must be enrolled or expecting to enroll full or part-time at a two-year or four-year institution or university; resident of Washington and studying in Washington. Available to U.S. citizens.

Application Requirements: Application, essay, references, transcript, bilingual verification, if applicable. *Deadline:* October 15.

Contact: Mary Knutson, Program Coordinator
Washington Higher Education Coordinating Board
917 Lakeridge Way, SW, PO Box 43430
Olympia, WA 98504-3430
Phone: 360-753-7800
Fax: 360-753-7808
E-mail: futureteachers@hecb.wa.gov

WEST VIRGINIA HIGHER EDUCATION POLICY COMMISSION-OFFICE OF FINANCIAL AID AND OUTREACH SERVICES http://www.hepc.wvnet.edu

UNDERWOOD-SMITH TEACHER SCHOLARSHIP PROGRAM

For West Virginia residents at West Virginia institutions pursuing teaching careers. Must have a 3.25 GPA after completion of two years of course work. Must teach two years in West Virginia public schools for each year the award is received. Recipients will be required to sign an agreement acknowledging an understanding of the program's requirements and their willingness to repay the award if appropriate teaching service is not rendered.

Academic Fields/Career Goals: Education.

Award: Scholarship for use in junior, senior, or graduate years; renewable. *Number:* 53. *Amount:* $1620–$5000.

Eligibility Requirements: Applicant must be enrolled or expecting to enroll full-time at a four-year institution or university; resident of West Virginia and studying in West Virginia. Available to U.S. citizens.

Application Requirements: Application, essay, references. *Deadline:* March 1.

Contact: Michelle Wicks, Scholarship Coordinator
West Virginia Higher Education Policy Commission-Office of Financial Aid and Outreach Services
1018 Kanawha Boulevard East, Suite 700
Charleston, WV 25301
Phone: 304-558-4618
Fax: 304-558-4622
E-mail: wicks@hepc.wvnet.edu

WISCONSIN CONGRESS OF PARENTS AND TEACHERS, INC.

BROOKMIRE-HASTINGS SCHOLARSHIPS

One-time award to graduating high school seniors from Wisconsin public schools. Must pursue a degree in education. High school must have an active PTA in good standing of the Wisconsin PTA.

Academic Fields/Career Goals: Education; Special Education.

Award: Scholarship for use in freshman year; not renewable. *Number:* 2. *Amount:* $1000.

Eligibility Requirements: Applicant must be high school student; planning to enroll or expecting to enroll full-time at a four-year institution and resident of Wisconsin. Available to U.S. citizens.

Application Requirements: Application, essay, interview, references, transcript. *Deadline:* January 15.

Contact: Kim Schwantes, Executive Administrator
Wisconsin Congress of Parents and Teachers, Inc.
4797 Hayes Road, Suite 2
Madison, WI 53704-3256

WISCONSIN MATHEMATICS COUNCIL, INC. http://www.wismath.org

ARNE ENGEBRETSEN WISCONSIN MATHEMATICS COUNCIL SCHOLARSHIP

Scholarship for Wisconsin high school senior who is planning to study mathematics education and teach mathematics at K-12 level.

Academic Fields/Career Goals: Education; Mathematics.

Award: Scholarship for use in freshman year; not renewable. *Number:* 1. *Amount:* $1500.

Eligibility Requirements: Applicant must be high school student; planning to enroll or expecting to enroll full-time at a four-year institution or university and resident of Wisconsin. Available to U.S. citizens.

Application Requirements: Application, essay, resume, references, transcript. *Deadline:* March 1.

Contact: Wisconsin Mathematics Council, Inc.
142 North Main Street
Thiensville, WI 53092
Phone: 262-242-9418
Fax: 262-242-1862
E-mail: wismath@execpc.com

ETHEL A. NEIJAHR WISCONSIN MATHEMATICS COUNCIL SCHOLARSHIP

Scholarship for a Wisconsin resident who is currently enrolled in a Wisconsin institution studying mathematics education. Minimum GPA of 3.0 required.

Academic Fields/Career Goals: Education; Mathematics.

Award: Scholarship for use in junior, senior, or graduate years; not renewable. *Number:* 1. *Amount:* $1500.

Eligibility Requirements: Applicant must be enrolled or expecting to enroll full-time at a four-year institution or university; resident of Wisconsin and studying in Wisconsin. Applicant must have 3.0 GPA or higher. Available to U.S. citizens.

Application Requirements: Application, essay, resume, references, transcript. *Deadline:* March 1.

Contact: Wisconsin Mathematics Council, Inc.
142 North Main Street
Thiensville, WI 53092
Phone: 262-242-9418
Fax: 262-242-1862
E-mail: wismath@execpc.com

SISTER MARY PETRONIA VAN STRATEN WISCONSIN MATHEMATICS COUNCIL SCHOLARSHIP

Scholarship for a Wisconsin resident who is currently enrolled in a Wisconsin institution studying mathematics education. Minimum GPA of 3.0 required.

Academic Fields/Career Goals: Education; Mathematics.

Award: Scholarship for use in junior, senior, or graduate years; not renewable. *Number:* 1. *Amount:* $1500.

Eligibility Requirements: Applicant must be enrolled or expecting to enroll full-time at a four-year institution or university; resident of Wisconsin and studying in Wisconsin. Applicant must have 3.0 GPA or higher. Available to U.S. citizens.

Application Requirements: Application, essay, resume, references, transcript. *Deadline:* March 1.

Contact: Wisconsin Mathematics Council, Inc.
142 North Main Street
Thiensville, WI 53092
Phone: 262-242-9418
Fax: 262-242-1862
E-mail: wismath@execpc.com

WOMEN BAND DIRECTORS INTERNATIONAL http://womenbanddirectors.org

GLADYS STONE WRIGHT SCHOLARSHIP

One-time award for women instrumental music majors enrolled in a four-year institution. Applicants must be working toward a degree in music education with the intention of becoming a band director. Merit-based.

Academic Fields/Career Goals: Education; Music; Performing Arts.

Award: Scholarship for use in freshman, sophomore, junior, senior, or graduate years; not renewable. *Number:* 1. *Amount:* $300.

Eligibility Requirements: Applicant must be enrolled or expecting to enroll full-time at a four-year institution or university; female and must have an interest in music/singing. Applicant must have 3.0 GPA or higher. Available to U.S. and non-U.S. citizens.

Application Requirements: Application, essay, financial need analysis, photo, resume, references, self-addressed stamped envelope, transcript. *Deadline:* December 1.

Contact: Linda Moorhouse, Associate Director of Bands
Women Band Directors International
292 Band Hall, Louisiana State University
Baton Rouge, LA 70803
Phone: 225-578-2384
Fax: 225-578-4693
E-mail: moorhous@lsu.edu

HELEN MAY BULTER MEMORIAL SCHOLARSHIP

One-time award for women instrumental music majors enrolled in a four-year institution. Applicants must be working toward a degree in music education with the intention of becoming a band director. Merit-based.

Academic Fields/Career Goals: Education; Music; Performing Arts.

Award: Scholarship for use in freshman, sophomore, junior, senior, or graduate years; not renewable. *Number:* 1. *Amount:* $300.

Eligibility Requirements: Applicant must be enrolled or expecting to enroll full-time at a four-year institution or university; female and must have an interest in music/singing. Applicant must have 3.0 GPA or higher. Available to U.S. and non-U.S. citizens.

Application Requirements: Application, essay, financial need analysis, photo, resume, references, self-addressed stamped envelope, transcript. *Deadline:* December 1.

Contact: Linda Moorhouse, Associate Director of Bands
Women Band Directors International
292 Band Hall, Louisiana State University
Baton Rouge, LA 70803
Phone: 225-578-2384
Fax: 225-578-4693
E-mail: moorhous@lsu.edu

MARTHA ANN STARK MEMORIAL SCHOLARSHIP

One-time award for a woman college student who demonstrates outstanding contributions to bands and band music. Must be pursuing a major in music education and plan to become a band director. Merit-based. Must have a 3.0 GPA.

Academic Fields/Career Goals: Education; Music; Performing Arts.

Award: Scholarship for use in freshman, sophomore, junior, or senior years; not renewable. *Number:* 1. *Amount:* $300.

Eligibility Requirements: Applicant must be enrolled or expecting to enroll full-time at a four-year institution or university; female and must have an interest in music/singing. Applicant must have 3.0 GPA or higher. Available to U.S. and non-U.S. citizens.

Application Requirements: Application, essay, financial need analysis, photo, resume, references, self-addressed stamped envelope, transcript. *Deadline:* December 1.

Contact: Linda Moorhouse, Associate Director of Bands
Women Band Directors International
292 Band Hall, Louisiana State University
Baton Rouge, LA 70803
Phone: 225-578-2384
Fax: 225-578-4693
E-mail: moorhous@lsu.edu

MUSIC TECHNOLOGY SCHOLARSHIP

One-time award of $300. Student must be able to demonstrate the use of incorporation of music technology. Applicants must be working toward a degree in music education with the intention of becoming a band director.

Academic Fields/Career Goals: Education; Music; Performing Arts.

Award: Scholarship for use in freshman, sophomore, junior, senior, or graduate years; not renewable. *Number:* 1. *Amount:* $300.

Eligibility Requirements: Applicant must be enrolled or expecting to enroll full-time at a four-year institution or university; female and must have an interest in music/singing. Applicant must have 3.0 GPA or higher. Available to U.S. and non-U.S. citizens.

Application Requirements: Application, essay, financial need analysis, photo, resume, references, self-addressed stamped envelope, transcript. *Deadline:* December 1.

Contact: Linda Moorhouse, Associate Director of Bands
Women Band Directors International
292 Band Hall, Louisiana State University
Baton Rouge, LA 70803
Phone: 225-578-2384
Fax: 225-578-4693
E-mail: moorhous@lsu.edu

VOLKWEIN MEMORIAL SCHOLARSHIP

One-time award for women instrumental music majors enrolled in a four-year institution. Applicants must be working toward a degree in music education with the intention of becoming a band director. Merit-based. Must have a 3.0 GPA.

Academic Fields/Career Goals: Education; Music; Performing Arts.

Award: Scholarship for use in freshman, sophomore, junior, senior, or graduate years; not renewable. *Number:* 1. *Amount:* $300.

Eligibility Requirements: Applicant must be enrolled or expecting to enroll full-time at a four-year institution or university; female and must have an interest in music/singing. Applicant must have 3.0 GPA or higher. Available to U.S. and non-U.S. citizens.

Application Requirements: Application, essay, financial need analysis, photo, resume, references, self-addressed stamped envelope, transcript. *Deadline:* December 1.

Contact: Linda Moorhouse, Associate Director of Bands
Women Band Directors International
292 Band Hall, Louisiana State University
Baton Rouge, LA 70803
Phone: 225-578-2384
Fax: 225-578-4693
E-mail: moorhous@lsu.edu

ZETA PHI BETA SORORITY, INC. NATIONAL EDUCATIONAL FOUNDATION http://www.zphib1920.org

ISABEL M. HERSON SCHOLARSHIP IN EDUCATION

Scholarships available for graduate or undergraduate students enrolled in a degree program in either elementary or secondary education. Award for full-time study for one academic year. See Web site for additional information and application: http://www.zphib1920.org.

Academic Fields/Career Goals: Education.

Award: Scholarship for use in freshman, sophomore, junior, senior, or graduate years; not renewable. *Number:* varies. *Amount:* $500–$1000.

Eligibility Requirements: Applicant must be enrolled or expecting to enroll full-time at a four-year institution or university. Available to U.S. citizens.

Application Requirements: Application, essay, references, transcript. *Deadline:* February 1.

Contact: Cheryl Williams, National Second Vice President
Zeta Phi Beta Sorority, Inc. National Educational Foundation
1734 New Hampshire Avenue, NW
Washington, DC 20009-2595
Fax: 318-631-4028
E-mail: 2ndanti@zphib1920.org

ELECTRICAL ENGINEERING/ ELECTRONICS

AACE INTERNATIONAL http://www.aacei.org

AACE INTERNATIONAL COMPETITIVE SCHOLARSHIP

• *See page 73*

AEA-OREGON COUNCIL http://www.ous.edu/ecs/scholarships

AEA- OREGON COUNCIL TECHNOLOGY SCHOLARSHIP PROGRAM

• *See page 136*

AMERICAN COUNCIL OF ENGINEERING COMPANIES OF PENNSYLVANIA (ACEC/PA) http://www.acecpa.org

ENGINEERING SCHOLARSHIP

• *See page 136*

AMERICAN INSTITUTE OF AERONAUTICS AND ASTRONAUTICS http://www.aiaa.org

AIAA UNDERGRADUATE SCHOLARSHIP

• *See page 66*

AMERICAN PUBLIC POWER ASSOCIATION

http://www.appanet.org

DEMONSTRATION OF ENERGY EFFICIENT DEVELOPMENTS SCHOLARSHIP

DEED scholarships support education in energy-related fields and increase awareness about career opportunities in public power. Applicant must be currently attending an accredited college or university. Application deadlines are January 15 and July 15.

Academic Fields/Career Goals: Electrical Engineering/Electronics; Energy and Power Engineering; Engineering/Technology; Engineering-Related Technologies.

Award: Scholarship for use in sophomore, junior, or senior years; not renewable. *Number:* 10. *Amount:* $4000.

Eligibility Requirements: Applicant must be enrolled or expecting to enroll full or part-time at a two-year or four-year or technical institution or university. Available to U.S. and non-U.S. citizens.

Application Requirements: Application, transcript, answers to 7 application questions. *Deadline:* varies.

Contact: Bethany Luna, Policy, Broadband and Engineering Services Associate
American Public Power Association
2301 M Street, NW
Washington, DC 20037-1484
Phone: 202-467-2993
Fax: 202-467-2992
E-mail: deed@appanet.org

AMERICAN PUBLIC TRANSPORTATION FOUNDATION

http://www.apta.com

DONALD C. HYDE ESSAY PROGRAM

• *See page 149*

JACK GILSTRAP SCHOLARSHIP

• *See page 149*

LOUIS T. KLAUDER SCHOLARSHIP

• *See page 150*

PARSONS BRINCKERHOFF-JIM LAMMIE SCHOLARSHIP

• *See page 150*

TRANSIT HALL OF FAME SCHOLARSHIP AWARD PROGRAM

• *See page 150*

AMERICAN SOCIETY OF HEATING, REFRIGERATING, AND AIR CONDITIONING ENGINEERS, INC.

http://www.ashrae.org

ALWIN B. NEWTON SCHOLARSHIP FUND

For full-time studies relating to heating, refrigeration, and air conditioning. Must be for an ABET-accredited program. Minimum 3.0 GPA required. Character, leadership ability and potential service to the HVAC and/or refrigeration profession are considered in selection process.

Academic Fields/Career Goals: Electrical Engineering/Electronics; Engineering/Technology; Heating, Air-Conditioning, and Refrigeration Mechanics; Mechanical Engineering; Trade/Technical Specialties.

Award: Scholarship for use in sophomore, junior, or senior years; not renewable. *Number:* 1. *Amount:* $3000.

Eligibility Requirements: Applicant must be enrolled or expecting to enroll full-time at a four-year institution or university and must have an interest in leadership. Applicant must have 3.0 GPA or higher.

Application Requirements: Application, financial need analysis, references, transcript. *Deadline:* December 1.

Contact: Scholarship Administrator
American Society of Heating, Refrigerating, and Air Conditioning Engineers, Inc.
1791 Tullie Circle, NE
Atlanta, GA 30329
Phone: 404-636-8400
Fax: 404-321-5478

REUBEN TRANE SCHOLARSHIP

Two-year scholarship for full-time study in heating, refrigerating, and air conditioning. Recipient awarded $5000 each year for two years in an ABET-accredited program. Applicant must have two years remaining in undergraduate study. Minimum 3.0 GPA required.

Academic Fields/Career Goals: Electrical Engineering/Electronics; Heating, Air-Conditioning, and Refrigeration Mechanics; Mechanical Engineering; Trade/Technical Specialties.

Award: Scholarship for use in sophomore or junior years; renewable. *Number:* 4. *Amount:* $5000.

Eligibility Requirements: Applicant must be enrolled or expecting to enroll full-time at a four-year institution or university. Applicant must have 3.0 GPA or higher.

Application Requirements: Application, financial need analysis, references, transcript. *Deadline:* December 1.

Contact: Scholarship Administrator
American Society of Heating, Refrigerating, and Air Conditioning Engineers, Inc.
1791 Tullie Circle, NE
Atlanta, GA 30329
Phone: 404-636-8400
Fax: 404-321-5478

AMERICAN SOCIETY OF NAVAL ENGINEERS

http://www.navalengineers.org

AMERICAN SOCIETY OF NAVAL ENGINEERS SCHOLARSHIP

• *See page 66*

ARMED FORCES COMMUNICATIONS AND ELECTRONICS ASSOCIATION, EDUCATIONAL FOUNDATION

http://www.afcea.org

AFCEA SCHOLARSHIP FOR WORKING PROFESSIONALS

• *See page 96*

AFCEA SGT. JEANNETTE L. WINTERS, USMC MEMORIAL SCHOLARSHIP

• *See page 168*

AFCEA/LOCKHEED MARTIN ORINCON IT SCHOLARSHIP

• *See page 169*

ARMED FORCES COMMUNICATIONS AND ELECTRONICS ASSOCIATION EDUCATIONAL FOUNDATION DISTANCE-LEARNING SCHOLARSHIP

• *See page 169*

ARMED FORCES COMMUNICATIONS AND ELECTRONICS ASSOCIATION GENERAL EMMETT PAIGE SCHOLARSHIP

• *See page 169*

ARMED FORCES COMMUNICATIONS AND ELECTRONICS ASSOCIATION GENERAL JOHN A. WICKHAM SCHOLARSHIP

• *See page 169*

ARMED FORCES COMMUNICATIONS AND ELECTRONICS ASSOCIATION ROTC SCHOLARSHIP PROGRAM

• *See page 96*

ARRL FOUNDATION, INC.

http://www.arrl.org/arrlf/scholgen.html

CHARLES N. FISHER MEMORIAL SCHOLARSHIP

• *See page 66*

DR. JAMES L. LAWSON MEMORIAL SCHOLARSHIP

• *See page 157*

EARL I. ANDERSON SCHOLARSHIP

Award for students in electronic engineering or related technical field. Students must be amateur radio operators and members of the American Radio Relay League. Preference given to students who reside and attend classes in Illinois, Indiana, Michigan, or Florida.

Academic Fields/Career Goals: Electrical Engineering/Electronics.

Award: Scholarship for use in freshman, sophomore, junior, or senior years; not renewable. *Number:* 3. *Amount:* $1250.

Eligibility Requirements: Applicant must be enrolled or expecting to enroll at an institution or university and must have an interest in amateur radio. Applicant or parent of applicant must be member of American Radio Relay League.

Application Requirements: Application, transcript. *Deadline:* February 1.

Contact: Mary Lau, Scholarship Director
ARRL Foundation, Inc.
225 Main Street
Newington, CT 06111-4845

EDMOND A. METZGER SCHOLARSHIP

Scholarship for undergraduate or graduate students who are licensed amateur radio operators, novice minimum. Applicants must be electrical engineering students and members of the Amateur Radio Relay League. Must reside in Illinois, Indiana, or Wisconsin and attend a school in those states.

Academic Fields/Career Goals: Electrical Engineering/Electronics.

Award: Scholarship for use in freshman, sophomore, junior, senior, or graduate years; not renewable. *Number:* 1. *Amount:* $500.

Eligibility Requirements: Applicant must be enrolled or expecting to enroll at an institution or university; resident of Illinois, Indiana, or Wisconsin; studying in Illinois, Indiana, or Wisconsin and must have an interest in amateur radio. Applicant or parent of applicant must be member of American Radio Relay League.

Application Requirements: Application, transcript. *Deadline:* February 1.

Contact: Mary Lau, Scholarship Director
ARRL Foundation, Inc.
225 Main Street
Newington, CT 06111-4845

FRED R. MCDANIEL MEMORIAL SCHOLARSHIP
• *See page 157*

IRVING W. COOK, WA0CGS, SCHOLARSHIP
• *See page 67*

L. PHIL WICKER SCHOLARSHIP
• *See page 157*

MISSISSIPPI SCHOLARSHIP
• *See page 67*

PAUL AND HELEN L. GRAUER SCHOLARSHIP
• *See page 67*

PERRY F. HADLOCK MEMORIAL SCHOLARSHIP

For students licensed as technicians pursuing an electrical or electronics engineering degree. Preference given to students attending Clarkson University, Potsdam, New York, and those pursuing a bachelor's or higher degree.

Academic Fields/Career Goals: Electrical Engineering/Electronics.

Award: Scholarship for use in freshman, sophomore, junior, senior, or graduate years; not renewable. *Number:* 1. *Amount:* $2000.

Eligibility Requirements: Applicant must be enrolled or expecting to enroll at a four-year institution or university and must have an interest in amateur radio. Available to U.S. citizens.

Application Requirements: Application, transcript. *Deadline:* February 1.

Contact: Mary Lau, Scholarship Director
ARRL Foundation, Inc.
225 Main Street
Newington, CT 06111-4845

PHD ARA SCHOLARSHIP
• *See page 157*

ASSOCIATED BUILDERS AND CONTRACTORS SCHOLARSHIP PROGRAM http://www.abc.org

TRIMMER EDUCATION FOUNDATION SCHOLARSHIPS FOR CONSTRUCTION MANAGEMENT
• *See page 151*

ASSOCIATION FOR FACILITIES ENGINEERING (AFE)

ASSOCIATION FOR FACILITIES ENGINEERING CEDAR VALLEY CHAPTER # 132 SCHOLARSHIP
• *See page 97*

ASSOCIATION FOR IRON AND STEEL TECHNOLOGY http://www.aist.org/foundation/scholarships.htm

ASSOCIATION FOR IRON AND STEEL TECHNOLOGY DAVID H. SAMSON SCHOLARSHIP
• *See page 139*

ASSOCIATION FOR IRON AND STEEL TECHNOLOGY OHIO VALLEY CHAPTER SCHOLARSHIP
• *See page 112*

ASSOCIATION OF FEDERAL COMMUNICATIONS CONSULTING ENGINEERS

ASSOCIATION OF FEDERAL COMMUNICATIONS CONSULTING ENGINEERS SCHOLARSHIP FUND
• *See page 158*

ASSOCIATION OF THE OLD CROWS http://www.crows.org

ASSOCIATION OF OLD CROWS CHAPTER SCHOLARSHIP PROGRAM

Assists in the education of students in electrical engineering and the hard sciences who are likely to pursue careers in electronic defense.

Academic Fields/Career Goals: Electrical Engineering/Electronics.

Award: Scholarship for use in freshman, sophomore, junior, or senior years; not renewable. *Number:* 1–21. *Amount:* $500–$1000.

Eligibility Requirements: Applicant must be enrolled or expecting to enroll full-time at an institution or university. Available to U.S. citizens.

Application Requirements: Application. *Deadline:* Continuous.

Contact: Andrew Vittoria, Membership Director
Association of the Old Crows
1000 North Payne Street
Alexandria, VA 22314-1652
Phone: 703-549-1600
Fax: 703-549-2589
E-mail: vittoria@crows.org

ASTRONAUT SCHOLARSHIP FOUNDATION http://www.astronautscholarship.org

ASTRONAUT SCHOLARSHIP FOUNDATION
• *See page 68*

AUTOMOTIVE HALL OF FAME http://www.automotivehalloffame.org

AUTOMOTIVE HALL OF FAME EDUCATIONAL FUNDS
• *See page 140*

CATCHING THE DREAM

TRIBAL BUSINESS MANAGEMENT PROGRAM (TBM)
• *See page 38*

CENTRAL INTELLIGENCE AGENCY http://www.cia.gov

CENTRAL INTELLIGENCE AGENCY UNDERGRADUATE SCHOLARSHIP PROGRAM
• *See page 39*

CHAVERIM OF DELAWARE VALLEY, INC.

K2UK JEWISH RADIO MEMORIAL SCHOLARSHIP

Two $1000 scholarships are given to full-time students pursuing a degree in electronics, electrical engineering. Student must be of Hebrew descent. Award is based upon academic achievement, civic activities, Jewish heritage, need, and participation in amateur radio, with FCC license. Must have letter of acceptance from technical institute, college, or university.

Chaverim of Delaware Valley, Inc. (continued)

Academic Fields/Career Goals: Electrical Engineering/Electronics; Engineering/Technology; Trade/Technical Specialties.

Award: Scholarship for use in freshman, sophomore, junior, senior, or graduate years; not renewable. *Number:* 2. *Amount:* $1000.

Eligibility Requirements: Applicant must be Jewish; of Hebrew heritage; enrolled or expecting to enroll full-time at a four-year or technical institution or university and must have an interest in amateur radio. Applicant must have 3.0 GPA or higher. Available to U.S. citizens.

Application Requirements: Application, financial need analysis, references, self-addressed stamped envelope, test scores, transcript, copy of IRS 1040 Forms, copy of FCC radio amateur license. *Deadline:* June 15.

Contact: Sidney Abbott, Scholarship Chairman
Chaverim of Delaware Valley, Inc.
21 Sussex Drive
Willingboro, NJ 08046-1407
Phone: 609-877-0263
E-mail: sid604@aol.com

COMTO-BOSTON CHAPTER http://www.bostoncomto.org

COMTO BOSTON/GARRETT A. MORGAN SCHOLARSHIP
• *See page 75*

CONNECTICUT BUILDING CONGRESS http://www.cbc-ct.org

CONNECTICUT BUILDING CONGRESS SCHOLARSHIP FUND
• *See page 75*

CONNECTICUT STUDENT LOAN FOUNDATION http://www.cslf.com

CONNECTICUT INNOVATIONS TECHNOLOGY SCHOLAR PROGRAM
• *See page 113*

CUBAN AMERICAN NATIONAL FOUNDATION

MAS FAMILY SCHOLARSHIPS
• *See page 123*

EAST LOS ANGELES COMMUNITY UNION (TELACU) EDUCATION FOUNDATION

TELACU ENGINEERING AWARD
• *See page 141*

FLORIDA EDUCATIONAL FACILITIES PLANNERS' ASSOCIATION http://www.fefpa.org

FEFPA ASSISTANTSHIP
• *See page 76*

GEORGE BIRD GRINNELL AMERICAN INDIAN FUND

AL QOYAWAYMA AWARD
• *See page 141*

HAROLD B. & DOROTHY A. SNYDER FOUNDATION, INC.

HAROLD B. AND DOROTHY A. SNYDER FOUNDATION, INC., PROGRAM
• *See page 141*

HAWAIIAN LODGE, F.& A. M. http://www.hawaiianlodge.org/

HAWAIIAN LODGE SCHOLARSHIPS
• *See page 76*

HISPANIC COLLEGE FUND, INC. http://www.hispanicfund.org

DENNY'S/HISPANIC COLLEGE FUND SCHOLARSHIP
• *See page 41*

DEPARTMENT OF ENERGY SCHOLARSHIP PROGRAM
• *See page 125*

HISPANIC COLLEGE FUND/INROADS/SPRINT SCHOLARSHIP PROGRAM
• *See page 125*

LOCKHEED MARTIN SCHOLARSHIP PROGRAM
• *See page 141*

NATIONAL HISPANIC EXPLORERS SCHOLARSHIP PROGRAM
• *See page 69*

HISPANIC ENGINEER NATIONAL ACHIEVEMENT AWARDS CORPORATION (HENAAC) http://www.henaac.org

HISPANIC ENGINEER NATIONAL ACHIEVEMENT AWARDS CORPORATION SCHOLARSHIP PROGRAM
• *See page 99*

HISPANIC SCHOLARSHIP FUND http://www.hsf.net

HSF/GENERAL MOTORS SCHOLARSHIP
• *See page 126*

HSF/SOCIETY OF HISPANIC PROFESSIONAL ENGINEERS, INC. SCHOLARSHIP PROGRAM
• *See page 152*

ILLUMINATING ENGINEERING SOCIETY OF NORTH AMERICA–GOLDEN GATE SECTION http://www.iesgg.org

ALAN LUCAS MEMORIAL EDUCATIONAL SCHOLARSHIP
• *See page 77*

ROBERT W. THUNEN MEMORIAL SCHOLARSHIPS
• *See page 77*

INDEPENDENT LABORATORIES INSTITUTE SCHOLARSHIP ALLIANCE http://www.acil.org

INDEPENDENT LABORATORIES INSTITUTE SCHOLARSHIP ALLIANCE
• *See page 69*

INNOVATION AND SCIENCE COUNCIL OF BRITISH COLUMBIA http://www.scbc.org

IBM SCHOLARSHIP
• *See page 171*

INSTRUMENTATION, SYSTEMS, AND AUTOMATION SOCIETY (ISA) http://www.isa.org

INSTRUMENTATION, SYSTEMS, AND AUTOMATION SOCIETY (ISA) SCHOLARSHIP PROGRAM
• *See page 99*

INTERNATIONAL SOCIETY FOR OPTICAL ENGINEERING-SPIE http://www.spie.org/info/scholarships

SPIE EDUCATIONAL SCHOLARSHIPS IN OPTICAL SCIENCE AND ENGINEERING
• *See page 70*

JORGE MAS CANOSA FREEDOM FOUNDATION

MAS FAMILY SCHOLARSHIP AWARD
• *See page 126*

KOREAN-AMERICAN SCIENTISTS AND ENGINEERS ASSOCIATION http://www.ksea.org

KSEA SCHOLARSHIPS

Award for undergraduate or graduate Korean-American students majoring in science, engineering, or related fields. Must be a member of KSEA. Two scholarships are reserved for women. Application deadline is February 15. See Web site at http://www.ksea.org for further details.

Academic Fields/Career Goals: Electrical Engineering/Electronics; Engineering/Technology; Engineering-Related Technologies; Science, Technology, and Society.

Award: Scholarship for use in freshman, sophomore, junior, senior, or graduate years; not renewable. *Number:* varies. *Amount:* $1000.

Eligibility Requirements: Applicant must be of Korean heritage and enrolled or expecting to enroll full-time at a two-year or four-year institution or university. Applicant or parent of applicant must be member of Korean-American Scientists and Engineers Association. Available to U.S. citizens.

Application Requirements: Application, essay, resume, references, transcript. *Deadline:* February 15.

Contact: KSEA Scholarships
Korean-American Scientists and Engineers Association
1952 Gallows Road, Suite 300
Vienna, VA 22182
Phone: 703-748-1221
Fax: 703-748-1331
E-mail: sejong@ksea.org

LOS ANGELES COUNCIL OF BLACK PROFESSIONAL ENGINEERS http://www.lablackengineers.org/scholarships.html

AL-BEN SCHOLARSHIP FOR ACADEMIC INCENTIVE
• *See page 142*

AL-BEN SCHOLARSHIP FOR PROFESSIONAL MERIT
• *See page 142*

AL-BEN SCHOLARSHIP FOR SCHOLASTIC ACHIEVEMENT
• *See page 143*

LUCENT TECHNOLOGIES FOUNDATION http://www.iie.org/programs/lucent

LUCENT GLOBAL SCIENCE SCHOLARS PROGRAM
• *See page 70*

MICHIGAN SOCIETY OF PROFESSIONAL ENGINEERS http://www.michiganspe.org

MICHIGAN SOCIETY OF PROFESSIONAL ENGINEERS UNDESIGNATED GRANT
• *See page 143*

MICHIGAN SOCIETY OF PROFESSIONAL ENGINEERS 1980 NATIONAL SOCIETY OF PROFESSIONAL ENGINEERS ANNUAL MEETING COMMITTEE GRANT
• *See page 143*

MICHIGAN SOCIETY OF PROFESSIONAL ENGINEERS AUXILIARY GRANT
• *See page 143*

MICHIGAN SOCIETY OF PROFESSIONAL ENGINEERS HARRY R. BALL, P.E. GRANT
• *See page 144*

MICHIGAN SOCIETY OF PROFESSIONAL ENGINEERS KENNETH B. FISHBECK, P.E. MEMORIAL GRANT
• *See page 144*

MICHIGAN SOCIETY OF PROFESSIONAL ENGINEERS SCHOLARSHIP TRUST GRANT
• *See page 144*

ROBERT E. FOLMSBEE, P.E. MEMORIAL GRANT
• *See page 153*

MICRON TECHNOLOGY FOUNDATION, INC. http://www.micron.com/scholars

MICRON SCIENCE AND TECHNOLOGY SCHOLARS PROGRAM
• *See page 144*

NAMEPA NATIONAL SCHOLARSHIP FOUNDATION http://www.namepa.org

NATIONAL ASSOCIATION OF MINORITY ENGINEERING PROGRAM ADMINISTRATORS NATIONAL SCHOLARSHIP FUND
• *See page 101*

NASA DELAWARE SPACE GRANT CONSORTIUM http://www.delspace.org

NASA DELAWARE SPACE GRANT UNDERGRADUATE TUITION SCHOLARSHIP
• *See page 70*

NASA IDAHO SPACE GRANT CONSORTIUM http://www.uidaho.edu/nasa_isgc

NASA IDAHO SPACE GRANT CONSORTIUM SCHOLARSHIP PROGRAM
• *See page 71*

NASA NEBRASKA SPACE GRANT CONSORTIUM http://nasa.unomaha.edu

NASA NEBRASKA SPACE GRANT
• *See page 101*

NASA NEVADA SPACE GRANT CONSORTIUM http://www.unr.edu/spacegrant

UNIVERSITY AND COMMUNITY COLLEGE SYSTEM OF NEVADA NASA SPACE GRANT AND FELLOWSHIP PROGRAM
• *See page 101*

NATIONAL ASSOCIATION OF WOMEN IN CONSTRUCTION http://nawic.org

NAWIC UNDERGRADUATE SCHOLARSHIPS
• *See page 77*

NATIONAL SECURITY AGENCY http://www.nsa.gov

NATIONAL SECURITY AGENCY STOKES EDUCATIONAL SCHOLARSHIP PROGRAM
• *See page 172*

NATIONAL SOCIETY OF PROFESSIONAL ENGINEERS http://www.nspe.org

MAUREEN L. AND HOWARD N. BLITMAN, PE SCHOLARSHIP TO PROMOTE DIVERSITY IN ENGINEERING
• *See page 145*

NATIONAL SOCIETY OF PROFESSIONAL ENGINEERS/AUXILIARY SCHOLARSHIP
• *See page 145*

PAUL H. ROBBINS HONORARY SCHOLARSHIP
• *See page 145*

PROFESSIONAL ENGINEERS IN INDUSTRY SCHOLARSHIP
• *See page 145*

VIRGINIA HENRY MEMORIAL SCHOLARSHIP
• *See page 146*

OREGON STUDENT ASSISTANCE COMMISSION http://www.osac.state.or.us

AMERICAN COUNCIL OF ENGINEERING COMPANIES OF OREGON SCHOLARSHIP

• *See page 146*

KEY TECHNOLOGY SCHOLARSHIP

Scholarship for graduating high school seniors who reside in Crook, Deschutes, Jackson, Jefferson, Josephine, or Umatilla County, Oregon, or WallaWalla County, Washington. Must have 3.0 GPA and major in engineering or electronics. Dependents of Key employees are given preference. Deadline is March 1.

Academic Fields/Career Goals: Electrical Engineering/Electronics; Engineering/Technology.

Award: Scholarship for use in freshman, sophomore, junior, or senior years; renewable. *Number:* varies. *Amount:* $500.

Eligibility Requirements: Applicant must be enrolled or expecting to enroll at an institution or university and resident of Oregon or Washington. Applicant must have 3.0 GPA or higher. Available to U.S. citizens.

Application Requirements: Application. *Deadline:* March 1.

Contact: Director of Grant Programs
Oregon Student Assistance Commission
1500 Valley River Drive, Suite 100
Eugene, OR 97401-7020
Phone: 800-452-8807 Ext. 7395
E-mail: awardinfo@mercury.osac.state.or.us

MENTOR GRAPHICS SCHOLARSHIP

• *See page 172*

PROFESSIONAL CONSTRUCTION ESTIMATORS ASSOCIATION http://www.pcea.org

TED WILSON MEMORIAL SCHOLARSHIP FOUNDATION

• *See page 188*

ROBERT H. MOLLOHAN FAMILY CHARITABLE FOUNDATION, INC. http://www.mollohanfoundation.org

HIGH TECHNOLOGY SCHOLARS PROGRAM

• *See page 117*

ROCKY MOUNTAIN COAL MINING INSTITUTE http://www.rmcmi.org

ROCKY MOUNTAIN COAL MINING INSTITUTE SCHOLARSHIP

• *See page 146*

SOCIETY OF AUTOMOTIVE ENGINEERS http://www.sae.org/students/stuschol.htm

BMW/SAE ENGINEERING SCHOLARSHIP

• *See page 105*

EDWARD D. HENDRICKSON/SAE ENGINEERING SCHOLARSHIP

• *See page 105*

TMC/SAE DONALD D. DAWSON TECHNICAL SCHOLARSHIP

• *See page 105*

SOCIETY OF HISPANIC PROFESSIONAL ENGINEERS FOUNDATION http://www.shpefoundation.org

SOCIETY OF HISPANIC PROFESSIONAL ENGINEERS FOUNDATION

• *See page 146*

SOCIETY OF MANUFACTURING ENGINEERS EDUCATION FOUNDATION http://www.sme.org/foundation

WILLIAM E. WEISEL SCHOLARSHIP FUND

Must be full-time undergraduate student enrolled in a degree engineering or technology program in the United States or Canada and must be seeking a career in robotics or automated systems used in manufacturing. Candidates will also be considered which are seeking a career in robotics for use in the medical field. Must have completed a minimum of 30 college credit hours. Minimum GPA of 3.5 is required.

Academic Fields/Career Goals: Electrical Engineering/Electronics; Engineering/Technology; Mechanical Engineering; Trade/Technical Specialties.

Award: Scholarship for use in sophomore, junior, or senior years; not renewable. *Number:* 1. *Amount:* $1000.

Eligibility Requirements: Applicant must be enrolled or expecting to enroll full-time at an institution or university. Applicant must have 3.5 GPA or higher. Available to U.S. and Canadian citizens.

Application Requirements: Essay, resume, references, transcript. *Deadline:* February 1.

Contact: Cindy Monzon, Program Coordinator
Society of Manufacturing Engineers Education Foundation
One SME Drive
PO Box 930
Dearborn, MI 48121-0930
Phone: 313-271-1500 Ext. 1707
Fax: 313-240-6095
E-mail: monzcyn@sme.org

SOCIETY OF MEXICAN AMERICAN ENGINEERS AND SCIENTISTS http://www.maes-natl.org

GRE AND GRADUATE APPLICATIONS WAIVER

• *See page 72*

SOCIETY OF PLASTICS ENGINEERS (SPE) FOUNDATION http://www.4spe.org

FLEMING/BASZCAK SCHOLARSHIP

• *See page 147*

SOCIETY OF PLASTICS ENGINEERS SCHOLARSHIP PROGRAM

• *See page 147*

SOCIETY OF WOMEN ENGINEERS http://www.swe.org/scholarships

AGILENT MENTORING SCHOLARSHIP

• *See page 172*

BECHTEL CORPORATION SCHOLARSHIP

• *See page 155*

BERTHA LAMME MEMORIAL SCHOLARSHIP

One $1200 scholarship for entering freshman pursuing electrical engineering degree.

Academic Fields/Career Goals: Electrical Engineering/Electronics.

Award: Scholarship for use in freshman year; not renewable. *Number:* 1. *Amount:* $1200.

Eligibility Requirements: Applicant must be enrolled or expecting to enroll full-time at a four-year institution or university and female. Applicant must have 3.5 GPA or higher. Available to U.S. citizens.

Application Requirements: Application. *Deadline:* May 15.

Contact: Program Coordinator
Society of Women Engineers
230 East Ohio Street, Suite 400
Chicago, IL 60611-3265
Phone: 312-596-5223
Fax: 312-644-8557
E-mail: hq@swe.org

DAIMLER CHRYSLER CORPORATION SCHOLARSHIP

Renewable award for entering female sophomore majoring in mechanical or electrical engineering at an accredited school. Applicants must have minimum 3.0 GPA. Must be active contributor to and supporter of Society of Women Engineers. Must be U.S. citizen. Deadline: February 1.

Academic Fields/Career Goals: Electrical Engineering/Electronics; Mechanical Engineering.

Award: Scholarship for use in sophomore year; renewable. *Number:* 1. *Amount:* $2000.

Eligibility Requirements: Applicant must be enrolled or expecting to enroll full-time at a four-year institution and female. Applicant or parent of applicant must be member of Society of Women Engineers. Applicant must have 3.0 GPA or higher. Available to U.S. citizens.

Application Requirements: Application, essay, references, self-addressed stamped envelope, test scores, transcript. *Deadline:* February 1.

Contact: Program Coordinator
Society of Women Engineers
230 East Ohio Street, Suite 400
Chicago, IL 60611-3265
Phone: 312-596-5223
Fax: 312-644-8557
E-mail: hq@swe.org

DELL COMPUTER CORPORATION SCHOLARSHIPS
• *See page 173*

GENERAL MOTORS FOUNDATION UNDERGRADUATE SCHOLARSHIPS
• *See page 147*

GUIDANT CORPORATION SCHOLARSHIP
• *See page 173*

LOCKHEED AERONAUTICS COMPANY SCHOLARSHIPS

Two $1000 scholarships for entering female juniors majoring in electrical or mechanical engineering. One scholarship for each major. Minimum 3.5 GPA required. Application deadline is February 1.

Academic Fields/Career Goals: Electrical Engineering/Electronics; Mechanical Engineering.

Award: Scholarship for use in junior year; not renewable. *Number:* 2. *Amount:* $1000.

Eligibility Requirements: Applicant must be enrolled or expecting to enroll full-time at a four-year institution or university and female. Applicant must have 3.5 GPA or higher. Available to U.S. and non-U.S. citizens.

Application Requirements: Application, essay, references, self-addressed stamped envelope, test scores, transcript. *Deadline:* February 1.

Contact: Program Coordinator
Society of Women Engineers
230 East Ohio Street, Suite 400
Chicago, IL 60611-3265
Phone: 312-596-5223
Fax: 312-644-8557
E-mail: hq@swe.org

NORTHROP GRUMMAN CORPORATION SCHOLARSHIPS
• *See page 106*

SOUTH DAKOTA RETAILERS ASSOCIATION http://www.sdra.org

SOUTH DAKOTA RETAILERS ASSOCIATION SCHOLARSHIP PROGRAM
• *See page 47*

TEXAS ENGINEERING FOUNDATION http://www.tspe.org

TEXAS SOCIETY OF PROFESSIONAL ENGINEERS (TSPE) REGIONAL SCHOLARSHIPS
• *See page 148*

UNITED NEGRO COLLEGE FUND http://www.uncf.org

CDM SCHOLARSHIP/INTERNSHIP
• *See page 155*

CISCO/UNCF SCHOLARS PROGRAM
• *See page 175*

DELL/UNCF CORPORATE SCHOLARS PROGRAM
• *See page 131*

ROCKWELL/UNCF CORPORATE SCHOLARS PROGRAM
• *See page 133*

SBC FOUNDATION SCHOLARSHIP
• *See page 133*

SPRINT SCHOLARSHIP/INTERNSHIP
• *See page 50*

UNCF/SPRINT SCHOLARS PROGRAM
• *See page 50*

WEYERHAEUSER/UNCF CORPORATE SCHOLARS
• *See page 134*

UNIVERSITIES SPACE RESEARCH ASSOCIATION http://www.usra.edu/hq/scholarships/overview.shtml

UNIVERSITIES SPACE RESEARCH ASSOCIATION SCHOLARSHIP PROGRAM
• *See page 72*

UTAH SOCIETY OF PROFESSIONAL ENGINEERS http://www.uspeonline.com

UTAH SOCIETY OF PROFESSIONAL ENGINEERS SCHOLARSHIP
• *See page 148*

VERTICAL FLIGHT FOUNDATION http://www.vtol.org

VERTICAL FLIGHT FOUNDATION SCHOLARSHIP
• *See page 108*

WEST VIRGINIA HIGHER EDUCATION POLICY COMMISSION-OFFICE OF FINANCIAL AID AND OUTREACH SERVICES http://www.hepc.wvnet.edu

WEST VIRGINIA ENGINEERING, SCIENCE & TECHNOLOGY SCHOLARSHIP PROGRAM

For students attending West Virginia institutions full-time pursuing a career in engineering, science, or technology. Must have a 3.0 GPA on a 4.0 scale. Must work in the fields of engineering, science, or technology in West Virginia one year for each year the award is received.

Academic Fields/Career Goals: Electrical Engineering/Electronics; Engineering/Technology; Engineering-Related Technologies; Science, Technology, and Society.

Award: Scholarship for use in freshman, sophomore, junior, or senior years; renewable. *Number:* 250. *Amount:* up to $3000.

Eligibility Requirements: Applicant must be enrolled or expecting to enroll full-time at a two-year or four-year or technical institution or university and studying in West Virginia. Applicant must have 3.0 GPA or higher. Available to U.S. citizens.

Application Requirements: Application, essay, test scores, transcript. *Deadline:* March 1.

Contact: Michelle Wicks, Scholarship Coordinator
West Virginia Higher Education Policy Commission-Office of Financial Aid and Outreach Services
1018 Kanawha Boulevard East, Suite 700
Charleston, WV 25301
Phone: 304-558-4618
Fax: 304-558-4622
E-mail: wicks@hepc.wvnet.edu

WOMEN IN AVIATION, INTERNATIONAL http://www.wai.org

DELTA AIR LINES ENGINEERING SCHOLARSHIP
• *See page 108*

XEROX http://xerox.com

TECHNICAL MINORITY SCHOLARSHIP
• *See page 148*

ENERGY AND POWER ENGINEERING

AMERICAN PUBLIC POWER ASSOCIATION http://www.appanet.org

DEMONSTRATION OF ENERGY EFFICIENT DEVELOPMENTS SCHOLARSHIP

• See page 218

AMERICAN SOCIETY OF NAVAL ENGINEERS http://www.navalengineers.org

AMERICAN SOCIETY OF NAVAL ENGINEERS SCHOLARSHIP

• See page 66

ASSOCIATION FOR IRON AND STEEL TECHNOLOGY http://www.aist.org/foundation/scholarships.htm

ASSOCIATION FOR IRON AND STEEL TECHNOLOGY DAVID H. SAMSON SCHOLARSHIP

• See page 139

HANDS-ON! PROJECTS/HYDRO POWER CONTEST http://users.rcn.com/hands-on/hydro/contest.html

HYDRO POWER CONTEST

Scholarship awards are presented to winners in two categories of an engineering competition. Winners must design, build, and submit for testing a device that converts the potential energy contained in water into mechanical power. Contestants may compete in either power or efficiency categories, or both. Application fee is $20. Deadline is June 1.

Academic Fields/Career Goals: Energy and Power Engineering; Hydrology.

Award: Scholarship for use in freshman, sophomore, junior, senior, or graduate years; not renewable. *Number:* 6–10. *Amount:* $500–$2500.

Eligibility Requirements: Applicant must be enrolled or expecting to enroll full-time at a two-year or four-year or technical institution or university. Available to U.S. and non-U.S. citizens.

Application Requirements: Applicant must enter a contest, transcript. *Fee:* $20. *Deadline:* June 1.

Contact: Michael Coates, Administrator
Hands-on! Projects/Hydro Power Contest
9 Mayflower Road
Northborough, MA 01532
Phone: 508-351-6023
Fax: 508-351-6023
E-mail: hands-on@rcn.com

HAWAIIAN LODGE, F.& A. M. http://www.hawaiianlodge.org/

HAWAIIAN LODGE SCHOLARSHIPS

• See page 76

HISPANIC COLLEGE FUND, INC. http://www.hispanicfund.org

DEPARTMENT OF ENERGY SCHOLARSHIP PROGRAM

• See page 125

LOCKHEED MARTIN SCHOLARSHIP PROGRAM

• See page 141

NASA WEST VIRGINIA SPACE GRANT CONSORTIUM http://www.nasa.wvu.edu

WEST VIRGINIA SPACE GRANT CONSORTIUM UNDERGRADUATE SCHOLARSHIP PROGRAM

• See page 102

ROBERT H. MOLLOHAN FAMILY CHARITABLE FOUNDATION, INC. http://www.mollohanfoundation.org

HIGH TECHNOLOGY SCHOLARS PROGRAM

• See page 117

UNITED NEGRO COLLEGE FUND http://www.uncf.org

CON EDISON SCHOLARSHIP

• See page 49

NORTHEAST UTILITIES SYSTEM SCHOLARSHIP PROGRAM

• See page 132

UTAH SOCIETY OF PROFESSIONAL ENGINEERS http://www.uspeonline.com

UTAH SOCIETY OF PROFESSIONAL ENGINEERS SCHOLARSHIP

• See page 148

ENGINEERING-RELATED TECHNOLOGIES

AACE INTERNATIONAL http://www.aacei.org

AACE INTERNATIONAL COMPETITIVE SCHOLARSHIP

• See page 73

AEA-OREGON COUNCIL http://www.ous.edu/ecs/scholarships

AEA- OREGON COUNCIL TECHNOLOGY SCHOLARSHIP PROGRAM

• See page 136

AMERICAN COUNCIL OF ENGINEERING COMPANIES OF PENNSYLVANIA (ACEC/PA) http://www.acecpa.org

ENGINEERING SCHOLARSHIP

• See page 136

AMERICAN INDIAN SCIENCE AND ENGINEERING SOCIETY http://www.aises.org

GENERAL MOTORS ENGINEERING SCHOLARSHIP

A $3000 scholarship will be given to a current AISES member. Must be a member of an American-Indian Tribe or otherwise be considered to be an American-Indian by the tribe with which affiliation is claimed. Must maintain a 3.0 GPA.

Academic Fields/Career Goals: Engineering-Related Technologies.

Award: Scholarship for use in freshman, sophomore, junior, senior, or graduate years; not renewable. *Number:* varies. *Amount:* $3000.

Eligibility Requirements: Applicant must be American Indian/Alaska Native and enrolled or expecting to enroll full-time at a four-year institution or university. Applicant must have 3.0 GPA or higher. Available to U.S. citizens.

Application Requirements: Application, essay. *Deadline:* June 15.

Contact: Scholarship Information
American Indian Science and Engineering Society
PO Box 9828
Albuquerque, NM 87119-9828
Phone: 505-765-1052
Fax: 505-765-5608
E-mail: info@aises.org

HENRY RODRIGUEZ RECLAMATION COLLEGE SCHOLARSHIP AND INTERNSHIP

A $5000 scholarship will be given to a current AISES member. Must be enrolled full time in an accredited college or university. Must agree to serve an eight- to ten-week paid internship with the Bureau of Reclamation prior to graduation. Must maintain a 2.5 GPA. Must be seeking a BA in engineering or science, relating to water resources or an environmentally-related field.

Academic Fields/Career Goals: Engineering-Related Technologies; Environmental Science; Natural Resources; Natural Sciences.

Award: Scholarship for use in freshman, sophomore, junior, or senior years; renewable. *Number:* varies. *Amount:* $5000.

Eligibility Requirements: Applicant must be enrolled or expecting to enroll full-time at a four-year institution or university. Applicant must have 2.5 GPA or higher.

Application Requirements: Application, essay. *Deadline:* June 15.

Contact: Scholarship Information
American Indian Science and Engineering Society
PO Box 9828
Albuquerque, NM 87119-9828
Phone: 505-765-1052
Fax: 505-765-5608
E-mail: info@aises.org

AMERICAN PUBLIC POWER ASSOCIATION http://www.appanet.org

DEMONSTRATION OF ENERGY EFFICIENT DEVELOPMENTS SCHOLARSHIP

• *See page 218*

AMERICAN PUBLIC TRANSPORTATION FOUNDATION http://www.apta.com

DONALD C. HYDE ESSAY PROGRAM

• *See page 149*

JACK GILSTRAP SCHOLARSHIP

• *See page 149*

LOUIS T. KLAUDER SCHOLARSHIP

• *See page 150*

PARSONS BRINCKERHOFF-JIM LAMMIE SCHOLARSHIP

• *See page 150*

TRANSIT HALL OF FAME SCHOLARSHIP AWARD PROGRAM

• *See page 150*

AMERICAN SOCIETY OF HEATING, REFRIGERATING, AND AIR CONDITIONING ENGINEERS, INC. http://www.ashrae.org

ASHRAE MEMORIAL SCHOLARSHIP

One-time $3000 award for full-time study in hearing, ventilating, refrigeration, and air conditioning in an ABET-accredited program at an accredited school. Submit letter of recommendation from a professor or faculty adviser and two letters of recommendation from individuals familiar with the applicant's character, accomplishments, and likelihood of success in the HVAC and/or refrigeration industry. Applicants must have at least one full year of remaining study.

Academic Fields/Career Goals: Engineering/Technology; Engineering-Related Technologies; Heating, Air-Conditioning, and Refrigeration Mechanics; Trade/Technical Specialties.

Award: Scholarship for use in sophomore, junior, or senior years; not renewable. *Number:* 1. *Amount:* $3000.

Eligibility Requirements: Applicant must be enrolled or expecting to enroll full-time at a four-year institution or university. Applicant must have 3.0 GPA or higher.

Application Requirements: Application, financial need analysis, references, transcript. *Deadline:* December 1.

Contact: Scholarship Administrator
American Society of Heating, Refrigerating, and Air Conditioning Engineers, Inc.
1791 Tullie Circle, NE
Atlanta, GA 30329
Phone: 404-636-8400
Fax: 404-321-5478

ASHRAE SCHOLARSHIPS

One-time, $3000 award for full-time study in heating, ventilating, refrigeration, and air conditioning in an ABET-accredited program at an accredited school. Submit letter of recommendation from a professor or faculty adviser and two letters of recommendation from individuals familiar with the applicant's character, accomplishments, and likelihood of success in the HVAC and/or refrigeration industry. Applicants must have at least one full year of remaining study.

Academic Fields/Career Goals: Engineering/Technology; Engineering-Related Technologies; Heating, Air-Conditioning, and Refrigeration Mechanics; Trade/Technical Specialties.

Award: Scholarship for use in sophomore, junior, or senior years; not renewable. *Number:* 2. *Amount:* $3000.

Eligibility Requirements: Applicant must be enrolled or expecting to enroll full-time at a four-year institution or university and must have an interest in leadership. Applicant must have 3.0 GPA or higher.

Application Requirements: Application, financial need analysis, references, transcript. *Deadline:* December 1.

Contact: Scholarship Administrator
American Society of Heating, Refrigerating, and Air Conditioning Engineers, Inc.
1791 Tullie Circle, NE
Atlanta, GA 30329
Phone: 404-636-8400
Fax: 404-321-5478

DUANE HANSON SCHOLARSHIP

One-time $3000 award for full-time study in heating, ventilating, refrigeration, and air conditioning in an ABET-accredited program at an accredited school. Submit letter of recommendation from a professor or faculty adviser and two letters of recommendation from individuals familiar with the applicant's character, accomplishments, and likelihood of success in the HVAC and/or refrigeration industry. Applicants must have at least one full year of remaining study.

Academic Fields/Career Goals: Engineering-Related Technologies; Heating, Air-Conditioning, and Refrigeration Mechanics; Trade/Technical Specialties.

Award: Scholarship for use in sophomore, junior, or senior years; not renewable. *Number:* 1. *Amount:* $3000.

Eligibility Requirements: Applicant must be enrolled or expecting to enroll full-time at a four-year institution or university. Applicant must have 3.0 GPA or higher.

Application Requirements: Application, financial need analysis, references, transcript. *Deadline:* December 1.

Contact: Scholarship Administrator
American Society of Heating, Refrigerating, and Air Conditioning Engineers, Inc.
1791 Tullie Circle, NE
Atlanta, GA 30329
Phone: 404-636-8400
Fax: 404-321-5478

HENRY ADAMS SCHOLARSHIP

One-time $3000 award for full-time study in heating, ventilating, refrigeration, and air conditioning in an ABET-accredited program at an accredited school. Submit letter of recommendation from a professor or faculty adviser and two letters of recommendation from individuals familiar with the applicant's character, accomplishments, and likelihood of success in the HVAC and/or refrigeration industry. Applicants must have at least one full year of remaining study.

Academic Fields/Career Goals: Engineering/Technology; Engineering-Related Technologies; Heating, Air-Conditioning, and Refrigeration Mechanics; Trade/Technical Specialties.

Award: Scholarship for use in sophomore, junior, or senior years; not renewable. *Number:* 1. *Amount:* $3000.

Eligibility Requirements: Applicant must be enrolled or expecting to enroll full-time at a four-year institution and must have an interest in leadership. Applicant must have 3.0 GPA or higher.

American Society of Heating, Refrigerating, and Air Conditioning Engineers, Inc. (continued)

Application Requirements: Application, financial need analysis, references, transcript. *Deadline:* December 1.

Contact: Scholarship Administrator
American Society of Heating, Refrigerating, and Air Conditioning Engineers, Inc.
1791 Tullie Circle, NE
Atlanta, GA 30329
Phone: 404-636-8400
Fax: 404-321-5478

AMERICAN SOCIETY OF MECHANICAL ENGINEERS (ASME INTERNATIONAL)

http://www.asme.org/education/enged/aid

AMERICAN SOCIETY OF MECHANICAL ENGINEERS WILLIAM E. COOPER SCHOLARSHIPS

Scholarships available for students pursuing a baccalaureate degree in mechanical engineering or mechanical engineering technology. Must be in junior or senior year. Must be an ASME student member. Deadline is March 15.

Academic Fields/Career Goals: Engineering-Related Technologies; Mechanical Engineering.

Award: Scholarship for use in junior or senior years. *Number:* 2. *Amount:* $2500.

Eligibility Requirements: Applicant must be enrolled or expecting to enroll at a four-year institution or university. Available to U.S. and non-U.S. citizens.

Application Requirements: Application, financial need analysis, transcript. *Deadline:* March 15.

Contact: Theresa Oluwanifise, Administrative Assistant
American Society of Mechanical Engineers (ASME International)
3 Park Avenue
New York, NY 10016
Phone: 212-591-8131
Fax: 212-591-7143
E-mail: oluwanifiset@asme.org

AMERICAN WELDING SOCIETY

http://www.aws.org/foundation

AIRGAS JERRY BAKER SCHOLARSHIP

Awarded to full-time undergraduate pursuing a minimum four-year degree in welding engineering or welding engineering technology.

Academic Fields/Career Goals: Engineering-Related Technologies; Trade/Technical Specialties.

Award: Scholarship for use in sophomore, junior, or senior years; not renewable. *Number:* 1. *Amount:* $2500.

Eligibility Requirements: Applicant must be age 18 and enrolled or expecting to enroll full-time at a four-year institution. Applicant must have 3.0 GPA or higher. Available to U.S. and Canadian citizens.

Application Requirements: Application, autobiography, financial need analysis, references, transcript. *Deadline:* January 15.

Contact: Ms. Neida Herrera, Development Coordinator
American Welding Society
550 Northwest Le Jeune Road
Miami, FL 33126
Phone: 305-443-9353 Ext. 461
Fax: 305-443-7559
E-mail: neida@aws.org

AIRGAS-TERRY JARVIS MEMORIAL SCHOLARSHIP

Award for a full-time undergraduate pursuing a minimum four-year degree in welding engineering or welding engineering technology. Must have a minimum 2.8 overall GPA with a 3.0 GPA in engineering courses. Priority given to applicants residing or attending school in Florida, Georgia, or Alabama.

Academic Fields/Career Goals: Engineering/Technology; Engineering-Related Technologies; Trade/Technical Specialties.

Award: Scholarship for use in sophomore, junior, or senior years; not renewable. *Number:* 1. *Amount:* $2500.

Eligibility Requirements: Applicant must be age 18 and enrolled or expecting to enroll full-time at a four-year institution. Applicant must have 3.0 GPA or higher. Available to U.S. and Canadian citizens.

Application Requirements: Application, autobiography, essay, financial need analysis, references, transcript. *Deadline:* January 15.

Contact: Ms. Neida Herrera, Development Coordinator
American Welding Society
550 Northwest Le Jeune Road
Miami, FL 33126
Phone: 800-443-9353 Ext. 461
Fax: 305-443-7559
E-mail: neida@aws.org

AMERICAN WELDING SOCIETY DISTRICT SCHOLARSHIP PROGRAM

Award for students in vocational training, community college, or a degree program in welding or a related field of study. Applicants must be high school graduates or equivalent. Must reside in the U.S. and attend a U.S. institution. Recipients may reapply. Must include personal statement of career goals. Also must rank in upper half of class or have a minimum GPA of 2.5.

Academic Fields/Career Goals: Engineering-Related Technologies; Trade/Technical Specialties.

Award: Scholarship for use in freshman, sophomore, junior, or senior years; not renewable. *Number:* 66–150. *Amount:* $500–$1000.

Eligibility Requirements: Applicant must be age 18 and enrolled or expecting to enroll full or part-time at a two-year or four-year or technical institution or university. Applicant must have 2.5 GPA or higher. Available to U.S. and non-U.S. citizens.

Application Requirements: Application, autobiography, financial need analysis, photo, transcript. *Deadline:* March 1.

Contact: Mrs. Nazdhia Prado-Pulido, Foundation Associate
American Welding Society
550 Northwest Le Jeune Road
Miami, FL 33126
Phone: 800-443-9353 Ext. 250
Fax: 305-443-7559
E-mail: nprado-pulido@aws.org

AMERICAN WELDING SOCIETY INTERNATIONAL SCHOLARSHIP

Award for full-time international students pursuing a bachelor's degree or equivalent in a welding or related field of study. Applicant must have completed at least one year of welding or related field of study at a baccalaureate degree-granting institution and be in the top 20 percent of that institution's grading system. Scholarship not available for students residing in Canada, Mexico, or the U.S. For more information see Web site: http://www.aws.org/foundation.

Academic Fields/Career Goals: Engineering/Technology; Engineering-Related Technologies; Trade/Technical Specialties.

Award: Scholarship for use in freshman, sophomore, junior, or senior years; not renewable. *Number:* up to 1. *Amount:* up to $2500.

Eligibility Requirements: Applicant must be enrolled or expecting to enroll full-time at a four-year institution or university. Available to citizens of countries other than the U.S. or Canada.

Application Requirements: Application, essay, references, transcript. *Deadline:* April 1.

Contact: Neida Herrera, Development Coordinator
American Welding Society
550 Northwest Le Jeune Road
Miami, FL 33126
Phone: 305-443-9353 Ext. 461
Fax: 305-443-7559
E-mail: neida@aws.org

DONALD AND JEAN CLEVELAND-WILLAMETTE VALLEY SECTION SCHOLARSHIP

• *See page 150*

DONALD F. HASTINGS SCHOLARSHIP

Award for undergraduate pursuing a four-year degree either full-time or part-time in welding engineering or welding engineering technology. Priority will be given to welding engineering students. Preference given to students residing or attending school in California or Ohio. Submit copy of proposed curriculum. Must rank in upper half of class or have a minimum GPA of 2.5. Also include acceptance letter.

Academic Fields/Career Goals: Engineering/Technology; Engineering-Related Technologies; Trade/Technical Specialties.

Award: Scholarship for use in sophomore, junior, or senior years; not renewable. *Number:* 1. *Amount:* $3000.

Eligibility Requirements: Applicant must be enrolled or expecting to enroll full or part-time at a four-year institution. Applicant must have 2.5 GPA or higher. Available to U.S. citizens.

Application Requirements: Application, autobiography, financial need analysis, references, transcript. *Deadline:* January 15.

Contact: Ms. Neida Herrera, Development Coordinator
American Welding Society
550 Northwest Le Jeune Road
Miami, FL 33126
Phone: 800-443-9353 Ext. 461
Fax: 305-443-7559
E-mail: neida@aws.org

EDWARD J. BRADY MEMORIAL SCHOLARSHIP

Award for an undergraduate pursuing a four-year degree either full-time or part-time in welding engineering or welding engineering technology. Priority given to welding engineering students. Submit a letter of reference indicating previous hands-on experience, a copy of proposed curriculum, and an acceptance letter. Must have minimum 2.5 GPA.

Academic Fields/Career Goals: Engineering/Technology; Engineering-Related Technologies; Trade/Technical Specialties.

Award: Scholarship for use in sophomore, junior, or senior years; not renewable. *Number:* 1. *Amount:* $2500.

Eligibility Requirements: Applicant must be age 18 and enrolled or expecting to enroll full or part-time at a four-year institution. Applicant must have 2.5 GPA or higher. Available to U.S. citizens.

Application Requirements: Application, autobiography, essay, financial need analysis, references, transcript. *Deadline:* January 15.

Contact: Ms. Neida Herrera, Development Coordinator
American Welding Society
550 Northwest Le Jeune Road
Miami, FL 33126
Phone: 800-443-9353 Ext. 461
Fax: 305-443-7559
E-mail: neida@aws.org

HOWARD E. ADKINS MEMORIAL SCHOLARSHIP

Award for a full-time junior or senior in welding engineering or welding engineering technology. Preference to welding engineering students and those residing or attending school in Wisconsin or Kentucky. Must have at least 3.2 GPA in engineering, scientific, and technical subjects and a 2.8 GPA overall. No financial need is required to apply. Award may be granted a maximum of two years. Reapply each year. Submit copy of proposed curriculum and an acceptance letter.

Academic Fields/Career Goals: Engineering/Technology; Engineering-Related Technologies; Trade/Technical Specialties.

Award: Scholarship for use in junior or senior years; not renewable. *Number:* 1. *Amount:* $2500.

Eligibility Requirements: Applicant must be age 18 and enrolled or expecting to enroll full-time at a four-year institution. Available to U.S. citizens.

Application Requirements: Application, autobiography, essay, references, transcript. *Deadline:* January 15.

Contact: Ms. Neida Herrera, Development Coordinator
American Welding Society
550 Northwest Le Jeune Road
Miami, FL 33126
Phone: 800-443-9353 Ext. 461
Fax: 305-443-7559
E-mail: neida@aws.org

ILLINOIS TOOL WORKS WELDING COMPANIES SCHOLARSHIP

Two awards of $3000 each are available for undergraduate students who will be seniors in a four-year bachelors degree in welding engineering technology or welding engineering. Applicant must be U.S. citizen planning to attend a U.S. institution and have a minimum 3.0 GPA. Priority given to students attending Ferris State University, exhibit a strong interest in welding equipment and have prior work experience in the welding equipment field. Application deadline is January 15. For more information see http://www.aws.org/foundation.

Academic Fields/Career Goals: Engineering/Technology; Engineering-Related Technologies; Trade/Technical Specialties.

Award: Scholarship for use in senior year; not renewable. *Number:* 2. *Amount:* $3000.

Eligibility Requirements: Applicant must be age 18 and enrolled or expecting to enroll full or part-time at a four-year institution or university. Applicant must have 3.0 GPA or higher. Available to U.S. citizens.

Application Requirements: Application. *Deadline:* January 15.

Contact: Neida Herrera, Development Coordinator
American Welding Society
550 Northwest Le Jeune Road
Miami, FL 33126
Phone: 305-443-9353 Ext. 461
Fax: 305-443-7559
E-mail: neida@aws.org

JOHN C. LINCOLN MEMORIAL SCHOLARSHIP

Award for an undergraduate pursuing a four-year degree either full time or part time in engineering or welding engineering technology. Priority given to welding engineering students. Applicant must have a minimum 2.5 overall grade point average. Proof of financial need is required to qualify.

Academic Fields/Career Goals: Engineering/Technology; Engineering-Related Technologies; Trade/Technical Specialties.

Award: Scholarship for use in sophomore, junior, or senior years; not renewable. *Number:* 1. *Amount:* $2500.

Eligibility Requirements: Applicant must be enrolled or expecting to enroll full or part-time at a four-year institution. Applicant must have 2.5 GPA or higher. Available to U.S. citizens.

Application Requirements: Application, autobiography, financial need analysis, references, transcript. *Deadline:* January 15.

Contact: Ms. Neida Herrera, Development Coordinator
American Welding Society
550 Northwest Le Jeune Road
Miami, FL 33126
Phone: 800-443-9353 Ext. 461
Fax: 305-443-7559
E-mail: neida@aws.org

MATSUO BRIDGE COMPANY, LTD., OF JAPAN SCHOLARSHIP

• *See page 151*

PRAXAIR INTERNATIONAL SCHOLARSHIP

Award for a full-time student demonstrating leadership and pursuing a four-year degree in welding engineering or welding engineering technology. Priority given to welding engineering students. Must be a U.S. or Canadian citizen. Financial need is not required. Must have minimum 2.5 GPA.

Academic Fields/Career Goals: Engineering/Technology; Engineering-Related Technologies; Trade/Technical Specialties.

Award: Scholarship for use in sophomore, junior, or senior years; not renewable. *Number:* 1. *Amount:* $2500.

Eligibility Requirements: Applicant must be enrolled or expecting to enroll full-time at a four-year institution. Applicant must have 2.5 GPA or higher. Available to U.S. and Canadian citizens.

American Welding Society (continued)

Application Requirements: Application, autobiography, financial need analysis, references, transcript. *Deadline:* January 15.

Contact: Ms. Neida Herrera, Development Coordinator
American Welding Society
550 Northwest Le Jeune Road
Miami, FL 33126
Phone: 800-443-9353 Ext. 461
Fax: 305-443-7559
E-mail: neida@aws.org

WILLIAM A. AND ANN M. BROTHERS SCHOLARSHIP

Awarded to a full-time undergraduate pursuing a bachelor's degree in welding or welding-related program at an accredited university.

Academic Fields/Career Goals: Engineering-Related Technologies; Trade/Technical Specialties.

Award: Scholarship for use in sophomore, junior, or senior years; not renewable. *Number:* 1. *Amount:* $2500.

Eligibility Requirements: Applicant must be age 18 and enrolled or expecting to enroll full-time at a four-year institution. Applicant must have 2.5 GPA or higher. Available to U.S. citizens.

Application Requirements: Application, autobiography, financial need analysis, references, transcript. *Deadline:* January 15.

Contact: Ms. Neida Herrera, Development Coordinator
American Welding Society
550 Northwest Le Jeune Road
Miami, FL 33126
Phone: 305-443-9353 Ext. 461
Fax: 305-443-7559
E-mail: neida@aws.org

WILLIAM B. HOWELL MEMORIAL SCHOLARSHIP

Awarded to a full-time undergraduate student pursuing a minimum four-year degree in a welding program at an accredited university. Priority will be given to those individuals residing or attending schools in the state of Florida, Michigan, and Ohio. Minimum 2.5 GPA required.

Academic Fields/Career Goals: Engineering/Technology; Engineering-Related Technologies; Trade/Technical Specialties.

Award: Scholarship for use in sophomore, junior, or senior years; not renewable. *Number:* 1. *Amount:* $2500.

Eligibility Requirements: Applicant must be age 18 and enrolled or expecting to enroll full-time at a four-year institution. Applicant must have 2.5 GPA or higher. Available to U.S. citizens.

Application Requirements: Application, autobiography, essay, financial need analysis, references, transcript. *Deadline:* January 15.

Contact: Ms. Neida Herrera, Development Coordinator
American Welding Society
550 NW Le Jeune Road
Miami, FL 33126
Phone: 305-443-9353 Ext. 461
E-mail: neida@aws.org

ARMED FORCES COMMUNICATIONS AND ELECTRONICS ASSOCIATION, EDUCATIONAL FOUNDATION http://www.afcea.org

VICE ADMIRAL JERRY O. TUTTLE, USN (RET.) AND MRS. BARBARA A. TUTTLE SCIENCE AND TECHNOLOGY SCHOLARSHIP

Candidate must be a U.S. citizen enrolled in a technology-related field and be a sophomore or junior at the time of application. Primary consideration will be given to military enlisted candidates.

Academic Fields/Career Goals: Engineering/Technology; Engineering-Related Technologies; Science, Technology, and Society.

Award: Scholarship for use in sophomore or junior years; not renewable. *Number:* varies. *Amount:* $2000.

Eligibility Requirements: Applicant must be enrolled or expecting to enroll full-time at a four-year or technical institution or university. Available to U.S. citizens.

Application Requirements: Application, references, transcript. *Deadline:* November 1.

Contact: Norma Corrales, Director, Scholarships and Award Programs
Armed Forces Communications and Electronics Association, Educational Foundation
4400 Fair Lakes Court
Fairfax, VA 22033-3899
Phone: 703-631-6149
Fax: 703-631-4693
E-mail: scholarship@afcea.org

ARRL FOUNDATION, INC. http://www.arrl.org/arrlf/scholgen.html

HENRY BROUGHTON, K2AE MEMORIAL SCHOLARSHIP

• *See page 67*

ASSOCIATED BUILDERS AND CONTRACTORS SCHOLARSHIP PROGRAM http://www.abc.org

TRIMMER EDUCATION FOUNDATION SCHOLARSHIPS FOR CONSTRUCTION MANAGEMENT

• *See page 151*

ASSOCIATION FOR FACILITIES ENGINEERING (AFE)

ASSOCIATION FOR FACILITIES ENGINEERING CEDAR VALLEY CHAPTER # 132 SCHOLARSHIP

• *See page 97*

ASSOCIATION FOR IRON AND STEEL TECHNOLOGY http://www.aist.org/foundation/scholarships.htm

ASSOCIATION FOR IRON AND STEEL TECHNOLOGY OHIO VALLEY CHAPTER SCHOLARSHIP

• *See page 112*

ASSOCIATION OF ENGINEERING GEOLOGISTS http://www.aegweb.org

MARLIAVE FUND

• *See page 189*

ASTRONAUT SCHOLARSHIP FOUNDATION http://www.astronautscholarship.org

ASTRONAUT SCHOLARSHIP FOUNDATION

• *See page 68*

AUTOMOTIVE HALL OF FAME http://www.automotivehalloffame.org

AUTOMOTIVE HALL OF FAME EDUCATIONAL FUNDS

• *See page 140*

BUSINESS AND PROFESSIONAL WOMEN'S FOUNDATION http://www.bpwusa.org

BPW CAREER ADVANCEMENT SCHOLARSHIP PROGRAM FOR WOMEN

• *See page 112*

CATCHING THE DREAM

TRIBAL BUSINESS MANAGEMENT PROGRAM (TBM)

• *See page 38*

COMTO-BOSTON CHAPTER http://www.bostoncomto.org

COMTO BOSTON/GARRETT A. MORGAN SCHOLARSHIP

• *See page 75*

CONNECTICUT BUILDING CONGRESS http://www.cbc-ct.org

CONNECTICUT BUILDING CONGRESS SCHOLARSHIP FUND
• *See page 75*

CUBAN AMERICAN NATIONAL FOUNDATION

MAS FAMILY SCHOLARSHIPS
• *See page 123*

DELAWARE SOLID WASTE AUTHORITY http://www.dswa.com

DELAWARE SOLID WASTE AUTHORITY SCHOLARSHIP
• *See page 113*

DESK AND DERRICK EDUCATIONAL TRUST http://www.addc.org

DESK AND DERRICK EDUCATIONAL TRUST
• *See page 69*

EAST LOS ANGELES COMMUNITY UNION (TELACU) EDUCATION FOUNDATION

TELACU ENGINEERING AWARD
• *See page 141*

FLORIDA EDUCATIONAL FACILITIES PLANNERS' ASSOCIATION http://www.fefpa.org

FEFPA ASSISTANTSHIP
• *See page 76*

FOUNDATION OF THE WALL AND CEILING INDUSTRY http://www.awci.org/thefoundation.shtml

FOUNDATION OF THE WALL AND CEILING INDUSTRY SCHOLARSHIP PROGRAM
• *See page 76*

GEORGE BIRD GRINNELL AMERICAN INDIAN FUND

AL QOYAWAYMA AWARD
• *See page 141*

GRAND RAPIDS COMMUNITY FOUNDATION http://www.grfoundation.org

ECONOMIC CLUB OF GRAND RAPIDS BUSINESS STUDY ABROAD SCHOLARSHIP
• *See page 41*

HAROLD B. & DOROTHY A. SNYDER FOUNDATION, INC.

HAROLD B. AND DOROTHY A. SNYDER FOUNDATION, INC., PROGRAM
• *See page 141*

HAWAIIAN LODGE, F.& A. M. http://www.hawaiianlodge.org/

HAWAIIAN LODGE SCHOLARSHIPS
• *See page 76*

HISPANIC COLLEGE FUND, INC. http://www.hispanicfund.org

BURLINGTON NORTHERN SANTA FE FOUNDATION/HISPANIC COLLEGE FUND SCHOLARSHIP PROGRAM
• *See page 41*

DENNY'S/HISPANIC COLLEGE FUND SCHOLARSHIP
• *See page 41*

DEPARTMENT OF ENERGY SCHOLARSHIP PROGRAM
• *See page 125*

HISPANIC COLLEGE FUND/INROADS/SPRINT SCHOLARSHIP PROGRAM
• *See page 125*

LOCKHEED MARTIN SCHOLARSHIP PROGRAM
• *See page 141*

M & T BANK/ HISPANIC COLLEGE FUND SCHOLARSHIP PROGRAM
• *See page 42*

NATIONAL HISPANIC EXPLORERS SCHOLARSHIP PROGRAM
• *See page 69*

HISPANIC SCHOLARSHIP FUND http://www.hsf.net

HSF/GENERAL MOTORS SCHOLARSHIP
• *See page 126*

HSF/SOCIETY OF HISPANIC PROFESSIONAL ENGINEERS, INC. SCHOLARSHIP PROGRAM
• *See page 152*

ILLUMINATING ENGINEERING SOCIETY OF NORTH AMERICA http://www.iesna.org

ROBERT W. THUNEN MEMORIAL SCHOLARSHIPS
• *See page 77*

INDEPENDENT LABORATORIES INSTITUTE SCHOLARSHIP ALLIANCE http://www.acil.org

INDEPENDENT LABORATORIES INSTITUTE SCHOLARSHIP ALLIANCE
• *See page 69*

INSTRUMENTATION, SYSTEMS, AND AUTOMATION SOCIETY (ISA) http://www.isa.org

INSTRUMENTATION, SYSTEMS, AND AUTOMATION SOCIETY (ISA) SCHOLARSHIP PROGRAM
• *See page 99*

INTERNATIONAL FACILITY MANAGEMENT ASSOCIATION FOUNDATION http://www.ifma.org

IFMA FOUNDATION SCHOLARSHIPS
• *See page 77*

INTERNATIONAL SOCIETY FOR OPTICAL ENGINEERING-SPIE http://www.spie.org/info/scholarships

SPIE EDUCATIONAL SCHOLARSHIPS IN OPTICAL SCIENCE AND ENGINEERING
• *See page 70*

JORGE MAS CANOSA FREEDOM FOUNDATION

MAS FAMILY SCHOLARSHIP AWARD
• *See page 126*

KCNC-TV CHANNEL 4 NEWS http://www.news4colorado.com

NEWS 4 PETER ROGOT MEDIA SCHOLARSHIP
• *See page 161*

KOREAN-AMERICAN SCIENTISTS AND ENGINEERS ASSOCIATION http://www.ksea.org

KSEA SCHOLARSHIPS
• *See page 221*

LOS ANGELES COUNCIL OF BLACK PROFESSIONAL ENGINEERS http://www.lablackengineers.org/scholarships.html

AL-BEN SCHOLARSHIP FOR ACADEMIC INCENTIVE
• *See page 142*

AL-BEN SCHOLARSHIP FOR PROFESSIONAL MERIT
• *See page 142*

AL-BEN SCHOLARSHIP FOR SCHOLASTIC ACHIEVEMENT
• *See page 143*

LUCENT TECHNOLOGIES FOUNDATION http://www.iie.org/programs/lucent

LUCENT GLOBAL SCIENCE SCHOLARS PROGRAM

• *See page 70*

MAINE SOCIETY OF PROFESSIONAL ENGINEERS

MAINE SOCIETY OF PROFESSIONAL ENGINEERS VERNON T. SWAINE-ROBERT E. CHUTE SCHOLARSHIP

Non-renewable scholarship for full-time study for freshmen only. Must be a Maine resident. Deadline: March 1.

Academic Fields/Career Goals: Engineering/Technology; Engineering-Related Technologies.

Award: Scholarship for use in freshman year; not renewable. *Number:* 1–2. *Amount:* $1500.

Eligibility Requirements: Applicant must be enrolled or expecting to enroll full-time at a four-year institution or university and resident of Maine. Available to U.S. citizens.

Application Requirements: Application, essay, interview, references, self-addressed stamped envelope, test scores, transcript. *Deadline:* March 1.

Contact: Robert G. Martin
Maine Society of Professional Engineers
RRI Box 70
Belgrade, ME 04917
Phone: 207-495-2244
E-mail: rgmglads@twi.net

MICRON TECHNOLOGY FOUNDATION, INC. http://www.micron.com/scholars

MICRON SCIENCE AND TECHNOLOGY SCHOLARS PROGRAM

• *See page 144*

MINERALS, METALS, AND MATERIALS SOCIETY (TMS) http://www.tms.org

TMS J. KEITH BRIMACOMBE PRESIDENTIAL SCHOLARSHIP

One award of $5000 for a Minerals, Metals, and Materials Society student member who is an undergraduate student majoring in metallurgical engineering, materials science and engineering, or minerals processing/extraction programs. $1000 travel stipend for recipient to attend the TMS Annual Banquet to formally receive scholarship.

Academic Fields/Career Goals: Engineering/Technology; Engineering-Related Technologies; Materials Science, Engineering, and Metallurgy.

Award: Scholarship for use in freshman, sophomore, junior, or senior years; not renewable. *Number:* 1. *Amount:* $5000.

Eligibility Requirements: Applicant must be enrolled or expecting to enroll full-time at a four-year institution. Applicant must have 2.5 GPA or higher. Available to U.S. and non-U.S. citizens.

Application Requirements: Application, essay, references, transcript. *Deadline:* May 1.

Contact: Diane Scheuring, Membership and Marketing Coordinator
Minerals, Metals, and Materials Society (TMS)
184 Thorn Hill Road
Warrendale, PA 15086
Phone: 724-776-9000 Ext. 220
Fax: 724-776-3770
E-mail: dscheuring@tms.org

TMS OUTSTANDING STUDENT PAPER CONTEST-UNDERGRADUATE

Two prizes for essays on global or national issues, as well as technical research papers. Metallurgy or materials science papers will be considered. Applicants must be TMS student members or include completed membership application with dues payment and essay to become eligible. Submit one entry per student. Prize includes cash and travel expenses.

Academic Fields/Career Goals: Engineering/Technology; Engineering-Related Technologies; Materials Science, Engineering, and Metallurgy.

Award: Prize for use in freshman, sophomore, junior, or senior years; not renewable. *Number:* 2. *Amount:* $500–$1000.

Eligibility Requirements: Applicant must be enrolled or expecting to enroll full-time at a four-year institution. Available to U.S. and non-U.S. citizens.

Application Requirements: Essay. *Deadline:* May 1.

Contact: Diane Schuering, Membership and Marketing Coordinator
Minerals, Metals, and Materials Society (TMS)
184 Thorn Hill Road
Warrendale, PA 15086
Phone: 724-776-9000 Ext. 220
Fax: 724-776-3770
E-mail: dscheuring@tms.org

TMS/EMPMD GILBERT CHIN SCHOLARSHIP

Award of $2000 to a TMS student member who is a college undergraduate studying subjects in relation to electronic, magnetic, and/or photonic materials. Preference given to juniors and seniors enrolled full-time in a program that includes the study of electronic materials. An additional $500 travel award for recipient to attend the TMS Annual Meeting to accept award.

Academic Fields/Career Goals: Engineering/Technology; Engineering-Related Technologies; Materials Science, Engineering, and Metallurgy.

Award: Scholarship for use in freshman, sophomore, junior, or senior years; not renewable. *Number:* 1. *Amount:* $2000.

Eligibility Requirements: Applicant must be enrolled or expecting to enroll full-time at a four-year institution. Available to U.S. and non-U.S. citizens.

Application Requirements: Application, essay, references, transcript. *Deadline:* May 1.

Contact: Diane Scheuring, Membership and Marketing Coordinator
Minerals, Metals, and Materials Society (TMS)
184 Thorn Hill Road
Warrendale, PA 15086
Phone: 724-776-9000 Ext. 220
Fax: 724-776-3770
E-mail: dscheuring@tms.org

TMS/EPD SCHOLARSHIP

Four awards of $2000 for TMS student members majoring in the extraction and processing of materials. Preference given to college seniors enrolled full-time in a program relating to the extraction and processing of minerals, metals, and materials. Recipients are given the opportunity to select up to five Extraction and Processing Division-sponsored conference proceedings or textbooks to be donated to the recipient's college/university in his/her name.

Academic Fields/Career Goals: Engineering/Technology; Engineering-Related Technologies; Materials Science, Engineering, and Metallurgy.

Award: Scholarship for use in freshman, sophomore, junior, or senior years; not renewable. *Number:* 4. *Amount:* $2000.

Eligibility Requirements: Applicant must be enrolled or expecting to enroll full-time at a four-year institution. Available to U.S. and non-U.S. citizens.

Application Requirements: Application, essay, references, transcript. *Deadline:* May 1.

Contact: Diane Scheuring, Membership and Marketing Coordinator
Minerals, Metals, and Materials Society (TMS)
184 Thorn Hill Road
Warrendale, PA 15086
Phone: 724-776-9000 Ext. 220
Fax: 724-776-3770
E-mail: dscheuring@tms.org

TMS/INTERNATIONAL SYMPOSIUM ON SUPERALLOYS SCHOLARSHIP PROGRAM

Two awards of $2000 for undergraduate and graduate student member of TMS majoring in metallurgy, materials science and engineering, or materials processing/extraction programs. Preference given to students pursuing a curriculum/career in superalloys. Scholarship will be awarded at the TMS Fall Conference.

Academic Fields/Career Goals: Engineering/Technology; Engineering-Related Technologies; Materials Science, Engineering, and Metallurgy.

Award: Scholarship for use in freshman, sophomore, junior, senior, or graduate years; not renewable. *Number:* 2. *Amount:* $2000.

Eligibility Requirements: Applicant must be enrolled or expecting to enroll full-time at a four-year institution. Available to U.S. and non-U.S. citizens.

Application Requirements: Application, essay, references, transcript. *Deadline:* May 1.

Contact: Diane Scheuring, Membership and Marketing Coordinator
Minerals, Metals, and Materials Society (TMS)
184 Thorn Hill Road
Warrendale, PA 15086
Phone: 724-776-9000 Ext. 220
Fax: 724-776-3770
E-mail: dscheuring@tms.org

TMS/LMD SCHOLARSHIP PROGRAM

Three awards of $4000 for undergraduate TMS student members majoring in the study of non-ferrous metallurgy. Preference given to juniors and seniors enrolled full-time in a non-ferrous metallurgy program, and to individuals who have participated in a relevant industrial co-op program. Recipients are given the opportunity of selecting up to $300 in Light Metals Division-sponsored conference proceedings or textbooks to be donated to the recipient's college/university library in his/her name.

Academic Fields/Career Goals: Engineering/Technology; Engineering-Related Technologies; Materials Science, Engineering, and Metallurgy.

Award: Scholarship for use in freshman, sophomore, junior, or senior years; not renewable. *Number:* 3. *Amount:* $4000.

Eligibility Requirements: Applicant must be enrolled or expecting to enroll full-time at a four-year institution. Available to U.S. and non-U.S. citizens.

Application Requirements: Application, essay, references, transcript. *Deadline:* May 1.

Contact: Diane Scheuring, Membership and Marketing Coordinator
Minerals, Metals, and Materials Society (TMS)
184 Thorn Hill Road
Warrendale, PA 15086
Phone: 724-776-9000 Ext. 220
Fax: 724-776-3770
E-mail: dscheuring@tms.org

TMS/STRUCTURAL MATERIALS DIVISION SCHOLARSHIP

Two awards of $2500 for TMS student members who are undergraduates majoring in materials science and engineering or physical metallurgy. Recipient will be given $500 in travel expenses to the TMS Annual Meeting to accept his/her award. Preference given to seniors enrolled full time in an engineering program relating to the structure, property, and processing of materials.

Academic Fields/Career Goals: Engineering/Technology; Engineering-Related Technologies; Materials Science, Engineering, and Metallurgy.

Award: Scholarship for use in freshman, sophomore, junior, or senior years; not renewable. *Number:* 2. *Amount:* $2500.

Eligibility Requirements: Applicant must be enrolled or expecting to enroll full-time at a four-year institution. Available to U.S. and non-U.S. citizens.

Application Requirements: Application, essay, references, transcript. *Deadline:* May 1.

Contact: Diane Scheuring, Membership and Marketing Coordinator
Minerals, Metals, and Materials Society (TMS)
184 Thorn Hill Road

Warrendale, PA 15086
Phone: 724-776-9000 Ext. 220
Fax: 724-776-3770
E-mail: dscheuring@tms.org

NAMEPA NATIONAL SCHOLARSHIP FOUNDATION http://www.namepa.org

NATIONAL ASSOCIATION OF MINORITY ENGINEERING PROGRAM ADMINISTRATORS NATIONAL SCHOLARSHIP FUND

• *See page 101*

NASA DELAWARE SPACE GRANT CONSORTIUM http://www.delspace.org

NASA DELAWARE SPACE GRANT UNDERGRADUATE TUITION SCHOLARSHIP

• *See page 70*

NASA NEBRASKA SPACE GRANT CONSORTIUM http://nasa.unomaha.edu

NASA NEBRASKA SPACE GRANT

• *See page 101*

NASA VERMONT SPACE GRANT CONSORTIUM http://www.emba.uvm.edu/vsgc

VERMONT SPACE GRANT CONSORTIUM SCHOLARSHIP PROGRAM

• *See page 71*

NASA WEST VIRGINIA SPACE GRANT CONSORTIUM http://www.nasa.wvu.edu

WEST VIRGINIA SPACE GRANT CONSORTIUM UNDERGRADUATE SCHOLARSHIP PROGRAM

• *See page 102*

NATIONAL ASSOCIATION FOR THE ADVANCEMENT OF COLORED PEOPLE http://www.naacp.org

HUBERTUS W.V. WILLEMS SCHOLARSHIP FOR MALE STUDENTS

• *See page 144*

LOUIS STOKES SCIENCE AND TECHNOLOGY AWARD

• *See page 114*

NATIONAL ASSOCIATION OF WATER COMPANIES http://www.nawc.org

J.J. BARR SCHOLARSHIP

• *See page 115*

NATIONAL ASSOCIATION OF WOMEN IN CONSTRUCTION http://nawic.org

NAWIC UNDERGRADUATE SCHOLARSHIPS

• *See page 77*

NATIONAL INVENTORS HALL OF FAME http://www.invent.org/collegiate

COLLEGIATE INVENTORS COMPETITION - GRAND PRIZE

• *See page 71*

COLLEGIATE INVENTORS COMPETITION FOR UNDERGRADUATE STUDENTS

• *See page 71*

NATIONAL SOCIETY OF PROFESSIONAL ENGINEERS http://www.nspe.org

MAUREEN L. AND HOWARD N. BLITMAN, PE SCHOLARSHIP TO PROMOTE DIVERSITY IN ENGINEERING

• *See page 145*

NATIONAL SOCIETY OF PROFESSIONAL ENGINEERS/AUXILIARY SCHOLARSHIP

• *See page 145*

PAUL H. ROBBINS HONORARY SCHOLARSHIP

• *See page 145*

PROFESSIONAL ENGINEERS IN INDUSTRY SCHOLARSHIP

• *See page 145*

VIRGINIA HENRY MEMORIAL SCHOLARSHIP

• *See page 146*

NATIONAL STONE, SAND AND GRAVEL ASSOCIATION (NSSGA) http://www.nssga.org

BARRY K. WENDT MEMORIAL SCHOLARSHIP

Restricted to a student in an engineering school who plans to pursue a career in the aggregates industry. One-time award for full-time students attending a four-year college or university.

Academic Fields/Career Goals: Engineering-Related Technologies.

Award: Scholarship for use in freshman, sophomore, junior, or senior years; not renewable. *Number:* 1. *Amount:* $2500.

Eligibility Requirements: Applicant must be enrolled or expecting to enroll full-time at a four-year institution or university. Available to U.S. and non-U.S. citizens.

Application Requirements: Application, essay, references, transcript. *Deadline:* April 30.

Contact: Wendt Memorial Scholarship Committee, c/o NSSGA
National Stone, Sand and Gravel Association (NSSGA)
2101 Wilson Boulevard, Suite 100
Arlington, VA 22201-3062
Phone: 703-525-8788
Fax: 703-525-7782
E-mail: info@nssga.org

NSSGA SCHOLARSHIP

This program is restricted to students intending to pursue a career in the aggregates industry. One-time award for full-time students attending a four-year college or university. Studies must be related to mining engineering.

Academic Fields/Career Goals: Engineering-Related Technologies.

Award: Scholarship for use in freshman, sophomore, junior, or senior years; not renewable. *Number:* 10. *Amount:* $2500.

Eligibility Requirements: Applicant must be enrolled or expecting to enroll full-time at a four-year institution or university. Available to U.S. and non-U.S. citizens.

Application Requirements: Application, essay, references, transcript. *Deadline:* April 30.

Contact: Vice President for Operations
National Stone, Sand and Gravel Association (NSSGA)
2101 Wilson Boulevard, Suite 100
Arlington, VA 22201-3062
Phone: 703-525-8788
Fax: 703-525-7782
E-mail: info@nssga.org

OREGON STUDENT ASSISTANCE COMMISSION http://www.osac.state.or.us

AMERICAN COUNCIL OF ENGINEERING COMPANIES OF OREGON SCHOLARSHIP

• *See page 146*

PLASTICS INSTITUTE OF AMERICA http://www.plasticsinstitute.org

PLASTICS PIONEERS SCHOLARSHIPS

Financial grants awarded to undergraduate students needing help in their education expenses to enter into a full-time career in any and all segments of the plastics industry, with emphasis on "hands on" participation in the many fields where members of the Plastics Pioneers Association have spent their professional years. Applicants must be U.S. citizens.

Academic Fields/Career Goals: Engineering/Technology; Engineering-Related Technologies; Materials Science, Engineering, and Metallurgy; Trade/Technical Specialties.

Award: Scholarship for use in freshman, sophomore, junior, or senior years; renewable. *Number:* 30–40. *Amount:* $1500.

Eligibility Requirements: Applicant must be enrolled or expecting to enroll full or part-time at a two-year or four-year or technical institution. Available to U.S. citizens.

Application Requirements: Application, essay, references, transcript. *Deadline:* April 1.

Contact: Aldo Crugnola, Executive Director
Plastics Institute of America
333 Aiken Street
Lowell, MA 01854
Phone: 978-934-2575
Fax: 978-459-9420
E-mail: pia@uml.edu

PLUMBING-HEATING-COOLING CONTRACTORS ASSOCIATION EDUCATION FOUNDATION http://www.phccweb.org

BRADFORD WHITE CORPORATION SCHOLARSHIP

• *See page 79*

DELTA FAUCET COMPANY SCHOLARSHIP PROGRAM

• *See page 79*

PHCC EDUCATIONAL FOUNDATION NEED-BASED SCHOLARSHIP

• *See page 79*

PHCC EDUCATIONAL FOUNDATION SCHOLARSHIP PROGRAM

• *See page 79*

ROBERT H. MOLLOHAN FAMILY CHARITABLE FOUNDATION, INC. http://www.mollohanfoundation.org

HIGH TECHNOLOGY SCHOLARS PROGRAM

• *See page 117*

SOCIETY FOR TECHNICAL COMMUNICATION http://www.stc.org

SOCIETY FOR TECHNICAL COMMUNICATION SCHOLARSHIP PROGRAM

• *See page 165*

SOCIETY OF AUTOMOTIVE ENGINEERS http://www.sae.org/students/stuschol.htm

BMW/SAE ENGINEERING SCHOLARSHIP

• *See page 105*

DETROIT SECTION SAE TECHNICAL SCHOLARSHIP

Renewable scholarship for high school seniors with a minimum 3.0 GPA, SAT of 1200 or 28 ACT enrolled in a two or four year engineering or science program. Must be a child or grandchild of a Detroit SAE member. Application should be retrieved from SAE Web site http://www.sae.org/students/stuschol.htm.

Academic Fields/Career Goals: Engineering/Technology; Engineering-Related Technologies; Science, Technology, and Society.

Award: Scholarship for use in freshman, sophomore, junior, or senior years; renewable. *Number:* 1. *Amount:* $2500.

Eligibility Requirements: Applicant must be high school student and planning to enroll or expecting to enroll full-time at a two-year or four-year institution or university. Applicant or parent of applicant must be member of Society of Automotive Engineers. Applicant must have 3.0 GPA or higher. Available to U.S. citizens.

Application Requirements: Application, financial need analysis, test scores, transcript. *Fee:* $6. *Deadline:* December 1.

Contact: Connie Harnish, SAE Customer Service
Society of Automotive Engineers
400 Commonwealth Drive
Warrendale, PA 15096-0001
Phone: 724-776-4970
E-mail: customerservice@sae.org

EDWARD D. HENDRICKSON/SAE ENGINEERING SCHOLARSHIP

• *See page 105*

RALPH K. HILLQUIST HONORARY SAE SCHOLARSHIP

Non-renewable scholarship for university juniors with a minimum 3.0 GPA. Must have a declared major in mechanical or automotive-related engineering.

Preference given to those with studies related to noise and vibration. Application should be retrieved from the SAE Web site http://www.sae.org/students/stuschol.htm.

Academic Fields/Career Goals: Engineering/Technology; Engineering-Related Technologies; Mechanical Engineering.

Award: Scholarship for use in junior year; not renewable. *Number:* 1. *Amount:* $1000.

Eligibility Requirements: Applicant must be enrolled or expecting to enroll full-time at an institution or university. Applicant must have 3.0 GPA or higher. Available to U.S. citizens.

Application Requirements: *Deadline:* February 1.

Contact: Connie Harnish, SAE Customer Service
Society of Automotive Engineers
400 Commonwealth Drive
Warrendale, PA 15096-0001
Phone: 724-776-4970
E-mail: customerservice@sae.org

SAE WILLIAM G. BELFREY MEMORIAL GRANT

Non-renewable grant for university juniors at a Canadian university enrolled in a mobility-related engineering discipline. Must be a Canadian citizen. Application should be retrieved from SAE Web site http://www.sae.org/students/stuschol.htm

Academic Fields/Career Goals: Engineering/Technology; Engineering-Related Technologies.

Award: Grant for use in junior year. *Number:* 1. *Amount:* $1000.

Eligibility Requirements: Applicant must be enrolled or expecting to enroll full-time at an institution or university. Available to Canadian citizens.

Application Requirements: Application, essay, resume, references, transcript. *Deadline:* April 1.

Contact: Connie Harnish, SAE Customer Service
Society of Automotive Engineers
400 Commonwealth Drive
Warrendale, PA 15096-0001
Phone: 724-776-4970
E-mail: customerservice@sae.org

TMC/SAE DONALD D. DAWSON TECHNICAL SCHOLARSHIP

• *See page 105*

YANMAR/SAE SCHOLARSHIP

Eligible applicants will be citizens of North America (U.S., Canada, Mexico) and will be entering their junior year of undergraduate engineering or enrolled in a postgraduate engineering or related science program. Applicants must be pursuing a course of study or research related to the conservation of energy in transportation, agriculture, construction, and power generation. Emphasis will be placed on research or study related to the internal combustion engine. Application should be retrieved from the SAE Web site at http://www.sae.org/students/stuschol.htm.

Academic Fields/Career Goals: Engineering/Technology; Engineering-Related Technologies; Materials Science, Engineering, and Metallurgy; Mechanical Engineering.

Award: Scholarship for use in junior, senior, or graduate years; renewable. *Number:* 1. *Amount:* $1000.

Eligibility Requirements: Applicant must be Canadian or Mexican citizen and enrolled or expecting to enroll full-time at an institution or university. Available to U.S. and non-U.S. citizens.

Application Requirements: Application, essay, self-addressed stamped envelope, test scores, transcript. *Deadline:* April 1.

Contact: Connie Harnish, SAE Customer Service
Society of Automotive Engineers
400 Commonwealth Drive
Warrendale, PA 15096-0001
Phone: 724-776-4970
E-mail: customerservice@sae.org

SOCIETY OF BROADCAST ENGINEERS, INC. http://www.sbe.org

ROBERT GREENBERG/HAROLD E. ENNES SCHOLARSHIP FUND AND ENNES EDUCATIONAL FOUNDATION BROADCAST TECHNOLOGY SCHOLARSHIP

Merit-based awards for undergraduate students to study the technical aspects of broadcast engineering. Students should apply as high school senior or college freshman and may use the award for a two- or four-year college or university program. One-time award of $1000.

Academic Fields/Career Goals: Engineering/Technology; Engineering-Related Technologies; TV/Radio Broadcasting.

Award: Scholarship for use in freshman, sophomore, junior, or senior years; not renewable. *Number:* 3. *Amount:* $1000.

Eligibility Requirements: Applicant must be enrolled or expecting to enroll full-time at a two-year or four-year institution or university. Applicant must have 3.0 GPA or higher. Available to U.S. and Canadian citizens.

Application Requirements: Application, essay, references, self-addressed stamped envelope, transcript. *Deadline:* July 1.

Contact: Linda Baun, Certification Director
Society of Broadcast Engineers, Inc.
9247 North Meridian, Suite 305
Indianapolis, IN 46260
Phone: 317-846-9000
Fax: 317-846-9120

SOCIETY OF HISPANIC PROFESSIONAL ENGINEERS FOUNDATION http://www.shpefoundation.org

SOCIETY OF HISPANIC PROFESSIONAL ENGINEERS FOUNDATION

• *See page 146*

SOCIETY OF MEXICAN AMERICAN ENGINEERS AND SCIENTISTS http://www.maes-natl.org

GRE AND GRADUATE APPLICATIONS WAIVER

• *See page 72*

SOCIETY OF WOMEN ENGINEERS http://www.swe.org/scholarships

ARIZONA SECTION SCHOLARSHIP

Two scholarships given to freshmen who are either residents of Arizona or attending a school in that state. Must be studying an engineering related field. Deadline: May 15. Minimum 3.5 GPA required.

Academic Fields/Career Goals: Engineering/Technology; Engineering-Related Technologies.

Award: Scholarship for use in freshman year; not renewable. *Number:* 2. *Amount:* $1000.

Eligibility Requirements: Applicant must be high school student; planning to enroll or expecting to enroll full-time at a two-year or four-year institution or university and female. Applicant must have 3.5 GPA or higher.

Application Requirements: Application, essay, references, self-addressed stamped envelope, test scores, transcript. *Deadline:* May 15.

Contact: Program Coordinator
Society of Women Engineers
230 East Ohio Street, Suite 400
Chicago, IL 60611-3265
Phone: 312-596-5223
Fax: 312-644-8557
E-mail: hq@swe.org

GENERAL MOTORS FOUNDATION UNDERGRADUATE SCHOLARSHIPS

• *See page 147*

GUIDANT CORPORATION SCHOLARSHIP

• *See page 173*

SOLE - THE INTERNATIONAL LOGISTICS SOCIETY http://www.sole.org

LOGISTICS EDUCATION FOUNDATION SCHOLARSHIP

One-time award for students enrolled in a program of study in logistics. Must have minimum 3.0 GPA. Submit transcript and references with application.

Academic Fields/Career Goals: Engineering-Related Technologies.

Award: Scholarship for use in sophomore, junior, senior, or graduate years; not renewable. *Number:* 5–10. *Amount:* $1000–$3000.

Eligibility Requirements: Applicant must be enrolled or expecting to enroll full-time at a four-year institution or university. Applicant must have 3.0 GPA or higher. Available to U.S. and non-U.S. citizens.

Application Requirements: Application, references, transcript. *Deadline:* May 15.

Contact: Scholarship Coordinator
SOLE - The International Logistics Society
8100 Professional Place, Suite 111
Hyattsville, MD 20785
E-mail: solehq@erols.com

TAG AND LABEL MANUFACTURERS INSTITUTE, INC. http://www.tlmi.com

TAG AND LABEL MANUFACTURERS, INC., SCHOLARSHIP FUND

TLMI offers six $5000 scholarships annually to qualified junior and senior undergraduates. Applicant must demonstrate interest in entering the tag and label industry. Minimum 3.0 GPA required.

Academic Fields/Career Goals: Engineering-Related Technologies; Flexography; Graphics/Graphic Arts/Printing.

Award: Scholarship for use in junior or senior years; renewable. *Number:* 6. *Amount:* $5000.

Eligibility Requirements: Applicant must be enrolled or expecting to enroll full-time at a four-year institution or university. Applicant must have 3.0 GPA or higher. Available to U.S. and Canadian citizens.

Application Requirements: Application, autobiography, interview, portfolio, resume, references, transcript. *Deadline:* March 31.

Contact: Karen Planz, Office Manager
Tag and Label Manufacturers Institute, Inc.
Scholarship Committee
40 Shuman Boulevard, Suite 295
Naperville, IL 60563-8465
Phone: 630-357-9222 Ext. 11
Fax: 630-357-0192
E-mail: office@thmi.com

UNITED NEGRO COLLEGE FUND http://www.uncf.org

NORTHEAST UTILITIES SYSTEM SCHOLARSHIP PROGRAM

• *See page 132*

UNCF/SPRINT SCHOLARS PROGRAM

• *See page 50*

WEST VIRGINIA HIGHER EDUCATION POLICY COMMISSION-OFFICE OF FINANCIAL AID AND OUTREACH SERVICES http://www.hepc.wvnet.edu

WEST VIRGINIA ENGINEERING, SCIENCE & TECHNOLOGY SCHOLARSHIP PROGRAM

• *See page 223*

XEROX http://xerox.com

TECHNICAL MINORITY SCHOLARSHIP

• *See page 148*

ENGINEERING/TECHNOLOGY

AACE INTERNATIONAL http://www.aacei.org

AACE INTERNATIONAL COMPETITIVE SCHOLARSHIP

• *See page 73*

ACI INTERNATIONAL/CONCRETE RESEARCH AND EDUCATION FOUNDATION (CONREF) http://www.concrete.org

PETER D. COURTOIS CONCRETE CONSTRUCTION SCHOLARSHIP

• *See page 73*

AEA-OREGON COUNCIL http://www.ous.edu/ecs/scholarships

AEA- OREGON COUNCIL TECHNOLOGY SCHOLARSHIP PROGRAM

• *See page 136*

AIR AND WASTE MANAGEMENT ASSOCIATION-CONNECTICUT CHAPTER http://www.awma-nes.org/

AIR AND WASTE MANAGEMENT ASSOCIATION-CONNECTICUT CHAPTER SCHOLARSHIP

• *See page 111*

AIR TRAFFIC CONTROL ASSOCIATION, INC. http://www.atca.org

AIR TRAFFIC CONTROL ASSOCIATION SCHOLARSHIP

• *See page 92*

AMERICAN ASSOCIATION OF CEREAL CHEMISTS http://www.aaccnet.org

UNDERGRADUATE SCHOLARSHIP AWARD

One-time award to encourage scholastically outstanding undergraduate students in academic preparation for a career in grain-based food science and technology, and to attract and encourage outstanding students to enter the field of grain-based food science and technology. Must be AACC member. Minimum 3.0 GPA required. Application must be submitted to AACC by March 1.

Academic Fields/Career Goals: Engineering/Technology; Food Science/Nutrition.

Award: Scholarship for use in junior or senior years; not renewable. *Number:* up to 15. *Amount:* $1000–$2000.

Eligibility Requirements: Applicant must be enrolled or expecting to enroll full-time at a four-year institution or university. Applicant must have 3.0 GPA or higher. Available to U.S. and non-U.S. citizens.

Application Requirements: Application, essay, references, transcript. *Deadline:* March 1.

Contact: Linda Schmitt, Scholarship Coordinator
American Association of Cereal Chemists
3340 Pilot Knob Road
St. Paul, MN 55121-2097
Phone: 651-994-3828
Fax: 651-454-0766
E-mail: lschmitt@scisoc.org

AMERICAN CHEMICAL SOCIETY, RUBBER DIVISION http://www.rubber.org/awards/scholarships.htm

AMERICAN CHEMICAL SOCIETY, RUBBER DIVISION-UNDERGRADUATE SCHOLARSHIP

• *See page 136*

AMERICAN COUNCIL OF ENGINEERING COMPANIES OF PENNSYLVANIA (ACEC/PA) http://www.acecpa.org

ENGINEERING SCHOLARSHIP

• *See page 136*

AMERICAN ELECTROPLATERS AND SURFACE FINISHERS SOCIETY http://www.aesf.org

AMERICAN ELECTROPLATERS AND SURFACE FINISHERS SCHOLARSHIPS

• *See page 136*

AMERICAN INSTITUTE OF AERONAUTICS AND ASTRONAUTICS http://www.aiaa.org

AIAA UNDERGRADUATE SCHOLARSHIP

• *See page 66*

AMERICAN INSTITUTE OF ARCHITECTS, NEW YORK CHAPTER http://www.aiany.org

HASKELL AWARDS FOR STUDENTS IN ARCHITECTURAL JOURNALISM

• *See page 74*

AMERICAN LEGION, DEPARTMENT OF KANSAS

CHARLES W. AND ANNETTE HILL SCHOLARSHIP

• *See page 120*

AMERICAN METEOROLOGICAL SOCIETY http://www.ametsoc.org/AMS

AMERICAN METEOROLOGICAL SOCIETY INDUSTRY UNDERGRADUATE SCHOLARSHIPS

• *See page 66*

AMERICAN NUCLEAR SOCIETY http://www.ans.org

AMERICAN NUCLEAR SOCIETY ENVIRONMENTAL SCIENCES DIVISION SCHOLARSHIP

Must be at least an entering junior enrolled in a course of study relating to a degree in nuclear science, nuclear engineering, or a nuclear-related field. One-time award for U.S. citizen or permanent resident. Must be enrolled in a U.S. institution. Student must be pursuing a degree in a discipline related to the environmental sciences. Application available at Web site: http://www.ans.org.

Academic Fields/Career Goals: Engineering/Technology; Nuclear Science.

Award: Scholarship for use in junior or senior years; not renewable. *Number:* 1. *Amount:* $2000.

Eligibility Requirements: Applicant must be enrolled or expecting to enroll full-time at a four-year institution. Available to U.S. citizens.

Application Requirements: Application, references, transcript. *Deadline:* February 1.

Contact: Scholarship Coordinator
American Nuclear Society
555 North Kensington Avenue
La Grange Park, IL 60526
Phone: 708-352-6611
Fax: 708-352-0499
E-mail: outreach@ans.org

AMERICAN NUCLEAR SOCIETY JAMES R. VOGT SCHOLARSHIP

One-time award for juniors, seniors, and first-year graduate students enrolled or proposing research in radio-analytical or analytical application of nuclear science. Check "Vogt" box for this one-time award. Must be U.S. citizen or permanent resident. Application available at Web site: http://www.ans.org.

Academic Fields/Career Goals: Engineering/Technology; Nuclear Science.

Award: Scholarship for use in junior, senior, or graduate years; not renewable. *Number:* 1. *Amount:* $2000–$3000.

Eligibility Requirements: Applicant must be enrolled or expecting to enroll full-time at a four-year institution. Available to U.S. citizens.

Application Requirements: Application, references, transcript. *Deadline:* February 1.

Contact: Scholarship Coordinator
American Nuclear Society
555 North Kensington Avenue
La Grange Park, IL 60526
Phone: 708-352-6611
Fax: 708-352-0499
E-mail: outreach@ans.org

AMERICAN NUCLEAR SOCIETY OPERATIONS AND POWER SCHOLARSHIP

Must be at least an entering junior enrolled in a program leading to a degree in nuclear science, nuclear engineering, or a nuclear-related field. One-time award for a U.S. citizen or permanent resident. Application available at Web site: http://www.ans.org.

Academic Fields/Career Goals: Engineering/Technology; Nuclear Science.

Award: Scholarship for use in junior or senior years; not renewable. *Number:* 1. *Amount:* $2500.

Eligibility Requirements: Applicant must be enrolled or expecting to enroll at an institution or university. Available to U.S. citizens.

Application Requirements: Application, references, transcript. *Deadline:* February 1.

Contact: Scholarship Coordinator
American Nuclear Society
555 North Kensington Avenue
La Grange Park, IL 60526
Phone: 708-352-6611
Fax: 708-352-0499
E-mail: outreach@ans.org

AMERICAN NUCLEAR SOCIETY UNDERGRADUATE SCHOLARSHIPS

One-time award for students who have completed at least one year of a four-year nuclear science or nuclear engineering or nuclear-related program. Must be sponsored by ANS member or branch. Must be U.S. citizen or permanent resident. Application available at Web site: http://www.ans.org.

Academic Fields/Career Goals: Engineering/Technology; Nuclear Science.

Award: Scholarship for use in sophomore, junior, or senior years; not renewable. *Number:* 1–21. *Amount:* $2000.

Eligibility Requirements: Applicant must be enrolled or expecting to enroll full-time at a four-year institution. Available to U.S. citizens.

Application Requirements: Application, references, transcript. *Deadline:* February 1.

Contact: Scholarship Coordinator
American Nuclear Society
555 North Kensington Avenue
La Grange Park, IL 60526
Phone: 708-352-6611
Fax: 708-352-0499
E-mail: outreach@ans.org

DECOMMISSIONING, DECONTAMINATION, AND REUTILIZATION SCHOLARSHIP

For undergraduate student associated with decommissioning/decontamination nuclear facilities, management/characterization of nuclear waste, or environmental restoration. Application available at Web site. Must be a U.S. citizen enrolled in a U.S. school. Student will join the American Nuclear Society. Applicants are required to submit a brief essay discussing the importance of some aspect of decommissioning, decontamination, and reutilization to the future of the nuclear field.

Academic Fields/Career Goals: Engineering/Technology; Nuclear Science.

Award: Scholarship for use in sophomore, junior, or senior years; not renewable. *Number:* 1. *Amount:* $2000.

Eligibility Requirements: Applicant must be enrolled or expecting to enroll full-time at a four-year institution and must have an interest in designated field specified by sponsor. Available to U.S. citizens.

Application Requirements: Application, essay, references, transcript. *Deadline:* February 1.

Contact: Scholarship Coordinator
American Nuclear Society
555 North Kensington Avenue
La Grange Park, IL 60526
Phone: 708-352-6611
Fax: 708-352-0499
E-mail: outreach@ans.org

DELAYED EDUCATION FOR WOMEN SCHOLARSHIPS

One-time award is to enable mature women whose formal studies in nuclear science, nuclear engineering, or related fields have been delayed or interrupted at least one year. Must be U.S. citizen or permanent resident in a four-year program. Application available at Web site: http://www.ans.org.

Academic Fields/Career Goals: Engineering/Technology; Nuclear Science.

Award: Scholarship for use in freshman, sophomore, junior, or senior years; not renewable. *Number:* 1. *Amount:* $3500.

Eligibility Requirements: Applicant must be enrolled or expecting to enroll full-time at a four-year institution and female. Applicant must have 2.5 GPA or higher. Available to U.S. citizens.

Application Requirements: Application, financial need analysis, references, transcript. *Deadline:* February 1.

Contact: Scholarship Coordinator
American Nuclear Society
555 North Kensington Avenue
La Grange Park, IL 60526
Phone: 708-352-6611
Fax: 708-352-0499
E-mail: outreach@ans.org

JOHN AND MURIEL LANDIS SCHOLARSHIP AWARDS

One-time award for undergraduate and graduate study in nuclear engineering or nuclear-related field. Must have greater than average financial need or be educationally disadvantaged and be nominated by ANS member. Must be U.S. citizen or permanent resident. Application available at Web site: http://www.ans.org.

Academic Fields/Career Goals: Engineering/Technology; Nuclear Science.

Award: Scholarship for use in freshman, sophomore, junior, senior, or graduate years; not renewable. *Number:* 1–8. *Amount:* $3500.

Eligibility Requirements: Applicant must be enrolled or expecting to enroll at a four-year institution. Available to U.S. citizens.

Application Requirements: Application, financial need analysis, references, transcript. *Deadline:* February 1.

Contact: Scholarship Coordinator
American Nuclear Society
555 North Kensington Avenue
La Grange Park, IL 60526
Phone: 708-352-6611
Fax: 708-352-0469
E-mail: outreach@ans.org

JOHN R. LAMARSH SCHOLARSHIP

One-time award for an entering junior or senior in program leading to degree in nuclear science, nuclear engineering, or a nuclear-related field. Must be sponsored by the ANS and be a U.S. citizen or permanent resident. Application available at Web site: http://www.ans.org.

Academic Fields/Career Goals: Engineering/Technology; Nuclear Science.

Award: Scholarship for use in junior or senior years; not renewable. *Number:* 1. *Amount:* $2000.

Eligibility Requirements: Applicant must be enrolled or expecting to enroll at a four-year institution. Available to U.S. citizens.

Application Requirements: Application, references, transcript. *Deadline:* February 1.

Contact: Scholarship Coordinator
American Nuclear Society
555 North Kensington Avenue
La Grange Park, IL 60526
Phone: 708-352-6611
Fax: 708-352-0499
E-mail: outreach@ans.org

JOSEPH R. DIETRICH SCHOLARSHIP

One-time award for an entering junior or senior in program leading to degree in nuclear science, nuclear engineering, or a nuclear-related field. Must be sponsored by the ANS and be a U.S. citizen or permanent resident. Application available at Web site: http://www.ans.org.

Academic Fields/Career Goals: Engineering/Technology; Nuclear Science.

Award: Scholarship for use in junior or senior years; not renewable. *Number:* 1. *Amount:* $2000.

Eligibility Requirements: Applicant must be enrolled or expecting to enroll at a four-year institution. Available to U.S. citizens.

Application Requirements: Application, references, transcript. *Deadline:* February 1.

Contact: Scholarship Coordinator
American Nuclear Society
555 North Kensington Avenue
La Grange Park, IL 60526
Phone: 708-352-6611
Fax: 708-352-0499
E-mail: outreach@ans.org

AMERICAN PUBLIC POWER ASSOCIATION http://www.appanet.org

DEMONSTRATION OF ENERGY EFFICIENT DEVELOPMENTS SCHOLARSHIP

• *See page 218*

AMERICAN PUBLIC TRANSPORTATION FOUNDATION http://www.apta.com

DONALD C. HYDE ESSAY PROGRAM

• *See page 149*

JACK GILSTRAP SCHOLARSHIP

• *See page 149*

LOUIS T. KLAUDER SCHOLARSHIP

• *See page 150*

PARSONS BRINCKERHOFF-JIM LAMMIE SCHOLARSHIP

• *See page 150*

TRANSIT HALL OF FAME SCHOLARSHIP AWARD PROGRAM

• *See page 150*

AMERICAN SOCIETY OF AGRICULTURAL ENGINEERS http://www.asae.org

AMERICAN SOCIETY OF AGRICULTURAL ENGINEERS STUDENT ENGINEER OF THE YEAR SCHOLARSHIP

Award for engineering undergraduate student in the U.S. or Canada. Must be active student member of the American Society of Agricultural Engineers. Write for more information and special application procedures. One-time award of $1000. Must have completed one year of school, and must submit paper titled "My Goals in the Engineering Profession."

Academic Fields/Career Goals: Engineering/Technology.

Award: Scholarship for use in sophomore or junior years; not renewable. *Number:* 1. *Amount:* $1000.

Eligibility Requirements: Applicant must be enrolled or expecting to enroll at a four-year institution or university. Applicant must have 3.0 GPA or higher. Available to U.S. and Canadian citizens.

Application Requirements: Application, essay, references. *Deadline:* February 16.

Contact: Carol Flautt, Scholarship Program
American Society of Agricultural Engineers
2950 Niles Road
St. Joseph, MI 49085
Phone: 269-428-6336
Fax: 269-429-3852
E-mail: flautt@asae.org

AMERICAN SOCIETY OF CERTIFIED ENGINEERING TECHNICIANS http://www.ascet.org

AMERICAN SOCIETY OF CERTIFIED ENGINEERING TECHNICIANS SMALL CASH GRANT

Award designed to provide financial assistance to high school seniors who will enter an engineering technology program following high school graduation. Must be U.S. citizen. Application deadline is April 1.

Academic Fields/Career Goals: Engineering/Technology.

Award: Grant for use in freshman year; not renewable. *Number:* 4. *Amount:* $100.

Eligibility Requirements: Applicant must be high school student and planning to enroll or expecting to enroll full or part-time at a two-year or four-year or technical institution or university. Available to U.S. citizens.

Application Requirements: Application, references, transcript. *Deadline:* April 1.

Contact: Kurt H. Schuler, General Manager
American Society of Certified Engineering Technicians
PO Box 1348
Flowery Branch, GA 30542-0023
Phone: 770-967-9173
Fax: 770-967-8049
E-mail: kurt_schuler@ascet.org

JOSEPH C. JOHNSON MEMORIAL GRANT

The Joseph C. Johnson Memorial Grant is a $750 award given to qualified applicants in order to offset the cost of tuition, books and lab fees. Applicant must be an American citizen or a legal resident of the country in which the applicant is currently living, as well as be either a student, certified, regular, registered or associate member of ASCET. Student must be enrolled in an engineering technology program. For further information, visit http://www.ascet.org.

Academic Fields/Career Goals: Engineering/Technology.

Award: Grant for use in sophomore or senior years; not renewable. *Number:* 1. *Amount:* $750.

Eligibility Requirements: Applicant must be enrolled or expecting to enroll full or part-time at a two-year or four-year institution or university. Applicant must have 3.0 GPA or higher. Available to U.S. citizens.

Application Requirements: Application, financial need analysis, references, transcript. *Deadline:* varies.

Contact: Kurt Schuler, General Manager
American Society of Certified Engineering Technicians
PO Box 1348
Flowery Branch, GA 30542-0023
Phone: 770-967-9173
Fax: 770-967-8049
E-mail: kurt_schuler@ascet.org

JOSEPH M. PARISH MEMORIAL GRANT

The Joseph M. Parish Memorial Grant will be awarded to a student in the amount of $500 to be used to offset the cost of tuition, books and lab fees. Applicant must be a student member of ASCET and be an American citizen or a legal resident of the country in which the applicant is currently living. The award will be given to full time students enrolled in an engineering technology program; students pursuing a B.S. degree in Engineering are not eligible for this grant. For more information, visit http://www.ascet.org.

Academic Fields/Career Goals: Engineering/Technology.

Award: Grant for use in sophomore or senior years; not renewable. *Number:* 1. *Amount:* $500.

Eligibility Requirements: Applicant must be enrolled or expecting to enroll full-time at a two-year or four-year institution. Applicant must have 3.0 GPA or higher. Available to U.S. citizens.

Application Requirements: Application, financial need analysis. *Deadline:* varies.

Contact: Kurt Schuler, General Manager
American Society of Certified Engineering Technicians
PO Box 1348
Flowery Branch, GA 30542-0023
Phone: 770-967-9173
Fax: 770-967-8049
E-mail: kurt_schuler@ascet.org

AMERICAN SOCIETY OF HEATING, REFRIGERATING, AND AIR CONDITIONING ENGINEERS, INC.

http://www.ashrae.org

ALWIN B. NEWTON SCHOLARSHIP FUND

• *See page 218*

AMERICAN SOCIETY OF HEATING, REFRIGERATION, AND AIR CONDITIONING ENGINEERING TECHNOLOGY SCHOLARSHIP

• *See page 66*

ASHRAE REGION VIII SCHOLARSHIP

One-time award to qualified engineering students enrolled full-time in an ABET-accredited program. Minimum 3.0 GPA required. Must study in Arkansas, Louisiana, Texas, Oklahoma or Mexico.

Academic Fields/Career Goals: Engineering/Technology; Heating, Air-Conditioning, and Refrigeration Mechanics.

Award: Scholarship for use in sophomore, junior, or senior years; not renewable. *Number:* 1. *Amount:* $3000.

Eligibility Requirements: Applicant must be enrolled or expecting to enroll full-time at a four-year institution or university and studying in Arkansas, Louisiana, Oklahoma, or Texas. Applicant must have 3.0 GPA or higher. Available to U.S. citizens.

Application Requirements: Application, financial need analysis, references, transcript. *Deadline:* December 1.

Contact: Scholarship Administrator
American Society of Heating, Refrigerating, and Air Conditioning Engineers, Inc.
1791 Tullie Circle, NE
Atlanta, GA 30329
Phone: 404-636-8400
Fax: 404-321-5478

ASHRAE MEMORIAL SCHOLARSHIP

• *See page 225*

ASHRAE REGION IV BENNY BOOTLE SCHOLARSHIP

One-time award to full-time engineering student enrolled in ABET-accredited program. Minimum 3.0 GPA required. Must study in North Carolina, South Carolina or Georgia.

Academic Fields/Career Goals: Engineering/Technology; Heating, Air-Conditioning, and Refrigeration Mechanics.

Award: Scholarship for use in sophomore, junior, or senior years; not renewable. *Number:* 1. *Amount:* $3000.

Eligibility Requirements: Applicant must be enrolled or expecting to enroll full-time at a four-year institution or university and studying in Georgia, North Carolina, or South Carolina. Applicant must have 3.0 GPA or higher. Available to U.S. citizens.

Application Requirements: Application, financial need analysis, references, transcript. *Deadline:* December 1.

Contact: Scholarship Administrator
American Society of Heating, Refrigerating, and Air Conditioning Engineers, Inc.
1791 Tullie Circle, NE
Atlanta, GA 30329
Phone: 404-636-8400
Fax: 404-321-5478

ASHRAE SCHOLARSHIPS

• *See page 225*

HENRY ADAMS SCHOLARSHIP

• *See page 225*

AMERICAN SOCIETY OF MECHANICAL ENGINEERS (ASME INTERNATIONAL)

http://www.asme.org/education/enged/aid

AMERICAN SOCIETY OF MECHANICAL ENGINEERS FOUNDATION SCHOLARSHIP

Award for college juniors and seniors who are members of the American Society of Mechanical Engineers. Must be pursuing studies in a mechanical

American Society of Mechanical Engineers (ASME International) (continued)

engineering, mechanical engineering technology, or related program. There are no geographic or citizenship limitations. Applications are available online: http://www.asme.org/education/enged/aid.

Academic Fields/Career Goals: Engineering/Technology; Mechanical Engineering.

Award: Scholarship for use in junior or senior years; not renewable. *Number:* up to 15. *Amount:* up to $1500.

Eligibility Requirements: Applicant must be enrolled or expecting to enroll full-time at a four-year institution or university. Available to U.S. and non-U.S. citizens.

Application Requirements: Application, essay, financial need analysis, references, self-addressed stamped envelope, transcript. *Deadline:* March 15.

Contact: Ms. Theresa Oluwanifise, Administrative Assistant
American Society of Mechanical Engineers (ASME International)
3 Park Avenue
New York, NY 10016-5990
Phone: 212-591-8131
Fax: 212-591-7143
E-mail: oluwanifiset@asme.org

AMERICAN SOCIETY OF NAVAL ENGINEERS http://www.navalengineers.org

AMERICAN SOCIETY OF NAVAL ENGINEERS SCHOLARSHIP
• *See page 66*

AMERICAN WELDING SOCIETY http://www.aws.org/foundation

AIRGAS-TERRY JARVIS MEMORIAL SCHOLARSHIP
• *See page 226*

AMERICAN WELDING SOCIETY INTERNATIONAL SCHOLARSHIP
• *See page 226*

DONALD F. HASTINGS SCHOLARSHIP
• *See page 226*

EDWARD J. BRADY MEMORIAL SCHOLARSHIP
• *See page 227*

HOWARD E. ADKINS MEMORIAL SCHOLARSHIP
• *See page 227*

ILLINOIS TOOL WORKS WELDING COMPANIES SCHOLARSHIP
• *See page 227*

JOHN C. LINCOLN MEMORIAL SCHOLARSHIP
• *See page 227*

MATSUO BRIDGE COMPANY, LTD., OF JAPAN SCHOLARSHIP
• *See page 151*

MILLER ELECTRIC IYSC SCHOLARSHIP

Applicant must compete in the National Skills USA-VICA Competition for Welding, and advance to the AWS Weld Trials at the AWS International Welding and Fabricating Exposition and Convention, which is held on a bi-annual basis. For additional information, see Web site: http://www.aws.org/foundation.

Academic Fields/Career Goals: Engineering/Technology; Trade/Technical Specialties.

Award: Scholarship for use in freshman, sophomore, junior, senior, graduate, or postgraduate years; renewable. *Number:* up to 1. *Amount:* $1000–$10,000.

Eligibility Requirements: Applicant must be enrolled or expecting to enroll full or part-time at an institution or university. Available to U.S. citizens.

Application Requirements: Applicant must enter a contest. *Deadline:* varies.

Contact: Neida Herrera, Development Coordinator
American Welding Society
550 Northwest Le Jeune Road
Miami, FL 33126
Phone: 305-443-9353 Ext. 461
Fax: 305-443-7559
E-mail: neida@aws.org

PRAXAIR INTERNATIONAL SCHOLARSHIP
• *See page 227*

WILLIAM B. HOWELL MEMORIAL SCHOLARSHIP
• *See page 228*

ARMED FORCES COMMUNICATIONS AND ELECTRONICS ASSOCIATION, EDUCATIONAL FOUNDATION http://www.afcea.org

AFCEA SCHOLARSHIP FOR WORKING PROFESSIONALS
• *See page 96*

AFCEA SGT. JEANNETTE L. WINTERS, USMC MEMORIAL SCHOLARSHIP
• *See page 168*

AFCEA/LOCKHEED MARTIN ORINCON IT SCHOLARSHIP
• *See page 169*

ARMED FORCES COMMUNICATIONS AND ELECTRONICS ASSOCIATION EDUCATIONAL FOUNDATION DISTANCE-LEARNING SCHOLARSHIP
• *See page 169*

ARMED FORCES COMMUNICATIONS AND ELECTRONICS ASSOCIATION GENERAL EMMETT PAIGE SCHOLARSHIP
• *See page 169*

ARMED FORCES COMMUNICATIONS AND ELECTRONICS ASSOCIATION GENERAL JOHN A. WICKHAM SCHOLARSHIP
• *See page 169*

ARMED FORCES COMMUNICATIONS AND ELECTRONICS ASSOCIATION ROTC SCHOLARSHIP PROGRAM
• *See page 96*

VICE ADMIRAL JERRY O. TUTTLE, USN (RET.) AND MRS. BARBARA A. TUTTLE SCIENCE AND TECHNOLOGY SCHOLARSHIP
• *See page 228*

ARRL FOUNDATION, INC. http://www.arrl.org/arrlf/scholgen.html

CHARLES N. FISHER MEMORIAL SCHOLARSHIP
• *See page 66*

IRVING W. COOK, WA0CGS, SCHOLARSHIP
• *See page 67*

MISSISSIPPI SCHOLARSHIP
• *See page 67*

PAUL AND HELEN L. GRAUER SCHOLARSHIP
• *See page 67*

PHD ARA SCHOLARSHIP
• *See page 157*

WILLIAM R. GOLDFARB MEMORIAL SCHOLARSHIP
• *See page 121*

ASIAN PACIFIC AMERICAN HERITAGE COUNCIL http://www.apahc.org

ASIAN PACIFIC AMERICAN HERITAGE COUNCIL SCHOLARSHIP
• *See page 121*

ASM MATERIALS EDUCATION FOUNDATION http://www.asminternational.org

ASM MATERIALS EDUCATION FOUNDATION SCHOLARSHIPS

Twelve awards of $1000 for student members of ASM International studying metallurgy or materials engineering. Must have completed at least one year of college to apply. Award is based on merit; financial need is not considered.

Academic Fields/Career Goals: Engineering/Technology; Materials Science, Engineering, and Metallurgy.

Award: Scholarship for use in sophomore, junior, or senior years; not renewable. *Number:* 12. *Amount:* $1000.

Eligibility Requirements: Applicant must be enrolled or expecting to enroll full-time at a four-year institution or university. Applicant or parent of applicant must be member of ASM International. Available to U.S. and non-U.S. citizens.

Application Requirements: Application, essay, photo, references, transcript. *Deadline:* May 1.

Contact: Pergentina Deatherage, Administrator, Foundation Programs
ASM Materials Education Foundation
9639 Kinsman Road
Materials Park, OH 44073-0002
Phone: 440-338-5151
Fax: 440-338-4634
E-mail: jdeather@asminternational.org

ASM OUTSTANDING SCHOLARS AWARDS

Three awards of $2000 for student members of ASM International studying metallurgy or materials science and engineering. Must have completed at least one year of college to apply. Awards are merit-based; financial need is not considered.

Academic Fields/Career Goals: Engineering/Technology; Materials Science, Engineering, and Metallurgy.

Award: Scholarship for use in sophomore, junior, or senior years; not renewable. *Number:* 3. *Amount:* $2000.

Eligibility Requirements: Applicant must be enrolled or expecting to enroll full-time at a four-year institution or university. Applicant or parent of applicant must be member of ASM International. Available to U.S. and non-U.S. citizens.

Application Requirements: Application, essay, photo, references, transcript. *Deadline:* May 1.

Contact: Pergentina Deatherage, Administrator, Foundation Programs
ASM Materials Education Foundation
9639 Kinsman Road
Materials Park, OH 44073-0002
Phone: 440-338-5151
Fax: 440-338-4634

EDWARD J. DULIS SCHOLARSHIP

Award of $1500 for student members of ASM International studying metallurgy or materials science and engineering. Must have completed at least one year of college to apply. Award is merit based; financial need is not considered.

Academic Fields/Career Goals: Engineering/Technology; Materials Science, Engineering, and Metallurgy.

Award: Scholarship for use in sophomore, junior, or senior years; not renewable. *Number:* 1. *Amount:* $1500.

Eligibility Requirements: Applicant must be enrolled or expecting to enroll full-time at an institution or university. Applicant or parent of applicant must be member of ASM International. Available to U.S. and Canadian citizens.

Application Requirements: Application, photo, references, transcript. *Deadline:* May 1.

Contact: Pergentina Deatherage, Administrator, Foundation Programs
ASM Materials Education Foundation
9639 Kinsman Road
Materials Park, OH 44073-0002
Phone: 440-338-5151
Fax: 440-338-4634

GEORGE A. ROBERTS SCHOLARSHIP

Seven awards for college juniors or seniors studying metallurgy or materials engineering in North America. Applicants must be student members of ASM International. Awards based on need, interest in field, academics, and character.

Academic Fields/Career Goals: Engineering/Technology; Materials Science, Engineering, and Metallurgy.

Award: Scholarship for use in junior or senior years; not renewable. *Number:* 7. *Amount:* $6000.

Eligibility Requirements: Applicant must be enrolled or expecting to enroll full-time at an institution or university. Applicant or parent of applicant must be member of ASM International. Available to U.S. and Canadian citizens.

Application Requirements: Application, essay, financial need analysis, photo, references, transcript. *Deadline:* May 1.

Contact: Pergentina Deatherage, Administrator, Foundation Programs
ASM Materials Education Foundation
9639 Kinsman Road
Materials Park, OH 44073-0002
Phone: 440-338-5151
Fax: 440-338-4634

JOHN M. HANIAK SCHOLARSHIP

Award for student members of ASM International studying metallurgy or materials science and engineering. Must have completed at least one year of college to apply. Award is merit based; financial need is not considered.

Academic Fields/Career Goals: Engineering/Technology; Materials Science, Engineering, and Metallurgy.

Award: Scholarship for use in sophomore, junior, or senior years; not renewable. *Number:* 1. *Amount:* $1500.

Eligibility Requirements: Applicant must be enrolled or expecting to enroll full-time at a four-year institution or university. Applicant or parent of applicant must be member of ASM International. Available to U.S. and non-U.S. citizens.

Application Requirements: Application, essay, references, self-addressed stamped envelope, transcript. *Deadline:* May 1.

Contact: Pergentina Deatherage, Administrator, Foundation Programs
ASM Materials Education Foundation
9639 Kinsman Road
Materials Park, OH 44073-0002
Phone: 440-338-5151
Fax: 440-338-4634

NICHOLAS J. GRANT SCHOLARSHIP

Full tuition for student member of ASM International studying metallurgy or materials science and engineering. Must have completed first two years of college at a North American university. Must demonstrate financial need.

Academic Fields/Career Goals: Engineering/Technology; Materials Science, Engineering, and Metallurgy.

Award: Scholarship for use in junior or senior years; not renewable. *Number:* 1. *Amount:* varies.

Eligibility Requirements: Applicant must be enrolled or expecting to enroll full-time at an institution or university. Applicant or parent of applicant must be member of ASM International. Available to U.S. and Canadian citizens.

Application Requirements: Application, essay, financial need analysis, photo, references, transcript. *Deadline:* May 1.

Contact: Pergentina Deatherage, Administrator, Foundation Programs
ASM Materials Education Foundation
9639 Kinsman Road
Materials Park, OH 44073-0002

WILLIAM P. WOODSIDE FOUNDER'S SCHOLARSHIP

Award for college junior or senior studying metallurgy or materials engineering in North America. Must be a student member of ASM International. Award based on need, interest in field, academics, and character. Scholarship covers full tuition up to $10,000.

ASM Materials Education Foundation (continued)

Academic Fields/Career Goals: Engineering/Technology; Materials Science, Engineering, and Metallurgy.

Award: Scholarship for use in junior or senior years; not renewable. *Number:* 1. *Amount:* up to $10,000.

Eligibility Requirements: Applicant must be enrolled or expecting to enroll full-time at an institution or university. Applicant or parent of applicant must be member of ASM International.

Application Requirements: Application, essay, financial need analysis, photo, references, transcript. *Deadline:* May 1.

Contact: Pergentina Deatherage, Administrator, Foundation Programs
ASM Materials Education Foundation
9639 Kinsman Road
Materials Park, OH 44073-0002
Phone: 440-338-5151
Fax: 440-338-4634

ASPRS, THE IMAGING AND GEOSPATIAL INFORMATION SOCIETY http://www.asprs.org

ROBERT E. ALTENHOFEN MEMORIAL SCHOLARSHIP
• *See page 67*

SPACE IMAGING AWARD FOR APPLICATION OF HIGH RESOLUTION DIGITAL SATELLITE IMAGERY
• *See page 67*

Z/I IMAGING SCHOLARSHIP
• *See page 68*

ASSOCIATED BUILDERS AND CONTRACTORS SCHOLARSHIP PROGRAM http://www.abc.org

TRIMMER EDUCATION FOUNDATION SCHOLARSHIPS FOR CONSTRUCTION MANAGEMENT
• *See page 151*

ASSOCIATED GENERAL CONTRACTORS EDUCATION AND RESEARCH FOUNDATION http://www.agcfoundation.org

AGC EDUCATION AND RESEARCH FOUNDATION UNDERGRADUATE SCHOLARSHIPS
• *See page 151*

ASSOCIATION FOR FACILITIES ENGINEERING (AFE)

ASSOCIATION FOR FACILITIES ENGINEERING CEDAR VALLEY CHAPTER # 132 SCHOLARSHIP
• *See page 97*

ASSOCIATION FOR IRON AND STEEL TECHNOLOGY http://www.aist.org/foundation/scholarships.htm

AIST ALFRED B. GLOSSBRENNER AND JOHN KLUSCH SCHOLARSHIPS

Scholarship intended to award high school senior who plans on pursuing degree in metallurgy or engineering. Student must have previous academic excellence in science courses. Applicant must be a dependent of a AIST Northeastern Ohio Chapter member.

Academic Fields/Career Goals: Engineering/Technology; Materials Science, Engineering, and Metallurgy.

Award: Scholarship for use in freshman, sophomore, junior, or senior years; not renewable. *Number:* 2. *Amount:* $1000.

Eligibility Requirements: Applicant must be high school student; planning to enroll or expecting to enroll full-time at a four-year institution or university and must have an interest in leadership. Available to U.S. citizens.

Application Requirements: Application, essay, resume, references, transcript. *Deadline:* March 26.

Contact: Michael D. Hickman, Section Secretary, AIST Canton Section
Association for Iron and Steel Technology
PO Box 2657, 22831 East State Street
Alliance, OH 44601

ASSOCIATION FOR IRON AND STEEL TECHNOLOGY DAVID H. SAMSON SCHOLARSHIP
• *See page 139*

ASSOCIATION FOR IRON AND STEEL TECHNOLOGY MIDWEST CHAPTER BETTY MCKERN SCHOLARSHIP

Scholarship will be awarded to a graduating female high school senior, or undergraduate freshman, sophomore, or junior enrolled in a fully AIST accredited college or university. Applicant must be in good academic standing. Applicant must be a dependent of an AIST Midwest Chapter member.

Academic Fields/Career Goals: Engineering/Technology.

Award: Scholarship for use in freshman, sophomore, or junior years; not renewable. *Number:* 1. *Amount:* $2500.

Eligibility Requirements: Applicant must be enrolled or expecting to enroll full-time at a four-year institution or university and female. Available to U.S. citizens.

Application Requirements: Application, essay, references, transcript. *Deadline:* May 15.

Contact: Michael Heaney, Division Manager Maintenance and Engineering, ISG Indiana Harbor
Association for Iron and Steel Technology
3001 Dickey Road
East Chicago, IN 46312

ASSOCIATION FOR IRON AND STEEL TECHNOLOGY MIDWEST CHAPTER DON NELSON SCHOLARSHIP

One scholarship will be awarded to a graduating high school senior, or undergraduate freshman, sophomore or junior enrolled in a fully AIST accredited college or university. Applicant must be in good academic standing. Applicant must be a dependent of an AIST Midwest Chapter member.

Academic Fields/Career Goals: Engineering/Technology.

Award: Scholarship for use in freshman, sophomore, or junior years; not renewable. *Number:* 1. *Amount:* $2500.

Eligibility Requirements: Applicant must be enrolled or expecting to enroll full-time at a four-year institution or university. Available to U.S. citizens.

Application Requirements: Application, essay, references, transcript. *Deadline:* May 15.

Contact: Michael Heaney, Division Manager Maintenance and Engineering, ISG Indiana Harbor
Association for Iron and Steel Technology
3001 Dickey Road
East Chicago, IN 46312

ASSOCIATION FOR IRON AND STEEL TECHNOLOGY MIDWEST CHAPTER ENGINEERING SCHOLARSHIP

Two four-year $1000 scholarships will be awarded to graduating high school senior, or undergraduate freshman, sophomore, or junior enrolled in a fully AIST accredited college or university. Applicant must be in good academic standing. Applicant must be a dependent of an AIST Midwest Chapter member.

Academic Fields/Career Goals: Engineering/Technology.

Award: Scholarship for use in freshman, sophomore, or junior years; renewable. *Number:* 2. *Amount:* $1000.

Eligibility Requirements: Applicant must be enrolled or expecting to enroll full-time at a four-year institution or university. Available to U.S. citizens.

Application Requirements: Application, essay, references, transcript. *Deadline:* May 15.

Contact: Michael Heaney, Division Manager Maintenance and Engineering, ISG Indiana Harbor
Association for Iron and Steel Technology
3001 Dickey Road
East Chicago, IN 46312

ASSOCIATION FOR IRON AND STEEL TECHNOLOGY MIDWEST CHAPTER JACK GILL SCHOLARSHIP

Scholarship will be awarded to a graduating high school senior, or undergraduate freshman, sophomore, or junior enrolled in a fully AIST accredited college or university. Applicant must be in good academic standing. Applicant must be a dependent of an AIST Midwest Chapter member.

Academic Fields/Career Goals: Engineering/Technology.

Award: Scholarship for use in freshman, sophomore, or junior years; not renewable. *Number:* 1. *Amount:* $2500.

Eligibility Requirements: Applicant must be enrolled or expecting to enroll full-time at a four-year institution or university. Available to U.S. citizens.

Application Requirements: Application, essay, references, transcript. *Deadline:* May 15.

Contact: Michael Heaney, Division Manager Maintenance and Engineering, ISG Indiana Harbor
Association for Iron and Steel Technology
3001 Dickey Road
East Chicago, IN 46312

ASSOCIATION FOR IRON AND STEEL TECHNOLOGY MIDWEST CHAPTER MEL NICKEL SCHOLARSHIP

Scholarship will be awarded to a graduating high school senior, or undergraduate freshman, sophomore or junior enrolled in a fully AIST accredited college or university. Applicant must be in good academic standing. Applicant must be a dependent of an AIST Midwest Chapter member.

Academic Fields/Career Goals: Engineering/Technology.

Award: Scholarship for use in freshman, sophomore, or junior years; not renewable. *Number:* 1. *Amount:* $2500.

Eligibility Requirements: Applicant must be enrolled or expecting to enroll full-time at a four-year institution or university. Available to U.S. citizens.

Application Requirements: Application, essay, references, transcript. *Deadline:* May 15.

Contact: Michael Heaney, Division Manager Maintenance and Engineering, ISG Indiana Harbor
Association for Iron and Steel Technology
3001 Dickey Road
East Chicago, IN 46312

ASSOCIATION FOR IRON AND STEEL TECHNOLOGY NATIONAL MERIT SCHOLARSHIP

Scholarship of $2000 per year, renewable for up to four years, for sons and daughters of AIST members in good standing who have qualified as a semifinalist in the National Merit Scholarship competition. For more information visit National Merit Scholarship Corporation Web site: http://www.nationalmerit.org and AIST Web site: http://www.aist.org/foundation/scholarships.htm

Academic Fields/Career Goals: Engineering/Technology; Materials Science, Engineering, and Metallurgy.

Award: Scholarship for use in freshman, sophomore, junior, or senior years; renewable. *Number:* 1. *Amount:* $2000.

Eligibility Requirements: Applicant must be high school student and planning to enroll or expecting to enroll full-time at a four-year institution or university. Available to U.S. citizens.

Application Requirements: References, test scores, transcript, National Merit Scholarship semi-finalist.

Contact: Program Coordinator
Association for Iron and Steel Technology
186 Thorn Hill Road
Warrendale, PA 15086-7528
Phone: 724-776-6040 Ext. 621
Fax: 724-776-0430

ASSOCIATION FOR IRON AND STEEL TECHNOLOGY NORTHWEST MEMBER CHAPTER SCHOLARSHIP

Scholarships available to encourage a Pacific Northwest area student to prepare for a career in engineering. Must be the child, grandchild, spouse, or niece/nephew of a member in good standing of the AIST Northwest Member Chapter. Award based on academic achievements in science projects in chemistry, mathematics, and physics. Application forms may be obtained by writing to: The Secretary, AIST Member Chapter. Applications are to be returned by registered mail to the same address by June 15.

Academic Fields/Career Goals: Engineering/Technology; Materials Science, Engineering, and Metallurgy.

Award: Scholarship for use in freshman, sophomore, junior, or senior years; not renewable. *Number:* 2. *Amount:* $1000.

Eligibility Requirements: Applicant must be enrolled or expecting to enroll full or part-time at a four-year institution or university. Available to U.S. citizens.

Application Requirements: Application. *Deadline:* June 15.

Contact: Gerardo Giraldo, Secretary-Treasurer Northwest Chapter
Association for Iron and Steel Technology
c/o Nucor Steel Seattle, Inc., Washington Steel Division
2424 Southwest Andover Street
Seattle, WA 98106-1100
Phone: 206-933-2245
Fax: 206-933-2207
E-mail: gerry.giraldo@nucor-seattle.com

ASSOCIATION FOR IRON AND STEEL TECHNOLOGY OHIO VALLEY CHAPTER SCHOLARSHIP

• *See page 112*

ASSOCIATION FOR IRON AND STEEL TECHNOLOGY PITTSBURGH CHAPTER SCHOLARSHIP

Scholarships available for children and grandchildren (natural, step, adopted, or ward), or spouse of a member in good standing of the Pittsburgh Member Chapter. Applicant must be a high school senior or currently enrolled undergraduate preparing for a career in engineering or metallurgy. Application and guidelines on Web site: http://www.aist.org/chapters/mc_pittsburgh_scholar.htm. Completed applications are to be returned by registered mail to scholarship contact postmarked no later than May 31.

Academic Fields/Career Goals: Engineering/Technology; Materials Science, Engineering, and Metallurgy.

Award: Scholarship for use in freshman, sophomore, junior, or senior years; not renewable. *Number:* 2. *Amount:* $2500.

Eligibility Requirements: Applicant must be enrolled or expecting to enroll full-time at a four-year institution or university. Available to U.S. citizens.

Application Requirements: Application, essay. *Deadline:* May 31.

Contact: Paul D. Conley, Pittsburgh Chapter AIST
Association for Iron and Steel Technology
100 River Road
Brackenridge, PA 15014-1597

ASSOCIATION FOR IRON AND STEEL TECHNOLOGY SOUTHEAST MEMBER CHAPTER SCHOLARSHIP

Scholarship for children, stepchildren, grandchildren, or spouse of active Southeast Chapter members who are pursuing a career in engineering, the sciences, or other majors relating to iron and steel production. Awarded based on SAT and ACT scores, consideration will be given for extra-curricular activities and the essay. Students may reapply for the scholarship each year for their term of college. Applications available by writing Chapter Secretary. Additional information on Web site: http://www.aist.org/chapters/mc_southeast_scholar_guidelines.htm.

Academic Fields/Career Goals: Engineering/Technology; Materials Science, Engineering, and Metallurgy.

Award: Scholarship for use in freshman, sophomore, junior, or senior years; renewable. *Number:* 1. *Amount:* $1000.

Eligibility Requirements: Applicant must be enrolled or expecting to enroll full or part-time at a four-year institution or university. Available to U.S. citizens.

Association for Iron and Steel Technology (continued)

Application Requirements: Application, essay, test scores. *Deadline:* July 30.

Contact: Mike Hutson, AIST Southeast Chapter Sectetary
Association for Iron and Steel Technology
803 Floyd Street
Kings Mountain, NC 29086
Phone: 704-730-8320
Fax: 704-730-8321
E-mail: mike@johnhutsoncompany.com

ASSOCIATION FOR WOMEN IN SCIENCE EDUCATIONAL FOUNDATION http://www.awis.org/ed_foundation.html

ASSOCIATION FOR WOMEN IN SCIENCE COLLEGE SCHOLARSHIP

• *See page 63*

ASSOCIATION OF ENGINEERING GEOLOGISTS http://www.aegweb.org

MARLIAVE FUND

• *See page 189*

ASSOCIATION OF FEDERAL COMMUNICATIONS CONSULTING ENGINEERS

ASSOCIATION OF FEDERAL COMMUNICATIONS CONSULTING ENGINEERS SCHOLARSHIP FUND

• *See page 158*

ASSOCIATION OF STATE DAM SAFETY OFFICIALS http://www.damsafety.org

ASSOCIATION OF STATE DAM SAFETY OFFICIALS UNDERGRADUATE SCHOLARSHIP

• *See page 152*

AUTOMOTIVE HALL OF FAME http://www.automotivehalloffame.org

AUTOMOTIVE HALL OF FAME EDUCATIONAL FUNDS

• *See page 140*

BARRY M. GOLDWATER SCHOLARSHIP AND EXCELLENCE IN EDUCATION FOUNDATION http://www.act.org/goldwater

BARRY M. GOLDWATER SCHOLARSHIP AND EXCELLENCE IN EDUCATION PROGRAM

• *See page 68*

BOYS AND GIRLS CLUBS OF GREATER SAN DIEGO http://www.sdyouth.org

SPENCE REESE SCHOLARSHIP FUND

Renewable scholarship for graduating male high school seniors in U.S. with minimum 2.5 GPA. For study of law, medicine, engineering, and political science. Application fee: $10. Based on academic ability, financial need, and character.

Academic Fields/Career Goals: Engineering/Technology; Health and Medical Sciences; Law/Legal Services; Political Science.

Award: Scholarship for use in freshman, sophomore, junior, or senior years; renewable. *Number:* 4. *Amount:* $2000.

Eligibility Requirements: Applicant must be high school student; age 20 or under; planning to enroll or expecting to enroll full-time at a four-year institution or university and male. Applicant must have 2.5 GPA or higher. Available to U.S. citizens.

Application Requirements: Application, financial need analysis, interview, self-addressed stamped envelope, test scores, transcript. *Fee:* $10. *Deadline:* April 15.

Contact: Jean Pilley, Scholarship Coordinator
Boys and Girls Clubs of Greater San Diego
4635 Clairemont Mesa Boulevard
San Diego, CA 92117
Phone: 619-298-3520
Fax: 619-298-3615
E-mail: bgcsandiego@yahoo.com

BUSINESS AND PROFESSIONAL WOMEN'S FOUNDATION http://www.bpwusa.org

BPW CAREER ADVANCEMENT SCHOLARSHIP PROGRAM FOR WOMEN

• *See page 112*

CALIFORNIA SEA GRANT COLLEGE PROGRAM http://www-csgc.ucsd.edu

JOHN D. ISSACS SCHOLARSHIP

• *See page 113*

CATCHING THE DREAM

MATH, ENGINEERING, SCIENCE, BUSINESS, EDUCATION, COMPUTERS SCHOLARSHIPS

• *See page 121*

TRIBAL BUSINESS MANAGEMENT PROGRAM (TBM)

• *See page 38*

CHAVERIM OF DELAWARE VALLEY, INC.

K2UK JEWISH RADIO MEMORIAL SCHOLARSHIP

• *See page 219*

CIRI FOUNDATION http://www.ciri.com/tcf

KIRBY MCDONALD EDUCATION ENDOWMENT SCHOLARSHIP FUND

• *See page 122*

COLLEGEBOUND FOUNDATION http://www.collegeboundfoundation.org

DR. FREEMAN A. HRABOWSKI, III SCHOLARSHIP

Award for Baltimore City public high school graduates. Please see Web site: http://www.collegeboundfoundation.org for complete information on application process. Must major in field of mathematics and/or science/technology, minimum GPA of 3.0. Must apply for CollegeBound Competitive Scholarship/Last-Dollar Grant. Preference given to students attending a Maryland university.

Academic Fields/Career Goals: Engineering/Technology; Mathematics.

Award: Scholarship for use in freshman, sophomore, junior, or senior years; renewable. *Number:* 1. *Amount:* $1500.

Eligibility Requirements: Applicant must be enrolled or expecting to enroll full-time at a two-year or four-year institution or university and resident of Maryland. Applicant must have 3.0 GPA or higher. Available to U.S. citizens.

Application Requirements: Application, financial need analysis, references, transcript, financial aid award letters, Student Aid Report. *Deadline:* March 19.

Contact: April Bell, Associate Program Director
CollegeBound Foundation
300 Water Street, Suite 300
Baltimore, MD 21202
Phone: 410-783-2905 Ext. 208
Fax: 410-727-5786
E-mail: abell@collegeboundfoundation.org

GEORGE V. MCGOWAN SCHOLARSHIP

Award for Baltimore City public high school graduates. Please see Web site: http://www.collegeboundfoundation.org for complete information on application process. Must major in engineering, have a cumulative GPA of 3.0 or better, and combined SAT score of 1000. Preference given to students who attend a Maryland university. Must complete and return CollegeBound/Competitive Scholarship/Last-Dollar Grant Application.

Academic Fields/Career Goals: Engineering/Technology.

Award: Scholarship for use in freshman, sophomore, junior, or senior years; renewable. *Number:* 1. *Amount:* $1500.

Eligibility Requirements: Applicant must be enrolled or expecting to enroll full-time at a two-year or four-year institution or university and resident of Maryland. Applicant must have 3.0 GPA or higher. Available to U.S. citizens.

Application Requirements: Application, financial need analysis, references, transcript, financial aid letters, Student Aid Report. *Deadline:* March 19.

Contact: April Bell, Associate Program Director
CollegeBound Foundation
300 Water Street, Suite 300
Baltimore, MD 21202
Phone: 410-783-2905 Ext. 208
Fax: 410-727-5786
E-mail: abell@collegeboundfoundation.org

NATIONAL AQUARIUM IN BALTIMORE HENRY HALL SCHOLARSHIP
• *See page 113*

COMTO-BOSTON CHAPTER http://www.bostoncomto.org

COMTO BOSTON/GARRETT A. MORGAN SCHOLARSHIP
• *See page 75*

CONNECTICUT BUILDING CONGRESS http://www.cbc-ct.org

CONNECTICUT BUILDING CONGRESS SCHOLARSHIP FUND
• *See page 75*

CONNECTICUT STUDENT LOAN FOUNDATION http://www.cslf.com

CONNECTICUT INNOVATIONS TECHNOLOGY SCHOLAR PROGRAM
• *See page 113*

CUBAN AMERICAN NATIONAL FOUNDATION

MAS FAMILY SCHOLARSHIPS
• *See page 123*

EAA AVIATION FOUNDATION, INC. http://www.eaa.org

PAYZER SCHOLARSHIP
• *See page 98*

EAST LOS ANGELES COMMUNITY UNION (TELACU) EDUCATION FOUNDATION

TELACU ENGINEERING AWARD
• *See page 141*

ELECTRONIC DOCUMENT SYSTEMS FOUNDATION http://www.edsf.org

ELECTRONIC DOCUMENT SYSTEMS FOUNDATION SCHOLARSHIP AWARDS
• *See page 159*

ENGINEERS FOUNDATION OF OHIO http://www.ohioengineer.com

ENGINEERS FOUNDATION OF OHIO ENGINEERING SCHOLARSHIPS

Award available to full-time, undergraduate students enrolled or planning to enroll in an ABET-accredited engineering program in an Ohio school or university. Minimum ACT or SAT required. ACT: math-29, English-25, SAT: math-600, verbal-500. Minimum 3.0 GPA required. Must be an Ohio resident and U.S. citizen. Application deadline is in mid-December. Call or go to the Web site for the exact date.

Academic Fields/Career Goals: Engineering/Technology.

Award: Scholarship for use in freshman, sophomore, junior, or senior years; renewable. *Number:* 10–14. *Amount:* $500–$2500.

Eligibility Requirements: Applicant must be enrolled or expecting to enroll full-time at a four-year institution or university; resident of Ohio and studying in Ohio. Applicant must have 3.0 GPA or higher. Available to U.S. citizens.

Application Requirements: Application, essay, references, test scores, transcript. *Deadline:* varies.

Contact: Pam McClure, Manager of Administration
Engineers Foundation of Ohio
4795 Evanswood Drive, Suite 201
Columbus, OH 43229-7216
Phone: 614-846-1177
Fax: 614-846-1131
E-mail: ospe@iwaynet.net

FISHER BROADCASTING COMPANY http://www.fisherbroadcasting.com/

FISHER BROADCASTING, INC., SCHOLARSHIP FOR MINORITIES
• *See page 159*

FLORIDA EDUCATIONAL FACILITIES PLANNERS' ASSOCIATION http://www.fefpa.org

FEFPA ASSISTANTSHIP
• *See page 76*

FOUNDATION OF THE WALL AND CEILING INDUSTRY http://www.awci.org/thefoundation.shtml

FOUNDATION OF THE WALL AND CEILING INDUSTRY SCHOLARSHIP PROGRAM
• *See page 76*

GEORGE BIRD GRINNELL AMERICAN INDIAN FUND

AL QOYAWAYMA AWARD
• *See page 141*

GERMAN ACADEMIC EXCHANGE SERVICE (DAAD) http://www.daad.org

HIGH-TECH IN OLD MUNICH

Grant offers opportunity for engineering students with beginning and advanced language skills to study during the summer at TU Munchen. Open to second- and third-year students enrolled full time at an accredited university or college in the U.S. or Canada. Must be U.S. or Canadian citizen or permanent resident. Minimum of one semester of college German or equivalent required. Deadline: March 24.

Academic Fields/Career Goals: Engineering/Technology.

Award: Grant for use in sophomore, junior, or senior years; not renewable. *Number:* 30. *Amount:* $1800.

Eligibility Requirements: Applicant must be enrolled or expecting to enroll full-time at a four-year institution or university and must have an interest in German language. Available to U.S. and Canadian citizens.

Application Requirements: Application, essay, resume, references, transcript. *Deadline:* March 24.

Contact: German Academic Exchange Service (DAAD)
871 United Nations Plaza
New York, NY 10017
Phone: 212-758-3223
Fax: 212-755-5780
E-mail: daadny@daad.org

GOLDEN KEY INTERNATIONAL HONOUR SOCIETY http://www.goldenkey.org

ENGINEERING ACHIEVEMENT AWARD

Applicants will be asked to respond to a problem posed by an honorary member within discipline. One winner will receive a $1000 award. The second

Golden Key International Honour Society (continued)

place applicant will receive $750 and the third place applicant will receive $500. See Web site for more information: http://goldenkey.gsu.edu.

Academic Fields/Career Goals: Engineering/Technology.

Award: Prize for use in junior, senior, graduate, or postgraduate years; not renewable. *Number:* 3. *Amount:* $500–$1000.

Eligibility Requirements: Applicant must be enrolled or expecting to enroll full or part-time at an institution or university.

Application Requirements: Application, applicant must enter a contest, essay, references, transcript. *Deadline:* March 1.

Contact: Member Services
Golden Key International Honour Society
621 North Avenue, NE
Suite C-100
Atlanta, GA 30308
Phone: 404-377-2400
Fax: 678-420-6757
E-mail: scholarships@goldenkey.org

GRAND RAPIDS COMMUNITY FOUNDATION http://www.grfoundation.org

ECONOMIC CLUB OF GRAND RAPIDS BUSINESS STUDY ABROAD SCHOLARSHIP

• *See page 41*

GREATER KANAWHA VALLEY FOUNDATION http://www.tgkvf.org

MATH AND SCIENCE SCHOLARSHIP

Awarded to students pursuing a degree in math, science or engineering at any accredited college or university. For purposes of this Fund, science shall include chemistry, physics, biology and other scientific fields. Scholarships are awarded for one or more years. May apply for two Foundation scholarships but will only be chosen for one. Must be a resident of West Virginia.

Academic Fields/Career Goals: Engineering/Technology; Physical Sciences and Math; Science, Technology, and Society.

Award: Scholarship for use in freshman, sophomore, junior, or senior years; renewable. *Number:* 1. *Amount:* $1000.

Eligibility Requirements: Applicant must be enrolled or expecting to enroll full-time at a four-year institution or university and resident of West Virginia. Applicant must have 2.5 GPA or higher. Available to U.S. citizens.

Application Requirements: Application, essay, financial need analysis, references, transcript, IRS 1040 form. *Deadline:* February 17.

Contact: Susan Hoover, Scholarship Coordinator
Greater Kanawha Valley Foundation
PO Box 3041
Charleston, WV 25331
Phone: 304-346-3620
Fax: 304-346-3640

HAROLD B. & DOROTHY A. SNYDER FOUNDATION, INC.

HAROLD B. AND DOROTHY A. SNYDER FOUNDATION, INC., PROGRAM

• *See page 141*

HAWAIIAN LODGE, F.& A. M. http://www.hawaiianlodge.org/

HAWAIIAN LODGE SCHOLARSHIPS

• *See page 76*

HISPANIC COLLEGE FUND, INC. http://www.hispanicfund.org

BURLINGTON NORTHERN SANTA FE FOUNDATION/HISPANIC COLLEGE FUND SCHOLARSHIP PROGRAM

• *See page 41*

DENNY'S/HISPANIC COLLEGE FUND SCHOLARSHIP

• *See page 41*

DEPARTMENT OF ENERGY SCHOLARSHIP PROGRAM

• *See page 125*

HISPANIC COLLEGE FUND/INROADS/SPRINT SCHOLARSHIP PROGRAM

• *See page 125*

ICI EDUCATIONAL FOUNDATION SCHOLARSHIP PROGRAM

• *See page 42*

LOCKHEED MARTIN SCHOLARSHIP PROGRAM

• *See page 141*

M & T BANK/ HISPANIC COLLEGE FUND SCHOLARSHIP PROGRAM

• *See page 42*

NATIONAL HISPANIC EXPLORERS SCHOLARSHIP PROGRAM

• *See page 69*

7-ELEVEN SCHOLARSHIP PROGRAM

• *See page 126*

HISPANIC ENGINEER NATIONAL ACHIEVEMENT AWARDS CORPORATION (HENAAC) http://www.henaac.org

HISPANIC ENGINEER NATIONAL ACHIEVEMENT AWARDS CORPORATION SCHOLARSHIP PROGRAM

• *See page 99*

HISPANIC SCHOLARSHIP FUND http://www.hsf.net

HSF/GENERAL MOTORS SCHOLARSHIP

• *See page 126*

HSF/SOCIETY OF HISPANIC PROFESSIONAL ENGINEERS, INC. SCHOLARSHIP PROGRAM

• *See page 152*

ILLINOIS SOCIETY OF PROFESSIONAL ENGINEERS http://www.ilspe.com

ILLINOIS SOCIETY OF PROFESSIONAL ENGINEERS ADVANTAGE AWARD/FOUNDATION SCHOLARSHIP

Applicant must be son or daughter of ISPE member in good standing and attend an Illinois university approved by the Accreditation Board of Engineering. Applicant must be at least a junior at the approved university. Engineering technology students are not eligible. Application deadline is January 31. Required essay must address why applicant wishes to become a professional engineer. Must have a "B" average.

Academic Fields/Career Goals: Engineering/Technology.

Award: Scholarship for use in junior or senior years; not renewable. *Number:* 1. *Amount:* $1200.

Eligibility Requirements: Applicant must be enrolled or expecting to enroll at an institution or university and studying in Illinois. Available to U.S. citizens.

Application Requirements: Application, essay, references, transcript. *Deadline:* January 31.

Contact: Illinois Society of Professional Engineers
300 West Edwards, Suite 201-B
Springfield, IL 62704
E-mail: info@ilspe.com

ILLINOIS SOCIETY OF PROFESSIONAL ENGINEERS/PEPPY MOLDOVAN MEMORIAL AWARD

Applicant must be female engineering student enrolled as a sophomore at a specified Illinois college or university. Applicant must be accepted at an accredited Illinois university.

Academic Fields/Career Goals: Engineering/Technology.

Award: Scholarship for use in sophomore, junior, or senior years. *Number:* 1. *Amount:* $1000.

Eligibility Requirements: Applicant must be enrolled or expecting to enroll at a two-year or four-year institution; female and studying in Illinois. Available to U.S. citizens.

Application Requirements: Application, essay, resume, references, transcript. *Deadline:* April 16.

Contact: Illinois Society of Professional Engineers
300 West Edwards, Suite 201-B
Springfield, IL 62704
E-mail: info@ilspe.com

LLINOIS SOCIETY OF PROFESSIONAL ENGINEERS/MELVIN E. AMSTUTZ MEMORIAL AWARD

Applicant must attend an Illinois university approved by the Accreditation Board of Engineering. Applicant must be at least a junior in university he or she attends, and must prove financial need. Engineering technology students are not eligible. Application deadline is January 31. Essay must address why applicant wishes to become a professional engineer. Must have a "B" average.

Academic Fields/Career Goals: Engineering/Technology.

Award: Scholarship for use in junior or senior years; not renewable. *Number:* 1. *Amount:* $1500.

Eligibility Requirements: Applicant must be enrolled or expecting to enroll at an institution or university and studying in Illinois. Available to U.S. citizens.

Application Requirements: Application, essay, financial need analysis, references. *Deadline:* January 31.

Contact: Illinois Society of Professional Engineers
300 West Edwards, Suite 201-B
Springfield, IL 62704
E-mail: info@ilspe.com

ILLUMINATING ENGINEERING SOCIETY OF NORTH AMERICA http://www.iesna.org

ROBERT W. THUNEN MEMORIAL SCHOLARSHIPS

• *See page 77*

INDEPENDENT LABORATORIES INSTITUTE SCHOLARSHIP ALLIANCE http://www.acil.org

INDEPENDENT LABORATORIES INSTITUTE SCHOLARSHIP ALLIANCE

• *See page 69*

INDIANA SOCIETY OF PROFESSIONAL ENGINEERS http://www.indspe.org

INDIANA ENGINEERING SCHOLARSHIP

Award for Indiana resident who attends an Indiana educational institution, or commutes daily to a school outside Indiana. Applicant must have accrued the minimum of one-half the credits required for an undergraduate ABET accredited engineering degree. For details and an application visit Web site: http://indspe.org.

Academic Fields/Career Goals: Engineering/Technology.

Award: Scholarship for use in junior or senior years; not renewable. *Number:* 3. *Amount:* $750.

Eligibility Requirements: Applicant must be enrolled or expecting to enroll full-time at an institution or university; resident of Indiana and studying in Indiana. Available to U.S. citizens.

Application Requirements: Application, interview, references, transcript. *Deadline:* May 1.

Contact: Indiana Society of Professional Engineers
PO Box 20806
Indianapolis, IN 46220
Phone: 317-255-2267
Fax: 317-255-2530

INSTITUTE OF INDUSTRIAL ENGINEERS http://www.iienet.org

A.O. PUTNAM MEMORIAL SCHOLARSHIP

One-time award for industrial engineering undergraduates at four-year accredited institutions. Applicants must be members of the Institute of Industrial Engineers, have a 3.4 GPA, and be nominated by a department head by November 15. Priority given to students who have demonstrated an interest in management consulting.

Academic Fields/Career Goals: Engineering/Technology.

Award: Scholarship for use in junior or senior years; not renewable. *Number:* 1. *Amount:* $400.

Eligibility Requirements: Applicant must be enrolled or expecting to enroll full-time at a four-year institution or university. Applicant or parent of applicant must be member of Institute of Industrial Engineers. Available to U.S. and non-U.S. citizens.

Application Requirements: Application, references, transcript, nomination. *Deadline:* November 15.

Contact: Sherry Richards, Chapter Operations Assistant
Institute of Industrial Engineers
25 Technology Park
Norcross, GA 30092-2988
Phone: 770-449-0461 Ext. 118
Fax: 770-263-8532
E-mail: srichards@iienet.org

C.B. GAMBRELL UNDERGRADUATE SCHOLARSHIP

One-time award for undergraduate industrial engineering students who are U.S. citizens graduated from a U.S. high school with a class standing above freshman level in an ABET accredited IE program. Must be a member of Industrial Engineers, have a minimum GPA of 3.4, and be nominated by a department head.

Academic Fields/Career Goals: Engineering/Technology.

Award: Scholarship for use in sophomore, junior, or senior years; not renewable. *Number:* 1. *Amount:* $400.

Eligibility Requirements: Applicant must be enrolled or expecting to enroll full-time at a four-year institution or university. Applicant or parent of applicant must be member of Institute of Industrial Engineers. Available to U.S. citizens.

Application Requirements: References, nomination. *Deadline:* November 15.

Contact: Sherry Richards, Chapter Operations Assistant
Institute of Industrial Engineers
25 Technology Park
Norcross, GA 30092-2988
Phone: 770-449-0461 Ext. 118
Fax: 770-263-8532
E-mail: srichards@iienet.org

DWIGHT D. GARDNER SCHOLARSHIP

Scholarship of $1500 for undergraduate students enrolled in any school in the U.S. and its territories, Canada, and Mexico, provided the school's engineering program or equivalent is accredited by an agency recognized by IIE and the student is pursuing a course of study in industrial engineering. Must be an IIE member and have minimum 3.4 GPA. Must be nominated.

Academic Fields/Career Goals: Engineering/Technology.

Award: Scholarship for use in freshman, sophomore, or junior years; not renewable. *Number:* 2. *Amount:* $1500.

Eligibility Requirements: Applicant must be enrolled or expecting to enroll full-time at a four-year institution or university. Applicant or parent of applicant must be member of Institute of Industrial Engineers. Available to U.S. and non-U.S. citizens.

Application Requirements: Application, essay, financial need analysis, references, transcript, nomination. *Deadline:* November 15.

Contact: Sherry Richards, Chapter Operations Assistant
Institute of Industrial Engineers
25 Technology Park
Norcross, GA 30092-2988
Phone: 770-449-0461 Ext. 118
Fax: 770-263-8532
E-mail: srichards@iienet.org

IIE COUNCIL OF FELLOWS UNDERGRADUATE SCHOLARSHIP

Awards to undergraduate students enrolled in any school in the U.S. and its territories, Canada, and Mexico, provided the school's engineering program or equivalent is accredited by an agency recognized by IIE and the student is

Institute of Industrial Engineers (continued)

pursuing a course of study in industrial engineering. Must be IIE member and have minimum 3.4 GPA. Write to IIE Headquarters to obtain application form.

Academic Fields/Career Goals: Engineering/Technology.

Award: Scholarship for use in sophomore or junior years; not renewable. *Amount:* $600.

Eligibility Requirements: Applicant must be enrolled or expecting to enroll full-time at a four-year institution or university. Applicant or parent of applicant must be member of Institute of Industrial Engineers. Available to U.S. and non-U.S. citizens.

Application Requirements: Application. *Deadline:* November 15.

Contact: Sherry Richards, Chapter Operations Assistant
Institute of Industrial Engineers
25 Technology Park
Norcross, GA 30092-2988
Phone: 770-449-0461 Ext. 118
Fax: 770-263-8532
E-mail: srichards@iienet.org

MARVIN MUNDEL MEMORIAL SCHOLARSHIP

Scholarship awarded to undergraduate students enrolled in any school in the U.S., Canada, or Mexico with an accredited industrial engineering program. Priority given to students who have demonstrated an interest in work measurement and methods engineering. Must be active Institute members with 3.4 GPA or above. Must be nominated by department head or faculty adviser.

Academic Fields/Career Goals: Engineering/Technology.

Award: Scholarship for use in freshman, sophomore, junior, or senior years; not renewable. *Amount:* $600.

Eligibility Requirements: Applicant must be enrolled or expecting to enroll at a four-year institution or university. Applicant or parent of applicant must be member of Institute of Industrial Engineers. Available to U.S. citizens.

Application Requirements: Application, nomination. *Deadline:* November 15.

Contact: Sherry Richards, Chapter Operations Assistant
Institute of Industrial Engineers
25 Technology Park
Norcross, GA 30092-2988
Phone: 770-449-0461 Ext. 118
Fax: 770-263-8532
E-mail: srichards@iienet.org

UPS SCHOLARSHIP FOR FEMALE STUDENTS

One-time award for female undergraduate students enrolled at any school in the U.S., Canada, or Mexico in an industrial engineering program. Must be a member of Institute of Industrial Engineers, have a minimum GPA of 3.4, and be nominated by a department head.

Academic Fields/Career Goals: Engineering/Technology.

Award: Scholarship for use in freshman, sophomore, junior, or senior years; not renewable. *Number:* 1. *Amount:* $4000.

Eligibility Requirements: Applicant must be enrolled or expecting to enroll full-time at a four-year institution or university and female. Applicant or parent of applicant must be member of Institute of Industrial Engineers. Available to U.S. and non-U.S. citizens.

Application Requirements: Application, references, transcript, nomination. *Deadline:* November 15.

Contact: Sherry Richards, Chapter Operations Assistant
Institute of Industrial Engineers
25 Technology Park
Norcross, GA 30092-2988
Phone: 770-449-0461 Ext. 118
Fax: 770-263-8532
E-mail: srichards@iienet.org

UPS SCHOLARSHIP FOR MINORITY STUDENTS

One-time award for minority undergraduate students enrolled at any school in the U.S., Canada, or Mexico in an industrial engineering program. Must be a member of Institute of Industrial Engineers, have minimum GPA of 3.4, and be nominated by a department head.

Academic Fields/Career Goals: Engineering/Technology.

Award: Scholarship for use in freshman, sophomore, junior, or senior years; not renewable. *Number:* varies. *Amount:* $4000.

Eligibility Requirements: Applicant must be American Indian/Alaska Native, Asian/Pacific Islander, Black (non-Hispanic), or Hispanic and enrolled or expecting to enroll at a four-year institution or university. Applicant or parent of applicant must be member of Institute of Industrial Engineers. Available to U.S. and non-U.S. citizens.

Application Requirements: Application, references, transcript, nomination. *Deadline:* November 15.

Contact: Sherry Richards, Chapter Operations Assistant
Institute of Industrial Engineers
25 Technology Park
Norcross, GA 30092-2988
Phone: 770-449-0461 Ext. 118
Fax: 770-263-8532
E-mail: srichards@iienet.org

INSTRUMENTATION, SYSTEMS, AND AUTOMATION SOCIETY (ISA) http://www.isa.org

INSTRUMENTATION, SYSTEMS, AND AUTOMATION SOCIETY (ISA) SCHOLARSHIP PROGRAM

• *See page 99*

INTERNATIONAL SOCIETY FOR OPTICAL ENGINEERING-SPIE http://www.spie.org/info/scholarships

SPIE EDUCATIONAL SCHOLARSHIPS IN OPTICAL SCIENCE AND ENGINEERING

• *See page 70*

INTERNATIONAL TECHNOLOGY EDUCATION ASSOCIATION http://www.iteawww.org

INTERNATIONAL TECHNOLOGY EDUCATION ASSOCIATION UNDERGRADUATE SCHOLARSHIP IN TECHNOLOGY EDUCATION

A scholarship for undergraduate students pursuing a degree in technology education/technological studies. Applicants must be members of the Association.

Academic Fields/Career Goals: Engineering/Technology.

Award: Scholarship for use in freshman, sophomore, or junior years; not renewable. *Number:* 3. *Amount:* $1000.

Eligibility Requirements: Applicant must be enrolled or expecting to enroll full-time at a four-year institution or university. Applicant or parent of applicant must be member of International Technology Education Association. Applicant must have 2.5 GPA or higher. Available to U.S. and non-U.S. citizens.

Application Requirements: Application, resume, references, transcript. *Deadline:* December 1.

Contact: Barbara Mongold, Undergraduate Scholarship Committee
International Technology Education Association
1914 Association Drive, Suite 201
Reston, VA 20191
Phone: 703-860-2100
Fax: 703-860-0353
E-mail: iteaordr@iris.org

INTERNATIONAL UNION OF ELECTRONIC, ELECTRICAL, SALARIED, MACHINE, AND FURNITURE WORKERS-CWA http://www.iue-cwa.org

DAVID J. FITZMAURICE ENGINEERING SCHOLARSHIP

One award for a student whose parent or grandparent is a member of the IUE-CWA. Applicant must be pursuing undergraduate engineering degree. Submit family financial status form with application. One-time award of $2000.

Academic Fields/Career Goals: Engineering/Technology.

Award: Scholarship for use in freshman, sophomore, junior, or senior years; not renewable. *Number:* 1. *Amount:* $2000.

Eligibility Requirements: Applicant must be enrolled or expecting to enroll full-time at a two-year or four-year or technical institution or university. Applicant or parent of applicant must be member of International Union of Electronic, Electrical, Salaries, Machine and Furniture Workers. Available to U.S. citizens.

Application Requirements: Application, essay, financial need analysis, references, test scores, transcript. *Deadline:* March 31.

Contact: Trudy Humphrey, Director
International Union of Electronic, Electrical, Salaried, Machine, and Furniture Workers-CWA
501 3rd Street, NW
Washington, DC 20001
Phone: 202-434-9591
Fax: 202-434-1252
E-mail: thumphrey@cwa-union.org

JEWISH FEDERATION OF METROPOLITAN CHICAGO (JFMC) http://www.jvschicago.org

JEWISH FEDERATION OF METROPOLITAN CHICAGO ACADEMIC SCHOLARSHIP PROGRAM

• *See page 185*

KCNC-TV CHANNEL 4 NEWS http://www.news4colorado.com

NEWS 4 PETER ROGOT MEDIA SCHOLARSHIP

• *See page 161*

KOREAN-AMERICAN SCIENTISTS AND ENGINEERS ASSOCIATION http://www.ksea.org

KSEA SCHOLARSHIPS

• *See page 221*

LEAGUE OF UNITED LATIN AMERICAN CITIZENS NATIONAL EDUCATIONAL SERVICE CENTERS, INC. http://www.lnesc.org

GE/LULAC SCHOLARSHIP

• *See page 127*

GM/LULAC SCHOLARSHIP

Renewable award for minority students who are pursuing an undergraduate degree in engineering at an accredited college or university. Must maintain a minimum 3.0 GPA. Selection is based in part on the likelihood of pursuing a successful career in engineering. Application deadline is July 15.

Academic Fields/Career Goals: Engineering/Technology.

Award: Scholarship for use in freshman, sophomore, junior, or senior years; renewable. *Number:* 20. *Amount:* $2000.

Eligibility Requirements: Applicant must be Hispanic and enrolled or expecting to enroll full-time at a four-year institution or university. Applicant must have 3.0 GPA or higher.

Application Requirements: Application, references, transcript. *Deadline:* July 15.

Contact: Scholarship Administrator
League of United Latin American Citizens National Educational Service Centers, Inc.
2000 L Street, NW
Suite 610
Washington, DC 20036

LOS ANGELES COUNCIL OF BLACK PROFESSIONAL ENGINEERS http://www.lablackengineers.org/scholarships.html

AL-BEN SCHOLARSHIP FOR ACADEMIC INCENTIVE

• *See page 142*

AL-BEN SCHOLARSHIP FOR PROFESSIONAL MERIT

• *See page 142*

AL-BEN SCHOLARSHIP FOR SCHOLASTIC ACHIEVEMENT

• *See page 143*

LUCENT TECHNOLOGIES FOUNDATION http://www.iie.org/programs/lucent

LUCENT GLOBAL SCIENCE SCHOLARS PROGRAM

• *See page 70*

MAINE SOCIETY OF PROFESSIONAL ENGINEERS

MAINE SOCIETY OF PROFESSIONAL ENGINEERS VERNON T. SWAINE-ROBERT E. CHUTE SCHOLARSHIP

• *See page 230*

MARION D. AND EVA S. PEEPLES FOUNDATION TRUST SCHOLARSHIP PROGRAM http://www.jccf.org

MARION D. AND EVA S. PEEPLES SCHOLARSHIPS

• *See page 205*

MARYLAND ASSOCIATION OF PRIVATE COLLEGES AND CAREER SCHOOLS http://www.mapccs.org

MARYLAND ASSOCIATION OF PRIVATE COLLEGES AND CAREER SCHOOLS SCHOLARSHIP

• *See page 127*

MICHIGAN SOCIETY OF PROFESSIONAL ENGINEERS http://www.michiganspe.org

ANTHONY C. FORTUNSKI, P.E. MEMORIAL GRANT

• *See page 143*

MICHIGAN SOCIETY OF PROFESSIONAL ENGINEERS UNDESIGNATED GRANT

• *See page 143*

MICHIGAN SOCIETY OF PROFESSIONAL ENGINEERS 1980 NATIONAL SOCIETY OF PROFESSIONAL ENGINEERS ANNUAL MEETING COMMITTEE GRANT

• *See page 143*

MICHIGAN SOCIETY OF PROFESSIONAL ENGINEERS AUXILIARY GRANT

• *See page 143*

MICHIGAN SOCIETY OF PROFESSIONAL ENGINEERS HARRY R. BALL, P.E. GRANT

• *See page 144*

MICHIGAN SOCIETY OF PROFESSIONAL ENGINEERS KENNETH B. FISHBECK, P.E. MEMORIAL GRANT

• *See page 144*

MICHIGAN SOCIETY OF PROFESSIONAL ENGINEERS SCHOLARSHIP TRUST GRANT

• *See page 144*

MSPE AUXILIARY GRANT FOR UNDERGRADUATE STUDY

• *See page 153*

ROBERT E. FOLMSBEE, P.E. MEMORIAL GRANT

• *See page 153*

MICRON TECHNOLOGY FOUNDATION, INC. http://www.micron.com/scholars

MICRON SCIENCE AND TECHNOLOGY SCHOLARS PROGRAM

• *See page 144*

MIDWEST ROOFING CONTRACTORS ASSOCIATION http://www.mrca.org

MRCA FOUNDATION SCHOLARSHIP PROGRAM

• *See page 70*

MINERALS, METALS, AND MATERIALS SOCIETY (TMS) http://www.tms.org

TMS J. KEITH BRIMACOMBE PRESIDENTIAL SCHOLARSHIP

• *See page 230*

TMS OUTSTANDING STUDENT PAPER CONTEST-UNDERGRADUATE

• *See page 230*

TMS/EMPMD GILBERT CHIN SCHOLARSHIP
• *See page 230*

TMS/EPD SCHOLARSHIP
• *See page 230*

TMS/INTERNATIONAL SYMPOSIUM ON SUPERALLOYS SCHOLARSHIP PROGRAM
• *See page 230*

TMS/LMD SCHOLARSHIP PROGRAM
• *See page 231*

TMS/STRUCTURAL MATERIALS DIVISION SCHOLARSHIP
• *See page 231*

NAMEPA NATIONAL SCHOLARSHIP FOUNDATION http://www.namepa.org

NATIONAL ASSOCIATION OF MINORITY ENGINEERING PROGRAM ADMINISTRATORS NATIONAL SCHOLARSHIP FUND
• *See page 101*

NASA DELAWARE SPACE GRANT CONSORTIUM http://www.delspace.org

NASA DELAWARE SPACE GRANT UNDERGRADUATE TUITION SCHOLARSHIP
• *See page 70*

NASA IDAHO SPACE GRANT CONSORTIUM http://www.uidaho.edu/nasa_isgc

NASA IDAHO SPACE GRANT CONSORTIUM SCHOLARSHIP PROGRAM
• *See page 71*

NASA MINNESOTA SPACE GRANT CONSORTIUM http://www.aem.umn.edu/msgc

MINNESOTA SPACE GRANT CONSORTIUM
• *See page 101*

NASA MONTANA SPACE GRANT CONSORTIUM http://www.spacegrant.montana.edu

MONTANA SPACE GRANT SCHOLARSHIP PROGRAM
• *See page 101*

NASA NEBRASKA SPACE GRANT CONSORTIUM http://nasa.unomaha.edu

NASA NEBRASKA SPACE GRANT
• *See page 101*

NASA NEVADA SPACE GRANT CONSORTIUM http://www.unr.edu/spacegrant

UNIVERSITY AND COMMUNITY COLLEGE SYSTEM OF NEVADA NASA SPACE GRANT AND FELLOWSHIP PROGRAM
• *See page 101*

NASA VERMONT SPACE GRANT CONSORTIUM http://www.emba.uvm.edu/vsgc

VERMONT SPACE GRANT CONSORTIUM SCHOLARSHIP PROGRAM
• *See page 71*

NASA VIRGINIA SPACE GRANT CONSORTIUM http://www.vsgc.odu.edu

VIRGINIA SPACE GRANT CONSORTIUM COMMUNITY COLLEGE SCHOLARSHIPS
• *See page 102*

VIRGINIA SPACE GRANT CONSORTIUM TEACHER EDUCATION SCHOLARSHIPS
• *See page 102*

NASA WEST VIRGINIA SPACE GRANT CONSORTIUM http://www.nasa.wvu.edu

WEST VIRGINIA SPACE GRANT CONSORTIUM UNDERGRADUATE SCHOLARSHIP PROGRAM
• *See page 102*

NATIONAL ACTION COUNCIL FOR MINORITIES IN ENGINEERING-NACME, INC. http://www.nacme.org

NACME SCHOLARS PROGRAM

Renewable award for African-American, American-Indian, or Latino student enrolled in a baccalaureate engineering program. Must attend an ABET-accredited institution full-time and complete one semester with a minimum 2.7 GPA. Must be a U.S. citizen. Award money is given to participating institutions who select applicants and disperse funds. Check Web site for details. http://www.nacme.org

Academic Fields/Career Goals: Engineering/Technology.

Award: Scholarship for use in freshman, sophomore, junior, or senior years; renewable. *Number:* varies. *Amount:* varies.

Eligibility Requirements: Applicant must be American Indian/Alaska Native, Black (non-Hispanic), or Hispanic and enrolled or expecting to enroll full-time at a four-year institution or university. Available to U.S. citizens.

Application Requirements: Application, financial need analysis, references. *Deadline:* Continuous.

Contact: National Action Council for Minorities in Engineering-NACME, Inc.
The Empire State Building, 350 Fifth Avenue, Suite 2212
New York, NY 10118-2299
E-mail: scholarships@nacme.org

NACME/NASA SPACE STATION ENGINEERING SCHOLARS PROGRAM

Scholarships available for applicants attending designated minority institutions. Must have a minimum 3.0 GPA and pursue studies in engineering. Must demonstrate financial need and have earned no more than 39 credit hours. Check Web site for details. http://www.nacme.org

Academic Fields/Career Goals: Engineering/Technology.

Award: Scholarship for use in freshman, sophomore, junior, or senior years; renewable. *Number:* varies. *Amount:* varies.

Eligibility Requirements: Applicant must be enrolled or expecting to enroll full-time at a four-year institution or university. Applicant must have 3.0 GPA or higher. Available to U.S. citizens.

Application Requirements: Application. *Deadline:* Continuous.

Contact: National Action Council for Minorities in Engineering-NACME, Inc.
The Empire State Building, 350 Fifth Avenue, Suite 2212
New York, NY 10118-2299
E-mail: scholarships@nacme.org

NATIONAL ASSOCIATION OF WATER COMPANIES-NEW JERSEY CHAPTER

NATIONAL ASSOCIATION OF WATER COMPANIES-NEW JERSEY CHAPTER SCHOLARSHIP
• *See page 115*

NATIONAL ASSOCIATION OF WOMEN IN CONSTRUCTION http://nawic.org

NAWIC UNDERGRADUATE SCHOLARSHIPS
• *See page 77*

NATIONAL FEDERATION OF THE BLIND http://www.nfb.org

HOWARD BROWN RICKARD SCHOLARSHIP
• *See page 78*

NATIONAL INSTITUTE OF BUILDING SCIENCES, MULTIHAZARD MITIGATION COUNCIL http://www.nibs.org

ARCHITECTURE, CONSTRUCTION, AND ENGINEERING MENTOR PROGRAM SCHOLARSHIPS
• *See page 78*

NATIONAL INVENTORS HALL OF FAME http://www.invent.org/collegiate

COLLEGIATE INVENTORS COMPETITION - GRAND PRIZE
• *See page 71*

COLLEGIATE INVENTORS COMPETITION FOR UNDERGRADUATE STUDENTS
• *See page 71*

NATIONAL SOCIETY OF PROFESSIONAL ENGINEERS http://www.nspe.org

MAUREEN L. AND HOWARD N. BLITMAN, PE SCHOLARSHIP TO PROMOTE DIVERSITY IN ENGINEERING
• *See page 145*

NATIONAL SOCIETY OF PROFESSIONAL ENGINEERS/AUXILIARY SCHOLARSHIP
• *See page 145*

PAUL H. ROBBINS HONORARY SCHOLARSHIP
• *See page 145*

PROFESSIONAL ENGINEERS IN INDUSTRY SCHOLARSHIP
• *See page 145*

VIRGINIA HENRY MEMORIAL SCHOLARSHIP
• *See page 146*

NATIONAL URBAN LEAGUE http://www.nul.org

BLACK EXECUTIVE EXCHANGE PROGRAM JERRY BARTOW SCHOLARSHIP FUND
• *See page 128*

NEW JERSEY ACADEMY OF SCIENCE http://www.njas.org

NEW JERSEY ACADEMY OF SCIENCE RESEARCH GRANTS-IN-AID TO HIGH SCHOOL STUDENTS
• *See page 116*

NEW YORK STATE EDUCATION DEPARTMENT http://www.highered.nysed.gov

REGENTS PROFESSIONAL OPPORTUNITY SCHOLARSHIP
• *See page 45*

NORTH DAKOTA DEPARTMENT OF TRANSPORTATION http://www.state.nd.us/dot/

NORTH DAKOTA DEPARTMENT OF TRANSPORTATION ENGINEERING GRANT
• *See page 154*

OREGON STUDENT ASSISTANCE COMMISSION http://www.osac.state.or.us

HOMESTEAD CAPITAL HOUSING SCHOLARSHIP
• *See page 46*

HOWARD VOLLUM AMERICAN INDIAN SCHOLARSHIP
• *See page 172*

KEY TECHNOLOGY SCHOLARSHIP
• *See page 222*

PLASTICS INSTITUTE OF AMERICA http://www.plasticsinstitute.org

PLASTICS PIONEERS SCHOLARSHIPS
• *See page 232*

PLUMBING-HEATING-COOLING CONTRACTORS ASSOCIATION EDUCATION FOUNDATION http://www.phccweb.org

BRADFORD WHITE CORPORATION SCHOLARSHIP
• *See page 79*

DELTA FAUCET COMPANY SCHOLARSHIP PROGRAM
• *See page 79*

PHCC EDUCATIONAL FOUNDATION NEED-BASED SCHOLARSHIP
• *See page 79*

PHCC EDUCATIONAL FOUNDATION SCHOLARSHIP PROGRAM
• *See page 79*

PNC BANK TRUST DEPARTMENT

H. FLETCHER BROWN SCHOLARSHIP
• *See page 187*

PROFESSIONAL CONSTRUCTION ESTIMATORS ASSOCIATION http://www.pcea.org

TED WILSON MEMORIAL SCHOLARSHIP FOUNDATION
• *See page 188*

ROBERT H. MOLLOHAN FAMILY CHARITABLE FOUNDATION, INC. http://www.mollohanfoundation.org

HIGH TECHNOLOGY SCHOLARS PROGRAM
• *See page 117*

ROCKY MOUNTAIN COAL MINING INSTITUTE http://www.rmcmi.org

ROCKY MOUNTAIN COAL MINING INSTITUTE SCHOLARSHIP
• *See page 146*

SOCIETY FOR IMAGING SCIENCE AND TECHNOLOGY http://www.imaging.org

RAYMOND DAVIS SCHOLARSHIP

Award available to an undergraduate junior or senior or graduate student enrolled full-time in an accredited program of photographic, imaging science or engineering. Minimum award is $1000. Applications processed between October 15 and December 15 only.

Academic Fields/Career Goals: Engineering/Technology; Physical Sciences and Math.

Award: Scholarship for use in junior, senior, or graduate years; not renewable. *Number:* 1–2. *Amount:* $1000.

Eligibility Requirements: Applicant must be enrolled or expecting to enroll full-time at a four-year institution or university. Available to U.S. citizens.

Application Requirements: Application, autobiography, references, transcript. *Deadline:* December 15.

Contact: Coordinator of Members/Customer Service
Society for Imaging Science and Technology
7003 Kilworth Lane
Springfield, VA 22151

SOCIETY OF AUTOMOTIVE ENGINEERS http://www.sae.org/students/stuschol.htm

BMW/SAE ENGINEERING SCHOLARSHIP
• *See page 105*

DETROIT SECTION SAE TECHNICAL SCHOLARSHIP
• *See page 232*

EDWARD D. HENDRICKSON/SAE ENGINEERING SCHOLARSHIP

• *See page 105*

FRED M. YOUNG SR./SAE ENGINEERING SCHOLARSHIP

Renewable scholarship for student enrolled in an ABET-accredited engineering program. Must have 3.75 GPA, rank in the 90th percentile in both math and verbal on SAT or composite ACT scores. A 3.0 GPA and continued engineering enrollment must be maintained to renew scholarship. Application should be retrieved from the SAE Web site at http://www.sae.org/students/stuschol.htm

Academic Fields/Career Goals: Engineering/Technology.

Award: Scholarship for use in freshman, sophomore, junior, or senior years; renewable. *Number:* 1. *Amount:* $1000.

Eligibility Requirements: Applicant must be enrolled or expecting to enroll full-time at a four-year institution or university. Available to U.S. citizens.

Application Requirements: Application, essay, test scores, transcript. *Fee:* $6. *Deadline:* December 1.

Contact: Connie Harnish, SAE Customer Service
Society of Automotive Engineers
400 Commonwealth Drive
Warrendale, PA 15096-0001
Phone: 724-776-4970
E-mail: customerservice@sae.org

INFORMATION HANDLING SERVICES, INC./SAE WOMEN ENGINEERS COMMITTEE SCHOLARSHIP

One-time award for women accepted into an accredited engineering program. Scholarship is for freshman year only and applicants must have a minimum 3.0 GPA. Application should be retrieved from the SAE Web site at http://www.sae.org/students/stuschol.htm

Academic Fields/Career Goals: Engineering/Technology.

Award: Scholarship for use in freshman year; not renewable. *Number:* 1. *Amount:* $1500.

Eligibility Requirements: Applicant must be high school student; planning to enroll or expecting to enroll at a four-year institution and female. Applicant must have 3.0 GPA or higher. Available to U.S. citizens.

Application Requirements: *Fee:* $6. *Deadline:* December 1.

Contact: Connie Harnish, SAE Customer Service
Society of Automotive Engineers
400 Commonwealth Drive
Warrendale, PA 15096-0001
Phone: 724-776-4970
E-mail: customerservice@sae.org

MERCEDES-BENZ U.S. INTERNATIONAL/SAE SCHOLARSHIP

One-time award for those studying manufacturing engineering or a mobility-related engineering discipline. Must be an Alabama resident about to enter senior year at an Alabama institution. Selection will be based on academic and leadership achievement, major course of study, essay, and intent to pursue a career in manufacturing engineering following graduation. Application should be retrieved from the SAE Web site at http://www.sae.org/students/stuschol.htm

Academic Fields/Career Goals: Engineering/Technology.

Award: Scholarship for use in junior year; not renewable. *Number:* 1. *Amount:* $2500.

Eligibility Requirements: Applicant must be enrolled or expecting to enroll at a four-year institution or university; resident of Alabama and studying in Alabama. Available to U.S. citizens.

Application Requirements: Application, essay, test scores, transcript. *Fee:* $6. *Deadline:* April 1.

Contact: Connie Harnish, SAE Customer Service
Society of Automotive Engineers
400 Commonwealth Drive
Warrendale, PA 15096-0001
Phone: 724-776-4970
E-mail: customerservice@sae.org

RALPH K. HILLQUIST HONORARY SAE SCHOLARSHIP

• *See page 232*

SAE BALTIMORE SECTION BILL BRUBAKER SCHOLARSHIP

Non-renewable scholarship for any family member of a member of Baltimore SAE or any high school senior accepted to an engineering university in Maryland.

Academic Fields/Career Goals: Engineering/Technology.

Award: Scholarship for use in freshman year; not renewable. *Number:* 1. *Amount:* $1000.

Eligibility Requirements: Applicant must be enrolled or expecting to enroll at an institution or university. Applicant or parent of applicant must be member of Society of Automotive Engineers. Available to U.S. citizens.

Application Requirements: Application, essay, resume, transcript. *Deadline:* May 10.

Contact: Rich Bechtold
Society of Automotive Engineers
5400 Thunder Hill Road
Columbia, MD 21045
Phone: 410-997-1282
E-mail: RLBechtold@aol.com

SAE LONG TERM MEMBER SPONSORED SCHOLARSHIP

One-time award for SAE student member who will be entering the senior year of undergraduate engineering studies. The scholarship will be awarded purely on the basis of the student's support for SAE and its programs. GPA is not a determining factor. Application deadline is April 1.

Academic Fields/Career Goals: Engineering/Technology.

Award: Scholarship for use in junior year; not renewable. *Amount:* $1000.

Eligibility Requirements: Applicant must be enrolled or expecting to enroll at a four-year institution. Applicant or parent of applicant must be member of Society of Automotive Engineers.

Application Requirements: Application, references. *Deadline:* April 1.

Contact: Connie Harnish, SAE Customer Service
Society of Automotive Engineers
400 Commonwealth Drive
Warrendale, PA 15096-0001
Phone: 724-776-4970
E-mail: customerservice@sae.org

SAE WILLIAM G. BELFREY MEMORIAL GRANT

• *See page 233*

TAU BETA PI/SAE ENGINEERING SCHOLARSHIP

Merit-based award given to top-ranking candidates pursuing an accredited engineering program. Award is for freshman year only. Must have 3.75 GPA and rank in the 90th percentile in both math and verbal for SAT scores or for composite ACT scores. Application should be retrieved from the SAE Web site at http://www.sae.org/students/stuschol.htm

Academic Fields/Career Goals: Engineering/Technology.

Award: Scholarship for use in freshman year; not renewable. *Number:* 6. *Amount:* $1000.

Eligibility Requirements: Applicant must be high school student and planning to enroll or expecting to enroll at a four-year institution or university. Available to U.S. citizens.

Application Requirements: Application, essay, test scores, transcript. *Fee:* $6. *Deadline:* December 1.

Contact: Connie Harnish, SAE Customer Service
Society of Automotive Engineers
400 Commonwealth Drive
Warrendale, PA 15096-0001
Phone: 724-776-4970
E-mail: customerservice@sae.org

TMC/SAE DONALD D. DAWSON TECHNICAL SCHOLARSHIP

• *See page 105*

YANMAR/SAE SCHOLARSHIP
• *See page 233*

SOCIETY OF BROADCAST ENGINEERS, INC. http://www.sbe.org

ROBERT GREENBERG/HAROLD E. ENNES SCHOLARSHIP FUND AND ENNES EDUCATIONAL FOUNDATION BROADCAST TECHNOLOGY SCHOLARSHIP
• *See page 233*

SOCIETY OF HISPANIC PROFESSIONAL ENGINEERS FOUNDATION http://www.shpefoundation.org

SOCIETY OF HISPANIC PROFESSIONAL ENGINEERS FOUNDATION
• *See page 146*

SOCIETY OF MANUFACTURING ENGINEERS EDUCATION FOUNDATION http://www.sme.org/foundation

ALBERT E. WISCHMEYER MEMORIAL SCHOLARSHIP AWARD

One-time award supports two scholarships of at least $1900 each. Applicants must be residents of Western New York State (West of Interstate 81), graduating high school seniors or current undergraduate students enrolled in an accredited degree program in manufacturing engineering, manufacturing engineering technology or mechanical technology. Applicants must plan to attend a college or university in New York State and have an overall minimum GPA of 3.0.

Academic Fields/Career Goals: Engineering/Technology.

Award: Scholarship for use in freshman, sophomore, junior, or senior years; not renewable. *Number:* 2. *Amount:* $1900.

Eligibility Requirements: Applicant must be enrolled or expecting to enroll full-time at a four-year institution or university; resident of New York and studying in New York. Applicant must have 3.0 GPA or higher.

Application Requirements: Application, essay, resume, references, transcript. *Deadline:* February 1.

Contact: Cindy Monzon, Program Coordinator
Society of Manufacturing Engineers Education Foundation
One SME Drive
PO Box 930
Dearborn, MI 48121-0930
Phone: 313-271-1500 Ext. 1707
Fax: 313-240-6095
E-mail: monzcyn@sme.org

ARTHUR AND GLADYS CERVENKA SCHOLARSHIP AWARD

One-time award to full-time students enrolled in a degree program in manufacturing engineering or technology. Preference given to students attending a Florida institution. Must have completed a minimum of 30 college credit hours. Minimum 3.0 GPA required.

Academic Fields/Career Goals: Engineering/Technology.

Award: Scholarship for use in sophomore, junior, or senior years; not renewable. *Number:* 1. *Amount:* $1250.

Eligibility Requirements: Applicant must be enrolled or expecting to enroll full-time at a four-year institution or university. Applicant must have 3.0 GPA or higher.

Application Requirements: Application, essay, resume, references, transcript. *Deadline:* February 1.

Contact: Cindy Monzon, Program Coordinator
Society of Manufacturing Engineers Education Foundation
One SME Drive
PO Box 930
Dearborn, MI 48121-0930
Phone: 313-271-1500 Ext. 1707
Fax: 313-240-6095
E-mail: monzcyn@sme.org

CATERPILLAR SCHOLARS AWARD FUND

Supports five one-time scholarships of $2000 each for full-time students enrolled in a manufacturing engineering program. Minority applicants may apply as incoming freshmen. Applicants must have an overall minimum GPA of 3.0 on a 4.0 scale.

Academic Fields/Career Goals: Engineering/Technology.

Award: Scholarship for use in freshman, sophomore, junior, or senior years; not renewable. *Number:* 5. *Amount:* $2000.

Eligibility Requirements: Applicant must be enrolled or expecting to enroll full-time at a four-year institution or university. Applicant must have 3.0 GPA or higher.

Application Requirements: Application, essay, references, transcript. *Deadline:* February 1.

Contact: Cindy Monzon, Program Coordinator
Society of Manufacturing Engineers Education Foundation
One SME Drive
PO Box 930
Dearborn, MI 48121-0930
Phone: 313-271-1500 Ext. 1707
Fax: 313-240-6095
E-mail: monzcyn@sme.org

CHAPTER 4 LAWRENCE A. WACKER MEMORIAL SCHOLARSHIP

Two one-time awards available to full-time students. One scholarship will be granted to a graduating high school senior and the other will be granted to a current undergraduate student. Students must be enrolled in or accepted to a degree program in manufacturing, mechanical or industrial engineering at a college or university in the state of Wisconsin. All applicants must have a GPA of 3.0 or better on a 4.0 scale.

Academic Fields/Career Goals: Engineering/Technology.

Award: Scholarship for use in freshman, sophomore, junior, or senior years; not renewable. *Number:* 2. *Amount:* $1500.

Eligibility Requirements: Applicant must be enrolled or expecting to enroll full-time at a four-year institution or university and studying in Wisconsin. Applicant must have 3.0 GPA or higher.

Application Requirements: Application, essay, resume, references, transcript. *Deadline:* February 1.

Contact: Cindy Monzon, Program Coordinator
Society of Manufacturing Engineers Education Foundation
One SME Drive
PO Box 930
Dearborn, MI 48121-0930
Phone: 313-271-1500 Ext. 1707
Fax: 313-240-6095
E-mail: monzcyn@sme.org

CLINTON J. HELTON MANUFACTURING SCHOLARSHIP AWARD FUND

One-time award to full-time students enrolled in a degree program in manufacturing engineering or technology at one of the following institutions: Colorado State University, University of Colorado-all campuses. Applicants must possess an overall minimum GPA of 3.3.

Academic Fields/Career Goals: Engineering/Technology; Trade/Technical Specialties.

Award: Scholarship for use in freshman, sophomore, junior, or senior years. *Number:* 1. *Amount:* $3500.

Eligibility Requirements: Applicant must be enrolled or expecting to enroll full-time at an institution or university and studying in Colorado.

Application Requirements: *Deadline:* February 1.

Contact: Cindy Monzon, Program Coordinator
Society of Manufacturing Engineers Education Foundation
One SME Drive
PO Box 930
Dearborn, MI 48121-0930
Phone: 313-271-1500 Ext. 1707
Fax: 313-240-6095
E-mail: monzcyn@sme.org

CONNIE AND ROBERT T. GUNTER SCHOLARSHIP

One-time award for full-time undergraduate student attending Georgia Institute of Technology, Georgia Southern College, or Southern College of Technology and enrolled in a degree program in manufacturing engineering or manufacturing engineering technology. Must have minimum 3.5 GPA and have completed at least thirty college credit hours. One-time award of $1000. Must submit application cover sheet and resume.

Academic Fields/Career Goals: Engineering/Technology.

Award: Scholarship for use in sophomore, junior, or senior years; not renewable. *Number:* 1. *Amount:* $1000.

Eligibility Requirements: Applicant must be enrolled or expecting to enroll full-time at a four-year institution and studying in Georgia. Applicant must have 3.5 GPA or higher. Available to U.S. citizens.

Application Requirements: Application, essay, resume, references, transcript. *Deadline:* February 1.

Contact: Cindy Monzon, Program Coordinator
Society of Manufacturing Engineers Education Foundation
One SME Drive
PO Box 930
Dearborn, MI 48121-0930
Phone: 313-271-1500 Ext. 1707
Fax: 313-240-6095
E-mail: monzcyn@sme.org

DETROIT CHAPTER ONE-FOUNDING CHAPTER SCHOLARSHIP

Three annual awards of at least $1000 each, will be available in each of the following: associate degree and equivalent, baccalaureate degree and graduate degree programs. Minimum GPA of 3.0 is required. Must be undergraduate or graduate student enrolled in a manufacturing engineering or technology program at one of the sponsored institutions and be a member in good standing of their SME Student Chapter.

Academic Fields/Career Goals: Engineering/Technology.

Award: Scholarship for use in sophomore, junior, senior, or graduate years; not renewable. *Number:* 3. *Amount:* $1000.

Eligibility Requirements: Applicant must be enrolled or expecting to enroll full or part-time at a two-year or four-year institution or university and studying in Michigan. Applicant must have 3.0 GPA or higher.

Application Requirements: Application, references. *Deadline:* February 1.

Contact: Cindy Monzon, Program Coordinator
Society of Manufacturing Engineers Education Foundation
One SME Drive
PO Box 930
Dearborn, MI 48121-0930
Phone: 313-271-1500 Ext. 1707
Fax: 313-240-6095
E-mail: monzcyn@sme.org

DIRECTOR'S SCHOLARSHIP AWARD

One-time award for full-time undergraduate students enrolled in a manufacturing degree program in the U.S. or Canada. Must have completed 30 college credit hours. Minimum 3.5 GPA required. Preference given to students who demonstrate leadership skills.

Academic Fields/Career Goals: Engineering/Technology.

Award: Scholarship for use in sophomore, junior, or senior years; not renewable. *Number:* 1. *Amount:* $5000.

Eligibility Requirements: Applicant must be enrolled or expecting to enroll full-time at a four-year institution or university and must have an interest in leadership. Applicant must have 3.5 GPA or higher.

Application Requirements: Application, essay, resume, references, transcript. *Deadline:* February 1.

Contact: Cindy Monzon, Program Coordinator
Society of Manufacturing Engineers Education Foundation
One SME Drive
PO Box 930
Dearborn, MI 48121-0930
Phone: 313-271-1500 Ext. 1707
Fax: 313-240-6095
E-mail: monzcyn@sme.org

DOWNRIVER DETROIT CHAPTER 198 SCHOLARSHIP

One-time award for an individual seeking an associate's degree, bachelor's degree, or graduate degree in manufacturing, mechanical or industrial engineering, engineering technology, or industrial technology at an accredited public or private college or university in Michigan. Applicants must have a minimum GPA of 2.5. Preference is given to applicants who are a child or grandchild of a current SME Downriver Chapter No. 198 member, a member of its student chapter, or a Michigan resident.

Academic Fields/Career Goals: Engineering/Technology; Industrial Design; Mechanical Engineering; Trade/Technical Specialties.

Award: Scholarship for use in freshman, sophomore, junior, senior, or graduate years. *Number:* 1. *Amount:* $1000.

Eligibility Requirements: Applicant must be enrolled or expecting to enroll at a two-year or four-year institution or university and studying in Michigan. Applicant must have 2.5 GPA or higher.

Application Requirements: *Deadline:* February 1.

Contact: Cindy Monzon, Program Coordinator
Society of Manufacturing Engineers Education Foundation
One SME Drive
PO Box 930
Dearborn, MI 48121-0930
Phone: 313-271-1500 Ext. 1707
Fax: 313-240-6095
E-mail: monzcyn@sme.org

E. WAYNE KAY CO-OP SCHOLARSHIP

Two $2500 awards for full-time students enrolled in a manufacturing engineering or technology co-op program at an accredited college or university. Minimum 3.0 GPA required. Must have completed a minimum of 30 college credit hours.

Academic Fields/Career Goals: Engineering/Technology.

Award: Scholarship for use in sophomore, junior, or senior years; not renewable. *Number:* 2. *Amount:* $2500.

Eligibility Requirements: Applicant must be enrolled or expecting to enroll full-time at an institution or university. Applicant must have 3.0 GPA or higher. Available to U.S. and non-U.S. citizens.

Application Requirements: Application, essay, references, transcript. *Deadline:* February 1.

Contact: Cindy Monzon, Program Coordinator
Society of Manufacturing Engineers Education Foundation
One SME Drive
PO Box 930
Dearborn, MI 48121-0930
Phone: 313-271-1500 Ext. 1707
Fax: 313-240-6095
E-mail: monzcyn@sme.org

E. WAYNE KAY COMMUNITY COLLEGE SCHOLARSHIP AWARD

One-time award to full-time students enrolled at an accredited community college or trade school which offers programs in manufacturing or closely related field in the U.S. or Canada. Minimum GPA of 3.0 required. Must have less than 60 college credit hours and seeking a career in manufacturing engineering or technology.

Academic Fields/Career Goals: Engineering/Technology; Trade/Technical Specialties.

Award: Scholarship for use in freshman or sophomore years; not renewable. *Number:* 3. *Amount:* $1000.

Eligibility Requirements: Applicant must be enrolled or expecting to enroll full-time at a two-year or technical institution. Applicant must have 3.0 GPA or higher.

Application Requirements: Application, essay, resume, references, transcript. *Deadline:* February 1.

Contact: Cindy Monzon, Program Coordinator
Society of Manufacturing Engineers Education Foundation
One SME Drive
PO Box 930
Dearborn, MI 48121-0930
Phone: 313-271-1500 Ext. 1707
Fax: 313-240-6095
E-mail: monzcyn@sme.org

E. WAYNE KAY SCHOLARSHIP

Award for full-time undergraduate study in manufacturing engineering and manufacturing technology. Must have minimum 3.0 GPA. Submit transcript, essay, references, application cover sheet, and statement letter with resume. One-time award of $2500. Must have completed a minimum of 30 college credit hours.

Academic Fields/Career Goals: Engineering/Technology; Trade/Technical Specialties.

Award: Scholarship for use in sophomore, junior, or senior years; not renewable. *Number:* 10. *Amount:* $2500.

Eligibility Requirements: Applicant must be enrolled or expecting to enroll full-time at an institution or university. Applicant must have 3.0 GPA or higher. Available to U.S. and Canadian citizens.

Application Requirements: Application, essay, resume, references, transcript. *Deadline:* February 1.

Contact: Cindy Monzon, Program Coordinator
Society of Manufacturing Engineers Education Foundation
One SME Drive
PO Box 930
Dearborn, MI 48121-0930
Phone: 313-271-1500 Ext. 1707
Fax: 313-240-6095
E-mail: monzcyn@sme.org

EDWARD S. ROTH MANUFACTURING ENGINEERING SCHOLARSHIP

Awarded to a graduating high school senior, a current full time undergraduate or graduate student enrolled in an accredited four-year degree program in manufacturing engineering at a sponsored ABET accredited school. Minimum GPA of 3.0 and be a U.S. citizen. Preferences will be given to students demonstrating financial need, minority students, and students participating in a Co-Op program. The top three applications will be sent to Mr. and Mrs. Roth for final selection.

Academic Fields/Career Goals: Engineering/Technology.

Award: Scholarship for use in freshman, sophomore, junior, senior, or graduate years; not renewable. *Number:* 1. *Amount:* $2500.

Eligibility Requirements: Applicant must be enrolled or expecting to enroll full-time at a four-year institution or university and studying in California, Florida, Illinois, Massachusetts, Minnesota, Ohio, Texas, or Utah. Applicant must have 3.0 GPA or higher. Available to U.S. citizens.

Application Requirements: Application, interview. *Deadline:* February 1.

Contact: Cindy Monzon, Program Coordinator
Society of Manufacturing Engineers Education Foundation
One SME Drive
PO Box 930
Dearborn, MI 48121-0930
Phone: 313-271-1500 Ext. 1707
Fax: 313-240-6095
E-mail: monzcyn@sme.org

FORT WAYNE CHAPTER 56 SCHOLARSHIP

One-time award for an individual seeking an associate's degree, bachelor's degree, or graduate degree in manufacturing, mechanical or industrial engineering, engineering technology, or industrial technology at an accredited public or private college or university in Indiana. Applicants must have a minimum GPA of 2.5. Preference given to applicants who are a child or grandchild of a current SME Fort Wayne Chapter No. 56 member, a member of its student chapter, or an Indiana resident.

Academic Fields/Career Goals: Engineering/Technology; Industrial Design; Mechanical Engineering; Trade/Technical Specialties.

Award: Scholarship for use in freshman, sophomore, junior, senior, or graduate years. *Number:* 4. *Amount:* $1000.

Eligibility Requirements: Applicant must be enrolled or expecting to enroll at a two-year or four-year institution or university and studying in Indiana. Applicant must have 2.5 GPA or higher.

Application Requirements: *Deadline:* February 1.

Contact: Cindy Monzon, Program Coordinator
Society of Manufacturing Engineers Education Foundation
One SME Drive
PO Box 930
Dearborn, MI 48121-0930
Phone: 313-271-1500 Ext. 1707
Fax: 313-240-6095
E-mail: monzcyn@sme.org

GUILIANO MAZZETTI SCHOLARSHIP AWARD

One-time award available to full-time students enrolled in a degree program in manufacturing engineering or technology in the U.S. or Canada. Must have completed a minimum of 30 college credit hours. Minimum GPA of 3.0 required.

Academic Fields/Career Goals: Engineering/Technology.

Award: Scholarship for use in sophomore, junior, or senior years; not renewable. *Number:* 2. *Amount:* $1500.

Eligibility Requirements: Applicant must be enrolled or expecting to enroll full-time at a four-year institution or university. Applicant must have 3.0 GPA or higher.

Application Requirements: Application, essay, resume, references, transcript. *Deadline:* February 1.

Contact: Cindy Monzon, Program Coordinator
Society of Manufacturing Engineers Education Foundation
One SME Drive
PO Box 930
Dearborn, MI 48121-0930
Phone: 313-271-1500 Ext. 1707
Fax: 313-240-6095
E-mail: monzcyn@sme.org

KALAMAZOO CHAPTER 116-ROSCOE DOUGLAS MEMORIAL SCHOLARSHIP AWARD

Scholarship to full-time undergraduate students enrolled in a degree program in manufacturing, engineering, or technology at one of the sponsored Michigan institutions. Minimum GPA of 3.0 required. Must have completed a minimum of 30 college credit hours.

Academic Fields/Career Goals: Engineering/Technology.

Award: Scholarship for use in sophomore, junior, or senior years; not renewable. *Number:* 1. *Amount:* $1500.

Eligibility Requirements: Applicant must be enrolled or expecting to enroll full-time at a four-year institution or university and studying in Michigan. Applicant must have 3.0 GPA or higher.

Application Requirements: Application. *Deadline:* February 1.

Contact: Cindy Monzon, Program Coordinator
Society of Manufacturing Engineers Education Foundation
One SME Drive
PO Box 930
Dearborn, MI 48121-0930
Phone: 313-271-1500 Ext. 1707
Fax: 313-240-6095
E-mail: monzcyn@sme.org

MYRTLE AND EARL WALKER SCHOLARSHIP FUND

One-time award for students seeking a career in manufacturing engineering or technology who have completed at least 15 credit hours or one semester.

Society of Manufacturing Engineers Education Foundation (continued)

Must have minimum 3.5 GPA. Submit application cover sheet, resume, transcript, essay, references, and statement of career goals.

Academic Fields/Career Goals: Engineering/Technology; Trade/Technical Specialties.

Award: Scholarship for use in sophomore, junior, or senior years; not renewable. *Number:* 25. *Amount:* $1000.

Eligibility Requirements: Applicant must be enrolled or expecting to enroll full-time at a two-year or four-year or technical institution or university. Applicant must have 3.5 GPA or higher. Available to U.S. and Canadian citizens.

Application Requirements: Application, essay, resume, references, transcript. *Deadline:* February 1.

Contact: Cindy Monzon, Program Coordinator
Society of Manufacturing Engineers Education Foundation
One SME Drive
PO Box 930
Dearborn, MI 48121-0930
Phone: 313-271-1500 Ext. 1707
Fax: 313-240-6095
E-mail: monzcyn@sme.org

NORTH CENTRAL REGION 9 SCHOLARSHIP

Award to a full-time student enrolled in a manufacturing, mechanical, or industrial engineering degree program in North Central Region 9 (Iowa, Minnesota, Nebraska, North Dakota, South Dakota, Wisconsin, and the upper peninsula of Michigan). Applicants must have a 3.0 GPA. Preference will be given to North Central Region 9 members and their family members and to residents of the states in North Central Region 9.

Academic Fields/Career Goals: Engineering/Technology; Industrial Design; Mechanical Engineering; Trade/Technical Specialties.

Award: Scholarship for use in freshman, sophomore, junior, or senior years. *Number:* 1. *Amount:* $1000.

Eligibility Requirements: Applicant must be enrolled or expecting to enroll full-time at an institution or university and studying in Iowa, Michigan, Minnesota, Nebraska, North Dakota, South Dakota, or Wisconsin. Applicant must have 3.0 GPA or higher.

Application Requirements: *Deadline:* February 1.

Contact: Cindy Monzon, Program Coordinator
Society of Manufacturing Engineers Education Foundation
One SME Drive
PO Box 930
Dearborn, MI 48121-0930
Phone: 313-271-1500 Ext. 1707
Fax: 313-240-6095
E-mail: monzcyn@sme.org

PHOENIX CHAPTER 67 SCHOLARSHIP

Award for a high school senior who plans on enrolling in a manufacturing program technology or manufacturing technology program or an undergraduate student enrolled in a manufacturing engineering technology, manufacturing technology, industrial technology, or closely related program at an accredited college or university in Arizona. Applicants must have an overall GPA of 2.5 and a 3.0 GPA in their manufacturing courses.

Academic Fields/Career Goals: Engineering/Technology; Industrial Design; Mechanical Engineering; Trade/Technical Specialties.

Award: Scholarship for use in freshman, sophomore, junior, or senior years. *Number:* 1. *Amount:* $1000.

Eligibility Requirements: Applicant must be enrolled or expecting to enroll at a two-year or four-year institution or university and studying in Arizona. Applicant must have 2.5 GPA or higher.

Application Requirements: *Deadline:* February 1.

Contact: Cindy Monzon, Program Coordinator
Society of Manufacturing Engineers Education Foundation
One SME Drive
PO Box 930
Dearborn, MI 48121-0930
Phone: 313-271-1500 Ext. 1707
Fax: 313-240-6095
E-mail: monzcyn@sme.org

SME CORPORATE SCHOLARS

Award to full-time students enrolled in a degree program in manufacturing engineering or technology in the United States or Canada. Applicants must have an overall GPA of 3.0.

Academic Fields/Career Goals: Engineering/Technology; Trade/Technical Specialties.

Award: Scholarship for use in freshman, sophomore, junior, or senior years. *Number:* varies. *Amount:* $1000–$5000.

Eligibility Requirements: Applicant must be enrolled or expecting to enroll full-time at an institution or university. Applicant must have 3.0 GPA or higher.

Application Requirements: *Deadline:* February 1.

Contact: Cindy Monzon, Program Coordinator
Society of Manufacturing Engineers Education Foundation
One SME Drive
PO Box 930
Dearborn, MI 48121-0930
Phone: 313-271-1500 Ext. 1707
Fax: 313-240-6095
E-mail: monzcyn@sme.org

SME FAMILY SCHOLARSHIP

Three scholarships awarded to children or grandchildren of Society of Manufacturing Engineers members. Must be graduating high school senior planning to pursue full-time studies for an undergraduate degree in manufacturing engineering, manufacturing engineering technology, or a closely related engineering study at an accredited college or university. Undergraduate students must have completed 30 credit hours. Minimum GPA of 3.0 and SAT score of 1000 required, or ACT score of 21.

Academic Fields/Career Goals: Engineering/Technology.

Award: Scholarship for use in freshman, sophomore, junior, or senior years; renewable. *Number:* 3. *Amount:* $5000–$20,000.

Eligibility Requirements: Applicant must be enrolled or expecting to enroll full-time at a four-year institution or university. Applicant must have 3.0 GPA or higher. Available to U.S. and non-U.S. citizens.

Application Requirements: Application, essay, resume, references, test scores, transcript. *Deadline:* February 1.

Contact: Cindy Monzon, Program Coordinator
Society of Manufacturing Engineers Education Foundation
One SME Drive
PO Box 930
Dearborn, MI 48121-0930
Phone: 313-271-1500 Ext. 1707
Fax: 313-240-6095
E-mail: monzcyn@sme.org

ST. LOUIS CHAPTER NO. 17 SCHOLARSHIP FUND

Award for undergraduates pursuing studies in manufacturing engineering or industrial technology. Must attend an approved institution with a student chapter of the Society of Manufacturing Engineers, sponsored by St. Louis Chapter Number 17. One-time award of $1000. Award based on merit. Submit application cover sheet and resume. Must rank in upper quarter of class or have minimum GPA of 3.5.

Academic Fields/Career Goals: Engineering/Technology.

Award: Scholarship for use in freshman, sophomore, junior, or senior years; not renewable. *Number:* 4. *Amount:* $1000.

Eligibility Requirements: Applicant must be enrolled or expecting to enroll full-time at a two-year or four-year institution or university and studying in Illinois or Missouri. Applicant must have 3.5 GPA or higher. Available to U.S. and Canadian citizens.

Application Requirements: Application, essay, resume, references, transcript. *Deadline:* February 1.

Contact: Cindy Monzon, Program Coordinator
Society of Manufacturing Engineers Education Foundation
One SME Drive
PO Box 930
Dearborn, MI 48121-0930
Phone: 313-271-1500 Ext. 1707
Fax: 313-240-6095
E-mail: monzcyn@sme.org

WAYNE KAY HIGH SCHOOL SCHOLARSHIP

Two awards for up to $2500 each for two years as follows: $1000 for first year and renewable for $1500 for second year, based on academic excellence and career path. Must be graduating high school seniors who commit to enroll in manufacturing engineering or technology program at an accredited college or university as a full-time freshman in the current summer or full semester. Minimum 3.0 GPA required.

Academic Fields/Career Goals: Engineering/Technology.

Award: Scholarship for use in freshman year; renewable. *Number:* 2. *Amount:* up to $2500.

Eligibility Requirements: Applicant must be high school student and planning to enroll or expecting to enroll full-time at a four-year institution or university. Applicant must have 3.0 GPA or higher. Available to U.S. and non-U.S. citizens.

Application Requirements: Application, essay, references, transcript. *Deadline:* February 1.

Contact: Cindy Monzon, Program Coordinator
Society of Manufacturing Engineers Education Foundation
One SME Drive
PO Box 930
Dearborn, MI 48121-0930
Phone: 313-271-1500 Ext. 1707
Fax: 313-240-6095
E-mail: monzcyn@sme.org

WICHITA CHAPTER 52 SCHOLARSHIP

Award for an individual seeking an associate's degree, bachelor's degree, or graduate degree in manufacturing, mechanical or industrial engineering, engineering technology, or industrial technology at an accredited public or private college or university in Kansas. Applicants must have a minimum GPA of 2.5. Preference given to applicants who are a relative of a current SME Wichita Chapter No. 52 member or a Kansas resident.

Academic Fields/Career Goals: Engineering/Technology; Industrial Design; Mechanical Engineering; Trade/Technical Specialties.

Award: Scholarship for use in freshman, sophomore, junior, senior, or graduate years. *Number:* 1. *Amount:* $1000.

Eligibility Requirements: Applicant must be enrolled or expecting to enroll at a two-year or four-year institution or university and studying in Kansas. Applicant must have 2.5 GPA or higher.

Application Requirements: *Deadline:* February 1.

Contact: Cindy Monzon, Program Coordinator
Society of Manufacturing Engineers Education Foundation
One SME Drive
PO Box 930
Dearborn, MI 48121-0930
Phone: 313-271-1500 Ext. 1707
Fax: 313-240-6095
E-mail: monzcyn@sme.org

WILLIAM E. WEISEL SCHOLARSHIP FUND

• *See page 222*

SOCIETY OF MEXICAN AMERICAN ENGINEERS AND SCIENTISTS http://www.maes-natl.org

GRE AND GRADUATE APPLICATIONS WAIVER

• *See page 72*

SOCIETY OF NAVAL ARCHITECTS & MARINE ENGINEERS http://www.sname.org

SOCIETY OF NAVAL ARCHITECTS AND MARINE ENGINEERS UNDERGRADUATE SCHOLARSHIPS

These scholarships are open to U.S. and Canadian citizens studying toward a degree in naval architecture, marine engineering, ocean engineering or marine industry-related fields at an approved school. Must be nominated by school. Applicants must be entering their junior or senior year and must be a member of the Society at the time of the award. For more information visit Web site at http://www.sname.org.

Academic Fields/Career Goals: Engineering/Technology; Marine/Ocean Engineering.

Award: Scholarship for use in junior or senior years; not renewable. *Number:* varies. *Amount:* up to $2000.

Eligibility Requirements: Applicant must be enrolled or expecting to enroll at a four-year institution or university. Available to U.S. and Canadian citizens.

Application Requirements: Nomination. *Deadline:* May 1.

Contact: Scott McClure, Chairman, Scholarship Committee
Society of Naval Architects & Marine Engineers
601 Pavonia Avenue
Jersey City, NJ 07306
Phone: 713-789-1840
Fax: 713-789-1347
E-mail: scottm@acma-inc.com

SOCIETY OF PETROLEUM ENGINEERS http://www.spe.org

GUS ARCHIE MEMORIAL SCHOLARSHIPS

Renewable award for high school seniors planning to enroll in a petroleum engineering degree program at a four-year institution. Must have minimum 3.5 GPA.

Academic Fields/Career Goals: Engineering/Technology.

Award: Scholarship for use in freshman, sophomore, junior, or senior years; renewable. *Amount:* $5000.

Eligibility Requirements: Applicant must be high school student and planning to enroll or expecting to enroll full-time at a four-year institution or university. Applicant must have 3.5 GPA or higher. Available to U.S. and non-U.S. citizens.

Application Requirements: Application, autobiography, financial need analysis, photo, references, transcript. *Deadline:* April 30.

Contact: Tom Whipple, Professional Development Manager
Society of Petroleum Engineers
PO Box 833836
Richardson, TX 75083
Phone: 972-952-9452
Fax: 972-952-9435
E-mail: twhipple@spe.org

SOCIETY OF PLASTICS ENGINEERS (SPE) FOUNDATION http://www.4spe.org

FLEMING/BASZCAK SCHOLARSHIP

• *See page 147*

SOCIETY OF PLASTICS ENGINEERS SCHOLARSHIP PROGRAM

• *See page 147*

SOCIETY OF WOMEN ENGINEERS http://www.swe.org/scholarships

ADMIRAL GRACE MURRAY HOPPER MEMORIAL SCHOLARSHIP

Scholarships for female freshmen entering the study of engineering in a four-year program. Must attend an ABET-accredited or SWE-approved school and have minimum GPA of 3.5. Five one-time awards of $1000 each. Deadline: May 15.

Academic Fields/Career Goals: Engineering/Technology.

Award: Scholarship for use in freshman year; not renewable. *Number:* 5. *Amount:* $1000.

Eligibility Requirements: Applicant must be high school student; planning to enroll or expecting to enroll full-time at a four-year

Society of Women Engineers (continued)

institution or university and female. Applicant must have 3.5 GPA or higher. Available to U.S. and non-U.S. citizens.

Application Requirements: Application, essay, self-addressed stamped envelope, test scores, transcript. *Deadline:* May 15.

Contact: Program Coordinator
Society of Women Engineers
230 East Ohio Street, Suite 400
Chicago, IL 60611-3265
Phone: 312-596-5223
Fax: 312-644-8557
E-mail: hq@swe.org

ADOBE SYSTEMS COMPUTER SCIENCE SCHOLARSHIP

Two scholarships available to female engineering students in junior or senior year. Must have 3.0 GPA. Preference given to students attending selected schools in the San Francisco Bay area.

Academic Fields/Career Goals: Engineering/Technology.

Award: Scholarship for use in junior or senior years. *Number:* 2. *Amount:* $1500–$2000.

Eligibility Requirements: Applicant must be enrolled or expecting to enroll at a four-year institution or university and female. Applicant must have 3.0 GPA or higher. Available to U.S. citizens.

Application Requirements: Application, references, self-addressed stamped envelope, transcript. *Deadline:* February 1.

Contact: Program Coordinator
Society of Women Engineers
230 East Ohio Street, Suite 400
Chicago, IL 60611-3265
Phone: 312-596-5223
Fax: 312-644-8557
E-mail: hq@swe.org

AGILENT MENTORING SCHOLARSHIP

• *See page 172*

ANNE MAUREEN WHITNEY BARROW MEMORIAL SCHOLARSHIP

One award for a female undergraduate entering an engineering or engineering technology degree program. Must have a minimum 3.5 GPA. Send self-addressed stamped envelope for application. Renewable award of $5000. Deadline: May 15 for freshman and February 1 for sophomores, juniors, and seniors.

Academic Fields/Career Goals: Engineering/Technology.

Award: Scholarship for use in freshman, sophomore, junior, or senior years; renewable. *Number:* 1. *Amount:* $5000.

Eligibility Requirements: Applicant must be enrolled or expecting to enroll full-time at a four-year institution or university and female. Applicant must have 3.5 GPA or higher. Available to U.S. and non-U.S. citizens.

Application Requirements: Application, essay, references, self-addressed stamped envelope, test scores, transcript. *Deadline:* varies.

Contact: Program Coordinator
Society of Women Engineers
230 East Ohio Street, Suite 400
Chicago, IL 60611-3265
Phone: 312-596-5223
Fax: 312-644-8557
E-mail: hq@swe.org

ARIZONA SECTION SCHOLARSHIP

• *See page 233*

B.J. HARROD SCHOLARSHIP

Two $1500 awards made to an incoming female freshman majoring in engineering. Deadline for application is May 15.

Academic Fields/Career Goals: Engineering/Technology.

Award: Scholarship for use in freshman year; not renewable. *Number:* 2. *Amount:* $1500.

Eligibility Requirements: Applicant must be high school student; planning to enroll or expecting to enroll full-time at a two-year or four-year institution or university and female. Applicant must have 3.5 GPA or higher. Available to U.S. and non-U.S. citizens.

Application Requirements: Application, essay, references, self-addressed stamped envelope, test scores, transcript. *Deadline:* May 15.

Contact: Program Coordinator
Society of Women Engineers
230 East Ohio Street, Suite 400
Chicago, IL 60611-3265
Phone: 312-596-5223
Fax: 312-644-8557
E-mail: hq@swe.org

B.K. KRENZER MEMORIAL REENTRY SCHOLARSHIP

Preference is given to degreed female engineers desiring to return to the workforce following a period of temporary retirement. Recipients may be entering any year of an engineering program, undergraduate or graduate, as full-time or part-time students. Applicants must have been out of the engineering job market as well as out of school for a minimum of two years. Deadline: May 15.

Academic Fields/Career Goals: Engineering/Technology.

Award: Scholarship for use in freshman, sophomore, junior, senior, or graduate years; not renewable. *Number:* 1. *Amount:* $2000.

Eligibility Requirements: Applicant must be enrolled or expecting to enroll at a two-year or four-year or technical institution or university and female. Applicant must have 3.5 GPA or higher. Available to U.S. and non-U.S. citizens.

Application Requirements: Application, essay, references, self-addressed stamped envelope, test scores, transcript. *Deadline:* May 15.

Contact: Program Coordinator
Society of Women Engineers
230 East Ohio Street, Suite 400
Chicago, IL 60611-3265
Phone: 312-596-5223
Fax: 312-644-8557
E-mail: hq@swe.org

BECHTEL CORPORATION SCHOLARSHIP

• *See page 155*

CATERPILLAR, INC. SCHOLARSHIP

Three $2400 scholarships awarded to undergraduate and graduate students studying engineering. Must be U.S. citizen or authorized to work in the United States. Must have minimum 2.8 GPA.

Academic Fields/Career Goals: Engineering/Technology.

Award: Scholarship for use in freshman, sophomore, junior, senior, or graduate years; not renewable. *Number:* 3. *Amount:* $2400.

Eligibility Requirements: Applicant must be enrolled or expecting to enroll full-time at a four-year institution or university and female. Available to U.S. citizens.

Application Requirements: Application. *Deadline:* varies.

Contact: Program Coordinator
Society of Women Engineers
230 East Ohio Street, Suite 400
Chicago, IL 60611-3265
Phone: 312-596-5223
Fax: 312-644-8557
E-mail: hq@swe.org

CHEVRON TEXACO CORPORATION SCHOLARSHIPS

• *See page 147*

COLUMBIA RIVER SECTION SCHOLARSHIPS

Scholarships available to students attending University of Portland, Portland State University, or Oregon Institute of Technology or a transfer student from an Oregon or Southwest Washington community college planning on pursuing an engineering degree at one of those schools.

Academic Fields/Career Goals: Engineering/Technology.

Award: Scholarship for use in freshman, sophomore, junior, or senior years; not renewable. *Number:* 6. *Amount:* $300–$750.

Eligibility Requirements: Applicant must be enrolled or expecting to enroll full-time at a two-year or four-year institution or university; female and studying in Oregon or Washington. Applicant must have 2.5 GPA or higher. Available to U.S. citizens.

Application Requirements: Application. *Deadline:* April 15.

Contact: Jennifer Belknap, Scholarship Chair
E-mail: Jennifer_Belknap@URSCorp.com

DAVID SARNOFF RESEARCH CENTER SCHOLARSHIP

• *See page 173*

DELL COMPUTER CORPORATION SCHOLARSHIPS

• *See page 173*

DELPHI SCHOLARSHIP

Scholarship for female engineering students in sophomore or junior year. Limited to students at Michigan State University, University of Michigan, Purdue University at West Lafayette, Kettering University, University of Dayton.

Academic Fields/Career Goals: Engineering/Technology.

Award: Scholarship for use in sophomore or junior years. *Number:* 2. *Amount:* $2500.

Eligibility Requirements: Applicant must be enrolled or expecting to enroll full-time at an institution or university; female and studying in Indiana, Michigan, or Ohio. Applicant must have 3.0 GPA or higher. Available to U.S. citizens.

Application Requirements: Application, references, self-addressed stamped envelope, transcript. *Deadline:* February 1.

Contact: Program Coordinator
Society of Women Engineers
230 East Ohio Street, Suite 400
Chicago, IL 60611-3265
Phone: 312-596-5223
Fax: 312-644-8557
E-mail: hq@swe.org

DOROTHY LEMKE HOWARTH SCHOLARSHIPS

Scholarship awarded to entering female sophomore students in engineering who are U.S. citizens attending a four-year institution. Send self-addressed stamped envelope for more information. Must have minimum 3.0 GPA. Five one-time awards of $2000 each. Deadline: February 1.

Academic Fields/Career Goals: Engineering/Technology.

Award: Scholarship for use in sophomore year; not renewable. *Number:* 5. *Amount:* $2000.

Eligibility Requirements: Applicant must be enrolled or expecting to enroll at a four-year institution or university and female. Applicant must have 3.0 GPA or higher. Available to U.S. citizens.

Application Requirements: Application, essay, references, self-addressed stamped envelope, test scores, transcript. *Deadline:* February 1.

Contact: Program Coordinator
Society of Women Engineers
230 East Ohio Street, Suite 400
Chicago, IL 60611-3265
Phone: 312-596-5223
Fax: 312-644-8557
E-mail: hq@swe.org

DOROTHY M. AND EARL S. HOFFMAN SCHOLARSHIP

Renewable 3-year scholarship for female freshman engineering students. Must have minimum 3.5 GPA. Preference given to students at Bucknell University and Rensselaer Polytechnic University.

Academic Fields/Career Goals: Engineering/Technology.

Award: Scholarship for use in freshman year; renewable. *Number:* 3. *Amount:* $3000.

Eligibility Requirements: Applicant must be high school student; planning to enroll or expecting to enroll full-time at a four-year institution or university and female. Applicant must have 3.5 GPA or higher. Available to U.S. citizens.

Application Requirements: Application, references, self-addressed stamped envelope, transcript. *Deadline:* May 15.

Contact: Program Coordinator
Society of Women Engineers
230 East Ohio Street, Suite 400
Chicago, IL 60611-3265
Phone: 312-596-5223
Fax: 312-644-8557
E-mail: hq@swe.org

DOROTHY MORRIS SCHOLARSHIP

One $1000 scholarship available to graduate of New Jersey high school. Must be U.S. citizen.

Academic Fields/Career Goals: Engineering/Technology.

Award: Scholarship for use in sophomore, junior, or senior years; not renewable. *Number:* 1. *Amount:* $1000.

Eligibility Requirements: Applicant must be enrolled or expecting to enroll full-time at a four-year institution or university and female. Applicant must have 3.0 GPA or higher. Available to U.S. citizens.

Application Requirements: Application. *Deadline:* February 1.

Contact: Program Coordinator
Society of Women Engineers
230 East Ohio Street, Suite 400
Chicago, IL 60611-3265
Phone: 312-596-5223
Fax: 312-644-8557
E-mail: hq@swe.org

ELECTRONICS FOR IMAGING (EFI) SCHOLARSHIPS

Four scholarships available to female engineering students in sophomore, junior, senior year, and graduate study. Preference given to students attending selected schools in the San Francisco Bay area.

Academic Fields/Career Goals: Engineering/Technology.

Award: Scholarship for use in sophomore, junior, senior, or graduate years. *Number:* 4. *Amount:* $4000.

Eligibility Requirements: Applicant must be enrolled or expecting to enroll full-time at a four-year institution or university and female. Applicant must have 3.0 GPA or higher. Available to U.S. citizens.

Application Requirements: Application, references, self-addressed stamped envelope, transcript. *Deadline:* February 1.

Contact: Program Coordinator
Society of Women Engineers
230 East Ohio Street, Suite 400
Chicago, IL 60611-3265
Phone: 312-596-5223
Fax: 312-644-8557
E-mail: hq@swe.org

ELECTRONICS FOR IMAGING SCHOLARSHIP

Four $4000 scholarships available to female sophomore, junior, and senior undergraduate engineering students.

Academic Fields/Career Goals: Engineering/Technology.

Award: Scholarship for use in sophomore, junior, senior, or graduate years; not renewable. *Number:* 4. *Amount:* $4000.

Eligibility Requirements: Applicant must be enrolled or expecting to enroll full-time at a four-year institution or university and female. Applicant must have 3.0 GPA or higher. Available to U.S. citizens.

Society of Women Engineers (continued)

Application Requirements: Application. *Deadline:* February 1.

Contact: Program Coordinator
Society of Women Engineers
230 East Ohio Street, Suite 400
Chicago, IL 60611-3265
Phone: 312-596-5223
Fax: 312-644-8557
E-mail: hq@swe.org

EXELON SCHOLARSHIP

One $1000 scholarship for entering freshman pursuing engineering degree.

Academic Fields/Career Goals: Engineering/Technology.

Award: Scholarship for use in freshman year; not renewable. *Number:* 1. *Amount:* $1000.

Eligibility Requirements: Applicant must be enrolled or expecting to enroll full-time at a four-year institution or university and female. Applicant must have 3.5 GPA or higher. Available to U.S. citizens.

Application Requirements: Application. *Deadline:* May 15.

Contact: Program Coordinator
Society of Women Engineers
230 East Ohio Street, Suite 400
Chicago, IL 60611-3265
Phone: 312-596-5223
Fax: 312-644-8557
E-mail: hq@swe.org

FORD MOTOR COMPANY SCHOLARSHIP

One $1000 scholarship will be awarded to a female student studying engineering. Eligible applicants will be sophomores demonstrating leadership qualities.

Academic Fields/Career Goals: Engineering/Technology.

Award: Scholarship for use in sophomore year; not renewable. *Number:* 1. *Amount:* $1000.

Eligibility Requirements: Applicant must be enrolled or expecting to enroll at an institution or university; female and must have an interest in leadership. Applicant must have 3.5 GPA or higher. Available to U.S. citizens.

Application Requirements: Application, references, self-addressed stamped envelope, transcript. *Deadline:* February 1.

Contact: Program Coordinator
Society of Women Engineers
230 East Ohio Street, Suite 400
Chicago, IL 60611-3265
Phone: 312-596-5223
Fax: 312-644-8557
E-mail: hq@swe.org

GENERAL ELECTRIC FOUNDATION SCHOLARSHIP

Renewable award for outstanding women engineering students. Renewable for three years with continued academic achievement. Send self-addressed stamped envelope for more information. Must be U.S. citizen. Three scholarships at $1000 each. Must have a minimum 3.5 GPA. Deadline: May 15.

Academic Fields/Career Goals: Engineering/Technology.

Award: Scholarship for use in freshman year; renewable. *Number:* 3. *Amount:* $1000.

Eligibility Requirements: Applicant must be high school student; planning to enroll or expecting to enroll at a four-year institution or university and female. Applicant must have 3.5 GPA or higher. Available to U.S. citizens.

Application Requirements: Application, essay, references, self-addressed stamped envelope, test scores, transcript. *Deadline:* May 15.

Contact: Program Coordinator
Society of Women Engineers
230 East Ohio Street, Suite 400
Chicago, IL 60611-3265
Phone: 312-596-5223
Fax: 312-644-8557
E-mail: hq@swe.org

GENERAL ELECTRIC WOMEN'S NETWORK SCHOLARSHIP

Thirteen $2425 scholarships available to undergraduate sophomores, juniors, and seniors studying engineering. Must be U.S. citizen.

Academic Fields/Career Goals: Engineering/Technology.

Award: Scholarship for use in sophomore, junior, or senior years; not renewable. *Number:* 13. *Amount:* $2425.

Eligibility Requirements: Applicant must be enrolled or expecting to enroll full-time at a four-year institution or university and female. Applicant must have 3.0 GPA or higher. Available to U.S. citizens.

Application Requirements: Application. *Deadline:* February 1.

Contact: Program Coordinator
Society of Women Engineers
230 East Ohio Street, Suite 400
Chicago, IL 60611-3265
Phone: 312-596-5223
Fax: 312-644-8557
E-mail: hq@swe.org

GENERAL MOTORS FOUNDATION UNDERGRADUATE SCHOLARSHIPS

• *See page 147*

GUIDANT CORPORATION SCHOLARSHIP

• *See page 173*

IVY PARKER MEMORIAL SCHOLARSHIP

One-time award for female engineering major. Must be in junior or senior year and have a minimum 3.0 GPA. Selection also based on financial need. Deadline: February 1.

Academic Fields/Career Goals: Engineering/Technology.

Award: Scholarship for use in junior or senior years; not renewable. *Number:* 1. *Amount:* $2500.

Eligibility Requirements: Applicant must be enrolled or expecting to enroll at a four-year institution or university and female. Applicant must have 3.0 GPA or higher. Available to U.S. citizens.

Application Requirements: Application, financial need analysis, references, self-addressed stamped envelope, transcript. *Deadline:* February 1.

Contact: Program Coordinator
Society of Women Engineers
230 East Ohio Street, Suite 400
Chicago, IL 60611-3265
Phone: 312-596-5223
Fax: 312-644-8557
E-mail: hq@swe.org

JUDITH RESNIK MEMORIAL SCHOLARSHIP

• *See page 106*

LILIAN MOLLER GILBRETH SCHOLARSHIP

One award for college junior or senior female engineering student. Must be a U.S. citizen and possess outstanding potential demonstrated by achievement. Send self-addressed stamped envelope for application. One-time award of $6000. Must rank in upper third of class or have a minimum GPA of 3.0. Deadline: February 1.

Academic Fields/Career Goals: Engineering/Technology.

Award: Scholarship for use in junior or senior years; not renewable. *Number:* 1. *Amount:* $6000.

Eligibility Requirements: Applicant must be enrolled or expecting to enroll at a four-year institution or university and female. Applicant must have 3.0 GPA or higher. Available to U.S. citizens.

Application Requirements: Application, essay, references, self-addressed stamped envelope, test scores, transcript. *Deadline:* February 1.

Contact: Program Coordinator
Society of Women Engineers
230 East Ohio Street, Suite 400
Chicago, IL 60611-3265
Phone: 312-596-5223
Fax: 312-644-8557
E-mail: hq@swe.org

LOCKHEED-MARTIN CORPORATION SCHOLARSHIPS

Two $3000 scholarships awarded to female incoming freshmen majoring in engineering. Minimum 3.5 GPA required. Deadline for application is May 15.

Academic Fields/Career Goals: Engineering/Technology.

Award: Scholarship for use in freshman year; not renewable. *Number:* 2. *Amount:* $3000.

Eligibility Requirements: Applicant must be enrolled or expecting to enroll full-time at a four-year institution or university and female. Applicant must have 3.5 GPA or higher. Available to U.S. and non-U.S. citizens.

Application Requirements: Application, essay, references, self-addressed stamped envelope, test scores, transcript. *Deadline:* May 15.

Contact: Program Coordinator
Society of Women Engineers
230 East Ohio Street, Suite 400
Chicago, IL 60611-3265
Phone: 312-596-5223
Fax: 312-644-8557
E-mail: hq@swe.org

LYDIA I. PICKUP MEMORIAL SCHOLARSHIP

• *See page 173*

MASWE MEMORIAL SCHOLARSHIP

Four $2000 awards for female engineering students who are sophomores, juniors, or seniors in college. Must be U.S. citizens and have minimum 3.0 GPA. Send self-addressed stamped envelope for application. Selection also based on financial need. Deadline: February 1.

Academic Fields/Career Goals: Engineering/Technology.

Award: Scholarship for use in sophomore, junior, or senior years; not renewable. *Number:* 4. *Amount:* $2000.

Eligibility Requirements: Applicant must be enrolled or expecting to enroll at a four-year institution or university and female. Applicant must have 3.0 GPA or higher. Available to U.S. citizens.

Application Requirements: Application, essay, financial need analysis, self-addressed stamped envelope, test scores, transcript. *Deadline:* February 1.

Contact: Program Coordinator
Society of Women Engineers
230 East Ohio Street, Suite 400
Chicago, IL 60611-3265
Phone: 312-596-5223
Fax: 312-644-8557
E-mail: hq@swe.org

MERIDITH THOMS MEMORIAL SCHOLARSHIP

Renewable award available to female engineering majors. Minimum 3.0 GPA required. Must be in ABET-accredited engineering program at SWE-approved colleges and universities.

Academic Fields/Career Goals: Engineering/Technology.

Award: Scholarship for use in sophomore, junior, or senior years; renewable. *Number:* 6. *Amount:* $2000.

Eligibility Requirements: Applicant must be enrolled or expecting to enroll at a four-year institution or university and female. Applicant must have 3.0 GPA or higher.

Application Requirements: Application, references, self-addressed stamped envelope, test scores, transcript. *Deadline:* February 1.

Contact: Program Coordinator
Society of Women Engineers
230 East Ohio Street, Suite 400
Chicago, IL 60611-3265
Phone: 312-596-5223
Fax: 312-644-8557
E-mail: hq@swe.org

MINNESOTA SWE SECTION SCHOLARSHIP

Applicants must be undergraduate juniors or seniors at an accredited engineering program attending a Minnesota, North Dakota, or South Dakota school. Applicants judged on potential to succeed as engineer, communication skills, extracurricular activities, community involvement or leadership skills, demonstration of work experience and success, and academic excellence.

Academic Fields/Career Goals: Engineering/Technology.

Award: Scholarship for use in junior or senior years; not renewable. *Number:* 1. *Amount:* $750.

Eligibility Requirements: Applicant must be enrolled or expecting to enroll at a four-year institution or university; female and studying in Minnesota, North Dakota, or South Dakota. Available to U.S. citizens.

Application Requirements: Application. *Deadline:* March 15.

Contact: Naomi Brill
Phone: 651-636-8676
E-mail: nbrill323@yahoo.com

NEW JERSEY SCHOLARSHIP

Award granted to female New Jersey resident majoring in engineering. Available to incoming freshman. Minimum 3.5 GPA required. Application deadline is May 15.

Academic Fields/Career Goals: Engineering/Technology.

Award: Scholarship for use in freshman year; not renewable. *Number:* 1. *Amount:* $1500.

Eligibility Requirements: Applicant must be enrolled or expecting to enroll full-time at an institution or university; female and resident of New Jersey. Applicant must have 3.5 GPA or higher. Available to U.S. citizens.

Application Requirements: Application, essay, references, self-addressed stamped envelope, test scores, transcript. *Deadline:* May 15.

Contact: Program Coordinator
Society of Women Engineers
230 East Ohio Street, Suite 400
Chicago, IL 60611-3265
Phone: 312-596-5223
Fax: 312-644-8557
E-mail: hq@swe.org

NORTHROP GRUMMAN CORPORATION SCHOLARSHIPS

• *See page 106*

OLIVE LYNN SALEMBIER SCHOLARSHIP

One $2000 award for female students entering any undergraduate or graduate year as full- or part-time students. Applicants must have been out of the engineering job market as well as out of school for a minimum of two years. Application deadline is May 15.

Academic Fields/Career Goals: Engineering/Technology.

Award: Scholarship for use in freshman, sophomore, junior, senior, or graduate years; not renewable. *Number:* 1. *Amount:* $2000.

Eligibility Requirements: Applicant must be enrolled or expecting to enroll full or part-time at a four-year institution or university and female. Applicant must have 3.5 GPA or higher.

Society of Women Engineers (continued)

Application Requirements: Application, essay, references, self-addressed stamped envelope, test scores, transcript. *Deadline:* May 15.

Contact: Program Coordinator
Society of Women Engineers
230 East Ohio Street, Suite 400
Chicago, IL 60611-3265
Phone: 312-596-5223
Fax: 312-644-8557
E-mail: hq@swe.org

PAST PRESIDENTS SCHOLARSHIPS

Two $1500 awards offered to female undergraduate or graduate students majoring in engineering. Minimum 3.0 GPA required. Must be U.S. citizen. Deadline: February 1.

Academic Fields/Career Goals: Engineering/Technology.

Award: Scholarship for use in sophomore, junior, senior, or graduate years; renewable. *Number:* 2. *Amount:* $1500.

Eligibility Requirements: Applicant must be enrolled or expecting to enroll full-time at a four-year institution or university and female. Applicant must have 3.0 GPA or higher. Available to U.S. citizens.

Application Requirements: Application, essay, references, self-addressed stamped envelope, test scores, transcript. *Deadline:* February 1.

Contact: Program Coordinator
Society of Women Engineers
230 East Ohio Street, Suite 400
Chicago, IL 60611-3265
Phone: 312-596-5223
Fax: 312-644-8557
E-mail: hq@swe.org

ROCKWELL AUTOMATION SCHOLARSHIP

One-time award available to female engineering major. Must be in junior year and have a minimum 3.5 GPA. Must have demonstrated leadership potential. Underrepresented group preferred. Deadline: February 1.

Academic Fields/Career Goals: Engineering/Technology.

Award: Scholarship for use in junior year; not renewable. *Number:* 2. *Amount:* $3000.

Eligibility Requirements: Applicant must be enrolled or expecting to enroll full-time at a four-year institution or university; female and must have an interest in leadership. Applicant must have 3.5 GPA or higher. Available to U.S. citizens.

Application Requirements: Application, references, self-addressed stamped envelope, transcript. *Deadline:* February 1.

Contact: Program Coordinator
Society of Women Engineers
230 East Ohio Street, Suite 400
Chicago, IL 60611-3265
Phone: 312-596-5223
Fax: 312-644-8557
E-mail: hq@swe.org

SUSAN MISZKOWITZ MEMORIAL SCHOLARSHIP

One $1000 scholarship available to undergraduate sophomore, junior, or senior studying engineering.

Academic Fields/Career Goals: Engineering/Technology.

Award: Scholarship for use in sophomore, junior, or senior years; not renewable. *Number:* 1. *Amount:* $1000.

Eligibility Requirements: Applicant must be enrolled or expecting to enroll full-time at a four-year institution or university and female. Applicant must have 3.0 GPA or higher. Available to U.S. citizens.

Application Requirements: Application. *Deadline:* February 1.

Contact: Program Coordinator
Society of Women Engineers
230 East Ohio Street, Suite 400
Chicago, IL 60611-3265
Phone: 312-596-5223
Fax: 312-644-8557
E-mail: hq@swe.org

SWE BALTIMORE-WASHINGTON SECTION SCHOLARSHIPS

• **See page 173**

SWE BATON ROUGE SECTION SCHOLARSHIPS

• **See page 174**

SWE CALIFORNIA GOLDEN GATE SECTION SCHOLARSHIPS

• **See page 174**

SWE CALIFORNIA SANTA CLARA VALLEY SECTION SCHOLARSHIP

Applicant must plan to attend school full time in the fall next year and plan to attend a four or five year baccalaureate program or an advanced degree program. Applicant must attend school or be a permanent resident in the South San Francisco Bay Area. Please see Web site for more details: http://www.swe-goldenwest.org/scvs/www/index.htm

Academic Fields/Career Goals: Engineering/Technology.

Award: Scholarship for use in freshman, sophomore, junior, senior, or graduate years; not renewable. *Number:* 20. *Amount:* $1000.

Eligibility Requirements: Applicant must be enrolled or expecting to enroll full-time at a four-year institution or university; female and resident of California. Available to U.S. citizens.

Application Requirements: Application. *Deadline:* varies.

Contact: Tassanee Paya Kapan
E-mail: tassanee_payakapan@agilent.com

SWE CHICAGO REGIONAL SECTION SCHOLARSHIPS

Scholarship for first-year, reentry, or transfer student in undergraduate engineering degree program. Must be accepted into accredited university for following fall semester. Applications available at Web site: http://www.iit.edu/~swe-chi

Academic Fields/Career Goals: Engineering/Technology.

Award: Scholarship for use in freshman, sophomore, junior, or senior years; not renewable. *Number:* varies. *Amount:* varies.

Eligibility Requirements: Applicant must be enrolled or expecting to enroll at a four-year institution or university and female. Available to U.S. citizens.

Application Requirements: Application, essay. *Deadline:* varies.

Contact: SWE Chicago Regional Scholarships
Society of Women Engineers
PO Box 95525
Palatine, IL 60095-0525

SWE CONNECTICUT SECTION JEAN R. BEERS SCHOLARSHIP

• **See page 174**

SWE FLORIDA SPACE COAST SECTION SCHOLARSHIP

One or more awards of $1000 to entering freshman within the counties served by the Section.

Academic Fields/Career Goals: Engineering/Technology.

Award: Scholarship for use in freshman year; not renewable. *Number:* 1. *Amount:* $1000.

Eligibility Requirements: Applicant must be enrolled or expecting to enroll at a four-year institution; female; resident of Florida and studying in Florida. Available to U.S. citizens.

Application Requirements: Application. *Deadline:* varies.

Contact: Donna Ware
E-mail: donna.ware@lmco.com

SWE GREATER NEW ORLEANS SECTION SCHOLARSHIP

• *See page 174*

SWE LEHIGH VALLEY SECTION SCHOLARSHIP

Applicants must be female graduating high school seniors, within the Lehigh Valley Section, planning on attending an ABET-accredited college or university in the following fall semester.

Academic Fields/Career Goals: Engineering/Technology.

Award: Scholarship for use in freshman year; not renewable. *Number:* varies. *Amount:* $1000.

Eligibility Requirements: Applicant must be high school student; planning to enroll or expecting to enroll at a four-year institution or university; female; resident of Pennsylvania and must have an interest in leadership. Available to U.S. citizens.

Application Requirements: Application, proof of acceptance. *Deadline:* April 15.

Contact: Amy Holovaty
Phone: 610-481-5317
E-mail: holovaam@apci.com

SWE SOUTHWEST IDAHO SECTION SCHOLARSHIP

Applicant must be female high school senior resident of Southwest Idaho planning to attend an engineering program. Must plan on attending a five year program at an ABET-accredited engineering program.

Academic Fields/Career Goals: Engineering/Technology.

Award: Scholarship for use in freshman year; not renewable. *Number:* varies. *Amount:* varies.

Eligibility Requirements: Applicant must be enrolled or expecting to enroll full or part-time at a four-year institution; female and resident of Idaho. Available to U.S. citizens.

Application Requirements: Application, essay. *Deadline:* varies.

Contact: Barbara Gaston
Phone: 208-396-4873

SWE ST. LOUIS SCHOLARSHIP

One $500 scholarship will be awarded to an entering sophomore, junior, or senior undergraduate student, or a graduate student attending one of the following colleges/universities: Southern Illinois University, Parks College of Engineering and Aviation, St. Louis University, University of Missouri, or Washington University. Must be SWE student member.

Academic Fields/Career Goals: Engineering/Technology.

Award: Scholarship for use in sophomore, junior, senior, or graduate years; not renewable. *Number:* 1. *Amount:* $500.

Eligibility Requirements: Applicant must be enrolled or expecting to enroll at an institution or university; female and studying in Illinois or Missouri. Applicant or parent of applicant must be member of Society of Women Engineers. Available to U.S. citizens.

Application Requirements: Application. *Deadline:* varies.

Contact: Heidi Houghton
Phone: 618-583-1343
E-mail: Heidi.Houghton@swe.org

WILLAMETTE VALLEY SECTION MARTINA TESTA MEMORIAL SCHOLARSHIP

Applicant must be female graduating high school senior planning on pursuing an engineering baccalaureate degree at an ABET-accredited school.

Academic Fields/Career Goals: Engineering/Technology.

Award: Scholarship for use in freshman year; not renewable. *Number:* 1. *Amount:* $1000.

Eligibility Requirements: Applicant must be high school student; planning to enroll or expecting to enroll at a four-year institution or university; female and resident of Oregon. Available to U.S. citizens.

Application Requirements: Application. *Deadline:* varies.

Contact: SWE-WVS
Society of Women Engineers
PO Box 576
Corvallis, OR 97339-0576

SOCIETY OF WOMEN ENGINEERS - DALLAS SECTION

http://www.dallaswe.org

FRESHMAN ENGINEERING SCHOLARSHIP FOR DALLAS WOMEN

Scholarship for freshman women pursuing a degree in engineering. Applicant must be a Texas resident. Deadline is May 15. Please refer to Web site for further details: http://www.dallaswe.org

Academic Fields/Career Goals: Engineering/Technology.

Award: Scholarship for use in freshman year; not renewable. *Number:* 2. *Amount:* $500.

Eligibility Requirements: Applicant must be high school student; planning to enroll or expecting to enroll full-time at a four-year institution or university; female and resident of Texas. Available to U.S. citizens.

Application Requirements: Application, financial need analysis, references, confirmation of enrollment. *Deadline:* May 15.

Contact: LuAnne Beckley, Dallas SWE Scholarship Chair
Society of Women Engineers - Dallas Section
SWE - Dallas Section
PO Box 85022
Richardson, TX 75085-2022

SOCIETY OF WOMEN ENGINEERS - TWIN TIERS SECTION

http://www.swetwintiers.org

SOCIETY OF WOMEN ENGINEERS - TWIN TIERS SECTION SCHOLARSHIP

• *See page 174*

SOCIETY OF WOMEN ENGINEERS-ROCKY MOUNTAIN SECTION

http://www.swe.org

SOCIETY OF WOMEN ENGINEERS-ROCKY MOUNTAIN SECTION SCHOLARSHIP PROGRAM

• *See page 174*

SPECIALTY EQUIPMENT MARKET ASSOCIATION

http://www.sema.org

SPECIALTY EQUIPMENT MARKET ASSOCIATION MEMORIAL SCHOLARSHIP FUND

Scholarship for higher education in the automotive field. Several one-time awards of $2000 each. All applicants must be attending a U.S. institution. For further details visit Web site: http://www.sema.org.

Academic Fields/Career Goals: Engineering/Technology; Trade/Technical Specialties.

Award: Scholarship for use in freshman, sophomore, junior, senior, or graduate years; not renewable. *Number:* varies. *Amount:* $2000.

Eligibility Requirements: Applicant must be enrolled or expecting to enroll full-time at a two-year or four-year or technical institution or university and must have an interest in automotive. Available to U.S. and non-U.S. citizens.

Application Requirements: Application, essay, photo, references, self-addressed stamped envelope, transcript. *Deadline:* May 31.

Contact: Pat Talaska, Director, Educational Services
Specialty Equipment Market Association
PO Box 4910
Diamond Bar, CA 91765-4910
Phone: 909-396-0289 Ext. 137
Fax: 909-860-0184
E-mail: patt@sema.org

TAU BETA PI ASSOCIATION

http://www.tbp.org/

TAU BETA PI SCHOLARSHIP PROGRAM

One-time award for initiated members of Tau Beta Pi in their senior year of full-time undergraduate engineering study. Submit application and two letters of recommendation. Contact for complete details or visit http://www.tbp.org.

Academic Fields/Career Goals: Engineering/Technology.

Award: Scholarship for use in senior year; not renewable. *Number:* 30–50. *Amount:* $2000.

Eligibility Requirements: Applicant must be enrolled or expecting to enroll full-time at a four-year institution or university. Applicant or

Tau Beta Pi Association (continued)

parent of applicant must be member of Tau Beta Pi Association. Applicant must have 3.5 GPA or higher. Available to U.S. and non-U.S. citizens.

Application Requirements: Application, references. *Deadline:* March 1.

Contact: D. Stephen Pierre, Jr., Director of Fellowships
Tau Beta Pi Association
PO Box 2697
Knoxville, TN 37901-2697
Fax: 334-694-2310
E-mail: dspierre@southernco.com

TEXAS ENGINEERING FOUNDATION http://www.tspe.org

TEXAS SOCIETY OF PROFESSIONAL ENGINEERS (TSPE) REGIONAL SCHOLARSHIPS

• See page 148

TRIANGLE EDUCATION FOUNDATION http://www.triangle.org

KAPADIA SCHOLARSHIPS

One-time award for active members of the Triangle Fraternity. Must be full-time, male students who have completed at least one year of study at the college level. Must be majoring in an engineering program and have at least a 3.0 GPA. Preference given to members of the Zoroastrian religion.

Academic Fields/Career Goals: Engineering/Technology.

Award: Scholarship for use in junior, senior, or graduate years; not renewable. *Number:* varies. *Amount:* $1500–$5000.

Eligibility Requirements: Applicant must be a member of the specified denomination; enrolled or expecting to enroll full-time at an institution or university and male. Applicant must have 3.0 GPA or higher. Available to U.S. and non-U.S. citizens.

Application Requirements: Application, essay, financial need analysis, references, self-addressed stamped envelope, transcript. *Deadline:* May 1.

Contact: Scott Bova, Administrative Assistant
Triangle Education Foundation
120 South Center Street
Plainfield, IN 46168
Phone: 317-837-9641
Fax: 317-837-9042
E-mail: sbova@triangle.org

SEVCIK SCHOLARSHIP

One-time award for active member of the Triangle Fraternity. Must be full-time male student who has completed at least two full academic years of school. Minimum 3.0 GPA. Preference to minority students and Ohio State undergraduates who are engineering majors. Application must be postmarked by April 30. Further information available at Web site http://www.triangle.org.

Academic Fields/Career Goals: Engineering/Technology.

Award: Scholarship for use in junior or senior years; not renewable. *Number:* 1. *Amount:* $1000.

Eligibility Requirements: Applicant must be American Indian/Alaska Native, Asian/Pacific Islander, Black (non-Hispanic), or Hispanic; enrolled or expecting to enroll full-time at a four-year institution or university and male. Applicant must have 3.0 GPA or higher.

Application Requirements: Application, essay, financial need analysis, references, self-addressed stamped envelope, transcript. *Deadline:* April 30.

Contact: Scott Bova, Chief Operating Officer
Triangle Education Foundation
120 South Center Street
Plainfield, IN 46168-1214
Phone: 317-837-9641
Fax: 317-837-9642
E-mail: sbova@triangle.org

UNITED NEGRO COLLEGE FUND http://www.uncf.org

ACCENTURE SCHOLARSHIP

• See page 175

ALFRED L. CHISHOLM SCHOLARSHIP

• See page 175

BATTELLE SCHOLARS PROGRAM

Scholarship for students from central Ohio attending a UNCF member college or university. Please visit Web site for more information: http://www.uncf.org.

Academic Fields/Career Goals: Engineering/Technology.

Award: Scholarship for use in junior year. *Number:* varies. *Amount:* $1000.

Eligibility Requirements: Applicant must be Black (non-Hispanic); enrolled or expecting to enroll at a four-year institution or university and resident of Ohio. Applicant must have 3.0 GPA or higher. Available to U.S. citizens.

Application Requirements: Application, financial need analysis, FAFSA, SAR. *Deadline:* varies.

Contact: Program Services Department
United Negro College Fund
8260 Willow Oaks Corporate Drive
Fairfax, VA 22031

BOOZ, ALLEN & HAMILTON/WILLIAM F. STASIOR INTERNSHIP

• See page 130

CARDINAL HEALTH SCHOLARSHIP

• See page 48

CARTER AND BURGESS SCHOLARSHIP

Scholarship awarded to a student majoring in engineering, who also attends a UNCF member college or university. Must be a resident of Ft. Worth, Texas. Please visit Web site for more information: http://www.uncf.org.

Academic Fields/Career Goals: Engineering/Technology.

Award: Scholarship for use in freshman, sophomore, junior, senior, or graduate years; renewable. *Number:* varies. *Amount:* varies.

Eligibility Requirements: Applicant must be Black (non-Hispanic); enrolled or expecting to enroll at a four-year institution or university and resident of Texas. Applicant must have 2.5 GPA or higher.

Application Requirements: Application, financial need analysis, FAFSA, SAR. *Deadline:* varies.

Contact: Program Services Department
United Negro College Fund
8260 Willow Oaks Corporate Drive
Fairfax, VA 22031

CASTLE ROCK FOUNDATION SCHOLARSHIP

• See page 131

CDM SCHOLARSHIP/INTERNSHIP

• See page 155

CHEVRON/TEXACO SCHOLARS PROGRAM

• See page 155

CHRYSLER CORPORATION SCHOLARSHIP

• See page 175

CON EDISON SCHOLARSHIP

• See page 49

DELL/UNCF CORPORATE SCHOLARS PROGRAM

• See page 131

EMERSON ELECTRIC COMPANY SCHOLARSHIP

• See page 49

FORD/UNCF CORPORATE SCHOLARS PROGRAM

• See page 49

GENERAL MILLS SCHOLARS PROGRAM/INTERNSHIP
• *See page 50*

GILBANE SCHOLARSHIP/INTERNSHIP

Scholarship provides up to $5000 in financial assistance after students have completed a paid summer internship program. Applicants must be Pennsylvania residents majoring in engineering at a UNCF member college or university. Minimum 2.5 GPA required. Prospective applicants should complete the Student Profile found at Web site: http://www.uncf.org

Academic Fields/Career Goals: Engineering/Technology.

Award: Scholarship for use in sophomore or junior years; not renewable. *Amount:* up to $5000.

Eligibility Requirements: Applicant must be Black (non-Hispanic); enrolled or expecting to enroll full-time at a four-year institution or university and resident of Pennsylvania. Applicant must have 2.5 GPA or higher. Available to U.S. citizens.

Application Requirements: Application, financial need analysis. *Deadline:* January 30.

Contact: Program Services Department
United Negro College Fund
8260 Willow Oaks Corporate Drive
Fairfax, VA 22031

KODAK ENGINEERING EXCELLENCE PROGRAM SCHOLARSHIP
• *See page 176*

MAYTAG COMPANY SCHOLARSHIP
• *See page 132*

NORTHEAST UTILITIES SYSTEM SCHOLARSHIP PROGRAM
• *See page 132*

PECO ENERGY SCHOLARSHIP
• *See page 50*

SBC FOUNDATION SCHOLARSHIP
• *See page 133*

SBC PACIFIC BELL FOUNDATION SCHOLARSHIP
• *See page 133*

SOUTHWESTERN BELL CORPORATION SCHOLARSHIP
• *See page 133*

SPRINT SCHOLARSHIP/INTERNSHIP
• *See page 50*

TRW INFORMATION TECHNOLOGY MINORITY SCHOLARSHIP
• *See page 176*

UNCF/ORACLE SCHOLARS/INTERNS PROGRAM
• *See page 50*

UNCF/SPRINT SCHOLARS PROGRAM
• *See page 50*

WEYERHAEUSER/UNCF CORPORATE SCHOLARS
• *See page 134*

WM. WRIGLEY, JR. COMPANY SCHOLARS PROGRAM
• *See page 134*

UNIVERSITIES SPACE RESEARCH ASSOCIATION http://www.usra.edu/hq/scholarships/overview.shtml

UNIVERSITIES SPACE RESEARCH ASSOCIATION SCHOLARSHIP PROGRAM
• *See page 72*

UTAH SOCIETY OF PROFESSIONAL ENGINEERS http://www.uspeonline.com

UTAH SOCIETY OF PROFESSIONAL ENGINEERS SCHOLARSHIP
• *See page 148*

VIRGINIA BUSINESS AND PROFESSIONAL WOMEN'S FOUNDATION http://www.bpwva.advocate.net/foundation.htm

WOMEN IN SCIENCE AND TECHNOLOGY SCHOLARSHIP
• *See page 119*

WEST VIRGINIA HIGHER EDUCATION POLICY COMMISSION-OFFICE OF FINANCIAL AID AND OUTREACH SERVICES http://www.hepc.wvnet.edu

WEST VIRGINIA ENGINEERING, SCIENCE & TECHNOLOGY SCHOLARSHIP PROGRAM
• *See page 223*

WISCONSIN SOCIETY OF PROFESSIONAL ENGINEERS http://www.wspe.org

WISCONSIN SOCIETY OF PROFESSIONAL ENGINEERS SCHOLARSHIPS

One-time award for students pursuing full-time study in engineering. Must be a Wisconsin resident and have a minimum GPA of 3.0. Application deadline is December 15.

Academic Fields/Career Goals: Engineering/Technology.

Award: Scholarship for use in freshman, junior, or senior years; not renewable. *Number:* 4. *Amount:* $1000–$1500.

Eligibility Requirements: Applicant must be enrolled or expecting to enroll full-time at a four-year institution or university and resident of Wisconsin. Applicant must have 3.0 GPA or higher. Available to U.S. and non-U.S. citizens.

Application Requirements: Application, essay, references, self-addressed stamped envelope, test scores, transcript. *Deadline:* December 15.

Contact: Office Manager
Wisconsin Society of Professional Engineers
7044 South 13th Street
Oak Creek, WI 53154
Fax: 414-768-8001
E-mail: e.grochowski@wspe.org

XEROX http://xerox.com

TECHNICAL MINORITY SCHOLARSHIP
• *See page 148*

ENVIRONMENTAL SCIENCE

AMERICAN INDIAN SCIENCE AND ENGINEERING SOCIETY http://www.aises.org

HENRY RODRIGUEZ RECLAMATION COLLEGE SCHOLARSHIP AND INTERNSHIP
• *See page 224*

AMERICAN SOCIETY OF SAFETY ENGINEERS (ASSE) FOUNDATION http://www.asse.org/foundat.htm

UNITED PARCEL SERVICE DIVERSITY SCHOLARSHIP PROGRAM

Two one-time awards available to minority ethnic or racial group students pursuing an undergraduate degree full-time in occupational safety, health, or environment. Must be an ASSE member, a U.S. citizen, and have a minimum 3.25 GPA. Recommendation by a safety faculty member required. Deadline is December 1.

Academic Fields/Career Goals: Environmental Science; Health and Medical Sciences; Occupational Safety and Health.

Award: Scholarship for use in junior or senior years; not renewable. *Number:* 2. *Amount:* $3000–$4000.

Eligibility Requirements: Applicant must be American Indian/Alaska Native, Asian/Pacific Islander, Black (non-Hispanic), or Hispanic and enrolled or expecting to enroll full-time at an institution or university. Applicant or parent of applicant must be member of American Society of Safety Engineers. Available to U.S. citizens.

American Society of Safety Engineers (ASSE) Foundation (continued)

Application Requirements: Application, essay, references, transcript. *Deadline:* December 1.

Contact: Customer Service Department
American Society of Safety Engineers (ASSE) Foundation
1800 East Oakton Street
Des Plaines, IL 60018
Phone: 847-699-2929
Fax: 847-296-3769
E-mail: customerservice@asse.org

ASSOCIATION FOR IRON AND STEEL TECHNOLOGY http://www.aist.org/foundation/scholarships.htm

ASSOCIATION FOR IRON AND STEEL TECHNOLOGY OHIO VALLEY CHAPTER SCHOLARSHIP

• *See page 112*

ASSOCIATION OF CALIFORNIA WATER AGENCIES http://www.acwanet.com

ASSOCIATION OF CALIFORNIA WATER AGENCIES SCHOLARSHIPS

• *See page 68*

CLAIR A. HILL SCHOLARSHIP

• *See page 68*

AUDUBON SOCIETY OF WESTERN PENNSYLVANIA http://www.aswp.org

BEULAH FREY ENVIRONMENTAL SCHOLARSHIP

Scholarship available to high school seniors pursuing studies in the Environmental and Natural Sciences. Must be a U.S. citizen and resident of Pennsylvania. Essay required. Application deadline is March 31.

Academic Fields/Career Goals: Environmental Science; Natural Sciences.

Award: Scholarship for use in freshman year; not renewable. *Number:* 1–2. *Amount:* $1000.

Eligibility Requirements: Applicant must be high school student; planning to enroll or expecting to enroll full-time at a four-year institution or university and resident of Pennsylvania. Available to U.S. citizens.

Application Requirements: Application, essay, references, test scores, transcript. *Deadline:* March 31.

Contact: Audubon Society of Western Pennsylvania
614 Dorseyville Road
Pittsburgh, PA 15238

CALAVERAS BIG TREES ASSOCIATION http://www.bigtrees.org

EMILY M. HEWITT MEMORIAL SCHOLARSHIP

Scholarships for promising California undergraduate and graduate students who have shown an educational and career commitment to the study of environment and the need to practice conservation.

Academic Fields/Career Goals: Environmental Science; Natural Resources.

Award: Scholarship for use in sophomore, junior, senior, graduate, or postgraduate years; not renewable. *Number:* 1. *Amount:* $500.

Eligibility Requirements: Applicant must be enrolled or expecting to enroll full-time at a two-year or four-year institution or university and studying in California.

Application Requirements: Application, transcript. *Deadline:* May 4.

Contact: Dick Watson, Vice President
Calaveras Big Trees Association
PO Box 1196
Arnold, CA 95223-1196
Phone: 209-795-3840
Fax: 209-795-6680
E-mail: cbtuc@goldrush.com

CALIFORNIA WATER AWARENESS CAMPAIGN http://www.wateraware.org

CALIFORNIA WATER AWARENESS CAMPAIGN WATER SCHOLAR

• *See page 57*

CANADIAN RECREATIONAL CANOEING ASSOCIATION http://www.paddlingcanada.com

BILL MASON MEMORIAL SCHOLARSHIP FUND

• *See page 57*

COLLEGEBOUND FOUNDATION http://www.collegeboundfoundation.org

NATIONAL AQUARIUM IN BALTIMORE HENRY HALL SCHOLARSHIP

• *See page 113*

DOGRIB TREATY 11 SCHOLARSHIP COMMITTEE http://www.dt11sc.ca

FRANCIS BLACKDUCK MEMORIAL "STRONG LIKE TWO PEOPLE" AWARDS

Award for students of Dogrib ancestry enrolled in either college, university, or technical school with a major in environmental studies or natural resources sciences/technologies. Preference will be given to individuals who are able to speak fluently in both Dogrib and English.

Academic Fields/Career Goals: Environmental Science; Natural Resources.

Award: Scholarship for use in freshman, sophomore, junior, or senior years. *Number:* 2. *Amount:* $371.

Eligibility Requirements: Applicant must be enrolled or expecting to enroll at a two-year or four-year or technical institution or university.

Application Requirements: Application, transcript. *Deadline:* varies.

Contact: Morven MacPherson, Post Secondary Student Support Coordinator
Dogrib Treaty 11 Scholarship Committee
c/o CJBRHS
Bag #1
Rae-Edzo, NT X0E 0Y0
Canada
Phone: 867-371-3815
Fax: 867-371-3813
E-mail: morvenm@dogrib.net

FRIENDS OF THE FRELINGHUYSEN ARBORETUM http://arboretumfriends.org

BENJAMIN C. BLACKBURN SCHOLARSHIP

One-time award for college undergraduates and graduate students who are pursuing degrees in horticulture, landscape architecture, or environmental studies. Must be a U.S. citizen and New Jersey resident. Must have minimum 3.0 GPA.

Academic Fields/Career Goals: Environmental Science; Horticulture/Floriculture; Landscape Architecture; Natural Resources.

Award: Scholarship for use in sophomore, junior, senior, or graduate years; not renewable. *Number:* 1. *Amount:* $5000.

Eligibility Requirements: Applicant must be enrolled or expecting to enroll full-time at a two-year or four-year institution or university and resident of New Jersey. Applicant must have 3.0 GPA or higher. Available to U.S. citizens.

Application Requirements: Application, essay, references, transcript. *Deadline:* varies.

Contact: Dorothy Hennessey, Scholarship Chairman
Friends of the Frelinghuysen Arboretum
53 East Hanover Avenue
PO Box 1295
Morristown, NJ 07962-1295
Phone: 973-326-7603
Fax: 973-644-9627

HISPANIC COLLEGE FUND, INC. http://www.hispanicfund.org

DEPARTMENT OF ENERGY SCHOLARSHIP PROGRAM
• *See page 125*

INTERNATIONAL ASSOCIATION OF GREAT LAKES RESEARCH http://www.iaglr.org

PAUL W. RODGERS SCHOLARSHIP
• *See page 190*

KENTUCKY NATURAL RESOURCES AND ENVIRONMENTAL PROTECTION CABINET http://www.uky.edu/waterresources

CONSERVATION OF NATURAL RESOURCES SCHOLARSHIP
• *See page 58*

CONSERVATION OF NATURAL RESOURCES SCHOLARSHIP FOR NONTRADITIONAL STUDENTS
• *See page 58*

GEORGE R. CRAFTON SCHOLARSHIP
• *See page 59*

NASA VIRGINIA SPACE GRANT CONSORTIUM http://www.vsgc.odu.edu

VIRGINIA SPACE GRANT CONSORTIUM TEACHER EDUCATION SCHOLARSHIPS
• *See page 102*

NASA WEST VIRGINIA SPACE GRANT CONSORTIUM http://www.nasa.wvu.edu

WEST VIRGINIA SPACE GRANT CONSORTIUM UNDERGRADUATE SCHOLARSHIP PROGRAM
• *See page 102*

NATIONAL GARDEN CLUBS, INC. http://www.gardenclub.org

NATIONAL GARDEN CLUBS, INC. SCHOLARSHIP PROGRAM
• *See page 60*

NATIONAL INVENTORS HALL OF FAME http://www.invent.org/collegiate

COLLEGIATE INVENTORS COMPETITION - GRAND PRIZE
• *See page 71*

COLLEGIATE INVENTORS COMPETITION FOR UNDERGRADUATE STUDENTS
• *See page 71*

NATIONAL SAFETY COUNCIL http://www.cshema.org

CAMPUS SAFETY, HEALTH AND ENVIRONMENTAL MANAGEMENT ASSOCIATION SCHOLARSHIP AWARD PROGRAM

One $2000 scholarship, to encourage the study of safety and environmental management, is available to full-time undergraduate or graduate students in all majors/disciplines. Submit application, transcript, and essay by March 31 deadline. Information and application available at CSHEMA's Web site: http://www.cshema.org.

Academic Fields/Career Goals: Environmental Science; Occupational Safety and Health.

Award: Scholarship for use in freshman, sophomore, junior, senior, or graduate years; not renewable. *Number:* 1. *Amount:* $2000.

Eligibility Requirements: Applicant must be enrolled or expecting to enroll full-time at a four-year institution or university. Available to U.S. and Canadian citizens.

Application Requirements: Application, essay, transcript. *Deadline:* March 31.

Contact: Application available at Web site.

NEW JERSEY DIVISION OF FISH AND WILDLIFE/NJ CHAPTER OF THE WILDLIFE SOCIETY http://www.njfishandwildlife.com

RUSSELL A. COOKINGHAM SCHOLARSHIP
• *See page 116*

OHIO ACADEMY OF SCIENCE/OHIO ENVIRONMENTAL EDUCATION FUND http://www.ohiosci.org

OEEF SCHOLARSHIP

Merit-based, non-renewable, tuition-only scholarships given to undergraduate students admitted to Ohio state or private colleges and universities who can demonstrate their knowledge and commitment to careers in environmental sciences or environmental engineering. Must be in their final year of a program in a two-year or four-year institution. Sophomores in a four-year institution are not eligible.

Academic Fields/Career Goals: Environmental Science.

Award: Scholarship for use in sophomore or senior years; not renewable. *Number:* 18. *Amount:* $1250–$2500.

Eligibility Requirements: Applicant must be enrolled or expecting to enroll full or part-time at a two-year or four-year institution or university; resident of Ohio and studying in Ohio. Applicant must have 3.0 GPA or higher. Available to U.S. citizens.

Application Requirements: Application, essay, resume, references, self-addressed stamped envelope, transcript. *Deadline:* July 1.

Contact: Mr. Lynn E. Elfner, CEO
Ohio Academy of Science/Ohio Environmental Education Fund
1500 West Third Avenue, Suite 228
Columbus, OH 43212-2817
Phone: 614-488-2228
Fax: 614-488-7629
E-mail: oas@iwaynet.net

PENNSYLVANIA ASSOCIATION OF CONSERVATION DISTRICTS AUXILIARY http://www.blairconservationdistrict.org

PACD AUXILIARY SCHOLARSHIPS
• *See page 55*

SOCIETY OF MEXICAN AMERICAN ENGINEERS AND SCIENTISTS http://www.maes-natl.org

GRE AND GRADUATE APPLICATIONS WAIVER
• *See page 72*

TEXAS OUTDOOR WRITERS ASSOCIATION http://www.towa.org

TEXAS OUTDOOR WRITERS ASSOCIATION SCHOLARSHIP
• *See page 165*

UNITED NEGRO COLLEGE FUND http://www.uncf.org

WEYERHAEUSER/UNCF CORPORATE SCHOLARS
• *See page 134*

EUROPEAN STUDIES

AMERICAN HISTORICAL ASSOCIATION http://www.theaha.org

GEORGE L. MOSSE PRIZE

Prize to recognize outstanding major work of scholarly distinction, creativity, and originality in the intellectual and cultural history of Europe since the Renaissance. Copies of work must be sent to each committee member. See Web site (http://www.theaha.org) for names and mailing addresses. Applicant must be a published author.

Academic Fields/Career Goals: European Studies; History.

American Historical Association (continued)

Award: Prize for use in freshman, sophomore, junior, senior, graduate, or postgraduate years; not renewable. *Number:* 1. *Amount:* varies.

Eligibility Requirements: Applicant must be enrolled or expecting to enroll at an institution or university.

Application Requirements: Applicant must enter a contest, copies of work. *Deadline:* May 17.

Contact: Book Prize Administrator
American Historical Association
400 A Street, SE
Washington, DC 20003
E-mail: aha@theaha.org

GEORGE LOUIS BEER PRIZE

Prize for best recent work on any phase of European international history since 1895. Applicant must be published author and U.S. citizen. Based on research, accuracy, originality, and literary merit. Copies of entries must be sent to each committee member. Refer to Web site (http://www.theaha.org) for names and mailing address.

Academic Fields/Career Goals: European Studies; History; Humanities.

Award: Prize for use in freshman, sophomore, junior, senior, graduate, or postgraduate years; not renewable. *Number:* 1. *Amount:* $250–$1000.

Eligibility Requirements: Applicant must be enrolled or expecting to enroll at an institution or university and must have an interest in writing. Available to U.S. citizens.

Application Requirements: Applicant must enter a contest, copies of book. *Deadline:* May 17.

Contact: Book Prize Administrator
American Historical Association
400 A Street, SE
Washington, DC 20003
E-mail: aha@theaha.org

LEO GERSHOY AWARD

Annual award for best recent book published in English on 17th- and 18th-century western European history. Copies of entries must be sent to each committee member. See Web site (http://www.theaha.org) for names and mailing addresses.

Academic Fields/Career Goals: European Studies; History.

Award: Prize for use in freshman, sophomore, junior, senior, graduate, or postgraduate years; not renewable. *Number:* 1. *Amount:* varies.

Eligibility Requirements: Applicant must be enrolled or expecting to enroll at an institution or university and must have an interest in writing. Available to U.S. citizens.

Application Requirements: Applicant must enter a contest, copies of book. *Deadline:* May 17.

Contact: Book Prize Administrator
American Historical Association
400 A Street, SE
Washington, DC 20003
E-mail: aha@theaha.org

AMERICAN SCHOOLS OF ORIENTAL RESEARCH (ASOR)
http://www.asor.org

CYPRUS AMERICAN ARCHAEOLOGICAL RESEARCH INSTITUTE HELENA WYLDE AND STUART SWINY FELLOWSHIP

• *See page 73*

CULTURE CONNECTION
http://www.thecultureconnection.com

CULTURE CONNECTION FOUNDATION SCHOLARSHIP

• *See page 52*

GERMAN ACADEMIC EXCHANGE SERVICE (DAAD)
http://www.daad.org

GERMAN ACADEMIC EXCHANGE INFORMATION VISITS

Grants worth 430 Euros are available for an information visit of 7 to 12 days to groups of 10 to 15 students, accompanied by a faculty member. The purpose of this program is to increase the knowledge of specific German subjects and institutions within the framework of an academic study tour. Preference will be given to groups with a homogeneous academic background. Tours cannot be funded during July and August and between December and January 8. Application should reach DAAD New York at least six months before beginning date of planned visit.

Academic Fields/Career Goals: European Studies; German Studies.

Award: Grant for use in junior, senior, or graduate years; not renewable.

Eligibility Requirements: Applicant must be enrolled or expecting to enroll at an institution or university. Available to U.S. and Canadian citizens.

Application Requirements: Application. *Deadline:* Continuous.

Contact: German Academic Exchange Service (DAAD)
871 United Nations Plaza
New York, NY 10017
Phone: 212-758-3223
Fax: 212-755-5780
E-mail: daadny@daad.org

FASHION DESIGN

OREGON STUDENT ASSISTANCE COMMISSION
http://www.osac.state.or.us

FASHION GROUP INTERNATIONAL OF PORTLAND SCHOLARSHIP

One-time award for Oregon residents planning to pursue a career in a fashion-related field. Must be enrolled at least half-time at the sophomore or higher level. Minimum GPA of 3.0 required. Semifinalists will be interviewed in Portland. Must attend college in Oregon, Washington, California, or Idaho.

Academic Fields/Career Goals: Fashion Design.

Award: Scholarship for use in sophomore, junior, or senior years; not renewable. *Number:* 5. *Amount:* $1500.

Eligibility Requirements: Applicant must be enrolled or expecting to enroll full or part-time at a four-year institution; resident of Oregon and studying in California, Idaho, Oregon, or Washington. Applicant must have 3.0 GPA or higher. Available to U.S. citizens.

Application Requirements: Application, essay, financial need analysis, interview, references, transcript, activity chart. *Deadline:* March 1.

Contact: Director of Grant Programs
Oregon Student Assistance Commission
1500 Valley River Drive, Suite 100
Eugene, OR 97401-7020
Phone: 800-452-8807 Ext. 7395
E-mail: awardinfo@mercury.osac.state.or.us

WORLDSTUDIO FOUNDATION
http://www.worldstudio.org

WORLDSTUDIO FOUNDATION SCHOLARSHIP PROGRAM

• *See page 80*

FILMMAKING/VIDEO

ACADEMY FOUNDATION OF THE ACADEMY OF MOTION PICTURE ARTS AND SCIENCES
http://www.oscars.org/saa

ACADEMY OF MOTION PICTURE STUDENT ACADEMY AWARD-HONORARY FOREIGN FILM

One award is given to an applicant from an institution outside the U.S. and a member of CILECT. Applications are limited to one per school, per year. Visit Web site for applications: http://www.oscars.org/saa.

Academic Fields/Career Goals: Filmmaking/Video.

Award: Prize for use in freshman, sophomore, junior, senior, or graduate years; not renewable. *Number:* 1. *Amount:* $1000.

Eligibility Requirements: Applicant must be enrolled or expecting to enroll at a four-year institution or university.

Application Requirements: Application, applicant must enter a contest, self-addressed stamped envelope, film or digital betacam tape. *Deadline:* March 19.

Contact: Richard Miller, Awards Administration Director
Academy Foundation of the Academy of Motion Picture Arts and Sciences
8949 Wilshire Boulevard
Beverly Hills, CA 90211-1972
E-mail: rmiller@oscars.org

ACADEMY OF MOTION PICTURES STUDENT ACADEMY AWARDS

Available to students who have made a narrative, documentary, alternative, or animated film of up to sixty minutes within the curricular structure of an accredited college or university. Initial entry must be on 1/2 inch VHS tape. 16mm or larger format print or digital betacam tape required for further rounds. Prizes awarded in four categories. Each category awards Gold ($5000), Silver ($3000), and Bronze ($2000). Visit Web site for details and application (http://www.oscars.org/saa).

Academic Fields/Career Goals: Filmmaking/Video.

Award: Prize for use in freshman, sophomore, junior, senior, or graduate years; not renewable. *Number:* 3–12. *Amount:* $2000–$5000.

Eligibility Requirements: Applicant must be enrolled or expecting to enroll full-time at a two-year or four-year institution or university. Available to U.S. and non-U.S. citizens.

Application Requirements: Application, applicant must enter a contest, VHS tape. *Deadline:* April 1.

Contact: Richard Miller, Awards Administration Director
Academy Foundation of the Academy of Motion Picture Arts and Sciences
8949 Wilshire Boulevard
Beverly Hills, CA 90211-1972
Phone: 310-247-3000 Ext. 129
Fax: 310-859-9619
E-mail: rmiller@oscars.org

ACADEMY OF TELEVISION ARTS AND SCIENCES FOUNDATION http://www.emmys.tv/foundation

ACADEMY OF TELEVISION ARTS AND SCIENCES COLLEGE TELEVISION AWARDS

• *See page 84*

ADC RESEARCH INSTITUTE http://www.adc.org

JACK SHAHEEN MASS COMMUNICATIONS SCHOLARSHIP AWARD

• *See page 156*

ADVERTISING FEDERATION OF FORT WAYNE, INC. http://adfedfortwayne.org

ADVERTISING FEDERATION OF FORT WAYNE, INC., SCHOLARSHIP

• *See page 156*

AMERICAN AUTOMOBILE ASSOCIATION http://aaapublicaffairs.com

NATIONAL SENIOR HIGH COMMUNICATION CONTEST

Contest for graduating high school seniors. Competition areas include graphic arts, writing, and audiovisual. Contact local AAA or CAA for details.

Academic Fields/Career Goals: Filmmaking/Video; Graphics/Graphic Arts/Printing; Literature/English/Writing.

Award: Scholarship for use in freshman, sophomore, junior, or senior years; not renewable. *Number:* 30–40. *Amount:* $100–$5000.

Eligibility Requirements: Applicant must be high school student and planning to enroll or expecting to enroll full or part-time at a two-year or four-year or technical institution or university. Available to U.S. and Canadian citizens.

Application Requirements: Applicant must enter a contest. *Deadline:* January 27.

Contact: Shawn Rudd, Educational Technologist
American Automobile Association
1000 AAA Drive
Heathrow, FL 32746-5063
Phone: 407-444-7073
Fax: 407-444-7150
E-mail: srudd@national.aaa.com

AMERICAN HISTORICAL ASSOCIATION http://www.theaha.org

JOHN E. O'CONNOR FILM AWARD

Award to recognize outstanding interpretations of history on film and video. Copies must be sent to each committee member. See Web site (http://www.theaha.org) for names and mailing addresses, and further details.

Academic Fields/Career Goals: Filmmaking/Video; History; Humanities.

Award: Prize for use in freshman, sophomore, junior, senior, graduate, or postgraduate years; not renewable. *Number:* 1. *Amount:* varies.

Eligibility Requirements: Applicant must be enrolled or expecting to enroll at an institution or university. Available to U.S. citizens.

Application Requirements: Applicant must enter a contest, copies of video or film. *Deadline:* June 2.

Contact: Administrative Assistant
American Historical Association
400 A Street, SE
Washington, DC 20003
E-mail: aha@theaha.org

BOSTON FILM AND VIDEO FOUNDATION

NEW ENGLAND FILM AND VIDEO FESTIVAL AWARDS

One-time film and video awards available to students who are residents of New England or upstate New York. Must be U.S. citizen. Application fee of $25.

Academic Fields/Career Goals: Filmmaking/Video.

Award: Prize for use in freshman, sophomore, junior, or senior years; not renewable. *Number:* 9–15. *Amount:* $250–$5000.

Eligibility Requirements: Applicant must be enrolled or expecting to enroll full or part-time at a two-year or four-year institution or university and resident of Connecticut, Maine, Massachusetts, New Hampshire, New York, Rhode Island, or Vermont. Available to U.S. citizens.

Application Requirements: Application, applicant must enter a contest, driver's license, photo. *Fee:* $25. *Deadline:* November 15.

Contact: Sandra Sullivan, Festival Co-director
Boston Film and Video Foundation
119 Braintree Street, Box 159, Suite 104
Boston, MA 02134
Phone: 617-783-9241 Ext. 12
Fax: 617-783-4368
E-mail: festival@bfvf.org

CHARLES & LUCILLE KING FAMILY FOUNDATION, INC. http://www.kingfoundation.org

CHARLES AND LUCILLE KING FAMILY FOUNDATION SCHOLARSHIPS

• *See page 159*

GOLDEN KEY INTERNATIONAL HONOUR SOCIETY http://www.goldenkey.org

PERFORMING ARTS SHOWCASE

$1000 will be awarded in each of the following six categories: vocal performance, dance, drama, original musical composition, filmmaking, instrumental performance. See Web site for more information: http://goldenkey.gsu.edu.

Academic Fields/Career Goals: Filmmaking/Video; Music; Performing Arts.

Golden Key International Honour Society (continued)

Award: Scholarship for use in junior, senior, graduate, or postgraduate years; not renewable. *Number:* 6. *Amount:* $1000.

Eligibility Requirements: Applicant must be enrolled or expecting to enroll at an institution or university. Available to U.S. and non-U.S. citizens.

Application Requirements: Application, applicant must enter a contest, videotaped performance. *Deadline:* March 1.

Contact: Member Services
Golden Key International Honour Society
621 North Avenue, NE
Suite C-100
Atlanta, GA 30308
Phone: 404-377-2400
Fax: 678-420-6757
E-mail: scholarships@goldenkey.org

ILLUMINATING ENGINEERING SOCIETY OF NORTH AMERICA–GOLDEN GATE SECTION http://www.iesgg.org

ALAN LUCAS MEMORIAL EDUCATIONAL SCHOLARSHIP
• *See page 77*

ROBERT W. THUNEN MEMORIAL SCHOLARSHIPS
• *See page 77*

INSTITUTE FOR HUMANE STUDIES http://www.theihs.org

FILM AND FICTION SCHOLARSHIP
• *See page 87*

KCNC-TV CHANNEL 4 NEWS http://www.news4colorado.com

NEWS 4 PETER ROGOT MEDIA SCHOLARSHIP
• *See page 161*

MEDIA ACTION NETWORK FOR ASIAN AMERICANS http://www.manaa.org

MANAA MEDIA SCHOLARSHIPS FOR ASIAN AMERICAN STUDENTS
• *See page 89*

NATIONAL FOUNDATION FOR ADVANCEMENT IN THE ARTS http://www.artsawards.org

ARTS RECOGNITION AND TALENT SEARCH (ARTS)
• *See page 89*

NATIONAL WRITERS ASSOCIATION FOUNDATION http://www.nationalwriters.com

NATIONAL WRITERS ASSOCIATION FOUNDATION SCHOLARSHIPS
• *See page 162*

OUTDOOR WRITERS ASSOCIATION OF AMERICA http://www.owaa.org

OUTDOOR WRITERS ASSOCIATION OF AMERICA BODIE MCDOWELL SCHOLARSHIP AWARD
• *See page 163*

PHI DELTA THETA EDUCATIONAL FOUNDATION http://phideltatheta.org

FRANCIS D. LYON SCHOLARSHIPS

Program run in the honor of Francis D. Lyon who had a distinguished motion picture and television career as a film editor, director, and producer. One-time scholarship for undergraduate junior or senior, graduate, or post-graduate student. Applicants must be pursuing a filmmaking career.

Academic Fields/Career Goals: Filmmaking/Video.

Award: Scholarship for use in junior, senior, graduate, or postgraduate years; not renewable. *Number:* 2. *Amount:* $2000–$3000.

Eligibility Requirements: Applicant must be enrolled or expecting to enroll full-time at a four-year institution or university. Available to U.S. and non-U.S. citizens.

Application Requirements: Application, essay, photo, references, transcript. *Deadline:* March 15.

Contact: Carmalieta Jenkins, Assistant to the President
Phi Delta Theta Educational Foundation
2 South Campus Avenue
Oxford, OH 45056-1872
Phone: 513-523-6966
Fax: 513-523-9200
E-mail: carmalieta@phideltatheta.org

POLISH ARTS CLUB OF BUFFALO SCHOLARSHIP FOUNDATION

POLISH ARTS CLUB OF BUFFALO SCHOLARSHIP FOUNDATION TRUST
• *See page 84*

PRINCESS GRACE FOUNDATION-USA http://www.pgfusa.com

PRINCESS GRACE SCHOLARSHIPS IN DANCE, THEATER, AND FILM

Scholarships are offered as follows: Dance: for any year of training after the first year; Theater: for last year of study in acting, directing, designing; Film: for senior/master's thesis projects. Must be a U.S. citizen or permanent resident. Must include a video and nominator's statements. Deadlines: Theater: March 31, Dance: April 30, and Film: June 1. Refer to Web site for application: http://www.pgfusa.com.

Academic Fields/Career Goals: Filmmaking/Video; Performing Arts.

Award: Scholarship for use in senior, or graduate years; not renewable. *Number:* 15–20. *Amount:* $5000–$25,000.

Eligibility Requirements: Applicant must be enrolled or expecting to enroll full-time at a four-year institution or university. Available to U.S. citizens.

Application Requirements: Application, essay, photo, portfolio, resume, references, self-addressed stamped envelope, nomination. *Deadline:* varies.

Contact: Christine Giancatarino, Executive Director
Princess Grace Foundation-USA
150 East 58th Street, 25th Floor
New York, NY 10155
Phone: 212-317-1470
Fax: 212-317-1473

RHODE ISLAND FOUNDATION http://www.rifoundation.org

RHODE ISLAND ADVERTISING SCHOLARSHIP

One-time award for a Rhode Island resident with an advertising-related major who intends to pursue a career in advertising, public relations, marketing, graphic design, film, or broadcast production. Must be a college sophomore or above.

Academic Fields/Career Goals: Filmmaking/Video; Graphics/Graphic Arts/Printing; TV/Radio Broadcasting.

Award: Scholarship for use in sophomore, junior, or senior years; not renewable. *Number:* 1. *Amount:* $5000.

Eligibility Requirements: Applicant must be enrolled or expecting to enroll full or part-time at a four-year institution and resident of Rhode Island.

Application Requirements: Application, financial need analysis, references, self-addressed stamped envelope, transcript. *Deadline:* April 30.

Contact: Scholarship Coordinator
Rhode Island Foundation
1 Union Station
Providence, RI 02903
Phone: 401-274-4564
Fax: 401-272-1359

SAN FRANCISCO FOUNDATION http://www.sff.org

PHELAN ART AWARD IN FILMMAKING

Award presented in every even-numbered year to recognize achievement in filmmaking. Must have been born in California, but need not be a current resident. Applicants must provide a copy of their birth certificate with their application. This award is not a scholarship. See Web site at http://www.sff.org for further information and deadlines.

Academic Fields/Career Goals: Filmmaking/Video.

Award: Prize for use in freshman, sophomore, junior, senior, graduate, or postgraduate years; not renewable. *Number:* 1. *Amount:* $2500–$7500.

Eligibility Requirements: Applicant must be enrolled or expecting to enroll at an institution or university. Available to U.S. citizens.

Application Requirements: Application, applicant must enter a contest, self-addressed stamped envelope. *Deadline:* varies.

Contact: Art Awards Coordinator
San Francisco Foundation
225 Bush Street, Suite 500
San Francisco, CA 94104
Phone: 415-733-8500

PHELAN ART AWARD IN VIDEO

Award presented in every even-numbered year to recognize achievement in video. Must have been born in California, but need not be a current resident. Applicants must provide a copy of their birth certificates with their application. This award is not a scholarship. See Web site at http://www.sff.org for further information and deadlines.

Academic Fields/Career Goals: Filmmaking/Video.

Award: Prize for use in freshman, sophomore, junior, senior, graduate, or postgraduate years; not renewable. *Number:* 1–2. *Amount:* $2500–$7500.

Eligibility Requirements: Applicant must be enrolled or expecting to enroll at an institution or university. Available to U.S. citizens.

Application Requirements: Application, applicant must enter a contest, self-addressed stamped envelope. *Deadline:* varies.

Contact: Art Awards Coordinator
San Francisco Foundation
225 Bush Street, Suite 500
San Francisco, CA 94104
Phone: 415-733-8500

TELETOON http://www.teletoon.com

TELETOON ANIMATION SCHOLARSHIP AWARD COMPETITION

• *See page 90*

UNIVERSITY FILM AND VIDEO ASSOCIATION http://www.ufva.org

UNIVERSITY FILM AND VIDEO ASSOCIATION CAROLE FIELDING STUDENT GRANTS

Up to $5000 is available for production grants in narrative, documentary, experimental, new-media/installation, or animation. Up to $1000 is available for grants in research. Applicant must be sponsored by a faculty person who is an active member of the University Film and Video Association. Fifty percent of award distributed upon completion of project.

Academic Fields/Career Goals: Filmmaking/Video.

Award: Grant for use in freshman, sophomore, junior, senior, or graduate years; not renewable. *Number:* up to 5. *Amount:* $1000–$5000.

Eligibility Requirements: Applicant must be enrolled or expecting to enroll full or part-time at a two-year or four-year institution or university. Available to U.S. and non-U.S. citizens.

Application Requirements: Application, essay, resume, references, project description, budget. *Deadline:* January 1.

Contact: Prof. Robert Johnson, Jr., Chair, Carole Fielding Grants
University Film and Video Association
Framingham State College, 100 State Street
Framingham, MA 01701-9101
Phone: 508-626-4684
Fax: 508-626-4847
E-mail: rjohnso@frc.mass.edu

WORLDFEST INTERNATIONAL FILM AND VIDEO FESTIVAL http://www.worldfest.org

WORLDFEST STUDENT FILM AWARD

This is a cash award program for student films, both shorts and features. Film must be entered into the Worldfest International Film and Video Festival by December 15 to be considered for an award. Application fee is $45. Entry form available on Web site: http://worldfest.org.

Academic Fields/Career Goals: Filmmaking/Video.

Award: Prize for use in freshman, sophomore, junior, senior, or graduate years; not renewable. *Number:* 10. *Amount:* $1000–$10,000.

Eligibility Requirements: Applicant must be enrolled or expecting to enroll full or part-time at a two-year or four-year or technical institution or university. Available to U.S. and non-U.S. citizens.

Application Requirements: Application, applicant must enter a contest, film/tape entry. *Fee:* $45. *Deadline:* December 15.

Contact: Hunter Todd, Executive Director
Worldfest International Film and Video Festival
PO Box 56566
Houston, TX 77256-6566
Phone: 713-965-9955
Fax: 713-965-9960
E-mail: mail@worldfest.org

WORLDSTUDIO FOUNDATION http://www.worldstudio.org

WORLDSTUDIO FOUNDATION SCHOLARSHIP PROGRAM

• *See page 80*

FIRE SCIENCES

INDEPENDENT LABORATORIES INSTITUTE SCHOLARSHIP ALLIANCE http://www.acil.org

INDEPENDENT LABORATORIES INSTITUTE SCHOLARSHIP ALLIANCE

• *See page 69*

INTERNATIONAL ASSOCIATION OF ARSON INVESTIGATORS EDUCATIONAL FOUNDATION, INC. http://www.fire-investigators.org/

JOHN CHARLES WILSON SCHOLARSHIP

One-time award to members in good standing of IAAI or the immediate family of a member or must be sponsored by an IAAI member. Must enroll or plan to enroll full-time in an accredited college or university that offers courses in police, fire sciences, or any arson investigation-related field. Application available at Web site. Deadline is February 15.

Academic Fields/Career Goals: Fire Sciences; Law Enforcement/Police Administration.

Award: Scholarship for use in freshman, sophomore, junior, senior, or graduate years; not renewable. *Number:* 5–10. *Amount:* $500–$1000.

Eligibility Requirements: Applicant must be enrolled or expecting to enroll full-time at a two-year or four-year institution or university. Available to U.S. and non-U.S. citizens.

Application Requirements: Application, essay, references, transcript. *Deadline:* February 15.

Contact: Marsha Sipes, Office Manager
International Association of Arson Investigators Educational Foundation, Inc.
12770 Boenker Road
Bridgeton, MO 63044
Phone: 314-739-4224
Fax: 314-739-4219
E-mail: iaai@firearson.com

LEARNING FOR LIFE http://www.learning-for-life.org/exploring

INTERNATIONAL ASSOCIATIONS OF FIRE CHIEFS FOUNDATION SCHOLARSHIP

The International Association of Fire Chiefs Foundation coordinates a yearly $500 scholarship program to assist Explorers in pursuing a career in the fire

Learning for Life (continued)

sciences. For more information visit http://www.learning-for-life.org/exploring. Applicant must be younger than 21 years of age.

Academic Fields/Career Goals: Fire Sciences.

Award: Scholarship for use in freshman, sophomore, junior, or senior years; not renewable. *Number:* 1. *Amount:* $500.

Eligibility Requirements: Applicant must be age 20 or under and enrolled or expecting to enroll full-time at a four-year institution. Available to U.S. citizens.

Application Requirements: Application, essay, references, transcript. *Deadline:* July 1.

Contact: Learning for Life
1325 West Walnut Hill Lane, Sum 310
PO Box 152079
Irving, TX 75015-2079
Phone: 972-580-2000

MARYLAND HIGHER EDUCATION COMMISSION http://www.mhec.state.md.us

FIREFIGHTER, AMBULANCE, AND RESCUE SQUAD MEMBER TUITION REIMBURSEMENT PROGRAM-MARYLAND

Award intended to reimburse members of rescue organizations serving Maryland communities for tuition costs of course work towards a degree or certificate in fire service or medical technology. Must attend a two- or four-year school in Maryland. Minimum 2.0 GPA.

Academic Fields/Career Goals: Fire Sciences; Health and Medical Sciences; Trade/Technical Specialties.

Award: Scholarship for use in freshman, sophomore, junior, or senior years; not renewable. *Number:* 100–300. *Amount:* $200–$4000.

Eligibility Requirements: Applicant must be enrolled or expecting to enroll full or part-time at a two-year or four-year institution or university; resident of Maryland and studying in Maryland. Applicant or parent of applicant must have employment or volunteer experience in police/firefighting. Available to U.S. citizens.

Application Requirements: Application, transcript. *Deadline:* July 1.

Contact: Gerrie Rogers, Office of Student Financial Assistance
Maryland Higher Education Commission
839 Bestgate Road, Suite 400
Annapolis, MD 21401-3013
Phone: 410-260-4574
Fax: 410-260-3203
E-mail: ofsamail@mhec.state.md.us

FLEXOGRAPHY

TAG AND LABEL MANUFACTURERS INSTITUTE, INC. http://www.tlmi.com

TAG AND LABEL MANUFACTURERS, INC., SCHOLARSHIP FUND

• *See page 234*

FOOD SCIENCE/NUTRITION

ALASKA COMMISSION ON POSTSECONDARY EDUCATION http://www.state.ak.us/acpe/

A.W. "WINN" BRINDLE MEMORIAL EDUCATION LOANS

• *See page 52*

AMERICAN ASSOCIATION OF CEREAL CHEMISTS http://www.aaccnet.org

UNDERGRADUATE SCHOLARSHIP AWARD

• *See page 234*

AMERICAN DIETETIC ASSOCIATION http://www.eatright.org

AMERICAN DIETETIC ASSOCIATION FOUNDATION SCHOLARSHIP PROGRAM

ADAF scholarships are available for undergraduate and graduate students enrolled in programs, including dietetic internships, preparing for entry to dietetics practice as well as dietetics professionals engaged in continuing education at the graduate level. Scholarship funds are provided by many state dietetic associations, dietetic practice groups, past ADA leaders, and corporate donors. All scholarships require ADA membership. Details available on Web site http://www.eatright.org.

Academic Fields/Career Goals: Food Science/Nutrition.

Award: Scholarship for use in sophomore, junior, senior, graduate, or postgraduate years; not renewable. *Number:* 200. *Amount:* $500–$5000.

Eligibility Requirements: Applicant must be enrolled or expecting to enroll full or part-time at a two-year or four-year institution or university. Applicant or parent of applicant must be member of American Dietetic Association. Available to U.S. citizens.

Application Requirements: Application, essay, financial need analysis, references, transcript. *Deadline:* February 15.

Contact: Eva Donovan, Education Coordinator
American Dietetic Association
120 South Riverside Plaza, Suite 2000
Chicago, IL 60606-6695
Phone: 312-899-0040 Ext. 4876
Fax: 312-899-4817
E-mail: education@eatright.org

AMERICAN INSTITUTE OF WINE AND FOOD-PACIFIC NORTHWEST CHAPTER http://www.aiwf.org

CULINARY, VINIFERA, AND HOSPITALITY SCHOLARSHIP

One-time award available to residents of Washington State. Must be enrolled full-time in an accredited culinary, vinifera, or hospitality program in Washington State. Must have completed two years. Minimum 3.0 GPA required.

Academic Fields/Career Goals: Food Science/Nutrition; Food Service/Hospitality; Hospitality Management.

Award: Scholarship for use in junior year; not renewable. *Number:* 1–2. *Amount:* $1000–$2000.

Eligibility Requirements: Applicant must be enrolled or expecting to enroll full-time at a four-year or technical institution; resident of Washington and studying in Washington. Applicant must have 3.0 GPA or higher. Available to U.S. and non-U.S. citizens.

Application Requirements: Application, essay, references. *Deadline:* Continuous.

Contact: See Web site.

AMERICAN SOCIETY FOR ENOLOGY AND VITICULTURE http://www.asev.org

AMERICAN SOCIETY FOR ENOLOGY AND VITICULTURE SCHOLARSHIPS

• *See page 56*

ASSOCIATION FOR FOOD AND DRUG OFFICIALS http://www.afdo.org

ASSOCIATION FOR FOOD AND DRUG OFFICIALS SCHOLARSHIP FUND

$1500 scholarship for students in their third or fourth year of college/university who have demonstrated a desire for a career in research, regulatory work, quality control, or teaching in an area related to some aspect of food, drugs, or consumer products safety. Minimum 3.0 GPA required in first two years of undergraduate study. For further information, visit Web site at http://www.afdo.org.

Academic Fields/Career Goals: Food Science/Nutrition.

Award: Scholarship for use in junior or senior years; not renewable. *Number:* 2. *Amount:* $1500.

Eligibility Requirements: Applicant must be enrolled or expecting to enroll at a four-year institution or university. Applicant must have 3.0 GPA or higher. Available to U.S. citizens.

Application Requirements: Application, essay, references, transcript. *Deadline:* February 1.

Contact: Association for Food and Drug Officials
2550 Kingston Road
Suite 311
York, PA 17402

CALIFORNIA ADOLESCENT NUTRITION AND FITNESS (CANFIT) PROGRAM http://www.canfit.org

CALIFORNIA ADOLESCENT NUTRITION AND FITNESS (CANFIT) PROGRAM SCHOLARSHIP

Award for undergraduate and graduate African-American, American-Indian/Alaska Native, Asian/Pacific Islander or Latino/Hispanic students who express financial need and are studying nutrition, physical fitness, or culinary arts in California. Minimum GPA of 2.5. Must be California resident. Application deadline: March 31. Please see Web site for essay topic: http://www.canfit.org.

Academic Fields/Career Goals: Food Science/Nutrition; Food Service/Hospitality; Health and Medical Sciences; Sports-related.

Award: Scholarship for use in junior, senior, graduate, or postgraduate years; not renewable. *Number:* 10–15. *Amount:* $500–$1500.

Eligibility Requirements: Applicant must be American Indian/Alaska Native, Asian/Pacific Islander, Black (non-Hispanic), or Hispanic; enrolled or expecting to enroll full or part-time at a four-year or technical institution or university; resident of California and studying in California. Applicant must have 2.5 GPA or higher. Available to U.S. citizens.

Application Requirements: Application, essay, financial need analysis, photo, references, transcript, letter by applicant about themselves. *Deadline:* March 31.

Contact: CANFit Scholarship Program
California Adolescent Nutrition and Fitness (CANFit) Program
2140 Shattuck Avenue, Suite 610
Berkeley, CA 94704
Phone: 510-644-1533
Fax: 510-644-1535
E-mail: info@canfit.org

CHILD NUTRITION FOUNDATION http://www.asfsa.org

NANCY CURRY SCHOLARSHIP

Scholarship assists members of the American School Food Service Association and their dependents to pursue educational and career advancement in school foodservice or child nutrition.

Academic Fields/Career Goals: Food Science/Nutrition; Food Service/Hospitality.

Award: Scholarship for use in freshman, sophomore, junior, senior, or graduate years; not renewable. *Number:* 1. *Amount:* $1000.

Eligibility Requirements: Applicant must be enrolled or expecting to enroll full or part-time at a two-year or four-year or technical institution or university. Applicant or parent of applicant must be member of American School Food Service Association. Applicant or parent of applicant must have employment or volunteer experience in food service. Applicant must have 3.0 GPA or higher. Available to U.S. citizens.

Application Requirements: Application, essay, resume, references, transcript, proof of enrollment. *Deadline:* April 15.

Contact: Ruth O'Brien, Scholarship Manager
Child Nutrition Foundation
700 South Washington Street, Suite 300
Alexandria, VA 22314
Phone: 703-739-3900 Ext. 150

SCHWAN'S FOOD SERVICE SCHOLARSHIP

Program is designed to assist members of the American School Food Service Association and their dependents as they pursue educational advancement in the field of child nutrition.

Academic Fields/Career Goals: Food Science/Nutrition; Food Service/Hospitality.

Award: Scholarship for use in freshman,,sophomore, junior, senior, or graduate years; not renewable. *Number:* 50–60. *Amount:* $100–$1000.

Eligibility Requirements: Applicant must be enrolled or expecting to enroll full or part-time at a two-year or four-year or technical institution or university. Applicant or parent of applicant must be member of American School Food Service Association. Applicant or parent of applicant must have employment or volunteer experience in food service. Applicant must have 2.5 GPA or higher. Available to U.S. citizens.

Application Requirements: Application, essay, resume, references, transcript, proof of enrollment. *Deadline:* April 15.

Contact: Ruth O'Brien, Scholarship Manager
Child Nutrition Foundation
700 South Washington Street, Suite 300
Alexandria, VA 22314
Phone: 703-739-3900 Ext. 150
E-mail: robrien@asfsa.org

CULINARY TRUST http://www.iacpfoundation.org

CULINARY TRUST SCHOLARSHIP PROGRAM FOR CULINARY STUDY AND RESEARCH

Scholarships for beginning students, continuing education, culinary professionals and independent research. Applicants must have at least two years of food service experience (paid, volunteer, or combination of both), a minimum 3.0 GPA and write an essay. There is a $25 application fee.

Academic Fields/Career Goals: Food Science/Nutrition; Food Service/Hospitality.

Award: Scholarship for use in freshman, sophomore, junior, senior, graduate, or postgraduate years; not renewable. *Number:* 21. *Amount:* $1000–$5000.

Eligibility Requirements: Applicant must be enrolled or expecting to enroll full or part-time at a two-year or four-year or technical institution or university. Applicant or parent of applicant must have employment or volunteer experience in food service. Applicant must have 3.0 GPA or higher. Available to U.S. and non-U.S. citizens.

Application Requirements: Application, essay, interview, references, transcript. *Fee:* $25. *Deadline:* December 15.

Contact: Trina Gribbins, Director of Administration
Culinary Trust
304 West Liberty Street, Suite 201
Louisville, KY 40202-3068
Phone: 502-581-9786 Ext. 264
Fax: 502-589-3602
E-mail: tgribbins@hqtrs.com

HERB SOCIETY OF AMERICA http://www.herbsociety.org

HERB SOCIETY RESEARCH GRANTS

• *See page 69*

HISPANIC COLLEGE FUND, INC. http://www.hispanicfund.org

NATIONAL HISPANIC EXPLORERS SCHOLARSHIP PROGRAM

• *See page 69*

ILLINOIS RESTAURANT ASSOCIATION EDUCATIONAL FOUNDATION http://www.illinoisrestaurants.org

ILLINOIS RESTAURANT ASSOCIATION EDUCATIONAL FOUNDATION SCHOLARSHIPS

• *See page 180*

INSTITUTE OF FOOD TECHNOLOGISTS http://www.ift.org

INSTITUTE OF FOOD TECHNOLOGISTS FOOD ENGINEERING DIVISION JUNIOR/SENIOR SCHOLARSHIP

One-time award for junior or senior level students in an Institute of Food Technologists approved program, with demonstrated intent to pursue professional activities in food science or food technology. Submit recommendation. Applications must be sent to department head of educational institution, not IFT.

Academic Fields/Career Goals: Food Science/Nutrition.

Institute of Food Technologists (continued)

Award: Scholarship for use in sophomore, junior, or senior years; not renewable. *Number:* 61. *Amount:* $1000–$2250.

Eligibility Requirements: Applicant must be enrolled or expecting to enroll at a four-year institution or university. Available to U.S. citizens.

Application Requirements: Application, references, transcript. *Deadline:* February 1.

Contact: Administrator
Institute of Food Technologists
525 West Van Buren Street, Suite 1000
Chicago, IL 60607
Phone: 312-782-8424
Fax: 312-782-8348

INSTITUTE OF FOOD TECHNOLOGISTS FRESHMAN SCHOLARSHIPS

Twenty-four awards for scholastically outstanding high school graduates or seniors entering college in an approved four-year program in food sciences or technology. Program must be approved by Institute of Food Technologists Education Committee. Submit application to head of college. Merit-based, one-time award of $1000-$1500.

Academic Fields/Career Goals: Food Science/Nutrition.

Award: Scholarship for use in freshman year; not renewable. *Number:* 24. *Amount:* $1000–$1500.

Eligibility Requirements: Applicant must be enrolled or expecting to enroll full-time at a four-year institution or university. Applicant must have 3.5 GPA or higher. Available to U.S. and non-U.S. citizens.

Application Requirements: Application, references, transcript. *Deadline:* February 15.

Contact: Administrator
Institute of Food Technologists
525 West Van Buren Street, Suite 1000
Chicago, IL 60607
Phone: 312-782-8424
Fax: 312-782-8348

INSTITUTE OF FOOD TECHNOLOGISTS QUALITY ASSURANCE DIVISION JUNIOR/SENIOR SCHOLARSHIPS

One-time award for college juniors and seniors who are taking or have taken a course in quality assurance and have demonstrated an interest in the quality assurance area. Submit recommendation. Applications must be sent to department head of educational institution, not IFT.

Academic Fields/Career Goals: Food Science/Nutrition.

Award: Scholarship for use in junior or senior years; not renewable. *Number:* 2. *Amount:* $2000.

Eligibility Requirements: Applicant must be enrolled or expecting to enroll at a four-year institution. Available to U.S. citizens.

Application Requirements: Application, references, transcript. *Deadline:* February 1.

Contact: Administrator
Institute of Food Technologists
525 West Van Buren Street, Suite 1000
Chicago, IL 60607
Phone: 312-782-8424
Fax: 312-782-8348

INSTITUTE OF FOOD TECHNOLOGISTS SOPHOMORE SCHOLARSHIPS

Twenty-two awards available to college freshmen for use in sophomore year. Applicants must major in food science or food technology in a four-year Institute of Food Technologists Education Committee-approved program and have a 2.5 GPA. One-time award of $1000. Applications must be submitted to the department head of educational institution.

Academic Fields/Career Goals: Food Science/Nutrition.

Award: Scholarship for use in sophomore year; not renewable. *Number:* 22. *Amount:* $1000.

Eligibility Requirements: Applicant must be enrolled or expecting to enroll full-time at a four-year institution or university. Applicant must have 2.5 GPA or higher. Available to U.S. citizens.

Application Requirements: Application, references, transcript. *Deadline:* March 1.

Contact: Administrator
Institute of Food Technologists
525 West Van Buren Street, Suite 1000
Chicago, IL 60607
Phone: 312-782-8424
Fax: 312-782-8348

INSTITUTE OF FOOD TECHNOLOGISTS/MASTER FOODS USA UNDERGRADUATE MENTORED SCHOLARSHIP

Mentored scholarships available for students from a minority group pursuing studies in Food Science. Must have a 3.0 GPA. Deadline is June 1.

Academic Fields/Career Goals: Food Science/Nutrition.

Award: Scholarship for use in freshman, sophomore, junior, or senior years; renewable. *Number:* 7. *Amount:* $4000.

Eligibility Requirements: Applicant must be American Indian/Alaska Native, Asian/Pacific Islander, Black (non-Hispanic), or Hispanic and enrolled or expecting to enroll at a two-year or four-year institution. Applicant must have 3.0 GPA or higher.

Application Requirements: Application, test scores. *Deadline:* June 1.

Contact: Administrator
Institute of Food Technologists
525 West Van Buren Street
Suite 1000
Chicago, IL 60607
Phone: 312-782-8424
Fax: 312-782-8348

INTERNATIONAL FOODSERVICE EDITORIAL COUNCIL http://www.ifec-is-us.com

INTERNATIONAL FOODSERVICE EDITORIAL COUNCIL COMMUNICATIONS SCHOLARSHIP

• *See page 160*

JAMES BEARD FOUNDATION, INC. http://www.jamesbeard.org

AAA FIVE DIAMOND SCHOLARSHIP

One-time award towards tuition at an accredited culinary school of the applicant's choice. Must submit a 500-word essay on culinary goals and how this scholarship can help attain them. Candidates must demonstrate a strong commitment to the culinary arts, an exceptional academic or work record, and financial need. See Web site at http://www.jamesbeard.org for further details.

Academic Fields/Career Goals: Food Science/Nutrition.

Award: Scholarship for use in freshman, sophomore, junior, senior, or graduate years; not renewable. *Number:* 1. *Amount:* $5000.

Eligibility Requirements: Applicant must be enrolled or expecting to enroll at an institution or university. Available to U.S. and non-U.S. citizens.

Application Requirements: Application, essay, financial need analysis, references, transcript. *Deadline:* May 1.

Contact: Caroline Stuart, Scholarship Director
James Beard Foundation, Inc.
167 West 12th Street
New York, NY 10011
Phone: 212-675-4984 Ext. 311
Fax: 212-645-1438
E-mail: jamesbeardfound@hotmail.com

AMERICAN EXPRESS BEACON SCHOLARSHIP

Two $2000 awards toward tuition at an accredited culinary school of student's choice. See Web site http://www.jamesbeard.org for further details.

Academic Fields/Career Goals: Food Science/Nutrition.

Award: Scholarship for use in freshman, sophomore, junior, senior, or graduate years; not renewable. *Number:* 2. *Amount:* $2000.

Eligibility Requirements: Applicant must be enrolled or expecting to enroll at an institution or university. Available to U.S. and non-U.S. citizens.

Application Requirements: Application, essay, financial need analysis, references, transcript. *Deadline:* May 1.

Contact: Caroline Stuart, Scholarship Director
James Beard Foundation, Inc.
167 West 12th Street
New York, NY 10011
Phone: 212-675-4984 Ext. 311
Fax: 212-645-1438
E-mail: jamesbeardfound@hotmail.com

ARTIE CUTLER MEMORIAL SCHOLARSHIP

One-time award towards tuition at an accredited culinary school of student's choice. Applicant must submit a 500-word essay on culinary goals and how this scholarship can help attain them. Candidates must demonstrate a strong commitment to the culinary arts, an exceptional academic or work record, and financial need. See Web site at http://www.jamesbeard.org for further details.

Academic Fields/Career Goals: Food Science/Nutrition.

Award: Scholarship for use in freshman, sophomore, junior, senior, or graduate years; not renewable. *Number:* 1. *Amount:* $4000.

Eligibility Requirements: Applicant must be enrolled or expecting to enroll at an institution or university. Available to U.S. and non-U.S. citizens.

Application Requirements: Application, essay, financial need analysis, references, transcript. *Deadline:* May 1.

Contact: Caroline Stuart, Scholarship Director
James Beard Foundation, Inc.
167 West 12th Street
New York, NY 10011
Phone: 212-675-4984 Ext. 311
Fax: 212-645-1438
E-mail: jamesbeardfound@hotmail.com

BECOMING A CHEF SCHOLARSHIP

One-time award towards tuition at an accredited culinary school of student's choice. Candidates must demonstrate a strong commitment to the culinary arts, an exceptional academic or work record, and financial need. See Web site at http://www.jamesbeard.org for further details.

Academic Fields/Career Goals: Food Science/Nutrition.

Award: Scholarship for use in freshman, sophomore, junior, senior, or graduate years; not renewable. *Number:* 1. *Amount:* $1000.

Eligibility Requirements: Applicant must be enrolled or expecting to enroll at an institution or university. Available to U.S. and non-U.S. citizens.

Application Requirements: Application, essay, financial need analysis, references, transcript. *Deadline:* May 1.

Contact: Caroline Stuart, Scholarship Director
James Beard Foundation, Inc.
167 West 12th Street
New York, NY 10011
Phone: 212-675-4984 Ext. 311
Fax: 212-645-1438
E-mail: jamesbeardfound@hotmail.com

BERN LAXER MEMORIAL SCHOLARSHIP

Scholarships of $2000 toward tuition for students seeking careers in food service and hospitality management. One scholarship given in each of three programs: Culinary, Hospitality Management, and Viticulture/Oenology. Program and school must be accredited in accordance with the James Beard Foundation scholarship criteria. Applicants must be residents of Florida and substantiate; have a high school diploma or the equivalent; have a minimum of one-year culinary experience either as a student or employee, and submit a minimum 500-word essay. See Web site at http://www.jamesbeard.org for further details.

Academic Fields/Career Goals: Food Science/Nutrition.

Award: Scholarship for use in freshman, sophomore, junior, senior, or graduate years; not renewable. *Number:* 3. *Amount:* $2000.

Eligibility Requirements: Applicant must be enrolled or expecting to enroll at an institution or university and resident of Florida. Available to U.S. and non-U.S. citizens.

Application Requirements: Application, essay, financial need analysis, references, transcript. *Deadline:* May 1.

Contact: Caroline Stuart, Scholarship Director
James Beard Foundation, Inc.
167 West 12th Street
New York, NY 10011
Phone: 212-675-4984 Ext. 311
Fax: 212-645-1438
E-mail: jamesbeardfound@hotmail.com

BRYAN CLOSE POLO GRILL SCHOLARSHIP

One-time award towards tuition at an accredited culinary school of student's choice. Applicant must be a resident of Oklahoma and have had at least one year of culinary experience. Candidates must demonstrate a strong commitment to the culinary arts, an exceptional academic or work record, and financial need. See Web site at http://www.jamesbeard.org for further details.

Academic Fields/Career Goals: Food Science/Nutrition.

Award: Scholarship for use in freshman, sophomore, junior, senior, or graduate years; not renewable. *Number:* 4. *Amount:* up to $1000.

Eligibility Requirements: Applicant must be enrolled or expecting to enroll at an institution or university and resident of Oklahoma. Available to U.S. and non-U.S. citizens.

Application Requirements: Application, essay, financial need analysis, references, transcript. *Deadline:* May 1.

Contact: Caroline Stuart, Scholarship Director
James Beard Foundation, Inc.
167 West 12th Street
New York, NY 10011
Phone: 212-675-4984 Ext. 311
Fax: 212-645-1438
E-mail: jamesbeardfound@hotmail.com

DANA CAMPBELL MEMORIAL SCHOLARSHIP

Scholarship for $2000 awarded to an applicant with career interests in food journalism who is in his/her second or third year in an accredited bachelor degree program in journalism or a food-related curriculum. Must be resident of a "Southern" state within the Southern Living readership area (Alabama, Florida, Georgia, North Carolina, South Carolina, Louisiana, Virginia, Arkansas, Texas, Mississippi, Kentucky, Maryland, Missouri, Oklahoma, West Virginia, or Delaware) and substantiate residency. The scholarship recipient will also be considered for an internship at Southern Living. See Web site at http://www.jamesbeard.org for further details.

Academic Fields/Career Goals: Food Science/Nutrition.

Award: Scholarship for use in sophomore or junior years; not renewable. *Number:* 1. *Amount:* $2000.

Eligibility Requirements: Applicant must be enrolled or expecting to enroll at a four-year institution or university and resident of Alabama, Arkansas, Delaware, Florida, Georgia, Kentucky, Louisiana, Maryland, Mississippi, Missouri, North Carolina, Oklahoma, South Carolina, Texas, or Virginia. Available to U.S. and non-U.S. citizens.

Application Requirements: Application, essay, financial need analysis, references, transcript. *Deadline:* May 1.

Contact: Caroline Stuart, Scholarship Director
James Beard Foundation, Inc.
167 West 12th Street
New York, NY 10011
Phone: 212-675-4984 Ext. 311
Fax: 212-645-1438
E-mail: jamesbeardfound@hotmail.com

DAVID EDGCUMBE SCHOLARSHIP

One-time award towards tuition for a beginning student interested in teaching in the culinary field. Applicant must have a high school diploma or equivalent. Candidates must demonstrate a strong commitment to the culinary arts, an exceptional academic or work record, and financial need. See Web site at http://www.jamesbeard.org for further details.

Academic Fields/Career Goals: Food Science/Nutrition.

Award: Scholarship for use in freshman year; not renewable. *Number:* 1. *Amount:* $1000.

Eligibility Requirements: Applicant must be enrolled or expecting to enroll at an institution or university. Available to U.S. and non-U.S. citizens.

Application Requirements: Application, essay, financial need analysis, references, transcript. *Deadline:* May 1.

Contact: Caroline Stuart, Scholarship Director
James Beard Foundation, Inc.
167 West 12th Street
New York, NY 10011
Phone: 212-675-4984 Ext. 311
Fax: 212-645-1438
E-mail: jamesbeardfound@hotmail.com

FIRE SCHOLARSHIP

One $2,500 scholarship towards tuition at an accredited school of student's choice. See Web site at http://www.jamesbeard.org for further details.

Academic Fields/Career Goals: Food Science/Nutrition.

Award: Scholarship for use in freshman, sophomore, junior, senior, or graduate years; not renewable. *Number:* 1. *Amount:* $2500.

Eligibility Requirements: Applicant must be enrolled or expecting to enroll at an institution or university. Available to U.S. and non-U.S. citizens.

Application Requirements: Application, essay, financial need analysis, references, transcript. *Deadline:* May 1.

Contact: Caroline Stuart, Scholarship Director
James Beard Foundation, Inc.
167 West 12th Street
New York, NY 10011
Phone: 212-675-4984 Ext. 311
Fax: 212-645-1438
E-mail: jamesbeardfound@hotmail.com

GINO COFACCI MEMORIAL SCHOLARSHIP

One-time award towards tuition for foreign culinary education. Applicant must have applied for an extensive culinary course. Approval of the course is at the discretion of the James Beard Foundation scholarship committee. Candidates must demonstrate a strong commitment to the culinary arts, an exceptional academic or work record, and financial need. See Web site at http://www.jamesbeard.org for further details.

Academic Fields/Career Goals: Food Science/Nutrition.

Award: Scholarship for use in freshman, sophomore, junior, senior, or graduate years; not renewable. *Number:* 1. *Amount:* $1000.

Eligibility Requirements: Applicant must be enrolled or expecting to enroll at an institution or university. Available to U.S. and non-U.S. citizens.

Application Requirements: Application, essay, financial need analysis, references, transcript. *Deadline:* May 1.

Contact: Caroline Stuart, Scholarship Director
James Beard Foundation, Inc.
167 West 12th Street
New York, NY 10011
Phone: 212-675-4984 Ext. 311
Fax: 212-645-1438
E-mail: jamesbeardfound@hotmail.com

JAMES BEARD FOUNDATION GENERAL SCHOLARSHIPS

One-time award towards tuition at an accredited culinary school of student's choice. The amount of each scholarship will be at the discretion of the James Beard Foundation scholarship committee. Candidates must demonstrate a strong commitment to the culinary arts, an exceptional academic or work record, and financial need. See Web site at http://www.jamesbeard.org for further details.

Academic Fields/Career Goals: Food Science/Nutrition.

Award: Scholarship for use in freshman, sophomore, junior, senior, or graduate years; not renewable. *Number:* up to 50. *Amount:* $1000–$2000.

Eligibility Requirements: Applicant must be enrolled or expecting to enroll at an institution or university. Available to U.S. and non-U.S. citizens.

Application Requirements: Application, essay, financial need analysis, references, transcript. *Deadline:* May 1.

Contact: Caroline Stuart, Scholarship Director
James Beard Foundation, Inc.
167 West 12th Street
New York, NY 10011
Phone: 212-675-4984 Ext. 311
Fax: 212-645-1438
E-mail: jamesbeardfound@hotmail.com

JER-NE RESTAURANT AND BAR SCHOLARSHIP

Scholarship for $3200 toward tuition at an accredited culinary school of student's choice. See Web site at http://www.jamesbeard.org for further details.

Academic Fields/Career Goals: Food Science/Nutrition.

Award: Scholarship for use in freshman, sophomore, junior, senior, or graduate years; not renewable. *Number:* 1. *Amount:* $3200.

Eligibility Requirements: Applicant must be enrolled or expecting to enroll at an institution or university. Available to U.S. and non-U.S. citizens.

Application Requirements: Application, essay, financial need analysis, references, transcript. *Deadline:* May 1.

Contact: Caroline Stuart, Scholarship Director
James Beard Foundation, Inc.
167 West 12th Street
New York, NY 10011
Phone: 212-675-4984 Ext. 311
Fax: 212-645-1438
E-mail: jamesbeardfound@hotmail.com

LA TOQUE SCHOLARSHIP

Scholarship for $3000 toward tuition at an accredited culinary school of the student's choice. See Web site at http://www.jamesbeard.org for further details.

Academic Fields/Career Goals: Food Science/Nutrition.

Award: Scholarship for use in freshman, sophomore, junior, senior, or graduate years; not renewable. *Number:* 1. *Amount:* $3000.

Eligibility Requirements: Applicant must be enrolled or expecting to enroll at an institution or university. Available to U.S. and non-U.S. citizens.

Application Requirements: Application, essay, financial need analysis, references, transcript. *Deadline:* May 1.

Contact: Caroline Stuart, Scholarship Director
James Beard Foundation, Inc.
167 West 12th Street
New York, NY 10011
Phone: 212-675-4984 Ext. 311
Fax: 212-645-1438
E-mail: jamesbeardfound@hotmail.com

LAS CANARIAS SCHOLARSHIP

Scholarship for $3700 toward tuition at an accredited culinary school of student's choice. See Web site at http://www.jamesbeard.org for further details.

Academic Fields/Career Goals: Food Science/Nutrition.

Award: Scholarship for use in freshman, sophomore, junior, senior, or graduate years; not renewable. *Number:* 1. *Amount:* $3700.

Eligibility Requirements: Applicant must be enrolled or expecting to enroll at an institution or university. Available to U.S. and non-U.S. citizens.

Application Requirements: Application, essay, financial need analysis, references, transcript. *Deadline:* May 1.

Contact: Caroline Stuart, Scholarship Director
James Beard Foundation, Inc.
167 West 12th Street
New York, NY 10011
Phone: 212-675-4984 Ext. 311
Fax: 212-645-1438
E-mail: jamesbeardfound@hotmail.com

PETER KUMP MEMORIAL SCHOLARSHIP

One-time award towards tuition at an accredited or licensed culinary school of student's choice. Applicant must submit a 500-word essay on culinary goals and how this scholarship can help attain them. Candidates must demonstrate a strong commitment to the culinary arts, an exceptional academic or work record, and financial need. See Web site at http://www.jamesbeard.org for further details.

Academic Fields/Career Goals: Food Science/Nutrition.

Award: Scholarship for use in freshman year; not renewable. *Number:* 1. *Amount:* $5000.

Eligibility Requirements: Applicant must be high school student and planning to enroll or expecting to enroll at an institution or university. Applicant must have 3.5 GPA or higher. Available to U.S. and non-U.S. citizens.

Application Requirements: Application, essay, financial need analysis, references, transcript. *Deadline:* May 1.

Contact: Caroline Stuart, Scholarship Director
James Beard Foundation, Inc.
167 West 12th Street
New York, NY 10011
Phone: 212-675-4984 Ext. 311
Fax: 212-645-1438
E-mail: jamesbeardfound@hotmail.com

SIA'S SCHOLARSHIP

One-time award towards tuition at an accredited culinary school. Applicant must be from Georgia, Louisiana or Texas. Applicant must be finishing the first year or beginning the second year of a minimum two-year program at an accredited culinary school. Applicant must submit a 500-word essay on their culinary goals and how this scholarship can help to attain them. See Web site at http://www.jamesbeard.org for further details.

Academic Fields/Career Goals: Food Science/Nutrition.

Award: Scholarship for use in sophomore, junior, or senior years; not renewable. *Number:* 1. *Amount:* $3500.

Eligibility Requirements: Applicant must be enrolled or expecting to enroll at an institution or university and resident of Georgia, Louisiana, or Texas. Available to U.S. and non-U.S. citizens.

Application Requirements: Application, essay, financial need analysis, references, transcript. *Deadline:* May 1.

Contact: Caroline Stuart, Scholarship Director
James Beard Foundation, Inc.
167 West 12th Street
New York, NY 10011
Phone: 212-675-4984 Ext. 311
Fax: 212-645-1438
E-mail: jamesbeardfound@hotmail.com

TRIBUTE RESTAURANT SCHOLARSHIP

One-time award towards tuition at an accredited culinary school of the student's choice. Candidates must demonstrate a strong commitment to the culinary arts, an exceptional academic or work record, and financial need. See Web site at http://www.jamesbeard.org for further details.

Academic Fields/Career Goals: Food Science/Nutrition.

Award: Scholarship for use in freshman, sophomore, junior, senior, or graduate years; not renewable. *Number:* 1. *Amount:* $3750.

Eligibility Requirements: Applicant must be enrolled or expecting to enroll at an institution or university. Available to U.S. and non-U.S. citizens.

Application Requirements: Application, essay, financial need analysis, references, transcript. *Deadline:* May 1.

Contact: Caroline Stuart, Scholarship Director
James Beard Foundation, Inc.
167 West 12th Street
New York, NY 10011
Phone: 212-675-4984 Ext. 311
Fax: 212-645-1438
E-mail: jamesbeardfound@hotmail.com

TRU SCHOLARSHIP

Scholarship for $3700 toward tuition at an accredited culinary school of the student's choice. See Web site at http://www.jamesbeard.org for further details.

Academic Fields/Career Goals: Food Science/Nutrition.

Award: Scholarship for use in freshman, sophomore, junior, senior, or graduate years; not renewable. *Number:* 1. *Amount:* $3700.

Eligibility Requirements: Applicant must be enrolled or expecting to enroll at an institution or university. Available to U.S. and non-U.S. citizens.

Application Requirements: Application, essay, financial need analysis, references, transcript. *Deadline:* May 1.

Contact: Caroline Stuart, Scholarship Director
James Beard Foundation, Inc.
167 West 12th Street
New York, NY 10011
Phone: 212-675-4984 Ext. 311
Fax: 212-645-1438
E-mail: jamesbeardfound@hotmail.com

WALLY JOE SCHOLARSHIP

One-time award towards tuition at an accredited culinary school for applicants who are residents of Mississippi, Tennessee, Arkansas or Louisiana. Candidates must demonstrate a strong commitment to the culinary arts, an exceptional academic or work record, and financial need. See Web site at http://www.jamesbeard.org for further details.

Academic Fields/Career Goals: Food Science/Nutrition.

Award: Scholarship for use in freshman, sophomore, junior, senior, or graduate years; not renewable. *Number:* 2. *Amount:* $1500.

Eligibility Requirements: Applicant must be enrolled or expecting to enroll at an institution or university and resident of Alaska, Louisiana, Mississippi, or Tennessee. Available to U.S. and non-U.S. citizens.

Application Requirements: Application, essay, financial need analysis, references, transcript. *Deadline:* May 1.

Contact: Caroline Stuart, Scholarship Director
James Beard Foundation, Inc.
167 West 12th Street
New York, NY 10011
Phone: 212-675-4984 Ext. 311
Fax: 212-645-1438
E-mail: jamesbeardfound@hotmail.com

KENTUCKY RESTAURANT ASSOCIATION EDUCATIONAL FOUNDATION

http://www.kyra.org/

KENTUCKY RESTAURANT ASSOCIATION EDUCATIONAL FOUNDATION SCHOLARSHIP

Renewable award to Kentucky residents enrolled in a food service program. Submit application, transcript, and references. Application deadlines are January 1 and July 1.

Academic Fields/Career Goals: Food Science/Nutrition; Food Service/Hospitality; Hospitality Management.

Kentucky Restaurant Association Educational Foundation (continued)

Award: Scholarship for use in freshman, sophomore, junior, senior, graduate, or postgraduate years; renewable. *Number:* 30–40. *Amount:* $500–$1500.

Eligibility Requirements: Applicant must be enrolled or expecting to enroll full-time at a two-year or four-year or technical institution or university and resident of Kentucky. Available to U.S. citizens.

Application Requirements: Application, references, transcript, letters from school and employer. *Deadline:* varies.

Contact: Betsy Byrd, Director of Member Relations
Kentucky Restaurant Association Educational Foundation
133 Evergreen Road, Suite 201
Louisville, KY 40243
Phone: 502-896-0464
Fax: 502-896-0465
E-mail: info@kyra.org

MAINE SCHOOL FOOD SERVICE ASSOCIATION (MSFSA) http://www.msfsa.com

SCHOLARSHIP OF THE MAINE SCHOOL FOOD SERVICE ASSOCIATION

Awarded to students from Maine enrolling in nutrition or culinary arts. It is also available to employees of school nutrition programs wishing to continue their education. Applicant must be attending an institution in Maine.

Academic Fields/Career Goals: Food Science/Nutrition; Food Service/Hospitality; Home Economics; Hospitality Management; Trade/Technical Specialties.

Award: Scholarship for use in freshman, sophomore, junior, or senior years; not renewable. *Number:* 1–4. *Amount:* $300–$1200.

Eligibility Requirements: Applicant must be enrolled or expecting to enroll full or part-time at a two-year or four-year or technical institution; resident of Maine and studying in Maine. Available to U.S. citizens.

Application Requirements: Application, essay, references, transcript. *Deadline:* May 1.

Contact: Kathleen Civiello, Education Committee Chair, MSFSA Professional Development
Maine School Food Service Association (MSFSA)
166 Connecticut Avenue
Millinocket, ME 04462
Phone: 207-723-9906
Fax: 207-723-6410
E-mail: civijk@prexar.com

MARIN EDUCATION FUND http://www.marineducationfund.org

GOLDMAN FAMILY FUND, NEW LEADER SCHOLARSHIP

• *See page 186*

MARION D. AND EVA S. PEEPLES FOUNDATION TRUST SCHOLARSHIP PROGRAM http://www.jccf.org

MARION D. AND EVA S. PEEPLES SCHOLARSHIPS

• *See page 205*

MARYLAND ASSOCIATION OF PRIVATE COLLEGES AND CAREER SCHOOLS http://www.mapccs.org

MARYLAND ASSOCIATION OF PRIVATE COLLEGES AND CAREER SCHOOLS SCHOLARSHIP

• *See page 127*

MASTER BREWERS ASSOCIATION OF THE AMERICAS http://www.mbaa.com

MASTER BREWERS ASSOCIATION OF THE AMERICAS

• *See page 59*

MINNESOTA SOYBEAN RESEARCH AND PROMOTION COUNCIL http://mnsoybean.org

MINNESOTA SOYBEAN RESEARCH AND PROMOTION COUNCIL YOUTH SOYBEAN SCHOLARSHIP

• *See page 54*

NATIONAL DAIRY SHRINE http://www.dairyshrine.org

NATIONAL DAIRY SHRINE/DAIRY MARKETING, INC. MILK MARKETING SCHOLARSHIPS

• *See page 60*

NDS STUDENT RECOGNITION CONTEST

• *See page 54*

NATIONAL POTATO COUNCIL WOMEN'S AUXILIARY http://www.nationalpotatocouncil.org

POTATO INDUSTRY SCHOLARSHIP

• *See page 55*

NATIONAL POULTRY AND FOOD DISTRIBUTORS ASSOCIATION http://www.npfda.org

NATIONAL POULTRY AND FOOD DISTRIBUTORS ASSOCIATION SCHOLARSHIP FOUNDATION

• *See page 55*

OREGON STUDENT ASSISTANCE COMMISSION http://www.osac.state.or.us

OREGON WINE BROTHERHOOD SCHOLARSHIP

• *See page 180*

RESOURCE CENTER http://www.resourcecenterscholarshipinfo.com

MARIE BLAHA MEDICAL GRANT

• *See page 64*

SOUTHWEST STUDENT SERVICES CORPORATION http://www.sssc.com

ANNE LINDEMAN MEMORIAL SCHOLARSHIP

• *See page 117*

TEXAS ELECTRIC CO-OP, INC. http://www.texas-ec.org

ANN LANE HOME ECONOMICS SCHOLARSHIP

Award for graduating high school member of a local Family, Career, and Community Leaders of America, Texas Association chapter. Minimum GPA of 2.5. Include a 250-word essay on "The Role of the Homemaker" and two letters of recommendation. Must attend a Texas institution. Merit-based. One-time scholarship of $1000.

Academic Fields/Career Goals: Food Science/Nutrition; Food Service/Hospitality; Home Economics.

Award: Scholarship for use in freshman year; not renewable. *Number:* 1. *Amount:* $1000.

Eligibility Requirements: Applicant must be high school student; planning to enroll or expecting to enroll full-time at a two-year or four-year or technical institution or university; resident of Texas and studying in Texas. Applicant or parent of applicant must be member of Family, Career and Community Leaders of America. Applicant must have 2.5 GPA or higher. Available to U.S. citizens.

Application Requirements: Application, essay, financial need analysis, photo, references, test scores, transcript. *Deadline:* March 1.

Contact: Esther Dominguez, Administrative Assistant for Member Services
Texas Electric Co-Op, Inc.
2550 South IH 35
Austin, TX 78704
Phone: 512-454-0311
Fax: 512-486-6215
E-mail: edomingz@texas-ec.org

UNITED AGRIBUSINESS LEAGUE http://www.ual.org

UNITED AGRIBUSINESS LEAGUE SCHOLARSHIP PROGRAM
• *See page 56*

UNITED AGRICULTURAL BENEFIT TRUST SCHOLARSHIP
• *See page 56*

UNITED DAUGHTERS OF THE CONFEDERACY http://www.hqudc.org

WALTER REED SMITH SCHOLARSHIP
• *See page 130*

UNITED NEGRO COLLEGE FUND http://www.uncf.org

CARGILL SCHOLARSHIP PROGRAM
• *See page 49*

FOOD SERVICE/HOSPITALITY

AMERICAN CULINARY FEDERATION http://www.acfchefs.org

AMERICAN ACADEMY OF CHEFS CHAINE DES ROTISSEURS SCHOLARSHIP

One-time award to exemplary students currently enrolled in a full-time two-year culinary program. Must have completed a grading or marking period. Deadline is December 1.

Academic Fields/Career Goals: Food Service/Hospitality.

Award: Scholarship for use in freshman or sophomore years; not renewable. *Number:* 20. *Amount:* $1000.

Eligibility Requirements: Applicant must be enrolled or expecting to enroll full-time at a two-year or technical institution.

Application Requirements: Application, references, transcript. *Deadline:* December 1.

Contact: Member Services Center
American Culinary Federation
180 Carter Place Way
St. Augustine, FL 32095
Phone: 800-624-9458
Fax: 904-825-4758

AMERICAN ACADEMY OF CHEFS CHAIR'S SCHOLARSHIP

One-time award to exemplary students currently enrolled in a full-time two- or four-year culinary program. Must have a career goal of becoming a chef or pastry chef. Deadline is July 1.

Academic Fields/Career Goals: Food Service/Hospitality.

Award: Scholarship for use in freshman, sophomore, junior, or senior years; not renewable. *Number:* 10. *Amount:* $1000.

Eligibility Requirements: Applicant must be enrolled or expecting to enroll full-time at a two-year or four-year or technical institution.

Application Requirements: Application, references, transcript. *Deadline:* July 1.

Contact: Member Services Center
American Culinary Federation
180 Carter Place Way
St. Augustine, FL 32095
Phone: 800-624-9458
Fax: 904-825-4758

AMERICAN INSTITUTE OF WINE AND FOOD-PACIFIC NORTHWEST CHAPTER http://www.aiwf.org

CULINARY, VINIFERA, AND HOSPITALITY SCHOLARSHIP
• *See page 270*

CALIFORNIA ADOLESCENT NUTRITION AND FITNESS (CANFIT) PROGRAM http://www.canfit.org

CALIFORNIA ADOLESCENT NUTRITION AND FITNESS (CANFIT) PROGRAM SCHOLARSHIP
• *See page 271*

CHILD NUTRITION FOUNDATION http://www.asfsa.org

NANCY CURRY SCHOLARSHIP
• *See page 271*

SCHWAN'S FOOD SERVICE SCHOLARSHIP
• *See page 271*

CULINARY TRUST http://www.iacpfoundation.org

CULINARY TRUST SCHOLARSHIP PROGRAM FOR CULINARY STUDY AND RESEARCH
• *See page 271*

DECA (DISTRIBUTIVE EDUCATION CLUBS OF AMERICA) http://www.deca.org

HARRY A. APPLEGATE SCHOLARSHIP
• *See page 123*

GOLDEN GATE RESTAURANT ASSOCIATION http://www.ggra.org

GOLDEN GATE RESTAURANT ASSOCIATION SCHOLARSHIP FOUNDATION

One-time award for any student pursuing a food service degree at a 501(c)(3) institution, or institutions approved by the Board of Trustees. California residency and personal interview in San Francisco is required. Minimum GPA of 2.75 required. Write for further information.

Academic Fields/Career Goals: Food Service/Hospitality; Hospitality Management.

Award: Scholarship for use in freshman, sophomore, junior, or senior years; not renewable. *Number:* 1–15. *Amount:* $1000–$3000.

Eligibility Requirements: Applicant must be enrolled or expecting to enroll full or part-time at a two-year or four-year or technical institution or university and resident of California. Available to U.S. citizens.

Application Requirements: Application, essay, financial need analysis, interview, references, transcript. *Deadline:* March 31.

Contact: Donnalyn Murphy, Scholarship Coordinator
Golden Gate Restaurant Association
120 Montgomery Street, Suite 1280
San Francisco, CA 94104
Phone: 415-781-5348 Ext. 812
Fax: 415-781-3925
E-mail: administration@ggra.org

ILLINOIS RESTAURANT ASSOCIATION EDUCATIONAL FOUNDATION http://www.illinoisrestaurants.org

ILLINOIS RESTAURANT ASSOCIATION EDUCATIONAL FOUNDATION SCHOLARSHIPS
• *See page 180*

INTERNATIONAL EXECUTIVE HOUSEKEEPERS ASSOCIATION http://www.ieha.org

INTERNATIONAL EXECUTIVE HOUSEKEEPERS EDUCATIONAL FOUNDATION

Award for students planning careers in the area of facilities management. Must be enrolled in IEHA-approved courses at a participating college or university. One-time award of up to $800. Must be a member of IEHA.

Academic Fields/Career Goals: Food Service/Hospitality; Home Economics; Horticulture/Floriculture; Trade/Technical Specialties.

Award: Scholarship for use in freshman, sophomore, junior, or senior years; not renewable. *Number:* 10. *Amount:* up to $800.

Eligibility Requirements: Applicant must be enrolled or expecting to enroll full or part-time at a two-year or four-year or technical institution or university and must have an interest in designated field specified by sponsor. Applicant or parent of applicant must be member of International Executive Housekeepers Association.

Application Requirements: Application, essay, transcript. *Deadline:* January 10.

Contact: Beth Risinger, CEO/Executive Director
International Executive Housekeepers Association
1001 Eastwind Drive, Suite 301
Westerville, OH 43081-3361
Phone: 800-200-6342
Fax: 614-895-1248
E-mail: excel@ieha.org

INTERNATIONAL FOOD SERVICE EXECUTIVES ASSOCIATION http://www.ifsea.com

WORTHY GOAL SCHOLARSHIP FUND

Scholarships to assist individuals in receiving food service management or vocational training beyond high school. Applicant must be enrolled or accepted as full-time student in a food service related major for the fall term following the award.

Academic Fields/Career Goals: Food Service/Hospitality.

Award: Scholarship for use in freshman, sophomore, junior, senior, or graduate years; not renewable. *Number:* 15. *Amount:* up to $1000.

Eligibility Requirements: Applicant must be enrolled or expecting to enroll full-time at a two-year or four-year or technical institution or university. Available to U.S. and non-U.S. citizens.

Application Requirements: Essay, references, transcript, financial statement summary, work experience documentation. *Deadline:* February 1.

Contact: Scholarship Chairperson
International Food Service Executives Association
2609 Surfwood Drive
Las Vegas, NV 89128
E-mail: hq@ifsea.com

INTERNATIONAL FOODSERVICE EDITORIAL COUNCIL http://www.ifec-is-us.com

INTERNATIONAL FOODSERVICE EDITORIAL COUNCIL COMMUNICATIONS SCHOLARSHIP

• *See page 160*

KENTUCKY RESTAURANT ASSOCIATION EDUCATIONAL FOUNDATION http://www.kyra.org/

KENTUCKY RESTAURANT ASSOCIATION EDUCATIONAL FOUNDATION SCHOLARSHIP

• *See page 275*

MAINE SCHOOL FOOD SERVICE ASSOCIATION (MSFSA) http://www.msfsa.com

SCHOLARSHIP OF THE MAINE SCHOOL FOOD SERVICE ASSOCIATION

• *See page 276*

MISSOURI TRAVEL COUNCIL http://www.missouritravel.com

MISSOURI TRAVEL COUNCIL TOURISM SCHOLARSHIP

One-time award for Missouri resident pursuing a hospitality related major such as hotel/restaurant management, parks and recreation, etc. Applicant must be currently enrolled in an accredited college or university in the State of Missouri. Selection based on essay, GPA, community involvement, academic activities, and hospitality-related experience.

Academic Fields/Career Goals: Food Service/Hospitality; Hospitality Management; Travel/Tourism.

Award: Scholarship for use in freshman, sophomore, junior, or senior years; not renewable. *Number:* 2. *Amount:* $1000.

Eligibility Requirements: Applicant must be enrolled or expecting to enroll full-time at a two-year or four-year or technical institution or university; resident of Missouri and studying in Missouri. Applicant must have 3.0 GPA or higher. Available to U.S. citizens.

Application Requirements: Application, essay, transcript. *Deadline:* February 15.

Contact: Pat Amick, Executive Director
Missouri Travel Council
204 East High Street
Jefferson City, MO 65101-3287
Phone: 573-636-2814
Fax: 573-636-5783
E-mail: pamick@sockets.net

NATIONAL ASSOCIATION OF COLLEGE AND UNIVERSITY FOOD SERVICES http://www.nacufs.org

CLARK E. DEHAVEN SCHOLARSHIP

Scholarships available to students currently enrolled full-time in a program that will lead to an undergraduate degree in a field of study designed to prepare students for careers in food service or related areas. College must be a member of NACUFS. Open to U.S. and Canadian citizens with a 2.75 minimum GPA. Deadline is February 15.

Academic Fields/Career Goals: Food Service/Hospitality.

Award: Scholarship for use in sophomore, junior, or senior years. *Number:* up to 4. *Amount:* up to $2674.

Eligibility Requirements: Applicant must be enrolled or expecting to enroll full-time at a two-year or four-year institution. Available to U.S. and Canadian citizens.

Application Requirements: Application, financial need analysis, resume, references, transcript. *Deadline:* February 15.

NATIONAL POULTRY AND FOOD DISTRIBUTORS ASSOCIATION http://www.npfda.org

NATIONAL POULTRY AND FOOD DISTRIBUTORS ASSOCIATION SCHOLARSHIP FOUNDATION

• *See page 55*

NATIONAL RESTAURANT ASSOCIATION EDUCATIONAL FOUNDATION http://www.nraef.org

NATIONAL RESTAURANT ASSOCIATION EDUCATIONAL FOUNDATION PROFESSIONAL DEVELOPMENT SCHOLARSHIP FOR EDUCATORS

For restaurant and food service educators who want to complement classroom time with hands-on operational professional development. Applicants must be full-time educators of a restaurant and foodservice-related program in a secondary or post-secondary school. See Web site: http://www.nraef.org for application and details.

Academic Fields/Career Goals: Food Service/Hospitality.

Award: Scholarship for use in junior, senior, graduate, or postgraduate years; not renewable. *Number:* varies. *Amount:* up to $1500.

Eligibility Requirements: Applicant must be enrolled or expecting to enroll full-time at a two-year or four-year institution or university. Applicant or parent of applicant must have employment or volunteer experience in food service. Applicant must have 3.0 GPA or higher. Available to U.S. citizens.

Application Requirements: Application, references. *Deadline:* March 15.

Contact: Emilee N. Rogan, Director, Scholarship Program
National Restaurant Association Educational Foundation
175 West Jackson Boulevard, Suite 1500
Chicago, IL 60604-2702
Phone: 800-765-2122 Ext. 780
Fax: 312-715-1362
E-mail: scholars@foodtrain.org

NATIONAL RESTAURANT ASSOCIATION EDUCATIONAL FOUNDATION UNDERGRADUATE SCHOLARSHIPS FOR COLLEGE STUDENTS

This scholarship is awarded to college students who have demonstrated a commitment to both postsecondary hospitality education and to a career in the industry with 750 hours of industry work experience. Must have a 2.75 GPA, and be enrolled for a full academic term for the school year beginning in fall. For application and further details visit Web site: http://nraef.org.

Academic Fields/Career Goals: Food Service/Hospitality.

Award: Scholarship for use in sophomore, junior, or senior years; not renewable. *Number:* 159–200. *Amount:* $2000.

Eligibility Requirements: Applicant must be enrolled or expecting to enroll full-time at an institution or university. Applicant or parent of applicant must have employment or volunteer experience in food service. Available to U.S. citizens.

Application Requirements: Application, essay, transcript. *Deadline:* varies.

Contact: Dalilah Torres-Ramos, Scholarship Program Specialist
National Restaurant Association Educational Foundation
175 West Jackson Boulevard
Suite 1500
Chicago, IL 60604-2702
Phone: 800-765-2122 Ext. 385
Fax: 312-566-9733
E-mail: dramos@foodtrain.org

NATIONAL RESTAURANT ASSOCIATION EDUCATIONAL FOUNDATION UNDERGRADUATE SCHOLARSHIPS FOR HIGH SCHOOL SENIORS

This scholarship is awarded to high school students who have demonstrated a commitment to both postsecondary hospitality education and to a career in the industry. Must have 250 hours of industry experience, age 17-19 with a 2.75 GPA.

Academic Fields/Career Goals: Food Service/Hospitality.

Award: Scholarship for use in freshman year; not renewable. *Number:* 50–100. *Amount:* $2000.

Eligibility Requirements: Applicant must be high school student; age 17-19 and planning to enroll or expecting to enroll full-time at an institution or university. Applicant or parent of applicant must have employment or volunteer experience in food service.

Application Requirements: Application, essay, references, transcript, letter of acceptance. *Deadline:* April 16.

Contact: Dalilah Torres-Ramos, Scholarship Program Specialist
National Restaurant Association Educational Foundation
175 West Jackson Boulevard
Suite 1500
Chicago, IL 60604-2702
Phone: 800-765-2122 Ext. 385
Fax: 312-566-9733
E-mail: dramos@foodtrain.org

PROSTART® NATIONAL CERTIFICATE OF ACHIEVEMENT SCHOLARSHIP

For high school junior and senior students who have earned Pro Start National Certificate of Achievement and are continuing their education in a restaurant or foodservice program. For application and details visit Web site: http://nraef.org.

Academic Fields/Career Goals: Food Service/Hospitality.

Award: Scholarship for use in freshman, sophomore, junior, or senior years; not renewable. *Number:* varies. *Amount:* up to $2000.

Eligibility Requirements: Applicant must be high school student and planning to enroll or expecting to enroll at a two-year or four-year or technical institution.

Application Requirements: Application. *Deadline:* August 16.

Contact: Dalilah Torres-Ramos, Scholarship Program Specialist
National Restaurant Association Educational Foundation
175 West Jackson Boulevard
Suite 1500
Chicago, IL 60604-2702
Phone: 800-765-2122 Ext. 385
Fax: 312-566-9733
E-mail: dramos@foodtrain.org

NATIONAL TOURISM FOUNDATION

http://www.ntfonline.org

CLEVELAND LEGACY I AND II SCHOLARSHIP AWARDS

Award for Ohio residents pursuing travel and tourism studies. Must be enrolled full time in two- or four-year institution. Minimum 3.0 GPA required. Submit resume.

Academic Fields/Career Goals: Food Service/Hospitality; Hospitality Management; Travel/Tourism.

Award: Scholarship for use in freshman, sophomore, junior, or senior years; not renewable. *Number:* 1. *Amount:* $1000.

Eligibility Requirements: Applicant must be enrolled or expecting to enroll full-time at a two-year or four-year institution or university and resident of Ohio. Applicant must have 3.0 GPA or higher. Available to U.S. citizens.

Application Requirements: Application, essay, resume, references, transcript. *Deadline:* May 10.

Contact: Michelle Gorin, Projects Coordinator
National Tourism Foundation
546 East Main Street
Lexington, KY 40508-3071
Phone: 800-682-8886
Fax: 859-226-4437
E-mail: michelle.gorin@ntastaff.com

NEW HORIZONS KATHY LE TARTE SCHOLARSHIP

One $1000 scholarship awarded to an undergraduate student entering his or her junior year of study. Applicant must be enrolled in a tourism-related program at an accredited four-year college or university. Must have minimum 3.0 GPA. Applicant must be Michigan resident. Please refer to Web site for further details: http://www.ntfonline.org

Academic Fields/Career Goals: Food Service/Hospitality; Hospitality Management; Travel/Tourism.

Award: Scholarship for use in junior year; not renewable. *Number:* 1. *Amount:* $1000.

Eligibility Requirements: Applicant must be enrolled or expecting to enroll full-time at a four-year institution or university and resident of Michigan. Applicant must have 3.0 GPA or higher. Available to U.S. citizens.

Application Requirements: Application, essay, resume, references, transcript. *Deadline:* May 10.

Contact: Michelle Gorin, Projects Coordinator
National Tourism Foundation
546 East Main Street
Lexington, KY 40508-3071
Phone: 800-682-8886
Fax: 859-226-4437
E-mail: michelle.gorin@ntastaff.com

PAT AND JIM HOST SCHOLARSHIP

Award for students who have a degree emphasis in a travel and tourism related field. Must maintain a 3.0 GPA for renewal. Application deadline is May 10.

Academic Fields/Career Goals: Food Service/Hospitality; Hospitality Management; Travel/Tourism.

Award: Scholarship for use in freshman, sophomore, junior, or senior years; renewable. *Number:* 1. *Amount:* $2000.

Eligibility Requirements: Applicant must be enrolled or expecting to enroll full-time at a four-year institution and studying in Kentucky. Applicant must have 3.0 GPA or higher. Available to U.S. citizens.

Application Requirements: Application, essay, resume, references, transcript. *Deadline:* May 10.

Contact: Michelle Gorin, Projects Coordinator
National Tourism Foundation
546 East Main Street
Lexington, KY 40508-3071
Phone: 800-682-8886
Fax: 859-226-4437
E-mail: michelle.gorin@ntastaff.com

SOCIETIE DES CASINOS DU QUEBEC SCHOLARSHIP

Award for resident of Quebec who is pursuing travel and tourism studies. May attend a four-year college or university. Minimum 3.0 GPA required.

Academic Fields/Career Goals: Food Service/Hospitality; Hospitality Management; Travel/Tourism.

Award: Scholarship for use in freshman or sophomore years; not renewable. *Number:* 1. *Amount:* $1000.

Eligibility Requirements: Applicant must be enrolled or expecting to enroll full-time at a four-year institution or university and resident of Quebec. Applicant must have 3.0 GPA or higher.

Application Requirements: Application, essay, resume, references, transcript. *Deadline:* May 10.

Contact: Michelle Gorin, Projects Coordinator
National Tourism Foundation
546 East Main Street
Lexington, KY 40508-3071
Phone: 800-682-8886
Fax: 859-226-4437
E-mail: michelle.gorin@ntastaff.com

TAMPA, HILLSBOROUGH LEGACY SCHOLARSHIP

One-time award for Florida resident who is pursuing studies in travel and tourism. Must attend a Florida college or university. Minimum 3.0 GPA required.

Academic Fields/Career Goals: Food Service/Hospitality; Hospitality Management; Travel/Tourism.

Award: Scholarship for use in freshman, sophomore, junior, or senior years; not renewable. *Number:* 1. *Amount:* $1000.

Eligibility Requirements: Applicant must be enrolled or expecting to enroll full-time at a four-year institution or university; resident of Florida and studying in Florida. Applicant must have 3.0 GPA or higher. Available to U.S. citizens.

Application Requirements: Application, essay, resume, references, transcript. *Deadline:* May 10.

Contact: Michelle Gorin, Projects Coordinator
National Tourism Foundation
546 East Main Street
Lexington, KY 40508-3071
Phone: 800-682-8886
Fax: 859-226-4437
E-mail: michelle.gorin@ntastaff.com

TAUCK SCHOLARS SCHOLARSHIPS

Four undergraduate scholarships awarded to students entering their sophomore or junior years of study in travel and tourism-related degrees. Applicants will receive $3000 over two years; $1500 awarded first year and $1500 awarded the following year. Must have minimum 3.0 GPA. Please refer to Web site for further details: http://www.ntfonline.org

Academic Fields/Career Goals: Food Service/Hospitality; Hospitality Management; Travel/Tourism.

Award: Scholarship for use in sophomore or junior years; renewable. *Number:* 4. *Amount:* $3000.

Eligibility Requirements: Applicant must be enrolled or expecting to enroll at a two-year or four-year institution or university. Applicant must have 3.0 GPA or higher. Available to U.S. citizens.

Application Requirements: Application, essay, resume, references, transcript. *Deadline:* May 10.

Contact: Michelle Gorin, Projects Coordinator
National Tourism Foundation
546 East Main Street
Lexington, KY 40508-3071
Phone: 800-682-8886
Fax: 859-226-4437
E-mail: michelle.gorin@ntastaff.com

TULSA SCHOLARSHIP AWARDS

Scholarship for Oklahoma residents pursuing travel and tourism studies. Must be a college junior or senior enrolled in an Oklahoma four-year institution. Minimum 3.0 GPA required. Submit resume. One-time award of $500.

Academic Fields/Career Goals: Food Service/Hospitality; Hospitality Management; Travel/Tourism.

Award: Scholarship for use in junior or senior years; not renewable. *Number:* 1. *Amount:* $500.

Eligibility Requirements: Applicant must be enrolled or expecting to enroll full-time at a four-year institution or university; resident of Oklahoma and studying in Oklahoma. Applicant must have 3.0 GPA or higher. Available to U.S. citizens.

Application Requirements: Application, essay, resume, references, transcript. *Deadline:* May 10.

Contact: Michelle Gorin, Projects Coordinator
National Tourism Foundation
546 East Main Street
Lexington, KY 40508-3071
Phone: 800-682-8886
Fax: 859-226-4437
E-mail: michelle.gorin@ntastaff.com

YELLOW RIBBON SCHOLARSHIP

Scholarship for residents of North America with physical or sensory disabilities who are pursuing travel and tourism studies in a North American institution. Must be entering postsecondary education with a minimum 3.0 GPA or must be maintaining at least a 2.5 GPA at college level. Submit resume. One-time award of $2500. Must submit an essay explaining how applicant plans to utilize his or her education in making a career in travel and tourism.

Academic Fields/Career Goals: Food Service/Hospitality; Hospitality Management; Travel/Tourism.

Award: Scholarship for use in freshman, sophomore, junior, or senior years; not renewable. *Number:* 1. *Amount:* $2500.

Eligibility Requirements: Applicant must be enrolled or expecting to enroll full-time at a two-year or four-year institution or university. Applicant must be hearing impaired, physically disabled, or visually impaired. Applicant must have 3.0 GPA or higher. Available to U.S. and Canadian citizens.

Application Requirements: Application, essay, resume, references, transcript. *Deadline:* May 10.

Contact: Michelle Gorin, Projects Coordinator
National Tourism Foundation
546 East Main Street
Lexington, KY 40508-3071
Phone: 800-682-8886
Fax: 859-226-4437
E-mail: michelle.gorin@ntastaff.com

NETWORK OF EXECUTIVE WOMEN IN HOSPITALITY

http://www.newh.org

NETWORK OF EXECUTIVE WOMEN IN HOSPITALITY, INC. SCHOLARSHIP

• *See page 78*

SOUTH DAKOTA RETAILERS ASSOCIATION http://www.sdra.org

SOUTH DAKOTA RETAILERS ASSOCIATION SCHOLARSHIP PROGRAM

• *See page 47*

TEXAS ELECTRIC CO-OP, INC. http://www.texas-ec.org

ANN LANE HOME ECONOMICS SCHOLARSHIP

• *See page 276*

UNITED NEGRO COLLEGE FUND http://www.uncf.org

FLOWERS INDUSTRIES SCHOLARSHIP

• *See page 131*

HILTON HOTELS SCHOLARSHIP

Award for students majoring in hospitality or restaurant management. Must have a 2.6 GPA. Please visit Web site for more information: http://www.uncf.org.

Academic Fields/Career Goals: Food Service/Hospitality; Hospitality Management.

Award: Scholarship for use in freshman, sophomore, junior, senior, or graduate years. *Number:* varies. *Amount:* varies.

Eligibility Requirements: Applicant must be Black (non-Hispanic) and enrolled or expecting to enroll at a two-year or four-year institution or university.

Application Requirements: Application, essay, financial need analysis, transcript, FAFSA, SAR. *Deadline:* November 30.

Contact: Program Services Department
United Negro College Fund
8260 Willow Oaks Corporate Drive
Fairfax, VA 22031

WOMEN GROCERS OF AMERICA http://www.nationalgrocers.org

MARY MACEY SCHOLARSHIP

• *See page 61*

FOREIGN LANGUAGE

ACL/NJCL NATIONAL LATIN EXAM http://www.nle.org

NATIONAL LATIN EXAM SCHOLARSHIP

Applications for the $1000 scholarships are mailed to gold medal winners in Latin III-IV Prose, III-IV Poetry, or Latin V-VI who are high school seniors. Applicants must agree to take at least one year of Latin or classical Greek in college.

Academic Fields/Career Goals: Foreign Language.

Award: Scholarship for use in freshman, sophomore, junior, senior, or graduate years; renewable. *Number:* 20. *Amount:* $1000.

Eligibility Requirements: Applicant must be high school student; planning to enroll or expecting to enroll full-time at a two-year or four-year institution or university and must have an interest in Greek language or Latin language. Available to U.S. and non-U.S. citizens.

Application Requirements: Application, applicant must enter a contest, essay, test scores, transcript. *Fee:* $3. *Deadline:* January 10.

Contact: Jane Hall, Chair
ACL/NJCL National Latin Exam
Mary Washington College
1301 College Avenue
Fredericksburg, VA 22401
Phone: 888-378-7721
Fax: 540-654-1567
E-mail: nle@mwc.edu

ALBERTA HERITAGE SCHOLARSHIP FUND/ ALBERTA SCHOLARSHIP PROGRAMS http://www.alis.gov.ab.ca/scholarships

LANGUAGES IN TEACHER EDUCATION SCHOLARSHIPS

• *See page 194*

ALPHA MU GAMMA, THE NATIONAL COLLEGIATE FOREIGN LANGUAGE SOCIETY http://www.lacitycollege.edu

NATIONAL ALPHA MU GAMMA SCHOLARSHIPS

One-time award to student members of Alpha Mu Gamma with a minimum 3.5 GPA who plan to continue study of a foreign language. Must participate in a national scholarship competition. Apply through local chapter advisers. Freshmen are not eligible. Must submit copy of Alpha Mu Gamma membership certificate. Can study overseas if part of his/her school program.

Academic Fields/Career Goals: Foreign Language.

Award: Scholarship for use in sophomore, junior, senior, graduate, or postgraduate years; not renewable. *Number:* 5. *Amount:* $200–$500.

Eligibility Requirements: Applicant must be enrolled or expecting to enroll full or part-time at a two-year or four-year institution or university. Applicant or parent of applicant must be member of Alpha Mu Gamma. Applicant must have 3.5 GPA or higher. Available to U.S. and non-U.S. citizens.

Application Requirements: Application, applicant must enter a contest, essay, references, transcript, a photocopy of Full Member Certificate. *Deadline:* February 1.

Contact: Local chapter advisor
Alpha Mu Gamma, The National Collegiate Foreign Language Society
855 North Vermont Avenue
Los Angeles, CA 90029

AMERICAN CLASSICAL LEAGUE/NATIONAL JUNIOR CLASSICAL LEAGUE http://www.aclclassics.org

NATIONAL JUNIOR CLASSICAL LEAGUE SCHOLARSHIP

This one-time award is available to graduating high school seniors who are members of the Junior Classical League. Preference is given to students who plan to major in the classics.

Academic Fields/Career Goals: Foreign Language; Humanities.

Award: Scholarship for use in freshman year; not renewable. *Number:* 7. *Amount:* $1000–$1500.

Eligibility Requirements: Applicant must be high school student; age 20 or under; planning to enroll or expecting to enroll at a two-year or four-year institution or university and must have an interest in foreign language. Applicant or parent of applicant must be member of Junior Classical League.

Application Requirements: Application, essay, references, transcript. *Deadline:* May 1.

Contact: Geri Dutra, Administrator
American Classical League/National Junior Classical League
Miami University
422 Wells Mill Drive
Oxford, OH 45056
Phone: 513-529-7741
Fax: 513-529-7742
E-mail: info@aclclassics.org

AMERICAN HISTORICAL ASSOCIATION http://www.theaha.org

HELEN AND HOWARD MARRARO PRIZE

Award for best book or article published on Italian history, Italian cultural history, or Italian-American relations. Three copies of work, curriculum vitae and bibliography must be sent to each committee member. Refer to Web site (http://www.theaha.org) for names and mailing addresses.

Academic Fields/Career Goals: Foreign Language; History; Humanities.

Award: Prize for use in freshman, sophomore, junior, senior, graduate, or postgraduate years; not renewable. *Number:* 1. *Amount:* varies.

Eligibility Requirements: Applicant must be enrolled or expecting to enroll at an institution or university and must have an interest in writing. Available to U.S. citizens.

American Historical Association (continued)

Application Requirements: Applicant must enter a contest, resume, bibliography. *Deadline:* May 17.

Contact: Book Prize Administrator
American Historical Association
400 A Street, SE
Washington, DC 20003
E-mail: aha@theaha.org

JOHN K. FAIRBANK PRIZE FOR EAST ASIAN HISTORY

• *See page 80*

PREMIO DEL REY PRIZE

Biannual award for recent distinguished book in English on early Spanish history, 500-1516 A.D. Must be of high scholarly nature. Copies of book must be sent to each committee member. See Web site (http://www.theaha.org) for names and mailing addresses.

Academic Fields/Career Goals: Foreign Language; History; Humanities.

Award: Prize for use in freshman, sophomore, junior, senior, graduate, or postgraduate years; not renewable. *Number:* 1. *Amount:* up to $1000.

Eligibility Requirements: Applicant must be enrolled or expecting to enroll at an institution or university and must have an interest in writing.

Application Requirements: Applicant must enter a contest, copies of book. *Deadline:* May 17.

Contact: Book Prize Administrator
American Historical Association
400 A Street, SE
Washington, DC 20003
E-mail: aha@theaha.org

AMERICAN PHILOLOGICAL ASSOCIATION http://www.apaclassics.org

MINORITY STUDENT SUMMER SCHOLARSHIP

• *See page 85*

ARKANSAS DEPARTMENT OF HIGHER EDUCATION http://www.arscholarships.com

EMERGENCY SECONDARY EDUCATION LOAN PROGRAM

• *See page 111*

ASSOCIATION OF TEACHERS OF JAPANESE BRIDGING CLEARINGHOUSE FOR STUDY ABROAD IN JAPAN http://www.colorado.edu/ealld/atj/Bridging/scholarships.html

BRIDGING SCHOLARSHIPS

Scholarships for U.S. students studying in Japan on semester or year-long programs. Deadlines are April 5 and October 5.

Academic Fields/Career Goals: Foreign Language.

Award: Scholarship for use in sophomore, junior, or senior years; not renewable. *Number:* 40–80. *Amount:* $2500–$4000.

Eligibility Requirements: Applicant must be enrolled or expecting to enroll full-time at a two-year or four-year institution or university. Available to U.S. citizens.

Application Requirements: Application, essay, references, transcript. *Deadline:* varies.

Contact: Susan Schmidt, Executive Director
Association of Teachers of Japanese Bridging Clearinghouse for Study Abroad in Japan
279 UCB
Boulder, CO 80309-0279
Phone: 303-492-5487
Fax: 303-492-5856
E-mail: atj@colorado.edu

CENTRAL INTELLIGENCE AGENCY http://www.cia.gov

CENTRAL INTELLIGENCE AGENCY UNDERGRADUATE SCHOLARSHIP PROGRAM

• *See page 39*

COMMUNITY FOUNDATION FOR PALM BEACH AND MARTIN COUNTIES, INC. http://www.yourcommunityfoundation.org

STEPHEN MADRY PECK, JR. MEMORIAL SCHOLARSHIP

African-American student, high achiever in French or Spanish as a second language. College applicant with goal of pursuing a major or minor in French or Spanish language or culture. Martin and Palm Beach County residents only.

Academic Fields/Career Goals: Foreign Language.

Award: Scholarship for use in freshman year; not renewable. *Number:* 1. *Amount:* $750–$2500.

Eligibility Requirements: Applicant must be Black (non-Hispanic); high school student; planning to enroll or expecting to enroll full-time at a four-year institution or university and resident of Florida. Available to U.S. citizens.

Application Requirements: Application, financial need analysis. *Deadline:* March 1.

Contact: Carolyn Jenco, Grants Manager/Scholarship Coordinator
Community Foundation for Palm Beach and Martin Counties, Inc.
700 South Dixie Highway
Suite 200
West Palm Beach, FL 33401

CULTURE CONNECTION http://www.thecultureconnection.com

CULTURE CONNECTION FOUNDATION SCHOLARSHIP

• *See page 52*

DONALD KEENE CENTER OF JAPANESE CULTURE http://www.columbia.edu/cu/ealac/dkc

JAPAN-U.S. FRIENDSHIP COMMISSION PRIZE FOR THE TRANSLATION OF JAPANESE LITERATURE

The Donald Keene Center of Japanese Culture offers an annual $2500 prize for translation of a work of classical Japanese literature into English and a $2500 prize for translation of a work of modern Japanese literature into English. To qualify, works must be book-length translations of Japanese literary works: novels, collections of short stories, literary essays, memoirs, drama, or poetry.

Academic Fields/Career Goals: Foreign Language.

Award: Prize for use in freshman, sophomore, junior, senior, graduate, or postgraduate years; not renewable. *Number:* up to 2. *Amount:* $2500.

Eligibility Requirements: Applicant must be enrolled or expecting to enroll at an institution or university. Available to U.S. and non-U.S. citizens.

Application Requirements: Application, applicant must enter a contest, resume, seven copies of book-length manuscript or published book. *Deadline:* February 1.

Contact: Yurika Kurakata, Associate Director
Donald Keene Center of Japanese Culture
Columbia University, 507 Kent Hall
New York, NY 10027
Phone: 212-854-5036
Fax: 212-854-4019
E-mail: donald-keene-center@columbia.edu

GREATER KANAWHA VALLEY FOUNDATION http://www.tgkvf.org

WEST VIRGINIA BROADCASTERS ASSOCIATION FUND

• *See page 159*

JAPAN STUDIES SCHOLARSHIP FOUNDATION COMMITTEE

JAPAN STUDIES SCHOLARSHIP

Two $1500 awards for residents of Northern or Central California and Nevada who are currently enrolled sophomore, junior or senior students studying or researching Japanese culture, language, or Japan-U.S. relations. Must attend an award ceremony in August.

Academic Fields/Career Goals: Foreign Language; International Studies; Social Sciences.

Award: Scholarship for use in sophomore, junior, or senior years; not renewable. *Number:* 2. *Amount:* $1500.

Eligibility Requirements: Applicant must be enrolled or expecting to enroll full-time at a four-year institution or university and resident of California or Nevada. Available to U.S. citizens.

Application Requirements: Application, transcript. *Deadline:* May 7.

Contact: Ms. Takahashi, Senior Education Coordinator
Japan Studies Scholarship Foundation Committee
c/o Japan Information Center
50 Freemont Street, Suite 2200
San Francisco, CA 94105
Phone: 415-356-2461
E-mail: education@cgjsf.org

KLINGON LANGUAGE INSTITUTE http://www.kli.org/scholarship/

KOR MEMORIAL SCHOLARSHIP

Scholarship for undergraduate or graduate student in a program leading to a degree in a field of language study. Instructions for applying are at the Web site only: http://www.kli.org/scholarship. Must send application materials by mail as instructed.

Academic Fields/Career Goals: Foreign Language.

Award: Scholarship for use in sophomore, junior, senior, or graduate years; not renewable. *Number:* 1. *Amount:* $500.

Eligibility Requirements: Applicant must be enrolled or expecting to enroll full-time at a four-year institution or university and must have an interest in foreign language. Available to U.S. citizens.

Application Requirements: Application, resume, references, nominating letter from chair, head, or dean; statement of goals. *Deadline:* June 1.

Contact: Information at Web site.
Klingon Language Institute
PO Box 634
Flourtown, PA 19031

KOSCIUSZKO FOUNDATION http://www.kosciuszkofoundation.org

YEAR ABROAD PROGRAM IN POLAND

• *See page 82*

NATIONAL FEDERATION OF THE BLIND http://www.nfb.org

MICHAEL AND MARIE MARUCCI SCHOLARSHIP

One-time award for students who are legally blind and pursuing full-time studies in the U.S. Must be studying a foreign language or comparative literature; pursuing a degree in history, geography, or political science with a concentration in international studies; or majoring in any other discipline that includes study abroad. Must also show competency in a foreign language.

Academic Fields/Career Goals: Foreign Language; History; International Studies; Literature/English/Writing; Political Science.

Award: Scholarship for use in freshman, sophomore, junior, or senior years; not renewable. *Number:* 1. *Amount:* $5000.

Eligibility Requirements: Applicant must be enrolled or expecting to enroll full-time at an institution or university. Applicant must be visually impaired. Available to U.S. citizens.

Application Requirements: Application, essay, financial need analysis, references, transcript. *Deadline:* March 31.

Contact: Peggy Elliott, Chairman
National Federation of the Blind
805 Fifth Avenue
Grinnell, IA 50112
Phone: 641-236-3366
E-mail: delliott@pcpartner.net

NATIONAL SECURITY AGENCY http://www.nsa.gov

NATIONAL SECURITY AGENCY STOKES EDUCATIONAL SCHOLARSHIP PROGRAM

• *See page 172*

NEW HAMPSHIRE POSTSECONDARY EDUCATION COMMISSION http://www.state.nh.us/postsecondary

WORKFORCE INCENTIVE PROGRAM

• *See page 208*

NORWICH JUBILEE ESPERANTO FOUNDATION http://www.esperanto.org/uk/nojef/index.htm

TRAVEL GRANTS

Fluency in the Esperanto language is essential. Applicants must have arranged to visit an approved Esperanto conference or other venue abroad. Non-Britons must have arranged to lecture or speak informally in at least one British Esperanto club or similar venue. Preference to non-Britons whose native language is not English.

Academic Fields/Career Goals: Foreign Language.

Award: Grant for use in freshman, sophomore, junior, senior, or graduate years; not renewable. *Number:* 1–20. *Amount:* $64–$1600.

Eligibility Requirements: Applicant must be age 26 or under; enrolled or expecting to enroll full or part-time at a two-year or four-year or technical institution or university and must have an interest in foreign language. Available to U.S. and non-U.S. citizens.

Application Requirements: Application, essay, references. *Deadline:* Continuous.

Contact: Dr. K. M. Hall
Norwich Jubilee Esperanto Foundation
37 Granville Court
Oxford OX3 0HS
United Kingdom

ROTARY FOUNDATION OF ROTARY INTERNATIONAL http://www.rotary.org

ROTARY FOUNDATION CULTURAL AMBASSADORIAL SCHOLARSHIP

One-time award funds three or six months (depending on availability through sponsoring Rotary district) of intensive language study and cultural immersion abroad. Applicant must have completed at least two years of university course work or one year in proposed language of study. Application through local Rotary club; appearances before clubs required during award period. Applications accepted March through July. See Web site at http://www.rotary.org for updated information.

Academic Fields/Career Goals: Foreign Language.

Award: Scholarship for use in junior, senior, or graduate years; not renewable. *Number:* 150–200. *Amount:* $12,000–$19,000.

Eligibility Requirements: Applicant must be enrolled or expecting to enroll at an institution or university and must have an interest in leadership. Available to U.S. and non-U.S. citizens.

Application Requirements: Application, autobiography, essay, interview, references, transcript. *Deadline:* varies.

Contact: Scholarship Program
Rotary Foundation of Rotary International
1560 Sherman Avenue
Evanston, IL 60201
Phone: 847-866-4459

SOCIEDAD HONORARIA HISPÁNICA http://www.sociedadhonorariahispanica.org

JOSEPH S. ADAMS SCHOLARSHIP

Applicants must be members of the Sociedad Honoraria Hispánica and a high school senior. Must have major/career interest in Spanish/Portuguese. Applicants must demonstrate high academic achievement, depth of character, leadership, patriotism, seriousness of purpose. Award available to citizens of other countries as long as they are members of the Sacred Honoraria Hispánica. For information contact local sponsor of Sociedad Honoraria Hispánica. For high school students only.

Academic Fields/Career Goals: Foreign Language.

Award: Scholarship for use in freshman year; not renewable. *Number:* 48. *Amount:* $1000–$2000.

Eligibility Requirements: Applicant must be high school student; planning to enroll or expecting to enroll full-time at a two-year or four-year institution or university and must have an interest in Portuguese language or Spanish language. Available to U.S. and non-U.S. citizens.

Application Requirements: Application. *Deadline:* February 15.

Contact: local sponsor of SHH at high school

SONOMA CHAMBOLLE-MUSIGNY SISTER CITIES

HENRI CARDINAUX MEMORIAL SCHOLARSHIP

• *See page 83*

FUNERAL SERVICES/MORTUARY SCIENCE

AMERICAN BOARD OF FUNERAL SERVICE EDUCATION http://www.abfse.org

AMERICAN BOARD OF FUNERAL SERVICE EDUCATION SCHOLARSHIPS

One-time award for U.S. citizens who are currently enrolled in and have completed at least one term of study in an accredited funeral science education program. Application deadlines are mid-March and mid-September. For more details see Web site: http//www.abfse.org.

Academic Fields/Career Goals: Funeral Services/Mortuary Science.

Award: Scholarship for use in freshman, sophomore, junior, or senior years; not renewable. *Number:* 50. *Amount:* $250–$500.

Eligibility Requirements: Applicant must be enrolled or expecting to enroll at a two-year or four-year institution or university. Available to U.S. citizens.

Application Requirements: Application, essay, financial need analysis, references, transcript. *Deadline:* varies.

Contact: Scholarship Administrator
American Board of Funeral Service Education
38 Florida Avenue
Portland, ME 04103
Phone: 207-878-6530
Fax: 207-797-7686
E-mail: gconnic1@maine.rr.com

HILGENFELD FOUNDATION FOR MORTUARY SCIENCE EDUCATION

MORTUARY SCIENCE SCHOLARSHIP

Renewable award for undergraduate and graduate students enrolled in a mortuary science program. Must have completed freshman year. Minimum 3.0 GPA required. Must be a U.S. citizen.

Academic Fields/Career Goals: Funeral Services/Mortuary Science.

Award: Scholarship for use in sophomore, junior, senior, or graduate years; renewable. *Number:* 12–15. *Amount:* $200–$500.

Eligibility Requirements: Applicant must be enrolled or expecting to enroll full or part-time at a four-year or technical institution or university. Applicant must have 3.0 GPA or higher. Available to U.S. citizens.

Application Requirements: Application. *Deadline:* Continuous.

Contact: Dr. Chester Gromacki, President
Hilgenfeld Foundation for Mortuary Science Education
PO Box 4311
Fullerton, CA 92831

ILLINOIS FUNERAL DIRECTORS ASSOCIATION http://www.ifda.org

ILLINOIS FUNERAL DIRECTORS ASSOCIATION SCHOLARSHIPS

Award for Illinois residents attending a two-year or four-year mortuary service program in Illinois. Open to students at the sophomore level. Must be a U.S. citizen. Minimum 3.5 GPA required. Write for application deadline. One-time award of $750. Must be recommended by school.

Academic Fields/Career Goals: Funeral Services/Mortuary Science.

Award: Scholarship for use in sophomore year; not renewable. *Number:* 12. *Amount:* $750.

Eligibility Requirements: Applicant must be enrolled or expecting to enroll full-time at a two-year or four-year institution; resident of Illinois and studying in Illinois. Applicant must have 3.5 GPA or higher. Available to U.S. citizens.

Application Requirements: Application. *Deadline:* varies.

Contact: Paul Dixon, Executive Director
Illinois Funeral Directors Association
215 South Grand Avenue West
Springfield, IL 62704
Phone: 217-525-2000
Fax: 217-525-8342
E-mail: info@ifda.org

INTERNATIONAL ORDER OF THE GOLDEN RULE http://www.ogr.org

INTERNATIONAL ORDER OF THE GOLDEN RULE AWARD OF EXCELLENCE

One-time scholarship for mortuary science students to prepare for a career in funeral service. Must be enrolled in a mortuary science degree program at an accredited mortuary school. Deadline is October 15. Minimum 3.0 GPA required.

Academic Fields/Career Goals: Funeral Services/Mortuary Science.

Award: Scholarship for use in freshman, sophomore, junior, or senior years; not renewable. *Number:* 1–3. *Amount:* $500–$3000.

Eligibility Requirements: Applicant must be enrolled or expecting to enroll full or part-time at a two-year or four-year or technical institution or university. Applicant must have 3.0 GPA or higher. Available to U.S. and non-U.S. citizens.

Application Requirements: Application, essay, financial need analysis, transcript. *Deadline:* October 15.

Contact: Mr. Mark Allen, Director of Education
International Order of the Golden Rule
13523 Lake Front Drive
Bridgeton, MO 63045
Phone: 314-209-7142
Fax: 314-209-1289
E-mail: malllen@ogr.org

MISSOURI FUNERAL DIRECTOR'S ASSOCIATION http://mofda.org

MISSOURI FUNERAL DIRECTORS ASSOCIATION SCHOLARSHIPS

Available to Missouri residents pursuing a career in funeral services/mortuary science. Minimum 3.0 GPA required. Application deadline is October 15.

Academic Fields/Career Goals: Funeral Services/Mortuary Science.

Award: Scholarship for use in junior or senior years; not renewable. *Number:* 3–4. *Amount:* $500–$1000.

Eligibility Requirements: Applicant must be enrolled or expecting to enroll full-time at a two-year or four-year institution and resident of Missouri. Applicant must have 3.0 GPA or higher. Available to U.S. citizens.

Application Requirements: Application, essay, financial need analysis, references, test scores, transcript. *Deadline:* October 15.

Contact: Ms. Sherry L. Anderson, Executive Director
Missouri Funeral Director's Association
PO Box 104688
Jefferson City, MO 65110
Phone: 573-635-1661
Fax: 573-635-9494

MONTANA FUNERAL DIRECTORS ASSOCIATION

MONTANA FUNERAL SERVICE SCHOLARSHIP

One-time $1000 award for full-time mortuary science student intending to return to Montana following graduation. Must be a U.S. citizen and resident of Montana.

Academic Fields/Career Goals: Funeral Services/Mortuary Science.

Award: Scholarship for use in freshman or sophomore years; not renewable. *Number:* 1–2. *Amount:* $1000.

Eligibility Requirements: Applicant must be enrolled or expecting to enroll full-time at a two-year or four-year institution and resident of Montana. Available to U.S. citizens.

Application Requirements: Application, transcript. *Deadline:* May 1.

Contact: Steven Yeakel, Executive Director
Montana Funeral Directors Association
PO Box 4267
Helena, MT 59604-4267
Phone: 406-449-7244
Fax: 406-443-0979
E-mail: mfda@sy-key.com

WALLACE S. AND WILMA K. LAUGHLIN FOUNDATION TRUST

WALLACE S. AND WILMA K. LAUGHLIN SCHOLARSHIP

Scholarships for Nebraska students entering mortuary science programs in order to become a licensed funeral director. Must be U.S. citizen. Must be high school graduate. Application deadline June 30.

Academic Fields/Career Goals: Funeral Services/Mortuary Science.

Award: Scholarship for use in junior or senior years; not renewable. *Number:* up to 4. *Amount:* $1000.

Eligibility Requirements: Applicant must be enrolled or expecting to enroll full-time at a two-year institution and resident of Nebraska. Available to U.S. citizens.

Application Requirements: Application, financial need analysis, interview, references, transcript. *Deadline:* June 30.

Contact: Leo Seger, President, Nebraska Funeral Directors Association
Wallace S. and Wilma K. Laughlin Foundation Trust
6000 South 58th Street, Suite B
Lincoln, NE 68516
Phone: 402-423-8900
Fax: 402-420-9716
E-mail: segerfh@morcomm.net

GEMOLOGY

MINERALOGICAL SOCIETY OF AMERICA http://www.minsocam.org

MINERALOGICAL SOCIETY OF AMERICA-GRANT FOR STUDENT RESEARCH IN MINERALOGY AND PETROLOGY

• *See page 190*

MINERALOGY SOCIETY OF AMERICA-GRANT FOR RESEARCH IN CRYSTALLOGRAPHY

• *See page 191*

GEOGRAPHY

ASSOCIATION FOR IRON AND STEEL TECHNOLOGY http://www.aist.org/foundation/scholarships.htm

ASSOCIATION FOR IRON AND STEEL TECHNOLOGY OHIO VALLEY CHAPTER SCHOLARSHIP

• *See page 112*

CANADIAN RECREATIONAL CANOEING ASSOCIATION http://www.paddlingcanada.com

BILL MASON MEMORIAL SCHOLARSHIP FUND

• *See page 57*

CENTRAL INTELLIGENCE AGENCY http://www.cia.gov

CENTRAL INTELLIGENCE AGENCY UNDERGRADUATE SCHOLARSHIP PROGRAM

• *See page 39*

HARVARD TRAVELLERS CLUB

HARVARD TRAVELLERS CLUB GRANTS

• *See page 73*

INNOVATION AND SCIENCE COUNCIL OF BRITISH COLUMBIA http://www.scbc.org

PAUL AND HELEN TRUSSEL SCIENCE AND TECHNOLOGY SCHOLARSHIP

• *See page 69*

MORRIS K. UDALL FOUNDATION http://www.udall.gov

MORRIS K. UDALL SCHOLARS

• *See page 59*

NATIONAL FISH AND WILDLIFE FOUNDATION http://www.nfwf.org

BUDWEISER CONSERVATION SCHOLARSHIP PROGRAM

• *See page 115*

GERMAN STUDIES

GERMAN ACADEMIC EXCHANGE SERVICE (DAAD) http://www.daad.org

GERMAN ACADEMIC EXCHANGE INFORMATION VISITS

• *See page 266*

GRAPHICS/GRAPHIC ARTS/PRINTING

ADVERTISING FEDERATION OF FORT WAYNE, INC. http://adfedfortwayne.org

ADVERTISING FEDERATION OF FORT WAYNE, INC., SCHOLARSHIP

• *See page 156*

AMERICAN AUTOMOBILE ASSOCIATION http://aaapublicaffairs.com

NATIONAL SENIOR HIGH COMMUNICATION CONTEST

• *See page 267*

ART INSTITUTES http://www.artinstitutes.edu

NATIONAL POSTER DESIGN CONTEST

Graphic design competition for high school seniors who are interested in pursuing a career in design. Competition winners receive tuition scholarships at The Art Institutes location they have chosen to attend. Students should

Art Institutes (continued)

submit work that shows an understanding of the specified theme "Life is Better with Art in it", basic design concepts, and development of a "design eye".

Academic Fields/Career Goals: Graphics/Graphic Arts/Printing.

Award: Scholarship for use in freshman, sophomore, junior, or senior years; renewable. *Number:* 10. *Amount:* $2000–$25,000.

Eligibility Requirements: Applicant must be high school student and planning to enroll or expecting to enroll full-time at a technical institution.

Application Requirements: Application, applicant must enter a contest, 35mm slide of work. *Deadline:* February 14.

Contact: Julie Walsh, Admissions Department
Art Institutes
210 6th Avenue
Suite 3300
Pittsburgh, PA 15222
Phone: 800-275-2440
Fax: 412-456-2305
E-mail: webadmin@aii.edu

CENTRAL INTELLIGENCE AGENCY http://www.cia.gov

CENTRAL INTELLIGENCE AGENCY UNDERGRADUATE SCHOLARSHIP PROGRAM

• *See page 39*

DALLAS-FORT WORTH ASSOCIATION OF BLACK COMMUNICATORS http://www.dfwabc.org

FUTURE JOURNALISTS SCHOLARSHIP PROGRAM

• *See page 159*

ELECTRONIC DOCUMENT SYSTEMS FOUNDATION http://www.edsf.org

ELECTRONIC DOCUMENT SYSTEMS FOUNDATION SCHOLARSHIP AWARDS

• *See page 159*

GOLDEN KEY INTERNATIONAL HONOUR SOCIETY http://www.goldenkey.org

ART INTERNATIONAL AWARD

• *See page 87*

HISPANIC COLLEGE FUND, INC. http://www.hispanicfund.org

DENNY'S/HISPANIC COLLEGE FUND SCHOLARSHIP

• *See page 41*

INTERNATIONAL FOODSERVICE EDITORIAL COUNCIL http://www.ifec-is-us.com

INTERNATIONAL FOODSERVICE EDITORIAL COUNCIL COMMUNICATIONS SCHOLARSHIP

• *See page 160*

KNIGHT RIDDER http://www.kri.com

KNIGHT RIDDER MINORITY SCHOLARSHIP PROGRAM

• *See page 126*

MAINE GRAPHICS ARTS ASSOCIATION

MAINE GRAPHICS ART ASSOCIATION

Scholarship for Maine high school students majoring in graphic arts at any university. Submit transcript and references with application. One-time award.

Academic Fields/Career Goals: Graphics/Graphic Arts/Printing.

Award: Scholarship for use in freshman year; not renewable. *Number:* up to 20. *Amount:* $100–$500.

Eligibility Requirements: Applicant must be high school student; planning to enroll or expecting to enroll full-time at an institution or university and resident of Maine.

Application Requirements: Application, references, transcript. *Deadline:* May 15.

Contact: Angie Dougherty, Director
Maine Graphics Arts Association
PO Box 874
Auburn, ME 04212-0874
Phone: 207-883-3083
Fax: 207-883-3158

MAINE MEDIA WOMEN SCHOLARSHIPS COMMITTEE http://www.mainemediawomen.org/scholarships.html

MAINE MEDIA WOMEN'S SCHOLARSHIP

• *See page 88*

NEW ENGLAND PRINTING AND PUBLISHING COUNCIL

NEW ENGLAND GRAPHIC ARTS SCHOLARSHIP

For high school senior or college student who is a resident of New England. Assists students in continuing their education in a two- or four-year program leading to a graphic arts degree. Renewable for up to four years if student maintains a 2.5 GPA.

Academic Fields/Career Goals: Graphics/Graphic Arts/Printing.

Award: Scholarship for use in freshman, sophomore, junior, or senior years; renewable. *Number:* varies. *Amount:* $1300–$2000.

Eligibility Requirements: Applicant must be enrolled or expecting to enroll full-time at a two-year or four-year institution or university and resident of Connecticut, Maine, Massachusetts, New Hampshire, Rhode Island, or Vermont. Applicant must have 2.5 GPA or higher. Available to U.S. citizens.

Application Requirements: Application, financial need analysis, test scores, transcript. *Deadline:* May 31.

Contact: Kurt Drescher, Scholarship Chair
New England Printing and Publishing Council
PO Box 593
Reading, MA 01867-0218
Phone: 781-944-1116
Fax: 781-944-3905

PRINT AND GRAPHIC SCHOLARSHIP FOUNDATION http://www.pgsf.org

PRINT AND GRAPHICS SCHOLARSHIPS

Applicant must be interested in a career in graphic communications, printing technology, printing management, or publishing. Must have and maintain a 3.0 cumulative GPA. Selection based on academic record, class rank, recommendations, biographical information and extracurricular activities. Deadline for high school students is March 1 and April 1 for enrolled college students. Award available to citizens outside U.S. as long as they are attending a U.S. institution. Application may be obtained from Web site http://www.pgsf.org and may be submitted between November 1 and April 1.

Academic Fields/Career Goals: Graphics/Graphic Arts/Printing.

Award: Scholarship for use in freshman, sophomore, junior, senior, or graduate years; renewable. *Number:* 200–300. *Amount:* $500–$3000.

Eligibility Requirements: Applicant must be enrolled or expecting to enroll full-time at a two-year or four-year or technical institution or university and must have an interest in designated field specified by sponsor. Applicant must have 3.0 GPA or higher. Available to U.S. and non-U.S. citizens.

Application Requirements: Application, essay, references, self-addressed stamped envelope, test scores, transcript. *Deadline:* varies.

Contact: Bernadine Eckert, Scholarship Administrator
Print and Graphic Scholarship Foundation
200 Deer Run Road
Sewickley, PA 15143-2600
Phone: 412-741-6860
Fax: 412-741-2311
E-mail: pgsf@gatf.org

PRINTING INDUSTRY OF MINNESOTA EDUCATION FOUNDATION http://www.pimn.org

PRINTING INDUSTRY OF MINNESOTA EDUCATION FOUNDATION SCHOLARSHIP FUND

The PIMEF offers $1,000-2,000 renewable scholarships to full-time students enrolled in two- or four-year institutions and technical colleges offering degrees in the print communications discipline. Applicant must be a Minnesota resident and be committed to a career in the print communications industry. Minimum 3.0 GPA required. Priority given to children of PIM member company employees.

Academic Fields/Career Goals: Graphics/Graphic Arts/Printing.

Award: Scholarship for use in freshman, sophomore, junior, or senior years; renewable. *Number:* 10–15. *Amount:* $1000–$2000.

Eligibility Requirements: Applicant must be enrolled or expecting to enroll full-time at a two-year or four-year or technical institution; resident of Minnesota and studying in Minnesota, New York, or Wisconsin. Applicant must have 3.0 GPA or higher. Available to U.S. citizens.

Application Requirements: Application, essay, references, test scores, transcript, copy of college admission form, proof of admission. *Deadline:* April 15.

Contact: Lisa Elfrink, Scholarship Fund Program Coordinator
Printing Industry of Minnesota Education Foundation
2829 University Avenue SE, Suite 750
Minneapolis, MN 55414-3248
Phone: 612-379-6014
Fax: 612-379-6030
E-mail: lelfrink@pimn.org

RHODE ISLAND FOUNDATION http://www.rifoundation.org

RHODE ISLAND ADVERTISING SCHOLARSHIP

• *See page 268*

ROBERT H. MOLLOHAN FAMILY CHARITABLE FOUNDATION, INC. http://www.mollohanfoundation.org

MARY OLIVE EDDY JONES ART SCHOLARSHIP

• *See page 84*

SAN FRANCISCO FOUNDATION http://www.sff.org

PHELAN AWARD IN PRINTMAKING

Award presented in every odd-numbered year to recognize achievement in printmaking. Must have been born in California, but need not be a current resident. Applicants must provide a copy of their birth certificate with their application. This award is not a scholarship. See Web site at http://www.sff.org for further information and deadlines.

Academic Fields/Career Goals: Graphics/Graphic Arts/Printing.

Award: Prize for use in freshman, sophomore, junior, senior, graduate, or postgraduate years; not renewable. *Number:* 3. *Amount:* $2500.

Eligibility Requirements: Applicant must be enrolled or expecting to enroll at an institution or university. Available to U.S. citizens.

Application Requirements: Application, applicant must enter a contest, self-addressed stamped envelope. *Deadline:* varies.

Contact: Art Awards Coordinator
San Francisco Foundation
225 Bush Street, Suite 500
San Francisco, CA 94104
Phone: 415-733-8500

SOUTH DAKOTA RETAILERS ASSOCIATION http://www.sdra.org

SOUTH DAKOTA RETAILERS ASSOCIATION SCHOLARSHIP PROGRAM

• *See page 47*

TAG AND LABEL MANUFACTURERS INSTITUTE, INC. http://www.tlmi.com

TAG AND LABEL MANUFACTURERS, INC., SCHOLARSHIP FUND

• *See page 234*

WORLDSTUDIO FOUNDATION http://www.worldstudio.org

WORLDSTUDIO FOUNDATION SCHOLARSHIP PROGRAM

• *See page 80*

HEALTH ADMINISTRATION

ALBERTA HERITAGE SCHOLARSHIP FUND/ ALBERTA SCHOLARSHIP PROGRAMS http://www.alis.gov.ab.ca/scholarships

ALBERTA HERITAGE SCHOLARSHIP FUND ABORIGINAL HEALTH CAREERS BURSARY

• *See page 111*

AMERICAN INDIAN SCIENCE AND ENGINEERING SOCIETY http://www.aises.org

BURLINGTON NORTHERN SANTA FE FOUNDATION SCHOLARSHIP

• *See page 65*

AMERICAN SOCIETY OF RADIOLOGIC TECHNOLOGISTS EDUCATION AND RESEARCH FOUNDATION http://www.asrt.org

ISADORE N. STERN SCHOLARSHIP

Open to ASRT members only who are certificate, undergraduate or graduate students. Must have ASRT, ARRT registered/unrestricted state license, and must have worked in the radiological sciences profession for at least one year in the past five years. Sponsored in conjunction with E-Z-EM, Inc.

Academic Fields/Career Goals: Health Administration; Health and Medical Sciences; Health Information Management/Technology.

Award: Scholarship for use in freshman, sophomore, junior, senior, or graduate years; not renewable. *Number:* 10. *Amount:* $1000.

Eligibility Requirements: Applicant must be enrolled or expecting to enroll full or part-time at a two-year or four-year or technical institution or university. Available to U.S. and non-U.S. citizens.

Application Requirements: Application, essay, financial need analysis, resume, references. *Deadline:* February 1.

Contact: Phelosha Collaros, Development Officer
American Society of Radiologic Technologists Education and Research Foundation
15000 Central Avenue, SE
Albuquerque, NM 87123-3917
Phone: 505-298-4500 Ext. 2541
Fax: 505-298-5063
E-mail: foundation@asrt.org

SIEMENS SCHOLAR AWARD

Open to ASRT members only who are undergraduate or graduate students. Must have ARRT registered/unrestricted state license, and must have worked in the radiologic sciences profession for at least one year in the past five years. Sponsored in conjunction with Seimen's Medical-Oncology Care Systems.

Academic Fields/Career Goals: Health Administration; Health and Medical Sciences; Health Information Management/Technology.

Award: Scholarship for use in freshman, sophomore, junior, senior, or graduate years; not renewable. *Number:* 1. *Amount:* $3000.

Eligibility Requirements: Applicant must be enrolled or expecting to enroll full or part-time at a four-year institution or university. Available to U.S. and non-U.S. citizens.

Application Requirements: Application, essay, financial need analysis, resume, references. *Deadline:* February 1.

Contact: Phelosha Collaros, Development Officer
American Society of Radiologic Technologists Education and Research Foundation
15000 Central Avenue, SE
Albuquerque, NM 87123-3917
Phone: 505-298-4500 Ext. 2541
Fax: 505-298-5063
E-mail: foundation@asrt.org

BETHESDA LUTHERAN HOMES AND SERVICES, INC. http://www.blhs.org

DEVELOPMENTAL DISABILITIES SCHOLASTIC ACHIEVEMENT SCHOLARSHIP FOR LUTHERAN COLLEGE STUDENTS

• *See page 184*

CANADIAN SOCIETY FOR MEDICAL LABORATORY SCIENCE http://www.csmls.org

E.V. BOOTH SCHOLARSHIP AWARD

This fund was established to assist CSMLS members in fulfilling their vision of achieving university level education in the medical laboratory sciences. One-time award of CAN$500. Must be a Canadian citizen.

Academic Fields/Career Goals: Health Administration; Health and Medical Sciences; Health Information Management/Technology.

Award: Scholarship for use in freshman, sophomore, junior, or senior years; not renewable. *Number:* 2. *Amount:* $371.

Eligibility Requirements: Applicant must be Canadian citizen and enrolled or expecting to enroll full or part-time at an institution or university. Applicant or parent of applicant must be member of Canadian Society for Medical Laboratory Science.

Application Requirements: Application, financial need analysis, self-addressed stamped envelope, transcript. *Deadline:* April 1.

Contact: Lynn Zehr, Executive Assistant
Canadian Society for Medical Laboratory Science
PO Box 2830 LCDI
Hamilton, ON L8N 3N8
Canada
Phone: 905-528-8642 Ext. 12
Fax: 905-528-4968
E-mail: lzehr@csmls.org

CONGRESSIONAL BLACK CAUCUS SPOUSES PROGRAM http://cbcfinc.org

CONGRESSIONAL BLACK CAUCUS SPOUSES HEALTH INITIATIVE

Award made to students who reside or attend school in a congressional district represented by an African-American member of Congress. Must be full-time undergraduate enrolled in health-related program. Minimum 2.5 GPA required. Contact the congressional office in the appropriate district for information and applications. Visit http://www.cbcfinc.org for a list of district offices.

Academic Fields/Career Goals: Health Administration; Health and Medical Sciences; Health Information Management/Technology.

Award: Scholarship for use in freshman, sophomore, junior, or senior years; renewable. *Number:* 200. *Amount:* $500–$4000.

Eligibility Requirements: Applicant must be enrolled or expecting to enroll full-time at a two-year or four-year or technical institution or university. Applicant must have 2.5 GPA or higher. Available to U.S. citizens.

Application Requirements: Application, essay, financial need analysis, interview, photo, references, transcript. *Deadline:* Continuous.

Contact: Appropriate Congressional District Office

GREATER KANAWHA VALLEY FOUNDATION http://www.tgkvf.org

WILLARD H. ERWIN, JR. MEMORIAL SCHOLARSHIP FUND

• *See page 125*

HEALTH RESEARCH COUNCIL OF NEW ZEALAND http://www.hrc.govt.nz

PACIFIC HEALTH WORKFORCE AWARD

Intended to provide one year of support for students studying towards a health or health-related qualification. The eligible courses of study are: health, health administration, or a recognized qualification aligned with the Pacific Island. Priority given to management training, medical, and nursing students. Applicants should be New Zealand citizens or hold residency in New Zealand at the time of application and be of Pacific Island descent. May only be enrolled at New Zealand Universities or other approved New Zealand tertiary institutions.

Academic Fields/Career Goals: Health Administration; Health and Medical Sciences; Health Information Management/Technology; Nursing.

Award: Scholarship for use in freshman, sophomore, junior, senior, graduate, or postgraduate years; not renewable. *Amount:* $10,000.

Eligibility Requirements: Applicant must be New Zealander citizen; Asian/Pacific Islander and enrolled or expecting to enroll full-time at a two-year or four-year institution or university.

Application Requirements: Application, essay, financial need analysis, references, transcript, curriculum vitae. *Deadline:* October 10.

Contact: Health Research Council of New Zealand
PO Box 5541
Wellesley Street
Auckland 1036
New Zealand
Phone: 64-9-3798227
Fax: 64-9-377 9988

PACIFIC MENTAL HEALTH WORK FORCE AWARD

Intended to provide one year of support for students studying towards a mental health or mental health-related qualification. Eligible courses of study include: nursing, psychology, health, health administration or a recognized qualification aligned with the Pacific Island mental health priority areas. Applicants should be New Zealand citizens or hold residency in New Zealand at the time of application and be of Pacific Island descent. May only be enrolled at New Zealand Universities or other approved New Zealand tertiary institutions.

Academic Fields/Career Goals: Health Administration; Health and Medical Sciences; Health Information Management/Technology; Nursing.

Award: Scholarship for use in freshman, sophomore, junior, senior, graduate, or postgraduate years; not renewable. *Amount:* $10,000.

Eligibility Requirements: Applicant must be New Zealander citizen; Asian/Pacific Islander and enrolled or expecting to enroll full-time at a two-year or four-year institution or university.

Application Requirements: Application, essay, financial need analysis, references, transcript, curriculum vitae. *Deadline:* October 1.

Contact: Health Research Council of New Zealand
PO Box 5541
Wellesley Street
Auckland 1036
New Zealand
Phone: 64-9-3798227
Fax: 64-9-377 9988

HEALTHCARE INFORMATION AND MANAGEMENT SYSTEMS SOCIETY FOUNDATION http://www.himss.org

HIMSS FOUNDATION SCHOLARSHIP PROGRAM

One-time award available to undergraduate (junior level or higher), Management Engineering student (junior level or higher), graduate, or PhD candidate. Given for academic excellence and the potential for future leadership in the health care information and management systems industry. Must be full-time student and a member of HIMSS.

Academic Fields/Career Goals: Health Administration; Health and Medical Sciences; Health Information Management/Technology; Science, Technology, and Society.

Award: Scholarship for use in junior, senior, graduate, or postgraduate years; renewable. *Number:* 3–5. *Amount:* $5000.

Eligibility Requirements: Applicant must be enrolled or expecting to enroll full-time at a four-year institution or university. Applicant or parent of applicant must be member of Healthcare Information and Management Systems Society. Available to U.S. and non-U.S. citizens.

Application Requirements: Application, autobiography, essay, photo, resume, references, transcript. *Deadline:* October 1.

Contact: Betty Sanders, Member Relations Coordinator
Healthcare Information and Management Systems Society Foundation
230 East Ohio, Suite 500
Chicago, IL 60611
Phone: 312-915-9269
Fax: 312-664-6143
E-mail: bsanders@himss.org

MARIN EDUCATION FUND http://www.marineducationfund.org

GOLDMAN FAMILY FUND, NEW LEADER SCHOLARSHIP
• *See page 186*

NORTH CAROLINA STATE EDUCATION ASSISTANCE AUTHORITY http://www.cfnc.org

NORTH CAROLINA STUDENT LOAN PROGRAM FOR HEALTH, SCIENCE, AND MATHEMATICS
• *See page 187*

ORDEAN FOUNDATION

ORDEAN LOAN PROGRAM
• *See page 45*

RESOURCE CENTER http://www.resourcecenterscholarshipinfo.com

MARIE BLAHA MEDICAL GRANT
• *See page 64*

VIRGINIA SOCIETY OF HEALTHCARE HR ADMINISTRATION

VIRGINIA SOCIETY FOR HEALTHCARE HUMAN RESOURCES ADMINISTRATION SCHOLARSHIP

One-time award to a deserving junior, senior, or graduate student to promote and encourage excellence in the practice of healthcare human resources management in the State of Virginia. Award only available to Virginia residents who have an interest in healthcare, specifically Human Resources Administration. Must study in Virginia.

Academic Fields/Career Goals: Health Administration.

Award: Scholarship for use in junior, senior, or graduate years; not renewable. *Number:* 1. *Amount:* $1000.

Eligibility Requirements: Applicant must be enrolled or expecting to enroll full or part-time at a four-year institution or university; resident of Virginia and studying in Virginia.

Application Requirements: Application, autobiography, references, transcript. *Deadline:* August 15.

Contact: Janice S. Gibbs, Assistant Director of Human Resources
Virginia Society of Healthcare HR Administration
2800 Godwin Boulevard
Suffolk, VA 23434
Phone: 757-934-4602
Fax: 757-934-4414
E-mail: jgibbs@obic.com

WOMEN OF THE EVANGELICAL LUTHERAN CHURCH IN AMERICA http://www.elca.org/wo

HEALTH SERVICES SCHOLARSHIP FOR WOMEN STUDYING ABROAD

Scholarships provided for ELCA women studying for service in health professions associated with ELCA projects abroad. Must be at least 21 years old and hold membership in the ELCA. Must have experienced an interruption in education of two or more years since the completion of high school. For more details see Web site: http://www.elca.org/wo.

Academic Fields/Career Goals: Health Administration; Health and Medical Sciences; Health Information Management/Technology.

Award: Scholarship for use in freshman, sophomore, junior, senior, or graduate years; not renewable. *Number:* 3. *Amount:* up to $1200.

Eligibility Requirements: Applicant must be Lutheran; age 21; enrolled or expecting to enroll at an institution or university and female. Available to U.S. citizens.

Application Requirements: *Deadline:* February 15.

Contact: Application available at Web site.

HEALTH AND MEDICAL SCIENCES

ALBERTA HERITAGE SCHOLARSHIP FUND/ ALBERTA SCHOLARSHIP PROGRAMS http://www.alis.gov.ab.ca/scholarships

ALBERTA HERITAGE SCHOLARSHIP FUND ABORIGINAL HEALTH CAREERS BURSARY
• *See page 111*

ALICE M. YARNOLD AND SAMUEL YARNOLD SCHOLARSHIP TRUST

ALICE M. AND SAMUEL YARNOLD SCHOLARSHIP

Must be a New Hampshire resident attending school in any state; applicant must already have begun postsecondary education (graduating high school seniors not eligible); must major in medicine, nursing or health-related field but not in management within those fields. Applicants are required to reapply.

Academic Fields/Career Goals: Health and Medical Sciences; Nursing; Therapy/Rehabilitation.

Award: Scholarship for use in sophomore, junior, senior, graduate, or postgraduate years; not renewable. *Number:* 20–30. *Amount:* $1000–$3000.

Eligibility Requirements: Applicant must be enrolled or expecting to enroll full or part-time at a two-year or four-year or technical institution or university and resident of New Hampshire. Available to U.S. citizens.

Application Requirements: Application, essay, financial need analysis, references, transcript. *Deadline:* May 10.

Contact: Ms. Jacqueline Lambert, Assistant to Trustees of Yarnold Trust
Alice M. Yarnold and Samuel Yarnold Scholarship Trust
180 Locust Street
Dover, NH 03820
Phone: 603-749-5535
Fax: 603-749-1187

AMERICAN ASSOCIATION FOR HEALTH EDUCATION http://www.aahperd.org/aahe

AMERICAN ASSOCIATION FOR HEALTH EDUCATION SCHOLARSHIP
• *See page 194*

AMERICAN FEDERATION OF TEACHERS http://www.aft.org

ROBERT G. PORTER SCHOLARS PROGRAM-AFT DEPENDENTS
• *See page 194*

ROBERT G. PORTER SCHOLARS PROGRAM-AFT MEMBERS
• *See page 194*

AMERICAN FOUNDATION FOR PHARMACEUTICAL EDUCATION http://www.afpenet.org

AMERICAN ASSOCIATION OF PHARMACEUTICAL SCIENTISTS GATEWAY SCHOLARSHIP PROGRAM

Awards of $4500 for research project, $500 to attend AAPS Annual Meeting. To encourage students to undertake pre-professional or undergraduate degree research experience. Letter from faculty sponsor and one other faculty member, official transcript, and test scores required. May be used in sophomore, junior, or senior year, or in last 3 years of PharmD program.

Academic Fields/Career Goals: Health and Medical Sciences.

Award: Scholarship for use in sophomore, junior, or senior years; renewable. *Number:* up to 16. *Amount:* up to $5000.

American Foundation for Pharmaceutical Education (continued)

Eligibility Requirements: Applicant must be enrolled or expecting to enroll full-time at an institution or university.

Application Requirements: Application, references, test scores, transcript. *Deadline:* January 28.

Contact: Robert M. Bachman, President
American Foundation for Pharmaceutical Education
One Church Street, Suite 202
Rockville, MD 20850
Phone: 301-738-2160
Fax: 301-738-2161

AMERICAN INDIAN SCIENCE AND ENGINEERING SOCIETY http://www.aises.org

A.T. ANDERSON MEMORIAL SCHOLARSHIP

• *See page 65*

AMERICAN LEGION AUXILIARY, DEPARTMENT OF ARIZONA

AMERICAN LEGION AUXILIARY DEPARTMENT OF ARIZONA HEALTH CARE OCCUPATION SCHOLARSHIPS

Award for Arizona residents enrolled at an institution in Arizona that awards degree or certificate in health occupations. Preference given to an immediate family member of a veteran. Must be a U.S. citizen and Arizona resident for at least one year.

Academic Fields/Career Goals: Health and Medical Sciences.

Award: Scholarship for use in freshman, sophomore, junior, or senior years; not renewable. *Amount:* $400.

Eligibility Requirements: Applicant must be enrolled or expecting to enroll full-time at a two-year or four-year institution or university; resident of Arizona and studying in Arizona. Available to U.S. citizens.

Application Requirements: Application, autobiography, essay, financial need analysis, photo, references, test scores, transcript. *Deadline:* May 15.

Contact: Department Secretary and Treasurer
American Legion Auxiliary, Department of Arizona
4701 North 19th Avenue, Suite 100
Phoenix, AZ 85015-3727
Phone: 602-241-1080
Fax: 602-604-9640
E-mail: amlegauxaz@mcleodusa.net

AMERICAN LEGION AUXILIARY, DEPARTMENT OF MAINE

AMERICAN LEGION AUXILIARY DEPARTMENT OF MAINE PAST PRESIDENTS' PARLEY NURSES SCHOLARSHIP

One-time award for child, grandchild, sister, or brother of veteran. Must be resident of Maine age 18 and over wishing to continue education at accredited school in medical field. Must submit photo, doctor's statement, and evidence of civic activity. Minimum 3.5 GPA required.

Academic Fields/Career Goals: Health and Medical Sciences.

Award: Scholarship for use in freshman, sophomore, junior, or senior years; not renewable. *Number:* 1. *Amount:* $300.

Eligibility Requirements: Applicant must be age 18; enrolled or expecting to enroll at a two-year or four-year or technical institution or university and resident of Maine. Applicant or parent of applicant must have employment or volunteer experience in community service. Applicant must have 3.5 GPA or higher. Applicant or parent must meet one or more of the following requirements: general military experience; retired from active duty; disabled or killed as a result of military service; prisoner of war; or missing in action.

Application Requirements: Application, photo, references, transcript. *Deadline:* April 30.

Contact: Ms. Madeline Sweet, Secretary
American Legion Auxiliary, Department of Maine
PO Box 887
Bucksport, ME 04416-0887

AMERICAN LEGION AUXILIARY, DEPARTMENT OF MICHIGAN http://www.michalaux.org

MEDICAL CAREER SCHOLARSHIP

Award for training in Michigan as registered nurse, licensed practical nurse, physical therapist, respiratory therapist, or any medical career. Must be child, grandchild, great-grandchild, wife, or widow of honorably discharged or deceased veteran who has served during eligibility dates for American Legion membership. Must be Michigan resident attending a Michigan school.

Academic Fields/Career Goals: Health and Medical Sciences; Nursing; Therapy/Rehabilitation.

Award: Scholarship for use in freshman year; not renewable. *Number:* 5–20. *Amount:* $500.

Eligibility Requirements: Applicant must be enrolled or expecting to enroll full or part-time at a two-year or four-year or technical institution or university; resident of Michigan and studying in Michigan. Applicant must have 3.5 GPA or higher. Available to U.S. citizens. Applicant or parent must meet one or more of the following requirements: general military experience; retired from active duty; disabled or killed as a result of military service; prisoner of war; or missing in action.

Application Requirements: Application, financial need analysis, references, transcript. *Deadline:* March 15.

Contact: Leisa Eldred, Scholarship Coordinator
American Legion Auxiliary, Department of Michigan
212 North Verlinden Avenue
Lansing, MI 48915
Phone: 517-371-4720 Ext. 19
Fax: 517-371-2401
E-mail: michalaux@voyager.net

AMERICAN LEGION AUXILIARY, DEPARTMENT OF MINNESOTA

AMERICAN LEGION AUXILIARY DEPARTMENT OF MINNESOTA PAST PRESIDENT PARLEY HEALTH CARE SCHOLARSHIP

One-time $750 award for American Legion Auxiliary Department of Minnesota member of at least three years who is needy and deserving, to begin or continue education in any phase of the health care field. Must be a Minnesota resident, attend a vocational or postsecondary institution and maintain at least a C average in school.

Academic Fields/Career Goals: Health and Medical Sciences.

Award: Scholarship for use in freshman, sophomore, junior, or senior years; not renewable. *Number:* up to 3. *Amount:* $750.

Eligibility Requirements: Applicant must be enrolled or expecting to enroll at a two-year or four-year or technical institution or university; resident of Minnesota and studying in Minnesota. Applicant or parent of applicant must be member of American Legion or Auxiliary.

Application Requirements: Application, financial need analysis. *Deadline:* March 15.

Contact: Eleanor Johnson, Executive Secretary
American Legion Auxiliary, Department of Minnesota
State Veterans Service Building, 20 W 12th Street, Room 314
St. Paul, MN 55155
Phone: 651-224-7634
Fax: 651-224-5243

AMERICAN LEGION AUXILIARY, DEPARTMENT OF TEXAS

AMERICAN LEGION AUXILIARY, DEPARTMENT OF TEXAS PAST PRESIDENT'S PARLEY MEDICAL SCHOLARSHIP

Scholarships available for full-time students pursuing studies in human health care. Must be a resident of Texas. Must be a veteran or child, grandchild, great grandchild of a veteran who served in the Armed Forces during period of eligibility. For specific details and application contact your local American Legion Auxiliary unit. Deadline is May 1.

Academic Fields/Career Goals: Health and Medical Sciences.

Award: Scholarship for use in freshman, sophomore, junior, senior, graduate, or postgraduate years; not renewable. *Number:* varies. *Amount:* $500.

Eligibility Requirements: Applicant must be enrolled or expecting to enroll full-time at a two-year or four-year or technical institution or university and resident of Texas. Available to U.S. citizens. Applicant or parent must meet one or more of the following requirements: general military experience; retired from active duty; disabled or killed as a result of military service; prisoner of war; or missing in action.

Application Requirements: Application, financial need analysis, photo, references, self-addressed stamped envelope, transcript, letter stating qualifications and intentions. *Deadline:* May 1.

Contact: American Legion Auxiliary, Department of Texas
3401 Ed Bluestein Boulevard, Suite 200
Austin, TX 78721-2902
Fax: 512-476-7278

AMERICAN LEGION AUXILIARY, DEPARTMENT OF WYOMING

PAST PRESIDENTS PARLEY HEALTH CARE SCHOLARSHIP

• *See page 183*

AMERICAN MEDICAL TECHNOLOGISTS http://www.amt1.com

AMERICAN MEDICAL TECHNOLOGISTS STUDENT SCHOLARSHIP

• *See page 183*

AMERICAN OCCUPATIONAL THERAPY FOUNDATION, INC. http://www.aotf.org

AMERICAN OCCUPATIONAL THERAPY FOUNDATION STATE ASSOCIATION SCHOLARSHIPS

Awards offered at the American Occupational Therapy Foundation state association level for study leading to associate, baccalaureate and graduate degrees in occupational therapy. Must be an AOTF member. Requirements vary by state. See Web site at http://www.aotf.org for further details. Application deadline is January 15.

Academic Fields/Career Goals: Health and Medical Sciences; Therapy/Rehabilitation.

Award: Scholarship for use in freshman, sophomore, junior, senior, or graduate years; not renewable. *Number:* up to 38. *Amount:* $250–$2000.

Eligibility Requirements: Applicant must be enrolled or expecting to enroll full or part-time at a two-year or four-year institution or university. Applicant or parent of applicant must be member of American Occupational Therapy Association. Available to U.S. citizens.

Application Requirements: Application, essay, financial need analysis, references, transcript. *Deadline:* January 15.

Contact: Jane Huntington, Scholarship Coordinator
American Occupational Therapy Foundation, Inc.
4720 Montgomery Lane
PO Box 31220
Bethesda, MD 20824-1220
Phone: 301-652-6611 Ext. 2550
Fax: 301-656-3620

CARLOTTA WELLES SCHOLARSHIP

Award for study leading to an occupational therapy assistant degree at an accredited institution. Must be a member of the American Occupational Therapy Association. Application deadline is January 15.

Academic Fields/Career Goals: Health and Medical Sciences; Therapy/Rehabilitation.

Award: Scholarship for use in sophomore year; not renewable. *Number:* varies. *Amount:* $500.

Eligibility Requirements: Applicant must be enrolled or expecting to enroll full-time at a two-year institution. Applicant or parent of applicant must be member of American Occupational Therapy Association. Available to U.S. citizens.

Application Requirements: Application, essay, financial need analysis, references, transcript. *Deadline:* January 15.

Contact: Jane Huntington, Scholarship Coordinator
American Occupational Therapy Foundation, Inc.
4720 Montgomery Lane
PO Box 31220
Bethesda, MD 20824-1220
Phone: 301-652-6611 Ext. 2550
Fax: 301-656-3620

FLORENCE WOOD/ARKANSAS OCCUPATIONAL THERAPY ASSOCIATION SCHOLARSHIP

One scholarship of $500 to an Arkansas resident enrolled in an accredited occupational therapy educational program in Arkansas.

Academic Fields/Career Goals: Health and Medical Sciences; Therapy/Rehabilitation.

Award: Scholarship for use in junior, senior, or graduate years; not renewable. *Number:* 1. *Amount:* $500.

Eligibility Requirements: Applicant must be enrolled or expecting to enroll full or part-time at a two-year or four-year or technical institution or university; resident of Arkansas and studying in Arkansas. Available to U.S. citizens.

Application Requirements: Application, essay, financial need analysis, references, transcript. *Deadline:* January 15.

Contact: Jane Huntington, Scholarship Coordinator
American Occupational Therapy Foundation, Inc.
4720 Montgomery Lane, PO Box 31220
Bethesda, MD 20824
Phone: 301-652-6611 Ext. 2550
Fax: 301-656-3620
E-mail: jhuntington@aotf.org

KAPPA DELTA PHI SCHOLARSHIP FOR OCCUPATIONAL THERAPY ASSISTANT

Award for study leading to an occupational therapy assistant degree at an accredited institution. Must be a member of the American Occupational Therapy Association. Application deadline is January 15.

Academic Fields/Career Goals: Health and Medical Sciences; Therapy/Rehabilitation.

Award: Scholarship for use in sophomore year; not renewable. *Number:* 2. *Amount:* $500.

Eligibility Requirements: Applicant must be enrolled or expecting to enroll full-time at a two-year institution. Applicant or parent of applicant must be member of American Occupational Therapy Association. Available to U.S. citizens.

Application Requirements: Application, essay, financial need analysis, references, transcript. *Deadline:* January 15.

Contact: Jane Huntington, Scholarship Coordinator
American Occupational Therapy Foundation, Inc.
4720 Montgomery Lane
PO Box 31220
Bethesda, MD 20824-1220
Phone: 301-652-6611 Ext. 2550
Fax: 301-656-3620

AMERICAN PHYSICAL THERAPY ASSOCIATION http://www.apta.org

MINORITY SCHOLARSHIP AWARD FOR ACADEMIC EXCELLENCE IN PHYSICAL THERAPY

Scholarships available to minority students enrolled in their final year of an accredited physical therapy program. All application material must be received by December 1. Information on Web site http://www.apta.org.

Academic Fields/Career Goals: Health and Medical Sciences.

Award: Scholarship for use in senior year; not renewable. *Number:* varies. *Amount:* $5000.

Eligibility Requirements: Applicant must be American Indian/Alaska Native, Asian/Pacific Islander, Black (non-Hispanic), or Hispanic and enrolled or expecting to enroll at a four-year institution or university. Available to U.S. citizens.

American Physical Therapy Association (continued)

Application Requirements: Application, essay, resume, references, transcript, original plus 6 copies. *Deadline:* December 1.

Contact: Eva King, Assistant to the Director
American Physical Therapy Association
1111 North Fairfax Street
Alexandria, VA 22314-1488
Phone: 800-999-2782 Ext. 3144
E-mail: evaking@apta.org

MINORITY SCHOLARSHIP AWARD FOR ACADEMIC EXCELLENCE-PHYSICAL THERAPIST ASSISTANT

Scholarships available for minority students enrolled in the final year of an accredited physical therapist assistant program. All material must be received by December 1. Information and application is available on Web site http://www.apta.org.

Academic Fields/Career Goals: Health and Medical Sciences.

Award: Scholarship for use in senior year; not renewable. *Number:* varies. *Amount:* $2000.

Eligibility Requirements: Applicant must be American Indian/Alaska Native, Asian/Pacific Islander, Black (non-Hispanic), or Hispanic and enrolled or expecting to enroll at a four-year institution or university. Available to U.S. citizens.

Application Requirements: Application, essay, resume, references, transcript, 1 original, six copies. *Deadline:* December 1.

Contact: Eva King, Assistant to the Director
American Physical Therapy Association
1111 North Fairfax Street
Alexandria, VA 22314-1488
Phone: 800-999-2782 Ext. 3144
E-mail: evaking@apta.org

AMERICAN PSYCHOLOGICAL ASSOCIATION

http://www.apa.org/mfp

MINORITY AGING NETWORK IN PSYCHOLOGY SUMMER INSTITUTE ON AGING

One week institute/retreat designed to introduce students to aging research in the field of psychology through didactic seminars, group mentoring and multimedia exercises. Summer Institute provided to students at no cost. Applications available at Web site. Minorities are encouraged to apply.

Academic Fields/Career Goals: Health and Medical Sciences; Psychology; Social Sciences; Social Services.

Award: Scholarship for use in junior, senior, or graduate years; not renewable. *Number:* 10–12. *Amount:* varies.

Eligibility Requirements: Applicant must be enrolled or expecting to enroll full-time at a four-year institution or university. Available to U.S. citizens.

Application Requirements: Application, essay, financial need analysis, references, transcript. *Deadline:* March 15.

Contact: Dr. Kim Nickerson, Program Assistant Director
American Psychological Association
750 First Street, NE
Washington, DC 20002-4242
Phone: 202-336-6027
Fax: 202-336-6012
E-mail: mfp@apa.org

AMERICAN RESPIRATORY CARE FOUNDATION

http://www.arcfoundation.org

JIMMY A. YOUNG MEMORIAL EDUCATION RECOGNITION AWARD

Award available to undergraduate minority students studying respiratory care at an American Medical Association-approved institution. Submit letters of recommendation and a paper on a respiratory care topic. Must have a minimum 3.0 GPA. One-time award of up to $1000.

Academic Fields/Career Goals: Health and Medical Sciences; Therapy/Rehabilitation.

Award: Prize for use in freshman, sophomore, junior, or senior years; not renewable. *Number:* 1. *Amount:* up to $1000.

Eligibility Requirements: Applicant must be American Indian/Alaska Native, Asian/Pacific Islander, Black (non-Hispanic), or Hispanic and enrolled or expecting to enroll full or part-time at a two-year or four-year or technical institution or university. Applicant must have 3.0 GPA or higher.

Application Requirements: Application, references, transcript, paper on respiratory care topic. *Deadline:* May 31.

Contact: Jill Nelson, Administrative Coordinator
American Respiratory Care Foundation
9425 North MacArthur Boulevard, Suite 100
Irving, TX 75063-4706
Phone: 972-243-2272
Fax: 972-484-2720
E-mail: info@arcfoundation.org

MORTON B. DUGGAN, JR. MEMORIAL EDUCATION RECOGNITION AWARD

Award for students with a minimum 3.0 GPA enrolled in an American Medical Association-approved respiratory care program. Must be U.S. citizen or permanent resident. Need proof of college enrollment. Submit an original referenced paper on respiratory care. Preference given to Georgia and South Carolina residents. One-time merit-based award of $1000 plus airfare, registration to AARC Congress, and one night's lodging.

Academic Fields/Career Goals: Health and Medical Sciences; Therapy/Rehabilitation.

Award: Prize for use in freshman, sophomore, junior, or senior years; not renewable. *Number:* 1. *Amount:* up to $1000.

Eligibility Requirements: Applicant must be enrolled or expecting to enroll full or part-time at a two-year or four-year or technical institution or university. Applicant must have 3.0 GPA or higher. Available to U.S. and non-U.S. citizens.

Application Requirements: Application, references, transcript, paper on respiratory care. *Deadline:* May 31.

Contact: Jill Nelson, Administrative Coordinator
American Respiratory Care Foundation
9425 North MacArthur Boulevard, Suite 100
Irving, TX 75063-4706
Phone: 972-243-2272
Fax: 972-484-2720
E-mail: info@arcfoundation.org

NBRC/AMP ROBERT M. LAWRENCE, MD, EDUCATION RECOGNITION AWARD

Merit-based award to third- or fourth-year student with a minimum 3.0 GPA, enrolled in accredited undergraduate respiratory therapy program. Submit proof of enrollment, original paper on some aspect of respiratory care, and original 1200-word essay on how this award will assist the applicant in reaching the objective of a degree and the ultimate goal of leadership in health care.

Academic Fields/Career Goals: Health and Medical Sciences; Therapy/Rehabilitation.

Award: Prize for use in junior or senior years; not renewable. *Number:* 1. *Amount:* up to $2500.

Eligibility Requirements: Applicant must be enrolled or expecting to enroll full or part-time at a four-year institution or university. Applicant must have 3.0 GPA or higher. Available to U.S. and non-U.S. citizens.

Application Requirements: Application, essay, references, transcript, paper on respiratory care. *Deadline:* May 31.

Contact: Jill Nelson, Administrative Coordinator
American Respiratory Care Foundation
9425 North MacArthur Boulevard, Suite 100
Irving, TX 75063-4706
Phone: 972-243-2272
Fax: 972-484-2720
E-mail: info@arcfoundation.org

NBRC/AMP WILLIAM W. BURGIN, MD EDUCATION RECOGNITION AWARD

Merit-based award for second-year students enrolled in an accredited respiratory therapy program leading to an associate degree. Minimum GPA of

3.0 required. Submit an original referenced paper on some aspect of respiratory care and an original essay of at least 1200 words describing how the award will assist applicant in attaining career objective.

Academic Fields/Career Goals: Health and Medical Sciences; Therapy/Rehabilitation.

Award: Prize for use in sophomore year; not renewable. *Number:* 1. *Amount:* up to $2500.

Eligibility Requirements: Applicant must be enrolled or expecting to enroll full or part-time at a two-year institution. Applicant must have 3.0 GPA or higher. Available to U.S. and non-U.S. citizens.

Application Requirements: Application, essay, references, transcript, paper on respiratory care. *Deadline:* May 31.

Contact: Jill Nelson, Administrative Coordinator
American Respiratory Care Foundation
9425 North MacArthur Boulevard, Suite 100
Irving, TX 75063-4706
Phone: 972-243-2272
Fax: 972-484-2720
E-mail: info@arcfoundation.org

SEPRACOR ACHIEVEMENT AWARD FOR EXCELLENCE IN PULMONARY DISEASE STATE MANAGEMENT

One-time award to recognize achievement in respiratory therapy and other disease state management.

Academic Fields/Career Goals: Health and Medical Sciences; Therapy/Rehabilitation.

Award: Prize for use in freshman, sophomore, junior, senior, graduate, or postgraduate years; not renewable. *Number:* 1. *Amount:* up to $2500.

Eligibility Requirements: Applicant must be enrolled or expecting to enroll at an institution or university. Applicant or parent of applicant must have employment or volunteer experience in designated career field. Available to U.S. and non-U.S. citizens.

Application Requirements: References, curriculum vitae. *Deadline:* May 31.

Contact: Jill Nelson, Administrative Coordinator
American Respiratory Care Foundation
9425 North MacArthur Boulevard, Suite 100
Irving, TX 75063-4706
Phone: 972-243-2272
Fax: 972-484-2720
E-mail: info@arcfoundation.org

AMERICAN SOCIETY FOR CLINICAL PATHOLOGY http://www.ascp.org

AMERICAN SOCIETY FOR CLINICAL PATHOLOGY SCHOLARSHIPS

One-time award for students in the final clinical year of study in a NAACLS or CAAHEP college or university MT, MLT, CT, HT or HTL program. Must be U.S. citizen or permanent resident. Submit three references and two self-addressed stamped envelopes.

Academic Fields/Career Goals: Health and Medical Sciences.

Award: Scholarship for use in senior year; not renewable. *Number:* 30–40. *Amount:* $1000.

Eligibility Requirements: Applicant must be enrolled or expecting to enroll full-time at a four-year institution or university. Applicant must have 3.0 GPA or higher. Available to U.S. citizens.

Application Requirements: Application, essay, references, self-addressed stamped envelope, transcript. *Deadline:* October 31.

Contact: Customer Service
American Society for Clinical Pathology
2100 West Harrison Street
Chicago, IL 60612
Phone: 312-738-1336

AMERICAN SOCIETY FOR CLINICAL LABORATORY SCIENCE http://www.ascls.org

ASCLS FORUM FOR CONCERNS OF MINORITIES SCHOLARSHIP

• *See page 139*

ASCLS REGION II PENNSYLVANIA SOCIETY FOR CLINICAL LABORATORY SCIENCE MERCEDES T. COLE MEMORIAL SCHOLARSHIP

One $1000 scholarship will be awarded to a student who is an ASCLS member with Pennsylvania as their constituent society. Applicant must be enrolled in a NAACLS accredited program at time of application and attend the laboratory technology program for the duration of the scholarship. Please refer to Web site for further information and application: http://www.pscls.org.

Academic Fields/Career Goals: Health and Medical Sciences.

Award: Scholarship for use in freshman, sophomore, junior, or senior years. *Number:* 1. *Amount:* $1000.

Eligibility Requirements: Applicant must be enrolled or expecting to enroll at a two-year or four-year or technical institution or university. Applicant or parent of applicant must be member of American Society for Clinical Laboratory Science. Available to U.S. citizens.

Application Requirements: Application, essay, references, transcript, proof of enrollment. *Deadline:* December 1.

Contact: See Web site.

ASCLS REGION II PENNSYLVANIA SOCIETY FOR CLINICAL LABORATORY SCIENCE SANDRA L. KEENER MEMORIAL CONTINUING EDUCATIONSHIP

Scholarship awards up to $150 for non-members, and up to $250 to PSCLS members for continuing education in clinical laboratory science. Applicants must be currently employed in the discipline or previously employed in the discipline and wish to return. Please refer to Web site for further information and application: http://www.pscls.org.

Academic Fields/Career Goals: Health and Medical Sciences.

Award: Scholarship for use in freshman, sophomore, junior, senior, graduate, or postgraduate years; not renewable. *Number:* varies. *Amount:* $150–$250.

Eligibility Requirements: Applicant must be enrolled or expecting to enroll at a two-year or four-year or technical institution or university. Available to U.S. citizens.

Application Requirements: Application, transcript. *Deadline:* Continuous.

Contact: See Web site.

ASCLS REGION II VIRGINIA SOCIETY FOR CLINICAL LABORATORY SCIENCE SCHOLARSHIPS

One $500 scholarship available to a clinical laboratory student in his or her final year of study. Applicant must be in their final clinical year in an accredited CLS/MT, CLT/MLT, cytology, or histology program. Must attend program within Commonwealth of Virginia. Please refer to Web site for further information and application: http://www.rscls.vavalleyweb.com.

Academic Fields/Career Goals: Health and Medical Sciences.

Award: Scholarship for use in senior year; not renewable. *Number:* 1. *Amount:* $500.

Eligibility Requirements: Applicant must be enrolled or expecting to enroll at a four-year institution or university and studying in Virginia. Available to U.S. citizens.

Application Requirements: Application, financial need analysis, references, transcript. *Deadline:* varies.

Contact: Shirley Jenkins
E-mail: shirley.jenkins@mjh.org

ASCLS REGION IV OHIO SOCIETY FOR CLINICAL LABORATORY SCIENCE GERALDINE DIEBLER/STELLA GRIFFIN AWARD

One scholarship available to a student enrolled in a clinical laboratory science curriculum. Award may be used for freshman year through clinical year of program. Applicant must be a permanent resident of Ohio from the Akron,

American Society for Clinical Laboratory Science (continued)

Canton, and Steubenville areas. Must have minimum 2.5 GPA. Please refer to Web site for further information and application: http://www/oscls.com.

Academic Fields/Career Goals: Health and Medical Sciences.

Award: Scholarship for use in freshman, sophomore, junior, or senior years; not renewable. *Number:* 1. *Amount:* $1000.

Eligibility Requirements: Applicant must be enrolled or expecting to enroll at a four-year institution or university and resident of Ohio. Applicant must have 2.5 GPA or higher. Available to U.S. citizens.

Application Requirements: Application, financial need analysis, references, transcript, personal statement. *Deadline:* May 15.

Contact: Rose Ann Crawford, Scholarship Committee Chair
American Society for Clinical Laboratory Science
529 Tammery Drive
Tallmadge, OH 44278-3033
Phone: 330-344-6256
E-mail: RAC529@hotmail.com

ASCLS REGION IV OHIO SOCIETY FOR CLINICAL LABORATORY SCIENCE STELLA GRIFFIN MEMORIAL SCHOLARSHIP

One scholarship available to a student enrolled in a clinical laboratory science curriculum. Award may be used for freshman year through clinical year of program. Applicant must be a permanent resident of Ohio with a minimum 2.5 GPA. Please refer to Web site for further information and application: http://www.oscls.com.

Academic Fields/Career Goals: Health and Medical Sciences.

Award: Scholarship for use in freshman, sophomore, junior, or senior years; not renewable. *Number:* 1. *Amount:* $1000.

Eligibility Requirements: Applicant must be enrolled or expecting to enroll at a four-year institution or university and resident of Ohio. Applicant must have 2.5 GPA or higher. Available to U.S. citizens.

Application Requirements: Application, financial need analysis, references, transcript, personal statement. *Deadline:* May 15.

Contact: Rose Ann Crawford, Scholarship Committee Chair
American Society for Clinical Laboratory Science
529 Tammery Drive
Tallmadge, OH 44278-3033
Phone: 330-344-6256
E-mail: rac529@hotmail.com

ASCLS REGION IX CLINICAL LABORATORY SCIENTISTS OF ALASKA SHARON O'MEARA CONTINUING EDUCATION SCHOLARSHIP FUND

• *See page 139*

ASCLS REGION VI MISSOURI ORGANIZATION FOR CLINICAL LABORATORY SCIENCE EDUCATION SCHOLARSHIP

• *See page 139*

AMERICAN SOCIETY OF RADIOLOGIC TECHNOLOGISTS EDUCATION AND RESEARCH FOUNDATION

http://www.asrt.org

ISADORE N. STERN SCHOLARSHIP

• *See page 287*

JERMAN-CAHOON STUDENT SCHOLARSHIP

Merit Scholarship for certificate or undergraduate students. Must have completed at least one semester in the Radiological Sciences to apply. Financial need is a factor. Requirements include 3.0 GPA, recommendation and 450-500 word essay.

Academic Fields/Career Goals: Health and Medical Sciences.

Award: Scholarship for use in freshman, sophomore, or junior years; not renewable. *Number:* 3. *Amount:* $2500.

Eligibility Requirements: Applicant must be enrolled or expecting to enroll full or part-time at a two-year or four-year or technical institution or university. Applicant must have 3.0 GPA or higher. Available to U.S. citizens.

Application Requirements: Application, essay, financial need analysis, references, transcript. *Deadline:* February 1.

Contact: Phelosha Collaros, Development Officer
American Society of Radiologic Technologists Education and Research Foundation
15000 Central Avenue, SE
Albuquerque, NM 87123-3917
Phone: 505-298-4500 Ext. 2541
Fax: 505-298-5063
E-mail: foundation@asrt.org

ROYCE OSBORN MINORITY STUDENT SCHOLARSHIP

Minority scholarship for certificate or undergraduate students. Must have completed at least one semester in the Radiologic Sciences to apply. Financial need is a factor. Requirements include 3.0 GPA, recommendation, and 450-500 word essay.

Academic Fields/Career Goals: Health and Medical Sciences.

Award: Scholarship for use in freshman, sophomore, or junior years; not renewable. *Number:* 5. *Amount:* $4000.

Eligibility Requirements: Applicant must be American Indian/Alaska Native, Asian/Pacific Islander, Black (non-Hispanic), or Hispanic and enrolled or expecting to enroll full or part-time at a two-year or four-year or technical institution or university. Applicant must have 3.0 GPA or higher. Available to U.S. citizens.

Application Requirements: Application, essay, financial need analysis, references, transcript. *Deadline:* February 1.

Contact: Phelosha Collaros, Development Officer
American Society of Radiologic Technologists Education and Research Foundation
15000 Central Avenue, SE
Albuquerque, NM 87123-3917
Phone: 505-298-4500 Ext. 2541
Fax: 505-298-5063
E-mail: foundation@asrt.org

SIEMENS SCHOLAR AWARD

• *See page 287*

VARIAN RADIATION THERAPY STUDENT SCHOLARSHIP

Merit Scholarship for undergraduate or certificate students accepted or enrolled in a Radiation Therapy Program. Financial need is a factor. Requirements include 3.0 GPA, recommendation and 450-500 word essay. Sponsored in conjunction with Varian Oncology Systems.

Academic Fields/Career Goals: Health and Medical Sciences.

Award: Scholarship for use in freshman, sophomore, or junior years; not renewable. *Number:* 11. *Amount:* $5000.

Eligibility Requirements: Applicant must be enrolled or expecting to enroll full or part-time at a two-year or four-year or technical institution or university. Applicant must have 3.0 GPA or higher. Available to U.S. citizens.

Application Requirements: Application, essay, financial need analysis, references, transcript. *Deadline:* February 1.

Contact: Phelosha Collaros, Development Officer
American Society of Radiologic Technologists Education and Research Foundation
15000 Central Avenue, SE
Albuquerque, NM 87123-3917
Phone: 505-298-4500 Ext. 2541
Fax: 505-298-5063
E-mail: foundation@asrt.org

AMERICAN SOCIETY OF SAFETY ENGINEERS (ASSE) FOUNDATION

http://www.asse.org/foundat.htm

UNITED PARCEL SERVICE DIVERSITY SCHOLARSHIP PROGRAM

• *See page 263*

ARKANSAS DEPARTMENT OF HIGHER EDUCATION

http://www.arscholarships.com

ARKANSAS HEALTH EDUCATION GRANT PROGRAM (ARHEG)

• *See page 62*

ARRL FOUNDATION, INC. http://www.arrl.org/arrlf/scholgen.html

WILLIAM R. GOLDFARB MEMORIAL SCHOLARSHIP

• *See page 121*

ASSOCIATED MEDICAL SERVICES, INC. http://www.ams-inc.on.ca

ASSOCIATED MEDICAL SERVICES, INC. HANNAH STUDENTSHIP

Studentships available to undergraduate students who are Canadian citizens or permanent residents. Research must be done at a Canadian university and limited to the study of health, disease, or medicine. Studentship limited to three months. Deadline is January 15. Information is available on Web site: http://www.ams-inc.on.ca.

Academic Fields/Career Goals: Health and Medical Sciences.

Award: Grant for use in freshman, sophomore, junior, or senior years. *Number:* 1–10. *Amount:* up to $3366.

Eligibility Requirements: Applicant must be Canadian citizen; enrolled or expecting to enroll at a four-year institution or university and studying in Alberta, British Columbia, Manitoba, New Brunswick, Newfoundland, North West Territories, Nova Scotia, Prince Edward Island, Quebec, Saskatchewan, or Yukon.

Application Requirements: Application, references, transcript, ethics certificate. *Deadline:* January 15.

Contact: Margaret Phillips, Grants Officer
Associated Medical Services, Inc.
162 Cumberland Street
Suite 228
Toronto, ON M5R 3N5
Canada
Phone: 416-924-3368
Fax: 416-323-3338
E-mail: grantsof@ams-inc.on.ca

ASSOCIATION OF SURGICAL TECHNOLOGISTS http://www.ast.org

SURGICAL TECHNOLOGY SCHOLARSHIPS

The scholarship is to encourage and reward educational excellence and need demonstrated by surgical technology students.

Academic Fields/Career Goals: Health and Medical Sciences.

Award: Scholarship for use in freshman or sophomore years; not renewable. *Number:* 5–10. *Amount:* $500–$2500.

Eligibility Requirements: Applicant must be enrolled or expecting to enroll full-time at a two-year or technical institution. Applicant must have 3.5 GPA or higher. Available to U.S. and non-U.S. citizens.

Application Requirements: Application, essay, financial need analysis, references, self-addressed stamped envelope, transcript. *Deadline:* April 1.

Contact: Karen Ludwig, Director of Publishing-Association of Surgical Technologists
Association of Surgical Technologists
7108-C South Alton Way
Centennial, CO 80112-2106
Phone: 303-694-9130 Ext. 224
Fax: 303-694-9169

THOMSON DELMAR LEARNING SURGICAL TECHNOLOGY SCHOLARSHIP

Award available to a student in CAAHEP-accredited program. Must have a 2.5 GPA. See Web site for more information http://www.ast.org

Academic Fields/Career Goals: Health and Medical Sciences.

Award: Scholarship for use in freshman, sophomore, junior, or senior years; not renewable. *Number:* up to 1. *Amount:* up to $1000.

Eligibility Requirements: Applicant must be enrolled or expecting to enroll at a two-year or technical institution. Applicant must have 2.5 GPA or higher.

Application Requirements: Application, essay, references, self-addressed stamped envelope, transcript, course fee schedule. *Deadline:* April 1.

Contact: AST Education Department
Association of Surgical Technologists
7108-C South Alton Way
Centennial, CO 80112-2106

BECA FOUNDATION, INC.

ALICE NEWELL JOSLYN MEDICAL FUND

• *See page 183*

BETHESDA LUTHERAN HOMES AND SERVICES, INC. http://www.blhs.org

DEVELOPMENTAL DISABILITIES SCHOLASTIC ACHIEVEMENT SCHOLARSHIP FOR LUTHERAN COLLEGE STUDENTS

• *See page 184*

BOYS AND GIRLS CLUBS OF GREATER SAN DIEGO http://www.sdyouth.org

SPENCE REESE SCHOLARSHIP FUND

• *See page 242*

BRITISH COLUMBIA MINISTRY OF ADVANCED EDUCATION http://www.aved.gov.bc.ca/

LOAN FORGIVENESS PROGRAM FOR NURSES, DOCTORS, MIDWIVES, AND PHARMACISTS

Loans to nursing, medical, midwifery, and pharmacy students from the British Columbia Ministry of Advanced Education will be forgiven at a rate of 33% per every year of service in a underprivileged or rural area of British Columbia. Three years of service will be rewarded with complete forgiveness of the loan. Must be Canadian. Must have graduated from a post-secondary institution with BC student loans in August 2000, or later. For more information, see Web site: http://www.aved.gov.bc.ca/.

Academic Fields/Career Goals: Health and Medical Sciences; Nursing; Pharmacy.

Award: Forgivable loan for use in freshman, sophomore, junior, senior, or graduate years; renewable. *Number:* varies. *Amount:* varies.

Eligibility Requirements: Applicant must be enrolled or expecting to enroll at a two-year or four-year institution or university. Available to Canadian citizens.

Application Requirements: Application, transcript. *Deadline:* Continuous.

Contact: Loan Remission and Management Unit
British Columbia Ministry of Advanced Education
PO Box 9173
Stn Prov Govt
Victoria, BC V8W 9H7
Canada
Phone: 800-561-1818

BUREAU OF HEALTH PROFESSIONS http://nhsc.bhpr.hrsa.gov/members/scholars/

NATIONAL HEALTH SERVICE CORPS SCHOLARSHIP PROGRAM

Federal scholarships for U.S. citizens pursuing allopathic (MD) or osteopathic (DO) medicine, dentistry, family nurse practitioner, nurse midwifery, or physician assistant education. Two-year to four-year service commitment required. Scholarship includes tuition, fees, monthly stipends, and payment for educational expenses. Monthly stipend is taxable. Federal income tax only withheld from monthly stipend. Application deadline: March 26.

Academic Fields/Career Goals: Health and Medical Sciences; Nursing.

Award: Scholarship for use in freshman, sophomore, junior, senior, or graduate years; renewable. *Number:* 200–300. *Amount:* $67,500–$135,000.

Eligibility Requirements: Applicant must be enrolled or expecting to enroll full-time at a four-year institution or university. Available to U.S. citizens.

Bureau of Health Professions (continued)

Application Requirements: Application, interview. *Deadline:* March 26.

Contact: c/o IQ Solutions Information Specialist
Bureau of Health Professions
11300 Rockville Pike, Suite 801
Rockville, MD 20852
Phone: 800-638-0824

BUSINESS AND PROFESSIONAL WOMEN'S FOUNDATION http://www.bpwusa.org

BPW CAREER ADVANCEMENT SCHOLARSHIP PROGRAM FOR WOMEN

• *See page 112*

CALIFORNIA ADOLESCENT NUTRITION AND FITNESS (CANFIT) PROGRAM http://www.canfit.org

CALIFORNIA ADOLESCENT NUTRITION AND FITNESS (CANFIT) PROGRAM SCHOLARSHIP

• *See page 271*

CANADIAN SOCIETY FOR MEDICAL LABORATORY SCIENCE http://www.csmls.org

CANADIAN SOCIETY OF LABORATORY TECHNOLOGISTS STUDENT SCHOLARSHIP PROGRAM

Six awards available to students enrolled in their final year of general medical laboratory technology, cytotechnology, or clinical genetic studies. Must be student member of Canadian Society for Medical Laboratory Science, and Canadian citizen or permanent resident of Canada. One-time award of CAN$500. Deadline: April 1 for clinical genetics, November 1 for all other.

Academic Fields/Career Goals: Health and Medical Sciences.

Award: Scholarship for use in senior, or graduate years; not renewable. *Number:* 6. *Amount:* $371.

Eligibility Requirements: Applicant must be Canadian citizen and enrolled or expecting to enroll full-time at a technical institution. Applicant or parent of applicant must be member of Canadian Society for Medical Laboratory Science.

Application Requirements: Application, financial need analysis, references, self-addressed stamped envelope, transcript. *Deadline:* varies.

Contact: Lynn Zehr, Executive Assistant
Canadian Society for Medical Laboratory Science
LCD 1, PO Box 2830
Hamilton, ON L8N 3N8
Canada
Phone: 905-528-8642 Ext. 12
Fax: 905-528-4968
E-mail: lzehr@csmis.org

E.V. BOOTH SCHOLARSHIP AWARD

• *See page 288*

CIRI FOUNDATION http://www.ciri.com/tcf

ROY M. HUHNDORF HEALTH SCIENCES ENDOWMENT SCHOLARSHIP FUND

To encourage students seeking an undergraduate or graduate degree particularly in health services. Applicant must be Alaska Native student. For details see Web site: http://www.ciri.com/tcf.

Academic Fields/Career Goals: Health and Medical Sciences.

Award: Scholarship for use in freshman, sophomore, junior, senior, or graduate years; not renewable. *Number:* varies. *Amount:* varies.

Eligibility Requirements: Applicant must be enrolled or expecting to enroll full-time at a two-year or four-year institution or university.

Application Requirements: Application, essay, references, transcript, proof of eligibility, birth certificate or adoption decree. *Deadline:* June 1.

Contact: CIRI Foundation
2600 Cordova Street, Suite 206
Anchorage, AK 99503
Phone: 907-263-5582
Fax: 907-263-5588
E-mail: tcf@ciri.com

CONGRESSIONAL BLACK CAUCUS SPOUSES PROGRAM http://cbcfinc.org

CONGRESSIONAL BLACK CAUCUS SPOUSES HEALTH INITIATIVE

• *See page 288*

FOUNDATION FOR SURGICAL TECHNOLOGY http://www.ffst.org

FOUNDATION FOR SURGICAL TECHNOLOGY SCHOLARSHIP FUND

Scholarships available for students who are currently enrolled in a CAAHEP-accredited surgical technology program. Must be preparing for a career as a surgical technologist. 3.0 GPA is required. One-time award valued from $500 upwards, which varies from year to year . Applicant must be selected by sponsoring institution. Visit Web site for more information.

Academic Fields/Career Goals: Health and Medical Sciences.

Award: Scholarship for use in freshman, sophomore, junior, or senior years; not renewable. *Number:* 5–10. *Amount:* $500–$2500.

Eligibility Requirements: Applicant must be enrolled or expecting to enroll full or part-time at a two-year or four-year or technical institution or university. Applicant must have 3.0 GPA or higher. Available to U.S. and non-U.S. citizens.

Application Requirements: Application, financial need analysis, references, transcript. *Deadline:* April 1.

Contact: Karen Ludwig
Foundation for Surgical Technology
7108-C South Alton Way
Englewood, CO 80112-2106
Phone: 303-694-9130 Ext. 224
Fax: 303-694-9169

GENERAL FEDERATION OF WOMEN'S CLUBS OF MASSACHUSETTS

CATHERINE E. PHILBIN SCHOLARSHIP

One scholarship of $500 will be awarded to a graduate or undergraduate student studying public health. Eligible applicants will be residents of Massachusetts. Along with the application, students must send a personal statement of no more than 500 words addressing professional goals and financial need.

Academic Fields/Career Goals: Health and Medical Sciences.

Award: Scholarship for use in freshman, sophomore, junior, senior, or graduate years; not renewable. *Number:* 1. *Amount:* $500.

Eligibility Requirements: Applicant must be enrolled or expecting to enroll full-time at a two-year or four-year institution or university and resident of Massachusetts. Available to U.S. citizens.

Application Requirements: Application, essay, references, transcript. *Deadline:* March 1.

Contact: Jane Howard, Scholarship Chairperson
General Federation of Women's Clubs of Massachusetts
PO Box 679
Sudbury, MA 01776-0679
Phone: 978-443-4569

GOVERNOR'S OFFICE

GOVERNOR'S OPPORTUNITY SCHOLARSHIP

• *See page 124*

GREATER KANAWHA VALLEY FOUNDATION http://www.tgkvf.org

NICHOLAS AND MARY AGNES TRIVILLIAN MEMORIAL SCHOLARSHIP FUND

Renewable award for West Virginia residents pursuing medical or pharmacy programs. Must show financial need and academic merit. For more information, contact address below. May apply for two Foundation scholarships but will only be chosen for one.

Academic Fields/Career Goals: Health and Medical Sciences.

Award: Scholarship for use in junior, senior, or graduate years; renewable. *Number:* 33. *Amount:* $1000.

Eligibility Requirements: Applicant must be enrolled or expecting to enroll at a four-year institution or university and resident of West Virginia. Applicant must have 2.5 GPA or higher. Available to U.S. citizens.

Application Requirements: Application, essay, financial need analysis, references, self-addressed stamped envelope, test scores, transcript. *Deadline:* February 17.

Contact: Susan Hoover, Scholarship Coordinator
Greater Kanawha Valley Foundation
PO Box 3041
Charleston, WV 25331
Phone: 304-346-3620
Fax: 304-346-3640

HAWAIIAN LODGE, F.& A. M. http://www.hawaiianlodge.org/

HAWAIIAN LODGE SCHOLARSHIPS

• *See page 76*

HEALTH PROFESSIONS EDUCATION FOUNDATION http://www.healthprofessions.ca.gov

HEALTH PROFESSIONS EDUCATION SCHOLARSHIP PROGRAM

• *See page 184*

KAISER PERMANENTE ALLIED HEALTHCARE SCHOLARSHIP

One-time award to all students enrolled in or accepted to California accredited allied health education programs for school related expenses. Priority is given to students enrolled in the following fields: medical imaging, occupational therapy, physical therapy, respiratory care, social work, pharmacy, pharmacy technician, medical laboratory technologist, surgical technician, ultrasound technician and diagnostic medical sonography. Eligible applicants may receive up to $2,500 per year in financial assistance. Deadlines: March 24 and September 9. Must be resident of CA and U.S. citizen.

Academic Fields/Career Goals: Health and Medical Sciences; Social Services; Therapy/Rehabilitation.

Award: Scholarship for use in freshman, sophomore, junior, or senior years; not renewable. *Number:* 20–40. *Amount:* $2000–$2500.

Eligibility Requirements: Applicant must be enrolled or expecting to enroll full or part-time at a two-year or four-year or technical institution or university; resident of California and studying in California. Available to U.S. citizens.

Application Requirements: Application, driver's license, financial need analysis, references, transcript. *Deadline:* varies.

Contact: Sondra Jacobs, Program Officer
Health Professions Education Foundation
818 K Street, Suite 210
Sacramento, CA 95814
Phone: 916-324-6500

YOUTH FOR ADOLESCENT PREGNANCY PREVENTION LEADERSHIP RECOGNITION PROGRAM

The Youth for Adolescent Pregnancy Prevention (YAPP) Leadership Recognition Program (LRP) will recognize youths throughout California who have made an outstanding contribution to their communities by promoting healthy adolescent sexuality and teen pregnancy prevention. Youths selected to receive this scholarship award will receive up to $5,000 per year for up to five years to assist them in pursing careers in the health field (e.g., medicine, ancillary services, dentistry, mental health). Must be resident of CA and U.S. citizen between the ages of 16-24.

Academic Fields/Career Goals: Health and Medical Sciences; Nursing.

Award: Scholarship for use in freshman, sophomore, junior, or senior years; not renewable. *Number:* 8. *Amount:* $5000–$25,000.

Eligibility Requirements: Applicant must be age 16-24; enrolled or expecting to enroll full or part-time at a two-year or four-year or technical institution or university; resident of California and studying in California. Available to U.S. citizens.

Application Requirements: Application, financial need analysis, interview, photo, references, transcript, 2 copies of application. *Deadline:* January 23.

Contact: Charles Gray, Project Officer
Health Professions Education Foundation
818 K Street, Suite 210
Sacramento, CA 95814
Phone: 916-324-6500
Fax: 916-324-6585
E-mail: cgray@oshpd.state.ca.us

HEALTH RESEARCH COUNCIL OF NEW ZEALAND http://www.hrc.govt.nz

PACIFIC HEALTH WORKFORCE AWARD

• *See page 288*

PACIFIC MENTAL HEALTH WORK FORCE AWARD

• *See page 288*

HEALTHCARE INFORMATION AND MANAGEMENT SYSTEMS SOCIETY FOUNDATION http://www.himss.org

HIMSS FOUNDATION SCHOLARSHIP PROGRAM

• *See page 288*

HERB SOCIETY OF AMERICA http://www.herbsociety.org

HERB SOCIETY RESEARCH GRANTS

• *See page 69*

ILLINOIS STUDENT ASSISTANCE COMMISSION (ISAC) http://www.collegezone.org

ILLINOIS DEPARTMENT OF PUBLIC HEALTH CENTER FOR RURAL HEALTH ALLIED HEALTH CARE PROFESSIONAL SCHOLARSHIP PROGRAM

Scholarship for Illinois students studying to be a nurse practitioner, physician assistant, or certified nurse midwife. Funding available for up to two years. Must fulfill an obligation to practice full-time in a designated shortage area as an allied healthcare professional in Illinois for one year for each year of scholarship funding. Failure to fulfill the obligation will require repayment to the state three times the amount of the scholarship received for each unfulfilled year of obligation plus 7% interest per year.

Academic Fields/Career Goals: Health and Medical Sciences.

Award: Scholarship for use in freshman, sophomore, junior, or senior years; renewable. *Number:* 20. *Amount:* $7500–$15,000.

Eligibility Requirements: Applicant must be enrolled or expecting to enroll at a two-year or four-year institution or university and resident of Illinois. Available to U.S. citizens.

Application Requirements: Application.

Contact: Marcia Franklin, Department of Public Health
Phone: 217-782-1624

ILLINOIS DEPARTMENT OF PUBLIC HEALTH CENTER FOR RURAL HEALTH NURSING EDUCATION SCHOLARSHIP PROGRAM

Scholarship for Illinois students pursuing a certificate, diploma, or degree in nursing and demonstrating financial need. Scholarship provides up to four years of financial aid in return for full-or part-time employment as a licensed practical or registered nurse in Illinois upon graduation. Must remain employed in Illinois for a period equivalent to the educational time that was supported by the scholarship. Application deadline is May 31.

Academic Fields/Career Goals: Health and Medical Sciences; Nursing.

Illinois Student Assistance Commission (ISAC) (continued)

Award: Scholarship for use in freshman, sophomore, junior, or senior years; renewable. *Number:* varies. *Amount:* varies.

Eligibility Requirements: Applicant must be enrolled or expecting to enroll at a two-year or four-year institution or university and resident of Illinois. Available to U.S. citizens.

Application Requirements: Application, financial need analysis. *Deadline:* May 31.

Contact: College Zone Counselor
Illinois Student Assistance Commission (ISAC)
1755 Lake Cook Road
Deerfield, IL 60015-5209
Phone: 800-899-4722
E-mail: collegezone@isac.org

INDIAN HEALTH SERVICES, UNITED STATES DEPARTMENT OF HEALTH AND HUMAN SERVICES http://www.ihs.gov

INDIAN HEALTH SERVICE HEALTH PROFESSIONS PRE-GRADUATE SCHOLARSHIPS

• *See page 185*

INTERNATIONAL ORDER OF THE KING'S DAUGHTERS AND SONS http://www.iokds.org

HEALTH CAREERS SCHOLARSHIP

• *See page 185*

J.D. ARCHBOLD MEMORIAL HOSPITAL http://www.archbold.org

ARCHBOLD SCHOLARSHIP PROGRAM

Service cancelable loan awarded for a clinical degree. Awarded to residents of Southwest Georgia and North Florida. Specific clinical degree may vary, depending on need in area. Must agree to full-time employment for 1-3 years upon graduation.

Academic Fields/Career Goals: Health and Medical Sciences; Nursing.

Award: Forgivable loan for use in junior year; not renewable. *Number:* 50. *Amount:* $600–$6000.

Eligibility Requirements: Applicant must be enrolled or expecting to enroll full or part-time at a two-year or four-year or technical institution or university and resident of Florida or Georgia. Available to U.S. citizens.

Application Requirements: Application, interview, transcript. *Deadline:* Continuous.

Contact: Donna McMillan, Education Coordinator
J.D. Archbold Memorial Hospital
PO Box 1018
Thomasville, GA 31799
Phone: 229-228-2795
Fax: 229-228-8584

JEWISH FEDERATION OF METROPOLITAN CHICAGO (JFMC) http://www.jvschicago.org

JEWISH FEDERATION OF METROPOLITAN CHICAGO ACADEMIC SCHOLARSHIP PROGRAM

• *See page 185*

JEWISH FOUNDATION FOR EDUCATION OF WOMEN http://www.jfew.org

SCHOLARSHIP PROGRAM FOR FORMER SOVIET UNION EMIGRES TRAINING IN THE HEALTH SCIENCES

• *See page 186*

LADIES AUXILIARY TO THE VETERANS OF FOREIGN WARS, DEPARTMENT OF MAINE

FRANCIS L. BOOTH MEDICAL SCHOLARSHIP SPONSORED BY LAVFW DEPARTMENT OF MAINE

Award for an undergraduate student majoring in the field of medicine who has a parent or grandparent who is a member of the Maine VFW or VFW auxiliary.

Academic Fields/Career Goals: Health and Medical Sciences; Humanities; Nursing; Therapy/Rehabilitation.

Award: Scholarship for use in freshman, sophomore, junior, or senior years; not renewable. *Number:* 1. *Amount:* $1000.

Eligibility Requirements: Applicant must be enrolled or expecting to enroll full-time at a four-year institution or university. Applicant or parent of applicant must be member of Veterans of Foreign Wars or Auxiliary. Applicant must have 3.0 GPA or higher. Available to U.S. citizens.

Application Requirements: Application, financial need analysis, resume, references, transcript. *Deadline:* March 1.

Contact: Janice Gaskill, Senior Vice President
Ladies Auxiliary to the Veterans of Foreign Wars, Department of Maine
PO Box 66
Passadumkeag, ME 04475
Phone: 207-723-4000

LINCOLN COMMUNITY FOUNDATION http://www.lcf.org

BRYAN/LGH MEDICAL CENTER WEST AUXILIARY SENIOR VOLUNTEER SCHOLARSHIP

Scholarship for student who is pursuing a health-related degree and has volunteered at least 100 hours at Bryan/LGH Medical Center West in Lincoln, NE.

Academic Fields/Career Goals: Health and Medical Sciences.

Award: Scholarship for use in freshman, sophomore, junior, or senior years; not renewable. *Number:* 1. *Amount:* $1000.

Eligibility Requirements: Applicant must be enrolled or expecting to enroll full-time at a two-year or four-year or technical institution or university and resident of Nebraska. Applicant must have 2.5 GPA or higher. Available to U.S. citizens.

Application Requirements: Application, essay, test scores, transcript, verification of volunteer hours. *Deadline:* April 15.

Contact: Application available at Web site.

MARIN EDUCATION FUND http://www.marineducationfund.org

GOLDMAN FAMILY FUND, NEW LEADER SCHOLARSHIP

• *See page 186*

MARYLAND HIGHER EDUCATION COMMISSION http://www.mhec.state.md.us

DEVELOPMENTAL DISABILITIES, MENTAL HEALTH, CHILD WELFARE AND JUVENILE JUSTICE WORKFORCE TUITION ASSISTANCE PROGRAM

Provides tuition assistance to students who are service employees who provide direct support or care to individuals with developmental disabilities or mental disorders. Must be a Maryland resident attending a Maryland college. Minimum 2.0 GPA.

Academic Fields/Career Goals: Health and Medical Sciences; Nursing; Social Services; Special Education; Therapy/Rehabilitation.

Award: Forgivable loan for use in freshman, sophomore, junior, senior, or graduate years; renewable. *Number:* 300–400. *Amount:* $500–$3000.

Eligibility Requirements: Applicant must be enrolled or expecting to enroll full or part-time at a two-year or four-year institution or university; resident of Maryland and studying in Maryland. Applicant or parent of applicant must have employment or volunteer experience in designated career field. Available to U.S. citizens.

Application Requirements: Application, transcript. *Deadline:* July 1.

Contact: Gerrie Rogers, Office of Student Financial Assistance
Maryland Higher Education Commission
839 Bestgate Road, Suite 400
Annapolis, MD 21401
Phone: 410-260-4574
Fax: 410-260-3203
E-mail: osfamail@mhec.state.md.us

FIREFIGHTER, AMBULANCE, AND RESCUE SQUAD MEMBER TUITION REIMBURSEMENT PROGRAM-MARYLAND

• *See page 270*

GRADUATE AND PROFESSIONAL SCHOLARSHIP PROGRAM-MARYLAND

• *See page 186*

MENTAL HEALTH ASSOCIATION IN NEW YORK STATE, INC. http://www.mhanys.org

EDNA AIMES SCHOLARSHIP

One-time award for individuals studying the prevention and treatment of mental illness and the promotion of mental health. Must be a New York resident attending a New York four-year institution. Application deadline is April 15.

Academic Fields/Career Goals: Health and Medical Sciences; Pharmacy; Psychology; Public Health.

Award: Scholarship for use in junior, senior, or graduate years; not renewable. *Number:* 1–3. *Amount:* $2000–$2500.

Eligibility Requirements: Applicant must be enrolled or expecting to enroll full-time at a four-year institution or university; resident of New York and studying in New York. Available to U.S. and non-U.S. citizens.

Application Requirements: Application, essay, references, transcript, demonstrate financial need, personal statement. *Deadline:* April 15.

Contact: Lillian Lasher, Administrative Assistant
Mental Health Association in New York State, Inc.
194 Washington Avenue, Suite 415
Albany, NY 12210
Phone: 518-434-0439 Ext. 22
Fax: 518-427-8676
E-mail: llasher@mhanys.org

MINNESOTA DEPARTMENT OF HEALTH http://www.health.state.mn.us

MINNESOTA NURSES LOAN FORGIVENESS PROGRAM

This program offers loan repayment to registered nurse and licensed practical nurse students who agree to practice in a Minnesota nursing home or an Intermediate Care Facility for persons with mental retardation for a minimum 3-year service obligation after completion of training. Candidates must apply while still in school.

Academic Fields/Career Goals: Health and Medical Sciences; Nursing.

Award: Grant for use in freshman, sophomore, junior, or senior years; not renewable. *Number:* 25–35. *Amount:* $3000–$4000.

Eligibility Requirements: Applicant must be enrolled or expecting to enroll full or part-time at a two-year or four-year or technical institution or university. Available to U.S. citizens.

Application Requirements: Application, essay, resume. *Deadline:* Continuous.

Contact: Karen Welter
Minnesota Department of Health
121 East Seventh Place, Suite 460, PO Box 64975
St. Paul, MN 55164-0975
Phone: 651-282-6302
E-mail: karen.welter@health.state.mn.us

MISSISSIPPI STATE STUDENT FINANCIAL AID http://www.mississippiuniversities.com

MISSISSIPPI HEALTH CARE PROFESSIONS LOAN/SCHOLARSHIP PROGRAM

Renewable award for junior and senior undergraduates studying psychology, speech pathology or occupational therapy. Must be Mississippi residents attending four-year universities in Mississippi. Must fulfill work obligation in Mississippi or pay back as loan. Renewable award for graduate student enrolled in physical therapy.

Academic Fields/Career Goals: Health and Medical Sciences; Psychology; Therapy/Rehabilitation.

Award: Forgivable loan for use in junior, senior, or graduate years; renewable. *Number:* varies. *Amount:* $1500–$6000.

Eligibility Requirements: Applicant must be enrolled or expecting to enroll full-time at a four-year institution or university; resident of Mississippi and studying in Mississippi. Available to U.S. citizens.

Application Requirements: Application, driver's license, references, transcript. *Deadline:* March 31.

Contact: Susan Eckels, Program Administrator
Mississippi State Student Financial Aid
3825 Ridgewood Road
Jackson, MS 39211-6453
Phone: 601-432-6997
E-mail: sme@ihl.state.ms.us

MISSOURI DEPARTMENT OF HEALTH AND SENIOR SERVICES http://www.dhss.state.mo.us

PRIMARY CARE RESOURCE INITIATIVE FOR MISSOURI LOAN PROGRAM

• *See page 186*

NASA IDAHO SPACE GRANT CONSORTIUM http://www.uidaho.edu/nasa_isgc

NASA IDAHO SPACE GRANT CONSORTIUM SCHOLARSHIP PROGRAM

• *See page 71*

NASA VERMONT SPACE GRANT CONSORTIUM http://www.emba.uvm.edu/vsgc

VERMONT SPACE GRANT CONSORTIUM SCHOLARSHIP PROGRAM

• *See page 71*

NATIONAL AMBUCS, INC. http://www.ambucs.com

AMBUCS SCHOLARS-SCHOLARSHIPS FOR THERAPISTS

Scholarships are open to students who are U.S. citizens at a junior level or above in college. Must be enrolled in an accredited program by the appropriate health therapy profession authority in physical therapy, occupational therapy, speech-language pathology, or audiology and must demonstrate a financial need. Application available on Web site at http://www.ambucs.com. Paper applications are not accepted.

Academic Fields/Career Goals: Health and Medical Sciences; Therapy/Rehabilitation.

Award: Scholarship for use in junior, senior, graduate, or postgraduate years; not renewable. *Number:* 300. *Amount:* $500–$6000.

Eligibility Requirements: Applicant must be enrolled or expecting to enroll full-time at a four-year institution or university. Available to U.S. citizens.

Application Requirements: Application, essay, financial need analysis, enrollment certification form. *Deadline:* April 15.

Contact: Janice Blankenship, Scholarship Coordinator
National AMBUCS, Inc.
PO Box 5127
High Point, NC 27262
Phone: 336-869-2166
Fax: 336-887-8451
E-mail: janiceb@ambucs.com

NATIONAL ATHLETIC TRAINERS' ASSOCIATION RESEARCH AND EDUCATION FOUNDATION http://www.natafoundation.org

NATIONAL ATHLETIC TRAINER'S ASSOCIATION RESEARCH AND EDUCATION FOUNDATION SCHOLARSHIP PROGRAM

One-time award available to full-time students who are members of NATA. Minimum 3.2 GPA required. Open to undergraduate upperclassmen and graduate/post-graduate students.

National Athletic Trainers' Association Research and Education Foundation (continued)

Academic Fields/Career Goals: Health and Medical Sciences; Health Information Management/Technology; Sports-related; Therapy/Rehabilitation.

Award: Scholarship for use in junior, senior, graduate, or postgraduate years; not renewable. *Number:* 55–60. *Amount:* $2000.

Eligibility Requirements: Applicant must be enrolled or expecting to enroll full-time at a four-year institution or university. Available to U.S. and non-U.S. citizens.

Application Requirements: Application, essay, references, transcript. *Deadline:* February 10.

Contact: Barbara Niland, Scholarship Coordinator
National Athletic Trainers' Association Research and Education Foundation
2952 Stemmons Freeway, Suite 200
Dallas, TX 75247-6103
Phone: 214-637-6282 Ext. 121
Fax: 214-637-2206
E-mail: barbara@nata.org

NATIONAL COMMUNITY PHARMACIST ASSOCIATION (NCPA) FOUNDATION http://www.ncpanet.org

NATIONAL COMMUNITY PHARMACIST ASSOCIATION FOUNDATION PRESIDENTIAL SCHOLARSHIP

Scholarship for student members of NCPA who are full-time pharmacy students at an accredited U.S. school of pharmacy. Based on academic achievement and leadership qualities. Submit resume and curriculum vitae with application. Application deadline is March 1. One-time award of up to $2000 for college juniors and seniors.

Academic Fields/Career Goals: Health and Medical Sciences.

Award: Scholarship for use in junior or senior years; not renewable. *Number:* up to 15. *Amount:* up to $2000.

Eligibility Requirements: Applicant must be enrolled or expecting to enroll full-time at a four-year institution or university. Applicant must have 2.5 GPA or higher. Available to U.S. citizens.

Application Requirements: Application, essay, resume, references, transcript. *Deadline:* March 1.

Contact: Yulanda Slade, Administrative Assistant
National Community Pharmacist Association (NCPA) Foundation
205 Daingerfield Road
Alexandria, VA 22314
Phone: 703-683-8200
Fax: 703-683-3619

NATIONAL FEDERATION OF THE BLIND http://www.nfb.org

HOWARD BROWN RICKARD SCHOLARSHIP

• *See page 78*

NATIONAL INSTITUTES OF HEALTH http://ugsp.info.nih.gov

NIH UNDERGRADUATE SCHOLARSHIP PROGRAM FOR STUDENTS FROM DISADVANTAGED BACKGROUNDS

• *See page 116*

NATIONAL INVENTORS HALL OF FAME http://www.invent.org/collegiate

COLLEGIATE INVENTORS COMPETITION - GRAND PRIZE

• *See page 71*

COLLEGIATE INVENTORS COMPETITION FOR UNDERGRADUATE STUDENTS

• *See page 71*

NATIONAL OSTEOPOROSIS FOUNDATION http://www.nof.org/grants

NATIONAL OSTEOPOROSIS FOUNDATION STUDENT FELLOWSHIP GRANTS

Applicants must have high school or undergraduate degree with interest in pursuing a PhD, MD or equivalent degree. Post-doctoral fellowships may be awarded to persons who have received doctoral degrees under special circumstances. Please refer to Web site for further details: http://www.nof.org/grants/index.htm

Academic Fields/Career Goals: Health and Medical Sciences.

Award: Grant for use in freshman, sophomore, junior, or senior years; not renewable. *Number:* 5. *Amount:* $3000.

Eligibility Requirements: Applicant must be enrolled or expecting to enroll full or part-time at an institution or university. Available to U.S. and non-U.S. citizens.

Application Requirements: Application, resume, references. *Deadline:* December 15.

Contact: Harriet Shapiro, Director of Patient and Professional Education
National Osteoporosis Foundation
1232 22nd Street, NW
Washington, DC 20037-1292
Phone: 202-223-2226
Fax: 202-223-2237
E-mail: harriet@nof.org

NEW JERSEY ACADEMY OF SCIENCE http://www.njas.org

NEW JERSEY ACADEMY OF SCIENCE RESEARCH GRANTS-IN-AID TO HIGH SCHOOL STUDENTS

• *See page 116*

NEW MEXICO COMMISSION ON HIGHER EDUCATION http://www.nmche.org

ALLIED HEALTH STUDENT LOAN PROGRAM-NEW MEXICO

• *See page 186*

NEW YORK STATE EDUCATION DEPARTMENT http://www.highered.nysed.gov

REGENTS PROFESSIONAL OPPORTUNITY SCHOLARSHIP

• *See page 45*

NORTH CAROLINA STATE EDUCATION ASSISTANCE AUTHORITY http://www.cfnc.org

NORTH CAROLINA STUDENT LOAN PROGRAM FOR HEALTH, SCIENCE, AND MATHEMATICS

• *See page 187*

NORTON HEALTHCARE http://www.nortonhealthcare.com

NORTON HEALTHCARE SCHOLARS–METROPOLITAN COLLEGE

For books, housing, and tuition for students interested in nursing and allied health careers who attend University of Louisville, Jefferson Community College, and Jefferson Technical College. Students agree to work part-time for United Parcel Service (UPS) for 12 months, receiving at least $8.50/hour and health benefits. After 12 months in program they may work for Norton Healthcare part-time or just continue their studies full-time. Must agree to work for Norton Healthcare upon graduation, one year for each year of tuition they received.

Academic Fields/Career Goals: Health and Medical Sciences; Nursing; Pharmacy; Radiology.

Award: Forgivable loan for use in freshman, sophomore, junior, or senior years. *Number:* up to 100. *Amount:* up to $6000.

Eligibility Requirements: Applicant must be enrolled or expecting to enroll full or part-time at a two-year or four-year or technical institution or university and studying in Kentucky. Available to U.S. citizens.

Application Requirements: Application.

Contact: Debra Rayman, Manager of Workforce Development
Norton Healthcare
PO Box 35070
Louisville, KY 40202
Phone: 502-629-4955
Fax: 502-629-8621
E-mail: debra.rayman@nortonhealthcare.org

NORTON HEALTHCARE SCHOLARS–PRIVATE COLLEGES AND UNIVERSITIES

Forgivable loan for books, housing, and tuition for private colleges and universities in the Louisville area for students majoring in healthcare disciplines such as nursing, pharmacy, radiographic technology and medical, laboratory, and surgical technology. Must agree to work for Norton Healthcare upon graduation, one year for each year of tuition received.

Academic Fields/Career Goals: Health and Medical Sciences; Nursing; Pharmacy; Radiology.

Award: Forgivable loan for use in freshman, sophomore, junior, or senior years; renewable. *Number:* up to 100. *Amount:* up to $6000.

Eligibility Requirements: Applicant must be enrolled or expecting to enroll full-time at a two-year or four-year institution or university and studying in Kentucky. Available to U.S. citizens.

Application Requirements: Application.

Contact: Debra Rayman, Manager of Workforce Development
Norton Healthcare
PO Box 35070
Louisville, KY 40202
Phone: 502-629-4955
Fax: 502-629-8621
E-mail: debra.rayman@nortonhealthcare.org

ONS FOUNDATION http://www.ons.org

ONS FOUNDATION NURSING OUTCOMES RESEARCH GRANT

One grant for a registered nurse actively involved in some aspect of cancer patient care, education, or research. Award to be used to support research. Research must be clinically focused. One-time award of $7500. Deadline: November 1.

Academic Fields/Career Goals: Health and Medical Sciences; Nursing.

Award: Grant for use in junior, senior, graduate, or postgraduate years; not renewable. *Number:* 1. *Amount:* $7500.

Eligibility Requirements: Applicant must be enrolled or expecting to enroll at an institution or university. Applicant or parent of applicant must have employment or volunteer experience in designated career field. Available to U.S. citizens.

Application Requirements: Application. *Deadline:* November 1.

Contact: ONS Foundation
125 Enterprise Drive
Pittsburgh, PA 15275
Phone: 412-859-6100
E-mail: foundation@ons.org

ONS FOUNDATION ONCOLOGY NURSING SOCIETY RESEARCH GRANT

One grant for a registered nurse actively involved in some aspect of cancer patient care, education, or research. Award to be used to support research. Research must be clinically focused. One-time award of $10,000. Deadline: November 1.

Academic Fields/Career Goals: Health and Medical Sciences; Nursing.

Award: Grant for use in junior, senior, graduate, or postgraduate years; not renewable. *Number:* 1. *Amount:* $10,000.

Eligibility Requirements: Applicant must be enrolled or expecting to enroll at an institution or university. Applicant or parent of applicant must have employment or volunteer experience in designated career field.

Application Requirements: Application. *Deadline:* November 1.

Contact: ONS Foundation
125 Enterprise Drive
Pittsburgh, PA 15275
Phone: 412-859-6100
E-mail: foundation@ons.org

OREGON STUDENT ASSISTANCE COMMISSION http://www.osac.state.or.us

FRIENDS OF OREGON STUDENTS SCHOLARSHIP

• *See page 209*

LAWRENCE R. FOSTER MEMORIAL SCHOLARSHIP

One-time award to students enrolled or planning to enroll in a public health degree program. First preference given to those working in the public health field and those pursuing a graduate degree in public health. Undergraduates entering junior or senior year health programs may apply if seeking a public health career, and not private practice. Prefer applicants from diverse cultures. Must provide 3 references. Additional essay required. Must be resident of Oregon.

Academic Fields/Career Goals: Health and Medical Sciences.

Award: Scholarship for use in junior, senior, graduate, or postgraduate years; not renewable. *Number:* 6. *Amount:* $4167.

Eligibility Requirements: Applicant must be enrolled or expecting to enroll at a four-year institution and resident of Oregon. Available to U.S. citizens.

Application Requirements: Application, essay, financial need analysis, references, transcript, activity chart. *Deadline:* March 1.

Contact: Director of Grant Programs
Oregon Student Assistance Commission
1500 Valley River Drive, Suite 100
Eugene, OR 97401-7020
Phone: 800-452-8807 Ext. 7395
E-mail: awardinfo@mercury.osac.state.or.us

MARION A. LINDEMAN SCHOLARSHIP

One-time award for Willamette View employees who have completed one or more years of service as Certified Nurses Assistants or nursing staff members. Must pursue a degree or certification in nursing; speech, physical or occupational therapy or other health-related fields.

Academic Fields/Career Goals: Health and Medical Sciences; Nursing; Therapy/Rehabilitation.

Award: Scholarship for use in freshman, sophomore, junior, or senior years; not renewable.

Eligibility Requirements: Applicant must be enrolled or expecting to enroll full or part-time at a two-year or four-year institution and resident of Oregon. Applicant or parent of applicant must have employment or volunteer experience in designated career field. Available to U.S. citizens.

Application Requirements: Application, essay, financial need analysis, references, transcript, activity chart. *Deadline:* March 1.

Contact: Director of Grant Programs
Oregon Student Assistance Commission
1500 Valley River Drive, Suite 100
Eugene, OR 97401-7020
Phone: 800-452-8807 Ext. 7395
E-mail: awardinfo@mercury.osac.state.or.us

PACERS FOUNDATION, INC. http://www.pacersfoundation.org

LINDA CRAIG MEMORIAL SCHOLARSHIP

Scholarship presented by St. Vincent Sports Medicine is for currently-enrolled juniors and seniors with declared majors of medicine, sports medicine, and/or physical therapy. Students must have completed at least 4 semesters and attend a school in Indiana. Minimum 3.0 GPA required.

Academic Fields/Career Goals: Health and Medical Sciences; Sports-related; Therapy/Rehabilitation.

Award: Scholarship for use in junior or senior years; not renewable. *Number:* 2–2. *Amount:* $2000.

Pacers Foundation, Inc. (continued)

Eligibility Requirements: Applicant must be enrolled or expecting to enroll full-time at a two-year or four-year institution or university and studying in Indiana. Applicant must have 3.0 GPA or higher. Available to U.S. citizens.

Application Requirements: Application, essay, references, transcript. *Deadline:* March 1.

Contact: Sarah Furimsky, Coordinator
Pacers Foundation, Inc.
125 South Pennsylvania Street
Indianapolis, IN 46204
Phone: 317-917-2864
Fax: 317-917-2599
E-mail: foundation@pacers.com

PHYSICIAN ASSISTANT FOUNDATION http://www.aapa.org

PHYSICIAN ASSISTANT FOUNDATION ANNUAL SCHOLARSHIP

One-time award for student members of the American Academy of Physician Assistants enrolled in an ARC PA accredited physician assistant program. Award based on financial need, academic achievement, and goals. Must submit two passport-type photographs for promotional reasons.

Academic Fields/Career Goals: Health and Medical Sciences.

Award: Scholarship for use in junior or senior years; not renewable. *Number:* 50–75. *Amount:* $2000.

Eligibility Requirements: Applicant must be enrolled or expecting to enroll full or part-time at a two-year or four-year institution or university. Applicant or parent of applicant must be member of American Academy of Physicians Assistants. Available to U.S. and non-U.S. citizens.

Application Requirements: Application, essay, financial need analysis, photo, transcript. *Deadline:* February 1.

Contact: Physician Assistant Foundation
950 North Washington Street
Alexandria, VA 22304-1552
Phone: 703-836-2272
Fax: 703-684-1924

PILOT INTERNATIONAL FOUNDATION http://www.pilotinternational.org

PILOT INTERNATIONAL FOUNDATION RUBY NEWHALL MEMORIAL SCHOLARSHIP

Scholarship available to international students for study in the United States or Canada. Applicant must have visa or green card. Application deadline is February 15.

Academic Fields/Career Goals: Health and Medical Sciences; Nursing; Psychology; Special Education; Therapy/Rehabilitation.

Award: Scholarship for use in freshman, sophomore, junior, senior, or graduate years; not renewable. *Number:* varies. *Amount:* varies.

Eligibility Requirements: Applicant must be enrolled or expecting to enroll full or part-time at a two-year or four-year or technical institution or university. Applicant must have 3.0 GPA or higher. Available to Canadian and non-U.S. citizens.

Application Requirements: Application, essay, financial need analysis, references, self-addressed stamped envelope, transcript, visa or F1 status. *Deadline:* February 15.

Contact: Jennifer Overbay, Foundation Services Director
Pilot International Foundation
PO Box 5600
Macon, GA 31208-5600
Phone: 478-743-2245
Fax: 478-743-2912
E-mail: pifinfo@pilothq.org

PILOT INTERNATIONAL FOUNDATION SCHOLARSHIP PROGRAM

Scholarship program for undergraduate students preparing for a career helping those with brain related disorders or disabilities. Applicant must have visa or green card.

Academic Fields/Career Goals: Health and Medical Sciences; Nursing; Psychology; Special Education; Therapy/Rehabilitation.

Award: Scholarship for use in freshman, sophomore, junior, or senior years; not renewable. *Number:* varies. *Amount:* varies.

Eligibility Requirements: Applicant must be enrolled or expecting to enroll full or part-time at a two-year or four-year or technical institution or university. Applicant must have 3.0 GPA or higher. Available to U.S. and non-U.S. citizens.

Application Requirements: Application, essay, financial need analysis, references, self-addressed stamped envelope, transcript, visa or F1 status. *Deadline:* February 15.

Contact: Jennifer Overbay, Foundation Services Director
Pilot International Foundation
PO Box 5600
Macon, GA 31208-5600
Phone: 478-743-2245
Fax: 478-743-2912
E-mail: pifinfo@pilothq.org

PILOT INTERNATIONAL FOUNDATION/LIFELINE SCHOLARSHIP PROGRAM

Scholarship program is for graduate or undergraduate students preparing for a second career, re-entering the job market, or obtaining additional training in their current field. The career path must pertain to assisting those with brain related disorders or disabilities. Applicant must have visa or green card.

Academic Fields/Career Goals: Health and Medical Sciences; Nursing; Psychology; Special Education; Therapy/Rehabilitation.

Award: Scholarship for use in freshman, sophomore, junior, senior, or graduate years; not renewable. *Number:* varies. *Amount:* varies.

Eligibility Requirements: Applicant must be enrolled or expecting to enroll full or part-time at a two-year or four-year or technical institution or university. Applicant must have 3.0 GPA or higher. Available to U.S. and non-U.S. citizens.

Application Requirements: Application, essay, financial need analysis, references, self-addressed stamped envelope, transcript, visa or F1 status. *Deadline:* February 15.

Contact: Jennifer Overbay, Foundation Services Director
Pilot International Foundation
PO Box 5600
Macon, GA 31208-5600
Phone: 478-743-2245
Fax: 478-743-2912
E-mail: pifinfo@pilothq.org

PNC BANK TRUST DEPARTMENT

H. FLETCHER BROWN SCHOLARSHIP

• *See page 187*

RESOURCE CENTER http://www.resourcecenterscholarshipinfo.com

MARIE BLAHA MEDICAL GRANT

• *See page 64*

SOCIETY FOR APPLIED ANTHROPOLOGY http://www.sfaa.net

PETER KONG-MING NEW STUDENT PRIZE

Prize awarded for SFAA's annual student research competition in the applied social and behavioral sciences. The issue of research question should be in the domain of health care or human services (broadly construed). The winner of the competition will receive a cash prize of $1000, a crystal trophy, and travel funds to attend the annual meeting of the SFAA. For more details, see Web site at http://www.sfaa.net

Academic Fields/Career Goals: Health and Medical Sciences; Social Sciences.

Award: Prize for use in freshman, sophomore, junior, senior, or graduate years; not renewable. *Number:* 1–3. *Amount:* $100–$1000.

Eligibility Requirements: Applicant must be enrolled or expecting to enroll full or part-time at a two-year or four-year institution or university. Available to U.S. and non-U.S. citizens.

Application Requirements: Applicant must enter a contest, manuscript. *Deadline:* December 31.

Contact: Program Director
Society for Applied Anthropology
PO Box 2436
Oklahoma City, OK 73101
Phone: 405-843-5113
Fax: 405-843-8553
E-mail: info@sfaa.net

SOCIETY OF NUCLEAR MEDICINE http://www.snm.org

PAUL COLE SCHOLARSHIP

One-time award for students of nuclear medicine technology at a two- or four-year institution. Academic merit considered. Minimum 2.5 GPA required. Application must be submitted by program director on behalf of the student. Please see Web site: http://www.snm.org for more information and application.

Academic Fields/Career Goals: Health and Medical Sciences; Nuclear Science.

Award: Scholarship for use in freshman, sophomore, junior, or senior years; not renewable. *Number:* 24. *Amount:* $1000.

Eligibility Requirements: Applicant must be enrolled or expecting to enroll full or part-time at a two-year or four-year institution. Applicant must have 2.5 GPA or higher. Available to U.S. and Canadian citizens.

Application Requirements: Application, essay, references, transcript. *Deadline:* October 15.

Contact: Travis Stiltner, Manager, Leadership Services
Society of Nuclear Medicine
1850 Samuel Morse Drive
Reston, VA 20190
Phone: 703-708-9000
Fax: 703-708-9015

SOCIETY OF TOXICOLOGY http://www.toxicology.org

MINORITY UNDERGRADUATE STUDENT AWARDS

• *See page 117*

SOUTHWEST STUDENT SERVICES CORPORATION http://www.sssc.com

ANNE LINDEMAN MEMORIAL SCHOLARSHIP

• *See page 117*

STATE OF GEORGIA http://www.gsfc.org

SERVICE-CANCELABLE STAFFORD LOAN-GEORGIA

• *See page 187*

SUBURBAN HOSPITAL HEALTHCARE SYSTEM http://www.suburbanhospital.org

SUBURBAN HOSPITAL HEALTHCARE SYSTEM SCHOLARSHIP

Award to students pursuing heath care-related careers. Must be resident of Maryland, Virginia, Washington, D.C. Employment/volunteer experience in a health care-related environment is preferred. Minimum 2.5 GPA required. Deadline: April 21.

Academic Fields/Career Goals: Health and Medical Sciences; Nursing; Therapy/Rehabilitation.

Award: Scholarship for use in junior or senior years; not renewable. *Number:* varies. *Amount:* up to $5000.

Eligibility Requirements: Applicant must be enrolled or expecting to enroll full or part-time at a two-year or four-year institution or university; resident of District of Columbia, Maryland, or Virginia and studying in District of Columbia, Maryland, or Virginia. Applicant must have 2.5 GPA or higher. Available to U.S. citizens.

Application Requirements: Application, essay, interview, references, self-addressed stamped envelope, transcript, proof of enrollment in good standing. *Deadline:* April 21.

Contact: Ms. Charmaine Williams, Manager, Employee Relations
Suburban Hospital Healthcare System
Human Resources Department, 8600 Old Georgetown Road
Bethesda, MD 20814-1497
Phone: 301-896-3795
Fax: 301-897-1339

TEXAS HIGHER EDUCATION COORDINATING BOARD http://www.collegefortexans.com

OUTSTANDING RURAL SCHOLAR PROGRAM

Award enables rural communities to sponsor a student going into health professions. The students must agree to work in that community once they receive their degree. Must be Texas resident entering a Texas institution on a full-time basis. Must demonstrate financial need.

Academic Fields/Career Goals: Health and Medical Sciences.

Award: Scholarship for use in freshman, sophomore, junior, or senior years; renewable. *Number:* varies. *Amount:* varies.

Eligibility Requirements: Applicant must be enrolled or expecting to enroll full-time at a four-year institution or university; resident of Texas and studying in Texas. Applicant must have 3.0 GPA or higher.

Application Requirements: Application, financial need analysis, transcript, nomination. *Deadline:* varies.

Contact: Center for Rural Health Initiatives
Texas Higher Education Coordinating Board
PO Drawer 1708
Austin, TX 78767
Phone: 512-479-8891
E-mail: grantinfo@thecb.state.tx.us

THE EDUCATION PARTNERSHIP http://www.edpartnership.org

PROVIDENCE MEDICAL ASSOCIATION SCHOLARSHIPS

For students who are pursuing a post-secondary education in a health-related field. Must be a graduate of a Providence high school from 1986 to present. Application deadline is June 1.

Academic Fields/Career Goals: Health and Medical Sciences.

Award: Scholarship for use in freshman, sophomore, junior, or senior years; not renewable. *Number:* 3. *Amount:* $500.

Eligibility Requirements: Applicant must be enrolled or expecting to enroll full-time at a two-year or four-year institution or university and resident of Rhode Island. Applicant must have 2.5 GPA or higher. Available to U.S. citizens.

Application Requirements: Application, essay, financial need analysis, references, test scores, transcript. *Deadline:* June 1.

Contact: Keturah Johnson, Scholarships and Communications Coordinator
The Education Partnership
345 South Main Street
Providence, RI 02903
Phone: 401-331-5222 Ext. 112
Fax: 401-331-1659
E-mail: kjohnson@edpartnership.org

TUBERCULOSIS ASSOCIATION OF OHIO COUNTY http://www.tboc.org

DR. WILLIAM J. STEGER SCHOLARSHIP AWARDS

Award for students who are residents of Ohio, Marshall, Brooke, Wetzel, Tyler, and Hancock counties in West Virginia and Belmont county in Ohio. Must be enrolled in respiratory care programs at designated West Virginia institutions. Submit application, financial aid forms, and references. Write or email for more information. Scholarship reverts to loan if students do not practice respiratory therapy in designated areas.

Academic Fields/Career Goals: Health and Medical Sciences; Therapy/Rehabilitation.

Award: Scholarship for use in freshman, sophomore, junior, or senior years; not renewable. *Number:* varies. *Amount:* varies.

Tuberculosis Association of Ohio County (continued)

Eligibility Requirements: Applicant must be enrolled or expecting to enroll full-time at a two-year or four-year institution or university; resident of Ohio or West Virginia and studying in West Virginia. Available to U.S. citizens.

Application Requirements: Application, financial need analysis, references, transcript. *Deadline:* Continuous.

Contact: Scholarship Director
Tuberculosis Association of Ohio County
90 16th Street
Wheeling, WV 26003
Phone: 304-233-0640

UNITED NEGRO COLLEGE FUND http://www.uncf.org

ALTON AND DOROTHY HIGGINS, MD SCHOLARSHIP

Scholarship available for junior, senior, or pre-medicine graduate students attending a UNCF member college or university or Morehouse School of Medicine. 3.0 GPA is required. Prospective applicants should complete the Student Profile found at Web site: http://www.uncf.org.

Academic Fields/Career Goals: Health and Medical Sciences.

Award: Scholarship for use in junior, senior, or graduate years; not renewable. *Amount:* $5000–$10,000.

Eligibility Requirements: Applicant must be Black (non-Hispanic) and enrolled or expecting to enroll at a four-year institution or university. Applicant must have 3.0 GPA or higher.

Application Requirements: Application. *Deadline:* varies.

Contact: Program Services Department
United Negro College Fund
8260 Willow Oaks Corporate Drive
Fairfax, VA 22031

BIGWOOD MEMORIAL FUND

Scholarship awarded to students attending UNCF member colleges and universities who plan on pursuing careers in health care. Please visit Web site for more information: http://www.uncf.org.

Academic Fields/Career Goals: Health and Medical Sciences; Nursing.

Award: Scholarship for use in freshman, sophomore, junior, senior, or graduate years. *Number:* varies. *Amount:* $1000–$5000.

Eligibility Requirements: Applicant must be Black (non-Hispanic) and enrolled or expecting to enroll at a four-year institution or university. Applicant must have 2.5 GPA or higher. Available to U.S. citizens.

Application Requirements: Application, financial need analysis, FAFSA, SAR. *Deadline:* varies.

Contact: Program Services Department
United Negro College Fund
8260 Willow Oaks Corporate Drive
Fairfax, VA 22031

CHARLES E. CULPEPPER SCHOLARSHIP

Scholarship awarded to students attending UNCF member colleges and universities who are completing the Fisk Pre-Medicine program. Please visit Web site for more information: http://www.uncf.org.

Academic Fields/Career Goals: Health and Medical Sciences; Science, Technology, and Society.

Award: Scholarship for use in freshman, sophomore, junior, senior, or graduate years. *Number:* varies. *Amount:* $1000.

Eligibility Requirements: Applicant must be Black (non-Hispanic) and enrolled or expecting to enroll at a four-year institution or university. Applicant must have 3.0 GPA or higher.

Application Requirements: Application, financial need analysis, FAFSA, SAR. *Deadline:* varies.

Contact: Program Services Department
United Negro College Fund
8260 Willow Oaks Corporate Drive
Fairfax, VA 22031

DR. JAMES M. ROSIN SCHOLARSHIP

Scholarships available to African American students who are pursuing a bachelor of science degree pertaining to the health sciences field. Must have a minimum 3.0 GPA. Information available on Web site: http://www.uncf.org.

Academic Fields/Career Goals: Health and Medical Sciences.

Award: Scholarship for use in freshman, sophomore, junior, or senior years; renewable. *Number:* varies. *Amount:* $5000.

Eligibility Requirements: Applicant must be Black (non-Hispanic) and enrolled or expecting to enroll at a four-year institution or university. Applicant must have 3.0 GPA or higher.

Application Requirements: Application, financial need analysis, FAFSA, SAR. *Deadline:* varies.

Contact: Program Services Department
United Negro College Fund
8260 Willow Oaks Corporate Drive
Fairfax, VA 22031

EARL AND PATRICIA ARMSTRONG SCHOLARSHIP

• *See page 118*

HARRY C. JAECKER SCHOLARSHIP

Award for pre-medical students attending a UNCF member college or university. Minimum 2.5 GPA required. Prospective applicants should complete the Student Profile found at Web site: http://www.uncf.org.

Academic Fields/Career Goals: Health and Medical Sciences.

Award: Scholarship for use in freshman, sophomore, junior, or senior years; not renewable. *Amount:* $2000–$5000.

Eligibility Requirements: Applicant must be Black (non-Hispanic) and enrolled or expecting to enroll at a four-year institution or university. Applicant must have 2.5 GPA or higher. Available to U.S. citizens.

Application Requirements: Application, financial need analysis. *Deadline:* varies.

Contact: Program Services Department
United Negro College Fund
8260 Willow Oaks Corporate Drive
Fairfax, VA 22031

MERCK SCIENCE INITIATIVE

• *See page 118*

RAYMOND W. CANNON MEMORIAL SCHOLARSHIP PROGRAM

Must be nominated by financial aid director at the UNCF college. Available to students majoring in pharmacy or pre-law who have demonstrated leadership in high school and college. Prospective applicants should complete the Student Profile found at Web site: http://www.uncf.org.

Academic Fields/Career Goals: Health and Medical Sciences; Law/Legal Services.

Award: Scholarship for use in junior year; not renewable. *Amount:* $2000–$5000.

Eligibility Requirements: Applicant must be Black (non-Hispanic) and enrolled or expecting to enroll at a four-year institution or university. Applicant must have 2.5 GPA or higher.

Application Requirements: Application, financial need analysis. *Deadline:* Continuous.

Contact: Program Services Department
United Negro College Fund
8260 Willow Oaks Corporate Drive
Fairfax, VA 22031

SODEXHO SCHOLARSHIP

Award available to incoming freshmen attending historically black colleges and universities. Must major in nursing, social work, political science, community development, or other related health disciplines. Must demonstrate leadership abilities. Minimum GPA of 3.0. Please visit Web site for more information: http://www.uncf.org

Academic Fields/Career Goals: Health and Medical Sciences; Nursing; Political Science; Social Services.

Award: Scholarship for use in freshman, sophomore, junior, or senior years; renewable. *Number:* varies. *Amount:* up to $3500.

Eligibility Requirements: Applicant must be Black (non-Hispanic); high school student and planning to enroll or expecting to enroll at an institution or university. Applicant must have 3.0 GPA or higher.

Application Requirements: Application, financial need analysis, references, transcript, FAFSA, SAR. *Deadline:* August 22.

Contact: Annette Singletary, Senior Program Manager
United Negro College Fund
8260 Willow Oaks Corporate Drive
Fairfax, VA 22031
Phone: 800-331-2244

WYETH SCHOLARSHIP
• *See page 119*

UNITED STATES PUBLIC HEALTH SERVICE - HEALTH RESOURCES AND SERVICES ADMINISTRATION, BUREAU OF HEALTH PROFESSIONS http://bhpr.hrsa.gov/dsa

HEALTH RESOURCES AND SERVICES ADMINISTRATION-BUREAU OF HEALTH PROFESSIONS SCHOLARSHIPS FOR DISADVANTAGED STUDENTS
• *See page 187*

UNIVERSITY OF MEDICINE AND DENTISTRY OF NJ SCHOOL OF OSTEOPATHIC MEDICINE http://www.umdnj.edu/studentfinancialaid

NEW JERSEY EDUCATIONAL OPPORTUNITY FUND GRANTS
• *See page 187*

VIRGINIA BUSINESS AND PROFESSIONAL WOMEN'S FOUNDATION http://www.bpwva.advocate.net/foundation.htm

WOMEN IN SCIENCE AND TECHNOLOGY SCHOLARSHIP
• *See page 119*

WASHINGTON HIGHER EDUCATION COORDINATING BOARD http://www.hecb.wa.gov

HEALTH PROFESSIONAL LOAN REPAYMENT AND SCHOLARSHIP PROGRAMS
• *See page 188*

WASHINGTON STATE ENVIRONMENTAL HEALTH ASSOCIATION http://www.wseha.org/

CIND M. TRESER MEMORIAL SCHOLARSHIP PROGRAM

Scholarships are available for undergraduate students pursuing a major in environmental health or related science and intending to practice environmental health. Must be a resident of Washington. For more details see Web site: http://www.wseha.org.

Academic Fields/Career Goals: Health and Medical Sciences.

Award: Scholarship for use in sophomore, junior, or senior years; not renewable. *Number:* 1. *Amount:* $1000.

Eligibility Requirements: Applicant must be enrolled or expecting to enroll full-time at a two-year or four-year institution or university and resident of Washington. Available to U.S. citizens.

Application Requirements: Application, references, transcript. *Deadline:* March 15.

Contact: Charles Treser, WSEHA Scholarships Committee Chair
Washington State Environmental Health Association
3045 Northwest 57th Street
Seattle, WA 98107
Phone: 206-616-2097
Fax: 206-543-8123
E-mail: ctreser@u.washington.edu

WOMEN OF THE EVANGELICAL LUTHERAN CHURCH IN AMERICA http://www.elca.org/wo

HEALTH SERVICES SCHOLARSHIP FOR WOMEN STUDYING ABROAD
• *See page 289*

ZETA PHI BETA SORORITY, INC. NATIONAL EDUCATIONAL FOUNDATION http://www.zphib1920.org

S. EVELYN LEWIS MEMORIAL SCHOLARSHIP IN MEDICAL HEALTH SCIENCES

Scholarships available for graduate or undergraduate women enrolled in a program leading to a degree in medicine or health sciences. Must be a full-time student. See Web site for information and application: http://www.zphib1920.org.

Academic Fields/Career Goals: Health and Medical Sciences.

Award: Scholarship for use in freshman, sophomore, junior, or senior years; not renewable. *Number:* varies. *Amount:* $500–$1000.

Eligibility Requirements: Applicant must be enrolled or expecting to enroll full-time at a four-year institution or university and female. Available to U.S. citizens.

Application Requirements: Application, essay, references, transcript. *Deadline:* February 1.

Contact: Cheryl Williams, National Second Vice President
Zeta Phi Beta Sorority, Inc. National Educational Foundation
1734 New Hampshire Avenue, NW
Washington, DC 20009-2595
Fax: 318-631-4028
E-mail: 2ndanti@zphib1920.org

HEALTH INFORMATION MANAGEMENT/TECHNOLOGY

AMERICAN HEALTH INFORMATION MANAGEMENT ASSOCIATION/FOUNDATION OF RESEARCH AND EDUCATION http://www.ahima.org

FOUNDATION OF RESEARCH AND EDUCATION UNDERGRADUATE MERIT SCHOLARSHIPS

Multiple scholarships for undergraduate Health Information Management students. One standard application for all available scholarships. Must have a 3.0 GPA. Applications can be downloaded at http://www.ahima.org. Must be a member of AHIMA.

Academic Fields/Career Goals: Health Information Management/Technology.

Award: Scholarship for use in freshman, sophomore, junior, senior, graduate, or postgraduate years; not renewable. *Number:* 40–60. *Amount:* $1000–$5000.

Eligibility Requirements: Applicant must be enrolled or expecting to enroll full or part-time at a two-year or four-year or technical institution or university. Applicant or parent of applicant must be member of American Health Information Management Association. Applicant must have 3.0 GPA or higher. Available to U.S. and non-U.S. citizens.

Application Requirements: Application, essay, references, transcript. *Deadline:* May 30.

Contact: Donor Relations and Grants Associate
American Health Information Management Association/Foundation of Research and Education
233 North Michigan Avenue, Suite 2150
Chicago, IL 60601-5800
Phone: 312-233-1100
E-mail: fore@ahima.org

AMERICAN SOCIETY OF RADIOLOGIC TECHNOLOGISTS EDUCATION AND RESEARCH FOUNDATION http://www.asrt.org

ISADORE N. STERN SCHOLARSHIP
• *See page 287*

SIEMENS SCHOLAR AWARD
• *See page 287*

BETHESDA LUTHERAN HOMES AND SERVICES, INC. http://www.blhs.org

DEVELOPMENTAL DISABILITIES SCHOLASTIC ACHIEVEMENT SCHOLARSHIP FOR LUTHERAN COLLEGE STUDENTS
• *See page 184*

CANADIAN SOCIETY FOR MEDICAL LABORATORY SCIENCE http://www.csmls.org

E.V. BOOTH SCHOLARSHIP AWARD
• *See page 288*

CONGRESSIONAL BLACK CAUCUS SPOUSES PROGRAM http://cbcfinc.org

CONGRESSIONAL BLACK CAUCUS SPOUSES HEALTH INITIATIVE
• *See page 288*

HEALTH RESEARCH COUNCIL OF NEW ZEALAND http://www.hrc.govt.nz

PACIFIC HEALTH WORKFORCE AWARD
• *See page 288*

PACIFIC MENTAL HEALTH WORK FORCE AWARD
• *See page 288*

HEALTHCARE INFORMATION AND MANAGEMENT SYSTEMS SOCIETY FOUNDATION http://www.himss.org

HIMSS FOUNDATION SCHOLARSHIP PROGRAM
• *See page 288*

MARIN EDUCATION FUND http://www.marineducationfund.org

GOLDMAN FAMILY FUND, NEW LEADER SCHOLARSHIP
• *See page 186*

NATIONAL ATHLETIC TRAINERS' ASSOCIATION RESEARCH AND EDUCATION FOUNDATION http://www.natafoundation.org

NATIONAL ATHLETIC TRAINER'S ASSOCIATION RESEARCH AND EDUCATION FOUNDATION SCHOLARSHIP PROGRAM
• *See page 299*

NATIONAL STRENGTH AND CONDITIONING ASSOCIATION http://www.nsca-lift.org

GNC NUTRITION RESEARCH GRANT

GNC sponsors this nutrition based research grant. The purpose of the project must fall within the mission of the NSCA. Applicant must submit: cover letter, abstract, proposal, itemized budget, "Human Subject Consent Form," and proof of institutional review board approval, and abbreviated vitae of faculty co-investigator. Please refer to Web site for further details: http://www.nsca-lift.org

Academic Fields/Career Goals: Health Information Management/ Technology; Sports-related; Therapy/Rehabilitation.

Award: Grant for use in junior, senior, or graduate years; not renewable. *Number:* 1. *Amount:* up to $2500.

Eligibility Requirements: Applicant must be enrolled or expecting to enroll full-time at a four-year institution or university. Applicant or parent of applicant must be member of National Strength and Conditioning Association. Available to U.S. and non-U.S. citizens.

Application Requirements: Application, references, transcript, abstract, proposal, itemized budget, time schedule, consent form, vitae of faculty co-investigator. *Deadline:* March 15.

Contact: Karri Baker, Membership Director
National Strength and Conditioning Association
PO Box 9908
Colorado Springs, CO 80932-0908
Phone: 719-632-6722
Fax: 719-632-6367
E-mail: foundation@nsca-lift.org

NATIONAL STRENGTH AND CONDITIONING ASSOCIATION CHALLENGE SCHOLARSHIP

One-time award for undergraduate or graduate students in strength and conditioning-related fields. Must be NSCA member for at least one year prior to the application deadline of March 15. Submit resume, cover letter, and 500-word essay outlining course of study, career goals, and financial need. Please see Web site for further details: http://www.nsca-lift.org

Academic Fields/Career Goals: Health Information Management/ Technology; Sports-related; Therapy/Rehabilitation.

Award: Scholarship for use in freshman, sophomore, junior, senior, or graduate years; not renewable. *Number:* 1–12. *Amount:* $1000.

Eligibility Requirements: Applicant must be enrolled or expecting to enroll full-time at a two-year or four-year institution or university. Applicant or parent of applicant must be member of National Strength and Conditioning Association. Available to U.S. and non-U.S. citizens.

Application Requirements: Application, essay, financial need analysis, photo, resume, references, transcript. *Deadline:* March 15.

Contact: Karri Baker, Membership Director
National Strength and Conditioning Association
1885 Bob Johnson Drive
Colorado Springs, CO 80906-4000
Phone: 719-632-6722
Fax: 719-632-6367
E-mail: foundation@nsca-lift.org

NATIONAL STRENGTH AND CONDITIONING ASSOCIATION HIGH SCHOOL SCHOLARSHIP

One-time award to high school seniors preparing to enter college. Must demonstrate acceptance into an accredited institution and intention to graduate with a degree in a strength and conditioning field. Minimum 3.0 GPA required. Must be a member of NCSA. Please see Web site for further details: http://www.nsca-lift.org

Academic Fields/Career Goals: Health Information Management/ Technology; Sports-related; Therapy/Rehabilitation.

Award: Scholarship for use in freshman year; not renewable. *Number:* 1–2. *Amount:* $1000.

Eligibility Requirements: Applicant must be high school student and planning to enroll or expecting to enroll full-time at a four-year institution or university. Applicant or parent of applicant must be member of National Strength and Conditioning Association. Applicant must have 3.0 GPA or higher. Available to U.S. and non-U.S. citizens.

Application Requirements: Application, essay, references, transcript, letter of acceptance. *Deadline:* March 15.

Contact: Karri Baker, Membership Director
National Strength and Conditioning Association
1885 Bob Johnson Drive
Colorado Springs, CO 80906-4000
Phone: 719-632-6722
Fax: 719-632-6367
E-mail: foundation@nsca-lift.org

NATIONAL STRENGTH AND CONDITIONING ASSOCIATION UNDERGRADUATE RESEARCH GRANT

One-time award for undergraduate research in strength and conditioning. Maximum award is $1500 (overhead costs are not supported). The purpose of the project should fall within the mission of the NSCA. Must be a NSCA member. Applications are due March 15. Please refer to Web site for further details: http://www.nsca-lift.org

Academic Fields/Career Goals: Health Information Management/Technology; Sports-related; Therapy/Rehabilitation.

Award: Grant for use in freshman, sophomore, junior, or senior years; not renewable. *Number:* 1–3. *Amount:* $500–$1500.

Eligibility Requirements: Applicant must be enrolled or expecting to enroll full-time at a four-year institution or university. Applicant or parent of applicant must be member of National Strength and Conditioning Association. Available to U.S. and non-U.S. citizens.

Application Requirements: Application, essay, financial need analysis, photo, resume, references, transcript, proposal, abstract, itemized budget. *Deadline:* March 15.

Contact: Karri Baker, Membership Director
National Strength and Conditioning Association
1885 Bob Johnson Drive
Colorado Springs, CO 80906-4000
Phone: 719-632-6722
Fax: 719-632-6367
E-mail: foundation@nsca-lift.org

NATIONAL STRENGTH AND CONDITIONING ASSOCIATION WOMEN'S SCHOLARSHIP

This scholarship is designed to encourage women, ages 17 and older, to enter into the field of strength and conditioning. Please refer to Web site for further details: http://www.nsca-lift.org

Academic Fields/Career Goals: Health Information Management/Technology; Sports-related; Therapy/Rehabilitation.

Award: Scholarship for use in freshman, sophomore, junior, senior, or graduate years; not renewable. *Number:* 1–2. *Amount:* $1000.

Eligibility Requirements: Applicant must be age 17; enrolled or expecting to enroll full-time at a two-year or four-year institution or university and female. Applicant or parent of applicant must be member of National Strength and Conditioning Association. Available to U.S. and non-U.S. citizens.

Application Requirements: Application, essay, resume, references, transcript. *Deadline:* March 15.

Contact: Karri Baker, Membership Director
National Strength and Conditioning Association
1885 Bob Johnson Drive
Colorado Springs, CO 80906-4000
Phone: 719-632-6722
Fax: 719-632-6367
E-mail: foundation@nsca-lift.org

NSCA MINORITY SCHOLARSHIP

This scholarship is designed to encourage minorities, ages 17 and older, to enter into the field of strength and conditioning. Please refer to Web site for further details: http://www.nsca-lift.org

Academic Fields/Career Goals: Health Information Management/Technology; Sports-related; Therapy/Rehabilitation.

Award: Scholarship for use in freshman, sophomore, junior, senior, or graduate years; not renewable. *Number:* 1–2. *Amount:* $1000.

Eligibility Requirements: Applicant must be American Indian/Alaska Native, Asian/Pacific Islander, Black (non-Hispanic), or Hispanic; age 17 and enrolled or expecting to enroll full-time at a two-year or four-year institution or university. Applicant or parent of applicant must be member of National Strength and Conditioning Association. Available to U.S. and non-U.S. citizens.

Application Requirements: Application, essay, resume, references, transcript. *Deadline:* March 15.

Contact: Karri Baker, Membership Director
National Strength and Conditioning Association
PO Box 9908
Colorado Springs, CO 80932-0908
Phone: 719-632-6722
Fax: 719-632-6367
E-mail: foundation@nsca-lift.org

POWER SYSTEMS PROFESSIONAL SCHOLARSHIP

One-time award for students in pursuit of a career as a strength and conditioning coach. Submit letter of application, resume, transcripts, and 500-word essay outlining career goals and objectives. Must be a member of National Strength and Conditioning Association. Please refer to Web site for further details: http://www.nsca-lift.org

Academic Fields/Career Goals: Health Information Management/Technology; Sports-related; Therapy/Rehabilitation.

Award: Scholarship for use in freshman, sophomore, junior, or senior years; not renewable. *Number:* 1. *Amount:* $1000.

Eligibility Requirements: Applicant must be enrolled or expecting to enroll full-time at a four-year institution or university. Applicant or parent of applicant must be member of National Strength and Conditioning Association. Available to U.S. and non-U.S. citizens.

Application Requirements: Application, essay, photo, resume, references, transcript. *Deadline:* March 15.

Contact: Karri Baker, Membership Director
National Strength and Conditioning Association
1885 Bob Johnson Drive
Colorado Springs, CO 80906-4000
Phone: 719-632-6722
Fax: 719-632-6367
E-mail: foundation@nsca-lift.org

ORDEAN FOUNDATION

ORDEAN LOAN PROGRAM

• *See page 45*

WOMEN OF THE EVANGELICAL LUTHERAN CHURCH IN AMERICA http://www.elca.org/wo

HEALTH SERVICES SCHOLARSHIP FOR WOMEN STUDYING ABROAD

• *See page 289*

HEATING, AIR-CONDITIONING, AND REFRIGERATION MECHANICS

AMERICAN SOCIETY OF HEATING, REFRIGERATING, AND AIR CONDITIONING ENGINEERS, INC. http://www.ashrae.org

ALWIN B. NEWTON SCHOLARSHIP FUND

• *See page 218*

AMERICAN SOCIETY OF HEATING, REFRIGERATION, AND AIR CONDITIONING ENGINEERING TECHNOLOGY SCHOLARSHIP

• *See page 66*

ASHRAE REGION VIII SCHOLARSHIP

• *See page 237*

ASHRAE MEMORIAL SCHOLARSHIP

• *See page 225*

ASHRAE REGION IV BENNY BOOTLE SCHOLARSHIP

• *See page 237*

ASHRAE SCHOLARSHIPS

• *See page 225*

DUANE HANSON SCHOLARSHIP

• *See page 225*

HENRY ADAMS SCHOLARSHIP

• *See page 225*

REUBEN TRANE SCHOLARSHIP

• *See page 218*

CONNECTICUT BUILDING CONGRESS http://www.cbc-ct.org

CONNECTICUT BUILDING CONGRESS SCHOLARSHIP FUND

• *See page 75*

HISPANIC COLLEGE FUND, INC. http://www.hispanicfund.org

EL NUEVO CONSTRUCTOR SCHOLARSHIP PROGRAM
• See page 76

INSTRUMENTATION, SYSTEMS, AND AUTOMATION SOCIETY (ISA) http://www.isa.org

INSTRUMENTATION, SYSTEMS, AND AUTOMATION SOCIETY (ISA) SCHOLARSHIP PROGRAM
• See page 99

MIDWEST ROOFING CONTRACTORS ASSOCIATION http://www.mrca.org

MRCA FOUNDATION SCHOLARSHIP PROGRAM
• See page 70

PLUMBING-HEATING-COOLING CONTRACTORS ASSOCIATION EDUCATION FOUNDATION http://www.phccweb.org

BRADFORD WHITE CORPORATION SCHOLARSHIP
• See page 79

DELTA FAUCET COMPANY SCHOLARSHIP PROGRAM
• See page 79

PHCC EDUCATIONAL FOUNDATION NEED-BASED SCHOLARSHIP
• See page 79

PHCC EDUCATIONAL FOUNDATION SCHOLARSHIP PROGRAM
• See page 79

PROFESSIONAL CONSTRUCTION ESTIMATORS ASSOCIATION http://www.pcea.org

TED WILSON MEMORIAL SCHOLARSHIP FOUNDATION
• See page 188

SOUTH DAKOTA RETAILERS ASSOCIATION http://www.sdra.org

SOUTH DAKOTA RETAILERS ASSOCIATION SCHOLARSHIP PROGRAM
• See page 47

HISTORIC PRESERVATION AND CONSERVATION

AMERICAN SCHOOL OF CLASSICAL STUDIES AT ATHENS http://www.ascsa.edu.gr

ASCSA SUMMER SESSIONS
• See page 65

COSTUME SOCIETY OF AMERICA http://www.costumesocietyamerica.com

ADELE FILENE TRAVEL AWARD
• See page 81

STELLA BLUM RESEARCH GRANT
• See page 81

GEORGIA TRUST FOR HISTORIC PRESERVATION http://www.georgiatrust.org

GEORGIA TRUST FOR HISTORIC PRESERVATION SCHOLARSHIP

Each year, the Trust awards two $1,000 scholarships to encourage the study of historic preservation and related fields. Recipients are chosen on the basis of leadership and academic achievement. Applicants must be residents of Georgia enrolled in an accredited Georgia institution. A GPA of 3.0 is required.

Academic Fields/Career Goals: Historic Preservation and Conservation.

Award: Scholarship for use in freshman, sophomore, junior, senior, or graduate years; not renewable. *Number:* 2. *Amount:* $1000.

Eligibility Requirements: Applicant must be enrolled or expecting to enroll full-time at a four-year institution or university; resident of Georgia and studying in Georgia. Applicant must have 3.0 GPA or higher. Available to U.S. citizens.

Application Requirements: Application, essay, resume, references, transcript. *Deadline:* February 1.

Contact: Manager, Heritage Education
Georgia Trust for Historic Preservation
1516 Peachtree Street, NW
Atlanta, GA 30309
Phone: 404-881-9980
Fax: 404-875-2205
E-mail: info@georgiatrust.org

HARRY S. TRUMAN LIBRARY INSTITUTE http://www.trumanlibrary.org

HARRY S. TRUMAN LIBRARY INSTITUTE UNDERGRADUATE STUDENT GRANT
• See page 192

HISTORY

AMERICAN HISTORICAL ASSOCIATION http://www.theaha.org

AHA PRIZE IN ATLANTIC HISTORY

Prize for books that explore aspects of integration of Atlantic worlds before the 20th century. Only books of high scholarly and literary merit will be considered. Copies of book must be sent to each committee member. See Web site (http://www.theaha.org) for names and mailing addresses. Applicant must be a published author.

Academic Fields/Career Goals: History.

Award: Prize for use in freshman, sophomore, junior, senior, graduate, or postgraduate years; not renewable. *Number:* 1. *Amount:* varies.

Eligibility Requirements: Applicant must be enrolled or expecting to enroll at an institution or university.

Application Requirements: Copies of book. *Deadline:* May 17.

Contact: Book Prize Administrator
American Historical Association
400 A Street, SE
Washington, DC 20003
E-mail: aha@theaha.org

ALBERT J. BEVERIDGE AWARD

Annual prize for best recent book in English on the history of Canada, Latin America, or the U.S. from 1492 to present. Five copies required. Copies of entries must be sent to each committee member. Refer to Web site (http://www.theaha.org) for names and mailing addresses. Applicant must be a published author.

Academic Fields/Career Goals: History.

Award: Prize for use in freshman, sophomore, junior, senior, graduate, or postgraduate years; not renewable. *Number:* 1. *Amount:* varies.

Eligibility Requirements: Applicant must be enrolled or expecting to enroll at an institution or university and must have an interest in writing.

Application Requirements: Applicant must enter a contest. *Deadline:* May 15.

Contact: Book Prize Administrator
American Historical Association
400 A Street, SE
Washington, DC 20003
E-mail: aha@theaha.org

GEORGE L. MOSSE PRIZE
• See page 265

GEORGE LOUIS BEER PRIZE
• *See page 266*

HELEN AND HOWARD MARRARO PRIZE
• *See page 281*

HERBERT BAXTER ADAMS PRIZE

Annual prize for distinguished recent book on European history. Books on ancient, medieval, or early modern European history to 1815 are eligible. Must be author's first substantial work. Must be citizen or permanent resident of the U.S. or Canada. Copies of entries must be sent to each committee member. Refer to Web site (http://www.theaha.org) for names and mailing addresses.

Academic Fields/Career Goals: History; Humanities.

Award: Prize for use in freshman, sophomore, junior, senior, graduate, or postgraduate years; not renewable. *Number:* 1. *Amount:* varies.

Eligibility Requirements: Applicant must be enrolled or expecting to enroll at an institution or university and must have an interest in writing. Available to U.S. and Canadian citizens.

Application Requirements: Applicant must enter a contest, copies of book. *Deadline:* May 17.

Contact: Book Prize Administrator
American Historical Association
400 A Street, SE
Washington, DC 20003
E-mail: aha@theaha.org

J. RUSSELL MAJOR PRIZE

Prize to recognize best work in English on any aspect of French history. Copies of book must be sent to each committee member. See Web site (http://www.theaha.org) for names and mailing addresses.

Academic Fields/Career Goals: History.

Award: Prize for use in freshman, sophomore, junior, senior, graduate, or postgraduate years; not renewable. *Number:* 1. *Amount:* varies.

Eligibility Requirements: Applicant must be enrolled or expecting to enroll at an institution or university.

Application Requirements: Applicant must enter a contest, copies of book. *Deadline:* May 17.

Contact: Book Prize Administrator
American Historical Association
400 A Street, SE
Washington, DC 20003
E-mail: aha@theaha.org

JAMES HARVEY ROBINSON PRIZE

Honorific, biannual award for teaching aid that reflects most outstanding contribution to teaching of history. Copies of item must be sent to each committee member. See Web site (http://www.theaha.org) for names and mailing addresses.

Academic Fields/Career Goals: History; Humanities.

Award: Prize for use in freshman, sophomore, junior, senior, graduate, or postgraduate years; not renewable. *Number:* 1. *Amount:* varies.

Eligibility Requirements: Applicant must be enrolled or expecting to enroll at an institution or university. Applicant or parent of applicant must have employment or volunteer experience in teaching. Available to U.S. citizens.

Application Requirements: Applicant must enter a contest, copies of submission. *Deadline:* May 17.

Contact: Book Prize Administrator
American Historical Association
400 A Street, SE
Washington, DC 20003
E-mail: aha@theaha.org

JAMES HENRY BREASTED PRIZE

Annual award for best recent book in English on any field of history prior to 1000 A.D. Copies of entries must be sent to each committee member. Refer to Web site (http://www.theaha.org) for names, mailing addresses, and complete details.

Academic Fields/Career Goals: History; Humanities.

Award: Prize for use in freshman, sophomore, junior, senior, graduate, or postgraduate years; not renewable. *Number:* 1. *Amount:* varies.

Eligibility Requirements: Applicant must be enrolled or expecting to enroll at an institution or university and must have an interest in writing. Available to U.S. citizens.

Application Requirements: Applicant must enter a contest, copies of entries. *Deadline:* May 15.

Contact: Book Prize Administrator
American Historical Association
400 A Street, SE
Washington, DC 20003
E-mail: aha@theaha.org

JOAN KELLY MEMORIAL PRIZE IN WOMEN'S HISTORY

Award for outstanding recent book on women's history and/or feminist theory. Books should address the interrelationship between women and the historical process. Copies must be sent to each committee member. Refer to Web site (http://www.theaha.org) for names and mailing addresses. Applicant must be a published author.

Academic Fields/Career Goals: History; Humanities; Social Sciences; Women's Studies.

Award: Prize for use in freshman, sophomore, junior, senior, graduate, or postgraduate years; not renewable. *Number:* 1. *Amount:* varies.

Eligibility Requirements: Applicant must be enrolled or expecting to enroll at an institution or university and must have an interest in writing. Available to U.S. citizens.

Application Requirements: Applicant must enter a contest, copies of entries. *Deadline:* May 17.

Contact: Book Prize Administrator
American Historical Association
400 A Street, SE
Washington, DC 20003
E-mail: aha@theaha.org

JOHN E. FAGG PRIZE

Recognizes the best publication in the history of Spain, Portugal, or Latin America. Will be awarded annually through 2011. Applicant must be a published author.

Academic Fields/Career Goals: History.

Award: Prize for use in freshman, sophomore, junior, senior, graduate, or postgraduate years; not renewable. *Number:* 1. *Amount:* varies.

Eligibility Requirements: Applicant must be enrolled or expecting to enroll at an institution or university and must have an interest in writing. Available to U.S. and non-U.S. citizens.

Application Requirements: Applicant must enter a contest. *Deadline:* May 15.

Contact: Book Prize Administrator
American Historical Association
400 A Street, SE
Washington, DC 20003
Phone: 202-544-2422 Ext. 104
Fax: 202-544-8307
E-mail: aha@theaha.org

JOHN E. O'CONNOR FILM AWARD
• *See page 267*

JOHN H. DUNNING PRIZE

Biannual prize awarded to a young scholar for an outstanding monograph in manuscript or in print on any subject relating to U.S. history. Refer to Web site (http://www.theaha.org) for more information.

Academic Fields/Career Goals: History; Humanities.

Award: Prize for use in freshman, sophomore, junior, senior, graduate, or postgraduate years; not renewable. *Number:* 1. *Amount:* varies.

Eligibility Requirements: Applicant must be enrolled or expecting to enroll at an institution or university and must have an interest in writing.

American Historical Association (continued)

Application Requirements: Applicant must enter a contest, copies of entries. *Deadline:* May 17.

Contact: Book Prize Administrator
American Historical Association
400 A Street, SE
Washington, DC 20003
E-mail: aha@theaha.org

JOHN K. FAIRBANK PRIZE FOR EAST ASIAN HISTORY
• *See page 80*

LEO GERSHOY AWARD
• *See page 266*

LITTLETON-GRISWOLD PRIZE

Annual prize for the best recent book on the history of American law and society. Copies of book must be sent to each committee member. Refer to Web site (http://www.theaha.org) for names and mailing addresses.

Academic Fields/Career Goals: History; Humanities; Law/Legal Services; Political Science; Social Sciences.

Award: Prize for use in freshman, sophomore, junior, senior, graduate, or postgraduate years; not renewable. *Number:* 1. *Amount:* varies.

Eligibility Requirements: Applicant must be enrolled or expecting to enroll at an institution or university and must have an interest in writing. Available to U.S. citizens.

Application Requirements: Applicant must enter a contest, copies of book. *Deadline:* May 17.

Contact: Book Prize Administrator
American Historical Association
400 A Street, SE
Washington, DC 20003
E-mail: aha@theaha.org

MORRIS D. FORKOSCH PRIZE

Prize to recognize best book in English in the field of British history since 1485. Topic rotates yearly between British Imperial or Commonwealth history and British history. Copies of book must be sent to each committee member. See Web site (http://www.theaha.org) for names, mailing addresses, and updated information.

Academic Fields/Career Goals: History.

Award: Prize for use in freshman, sophomore, junior, senior, graduate, or postgraduate years; not renewable. *Number:* 1. *Amount:* varies.

Eligibility Requirements: Applicant must be enrolled or expecting to enroll at an institution or university.

Application Requirements: Applicant must enter a contest, copies of book. *Deadline:* May 17.

Contact: Book Prize Administrator
American Historical Association
400 A Street, SE
Washington, DC 20003
E-mail: aha@theaha.org

PAUL BIRDSALL PRIZE

Biannual prize for major book in European military and strategic history since 1870. Technical study ineligible. Preference given to younger academics. Must be U.S. or Canadian citizen. Copies of entries must be sent to each committee member. Refer to Web site (http://www.theaha.org) for names and mailing addresses.

Academic Fields/Career Goals: History; Humanities.

Award: Prize for use in freshman, sophomore, junior, senior, graduate, or postgraduate years; not renewable. *Number:* 1. *Amount:* varies.

Eligibility Requirements: Applicant must be enrolled or expecting to enroll at an institution or university and must have an interest in writing. Available to U.S. and Canadian citizens.

Application Requirements: Applicant must enter a contest, copies of entry. *Deadline:* May 17.

Contact: Book Prize Administrator
American Historical Association
400 A Street, SE
Washington, DC 20003
E-mail: aha@theaha.org

PREMIO DEL REY PRIZE
• *See page 282*

WESLEY-LOGAN PRIZE
• *See page 52*

AMERICAN PHILOLOGICAL ASSOCIATION http://www.apaclassics.org

MINORITY STUDENT SUMMER SCHOLARSHIP
• *See page 85*

AMERICAN SCHOOL OF CLASSICAL STUDIES AT ATHENS http://www.ascsa.edu.gr

ASCSA SUMMER SESSIONS
• *See page 65*

CANADIAN INSTITUTE OF UKRAINIAN STUDIES http://www.ualberta.ca/cius/

LEO J. KRYSA UNDERGRADUATE SCHOLARSHIP
• *See page 80*

COLLEGEBOUND FOUNDATION http://www.collegeboundfoundation.org

DECATUR H. MILLER SCHOLARSHIP

Award for Baltimore City public high school graduates. Please see Web site: http://www.collegeboundfoundation.org for complete information on application process. Must major in political science, history, or pre-law. Minimum GPA of 3.0, SAT score of 1100. Preference given to students who plan to enter law school. Must submit CollegeBound Competitive Scholarship/Last-Dollar Grant Application.

Academic Fields/Career Goals: History; Law/Legal Services; Political Science.

Award: Scholarship for use in freshman, sophomore, junior, or senior years; renewable. *Number:* 1. *Amount:* $1500.

Eligibility Requirements: Applicant must be enrolled or expecting to enroll full-time at a two-year or four-year institution or university and resident of Maryland. Applicant must have 3.0 GPA or higher. Available to U.S. citizens.

Application Requirements: Application, financial need analysis, references, transcript, financial aid award letters, Student Aid Report. *Deadline:* March 19.

Contact: April Bell, Associate Program Director
CollegeBound Foundation
300 Water Street, Suite 300
Baltimore, MD 21202
Phone: 410-783-2905 Ext. 208
Fax: 410-727-5786
E-mail: abell@collegeboundfoundation.org

COSTUME SOCIETY OF AMERICA http://www.costumesocietyamerica.com

ADELE FILENE TRAVEL AWARD
• *See page 81*

STELLA BLUM RESEARCH GRANT
• *See page 81*

HARRY S. TRUMAN LIBRARY INSTITUTE http://www.trumanlibrary.org

HARRY S. TRUMAN LIBRARY INSTITUTE UNDERGRADUATE STUDENT GRANT

• *See page 192*

HARVARD TRAVELLERS CLUB

HARVARD TRAVELLERS CLUB GRANTS

• *See page 73*

HUGH FULTON BYAS MEMORIAL FUNDS, INC.

HUGH FULTON BYAS MEMORIAL GRANT

Grants for United Kingdom citizens who are full-time students intending to pursue a course of study in the United States devoted to world peace, journalism, Anglo-American relations, or the creative arts.

Academic Fields/Career Goals: History; International Migration; Journalism; Peace and Conflict Studies.

Award: Grant for use in sophomore, junior, senior, graduate, or postgraduate years; renewable. *Number:* 3–10. *Amount:* $1000–$25,000.

Eligibility Requirements: Applicant must be English citizen and enrolled or expecting to enroll full-time at a four-year institution or university. Available to citizens of countries other than the U.S. or Canada.

Application Requirements: Application, essay, financial need analysis, photo, self-addressed stamped envelope, transcript, United Kingdom passport. *Deadline:* Continuous.

Contact: Linda Maffei, Administrator
Hugh Fulton Byas Memorial Funds, Inc.
261 Bradley Street
New Haven, CT 06511
Phone: 203-777-8356
Fax: 203-562-6288

JEWISH FAMILY AND CHILDREN'S SERVICES http://www.jfcs.org

ZISOVICH JEWISH STUDIES SCHOLARSHIP FUND TO TEACH THE HOLOCAUST

• *See page 204*

MORRIS K. UDALL FOUNDATION http://www.udall.gov

MORRIS K. UDALL SCHOLARS

• *See page 59*

NATIONAL FEDERATION OF THE BLIND http://www.nfb.org

MICHAEL AND MARIE MARUCCI SCHOLARSHIP

• *See page 283*

NATIONAL SOCIETY DAUGHTERS OF THE AMERICAN REVOLUTION http://www.dar.org

NATIONAL SOCIETY DAUGHTERS OF THE AMERICAN REVOLUTION AMERICAN HISTORY SCHOLARSHIP

For graduating high school seniors planning to major in U.S. history at a four-year institution. Must submit a DAR sponsorship letter from local chapter and financial need form from parents. Application deadline: February 1. Merit based. Must submit self-addressed stamped envelope to be considered. Contact state chairman.

Academic Fields/Career Goals: History.

Award: Scholarship for use in freshman, sophomore, junior, or senior years; renewable. *Number:* 1–3. *Amount:* up to $2000.

Eligibility Requirements: Applicant must be high school student and planning to enroll or expecting to enroll at a four-year institution. Applicant or parent of applicant must be member of Daughters of the American Revolution. Applicant must have 3.0 GPA or higher. Available to U.S. and non-U.S. citizens.

Application Requirements: Application, essay, financial need analysis, references, self-addressed stamped envelope, test scores, transcript. *Deadline:* February 1.

Contact: Office of Committees, Scholarship
National Society Daughters of the American Revolution
1776 D Street, NW
Washington, DC 20006-5392

NATIONAL SOCIETY DAUGHTERS OF THE AMERICAN REVOLUTION ENID HALL GRISWOLD MEMORIAL SCHOLARSHIP

• *See page 193*

NEW JERSEY HISTORICAL COMMISSION http://www.state.nj.us/state/history/grants.html

NEW JERSEY HISTORICAL COMMISSION MINI-GRANTS

Grants available to support small projects which are relatively inexpensive and support the mission of the New Jersey Historical Commission. The regular rules for project grants apply (see Web site), however, there is no deadline; they are reviewed bimonthly in January, March, May, August, October, and December.

Academic Fields/Career Goals: History.

Award: Grant for use in freshman, sophomore, junior, senior, graduate, or postgraduate years; not renewable. *Amount:* up to $3000.

Eligibility Requirements: Applicant must be enrolled or expecting to enroll at a two-year or four-year or technical institution or university. Available to U.S. citizens.

Application Requirements: Application, proposal. *Deadline:* Continuous.

Contact: Mary Murrin, Director, Grants Program
New Jersey Historical Commission
Attn: Grants and Prizes
225 West State Street, PO Box 305
Trenton, NJ 08625-0305
Phone: 609-984-0954
Fax: 609-633-8168
E-mail: mary.murrin@sos.state.nj.us

RICHARD G. MCCORMICK PRIZE

Award to the author of an outstanding book on New Jersey history published during the preceding two years. Offered only in odd-numbered years. Nomination form is on the Web site. Must be nominated.

Academic Fields/Career Goals: History.

Award: Prize for use in freshman, sophomore, junior, senior, graduate, or postgraduate years; not renewable. *Number:* 1. *Amount:* $1000.

Eligibility Requirements: Applicant must be enrolled or expecting to enroll at an institution or university. Available to U.S. citizens.

Application Requirements: Application, nomination, one copy of book. *Deadline:* January 2.

Contact: Mary Murrin, Director, Grants Program
New Jersey Historical Commission
Attn: Grants and Prizes
225 West State Street, PO Box 305
Trenton, NJ 08625-0305
Phone: 609-984-0954
Fax: 609-633-8168
E-mail: mary.murrin@sos.state.nj.us

ORGANIZATION OF AMERICAN HISTORIANS http://www.oah.org

BINKLEY-STEPHENSON AWARD

• *See page 62*

PHI ALPHA THETA HISTORY HONOR SOCIETY, INC. http://www.phialphatheta.org

PHI ALPHA THETA PAPER PRIZES

$300 prize for best graduate student paper, $250 prize for best undergraduate paper, and four $250 prizes for either graduate or undergraduate papers. All applicants must be members of Phi Alpha Theta. Deadline is July 1.

Phi Alpha Theta History Honor Society, Inc. (continued)

Academic Fields/Career Goals: History.

Award: Prize for use in freshman, sophomore, junior, senior, or graduate years; not renewable. *Number:* 6. *Amount:* $250–$300.

Eligibility Requirements: Applicant must be enrolled or expecting to enroll full-time at a four-year institution or university. Applicant must have 3.0 GPA or higher. Available to U.S. and non-U.S. citizens.

Application Requirements: Applicant must enter a contest, essay, references. *Deadline:* July 1.

Contact: Graydon A. Tunstall, Jr., Executive Director
Phi Alpha Theta History Honor Society, Inc.
University of South Florida, 4202 East Fowler Avenue, SOC107
Tampa, FL 33620-8100
Phone: 813-974-6249
Fax: 813-974-8215
E-mail: phialpha@phialphatheta.org

PHI ALPHA THETA WORLD HISTORY ASSOCIATION PAPER PRIZE

One undergraduate and one graduate-level prize for papers examining any historical issue with global implications (for example: exchange or interchange of cultures, comparison of civilizations or cultures). This is a joint award with the World History Association. Must be a member of the World History Association or Phi Alpha Theta. Paper must have been composed while enrolled at an accredited college or university. Must send in 2 copies of paper along with professor's letter. Deadline is August 15.

Academic Fields/Career Goals: History.

Award: Prize for use in freshman, sophomore, junior, senior, or graduate years; not renewable. *Number:* 2. *Amount:* $200.

Eligibility Requirements: Applicant must be enrolled or expecting to enroll full-time at a four-year institution or university. Applicant must have 3.0 GPA or higher. Available to U.S. and non-U.S. citizens.

Application Requirements: Essay, 2 copies of paper, abstract, letter from faculty member. *Deadline:* August 15.

Contact: Graydon A. Tunstall, Jr., Executive Director
Phi Alpha Theta History Honor Society, Inc.
University of South Florida, 4202 East Fowler Avenue, SOC107
Tampa, FL 33620-8100
Phone: 813-974-6249
Fax: 813-974-8215
E-mail: phialpha@phialphatheta.org

PHI ALPHA THETA/WESTERN FRONT ASSOCIATION PAPER PRIZE

Essay competition available to full-time undergraduate members of Phi Alpha Theta. The paper must be from 12 to 15 typed pages and must address the American experience in World War I, dealing with virtually any aspect of American involvement during the period from 1912 (Second Moroccan Crisis) to 1924 (Dawes Plan). Primary source material must be used. For further details visit Web site: http://www.phialphatheta.org/awards2.htm.

Academic Fields/Career Goals: History.

Award: Prize for use in freshman, sophomore, junior, or senior years; not renewable. *Number:* 1. *Amount:* $700.

Eligibility Requirements: Applicant must be enrolled or expecting to enroll full-time at a four-year institution or university. Applicant must have 3.0 GPA or higher. Available to U.S. and non-U.S. citizens.

Application Requirements: Applicant must enter a contest, essay, disk containing file of paper and cover letter. *Deadline:* December 3.

Contact: Graydon Tunstall, Jr., Executive Director
Phi Alpha Theta History Honor Society, Inc.
University of South Florida
4202 East Fowler Avenue SOC107
Tampa, FL 33620-8100
Phone: 813-974-6249
Fax: 813-974-8215
E-mail: phialpha@phialphatheta.org

SOUTHERN BAPTIST HISTORICAL LIBRARY AND ARCHIVES http://www.sbhla.org

LYNN E. MAY, JR. STUDY GRANT

Grants to assist researchers (graduate students, college and seminary professors, historians, and other writers) with travel and research costs related to research in the Southern Baptist Historical Library and Archives.

Academic Fields/Career Goals: History; Religion/Theology.

Award: Grant for use in junior, senior, graduate, or postgraduate years; not renewable. *Number:* 8–10. *Amount:* $500–$750.

Eligibility Requirements: Applicant must be enrolled or expecting to enroll full or part-time at a two-year or four-year institution or university and studying in Tennessee. Available to U.S. and non-U.S. citizens.

Application Requirements: Application, references. *Deadline:* April 1.

Contact: Bill Sumners, Director
Southern Baptist Historical Library and Archives
901 Commerce Street, Suite 400
Nashville, TN 37203-3630
Phone: 615-244-0344

TOPSFIELD HISTORICAL SOCIETY http://www.topsfieldhistory.org

JOHN KIMBALL, JR. MEMORIAL TRUST SCHOLARSHIP PROGRAM FOR THE STUDY OF HISTORY

For tuition, books, and other educational and research expenses to undergraduate and graduate students, as well as college, university, and graduate school instructors and professors who have excelled in, and/or have a passion for, the study of history and related disciplines, and who reside in, or have a substantial connection to Topsfield, Massachusetts.

Academic Fields/Career Goals: History.

Award: Grant for use in freshman, sophomore, junior, senior, graduate, or postgraduate years; not renewable. *Number:* 5–20. *Amount:* $250–$5000.

Eligibility Requirements: Applicant must be enrolled or expecting to enroll full or part-time at a two-year or four-year institution or university. Available to U.S. and non-U.S. citizens.

Application Requirements: Application. *Deadline:* May 15.

Contact: Norman Isler, President
Topsfield Historical Society
PO Box 323
Topsfield, MA 01983
Phone: 978-887-9724
Fax: 978-887-0185
E-mail: nisler@verizon.net

UNITED DAUGHTERS OF THE CONFEDERACY http://www.hqudc.org

HELEN JAMES BREWER SCHOLARSHIP

Award for full-time undergraduate student who is a descendant of a Confederate soldier, sailor or marine. Must be from Alabama, Florida, Georgia, South Carolina, Tennessee or Virginia. Recipient must be enrolled in an accredited college or university and studying Southern history and literature. Must be a member or former member of the Children of the Confederacy. Minimum 3.0 GPA. Submit letter of endorsement from sponsoring chapter of the United Daughters of the Confederacy. Please refer to Web site for further details: http://www.hqudc.org

Academic Fields/Career Goals: History; Literature/English/Writing.

Award: Scholarship for use in freshman, sophomore, junior, or senior years; renewable. *Number:* 1–2. *Amount:* $800–$1000.

Eligibility Requirements: Applicant must be enrolled or expecting to enroll full-time at a four-year institution or university and resident of Alabama, Florida, Georgia, South Carolina, Tennessee, or Virginia. Applicant or parent of applicant must be member of United Daughters of the Confederacy. Applicant must have 3.0 GPA or higher. Available to U.S. citizens.

Application Requirements: Application, essay, financial need analysis, photo, references, self-addressed stamped envelope, transcript. *Deadline:* February 15.

Contact: Second Vice President General
United Daughters of the Confederacy
328 North Boulevard
Richmond, VA 23220-4057
Phone: 804-355-1636

UNITED NEGRO COLLEGE FUND http://www.uncf.org

C-SPAN SCHOLARSHIP PROGRAM

• *See page 166*

CATHERINE W. PIERCE SCHOLARSHIP

• *See page 91*

HOME ECONOMICS

COSTUME SOCIETY OF AMERICA http://www.costumesocietyamerica.com

ADELE FILENE TRAVEL AWARD

• *See page 81*

STELLA BLUM RESEARCH GRANT

• *See page 81*

FAMILY, CAREER AND COMMUNITY LEADERS OF AMERICA-TEXAS ASSOCIATION http://www.texasfccla.org

C.J. DAVIDSON SCHOLARSHIP FOR FCCLA

Scholarships are available to outstanding members of the Texas FCCLA. $900 is awarded per semester and will be continued for eight straight semesters if recipients remain eligible. Applicants should visit the Web site (http://www.texasfccla.org) or write to Texas FCCLA for complete information, submission guidelines, and restrictions.

Academic Fields/Career Goals: Home Economics.

Award: Scholarship for use in freshman, sophomore, junior, or senior years; renewable. *Number:* 10. *Amount:* $1800.

Eligibility Requirements: Applicant must be high school student; planning to enroll or expecting to enroll full-time at a four-year institution or university; single; resident of Texas and studying in Texas. Applicant or parent of applicant must be member of Family, Career and Community Leaders of America. Applicant must have 2.5 GPA or higher. Available to U.S. citizens.

Application Requirements: Application, essay, references, test scores, transcript. *Deadline:* March 1.

Contact: FCCLA Staff
Family, Career and Community Leaders of America-Texas Association
3530 Bee Caves Road, #101
Austin, TX 78746-9616
Phone: 512-306-0099
Fax: 512-306-0041
E-mail: fccla@texasfccla.org

FCCLA HOUSTON LIVESTOCK SHOW AND RODEO SCHOLARSHIP

Ten, four-year $10,000 scholarships to be awarded to outstanding members of the Texas FCCLA. Applicants should visit the Web site (http://www.texasfccla.org) or write to Texas FCCLA for complete information, submission guidelines, and restrictions. Minimum 3.5 GPA required. Must be Texas resident and attend a Texas institution.

Academic Fields/Career Goals: Home Economics.

Award: Scholarship for use in freshman, sophomore, junior, or senior years; not renewable. *Number:* 10. *Amount:* $10,000.

Eligibility Requirements: Applicant must be high school student; planning to enroll or expecting to enroll full-time at a four-year institution or university; resident of Texas and studying in Texas. Applicant or parent of applicant must be member of Family, Career and Community Leaders of America. Applicant must have 3.5 GPA or higher. Available to U.S. citizens.

Application Requirements: Application, essay, photo, references, test scores, transcript. *Deadline:* March 1.

Contact: FCCLA Staff
Family, Career and Community Leaders of America-Texas Association
3530 Bee Caves Road, #101
Austin, TX 78746-9616
Phone: 512-306-0099
Fax: 512-306-0041
E-mail: fccla@texasfccla.org

FCCLA REGIONAL SCHOLARSHIPS

• *See page 123*

FCCLA TEXAS FARM BUREAU SCHOLARSHIP

• *See page 123*

INTERNATIONAL EXECUTIVE HOUSEKEEPERS ASSOCIATION http://www.ieha.org

INTERNATIONAL EXECUTIVE HOUSEKEEPERS EDUCATIONAL FOUNDATION

• *See page 277*

MAINE SCHOOL FOOD SERVICE ASSOCIATION (MSFSA) http://www.msfsa.com

SCHOLARSHIP OF THE MAINE SCHOOL FOOD SERVICE ASSOCIATION

• *See page 276*

MARYLAND ASSOCIATION OF PRIVATE COLLEGES AND CAREER SCHOOLS http://www.mapccs.org

MARYLAND ASSOCIATION OF PRIVATE COLLEGES AND CAREER SCHOOLS SCHOLARSHIP

• *See page 127*

NATIONAL POULTRY AND FOOD DISTRIBUTORS ASSOCIATION http://www.npfda.org

NATIONAL POULTRY AND FOOD DISTRIBUTORS ASSOCIATION SCHOLARSHIP FOUNDATION

• *See page 55*

TEXAS ELECTRIC CO-OP, INC. http://www.texas-ec.org

ANN LANE HOME ECONOMICS SCHOLARSHIP

• *See page 276*

UNITED DAUGHTERS OF THE CONFEDERACY http://www.hqudc.org

WALTER REED SMITH SCHOLARSHIP

• *See page 130*

HORTICULTURE/FLORICULTURE

ALABAMA GOLF COURSE SUPERINTENDENTS ASSOCIATION http://www.agcsa.org

ALABAMA GOLF COURSE SUPERINTENDENT'S ASSOCIATION'S DONNIE ARTHUR MEMORIAL SCHOLARSHIP

One-time award for students majoring in agriculture with an emphasis on turfgrass management. Must have a minimum 2.0 GPA. Application deadline is September 30.

Academic Fields/Career Goals: Horticulture/Floriculture.

Award: Scholarship for use in freshman, sophomore, junior, or senior years; not renewable. *Number:* 2. *Amount:* $1000.

Eligibility Requirements: Applicant must be enrolled or expecting to enroll full-time at a two-year or four-year institution or university. Available to U.S. and non-U.S. citizens.

Alabama Golf Course Superintendents Association (continued)

Application Requirements: Application, essay, transcript. *Deadline:* September 30.

Contact: Melanie Bonds, Executive Secretary
Alabama Golf Course Superintendents Association
PO Box 661214
Birmingham, AL 35266-1214
Phone: 205-979-5225
Fax: 205-967-1466
E-mail: melaniebonds@mindspring.com

AMERICAN FLORAL ENDOWMENT http://www.endowment.org

HAROLD F. WILKINS SCHOLARSHIP PROGRAM

• *See page 119*

MOSMILLER SCHOLAR PROGRAM

• *See page 119*

VICTOR AND MARGARET BALL PROGRAM

• *See page 119*

AMERICAN NURSERY AND LANDSCAPE ASSOCIATION http://www.anla.org/research

ANLA NATIONAL SCHOLARSHIP ENDOWMENT-USREY FAMILY SCHOLARSHIP

Award for students who are enrolled in accredited undergraduate or graduate landscape/horticulture program. Must attend a California school. Preference given to applicants who plan to work within the industry. Must have a minimum 2.5 GPA.

Academic Fields/Career Goals: Horticulture/Floriculture; Landscape Architecture.

Award: Scholarship for use in sophomore, junior, senior, graduate, or postgraduate years; not renewable. *Number:* 1. *Amount:* $1000–$1500.

Eligibility Requirements: Applicant must be enrolled or expecting to enroll full-time at a two-year or four-year or technical institution or university and studying in California. Applicant must have 2.5 GPA or higher. Available to U.S. and non-U.S. citizens.

Application Requirements: Application, essay, financial need analysis, references, transcript. *Deadline:* April 1.

Contact: Research Communications and Grants Manager
American Nursery and Landscape Association
1000 Vermont Street, NW, Suite 300
Washington, DC 20005
Phone: 202-789-2900 Ext. 3014
Fax: 202-789-1893
E-mail: hriresearch@anla.org

CARVILLE M. AKEHURST MEMORIAL SCHOLARSHIP

Scholarship to resident of Maryland, Virginia, or West Virginia, for full-time study of horticulture/landscape. Applicant must have minimum 3.0 GPA.

Academic Fields/Career Goals: Horticulture/Floriculture; Landscape Architecture.

Award: Scholarship for use in junior, senior, or graduate years; not renewable. *Number:* 1–2. *Amount:* $1000.

Eligibility Requirements: Applicant must be enrolled or expecting to enroll full-time at a two-year or four-year institution or university and resident of Maryland, Virginia, or West Virginia. Applicant must have 3.0 GPA or higher. Available to U.S. citizens.

Application Requirements: Application, essay, financial need analysis, resume, references, transcript. *Deadline:* April 1.

Contact: Teresa Jodon, Endowment Program Administrator
American Nursery and Landscape Association
HRI
1000 Vermont Avenue, NW, Suite 300
Washington, DC 20005-4914
Phone: 202-789-5980 Ext. 3014
Fax: 202-789-1893
E-mail: hriresearch@anla.org

HORTICULTURE RESEARCH INSTITUTE TIMOTHY BIGELOW SCHOLARSHIP

Award for students who are enrolled in accredited undergraduate or graduate landscape/horticulture program. Must be resident of Connecticut, Maine, Massachusetts, New Hampshire, Rhode Island, or Vermont. Undergraduates must have a GPA of 2.25; graduate students, 3.0. Financial need, desire to work in nursery industry are factors. Deadline: April 1.

Academic Fields/Career Goals: Horticulture/Floriculture; Landscape Architecture.

Award: Scholarship for use in sophomore, junior, senior, or graduate years; not renewable. *Number:* varies. *Amount:* $1500–$2500.

Eligibility Requirements: Applicant must be enrolled or expecting to enroll full-time at a two-year or four-year institution or university and resident of Connecticut, Maine, Massachusetts, New Hampshire, Rhode Island, or Vermont. Available to U.S. and non-U.S. citizens.

Application Requirements: Application, essay, financial need analysis, references, transcript. *Deadline:* April 1.

Contact: Research Funding/Grants Manager
American Nursery and Landscape Association
1000 Vermont Street, NW, Suite 300
Washington, DC 20005
Phone: 202-789-2900 Ext. 3014
Fax: 202-789-1893
E-mail: hriresearch@anla.org

SPRING MEADOW NURSERY SCHOLARSHIP

Scholarship for the full-time study of horticulture or landscape architecture. Applicant must have minimum 2.5 GPA.

Academic Fields/Career Goals: Horticulture/Floriculture; Landscape Architecture.

Award: Scholarship for use in freshman, sophomore, junior, senior, or graduate years; not renewable. *Number:* 1–2. *Amount:* $1000–$1500.

Eligibility Requirements: Applicant must be enrolled or expecting to enroll full-time at a two-year or four-year or technical institution or university. Applicant must have 2.5 GPA or higher. Available to U.S. and Canadian citizens.

Application Requirements: Application, essay, financial need analysis, resume, references, transcript. *Deadline:* April 1.

Contact: Teresa Jodon, Endowment Program Administrator
American Nursery and Landscape Association
HRI
1000 Vermont Avenue, NW, Suite 300
Washington, DC 20005-4914
Phone: 202-789-5980 Ext. 3014
Fax: 202-789-1893
E-mail: hriresearch@anla.org

AMERICAN SOCIETY FOR ENOLOGY AND VITICULTURE http://www.asev.org

AMERICAN SOCIETY FOR ENOLOGY AND VITICULTURE SCHOLARSHIPS

• *See page 56*

ARIZONA NURSERY ASSOCIATION http://www.azna.org

ARIZONA NURSERY ASSOCIATION FOUNDATION SCHOLARSHIP

Provides research grants and scholarships for the green industry. Application deadline is April 15. Applicant must be an Arizona resident currently or planning to be enrolled in a horticultural related curriculum at an Arizona university, community college, or continuing education program. See Web site for further details: http://www.azna.org

Academic Fields/Career Goals: Horticulture/Floriculture.

Award: Scholarship for use in freshman, sophomore, junior, senior, graduate, or postgraduate years; not renewable. *Number:* 12–15. *Amount:* $500–$3000.

Eligibility Requirements: Applicant must be enrolled or expecting to enroll full or part-time at a two-year or four-year or technical institution or university. Available to U.S. and non-U.S. citizens.

Application Requirements: Application, references, transcript. *Deadline:* April 15.

Contact: Cheryl Goar, Executive Director
Arizona Nursery Association
1430 West Broadway
Suite A-180
Tempe, AZ 85282
Phone: 480-966-1610
Fax: 480-966-0923
E-mail: cgoar@azna.org

COMMUNITY FOUNDATION FOR PALM BEACH AND MARTIN COUNTIES, INC. http://www.yourcommunityfoundation.org

MILTON J. BOONE HORTICULTURAL SCHOLARSHIP

Scholarship awarded to graduating senior in high school, or returning student to the pursuit of Horticultural studies. Restricted to residents of Palm Beach or Martin County. Applications available online http://www.yourcommunityfoundation.org. Deadline is March 1.

Academic Fields/Career Goals: Horticulture/Floriculture.

Award: Scholarship for use in freshman year; not renewable. *Number:* varies. *Amount:* varies.

Eligibility Requirements: Applicant must be enrolled or expecting to enroll at a four-year institution or university and resident of Florida. Available to U.S. citizens.

Application Requirements: Application, financial need analysis. *Deadline:* March 1.

Contact: Carolyn Jenco, Grants Manager/Scholarship Coordinator
Community Foundation for Palm Beach and Martin Counties, Inc.
700 South Dixie Highway
Suite 200
West Palm Beach, FL 33401

CONNECTICUT NURSERYMEN'S FOUNDATION, INC.

CONNECTICUT NURSERYMEN'S FOUNDATION, INC. SCHOLARSHIPS

Award to graduating high school seniors or preparatory school graduates who will enter college in the fall semester, majoring in horticulture, landscape design, or nursery management. This award is renewable for up to four years. Must be a resident of Connecticut and a U.S. citizen. Deadline: March 15. Minimum 2.5 GPA required.

Academic Fields/Career Goals: Horticulture/Floriculture; Landscape Architecture.

Award: Scholarship for use in freshman year; renewable. *Number:* 1. *Amount:* $5000.

Eligibility Requirements: Applicant must be enrolled or expecting to enroll full-time at a two-year or four-year institution or university and resident of Connecticut. Applicant must have 2.5 GPA or higher. Available to U.S. citizens.

Application Requirements: Application, financial need analysis, interview, references, test scores, transcript. *Deadline:* March 15.

Contact: Michael D. Johnson, Financial Coordinator
Connecticut Nurserymen's Foundation, Inc.
888 Summer Hill Road
Madison, CT 06443
Phone: 203-421-3055
Fax: 203-421-5189

FEDERATED GARDEN CLUBS OF CONNECTICUT

FEDERATED GARDEN CLUBS OF CONNECTICUT, INC.

• *See page 113*

FIRST–FLORICULTURE INDUSTRY RESEARCH AND SCHOLARSHIP TRUST http://www.firstinfloriculture.org

BALL HORTICULTURAL COMPANY SCHOLARSHIP

Award open to undergraduates entering junior or senior year at a four-year college or university in the U.S. or Canada. Must be studying horticulture or a related field and intend to pursue a career in commercial floriculture. To apply you must register with lunch-money.com, which is partnering with FIRST to make the application process easier. You only need to fill out one application online, and there is a link to lunch-money.com from the FIRST Web site: http://www.firstinfloriculture.org/schl_req_app.htm. In addition to the application, you must submit two letters of recommendation and transcripts via email to: scholarships@firstinfloriculture.org. Application deadline is May 1.

Academic Fields/Career Goals: Horticulture/Floriculture.

Award: Scholarship for use in junior or senior years; not renewable. *Number:* 1. *Amount:* $1000.

Eligibility Requirements: Applicant must be enrolled or expecting to enroll at a four-year institution or university. Applicant must have 3.0 GPA or higher. Available to U.S. and non-U.S. citizens.

Application Requirements: Application, references, transcript. *Deadline:* May 1.

Contact: Scholarship Information
FIRST–Floriculture Industry Research and Scholarship Trust
PO Box 280
East Lansing, MI 48826-0280
E-mail: scholarship@firstinfloriculture.org

BARBARA CARLSON SCHOLARSHIP

Award open to undergraduates or graduates studying horticulture or a related major at a four-year college or university in the U.S. or Canada. For students interested in interning or working for public gardens. Must have a career interest in horticulture. To apply you must register with lunch-money.com, which is partnering with FIRST to make the application process easier. You only need to fill out one application online, and there is a link to lunch-money.com from the FIRST Web site: http://www.firstinfloriculture.org/schl_req_app.htm In addition to the application, you must submit two letters of recommendation and transcripts via email to: scholarships@firstinfloriculture.org. Application deadline is May 1.

Academic Fields/Career Goals: Horticulture/Floriculture.

Award: Scholarship for use in sophomore, junior, senior, or graduate years; not renewable. *Number:* 1. *Amount:* $1000.

Eligibility Requirements: Applicant must be enrolled or expecting to enroll at a four-year institution or university. Applicant or parent of applicant must have employment or volunteer experience in designated career field. Applicant must have 3.0 GPA or higher. Available to U.S. and non-U.S. citizens.

Application Requirements: Application, references, transcript. *Deadline:* May 1.

Contact: Scholarship Information
FIRST–Floriculture Industry Research and Scholarship Trust
PO Box 280
East Lansing, MI 48826-0280
E-mail: scholarship@firstinfloriculture.org

BUD OHLMAN SCHOLARSHIP

Award available for student studying horticulture at a U.S. or Canadian institution with career goal of becoming a bedding plant grower for an established business. Minimum GPA of 3.0 required. To apply you must register with lunch-money.com, which is partnering with FIRST to make the application process easier. You only need to fill out one application online, and there is a link to lunch-money.com from the FIRST Web site: http://www.firstinfloriculture.org/schl_req_app.htm In addition to the application, you must submit two letters of recommendation and transcripts via email to: scholarships@firstinfloriculture.org. Application deadline is May 1.

Academic Fields/Career Goals: Horticulture/Floriculture.

Award: Scholarship for use in junior or senior years; not renewable. *Number:* 1. *Amount:* $1000.

Eligibility Requirements: Applicant must be enrolled or expecting to enroll at a four-year institution or university. Applicant must have 3.0 GPA or higher. Available to U.S. and non-U.S. citizens.

FIRST–Floriculture Industry Research and Scholarship Trust (continued)

Application Requirements: Application, references, transcript. *Deadline:* May 1.

Contact: Scholarship Information
FIRST–Floriculture Industry Research and Scholarship Trust
PO Box 280
East Lansing, MI 48826-0280
E-mail: scholarship@firstinfloriculture.org

CARL F. DEITZ MEMORIAL SCHOLARSHIP

One-time award available to undergraduate horticulture or related majors at a four-year institution in the U.S. or Canada who have a career interest in horticultural allied trades. Must have completed one year of study. Minimum 3.0 GPA required. To apply you must register with lunch-money.com, which is partnering with FIRST to make the application process easier. You only need to fill out one application online, and there is a link to lunch-money.com from the FIRST Web site: http://www.firstinfloriculture.org/schl_req_app.htm In addition to the application, you must submit two letters of recommendation and transcripts via email to: scholarships@firstinfloriculture.org. Application deadline is May 1.

Academic Fields/Career Goals: Horticulture/Floriculture.

Award: Scholarship for use in sophomore or senior years; not renewable. *Number:* 1. *Amount:* $1000.

Eligibility Requirements: Applicant must be enrolled or expecting to enroll at a four-year institution or university. Applicant must have 3.0 GPA or higher. Available to U.S. and non-U.S. citizens.

Application Requirements: Application, references, transcript. *Deadline:* May 1.

Contact: Scholarship Information
FIRST–Floriculture Industry Research and Scholarship Trust
PO Box 280
East Lansing, MI 48826-0280
E-mail: scholarship@firstinfloriculture.org

DOSATRON INTERNATIONAL, INC., SCHOLARSHIP

Award open to upper-level undergraduates or graduates studying horticulture or a related major at a four-year college or university in the U.S. or Canada. Must have interest in floriculture production, with a career goal to work in a greenhouse environment. Minimum GPA of 3.0 required. To apply you must register with lunch-money.com, which is partnering with FIRST to make the application process easier. You only need to fill out one application online, and there is a link to lunch-money.com from the FIRST Web site: http://www.firstinfloriculture.org/schl_req_app.htm In addition to the application, you must submit two letters of recommendation and transcripts via email to: scholarships@firstinfloriculture.org. Application deadline is May 1.

Academic Fields/Career Goals: Horticulture/Floriculture.

Award: Scholarship for use in junior, senior, or graduate years; not renewable. *Number:* 1. *Amount:* $1000.

Eligibility Requirements: Applicant must be enrolled or expecting to enroll at a four-year institution or university. Applicant must have 3.0 GPA or higher. Available to U.S. and non-U.S. citizens.

Application Requirements: Application, references, transcript. *Deadline:* May 1.

Contact: Scholarship Information
FIRST–Floriculture Industry Research and Scholarship Trust
PO Box 280
East Lansing, MI 48826-0280
E-mail: scholarship@firstinfloriculture.org

EARL DEDMAN MEMORIAL SCHOLARSHIP

Award available to students from the Northwest area of the U.S. who are undergraduates studying horticulture or a related subject at a four-year college or university in the U.S. or Canada. Must intend to pursue a career as a greenhouse grower. Minimum GPA of 3.0 required. To apply you must register with lunch-money.com, which is partnering with FIRST to make the application process easier. You only need to fill out one application online, and there is a link to lunch-money.com from the FIRST Web site: http://www.firstinfloriculture.org/schl_req_app.htm In addition to the application, you must submit two letters of recommendation and transcripts via email to: scholarships@firstinfloriculture.org. Application deadline is May 1.

Academic Fields/Career Goals: Horticulture/Floriculture.

Award: Scholarship for use in sophomore, junior, or senior years; not renewable. *Number:* 1. *Amount:* $1000.

Eligibility Requirements: Applicant must be enrolled or expecting to enroll at a four-year institution or university. Applicant must have 3.0 GPA or higher. Available to U.S. and non-U.S. citizens.

Application Requirements: Application, references, transcript. *Deadline:* May 1.

Contact: Scholarship Information
FIRST–Floriculture Industry Research and Scholarship Trust
PO Box 280
East Lansing, MI 48826-0280
E-mail: scholarship@firstinfloriculture.org

ECKE FAMILY SCHOLARSHIP

Award available to students entering junior or senior year at a four-year college or university in the U.S. or Canada. Must be studying horticulture or a related field and intend to pursue a career in production floriculture. Minimum GPA of 3.0 required. To apply you must register with lunch-money.com, which is partnering with FIRST to make the application process easier. You only need to fill out one application online, and there is a link to lunch-money.com from the FIRST Web site: http://www.firstinfloriculture.org/schl_req_app.htm In addition to the application, you must submit two letters of recommendation and transcripts via email to: scholarships@firstinfloriculture.org. Application deadline is May 1.

Academic Fields/Career Goals: Horticulture/Floriculture.

Award: Scholarship for use in junior or senior years; not renewable. *Number:* 1. *Amount:* $1000.

Eligibility Requirements: Applicant must be enrolled or expecting to enroll at a four-year institution or university. Applicant must have 3.0 GPA or higher. Available to U.S. and non-U.S. citizens.

Application Requirements: Application, references, transcript. *Deadline:* May 1.

Contact: Scholarship Information
FIRST–Floriculture Industry Research and Scholarship Trust
PO Box 280
Lansing, MI 48826-0280
E-mail: scholarship@firstinfloriculture.org

ED MARKHAM INTERNATIONAL SCHOLARSHIP

Award open to undergraduates or graduates studying horticulture or a related major at a four-year college or university in the U.S. or Canada. For students who wish to further their understanding of domestic and international marketing through international horticultural related study, work, or travel. Minimum GPA of 3.0 required. To apply you must register with lunch-money.com, which is partnering with FIRST to make the application process easier. You only need to fill out one application online, and there is a link to lunch-money.com from the FIRST Web site: http://www.firstinfloriculture.org/schl_req_app.htm In addition to the application, you must submit two letters of recommendation and transcripts via email to: scholarships@firstinfloriculture.org. Application deadline is May 1.

Academic Fields/Career Goals: Horticulture/Floriculture.

Award: Scholarship for use in sophomore, junior, senior, or graduate years; not renewable. *Number:* 1. *Amount:* $1000.

Eligibility Requirements: Applicant must be enrolled or expecting to enroll at a four-year institution or university. Applicant must have 3.0 GPA or higher. Available to U.S. and non-U.S. citizens.

Application Requirements: Application, references, transcript. *Deadline:* May 1.

Contact: Scholarship Information
FIRST–Floriculture Industry Research and Scholarship Trust
PO Box 280
East Lansing, MI 48826-0280
E-mail: scholarship@firstinfloriculture.org

FRAN JOHNSON SCHOLARSHIP FOR NON-TRADITIONAL STUDENTS

One-time scholarship for graduate/undergraduate pursuing a degree in floriculture at a U.S. or Canadian institution who has been out of school for at least five years and is now reentering a program. Must have specific interest in bedding plants/floral crops. Send photo with application. To apply you must register with lunch-money.com, which is partnering with FIRST to make the application process easier. You only need to fill out one application online, and there is a link to lunch-money.com from the FIRST Web site: http://www.firstinfloriculture.org/schl_req_app.htm In addition to the application, you must submit two letters of recommendation and transcripts via email to: scholarships@firstinfloriculture.org. Application deadline is May 1.

Academic Fields/Career Goals: Horticulture/Floriculture.

Award: Scholarship for use in freshman, sophomore, junior, senior, or graduate years; not renewable. *Number:* 1. *Amount:* $500–$1000.

Eligibility Requirements: Applicant must be enrolled or expecting to enroll at a four-year institution or university. Available to U.S. and non-U.S. citizens.

Application Requirements: Application, photo, references, transcript. *Deadline:* May 1.

Contact: Scholarship Information
FIRST–Floriculture Industry Research and Scholarship Trust
PO Box 280
East Lansing, MI 48826-0280
E-mail: scholarship@firstinfloriculture.org

HAROLD BETTINGER MEMORIAL SCHOLARSHIP

• *See page 53*

JACOB VAN NAMEN/VANS MARKETING SCHOLARSHIP

• *See page 53*

JAMES BRIDENBAUGH MEMORIAL SCHOLARSHIP

Award open to students in sophomore, junior, and senior year at a four-year college or university in the U.S. or Canada. Must be studying horticulture or a related field and intend to pursue a career in floral design and marketing of fresh flowers and plants. Minimum GPA of 3.0 required. To apply you must register with lunch-money.com, which is partnering with FIRST to make the application process easier. You only need to fill out one application online, and there is a link to lunch-money.com from the FIRST Web site: http://www.firstinfloriculture.org/schl_req_app.htm In addition to the application, you must submit two letters of recommendation and transcripts via email to: scholarships@firstinfloriculture.org. Application deadline is May 1.

Academic Fields/Career Goals: Horticulture/Floriculture.

Award: Scholarship for use in sophomore, junior, or senior years; not renewable. *Number:* 1. *Amount:* $1000.

Eligibility Requirements: Applicant must be enrolled or expecting to enroll at a four-year institution or university. Applicant must have 3.0 GPA or higher. Available to U.S. and non-U.S. citizens.

Application Requirements: Application, references, transcript. *Deadline:* May 1.

Contact: Scholarship Information
FIRST–Floriculture Industry Research and Scholarship Trust
PO Box 280
East Lansing, MI 48826-0280
E-mail: scholarship@firstinfloriculture.org

JAMES RATHMELL, JR. MEMORIAL SCHOLARSHIP

One scholarship available to upper-level undergraduate or graduate student at a four-year institution in the U.S. or Canada who plans to engage in a work-study program outside the country for at least six months in the field of floriculture or horticulture. Minimum 3.0 GPA required. Submit letter of invitation from host country. To apply you must register with lunch-money.com, which is partnering with FIRST to make the application process easier. You only need to fill out one application online, and there is a link to lunch-money.com from the FIRST Web site: http://www.firstinfloriculture.org/schl_req_app.htm In addition to the application, you must submit two letters of recommendation and transcripts via email to: scholarships@firstinfloriculture.org. Application deadline is May 1.

Academic Fields/Career Goals: Horticulture/Floriculture.

Award: Scholarship for use in junior, senior, or graduate years; not renewable. *Number:* 1. *Amount:* up to $2500.

Eligibility Requirements: Applicant must be enrolled or expecting to enroll at a four-year institution or university. Applicant must have 3.0 GPA or higher. Available to U.S. and non-U.S. citizens.

Application Requirements: Application, references, transcript. *Deadline:* May 1.

Contact: Scholarship Information
FIRST–Floriculture Industry Research and Scholarship Trust
PO Box 280
East Lansing, MI 48826-0280
E-mail: scholarship@firstinfloriculture.org

JIM PERRY/HOLDEN L. BETTINGER SCHOLARSHIP

Award for vocational students in a one- or two-year program in the U.S. or Canada who intend to become a grower or greenhouse manager. Minimum GPA of 3.0 required. To apply you must register with lunch-money.com, which is partnering with FIRST to make the application process easier. You only need to fill out one application online, and there is a link to lunch-money.com from the FIRST Web site: http://www.firstinfloriculture.org/schl_req_app.htm In addition to the application, you must submit two letters of recommendation and transcripts via email to: scholarships@firstinfloriculture.org. Application deadline is May 1.

Academic Fields/Career Goals: Horticulture/Floriculture.

Award: Scholarship for use in freshman or sophomore years; not renewable. *Number:* 1. *Amount:* $1000.

Eligibility Requirements: Applicant must be enrolled or expecting to enroll at a two-year or four-year or technical institution or university. Applicant must have 3.0 GPA or higher. Available to U.S. and non-U.S. citizens.

Application Requirements: Application, references, transcript. *Deadline:* May 1.

Contact: Scholarship Information
FIRST–Floriculture Industry Research and Scholarship Trust
PO Box 280
East Lansing, MI 48826-0280
E-mail: scholarship@firstinfloriculture.org

JOHN HOLDEN MEMORIAL VOCATIONAL SCHOLARSHIP

Award open to vocational students in a one- or two-year program in an institution in the U.S. or Canada. Must be studying horticulture or a related field and intend to pursue a career as a grower or greenhouse manager. Minimum GPA of 3.0 required. To apply you must register with lunch-money.com, which is partnering with FIRST to make the application process easier. You only need to fill out one application online, and there is a link to lunch-money.com from the FIRST Web site: http://www.firstinfloriculture.org/schl_req_app.htm In addition to the application, you must submit two letters of recommendation and transcripts via email to: scholarships@firstinfloriculture.org. Application deadline is May 1.

Academic Fields/Career Goals: Horticulture/Floriculture.

Award: Scholarship for use in freshman or sophomore years; not renewable. *Number:* 1. *Amount:* $1000.

Eligibility Requirements: Applicant must be enrolled or expecting to enroll at a two-year or four-year or technical institution or university. Applicant must have 3.0 GPA or higher. Available to U.S. and non-U.S. citizens.

Application Requirements: Application, references, transcript. *Deadline:* May 1.

Contact: Scholarship Information
FIRST–Floriculture Industry Research and Scholarship Trust
PO Box 280
East Lansing, MI 48826-0280
E-mail: scholarship@firstinfloriculture.org

JOHN L. TOMASOVIC, SR., SCHOLARSHIP

Award for student pursuing career in horticulture at a U.S. or Canadian school. Special consideration for financial need and grade point average between 3.0 and 3.5. To apply you must register with lunch-money.com, which is partnering with FIRST to make the application process easier. You only need to fill out one application online, and there is a link to lunch-money.com from the FIRST Web site: http://www.firstinfloriculture.org/schl_req_app.htm In addition to the application, you must submit two letters of recommendation and transcripts via email to: scholarships@firstinfloriculture.org. Application deadline is May 1.

FIRST–Floriculture Industry Research and Scholarship Trust (continued)

Academic Fields/Career Goals: Horticulture/Floriculture.

Award: Scholarship for use in sophomore, junior, senior, or graduate years; not renewable. *Number:* 1. *Amount:* $1000–$2000.

Eligibility Requirements: Applicant must be enrolled or expecting to enroll at a four-year institution or university. Applicant must have 3.0 GPA or higher. Available to U.S. and non-U.S. citizens.

Application Requirements: Application, financial need analysis, references, transcript. *Deadline:* May 1.

Contact: Scholarship Information
FIRST–Floriculture Industry Research and Scholarship Trust
PO Box 280
East Lansing, MI 48826-0280
E-mail: scholarship@firstinfloriculture.org

LEONARD BETTINGER SCHOLARSHIP

Award open to vocational students in a one- or two-year program in an institution in the U.S. or Canada. Must be studying horticulture or a related field and intend to pursue a career as a grower or greenhouse manager. Minimum GPA of 3.0 required. To apply you must register with lunch-money.com, which is partnering with FIRST to make the application process easier. You only need to fill out one application online, and there is a link to lunch-money.com from the FIRST Web site: http://www.firstinfloriculture.org/schl_req_app.htm In addition to the application, you must submit two letters of recommendation and transcripts via email to: scholarships@firstinfloriculture.org. Application deadline is May 1.

Academic Fields/Career Goals: Horticulture/Floriculture.

Award: Scholarship for use in freshman or sophomore years; not renewable. *Number:* 1. *Amount:* $1000.

Eligibility Requirements: Applicant must be enrolled or expecting to enroll at a two-year or four-year or technical institution or university. Applicant must have 3.0 GPA or higher. Available to U.S. and non-U.S. citizens.

Application Requirements: Application, references, transcript. *Deadline:* May 1.

Contact: Scholarship Information
FIRST–Floriculture Industry Research and Scholarship Trust
PO Box 280
East Lansing, MI 48826-0280
E-mail: scholarship@firstinfloriculture.org

LONG ISLAND FLOWER GROWERS SCHOLARSHIP

Award for a horticulture student from Long Island studying commercial horticulture in a two- or four-year college or university in the U.S. or Canada. Minimum GPA of 3.0 required. To apply you must register with lunch-money.com, which is partnering with FIRST to make the application process easier. You only need to fill out one application online, and there is a link to lunch-money.com from the FIRST Web site: http://www.firstinfloriculture.org/schl_req_app.htm In addition to the application, you must submit two letters of recommendation and transcripts via email to: scholarships@firstinfloriculture.org. Application deadline is May 1.

Academic Fields/Career Goals: Horticulture/Floriculture.

Award: Scholarship for use in sophomore, junior, or senior years; not renewable. *Number:* 1. *Amount:* $1000.

Eligibility Requirements: Applicant must be enrolled or expecting to enroll at a two-year or four-year institution or university and resident of New York. Applicant must have 3.0 GPA or higher. Available to U.S. and non-U.S. citizens.

Application Requirements: Application, references, transcript. *Deadline:* May 1.

Contact: Scholarship Information
FIRST–Floriculture Industry Research and Scholarship Trust
PO Box 280
East Lansing, MI 48826-0280
E-mail: scholarship@firstinfloriculture.org

NATIONAL GREENHOUSE MANUFACTURERS ASSOCIATION SCHOLARSHIP

Scholarship targets students majoring in horticulture and bioengineering or the equivalent. Must be at least a junior at an accredited four-year college in the U.S. or Canada. Minimum GPA of 3.0 required. To apply you must register with lunch-money.com, which is partnering with FIRST to make the application process easier. You only need to fill out one application online, and there is a link to lunch-money.com from the FIRST Web site: http://www.firstinfloriculture.org/schl_req_app.htm In addition to the application, you must submit two letters of recommendation and transcripts via email to: scholarships@firstinfloriculture.org. Application deadline is May 1.

Academic Fields/Career Goals: Horticulture/Floriculture.

Award: Scholarship for use in junior or senior years; not renewable. *Number:* 1. *Amount:* $1000.

Eligibility Requirements: Applicant must be enrolled or expecting to enroll full or part-time at a four-year institution or university. Applicant must have 3.0 GPA or higher. Available to U.S. and non-U.S. citizens.

Application Requirements: Application, references, transcript. *Deadline:* May 1.

Contact: Scholarship Information
FIRST–Floriculture Industry Research and Scholarship Trust
PO Box 280
East Lansing, MI 48826-0280
E-mail: scholarship@firstinfloriculture.org

PARIS FRACASSO PRODUCTION FLORICULTURE SCHOLARSHIP

Award open to undergraduates entering junior or senior year at a four-year college or university in the U.S. or Canada. Must be studying horticulture or a related major and intend to pursue a career in floriculture production. Minimum GPA of 3.0 required. To apply you must register with lunch-money.com, which is partnering with FIRST to make the application process easier. You only need to fill out one application online, and there is a link to lunch-money.com from the FIRST Web site: http://www.firstinfloriculture.org/schl_req_app.htm In addition to the application, you must submit two letters of recommendation and transcripts via email to: scholarships@firstinfloriculture.org. Application deadline is May 1.

Academic Fields/Career Goals: Horticulture/Floriculture.

Award: Scholarship for use in junior or senior years; not renewable. *Number:* 1. *Amount:* $2000.

Eligibility Requirements: Applicant must be enrolled or expecting to enroll at a four-year institution or university. Applicant must have 3.0 GPA or higher. Available to U.S. and non-U.S. citizens.

Application Requirements: Application, references, transcript. *Deadline:* May 1.

Contact: Scholarship Information
FIRST–Floriculture Industry Research and Scholarship Trust
PO Box 280
East Lansing, MI 48826-0280
E-mail: scholarship@firstinfloriculture.org

RICHARD E. BARRETT SCHOLARSHIP

Scholarship available for student pursuing a career in research and/or education in horticulture at a U.S. or Canadian institution. Minimum GPA of 3.0 required. To apply you must register with lunch-money.com, which is partnering with FIRST to make the application process easier. You only need to fill out one application online, and there is a link to lunch-money.com from the FIRST Web site: http://www.firstinfloriculture.org/schl_req_app.htm In addition to the application, you must submit two letters of recommendation and transcripts via email to: scholarships@firstinfloriculture.org. Application deadline is May 1.

Academic Fields/Career Goals: Horticulture/Floriculture.

Award: Scholarship for use in junior, senior, or graduate years; not renewable. *Number:* 1. *Amount:* $1000.

Eligibility Requirements: Applicant must be enrolled or expecting to enroll at a four-year institution or university. Applicant must have 3.0 GPA or higher. Available to U.S. and non-U.S. citizens.

Application Requirements: Application, references, transcript.
Deadline: May 1.

Contact: Scholarship Information
FIRST–Floriculture Industry Research and Scholarship Trust
PO Box 280
East Lansing, MI 48826-0280
E-mail: scholarship@firstinfloriculture.org

SEED COMPANIES SCHOLARSHIP

Award open to undergraduates entering junior or senior year at a four-year college or university in the U.S. or Canada, as well as to graduate students. Must be studying horticulture or a related field and intend to pursue a career in the seed industry in research, sales, breeding or marketing. Minimum GPA of 3.0 required. To apply you must register with lunch-money.com, which is partnering with FIRST to make the application process easier. You only need to fill out one application online, and there is a link to lunch-money.com from the FIRST Web site: http://www.firstinfloriculture.org/schl_req_app.htm In addition to the application, you must submit two letters of recommendation and transcripts via email to: scholarships@firstinfloriculture.org. Application deadline is May 1.

Academic Fields/Career Goals: Horticulture/Floriculture.

Award: Scholarship for use in junior, senior, or graduate years; not renewable. *Number:* 1. *Amount:* $1000.

Eligibility Requirements: Applicant must be enrolled or expecting to enroll at a four-year institution or university. Applicant must have 3.0 GPA or higher. Available to U.S. and non-U.S. citizens.

Application Requirements: Application, references, transcript.
Deadline: May 1.

Contact: Scholarship Information
FIRST–Floriculture Industry Research and Scholarship Trust
PO Box 280
East Lansing, MI 48826-0280
E-mail: scholarship@firstinfloriculture.org

SOUTHEAST GREENHOUSE CONFERENCE SCHOLARSHIP

Award available to students studying horticulture at a college or university in one of the following states: Alabama, Florida, Georgia, North Carolina, South Carolina, Tennessee, or Virginia. Minimum GPA of 3.0 required. To apply you must register with lunch-money.com, which is partnering with FIRST to make the application process easier. You only need to fill out one application online, and there is a link to lunch-money.com from the FIRST Web site: http://www.firstinfloriculture.org/schl_req_app.htm In addition to the application, you must submit two letters of recommendation and transcripts via email to: scholarships@firstinfloriculture.org. Application deadline is May 1.

Academic Fields/Career Goals: Horticulture/Floriculture.

Award: Scholarship for use in sophomore, junior, senior, or graduate years; not renewable. *Number:* 1. *Amount:* $1000.

Eligibility Requirements: Applicant must be enrolled or expecting to enroll at a four-year institution or university and studying in Alabama, Florida, Georgia, North Carolina, South Carolina, Tennessee, or Virginia. Applicant must have 3.0 GPA or higher. Available to U.S. and non-U.S. citizens.

Application Requirements: Application, references, transcript.
Deadline: May 1.

Contact: Scholarship Information
FIRST–Floriculture Industry Research and Scholarship Trust
PO Box 280
East Lansing, MI 48826-0280
E-mail: scholarship@firstinfloriculture.org

TOLEDO AREA FLOWER AND VEGETABLE GROWERS ASSOCIATION SCHOLARSHIP

Award available to students from Ohio, preferably northwestern Ohio, who are majoring in horticulture or related field and are attending Ohio State University or OSU Agricultural Technical Institute. Minimum GPA of 3.0 required. To apply you must register with lunch-money.com, which is partnering with FIRST to make the application process easier. You only need to fill out one application online, and there is a link to lunch-money.com from the FIRST Web site: http://www.firstinfloriculture.org/schl_req_app.htm In addition to the application, you must submit two letters of recommendation and transcripts via email to: scholarships@firstinfloriculture.org. Application deadline is May 1.

Academic Fields/Career Goals: Horticulture/Floriculture.

Award: Scholarship for use in sophomore, junior, or senior years; not renewable. *Number:* 1. *Amount:* $1000.

Eligibility Requirements: Applicant must be enrolled or expecting to enroll at a four-year institution or university; resident of Ohio and studying in Ohio. Applicant must have 3.0 GPA or higher. Available to U.S. and non-U.S. citizens.

Application Requirements: Application, references, transcript.
Deadline: May 1.

Contact: Scholarship Information
FIRST–Floriculture Industry Research and Scholarship Trust
PO Box 280
East Lansing, MI 48826-0280
E-mail: scholarship@firstinfloriculture.org

WESTERN MICHIGAN GREENHOUSE ASSOCIATION SCHOLARSHIP

Award available to a student from Michigan who is studying commercial horticulture at a four-year college or university in the U.S. or Canada. Minimum GPA of 3.0 required. To apply you must register with lunch-money.com, which is partnering with FIRST to make the application process easier. You only need to fill out one application online, and there is a link to lunch-money.com from the FIRST Web site: http://www.firstinfloriculture.org/schl_req_app.htm In addition to the application, you must submit two letters of recommendation and transcripts via email to: scholarships@firstinfloriculture.org. Application deadline is May 1.

Academic Fields/Career Goals: Horticulture/Floriculture.

Award: Scholarship for use in sophomore, junior, senior, or graduate years; not renewable. *Number:* 1. *Amount:* $1000.

Eligibility Requirements: Applicant must be enrolled or expecting to enroll at a four-year institution or university and resident of Michigan. Applicant must have 3.0 GPA or higher. Available to U.S. and non-U.S. citizens.

Application Requirements: Application, references, transcript.
Deadline: May 1.

Contact: Scholarship Information
FIRST–Floriculture Industry Research and Scholarship Trust
PO Box 280
East Lansing, MI 48826-0280
E-mail: scholarship@firstinfloriculture.org

FRIENDS OF THE FRELINGHUYSEN ARBORETUM http://arboretumfriends.org

BENJAMIN C. BLACKBURN SCHOLARSHIP

• *See page 264*

FUHRMANN ORCHARDS

KARL "PETE" FUHRMANN IV MEMORIAL SCHOLARSHIP

• *See page 53*

GARDEN CLUB OF AMERICA http://www.gcamerica.org

JOAN K. HUNT AND RACHEL M. HUNT SUMMER SCHOLARSHIP IN FIELD BOTANY

The purpose of this scholarship is to promote the awareness of the importance of botany to horticulture. Study must be in any one of the 50 states of the U.S. Preference is given to undergraduates. For more details and an application visit Web site: http://www.gcamerica.org.

Academic Fields/Career Goals: Horticulture/Floriculture.

Award: Scholarship for use in freshman, sophomore, junior, senior, or graduate years. *Number:* 1. *Amount:* up to $1500.

Eligibility Requirements: Applicant must be enrolled or expecting to enroll at a four-year institution or university.

Application Requirements: *Deadline:* February 1.

Contact: Garden Club of America
Scholarship Committee
14 East 60th Street
New York, NY 10022-1002

KATHARINE M. GROSSCUP SCHOLARSHIP

Several scholarships available to college juniors, seniors, and graduate students studying horticulture or related fields. Preference given to students from Ohio, Pennsylvania, West Virginia, Michigan, Indiana, and Kentucky. One-time award of up to $3000. Application on GCA Web site: http://www.gcamerica.org.

Academic Fields/Career Goals: Horticulture/Floriculture.

Award: Scholarship for use in junior, senior, or graduate years; not renewable. *Number:* 1–3. *Amount:* up to $3000.

Eligibility Requirements: Applicant must be enrolled or expecting to enroll at an institution or university. Available to U.S. citizens.

Application Requirements: Application, interview, references, self-addressed stamped envelope, transcript. *Deadline:* February 1.

Contact: Nancy Stevenson, Scholarship Administrator
Garden Club of America
Cleveland Botanical Garden, 11030 East Boulevard
Cleveland, OH 44106
Fax: 216-721-2056

LOY MCCANDLESS MARKS SCHOLARSHIP IN TROPICAL ORNAMENTAL HORTICULTURE

• *See page 114*

GOLF COURSE SUPERINTENDENTS ASSOCIATION OF AMERICA http://www.gcsaa.org

GCSAA SCHOLARS COMPETITION

For outstanding students planning careers in golf course management. Must be full-time college undergraduates currently enrolled in a two-year or more accredited program related to golf course management and have completed one year of program. Must be member of GCSAA.

Academic Fields/Career Goals: Horticulture/Floriculture.

Award: Scholarship for use in sophomore, junior, or senior years; not renewable. *Number:* varies. *Amount:* $500–$6000.

Eligibility Requirements: Applicant must be enrolled or expecting to enroll full-time at a two-year or four-year institution or university. Applicant or parent of applicant must be member of Golf Course Superintendents Association of America. Available to U.S. and non-U.S. citizens.

Application Requirements: Application, essay, references, transcript. *Deadline:* June 1.

Contact: Pam Smith, Scholarship/Student Programs Manager
Golf Course Superintendents Association of America
1421 Research Park Drive
Lawrence, KS 66049-3859
Phone: 800-472-7878 Ext. 678
Fax: 785-832-4449
E-mail: psmith@gcsaa.org

GOLF COURSE SUPERINTENDENTS ASSOCIATION OF AMERICA STUDENT ESSAY CONTEST

• *See page 53*

SCOTTS COMPANY SCHOLARS PROGRAM

The Scotts Company Scholars Program was developed by the Scotts Company in cooperation with The Environmental Institute for Golf to offer education and employment opportunities to students interested in pursuing a career in the "green industry." Students from diverse ethnic, cultural and socioeconomic backgrounds will be considered for judging. Must be a graduating high school senior or freshman, sophomore, or junior in college. Graduating high school seniors must attach a letter of college acceptance to application.

Academic Fields/Career Goals: Horticulture/Floriculture.

Award: Scholarship for use in freshman, sophomore, junior, or senior years; not renewable. *Number:* up to 7. *Amount:* $500–$2500.

Eligibility Requirements: Applicant must be enrolled or expecting to enroll full-time at a two-year or four-year or technical institution or university. Available to U.S. and non-U.S. citizens.

Application Requirements: Application, essay, references, transcript. *Deadline:* March 1.

Contact: Pam Smith, Scholarship/Student Programs Manager
Golf Course Superintendents Association of America
1421 Research Park Drive
Lawrence, KS 66049-3859
Phone: 800-472-7878 Ext. 678
Fax: 785-832-4449
E-mail: psmith@gcsaa.org

HERB SOCIETY OF AMERICA http://www.herbsociety.org

HERB SOCIETY RESEARCH GRANTS

• *See page 69*

HERB SOCIETY OF AMERICA, WESTERN RESERVE UNIT http://www.herbsociety.org

FRANCIS SYLVIA ZVERINA SCHOLARSHIP

Awards are given to needy students who plan a career in horticulture or related field. Preference will be given to applicants whose horticultural career goals involve teaching, research, or work in the public or nonprofit sector, such as public gardens, botanical gardens, parks, arboreta, city planning, public education, and awareness.

Academic Fields/Career Goals: Horticulture/Floriculture; Landscape Architecture.

Award: Scholarship for use in junior or senior years; not renewable. *Number:* 1–3. *Amount:* $2000–$5000.

Eligibility Requirements: Applicant must be enrolled or expecting to enroll full or part-time at a four-year institution or university. Available to U.S. citizens.

Application Requirements: Application, essay, references, transcript. *Deadline:* April 15.

Contact: Mrs. Shirley Ricketts, Unit Chair
Herb Society of America, Western Reserve Unit
2922 Somerton Road
Cleveland Heights, OH 44118
Phone: 216-932-5287

WESTERN RESERVE HERB SOCIETY SCHOLARSHIP

Awards are given to needy students who plan a career in horticulture or related field. Preference will be given to applicants whose horticultural career goals involve teaching, research, or work in the public or nonprofit sector, such as public gardens, botanical gardens, parks, arboreta, city planning, public education and awareness.

Academic Fields/Career Goals: Horticulture/Floriculture; Landscape Architecture.

Award: Scholarship for use in sophomore, junior, or senior years; not renewable. *Number:* 1–3. *Amount:* $1000–$2000.

Eligibility Requirements: Applicant must be enrolled or expecting to enroll full or part-time at a four-year institution or university and resident of Ohio. Available to U.S. citizens.

Application Requirements: Application, essay, references, transcript. *Deadline:* April 15.

Contact: Mrs. Shirley Ricketts, Unit Chair
Herb Society of America, Western Reserve Unit
2922 Somerton Road
Cleveland Heights, OH 44118
Phone: 216-932-5287

INTERNATIONAL EXECUTIVE HOUSEKEEPERS ASSOCIATION http://www.ieha.org

INTERNATIONAL EXECUTIVE HOUSEKEEPERS EDUCATIONAL FOUNDATION

• *See page 277*

JOSEPH SHINODA MEMORIAL SCHOLARSHIP FOUNDATION http://www.shinodascholarship.org

JOSEPH SHINODA MEMORIAL SCHOLARSHIP

One-time award for undergraduates in accredited colleges and universities. Must be furthering their education in the field of floriculture (production, distribution, research, or retail). Deadline is March 30.

Academic Fields/Career Goals: Horticulture/Floriculture.

Award: Scholarship for use in sophomore, junior, or senior years; not renewable. *Number:* 10–20. *Amount:* $250–$3000.

Eligibility Requirements: Applicant must be enrolled or expecting to enroll full-time at a four-year institution or university and must have an interest in designated field specified by sponsor. Available to U.S. and non-U.S. citizens.

Application Requirements: Application, essay, financial need analysis, photo, references, transcript. *Deadline:* March 30.

Contact: Virginia Walter, Professor, Horticulture and Crop Science Department
Joseph Shinoda Memorial Scholarship Foundation
Cal Poly State University
San Luis Obispo, CA 93407
Phone: 805-756-2897
E-mail: vwalter@calpoly.edu

LANDSCAPE ARCHITECTURE FOUNDATION http://www.LAprofession.org

LANDSCAPE ARCHITECTURE FOUNDATION/CALIFORNIA LANDSCAPE ARCHITECTURE STUDENT FUND UNIVERSITY SCHOLARSHIP PROGRAM

Nonrenewable scholarship for students continuing to study landscape architecture in California. Based on financial need and commitment to profession.

Academic Fields/Career Goals: Horticulture/Floriculture; Landscape Architecture.

Award: Scholarship for use in junior or senior years; not renewable. *Number:* 6. *Amount:* $1500.

Eligibility Requirements: Applicant must be enrolled or expecting to enroll at a four-year institution and studying in California. Available to U.S. citizens.

Application Requirements: Application, financial need analysis, references. *Deadline:* April 1.

Contact: Ron Figura, Project Manager
Landscape Architecture Foundation
818 18th Street, NW
Suite 810
Washington, DC 20006
Phone: 202-331-7070 Ext. 10
Fax: 202-331-7079
E-mail: rfigura@lafoundation.org

MAINE STATE FLORIST AND GROWERS ASSOCIATION

MAINE STATE FLORIST AND GROWERS ASSOCIATION SCHOLARSHIP

One-time award to promote horticulture and floriculture in Maine. Must be Maine resident. For use at a two- or four-year institution. Minimum 3.0 GPA required. Application deadline is April 1.

Academic Fields/Career Goals: Horticulture/Floriculture.

Award: Scholarship for use in freshman, sophomore, junior, or senior years; not renewable. *Number:* up to 2. *Amount:* $500.

Eligibility Requirements: Applicant must be enrolled or expecting to enroll full or part-time at a two-year or four-year or technical institution or university and resident of Maine. Applicant must have 3.0 GPA or higher. Available to U.S. citizens.

Application Requirements: Application, autobiography, essay, test scores. *Deadline:* April 1.

Contact: Janet Black, President
Maine State Florist and Growers Association
2 Mechanic Street, PO Box 207
Bethel, ME 04217

MONTANA FEDERATION OF GARDEN CLUBS

LIFE MEMBER MONTANA FEDERATION OF GARDEN CLUBS SCHOLARSHIP

• *See page 114*

NATIONAL GARDEN CLUBS, INC. http://www.gardenclub.org

NATIONAL GARDEN CLUBS, INC. SCHOLARSHIP PROGRAM

• *See page 60*

PENNSYLVANIA ASSOCIATION OF CONSERVATION DISTRICTS AUXILIARY http://www.blairconservationdistrict.org

PACD AUXILIARY SCHOLARSHIPS

• *See page 55*

PROFESSIONAL GROUNDS MANAGEMENT SOCIETY http://www.pgms.org

ANNE SEAMAN PROFESSIONAL GROUNDS MANAGEMENT SOCIETY MEMORIAL SCHOLARSHIP

• *See page 61*

SOIL AND WATER CONSERVATION SOCIETY-NEW JERSEY CHAPTER http://www.geocities.com/njswcs

EDWARD R. HALL SCHOLARSHIP

• *See page 55*

TURF AND ORNAMENTAL COMMUNICATION ASSOCIATION http://www.toca.org

TURF AND ORNAMENTAL COMMUNICATORS ASSOCIATION SCHOLARSHIP PROGRAM

• *See page 118*

UNITED AGRIBUSINESS LEAGUE http://www.ual.org

UNITED AGRIBUSINESS LEAGUE SCHOLARSHIP PROGRAM

• *See page 56*

UNITED AGRICULTURAL BENEFIT TRUST SCHOLARSHIP

• *See page 56*

HOSPITALITY MANAGEMENT

AMERICAN HOTEL AND LODGING EDUCATIONAL FOUNDATION http://www.ahlef.org

AMERICAN EXPRESS SCHOLARSHIP PROGRAM

Award for hotel employees of American Hotel and Lodging Association member properties and their dependents. For full- and part-time students in undergraduate program leading to degree in hospitality management. Must be employed at hotel, complete appropriate application, and submit copy of college curriculum and IRS 1040 form. Deadline: May 1. Application available at Web site: http://www.ahlef.org.

Academic Fields/Career Goals: Hospitality Management.

Award: Scholarship for use in freshman, sophomore, junior, or senior years; not renewable. *Number:* varies. *Amount:* $500–$2000.

Eligibility Requirements: Applicant must be enrolled or expecting to enroll full or part-time at a two-year or four-year institution or university. Applicant or parent of applicant must have employment or volunteer experience in hospitality/hotel administration/operations.

Application Requirements: Application, essay, financial need analysis, transcript. *Deadline:* May 1.

Contact: Crystal Hammond, Manager of Foundation Programs
American Hotel and Lodging Educational Foundation
1201 New York Avenue, NW, Suite 600
Washington, DC 20005-3931
Phone: 202-289-3188
Fax: 202-289-3199
E-mail: chammond@ahlef.org

ECOLAB SCHOLARSHIP PROGRAM

Award for students enrolled full-time in U.S. baccalaureate or associate program leading to degree in hospitality management. Must complete

American Hotel and Lodging Educational Foundation (continued)

appropriate application and submit copy of college curriculum and IRS 1040 form. Deadline: June 1. Application available at Web site: http://www.ahlef.org.

Academic Fields/Career Goals: Hospitality Management.

Award: Scholarship for use in freshman, sophomore, junior, or senior years; not renewable. *Number:* varies. *Amount:* $1000–$2000.

Eligibility Requirements: Applicant must be enrolled or expecting to enroll full-time at a two-year or four-year institution or university.

Application Requirements: Application, essay, financial need analysis, transcript. *Deadline:* June 1.

Contact: Crystal Hammond, Coordinator of Foundation Programs
American Hotel and Lodging Educational Foundation
1201 New York Avenue, SW, Suite 600
Washington, DC 20005-3931
Phone: 202-289-3188
Fax: 202-289-3199
E-mail: chammond@ahlef.org

AMERICAN INSTITUTE OF WINE AND FOOD-PACIFIC NORTHWEST CHAPTER http://www.aiwf.org

CULINARY, VINIFERA, AND HOSPITALITY SCHOLARSHIP

• *See page 270*

CLUB FOUNDATION http://www.clubfoundation.org

STUDENT SCHOLARSHIP PROGRAM

Candidates must be actively seeking a managerial career in the private club industry and currently attending an accredited four-year college or university. Individual must have completed his/her freshman year and be enrolled full-time for the following year. Also, candidate must have achieved and continue to maintain a grade point average of at least 2.5 on a 4.0 scale, or 4.5 on a 6.0 scale.

Academic Fields/Career Goals: Hospitality Management.

Award: Scholarship for use in sophomore, junior, or senior years; not renewable. *Number:* 2. *Amount:* $2500.

Eligibility Requirements: Applicant must be enrolled or expecting to enroll full-time at a four-year institution or university. Applicant must have 2.5 GPA or higher. Available to U.S. citizens.

Application Requirements: Application, essay, resume, references, self-addressed stamped envelope, transcript. *Deadline:* April 16.

Contact: Rhonda Schaver, Manager, Administration and Scholarship Programs
Club Foundation
1733 King Street
Alexandria, VA 22314
Phone: 703-739-9500 Ext. 301
Fax: 703-739-0124
E-mail: schaverr@clubfoundation.org

GOLDEN GATE RESTAURANT ASSOCIATION http://www.ggra.org

GOLDEN GATE RESTAURANT ASSOCIATION SCHOLARSHIP FOUNDATION

• *See page 277*

HAWAII HOTEL AND LODGING ASSOCIATION http://www.hawaiihotels.org

R.W. BOB HOLDEN SCHOLARSHIP

One $500 award for student attending or planning to attend an accredited university or college in Hawaii majoring in hotel management. Must be Hawaii resident and have a minimum 3.0 GPA.

Academic Fields/Career Goals: Hospitality Management; Travel/Tourism.

Award: Scholarship for use in sophomore, junior, senior, or graduate years; not renewable. *Number:* 1–5. *Amount:* $500.

Eligibility Requirements: Applicant must be enrolled or expecting to enroll full-time at a two-year or four-year institution or university; resident of Hawaii and studying in Hawaii. Applicant must have 3.0 GPA or higher. Available to U.S. and non-U.S. citizens.

Application Requirements: Application, autobiography, driver's license, essay, photo, references, transcript. *Deadline:* July 1.

Contact: Naomi Kanna, Director of Membership Services
Hawaii Hotel and Lodging Association
2250 Kalakaua Avenue, Suite 404-4
Honolulu, HI 96815
Phone: 808-923-0407
Fax: 808-924-3843
E-mail: hha@hawaiihotels.org

HISPANIC COLLEGE FUND, INC. http://www.hispanicfund.org

DENNY'S/HISPANIC COLLEGE FUND SCHOLARSHIP

• *See page 41*

HOSPITALITY SALES AND MARKETING ASSOCIATION INTERNATIONAL FOUNDATION http://www.hsmai.org

HOSPITALITY SALES AND MARKETING ASSOCIATION INTERNATIONAL FOUNDATION STUDENT SCHOLARSHIPS

One-time award for full-time undergraduate students interested in pursuing a career in hospitality sales and marketing. Application deadline is March 3.

Academic Fields/Career Goals: Hospitality Management; Travel/Tourism.

Award: Scholarship for use in freshman, sophomore, junior, senior, graduate, or postgraduate years; not renewable. *Number:* 2–4. *Amount:* $500–$2000.

Eligibility Requirements: Applicant must be enrolled or expecting to enroll full-time at a two-year or four-year institution or university. Available to U.S. and non-U.S. citizens.

Application Requirements: Application, references. *Deadline:* March 3.

Contact: Jason Smith, Director of Communications
Hospitality Sales and Marketing Association International Foundation
8201 Greensboro Drive, #300
McLean, VA 22102
Phone: 703-610-9024
Fax: 703-610-9005
E-mail: jsmith@hsmai.org

ILLINOIS RESTAURANT ASSOCIATION EDUCATIONAL FOUNDATION http://www.illinoisrestaurants.org

ILLINOIS RESTAURANT ASSOCIATION EDUCATIONAL FOUNDATION SCHOLARSHIPS

• *See page 180*

INTERNATIONAL AIRLINES TRAVEL AGENT NETWORK http://www.iatan.org

INTERNATIONAL AIRLINES TRAVEL AGENT NETWORK RONALD A. SANTANA MEMORIAL FOUNDATION

The IATAN Foundation provides scholarships annually to individuals who are interested in pursuing or enhancing their careers in travel. The IATAN Foundation was established in memory of the late Ronald A. Santana, IATAN former Board member, to continue his dedication and tireless efforts toward the education of travel agents.

Academic Fields/Career Goals: Hospitality Management; Travel/Tourism.

Award: Scholarship for use in freshman, sophomore, junior, senior, or graduate years; not renewable. *Number:* 2–14. *Amount:* $500–$2500.

Eligibility Requirements: Applicant must be age 17 and enrolled or expecting to enroll full or part-time at a two-year or four-year or technical institution or university. Available to U.S. citizens.

Application Requirements: Application, essay, resume, references, transcript. *Deadline:* April 1.

Contact: Jodi Viola, Manager, Marketing & Education Programs
International Airlines Travel Agent Network
300 Garden City Plaza, Suite 342
Garden City, NY 11530
Phone: 516-663-6012
Fax: 516-747-4462
E-mail: violaj@iata.org

INTERNATIONAL FOODSERVICE EDITORIAL COUNCIL http://www.ifec-is-us.com

INTERNATIONAL FOODSERVICE EDITORIAL COUNCIL COMMUNICATIONS SCHOLARSHIP

• *See page 160*

KENTUCKY RESTAURANT ASSOCIATION EDUCATIONAL FOUNDATION http://www.kyra.org/

KENTUCKY RESTAURANT ASSOCIATION EDUCATIONAL FOUNDATION SCHOLARSHIP

• *See page 275*

MAINE SCHOOL FOOD SERVICE ASSOCIATION (MSFSA) http://www.msfsa.com

SCHOLARSHIP OF THE MAINE SCHOOL FOOD SERVICE ASSOCIATION

• *See page 276*

MISSOURI TRAVEL COUNCIL http://www.missouritravel.com

MISSOURI TRAVEL COUNCIL TOURISM SCHOLARSHIP

• *See page 278*

NATIONAL TOURISM FOUNDATION http://www.ntfonline.org

ACADEMY OF TRAVEL AND TOURISM SCHOLARSHIPS

One $500 scholarship award to a graduating high school senior planning to attend accredited post-secondary education tourism-related program. Applicant must be completing senior year of high school at Academy of Travel and Tourism location. Each academy may submit most qualified student. Please refer to Web site for further details: http://www.ntfonline.org

Academic Fields/Career Goals: Hospitality Management; Political Science; Travel/Tourism.

Award: Scholarship for use in freshman year; not renewable. *Number:* 1. *Amount:* $500.

Eligibility Requirements: Applicant must be high school student and planning to enroll or expecting to enroll at a two-year or four-year institution or university. Applicant must have 3.0 GPA or higher. Available to U.S. citizens.

Application Requirements: Application, essay, resume, references. *Deadline:* May 10.

Contact: Michelle Gorin, Projects Coordinator
National Tourism Foundation
546 East Main Street
Lexington, KY 40508-3071
Phone: 800-682-8886
Fax: 859-226-4437
E-mail: michelle.gorin@ntastaff.com

CLEVELAND LEGACY I AND II SCHOLARSHIP AWARDS

• *See page 279*

NEW HORIZONS KATHY LE TARTE SCHOLARSHIP

• *See page 279*

PAT AND JIM HOST SCHOLARSHIP

• *See page 279*

SOCIETIE DES CASINOS DU QUEBEC SCHOLARSHIP

• *See page 280*

TAMPA, HILLSBOROUGH LEGACY SCHOLARSHIP

• *See page 280*

TAUCK SCHOLARS SCHOLARSHIPS

• *See page 280*

TULSA SCHOLARSHIP AWARDS

• *See page 280*

YELLOW RIBBON SCHOLARSHIP

• *See page 280*

NETWORK OF EXECUTIVE WOMEN IN HOSPITALITY http://www.newh.org

NETWORK OF EXECUTIVE WOMEN IN HOSPITALITY, INC. SCHOLARSHIP

• *See page 78*

SOUTH DAKOTA RETAILERS ASSOCIATION http://www.sdra.org

SOUTH DAKOTA RETAILERS ASSOCIATION SCHOLARSHIP PROGRAM

• *See page 47*

UNITED NEGRO COLLEGE FUND http://www.uncf.org

AMERICAN HOTEL FOUNDATION SCHOLARSHIP

Scholarship available to hotel management majors attending UNCF member colleges and universities. 2.5 GPA required. Prospective applicants should complete the Student Profile found at Web site: http://www.uncf.org.

Academic Fields/Career Goals: Hospitality Management.

Award: Scholarship for use in freshman, sophomore, junior, or senior years; not renewable. *Amount:* $1500.

Eligibility Requirements: Applicant must be Black (non-Hispanic) and enrolled or expecting to enroll at a four-year institution or university. Applicant must have 2.5 GPA or higher.

Application Requirements: Application. *Deadline:* Continuous.

Contact: Program Services Department
United Negro College Fund
8260 Willow Oaks Corporate Drive
Fairfax, VA 22031

EMERSON ELECTRIC COMPANY SCHOLARSHIP

• *See page 49*

HILTON HOTELS SCHOLARSHIP

• *See page 281*

HUMANITIES

AMERICAN CLASSICAL LEAGUE/NATIONAL JUNIOR CLASSICAL LEAGUE http://www.aclclassics.org

NATIONAL JUNIOR CLASSICAL LEAGUE SCHOLARSHIP

• *See page 281*

AMERICAN HISTORICAL ASSOCIATION http://www.theaha.org

GEORGE LOUIS BEER PRIZE

• *See page 266*

HELEN AND HOWARD MARRARO PRIZE

• *See page 281*

HERBERT BAXTER ADAMS PRIZE

• *See page 309*

JAMES HARVEY ROBINSON PRIZE

• *See page 309*

JAMES HENRY BREASTED PRIZE

• *See page 309*

JOAN KELLY MEMORIAL PRIZE IN WOMEN'S HISTORY
• *See page 309*

JOHN E. O'CONNOR FILM AWARD
• *See page 267*

JOHN H. DUNNING PRIZE
• *See page 309*

JOHN K. FAIRBANK PRIZE FOR EAST ASIAN HISTORY
• *See page 80*

LITTLETON-GRISWOLD PRIZE
• *See page 310*

PAUL BIRDSALL PRIZE
• *See page 310*

PREMIO DEL REY PRIZE
• *See page 282*

WESLEY-LOGAN PRIZE
• *See page 52*

AMERICAN LEGION AUXILIARY, DEPARTMENT OF WASHINGTON http://www.walegion-aux.org

FLORENCE LEMCKE MEMORIAL SCHOLARSHIP IN FINE ARTS
• *See page 84*

AMERICAN PHILOLOGICAL ASSOCIATION http://www.apaclassics.org

MINORITY STUDENT SUMMER SCHOLARSHIP
• *See page 85*

AMERICAN SCHOOL OF CLASSICAL STUDIES AT ATHENS http://www.ascsa.edu.gr

ASCSA SUMMER SESSIONS
• *See page 65*

ASPEN INSTITUTE http://www.nonprofitresearch.org/

WILLIAM RANDOLPH HEARST ENDOWED SCHOLARSHIP FOR MINORITY STUDENTS

Scholarships will be awarded to minority students who demonstrate outstanding research skills, a background in social sciences or humanities, excellent writing and communication skills, and financial need. There is no application; send a letter of interest, resume, transcript, a letter from the appropriate college or university financial aid officer certifying demonstrated financial need, and two letters of reference. Deadline is March 15.

Academic Fields/Career Goals: Humanities; Social Sciences.

Award: Scholarship for use in freshman, sophomore, junior, senior, or graduate years; not renewable. *Number:* 1. *Amount:* $2500–$5000.

Eligibility Requirements: Applicant must be American Indian/Alaska Native, Asian/Pacific Islander, Black (non-Hispanic), or Hispanic and enrolled or expecting to enroll at an institution or university. Available to U.S. citizens.

Application Requirements: Essay, financial need analysis, resume, references, transcript. *Deadline:* March 15.

Contact: Aspen Institute
One Dupont Circle, NW, Suite 700
Washington, DC 20036

BETHESDA LUTHERAN HOMES AND SERVICES, INC. http://www.blhs.org

DEVELOPMENTAL DISABILITIES SCHOLASTIC ACHIEVEMENT SCHOLARSHIP FOR LUTHERAN COLLEGE STUDENTS
• *See page 184*

BUSINESS AND PROFESSIONAL WOMEN'S FOUNDATION http://www.bpwusa.org

BPW CAREER ADVANCEMENT SCHOLARSHIP PROGRAM FOR WOMEN
• *See page 112*

CANADIAN INSTITUTE OF UKRAINIAN STUDIES http://www.ualberta.ca/cius/

LEO J. KRYSA UNDERGRADUATE SCHOLARSHIP
• *See page 80*

CATCHING THE DREAM

MATH, ENGINEERING, SCIENCE, BUSINESS, EDUCATION, COMPUTERS SCHOLARSHIPS
• *See page 121*

NATIVE AMERICAN LEADERSHIP IN EDUCATION (NALE)
• *See page 122*

CHINESE HISTORICAL SOCIETY OF SOUTHERN CALIFORNIA http://www.chssc.org

CHSSC SCHOLARSHIP AWARD

$1000 scholarship is offered to a deserving full-time student in southern California who demonstrates strong interest in Chinese American studies in humanities or social sciences. Deadline is March 12.

Academic Fields/Career Goals: Humanities; Social Sciences.

Award: Scholarship for use in sophomore, junior, senior, or graduate years; not renewable. *Number:* 1–2. *Amount:* $1000.

Eligibility Requirements: Applicant must be enrolled or expecting to enroll full-time at a four-year institution or university; resident of California and studying in California. Applicant must have 3.0 GPA or higher. Available to U.S. and non-U.S. citizens.

Application Requirements: Application, essay, financial need analysis, interview, references. *Deadline:* March 12.

Contact: Susie Ling, Scholarship Chair
Chinese Historical Society of Southern California
Attn: Scholarship Chair
PO Box 862647
Los Angeles, CA 90086-2647
Phone: 323-222-0856
E-mail: shling@pasadena.edu

HARVARD TRAVELLERS CLUB

HARVARD TRAVELLERS CLUB GRANTS
• *See page 73*

IRISH-AMERICAN CULTURAL INSTITUTE http://www.iaci-usa.org

IRISH RESEARCH FUNDS
• *See page 82*

JACK J. ISGUR FOUNDATION

JACK J. ISGUR FOUNDATION SCHOLARSHIP
• *See page 87*

LADIES AUXILIARY TO THE VETERANS OF FOREIGN WARS, DEPARTMENT OF MAINE

FRANCIS L. BOOTH MEDICAL SCHOLARSHIP SPONSORED BY LAVFW DEPARTMENT OF MAINE
• *See page 298*

NATIONAL FEDERATION OF THE BLIND http://www.nfb.org

NATIONAL FEDERATION OF THE BLIND HUMANITIES SCHOLARSHIP

One-time award for full-time postsecondary study in the humanities (art, English, foreign languages, history, philosophy, or religion) for students who are legally blind. Must submit recommendation from state officer of National Federation of the Blind. Based on academic excellence, service to the community, and financial need. May reapply. Must attend school in U.S.

Academic Fields/Career Goals: Humanities.

Award: Scholarship for use in freshman, sophomore, junior, or senior years; not renewable. *Number:* 1. *Amount:* $3000.

Eligibility Requirements: Applicant must be enrolled or expecting to enroll full-time at a two-year or four-year institution or university. Applicant or parent of applicant must have employment or volunteer experience in community service. Applicant must be visually impaired. Applicant must have 3.5 GPA or higher. Available to U.S. and non-U.S. citizens.

Application Requirements: Application, autobiography, essay, financial need analysis, references, transcript. *Deadline:* March 31.

Contact: Peggy Elliot, Chairman, Scholarship Committee
National Federation of the Blind
805 Fifth Avenue
Grinnell, IA 50112
Phone: 641-236-3366

POLISH ARTS CLUB OF BUFFALO SCHOLARSHIP FOUNDATION

POLISH ARTS CLUB OF BUFFALO SCHOLARSHIP FOUNDATION TRUST

• *See page 84*

UNITED NEGRO COLLEGE FUND http://www.uncf.org

JACQUELINE FEIGENSON SCHOLARSHIP

• *See page 91*

MCCLARE FAMILY TRUST SCHOLARSHIP

Scholarship for college freshmen majoring in the humanities with an interest in English literature. Must attend UNCF member institution. Information on Web site http://www.uncf.org.

Academic Fields/Career Goals: Humanities.

Award: Scholarship for use in freshman year; renewable. *Number:* varies. *Amount:* varies.

Eligibility Requirements: Applicant must be Black (non-Hispanic) and enrolled or expecting to enroll at a four-year institution or university. Applicant must have 3.0 GPA or higher.

Application Requirements: Application, financial need analysis, FAFSA. *Deadline:* October 29.

Contact: Program Services Department
United Negro College Fund
8260 Willow Oaks Corporate Drive
Fairfax, VA 22031

HYDROLOGY

ASSOCIATION OF CALIFORNIA WATER AGENCIES http://www.acwanet.com

ASSOCIATION OF CALIFORNIA WATER AGENCIES SCHOLARSHIPS

• *See page 68*

CLAIR A. HILL SCHOLARSHIP

• *See page 68*

CALIFORNIA WATER AWARENESS CAMPAIGN http://www.wateraware.org

CALIFORNIA WATER AWARENESS CAMPAIGN WATER SCHOLAR

• *See page 57*

HANDS-ON! PROJECTS/HYDRO POWER CONTEST http://users.rcn.com/hands-on/hydro/contest.html

HYDRO POWER CONTEST

• *See page 224*

INTERNATIONAL ASSOCIATION OF GREAT LAKES RESEARCH http://www.iaglr.org

PAUL W. RODGERS SCHOLARSHIP

• *See page 190*

INDUSTRIAL DESIGN

HISPANIC COLLEGE FUND, INC. http://www.hispanicfund.org

EL NUEVO CONSTRUCTOR SCHOLARSHIP PROGRAM

• *See page 76*

INDUSTRIAL DESIGNERS SOCIETY OF AMERICA http://www.idsa.org

INDUSTRIAL DESIGNERS SOCIETY OF AMERICA UNDERGRADUATE SCHOLARSHIP

One-time award to a U.S. citizen or permanent U.S. resident currently enrolled in an industrial design program. Must submit 20 visual examples of work and study full-time.

Academic Fields/Career Goals: Industrial Design.

Award: Scholarship for use in junior year; not renewable. *Number:* 2. *Amount:* $1000–$2000.

Eligibility Requirements: Applicant must be enrolled or expecting to enroll full-time at a four-year institution or university. Applicant must have 3.0 GPA or higher. Available to U.S. citizens.

Application Requirements: Application, references, transcript. *Deadline:* varies.

Contact: Diana McMillan, Executive Assistant
Industrial Designers Society of America
45195 Business Court, Suite 250
Dulles, VA 20166
Phone: 703-707-6000
Fax: 703-787-8501
E-mail: dianam@idsa.org

INTERNATIONAL FURNISHINGS AND DESIGN ASSOCIATION http://www.ifdaef.org/scholarships.html

RUTH CLARK SCHOLARSHIP

• *See page 87*

INTERNATIONAL HOUSEWARES ASSOCIATION http://www.housewares.org

STUDENT DESIGN COMPETITION

Prizes awarded to full-time students enrolled in a degree program for industrial design at a U.S. college. Must design a housewares project according to specified guidelines. Must call to obtain entry form. Details on Web site: http://www.ifpte.org

Academic Fields/Career Goals: Industrial Design.

Award: Prize for use in freshman, sophomore, junior, or senior years; not renewable. *Number:* 3–7. *Amount:* $1000–$2500.

Eligibility Requirements: Applicant must be enrolled or expecting to enroll full-time at a four-year institution or university. Available to U.S. and non-U.S. citizens.

Application Requirements: Applicant must enter a contest, entry form, drawings, slides. *Deadline:* December 30.

Contact: Victoria Matranga, Design Programs Coordinator
International Housewares Association
6400 Shafer Court, Suite 650
Rosemont, IL 60018
Phone: 847-692-0136
Fax: 847-292-4211
E-mail: vmatranga@housewares.org

SOCIETY OF MANUFACTURING ENGINEERS EDUCATION FOUNDATION http://www.sme.org/foundation

DOWNRIVER DETROIT CHAPTER 198 SCHOLARSHIP

• *See page 252*

FORT WAYNE CHAPTER 56 SCHOLARSHIP

• *See page 253*

Industrial Design

NORTH CENTRAL REGION 9 SCHOLARSHIP
• *See page 254*

PHOENIX CHAPTER 67 SCHOLARSHIP
• *See page 254*

WICHITA CHAPTER 52 SCHOLARSHIP
• *See page 255*

SOCIETY OF PLASTICS ENGINEERS (SPE) FOUNDATION http://www.4spe.org

FLEMING/BASZCAK SCHOLARSHIP
• *See page 147*

SOCIETY OF PLASTICS ENGINEERS SCHOLARSHIP PROGRAM
• *See page 147*

WORLDSTUDIO FOUNDATION http://www.worldstudio.org

WORLDSTUDIO FOUNDATION SCHOLARSHIP PROGRAM
• *See page 80*

INSURANCE AND ACTUARIAL SCIENCE

ACTUARIAL FOUNDATION http://www.actuarialfoundation.org

WOODDY SCHOLARSHIPS

One time award for actuarial students in their senior year. Must rank in the top quarter of their class and have successfully completed an actuarial examination. Must be recommended by a professor from their school. Application deadline is June 25. See Web site at http://www.beanactuary.org for further details.

Academic Fields/Career Goals: Insurance and Actuarial Science.

Award: Scholarship for use in senior year; not renewable. *Number:* 4. *Amount:* $2000.

Eligibility Requirements: Applicant must be enrolled or expecting to enroll full-time at a four-year institution or university. Applicant must have 3.5 GPA or higher. Available to U.S. and non-U.S. citizens.

Application Requirements: Application, essay, references. *Deadline:* June 25.

Contact: Diane Rutherford, Actuarial Education and Research Fund
Actuarial Foundation
475 North Martingale Road, Suite 600
Schaumburg, IL 60173-2226
Phone: 847-706-3600
E-mail: diane.rutherford@actfnd.org

CASUALTY ACTUARIAL SOCIETY http://www.casact.org

CASUALTY ACTUARIAL SOCIETY TRUST SCHOLARSHIP

Scholarships for students in U.S. and Canadian institutions who are pursuing studies in actuarial science and plan to enter the property/casualty actuarial profession. Must be full-time student demonstrating high scholastic achievement and strong interest in mathematics or a mathematics-related field. Must submit a one-page essay on why you are interested in becoming a casualty actuary. Must submit two nomination forms from instructors and/or advisors at your institution. Applications and information available on Web site: http://www.casact.org/academ.

Academic Fields/Career Goals: Insurance and Actuarial Science; Mathematics.

Award: Scholarship for use in freshman, sophomore, junior, or senior years. *Number:* up to 3. *Amount:* $1500.

Eligibility Requirements: Applicant must be enrolled or expecting to enroll full-time at a four-year institution or university. Available to U.S. and Canadian citizens.

Application Requirements: Application, essay, references, transcript. *Deadline:* May 1.

Contact: Scholarship Coordinator
Casualty Actuarial Society
1100 North Glebe Road, Suite 600
Arlington, VA 22201-4798
Phone: 703-276-3100
Fax: 703-276-3108
E-mail: office@casact.org

CASUALTY ACTUARIES OF THE SOUTHEAST http://www.casact.org/affiliates/case/scholarmemo.htm

CASUALTY ACTUARIES OF THE SOUTHEAST SCHOLARSHIP PROGRAM

Scholarships available for undergraduate students in the southeastern states for the study of actuarial science. Must be studying in one of the following states: Alabama, Arkansas, Florida, Georgia, Kentucky, Louisiana, Mississippi, North Carolina, South Carolina, Tennessee, or Virginia. See Web site: http://www.casact.org/affiliates/case/scholarmemo.htm for information and application form and evaluation and recommendation form.

Academic Fields/Career Goals: Insurance and Actuarial Science.

Award: Scholarship for use in sophomore, junior, or senior years; not renewable. *Number:* 1. *Amount:* $1000.

Eligibility Requirements: Applicant must be enrolled or expecting to enroll full-time at a four-year institution or university and studying in Alabama, Arkansas, Florida, Georgia, Kentucky, Louisiana, Michigan, North Carolina, South Carolina, Tennessee, or Virginia. Available to U.S. citizens.

Application Requirements: Application, Evaluation and Recommendation Form.

Contact: Application and information on Web site.
Casualty Actuaries of the Southeast
Tillinghast-Towers Perrin, One Alliance Center
3500 Lenox Road, Suite 900
Atlanta, GA 30326-4238

NATIONAL ASSOCIATION OF INSURANCE WOMEN EDUCATION FOUNDATION http://www.naiw-foundation.org

NAIW COLLEGE SCHOLARSHIP

Award available to student seeking bachelor degree or higher with a major or minor in insurance and/or risk management and/or actuarial science. Must have completed two insurance, actuarial or risk management-related courses. Must be completing second year of college and have a minimum 3.0 GPA. Deadline is March 1.

Academic Fields/Career Goals: Insurance and Actuarial Science.

Award: Scholarship for use in sophomore, junior, senior, or graduate years; not renewable. *Number:* varies. *Amount:* $1000–$4000.

Eligibility Requirements: Applicant must be enrolled or expecting to enroll full or part-time at a four-year institution or university. Applicant must have 3.0 GPA or higher.

Application Requirements: Application, essay, references, transcript. *Deadline:* March 1.

Contact: Billie Sleet, Executive Director
National Association of Insurance Women Education Foundation
5310 East 31st Street, #302
Tulsa, OK 74135
Phone: 918-622-1816
Fax: 918-622-1821
E-mail: foundation@naiwfoundation.org

NAIW EDUCATION FOUNDATION PROFESSIONAL SCHOLARSHIP
• *See page 128*

SOCIETY OF ACTUARIES http://www.soa.org

ACTUARIAL SCHOLARSHIPS FOR MINORITY STUDENTS

Award for minority students at the undergraduate or graduate level pursuing an actuarial career. Amount based on merit and individual need. Must be U.S. citizen or permanent resident. Recipients receive an additional $500 for each actuarial exam passed. Application deadline is April 15. See Web site at http://www.beanactuary.org for further details.

Academic Fields/Career Goals: Insurance and Actuarial Science.

Award: Scholarship for use in freshman, sophomore, junior, senior, or graduate years; not renewable. *Number:* varies. *Amount:* $500–$5000.

Eligibility Requirements: Applicant must be American Indian/Alaska Native, Asian/Pacific Islander, Black (non-Hispanic), or Hispanic and enrolled or expecting to enroll full-time at a four-year institution or university. Available to U.S. and non-U.S. citizens.

Application Requirements: Application, financial need analysis, transcript. *Deadline:* April 15.

Contact: Minority Scholarship Coordinator
Society of Actuaries
475 North Martingale Road, Suite 600
Schaumburg, IL 60173-2226
Phone: 847-706-3500
E-mail: sparker@soa.org

SPENCER EDUCATIONAL FOUNDATION, INC. http://www.spencered.org

SPENCER RISK MANAGEMENT AND INSURANCE SCHOLARSHIP

Scholarship awarded to full- or part-time students interested in risk management/insurance studies. Student must retain 3.3 GPA or higher. Please refer to Web site for further details: http://www.spencer.org.

Academic Fields/Career Goals: Insurance and Actuarial Science.

Award: Scholarship for use in sophomore, junior, senior, or graduate years; renewable. *Number:* 10–20. *Amount:* $5000–$10,000.

Eligibility Requirements: Applicant must be enrolled or expecting to enroll full or part-time at a four-year institution or university. Available to U.S. and non-U.S. citizens.

Application Requirements: Application, essay, resume, references, transcript. *Deadline:* varies.

Contact: Angela Sabatino, Secretary and Foundation Administrator
Spencer Educational Foundation, Inc.
655 Third Avenue
New York, NY 10017-5637
Phone: 212-655-6223
Fax: 212-655-6044
E-mail: asabatino@rims.org

INTERIOR DESIGN

AMERICAN SOCIETY OF INTERIOR DESIGNERS (ASID) EDUCATION FOUNDATION, INC. http://www.asid.org

ASID EDUCATIONAL FOUNDATION/IRENE WINIFRED ENO GRANT

Provides financial assistance to individuals or groups engaged in the creation of an educational program(s) or an interior design research project dedicated to health, safety, and welfare. The grant will be awarded on the basis of the project description, breakdown of potential use of funds, and the marketing plan for the use/distribution of the end product of the project. The grant is open to students, educators, interior design practitioners, institutions, or other interior design-related groups.

Academic Fields/Career Goals: Interior Design.

Award: Grant for use in freshman, sophomore, junior, senior, graduate, or postgraduate years. *Number:* 1. *Amount:* $1000.

Eligibility Requirements: Applicant must be enrolled or expecting to enroll at an institution or university. Available to U.S. citizens.

Application Requirements: Application. *Deadline:* March 31.

Contact: American Society of Interior Designers (ASID) Education Foundation, Inc.
608 Massachusetts Avenue, NE
Washington, DC 20002-6006
Phone: 202-546-3480
Fax: 202-546-3240
E-mail: education@asid.org

ASID EDUCATIONAL FOUNDATION/JOEL POLSKY ACADEMIC ACHIEVEMENT AWARD

Awarded to recognize an outstanding undergraduate or graduate student's interior design research or thesis project. Research papers or doctoral and master's thesis should address such interior design topics as educational research, behavioral science, business practice, design process, theory, or technical subjects.

Academic Fields/Career Goals: Interior Design.

Award: Prize for use in freshman, sophomore, junior, senior, or graduate years. *Number:* 1. *Amount:* $1000.

Eligibility Requirements: Applicant must be enrolled or expecting to enroll at an institution or university. Available to U.S. citizens.

Application Requirements: Application, references. *Deadline:* March 31.

Contact: American Society of Interior Designers (ASID) Education Foundation, Inc.
608 Massachusetts Avenue, NE
Washington, DC 20002-6006
Phone: 202-546-3480
Fax: 202-546-3240
E-mail: education@asid.org

ASID EDUCATIONAL FOUNDATION/YALE R. BURGE COMPETITION

Open to all students in their final years of undergraduate study enrolled in at least a three-year program of interior design. The competition is designed to encourage students to seriously plan their portfolios. Portfolio components, submitted on slides, may be as few as eight, but are not to exceed 12. Judges will evaluate presentation skills, design and planning competency, and conceptual creativity.

Academic Fields/Career Goals: Interior Design.

Award: Prize for use in senior year. *Number:* 1. *Amount:* $750.

Eligibility Requirements: Applicant must be enrolled or expecting to enroll at an institution or university. Available to U.S. citizens.

Application Requirements: Application, applicant must enter a contest, portfolio. *Fee:* $10. *Deadline:* March 31.

Contact: American Society of Interior Designers (ASID) Education Foundation, Inc.
608 Massachusetts Avenue, NE
Washington, DC 20002-6006
Phone: 202-546-3480
Fax: 202-546-3240
E-mail: education@asid.org

ASSOCIATION FOR WOMEN IN ARCHITECTURE FOUNDATION http://www.awa-la.org

ASSOCIATION FOR WOMEN IN ARCHITECTURE SCHOLARSHIP

• *See page 75*

ILLUMINATING ENGINEERING SOCIETY OF NORTH AMERICA http://www.iesna.org

ROBERT W. THUNEN MEMORIAL SCHOLARSHIPS

• *See page 77*

ILLUMINATING ENGINEERING SOCIETY OF NORTH AMERICA–GOLDEN GATE SECTION http://www.iesgg.org

ALAN LUCAS MEMORIAL EDUCATIONAL SCHOLARSHIP

• *See page 77*

ROBERT W. THUNEN MEMORIAL SCHOLARSHIPS

• *See page 77*

INTERNATIONAL FURNISHINGS AND DESIGN ASSOCIATION http://www.ifdaef.org/scholarships.html

CHARLES D. MAYO SCHOLARSHIP

Scholarship available to students studying interior design and the related fields of the home furnishings and design industry. Award of $1,000 to full-time student. Applicant does not have to be IFDA student member.

International Furnishings and Design Association (continued)

Applicant must submit 300-500 word essay explaining future plans and goals, indicating why they believe that they are deserving of this award. Decision based upon student's academic achievement, awards and accomplishments, future plans and goals, and letter of recommendation.

Academic Fields/Career Goals: Interior Design; Trade/Technical Specialties.

Award: Scholarship for use in sophomore, junior, or senior years; not renewable. *Number:* 1. *Amount:* $1000.

Eligibility Requirements: Applicant must be enrolled or expecting to enroll full-time at a two-year or four-year or technical institution or university. Available to U.S. and non-U.S. citizens.

Application Requirements: Application, essay, references, transcript. *Deadline:* March 31.

Contact: Dr. Nancy Wolford, Director of Grants and Scholarships
International Furnishings and Design Association
16171 Jasmine Way
Los Gatos, CA 95032-3630
Phone: 408-356-2465
E-mail: nlwolford@earthlink.net

IFDA STUDENT SCHOLARSHIP

Scholarship available to students studying interior design and the related fields of the home furnishings and design industry. Award of $1,500 to full-time student. Applicant must be IFDA student member. Applicant must submit 300-500 word essay explaining why they joined IFDA, discuss future plans and goals, and indicate why they are deserving of this award. Decision based upon student's academic achievement, awards and accomplishments, future plans and goals, and letter of recommendation.

Academic Fields/Career Goals: Interior Design; Trade/Technical Specialties.

Award: Scholarship for use in sophomore, junior, or senior years; not renewable. *Number:* 1–2. *Amount:* $1500.

Eligibility Requirements: Applicant must be enrolled or expecting to enroll full-time at a two-year or four-year or technical institution or university. Available to U.S. and non-U.S. citizens.

Application Requirements: Application, essay, references, transcript. *Deadline:* March 31.

Contact: Dr. Nancy Wolford, Director of Grants and Scholarships
International Furnishings and Design Association
16171 Jasmine Way
Los Gatos, CA 95032-3630
Phone: 408-356-2465
E-mail: nlwolford@earthlink.net

NATIONAL ASSOCIATION OF WOMEN IN CONSTRUCTION http://nawic.org

NAWIC UNDERGRADUATE SCHOLARSHIPS

• *See page 77*

NETWORK OF EXECUTIVE WOMEN IN HOSPITALITY http://www.newh.org

NETWORK OF EXECUTIVE WOMEN IN HOSPITALITY, INC. SCHOLARSHIP

• *See page 78*

NEW YORK STATE EDUCATION DEPARTMENT http://www.highered.nysed.gov

REGENTS PROFESSIONAL OPPORTUNITY SCHOLARSHIP

• *See page 45*

SOUTH DAKOTA RETAILERS ASSOCIATION http://www.sdra.org

SOUTH DAKOTA RETAILERS ASSOCIATION SCHOLARSHIP PROGRAM

• *See page 47*

WORLDSTUDIO FOUNDATION http://www.worldstudio.org

WORLDSTUDIO FOUNDATION SCHOLARSHIP PROGRAM

• *See page 80*

INTERNATIONAL MIGRATION

HUGH FULTON BYAS MEMORIAL FUNDS, INC.

HUGH FULTON BYAS MEMORIAL GRANT

• *See page 311*

INTERNATIONAL STUDIES

ARRL FOUNDATION, INC. http://www.arrl.org/arrlf/scholgen.html

DONALD RIEBHOFF MEMORIAL SCHOLARSHIP

One $1000 award available to students with a Technician Class license for radio operation. Must be pursuing a baccalaureate or higher degree in international studies at any accredited institution above the high school level. Must be an ARRL member.

Academic Fields/Career Goals: International Studies.

Award: Scholarship for use in freshman, sophomore, junior, senior, or graduate years; not renewable. *Number:* 1. *Amount:* $1000.

Eligibility Requirements: Applicant must be enrolled or expecting to enroll at a four-year institution or university and must have an interest in amateur radio. Applicant or parent of applicant must be member of American Radio Relay League.

Application Requirements: Application, transcript. *Deadline:* February 1.

Contact: Mary Lau, Scholarship Director
ARRL Foundation, Inc.
225 Main Street
Newington, CT 06111-4845

CENTRAL INTELLIGENCE AGENCY http://www.cia.gov

CENTRAL INTELLIGENCE AGENCY UNDERGRADUATE SCHOLARSHIP PROGRAM

• *See page 39*

CULTURE CONNECTION http://www.thecultureconnection.com

CULTURE CONNECTION FOUNDATION SCHOLARSHIP

• *See page 52*

JAPAN STUDIES SCHOLARSHIP FOUNDATION COMMITTEE

JAPAN STUDIES SCHOLARSHIP

• *See page 283*

NATIONAL FEDERATION OF THE BLIND http://www.nfb.org

MICHAEL AND MARIE MARUCCI SCHOLARSHIP

• *See page 283*

WATERBURY FOUNDATION http://www.waterburyfoundation.org

MALCOLM BALDRIGE SCHOLARSHIP

• *See page 134*

JOURNALISM

ACADEMY OF TELEVISION ARTS AND SCIENCES FOUNDATION http://www.emmys.tv/foundation

ACADEMY OF TELEVISION ARTS AND SCIENCES COLLEGE TELEVISION AWARDS

• *See page 84*

ADC RESEARCH INSTITUTE http://www.adc.org

JACK SHAHEEN MASS COMMUNICATIONS SCHOLARSHIP AWARD

• *See page 156*

AMERICAN INSTITUTE OF POLISH CULTURE, INC. http://www.ampolinstitute.org

HARRIET IRSAY SCHOLARSHIP GRANT

• *See page 156*

AMERICAN LEGION, PRESS CLUB OF NEW JERSEY

AMERICAN LEGION PRESS CLUB OF NEW JERSEY AND POST 170 ARTHUR DEHARDT MEMORIAL SCHOLARSHIP

• *See page 156*

AMERICAN QUARTER HORSE FOUNDATION (AQHF) http://www.aqha.org/aqhya

AQHF JOURNALISM OR COMMUNICATIONS SCHOLARSHIP

• *See page 157*

ARRL FOUNDATION, INC. http://www.arrl.org/arrlf/scholgen.html

PHD ARA SCHOLARSHIP

• *See page 157*

ASIAN AMERICAN JOURNALISTS ASSOCIATION http://www.aaja.org

ASIAN-AMERICAN JOURNALISTS ASSOCIATION SCHOLARSHIP

• *See page 157*

MARY MOY QUAN ING MEMORIAL SCHOLARSHIP AWARD

One-time award for a deserving high school senior for undergraduate study. Must intend to pursue a journalism career and must show a commitment to the Asian-American community. One-time award of up to $1500. Visit Web site http://www.aaja.org for application and details.

Academic Fields/Career Goals: Journalism.

Award: Scholarship for use in freshman year; not renewable. *Number:* 1. *Amount:* up to $1500.

Eligibility Requirements: Applicant must be high school student; planning to enroll or expecting to enroll full-time at a two-year or four-year institution and must have an interest in writing.

Application Requirements: Application, essay, financial need analysis, resume, references, transcript. *Deadline:* varies.

Contact: Lila Chwee, Student Programs Coordinator
Asian American Journalists Association
1182 Market Street, Suite 320
San Francisco, CA 94102
Phone: 415-346-2051
Fax: 415-346-6343
E-mail: programs@aaja.org

MINORU YASUI MEMORIAL SCHOLARSHIP AWARD

One-time award for a promising Asian undergraduate male who will pursue a broadcasting career. For use at an accredited two- or four-year institution. One-time award of $1500. Visit Web site http://www.aaja.org for application and details.

Academic Fields/Career Goals: Journalism; TV/Radio Broadcasting.

Award: Scholarship for use in freshman, sophomore, junior, or senior years; not renewable. *Number:* 1. *Amount:* $1500.

Eligibility Requirements: Applicant must be Asian/Pacific Islander; enrolled or expecting to enroll full-time at a two-year or four-year institution or university and male.

Application Requirements: Application, essay, financial need analysis, resume, references, transcript. *Deadline:* varies.

Contact: Lila Chwee, Student Programs Coordinator
Asian American Journalists Association
1182 Market Street, Suite 320
San Francisco, CA 94102
Phone: 415-346-2051 Ext. 102
Fax: 415-346-6343
E-mail: programs@aaja.org

NATIONAL ASIAN-AMERICAN JOURNALISTS ASSOCIATION NEWHOUSE SCHOLARSHIP

One-time award for high school seniors and college students who plan to or are currently enrolled in a journalism program at any two- or four-year postsecondary institution. Up to $5000 awarded. Scholarship awardees will be eligible for summer internships with a Newhouse publication. Applicants from underrepresented Asian Pacific American groups including Vietnamese, Hmong, Cambodians, and other Southeast Asians, South Asians, and Pacific Islanders are especially encouraged. Visit Web site: http://www.aaja.org for application and details.

Academic Fields/Career Goals: Journalism.

Award: Scholarship for use in freshman, sophomore, junior, or senior years; not renewable. *Number:* up to 5. *Amount:* up to $5000.

Eligibility Requirements: Applicant must be enrolled or expecting to enroll full-time at a two-year or four-year institution or university.

Application Requirements: Application, essay, financial need analysis, resume, references, transcript. *Deadline:* varies.

Contact: Lila Chwee, Student Programs Coordinator
Asian American Journalists Association
1182 Market Street, Suite 320
San Francisco, CA 94102
Phone: 415-346-2051 Ext. 102
Fax: 415-346-6343
E-mail: programs@aaja.org

ASSOCIATED PRESS http://www.aptra.org

ASSOCIATED PRESS TELEVISION/RADIO ASSOCIATION-CLETE ROBERTS JOURNALISM SCHOLARSHIP AWARDS

Award for college undergraduates and graduate students studying in California or Nevada and pursuing careers in broadcast journalism. Please submit application, references, and examples of broadcast-related work. Email for application to shughes@nbc3.com. One-time award of $1500.

Academic Fields/Career Goals: Journalism; TV/Radio Broadcasting.

Award: Scholarship for use in freshman, sophomore, junior, senior, or graduate years; not renewable. *Number:* 3. *Amount:* $1500.

Eligibility Requirements: Applicant must be enrolled or expecting to enroll full-time at a two-year or four-year institution or university and studying in California or Nevada. Available to U.S. citizens.

Application Requirements: Application, references. *Deadline:* December 12.

Contact: Rachel Ambrose, CA-NV Broadcast Editor
Associated Press
221 South Figueroa Street, #300
Los Angeles, CA 90012
Phone: 213-626-1200
Fax: 213-346-0200
E-mail: rambrose@ap.org

KATHRYN DETTMAN MEMORIAL JOURNALISM SCHOLARSHIP

One-time $1500 award for broadcast journalism students, enrolled at a California or Nevada college or university. Submit entry form and examples of broadcast-related work. Email for application to shughes@nbc3.com. Application deadline: December 11.

Academic Fields/Career Goals: Journalism; TV/Radio Broadcasting.

Award: Scholarship for use in freshman, sophomore, junior, or senior years; not renewable. *Number:* 4. *Amount:* $1500.

Associated Press (continued)

Eligibility Requirements: Applicant must be enrolled or expecting to enroll at a four-year institution or university and studying in California or Nevada. Available to U.S. citizens.

Application Requirements: Application. *Deadline:* December 11.

Contact: Rachel Ambrose, CA-NV Broadcast Editor
Associated Press
221 South Figueroa Street, #300
Los Angeles, CA 90012
Phone: 213-626-1200
Fax: 213-346-0200
E-mail: rambrose@ap.org

ASSOCIATION FOR EDUCATION IN JOURNALISM AND MASS COMMUNICATIONS http://www.aejmc.org

MARY A. GARDNER SCHOLARSHIP

Award is available for an outstanding college journalism student who is an incoming junior or senior with full-time enrollment in a college undergraduate news editorial program. The student must have a minimum GPA of 3.0 and a demonstrable interest in pursuing a career in news reporting and/or editing.

Academic Fields/Career Goals: Journalism.

Award: Scholarship for use in junior or senior years; not renewable. *Number:* 1. *Amount:* $300–$500.

Eligibility Requirements: Applicant must be enrolled or expecting to enroll full-time at a four-year institution or university. Applicant must have 3.0 GPA or higher. Available to U.S. and non-U.S. citizens.

Application Requirements: Essay, references, self-addressed stamped envelope, transcript, copies/clippings or other journalistic accomplishments. *Deadline:* April 1.

Contact: Janet Harley, Office Assistant
Association for Education in Journalism and Mass Communications
234 Outlet Pointe Boulevard, Suite A
Columbia, SC 29210
Phone: 803-798-0271
Fax: 803-772-3509
E-mail: janet@aejmc.org

ATLANTA PRESS CLUB, INC. http://www.atlpressclub.org

ATLANTA PRESS CLUB JOURNALISM SCHOLARSHIP PROGRAM

• *See page 158*

BOWEN FOUNDATION http://www.emmabowenfoundation.com

EMMA L. BOWEN FOUNDATION FOR MINORITY INTERESTS IN MEDIA

• *See page 158*

CALIFORNIA CHICANO NEWS MEDIA ASSOCIATION (CCNMA) http://www.ccnma.org

JOEL GARCIA MEMORIAL SCHOLARSHIP

• *See page 158*

CANADIAN ASSOCIATION OF BROADCASTERS http://www.cab-acr.ca

JIM ALLARD BROADCAST JOURNALISM SCHOLARSHIP

This CAN$2,500 scholarship is awarded annually to aspiring broadcasters enrolled in broadcast journalism courses at a Canadian college or university. The award is given to the student who best combines academic achievement with natural talent. Must be a Canadian citizen.

Academic Fields/Career Goals: Journalism; TV/Radio Broadcasting.

Award: Scholarship for use in freshman, sophomore, junior, senior, or graduate years; not renewable. *Number:* 1. *Amount:* $1857.

Eligibility Requirements: Applicant must be Canadian citizen; enrolled or expecting to enroll full or part-time at a two-year or four-year institution or university; studying in Alberta, British Columbia, Manitoba, New Brunswick, Newfoundland, North West Territories, Nova Scotia, Ontario, Prince Edward Island, Quebec, Saskatchewan, or Yukon and must have an interest in leadership.

Application Requirements: Application, essay, references. *Deadline:* June 30.

Contact: Vanessa Dewson, Special Events and Projects Coordinator
Canadian Association of Broadcasters
PO Box 627, Station B
Ottawa, ON K1P 5S2
Canada
Phone: 613-233-4035 Ext. 309
Fax: 613-233-6961
E-mail: vdewson@cab-acr.ca

CANADIAN PRESS http://www.cp.org

GIL PURCELL MEMORIAL JOURNALISM SCHOLARSHIP FOR NATIVE CANADIANS

Award for Aboriginal Canadians (status or non-status Indian, Metis, or Inuit) who are pursuing post-secondary studies and intend to work in the field of journalism.

Academic Fields/Career Goals: Journalism.

Award: Scholarship for use in freshman, sophomore, junior, senior, graduate, or postgraduate years; not renewable. *Number:* 1. *Amount:* $3268.

Eligibility Requirements: Applicant must be of Canadian heritage and Canadian citizen; American Indian/Alaska Native and enrolled or expecting to enroll full-time at a four-year institution or university.

Application Requirements: Application, interview, resume. *Deadline:* November 15.

Contact: Paul Woods, Director of Human Resources
Canadian Press
36 King Street East
Toronto, ON M5C 2L9
Canada
Phone: 416-507-2133
Fax: 416-507-2033
E-mail: pwoods@cp.org

CHARLOTTE OBSERVER

CHARLOTTE OBSERVER MINORITY SCHOLARSHIPS

• *See page 122*

CONNECTICUT CHAPTER OF SOCIETY OF PROFESSIONAL JOURNALISTS http://www.ctspj.org

CONNECTICUT SPJ BOB EDDY SCHOLARSHIP PROGRAM

One-time award for college junior or senior planning a career in journalism. Must be a Connecticut resident attending a four-year college or any student attending a four-year college in Connecticut. Information available from February 1 to April 14.

Academic Fields/Career Goals: Journalism; Photojournalism/Photography.

Award: Scholarship for use in junior or senior years; not renewable. *Number:* 4. *Amount:* $500–$2500.

Eligibility Requirements: Applicant must be enrolled or expecting to enroll full-time at a four-year institution and must have an interest in writing. Available to U.S. and non-U.S. citizens.

Application Requirements: Application, essay, financial need analysis, transcript. *Deadline:* April 14.

Contact: Debra Estock, Scholarship Committee Chairman
Connecticut Chapter of Society of Professional Journalists
71 Kenwood Avenue
Fairfield, CT 06430
Phone: 203-255-2127
E-mail: destock963@aol.com

CUBAN AMERICAN NATIONAL FOUNDATION

MAS FAMILY SCHOLARSHIPS

• *See page 123*

DALLAS-FORT WORTH ASSOCIATION OF BLACK COMMUNICATORS http://www.dfwabc.org

FUTURE JOURNALISTS SCHOLARSHIP PROGRAM

• *See page 159*

FISHER BROADCASTING COMPANY http://www.fisherbroadcasting.com/

FISHER BROADCASTING, INC., SCHOLARSHIP FOR MINORITIES

• *See page 159*

FREEDOM FORUM http://www.freedomforum.org

AL NEUHARTH FREE SPIRIT SCHOLARSHIP

One-time award for high school seniors interested in pursuing a career in journalism. Must be actively involved in high school journalism and demonstrate qualities such as being a visionary, an innovative leader, an entrepreneur, or a courageous achiever. Deadline is October 15. See Web site at http://www.freedomforum.org for further information.

Academic Fields/Career Goals: Journalism.

Award: Scholarship for use in freshman year; not renewable. *Number:* 102. *Amount:* $1000.

Eligibility Requirements: Applicant must be high school student and planning to enroll or expecting to enroll at an institution or university.

Application Requirements: Application, essay, photo, references, transcript, sample of journalistic work. *Deadline:* October 15.

Contact: Freedom Forum
1101 Wilson Boulevard
Arlington, VA 22209

CHIPS QUINN SCHOLARS PROGRAM

One-time award for students of color who are college juniors, seniors, or recent graduates. Must have a definite interest in print journalism as a career. Award requires paid internship. Applicants may be nominated by their schools, by newspaper editors, or by direct application with supporting letters of endorsement. Deadline is October 15. See Web site at http://www.freedomforum.org for further information.

Academic Fields/Career Goals: Journalism.

Award: Scholarship for use in junior or senior years; not renewable. *Number:* 75. *Amount:* $1000.

Eligibility Requirements: Applicant must be American Indian/Alaska Native, Asian/Pacific Islander, Black (non-Hispanic), or Hispanic and enrolled or expecting to enroll at a four-year institution or university.

Application Requirements: Application, essay, photo, portfolio, resume, references, transcript. *Deadline:* October 15.

Contact: Karen Catone, Director
Freedom Forum
1101 Wilson Boulevard
Arlington, VA 22209
Phone: 703-284-2863
Fax: 703-284-3543
E-mail: chipsquinnscholars@freedomforum.org

FUND FOR AMERICAN STUDIES http://www.tfas.org

ECONOMIC JOURNALISM AWARD

• *See page 192*

MOLLENHOFF AWARD FOR INVESTIGATIVE JOURNALISM

One-time award for a newspaper reporter or a team of reporters for groundbreaking work in investigative reporting. Multiple entries may be submitted, but no more than 20 stories per entry should be included. Entry deadline is March 15. See Web site at http://www.tfas.org for further information.

Academic Fields/Career Goals: Journalism.

Award: Prize for use in freshman, sophomore, junior, senior, or graduate years; not renewable. *Number:* 1. *Amount:* $5000.

Eligibility Requirements: Applicant must be enrolled or expecting to enroll at an institution or university. Available to U.S. citizens.

Application Requirements: Application, portfolio. *Deadline:* March 15.

Contact: Steve Slattery, Vice President of Programs
Fund for American Studies
1706 New Hampshire Avenue, NW
Washington, DC 20009
Phone: 202-986-0384
Fax: 202-986-8930
E-mail: sslattery@tfas.org

GEORGIA PRESS EDUCATIONAL FOUNDATION, INC. http://www.gapress.org

GEORGIA PRESS EDUCATIONAL FOUNDATION SCHOLARSHIPS

One-time awards to Georgia high school seniors and college undergraduates. Based on prior interest in newspaper journalism. Must be recommended by high school counselor, professor, and/or Georgia Press Educational Foundation member. Must reside and attend school in Georgia. Application deadline is February 1.

Academic Fields/Career Goals: Journalism.

Award: Scholarship for use in freshman, sophomore, junior, or senior years; not renewable. *Number:* 20. *Amount:* $500–$1500.

Eligibility Requirements: Applicant must be enrolled or expecting to enroll full-time at a two-year or four-year institution or university; resident of Georgia; studying in Georgia and must have an interest in writing. Applicant must have 2.5 GPA or higher. Available to U.S. citizens.

Application Requirements: Application, financial need analysis, photo, references, test scores, transcript. *Deadline:* February 1.

Contact: Ali Garrett
Georgia Press Educational Foundation, Inc.
3066 Mercer University Drive, Suite 200
Atlanta, GA 30341-4137
Phone: 770-454-6776
Fax: 770-454-6778

HUGH FULTON BYAS MEMORIAL FUNDS, INC.

HUGH FULTON BYAS MEMORIAL GRANT

• *See page 311*

INDIANA BROADCASTERS ASSOCIATION http://www.indianabroadcasters.org

INDIANA BROADCASTERS FOUNDATION SCHOLARSHIP

Must be majoring in broadcasting, electronic media or journalism. Must maintain a 3.0 GPA and be a resident of Indiana. One-time award for full-time undergraduate study in Indiana.

Academic Fields/Career Goals: Journalism; TV/Radio Broadcasting.

Award: Scholarship for use in freshman, sophomore, junior, or senior years; not renewable. *Number:* up to 14. *Amount:* $500–$2000.

Eligibility Requirements: Applicant must be high school student; planning to enroll or expecting to enroll full-time at a two-year or four-year or technical institution or university; resident of Indiana and studying in Indiana. Applicant must have 3.0 GPA or higher. Available to U.S. and non-U.S. citizens.

Application Requirements: Application, essay, references, transcript. *Deadline:* March 2.

Contact: Gwen C. Piening, Scholarship Administrator
Indiana Broadcasters Association
3003 East 98th Street, Suite 161
Indianapolis, IN 46280
Phone: 317-573-0119
Fax: 317-573-0895
E-mail: indba@aol.com

INDIANAPOLIS ASSOCIATION OF BLACK JOURNALISTS http://www.iabj.org

LYNN DEAN FORD IABJ SCHOLARSHIP AWARDS

• *See page 160*

INTERNATIONAL FOODSERVICE EDITORIAL COUNCIL http://www.ifec-is-us.com

INTERNATIONAL FOODSERVICE EDITORIAL COUNCIL COMMUNICATIONS SCHOLARSHIP

• *See page 160*

JOHN BAYLISS BROADCAST FOUNDATION http://www.baylissfoundation.org

JOHN BAYLISS BROADCAST RADIO SCHOLARSHIP

• *See page 160*

JOHN M. WILL MEMORIAL SCHOLARSHIP FOUNDATION

HEARIN-CHANDLER JOURNALISM SCHOLARSHIP

Scholarship for residents of Mobile, Baldwin, Escambia, Clarke, Conecuh, Washington, and Monroe counties in Alabama; Santa Rosa and Escambia counties in Florida; George and Jackson counties in Mississippi. For full-time journalism study, leading to a degree, at a regionally accredited institution. Applicant may be a high school senior, college student, or practicing journalist.

Academic Fields/Career Goals: Journalism.

Award: Scholarship for use in freshman, sophomore, junior, or senior years; not renewable. *Number:* 1. *Amount:* $5000.

Eligibility Requirements: Applicant must be enrolled or expecting to enroll full-time at a four-year institution or university; resident of Alabama, Florida, or Mississippi and must have an interest in writing. Available to U.S. citizens.

Application Requirements: Application, essay, interview, portfolio, references, transcript. *Deadline:* varies.

Contact: William Holman, II
John M. Will Memorial Scholarship Foundation
PO Box 290
Mobile, AL 36601

JOHN M. WILL JOURNALISM SCHOLARSHIP

Scholarship for residents of Mobile, Baldwin, Escambia, Clarke, Conecuh, Washington, and Monroe counties in Alabama; Santa Rosa and Escambia counties in Florida; George and Jackson counties in Mississippi. For full-time journalism study at a regionally accredited institution. Applicant may be high school senior, college student, or practicing journalist.

Academic Fields/Career Goals: Journalism.

Award: Scholarship for use in freshman, sophomore, junior, or senior years; not renewable. *Number:* 1. *Amount:* $3000.

Eligibility Requirements: Applicant must be enrolled or expecting to enroll full-time at a four-year institution or university; resident of Alabama, Florida, or Mississippi and must have an interest in writing. Available to U.S. citizens.

Application Requirements: Application, essay, interview, portfolio, references, transcript. *Deadline:* varies.

Contact: William Holman, II, Secretary of Foundation
John M. Will Memorial Scholarship Foundation
PO Box 290
Mobile, AL 36601

JORGE MAS CANOSA FREEDOM FOUNDATION

MAS FAMILY SCHOLARSHIP AWARD

• *See page 126*

JOURNALISM EDUCATION ASSOCIATION http://www.jea.org

NATIONAL HIGH SCHOOL JOURNALIST OF THE YEAR/SISTER RITA JEANNE SCHOLARSHIPS

• *See page 160*

KANSAS CITY STAR http://www.kcstar.com

ERNEST HEMINGWAY WRITING AWARDS

Four scholarships of $2500 will be awarded to high school students who work for their school newspaper. Students must plan to enroll in an accredited college or university. Applications should be accompanied by writing samples or clips from the newspaper. Eligible applicants will be United States citizens. The deadline is January 15.

Academic Fields/Career Goals: Journalism.

Award: Scholarship for use in freshman, sophomore, junior, or senior years; not renewable. *Number:* 4. *Amount:* $2500.

Eligibility Requirements: Applicant must be high school student and planning to enroll or expecting to enroll full-time at a two-year or four-year institution or university. Available to U.S. citizens.

Application Requirements: Application, mounted samples of writing. *Deadline:* January 15.

Contact: Lisa Lopez, Administrative Assistant
Kansas City Star
1729 Grand Boulevard
Kansas City, MO 64108
Phone: 816-234-4907
Fax: 816-234-4876
E-mail: llopez@kcstar.com

KCNC-TV CHANNEL 4 NEWS http://www.news4colorado.com

NEWS 4 PETER ROGOT MEDIA SCHOLARSHIP

• *See page 161*

KNIGHT RIDDER http://www.kri.com

KNIGHT RIDDER MINORITY SCHOLARSHIP PROGRAM

• *See page 126*

LEXINGTON HERALD-LEADER http://www.kentucky.com

LEXINGTON HERALD-LEADER/KNIGHT RIDDER MINORITY SCHOLARSHIPS

• *See page 127*

MAINE MEDIA WOMEN SCHOLARSHIPS COMMITTEE http://www.mainemediawomen.org/scholarships.html

MAINE MEDIA WOMEN'S SCHOLARSHIP

• *See page 88*

MISSISSIPPI PRESS ASSOCIATION EDUCATION FOUNDATION http://www.mspress.org/foundation/

MISSISSIPPI PRESS ASSOCIATION EDUCATION FOUNDATION SCHOLARSHIP

The Mississippi Press Association Education Foundation annually offers $1,000 ($500 per semester) scholarships to qualified students enrolled in print journalism, and who are residents of Mississippi. The recipient who maintains a 3.0 GPA, and submits proof of summer internship, will be eligible to continue the scholarship for his/her following year. Total value of the scholarship can be as much as $4,000 when awarded to an upcoming freshman who remains qualified throughout their four years of print journalism education.

Academic Fields/Career Goals: Journalism.

Award: Scholarship for use in freshman, sophomore, junior, or senior years; renewable. *Number:* 2. *Amount:* $1000.

Eligibility Requirements: Applicant must be enrolled or expecting to enroll full-time at a two-year or four-year institution or university; resident of Mississippi and studying in Mississippi. Applicant must have 3.0 GPA or higher. Available to U.S. citizens.

Application Requirements: Application, references, sample of work. *Deadline:* April 1.

Contact: Scholarship Coordinator
Mississippi Press Association Education Foundation
351 Edgewood Terrace
Jackson, MS 39206
Phone: 601-981-3060
Fax: 601-981-3676
E-mail: foundation@mspress.org

NATIONAL ASSOCIATION OF BLACK JOURNALISTS http://www.nabj.org

ALLISON FISHER SCHOLARSHIP

Available to any African-American student who is currently attending an accredited university. Must be majoring in print journalism and maintain a 3.0 GPA. Recipient will attend NABJ convention and participate in mentor program. Previous NABJ scholarship winners not eligible. Must be NABJ member before award.

Academic Fields/Career Goals: Journalism.

Award: Scholarship for use in freshman, sophomore, junior, senior, or graduate years; not renewable. *Number:* 1. *Amount:* $2500.

Eligibility Requirements: Applicant must be Black (non-Hispanic) and enrolled or expecting to enroll at an institution or university. Applicant must have 3.0 GPA or higher.

Application Requirements: Autobiography, references, proof of enrollment. *Deadline:* April 30.

Contact: Warren Paul, Media Instructor/Program Associate
National Association of Black Journalists
8701-A Adelphi Road
Adelphi, MD 20783-1716
Phone: 301-445-7100 Ext. 108
Fax: 301-445-7101

GERALD BOYD/ROBIN STONE NON-SUSTAINING SCHOLARSHIP

One-time scholarship is open to any African-American student who is currently enrolled in an accredited four-year institution. Must be enrolled as an undergraduate or graduate student and maintain a 3.0 GPA. Major must be in print journalism. Must be NABJ member before award.

Academic Fields/Career Goals: Journalism.

Award: Scholarship for use in freshman, sophomore, junior, senior, or graduate years; not renewable. *Number:* 1. *Amount:* $2500.

Eligibility Requirements: Applicant must be Black (non-Hispanic) and enrolled or expecting to enroll full-time at a four-year institution. Applicant must have 3.0 GPA or higher. Available to U.S. citizens.

Application Requirements: Application, essay, photo, references, transcript, six samples of work. *Deadline:* April 30.

Contact: Warren J. Paul, Media Institute Program Associate
National Association of Black Journalists
8701-A Adelphi Road
Adelphi, MD 20783
Phone: 301-445-7100 Ext. 108
Fax: 301-445-7101
E-mail: warren@nabj.org

NATIONAL ASSOCIATION OF BLACK JOURNALISTS AND NEWHOUSE FOUNDATION SCHOLARSHIP

Renewable award for African-American high school seniors planning to attend an accredited four-year college or university and major in journalism. Minimum 3.0 GPA required. Summer internship also required. Submit work sample and autobiography with application. Recipients attend NABJ convention and participate in mentor program. Must be NABJ member before award.

Academic Fields/Career Goals: Journalism.

Award: Scholarship for use in junior or senior years; renewable. *Number:* 2. *Amount:* $5000.

Eligibility Requirements: Applicant must be Black (non-Hispanic); high school student; planning to enroll or expecting to enroll full-time at a four-year institution and must have an interest in writing. Applicant must have 3.0 GPA or higher.

Application Requirements: Application, autobiography, essay, interview, references, transcript. *Deadline:* April 30.

Contact: Program and Exposition Coordinator
National Association of Black Journalists
8701-A Adelphi Road
Adelphi, MD 20783-1716
Phone: 301-445-7100 Ext. 109
Fax: 301-445-7101

NATIONAL ASSOCIATION OF BLACK JOURNALISTS NON-SUSTAINING SCHOLARSHIP AWARDS

One-time award for African-American college students attending a four-year institution and majoring in journalism. Minimum 2.5 GPA required. Submit letter from adviser, work sample, autobiography, resume, and photo with application. Recipient will attend NABJ convention and participate in mentor program. Previous NABJ scholarship winners not eligible. Must be NABJ member before award.

Academic Fields/Career Goals: Journalism; Photojournalism/Photography; TV/Radio Broadcasting.

Award: Scholarship for use in freshman, sophomore, junior, or senior years; not renewable. *Number:* 10. *Amount:* $2500.

Eligibility Requirements: Applicant must be Black (non-Hispanic); enrolled or expecting to enroll at a four-year institution or university and must have an interest in writing. Applicant must have 2.5 GPA or higher.

Application Requirements: Application, autobiography, photo, references, transcript, proof of enrollment. *Deadline:* April 30.

Contact: Program and Exposition Coordinator
National Association of Black Journalists
8701-A Adelphi Road
Adelphi, MD 20783-1716
Phone: 301-445-7100 Ext. 109
Fax: 301-445-7101

NATIONAL ASSOCIATION OF HISPANIC JOURNALISTS (NAHJ) http://www.nahj.org

ABC NEWS/JOANNA BISTANY MEMORIAL SCHOLARSHIP

This scholarship will be awarded to students who are pursuing careers as reporters or producers in the English-language television news industry. Students may major in any subject, but must demonstrate a sincere desire to pursue a career in this field. Students will be required to submit an essay and work samples. Applications must be postmarked on or before the final Friday in January of each year. Recipients will be given an opportunity to intern with ABC News. Applications available only at Web site: http://www.nahj.org.

Academic Fields/Career Goals: Journalism; TV/Radio Broadcasting.

Award: Scholarship for use in freshman, sophomore, junior, senior, or graduate years; not renewable. *Number:* 2. *Amount:* $5000.

Eligibility Requirements: Applicant must be enrolled or expecting to enroll full-time at a two-year or four-year institution or university. Available to U.S. citizens.

Application Requirements: Application, autobiography, essay, financial need analysis, resume, references, transcript, work samples. *Deadline:* January 28.

Contact: Nancy Tita, Educational Programs Manager
National Association of Hispanic Journalists (NAHJ)
1000 National Press Building
529 14th Street, NW, Suite 1000
Washington, DC 20045-2001
Phone: 202-662-7145
Fax: 202-662-7144
E-mail: ntita@nahj.org

GERALDO RIVERA SCHOLARSHIP

Awards available to college undergraduates and graduate students pursuing careers in English- or Spanish-language TV broadcast journalism. Applications only available at Web site: http://www.nahj.org.

Academic Fields/Career Goals: Journalism; TV/Radio Broadcasting.

Award: Scholarship for use in freshman, sophomore, junior, senior, or graduate years; not renewable. *Amount:* $1000–$5000.

Eligibility Requirements: Applicant must be enrolled or expecting to enroll full-time at a two-year or four-year institution or university.

National Association of Hispanic Journalists (NAHJ) (continued)

Application Requirements: *Deadline:* January 28.

Contact: Nancy Tita, Educational Programs Manager
National Association of Hispanic Journalists (NAHJ)
1000 National Press Building
529 14th Street, NW, Suite 1000
Washington, DC 20045-2001
Phone: 202-662-7145
Fax: 202-662-7144
E-mail: ntita@nahj.org

MARIA ELENA SALINAS SCHOLARSHIP

One-time scholarship for high school seniors, college undergraduates, and first-year graduate students who are pursuing careers in Spanish-language broadcast (radio or TV) journalism. Students may major or plan to major in any subject, but must demonstrate a sincere desire to pursue a career in this field. Must submit essays and demo tapes (audio or video) in Spanish. Scholarship includes the opportunity to serve an internship with Univision Spanish-language television news network. Applications must be postmarked on or before the final Friday in January of each year. Applications available only at Web site: http://www.nahj.org.

Academic Fields/Career Goals: Journalism; TV/Radio Broadcasting.

Award: Scholarship for use in freshman, sophomore, junior, senior, or graduate years; not renewable. *Number:* 2. *Amount:* $5000.

Eligibility Requirements: Applicant must be enrolled or expecting to enroll full-time at a two-year or four-year institution or university and must have an interest in Spanish language. Available to U.S. citizens.

Application Requirements: Application, autobiography, essay, financial need analysis, resume, references, transcript. *Deadline:* January 28.

Contact: Nancy Tita, Educational Programs Manager
National Association of Hispanic Journalists (NAHJ)
1000 National Press Building
529 14th Street, NW, Suite 1000
Washington, DC 20045-2001
Phone: 202-662-7145
Fax: 202-662-7144
E-mail: ntita@nahj.org

NATIONAL ASSOCIATION OF HISPANIC JOURNALISTS SCHOLARSHIP

• *See page 161*

NEWHOUSE SCHOLARSHIP PROGRAM

Two-year ($5000 annually) award for students who are pursuing careers in the newspaper industry as reporters, editors, graphic artists, or photojournalists. Students must be current college sophomores to be eligible. Recipient is expected to participate in summer internship at a Newhouse newspaper following their junior year. Students must submit resume and writing samples. Applications must be postmarked on or before final Friday in January. Applications available only at Web site http://www.nahj.org. Program provides a stipend to attend NAHJ's annual convention.

Academic Fields/Career Goals: Journalism.

Award: Scholarship for use in sophomore year; not renewable. *Number:* 2. *Amount:* $5000.

Eligibility Requirements: Applicant must be enrolled or expecting to enroll full-time at a two-year or four-year institution. Available to U.S. citizens.

Application Requirements: Application, essay, financial need analysis, resume, references, transcript, work samples. *Deadline:* January 28.

Contact: Nancy Tita, Educational Programs Manager
National Association of Hispanic Journalists (NAHJ)
1000 National Press Building
529 14th Street, NW, Suite 1000
Washington, DC 20045-2001
Phone: 202-662-7145
Fax: 202-662-7144
E-mail: ntita@nahj.org

WASHINGTON POST YOUNG JOURNALISTS SCHOLARSHIP

Four-year award of $10,000 for high school seniors in the metropolitan Washington DC area. Contact Educational Programs Manager for application and information.

Academic Fields/Career Goals: Journalism.

Award: Scholarship for use in freshman year; not renewable. *Number:* 1. *Amount:* $10,000.

Eligibility Requirements: Applicant must be high school student; planning to enroll or expecting to enroll full-time at a four-year institution or university and resident of District of Columbia, Maryland, or Virginia. Available to U.S. citizens.

Application Requirements: Application.

Contact: Nancy Tita, Educational Programs Manager
National Association of Hispanic Journalists (NAHJ)
1000 National Press Building
529 14th Street, NW, Suite 1000
Washington, DC 20045-2001
Phone: 202-662-7145
Fax: 202-662-7144
E-mail: ntita@nahj.org

NATIONAL GAY AND LESBIAN TASK FORCE http://www.ngltf.org/about/messenger.htm

NATIONAL GAY AND LESBIAN TASK FORCE MESSENGER-ANDERSON JOURNALISM SCHOLARSHIP

• *See page 162*

NATIONAL INSTITUTE FOR LABOR RELATIONS RESEARCH http://www.nilrr.org

NATIONAL INSTITUTE FOR LABOR RELATIONS RESEARCH WILLIAM B. RUGGLES JOURNALISM SCHOLARSHIP

• *See page 162*

NATIONAL STONE, SAND AND GRAVEL ASSOCIATION (NSSGA) http://www.nssga.org

JENNIFER CURTIS BYLER SCHOLARSHIP FOR THE STUDY OF PUBLIC AFFAIRS

• *See page 162*

NATIONAL WRITERS ASSOCIATION FOUNDATION http://www.nationalwriters.com

NATIONAL WRITERS ASSOCIATION FOUNDATION SCHOLARSHIPS

• *See page 162*

NATIVE AMERICAN JOURNALISTS ASSOCIATION http://www.naja.com

NATIVE AMERICAN JOURNALISTS ASSOCIATION SCHOLARSHIPS

Applicants must have proof of tribal association. Send cover letter, letters of reference, and work samples with application. Financial need considered. One-time award for undergraduate study leading to journalism career at accredited colleges and universities. Applicants must be current members of Native-American Journalists Association or may join at time of application.

Academic Fields/Career Goals: Journalism.

Award: Scholarship for use in freshman, sophomore, junior, senior, or graduate years; not renewable. *Number:* 10–14. *Amount:* $500–$3000.

Eligibility Requirements: Applicant must be American Indian/Alaska Native; high school student; planning to enroll or expecting to enroll full-time at a two-year or four-year institution and must have an interest in writing. Applicant must have 2.5 GPA or higher. Available to U.S. and Canadian citizens.

Application Requirements: Application, driver's license, essay, financial need analysis, interview, photo, portfolio, resume, references, test scores, transcript. *Deadline:* March 31.

Contact: Ron Walters, Executive Director
Native American Journalists Association
Al Neuharth Media Center
555 North Dakota Street
Vermillion, SD 57069
Phone: 605-677-5282
Fax: 866-694-4264
E-mail: info@naja.com

NEBRASKA PRESS ASSOCIATION http://www.nebpress.com/

NEBRASKA PRESS ASSOCIATION FOUNDATION, INC., SCHOLARSHIP

Award for graduates of Nebraska high schools who have a minimum GPA of 2.5 and are enrolled or planning to enroll in programs in Nebraska colleges or universities leading to careers in print journalism. Two to four awards of $1250. Deadline: March 8.

Academic Fields/Career Goals: Journalism; Photojournalism/Photography.

Award: Scholarship for use in freshman, sophomore, junior, or senior years; not renewable. *Number:* 2–4. *Amount:* $1250.

Eligibility Requirements: Applicant must be enrolled or expecting to enroll full-time at a four-year institution or university; resident of Nebraska and studying in Nebraska. Applicant must have 2.5 GPA or higher. Available to U.S. citizens.

Application Requirements: Application, financial need analysis. *Deadline:* March 8.

Contact: Allen Beermann, Executive Director
Nebraska Press Association
845 S Street
Lincoln, NE 68508-1226
Phone: 402-476-2851
Fax: 402-476-2942
E-mail: nebpress@nebpress.com

NEW JERSEY PRESS FOUNDATION http://www.njpa.org/foundation

BERNARD KILGORE MEMORIAL SCHOLARSHIP FOR THE NJ HIGH SCHOOL JOURNALIST OF THE YEAR

Program co-sponsored with the Garden State Scholastic Press Association. Winning student is nominated to the Journalism Education Association for the National High School Journalist of the Year Competition. Must be in high school with plans of entering a four-year college or university on a full-time basis. Deadline is February 15. Minimum 3.0 GPA required.

Academic Fields/Career Goals: Journalism.

Award: Scholarship for use in freshman year; not renewable. *Number:* 1. *Amount:* $5000.

Eligibility Requirements: Applicant must be high school student; planning to enroll or expecting to enroll full-time at a four-year institution or university and resident of New Jersey. Applicant must have 3.0 GPA or higher. Available to U.S. citizens.

Application Requirements: Application, essay, portfolio, references, transcript. *Deadline:* February 15.

Contact: Thomas Engleman, Director
New Jersey Press Foundation
840 Bear Tavern Road, Suite 305
West Trenton, NJ 08628-1019
Phone: 609-406-0600 Ext. 19
Fax: 609-406-0300
E-mail: foundation@njpa.org

NEW YORK WOMEN IN COMMUNICATIONS, INC., FOUNDATION http://www.nywici.org/foundation/index.html

NEW YORK WOMEN IN COMMUNICATIONS, INC. FOUNDATION SCHOLARSHIP PROGRAM

• *See page 163*

NEWSPAPER GUILD-CWA http://www.newsguild.org

DAVID S. BARR AWARD

For their journalistic achievements and to encourage young journalists to focus on issues of social justice, one $500 award will be given to a graduating high school senior and one $1500 award will be given to a college student. For application and more details see Web site: http://www.newguild.org.

Academic Fields/Career Goals: Journalism.

Award: Scholarship for use in freshman, sophomore, junior, or senior years; not renewable. *Number:* up to 2. *Amount:* $500–$1500.

Eligibility Requirements: Applicant must be enrolled or expecting to enroll full or part-time at an institution or university. Available to U.S. and Canadian citizens.

Application Requirements: Application. *Deadline:* January 30.

Contact: The Newspaper Guild-Communication Workers of America
Newspaper Guild-CWA
503 Third Street, NW, Suite 250
Washington, DC 20001

NORTHWEST JOURNALISTS OF COLOR http://www.aajaseattle.org

NORTHWEST JOURNALISTS OF COLOR SCHOLARSHIP

One-time award for Washington state high school and college students seeking careers in journalism. Must be an undergraduate enrolled in an accredited college or university or a senior in high school. Must be Asian-American, African-American, Native-American or Latino. Application deadline is May 3.

Academic Fields/Career Goals: Journalism.

Award: Scholarship for use in freshman, sophomore, junior, or senior years; not renewable. *Number:* 1–6. *Amount:* $250–$1000.

Eligibility Requirements: Applicant must be American Indian/Alaska Native, Asian/Pacific Islander, Black (non-Hispanic), or Hispanic; enrolled or expecting to enroll full-time at a two-year or four-year or technical institution or university and resident of Washington. Applicant must have 2.5 GPA or higher. Available to U.S. citizens.

Application Requirements: Application, essay, financial need analysis, references, transcript, work samples. *Deadline:* May 3.

Contact: Lori Matsukawa, Scholarship Coordinator
Northwest Journalists of Color
c/o King TV
333 Dexter Avenue North
Seattle, WA 98109
Phone: 206-448-3853
Fax: 206-448-4525
E-mail: lmatsukawa@king5.com

OHIO NEWSPAPERS FOUNDATION http://www.ohionews.org

HAROLD K. DOUTHIT SCHOLARSHIP

A $1,000 scholarship will be awarded to a northern Ohio high school senior who plans to pursue a newspaper journalism career. Applicants must be enrolled in a high school in Cuyahoga, Lorain, Huron, Erie, Wood, Geauge, Sandusky, Ottawa, or Lucas County. The applicant must be enrolled in an accredited Ohio college or university at the time the award is distributed. A minimum high school GPA of 3.0 (B) is required.

Academic Fields/Career Goals: Journalism.

Award: Scholarship for use in freshman year; not renewable. *Number:* 1. *Amount:* $1000.

Eligibility Requirements: Applicant must be high school student; planning to enroll or expecting to enroll at an institution or university; resident of Ohio and studying in Ohio. Applicant must have 3.0 GPA or higher. Available to U.S. citizens.

Ohio Newspapers Foundation (continued)

Application Requirements: Application, autobiography, financial need analysis, references, transcript. *Deadline:* March 31.

Contact: Kathleen Pouliot, Secretary
Ohio Newspapers Foundation
1335 Dublin Road, Suite 216-B
Columbus, OH 43215-7038
Phone: 614-486-6677
Fax: 614-486-4940
E-mail: kpouliot@ohionews.org

OHIO NEWSPAPERS FOUNDATION MINORITY SCHOLARSHIP

Three $1,500 scholarships will be awarded to minority high school seniors who plan to pursue a newspaper journalism career. Applicants must be enrolled in an accredited Ohio college or university. A minimum high school GPA of 2.5 (C+) is required. Applicants must be African-American, Hispanic, Asian-American or American-Indian.

Academic Fields/Career Goals: Journalism.

Award: Scholarship for use in freshman year; not renewable. *Number:* 3. *Amount:* $1500.

Eligibility Requirements: Applicant must be American Indian/Alaska Native, Asian/Pacific Islander, Black (non-Hispanic), or Hispanic; high school student; planning to enroll or expecting to enroll at an institution or university; resident of Ohio and studying in Ohio. Applicant must have 2.5 GPA or higher. Available to U.S. citizens.

Application Requirements: Application, autobiography, essay, transcript. *Deadline:* March 31.

Contact: Kathleen Pouliot, Secretary
Ohio Newspapers Foundation
1335 Dublin Road, Suite 216-B
Columbus, OH 43215-7038
Phone: 614-486-6677
Fax: 614-486-4940
E-mail: kpouliot@ohionews.org

OHIO NEWSPAPERS FOUNDATION UNIVERSITY JOURNALISM SCHOLARSHIP

A $1,500 scholarship will be awarded to a student who is enrolled in an Ohio college or university who is majoring in journalism or equivalent degree program. Applicants are not limited to, but preference will be given to students demonstrating a career commitment to newspaper journalism. A minimum GPA of 2.5 (C+) is required. Applicants must be sophomore, junior, or senior.

Academic Fields/Career Goals: Journalism.

Award: Scholarship for use in sophomore, junior, or senior years; not renewable. *Number:* 1. *Amount:* $1500.

Eligibility Requirements: Applicant must be enrolled or expecting to enroll at an institution or university; resident of Ohio and studying in Ohio. Applicant must have 2.5 GPA or higher. Available to U.S. citizens.

Application Requirements: Application, autobiography, essay, references, transcript. *Deadline:* March 31.

Contact: Kathleen Pouliot, Secretary
Ohio Newspapers Foundation
1335 Dublin Road, Suite 216-B
Columbus, OH 43215-7038
Phone: 614-486-6677
Fax: 614-486-4940
E-mail: kpouliot@ohionews.org

OREGON ASSOCIATION OF BROADCASTERS

http://www.theoab.org

OAB BROADCAST SCHOLARSHIP

• *See page 163*

OREGON STUDENT ASSISTANCE COMMISSION

http://www.osac.state.or.us

ENTERCOM PORTLAND RADIO SCHOLARSHIP FUND

Awards for residents of Clackamas, Multnomah, Washington, or Yamhill Counties in Oregon or Clark County, Washington. Award for the study of broadcasting or journalism at the undergraduate level. One-time award.

Academic Fields/Career Goals: Journalism; TV/Radio Broadcasting.

Award: Scholarship for use in freshman, sophomore, junior, or senior years; not renewable. *Number:* varies. *Amount:* $500.

Eligibility Requirements: Applicant must be enrolled or expecting to enroll at a two-year or four-year institution and resident of Oregon or Washington. Available to U.S. citizens.

Application Requirements: Application, essay, financial need analysis, test scores, transcript, activity chart. *Deadline:* March 1.

Contact: Director of Grant Programs
Oregon Student Assistance Commission
1500 Valley River Drive, Suite 100
Eugene, OR 97401-7020
Phone: 800-452-8807 Ext. 7395
E-mail: awardinfo@mercury.osac.state.or.us

JACKSON FOUNDATION JOURNALISM SCHOLARSHIP

One-time award for graduates of Oregon high schools pursuing a major in journalism. Must be enrolled in an Oregon college.

Academic Fields/Career Goals: Journalism.

Award: Scholarship for use in freshman year; not renewable. *Number:* 7. *Amount:* $1429.

Eligibility Requirements: Applicant must be high school student; planning to enroll or expecting to enroll at a four-year institution; resident of Oregon and studying in Oregon. Available to U.S. citizens.

Application Requirements: Application, essay, financial need analysis, references, transcript, activity chart. *Deadline:* March 1.

Contact: Director of Grant Programs
Oregon Student Assistance Commission
1500 Valley River Drive, Suite 100
Eugene, OR 97401-7020
Phone: 800-452-8807 Ext. 7395
E-mail: awardinfo@mercury.osac.state.or.us

MARK HASS JOURNALISM AWARD

One-time award for journalism majors who are graduating Oregon high school seniors and college undergraduates. Visit Web site http://www.osac.state.or.us for application procedures, requirements, and deadlines.

Academic Fields/Career Goals: Journalism.

Award: Scholarship for use in freshman, sophomore, junior, or senior years; not renewable. *Number:* 1. *Amount:* $1000.

Eligibility Requirements: Applicant must be enrolled or expecting to enroll at an institution or university and resident of Oregon. Available to U.S. citizens.

Application Requirements: Application, essay, financial need analysis, references, transcript, activity chart. *Deadline:* March 1.

Contact: Director of Grant Programs
Oregon Student Assistance Commission
1500 Valley River Drive, Suite 100
Eugene, OR 97401-7020
Phone: 800-452-8807 Ext. 7395
E-mail: awardinfo@mercury.osac.state.or.us

OUTDOOR WRITERS ASSOCIATION OF AMERICA

http://www.owaa.org

OUTDOOR WRITERS ASSOCIATION OF AMERICA BODIE MCDOWELL SCHOLARSHIP AWARD

• *See page 163*

OVERSEAS PRESS CLUB FOUNDATION http://www.opcofamerica.org

OVERSEAS PRESS CLUB FOUNDATION SCHOLARSHIPS

Students who aspire to become foreign correspondents are asked to write an essay of no more than 500 words concentrating on an area of the world or an international issue that is in keeping with the applicant's interest. It can be in the form of a story, news analysis, or a traditional essay. Must be studying at an American college or university. Application deadline is December 1.

Academic Fields/Career Goals: Journalism.

Award: Scholarship for use in freshman, sophomore, junior, senior, or graduate years; not renewable. *Number:* 12. *Amount:* $2000.

Eligibility Requirements: Applicant must be enrolled or expecting to enroll full or part-time at a two-year or four-year institution or university. Available to U.S. and non-U.S. citizens.

Application Requirements: Applicant must enter a contest, autobiography, essay, resume. *Deadline:* December 1.

Contact: William J. Holstein, President
Overseas Press Club Foundation
40 West 45th Street
New York, NY 10036
Phone: 212-626-9220
Fax: 212-626-9210
E-mail: foundation@opcofamerica.org

PHILADELPHIA ASSOCIATION OF BLACK JOURNALISTS http://www.pabj.org

PHILADELPHIA ASSOCIATION OF BLACK JOURNALISTS SCHOLARSHIP

One-time award available to African-American high school students interested in becoming journalists. Must have a 2.5 GPA.

Academic Fields/Career Goals: Journalism.

Award: Scholarship for use in freshman year; not renewable. *Number:* 2–4. *Amount:* $500–$1000.

Eligibility Requirements: Applicant must be Black (non-Hispanic); high school student; planning to enroll or expecting to enroll full-time at a four-year institution or university; resident of Pennsylvania and must have an interest in writing. Applicant must have 2.5 GPA or higher. Available to U.S. citizens.

Application Requirements: Application, autobiography, essay, references, transcript. *Deadline:* April 30.

Contact: Nia Neeks, General Assignment Reporter
Philadelphia Association of Black Journalists
c/o Philadelphia Tribune, 520 South 16th Street
Philadelphia, PA 19146
Phone: 215-893-4080
Fax: 215-893-5767
E-mail: browngirl@msn.com

POLISH ARTS CLUB OF BUFFALO SCHOLARSHIP FOUNDATION

POLISH ARTS CLUB OF BUFFALO SCHOLARSHIP FOUNDATION TRUST

• *See page 84*

PRESS WOMEN OF TEXAS

PRESS WOMEN OF TEXAS ROVING SCHOLARSHIP

• *See page 163*

QUILL AND SCROLL FOUNDATION http://www.uiowa.edu/~quill-sc

EDWARD J. NELL MEMORIAL SCHOLARSHIP IN JOURNALISM

Merit-based award for high school seniors planning to major in journalism. Must have won a National Quill and Scroll Writing Award or a Photography or Yearbook Excellence contest. Entry forms available from journalism adviser or Quill and Scroll. Must rank in upper third of class or have a minimum 3.0 GPA.

Academic Fields/Career Goals: Journalism.

Award: Scholarship for use in freshman year; not renewable. *Number:* 8–10. *Amount:* $500–$1500.

Eligibility Requirements: Applicant must be high school student; planning to enroll or expecting to enroll full-time at a four-year institution or university and must have an interest in photography/photogrammetry/filmmaking or writing. Applicant must have 3.0 GPA or higher. Available to U.S. citizens.

Application Requirements: Application, essay, photo, references, self-addressed stamped envelope, test scores, transcript. *Deadline:* May 10.

Contact: Richard Johns, Executive Director
Quill and Scroll Foundation
312 WSSH, School of Journalism
Iowa City, IA 52242-1528
Phone: 319-335-3321
Fax: 319-335-5210
E-mail: quill-scroll@uiowa.edu

R/A B. MEMORIAL SCHOLARSHIPS, USA

ROBERT BILMANIS AND DR. ALFRED BILMANIS MEMORIAL SCHOLARSHIP

One-time award offered to a qualifying full-time student of Latvian heritage who has selected "investigative journalism" as a career and has enrolled in sophomore year or later in a four-year college or university. Selection criteria will include a thesis on the history of Latvia as specified by the sponsor.

Academic Fields/Career Goals: Journalism.

Award: Scholarship for use in sophomore, junior, senior, or graduate years; not renewable. *Number:* 1. *Amount:* $2000.

Eligibility Requirements: Applicant must be of Latvian heritage and enrolled or expecting to enroll full-time at a four-year institution or university. Available to U.S. and non-U.S. citizens.

Application Requirements: Application, autobiography, essay, references, self-addressed stamped envelope, transcript. *Deadline:* July 1.

Contact: Juris Bilmanis, Sponsor
R/A B. Memorial Scholarships, USA
12465 Potomac View Road
Newburg, MD 20664-6309
Phone: 301-259-0414
E-mail: juris2@aol.com

RADIO-TELEVISION NEWS DIRECTORS ASSOCIATION AND FOUNDATION http://www.rtndf.org

CAROLE SIMPSON SCHOLARSHIP

• *See page 164*

ED BRADLEY SCHOLARSHIP

• *See page 164*

KEN KASHIWAHARA SCHOLARSHIP

• *See page 164*

LOU AND CAROLE PRATO SPORTS REPORTING SCHOLARSHIP

• *See page 164*

MIKE REYNOLDS $1,000 SCHOLARSHIP

• *See page 164*

PRESIDENT'S $2500 SCHOLARSHIP

• *See page 164*

SACRAMENTO BEE http://www.sacbee.com/scholarships

SACRAMENTO BEE JOURNALISM SCHOLARSHIP PROGRAM

The Sacramento Bee Journalism Scholarship Program is for graduating high school seniors, and college students pursuing careers in the newspaper business. Applicants and recipients must reside in the Sacramento region.

Academic Fields/Career Goals: Journalism.

Award: Scholarship for use in senior year; not renewable. *Number:* up to 16. *Amount:* $1500–$2500.

Eligibility Requirements: Applicant must be enrolled or expecting to enroll full-time at a four-year institution or university and resident of California. Applicant must have 3.0 GPA or higher. Available to U.S. citizens.

Sacramento Bee (continued)

Application Requirements: Application, autobiography, essay, financial need analysis, photo, portfolio, resume, references, transcript. *Deadline:* January 17.

Contact: Cathy Rodriguez, Public Affairs Representative
Sacramento Bee
2100 Q Street
Sacramento, CA 95816
Phone: 916-321-1880
Fax: 916-321-1783
E-mail: crodriguez@sacbee.com

SEATTLE POST-INTELLIGENCER http://www.seattlepi.com

BOBBI MCCALLUM MEMORIAL SCHOLARSHIP

Scholarship is available to junior and senior college women from a Washington state university who have an interest in print journalism. Submit clips of published stories with transcripts, financial need analysis, application, and two letters of recommendation. Must be a Washington resident. Submit only questions through email. Applications must be mailed.

Academic Fields/Career Goals: Journalism.

Award: Scholarship for use in junior or senior years; not renewable. *Number:* 1. *Amount:* $1000.

Eligibility Requirements: Applicant must be enrolled or expecting to enroll full or part-time at a four-year institution; female; resident of Washington and studying in Washington. Applicant must have 3.0 GPA or higher. Available to U.S. citizens.

Application Requirements: Application, financial need analysis, portfolio, resume, references, transcript. *Deadline:* April 1.

Contact: Janet Grimley, Assistant Managing Editor
Seattle Post-Intelligencer
PO Box 1909
Seattle, WA 98111
Phone: 206-448-8316
Fax: 206-448-8305
E-mail: janetgrimley@seattlep-i.com

SOCIETY OF PROFESSIONAL JOURNALISTS, LOS ANGELES CHAPTER http://www.spj.org/losangeles

BILL FARR SCHOLARSHIP

Awards are available to a student who is either a resident of Los Angeles, Ventura or Orange counties or is enrolled at a university in one of those three California counties. Must have completed sophomore year and be enrolled in or accepted to a journalism program. Application deadline is April 15.

Academic Fields/Career Goals: Journalism.

Award: Scholarship for use in junior, senior, or graduate years; not renewable. *Number:* 1. *Amount:* $500–$1000.

Eligibility Requirements: Applicant must be enrolled or expecting to enroll full-time at a four-year institution or university. Available to U.S. citizens.

Application Requirements: Application, essay, resume, work samples. *Deadline:* April 15.

Contact: Christopher Burnett, Scholarship Chair
Society of Professional Journalists, Los Angeles Chapter
c/o Department of Journalism, California State University, Long Beach
1250 Bellflower
Long Beach, CA 90840
Phone: 562-985-5779
E-mail: cburnett@csulb.edu

CARL GREENBERG SCHOLARSHIP

Awards are available to a student who is either a resident of Los Angeles, Ventura or Orange counties or is enrolled at a university in one of those three California counties. Must have completed sophomore year and be enrolled in or accepted to an investigative or political journalism program. Application deadline is April 15.

Academic Fields/Career Goals: Journalism.

Award: Scholarship for use in junior, senior, or graduate years; not renewable. *Number:* 1. *Amount:* $1000.

Eligibility Requirements: Applicant must be enrolled or expecting to enroll full-time at a four-year institution or university. Available to U.S. citizens.

Application Requirements: Application, essay, resume, work samples. *Deadline:* April 15.

Contact: Christopher Burnett, Scholarship Chair
Society of Professional Journalists, Los Angeles Chapter
c/o Department of Journalism, California State University, Long Beach
1250 Bellflower
Long Beach, CA 90840
Phone: 562-985-5779
E-mail: cburnett@csulb.edu

HELEN JOHNSON SCHOLARSHIP

Awards are available to a student who is a resident of Los Angeles, Ventura or Orange counties or is enrolled at a university in one of those three California counties. Must have completed sophomore year and be enrolled in or accepted to a broadcast journalism program. Application deadline is April 15.

Academic Fields/Career Goals: Journalism; TV/Radio Broadcasting.

Award: Scholarship for use in junior, senior, or graduate years; not renewable. *Number:* 1. *Amount:* $500–$1000.

Eligibility Requirements: Applicant must be enrolled or expecting to enroll full-time at a four-year institution or university. Available to U.S. citizens.

Application Requirements: Application, essay, resume, work samples. *Deadline:* April 15.

Contact: Christopher Burnett, Scholarship Chair
Society of Professional Journalists, Los Angeles Chapter
c/o Department of Journalism, California State University, Long Beach
1250 Bellflower
Long Beach, CA 90840
Phone: 562-985-5779
E-mail: cburnett@csulb.edu

KEN INOUYE SCHOLARSHIP

Awards are available to a minority student who is either a resident of Los Angeles, Ventura or Orange counties or is enrolled at a university in one of those three California counties. Must have completed sophomore year and be enrolled in or accepted to a journalism program. Application deadline is April 15.

Academic Fields/Career Goals: Journalism.

Award: Scholarship for use in junior, senior, or graduate years; not renewable. *Number:* 1. *Amount:* $500–$1000.

Eligibility Requirements: Applicant must be American Indian/Alaska Native, Asian/Pacific Islander, Black (non-Hispanic), or Hispanic and enrolled or expecting to enroll full-time at a four-year institution or university. Available to U.S. citizens.

Application Requirements: Application, essay, resume, work samples. *Deadline:* April 15.

Contact: Christopher Burnett, Scholarship Chair
Society of Professional Journalists, Los Angeles Chapter
c/o Department of Journalism, California State University, Long Beach
1250 Bellflower
Long Beach, CA 90840
Phone: 562-985-5779
E-mail: cburnett@csulb.edu

SOCIETY OF PROFESSIONAL JOURNALISTS-SOUTH FLORIDA CHAPTER

GARTH REEVES, JR. MEMORIAL SCHOLARSHIPS

• *See page 165*

SOIL AND WATER CONSERVATION SOCIETY-NEW JERSEY CHAPTER http://www.geocities.com/njswcs

EDWARD R. HALL SCHOLARSHIP
• See page 55

SOUTH CAROLINA PRESS ASSOCIATION FOUNDATION http://www.scpress.org

SOUTH CAROLINA PRESS ASSOCIATION FOUNDATION NEWSPAPER SCHOLARSHIPS

Renewable award for students entering junior year at a South Carolina institution. Based on grades, journalistic activities in college, and recommendations. Must agree to work in the newspaper field for two years after graduation or repay as loan.

Academic Fields/Career Goals: Journalism.

Award: Forgivable loan for use in junior or senior years; renewable. *Number:* up to 3. *Amount:* $4000–$5500.

Eligibility Requirements: Applicant must be enrolled or expecting to enroll full-time at a four-year institution and studying in South Carolina. Available to U.S. and non-U.S. citizens.

Application Requirements: Application, essay, portfolio, resume, references, transcript. *Deadline:* January 1.

Contact: Jennifer Roberts, Assistant Director
South Carolina Press Association Foundation
PO Box 11429
Columbia, SC 29211-1429
Phone: 803-750-9561
Fax: 803-551-0903
E-mail: jroberts@scpress.org

TEXAS GRIDIRON CLUB, INC. http://www.spjfw.org

TEXAS GRIDIRON CLUB SCHOLARSHIPS
• See page 165

UNITED METHODIST COMMUNICATIONS http://www.umcom.org/scholarships

LEONARD M. PERRYMAN COMMUNICATIONS SCHOLARSHIP FOR ETHNIC MINORITY STUDENTS
• See page 166

UNITED NEGRO COLLEGE FUND http://www.uncf.org

BEST BUY ENTERPRISE EMPLOYEE SCHOLARSHIP
• See page 48

C-SPAN SCHOLARSHIP PROGRAM
• See page 166

CBS CAREER HORIZONS SCHOLARSHIP PROGRAM
• See page 166

11-ALIVE COMMUNITY SERVICE SCHOLARSHIP TEST
• See page 166

READER'S DIGEST SCHOLARSHIP
• See page 167

UNCF/SPRINT SCHOLARS PROGRAM
• See page 50

VALLEY PRESS CLUB

VALLEY PRESS CLUB SCHOLARSHIPS, THE REPUBLICAN SCHOLARSHIP; PHOTOJOURNALISM SCHOLARSHIP, CHANNEL 22 SCHOLARSHIP
• See page 167

WASHINGTON NEWS COUNCIL http://www.wanewscouncil.org

DICK LARSEN SCHOLARSHIP PROGRAM
• See page 167

HERB ROBINSON SCHOLARSHIP PROGRAM
• See page 168

WASHINGTON THOROUGHBRED FOUNDATION http://www.washingtonthoroughbred.com

THOROUGHBRED HORSE RACING'S UNITED SCHOLARSHIP TRUST
• See page 64

LANDSCAPE ARCHITECTURE

AMERICAN INSTITUTE OF ARCHITECTS, NEW YORK CHAPTER http://www.aiany.org

HASKELL AWARDS FOR STUDENTS IN ARCHITECTURAL JOURNALISM
• See page 74

AMERICAN NURSERY AND LANDSCAPE ASSOCIATION http://www.anla.org/research

ANLA NATIONAL SCHOLARSHIP ENDOWMENT-USREY FAMILY SCHOLARSHIP
• See page 314

CARVILLE M. AKEHURST MEMORIAL SCHOLARSHIP
• See page 314

HORTICULTURE RESEARCH INSTITUTE TIMOTHY BIGELOW SCHOLARSHIP
• See page 314

SPRING MEADOW NURSERY SCHOLARSHIP
• See page 314

ASSOCIATION FOR WOMEN IN ARCHITECTURE FOUNDATION http://www.awa-la.org

ASSOCIATION FOR WOMEN IN ARCHITECTURE SCHOLARSHIP
• See page 75

CALIFORNIA WATER AWARENESS CAMPAIGN http://www.wateraware.org

CALIFORNIA WATER AWARENESS CAMPAIGN WATER SCHOLAR
• See page 57

CONNECTICUT BUILDING CONGRESS http://www.cbc-ct.org

CONNECTICUT BUILDING CONGRESS SCHOLARSHIP FUND
• See page 75

CONNECTICUT NURSERYMEN'S FOUNDATION, INC.

CONNECTICUT NURSERYMEN'S FOUNDATION, INC. SCHOLARSHIPS
• See page 315

FEDERATED GARDEN CLUBS OF CONNECTICUT

FEDERATED GARDEN CLUBS OF CONNECTICUT, INC.
• See page 113

FLORIDA EDUCATIONAL FACILITIES PLANNERS' ASSOCIATION http://www.fefpa.org

FEFPA ASSISTANTSHIP
• See page 76

FRIENDS OF THE FRELINGHUYSEN ARBORETUM http://arboretumfriends.org

BENJAMIN C. BLACKBURN SCHOLARSHIP
• See page 264

HERB SOCIETY OF AMERICA http://www.herbsociety.org

HERB SOCIETY RESEARCH GRANTS
• See page 69

HERB SOCIETY OF AMERICA, WESTERN RESERVE UNIT http://www.herbsociety.org

FRANCIS SYLVIA ZVERINA SCHOLARSHIP

• *See page 320*

WESTERN RESERVE HERB SOCIETY SCHOLARSHIP

• *See page 320*

LANDSCAPE ARCHITECTURE FOUNDATION http://www.LAprofession.org

HAWAII CHAPTER/DAVID T. WOOLSEY SCHOLARSHIP

One-time award of $1000 in memory of David T. Woolsey provides funds for a third-, fourth-, fifth-year, or graduate student in landscape architecture from Hawaii. Must submit three 8x10 photographs of design work. Must include record of Hawaii residency.

Academic Fields/Career Goals: Landscape Architecture.

Award: Scholarship for use in junior, senior, or graduate years; not renewable. *Number:* 1. *Amount:* $1000.

Eligibility Requirements: Applicant must be enrolled or expecting to enroll at a four-year institution and resident of Hawaii. Available to U.S. citizens.

Application Requirements: Application, autobiography, essay, financial need analysis, references, photos of work, proof of Hawaii residency. *Deadline:* April 1.

Contact: Ron Figura, Project Manager
Landscape Architecture Foundation
818 18th Street, NW
Suite 810
Washington, DC 20006
Phone: 202-331-7070 Ext. 10
Fax: 202-331-7079
E-mail: rfigura@lafoundation.org

LANDSCAPE ARCHITECTURE FOUNDATION/CALIFORNIA LANDSCAPE ARCHITECTURAL STUDENT FUND SCHOLARSHIPS PROGRAM

Nonrenewable scholarships for students continuing degree program in landscape architecture at eligible institution in California. Based on financial need and commitment to profession.

Academic Fields/Career Goals: Landscape Architecture.

Award: Scholarship for use in freshman, sophomore, junior, or senior years; not renewable. *Number:* 10. *Amount:* $500.

Eligibility Requirements: Applicant must be enrolled or expecting to enroll at a four-year institution or university and studying in California. Available to U.S. citizens.

Application Requirements: Application, financial need analysis, references. *Deadline:* April 1.

Contact: Ron Figura, Project Manager
Landscape Architecture Foundation
818 18th Street, NW
Suite 810
Washington, DC 20006
Phone: 202-331-7070 Ext. 10
Fax: 202-331-7079
E-mail: rfigura@lafoundation.org

LANDSCAPE ARCHITECTURE FOUNDATION/CALIFORNIA LANDSCAPE ARCHITECTURE STUDENT FUND UNIVERSITY SCHOLARSHIP PROGRAM

• *See page 321*

RAIN BIRD COMPANY SCHOLARSHIP

One-time need-based award for student in final two years of undergraduate study in landscape architecture. 300-word essay on career goals and how recipient will contribute to the advancement of the profession is required.

Academic Fields/Career Goals: Landscape Architecture.

Award: Scholarship for use in junior or senior years; not renewable. *Number:* 1. *Amount:* $1000.

Eligibility Requirements: Applicant must be enrolled or expecting to enroll at a four-year institution or university.

Application Requirements: Application, essay, financial need analysis, references. *Deadline:* April 1.

Contact: Ron Figura, Project Manager
Landscape Architecture Foundation
818 18th Street, NW
Suite 810
Washington, DC 20006
Phone: 202-331-7070 Ext. 10
Fax: 202-331-7079
E-mail: rfigura@lafoundation.org

RAYMOND E. PAGE SCHOLARSHIP

Nonrenewable award for any student majoring in landscape architecture in need of financial assistance. Two-page essay describing student's need and how the award will be used is required.

Academic Fields/Career Goals: Landscape Architecture.

Award: Scholarship for use in freshman, sophomore, junior, or senior years; not renewable. *Number:* 1. *Amount:* $1000.

Eligibility Requirements: Applicant must be enrolled or expecting to enroll at a four-year institution or university.

Application Requirements: Application, essay, financial need analysis, references. *Deadline:* April 1.

Contact: Ron Figura, Project Manager
Landscape Architecture Foundation
818 18th Street, NW
Suite 810
Washington, DC 20006
Phone: 202-331-7070 Ext. 10
Fax: 202-331-7079
E-mail: rfigura@lafoundation.org

MONTANA FEDERATION OF GARDEN CLUBS

LIFE MEMBER MONTANA FEDERATION OF GARDEN CLUBS SCHOLARSHIP

• *See page 114*

NATIONAL ASSOCIATION OF WOMEN IN CONSTRUCTION http://nawic.org

NAWIC UNDERGRADUATE SCHOLARSHIPS

• *See page 77*

NATIONAL GARDEN CLUBS, INC. http://www.gardenclub.org

NATIONAL GARDEN CLUBS, INC. SCHOLARSHIP PROGRAM

• *See page 60*

NATIONAL STONE, SAND AND GRAVEL ASSOCIATION (NSSGA) http://www.nssga.org

AMERICAN SOCIETY OF LANDSCAPE ARCHITECTS/NSSGA STUDENT COMPETITION

Students must design a reclamation project using an abandoned quarry or sand and gravel mine. Students are encouraged to research their state reclamation laws and regulations as well as local zoning ordinances. These may affect their proposed project. Groups submitting entries may have no more than three members. Contest format: First prize winner receives $3,400, second prize $1,600, third prize $1,000.

Academic Fields/Career Goals: Landscape Architecture.

Award: Prize for use in senior, or graduate years; not renewable. *Number:* 3. *Amount:* $1000–$3400.

Eligibility Requirements: Applicant must be enrolled or expecting to enroll full-time at a four-year institution or university. Available to U.S. and non-U.S. citizens.

Application Requirements: Application, applicant must enter a contest, essay, transcript, project design boards. *Deadline:* May 15.

Contact: ASCA/NSSGA Student Competition
National Stone, Sand and Gravel Association (NSSGA)
2101 Wilson Boulevard, Suite 100
Arlington, VA 22201-3062
Phone: 703-525-8788
Fax: 703-525-7782
E-mail: info@nssga.org

NETWORK OF EXECUTIVE WOMEN IN HOSPITALITY http://www.newh.org

NETWORK OF EXECUTIVE WOMEN IN HOSPITALITY, INC. SCHOLARSHIP
• *See page 78*

NEW YORK STATE EDUCATION DEPARTMENT http://www.highered.nysed.gov

REGENTS PROFESSIONAL OPPORTUNITY SCHOLARSHIP
• *See page 45*

PROFESSIONAL CONSTRUCTION ESTIMATORS ASSOCIATION http://www.pcea.org

TED WILSON MEMORIAL SCHOLARSHIP FOUNDATION
• *See page 188*

PROFESSIONAL GROUNDS MANAGEMENT SOCIETY http://www.pgms.org

ANNE SEAMAN PROFESSIONAL GROUNDS MANAGEMENT SOCIETY MEMORIAL SCHOLARSHIP
• *See page 61*

UNITED AGRIBUSINESS LEAGUE http://www.ual.org

UNITED AGRIBUSINESS LEAGUE SCHOLARSHIP PROGRAM
• *See page 56*

UNITED AGRICULTURAL BENEFIT TRUST SCHOLARSHIP
• *See page 56*

WORLDSTUDIO FOUNDATION http://www.worldstudio.org

WORLDSTUDIO FOUNDATION SCHOLARSHIP PROGRAM
• *See page 80*

LAW ENFORCEMENT/POLICE ADMINISTRATION

ALASKA STATE TROOPERS http://www.dps.state.ak.us/ast

MICHAEL MURPHY MEMORIAL SCHOLARSHIP LOAN FUND
• *See page 177*

ALBERTA HERITAGE SCHOLARSHIP FUND/ ALBERTA SCHOLARSHIP PROGRAMS http://www.alis.gov.ab.ca/scholarships

ROBERT C. CARSON MEMORIAL BURSARY
• *See page 177*

AMERICAN SOCIETY OF CRIMINOLOGY http://www.ASC41.com

AMERICAN SOCIETY OF CRIMINOLOGY GENE CARTE STUDENT PAPER COMPETITION
• *See page 178*

CONNECTICUT ASSOCIATION OF WOMEN POLICE http://www.cawp.net

CONNECTICUT ASSOCIATION OF WOMEN POLICE SCHOLARSHIP
• *See page 178*

FLORIDA POLICE CORPS http://www.floridapolicecorps.com

FLORIDA POLICE CORPS SCHOLARSHIPS
• *See page 178*

GOVERNOR'S OFFICE

GOVERNOR'S OPPORTUNITY SCHOLARSHIP
• *See page 124*

ILLINOIS POLICE CORPS http://www.ptb.state.il.us/police_corps/index.shtml

ILLINOIS POLICE CORPS SCHOLARSHIP

Scholarships available for students seeking careers in law enforcement. Up to $15,000 for tuition or reimbursement of educational expenses. Must agree to commit to four years of employment with a participating Illinois law enforcement agency. Check Web site for updated information on available funding, application, and requirements: http://www.ptb.state.il.us/policecorps/default.html

Academic Fields/Career Goals: Law Enforcement/Police Administration.

Award: Scholarship for use in junior or senior years. *Number:* 10. *Amount:* up to $23,000.

Eligibility Requirements: Applicant must be enrolled or expecting to enroll at a four-year institution or university. Applicant must have 2.5 GPA or higher. Available to U.S. citizens.

Application Requirements: Application, driver's license, interview, references, transcript. *Deadline:* Continuous.

Contact: Cynthia Bowman, Scholarship Committee
Illinois Police Corps
600 South Second Street, Suite 300
Springfield, IL 62704-2542
Phone: 309-298-3350
Fax: 309-298-2515
E-mail: policecorps@wiu.edu

INDIANA SHERIFFS' ASSOCIATION

INDIANA SHERIFFS' ASSOCIATION SCHOLARSHIP PROGRAM
• *See page 178*

INTERNATIONAL ASSOCIATION OF ARSON INVESTIGATORS EDUCATIONAL FOUNDATION, INC. http://www.fire-investigators.org/

JOHN CHARLES WILSON SCHOLARSHIP
• *See page 269*

LEARNING FOR LIFE http://www.learning-for-life.org/exploring

BUREAU OF ALCOHOL, TOBACCO, FIREARMS AND EXPLOSIVES SCHOLARSHIP-LAW ENFORCEMENT

As part of the Learning for Life-Exploring Program the ATFRA Scholarships are presented every even-numbered year to Law Enforcement Explorers whose achievements reflect the high degree of motivation, commitment, and community concern that epitomizes the law enforcement profession. For more information visit Web site http://www.learning-for-life.org/exploring. Applicant must be younger than 21 years of age.

Academic Fields/Career Goals: Law Enforcement/Police Administration.

Award: Scholarship for use in freshman, sophomore, junior, or senior years; not renewable. *Number:* 2. *Amount:* $1000.

Eligibility Requirements: Applicant must be age 20 or under and enrolled or expecting to enroll full-time at a two-year or four-year institution or university. Available to U.S. citizens.

Learning for Life (continued)

Application Requirements: Application, essay, references, transcript. *Deadline:* varies.

Contact: Learning for Life
1325 West Walnut Hill Lane, Sum 310
PO Box 152079
Irving, TX 75015-2079
Phone: 972-580-2000

CAPTAIN JAMES J. REGAN SCHOLARSHIP

The National Technical Investigators Association presents two one-time $500 scholarships annually. Criteria include academic record, leadership, extracurricular activities, and a personal statement on "What significance I place on a technical background in law enforcement." For more information visit http://www.learning-for-life.org/exploring. Applicant must be younger than 21 years of age.

Academic Fields/Career Goals: Law Enforcement/Police Administration.

Award: Scholarship for use in freshman, sophomore, junior, or senior years; not renewable. *Number:* 2. *Amount:* $500.

Eligibility Requirements: Applicant must be age 20 or under and enrolled or expecting to enroll full-time at a four-year institution or university. Available to U.S. citizens.

Application Requirements: Application, essay, references, transcript. *Deadline:* varies.

Contact: Learning for Life
1325 West Walnut Hill Lane, Sum 310
PO Box 152079
Irving, TX 75015-2079
Phone: 972-580-2000

DEA DRUG ABUSE PREVENTION SERVICE AWARDS

The DEA Drug Abuse Prevention Service Award consists of an engraved plaque and a $1,000 award, which will be presented in recognition of "an act or actions representing a contribution of outstanding service in drug abuse prevention." For more information visit http://www.learning-for-life.org/exploring. Applicant must be younger than 21 years of age.

Academic Fields/Career Goals: Law Enforcement/Police Administration.

Award: Prize for use in freshman, sophomore, junior, or senior years; not renewable. *Number:* 1. *Amount:* $1000.

Eligibility Requirements: Applicant must be age 20 or under; enrolled or expecting to enroll full-time at an institution or university and must have an interest in designated field specified by sponsor. Available to U.S. citizens.

Application Requirements: Application. *Deadline:* varies.

Contact: Learning for Life
1325 West Walnut Hill Lane, Sum 310
PO Box 152079
Irving, TX 75015-2079
Phone: 972-580-2000

FEDERAL CRIMINAL INVESTIGATORS' SERVICE AWARD

Federal Investigators Association recognizes Explorers who render outstanding service to law enforcement agencies with a $500 U.S. Savings bond and plaque. Please visit Web site http://www.learning-for-life.org/exploring for information and application. Applicant must be younger than 21 years of age.

Academic Fields/Career Goals: Law Enforcement/Police Administration.

Award: Prize for use in freshman, sophomore, junior, or senior years; not renewable. *Number:* varies. *Amount:* $500.

Eligibility Requirements: Applicant must be age 20 or under and enrolled or expecting to enroll at an institution or university. Available to U.S. citizens.

Application Requirements: Application. *Deadline:* varies.

Contact: Learning for Life
1325 West Walnut Hill Lane, Sum 310
PO Box 152079
Irving, TX 75015-2079
Phone: 972-580-2000

FLOYD BORING AWARD

The director of the U.S. Secret Service presents two scholarships annually to a law enforcement Explorer whose achievements reflect the high degree of motivation, commitment, and community concern that epitomizes the law enforcement profession. For more information visit http://www.learning-for-life.org/exploring. Applicant must be younger than 21 years of age.

Academic Fields/Career Goals: Law Enforcement/Police Administration.

Award: Scholarship for use in freshman, sophomore, junior, or senior years; not renewable. *Number:* 2. *Amount:* $2000.

Eligibility Requirements: Applicant must be age 20 or under and enrolled or expecting to enroll full-time at a four-year institution or university. Available to U.S. citizens.

Application Requirements: Application, essay, photo, references, transcript. *Deadline:* varies.

Contact: Learning for Life
1325 West Walnut Hill Lane, Sum 310
PO Box 152079
Irving, TX 75015-2079
Phone: 972-580-2000

SHERYL A. HORAK MEMORIAL SCHOLARSHIP

One-time, $1,000 scholarship based on merit. For more information visit http://www.learning-for-life.org/exploring. Applicant must be younger than 21 years of age.

Academic Fields/Career Goals: Law Enforcement/Police Administration.

Award: Scholarship for use in freshman, sophomore, junior, or senior years; not renewable. *Number:* 1–2. *Amount:* $1000.

Eligibility Requirements: Applicant must be age 20 or under and enrolled or expecting to enroll full-time at a two-year or four-year institution or university. Available to U.S. citizens.

Application Requirements: Application, essay, photo, references, transcript. *Deadline:* varies.

Contact: Learning for Life
1325 West Walnut Hill Lane, Sum 310
PO Box 152079
Irving, TX 75015-2079
Phone: 972-580-2000

MISSISSIPPI POLICE CORPS http://www.mississippipolicecorps.org

MISSISSIPPI POLICE CORPS SCHOLARSHIP

• *See page 178*

MISSOURI POLICE CORPS http://www.mocorps.org

MISSOURI POLICE CORPS FUND

• *See page 179*

NATIONAL BLACK POLICE ASSOCIATION http://www.blackpolice.org

ALPHONSO DEAL SCHOLARSHIP AWARD

• *See page 179*

NORTH CAROLINA POLICE CORPS http://www.ncpolicecorps.org

NORTH CAROLINA POLICE CORPS SCHOLARSHIP

• *See page 179*

NORTH CAROLINA STATE EDUCATION ASSISTANCE AUTHORITY http://www.cfnc.org

NORTH CAROLINA SHERIFFS' ASSOCIATION UNDERGRADUATE CRIMINAL JUSTICE SCHOLARSHIPS
• *See page 179*

SOUTH DAKOTA RETAILERS ASSOCIATION http://www.sdra.org

SOUTH DAKOTA RETAILERS ASSOCIATION SCHOLARSHIP PROGRAM
• *See page 47*

UTAH POLICE CORPS http://www.policecorps.utah.gov

UTAH POLICE CORPS SCHOLARSHIP PROGRAM

Once accepted into this program we will pay up to $7500 per academic year for a degree with any major. Years completed before acceptance into our program are reimbursed for a total of up to $15,000. Students must attend and pass our police training academy and complete four years with one of Utah's sponsoring law enforcement agencies.

Academic Fields/Career Goals: Law Enforcement/Police Administration.

Award: Scholarship for use in senior, graduate, or postgraduate years; renewable. *Number:* 30. *Amount:* $7500–$15,000.

Eligibility Requirements: Applicant must be enrolled or expecting to enroll full-time at a four-year institution or university. Available to U.S. citizens.

Application Requirements: Application, autobiography, driver's license, interview, photo, resume, references, test scores, transcript. *Deadline:* Continuous.

Contact: Arlene Bobowski, Office Specialist
Utah Police Corps
4525 South 2700 West
Salt Lake City, UT 84119-1775
Phone: 801-965-4650
Fax: 801-965-4292
E-mail: abobowski@utah.gov

LAW/LEGAL SERVICES

ALBERTA HERITAGE SCHOLARSHIP FUND/ ALBERTA SCHOLARSHIP PROGRAMS http://www.alis.gov.ab.ca/scholarships

ROBERT C. CARSON MEMORIAL BURSARY
• *See page 177*

AMERICAN CRIMINAL JUSTICE ASSOCIATION-LAMBDA ALPHA EPSILON http://www.acjalae.org

AMERICAN CRIMINAL JUSTICE ASSOCIATION-LAMBDA ALPHA EPSILON NATIONAL SCHOLARSHIP
• *See page 177*

AMERICAN HISTORICAL ASSOCIATION http://www.theaha.org

LITTLETON-GRISWOLD PRIZE
• *See page 310*

AMERICAN SOCIETY OF CRIMINOLOGY http://www.ASC41.com

AMERICAN SOCIETY OF CRIMINOLOGY GENE CARTE STUDENT PAPER COMPETITION
• *See page 178*

ASIAN PACIFIC AMERICAN HERITAGE COUNCIL http://www.apahc.org

ASIAN PACIFIC AMERICAN HERITAGE COUNCIL SCHOLARSHIP
• *See page 121*

BOYS AND GIRLS CLUBS OF GREATER SAN DIEGO http://www.sdyouth.org

SPENCE REESE SCHOLARSHIP FUND
• *See page 242*

BUSINESS AND PROFESSIONAL WOMEN'S FOUNDATION http://www.bpwusa.org

BPW CAREER ADVANCEMENT SCHOLARSHIP PROGRAM FOR WOMEN
• *See page 112*

CIRI FOUNDATION http://www.ciri.com/tcf

JOHN N. COLBERG ENDOWMENT SCHOLARSHIP FUND

To encourage students seeking an undergraduate or graduate degree in law. Applicant must be Alaska Native student, with a 2.5 GPA or better. For more details see Web site: http://www.ciri.com/tcf.

Academic Fields/Career Goals: Law/Legal Services.

Award: Scholarship for use in freshman, sophomore, junior, senior, or graduate years; not renewable. *Number:* varies. *Amount:* varies.

Eligibility Requirements: Applicant must be enrolled or expecting to enroll full-time at a two-year or four-year institution or university. Applicant must have 2.5 GPA or higher.

Application Requirements: Application, essay, references, transcript, proof of eligibility, birth certificate or adoption decree. *Deadline:* June 1.

Contact: CIRI Foundation
2600 Cordova Street, Suite 206
Anchorage, AK 99503
Phone: 907-263-5582
Fax: 907-263-5588
E-mail: tcf@ciri.com

LAWRENCE MATSON MEMORIAL ENDOWMENT SCHOLARSHIP FUND
• *See page 86*

COLLEGEBOUND FOUNDATION http://www.collegeboundfoundation.org

DECATUR H. MILLER SCHOLARSHIP
• *See page 310*

JEANETTE R. WOLMAN SCHOLARSHIP

Award for Baltimore City public high school graduates. Please see Web site: http://www.collegeboundfoundation.org for complete information on application process. Must major in pre-law, social work or a field that focuses on child advocacy. Minimum GPA of 3.0. Must submit CollegeBound Competitive Scholarship/Last-Dollar Grant Application.

Academic Fields/Career Goals: Law/Legal Services; Social Sciences.

Award: Scholarship for use in freshman, sophomore, junior, or senior years; renewable. *Number:* 1. *Amount:* $500.

Eligibility Requirements: Applicant must be enrolled or expecting to enroll full-time at a two-year or four-year institution or university and resident of Maryland. Applicant must have 3.0 GPA or higher. Available to U.S. citizens.

Application Requirements: Application, financial need analysis, transcript, financial aid award letters, Student Aid Report. *Deadline:* March 19.

Contact: April Bell, Associate Program Director
CollegeBound Foundation
300 Water Street, Suite 300
Baltimore, MD 21202
Phone: 410-783-2905 Ext. 208
Fax: 410-727-5786
E-mail: abell@collegeboundfoundation.org

CULTURE CONNECTION http://www.thecultureconnection.com

CULTURE CONNECTION FOUNDATION SCHOLARSHIP
• *See page 52*

GRAND RAPIDS COMMUNITY FOUNDATION http://www.grfoundation.org

WARNER NORCROSS AND JUDD LLP SCHOLARSHIP FOR MINORITY STUDENTS

Financial assistance to students who are residents of Michigan, or attend a college/university/vocational school in Michigan, and are of racial and ethnic minority heritage pursuing a career in law, paralegal, or a legal secretarial program. Law school scholarship ($5000), paralegal scholarship ($2000), legal secretary scholarship ($1000). Refer to Web site for details and an application.

Academic Fields/Career Goals: Law/Legal Services.

Award: Scholarship for use in freshman, sophomore, junior, or senior years; not renewable. *Number:* up to 3. *Amount:* $1000–$5000.

Eligibility Requirements: Applicant must be American Indian/Alaska Native, Asian/Pacific Islander, Black (non-Hispanic), or Hispanic and enrolled or expecting to enroll at a two-year or four-year institution or university. Applicant must have 2.5 GPA or higher.

Application Requirements: Application, essay, financial need analysis, references, transcript. *Deadline:* April 1.

Contact: See Web site.

GREATER KANAWHA VALLEY FOUNDATION http://www.tgkvf.org

BERNICE PICKINS PARSONS FUND

Renewable award open to students pursuing education or training in the fields of library science, nursing and paraprofessional training in the legal field. May apply for two Foundation scholarships, but will only be chosen for one. Grant based on financial need. Must be a resident of West Virginia.

Academic Fields/Career Goals: Law/Legal Services; Library and Information Sciences; Nursing.

Award: Grant for use in freshman, sophomore, junior, or senior years; renewable. *Number:* 7. *Amount:* $1000.

Eligibility Requirements: Applicant must be enrolled or expecting to enroll full-time at a four-year institution or university and resident of West Virginia. Applicant must have 2.5 GPA or higher. Available to U.S. citizens.

Application Requirements: Application, essay, financial need analysis, references, self-addressed stamped envelope, test scores, transcript. *Deadline:* February 17.

Contact: Susan Hoover, Scholarship Coordinator
Greater Kanawha Valley Foundation
PO Box 3041
Charleston, WV 25331
Phone: 304-346-3620
Fax: 304-346-3640
E-mail: shoover@tgkvf.org

JEWISH FEDERATION OF METROPOLITAN CHICAGO (JFMC) http://www.jvschicago.org

JEWISH FEDERATION OF METROPOLITAN CHICAGO ACADEMIC SCHOLARSHIP PROGRAM

• *See page 185*

LINCOLN COMMUNITY FOUNDATION http://www.lcf.org

LAWRENCE "LARRY" FRAZIER MEMORIAL SCHOLARSHIP

• *See page 100*

MARYLAND HIGHER EDUCATION COMMISSION http://www.mhec.state.md.us

GRADUATE AND PROFESSIONAL SCHOLARSHIP PROGRAM-MARYLAND

• *See page 186*

JANET L. HOFFMANN LOAN ASSISTANCE REPAYMENT PROGRAM

• *See page 206*

NATIONAL ASSOCIATION OF WATER COMPANIES http://www.nawc.org

J.J. BARR SCHOLARSHIP

• *See page 115*

NATIONAL ASSOCIATION OF WATER COMPANIES-NEW JERSEY CHAPTER

NATIONAL ASSOCIATION OF WATER COMPANIES-NEW JERSEY CHAPTER SCHOLARSHIP

• *See page 115*

NATIONAL BLACK POLICE ASSOCIATION http://www.blackpolice.org

ALPHONSO DEAL SCHOLARSHIP AWARD

• *See page 179*

NATIONAL FEDERATION OF PARALEGAL ASSOCIATIONS, INC. (NFPA) http://www.paralegals.org

NATIONAL FEDERATION OF PARALEGAL ASSOCIATES, INC. WEST SCHOLARSHIP

Paralegal scholarship. Minimum GPA of 3.0 required. Application deadline is February 1.

Academic Fields/Career Goals: Law/Legal Services.

Award: Scholarship for use in freshman, sophomore, junior, senior, graduate, or postgraduate years; not renewable. *Number:* 2. *Amount:* $1500–$3500.

Eligibility Requirements: Applicant must be enrolled or expecting to enroll full or part-time at a two-year or four-year or technical institution or university. Applicant must have 3.0 GPA or higher. Available to U.S. and non-U.S. citizens.

Application Requirements: Application, essay, references, transcript. *Deadline:* February 1.

Contact: Teri Nelson
National Federation of Paralegal Associations, Inc. (NFPA)
2517 Eastlake
Seattle, WA 98102
Phone: 206-652-4120
Fax: 206-652-4122
E-mail: info@paralegals.org

NATIONAL FEDERATION OF THE BLIND http://www.nfb.org

HOWARD BROWN RICKARD SCHOLARSHIP

• *See page 78*

NEW YORK STATE EDUCATION DEPARTMENT http://www.highered.nysed.gov

REGENTS PROFESSIONAL OPPORTUNITY SCHOLARSHIP

• *See page 45*

PNC BANK TRUST DEPARTMENT

H. FLETCHER BROWN SCHOLARSHIP

• *See page 187*

TKE EDUCATIONAL FOUNDATION http://www.tkefoundation.org

HARRY J. DONNELLY MEMORIAL SCHOLARSHIP

• *See page 47*

UNITED NEGRO COLLEGE FUND http://www.uncf.org

RAYMOND W. CANNON MEMORIAL SCHOLARSHIP PROGRAM

• *See page 304*

UNCF/PFIZER CORPORATE SCHOLARS PROGRAM

• *See page 64*

LIBRARY AND INFORMATION SCIENCES

ALICE L. HALTOM EDUCATIONAL FUND http://www.alhef.org

ALICE L. HALTOM EDUCATIONAL FUND SCHOLARSHIP

• *See page 168*

AMERICAN SOCIETY FOR INFORMATION SCIENCE AND TECHNOLOGY http://www.asis.org

JOHN WILEY & SONS BEST JASIST PAPER AWARD

• *See page 168*

GREATER KANAWHA VALLEY FOUNDATION http://www.tgkvf.org

BERNICE PICKINS PARSONS FUND

• *See page 344*

IDAHO LIBRARY ASSOCIATION http://www.idaholibraries.org

IDAHO LIBRARY ASSOCIATION LIBRARY SCIENCE SCHOLARSHIPS

One-time award for students studying library science. Must be a member of the Idaho Library Association. Must be a resident of Idaho.

Academic Fields/Career Goals: Library and Information Sciences.

Award: Scholarship for use in freshman, sophomore, junior, senior, or graduate years; not renewable. *Number:* 2–6. *Amount:* $100–$500.

Eligibility Requirements: Applicant must be enrolled or expecting to enroll full or part-time at a two-year or four-year institution or university and resident of Idaho. Applicant or parent of applicant must be member of Idaho Library Association. Available to U.S. and non-U.S. citizens.

Application Requirements: Application, essay, resume, references. *Deadline:* September 1.

Contact: Wayne Gunter, Chairperson, Scholarships, Recruitment and Awards
Idaho Library Association
1407 Cedar Street
Sandpoint, ID 83864-2052
Phone: 208-263-6930 Ext. 208
Fax: 208-263-8320
E-mail: wayne@ebcl.lib.id.us

INDIANA LIBRARY FEDERATION http://www.ilfonline.org

AIME SCHOLARSHIP FUND

Scholarships are provided for undergraduate or graduate students entering or currently enrolled in a program to receive educational certification in the field of School Library Media Services. For more details see Web site: http://www.ilfonline.org.

Academic Fields/Career Goals: Library and Information Sciences.

Award: Scholarship for use in freshman, sophomore, junior, senior, or graduate years; not renewable. *Number:* varies. *Amount:* up to $500.

Eligibility Requirements: Applicant must be enrolled or expecting to enroll at an institution or university. Available to U.S. citizens.

Application Requirements: Application. *Deadline:* January 3.

Contact: Application available at Web site.

PENNSYLVANIA LIBRARY ASSOCIATION http://www.palibraries.org

BRODART/PENNSYLVANIA LIBRARY ASSOCIATION UNDERGRADUATE SCHOLARSHIP GRANT

Applicant must be enrolled in a state certified institution and must complete a minimum of 3 credits in library science courses leading to state certification. Credits must be completed during the summer session or academic year (September through May) which begins the year of the scholarship award.

Academic Fields/Career Goals: Library and Information Sciences.

Award: Scholarship for use in freshman, sophomore, junior, or senior years; not renewable. *Number:* varies. *Amount:* up to $2000.

Eligibility Requirements: Applicant must be enrolled or expecting to enroll full or part-time at a two-year or four-year institution or university; resident of Pennsylvania and studying in Pennsylvania. Available to U.S. citizens.

Application Requirements: Application. *Deadline:* May 15.

Contact: Ellen Wharton, Administrative Assistant
Pennsylvania Library Association
220 Cumberland Parkway, Suite 10
Mechanicsburg, PA 17055-5683
Phone: 717-766-7663
Fax: 717-766-5440
E-mail: ellen@palibraries.org

SPECIAL LIBRARIES ASSOCIATION http://www.sla.org

SPECIAL LIBRARIES ASSOCIATION SCHOLARSHIP

Up to three scholarships available to graduating college seniors and master's candidates enrolled in a program for library science. May be used for tuition, fees, research, and other related costs. Members of SLA preferred. One-time awards of $6000 each.

Academic Fields/Career Goals: Library and Information Sciences.

Award: Scholarship for use in senior, or graduate years; not renewable. *Number:* up to 3. *Amount:* $6000.

Eligibility Requirements: Applicant must be enrolled or expecting to enroll full or part-time at a four-year institution or university. Available to U.S. citizens.

Application Requirements: Application, essay, financial need analysis, interview, references, test scores, transcript. *Deadline:* October 31.

Contact: Diana Gonzalez, Membership Coordinator
Special Libraries Association
1700 18th Street, NW
Washington, DC 20009-2514
Phone: 202-234-4700 Ext. 671
Fax: 202-265-9317

UNITED NEGRO COLLEGE FUND http://www.uncf.org

C-SPAN SCHOLARSHIP PROGRAM

• *See page 166*

LITERATURE/ENGLISH/WRITING

ACTORS THEATRE OF LOUISVILLE

NATIONAL TEN MINUTE PLAY CONTEST

Writers from across the country compete for prizes by submitting short plays (10 pages or less). Plays are considered for our annual Apprentice Showcase, The Humana Festival of New American Plays and the $1000 Heideman Award. Must be U.S. citizen. Deadline is December 1.

Academic Fields/Career Goals: Literature/English/Writing.

Award: Prize for use in freshman, sophomore, junior, senior, or graduate years; not renewable. *Number:* 1. *Amount:* $1000.

Eligibility Requirements: Applicant must be enrolled or expecting to enroll full or part-time at a two-year or four-year or technical institution or university. Available to U.S. citizens.

Application Requirements: Applicant must enter a contest. *Deadline:* December 1.

Contact: Tanya Palmer, Literary Manager
Actors Theatre of Louisville
316 West Main Street
Louisville, KY 40202-4218
Phone: 502-584-1265 Ext. 3033
Fax: 502-561-3300
E-mail: tpalmer@actorstheatre.org

AIM MAGAZINE SHORT STORY CONTEST http://www.aimmagazine.org

AMERICA'S INTERCULTURAL MAGAZINE (AIM) SHORT STORY CONTEST

Short fiction award for a previously unpublished story that embodies our goal of furthering the brotherhood of man through the written word. Proof that

Aim Magazine Short Story Contest (continued)

people from different racial/ethnic backgrounds are more alike than they are different. Maximum length 4,000 words. Story should not moralize. August 15 is deadline.

Academic Fields/Career Goals: Literature/English/Writing.

Award: Prize for use in freshman, sophomore, junior, senior, or graduate years; not renewable. *Number:* 1–2. *Amount:* $75–$100.

Eligibility Requirements: Applicant must be enrolled or expecting to enroll at a two-year or four-year or technical institution or university.

Application Requirements: Applicant must enter a contest. *Deadline:* August 15.

Contact: Mark Boone, Fiction Editor
Aim Magazine Short Story Contest
PO Box 1174
Maywood, IL 60153

ALLIANCE FOR YOUNG ARTISTS AND WRITERS, INC. http://www.artandwriting.org

SCHOLASTIC ART AND WRITING AWARDS-ART SECTION

• *See page 85*

SCHOLASTIC ART AND WRITING AWARDS-WRITING SECTION SCHOLARSHIP

• *See page 85*

AMERICAN AUTOMOBILE ASSOCIATION http://aaapublicaffairs.com

NATIONAL SENIOR HIGH COMMUNICATION CONTEST

• *See page 267*

AMERICAN FOUNDATION FOR THE BLIND http://www.afb.org

R.L. GILLETTE SCHOLARSHIP

Award for legally blind female students who are enrolled in a four-year undergraduate program in music or literature. For additional information, refer to Web site: http://www.afb.org.

Academic Fields/Career Goals: Literature/English/Writing; Music.

Award: Scholarship for use in freshman, sophomore, junior, or senior years; not renewable. *Number:* up to 2. *Amount:* up to $1000.

Eligibility Requirements: Applicant must be enrolled or expecting to enroll full-time at a four-year institution or university and female. Applicant must be visually impaired. Available to U.S. citizens.

Application Requirements: Application, essay, financial need analysis, references, transcript, performance tape, creative writing sample evidence of legal blindness. *Deadline:* April 30.

Contact: Information Center
American Foundation for the Blind
11 Penn Plaza, Suite 300
New York, NY 10001
Phone: 212-502-7661
Fax: 212-502-7771
E-mail: afbinfo@afb.net

AMERICAN LEGION AUXILIARY, DEPARTMENT OF WASHINGTON http://www.walegion-aux.org

FLORENCE LEMCKE MEMORIAL SCHOLARSHIP IN FINE ARTS

• *See page 84*

AMY LOWELL POETRY TRAVELING SCHOLARSHIP TRUST http://www.amylowell.org

AMY LOWELL POETRY TRAVELING SCHOLARSHIP

The Amy Lowell Poetry Traveling Scholarship awards a scholarship each year to a poet of American birth. Upon acceptance, the recipient agrees to spend one year outside the continent of North America in a place deemed by the recipient suitable to advance the art of poetry. At the end of the year, the recipient shall submit at least three poems for consideration by the trust's committee. Application request deadline is October 1. Application submission deadline is October 15. For additional information visit Web site: http://www.amylowell.org

Academic Fields/Career Goals: Literature/English/Writing.

Award: Scholarship for use in freshman, sophomore, junior, senior, graduate, or postgraduate years; not renewable. *Number:* 1. *Amount:* $37,000.

Eligibility Requirements: Applicant must be enrolled or expecting to enroll at a two-year or four-year or technical institution or university. Available to U.S. citizens.

Application Requirements: Application, applicant must enter a contest, poetry sample. *Deadline:* October 15.

Contact: Pearl Bell, Trust Administrator
Amy Lowell Poetry Traveling Scholarship Trust
Exchange Place
Boston, MA 02109-2891
Phone: 617-248-5000
Fax: 617-248-4000

ATLANTA PRESS CLUB, INC. http://www.atlpressclub.org

ATLANTA PRESS CLUB JOURNALISM SCHOLARSHIP PROGRAM

• *See page 158*

CASE WESTERN RESERVE UNIVERSITY http://www.cwru.edu/artsci/thtr

MARC A. KLEIN PLAYWRIGHT AWARD

Annual competition among student playwrights with cash award of $1000. Play receives a full mainstage production. Contact Department of Theater Arts for application; playwrights must be enrolled at an American college or university.

Academic Fields/Career Goals: Literature/English/Writing; Performing Arts.

Award: Prize for use in freshman, sophomore, junior, senior, or graduate years; not renewable. *Number:* 1. *Amount:* $1000.

Eligibility Requirements: Applicant must be enrolled or expecting to enroll at a four-year institution or university.

Application Requirements: Application, play. *Deadline:* December 1.

Contact: Scarlett Grala, Departmental Assistant IV
Case Western Reserve University
CWRU Department of Theater Arts
10900 Euclid Avenue
Cleveland, OH 44106-7077
Phone: 216-368-4868
Fax: 216-368-5184
E-mail: ksg@po.cwru.edu

CENTER FOR LESBIAN AND GAY STUDIES (C.L.A.G.S.) http://www.clags.org

CENTER FOR GAY AND LESBIAN STUDIES UNDERGRADUATE PAPER AWARDS

A cash prize of $250 will be awarded to the best paper written in a CUNY or SUNY undergraduate class on a topic related to gay, lesbian, bisexual, queer, or transgender experiences. Essays should be between 15 and 50 pages, well thought-out, and fully realized.

Academic Fields/Career Goals: Literature/English/Writing; Social Sciences.

Award: Prize for use in freshman, sophomore, junior, or senior years; not renewable. *Number:* 1. *Amount:* $250.

Eligibility Requirements: Applicant must be enrolled or expecting to enroll full or part-time at an institution or university; resident of New York and studying in New York. Available to U.S. and non-U.S. citizens.

Application Requirements: Applicant must enter a contest, essay. *Deadline:* June 1.

Contact: Lavelle Porter, Office Staff
Center for Lesbian and Gay Studies (C.L.A.G.S.)
365 Fifth Avenue
Room 7115
New York, NY 10016
Phone: 212-817-1955
Fax: 212-817-1567
E-mail: clags@gc.cuny.edu

CIRI FOUNDATION http://www.ciri.com/tcf

CIRI FOUNDATION SUSIE QIMMIQSAK BEVINS ENDOWMENT SCHOLARSHIP FUND

• *See page 86*

CULTURAL FELLOWSHIP GRANTS

Applicant must be accepted or enrolled in a seminar or conference that is accredited, authorized, or approved by the CIRI Foundation. May reapply each quarter until grant cap is reached and may reapply the following year. Must be Alaska Native Student, CIRI original enrollee, or descendant. Award is intended to encourage applicants in perpetuating and transmitting the visual, literary, and performing arts of Alaska's first people. Application deadlines are March 31, June 30, September 30, and December 1.

Academic Fields/Career Goals: Literature/English/Writing; Performing Arts.

Award: Grant for use in freshman, sophomore, junior, senior, graduate, or postgraduate years; not renewable. *Number:* varies. *Amount:* up to $500.

Eligibility Requirements: Applicant must be age 18 and enrolled or expecting to enroll full or part-time at a two-year or four-year institution or university. Applicant must have 2.5 GPA or higher.

Application Requirements: Application, essay, references, transcript, proof of eligibility, birth certificate or adoption decree. *Deadline:* varies.

Contact: CIRI Foundation
2600 Cordova Street, Suite 206
Anchorage, AK 99503
Phone: 907-263-5582
Fax: 907-263-5588
E-mail: tcf@ciri.com

GUIDEPOSTS MAGAZINE http://www.guideposts.com

GUIDEPOSTS YOUNG WRITER'S CONTEST

Entrants must be either a high school junior or senior. Submit a first-person story about a memorable or moving experience; story must be a true personal experience of the writer. Authors of top ten manuscripts receive a scholarship. First Prize: $10,000; Second Prize: $8,000; Third Prize: $6,000; Fourth Prize: $4,000; Fifth Prize: $3,000; Sixth through Tenth Prizes: $1,000; Eleventh through Twentieth Prizes receive $250 gift certificate for college supplies. The deadline is the Monday before Thanksgiving.

Academic Fields/Career Goals: Literature/English/Writing.

Award: Scholarship for use in freshman year; not renewable. *Number:* 20. *Amount:* $250–$10,000.

Eligibility Requirements: Applicant must be high school student and planning to enroll or expecting to enroll full or part-time at a two-year or four-year or technical institution or university. Available to U.S. and non-U.S. citizens.

Application Requirements: Applicant must enter a contest, manuscript (maximum 1200 words). *Deadline:* varies.

Contact: Christine Pisani, Secretary
GUIDEPOSTS Magazine
16 East 34th Street, 21st Floor
New York, NY 10016
Phone: 212-251-8107
Fax: 212-684-1311
E-mail: cpisani@guideposts.org

HERB SOCIETY OF AMERICA http://www.herbsociety.org

HERB SOCIETY RESEARCH GRANTS

• *See page 69*

INSTITUTE FOR HUMANE STUDIES http://www.theihs.org

FILM AND FICTION SCHOLARSHIP

• *See page 87*

INTERNATIONAL FOODSERVICE EDITORIAL COUNCIL http://www.ifec-is-us.com

INTERNATIONAL FOODSERVICE EDITORIAL COUNCIL COMMUNICATIONS SCHOLARSHIP

• *See page 160*

JACK J. ISGUR FOUNDATION

JACK J. ISGUR FOUNDATION SCHOLARSHIP

• *See page 87*

LAMBDA IOTA TAU, COLLEGE LITERATURE HONOR SOCIETY http://www.bsu.edu/csh/english/undergraduate/lit/

LAMBDA IOTA TAU LITERATURE SCHOLARSHIP

Scholarships for members of Lambda Iota Tau who are pursuing the study of literature. Must be nominated by chapter sponsor and have 3.5 GPA. Must be an initiated member of Lambda Iota Tau.

Academic Fields/Career Goals: Literature/English/Writing.

Award: Scholarship for use in sophomore, junior, senior, graduate, or postgraduate years; not renewable. *Number:* 3. *Amount:* $1000.

Eligibility Requirements: Applicant must be enrolled or expecting to enroll full-time at a two-year or four-year institution or university. Applicant must have 3.5 GPA or higher. Available to U.S. and non-U.S. citizens.

Application Requirements: Application, essay, references. *Deadline:* June 30.

Contact: Bruce Hozeski, Executive Secretary/Treasurer
Lambda Iota Tau, College Literature Honor Society
Ball State University Department of English
2000 West University Avenue
Muncie, IN 47306-0460
Phone: 765-285-8456
Fax: 765-285-3765
E-mail: bhozeski@bsu.edu

MAINE MEDIA WOMEN SCHOLARSHIPS COMMITTEE http://www.mainemediawomen.org/scholarships.html

MAINE MEDIA WOMEN'S SCHOLARSHIP

• *See page 88*

NATIONAL FEDERATION OF THE BLIND http://www.nfb.org

MICHAEL AND MARIE MARUCCI SCHOLARSHIP

• *See page 283*

NATIONAL FOUNDATION FOR ADVANCEMENT IN THE ARTS http://www.artsawards.org

ARTS RECOGNITION AND TALENT SEARCH (ARTS)

• *See page 89*

NATIONAL WRITERS ASSOCIATION FOUNDATION http://www.nationalwriters.com

NATIONAL WRITERS ASSOCIATION FOUNDATION SCHOLARSHIPS

• *See page 162*

OREGON STUDENT ASSISTANCE COMMISSION http://www.osac.state.or.us

SEHAR SALEHA AHMAD MEMORIAL SCHOLARSHIP

Available to Oregon high school graduates. Award open to students majoring in English. Preference given to females. Minimum 3.5 GPA required.

Academic Fields/Career Goals: Literature/English/Writing.

Oregon Student Assistance Commission (continued)

Award: Scholarship for use in freshman year; renewable. *Number:* varies. *Amount:* $500.

Eligibility Requirements: Applicant must be high school student; planning to enroll or expecting to enroll at an institution or university and resident of Oregon. Applicant must have 3.5 GPA or higher.

Application Requirements: Application, essay, financial need analysis, references, transcript, activity chart. *Deadline:* March 1.

Contact: Director of Grant Programs
Oregon Student Assistance Commission
1500 Valley River Drive, Suite 100
Eugene, OR 97401-7020
Phone: 800-452-8807 Ext. 7395
E-mail: awardinfo@mercury.osac.state.or.us

OUTDOOR WRITERS ASSOCIATION OF AMERICA http://www.owaa.org

OUTDOOR WRITERS ASSOCIATION OF AMERICA BODIE MCDOWELL SCHOLARSHIP AWARD

• *See page 163*

PLAYWRIGHTS' CENTER http://www.pwcenter.org

MANY VOICES RESIDENCY PROGRAM

The Playwrights' Center's Many Voices programs enrich the American theater by offering playwriting residencies to artists of color. Must be U.S. citizen.

Academic Fields/Career Goals: Literature/English/Writing.

Award: Grant for use in freshman, sophomore, junior, senior, graduate, or postgraduate years; not renewable. *Number:* 8. *Amount:* $1200–$2000.

Eligibility Requirements: Applicant must be American Indian/Alaska Native, Asian/Pacific Islander, Black (non-Hispanic), or Hispanic; enrolled or expecting to enroll full or part-time at a two-year or four-year or technical institution or university; resident of Minnesota; studying in Minnesota and must have an interest in writing. Available to U.S. citizens.

Application Requirements: Application. *Deadline:* July 31.

Contact: Stacey Parshall, Many Voices Coordinator
Playwrights' Center
2301 Franklin Avenue East
Minneapolis, MN 55406
Phone: 612-332-7481 Ext. 10
Fax: 612-332-6037
E-mail: staceyp@pwcenter.org

UNITED DAUGHTERS OF THE CONFEDERACY http://www.hqudc.org

HELEN JAMES BREWER SCHOLARSHIP

• *See page 312*

UNITED NEGRO COLLEGE FUND http://www.uncf.org

BRYANT GUMBEL/WALT DISNEY WORLD CELEBRITY GOLF TOURNAMENT SCHOLARSHIP PROGRAM

• *See page 166*

JANET JACKSON/RHYTHM NATION SCHOLARSHIP

• *See page 91*

MICHAEL JACKSON SCHOLARSHIP

• *See page 167*

READER'S DIGEST SCHOLARSHIP

• *See page 167*

TOYOTA SCHOLARSHIP

• *See page 133*

WAVERLY COMMUNITY HOUSE, INC. http://waverlycomm.com

F. LAMMOT BELIN ARTS SCHOLARSHIP

• *See page 80*

WILLA CATHER FOUNDATION http://www.willacather.org

NORMA ROSS WALTER SCHOLARSHIP

Awarded yearly to a Nebraska female high school graduate. Must major in English at any accredited college or university. Must have a minimum 3.0 GPA. Deadline is January 31.

Academic Fields/Career Goals: Literature/English/Writing.

Award: Scholarship for use in freshman year; not renewable. *Number:* 1. *Amount:* $1000.

Eligibility Requirements: Applicant must be enrolled or expecting to enroll full-time at a four-year institution or university; female and resident of Nebraska. Applicant must have 3.0 GPA or higher. Available to U.S. citizens.

Application Requirements: Application, essay, portfolio, references, test scores, transcript. *Deadline:* January 31.

Contact: Betty Kort, Executive Director
Willa Cather Foundation
413 North Webster
Red Cloud, NE 68970
Phone: 402-746-2653
Fax: 402-746-2652
E-mail: bkort@gpcom.net

MARINE BIOLOGY

CALIFORNIA SEA GRANT COLLEGE PROGRAM http://www-csgc.ucsd.edu

JOHN D. ISSACS SCHOLARSHIP

• *See page 113*

CANADIAN RECREATIONAL CANOEING ASSOCIATION http://www.paddlingcanada.com

BILL MASON MEMORIAL SCHOLARSHIP FUND

• *See page 57*

INTERNATIONAL ASSOCIATION OF GREAT LAKES RESEARCH http://www.iaglr.org

PAUL W. RODGERS SCHOLARSHIP

• *See page 190*

LOUISIANA OFFICE OF STUDENT FINANCIAL ASSISTANCE http://www.osfa.state.la.us

ROCKEFELLER STATE WILDLIFE SCHOLARSHIP

• *See page 63*

MARINE/OCEAN ENGINEERING

AMERICAN SOCIETY OF NAVAL ENGINEERS http://www.navalengineers.org

AMERICAN SOCIETY OF NAVAL ENGINEERS SCHOLARSHIP

• *See page 66*

ASSOCIATION FOR IRON AND STEEL TECHNOLOGY http://www.aist.org/foundation/scholarships.htm

ASSOCIATION FOR IRON AND STEEL TECHNOLOGY DAVID H. SAMSON SCHOLARSHIP

• *See page 139*

SOCIETY OF NAVAL ARCHITECTS & MARINE ENGINEERS http://www.sname.org

SOCIETY OF NAVAL ARCHITECTS AND MARINE ENGINEERS UNDERGRADUATE SCHOLARSHIPS
• *See page 255*

MATERIALS SCIENCE, ENGINEERING, AND METALLURGY

ACI INTERNATIONAL/CONCRETE RESEARCH AND EDUCATION FOUNDATION (CONREF) http://www.concrete.org

PETER D. COURTOIS CONCRETE CONSTRUCTION SCHOLARSHIP
• *See page 73*

AEA-OREGON COUNCIL http://www.ous.edu/ecs/scholarships

AEA- OREGON COUNCIL TECHNOLOGY SCHOLARSHIP PROGRAM
• *See page 136*

AMERICAN CHEMICAL SOCIETY http://www.chemistry.org/scholars

AMERICAN CHEMICAL SOCIETY SCHOLARS PROGRAM
• *See page 136*

AMERICAN CHEMICAL SOCIETY, RUBBER DIVISION http://www.rubber.org/awards/scholarships.htm

AMERICAN CHEMICAL SOCIETY, RUBBER DIVISION-UNDERGRADUATE SCHOLARSHIP
• *See page 136*

AMERICAN COUNCIL OF ENGINEERING COMPANIES OF PENNSYLVANIA (ACEC/PA) http://www.acecpa.org

ENGINEERING SCHOLARSHIP
• *See page 136*

AMERICAN ELECTROPLATERS AND SURFACE FINISHERS SOCIETY http://www.aesf.org

AMERICAN ELECTROPLATERS AND SURFACE FINISHERS SCHOLARSHIPS
• *See page 136*

AMERICAN INSTITUTE OF AERONAUTICS AND ASTRONAUTICS http://www.aiaa.org

AIAA UNDERGRADUATE SCHOLARSHIP
• *See page 66*

AMERICAN SOCIETY OF NAVAL ENGINEERS http://www.navalengineers.org

AMERICAN SOCIETY OF NAVAL ENGINEERS SCHOLARSHIP
• *See page 66*

AMERICAN WELDING SOCIETY http://www.aws.org/foundation

ARSHAM AMIRIKIAN ENGINEERING SCHOLARSHIP
• *See page 150*

DONALD AND JEAN CLEVELAND-WILLAMETTE VALLEY SECTION SCHOLARSHIP
• *See page 150*

ASM MATERIALS EDUCATION FOUNDATION http://www.asminternational.org

ASM MATERIALS EDUCATION FOUNDATION SCHOLARSHIPS
• *See page 239*

ASM OUTSTANDING SCHOLARS AWARDS
• *See page 239*

EDWARD J. DULIS SCHOLARSHIP
• *See page 239*

GEORGE A. ROBERTS SCHOLARSHIP
• *See page 239*

JOHN M. HANIAK SCHOLARSHIP
• *See page 239*

NICHOLAS J. GRANT SCHOLARSHIP
• *See page 239*

WILLIAM P. WOODSIDE FOUNDER'S SCHOLARSHIP
• *See page 239*

ASSOCIATION FOR FACILITIES ENGINEERING (AFE)

ASSOCIATION FOR FACILITIES ENGINEERING CEDAR VALLEY CHAPTER # 132 SCHOLARSHIP
• *See page 97*

ASSOCIATION FOR IRON AND STEEL TECHNOLOGY http://www.aist.org/foundation/scholarships.htm

AIST ALFRED B. GLOSSBRENNER AND JOHN KLUSCH SCHOLARSHIPS
• *See page 240*

ASSOCIATION FOR IRON AND STEEL TECHNOLOGY BALTIMORE CHAPTER SCHOLARSHIP

Scholarship for Baltimore Chapter area high school seniors or currently enrolled undergraduate students pursuing a career in engineering or metallurgy. Must be the child, grandchild, or spouse of a member of the Baltimore Chapter of AIST. Student may reapply each year for the term of their college education. Information and application available on Web site: http://www.aist.org/chapters/mc_baltimore_scholar.htm

Academic Fields/Career Goals: Materials Science, Engineering, and Metallurgy.

Award: Scholarship for use in freshman, sophomore, junior, or senior years; not renewable. *Number:* 1. *Amount:* $1500.

Eligibility Requirements: Applicant must be enrolled or expecting to enroll full-time at a four-year institution or university. Available to U.S. citizens.

Application Requirements: Application, essay, test scores, transcript. *Deadline:* April 30.

Contact: Thomas Russo, AIST Baltimore Member Chapter Scholarships/Division Manager Steelmaking
Association for Iron and Steel Technology
5111 North Point Boulevard
Sparrows Point, MD 21219-1014

ASSOCIATION FOR IRON AND STEEL TECHNOLOGY BENJAMIN F. FAIRLESS SCHOLARSHIP

Scholarships available to students of metallurgy, metallurgical engineering, or materials science, who have a genuine interest in a career in ferrous related industries as demonstrated by an internship, co-op, or related experience or who have plans to pursue such experiences during college. Student may apply after first term of freshman year of college and must join the AIST at the student rate. The Web site contains further information.

Academic Fields/Career Goals: Materials Science, Engineering, and Metallurgy.

Award: Scholarship for use in freshman, sophomore, junior, or senior years; not renewable. *Number:* 2. *Amount:* $2000.

Eligibility Requirements: Applicant must be enrolled or expecting to enroll full-time at a four-year institution or university and must have an interest in leadership. Applicant must have 3.0 GPA or higher. Available to U.S. and non-U.S. citizens.

Association for Iron and Steel Technology (continued)

Application Requirements: Application, essay, resume, references, transcript. *Deadline:* April 30.

Contact: Program Coordinator
Association for Iron and Steel Technology
186 Thorn Hill Road
Warrendale, PA 15086-7528
Phone: 724-776-6040 Ext. 621
Fax: 724-776-0430

ASSOCIATION FOR IRON AND STEEL TECHNOLOGY DAVID H. SAMSON SCHOLARSHIP

• *See page 139*

ASSOCIATION FOR IRON AND STEEL TECHNOLOGY FERROUS METALLURGY EDUCATION TODAY (FEMET)

Scholarship/internship to provide incentive for students to become involved in the steel industry. Each recipient is awarded $5000 in their junior year, a paid summer internship with a North American steel company between junior and senior year, and $5000 toward senior year tuition. Must be enrolled full-time in metallurgy or materials science program at an accredited North American University. For more information call or email scholarship contact.

Academic Fields/Career Goals: Materials Science, Engineering, and Metallurgy.

Award: Scholarship for use in junior or senior years; not renewable. *Number:* 10. *Amount:* $5000.

Eligibility Requirements: Applicant must be enrolled or expecting to enroll full-time at a four-year institution or university. Applicant must have 3.0 GPA or higher. Available to U.S. citizens.

Application Requirements: Application, essay, resume, references, transcript.

Contact: B. V. Lakshminarayana
Phone: 202-452-7143
E-mail: blakshmi@steel.org

ASSOCIATION FOR IRON AND STEEL TECHNOLOGY NATIONAL MERIT SCHOLARSHIP

• *See page 241*

ASSOCIATION FOR IRON AND STEEL TECHNOLOGY NORTHWEST MEMBER CHAPTER SCHOLARSHIP

• *See page 241*

ASSOCIATION FOR IRON AND STEEL TECHNOLOGY OHIO VALLEY CHAPTER SCHOLARSHIP

• *See page 112*

ASSOCIATION FOR IRON AND STEEL TECHNOLOGY PITTSBURGH CHAPTER SCHOLARSHIP

• *See page 241*

ASSOCIATION FOR IRON AND STEEL TECHNOLOGY RONALD E. LINCOLN SCHOLARSHIP

Scholarship available to students of metallurgy, metallurgical engineering, or materials science, who have a genuine interest in a career in ferrous related industries as demonstrated by an internship, co-op, or related experience or who have plans to pursue such experiences during college. Student may apply after first term of freshman year of college and must join the AIST at the student rate. The Web site contains further information.

Academic Fields/Career Goals: Materials Science, Engineering, and Metallurgy.

Award: Scholarship for use in freshman, sophomore, junior, or senior years; not renewable. *Number:* 1. *Amount:* $2000.

Eligibility Requirements: Applicant must be enrolled or expecting to enroll full-time at a four-year institution or university and must have an interest in leadership. Applicant must have 3.0 GPA or higher. Available to U.S. and non-U.S. citizens.

Application Requirements: Application, essay, resume, references, transcript. *Deadline:* April 30.

Contact: Program Coordinator
Association for Iron and Steel Technology
186 Thorn Hill Road
Warrendale, PA 15086-7528
Phone: 724-776-6040 Ext. 621
Fax: 724-776-0430

ASSOCIATION FOR IRON AND STEEL TECHNOLOGY SOUTHEAST MEMBER CHAPTER SCHOLARSHIP

• *See page 241*

ASSOCIATION FOR IRON AND STEEL TECHNOLOGY WILLY KORF MEMORIAL SCHOLARSHIP

Scholarships available to students of metallurgy, metallurgical engineering, or materials science, who have a genuine interest in a career in ferrous related industries as demonstrated by an internship, co-op, or related experience or who have plans to pursue such experiences during college. Student may apply at first term of freshman year of college and must join the AIST at the student rate. The Web site contains further information.

Academic Fields/Career Goals: Materials Science, Engineering, and Metallurgy.

Award: Scholarship for use in freshman, sophomore, junior, or senior years; not renewable. *Number:* 2. *Amount:* $2000.

Eligibility Requirements: Applicant must be enrolled or expecting to enroll full-time at a four-year institution or university and must have an interest in leadership. Applicant must have 3.0 GPA or higher. Available to U.S. and non-U.S. citizens.

Application Requirements: Application, essay, resume, references, transcript. *Deadline:* April 30.

Contact: Program Coordinator
Association for Iron and Steel Technology
186 Thorn Hill Road
Warrendale, PA 15086-7528
Phone: 724-776-6040 Ext. 621
Fax: 724-776-0430

ASSOCIATION FOR WOMEN IN SCIENCE EDUCATIONAL FOUNDATION

http://www.awis.org/ed_foundation.html

ASSOCIATION FOR WOMEN IN SCIENCE COLLEGE SCHOLARSHIP

• *See page 63*

ASTRONAUT SCHOLARSHIP FOUNDATION

http://www.astronautscholarship.org

ASTRONAUT SCHOLARSHIP FOUNDATION

• *See page 68*

BARRY M. GOLDWATER SCHOLARSHIP AND EXCELLENCE IN EDUCATION FOUNDATION

http://www.act.org/goldwater

BARRY M. GOLDWATER SCHOLARSHIP AND EXCELLENCE IN EDUCATION PROGRAM

• *See page 68*

CONNECTICUT STUDENT LOAN FOUNDATION

http://www.cslf.com

CONNECTICUT INNOVATIONS TECHNOLOGY SCHOLAR PROGRAM

• *See page 113*

FOUNDATION OF THE WALL AND CEILING INDUSTRY

http://www.awci.org/thefoundation.shtml

FOUNDATION OF THE WALL AND CEILING INDUSTRY SCHOLARSHIP PROGRAM

• *See page 76*

GEORGE BIRD GRINNELL AMERICAN INDIAN FUND

AL QOYAWAYMA AWARD
• *See page 141*

H.H. HARRIS FOUNDATION http://www.afsinc.org

H.H. HARRIS FOUNDATION ANNUAL SCHOLARSHIP

Scholarships averaging $1200 will be awarded to students and professionals in the metallurgical and casting of metals field who are U.S. citizens. For more details see Web site: http://www.afsinc.org. Deadline is June 30.

Academic Fields/Career Goals: Materials Science, Engineering, and Metallurgy.

Award: Scholarship for use in freshman, sophomore, junior, senior, graduate, or postgraduate years; not renewable. *Amount:* $500–$5000.

Eligibility Requirements: Applicant must be enrolled or expecting to enroll full or part-time at an institution or university. Available to U.S. citizens.

Application Requirements: Application, references. *Deadline:* June 30.

Contact: H.H. Harris Foundation
30 South Wacker Drive, Suite 2300
Chicago, IL 60606
Fax: 312-346-0904
E-mail: johnHH@aol.com

HISPANIC COLLEGE FUND, INC. http://www.hispanicfund.org

DEPARTMENT OF ENERGY SCHOLARSHIP PROGRAM
• *See page 125*

LOCKHEED MARTIN SCHOLARSHIP PROGRAM
• *See page 141*

HISPANIC ENGINEER NATIONAL ACHIEVEMENT AWARDS CORPORATION (HENAAC) http://www.henaac.org

HISPANIC ENGINEER NATIONAL ACHIEVEMENT AWARDS CORPORATION SCHOLARSHIP PROGRAM
• *See page 99*

INDEPENDENT LABORATORIES INSTITUTE SCHOLARSHIP ALLIANCE http://www.acil.org

INDEPENDENT LABORATORIES INSTITUTE SCHOLARSHIP ALLIANCE
• *See page 69*

INTERNATIONAL SOCIETY FOR OPTICAL ENGINEERING-SPIE http://www.spie.org/info/scholarships

SPIE EDUCATIONAL SCHOLARSHIPS IN OPTICAL SCIENCE AND ENGINEERING
• *See page 70*

JORGE MAS CANOSA FREEDOM FOUNDATION

MAS FAMILY SCHOLARSHIP AWARD
• *See page 126*

KENTUCKY NATURAL RESOURCES AND ENVIRONMENTAL PROTECTION CABINET http://www.uky.edu/waterresources

ENVIRONMENTAL PROTECTION SCHOLARSHIPS
• *See page 142*

LOS ANGELES COUNCIL OF BLACK PROFESSIONAL ENGINEERS http://www.lablackengineers.org/scholarships.html

AL-BEN SCHOLARSHIP FOR ACADEMIC INCENTIVE
• *See page 142*

AL-BEN SCHOLARSHIP FOR PROFESSIONAL MERIT
• *See page 142*

AL-BEN SCHOLARSHIP FOR SCHOLASTIC ACHIEVEMENT
• *See page 143*

MAINE METAL PRODUCTS ASSOCIATION http://www.maine-metals.org

MAINE METAL PRODUCTS ASSOCIATION SCHOLARSHIP PROGRAM

MMPA offers scholarship awards to individuals seeking postsecondary education in the metal trades/precision manufacturing field of study. Any Maine student or worker can apply for tuition assistance at any Maine institute of higher learning. Special awards are also available.

Academic Fields/Career Goals: Materials Science, Engineering, and Metallurgy; Mechanical Engineering; Trade/Technical Specialties.

Award: Scholarship for use in freshman, sophomore, junior, or senior years; not renewable. *Number:* up to 15. *Amount:* $500–$1500.

Eligibility Requirements: Applicant must be enrolled or expecting to enroll full or part-time at a two-year or four-year or technical institution or university; resident of Maine and studying in Maine. Applicant must have 2.5 GPA or higher. Available to U.S. citizens.

Application Requirements: Application, essay, references, transcript. *Deadline:* June 1.

Contact: Laurie Cook, Office Manager
Maine Metal Products Association
28 Stroudwater Street, Suite 4
Westbrook, ME 04092
Phone: 207-854-2153
Fax: 207-854-3865
E-mail: mmpa@ime.net

MICRON TECHNOLOGY FOUNDATION, INC. http://www.micron.com/scholars

MICRON SCIENCE AND TECHNOLOGY SCHOLARS PROGRAM
• *See page 144*

MIDWEST ROOFING CONTRACTORS ASSOCIATION http://www.mrca.org

MRCA FOUNDATION SCHOLARSHIP PROGRAM
• *See page 70*

MINERALOGICAL SOCIETY OF AMERICA http://www.minsocam.org

MINERALOGY SOCIETY OF AMERICA-GRANT FOR RESEARCH IN CRYSTALLOGRAPHY
• *See page 191*

MINERALS, METALS, AND MATERIALS SOCIETY (TMS) http://www.tms.org

TMS J. KEITH BRIMACOMBE PRESIDENTIAL SCHOLARSHIP
• *See page 230*

TMS OUTSTANDING STUDENT PAPER CONTEST-UNDERGRADUATE
• *See page 230*

TMS/EMPMD GILBERT CHIN SCHOLARSHIP
• *See page 230*

TMS/EPD SCHOLARSHIP
• *See page 230*

TMS/INTERNATIONAL SYMPOSIUM ON SUPERALLOYS SCHOLARSHIP PROGRAM
• *See page 230*

TMS/LMD SCHOLARSHIP PROGRAM
• *See page 231*

TMS/STRUCTURAL MATERIALS DIVISION SCHOLARSHIP
• *See page 231*

NAMEPA NATIONAL SCHOLARSHIP FOUNDATION http://www.namepa.org

NATIONAL ASSOCIATION OF MINORITY ENGINEERING PROGRAM ADMINISTRATORS NATIONAL SCHOLARSHIP FUND
• See page 101

NASA VERMONT SPACE GRANT CONSORTIUM http://www.emba.uvm.edu/vsgc

VERMONT SPACE GRANT CONSORTIUM SCHOLARSHIP PROGRAM
• See page 71

NATIONAL INVENTORS HALL OF FAME http://www.invent.org/collegiate

COLLEGIATE INVENTORS COMPETITION - GRAND PRIZE
• See page 71

COLLEGIATE INVENTORS COMPETITION FOR UNDERGRADUATE STUDENTS
• See page 71

NATIONAL SOCIETY OF PROFESSIONAL ENGINEERS http://www.nspe.org

MAUREEN L. AND HOWARD N. BLITMAN, PE SCHOLARSHIP TO PROMOTE DIVERSITY IN ENGINEERING
• See page 145

NATIONAL SOCIETY OF PROFESSIONAL ENGINEERS/AUXILIARY SCHOLARSHIP
• See page 145

PAUL H. ROBBINS HONORARY SCHOLARSHIP
• See page 145

PROFESSIONAL ENGINEERS IN INDUSTRY SCHOLARSHIP
• See page 145

VIRGINIA HENRY MEMORIAL SCHOLARSHIP
• See page 146

PLASTICS INSTITUTE OF AMERICA http://www.plasticsinstitute.org

PLASTICS PIONEERS SCHOLARSHIPS
• See page 232

SOCIETY FOR MINING, METALLURGY AND EXPLORATION - CENTRAL WYOMING SECTION

COATES, WOLFF, RUSSELL MINING INDUSTRY SCHOLARSHIP
• See page 71

SOCIETY OF AUTOMOTIVE ENGINEERS http://www.sae.org/students/stuschol.htm

BMW/SAE ENGINEERING SCHOLARSHIP
• See page 105

EDWARD D. HENDRICKSON/SAE ENGINEERING SCHOLARSHIP
• See page 105

TMC/SAE DONALD D. DAWSON TECHNICAL SCHOLARSHIP
• See page 105

YANMAR/SAE SCHOLARSHIP
• See page 233

SOCIETY OF HISPANIC PROFESSIONAL ENGINEERS FOUNDATION http://www.shpefoundation.org

SOCIETY OF HISPANIC PROFESSIONAL ENGINEERS FOUNDATION
• See page 146

SOCIETY OF PLASTICS ENGINEERS (SPE) FOUNDATION http://www.4spe.org

FLEMING/BASZCAK SCHOLARSHIP
• See page 147

SOCIETY OF PLASTICS ENGINEERS SCHOLARSHIP PROGRAM
• See page 147

SOCIETY OF WOMEN ENGINEERS http://www.swe.org/scholarships

GUIDANT CORPORATION SCHOLARSHIP
• See page 173

NORTHROP GRUMMAN CORPORATION SCHOLARSHIPS
• See page 106

SOIL AND WATER CONSERVATION SOCIETY-NEW JERSEY CHAPTER http://www.geocities.com/njswcs

EDWARD R. HALL SCHOLARSHIP
• See page 55

UNIVERSITIES SPACE RESEARCH ASSOCIATION http://www.usra.edu/hq/scholarships/overview.shtml

UNIVERSITIES SPACE RESEARCH ASSOCIATION SCHOLARSHIP PROGRAM
• See page 72

XEROX http://xerox.com

TECHNICAL MINORITY SCHOLARSHIP
• See page 148

MATHEMATICS

CASUALTY ACTUARIAL SOCIETY http://www.casact.org

CASUALTY ACTUARIAL SOCIETY TRUST SCHOLARSHIP
• See page 326

COLLEGEBOUND FOUNDATION http://www.collegeboundfoundation.org

DR. FREEMAN A. HRABOWSKI, III SCHOLARSHIP
• See page 242

WISCONSIN MATHEMATICS COUNCIL, INC. http://www.wismath.org

ARNE ENGEBRETSEN WISCONSIN MATHEMATICS COUNCIL SCHOLARSHIP
• See page 216

ETHEL A. NEIJAHR WISCONSIN MATHEMATICS COUNCIL SCHOLARSHIP
• See page 216

SISTER MARY PETRONIA VAN STRATEN WISCONSIN MATHEMATICS COUNCIL SCHOLARSHIP
• See page 216

MECHANICAL ENGINEERING

AACE INTERNATIONAL http://www.aacei.org

AACE INTERNATIONAL COMPETITIVE SCHOLARSHIP
• See page 73

AEA-OREGON COUNCIL http://www.ous.edu/ecs/scholarships

AEA- OREGON COUNCIL TECHNOLOGY SCHOLARSHIP PROGRAM
• See page 136

AMERICAN CHEMICAL SOCIETY, RUBBER DIVISION http://www.rubber.org/awards/scholarships.htm

AMERICAN CHEMICAL SOCIETY, RUBBER DIVISION-UNDERGRADUATE SCHOLARSHIP
• See page 136

AMERICAN COUNCIL OF ENGINEERING COMPANIES OF PENNSYLVANIA (ACEC/PA) http://www.acecpa.org

ENGINEERING SCHOLARSHIP
• See page 136

AMERICAN INSTITUTE OF AERONAUTICS AND ASTRONAUTICS http://www.aiaa.org

AIAA UNDERGRADUATE SCHOLARSHIP
• See page 66

AMERICAN PUBLIC TRANSPORTATION FOUNDATION http://www.apta.com

DONALD C. HYDE ESSAY PROGRAM
• See page 149

JACK GILSTRAP SCHOLARSHIP
• See page 149

LOUIS T. KLAUDER SCHOLARSHIP
• See page 150

PARSONS BRINCKERHOFF-JIM LAMMIE SCHOLARSHIP
• See page 150

TRANSIT HALL OF FAME SCHOLARSHIP AWARD PROGRAM
• See page 150

AMERICAN SOCIETY OF HEATING, REFRIGERATING, AND AIR CONDITIONING ENGINEERS, INC. http://www.ashrae.org

ALWIN B. NEWTON SCHOLARSHIP FUND
• See page 218

REUBEN TRANE SCHOLARSHIP
• See page 218

AMERICAN SOCIETY OF MECHANICAL ENGINEERS (ASME INTERNATIONAL) http://www.asme.org/education/enged/aid

AMERICAN SOCIETY OF MECHANICAL ENGINEERS FOUNDATION SCHOLARSHIP
• See page 237

AMERICAN SOCIETY OF MECHANICAL ENGINEERS HIGH SCHOOL SCHOLARSHIPS

Scholarships available for high school students pursuing a degree in mechanical engineering. Must have a minimum 3.0 GPA. Application deadline is March 15.

Academic Fields/Career Goals: Mechanical Engineering.

Award: Scholarship for use in freshman year; not renewable. *Number:* 2. *Amount:* $1000.

Eligibility Requirements: Applicant must be high school student and planning to enroll or expecting to enroll at a four-year institution or university. Applicant must have 3.0 GPA or higher.

Application Requirements: Application, essay, references, transcript. *Deadline:* March 15.

Contact: Theresa Oluwanifise, Administrative Assistant
American Society of Mechanical Engineers (ASME International)
3 Park Avenue
New York, NY 10016
Phone: 212-591-8131
Fax: 212-591-7143
E-mail: oluwanifiset@asme.org

AMERICAN SOCIETY OF MECHANICAL ENGINEERS PETROLEUM DIVISION STUDENT SCHOLARSHIP PROGRAM

Scholarships available to ASME student members interested in any phase of the petroleum industry, including drilling completions, facilities, pipelines, rigs, operations, materials, equipment manufacturing, plant design and operation, maintenance, environmental protection, and innovations. For further details visit Web site at http://www.asme-petroleumdiv.org/students/scholarshipsbody.htm.

Academic Fields/Career Goals: Mechanical Engineering.

Award: Prize for use in junior or senior years; not renewable. *Number:* 5. *Amount:* $2000.

Eligibility Requirements: Applicant must be enrolled or expecting to enroll at a two-year or four-year institution or university. Applicant must have 2.5 GPA or higher.

Application Requirements: Application, essay, references, transcript. *Deadline:* March 15.

Contact: Manny Mones, Student Scholarship Program
American Society of Mechanical Engineers (ASME International)
11757 Katy Freeway, Suite 865
Houston, TX 77079
Phone: 281-493-3491
Fax: 281-493-3493

AMERICAN SOCIETY OF MECHANICAL ENGINEERS SOLID WASTE PROCESSING DIVISION UNDERGRADUATE SCHOLARSHIP

One undergraduate scholarship available for study at North American colleges and universities with established programs in solid waste management. Award is divided equally between the student and the school. Must be a member of the American Society of Mechanical Engineers.

Academic Fields/Career Goals: Mechanical Engineering.

Award: Scholarship for use in sophomore, junior, or senior years; not renewable. *Number:* 1. *Amount:* $3000.

Eligibility Requirements: Applicant must be enrolled or expecting to enroll full-time at a four-year institution or university. Available to U.S. and non-U.S. citizens.

Application Requirements: Application, essay, references, transcript. *Deadline:* June 10.

Contact: Elio Manes, Senior Manager
American Society of Mechanical Engineers (ASME International)
3 Park Avenue
New York, NY 10016-5990
Phone: 212-591-7797
Fax: 212-591-7671
E-mail: manese@asme.org

AMERICAN SOCIETY OF MECHANICAL ENGINEERS WILLIAM E. COOPER SCHOLARSHIPS
• See page 226

AMERICAN SOCIETY OF MECHANICAL ENGINEERS/FIRST ROBOTICS COMPETITION SCHOLARSHIP

Seven $5,000 scholarships to graduating high school seniors who are members of a FIRST Robotics Competition. Must be planning to enroll no later than the fall semester following high school graduation in an ABET-accredited or substantially equivalent mechanical engineering or mechanical engineering technology program. ASME does not accept applications directly from students for this program. Students must be nominated by ASME members involved with FIRST teams. Nomination postmark deadline: March 1.

Academic Fields/Career Goals: Mechanical Engineering.

Award: Scholarship for use in freshman year; not renewable. *Number:* 7. *Amount:* $5000.

Eligibility Requirements: Applicant must be high school student and planning to enroll or expecting to enroll full-time at a four-year institution or university.

Application Requirements: Applicant must enter a contest, financial need analysis, transcript, nomination letter. *Deadline:* March 1.

Contact: Theresa Oluwanifise, Administrative Assistant
American Society of Mechanical Engineers (ASME International)
3 Park Avenue
New York, NY 10016
Phone: 212-591-8131
Fax: 212-591-7143
E-mail: oluwanifiset@asme.org

F.W. "BEICH" BEICHLEY SCHOLARSHIP

One-time award for college juniors and seniors who are members of the American Society of Mechanical Engineers. Must be attending a four-year institution and pursuing studies in mechanical engineering or mechanical engineering technology. Application available online http://www.asme.org/education/enged/aid.

Academic Fields/Career Goals: Mechanical Engineering.

Award: Scholarship for use in junior or senior years; not renewable. *Number:* 1. *Amount:* $2000.

Eligibility Requirements: Applicant must be enrolled or expecting to enroll full-time at a four-year institution or university. Available to U.S. citizens.

Application Requirements: Application, essay, financial need analysis, references, self-addressed stamped envelope, transcript. *Deadline:* March 15.

Contact: Ms. Theresa Oluwanifise, Administrative Assistant
American Society of Mechanical Engineers (ASME International)
3 Park Avenue
New York, NY 10016-5990
Phone: 212-591-8131
Fax: 212-591-7143
E-mail: oluwanifiset@asme.org

FRANK WILLIAM AND DOROTHY GIVEN MILLER SCHOLARSHIP

Award for college juniors and seniors who are members of the American Society of Mechanical Engineers. Must be attending a four-year institution in North America and pursuing studies in mechanical engineering or mechanical engineering technology. Must be a U.S. citizen, or North American resident. Application available online http://www.asme.org/education/enged/aid.

Academic Fields/Career Goals: Mechanical Engineering.

Award: Scholarship for use in junior or senior years; not renewable. *Number:* 2. *Amount:* $1500.

Eligibility Requirements: Applicant must be enrolled or expecting to enroll full-time at a four-year institution or university. Available to U.S. citizens.

Application Requirements: Application, essay, financial need analysis, references, self-addressed stamped envelope, transcript. *Deadline:* March 15.

Contact: Ms. Theresa Oluwanifise, Administrative Assistant
American Society of Mechanical Engineers (ASME International)
3 Park Avenue
New York, NY 10016-5990
Phone: 212-591-8131
Fax: 212-591-7143
E-mail: oluwanifiset@asme.org

GARLAND DUNCAN SCHOLARSHIP

Award for college juniors and seniors who are members of the American Society of Mechanical Engineers. Must be enrolled at a four-year college or university and pursuing studies in mechanical engineering or mechanical engineering technology in the U.S. Application available online http://www.asme.org/education/enged/aid

Academic Fields/Career Goals: Mechanical Engineering.

Award: Scholarship for use in junior or senior years; not renewable. *Number:* up to 2. *Amount:* up to $3500.

Eligibility Requirements: Applicant must be enrolled or expecting to enroll full-time at a four-year institution or university. Available to U.S. and non-U.S. citizens.

Application Requirements: Application, essay, financial need analysis, references, self-addressed stamped envelope, transcript. *Deadline:* March 15.

Contact: Ms. Theresa Oluwanifise, Administrative Assistant
American Society of Mechanical Engineers (ASME International)
3 Park Avenue
New York, NY 10016-5990
Phone: 212-591-8131
Fax: 212-591-7143
E-mail: oluwanifiset@asme.org

JOHN AND ELSA GRACIK SCHOLARSHIPS

Award for college undergraduates enrolled or enrolling in a mechanical engineering or related program. Must be a U.S. citizen and a member of the American Society of Mechanical Engineers. Application available online http://www.asme.org/education/enged/aid

Academic Fields/Career Goals: Mechanical Engineering.

Award: Scholarship for use in freshman, sophomore, junior, or senior years; not renewable. *Number:* up to 18. *Amount:* $1500.

Eligibility Requirements: Applicant must be enrolled or expecting to enroll full-time at a four-year institution or university. Available to U.S. citizens.

Application Requirements: Application, essay, financial need analysis, references, self-addressed stamped envelope, transcript. *Deadline:* March 15.

Contact: Ms. Theresa Oluwanifise, Administrative Assistant
American Society of Mechanical Engineers (ASME International)
3 Park Avenue
New York, NY 10016-5990
Phone: 212-591-8131
Fax: 212-591-7143
E-mail: oluwanifiset@asme.org

KENNETH ANDREW ROE SCHOLARSHIP

Award for college juniors and seniors who are members of the American Society of Mechanical Engineers. Must be a U.S. citizen and North American resident. Must be pursuing studies in an ABET-accredited mechanical engineering or mechanical engineering technology program. Application available online http://www.asme.org/education/enged/aid

Academic Fields/Career Goals: Mechanical Engineering.

Award: Scholarship for use in junior or senior years; not renewable. *Number:* 1. *Amount:* $10,000.

Eligibility Requirements: Applicant must be enrolled or expecting to enroll full-time at a four-year institution or university. Available to U.S. citizens.

Application Requirements: Application, essay, financial need analysis, references, self-addressed stamped envelope, transcript. *Deadline:* March 15.

Contact: Ms. Theresa Oluwanifise, Administrative Assistant
American Society of Mechanical Engineers (ASME International)
3 Park Avenue
New York, NY 10016-5990
Phone: 212-591-8131
Fax: 212-591-7143
E-mail: oluwanifiset@asme.org

MELVIN R. GREEN SCHOLARSHIP

Award for college juniors and seniors who are members of the American Society of Mechanical Engineers. Must be enrolled at a four-year college or university, and pursuing studies in mechanical engineering or mechanical engineering technology. Application available online http://www.asme.org/education/enged/aid

Academic Fields/Career Goals: Mechanical Engineering.

Award: Scholarship for use in junior or senior years; not renewable. *Number:* up to 2. *Amount:* up to $3500.

Eligibility Requirements: Applicant must be enrolled or expecting to enroll full-time at a four-year institution or university. Available to U.S. and non-U.S. citizens.

Application Requirements: Application, essay, financial need analysis, references, self-addressed stamped envelope, transcript. *Deadline:* March 15.

Contact: Ms. Theresa Oluwanifise, Administrative Assistant
American Society of Mechanical Engineers (ASME International)
3 Park Avenue
New York, NY 10016-5990
Phone: 212-591-8131
Fax: 212-591-7143
E-mail: oluwanifiset@asme.org

ROBERT F. SAMMATARO PRESSURE VESSELS AND PIPING DIVISION MEMORIAL SCHOLARSHIP

One (1) $1,000 scholarship to an ASME student member, preferably with an interest in pressure vessels and piping. Must be U.S. citizen. Deadline: March 15. Application available online: http://www.asme.org/education/enged/aid

Academic Fields/Career Goals: Mechanical Engineering.

Award: Scholarship for use in sophomore, junior, or senior years; not renewable. *Number:* up to 1. *Amount:* up to $1000.

Eligibility Requirements: Applicant must be enrolled or expecting to enroll full-time at a four-year institution or university. Available to U.S. citizens.

Application Requirements: Application, essay, financial need analysis, references, transcript. *Deadline:* March 15.

Contact: Theresa Oluwanifise, Administrative Assistant
American Society of Mechanical Engineers (ASME International)
3 Park Avenue
New York, NY 10016
Phone: 212-591-8131
Fax: 212-591-7143
E-mail: oluwanifiset@asme.org

WILLIAM J. AND MARIJANE E. ADAMS SCHOLARSHIP

Award for student with a minimum 2.5 GPA who is at least a sophomore and attends a college or university in ASME Region IX (California, Nevada, and Hawaii). Must be pursuing studies in mechanical engineering or mechanical engineering technology and demonstrate special interest in product development and design. Must be a member of the American Society of Mechanical Engineers. Application available online: http://www.asme.org/education/enged/aid

Academic Fields/Career Goals: Mechanical Engineering.

Award: Scholarship for use in sophomore, junior, or senior years; not renewable. *Number:* 1. *Amount:* $2000.

Eligibility Requirements: Applicant must be enrolled or expecting to enroll full-time at a four-year institution or university and studying in California, Hawaii, or Nevada. Applicant must have 2.5 GPA or higher. Available to U.S. citizens.

Application Requirements: Application, essay, financial need analysis, references, self-addressed stamped envelope, transcript. *Deadline:* March 15.

Contact: Ms. Theresa Oluwanifise, Administrative Assistant
American Society of Mechanical Engineers (ASME International)
3 Park Avenue
New York, NY 10016-5990
Phone: 212-591-8131
Fax: 212-591-7143
E-mail: oluwanifiset@asme.org

AMERICAN SOCIETY OF MECHANICAL ENGINEERS AUXILIARY, INC. http://www.asme.org

AGNES MALAKATE KEZIOS SCHOLARSHIP

Available to college juniors for use in final year at a four-year college. Five-year students may apply in fourth year. Must be majoring in mechanical engineering, be member of a student section of ASME (if available), and exhibit leadership values. Must be a U.S. citizen enrolled in a college/university in the U.S. that has ABET-accreditation.

Academic Fields/Career Goals: Mechanical Engineering.

Award: Scholarship for use in senior year; not renewable. *Number:* varies. *Amount:* up to $2000.

Eligibility Requirements: Applicant must be enrolled or expecting to enroll full-time at a four-year institution. Available to U.S. citizens.

Application Requirements: Application, autobiography, financial need analysis, references, self-addressed stamped envelope, transcript. *Deadline:* March 15.

Contact: Alverta Cover
American Society of Mechanical Engineers Auxiliary, Inc.
5425 Caldwell Mill Road
Birmingham, AL 35242
Phone: 205-991-6109
E-mail: undergradauxsch@asme.org

ALLEN J. BALDWIN SCHOLARSHIP

Available to college juniors for use in final year at a four-year college. Five-year students may apply in fourth year. Must be majoring in mechanical engineering, be member of a student section of ASME (if available), and exhibit leadership values. Must be U.S. citizen enrolled in a college/university in the U.S. that has ABET-accreditation.

Academic Fields/Career Goals: Mechanical Engineering.

Award: Scholarship for use in senior year; not renewable. *Number:* varies. *Amount:* up to $2000.

Eligibility Requirements: Applicant must be enrolled or expecting to enroll full-time at a four-year institution. Available to U.S. citizens.

Application Requirements: Application, autobiography, financial need analysis, references, self-addressed stamped envelope, transcript. *Deadline:* March 15.

Contact: Alverta Cover
American Society of Mechanical Engineers Auxiliary, Inc.
5425 Caldwell Mill Road
Birmingham, AL 35242
Phone: 205-991-6109
E-mail: undergradauxsch@asme.org

AMERICAN SOCIETY OF MECHANICAL ENGINEERS-AMERICAN SOCIETY OF MECHANICAL ENGINEERS AUXILIARY FIRST CLARKE SCHOLARSHIP

Scholarships available for high school seniors only, who are active on FIRST teams. Applicant must be a member or nominated by a member of ASME or ASME Auxiliary . Must enroll full time in an ABET accredited mechanical engineering or mechanical engineering technology program.

Academic Fields/Career Goals: Mechanical Engineering.

Award: Scholarship for use in freshman year. *Number:* 7. *Amount:* $5000.

Eligibility Requirements: Applicant must be high school student and planning to enroll or expecting to enroll full-time at a four-year institution or university.

Application Requirements: Application, financial need analysis, transcript. *Deadline:* March 1.

Contact: David Soukup
American Society of Mechanical Engineers Auxiliary, Inc.
Three Park Avenue, 23-W1
New York, NY 10016-5990
Phone: 800-843-2763
Fax: 212-591-7143
E-mail: soukupd@asme.org

BERNA LOU CARTWRIGHT SCHOLARSHIP

Available to college juniors for use in final year at a four-year college. Five-year students may apply in fourth year. Must be majoring in mechanical engineering, be member of a student section of ASME (if available), and exhibit leadership values. Must be a U.S. citizen enrolled in a college/university in the U.S. that has ABET-accreditation.

Academic Fields/Career Goals: Mechanical Engineering.

Award: Scholarship for use in senior year; not renewable. *Number:* 2–10. *Amount:* up to $2000.

Eligibility Requirements: Applicant must be enrolled or expecting to enroll at a four-year institution or university and must have an interest in leadership. Available to U.S. citizens.

Application Requirements: Application, autobiography, financial need analysis, references, self-addressed stamped envelope, transcript. *Deadline:* March 15.

Contact: Alverta Cover
American Society of Mechanical Engineers Auxiliary, Inc.
5425 Caldwell Mill Road
Birmingham, AL 35242
Phone: 205-991-6109
E-mail: undergradauxsch@asme.org

SYLVIA W. FARNY SCHOLARSHIP

One-time awards of $2000 to ASME student members for the final year of undergraduate study in mechanical engineering. Must be a U.S. citizen enrolled in a college/university in the U.S. that has ABET-accreditation.

American Society of Mechanical Engineers Auxiliary, Inc. (continued)

Academic Fields/Career Goals: Mechanical Engineering.

Award: Scholarship for use in senior year; not renewable. *Number:* 2–10. *Amount:* up to $2000.

Eligibility Requirements: Applicant must be enrolled or expecting to enroll full-time at a four-year institution or university. Available to U.S. citizens.

Application Requirements: Application, references, transcript. *Deadline:* March 15.

Contact: Alverta Cover
American Society of Mechanical Engineers Auxiliary, Inc.
5425 Caldwell Mill Road
Birmingham, AL 35242
Phone: 205-991-6109
E-mail: undergradauxsch@asme.org

AMERICAN SOCIETY OF NAVAL ENGINEERS http://www.navalengineers.org

AMERICAN SOCIETY OF NAVAL ENGINEERS SCHOLARSHIP
• *See page 66*

ASSOCIATED BUILDERS AND CONTRACTORS SCHOLARSHIP PROGRAM http://www.abc.org

TRIMMER EDUCATION FOUNDATION SCHOLARSHIPS FOR CONSTRUCTION MANAGEMENT
• *See page 151*

ASSOCIATION FOR FACILITIES ENGINEERING (AFE)

ASSOCIATION FOR FACILITIES ENGINEERING CEDAR VALLEY CHAPTER # 132 SCHOLARSHIP
• *See page 97*

ASSOCIATION FOR WOMEN IN SCIENCE EDUCATIONAL FOUNDATION http://www.awis.org/ed_foundation.html

ASSOCIATION FOR WOMEN IN SCIENCE COLLEGE SCHOLARSHIP
• *See page 63*

ASTRONAUT SCHOLARSHIP FOUNDATION http://www.astronautscholarship.org

ASTRONAUT SCHOLARSHIP FOUNDATION
• *See page 68*

AUTOMOTIVE HALL OF FAME http://www.automotivehalloffame.org

AUTOMOTIVE HALL OF FAME EDUCATIONAL FUNDS
• *See page 140*

BARRY M. GOLDWATER SCHOLARSHIP AND EXCELLENCE IN EDUCATION FOUNDATION http://www.act.org/goldwater

BARRY M. GOLDWATER SCHOLARSHIP AND EXCELLENCE IN EDUCATION PROGRAM
• *See page 68*

COMTO-BOSTON CHAPTER http://www.bostoncomto.org

COMTO BOSTON/GARRETT A. MORGAN SCHOLARSHIP
• *See page 75*

CONNECTICUT BUILDING CONGRESS http://www.cbc-ct.org

CONNECTICUT BUILDING CONGRESS SCHOLARSHIP FUND
• *See page 75*

CONNECTICUT STUDENT LOAN FOUNDATION http://www.cslf.com

CONNECTICUT INNOVATIONS TECHNOLOGY SCHOLAR PROGRAM
• *See page 113*

CUBAN AMERICAN NATIONAL FOUNDATION

MAS FAMILY SCHOLARSHIPS
• *See page 123*

EAST LOS ANGELES COMMUNITY UNION (TELACU) EDUCATION FOUNDATION

TELACU ENGINEERING AWARD
• *See page 141*

FLORIDA EDUCATIONAL FACILITIES PLANNERS' ASSOCIATION http://www.fefpa.org

FEFPA ASSISTANTSHIP
• *See page 76*

GEORGE BIRD GRINNELL AMERICAN INDIAN FUND

AL QOYAWAYMA AWARD
• *See page 141*

HAROLD B. & DOROTHY A. SNYDER FOUNDATION, INC.

HAROLD B. AND DOROTHY A. SNYDER FOUNDATION, INC., PROGRAM
• *See page 141*

HISPANIC COLLEGE FUND, INC. http://www.hispanicfund.org

DEPARTMENT OF ENERGY SCHOLARSHIP PROGRAM
• *See page 125*

HISPANIC COLLEGE FUND/INROADS/SPRINT SCHOLARSHIP PROGRAM
• *See page 125*

HISPANIC ENGINEER NATIONAL ACHIEVEMENT AWARDS CORPORATION (HENAAC) http://www.henaac.org

HISPANIC ENGINEER NATIONAL ACHIEVEMENT AWARDS CORPORATION SCHOLARSHIP PROGRAM
• *See page 99*

HISPANIC SCHOLARSHIP FUND http://www.hsf.net

HSF/GENERAL MOTORS SCHOLARSHIP
• *See page 126*

HSF/SOCIETY OF HISPANIC PROFESSIONAL ENGINEERS, INC. SCHOLARSHIP PROGRAM
• *See page 152*

INDEPENDENT LABORATORIES INSTITUTE SCHOLARSHIP ALLIANCE http://www.acil.org

INDEPENDENT LABORATORIES INSTITUTE SCHOLARSHIP ALLIANCE
• *See page 69*

INSTRUMENTATION, SYSTEMS, AND AUTOMATION SOCIETY (ISA) http://www.isa.org

INSTRUMENTATION, SYSTEMS, AND AUTOMATION SOCIETY (ISA) SCHOLARSHIP PROGRAM
• *See page 99*

INTERNATIONAL SOCIETY FOR OPTICAL ENGINEERING-SPIE http://www.spie.org/info/scholarships

SPIE EDUCATIONAL SCHOLARSHIPS IN OPTICAL SCIENCE AND ENGINEERING
• *See page 70*

JORGE MAS CANOSA FREEDOM FOUNDATION

MAS FAMILY SCHOLARSHIP AWARD
• *See page 126*

LOS ANGELES COUNCIL OF BLACK PROFESSIONAL ENGINEERS http://www.lablackengineers.org/scholarships.html

AL-BEN SCHOLARSHIP FOR ACADEMIC INCENTIVE
• *See page 142*

AL-BEN SCHOLARSHIP FOR PROFESSIONAL MERIT
• *See page 142*

AL-BEN SCHOLARSHIP FOR SCHOLASTIC ACHIEVEMENT
• *See page 143*

MAINE METAL PRODUCTS ASSOCIATION http://www.maine-metals.org

MAINE METAL PRODUCTS ASSOCIATION SCHOLARSHIP PROGRAM
• *See page 351*

MICHIGAN SOCIETY OF PROFESSIONAL ENGINEERS http://www.michiganspe.org

ANTHONY C. FORTUNSKI, P.E. MEMORIAL GRANT
• *See page 143*

MICHIGAN SOCIETY OF PROFESSIONAL ENGINEERS UNDESIGNATED GRANT
• *See page 143*

MICHIGAN SOCIETY OF PROFESSIONAL ENGINEERS 1980 NATIONAL SOCIETY OF PROFESSIONAL ENGINEERS ANNUAL MEETING COMMITTEE GRANT
• *See page 143*

MICHIGAN SOCIETY OF PROFESSIONAL ENGINEERS AUXILIARY GRANT
• *See page 143*

MICHIGAN SOCIETY OF PROFESSIONAL ENGINEERS HARRY R. BALL, P.E. GRANT
• *See page 144*

MICHIGAN SOCIETY OF PROFESSIONAL ENGINEERS KENNETH B. FISHBECK, P.E. MEMORIAL GRANT
• *See page 144*

MICHIGAN SOCIETY OF PROFESSIONAL ENGINEERS SCHOLARSHIP TRUST GRANT
• *See page 144*

MICRON TECHNOLOGY FOUNDATION, INC. http://www.micron.com/scholars

MICRON SCIENCE AND TECHNOLOGY SCHOLARS PROGRAM
• *See page 144*

MIDWEST ROOFING CONTRACTORS ASSOCIATION http://www.mrca.org

MRCA FOUNDATION SCHOLARSHIP PROGRAM
• *See page 70*

NAMEPA NATIONAL SCHOLARSHIP FOUNDATION http://www.namepa.org

NATIONAL ASSOCIATION OF MINORITY ENGINEERING PROGRAM ADMINISTRATORS NATIONAL SCHOLARSHIP FUND
• *See page 101*

NASA DELAWARE SPACE GRANT CONSORTIUM http://www.delspace.org

NASA DELAWARE SPACE GRANT UNDERGRADUATE TUITION SCHOLARSHIP
• *See page 70*

NATIONAL ASSOCIATION OF WOMEN IN CONSTRUCTION http://nawic.org

NAWIC UNDERGRADUATE SCHOLARSHIPS
• *See page 77*

NATIONAL SOCIETY OF PROFESSIONAL ENGINEERS http://www.nspe.org

MAUREEN L. AND HOWARD N. BLITMAN, PE SCHOLARSHIP TO PROMOTE DIVERSITY IN ENGINEERING
• *See page 145*

NATIONAL SOCIETY OF PROFESSIONAL ENGINEERS/AUXILIARY SCHOLARSHIP
• *See page 145*

PAUL H. ROBBINS HONORARY SCHOLARSHIP
• *See page 145*

PROFESSIONAL ENGINEERS IN INDUSTRY SCHOLARSHIP
• *See page 145*

VIRGINIA HENRY MEMORIAL SCHOLARSHIP
• *See page 146*

NEW JERSEY ACADEMY OF SCIENCE http://www.njas.org

NEW JERSEY ACADEMY OF SCIENCE RESEARCH GRANTS-IN-AID TO HIGH SCHOOL STUDENTS
• *See page 116*

OREGON STUDENT ASSISTANCE COMMISSION http://www.osac.state.or.us

AMERICAN COUNCIL OF ENGINEERING COMPANIES OF OREGON SCHOLARSHIP
• *See page 146*

PLUMBING-HEATING-COOLING CONTRACTORS ASSOCIATION EDUCATION FOUNDATION http://www.phccweb.org

BRADFORD WHITE CORPORATION SCHOLARSHIP
• *See page 79*

DELTA FAUCET COMPANY SCHOLARSHIP PROGRAM
• *See page 79*

PHCC EDUCATIONAL FOUNDATION NEED-BASED SCHOLARSHIP
• *See page 79*

PHCC EDUCATIONAL FOUNDATION SCHOLARSHIP PROGRAM
• *See page 79*

PROFESSIONAL CONSTRUCTION ESTIMATORS ASSOCIATION http://www.pcea.org

TED WILSON MEMORIAL SCHOLARSHIP FOUNDATION
• *See page 188*

ROBERT H. MOLLOHAN FAMILY CHARITABLE FOUNDATION, INC. http://www.mollohanfoundation.org

HIGH TECHNOLOGY SCHOLARS PROGRAM
• *See page 117*

ROCKY MOUNTAIN COAL MINING INSTITUTE http://www.rmcmi.org

ROCKY MOUNTAIN COAL MINING INSTITUTE SCHOLARSHIP
• *See page 146*

SKIDMORE, OWINGS, AND MERRILL FOUNDATION http://www.somfoundation.som.com

BUILDING SYSTEMS TECHNOLOGY RESEARCH GRANT

One-time award intended to encourage mechanical engineering students to continue preparation for service in the building systems technology industry. Typical expenditures include living expenses, travel to research project sites, experimental equipment and supplies. The intent is to expand the imagination of young engineers in the design and engineering of building systems. Students should apply for this award through the American Society of Heating, Refrigerating and Air-Conditioning Engineers. See Web site at http://www.ashrae.org under "The Student Zone" for eligibility and deadline information.

Academic Fields/Career Goals: Mechanical Engineering.

Award: Grant for use in senior, or graduate years; not renewable. *Number:* 1. *Amount:* $7500.

Eligibility Requirements: Applicant must be enrolled or expecting to enroll full or part-time at an institution or university. Available to U.S. and non-U.S. citizens.

Application Requirements: Application, applicant must enter a contest, references.

Contact: Skidmore, Owings, and Merrill Foundation
1791 Tullie Circle, NE
Atlanta, GA 30324
Phone: 404-636-8400
Fax: 404-321-5478

SOCIETY FOR MINING, METALLURGY AND EXPLORATION - CENTRAL WYOMING SECTION

COATES, WOLFF, RUSSELL MINING INDUSTRY SCHOLARSHIP
• *See page 71*

SOCIETY OF AUTOMOTIVE ENGINEERS http://www.sae.org/students/stuschol.htm

BMW/SAE ENGINEERING SCHOLARSHIP
• *See page 105*

EDWARD D. HENDRICKSON/SAE ENGINEERING SCHOLARSHIP
• *See page 105*

RALPH K. HILLQUIST HONORARY SAE SCHOLARSHIP
• *See page 232*

TMC/SAE DONALD D. DAWSON TECHNICAL SCHOLARSHIP
• *See page 105*

YANMAR/SAE SCHOLARSHIP
• *See page 233*

SOCIETY OF HISPANIC PROFESSIONAL ENGINEERS FOUNDATION http://www.shpefoundation.org

SOCIETY OF HISPANIC PROFESSIONAL ENGINEERS FOUNDATION
• *See page 146*

SOCIETY OF MANUFACTURING ENGINEERS EDUCATION FOUNDATION http://www.sme.org/foundation

DOWNRIVER DETROIT CHAPTER 198 SCHOLARSHIP
• *See page 252*

FORT WAYNE CHAPTER 56 SCHOLARSHIP
• *See page 253*

NORTH CENTRAL REGION 9 SCHOLARSHIP
• *See page 254*

PHOENIX CHAPTER 67 SCHOLARSHIP
• *See page 254*

WICHITA CHAPTER 52 SCHOLARSHIP
• *See page 255*

WILLIAM E. WEISEL SCHOLARSHIP FUND
• *See page 222*

SOCIETY OF PLASTICS ENGINEERS (SPE) FOUNDATION http://www.4spe.org

FLEMING/BASZCAK SCHOLARSHIP
• *See page 147*

SOCIETY OF PLASTICS ENGINEERS SCHOLARSHIP PROGRAM
• *See page 147*

SOCIETY OF WOMEN ENGINEERS http://www.swe.org/scholarships

AGILENT MENTORING SCHOLARSHIP
• *See page 172*

BECHTEL CORPORATION SCHOLARSHIP
• *See page 155*

CHEVRON TEXACO CORPORATION SCHOLARSHIPS
• *See page 147*

DAIMLER CHRYSLER CORPORATION SCHOLARSHIP
• *See page 222*

DELL COMPUTER CORPORATION SCHOLARSHIPS
• *See page 173*

DUPONT COMPANY SCHOLARSHIPS
• *See page 147*

GENERAL MOTORS FOUNDATION UNDERGRADUATE SCHOLARSHIPS
• *See page 147*

GUIDANT CORPORATION SCHOLARSHIP
• *See page 173*

LOCKHEED AERONAUTICS COMPANY SCHOLARSHIPS
• *See page 223*

NORTHROP GRUMMAN CORPORATION SCHOLARSHIPS
• *See page 106*

TEXAS ENGINEERING FOUNDATION http://www.tspe.org

TEXAS SOCIETY OF PROFESSIONAL ENGINEERS (TSPE) REGIONAL SCHOLARSHIPS
• *See page 148*

UNITED NEGRO COLLEGE FUND http://www.uncf.org

CARGILL SCHOLARSHIP PROGRAM
• *See page 49*

CHEVRON/TEXACO SCHOLARS PROGRAM
• *See page 155*

CON EDISON SCHOLARSHIP
• *See page 49*

SBC FOUNDATION SCHOLARSHIP
• *See page 133*

UPS CORPORATE SCHOLARS PROGRAM/INTERNSHIP
• *See page 134*

UNIVERSITIES SPACE RESEARCH ASSOCIATION http://www.usra.edu/hq/scholarships/overview.shtml

UNIVERSITIES SPACE RESEARCH ASSOCIATION SCHOLARSHIP PROGRAM
• *See page 72*

UTAH SOCIETY OF PROFESSIONAL ENGINEERS http://www.uspeonline.com

UTAH SOCIETY OF PROFESSIONAL ENGINEERS SCHOLARSHIP
• *See page 148*

VERTICAL FLIGHT FOUNDATION http://www.vtol.org

VERTICAL FLIGHT FOUNDATION SCHOLARSHIP
• *See page 108*

WOMEN IN AVIATION, INTERNATIONAL http://www.wai.org

DELTA AIR LINES ENGINEERING SCHOLARSHIP
• See page 108

WYOMING TRUCKING ASSOCIATION

WYOMING TRUCKING ASSOCIATION TRUST FUND SCHOLARSHIP
• See page 135

XEROX http://xerox.com

TECHNICAL MINORITY SCHOLARSHIP
• See page 148

METEOROLOGY/ATMOSPHERIC SCIENCE

ALABAMA STATE DEPARTMENT OF EDUCATION http://www.alsde.edu

MATH AND SCIENCE SCHOLARSHIP PROGRAM FOR ALABAMA TEACHERS
• See page 111

AMERICAN INDIAN SCIENCE AND ENGINEERING SOCIETY http://www.aises.org

A.T. ANDERSON MEMORIAL SCHOLARSHIP
• See page 65

BURLINGTON NORTHERN SANTA FE FOUNDATION SCHOLARSHIP
• See page 65

ENVIRONMENTAL PROTECTION AGENCY TRIBAL LANDS ENVIRONMENTAL SCIENCE SCHOLARSHIP
• See page 111

AMERICAN METEOROLOGICAL SOCIETY http://www.ametsoc.org/AMS

AMERICAN METEOROLOGICAL SOCIETY 75TH ANNIVERSARY SCHOLARSHIP

Award for full-time college juniors and seniors majoring in atmospheric or related oceanic and hydrologic sciences. Must be enrolled at a U.S. institution. Cumulative GPA of 3.25 required. One-time award of $2000.

Academic Fields/Career Goals: Meteorology/Atmospheric Science.

Award: Scholarship for use in junior or senior years; not renewable. *Number:* 13. *Amount:* $2000.

Eligibility Requirements: Applicant must be enrolled or expecting to enroll full-time at an institution or university. Available to U.S. citizens.

Application Requirements: Application, essay, references, transcript. *Deadline:* February 13.

Contact: Donna Fernandez, Fellowship/Scholarship Coordinator
American Meteorological Society
45 Beacon Street
Boston, MA 02108-3693
Phone: 617-227-2426 Ext. 246
Fax: 617-742-8718
E-mail: dfernand@ametsoc.org

AMERICAN METEOROLOGICAL SOCIETY DR. PEDRO GRAU UNDERGRADUATE SCHOLARSHIP

Award for full-time college juniors and seniors majoring in atmospheric or related oceanic and hydrologic sciences. Must be enrolled at a U.S. institution. Cumulative GPA of 3.25 required. One-time award of $2500.

Academic Fields/Career Goals: Meteorology/Atmospheric Science.

Award: Scholarship for use in junior or senior years; not renewable. *Number:* varies. *Amount:* $2500.

Eligibility Requirements: Applicant must be enrolled or expecting to enroll full-time at a two-year or four-year institution or university. Available to U.S. citizens.

Application Requirements: Application, essay, references, transcript. *Deadline:* February 13.

Contact: Donna Fernandez, Fellowship/Scholarship Coordinator
American Meteorological Society
45 Beacon Street
Boston, MA 02108-3693
Phone: 617-227-2426 Ext. 246
Fax: 617-742-8718
E-mail: dfernand@ametsoc.org

AMERICAN METEOROLOGICAL SOCIETY HOWARD H. HANKS, JR. METEOROLOGICAL SCHOLARSHIP

Award for college juniors and seniors majoring in atmospheric or related oceanic and hydrologic sciences. Must be enrolled full-time at a U.S. institution with a 3.25 cumulative GPA. U.S. citizenship required. One-time award of $700.

Academic Fields/Career Goals: Meteorology/Atmospheric Science.

Award: Scholarship for use in junior or senior years; not renewable. *Number:* varies. *Amount:* $700.

Eligibility Requirements: Applicant must be enrolled or expecting to enroll full-time at a four-year institution. Available to U.S. citizens.

Application Requirements: Application, essay, references, transcript. *Deadline:* February 13.

Contact: Donna Fernandez, Fellowship/Scholarship Coordinator
American Meteorological Society
45 Beacon Street
Boston, MA 02108-3693
Phone: 617-227-2426 Ext. 246
Fax: 617-742-8718
E-mail: dfernand@ametsoc.org

AMERICAN METEOROLOGICAL SOCIETY HOWARD T. ORVILLE METEOROLOGY SCHOLARSHIP

One-time award for college juniors and seniors majoring in atmospheric or related oceanic and hydrologic sciences. Must be enrolled full-time at a U.S. institution with a 3.25 cumulative GPA.

Academic Fields/Career Goals: Meteorology/Atmospheric Science.

Award: Scholarship for use in junior or senior years; not renewable. *Number:* varies. *Amount:* $5000.

Eligibility Requirements: Applicant must be enrolled or expecting to enroll full-time at an institution or university. Available to U.S. citizens.

Application Requirements: Application, essay, references, transcript. *Deadline:* February 13.

Contact: Donna Fernandez, Fellowship/Scholarship Coordinator
American Meteorological Society
45 Beacon Street
Boston, MA 02108-3693
Phone: 617-227-2426 Ext. 246
Fax: 617-742-8718
E-mail: dfernand@ametsoc.org

AMERICAN METEOROLOGICAL SOCIETY INDUSTRY UNDERGRADUATE SCHOLARSHIPS
• See page 66

AMERICAN METEOROLOGICAL SOCIETY MARK J. SCHROEDER SCHOLARSHIP IN METEOROLOGY

Award for full-time college juniors and seniors majoring in atmospheric or related oceanic and hydrologic sciences. Must be enrolled at a U.S. institution and demonstrate financial need. Cumulative GPA of 3.25 is required.

Academic Fields/Career Goals: Meteorology/Atmospheric Science.

Award: Scholarship for use in junior or senior years; not renewable. *Number:* varies. *Amount:* varies.

American Meteorological Society (continued)

Eligibility Requirements: Applicant must be enrolled or expecting to enroll full-time at an institution or university. Available to U.S. citizens.

Application Requirements: Application, essay, financial need analysis, references, transcript. *Deadline:* February 13.

Contact: Donna Fernandez, Fellowship/Scholarship Coordinator
American Meteorological Society
45 Beacon Street
Boston, MA 02108-3693
Phone: 617-227-2426 Ext. 246
Fax: 617-742-8718
E-mail: dfernand@ametsoc.org

AMERICAN METEOROLOGICAL SOCIETY RICHARD AND HELEN HAGEMEYER SCHOLARSHIP

Award for full-time college juniors and seniors majoring in atmospheric or related oceanic and hydrologic sciences. Must be enrolled at a U.S. institution. Cumulative GPA of 3.25 is required. One-time award of $3000.

Academic Fields/Career Goals: Meteorology/Atmospheric Science.

Award: Scholarship for use in junior or senior years; not renewable. *Number:* varies. *Amount:* $3000.

Eligibility Requirements: Applicant must be enrolled or expecting to enroll full-time at an institution or university. Available to U.S. citizens.

Application Requirements: Application, essay, references, transcript. *Deadline:* February 13.

Contact: Donna Fernandez, Fellowship/Scholarship Coordinator
American Meteorological Society
45 Beacon Street
Boston, MA 02108-3693
Phone: 617-227-2426 Ext. 246
Fax: 617-742-8718
E-mail: dfernand@ametsoc.org

AMERICAN METEOROLOGICAL SOCIETY WERNER A. BAUM UNDERGRADUATE SCHOLARSHIP

Award for full-time college juniors and seniors majoring in atmospheric or related oceanic and hydrologic sciences. Must be enrolled at a U.S. institution and demonstrate financial need. Cumulative GPA of 3.25 is required. One-time award of $5000.

Academic Fields/Career Goals: Meteorology/Atmospheric Science.

Award: Scholarship for use in junior or senior years; not renewable. *Number:* varies. *Amount:* $5000.

Eligibility Requirements: Applicant must be enrolled or expecting to enroll full-time at an institution or university. Available to U.S. citizens.

Application Requirements: Application, essay, financial need analysis, references, transcript. *Deadline:* February 13.

Contact: Donna Fernandez, Fellowship/Scholarship Coordinator
American Meteorological Society
45 Beacon Street
Boston, MA 02108-3693
Phone: 617-227-2426 Ext. 246
Fax: 617-742-8718
E-mail: dfernand@ametsoc.org

AMERICAN METEOROLOGICAL SOCIETY/INDUSTRY MINORITY SCHOLARSHIPS

Two-year scholarships of $3000 per year for minority students entering their freshman year of college. Must plan to pursue careers in the atmospheric and related oceanic and hydrologic sciences. Must be U.S. citizen or permanent resident to apply.

Academic Fields/Career Goals: Meteorology/Atmospheric Science.

Award: Scholarship for use in freshman year; not renewable. *Number:* varies. *Amount:* $3000.

Eligibility Requirements: Applicant must be American Indian/Alaska Native, Asian/Pacific Islander, Black (non-Hispanic), or Hispanic; high school student and planning to enroll or expecting to enroll full-time at a four-year institution or university. Available to U.S. citizens.

Application Requirements: Application, references, test scores, transcript. *Deadline:* February 13.

Contact: Donna Fernandez, Fellowship/Scholarship Coordinator
American Meteorological Society
45 Beacon Street
Boston, MA 02108-3693
Phone: 617-227-2426 Ext. 246
Fax: 617-742-8718
E-mail: dfernand@ametsoc.org

ETHAN AND ALLAN MURPHY MEMORIAL SCHOLARSHIP

Award for full-time college juniors and seniors majoring in atmospheric or related oceanic and hydrologic science. Must show clear intent to make the atmospheric or related sciences a career. Must be enrolled in an accredited U.S. institution. Minimum 3.25 GPA required.

Academic Fields/Career Goals: Meteorology/Atmospheric Science.

Award: Scholarship for use in junior or senior years; not renewable. *Number:* varies. *Amount:* $2000.

Eligibility Requirements: Applicant must be enrolled or expecting to enroll full-time at an institution or university. Available to U.S. citizens.

Application Requirements: Application, essay, references, transcript. *Deadline:* February 13.

Contact: Donna Fernandez, Fellowship/Scholarship Coordinator
American Meteorological Society
45 Beacon Street
Boston, MA 02108-3693
Phone: 617-227-2426 Ext. 246
Fax: 617-742-8718
E-mail: amsinfo@ametsoc.org

FATHER JAMES B. MACELWANE ANNUAL AWARDS

Available to enrolled undergraduates who submit a paper on a phase of atmospheric sciences with a statement from a supervisor on the student's original contribution to the work. Minimum 3.0 GPA required. No more than two students from any one institution may enter papers in one contest. Must submit letter from department head or faculty member confirming applicant's undergraduate status and paper's originality.

Academic Fields/Career Goals: Meteorology/Atmospheric Science.

Award: Prize for use in freshman, sophomore, junior, or senior years; not renewable. *Number:* 1. *Amount:* up to $300.

Eligibility Requirements: Applicant must be enrolled or expecting to enroll at a four-year institution. Applicant must have 3.0 GPA or higher. Available to U.S. citizens.

Application Requirements: Applicant must enter a contest, essay, references, letter of application. *Deadline:* June 11.

Contact: Donna Fernandez, Fellowship/Scholarship Coordinator
American Meteorological Society
45 Beacon Street
Boston, MA 02108-3693
Phone: 617-227-2426 Ext. 246
Fax: 617-742-8718
E-mail: dfernand@ametsoc.org

GUILLERMO SALAZAR RODRIGUES SCHOLARSHIP

Award for full-time college juniors and seniors majoring in atmospheric or related oceanic and hydrologic science. Must show clear intent to make the atmospheric or related sciences a career. Must be enrolled in an accredited U.S. institution. Minimum 3.25 GPA required.

Academic Fields/Career Goals: Meteorology/Atmospheric Science.

Award: Scholarship for use in junior or senior years; not renewable. *Number:* varies. *Amount:* $2500.

Eligibility Requirements: Applicant must be enrolled or expecting to enroll at an institution or university. Available to U.S. citizens.

Application Requirements: Application, essay, references, transcript. *Deadline:* February 13.

Contact: Donna Fernandez, Fellowship/Scholarship Coordinator
American Meteorological Society
45 Beacon Street
Boston, MA 02108-3693
Phone: 617-227-2426 Ext. 246
Fax: 617-742-8718
E-mail: amsinfo@ametsoc.org

JOHN R. HOPE SCHOLARSHIP

Award for full-time college juniors and seniors majoring in atmospheric or related oceanic and hydrologic science. Must show clear intent to make the atmospheric or related science a career. Minimum 3.25 GPA required. Must be enrolled in an accredited U.S. institution.

Academic Fields/Career Goals: Meteorology/Atmospheric Science.

Award: Scholarship for use in junior or senior years; not renewable. *Number:* varies. *Amount:* $2500.

Eligibility Requirements: Applicant must be enrolled or expecting to enroll full-time at an institution or university. Available to U.S. citizens.

Application Requirements: Application, essay, references, transcript. *Deadline:* February 13.

Contact: Donna Fernandez, Fellowship/Scholarship Coordinator
American Meteorological Society
45 Beacon Street
Boston, MA 02108-3693
Phone: 617-227-2426 Ext. 246
Fax: 617-742-8718
E-mail: amsinfo@ametsoc.org

LOREN W. CROW SCHOLARSHIP

One-time award for college juniors and seniors who are majoring in atmospheric or related oceanic and hydrologic sciences. Must be enrolled full-time at a U.S. institution with a 3.25 GPA. Must be a U.S. citizen.

Academic Fields/Career Goals: Meteorology/Atmospheric Science.

Award: Scholarship for use in junior or senior years; not renewable. *Number:* varies. *Amount:* $2000.

Eligibility Requirements: Applicant must be enrolled or expecting to enroll at an institution or university. Available to U.S. citizens.

Application Requirements: Application, essay, references, transcript. *Deadline:* February 13.

Contact: Donna Fernandez, Fellowship/Scholarship Coordinator
American Meteorological Society
45 Beacon Street
Boston, MA 02108-3693
Phone: 617-227-2426 Ext. 246
Fax: 617-742-8718
E-mail: amsinfo@ametsoc.org

ASSOCIATION FOR WOMEN IN SCIENCE EDUCATIONAL FOUNDATION http://www.awis.org/ed_foundation.html

ASSOCIATION FOR WOMEN IN SCIENCE COLLEGE SCHOLARSHIP

• *See page 63*

ASTRONAUT SCHOLARSHIP FOUNDATION http://www.astronautscholarship.org

ASTRONAUT SCHOLARSHIP FOUNDATION

• *See page 68*

GARDEN CLUB OF AMERICA http://www.gcamerica.org

GARDEN CLUB OF AMERICA AWARDS FOR SUMMER ENVIRONMENTAL STUDIES

• *See page 58*

INNOVATION AND SCIENCE COUNCIL OF BRITISH COLUMBIA http://www.scbc.org

PAUL AND HELEN TRUSSEL SCIENCE AND TECHNOLOGY SCHOLARSHIP

• *See page 69*

NASA DELAWARE SPACE GRANT CONSORTIUM http://www.delspace.org

NASA DELAWARE SPACE GRANT UNDERGRADUATE TUITION SCHOLARSHIP

• *See page 70*

NASA NEVADA SPACE GRANT CONSORTIUM http://www.unr.edu/spacegrant

UNIVERSITY AND COMMUNITY COLLEGE SYSTEM OF NEVADA NASA SPACE GRANT AND FELLOWSHIP PROGRAM

• *See page 101*

NASA VERMONT SPACE GRANT CONSORTIUM http://www.emba.uvm.edu/vsgc

VERMONT SPACE GRANT CONSORTIUM SCHOLARSHIP PROGRAM

• *See page 71*

NASA WEST VIRGINIA SPACE GRANT CONSORTIUM http://www.nasa.wvu.edu

WEST VIRGINIA SPACE GRANT CONSORTIUM UNDERGRADUATE SCHOLARSHIP PROGRAM

• *See page 102*

NEW JERSEY ACADEMY OF SCIENCE http://www.njas.org

NEW JERSEY ACADEMY OF SCIENCE RESEARCH GRANTS-IN-AID TO HIGH SCHOOL STUDENTS

• *See page 116*

TKE EDUCATIONAL FOUNDATION http://www.tkefoundation.org

CARROL C. HALL MEMORIAL SCHOLARSHIP

• *See page 72*

MILITARY AND DEFENSE STUDIES

HISPANIC COLLEGE FUND, INC. http://www.hispanicfund.org

LOCKHEED MARTIN SCHOLARSHIP PROGRAM

• *See page 141*

MUSEUM STUDIES

AMERICAN SCHOOL OF CLASSICAL STUDIES AT ATHENS http://www.ascsa.edu.gr

ASCSA SUMMER SESSIONS

• *See page 65*

COSTUME SOCIETY OF AMERICA http://www.costumesocietyamerica.com

ADELE FILENE TRAVEL AWARD

• *See page 81*

STELLA BLUM RESEARCH GRANT

• *See page 81*

MINERALOGICAL SOCIETY OF AMERICA http://www.minsocam.org

MINERALOGICAL SOCIETY OF AMERICA-GRANT FOR STUDENT RESEARCH IN MINERALOGY AND PETROLOGY

• *See page 190*

MINERALOGY SOCIETY OF AMERICA-GRANT FOR RESEARCH IN CRYSTALLOGRAPHY

• *See page 191*

MUSIC

AMERICAN COLLEGE OF MUSICIANS/NATIONAL GUILD OF PIANO TEACHERS http://www.pianoguild.com

AMERICAN COLLEGE OF MUSICIANS/NATIONAL GUILD OF PIANO TEACHERS 200-DOLLAR SCHOLARSHIPS

Available only to student affiliate members who have participated in National Guild of Piano Teachers auditions over a ten-year period. Must be sponsored by Guild member. Contact American College of Musicians for more information.

Academic Fields/Career Goals: Music.

Award: Scholarship for use in freshman, sophomore, junior, or senior years; not renewable. *Number:* 150. *Amount:* $200.

Eligibility Requirements: Applicant must be enrolled or expecting to enroll full-time at a two-year or four-year or technical institution or university. Applicant or parent of applicant must be member of American College of Musicians. Available to U.S. and non-U.S. citizens.

Application Requirements: Application, test scores. *Deadline:* September 15.

Contact: Ms. Pat McCabe, Scholarship Coordinator
American College of Musicians/National Guild of Piano Teachers
808 Rio Grande
Austin, TX 78767-1807
Phone: 512-478-5775
E-mail: ngpt@aol.com

AMERICAN FOUNDATION FOR THE BLIND http://www.afb.org

R.L. GILLETTE SCHOLARSHIP

• *See page 346*

AMERICAN LEGION, DEPARTMENT OF KANSAS

MUSIC COMMITTEE SCHOLARSHIP

One-time award open to a high school senior or college freshman or sophomore. Must be used at an approved Kansas university or college. Must major or minor in music. Write for more information.

Academic Fields/Career Goals: Music; Performing Arts.

Award: Scholarship for use in freshman or sophomore years; not renewable. *Number:* 1. *Amount:* $1000.

Eligibility Requirements: Applicant must be enrolled or expecting to enroll at a four-year institution or university; studying in Kansas and must have an interest in music/singing. Available to U.S. citizens.

Application Requirements: Application, financial need analysis, photo, references, transcript. *Deadline:* February 15.

Contact: Scholarship Administrator
American Legion, Department of Kansas
1314 Southwest Topeka Boulevard
Topeka, KS 66612-1886

AMERICAN MUSICOLOGICAL SOCIETY http://www.ams-net.org

MINORITY TRAVEL FUND AWARD

Award for promising minority undergraduates and terminal masters degree candidates who are considering graduate work toward a doctorate in music. Award is to help cover travel expenses to the AMS annual conference. See Web site for more information http://www.ams-net.org.

Academic Fields/Career Goals: Music.

Award: Grant for use in freshman, sophomore, junior, senior, or graduate years; not renewable. *Number:* varies. *Amount:* varies.

Eligibility Requirements: Applicant must be American Indian/Alaska Native, Asian/Pacific Islander, Black (non-Hispanic), or Hispanic and enrolled or expecting to enroll at a four-year institution or university. Available to U.S. citizens.

Application Requirements: Application, autobiography, references. *Deadline:* October 11.

Contact: American Musicological Society
201 South 34th Street
Philadelphia, PA 19104-6313

AMERICAN SOCIETY OF COMPOSERS, AUTHORS, AND PUBLISHERS FOUNDATION http://www.ascap.com

AMERICAN SOCIETY OF COMPOSERS, AUTHORS, AND PUBLISHERS FOUNDATION RUDOLF NISSIM AWARD

One-time $5000 prize for member of American Society of Composers, Authors, and Publishers entering a music composition which has not been professionally premiered, for large ensemble requiring a conductor. Please submit biography, a copy of an original musical score (tape or CD) of musical composition, and self-addressed stamped envelope.

Academic Fields/Career Goals: Music.

Award: Prize for use in freshman, sophomore, junior, senior, graduate, or postgraduate years; not renewable. *Number:* 1. *Amount:* $5000.

Eligibility Requirements: Applicant must be enrolled or expecting to enroll at an institution or university and must have an interest in music. Applicant or parent of applicant must be member of American Society of Composers, Authors, and Publishers. Available to U.S. and non-U.S. citizens.

Application Requirements: Application, applicant must enter a contest, autobiography, self-addressed stamped envelope, music score. *Deadline:* November 15.

Contact: Frances Richard, Vice President and Director of Concert Music
American Society of Composers, Authors, and Publishers Foundation
One Lincoln Plaza
New York, NY 10023
Phone: 212-621-6327
Fax: 212-621-6504
E-mail: frichard@ascap.com

ASCAP FOUNDATION MORTON GOULD YOUNG COMPOSER AWARDS

Cash prizes for U.S. citizens or permanent residents or those with U.S. student visas, up to age 30 as of December 31. Applicants must be composers and must submit score, with tape or CD recording, for competition. Original concert music of any style will be considered. Works that have earned national prizes are ineligible, as are arrangements.

Academic Fields/Career Goals: Music.

Award: Prize for use in freshman, sophomore, junior, senior, graduate, or postgraduate years; not renewable. *Number:* 20–25. *Amount:* $250–$2500.

Eligibility Requirements: Applicant must be age 30 or under; enrolled or expecting to enroll at a two-year or four-year or technical institution or university and must have an interest in music. Available to U.S. and non-U.S. citizens.

Application Requirements: Application, applicant must enter a contest, autobiography, self-addressed stamped envelope, music score. *Deadline:* March 1.

Contact: Frances Richard, Vice President and Director of Concert Music
American Society of Composers, Authors, and Publishers Foundation
One Lincoln Plaza
New York, NY 10023
Phone: 212-621-6327
Fax: 212-621-6504
E-mail: frichard@ascap.com

ASCAP FOUNDATION YOUNG JAZZ COMPOSER AWARD

Cash prizes for U.S. citizens or permanent presidents up to age 30 as of December 31. Applicants must be jazz composers and must submit score of one original work (no arrangements). Tape or electronic realization may accompany score. Works that have earned national prizes are ineligible.

Academic Fields/Career Goals: Music.

Award: Prize for use in freshman, sophomore, junior, senior, graduate, or postgraduate years; not renewable.

Eligibility Requirements: Applicant must be age 30 or under; enrolled or expecting to enroll full or part-time at a two-year or four-year or technical institution or university and must have an interest in music. Available to U.S. citizens.

Application Requirements: Application, applicant must enter a contest, autobiography, self-addressed stamped envelope, score of one original composition. *Deadline:* October 1.

Contact: Frances Richard, Vice President and Director of Concert Music
American Society of Composers, Authors, and Publishers Foundation
ASCAP Building
One Lincoln Plaza
New York, NY 10023-2399
Phone: 212-621-6327
Fax: 212-621-6504
E-mail: frichard@ascap.com

BEEM FOUNDATION FOR THE ADVANCEMENT OF MUSIC http://www.beemfoundation.org

BEEM FOUNDATION SCHOLARSHIP

Competition for excellence in the performance of vocal or instrumental music. Awarded to talented music students of Southern California.

Academic Fields/Career Goals: Music.

Award: Scholarship for use in freshman, sophomore, junior, senior, or graduate years; not renewable. *Number:* 3. *Amount:* $1000–$5000.

Eligibility Requirements: Applicant must be age 25 or under; enrolled or expecting to enroll full-time at an institution or university and resident of California. Available to U.S. citizens.

Application Requirements: Application, applicant must enter a contest, photo, resume, transcript. *Deadline:* May 2.

Contact: BEEM Foundation Scholarship
BEEM Foundation for the Advancement of Music
3864 Grayburn Avenue
Los Angeles, CA 90008

CALIFORNIA ALLIANCE FOR ARTS EDUCATION (CAAE) http://www.artsed411.org

EMERGING YOUNG ARTIST AWARDS

• *See page 86*

CHAFFER SCHOLARSHIP TRUST

CHAFFER SCHOLARSHIP TRUST

The Chaffer Trust is designated for university music majors in their junior, senior, or graduate school years attending Idaho institutions, or are Idahoans attending school out-of-state. They must major in piano, organ, or harpsichord, or Music Education with their main instrument one of the three mentioned. Trust awards are for a maximum of 2 years.

Academic Fields/Career Goals: Music.

Award: Scholarship for use in junior, senior, graduate, or postgraduate years; renewable. *Number:* 22–25. *Amount:* $700–$4800.

Eligibility Requirements: Applicant must be enrolled or expecting to enroll full-time at a four-year institution or university and must have an interest in music. Available to U.S. and non-U.S. citizens.

Application Requirements: Application, tape or CD of applicant playing 3 piano/organ/harpsichord pieces from 3 different music periods. *Deadline:* April 1.

Contact: Gay Pool, Chairman of Chaffer Trust
Chaffer Scholarship Trust
c/o Wells Fargo Bank
119 North Ninth Street, PO Box 2618
Boise, ID 83701
Phone: 208-383-9216
E-mail: gpiano83712@earthlink.net

CHOPIN FOUNDATION OF THE UNITED STATES http://www.chopin.org

CHOPIN FOUNDATION OF THE UNITED STATES SCHOLARSHIP

Program aimed to help young American pianists to continue their piano education. Award(s) are available to students between ages 14 to 17 whose field of study is music and whose major is piano. Renewable for up to four years. Students will be assisted in preparing to qualify for the American National Chopin Piano Competition. Must be U.S. citizen or legal resident. Award based on performance of F. Chopin's required repertoire. Registration fee is $25.

Academic Fields/Career Goals: Music; Performing Arts.

Award: Scholarship for use in freshman year; renewable. *Number:* 10. *Amount:* $1000.

Eligibility Requirements: Applicant must be age 14-17; enrolled or expecting to enroll full or part-time at an institution or university and must have an interest in music. Available to U.S. citizens.

Application Requirements: Application, applicant must enter a contest, references, recording. *Fee:* $25. *Deadline:* February 15.

Contact: Ms. Jadwiga Gewert, Executive Director
Chopin Foundation of the United States
1440 79th Street Causeway, Suite 117
Miami, FL 33141
Phone: 305-868-0624
Fax: 305-865-5150
E-mail: info@chopin.org

COMMUNITY FOUNDATION OF CAPE COD http://www.capecodfoundation.org

RICHARD AND ETHEL KOFF MEMORIAL SCHOLARSHIP FUND

Richard & Ethel Koff Memorial Scholarship Fund provides four-year scholarships to graduating seniors from the greater Barnstable area intending to further their education in the field of music. For more details see Web site: http://www.capecodfoundation.org.

Academic Fields/Career Goals: Music.

Award: Scholarship for use in freshman, sophomore, junior, or senior years; renewable. *Number:* 1. *Amount:* $1000–$4000.

Eligibility Requirements: Applicant must be high school student; planning to enroll or expecting to enroll full-time at a four-year institution or university and resident of Massachusetts. Available to U.S. citizens.

Application Requirements: Application, essay, financial need analysis, references, test scores, transcript. *Deadline:* April 1.

Contact: Pauline Greenberg, Scholarship Associate
Community Foundation of Cape Cod
PO Box 406
259 Willow Street
Yarmouthport, MA 02675
Phone: 508-790-3040
Fax: 508-790-4069
E-mail: pgreenberg@capecodfoundation.org

DELTA OMICRON INTERNATIONAL MUSIC FRATERNITY/DELTA OMICRON FOUNDATION, INC. http://delta-omicron.org

EDUCATIONAL GRANTS IN MUSIC

Twenty one-time $500 grants available to those studying music at a four-year college or university. Must have a minimum 2.5 GPA. Deadline: March 31. Must be a member of Delta Omicron International Music Fraternity.

Delta Omicron International Music Fraternity/Delta Omicron Foundation, Inc. (continued)

Academic Fields/Career Goals: Music.

Award: Grant for use in freshman, sophomore, junior, senior, graduate, or postgraduate years; not renewable. *Number:* 20. *Amount:* $500.

Eligibility Requirements: Applicant must be enrolled or expecting to enroll full or part-time at a four-year institution or university and must have an interest in music. Applicant must have 2.5 GPA or higher. Available to U.S. and non-U.S. citizens.

Application Requirements: Application, resume, references. *Deadline:* March 31.

Contact: Dr. Kay Wideman, President
Delta Omicron International Music Fraternity/Delta Omicron Foundation, Inc.
503 Greystone Lane
Douglasville, GA 30134
Phone: 770-920-2417
E-mail: widemans@bellsouth.net

SUMMER MUSIC SCHOLARSHIPS

Seven $500 awards for summer music workshops. Open to Delta Omicron members in good standing. Must be at least 16 years old. Deadline: March 31.

Academic Fields/Career Goals: Music.

Award: Scholarship for use in freshman, sophomore, junior, senior, graduate, or postgraduate years; not renewable. *Number:* 7. *Amount:* $500.

Eligibility Requirements: Applicant must be age 16; enrolled or expecting to enroll full or part-time at a two-year or four-year institution or university and must have an interest in music or music/singing. Available to U.S. and non-U.S. citizens.

Application Requirements: Application, references. *Deadline:* March 31.

Contact: Michelle A. May, Chair, Rotating Grants and Summer Scholarships
Delta Omicron International Music Fraternity/Delta Omicron Foundation, Inc.
1635 West Boston Boulevard
Detroit, MI 48206
Phone: 313-865-1149
Fax: 313-965-0868
E-mail: maybiz@aol.com

GENERAL FEDERATION OF WOMEN'S CLUBS OF MASSACHUSETTS

DORCHESTER WOMEN'S CLUB SCHOLARSHIP

Scholarship for major in voice. Must submit letter of endorsement from president of the sponsoring General Federation of Women's Clubs of Massachusetts and personal statement of no more than 500 words addressing professional goals and financial need. Audition required. Must be a Massachusetts resident.

Academic Fields/Career Goals: Music; Performing Arts.

Award: Scholarship for use in freshman, sophomore, junior, or senior years; not renewable. *Number:* 1. *Amount:* $500.

Eligibility Requirements: Applicant must be enrolled or expecting to enroll full-time at a four-year institution or university; resident of Massachusetts and must have an interest in music/singing.

Application Requirements: Application, applicant must enter a contest, autobiography, interview, references, self-addressed stamped envelope, transcript. *Deadline:* February 1.

Contact: June Alfano, Chairperson
General Federation of Women's Clubs of Massachusetts
PO Box 679
Sudbury, MA 01776-0679
Phone: 978-443-4569
E-mail: joaheart@attbi.com

GENERAL FEDERATION OF WOMEN'S CLUBS OF MASSACHUSETTS MUSIC SCHOLARSHIP

• *See page 201*

GOLDEN KEY INTERNATIONAL HONOUR SOCIETY http://www.goldenkey.org

PERFORMING ARTS SHOWCASE

• *See page 267*

GRAND RAPIDS COMMUNITY FOUNDATION http://www.grfoundation.org

LLEWELLYN L. CAYVAN STRING INSTRUMENT SCHOLARSHIP

For undergraduate students studying the violin, the viola, the violoncello, and/or the bass viol. Refer to Web site for application and details: http://www.grfoundation.org

Academic Fields/Career Goals: Music.

Award: Scholarship for use in freshman, sophomore, junior, or senior years. *Number:* varies. *Amount:* varies.

Eligibility Requirements: Applicant must be enrolled or expecting to enroll at an institution or university and resident of Michigan.

Application Requirements: Application, essay, references, transcript. *Deadline:* April 1.

Contact: See Web site.

INTERNATIONALER MUSIKWETTBEWERB http://www.ard-musikwettbewerb.de

INTERNATIONAL MUSIC COMPETITION OF THE ARD MUNICH

Twelve prizes will be awarded at the International Music Competition of the ARD Munich. The competition is held annually in September. Prizes are awarded in various categories.

Academic Fields/Career Goals: Music.

Award: Prize for use in senior, or graduate years; not renewable. *Number:* 12. *Amount:* $5000–$10,000.

Eligibility Requirements: Applicant must be age 20-29 and enrolled or expecting to enroll full or part-time at an institution or university. Available to U.S. and non-U.S. citizens.

Application Requirements: Application, applicant must enter a contest, references. *Fee:* $80. *Deadline:* April 20.

Contact: Ingeborg Krause, Head of Organization
Internationaler Musikwettbewerb
Bayerischer Rundfink
Munich 80300
Germany
Phone: 49-89-5900247
Fax: 49-89-5900357
E-mail: ard.musikwettbewerb@brnet.de

JACK J. ISGUR FOUNDATION

JACK J. ISGUR FOUNDATION SCHOLARSHIP

• *See page 87*

MELLON NEW ENGLAND

SUSAN GLOVER HITCHCOCK SCHOLARSHIP

Award for women who are majoring in music. Must be a Massachusetts resident. Application deadline is April 15.

Academic Fields/Career Goals: Music.

Award: Scholarship for use in freshman, sophomore, junior, or senior years; not renewable. *Number:* varies. *Amount:* $500–$800.

Eligibility Requirements: Applicant must be enrolled or expecting to enroll full-time at a two-year or four-year or technical institution or university; female and resident of Massachusetts. Available to U.S. citizens.

Application Requirements: Application, essay, transcript. *Deadline:* April 15.

Contact: Sandra Brown-McMullen, Vice President
Mellon New England
One Boston Place, 024-0084
Boston, MA 02108
Phone: 617-722-3891

NATIONAL ASSOCIATION OF PASTORAL MUSICIANS http://www.npm.org

ELAINE RENDLER-RENE DOSOGNE-GEORGETOWN CHORALE SCHOLARSHIP

Award for students pursuing studies related to the field of pastoral music. Applicant must intend to work at least two years in the field of pastoral music following graduation or program completion. Must submit applicant's definition of "pastoral music," description of talents and previous experience, and a 5-minute performance cassette or applicant's choir ensemble. Applicant must be a member of NPM.

Academic Fields/Career Goals: Music; Religion/Theology.

Award: Scholarship for use in junior, senior, graduate, or postgraduate years; not renewable. *Number:* 1. *Amount:* $1000.

Eligibility Requirements: Applicant must be enrolled or expecting to enroll full or part-time at a two-year or four-year or technical institution or university and must have an interest in music/singing. Available to U.S. and non-U.S. citizens.

Application Requirements: Application, essay, financial need analysis, resume, references, tape of performance. *Deadline:* March 1.

Contact: Scholarship Department
National Association of Pastoral Musicians
962 Wayne Avenue, Suite 210
Silver Spring, MD 20910
Phone: 240-247-3000
Fax: 240-247-3001
E-mail: npmsing@npm.org

FUNK FAMILY MEMORIAL SCHOLARSHIP

Award for students pursuing studies related to the field of pastoral music. Applicant must intend to work at least two years in the field of pastoral music following graduation or program completion. Must submit applicant's definition of "pastoral music," description of talents and previous experience, and a 5-minute performance cassette of applicant's choir ensemble. Applicant must be a member of NPM.

Academic Fields/Career Goals: Music; Religion/Theology.

Award: Scholarship for use in senior, graduate, or postgraduate years; not renewable. *Number:* 1. *Amount:* $1000.

Eligibility Requirements: Applicant must be enrolled or expecting to enroll full or part-time at a two-year or four-year or technical institution or university and must have an interest in music/singing. Available to U.S. and non-U.S. citizens.

Application Requirements: Application, essay, financial need analysis, resume, references, tape of performance. *Deadline:* March 1.

Contact: Scholarship Department
National Association of Pastoral Musicians
962 Wayne Avenue, Suite 210
Silver Spring, MD 20910
Phone: 240-247-3000
Fax: 240-247-3001
E-mail: npmsing@npm.org

GIA PUBLICATION PASTORAL MUSICIAN SCHOLARSHIP

Award for students pursuing studies related to the field of pastoral music. Applicant must intend to work at least two years in the field of pastoral music following graduation or program completion. Must submit applicant's definition of "pastoral music," description of talents and previous experience, and a 5-minute performance cassette of applicant's choir/ensemble. Applicant must be a member of NPM.

Academic Fields/Career Goals: Music; Religion/Theology.

Award: Scholarship for use in senior, graduate, or postgraduate years; not renewable. *Number:* 1. *Amount:* $1500.

Eligibility Requirements: Applicant must be enrolled or expecting to enroll full or part-time at a two-year or four-year or technical institution or university and must have an interest in music/singing. Available to U.S. and non-U.S. citizens.

Application Requirements: Application, essay, financial need analysis, resume, references, tape of performance. *Deadline:* March 1.

Contact: Scholarship Department
National Association of Pastoral Musicians
962 Wayne Avenue, Suite 210
Silver Spring, MD 20910
Phone: 240-247-3000
Fax: 240-247-3001
E-mail: npmsing@npm.org

MUSONICS SCHOLARSHIP

Award for students pursuing studies related to the field of pastoral music. Applicant must intend to work at least two years in the field of pastoral music following graduation or program completion. Must submit applicant's definition of "pastoral music," description of talents and previous experience, and a 5-minute performance cassette of applicant's choir/ensemble. Applicant must be a member of NPM.

Academic Fields/Career Goals: Music; Religion/Theology.

Award: Scholarship for use in senior, graduate, or postgraduate years; not renewable. *Number:* 1. *Amount:* $2000.

Eligibility Requirements: Applicant must be enrolled or expecting to enroll full or part-time at a two-year or four-year or technical institution or university and must have an interest in music/singing. Available to U.S. and non-U.S. citizens.

Application Requirements: Application, essay, financial need analysis, resume, references, tape of performance. *Deadline:* March 1.

Contact: Scholarship Department
National Association of Pastoral Musicians
962 Wayne Avenue, Suite 210
Silver Spring, MD 20910
Phone: 240-247-3000
Fax: 240-247-3001
E-mail: npmsing@npm.org

NATIONAL ASSOCIATION OF PASTORAL MUSICIANS MEMBERS' SCHOLARSHIP

Award for students pursuing studies related to the field of pastoral music. Applicant must intend to work at least two years in the field of pastoral music following graduation or program completion. Must submit applicant's definition of "pastoral music," description of talents and previous experience, and a 5-minute performance cassette of applicant's choir/ensemble. Applicant must be a member of NPM.

Academic Fields/Career Goals: Music; Religion/Theology.

Award: Scholarship for use in senior, graduate, or postgraduate years; not renewable. *Number:* 1. *Amount:* $2000–$10,000.

Eligibility Requirements: Applicant must be enrolled or expecting to enroll full or part-time at a two-year or four-year or technical institution or university and must have an interest in music/singing. Available to U.S. and non-U.S. citizens.

Application Requirements: Application, essay, financial need analysis, resume, references, tape of performance. *Deadline:* March 1.

Contact: Scholarship Department
National Association of Pastoral Musicians
962 Wayne Avenue, Suite 210
Silver Spring, MD 20910
Phone: 240-247-3000
Fax: 240-247-3001
E-mail: npmsing@npm.org

NPM KOINONIA/BOARD OF DIRECTORS SCHOLARSHIP

Awards for students pursuing studies related to the field of pastoral music. Applicant must intend to work at least two years in the field of pastoral music following graduation or program completion. Must submit applicant's

National Association of Pastoral Musicians (continued)

definition of "pastoral music", description of talents and previous experience, and a 5-minute performance cassette of applicant's choir/ensemble. Applicant must be a member of NPM.

Academic Fields/Career Goals: Music; Religion/Theology.

Award: Scholarship for use in senior, graduate, or postgraduate years; not renewable. *Number:* 2. *Amount:* $2000–$2500.

Eligibility Requirements: Applicant must be enrolled or expecting to enroll full or part-time at a two-year or four-year or technical institution or university and must have an interest in music/singing. Available to U.S. and non-U.S. citizens.

Application Requirements: Application, essay, financial need analysis, resume, references. *Deadline:* March 1.

Contact: Scholarship Department
National Association of Pastoral Musicians
962 Wayne Avenue, Suite 210
Silver Spring, MD 20910
Phone: 240-247-3000
Fax: 240-247-3001

NPM PERROT SCHOLARSHIP

Award for students pursuing studies related to the field of pastoral music. Applicant must intend to work at least two years in the field of pastoral music following graduation or program completion. Must submit applicant's definition of "pastoral music," description of talents and previous experience, and a 5-minute performance cassette of applicant's choir/ensemble. Applicant must be member of NPM.

Academic Fields/Career Goals: Music; Religion/Theology.

Award: Scholarship for use in senior, graduate, or postgraduate years; not renewable. *Number:* 1. *Amount:* $2000.

Eligibility Requirements: Applicant must be enrolled or expecting to enroll full or part-time at a two-year or four-year or technical institution or university. Available to U.S. and non-U.S. citizens.

Application Requirements: Application, essay, financial need analysis, resume, references, tape of performance. *Deadline:* March 1.

Contact: Scholarship Department
National Association of Pastoral Musicians
962 Wayne Avenue, Suite 210
Silver Spring, MD 20910
Phone: 240-247-3000
Fax: 240-247-3001

OREGON CATHOLIC PRESS SCHOLARSHIP

Award for students pursuing studies related to the field of pastoral music. Applicant must intend to work at least two years in the field of pastoral music following graduation or program completion. Must submit applicant's definition of "pastoral music," description of talents and previous experience, and a 5 minute performance cassette of applicant's choir/ensemble. Applicant must be a member of NPM.

Academic Fields/Career Goals: Music; Religion/Theology.

Award: Scholarship for use in senior, graduate, or postgraduate years; not renewable. *Number:* 1. *Amount:* $1500.

Eligibility Requirements: Applicant must be enrolled or expecting to enroll full or part-time at a two-year or four-year or technical institution or university and must have an interest in music/singing. Available to U.S. and non-U.S. citizens.

Application Requirements: Application, essay, financial need analysis, resume, references, tape of performance. *Deadline:* March 1.

Contact: Scholarship Department
National Association of Pastoral Musicians
962 Wayne Avenue, Suite 210
Silver Spring, MD 20910
Phone: 240-247-3000
Fax: 240-247-3001
E-mail: npmsing@npm.org

PALUCH FAMILY FOUNDATION/WORLD LIBRARY PUBLICATIONS SCHOLARSHIP

Award for students pursuing studies related to the field of pastoral music. Applicant must intend to work at least two years in the field of pastoral music following graduation or program completion. Must submit applicant's definition of "pastoral music", description of talents and previous experience, and a 5-minute performance cassette of applicant's choir/ensemble. Applicant must be a member of NPM.

Academic Fields/Career Goals: Music; Religion/Theology.

Award: Scholarship for use in senior, graduate, or postgraduate years; not renewable. *Number:* 1. *Amount:* $2000.

Eligibility Requirements: Applicant must be enrolled or expecting to enroll full or part-time at a two-year or four-year or technical institution or university and must have an interest in music/singing. Available to U.S. and non-U.S. citizens.

Application Requirements: Application, essay, financial need analysis, resume, references, tape of performance. *Deadline:* March 1.

Contact: Scholarship Department
National Association of Pastoral Musicians
962 Wayne Avenue, Suite 210
Silver Spring, MD 20910
Phone: 240-247-3000
Fax: 240-247-3001
E-mail: npmsing@npm.org

NATIONAL FOUNDATION FOR ADVANCEMENT IN THE ARTS http://www.artsawards.org

ASTRAL CAREER GRANT

Award available to those pursuing music and dance. Must be U.S. citizen or permanent resident. One-time award. Music applicants must be vocalists, composers or pianists, while dance applicants must be ballet dancers or choreographers.

Academic Fields/Career Goals: Music; Performing Arts.

Award: Grant for use in freshman, sophomore, junior, or senior years; not renewable. *Number:* 8–12. *Amount:* $200–$250.

Eligibility Requirements: Applicant must be enrolled or expecting to enroll part-time at an institution or university. Available to U.S. and non-U.S. citizens.

Application Requirements: Application, autobiography, essay, financial need analysis, portfolio, resume, references, self-addressed stamped envelope, transcript. *Deadline:* Continuous.

Contact: Programs Department
National Foundation for Advancement in the Arts
444 Brickell Avenue, Suite R14
Miami, FL 33133
Phone: 800-970-2787 Ext. 33
Fax: 305-377-1149
E-mail: nfaa@nfaa.org

NATIONAL GUILD OF COMMUNITY SCHOOLS OF THE ARTS http://www.nationalguild.org

YOUNG COMPOSERS AWARDS

Applicant must send an original classical or jazz musical composition. Must be ages 13-18 and a U.S. or Canadian resident in either school music program or private program. Submit four copies of work and certification by teacher with $15 check. One-time award of $250-$1000.

Academic Fields/Career Goals: Music; Performing Arts.

Award: Prize for use in freshman year; not renewable. *Number:* 4. *Amount:* $250–$1000.

Eligibility Requirements: Applicant must be high school student; age 13-18; planning to enroll or expecting to enroll full-time at an institution or university and must have an interest in music/singing. Available to U.S. and non-U.S. citizens.

Application Requirements: Application, applicant must enter a contest, composition manuscripts. *Fee:* $15. *Deadline:* April 14.

Contact: Carissa Reddick, YCA Coordinator
National Guild of Community Schools of the Arts
The Hartt School Community Division, University of Hartford, 200 Bloomfield Avenue
West Hartford, CT 06117
Phone: 860-768-7768 Ext. 8558
Fax: 860-768-4777
E-mail: youngcomp@hartford.edu

RHODE ISLAND FOUNDATION http://www.rifoundation.org

BACH ORGAN AND KEYBOARD SCHOLARSHIP FUND

For organ or keyboard musicians attending four-year colleges and universities. Applicants must demonstrate good grades and financial need. Must include music tape. Must be Rhode Island resident attending college as a music major.

Academic Fields/Career Goals: Music.

Award: Scholarship for use in freshman, sophomore, junior, or senior years; renewable. *Number:* 1–3. *Amount:* $300–$1000.

Eligibility Requirements: Applicant must be enrolled or expecting to enroll full-time at a four-year institution or university; resident of Rhode Island and must have an interest in music/singing.

Application Requirements: Application, financial need analysis, references, self-addressed stamped envelope, transcript. *Deadline:* June 4.

Contact: Libby Monahan, Scholarship Coordinator
Rhode Island Foundation
1 Union Station
Providence, RI 02903
Phone: 401-274-4564
Fax: 401-272-1359

CONSTANT MEMORIAL SCHOLARSHIP FOR AQUIDNECK ISLAND RESIDENTS

• *See page 90*

SIGMA ALPHA IOTA PHILANTHROPIES, INC. http://www.sai-national.org

SIGMA ALPHA IOTA MUSIC THERAPY SCHOLARSHIP

One-time award offered yearly for undergraduate and graduate members of SAI who have completed two years in music therapy training at a university approved by the American Music Therapy Association. Contact local chapter for further information. Application fee: $25.

Academic Fields/Career Goals: Music; Therapy/Rehabilitation.

Award: Scholarship for use in junior, senior, or graduate years; not renewable. *Number:* 1. *Amount:* $1000.

Eligibility Requirements: Applicant must be enrolled or expecting to enroll full-time at a four-year institution or university; female and must have an interest in music/singing. Available to U.S. and non-U.S. citizens.

Application Requirements: Application, essay, references, transcript. *Fee:* $25. *Deadline:* March 15.

Contact: Ms. Ruth Sieber Johnson, Executive Director of SAI
Sigma Alpha Iota Philanthropies, Inc.
34 Wall Street, Suite 515
Asheville, NC 28801-2710
Phone: 828-251-0606
Fax: 828-251-0644
E-mail: nh@sai-national.org

SIGMA ALPHA IOTA PHILANTHROPIES UNDERGRADUATE PERFORMANCE SCHOLARSHIPS

Award offered triennially for female SAI members in freshman, sophomore or junior year in voice; keyboard and percussion; strings; winds and brass. Winners perform at national convention. Must submit tape with required repertoire. Consult local chapter for details. Four one-time scholarships of $1500. Application fee: $25.

Academic Fields/Career Goals: Music; Performing Arts.

Award: Scholarship for use in freshman, sophomore, or junior years; not renewable. *Number:* 4. *Amount:* $1500.

Eligibility Requirements: Applicant must be enrolled or expecting to enroll full-time at a four-year institution or university; female and must have an interest in music/singing. Available to U.S. and non-U.S. citizens.

Application Requirements: Application, applicant must enter a contest, essay, references, transcript, audio tape. *Fee:* $25. *Deadline:* March 15.

Contact: Ms. Ruth Sieber Johnson, Executive Director of SAI
Sigma Alpha Iota Philanthropies, Inc.
34 Wall Street, Suite 515
Asheville, NC 28801-2710
Phone: 828-251-0606
Fax: 828-251-0644
E-mail: nh@sai-national.org

SIGMA ALPHA IOTA SUMMER MUSIC SCHOLARSHIPS IN THE U.S. OR ABROAD

One-time award for use at summer music programs in the U.S. or abroad. Must be a member of SAI and accepted by the summer music program. Contact local chapter for details. Application fee: $25.

Academic Fields/Career Goals: Music; Performing Arts.

Award: Scholarship for use in freshman, sophomore, junior, or senior years; not renewable. *Number:* 5. *Amount:* up to $1000.

Eligibility Requirements: Applicant must be enrolled or expecting to enroll full-time at a four-year institution or university; female and must have an interest in music/singing. Available to U.S. and non-U.S. citizens.

Application Requirements: Application, essay. *Fee:* $25. *Deadline:* March 15.

Contact: Ms. Ruth Sieber Johnson, Executive Director of SAI
Sigma Alpha Iota Philanthropies, Inc.
34 Wall Street, Suite 515
Asheville, NC 28801-2710
Phone: 828-251-0606
Fax: 828-251-0644
E-mail: nh@sai-national.org

SIGMA ALPHA IOTA VISUALLY IMPAIRED SCHOLARSHIP

• *See page 211*

UNICO NATIONAL, INC http://www.unico.org

THEODORE MAZZA SCHOLARSHIP

• *See page 79*

UNITED NEGRO COLLEGE FUND http://www.uncf.org

ELLA FITZGERALD CHARITABLE FOUNDATION SCHOLARSHIP

Scholarship for students majoring in music and attending a UNCF member college or university. Minimum 2.5 GPA required. Prospective applicants should complete the Student Profile found at Web site: http://www.uncf.org.

Academic Fields/Career Goals: Music; Performing Arts.

Award: Scholarship for use in freshman, sophomore, junior, or senior years; not renewable.

Eligibility Requirements: Applicant must be Black (non-Hispanic) and enrolled or expecting to enroll at a four-year institution or university. Applicant must have 2.5 GPA or higher.

Application Requirements: Application, financial need analysis. *Deadline:* Continuous.

Contact: Program Services Department
United Negro College Fund
8260 Willow Oaks Corporate Drive
Fairfax, VA 22031

WAVERLY COMMUNITY HOUSE, INC. http://waverlycomm.com

F. LAMMOT BELIN ARTS SCHOLARSHIP
• *See page 80*

WOMEN BAND DIRECTORS INTERNATIONAL http://womenbanddirectors.org

GLADYS STONE WRIGHT SCHOLARSHIP
• *See page 216*

HELEN MAY BULTER MEMORIAL SCHOLARSHIP
• *See page 216*

MARTHA ANN STARK MEMORIAL SCHOLARSHIP
• *See page 217*

MUSIC TECHNOLOGY SCHOLARSHIP
• *See page 217*

VOLKWEIN MEMORIAL SCHOLARSHIP
• *See page 217*

NATURAL RESOURCES

AIR AND WASTE MANAGEMENT ASSOCIATION-CONNECTICUT CHAPTER http://www.awma-nes.org/

AIR AND WASTE MANAGEMENT ASSOCIATION-CONNECTICUT CHAPTER SCHOLARSHIP
• *See page 111*

ALASKA COMMISSION ON POSTSECONDARY EDUCATION http://www.state.ak.us/acpe/

A.W. "WINN" BRINDLE MEMORIAL EDUCATION LOANS
• *See page 52*

AMERICAN GROUND WATER TRUST http://www.agwt.org

AMERICAN GROUND WATER TRUST-AMTROL, INC. SCHOLARSHIP
• *See page 149*

AMERICAN GROUND WATER TRUST-CLAUDE LAVAL CORPORATION THE BEN EVERSON SCHOLARSHIP
• *See page 149*

AMERICAN INDIAN SCIENCE AND ENGINEERING SOCIETY http://www.aises.org

A.T. ANDERSON MEMORIAL SCHOLARSHIP
• *See page 65*

HENRY RODRIGUEZ RECLAMATION COLLEGE SCHOLARSHIP AND INTERNSHIP
• *See page 224*

AMERICAN WATER RESOURCES ASSOCIATION http://www.awra.org/student/herbert.html

RICHARD A. HERBERT MEMORIAL SCHOLARSHIP

There are two scholarships: one for full-time undergraduate student working toward his/her first undergraduate degree and enrolled in a program related to water resources. One is for full-time graduate student enrolled in a program relating to water resources. All applicants must be national AWRA members.

Academic Fields/Career Goals: Natural Resources.

Award: Scholarship for use in freshman, sophomore, junior, senior, or graduate years; not renewable. *Number:* 2. *Amount:* up to $2000.

Eligibility Requirements: Applicant must be enrolled or expecting to enroll full-time at a four-year institution or university. Available to U.S. and non-U.S. citizens.

Application Requirements: Application, essay, references, transcript. *Deadline:* April 30.

Contact: Harriett Bayse, Director of Marketing
American Water Resources Association
4 West Federal Street
PO Box 1626
Middleburg, VA 20118-1626
Phone: 540-687-8390
E-mail: info@awra.org

APICS EDUCATIONAL AND RESEARCH FOUNDATION, INC. http://www.apics.org

DONALD W. FOGARTY INTERNATIONAL STUDENT PAPER COMPETITION
• *See page 120*

ARCTIC INSTITUTE OF NORTH AMERICA http://www.ucalgary.ca/aina

JIM BOURQUE SCHOLARSHIP
• *See page 196*

ARIZONA HYDROLOGICAL SOCIETY http://www.azhydrosoc.org

ARIZONA HYDROLOGICAL SURVEY STUDENT SCHOLARSHIP
• *See page 189*

ASSOCIATION OF CALIFORNIA WATER AGENCIES http://www.acwanet.com

ASSOCIATION OF CALIFORNIA WATER AGENCIES SCHOLARSHIPS
• *See page 68*

CLAIR A. HILL SCHOLARSHIP
• *See page 68*

BAT CONSERVATION INTERNATIONAL http://www.batcon.org

BAT CONSERVATION INTERNATIONAL STUDENT SCHOLARSHIP PROGRAM
• *See page 112*

CALAVERAS BIG TREES ASSOCIATION http://www.bigtrees.org

EMILY M. HEWITT MEMORIAL SCHOLARSHIP
• *See page 264*

CALIFORNIA GROUNDWATER ASSOCIATION http://www.groundh2o.org

CALIFORNIA GROUNDWATER ASSOCIATION SCHOLARSHIP
• *See page 190*

CALIFORNIA SEA GRANT COLLEGE PROGRAM http://www-csgc.ucsd.edu

JOHN D. ISSACS SCHOLARSHIP
• *See page 113*

CALIFORNIA WATER AWARENESS CAMPAIGN http://www.wateraware.org

CALIFORNIA WATER AWARENESS CAMPAIGN WATER SCHOLAR
• *See page 57*

CANADIAN RECREATIONAL CANOEING ASSOCIATION http://www.paddlingcanada.com

BILL MASON MEMORIAL SCHOLARSHIP FUND
• *See page 57*

CONSERVATION FEDERATION OF MISSOURI http://www.confedmo.com

CHARLES P. BELL CONSERVATION SCHOLARSHIP

• *See page 113*

DELAWARE SOLID WASTE AUTHORITY http://www.dswa.com

DELAWARE SOLID WASTE AUTHORITY SCHOLARSHIP

• *See page 113*

DESK AND DERRICK EDUCATIONAL TRUST http://www.addc.org

DESK AND DERRICK EDUCATIONAL TRUST

• *See page 69*

DOGRIB TREATY 11 SCHOLARSHIP COMMITTEE http://www.dt11sc.ca

FRANCIS BLACKDUCK MEMORIAL "STRONG LIKE TWO PEOPLE" AWARDS

• *See page 264*

FRIENDS OF THE FRELINGHUYSEN ARBORETUM http://arboretumfriends.org

BENJAMIN C. BLACKBURN SCHOLARSHIP

• *See page 264*

GARDEN CLUB OF AMERICA http://www.gcamerica.org

FRANCES M. PEACOCK SCHOLARSHIP FOR NATIVE BIRD HABITAT

One scholarship available to a college senior or graduate student to study habitat related issues to benefit endangered bird species.

Academic Fields/Career Goals: Natural Resources.

Award: Scholarship for use in senior, or graduate years; not renewable. *Number:* 1. *Amount:* $4000.

Eligibility Requirements: Applicant must be enrolled or expecting to enroll at a four-year institution or university. Available to U.S. citizens.

Application Requirements: Application, essay, references, self-addressed stamped envelope, budget. *Deadline:* January 15.

Contact: Scott Sutcliffe, Associate Director
Garden Club of America
Cornell Lab of Ornithology, 159 Sapsucker Woods Road
Ithaca, NY 14850
Fax: 607-254-2415
E-mail: Lh17@cornell.edu

GARDEN CLUB OF AMERICA AWARDS FOR SUMMER ENVIRONMENTAL STUDIES

• *See page 58*

HISPANIC COLLEGE FUND, INC. http://www.hispanicfund.org

DEPARTMENT OF ENERGY SCHOLARSHIP PROGRAM

• *See page 125*

INDIANA WILDLIFE FEDERATION ENDOWMENT http://indianawildlife.org

CHARLES A. HOLT INDIANA WILDLIFE FEDERATION ENDOWMENT SCHOLARSHIP

A $1000 scholarship will be awarded to an Indiana resident accepted for the study or already enrolled for the study of resource conservation or environmental education at the undergraduate level. For more details see Web site: http://www.indianawildlife.org.

Academic Fields/Career Goals: Natural Resources.

Award: Scholarship for use in sophomore, junior, or senior years; not renewable. *Number:* 1. *Amount:* $1000.

Eligibility Requirements: Applicant must be enrolled or expecting to enroll full-time at a four-year institution or university; resident of Indiana and studying in Indiana. Available to U.S. citizens.

Application Requirements: Application. *Deadline:* April 30.

Contact: Application available at Web site.

INNOVATION AND SCIENCE COUNCIL OF BRITISH COLUMBIA http://www.scbc.org

PAUL AND HELEN TRUSSEL SCIENCE AND TECHNOLOGY SCHOLARSHIP

• *See page 69*

INTERNATIONAL ASSOCIATION OF GREAT LAKES RESEARCH http://www.iaglr.org

PAUL W. RODGERS SCHOLARSHIP

• *See page 190*

INTERTRIBAL TIMBER COUNCIL http://www.itcnet.org

TRUMAN D. PICARD SCHOLARSHIP

• *See page 54*

KENTUCKY NATURAL RESOURCES AND ENVIRONMENTAL PROTECTION CABINET http://www.uky.edu/waterresources

CONSERVATION OF NATURAL RESOURCES SCHOLARSHIP

• *See page 58*

CONSERVATION OF NATURAL RESOURCES SCHOLARSHIP FOR NONTRADITIONAL STUDENTS

• *See page 58*

GEORGE R. CRAFTON SCHOLARSHIP

• *See page 59*

LOUISIANA OFFICE OF STUDENT FINANCIAL ASSISTANCE http://www.osfa.state.la.us

ROCKEFELLER STATE WILDLIFE SCHOLARSHIP

• *See page 63*

MAINE CAMPGROUND OWNERS ASSOCIATION http://www.campmaine.com

MAINE CAMPGROUND OWNERS ASSOCIATION SCHOLARSHIP

One-time award of $500 to a Maine resident pursuing a career in outdoor recreation. Must have completed one year of study and have a GPA of at least 2.5. Application deadline is March 29.

Academic Fields/Career Goals: Natural Resources; Recreation, Parks, Leisure Studies.

Award: Scholarship for use in sophomore, junior, senior, graduate, or postgraduate years; not renewable. *Number:* 1–2. *Amount:* $500.

Eligibility Requirements: Applicant must be enrolled or expecting to enroll at a two-year or four-year or technical institution or university and resident of Maine. Applicant must have 2.5 GPA or higher.

Application Requirements: Application, essay, financial need analysis, transcript. *Deadline:* March 29.

Contact: Jeffrey Rowe, Executive Director
Maine Campground Owners Association
655 Main Street
Lewiston, ME 04240
Phone: 207-782-5874
Fax: 207-782-4497
E-mail: info@campmaine.com

MINERALOGICAL SOCIETY OF AMERICA http://www.minsocam.org

MINERALOGICAL SOCIETY OF AMERICA-GRANT FOR STUDENT RESEARCH IN MINERALOGY AND PETROLOGY

• *See page 190*

MINERALOGY SOCIETY OF AMERICA-GRANT FOR RESEARCH IN CRYSTALLOGRAPHY
• *See page 191*

MORRIS K. UDALL FOUNDATION http://www.udall.gov

MORRIS K. UDALL SCHOLARS
• *See page 59*

NATIONAL ASSOCIATION OF WATER COMPANIES http://www.nawc.org

J.J. BARR SCHOLARSHIP
• *See page 115*

NATIONAL ASSOCIATION OF WATER COMPANIES-NEW JERSEY CHAPTER

NATIONAL ASSOCIATION OF WATER COMPANIES-NEW JERSEY CHAPTER SCHOLARSHIP
• *See page 115*

NATIONAL FEDERATION OF THE BLIND http://www.nfb.org

HOWARD BROWN RICKARD SCHOLARSHIP
• *See page 78*

NATIONAL FISH AND WILDLIFE FOUNDATION http://www.nfwf.org

BUDWEISER CONSERVATION SCHOLARSHIP PROGRAM
• *See page 115*

NEW ENGLAND WATER WORKS ASSOCIATION http://www.newwa.org

NEW ENGLAND WATER WORKS SCHOLARSHIPS
• *See page 154*

NEW JERSEY DIVISION OF FISH AND WILDLIFE/NJ CHAPTER OF THE WILDLIFE SOCIETY http://www.njfishandwildlife.com

RUSSELL A. COOKINGHAM SCHOLARSHIP
• *See page 116*

OREGON STUDENT ASSISTANCE COMMISSION http://www.osac.state.or.us

OREGON FOUNDATION FOR BLACKTAIL DEER OUTDOOR AND WILDLIFE SCHOLARSHIP
• *See page 116*

ROYDEN M. BODLEY SCHOLARSHIP
• *See page 63*

PENNSYLVANIA ASSOCIATION OF CONSERVATION DISTRICTS AUXILIARY http://www.blairconservationdistrict.org

PACD AUXILIARY SCHOLARSHIPS
• *See page 55*

RAILWAY TIE ASSOCIATION http://www.rta.org

JOHN MABRY FORESTRY SCHOLARSHIP

One-time award to potential forestry industry leaders. Open to junior and senior undergraduates who will be enrolled in accredited forestry schools. Applications reviewed with emphasis on leadership qualities, career objectives, scholastic achievement, and financial need. Application deadline is June 30.

Academic Fields/Career Goals: Natural Resources.

Award: Scholarship for use in junior or senior years; not renewable. *Number:* 2. *Amount:* $1250.

Eligibility Requirements: Applicant must be enrolled or expecting to enroll full-time at a four-year institution or university. Available to U.S. and Canadian citizens.

Application Requirements: Application, autobiography, essay, references, transcript. *Deadline:* June 30.

Contact: Debbie Corallo, Administrator
Railway Tie Association
115 Commerce Drive, Suite C
Fayetteville, GA 30214
Phone: 770-460-5553
Fax: 770-460-5573
E-mail: ties@rta.org

RECREATIONAL BOATING INDUSTRIES EDUCATIONAL FOUNDATION http://mbia.org

RECREATIONAL BOATING INDUSTRIES EDUCATIONAL FOUNDATION SCHOLARSHIPS
• *See page 117*

ROCKY MOUNTAIN ELK FOUNDATION http://www.rmef.org

WILDLIFE LEADERSHIP AWARDS
• *See page 117*

SAEMS - SOUTHERN ARIZONA ENVIRONMENTAL MANAGEMENT SOCIETY http://www.saems.org

ENVIRONMENTAL SCHOLARSHIPS

Applicant must be a student in any accredited Southern Arizona college or university. Student must have a minimum GPA of 2.5 or be a full- or part-time student and plan on pursuing a career in the environmental arena.

Academic Fields/Career Goals: Natural Resources.

Award: Scholarship for use in freshman, sophomore, junior, or senior years; not renewable. *Number:* 2. *Amount:* up to $3000.

Eligibility Requirements: Applicant must be enrolled or expecting to enroll full or part-time at a two-year or four-year institution or university and studying in Arizona. Applicant must have 2.5 GPA or higher. Available to U.S. and non-U.S. citizens.

Application Requirements: Application, essay, interview. *Deadline:* March 15.

Contact: Dan Uthe, Scholarship Committee Chair
SAEMS - Southern Arizona Environmental Management Society
PO Box 41433
Tucson, AZ 85717
Phone: 520-791-4014
Fax: 520-791-5346
E-mail: duthe1@ci.tucson.az.us

SOCIETY FOR MINING, METALLURGY AND EXPLORATION - CENTRAL WYOMING SECTION

COATES, WOLFF, RUSSELL MINING INDUSTRY SCHOLARSHIP
• *See page 71*

SOCIETY FOR RANGE MANAGEMENT http://www.rangelands.org

MASONIC RANGE SCIENCE SCHOLARSHIP
• *See page 55*

SOIL AND WATER CONSERVATION SOCIETY http://www.swcs.org

DONALD A. WILLIAMS SCHOLARSHIP SOIL CONSERVATION SCHOLARSHIP
• *See page 191*

SWCS MELVILLE H. COHEE STUDENT LEADER CONSERVATION SCHOLARSHIP
• *See page 61*

SOIL AND WATER CONSERVATION SOCIETY-NEW JERSEY CHAPTER http://www.geocities.com/njswcs

EDWARD R. HALL SCHOLARSHIP
• *See page 55*

SOUTH DAKOTA BOARD OF REGENTS http://www.ris.sdbor.edu

SOUTH DAKOTA BOARD OF REGENTS BJUGSTAD SCHOLARSHIP
• *See page 55*

TEXAS OUTDOOR WRITERS ASSOCIATION http://www.towa.org

TEXAS OUTDOOR WRITERS ASSOCIATION SCHOLARSHIP
• *See page 165*

UNITED NEGRO COLLEGE FUND http://www.uncf.org

MALCOLM PIRNIE, INC. SCHOLARS PROGRAM
• *See page 148*

MELLON ECOLOGY PROGRAM (S.E.E.D.S)

Program gives minority students exposure to research in ecology and ecology-related careers. Must attend a UNCF member college or university. Prospective applicants should complete the Student Profile found at Web site: http://www.uncf.org.

Academic Fields/Career Goals: Natural Resources.

Award: Scholarship for use in freshman, sophomore, junior, or senior years; not renewable.

Eligibility Requirements: Applicant must be Black (non-Hispanic) and enrolled or expecting to enroll at a four-year institution or university.

Application Requirements: Application, financial need analysis. *Deadline:* Continuous.

Contact: Program Services Department
United Negro College Fund
8260 Willow Oaks Corporate Drive
Fairfax, VA 22031

WEYERHAEUSER/UNCF CORPORATE SCHOLARS
• *See page 134*

UNITED STATES ENVIRONMENTAL PROTECTION AGENCY http://www.epa.gov/enviroed/students.html

NATIONAL NETWORK FOR ENVIRONMENTAL MANAGEMENT STUDIES FELLOWSHIP

The NNEMS Fellowship Program is designed to provide undergraduate and graduate students with research opportunities at one of EPA's facilities nationwide. EPA awards approximately 40 NNEMS fellowships per year. Selected students receive a stipend for performing their research project. EPA develops an annual catalog of research projects available for student application. Submit a complete application package as described in the annual catalog. Minimum 3.0 GPA required.

Academic Fields/Career Goals: Natural Resources.

Award: Grant for use in freshman, sophomore, junior, senior, or graduate years; not renewable. *Number:* 35–40. *Amount:* $6000–$10,000.

Eligibility Requirements: Applicant must be enrolled or expecting to enroll full or part-time at a two-year or four-year institution or university. Applicant must have 3.0 GPA or higher. Available to U.S. citizens.

Application Requirements: Application, applicant must enter a contest, resume, references, transcript, application package. *Deadline:* January 26.

Contact: Sheri Jojokian, Environmental Education Specialist
United States Environmental Protection Agency
Office of Environmental Education, 1200 Pennsylvania Avenue, NW (1704A)
Washington, DC 20460
Phone: 800-358-8769
E-mail: jojokian.sheri@epa.gov

WILSON ORNITHOLOGICAL SOCIETY http://www.ummz.lsa.umich.edu/birds/wosawards.html

GEORGE A. HALL / HAROLD F. MAYFIELD AWARD
• *See page 64*

PAUL A. STEWART AWARDS
• *See page 64*

NATURAL SCIENCES

AIR AND WASTE MANAGEMENT ASSOCIATION-CONNECTICUT CHAPTER http://www.awma-nes.org/

AIR AND WASTE MANAGEMENT ASSOCIATION-CONNECTICUT CHAPTER SCHOLARSHIP
• *See page 111*

ALABAMA STATE DEPARTMENT OF EDUCATION http://www.alsde.edu

MATH AND SCIENCE SCHOLARSHIP PROGRAM FOR ALABAMA TEACHERS
• *See page 111*

AMERICAN CHEMICAL SOCIETY http://www.chemistry.org/scholars

AMERICAN CHEMICAL SOCIETY SCHOLARS PROGRAM
• *See page 136*

AMERICAN INDIAN SCIENCE AND ENGINEERING SOCIETY http://www.aises.org

A.T. ANDERSON MEMORIAL SCHOLARSHIP
• *See page 65*

BURLINGTON NORTHERN SANTA FE FOUNDATION SCHOLARSHIP
• *See page 65*

ENVIRONMENTAL PROTECTION AGENCY TRIBAL LANDS ENVIRONMENTAL SCIENCE SCHOLARSHIP
• *See page 111*

HENRY RODRIGUEZ RECLAMATION COLLEGE SCHOLARSHIP AND INTERNSHIP
• *See page 224*

AMERICAN ORNITHOLOGISTS' UNION http://www.aou.org

AMERICAN ORNITHOLOGISTS' UNION RESEARCH AWARDS
• *See page 62*

ARCTIC INSTITUTE OF NORTH AMERICA http://www.ucalgary.ca/aina

JIM BOURQUE SCHOLARSHIP
• *See page 196*

ARRL FOUNDATION, INC. http://www.arrl.org/arrlf/scholgen.html

WILLIAM R. GOLDFARB MEMORIAL SCHOLARSHIP
• *See page 121*

ASSOCIATION FOR WOMEN IN SCIENCE EDUCATIONAL FOUNDATION http://www.awis.org/ed_foundation.html

ASSOCIATION FOR WOMEN IN SCIENCE COLLEGE SCHOLARSHIP
• *See page 63*

ASSOCIATION OF CALIFORNIA WATER AGENCIES http://www.acwanet.com

ASSOCIATION OF CALIFORNIA WATER AGENCIES SCHOLARSHIPS
• *See page 68*

CLAIR A. HILL SCHOLARSHIP
• *See page 68*

AUDUBON SOCIETY OF WESTERN PENNSYLVANIA http://www.aswp.org

BEULAH FREY ENVIRONMENTAL SCHOLARSHIP
• *See page 264*

BARRY M. GOLDWATER SCHOLARSHIP AND EXCELLENCE IN EDUCATION FOUNDATION http://www.act.org/goldwater

BARRY M. GOLDWATER SCHOLARSHIP AND EXCELLENCE IN EDUCATION PROGRAM
• *See page 68*

BAT CONSERVATION INTERNATIONAL http://www.batcon.org

BAT CONSERVATION INTERNATIONAL STUDENT SCHOLARSHIP PROGRAM
• *See page 112*

CALIFORNIA SEA GRANT COLLEGE PROGRAM http://www-csgc.ucsd.edu

JOHN D. ISSACS SCHOLARSHIP
• *See page 113*

CANADIAN RECREATIONAL CANOEING ASSOCIATION http://www.paddlingcanada.com

BILL MASON MEMORIAL SCHOLARSHIP FUND
• *See page 57*

CONNECTICUT STUDENT LOAN FOUNDATION http://www.cslf.com

CONNECTICUT INNOVATIONS TECHNOLOGY SCHOLAR PROGRAM
• *See page 113*

DESK AND DERRICK EDUCATIONAL TRUST http://www.addc.org

DESK AND DERRICK EDUCATIONAL TRUST
• *See page 69*

EXPLORERS CLUB http://www.explorers.org

YOUTH ACTIVITY FUND

Award given to college students or high school students pursuing a research project in the field of science. Applicants must have two letters of recommendation, one-page description of project, and a budget or plan.

Academic Fields/Career Goals: Natural Sciences; Science, Technology, and Society.

Award: Grant for use in freshman, sophomore, junior, or senior years; not renewable. *Number:* 10–15. *Amount:* $500–$1500.

Eligibility Requirements: Applicant must be enrolled or expecting to enroll at an institution or university.

Application Requirements: Application, essay, references. *Deadline:* February 13.

Contact: Suzi Zetkus, Administrative Assistant
Explorers Club
46 East 70th Street
New York, NY 10021
Phone: 212-628-8383
Fax: 212-288-4449

HARVARD TRAVELLERS CLUB

HARVARD TRAVELLERS CLUB GRANTS
• *See page 73*

HISPANIC COLLEGE FUND, INC. http://www.hispanicfund.org

DEPARTMENT OF ENERGY SCHOLARSHIP PROGRAM
• *See page 125*

INNOVATION AND SCIENCE COUNCIL OF BRITISH COLUMBIA http://www.scbc.org

PAUL AND HELEN TRUSSEL SCIENCE AND TECHNOLOGY SCHOLARSHIP
• *See page 69*

INTERNATIONAL ASSOCIATION OF GREAT LAKES RESEARCH http://www.iaglr.org

PAUL W. RODGERS SCHOLARSHIP
• *See page 190*

MID-COAST AUDUBON SOCIETY http://www.midcoastaudubon.org

JEAN BOYER HAMLIN SCHOLARSHIP IN ORNITHOLOGY
• *See page 63*

MIDWEST ROOFING CONTRACTORS ASSOCIATION http://www.mrca.org

MRCA FOUNDATION SCHOLARSHIP PROGRAM
• *See page 70*

MINERALOGICAL SOCIETY OF AMERICA http://www.minsocam.org

MINERALOGICAL SOCIETY OF AMERICA-GRANT FOR STUDENT RESEARCH IN MINERALOGY AND PETROLOGY
• *See page 190*

MINERALOGY SOCIETY OF AMERICA-GRANT FOR RESEARCH IN CRYSTALLOGRAPHY
• *See page 191*

NASA NEBRASKA SPACE GRANT CONSORTIUM http://nasa.unomaha.edu

NASA NEBRASKA SPACE GRANT
• *See page 101*

NASA VERMONT SPACE GRANT CONSORTIUM http://www.emba.uvm.edu/vsgc

VERMONT SPACE GRANT CONSORTIUM SCHOLARSHIP PROGRAM
• *See page 71*

NASA WEST VIRGINIA SPACE GRANT CONSORTIUM http://www.nasa.wvu.edu

WEST VIRGINIA SPACE GRANT CONSORTIUM UNDERGRADUATE SCHOLARSHIP PROGRAM
• *See page 102*

NATIONAL FISH AND WILDLIFE FOUNDATION http://www.nfwf.org

BUDWEISER CONSERVATION SCHOLARSHIP PROGRAM
• *See page 115*

NATIONAL INSTITUTE OF GENERAL MEDICAL SCIENCES, NATIONAL INSTITUTE OF HEALTH http://www.nigms.nih.gov

*MARC UNDERGRADUATE STUDENT TRAINING IN ACADEMIC RESEARCH U*STAR AWARDS*
• *See page 115*

NEW JERSEY ACADEMY OF SCIENCE http://www.njas.org

NEW JERSEY ACADEMY OF SCIENCE RESEARCH GRANTS-IN-AID TO HIGH SCHOOL STUDENTS
• *See page 116*

OREGON STUDENT ASSISTANCE COMMISSION http://www.osac.state.or.us

OREGON FOUNDATION FOR BLACKTAIL DEER OUTDOOR AND WILDLIFE SCHOLARSHIP
• *See page 116*

ROYDEN M. BODLEY SCHOLARSHIP
• *See page 63*

POLANKI, POLISH WOMEN'S CULTURAL CLUB OF MILWAUKEE, WISCONSIN, U.S.A. http://www.polanki.org/

COPERNICUS AWARD

Award to a student of Polish heritage who is an outstanding student in a science field. Applicants must be college juniors, seniors, or graduate students and must be Wisconsin residents or attend college in Wisconsin. Successful applicants will usually have a GPA of 3.0.

Academic Fields/Career Goals: Natural Sciences; Physical Sciences and Math.

Award: Scholarship for use in junior, senior, or graduate years. *Number:* 1. *Amount:* $500–$1000.

Eligibility Requirements: Applicant must be of Polish heritage and enrolled or expecting to enroll at a four-year institution or university. Available to U.S. citizens.

Application Requirements: Application, transcript. *Deadline:* March 1.

Contact: Ewa Barczyk-Pease
Polanki, Polish Women's Cultural Club
of Milwaukee, Wisconsin, U.S.A.
4160 South 1st Street
Milwaukee, WI 53207
Phone: 414-963-1098
E-mail: polanki@polanki.org

SOCIETY FOR MINING, METALLURGY AND EXPLORATION - CENTRAL WYOMING SECTION

COATES, WOLFF, RUSSELL MINING INDUSTRY SCHOLARSHIP
• *See page 71*

SOCIETY OF HISPANIC PROFESSIONAL ENGINEERS FOUNDATION http://www.shpefoundation.org

SOCIETY OF HISPANIC PROFESSIONAL ENGINEERS FOUNDATION
• *See page 146*

SOIL AND WATER CONSERVATION SOCIETY http://www.swcs.org

DONALD A. WILLIAMS SCHOLARSHIP SOIL CONSERVATION SCHOLARSHIP
• *See page 191*

SWCS MELVILLE H. COHEE STUDENT LEADER CONSERVATION SCHOLARSHIP
• *See page 61*

SOIL AND WATER CONSERVATION SOCIETY-NEW JERSEY CHAPTER http://www.geocities.com/njswcs

EDWARD R. HALL SCHOLARSHIP
• *See page 55*

NEAR AND MIDDLE EAST STUDIES

AMERICAN SCHOOL OF CLASSICAL STUDIES AT ATHENS http://www.ascsa.edu.gr

ASCSA SUMMER SESSIONS
• *See page 65*

AMERICAN SCHOOLS OF ORIENTAL RESEARCH (ASOR) http://www.asor.org

CYPRUS AMERICAN ARCHAEOLOGICAL RESEARCH INSTITUTE HELENA WYLDE AND STUART SWINY FELLOWSHIP
• *See page 73*

NUCLEAR SCIENCE

AMERICAN INDIAN SCIENCE AND ENGINEERING SOCIETY http://www.aises.org

A.T. ANDERSON MEMORIAL SCHOLARSHIP
• *See page 65*

BURLINGTON NORTHERN SANTA FE FOUNDATION SCHOLARSHIP
• *See page 65*

AMERICAN NUCLEAR SOCIETY http://www.ans.org

AMERICAN NUCLEAR SOCIETY ENVIRONMENTAL SCIENCES DIVISION SCHOLARSHIP
• *See page 235*

AMERICAN NUCLEAR SOCIETY JAMES R. VOGT SCHOLARSHIP
• *See page 235*

AMERICAN NUCLEAR SOCIETY OPERATIONS AND POWER SCHOLARSHIP
• *See page 235*

AMERICAN NUCLEAR SOCIETY UNDERGRADUATE SCHOLARSHIPS
• *See page 235*

DECOMMISSIONING, DECONTAMINATION, AND REUTILIZATION SCHOLARSHIP
• *See page 235*

DELAYED EDUCATION FOR WOMEN SCHOLARSHIPS
• *See page 236*

JOHN AND MURIEL LANDIS SCHOLARSHIP AWARDS
• *See page 236*

JOHN R. LAMARSH SCHOLARSHIP
• *See page 236*

JOSEPH R. DIETRICH SCHOLARSHIP
• *See page 236*

AMERICAN SOCIETY OF NAVAL ENGINEERS http://www.navalengineers.org

AMERICAN SOCIETY OF NAVAL ENGINEERS SCHOLARSHIP
• *See page 66*

ARIZONA HYDROLOGICAL SOCIETY http://www.azhydrosoc.org

ARIZONA HYDROLOGICAL SURVEY STUDENT SCHOLARSHIP
• *See page 189*

ASSOCIATION FOR WOMEN IN SCIENCE EDUCATIONAL FOUNDATION http://www.awis.org/ed_foundation.html

ASSOCIATION FOR WOMEN IN SCIENCE COLLEGE SCHOLARSHIP
• *See page 63*

BARRY M. GOLDWATER SCHOLARSHIP AND EXCELLENCE IN EDUCATION FOUNDATION http://www.act.org/goldwater

BARRY M. GOLDWATER SCHOLARSHIP AND EXCELLENCE IN EDUCATION PROGRAM

• See page 68

DESK AND DERRICK EDUCATIONAL TRUST http://www.addc.org

DESK AND DERRICK EDUCATIONAL TRUST

• See page 69

HISPANIC COLLEGE FUND, INC. http://www.hispanicfund.org

DEPARTMENT OF ENERGY SCHOLARSHIP PROGRAM

• See page 125

HISPANIC ENGINEER NATIONAL ACHIEVEMENT AWARDS CORPORATION (HENAAC) http://www.henaac.org

HISPANIC ENGINEER NATIONAL ACHIEVEMENT AWARDS CORPORATION SCHOLARSHIP PROGRAM

• See page 99

INNOVATION AND SCIENCE COUNCIL OF BRITISH COLUMBIA http://www.scbc.org

PAUL AND HELEN TRUSSEL SCIENCE AND TECHNOLOGY SCHOLARSHIP

• See page 69

MORRIS K. UDALL FOUNDATION http://www.udall.gov

MORRIS K. UDALL SCHOLARS

• See page 59

NASA WEST VIRGINIA SPACE GRANT CONSORTIUM http://www.nasa.wvu.edu

WEST VIRGINIA SPACE GRANT CONSORTIUM UNDERGRADUATE SCHOLARSHIP PROGRAM

• See page 102

SOCIETY OF HISPANIC PROFESSIONAL ENGINEERS FOUNDATION http://www.shpefoundation.org

SOCIETY OF HISPANIC PROFESSIONAL ENGINEERS FOUNDATION

• See page 146

SOCIETY OF NUCLEAR MEDICINE http://www.snm.org

PAUL COLE SCHOLARSHIP

• See page 303

UNIVERSITIES SPACE RESEARCH ASSOCIATION http://www.usra.edu/hq/scholarships/overview.shtml

UNIVERSITIES SPACE RESEARCH ASSOCIATION SCHOLARSHIP PROGRAM

• See page 72

NURSING

ALBERTA HERITAGE SCHOLARSHIP FUND/ ALBERTA SCHOLARSHIP PROGRAMS http://www.alis.gov.ab.ca/scholarships

ALBERTA HERITAGE SCHOLARSHIP FUND ABORIGINAL HEALTH CAREERS BURSARY

• See page 111

ALICE M. YARNOLD AND SAMUEL YARNOLD SCHOLARSHIP TRUST

ALICE M. AND SAMUEL YARNOLD SCHOLARSHIP

• See page 289

AMERICAN ASSOCIATION OF CRITICAL-CARE NURSES (AACN) http://www.aacn.org

AACN EDUCATIONAL ADVANCEMENT SCHOLARSHIPS-BSN COMPLETION

Award for juniors and seniors currently enrolled in a nursing program accredited by State Board of Nursing. Must be AACN member with active RN license who is currently or has recently worked in critical care. Must have 3.0 GPA. Supports RN members completing a baccalaureate degree in nursing. Student may only receive award a maximum of two times.

Academic Fields/Career Goals: Nursing.

Award: Scholarship for use in junior or senior years; not renewable. *Number:* 50–100. *Amount:* $1500.

Eligibility Requirements: Applicant must be enrolled or expecting to enroll full or part-time at a four-year institution or university. Applicant or parent of applicant must be member of American Association of Critical Care Nurses. Applicant or parent of applicant must have employment or volunteer experience in designated career field. Applicant must have 3.0 GPA or higher. Available to U.S. and Canadian citizens.

Application Requirements: Application, essay, transcript, verification of critical care experience. *Deadline:* April 1.

Contact: Lisa Mynes, Member Relations and Services Specialist
American Association of Critical-Care Nurses (AACN)
101 Columbia
Aliso Viejo, CA 92656
Phone: 800-899-2226
Fax: 949-448-5502
E-mail: lisa.mynes@aacn.org

AMERICAN ASSOCIATION OF NEUROSCIENCE NURSES http://www.aann.org

NEUROSCIENCE NURSING FOUNDATION SCHOLARSHIP

Scholarship available for registered nurse to attend an NLN accredited school. Submit letter of school acceptance along with application, transcript, and copy of current RN license.

Academic Fields/Career Goals: Nursing.

Award: Scholarship for use in freshman, sophomore, junior, senior, or graduate years; not renewable. *Number:* varies. *Amount:* $1500.

Eligibility Requirements: Applicant must be enrolled or expecting to enroll at a two-year or four-year institution or university. Applicant must have 3.0 GPA or higher. Available to U.S. citizens.

Application Requirements: Application, transcript, letter of school acceptance. *Deadline:* January 15.

Contact: NNF Scholarship Programs
American Association of Neuroscience Nurses
4700 West Lake Avenue
Glenview, IL 60025-1485

AMERICAN LEGION AUXILIARY, DEPARTMENT OF ARIZONA

AMERICAN LEGION AUXILIARY DEPARTMENT OF ARIZONA NURSES' SCHOLARSHIPS

Award for Arizona residents enrolled in their second year at an institution in Arizona awarding degree as a registered nurse. Preference given to immediate family member of a veteran. Must be a U.S. citizen and resident of Arizona for one year.

Academic Fields/Career Goals: Nursing.

Award: Scholarship for use in sophomore, junior, or senior years; not renewable. *Amount:* $500.

Eligibility Requirements: Applicant must be enrolled or expecting to enroll full-time at a two-year or four-year institution or university; resident of Arizona and studying in Arizona. Available to U.S. citizens.

Application Requirements: Application, autobiography, essay, financial need analysis, photo, references, test scores, transcript. *Deadline:* May 15.

Contact: Department Secretary and Treasurer
American Legion Auxiliary, Department of Arizona
4701 North 19th Avenue, Suite 100
Phoenix, AZ 85015-3727
Phone: 602-241-1080
Fax: 602-604-9640
E-mail: amlegauxaz@mcleodusa.net

AMERICAN LEGION AUXILIARY, DEPARTMENT OF ARKANSAS

AMERICAN LEGION AUXILIARY DEPARTMENT OF ARKANSAS NURSE SCHOLARSHIP

One-time award for Arkansas residents who are the children of veterans who served during eligibility dates for membership. Must attend nursing program in Arkansas. Open to high school seniors. Must complete 1,000-word essay entitled "What my country's flag means to me." Contact local American Legion Auxiliary.

Academic Fields/Career Goals: Nursing.

Award: Scholarship for use in freshman year; not renewable. *Number:* 1. *Amount:* $500.

Eligibility Requirements: Applicant must be high school student; planning to enroll or expecting to enroll full-time at a two-year or four-year or technical institution or university; resident of Arkansas and studying in Arkansas. Available to U.S. citizens. Applicant or parent must meet one or more of the following requirements: general military experience; retired from active duty; disabled or killed as a result of military service; prisoner of war; or missing in action.

Application Requirements: Application, essay, financial need analysis, references, self-addressed stamped envelope, test scores, transcript, copy of veteran discharge papers - branch of service, dates of service, DD Form 214.. *Deadline:* March 1.

Contact: Department Secretary
American Legion Auxiliary, Department of Arkansas
1415 West 7th Street
Little Rock, AR 72201
Phone: 501-374-5836

AMERICAN LEGION AUXILIARY, DEPARTMENT OF COLORADO

AMERICAN LEGION AUXILIARY DEPARTMENT OF COLORADO PAST PRESIDENT PARLEY NURSES SCHOLARSHIP

Nonrenewable scholarship for veterans or their dependents to pursue nursing degree at an accredited institution. Service must have been during time of eligibility for American Legion membership. Must be U.S. citizen and a Colorado resident.

Academic Fields/Career Goals: Nursing.

Award: Scholarship for use in freshman, sophomore, junior, or senior years; not renewable. *Number:* 1–3. *Amount:* $500–$1000.

Eligibility Requirements: Applicant must be enrolled or expecting to enroll full-time at a two-year or four-year institution or university and resident of Colorado. Available to U.S. citizens. Applicant must have general military experience.

Application Requirements: Application, essay, financial need analysis, photo, references, test scores, transcript. *Deadline:* April 15.

Contact: Department Secretary/Treasurer
American Legion Auxiliary, Department of Colorado
7465 East First Avenue, Suite D
Denver, CO 80230
Phone: 303-367-5388

AMERICAN LEGION AUXILIARY, DEPARTMENT OF IDAHO

AMERICAN LEGION AUXILIARY, DEPARTMENT OF IDAHO NURSING SCHOLARSHIP

Scholarship available to veterans or the children of veterans who are majoring in nursing. Applicants must be 17-35 years of age and residents of Idaho for five years prior to applying. One-time award of $750.

Academic Fields/Career Goals: Nursing.

Award: Scholarship for use in freshman, sophomore, junior, or senior years; not renewable. *Number:* 1. *Amount:* $750.

Eligibility Requirements: Applicant must be age 17-35; enrolled or expecting to enroll full-time at an institution or university and resident of Idaho. Applicant or parent must meet one or more of the following requirements: general military experience; retired from active duty; disabled or killed as a result of military service; prisoner of war; or missing in action.

Application Requirements: Application, financial need analysis, photo, references, self-addressed stamped envelope, transcript. *Deadline:* March 15.

Contact: Connie Evans, Secretary and Treasurer
American Legion Auxiliary, Department of Idaho
905 South Warren Street
Boise, ID 83706-3825
Phone: 208-342-7066
Fax: 208-342-0855
E-mail: idalegionaux@earthlink.net

AMERICAN LEGION AUXILIARY, DEPARTMENT OF INDIANA

AMERICAN LEGION AUXILIARY DEPARTMENT OF INDIANA PAST PRESIDENT PARLEY NURSES SCHOLARSHIP

Renewable scholarship for graduating high school senior female who is a child, grandchild, or great-grandchild of veteran who served during American Legion eligibility dates. Must be Indiana resident enrolled full-time in accredited undergraduate nursing program in Indiana.

Academic Fields/Career Goals: Nursing.

Award: Scholarship for use in freshman year; renewable. *Number:* 1. *Amount:* $500.

Eligibility Requirements: Applicant must be high school student; planning to enroll or expecting to enroll full-time at a two-year or four-year or technical institution or university; female; resident of Indiana and studying in Indiana. Available to U.S. citizens. Applicant or parent must meet one or more of the following requirements: general military experience; retired from active duty; disabled or killed as a result of military service; prisoner of war; or missing in action.

Application Requirements: Application, references, self-addressed stamped envelope, transcript. *Deadline:* April 1.

Contact: Ms. Sue Liford, Department Secretary and Treasurer
American Legion Auxiliary, Department of Indiana
777 North Meridian, Room 107
Indianapolis, IN 46204

AMERICAN LEGION AUXILIARY, DEPARTMENT OF IOWA

http://www.ialegion.org/ala

M.V. MCCRAE MEMORIAL NURSES SCHOLARSHIP

One-time award available to the child of an Iowa American Legion Post member or Iowa American Legion Auxiliary Unit member. Award is for full-time study in accredited nursing program. Must be U.S. citizen and Iowa resident. Must attend an Iowa institution.

Academic Fields/Career Goals: Nursing.

Award: Scholarship for use in freshman year; not renewable. *Number:* 1. *Amount:* $400.

Eligibility Requirements: Applicant must be enrolled or expecting to enroll full or part-time at a two-year or four-year institution or university; resident of Iowa and studying in Iowa. Applicant or parent of applicant must be member of American Legion or Auxiliary. Available to U.S. citizens. Applicant or parent must meet one or more of the following requirements: general military experience; retired from active duty; disabled or killed as a result of military service; prisoner of war; or missing in action.

American Legion Auxiliary, Department of Iowa (continued)

Application Requirements: Application, autobiography, essay, financial need analysis, photo, references, self-addressed stamped envelope, test scores, transcript. *Deadline:* June 1.

Contact: Marlene Valentine, Secretary/Treasurer
American Legion Auxiliary, Department of Iowa
720 Lyon Street
Des Moines, IA 50309
Phone: 515-282-7987
Fax: 515-282-7583

AMERICAN LEGION AUXILIARY, DEPARTMENT OF MARYLAND

AMERICAN LEGION AUXILIARY DEPARTMENT OF MARYLAND PAST PRESIDENT'S PARLEY NURSING SCHOLARSHIP

Nonrenewable scholarship for natural or stepdaughter, granddaughter, or great-granddaughter of former serviceman or woman to pursue a degree in nursing. Must be a resident of Maryland and U.S. citizen. Need recommendation from high school official, minister, or rabbi. Must apply to Maryland American Legion Auxiliary.

Academic Fields/Career Goals: Nursing.

Award: Scholarship for use in freshman, sophomore, junior, or senior years; not renewable. *Number:* 1. *Amount:* $2000.

Eligibility Requirements: Applicant must be high school student; planning to enroll or expecting to enroll full-time at a two-year or four-year institution or university; female and resident of Maryland. Available to U.S. citizens. Applicant or parent must meet one or more of the following requirements: general military experience; retired from active duty; disabled or killed as a result of military service; prisoner of war; or missing in action.

Application Requirements: Application, essay, references, transcript. *Deadline:* May 1.

Contact: Ms. Anna Thompson, Department Secretary
American Legion Auxiliary, Department of Maryland
1589 Sulphur Spring Road, Suite 105
Baltimore, MD 21227
Phone: 410-242-9519
Fax: 410-242-9553
E-mail: anna@alamd.org

AMERICAN LEGION AUXILIARY, DEPARTMENT OF MASSACHUSETTS

AMERICAN LEGION AUXILIARY DEPARTMENT OF MASSACHUSETTS PAST PRESIDENT'S PARLEY SCHOLARSHIP

One-time award for Massachusetts residents who are children of living or deceased veterans. Must enroll or be enrolled in a nursing program. Must not be eligible for state or federal scholarships.

Academic Fields/Career Goals: Nursing.

Award: Scholarship for use in freshman, sophomore, junior, or senior years; not renewable. *Number:* 1. *Amount:* $200.

Eligibility Requirements: Applicant must be age 16-22; enrolled or expecting to enroll full-time at a four-year institution or university and resident of Massachusetts. Applicant or parent must meet one or more of the following requirements: general military experience; retired from active duty; disabled or killed as a result of military service; prisoner of war; or missing in action.

Application Requirements: Application, financial need analysis, transcript. *Deadline:* April 10.

Contact: Beverly Monaco, Secretary and Treasurer
American Legion Auxiliary, Department of Massachusetts
546-2 State House
Boston, MA 02133
Phone: 617-727-2958

AMERICAN LEGION AUXILIARY, DEPARTMENT OF MASSACHUSETTS DEPARTMENT PRESIDENT'S SCHOLARSHIP

One-time award for Massachusetts residents who are children/grand-children of living or deceased veterans.

Academic Fields/Career Goals: Nursing.

Award: Scholarship for use in freshman, sophomore, junior, or senior years; not renewable. *Number:* 11. *Amount:* $100–$500.

Eligibility Requirements: Applicant must be age 16-22; enrolled or expecting to enroll full-time at an institution or university and resident of Massachusetts. Applicant or parent must meet one or more of the following requirements: general military experience; retired from active duty; disabled or killed as a result of military service; prisoner of war; or missing in action.

Application Requirements: Application, financial need analysis, transcript. *Deadline:* April 10.

Contact: Beverly Monaco, Secretary and Treasurer
American Legion Auxiliary, Department of Massachusetts
546-2 State House
Boston, MA 02133
Phone: 617-727-2958

AMERICAN LEGION AUXILIARY, DEPARTMENT OF MICHIGAN http://www.michalaux.org

MEDICAL CAREER SCHOLARSHIP

• *See page 290*

AMERICAN LEGION AUXILIARY, DEPARTMENT OF MISSOURI

PAST PRESIDENTS PARLEY SCHOLARSHIP-MISSOURI

$500 scholarship awarded to high school graduate who has chosen to study nursing. $250 will be awarded each semester upon receipt of verification from the college that student is enrolled. The applicant must be a resident of Missouri and a member of a veteran's family. The applicant must be validated by the sponsoring unit. Check with sponsoring unit for details on required recommendation letters.

Academic Fields/Career Goals: Nursing.

Award: Scholarship for use in freshman year; renewable. *Number:* 1. *Amount:* $500–$1000.

Eligibility Requirements: Applicant must be high school student; planning to enroll or expecting to enroll at a two-year or four-year or technical institution or university and resident of Missouri. Applicant or parent of applicant must be member of American Legion or Auxiliary. Available to U.S. citizens. Applicant or parent must meet one or more of the following requirements: general military experience; retired from active duty; disabled or killed as a result of military service; prisoner of war; or missing in action.

Application Requirements: Application, photo. *Deadline:* April 1.

Contact: Kim Merchant, Department Secretary/Treasurer
American Legion Auxiliary, Department of Missouri
600 Ellis Boulevard
Jefferson City, MO 65101-1615
Phone: 573-636-9133
Fax: 573-635-3467
E-mail: dptmoala@socket.net

AMERICAN LEGION AUXILIARY, DEPARTMENT OF NEBRASKA

AMERICAN LEGION AUXILIARY DEPARTMENT OF NEBRASKA NURSE'S GIFT TUITION SCHOLARSHIP

One-time scholarship for Nebraska resident who is a veteran or a child of a veteran who served in the Armed Forces during dates of eligibility for American Legion membership. Proof of enrollment in nursing program at eligible institution required. Must rank in upper third of class or have a minimum 3.0 GPA.

Academic Fields/Career Goals: Nursing.

Award: Scholarship for use in freshman, sophomore, junior, or senior years; not renewable. *Number:* 1–20. *Amount:* $200–$400.

Eligibility Requirements: Applicant must be enrolled or expecting to enroll full-time at a two-year or four-year institution or university and resident of Nebraska. Applicant must have 3.0 GPA or higher. Available to U.S. citizens. Applicant or parent must meet one or more of the following requirements: general military experience; retired from active duty; disabled or killed as a result of military service; prisoner of war; or missing in action.

Application Requirements: Application, essay, financial need analysis, references, test scores, transcript. *Deadline:* April 1.

Contact: Terry Walker, Department Secretary
American Legion Auxiliary, Department of Nebraska
PO Box 5227
Lincoln, NE 68505
Phone: 402-466-1808
Fax: 402-466-0182
E-mail: neaux@alltel.net

AMERICAN LEGION AUXILIARY DEPARTMENT OF NEBRASKA PRACTICAL NURSE SCHOLARSHIP

Nonrenewable scholarship for a veteran or a child of a veteran who served in the Armed Forces during dates of eligibility for American Legion membership. For full-time undergraduate study toward nursing degree at eligible institution. Must be a Nebraska resident. Must rank in upper third of class or have a minimum 3.0 GPA.

Academic Fields/Career Goals: Nursing.

Award: Scholarship for use in freshman, sophomore, junior, or senior years; not renewable. *Number:* 1–3. *Amount:* $200–$400.

Eligibility Requirements: Applicant must be enrolled or expecting to enroll full-time at a two-year or four-year institution or university and resident of Nebraska. Applicant must have 3.0 GPA or higher. Applicant or parent must meet one or more of the following requirements: general military experience; retired from active duty; disabled or killed as a result of military service; prisoner of war; or missing in action.

Application Requirements: Application, essay, financial need analysis, references, test scores, transcript. *Deadline:* April 1.

Contact: Terry Walker, Department Secretary
American Legion Auxiliary, Department of Nebraska
PO Box 5227
Lincoln, NE 68505
Phone: 402-466-1808
Fax: 402-466-0182
E-mail: neaux@alltel.net

AMERICAN LEGION AUXILIARY, DEPARTMENT OF NEW JERSEY http://www.alanj.thisnation.net/contact.html

AMERICAN LEGION AUXILIARY DEPARTMENT OF NEW JERSEY PAST PRESIDENT'S PARLEY NURSES SCHOLARSHIP

One-time award for New Jersey residents of at least three years who are high school seniors and the child or grandchild of an honorably discharged veteran of U.S. Armed Forces. Must enroll in a nursing program. Contact local American Legion Auxiliary.

Academic Fields/Career Goals: Nursing.

Award: Scholarship for use in freshman year; not renewable. *Number:* varies. *Amount:* varies.

Eligibility Requirements: Applicant must be high school student; planning to enroll or expecting to enroll at a two-year or four-year or technical institution or university and resident of New Jersey. Available to U.S. citizens. Applicant or parent must meet one or more of the following requirements: general military experience; retired from active duty; disabled or killed as a result of military service; prisoner of war; or missing in action.

Application Requirements: Application, financial need analysis, test scores, transcript. *Deadline:* March 15.

Contact: Lucille Miller, Scholarship Coordinator
American Legion Auxiliary, Department of New Jersey
1540 Kuser Road, Suite A-8
Hamilton, NJ 08619
Phone: 609-581-9580
Fax: 609-581-8429
E-mail: newjerseyala@juno.com

AMERICAN LEGION AUXILIARY, DEPARTMENT OF NEW MEXICO

AMERICAN LEGION AUXILIARY DEPARTMENT OF NEW MEXICO PAST PRESIDENT PARLEY NURSES SCHOLARSHIP

Scholarship available to children of veterans who served in the Armed Forces during the eligibility dates for American Legion membership. Must be New Mexico resident, high school senior, and in pursuit of a nursing degree full-time at an accredited institution. One-time award of $250. Must be U.S. citizen.

Academic Fields/Career Goals: Nursing.

Award: Scholarship for use in freshman, sophomore, junior, or senior years; not renewable. *Number:* 1. *Amount:* $250.

Eligibility Requirements: Applicant must be high school student; planning to enroll or expecting to enroll full-time at an institution or university and resident of New Mexico. Available to U.S. citizens. Applicant or parent must meet one or more of the following requirements: general military experience; retired from active duty; disabled or killed as a result of military service; prisoner of war; or missing in action.

Application Requirements: Application, essay, references, self-addressed stamped envelope, transcript. *Deadline:* March 1.

Contact: Loreen Jorgensen, Scholarship Director
American Legion Auxiliary, Department of New Mexico
1215 Mountain Road, NE
Albuquerque, NM 87102
Phone: 505-242-9918

AMERICAN LEGION AUXILIARY, DEPARTMENT OF NORTH DAKOTA

AMERICAN LEGION AUXILIARY DEPARTMENT OF NORTH DAKOTA PAST PRESIDENT'S PARLEY NURSES' SCHOLARSHIP

One-time award for North Dakota resident who is the child, grandchild, or great-grandchild of a member of the American Legion or Auxiliary. Must be a graduate of a North Dakota high school and attending a nursing program in North Dakota. A minimum 2.5 GPA is required.

Academic Fields/Career Goals: Nursing.

Award: Scholarship for use in freshman, sophomore, junior, or senior years; not renewable. *Number:* 5. *Amount:* $350.

Eligibility Requirements: Applicant must be enrolled or expecting to enroll full or part-time at a two-year or four-year institution or university; resident of North Dakota and studying in North Dakota. Applicant or parent of applicant must be member of American Legion or Auxiliary. Applicant must have 2.5 GPA or higher. Available to U.S. citizens. Applicant or parent must meet one or more of the following requirements: general military experience; retired from active duty; disabled or killed as a result of military service; prisoner of war; or missing in action.

Application Requirements: Application, autobiography, essay, financial need analysis, self-addressed stamped envelope, test scores, transcript. *Deadline:* May 15.

Contact: Donna Rice, Education Chairman
American Legion Auxiliary, Department of North Dakota
201 Kennedy Avenue
Maddock, ND 58348
Phone: 701-742-2647

AMERICAN LEGION AUXILIARY, DEPARTMENT OF OHIO

AMERICAN LEGION AUXILIARY DEPARTMENT OF OHIO PAST PRESIDENT'S PARLEY NURSES' SCHOLARSHIP

One-time award for Ohio residents who are the children or grandchildren of a veteran, living or deceased. Must enroll or be enrolled in a nursing program. Application requests must be received by May 1.

Academic Fields/Career Goals: Nursing.

Award: Scholarship for use in freshman, sophomore, junior, or senior years; not renewable. *Number:* 15–20. *Amount:* $300–$500.

Eligibility Requirements: Applicant must be enrolled or expecting to enroll full-time at a two-year or four-year institution or university and resident of Ohio. Available to U.S. citizens. Applicant or parent must meet one or more of the following requirements: general military experience; retired from active duty; disabled or killed as a result of military service; prisoner of war; or missing in action.

American Legion Auxiliary, Department of Ohio (continued)

Application Requirements: Application, references. *Deadline:* May 1.

Contact: Reva McClure, Scholarship Coordinator
American Legion Auxiliary, Department of Ohio
PO Box 2760
Zanesville, OH 43702-2760
Phone: 740-452-8245
Fax: 740-452-2620
E-mail: ala_pam@rrohio.com

AMERICAN LEGION AUXILIARY, DEPARTMENT OF OREGON

AMERICAN LEGION AUXILIARY DEPARTMENT OF OREGON NURSES SCHOLARSHIP

One-time award for Oregon residents entering their freshman year who are the children of veterans who served during eligibility dates for American Legion membership. Must enroll in a nursing program. Contact local units for application.

Academic Fields/Career Goals: Nursing.

Award: Scholarship for use in freshman year; not renewable. *Number:* 1. *Amount:* $1500.

Eligibility Requirements: Applicant must be enrolled or expecting to enroll at an institution or university and resident of Oregon. Available to U.S. citizens. Applicant or parent must meet one or more of the following requirements: general military experience; retired from active duty; disabled or killed as a result of military service; prisoner of war; or missing in action.

Application Requirements: Application, financial need analysis, interview, transcript. *Deadline:* May 1.

Contact: Pat Calhoun-Floren, Secretary
American Legion Auxiliary, Department of Oregon
PO Box 1730
Wilsonville, OR 97070
Phone: 503-682-3162
Fax: 503-695-5008

AMERICAN LEGION AUXILIARY, DEPARTMENT OF PENNSYLVANIA

AMERICAN LEGION AUXILIARY DEPARTMENT OF PENNSYLVANIA PAST DEPARTMENT PRESIDENT'S MEMORIAL SCHOLARSHIP

Nonrenewable scholarship for children or grandchildren of veterans. Must be U.S. citizen and Pennsylvania resident. For high school seniors who are planning to attend a Pennsylvania school to study nursing. Award is $400 each year. Contact local American Legion unit for details.

Academic Fields/Career Goals: Nursing.

Award: Scholarship for use in freshman, sophomore, or junior years; not renewable. *Number:* 1. *Amount:* $400.

Eligibility Requirements: Applicant must be high school student; planning to enroll or expecting to enroll full-time at an institution or university; resident of Pennsylvania and studying in Pennsylvania. Available to U.S. citizens. Applicant or parent must meet one or more of the following requirements: general military experience; retired from active duty; disabled or killed as a result of military service; prisoner of war; or missing in action.

Application Requirements: Application. *Deadline:* March 15.

Contact: Colleen Watson, Executive Secretary and Treasurer
American Legion Auxiliary, Department of Pennsylvania
PO Box 2643
Harrisburg, PA 17105
Phone: 717-763-7545

AMERICAN LEGION AUXILIARY, DEPARTMENT OF SOUTH DAKOTA

LOIS HALLBERG NURSE'S SCHOLARSHIP

Award for residents of South Dakota who are graduates of an accredited high school and interested in a career in nursing. Must be a veteran's or auxiliary member's child or grandchild. One-time award of $500.

Academic Fields/Career Goals: Nursing.

Award: Scholarship for use in freshman year; not renewable. *Number:* 2. *Amount:* $500.

Eligibility Requirements: Applicant must be enrolled or expecting to enroll at an institution or university and resident of South Dakota. Applicant or parent of applicant must be member of American Legion or Auxiliary. Applicant or parent must meet one or more of the following requirements: general military experience; retired from active duty; disabled or killed as a result of military service; prisoner of war; or missing in action.

Application Requirements: Application, essay, financial need analysis, references. *Deadline:* March 1.

Contact: Patricia Coyle, Executive Secretary
American Legion Auxiliary, Department of South Dakota
PO Box 117
Huron, SD 57350
Phone: 605-353-1793
Fax: 605-352-0336
E-mail: sdlegionaux@msn.com

AMERICAN LEGION AUXILIARY, DEPARTMENT OF WASHINGTON http://www.walegion-aux.org

MARGARITE MCALPIN NURSE'S SCHOLARSHIP

One award for a child or grandchild of a veteran pursuing an education in nursing. May be a high school senior or an enrolled nursing student. Submit a brief statement of military service of veteran parent or grandparent. For Washington residents. One-time award of $500.

Academic Fields/Career Goals: Nursing.

Award: Scholarship for use in freshman year; not renewable. *Number:* 1. *Amount:* $500.

Eligibility Requirements: Applicant must be enrolled or expecting to enroll at an institution or university and resident of Washington. Available to U.S. citizens. Applicant or parent must meet one or more of the following requirements: general military experience; retired from active duty; disabled or killed as a result of military service; prisoner of war; or missing in action.

Application Requirements: Application, autobiography, essay, financial need analysis, references, transcript. *Deadline:* April 1.

Contact: Lois Boyle, Education Chairman
American Legion Auxiliary, Department of Washington
PO Box 5867
Lacey, WA 98509-5867
Phone: 360-456-5995
Fax: 360-491-7442
E-mail: alawash@qwest.net

AMERICAN LEGION AUXILIARY, DEPARTMENT OF WISCONSIN http://www.amlegionauxwi.org

REGISTERED NURSE SCHOLARSHIP

One-time award of $750. Applicant must be in nursing school or have positive acceptance to an accredited hospital or university registered nursing program. Applicant must be a daughter, son, wife, or widow of a veteran. Granddaughters and great-granddaughters of veterans who are auxiliary members may also apply. Must send with completed application: certification of an American Legion Auxiliary Unit President, copy of proof that veteran was in service (i.e. discharge papers), letters of recommendation, transcripts, and essay. Must have minimum 3.5 GPA, show financial need, and be a resident of Wisconsin. Refer questions to Department Secretary, (608) 745-0124. Applications available on Web site: http://www.legion-aux.org.

Academic Fields/Career Goals: Nursing.

Award: Scholarship for use in freshman, sophomore, junior, senior, or graduate years; not renewable. *Number:* 2. *Amount:* $750.

Eligibility Requirements: Applicant must be enrolled or expecting to enroll full or part-time at a technical institution or university and resident of Wisconsin. Applicant or parent of applicant must be member of American Legion or Auxiliary. Applicant must have 3.5 GPA or higher. Available to U.S. citizens.

Application Requirements: Application, essay, financial need analysis, references, transcript. *Deadline:* March 15.

Contact: Kim Henderson, Scholarship Information
American Legion Auxiliary, Department of Wisconsin
PO Box 140
Portage, WI 53901-0140
Phone: 608-745-0124
Fax: 608-745-1947
E-mail: membership@amlegionauxwi.org

AMERICAN LEGION AUXILIARY, DEPARTMENT OF WYOMING

PAST PRESIDENTS PARLEY HEALTH CARE SCHOLARSHIP

• *See page 183*

AMERICAN LEGION, DEPARTMENT OF KANSAS

HOBBLE (LPN) NURSING SCHOLARSHIP

This is an outright grant of $300 (payable one time) at the start of the first semester, awarded only upon acceptance and verification of enrollment by the scholarship winner in an accredited Kansas school which awards a diploma for Licensed Practical Nursing (LPN). The applicant must have attained the age of 18 prior to taking the Kansas State Board Examination. The scholarship will be awarded to an individual who is both qualified and in need of financial aid.

Academic Fields/Career Goals: Nursing.

Award: Scholarship for use in freshman year; not renewable. *Number:* 1. *Amount:* $300.

Eligibility Requirements: Applicant must be age 18; enrolled or expecting to enroll at a two-year or four-year institution; resident of Kansas and studying in Kansas. Available to U.S. citizens.

Application Requirements: Application, financial need analysis, photo, references. *Deadline:* February 15.

Contact: Scholarship Administrator
American Legion, Department of Kansas
1314 Southwest Topeka Boulevard
Topeka, KS 66612-1886

AMERICAN LEGION, DEPARTMENT OF MISSOURI http://www.missourilegion.org

M.D. "JACK" MURPHY MEMORIAL SCHOLARSHIP

One-time award for a single Missouri resident who wants to further their education in the field of nursing. Should be at least 18. Must be a dependent child or grandchild of a Missouri veteran.

Academic Fields/Career Goals: Nursing.

Award: Scholarship for use in freshman or sophomore years; renewable. *Number:* 1. *Amount:* $750.

Eligibility Requirements: Applicant must be age 18; enrolled or expecting to enroll full-time at a four-year institution or university; single and resident of Missouri. Available to U.S. citizens. Applicant or parent must meet one or more of the following requirements: general military experience; retired from active duty; disabled or killed as a result of military service; prisoner of war; or missing in action.

Application Requirements: Application, financial need analysis, test scores. *Deadline:* April 20.

Contact: Scholarship Information
American Legion, Department of Missouri
PO Box 179
Jefferson City, MO 65102-0179
Phone: 573-893-2353
Fax: 573-893-2980

AMERICAN LEGION, EIGHT AND FORTY http://www.legion.org

EIGHT & FORTY LUNG AND RESPIRATORY DISEASE NURSING SCHOLARSHIP FUND

Available to registered nurses with work experience who are taking courses leading to full-time employment in lung or respiratory disease nursing and teaching. Candidates should have proven leadership qualities in emergency situations.

Academic Fields/Career Goals: Nursing.

Award: Scholarship for use in junior, senior, or graduate years; not renewable. *Number:* 20–25. *Amount:* $3000.

Eligibility Requirements: Applicant must be enrolled or expecting to enroll full or part-time at a four-year institution or university and must have an interest in leadership. Available to U.S. citizens.

Application Requirements: Application, references, transcript. *Deadline:* May 15.

Contact: Program Administrator
American Legion, Eight and Forty
PO Box 1055
Indianapolis, IN 46206-1055

AMERICAN NEPHROLOGY NURSES' ASSOCIATION http://www.annanurse.org

ABBOTT/PAMELA BALZER CAREER MOBILITY SCHOLARSHIP

Scholarships available to support qualified ANNA members, minimum two years membership, in the pursuit of either a BSN or advanced degree in nursing that will enhance their nephrology nursing practice. Deadline is October 15. Details on Web. http://www.annanurse.org.

Academic Fields/Career Goals: Nursing.

Award: Scholarship for use in junior, senior, graduate, or postgraduate years; not renewable. *Number:* 1. *Amount:* $2500.

Eligibility Requirements: Applicant must be enrolled or expecting to enroll full or part-time at a four-year institution or university. Applicant or parent of applicant must be member of American Nephrology Nurses' Association. Applicant or parent of applicant must have employment or volunteer experience in designated career field.

Application Requirements: Application, essay, references, transcript, eligibility documentation, acceptance letter. *Deadline:* October 15.

Contact: Charlotte Thomas-Hawkins, American Nephrology Nurses' Association
American Nephrology Nurses' Association
East Holly Avenue
Box 56
Pitman, NJ 08071-0056
Phone: 856-256-2320
Fax: 856-589-7463
E-mail: anna@ajj.com

AMERICAN NEPHROLOGY NURSES' ASSOCIATION AMERICAN REGENT CAREER MOBILITY SCHOLARSHIP

Scholarships available to support qualified ANNA members in the pursuit of either a BSN or advanced degree in nursing that will enhance their nephrology nursing practice. Deadline is October 15. Details on Web. http://www.annanurse.org.

Academic Fields/Career Goals: Nursing.

Award: Scholarship for use in junior, senior, graduate, or postgraduate years; not renewable. *Number:* 1. *Amount:* $2000.

Eligibility Requirements: Applicant must be enrolled or expecting to enroll full or part-time at a four-year institution or university. Applicant or parent of applicant must be member of American Nephrology Nurses' Association. Applicant or parent of applicant must have employment or volunteer experience in designated career field.

Application Requirements: Application, essay, references, transcript, eligibility documentation, acceptance letter. *Deadline:* October 15.

Contact: Charlotte Thomas-Hawkins, American Nephrology Nurses' Association
American Nephrology Nurses' Association
East Holly Avenue
Box 56
Pitman, NJ 08071-0056
Phone: 856-256-2320
Fax: 856-589-7463
E-mail: anna@ajj.com

AMERICAN NEPHROLOGY NURSES' ASSOCIATION AMGEN CAREER MOBILITY SCHOLARSHIP

Scholarships available to support qualified ANNA members in the pursuit of either a BSN or advanced degree in nursing that will enhance their nephrology nursing practice. Deadline is October 15. Details on Web http://www.annanurse.org.

Academic Fields/Career Goals: Nursing.

Award: Scholarship for use in junior, senior, graduate, or postgraduate years; not renewable. *Number:* 1. *Amount:* $2500.

Eligibility Requirements: Applicant must be enrolled or expecting to enroll full or part-time at a four-year institution or university. Applicant or parent of applicant must be member of American Nephrology Nurses' Association. Applicant or parent of applicant must have employment or volunteer experience in designated career field.

Application Requirements: Application, essay, references, transcript, eligibility documentation, acceptance letter. *Deadline:* October 15.

Contact: Charlotte Thomas-Hawkins, American Nephrology Nurses' Association
American Nephrology Nurses' Association
East Holly Avenue
Box 56
Pitman, NJ 08071-0056
Phone: 856-256-2320
Fax: 856-589-7463
E-mail: anna@ajj.com

AMERICAN NEPHROLOGY NURSES' ASSOCIATION ANTHONY J. JANETTI, INC. CAREER MOBILITY SCHOLARSHIP

Scholarships available to support qualified ANNA members in the pursuit of either a BSN or advanced degree in nursing that will enhance their nephrology nursing practice. Deadline is October 15. Details on the Web http://www.annanurse.org.

Academic Fields/Career Goals: Nursing.

Award: Scholarship for use in junior, senior, graduate, or postgraduate years; not renewable. *Number:* 1. *Amount:* up to $2000.

Eligibility Requirements: Applicant must be enrolled or expecting to enroll at a four-year institution or university. Applicant or parent of applicant must be member of American Nephrology Nurses' Association. Applicant or parent of applicant must have employment or volunteer experience in designated career field.

Application Requirements: Application, essay, references, transcript, eligibility documentation, letter of acceptance. *Deadline:* October 15.

Contact: Charlotte Thomas-Hawkins, American Nephrology Nurses' Association
American Nephrology Nurses' Association
East Holly Avenue
Box 56
Pitman, NJ 08071-0056
Phone: 856-256-2320
Fax: 856-589-7463
E-mail: anna@ajj.com

AMERICAN NEPHROLOGY NURSES' ASSOCIATION BIOETHICS GRANT

Grant available to provide funding for one qualified ANNA member to support education in basic philosophical theory, as well as current concepts and issues in healthcare science-related ethics. Must currently be employed as a nephrology nurse. Deadline is October 15. Details available at Web site: http://www.annanurse.org.

Academic Fields/Career Goals: Nursing.

Award: Grant for use in junior, senior, graduate, or postgraduate years; not renewable. *Number:* 1. *Amount:* up to $2400.

Eligibility Requirements: Applicant must be enrolled or expecting to enroll full or part-time at a four-year institution or university. Applicant or parent of applicant must be member of American Nephrology Nurses' Association. Applicant or parent of applicant must have employment or volunteer experience in designated career field.

Application Requirements: Application, essay, references, transcript, eligibility documentation. *Deadline:* October 15.

Contact: Charlotte Thomas-Hawkins, American Nephrology Nurses' Association
American Nephrology Nurses' Association
East Holly Avenue
Box 56
Pitman, NJ 08071-0056
Phone: 856-256-2320
Fax: 856-589-7463
E-mail: anna@ajj.com

AMERICAN NEPHROLOGY NURSES' ASSOCIATION CAREER MOBILITY SCHOLARSHIP

Scholarships available to support qualified ANNA members, minimum two years, in the pursuit of either BSN or advanced degrees in nursing that will enhance their nephrology nursing practice. Must be accepted or enrolled in baccalaureate or higher degree program in nursing. Details on Web http://www.annanurse.org

Academic Fields/Career Goals: Nursing.

Award: Scholarship for use in junior, senior, graduate, or postgraduate years; not renewable. *Number:* 5. *Amount:* $2000.

Eligibility Requirements: Applicant must be enrolled or expecting to enroll full or part-time at a four-year institution or university. Applicant or parent of applicant must be member of American Nephrology Nurses' Association. Applicant or parent of applicant must have employment or volunteer experience in designated career field.

Application Requirements: Application, essay, references, transcript, eligibility documentation, acceptance letter. *Deadline:* October 15.

Contact: Charlotte Thomas-Hawkins, American Nephrology Nurses' Association
American Nephrology Nurses' Association
East Holly Avenue
Box 56
Pitman, NJ 08071-0056
Phone: 856-256-2320
Fax: 856-589-7463
E-mail: anna@ajj.com

AMERICAN NEPHROLOGY NURSES' ASSOCIATION GE OSMONICS MEDICAL SYSTEMS CAREER MOBILITY SCHOLARSHIP

Scholarships available to support qualified ANNA members in the pursuit of either BSN or advanced degrees in nursing that will enhance their nephrology nursing practice. Deadline is October 15. Details on Web. http://www.annanurse.org.

Academic Fields/Career Goals: Nursing.

Award: Scholarship for use in junior, senior, graduate, or postgraduate years; not renewable. *Number:* 2. *Amount:* $2500.

Eligibility Requirements: Applicant must be enrolled or expecting to enroll full or part-time at a four-year institution or university. Applicant or parent of applicant must be member of American Nephrology Nurses' Association. Applicant or parent of applicant must have employment or volunteer experience in designated career field.

Application Requirements: Application, essay, references, transcript, eligibility documentation, letter of acceptance. *Deadline:* October 15.

Contact: Charlotte Thomas-Hawkins, American Nephrology Nurses' Association
American Nephrology Nurses' Association
East Holly Avenue
Box 56
Pitman, NJ 08071-0056
Phone: 856-256-2320
Fax: 856-589-7463
E-mail: anna@ajj.com

AMERICAN NEPHROLOGY NURSES' ASSOCIATION NNCC CAREER MOBILITY SCHOLARSHIP

Scholarships available for qualified ANNA members who are certified nephrology nurses, or certified dialysis nurse in the pursuit of a BSN or advanced degree in nursing. Deadline is October 15. Details on Web. http://www.annanurse.org.

Academic Fields/Career Goals: Nursing.

Award: Scholarship for use in junior, senior, graduate, or postgraduate years. *Number:* 3. *Amount:* $2000.

Eligibility Requirements: Applicant must be enrolled or expecting to enroll full or part-time at a four-year institution or university. Applicant or parent of applicant must be member of American Nephrology Nurses' Association. Applicant or parent of applicant must have employment or volunteer experience in designated career field.

Application Requirements: Application, essay, references, transcript, eligibility documentation, letter of acceptance. *Deadline:* October 15.

Contact: Charlotte Thomas-Hawkins, American Nephrology Nurses' Association
American Nephrology Nurses' Association
East Holly Avenue
Box 56
Pitman, NJ 08071-0056
Phone: 856-256-2320
Fax: 856-589-7463
E-mail: anna@ajj.com

AMERICAN NEPHROLOGY NURSES' ASSOCIATION WATSON PHARMA, INC. CAREER MOBILITY SCHOLARSHIP

Scholarships available to support qualified ANNA members in the pursuit of either a BSN or advanced degree in nursing that will enhance their nephrology nursing practice. Deadline is October 15. Details on Web. http://www.annanurse.org.

Academic Fields/Career Goals: Nursing.

Award: Scholarship for use in junior, senior, graduate, or postgraduate years; not renewable. *Number:* 1. *Amount:* $2500.

Eligibility Requirements: Applicant must be enrolled or expecting to enroll full or part-time at a four-year institution or university. Applicant or parent of applicant must be member of American Nephrology Nurses' Association. Applicant or parent of applicant must have employment or volunteer experience in designated career field.

Application Requirements: Application, essay, references, transcript, eligibility documentation, letter of acceptance. *Deadline:* October 15.

Contact: Charlotte Thomas-Hawkins, American Nephrology Nurses' Association
American Nephrology Nurses' Association
East Holly Avenue
Box 56
Pitman, NJ 08071-0056
Phone: 856-256-2320
Fax: 856-589-7463
E-mail: anna@ajj.com

AMERICAN QUARTER HORSE FOUNDATION (AQHF) http://www.aqha.org/aqhya

AQHF EDUCATION OR NURSING SCHOLARSHIP

• *See page 196*

AMVETS DEPARTMENT OF ILLINOIS http://www.amvets.com

ILLINOIS AMVETS SAD SACKS NURSING SCHOLARSHIPS

Applicant must be a resident of Illinois and accepted for training at an approved school of nursing in Illinois. Preference given to child of deceased veteran and/or student nurse in training in the order: third-, second-, first-year student. Submit IRS 1040 form.

Academic Fields/Career Goals: Nursing.

Award: Scholarship for use in freshman, sophomore, or junior years; not renewable. *Number:* 2–3. *Amount:* $500–$750.

Eligibility Requirements: Applicant must be age 18; enrolled or expecting to enroll full-time at a two-year or four-year or technical institution or university; resident of Illinois and studying in Illinois. Available to U.S. citizens.

Application Requirements: Application, financial need analysis, references, test scores, transcript, IRS 1040 form. *Deadline:* March 1.

Contact: Sara Van Dyke, Scholarship Director
AMVETS Department of Illinois
2200 South Sixth Street
Springfield, IL 62703-3496
Phone: 217-528-4713
Fax: 217-528-9896
E-mail: scholarship@amvetsillinois.com

ARRL FOUNDATION, INC. http://www.arrl.org/arrlf/scholgen.html

WILLIAM R. GOLDFARB MEMORIAL SCHOLARSHIP

• *See page 121*

ASSOCIATION OF PERI-OPERATIVE REGISTERED NURSES http://www.aorn.org

ASSOCIATION OF PERI-OPERATIVE REGISTERED NURSES

Applicant must be an RN and a member of AORN for twelve consecutive months to apply for a scholarship for an advanced degree. Recipients may reapply. Amount and number of one-time awards vary. Minimum 3.0 GPA required. Must be pursuing studies in nursing. Students working toward their RN need not be members of AORN. Applicants must be U.S. citizen or legal resident. See Web site: http://www.aorn.org for application and further details

Academic Fields/Career Goals: Nursing.

Award: Scholarship for use in freshman, sophomore, junior, senior, graduate, or postgraduate years; not renewable. *Number:* varies. *Amount:* varies.

Eligibility Requirements: Applicant must be enrolled or expecting to enroll full or part-time at a two-year or four-year institution or university. Applicant or parent of applicant must be member of Association of Operating Room Nurses. Applicant must have 3.0 GPA or higher. Available to U.S. citizens.

Application Requirements: Application, essay, transcript. *Deadline:* May 1.

Contact: Ingrid Bendzsa, Executive Assistant
Association of Peri-Operative Registered Nurses
2170 South Parker Road
Suite 300
Denver, CO 80231
Phone: 800-755-2676 Ext. 328
Fax: 303-755-4219
E-mail: ibendzsa@aorn.org

BECA FOUNDATION, INC.

ALICE NEWELL JOSLYN MEDICAL FUND

• *See page 183*

BETHESDA LUTHERAN HOMES AND SERVICES, INC. http://www.blhs.org

NURSING SCHOLASTIC ACHIEVEMENT SCHOLARSHIP FOR LUTHERAN COLLEGE STUDENTS

One-time award for college nursing students with minimum 3.0 GPA who are Lutheran and have completed the sophomore year of a four-year nursing program or one year of a two-year nursing program. Must be interested in working with people with developmental disabilities. Awards of up to $1500.

Academic Fields/Career Goals: Nursing.

Award: Scholarship for use in sophomore, junior, senior, or graduate years; not renewable. *Number:* 1–3. *Amount:* up to $1500.

Eligibility Requirements: Applicant must be Lutheran and enrolled or expecting to enroll full-time at a two-year or four-year institution or university. Applicant must have 3.0 GPA or higher. Available to U.S. and Canadian citizens.

Bethesda Lutheran Homes and Services, Inc. (continued)

Application Requirements: Application, autobiography, essay, references, transcript. *Deadline:* March 15.

Contact: Thomas Heuer, Coordinator, Outreach Programs and Services
Bethesda Lutheran Homes and Services, Inc.
National Christian Resource Center, 600 Hoffmann Drive
Watertown, WI 53094-6294
Phone: 920-261-3050 Ext. 4449
Fax: 920-262-6513
E-mail: theuer@blhs.org

BRITISH COLUMBIA MINISTRY OF ADVANCED EDUCATION http://www.aved.gov.bc.ca/

LOAN FORGIVENESS PROGRAM FOR NURSES, DOCTORS, MIDWIVES, AND PHARMACISTS

• *See page 295*

BUREAU OF HEALTH PROFESSIONS http://nhsc.bhpr.hrsa.gov/members/scholars/

NATIONAL HEALTH SERVICE CORPS SCHOLARSHIP PROGRAM

• *See page 295*

CONNECTICUT LEAGUE FOR NURSING http://www.ctleaguefornursing.org

CONNECTICUT LEAGUE FOR NURSING SCHOLARSHIP

For Connecticut residents entering final year of two- or four-year NLN-accredited program in a Connecticut nursing school that is a Connecticut League for Nursing member. Graduate students must have completed twenty credits in an accredited program. Based on academic merit and promise. Must have minimum 2.5 GPA. Deadline: October 15.

Academic Fields/Career Goals: Nursing.

Award: Scholarship for use in sophomore, senior, or graduate years; not renewable. *Number:* 2. *Amount:* $1000.

Eligibility Requirements: Applicant must be enrolled or expecting to enroll full-time at a two-year or four-year institution or university; resident of Connecticut and studying in Connecticut. Applicant must have 2.5 GPA or higher. Available to U.S. citizens.

Application Requirements: Application, financial need analysis, references, transcript. *Deadline:* October 15.

Contact: Diantha McMorrow, Executive Director
Connecticut League for Nursing
PO Box 365
Wallingford, CT 06492
Phone: 203-265-4248
Fax: 203-265-5311
E-mail: cln@chime.net

DANISH SISTERHOOD OF AMERICA

ELIZABETH GARDE NURSING SCHOLARSHIP

One-time award for student seeking to be in the medical profession. Must be a member of the Danish Sisterhood of America or be a son or daughter of a member. Minimum GPA of 3.0. Write for further details.

Academic Fields/Career Goals: Nursing.

Award: Scholarship for use in freshman, sophomore, junior, senior, graduate, or postgraduate years; not renewable. *Number:* 1. *Amount:* $850.

Eligibility Requirements: Applicant must be enrolled or expecting to enroll at a four-year institution. Applicant or parent of applicant must be member of Danish Sisterhood of America. Applicant must have 3.0 GPA or higher. Available to U.S. citizens.

Application Requirements: Application. *Deadline:* February 28.

Contact: Melanie Berg, Chairperson
Danish Sisterhood of America
10911 B. Glen Acres Drive South
Seattle, WA 98168
Phone: 206-243-1728

DELAWARE HIGHER EDUCATION COMMISSION http://www.doe.state.de.us/high-ed

DELAWARE NURSING INCENTIVE SCHOLARSHIP LOAN

Award for Delaware residents pursuing a nursing career. Must be repaid with nursing practice at a Delaware state-owned hospital. Based on academic merit. Must have minimum 2.5 GPA. Renewable for up to four years.

Academic Fields/Career Goals: Nursing.

Award: Forgivable loan for use in freshman, sophomore, junior, or senior years; renewable. *Number:* 1–40. *Amount:* $1000–$5000.

Eligibility Requirements: Applicant must be enrolled or expecting to enroll full-time at a two-year or four-year institution or university and resident of Delaware. Applicant must have 2.5 GPA or higher. Available to U.S. citizens.

Application Requirements: Application, essay, test scores, transcript. *Deadline:* March 31.

Contact: Donna Myers, Higher Education Analyst
Delaware Higher Education Commission
820 North French Street
5th Floor
Wilmington, DE 19711-3509
Phone: 302-577-3240
Fax: 302-577-6765
E-mail: dhec@doe.k12.de.us

DEMOCRATIC NURSING ORGANIZATION OF SOUTH AFRICA http://www.denosa.org.za

DEMOCRATIC NURSING ORGANIZATION OF SOUTH AFRICA STUDY FUND

Awards granted annually to members of DENOSA who are enrolled for postsecondary studies. Must have been member of DENOSA for three years. Must study in South Africa. The deadline is January 31.

Academic Fields/Career Goals: Nursing.

Award: Grant for use in freshman, sophomore, junior, or senior years; not renewable. *Number:* varies. *Amount:* varies.

Eligibility Requirements: Applicant must be enrolled or expecting to enroll full or part-time at a four-year or technical institution or university. Available to citizens of countries other than the U.S. or Canada.

Application Requirements: Application. *Deadline:* January 31.

Contact: Ms. Thembeka Gwagwa, Executive Director
Democratic Nursing Organization of South Africa
PO Box 1280
Pretoria 0001
South Africa
Phone: 27-12-3432315
Fax: 27-12-3440750
E-mail: info@denosa.org.za

EMERGENCY NURSES ASSOCIATION (ENA) FOUNDATION http://www.ena.org/foundation

ENA FOUNDATION UNDERGRADUATE SCHOLARSHIP

Award of up to $2000 to a registered nurse pursuing a baccalaureate degree in nursing. Applicants must be nurses currently licensed and members of ENA for a minimum of 12 months. All other applicants will not be considered. Application must be postmarked by June 1. Recipient will be notified August 1.

Academic Fields/Career Goals: Nursing.

Award: Scholarship for use in freshman, sophomore, junior, or senior years; not renewable. *Number:* 1. *Amount:* up to $2000.

Eligibility Requirements: Applicant must be enrolled or expecting to enroll full or part-time at a four-year institution or university. Applicant or parent of applicant must be member of Emergency Nurses Association. Available to U.S. and non-U.S. citizens.

Application Requirements: Application, transcript. *Deadline:* June 1.

Contact: Emergency Nurses Association (ENA) Foundation
915 Lee Street
Des Plaines, IL 60016-6569

FLORIDA DEPARTMENT OF HEALTH

NURSING SCHOLARSHIP PROGRAM

Provides financial assistance for Florida residents who are full- or part-time nursing students enrolled in an approved nursing program in Florida. Awards are for a maximum of two years and must be repaid through full-time service at an approved/designated site, in a medically underserved area in Florida.

Academic Fields/Career Goals: Nursing.

Award: Scholarship for use in junior, senior, or graduate years; renewable. *Number:* 15–30. *Amount:* $8000–$12,000.

Eligibility Requirements: Applicant must be enrolled or expecting to enroll full or part-time at a two-year or four-year institution or university; resident of Florida and studying in Florida. Available to U.S. and non-U.S. citizens.

Application Requirements: Application. *Deadline:* varies.

Contact: Thomas Gabriele, Program Coordinator
Florida Department of Health
Office of Public Health Nursing
4052 Bald Cypress Way, Mail Bin C-27
Tallahassee, FL 32399-1708
Phone: 800-342-8660 Ext. 3503
Fax: 850-922-6296

FOUNDATION OF THE NATIONAL STUDENT NURSES' ASSOCIATION http://www.nsna.org

BREAKTHROUGH TO NURSING SCHOLARSHIPS FOR RACIAL/ETHNIC MINORITIES

Available to minority students enrolled in nursing or pre-nursing programs. Awards based on need, scholarship, and health-related activities. Application fee of $10. Send self-addressed stamped envelope with two stamps along with application request. One-time award of $1000-$2000. Application available at Web site.

Academic Fields/Career Goals: Nursing.

Award: Scholarship for use in freshman, sophomore, junior, or senior years; not renewable. *Number:* 5. *Amount:* $1000–$2000.

Eligibility Requirements: Applicant must be American Indian/Alaska Native, Asian/Pacific Islander, Black (non-Hispanic), or Hispanic and enrolled or expecting to enroll at an institution or university. Available to U.S. citizens.

Application Requirements: Application, financial need analysis, self-addressed stamped envelope, transcript. *Fee:* $10. *Deadline:* January 22.

Contact: Application available at Web site.
E-mail: receptionist@nsna.org

FOUNDATION OF THE NATIONAL STUDENT NURSES' ASSOCIATION CAREER MOBILITY SCHOLARSHIP

One-time award open to registered nurses enrolled in program leading to a BA in nursing or licensed practical or vocational nurses enrolled in a program leading to licensure as a registered nurse. Submit copy of license. Application fee: $10. Send self-addressed stamped envelope.

Academic Fields/Career Goals: Nursing.

Award: Scholarship for use in freshman, sophomore, junior, or senior years; not renewable. *Number:* varies. *Amount:* $1000–$2000.

Eligibility Requirements: Applicant must be enrolled or expecting to enroll at an institution or university. Applicant or parent of applicant must have employment or volunteer experience in community service, designated career field, or helping handicapped. Available to U.S. citizens.

Application Requirements: Application, financial need analysis, self-addressed stamped envelope, transcript. *Fee:* $10. *Deadline:* January 22.

Contact: Application available at Web site.
E-mail: receptionist@nsna.org

FOUNDATION OF THE NATIONAL STUDENT NURSES' ASSOCIATION GENERAL SCHOLARSHIPS

One-time award for National Student Nurses' Association members and nonmembers enrolled in nursing programs leading to RN license. Based on need, academic ability, and health-related nursing school or community involvement. Send self-addressed stamped envelope with two stamps for application. Graduating high school seniors are not eligible.

Academic Fields/Career Goals: Nursing.

Award: Scholarship for use in freshman, sophomore, junior, or senior years; not renewable. *Number:* 50–100. *Amount:* $1000–$5000.

Eligibility Requirements: Applicant must be enrolled or expecting to enroll full-time at a two-year or four-year institution or university. Applicant must have 2.5 GPA or higher. Available to U.S. citizens.

Application Requirements: Application, financial need analysis, self-addressed stamped envelope, transcript. *Fee:* $10. *Deadline:* January 22.

Contact: Application available at Web site.
E-mail: receptionist@nsna.org

FOUNDATION OF THE NATIONAL STUDENT NURSES' ASSOCIATION SPECIALTY SCHOLARSHIP

One-time award available to students currently enrolled in a state-approved school of nursing or pre-nursing. Must have interest in a specialty area of nursing. Send self-addressed stamped envelope with two stamps for application. Application fee: $10.

Academic Fields/Career Goals: Nursing.

Award: Scholarship for use in freshman, sophomore, junior, or senior years; not renewable. *Number:* varies. *Amount:* $1000–$2000.

Eligibility Requirements: Applicant must be enrolled or expecting to enroll at an institution or university. Applicant or parent of applicant must have employment or volunteer experience in community service or helping handicapped. Available to U.S. citizens.

Application Requirements: Application, financial need analysis, self-addressed stamped envelope, transcript. *Fee:* $10. *Deadline:* January 22.

Contact: Application available at Web site.
E-mail: receptionist@nsna.org

PROMISE OF NURSING SCHOLARSHIP

For applicants attending nursing school in California, South Florida, Georgia, Illinois, Massachusetts, Michigan, New Jersey, Tennessee, or Dallas/Fort Worth Texas. For an application and further details visit Web site: http://www.nsna.org

Academic Fields/Career Goals: Nursing.

Award: Scholarship for use in freshman, sophomore, junior, or senior years. *Number:* varies. *Amount:* $1000–$2500.

Eligibility Requirements: Applicant must be enrolled or expecting to enroll at an institution or university and studying in California, Florida, Georgia, Illinois, Massachusetts, Michigan, New Jersey, Tennessee, or Texas.

Application Requirements: Application, transcript. *Fee:* $10. *Deadline:* January 22.

Contact: Scholarship Chairperson
Foundation of the National Student Nurses' Association
45 Main Street, Suite 606
Brooklyn, NY 11201
Phone: 718-210-0705
E-mail: receptionist@nsna.org

GOVERNOR'S OFFICE

GOVERNOR'S OPPORTUNITY SCHOLARSHIP

• *See page 124*

GREATER KANAWHA VALLEY FOUNDATION http://www.tgkvf.org

BERNICE PICKINS PARSONS FUND

• *See page 344*

ELEANORA G. WYLIE SCHOLARSHIP FUND FOR NURSING

Awarded to persons to attend any accredited college or university, with preference given to applicants pursuing a nursing education, either at the undergraduate or graduate level, or, specifically, in the broad field of

Greater Kanawha Valley Foundation (continued)

gerontology. May apply for two Foundation scholarships but will only be chosen for one. Must be a resident of West Virginia.

Academic Fields/Career Goals: Nursing.

Award: Scholarship for use in freshman, sophomore, junior, senior, or graduate years; renewable. *Number:* 1. *Amount:* $500.

Eligibility Requirements: Applicant must be enrolled or expecting to enroll full-time at a four-year institution or university and resident of West Virginia. Applicant must have 2.5 GPA or higher. Available to U.S. citizens.

Application Requirements: Application, essay, financial need analysis, references, transcript, IRS 1040 form. *Deadline:* February 17.

Contact: Susan Hoover, Scholarship Coordinator
Greater Kanawha Valley Foundation
PO Box 3041
Charleston, WV 25331
Phone: 304-346-3620
Fax: 304-346-3640

GUSTAVUS B. CAPITO FUND

Scholarships awarded to students who show financial need and are seeking education in nursing at any accredited college or university with a nursing program in West Virginia. Scholarships are awarded for one or more years. May apply for two Foundation scholarships but will only be chosen for one. Must be a resident of West Virginia.

Academic Fields/Career Goals: Nursing.

Award: Scholarship for use in freshman, sophomore, junior, or senior years; renewable. *Number:* 4. *Amount:* $1000.

Eligibility Requirements: Applicant must be enrolled or expecting to enroll full-time at a two-year or four-year institution or university; resident of West Virginia and studying in West Virginia. Applicant must have 2.5 GPA or higher.

Application Requirements: Application, essay, financial need analysis, references, transcript, IRS 1040 form. *Deadline:* February 17.

Contact: Susan Hoover, Scholarship Coordinator
Greater Kanawha Valley Foundation
PO Box 3041
Charleston, WV 25331
Phone: 304-346-3620
Fax: 304-346-3640

HAROLD B. & DOROTHY A. SNYDER FOUNDATION, INC.

HAROLD B. AND DOROTHY A. SNYDER FOUNDATION, INC., PROGRAM

• *See page 141*

HAVANA NATIONAL BANK, TRUSTEE

http://www.havanabank.com

MCFARLAND CHARITABLE NURSING SCHOLARSHIP

For registered nursing students only. Must sign contract obliging student to work in Havana, Illinois for two years for each year of funding or repay award with interest and liquidated damages. Submit test scores, essay, transcripts, references, financial need analysis, and autobiography with application. Preference given to local residents. GPA is an important consideration in selection.

Academic Fields/Career Goals: Nursing.

Award: Forgivable loan for use in freshman, sophomore, junior, senior, graduate, or postgraduate years; renewable. *Number:* 3–5. *Amount:* $1000–$15,000.

Eligibility Requirements: Applicant must be enrolled or expecting to enroll full-time at a two-year or four-year institution or university. Available to U.S. and non-U.S. citizens.

Application Requirements: Application, autobiography, essay, financial need analysis, interview, photo, references, test scores, transcript. *Deadline:* May 1.

Contact: Larry Thomson, Vice President and Senior Trust Officer
Havana National Bank, Trustee
PO Box 200
Havana, IL 62644
Phone: 309-543-3361
Fax: 309-543-3441

HCR MANOR CARE, INC.

HCR MANOR CARE NURSING SCHOLARSHIP PROGRAM

Nursing scholarships available for employees and non-employees of HCR Manor Care who want to continue or begin their nursing education. Non-employees must agree to work at an HCR Manor Care facility while they are going to school and after graduation.

Academic Fields/Career Goals: Nursing.

Award: Scholarship for use in freshman, sophomore, junior, or senior years; not renewable. *Number:* 40–50. *Amount:* $2000–$15,000.

Eligibility Requirements: Applicant must be enrolled or expecting to enroll full-time at a two-year or four-year or technical institution or university. Available to U.S. and non-U.S. citizens.

Application Requirements: Application, essay, financial need analysis, references. *Deadline:* varies.

Contact: Danzella Caldwell, Benefits Assistant
HCR Manor Care, Inc.
333 North Summit Street
Toledo, OH 43604
Phone: 419-254-5378
Fax: 419-254-5384
E-mail: dcaldwell@hcr-manorcare.com

HEALTH PROFESSIONS EDUCATION FOUNDATION

http://www.healthprofessions.ca.gov

ASSOCIATE DEGREE NURSING SCHOLARSHIP PROGRAM

One-time award to nursing students accepted to or enrolled in associate degree nursing programs and who agree to obtain a BSN at a nursing program in California within five years of obtaining an ADN. Eligible applicants may receive up to $8,000 per year in financial assistance. Deadlines: March 24 and September 9. Must be a resident of California. Minimum 2.0 GPA.

Academic Fields/Career Goals: Nursing.

Award: Scholarship for use in freshman or sophomore years; not renewable. *Number:* 15–30. *Amount:* $4000–$8000.

Eligibility Requirements: Applicant must be enrolled or expecting to enroll full or part-time at a two-year or technical institution or university; resident of California and studying in California. Available to U.S. citizens.

Application Requirements: Application, driver's license, financial need analysis, references, transcript. *Deadline:* varies.

Contact: Sondra Jacobs, Program Officer
Health Professions Education Foundation
818 K Street, Suite 210
Sacramento, CA 95814
Phone: 916-324-6500

CENTRAL VALLEY NURSING SCHOLARSHIP

One-time award for California residents studying nursing at a California institution. Scholarship is part of the Central Valley Nursing Work Force Diversity Initiative. Minimum 2.0 GPA. Application deadlines are March 26 and October 9.

Academic Fields/Career Goals: Nursing.

Award: Scholarship for use in freshman, sophomore, junior, senior, graduate, or postgraduate years; not renewable. *Number:* 90–140. *Amount:* $8000–$12,000.

Eligibility Requirements: Applicant must be enrolled or expecting to enroll full or part-time at a two-year or four-year or technical institution or university; resident of California and studying in California. Available to U.S. citizens.

Application Requirements: Application, driver's license, financial need analysis, transcript. *Deadline:* varies.

Contact: Charles Gray, Program Director
Health Professions Education Foundation
818 K Street, Suite 210
Sacramento, CA 95814
Phone: 916-324-6500

HEALTH PROFESSIONS EDUCATION SCHOLARSHIP PROGRAM

• *See page 184*

REGISTERED NURSE EDUCATION LOAN REPAYMENT PROGRAM

Repays governmental and commercial loans that were obtained for tuition expenses, books, equipment, and reasonable living expenses associated with attending college. In return for the repayment of educational debt, loan repayment recipients are required to practice full time in direct patient care in a medically underserved area or county health facility. Eligible applicants may receive up to $19,000 for repayment of educational debt. Deadlines: March 27 and September 11. Must be resident of CA and U.S. citizen.

Academic Fields/Career Goals: Nursing.

Award: Grant for use in senior, or postgraduate years; not renewable. *Number:* 50–70. *Amount:* $4000–$8000.

Eligibility Requirements: Applicant must be enrolled or expecting to enroll full or part-time at a four-year institution or university; resident of California and studying in California. Available to U.S. citizens.

Application Requirements: Application, driver's license, financial need analysis, references, transcript. *Deadline:* varies.

Contact: Monique Voss, Project Officer
Health Professions Education Foundation
818 K Street, Suite 210
Sacramento, CA 95814
Phone: 916-324-6500
Fax: 916-324-6585
E-mail: mvoss@oshpd.state.ca.us

RN EDUCATION SCHOLARSHIP PROGRAM

One-time award to nursing students accepted to or enrolled in baccalaureate degree nursing programs in California. Eligible applicants may receive up to $8,000 per year in financial assistance. Deadlines: March 29 and September 11. Must be resident of California and a U.S. citizen. Minimum 2.0 GPA.

Academic Fields/Career Goals: Nursing.

Award: Scholarship for use in freshman, sophomore, junior, or senior years; not renewable. *Number:* 50–70. *Amount:* $6000–$8000.

Eligibility Requirements: Applicant must be enrolled or expecting to enroll full or part-time at a four-year or technical institution or university; resident of California and studying in California. Available to U.S. citizens.

Application Requirements: Application, driver's license, financial need analysis, references, transcript. *Deadline:* varies.

Contact: Monique Voss, Project Officer
Health Professions Education Foundation
818 K Street, Suite 210
Sacramento, CA 95814
Phone: 916-324-6500
Fax: 916-324-6585
E-mail: mvoss@oshpd.state.ca.us

YOUTH FOR ADOLESCENT PREGNANCY PREVENTION LEADERSHIP RECOGNITION PROGRAM

• *See page 297*

HEALTH RESEARCH COUNCIL OF NEW ZEALAND http://www.hrc.govt.nz

PACIFIC HEALTH WORKFORCE AWARD

• *See page 288*

PACIFIC MENTAL HEALTH WORK FORCE AWARD

• *See page 288*

IDAHO STATE BOARD OF EDUCATION http://www.idahoboardofed.org

EDUCATION INCENTIVE LOAN FORGIVENESS CONTRACT-IDAHO

• *See page 203*

ILLINOIS NURSES ASSOCIATION http://www.illinoisnurses.org

SONNE SCHOLARSHIP

One-time award for up to $1500 available to nursing students. Funds may be used to cover tuition, fees, or any other cost encountered by students enrolled in Illinois state-approved nursing program. Award limited to U.S. citizens who are residents of Illinois. Minimum 2.5 GPA required.

Academic Fields/Career Goals: Nursing.

Award: Scholarship for use in sophomore, junior, or senior years; not renewable. *Number:* 1–4. *Amount:* $1000–$1500.

Eligibility Requirements: Applicant must be enrolled or expecting to enroll full-time at a four-year institution or university; resident of Illinois and studying in Illinois. Applicant must have 2.5 GPA or higher. Available to U.S. citizens.

Application Requirements: Application, essay, financial need analysis, references, transcript. *Deadline:* May 1.

Contact: Sharon Balark, Associate Director of Marketing and Membership
Illinois Nurses Association
105 West Adams, Suite 2101
Chicago, IL 60603
Phone: 312-419-2900
Fax: 312-419-2920

ILLINOIS STUDENT ASSISTANCE COMMISSION (ISAC) http://www.collegezone.org

ILLINOIS DEPARTMENT OF PUBLIC HEALTH CENTER FOR RURAL HEALTH NURSING EDUCATION SCHOLARSHIP PROGRAM

• *See page 297*

INDEPENDENT ORDER OF ODD FELLOWS

ODD FELLOWS AND REBEKAHS ELLEN F. WASHBURN NURSES TRAINING AWARD

Award based on need. Must attend an accredited nursing program in the State of Maine leading to a RN degree. Application deadline is April 15.

Academic Fields/Career Goals: Nursing.

Award: Grant for use in freshman, sophomore, junior, or senior years; not renewable. *Number:* 18–30. *Amount:* $150–$300.

Eligibility Requirements: Applicant must be enrolled or expecting to enroll full-time at a two-year or four-year or technical institution or university and studying in Maine. Available to U.S. and non-U.S. citizens.

Application Requirements: Application, financial need analysis, photo, references, test scores. *Deadline:* April 15.

Contact: Joyce Young, Chairperson
Independent Order of Odd Fellows
131 Queen Street Extension
Gorham, ME 04038
Phone: 207-839-4723

INDIANA HEALTH CARE FOUNDATION http://www.ihca.org

INDIANA HEALTH CARE FOUNDATION NURSING SCHOLARSHIP

One-time award of up to $1500 for Indiana residents studying nursing at an institution in Indiana, Ohio, Kentucky, Illinois or Michigan. Minimum 2.5 GPA. Application deadline May 1.

Academic Fields/Career Goals: Nursing.

Award: Scholarship for use in freshman, sophomore, junior, senior, graduate, or postgraduate years; not renewable. *Number:* varies. *Amount:* $750–$1500.

Eligibility Requirements: Applicant must be enrolled or expecting to enroll full or part-time at a two-year or four-year or technical

Indiana Health Care Foundation (continued)

institution or university; resident of Indiana and studying in Illinois, Indiana, Kentucky, Michigan, or Ohio. Applicant must have 2.5 GPA or higher. Available to U.S. citizens.

Application Requirements: Application, essay, interview, references, transcript. *Deadline:* May 1.

Contact: Tamara Noel, Executive Director
Indiana Health Care Foundation
One North Capitol, Suite 1115
Indianapolis, IN 46204
Phone: 317-636-6406
Fax: 877-561-3757
E-mail: tnoel@ihca.org

INTERNATIONAL ORDER OF THE KING'S DAUGHTERS AND SONS http://www.iokds.org

HEALTH CAREERS SCHOLARSHIP

• *See page 185*

J.D. ARCHBOLD MEMORIAL HOSPITAL http://www.archbold.org

ARCHBOLD SCHOLARSHIP PROGRAM

• *See page 298*

JEWISH FOUNDATION FOR EDUCATION OF WOMEN http://www.jfew.org

SCHOLARSHIP PROGRAM FOR FORMER SOVIET UNION EMIGRES TRAINING IN THE HEALTH SCIENCES

• *See page 186*

LADIES AUXILIARY TO THE VETERANS OF FOREIGN WARS, DEPARTMENT OF MAINE

FRANCIS L. BOOTH MEDICAL SCHOLARSHIP SPONSORED BY LAVFW DEPARTMENT OF MAINE

• *See page 298*

MARIN EDUCATION FUND http://www.marineducationfund.org

GOLDMAN FAMILY FUND, NEW LEADER SCHOLARSHIP

• *See page 186*

MARION D. AND EVA S. PEEPLES FOUNDATION TRUST SCHOLARSHIP PROGRAM http://www.jccf.org

MARION D. AND EVA S. PEEPLES SCHOLARSHIPS

• *See page 205*

MARYLAND HIGHER EDUCATION COMMISSION http://www.mhec.state.md.us

DEVELOPMENTAL DISABILITIES, MENTAL HEALTH, CHILD WELFARE AND JUVENILE JUSTICE WORKFORCE TUITION ASSISTANCE PROGRAM

• *See page 298*

GRADUATE AND PROFESSIONAL SCHOLARSHIP PROGRAM-MARYLAND

• *See page 186*

JANET L. HOFFMANN LOAN ASSISTANCE REPAYMENT PROGRAM

• *See page 206*

MARYLAND STATE NURSING SCHOLARSHIP AND LIVING EXPENSES GRANT

Renewable grant for Maryland residents enrolled in a two- or four-year Maryland institution nursing degree program. Recipients must agree to serve as a full-time nurse in a Maryland shortage area and must maintain a 3.0 GPA in college. Application deadline is June 30. Submit Free Application for Federal Student Aid.

Academic Fields/Career Goals: Nursing.

Award: Forgivable loan for use in freshman, sophomore, junior, senior, or graduate years; renewable. *Number:* up to 600. *Amount:* $200–$3000.

Eligibility Requirements: Applicant must be enrolled or expecting to enroll full or part-time at a two-year or four-year institution or university; resident of Maryland and studying in Maryland. Applicant must have 3.0 GPA or higher. Available to U.S. citizens.

Application Requirements: Application, financial need analysis, transcript. *Deadline:* June 30.

Contact: Marie Janiszewski, Office of Student Financial Assistance
Maryland Higher Education Commission
839 Bestgate Road, Suite 400
Annapolis, MD 21401-3013
Phone: 410-260-4569
Fax: 410-260-3203
E-mail: ofsamail@mhec.state.md.us

TUITION REDUCTION FOR NON-RESIDENT NURSING STUDENTS

Forgivable loan is available to nonresidents of Maryland who attend a two-year or four-year public institution in Maryland. The loan will be renewed provided student maintains academic requirements designated by institution attended. Loan recipient must agree to serve as a full-time nurse in a hospital or related institution for an equal amount of years as tuition was paid by Maryland Higher Education Commission. Loan recipient will pay tuition of Maryland resident.

Academic Fields/Career Goals: Nursing.

Award: Forgivable loan for use in freshman, sophomore, junior, or senior years; renewable. *Number:* varies. *Amount:* varies.

Eligibility Requirements: Applicant must be enrolled or expecting to enroll full or part-time at a two-year or four-year institution and studying in Maryland.

Application Requirements: Application. *Deadline:* varies.

Contact: Financial Aid Office of your school

MASSACHUSETTS OFFICE OF STUDENT FINANCIAL ASSISTANCE http://www.osfa.mass.edu

MASSACHUSETTS GILBERT MATCHING STUDENT GRANT PROGRAM

Must be permanent Massachusetts resident for at least one year and attending an independent, regionally accredited Massachusetts school or school of nursing full time. File the Free Application for Federal Student Aid after January 1. Contact college financial aid office for complete details and deadlines.

Academic Fields/Career Goals: Nursing.

Award: Grant for use in freshman, sophomore, junior, or senior years; not renewable. *Number:* varies. *Amount:* $200–$2500.

Eligibility Requirements: Applicant must be enrolled or expecting to enroll full-time at a four-year institution or university; resident of Massachusetts and studying in Massachusetts. Available to U.S. citizens.

Application Requirements: Financial need analysis, FAFSA. *Deadline:* varies.

Contact: College financial aid office

MICHIGAN BUREAU OF STUDENT FINANCIAL ASSISTANCE http://www.michigan.gov/mistudentaid

MICHIGAN NURSING SCHOLARSHIP

For students enrolled in an LPN, associate degree in nursing, or bachelor of science in nursing programs. Colleges determine application procedure and select recipients. Recipients must fulfill in-state work commitment or repay scholarship.

Academic Fields/Career Goals: Nursing.

Award: Scholarship for use in freshman, sophomore, junior, or senior years; renewable. *Number:* varies. *Amount:* up to $4000.

Eligibility Requirements: Applicant must be enrolled or expecting to enroll full or part-time at a two-year or four-year institution or university; resident of Michigan and studying in Michigan. Available to U.S. citizens.

Contact: Program Director
Michigan Bureau of Student Financial Assistance
PO Box 30466
Lansing, MI 48909-7966

MICHIGAN LEAGUE FOR NURSING http://www.michleaguenursing.org

NURSING STUDENT SCHOLARSHIP

One-time award for students who have completed at least one year of a nursing program or are continuing with undergraduate degree at a Michigan institution. Must have GPA of 2.0 or better. Scholarships of variable number and amount. Must be a resident of Michigan.

Academic Fields/Career Goals: Nursing.

Award: Scholarship for use in sophomore, junior, or senior years; not renewable. *Number:* up to 4. *Amount:* $500.

Eligibility Requirements: Applicant must be enrolled or expecting to enroll at a two-year or four-year institution; resident of Michigan and studying in Michigan. Available to U.S. citizens.

Application Requirements: Application, essay, transcript. *Deadline:* January 10.

Contact: Carole Stacy, Managing Director
Michigan League for Nursing
2410 Woodlake Drive
Suite 440
Okemos, MI 48864
Phone: 517-347-8091
E-mail: cstacy@mhc.org

MINNESOTA DEPARTMENT OF HEALTH http://www.health.state.mn.us

MINNESOTA NURSES LOAN FORGIVENESS PROGRAM

• *See page 299*

MINORITY NURSE MAGAZINE http://www.minoritynurse.com

MINORITY NURSE MAGAZINE SCHOLARSHIP PROGRAM

Scholarships to help academically excellent, financially needy racial and ethnic minority nursing students complete a BSN degree.

Academic Fields/Career Goals: Nursing.

Award: Scholarship for use in junior or senior years; not renewable. *Number:* 4. *Amount:* $500–$1000.

Eligibility Requirements: Applicant must be American Indian/Alaska Native, Asian/Pacific Islander, Black (non-Hispanic), or Hispanic and enrolled or expecting to enroll full or part-time at a four-year institution or university. Applicant must have 3.0 GPA or higher. Available to U.S. citizens.

Application Requirements: Application, essay, financial need analysis, references, transcript. *Deadline:* June 15.

Contact: Pam Chwedyk, Senior Editor/Editorial Manager
Minority Nurse Magazine
211 West Wacker Drive, Suite 900
Chicago, IL 60606
Phone: 312-525-3095
Fax: 312-429-3336
E-mail: pam.chwedyk@careermedia.com

MISSISSIPPI STATE STUDENT FINANCIAL AID http://www.mississippiuniversities.com

NURSING EDUCATION LOAN/SCHOLARSHIP-BSN

Renewable award for Mississippi undergraduates in junior or senior year pursuing nursing programs in Mississippi in order to earn BSN degree. Include transcript and references with application. Must agree to employment in professional nursing (patient care) in Mississippi.

Academic Fields/Career Goals: Nursing.

Award: Forgivable loan for use in junior or senior years; renewable. *Number:* varies. *Amount:* up to $8000.

Eligibility Requirements: Applicant must be enrolled or expecting to enroll full or part-time at a four-year institution or university; resident of Mississippi and studying in Mississippi. Applicant must have 2.5 GPA or higher. Available to U.S. citizens.

Application Requirements: Application, driver's license, financial need analysis, references, transcript. *Deadline:* March 31.

Contact: Board of Trustees
Mississippi State Student Financial Aid
3825 Ridgewood road
Jackson, MS 39211-6453

MISSOURI DEPARTMENT OF HEALTH AND SENIOR SERVICES http://www.dhss.state.mo.us

MISSOURI PROFESSIONAL AND PRACTICAL NURSING STUDENT LOAN PROGRAM

For Missouri residents attending institutions in Missouri. Forgivable loan for nursing student. Upon graduation, the student must work with a nonprofit Health Service program or at a nonprofit Health Service Public Agency in Missouri. Minimum 2.5 GPA required for applicants. Deadlines: 7/15 and 12/15.

Academic Fields/Career Goals: Nursing.

Award: Forgivable loan for use in freshman, sophomore, junior, senior, graduate, or postgraduate years; not renewable. *Number:* varies. *Amount:* up to $5000.

Eligibility Requirements: Applicant must be enrolled or expecting to enroll full-time at a two-year or four-year or technical institution or university; resident of Missouri and studying in Missouri. Applicant must have 2.5 GPA or higher. Available to U.S. and non-U.S. citizens.

Application Requirements: Application, driver's license. *Deadline:* varies.

Contact: Cindy Cox
Missouri Department of Health and Senior Services
PO Box 570
Jefferson City, MO 65102-0570
Phone: 573-751-6219
Fax: 573-522-8146
E-mail: coxc@dhss.mo.gov

PRIMARY CARE RESOURCE INITIATIVE FOR MISSOURI LOAN PROGRAM

• *See page 186*

NATIONAL BLACK NURSES ASSOCIATION, INC. http://www.nbna.org

AETNA SCHOLARSHIP

Scholarships available to nursing students with at least one year of program left for completion. Must be an active member of the National Black Nurses Association. Must demonstrate involvement in African-American community. Send self-addressed stamped envelope for application.

Academic Fields/Career Goals: Nursing.

Award: Scholarship for use in freshman, sophomore, junior, or senior years; not renewable. *Number:* 1–2. *Amount:* $500–$2000.

Eligibility Requirements: Applicant must be enrolled or expecting to enroll full or part-time at a two-year or four-year institution or university. Applicant or parent of applicant must be member of National Black Nurses' Association. Applicant or parent of applicant must have employment or volunteer experience in community service. Available to U.S. and non-U.S. citizens.

Application Requirements: Application, essay, photo, references, self-addressed stamped envelope, transcript. *Deadline:* April 15.

Contact: Scholarship Committee
National Black Nurses Association, Inc.
8360 Fenton Street, Suite 330
Silver Spring, MD 20910
Phone: 301-589-3200
Fax: 301-589-3223
E-mail: nbna@erols.com

DR. HILDA RICHARDS SCHOLARSHIP

Scholarships available to nursing students with at least one year of program left for completion. Must be an active member of the National Black Nurses

National Black Nurses Association, Inc. (continued)

Association at student rate of $35. Must demonstrate involvement in African-American community. Send self-addressed stamped envelope for application.

Academic Fields/Career Goals: Nursing.

Award: Scholarship for use in freshman, sophomore, junior, or senior years; not renewable. *Number:* 1–2. *Amount:* $500–$2000.

Eligibility Requirements: Applicant must be enrolled or expecting to enroll full or part-time at a two-year or four-year institution or university. Applicant or parent of applicant must be member of National Black Nurses' Association. Applicant or parent of applicant must have employment or volunteer experience in community service. Available to U.S. and non-U.S. citizens.

Application Requirements: Application, essay, photo, references, self-addressed stamped envelope, transcript. *Deadline:* April 15.

Contact: Scholarship Committee
National Black Nurses Association, Inc.
8360 Fenton Street, Suite 330
Silver Spring, MD 20910
Phone: 301-589-3200
Fax: 301-589-3223
E-mail: nbna@erols.com

DR. LAURANNE SAMS SCHOLARSHIP

Scholarships available to nursing students with at least one year of program left for completion. Must be an active member of National Black Nurses Association. Student membership is $35. Must demonstrate involvement in African-American community. Send self-addressed stamped envelope for application.

Academic Fields/Career Goals: Nursing.

Award: Scholarship for use in freshman, sophomore, junior, or senior years; not renewable. *Number:* 1–2. *Amount:* $500–$2000.

Eligibility Requirements: Applicant must be enrolled or expecting to enroll full or part-time at a two-year or four-year institution or university. Applicant or parent of applicant must be member of National Black Nurses' Association. Applicant or parent of applicant must have employment or volunteer experience in community service. Available to U.S. and non-U.S. citizens.

Application Requirements: Application, essay, photo, references, self-addressed stamped envelope, transcript. *Deadline:* April 15.

Contact: Scholarship Committee
National Black Nurses Association, Inc.
8360 Fenton Street, Suite 330
Silver Spring, MD 20910
Phone: 301-589-3200
Fax: 301-589-3223
E-mail: nbna@erols.com

KAISER PERMANENTE SCHOOL OF ANESTHESIA SCHOLARSHIP

Scholarship available to nursing students with an least one full year of program left for completion. Must be an active member of the National Black Nurses Association at the student rate of $35. Must demonstrate involvement in the African-American community. Send self-addressed envelope for application.

Academic Fields/Career Goals: Nursing.

Award: Scholarship for use in freshman, sophomore, junior, or senior years; not renewable. *Number:* 1–2. *Amount:* $500–$2000.

Eligibility Requirements: Applicant must be enrolled or expecting to enroll full or part-time at a two-year or four-year institution or university. Applicant or parent of applicant must be member of National Black Nurses' Association. Applicant or parent of applicant must have employment or volunteer experience in community service. Available to U.S. and non-U.S. citizens.

Application Requirements: Application, essay, photo, references, self-addressed stamped envelope, transcript. *Deadline:* April 15.

Contact: Scholarship Committee
National Black Nurses Association, Inc.
8360 Fenton Street, Suite 330
Silver Spring, MD 20910
Phone: 301-589-3200
Fax: 301-589-3223
E-mail: nbna@erols.com

MAYO FOUNDATIONS SCHOLARSHIP

Scholarships available to nursing students with at least one year of program left for completion. Must be an active member of the National Black Nurses Association at student rate of $35. Must demonstrate involvement in African-American community. Send self-addressed stamped envelope for application.

Academic Fields/Career Goals: Nursing.

Award: Scholarship for use in freshman, sophomore, junior, or senior years; not renewable. *Number:* 1–2. *Amount:* $500–$2000.

Eligibility Requirements: Applicant must be enrolled or expecting to enroll full or part-time at a two-year or four-year or technical institution or university. Applicant or parent of applicant must be member of National Black Nurses' Association. Applicant or parent of applicant must have employment or volunteer experience in community service. Available to U.S. and non-U.S. citizens.

Application Requirements: Application, essay, photo, references, self-addressed stamped envelope, transcript. *Deadline:* April 15.

Contact: Scholarship Committee
National Black Nurses Association, Inc.
8360 Fenton Street, Suite 330
Silver Spring, MD 20910
Phone: 301-589-3200
Fax: 301-589-3223
E-mail: nbna@erols.com

NBNA BOARD OF DIRECTORS SCHOLARSHIP

Scholarships for licensed persons who are members of National Black Nurses Association who are enrolled at an accredited school of nursing pursuing a bachelor's or advanced degree. Requires transcript, letter of recommendation from local chapter and school of nursing, and self-addressed stamped envelope. Must show evidence of involvement in African-American community. Student NBNA fee-$35. Must have at least one full year of school remaining.

Academic Fields/Career Goals: Nursing.

Award: Scholarship for use in sophomore, junior, senior, or graduate years; not renewable. *Number:* 1–2. *Amount:* $500–$2000.

Eligibility Requirements: Applicant must be enrolled or expecting to enroll full or part-time at a four-year institution or university. Applicant or parent of applicant must be member of National Black Nurses' Association. Applicant or parent of applicant must have employment or volunteer experience in community service. Available to U.S. and non-U.S. citizens.

Application Requirements: Application, essay, photo, references, self-addressed stamped envelope, transcript. *Deadline:* April 15.

Contact: Scholarship Committee
National Black Nurses Association, Inc.
8360 Fenton Street, Suite 330
Silver Spring, MD 20910
Phone: 301-589-3200
Fax: 301-589-3223
E-mail: nbna@erols.com

NURSING SPECTRUM SCHOLARSHIP

Scholarships available to nursing students with at least one year of program left for completion. Must be an active member of the National Black Nurses Association. Must demonstrate involvement in African-American community. Send self-addressed stamped envelope for application.

Academic Fields/Career Goals: Nursing.

Award: Scholarship for use in freshman, sophomore, junior, or senior years; not renewable. *Number:* 1–2. *Amount:* $500–$2000.

Eligibility Requirements: Applicant must be enrolled or expecting to enroll full or part-time at a two-year or four-year institution or university. Applicant or parent of applicant must be member of National Black Nurses' Association. Applicant or parent of applicant must have employment or volunteer experience in community service. Available to U.S. and non-U.S. citizens.

Application Requirements: Application, essay, photo, references, self-addressed stamped envelope, transcript. *Deadline:* April 15.

Contact: Scholarship Committee
National Black Nurses Association, Inc.
8360 Fenton Street, Suite 330
Silver Spring, MD 20910
Phone: 301-589-3200
Fax: 301-589-3223
E-mail: nbna@erols.com

NATIONAL SOCIETY DAUGHTERS OF THE AMERICAN REVOLUTION http://www.dar.org

NATIONAL SOCIETY DAUGHTERS OF THE AMERICAN REVOLUTION CAROLINE E. HOLT NURSING SCHOLARSHIPS

Nonrenewable award for undergraduate nursing students. Must be U.S. citizen. Need not be DAR member but must submit a letter of sponsorship from local chapter and a financial need form from parents. Award is merit-based. Deadlines: February 15 and August 15. Must submit self-addressed stamped envelope to be considered.

Academic Fields/Career Goals: Nursing.

Award: Scholarship for use in freshman, sophomore, junior, or senior years; not renewable. *Amount:* $500.

Eligibility Requirements: Applicant must be enrolled or expecting to enroll at a two-year or four-year institution. Applicant must have 3.0 GPA or higher. Available to U.S. citizens.

Application Requirements: Application, essay, financial need analysis, references, self-addressed stamped envelope, test scores, transcript. *Deadline:* varies.

Contact: Office of Committees, Scholarship
National Society Daughters of the American Revolution
1776 D Street, NW
Washington, DC 20006-5392

NATIONAL SOCIETY DAUGHTERS OF THE AMERICAN REVOLUTION MADELINE PICKETT (HALBERT) COGSWELL NURSING SCHOLARSHIP

Nonrenewable award for undergraduate nursing students. Must be eligible for membership in NSDAR through relationship to NSDAR, Sons of the Revolution, or DAR member. DAR member number must be included. Must be sponsored by a local chapter. Apply by February 15 or August 15. Must submit self-addressed stamped envelope to be considered.

Academic Fields/Career Goals: Nursing.

Award: Scholarship for use in freshman, sophomore, junior, or senior years; not renewable. *Number:* 7–10. *Amount:* $500.

Eligibility Requirements: Applicant must be enrolled or expecting to enroll at a two-year or four-year institution. Applicant or parent of applicant must be member of Daughters of the American Revolution. Applicant must have 3.0 GPA or higher. Available to U.S. citizens.

Application Requirements: Application, essay, financial need analysis, references, self-addressed stamped envelope, test scores, transcript. *Deadline:* varies.

Contact: Office of Committees, Scholarship
National Society Daughters of the American Revolution
1776 D Street, NW
Washington, DC 20006-5392

NATIONAL SOCIETY DAUGHTERS OF THE AMERICAN REVOLUTION MILDRED NUTTING NURSING SCHOLARSHIP

Nonrenewable award for undergraduate nursing students. Must be a U.S. citizen. Need not be a DAR member but must submit a letter of sponsorship from local chapter and a financial need form from parents. Deadlines: February 15 and August 15. Must submit a self-addressed stamped envelope to be considered. Preference will be given to candidates from the greater Lowell, MA area.

Academic Fields/Career Goals: Nursing.

Award: Scholarship for use in freshman, sophomore, junior, or senior years; not renewable. *Number:* varies. *Amount:* $500.

Eligibility Requirements: Applicant must be enrolled or expecting to enroll at a two-year or four-year institution. Applicant must have 3.0 GPA or higher. Available to U.S. citizens.

Application Requirements: Application, essay, financial need analysis, references, self-addressed stamped envelope, test scores, transcript. *Deadline:* varies.

Contact: Office of Committees, Scholarship
National Society Daughters of the American Revolution
1776 D Street, NW
Washington, DC 20006-5392

NATIONAL SOCIETY OF THE COLONIAL DAMES OF AMERICA

AMERICAN INDIAN NURSE SCHOLARSHIP AWARDS

Renewable award of $500 to $1500 per semester for Native American nursing student with minimum 2.5 GPA in an accredited nursing program within two years of completing courses. Applicant may also be a graduating high school student accepted in a nursing program. Must be full-time student with financial need not receiving Indian Health Service Scholarship and recommended by college.

Academic Fields/Career Goals: Nursing.

Award: Scholarship for use in freshman, sophomore, junior, senior, graduate, or postgraduate years; renewable. *Number:* 13–16. *Amount:* $500–$1500.

Eligibility Requirements: Applicant must be American Indian/Alaska Native and enrolled or expecting to enroll full-time at a two-year or four-year or technical institution or university. Applicant must have 2.5 GPA or higher. Available to U.S. citizens.

Application Requirements: Application, autobiography, financial need analysis, photo, references, transcript. *Deadline:* Continuous.

Contact: Mrs. Thomas Van Antwerp, Consultant
National Society of The Colonial Dames of America
1520 Lake Cove
Atlanta, GA 30338-3429
Phone: 770-352-0470
Fax: 770-671-0950
E-mail: vanant@bellsouth.net

NEW HAMPSHIRE POSTSECONDARY EDUCATION COMMISSION http://www.state.nh.us/postsecondary

WORKFORCE INCENTIVE PROGRAM

• *See page 208*

NEW MEXICO COMMISSION ON HIGHER EDUCATION http://www.nmche.org

ALLIED HEALTH STUDENT LOAN PROGRAM-NEW MEXICO

• *See page 186*

NURSING STUDENT LOAN-FOR-SERVICE PROGRAM

Award for New Mexico residents accepted or enrolled in nursing program at New Mexico public postsecondary institution. Must practice as nurse in designated health professional shortage area in New Mexico. Award dependent upon financial need but may not exceed $12,000. Deadline: July 1.

Academic Fields/Career Goals: Nursing.

Award: Forgivable loan for use in freshman, sophomore, junior, or senior years; not renewable. *Amount:* up to $12,000.

Eligibility Requirements: Applicant must be enrolled or expecting to enroll full or part-time at a two-year or four-year institution; resident of New Mexico and studying in New Mexico. Available to U.S. citizens.

New Mexico Commission on Higher Education (continued)

Application Requirements: Application, financial need analysis, FAFSA. *Deadline:* July 1.

Contact: Maria Barele, Financial Specialist
New Mexico Commission on Higher Education
PO Box 15910
Santa Fe, NM 87506-5910
Phone: 505-827-4026
Fax: 505-827-7392

NEW YORK STATE EDUCATION DEPARTMENT http://www.highered.nysed.gov

REGENTS PROFESSIONAL OPPORTUNITY SCHOLARSHIP

• See page 45

NEW YORK STATE GRANGE

JUNE GILL NURSING SCHOLARSHIP

One annual scholarship award to verified NYS Grange member pursuing a career in nursing. Selection based on verification of NYS Grange membership and enrollment in a nursing program, as well as applicant's career statement, academic records, and financial need. Payment made after successful completion of one term.

Academic Fields/Career Goals: Nursing.

Award: Scholarship for use in freshman, sophomore, junior, or senior years; not renewable. *Number:* 1. *Amount:* varies.

Eligibility Requirements: Applicant must be enrolled or expecting to enroll at a two-year or four-year institution and resident of New York. Applicant or parent of applicant must be member of Grange Association.

Application Requirements: Application, financial need analysis. *Deadline:* varies.

Contact: Ann Hall, Scholarship Chairperson
New York State Grange
100 Grange Place
Cortland, NY 13045
Phone: 607-756-7553
Fax: 607-756-7757
E-mail: nysgrange@nysgrange.com

NEWTON NURSE SCHOLARS RHODE ISLAND FOUNDATION http://northwesthealthcare.org

ALBERT AND FLORENCE NEWTON NURSE SCHOLARSHIP NEWTON FUND

For schools in Rhode Island only. Ascribes funds to: registered nurses seeking BS degree in nursing; senior nursing students in final year of education to become a registered nurse; registered nurses with BS degree seeking graduate degree; programs selected which are targeted to increase the availability of new registered nurses. Application deadlines: April 1 and October 1.

Academic Fields/Career Goals: Nursing.

Award: Scholarship for use in junior, senior, or graduate years; not renewable. *Number:* 5–20. *Amount:* $250–$2500.

Eligibility Requirements: Applicant must be enrolled or expecting to enroll full or part-time at a two-year or four-year institution or university and studying in Rhode Island. Available to U.S. and non-U.S. citizens.

Application Requirements: Application, essay, financial need analysis.

Contact: Beverly McGuire, CEO
Newton Nurse Scholars Rhode Island Foundation
1 Union Station
Providence, RI 02903
Phone: 401-949-3801
Fax: 401-949-5115
E-mail: bmcguire@northwesthealthcare.org

NORTH CAROLINA STATE EDUCATION ASSISTANCE AUTHORITY http://www.cfnc.org

NORTH CAROLINA STUDENT LOAN PROGRAM FOR HEALTH, SCIENCE, AND MATHEMATICS

• See page 187

NURSE EDUCATION SCHOLARSHIP LOAN PROGRAM (NESLP)

Must be U.S. citizen and North Carolina resident. Award available through financial aid offices of North Carolina colleges and universities that offer nurse education programs to prepare students for licensure in the state as LPN or RN. Recipients enter contract with the State of North Carolina to work full time as a licensed nurse. Loans not repaid through service must be repaid in cash. Award based upon financial need. Maximum award for students enrolled in Associate Degree Nursing and Practical Nurse Education programs is $3000. Maximum award for students enrolled in a Baccalaureate program is $5000.

Academic Fields/Career Goals: Nursing.

Award: Forgivable loan for use in freshman, sophomore, junior, or senior years; renewable. *Number:* varies. *Amount:* $3000–$5000.

Eligibility Requirements: Applicant must be enrolled or expecting to enroll at a four-year institution or university; resident of North Carolina and studying in North Carolina. Available to U.S. citizens.

Application Requirements: Application, financial need analysis. *Deadline:* Continuous.

Contact: Financial Aid Office

NURSE SCHOLARS PROGRAM—UNDERGRADUATE (NORTH CAROLINA)

Forgivable loans to residents of North Carolina who have gained full acceptance to a North Carolina institution of higher education that offers a nursing program. Must apply to the North Carolina State Education and Welfare division. Must serve as a registered nurse in North Carolina for one year for each year of funding. Minimum 3.0 GPA required. Amount of award is based upon type of nursing education sought.

Academic Fields/Career Goals: Nursing.

Award: Forgivable loan for use in freshman, sophomore, junior, or senior years; renewable. *Number:* up to 600. *Amount:* $3000–$5000.

Eligibility Requirements: Applicant must be enrolled or expecting to enroll full-time at a two-year or four-year institution or university; resident of North Carolina and studying in North Carolina. Applicant must have 3.0 GPA or higher. Available to U.S. citizens.

Application Requirements: Application, essay, references, test scores, transcript. *Deadline:* varies.

Contact: Christy Campbell, Manager-Health, Education and Welfare
North Carolina State Education Assistance Authority
PO Box 14223
Research Triangle Park, NC 27709-3663
Phone: 919-549-8614
Fax: 919-248-4687

NORTH DAKOTA BOARD OF NURSING http://www.ndbon.org

NORTH DAKOTA BOARD OF NURSING EDUCATION LOAN PROGRAM

One-time loan for North Dakota residents pursuing a nursing degree. Must sign repayment note agreeing to repay loan by nursing employment in North Dakota after graduation. Repayment rate is $1 per hour of employment. For juniors, seniors, and graduate students.

Academic Fields/Career Goals: Nursing.

Award: Forgivable loan for use in junior, senior, or graduate years; not renewable. *Number:* 30–35. *Amount:* $2000–$5000.

Eligibility Requirements: Applicant must be enrolled or expecting to enroll full or part-time at a two-year or four-year institution or university and resident of North Dakota. Applicant must have 2.5 GPA or higher. Available to U.S. citizens.

Application Requirements: Application, financial need analysis, references, transcript. *Fee:* $15. *Deadline:* July 1.

Contact: Ms. Constance Kalanek, Executive Director
North Dakota Board of Nursing
919 South 7th Street, Suite 504
Bismarck, ND 58504-5881
Phone: 701-328-9777
Fax: 701-328-9785
E-mail: executivedir@nbdon.org

NORTON HEALTHCARE http://www.nortonhealthcare.com

NORTON HEALTHCARE SCHOLARS–METROPOLITAN COLLEGE

• *See page 300*

NORTON HEALTHCARE SCHOLARS–PRIVATE COLLEGES AND UNIVERSITIES

• *See page 301*

NURSING FOUNDATION OF PENNSYLVANIA http://www.psna.org

PAULINE THOMPSON NURSING EDUCATION SCHOLARSHIP

One-time award for a nursing student who exemplifies academic achievement (minimum 3.0 GPA), leadership and community service as required in the criteria. A baccalaureate student may be in his/her junior year or in the beginning of his/her senior year. An associate degree student must be in his/her final year. Eligible applicants will be members of a state nurses association. Must be a resident of Pennsylvania.

Academic Fields/Career Goals: Nursing.

Award: Scholarship for use in sophomore, junior, or senior years; not renewable. *Number:* 5. *Amount:* up to $1000.

Eligibility Requirements: Applicant must be enrolled or expecting to enroll full-time at a two-year or four-year institution or university and resident of Pennsylvania. Applicant must have 3.0 GPA or higher. Available to U.S. citizens.

Application Requirements: Application, essay, references, transcript. *Deadline:* May 3.

Contact: Frances Manning, Executive Assistant
Nursing Foundation of Pennsylvania
2578 Interstate Drive, Suite 101
Harrisburg, PA 17110
Phone: 717-657-1222 Ext. 205
Fax: 717-657-3796
E-mail: fmanning@psna.org

ODD FELLOWS AND REBEKAHS

ODD FELLOWS AND REBEKAHS ELLEN F. WASHBURN NURSES TRAINING AWARD

Award for high school seniors and college undergraduates to attend an accredited Maine institution and pursue a registered nursing degree. Must have a minimum 2.5 GPA. Can reapply for award for up to four years.

Academic Fields/Career Goals: Nursing.

Award: Scholarship for use in freshman, sophomore, junior, or senior years; not renewable. *Number:* 15–30. *Amount:* $150–$400.

Eligibility Requirements: Applicant must be enrolled or expecting to enroll full or part-time at a two-year or four-year or technical institution or university and studying in Maine. Applicant must have 2.5 GPA or higher. Available to U.S. and non-U.S. citizens.

Application Requirements: Application, financial need analysis, photo, references. *Deadline:* April 15.

Contact: Scholarship Director
Odd Fellows and Rebekahs
131 Queen Street Extension
Gorham, ME 04638

ONS FOUNDATION http://www.ons.org

ONS FOUNDATION ETHNIC MINORITY BACHELOR'S SCHOLARSHIP

Three scholarships available to registered nurses with a demonstrated interest in oncology nursing. Must be currently enrolled in an undergraduate program at an NLN-accredited school, and must currently hold a license to practice as a registered nurse. Must be minority student who has not received any BA grants previously from ONF. One-time award of $2000. Deadline: February 1.

Academic Fields/Career Goals: Nursing.

Award: Scholarship for use in freshman, sophomore, junior, or senior years; not renewable. *Number:* 3. *Amount:* $2000.

Eligibility Requirements: Applicant must be American Indian/Alaska Native, Asian/Pacific Islander, Black (non-Hispanic), or Hispanic and enrolled or expecting to enroll full or part-time at a four-year institution or university. Applicant or parent of applicant must have employment or volunteer experience in designated career field. Available to U.S. citizens.

Application Requirements: Application, transcript. *Fee:* $5. *Deadline:* February 1.

Contact: ONS Foundation
125 Enterprise Drive
Pittsburgh, PA 15275
Phone: 412-859-6100
E-mail: foundation@ons.org

ONS FOUNDATION JOSH GOTTHEIL MEMORIAL BONE MARROW TRANSPLANT CAREER DEVELOPMENT AWARDS

Several awards available to any professional registered nurse for practice of bone marrow transplant nursing by providing financial assistance to continue education that will further professional goals or to supplement tuition in a bachelor's or master's program. Submit examples of contributions to BMT nursing. Four awards of $2000 each. Deadline: December 1.

Academic Fields/Career Goals: Nursing.

Award: Scholarship for use in freshman, sophomore, junior, senior, or graduate years; not renewable. *Number:* 4. *Amount:* $2000.

Eligibility Requirements: Applicant must be enrolled or expecting to enroll full or part-time at a four-year institution or university. Applicant or parent of applicant must have employment or volunteer experience in designated career field. Available to U.S. and non-U.S. citizens.

Application Requirements: Application, essay, resume, references. *Deadline:* December 1.

Contact: ONS Foundation
125 Enterprise Drive
Pittsburgh, PA 15275
Phone: 412-859-6100
E-mail: foundation@ons.org

ONS FOUNDATION NURSING OUTCOMES RESEARCH GRANT

• *See page 301*

ONS FOUNDATION ONCOLOGY NURSING SOCIETY RESEARCH GRANT

• *See page 301*

ONS FOUNDATION ROBERTA PIERCE SCOFIELD BACHELOR'S SCHOLARSHIPS

Three awards to improve oncology nursing by assisting registered nurses in furthering their education. Must be currently enrolled in an undergraduate nursing degree program at an NLN-accredited school of nursing and must hold a current license to practice as a registered nurse. One-time award of $2000. Deadline: February 1.

Academic Fields/Career Goals: Nursing.

Award: Scholarship for use in freshman, sophomore, junior, or senior years; not renewable. *Number:* 3. *Amount:* $2000.

Eligibility Requirements: Applicant must be enrolled or expecting to enroll full or part-time at a four-year institution or university. Applicant or parent of applicant must have employment or volunteer experience in designated career field.

Application Requirements: Application, transcript. *Fee:* $5. *Deadline:* February 1.

Contact: ONS Foundation
125 Enterprise Drive
Pittsburgh, PA 15275
Phone: 412-859-6100
E-mail: foundation@ons.org

ONS FOUNDATION/ONCOLOGY NURSING CERTIFICATION CORPORATION BACHELOR'S SCHOLARSHIPS

Ten awards to improve oncology nursing by assisting registered nurses in furthering their education. Must be currently enrolled in an undergraduate nursing degree program at an NLN-accredited school of nursing and must have a current license to practice as a registered nurse. One-time award of $2000. Deadline: February 1.

Academic Fields/Career Goals: Nursing.

Award: Scholarship for use in freshman year; not renewable. *Number:* 10. *Amount:* $2000.

Eligibility Requirements: Applicant must be enrolled or expecting to enroll full or part-time at a four-year institution or university. Applicant or parent of applicant must have employment or volunteer experience in designated career field.

Application Requirements: Application, transcript. *Fee:* $5. *Deadline:* February 1.

Contact: ONS Foundation
125 Enterprise Drive
Pittsburgh, PA 15275
Phone: 412-859-6100
E-mail: foundation@ons.org

ONS FOUNDATION/PEARL MOORE CAREER DEVELOPMENT AWARDS

Several awards to reward a professional staff nurse for meritorious practice by providing financial assistance to continue education. Must possess or be pursuing a BSN and be employed as a staff nurse with two years' oncology practice. Three awards of $2500 each. Deadline: December 1.

Academic Fields/Career Goals: Nursing.

Award: Scholarship for use in freshman, sophomore, junior, or senior years; not renewable. *Number:* 3. *Amount:* $2500.

Eligibility Requirements: Applicant must be enrolled or expecting to enroll at a four-year institution or university. Applicant or parent of applicant must have employment or volunteer experience in designated career field. Available to U.S. citizens.

Application Requirements: Application, autobiography, references. *Deadline:* December 1.

Contact: ONS Foundation
125 Enterprise Drive
Pittsburgh, PA 15275
Phone: 412-859-6100
E-mail: foundation@ons.org

ORDEAN FOUNDATION

ORDEAN LOAN PROGRAM

• *See page 45*

OREGON NURSES ASSOCIATION

http://www.oregonrn.org

ONF-SMITH EDUCATION SCHOLARSHIP

Award for nursing students enrolled in an undergraduate or graduate program in Oregon. RN recipients must be current ONA members. Non-RN recipients of the baccalaureate scholarship must join the nurses association in their state of residence upon graduation. Application deadline is February 28.

Academic Fields/Career Goals: Nursing.

Award: Scholarship for use in freshman, sophomore, junior, senior, or graduate years; not renewable. *Number:* 3. *Amount:* $1000.

Eligibility Requirements: Applicant must be enrolled or expecting to enroll at a four-year institution and studying in Oregon. Applicant must have 3.0 GPA or higher. Available to U.S. citizens.

Application Requirements: Application. *Deadline:* February 28.

Contact: Oregon Nurses Foundation
Oregon Nurses Association
18765 South West Boones Ferry Road, Suite 200
Tualatin, OR 97062

OREGON STUDENT ASSISTANCE COMMISSION

http://www.osac.state.or.us

BERTHA P. SINGER NURSES SCHOLARSHIP

Available to Oregon residents pursuing a nursing career. Must have at least a 3.0 GPA and attend a college or university in Oregon. Must have completed one year of undergraduate study. One-time award of $1000. Proof of enrollment in 3rd year of 4-year nursing degree program or 2nd year of a 2-year associate degree nursing program is required. (Transcripts not sufficient.) U.S. Bancorp employees, their children, or close relatives are not eligible.

Academic Fields/Career Goals: Nursing.

Award: Scholarship for use in sophomore, junior, senior, or graduate years; not renewable. *Number:* 23. *Amount:* $1087.

Eligibility Requirements: Applicant must be enrolled or expecting to enroll at a two-year or four-year institution or university; resident of Oregon and studying in Oregon. Applicant must have 3.0 GPA or higher. Available to U.S. citizens.

Application Requirements: Application, essay, financial need analysis, test scores, transcript. *Deadline:* March 1.

Contact: Director of Grant Programs
Oregon Student Assistance Commission
1500 Valley River Drive, Suite 100
Eugene, OR 97401-7020
Phone: 800-452-8807 Ext. 7395
E-mail: awardinfo@mercury.osac.state.or.us

FRANKS FOUNDATION SCHOLARSHIP

Award for graduating high school seniors with a minimum 2.5 GPA and college students with a minimum 2.0 GPA. Must major in nursing or theology. First preference: residents of Deschutes, Crook, or Jefferson Counties. Second preference: residents of Harney, Lake, Grant, and Klamath Counties. U.S. Bancorp employees and relatives ineligible.

Academic Fields/Career Goals: Nursing; Religion/Theology.

Award: Scholarship for use in freshman, sophomore, junior, senior, or graduate years; not renewable. *Number:* 22. *Amount:* $1023.

Eligibility Requirements: Applicant must be enrolled or expecting to enroll at an institution or university and resident of Oregon. Available to U.S. citizens.

Application Requirements: Application, essay, financial need analysis, transcript, activity chart. *Deadline:* March 1.

Contact: Director of Grant Programs
Oregon Student Assistance Commission
1500 Valley River Drive, Suite 100
Eugene, OR 97401-7020
Phone: 800-452-8807 Ext. 7395
E-mail: awardinfo@mercury.osac.state.or.us

MARION A. LINDEMAN SCHOLARSHIP

• *See page 301*

WALTER AND MARIE SCHMIDT SCHOLARSHIP

One-time scholarship available to a student who is enrolled or planning to enroll in a program of training to become a registered nurse. Applicants must submit an additional essay describing their desire to pursue a nursing career in geriatrics. U.S. Bancorp employees and their relatives are not eligible.

Academic Fields/Career Goals: Nursing.

Award: Scholarship for use in freshman or sophomore years; not renewable. *Number:* 33. *Amount:* $939.

Eligibility Requirements: Applicant must be enrolled or expecting to enroll full or part-time at a two-year or four-year institution and resident of Oregon. Available to U.S. citizens.

Application Requirements: Application, essay, financial need analysis, references, transcript, activity chart. *Deadline:* March 1.

Contact: Director of Grant Programs
Oregon Student Assistance Commission
1500 Valley River Drive, Suite 100
Eugene, OR 97401-7020
Phone: 800-452-8807 Ext. 7395
E-mail: awardinfo@mercury.osac.state.or.us

PILOT INTERNATIONAL FOUNDATION http://www.pilotinternational.org

PILOT INTERNATIONAL FOUNDATION RUBY NEWHALL MEMORIAL SCHOLARSHIP

• *See page 302*

PILOT INTERNATIONAL FOUNDATION SCHOLARSHIP PROGRAM

• *See page 302*

PILOT INTERNATIONAL FOUNDATION/LIFELINE SCHOLARSHIP PROGRAM

• *See page 302*

RESOURCE CENTER http://www.resourcecenterscholarshipinfo.com

MARIE BLAHA MEDICAL GRANT

• *See page 64*

RHODE ISLAND FOUNDATION http://www.rifoundation.org

ALBERT E. AND FLORENCE W. NEWTON NURSE SCHOLARSHIP

To benefit practicing nurses (RN's) enrolled in an accredited BSN program in Rhode Island. Renewable award. Must be a Rhode Island resident and beginning junior year or higher. Must have proof of nursing license. Deadlines: April 1 and October 1.

Academic Fields/Career Goals: Nursing.

Award: Scholarship for use in junior, senior, graduate, or postgraduate years; renewable. *Number:* varies. *Amount:* $500–$2500.

Eligibility Requirements: Applicant must be enrolled or expecting to enroll full or part-time at an institution or university; resident of Rhode Island and studying in Rhode Island. Applicant or parent of applicant must have employment or volunteer experience in designated career field.

Application Requirements: Application, financial need analysis, self-addressed stamped envelope, transcript. *Deadline:* varies.

Contact: Libby Monahan, Scholarship Coordinator
Rhode Island Foundation
One Union Station
Providence, RI 02903
Phone: 401-274-4564
Fax: 401-272-1359
E-mail: libbym@rifoundation.org

SOUTHWEST STUDENT SERVICES CORPORATION http://www.sssc.com

ANNE LINDEMAN MEMORIAL SCHOLARSHIP

• *See page 117*

STATE OF GEORGIA http://www.gsfc.org

DEPARTMENT OF HUMAN RESOURCES FEDERAL STAFFORD LOAN WITH THE SERVICE CANCELABLE LOAN OPTION

Forgivable loans of $4000 are awarded to current Department of Human Resources employees who will be enrolled in a baccalaureate or advanced nursing degree program at an eligible participating school in Georgia. Loans are cancelled upon two calendar years of service as a registered nurse for the Georgia DHR or any Georgia county board of health.

Academic Fields/Career Goals: Nursing.

Award: Forgivable loan for use in freshman, sophomore, junior, senior, or graduate years; not renewable. *Number:* varies. *Amount:* $4000.

Eligibility Requirements: Applicant must be enrolled or expecting to enroll full or part-time at a four-year institution or university; resident of Georgia and studying in Georgia. Available to U.S. citizens.

Application Requirements: Application, financial need analysis. *Deadline:* June 4.

Contact: Peggy Matthews, Manager/GSFA Originations
State of Georgia
2082 East Exchange Place, Suite 230
Tucker, GA 30084-5305
Phone: 770-724-9230
Fax: 770-724-9225
E-mail: peggy@gsfc.org

LADDERS IN NURSING CAREER SERVICE CANCELABLE LOAN PROGRAM

Forgivable loans of $3,000 are awarded to students who agree to serve for one calendar year at an approved site within the state of Georgia. Eligible applicants will be residents of Georgia who are studying nursing at a Georgia institution.

Academic Fields/Career Goals: Nursing.

Award: Forgivable loan for use in freshman, sophomore, junior, senior, or graduate years; not renewable. *Number:* varies. *Amount:* $3000.

Eligibility Requirements: Applicant must be enrolled or expecting to enroll full or part-time at a two-year or four-year or technical institution or university; resident of Georgia and studying in Georgia. Available to U.S. citizens.

Application Requirements: Application, financial need analysis. *Deadline:* June 3.

Contact: Peggy Matthews, Manager/GSFA Originations
State of Georgia
2082 East Exchange Place, Suite 230
Tucker, GA 30084-5305
Phone: 770-724-9230
Fax: 770-724-9225
E-mail: peggy@gsfc.org

NORTHEAST GEORGIA PILOT NURSE SERVICE CANCELABLE LOAN

Up to 100 forgivable loans between $2,500 and $4,500 will be awarded to undergraduate students who are residents of Georgia studying nursing at a four-year school in Georgia. Loans can be repaid by working as a nurse in northeast Georgia.

Academic Fields/Career Goals: Nursing.

Award: Forgivable loan for use in freshman, sophomore, junior, or senior years; not renewable. *Number:* up to 100. *Amount:* $2500–$4500.

Eligibility Requirements: Applicant must be enrolled or expecting to enroll full-time at a four-year institution; resident of Georgia and studying in Georgia. Available to U.S. citizens.

Application Requirements: Application, financial need analysis. *Deadline:* June 3.

Contact: Peggy Matthews, Manager/GSFA Originations
State of Georgia
2082 East Exchange Place, Suite 230
Tucker, GA 30084-5305
Phone: 770-724-9230
Fax: 770-724-9225
E-mail: peggy@gsfc.org

REGISTERED NURSE SERVICE CANCELABLE LOAN PROGRAM

Forgivable loans will be awarded to undergraduate students who are residents of Georgia studying nursing in a two-year or four-year school in Georgia. Loans can be repaid by working as a registered nurse in the state of Georgia.

Academic Fields/Career Goals: Nursing.

Award: Forgivable loan for use in freshman, sophomore, junior, or senior years; not renewable. *Number:* varies. *Amount:* $200–$4500.

Eligibility Requirements: Applicant must be enrolled or expecting to enroll full or part-time at a two-year or four-year institution; resident of Georgia and studying in Georgia. Available to U.S. citizens.

Application Requirements: Application, financial need analysis. *Deadline:* June 3.

Contact: Peggy Matthews, Manager/GSFA Originations
State of Georgia
2082 East Exchange Place, Suite 230
Tucker, GA 30084-5305
Phone: 770-724-9230
Fax: 770-724-9225
E-mail: peggy@gsfc.org

SERVICE-CANCELABLE STAFFORD LOAN-GEORGIA

• *See page 187*

STATE STUDENT ASSISTANCE COMMISSION OF INDIANA (SSACI) http://www.ssaci.in.gov

INDIANA NURSING SCHOLARSHIP FUND

Need-based tuition funding for nursing students enrolled full- or part-time at an eligible Indiana institution. Must be a U.S. citizen and an Indiana resident and have a minimum 2.0 GPA or meet the minimum requirements for the nursing program. Upon graduation, recipients must practice as a nurse in an Indiana health care setting for two years.

Academic Fields/Career Goals: Nursing.

Award: Scholarship for use in freshman, sophomore, junior, or senior years; not renewable. *Number:* 490–690. *Amount:* $200–$5000.

Eligibility Requirements: Applicant must be enrolled or expecting to enroll full or part-time at a two-year or four-year institution or university; resident of Indiana and studying in Indiana. Available to U.S. citizens.

Application Requirements: Application, financial need analysis. *Deadline:* Continuous.

Contact: Ms. Yvonne Heflin, Director, Special Programs
State Student Assistance Commission of Indiana (SSACI)
150 West Market Street, Suite 500
Indianapolis, IN 46204-2805
Phone: 317-232-2350
Fax: 317-232-3260

SUBURBAN HOSPITAL HEALTHCARE SYSTEM http://www.suburbanhospital.org

CASEY SCHOLARS PROGRAM

An award to students entering the nursing field and to current caregivers pursuing advanced and graduate training. Scholarship recipients will commit to work at Suburban Hospital for a period of time, generally a year, but may vary. A GPA of 3.0 is required. Applications are accepted in October and April.

Academic Fields/Career Goals: Nursing.

Award: Scholarship for use in freshman, sophomore, junior, senior, or graduate years. *Number:* varies. *Amount:* varies.

Eligibility Requirements: Applicant must be enrolled or expecting to enroll at an institution or university. Applicant must have 3.0 GPA or higher.

Application Requirements: Application, essay, interview, references, transcript. *Deadline:* varies.

Contact: Charmaine Williams, Manager, Employee Relations
Suburban Hospital Healthcare System
Human Resources Department
8600 Old Georgetown Road
Bethesda, MD 20814-1497
Phone: 301-896-3795
Fax: 301-897-1339
E-mail: cwilliams@suburbanhospital.org

SUBURBAN HOSPITAL HEALTHCARE SYSTEM SCHOLARSHIP

• *See page 303*

TEXAS HIGHER EDUCATION COORDINATING BOARD http://www.collegefortexans.com

PROFESSIONAL NURSING SCHOLARSHIPS

Several awards for Texas residents enrolled at least half-time in a nursing program leading to a professional degree at a Texas institution. Contact school financial aid office for further information.

Academic Fields/Career Goals: Nursing.

Award: Scholarship for use in freshman, sophomore, junior, or senior years; not renewable. *Number:* varies. *Amount:* up to $3000.

Eligibility Requirements: Applicant must be enrolled or expecting to enroll full or part-time at a four-year institution or university; resident of Texas and studying in Texas. Available to U.S. citizens.

Application Requirements: Application, financial need analysis, test scores, transcript. *Deadline:* varies.

Contact: Student Services Division
Texas Higher Education Coordinating Board
PO Box 12788
Austin, TX 78711-2788
Phone: 800-242-3062
E-mail: grantinfo@thecb.state.tx.us

VOCATIONAL NURSING SCHOLARSHIPS

Scholarships for Texas residents enrolled in a vocational nursing program at an institution in Texas. Deadline varies.

Academic Fields/Career Goals: Nursing.

Award: Scholarship for use in freshman or sophomore years; not renewable. *Number:* varies. *Amount:* up to $1500.

Eligibility Requirements: Applicant must be enrolled or expecting to enroll full or part-time at a four-year institution or university; resident of Texas and studying in Texas. Available to U.S. citizens.

Application Requirements: Application, financial need analysis, test scores, transcript. *Deadline:* varies.

Contact: Texas Higher Education Coordinating Board
PO Box 12788
Austin, TX 78711-2788
E-mail: grantinfo@thecb.state.tx.us

UNITED DAUGHTERS OF THE CONFEDERACY http://www.hqudc.org

PHOEBE PEMBER MEMORIAL SCHOLARSHIP

Award for full-time undergraduate student who is a descendant of a Confederate soldier enrolled in a School of Nursing. Must carry a minimum of 12 credit hours each semester and have a minimum 3.0 GPA. Submit letter of endorsement from sponsoring Chapter of the United Daughters of the Confederacy. Please refer to Web site for further details: http://www.hqudc.org

Academic Fields/Career Goals: Nursing.

Award: Scholarship for use in freshman, sophomore, junior, or senior years; renewable. *Number:* 1–2. *Amount:* $800–$1000.

Eligibility Requirements: Applicant must be enrolled or expecting to enroll full-time at a four-year institution or university. Applicant or parent of applicant must be member of United Daughters of the Confederacy. Applicant must have 3.0 GPA or higher. Available to U.S. citizens.

Application Requirements: Application, essay, financial need analysis, photo, references, self-addressed stamped envelope, transcript. *Deadline:* February 15.

Contact: Second Vice President General
United Daughters of the Confederacy
328 North Boulevard
Richmond, VA 23220-4057
Phone: 804-355-1636

WALTER REED SMITH SCHOLARSHIP

• *See page 130*

UNITED NEGRO COLLEGE FUND http://www.uncf.org

BIGWOOD MEMORIAL FUND

• *See page 304*

OSTINA AND HERMAN HARTFIELD SCHOLARSHIP

• *See page 118*

SODEXHO SCHOLARSHIP

• *See page 304*

UNITED STATES PUBLIC HEALTH SERVICE - HEALTH RESOURCES AND SERVICES ADMINISTRATION, BUREAU OF HEALTH PROFESSIONS http://bhpr.hrsa.gov/dsa

HEALTH RESOURCES AND SERVICES ADMINISTRATION-BUREAU OF HEALTH PROFESSIONS SCHOLARSHIPS FOR DISADVANTAGED STUDENTS

• *See page 187*

VIRGINIA DEPARTMENT OF HEALTH, OFFICE OF HEALTH POLICY AND PLANNING http://www.vdh.virginia.gov/primcare/index.asp

MARY MARSHALL PRACTICAL NURSING SCHOLARSHIPS

Award for practical nursing students who are Virginia residents. Must attend a nursing program in Virginia. Recipient must agree to work in Virginia after graduation. Minimum 3.0 GPA required. Recipients may reapply up to three years for an award.

Academic Fields/Career Goals: Nursing.

Award: Scholarship for use in freshman, sophomore, junior, or senior years; not renewable. *Number:* varies. *Amount:* $150–$500.

Eligibility Requirements: Applicant must be enrolled or expecting to enroll full or part-time at a two-year or technical institution; resident of Virginia and studying in Virginia. Applicant must have 3.0 GPA or higher. Available to U.S. citizens.

Application Requirements: Application, financial need analysis, references, transcript. *Deadline:* June 30.

Contact: Norma Marrin, Business Manager/Policy Analyst
Virginia Department of Health, Office of Health Policy and Planning
PO Box 2448
Richmond, VA 23218-2448
Phone: 804-864-7433
Fax: 804-864-7440
E-mail: norma.marrin@vdh.virginia.gov

MARY MARSHALL REGISTERED NURSING PROGRAM SCHOLARSHIPS

Award for registered nursing students who are Virginia residents. Must attend a nursing program in Virginia. Recipient must agree to work in Virginia after graduation. Minimum 3.0 GPA required. Recipient may reapply up to three years for an award.

Academic Fields/Career Goals: Nursing.

Award: Scholarship for use in freshman, sophomore, junior, or senior years; not renewable. *Number:* 60–100. *Amount:* $1200–$2000.

Eligibility Requirements: Applicant must be enrolled or expecting to enroll full or part-time at a two-year or four-year institution or university; resident of Virginia and studying in Virginia. Applicant must have 3.0 GPA or higher. Available to U.S. citizens.

Application Requirements: Application, financial need analysis, references, transcript. *Deadline:* June 30.

Contact: Norma Marrin, Business Manager/Policy Analyst
Virginia Department of Health, Office of Health Policy and Planning
PO Box 2448
Richmond, VA 23218-2448
Phone: 804-864-7433
Fax: 804-864-7440
E-mail: norma.marrin@vdh.virginia.gov

WASHINGTON HIGHER EDUCATION COORDINATING BOARD http://www.hecb.wa.gov

HEALTH PROFESSIONAL LOAN REPAYMENT AND SCHOLARSHIP PROGRAMS

• *See page 188*

WISCONSIN HIGHER EDUCATIONAL AIDS BOARD http://heab.state.wi.us

NURSING STUDENT LOAN PROGRAM

Provides forgivable loans to students enrolled in a nursing program. Must be a Wisconsin resident studying in Wisconsin. Application deadline is last day on which student is enrolled. Please refer to Web site for further details: http://heab.state.wi.us

Academic Fields/Career Goals: Nursing.

Award: Forgivable loan for use in freshman, sophomore, junior, or senior years; renewable. *Number:* 150–1800. *Amount:* $250–$3000.

Eligibility Requirements: Applicant must be enrolled or expecting to enroll full or part-time at a two-year or four-year or technical institution or university; resident of Wisconsin and studying in Wisconsin. Available to U.S. citizens.

Application Requirements: Application, financial need analysis.

Contact: Cindy Lehrman, Program Coordinator
Wisconsin Higher Educational Aids Board
PO Box 7885
Madison, WI 53707-7885
Phone: 608-267-2209
Fax: 608-267-2808
E-mail: cindy.lehrman@heab.state.wi.us

WISCONSIN LEAGUE FOR NURSING, INC. http://www2.cuw.edu/wln

NURSING SCHOLARSHIP FOR HIGH SCHOOL SENIORS

One scholarship for a Wisconsin high school senior who will be pursing a professional nursing career. The senior must have been accepted by a Wisconsin NLN accredited school of nursing, have financial need, demonstrate scholastic excellence and leadership potential. Contact the WLN office by mail to request an application.

Academic Fields/Career Goals: Nursing.

Award: Scholarship for use in freshman year; not renewable. *Number:* 1. *Amount:* $500.

Eligibility Requirements: Applicant must be high school student; planning to enroll or expecting to enroll full-time at a two-year or four-year institution or university; resident of Wisconsin and studying in Wisconsin. Available to U.S. citizens.

Application Requirements: Application, financial need analysis. *Deadline:* March 1.

Contact: Mary Ann Tanner, Administrative Secretary
Wisconsin League for Nursing, Inc.
PO Box 107
Long Lake, WI 54542-0107
Phone: 414-332-6271

WISCONSIN LEAGUE FOR NURSING INC., SCHOLARSHIP

One-time award for Wisconsin residents who have completed half of an accredited Wisconsin school of nursing program. Financial need of student must be demonstrated. Contact for additional information.

Academic Fields/Career Goals: Nursing.

Award: Scholarship for use in junior, senior, or graduate years; not renewable. *Number:* 12. *Amount:* $500.

Eligibility Requirements: Applicant must be enrolled or expecting to enroll full-time at a two-year or four-year or technical institution or university; resident of Wisconsin and studying in Wisconsin. Available to U.S. citizens.

Application Requirements: Application, financial need analysis. *Deadline:* March 1.

Contact: Mary Ann Tanner, Administrative Secretary
Wisconsin League for Nursing, Inc.
PO Box 107
Long Lake, WI 54542-0107
Phone: 414-332-6271

OCCUPATIONAL SAFETY AND HEALTH

AMERICAN SOCIETY OF SAFETY ENGINEERS (ASSE) FOUNDATION http://www.asse.org/foundat.htm

AMERICA RESPONDS MEMORIAL SCHOLARSHIP

One $1000 scholarship will be awarded to a student pursuing an undergraduate degree in occupational safety and health or a closely related field. Must have completed 60 semester hours and maintain at least a 3.2 GPA. Eligible applicants will be members of American Society of Safety Engineers.

Academic Fields/Career Goals: Occupational Safety and Health.

Award: Scholarship for use in junior or senior years; not renewable. *Number:* 1. *Amount:* $1000.

Eligibility Requirements: Applicant must be enrolled or expecting to enroll full-time at a four-year institution or university. Applicant or parent of applicant must be member of American Society of Safety Engineers.

Application Requirements: Application, essay, references. *Deadline:* December 1.

Contact: Customer Service Department
American Society of Safety Engineers (ASSE) Foundation
1800 East Oakton Street
Des Plaines, IL 60018
Phone: 847-699-2929
Fax: 847-296-3769
E-mail: customerservice@asse.org

ASSE-EDWIN P. GRANBERRY, JR. DISTINGUISHED SERVICE AWARD SCHOLARSHIP

Scholarships for students pursuing an undergraduate degree in occupational safety. Completion of at least 60 current semester hours and minimum GPA of 3.0 required. Deadline is December 1. ASSE student membership is required.

Academic Fields/Career Goals: Occupational Safety and Health.

Award: Scholarship for use in sophomore, junior, or senior years; not renewable. *Number:* 1. *Amount:* $2000.

Eligibility Requirements: Applicant must be enrolled or expecting to enroll full-time at a four-year institution or university. Applicant or parent of applicant must be member of American Society of Safety Engineers. Applicant must have 3.0 GPA or higher. Available to U.S. and non-U.S. citizens.

Application Requirements: Application, essay, references, transcript. *Deadline:* December 1.

Contact: Customer Service Department
American Society of Safety Engineers (ASSE) Foundation
1800 East Oakton Street
Des Plaines, IL 60018
Phone: 847-699-2929
Fax: 847-296-3769
E-mail: customerservice@asse.org

ASSE-GULF COAST PAST PRESIDENTS SCHOLARSHIP

One $1000 scholarship will be awarded to a part- or full-time student pursuing an undergraduate degree in occupational safety and health or a closely related field. Must have completed 60 semester hours and maintain at least a 3.2 GPA. American Society of Safety Engineers membership required if applicant is a part-time student.

Academic Fields/Career Goals: Occupational Safety and Health.

Award: Scholarship for use in junior or senior years; not renewable. *Number:* 1. *Amount:* $1000.

Eligibility Requirements: Applicant must be enrolled or expecting to enroll full or part-time at a four-year institution or university. Applicant or parent of applicant must be member of American Society of Safety Engineers.

Application Requirements: Application, essay, references. *Deadline:* December 1.

Contact: Customer Service Department
American Society of Safety Engineers (ASSE) Foundation
1800 East Oakton Street
Des Plaines, IL 60018
Phone: 847-699-2929
Fax: 847-296-3769
E-mail: customerservice@asse.org

ASSE-MARSH RISK CONSULTING SCHOLARSHIP

For students pursuing an undergraduate degree in occupational safety. Completion of at least 60 credit hours and minimum GPA of 3.0 required. Deadline is December 1.

Academic Fields/Career Goals: Occupational Safety and Health.

Award: Scholarship for use in junior or senior years; not renewable. *Number:* 1. *Amount:* $5000.

Eligibility Requirements: Applicant must be enrolled or expecting to enroll at a four-year institution or university. Applicant or parent of applicant must be member of American Society of Safety Engineers. Applicant must have 3.0 GPA or higher. Available to U.S. and non-U.S. citizens.

Application Requirements: Application, essay, references, transcript. *Deadline:* December 1.

Contact: Customer Service Department
American Society of Safety Engineers (ASSE) Foundation
1800 East Oakton Street
Des Plaines, IL 60018
Phone: 847-699-2929
Fax: 847-296-3769
E-mail: customerservice@asse.org

ASSE-REGION IV/EDWIN P. GRANBERRY SCHOLARSHIP

One $1000 scholarship will be awarded to a student pursuing an undergraduate degree in occupational safety and health or a closely related field. Must reside in the ASSE Region IV area (Louisiana, Alabama, Mississippi, Georgia, Florida, Puerto Rico or United States Virgin Islands). Natives of Region IV attending school elsewhere are also eligible. Must have completed 60 semester hours and maintain at least a 3.2 GPA. Eligible applicants will be members of American Society of Safety Engineers.

Academic Fields/Career Goals: Occupational Safety and Health.

Award: Scholarship for use in junior or senior years; not renewable. *Number:* 1. *Amount:* $1000.

Eligibility Requirements: Applicant must be enrolled or expecting to enroll full-time at a four-year institution or university. Applicant or parent of applicant must be member of American Society of Safety Engineers.

Application Requirements: Application, essay, references. *Deadline:* December 1.

Contact: Customer Service Department
American Society of Safety Engineers (ASSE) Foundation
1800 East Oakton Street
Des Plaines, IL 60018
Phone: 847-699-2929
Fax: 847-296-3769
E-mail: customerservice@asse.org

ASSE-UNITED PARCEL SERVICE SCHOLARSHIP

Scholarships for students pursuing a four-year BS or BA degree in occupational safety and health or related area (i.e. safety engineering, safety management, systems safety, environmental science, industrial hygiene, ergonomics, fire science or other related safety, health, or environmental program). Completion of at least 60 current semester hours and a minimum 3.0 GPA is required. Deadline: December 1.

Academic Fields/Career Goals: Occupational Safety and Health.

Award: Scholarship for use in junior or senior years; not renewable. *Amount:* $3000–$5000.

Eligibility Requirements: Applicant must be enrolled or expecting to enroll full-time at a four-year institution or university. Applicant or parent of applicant must be member of American Society of Safety Engineers. Applicant must have 3.0 GPA or higher. Available to U.S. and non-U.S. citizens.

Application Requirements: Application, essay, references, transcript. *Deadline:* December 1.

Contact: Customer Service Department
American Society of Safety Engineers (ASSE) Foundation
1800 East Oakton Street
Des Plaines, IL 60018
Phone: 847-699-2929
Fax: 847-296-3769
E-mail: customerservice@asse.org

BECHTEL FOUNDATION SCHOLARSHIP PROGRAM FOR SAFETY AND HEALTH

One $3000 scholarship for students pursuing an undergraduate degree in occupational safety and health, with an emphasis on construction safety. ASSE student membership required.

Academic Fields/Career Goals: Occupational Safety and Health.

Award: Scholarship for use in freshman, sophomore, junior, or senior years. *Number:* 1. *Amount:* $3000.

Eligibility Requirements: Applicant must be enrolled or expecting to enroll at an institution or university. Applicant or parent of applicant must be member of American Society of Safety Engineers.

Application Requirements: Application. *Deadline:* December 1.

Contact: Customer Service Department
American Society of Safety Engineers (ASSE) Foundation
1800 East Oakton Street
Des Plaines, IL 60018
Phone: 847-699-2929
Fax: 847-296-3769
E-mail: customerservice@asse.org

FORD MOTOR COMPANY SCHOLARSHIP-UNDERGRADUATE

For women pursuing an undergraduate degree in occupational safety. Completion of at least 60 current semester hours and minimum GPA of 3.0 required. Deadline is December 1.

Academic Fields/Career Goals: Occupational Safety and Health.

Award: Scholarship for use in junior or senior years; not renewable. *Number:* 3. *Amount:* $3375.

Eligibility Requirements: Applicant must be enrolled or expecting to enroll full-time at a four-year institution or university and female. Applicant or parent of applicant must be member of American Society of Safety Engineers. Applicant must have 3.0 GPA or higher. Available to U.S. and non-U.S. citizens.

Application Requirements: Application, essay, references, transcript. *Deadline:* December 1.

Contact: Customer Service Department
American Society of Safety Engineers (ASSE) Foundation
1800 East Oakton Street
Des Plaines, IL 60018
Phone: 847-699-2929
Fax: 847-296-3769
E-mail: customerservice@asse.org

GEORGIA CHAPTER OF ASSE ANNUAL SCHOLARSHIP

One $1000 scholarship will be awarded to a student pursuing an undergraduate degree in occupational safety and health or a closely related field. Student must reside in a county that is within the ASSE Georgia Chapter or be enrolled in a college or university within Georgia. Must have completed 60 semester hours and maintain at least a 3.2 GPA. Eligible applicants will be members of American Society of Safety Engineers.

Academic Fields/Career Goals: Occupational Safety and Health.

Award: Scholarship for use in junior or senior years; not renewable. *Number:* 1. *Amount:* $1000.

Eligibility Requirements: Applicant must be enrolled or expecting to enroll full-time at a four-year institution or university. Applicant or parent of applicant must be member of American Society of Safety Engineers.

Application Requirements: Application, essay, references. *Deadline:* December 1.

Contact: Customer Service Department
American Society of Safety Engineers (ASSE) Foundation
1800 East Oakton Street
Des Plaines, IL 60018
Phone: 847-699-2929
Fax: 847-296-3769
E-mail: customerservice@asse.org

GOLD COUNTRY SECTION AND REGION II SCHOLARSHIP

One $1000 scholarship for students pursuing an undergraduate or graduate degree in occupational safety and health or a closely related field. Students that reside within region II (MT,ID, WY, CO, UT, NV, AZ, NM) area will have priority on this award. ASSE student membership required.

Academic Fields/Career Goals: Occupational Safety and Health.

Award: Scholarship for use in freshman, sophomore, junior, senior, or graduate years. *Number:* 1. *Amount:* $1000.

Eligibility Requirements: Applicant must be enrolled or expecting to enroll at an institution or university. Applicant or parent of applicant must be member of American Society of Safety Engineers.

Application Requirements: Application. *Deadline:* December 1.

Contact: Customer Service Department
American Society of Safety Engineers (ASSE) Foundation
1800 East Oakton Street
Des Plaines, IL 60018
Phone: 847-699-2929
Fax: 847-296-3769
E-mail: customerservice@asse.org

LIBERTY MUTUAL SCHOLARSHIP

One $3000 scholarship for students pursuing an undergraduate degree in occupational safety and health or a closely related field. ASSE student membership required.

Academic Fields/Career Goals: Occupational Safety and Health.

Award: Scholarship for use in freshman, sophomore, junior, or senior years. *Number:* 1. *Amount:* $3000.

Eligibility Requirements: Applicant must be enrolled or expecting to enroll at an institution or university. Applicant or parent of applicant must be member of American Society of Safety Engineers.

Application Requirements: Application. *Deadline:* December 1.

Contact: Customer Service Department
American Society of Safety Engineers (ASSE) Foundation
1800 East Oakton Street
Des Plaines, IL 60018
Phone: 847-699-2929
Fax: 847-296-3769
E-mail: customerservice@asse.org

NORTHEASTERN ILLINOIS CHAPTER SCHOLARSHIP

One $2500 scholarship for students pursuing an undergraduate or graduate degree in occupational safety and health or a closely related field. Students attending school in the Northeastern Illinois region, including Illinois and Wisconsin have priority on this award. ASSE student membership required.

Academic Fields/Career Goals: Occupational Safety and Health.

Award: Scholarship for use in freshman, sophomore, junior, senior, or graduate years. *Number:* 1. *Amount:* $2500.

Eligibility Requirements: Applicant must be enrolled or expecting to enroll at an institution or university. Applicant or parent of applicant must be member of American Society of Safety Engineers.

American Society of Safety Engineers (ASSE) Foundation (continued)

Application Requirements: Application. *Deadline:* December 1.

Contact: Customer Service Department
American Society of Safety Engineers (ASSE) Foundation
1800 East Oakton Street
Des Plaines, IL 60018
Phone: 847-699-2929
Fax: 847-296-3769
E-mail: customerservice@asse.org

SCOTT DOMINGUEZ-CRATERS OF THE MOON SCHOLARSHIP

For part-or full-time students pursuing an undergraduate or graduate degree in occupational safety and health or a closely related field. Students that reside within the Craters of the Moon Chapter, Idaho, and Region II (MT, ID, WY, CO, UT, NV, AZ, NM) will have priority on this award. ASSE student membership required. For further information see Web site: http://www.asse.org/foundation.htm

Academic Fields/Career Goals: Occupational Safety and Health.

Award: Scholarship for use in freshman, sophomore, junior, senior, or graduate years. *Number:* 1. *Amount:* $1000.

Eligibility Requirements: Applicant must be enrolled or expecting to enroll at an institution or university. Applicant or parent of applicant must be member of American Society of Safety Engineers.

Application Requirements: Application. *Deadline:* December 1.

Contact: Customer Service Department
American Society of Safety Engineers (ASSE) Foundation
1800 East Oakton Street
Des Plaines, IL 60018
Phone: 847-699-2929
Fax: 847-296-3769
E-mail: customerservice@asse.org

UNITED PARCEL SERVICE DIVERSITY SCHOLARSHIP PROGRAM

• *See page 263*

NATIONAL ENVIRONMENTAL HEALTH ASSOCIATION/AMERICAN ACADEMY OF SANITARIANS http://www.neha.org

NATIONAL ENVIRONMENTAL HEALTH ASSOCIATION/AMERICAN ACADEMY OF SANITARIANS SCHOLARSHIP

One-time award for college juniors, seniors, and graduate students pursuing studies in environmental health sciences or public health. Undergraduates must be enrolled full-time in an approved program that is accredited by the Environmental Health Accreditation Council (EHAC) or a NEHA institutional/educational or sustaining member school. Graduate students must be enrolled full-time in a graduate program at a recognized college or university with a declared curriculum in EH science and/or public health.

Academic Fields/Career Goals: Occupational Safety and Health; Public Health.

Award: Scholarship for use in junior, senior, or graduate years; not renewable. *Number:* 3–4. *Amount:* $1000–$2000.

Eligibility Requirements: Applicant must be enrolled or expecting to enroll full-time at a four-year institution or university. Available to U.S. citizens.

Application Requirements: Application, references, transcript. *Deadline:* February 1.

Contact: Jim Balsamo, NEHA Liaison
National Environmental Health Association/American Academy of Sanitarians
720 South Colorado Boulevard
Suite 970-S
Denver, CO 80246-1925
Phone: 303-756-9090 Ext. 310
Fax: 303-691-9490
E-mail: mthomsen@neha.org

NATIONAL SAFETY COUNCIL http://www.cshema.org

CAMPUS SAFETY, HEALTH AND ENVIRONMENTAL MANAGEMENT ASSOCIATION SCHOLARSHIP AWARD PROGRAM

• *See page 265*

OCEANOGRAPHY

CANADIAN RECREATIONAL CANOEING ASSOCIATION http://www.paddlingcanada.com

BILL MASON MEMORIAL SCHOLARSHIP FUND

• *See page 57*

PEACE AND CONFLICT STUDIES

HUGH FULTON BYAS MEMORIAL FUNDS, INC.

HUGH FULTON BYAS MEMORIAL GRANT

• *See page 311*

MENNONITE EDUCATION AGENCY

RACIAL/ETHNIC LEADERSHIP EDUCATION (RELE)

One-time grant for underrepresented minorities (especially people of color) who are not part of a recognized associate group in the Mennonite Church.

Academic Fields/Career Goals: Peace and Conflict Studies; Religion/Theology.

Award: Grant for use in freshman, sophomore, junior, or senior years; not renewable. *Number:* 2–3. *Amount:* $500.

Eligibility Requirements: Applicant must be a member of the specified denomination; American Indian/Alaska Native, Asian/Pacific Islander, Black (non-Hispanic), or Hispanic and enrolled or expecting to enroll full or part-time at a two-year or four-year institution or university. Available to U.S. and Canadian citizens.

Application Requirements: Application, financial need analysis, references. *Deadline:* Continuous.

Contact: Lisa Heinz, Associate Director, Finance
Mennonite Education Agency
500 South Main Street
PO Box 1142
Elkhart, IN 46515-1142
Phone: 574-642-3164
Fax: 574-642-4863

UNITED STATES INSTITUTE OF PEACE http://www.usip.org

NATIONAL PEACE ESSAY CONTEST

Essay contest designed to have students research and write about international peace and conflict resolution. Topic changes yearly. State winners are invited to Washington, D.C. for the awards program. Deadline varies, usually end of January. Must be enrolled in a U.S. high school.

Academic Fields/Career Goals: Peace and Conflict Studies.

Award: Scholarship for use in freshman year; not renewable. *Number:* 50. *Amount:* $1000–$10,000.

Eligibility Requirements: Applicant must be high school student and planning to enroll or expecting to enroll full or part-time at a two-year or four-year institution or university. Available to U.S. citizens.

Application Requirements: Application, applicant must enter a contest, essay. *Deadline:* varies.

Contact: Contest Coordinator, Education Program
United States Institute of Peace
1200 17th Street, NW, 2nd Floor
Washington, DC 20036-3011
Phone: 202-457-3854
Fax: 202-429-6063
E-mail: essay_contest@usip.org

PERFORMING ARTS

ACADEMY OF TELEVISION ARTS AND SCIENCES FOUNDATION http://www.emmys.tv/foundation

ACADEMY OF TELEVISION ARTS AND SCIENCES COLLEGE TELEVISION AWARDS

• *See page 84*

AMERICAN ACCORDION MUSICOLOGICAL SOCIETY

AMERICAN ACCORDION MUSICOLOGICAL SOCIETY SCHOLARSHIP FUND

One-time award to encourage young musicians to continue their music education and to further the development of the accordion as a serious concert instrument. Award amounts vary. Write for details and application.

Academic Fields/Career Goals: Performing Arts.

Award: Scholarship for use in freshman, sophomore, junior, or senior years; not renewable. *Number:* varies. *Amount:* varies.

Eligibility Requirements: Applicant must be enrolled or expecting to enroll at a two-year or four-year or technical institution or university and must have an interest in music/singing. Available to U.S. citizens.

Application Requirements: Application, applicant must enter a contest. *Deadline:* Continuous.

Contact: Stanley Darrow, Scholarship Director
American Accordion Musicological Society
334 South Broadway
Pitman, NJ 08071
Phone: 856-854-6628

AMERICAN LEGION, DEPARTMENT OF KANSAS

MUSIC COMMITTEE SCHOLARSHIP

• *See page 362*

CALIFORNIA ALLIANCE FOR ARTS EDUCATION (CAAE) http://www.artsed411.org

EMERGING YOUNG ARTIST AWARDS

• *See page 86*

CASE WESTERN RESERVE UNIVERSITY http://www.cwru.edu/artsci/thtr

MARC A. KLEIN PLAYWRIGHT AWARD

• *See page 346*

CHOPIN FOUNDATION OF THE UNITED STATES http://www.chopin.org

CHOPIN FOUNDATION OF THE UNITED STATES SCHOLARSHIP

• *See page 363*

CIRI FOUNDATION http://www.ciri.com/tcf

CIRI FOUNDATION SUSIE QIMMIQSAK BEVINS ENDOWMENT SCHOLARSHIP FUND

• *See page 86*

CULTURAL FELLOWSHIP GRANTS

• *See page 347*

CLARICE SMITH PERFORMING ARTS CENTER AT MARYLAND http://www.claricesmithcenter.umd.edu

WILLIAM KAPELL INTERNATIONAL PIANO COMPETITION AND FESTIVAL

Quadrennial international piano competition for ages 18-31. $80 application fee. Competition takes place at the Clarice Smith Performing Arts Center at the University of Maryland July 16-25, 2003. Next competition will be in 2007.

Academic Fields/Career Goals: Performing Arts.

Award: Prize for use in freshman, sophomore, junior, senior, graduate, or postgraduate years; not renewable. *Number:* up to 12. *Amount:* $1000–$20,000.

Eligibility Requirements: Applicant must be age 18-31; enrolled or expecting to enroll at an institution or university and must have an interest in music. Available to U.S. and non-U.S. citizens.

Application Requirements: Application, applicant must enter a contest, autobiography, photo, portfolio, references, CD of performance. *Fee:* $80. *Deadline:* December 1.

Contact: Dr. Christopher Patton, Coordinator
Clarice Smith Performing Arts Center at Maryland
Suite 3800, University of Maryland
College Park, MD 20742-1625
Phone: 301-405-8174
Fax: 301-405-5977
E-mail: kapell@deans.umd.edu

CONGRESSIONAL BLACK CAUCUS SPOUSES PROGRAM http://cbcfinc.org

CONGRESSIONAL BLACK CAUCUS SPOUSES PERFORMING ARTS SCHOLARSHIP

Award made to students who reside or attend school in a congressional district represented by an African-American member of Congress. Must be full-time student enrolled in a performing arts program. Minimum 2.5 GPA required. Contact the congressional office in the appropriate district for information and applications. See http://www.cbcfinc.org for a list of district offices.

Academic Fields/Career Goals: Performing Arts.

Award: Scholarship for use in freshman, sophomore, junior, senior, graduate, or postgraduate years; not renewable. *Number:* 10. *Amount:* $3000.

Eligibility Requirements: Applicant must be enrolled or expecting to enroll full-time at a two-year or four-year or technical institution or university. Applicant must have 2.5 GPA or higher. Available to U.S. citizens.

Application Requirements: Application, essay, financial need analysis, interview, photo, references, transcript. *Deadline:* Continuous.

Contact: Appropriate Congressional District Office

CONTEMPORARY RECORD SOCIETY

CONTEMPORARY RECORD SOCIETY NATIONAL COMPETITION FOR PERFORMING ARTISTS

Applicant may submit one performance tape of varied length with each application. May use any number of instrumentalists and voices. First prize is commercial distribution of winner's recording. Application fee is $50. Submit self-addressed stamped envelope for application. Deadline: February 10.

Academic Fields/Career Goals: Performing Arts.

Award: Prize for use in freshman, sophomore, junior, senior, or graduate years; not renewable. *Number:* 1. *Amount:* $1500–$5000.

Eligibility Requirements: Applicant must be enrolled or expecting to enroll at an institution or university and must have an interest in music/singing. Available to U.S. and non-U.S. citizens.

Application Requirements: Application, applicant must enter a contest, autobiography, resume, references, self-addressed stamped envelope. *Fee:* $50. *Deadline:* February 10.

Contact: Administrative Assistant
Contemporary Record Society
724 Winchester Road
Broomall, PA 19008
Phone: 610-544-5920
Fax: 610-544-5921
E-mail: crsnews@verizon.net

COSTUME SOCIETY OF AMERICA http://www.costumesocietyamerica.com

ADELE FILENE TRAVEL AWARD

• *See page 81*

STELLA BLUM RESEARCH GRANT

• *See page 81*

DONNA REED FOUNDATION FOR THE PERFORMING ARTS http://www.donnareed.org

DONNA REED PERFORMING ARTS SCHOLARSHIPS

Three $4000 scholarships awarded to division finalists in acting, musical theatre, and vocal. Six $500 awards are given to second level winners, two in each division. Must be a graduating high school senior. To remain eligible, you must be attending an accredited postsecondary or approved program of study. Finalists will compete at the Donna Reed Festival in Iowa during the third week of June.

Academic Fields/Career Goals: Performing Arts.

Award: Scholarship for use in freshman year; not renewable. *Number:* up to 9. *Amount:* $500–$4000.

Eligibility Requirements: Applicant must be high school student and planning to enroll or expecting to enroll full-time at a two-year or four-year or technical institution or university. Available to U.S. and non-U.S. citizens.

Application Requirements: Application, applicant must enter a contest, video/audio tape, CD. *Fee:* $35. *Deadline:* March 1.

Contact: Donna Reed Foundation for the Performing Arts
1305 Broadway
Denison, IA 51442
Phone: 712-263-3334
Fax: 712-263-8026
E-mail: info@donnareed.org

GENERAL FEDERATION OF WOMEN'S CLUBS OF MASSACHUSETTS

DORCHESTER WOMEN'S CLUB SCHOLARSHIP

• *See page 364*

GENERAL FEDERATION OF WOMEN'S CLUBS OF MASSACHUSETTS MUSIC SCHOLARSHIP

• *See page 201*

GINA BACHAUER INTERNATIONAL PIANO FOUNDATION http://www.bachauer.com

GINA BACHAUER INTERNATIONAL ARTISTS PIANO COMPETITION AWARD

Piano competition sponsored every four years. Includes solo, and orchestral performances. Prizes include cash awards, concerts, CD recording, and residency in various countries. Submit birth certificate copy, passport copy, tapes of last two year's programs, and audition tape. May also audition live.

Academic Fields/Career Goals: Performing Arts.

Award: Prize for use in freshman, sophomore, junior, senior, graduate, or postgraduate years; not renewable. *Number:* 6. *Amount:* $600–$30,000.

Eligibility Requirements: Applicant must be enrolled or expecting to enroll at an institution or university and must have an interest in music/singing. Available to U.S. and non-U.S. citizens.

Application Requirements: Application, applicant must enter a contest, driver's license, photo, resume, tapes, passport and birth certificate copies. *Fee:* $75. *Deadline:* varies.

Contact: Paul Pollei, Artistic Director
Gina Bachauer International Piano Foundation
138 West Broadway Suite 220
Salt Lake City, UT 84101-1664
Phone: 801-297-4250
Fax: 801-521-9202
E-mail: gina@bachauer.com

GOLDEN KEY INTERNATIONAL HONOUR SOCIETY http://www.goldenkey.org

PERFORMING ARTS SHOWCASE

• *See page 267*

HILTON HEAD JAZZ SOCIETY http://www.hhjs.org

HILTON HEAD JAZZ SOCIETY SCHOLARSHIP AWARD

Award is for full-time college level or higher music students with a jazz emphasis. Award requires an audition tape or CD to be submitted with application. Visit Web site at http://www.hhjs.org for additional information.

Academic Fields/Career Goals: Performing Arts.

Award: Scholarship for use in freshman, sophomore, junior, senior, or graduate years; not renewable. *Number:* 1–3. *Amount:* $1500–$2500.

Eligibility Requirements: Applicant must be age 26 or under; enrolled or expecting to enroll full-time at a two-year or four-year or technical institution or university and must have an interest in music/singing. Available to U.S. and non-U.S. citizens.

Application Requirements: Application, applicant must enter a contest, references, audition tape or disc. *Deadline:* May 15.

Contact: Hilton Head Jazz Society
PO Box 22193
Hilton Head Island, SC 29925-2193
E-mail: nichhi@aol.com

HOSTESS COMMITTEE SCHOLARSHIPS/MISS AMERICA PAGEANT http://www.missamerica.org

EUGENIA VELLNER FISCHER AWARD FOR PERFORMING ARTS

Scholarship for Miss America contestants pursuing degree in performing arts. Award available to women who have competed within the Miss America system on the local, state, or national level from 1993 to the present, regardless of whether title was won. One or more scholarships are awarded annually, depending on qualifications of applicants. Applications must be received by June 30. Late or incomplete applications are not accepted.

Academic Fields/Career Goals: Performing Arts.

Award: Scholarship for use in freshman, sophomore, junior, senior, or graduate years; not renewable. *Number:* 1. *Amount:* up to $2000.

Eligibility Requirements: Applicant must be enrolled or expecting to enroll at a four-year institution or university; female and must have an interest in beauty pageant. Available to U.S. citizens.

Application Requirements: Application, essay, financial need analysis, references, transcript. *Deadline:* June 30.

Contact: See Web site.

ILLUMINATING ENGINEERING SOCIETY OF NORTH AMERICA http://www.iesna.org

ROBERT W. THUNEN MEMORIAL SCHOLARSHIPS

• *See page 77*

JACK J. ISGUR FOUNDATION

JACK J. ISGUR FOUNDATION SCHOLARSHIP

• *See page 87*

KOSCIUSZKO FOUNDATION http://www.kosciuszkofoundation.org

KOSCIUSZKO FOUNDATION CHOPIN PIANO COMPETITION

Three awards for students majoring or planning to major in piano studies who are between the ages of 16-22. Must submit recital program of at least 60-75 minutes. Live audition and $35 fee required. Must be U.S. citizen or full-time international student in the U.S. with valid visa.

Academic Fields/Career Goals: Performing Arts.

Award: Prize for use in freshman, sophomore, junior, or senior years; not renewable. *Number:* 3. *Amount:* $1500–$5000.

Eligibility Requirements: Applicant must be age 16-22; enrolled or expecting to enroll full or part-time at a four-year institution or university and must have an interest in music/singing. Available to U.S. citizens.

Application Requirements: Application, applicant must enter a contest, photo, references, curriculum vitae, proof of age. *Fee:* $35. *Deadline:* March 2.

Contact: Mr. Tom Pniewski, Director of Cultural Programs
Kosciuszko Foundation
15 East 65th Street
New York, NY 10021-6595
Phone: 212-734-2130
Fax: 212-628-4552
E-mail: tompkf@aol.com

KURT WEILL FOUNDATION FOR MUSIC http://www.kwf.org

LOTTE LENYA COMPETITION FOR SINGERS

The Lotte Lenya Competition for Singers exists to recognize excellence in the performance of music for the theater, including opera, operetta, and American musical theater. Applicants should contact the Foundation for more information.

Academic Fields/Career Goals: Performing Arts.

Award: Prize for use in freshman, sophomore, junior, senior, graduate, or postgraduate years; not renewable. *Number:* varies. *Amount:* varies.

Eligibility Requirements: Applicant must be age 32 or under; enrolled or expecting to enroll at an institution or university and must have an interest in music/singing. Available to U.S. and Canadian citizens.

Application Requirements: Application, applicant must enter a contest, audition. *Deadline:* January 15.

Contact: Carolyn Weber, Director for Program Administration
Kurt Weill Foundation for Music
7 East 20th Street
New York, NY 10003-1106
Phone: 212-505-5240
Fax: 212-353-9663
E-mail: kwfinfo@kwf.org

MIDLAND COMMUNITY THEATER http://www.mctmidland.org

MADEIRA SHANER SCHOLARSHIP

Available to freshman and sophomore students who are U. S. citizens and residents of Midland, Texas. Intended for those pursuing a career in the performing arts. Minimum 3.0 GPA. Application deadline: June 30.

Academic Fields/Career Goals: Performing Arts.

Award: Scholarship for use in freshman or sophomore years; not renewable. *Number:* 2–3. *Amount:* $1000.

Eligibility Requirements: Applicant must be enrolled or expecting to enroll full-time at an institution or university and resident of Texas. Applicant must have 3.0 GPA or higher. Available to U.S. citizens.

Application Requirements: Application. *Deadline:* June 30.

Contact: Chair, Scholarship Award Committee
Midland Community Theater
2000 West Wadley
Midland, TX 79705

NATIONAL FOUNDATION FOR ADVANCEMENT IN THE ARTS http://www.artsawards.org

ARTS RECOGNITION AND TALENT SEARCH (ARTS)

• *See page 89*

ASTRAL CAREER GRANT

• *See page 366*

NATIONAL GUILD OF COMMUNITY SCHOOLS OF THE ARTS http://www.nationalguild.org

YOUNG COMPOSERS AWARDS

• *See page 366*

NATIONAL OPERA ASSOCIATION http://www.noa.org

NOA VOCAL COMPETITION/ LEGACY AWARD PROGRAM

• *See page 89*

POLISH ARTS CLUB OF BUFFALO SCHOLARSHIP FOUNDATION

POLISH ARTS CLUB OF BUFFALO SCHOLARSHIP FOUNDATION TRUST

• *See page 84*

PRINCESS GRACE FOUNDATION-USA http://www.pgfusa.com

PRINCESS GRACE SCHOLARSHIPS IN DANCE, THEATER, AND FILM

• *See page 268*

SAN ANGELO SYMPHONY SOCIETY http://www.sanangelosymphony.org

SORANTIN YOUNG ARTIST AWARD

Prizes awarded to vocalists under 31 and pianists and instrumentalists under 28 in four categories: piano, vocal, strings, and instrumental. Overall winner will appear with the San Angelo Symphony Orchestra. Application fee of $90 is required.

Academic Fields/Career Goals: Performing Arts.

Award: Prize for use in freshman, sophomore, junior, senior, graduate, or postgraduate years; not renewable. *Number:* 5–12. *Amount:* $250–$1000.

Eligibility Requirements: Applicant must be enrolled or expecting to enroll full or part-time at a two-year or four-year institution or university and must have an interest in music/singing. Available to U.S. and non-U.S. citizens.

Application Requirements: Application, applicant must enter a contest. *Fee:* $90. *Deadline:* October 8.

Contact: Grace Torres, Executive Director
San Angelo Symphony Society
PO Box 5922
San Angelo, TX 76902-5922
Phone: 915-658-5877
Fax: 915-653-1045
E-mail: receptionist@sanangelosymphony.org

SIGMA ALPHA IOTA PHILANTHROPIES, INC. http://www.sai-national.org

SIGMA ALPHA IOTA PHILANTHROPIES UNDERGRADUATE PERFORMANCE SCHOLARSHIPS

• *See page 367*

SIGMA ALPHA IOTA PHILANTHROPIES UNDERGRADUATE SCHOLARSHIPS

• *See page 211*

SIGMA ALPHA IOTA SUMMER MUSIC SCHOLARSHIPS IN THE U.S. OR ABROAD

• *See page 367*

SIGMA ALPHA IOTA VISUALLY IMPAIRED SCHOLARSHIP

• *See page 211*

UNITED NEGRO COLLEGE FUND http://www.uncf.org

ELLA FITZGERALD CHARITABLE FOUNDATION SCHOLARSHIP

• *See page 367*

JANET JACKSON/RHYTHM NATION SCHOLARSHIP

• *See page 91*

JIMI HENDRIX ENDOWMENT FUND SCHOLARSHIP

Scholarship supports students majoring in music and attending a UNCF member college and university. Minimum 2.5 GPA required. Prospective applicants should complete the Student Profile found at Web site: http://www.uncf.org.

Academic Fields/Career Goals: Performing Arts.

Award: Scholarship for use in freshman, sophomore, junior, or senior years; not renewable. *Amount:* $2000–$5000.

Eligibility Requirements: Applicant must be Black (non-Hispanic) and enrolled or expecting to enroll at a four-year institution or university. Applicant must have 2.5 GPA or higher.

Application Requirements: Application, financial need analysis.

Contact: Program Services Department
United Negro College Fund
8260 Willow Oaks Corporate Drive
Fairfax, VA 22031

JOHN LENNON SCHOLARSHIP FUND

• *See page 167*

MICHAEL JACKSON SCHOLARSHIP
• *See page 167*

VSA ARTS http://www.vsarts.org

VSA ARTS-PANASONIC YOUNG SOLOIST AWARD

Musical performance competition for persons 25 and under with disabilities. One-time award of $5000. Submit audio or videotape of performance. Contact VSA arts for information and application materials. (TTY) 202-737-0645.

Academic Fields/Career Goals: Performing Arts.

Award: Scholarship for use in freshman, sophomore, junior, or senior years; not renewable. *Number:* 2. *Amount:* $5000.

Eligibility Requirements: Applicant must be age 25 or under; enrolled or expecting to enroll full or part-time at an institution or university and must have an interest in music/singing. Applicant must be hearing impaired, learning disabled, physically disabled, or visually impaired. Available to U.S. citizens.

Application Requirements: Application, applicant must enter a contest, autobiography, audition tape. *Deadline:* November 1.

Contact: Elena Widder, Director of Performing Arts
VSA arts
1300 Connecticut Avenue, NW, Suite 700
Washington, DC 20036
Phone: 800-933-8721
Fax: 202-737-0725

VSA ARTS-ROSEMARY KENNEDY INTERNATIONAL YOUNG SOLOIST AWARD

Musical performance for persons 25 and under with disabilities. One-time award of $1000. Submit audio or videotape of performance. Contact VSA arts for information and application materials.

Academic Fields/Career Goals: Performing Arts.

Award: Scholarship for use in freshman, sophomore, junior, or senior years; not renewable. *Number:* 2. *Amount:* $1000.

Eligibility Requirements: Applicant must be age 25 or under; enrolled or expecting to enroll full or part-time at an institution or university and must have an interest in music/singing. Applicant must be hearing impaired, learning disabled, physically disabled, or visually impaired. Available to Canadian and non-U.S. citizens.

Application Requirements: Application, applicant must enter a contest, autobiography, audio or video tape. *Deadline:* November 1.

Contact: Elena Widder, Director of Performing Arts
VSA arts
1300 Connecticut Avenue, NW, Suite 700
Washington, DC 20036
Phone: 800-933-8721
Fax: 202-737-0725

WAMSO-MINNESOTA ORCHESTRA VOLUNTEER ASSOCIATION http://www.wamso.org

YOUNG ARTIST COMPETITION

Created in 1956, the contest is designed to discover and encourage exceptional young talented musicians ages 15-26 through a regional competition. Applicants submit taped performances. From that group, selected participants compete in the semi-finals with finalists advancing to the last round. Applicant must play an instrument which has a permanent chair in the Minnesota orchestra. Only students or legal residents of Michigan, Minnesota, Iowa, Illinois, Kansas, Missouri, Nebraska, North Dakota, South Dakota, Indiana, Wisconsin, Ontario and Manitoba are eligible. Application fee is $65.

Academic Fields/Career Goals: Performing Arts.

Award: Prize for use in freshman, sophomore, junior, senior, graduate, or postgraduate years; not renewable. *Number:* 9–14. *Amount:* $500–$5250.

Eligibility Requirements: Applicant must be age 15-26; enrolled or expecting to enroll at an institution or university; resident of Illinois, Indiana, Iowa, Kansas, Manitoba, Michigan, Minnesota, Missouri, Nebraska, North Dakota, Ontario, South Dakota, or Wisconsin and must have an interest in music. Available to U.S. and non-U.S. citizens.

Application Requirements: Application, applicant must enter a contest, taped performance of specific repertoire. *Fee:* $65. *Deadline:* September 15.

Contact: YAC Chair
WAMSO-Minnesota Orchestra Volunteer Association
Orchestra Hall
1111 Nicollet Mall
Minneapolis, MN 55403-2477
Phone: 612-371-5654
Fax: 612-371-7176
E-mail: wamso@mnorch.org

WAVERLY COMMUNITY HOUSE, INC. http://waverlycomm.com

F. LAMMOT BELIN ARTS SCHOLARSHIP
• *See page 80*

WOMEN BAND DIRECTORS INTERNATIONAL http://womenbanddirectors.org

GLADYS STONE WRIGHT SCHOLARSHIP
• *See page 216*

HELEN MAY BULTER MEMORIAL SCHOLARSHIP
• *See page 216*

MARTHA ANN STARK MEMORIAL SCHOLARSHIP
• *See page 217*

MUSIC TECHNOLOGY SCHOLARSHIP
• *See page 217*

VOLKWEIN MEMORIAL SCHOLARSHIP
• *See page 217*

PHARMACY

AMERICAN PHARMACY SERVICES CORPORATION FOUNDATION FOR EDUCATION AND RESEARCH, INC. http://www.apscnet.com

AMERICAN PHARMACY SERVICES CORPORATION SCHOLARSHIP/LOAN

Forgivable loan available to students who have successfully completed the requirement of a pre-pharmacy curriculum and have been accepted into an accredited pharmacy school. Must be committed to independent pharmacy practice and upon graduation and licensure must accept a pharmacist position in a APSC member pharmacy to pay off their loan in four years of full-time employment. Selection for loan is based on academic record, personal characteristics management potential and interest in independent pharmacy. Must maintain a grade point average equal to "C". Application deadline July 15 for fall semester; November 15 for spring semester. For application and information see Web site: http://www.apscnet.com.

Academic Fields/Career Goals: Pharmacy.

Award: Forgivable loan for use in freshman, sophomore, junior, senior, or graduate years; renewable. *Number:* varies. *Amount:* up to $3000.

Eligibility Requirements: Applicant must be enrolled or expecting to enroll at an institution or university.

Application Requirements: Application, financial need analysis, references, transcript. *Deadline:* varies.

Contact: Teresa Doris, Program Director
American Pharmacy Services Corporation Foundation for Education and Research, Inc.
102 Enterprise Drive
Frankfort, KY 40601
Phone: 502-695-8899
Fax: 502-695-9912
E-mail: teresa@apscnet.com

BRITISH COLUMBIA MINISTRY OF ADVANCED EDUCATION http://www.aved.gov.bc.ca/

LOAN FORGIVENESS PROGRAM FOR NURSES, DOCTORS, MIDWIVES, AND PHARMACISTS

• See page 295

MENTAL HEALTH ASSOCIATION IN NEW YORK STATE, INC. http://www.mhanys.org

EDNA AIMES SCHOLARSHIP

• See page 299

NEW YORK STATE EDUCATION DEPARTMENT http://www.highered.nysed.gov

REGENTS PROFESSIONAL OPPORTUNITY SCHOLARSHIP

• See page 45

NORTON HEALTHCARE http://www.nortonhealthcare.com

NORTON HEALTHCARE SCHOLARS–METROPOLITAN COLLEGE

• See page 300

NORTON HEALTHCARE SCHOLARS–PRIVATE COLLEGES AND UNIVERSITIES

• See page 301

RESOURCE CENTER http://www.resourcecenterscholarshipinfo.com

MARIE BLAHA MEDICAL GRANT

• See page 64

UNITED NEGRO COLLEGE FUND http://www.uncf.org

CARDINAL HEALTH SCHOLARSHIP

• See page 48

CVS/PHARMACY SCHOLARSHIP

Scholarship awarded to undergraduate junior or senior enrolled in a pharmacy major. Applicant must attend school in the Washington, D. C. area or in Detroit, Michigan. Must have minimum 2.8 GPA. Please visit Web site for more information: http://www.uncf.org.

Academic Fields/Career Goals: Pharmacy.

Award: Scholarship for use in junior or senior years. *Number:* varies. *Amount:* $2000.

Eligibility Requirements: Applicant must be Black (non-Hispanic); enrolled or expecting to enroll at a four-year institution or university and studying in District of Columbia or Michigan.

Application Requirements: Application, financial need analysis, FAFSA, SAR. *Deadline:* varies.

Contact: Program Services Department
United Negro College Fund
8260 Willow Oaks Corporate Drive
Fairfax, VA 22031

OSTINA AND HERMAN HARTFIELD SCHOLARSHIP

• See page 118

WYETH SCHOLARSHIP

• See page 119

PHILOSOPHY

AMERICAN SCHOOL OF CLASSICAL STUDIES AT ATHENS http://www.ascsa.edu.gr

ASCSA SUMMER SESSIONS

• See page 65

PHOTOJOURNALISM/ PHOTOGRAPHY

ACADEMY OF TELEVISION ARTS AND SCIENCES FOUNDATION http://www.emmys.tv/foundation

ACADEMY OF TELEVISION ARTS AND SCIENCES COLLEGE TELEVISION AWARDS

• See page 84

AMERICAN LEGION, PRESS CLUB OF NEW JERSEY

AMERICAN LEGION PRESS CLUB OF NEW JERSEY AND POST 170 ARTHUR DEHARDT MEMORIAL SCHOLARSHIP

• See page 156

ASIAN AMERICAN JOURNALISTS ASSOCIATION http://www.aaja.org

ASIAN-AMERICAN JOURNALISTS ASSOCIATION SCHOLARSHIP

• See page 157

BOB BAXTER SCHOLARSHIP FOUNDATION

BOB BAXTER SCHOLARSHIP FOUNDATION

For New Jersey students intending to study press photography. Must be a high school senior or be enrolled in a school of photography. Applicants must be New Jersey residents. Submit portfolio of work, two letters of recommendation, and application form. Emphasis is on portfolio which should show a cross-section of the applicant's work.

Academic Fields/Career Goals: Photojournalism/Photography.

Award: Scholarship for use in freshman, sophomore, or junior years; renewable. *Number:* 2. *Amount:* $1000.

Eligibility Requirements: Applicant must be enrolled or expecting to enroll full-time at a two-year or four-year or technical institution or university; resident of New Jersey and must have an interest in photography/photogrammetry/filmmaking. Available to U.S. citizens.

Application Requirements: Application, portfolio, references. *Deadline:* April 30.

Contact: Jean-Rae Turner, Administrator
Bob Baxter Scholarship Foundation
c/o New Jersey Newsphotos, Hemisphere Center, Route 1
Newark, NJ 07114

CALIFORNIA CHICANO NEWS MEDIA ASSOCIATION (CCNMA) http://www.ccnma.org

JOEL GARCIA MEMORIAL SCHOLARSHIP

• See page 158

CONNECTICUT CHAPTER OF SOCIETY OF PROFESSIONAL JOURNALISTS http://www.ctspj.org

CONNECTICUT SPJ BOB EDDY SCHOLARSHIP PROGRAM

• See page 330

DALLAS-FORT WORTH ASSOCIATION OF BLACK COMMUNICATORS http://www.dfwabc.org

FUTURE JOURNALISTS SCHOLARSHIP PROGRAM

• See page 159

DAYTON FOUNDATION http://www.daytonfoundation.org

LARRY FULLERTON PHOTOJOURNALISM SCHOLARSHIP

One-time scholarship for Ohio resident pursuing career in photojournalism. Must have experience and submit examples of work. Award for use at an Ohio two- or four-year college or university. High school students are ineligible. For use in sophomore, junior or senior year. Minimum 2.5 GPA required. Must be U.S. citizen.

Academic Fields/Career Goals: Photojournalism/Photography.

Award: Scholarship for use in sophomore, junior, or senior years; not renewable. *Number:* 1–2. *Amount:* $500–$2500.

Dayton Foundation (continued)

Eligibility Requirements: Applicant must be enrolled or expecting to enroll full-time at a two-year or four-year institution or university; resident of Ohio; studying in Ohio and must have an interest in photography/photogrammetry/filmmaking. Applicant must have 2.5 GPA or higher. Available to U.S. citizens.

Application Requirements: Application, financial need analysis, portfolio, transcript, slide portfolio. *Deadline:* January 31.

Contact: Diane K. Timmons, Director of Grants and Programs
Dayton Foundation
2300 Kettering Tower
Dayton, OH 45423
Phone: 937-222-0410
Fax: 937-222-0636
E-mail: dtimmons@daytonfoundation.org

FISHER BROADCASTING COMPANY http://www.fisherbroadcasting.com/

FISHER BROADCASTING, INC., SCHOLARSHIP FOR MINORITIES
• *See page 159*

INDIANAPOLIS ASSOCIATION OF BLACK JOURNALISTS http://www.iabj.org

LYNN DEAN FORD IABJ SCHOLARSHIP AWARDS
• *See page 160*

INTERNATIONAL FOODSERVICE EDITORIAL COUNCIL http://www.ifec-is-us.com

INTERNATIONAL FOODSERVICE EDITORIAL COUNCIL COMMUNICATIONS SCHOLARSHIP
• *See page 160*

KCNC-TV CHANNEL 4 NEWS http://www.news4colorado.com

NEWS 4 PETER ROGOT MEDIA SCHOLARSHIP
• *See page 161*

MAINE MEDIA WOMEN SCHOLARSHIPS COMMITTEE http://www.mainemediawomen.org/scholarships.html

MAINE MEDIA WOMEN'S SCHOLARSHIP
• *See page 88*

NATIONAL ASSOCIATION OF BLACK JOURNALISTS http://www.nabj.org

NATIONAL ASSOCIATION OF BLACK JOURNALISTS NON-SUSTAINING SCHOLARSHIP AWARDS
• *See page 333*

VISUAL TASK FORCE SCHOLARSHIP

Scholarship available to African American students attending an accredited four-year college or university and majoring in visual journalism. Minimum 3.0 GPA required. Must be NABJ member before award.

Academic Fields/Career Goals: Photojournalism/Photography.

Award: Scholarship for use in freshman, sophomore, junior, senior, or graduate years. *Number:* 2. *Amount:* $1250.

Eligibility Requirements: Applicant must be Black (non-Hispanic) and enrolled or expecting to enroll at a four-year institution or university. Applicant must have 3.0 GPA or higher.

Application Requirements: *Deadline:* April 30.

Contact: Program and Exposition Coordinator
National Association of Black Journalists
8701-A Adelphi Road
Adelphi, MD 20783-1716
Phone: 301-445-7100
Fax: 301-445-7101

NATIONAL ASSOCIATION OF HISPANIC JOURNALISTS (NAHJ) http://www.nahj.org

NATIONAL ASSOCIATION OF HISPANIC JOURNALISTS SCHOLARSHIP
• *See page 161*

NATIONAL FOUNDATION FOR ADVANCEMENT IN THE ARTS http://www.artsawards.org

ARTS RECOGNITION AND TALENT SEARCH (ARTS)
• *See page 89*

NATIONAL PRESS PHOTOGRAPHERS FOUNDATION, INC. http://www.nppa.org

BOB EAST SCHOLARSHIP

Award of $2000 for applicant who is either an undergraduate in the first three and one-half years of college or is planning to pursue postgraduate work and offers indication of acceptance in such a program. Portfolio must include at least five single images in addition to a picture story. Award is chosen primarily on portfolio quality.

Academic Fields/Career Goals: Photojournalism/Photography.

Award: Scholarship for use in freshman, sophomore, junior, or senior years; not renewable. *Number:* 1. *Amount:* $2000.

Eligibility Requirements: Applicant must be enrolled or expecting to enroll full-time at a four-year institution. Available to U.S. citizens.

Application Requirements: Application, financial need analysis, portfolio, self-addressed stamped envelope, transcript. *Deadline:* March 1.

Contact: Chuck Fadely
National Press Photographers Foundation, Inc.
The Miami Herald, One Herald Plaza
Miami, FL 33132
Phone: 305-376-2015
E-mail: info@nppa.org

NATIONAL PRESS PHOTOGRAPHERS FOUNDATION STILL PHOTOGRAPHER SCHOLARSHIP

Award of $2000 for students who have completed one year at a four-year college or university having photojournalism courses. Applicant must be pursuing a bachelor's degree and must have at least one-half year of undergraduate schooling remaining at the time of award.

Academic Fields/Career Goals: Photojournalism/Photography.

Award: Scholarship for use in sophomore, junior, or senior years; not renewable. *Number:* 1. *Amount:* up to $2000.

Eligibility Requirements: Applicant must be enrolled or expecting to enroll full-time at a four-year institution or university. Available to U.S. citizens.

Application Requirements: Application, financial need analysis, portfolio, self-addressed stamped envelope, transcript. *Deadline:* March 1.

Contact: Bill Sanders
National Press Photographers Foundation, Inc.
640 Northwest 100 Way
Coral Springs, FL 33071
Phone: 954-341-9718

NATIONAL PRESS PHOTOGRAPHERS FOUNDATION TELEVISION NEWS SCHOLARSHIP

Award of $2000 for student enrolled in a four-year college or university having courses in TV news photojournalism. Applicant must be pursuing a bachelor's degree and be in his/her junior or senior year at the time of award. Submit entry form, biographical sketch, and videotape samples of work.

Academic Fields/Career Goals: Photojournalism/Photography; TV/Radio Broadcasting.

Award: Scholarship for use in junior or senior years; not renewable. *Number:* 1. *Amount:* up to $2000.

Eligibility Requirements: Applicant must be enrolled or expecting to enroll full-time at a four-year institution or university. Available to U.S. citizens.

Application Requirements: Application, autobiography, essay, financial need analysis, portfolio, references, self-addressed stamped envelope, transcript. *Deadline:* March 1.

Contact: Dave Hamer, NPPF Television News Scholarship Coordinator
National Press Photographers Foundation, Inc.
3702 North 53rd Street
Omaha, NE 68104
E-mail: 75271.1707@compuserve.com

REID BLACKBURN SCHOLARSHIP

Award of $2000 for a student who has completed one year of a photojournalism program at a four-year college or university in preparation for a bachelor's degree. Must have at least one-half year of undergraduate schooling remaining at time of award. The philosophy and goals statement is particularly important in this selection.

Academic Fields/Career Goals: Photojournalism/Photography.

Award: Scholarship for use in sophomore, junior, or senior years; not renewable. *Number:* 1. *Amount:* up to $2000.

Eligibility Requirements: Applicant must be enrolled or expecting to enroll full-time at a four-year institution or university. Available to U.S. citizens.

Application Requirements: Application, essay, financial need analysis, portfolio, self-addressed stamped envelope, transcript. *Deadline:* March 1.

Contact: Jeremiah Coughlan, Staff Photographer
National Press Photographers Foundation, Inc.
The Columbian, 701 West 8th Street
Vancouver, WA 98660
Phone: 360-694-3391
E-mail: coughlan@attbi.com

NATIONAL WRITERS ASSOCIATION FOUNDATION http://www.nationalwriters.com

NATIONAL WRITERS ASSOCIATION FOUNDATION SCHOLARSHIPS
• *See page 162*

NEBRASKA PRESS ASSOCIATION http://www.nebpress.com/

NEBRASKA PRESS ASSOCIATION FOUNDATION, INC., SCHOLARSHIP
• *See page 335*

OUTDOOR WRITERS ASSOCIATION OF AMERICA http://www.owaa.org

OUTDOOR WRITERS ASSOCIATION OF AMERICA BODIE MCDOWELL SCHOLARSHIP AWARD
• *See page 163*

SAN FRANCISCO FOUNDATION http://www.sff.org

PHELAN AWARD IN PHOTOGRAPHY

Award presented in every odd-numbered year to recognize achievement in photography. Must have been born in California, but need not be a current resident. Applicants must provide a copy of their birth certificate with their application. This award is not a scholarship. See Web site at http://sff.org for further information and deadlines.

Academic Fields/Career Goals: Photojournalism/Photography.

Award: Prize for use in freshman, sophomore, junior, senior, graduate, or postgraduate years; not renewable. *Number:* 3. *Amount:* $2500.

Eligibility Requirements: Applicant must be enrolled or expecting to enroll at an institution or university. Available to U.S. citizens.

Application Requirements: Application, applicant must enter a contest, self-addressed stamped envelope. *Deadline:* varies.

Contact: Art Awards Coordinator
San Francisco Foundation
225 Bush Street, Suite 500
San Francisco, CA 94104
Phone: 415-733-8500

TEXAS GRIDIRON CLUB, INC. http://www.spjfw.org

TEXAS GRIDIRON CLUB SCHOLARSHIPS
• *See page 165*

UNITED METHODIST COMMUNICATIONS http://www.umcom.org/scholarships

LEONARD M. PERRYMAN COMMUNICATIONS SCHOLARSHIP FOR ETHNIC MINORITY STUDENTS
• *See page 166*

VALLEY PRESS CLUB

VALLEY PRESS CLUB SCHOLARSHIPS, THE REPUBLICAN SCHOLARSHIP; PHOTOJOURNALISM SCHOLARSHIP, CHANNEL 22 SCHOLARSHIP
• *See page 167*

PHYSICAL SCIENCES AND MATH

AIR AND WASTE MANAGEMENT ASSOCIATION-CONNECTICUT CHAPTER http://www.awma-nes.org/

AIR AND WASTE MANAGEMENT ASSOCIATION-CONNECTICUT CHAPTER SCHOLARSHIP
• *See page 111*

ALABAMA STATE DEPARTMENT OF EDUCATION http://www.alsde.edu

MATH AND SCIENCE SCHOLARSHIP PROGRAM FOR ALABAMA TEACHERS
• *See page 111*

AMERICAN INDIAN SCIENCE AND ENGINEERING SOCIETY http://www.aises.org

A.T. ANDERSON MEMORIAL SCHOLARSHIP
• *See page 65*

BURLINGTON NORTHERN SANTA FE FOUNDATION SCHOLARSHIP
• *See page 65*

ENVIRONMENTAL PROTECTION AGENCY TRIBAL LANDS ENVIRONMENTAL SCIENCE SCHOLARSHIP
• *See page 111*

AMERICAN INSTITUTE OF AERONAUTICS AND ASTRONAUTICS http://www.aiaa.org

AIAA UNDERGRADUATE SCHOLARSHIP
• *See page 66*

AMERICAN LEGION, DEPARTMENT OF KANSAS

CHARLES W. AND ANNETTE HILL SCHOLARSHIP
• *See page 120*

AMERICAN LEGION, DEPARTMENT OF MARYLAND http://mdlegion.org

AMERICAN LEGION DEPARTMENT OF MARYLAND MATH-SCIENCE SCHOLARSHIP

Scholarship for study in math or the sciences. Must be a Maryland resident and the dependent child of a veteran. Must submit essay, financial need analysis, and transcript with application. Nonrenewable award for freshman year. Application available on Web site: http://mdlegion.org.

Academic Fields/Career Goals: Physical Sciences and Math.

Award: Scholarship for use in freshman year; not renewable. *Number:* 1. *Amount:* $500.

Eligibility Requirements: Applicant must be high school student; planning to enroll or expecting to enroll full-time at a two-year or four-year institution and resident of Maryland. Available to U.S. citizens. Applicant or parent must meet one or more of the following

American Legion, Department of Maryland (continued)

requirements: general military experience; retired from active duty; disabled or killed as a result of military service; prisoner of war; or missing in action.

Application Requirements: Application, essay, financial need analysis, transcript. *Deadline:* March 31.

Contact: Thomas Davis, Department Adjutant
American Legion, Department of Maryland
101 North Gay, Room E
Baltimore, MD 21202
Phone: 410-752-3104

AMERICAN METEOROLOGICAL SOCIETY http://www.ametsoc.org/AMS

AMERICAN METEOROLOGICAL SOCIETY INDUSTRY UNDERGRADUATE SCHOLARSHIPS

• *See page 66*

AMERICAN PHYSICAL SOCIETY http://www.aps.org/educ/com/index.html

AMERICAN PHYSICAL SOCIETY SCHOLARSHIP FOR MINORITY UNDERGRADUATE PHYSICS MAJORS

One-time award for high school seniors, college freshmen and sophomores planning to major in physics. Must be African-American, Hispanic, or Native-American. Must be a U.S. citizen or a legal resident. For legal residents, a copy of alien registration card is required. Deadline for application is the first Friday in February.

Academic Fields/Career Goals: Physical Sciences and Math.

Award: Scholarship for use in freshman or sophomore years; not renewable. *Number:* 20–25. *Amount:* $2000–$3000.

Eligibility Requirements: Applicant must be American Indian/Alaska Native, Black (non-Hispanic), or Hispanic and enrolled or expecting to enroll full-time at a two-year or four-year institution or university. Available to U.S. citizens.

Application Requirements: Application, essay, references, test scores, transcript. *Deadline:* varies.

Contact: Arlene Modeste Knowles, Scholarship Administrator
American Physical Society
One Physics Ellipse
College Park, MD 20740
Phone: 301-209-3232
Fax: 301-209-0865
E-mail: knowles@aps.org

AMERICAN SOCIETY OF NAVAL ENGINEERS http://www.navalengineers.org

AMERICAN SOCIETY OF NAVAL ENGINEERS SCHOLARSHIP

• *See page 66*

ARIZONA HYDROLOGICAL SOCIETY http://www.azhydrosoc.org

ARIZONA HYDROLOGICAL SURVEY STUDENT SCHOLARSHIP

• *See page 189*

ARKANSAS DEPARTMENT OF HIGHER EDUCATION http://www.arscholarships.com

EMERGENCY SECONDARY EDUCATION LOAN PROGRAM

• *See page 111*

ARMED FORCES COMMUNICATIONS AND ELECTRONICS ASSOCIATION, EDUCATIONAL FOUNDATION http://www.afcea.org

AFCEA SCHOLARSHIP FOR WORKING PROFESSIONALS

• *See page 96*

AFCEA SGT. JEANNETTE L. WINTERS, USMC MEMORIAL SCHOLARSHIP

• *See page 168*

AFCEA/LOCKHEED MARTIN ORINCON IT SCHOLARSHIP

• *See page 169*

ARMED FORCES COMMUNICATIONS AND ELECTRONICS ASSOCIATION GENERAL EMMETT PAIGE SCHOLARSHIP

• *See page 169*

ARMED FORCES COMMUNICATIONS AND ELECTRONICS ASSOCIATION GENERAL JOHN A. WICKHAM SCHOLARSHIP

• *See page 169*

ARMED FORCES COMMUNICATIONS AND ELECTRONICS ASSOCIATION ROTC SCHOLARSHIP PROGRAM

• *See page 96*

ASPRS, THE IMAGING AND GEOSPATIAL INFORMATION SOCIETY http://www.asprs.org

SPACE IMAGING AWARD FOR APPLICATION OF HIGH RESOLUTION DIGITAL SATELLITE IMAGERY

• *See page 67*

Z/I IMAGING SCHOLARSHIP

• *See page 68*

ASSOCIATION FOR IRON AND STEEL TECHNOLOGY http://www.aist.org/foundation/scholarships.htm

ASSOCIATION FOR IRON AND STEEL TECHNOLOGY OHIO VALLEY CHAPTER SCHOLARSHIP

• *See page 112*

ASSOCIATION FOR WOMEN GEOSCIENTISTS, PUGET SOUND CHAPTER http://www.awg.org/

PUGET SOUND CHAPTER SCHOLARSHIP

• *See page 189*

ASSOCIATION FOR WOMEN IN MATHEMATICS http://www.awm-math.org/

ALICE T. SCHAFER MATHEMATICS PRIZE FOR EXCELLENCE IN MATHEMATICS BY AN UNDERGRADUATE WOMAN

One-time merit award for women undergraduates in the math field. Based on quality of performance in math courses and special programs, ability to work independently, interest in math, and performance in competitions. Must be nominated by professor or adviser.

Academic Fields/Career Goals: Physical Sciences and Math.

Award: Prize for use in freshman, sophomore, junior, or senior years; not renewable. *Number:* 1–6. *Amount:* $250–$1000.

Eligibility Requirements: Applicant must be enrolled or expecting to enroll at a four-year institution or university and female. Available to U.S. citizens.

Application Requirements: References, transcript, nomination. *Deadline:* October 1.

Contact: Dawn V. Wheeler, Director of Marketing
Association for Women in Mathematics
4114 Computer and Space Sciences Building
College Park, MD 20742-2461
E-mail: awn@math.umd.edu

ASSOCIATION FOR WOMEN IN SCIENCE EDUCATIONAL FOUNDATION http://www.awis.org/ed_foundation.html

ASSOCIATION FOR WOMEN IN SCIENCE COLLEGE SCHOLARSHIP

• *See page 63*

AWIS KIRSTEN R. LORENTZEN AWARD IN PHYSICS

• *See page 189*

BARRY M. GOLDWATER SCHOLARSHIP AND EXCELLENCE IN EDUCATION FOUNDATION http://www.act.org/goldwater

BARRY M. GOLDWATER SCHOLARSHIP AND EXCELLENCE IN EDUCATION PROGRAM

• See page 68

BUSINESS AND PROFESSIONAL WOMEN'S FOUNDATION http://www.bpwusa.org

BPW CAREER ADVANCEMENT SCHOLARSHIP PROGRAM FOR WOMEN

• See page 112

CATCHING THE DREAM

MATH, ENGINEERING, SCIENCE, BUSINESS, EDUCATION, COMPUTERS SCHOLARSHIPS

• See page 121

NATIVE AMERICAN LEADERSHIP IN EDUCATION (NALE)

• See page 122

CONNECTICUT STUDENT LOAN FOUNDATION http://www.cslf.com

CONNECTICUT INNOVATIONS TECHNOLOGY SCHOLAR PROGRAM

• See page 113

DAYTON FOUNDATION http://www.daytonfoundation.org

THRYSA FRAZIER SVAGER SCHOLARSHIP

Scholarship for African-American female students majoring in mathematics and attending Central State University, Wilberforce University, Wright State University, University of Dayton, Howard University or Spelman College. Must maintain average grade of "B" or better. Application deadline is May 1.

Academic Fields/Career Goals: Physical Sciences and Math.

Award: Scholarship for use in sophomore, junior, or senior years; renewable. *Number:* 1–3. *Amount:* $2000.

Eligibility Requirements: Applicant must be Black (non-Hispanic); enrolled or expecting to enroll full-time at a four-year institution or university and female. Applicant must have 3.0 GPA or higher. Available to U.S. citizens.

Application Requirements: Application, essay, transcript. *Deadline:* May 1.

Contact: Diane K. Timmons, Director of Grants and Programs
Dayton Foundation
2300 Kettering Tower
Dayton, OH 45423
Phone: 937-222-0410
Fax: 937-222-0636
E-mail: dtimmons@daytonfoundation.org

EAA AVIATION FOUNDATION, INC. http://www.eaa.org

PAYZER SCHOLARSHIP

• See page 98

GARDEN CLUB OF AMERICA http://www.gcamerica.org

GARDEN CLUB OF AMERICA AWARDS FOR SUMMER ENVIRONMENTAL STUDIES

• See page 58

GRAND RAPIDS COMMUNITY FOUNDATION http://www.grfoundation.org

ECONOMIC CLUB OF GRAND RAPIDS BUSINESS STUDY ABROAD SCHOLARSHIP

• See page 41

GREATER KANAWHA VALLEY FOUNDATION http://www.tgkvf.org

MATH AND SCIENCE SCHOLARSHIP

• See page 244

HISPANIC COLLEGE FUND, INC. http://www.hispanicfund.org

LOCKHEED MARTIN SCHOLARSHIP PROGRAM

• See page 141

HISPANIC SCHOLARSHIP FUND http://www.hsf.net

HSF/SOCIETY OF HISPANIC PROFESSIONAL ENGINEERS, INC. SCHOLARSHIP PROGRAM

• See page 152

INDEPENDENT LABORATORIES INSTITUTE SCHOLARSHIP ALLIANCE http://www.acil.org

INDEPENDENT LABORATORIES INSTITUTE SCHOLARSHIP ALLIANCE

• See page 69

INNOVATION AND SCIENCE COUNCIL OF BRITISH COLUMBIA http://www.scbc.org

IBM SCHOLARSHIP

• See page 171

PAUL AND HELEN TRUSSEL SCIENCE AND TECHNOLOGY SCHOLARSHIP

• See page 69

JEWISH FEDERATION OF METROPOLITAN CHICAGO (JFMC) http://www.jvschicago.org

JEWISH FEDERATION OF METROPOLITAN CHICAGO ACADEMIC SCHOLARSHIP PROGRAM

• See page 185

LOS ANGELES COUNCIL OF BLACK PROFESSIONAL ENGINEERS http://www.lablackengineers.org/scholarships.html

AL-BEN SCHOLARSHIP FOR ACADEMIC INCENTIVE

• See page 142

AL-BEN SCHOLARSHIP FOR PROFESSIONAL MERIT

• See page 142

AL-BEN SCHOLARSHIP FOR SCHOLASTIC ACHIEVEMENT

• See page 143

LUCENT TECHNOLOGIES FOUNDATION http://www.iie.org/programs/lucent

LUCENT GLOBAL SCIENCE SCHOLARS PROGRAM

• See page 70

MICRON TECHNOLOGY FOUNDATION, INC. http://www.micron.com/scholars

MICRON SCIENCE AND TECHNOLOGY SCHOLARS PROGRAM

• See page 144

MINERALOGICAL SOCIETY OF AMERICA http://www.minsocam.org

MINERALOGICAL SOCIETY OF AMERICA-GRANT FOR STUDENT RESEARCH IN MINERALOGY AND PETROLOGY

• See page 190

MINERALOGY SOCIETY OF AMERICA-GRANT FOR RESEARCH IN CRYSTALLOGRAPHY

• See page 191

NASA DELAWARE SPACE GRANT CONSORTIUM http://www.delspace.org

NASA DELAWARE SPACE GRANT UNDERGRADUATE TUITION SCHOLARSHIP

• See page 70

NASA IDAHO SPACE GRANT CONSORTIUM http://www.uidaho.edu/nasa_isgc

NASA IDAHO SPACE GRANT CONSORTIUM SCHOLARSHIP PROGRAM
• *See page 71*

NASA MINNESOTA SPACE GRANT CONSORTIUM http://www.aem.umn.edu/msgc

MINNESOTA SPACE GRANT CONSORTIUM
• *See page 101*

NASA NEBRASKA SPACE GRANT CONSORTIUM http://nasa.unomaha.edu

NASA NEBRASKA SPACE GRANT
• *See page 101*

NASA NEVADA SPACE GRANT CONSORTIUM http://www.unr.edu/spacegrant

UNIVERSITY AND COMMUNITY COLLEGE SYSTEM OF NEVADA NASA SPACE GRANT AND FELLOWSHIP PROGRAM
• *See page 101*

NASA VERMONT SPACE GRANT CONSORTIUM http://www.emba.uvm.edu/vsgc

VERMONT SPACE GRANT CONSORTIUM SCHOLARSHIP PROGRAM
• *See page 71*

NASA VIRGINIA SPACE GRANT CONSORTIUM http://www.vsgc.odu.edu

VIRGINIA SPACE GRANT CONSORTIUM TEACHER EDUCATION SCHOLARSHIPS
• *See page 102*

NASA WEST VIRGINIA SPACE GRANT CONSORTIUM http://www.nasa.wvu.edu

WEST VIRGINIA SPACE GRANT CONSORTIUM UNDERGRADUATE SCHOLARSHIP PROGRAM
• *See page 102*

NATIONAL ASSOCIATION FOR THE ADVANCEMENT OF COLORED PEOPLE http://www.naacp.org

HUBERTUS W.V. WILLEMS SCHOLARSHIP FOR MALE STUDENTS
• *See page 144*

LOUIS STOKES SCIENCE AND TECHNOLOGY AWARD
• *See page 114*

NATIONAL ASSOCIATION OF WATER COMPANIES-NEW JERSEY CHAPTER

NATIONAL ASSOCIATION OF WATER COMPANIES-NEW JERSEY CHAPTER SCHOLARSHIP
• *See page 115*

NATIONAL FEDERATION OF THE BLIND http://www.nfb.org

HOWARD BROWN RICKARD SCHOLARSHIP
• *See page 78*

NATIONAL INVENTORS HALL OF FAME http://www.invent.org/collegiate

COLLEGIATE INVENTORS COMPETITION - GRAND PRIZE
• *See page 71*

COLLEGIATE INVENTORS COMPETITION FOR UNDERGRADUATE STUDENTS
• *See page 71*

NATIONAL SECURITY AGENCY http://www.nsa.gov

NATIONAL SECURITY AGENCY STOKES EDUCATIONAL SCHOLARSHIP PROGRAM
• *See page 172*

NATIONAL SOCIETY OF BLACK PHYSICISTS http://www.nsbp.org

HARVEY WASHINGTON BANKS SCHOLARSHIP IN ASTRONOMY

One-time scholarship for student majoring in physics. Application available on Web site: http://www.nsbp.org

Academic Fields/Career Goals: Physical Sciences and Math.

Award: Scholarship for use in freshman, sophomore, junior, or senior years; not renewable. *Number:* 1. *Amount:* $1000.

Eligibility Requirements: Applicant must be enrolled or expecting to enroll full-time at a four-year institution. Available to U.S. citizens.

Application Requirements: Application, essay, references, transcript. *Deadline:* January 10.

Contact: Dr. Kennedy Reed, Scholarship Chairman
National Society of Black Physicists
6704G Lee Highway
Arlington, VA 22205
Phone: 703-536-4207
Fax: 703-536-4203
E-mail: scholarships@nsbp.org

MICHAEL P. ANDERSON SCHOLARSHIP IN SPACE SCIENCE

One-time scholarship for student majoring in physics. Application available on Web site: http://www.nsbp.org

Academic Fields/Career Goals: Physical Sciences and Math.

Award: Scholarship for use in freshman, sophomore, junior, or senior years; not renewable. *Number:* 1. *Amount:* $1000.

Eligibility Requirements: Applicant must be enrolled or expecting to enroll full-time at a four-year institution. Available to U.S. citizens.

Application Requirements: Application, essay, references, transcript. *Deadline:* January 10.

Contact: Dr. Kennedy Reed, Scholarship Chairman
National Society of Black Physicists
6704G Lee Highway
Arlington, VA 22205
Phone: 703-536-4207
Fax: 703-536-4203
E-mail: scholarships@nsbp.org

NATIONAL SOCIETY OF BLACK PHYSICISTS AND LAWRENCE LIVERMORE NATIONAL LIBRARY UNDERGRADUATE SCHOLARSHIP

Scholarship is available to graduating high school seniors and undergraduate students enrolled in a physics major. Scholarship is renewable up to four years if student maintains a 3.0 GPA and remains a physics major. Student required to intern one summer during scholarship period at Lawrence Livermore National Library. Application available on Web site: http://www.nsbp.org

Academic Fields/Career Goals: Physical Sciences and Math.

Award: Scholarship for use in freshman, sophomore, junior, or senior years; renewable. *Number:* 1. *Amount:* $5000.

Eligibility Requirements: Applicant must be enrolled or expecting to enroll full-time at a four-year institution. Applicant must have 3.0 GPA or higher. Available to U.S. citizens.

Application Requirements: Application, essay, references, transcript. *Deadline:* January 10.

Contact: Dr. Kennedy Reed, Scholarship Chairman
National Society of Black Physicists
6704G Lee Highway
Arlington, VA 22205
Phone: 703-536-4207
Fax: 703-536-4203
E-mail: scholarships@nsbp.org

RONALD E. MCNAIR SCHOLARSHIP IN SPACE AND OPTICAL PHYSICS

One-time scholarship for students majoring in physics. Application available on Web site: http://www.nsbp.org

Academic Fields/Career Goals: Physical Sciences and Math.

Award: Scholarship for use in freshman, sophomore, junior, or senior years; not renewable. *Number:* 1. *Amount:* $1000.

Eligibility Requirements: Applicant must be enrolled or expecting to enroll full-time at a four-year institution. Available to U.S. citizens.

Application Requirements: Application, essay, references, transcript. *Deadline:* January 10.

Contact: Dr. Kennedy Reed, Scholarship Chairman
National Society of Black Physicists
6704G Lee Highway
Arlington, VA 22205
Phone: 703-536-4207
Fax: 703-536-4203
E-mail: scholarships@nsbp.org

WALTER SAMUEL MCAFEE SCHOLARSHIP IN SPACE PHYSICS

One-time scholarship for student majoring in physics. Application available on Web site: http://www.nsbp.org

Academic Fields/Career Goals: Physical Sciences and Math.

Award: Scholarship for use in freshman, sophomore, junior, or senior years; not renewable. *Number:* 1. *Amount:* $1000.

Eligibility Requirements: Applicant must be enrolled or expecting to enroll full-time at a four-year institution. Available to U.S. citizens.

Application Requirements: Application, essay, references, transcript. *Deadline:* January 10.

Contact: Dr. Kennedy Reed, Scholarship Chairman
National Society of Black Physicists
6704G Lee Highway
Arlington, VA 22205
Phone: 703-536-4207
Fax: 703-536-4203
E-mail: scholarships@nsbp.org

WILLIE HOBBS MOORE, HARRY L. MORRISON, AND ARTHUR B.C. WALKER PHYSICS SCHOLARSHIPS

Scholarships are intended for undergraduate physics majors in their junior or senior year of college. Student should apply as a sophomore or junior. Application available on Web site: http://www.nsbp.org

Academic Fields/Career Goals: Physical Sciences and Math.

Award: Scholarship for use in sophomore or junior years; not renewable. *Number:* 3. *Amount:* $1000.

Eligibility Requirements: Applicant must be enrolled or expecting to enroll full-time at a four-year institution. Available to U.S. citizens.

Application Requirements: Application, essay, references, transcript. *Deadline:* January 10.

Contact: Dr. Kennedy Reed, Scholarship Chairman
National Society of Black Physicists
6704G Lee Highway
Arlington, VA 22205
Phone: 703-536-4207
Fax: 703-536-4203
E-mail: scholarships@nsbp.org

NEW JERSEY ACADEMY OF SCIENCE http://www.njas.org

NEW JERSEY ACADEMY OF SCIENCE RESEARCH GRANTS-IN-AID TO HIGH SCHOOL STUDENTS

• See page 116

NORTH CAROLINA STATE EDUCATION ASSISTANCE AUTHORITY http://www.cfnc.org

NORTH CAROLINA STUDENT LOAN PROGRAM FOR HEALTH, SCIENCE, AND MATHEMATICS

• See page 187

OREGON STUDENT ASSISTANCE COMMISSION http://www.osac.state.or.us

HOWARD VOLLUM AMERICAN INDIAN SCHOLARSHIP

• See page 172

PNC BANK TRUST DEPARTMENT

H. FLETCHER BROWN SCHOLARSHIP

• See page 187

POLANKI, POLISH WOMEN'S CULTURAL CLUB OF MILWAUKEE, WISCONSIN, U.S.A. http://www.polanki.org/

COPERNICUS AWARD

• See page 373

ROBERT H. MOLLOHAN FAMILY CHARITABLE FOUNDATION, INC. http://www.mollohanfoundation.org

HIGH TECHNOLOGY SCHOLARS PROGRAM

• See page 117

SOCIETY FOR IMAGING SCIENCE AND TECHNOLOGY http://www.imaging.org

RAYMOND DAVIS SCHOLARSHIP

• See page 249

SOCIETY OF WOMEN ENGINEERS http://www.swe.org/scholarships

SWE CALIFORNIA GOLDEN GATE SECTION SCHOLARSHIPS

• See page 174

SWE CONNECTICUT SECTION JEAN R. BEERS SCHOLARSHIP

• See page 174

TEXAS HIGHER EDUCATION COORDINATING BOARD http://www.collegefortexans.com

FIREFIGHTER EXEMPTION PROGRAM-TEXAS

• See page 72

TKE EDUCATIONAL FOUNDATION http://www.tkefoundation.org

CARROL C. HALL MEMORIAL SCHOLARSHIP

• See page 72

FRANCIS J. FLYNN MEMORIAL SCHOLARSHIP

• See page 214

UNITED NEGRO COLLEGE FUND http://www.uncf.org

ALFRED L. CHISHOLM SCHOLARSHIP

• See page 175

BOOZ, ALLEN & HAMILTON/WILLIAM F. STASIOR INTERNSHIP

• See page 130

HEINZ ENVIRONMENTAL FELLOWS PROGRAM

• See page 118

HOUSEHOLD INTERNATIONAL CORPORATE SCHOLARS

• See page 131

MERCK SCIENCE INITIATIVE

• See page 118

PECO ENERGY SCHOLARSHIP

• See page 50

SOUTHWESTERN BELL CORPORATION SCHOLARSHIP

• See page 133

SPRINT SCHOLARSHIP/INTERNSHIP

• See page 50

WYETH SCHOLARSHIP
• *See page 119*

UNIVERSITIES SPACE RESEARCH ASSOCIATION http://www.usra.edu/hq/scholarships/overview.shtml

UNIVERSITIES SPACE RESEARCH ASSOCIATION SCHOLARSHIP PROGRAM
• *See page 72*

VIRGINIA BUSINESS AND PROFESSIONAL WOMEN'S FOUNDATION http://www.bpwva.advocate.net/foundation.htm

WOMEN IN SCIENCE AND TECHNOLOGY SCHOLARSHIP
• *See page 119*

WISCONSIN FOUNDATION FOR INDEPENDENT COLLEGES, INC. http://www.wficweb.org

SENTRY 21 CLUB SCHOLARSHIP
• *See page 135*

XEROX http://xerox.com

TECHNICAL MINORITY SCHOLARSHIP
• *See page 148*

POLITICAL SCIENCE

AMERICAN FEDERATION OF STATE, COUNTY, AND MUNICIPAL EMPLOYEES http://www.afscme.org

JERRY CLARK MEMORIAL SCHOLARSHIP

Renewable award for a student majoring in political science for his or her junior and senior years of study. Must be a child of an AFSCME member. The recipient also will be given the opportunity to intern at the International Union headquarters. Minimum 3.0 GPA required. Once awarded, the scholarship will be renewed for the senior year provided the student remains enrolled full-time as a political science major. See Web site at http://www.afscme.org for further details. Application deadline is July 1.

Academic Fields/Career Goals: Political Science.

Award: Scholarship for use in junior or senior years; renewable. *Number:* 1. *Amount:* $10,000.

Eligibility Requirements: Applicant must be enrolled or expecting to enroll full-time at a four-year institution or university. Applicant or parent of applicant must be member of American Federation of State, County, and Municipal Employees. Applicant must have 3.0 GPA or higher. Available to U.S. citizens.

Application Requirements: Application, transcript. *Deadline:* July 1.

Contact: Genevieve Marcus, Scholarship Coordinator
American Federation of State, County, and Municipal Employees
1625 L Street, NW
Washington, DC 20036
Phone: 202-429-1250
Fax: 202-429-1272

AMERICAN HISTORICAL ASSOCIATION http://www.theaha.org

LITTLETON-GRISWOLD PRIZE
• *See page 310*

AMERICAN LEGION AUXILIARY, DEPARTMENT OF ARIZONA

AMERICAN LEGION AUXILIARY DEPARTMENT OF ARIZONA WILMA HOYAL-MAXINE CHILTON MEMORIAL SCHOLARSHIP

Annual scholarship to a student in second year or higher in one of the three state universities in Arizona. Must be enrolled in a program of study in political science, public programs, or special education. Must be a citizen of the U.S. and of Arizona for at least one year. Honorably discharged veterans or immediate family members are given preference.

Academic Fields/Career Goals: Political Science; Public Policy and Administration; Social Services; Special Education.

Award: Scholarship for use in sophomore, junior, senior, graduate, or postgraduate years; not renewable. *Number:* 1. *Amount:* $1000.

Eligibility Requirements: Applicant must be enrolled or expecting to enroll full-time at a two-year or four-year institution or university; resident of Arizona and studying in Arizona. Available to U.S. citizens.

Application Requirements: Application, autobiography, essay, financial need analysis, photo, references, test scores, transcript. *Deadline:* May 15.

Contact: Barbara Matteson, Department Secretary and Treasurer
American Legion Auxiliary, Department of Arizona
4701 North 19th Avenue, Suite 100
Phoenix, AZ 85015-3727
Phone: 602-241-1080
Fax: 602-604-9640
E-mail: amlegauxaz@mcleodusa.net

BOYS AND GIRLS CLUBS OF GREATER SAN DIEGO http://www.sdyouth.org

SPENCE REESE SCHOLARSHIP FUND
• *See page 242*

CENTRAL INTELLIGENCE AGENCY http://www.cia.gov

CENTRAL INTELLIGENCE AGENCY UNDERGRADUATE SCHOLARSHIP PROGRAM
• *See page 39*

COLLEGEBOUND FOUNDATION http://www.collegeboundfoundation.org

DECATUR H. MILLER SCHOLARSHIP
• *See page 310*

CUBAN AMERICAN NATIONAL FOUNDATION

MAS FAMILY SCHOLARSHIPS
• *See page 123*

GOVERNMENT FINANCE OFFICERS ASSOCIATION http://www.GFOA.org

MINORITIES IN GOVERNMENT FINANCE SCHOLARSHIP
• *See page 41*

GOVERNOR'S OFFICE

GOVERNOR'S OPPORTUNITY SCHOLARSHIP
• *See page 124*

HARRY S. TRUMAN LIBRARY INSTITUTE http://www.trumanlibrary.org

HARRY S. TRUMAN LIBRARY INSTITUTE UNDERGRADUATE STUDENT GRANT
• *See page 192*

MORRIS K. UDALL FOUNDATION http://www.udall.gov

MORRIS K. UDALL SCHOLARS
• *See page 59*

NATIONAL FEDERATION OF THE BLIND http://www.nfb.org

MICHAEL AND MARIE MARUCCI SCHOLARSHIP
• *See page 283*

NATIONAL FISH AND WILDLIFE FOUNDATION http://www.nfwf.org

BUDWEISER CONSERVATION SCHOLARSHIP PROGRAM
• *See page 115*

NATIONAL SOCIETY DAUGHTERS OF THE AMERICAN REVOLUTION http://www.dar.org

NATIONAL SOCIETY DAUGHTERS OF THE AMERICAN REVOLUTION ENID HALL GRISWOLD MEMORIAL SCHOLARSHIP

• *See page 193*

NATIONAL STONE, SAND AND GRAVEL ASSOCIATION (NSSGA) http://www.nssga.org

JENNIFER CURTIS BYLER SCHOLARSHIP FOR THE STUDY OF PUBLIC AFFAIRS

• *See page 162*

NATIONAL TOURISM FOUNDATION http://www.ntfonline.org

ACADEMY OF TRAVEL AND TOURISM SCHOLARSHIPS

• *See page 323*

TKE EDUCATIONAL FOUNDATION http://www.tkefoundation.org

BRUCE B. MELCHERT SCHOLARSHIP

One-time award of $400 given to an undergraduate member of Tau Kappa Epsilon with sophomore, junior, or senior standing. Applicant must be pursuing a degree in political science or government and have a record of leadership within his fraternity and other campus organizations. Should have as a goal to serve in a political or government position. Recent head and shoulders photograph must be submitted with application. Minimum 3.0 GPA required.

Academic Fields/Career Goals: Political Science.

Award: Scholarship for use in sophomore, junior, or senior years; not renewable. *Number:* 1. *Amount:* $400.

Eligibility Requirements: Applicant must be enrolled or expecting to enroll full-time at a four-year institution or university; male and must have an interest in leadership. Applicant must have 3.0 GPA or higher. Available to U.S. and non-U.S. citizens.

Application Requirements: Application, essay, photo, transcript. *Deadline:* May 15.

Contact: Tim Taschwer, President/CEO
TKE Educational Foundation
8645 Founders Road
Indianapolis, IN 46268-1393
Phone: 317-872-6533
Fax: 317-875-8353
E-mail: tef@tkehq.org

UNITED NEGRO COLLEGE FUND http://www.uncf.org

C-SPAN SCHOLARSHIP PROGRAM

• *See page 166*

SODEXHO SCHOLARSHIP

• *See page 304*

WASHINGTON NEWS COUNCIL http://www.wanewscouncil.org

DICK LARSEN SCHOLARSHIP PROGRAM

• *See page 167*

HERB ROBINSON SCHOLARSHIP PROGRAM

• *See page 168*

WISCONSIN FOUNDATION FOR INDEPENDENT COLLEGES, INC. http://www.wficweb.org

WE ENERGIES SCHOLARSHIP

• *See page 52*

PSYCHOLOGY

AMERICAN PSYCHOLOGICAL ASSOCIATION http://www.apa.org/mfp

MINORITY AGING NETWORK IN PSYCHOLOGY SUMMER INSTITUTE ON AGING

• *See page 292*

ASSOCIATION FOR WOMEN IN PSYCHOLOGY/ AMERICAN PSYCHOLOGICAL ASSOCIATION DIVISION 35

ANNUAL PRIZE FOR PSYCHOLOGICAL RESEARCH ON WOMEN AND GENDER BY GRADUATE OR UNDERGRADUATE STUDENTS

This prize recognizes outstanding psychology research on women or gender conducted by undergraduate or graduate students.

Academic Fields/Career Goals: Psychology.

Award: Prize for use in freshman, sophomore, junior, senior, or graduate years; not renewable. *Number:* 1. *Amount:* $200.

Eligibility Requirements: Applicant must be enrolled or expecting to enroll full or part-time at a four-year institution or university. Available to U.S. and non-U.S. citizens.

Application Requirements: Applicant must enter a contest, research paper. *Deadline:* April 1.

Contact: Britain Scott, Award Chair
Association for Women in Psychology/American Psychological Association Division 35
LL56 JRC
2115 Summit Avenue
St. Paul, MN 55105
Phone: 651-962-5039
E-mail: bascott@stthomas.edu

JEWISH FEDERATION OF METROPOLITAN CHICAGO (JFMC) http://www.jvschicago.org

JEWISH FEDERATION OF METROPOLITAN CHICAGO ACADEMIC SCHOLARSHIP PROGRAM

• *See page 185*

MENTAL HEALTH ASSOCIATION IN NEW YORK STATE, INC. http://www.mhanys.org

EDNA AIMES SCHOLARSHIP

• *See page 299*

MISSISSIPPI STATE STUDENT FINANCIAL AID http://www.mississippiuniversities.com

CRITICAL NEEDS TEACHER LOAN/SCHOLARSHIP

• *See page 206*

MISSISSIPPI HEALTH CARE PROFESSIONS LOAN/SCHOLARSHIP PROGRAM

• *See page 299*

NEW YORK STATE EDUCATION DEPARTMENT http://www.highered.nysed.gov

REGENTS PROFESSIONAL OPPORTUNITY SCHOLARSHIP

• *See page 45*

PILOT INTERNATIONAL FOUNDATION http://www.pilotinternational.org

PILOT INTERNATIONAL FOUNDATION RUBY NEWHALL MEMORIAL SCHOLARSHIP

• *See page 302*

PILOT INTERNATIONAL FOUNDATION SCHOLARSHIP PROGRAM

• *See page 302*

PILOT INTERNATIONAL FOUNDATION/LIFELINE SCHOLARSHIP PROGRAM

• *See page 302*

SUNSHINE LADY FOUNDATION, INC. http://www.sunshineladyfdn.org

COUNSELOR, ADVOCATE, AND SUPPORT STAFF SCHOLARSHIP PROGRAM
• See page 47

UNITED NEGRO COLLEGE FUND http://www.uncf.org

ROCKWELL/UNCF CORPORATE SCHOLARS PROGRAM
• See page 133

PUBLIC HEALTH

ASIAN PACIFIC AMERICAN HERITAGE COUNCIL http://www.apahc.org

ASIAN PACIFIC AMERICAN HERITAGE COUNCIL SCHOLARSHIP
• See page 121

MENTAL HEALTH ASSOCIATION IN NEW YORK STATE, INC. http://www.mhanys.org

EDNA AIMES SCHOLARSHIP
• See page 299

NATIONAL ENVIRONMENTAL HEALTH ASSOCIATION/AMERICAN ACADEMY OF SANITARIANS http://www.neha.org

NATIONAL ENVIRONMENTAL HEALTH ASSOCIATION/AMERICAN ACADEMY OF SANITARIANS SCHOLARSHIP
• See page 398

WASHINGTON HIGHER EDUCATION COORDINATING BOARD http://www.hecb.wa.gov

HEALTH PROFESSIONAL LOAN REPAYMENT AND SCHOLARSHIP PROGRAMS
• See page 188

PUBLIC POLICY AND ADMINISTRATION

AMERICAN LEGION AUXILIARY, DEPARTMENT OF ARIZONA

AMERICAN LEGION AUXILIARY DEPARTMENT OF ARIZONA WILMA HOYAL-MAXINE CHILTON MEMORIAL SCHOLARSHIP
• See page 410

RADIOLOGY

NORTON HEALTHCARE http://www.nortonhealthcare.com

NORTON HEALTHCARE SCHOLARS–METROPOLITAN COLLEGE
• See page 300

NORTON HEALTHCARE SCHOLARS–PRIVATE COLLEGES AND UNIVERSITIES
• See page 301

REAL ESTATE

APPRAISAL INSTITUTE http://www.appraisalinstitute.org

APPRAISAL INSTITUTE EDUCATIONAL SCHOLARSHIP PROGRAM

Award available to racial, ethnic and gender groups underrepresented in real estate appraisal or allied field, and to those who are disabled. Minimum 2.5 GPA required. Must demonstrate financial need.

Academic Fields/Career Goals: Real Estate.

Award: Scholarship for use in sophomore, junior, senior, or graduate years; not renewable. *Number:* up to 10. *Amount:* up to $1000.

Eligibility Requirements: Applicant must be enrolled or expecting to enroll full or part-time at a two-year or four-year institution or university. Applicant must have 2.5 GPA or higher. Available to U.S. and non-U.S. citizens.

Application Requirements: Application, essay, financial need analysis, references, transcript. *Deadline:* April 15.

Contact: Project Coordinator
Appraisal Institute
550 West Van Buren Street, Suite 1000
Chicago, IL 60607
Phone: 312-335-4121
Fax: 312-335-4200
E-mail: sbarnes@appraisalinstitute.org

ILLINOIS REAL ESTATE EDUCATIONAL FOUNDATION http://www.illinoisrealtor.org

ILLINOIS REAL ESTATE EDUCATIONAL FOUNDATION ACADEMIC SCHOLARSHIPS

Awards for Illinois residents attending an accredited two- or four-year junior college, college, or university in Illinois. Must have completed 30 college credit hours and be pursuing a degree with an emphasis in real estate. Must be a U.S. citizen. Minimum scholarship amount is $1000.

Academic Fields/Career Goals: Real Estate.

Award: Scholarship for use in sophomore, junior, or senior years; not renewable. *Number:* varies. *Amount:* $1000.

Eligibility Requirements: Applicant must be enrolled or expecting to enroll full-time at a two-year or four-year institution or university; resident of Illinois and studying in Illinois. Available to U.S. citizens.

Application Requirements: Application, essay, interview, references, transcript. *Deadline:* April 1.

Contact: Administrative Assistant
Illinois Real Estate Educational Foundation
3180 Adloff Lane
Springfield, IL 62703-9451
Phone: 217-529-2600
Fax: 217-529-3904

THOMAS F. SEAY SCHOLARSHIP

Minimum $2000 award to students pursuing a degree with an emphasis in real estate. Must be a U.S. citizen and attending any accredited U.S. college or university full-time. Must have completed at least 30 college credit hours. Minimum 3.5 GPA required.

Academic Fields/Career Goals: Real Estate.

Award: Scholarship for use in sophomore, junior, or senior years; not renewable. *Number:* varies. *Amount:* $2000.

Eligibility Requirements: Applicant must be enrolled or expecting to enroll full-time at a four-year institution or university. Applicant must have 3.5 GPA or higher. Available to U.S. citizens.

Application Requirements: Application, essay, interview, references, transcript. *Deadline:* April 1.

Contact: Administrative Assistant
Illinois Real Estate Educational Foundation
3180 Adloff Lane
Springfield, IL 62703
Phone: 217-529-2600
Fax: 217-529-3904

INSTITUTE OF REAL ESTATE MANAGEMENT FOUNDATION http://www.irem.org

GEORGE M. BROOKER COLLEGIATE SCHOLARSHIP FOR MINORITIES

One-time award for minority college juniors, seniors, and graduate students who are U.S. citizens and are committed to a career in real estate, specifically real estate management. Must have a minimum GPA of 3.0. Deadline is March 31.

Academic Fields/Career Goals: Real Estate.

Award: Scholarship for use in junior, senior, or graduate years; not renewable. *Number:* up to 3. *Amount:* $1000–$2500.

Eligibility Requirements: Applicant must be American Indian/Alaska Native, Asian/Pacific Islander, Black (non-Hispanic), or Hispanic and enrolled or expecting to enroll full-time at a four-year institution or university. Applicant must have 3.0 GPA or higher. Available to U.S. citizens.

Application Requirements: Application, essay, interview, references, transcript. *Deadline:* March 31.

Contact: Kimberly Holmes, Foundation Administrator
Institute of Real Estate Management Foundation
430 North Michigan Avenue, 7th Floor
Chicago, IL 60611-4090
Phone: 312-329-6008
Fax: 312-410-7908
E-mail: foundatn@irem.org

NEW JERSEY ASSOCIATION OF REALTORS

NEW JERSEY ASSOCIATION OF REALTORS EDUCATIONAL FOUNDATION SCHOLARSHIP PROGRAM

One-time awards for New Jersey residents who are high school seniors, college undergraduates, or graduate students pursuing studies in real estate or allied fields. Preference to students considering a career in real estate. Must be member of NJAR or relative of a member. Selected candidates are interviewed in June. Must be a U.S. citizen.

Academic Fields/Career Goals: Real Estate.

Award: Scholarship for use in freshman, sophomore, junior, senior, or graduate years; not renewable. *Number:* 20. *Amount:* $1000–$2000.

Eligibility Requirements: Applicant must be enrolled or expecting to enroll full-time at a four-year institution or university and resident of New Jersey. Available to U.S. citizens.

Application Requirements: Application, essay, financial need analysis, interview, transcript. *Deadline:* April 25.

Contact: Diane Hatley, Educational Foundation
New Jersey Association of Realtors
PO Box 2098
Edison, NJ 08818
Phone: 732-494-5616
Fax: 732-494-4723

OREGON STUDENT ASSISTANCE COMMISSION http://www.osac.state.or.us

HOMESTEAD CAPITAL HOUSING SCHOLARSHIP

• *See page 46*

RECREATION, PARKS, LEISURE STUDIES

AMERICAN ALLIANCE FOR HEALTH, PHYSICAL EDUCATION, RECREATION AND DANCE http://www.aahperd.org

ROBERT W. CRAWFORD STUDENT LITERARY AWARD

Award for writing excellence recognizes an undergraduate or graduate student enrolled or majoring in recreation, parks, and leisure studies at an accredited university, college, or community college. Manuscripts must be related to parks, recreation, and leisure to be eligible.

Academic Fields/Career Goals: Recreation, Parks, Leisure Studies.

Award: Scholarship for use in freshman, sophomore, junior, senior, or graduate years; not renewable. *Number:* 2. *Amount:* $500.

Eligibility Requirements: Applicant must be enrolled or expecting to enroll full or part-time at a two-year or four-year institution or university. Available to U.S. and non-U.S. citizens.

Application Requirements: Application, essay, resume, faculty sponsor. *Deadline:* April 15.

Contact: Vicki Clary, Program Coordinator
American Alliance for Health, Physical Education, Recreation and Dance
1900 Association Drive
Reston, VA 20191
Phone: 703-476-3472
Fax: 703-476-9527
E-mail: aalr@aahperd.org

CANADIAN RECREATIONAL CANOEING ASSOCIATION http://www.paddlingcanada.com

BILL MASON MEMORIAL SCHOLARSHIP FUND

• *See page 57*

MAINE CAMPGROUND OWNERS ASSOCIATION http://www.campmaine.com

MAINE CAMPGROUND OWNERS ASSOCIATION SCHOLARSHIP

• *See page 369*

RELIGION/THEOLOGY

AMERICAN SCHOOL OF CLASSICAL STUDIES AT ATHENS http://www.ascsa.edu.gr

ASCSA SUMMER SESSIONS

• *See page 65*

BANK OF AMERICA

WILLIAM HEATH EDUCATION SCHOLARSHIP FOR MINISTERS, PRIESTS AND MISSIONARIES

One-time award available to male students who are graduates from a high school in Alabama, Florida, Georgia, Kentucky, Louisiana, Maryland, Mississippi, North Carolina, South Carolina, Tennessee, Virginia or West Virginia. Students must be under age 35 and pursuing an undergraduate or graduate degree in order to serve in the ministry, as a missionary or as a social worker. Primary consideration is given to those candidates who are of the Methodist or Episcopalian denominations.

Academic Fields/Career Goals: Religion/Theology; Social Services.

Award: Scholarship for use in sophomore, junior, senior, or graduate years; not renewable. *Amount:* $100–$350.

Eligibility Requirements: Applicant must be Episcopalian or Methodist; age 35 or under; enrolled or expecting to enroll full or part-time at a two-year or four-year institution or university; male and resident of Alabama, Florida, Georgia, Kentucky, Louisiana, Maryland, Mississippi, North Carolina, South Carolina, Tennessee, Virginia, or West Virginia. Available to U.S. citizens.

Application Requirements: Application, essay, references, transcript, high school diploma, birth certificate. *Deadline:* June 30.

Contact: Lori J. Nichols, Relationship Associate
Bank of America
600 Cleveland Street, 3rd Floor
Clearwater, FL 33755
Phone: 727-298-5935
Fax: 727-298-5940
E-mail: lori.j.nichols@bankofamerica.com

BROSS PRIZE FOUNDATION

BROSS PRIZE

The Bross Prize is a scholarly award presented once every ten years to the author who, in the opinion of a panel of judges, has written the best book or treatise on the relation between any discipline or topic of investigation and the Christian religion. Next deadline: September 1, 2010.

Academic Fields/Career Goals: Religion/Theology.

Award: Prize for use in freshman, sophomore, junior, senior, graduate, or postgraduate years; not renewable. *Number:* 1. *Amount:* $4000–$15,000.

Bross Prize Foundation (continued)

Eligibility Requirements: Applicant must be enrolled or expecting to enroll full or part-time at a two-year or four-year or technical institution or university. Available to U.S. and non-U.S. citizens.

Application Requirements: Applicant must enter a contest, manuscript (minimum of 50,000 words). *Deadline:* September 1.

Contact: Ronald H. Miller
Bross Prize Foundation
555 North Sheridan Road, Religion Department
Lake Forest, IL 60045
Phone: 847-735-5175
E-mail: rmiller@lfc.edu

CATHOLIC KNIGHTS OF AMERICA http://ckoa.com

VOCATIONAL SCHOLARSHIP PROGRAM

Vocational scholarships are available for qualifying men and women seeking to enter Roman Catholic religious life. Enrollment in an accredited educational institute is a must. Religious activities, financial need and recommendation by the church are considered when selecting scholarship winners. Minimum 2.5 GPA required. Applicant must not be married.

Academic Fields/Career Goals: Religion/Theology; Social Services.

Award: Grant for use in freshman, sophomore, junior, senior, or graduate years; not renewable. *Number:* 5–12. *Amount:* $100–$250.

Eligibility Requirements: Applicant must be Roman Catholic; enrolled or expecting to enroll full-time at a four-year institution or university; single and resident of Arkansas, District of Columbia, Indiana, Louisiana, Missouri, New Mexico, Ohio, Pennsylvania, Tennessee, Texas, or West Virginia. Applicant must have 2.5 GPA or higher. Available to U.S. citizens.

Application Requirements: Application, essay, financial need analysis, references. *Deadline:* May 1.

Contact: Christina Knott, Fraternal Communications Supervisor
Catholic Knights of America
3525 Hampton Avenue
St. Louis, MO 63139-1908
Phone: 314-351-1029 Ext. 12
Fax: 314-351-9937
E-mail: christina.knott@ckoa.com

DISCIPLES OF CHRIST HOMELAND MINISTRIES http://www.discipleshomemissions.org

DAVID TAMOTSU KAGIWADA MEMORIAL SCHOLARSHIP

$2000 scholarship available to Asian-American ministerial students. Must be a member of the Christian Church (Disciples of Christ), demonstrate financial need, have a C+ average, be a full-time student, and be under care of a regional Commission on the Ministry. Application may be submitted electronically. Deadline March 15.

Academic Fields/Career Goals: Religion/Theology.

Award: Scholarship for use in freshman, sophomore, junior, or senior years; not renewable. *Number:* varies. *Amount:* $2000.

Eligibility Requirements: Applicant must be Disciple of Christ; Asian/Pacific Islander and enrolled or expecting to enroll full-time at a two-year or four-year institution or university. Applicant must have 2.5 GPA or higher. Available to U.S. citizens.

Application Requirements: Application, financial need analysis, references, transcript. *Deadline:* March 15.

Contact: Administrative Assistant
Disciples of Christ Homeland Ministries
PO Box 1986
Indianapolis, IN 46206-1986
Phone: 888-346-2631
Fax: 317-635-4426
E-mail: gdurham@dhm.disciples.org

DISCIPLE CHAPLAINS' SCHOLARSHIP

$2000 scholarship available to first year seminarians. Must be a member of the Christian Church (Disciples of Christ), demonstrate financial need, have a C+ average, be a full-time student, and be under the care of a regional Commission on the Ministry. Application may be submitted electronically. Deadline March 15.

Academic Fields/Career Goals: Religion/Theology.

Award: Scholarship for use in freshman year; not renewable. *Number:* varies. *Amount:* $2000.

Eligibility Requirements: Applicant must be Disciple of Christ and enrolled or expecting to enroll full-time at an institution or university. Applicant must have 2.5 GPA or higher. Available to U.S. and non-U.S. citizens.

Application Requirements: Application, financial need analysis, references, transcript. *Deadline:* March 15.

Contact: Administrative Assistant
Disciples of Christ Homeland Ministries
PO Box 1986
Indianapolis, IN 46206-1986
Phone: 888-346-2631
Fax: 317-635-4426
E-mail: gdurham@dhm.disciples.org

EDWIN G. AND LAURETTA M. MICHAEL SCHOLARSHIP

$2000 scholarship available to ministers' wives. Must be a member of the Christian Church (Disciples of Christ), demonstrate financial need, have a C+ average, be a full-time student, and be under the care of a regional Commission on the Ministry. Application may be submitted electronically. Deadline March 15.

Academic Fields/Career Goals: Religion/Theology.

Award: Scholarship for use in freshman, sophomore, junior, or senior years; not renewable. *Number:* varies. *Amount:* $2000.

Eligibility Requirements: Applicant must be Disciple of Christ; enrolled or expecting to enroll full-time at a two-year or four-year institution or university and married female. Applicant must have 2.5 GPA or higher. Available to U.S. and non-U.S. citizens.

Application Requirements: Application, financial need analysis, references, transcript. *Deadline:* March 15.

Contact: Administrative Assistant
Disciples of Christ Homeland Ministries
PO Box 1986
Indianapolis, IN 46206-1986
Phone: 888-346-2631
Fax: 317-635-4426
E-mail: gdurham@dhm.disciples.org

KATHERINE J. SHUTZE MEMORIAL SCHOLARSHIP

$2000 scholarship available to female seminary students. Must be a member of the Christian Church (Disciples of Christ), demonstrate financial need, have a C+ average, be a full-time student, and be under the care of a regional Commission on the Ministry. Application may be submitted electronically. Deadline March 15.

Academic Fields/Career Goals: Religion/Theology.

Award: Scholarship for use in freshman, sophomore, junior, or senior years; not renewable. *Number:* varies. *Amount:* $2000.

Eligibility Requirements: Applicant must be Disciple of Christ; enrolled or expecting to enroll full-time at an institution or university and female. Applicant must have 2.5 GPA or higher. Available to U.S. and non-U.S. citizens.

Application Requirements: Application, financial need analysis, references, transcript. *Deadline:* March 15.

Contact: Administrative Assistant
Disciples of Christ Homeland Ministries
PO Box 1986
Indianapolis, IN 46206-1986
Phone: 888-346-2631
Fax: 317-635-4426
E-mail: gdurham@dhm.disciples.org

ROWLEY/MINISTERIAL EDUCATION SCHOLARSHIP

$2000 scholarship available to seminary students preparing for the ministry. Must be a member of the Christian Church (Disciples of Christ), demonstrate financial need, have a C+ average, be a full-time student and be under the care of a regional Commission on the Ministry. Application may be submitted electronically. Deadline March 15.

Academic Fields/Career Goals: Religion/Theology.

Award: Scholarship for use in freshman, sophomore, junior, senior, or graduate years; not renewable. *Number:* varies. *Amount:* $2000.

Eligibility Requirements: Applicant must be Disciple of Christ and enrolled or expecting to enroll full-time at a two-year or four-year institution or university. Applicant must have 2.5 GPA or higher. Available to U.S. and non-U.S. citizens.

Application Requirements: Application, financial need analysis, references, transcript. *Deadline:* March 15.

Contact: Administrative Assistant
Disciples of Christ Homeland Ministries
PO Box 1986
Indianapolis, IN 46206-1986
Phone: 888-346-2631
Fax: 317-635-4426
E-mail: gdurham@dhm.disciples.org

STAR SUPPORTER SCHOLARSHIP/LOAN

Scholarships in the form of forgivable loans are available to Black/African-Americans preparing for ministry. One year of full-time professional ministry reduces loan by one third. Three years of service repays loan. Must be member of the Christian Church (Disciples of Christ), have a C+ average, demonstrate financial need, be a full-time student in an accredited school or seminary and be under the care of a regional Commission on the Ministry. Application may be submitted electronically. Deadline March 15.

Academic Fields/Career Goals: Religion/Theology.

Award: Forgivable loan for use in freshman, sophomore, junior, or senior years; not renewable. *Number:* varies. *Amount:* $2000.

Eligibility Requirements: Applicant must be Disciple of Christ; Black (non-Hispanic) and enrolled or expecting to enroll full-time at a two-year or four-year institution or university. Applicant must have 2.5 GPA or higher. Available to U.S. citizens.

Application Requirements: Application, financial need analysis, references, transcript. *Deadline:* March 15.

Contact: Administrative Assistant
Disciples of Christ Homeland Ministries
PO Box 1986
Indianapolis, IN 46206-1986
Phone: 888-346-2631
Fax: 317-635-4426
E-mail: gdurham@dhm.disciples.org

ED E. AND GLADYS HURLEY FOUNDATION

ED E. AND GLADYS HURLEY FOUNDATION SCHOLARSHIP

The Hurley Foundation provides scholarships (maximum of $1,000/year per student) to worthy and deserving young men and women, residing in any state, who wish to study at a school within the State of Texas to become ministers, missionaries or religious workers of the Protestant faith. Contact institution's financial aid office for more information.

Academic Fields/Career Goals: Religion/Theology.

Award: Scholarship for use in freshman, sophomore, junior, senior, graduate, or postgraduate years; not renewable. *Number:* 100–150. *Amount:* up to $1000.

Eligibility Requirements: Applicant must be Protestant; enrolled or expecting to enroll full or part-time at a two-year or four-year institution or university and studying in Texas. Available to U.S. citizens.

Application Requirements: Application, financial need analysis, references. *Deadline:* April 30.

Contact: Financial Aid Office at school for application

FIRST PRESBYTERIAN CHURCH http://www.firstchurchtulsa.org

FIRST PRESBYTERIAN CHURCH SCHOLARSHIP PROGRAM

Awards to students pursuing full-time study at an accredited college, university or seminary. Preference given to church members in Tulsa, East Oklahoma, Synod of Sun, and at-large. Minimum 2.0 GPA. Must be a communicant member of the Presbyterian Church (U.S.A.).

Academic Fields/Career Goals: Religion/Theology.

Award: Scholarship for use in freshman, sophomore, junior, senior, or graduate years; not renewable. *Number:* 3–5. *Amount:* $500–$2000.

Eligibility Requirements: Applicant must be Presbyterian and enrolled or expecting to enroll full-time at a four-year institution or university. Available to U.S. citizens.

Application Requirements: Application, financial need analysis, interview, references, transcript. *Deadline:* April 15.

Contact: Tonye Briscoe, Administrative Assistant
First Presbyterian Church
709 South Boston Avenue
Tulsa, OK 74119-1629
Phone: 918-584-4701 Ext. 240
Fax: 918-584-5233
E-mail: tbriscoe@firstchurchtulsa.org

GRAND CHAPTER OF CALIFORNIA-ORDER OF THE EASTERN STAR http://www.oescal.org

SCHOLARSHIPS FOR EDUCATION, BUSINESS AND RELIGION

• *See page 125*

HAROLD B. & DOROTHY A. SNYDER FOUNDATION, INC.

HAROLD B. AND DOROTHY A. SNYDER FOUNDATION, INC., PROGRAM

• *See page 141*

JEWISH FEDERATION OF METROPOLITAN CHICAGO (JFMC) http://www.jvschicago.org

JEWISH FEDERATION OF METROPOLITAN CHICAGO ACADEMIC SCHOLARSHIP PROGRAM

• *See page 185*

MARY E. BIVINS FOUNDATION http://www.bivinsfoundation.org

MARY E. BIVINS RELIGIOUS SCHOLARSHIP

Scholarships provided to individuals who are permanent residents of the Texas Panhandle pursuing an undergraduate or graduate degree in a field preparing them to preach the Christian religion. Write for details.

Academic Fields/Career Goals: Religion/Theology.

Award: Scholarship for use in freshman, sophomore, junior, senior, or graduate years; not renewable. *Number:* 50–75. *Amount:* up to $3000.

Eligibility Requirements: Applicant must be Christian; enrolled or expecting to enroll full-time at a two-year or four-year institution or university and resident of Texas. Applicant must have 2.5 GPA or higher. Available to U.S. citizens.

Application Requirements: Application, essay, references, test scores, transcript, proof of residence. *Deadline:* varies.

Contact: Linda Pitner, Grant and Scholarship Program Coordinator
Mary E. Bivins Foundation
PO Box 1727
Amarillo, TX 79105
Phone: 806-379-9400
Fax: 806-379-9404
E-mail: linda@bivinsfoundation.org

MEMORIAL FOUNDATION FOR JEWISH CULTURE http://www.mfjc.org

MEMORIAL FOUNDATION FOR JEWISH CULTURE INTERNATIONAL SCHOLARSHIP PROGRAM FOR COMMUNITY SERVICE

• *See page 82*

MENNONITE EDUCATION AGENCY

RACIAL/ETHNIC LEADERSHIP EDUCATION (RELE)

• *See page 398*

NATIONAL ASSOCIATION OF PASTORAL MUSICIANS http://www.npm.org

ELAINE RENDLER-RENE DOSOGNE-GEORGETOWN CHORALE SCHOLARSHIP
• See page 365

FUNK FAMILY MEMORIAL SCHOLARSHIP
• See page 365

GIA PUBLICATION PASTORAL MUSICIAN SCHOLARSHIP
• See page 365

MUSONICS SCHOLARSHIP
• See page 365

NATIONAL ASSOCIATION OF PASTORAL MUSICIANS MEMBERS' SCHOLARSHIP
• See page 365

NPM KOINONIA/BOARD OF DIRECTORS SCHOLARSHIP
• See page 365

NPM PERROT SCHOLARSHIP
• See page 366

OREGON CATHOLIC PRESS SCHOLARSHIP
• See page 366

PALUCH FAMILY FOUNDATION/WORLD LIBRARY PUBLICATIONS SCHOLARSHIP
• See page 366

OREGON STUDENT ASSISTANCE COMMISSION http://www.osac.state.or.us

FRANKS FOUNDATION SCHOLARSHIP
• See page 392

SOUTHERN BAPTIST HISTORICAL LIBRARY AND ARCHIVES http://www.sbhla.org

LYNN E. MAY, JR. STUDY GRANT
• See page 312

UNITED METHODIST CHURCH http://www.umc.org/

ERNEST AND EURICE MILLER BASS SCHOLARSHIP FUND

One-time award for undergraduate student enrolled at an accredited institution and entering United Methodist Church ministry as a deacon or elder. Must be an active member of United Methodist Church for at least one year. Merit-based award. Minimum 3.0 GPA required.

Academic Fields/Career Goals: Religion/Theology.

Award: Scholarship for use in freshman, sophomore, junior, or senior years; not renewable. *Number:* 55–60. *Amount:* $800–$1000.

Eligibility Requirements: Applicant must be Methodist and enrolled or expecting to enroll full-time at a two-year or four-year institution or university. Applicant must have 3.0 GPA or higher. Available to U.S. citizens.

Application Requirements: Application, essay, references, transcript. *Deadline:* June 1.

Contact: Patti J. Zimmerman, Scholarships Administrator
United Methodist Church
PO Box 34007
Nashville, TN 37203-0007
Phone: 615-340-7344
E-mail: pzimmer@gbhem.org

UNITED METHODIST COMMUNICATIONS http://www.umcom.org/scholarships

LEONARD M. PERRYMAN COMMUNICATIONS SCHOLARSHIP FOR ETHNIC MINORITY STUDENTS
• See page 166

UNITED NEGRO COLLEGE FUND http://www.uncf.org

DR. JOE RATLIFF CHALLENGE SCHOLARSHIP

Scholarship awarded to students attending a UNCF member college or university who are majoring in religion/theological studies. Minimum 2.5 GPA required. Prospective applicants should complete the Student Profile found at Web site: http://www.uncf.org.

Academic Fields/Career Goals: Religion/Theology.

Award: Scholarship for use in freshman, sophomore, junior, or senior years; not renewable. *Amount:* up to $3000.

Eligibility Requirements: Applicant must be Black (non-Hispanic) and enrolled or expecting to enroll at a four-year institution or university. Applicant must have 2.5 GPA or higher.

Application Requirements: Application, financial need analysis. *Deadline:* Continuous.

Contact: Program Services Department
United Negro College Fund
8260 Willow Oaks Corporate Drive
Fairfax, VA 22031

UNITED SOCIETY OF FRIENDS WOMEN, INC.

JOHN SARRIN SCHOLARSHIP FUND

Scholarship provided for those studying for full-time Christian ministry who are members of the Friends (Quaker) Church, or children of friends ministers in under-graduate studies.

Academic Fields/Career Goals: Religion/Theology.

Award: Scholarship for use in freshman, sophomore, junior, senior, or graduate years; not renewable. *Number:* varies. *Amount:* $250–$2000.

Eligibility Requirements: Applicant must be Friends and enrolled or expecting to enroll full or part-time at a two-year or four-year or technical institution or university. Applicant or parent of applicant must have employment or volunteer experience in designated career field. Available to U.S. and non-U.S. citizens.

Application Requirements: Application, photo, transcript. *Deadline:* January 1.

Contact: Winifred Enyart
United Society of Friends Women, Inc.
1730 Hickory Lane
Greenfield, IN 46140-2529
Phone: 317-462-3861

SCIENCE, TECHNOLOGY, AND SOCIETY

AMERICAN CHEMICAL SOCIETY, RUBBER DIVISION http://www.rubber.org/awards/scholarships.htm

AMERICAN CHEMICAL SOCIETY, RUBBER DIVISION-UNDERGRADUATE SCHOLARSHIP
• See page 136

AMERICAN INSTITUTE OF AERONAUTICS AND ASTRONAUTICS http://www.aiaa.org

AIAA UNDERGRADUATE SCHOLARSHIP
• See page 66

ARIZONA HYDROLOGICAL SOCIETY http://www.azhydrosoc.org

ARIZONA HYDROLOGICAL SURVEY STUDENT SCHOLARSHIP
• See page 189

ARMED FORCES COMMUNICATIONS AND ELECTRONICS ASSOCIATION, EDUCATIONAL FOUNDATION http://www.afcea.org

VICE ADMIRAL JERRY O. TUTTLE, USN (RET.) AND MRS. BARBARA A. TUTTLE SCIENCE AND TECHNOLOGY SCHOLARSHIP
• See page 228

CATCHING THE DREAM

MATH, ENGINEERING, SCIENCE, BUSINESS, EDUCATION, COMPUTERS SCHOLARSHIPS
• See page 121

NATIVE AMERICAN LEADERSHIP IN EDUCATION (NALE)
• See page 122

EXPLORERS CLUB http://www.explorers.org

YOUTH ACTIVITY FUND
• See page 372

GEORGE BIRD GRINNELL AMERICAN INDIAN FUND

AL QOYAWAYMA AWARD
• See page 141

GOVERNOR'S OFFICE

GOVERNOR'S OPPORTUNITY SCHOLARSHIP
• See page 124

GREATER KANAWHA VALLEY FOUNDATION http://www.tgkvf.org

MATH AND SCIENCE SCHOLARSHIP
• See page 244

HEALTHCARE INFORMATION AND MANAGEMENT SYSTEMS SOCIETY FOUNDATION http://www.himss.org

HIMSS FOUNDATION SCHOLARSHIP PROGRAM
• See page 288

HISPANIC SCHOLARSHIP FUND http://www.hsf.net

HSF/SOCIETY OF HISPANIC PROFESSIONAL ENGINEERS, INC. SCHOLARSHIP PROGRAM
• See page 152

INNOVATION AND SCIENCE COUNCIL OF BRITISH COLUMBIA http://www.scbc.org

IBM SCHOLARSHIP
• See page 171

PAUL AND HELEN TRUSSEL SCIENCE AND TECHNOLOGY SCHOLARSHIP
• See page 69

KOREAN-AMERICAN SCIENTISTS AND ENGINEERS ASSOCIATION http://www.ksea.org

KSEA SCHOLARSHIPS
• See page 221

MICRON TECHNOLOGY FOUNDATION, INC. http://www.micron.com/scholars

MICRON SCIENCE AND TECHNOLOGY SCHOLARS PROGRAM
• See page 144

MIDWEST ROOFING CONTRACTORS ASSOCIATION http://www.mrca.org

MRCA FOUNDATION SCHOLARSHIP PROGRAM
• See page 70

NASA DELAWARE SPACE GRANT CONSORTIUM http://www.delspace.org

NASA DELAWARE SPACE GRANT UNDERGRADUATE TUITION SCHOLARSHIP
• See page 70

NASA IDAHO SPACE GRANT CONSORTIUM http://www.uidaho.edu/nasa_isgc

NASA IDAHO SPACE GRANT CONSORTIUM SCHOLARSHIP PROGRAM
• See page 71

NASA NEBRASKA SPACE GRANT CONSORTIUM http://nasa.unomaha.edu

NASA NEBRASKA SPACE GRANT
• See page 101

NEW JERSEY ACADEMY OF SCIENCE http://www.njas.org

NEW JERSEY ACADEMY OF SCIENCE RESEARCH GRANTS-IN-AID TO HIGH SCHOOL STUDENTS
• See page 116

PENNSYLVANIA HIGHER EDUCATION ASSISTANCE AGENCY http://www.pheaa.org

NEW ECONOMY TECHNOLOGY SCHOLARSHIPS

Renewable award for Pennsylvania residents pursuing a degree in science or technology at a PHEAA-approved Pennsylvania school. Must maintain minimum 3.0 GPA. Must commence employment in Pennsylvania in field related to student's program within one year after completion of studies. Must work one year for each year scholarship was awarded.

Academic Fields/Career Goals: Science, Technology, and Society.

Award: Scholarship for use in freshman, sophomore, junior, or senior years; renewable. *Number:* varies. *Amount:* up to $3000.

Eligibility Requirements: Applicant must be enrolled or expecting to enroll full or part-time at a two-year or four-year or technical institution; resident of Pennsylvania and studying in Pennsylvania. Applicant must have 3.0 GPA or higher.

Application Requirements: Application, FAFSA. *Deadline:* December 31.

Contact: PHEAA State Grant and Special Programs Division
Pennsylvania Higher Education Assistance Agency
1200 North Seventh Street
Harrisburg, PA 17102-1444
Phone: 800-692-7392

SEASPACE, INC. http://www.seaspace.org

SEASPACE SCHOLARSHIP PROGRAM

One-time award open to college junior/senior or graduate students pursuing degrees in the marine/aquatic sciences. Must be enrolled full-time with a minimum overall GPA of 3.3/4.0. Must be enrolled in an accredited U.S. institution. Must demonstrate financial need.

Academic Fields/Career Goals: Science, Technology, and Society.

Award: Scholarship for use in junior, senior, or graduate years; not renewable. *Number:* 10–15. *Amount:* $500–$3000.

Eligibility Requirements: Applicant must be enrolled or expecting to enroll full-time at a four-year institution or university. Available to U.S. and non-U.S. citizens.

Application Requirements: Application, financial need analysis, self-addressed stamped envelope, transcript. *Deadline:* February 1.

Contact: Carolyn Peterson, Scholarship Co-Chair
Seaspace, Inc.
PO Box 3753
Houston, TX 77253-3753
E-mail: sscholarships@piovere.com

SOCIETY OF AUTOMOTIVE ENGINEERS http://www.sae.org/students/stuschol.htm

DETROIT SECTION SAE TECHNICAL SCHOLARSHIP
• See page 232

SOCIETY OF HISPANIC PROFESSIONAL ENGINEERS FOUNDATION http://www.shpefoundation.org

SOCIETY OF HISPANIC PROFESSIONAL ENGINEERS FOUNDATION
• See page 146

SOCIETY OF MEXICAN AMERICAN ENGINEERS AND SCIENTISTS http://www.maes-natl.org

GRE AND GRADUATE APPLICATIONS WAIVER
• See page 72

UNITED NEGRO COLLEGE FUND http://www.uncf.org

CHARLES E. CULPEPPER SCHOLARSHIP
• See page 304

UNIVERSITIES SPACE RESEARCH ASSOCIATION http://www.usra.edu/hq/scholarships/overview.shtml

UNIVERSITIES SPACE RESEARCH ASSOCIATION SCHOLARSHIP PROGRAM
• See page 72

VIRGINIA BUSINESS AND PROFESSIONAL WOMEN'S FOUNDATION http://www.bpwva.advocate.net/foundation.htm

WOMEN IN SCIENCE AND TECHNOLOGY SCHOLARSHIP
• See page 119

WEST VIRGINIA HIGHER EDUCATION POLICY COMMISSION-OFFICE OF FINANCIAL AID AND OUTREACH SERVICES http://www.hepc.wvnet.edu

WEST VIRGINIA ENGINEERING, SCIENCE & TECHNOLOGY SCHOLARSHIP PROGRAM
• See page 223

SOCIAL SCIENCES

AMERICAN ASSOCIATION FOR PUBLIC OPINION RESEARCH http://www.aapor.org

SEYMOUR SUDMAN STUDENT PAPER PRIZE

One-time award open to undergraduate or graduate students for a paper broadly related to the study of public opinion or to the theory and methods of survey and market research. Entries should be 15 to 25 pages in length. For more information see Web site at http://www.aapor.org. Application deadline is December 12.

Academic Fields/Career Goals: Social Sciences.

Award: Prize for use in freshman, sophomore, junior, senior, or graduate years; not renewable. *Number:* 1. *Amount:* $500.

Eligibility Requirements: Applicant must be enrolled or expecting to enroll full-time at a two-year or four-year institution or university. Available to U.S. and non-U.S. citizens.

Application Requirements: *Deadline:* December 12.

Contact: Michael Flanagan, Executive Coordinator
American Association for Public Opinion Research
8310 Nieman Road
Lenexa, KS 66214-1579
Phone: 913-495-4470
Fax: 913-599-5340
E-mail: mflanagan@goamp.com

AMERICAN CRIMINAL JUSTICE ASSOCIATION-LAMBDA ALPHA EPSILON http://www.acjalae.org

AMERICAN CRIMINAL JUSTICE ASSOCIATION-LAMBDA ALPHA EPSILON NATIONAL SCHOLARSHIP
• See page 177

AMERICAN HISTORICAL ASSOCIATION http://www.theaha.org

JOAN KELLY MEMORIAL PRIZE IN WOMEN'S HISTORY
• See page 309

LITTLETON-GRISWOLD PRIZE
• See page 310

AMERICAN PSYCHOLOGICAL ASSOCIATION http://www.apa.org/mfp

MINORITY AGING NETWORK IN PSYCHOLOGY SUMMER INSTITUTE ON AGING
• See page 292

AMERICAN SOCIETY OF CRIMINOLOGY http://www.ASC41.com

AMERICAN SOCIETY OF CRIMINOLOGY GENE CARTE STUDENT PAPER COMPETITION
• See page 178

ASPEN INSTITUTE http://www.nonprofitresearch.org/

WILLIAM RANDOLPH HEARST ENDOWED SCHOLARSHIP FOR MINORITY STUDENTS
• See page 324

BUSINESS AND PROFESSIONAL WOMEN'S FOUNDATION http://www.bpwusa.org

BPW CAREER ADVANCEMENT SCHOLARSHIP PROGRAM FOR WOMEN
• See page 112

CANADIAN INSTITUTE OF UKRAINIAN STUDIES http://www.ualberta.ca/cius/

LEO J. KRYSA UNDERGRADUATE SCHOLARSHIP
• See page 80

CATCHING THE DREAM

MATH, ENGINEERING, SCIENCE, BUSINESS, EDUCATION, COMPUTERS SCHOLARSHIPS
• See page 121

CENTER FOR LESBIAN AND GAY STUDIES (C.L.A.G.S.) http://www.clags.org

CENTER FOR GAY AND LESBIAN STUDIES UNDERGRADUATE PAPER AWARDS
• See page 346

CHINESE HISTORICAL SOCIETY OF SOUTHERN CALIFORNIA http://www.chssc.org

CHSSC SCHOLARSHIP AWARD
• See page 324

CIRI FOUNDATION http://www.ciri.com/tcf

LAWRENCE MATSON MEMORIAL ENDOWMENT SCHOLARSHIP FUND
• See page 86

COLLEGEBOUND FOUNDATION http://www.collegeboundfoundation.org

JEANETTE R. WOLMAN SCHOLARSHIP
• See page 343

IRISH-AMERICAN CULTURAL INSTITUTE http://www.iaci-usa.org

IRISH RESEARCH FUNDS
• See page 82

JAPAN STUDIES SCHOLARSHIP FOUNDATION COMMITTEE

JAPAN STUDIES SCHOLARSHIP
• See page 283

MARIN EDUCATION FUND http://www.marineducationfund.org

GOLDMAN FAMILY FUND, NEW LEADER SCHOLARSHIP
• See page 186

NATIONAL BLACK POLICE ASSOCIATION

http://www.blackpolice.org

ALPHONSO DEAL SCHOLARSHIP AWARD

• *See page 179*

NATIONAL INSTITUTES OF HEALTH

http://ugsp.info.nih.gov

NIH UNDERGRADUATE SCHOLARSHIP PROGRAM FOR STUDENTS FROM DISADVANTAGED BACKGROUNDS

• *See page 116*

NEW JERSEY ACADEMY OF SCIENCE

http://www.njas.org

NEW JERSEY ACADEMY OF SCIENCE RESEARCH GRANTS-IN-AID TO HIGH SCHOOL STUDENTS

• *See page 116*

NEW MEXICO COMMISSION ON HIGHER EDUCATION

http://www.nmche.org

ALLIED HEALTH STUDENT LOAN PROGRAM-NEW MEXICO

• *See page 186*

ORGONE BIOPHYSICAL RESEARCH LABORATORY

http://www.orgonelab.org

LOU HOCHBERG AWARDS

Awards granted for the following: university theses and dissertations, university/college essays, and high school essays; university thesis/dissertation research improvement and implementation grants; outstanding research and journalism. Must focus upon the social aspects of the discoveries of Wilhelm Reich.

Academic Fields/Career Goals: Social Sciences.

Award: Prize for use in freshman, sophomore, junior, senior, graduate, or postgraduate years; renewable. *Number:* 2–4. *Amount:* $200–$1500.

Eligibility Requirements: Applicant must be enrolled or expecting to enroll full or part-time at a two-year or four-year or technical institution or university. Available to U.S. and non-U.S. citizens.

Application Requirements: Applicant must enter a contest, transcript, photocopy of student I.D.. *Deadline:* Continuous.

Contact: Dr. James DeMeo, Director, Hochberg Awards
Orgone Biophysical Research Laboratory
PO Box 1148
Ashland, OR 97520
Phone: 541-552-0118
Fax: 541-552-0118
E-mail: info@orgonelab.org

PARAPSYCHOLOGY FOUNDATION

http://www.parapsychology.org

CHARLES T. AND JUDITH A. TART STUDENT INCENTIVE

An annual incentive award to promote the research of an undergraduate or graduate student who shows dedication to work within parapsychology. For more details see Web site: http://www.parapsychology.org.

Academic Fields/Career Goals: Social Sciences.

Award: Scholarship for use in freshman, sophomore, junior, senior, or graduate years; not renewable. *Number:* 1. *Amount:* $500.

Eligibility Requirements: Applicant must be enrolled or expecting to enroll at an institution or university. Available to U.S. citizens.

Application Requirements: Application, essay, references, transcript. *Deadline:* November 15.

Contact: Director of Library
Parapsychology Foundation
PO Box 1562
New York, NY 10021-0043
E-mail: office@parapsychology.org

EILEEN J. GARRETT SCHOLARSHIP FOR PARAPSYCHOLOGICAL RESEARCH

Applicants must show an academic interest in the science of parapsychology through research, term papers, and courses for which credit was received. Those with only a general interest will not be considered. Visit Web site for additional information.

Academic Fields/Career Goals: Social Sciences.

Award: Scholarship for use in freshman, sophomore, junior, senior, or graduate years; not renewable. *Number:* 1. *Amount:* $3000.

Eligibility Requirements: Applicant must be enrolled or expecting to enroll at an institution or university.

Application Requirements: Application, essay, references, transcript. *Deadline:* July 15.

Contact: Director of Library
Parapsychology Foundation
PO Box 1562
New York, NY 10021-0043
E-mail: office@parapsychology.org

SOCIETY FOR APPLIED ANTHROPOLOGY

http://www.sfaa.net

DEL JONES MEMORIAL TRAVEL AWARD

Travel grants of $500 are available for students to attend the annual meeting of the Society. The Society seeks to achieve greater diversity in its programs and activities, and the award is directed toward increasing the participation of African Americans in the annual meeting program. For more details see Web site: http://www.sfaa.net

Academic Fields/Career Goals: Social Sciences.

Award: Grant for use in freshman, sophomore, junior, senior, or graduate years; not renewable. *Number:* 2. *Amount:* $500.

Eligibility Requirements: Applicant must be Black (non-Hispanic) and enrolled or expecting to enroll full or part-time at a two-year or four-year institution or university. Available to U.S. and non-U.S. citizens.

Application Requirements: Applicant must enter a contest, paper abstract and written statement. *Deadline:* January 23.

Contact: Program Director
Society for Applied Anthropology
PO Box 2436
Oklahoma City, OK 73101
Phone: 405-843-5113
Fax: 405-843-8553
E-mail: info@sfaa.net

EDWARD H. AND ROSAMUND B. SPICER TRAVEL AWARD

Two travel grants of $500 are awarded to students who meet the eligibility qualifications. The awards are for the students to attend and participate in the SFAA annual meeting. The award's purpose is to further the maturation of students in the social sciences, both intellectually and practically. For more details, see Web site: http://www.sfaa.net.

Academic Fields/Career Goals: Social Sciences.

Award: Prize for use in sophomore, junior, or senior years; not renewable. *Number:* 2. *Amount:* $500.

Eligibility Requirements: Applicant must be enrolled or expecting to enroll full or part-time at a two-year or four-year institution or university. Available to U.S. and non-U.S. citizens.

Application Requirements: Applicant must enter a contest, paper abstract and written statement. *Deadline:* January 23.

Contact: Program Director
Society for Applied Anthropology
PO Box 2436
Oklahoma City, OK 73101
Phone: 405-843-5113
Fax: 405-843-8553
E-mail: info@sfaa.net

PETER KONG-MING NEW STUDENT PRIZE

• *See page 302*

SOUTHWEST STUDENT SERVICES CORPORATION http://www.sssc.com

ANNE LINDEMAN MEMORIAL SCHOLARSHIP
• *See page 117*

SUNSHINE LADY FOUNDATION, INC. http://www.sunshineladyfdn.org

COUNSELOR, ADVOCATE, AND SUPPORT STAFF SCHOLARSHIP PROGRAM
• *See page 47*

SOCIAL SERVICES

ALASKA STATE TROOPERS http://www.dps.state.ak.us/ast

MICHAEL MURPHY MEMORIAL SCHOLARSHIP LOAN FUND
• *See page 177*

AMERICAN LEGION AUXILIARY, DEPARTMENT OF ARIZONA

AMERICAN LEGION AUXILIARY DEPARTMENT OF ARIZONA WILMA HOYAL-MAXINE CHILTON MEMORIAL SCHOLARSHIP
• *See page 410*

AMERICAN PSYCHOLOGICAL ASSOCIATION http://www.apa.org/mfp

MINORITY AGING NETWORK IN PSYCHOLOGY SUMMER INSTITUTE ON AGING
• *See page 292*

BANK OF AMERICA

WILLIAM HEATH EDUCATION SCHOLARSHIP FOR MINISTERS, PRIESTS AND MISSIONARIES
• *See page 413*

BETHESDA LUTHERAN HOMES AND SERVICES, INC. http://www.blhs.org

DEVELOPMENTAL DISABILITIES SCHOLASTIC ACHIEVEMENT SCHOLARSHIP FOR LUTHERAN COLLEGE STUDENTS
• *See page 184*

CATHOLIC KNIGHTS OF AMERICA http://ckoa.com

VOCATIONAL SCHOLARSHIP PROGRAM
• *See page 414*

CONTINENTAL SOCIETY, DAUGHTERS OF INDIAN WARS

CONTINENTAL SOCIETY, DAUGHTERS OF INDIAN WARS SCHOLARSHIP
• *See page 199*

HEALTH PROFESSIONS EDUCATION FOUNDATION http://www.healthprofessions.ca.gov

KAISER PERMANENTE ALLIED HEALTHCARE SCHOLARSHIP
• *See page 297*

JEWISH FEDERATION OF METROPOLITAN CHICAGO (JFMC) http://www.jvschicago.org

JEWISH FEDERATION OF METROPOLITAN CHICAGO ACADEMIC SCHOLARSHIP PROGRAM
• *See page 185*

MARIN EDUCATION FUND http://www.marineducationfund.org

GOLDMAN FAMILY FUND, NEW LEADER SCHOLARSHIP
• *See page 186*

MARYLAND HIGHER EDUCATION COMMISSION http://www.mhec.state.md.us

DEVELOPMENTAL DISABILITIES, MENTAL HEALTH, CHILD WELFARE AND JUVENILE JUSTICE WORKFORCE TUITION ASSISTANCE PROGRAM
• *See page 298*

GRADUATE AND PROFESSIONAL SCHOLARSHIP PROGRAM-MARYLAND
• *See page 186*

JANET L. HOFFMANN LOAN ASSISTANCE REPAYMENT PROGRAM
• *See page 206*

MEMORIAL FOUNDATION FOR JEWISH CULTURE http://www.mfjc.org

MEMORIAL FOUNDATION FOR JEWISH CULTURE INTERNATIONAL SCHOLARSHIP PROGRAM FOR COMMUNITY SERVICE
• *See page 82*

NATIONAL BLACK POLICE ASSOCIATION http://www.blackpolice.org

ALPHONSO DEAL SCHOLARSHIP AWARD
• *See page 179*

NEW YORK STATE EDUCATION DEPARTMENT http://www.highered.nysed.gov

REGENTS PROFESSIONAL OPPORTUNITY SCHOLARSHIP
• *See page 45*

ORDEAN FOUNDATION

ORDEAN LOAN PROGRAM
• *See page 45*

OREGON STUDENT ASSISTANCE COMMISSION http://www.osac.state.or.us

FRIENDS OF OREGON STUDENTS SCHOLARSHIP
• *See page 209*

RESOURCE CENTER http://www.resourcecenterscholarshipinfo.com

MARIE BLAHA MEDICAL GRANT
• *See page 64*

SOUTHWEST STUDENT SERVICES CORPORATION http://www.sssc.com

ANNE LINDEMAN MEMORIAL SCHOLARSHIP
• *See page 117*

SUNSHINE LADY FOUNDATION, INC. http://www.sunshineladyfdn.org

COUNSELOR, ADVOCATE, AND SUPPORT STAFF SCHOLARSHIP PROGRAM
• *See page 47*

UNITED COMMUNITY SERVICES FOR WORKING FAMILIES http://www.workingfamilies.com

TED BRICKER SCHOLARSHIP

One-time award available to child of a union member who is a parent or guardian. Must be a resident of Pennsylvania. Must submit essay that is clear, concise, persuasive and shows a commitment to the community. Application deadline is June 30.

Academic Fields/Career Goals: Social Services.

Award: Scholarship for use in freshman year; not renewable. *Number:* 1. *Amount:* $500.

Eligibility Requirements: Applicant must be high school student; planning to enroll or expecting to enroll full-time at a four-year institution or university and resident of Pennsylvania. Applicant or parent of applicant must be member of AFL-CIO. Applicant or parent of applicant must have employment or volunteer experience in community service. Available to U.S. citizens.

Application Requirements: Application, essay, financial need analysis, transcript. *Deadline:* June 30.

Contact: Ruth Mathews, Executive Director
United Community Services for Working Families
116 North 5th Street
Reading, PA 19601
Phone: 610-374-3319
Fax: 610-374-6521
E-mail: ucswf1@enter.net

UNITED NEGRO COLLEGE FUND http://www.uncf.org

FANNIE MAE FOUNDATION SCHOLARSHIP

Scholarship benefits 12 students pursuing careers in the fields of housing and community development. Must attend UNCF member college or university or Benedict College, Bethune-Cookman College, Johnson C. Smith University, LeMoyne-Owen College, or Morris Brown College. Minimum 3.0 GPA required. Prospective applicants should complete the Student Profile found at Web site: http://www.uncf.org.

Academic Fields/Career Goals: Social Services.

Award: Scholarship for use in junior year; not renewable. *Number:* 12.

Eligibility Requirements: Applicant must be Black (non-Hispanic) and enrolled or expecting to enroll at a four-year institution or university. Applicant must have 3.0 GPA or higher.

Application Requirements: Application, financial need analysis. *Deadline:* October 10.

Contact: Program Services Department
United Negro College Fund
8260 Willow Oaks Corporate Drive
Fairfax, VA 22031

SODEXHO SCHOLARSHIP

• See page 304

SPECIAL EDUCATION

ALBERTA HERITAGE SCHOLARSHIP FUND/ ALBERTA SCHOLARSHIP PROGRAMS http://www.alis.gov.ab.ca/scholarships

ANNA AND JOHN KOLESAR MEMORIAL SCHOLARSHIPS

• See page 194

AMERICAN FEDERATION OF TEACHERS http://www.aft.org

ROBERT G. PORTER SCHOLARS PROGRAM-AFT MEMBERS

• See page 194

AMERICAN LEGION AUXILIARY, DEPARTMENT OF ARIZONA

AMERICAN LEGION AUXILIARY DEPARTMENT OF ARIZONA WILMA HOYAL-MAXINE CHILTON MEMORIAL SCHOLARSHIP

• See page 410

ARC OF WASHINGTON TRUST FUND http://www.arcwa.org

ARC OF WASHINGTON TRUST FUND STIPEND PROGRAM

Stipends of up to $5000 will be awarded to upper division or graduate students in schools in the states of Washington, Alaska, Oregon or Idaho. Applicants must have a demonstrated interest in the field of mental retardation. The application can be downloaded from the Web site: http://www.arcwa.org.

Academic Fields/Career Goals: Special Education.

Award: Scholarship for use in junior, senior, graduate, or postgraduate years; not renewable. *Number:* 1–8. *Amount:* $5000.

Eligibility Requirements: Applicant must be enrolled or expecting to enroll full-time at a four-year institution or university and studying in Alaska, Idaho, Oregon, or Washington. Available to U.S. and non-U.S. citizens.

Application Requirements: Application, autobiography, essay, references, transcript. *Deadline:* February 28.

Contact: Neal Lessenger, Secretary
ARC of Washington Trust Fund
PO Box 27028
Seattle, WA 98165-1428
Phone: 206-363-2206
E-mail: arcwatrust@msn.com

ARKANSAS DEPARTMENT OF HIGHER EDUCATION http://www.arscholarships.com

EMERGENCY SECONDARY EDUCATION LOAN PROGRAM

• See page 111

BETHESDA LUTHERAN HOMES AND SERVICES, INC. http://www.blhs.org

DEVELOPMENTAL DISABILITIES SCHOLASTIC ACHIEVEMENT SCHOLARSHIP FOR LUTHERAN COLLEGE STUDENTS

• See page 184

CONNECTICUT DEPARTMENT OF HIGHER EDUCATION http://www.ctdhe.org

CONNECTICUT SPECIAL EDUCATION TEACHER INCENTIVE GRANT

Renewable award for upper-level undergraduates or graduate students in special education programs. Must be in a program at a Connecticut college or university, or be a Connecticut resident enrolled in an approved out-of-state program. Priority is placed on minority and bilingual candidates. Application deadline is October 1. Must be nominated by the education dean of institution attended.

Academic Fields/Career Goals: Special Education.

Award: Grant for use in junior, senior, or graduate years; renewable. *Number:* varies. *Amount:* $2000–$5000.

Eligibility Requirements: Applicant must be enrolled or expecting to enroll full or part-time at a four-year institution or university.

Application Requirements: Application. *Deadline:* October 1.

Contact: John Siegrist, Financial Aid Office
Connecticut Department of Higher Education
61 Woodland Street
Hartford, CT 06105-2326
Phone: 860-947-1855
Fax: 860-947-1311

ILLINOIS STUDENT ASSISTANCE COMMISSION (ISAC) http://www.collegezone.org

ILLINOIS SPECIAL EDUCATION TEACHER TUITION WAIVER

Tuition waiver for up to four years for Illinois teacher or student pursuing a career in special education. Must be enrolled in an eligible Illinois institution and seeking certification in any area of special education. Must teach in Illinois for two years upon gaining certification.

Academic Fields/Career Goals: Special Education.

Award: Forgivable loan for use in freshman, sophomore, junior, senior, or graduate years; renewable. *Number:* 250.

Eligibility Requirements: Applicant must be enrolled or expecting to enroll at a four-year institution or university; resident of Illinois and studying in Illinois. Available to U.S. citizens.

Application Requirements: Application. *Deadline:* March 1.

Contact: College Zone Counselor
Illinois Student Assistance Commission (ISAC)
1755 Lake Cook Road
Deerfield, IL 60015-5209
Phone: 800-899-4722
E-mail: collegezone@isac.org

MINORITY TEACHERS OF ILLINOIS SCHOLARSHIP PROGRAM
• *See page 203*

KENTUCKY HIGHER EDUCATION ASSISTANCE AUTHORITY (KHEAA) http://www.kheaa.com

MINORITY EDUCATOR RECRUITMENT AND RETENTION SCHOLARSHIP
• *See page 205*

MARYLAND HIGHER EDUCATION COMMISSION http://www.mhec.state.md.us

DEVELOPMENTAL DISABILITIES, MENTAL HEALTH, CHILD WELFARE AND JUVENILE JUSTICE WORKFORCE TUITION ASSISTANCE PROGRAM
• *See page 298*

NATIONAL INSTITUTE FOR LABOR RELATIONS RESEARCH http://www.nilrr.org

APPLEGATE/JACKSON/PARKS FUTURE TEACHER SCHOLARSHIP
• *See page 208*

NEW HAMPSHIRE POSTSECONDARY EDUCATION COMMISSION http://www.state.nh.us/postsecondary

WORKFORCE INCENTIVE PROGRAM
• *See page 208*

ORDER OF THE ALHAMBRA http://www.orderalhambra.org

ORDER OF THE ALHAMBRA SCHOLARSHIP FUND

Award for students planning to become teachers of developmentally disabled. Must be used in junior and senior years of college. Submit letter from college verifying course of study. Deadlines: January 1 and July 1.

Academic Fields/Career Goals: Special Education.

Award: Scholarship for use in junior or senior years; renewable. *Number:* 75–100. *Amount:* $400.

Eligibility Requirements: Applicant must be enrolled or expecting to enroll full-time at a four-year institution or university. Available to U.S. and Canadian citizens.

Application Requirements: Application, self-addressed stamped envelope. *Deadline:* varies.

Contact: Roger J. Reid, Executive Director
Order of the Alhambra
4200 Leeds Avenue
Baltimore, MD 21229-5421
Phone: 410-242-0660
Fax: 410-536-5729
E-mail: salaamone@att.net

OREGON STUDENT ASSISTANCE COMMISSION http://www.osac.state.or.us

JAMES CARLSON MEMORIAL SCHOLARSHIP
• *See page 210*

PILOT INTERNATIONAL FOUNDATION http://www.pilotinternational.org

PILOT INTERNATIONAL FOUNDATION RUBY NEWHALL MEMORIAL SCHOLARSHIP
• *See page 302*

PILOT INTERNATIONAL FOUNDATION SCHOLARSHIP PROGRAM
• *See page 302*

PILOT INTERNATIONAL FOUNDATION/LIFELINE SCHOLARSHIP PROGRAM
• *See page 302*

SOUTH CAROLINA STUDENT LOAN CORPORATION http://www.slc.sc.edu

SOUTH CAROLINA TEACHER LOAN PROGRAM
• *See page 211*

SOUTHWEST STUDENT SERVICES CORPORATION http://www.sssc.com

ANNE LINDEMAN MEMORIAL SCHOLARSHIP
• *See page 117*

STATE COUNCIL OF HIGHER EDUCATION FOR VIRGINIA http://www.schev.edu

HIGHER EDUCATION TEACHER ASSISTANCE PROGRAM
• *See page 212*

STATE STUDENT ASSISTANCE COMMISSION OF INDIANA (SSACI) http://www.ssaci.in.gov

INDIANA MINORITY TEACHER AND SPECIAL EDUCATION SERVICES SCHOLARSHIP PROGRAM
• *See page 213*

TENNESSEE STUDENT ASSISTANCE CORPORATION http://www.state.tn.us/tsac

MINORITY TEACHING FELLOWS PROGRAM/TENNESSEE
• *See page 213*

UTAH STATE OFFICE OF EDUCATION http://www.usoe.k12.ut.us/cert/scholarships/scholars.htm

T.H. BELL TEACHING INCENTIVE LOAN-UTAH
• *See page 215*

WISCONSIN CONGRESS OF PARENTS AND TEACHERS, INC.

BROOKMIRE-HASTINGS SCHOLARSHIPS
• *See page 216*

WISCONSIN HIGHER EDUCATIONAL AIDS BOARD http://heab.state.wi.us

TEACHER OF THE VISUALLY IMPAIRED LOAN PROGRAM

Provides forgivable loans to students who enroll in programs that lead to be certified as a teacher of the visually impaired or an orientation and mobility instructor. Must be a Wisconsin resident. For study in Wisconsin, Illinois, Iowa, Michigan, and Minnesota. Please refer to Web site for further details: http://heab.state.wi.us

Academic Fields/Career Goals: Special Education.

Award: Forgivable loan for use in freshman, sophomore, junior, senior, graduate, or postgraduate years; not renewable. *Number:* varies. *Amount:* $250–$10,000.

Eligibility Requirements: Applicant must be enrolled or expecting to enroll full or part-time at a two-year or four-year or technical institution or university; resident of Wisconsin and studying in Illinois, Iowa, Michigan, Minnesota, or Wisconsin. Available to U.S. citizens.

Application Requirements: Application, financial need analysis. *Deadline:* Continuous.

Contact: John Whitt, Program Coordinator
Wisconsin Higher Educational Aids Board
PO Box 7885
Madison, WI 53707-7885
Phone: 608-266-0888
Fax: 608-267-2808
E-mail: john.whitt@heab.state.wi.us

YES I CAN FOUNDATION FOR EXCEPTIONAL CHILDREN http://www.cec.sped.org

COUNCIL FOR EXCEPTIONAL CHILDREN STUDENT GRADUATION AWARDS

Award given to a graduating undergraduate and graduate student who are members of the CEC. Must have a 3.0 GPA.

Academic Fields/Career Goals: Special Education.

Award: Prize for use in senior, or graduate years; not renewable. *Number:* 2. *Amount:* $500.

Eligibility Requirements: Applicant must be enrolled or expecting to enroll at a four-year institution or university. Applicant must have 3.0 GPA or higher. Available to U.S. and Canadian citizens.

Application Requirements: Essay, references, transcript. *Deadline:* November 5.

Contact: Yes I Can Foundation for Exceptional Children
1110 North Glebe Road
Suite 300
Arlington, VA 22201

SPORTS-RELATED

CALIFORNIA ADOLESCENT NUTRITION AND FITNESS (CANFIT) PROGRAM http://www.canfit.org

CALIFORNIA ADOLESCENT NUTRITION AND FITNESS (CANFIT) PROGRAM SCHOLARSHIP

• *See page 271*

CONNECTICUT ASSOCIATION FOR HEALTH, PHYSICAL EDUCATION, RECREATION AND DANCE http://www.ctahperd.org

GIBSON-LAEMEL CAHPERD SCHOLARSHIP

• *See page 199*

MARY BENEVENTO CAHPERD SCHOLARSHIP

• *See page 199*

NATIONAL ATHLETIC TRAINERS' ASSOCIATION RESEARCH AND EDUCATION FOUNDATION http://www.natafoundation.org

NATIONAL ATHLETIC TRAINER'S ASSOCIATION RESEARCH AND EDUCATION FOUNDATION SCHOLARSHIP PROGRAM

• *See page 299*

NATIONAL STRENGTH AND CONDITIONING ASSOCIATION http://www.nsca-lift.org

GNC NUTRITION RESEARCH GRANT

• *See page 306*

NATIONAL STRENGTH AND CONDITIONING ASSOCIATION CHALLENGE SCHOLARSHIP

• *See page 306*

NATIONAL STRENGTH AND CONDITIONING ASSOCIATION HIGH SCHOOL SCHOLARSHIP

• *See page 306*

NATIONAL STRENGTH AND CONDITIONING ASSOCIATION UNDERGRADUATE RESEARCH GRANT

• *See page 306*

NATIONAL STRENGTH AND CONDITIONING ASSOCIATION WOMEN'S SCHOLARSHIP

• *See page 307*

NSCA MINORITY SCHOLARSHIP

• *See page 307*

POWER SYSTEMS PROFESSIONAL SCHOLARSHIP

• *See page 307*

PACERS FOUNDATION, INC. http://www.pacersfoundation.org

LINDA CRAIG MEMORIAL SCHOLARSHIP

• *See page 301*

PI LAMBDA THETA, INC. http://www.pilambda.org

TOBIN SORENSON PHYSICAL EDUCATION SCHOLARSHIP

The Tobin Sorenson Scholarship provides $1000 for tuition to an outstanding student who intends to pursue a career at the K-12 level as a physical education teacher, adaptive physical education teacher, coach, recreational therapist, dance therapist, or similar professional focusing on teaching the knowledge and use of the human body. Awarded in odd years only. Minimum 3.5 GPA required.

Academic Fields/Career Goals: Sports-related; Therapy/Rehabilitation.

Award: Scholarship for use in sophomore, junior, senior, or graduate years; not renewable. *Number:* 1. *Amount:* $1000.

Eligibility Requirements: Applicant must be enrolled or expecting to enroll full or part-time at a two-year or four-year institution or university. Applicant must have 3.5 GPA or higher. Available to U.S. and non-U.S. citizens.

Application Requirements: Application, resume, references, transcript. *Deadline:* February 10.

Contact: Ellen Mills, Controller
Pi Lambda Theta, Inc.
4101 East 3rd Street, PO Box 6626
Bloomington, IN 47407-6626
Phone: 812-339-3411
Fax: 812-339-3462
E-mail: ellen@pilambda.org

WOMEN'S SPORTS FOUNDATION http://www.womenssportsfoundation.org

LINDA RIDDLE/SGMA SCHOLARSHIP

One-time award for female high school seniors entering a two- or four-year college. Provides female athletes of limited financial means the opportunity to pursue their sport in addition to their college studies. Minimum GPA 3.5. Must be a U.S. citizen.

Academic Fields/Career Goals: Sports-related.

Award: Scholarship for use in freshman year; not renewable. *Number:* 1–10. *Amount:* $1500.

Eligibility Requirements: Applicant must be high school student; planning to enroll or expecting to enroll full-time at a two-year or four-year institution or university; female and must have an interest in athletics/sports. Applicant must have 3.5 GPA or higher. Available to U.S. citizens.

Application Requirements: Application, essay, financial need analysis, references, transcript. *Deadline:* December 1.

Contact: Women's Sports Foundation
Eisenhower Park
East Meadow, NY 11554
Phone: 800-227-3988
E-mail: wosport@aol.com

SURVEYING; SURVEYING TECHNOLOGY, CARTOGRAPHY, OR GEOGRAPHIC INFORMATION SCIENCE

AMERICAN CONGRESS ON SURVEYING AND MAPPING http://www.acsm.net

ACSM FELLOWS SCHOLARSHIP

One-time award available to a student with a junior or higher standing in any ACSM discipline. Must be ACSM member.

Academic Fields/Career Goals: Surveying; Surveying Technology, Cartography, or Geographic Information Science.

Award: Scholarship for use in junior or senior years; not renewable. *Amount:* $2000.

Eligibility Requirements: Applicant must be enrolled or expecting to enroll at a four-year institution. Applicant or parent of applicant must be member of American Congress on Surveying and Mapping.

Application Requirements: Application, essay, references, transcript. *Deadline:* December 1.

Contact: Scholarship Information
American Congress on Surveying and Mapping
6 Montgomery Village Avenue
Suite 403
Gaithersburg, MD 20879

AMERICAN ASSOCIATION FOR GEODETIC SURVEYING JOSEPH F. DRACUP SCHOLARSHIP AWARD

Award for students enrolled in four-year degree program in surveying. Preference given to applicants from programs with significant focus on geodetric surveying. Must be ACSM member.

Academic Fields/Career Goals: Surveying; Surveying Technology, Cartography, or Geographic Information Science.

Award: Scholarship for use in freshman, sophomore, junior, or senior years; not renewable. *Amount:* $2000.

Eligibility Requirements: Applicant must be enrolled or expecting to enroll at a four-year institution or university. Applicant or parent of applicant must be member of American Congress on Surveying and Mapping.

Application Requirements: Application, essay, references, transcript. *Deadline:* December 1.

Contact: Scholarship Information
American Congress on Surveying and Mapping
6 Montgomery Village Avenue
Suite 403
Gaithersburg, MD 20879

BERNTSEN INTERNATIONAL SCHOLARSHIP IN SURVEYING

Award for students enrolled in four-year degree program in surveying, or in closely-related degree program, such as geomatics or surveying engineering. Award funded by Berntsen International, Inc. Must be ACSM member.

Academic Fields/Career Goals: Surveying; Surveying Technology, Cartography, or Geographic Information Science.

Award: Scholarship for use in freshman, sophomore, junior, or senior years; not renewable. *Amount:* $1500.

Eligibility Requirements: Applicant must be enrolled or expecting to enroll at a four-year institution or university. Applicant or parent of applicant must be member of American Congress on Surveying and Mapping.

Application Requirements: Application, essay, references, transcript. *Deadline:* December 1.

Contact: Scholarship Information
American Congress on Surveying and Mapping
6 Montgomery Village Avenue
Suite 403
Gaithersburg, MD 20879

BERNTSEN INTERNATIONAL SCHOLARSHIP IN SURVEYING TECHNOLOGY

Award of $500 for students enrolled in a two-year degree program in surveying technology. For U.S. study only. Must be a member of the American Congress on Surveying and Mapping. Contact for further information.

Academic Fields/Career Goals: Surveying; Surveying Technology, Cartography, or Geographic Information Science.

Award: Scholarship for use in freshman or sophomore years; not renewable. *Amount:* $500.

Eligibility Requirements: Applicant must be enrolled or expecting to enroll at a two-year institution. Applicant or parent of applicant must be member of American Congress on Surveying and Mapping.

Application Requirements: Application, essay, references, transcript. *Deadline:* December 1.

Contact: Scholarship Information
American Congress on Surveying and Mapping
6 Montgomery Village Avenue
Suite 403
Gaithersburg, MD 20879

CADY MCDONNELL MEMORIAL SCHOLARSHIP

Award of $1000 for female surveying student. Must be a resident of one of the following western states: Alaska, Arizona, California, Colorado, Hawaii, Idaho, Montana, Nevada, New Mexico, Oregon, Utah, Washington, and Wyoming. Must provide proof of legal home residence and be a member of the American Congress on Surveying and Mapping.

Academic Fields/Career Goals: Surveying; Surveying Technology, Cartography, or Geographic Information Science.

Award: Scholarship for use in freshman, sophomore, junior, or senior years; not renewable. *Number:* 1. *Amount:* $1000.

Eligibility Requirements: Applicant must be enrolled or expecting to enroll full or part-time at a two-year or four-year institution or university; female and resident of Alaska, Arizona, California, Colorado, Hawaii, Idaho, Montana, Nevada, New Mexico, Oregon, Utah, Washington, or Wyoming. Applicant or parent of applicant must be member of American Congress on Surveying and Mapping.

Application Requirements: Application, essay, references, transcript. *Deadline:* December 1.

Contact: Scholarship Information
American Congress on Surveying and Mapping
6 Montgomery Village Avenue
Suite 403
Gaithersburg, MD 20879

CARTOGRAPHY AND GEOGRAPHIC INFORMATION SOCIETY SCHOLARSHIP

Award of $1000 for a member of the American Congress on Surveying and Mapping studying cartography or geographic information science. Preference given to undergraduates with junior or senior standing. Contact for further information. Must be ACSM member.

Academic Fields/Career Goals: Surveying; Surveying Technology, Cartography, or Geographic Information Science.

Award: Scholarship for use in freshman, sophomore, junior, senior, or graduate years; not renewable. *Amount:* $1000.

Eligibility Requirements: Applicant must be enrolled or expecting to enroll full-time at an institution or university. Applicant or parent of applicant must be member of American Congress on Surveying and Mapping.

Application Requirements: Application, essay, references, transcript. *Deadline:* December 1.

Contact: Scholarship Information
American Congress on Surveying and Mapping
6 Montgomery Village Avenue
Suite 403
Gaithersburg, MD 20879

NATIONAL SOCIETY OF PROFESSIONAL SURVEYORS BOARD OF GOVERNORS SCHOLARSHIP

Award available to student enrolled in surveying program entering junior year of study at four-year institution. Minimum 3.0 GPA required. Must be ACSM member.

Academic Fields/Career Goals: Surveying; Surveying Technology, Cartography, or Geographic Information Science.

Award: Scholarship for use in junior year; not renewable. *Amount:* $1000.

Eligibility Requirements: Applicant must be enrolled or expecting to enroll full or part-time at a two-year or four-year institution or university. Applicant or parent of applicant must be member of American Congress on Surveying and Mapping. Applicant must have 3.0 GPA or higher.

Application Requirements: Application, essay, references, transcript. *Deadline:* December 1.

Contact: Scholarship Information
American Congress on Surveying and Mapping
6 Montgomery Village Avenue
Suite 403
Gaithersburg, MD 20879

NATIONAL SOCIETY OF PROFESSIONAL SURVEYORS FOR EQUAL OPPORTUNITY/MARY FEINDT SCHOLARSHIP

Award available to female members of ACSM. Applicants must be enrolled in a four-year degree program in a surveying and mapping curriculum in the U.S..

Academic Fields/Career Goals: Surveying; Surveying Technology, Cartography, or Geographic Information Science.

Award: Scholarship for use in freshman, sophomore, junior, or senior years; not renewable. *Amount:* $1000.

Eligibility Requirements: Applicant must be enrolled or expecting to enroll at a four-year institution or university and female. Applicant or parent of applicant must be member of American Congress on Surveying and Mapping.

Application Requirements: Application, essay, references, transcript. *Deadline:* December 1.

Contact: Scholarship Information
American Congress on Surveying and Mapping
6 Montgomery Village Avenue
Suite 403
Gaithersburg, MD 20879

NATIONAL SOCIETY OF PROFESSIONAL SURVEYORS SCHOLARSHIPS

Award recognizes outstanding students enrolled full-time in undergraduate surveying program. Must be ACSM member.

Academic Fields/Career Goals: Surveying; Surveying Technology, Cartography, or Geographic Information Science.

Award: Scholarship for use in freshman, sophomore, junior, or senior years; not renewable. *Number:* 2. *Amount:* $1000.

Eligibility Requirements: Applicant must be enrolled or expecting to enroll full-time at a four-year institution or university. Applicant or parent of applicant must be member of American Congress on Surveying and Mapping.

Application Requirements: Application, essay, references, transcript. *Deadline:* December 1.

Contact: Scholarship Information
American Congress on Surveying and Mapping
6 Montgomery Village Avenue
Suite 403
Gaithersburg, MD 20879

NETTIE DRACUP MEMORIAL SCHOLARSHIP

Award for undergraduate student enrolled in geodetic surveying at an accredited college or university. Must be U.S. citizen. Must be ACSM member.

Academic Fields/Career Goals: Surveying; Surveying Technology, Cartography, or Geographic Information Science.

Award: Scholarship for use in freshman, sophomore, junior, or senior years; not renewable. *Amount:* $2000.

Eligibility Requirements: Applicant must be enrolled or expecting to enroll at a four-year institution or university. Applicant or parent of applicant must be member of American Congress on Surveying and Mapping. Available to U.S. citizens.

Application Requirements: Application, essay, financial need analysis, references, transcript. *Deadline:* December 1.

Contact: Scholarship Information
American Congress on Surveying and Mapping
6 Montgomery Village Avenue
Suite 403
Gaithersburg, MD 20879

SCHONSTEDT SCHOLARSHIP IN SURVEYING

Award preference given to applicants with junior or senior standing. Award sponsored by Schonstedt Instrument Company. Schonstedt donates magnetic locator to surveying program at each recipient's school. Must be ACSM member.

Academic Fields/Career Goals: Surveying; Surveying Technology, Cartography, or Geographic Information Science.

Award: Scholarship for use in freshman, sophomore, junior, or senior years; not renewable. *Number:* 2. *Amount:* $1500.

Eligibility Requirements: Applicant must be enrolled or expecting to enroll at a four-year institution or university. Applicant or parent of applicant must be member of American Congress on Surveying and Mapping.

Application Requirements: Application, essay, references, transcript. *Deadline:* December 1.

Contact: Scholarship Information
American Congress on Surveying and Mapping
6 Montgomery Village Avenue
Suite 403
Gaithersburg, MD 20879

ARIZONA HYDROLOGICAL SOCIETY http://www.azhydrosoc.org

ARIZONA HYDROLOGICAL SURVEY STUDENT SCHOLARSHIP

• *See page 189*

ASSOCIATED GENERAL CONTRACTORS OF AMERICA-NEW YORK STATE CHAPTER http://www.agcnys.org

ASSOCIATED GENERAL CONTRACTORS OF AMERICA-NEW YORK STATE CHAPTER SCHOLARSHIP PROGRAM

• *See page 151*

ASSOCIATION OF CALIFORNIA WATER AGENCIES http://www.acwanet.com

ASSOCIATION OF CALIFORNIA WATER AGENCIES SCHOLARSHIPS

• *See page 68*

CLAIR A. HILL SCHOLARSHIP

• *See page 68*

CENTRAL INTELLIGENCE AGENCY http://www.cia.gov

CENTRAL INTELLIGENCE AGENCY UNDERGRADUATE SCHOLARSHIP PROGRAM

• *See page 39*

COMTO-BOSTON CHAPTER http://www.bostoncomto.org

COMTO BOSTON/GARRETT A. MORGAN SCHOLARSHIP

• *See page 75*

MIDWEST ROOFING CONTRACTORS ASSOCIATION http://www.mrca.org

MRCA FOUNDATION SCHOLARSHIP PROGRAM

• *See page 70*

NATIONAL FISH AND WILDLIFE FOUNDATION http://www.nfwf.org

BUDWEISER CONSERVATION SCHOLARSHIP PROGRAM

• *See page 115*

OREGON STUDENT ASSISTANCE COMMISSION http://www.osac.state.or.us

PROFESSIONAL LAND SURVEYORS OF OREGON SCHOLARSHIPS

One-time award for sophomores or above enrolled in course of study leading to land-surveying career. Community college applicants must intend to transfer to four-year college. Oregon colleges only. Applicants must intend to take Fundamentals of Land Surveying exam. Additional essay stating education/career goals and their relation to land surveying is required.

Academic Fields/Career Goals: Surveying; Surveying Technology, Cartography, or Geographic Information Science.

Award: Scholarship for use in sophomore, junior, or senior years; not renewable. *Number:* 5. *Amount:* $1600.

Eligibility Requirements: Applicant must be enrolled or expecting to enroll at a four-year institution; resident of Oregon and studying in Oregon. Available to U.S. citizens.

Oregon Student Assistance Commission (continued)

Application Requirements: Application, essay, financial need analysis, references, transcript, activity chart. *Deadline:* March 1.

Contact: Director of Grant Programs
Oregon Student Assistance Commission
1500 Valley River Drive, Suite 100
Eugene, OR 97401-7020
Phone: 800-452-8807 Ext. 7395
E-mail: awardinfo@mercury.osac.state.or.us

PROFESSIONAL CONSTRUCTION ESTIMATORS ASSOCIATION http://www.pcea.org

TED WILSON MEMORIAL SCHOLARSHIP FOUNDATION
• *See page 188*

SOIL AND WATER CONSERVATION SOCIETY-NEW JERSEY CHAPTER http://www.geocities.com/njswcs

EDWARD R. HALL SCHOLARSHIP
• *See page 55*

THERAPY/REHABILITATION

ALBERTA HERITAGE SCHOLARSHIP FUND/ ALBERTA SCHOLARSHIP PROGRAMS http://www.alis.gov.ab.ca/scholarships

ALBERTA HERITAGE SCHOLARSHIP FUND ABORIGINAL HEALTH CAREERS BURSARY
• *See page 111*

ALICE M. YARNOLD AND SAMUEL YARNOLD SCHOLARSHIP TRUST

ALICE M. AND SAMUEL YARNOLD SCHOLARSHIP
• *See page 289*

AMERICAN FOUNDATION FOR THE BLIND http://www.afb.org

DELTA GAMMA FOUNDATION FLORENCE MARGARET HARVEY MEMORIAL SCHOLARSHIP
• *See page 195*

RUDOLPH DILLMAN MEMORIAL SCHOLARSHIP
• *See page 195*

AMERICAN LEGION AUXILIARY, DEPARTMENT OF MICHIGAN http://www.michalaux.org

MEDICAL CAREER SCHOLARSHIP
• *See page 290*

AMERICAN LEGION AUXILIARY, DEPARTMENT OF WYOMING

PAST PRESIDENTS PARLEY HEALTH CARE SCHOLARSHIP
• *See page 183*

AMERICAN OCCUPATIONAL THERAPY FOUNDATION, INC. http://www.aotf.org

AMERICAN OCCUPATIONAL THERAPY FOUNDATION STATE ASSOCIATION SCHOLARSHIPS
• *See page 291*

CARLOTTA WELLES SCHOLARSHIP
• *See page 291*

FLORENCE WOOD/ARKANSAS OCCUPATIONAL THERAPY ASSOCIATION SCHOLARSHIP
• *See page 291*

KAPPA DELTA PHI SCHOLARSHIP FOR OCCUPATIONAL THERAPY ASSISTANT
• *See page 291*

AMERICAN RESPIRATORY CARE FOUNDATION http://www.arcfoundation.org

JIMMY A. YOUNG MEMORIAL EDUCATION RECOGNITION AWARD
• *See page 292*

MORTON B. DUGGAN, JR. MEMORIAL EDUCATION RECOGNITION AWARD
• *See page 292*

NBRC/AMP ROBERT M. LAWRENCE, MD, EDUCATION RECOGNITION AWARD
• *See page 292*

NBRC/AMP WILLIAM W. BURGIN, MD EDUCATION RECOGNITION AWARD
• *See page 292*

SEPRACOR ACHIEVEMENT AWARD FOR EXCELLENCE IN PULMONARY DISEASE STATE MANAGEMENT
• *See page 293*

BECA FOUNDATION, INC.

ALICE NEWELL JOSLYN MEDICAL FUND
• *See page 183*

BETHESDA LUTHERAN HOMES AND SERVICES, INC. http://www.blhs.org

DEVELOPMENTAL DISABILITIES SCHOLASTIC ACHIEVEMENT SCHOLARSHIP FOR LUTHERAN COLLEGE STUDENTS
• *See page 184*

GENERAL FEDERATION OF WOMEN'S CLUBS OF MASSACHUSETTS

GENERAL FEDERATION OF WOMEN'S CLUBS OF MASSACHUSETTS MUSIC SCHOLARSHIP
• *See page 201*

HEALTH PROFESSIONS EDUCATION FOUNDATION http://www.healthprofessions.ca.gov

KAISER PERMANENTE ALLIED HEALTHCARE SCHOLARSHIP
• *See page 297*

INTERNATIONAL ORDER OF THE KING'S DAUGHTERS AND SONS http://www.iokds.org

HEALTH CAREERS SCHOLARSHIP
• *See page 185*

JEWISH FOUNDATION FOR EDUCATION OF WOMEN http://www.jfew.org

SCHOLARSHIP PROGRAM FOR FORMER SOVIET UNION EMIGRES TRAINING IN THE HEALTH SCIENCES
• *See page 186*

LADIES AUXILIARY TO THE VETERANS OF FOREIGN WARS, DEPARTMENT OF MAINE

FRANCIS L. BOOTH MEDICAL SCHOLARSHIP SPONSORED BY LAVFW DEPARTMENT OF MAINE
• *See page 298*

MARIN EDUCATION FUND http://www.marineducationfund.org

GOLDMAN FAMILY FUND, NEW LEADER SCHOLARSHIP
• *See page 186*

MARYLAND HIGHER EDUCATION COMMISSION http://www.mhec.state.md.us

DEVELOPMENTAL DISABILITIES, MENTAL HEALTH, CHILD WELFARE AND JUVENILE JUSTICE WORKFORCE TUITION ASSISTANCE PROGRAM

• See page 298

JANET L. HOFFMANN LOAN ASSISTANCE REPAYMENT PROGRAM

• See page 206

PHYSICAL AND OCCUPATIONAL THERAPISTS AND ASSISTANTS GRANT PROGRAM

For Maryland residents training as physical, occupational therapists or therapy assistants at Maryland postsecondary institutions. Recipients must provide one year of service for each full, or partial, year of award. Service must be to handicapped children in a Maryland facility that has, or accommodates and provides services to, such children. Minimum 2.0 GPA.

Academic Fields/Career Goals: Therapy/Rehabilitation.

Award: Forgivable loan for use in freshman, sophomore, junior, senior, or graduate years; renewable. *Number:* up to 10. *Amount:* up to $2000.

Eligibility Requirements: Applicant must be enrolled or expecting to enroll full-time at a two-year or four-year institution or university; resident of Maryland and studying in Maryland. Available to U.S. citizens.

Application Requirements: Application, transcript. *Deadline:* July 1.

Contact: Gerrie Rogers, Office of Student Financial Assistance
Maryland Higher Education Commission
839 Bestgate Road, Suite 400
Annapolis, MD 21401
Phone: 410-260-4574
Fax: 410-260-3203
E-mail: ssamail@mhec.state.md.us

MASSAGE MAGAZINE http://www.massagemag.com/schoolsProgram/scholarship.htm

MASSAGE MAGAZINE'S SCHOLARSHIP PROGRAM

Scholarships are awarded based on financial need and will only be available for programs in schools participating in the Massage Magazine Schools Program. Applicant must be currently enrolled in an approved program and have completed a minimum of 90 hours of training with a "B" average.

Academic Fields/Career Goals: Therapy/Rehabilitation.

Award: Scholarship for use in freshman or sophomore years; not renewable. *Number:* 5. *Amount:* $1000.

Eligibility Requirements: Applicant must be enrolled or expecting to enroll full or part-time at a technical institution. Applicant must have 3.0 GPA or higher. Available to U.S. and non-U.S. citizens.

Application Requirements: Application, essay, financial need analysis, references, transcript. *Deadline:* varies.

Contact: Jami Harless, Schools Program Manager
Massage Magazine
1636 West First Avenue, Suite 100
Spokane, WA 99204
Phone: 509-324-8117
Fax: 509-324-8606
E-mail: schools@massagemag.com

MISSISSIPPI STATE STUDENT FINANCIAL AID http://www.mississippiuniversities.com

CRITICAL NEEDS TEACHER LOAN/SCHOLARSHIP

• See page 206

MISSISSIPPI HEALTH CARE PROFESSIONS LOAN/SCHOLARSHIP PROGRAM

• See page 299

NATIONAL AMBUCS, INC. http://www.ambucs.com

AMBUCS SCHOLARS-SCHOLARSHIPS FOR THERAPISTS

• See page 299

NATIONAL ATHLETIC TRAINERS' ASSOCIATION RESEARCH AND EDUCATION FOUNDATION http://www.natafoundation.org

NATIONAL ATHLETIC TRAINER'S ASSOCIATION RESEARCH AND EDUCATION FOUNDATION SCHOLARSHIP PROGRAM

• See page 299

NATIONAL SOCIETY DAUGHTERS OF THE AMERICAN REVOLUTION http://www.dar.org

NATIONAL SOCIETY DAUGHTERS OF THE AMERICAN REVOLUTION MEDICAL OCCUPATIONAL THERAPY SCHOLARSHIPS

Nonrenewable award for students of physical or occupational therapy. Must be U.S. citizen sponsored by local DAR chapter. Award based on merit. Obtain list of local chapters from NSDAR. Deadlines: February 15 and August 15. Must submit self-addressed stamped envelope to be considered.

Academic Fields/Career Goals: Therapy/Rehabilitation.

Award: Scholarship for use in freshman, sophomore, junior, or senior years; not renewable. *Number:* 20. *Amount:* $500.

Eligibility Requirements: Applicant must be enrolled or expecting to enroll at a two-year or four-year institution. Applicant must have 3.0 GPA or higher. Available to U.S. citizens.

Application Requirements: Application, essay, financial need analysis, references, self-addressed stamped envelope, test scores, transcript. *Deadline:* varies.

Contact: Office of Committees, Scholarship
National Society Daughters of the American Revolution
1776 D Street, NW
Washington, DC 20006-5392

NATIONAL STRENGTH AND CONDITIONING ASSOCIATION http://www.nsca-lift.org

GNC NUTRITION RESEARCH GRANT

• See page 306

NATIONAL STRENGTH AND CONDITIONING ASSOCIATION CHALLENGE SCHOLARSHIP

• See page 306

NATIONAL STRENGTH AND CONDITIONING ASSOCIATION HIGH SCHOOL SCHOLARSHIP

• See page 306

NATIONAL STRENGTH AND CONDITIONING ASSOCIATION UNDERGRADUATE RESEARCH GRANT

• See page 306

NATIONAL STRENGTH AND CONDITIONING ASSOCIATION WOMEN'S SCHOLARSHIP

• See page 307

NSCA MINORITY SCHOLARSHIP

• See page 307

POWER SYSTEMS PROFESSIONAL SCHOLARSHIP

• See page 307

NEW MEXICO COMMISSION ON HIGHER EDUCATION http://www.nmche.org

ALLIED HEALTH STUDENT LOAN PROGRAM-NEW MEXICO

• See page 186

NORTH CAROLINA STATE EDUCATION ASSISTANCE AUTHORITY http://www.cfnc.org

NORTH CAROLINA STUDENT LOAN PROGRAM FOR HEALTH, SCIENCE, AND MATHEMATICS

• See page 187

OREGON STUDENT ASSISTANCE COMMISSION http://www.osac.state.or.us

MARION A. LINDEMAN SCHOLARSHIP

• See page 301

PACERS FOUNDATION, INC. http://www.pacersfoundation.org

LINDA CRAIG MEMORIAL SCHOLARSHIP
• *See page 301*

PI LAMBDA THETA, INC. http://www.pilambda.org

TOBIN SORENSON PHYSICAL EDUCATION SCHOLARSHIP
• *See page 423*

PILOT INTERNATIONAL FOUNDATION http://www.pilotinternational.org

PILOT INTERNATIONAL FOUNDATION RUBY NEWHALL MEMORIAL SCHOLARSHIP
• *See page 302*

PILOT INTERNATIONAL FOUNDATION SCHOLARSHIP PROGRAM
• *See page 302*

PILOT INTERNATIONAL FOUNDATION/LIFELINE SCHOLARSHIP PROGRAM
• *See page 302*

RESOURCE CENTER http://www.resourcecenterscholarshipinfo.com

MARIE BLAHA MEDICAL GRANT
• *See page 64*

SIGMA ALPHA IOTA PHILANTHROPIES, INC. http://www.sai-national.org

SIGMA ALPHA IOTA MUSIC THERAPY SCHOLARSHIP
• *See page 367*

SOUTHWEST STUDENT SERVICES CORPORATION http://www.sssc.com

ANNE LINDEMAN MEMORIAL SCHOLARSHIP
• *See page 117*

STATE OF GEORGIA http://www.gsfc.org

SERVICE-CANCELABLE STAFFORD LOAN-GEORGIA
• *See page 187*

STATE STUDENT ASSISTANCE COMMISSION OF INDIANA (SSACI) http://www.ssaci.in.gov

INDIANA MINORITY TEACHER AND SPECIAL EDUCATION SERVICES SCHOLARSHIP PROGRAM
• *See page 213*

SUBURBAN HOSPITAL HEALTHCARE SYSTEM http://www.suburbanhospital.org

SUBURBAN HOSPITAL HEALTHCARE SYSTEM SCHOLARSHIP
• *See page 303*

SUNSHINE LADY FOUNDATION, INC. http://www.sunshineladyfdn.org

COUNSELOR, ADVOCATE, AND SUPPORT STAFF SCHOLARSHIP PROGRAM
• *See page 47*

TUBERCULOSIS ASSOCIATION OF OHIO COUNTY http://www.tboc.org

DR. WILLIAM J. STEGER SCHOLARSHIP AWARDS
• *See page 303*

UNITED STATES DEPARTMENT OF EDUCATION, REHABILITATION SERVICES ADMINISTRATION http://www.ed.gov/students/college/aid/rehab/index.html

REHABILITATION TRAINING PROGRAM SCHOLARSHIP

RSA Scholarships are provided by colleges and universities receiving RSA training grants. Eligible students are generally full-time undergraduate or graduate students in training programs related to rehabilitation. Upon graduation, students must work for a state or nonprofit rehabilitation organization for two years for each year of assistance received. College or university sets criteria and application fee. Many universities with scholarship funds can be found at the following Web site: http://www.ed.gov/students/college/aid/rehab/index.html

Academic Fields/Career Goals: Therapy/Rehabilitation.

Award: Scholarship for use in freshman, sophomore, junior, senior, or graduate years; not renewable. *Number:* varies. *Amount:* varies.

Eligibility Requirements: Applicant must be enrolled or expecting to enroll full-time at a four-year institution or university. Available to U.S. citizens.

Application Requirements: Application. *Deadline:* Continuous.

Contact: Rehabilitation Training Program
United States Department of Education, Rehabilitation Services Administration
Division of Resource Development, 330 C Street, SW
Washington, DC 20202-2649
Phone: 202-205-8926
Fax: 202-260-0723

UNITED STATES PUBLIC HEALTH SERVICE - HEALTH RESOURCES AND SERVICES ADMINISTRATION, BUREAU OF HEALTH PROFESSIONS http://bhpr.hrsa.gov/dsa

HEALTH RESOURCES AND SERVICES ADMINISTRATION-BUREAU OF HEALTH PROFESSIONS SCHOLARSHIPS FOR DISADVANTAGED STUDENTS
• *See page 187*

TRADE/TECHNICAL SPECIALTIES

AIRCRAFT ELECTRONICS ASSOCIATION EDUCATIONAL FOUNDATION http://www.aea.net

BUD GLOVER MEMORIAL SCHOLARSHIP
• *See page 92*

FIELD AVIATION CO., INC., SCHOLARSHIP
• *See page 93*

LOWELL GAYLOR MEMORIAL SCHOLARSHIP
• *See page 94*

MONTE MITCHELL GLOBAL SCHOLARSHIP
• *See page 94*

PLANE AND PILOT MAGAZINE/GARMIN SCHOLARSHIP
• *See page 94*

AMERICAN LEGION, DEPARTMENT OF PENNSYLVANIA http://www.pa-legion.com

ROBERT W. VALIMONT ENDOWMENT FUND SCHOLARSHIP (PART II)

Scholarships for any Pennsylvania high school senior seeking admission to a two-year college, post-high school trade/technical school, or training program. Must attend school in Pennsylvania. Continuation of award is based on grades. Renewable award of $600. Number of awards varies from year to year. Membership in an American Legion post in Pennsylvania is not required, but it must be documented if it does apply.

Academic Fields/Career Goals: Trade/Technical Specialties.

Award: Scholarship for use in freshman or sophomore years; renewable. *Amount:* $600.

Eligibility Requirements: Applicant must be high school student; planning to enroll or expecting to enroll full-time at a two-year or

technical institution; resident of Pennsylvania and studying in Pennsylvania. Applicant must have 2.5 GPA or higher. Available to U.S. citizens.

Application Requirements: Application, financial need analysis, test scores, transcript. *Deadline:* May 1.

Contact: Debra Bellis, Scholarship Secretary
American Legion, Department of Pennsylvania
PO Box 2324
Harrisburg, PA 17105-2324
Phone: 717-730-9100
Fax: 717-975-2836
E-mail: hq@pa-legion.com

AMERICAN SOCIETY OF HEATING, REFRIGERATING, AND AIR CONDITIONING ENGINEERS, INC. http://www.ashrae.org

ALWIN B. NEWTON SCHOLARSHIP FUND
• *See page 218*

AMERICAN SOCIETY OF HEATING, REFRIGERATION, AND AIR CONDITIONING ENGINEERING TECHNOLOGY SCHOLARSHIP
• *See page 66*

ASHRAE MEMORIAL SCHOLARSHIP
• *See page 225*

ASHRAE SCHOLARSHIPS
• *See page 225*

DUANE HANSON SCHOLARSHIP
• *See page 225*

HENRY ADAMS SCHOLARSHIP
• *See page 225*

REUBEN TRANE SCHOLARSHIP
• *See page 218*

AMERICAN WELDING SOCIETY http://www.aws.org/foundation

AIRGAS JERRY BAKER SCHOLARSHIP
• *See page 226*

AIRGAS-TERRY JARVIS MEMORIAL SCHOLARSHIP
• *See page 226*

AMERICAN WELDING SOCIETY DISTRICT SCHOLARSHIP PROGRAM
• *See page 226*

AMERICAN WELDING SOCIETY INTERNATIONAL SCHOLARSHIP
• *See page 226*

ARSHAM AMIRIKIAN ENGINEERING SCHOLARSHIP
• *See page 150*

DONALD AND JEAN CLEVELAND-WILLAMETTE VALLEY SECTION SCHOLARSHIP
• *See page 150*

DONALD F. HASTINGS SCHOLARSHIP
• *See page 226*

EDWARD J. BRADY MEMORIAL SCHOLARSHIP
• *See page 227*

HOWARD E. ADKINS MEMORIAL SCHOLARSHIP
• *See page 227*

ILLINOIS TOOL WORKS WELDING COMPANIES SCHOLARSHIP
• *See page 227*

JOHN C. LINCOLN MEMORIAL SCHOLARSHIP
• *See page 227*

MATSUO BRIDGE COMPANY, LTD., OF JAPAN SCHOLARSHIP
• *See page 151*

MILLER ELECTRIC IYSC SCHOLARSHIP
• *See page 238*

PRAXAIR INTERNATIONAL SCHOLARSHIP
• *See page 227*

WILLIAM A. AND ANN M. BROTHERS SCHOLARSHIP
• *See page 228*

WILLIAM B. HOWELL MEMORIAL SCHOLARSHIP
• *See page 228*

ARRL FOUNDATION, INC. http://www.arrl.org/arrlf/scholgen.html

CHARLES N. FISHER MEMORIAL SCHOLARSHIP
• *See page 66*

IRVING W. COOK, WA0CGS, SCHOLARSHIP
• *See page 67*

MISSISSIPPI SCHOLARSHIP
• *See page 67*

PAUL AND HELEN L. GRAUER SCHOLARSHIP
• *See page 67*

ASSOCIATED GENERAL CONTRACTORS EDUCATION AND RESEARCH FOUNDATION http://www.agcfoundation.org

AGC EDUCATION AND RESEARCH FOUNDATION UNDERGRADUATE SCHOLARSHIPS
• *See page 151*

ASSOCIATION FOR FACILITIES ENGINEERING (AFE)

ASSOCIATION FOR FACILITIES ENGINEERING CEDAR VALLEY CHAPTER # 132 SCHOLARSHIP
• *See page 97*

AUTOMOTIVE HALL OF FAME http://www.automotivehalloffame.org

AUTOMOTIVE HALL OF FAME EDUCATIONAL FUNDS
• *See page 140*

CHAVERIM OF DELAWARE VALLEY, INC.

K2UK JEWISH RADIO MEMORIAL SCHOLARSHIP
• *See page 219*

CIRI FOUNDATION http://www.ciri.com/tcf

VOCATIONAL TRAINING GRANTS

Up to $3000 per calendar year for courses of study on a part-time basis to upgrade job skills or for students in post-secondary vocational training or apprenticeship. Must be Alaska Native Student. Minimum 2.5 GPA required. Deadlines: March 31, June 30, September 30, December 1.

Academic Fields/Career Goals: Trade/Technical Specialties.

Award: Grant for use in freshman, sophomore, junior, senior, graduate, or postgraduate years; not renewable. *Amount:* up to $3000.

Eligibility Requirements: Applicant must be enrolled or expecting to enroll part-time at a two-year or four-year or technical institution or university. Applicant must have 2.5 GPA or higher.

Application Requirements: Application, essay, references, transcript, proof of eligibility, birth certificate or adoption decree. *Deadline:* varies.

Contact: CIRI Foundation
2600 Cordova Street, Suite 206
Anchorage, AK 99503
Phone: 907-263-5582
Fax: 907-263-5588
E-mail: tcf@ciri.com

CONNECTICUT BUILDING CONGRESS http://www.cbc-ct.org

CONNECTICUT BUILDING CONGRESS SCHOLARSHIP FUND
• *See page 75*

DATATEL, INC. http://www.datatel.com/dsf

NANCY GOODHUE LYNCH SCHOLARSHIP

For any undergraduate student in an Information Technology curriculum program. Applicant must attend a Datatel client institution. Completed applications must be submitted by January 31.

Academic Fields/Career Goals: Trade/Technical Specialties.

Award: Scholarship for use in freshman, sophomore, junior, or senior years; not renewable. *Number:* 2. *Amount:* $2500.

Eligibility Requirements: Applicant must be enrolled or expecting to enroll full or part-time at a two-year or four-year or technical institution or university. Available to U.S. and non-U.S. citizens.

Application Requirements: Application, essay, references, transcript. *Deadline:* January 31.

Contact: Marissa Solis, Project Leader
Datatel, Inc.
4375 Fair Lakes Court
Fairfax, VA 22033
Phone: 800-486-4332
Fax: 703-968-4573
E-mail: scholars@datatel.com

FEDERATION OF AMERICAN CONSUMERS AND TRAVELERS http://www.fact-org.org

FEDERATION OF AMERICAN CONSUMERS AND TRAVELERS TRADE SCHOOL SCHOLARSHIP

There is $5000 available for students needing funds to attend a trade school or technical college. The amount of the awards is to be determined each year by the committee and will be based on the tuition costs and number of applicants. For more information, visit http://www.fact-org.org.

Academic Fields/Career Goals: Trade/Technical Specialties.

Award: Scholarship for use in freshman, sophomore, junior, or senior years; not renewable. *Number:* varies. *Amount:* up to $5000.

Eligibility Requirements: Applicant must be enrolled or expecting to enroll full-time at a technical institution. Available to U.S. citizens.

Application Requirements: Application, autobiography, essay, references, test scores, transcript. *Deadline:* January 15.

Contact: Vicki Rolens, Managing Director
Federation of American Consumers and Travelers
PO Box 104
Edwardsville, IL 62025
Phone: 800-872-3228
Fax: 618-656-5369
E-mail: gmsfact@aol.com

GREATER KANAWHA VALLEY FOUNDATION http://www.tgkvf.org

WEST VIRGINIA BROADCASTERS ASSOCIATION FUND
• *See page 159*

INTERNATIONAL EXECUTIVE HOUSEKEEPERS ASSOCIATION http://www.ieha.org

INTERNATIONAL EXECUTIVE HOUSEKEEPERS EDUCATIONAL FOUNDATION
• *See page 277*

INTERNATIONAL FURNISHINGS AND DESIGN ASSOCIATION http://www.ifdaef.org/scholarships.html

CHARLES D. MAYO SCHOLARSHIP
• *See page 327*

IFDA STUDENT SCHOLARSHIP
• *See page 328*

MAINE METAL PRODUCTS ASSOCIATION http://www.maine-metals.org

MAINE METAL PRODUCTS ASSOCIATION SCHOLARSHIP PROGRAM
• *See page 351*

MAINE SCHOOL FOOD SERVICE ASSOCIATION (MSFSA) http://www.msfsa.com

SCHOLARSHIP OF THE MAINE SCHOOL FOOD SERVICE ASSOCIATION
• *See page 276*

MARION D. AND EVA S. PEEPLES FOUNDATION TRUST SCHOLARSHIP PROGRAM http://www.jccf.org

MARION D. AND EVA S. PEEPLES SCHOLARSHIPS
• *See page 205*

MARYLAND ASSOCIATION OF PRIVATE COLLEGES AND CAREER SCHOOLS http://www.mapccs.org

MARYLAND ASSOCIATION OF PRIVATE COLLEGES AND CAREER SCHOOLS SCHOLARSHIP
• *See page 127*

MARYLAND HIGHER EDUCATION COMMISSION http://www.mhec.state.md.us

FIREFIGHTER, AMBULANCE, AND RESCUE SQUAD MEMBER TUITION REIMBURSEMENT PROGRAM-MARYLAND
• *See page 270*

MIDWEST ROOFING CONTRACTORS ASSOCIATION http://www.mrca.org

MRCA FOUNDATION SCHOLARSHIP PROGRAM
• *See page 70*

NATIONAL ASSOCIATION OF WATER COMPANIES-NEW JERSEY CHAPTER

NATIONAL ASSOCIATION OF WATER COMPANIES-NEW JERSEY CHAPTER SCHOLARSHIP
• *See page 115*

NATIONAL ASSOCIATION OF WOMEN IN CONSTRUCTION http://nawic.org

NAWIC UNDERGRADUATE SCHOLARSHIPS
• *See page 77*

PLASTICS INSTITUTE OF AMERICA http://www.plasticsinstitute.org

PLASTICS PIONEERS SCHOLARSHIPS
• *See page 232*

PLUMBING-HEATING-COOLING CONTRACTORS ASSOCIATION EDUCATION FOUNDATION http://www.phccweb.org

BRADFORD WHITE CORPORATION SCHOLARSHIP
• *See page 79*

DELTA FAUCET COMPANY SCHOLARSHIP PROGRAM
• *See page 79*

PHCC EDUCATIONAL FOUNDATION NEED-BASED SCHOLARSHIP
• *See page 79*

PHCC EDUCATIONAL FOUNDATION SCHOLARSHIP PROGRAM
• *See page 79*

PROFESSIONAL AVIATION MAINTENANCE FOUNDATION http://www.pama.org

PROFESSIONAL AVIATION MAINTENANCE FOUNDATION STUDENT SCHOLARSHIP PROGRAM

For students enrolled in an airframe and power plant licensing program. Must have a B average and have completed 25% of the program. Must reapply each year. Apply after July 1 and until October 31. For more details see Web site: http://www.pama.org.

Academic Fields/Career Goals: Trade/Technical Specialties.

Award: Scholarship for use in sophomore, junior, or senior years; not renewable. *Number:* 10–30. *Amount:* $1000.

Eligibility Requirements: Applicant must be enrolled or expecting to enroll at a two-year or four-year or technical institution or university. Applicant must have 3.0 GPA or higher. Available to U.S. and non-U.S. citizens.

Application Requirements: Application, financial need analysis, references, self-addressed stamped envelope, transcript. *Deadline:* October 31.

Contact: Scholarship Program Director, PAMA
Phone: 866-865-PAMA
Fax: 703-417-8801
E-mail: hq@pama.org

SOCIETY OF MANUFACTURING ENGINEERS EDUCATION FOUNDATION http://www.sme.org/foundation

CLINTON J. HELTON MANUFACTURING SCHOLARSHIP AWARD FUND
• *See page 251*

DOWNRIVER DETROIT CHAPTER 198 SCHOLARSHIP
• *See page 252*

E. WAYNE KAY COMMUNITY COLLEGE SCHOLARSHIP AWARD
• *See page 252*

E. WAYNE KAY SCHOLARSHIP
• *See page 253*

FORT WAYNE CHAPTER 56 SCHOLARSHIP
• *See page 253*

MYRTLE AND EARL WALKER SCHOLARSHIP FUND
• *See page 253*

NORTH CENTRAL REGION 9 SCHOLARSHIP
• *See page 254*

PHOENIX CHAPTER 67 SCHOLARSHIP
• *See page 254*

SME CORPORATE SCHOLARS
• *See page 254*

WICHITA CHAPTER 52 SCHOLARSHIP
• *See page 255*

WILLIAM E. WEISEL SCHOLARSHIP FUND
• *See page 222*

SOCIETY OF PLASTICS ENGINEERS (SPE) FOUNDATION http://www.4spe.org

FLEMING/BASZCAK SCHOLARSHIP
• *See page 147*

SOCIETY OF PLASTICS ENGINEERS SCHOLARSHIP PROGRAM
• *See page 147*

SOUTH DAKOTA RETAILERS ASSOCIATION http://www.sdra.org

SOUTH DAKOTA RETAILERS ASSOCIATION SCHOLARSHIP PROGRAM
• *See page 47*

SPECIALTY EQUIPMENT MARKET ASSOCIATION http://www.sema.org

SPECIALTY EQUIPMENT MARKET ASSOCIATION MEMORIAL SCHOLARSHIP FUND
• *See page 261*

STATE OF GEORGIA http://www.gsfc.org

INTELLECTUAL CAPITAL PARTNERSHIP PROGRAM, ICAPP

Forgivable loans will be awarded to undergraduate students who are residents of Georgia studying high-tech related fields at a Georgia institution. Repayment for every $2500 that is awarded is one-year service in a high-tech field in Georgia. Can be enrolled in a certificate or degree program.

Academic Fields/Career Goals: Trade/Technical Specialties.

Award: Forgivable loan for use in freshman, sophomore, junior, or senior years; not renewable. *Number:* up to 328. *Amount:* $7000–$10,000.

Eligibility Requirements: Applicant must be enrolled or expecting to enroll full or part-time at a two-year or four-year institution or university; resident of Georgia and studying in Georgia. Available to U.S. citizens.

Application Requirements: Application, financial need analysis. *Deadline:* June 3.

Contact: Peggy Matthews, Manager/GSFA Originations
State of Georgia
2082 East Exchange Place, Suite 230
Tucker, GA 30084-5305
Phone: 770-724-9230
Fax: 770-724-9225
E-mail: peggy@gsfc.org

TEXAS HIGHER EDUCATION COORDINATING BOARD http://www.collegefortexans.com

FIREFIGHTER EXEMPTION PROGRAM-TEXAS
• *See page 72*

WOMEN IN LOGISTICS, NORTHERN CALIFORNIA http://www.womeninlogistics.org

WOMEN IN LOGISTICS SCHOLARSHIP
• *See page 135*

WOMEN'S JEWELRY ASSOCIATION http://www.womensjewelry.org

WOMEN'S JEWELRY ASSOCIATION SCHOLARSHIP PROGRAM

Program is designed to encourage talented female students and help support their studies in the jewelry field. Applicants required to submit original drawings of their jewelry designs.

Academic Fields/Career Goals: Trade/Technical Specialties.

Award: Scholarship for use in freshman, sophomore, junior, senior, graduate, or postgraduate years; not renewable. *Number:* 5–15. *Amount:* $500–$5000.

Eligibility Requirements: Applicant must be enrolled or expecting to enroll full or part-time at a two-year or four-year or technical institution or university; female and must have an interest in designated field specified by sponsor. Available to U.S. citizens.

Application Requirements: Application, essay, portfolio, references, transcript. *Deadline:* June 1.

Contact: Gillian Schultz, Scholarship Committee
Women's Jewelry Association
373 Route 46 West, Building E, Suite 215
Fairfield, NJ 07004
Phone: 973-575-7190
Fax: 973-575-1445
E-mail: info@womensjewelry.org

WYOMING TRUCKING ASSOCIATION

WYOMING TRUCKING ASSOCIATION TRUST FUND SCHOLARSHIP
• *See page 135*

TRANSPORTATION

AMERICAN PUBLIC TRANSPORTATION FOUNDATION http://www.apta.com

DAN REICHARD SCHOLARSHIP
• *See page 120*

DONALD C. HYDE ESSAY PROGRAM
• *See page 149*

JACK GILSTRAP SCHOLARSHIP
• *See page 149*

LOUIS T. KLAUDER SCHOLARSHIP
• *See page 150*

PARSONS BRINCKERHOFF-JIM LAMMIE SCHOLARSHIP
• *See page 150*

TRANSIT HALL OF FAME SCHOLARSHIP AWARD PROGRAM
• *See page 150*

ASSOCIATED GENERAL CONTRACTORS OF AMERICA-NEW YORK STATE CHAPTER http://www.agcnys.org

ASSOCIATED GENERAL CONTRACTORS OF AMERICA-NEW YORK STATE CHAPTER SCHOLARSHIP PROGRAM
• *See page 151*

COMTO-BOSTON CHAPTER http://www.bostoncomto.org

COMTO BOSTON/GARRETT A. MORGAN SCHOLARSHIP
• *See page 75*

NASA NEBRASKA SPACE GRANT CONSORTIUM http://nasa.unomaha.edu

NASA NEBRASKA SPACE GRANT
• *See page 101*

NASA VERMONT SPACE GRANT CONSORTIUM http://www.emba.uvm.edu/vsgc

VERMONT SPACE GRANT CONSORTIUM SCHOLARSHIP PROGRAM
• *See page 71*

NATIONAL CUSTOMS BROKERS AND FORWARDERS ASSOCIATION OF AMERICA http://www.ncbfaa.org

NATIONAL CUSTOMS BROKERS AND FORWARDERS ASSOCIATION OF AMERICA SCHOLARSHIP AWARD

One-time award for employees of NCBFAA member organizations and their children. Must be studying transportation logistics or international trade full time. Minimum 2.5 GPA. Application deadline is in February.

Academic Fields/Career Goals: Transportation.

Award: Scholarship for use in freshman, sophomore, junior, senior, graduate, or postgraduate years; not renewable. *Number:* 1. *Amount:* $5000.

Eligibility Requirements: Applicant must be enrolled or expecting to enroll full-time at a four-year institution. Applicant or parent of applicant must have employment or volunteer experience in customs broker. Applicant must have 2.5 GPA or higher. Available to U.S. citizens.

Application Requirements: Application, essay, resume, letter from member. *Deadline:* varies.

Contact: Tom Mathers, Director of Communication
National Customs Brokers and Forwarders Association of America
1200 18th Street, NW
Suite 901
Washington, DC 20036
Phone: 202-466-0222

NINETY-NINES, SAN FERNANDO VALLEY CHAPTER/VAN NUYS AIRPORT http://sfv99s.org

SAN FERNANDO VALLEY CHAPTER OF THE NINETY-NINES CAREER SCHOLARSHIP
• *See page 104*

TRANSPORTATION CLUBS INTERNATIONAL http://www.transportationclubsinternational.com

ALICE GLAISYER WARFIELD MEMORIAL SCHOLARSHIP
• *See page 106*

DENNY LYDIC SCHOLARSHIP
• *See page 106*

TEXAS TRANSPORTATION SCHOLARSHIP
• *See page 106*

TRANSPORTATION CLUBS INTERNATIONAL CHARLOTTE WOODS SCHOLARSHIP
• *See page 107*

TRANSPORTATION CLUBS INTERNATIONAL FRED A. HOOPER MEMORIAL SCHOLARSHIP
• *See page 107*

TRANSPORTATION CLUBS INTERNATIONAL GINGER AND FRED DEINES CANADA SCHOLARSHIP
• *See page 107*

TRANSPORTATION CLUBS INTERNATIONAL GINGER AND FRED DEINES MEXICO SCHOLARSHIP
• *See page 107*

TRUCKLOAD CARRIERS ASSOCIATION http://www.truckload.org

TRUCKLOAD CARRIERS ASSOCIATION SCHOLARSHIP FUND
• *See page 130*

WOMEN IN LOGISTICS, NORTHERN CALIFORNIA http://www.womeninlogistics.org

WOMEN IN LOGISTICS SCHOLARSHIP
• *See page 135*

WYOMING TRUCKING ASSOCIATION

WYOMING TRUCKING ASSOCIATION TRUST FUND SCHOLARSHIP
• *See page 135*

TRAVEL/TOURISM

AMERICAN SOCIETY OF TRAVEL AGENTS (ASTA) FOUNDATION http://www.astanet.com

AMERICAN EXPRESS TRAVEL SCHOLARSHIP

Candidate must be enrolled in a travel or tourism program in either a two- or four-year college or university or proprietary travel school. Must write 500-word essay on student's view of travel industry's future. Merit-based. Award criteria subject to change. Contact ASTA Foundation for more information, or visit Web site: http://www.astanet.com/education/edu_scholarships.asp. Minimum 2.5 GPA required.

Academic Fields/Career Goals: Travel/Tourism.

Award: Scholarship for use in freshman, sophomore, junior, or senior years; not renewable. *Number:* 1. *Amount:* varies.

Eligibility Requirements: Applicant must be Canadian citizen and enrolled or expecting to enroll full or part-time at a two-year or four-year or technical institution. Applicant must have 2.5 GPA or higher. Available to U.S. and Canadian citizens.

Application Requirements: Application, driver's license, essay, references, transcript. *Deadline:* varies.

Contact: Verlette Mitchell, Manager
American Society of Travel Agents (ASTA) Foundation
1101 King Street
Alexandria, VA 22314-2187
Phone: 703-739-8721
Fax: 703-684-8319
E-mail: scholarship@astahq.com

ARIZONA CHAPTER GOLD SCHOLARSHIP

One-time award for college undergraduates who are Arizona residents pursuing a travel or tourism degree at a four-year Arizona institution. Freshmen are not eligible. Must submit essay on career plans and interests. Write for application by sending a self-addressed stamped business size envelope or go to http://www.astanet.com for requirements and an application. Minimum 2.5 GPA required.

Academic Fields/Career Goals: Travel/Tourism.

Award: Scholarship for use in sophomore, junior, or senior years; not renewable. *Number:* 1. *Amount:* $3000.

Eligibility Requirements: Applicant must be enrolled or expecting to enroll full or part-time at a four-year institution or university; resident of Arizona and studying in Arizona. Applicant or parent of applicant must have employment or volunteer experience in designated career field. Applicant must have 2.5 GPA or higher. Available to U.S. and non-U.S. citizens.

Application Requirements: Application, driver's license, essay, references, transcript. *Deadline:* varies.

Contact: Verlette Mitchell, Manager
American Society of Travel Agents (ASTA) Foundation
1101 King Street
Alexandria, VA 22314-2187
Phone: 703-739-8721
Fax: 703-684-8319
E-mail: scholarship@astahq.com

DONALD ESTEY SCHOLARSHIP FUND-ROCKY MOUNTAIN CHAPTER

One-time award for travel professionals or students in industry training programs. If professional, must be affiliated with the American Society of Travel Agents Rocky Mountain Chapter. Students are not required to be members of ASTA, but must have letter of recommendation from ASTA Rocky Mountain Chapter. Must be Colorado, Utah, or Wyoming resident. Visit Web site: http://www.astanet.com for requirements, application, and deadlines.

Academic Fields/Career Goals: Travel/Tourism.

Award: Scholarship for use in freshman, sophomore, junior, or senior years; not renewable. *Number:* 4. *Amount:* varies.

Eligibility Requirements: Applicant must be enrolled or expecting to enroll full or part-time at a two-year or technical institution; resident of Colorado, Utah, or Wyoming and studying in Colorado, Utah, or Wyoming. Applicant or parent of applicant must be member of American Society of Travel Agents. Applicant or parent of applicant must have employment or volunteer experience in designated career field. Available to U.S. citizens.

Application Requirements: Application, driver's license, financial need analysis, references, test scores, transcript. *Deadline:* Continuous.

Contact: Verlette Mitchell, Manager
American Society of Travel Agents (ASTA) Foundation
1101 King Street
Alexandria, VA 22314-2187
Phone: 703-739-8721
Fax: 703-684-8319
E-mail: scholarship@astahq.com

GEORGE REINKE SCHOLARSHIPS

For a student enrolled in proprietary travel school or junior college in a travel agent training program. Applicant must write a 500-word essay on career goals in the travel or tourism industry. Go to Web site (http://www.astanet.com) for requirements and an application. Two deadlines per year.

Academic Fields/Career Goals: Travel/Tourism.

Award: Scholarship for use in sophomore, junior, or senior years; not renewable. *Number:* 2–5. *Amount:* $2000.

Eligibility Requirements: Applicant must be enrolled or expecting to enroll full or part-time at a two-year or technical institution. Applicant or parent of applicant must have employment or volunteer experience in designated career field. Applicant must have 2.5 GPA or higher. Available to U.S. citizens.

Application Requirements: Application, driver's license, essay, references, transcript. *Deadline:* varies.

Contact: Verlette Mitchell, Manager
American Society of Travel Agents (ASTA) Foundation
1101 King Street
Alexandria, VA 22314-2187
Phone: 703-739-8721
Fax: 703-684-8319
E-mail: scholarship@astahq.com

HEALY SCHOLARSHIP

One-time award for a college undergraduate pursuing a travel or tourism degree. Must submit essay suggesting improvements for the travel industry. Go to http://www.astanet.com for requirements and an application. Must attend an institution in the U.S. or Canada. Minimum 2.5 GPA required.

Academic Fields/Career Goals: Travel/Tourism.

Award: Scholarship for use in freshman, sophomore, junior, or senior years; not renewable. *Number:* 1. *Amount:* $2000.

Eligibility Requirements: Applicant must be enrolled or expecting to enroll full or part-time at a four-year institution or university. Applicant must have 2.5 GPA or higher. Available to U.S. and Canadian citizens.

Application Requirements: Application, driver's license, essay, references, self-addressed stamped envelope, transcript. *Deadline:* varies.

Contact: Verlette Mitchell, Manager
American Society of Travel Agents (ASTA) Foundation
1101 King Street
Alexandria, VA 22314-2187
Phone: 703-739-8721
Fax: 703-684-8319
E-mail: scholarship@astahq.com

HOLLAND-AMERICA LINE WESTOURS SCHOLARSHIPS

Students must write 500-word essay on the future of the cruise industry and must be enrolled in travel or tourism program at a two- or four-year college or proprietary travel school. Go to http://www.astanet.com for requirements and an application form. Minimum 2.5 GPA required.

Academic Fields/Career Goals: Travel/Tourism.

Award: Scholarship for use in freshman, sophomore, junior, or senior years; not renewable. *Number:* 2. *Amount:* $3000.

Eligibility Requirements: Applicant must be enrolled or expecting to enroll full or part-time at a two-year or four-year or technical institution or university. Applicant or parent of applicant must have employment or volunteer experience in designated career field or hospitality/hotel administration/operations. Applicant must have 2.5 GPA or higher.

Application Requirements: Application, driver's license, essay, references, transcript. *Deadline:* varies.

Contact: Verlette Mitchell, Manager
American Society of Travel Agents (ASTA) Foundation
1101 King Street
Alexandria, VA 22314-2187
Phone: 703-739-8721
Fax: 703-684-8319
E-mail: scholarship@astahq.com

JOHN HJORTH SCHOLARSHIP FUND-SAN DIEGO CHAPTER

One-time award for travel professionals working for an agency that is a member of American Society of Travel Agents' San Diego Chapter. Provides

American Society of Travel Agents (ASTA) Foundation (continued)

support for employees to further education in travel and tourism. Go to http://www.astanet.com for requirements and an application form.

Academic Fields/Career Goals: Travel/Tourism.

Award: Scholarship for use in freshman, sophomore, junior, senior, or graduate years; not renewable. *Number:* 3. *Amount:* $250.

Eligibility Requirements: Applicant must be enrolled or expecting to enroll full or part-time at a technical institution and resident of California. Applicant or parent of applicant must be member of American Society of Travel Agents. Applicant or parent of applicant must have employment or volunteer experience in designated career field. Available to U.S. citizens.

Application Requirements: Application, essay, references. *Deadline:* Continuous.

Contact: Verlette Mitchell, Manager
American Society of Travel Agents (ASTA) Foundation
1101 King Street
Alexandria, VA 22314-2187
Phone: 703-739-8721
Fax: 703-684-8319
E-mail: scholarship@astahq.com

JOSEPH R. STONE SCHOLARSHIPS

One-time award for high school senior or college undergraduate pursuing a travel or tourism degree. Must have a parent in the industry and proof of employment. Must submit 500-word essay explaining career goals. Go to http://www.astanet.com for requirements and an application form. Minimum 2.5 GPA required.

Academic Fields/Career Goals: Travel/Tourism.

Award: Scholarship for use in freshman, sophomore, junior, or senior years; not renewable. *Number:* 3. *Amount:* $2400.

Eligibility Requirements: Applicant must be enrolled or expecting to enroll full or part-time at a four-year institution or university. Applicant or parent of applicant must be member of American Society of Travel Agents. Applicant or parent of applicant must have employment or volunteer experience in designated career field. Applicant must have 2.5 GPA or higher. Available to U.S. and Canadian citizens.

Application Requirements: Application, essay, references, transcript. *Deadline:* varies.

Contact: Verlette Mitchell, Manager
American Society of Travel Agents (ASTA) Foundation
1101 King Street
Alexandria, VA 22314-2187
Phone: 703-739-8721
Fax: 703-684-8319
E-mail: scholarship@astahq.com

NANCY STEWART SCHOLARSHIP FUND-ALLEGHENY CHAPTER

One-time award for travel professionals working for an agency that is a member of American Society of Travel Agents' Allegheny Chapter. Applicant must be Pennsylvania resident. Provides support for employees to further education in travel and tourism. Go to http://www.astanet.com for requirements and an application form.

Academic Fields/Career Goals: Travel/Tourism.

Award: Scholarship for use in freshman year; not renewable. *Number:* 3. *Amount:* $400.

Eligibility Requirements: Applicant must be enrolled or expecting to enroll part-time at a technical institution and resident of Pennsylvania. Applicant or parent of applicant must be member of American Society of Travel Agents. Applicant or parent of applicant must have employment or volunteer experience in designated career field. Available to U.S. citizens.

Application Requirements: Application, essay, references. *Deadline:* Continuous.

Contact: Verlette Mitchell, Manager
American Society of Travel Agents (ASTA) Foundation
1101 King Street
Alexandria, VA 22314-2187
Phone: 703-739-8721
Fax: 703-684-8319
E-mail: scholarship@astahq.com

NORTHERN CALIFORNIA CHAPTER RICHARD EPPING SCHOLARSHIP

Merit-based award for residents of northern California or northern Nevada who are attending school in the same area. Submit 500-word essay on desire for travel or tourism career. Go to http://www.astanet.com for requirements and an application. Minimum 2.5 GPA required.

Academic Fields/Career Goals: Travel/Tourism.

Award: Scholarship for use in freshman year; not renewable. *Number:* 1. *Amount:* $2000.

Eligibility Requirements: Applicant must be enrolled or expecting to enroll full or part-time at a two-year or four-year or technical institution or university; resident of California or Nevada and studying in California or Nevada. Applicant must have 2.5 GPA or higher. Available to U.S. citizens.

Application Requirements: Application, essay, references, transcript. *Deadline:* varies.

Contact: Verlette Mitchell, Manager
American Society of Travel Agents (ASTA) Foundation
1101 King Street
Alexandria, VA 22314-2187
Phone: 703-739-8721
Fax: 703-684-8319
E-mail: scholarship@astahq.com

ORANGE COUNTY CHAPTER/HARRY JACKSON SCHOLARSHIP FUND

One-time award for California residents enrolled in a travel related program. Must be a member of the American Society of Travel Agents and pursuing a career in the travel industry. Go to http://www.astanet.com for requirements and an application form.

Academic Fields/Career Goals: Travel/Tourism.

Award: Scholarship for use in freshman year; not renewable. *Number:* varies. *Amount:* $250–$2000.

Eligibility Requirements: Applicant must be enrolled or expecting to enroll full or part-time at a technical institution and resident of California. Applicant or parent of applicant must be member of American Society of Travel Agents. Applicant or parent of applicant must have employment or volunteer experience in designated career field. Available to U.S. citizens.

Application Requirements: Application, financial need analysis, references, transcript. *Deadline:* Continuous.

Contact: Verlette Mitchell, Manager
American Society of Travel Agents (ASTA) Foundation
1101 King Street
Alexandria, VA 22314-2187
Phone: 703-739-8721
Fax: 703-684-8319
E-mail: scholarship@astahq.com

PACIFIC NORTHWEST CHAPTER-WILLIAM HUNT SCHOLARSHIP FUND

One-time award for travel professionals who are members or employees of American Society of Travel Agents member organizations in the Oregon or Pacific Northwest Chapters. Must be a resident of and studying in one of the following states: Alaska, Idaho, Montana, Oregon, or Washington. Must be pursuing a certificate or diploma in travel or tourism. Please visit Web site http://www.astanet.com for updated information.

Academic Fields/Career Goals: Travel/Tourism.

Award: Scholarship for use in freshman year; not renewable. *Number:* 3. *Amount:* $200–$1000.

Eligibility Requirements: Applicant must be enrolled or expecting to enroll full or part-time at a two-year or four-year or technical institution and resident of Alaska, Idaho, Montana, Oregon, or Washington. Applicant or parent of applicant must be member of American Society of Travel Agents. Applicant or parent of applicant must have employment or volunteer experience in designated career field. Available to U.S. citizens.

Application Requirements: Application, essay, references. *Deadline:* Continuous.

Contact: Verlette Mitchell, Manager
American Society of Travel Agents (ASTA) Foundation
1101 King Street
Alexandria, VA 22314-2187
Phone: 703-739-8721
Fax: 703-684-8319
E-mail: scholarship@astahq.com

PRINCESS CRUISES AND PRINCESS TOURS SCHOLARSHIP

Merit-based award for student accepted or enrolled as an undergraduate in a travel or tourism program. Submit 300-word essay on two features cruise ships will need to offer passengers in the next ten years. Go to http://www.astanet.com for requirements and an application form. Minimum 2.5 GPA required.

Academic Fields/Career Goals: Travel/Tourism.

Award: Scholarship for use in freshman, sophomore, junior, or senior years; not renewable. *Number:* 2. *Amount:* $2000.

Eligibility Requirements: Applicant must be enrolled or expecting to enroll full or part-time at a two-year or four-year or technical institution or university. Applicant must have 2.5 GPA or higher. Available to U.S. and non-U.S. citizens.

Application Requirements: Application, essay, references, transcript. *Deadline:* varies.

Contact: Verlette Mitchell, Manager
American Society of Travel Agents (ASTA) Foundation
1101 King Street
Alexandria, VA 22314-2187
Phone: 703-739-8721
Fax: 703-684-8319
E-mail: scholarship@astahq.com

SOUTHEAST AMERICAN SOCIETY OF TRAVEL AGENTS CHAPTER SCHOLARSHIP

One-time award for active or associate members of the Southeast Chapter of American Society of Travel Agents. Must be resident of and studying in one of the following states: Alabama, Georgia, Kentucky, Louisiana, Mississippi, North Carolina, South Carolina, or Tennessee. Must have minimum two years experience in travel industry. Must complete ICTA course within three years and complete each of the four courses for CTE certification. Go to http://www.astanet.com for requirements and an application form.

Academic Fields/Career Goals: Travel/Tourism.

Award: Scholarship for use in freshman year; not renewable. *Number:* 6. *Amount:* $350.

Eligibility Requirements: Applicant must be enrolled or expecting to enroll part-time at a technical institution; resident of Alabama, Georgia, Kentucky, Louisiana, Mississippi, North Carolina, South Carolina, or Tennessee and studying in Alabama, Georgia, Kentucky, Louisiana, Mississippi, North Carolina, South Carolina, or Tennessee. Applicant or parent of applicant must be member of American Society of Travel Agents. Applicant or parent of applicant must have employment or volunteer experience in designated career field. Applicant must have 2.5 GPA or higher. Available to U.S. citizens.

Application Requirements: Application, references. *Deadline:* Continuous.

Contact: Verlette Mitchell, Manager
American Society of Travel Agents (ASTA) Foundation
1101 King Street
Alexandria, VA 22314-2187
Phone: 703-739-8721
Fax: 703-684-8319
E-mail: scholarship@astahq.com

SOUTHERN CALIFORNIA CHAPTER/PLEASANT HAWAIIAN HOLIDAYS SCHOLARSHIP

Two awards for students pursuing travel or tourism degrees. One award given to student attending college in southern California, and one award given to a student attending school anywhere in the U.S. If an insufficient number of qualified southern California applicants is received, then both awards may be given to students enrolled anywhere in the U.S. Applicant must be U.S. citizens. Please go to http://www.astanet.com for requirements and an application form. Minimum 2.5 GPA required.

Academic Fields/Career Goals: Travel/Tourism.

Award: Scholarship for use in freshman, sophomore, junior, or senior years; not renewable. *Number:* 2. *Amount:* $2500.

Eligibility Requirements: Applicant must be enrolled or expecting to enroll full or part-time at a four-year institution or university. Applicant must have 2.5 GPA or higher. Available to U.S. citizens.

Application Requirements: Application, essay, references, transcript. *Deadline:* varies.

Contact: Verlette Mitchell, Manager
American Society of Travel Agents (ASTA) Foundation
1101 King Street
Alexandria, VA 22314-2187
Phone: 703-739-8721
Fax: 703-684-8319
E-mail: scholarship@astahq.com

STAN AND LEONE POLLARD SCHOLARSHIPS

Available to a person re-entering the job market. Must be enrolled in a travel or tourism curriculum at a proprietary travel school or junior college. Go to Web site (http://www.astanet.com) for requirements and an application form. Scholarships are awarded twice each year.

Academic Fields/Career Goals: Travel/Tourism.

Award: Scholarship for use in freshman or sophomore years; not renewable. *Number:* 2. *Amount:* $2000.

Eligibility Requirements: Applicant must be enrolled or expecting to enroll full or part-time at a two-year or technical institution. Applicant must have 2.5 GPA or higher. Available to U.S. and Canadian citizens.

Application Requirements: Application, essay, references, transcript. *Deadline:* varies.

Contact: Verlette Mitchell, Manager
American Society of Travel Agents (ASTA) Foundation
1101 King Street
Alexandria, VA 22314-2187
Phone: 703-739-8721
Fax: 703-684-8319
E-mail: scholarship@astahq.com

CANADIAN RECREATIONAL CANOEING ASSOCIATION **http://www.paddlingcanada.com**

BILL MASON MEMORIAL SCHOLARSHIP FUND

• *See page 57*

CATCHING THE DREAM

TRIBAL BUSINESS MANAGEMENT PROGRAM (TBM)

• *See page 38*

HAWAII HOTEL AND LODGING ASSOCIATION **http://www.hawaiihotels.org**

R.W. BOB HOLDEN SCHOLARSHIP

• *See page 322*

HOSPITALITY SALES AND MARKETING ASSOCIATION INTERNATIONAL FOUNDATION **http://www.hsmai.org**

HOSPITALITY SALES AND MARKETING ASSOCIATION INTERNATIONAL FOUNDATION STUDENT SCHOLARSHIPS

• *See page 322*

INTERNATIONAL AIRLINES TRAVEL AGENT NETWORK http://www.iatan.org

INTERNATIONAL AIRLINES TRAVEL AGENT NETWORK RONALD A. SANTANA MEMORIAL FOUNDATION
• See page 322

INTERNATIONAL FOODSERVICE EDITORIAL COUNCIL http://www.ifec-is-us.com

INTERNATIONAL FOODSERVICE EDITORIAL COUNCIL COMMUNICATIONS SCHOLARSHIP
• See page 160

MISSOURI TRAVEL COUNCIL http://www.missouritravel.com

MISSOURI TRAVEL COUNCIL TOURISM SCHOLARSHIP
• See page 278

NATIONAL TOURISM FOUNDATION http://www.ntfonline.org

ACADEMY OF TRAVEL AND TOURISM SCHOLARSHIPS
• See page 323

CLEVELAND LEGACY I AND II SCHOLARSHIP AWARDS
• See page 279

NEW HORIZONS KATHY LE TARTE SCHOLARSHIP
• See page 279

PAT AND JIM HOST SCHOLARSHIP
• See page 279

SOCIETIE DES CASINOS DU QUEBEC SCHOLARSHIP
• See page 280

TAMPA, HILLSBOROUGH LEGACY SCHOLARSHIP
• See page 280

TAUCK SCHOLARS SCHOLARSHIPS
• See page 280

TULSA SCHOLARSHIP AWARDS
• See page 280

YELLOW RIBBON SCHOLARSHIP
• See page 280

NETWORK OF EXECUTIVE WOMEN IN HOSPITALITY http://www.newh.org

NETWORK OF EXECUTIVE WOMEN IN HOSPITALITY, INC. SCHOLARSHIP
• See page 78

RECREATIONAL BOATING INDUSTRIES EDUCATIONAL FOUNDATION http://mbia.org

RECREATIONAL BOATING INDUSTRIES EDUCATIONAL FOUNDATION SCHOLARSHIPS
• See page 117

SOUTH DAKOTA RETAILERS ASSOCIATION http://www.sdra.org

SOUTH DAKOTA RETAILERS ASSOCIATION SCHOLARSHIP PROGRAM
• See page 47

TV/RADIO BROADCASTING

ACADEMY OF TELEVISION ARTS AND SCIENCES FOUNDATION http://www.emmys.tv/foundation

ACADEMY OF TELEVISION ARTS AND SCIENCES COLLEGE TELEVISION AWARDS
• See page 84

ADC RESEARCH INSTITUTE http://www.adc.org

JACK SHAHEEN MASS COMMUNICATIONS SCHOLARSHIP AWARD
• See page 156

ADVERTISING FEDERATION OF FORT WAYNE, INC. http://adfedfortwayne.org

ADVERTISING FEDERATION OF FORT WAYNE, INC., SCHOLARSHIP
• See page 156

AMERICAN LEGION, PRESS CLUB OF NEW JERSEY

AMERICAN LEGION PRESS CLUB OF NEW JERSEY AND POST 170 ARTHUR DEHARDT MEMORIAL SCHOLARSHIP
• See page 156

ASIAN AMERICAN JOURNALISTS ASSOCIATION http://www.aaja.org

ASIAN-AMERICAN JOURNALISTS ASSOCIATION SCHOLARSHIP
• See page 157

MINORU YASUI MEMORIAL SCHOLARSHIP AWARD
• See page 329

ASSOCIATED PRESS http://www.aptra.org

ASSOCIATED PRESS TELEVISION/RADIO ASSOCIATION-CLETE ROBERTS JOURNALISM SCHOLARSHIP AWARDS
• See page 329

KATHRYN DETTMAN MEMORIAL JOURNALISM SCHOLARSHIP
• See page 329

ATLANTA PRESS CLUB, INC. http://www.atlpressclub.org

ATLANTA PRESS CLUB JOURNALISM SCHOLARSHIP PROGRAM
• See page 158

BOWEN FOUNDATION http://www.emmabowenfoundation.com

EMMA L. BOWEN FOUNDATION FOR MINORITY INTERESTS IN MEDIA
• See page 158

CALIFORNIA CHICANO NEWS MEDIA ASSOCIATION (CCNMA) http://www.ccnma.org

JOEL GARCIA MEMORIAL SCHOLARSHIP
• See page 158

CANADIAN ASSOCIATION OF BROADCASTERS http://www.cab-acr.ca

JIM ALLARD BROADCAST JOURNALISM SCHOLARSHIP
• See page 330

RUTH HANCOCK MEMORIAL SCHOLARSHIP
• See page 158

CHARLES & LUCILLE KING FAMILY FOUNDATION, INC. http://www.kingfoundation.org

CHARLES AND LUCILLE KING FAMILY FOUNDATION SCHOLARSHIPS
• See page 159

CIRI FOUNDATION http://www.ciri.com/tcf

CAP LATHROP SCHOLARSHIP PROGRAM

Applicants should plan to work in the broadcast/telecommunications industry in Alaska upon completion of the academic degree. One-time award to full-time student. Must be Native American Student. Minimum 3.0 GPA required. For more details see Web site: http://www.ciri.com/tcf.

Academic Fields/Career Goals: TV/Radio Broadcasting.

Award: Scholarship for use in freshman, sophomore, junior, senior, or graduate years; not renewable. *Number:* varies. *Amount:* $3500.

Eligibility Requirements: Applicant must be American Indian/Alaska Native and enrolled or expecting to enroll full-time at a two-year or four-year institution or university. Applicant must have 3.0 GPA or higher. Available to U.S. citizens.

Application Requirements: Application, references, transcript, statement of purpose. *Deadline:* June 1.

Contact: CIRI Foundation
2600 Cordova Street, Suite 206
Anchorage, AK 99503
Phone: 907-263-5582
Fax: 907-263-5588
E-mail: tcf@ciri.com

DALLAS-FORT WORTH ASSOCIATION OF BLACK COMMUNICATORS http://www.dfwabc.org

FUTURE JOURNALISTS SCHOLARSHIP PROGRAM
• *See page 159*

FISHER BROADCASTING COMPANY http://www.fisherbroadcasting.com/

FISHER BROADCASTING, INC., SCHOLARSHIP FOR MINORITIES
• *See page 159*

GREATER KANAWHA VALLEY FOUNDATION http://www.tgkvf.org

WEST VIRGINIA BROADCASTERS ASSOCIATION FUND
• *See page 159*

ILLUMINATING ENGINEERING SOCIETY OF NORTH AMERICA http://www.iesna.org

ROBERT W. THUNEN MEMORIAL SCHOLARSHIPS
• *See page 77*

INDIANA BROADCASTERS ASSOCIATION http://www.indianabroadcasters.org

INDIANA BROADCASTERS FOUNDATION SCHOLARSHIP
• *See page 331*

INDIANAPOLIS ASSOCIATION OF BLACK JOURNALISTS http://www.iabj.org

LYNN DEAN FORD IABJ SCHOLARSHIP AWARDS
• *See page 160*

JOHN BAYLISS BROADCAST FOUNDATION http://www.baylissfoundation.org

JOHN BAYLISS BROADCAST RADIO SCHOLARSHIP
• *See page 160*

KATU THOMAS R. DARGAN MINORITY SCHOLARSHIP http://www.katu.com

THOMAS R. DARGAN MINORITY SCHOLARSHIP
• *See page 161*

KCNC-TV CHANNEL 4 NEWS http://www.news4colorado.com

NEWS 4 PETER ROGOT MEDIA SCHOLARSHIP
• *See page 161*

MAINE MEDIA WOMEN SCHOLARSHIPS COMMITTEE http://www.mainemediawomen.org/scholarships.html

MAINE MEDIA WOMEN'S SCHOLARSHIP
• *See page 88*

MARYLAND ASSOCIATION OF PRIVATE COLLEGES AND CAREER SCHOOLS http://www.mapccs.org

MARYLAND ASSOCIATION OF PRIVATE COLLEGES AND CAREER SCHOOLS SCHOLARSHIP
• *See page 127*

MEDIA ACTION NETWORK FOR ASIAN AMERICANS http://www.manaa.org

MANAA MEDIA SCHOLARSHIPS FOR ASIAN AMERICAN STUDENTS
• *See page 89*

MINNESOTA BROADCASTERS ASSOCIATION http://www.minnesotabroadcasters.com

JAMES J. WYCHOR SCHOLARSHIP

One-time scholarships to Minnesota residents interested in broadcasting who are planning to enter broadcasting or other work in electronic media. Minimum 2.5 GPA is required. Application deadline is May 31. Submit proof of enrollment at an accredited postsecondary institution.

Academic Fields/Career Goals: TV/Radio Broadcasting.

Award: Scholarship for use in freshman, sophomore, junior, senior, or graduate years; not renewable. *Number:* 10. *Amount:* $1500.

Eligibility Requirements: Applicant must be enrolled or expecting to enroll full-time at a four-year institution or university; resident of Minnesota and must have an interest in designated field specified by sponsor. Applicant must have 2.5 GPA or higher. Available to U.S. citizens.

Application Requirements: Application, essay, references, transcript. *Deadline:* May 31.

Contact: Megan Eischen, Member Services Coordinator
Minnesota Broadcasters Association
3033 Excelsior Boulevard, Suite 301
Minneapolis, MN 55416-4675
Phone: 612-926-8123
Fax: 612-926-9761
E-mail: meischen@minnesotabroadcasters.com

NATIONAL ACADEMY OF TELEVISION ARTS AND SCIENCES http://www.emmyonline.org/emmy/scholr.html

NATIONAL ACADEMY OF TELEVISION ARTS AND SCIENCES JOHN CANNON MEMORIAL SCHOLARSHIP
• *See page 161*

TRUSTEE SCHOLARSHIP PROGRAM
• *See page 161*

NATIONAL ASSOCIATION OF BLACK JOURNALISTS http://www.nabj.org

NATIONAL ASSOCIATION OF BLACK JOURNALISTS NON-SUSTAINING SCHOLARSHIP AWARDS
• *See page 333*

NATIONAL ASSOCIATION OF HISPANIC JOURNALISTS (NAHJ) http://www.nahj.org

ABC NEWS/JOANNA BISTANY MEMORIAL SCHOLARSHIP
• *See page 333*

GERALDO RIVERA SCHOLARSHIP
• *See page 333*

MARIA ELENA SALINAS SCHOLARSHIP
• *See page 334*

NATIONAL ASSOCIATION OF HISPANIC JOURNALISTS SCHOLARSHIP
• *See page 161*

NATIONAL PRESS PHOTOGRAPHERS FOUNDATION, INC. http://www.nppa.org

NATIONAL PRESS PHOTOGRAPHERS FOUNDATION TELEVISION NEWS SCHOLARSHIP
• *See page 404*

NEW YORK WOMEN IN COMMUNICATIONS, INC., FOUNDATION http://www.nywici.org/foundation/index.html

NEW YORK WOMEN IN COMMUNICATIONS, INC. FOUNDATION SCHOLARSHIP PROGRAM
• *See page 163*

OREGON ASSOCIATION OF BROADCASTERS http://www.theoab.org

OAB BROADCAST SCHOLARSHIP
• *See page 163*

OREGON STUDENT ASSISTANCE COMMISSION http://www.osac.state.or.us

ENTERCOM PORTLAND RADIO SCHOLARSHIP FUND
• *See page 336*

OUTDOOR WRITERS ASSOCIATION OF AMERICA http://www.owaa.org

OUTDOOR WRITERS ASSOCIATION OF AMERICA BODIE MCDOWELL SCHOLARSHIP AWARD
• *See page 163*

RADIO-TELEVISION NEWS DIRECTORS ASSOCIATION AND FOUNDATION http://www.rtndf.org

CAROLE SIMPSON SCHOLARSHIP
• *See page 164*

ED BRADLEY SCHOLARSHIP
• *See page 164*

KEN KASHIWAHARA SCHOLARSHIP
• *See page 164*

LOU AND CAROLE PRATO SPORTS REPORTING SCHOLARSHIP
• *See page 164*

MIKE REYNOLDS $1,000 SCHOLARSHIP
• *See page 164*

PRESIDENT'S $2500 SCHOLARSHIP
• *See page 164*

RHODE ISLAND FOUNDATION http://www.rifoundation.org

RHODE ISLAND ADVERTISING SCHOLARSHIP
• *See page 268*

SOCIETY OF BROADCAST ENGINEERS, INC. http://www.sbe.org

ROBERT GREENBERG/HAROLD E. ENNES SCHOLARSHIP FUND AND ENNES EDUCATIONAL FOUNDATION BROADCAST TECHNOLOGY SCHOLARSHIP
• *See page 233*

SOCIETY OF PROFESSIONAL JOURNALISTS, LOS ANGELES CHAPTER http://www.spj.org/losangeles

HELEN JOHNSON SCHOLARSHIP
• *See page 338*

TEXAS GRIDIRON CLUB, INC. http://www.spjfw.org

TEXAS GRIDIRON CLUB SCHOLARSHIPS
• *See page 165*

UNITED METHODIST COMMUNICATIONS http://www.umcom.org/scholarships

LEONARD M. PERRYMAN COMMUNICATIONS SCHOLARSHIP FOR ETHNIC MINORITY STUDENTS
• *See page 166*

UNITED NEGRO COLLEGE FUND http://www.uncf.org

C-SPAN SCHOLARSHIP PROGRAM
• *See page 166*

VALLEY PRESS CLUB

VALLEY PRESS CLUB SCHOLARSHIPS, THE REPUBLICAN SCHOLARSHIP; PHOTOJOURNALISM SCHOLARSHIP, CHANNEL 22 SCHOLARSHIP
• *See page 167*

URBAN AND REGIONAL PLANNING

AMERICAN PLANNING ASSOCIATION http://www.planning.org

JUDITH MCMANUS PRICE SCHOLARSHIP

Scholarship available for women and minority students enrolled in degree programs in planning or a closely related field. Must demonstrate a genuine financial need. Deadline is April 30. Details on Web site: http://www.planning.org.

Academic Fields/Career Goals: Urban and Regional Planning.

Award: Scholarship for use in freshman, sophomore, junior, senior, or graduate years; not renewable. *Number:* 1. *Amount:* $2000–$4000.

Eligibility Requirements: Applicant must be American Indian/Alaska Native, Black (non-Hispanic), or Hispanic; enrolled or expecting to enroll at a four-year institution or university and female. Available to U.S. citizens.

Application Requirements: Application, financial need analysis, resume, references, transcript. *Deadline:* April 30.

Contact: Kriss Blank, Leadership Affairs Associate
American Planning Association
Minority Scholarship and Fellowship Programs
122 South Michigan Avenue, Suite 1600
Chicago, IL 60603-6107
Phone: 312-786-6722
Fax: 312-786-6727

CONNECTICUT CHAPTER OF THE AMERICAN PLANNING ASSOCIATION http://www.ccapa.org

DIANA DONALD SCHOLARSHIP

The Diana Donald Scholarship is available to Connecticut residents or students attending schools in Connecticut. Applicants must be enrolled in a graduate or undergraduate program in city planning or a closely related field.

Academic Fields/Career Goals: Urban and Regional Planning.

Award: Scholarship for use in freshman, sophomore, junior, senior, or graduate years; not renewable. *Number:* 1. *Amount:* $1000.

Eligibility Requirements: Applicant must be enrolled or expecting to enroll full-time at an institution or university. Available to U.S. and non-U.S. citizens.

Application Requirements: Application, essay, financial need analysis, references, transcript. *Deadline:* March 30.

Contact: Michael Piscitelli
Connecticut Chapter of the American Planning Association
City Planning Department, 165 Church Street, 5th Floor
New Haven, CT 06510
Phone: 203-946-7814

WOMEN'S STUDIES

AMERICAN HISTORICAL ASSOCIATION http://www.theaha.org

JOAN KELLY MEMORIAL PRIZE IN WOMEN'S HISTORY

• *See page 309*

NATIONAL CHAMBER OF COMMERCE FOR WOMEN http://fair-advantage.org

MILLIE BELAFONTE WRIGHT SCHOLARSHIP AND GRANT EVALUATION

• *See page 110*

SUNSHINE LADY FOUNDATION, INC. http://www.sunshineladyfdn.org

COUNSELOR, ADVOCATE, AND SUPPORT STAFF SCHOLARSHIP PROGRAM

• *See page 47*

NONACADEMIC/NONCAREER CRITERIA

CIVIC, PROFESSIONAL, SOCIAL, OR UNION AFFILIATION

AIR LINE PILOTS ASSOCIATION, INTERNATIONAL http://www.alpa.org

AIR LINE PILOTS ASSOCIATION SCHOLARSHIP PROGRAM

Four-year scholarship for children of medically retired, long-term disabled, or deceased pilot members of the Air Line Pilots Association. High school seniors may apply. Scholarship awards $3000 a year for four years. Minimum 3.0 GPA required. For undergraduate use.

Award: Scholarship for use in freshman, sophomore, junior, or senior years; renewable. *Number:* 1. *Amount:* $3000.

Eligibility Requirements: Applicant must be enrolled or expecting to enroll full-time at a four-year institution or university. Applicant or parent of applicant must be member of Airline Pilots Association. Applicant must have 3.0 GPA or higher. Available to U.S. and Canadian citizens.

Application Requirements: Application, financial need analysis, transcript. *Deadline:* April 1.

Contact: Janice Redden, Scholarship Program Manager
Air Line Pilots Association, International
1625 Massachusetts Avenue, NW
Washington, DC 20036

ALBERTA HERITAGE SCHOLARSHIP FUND/ ALBERTA SCHOLARSHIP PROGRAMS http://www.alis.gov.ab.ca/scholarships

BOYS AND GIRLS CLUB OF ALBERTA SCHOLARSHIPS

A CAN$500 scholarship is available to assist members of the Boys and Girls club pursue higher education. Candidates must be 24 years of age or younger, be current or former members of a Boys and Girls Club in Alberta and enrolled or planning to enroll full time in a postsecondary program. Must be a Canadian citizen or landed immigrant, and Alberta resident. For more details see Web site: http://www.alis.gov.ab.ca.

Award: Scholarship for use in freshman, sophomore, junior, or senior years; not renewable. *Number:* 3. *Amount:* $405.

Eligibility Requirements: Applicant must be age 24 or under; enrolled or expecting to enroll full-time at a two-year or four-year or technical institution or university and resident of Alberta. Applicant or parent of applicant must be member of Boys or Girls Club. Available to Canadian citizens.

Application Requirements: Application, references, transcript. *Deadline:* May 1.

Contact: Director
Alberta Heritage Scholarship Fund/Alberta Scholarship Programs
9940 106th Street, 9th Floor
Box 28000, Station Main
Edmonton, AB T5J 4R4
Canada
Phone: 780-427-8640
Fax: 780-422-4516
E-mail: heritage@gov.ab.ca

AMERICAN ASSOCIATION OF BIOANALYSTS http://www.aab.org

DAVID BIRENBAUM SCHOLARSHIP FUND

One-time award based on merit for associate members or dependents of members of the American Association of Bioanalysts for study in any discipline for any academic year. Submit two character references.

Award: Scholarship for use in freshman, sophomore, junior, senior, or graduate years; not renewable. *Number:* 1–5. *Amount:* varies.

Eligibility Requirements: Applicant must be enrolled or expecting to enroll full or part-time at a two-year or four-year or technical institution or university. Applicant or parent of applicant must be member of American Association of Bioanalysts. Available to U.S. and non-U.S. citizens.

Application Requirements: Application, essay, financial need analysis, references, transcript. *Deadline:* March 15.

Contact: Scholarship Coordinator
American Association of Bioanalysts
917 Locust Street, Suite 1100
St. Louis, MO 63101-1419
Phone: 314-241-1445
Fax: 314-241-1449

AMERICAN BOWLING CONGRESS http://www.bowl.com

CHUCK HALL STAR OF TOMORROW SCHOLARSHIP

Award is available to male, amateur bowlers 21 and under. Must be a high school senior or undergraduate student. Merit is taken into account as well. Minimum GPA of 2.50 is required. The award is $1,250 which is renewable for up to 3 years for a total of $5,000. Application deadline is November 15. Must be a member of YABA or ABC in good standing.

Award: Scholarship for use in freshman, sophomore, junior, or senior years; renewable. *Number:* 1. *Amount:* $1250.

Eligibility Requirements: Applicant must be age 21 or under; enrolled or expecting to enroll full or part-time at a two-year or four-year or technical institution or university; male and must have an interest in bowling. Applicant or parent of applicant must be member of Young American Bowling Alliance. Applicant must have 2.5 GPA or higher. Available to U.S. and Canadian citizens.

Application Requirements: Application, essay, references, self-addressed stamped envelope, transcript. *Deadline:* November 15.

Contact: Ed Gocha, Scholarship Administrator
American Bowling Congress
5301 South 76th Street
Greendale, WI 53129-1192
Phone: 800-514-2695 Ext. 3343
Fax: 414-421-3014
E-mail: egocha@bowlinginc.com

AMERICAN FEDERATION OF STATE, COUNTY, AND MUNICIPAL EMPLOYEES http://www.afscme.org

AMERICAN FEDERATION OF STATE, COUNTY, AND MUNICIPAL EMPLOYEES SCHOLARSHIP PROGRAM

Award for family dependents of American Federation of State, County, and Municipal Employees members. Must be a graduating high school senior planning to pursue postsecondary education at a four-year institution. Submit proof of parent's membership. Transcript and essay on what AFSCME has meant to my family must accompany application. Renewable award of $2000.

Award: Scholarship for use in freshman, sophomore, junior, or senior years; renewable. *Number:* 10. *Amount:* $2000.

Eligibility Requirements: Applicant must be high school student and planning to enroll or expecting to enroll full-time at a four-year institution or university. Applicant or parent of applicant must be member of American Federation of State, County, and Municipal Employees.

Application Requirements: Application, essay, references, test scores, transcript. *Deadline:* December 31.

Contact: Genevieve Marcus, Scholarship Coordinator
American Federation of State, County, and Municipal Employees
1625 L Street, NW
Washington, DC 20036
Phone: 202-429-1250
Fax: 202-429-1272

UNION PLUS CREDIT CARD SCHOLARSHIP PROGRAM

One-time award for AFSCME members, their spouses, and dependent children. Graduate students and grandchildren are not eligible. Members need not be AFSCME Advantage Union Plus credit cardholders to apply. Further information available at Web site http://www.afscme.org. Application deadline is January 31.

Award: Scholarship for use in freshman, sophomore, junior, or senior years; not renewable. *Number:* varies. *Amount:* $500–$4000.

Eligibility Requirements: Applicant must be enrolled or expecting to enroll at a two-year or four-year or technical institution. Applicant or parent of applicant must be member of American Federation of State, County, and Municipal Employees. Available to U.S. citizens.

Application Requirements: Application, autobiography, essay, references, transcript. *Deadline:* January 31.

Contact: Genevieve Marcus, Scholarship Coordinator
American Federation of State, County, and Municipal Employees
1625 L Street, NW
Washington, DC 20036
Phone: 202-429-1250
Fax: 202-429-1272

AMERICAN FEDERATION OF TEACHERS-NEW HAMPSHIRE FEDERATION OF TEACHERS http://www.nhft.org

NEW HAMPSHIRE FEDERATION OF TEACHERS SCHOLARSHIP

Award is based upon post academic performance and community service experiences. Financial need is also considered. Must be a U.S. citizen and a resident of New Hampshire. Must have a parent or guardian who is a member of the New Hampshire Federation of Teachers.

Award: Scholarship for use in freshman year; not renewable. *Number:* 1. *Amount:* $1000.

Eligibility Requirements: Applicant must be high school student; planning to enroll or expecting to enroll full or part-time at a two-year or four-year or technical institution or university and resident of New Hampshire. Applicant or parent of applicant must be member of New Hampshire Federation of Teachers. Available to U.S. citizens.

Application Requirements: Application, essay, financial need analysis, references, transcript. *Deadline:* April 15.

Contact: Cathy White, Associate Staff Representative
American Federation of Teachers-New Hampshire Federation of Teachers
553 Route 3A, Ruggles IV
Bow, NH 03304-3212
Phone: 603-223-0747
Fax: 603-226-0133
E-mail: cwhitenhft@conversent.net

AMERICAN FOREIGN SERVICE ASSOCIATION http://www.afsa.org

AMERICAN FOREIGN SERVICE ASSOCIATION (AFSA) FINANCIAL AID AWARD PROGRAM

Need-based financial aid scholarship program open to children whose parents are in the U.S. Government Foreign Service. Must attend a U.S. school full-time and maintain a "C" average. Children whose parents are in the military and international students are not eligible.

Award: Scholarship for use in freshman, sophomore, junior, or senior years; not renewable. *Number:* 50–60. *Amount:* $500–$3000.

Eligibility Requirements: Applicant must be enrolled or expecting to enroll full-time at a two-year or four-year or technical institution or university and single. Applicant or parent of applicant must be member of American Foreign Service Association. Applicant or parent of applicant must have employment or volunteer experience in U.S. government foreign service. Available to U.S. citizens.

Application Requirements: Application, financial need analysis, transcript, CSS Profile. *Deadline:* February 6.

Contact: Ms. Lori Dec, Scholarship Administrator
American Foreign Service Association
2101 E Street, NW
Washington, DC 20037
Phone: 202-944-5504
Fax: 202-338-6820
E-mail: dec@afsa.org

AMERICAN FOREIGN SERVICE ASSOCIATION (AFSA)/AAFSW MERIT AWARD PROGRAM

One-time award for a high school senior whose parent is a U.S. Government Foreign Service employee. Parent must be a member of AFSA or AAFSW. Children of military parents or international students are not eligible. Award based upon academic and artistic achievements of the applicant.

Award: Prize for use in freshman year; not renewable. *Number:* 6–15. *Amount:* $500–$1500.

Eligibility Requirements: Applicant must be high school student; planning to enroll or expecting to enroll full-time at an institution or university and single. Applicant or parent of applicant must be member of American Foreign Service Association. Applicant or parent of applicant must have employment or volunteer experience in U.S. government foreign service. Available to U.S. citizens.

Application Requirements: Application, essay, references, self-addressed stamped envelope, test scores, transcript. *Deadline:* February 6.

Contact: Ms. Lori Dec, Scholarship Administrator
American Foreign Service Association
2101 E Street, NW
Washington, DC 20037
Phone: 202-944-5504
Fax: 202-338-6820
E-mail: dec@afsa.org

AMERICAN GUILD OF ORGANISTS http://www.agohq.org

NATIONAL YOUNG ARTISTS COMPETITION IN ORGAN PERFORMANCE

Organ performance competition open to organists between 22 and 32 years of age who are members of the American Guild of Organists. Must submit birth certificate, two photos, 3 copies of cassette tape of program, and curriculum vitae. Four one-time awards of varying amounts. Application fee: $40.

Award: Prize for use in freshman, sophomore, junior, senior, or graduate years; not renewable. *Number:* 4. *Amount:* $500–$2000.

Eligibility Requirements: Applicant must be age 22-32; enrolled or expecting to enroll full or part-time at an institution or university and must have an interest in music. Applicant or parent of applicant must be member of American Guild of Organists.

Application Requirements: Application, applicant must enter a contest, autobiography, photo, resume, references, birth certificate, cassette tape of program. *Fee:* $40. *Deadline:* varies.

Contact: James Thomashower, Executive Director
American Guild of Organists
475 Riverside Drive, Suite 1260
New York, NY 10115
Phone: 212-870-2310
Fax: 212-870-2163
E-mail: info@agohq.org

AMERICAN LEGION AUXILIARY, DEPARTMENT OF COLORADO

AMERICAN LEGION AUXILIARY DEPARTMENT OF COLORADO DEPARTMENT PRESIDENT'S SCHOLARSHIP FOR JUNIOR MEMBERS

One-time award for members of the American Legion Junior Auxiliary who are residents of Colorado. Contact for more information.

American Legion Auxiliary, Department of Colorado (continued)

Award: Scholarship for use in freshman year; not renewable. *Number:* 1. *Amount:* $500.

Eligibility Requirements: Applicant must be high school student; planning to enroll or expecting to enroll full-time at a two-year or four-year institution or university; female and resident of Colorado. Applicant or parent of applicant must be member of American Legion or Auxiliary. Available to U.S. citizens. Applicant must have general military experience.

Application Requirements: Application, essay, references, test scores, transcript.

Contact: Department Secretary/Treasurer
American Legion Auxiliary, Department of Colorado
7465 East First Avenue, Suite D
Denver, CO 80230
Phone: 303-367-5388

AMERICAN LEGION AUXILIARY, DEPARTMENT OF CONNECTICUT

AMERICAN LEGION AUXILIARY DEPARTMENT OF CONNECTICUT MEMORIAL EDUCATIONAL GRANT

Half the number of grants awarded to children of veterans who are also residents of CT. Remaining grants awarded to child or grandchild of a member (or member at time of death) of the CT Departments of the American Legion /American Legion Auxiliary, regardless of residency; or are members of the CT Departments of the American Legion Auxiliary/Sons of the American Legion, regardless of residency. Contact local unit President. Must include list of community service activities.

Award: Grant for use in freshman, sophomore, junior, or senior years; not renewable. *Number:* 4. *Amount:* $500.

Eligibility Requirements: Applicant must be age 16-23 and enrolled or expecting to enroll full-time at a two-year or four-year or technical institution or university. Applicant or parent of applicant must be member of American Legion or Auxiliary. Available to U.S. citizens. Applicant or parent must meet one or more of the following requirements: general military experience; retired from active duty; disabled or killed as a result of military service; prisoner of war; or missing in action.

Application Requirements: Application, financial need analysis, references, self-addressed stamped envelope, transcript. *Deadline:* March 11.

Contact: Local Unit President
American Legion Auxiliary, Department of Connecticut
PO Box 266
Rocky Hill, CT 06067

AMERICAN LEGION AUXILIARY DEPARTMENT OF CONNECTICUT PAST PRESIDENT'S PARLEY MEMORIAL EDUCATION GRANT

Preference given to child or grandchild of ex-service woman, who was or is a member of the CT Departments of the American Legion/American Legion Auxiliary. In the event of a deficiency of preferred applicants, award may be granted to child or grandchild of a member of the CT Departments of the American Legion/American Legion Auxiliary or Sons of the American Legion. Minimum 5-year membership required, or 5 years prior to death. Contact local unit President. Must include list of community service activities.

Award: Grant for use in freshman, sophomore, junior, or senior years; not renewable. *Number:* 4. *Amount:* up to $500.

Eligibility Requirements: Applicant must be age 16-23 and enrolled or expecting to enroll at a two-year or four-year or technical institution or university. Applicant or parent of applicant must be member of American Legion or Auxiliary. Available to U.S. citizens. Applicant or parent must meet one or more of the following requirements: general military experience; retired from active duty; disabled or killed as a result of military service; prisoner of war; or missing in action.

Application Requirements: Application, financial need analysis, references, test scores, transcript, list of school and community activities. *Deadline:* March 1.

Contact: Local Unit President
American Legion Auxiliary, Department of Connecticut
PO Box 266
Rocky Hill, CT 06067

AMERICAN LEGION AUXILIARY, DEPARTMENT OF FLORIDA

AMERICAN LEGION AUXILIARY DEPARTMENT OF FLORIDA MEMORIAL SCHOLARSHIP

Scholarship for a member, daughter, or granddaughter of a member of Florida American Legion Auxiliary with minimum three years membership. Award for Florida resident for undergraduate study in Florida school. Minimum GPA 2.5.

Award: Scholarship for use in freshman, sophomore, junior, or senior years; renewable. *Number:* varies. *Amount:* $500–$1000.

Eligibility Requirements: Applicant must be enrolled or expecting to enroll full-time at a two-year or four-year or technical institution or university; female; resident of Florida and studying in Florida. Applicant or parent of applicant must be member of American Legion or Auxiliary. Applicant must have 2.5 GPA or higher. Available to U.S. citizens.

Application Requirements: Application, financial need analysis, references, transcript. *Deadline:* January 1.

Contact: Ms. Marie Mahoney, Department Secretary and Treasurer
American Legion Auxiliary, Department of Florida
PO Box 547917
Orlando, FL 32854-7917
Phone: 407-293-7411
Fax: 407-299-6522
E-mail: alaflorida@aol.com

AMERICAN LEGION AUXILIARY, DEPARTMENT OF KENTUCKY

MARY BARRETT MARSHALL SCHOLARSHIP

Must be high school or GED graduate. Must attend school in Kentucky and visit Auxiliary Unit to request scholarship. Must be five-year resident of Kentucky. Must be female relative of veteran eligible for American Legion membership.

Award: Scholarship for use in freshman, sophomore, junior, or senior years; renewable. *Number:* 1. *Amount:* $1000.

Eligibility Requirements: Applicant must be enrolled or expecting to enroll full or part-time at a two-year or four-year or technical institution or university; female; resident of Kentucky and studying in Kentucky. Applicant or parent of applicant must be member of American Legion or Auxiliary. Available to U.S. citizens. Applicant or parent must meet one or more of the following requirements: general military experience; retired from active duty; disabled or killed as a result of military service; prisoner of war; or missing in action.

Application Requirements: Application, financial need analysis, interview, references, test scores, transcript. *Deadline:* April 1.

Contact: Velma Greenleaf, Scholarship Chairman
American Legion Auxiliary, Department of Kentucky
1448 Leafdale Road
Hodgenville, KY 42748
Phone: 270-358-3341

AMERICAN LEGION AUXILIARY, DEPARTMENT OF MISSOURI

AMERICAN LEGION AUXILIARY MISSOURI STATE NATIONAL PRESIDENT'S SCHOLARSHIP

State-level award. Missouri Legion Auxiliary offers two $500 scholarships. To be eligible, applicant must complete 50 hours of community service during their high school years. Sponsoring Unit and Department must validate application. Applicant must be Missouri resident.

Award: Scholarship for use in freshman, sophomore, junior, or senior years; not renewable. *Number:* 2. *Amount:* $500.

Eligibility Requirements: Applicant must be enrolled or expecting to enroll at a two-year or four-year or technical institution or university and resident of Missouri. Applicant or parent of applicant must be member of American Legion or Auxiliary. Applicant or parent of applicant must have employment or volunteer experience in community service. Available to U.S. citizens. Applicant or parent must meet one or more of the following requirements: general military experience; retired from active duty; disabled or killed as a result of military service; prisoner of war; or missing in action.

Application Requirements: Application. *Deadline:* March 15.

Contact: Kim Merchant, Department Secretary/Treasurer
American Legion Auxiliary, Department of Missouri
600 Ellis Boulevard
Jefferson City, MO 65101-1615
Phone: 573-636-9133
Fax: 573-635-3467
E-mail: dptmoala@socket.net

LELA MURPHY SCHOLARSHIP

$500 scholarship for high school graduate. $250 will be awarded each semester. Applicant must be Missouri resident and the granddaughter or great-granddaughter of a living or deceased Auxiliary member. Sponsoring Unit and Department must validate application.

Award: Scholarship for use in freshman year; renewable. *Number:* 1. *Amount:* $500.

Eligibility Requirements: Applicant must be high school student; planning to enroll or expecting to enroll at a two-year or four-year or technical institution or university; female and resident of Missouri. Applicant or parent of applicant must be member of American Legion or Auxiliary. Available to U.S. citizens. Applicant or parent must meet one or more of the following requirements: general military experience; retired from active duty; disabled or killed as a result of military service; prisoner of war; or missing in action.

Application Requirements: Application. *Deadline:* March 15.

Contact: Kim Merchant, Department Secretary/Treasurer
American Legion Auxiliary, Department of Missouri
600 Ellis Boulevard
Jefferson City, MO 65101-1615
Phone: 573-636-9133
Fax: 573-635-3467
E-mail: dptmoala@socket.net

AMERICAN LEGION AUXILIARY, DEPARTMENT OF NEBRASKA

AMERICAN LEGION AUXILIARY DEPARTMENT OF NEBRASKA PRESIDENT'S SCHOLARSHIP FOR JUNIOR MEMBERS

One-time prize for female resident of Nebraska who has been entered into the National President's Scholarship for Junior Members and does not win at the national level. Must be in grades 9-12. Must rank in upper third of class or have a minimum 3.0 GPA.

Award: Prize for use in freshman year; not renewable. *Number:* 1. *Amount:* $200.

Eligibility Requirements: Applicant must be high school student; planning to enroll or expecting to enroll full-time at a two-year or four-year or technical institution or university; female and resident of Nebraska. Applicant or parent of applicant must be member of American Legion or Auxiliary. Applicant must have 3.0 GPA or higher.

Application Requirements: Application, applicant must enter a contest, financial need analysis, references, transcript. *Deadline:* April 1.

Contact: Terry Walker, Department Secretary
American Legion Auxiliary, Department of Nebraska
PO Box 5227
Lincoln, NE 68505
Phone: 402-466-1808
Fax: 402-466-0182
E-mail: neaux@alltel.net

RUBY PAUL CAMPAIGN FUND SCHOLARSHIP

One-time award for Nebraska residents who are children, grandchildren, or great-grandchildren of an American Legion Auxiliary member, or who have been members of the American Legion, American Legion Auxiliary, or Sons of the American Legion or Auxiliary for two years prior to application. Must rank in upper third of class or have minimum 3.0 GPA.

Award: Scholarship for use in freshman year; not renewable. *Number:* 1–3. *Amount:* $100–$300.

Eligibility Requirements: Applicant must be enrolled or expecting to enroll full-time at a two-year or four-year or technical institution or university and resident of Nebraska. Applicant or parent of applicant must be member of American Legion or Auxiliary. Applicant must have 3.0 GPA or higher. Applicant or parent must meet one or more of the following requirements: general military experience; retired from active duty; disabled or killed as a result of military service; prisoner of war; or missing in action.

Application Requirements: Application, essay, financial need analysis, references, test scores, transcript. *Deadline:* April 16.

Contact: Terry Walker, Department Secretary
American Legion Auxiliary, Department of Nebraska
PO Box 5227
Lincoln, NE 68505
Phone: 402-466-1808
Fax: 402-466-0182
E-mail: neaux@alltel.net

AMERICAN LEGION AUXILIARY, DEPARTMENT OF OREGON

AMERICAN LEGION AUXILIARY DEPARTMENT OF OREGON SPIRIT OF YOUTH SCHOLARSHIP

One-time award available to Oregon high school seniors. Must be a current female junior member of the American Legion Auxiliary with a three-year membership history. Apply through local units. $1000 available if won on national level.

Award: Scholarship for use in freshman year; not renewable. *Number:* 1. *Amount:* $300–$1000.

Eligibility Requirements: Applicant must be high school student; planning to enroll or expecting to enroll at an institution or university; female and resident of Oregon. Applicant or parent of applicant must be member of American Legion or Auxiliary. Available to U.S. citizens. Applicant or parent must meet one or more of the following requirements: general military experience; retired from active duty; disabled or killed as a result of military service; prisoner of war; or missing in action.

Application Requirements: Application, essay, financial need analysis, interview, references, transcript. *Deadline:* March 1.

Contact: Pat Calhoun-Floren, Secretary
American Legion Auxiliary, Department of Oregon
PO Box 1730
Wilsonville, OR 97070
Phone: 503-682-3162
Fax: 503-685-5008

AMERICAN LEGION AUXILIARY, DEPARTMENT OF SOUTH DAKOTA

AMERICAN LEGION AUXILIARY DEPARTMENT OF SOUTH DAKOTA COLLEGE SCHOLARSHIPS

Award to assist veterans' children or auxiliary members' children from South Dakota ages 16-22 to secure an education at a four-year school. Write for more information. One-time award of $500.

Award: Scholarship for use in freshman, sophomore, junior, or senior years; not renewable. *Number:* 2. *Amount:* $500.

Eligibility Requirements: Applicant must be age 16-22; enrolled or expecting to enroll full-time at a four-year institution and resident of South Dakota. Applicant or parent of applicant must be member of American Legion or Auxiliary. Applicant or parent must meet one or more of the following requirements: general military experience; retired from active duty; disabled or killed as a result of military service; prisoner of war; or missing in action.

American Legion Auxiliary, Department of South Dakota (continued)

Application Requirements: Application, essay, financial need analysis, references. *Deadline:* March 1.

Contact: Patricia Coyle, Executive Secretary
American Legion Auxiliary, Department of South Dakota
PO Box 117
Huron, SD 57350
Phone: 605-353-1793
Fax: 605-352-0336
E-mail: sdlegionaux@msn.com

AMERICAN LEGION AUXILIARY DEPARTMENT OF SOUTH DAKOTA THELMA FOSTER SCHOLARSHIP FOR SENIOR AUXILIARY MEMBERS

One award for a current senior member of the South Dakota American Legion Auxiliary who has been a member for three years. Applicant may be a high school senior or older and must be female. One-time award of $300 must be used within twelve months.

Award: Scholarship for use in freshman year; not renewable. *Number:* 1. *Amount:* $300.

Eligibility Requirements: Applicant must be enrolled or expecting to enroll at an institution or university; female and resident of South Dakota. Applicant or parent of applicant must be member of American Legion or Auxiliary. Applicant or parent must meet one or more of the following requirements: general military experience; retired from active duty; disabled or killed as a result of military service; prisoner of war; or missing in action.

Application Requirements: Application, essay, financial need analysis, references. *Deadline:* March 1.

Contact: Patricia Coyle, Executive Secretary
American Legion Auxiliary, Department of South Dakota
PO Box 117
Huron, SD 57350
Phone: 605-353-1793
Fax: 605-352-0336
E-mail: sdlegionaux@msn.com

AMERICAN LEGION AUXILIARY DEPARTMENT OF SOUTH DAKOTA THELMA FOSTER SCHOLARSHIPS FOR JUNIOR AUXILIARY MEMBERS

One award for junior member of the South Dakota American Legion Auxiliary who has held membership for the past three years and holds a membership card for the current year. Must be a senior in high school. One-time award of $300.

Award: Scholarship for use in freshman year; not renewable. *Number:* 1. *Amount:* $300.

Eligibility Requirements: Applicant must be high school student; planning to enroll or expecting to enroll at an institution or university; female and resident of South Dakota. Applicant or parent of applicant must be member of American Legion or Auxiliary. Applicant or parent must meet one or more of the following requirements: general military experience; retired from active duty; disabled or killed as a result of military service; prisoner of war; or missing in action.

Application Requirements: Application, essay, financial need analysis, references, transcript. *Deadline:* March 1.

Contact: Patricia Coyle, Executive Secretary
American Legion Auxiliary, Department of South Dakota
PO Box 117
Huron, SD 57350
Phone: 605-353-1793
Fax: 605-352-0336
E-mail: sdlegionaux@msn.com

AMERICAN LEGION AUXILIARY DEPARTMENT OF SOUTH DAKOTA VOCATIONAL SCHOLARSHIP

Award to assist veterans' children or auxiliary members' children from South Dakota ages 16-22 to secure a vocational education beyond the high school level. Write for more information. One-time award of $500.

Award: Scholarship for use in freshman or sophomore years; not renewable. *Number:* 2. *Amount:* $500.

Eligibility Requirements: Applicant must be age 16-22; enrolled or expecting to enroll at a technical institution; resident of South Dakota and studying in South Dakota. Applicant or parent of applicant must be member of American Legion or Auxiliary. Available to U.S. and Canadian citizens. Applicant or parent must meet one or more of the following requirements: general military experience; retired from active duty; disabled or killed as a result of military service; prisoner of war; or missing in action.

Application Requirements: Application, essay, financial need analysis, references. *Deadline:* March 1.

Contact: Patricia Coyle, Executive Secretary
American Legion Auxiliary, Department of South Dakota
PO Box 117
Huron, SD 57350
Phone: 605-353-1793
Fax: 605-352-0336
E-mail: sdlegionaux@msn.com

AMERICAN LEGION AUXILIARY, DEPARTMENT OF SOUTH DAKOTA SENIOR SCHOLARSHIP

Award for current senior member of South Dakota American Legion Auxiliary who has been a member for three years. $400 award, based on financial need.

Award: Scholarship for use in freshman year; not renewable. *Number:* 1. *Amount:* $400.

Eligibility Requirements: Applicant must be enrolled or expecting to enroll at a two-year or four-year or technical institution; female and resident of South Dakota. Applicant or parent of applicant must be member of American Legion or Auxiliary. Applicant or parent must meet one or more of the following requirements: general military experience; retired from active duty; disabled or killed as a result of military service; prisoner of war; or missing in action.

Application Requirements: Application, essay, financial need analysis, references, transcript. *Deadline:* March 1.

Contact: Patricia Coyle, Executive Secretary
American Legion Auxiliary, Department of South Dakota
PO Box 117
Huron, SD 57350
Phone: 605-353-1793
Fax: 605-352-0336
E-mail: sdlegionaux@msn.com

AMERICAN LEGION AUXILIARY, DEPARTMENT OF UTAH http://www.legion-aux.org

AMERICAN LEGION AUXILIARY NATIONAL PRESIDENTS SCHOLARSHIP

Scholarships available for graduating high school seniors. Must be a resident of Utah, a U.S. citizen and the direct descendant of a veteran.

Award: Scholarship for use in freshman year; not renewable. *Number:* varies. *Amount:* $250–$750.

Eligibility Requirements: Applicant must be high school student; planning to enroll or expecting to enroll full-time at a two-year or four-year or technical institution or university; single and resident of Utah. Applicant or parent of applicant must be member of American Legion or Auxiliary. Available to U.S. citizens. Applicant or parent must meet one or more of the following requirements: general military experience; retired from active duty; disabled or killed as a result of military service; prisoner of war; or missing in action.

Application Requirements: Application, essay, references, test scores, transcript. *Deadline:* February 15.

Contact: Chesney Galindo, Department Secretary
American Legion Auxiliary, Department of Utah
455 East 400 South, Suite 50
Salt Lake City, UT 84111
Phone: 801-539-1015
Fax: 801-521-9191
E-mail: utaux@aol.com

AMERICAN LEGION AUXILIARY, DEPARTMENT OF WISCONSIN http://www.amlegionauxwi.org

DELLA VAN DEUREN MEMORIAL SCHOLARSHIP

One-time award of $1000. For a student to qualify, the mother of the applicant or the applicant must be a member of an Auxiliary unit. Must send with completed application: certification of an American Legion Auxiliary Unit President, copy of proof that veteran was in service (i.e. discharge papers), letters of recommendation, transcripts, and essay. Must have minimum 3.5 GPA, show financial need, and be a resident of Wisconsin. Refer questions to Department Secretary, (608) 745-0124. Applications available on Web site: http://www.legion-aux.org.

Award: Scholarship for use in freshman, sophomore, junior, senior, or graduate years; not renewable. *Number:* 2. *Amount:* $1000.

Eligibility Requirements: Applicant must be enrolled or expecting to enroll full or part-time at a four-year institution or university and resident of Wisconsin. Applicant or parent of applicant must be member of American Legion or Auxiliary. Applicant must have 3.5 GPA or higher. Available to U.S. citizens.

Application Requirements: Application, essay, financial need analysis, references, transcript. *Deadline:* March 15.

Contact: Kim Henderson, Scholarship Information
American Legion Auxiliary, Department of Wisconsin
PO Box 140
Portage, WI 53901-0140
Phone: 608-745-0124
Fax: 608-745-1947
E-mail: membership@amlegionauxwi.org

H.S. AND ANGELINA LEWIS SCHOLARSHIPS

One-time award of $1000. Applicant must be a daughter, son, wife, or widow of a veteran. Granddaughters and great-granddaughters of veterans who are auxiliary members may also apply. Must send with completed application: certification of an American Legion Auxiliary Unit President, copy of proof that veteran was in service (i.e. discharge papers), letters of recommendation, transcripts and essay. Must have minimum 3.5 GPA, show financial need, and be a resident of Wisconsin. Refer questions to Department Secretary, (608) 745-0124. Applications available on Web site: http://www.legion-aux.org.

Award: Scholarship for use in freshman, sophomore, junior, senior, or graduate years; not renewable. *Number:* 6. *Amount:* $1000.

Eligibility Requirements: Applicant must be enrolled or expecting to enroll full or part-time at a four-year institution or university and resident of Wisconsin. Applicant or parent of applicant must be member of American Legion or Auxiliary. Applicant must have 3.5 GPA or higher. Available to U.S. citizens.

Application Requirements: Application, essay, financial need analysis, references, transcript. *Deadline:* March 15.

Contact: Kim Henderson, Scholarship Information
American Legion Auxiliary, Department of Wisconsin
PO Box 140
Portage, WI 53901-0140
Phone: 608-745-0124
Fax: 608-745-1947
E-mail: membership@amlegionauxwi.org

HEALTH CAREER SCHOLARSHIPS

One-time award of $750. Course of study need not be a four-year program. Hospital, university, or technical school program is acceptable. Applicant must be a daughter, son, wife, or widow of a veteran. Granddaughters and great-granddaughters of veterans who are auxiliary members may also apply. Must send with completed application: certification of an American Legion Auxiliary Unit President, copy of proof that veteran was in service (i.e. discharge papers), letters of recommendation, transcripts, and essay. Must have minimum 3.5 GPA, show financial need, and be a resident of Wisconsin. Refer questions to Department Secretary, (608) 745-0124. Applications available on Web site: http://www.legion-aux.org.

Award: Scholarship for use in freshman, sophomore, junior, or senior years; not renewable. *Number:* 2. *Amount:* $750.

Eligibility Requirements: Applicant must be enrolled or expecting to enroll full or part-time at a two-year or four-year or technical institution or university and resident of Wisconsin. Applicant or parent of applicant must be member of American Legion or Auxiliary. Applicant must have 3.5 GPA or higher. Available to U.S. citizens.

Application Requirements: Application, essay, financial need analysis, references, transcript. *Deadline:* March 15.

Contact: Kim Henderson, Scholarship Information
American Legion Auxiliary, Department of Wisconsin
PO Box 140
Portage, WI 53901-0140
Phone: 608-745-0124
Fax: 608-745-1947
E-mail: membership@amlegionauxwi.org

MERIT AND MEMORIAL SCHOLARSHIPS

One-time award of $1000. Applicant must be a daughter, son, wife, or widow of a veteran. Granddaughters and great granddaughters of veterans who are auxiliary members may also apply. Must send with completed application: certification of an American Legion Auxiliary Unit President, copy of proof that veteran was in service (i.e. discharge papers), letters of recommendation, transcripts, and essay. Must have minimum 3.5 GPA, show financial need, and be a resident of Wisconsin. Refer questions to Department Secretary, (608) 745-0124. Applications available on Web site: http://www.legion-aux.org.

Award: Scholarship for use in freshman, sophomore, junior, senior, or graduate years; not renewable. *Number:* 6. *Amount:* $1000.

Eligibility Requirements: Applicant must be enrolled or expecting to enroll full or part-time at a four-year institution or university and resident of Wisconsin. Applicant or parent of applicant must be member of American Legion or Auxiliary. Applicant must have 3.5 GPA or higher. Available to U.S. citizens.

Application Requirements: Application, essay, financial need analysis, references, transcript. *Deadline:* March 15.

Contact: Kim Henderson, Scholarship Information
American Legion Auxiliary, Department of Wisconsin
PO Box 140
Portage, WI 53901-0140
Phone: 608-745-0124
Fax: 608-745-1947
E-mail: membership@amlegionauxwi.org

STATE PRESIDENT'S SCHOLARSHIPS

One-time award of $1000. In order for student to qualify, the mother of the applicant or the applicant must be a member of an Auxiliary unit. Must send with completed application: certification of an American Legion Auxiliary Unit President, copy of proof that veteran was in service (i.e. discharge papers), letters of recommendation, transcripts, and essay. Must have minimum 3.5 GPA, show financial need, and be a resident of Wisconsin. Refer questions to Department Secretary, (608) 745-0124. Applications available on Web site: http://www.legion-aux.org.

Award: Scholarship for use in freshman, sophomore, junior, senior, or graduate years; not renewable. *Number:* 3. *Amount:* $1000.

Eligibility Requirements: Applicant must be enrolled or expecting to enroll full or part-time at a four-year institution or university and resident of Wisconsin. Applicant or parent of applicant must be member of American Legion or Auxiliary. Applicant must have 3.5 GPA or higher. Available to U.S. citizens.

Application Requirements: Application, essay, financial need analysis, references, transcript. *Deadline:* March 15.

Contact: Kim Henderson, Scholarship Information
American Legion Auxiliary, Department of Wisconsin
PO Box 140
Portage, WI 53901-0140
Phone: 608-745-0124
Fax: 608-745-1947
E-mail: membership@amlegionauxwi.org

AMERICAN LEGION AUXILIARY, NATIONAL HEADQUARTERS http://www.legion-aux.org

AMERICAN LEGION AUXILIARY GIRL SCOUT ACHIEVEMENT AWARD

One scholarship available to recipients of Girl Scout Gold Award. Must be active in religious institution and have received appropriate religious emblem,

American Legion Auxiliary, National Headquarters (continued)

Cadet or Senior Scout level. Must show practical citizenship in religious institution, community, and school. One-time award of $1000.

Award: Scholarship for use in freshman year; not renewable. *Number:* 1. *Amount:* $1000.

Eligibility Requirements: Applicant must be high school student; planning to enroll or expecting to enroll full-time at a two-year or four-year institution or university and female. Applicant or parent of applicant must be member of Girl Scouts. Applicant or parent of applicant must have employment or volunteer experience in community service. Available to U.S. and non-U.S. citizens.

Application Requirements: Application, applicant must enter a contest, essay, references, self-addressed stamped envelope, test scores, transcript. *Deadline:* February 11.

Contact: Department Secretary
American Legion Auxiliary, National Headquarters
777 North Meridian Street, 3rd Floor
Indianapolis, IN 46204-1189
Phone: 317-955-3845
Fax: 317-955-3884
E-mail: youthprog@legion-aux.org

AMERICAN LEGION AUXILIARY NON-TRADITIONAL STUDENTS SCHOLARSHIPS

One-time award for a student returning to the classroom after some period of time in which his/her formal schooling was interrupted or a student who has had at least one year of college and is in need of financial assistance to pursue an undergraduate degree. Must be a member of the American Legion, American Legion Auxiliary or Sons of the American Legion. One scholarship will be awarded per division.

Award: Scholarship for use in freshman, sophomore, junior, or senior years; not renewable. *Amount:* $1000.

Eligibility Requirements: Applicant must be enrolled or expecting to enroll full-time at a two-year or four-year or technical institution or university. Applicant or parent of applicant must be member of American Legion or Auxiliary. Available to U.S. citizens.

Application Requirements: Application. *Deadline:* March 10.

Contact: Department Secretary
American Legion Auxiliary, National Headquarters
777 North Meridian Street, 3rd Floor
Indianapolis, IN 46204-1189
Phone: 317-955-3853
Fax: 317-955-3884
E-mail: aef@legion-aux.org

AMERICAN LEGION AUXILIARY SPIRIT OF YOUTH SCHOLARSHIPS FOR JUNIOR MEMBERS

Renewable awards available to graduating high school seniors. Must be women and current junior members of the American Legion Auxiliary, with a three-year membership history. Students should apply through local chapter. Leadership considered.

Award: Scholarship for use in freshman, sophomore, junior, or senior years; renewable. *Number:* 5. *Amount:* $1000.

Eligibility Requirements: Applicant must be high school student; planning to enroll or expecting to enroll full-time at a four-year institution or university and female. Applicant or parent of applicant must be member of American Legion or Auxiliary. Available to U.S. and non-U.S. citizens.

Application Requirements: Application, essay, references, self-addressed stamped envelope, test scores, transcript. *Deadline:* March 10.

Contact: Department Secretary
American Legion Auxiliary, National Headquarters
777 North Meridian Street, 3rd Floor
Indianapolis, IN 46204-1189
Phone: 317-955-3853
Fax: 317-955-3884
E-mail: aef@legion-aux.org

AMERICAN LEGION, DEPARTMENT OF ARKANSAS http://www.arklegion.homestead.com

AMERICAN LEGION DEPARTMENT OF ARKANSAS COUDRET SCHOLARSHIP AWARD

Must be child, grandchild, or great-grandchild of American Legionnaire in good standing for two years. Two-year requirement is waived for Desert Storm and deceased veterans. One-time award for graduating Arkansas high school seniors.

Award: Scholarship for use in freshman year; not renewable. *Number:* 4. *Amount:* $500–$1000.

Eligibility Requirements: Applicant must be high school student; age 16-24; planning to enroll or expecting to enroll full or part-time at a two-year or four-year or technical institution or university and resident of Arkansas. Applicant or parent of applicant must be member of American Legion or Auxiliary. Applicant must have 2.5 GPA or higher. Available to U.S. citizens.

Application Requirements: Application, autobiography, essay, financial need analysis, photo, references, transcript. *Deadline:* March 15.

Contact: William Winchell, Department Adjutant
American Legion, Department of Arkansas
PO Box 3280
Little Rock, AR 72203-3280
Phone: 501-375-1104
Fax: 501-375-4236
E-mail: alegion@swbell.net

AMERICAN LEGION DEPARTMENT OF ARKANSAS PAST DEPARTMENT COMMANDER SCHOLARSHIP

Nonrenewable scholarship for rising college freshmen under 21 years of age. For child, grandchild or great-grandchild of an American Legionnaire, living or deceased.

Award: Scholarship for use in freshman year; not renewable. *Number:* 1. *Amount:* $500.

Eligibility Requirements: Applicant must be high school student; age 16-20; planning to enroll or expecting to enroll full or part-time at a two-year or four-year or technical institution or university and resident of Arkansas. Applicant or parent of applicant must be member of American Legion or Auxiliary. Applicant must have 2.5 GPA or higher. Available to U.S. citizens. Applicant or parent must meet one or more of the following requirements: general military experience; retired from active duty; disabled or killed as a result of military service; prisoner of war; or missing in action.

Application Requirements: Application, autobiography, essay, financial need analysis, photo, references, transcript. *Deadline:* March 15.

Contact: William Winchell, Department Adjutant
American Legion, Department of Arkansas
PO Box 3280
Little Rock, AR 72203-3280
Phone: 501-375-1104
Fax: 501-375-4236
E-mail: alegion@swbell.net

AMERICAN LEGION, DEPARTMENT OF IDAHO http://www.idaholegion.com

AMERICAN LEGION, DEPARTMENT OF IDAHO SCHOLARSHIP

One-time award of up to $500 for residents of Idaho studying at an Idaho institution. Minimum 2.5 GPA. Application deadline July 1.

Award: Scholarship for use in freshman year; not renewable. *Amount:* $300–$500.

Eligibility Requirements: Applicant must be high school student; planning to enroll or expecting to enroll full-time at a two-year or four-year or technical institution or university; single; resident of Idaho and studying in Idaho. Applicant or parent of applicant must be member of American Legion or Auxiliary. Applicant must have 2.5 GPA or higher. Available to U.S. citizens. Applicant or parent must meet one or more of the following requirements: general military experience; retired from active duty; disabled or killed as a result of military service; prisoner of war; or missing in action.

Application Requirements: Application, autobiography, financial need analysis, references, self-addressed stamped envelope, transcript. *Deadline:* July 1.

Contact: Terry Niles, Department Adjunct
American Legion, Department of Idaho
901 Warren Street
Boise, ID 83706-3825
Phone: 208-342-7061
Fax: 208-342-1964
E-mail: adj@idaholegion.com

AMERICAN LEGION, DEPARTMENT OF ILLINOIS http://www.illegion.org

AMERICAN LEGION, DEPARTMENT OF ILLINOIS SCHOLARSHIPS

Twenty $1000 scholarships for graduating students of Illinois high schools. May be used at any accredited college, university, trade or technical school. Applicant must be a child or grandchild of members of the American Legion Illinois. Awards will be based on academic merit and financial need. Applications available September 15 and must be returned prior to March 15.

Award: Scholarship for use in freshman year; not renewable. *Number:* 20. *Amount:* $1000.

Eligibility Requirements: Applicant must be high school student; planning to enroll or expecting to enroll full or part-time at a two-year or four-year or technical institution or university and resident of Illinois. Applicant or parent of applicant must be member of American Legion or Auxiliary. Available to U.S. citizens.

Application Requirements: Application, financial need analysis, photo, test scores, transcript. *Deadline:* March 14.

Contact: American Legion, Department of Illinois
PO Box 2910
Bloomington, IL 61702

AMERICAN LEGION, DEPARTMENT OF ILLINOIS, BOY SCOUT/ EXPLORER SCHOLARSHIP

Scholarship for a graduating high school senior who is a qualified senior Boy Scout or Explorer and a resident of Illinois. Must write a 500-word essay on Legion's Americanism and Boy Scout programs. Deadline: April 30.

Award: Scholarship for use in freshman year; not renewable. *Number:* 5. *Amount:* $200–$1000.

Eligibility Requirements: Applicant must be high school student; planning to enroll or expecting to enroll full or part-time at a two-year or four-year or technical institution or university and resident of Illinois. Applicant or parent of applicant must be member of Boy Scouts. Available to U.S. and non-U.S. citizens.

Application Requirements: Application, applicant must enter a contest, essay. *Deadline:* April 30.

Contact: American Legion Boy Scout Chairman, Department Headquarters
American Legion, Department of Illinois
PO Box 2910
Bloomington, IL 61702

AMERICAN LEGION, DEPARTMENT OF IOWA http://www.ialegion.org

AMERICAN LEGION DEPARTMENT OF IOWA EAGLE SCOUT OF THE YEAR SCHOLARSHIP

Three one-time award for Eagle Scouts who are residents of Iowa. Must be a high school student with minimum 2.5 GPA.

Award: Scholarship for use in freshman year; not renewable. *Number:* 3. *Amount:* $400–$2000.

Eligibility Requirements: Applicant must be high school student; planning to enroll or expecting to enroll full-time at a two-year or four-year institution or university; male and resident of Iowa. Applicant or parent of applicant must be member of Boy Scouts. Applicant must have 2.5 GPA or higher. Available to U.S. citizens.

Application Requirements: *Deadline:* February 1.

Contact: Program Director
American Legion, Department of Iowa
720 Lyon Street
Des Moines, IA 50309

AMERICAN LEGION, DEPARTMENT OF KANSAS

ALBERT M. LAPPIN SCHOLARSHIP

Scholarship for children of the members of Kansas American Legion or its Auxiliary. Membership has to have been active for the past three years. The children of deceased members are also eligible if parents' dues were paid up at time of death. Must be high school senior or college freshman or sophomore. Must use award at a Kansas college, university, or trade school.

Award: Scholarship for use in freshman or sophomore years; not renewable. *Number:* 1. *Amount:* $1000.

Eligibility Requirements: Applicant must be enrolled or expecting to enroll at a two-year or four-year or technical institution or university and studying in Kansas. Applicant or parent of applicant must be member of American Legion or Auxiliary. Available to U.S. citizens. Applicant or parent must meet one or more of the following requirements: general military experience; retired from active duty; disabled or killed as a result of military service; prisoner of war; or missing in action.

Application Requirements: Application, essay, financial need analysis, photo, transcript. *Deadline:* February 15.

Contact: Scholarship Administrator
American Legion, Department of Kansas
1314 Southwest Topeka Boulevard
Topeka, KS 66612-1886

HUGH A. SMITH SCHOLARSHIP FUND

Scholarship available to children of the Kansas American Legion or its Auxiliary members. Membership has to have been active for the past three years. Children of deceased members are also eligible if parents' dues were paid at time of death. Open to a high school senior or college freshman or sophomore. Award must be used at a Kansas university, college, or trade school. The applicant must be an average or better student scholastically, and must show a high school transcript with GPA.

Award: Scholarship for use in freshman or sophomore years; not renewable. *Number:* 1. *Amount:* $500.

Eligibility Requirements: Applicant must be enrolled or expecting to enroll at a two-year or four-year or technical institution or university and studying in Kansas. Applicant or parent of applicant must be member of American Legion or Auxiliary. Available to U.S. citizens. Applicant or parent must meet one or more of the following requirements: general military experience; retired from active duty; disabled or killed as a result of military service; prisoner of war; or missing in action.

Application Requirements: Application, financial need analysis, photo, references, transcript. *Deadline:* February 15.

Contact: Scholarship Administrator
American Legion, Department of Kansas
1314 Southwest Topeka Boulevard
Topeka, KS 66612-1886

NATIONAL HIGH SCHOOL ORATORICAL CONTEST

Oratorical contest open to students in 9th, 10th, 11th, and 12th grades of any accredited Kansas high school. Speech contests begin in January at post level and continue on to national competition. Contact local American Legion for deadlines.

Award: Prize for use in freshman year; not renewable. *Number:* 4. *Amount:* $150–$1500.

Eligibility Requirements: Applicant must be high school student; age 20 or under; planning to enroll or expecting to enroll at an institution or university; resident of Kansas and must have an interest in public speaking. Applicant or parent of applicant must be member of American Legion or Auxiliary. Available to U.S. citizens.

American Legion, Department of Kansas (continued)

Application Requirements: Application, applicant must enter a contest, photo, references.

Contact: Sallie Stewart, Scholarship Administrator
American Legion, Department of Kansas
1314 Southwest Topeka Boulevard
Topeka, KS 66612-1886

ROSEDALE POST 346 SCHOLARSHIP

Available to high school seniors, college level freshmen, or sophomores who are in need of educational assistance, and are enrolled or intend to enroll in an approved school located in the state of Kansas. The applicant must be the son or daughter of a veteran; the parent(s) must have been a member of the Kansas American Legion and/or Legion Auxiliary for the past three years. The sons or daughters of deceased members in either organization are also eligible if the parent's dues were paid up at the time of death. The applicant must be an average or better student scholastically.

Award: Scholarship for use in freshman or sophomore years; not renewable. *Number:* 2. *Amount:* $1500.

Eligibility Requirements: Applicant must be enrolled or expecting to enroll at a two-year or four-year or technical institution and studying in Kansas. Applicant or parent of applicant must be member of American Legion or Auxiliary. Available to U.S. citizens. Applicant or parent must meet one or more of the following requirements: general military experience; retired from active duty; disabled or killed as a result of military service; prisoner of war; or missing in action.

Application Requirements: Application, financial need analysis, photo, references, transcript. *Deadline:* February 15.

Contact: Scholarship Administrator
American Legion, Department of Kansas
1314 Southwest Topeka Boulevard
Topeka, KS 66612-1886

TED AND NORA ANDERSON SCHOLARSHIPS

Scholarship for children of American Legion or Auxiliary members. Must be high school seniors or college freshmen or sophomores. Scholarship for use at an approved Kansas college, university, or trade school. Must be Kansas resident.

Award: Scholarship for use in freshman or sophomore years; not renewable. *Number:* 4. *Amount:* $500.

Eligibility Requirements: Applicant must be enrolled or expecting to enroll at a two-year or four-year or technical institution or university; resident of Kansas and studying in Kansas. Applicant or parent of applicant must be member of American Legion or Auxiliary. Available to U.S. citizens. Applicant or parent must meet one or more of the following requirements: general military experience; retired from active duty; disabled or killed as a result of military service; prisoner of war; or missing in action.

Application Requirements: Application, financial need analysis, photo, references, transcript. *Deadline:* February 15.

Contact: Scholarship Administrator
American Legion, Department of Kansas
1314 Southwest Topeka Boulevard
Topeka, KS 66612-1886

AMERICAN LEGION, DEPARTMENT OF MAINE

JAMES V. DAY SCHOLARSHIP

One-time $500 award for a Maine resident whose parent is a member of the American Legion in Maine. Must be a U.S. citizen. Based on character and financial need. Minimum 2.5 GPA required.

Award: Scholarship for use in freshman, sophomore, junior, or senior years; not renewable. *Number:* 1. *Amount:* $500.

Eligibility Requirements: Applicant must be enrolled or expecting to enroll full-time at a two-year or four-year or technical institution or university and resident of Maine. Applicant or parent of applicant must be member of American Legion or Auxiliary. Applicant must have 2.5 GPA or higher. Available to U.S. citizens. Applicant or parent must meet one or more of the following requirements: general military experience; retired from active duty; disabled or killed as a result of military service; prisoner of war; or missing in action.

Application Requirements: Application, financial need analysis, references, transcript. *Deadline:* May 1.

Contact: Department Adjutant
American Legion, Department of Maine
PO Box 900
Waterville, ME 04903
Phone: 207-873-3229
Fax: 207-872-0501
E-mail: legionme@wtvl.net

AMERICAN LEGION, DEPARTMENT OF MINNESOTA http://www.mnlegion.org

AMERICAN LEGION DEPARTMENT OF MINNESOTA MEMORIAL SCHOLARSHIP

Scholarship available to Minnesota residents who are dependents of members of the Minnesota American Legion or Auxiliary. Award for study at a Minnesota institution or neighboring state with reciprocating agreement. One-time award of $500.

Award: Scholarship for use in freshman, sophomore, junior, or senior years; not renewable. *Number:* 6. *Amount:* $500.

Eligibility Requirements: Applicant must be enrolled or expecting to enroll full or part-time at a two-year or four-year or technical institution or university; resident of Minnesota and studying in Iowa, Minnesota, North Dakota, South Dakota, or Wisconsin. Applicant or parent of applicant must be member of American Legion or Auxiliary. Applicant must have 2.5 GPA or higher. Available to U.S. citizens. Applicant or parent must meet one or more of the following requirements: general military experience; retired from active duty; disabled or killed as a result of military service; prisoner of war; or missing in action.

Application Requirements: Application, essay, financial need analysis, references, transcript. *Deadline:* April 1.

Contact: Education and Scholarship Committee
American Legion, Department of Minnesota
20 West 12th Street, Room 300-A
St. Paul, MN 55155
Phone: 651-291-1800
Fax: 651-291-1057
E-mail: department@mnlegion.org

MINNESOTA LEGIONNAIRES INSURANCE TRUST

Scholarship for Minnesota residents who are veterans or dependents of veterans. Award for study at a Minnesota institution or neighboring state with reciprocating agreement. One-time award of $500. All applications must be approved and recommended by a post of the American Legion.

Award: Scholarship for use in sophomore, junior, or senior years; not renewable. *Number:* 3. *Amount:* $500.

Eligibility Requirements: Applicant must be enrolled or expecting to enroll full or part-time at a two-year or four-year or technical institution or university; resident of Minnesota and studying in Iowa, Minnesota, North Dakota, South Dakota, or Wisconsin. Applicant or parent of applicant must be member of American Legion or Auxiliary. Applicant must have 2.5 GPA or higher. Available to U.S. citizens. Applicant or parent must meet one or more of the following requirements: general military experience; retired from active duty; disabled or killed as a result of military service; prisoner of war; or missing in action.

Application Requirements: Application, essay, financial need analysis, references, transcript. *Deadline:* April 1.

Contact: Education and Scholarship Committee
American Legion, Department of Minnesota
20 West 12th Street, Room 300-A
St. Paul, MN 55155
Phone: 651-291-1800
Fax: 651-291-1057
E-mail: department@mnlegion.org

AMERICAN LEGION, DEPARTMENT OF MISSOURI http://www.missourilegion.org

CHARLES L. BACON MEMORIAL SCHOLARSHIP

One-time $500 award given to current members of the American Legion, American Legion Auxiliary, Sons of the American Legion or the descendant of a member of any of these organizations. Applicant must be under 21, not married, and must use scholarship as full-time student at accredited college or university. Applicant must be Missouri resident. Must submit proof of American Legion membership.

Award: Scholarship for use in freshman year; not renewable. *Number:* 2. *Amount:* $500.

Eligibility Requirements: Applicant must be age 20 or under; enrolled or expecting to enroll full-time at a four-year institution or university; single and resident of Missouri. Applicant or parent of applicant must be member of American Legion or Auxiliary. Available to U.S. citizens. Applicant or parent must meet one or more of the following requirements: general military experience; retired from active duty; disabled or killed as a result of military service; prisoner of war; or missing in action.

Application Requirements: Application, financial need analysis, test scores. *Deadline:* April 20.

Contact: Scholarship Information
American Legion, Department of Missouri
PO Box 179
Jefferson City, MO 65102
Phone: 573-893-2353
Fax: 573-893-2980

AMERICAN LEGION, DEPARTMENT OF NEBRASKA http://www.legion.org

MAYNARD JENSEN AMERICAN LEGION MEMORIAL SCHOLARSHIP

Scholarship for dependents or grandchildren of members, prisoner-of-war, missing-in-action veterans, killed-in-action veterans, or any deceased veterans of the American Legion. One-time award is based on academic achievement and financial need for Nebraska residents attending Nebraska institutions. Several scholarships of $500 each. Must have minimum 2.5 GPA and must submit school certification of GPA.

Award: Scholarship for use in freshman, sophomore, junior, or senior years; not renewable. *Number:* 1–10. *Amount:* $500.

Eligibility Requirements: Applicant must be enrolled or expecting to enroll full-time at a two-year or four-year or technical institution or university; resident of Nebraska and studying in Nebraska. Applicant or parent of applicant must be member of American Legion or Auxiliary. Applicant must have 2.5 GPA or higher. Available to U.S. citizens. Applicant or parent must meet one or more of the following requirements: general military experience; retired from active duty; disabled or killed as a result of military service; prisoner of war; or missing in action.

Application Requirements: Application, financial need analysis. *Deadline:* March 1.

Contact: Burdette Burkhart, Activities Director
American Legion, Department of Nebraska
PO Box 5205
Lincoln, NE 68505-0205
Phone: 402-464-6338
Fax: 402-464-6330
E-mail: actdirlegion@alltel.net

AMERICAN LEGION, DEPARTMENT OF NEW YORK http://www.ny.legion.org

AMERICAN LEGION DEPARTMENT OF NEW YORK DR. HANNAH K. VUOLO MEMORIAL SCHOLARSHIP

One-time scholarship for natural or adopted descendent of a New York Legionnaire. Must be graduating high school senior or high school graduate under 21 years. Must be accepted at recognized college or university. Must submit letter explaining why qualified for scholarship. One award of $250.

Award: Scholarship for use in freshman year; not renewable. *Number:* 1. *Amount:* $250.

Eligibility Requirements: Applicant must be age 20 or under and enrolled or expecting to enroll full-time at a two-year or four-year institution or university. Applicant or parent of applicant must be member of American Legion or Auxiliary. Applicant or parent of applicant must have employment or volunteer experience in community service. Applicant or parent must meet one or more of the following requirements: general military experience; retired from active duty; disabled or killed as a result of military service; prisoner of war; or missing in action.

Application Requirements: Application, financial need analysis, test scores, transcript. *Deadline:* May 1.

Contact: Richard Pedro, Department Adjutant
American Legion, Department of New York
112 State Street, Suite 400
Albany, NY 12207
Phone: 518-463-2215
Fax: 518-427-8443
E-mail: newyork@legion.org

AMERICAN LEGION, DEPARTMENT OF OHIO http://www.ohioamericanlegion.org

AMERICAN LEGION SCHOLARSHIP—OHIO

For descendants of Ohio Legionnaires only. Nonrenewable award for full-time study only. Must rank in upper third of class or have a minimum 3.0 GPA. Must include descendancy proofs. Deadline: April 15.

Award: Scholarship for use in freshman, sophomore, junior, or senior years; not renewable. *Number:* 15–20. *Amount:* $2000–$3000.

Eligibility Requirements: Applicant must be enrolled or expecting to enroll full-time at a two-year or four-year or technical institution or university. Applicant or parent of applicant must be member of American Legion or Auxiliary. Applicant must have 3.0 GPA or higher. Available to U.S. and non-U.S. citizens.

Application Requirements: Application, test scores, transcript. *Deadline:* April 15.

Contact: Donald Lanthorn, Service Director
American Legion, Department of Ohio
PO Box 8007
Delaware, OH 43015-8007
Phone: 740-362-7478
Fax: 740-362-1429
E-mail: dlanthorn@iwaynet.net

AMERICAN LEGION, DEPARTMENT OF PENNSYLVANIA http://www.pa-legion.com

JOSEPH P. GAVENONIS COLLEGE SCHOLARSHIP (PLAN I)

Scholarships for Pennsylvania residents seeking a four-year degree from a Pennsylvania college or university. Must be the child of a member of a Pennsylvania American Legion post. Must be a graduating high school senior. Award amount and number of awards determined annually. Renewable award. Must maintain 2.5 GPA in college.

Award: Scholarship for use in freshman, sophomore, junior, or senior years; renewable. *Amount:* $500–$1000.

Eligibility Requirements: Applicant must be high school student; planning to enroll or expecting to enroll full-time at a four-year institution or university; resident of Pennsylvania and studying in Pennsylvania. Applicant or parent of applicant must be member of American Legion or Auxiliary. Applicant must have 2.5 GPA or higher. Available to U.S. citizens.

Application Requirements: Application, financial need analysis, test scores, transcript. *Deadline:* May 1.

Contact: Debra Bellis, Scholarship Secretary
American Legion, Department of Pennsylvania
PO Box 2324
Harrisburg, PA 17105-2324
Phone: 717-730-9100
Fax: 717-975-2836
E-mail: hq@pa-legion.com

AMERICAN LEGION, DEPARTMENT OF TENNESSEE

AMERICAN LEGION DEPARTMENT OF TENNESSEE EAGLE SCOUT OF THE YEAR

One award for the Eagle Scout of the Year winner from Tennessee for use at any postsecondary institution in the U.S. One-time award of $1500 for Eagle Scouts 18 years old or younger.

Award: Scholarship for use in freshman year; not renewable. *Number:* 1. *Amount:* $1500.

Eligibility Requirements: Applicant must be high school student; age 15-18; planning to enroll or expecting to enroll full or part-time at a two-year or four-year or technical institution or university; male and resident of Tennessee. Applicant or parent of applicant must be member of Boy Scouts. Available to U.S. citizens.

Application Requirements: Application, photo, references. *Deadline:* March 1.

Contact: Darlene Burgess, Executive Assistant
American Legion, Department of Tennessee
215 Eighth Avenue North
Nashville, TN 37211
Phone: 615-254-0568
Fax: 615-255-1551

AMERICAN LEGION, DEPARTMENT OF VERMONT

AMERICAN LEGION EAGLE SCOUT OF THE YEAR

Awarded to the Boy Scout chosen for outstanding service to his religious institution, school, and community. Must receive the Eagle Scout Award and reside in Vermont.

Award: Scholarship for use in freshman year; not renewable. *Number:* 1. *Amount:* $1000.

Eligibility Requirements: Applicant must be high school student; planning to enroll or expecting to enroll at an institution or university and resident of Vermont. Applicant or parent of applicant must be member of Boy Scouts. Applicant or parent of applicant must have employment or volunteer experience in community service. Available to U.S. citizens.

Application Requirements: Application, photo. *Deadline:* March 1.

Contact: Richard Gray, Boy Scout Committee Chairman
American Legion, Department of Vermont
PO Box 396
Montpelier, VT 05601-0396
Phone: 802-223-7131
Fax: 802-223-0318
E-mail: alvt@sover.net

AMERICAN LEGION, DEPARTMENT OF WASHINGTON

http://www.walegion.org

AMERICAN LEGION DEPARTMENT OF WASHINGTON CHILDREN AND YOUTH SCHOLARSHIPS

One-time award for the son or daughter of a Washington American Legion or Auxiliary member, living or deceased. Must be high school senior planning to attend an accredited institution of higher education in Washington. Award based on need. Must be Washington resident.

Award: Scholarship for use in freshman year; not renewable. *Number:* 2. *Amount:* $1500–$2500.

Eligibility Requirements: Applicant must be high school student; planning to enroll or expecting to enroll full-time at an institution or university; resident of Washington and studying in Washington. Applicant or parent of applicant must be member of American Legion or Auxiliary. Available to U.S. citizens. Applicant or parent must meet one or more of the following requirements: general military experience; retired from active duty; disabled or killed as a result of military service; prisoner of war; or missing in action.

Application Requirements: Application, financial need analysis, transcript. *Deadline:* April 1.

Contact: Thomas Conner, Administrative Assistant
American Legion, Department of Washington
PO Box 3917
Lacey, WA 98509-3917
E-mail: tomal@qwest.net

AMERICAN LEGION, DEPARTMENT OF WEST VIRGINIA

WILLIAM F. "BILL" JOHNSON MEMORIAL SCHOLARSHIP SPONSORED BY SONS OF THE AMERICAN LEGION

Essay based on a different question each year. Award given second semester of college providing winner has passing grades first semester. Must be a resident of West Virginia and the child or grandchild of a member of The American Legion.

Award: Scholarship for use in freshman year; not renewable. *Number:* 1. *Amount:* $1000.

Eligibility Requirements: Applicant must be high school student; planning to enroll or expecting to enroll full-time at a two-year or four-year institution or university and resident of West Virginia. Applicant or parent of applicant must be member of American Legion or Auxiliary. Available to U.S. citizens. Applicant or parent must meet one or more of the following requirements: general military experience; retired from active duty; disabled or killed as a result of military service; prisoner of war; or missing in action.

Application Requirements: Application, essay, transcript. *Deadline:* March 15.

Contact: Melinda Sine, Executive Assistant
American Legion, Department of West Virginia
2016 Kanawha Boulevard East
Charleston, WV 25311
Phone: 304-343-7591
Fax: 304-343-7592
E-mail: wvlegion@aol.com

AMERICAN LEGION, DEPARTMENT OF WYOMING

E.A. BLACKMORE MEMORIAL SCHOLARSHIP

$1000 per year for four years will be awarded to the son, grandson, daughter or granddaughter of a member of the American Legion. Applicants must be residents of Wyoming and in the top 20% of their graduating high school class.

Award: Scholarship for use in freshman, sophomore, junior, or senior years; renewable. *Number:* 1. *Amount:* $1000.

Eligibility Requirements: Applicant must be high school student; age 17-18; planning to enroll or expecting to enroll full-time at a two-year or four-year institution or university and resident of Wyoming. Applicant or parent of applicant must be member of American Legion or Auxiliary. Available to U.S. citizens. Applicant or parent must meet one or more of the following requirements: general military experience; retired from active duty; disabled or killed as a result of military service; prisoner of war; or missing in action.

Application Requirements: Application, photo, resume, references, transcript. *Deadline:* May 1.

Contact: Julie Rust, Department Adjutant
American Legion, Department of Wyoming
1320 Hugur Avenue
Cheyenne, WY 82001
Phone: 307-634-3035
Fax: 307-635-7093
E-mail: wylegiondept@mcleodusa.net

AMERICAN LEGION, NATIONAL HEADQUARTERS

http://www.legion.org

AMERICAN LEGION NATIONAL HEADQUARTERS EAGLE SCOUT OF THE YEAR

Several scholarships for registered Eagle Scouts of American Legion-sponsored troops or American Legion families. Must be active in religious institution and have rendered outstanding school, community, and church service. Four one-time awards of $2500-$10,000. Applicant must be in high school and be at least 15 years old and no older than 18 years old.

Award: Scholarship for use in freshman, sophomore, junior, or senior years; not renewable. *Number:* 4. *Amount:* $2500–$10,000.

Eligibility Requirements: Applicant must be high school student; age 15-18; planning to enroll or expecting to enroll full-time at a four-year institution or university and male. Applicant or parent of applicant must be member of American Legion or Auxiliary or Boy Scouts.

Applicant or parent of applicant must have employment or volunteer experience in community service. Available to U.S. citizens.

Application Requirements: Application, essay, references, transcript. *Deadline:* March 1.

Contact: Michael Buss, Assistant Director
American Legion, National Headquarters
PO Box 1055
Indianapolis, IN 46206-1055
Phone: 317-630-1249
Fax: 317-630-1369
E-mail: acy@legion.org

AMERICAN POSTAL WORKERS UNION http://www.apwu.org

E.C. HALLBECK SCHOLARSHIP FUND

Scholarship for children of American Postal Workers Union members. Applicant must be a child, grandchild, stepchild, or legally adopted child of an active member, Retiree's Department member or deceased member of American Postal Workers Union. Must be a senior attending high school or other corresponding secondary school. Must be 18 years or older. Recipient must attend accredited college (community or university) as a full-time student. Scholarship will be $1000 for each year of four consecutive years of college. Scholarship will provide five area winners. For additional information and to download application go to Web site: http://www.apwu.org.

Award: Scholarship for use in freshman year; renewable. *Number:* 10. *Amount:* $1000.

Eligibility Requirements: Applicant must be high school student; age 18 and planning to enroll or expecting to enroll full-time at a two-year or four-year or technical institution or university. Applicant or parent of applicant must be member of American Postal Workers Union. Applicant or parent of applicant must have employment or volunteer experience in federal/postal service. Available to U.S. citizens.

Application Requirements: Application, references, test scores, transcript. *Deadline:* March 15.

Contact: Terry Stapleton, Secretary/Treasurer
American Postal Workers Union
1300 L Street, NW
Washington, DC 20005
Phone: 202-842-4215
Fax: 202-842-8530

VOCATIONAL SCHOLARSHIP PROGRAM

A scholarship for a child, grandchild, stepchild, or legally adopted child of an active member, Retiree's Department member, or deceased member of the American Postal Workers Union. Applicant must be a senior attending high school who plans on attending an accredited vocational school or community college vocational program as a full-time student. The award is $1000/yr. consecutively or until completion of the course, with the total not exceeding $3000. For additional information see Web site http://www.apwu.org

Award: Scholarship for use in freshman or sophomore years. *Number:* 1. *Amount:* $1000.

Eligibility Requirements: Applicant must be high school student and planning to enroll or expecting to enroll at a two-year or technical institution. Applicant or parent of applicant must be member of American Postal Workers Union. Applicant or parent of applicant must have employment or volunteer experience in federal/postal service.

Application Requirements: *Deadline:* March 15.

Contact: Terry Stapleton, Secretary/Treasurer
American Postal Workers Union
1300 L Street NW
Washington, DC 20005
Phone: 202-842-4215
Fax: 202-842-8530

AMERICAN QUARTER HORSE FOUNDATION (AQHF) http://www.aqha.org/aqhya

AMERICAN QUARTER HORSE FOUNDATION YOUTH SCHOLARSHIPS

$8,000 scholarships to AQHYA members who have belonged for three or more years. The recipient will receive $2,000 per year for four years. Minimum 2.5 GPA required.

Award: Scholarship for use in freshman, sophomore, junior, or senior years; renewable. *Number:* 1–25. *Amount:* $8000.

Eligibility Requirements: Applicant must be high school student and planning to enroll or expecting to enroll full-time at a two-year or four-year or technical institution or university. Applicant or parent of applicant must be member of American Quarter Horse Association. Applicant must have 2.5 GPA or higher. Available to U.S. and Canadian citizens.

Application Requirements: Application, financial need analysis, photo, references, transcript. *Deadline:* February 1.

Contact: Laura Owens, Scholarship Coordinator
American Quarter Horse Foundation (AQHF)
2601 I-40 East
Amarillo, TX 79104
Phone: 806-376-5181
Fax: 806-376-1005
E-mail: lowens@aqha.org

AQHF WORKING STUDENT SCHOLARSHIP

Must be member of AQHA or AQHYA who plans to work a minimum of 200 hours per school year. Recipient receives $2000 per year for a four-year degree plan. Minimum 2.5 GPA required.

Award: Scholarship for use in freshman, sophomore, junior, or senior years; renewable. *Number:* 1. *Amount:* $2000.

Eligibility Requirements: Applicant must be enrolled or expecting to enroll full-time at a two-year or four-year or technical institution or university. Applicant or parent of applicant must be member of American Quarter Horse Association. Applicant must have 2.5 GPA or higher. Available to U.S. and Canadian citizens.

Application Requirements: Application, financial need analysis, photo, references, transcript. *Deadline:* February 1.

Contact: Laura Owens, Scholarship Coordinator
American Quarter Horse Foundation (AQHF)
2601 I-40 East
Amarillo, TX 79104
Phone: 806-376-5181
Fax: 806-376-1005
E-mail: lowens@aqha.org

ARIZONA QUARTER HORSE YOUTH RACING SCHOLARSHIP

Renewable scholarship to a current AQHA or AQHYA member who lives in the state of Arizona. The recipient will receive $500 per year. Must be a full-time undergraduate. Minimum 2.5 GPA required.

Award: Scholarship for use in freshman or sophomore years; renewable. *Number:* 1. *Amount:* $500.

Eligibility Requirements: Applicant must be enrolled or expecting to enroll full-time at a two-year or four-year or technical institution or university and resident of Arizona. Applicant or parent of applicant must be member of American Quarter Horse Association. Applicant must have 2.5 GPA or higher. Available to U.S. citizens.

Application Requirements: Application, driver's license, financial need analysis, photo, references, transcript. *Deadline:* February 1.

Contact: Laura Owens, Scholarship Coordinator
American Quarter Horse Foundation (AQHF)
2601 I-40 East
Amarillo, TX 79104
Phone: 806-376-5181
Fax: 806-376-1005
E-mail: lowens@aqha.org

DR. GERALD O'CONNOR MICHIGAN SCHOLARSHIP

Must be current member of AQHA or AQHYA who lives in Michigan. Recipient receives $500 per year for a four-year degree plan. This scholarship is awarded every four years and will be available next in 2004. Minimum 2.5 GPA required.

Award: Scholarship for use in freshman, sophomore, junior, or senior years; renewable. *Number:* 1. *Amount:* $2000.

American Quarter Horse Foundation (AQHF) (continued)

Eligibility Requirements: Applicant must be enrolled or expecting to enroll full-time at a two-year or four-year or technical institution or university and resident of Michigan. Applicant or parent of applicant must be member of American Quarter Horse Association. Applicant must have 2.5 GPA or higher. Available to U.S. citizens.

Application Requirements: Application, driver's license, financial need analysis, photo, references, transcript. *Deadline:* February 1.

Contact: Laura Owens, Scholarship Coordinator
American Quarter Horse Foundation (AQHF)
2601 I-40 East
Amarillo, TX 79104
Phone: 806-376-5181
Fax: 806-376-1005
E-mail: lowens@aqha.org

EXCELLENCE IN EQUINE/AGRICULTURAL INVOLVEMENT SCHOLARSHIP

$25,000 scholarship to a current Member of AQHYA or AQHA from a farming or ranching family who exemplifies the qualities developed through a lifetime involvement with horses and agriculture. The recipient will receive $6,250 per year for a four-year degree plan if recipient maintains a 3.5 GPA.

Award: Scholarship for use in freshman, sophomore, junior, or senior years; renewable. *Number:* 1. *Amount:* $25,000.

Eligibility Requirements: Applicant must be enrolled or expecting to enroll full-time at a two-year or four-year or technical institution or university. Applicant or parent of applicant must be member of American Quarter Horse Association. Applicant or parent of applicant must have employment or volunteer experience in farming. Applicant must have 3.5 GPA or higher. Available to U.S. and Canadian citizens.

Application Requirements: Application, financial need analysis, photo, references, transcript, telephone interview. *Deadline:* February 1.

Contact: Laura Owens, Scholarship Coordinator
American Quarter Horse Foundation (AQHF)
2601 I-40 East
Amarillo, TX 79104
Phone: 806-376-5181
Fax: 806-376-1005
E-mail: lowens@aqha.org

FARM AND RANCH HERITAGE SCHOLARSHIP

$12,500 scholarship to current AQHYA or AQHA Members from farm or ranch backgrounds. The recipients will receive $3,125 per year for a four-year degree plan if the recipient maintains a 3.0 GPA.

Award: Scholarship for use in freshman, sophomore, junior, or senior years; renewable. *Number:* 1–2. *Amount:* $12,500.

Eligibility Requirements: Applicant must be enrolled or expecting to enroll full-time at a two-year or four-year or technical institution or university. Applicant or parent of applicant must be member of American Quarter Horse Association. Applicant or parent of applicant must have employment or volunteer experience in farming. Applicant must have 3.0 GPA or higher. Available to U.S. and Canadian citizens.

Application Requirements: Application, financial need analysis, photo, references, transcript. *Deadline:* February 1.

Contact: Laura Owens, Scholarship Coordinator
American Quarter Horse Foundation (AQHF)
2601 I-40 East
Amarillo, TX 79104
Phone: 806-376-5181
Fax: 806-376-1005
E-mail: lowens@aqha.org

GUY STOOPS MEMORIAL PROFESSIONAL HORSEMEN'S FAMILY SCHOLARSHIP

$500 will be awarded to the child of an AQHA Professional Horseman. Applicant must be AQHA member for three or more years. Minimum 2.5 GPA.

Award: Scholarship for use in freshman or sophomore years; renewable. *Number:* 1. *Amount:* $500.

Eligibility Requirements: Applicant must be enrolled or expecting to enroll full-time at a two-year or four-year or technical institution or university. Applicant or parent of applicant must be member of American Quarter Horse Association or Professional Horsemen Association. Applicant or parent of applicant must have employment or volunteer experience in designated career field. Applicant must have 2.5 GPA or higher. Available to U.S. and Canadian citizens.

Application Requirements: Application, financial need analysis, photo, references, transcript. *Deadline:* February 1.

Contact: Laura Owens, Scholarship Coordinator
American Quarter Horse Foundation (AQHF)
2601 I-40 East
Amarillo, TX 79104
Phone: 806-376-5181
Fax: 806-376-1005
E-mail: lowens@aqha.org

INDIANA QUARTER HORSE YOUTH SCHOLARSHIP

$500 scholarship to a current AQHYA member who lives in the state of Indiana. The recipient will receive $500 for one year. Minimum 2.5 GPA required.

Award: Scholarship for use in freshman, sophomore, junior, or senior years; not renewable. *Number:* 1. *Amount:* $500.

Eligibility Requirements: Applicant must be enrolled or expecting to enroll full-time at a two-year or four-year or technical institution or university and resident of Indiana. Applicant or parent of applicant must be member of American Quarter Horse Association. Applicant must have 2.5 GPA or higher. Available to U.S. citizens.

Application Requirements: Application, driver's license, financial need analysis, photo, references, transcript. *Deadline:* February 1.

Contact: Laura Owens, Scholarship Coordinator
American Quarter Horse Foundation (AQHF)
2601 I-40 East
Amarillo, TX 79104
Phone: 806-376-5181
Fax: 806-376-1005
E-mail: lowens@aqha.org

JOAN CAIN FLORIDA QUARTER HORSE YOUTH SCHOLARSHIP

$1,000 awarded to AQHA member from Florida. Minimum 2.5 GPA. Must be member of Florida Quarter Horse Youth Association.

Award: Scholarship for use in freshman, sophomore, junior, or senior years; renewable. *Number:* 1. *Amount:* $1000.

Eligibility Requirements: Applicant must be enrolled or expecting to enroll full-time at a two-year or four-year or technical institution or university and resident of Florida. Applicant or parent of applicant must be member of American Quarter Horse Association. Applicant must have 2.5 GPA or higher. Available to U.S. citizens.

Application Requirements: Application, driver's license, photo, references, transcript, membership card. *Deadline:* February 1.

Contact: Laura Owens, Scholarship Coordinator
American Quarter Horse Foundation (AQHF)
2601 I-40 East
Amarillo, TX 79104
Phone: 806-376-5181
Fax: 806-376-1005
E-mail: lowens@aqha.org

NEBRASKA QUARTER HORSE YOUTH SCHOLARSHIP

$2,000 scholarship to a current AQHYA Member who lives in the state of Nebraska. The recipient will receive $500 per year for a four-year degree plan. This scholarship is awarded every four years and will next be available in 2006.

Award: Scholarship for use in freshman, sophomore, junior, or senior years; renewable. *Number:* 1. *Amount:* $2000.

Eligibility Requirements: Applicant must be enrolled or expecting to enroll full-time at a two-year or four-year or technical institution or university and resident of Nebraska. Applicant or parent of applicant must be member of American Quarter Horse Association. Applicant must have 2.5 GPA or higher. Available to U.S. citizens.

Application Requirements: Application, driver's license, financial need analysis, photo, references, transcript. *Deadline:* February 1.

Contact: Laura Owens, Scholarship Coordinator
American Quarter Horse Foundation (AQHF)
2601 I-40 East
Amarillo, TX 79104
Phone: 806-376-5181
Fax: 806-376-1005
E-mail: lowens@aqha.org

RAY MELTON MEMORIAL VIRGINIA QUARTER HORSE YOUTH SCHOLARSHIP

Must be member of AQHA or AQHYA who resides in Virginia. Recipient receives $500 for one year. Minimum 2.5 GPA required.

Award: Scholarship for use in freshman, sophomore, junior, or senior years; renewable. *Number:* 1. *Amount:* $500.

Eligibility Requirements: Applicant must be enrolled or expecting to enroll full-time at a two-year or four-year or technical institution or university and resident of Virginia. Applicant or parent of applicant must be member of American Quarter Horse Association. Applicant must have 2.5 GPA or higher. Available to U.S. citizens.

Application Requirements: Application, driver's license, financial need analysis, photo, references, transcript. *Deadline:* February 1.

Contact: Laura Owens, Scholarship Coordinator
American Quarter Horse Foundation (AQHF)
2601 I-40 East
Amarillo, TX 79104
Phone: 806-376-5181
Fax: 806-376-1005
E-mail: lowens@aqha.org

SWAYZE WOODRUFF SCHOLARSHIP

Must be member of AQHA or AQHYA who resides in Alabama, Tennessee, Louisiana, Mississippi, or Arkansas. Recipient receives $2000 per year for four-year degree plan. Must be renewed annually.

Award: Scholarship for use in freshman, sophomore, junior, or senior years; renewable. *Number:* 1. *Amount:* $8000.

Eligibility Requirements: Applicant must be enrolled or expecting to enroll full-time at a two-year or four-year or technical institution or university and resident of Alabama, Arkansas, Louisiana, Mississippi, or Tennessee. Applicant or parent of applicant must be member of American Quarter Horse Association. Applicant must have 2.5 GPA or higher. Available to U.S. citizens.

Application Requirements: Application, driver's license, financial need analysis, photo, references, transcript. *Deadline:* February 1.

Contact: Laura Owens, Scholarship Coordinator
American Quarter Horse Foundation (AQHF)
2601 I-40 East
Amarillo, TX 79104
Phone: 806-376-5181
Fax: 806-376-1005
E-mail: lowens@aqha.org

AMERICAN SOCIETY OF ELECTRONEURODIAGNOSTIC TECHNOLOGISTS, INC. http://www.aset.org

AMERICAN SOCIETY OF ELECTRONEURODIAGNOSTIC TECHNOLOGISTS SCHOLARSHIPS

One-time award for members of the American Society of Electroneurodiagnostic Technologists to attend short courses and/or scientific programs at Society convention. Sophomores may apply if they were Society members in their freshman year. Write for more information.

Award: Scholarship for use in sophomore year; not renewable. *Number:* 6–10. *Amount:* $300–$500.

Eligibility Requirements: Applicant must be enrolled or expecting to enroll full or part-time at a two-year or technical institution. Applicant or parent of applicant must be member of American Society of Electroneurodiagnostic Technologists, Inc. Available to U.S. and non-U.S. citizens.

Application Requirements: Application, essay, references. *Deadline:* varies.

Contact: Sheila Navis, Executive Director
American Society of Electroneurodiagnostic Technologists, Inc.
426 West 42nd Street
Kansas City, MO 64111
Phone: 816-931-1120
Fax: 816-931-1145
E-mail: info@aset.org

AMERICAN SOCIETY OF TRAVEL AGENTS (ASTA) FOUNDATION http://www.astanet.com

ARIZONA CHAPTER DEPENDENT/EMPLOYEE MEMBERSHIP SCHOLARSHIP

One-time award for dependents of active members or employees of an American Society of Travel Agents member in Arizona. Major in travel and tourism is not required. Must be resident of Arizona. Submit proof of employment and membership, as well as a 500-word essay on career goals. Must attend Arizona institution. For requirements and an application form, visit Web site: http://www.astanet.com/education/edu_scholarships.asp. Minimum 2.5 GPA required.

Award: Scholarship for use in sophomore, junior, or senior years; not renewable. *Number:* 1. *Amount:* $1500.

Eligibility Requirements: Applicant must be enrolled or expecting to enroll full or part-time at a two-year or four-year institution or university; resident of Arizona and studying in Arizona. Applicant or parent of applicant must be member of American Society of Travel Agents. Applicant or parent of applicant must have employment or volunteer experience in designated career field. Applicant must have 2.5 GPA or higher. Available to U.S. citizens.

Application Requirements: Application, driver's license, essay, references, transcript. *Deadline:* varies.

Contact: Verlette Mitchell, Manager
American Society of Travel Agents (ASTA) Foundation
1101 King Street
Alexandria, VA 22314-2187
Phone: 703-739-8721
Fax: 703-684-8319
E-mail: scholarship@astahq.com

AMERICAN WATER SKI EDUCATIONAL FOUNDATION http://www.waterskihalloffame.com

AMERICAN WATER SKI EDUCATIONAL FOUNDATION SCHOLARSHIP

Six awards for incoming college sophomores through incoming seniors who are members of U.S.A Waterski. Based upon academics, leadership, extracurricular activities, recommendations, and financial need. One-time award of $1500.

Award: Scholarship for use in sophomore, junior, or senior years; not renewable. *Number:* 6. *Amount:* $1500.

Eligibility Requirements: Applicant must be enrolled or expecting to enroll full-time at a two-year or four-year institution and must have an interest in leadership. Applicant or parent of applicant must be member of USA Water Ski. Available to U.S. citizens.

Application Requirements: Application, essay, financial need analysis, references, transcript. *Deadline:* April 1.

Contact: Carole Lowe, Scholarship Director
American Water Ski Educational Foundation
1251 Holy Cow Road
Polk City, FL 33868-8200
Phone: 863-324-2472
Fax: 863-324-3996
E-mail: awsefhalloffame@cs.com

AMVETS AUXILIARY

AMVETS NATIONAL LADIES AUXILIARY SCHOLARSHIP

One-time award of up to $1000 for a member of AMVETS or the Auxiliary. Applicant may also be the family member of a member. Award for full-time study at any accredited U.S. institution. Minimum 2.5 GPA required.

Award: Scholarship for use in freshman, sophomore, junior, or senior years; not renewable. *Number:* 8–10. *Amount:* $500–$1000.

AMVETS Auxiliary (continued)

Eligibility Requirements: Applicant must be enrolled or expecting to enroll full-time at a two-year or four-year or technical institution or university. Applicant or parent of applicant must be member of AMVETS Auxiliary. Applicant must have 2.5 GPA or higher. Available to U.S. citizens.

Application Requirements: Application, essay, references, transcript. *Deadline:* June 1.

Contact: Scholarship Officer
AMVETS Auxiliary
4647 Forbes Boulevard
Lanham, MD 20706-4380
Phone: 301-459-6255
Fax: 877-726-8387

APPALOOSA HORSE CLUB-APPALOOSA YOUTH PROGRAM

http://www.appaloosa.com

APPALOOSA YOUTH EDUCATIONAL SCHOLARSHIPS

Applicants must be members or dependents of members of the Appaloosa Youth Association or Appaloosa Horse Club. Based on academics, leadership, sportsmanship, and horsemanship. Send picture with application.

Award: Scholarship for use in freshman, sophomore, junior, senior, or graduate years; not renewable. *Number:* 6–8. *Amount:* $1000.

Eligibility Requirements: Applicant must be enrolled or expecting to enroll full-time at a two-year or four-year institution or university and must have an interest in animal/agricultural competition or leadership. Applicant or parent of applicant must be member of Appaloosa Horse Club/Appaloosa Youth Association. Applicant must have 2.5 GPA or higher. Available to U.S. citizens.

Application Requirements: Application, essay, photo, references, test scores, transcript. *Deadline:* June 10.

Contact: Keeley Gant, AYF Coordinator
Appaloosa Horse Club-Appaloosa Youth Program
2720 Pullman Road
Moscow, ID 83843
Phone: 208-882-5578 Ext. 264
Fax: 208-882-8150
E-mail: aphc@appaloosa.com

ARBY'S FOUNDATION, BIG BROTHERS BIG SISTERS OF AMERICA

http://www.bbbsa.org

ARBY'S-BIG BROTHERS BIG SISTERS SCHOLARSHIP AWARD

Designed to assist exemplary high school students from low- and middle-income families. Applicants must be or have been a Little Brother or Little Sister in the Big Brothers or Big Sisters program. Write for more information. Merit considered. Renewable scholarships of up to $5000. Must rank in upper half of class or have a minimum 2.5 GPA.

Award: Scholarship for use in freshman year; renewable. *Number:* 2–10. *Amount:* $1000–$5000.

Eligibility Requirements: Applicant must be enrolled or expecting to enroll full-time at a two-year or four-year institution or university. Applicant or parent of applicant must be member of Big Brothers/Big Sisters. Applicant or parent of applicant must have employment or volunteer experience in community service. Applicant must have 2.5 GPA or higher. Available to U.S. citizens.

Application Requirements: Application, essay, financial need analysis, photo, references, test scores, transcript. *Deadline:* March 15.

Contact: Mr. Joseph Divensenso, Director of Corporate Partnerships
Arby's Foundation, Big Brothers Big Sisters of America
230 North 13th Street
Philadelphia, PA 19107
Phone: 215-567-7000
Fax: 215-567-0394
E-mail: rkearney@bbbsa.org

ARRL FOUNDATION, INC.

http://www.arrl.org/arrlf/scholgen.html

ALBERT H. HIX, W8AH, MEMORIAL SCHOLARSHIP

One-time award available to students who are licensed as general class or higher amateur radio operators and who live in the West Virginia section or the Roanoke Division or attend post-secondary school in West Virginia section. Minimum GPA of 3.0.

Award: Scholarship for use in freshman, sophomore, junior, or senior years; not renewable. *Number:* 1. *Amount:* $500.

Eligibility Requirements: Applicant must be enrolled or expecting to enroll at a two-year or four-year or technical institution or university and must have an interest in amateur radio. Applicant or parent of applicant must be member of American Radio Relay League. Applicant must have 3.0 GPA or higher. Available to U.S. citizens.

Application Requirements: Application. *Deadline:* February 1.

Contact: Mary Hobart, Foundation Secretary
ARRL Foundation, Inc.
225 Main Street
Newington, CT 06111-4845
Phone: 860-594-0397
E-mail: mhobart@arrl.org

IRARC MEMORIAL/JOSEPH P.RUBINO, WA4MMD, SCHOLARSHIP

Need-based award available to students who are licensed amateur radio operators. Residence in Brevard County, Florida preferred, Florida residence required. Must maintain 2.5 GPA and pursue undergraduate degree or electronic technician certification.

Award: Scholarship for use in freshman, sophomore, junior, or senior years; not renewable. *Number:* varies. *Amount:* $750.

Eligibility Requirements: Applicant must be enrolled or expecting to enroll at a two-year or four-year or technical institution or university; resident of Florida and must have an interest in amateur radio. Applicant or parent of applicant must be member of American Radio Relay League. Applicant must have 2.5 GPA or higher. Available to U.S. citizens.

Application Requirements: Application, financial need analysis, transcript. *Deadline:* February 1.

Contact: Mary Hobart, Foundation Secretary
ARRL Foundation, Inc.
225 Main Street
Newington, CT 06111-4845
Phone: 860-594-0397
E-mail: mhobart@arrl.org

TOM AND JUDITH COMSTOCK SCHOLARSHIP

One-time award for high school seniors who are members of the American Radio Relay League. Preference given to residents of Texas and Oklahoma. Must be licensed amateur radio operator. Must be accepted at a two- or four-year institution.

Award: Scholarship for use in freshman year; not renewable. *Number:* 1. *Amount:* $1000.

Eligibility Requirements: Applicant must be high school student; planning to enroll or expecting to enroll at a two-year or four-year institution or university and must have an interest in amateur radio. Applicant or parent of applicant must be member of American Radio Relay League. Applicant must have 2.5 GPA or higher.

Application Requirements: Application, transcript. *Deadline:* February 1.

Contact: Mary Lau, Scholarship Director
ARRL Foundation, Inc.
225 Main Street
Newington, CT 06111-4845

YANKEE CLIPPER CONTEST CLUB, INC. YOUTH SCHOLARSHIP

One-time award available to students who are licensed as general class or higher amateur radio operators and who live or attend college in the 175-mile radius of YCCC Center. Qualifying area includes all of MA, RI, CT and Long Island NY, most of VT and NH, portions of ME, eastern NY, and extreme north-eastern sections of PA and NJ.

Award: Scholarship for use in freshman, sophomore, junior, or senior years; not renewable. *Number:* 1. *Amount:* $1500–$2000.

Eligibility Requirements: Applicant must be enrolled or expecting to enroll at a two-year or four-year or technical institution or university and must have an interest in amateur radio. Applicant or parent of applicant must be member of American Radio Relay League. Available to U.S. citizens.

Application Requirements: Application, transcript. *Deadline:* February 1.

Contact: Mary Hobart, Foundation Secretary
ARRL Foundation, Inc.
225 Main Street
Newington, CT 06111-4845
Phone: 860-594-0397
E-mail: mhobart@arrl.org

YOU'VE GOT A FRIEND IN PENNSYLVANIA SCHOLARSHIP

One-time award available to students who are licensed as general amateur radio operators and who are members of the American Radio Relay League. Residents of Pennsylvania preferred.

Award: Scholarship for use in freshman, sophomore, junior, or senior years; not renewable. *Number:* 1. *Amount:* $1000.

Eligibility Requirements: Applicant must be enrolled or expecting to enroll at a two-year or four-year or technical institution or university and must have an interest in amateur radio. Applicant or parent of applicant must be member of American Radio Relay League.

Application Requirements: Application, transcript. *Deadline:* February 1.

Contact: Mary Lau, Scholarship Director
ARRL Foundation, Inc.
225 Main Street
Newington, CT 06111-4845

ASSOCIATION OF AMERICAN GEOGRAPHERS http://www.aag.org

ANNE U. WHITE FUND

Grants are available to AAG members who have held membership for at least two years. Must submit a summary of results no later then twelve months after receiving award. For more details see Web site: http://www.aag.org/grantsawards.

Award: Grant for use in freshman, sophomore, junior, senior, graduate, or postgraduate years; not renewable. *Number:* 6. *Amount:* $1000–$1500.

Eligibility Requirements: Applicant must be enrolled or expecting to enroll at a four-year institution or university. Applicant or parent of applicant must be member of Association of American Geographers. Available to U.S. citizens.

Application Requirements: Application, essay. *Deadline:* December 31.

Contact: Association of American Geographers
1710 16th Street NW
Washington, DC 20009-3198

AVIATION BOATSWAIN'S MATES ASSOCIATION http://www.abma-usn.org

AVIATION BOATSWAIN'S MATES ASSOCIATION ISABELLA M. GILLEN MEMORIAL SCHOLARSHIP

For undergraduate students who are dependents of active or deceased members of the Aviation Boatswain's Mates Association. Awards are based on character, motivation, and financial need. Membership identification number required. For further details, visit Web site: http://www.abma-usn.org/scholarship.htm

Award: Scholarship for use in freshman, sophomore, junior, or senior years; not renewable. *Number:* 1. *Amount:* $2500.

Eligibility Requirements: Applicant must be enrolled or expecting to enroll full-time at a two-year or four-year or technical institution or university and single. Applicant or parent of applicant must be member of Aviation Boatswain's Mates Association. Applicant must have 2.5 GPA or higher. Available to U.S. citizens.

Application Requirements: Application, financial need analysis, references, test scores, transcript. *Deadline:* June 1.

Contact: Lanny Vines, Scholarship Chairman
Aviation Boatswain's Mates Association
144 CR 1515
Alba, TX 75410
Phone: 903-473-4414
E-mail: abma30th@hotmail.com

BOY SCOUTS OF AMERICA, EAGLE SCOUT SERVICE http://www.scouting.org/nesa/scholar

ELKS NATIONAL FOUNDATION EAGLE SCOUT SCHOLARSHIP

Award is only available to Eagle Scouts. Must supply references from a scouting professional or a volunteer in scouting. Must be graduating high school senior. Renewable awards of $1000 to $2000 per year for four years. Visit Web site for application procedures. (http://www.scouting.org/nesa/scholar)

Award: Scholarship for use in freshman, sophomore, junior, or senior years; renewable. *Number:* up to 8. *Amount:* $1000–$2000.

Eligibility Requirements: Applicant must be high school student; planning to enroll or expecting to enroll full-time at a four-year institution and male. Applicant or parent of applicant must be member of Boy Scouts. Available to U.S. citizens.

Application Requirements: Application, financial need analysis, references, test scores, transcript. *Deadline:* February 28.

Contact: Ann Dimond, Manager
Boy Scouts of America, Eagle Scout Service
1325 West Walnut Hill Lane
Irving, TX 75038

MABLE AND LAWRENCE S. COOKE SCHOLARSHIP

One scholarship of up to $48,000 (up to $12,000 per year for four years) and four $20,000 scholarships ($5,000 a year for four years) are given annually. The Eagle Scout offered the scholarship must agree to specific conditions before acceptance. Please visit Web site for information and application. (http://www.scouting.org/nesa/scholar)

Award: Scholarship for use in freshman, sophomore, junior, or senior years; renewable. *Number:* up to 5. *Amount:* $5000–$12,000.

Eligibility Requirements: Applicant must be enrolled or expecting to enroll full-time at a four-year institution or university and male. Applicant or parent of applicant must be member of Boy Scouts. Applicant must have 3.0 GPA or higher.

Application Requirements: Application, essay, financial need analysis, references, test scores, transcript. *Deadline:* February 28.

Contact: Ann Dimond, Manager
Boy Scouts of America, Eagle Scout Service
1325 West Walnut Hill Lane
Box 152079
Irving, TX 75015-2079

NATIONAL EAGLE SCOUT HALL / MCELWAIN MERIT SCHOLARSHIP

Must be an Eagle Scout. Only graduating high school seniors through college juniors may apply. Application is available at the Web site. (http://www.scouting.org/nesa/scholar)

Award: Scholarship for use in freshman, sophomore, junior, or senior years; not renewable. *Number:* 60. *Amount:* $1000.

Eligibility Requirements: Applicant must be enrolled or expecting to enroll full-time at a four-year institution or university; male and must have an interest in leadership. Applicant or parent of applicant must be member of Boy Scouts. Available to U.S. citizens.

Application Requirements: Application, references. *Deadline:* February 28.

Contact: Ann Dimond, Manager
Boy Scouts of America, Eagle Scout Service
1325 West Walnut Hill Lane
Box 152079
Irving, TX 75015-2079

NATIONAL EAGLE SCOUT SCHOLARSHIP

Award for graduating high school males for use in undergraduate degree study. Must have SAT scores of at least 1090 and/or ACT scores of at least 26. Must be an Eagle Scout. Application is available at the Web site. (http://www.scouting.org/nesa/scholar)

Award: Scholarship for use in freshman, sophomore, junior, or senior years; not renewable. *Number:* varies. *Amount:* $3000.

Eligibility Requirements: Applicant must be high school student; planning to enroll or expecting to enroll full-time at a four-year institution or university and male. Applicant or parent of applicant must be member of Boy Scouts. Available to U.S. citizens.

Application Requirements: Application, financial need analysis, references, test scores, transcript. *Deadline:* February 28.

Contact: Ann Dimond, Manager
Boy Scouts of America, Eagle Scout Service
1325 West Walnut Hill Lane
Irving, TX 75038

BOY SCOUTS OF AMERICA/ORDER OF THE ARROW

E. URNER GOODMAN SCHOLARSHIP

Renewable aid to members of Order of the Arrow planning professional career with Boy Scouts. Submit 250 to 500-word essay on reasons for pursuing Boy Scouts of America career, proof of college acceptance for undergraduate study, and resume. Merit-based award.

Award: Scholarship for use in freshman, sophomore, junior, or senior years; renewable. *Number:* 3–6. *Amount:* $1000–$4000.

Eligibility Requirements: Applicant must be enrolled or expecting to enroll full-time at a four-year institution and male. Applicant or parent of applicant must be member of Boy Scouts or Order of the Arrow. Applicant must have 2.5 GPA or higher. Available to U.S. citizens.

Application Requirements: Application, autobiography, essay, photo, resume, references, self-addressed stamped envelope, test scores, transcript. *Deadline:* January 15.

Contact: Clyde Mayer, National Director
Boy Scouts of America/Order of the Arrow
1325 West Walnut Hill Lane
Irving, TX 75038-3008
Phone: 972-580-2438
Fax: 972-580-2399
E-mail: cmayer@netbsa.org

BOYS & GIRLS CLUBS OF AMERICA

http://www.bgca.org

BOYS & GIRLS CLUBS OF AMERICA NATIONAL YOUTH OF THE YEAR AWARD

This nonrenewable award is available to youths 14-18 who have been active members of their Boys Club or Girls Club for at least one year. Contact local club for nomination form. Minimum 3.0 GPA required. Must be nominated by local club.

Award: Scholarship for use in freshman, sophomore, junior, or senior years; not renewable. *Number:* 5. *Amount:* $5000–$10,000.

Eligibility Requirements: Applicant must be high school student; age 14-18; planning to enroll or expecting to enroll full or part-time at a two-year or four-year or technical institution; single and must have an interest in leadership. Applicant or parent of applicant must be member of Boys or Girls Club. Applicant must have 3.0 GPA or higher.

Application Requirements: Application, essay, interview, references. *Deadline:* varies.

Contact: Kelvin Davis, Program Services Director
Boys & Girls Clubs of America
1230 West Peachtree Street, NW
Atlanta, GA 30309

BOYS AND GIRLS CLUBS OF CHICAGO

http://www.bgcc.org

BOYS AND GIRLS CLUBS OF CHICAGO SCHOLARSHIPS

Boys and Girls Clubs of Chicago scholarships are awarded to graduating high school seniors who are local Club members. Scholarships are based upon academic achievement, Club involvement, financial need, and personal interviews. Students are asked to maintain their grades, seek internships and job opportunities, and lend guidance to younger children.

Award: Scholarship for use in freshman, sophomore, junior, or senior years; renewable. *Number:* varies. *Amount:* $3000–$5000.

Eligibility Requirements: Applicant must be high school student; planning to enroll or expecting to enroll full or part-time at a two-year or four-year or technical institution or university and resident of Illinois. Applicant or parent of applicant must be member of Boys or Girls Club. Applicant must have 2.5 GPA or higher. Available to U.S. citizens.

Contact: LaKesha Nelson, Project Director
Boys and Girls Clubs of Chicago
550 West Van Buren Street
Suite 350
Chicago, IL 60607
Phone: 312-235-8000
Fax: 312-427-4110
E-mail: lnelson@bgcc.org

BUFFALO AFL-CIO COUNCIL

AFL-CIO COUNCIL OF BUFFALO SCHOLARSHIP

One-time award of $1000 for a high school senior who is a son or daughter of a member of a local union affiliated with the Buffalo AFL-CIO Council. Must be a New York resident and use award for study in New York. Write for more information. March deadline.

Award: Scholarship for use in freshman year; not renewable. *Number:* 1. *Amount:* $500–$1000.

Eligibility Requirements: Applicant must be high school student; planning to enroll or expecting to enroll full-time at a two-year or four-year institution; resident of New York and studying in New York. Applicant or parent of applicant must be member of AFL-CIO. Available to U.S. and Canadian citizens.

Application Requirements: Application, essay, references, transcript. *Deadline:* March 14.

Contact: Scholarship Director
Buffalo AFL-CIO Council
295 Main Street
Buffalo, NY 14203
Phone: 716-852-0375
Fax: 716-855-1802

CALIFORNIA GRANGE FOUNDATION

http://www.grangeonline.org

CALIFORNIA GRANGE FOUNDATION SCHOLARSHIP

Scholarship program available for Grange members residing in California who wish to attend a higher institution of learning of their choice. Visit Web site for additional information and to download scholarship applications.

Award: Scholarship for use in freshman, sophomore, junior, or senior years; not renewable. *Number:* 5–15. *Amount:* $500–$1000.

Eligibility Requirements: Applicant must be enrolled or expecting to enroll full or part-time at a two-year or four-year or technical institution or university and resident of California. Applicant or parent of applicant must be member of Grange Association. Available to U.S. citizens.

Application Requirements: Application, financial need analysis, references, transcript. *Deadline:* May 1.

Contact: California Grange Foundation
2101 Stockton Boulevard
Sacremento, CA 95817
Phone: 916-454-5805
Fax: 916-739-8189

CALIFORNIA TEACHERS ASSOCIATION (CTA) http://www.cta.org

CALIFORNIA TEACHERS ASSOCIATION SCHOLARSHIP FOR DEPENDENT CHILDREN

Twenty-five $2000 scholarships for study in higher education awarded annually. Twenty-three provided by California Teachers Association; one provided by D. A. Weber Scholarship Fund for student attending continuation high school; and one provided by Ralph J. Flynn Memorial Fund. Must be dependent child of active, retired, or deceased member of California Teachers Association. Applications available in October.

Award: Scholarship for use in freshman, sophomore, junior, or senior years; not renewable. *Number:* 25. *Amount:* $2000.

Eligibility Requirements: Applicant must be enrolled or expecting to enroll full-time at a two-year or four-year or technical institution or university. Applicant or parent of applicant must be member of California Teachers Association. Applicant must have 3.0 GPA or higher.

Application Requirements: Application, essay, references, transcript. *Deadline:* February 16.

Contact: Human Rights Department
California Teachers Association (CTA)
PO Box 921
Burlingame, CA 94011-0921
Phone: 650-697-1400
E-mail: scholarships@cta.org

CALIFORNIA TEACHERS ASSOCIATION SCHOLARSHIP FOR MEMBERS

Must be an active member of California Teachers Association (including members working on an emergency credential). Available for study in a degree, credential, or graduate program.

Award: Scholarship for use in freshman, sophomore, junior, senior, or graduate years; not renewable. *Number:* 5. *Amount:* $2000.

Eligibility Requirements: Applicant must be enrolled or expecting to enroll full-time at an institution or university. Applicant or parent of applicant must be member of California Teachers Association. Applicant must have 3.0 GPA or higher.

Application Requirements: Application, essay, references, transcript. *Deadline:* February 16.

Contact: Human Rights Department
California Teachers Association (CTA)
PO Box 921
Burlingame, CA 94011-0921
Phone: 650-697-1400
E-mail: scholarships@cta.org

CATHOLIC KOLPING SOCIETY OF AMERICA http://www.kolping.org/scholar.htm

FATHER KREWITT SCHOLARSHIP

Scholarship based on an essay of 500 words on a specific topic selected by the board of the Kolping Society. Must be a member of the Kolping Society, or a child or grandchild of a member. Further information and application available at Web site: http://www.kolping.org. Application deadline is February 28.

Award: Scholarship for use in freshman, sophomore, junior, senior, or graduate years; not renewable. *Number:* 1. *Amount:* $1000.

Eligibility Requirements: Applicant must be Roman Catholic and enrolled or expecting to enroll full-time at a two-year or four-year or technical institution or university. Applicant or parent of applicant must be member of Catholic Kolping Society of America.

Application Requirements: Application, applicant must enter a contest, essay. *Deadline:* February 28.

Contact: Catholic Kolping Society of America
c/o Edward Farkas
9 East Eighth Street
Clifton, NJ 07011

CATHOLIC WORKMAN http://www.catholicworkman.org

CATHOLIC WORKMAN COLLEGE SCHOLARSHIPS

Award for members of the Catholic Workman Fraternal Society to continue their education. Must have minimum 2.5 GPA and demonstrate involvement within community. Available to members of all ages. Scholarship is either $500 or $1000, depending on year in college.

Award: Scholarship for use in freshman, sophomore, junior, or senior years; not renewable. *Number:* up to 20. *Amount:* $500–$1000.

Eligibility Requirements: Applicant must be a member of the specified denomination and enrolled or expecting to enroll full-time at a two-year or four-year or technical institution or university. Applicant or parent of applicant must be member of Catholic Workman Fraternal Society. Applicant or parent of applicant must have employment or volunteer experience in community service. Applicant must have 2.5 GPA or higher. Available to U.S. citizens.

Application Requirements: Application, essay, photo, references, transcript, ACT and/or SAT scores. *Deadline:* July 1.

Contact: Lenore Krava, Executive Secretary
Catholic Workman
1201 1st Street, NE
New Prague, MN 56071
Phone: 952-758-2229
Fax: 952-758-6221
E-mail: info@catholicworkman.org

CENTER FOR SCHOLARSHIP ADMINISTRATION http://www.scholarshipprograms.org

ANDERSON AREA SOCIETY FOR HUMAN RESOURCE MANAGEMENT SCHOLARSHIP PROGRAM

Non-renewable scholarship available to dependent children of members of AASHRM. For more details and an application, see Web site.

Award: Scholarship for use in freshman, sophomore, junior, or senior years; not renewable. *Number:* 1. *Amount:* $1000.

Eligibility Requirements: Applicant must be enrolled or expecting to enroll full-time at a two-year or four-year or technical institution or university. Applicant or parent of applicant must be member of Anderson Area Society for Human Resource Management. Applicant must have 3.0 GPA or higher.

Application Requirements: Application, essay, financial need analysis, references, transcript. *Deadline:* February 15.

Contact: Application available at Web site.

GREENVILLE AREA PERSONNEL ASSOCIATION WALTER L. MARTIN MEMORIAL SCHOLARSHIP PROGRAM

One-time award to dependent children of GAPA members. Financial need is not a consideration. For more details see the Web site.

Award: Scholarship for use in freshman, sophomore, junior, or senior years; not renewable. *Number:* varies. *Amount:* $1000.

Eligibility Requirements: Applicant must be enrolled or expecting to enroll full-time at a two-year or four-year or technical institution or university. Applicant or parent of applicant must be member of Greenville Area Personnel Association. Applicant must have 2.5 GPA or higher.

Application Requirements: Application, essay, references, transcript. *Deadline:* March 1.

Contact: Application available at Web site.

MICHELIN/TIA SCHOLARSHIPS

Renewable scholarships are available to qualified employees and dependent children of qualified employees of tire dealers who are members of the Tire Industry Association. For more details and an application see Web site: http://www.scholarshipprograms.org

Award: Scholarship for use in freshman, sophomore, junior, or senior years; renewable. *Number:* 3. *Amount:* $1250–$2500.

Eligibility Requirements: Applicant must be enrolled or expecting to enroll full-time at a two-year or four-year or technical institution or

Center for Scholarship Administration (continued)

university. Applicant or parent of applicant must be member of Tire Industry Association. Applicant must have 3.0 GPA or higher.

Application Requirements: Application, essay, references, transcript. *Deadline:* March 31.

Contact: Application available at Web site.

NATIONAL ASSOCIATION OF FOOD EQUIPMENT DEALERS, INC. SCHOLARSHIP

Non-renewable scholarships are available to the dependent children of qualified employees of NAFED dealers. See NAFED owner for more detailed information on additional criteria.

Award: Scholarship for use in freshman, sophomore, junior, or senior years; not renewable. *Number:* up to 1. *Amount:* $5000.

Eligibility Requirements: Applicant must be enrolled or expecting to enroll full-time at a two-year or four-year or technical institution or university. Applicant or parent of applicant must be member of National Association of Food Equipment Dealers. Applicant must have 3.0 GPA or higher.

Application Requirements: Application, essay, references, transcript. *Deadline:* February 15.

Contact: See NAFED owner.

CITIZENS FOR GLOBAL SOLUTIONS http://www.globalsolutions.org

HARLAN M. SMITH "BUILDERS OF A BETTER WORLD" SCHOLARSHIP COMPETITION

Essay competition for students whose goals have the potential to most closely contribute to the World Federalist Association's vision for a better world. Applicants must be between the ages of 18 and 25 and be members of Citizens for Global Solutions or children of members. Visit Web site at http://www.globalsolutions.org for further information.

Award: Prize for use in freshman, sophomore, junior, senior, graduate, or postgraduate years; not renewable. *Number:* 3–5. *Amount:* $500–$1500.

Eligibility Requirements: Applicant must be age 18-25 and enrolled or expecting to enroll full or part-time at a two-year or four-year institution or university. Applicant or parent of applicant must be member of World Federalist Association. Available to U.S. citizens.

Application Requirements: Essay, references, self-addressed stamped envelope. *Deadline:* October 26.

Contact: See Web site for details.

CIVIL AIR PATROL, USAF AUXILIARY http://www.capnhq.gov

CIVIL AIR PATROL ACADEMIC SCHOLARSHIPS

One-time $250-$1000 award for active members of the Civil Air Patrol to pursue undergraduate, graduate, or trade or technical education. Must be a current CAP member. Significant restrictions apply. Not open to the general public. Contact for further details.

Award: Scholarship for use in freshman, sophomore, junior, senior, or graduate years; not renewable. *Number:* up to 40. *Amount:* $250–$1000.

Eligibility Requirements: Applicant must be enrolled or expecting to enroll full-time at a four-year or technical institution or university. Applicant or parent of applicant must be member of Civil Air Patrol. Available to U.S. citizens.

Application Requirements: Application, essay, photo, resume, references, test scores, transcript. *Deadline:* January 31.

Contact: Tanjula Sankey, Assistant Program Manager
Civil Air Patrol, USAF Auxiliary
105 South Hansell Street, Building 714
Maxwell Air Force Base, AL 36112-6332
Phone: 334-953-8640
Fax: 334-953-6699
E-mail: cpr@capnhq.gov

COMMUNITY BANKER ASSOCIATION OF ILLINOIS http://www.cbai.com/scholarship.htm

COMMUNITY BANKER ASSOCIATION OF ILLINOIS CHILDREN OF COMMUNITY BANKING SCHOLARSHIP

Eligible Illinois community banks can submit one name for each $1,000 they have donated to the CBAI Foundation. Children of eligible community bankers and part-time bank employees entering freshman year of higher education are eligible. Winner determined by drawing. Must be Illinois resident.

Award: Scholarship for use in freshman year; not renewable. *Number:* 1. *Amount:* $1000–$4000.

Eligibility Requirements: Applicant must be high school student; planning to enroll or expecting to enroll full-time at a two-year or four-year or technical institution or university and resident of Illinois. Applicant or parent of applicant must be member of Community Banker Association of Illinois. Applicant or parent of applicant must have employment or volunteer experience in banking. Available to U.S. citizens.

Application Requirements: *Deadline:* August 15.

Contact: Andrea Cusick, Senior Vice President of Communications
Community Banker Association of Illinois
Attn: CBAI Foundation for Community Banking
901 Community Drive
Springfield, IL 62703-5184
Phone: 217-529-2265
Fax: 217-585-8738
E-mail: cbaicom@cbai.com

COMMUNITY FOUNDATION OF WESTERN MASSACHUSETTS http://www.communityfoundation.org

HORACE HILL SCHOLARSHIP

Scholarships are given to children or grandchildren of a member of the Springfield Newspapers' 25-Year Club. For more information or application visit http://www.communityfoundation.org.

Award: Scholarship for use in freshman, sophomore, junior, senior, or graduate years; not renewable. *Number:* 4. *Amount:* $600.

Eligibility Requirements: Applicant must be enrolled or expecting to enroll full or part-time at a two-year or four-year institution or university. Applicant or parent of applicant must be member of Springfield Newspaper 25-Year Club. Applicant or parent of applicant must have employment or volunteer experience in journalism. Available to U.S. citizens.

Application Requirements: Application, financial need analysis, transcript. *Deadline:* March 31.

Contact: Community Foundation of Western Massachusetts
1500 Main Street
PO Box 15769
Springfield, MA 01115

DANISH SISTERHOOD OF AMERICA

BETTY HANSEN CONTINUING EDUCATION GRANT

Grant is available to part-time students for use at any level, including community education classes. Must be a member of the Danish Sisterhood of America.

Award: Grant for use in freshman, sophomore, junior, or senior years; renewable. *Number:* up to 10. *Amount:* up to $500.

Eligibility Requirements: Applicant must be enrolled or expecting to enroll part-time at an institution or university. Applicant or parent of applicant must be member of Danish Sisterhood of America. Available to U.S. and Canadian citizens.

Application Requirements: Application. *Deadline:* varies.

Contact: Melanie Berg, Chairperson
Danish Sisterhood of America
10911 B. Glen Acres Drive South
Seattle, WA 98168
Phone: 206-243-1728

NATIONAL SCHOLARSHIP, MILDRED SORENSEN, OLGA CHRISTENSEN AND BETTY HANSEN SCHOLARSHIPS

One-time awards for full-time, postsecondary students who are members, or a son or daughter of members of the Danish Sisterhood of America. Candidates must have a minimum 2.5 GPA. Write for further details.

Award: Scholarship for use in freshman, sophomore, junior, or senior years; not renewable. *Number:* up to 12. *Amount:* $500–$1000.

Eligibility Requirements: Applicant must be enrolled or expecting to enroll full or part-time at a two-year or four-year or technical institution. Applicant or parent of applicant must be member of Danish Sisterhood of America. Applicant must have 2.5 GPA or higher.

Application Requirements: Application, references, test scores, transcript. *Deadline:* February 28.

Contact: Melanie Berg, Chairperson
Danish Sisterhood of America
10911 B. Glen Acres Drive South
Seattle, WA 98168

DAVIS-ROBERTS SCHOLARSHIP FUND, INC.

DAVIS-ROBERTS SCHOLARSHIPS

Renewable award to assist Demolays and Jobs Daughters in the state of Wyoming with their education, providing they are attending or planning to attend school full-time. Must submit letter from Chapter Dad or Bethel Guardian and photo.

Award: Scholarship for use in freshman, sophomore, junior, or senior years; renewable. *Number:* 3–5. *Amount:* $350–$1000.

Eligibility Requirements: Applicant must be enrolled or expecting to enroll full-time at a two-year or four-year or technical institution or university and resident of Wyoming. Applicant or parent of applicant must be member of Demolay or Jobs Daughters. Applicant must have 2.5 GPA or higher. Available to U.S. citizens.

Application Requirements: Application, essay, financial need analysis, photo, references, transcript. *Deadline:* June 15.

Contact: Gary Skillern, Secretary
Davis-Roberts Scholarship Fund, Inc.
PO Box 20645
Cheyenne, WY 82003
Phone: 307-632-0491

DELTA DELTA DELTA FOUNDATION http://www.tridelta.org

DELTA DELTA DELTA UNDERGRADUATE SCHOLARSHIP

One-time award based on academic achievement, campus, chapter, and community involvement. Any initiated sophomore or junior member in good-standing of Delta Delta Delta may apply. Application and information available at Web site http://www.tridelta.org.

Award: Scholarship for use in junior or senior years; not renewable. *Number:* 48–50. *Amount:* $500–$2000.

Eligibility Requirements: Applicant must be enrolled or expecting to enroll full-time at a four-year institution or university and single female. Applicant or parent of applicant must have employment or volunteer experience in community service. Available to U.S. citizens.

Application Requirements: Application, references, transcript. *Deadline:* February 1.

Contact: Laura Allen, Foundation Manager of Scholarships and Financial Services
Delta Delta Delta Foundation
PO Box 5987
Arlington, TX 76005
Phone: 817-633-8001
Fax: 817-652-0212
E-mail: lallen@trideltaeo.org

DELTA GAMMA FOUNDATION http://www.deltagamma.org

DELTA GAMMA FOUNDATION SCHOLARSHIPS

Award for initiated members of the Delta Gamma Fraternity. Must be female. Applicants must have completed three semesters or five quarters of college with a minimum 3.0 GPA. Must be active in campus, community, and chapter activities. Freshmen are ineligible. One-time award of $1000.

Award: Scholarship for use in sophomore, junior, or senior years; not renewable. *Number:* 150–175. *Amount:* $1000.

Eligibility Requirements: Applicant must be enrolled or expecting to enroll full-time at a four-year institution or university and female. Applicant must have 3.0 GPA or higher. Available to U.S. and Canadian citizens.

Application Requirements: Application, autobiography, essay, photo, references, self-addressed stamped envelope, transcript. *Deadline:* February 1.

Contact: Debbie Sayre, Assistant to the Development Director
Delta Gamma Foundation
3250 Riverside Drive, PO Box 21397
Columbus, OH 43221-0397
Phone: 614-481-8169
Fax: 614-481-0133
E-mail: debbie@deltagamma.org

DELTA PHI EPSILON EDUCATIONAL FOUNDATION http://www.dphie.org

DELTA PHI EPSILON EDUCATIONAL FOUNDATION GRANT

Scholarships are available to members and sons/daughters of members of Delta Phi Epsilon for graduate and undergraduate programs. Eligibility is based on academic achievement, recommendations and financial need.

Award: Grant for use in freshman, sophomore, junior, senior, or graduate years; not renewable. *Number:* 6–8. *Amount:* $1000.

Eligibility Requirements: Applicant must be enrolled or expecting to enroll full-time at a four-year institution or university. Available to U.S. and non-U.S. citizens.

Application Requirements: Application, autobiography, essay, financial need analysis, photo, references, transcript. *Deadline:* March 1.

Contact: Ellen Alper, Executive Director
Delta Phi Epsilon Educational Foundation
16A Worthington Drive
Maryland Heights, MO 63043
Phone: 314-275-2626
Fax: 314-275-2655
E-mail: ealper@dphie.org

DELTA SIGMA PI http://www.dspnet.org

UNDERGRADUATE SCHOLARSHIP

Must be a member of Delta Sigma Pi in good standing with at least one full semester or quarter of college remaining. Awarded in the fall.

Award: Scholarship for use in sophomore, junior, or senior years; not renewable. *Number:* 12. *Amount:* $500–$1250.

Eligibility Requirements: Applicant must be enrolled or expecting to enroll full-time at a four-year institution or university. Available to U.S. citizens.

Application Requirements: Application, essay, financial need analysis, references, transcript. *Deadline:* June 30.

Contact: Shanda Gray, Executive Vice President
Delta Sigma Pi
PO Box 230
Oxford, OH 45056-0230
Phone: 513-523-1907 Ext. 237
Fax: 513-523-7292
E-mail: sharda@dspnet.org

EASTERN ORTHODOX COMMITTEE ON SCOUTING http://www.eocs.org

EASTERN ORTHODOX COMMITTEE ON SCOUTING SCHOLARSHIPS

One-time award for high school seniors planning to attend a four-year institution. Must be a registered member of a Boy or Girl Scout unit, an Eagle Scout or Gold Award recipient, active member of an Eastern Orthodox Church, and recipient of the Alpha Omega religious award.

Award: Scholarship for use in freshman year; not renewable. *Number:* 2. *Amount:* $500–$1000.

Eastern Orthodox Committee on Scouting (continued)

Eligibility Requirements: Applicant must be Eastern Orthodox; high school student; planning to enroll or expecting to enroll full-time at a four-year institution and single. Applicant or parent of applicant must be member of Boy Scouts or Girl Scouts. Available to U.S. citizens.

Application Requirements: Application, autobiography, references, self-addressed stamped envelope, test scores, transcript. *Deadline:* May 15.

Contact: George Boulukos, Scholarship Chairman
Eastern Orthodox Committee on Scouting
862 Guy Lombardo Avenue
Freeport, NY 11520
Phone: 516-868-4050
Fax: 516-868-4052
E-mail: geobou@msn.com

ELKS GOLD AWARD SCHOLARSHIPS/GIRL SCOUTS OF THE USA http://www.gsusa.org

ELKS NATIONAL FOUNDATION GOLD AWARD SCHOLARSHIPS

Eight awards given annually to Gold Award recipients selected by the Girl Scouts of America. One girl from each Girl Scout Service area will receive a $6000 scholarship ($1500 per year). Must be a high school senior planning full-time undergraduate study. Contact the Girl Scout Council or visit Web site: http://www.girlscouts.org for information and applications. Deadlines vary per Council.

Award: Scholarship for use in freshman, sophomore, junior, or senior years; renewable. *Number:* 8. *Amount:* $6000.

Eligibility Requirements: Applicant must be high school student; planning to enroll or expecting to enroll full-time at a two-year or four-year institution or university and female. Applicant or parent of applicant must be member of Girl Scouts. Available to U.S. citizens.

Application Requirements: Application, applicant must enter a contest, autobiography, financial need analysis, references, transcript. *Deadline:* varies.

Contact: Kathleen Cullinan, Program Consultant
Elks Gold Award Scholarships/Girl Scouts of the USA
420 Fifth Avenue
New York, NY 10018
Phone: 212-852-8553
Fax: 212-852-6515
E-mail: kcullinan@girlscouts.org

ELKS NATIONAL FOUNDATION http://www.elks.org/enf

ELKS EMERGENCY EDUCATIONAL GRANTS

Grant available to children of Elks who are deceased or totally incapacitated. Applicants for the one-year, renewable awards must be unmarried, under the age of 23, be a full-time undergraduate student, and demonstrate financial need. Contact ENF for an application. Deadline between July 1 and December 31 of the academic year for which assistance is desired. Visit Web site at http://www.elks.org (keyword: scholarship).

Award: Grant for use in freshman, sophomore, junior, or senior years; renewable. *Number:* varies. *Amount:* $1000–$3000.

Eligibility Requirements: Applicant must be age 22 or under; enrolled or expecting to enroll full-time at a two-year or four-year or technical institution or university and single. Applicant or parent of applicant must be member of Elks Club. Available to U.S. citizens.

Application Requirements: Application, essay, financial need analysis, references, self-addressed stamped envelope, transcript. *Deadline:* December 31.

Contact: Jeannine Kunz, Program Coordinator
Elks National Foundation
2750 North Lakeview Avenue
Chicago, IL 60614-1889
Phone: 773-755-4732
Fax: 773-755-4733
E-mail: scholarships@elks.org

ELKS NATIONAL FOUNDATION LEGACY AWARDS

Up to five hundred $1000 one-year scholarships for children and grandchildren of Elks in good standing. Parent or grandparent must have been an Elk for two years. Contact local Elks Lodge for an application or send a SASE to Foundation or see home page (http://www.elks.org, keyword: scholarship). Deadline is January 9.

Award: Scholarship for use in freshman year; not renewable. *Number:* up to 500. *Amount:* $1000.

Eligibility Requirements: Applicant must be high school student and planning to enroll or expecting to enroll full-time at a two-year or four-year institution or university. Applicant or parent of applicant must be member of Elks Club. Available to U.S. citizens.

Application Requirements: Application, essay, references, self-addressed stamped envelope, test scores, transcript. *Deadline:* January 9.

Contact: Ms. Jeannine Kunz, Scholarship Coordinator
Elks National Foundation
2750 North Lakeview Avenue
Chicago, IL 60614-1889
Phone: 773-755-4732
Fax: 773-755-4733
E-mail: scholarship@elks.org

FEDERATION OF AMERICAN CONSUMERS AND TRAVELERS http://www.fact-org.org

FEDERATION OF AMERICAN CONSUMERS AND TRAVELERS CURRENT STUDENT SCHOLARSHIP

A minimum of one $10,000 scholarship and one $2,500 scholarship are given to students who are currently enrolled in an undergraduate college or university. Eligible applicants will be a member or the child or grandchild of a member of FACT. Awards are designed for the so-called "average" student. These funds are for the young man or woman who may never have made the honor roll or who did not excel on the athletic field and wants to obtain a higher education, but is all too often overlooked by other scholarship sources. For more information visit http://www.fact-org.org.

Award: Scholarship for use in freshman, sophomore, junior, or senior years; not renewable. *Number:* 2. *Amount:* $2500–$10,000.

Eligibility Requirements: Applicant must be enrolled or expecting to enroll full-time at a two-year or four-year institution or university. Applicant or parent of applicant must be member of Federation of American Consumers and Travelers. Available to U.S. citizens.

Application Requirements: Application, autobiography, essay, references, test scores, transcript. *Deadline:* January 15.

Contact: Vicki Rolens, Managing Director
Federation of American Consumers and Travelers
PO Box 104
Edwardsville, IL 62025
Phone: 800-872-3228
Fax: 618-656-5369
E-mail: gmsfact@aol.com

FEDERATION OF AMERICAN CONSUMERS AND TRAVELERS GRADUATING HIGH SCHOOL SENIOR SCHOLARSHIP

A minimum of one $10,000 scholarship and one $2,500 scholarship are given to graduating high school seniors. Eligible applicants will be a member or the child or grandchild of a member of FACT. Awards are designed for the so-called "average" student. These funds are for the young man or woman who may never have made the honor roll or who did not excel on the athletic field and wants to obtain a higher education, but is all too often overlooked by other scholarship sources. For more information visit http://www.fact-org.org.

Award: Scholarship for use in freshman, sophomore, junior, or senior years; not renewable. *Number:* 2. *Amount:* $2500–$10,000.

Eligibility Requirements: Applicant must be high school student and planning to enroll or expecting to enroll full-time at a two-year or four-year institution or university. Applicant or parent of applicant must be member of Federation of American Consumers and Travelers. Available to U.S. citizens.

Application Requirements: Application, autobiography, essay, references, test scores, transcript. *Deadline:* January 15.

Contact: Vicki Rolens, Managing Director
Federation of American Consumers and Travelers
PO Box 104
Edwardsville, IL 62025
Phone: 800-872-3228
Fax: 618-656-5369
E-mail: gmsfact@aol.com

FEDERATION OF AMERICAN CONSUMERS AND TRAVELERS RETURNING STUDENT SCHOLARSHIP

A minimum of one $10,000 scholarship and one $2,500 scholarship are given to people who graduated from high school four or more years ago and are now planning to enroll in an undergraduate college or university. Eligible applicants will be a member or the child or grandchild of a member of FACT. Awards are designed for the so-called "average" student. These funds are for the young man or woman who may never have made the honor roll or who did not excel on the athletic field and wants to obtain a higher education, but is all too often overlooked by other scholarship sources. For more information visit http://www.fact-org.org.

Award: Scholarship for use in freshman, sophomore, junior, or senior years; not renewable. *Number:* 2. *Amount:* $2500–$10,000.

Eligibility Requirements: Applicant must be enrolled or expecting to enroll full-time at a two-year or four-year institution or university. Applicant or parent of applicant must be member of Federation of American Consumers and Travelers. Available to U.S. citizens.

Application Requirements: Application, autobiography, essay, references, test scores, transcript. *Deadline:* January 15.

Contact: Vicki Rolens, Managing Director
Federation of American Consumers and Travelers
PO Box 104
Edwardsville, IL 62025
Phone: 800-872-3228
Fax: 618-656-5369
E-mail: gmsfact@aol.com

FLEET RESERVE ASSOCIATION http://www.fra.org

FLEET RESERVE ASSOCIATION SCHOLARSHIP

Dependent children/grandchildren and spouses of members in good standing of the Fleet Reserve Association or deceased while in aforementioned status, and member of the FRA may be eligible for up to $5000. Selection is based on financial need, academic standing, character and leadership qualities. Deadline: April 15. FRA members may access applications on Web site: http://www.fra.org/

Award: Scholarship for use in freshman, sophomore, junior, or senior years; not renewable. *Number:* 6. *Amount:* up to $5000.

Eligibility Requirements: Applicant must be enrolled or expecting to enroll full-time at a two-year or four-year institution or university and must have an interest in leadership. Applicant or parent of applicant must be member of Fleet Reserve Association/Auxiliary. Applicant must have 3.0 GPA or higher. Available to U.S. citizens. Applicant or parent must meet one or more of the following requirements: Coast Guard, Marine Corp, or Navy experience; retired from active duty; disabled or killed as a result of military service; prisoner of war; or missing in action.

Application Requirements: Application, essay, financial need analysis, references, test scores, transcript. *Deadline:* April 15.

Contact: Scholarship Administrator
Fleet Reserve Association
125 North West Street
Alexandria, VA 23214-2754
E-mail: fra@fra.org

OLIVER AND ESTHER R. HOWARD SCHOLARSHIP

Dependent children of members in good standing of the Fleet Reserve Association or the Ladies Auxiliary of the Fleet Reserve Association or a member in good standing at time of death. Recipient must pursue an undergraduate degree in postsecondary institution. Awards are alternated annually between female dependents (in even numbered years) and male dependents (in odd numbered years). Deadline: April 15.

Award: Scholarship for use in freshman, sophomore, junior, or senior years; not renewable. *Number:* 1. *Amount:* up to $235.

Eligibility Requirements: Applicant must be enrolled or expecting to enroll full-time at a two-year or four-year institution or university. Applicant or parent of applicant must be member of Fleet Reserve Association/Auxiliary. Applicant must have 3.0 GPA or higher. Available to U.S. citizens. Applicant or parent must meet one or more of the following requirements: Coast Guard, Marine Corp, or Navy experience; retired from active duty; disabled or killed as a result of military service; prisoner of war; or missing in action.

Application Requirements: Application, essay, financial need analysis, references, test scores, transcript. *Deadline:* April 15.

Contact: Scholarship Administrator
Fleet Reserve Association
125 North West Street
Alexandria, VA 22314-2754

FRATERNAL ORDER OF EAGLES

FRATERNAL ORDER OF EAGLES MEMORIAL FOUNDATION

Award for children of members of the Fraternal Order of Eagles and Ladies Auxiliary who died from injuries or diseases incurred or aggravated in line of duty. Grant may be renewed until a total of $30,000 is reached. May be used for cost of college, vocational school, fees, books, or course-related supplies. Eligible until 25 years of age unless married and self-supporting before then. Must maintain a "C" average. Contact for deadlines.

Award: Grant for use in freshman, sophomore, junior, or senior years; renewable. *Number:* varies. *Amount:* $6000.

Eligibility Requirements: Applicant must be age 25 or under and enrolled or expecting to enroll full or part-time at a two-year or four-year or technical institution or university. Applicant or parent of applicant must be member of Fraternal Order of Eagles. Available to U.S. citizens.

Application Requirements: Application. *Deadline:* varies.

Contact: Fraternal Order of Eagles
4710 14th Street West
Bradenton, FL 34207

GENERAL FEDERATION OF WOMEN'S CLUBS IN WYOMING

MARY N. BROOKS DAUGHTER/GRANDDAUGHTER SCHOLARSHIP

Award given yearly to a female high school graduate whose mother and/or grandmother is an active member in the General Federation of Women's Clubs in Wyoming. Must be a resident of Wyoming and preparing to attend any school of higher learning in the state of Wyoming. Award is based on scholarship, community/school involvement, and financial need. Minimum 3.0 GPA required.

Award: Scholarship for use in freshman, sophomore, junior, or senior years; not renewable. *Number:* 1–4. *Amount:* $500.

Eligibility Requirements: Applicant must be enrolled or expecting to enroll full-time at a two-year or four-year or technical institution or university; female; resident of Wyoming and studying in Wyoming. Applicant or parent of applicant must be member of General Federation of Women's Clubs in Wyoming. Applicant must have 3.0 GPA or higher. Available to U.S. citizens.

Application Requirements: Application, autobiography, financial need analysis, resume, references, transcript. *Deadline:* March 15.

Contact: Mrs. Norine Samuelson, Custodian, Scholarship Funds
General Federation of Women's Clubs in Wyoming
2005 Eagle Drive
Cheyenne, WY 82009
Phone: 307-638-9443
Fax: 307-433-1020
E-mail: samuelson63291@msn.com

GIRL SCOUTS OF GULFCOAST FLORIDA, INC. http://www.girlscoutsgulfcoastfl.org

GULFCOAST COLLEGE SCHOLARSHIP AWARD

Scholarships are provided for graduating high school seniors who are members of the Girl Scouts of Gulfcoast, Florida Senior Girl Scouts. Must have five years of continuous membership. Must be a resident of Florida.

Award: Scholarship for use in freshman or sophomore years; not renewable. *Number:* varies. *Amount:* $500–$1000.

Eligibility Requirements: Applicant must be high school student; planning to enroll or expecting to enroll full-time at a two-year or four-year institution or university; single female and resident of Florida. Applicant or parent of applicant must be member of Girl Scouts. Applicant must have 3.0 GPA or higher. Available to U.S. citizens.

Application Requirements: Application, autobiography, references, transcript. *Deadline:* February 15.

Contact: Sue Zimmerman, Director of Administrative Services
Girl Scouts of Gulfcoast Florida, Inc.
2909 Olympic Street
Sarasota, FL 34231
Phone: 941-921-5358
Fax: 941-923-5241
E-mail: suez@girlscoutsgulfcoastfl.org

GLASS, MOLDERS, POTTERY, PLASTICS AND ALLIED WORKERS INTERNATIONAL UNION http://www.gmpiu.org

GMP MEMORIAL SCHOLARSHIP PROGRAM

Eight $6000 scholarships will be awarded to the sons and daughters of members of the Glass, Molders, Pottery, Plastics, and Allied Workers International Union. Scholarships can be renewed for up to four years. For more details see Web site: http://www.gmpiu.org.

Award: Scholarship for use in freshman, sophomore, junior, or senior years; renewable. *Number:* 8. *Amount:* $6000.

Eligibility Requirements: Applicant must be high school student and planning to enroll or expecting to enroll full-time at a four-year institution or university. Applicant or parent of applicant must be member of Glass, Molders, Pottery, Plastics and Allied Workers International Union. Available to U.S. citizens.

Application Requirements: Application. *Deadline:* November 1.

Contact: Joseph Mitchell, Sr., International Secretary-Treasurer
Glass, Molders, Pottery, Plastics and Allied Workers International Union
608 East Baltimore Pike
PO Box 607
Media, PA 19063-0607
Phone: 610-565-5051
Fax: 610-565-0983
E-mail: gmpiu@ix.netcom.com

GOLDEN KEY INTERNATIONAL HONOUR SOCIETY http://www.goldenkey.org

GEICO ADULT SCHOLAR AWARD

Ten $1000 awards will be given to returning students in recognition of academic excellence while balancing additional responsibilities. Must have completed at least twelve undergraduate credits in the previous year. See Web site for more information: http://goldenkey.gsu.edu.

Award: Scholarship for use in junior or senior years; not renewable. *Number:* 10. *Amount:* $1000.

Eligibility Requirements: Applicant must be enrolled or expecting to enroll full or part-time at an institution or university. Applicant or parent of applicant must be member of Golden Key National Honor Society.

Application Requirements: Application, essay, references, transcript. *Deadline:* April 1.

Contact: Member Services
Golden Key International Honour Society
621 North Avenue, NE
Suite C-100
Atlanta, GA 30308
Phone: 404-377-2400
Fax: 678-420-6757
E-mail: scholarships@goldenkey.org

GOLDEN KEY RESEARCH TRAVEL GRANT

Ten travel grants of $500 each for the purpose of presentation of student research at a professional conference or student research symposium or for travel related to research needed for the completion of an honors thesis. See Web site for more information: http://goldenkey.gsu.edu. Deadlines are April 15 and October 15.

Award: Grant for use in junior or senior years; not renewable. *Number:* 10. *Amount:* $500.

Eligibility Requirements: Applicant must be enrolled or expecting to enroll at a four-year institution or university. Applicant or parent of applicant must be member of Golden Key National Honor Society.

Application Requirements: Application, essay, resume, transcript. *Deadline:* varies.

Contact: Member Services
Golden Key International Honour Society
621 North Avenue, NE
Suite C-100
Atlanta, GA 30308
Phone: 404-377-2400
Fax: 678-420-6757
E-mail: scholarships@goldenkey.org

GOLDEN KEY STUDY ABROAD SCHOLARSHIPS

Five $2000 scholarships will be awarded twice a year to assist student in the pursuit of a study abroad program. See Web site for more information: http://goldenkey.gsu.edu. Deadlines are April 15 and October 15.

Award: Scholarship for use in junior or senior years; not renewable. *Number:* 10. *Amount:* $2000.

Eligibility Requirements: Applicant must be enrolled or expecting to enroll at a four-year institution or university. Applicant or parent of applicant must be member of Golden Key National Honor Society.

Application Requirements: Application, essay, transcript. *Deadline:* varies.

Contact: Member Services
Golden Key International Honour Society
621 North Avenue, NE
Suite C-100
Atlanta, GA 30308
Phone: 404-377-2400
Fax: 678-420-6757
E-mail: scholarships@goldenkey.org

STUDENT SCHOLASTIC SHOWCASE

Four undergraduate students will receive $1000 and may have the opportunity to present their research or scholarly works at an international convention. See Web site for more information: http://goldenkey.gsu.edu.

Award: Scholarship for use in junior or senior years; not renewable. *Number:* 4. *Amount:* $1000.

Eligibility Requirements: Applicant must be enrolled or expecting to enroll at an institution or university. Applicant or parent of applicant must be member of Golden Key National Honor Society. Available to U.S. and non-U.S. citizens.

Application Requirements: Application, essay, references, transcript, copy of research. *Deadline:* March 1.

Contact: Member Services
Golden Key International Honour Society
621 North Avenue, NE
Suite C-100
Atlanta, GA 30308
Phone: 404-377-2400
Fax: 678-420-6757
E-mail: scholarships@goldenkey.org

UNDERGRADUATE SCHOLARSHIP

Two $500 scholarships are awarded at each chapter every year to members of Golden Key International Honour Society. Minimum 3.5 GPA required. Must be a member of Golden Key International Honour Society to be eligible for awards. Please visit Web site (http://goldenkey.gsu.edu) for more information. Offered in conjunction with the Ford Motor Company.

Award: Scholarship for use in junior or senior years; not renewable. *Number:* 690. *Amount:* $500–$700.

Eligibility Requirements: Applicant must be enrolled or expecting to enroll full-time at an institution or university. Applicant or parent of applicant must be member of Golden Key National Honor Society. Applicant must have 3.5 GPA or higher. Available to U.S. and non-U.S. citizens.

Application Requirements: Transcript. *Deadline:* varies.

Contact: Member Services
Golden Key International Honour Society
621 North Avenue, NE
Suite C-100
Atlanta, GA 30308
Phone: 404-377-2400
Fax: 678-420-6757
E-mail: scholarships@goldenkey.org

GOLF COURSE SUPERINTENDENTS ASSOCIATION OF AMERICA

http://www.gcsaa.org

GOLF COURSE SUPERINTENDENTS ASSOCIATION OF AMERICA LEGACY AWARD

Awards of $1500 for the children or grandchildren of Golf Course Superintendents Association of America members. Graduating high school seniors must attach a letter of acceptance to their application.

Award: Scholarship for use in freshman, sophomore, junior, senior, or graduate years; not renewable. *Number:* 20. *Amount:* $1500.

Eligibility Requirements: Applicant must be enrolled or expecting to enroll full-time at a two-year or four-year or technical institution or university. Applicant or parent of applicant must be member of Golf Course Superintendents Association of America. Available to U.S. and non-U.S. citizens.

Application Requirements: Application, essay, references, transcript. *Deadline:* April 15.

Contact: Pam Smith, Scholarship/Student Programs Manager
Golf Course Superintendents Association of America
1421 Research Park Drive
Lawrence, KS 66049-3859
Phone: 800-472-7878 Ext. 678
Fax: 785-832-4449
E-mail: psmith@gcsaa.org

JOSEPH S. GARSHE COLLEGIATE GRANT PROGRAM

Renewable award available to children/step children of GCSAA members for use at an accredited college or trade school.

Award: Scholarship for use in freshman or sophomore years; renewable. *Number:* 1. *Amount:* $2500.

Eligibility Requirements: Applicant must be high school student and planning to enroll or expecting to enroll full-time at a two-year or four-year or technical institution or university. Applicant or parent of applicant must be member of Golf Course Superintendents Association of America. Available to U.S. and non-U.S. citizens.

Application Requirements: Application, essay, transcript. *Deadline:* March 15.

Contact: Pam Smith, Scholarship Manager
Golf Course Superintendents Association of America
1421 Research Park Drive
Lawrence, KS 66049-3859
Phone: 800-472-7878 Ext. 678
Fax: 785-832-4449
E-mail: psmith@gcsaa.org

GRAPHIC COMMUNICATIONS INTERNATIONAL UNION

http://www.gciu.org

A.J. DEANDRADE SCHOLARSHIP PROGRAM

Program is open to dependents of Graphic Communications International Union members. Must be a graduating high school senior. The deadline is February 16. Award is payable at $500 a year for four years.

Award: Scholarship for use in freshman, sophomore, junior, or senior years; renewable. *Number:* 10. *Amount:* $500.

Eligibility Requirements: Applicant must be high school student and planning to enroll or expecting to enroll full-time at a four-year institution or university. Applicant or parent of applicant must be member of Graphic Communication International Union. Available to U.S. and Canadian citizens.

Application Requirements: Application, essay, references, test scores, transcript. *Deadline:* February 16.

Contact: Graphic Communications International Union
1900 L Street NW
Washington, DC 20036

HAWAII EDUCATION ASSOCIATION

http://www.heaed.com/

HAWAII EDUCATION ASSOCIATION HIGH SCHOOL STUDENT SCHOLARSHIP

Scholarship available to high school seniors planning on attending four-year college/university. Must be children of HEA members. Membership must be for at least one year.

Award: Scholarship for use in freshman year; not renewable. *Number:* 5. *Amount:* $1000.

Eligibility Requirements: Applicant must be high school student; planning to enroll or expecting to enroll full-time at a four-year institution or university and resident of Hawaii. Applicant or parent of applicant must be member of Hawaii Education Association. Applicant must have 3.0 GPA or higher. Available to U.S. citizens.

Application Requirements: Application, autobiography, financial need analysis, photo, references, transcript. *Deadline:* April 4.

Contact: George K. Kagehiro, Chairman
Hawaii Education Association
1649 Kalakaua Avenue
Honolulu, HI 96826-2494
Phone: 808-949-6657
Fax: 808-944-2032
E-mail: hea.office@heaed.com

HAWAII EDUCATION ASSOCIATION UNDERGRADUATE COLLEGE STUDENT SCHOLARSHIP

Scholarship available to children of HEA members. Membership must be for at least one year. Student must be currently attending college or university.

Award: Scholarship for use in freshman, sophomore, junior, or senior years; not renewable. *Number:* 4. *Amount:* $1000.

Eligibility Requirements: Applicant must be enrolled or expecting to enroll full-time at a four-year institution or university and resident of Hawaii. Applicant or parent of applicant must be member of Hawaii Education Association. Applicant must have 3.0 GPA or higher. Available to U.S. citizens.

Hawaii Education Association (continued)

Application Requirements: Application, autobiography, financial need analysis, photo, references, transcript. *Deadline:* April 4.

Contact: George K. Kagehiro, Chairman
Hawaii Education Association
1649 Kalakaua Avenue
Honolulu, HI 96826-2494
Phone: 808-949-6657
Fax: 808-944-2032
E-mail: hea.office@heaed.com

HEBREW IMMIGRANT AID SOCIETY http://www.hias.org

HEBREW IMMIGRANT AID SOCIETY SCHOLARSHIP AWARDS COMPETITION

Must be Hebrew Immigrant Aid Society-assisted refugee who came to the U.S. after January 1, 1992. Must have completed two semesters at a U.S. high school, college, or graduate school. Application and information are available at Web site http://www.hias.org. Applications will only be accepted online. Applications must be submitted by midnight of March 15.

Award: Scholarship for use in freshman, sophomore, junior, senior, or graduate years; not renewable. *Number:* 70–90. *Amount:* $1500.

Eligibility Requirements: Applicant must be enrolled or expecting to enroll full or part-time at a two-year or four-year or technical institution or university. Applicant or parent of applicant must be member of Hebrew Immigrant Aid Society. Available to U.S. citizens.

Application Requirements: Application, applicant must enter a contest, essay, financial need analysis, test scores, transcript. *Deadline:* March 15.

Contact: Amy Greenstein, Development Coordinator
Hebrew Immigrant Aid Society
333 Seventh Avenue
New York, NY 10001-5004
Phone: 212-613-1358
Fax: 212-967-4356
E-mail: scholarship@hias.org

HONOR SOCIETY OF PHI KAPPA PHI http://www.phikappaphi.org

LITERACY INITIATIVE GRANT COMPETITION

Grants up to $2500 will be awarded to Phi Kappa Phi members for projects relating to literacy. These projects should fulfill the spirit of volunteerism and community. For more details see Web site: http://www.phikappaphi.org.

Award: Grant for use in freshman, sophomore, junior, senior, graduate, or postgraduate years; not renewable. *Number:* varies. *Amount:* up to $2500.

Eligibility Requirements: Applicant must be enrolled or expecting to enroll at an institution or university. Applicant or parent of applicant must be member of Phi Kappa Phi. Available to U.S. and non-U.S. citizens.

Application Requirements: Application. *Deadline:* February 28.

Contact: Theresa Bard, Programs Coordinator
Honor Society of Phi Kappa Phi
Louisiana State University
PO Box 16000
Baton Rouge, LA 70893-6000
Phone: 225-388-4917 Ext. 13
Fax: 225-388-4900
E-mail: awards@phikappaphi.org

INTERNATIONAL CHEMICAL WORKERS UNION http://www.icwuc.org

WALTER L. MITCHELL MEMORIAL AWARDS

Award available to children of International Chemical Workers Union members. Applicants must be starting their freshman year of college. Application deadline is March 1.

Award: Grant for use in freshman year; not renewable. *Number:* 21. *Amount:* $1000.

Eligibility Requirements: Applicant must be enrolled or expecting to enroll full-time at a two-year or four-year or technical institution or university. Applicant or parent of applicant must be member of International Chemical Workers Union. Available to U.S. and non-U.S. citizens.

Application Requirements: Application, autobiography, test scores, transcript. *Deadline:* March 1.

Contact: Research and Education Director
International Chemical Workers Union
1655 West Market Street
Akron, OH 44313
Phone: 330-867-2444
Fax: 330-867-0544
E-mail: agreen@icwuc.org

INTERNATIONAL EXECUTIVE HOUSEKEEPERS ASSOCIATION http://www.ieha.org

INTERNATIONAL EXECUTIVE HOUSEKEEPERS ASSOCIATION EDUCATIONAL FOUNDATION AWARD

One-time award of $500 given for any year of full- or part-time undergraduate study. Must be a current member of IEHA.

Award: Scholarship for use in freshman, sophomore, junior, or senior years; not renewable. *Number:* 5–10. *Amount:* $500.

Eligibility Requirements: Applicant must be enrolled or expecting to enroll full or part-time at a two-year or four-year or technical institution or university. Applicant or parent of applicant must be member of International Executive Housekeepers Association.

Application Requirements: Application, essay, transcript. *Deadline:* January 31.

Contact: Beth Risinger, CEO/Executive Director
International Executive Housekeepers Association
Education Department, 1001 Eastwind Drive
Westerville, OH 43081-3361
Phone: 800-200-6342
Fax: 614-895-1248
E-mail: excel@ieha.org

INTERNATIONAL FEDERATION OF PROFESSIONAL AND TECHNICAL ENGINEERS http://www.ifpte.org

INTERNATIONAL FEDERATION OF PROFESSIONAL AND TECHNICAL ENGINEERS ANNUAL SCHOLARSHIP

IFPTE annual scholarships are open to high school seniors who have demonstrated academic achievement and service to their school and community. Only children or grandchildren of IFPTE members are eligible. Must be a U.S. or Canadian citizen.

Award: Scholarship for use in freshman year; not renewable. *Number:* 3. *Amount:* $1500.

Eligibility Requirements: Applicant must be high school student and planning to enroll or expecting to enroll full-time at a two-year or four-year or technical institution or university. Applicant or parent of applicant must be member of International Federation of Professional and Technical Engineers. Available to U.S. and Canadian citizens.

Application Requirements: Application, essay, references, transcript. *Deadline:* March 15.

Contact: Candace Rhett, Communications Representative
International Federation of Professional and Technical Engineers Scholarship
8630 Fenton Street, Suite 400
Silver Spring, MD 20910
Phone: 301-565-9016
Fax: 301-565-0018
E-mail: crhett@ifpte.org

INTERNATIONAL UNION OF ELECTRONIC, ELECTRICAL, SALARIED, MACHINE, AND FURNITURE WORKERS-CWA http://www.iue-cwa.org

CWA JOE BEIRNE FOUNDATION SCHOLARSHIP PROGRAM

Two-year scholarships, to be paid at the rate of $3000 annually to Communication Workers of America members, their spouses, children, and grandchildren (including dependents of laid-off, retired or deceased CWA members). A second-year award is contingent on academic accomplishment of the first year. No specific studies are required. Scholarship winners may pursue whatever courses they wish. Winner chosen by lottery drawing.

Award: Scholarship for use in freshman, sophomore, junior, or senior years; not renewable. *Number:* up to 30. *Amount:* $3000.

Eligibility Requirements: Applicant must be enrolled or expecting to enroll at a two-year or four-year institution or university. Applicant or parent of applicant must be member of AFL-CIO. Available to U.S. and Canadian citizens.

Application Requirements: Application, essay. *Deadline:* March 31.

Contact: Online application:
http://cwa-union.org/members/beirne/Application.asp

IUE-CWA INTERNATIONAL BRUCE VAN ESS SCHOLARSHIP

Scholarship available to all IUE-CWA members and employees and their children and grandchildren. Must be accepted for admission or enrolled as a full-time student. Deadline is March 31.

Award: Scholarship for use in freshman, sophomore, junior, or senior years; not renewable. *Number:* 1. *Amount:* $2500.

Eligibility Requirements: Applicant must be enrolled or expecting to enroll full-time at a two-year or four-year or technical institution or university. Applicant or parent of applicant must be member of International Union of Electronic, Electrical, Salaries, Machine and Furniture Workers.

Application Requirements: Application, essay, financial need analysis, references, test scores, transcript. *Deadline:* March 31.

Contact: Trudy Humphrey, Director
International Union of Electronic, Electrical, Salaried, Machine, and Furniture Workers-CWA
501 3rd Street, NW
Washington, DC 20001
Phone: 202-434-9591
Fax: 202-434-1252
E-mail: thumphrey@cwa-union.org

JAMES B. CAREY SCHOLARSHIP AWARD

Awards for students who are children or grandchildren of IUE-CWA members who are undergraduate students at accredited two-year, four-year, nursing, and technical schools.

Award: Scholarship for use in freshman, sophomore, junior, or senior years; not renewable. *Number:* 1–9. *Amount:* $1000.

Eligibility Requirements: Applicant must be enrolled or expecting to enroll full-time at a two-year or four-year or technical institution or university. Applicant or parent of applicant must be member of International Union of Electronic, Electrical, Salaries, Machine and Furniture Workers. Available to U.S. citizens.

Application Requirements: Application, essay, financial need analysis, references, test scores, transcript. *Deadline:* March 31.

Contact: Trudy Humphrey, Director
International Union of Electronic, Electrical, Salaried, Machine, and Furniture Workers-CWA
501 3rd Street, NW
Washington, DC 20001
Phone: 202-434-9591
Fax: 202-434-1252
E-mail: thumphrey@cwa-union.org

PAUL JENNINGS SCHOLARSHIP AWARD

One award for a student whose parent or grandparent is or has been a local union elected official. Families of full-time international union officers are not eligible. Submit family financial status form with application.

Award: Scholarship for use in freshman, sophomore, junior, or senior years; not renewable. *Number:* 1. *Amount:* $3000.

Eligibility Requirements: Applicant must be enrolled or expecting to enroll full-time at a two-year or four-year or technical institution or university. Applicant or parent of applicant must be member of International Union of Electronic, Electrical, Salaries, Machine and Furniture Workers. Available to U.S. citizens.

Application Requirements: Application, essay, financial need analysis, references, test scores, transcript. *Deadline:* March 31.

Contact: Trudy Humphrey, Director
International Union of Electronic, Electrical, Salaried, Machine, and Furniture Workers-CWA
501 3rd Street, NW
Washington, DC 20001
Phone: 202-434-9591
Fax: 202-434-1252
E-mail: thumphrey@cwa-union.org

WILLIE RUDD SCHOLARSHIP

One-time award available to all IUE-CWA members and employees and their children and grandchildren. Applicant must be accepted for admission or already enrolled as a full-time student at an accredited college or university, nursing or technical school offering college credit courses. All study must be completed at the undergraduate level. Application deadline is March 31.

Award: Scholarship for use in freshman, sophomore, junior, or senior years; not renewable. *Number:* 1. *Amount:* $1000.

Eligibility Requirements: Applicant must be enrolled or expecting to enroll full-time at a four-year or technical institution or university. Applicant or parent of applicant must be member of International Union of Electronic, Electrical, Salaries, Machine and Furniture Workers.

Application Requirements: Application, essay, financial need analysis, references, test scores, transcript. *Deadline:* March 31.

Contact: Trudy Humphrey, Director
International Union of Electronic, Electrical, Salaried, Machine, and Furniture Workers-CWA
501 3rd Street, NW
Washington, DC 20001
Phone: 202-434-9591
Fax: 202-434-1252
E-mail: thumphrey@cwa-union.org

ISIA EDUCATION FOUNDATION http://www.skateisi.org

ISIA EDUCATION FOUNDATION SCHOLARSHIP

Applicant must be a member of Ice Skating Institute (minimum of 4 years) and have participated in ISI-endorsed skating events. Scholarships will be awarded for full-time study only. Scholarship is non-renewable. Applicants must rank in upper third of class or have a minimum 3.0 GPA. Application deadline: March 1.

Award: Scholarship for use in freshman, sophomore, junior, or senior years; not renewable. *Number:* 2–4. *Amount:* $4000.

Eligibility Requirements: Applicant must be enrolled or expecting to enroll full-time at a two-year or four-year institution or university and must have an interest in designated field specified by sponsor. Applicant or parent of applicant must be member of Ice Skating Institute. Applicant must have 3.0 GPA or higher. Available to U.S. citizens.

Application Requirements: Application, essay, references, transcript, ice skating activities. *Deadline:* March 1.

Contact: Kathy Chase, Administrative Assistant
ISIA Education Foundation
17120 Dallas Parkway, Suite 140
Dallas, TX 75248
Phone: 972-735-8800
Fax: 972-735-8815
E-mail: kchase@skateisi.org

JAYCEE WAR MEMORIAL FUND

CHARLES FORD SCHOLARSHIP

One (1) scholarship awarded annually. Available to an active member of the Jaycees who wishes to return to a college or university to complete his or her formal education. Applicant must be a citizen of the United States, possess academic potential and leadership qualities, and show financial need. The scholarship is a one-time award of $2,500 sent directly to the recipient's college or university of choice.

Award: Scholarship for use in freshman, sophomore, junior, or senior years; not renewable. *Number:* 1. *Amount:* up to $2500.

Jaycee War Memorial Fund (continued)

Eligibility Requirements: Applicant must be age 21-40 and enrolled or expecting to enroll full or part-time at a four-year institution or university. Applicant or parent of applicant must be member of Jaycees. Applicant must have 3.0 GPA or higher. Available to U.S. citizens.

Application Requirements: Application, financial need analysis, self-addressed stamped envelope, transcript. *Fee:* $5. *Deadline:* March 1.

Contact: Scholarship Coordinator
Jaycee War Memorial Fund
PO Box 7
Tulsa, OK 74102-0007
Phone: 800-529-2337
Fax: 918-592-4372

THOMAS WOOD BALDRIDGE SCHOLARSHIP

Members of the Junior Chamber of Commerce organization (Jaycees) or immediate family members or descendents of a former Jaycee member are eligible to apply. Applicants must possess academic potential, leadership qualities, and show financial need. Application deadline is March 1. Send $5 application fee and self-addressed stamped envelope. Must be U.S. citizen.

Award: Scholarship for use in freshman, sophomore, junior, or senior years; not renewable. *Number:* 1. *Amount:* $3000.

Eligibility Requirements: Applicant must be enrolled or expecting to enroll full or part-time at a two-year or four-year or technical institution or university. Applicant or parent of applicant must be member of Jaycees. Applicant must have 3.0 GPA or higher. Available to U.S. citizens.

Application Requirements: Application, financial need analysis, self-addressed stamped envelope, transcript. *Fee:* $5. *Deadline:* March 1.

Contact: Scholarship Coordinator
Jaycee War Memorial Fund
PO Box 7
Tulsa, OK 74102-0007
Phone: 800-529-2337
Fax: 918-592-4372

JUNIOR ACHIEVEMENT http://www.ja.org

JUNIOR ACHIEVEMENT JOE FRANCOMANO SCHOLARSHIP

Renewable award to high school seniors who have demonstrated academic achievement, leadership skills, and financial need. May be used at any accredited postsecondary educational institution for any field of study resulting in a baccalaureate degree. Must have completed JA Company Program or JA Economics.

Award: Scholarship for use in freshman, sophomore, junior, or senior years; not renewable. *Number:* 1. *Amount:* $5000–$20,000.

Eligibility Requirements: Applicant must be high school student; planning to enroll or expecting to enroll full-time at a four-year institution or university and must have an interest in leadership. Applicant or parent of applicant must be member of Junior Achievement. Applicant must have 3.0 GPA or higher. Available to U.S. and Canadian citizens.

Application Requirements: Application, essay, financial need analysis, references, transcript. *Deadline:* February 1.

Contact: Steven Carruth, Scholarship and Curriculum Specialist
Junior Achievement
One Education Way
Colorado Springs, CO 80906-4477
Phone: 719-535-2954
Fax: 719-540-6175
E-mail: scarruth@ja.org

JUNIOR ACHIEVEMENT OFFICE DEPOT SCHOLARSHIP

One-time award to high school graduating seniors seeking a degree from an accredited postsecondary educational institution. Must demonstrate academic achievement and leadership skills. Must have completed a Junior Achievement program. Minimum 3.0 GPA required.

Award: Scholarship for use in freshman year; not renewable. *Number:* 5. *Amount:* $10,000.

Eligibility Requirements: Applicant must be high school student and planning to enroll or expecting to enroll full-time at a four-year institution or university. Applicant or parent of applicant must be member of Junior Achievement. Applicant must have 3.0 GPA or higher. Available to U.S. and Canadian citizens.

Application Requirements: Application, essay, references, transcript. *Deadline:* February 1.

Contact: Steven Carruth, Scholarship and Curriculum Specialist
Junior Achievement
One Education Way
Colorado Springs, CO 80906-4477
Phone: 719-535-2954
Fax: 719-540-6175
E-mail: scarruth@ja.org

KAPPA ALPHA THETA FOUNDATION http://www.kappaalphatheta.org

KAPPA ALPHA THETA FOUNDATION MERIT BASED SCHOLARSHIP PROGRAM

Foundation scholarships are awarded to either graduate or undergraduate members of Kappa Alpha Theta. All scholarships are merit-based. Application postmark date is February 1. Applications may be downloaded from the Web site or may be obtained by calling 1-888-526-1870 ext. 119.

Award: Scholarship for use in sophomore, junior, senior, graduate, or postgraduate years; not renewable. *Number:* 120–150. *Amount:* $1000–$10,000.

Eligibility Requirements: Applicant must be enrolled or expecting to enroll full or part-time at a four-year institution or university and female. Available to U.S. and non-U.S. citizens.

Application Requirements: Application, resume, references, transcript. *Deadline:* February 1.

Contact: Cindy Thoennes, Coordinator of Programs
Kappa Alpha Theta Foundation
8740 Founders Road
Indianapolis, IN 46268
Phone: 317-876-1870 Ext. 119
Fax: 317-876-1925
E-mail: cthoennes@kappaalphatheta.org

KAPPA ALPHA THETA FOUNDATION NAMED ENDOWMENT GRANT PROGRAM

The Kappa Alpha Theta Foundation Named Endowment Grant program was established to provide monies for undergraduate and alumna members of the Fraternity for leadership training and non-degree educational opportunities. Applications may be downloaded from the Web site. Application is due 90 days prior to event, workshop, or program.

Award: Grant for use in freshman, sophomore, junior, or senior years; not renewable. *Number:* up to 50. *Amount:* $100–$5000.

Eligibility Requirements: Applicant must be enrolled or expecting to enroll at an institution or university and female. Available to U.S. and non-U.S. citizens.

Application Requirements: Application, resume, references, budget, proposal, narrative. *Deadline:* Continuous.

Contact: Cindy Thoennes, Coordinator of Programs
Kappa Alpha Theta Foundation
8740 Founders Road
Indianapolis, IN 46268
Phone: 317-876-1870 Ext. 119
Fax: 317-876-1925
E-mail: cthoennes@kappaalphatheta.org

KAPPA SIGMA ENDOWMENT FUND http://www.ksendowmentfund.org/scholarship.html

SCHOLARSHIP-LEADERSHIP AWARDS PROGRAM

Scholarships are given to outstanding undergraduate Kappa Sigma members who excel in the classroom, on campus, and within the fraternity. Must have a 2.5 GPA. Applications can be downloaded at http://www.ksendowmentfund.org/scholarship.html.

Award: Scholarship for use in freshman, sophomore, junior, or senior years; not renewable. *Number:* 275–280. *Amount:* $500–$2500.

Eligibility Requirements: Applicant must be enrolled or expecting to enroll full-time at a four-year institution or university and male. Applicant must have 2.5 GPA or higher. Available to U.S. and non-U.S. citizens.

Application Requirements: Application, transcript. *Deadline:* October 15.

Contact: James Eldridge, Director of Annual Giving
Kappa Sigma Endowment Fund
PO Box 5643
Charlottesville, VA 22905-5643
Phone: 434-979-5733 Ext. 125
Fax: 434-296-5733
E-mail: jamese@imh.kappasigma.org

KNIGHTS OF COLUMBUS

FOURTH DEGREE PRO DEO AND PRO PATRIA (CANADA)

Renewable scholarships for members of Canadian Knights of Columbus councils and their children who are entering first year of study for baccalaureate degree. Based on academic excellence.

Award: Scholarship for use in freshman year; renewable. *Number:* 12. *Amount:* $1500.

Eligibility Requirements: Applicant must be Roman Catholic; Canadian citizen and enrolled or expecting to enroll full-time at a four-year institution. Applicant or parent of applicant must be member of Knights of Columbus. Applicant must have 3.0 GPA or higher.

Application Requirements: Application, autobiography, references, test scores, transcript. *Deadline:* May 1.

Contact: Rev. Donald Barry, Director of Scholarship Aid
Knights of Columbus
PO Box 1670
New Haven, CT 06507-0901
Phone: 203-752-4332
Fax: 203-752-4103

FOURTH DEGREE PRO DEO AND PRO PATRIA SCHOLARSHIPS

Renewable award available to students entering freshman year at a Catholic university or college. Applicant must be a member or child of a member of Knights of Columbus or Columbian Squires. Scholarships are awarded on the basis of academic excellence. Minimum 3.0 GPA required.

Award: Scholarship for use in freshman year; renewable. *Number:* 62. *Amount:* $1500.

Eligibility Requirements: Applicant must be Roman Catholic and enrolled or expecting to enroll full-time at a four-year institution. Applicant or parent of applicant must be member of Columbian Squires or Knights of Columbus. Applicant must have 3.0 GPA or higher. Available to U.S. citizens.

Application Requirements: Application, autobiography, essay, references, test scores, transcript. *Deadline:* March 1.

Contact: Rev. Donald Barry, Director of Scholarship Aid
Knights of Columbus
PO Box 1670
New Haven, CT 06507-0901
Phone: 203-752-4332
Fax: 203-752-4103

FRANCIS P. MATTHEWS AND JOHN E. SWIFT EDUCATIONAL TRUST SCHOLARSHIPS

Available to dependent children of Knights of Columbus who died or became permanently and totally disabled while in military service during a time of conflict, from a cause connected with military service, or as the result of criminal violence while in the performance of their duties as full-time law enforcement officers or firemen. The scholarship is awarded at a Catholic college and includes the amount not covered by other financial aid for tuition, room, board, books and fees.

Award: Scholarship for use in freshman, sophomore, junior, or senior years; renewable. *Number:* 1–4. *Amount:* varies.

Eligibility Requirements: Applicant must be Roman Catholic and enrolled or expecting to enroll full-time at a four-year institution. Applicant or parent of applicant must be member of Knights of Columbus. Applicant must have 2.5 GPA or higher. Available to U.S. and non-U.S. citizens.

Application Requirements: Application. *Deadline:* Continuous.

Contact: Rev. Donald Barry, Director of Scholarship Aid
Knights of Columbus
PO Box 1670
New Haven, CT 06507-0901
Phone: 203-752-4332
Fax: 203-752-4103

JOHN W. MC DEVITT (FOURTH DEGREE) SCHOLARSHIPS

Renewable scholarship for students entering freshman year at a Catholic college or university. Applicant must submit Pro Deo and Pro Patria Scholarship application. Must be a member or wife, son, or daughter of a member of the Knights of Columbus. Minimum 3.0 GPA required.

Award: Scholarship for use in freshman year; renewable. *Number:* 36. *Amount:* $1500.

Eligibility Requirements: Applicant must be Roman Catholic and enrolled or expecting to enroll full-time at a four-year institution. Applicant or parent of applicant must be member of Knights of Columbus. Applicant must have 3.0 GPA or higher. Available to U.S. citizens.

Application Requirements: Application, autobiography, references, test scores, transcript. *Deadline:* March 1.

Contact: Rev. Donald Barry, Director of Scholarship Aid
Knights of Columbus
PO Box 1670
New Haven, CT 06507-0901
Phone: 203-752-4332
Fax: 203-752-4103

PERCY J. JOHNSON ENDOWED SCHOLARSHIPS

Renewable scholarship for young men entering freshman year at a Catholic college or university. Applicants must submit Pro Deo and Pro Patria Scholarship application and a copy of Student Aid Report (SAR). Must be a member or a son of a member of the Knights of Columbus. Must also rank in upper third of class or have 3.0 GPA.

Award: Scholarship for use in freshman year; renewable. *Number:* 4–6. *Amount:* $1500.

Eligibility Requirements: Applicant must be Roman Catholic; enrolled or expecting to enroll full-time at a four-year institution and male. Applicant or parent of applicant must be member of Knights of Columbus. Applicant must have 3.0 GPA or higher. Available to U.S. citizens.

Application Requirements: Application, autobiography, financial need analysis, references, test scores, transcript. *Deadline:* March 1.

Contact: Rev. Donald Barry, Director of Scholarship Aid
Knights of Columbus
PO Box 1670
New Haven, CT 06507-0901
Phone: 203-752-4332
Fax: 203-752-4103

KNIGHTS OF LITHUANIA http://www.knightsoflithuania.com

KNIGHTS OF LITHUANIA NATIONAL SCHOLARSHIPS

Awards available only for members of the Knights of Lithuania with a minimum of two years of prior membership. Minimum 2.5 GPA required.

Award: Scholarship for use in freshman, sophomore, junior, senior, graduate, or postgraduate years; not renewable. *Number:* 3–6. *Amount:* $1000–$4000.

Eligibility Requirements: Applicant must be Roman Catholic; of Lithuanian heritage and enrolled or expecting to enroll full or part-time at a four-year institution or university. Applicant or parent of applicant must be member of Knights of Lithuania. Applicant must have 2.5 GPA or higher. Available to U.S. citizens.

Knights of Lithuania (continued)

Application Requirements: Application, essay, financial need analysis, photo, references, self-addressed stamped envelope, test scores, transcript. *Deadline:* June 15.

Contact: John Baltrus, Chairperson
Knights of Lithuania
118 Vine Street
Clairton, PA 15025
Phone: 412-855-9035
E-mail: baltru19@peoplepc.com

LADIES AUXILIARY OF THE FLEET RESERVE ASSOCIATION http://www.la-fra.org

ALLIE MAE ODEN MEMORIAL SCHOLARSHIP

Scholarships are given to the children/grandchildren of members of the FRA or LA FRA. Deadline is April 15. Selections are based on financial need, academic standing, character, and leadership qualities. Must be sponsored by a FRA member (living or deceased) in good standing.

Award: Scholarship for use in freshman, sophomore, junior, or senior years; not renewable. *Number:* varies. *Amount:* varies.

Eligibility Requirements: Applicant must be enrolled or expecting to enroll at an institution or university. Applicant or parent of applicant must be member of Fleet Reserve Association/Auxiliary. Available to U.S. citizens. Applicant or parent must meet one or more of the following requirements: Coast Guard, Marine Corp, or Navy experience; retired from active duty; disabled or killed as a result of military service; prisoner of war; or missing in action.

Application Requirements: Application, transcript. *Deadline:* April 15.

Contact: Scholarship Administrator
Ladies Auxiliary of the Fleet Reserve Association
125 North West Street
Alexandria, VA 22314-2754
Phone: 858-748-5190
E-mail: powaydick@webtu.net

LADIES AUXILIARY OF THE FLEET RESERVE ASSOCIATION SCHOLARSHIP

Scholarships are given to the daughters/granddaughters of U.S. Navy, Marine Corps, and Coast Guard personnel, active Fleet Reserve, Fleet Marine Corps Reserve, and Coast Guard Reserve, retired with pay or deceased. Deadline is April 15. Selections are based on financial need, academic standing, character, and leadership qualities. Must be sponsored by a FRA member in good standing.

Award: Scholarship for use in freshman, sophomore, junior, or senior years; not renewable. *Number:* varies. *Amount:* varies.

Eligibility Requirements: Applicant must be enrolled or expecting to enroll at an institution or university and female. Applicant or parent of applicant must be member of Fleet Reserve Association/Auxiliary. Available to U.S. citizens. Applicant or parent must meet one or more of the following requirements: Coast Guard, Marine Corp, or Navy experience; retired from active duty; disabled or killed as a result of military service; prisoner of war; or missing in action.

Application Requirements: Application, transcript. *Deadline:* April 15.

Contact: Scholarship Administrator
Ladies Auxiliary of the Fleet Reserve Association
125 North West Street
Alexandria, VA 22314-2754
Phone: 858-748-5190
E-mail: powaydick@webtu.net

LADIES AUXILIARY OF THE FLEET RESERVE ASSOCIATION- NATIONAL PRESIDENT'S SCHOLARSHIP

Scholarships are given to children/grandchildren of U.S. Navy, Marine Corps and Coast Guard personnel active Fleet Reserve, Fleet Marine Corps Reserve and Coast Guard Reserve, retired with pay or deceased. Selections are based on financial need, academic standing, character, and leadership qualities. Must be sponsored by a FRA member (living or deceased) in good standing.

Award: Scholarship for use in freshman, sophomore, junior, or senior years; not renewable. *Number:* 1. *Amount:* $1500.

Eligibility Requirements: Applicant must be enrolled or expecting to enroll at an institution or university. Applicant or parent of applicant must be member of Fleet Reserve Association/Auxiliary. Available to U.S. citizens. Applicant or parent must meet one or more of the following requirements: Coast Guard, Marine Corp, or Navy experience; retired from active duty; disabled or killed as a result of military service; prisoner of war; or missing in action.

Application Requirements: Application, transcript. *Deadline:* April 15.

Contact: Scholarship Administrator
Ladies Auxiliary of the Fleet Reserve Association
125 North West Street
Alexandria, VA 22314-2754
Phone: 858-748-5190
E-mail: powaydick@webtu.net

SAM ROSE MEMORIAL SCHOLARSHIP

Scholarships are given to the child/grandchild of a deceased FRA member or persons who were eligible to be FRA members at the time of death. Deadline is April 15. Selections are based on financial need, academic standing, character, and leadership qualities. Must be sponsored by a FRA member (living or deceased) in good standing.

Award: Scholarship for use in freshman, sophomore, junior, or senior years; not renewable. *Number:* varies. *Amount:* varies.

Eligibility Requirements: Applicant must be enrolled or expecting to enroll at an institution or university. Applicant or parent of applicant must be member of Fleet Reserve Association/Auxiliary. Available to U.S. citizens. Applicant or parent must meet one or more of the following requirements: Coast Guard, Marine Corp, or Navy experience; retired from active duty; disabled or killed as a result of military service; prisoner of war; or missing in action.

Application Requirements: Application, transcript. *Deadline:* April 15.

Contact: Scholarship Administrator
Ladies Auxiliary of the Fleet Reserve Association
125 North West Street
Alexandria, VA 22314-2754
Phone: 858-748-5190
E-mail: powaydick@webtu.net

LADIES AUXILIARY TO THE VETERANS OF FOREIGN WARS http://www.ladiesauxvfw.com

JUNIOR GIRLS SCHOLARSHIP PROGRAM

High school awards available to girls under 17 who have been members of Junior Girls Unit of Ladies Auxiliary for one year. Awards based on scholastic aptitude, participation in Junior Girls Unit, and school activities. Two one-time scholarships at $5000 and $10,000.

Award: Scholarship for use in freshman, sophomore, junior, or senior years; not renewable. *Number:* 2. *Amount:* $5000–$10,000.

Eligibility Requirements: Applicant must be high school student; age 13-16; planning to enroll or expecting to enroll full-time at a two-year or four-year or technical institution; single female and must have an interest in leadership. Applicant or parent of applicant must be member of Veterans of Foreign Wars or Auxiliary. Applicant must have 3.0 GPA or higher. Available to U.S. citizens.

Application Requirements: Application, applicant must enter a contest, references, transcript. *Deadline:* March 11.

Contact: Judy Millick, Administrator of Programs
Ladies Auxiliary to the Veterans of Foreign Wars
406 West 34th Street
Kansas City, MO 64111
Phone: 816-561-8655
Fax: 816-931-4753
E-mail: info@ladiesauxvfw.com

MINNESOTA AFL-CIO http://www.mnaflcio.org

BILL PETERSON SCHOLARSHIP

Scholarship available to union member, spouse, or dependent to attend a post-secondary institution. Local must have participated or made a donation to the Bill Peterson Golf Tournament. See Web site for additional information. http://www.mnaflcio.org

Award: Scholarship for use in freshman, sophomore, junior, or senior years; not renewable. *Number:* 14. *Amount:* $1000.

Eligibility Requirements: Applicant must be enrolled or expecting to enroll at a two-year or four-year or technical institution or university; resident of Minnesota and studying in Minnesota. Applicant or parent of applicant must be member of AFL-CIO. Available to U.S. citizens.

Application Requirements: Application, essay. *Deadline:* April 1.

Contact: Tim Geelan, Organizing Director
Minnesota AFL-CIO
175 Aurora Avenue
St. Paul, MN 55103
Phone: 651-227-7647
Fax: 651-227-3801
E-mail: tgeelan@qwest.net

MARTIN DUFFY ADULT LEARNER SCHOLARSHIP AWARD

Scholarship available for union members affiliated with the Minnesota AFL-CIO or the Minnesota Joint Council 32. May be used at any post-secondary institution in Minnesota. Deadline is April 30. Information available on Web site at http://www.mnaflcio.org.

Award: Scholarship for use in freshman, sophomore, junior, or senior years; not renewable. *Number:* 4. *Amount:* $500.

Eligibility Requirements: Applicant must be enrolled or expecting to enroll at a two-year or four-year or technical institution or university; resident of Minnesota and studying in Minnesota. Applicant or parent of applicant must be member of AFL-CIO. Available to U.S. citizens.

Application Requirements: Application. *Deadline:* April 30.

Contact: Tim Geelan, Organizing Director
Minnesota AFL-CIO
175 Aurora Avenue
St. Paul, MN 55103
Phone: 651-227-7647
Fax: 651-227-3801
E-mail: tgeelan@qwest.net

MINNESOTA AFL-CIO SCHOLARSHIPS

Must be attending a college or university located within the state of Minnesota. Applicant must have a parent or legal guardian who has held for a period of one year membership in a local union which is an affiliate of the Minnesota AFL-CIO. Winners are selected by lot. Academic eligibility based on a straight "B" average or better. See Web site (http://www.mnaflcio.org) for information and application.

Award: Scholarship for use in freshman year; not renewable. *Number:* up to 5. *Amount:* $1000.

Eligibility Requirements: Applicant must be high school student; planning to enroll or expecting to enroll full-time at a two-year or four-year or technical institution or university and studying in Minnesota. Applicant or parent of applicant must be member of AFL-CIO. Applicant must have 3.0 GPA or higher. Available to U.S. and non-U.S. citizens.

Application Requirements: Application, transcript. *Deadline:* May 1.

Contact: Tim Geelan, Organizing Director
Minnesota AFL-CIO
175 Aurora Avenue
St. Paul, MN 55103
Phone: 651-227-7647
Fax: 651-227-3801
E-mail: tgeelan@qwest.net

MODERN WOODMEN OF AMERICA http://www.modern-woodmen.org

MODERN WOODMEN OF AMERICA FRATERNAL COLLEGE SCHOLARSHIP PROGRAM

Available to high school seniors who have been beneficial members of Modern Woodmen of America for two years by September 30 of senior year. Selection based on scholarship, extracurricular activities, and character. Include photo. Renewable for four years. Must submit biographical questionnaire and a form from official of applicant's high school.

Award: Scholarship for use in freshman, sophomore, junior, or senior years; renewable. *Number:* up to 75. *Amount:* up to $4000.

Eligibility Requirements: Applicant must be high school student and planning to enroll or expecting to enroll full-time at a four-year institution or university. Applicant or parent of applicant must be member of Modern Woodmen. Applicant must have 2.5 GPA or higher. Available to U.S. citizens.

Application Requirements: Application, essay, photo, references, test scores, transcript. *Deadline:* January 1.

Contact: Byron Carlson, Fraternal Scholarship Administrator
Modern Woodmen of America
1701 1st Avenue
PO Box 2005
Rock Island, IL 61204

NATIONAL ALLIANCE OF POSTAL AND FEDERAL EMPLOYEES (NAPFE) http://www.napfe.com

ASHBY B. CARTER MEMORIAL SCHOLARSHIP FUND FOUNDERS AWARD

Scholarships available to high school seniors. Must be a U.S. citizen. Applicant must be a dependent of a NAPFE Labor Union member with a minimum three year membership. Application deadline is April 1.

Award: Scholarship for use in freshman year; not renewable. *Number:* 3. *Amount:* $3500–$5000.

Eligibility Requirements: Applicant must be high school student; age 17-18 and planning to enroll or expecting to enroll full-time at a four-year or technical institution or university. Applicant or parent of applicant must be member of National Alliance of Postal and Federal Employees. Available to U.S. citizens.

Application Requirements: Application, references, test scores, transcript. *Deadline:* April 1.

Contact: Melissa Jeffries-Stewart, Director
National Alliance of Postal and Federal Employees (NAPFE)
1628 11th Street, NW
Washington, DC 20001-5086
Phone: 202-939-6325 Ext. 239
Fax: 202-939-6389
E-mail: headquarters@napfe.org

ASHBY B. CARTER MEMORIAL SCHOLARSHIP FUND SCHOLARSHIP ACHIEVEMENT AWARD

Scholarships available to high school seniors. Must be a U.S. citizen. Applicant must be a dependent of a NAPFE Labor Union member with a minimum three year membership. Application deadline is April 1.

Award: Scholarship for use in freshman year. *Number:* 3. *Amount:* $1900–$3200.

Eligibility Requirements: Applicant must be high school student; age 17-18 and planning to enroll or expecting to enroll full-time at a four-year or technical institution or university. Applicant or parent of applicant must be member of National Alliance of Postal and Federal Employees. Available to U.S. citizens.

Application Requirements: Application, references, test scores, transcript. *Deadline:* April 1.

Contact: Melissa Jeffries-Stewart, Director
National Alliance of Postal and Federal Employees (NAPFE)
1628 11th Street, NW
Washington, DC 20001
Phone: 202-939-6325 Ext. 239
Fax: 202-939-6389
E-mail: headquarters@napfe.org

NATIONAL ASSOCIATION FOR THE ADVANCEMENT OF COLORED PEOPLE http://www.naacp.org

AGNES JONES JACKSON SCHOLARSHIP

Must be current NAACP member, citizen of United States, and enrolled full-time in accredited college. Graduating high school seniors and undergraduate students must have minimum 2.5 GPA. Graduate students must have 3.0 GPA and be full- or part-time. Must also demonstrate financial

National Association for the Advancement of Colored People (continued)

need. Must not have reached 25 years of age by the deadline of the last Friday in March. Undergraduate scholarship awards $1,500, graduate awards $2,500.

Award: Scholarship for use in freshman, sophomore, junior, senior, or graduate years; not renewable. *Number:* varies. *Amount:* $1500–$2500.

Eligibility Requirements: Applicant must be American Indian/Alaska Native, Asian/Pacific Islander, Black (non-Hispanic), or Hispanic; age 24 or under and enrolled or expecting to enroll full or part-time at a four-year institution or university. Applicant or parent of applicant must be member of National Association for the Advancement of Colored People. Available to U.S. citizens.

Application Requirements: Application, financial need analysis, references, transcript, evidence of NAACP membership. *Deadline:* varies.

Contact: Donna Lakins, Education Department, Scholarship Request
National Association for the Advancement of Colored People
4805 Mt. Hope Drive
Baltimore, MD 21215-3297
Phone: 410-580-5760
Fax: 410-585-1329

ROY WILKINS SCHOLARSHIP

One-time award of $1,000. Must be full-time freshman entering into accredited U.S. college. Must be U.S. citizen and have minimum 2.5 GPA. NAACP membership and participation is preferable. Application deadline is the last Friday in March.

Award: Scholarship for use in freshman year; not renewable. *Number:* varies. *Amount:* $1000.

Eligibility Requirements: Applicant must be American Indian/Alaska Native, Asian/Pacific Islander, Black (non-Hispanic), or Hispanic; high school student and planning to enroll or expecting to enroll full-time at a four-year institution or university. Applicant or parent of applicant must be member of National Association for the Advancement of Colored People. Applicant must have 2.5 GPA or higher. Available to U.S. citizens.

Application Requirements: Application, financial need analysis, references, transcript. *Deadline:* varies.

Contact: Donna Lakins, Education Department, Scholarship Request
National Association for the Advancement of Colored People
4805 Mt. Hope Drive
Baltimore, MD 21215-3297
Phone: 410-580-5760
Fax: 410-585-1329

NATIONAL ASSOCIATION OF ENERGY SERVICE COMPANIES

http://www.aesc.net

ASSOCIATION OF ENERGY SERVICE COMPANIES SCHOLARSHIP PROGRAM

Applicant must be the legal dependant of an employee from an AESC member company, or an employee. Dependants of company officers are not eligible. Must submit application to local AESC Chapter Chairman. Application must include ACT or SAT test scores.

Award: Scholarship for use in freshman, sophomore, or junior years; renewable. *Number:* varies.

Eligibility Requirements: Applicant must be enrolled or expecting to enroll at a two-year or four-year or technical institution or university. Applicant or parent of applicant must be member of Association of Energy Service Companies.

Application Requirements: Application, essay, test scores, transcript. *Deadline:* March 15.

Contact: Darla Eggleston, Administrative Assistant
National Association of Energy Service Companies
10200 Richmond Avenue
Suite 253
Houston, TX 77042
Phone: 800-692-0771
Fax: 713-781-7542
E-mail: deggleston@aesc.net

NATIONAL ASSOCIATION OF SECONDARY SCHOOL PRINCIPALS

http://www.principals.org

NATIONAL HONOR SOCIETY SCHOLARSHIPS

One-time award available only to high school seniors who are National Honor Society members, for use at an accredited two- or four-year college or university in the U.S. Based on outstanding scholarship, leadership, service, and character. Application fee $6. Contact school counselor or NHS chapter adviser. Minimum 3.0 GPA.

Award: Scholarship for use in freshman year; not renewable. *Number:* 200. *Amount:* $1000.

Eligibility Requirements: Applicant must be high school student and planning to enroll or expecting to enroll full-time at a two-year or four-year institution or university. Applicant or parent of applicant must be member of National Honor Society. Applicant must have 3.0 GPA or higher. Available to U.S. and non-U.S. citizens.

Application Requirements: Application, essay, references, test scores, transcript. *Fee:* $6. *Deadline:* January 23.

Contact: local school's NHS chapter adviser

NATIONAL BETA CLUB

http://www.betaclub.org

NATIONAL BETA CLUB SCHOLARSHIP

Applicant must be in 12th grade and a member of the National Beta Club. Must be nominated by school chapter of the National Beta Club, therefore, applications will not be sent to the individual students. Renewable and nonrenewable awards available. Contact school Beta Club sponsor for more information. Application fee: $10.

Award: Scholarship for use in freshman year; renewable. *Number:* 208. *Amount:* $1000–$3750.

Eligibility Requirements: Applicant must be high school student and planning to enroll or expecting to enroll full-time at a two-year or four-year institution or university. Applicant or parent of applicant must be member of National Beta Club.

Application Requirements: Application, essay, references, test scores, transcript. *Fee:* $10. *Deadline:* December 10.

Contact: Beta Club Sponsor (School Faculty Adviser)
National Beta Club
151 Beta Club Way
Spartanburg, SC 29306-3012

NATIONAL FOSTER PARENT ASSOCIATION

http://www.nfpainc.org/

NATIONAL FOSTER PARENT ASSOCIATION SCHOLARSHIP

Award for high school senior who will be entering first year of college, comparable education, or training program. Five $1000 awards, three for foster children currently in foster care with an NFPA member family, and one each for birth and adopted children of foster parents. NFPA family membership required ($35 membership fee).

Award: Scholarship for use in freshman year; not renewable. *Number:* 5. *Amount:* $1000.

Eligibility Requirements: Applicant must be high school student and planning to enroll or expecting to enroll full-time at a two-year or four-year or technical institution or university. Applicant or parent of applicant must be member of National Foster Parent Association. Available to U.S. citizens.

Application Requirements: Application, autobiography, essay, financial need analysis, photo, references, test scores, transcript. *Deadline:* March 31.

Contact: Karen Jorgenson, Administrator
National Foster Parent Association
7512 Stanich Avenue #6
Gig Harbor, WA 98335
Phone: 253-853-4000
Fax: 253-853-4001
E-mail: info@nfpainc.org

NATIONAL FRATERNAL SOCIETY OF THE DEAF http://www.nfsd.com

NATIONAL FRATERNAL SOCIETY OF THE DEAF SCHOLARSHIPS

Provides scholarship to cover room and board, tuition and/or fees. Applicants must be members of the NFSD for one full year and in a postsecondary program or ready to enter one as a full-time student.

Award: Scholarship for use in freshman, sophomore, junior, senior, graduate, or postgraduate years; not renewable. *Number:* 5. *Amount:* $1000.

Eligibility Requirements: Applicant must be enrolled or expecting to enroll full-time at a two-year or four-year institution or university. Applicant or parent of applicant must be member of National Fraternal Society of the Deaf. Available to U.S. citizens.

Application Requirements: Application, photo, references, transcript. *Deadline:* July 1.

Contact: Scholarship Information
National Fraternal Society of the Deaf
1118 South 6th Street
Springfield, IL 62703
Phone: 217-789-7429
Fax: 217-789-7489
E-mail: thefrat@nfsd.com

NATIONAL JUNIOR ANGUS ASSOCIATION http://www.njaa.info

ANGUS FOUNDATION SCHOLARSHIPS

Applicants must have at one time been a National Junior Angus Association member and must currently be a junior, regular or life member of the American Angus Association. Must be applied to undergraduate studies in any field. See Web site for further information and to download application.

Award: Scholarship for use in freshman, sophomore, junior, or senior years; not renewable. *Number:* 20. *Amount:* $1000–$3500.

Eligibility Requirements: Applicant must be age 25 or under and enrolled or expecting to enroll full-time at a two-year or four-year institution or university. Applicant or parent of applicant must be member of American Angus Association.

Application Requirements: Application, references, transcript. *Deadline:* May 13.

Contact: James Fisher, Director of Activities and Junior Activities
National Junior Angus Association
3201 Frederick Avenue
St. Joseph, MO 64506
Phone: 816-383-5100
Fax: 816-233-9703
E-mail: jfisher@angus.org

NATIONAL MILITARY INTELLIGENCE ASSOCIATION http://www.nmia.org/Scholarship.html

NATIONAL MILITARY INTELLIGENCE ASSOCIATION SCHOLARSHIP

One-time award for the dependent children of NMIA members pursuing an undergraduate degree. Award is based on merit. Must be a U.S. citizen. Minimum 3.0 GPA is required. Application deadline is November 1. Information on Web site at http://www.nmia.org.

Award: Scholarship for use in freshman, sophomore, junior, or senior years; not renewable. *Number:* 1–3. *Amount:* $1000.

Eligibility Requirements: Applicant must be enrolled or expecting to enroll full-time at a four-year institution. Applicant or parent of applicant must be member of National Military Intelligence Association. Applicant must have 3.0 GPA or higher. Available to U.S. citizens.

Application Requirements: Application, test scores. *Deadline:* November 1.

Contact: John Kuntzman, Executive Director
National Military Intelligence Association
9200 Centerway Road
Gaithersburg, MD 20879
Phone: 703-790-1428
Fax: 703-790-0337
E-mail: nmiascholarship@aol.com

NATIONAL RIFLE ASSOCIATION http://www.nrahq.org

JEANNE E. BRAY MEMORIAL SCHOLARSHIP PROGRAM

Renewable award of up to $2000 for dependent of NRA member who is a current full-time commissioned peace officer, an officer killed in the line of duty, a retired peace officer, or a peace officer disabled as a result of an incident occurring in the line of duty. Intended for full-time study. Minimum 2.5 GPA required.

Award: Scholarship for use in freshman, sophomore, junior, or senior years; renewable. *Number:* varies. *Amount:* up to $2000.

Eligibility Requirements: Applicant must be enrolled or expecting to enroll full-time at a two-year or four-year institution or university. Applicant or parent of applicant must be member of National Rifle Association. Applicant must have 2.5 GPA or higher. Available to U.S. citizens.

Application Requirements: Application, essay, references, test scores, transcript. *Deadline:* November 15.

Contact: Sandy Elkin, Grants Manager
National Rifle Association
11250 Waples Mill Road
Fairfax, VA 22030
Phone: 703-267-1131

NATIONAL ROOFING FOUNDATION http://www.nrca.net

NATIONAL ROOFING FOUNDATION/ROOFING INDUSTRY SCHOLARSHIP/GRANT

Scholarships are available only to the immediate families of National Roofing Contractors Association members and employees and immediate families of employees of NRCA Contractor Members. Must have 2.5 GPA or higher. Deadline is January 31.

Award: Scholarship for use in freshman, sophomore, junior, or senior years; renewable. *Number:* 1–4. *Amount:* up to $1000.

Eligibility Requirements: Applicant must be enrolled or expecting to enroll full-time at a two-year or four-year or technical institution or university. Applicant or parent of applicant must be member of National Roofing Contractors Association. Applicant must have 2.5 GPA or higher. Available to U.S. citizens.

Application Requirements: Application, references, transcript. *Deadline:* January 31.

Contact: Scholarship Coordinator
National Roofing Foundation
10255 West Higgins Road, Suite 600
Rosemont, IL 60018-5607
Phone: 847-299-9070
Fax: 847-299-1183
E-mail: nrca@nrca.net

NATIONAL SOCIETY DAUGHTERS OF THE AMERICAN REVOLUTION http://www.dar.org

NATIONAL SOCIETY DAUGHTERS OF THE AMERICAN REVOLUTION LILLIAN AND ARTHUR DUNN SCHOLARSHIP

These renewable awards are available to graduating high school seniors whose mothers are active members of the DAR. Must include DAR member number. Must be sponsored by DAR chapter. Awards based on scholarship, need, and commitment to field of study. Must submit self-addressed stamped envelope to be considered. Deadline is February 15.

Award: Scholarship for use in freshman, sophomore, junior, senior, or graduate years; renewable. *Number:* 4. *Amount:* $2000.

Eligibility Requirements: Applicant must be high school student and planning to enroll or expecting to enroll at a four-year institution or university. Applicant or parent of applicant must be member of Daughters of the American Revolution. Applicant must have 3.0 GPA or higher. Available to U.S. citizens.

Application Requirements: Application, essay, financial need analysis, references, self-addressed stamped envelope, test scores, transcript. *Deadline:* February 15.

Contact: Office of Committees, Scholarship
National Society Daughters of the American Revolution
1776 D Street, NW
Washington, DC 20006-5392

NATIONAL UNION OF PUBLIC AND GENERAL EMPLOYEES http://www.nupge.ca

SCHOLARSHIP FOR ABORIGINAL CANADIANS

Award for Aboriginal Canadian students who plan to enter the first year of a Canadian college or university and who are children or foster children of a member of the National Union of Public and General Employees. Must write a 750-1000-word essay on "the importance of quality public services in enhancing the quality of life of Aboriginal Canadians".

Award: Scholarship for use in freshman year. *Number:* 1. *Amount:* $1259.

Eligibility Requirements: Applicant must be of Canadian heritage and Canadian citizen; high school student; planning to enroll or expecting to enroll full-time at a four-year institution or university and studying in Alberta, British Columbia, Manitoba, New Brunswick, Newfoundland, North West Territories, Nova Scotia, Ontario, Prince Edward Island, Quebec, Saskatchewan, or Yukon. Applicant or parent of applicant must be member of National Union of Public and General Employees.

Application Requirements: Application, applicant must enter a contest, essay. *Deadline:* June 30.

Contact: Louise Trepanier, Scholarships
National Union of Public and General Employees
15 Auriga Drive
Nepean, ON K2E 1B7
Canada
Phone: 613-228-9800
Fax: 613-228-9801
E-mail: ltrep@nupge.ca

SCHOLARSHIP FOR VISIBLE MINORITIES

Award for first-year Canadian students who are, by race or color, in a visible minority and who are children or foster children of a member of the National Union of Public and General Employees. Must write a 750-1000-word essay on "the importance of quality public services in enhancing the quality of life of visible minorities".

Award: Scholarship for use in freshman year. *Number:* 1. *Amount:* $1259.

Eligibility Requirements: Applicant must be Canadian citizen; American Indian/Alaska Native, Asian/Pacific Islander, Black (non-Hispanic), or Hispanic; high school student; planning to enroll or expecting to enroll full-time at a four-year institution or university and studying in Alberta, British Columbia, Manitoba, New Brunswick, Newfoundland, North West Territories, Nova Scotia, Ontario, Prince Edward Island, Quebec, Saskatchewan, or Yukon. Applicant or parent of applicant must be member of National Union of Public and General Employees.

Application Requirements: Application, applicant must enter a contest, essay. *Deadline:* June 30.

Contact: Louise Trepanier, Scholarships
National Union of Public and General Employees
15 Auriga Drive
Nepean, ON K2E 1B7
Canada
Phone: 613-228-9800
Fax: 613-228-9801
E-mail: ltrep@nupge.ca

TERRY FOX MEMORIAL SCHOLARSHIP

Award for Canadian students with disabilities who plan to enter the first year of a Canadian college or university and who are the children or foster children of a member of the National Union of Public and General Employees. Must write a 750-1000-word essay on: "the importance of quality public services in enhancing the quality of life of people with disabilities".

Award: Scholarship for use in freshman year. *Number:* 1. *Amount:* $1259.

Eligibility Requirements: Applicant must be Canadian citizen; high school student; planning to enroll or expecting to enroll full-time at a four-year institution or university and studying in Alberta, British Columbia, Manitoba, New Brunswick, Newfoundland, North West Territories, Nova Scotia, Ontario, Prince Edward Island, Quebec, Saskatchewan, or Yukon. Applicant or parent of applicant must be member of National Union of Public and General Employees. Applicant must be hearing impaired, learning disabled, physically disabled, or visually impaired.

Application Requirements: Application, applicant must enter a contest, essay. *Deadline:* June 30.

Contact: Louise Trepanier, Scholarships
National Union of Public and General Employees
15 Auriga Drive
Nepean, ON K2E 1B7
Canada
Phone: 613-228-9800
Fax: 613-228-9801
E-mail: ltrep@nupge.ca

TOMMY DOUGLAS SCHOLARSHIP

Award for first-year students at a Canadian college or university who are children or foster children of members of National Union of Public and General Employees. Must write an essay on the topic: "How Tommy Douglas contributed to making Canada a more just and equitable society".

Award: Scholarship for use in freshman year. *Number:* 1. *Amount:* $1259.

Eligibility Requirements: Applicant must be Canadian citizen; high school student; planning to enroll or expecting to enroll full-time at a four-year institution or university and studying in Alberta, British Columbia, Manitoba, New Brunswick, Newfoundland, North West Territories, Nova Scotia, Ontario, Prince Edward Island, Quebec, Saskatchewan, or Yukon. Applicant or parent of applicant must be member of National Union of Public and General Employees.

Application Requirements: Application, applicant must enter a contest, essay. *Deadline:* June 30.

Contact: Louise Trepanier, Scholarships
National Union of Public and General Employees
15 Auriga Drive
Nepean, ON K2E 1B7
Canada
Phone: 613-228-9800
Fax: 613-228-9801
E-mail: ltrep@nupge.ca

NATIONAL WOMAN'S RELIEF CORPS

NATIONAL WOMAN'S RELIEF CORPS SCHOLARSHIP

For undergraduate study. Must be a member, relative, or descendant of a member of the Woman's Relief Corps. Application inquiries should be directed to the National Treasurer. Merit-based award. Minimum 3.0 GPA required. Student must reapply each year of undergraduate study.

Award: Scholarship for use in freshman, sophomore, junior, or senior years; not renewable. *Number:* 2–6. *Amount:* $200–$350.

Eligibility Requirements: Applicant must be enrolled or expecting to enroll full-time at a two-year or four-year or technical institution or university. Applicant or parent of applicant must be member of National Women's Relief Corps. Applicant must have 3.0 GPA or higher. Available to U.S. citizens.

Application Requirements: Application, financial need analysis, photo, references, self-addressed stamped envelope, transcript. *Deadline:* July 15.

Contact: Lurene Wentworth, National Treasurer
National Woman's Relief Corps
PO Box 165
New Durham, NH 03855-0165
Phone: 603-859-2861
E-mail: liwntwrth@aol.com

NATSO FOUNDATION http://www.natsofoundation.org

BILL MOON SCHOLARSHIP

Available to employees or dependents of NATSO-affiliated truckstops/travel plazas. Visit Web site at http://www.natsofoundation.org for additional information.

Award: Scholarship for use in freshman, sophomore, junior, senior, or graduate years; not renewable. *Number:* 5–12. *Amount:* $2500.

Eligibility Requirements: Applicant must be enrolled or expecting to enroll full or part-time at a two-year or four-year institution or university. Applicant or parent of applicant must be member of NATSO Foundation. Applicant or parent of applicant must have employment or volunteer experience in designated career field. Available to U.S. and non-U.S. citizens.

Application Requirements: Application, essay, financial need analysis, references, transcript, signature from employer. *Deadline:* varies.

Contact: Sharon Corigliano, Executive Director
NATSO Foundation
1199 North Fairfax Street, Suite 801
Alexandria, VA 22314
Phone: 703-549-2100
Fax: 703-684-9667
E-mail: foundation@natso.com

NEBRASKA DECA http://www.nedeca.org/scholarshipsandawards.htm

NEBRASKA DECA LEADERSHIP SCHOLARSHIP

For applicants who intend to pursue a full-time two-year or four-year course of study in a marketing or business-related field. Applicant must be active in DECA and involved in community service activities.

Award: Scholarship for use in freshman year; not renewable. *Number:* 2–6. *Amount:* $250–$500.

Eligibility Requirements: Applicant must be enrolled or expecting to enroll full-time at a two-year or four-year or technical institution or university and resident of Nebraska. Applicant or parent of applicant must be member of Distribution Ed Club or Future Business Leaders of America. Applicant must have 2.5 GPA or higher. Available to U.S. citizens.

Application Requirements: Application, essay, resume, references, transcript. *Deadline:* February 1.

Contact: Scholarship Administrator
Nebraska DECA
301 Centennial Mall South
PO Box 94987
Lincoln, NE 68509-4987
Phone: 402-471-4803
Fax: 402-471-8850
E-mail: scholarships@www.nedeca.org

NEW YORK STATE AFL-CIO http://www.nysaflcio.org

NEW YORK STATE AFL-CIO SCHOLARSHIP

Applicant must be a New York State high school graduate, planning to enroll in a New York state postsecondary school. Parent or guardian must be a member of a union affiliated with the NYS AFL-CIO. Must be accepted in a course of study in labor relations or a related field. Renewable award for $8000 ($2000 per year). Application deadline is May 1.

Award: Scholarship for use in freshman, sophomore, junior, or senior years; renewable. *Number:* 1. *Amount:* $2000.

Eligibility Requirements: Applicant must be high school student; planning to enroll or expecting to enroll full-time at a two-year or four-year or technical institution or university; resident of New York and studying in New York. Applicant or parent of applicant must be member of AFL-CIO. Available to U.S. citizens.

Application Requirements: Application, essay, references. *Deadline:* May 1.

Contact: Gary Duesberg, Education Director
New York State AFL-CIO
100 South Swan Street
Albany, NY 12210-1939
Phone: 518-436-8516
Fax: 518-436-8470
E-mail: garydues@aol.com

NEW YORK STATE GRANGE

SUSAN W. FREESTONE EDUCATION AWARD

Grants are for members of Junior Grange and Subordinate Grange in New York State. Students must enroll in an approved two- or four-year college in New York State. Second grants available with reapplication. Minimum 2.5 GPA required.

Award: Scholarship for use in freshman, sophomore, junior, or senior years; renewable. *Amount:* $500–$1000.

Eligibility Requirements: Applicant must be enrolled or expecting to enroll at a two-year or four-year institution; resident of New York and studying in New York. Applicant or parent of applicant must be member of Grange Association. Applicant must have 2.5 GPA or higher. Available to U.S. citizens.

Application Requirements: Application, financial need analysis, references, transcript. *Deadline:* April 15.

Contact: Ann Hall, Scholarship Chairperson
New York State Grange
100 Grange Place
Cortland, NY 13045
Phone: 607-756-7553
Fax: 607-756-7757
E-mail: nysgrange@nysgrange.com

NEW YORK STATE SOCIETY OF PROFESSIONAL ENGINEERS http://www.nysspe.org

NYSSPE-PAST OFFICERS' SCHOLARSHIP

Scholarship awarded to the child of a NYSSPE member, in the amount of $1000. Based on academic achievement. GPA of 3.6 or higher.

Award: Scholarship for use in freshman, sophomore, junior, or senior years; not renewable. *Number:* 1. *Amount:* $1000.

Eligibility Requirements: Applicant must be enrolled or expecting to enroll full-time at an institution or university. Applicant or parent of applicant must be member of New York State Society of Professional Engineers. Available to U.S. citizens.

Application Requirements: Application, essay, references, test scores, transcript. *Deadline:* December 1.

Contact: NYSSPE
New York State Society of Professional Engineers
RPI Technology Park, 385 Jordan Road
Troy, NY 12180
Phone: 518-283-7490
E-mail: jamiller@nysspe.org

NON COMMISSIONED OFFICERS ASSOCIATION (NCOA) http://www.ncoausa.org

NON-COMMISSIONED OFFICERS ASSOCIATION SCHOLARSHIPS

Awards for children and spouses of members of the Non-Commissioned Officers Association. Must be full-time student. Deadline is March 31. Children of members must be under age 25 to receive initial grant. Applicant must maintain 3.0 GPA for renewal.

Award: Scholarship for use in freshman, sophomore, junior, or senior years; renewable. *Number:* 16. *Amount:* $900–$1000.

Eligibility Requirements: Applicant must be age 24 or under and enrolled or expecting to enroll full-time at a four-year institution. Applicant or parent of applicant must be member of Non Commissioned Officers Association. Applicant must have 3.0 GPA or higher. Available to U.S. citizens.

Application Requirements: Application, autobiography, essay, references, test scores, transcript. *Deadline:* March 31.

Contact: Hilda Atkinson, Scholarship Department
Non Commissioned Officers Association (NCOA)
PO Box 33610
San Antonio, TX 78265-3610
Phone: 210-653-6161 Ext. 231
Fax: 210-637-3337
E-mail: hatkinso@ncoausa.org

NORTH EAST ROOFING EDUCATIONAL FOUNDATION http://www.nerca.org

NORTH EAST ROOFING EDUCATIONAL FOUNDATION SCHOLARSHIP

Applicants must be a member of NERCA, their employees, or their respective immediate family. Immediate family is defined as self, spouse, or child. The child may be natural, legally, adopted or a stepchild. Also must be a high school senior or graduate who plans to enroll in a full-time undergraduate course of study at an accredited two-year or four-year college, university, or vocational-technical school.

Award: Scholarship for use in freshman, sophomore, junior, or senior years; not renewable. *Number:* 4–5. *Amount:* up to $1500.

Eligibility Requirements: Applicant must be enrolled or expecting to enroll full or part-time at a two-year or four-year or technical institution or university. Applicant or parent of applicant must be member of National Roofing Contractors Association. Applicant or parent of applicant must have employment or volunteer experience in designated career field. Available to U.S. and Canadian citizens.

Application Requirements: Application, references, self-addressed stamped envelope, transcript. *Deadline:* April 1.

Contact: Ms. Kimberly Hurley, Foundation Coordinator
North East Roofing Educational Foundation
1400 Hancock Street, 7th Floor
Quincy, MA 02169
Phone: 617-472-5590
Fax: 617-479-1478
E-mail: khurley@nerca.org

NORTHEAST FRESH FOODS ALLIANCE http://www.neffa.com

NORTHEAST FRESH FOODS ALLIANCE SCHOLARSHIP AWARDS PROGRAM

The scholarship is available to graduating seniors who are employed, or whose parents are employed, by a Northeast Fresh Foods Alliance member company. Please refer to the Web site for further details: http://www.neffa.com.

Award: Scholarship for use in freshman year; not renewable. *Number:* 15–20. *Amount:* $500.

Eligibility Requirements: Applicant must be high school student and planning to enroll or expecting to enroll full-time at a two-year or four-year or technical institution or university. Applicant or parent of applicant must be member of Northeast Fresh Foods Alliance. Applicant or parent of applicant must have employment or volunteer experience in food service. Available to U.S. and Canadian citizens.

Application Requirements: Application, essay, references, transcript. *Deadline:* varies.

Contact: Andrea L. Walker, Executive Director
Northeast Fresh Foods Alliance
1189R North Main Street
Randolph, MA 02368
Phone: 781-963-9726
Fax: 781-963-5829
E-mail: andrea@neffa.com

NORTHEASTERN LOGGERS' ASSOCIATION, INC.

NORTHEASTERN LOGGERS' ASSOCIATION SCHOLARSHIPS

Scholarships available to those whose family belongs to the Northeastern Loggers' Association or whose family member is an employee of the Industrial and Associate Members of the Northeastern Loggers' Association. Must submit paper on topic of "What it means to grow up in the forest industry." Deadline: March 31.

Award: Scholarship for use in freshman, sophomore, junior, or senior years; not renewable. *Number:* 8. *Amount:* $500–$1000.

Eligibility Requirements: Applicant must be enrolled or expecting to enroll full-time at a two-year or four-year or technical institution or university and must have an interest in designated field specified by sponsor. Applicant or parent of applicant must be member of Northeastern Loggers Association. Available to U.S. and non-U.S. citizens.

Application Requirements: Application, essay, transcript. *Deadline:* March 31.

Contact: Mona Lincoln, Training and Safety Director
Northeastern Loggers' Association, Inc.
PO Box 69
Old Forge, NY 13420-0069
Phone: 315-369-3078
Fax: 315-369-3736
E-mail: mona@loggertraining.com

OHIO AMERICAN LEGION http://ohioamericanlegion.org

OHIO AMERICAN LEGION SCHOLARSHIPS

One-time award for full-time students attending accredited institution. Open to students of any postsecondary academic year. Must have minimum 3.0 GPA. Deadline April 15. Must be a member of the American Legion, a direct descendent of a Legionnaire (living or deceased), or surviving spouse or child of a deceased U.S. military person who died on active duty or of injuries received on active duty.

Award: Scholarship for use in freshman, sophomore, junior, or senior years; not renewable. *Number:* 15–18. *Amount:* $2000–$3000.

Eligibility Requirements: Applicant must be enrolled or expecting to enroll full-time at a two-year or four-year or technical institution or university. Applicant or parent of applicant must be member of American Legion or Auxiliary. Applicant must have 3.0 GPA or higher. Available to U.S. and non-U.S. citizens. Applicant or parent must meet one or more of the following requirements: general military experience; retired from active duty; disabled or killed as a result of military service; prisoner of war; or missing in action.

Application Requirements: Application, transcript. *Deadline:* April 15.

Contact: Donald Lanthorn, Service Director
Ohio American Legion
PO Box 8007
Delaware, OH 43015
Phone: 740-362-7478
Fax: 740-362-1429
E-mail: dlanthorn@iwaynet.net

OHIO CIVIL SERVICE EMPLOYEES ASSOCIATION http://www.ocsea.org

LES BEST SCHOLARSHIP

Up to twelve scholarships worth up to $1000 will be awarded to eligible union members, spouses and their dependent children. For more details see Web site: http://www.ocsea.org.

Award: Scholarship for use in freshman year; not renewable. *Number:* 8–12. *Amount:* $250–$1000.

Eligibility Requirements: Applicant must be enrolled or expecting to enroll full or part-time at a two-year or four-year or technical institution or university and resident of Ohio. Applicant or parent of applicant must be member of Ohio Civil Service Employee Association. Available to U.S. citizens.

Application Requirements: Application, essay, references, transcript, proof of enrollment. *Deadline:* April 2.

Contact: Les Best Scholarship Program
Ohio Civil Service Employees Association
390 Worthington Road, Suite A
Westerville, OH 43082-8331
Phone: 614-865-4740
Fax: 614-865-4777

OKLAHOMA ALUMNI & ASSOCIATES OF FHA, HERO AND FCCLA, INC. http://www.okfccla.org

OKLAHOMA ALUMNI & ASSOCIATES OF FHA, HERO AND FCCLA, INC. SCHOLARSHIP

Financial aid for academically promising FCCLA members who will be pursuing a post-secondary education. Must be a resident of Oklahoma, show financial need, minimum GPA of 3.0 required.

Award: Scholarship for use in freshman year; not renewable. *Number:* 2. *Amount:* $1000.

Eligibility Requirements: Applicant must be high school student; planning to enroll or expecting to enroll full-time at a two-year or

four-year or technical institution or university and resident of Oklahoma. Applicant or parent of applicant must be member of Family, Career and Community Leaders of America. Applicant must have 3.0 GPA or higher. Available to U.S. citizens.

Application Requirements: Application, essay, references, transcript. *Deadline:* March 1.

Contact: Denise Morris, State FCCLA Adviser
Oklahoma Alumni & Associates of FHA, HERO and FCCLA, Inc.
1500 West Seventh Avenue
Stillwater, OK 74074
Phone: 405-743-5467
Fax: 405-743-6809
E-mail: dmorr@okcareertech.org

OREGON STUDENT ASSISTANCE COMMISSION

http://www.osac.state.or.us

AFSCME: AMERICAN FEDERATION OF STATE, COUNTY, AND MUNICIPAL EMPLOYEES LOCAL 1724 SCHOLARSHIP

One-time award for active, laid-off, retired, or disabled members in good standing or spouses (including life partners and their children), natural children, stepchildren, or grandchildren of active, laid-off retired, disabled, or deceased members in good standing. Qualifying members must have been active in AFSCME Local 1724 one year or more as of March 1 of the year in which the scholarship application is filed, or have been a member one year or more preceding the date of layoff, death, disability, or retirement. Part-time enrollment (minimum six credit hours) will be considered, but only for active members, spouses (or life partners), or laid-off members.

Award: Scholarship for use in freshman, sophomore, junior, senior, or graduate years; not renewable. *Number:* 3. *Amount:* $667.

Eligibility Requirements: Applicant must be enrolled or expecting to enroll full or part-time at a four-year institution and resident of Oregon. Applicant or parent of applicant must be member of American Federation of State, County, and Municipal Employees. Available to U.S. citizens.

Application Requirements: Application, essay, financial need analysis, references, transcript, activity chart. *Deadline:* March 1.

Contact: Director of Grant Programs
Oregon Student Assistance Commission
1500 Valley River Drive, Suite 100
Eugene, OR 97401-7020
Phone: 800-452-8807 Ext. 7395
E-mail: awardinfo@mercury.osac.state.or.us

AFSCME: AMERICAN FEDERATION OF STATE, COUNTY, AND MUNICIPAL EMPLOYEES LOCAL 75 SCHOLARSHIP

One-time award for active, laid-off, retired, or disabled members in good standing or spouses (including life partners and their children), natural children, or grandchildren of active, laid-off, retired, disabled, or deceased members in good standing. Qualifying members must have been active in AFSCME Local 75 one year or more as of March 1 of the year in which the scholarship application is filed or have been a member one year or more preceding the date of layoff, death, disability, or retirement. Part-time enrollment (minimum six credit hours) will be considered, but only for active members, spouses (or life partners), or laid-off members. Additional essay required. College students must have minimum cumulative 2.5 GPA; graduating high school seniors must have minimum 3.0 GPA and combined achievement test scores of 1100+.

Award: Scholarship for use in freshman, sophomore, junior, senior, or graduate years; not renewable. *Number:* 6. *Amount:* $583.

Eligibility Requirements: Applicant must be enrolled or expecting to enroll full or part-time at an institution or university and resident of Oregon. Applicant or parent of applicant must be member of American Federation of State, County, and Municipal Employees. Available to U.S. citizens.

Application Requirements: Application, essay, financial need analysis, transcript, activity chart. *Deadline:* March 1.

Contact: Director of Grant Programs
Oregon Student Assistance Commission
1500 Valley River Drive, Suite 100
Eugene, OR 97401-7020
Phone: 800-452-8807 Ext. 7395
E-mail: awardinfo@mercury.osac.state.or.us

INTERNATIONAL BROTHERHOOD OF ELECTRICAL WORKERS LOCAL 280 SCHOLARSHIP

Scholarship available for children or grandchildren of active or retired members of IBEW Local 280 who are residents of Oregon. Not based on financial need. Deadline is March 1.

Award: Scholarship for use in freshman, sophomore, junior, or senior years; not renewable. *Number:* varies. *Amount:* $500.

Eligibility Requirements: Applicant must be enrolled or expecting to enroll at an institution or university and resident of Oregon. Applicant or parent of applicant must be member of International Brotherhood of Electrical Workers. Available to U.S. citizens.

Application Requirements: Application. *Deadline:* March 1.

Contact: Director of Grant Programs
Oregon Student Assistance Commission
1500 Valley River Drive, Suite 100
Eugene, OR 97401-7020
Phone: 800-452-8807 Ext. 7395
E-mail: awardinfo@mercury.osac.state.or.us

INTERNATIONAL UNION OF OPERATING ENGINEERS LOCAL 701 SCHOLARSHIP

Scholarship available for graduating high school seniors who are children of Local 701 members. Not based on financial need. Deadline is March 1.

Award: Scholarship for use in freshman year; not renewable. *Number:* varies. *Amount:* $500.

Eligibility Requirements: Applicant must be enrolled or expecting to enroll at an institution or university and resident of Oregon. Applicant or parent of applicant must be member of International Union of Operating Engineers.

Application Requirements: Application. *Deadline:* March 1.

Contact: Director of Grant Programs
Oregon Student Assistance Commission
1500 Valley River Drive, Suite 100
Eugene, OR 97401-7020
Phone: 800-452-8807 Ext. 7395
E-mail: awardinfo@mercury.osac.state.or.us

OREGON PUBLISHING COMPANY/HILLIARD SCHOLARSHIP

Available for graduating high school seniors who are members of the Prospective Gents Club of the Bridge Builders organization. Must be in the process of completing requirements for Bridge Builders "Rites of Passage Program." Automatically renewable upon volunteer service to Bridge Builders Program.

Award: Scholarship for use in freshman year; renewable. *Number:* 1. *Amount:* $2500.

Eligibility Requirements: Applicant must be high school student; planning to enroll or expecting to enroll at a four-year institution and resident of Oregon. Available to U.S. citizens.

Application Requirements: Application, essay, financial need analysis, references, transcript, activity chart. *Deadline:* March 1.

Contact: Director of Grant Programs
Oregon Student Assistance Commission
1500 Valley River Drive, Suite 100
Eugene, OR 97401-7020
Phone: 800-452-8807 Ext. 7395
E-mail: awardinfo@mercury.osac.state.or.us

OREGON STATE FISCAL ASSOCIATION SCHOLARSHIP

One-time award for OSFA members or their children. Members may enroll part-time and must study public administration, finance, economics, or related fields. Children of members must enroll full-time and may enter any program of study. Must be enrolled in an Oregon college.

Award: Scholarship for use in freshman, sophomore, junior, senior, or graduate years; not renewable. *Number:* 2. *Amount:* $500.

Eligibility Requirements: Applicant must be enrolled or expecting to enroll full or part-time at a two-year or four-year institution; resident of Oregon and studying in Oregon. Applicant or parent of applicant must be member of Oregon State Fiscal Association. Available to U.S. citizens.

Application Requirements: Application, essay, financial need analysis, references, transcript, activity chart. *Deadline:* March 1.

Contact: Director of Grant Programs
Oregon Student Assistance Commission
1500 Valley River Drive, Suite 100
Eugene, OR 97401-7020
Phone: 800-452-8807 Ext. 7395
E-mail: awardinfo@mercury.osac.state.or.us

TEAMSTERS CLYDE C. CROSBY/JOSEPH M. EDGAR MEMORIAL SCHOLARSHIP

One-time scholarship available for a graduating high school senior with a minimum 3.0 cumulative GPA who is a child, or dependent stepchild of an active, retired, disabled, or deceased member of local union affiliated with Teamsters #37. Member must have been active for at least one year. Award may be received for a maximum of twelve quarters.

Award: Scholarship for use in freshman, sophomore, junior, or senior years; renewable. *Number:* 2. *Amount:* $500.

Eligibility Requirements: Applicant must be high school student; planning to enroll or expecting to enroll full or part-time at an institution or university and resident of Oregon. Applicant or parent of applicant must be member of Teamsters. Applicant or parent of applicant must have employment or volunteer experience in designated career field. Applicant must have 3.0 GPA or higher. Available to U.S. citizens.

Application Requirements: Application, essay, financial need analysis, transcript, activity chart. *Deadline:* March 1.

Contact: Director of Grant Programs
Oregon Student Assistance Commission
1500 Valley River Drive, Suite 100
Eugene, OR 97401-7020
Phone: 800-452-8807 Ext. 7395
E-mail: awardinfo@mercury.osac.state.or.us

TEAMSTERS COUNCIL 37 FEDERAL CREDIT UNION SCHOLARSHIP

One-time award for members or dependents of Council #37 credit union who are active, retired, disabled, or deceased members of teamsters Joint Council #37. Members must have been active in local affiliated with Council for at least one year. Must be enrolled at least half-time in college and have cumulative GPA between 2.0 and 3.0. Contact for application requirements and deadlines.

Award: Scholarship for use in freshman, sophomore, junior, senior, or graduate years; not renewable. *Number:* 1. *Amount:* $1000.

Eligibility Requirements: Applicant must be enrolled or expecting to enroll full or part-time at a two-year or four-year institution and resident of Oregon. Applicant or parent of applicant must be member of Teamsters. Applicant or parent of applicant must have employment or volunteer experience in designated career field. Available to U.S. citizens.

Application Requirements: Application, essay, financial need analysis, references, transcript, activity chart. *Deadline:* March 1.

Contact: Director of Grant Programs
Oregon Student Assistance Commission
1500 Valley River Drive, Suite 100
Eugene, OR 97401-7020
Phone: 800-452-8807 Ext. 7395
E-mail: awardinfo@mercury.osac.state.or.us

TEAMSTERS LOCAL 305 SCHOLARSHIP

Graduating high school seniors who are children or dependent stepchildren of active, retired, disabled, or deceased members of Local 305 of the Joint Council of Teamsters #37. Members must have been active at least 1 year. Not based on financial need. Deadline is March 1.

Award: Scholarship for use in freshman, sophomore, junior, or senior years; renewable. *Number:* varies. *Amount:* $500.

Eligibility Requirements: Applicant must be enrolled or expecting to enroll at an institution or university and resident of Oregon. Applicant or parent of applicant must be member of Teamsters. Available to U.S. citizens.

Application Requirements: Application. *Deadline:* March 1.

Contact: Director of Grant Programs
Oregon Student Assistance Commission
1500 Valley River Drive, Suite 100
Eugene, OR 97401-7020
Phone: 800-452-8807 Ext. 7395
E-mail: awardinfo@mercury.osac.state.or.us

PAPER, ALLIED-INDUSTRIAL, CHEMICAL AND ENERGY WORKERS INTERNATIONAL UNION

http://www.paceunion.org

NICHOLAS C. VRATARIC SCHOLARSHIP FUND

Two scholarships worth $1000 each are available to PACE Members. The awards will be selected by a random drawing. Eligible applicants will be "active" members and submit a 500-word essay.

Award: Scholarship for use in freshman, sophomore, junior, or senior years; not renewable. *Number:* 2. *Amount:* $1000.

Eligibility Requirements: Applicant must be enrolled or expecting to enroll at a two-year or four-year or technical institution or university. Applicant or parent of applicant must be member of Paper, Allied Industrial, Chemical and Energy Workers International Union. Available to U.S. and Canadian citizens.

Application Requirements: Application, essay. *Deadline:* March 15.

Contact: Debi Taylor, Administrative Assistant II
Paper, Allied-Industrial, Chemical and Energy Workers International Union
PO Box 1475
Nashville, TN 37202-1475
Phone: 615-834-8590
Fax: 615-781-0428
E-mail: debitay@isdn.net

PACE SCHOLARSHIP AWARDS

Twenty $1000 awards available to the child of an active member of PACE International Union. One-time award for graduating high-school seniors.

Award: Scholarship for use in freshman year; not renewable. *Number:* up to 20. *Amount:* $1000.

Eligibility Requirements: Applicant must be high school student and planning to enroll or expecting to enroll full-time at a two-year or four-year or technical institution or university. Applicant or parent of applicant must be member of Paper, Allied Industrial, Chemical and Energy Workers International Union. Available to U.S. and Canadian citizens.

Application Requirements: Application, essay, financial need analysis, references, test scores, transcript. *Deadline:* March 15.

Contact: Debi Taylor, Administrative Assistant II
Paper, Allied-Industrial, Chemical and Energy Workers International Union
PO Box 1475
Nashville, TN 37202
Phone: 615-834-8590
Fax: 615-781-0428
E-mail: debitay@isdn.net

PARENTS WITHOUT PARTNERS INTERNATIONAL SCHOLARSHIP PROGRAM http://parentswithoutpartners.org

PARENTS WITHOUT PARTNERS INTERNATIONAL SCHOLARSHIP PROGRAM

Up to ten scholarships between $250 and $500 will be given to the children of members of Parents Without Partners. Must be a U.S. or Canadian citizen between 20 and 25. Application can be downloaded from the following Web site: http://parentswithoutpartners.org.

Award: Scholarship for use in freshman year; not renewable. *Number:* 10. *Amount:* $250–$500.

Eligibility Requirements: Applicant must be age 20-25 and enrolled or expecting to enroll full-time at a two-year or four-year or technical institution or university. Applicant or parent of applicant must be member of Parents Without Partners. Available to U.S. and Canadian citizens.

Application Requirements: Application, applicant must enter a contest, essay, references, transcript. *Deadline:* March 15.

Contact: Ann Willard, Scholarship Chair
Parents Without Partners International Scholarship Program
1737 Ridgemont Drive
Tuscaloosa, AL 35404
Phone: 205-553-3974
E-mail: gaewillard@aol.com

PENNSYLVANIA AFL-CIO http://www.paaflcio.org

PA AFL-CIO UNIONISM IN AMERICA ESSAY CONTEST

Contest consists of three categories: high school seniors, student currently attending an accredited post-secondary institution, and affiliated members attending an accredited post-secondary institution. Requirements: completed application form, 1,500-word essay, three references (one from a labor organization member). Three award levels in each category: 1st - $2,000; 2nd - $1,000; 3rd - $500. Must be a resident of Pennsylvania and a U.S. citizen.

Award: Prize for use in freshman, sophomore, junior, or senior years; not renewable. *Number:* 9. *Amount:* $500–$2000.

Eligibility Requirements: Applicant must be enrolled or expecting to enroll full-time at a two-year or four-year or technical institution or university and resident of Pennsylvania. Applicant or parent of applicant must be member of AFL-CIO. Available to U.S. citizens.

Application Requirements: Application, applicant must enter a contest, essay, references. *Deadline:* January 31.

Contact: Mr. Carl Dillinger, Education Director
Pennsylvania AFL-CIO
231 State Street
Harrisburg, PA 17101-1110
Phone: 717-231-2843
Fax: 717-238-8541
E-mail: cdillinger@paaflcio.org

PENNSYLVANIA FEDERATION OF DEMOCRATIC WOMEN, INC. http://www.pfdw.org

PENNSYLVANIA FEDERATION OF DEMOCRATIC WOMEN, INC. ANNUAL SCHOLARSHIP AWARDS

Scholarships for any female resident of Pennsylvania who is a student in the Junior class of an accredited college or university and is a registered Democrat. Applicants must possess a Democratic Party family background or be an active participant in activities of the Democratic Party.

Award: Scholarship for use in senior year; not renewable. *Number:* 5–6. *Amount:* $1000.

Eligibility Requirements: Applicant must be enrolled or expecting to enroll full-time at a four-year institution or university; female and resident of Pennsylvania. Applicant or parent of applicant must be member of Democratic Party.

Application Requirements: Application, essay, financial need analysis, references, transcript. *Deadline:* April 15.

Contact: Dr. Michele Bortner, PFDW President
Pennsylvania Federation of Democratic Women, Inc.
PO Box 86
York, PA 17405-0086
Phone: 717-845-3338
E-mail: bortner@suscom.net

PENNSYLVANIA YOUTH FOUNDATION http://www.pagrandlodge.org/pyf

PENNSYLVANIA YOUTH FOUNDATION SCHOLARSHIP

Grants for child, stepchild, grandchild, sibling, or dependent of a member in good standing of a Pennsylvania Masonic Lodge. Applicant must be high school graduate or high school senior who is pursuing a college education. Minimum GPA 3.0. Deadline March 15.

Award: Grant for use in freshman, sophomore, junior, or senior years; not renewable. *Number:* varies. *Amount:* $1000–$3000.

Eligibility Requirements: Applicant must be enrolled or expecting to enroll full-time at a two-year or four-year or technical institution or university and resident of Pennsylvania. Applicant or parent of applicant must be member of Freemasons. Applicant must have 3.0 GPA or higher. Available to U.S. citizens.

Application Requirements: Application, transcript. *Deadline:* March 15.

Contact: Executive Director, PA Youth Foundation
Pennsylvania Youth Foundation
1244 Bainbridge Road
Elizabethtown, PA 17022
E-mail: pyf@pagrandlodge.org

PHI KAPPA TAU FOUNDATION http://www.phikappatau.org/

PHI KAPPA TAU FOUNDATION SCHOLARSHIPS

Scholarship program is based on academic performance, chapter leadership, campus activities, community service, and recommendation letters. Candidates must be initiated members of Phi Kappa Tau Fraternity in good standing.

Award: Scholarship for use in sophomore, junior, senior, graduate, or postgraduate years; not renewable. *Number:* 20–25. *Amount:* $1000–$2250.

Eligibility Requirements: Applicant must be enrolled or expecting to enroll full or part-time at a four-year institution or university and male. Applicant must have 3.0 GPA or higher. Available to U.S. and non-U.S. citizens.

Application Requirements: Application, essay, photo, resume, references, transcript, chapter leadership. *Deadline:* April 1.

Contact: Bethany Deines, Director of Development
Phi Kappa Tau Foundation
5221 Morning Sun Road
Oxford, OH 45056
Phone: 513-523-4193
Fax: 513-524-4812
E-mail: badeines@phikappatau.org

PHI KAPPA THETA NATIONAL FOUNDATION http://www.phikaps.org

PHI KAPPA THETA NATIONAL FOUNDATION AWARD

Award for members of Phi Kappa Theta fraternity. To support education and opportunities for leadership of members in need. Deadline: April 30.

Award: Scholarship for use in sophomore, junior, or senior years; renewable. *Number:* 1–8. *Amount:* $250–$1500.

Eligibility Requirements: Applicant must be enrolled or expecting to enroll at a four-year institution and male. Available to U.S. and non-U.S. citizens.

Application Requirements: Application, transcript. *Deadline:* April 30.

Contact: Maria Mandel, Director of Development
Phi Kappa Theta National Foundation
9640 North Augusta Drive, Suite 420
Carmel, IN 46032-9602
Phone: 317-872-9934
Fax: 317-879-1889
E-mail: maria@phikaps.org

PHI SIGMA PI NATIONAL HONOR FRATERNITY http://www.phisigmapi.org

RICHARD CECIL TODD AND CLAUDA PENNOCK TODD TRIPOD SCHOLARSHIP

The purpose of this scholarship is to promote the future academic opportunity of brothers (members) of Phi Sigma Pi National Honor Fraternity who have excelled in embodying the ideals of scholarship, leadership, and fellowship. One-time award for full-time student, sophomore level or higher, with minimum 3.0 GPA.

Award: Scholarship for use in sophomore, junior, senior, graduate, or postgraduate years; not renewable. *Number:* 1. *Amount:* $1500.

Eligibility Requirements: Applicant must be enrolled or expecting to enroll full-time at a four-year institution or university. Applicant must have 3.0 GPA or higher. Available to U.S. and non-U.S. citizens.

Application Requirements: Application, autobiography, essay, references, transcript. *Deadline:* April 15.

Contact: Suzanne Schaffer, Executive Director
Phi Sigma Pi National Honor Fraternity
2119 Ambassador Circle
Lancaster, PA 17603
Phone: 717-299-4710
Fax: 717-390-3054
E-mail: sschaffer@phisigmapi.org

PONY OF THE AMERICAS CLUB http://www.poac.org

PONY OF THE AMERICAS SCHOLARSHIP

Two to four renewable awards that may be used for any year or any institution but must be for full-time undergraduate study. Application and transcript required. Deadline: June 1. Award restricted to those who have interest in animal or agricultural competition and active involvement in Pony of the Americas.

Award: Scholarship for use in freshman, sophomore, junior, or senior years; renewable. *Number:* 2–4. *Amount:* $500–$1000.

Eligibility Requirements: Applicant must be enrolled or expecting to enroll full-time at a two-year or four-year or technical institution or university and must have an interest in animal/agricultural competition. Applicant or parent of applicant must be member of Pony of the Americas Club. Available to U.S. and non-U.S. citizens.

Application Requirements: Application, autobiography, essay, transcript. *Deadline:* June 1.

Contact: Scholarship Endowment Fund
Pony of the Americas Club
5240 Elmwood Avenue
Indianapolis, IN 46203

PROFESSIONAL BOWLERS ASSOCIATION http://www.pba.com

PROFESSIONAL BOWLERS ASSOCIATION BILLY WELU MEMORIAL SCHOLARSHIP

One-time award available to a currently enrolled student who demonstrates outstanding academic and bowling achievement. Must be a member of YABA, WIBC, or ABC. Must have minimum 2.5 GPA.

Award: Scholarship for use in freshman, sophomore, junior, or senior years; not renewable. *Number:* 1. *Amount:* $1000.

Eligibility Requirements: Applicant must be enrolled or expecting to enroll full or part-time at an institution or university and must have an interest in bowling. Applicant or parent of applicant must be member of Young American Bowling Alliance. Applicant must have 2.5 GPA or higher.

Application Requirements: Application, essay, references, transcript. *Deadline:* May 31.

Contact: Bowling Scholarship Administrator
Professional Bowlers Association
719 Second Avenue, Suite 701
Seattle, WA 98104
Phone: 206-332-9688
Fax: 206-332-9722

PROFESSIONAL HORSEMEN'S SCHOLARSHIP FUND, INC. http://www.nationalpha.com/

PROFESSIONAL HORSEMEN'S SCHOLARSHIP FUND

Award for members of Professional Horsemen Association. Applicants must reapply after first year, for additional funds. Children of members are also eligible. Applicants must be full-time students attending a two- or four-year college or institution. Financial need is considered.

Award: Scholarship for use in freshman, sophomore, junior, senior, or graduate years; not renewable. *Number:* 8. *Amount:* $1000–$1500.

Eligibility Requirements: Applicant must be enrolled or expecting to enroll full-time at a two-year or four-year or technical institution or university. Applicant or parent of applicant must be member of Professional Horsemen Association. Available to U.S. citizens.

Application Requirements: Application, autobiography, financial need analysis, references, transcript. *Deadline:* July 1.

Contact: Professional Horsemen's Scholarship Fund, Inc.
204 Old Sleepy Hollow Road
Pleasantville, NY 10570

PROJECT BEST SCHOLARSHIP FUND http://projectbest.com

PROJECT BEST SCHOLARSHIP

Awards for employees or children or spouses of employees working for a company or labor union in the construction industry that is affiliated with Project BEST. Must be a resident of West Virginia, Pennsylvania, or Ohio and attend a West Virginia or Ohio postsecondary institution. Must be a U.S. citizen. One-time award of $1000 or $2000.

Award: Scholarship for use in freshman, sophomore, junior, senior, or graduate years; not renewable. *Number:* 11–22. *Amount:* $1000–$2000.

Eligibility Requirements: Applicant must be enrolled or expecting to enroll full-time at a two-year or four-year institution or university; resident of Ohio, Pennsylvania, or West Virginia and studying in Ohio or West Virginia. Applicant or parent of applicant must be member of AFL-CIO. Applicant or parent of applicant must have employment or volunteer experience in construction. Available to U.S. citizens.

Application Requirements: Application. *Deadline:* Continuous.

Contact: Mary Jo Klempa, Director
Project BEST Scholarship Fund
21 Armory Drive
Wheeling, WV 26003
Phone: 304-242-0520
Fax: 304-242-7261
E-mail: best2003@swave.net

RECORDING FOR THE BLIND & DYSLEXIC http://www.rfbd.org

MARION HUBER LEARNING THROUGH LISTENING AWARDS

One-time award presented to outstanding high school seniors with learning disabilities in recognition of extraordinary leadership, scholarship, enterprise, and service to others. Candidates must be registered with the Recording for the Blind & Dyslexic for at least one year prior to the filing date of February 21.

Award: Prize for use in freshman year; not renewable. *Number:* 6. *Amount:* $2000–$6000.

Eligibility Requirements: Applicant must be high school student; planning to enroll or expecting to enroll full-time at a two-year or four-year or technical institution or university and must have an interest in leadership. Applicant or parent of applicant must be member of Recording for the Blind and Dyslexic. Applicant or parent of applicant must have employment or volunteer experience in community service. Applicant must be learning disabled. Applicant must have 3.0 GPA or higher. Available to U.S. citizens.

Application Requirements: Application, essay, references, transcript. *Deadline:* February 21.

Contact: Public Affairs Office
Recording for the Blind & Dyslexic
20 Roszel Road
Princeton, NJ 08540-5443
Phone: 609-520-3044
Fax: 609-520-7990

MARY P. OENSLAGER SCHOLASTIC ACHIEVEMENT AWARDS

Awards for legally blind college seniors, awarded on basis of leadership, scholarship, enterprise, and service to others. Candidates must be registered with Recording for the Blind & Dyslexic for at least one year prior to filing date of February 21 and have an overall GPA of 3.0 or equivalent. Applicants need not plan to continue their education beyond a bachelor's degree.

Award: Prize for use in senior year; not renewable. *Number:* 9. *Amount:* $1000–$6000.

Eligibility Requirements: Applicant must be enrolled or expecting to enroll full-time at a four-year institution or university and must have an interest in leadership. Applicant or parent of applicant must be member of Recording for the Blind and Dyslexic. Applicant or parent of applicant must have employment or volunteer experience in community service. Applicant must be visually impaired. Applicant must have 3.0 GPA or higher. Available to U.S. citizens.

Application Requirements: Application, essay, references, transcript. *Deadline:* February 21.

Contact: Public Affairs Office
Recording for the Blind & Dyslexic
20 Roszel Road
Princeton, NJ 08540-5443
Phone: 866-520-3044
Fax: 609-520-7990

RESERVE OFFICERS ASSOCIATION OF THE US

http://www.roa.org

HENRY J. REILLY MEMORIAL SCHOLARSHIP-HIGH SCHOOL SENIORS AND FIRST YEAR FRESHMEN

Award for high school seniors or college freshmen who are children or grandchildren of active members of the Reserve Officers Association. Must demonstrate leadership, have minimum 3.0 GPA and 1250 on the SAT. One-time award of $500. Must submit sponsor verification. College freshmen must submit college transcript. Must be U.S. citizen.

Award: Scholarship for use in freshman, sophomore, or junior years; not renewable. *Number:* 25–50. *Amount:* $500.

Eligibility Requirements: Applicant must be enrolled or expecting to enroll full-time at a four-year institution or university and must have an interest in leadership. Applicant or parent of applicant must be member of Reserve Officers Association. Applicant must have 3.0 GPA or higher. Available to U.S. citizens. Applicant or parent must meet one or more of the following requirements: general military experience; retired from active duty; disabled or killed as a result of military service; prisoner of war; or missing in action.

Application Requirements: Application, essay, test scores, transcript, sponsor verification. *Deadline:* April 10.

Contact: Mrs. Mickey Hagen, Coordinator of Applications
Reserve Officers Association of the US
1 Constitution Avenue, NE
Washington, DC 20002-5655
Phone: 202-479-2200
Fax: 202-479-0416
E-mail: mhagen@roa.org

HENRY J. REILLY MEMORIAL UNDERGRADUATE SCHOLARSHIP PROGRAM FOR COLLEGE ATTENDEES

Award for members and children or grandchildren of members of the Reserve Officers Association or its Auxiliary. Must be 26 years old or younger and enrolled at an accredited four-year institution. Must submit sponsor verification. One-time award of $500. Minimum 3.0 GPA required. Submit SAT or ACT scores; contact for score requirements. Must be U.S. citizen.

Award: Scholarship for use in sophomore, junior, or senior years; not renewable. *Number:* 25–35. *Amount:* $500.

Eligibility Requirements: Applicant must be age 26 or under and enrolled or expecting to enroll full-time at a four-year institution or university. Applicant or parent of applicant must be member of Reserve Officers Association. Applicant must have 3.0 GPA or higher. Available to U.S. citizens. Applicant or parent must meet one or more of the following requirements: general military experience; retired from active duty; disabled or killed as a result of military service; prisoner of war; or missing in action.

Application Requirements: Application, essay, test scores, transcript, sponsor verification. *Deadline:* April 10.

Contact: Mrs. Mickey Hagen, Coordinator of Applications
Reserve Officers Association of the US
1 Constitution Avenue, NE
Washington, DC 20002-5655
Phone: 202-479-2200
Fax: 202-479-0416
E-mail: mhagen@roa.org

SCREEN ACTORS GUILD FOUNDATION

http://www.sagfoundation.org

SCREEN ACTORS GUILD FOUNDATION/JOHN L. DALES SCHOLARSHIP (TRANSITIONAL)

Award for Guild members and children of members. The member applying must have been a member in good standing for ten years. Member's lifetime gross income in Guild's jurisdiction must total $30,000.

Award: Scholarship for use in freshman, sophomore, junior, senior, or graduate years; not renewable. *Number:* varies. *Amount:* $3000–$5000.

Eligibility Requirements: Applicant must be enrolled or expecting to enroll full-time at a two-year or four-year institution or university. Applicant or parent of applicant must be member of Screen Actors' Guild. Applicant or parent of applicant must have employment or volunteer experience in designated career field. Available to U.S. citizens.

Application Requirements: Application, essay, financial need analysis, resume, references, test scores, transcript. *Deadline:* March 15.

Contact: Davidson Lloyd, Administrative Director
Screen Actors Guild Foundation
5757 Wilshire Boulevard, 7th Floor
Los Angeles, CA 90036-3600
Phone: 323-549-6649
Fax: 323-549-6710
E-mail: dlloyd@sag.org

SCREEN ACTORS GUILD FOUNDATION/JOHN L. DALES SCHOLARSHIP FUND (STANDARD)

Award for Guild members and children of members. The member applying must have been a member in good standing for five years and have $30,000 lifetime gross income in the Guild's jurisdiction. The parent of an applicant must have been a member in good standing for ten years and have a $60,000 lifetime gross income in the Guild's jurisdiction.

Award: Scholarship for use in freshman, sophomore, junior, senior, or graduate years; not renewable. *Number:* varies. *Amount:* $3000–$4000.

Eligibility Requirements: Applicant must be enrolled or expecting to enroll full-time at a two-year or four-year institution or university. Applicant or parent of applicant must be member of Screen Actors' Guild. Applicant or parent of applicant must have employment or volunteer experience in designated career field. Available to U.S. citizens.

Application Requirements: Application, essay, financial need analysis, resume, references, test scores, transcript. *Deadline:* March 15.

Contact: Davidson Lloyd, Administrative Director
Screen Actors Guild Foundation
5757 Wilshire Boulevard, 7th Floor
Los Angeles, CA 90036-3600
Phone: 323-549-6649
Fax: 323-549-6710
E-mail: dlloyd@sag.org

SECOND BOMBARDMENT ASSOCIATION

SECOND BOMBARDMENT ASSOCIATION SCHOLARSHIP

One-time award for children of members of the Second Bombardment Wing of the U.S. Air Force. Write for more information. Must attend a four-year postsecondary institution. Program is administered by Air Force Aid in Washington, D.C. Documentation must be submitted to them.

Award: Scholarship for use in freshman, sophomore, junior, senior, graduate, or postgraduate years; renewable. *Number:* 2. *Amount:* $1000.

Eligibility Requirements: Applicant must be enrolled or expecting to enroll full-time at a four-year institution or university. Applicant or

Second Bombardment Association (continued)

parent of applicant must be member of Second Bombardment Association. Available to U.S. and non-U.S. citizens. Applicant or parent must meet one or more of the following requirements: Air Force experience; retired from active duty; disabled or killed as a result of military service; prisoner of war; or missing in action.

Application Requirements: Application. *Deadline:* varies.

Contact: Air Force Aid Society
Second Bombardment Association
1745 Jefferson Davis Highway, Suite 202
Arlington, VA 22202-3410

SERVICE EMPLOYEES INTERNATIONAL UNION - CALIFORNIA STATE COUNCIL OF SERVICE EMPLOYEES http://www.seiu.org

CHARLES HARDY MEMORIAL SCHOLARSHIP AWARDS

Renewable $1000 award for California residents. For full-time study only. Deadline is in mid-March. Must be SEIU members or children of members. Membership must be for three continuous years as of September 1, 2001. For recent affiliates to SEIU, you must have been a member of your association for three years as of September 1, 2001. Download application at Web site (http://www.seiu.org) and take online union history test (open book).

Award: Scholarship for use in freshman year; renewable. *Number:* 1–4. *Amount:* $1000.

Eligibility Requirements: Applicant must be enrolled or expecting to enroll full-time at a two-year or four-year institution or university and resident of California. Applicant or parent of applicant must be member of Service Employees International Union. Applicant or parent of applicant must have employment or volunteer experience in designated career field. Available to U.S. citizens.

Application Requirements: Application, online test. *Deadline:* March 15.

Contact: SEIU-Scholarship Committee
Service Employees International Union - California State Council of Service Employees
1313 L Street NW
Washington, DC 20005
Phone: 800-846-1561

SIGMA CHI FOUNDATION http://www.sigmachi.org

GENERAL SCHOLARSHIP GRANTS

General scholarship grants available to qualified undergraduate brothers of Sigma Chi fraternity. All applicants must have completed three semesters (or four quarters) of undergraduate study to be considered for current year awards. Funds are available for tuition/fees payments only.

Award: Scholarship for use in sophomore, junior, or senior years; not renewable. *Number:* varies. *Amount:* $1000.

Eligibility Requirements: Applicant must be enrolled or expecting to enroll at an institution or university and male. Applicant must have 3.0 GPA or higher.

Application Requirements: Application, references, transcript. *Deadline:* May 1.

Contact: Chris Mashio, Associate Director of Education
Sigma Chi Foundation
1714 Hinman Avenue
Evanston, IL 60204
Phone: 847-869-3655
Fax: 847-869-4906
E-mail: chris.mashio@sigmachi.org

ORDER OF THE SCROLL AWARD

Awarded to undergraduates who have been nominated by their chapter mates for the outstanding direction of the chapter's educational program. Past winners were awarded due to their commitment to improving their chapter's academic performance and scholarship programming. Must be member of Sigma Chi. Funds are available for tuition/fees payments only.

Award: Prize for use in sophomore, junior, or senior years; not renewable. *Number:* varies. *Amount:* up to $750.

Eligibility Requirements: Applicant must be enrolled or expecting to enroll at an institution or university and male. Applicant must have 3.0 GPA or higher.

Application Requirements: Application, references, transcript. *Deadline:* May 1.

Contact: Chris Mashio, Associate Director of Education
Sigma Chi Foundation
1714 Hinman Avenue
Evanston, IL 60204
Phone: 847-869-3655
Fax: 847-869-4906
E-mail: chris.mashio@sigmachi.org

SLOVAK GYMNASTIC UNION SOKOL, USA

SLOVAK GYMNASTIC UNION SOKOL, USA/MILAN GETTING SCHOLARSHIP

Available to members of SOKOL, U.S.A who have been in good standing for at least three years. Must have plans to attend college. Renewable for a maximum of four years, based upon academic achievement. Minimum GPA 2.5 required.

Award: Scholarship for use in freshman, sophomore, junior, or senior years; renewable. *Number:* 4–8. *Amount:* $500.

Eligibility Requirements: Applicant must be high school student and planning to enroll or expecting to enroll full-time at a four-year institution. Applicant or parent of applicant must be member of SOKOL, USA. Applicant must have 2.5 GPA or higher.

Application Requirements: Application, references, transcript. *Deadline:* April 15.

Contact: Slovak Gymnastic Union SOKOL, USA
276 Prospect Street, Box 189
East Orange, NJ 07019

SOCIETY OF PHYSICS STUDENTS http://www.spsnational.org

SOCIETY OF PHYSICS STUDENTS OUTSTANDING STUDENT IN RESEARCH

$500 stipend, plus expenses paid to present research (undergraduate) at the International Conference of Physics Students; location is abroad, varies each year. $500 is also awarded to Society of Physics Students chapter. Available to members of the Society of Physics Students. More details visit: http://www.spsnational.org

Award: Prize for use in sophomore, junior, or senior years; not renewable. *Number:* 1–2. *Amount:* $1500–$2500.

Eligibility Requirements: Applicant must be enrolled or expecting to enroll full-time at a two-year or four-year institution or university. Applicant or parent of applicant must be member of Society of Physics Students. Available to U.S. and non-U.S. citizens.

Application Requirements: Application, references, abstract. *Deadline:* April 15.

Contact: SPS Secretary
Society of Physics Students
One Physics Ellipse
College Park, MD 20740
Phone: 301-209-3007
Fax: 301-209-0839
E-mail: sps@aip.org

SOCIETY OF PHYSICS STUDENTS PEGGY DIXON 2-YEAR COLLEGE SCHOLARSHIP

Scholarship available to Society of Physics Students (SPS) members. Award based on scholarship and/or need, and SPS participation. For more details visit Web site: http://www.spsnational.org

Award: Scholarship for use in junior year; not renewable. *Number:* 1. *Amount:* $1000.

Eligibility Requirements: Applicant must be enrolled or expecting to enroll at an institution or university. Applicant or parent of applicant must be member of Society of Physics Students.

Application Requirements: Application, financial need analysis, transcript. *Deadline:* February 15.

Contact: SPS Secretary
Society of Physics Students
1 Physics Ellipse
College Park, MD 20740-3843
Phone: 301-209-3007
Fax: 301-209-0839
E-mail: sps@aip.org

SOCIETY OF PHYSICS STUDENTS SCHOLARSHIPS

Scholarships available to Society of Physics Students (SPS) members. Award based on scholarship and/or need, and SPS participation. For more details visit: http://www.spsnational.org.

Award: Scholarship for use in sophomore, junior, or senior years; not renewable. *Number:* 17–22. *Amount:* $1000–$4000.

Eligibility Requirements: Applicant must be enrolled or expecting to enroll full-time at a four-year institution. Applicant or parent of applicant must be member of Society of Physics Students. Available to U.S. and non-U.S. citizens.

Application Requirements: Application, references, transcript. *Deadline:* February 15.

Contact: SPS Scholarship Committee
Society of Physics Students
One Physics Ellipse
College Park, MD 20740
Phone: 301-209-3007
Fax: 301-209-0839
E-mail: sps@aip.org

SONS OF NORWAY FOUNDATION http://www.sofn.com

ASTRID G. CATES AND MYRTLE BEINHAUER SCHOLARSHIP FUNDS

Merit and need-based award available to students ages 17 to 22 who are members, children, or grandchildren of members of the Sons of Norway. School transcript required. Financial need is key criterion for award. Must have minimum 3.0 GPA. One-time award of $500 to $750.

Award: Scholarship for use in freshman, sophomore, junior, or senior years; not renewable. *Number:* 6. *Amount:* $500–$750.

Eligibility Requirements: Applicant must be of Norwegian heritage; age 17-22 and enrolled or expecting to enroll at a two-year or four-year or technical institution or university. Applicant or parent of applicant must be member of Mutual Benefit Society. Applicant must have 3.0 GPA or higher. Available to U.S. citizens.

Application Requirements: Application, essay, financial need analysis, references, self-addressed stamped envelope, test scores, transcript. *Deadline:* March 1.

Contact: Administrative Director
Sons of Norway Foundation
1455 West Lake Street
Minneapolis, MN 55408-2666
Phone: 612-827-3611
Fax: 612-827-0658
E-mail: colson@sofn.com

TENNESSEE EDUCATION ASSOCIATION http://www.teateachers.org

TEA DON SAHLI-KATHY WOODALL SONS AND DAUGHTERS SCHOLARSHIP

This scholarship is available to a TEA member's child who is a high school senior, undergraduate or graduate student, and is planning to enroll, or is already enrolled, in a Tennessee college.

Award: Scholarship for use in freshman, sophomore, junior, senior, or graduate years; not renewable. *Number:* 1. *Amount:* $1000.

Eligibility Requirements: Applicant must be enrolled or expecting to enroll full-time at a four-year institution or university; resident of Tennessee and studying in Tennessee. Applicant or parent of applicant must be member of Tennessee Education Association. Applicant must have 3.0 GPA or higher. Available to U.S. citizens.

Application Requirements: Application, essay, financial need analysis, references, transcript, statement of income. *Deadline:* March 1.

Contact: Jeanette DeMain, Administrative Assistant
Tennessee Education Association
801 Second Avenue North
Nashville, TN 37201-1099
Phone: 615-242-8392
Fax: 615-259-4581
E-mail: jdemain@tea.nea.org

TEXAS AFL-CIO http://www.aflcio.org

TEXAS AFL-CIO SCHOLARSHIP PROGRAM

Award for sons or daughters of affiliated union members. Selection by testing or interview process. Fifteen one-time awards of $1000. Deadline: January 31. Applicant must be a graduating high school senior and Texas resident.

Award: Scholarship for use in freshman year; not renewable. *Number:* 15. *Amount:* $1000.

Eligibility Requirements: Applicant must be high school student; planning to enroll or expecting to enroll full-time at a two-year or four-year or technical institution or university and resident of Texas. Applicant or parent of applicant must be member of AFL-CIO.

Application Requirements: Application, essay, financial need analysis, interview, photo, test scores, transcript. *Deadline:* January 31.

Contact: Edward Sills, Director of Communications
Texas AFL-CIO
PO Box 12727
Education Department
Austin, TX 78711
Phone: 512-477-6195
E-mail: ed@texasflcio.org

TKE EDUCATIONAL FOUNDATION http://www.tkefoundation.org

ALL-TKE ACADEMIC TEAM RECOGNITION AND JOHN A. COURSON TOP SCHOLAR AWARD

One-time award given to full-time male students who are active members of Tau Kappa Epsilon with junior or senior standing. Candidates should be able to maintain excellent academic standing while making positive contributions to chapter, campus, and community. Top Scholar Award will be selected from All-TKE academic team and receive $1400 scholarship. Recent head and shoulders photograph must be submitted with application.

Award: Scholarship for use in junior or senior years; not renewable. *Number:* 10. *Amount:* $200–$1400.

Eligibility Requirements: Applicant must be enrolled or expecting to enroll full-time at a four-year institution or university; male and must have an interest in leadership. Applicant must have 3.5 GPA or higher. Available to U.S. and non-U.S. citizens.

Application Requirements: Application, photo, transcript. *Deadline:* February 18.

Contact: Tim Taschwer, President/CEO
TKE Educational Foundation
8645 Founders Road
Indianapolis, IN 46268-1393
Phone: 317-872-6533
Fax: 317-875-8353
E-mail: ttaschwe@tkehq.org

CANADIAN TKE SCHOLARSHIP

This scholarship is available to an undergraduate Teke who has been initiated into a Canadian TKE chapter and has demonstrated leadership qualities within the Fraternity and the campus community, while maintaining a good academic record.

Award: Scholarship for use in freshman, sophomore, junior, or senior years; not renewable. *Number:* 1. *Amount:* $200.

Eligibility Requirements: Applicant must be enrolled or expecting to enroll full-time at a four-year institution or university; male and must have an interest in leadership. Available to U.S. and non-U.S. citizens.

TKE Educational Foundation (continued)

Application Requirements: Application, essay, photo, transcript. *Deadline:* May 15.

Contact: Tim Taschwer, President/CEO
TKE Educational Foundation
8645 Founders Road
Indianapolis, IN 46268-1393
Phone: 317-872-6533
Fax: 317-875-8353
E-mail: tef@tkehq.org

CHARLES WALGREEN, JR. SCHOLARSHIP

Award is given in recognition of outstanding leadership, as demonstrated by an individual's activities and accomplishments within the chapter, on campus and in the community, while maintaining a good academic record. All initiated undergraduate members of TKE, in good standing with a cumulative GPA of 3.0 or higher, are eligible to apply.

Award: Scholarship for use in freshman, sophomore, junior, or senior years; not renewable. *Number:* 1. *Amount:* $950.

Eligibility Requirements: Applicant must be enrolled or expecting to enroll full-time at a four-year institution or university; male and must have an interest in leadership. Applicant must have 3.0 GPA or higher. Available to U.S. and non-U.S. citizens.

Application Requirements: Application, essay, photo, transcript. *Deadline:* May 15.

Contact: Tim Taschwer, President/CEO
TKE Educational Foundation
8645 Founders Road
Indianapolis, IN 46268-1393
Phone: 317-872-6533
Fax: 317-875-8353
E-mail: tef@tkehq.org

DONALD A. FISHER MEMORIAL SCHOLARSHIP

One-time award of $750 given to an undergraduate member of Tau Kappa Epsilon who has demonstrated leadership ability within his chapter, campus, or community. Must be a full-time student in good standing with a GPA of 2.5 or higher. Recent head and shoulders photograph must be submitted with application.

Award: Scholarship for use in freshman, sophomore, junior, or senior years; not renewable. *Number:* 1. *Amount:* $750.

Eligibility Requirements: Applicant must be enrolled or expecting to enroll full-time at a four-year institution or university; male and must have an interest in leadership. Applicant must have 2.5 GPA or higher. Available to U.S. and non-U.S. citizens.

Application Requirements: Application, essay, photo, transcript. *Deadline:* May 15.

Contact: Tim Taschwer, President/CEO
TKE Educational Foundation
8645 Founders Road
Indianapolis, IN 46268-1393
Phone: 317-872-6533
Fax: 317-875-8353
E-mail: tef@tkehq.org

DWAYNE R. WOERPEL MEMORIAL LEADERSHIP AWARD

An award available to an undergraduate Tau Kappa Epsilon member who is a full-time student and graduate of the TKE Leadership Academy. Applicants should have demonstrated leadership qualities in service to the Fraternity and to the civic and religious community while maintaining a 3.0 GPA or higher.

Award: Scholarship for use in freshman, sophomore, junior, or senior years; not renewable. *Number:* 1. *Amount:* $250.

Eligibility Requirements: Applicant must be enrolled or expecting to enroll full-time at a four-year institution or university; male and must have an interest in leadership. Applicant must have 3.0 GPA or higher. Available to U.S. and non-U.S. citizens.

Application Requirements: Application, essay, photo, transcript. *Deadline:* May 15.

Contact: Tim Taschwer, President/CEO
TKE Educational Foundation
8645 Founders Road
Indianapolis, IN 46268-1393
Phone: 317-872-6533
Fax: 317-875-8353
E-mail: tef@tkehq.org

ELMER AND DORIS SCHMITZ SR. MEMORIAL SCHOLARSHIP

One-time award of $250 given to an undergraduate member of Tau Kappa Epsilon from Wisconsin who has demonstrated leadership ability within his chapter, campus, or community. Must be a full-time student in good standing with a GPA of 2.5 or higher. Recent head and shoulders photograph must be submitted with application.

Award: Scholarship for use in freshman, sophomore, junior, or senior years; not renewable. *Number:* 1. *Amount:* $250.

Eligibility Requirements: Applicant must be enrolled or expecting to enroll full-time at a four-year institution or university; male; resident of Wisconsin and must have an interest in leadership. Applicant must have 2.5 GPA or higher. Available to U.S. and non-U.S. citizens.

Application Requirements: Application, essay, photo, transcript. *Deadline:* May 15.

Contact: Tim Taschwer, President/CEO
TKE Educational Foundation
8645 Founders Road
Indianapolis, IN 46268-1393
Phone: 317-872-6533
Fax: 317-875-8353
E-mail: tef@tkehq.org

EUGENE C. BEACH MEMORIAL SCHOLARSHIP

One-time award of $250 given to an undergraduate member of Tau Kappa Epsilon who has demonstrated leadership ability within his chapter, campus, or community. Must be a full-time student in good standing with a GPA of 2.5 or higher. Recent head and shoulders photograph must be submitted with application.

Award: Scholarship for use in freshman, sophomore, junior, or senior years; not renewable. *Number:* 1. *Amount:* $250.

Eligibility Requirements: Applicant must be enrolled or expecting to enroll full-time at a four-year institution or university; male and must have an interest in leadership. Applicant must have 2.5 GPA or higher. Available to U.S. and non-U.S. citizens.

Application Requirements: Application, essay, photo, transcript. *Deadline:* May 15.

Contact: Tim Taschwer, President/CEO
TKE Educational Foundation
8645 Founders Road
Indianapolis, IN 46268-1393
Phone: 317-872-6533
Fax: 317-875-8353
E-mail: tef@tkehq.org

J. RUSSEL SALSBURY MEMORIAL SCHOLARSHIP

One-time award of $250 given to an undergraduate member of Tau Kappa Epsilon who has demonstrated leadership ability within his chapter, campus, or community. Must be a full-time student in good standing with a GPA of 2.5 or higher. Recent head and shoulders photograph must be submitted with application.

Award: Scholarship for use in freshman, sophomore, junior, or senior years; not renewable. *Number:* 1. *Amount:* $250.

Eligibility Requirements: Applicant must be enrolled or expecting to enroll full-time at a four-year institution or university; male and must have an interest in leadership. Applicant must have 2.5 GPA or higher. Available to U.S. and non-U.S. citizens.

Application Requirements: Application, essay, photo, transcript. *Deadline:* May 15.

Contact: Tim Taschwer, President/CEO
TKE Educational Foundation
8645 Founders Road
Indianapolis, IN 46268-1393
Phone: 317-872-6533
Fax: 317-875-8353
E-mail: tef@tkehq.org

MICHAEL J. MORIN MEMORIAL SCHOLARSHIP

One-time award for any undergraduate member of Tau Kappa Epsilon who has demonstrated leadership capacity within his chapter, on campus or the community. Must have a cumulative GPA of 2.5 or higher and be a full-time student in good standing.

Award: Scholarship for use in freshman, sophomore, junior, or senior years; not renewable. *Number:* 1. *Amount:* $250.

Eligibility Requirements: Applicant must be enrolled or expecting to enroll full-time at a four-year institution or university; male and must have an interest in leadership. Applicant must have 2.5 GPA or higher. Available to U.S. and non-U.S. citizens.

Application Requirements: Application, essay, photo, transcript. *Deadline:* May 15.

Contact: Tim Taschwer, President/CEO
TKE Educational Foundation
8645 Founders Road
Indianapolis, IN 46268-1393
Phone: 317-872-6533
Fax: 317-875-8353
E-mail: tef@tkehq.org

MILES GRAY MEMORIAL SCHOLARSHIP

One-time award of $250 given to an undergraduate member of Tau Kappa Epsilon who has demonstrated leadership ability within his chapter, campus, or community. Must be a full-time student in good standing with a GPA of 2.5 or higher. Recent head and shoulders photograph must be submitted with application.

Award: Scholarship for use in freshman, sophomore, junior, or senior years; not renewable. *Number:* 1. *Amount:* $250.

Eligibility Requirements: Applicant must be enrolled or expecting to enroll full-time at a four-year institution or university; male and must have an interest in leadership. Applicant must have 2.5 GPA or higher. Available to U.S. and non-U.S. citizens.

Application Requirements: Application, essay, photo, transcript. *Deadline:* February 18.

Contact: Tim Taschwer, President/CEO
TKE Educational Foundation
8645 Founders Road
Indianapolis, IN 46268-1393
Phone: 317-872-6533
Fax: 317-875-8353
E-mail: tef@tkehq.org

RONALD REAGAN LEADERSHIP AWARD

One-time award of $1700 for initiated undergraduate member of Tau Kappa Epsilon, given in recognition of outstanding leadership, as demonstrated by activities and accomplishments within chapter, on campus, and in community. Must be a full-time student in good standing. Recent head and shoulders photograph must be submitted with application. Recipient required to attend official fraternity function to accept award.

Award: Scholarship for use in freshman, sophomore, junior, or senior years; not renewable. *Number:* 1. *Amount:* $1700.

Eligibility Requirements: Applicant must be enrolled or expecting to enroll full-time at a four-year institution or university; male and must have an interest in leadership. Applicant must have 3.0 GPA or higher. Available to U.S. and non-U.S. citizens.

Application Requirements: Application, essay, photo, transcript. *Deadline:* May 15.

Contact: Tim Taschwer, President/CEO
TKE Educational Foundation
8645 Founders Road
Indianapolis, IN 46268-1393
Phone: 317-872-6533
Fax: 317-875-8353
E-mail: tef@tkehq.org

T.J. SCHMITZ SCHOLARSHIP

Award of $350 for an initiated undergraduate member of TKE. Must be a full-time student in good standing with a minimum cumulative GPA of 2.5. Must have demonstrated leadership capability within chapter, campus, or community. Application deadline: May 15.

Award: Scholarship for use in freshman, sophomore, junior, or senior years; not renewable. *Number:* 1. *Amount:* $350.

Eligibility Requirements: Applicant must be enrolled or expecting to enroll full-time at an institution or university; male and must have an interest in leadership. Applicant must have 2.5 GPA or higher. Available to U.S. and non-U.S. citizens.

Application Requirements: Application, essay, photo, transcript. *Deadline:* May 15.

Contact: Tim Taschwer, President/CEO
TKE Educational Foundation
8645 Founders Road
Indianapolis, IN 46268-1393
Phone: 317-872-6533
Fax: 317-875-8353
E-mail: tef@tkehq.org

WALLACE MCCAULEY MEMORIAL SCHOLARSHIP

One-time $300 award to undergraduate member of Tau Kappa Epsilon with junior or senior standing. Must have demonstrated understanding of the importance of good alumni relations. Must have excelled in the development, promotion, and execution of programs which increase alumni contact, awareness, and participation in fraternity activities.

Award: Scholarship for use in junior or senior years; not renewable. *Number:* 1. *Amount:* $300.

Eligibility Requirements: Applicant must be enrolled or expecting to enroll full-time at a four-year institution or university; male and must have an interest in leadership. Available to U.S. and non-U.S. citizens.

Application Requirements: Application, essay, photo, transcript. *Deadline:* May 15.

Contact: Tim Taschwer, President/CEO
TKE Educational Foundation
8645 Founders Road
Indianapolis, IN 46268-1393
Phone: 317-872-6533
Fax: 317-875-8353
E-mail: tef@tkehq.org

WILLIAM V. MUSE SCHOLARSHIP

Award of $600 given to undergraduate member of Tau Kappa Epsilon who has completed at least 30 semester hours of course work. Applicant should demonstrate leadership within chapter and maintain 3.0 GPA. Preference given to members of Epsilon-Upsilon Chapter.

Award: Scholarship for use in junior or senior years; not renewable. *Number:* 1. *Amount:* $600.

Eligibility Requirements: Applicant must be enrolled or expecting to enroll full-time at a four-year institution or university; male and must have an interest in leadership. Applicant must have 3.0 GPA or higher. Available to U.S. and non-U.S. citizens.

TKE Educational Foundation (continued)

Application Requirements: Application, essay, photo, transcript. *Deadline:* May 15.

Contact: Tim Taschwer, President/CEO
TKE Educational Foundation
8645 Founders Road
Indianapolis, IN 46268-1393
Phone: 317-872-6533
Fax: 317-875-8353
E-mail: tef@tkehq.org

WILLIAM WILSON MEMORIAL SCHOLARSHIP

One-time award given to undergraduate member of Tau Kappa Epsilon with junior or senior standing. Must have demonstrated understanding of the importance of good alumni relations. Must have excelled in the development, promotion, and execution of programs which increase alumni contact, awareness, and participation in fraternity activities.

Award: Scholarship for use in junior or senior years; not renewable. *Number:* 1. *Amount:* $250.

Eligibility Requirements: Applicant must be enrolled or expecting to enroll full-time at a four-year institution or university; male and must have an interest in leadership. Available to U.S. and non-U.S. citizens.

Application Requirements: Application, essay, photo, transcript. *Deadline:* May 15.

Contact: Tim Taschwer, President/CEO
TKE Educational Foundation
8645 Founders Road
Indianapolis, IN 46268-1393
Phone: 317-872-6533
Fax: 317-875-8353
E-mail: tef@tkehq.org

UNION PLUS SCHOLARSHIP PROGRAM http://www.unionplus.org

UNION PLUS SCHOLARSHIP PROGRAM

One-time cash award for AFL-CIO union members, their spouses, or dependent children. Based upon academic achievement, character, leadership, career goals, social awareness, and financial need. Must be from Canada or U.S. including Puerto Rico. Members must download application from Web site http://www.unionplus.org. Applications are available from September 1 to January 15.

Award: Scholarship for use in freshman, sophomore, junior, or senior years; not renewable. *Number:* 110–130. *Amount:* $500–$4000.

Eligibility Requirements: Applicant must be enrolled or expecting to enroll full or part-time at a two-year or four-year or technical institution or university. Applicant or parent of applicant must be member of AFL-CIO. Available to U.S. and Canadian citizens.

Application Requirements: Application, essay, financial need analysis, references, test scores, transcript. *Deadline:* January 31.

Contact: See Web site for application and information.

UNITED COMMUNITY SERVICES FOR WORKING FAMILIES http://www.workingfamilies.com

RONALD LORAH MEMORIAL SCHOLARSHIP

One-time award available to a union member, spouse of a union member, or child of a union member. Must be a resident of Pennsylvania. Must submit essay that is clear, concise, persuasive and show an understanding of unions. Application deadline is July 23.

Award: Scholarship for use in freshman, sophomore, junior, or senior years; not renewable. *Number:* 1–1. *Amount:* $750–$1000.

Eligibility Requirements: Applicant must be enrolled or expecting to enroll full-time at a two-year or four-year or technical institution or university and resident of Pennsylvania. Applicant or parent of applicant must be member of AFL-CIO. Available to U.S. citizens.

Application Requirements: Application, essay, financial need analysis. *Deadline:* July 23.

Contact: Ruth Mathews, Executive Director
United Community Services for Working Families
116 North 5th Street
Reading, PA 19601
Phone: 610-374-3319
Fax: 610-374-6521
E-mail: ucswf1@enter.net

UNITED DAUGHTERS OF THE CONFEDERACY http://www.hqudc.org

ADMIRAL RAPHAEL SEMMES SCHOLARSHIP

Renewable award for undergraduate student who is a descendant of a Confederate soldier, sailor or marine. Must be enrolled in an accredited college or university and carry a minimum of 12 credit hours each semester. Minimum 3.0 GPA required. Submit letter of endorsement from sponsoring chapter of the United Daughters of the Confederacy. Please refer to Web site for further details: http://www.hqudc.org

Award: Scholarship for use in freshman, sophomore, junior, or senior years; renewable. *Number:* 1–2. *Amount:* $800–$1000.

Eligibility Requirements: Applicant must be enrolled or expecting to enroll full-time at a four-year institution or university. Applicant or parent of applicant must be member of United Daughters of the Confederacy. Applicant must have 3.0 GPA or higher. Available to U.S. citizens.

Application Requirements: Application, essay, financial need analysis, photo, references, self-addressed stamped envelope, transcript. *Deadline:* February 15.

Contact: Second Vice President General
United Daughters of the Confederacy
328 North Boulevard
Richmond, VA 23220-4057
Phone: 804-355-1636

BARBARA JACKSON SICHEL MEMORIAL SCHOLARSHIP

Renewable award for undergraduate student who is a descendant of a Confederate soldier, sailor or marine. Must be enrolled in an accredited college or university and carry a minimum of 12 credit hours each semester. Minimum of 3.0 GPA required. Submit a letter of endorsement from sponsoring Chapter of the United Daughters of the Confederacy. Please refer to Web site for further details: http://www.hqudc.org

Award: Scholarship for use in freshman, sophomore, junior, or senior years; renewable. *Number:* 1–2. *Amount:* $800–$1000.

Eligibility Requirements: Applicant must be enrolled or expecting to enroll full-time at a four-year institution or university. Applicant or parent of applicant must be member of United Daughters of the Confederacy. Applicant must have 3.0 GPA or higher. Available to U.S. citizens.

Application Requirements: Application, essay, financial need analysis, photo, references, self-addressed stamped envelope, transcript. *Deadline:* February 15.

Contact: Second Vice President General
United Daughters of the Confederacy
328 North Boulevard
Richmond, VA 23220-4057
Phone: 804-355-1636

CHARLOTTLE M. F. BENTLEY / NEW YORK CHAPTER 103 SCHOLARSHIP

Renewable award for undergraduate student who is a descendant of a Confederate soldier, sailor or marine. Must be enrolled in an accredited college or university and carry a minimum of 12 credit hours each semester. Minimum of 3.0 GPA required. Submit a letter of endorsement from sponsoring Chapter of the United Daughters of the Confederacy. Preference given to UDC and C of C members from New York. Please refer to Web site for further details: http://www.hqudc.org

Award: Scholarship for use in freshman, sophomore, junior, or senior years; renewable. *Number:* 1–2. *Amount:* $800–$1000.

Eligibility Requirements: Applicant must be enrolled or expecting to enroll full-time at a four-year institution or university. Applicant or parent of applicant must be member of United Daughters of the Confederacy. Applicant must have 3.0 GPA or higher. Available to U.S. citizens.

Application Requirements: Application, essay, financial need analysis, photo, references, self-addressed stamped envelope, transcript. *Deadline:* February 15.

Contact: Second Vice President General
United Daughters of the Confederacy
328 North Boulevard
Richmond, VA 23220-4057
Phone: 804-355-1636

CODY BACHMAN SCHOLARSHIP

Renewable award for undergraduate student who is a descendant of a Confederate soldier, sailor or marine. Must be enrolled in an accredited college or university and carry a minimum of 12 credit hours each semester. Minimum 3.0 GPA required. Submit letter of endorsement from sponsoring chapter of the United Daughters of the Confederacy. Please refer to Web site for further details: http://www.hqudc.org

Award: Scholarship for use in freshman, sophomore, junior, or senior years; renewable. *Number:* 1–2. *Amount:* $800–$1000.

Eligibility Requirements: Applicant must be enrolled or expecting to enroll full-time at a four-year institution or university. Applicant or parent of applicant must be member of United Daughters of the Confederacy. Applicant must have 3.0 GPA or higher. Available to U.S. citizens.

Application Requirements: Application, essay, financial need analysis, photo, references, self-addressed stamped envelope, transcript. *Deadline:* February 15.

Contact: Second Vice President General
United Daughters of the Confederacy
328 North Boulevard
Richmond, VA 23220-4057
Phone: 804-355-1636

CORA BELL WESLEY MEMORIAL SCHOLARSHIP

Renewable award for undergraduate student who is a descendant of a Confederate soldier, sailor or marine. Must be enrolled in an accredited college or university and carry a minimum of 12 credit hours each semester. Minimum 3.0 GPA required. Submit letter of endorsement from sponsoring chapter of the United Daughters of the Confederacy. Please refer to Web site for further details: http://www.hqudc.org

Award: Scholarship for use in freshman, sophomore, junior, or senior years; renewable. *Number:* 1–2. *Amount:* $800–$1000.

Eligibility Requirements: Applicant must be enrolled or expecting to enroll full-time at a four-year institution or university. Applicant or parent of applicant must be member of United Daughters of the Confederacy. Applicant must have 3.0 GPA or higher. Available to U.S. citizens.

Application Requirements: Application, essay, financial need analysis, photo, references, self-addressed stamped envelope, transcript. *Deadline:* February 15.

Contact: Second Vice President General
United Daughters of the Confederacy
328 North Boulevard
Richmond, VA 23220-4057
Phone: 804-355-1636

CORNELIA BRANCH STONE SCHOLARSHIP

Renewable award for undergraduate student who is a descendant of a Confederate soldier, sailor or marine. Must be enrolled in an accredited college or university and carry a minimum of 12 credit hours each semester. Minimum of 3.0 GPA required. Submit a letter of endorsement from sponsoring Chapter of the United Daughters of the Confederacy. Please refer to Web site for further details: http://www.hqudc.org

Award: Scholarship for use in freshman, sophomore, junior, or senior years; renewable. *Number:* 1–2. *Amount:* $800–$1000.

Eligibility Requirements: Applicant must be enrolled or expecting to enroll full-time at a four-year institution or university. Applicant or parent of applicant must be member of United Daughters of the Confederacy. Applicant must have 3.0 GPA or higher. Available to U.S. citizens.

Application Requirements: Application, essay, financial need analysis, photo, references, self-addressed stamped envelope, transcript. *Deadline:* February 15.

Contact: Second Vice President General
United Daughters of the Confederacy
328 North Boulevard
Richmond, VA 23220-4057
Phone: 804-355-1636

DAVID STEPHEN WYLIE SCHOLARSHIP

Renewable award for undergraduate student who is a descendant of a Confederate soldier, sailor or marine. Must be enrolled in an accredited college or university and carry a minimum of 12 credit hours each semester. Minimum 3.0 GPA required. Submit letter of endorsement from sponsoring chapter of the United Daughters of the Confederacy. Please refer to Web site for further details: http://www.hqudc.org

Award: Scholarship for use in freshman, sophomore, junior, or senior years; renewable. *Number:* 1–2. *Amount:* $800–$1000.

Eligibility Requirements: Applicant must be enrolled or expecting to enroll full-time at a four-year institution or university. Applicant or parent of applicant must be member of United Daughters of the Confederacy. Applicant must have 3.0 GPA or higher. Available to U.S. citizens.

Application Requirements: Application, essay, financial need analysis, photo, references, self-addressed stamped envelope, transcript. *Deadline:* February 15.

Contact: Second Vice President General
United Daughters of the Confederacy
328 North Boulevard
Richmond, VA 23220-4057
Phone: 804-355-1636

DOROTHY WILLIAMS SCHOLARSHIP

Renewable award for undergraduate student who is a descendant of a Confederate soldier, sailor or marine. Must be enrolled in an accredited college or university and carry a minimum of 12 credit hours each semester. Minimum 3.0 GPA required. Submit a letter of endorsement from sponsoring chapter of the United Daughters of the Confederacy. Please refer to Web site for further details: http://www.hqudc.org

Award: Scholarship for use in freshman, sophomore, junior, or senior years; renewable. *Number:* 1–2. *Amount:* $800–$1000.

Eligibility Requirements: Applicant must be enrolled or expecting to enroll full-time at a four-year institution or university. Applicant or parent of applicant must be member of United Daughters of the Confederacy. Applicant must have 3.0 GPA or higher. Available to U.S. citizens.

Application Requirements: Application, essay, financial need analysis, photo, references, self-addressed stamped envelope, transcript. *Deadline:* February 15.

Contact: Second Vice President General
United Daughters of the Confederacy
328 North Boulevard
Richmond, VA 23220-4057
Phone: 804-355-1636

ELIZABETH AND WALLACE KINGSBURY SCHOLARSHIP

Award for full-time undergraduate student who is a descendant of a Confederate soldier, studying at an accredited college or university and carrying a minimum of 12 credit hours each semester. Must have been a member of the Children of the Confederacy for a minimum of three years. Minimum 3.0 GPA required. Please refer to Web site for further details: http://www.hqudc.org

Award: Scholarship for use in freshman, sophomore, junior, or senior years; renewable. *Number:* 1–2. *Amount:* $800–$1000.

United Daughters of the Confederacy (continued)

Eligibility Requirements: Applicant must be enrolled or expecting to enroll full-time at a four-year institution or university. Applicant or parent of applicant must be member of United Daughters of the Confederacy. Applicant must have 3.0 GPA or higher. Available to U.S. citizens.

Application Requirements: Application, essay, financial need analysis, photo, references, self-addressed stamped envelope, transcript. *Deadline:* February 15.

Contact: Second Vice President General
United Daughters of the Confederacy
328 North Boulevard
Richmond, VA 23220-4057
Phone: 804-355-1636

GERTRUDE BOTTS-SAUCIER SCHOLARSHIP

Award for full-time undergraduate student who is a descendant of a Confederate soldier, sailor or marine. Must be from Texas, Mississippi or Louisiana. Must carry a minimum of 12 credit hours each semester and have a minimum 3.0 GPA. Submit letter of endorsement from sponsoring chapter of the United Daughters of the Confederacy. Please refer to Web site for further details: http://www.hqudc.org

Award: Scholarship for use in freshman, sophomore, junior, or senior years; renewable. *Number:* 1–2. *Amount:* $800–$1000.

Eligibility Requirements: Applicant must be enrolled or expecting to enroll full-time at a four-year institution or university and resident of Louisiana, Mississippi, or Texas. Applicant or parent of applicant must be member of United Daughters of the Confederacy. Applicant must have 3.0 GPA or higher. Available to U.S. citizens.

Application Requirements: Application, essay, financial need analysis, photo, references, self-addressed stamped envelope, transcript. *Deadline:* February 15.

Contact: Second Vice President General
United Daughters of the Confederacy
328 North Boulevard
Richmond, VA 23220-4057
Phone: 804-355-1636

HECTOR W. CHURCH SCHOLARSHIP

Renewable award for undergraduate student who is a descendant of a Confederate soldier, sailor or marine. Must be enrolled in an accredited college or university and carry a minimum of 12 credit hours each semester. Minimum of 3.0 GPA required. Submit letter of endorsement from sponsoring chapter of the United Daughters of the Confederacy. Please refer to Web site for further details: http://www.hqudc.org

Award: Scholarship for use in freshman, sophomore, junior, or senior years; renewable. *Number:* 1–5. *Amount:* $800–$1000.

Eligibility Requirements: Applicant must be enrolled or expecting to enroll full-time at a four-year institution or university. Applicant or parent of applicant must be member of United Daughters of the Confederacy. Applicant must have 3.0 GPA or higher. Available to U.S. citizens.

Application Requirements: Application, essay, financial need analysis, photo, references, self-addressed stamped envelope, transcript. *Deadline:* February 15.

Contact: Second Vice President General
United Daughters of the Confederacy
328 North Boulevard
Richmond, VA 23220-4057
Phone: 804-355-1636

HENRY CLAY DARSEY SCHOLARSHIP

Renewable award for undergraduate student who is a descendant of a Confederate soldier, sailor or marine. Must be enrolled in an accredited college or university and carry a minimum of 12 credit hours each semester. Minimum 3.0 GPA required. Submit letter of endorsement from sponsoring Chapter of the United Daughters of the Confederacy. Please refer to Web site for further details: http://www.hqudc.org

Award: Scholarship for use in freshman, sophomore, junior, or senior years; renewable. *Number:* 1–2. *Amount:* $800–$1000.

Eligibility Requirements: Applicant must be enrolled or expecting to enroll full-time at a four-year institution or university. Applicant or parent of applicant must be member of United Daughters of the Confederacy. Applicant must have 3.0 GPA or higher. Available to U.S. citizens.

Application Requirements: Application, essay, financial need analysis, photo, references, self-addressed stamped envelope, transcript. *Deadline:* February 15.

Contact: Second Vice President General
United Daughters of the Confederacy
328 North Boulevard
Richmond, VA 23220-4057
Phone: 804-355-1636

JANET B. SEIPPEL SCHOLARSHIP

Renewable award for undergraduate student who is a descendant of a Confederate soldier, sailor or marine. Must be enrolled in an accredited college or university and carry a minimum of 12 credit hours each semester. Minimum of 3.0 GPA required. Submit a letter of endorsement from sponsoring chapter of the United Daughters of the Confederacy. Please refer to Web site for further details: http://www.hqudc.org

Award: Scholarship for use in freshman, sophomore, junior, or senior years; renewable. *Number:* 1–2. *Amount:* $800–$1000.

Eligibility Requirements: Applicant must be enrolled or expecting to enroll full-time at a four-year institution or university. Applicant or parent of applicant must be member of United Daughters of the Confederacy. Applicant must have 3.0 GPA or higher. Available to U.S. citizens.

Application Requirements: Application, essay, financial need analysis, photo, references, self-addressed stamped envelope, transcript. *Deadline:* February 15.

Contact: Second Vice President General
United Daughters of the Confederacy
328 North Boulevard
Richmond, VA 23220-4057
Phone: 804-355-1636

LOLA B. CURRY SCHOLARSHIP

Award for full-time student from Alabama who is a descendant of a Confederate soldier. Must be enrolled in an accredited college or university in Alabama and carry a minimum of 12 credit hours each semester. Minimum 3.0 GPA required. Submit letter of endorsement from sponsoring chapter of the United Daughters of the Confederacy. Please refer to Web site for further details: http://www.hqudc.org

Award: Scholarship for use in freshman, sophomore, junior, or senior years; renewable. *Number:* 1–2. *Amount:* $800–$1000.

Eligibility Requirements: Applicant must be enrolled or expecting to enroll full-time at a four-year institution or university; resident of Alabama and studying in Alabama. Applicant or parent of applicant must be member of United Daughters of the Confederacy. Applicant must have 3.0 GPA or higher. Available to U.S. citizens.

Application Requirements: Application, essay, financial need analysis, photo, references, self-addressed stamped envelope, transcript. *Deadline:* February 15.

Contact: Second Vice President General
United Daughters of the Confederacy
328 North Boulevard
Richmond, VA 23220-4057
Phone: 804-355-1636

M. B. POPPENHEIM MEMORIAL SCHOLARSHIP

Renewable award for undergraduate student who is a descendant of a Confederate soldier, sailor or marine. Must be enrolled in an accredited college or university and carry a minimum of 12 credit hours each semester. Minimum 3.0 GPA required. Submit a letter of endorsement from sponsoring Chapter of the United Daughters of the Confederacy. Please refer to Web site for further details: http://www.hqudc.org

Award: Scholarship for use in freshman, sophomore, junior, or senior years; renewable. *Number:* 1–2. *Amount:* $800–$1000.

Eligibility Requirements: Applicant must be enrolled or expecting to enroll full-time at a four-year institution or university. Applicant or parent of applicant must be member of United Daughters of the Confederacy. Applicant must have 3.0 GPA or higher. Available to U.S. citizens.

Application Requirements: Application, essay, financial need analysis, photo, references, self-addressed stamped envelope, transcript. *Deadline:* February 15.

Contact: Second Vice President General
United Daughters of the Confederacy
328 North Boulevard
Richmond, VA 23220-4057
Phone: 804-355-1636

MAJOR MADISON BELL SCHOLARSHIP

Renewable award for undergraduate student who is a descendant of a Confederate soldier, sailor or marine. Must be enrolled in an accredited college or university and carry a minimum of 12 credit hours each semester. Minimum 3.0 GPA required. Submit letter of endorsement from sponsoring chapter of the United Daughters of the Confederacy. Please refer to Web site for further details: http://www.hqudc.org

Award: Scholarship for use in freshman, sophomore, junior, or senior years; renewable. *Number:* 1–2. *Amount:* $800–$1000.

Eligibility Requirements: Applicant must be enrolled or expecting to enroll full-time at a four-year institution or university. Applicant or parent of applicant must be member of United Daughters of the Confederacy. Applicant must have 3.0 GPA or higher. Available to U.S. citizens.

Application Requirements: Application, essay, financial need analysis, photo, references, self-addressed stamped envelope, transcript. *Deadline:* February 15.

Contact: Second Vice President General
United Daughters of the Confederacy
328 North Boulevard
Richmond, VA 23220-4057
Phone: 804-355-1636

MATTHEW FONTAINE MAURY SCHOLARSHIP

Renewable award for undergraduate student who is a descendant of a Confederate soldier, sailor or marine. Must be enrolled in an accredited college or university and carry a minimum of 12 credit hours each semester. Minimum 3.0 GPA required. Submit letter of endorsement from sponsoring Chapter of the United Daughters of the Confederacy. Please refer to Web site for further details: http://www.hqudc.org

Award: Scholarship for use in freshman, sophomore, junior, or senior years; renewable. *Number:* 1–2. *Amount:* $800–$1000.

Eligibility Requirements: Applicant must be enrolled or expecting to enroll full-time at a four-year institution or university. Applicant or parent of applicant must be member of United Daughters of the Confederacy. Applicant must have 3.0 GPA or higher. Available to U.S. citizens.

Application Requirements: Application, essay, financial need analysis, photo, references, self-addressed stamped envelope, transcript. *Deadline:* February 15.

Contact: Second Vice President General
United Daughters of the Confederacy
328 North Boulevard
Richmond, VA 23220-4057
Phone: 804-355-1636

MRS. ELLA M. FRANKLIN SCHOLARSHIP

Renewable award for undergraduate student who is a descendant of a Confederate soldier, sailor, or marine. Must be enrolled in an accredited college or university and carry a minimum of 12 credit hours each semester. Minimum 3.0 GPA required. Submit letter of endorsement from sponsoring chapter of the United Daughters of the Confederacy. Please refer to Web site for further details: http://www.hqudc.org

Award: Scholarship for use in freshman, sophomore, junior, or senior years; renewable. *Number:* 1–2. *Amount:* $800–$1000.

Eligibility Requirements: Applicant must be enrolled or expecting to enroll full-time at a four-year institution or university. Applicant or parent of applicant must be member of United Daughters of the Confederacy. Applicant must have 3.0 GPA or higher. Available to U.S. citizens.

Application Requirements: Application, essay, financial need analysis, photo, references, self-addressed stamped envelope, transcript. *Deadline:* February 15.

Contact: Second Vice President General
United Daughters of the Confederacy
328 North Boulevard
Richmond, VA 23220-4057
Phone: 804-355-1636

MRS. L. H. RAINES MEMORIAL SCHOLARSHIP

Renewable award for undergraduate student who is a descendant of a Confederate solider, sailor or marine. Must be enrolled in an accredited college or university and carry a minimum of 12 credit hours each semester. Minimum 3.0 GPA required. Submit letter of endorsement from sponsoring chapter of the United Daughters of the Confederacy. Please refer to Web site for further details: http://www.hqudc.org

Award: Scholarship for use in freshman, sophomore, junior, or senior years; renewable. *Number:* 1–2. *Amount:* $800–$1000.

Eligibility Requirements: Applicant must be enrolled or expecting to enroll full-time at a four-year institution or university. Applicant or parent of applicant must be member of United Daughters of the Confederacy. Applicant must have 3.0 GPA or higher. Available to U.S. citizens.

Application Requirements: Application, essay, financial need analysis, photo, references, self-addressed stamped envelope, transcript. *Deadline:* February 15.

Contact: Second Vice President General
United Daughters of the Confederacy
328 North Boulevard
Richmond, VA 23220-4057
Phone: 804-355-1636

S.A. CUNNINGHAM SCHOLARSHIP

Renewable award for undergraduate student who is a descendant of a Confederate soldier, sailor or marine. Must be enrolled in an accredited college or university and carry a minimum of 12 credit hours each semester. Minimum 3.0 GPA required. Submit letter of endorsement from sponsoring Chapter of the United Daughters of the Confederacy. Please refer to Web site for further details: http://www.hqudc.org

Award: Scholarship for use in freshman, sophomore, junior, or senior years; renewable. *Number:* 1–2. *Amount:* $800–$1000.

Eligibility Requirements: Applicant must be enrolled or expecting to enroll full-time at a four-year institution or university. Applicant or parent of applicant must be member of United Daughters of the Confederacy. Applicant must have 3.0 GPA or higher. Available to U.S. citizens.

Application Requirements: Application, essay, financial need analysis, photo, references, self-addressed stamped envelope, transcript. *Deadline:* February 15.

Contact: Second Vice President General
United Daughters of the Confederacy
328 North Boulevard
Richmond, VA 23220-4057
Phone: 804-355-1636

STONEWALL JACKSON SCHOLARSHIP

Renewable award for undergraduate student who is a descendant of a Confederate soldier, sailor or marine. Must be enrolled in an accredited college or university and carry a minimum of 12 credit hours each semester. Minimum 3.0 GPA required. Submit letter of endorsement from sponsoring Chapter of the United Daughters of the Confederacy. Please refer to Web site for further details: http://www.hqudc.org

United Daughters of the Confederacy (continued)

Award: Scholarship for use in freshman, sophomore, junior, or senior years; renewable. *Number:* 1–2. *Amount:* $800–$1000.

Eligibility Requirements: Applicant must be enrolled or expecting to enroll full-time at a four-year institution or university. Applicant or parent of applicant must be member of United Daughters of the Confederacy. Applicant must have 3.0 GPA or higher. Available to U.S. citizens.

Application Requirements: Application, essay, financial need analysis, photo, references, self-addressed stamped envelope, transcript. *Deadline:* February 15.

Contact: Second Vice President General
United Daughters of the Confederacy
328 North Boulevard
Richmond, VA 23220-4057
Phone: 804-355-1636

WINNIE DAVIS-CHILDREN OF THE CONFEDERACY SCHOLARSHIP

Award for full-time undergraduate student who is a descendant of a Confederate soldier, enrolled in an accredited college or university and carrying a minimum of 12 credit hours each semester. Recipient must be, or have been until age of 18, a participating member of the Children of the Confederacy and approved by the Third Vice President General. Minimum 3.0 GPA required. Please refer to Web site for further details: http://www.hqudc.org

Award: Scholarship for use in freshman, sophomore, junior, or senior years; renewable. *Number:* 1–2. *Amount:* $800–$1000.

Eligibility Requirements: Applicant must be enrolled or expecting to enroll full-time at a four-year institution or university. Applicant or parent of applicant must be member of United Daughters of the Confederacy. Applicant must have 3.0 GPA or higher. Available to U.S. citizens.

Application Requirements: Application, essay, financial need analysis, photo, references, self-addressed stamped envelope, transcript. *Deadline:* February 15.

Contact: Second Vice President General
United Daughters of the Confederacy
328 North Boulevard
Richmond, VA 23220-4057
Phone: 804-355-1636

UNITED FOOD AND COMMERCIAL WORKERS INTERNATIONAL UNION http://www.ufcw.org

JAMES A. SUFFRIDGE UNITED FOOD AND COMMERCIAL WORKERS SCHOLARSHIP PROGRAM

Scholarships available to graduating high school seniors during the specific program year. Must be a member of UFCW or the dependent of a UFCW member. Scholarship is disbursed over a four-year period of undergraduate study. Seven renewable awards of $4000 each. Preliminary applications due December 31; final applications due March 15.

Award: Scholarship for use in freshman, sophomore, junior, or senior years; renewable. *Number:* 7. *Amount:* $4000.

Eligibility Requirements: Applicant must be high school student; age 20 or under and planning to enroll or expecting to enroll full-time at a four-year institution. Applicant or parent of applicant must be member of United Food and Commercial Workers. Available to U.S. and Canadian citizens.

Application Requirements: Application, test scores, transcript. *Deadline:* March 15.

Contact: Yvonne Syphax, Assistant Director, Leadership Development Department
United Food and Commercial Workers International Union
1775 K Street, NW
Washington, DC 20006
Phone: 202-223-3111
Fax: 202-466-1587

UNITED NEGRO COLLEGE FUND http://www.uncf.org

CHURCH'S CHICKEN OPPORTUNITY SCHOLARSHIP

The child of a Church's Chicken employee is eligible to apply if he or she attends a UNCF member college or university. Minimum 3.0 GPA required. Prospective applicants should complete the Student Profile found at Web site: http://www.uncf.org.

Award: Scholarship for use in freshman, sophomore, junior, or senior years; not renewable. *Amount:* $2000–$4000.

Eligibility Requirements: Applicant must be Black (non-Hispanic) and enrolled or expecting to enroll full-time at a four-year institution or university. Applicant or parent of applicant must be affiliated with Church's Chicken. Applicant or parent of applicant must be member of National Academic Advising Association. Applicant must have 3.0 GPA or higher. Available to U.S. citizens.

Application Requirements: Application, financial need analysis. *Deadline:* Continuous.

Contact: Program Services Department
United Negro College Fund
8260 Willow Oaks Corporate Drive
Fairfax, VA 22031

UNITED STATES JUNIOR CHAMBER OF COMMERCE http://www.usjaycees.org

JAYCEE CHARLES R. FORD SCHOLARSHIP

One-time award of $2500 available to active members of Jaycee wishing to return to college to complete his/her formal education. Must be U.S. citizen, possess academic potential and leadership qualities and show financial need. To receive an application, send $5 application fee and self-addressed stamped envelope between July 1 and February 1.

Award: Scholarship for use in freshman, sophomore, junior, or senior years; not renewable. *Number:* 1. *Amount:* $2500.

Eligibility Requirements: Applicant must be enrolled or expecting to enroll at a two-year or four-year institution or university. Applicant or parent of applicant must be member of Jaycees. Available to U.S. citizens.

Application Requirements: Application, financial need analysis, self-addressed stamped envelope. *Fee:* $5. *Deadline:* varies.

Contact: Karen Fitzgerald, Data Entry
United States Junior Chamber of Commerce
PO Box 7
Tulsa, OK 74102
Phone: 918-584-2484
Fax: 918-584-4422
E-mail: customerservice@usjaycees.org

JAYCEE THOMAS WOOD BALDRIDGE SCHOLARSHIP

One-time award of $3000 available to a Jaycee, immediate family member, or a descendent of a Jaycee member. Must be U.S. citizen, possess academic potential and leadership qualities and show financial need. To receive an application, send $5 application fee and self-addressed stamped envelope between July 1 and February 1.

Award: Scholarship for use in freshman, sophomore, junior, or senior years; not renewable. *Number:* 1. *Amount:* $3000.

Eligibility Requirements: Applicant must be enrolled or expecting to enroll at a two-year or four-year institution or university. Applicant or parent of applicant must be member of Jaycees. Available to U.S. citizens.

Application Requirements: Application, financial need analysis, self-addressed stamped envelope. *Fee:* $5. *Deadline:* varies.

Contact: Karen Fitzgerald, Data Entry
United States Junior Chamber of Commerce
PO Box 7
Tulsa, OK 74102
Phone: 918-584-2484
Fax: 918-584-4422
E-mail: customerservice@usjaycees.org

UTILITY WORKERS UNION OF AMERICA http://www.uwua.org

UTILITY WORKERS UNION OF AMERICA SCHOLARSHIP AWARDS PROGRAM

Renewable award for high school juniors who are children of active members of the Utility Workers Union of America. Must take the Preliminary SAT National Merit Scholarship Qualifying Test in junior year and plan to enter college in the fall after high school graduation.

Award: Scholarship for use in freshman, sophomore, junior, or senior years; renewable. *Number:* 2. *Amount:* $500–$2000.

Eligibility Requirements: Applicant must be high school student and planning to enroll or expecting to enroll full-time at a four-year institution or university. Applicant or parent of applicant must be member of Utility Workers Union of America. Available to U.S. citizens.

Application Requirements: Application. *Deadline:* January 1.

Contact: Rosanna Farley, Office Manager
Utility Workers Union of America
815 16th Street, NW
Washington, DC 20006
Phone: 202-974-8200
Fax: 202-974-8201
E-mail: rfarley@aflcio.org

WESTERN FRATERNAL LIFE ASSOCIATION http://www.wflains.com

WESTERN FRATERNAL LIFE ASSOCIATION NATIONAL SCHOLARSHIP

Ten national scholarships will be awarded annually for up to $1,000 to qualified members attending college or vocational programs. Traditional and non-traditional students are eligible. Must be a WFLA member in good standing for two years prior to the application deadline. A member is an individual who has life insurance or an annuity with WFLA. High school seniors may apply. Members who are qualified for the National Scholarship may also qualify for 3 state scholarships and the NFCA's scholarship.

Award: Scholarship for use in freshman, sophomore, junior, or senior years; renewable. *Number:* 10. *Amount:* $500–$1000.

Eligibility Requirements: Applicant must be enrolled or expecting to enroll full-time at a two-year or four-year or technical institution or university. Applicant or parent of applicant must be member of Western Fraternal Life Association. Available to U.S. citizens.

Application Requirements: Application, driver's license, essay, references, test scores, transcript. *Deadline:* March 1.

Contact: Linda Grove, Fraternal Manager
Western Fraternal Life Association
1900 First Avenue NE
Cedar Rapids, IA 52402-5372
Phone: 877-935-2467
Fax: 319-363-8806
E-mail: lgrove@wflains.com

WOMEN'S INTERNATIONAL BOWLING CONGRESS http://www.bowl.com

ALBERTA E. CROWE STAR OF TOMORROW AWARD

Renewable award for a U.S. or Canadian female high school or college student who competes in the sport of bowling. Must be a current YABA or WIBC member in good standing. Must be younger than 22 years old. Minimum 2.5 GPA required. Deadline is October 1.

Award: Scholarship for use in freshman, sophomore, junior, or senior years; renewable. *Number:* 1. *Amount:* $1500.

Eligibility Requirements: Applicant must be age 21 or under; enrolled or expecting to enroll at an institution or university; female and must have an interest in bowling. Applicant or parent of applicant must be member of Young American Bowling Alliance. Applicant must have 2.5 GPA or higher. Available to U.S. and Canadian citizens.

Application Requirements: Application, essay, references, transcript. *Deadline:* October 1.

Contact: Ed Gocha, Manager of Smart Scholarship
Women's International Bowling Congress
5301 South 76th Street
Greendale, WI 53129-1192
Phone: 800-514-2695 Ext. 3343
Fax: 414-421-3013
E-mail: egocha@bowlinginc.com

WYOMING FARM BUREAU FEDERATION http://www.wyfb.org/

KING-LIVINGSTON SCHOLARSHIP

One-time award given to graduates of Wyoming high schools. Must attend a Wyoming junior college or the University of Wyoming. Minimum 2.5 GPA required. Applicant's family must be a current member of the Wyoming Farm Bureau. Deadline is March 1.

Award: Scholarship for use in freshman, sophomore, junior, senior, or graduate years; not renewable. *Number:* 1. *Amount:* $750.

Eligibility Requirements: Applicant must be enrolled or expecting to enroll at a two-year or four-year institution or university; resident of Wyoming and studying in Wyoming. Applicant or parent of applicant must be member of Wyoming Farm Bureau. Applicant must have 2.5 GPA or higher.

Application Requirements: Application, financial need analysis, photo, resume, references, transcript. *Deadline:* March 1.

Contact: Ellen Westbrook, Executive Secretary
Wyoming Farm Bureau Federation
931 Boulder Drive
Laramie, WY 82070
Phone: 307-721-7719
Fax: 307-721-7790
E-mail: ewestbrook@mwfbi.com

WYOMING FARM BUREAU CONTINUING EDUCATION SCHOLARSHIPS

Award to students attending a two-year college in Wyoming or the University of Wyoming. Must be a resident of Wyoming and applicant's family must be a current member of the Wyoming Farm Bureau. Applicants must submit at least two semesters of college grade transcripts. Freshmen must submit first semester grades and proof of enrollment in second semester. Minimum 2.5 GPA. Deadline is March 1.

Award: Scholarship for use in sophomore, junior, senior, or graduate years. *Number:* 3. *Amount:* $500.

Eligibility Requirements: Applicant must be enrolled or expecting to enroll at a four-year institution or university; resident of Wyoming and studying in Wyoming. Applicant or parent of applicant must be member of Wyoming Farm Bureau. Applicant must have 2.5 GPA or higher.

Application Requirements: Application, financial need analysis, photo, resume, references, transcript. *Deadline:* March 1.

Contact: Ellen Westbrook, Executive Secretary
Wyoming Farm Bureau Federation
931 Boulder Drive
Laramie, WY 82070
Phone: 307-721-7719
Fax: 307-721-7790
E-mail: ewestbrook@mwfbi.com

WYOMING FARM BUREAU FEDERATION SCHOLARSHIPS

Five $500 scholarships will be given to graduates of Wyoming high schools. Eligible candidates will be enrolled in a two-year college in Wyoming or the University of Wyoming and must have a minimum 2.5 GPA. Applicant's family should be current member of the Wyoming Farm Bureau Federation. Deadline: March 1.

Award: Scholarship for use in freshman, sophomore, junior, senior, or graduate years; not renewable. *Number:* 5. *Amount:* $500.

Eligibility Requirements: Applicant must be enrolled or expecting to enroll at a two-year or four-year institution or university; resident of

Wyoming Farm Bureau Federation (continued)

Wyoming and studying in Wyoming. Applicant or parent of applicant must be member of Wyoming Farm Bureau. Applicant must have 2.5 GPA or higher.

Application Requirements: Application, financial need analysis, photo, resume, references, transcript. *Deadline:* March 1.

Contact: Ellen Westbrook, Executive Secretary
Wyoming Farm Bureau Federation
931 Boulder Drive
Laramie, WY 82070
Phone: 307-721-7719
Fax: 307-721-7790
E-mail: ewestbrook@mwfbi.com

YOUNG AMERICAN BOWLING ALLIANCE (YABA) http://www.bowl.com

GIFT FOR LIFE SCHOLARSHIP

One-time award for high school students who compete in the sport of bowling. Minimum 2.0 GPA required. Must demonstrate financial need. Must be a member in good standing of YABA. Application deadline is April 1.

Award: Scholarship for use in freshman year; not renewable. *Number:* 12. *Amount:* $1000.

Eligibility Requirements: Applicant must be high school student; planning to enroll or expecting to enroll full-time at a two-year or four-year or technical institution or university and must have an interest in bowling. Applicant or parent of applicant must be member of Young American Bowling Alliance.

Application Requirements: Application, essay, financial need analysis, references. *Deadline:* April 1.

Contact: Young American Bowling Alliance (YABA)
5301 South 76th Street
Greendale, WI 53129
Phone: 800-514-2695 Ext. 3318
E-mail: egocha@bowlinginc.com

PEPSI-COLA YOUTH BOWLING CHAMPIONSHIPS

Awarded to members of the Young American Bowling Alliance. Must win state or provincial tournaments to be eligible for international championships. U.S. citizens abroad may participate through military affiliate. Application fee varies by state. Contact Youth Director at local bowling center.

Award: Scholarship for use in freshman, sophomore, junior, or senior years; not renewable. *Number:* 292. *Amount:* $500–$3000.

Eligibility Requirements: Applicant must be enrolled or expecting to enroll full or part-time at an institution or university and must have an interest in bowling. Applicant or parent of applicant must be member of Young American Bowling Alliance. Available to U.S. and non-U.S. citizens.

Application Requirements: Applicant must enter a contest. *Deadline:* February 28.

Contact: Young American Bowling Alliance (YABA)
5301 South 76th Street
Greendale, WI 53129-1192
Phone: 800-514-2695 Ext. 3318

CORPORATE AFFILIATION

ADMINISTRATIVE MANAGEMENT SERVICES (AMS) http://home.cogeco.ca/~chrisb7/AMS/amshome.html

DAIMLER CHRYSLER SCHOLARSHIP PROGRAM

Student must be graduating from final high school year and be enrolling in first year of a three- to four-year degree program. Twelve students are chosen based on academic performance, extracurricular activities, and community service. Once in the program they could be eligible for four awards as long as a "B" average is maintained on a full workload. Open to Canadian citizens who are dependents of employees of Daimler Chrysler Canada, Inc.

Award: Scholarship for use in freshman, sophomore, junior, or senior years; renewable. *Number:* 12. *Amount:* $743.

Eligibility Requirements: Applicant must be Canadian citizen; high school student and planning to enroll or expecting to enroll full-time at an institution or university. Applicant or parent of applicant must be affiliated with Daimler Chrysler Canada, Inc.. Applicant must have 3.0 GPA or higher.

Application Requirements: Application, autobiography, references, transcript. *Deadline:* April 30.

Contact: Request application via e-mail
E-mail: chrisb7@cogeco.ca

SYNCRUDE HIGHER EDUCATION EDUCATION AWARDS PROGRAM

Awarded to Canadian students enrolled in a program that involves a minimum of two years full-time study. Students could qualify for four awards at the undergraduate level and two years at the graduate or professional level as long as they are under 25 years of age. Awards may be held at the community college level for a maximum of two years. Must be a dependent of a Syncrude Canada, Inc., employee.

Award: Scholarship for use in freshman, sophomore, junior, senior, or graduate years; renewable. *Number:* varies. *Amount:* $1783.

Eligibility Requirements: Applicant must be Canadian citizen; age 24 or under and enrolled or expecting to enroll full-time at a two-year or technical institution or university. Applicant or parent of applicant must be affiliated with Syncrude Canada, Inc..

Application Requirements: Application, transcript. *Deadline:* November 15.

Contact: Request application via e-mail
E-mail: chrisb7@cogeco.ca

ALBERTA HERITAGE SCHOLARSHIP FUND/ ALBERTA SCHOLARSHIP PROGRAMS http://www.alis.gov.ab.ca/scholarships

ALBERTA HERITAGE SCHOLARSHIP FUND CANA SCHOLARSHIPS

Award to recognize and reward exceptional academic achievement of children of CANA Construction Company, Ltd. employees. Must be Alberta resident entering second or subsequent year of study at an eligible institution. One award of CAN$1500 and two awards of CAN$1000. Deadline: October 31.

Award: Scholarship for use in sophomore, junior, or senior years; not renewable. *Number:* 3. *Amount:* $811–$1216.

Eligibility Requirements: Applicant must be Canadian citizen; enrolled or expecting to enroll full-time at a two-year or four-year institution or university; resident of Alberta and studying in Alberta. Applicant or parent of applicant must be affiliated with CANA. Applicant must have 2.5 GPA or higher.

Application Requirements: Application, transcript. *Deadline:* October 31.

Contact: Alberta Heritage Scholarship Fund/Alberta Scholarship Programs
9940 106th Street, 9th Floor, Box 28000 Station Main
Edmonton, AB T5J 4R4
Canada
Phone: 780-427-8640
Fax: 780-422-4516
E-mail: heritage@gov.ab.ca

STREAM-FLO/MASTER FLO SCHOLARSHIPS

Two CAN$3000 scholarships are available to recognize exceptional academic achievement at the high school level of sons and daughters of Stream-Flo Industries Ltd., Master Flo Valve, Inc., and ERC Industries employees. For more details and deadlines see Web site: http://www.alis.gov.ab.ca.

Award: Scholarship for use in freshman year; not renewable. *Number:* 2. *Amount:* $2434.

Eligibility Requirements: Applicant must be high school student; planning to enroll or expecting to enroll full-time at a four-year or technical institution or university and studying in Alberta, British

Columbia, or Saskatchewan. Applicant or parent of applicant must be affiliated with Stream-Flo Industries Ltd.. Available to Canadian citizens.

Application Requirements: Application. *Deadline:* July 31.

Contact: Director
Alberta Heritage Scholarship Fund/Alberta Scholarship Programs
9940 106th Street, 9th Floor
Box 28000, Station Main
Edmonton, AB T5J 4R4
Canada
Phone: 780-427-8640
Fax: 780-422-4516
E-mail: heritage@gov.ab.ca

ALCOA FOUNDATION

ALCOA FOUNDATION SONS AND DAUGHTERS SCHOLARSHIP PROGRAM

Open to children of Alcoa, Inc., employees. Apply in senior year of high school through parent's employment location. Merit is considered. Application deadline third week in January.

Award: Scholarship for use in freshman, sophomore, junior, or senior years; renewable. *Number:* 100–150. *Amount:* $1500.

Eligibility Requirements: Applicant must be high school student and planning to enroll or expecting to enroll full-time at a two-year or four-year or technical institution or university. Applicant or parent of applicant must be affiliated with Alcoa, Inc.. Available to U.S. and non-U.S. citizens.

Application Requirements: Application, applicant must enter a contest, essay, references, test scores, transcript. *Deadline:* varies.

Contact: Ms. Carol Greco, Data Analyst
Alcoa Foundation
201 Isabella Street
Pittsburgh, PA 15212-5858
Phone: 412-553-4786
Fax: 412-553-4532
E-mail: carol.greco@alcoa.com

ARKANSAS COMMUNITY FOUNDATION, INC. http://www.arcf.org

MAVERICK SCHOLARSHIP FUND

Scholarship available only to employees and families of Maverick Transportation, Inc. See Web site for more information. (http://www.maverickusa.com).

Award: Scholarship for use in freshman, sophomore, junior, or senior years; not renewable. *Amount:* $500–$5000.

Eligibility Requirements: Applicant must be enrolled or expecting to enroll at an institution or university and resident of Arkansas. Applicant or parent of applicant must be affiliated with Maverick Transportation, Inc.. Available to U.S. citizens.

Application Requirements: Application. *Deadline:* March 15.

Contact: Maverick Transportation, Human Resources Department
Arkansas Community Foundation, Inc.
PO Box 15428
Little Rock, AR 72231

SCROLL TECHNOLOGIES SCHOLARSHIP FUND

Scholarship available only for children and stepchildren of Scroll Technologies employees. Contact for more information.

Award: Scholarship for use in freshman, sophomore, junior, or senior years; not renewable. *Amount:* $500–$5000.

Eligibility Requirements: Applicant must be enrolled or expecting to enroll at an institution or university and resident of Arkansas. Applicant or parent of applicant must be affiliated with Scroll Technologies. Available to U.S. citizens.

Application Requirements: Application. *Deadline:* March 15.

Contact: Scroll Technologies Human Resources Department
Arkansas Community Foundation, Inc.
1 Scroll Drive
Arkadelphia, AR 71913

BECU FOUNDATION http://www.becu.org

BECU FOUNDATION SCHOLARSHIP PROGRAM

The BECU Foundation extends the credit union philosophy of people helping people by offering educational support to Boeing Employees Credit Union members and their families. Scholarships will recognize and promote service in the school or community, leadership potential, and academic achievement.

Award: Scholarship for use in freshman, sophomore, junior, or senior years; not renewable. *Number:* 27. *Amount:* $2000.

Eligibility Requirements: Applicant must be enrolled or expecting to enroll full-time at a two-year or four-year or technical institution or university and must have an interest in leadership. Applicant or parent of applicant must be affiliated with Boeing Employees' Credit Union. Applicant must have 3.0 GPA or higher. Available to U.S. and non-U.S. citizens.

Application Requirements: Application, essay, references, transcript. *Deadline:* March 31.

Contact: Tara Cramer
BECU Foundation
PO Box 97050
Seattle, WA 98124-9750

BRIDGESTONE/FIRESTONE TRUST FUND

BRIDGESTONE/FIRESTONE TRUST FUND SCHOLARSHIPS

Award for sons and daughters of Bridgestone/Firestone, Inc., employees and retirees. Must be high school student in junior year. Must be a U.S. citizen. Must also meet all requirements for participation that are published in the PSAT/NMSQT Student Bulletin.

Award: Scholarship for use in freshman year; not renewable. *Number:* up to 50. *Amount:* $4000.

Eligibility Requirements: Applicant must be high school student and planning to enroll or expecting to enroll full-time at a four-year institution or university. Applicant or parent of applicant must be affiliated with Bridgestone/Firestone. Applicant or parent of applicant must have employment or volunteer experience in designated career field. Available to U.S. citizens.

Application Requirements: Application. *Deadline:* February 1.

Contact: Bernice Csaszar, Administrator
Bridgestone/Firestone Trust Fund
535 Marriott Drive
Nashville, TN 37214-0990
Phone: 615-937-1415
Fax: 615-937-1414
E-mail: bfstrustfund@bfusa.com

BUTLER MANUFACTURING COMPANY http://www.butlermfg.com

BUTLER MANUFACTURING COMPANY FOUNDATION SCHOLARSHIP PROGRAM

Award for high school seniors who are the children of full-time employees of Butler Manufacturing Company and its subsidiaries. Award is renewable for up to four years. Must enroll full-time and stay in upper half of class.

Award: Scholarship for use in freshman, sophomore, junior, or senior years; renewable. *Number:* 8. *Amount:* $2500.

Eligibility Requirements: Applicant must be high school student and planning to enroll or expecting to enroll full-time at a two-year or four-year institution. Applicant or parent of applicant must be affiliated with Butler Manufacturing Company. Available to U.S. and Canadian citizens.

Application Requirements: Application, essay, financial need analysis, references, test scores, transcript. *Deadline:* February 18.

Contact: Barbara Fay, Foundation Administrator
Butler Manufacturing Company
PO Box 419917
1540 Genessee, KCMO 64102
Kansas City, MO 64141
Phone: 816-968-3208
Fax: 816-968-6501
E-mail: blfay@butlermfg.org

CENTENNIAL SCHOLARSHIP FOR VOCATIONAL /TECHNICAL CERTIFICATION AND/OR ASSOCIATE DEGREE

Available to high school graduates up to age 21 who are financially dependent on a Butler-employed parent. The scholarship is awarded to students who plan to attend vocational/technical schools, junior colleges, or community colleges. Awards are renewed automatically up to one year based on satisfactory performance. Total award is $2000 ($1000 per year).

Award: Scholarship for use in freshman or sophomore years; renewable. *Number:* 2–20. *Amount:* $1000.

Eligibility Requirements: Applicant must be age 18-21 and enrolled or expecting to enroll full-time at a two-year or technical institution. Applicant or parent of applicant must be affiliated with Butler Manufacturing Company. Available to U.S. citizens.

Application Requirements: Application, essay, references, test scores, transcript. *Deadline:* February 18.

Contact: Barbara Fay, Foundation Administrator
Butler Manufacturing Company
PO Box 419917
1540 Genessee, KCMO 64102
Kansas City, MO 64141
Phone: 816-968-3208
Fax: 816-968-6501
E-mail: blfay@butlermfg.org

CENTER FOR SCHOLARSHIP ADMINISTRATION http://www.scholarshipprograms.org

BI-LO JOHN ROHALEY SCHOLARSHIP

Nonrenewable scholarships are available to associates of BI-LO who have had a minimum of one-year of service averaging 15 hours a week. For more details and an application, see Web site.

Award: Scholarship for use in freshman, sophomore, junior, or senior years; not renewable. *Number:* 3. *Amount:* $2000.

Eligibility Requirements: Applicant must be enrolled or expecting to enroll full-time at a two-year or four-year or technical institution or university. Applicant or parent of applicant must be affiliated with BI-LO.

Application Requirements: Application, essay, financial need analysis, references, transcript. *Deadline:* February 15.

Contact: Application available at Web site.

BONITZ (BILL ROGERS) SCHOLARSHIP

Renewable scholarships are for dependent children of qualified employees of Bonitz group of companies. For more details and an application, see Human Resources Manager at Bonitz of South Carolina.

Award: Scholarship for use in freshman, sophomore, junior, or senior years; renewable. *Number:* 1. *Amount:* up to $3000.

Eligibility Requirements: Applicant must be age 21 or under and enrolled or expecting to enroll full-time at a two-year or four-year or technical institution or university. Applicant or parent of applicant must be affiliated with Bonitz. Applicant must have 2.5 GPA or higher.

Application Requirements: Application, essay, financial need analysis, references, transcript. *Deadline:* February 15.

Contact: Center for Scholarship Administration
see Human Resources Manager at Bonitz of South Carolina

CARDINAL LOGISTICS MANAGEMENT, INC. SCHOLARSHIPS

Renewable scholarships are for dependent children of qualified employees of Cardinal Logistics Management, Inc. See the Human Resources Manager at Cardinal Logistics Management, Inc. for deadlines and more detailed information on additional criteria.

Award: Scholarship for use in freshman, sophomore, junior, or senior years; renewable. *Number:* 1. *Amount:* $2000.

Eligibility Requirements: Applicant must be age 22 or under; enrolled or expecting to enroll full-time at a four-year institution or university and single. Applicant or parent of applicant must be affiliated with Cardinal Logistic Management. Applicant must have 2.5 GPA or higher.

Application Requirements: Application, essay, references, transcript. *Deadline:* February 15.

Contact: See Human Resources Manager at Cardinal Logistics Mangement, Inc.

CARRIS SCHOLARSHIPS

Nonrenewable scholarships are for dependent children of qualified employees of Carris Financial Corporation. For more details and an application, see Web site: http://www.scholarshipprograms.org

Award: Scholarship for use in freshman, sophomore, junior, or senior years; not renewable. *Number:* up to 25. *Amount:* up to $2000.

Eligibility Requirements: Applicant must be enrolled or expecting to enroll full-time at a two-year or four-year or technical institution or university. Applicant or parent of applicant must be affiliated with Carris Financial Corporation.

Application Requirements: Application, essay, financial need analysis, references, transcript. *Deadline:* March 1.

Contact: Application available at Web site.

CONSOLIDATED SYSTEMS, INC. BILL ROGERS SCHOLARSHIP

Renewable scholarships are for dependent children of qualified employees of Consolidated Systems, Inc. who are on hourly payroll. See the Human Resources Manager for deadlines and more detailed information on additional criteria.

Award: Scholarship for use in freshman, sophomore, or junior years; renewable. *Number:* 1. *Amount:* $2000.

Eligibility Requirements: Applicant must be age 25 or under and enrolled or expecting to enroll full-time at a two-year or four-year or technical institution or university. Applicant or parent of applicant must be affiliated with Consolidation Systems, Inc..

Application Requirements: Application, essay, references, transcript. *Deadline:* February 15.

Contact: See Human Resources Manager at CSI.

CONSOLIDATED SYSTEMS, INC. THOMAS C. MEREDITH SCHOLARSHIP

Renewable scholarships are for dependent children of qualified employees of Consolidated Systems, Inc. who are on salaried payroll. See the Human Resources Manager for deadlines and more detailed information on additional criteria.

Award: Scholarship for use in freshman, sophomore, or junior years; renewable. *Number:* 1. *Amount:* $2000.

Eligibility Requirements: Applicant must be age 25 or under and enrolled or expecting to enroll full-time at a two-year or four-year or technical institution or university. Applicant or parent of applicant must be affiliated with Consolidation Systems, Inc..

Application Requirements: Application, essay, references, transcript. *Deadline:* February 15.

Contact: See Human Resources Manager at CSI.

DAN RIVER FOUNDATION SCHOLARSHIP

Renewable scholarships are for dependent children of qualified employees of Dan River, Inc. For more details and an application see Web site: http://www.scholarshipprograms.org

Award: Scholarship for use in freshman, sophomore, or junior years; renewable. *Number:* varies. *Amount:* up to $2000.

Eligibility Requirements: Applicant must be enrolled or expecting to enroll at a two-year or four-year institution or university. Applicant or parent of applicant must be affiliated with Dan River, Inc.. Applicant must have 2.5 GPA or higher.

Application Requirements: Application, essay, financial need analysis, references, transcript. *Deadline:* April 1.

Contact: Application available at Web site.

DELTA APPAREL, INC. SCHOLARSHIP

Renewable scholarships are for dependent children of qualified employees of Delta Apparel, Inc. See the Human Resources Manager for deadlines and more detailed information on additional criteria.

Award: Scholarship for use in freshman, sophomore, or junior years. *Number:* varies. *Amount:* $1000.

Eligibility Requirements: Applicant must be enrolled or expecting to enroll at a two-year or four-year or technical institution or university. Applicant or parent of applicant must be affiliated with Delta Apparel, Inc.. Applicant must have 2.5 GPA or higher.

Application Requirements: Application, essay, financial need analysis, references, transcript. *Deadline:* February 15.

Contact: See Human Resources Manager at Delta Apparel, Inc.

FLEXIBLE TECHNOLOGIES, INC. SCHOLARSHIPS

Renewable scholarships are for dependent children of qualified employees of Flexible Technologies, Inc. Must maintain a 2.5 GPA to continue to receive the scholarship. See the Human Resources Manager for deadlines and more detailed information on additional criteria.

Award: Scholarship for use in freshman, sophomore, or junior years; renewable. *Number:* 2. *Amount:* $2000.

Eligibility Requirements: Applicant must be high school student and planning to enroll or expecting to enroll full-time at a four-year institution or university. Applicant or parent of applicant must be affiliated with Flexible Technologies, Inc.. Applicant must have 2.5 GPA or higher.

Application Requirements: Application, essay, references, transcript. *Deadline:* February 15.

Contact: See Human Resources Manager.

LUCILLE P. AND EDWARD C. GILES FOUNDATION SCHOLARSHIPS

Renewable scholarships are available for dependent children or dependent grandchildren of qualified employees of Caraustar Industries, Inc. For more details and an application see Web site: http://www.scholarshipprograms.org

Award: Scholarship for use in freshman, sophomore, junior, senior, or graduate years; renewable. *Number:* varies. *Amount:* up to $6000.

Eligibility Requirements: Applicant must be enrolled or expecting to enroll at a two-year or four-year or technical institution or university. Applicant or parent of applicant must be affiliated with Caraustar Industries, Inc..

Application Requirements: Application, essay, financial need analysis, references, transcript. *Deadline:* February 15.

Contact: Application available at Web site.

MAYER SCHOLARSHIP FUND (LIBERTY HARDWARE MANUFACTURING COMPANY)

Renewable scholarships are available to dependent children of qualified employees of Liberty Hardware Manufacturing Company. See the Human Resources Manager for deadlines and more detailed information on additional criteria.

Award: Scholarship for use in freshman, sophomore, junior, or senior years; renewable. *Number:* 2. *Amount:* $2000.

Eligibility Requirements: Applicant must be age 24 or under; enrolled or expecting to enroll full-time at a two-year or four-year or technical institution or university and single. Applicant or parent of applicant must be affiliated with Liberty Hardware Manufacturing Company. Applicant must have 2.5 GPA or higher.

Application Requirements: Application, essay, financial need analysis, references, transcript. *Deadline:* March 30.

Contact: See Human Resources Manager.

MICHELIN NORTH AMERICA DEPENDENT SCHOLARSHIP

A renewable award for dependent children of qualified Michelin North America employees. Applicant must be unmarried and age 23 or younger. For more details see Web site.

Award: Scholarship for use in freshman, sophomore, junior, or senior years; renewable. *Number:* up to 15. *Amount:* $1000–$2500.

Eligibility Requirements: Applicant must be age 23 or under; enrolled or expecting to enroll full-time at a two-year or four-year or technical institution or university and single. Applicant or parent of applicant must be affiliated with Michelin North America. Applicant must have 3.0 GPA or higher.

Application Requirements: Application, essay, references, transcript. *Deadline:* March 30.

Contact: Application available at Web site.

MILLIKEN & COMPANY SCHOLARSHIP

Renewable scholarships are available to eligible associates or to dependent children of eligible associates of Milliken & Company. Must attend any private, accredited, four-year, not-for-profit, tax-free institution by federal statute (501) c (3) located in Georgia, New York, North Carolina or South Carolina. For more details and an application see Web site: http://www.scholarshipprograms.org

Award: Scholarship for use in freshman, sophomore, junior, or senior years; renewable. *Number:* up to 9. *Amount:* up to $5000.

Eligibility Requirements: Applicant must be enrolled or expecting to enroll at an institution or university and studying in Georgia, New York, North Carolina, or South Carolina. Applicant or parent of applicant must be affiliated with Milliken & Company.

Application Requirements: Application, essay, references, transcript. *Deadline:* February 15.

Contact: Application available at Web site.

SARA LEE BRANDED APPAREL SCHOLARSHIPS

Renewable scholarships are available to dependent children of qualified employees of Sara Lee Corporation. For more details and an application see Web site: http://www.scholarshipprograms.org

Award: Scholarship for use in freshman, sophomore, junior, or senior years; renewable. *Number:* varies. *Amount:* $1000–$3000.

Eligibility Requirements: Applicant must be age 24 or under; enrolled or expecting to enroll full-time at a two-year or four-year or technical institution or university and single. Applicant or parent of applicant must be affiliated with Sara Lee Corporation.

Application Requirements: Application, essay, financial need analysis, references, transcript. *Deadline:* March 1.

Contact: Application available at Web site.

SONOCO SCHOLARSHIP

Renewable scholarships are available to dependent children of qualified employees of Sonoco. For more details and an application see Web site: http://www.scholarshipprograms.org

Award: Scholarship for use in freshman, sophomore, junior, or senior years; renewable. *Number:* 10. *Amount:* $2000.

Eligibility Requirements: Applicant must be high school student and planning to enroll or expecting to enroll full-time at a four-year institution or university. Applicant or parent of applicant must be affiliated with Sonoco.

Application Requirements: Application, essay, financial need analysis, references, transcript. *Deadline:* February 15.

Contact: Application available at Web site.

SPARTANBURG AUTOMOTIVE, INC. SCHOLARSHIPS

Renewable scholarships are available to dependent children of qualified employees of Spartanburg Automotive, Inc. See the Human Resources Manager for more detailed information on additional criteria.

Award: Scholarship for use in freshman year; renewable. *Number:* varies. *Amount:* $1000.

Eligibility Requirements: Applicant must be high school student and planning to enroll or expecting to enroll full-time at a two-year or four-year or technical institution or university. Applicant or parent of applicant must be affiliated with Spartanburg Automotive, Inc..

Center for Scholarship Administration (continued)

Application Requirements: Application, essay, references, transcript. *Deadline:* February 15.

Contact: See Human Resources Manager.

SPARTANBURG STAINLESS PRODUCTS, INC. SCHOLARSHIP

Renewable scholarships are available to dependent children of qualified employees of Spartanburg Stainless Products, Inc. See the Human Resources Manager for more detailed information on additional criteria.

Award: Scholarship for use in freshman year; renewable. *Number:* varies. *Amount:* $1000.

Eligibility Requirements: Applicant must be high school student and planning to enroll or expecting to enroll full-time at a two-year or four-year or technical institution or university. Applicant or parent of applicant must be affiliated with Spartanburg Stainless Products, Inc..

Application Requirements: Application, essay, references, transcript. *Deadline:* February 15.

Contact: See Human Resources Manager.

STRATA MARKETING, INC. SCHOLARSHIP PROGRAM

One-time award for dependent children of Strata Marketing Inc. employees. The scholarships are for 25% of annual tuition up to $8000 each.

Award: Scholarship for use in freshman, sophomore, junior, or senior years; not renewable. *Number:* up to 3. *Amount:* up to $8000.

Eligibility Requirements: Applicant must be age 24 or under; enrolled or expecting to enroll full-time at a four-year institution or university and single. Applicant or parent of applicant must be affiliated with Strata Marketing, Inc.. Applicant must have 3.0 GPA or higher.

Application Requirements: Application, essay, references, transcript. *Deadline:* March 15.

Contact: Application available at Web site.

SUBWAY OF SOUTH CAROLINA SCHOLARSHIP

Non-renewable scholarships are available to qualified employees and dependent children of qualified employees of Subway of South Carolina. For more details and an application see Web site: http://www.scholarshipprograms.org

Award: Scholarship for use in freshman year; not renewable. *Number:* 10. *Amount:* $1000.

Eligibility Requirements: Applicant must be enrolled or expecting to enroll full-time at a two-year or four-year or technical institution or university. Applicant or parent of applicant must be affiliated with Subway.

Application Requirements: Application. *Deadline:* January 31.

Contact: Application available at Web site.

SUBWAY SCHOLARSHIPS

Non-renewable scholarships are available to qualified employees of Subway. For more details and an application see Web site: http://www.scholarshipprograms.org

Award: Scholarship for use in freshman, sophomore, junior, or senior years; not renewable. *Number:* varies. *Amount:* $1000.

Eligibility Requirements: Applicant must be enrolled or expecting to enroll full-time at a two-year or four-year or technical institution or university. Applicant or parent of applicant must be affiliated with Subway.

Application Requirements: Application, essay, references, transcript. *Deadline:* February 27.

Contact: Application available at Web site.

THYSSENKRUPP BUDD-UAW LOCAL 2383 VENDING MACHINE REVENUE COMMITTEE SCHOLARSHIP PROGRAM

Renewable award available to high school seniors who are dependent children of ThyssenKrupp Budd Shelbyville employees. See Web site for details.

Award: Scholarship for use in freshman, sophomore, junior, or senior years; renewable. *Number:* 7. *Amount:* $1000.

Eligibility Requirements: Applicant must be high school student and planning to enroll or expecting to enroll at a two-year or four-year or technical institution or university. Applicant or parent of applicant must be affiliated with ThyssenKrupp Budd Shelbyville.

Application Requirements: Application, essay, references, transcript. *Deadline:* February 15.

Contact: Application available at Web site.

TIETEX INTERNATIONAL SCHOLARSHIP

Renewable scholarships are available to the dependent children of employees of Teitex International. See the Human Resources Manager for more detailed information on additional criteria.

Award: Scholarship for use in freshman, sophomore, junior, or senior years; renewable. *Number:* varies. *Amount:* $1500.

Eligibility Requirements: Applicant must be high school student and planning to enroll or expecting to enroll full-time at a four-year institution or university. Applicant or parent of applicant must be affiliated with Teitex International.

Application Requirements: Application, essay, references, transcript. *Deadline:* February 15.

Contact: See Human Resources Manager.

TUPPERWARE U.S., INC. SCHOLARSHIP

Non-renewable scholarships are available to the dependent children of qualified associates of Tupperware U.S., Inc. See the Human Resources Advisor for more detailed information on additional criteria.

Award: Scholarship for use in freshman year; not renewable. *Number:* varies. *Amount:* $1000–$10,500.

Eligibility Requirements: Applicant must be high school student and planning to enroll or expecting to enroll full-time at a two-year or four-year or technical institution or university. Applicant or parent of applicant must be affiliated with Tupperware U.S., Inc..

Application Requirements: Application, essay, financial need analysis, references, transcript. *Deadline:* February 15.

Contact: See Human Resources Advisor.

UNIVERSAL AMERICAN FINANCIAL CORPORATION SCHOLARSHIP PROGRAM

One-time award available to dependent children of qualified Universal American Financial Corporation employees.

Award: Scholarship for use in freshman, sophomore, junior, or senior years; not renewable. *Number:* varies. *Amount:* up to $2000.

Eligibility Requirements: Applicant must be enrolled or expecting to enroll at a two-year or four-year or technical institution or university. Applicant or parent of applicant must be affiliated with Universal American Financial Corporation.

Application Requirements: Application, essay, financial need analysis, references, transcript. *Deadline:* February 15.

Contact: Application available at Web site.

WACHOVIA DEPENDENT SCHOLARSHIPS

Renewable scholarships are available to dependent children of qualified employees of Wachovia. For more details and an application see Web site: http://www.scholarshipprograms.org

Award: Scholarship for use in freshman, sophomore, junior, or senior years; renewable. *Number:* varies. *Amount:* up to $4000.

Eligibility Requirements: Applicant must be high school student; planning to enroll or expecting to enroll full-time at a four-year institution or university and single. Applicant or parent of applicant must be affiliated with Wachovia Bank. Applicant must have 3.0 GPA or higher.

Application Requirements: Application, essay, financial need analysis, references, transcript. *Deadline:* March 1.

Contact: Application available at Web site.

CHESAPEAKE CORPORATION FOUNDATION http://www.cskcorp.com

CHESAPEAKE CORPORATION FOUNDATION SCHOLARSHIP PROGRAM FOR CHESAPEAKE EMPLOYEES' CHILDREN

Award of up to $3,500 per academic year for up to four years to help finance the college education of outstanding sons and daughters of Chesapeake Corporation employees.

Award: Scholarship for use in freshman, sophomore, junior, or senior years; renewable. *Number:* 1. *Amount:* up to $3500.

Eligibility Requirements: Applicant must be high school student and planning to enroll or expecting to enroll full-time at a four-year institution or university. Applicant or parent of applicant must be affiliated with Chesapeake Corporation. Applicant or parent of applicant must have employment or volunteer experience in designated career field. Available to U.S. and non-Canadian citizens.

Application Requirements: Application, autobiography, essay, test scores, transcript. *Deadline:* November 14.

Contact: J. P. Causey, Jr., President
Chesapeake Corporation Foundation
PO Box 2350
Richmond, VA 23218
Phone: 804-697-1000
Fax: 804-697-1199

CLARA ABBOTT FOUNDATION http://clara.abbott.com/

SCHOLARSHIP PROGRAM

Scholarships are available to the children of Abbott Laboratories' employees and retirees. Must be under 29 years of age and planning to attend an accredited undergraduate program. Must reapply each year. Requirements: Completed application, copies of W2 and IRS 1040 form, and student's most recent grade report. Based on financial need. The deadline is the second Monday of December.

Award: Grant for use in freshman, sophomore, junior, or senior years; not renewable. *Number:* 4000. *Amount:* $500–$5000.

Eligibility Requirements: Applicant must be age 17-28 and enrolled or expecting to enroll full or part-time at a two-year or four-year or technical institution or university. Applicant or parent of applicant must be affiliated with Abbott Laboratories. Applicant or parent of applicant must have employment or volunteer experience in designated career field. Available to U.S. and non-U.S. citizens.

Application Requirements: Application, financial need analysis, transcript, copies of W2's, 1040's. *Deadline:* varies.

Contact: Kate O'Brian, Scholarship Coordinator
Clara Abbott Foundation
200 Abbott Park Road, D579, J37
Abbott Park, IL 60064
Phone: 847-935-8196
Fax: 847-938-6511
E-mail: jo.jakubowicz@abbott.com

COMMUNITY FOUNDATION OF WESTERN MASSACHUSETTS http://www.communityfoundation.org

DEERFIELD PLASTICS/BARKER FAMILY SCHOLARSHIP

Established by the Barker family for the children of employees of the former Deerfield Plastics.

Award: Scholarship for use in freshman, sophomore, junior, senior, or graduate years; not renewable. *Number:* 12. *Amount:* $1000–$3000.

Eligibility Requirements: Applicant must be enrolled or expecting to enroll full or part-time at a two-year or four-year institution or university and resident of Kentucky or Massachusetts. Applicant or parent of applicant must be affiliated with Deerfield Plastics. Applicant or parent of applicant must have employment or volunteer experience in designated career field. Available to U.S. citizens.

Application Requirements: Application, financial need analysis, transcript, personal statement. *Deadline:* March 31.

Contact: Community Foundation of Western Massachusetts
1500 Main Street, PO Box 15769
Springfield, MA 01115

DEMOLAY FOUNDATION INCORPORATED http://www.demolay.org

FRANK S. LAND SCHOLARSHIP

This scholarship is designed to be awarded to members of DeMolay International, who have not yet reached the age of 21, to assist in financing their education. Must be U.S. resident.

Award: Scholarship for use in freshman, sophomore, junior, or senior years; not renewable. *Number:* 10–15. *Amount:* $800.

Eligibility Requirements: Applicant must be age 21 or under; enrolled or expecting to enroll full or part-time at a two-year or four-year institution or university and male. Applicant or parent of applicant must be affiliated with DeMolay. Available to U.S. citizens.

Application Requirements: Application, references, self-addressed stamped envelope. *Deadline:* April 1.

Contact: DeMolay Foundation Incorporated
10200 NW Ambassador Drive
Kansas City, MO 64153
Phone: 800-DEM-OLAY
Fax: 816-891-9062
E-mail: news@demolay.org

DISTRICT OF COLUMBIA NATIONAL GUARD ENLISTED ASSOCIATION

DISTRICT OF COLUMBIA NATIONAL GUARD ENLISTED ASSOCIATION SCHOLARSHIP

Renewable scholarships available to residents of Washington D.C. Must be a member of the District of Columbia National Guard Enlisted Association or a dependent of member. Requires a GPA of 2.5 or greater. Application deadline varies.

Award: Scholarship for use in freshman, sophomore, junior, or senior years; renewable. *Number:* 4. *Amount:* $500.

Eligibility Requirements: Applicant must be enrolled or expecting to enroll full or part-time at a two-year or four-year institution or university and resident of District of Columbia. Applicant or parent of applicant must be affiliated with Daimler Chrysler Canada, Inc.. Applicant must have 2.5 GPA or higher. Available to U.S. citizens. Applicant or parent must meet one or more of the following requirements: Air Force National Guard or Army National Guard experience; retired from active duty; disabled or killed as a result of military service; prisoner of war; or missing in action.

Application Requirements: Application, autobiography, financial need analysis, references, transcript. *Deadline:* varies.

Contact: Scholarship Committee
District of Columbia National Guard Enlisted Association
2001 East Capitol Street, S.E.
Washington, DC 20003-1719

DONALDSON COMPANY http://www.donaldson.com

DONALDSON COMPANY, INC. SCHOLARSHIP PROGRAM

Scholarships for children of U.S. employees of Donaldson Company, Inc. Any form of accredited postsecondary education is eligible. Application deadline is March 12.

Award: Scholarship for use in freshman, sophomore, junior, or senior years; renewable. *Amount:* $1000–$3000.

Eligibility Requirements: Applicant must be enrolled or expecting to enroll full-time at a two-year or four-year or technical institution or university. Applicant or parent of applicant must be affiliated with Donaldson Company. Available to U.S. citizens.

Application Requirements: Application, essay, financial need analysis, references, transcript. *Deadline:* March 12.

Contact: Norm Linnell, Vice President, General Counsel, and Secretary
Donaldson Company
PO Box 1299
Minneapolis, MN 55440
Phone: 952-887-3631
Fax: 952-887-3005
E-mail: nlinnell@mail.donaldson.com

DUKE ENERGY CORPORATION http://www.duke-energy.com

DUKE ENERGY SCHOLARS PROGRAM

Scholarship is open to graduating high school seniors who are children of eligible employees and retirees of Duke Energy and its subsidiaries. Fifteen four-year scholarships of up to $20,000 and five $1,000 awards given annually. Recipients selected by 5-member outside committee.

Award: Scholarship for use in freshman, sophomore, junior, or senior years; renewable. *Number:* 20. *Amount:* $1000–$20,000.

Eligibility Requirements: Applicant must be high school student and planning to enroll or expecting to enroll full-time at a two-year or four-year or technical institution or university. Applicant or parent of applicant must be affiliated with Duke Energy Corporation. Available to U.S. and non-U.S. citizens.

Application Requirements: Application, autobiography, essay, financial need analysis, references, test scores, transcript. *Deadline:* December 1.

Contact: Celia Beam, Scholarship Administrator
Duke Energy Corporation
PO Box 1244
Charlotte, NC 28201-1244
Phone: 704-382-5544
Fax: 704-382-3553
E-mail: chbeam@duke-energy.com

EATON CORPORATION http://www.eaton.com

EATON CORPORATION HENRY R. TOWNE TRUST SCHOLARSHIP

Award for children of employees of the Eaton Corporation and its subsidiaries. Applicant must be junior in high school taking October PSAT. Renewable award of $1000 to $3000 depending upon financial need. Application deadline is December 31.

Award: Scholarship for use in freshman year; renewable. *Number:* 12. *Amount:* $1000–$3000.

Eligibility Requirements: Applicant must be high school student and planning to enroll or expecting to enroll full-time at a four-year institution. Applicant or parent of applicant must be affiliated with Eaton Corporation.

Application Requirements: Application. *Deadline:* December 31.

Contact: Mildred Neumann, Scholarship Coordinator
Eaton Corporation
Eaton Center
1111 Superior Avenue
Cleveland, OH 44114
Phone: 216-523-4354
Fax: 216-479-7354
E-mail: mildredneumann@eaton.com

GANNETT FOUNDATION http://www.gannettfoundation.org

GANNETT FOUNDATION/MADELYN P. JENNINGS SCHOLARSHIP AWARD

One-time awards for high school students whose parents are current full-time Gannett Company employees. Must be planning to attend a 4-year college or university for full-time study in the fall after graduation. Students must meet all requirements for participation in the National Merit Scholarship Program and take the PSAT/NMSQT in their junior year of high school. Application deadline is January 1 of applicant's junior year of high school. Call for application and information.

Award: Scholarship for use in freshman year; not renewable. *Number:* 12. *Amount:* $3000.

Eligibility Requirements: Applicant must be high school student and planning to enroll or expecting to enroll full-time at a four-year institution or university. Applicant or parent of applicant must be affiliated with Gannett Company, Inc.. Available to U.S. citizens.

Application Requirements: Application, test scores, PSAT/NMSQT. *Deadline:* January 1.

Contact: Collette Horton, Benefits Representative
Gannett Foundation
7950 Jones Branch Drive
McLean, VA 22107
Phone: 800-828-4414 Ext. 6254
E-mail: cnhorton@gannett.com

GRACO, INC. http://www.graco.com

DAVID A. KOCH SCHOLARSHIP

Three awards of $6000 (one for athletic achievement) for children of Graco employees with at least one year of company service. Award based on academics, financial need, and tuition costs. Candidate must be under 26 years of age.

Award: Scholarship for use in freshman, sophomore, junior, senior, or graduate years; not renewable. *Number:* 3. *Amount:* $6000.

Eligibility Requirements: Applicant must be age 26 or under and enrolled or expecting to enroll full-time at a two-year or four-year or technical institution or university. Applicant or parent of applicant must be affiliated with Graco, Inc.. Applicant or parent of applicant must have employment or volunteer experience in designated career field. Applicant must have 2.5 GPA or higher. Available to U.S. and non-U.S. citizens.

Application Requirements: Application, financial need analysis, test scores, transcript. *Deadline:* March 15.

Contact: Nancy Skaalrud, Legal Secretary and Foundation Coordinator
Graco, Inc.
PO Box 1441
Minneapolis, MN 55440-1441
Phone: 612-623-6684
Fax: 612-623-6944
E-mail: nskaalrud@graco.com

GRACO INC. SCHOLARSHIP PROGRAM

Renewable award for children of Graco employees under 26 years of age pursuing undergraduate or graduate education. Awards are based upon academics, financial need, and tuition costs. Submit transcripts, test scores, and financial need analysis with application.

Award: Scholarship for use in freshman, sophomore, junior, senior, or graduate years; renewable. *Number:* varies. *Amount:* $1500–$3500.

Eligibility Requirements: Applicant must be age 26 or under and enrolled or expecting to enroll full-time at a two-year or four-year or technical institution or university. Applicant or parent of applicant must be affiliated with Graco, Inc.. Applicant or parent of applicant must have employment or volunteer experience in designated career field. Applicant must have 2.5 GPA or higher. Available to U.S. and non-U.S. citizens.

Application Requirements: Application, financial need analysis, test scores, transcript. *Deadline:* March 15.

Contact: Nancy Skaalrud, Legal Secretary and Foundation Coordinator
Graco, Inc.
PO Box 1441
Minneapolis, MN 55440-1441
Phone: 612-623-6684
Fax: 612-623-6944
E-mail: nskaalrud@graco.com

HALTON FOUNDATION

HALTON SCHOLARS

Renewable scholarship available for full-time undergraduate or graduate study. Must be child of employee of Halton Company or related company. Selected on basis of merit and financial need.

Award: Scholarship for use in freshman, sophomore, junior, senior, graduate, or postgraduate years; renewable. *Number:* 1–5. *Amount:* $1260–$6499.

Eligibility Requirements: Applicant must be age 15-27; enrolled or expecting to enroll full-time at a two-year or four-year or technical institution or university and resident of Oregon or Washington. Applicant or parent of applicant must be affiliated with Halton Company. Applicant or parent of applicant must have employment or volunteer experience in designated career field. Available to U.S. and non-U.S. citizens.

Application Requirements: Application, applicant must enter a contest, essay, financial need analysis, interview, resume, test scores, transcript. *Deadline:* January 31.

Contact: Licia Bryant, Scholarship Administrator
Halton Foundation
PO Box 3377
Portland, OR 97208

HERMAN O. WEST FOUNDATION

HERMAN O. WEST FOUNDATION SCHOLARSHIP PROGRAM

Up to seven scholarships available to high school seniors who are legal dependents of a full-time West Pharmaceutical Services employee. Up to $2500 per year to pursue an undergraduate degree. Renewable for up to four years.

Award: Scholarship for use in freshman, sophomore, junior, or senior years; renewable. *Number:* up to 7. *Amount:* up to $2500.

Eligibility Requirements: Applicant must be high school student and planning to enroll or expecting to enroll full-time at a two-year or four-year institution or university. Applicant or parent of applicant must be affiliated with West Pharmaceuticals. Applicant or parent of applicant must have employment or volunteer experience in designated career field. Available to U.S. citizens.

Application Requirements: Application, essay, references, test scores, transcript. *Deadline:* February 28.

Contact: Maureen Goebel, Administrator
Herman O. West Foundation
101 Gordon Drive
Lionville, PA 19341-0645
Phone: 610-594-2945
Fax: 610-594-3011

HORMEL FOODS CORPORATION

HORMEL FOODS SCHOLARSHIP

College scholarships worth up to $3000. Must apply in your junior year of high school. Scholarships are renewable for up to four years. Must be the child of a Hormel Food employee or retiree. Must submit PSAT scores.

Award: Scholarship for use in freshman, sophomore, junior, or senior years; renewable. *Number:* 10. *Amount:* $1000–$3000.

Eligibility Requirements: Applicant must be high school student and planning to enroll or expecting to enroll full-time at a four-year institution or university. Applicant or parent of applicant must be affiliated with Hormel Foods Corporation. Available to U.S. citizens.

Application Requirements: Test scores. *Deadline:* January 10.

Contact: Ms. Julie Craven, Director of Corporate Communications
Hormel Foods Corporation
1 Hormel Place
Austin, MN 55912
Phone: 507-437-5345

HUMANA FOUNDATION http://www.humanafoundation.org/scholarship.asp

HUMANA FOUNDATION SCHOLARSHIP PROGRAM

Up to 75 scholarships are given to full-time undergraduate students. Eligible applicants must be under 25 and a United States citizen. The deadline is February 1. Must be a dependent of a Humana employee.

Award: Scholarship for use in freshman, sophomore, or junior years; renewable. *Number:* up to 75. *Amount:* $1250–$2500.

Eligibility Requirements: Applicant must be age 25 or under and enrolled or expecting to enroll full-time at a two-year or four-year institution. Applicant or parent of applicant must be affiliated with Humana Foundation. Available to U.S. citizens.

Application Requirements: Application, transcript. *Deadline:* February 1.

Contact: Charles Jackson, Program Manager
Humana Foundation
Attention: Scholarship Program, 500 West Main Street
Room 208
Louisville, KY 40202
Phone: 502-580-1245
Fax: 502-580-1256
E-mail: cjackson@humana.com

JOHNSON CONTROLS, INC. http://www.johnsoncontrols.com

JOHNSON CONTROLS FOUNDATION SCHOLARSHIP PROGRAM

Available to high school seniors who are children of Johnson Controls, Inc., employees. 20 one-time awards of $2000 and 25 renewable scholarships of $2000 a year for up to four years. Application deadline is last Friday in February.

Award: Scholarship for use in freshman, sophomore, junior, or senior years; renewable. *Number:* 45. *Amount:* $2000–$8000.

Eligibility Requirements: Applicant must be high school student and planning to enroll or expecting to enroll full-time at a four-year institution. Applicant or parent of applicant must be affiliated with Johnson Controls, Inc.. Applicant must have 3.0 GPA or higher. Available to U.S. citizens.

Application Requirements: Application, transcript.

Contact: Marlene Griffith, Human Resources Administration Coordinator
Johnson Controls, Inc.
5757 North Green Bay Avenue, X-46
Milwaukee, WI 53209
Phone: 414-524-2425

KINGSBURY CORPORATION

KINGSBURY FUND SCHOLARSHIPS

Up to three scholarships available to sons and daughters of Kingsbury Corporation employees. Must be a student in good standing, demonstrate leadership and good citizenship, be active in school affairs or have a part-time job, and establish a financial need. Renewable awards of $2000 each.

Award: Scholarship for use in freshman, sophomore, junior, or senior years; renewable. *Number:* 1–3. *Amount:* $2000.

Eligibility Requirements: Applicant must be enrolled or expecting to enroll full-time at a two-year or four-year or technical institution or university and must have an interest in leadership. Applicant or parent of applicant must be affiliated with Kingsbury Corporation. Applicant or parent of applicant must have employment or volunteer experience in designated career field.

Application Requirements: Application, essay, financial need analysis, references, transcript. *Deadline:* April 28.

Contact: Mary Ann Fleming, Scholarship Coordinator
Kingsbury Corporation
80 Laurel Street
Keene, NH 03431-4207
Phone: 603-352-5212

KNIGHT RIDDER http://www.kri.com

KNIGHT RIDDER MERIT SCHOLARSHIP PROGRAM

Renewable award for high school students who are sons or daughters of employees of Knight Ridder or its subsidiaries. Students must take the Preliminary SAT/National Merit Scholarship Qualifying Test. Winners will be chosen from a group of candidates who qualify as Merit Program Semifinalists, without regard to family financial circumstances. For further details, see Web site at http://www.kri.com.

Award: Scholarship for use in freshman, sophomore, junior, or senior years; renewable. *Number:* up to 3. *Amount:* $500–$2000.

Eligibility Requirements: Applicant must be high school student and planning to enroll or expecting to enroll full-time at a four-year institution or university. Applicant or parent of applicant must be affiliated with Knight Ridder. Available to U.S. citizens.

Knight Ridder (continued)

Application Requirements: Application, financial need analysis. *Deadline:* varies.

Contact: Cathy King, Director of Compensation
Knight Ridder
50 West San Fernando Street
San Jose, CA 95113
E-mail: cking@knightridder.com

KOHLER COMPANY http://www.kohler.com

KOHLER COMPANY COLLEGE SCHOLARSHIP

Renewable award for college-bound children of Kohler and its U.S. and Canadian subsidiary employees. High school students who are Kohler employees are also eligible. Scholarships are valued at $1500 per year.

Award: Scholarship for use in freshman, sophomore, junior, or senior years; renewable. *Number:* 21. *Amount:* $1500.

Eligibility Requirements: Applicant must be high school student and planning to enroll or expecting to enroll full-time at a two-year or four-year institution or university. Applicant or parent of applicant must be affiliated with Kohler Company. Available to U.S. and Canadian citizens.

Application Requirements: Application, references, test scores, transcript. *Deadline:* February 15.

Contact: Lynn Kulow, Senior Communication Specialist-Corporate Giving and Civic Services
Kohler Company
444 Highland Drive
Kohler, WI 53044
Phone: 920-457-4441
Fax: 920-457-9064
E-mail: lynn.kulow@kohler.com

NATIONAL ART MATERIALS TRADE ASSOCIATION http://www.namta.org

NATIONAL ART MATERIALS TRADE ASSOCIATION ACADEMIC SCHOLARSHIP

Two scholarships awarded to an employee or relative of a National Art Materials Trade Association member firm. Submit transcript, test scores, and essay with application. One-time award of $1500. Application deadline is April 1. For further details, see Web site at http://www.namta.org or email inquiries to scholarship@namta.org.

Award: Scholarship for use in freshman, sophomore, junior, senior, graduate, or postgraduate years; not renewable. *Number:* 2. *Amount:* $1500.

Eligibility Requirements: Applicant must be enrolled or expecting to enroll full-time at a two-year or four-year or technical institution or university. Applicant or parent of applicant must be affiliated with National Art Materials Trade Association. Available to U.S. and non-U.S. citizens.

Application Requirements: Application, essay, test scores, transcript. *Deadline:* April 1.

Contact: Ms. Katharine Coffey, Scholarship Coordinator
National Art Materials Trade Association
15806 Brookway Drive, Suite 300
Huntersville, NC 28078
Phone: 704-892-6244
Fax: 704-892-6247
E-mail: kcoffey@namta.org

NEW HAMPSHIRE FOOD INDUSTRIES EDUCATION FOUNDATION http://www.grocers.org

NEW HAMPSHIRE FOOD INDUSTRY SCHOLARSHIPS

The scholarships are one-time, non-renewable awards of $1,000. The purpose is to assist students who are employees or children of employees working for New Hampshire Grocers Association members.

Award: Scholarship for use in freshman, sophomore, junior, senior, or graduate years; not renewable. *Number:* 12. *Amount:* $1000.

Eligibility Requirements: Applicant must be enrolled or expecting to enroll full-time at a two-year or four-year or technical institution or university. Applicant or parent of applicant must be affiliated with New Hampshire Grocers Association member companies. Available to U.S. and non-U.S. citizens.

Application Requirements: Application, essay, references, test scores, transcript. *Deadline:* March 17.

Contact: John Dumais, Treasurer
New Hampshire Food Industries Education Foundation
110 Stark Street
Manchester, NH 03101-1977
Phone: 603-669-9333 Ext. 110
Fax: 603-623-1137
E-mail: dumais@grocers.org

OMNOVA SOLUTIONS FOUNDATION http://www.omnova.com

NATIONAL MERIT SCHOLARSHIPS FUNDED BY OMNOVA SOLUTIONS FOUNDATION

Awarded to children of Omnova Solutions employees only. Preliminary SAT or National Merit Scholarship Qualifying Test scores required. Test should be taken two years prior to high school graduation. Renewable award is for undergraduate study at an accredited four-year college or university. Deadline: December 24.

Award: Scholarship for use in freshman, sophomore, junior, or senior years; renewable. *Number:* 3. *Amount:* $500–$2000.

Eligibility Requirements: Applicant must be high school student and planning to enroll or expecting to enroll full-time at a four-year institution or university. Applicant or parent of applicant must be affiliated with Omnova Solutions. Available to U.S. citizens.

Application Requirements: Application, test scores. *Deadline:* December 24.

Contact: S. Theresa Carter, Director
Omnova Solutions Foundation
175 Ghent Road
Fairlawn, OH 44333-3300
Phone: 330-869-4289
Fax: 330-869-4345
E-mail: theresa.carter@omnova.com

OREGON STUDENT ASSISTANCE COMMISSION http://www.osac.state.or.us

A. VICTOR ROSENFELD SCHOLARSHIP

One-time award for children of employees of Calbag Metals, Portland, who have worked for that company for three years prior to the March 1 scholarship deadline.

Award: Scholarship for use in freshman, sophomore, junior, or senior years; not renewable. *Number:* 1. *Amount:* $1000.

Eligibility Requirements: Applicant must be enrolled or expecting to enroll at a four-year institution and resident of Oregon. Applicant or parent of applicant must be affiliated with Calbag Metals. Applicant or parent of applicant must have employment or volunteer experience in designated career field. Available to U.S. citizens.

Application Requirements: Application, essay, financial need analysis, references, transcript, activity chart. *Deadline:* March 1.

Contact: Director of Grant Programs
Oregon Student Assistance Commission
1500 Valley River Drive, Suite 100
Eugene, OR 97401-7020
Phone: 800-452-8807 Ext. 7395
E-mail: awardinfo@mercury.osac.state.or.us

ALBINA FUEL COMPANY SCHOLARSHIP

One scholarship available to a dependent child of a current Albina Fuel Company employee. The employee must have been employed for at least one full year as of October 1 prior to the scholarship deadline. One-time award.

Award: Scholarship for use in freshman, sophomore, junior, or senior years; not renewable. *Number:* 3. *Amount:* $1000.

Eligibility Requirements: Applicant must be enrolled or expecting to enroll at an institution or university and resident of Oregon. Applicant or parent of applicant must be affiliated with Albina Fuel Company.

Applicant or parent of applicant must have employment or volunteer experience in designated career field. Available to U.S. citizens.

Application Requirements: Application, essay, financial need analysis, transcript, activity chart. *Deadline:* March 1.

Contact: Director of Grant Programs
Oregon Student Assistance Commission
1500 Valley River Drive, Suite 100
Eugene, OR 97401-7020
Phone: 800-452-8807 Ext. 7395
E-mail: awardinfo@mercury.osac.state.or.us

BANK OF THE CASCADES SCHOLARSHIP

One-time award for employees or natural, adopted, or step children between the ages of 17 and 25 of current Bank of the Cascades employees. Children must be high school graduates with minimum 3.00 GPA. Employees must have been continuously employed at Bank of the Cascades for one year at no fewer than 20 hours per week as of the March 1 scholarship deadline. For use at Oregon colleges only. Children of Bank of the Cascades officers are not eligible.

Award: Scholarship for use in freshman, sophomore, junior, or senior years; not renewable. *Number:* varies. *Amount:* $500.

Eligibility Requirements: Applicant must be age 17-25; enrolled or expecting to enroll at an institution or university; resident of Oregon and studying in Oregon. Applicant or parent of applicant must be affiliated with Bank of the Cascades. Applicant must have 3.0 GPA or higher.

Application Requirements: Application, essay, financial need analysis, transcript. *Deadline:* March 1.

Contact: Director of Grant Programs
Oregon Student Assistance Commission
1500 Valley River Drive, Suite 100
Eugene, OR 97401-7020
Phone: 800-452-8807 Ext. 7395
E-mail: awardinfo@mercury.osac.state.or.us

BLUE HERON PAPER EMPLOYEE DEPENDENTS SCHOLARSHIP

Renewable award for children, grandchildren, and legal dependents (22 years old and under) of active Blue Heron Paper (formerly Smurfit Newsprint) employees. Must be employed with company at least one year.

Award: Scholarship for use in freshman, sophomore, junior, or senior years; renewable. *Number:* 1. *Amount:* $1750.

Eligibility Requirements: Applicant must be age 22 or under; enrolled or expecting to enroll at a four-year institution and resident of Oregon. Applicant or parent of applicant must be affiliated with Blue Heron Paper. Applicant or parent of applicant must have employment or volunteer experience in designated career field. Available to U.S. citizens.

Application Requirements: Application, essay, financial need analysis, references, transcript, activity chart. *Deadline:* March 1.

Contact: Director of Grant Programs
Oregon Student Assistance Commission
1500 Valley River Drive, Suite 100
Eugene, OR 97401-7020
Phone: 800-452-8807 Ext. 7395
E-mail: awardinfo@mercury.osac.state.or.us

DAN KONNIE MEMORIAL SCHOLARSHIP

Renewable award for graduating high school seniors who are children of Swanson Brothers Lumber Co. employees. Must be enrolled in a U.S. public college. Must be an Oregon resident.

Award: Scholarship for use in freshman year; renewable. *Number:* 19. *Amount:* $2000.

Eligibility Requirements: Applicant must be high school student; planning to enroll or expecting to enroll at a four-year institution and resident of Oregon. Applicant or parent of applicant must be affiliated with Swanson Brothers Lumber Company. Available to U.S. citizens.

Application Requirements: Application, essay, financial need analysis, references, transcript, activity chart. *Deadline:* March 1.

Contact: Director of Grant Programs
Oregon Student Assistance Commission
1500 Valley River Drive, Suite 100
Eugene, OR 97401-7020
Phone: 800-452-8807 Ext. 7395
E-mail: awardinfo@mercury.osac.state.or.us

ESSEX SCHOLARSHIP

One-time award for employees of Essex General Construction, Inc., or their children. Must be between the ages of 17 and 25. Qualifying children must be high school graduates or GED recipients. Qualifying employees must have been continuously employed at Essex for at least one year for at least 20 hours per week as of the March 1 scholarship deadline.

Award: Scholarship for use in freshman, sophomore, junior, or senior years; not renewable. *Number:* 1. *Amount:* $5000.

Eligibility Requirements: Applicant must be age 17-25; enrolled or expecting to enroll at an institution or university and resident of Oregon. Applicant or parent of applicant must be affiliated with Essex General Construction.

Application Requirements: Application, essay, financial need analysis, transcript. *Deadline:* March 1.

Contact: Director of Grant Programs
Oregon Student Assistance Commission
1500 Valley River Drive, Suite 100
Eugene, OR 97401-7020
Phone: 800-452-8807 Ext. 7395
E-mail: awardinfo@mercury.osac.state.or.us

GLENN JACKSON SCHOLARS SCHOLARSHIPS (OCF)

Award for graduating high school seniors who are dependents of employees or retirees of Oregon Department of Transportation or Parks and Recreation Department. Employees must have worked in their department at least three years. Award for maximum twelve undergraduate quarters or six quarters at a two-year institution. Must be U.S. citizen or permanent resident. Visit Web site (http://www.osac.state.or.us) for more details.

Award: Scholarship for use in freshman, sophomore, junior, or senior years; renewable. *Number:* 2. *Amount:* $2500.

Eligibility Requirements: Applicant must be high school student; planning to enroll or expecting to enroll at a four-year institution and resident of Oregon. Applicant or parent of applicant must be affiliated with Oregon Department of Transportation Parks and Recreation. Applicant or parent of applicant must have employment or volunteer experience in designated career field. Available to U.S. citizens.

Application Requirements: Application, essay, financial need analysis, references, transcript, activity chart. *Deadline:* March 1.

Contact: Director of Grant Programs
Oregon Student Assistance Commission
1500 Valley River Drive, Suite 100
Eugene, OR 97401-7020
Phone: 800-452-8807 Ext. 7395
E-mail: awardinfo@mercury.osac.state.or.us

MC GARRY MACHINE INC. SCHOLARSHIP

One-time award for employees or dependents of employees of McGarry Machine who are high school graduates or GED recipients enrolling at least half-time in college. Contact Web site http://www.osac.state.or.us for further information.

Award: Scholarship for use in freshman, sophomore, junior, senior, or graduate years; renewable. *Number:* varies. *Amount:* $500.

Eligibility Requirements: Applicant must be enrolled or expecting to enroll full or part-time at a four-year institution and resident of Oregon. Applicant or parent of applicant must be affiliated with McGarry Machine, Inc.. Applicant or parent of applicant must have employment or volunteer experience in designated career field. Available to U.S. citizens.

Oregon Student Assistance Commission (continued)

Application Requirements: Application, essay, financial need analysis, references, transcript, activity chart. *Deadline:* March 1.

Contact: Director of Grant Programs
Oregon Student Assistance Commission
1500 Valley River Drive, Suite 100
Eugene, OR 97401-7020
Phone: 800-452-8807 Ext. 7395
E-mail: awardinfo@mercury.osac.state.or.us

PACIFICSOURCE SCHOLARSHIP

One-time award for high school graduates or GED recipients between the ages of 17 and 25 who are the natural, adopted, or step children of PacificSource employees. Employee must have been continuously employed at PacificSource for at least two years at no fewer than 20 hours per week. Minimum 3.0 GPA. Children of PacificSource officers are not eligible to participate.

Award: Scholarship for use in freshman, sophomore, junior, or senior years; not renewable. *Number:* varies. *Amount:* $500.

Eligibility Requirements: Applicant must be age 17-25; enrolled or expecting to enroll at an institution or university and resident of Oregon. Applicant or parent of applicant must be affiliated with PacificSource. Applicant must have 3.0 GPA or higher.

Application Requirements: Application, essay, financial need analysis, transcript. *Deadline:* March 1.

Contact: Director of Grant Programs
Oregon Student Assistance Commission
1500 Valley River Drive, Suite 100
Eugene, OR 97401-7020
Phone: 800-452-8807 Ext. 7395
E-mail: awardinfo@mercury.osac.state.or.us

REED'S FUEL AND TRUCKING COMPANY SCHOLARSHIP

One-time award for dependents of Reed's employees who have been employed at least one year prior to deadline. Must attend a college or a university in Oregon and have minimum cumulative 2.5 GPA. Employees may enroll part time. Dependents must enroll full time.

Award: Scholarship for use in freshman, sophomore, junior, or senior years; not renewable. *Number:* 1. *Amount:* $500.

Eligibility Requirements: Applicant must be enrolled or expecting to enroll full or part-time at a two-year or four-year institution; resident of Oregon and studying in Oregon. Applicant or parent of applicant must be affiliated with Reeds Fuel and Trucking Company. Applicant or parent of applicant must have employment or volunteer experience in designated career field. Applicant must have 2.5 GPA or higher. Available to U.S. citizens.

Application Requirements: Application, essay, financial need analysis, references, transcript, activity chart. *Deadline:* March 1.

Contact: Director of Grant Programs
Oregon Student Assistance Commission
1500 Valley River Drive, Suite 100
Eugene, OR 97401-7020
Phone: 800-452-8807 Ext. 7395
E-mail: awardinfo@mercury.osac.state.or.us

RICHARD F. BRENTANO MEMORIAL SCHOLARSHIP

One-time award for legal dependents of Waste Control Systems Inc., and subsidiaries. Employees must be employed at least one year as of application deadline. Must be 24 years old or less, 26 years old for dependents entering U.S. Armed Forces directly from high school.

Award: Scholarship for use in freshman, sophomore, junior, or senior years; not renewable. *Number:* 9. *Amount:* $1417.

Eligibility Requirements: Applicant must be enrolled or expecting to enroll at a four-year institution and resident of Oregon. Applicant or parent of applicant must be affiliated with Waste Control Systems, Inc.. Available to U.S. citizens.

Application Requirements: Application, essay, financial need analysis, references, transcript, activity chart. *Deadline:* March 1.

Contact: Director of Grant Programs
Oregon Student Assistance Commission
1500 Valley River Drive, Suite 100
Eugene, OR 97401-7020
Phone: 800-452-8807 Ext. 7395
E-mail: awardinfo@mercury.osac.state.or.us

ROBERT D. FORSTER SCHOLARSHIP

One scholarship available to a dependent child of a Walsh Construction Co. employee who has completed 1,000 hours or more in each of three consecutive fiscal years. Award may be received for a maximum of twelve quarters of undergraduate study and may only be used at four-year colleges.

Award: Scholarship for use in freshman, sophomore, junior, or senior years; renewable. *Number:* 1. *Amount:* $2500.

Eligibility Requirements: Applicant must be enrolled or expecting to enroll at a four-year institution and resident of Oregon. Applicant or parent of applicant must be affiliated with Walsh Construction Company. Applicant or parent of applicant must have employment or volunteer experience in designated career field. Available to U.S. citizens.

Application Requirements: Application, essay, financial need analysis, references, transcript, activity chart. *Deadline:* March 1.

Contact: Director of Grant Programs
Oregon Student Assistance Commission
1500 Valley River Drive, Suite 100
Eugene, OR 97401-7020
Phone: 800-452-8807 Ext. 7395
E-mail: awardinfo@mercury.osac.state.or.us

ROGER W. EMMONS MEMORIAL SCHOLARSHIP

One scholarship available to a graduating Oregon high school senior who is a child or grandchild of an employee (for at least three years) of member of the Oregon Refuse and Recycling Association.

Award: Scholarship for use in freshman year; renewable. *Number:* 3. *Amount:* $1000.

Eligibility Requirements: Applicant must be high school student; planning to enroll or expecting to enroll at a four-year institution and resident of Oregon. Applicant or parent of applicant must be affiliated with Oregon Refuse and Recycling Association. Applicant or parent of applicant must have employment or volunteer experience in designated career field. Available to U.S. citizens.

Application Requirements: Application, essay, financial need analysis, references, transcript, activity chart. *Deadline:* March 1.

Contact: Director of Grant Programs
Oregon Student Assistance Commission
1500 Valley River Drive, Suite 100
Eugene, OR 97401-7020
Phone: 800-452-8807 Ext. 7395
E-mail: awardinfo@mercury.osac.state.or.us

ROSEBURG FOREST PRODUCTS SONS AND DAUGHTERS SCHOLARSHIP

Renewable award for legal dependents of employees of Roseburg Forest Products Co. Must be 21 years of age or younger. Qualifying parents must have been employees a minimum of 18 months prior to the March 1 deadline.

Award: Scholarship for use in freshman, sophomore, junior, or senior years; renewable. *Number:* varies. *Amount:* $2000–$5000.

Eligibility Requirements: Applicant must be age 21 or under; enrolled or expecting to enroll full-time at a two-year or four-year institution and resident of Oregon. Applicant or parent of applicant must be affiliated with Roseburg Forest Products. Applicant or parent of applicant must have employment or volunteer experience in designated career field. Available to U.S. citizens.

Application Requirements: Application, essay, financial need analysis, references, transcript, activity chart. *Deadline:* March 1.

Contact: Director of Grant Programs
Oregon Student Assistance Commission
1500 Valley River Drive, Suite 100
Eugene, OR 97401-7020
Phone: 800-452-8807 Ext. 7395
E-mail: awardinfo@mercury.osac.state.or.us

SP NEWSPRINT COMPANY, NEWBERG MILL, EMPLOYEE DEPENDENTS SCHOLARSHIP

One-time award available to children, grandchildren, legal dependents (22 years old and under) of active SP Newsprint Co., Newberg Mill employees. Age limit extended by years served to maximum age of 26 for those entering armed services directly from high school. Employees must be employed by the company at least one year. At least one award is for community colleges.

Award: Scholarship for use in freshman, sophomore, junior, or senior years; not renewable. *Number:* 9. *Amount:* $1667.

Eligibility Requirements: Applicant must be age 26 or under; enrolled or expecting to enroll at a two-year institution or university and resident of Oregon. Applicant or parent of applicant must be affiliated with SP Newsprint Company. Applicant or parent of applicant must have employment or volunteer experience in designated career field. Available to U.S. citizens.

Application Requirements: Application, essay, financial need analysis, references, transcript, activity chart. *Deadline:* March 1.

Contact: Director of Grant Programs
Oregon Student Assistance Commission
1500 Valley River Drive, Suite 100
Eugene, OR 97401-7020
Phone: 800-452-8807 Ext. 7395
E-mail: awardinfo@mercury.osac.state.or.us

STIMSON LUMBER COMPANY SCHOLARSHIP

Award for dependents of Stimson employees who are graduating seniors from accredited high school. Non-renewable scholarships available for two- or four-year colleges. Four-year scholarships renewable with minimum 2.7 cumulative GPA.

Award: Scholarship for use in freshman year; renewable. *Number:* 19. *Amount:* $1947.

Eligibility Requirements: Applicant must be high school student; planning to enroll or expecting to enroll at a two-year or four-year institution and resident of Oregon. Applicant or parent of applicant must be affiliated with Stimson Lumber Company. Applicant or parent of applicant must have employment or volunteer experience in designated career field. Available to U.S. citizens.

Application Requirements: Application, essay, financial need analysis, references, transcript, activity chart. *Deadline:* March 1.

Contact: Director of Grant Programs
Oregon Student Assistance Commission
1500 Valley River Drive, Suite 100
Eugene, OR 97401-7020
Phone: 800-452-8807 Ext. 7395
E-mail: awardinfo@mercury.osac.state.or.us

TAYLOR MADE LABELS SCHOLARSHIP

One-time award available to a child, grandchild or legal dependent (22 years of age and under) of an active employee of Taylor Made Label Company. Employee must have been employed by Taylor Made for a minimum of one year as of scholarship deadline.

Award: Scholarship for use in freshman, sophomore, junior, or senior years; not renewable. *Number:* varies. *Amount:* $500.

Eligibility Requirements: Applicant must be age 22 or under; enrolled or expecting to enroll at a four-year institution and resident of Oregon. Applicant or parent of applicant must be affiliated with Taylor Made Label Company. Applicant or parent of applicant must have employment or volunteer experience in designated career field. Available to U.S. citizens.

Application Requirements: Application, essay, financial need analysis, references, transcript, activity chart. *Deadline:* March 1.

Contact: Director of Grant Programs
Oregon Student Assistance Commission
1500 Valley River Drive, Suite 100
Eugene, OR 97401-7020
Phone: 800-452-8807 Ext. 7395
E-mail: awardinfo@mercury.osac.state.or.us

WALTER DAVIES SCHOLARSHIP

One-time award for U.S. Bancorp employees or employees' natural or adopted children. Must be Oregon high school graduates.

Award: Scholarship for use in freshman, sophomore, junior, or senior years; not renewable. *Number:* 38. *Amount:* $1529.

Eligibility Requirements: Applicant must be enrolled or expecting to enroll at a four-year institution and resident of Oregon. Applicant or parent of applicant must be affiliated with U.S. Bancorp. Available to U.S. citizens.

Application Requirements: Application, essay, financial need analysis, references, transcript, activity chart. *Deadline:* March 1.

Contact: Director of Grant Programs
Oregon Student Assistance Commission
1500 Valley River Drive, Suite 100
Eugene, OR 97401-7020
Phone: 800-452-8807 Ext. 7395
E-mail: awardinfo@mercury.osac.state.or.us

WILLETT AND MARGUERITE LAKE SCHOLARSHIP

Scholarship awards children, stepchildren, and grandchildren of current employees of Bonita Pioneer Packaging Company who have been employed by the company 2 years as of the March 1 scholarship deadline.

Award: Scholarship for use in freshman, sophomore, junior, senior, or graduate years; not renewable. *Number:* varies. *Amount:* $500.

Eligibility Requirements: Applicant must be enrolled or expecting to enroll at an institution or university and resident of Hawaii or Oregon. Applicant or parent of applicant must be affiliated with Mail-Well Envelope Company. Applicant or parent of applicant must have employment or volunteer experience in designated career field.

Application Requirements: Application, essay, financial need analysis, transcript, activity chart. *Deadline:* March 1.

Contact: Director of Grant Programs
Oregon Student Assistance Commission
1500 Valley River Drive, Suite 100
Eugene, OR 97401-7020
Phone: 800-452-8807 Ext. 7395
E-mail: awardinfo@mercury.osac.state.or.us

WOODARD FAMILY SCHOLARSHIP

Scholarships are available to employees and children of employees of Kimwood Corporation or Middlefield Estates. Applicants must have graduated from a U.S. high school. Awards may be used at Oregon colleges only, and may be received for a maximum of twelve quarters of undergraduate study.

Award: Scholarship for use in freshman, sophomore, junior, or senior years; renewable. *Number:* varies. *Amount:* $500.

Eligibility Requirements: Applicant must be enrolled or expecting to enroll at a two-year or four-year institution; resident of Oregon and studying in Oregon. Applicant or parent of applicant must be affiliated with Kimwood Corporation or Middlefield Village. Applicant or parent of applicant must have employment or volunteer experience in designated career field. Available to U.S. citizens.

Application Requirements: Application, essay, financial need analysis, references, transcript. *Deadline:* March 1.

Contact: Director of Grant Programs
Oregon Student Assistance Commission
1500 Valley River Drive, Suite 100
Eugene, OR 97401-7020
Phone: 800-452-8807 Ext. 7395
E-mail: awardinfo@mercury.osac.state.or.us

PROCTER & GAMBLE FUND http://www.pg.com

PROCTER & GAMBLE FUND SCHOLARSHIP COMPETITION FOR EMPLOYEES' CHILDREN

Award for high school seniors who are dependents of eligible employees, including deceased employees, and retirees of Procter and Gamble Company. All winners receive a one-time-only award of $2500. Deadline: January 15 of applicant's senior year of high school.

Award: Scholarship for use in freshman year; not renewable. *Number:* up to 250. *Amount:* $2500.

Eligibility Requirements: Applicant must be high school student and planning to enroll or expecting to enroll full-time at a two-year or four-year or technical institution or university. Applicant or parent of applicant must be affiliated with Procter & Gamble Company. Applicant or parent of applicant must have employment or volunteer experience in designated career field. Available to U.S. citizens.

Application Requirements: Application, applicant must enter a contest, essay, references, test scores, transcript. *Deadline:* January 15.

Contact: Tawnia True, Coordinator, P&G Employee Scholarship Fund
Procter & Gamble Fund
PO Box 599
Cincinnati, OH 45201-0599
Phone: 513-983-2139
Fax: 513-983-2173
E-mail: pgfund.im@pg.com

QUAKER CHEMICAL FOUNDATION (THE) http://www.quakerchem.com

QUAKER CHEMICAL FOUNDATION SCHOLARSHIPS

One-time award for high school seniors and college undergraduates who are dependents of Quaker Chemical employees. Must be a U.S. citizen and seeking a college degree to be eligible.

Award: Scholarship for use in freshman, sophomore, junior, or senior years; not renewable. *Number:* 1. *Amount:* $2000–$5000.

Eligibility Requirements: Applicant must be enrolled or expecting to enroll full-time at a four-year institution. Applicant or parent of applicant must be affiliated with Quaker Chemical Foundation. Applicant or parent of applicant must have employment or volunteer experience in designated career field. Available to U.S. citizens.

Application Requirements: Application, essay, references, test scores, transcript. *Deadline:* February 4.

Contact: Katherine Coughenour, Chair
Quaker Chemical Foundation (The)
901 Hector Street
Conshohocken, PA 19428
Phone: 610-832-4301
Fax: 610-832-4494

RHODE ISLAND FOUNDATION http://www.rifoundation.org

A.T. CROSS SCHOLARSHIP

Numerous scholarships available to children of full-time employees of A.T. Cross Company. Renewable. Must be Rhode Island resident.

Award: Scholarship for use in freshman, sophomore, junior, or senior years; renewable. *Number:* varies. *Amount:* $1000–$3000.

Eligibility Requirements: Applicant must be enrolled or expecting to enroll at an institution or university and resident of Rhode Island. Applicant or parent of applicant must be affiliated with A.T. Cross.

Application Requirements: Application, self-addressed stamped envelope. *Deadline:* May 14.

Contact: Kathleen Agostinelli, A. T. Cross Company
Rhode Island Foundation
One Albion Road
Lincoln, RI 02865
Phone: 401-335-8484

UNITED NEGRO COLLEGE FUND http://www.uncf.org

CHURCH'S CHICKEN OPPORTUNITY SCHOLARSHIP

• *See page 488*

KFC SCHOLARS PROGRAM

Award for KFC corporate or franchise employee who has at least one year of work experience with KFC and who wishes to pursue a Bachelor's degree in business management, computer sciences, or liberal arts at a UNCF institution. Must have a 3.0 GPA, be an employee in good standing, and have an unmet financial need.

Award: Scholarship for use in freshman, sophomore, junior, or senior years; renewable. *Number:* up to 1. *Amount:* varies.

Eligibility Requirements: Applicant must be enrolled or expecting to enroll at a four-year institution or university. Applicant or parent of applicant must be affiliated with Kentucky Fried Chicken. Applicant must have 3.0 GPA or higher.

Application Requirements: Application, essay, transcript. *Deadline:* April 1.

Contact: Program Services Department
United Negro College Fund
8260 Willow Oaks Corporate Drive
Fairfax, VA 22031

LEON JACKSON, JR. SCHOLARSHIP

Award for current UNCF employees who desire to return to school to complete their associate, undergraduate, or graduate education. Please see Web site for more information: http://www.uncf.org.

Award: Scholarship for use in freshman, sophomore, junior, senior, graduate, or postgraduate years; renewable. *Number:* up to 2. *Amount:* up to $2500.

Eligibility Requirements: Applicant must be enrolled or expecting to enroll full or part-time at a two-year or four-year institution or university. Applicant or parent of applicant must be affiliated with United Negro College Fund. Applicant must have 2.5 GPA or higher.

Application Requirements: Application, essay, financial need analysis, references, transcript, FAFSA, SAR. *Deadline:* May 31.

Contact: Annette Singletary, Senior Program Manager, United Negro College Fund, Inc.
United Negro College Fund
8260 Willow Oaks Corporate Drive
Fairfax, VA 22031

WAL-MART FOUNDATION http://www.walmartfoundation.org

WAL-MART ASSOCIATE SCHOLARSHIPS

Awards for college-bound high school seniors who work for Wal-Mart or whose parents are part-time Wal-Mart associates or have not been with the company for one year. Based on ACT or SAT scores, counselor recommendations, transcripts, class rank, activities, and financial need. One-time award of up to $2000. For use at an accredited two- or four-year U.S. institution.

Award: Scholarship for use in freshman year; not renewable. *Number:* 150–300. *Amount:* up to $2000.

Eligibility Requirements: Applicant must be high school student and planning to enroll or expecting to enroll full-time at a two-year or four-year institution or university. Applicant or parent of applicant must be affiliated with Wal-Mart Foundation. Applicant or parent of applicant must have employment or volunteer experience in designated career field. Available to U.S. citizens.

Application Requirements: Application, test scores, transcript, federal income tax return. *Deadline:* February 1.

Contact: Jenny Harral
Wal-Mart Foundation
702 Southwest 8th Street
Bentonville, AR 72716-0150
Phone: 800-530-9925
Fax: 501-273-6850

WAL-MART HIGHER REACH SCHOLARSHIP

For non-traditional students who have been employed full-time by Wal-Mart for at least a year by February 1. Award is based on financial need, academic record, essay, and job performance. Applications are available from each location personnel office in November.

Award: Scholarship for use in freshman, sophomore, junior, or senior years; not renewable. *Number:* varies. *Amount:* $500–$2000.

Eligibility Requirements: Applicant must be enrolled or expecting to enroll part-time at a two-year or four-year institution or university. Applicant or parent of applicant must be affiliated with Wal-Mart Foundation. Applicant or parent of applicant must have employment or volunteer experience in designated career field. Available to U.S. citizens.

Application Requirements: Application, essay, financial need analysis, references, transcript, job performance appraisal. *Deadline:* February 1.

Contact: Emmy Hardin, Program Coordinator
Wal-Mart Foundation
702 Southwest 8th Street
Bentonville, AR 72716-9002
Phone: 800-530-9925
Fax: 501-273-6850

WALTON FAMILY FOUNDATION SCHOLARSHIP

Award for high-school seniors who are children of a Wal-Mart associate who has been employed as a full-time associate for at least one year. $8000 undergraduate scholarship payable over four years. Must submit latest federal income tax return. Contact a member of Wal-Mart management for an application starting in November each year.

Award: Scholarship for use in freshman, sophomore, junior, or senior years; renewable. *Number:* 100–120. *Amount:* $8000.

Eligibility Requirements: Applicant must be high school student and planning to enroll or expecting to enroll full-time at a two-year or four-year institution or university. Applicant or parent of applicant must be affiliated with Wal-Mart Foundation. Available to U.S. citizens.

Application Requirements: Application, financial need analysis, test scores, transcript, federal income tax return. *Deadline:* February 1.

Contact: Jenny Harral
Wal-Mart Foundation
702 Southwest 8th Street
Bentonville, AR 72716-0150
Phone: 800-530-9925
Fax: 501-273-6850

WEYERHAEUSER COMPANY FOUNDATION

WEYERHAEUSER COMPANY FOUNDATION SCHOLARSHIPS

Renewable awards for children of Weyerhaeuser Company employees. Must apply by January 15 of senior year in high school.

Award: Scholarship for use in freshman year; renewable. *Number:* 65. *Amount:* $1000–$4000.

Eligibility Requirements: Applicant must be high school student and planning to enroll or expecting to enroll full-time at a two-year or four-year or technical institution. Applicant or parent of applicant must be affiliated with Weyerhauser Company.

Application Requirements: Application. *Deadline:* January 15.

Contact: Penny Paul, Program Manager
Weyerhaeuser Company Foundation
EC-22A8
PO Box 9777
Federal Way, WA 98063-9777
Phone: 253-924-2629
Fax: 253-924-3658

WILLITS FOUNDATION

WILLITS FOUNDATION SCHOLARSHIP PROGRAM

Renewable awards for children of full-time C. R. Bard, Inc., employees only. Children of Bard officers are not eligible. For domestic Bard branches only. Must be pursuing, or planning to pursue, full-time postsecondary studies in the year in which the application is made.

Award: Scholarship for use in freshman, sophomore, junior, or senior years; renewable. *Number:* 10. *Amount:* $1000–$5000.

Eligibility Requirements: Applicant must be enrolled or expecting to enroll full-time at a four-year institution or university. Applicant or parent of applicant must be affiliated with C.R. Bard, Inc.. Available to U.S. and Canadian citizens.

Application Requirements: Application, essay, photo, references, test scores, transcript. *Deadline:* March 1.

Contact: Ms. Linda Hrevnack, Program Manager
Willits Foundation
730 Central Avenue
Murray Hill, NJ 07974
Phone: 908-277-8182
Fax: 908-277-8098

EMPLOYMENT EXPERIENCE

A.W. BODINE-SUNKIST GROWERS, INC.

A.W. BODINE-SUNKIST MEMORIAL SCHOLARSHIP

Renewable award for undergraduate study for applicants whose family derives most of its income from the agriculture industry in Arizona or California. Award is based on minimum 2.7 GPA and financial need.

Award: Scholarship for use in freshman, sophomore, junior, or senior years; renewable. *Number:* 20. *Amount:* $2000.

Eligibility Requirements: Applicant must be enrolled or expecting to enroll full-time at a four-year institution and resident of Arizona or California. Applicant or parent of applicant must have employment or volunteer experience in agriculture.

Application Requirements: Application, essay, financial need analysis, references, test scores, transcript. *Deadline:* April 30.

Contact: Claire Smith, Scholarship Administrator
A.W. Bodine-Sunkist Growers, Inc.
PO Box 7888
Van Nuys, CA 91409-7888
Phone: 818-986-4800
Fax: 818-379-7511

AIR TRAFFIC CONTROL ASSOCIATION, INC. http://www.atca.org

BUCKINGHAM MEMORIAL SCHOLARSHIP

Scholarships granted to children of air traffic control specialists pursuing a bachelor's degree or higher in any course of study.

Award: Scholarship for use in freshman, sophomore, junior, senior, or graduate years; not renewable. *Number:* 2–4. *Amount:* $1000–$1500.

Eligibility Requirements: Applicant must be enrolled or expecting to enroll full or part-time at a four-year institution or university. Applicant or parent of applicant must have employment or volunteer experience in air traffic controller field. Available to U.S. citizens.

Application Requirements: Application, autobiography, essay, financial need analysis, references, transcript. *Deadline:* May 1.

Contact: James Crook, Vice President of Operations
Air Traffic Control Association, Inc.
2300 Clarendon Boulevard, Suite 711
Arlington, VA 22201-2302
Phone: 703-522-5717
Fax: 703-527-7251
E-mail: jim.crook@atca.org

ALABAMA COMMISSION ON HIGHER EDUCATION http://www.ache.state.al.us

POLICE OFFICERS AND FIREFIGHTERS SURVIVORS EDUCATION ASSISTANCE PROGRAM-ALABAMA

Provides tuition, fees, books, and supplies to dependents of full-time police officers and firefighters killed in the line of duty. Must attend any Alabama public college as an undergraduate. Must be Alabama resident. Renewable.

Award: Grant for use in freshman, sophomore, junior, or senior years; renewable. *Number:* 15–30. *Amount:* $2000–$5000.

Alabama Commission on Higher Education (continued)

Eligibility Requirements: Applicant must be enrolled or expecting to enroll full or part-time at a two-year or four-year or technical institution or university; single; resident of Alabama and studying in Alabama. Applicant or parent of applicant must have employment or volunteer experience in police/firefighting. Available to U.S. citizens.

Application Requirements: Application, transcript. *Deadline:* Continuous.

Contact: Dr. William Wall, Associate Executive Director for Student Assistance, ACHE
Alabama Commission on Higher Education
PO Box 302000
Montgomery, AL 36130-2000

ALBERTA HERITAGE SCHOLARSHIP FUND/ ALBERTA SCHOLARSHIP PROGRAMS http://www.alis.gov.ab.ca/scholarships

ALBERTA HERITAGE SCHOLARSHIP FUND HAL HARRISON MEMORIAL SCHOLARSHIP

Award for grade twelve student with highest marks who is enrolled full-time at a postsecondary institution. Must have one parent who is member in good standing with Alberta Volunteer Fire Fighters Association. Deadline: June 1. Must be a resident of Alberta, Canada. Must be ranked in upper third of class or have a minimum GPA of 3.0.

Award: Scholarship for use in freshman year; not renewable. *Number:* 1. *Amount:* $186.

Eligibility Requirements: Applicant must be Canadian citizen; high school student; planning to enroll or expecting to enroll full-time at a two-year or four-year or technical institution or university and resident of Alberta. Applicant or parent of applicant must have employment or volunteer experience in fire service. Applicant must have 3.0 GPA or higher.

Application Requirements: Application, transcript. *Deadline:* June 1.

Contact: Alberta Heritage Scholarship Fund/Alberta Scholarship Programs
9940 106th Street, 9th Floor, Box 28000 Station Main
Edmonton, AB T5J 4R4
Canada
Phone: 780-427-8640
Fax: 780-422-4516
E-mail: heritage@gov.ab.ca

ALLAINET CORPORATION http://www.allainet.com/ANET/index.html

PROJECT HIRE

Online recruiting program for creative, focused, service-minded college students in North America to work while completing college tuition-free. Must contact project through Web site: http://www.weblo.com/projecthire and complete the tasks assigned online during a 33-day period. Twelve winning candidates will receive salary, performance bonuses, college tuition, and comprehensive training programs. Registration deadline is February 28.

Award: Scholarship for use in freshman, sophomore, junior, senior, graduate, or postgraduate years; not renewable. *Number:* 12. *Amount:* up to $43,000.

Eligibility Requirements: Applicant must be enrolled or expecting to enroll full or part-time at a four-year institution or university. Applicant or parent of applicant must have employment or volunteer experience in community service. Available to U.S. and non-U.S. citizens.

Application Requirements: Application. *Deadline:* February 28.

Contact: Application and information at Web site.
Allainet Corporation
100-171 Nepean Street
Ottawa, ON K2P 0B4
CAN

AMERICAN FOREIGN SERVICE ASSOCIATION http://www.afsa.org

AMERICAN FOREIGN SERVICE ASSOCIATION (AFSA) FINANCIAL AID AWARD PROGRAM

• *See page 441*

AMERICAN FOREIGN SERVICE ASSOCIATION (AFSA)/AAFSW MERIT AWARD PROGRAM

• *See page 441*

AMERICAN LEGION AUXILIARY, DEPARTMENT OF MISSOURI

AMERICAN LEGION AUXILIARY MISSOURI STATE NATIONAL PRESIDENT'S SCHOLARSHIP

• *See page 442*

AMERICAN LEGION AUXILIARY, DEPARTMENT OF NORTH DAKOTA

AMERICAN LEGION AUXILIARY, NATIONAL PRESIDENT'S SCHOLARSHIP

Three division scholarships for children of veterans who served in the Armed Forces during eligible dates for American Legion membership. Must be U.S. citizen and a high school senior with a minimum 2.5 GPA. Must be entered by local American Legion Auxiliary Unit. Contact local Unit President. National Headquarters Web site: http://www.legion-aux.org.

Award: Scholarship for use in freshman year; not renewable. *Number:* 3. *Amount:* $1000–$2500.

Eligibility Requirements: Applicant must be high school student and planning to enroll or expecting to enroll full-time at a four-year institution or university. Applicant or parent of applicant must have employment or volunteer experience in community service. Applicant must have 2.5 GPA or higher. Available to U.S. citizens. Applicant or parent must meet one or more of the following requirements: general military experience; retired from active duty; disabled or killed as a result of military service; prisoner of war; or missing in action.

Application Requirements: Application, essay, financial need analysis, references, test scores, transcript, 50 hours voluntary service. *Deadline:* March 10.

Contact: Alice Carlson, Education Chairman
American Legion Auxiliary, Department of North Dakota
6422 Northeast 122nd Avenue
Lankin, ND 58250-9761
Phone: 701-593-6332

AMERICAN LEGION AUXILIARY, NATIONAL HEADQUARTERS http://www.legion-aux.org

AMERICAN LEGION AUXILIARY GIRL SCOUT ACHIEVEMENT AWARD

• *See page 445*

AMERICAN LEGION, DEPARTMENT OF NEW YORK http://www.ny.legion.org

AMERICAN LEGION DEPARTMENT OF NEW YORK DR. HANNAH K. VUOLO MEMORIAL SCHOLARSHIP

• *See page 449*

AMERICAN LEGION, DEPARTMENT OF VERMONT

AMERICAN LEGION EAGLE SCOUT OF THE YEAR

• *See page 450*

AMERICAN LEGION, NATIONAL HEADQUARTERS http://www.legion.org

AMERICAN LEGION NATIONAL HEADQUARTERS EAGLE SCOUT OF THE YEAR

• *See page 450*

AMERICAN POLICE HALL OF FAME AND MUSEUM http://aphf.org

AMERICAN POLICE HALL OF FAME EDUCATIONAL SCHOLARSHIP FUND

Award available for any son or daughter of a law enforcement officer killed in the line of duty. Submit name of officer, date of death, department, and state where he/she was killed. Must re-apply. Contact for application deadline.

Award: Scholarship for use in freshman, sophomore, junior, or senior years; not renewable. *Number:* varies. *Amount:* $1500.

Eligibility Requirements: Applicant must be enrolled or expecting to enroll at a two-year or four-year or technical institution or university. Applicant or parent of applicant must have employment or volunteer experience in police/firefighting. Available to U.S. citizens.

Application Requirements: Transcript, college acceptance letter. *Deadline:* Continuous.

Contact: Jim Gordon, Executive Editor
American Police Hall of Fame and Museum
6350 Horizon Drive
Titusville, FL 32780
Phone: 321-264-0911

AMERICAN POSTAL WORKERS UNION http://www.apwu.org

E.C. HALLBECK SCHOLARSHIP FUND

• *See page 451*

VOCATIONAL SCHOLARSHIP PROGRAM

• *See page 451*

AMERICAN QUARTER HORSE FOUNDATION (AQHF) http://www.aqha.org/aqhya

EXCELLENCE IN EQUINE/AGRICULTURAL INVOLVEMENT SCHOLARSHIP

• *See page 452*

FARM AND RANCH HERITAGE SCHOLARSHIP

• *See page 452*

GUY STOOPS MEMORIAL PROFESSIONAL HORSEMEN'S FAMILY SCHOLARSHIP

• *See page 452*

AMERICAN SOCIETY OF TRAVEL AGENTS (ASTA) FOUNDATION http://www.astanet.com

ARIZONA CHAPTER DEPENDENT/EMPLOYEE MEMBERSHIP SCHOLARSHIP

• *See page 453*

AVIS RENT-A-CAR SCHOLARSHIP

Scholarship specifically geared toward individuals who have already gained experience and/or training in the travel industry. Candidate must have a minimum of two years of full-time travel industry experience or an undergraduate degree in travel/tourism and must currently be employed in the travel industry. Must be enrolled in a minimum of two courses per semester in an accredited undergraduate or graduate level degree program in business, or equivalent degree program. The AVIS Scholarship offers one award of $2000. For more information go to: http://www.astanet.com/education/edu_scholarships.asp.

Award: Scholarship for use in freshman, sophomore, junior, senior, graduate, or postgraduate years; renewable. *Number:* 1. *Amount:* $2000.

Eligibility Requirements: Applicant must be enrolled or expecting to enroll full or part-time at a four-year institution or university. Applicant or parent of applicant must have employment or volunteer experience in designated career field or hospitality/hotel administration/operations. Applicant must have 3.0 GPA or higher. Available to U.S. and non-U.S. citizens.

Application Requirements: Application, driver's license, essay, references, transcript. *Deadline:* varies.

Contact: Verlette Mitchell, Manager
American Society of Travel Agents (ASTA) Foundation
1101 King Street
Alexandria, VA 22314-2187
Phone: 703-739-8721
Fax: 703-684-8319
E-mail: scholarship@astahq.com

AMERICAN TRAFFIC SAFETY SERVICES FOUNDATION http://www.atssa.com

ROADWAY WORKER MEMORIAL SCHOLARSHIP PROGRAM

One-time scholarship providing financial assistance for post-high school education to the children of roadway workers killed or permanently disabled in work zones, including mobile operations and the installation of roadway safety features or to the parents or legal guardians of such children. 200-word essay required. Applicant must explain reasons for wanting to continue education.

Award: Scholarship for use in freshman, sophomore, junior, or senior years; not renewable. *Number:* 2–5. *Amount:* up to $3000.

Eligibility Requirements: Applicant must be enrolled or expecting to enroll full or part-time at a two-year or four-year or technical institution or university. Applicant or parent of applicant must have employment or volunteer experience in roadway worker. Available to U.S. citizens.

Application Requirements: Application, essay, financial need analysis, references, transcript, 200 word statement. *Deadline:* February 28.

Contact: Melanie Myers, Foundation Director
American Traffic Safety Services Foundation
15 Riverside Parkway
Suite 100
Fredericksburg, VA 22406-1102
Phone: 540-368-1701
Fax: 540-368-1717
E-mail: melaniem@atssa.com

ARBY'S FOUNDATION, BIG BROTHERS BIG SISTERS OF AMERICA http://www.bbbsa.org

ARBY'S-BIG BROTHERS BIG SISTERS SCHOLARSHIP AWARD

• *See page 454*

ARKANSAS DEPARTMENT OF HIGHER EDUCATION http://www.arscholarships.com

LAW ENFORCEMENT OFFICERS' DEPENDENTS SCHOLARSHIP-ARKANSAS

For dependents, under 23 years old, of Arkansas law-enforcement officers killed or permanently disabled in the line of duty. Renewable award is a waiver of tuition, fees, and room at two- or four-year Arkansas institution. Submit birth certificate, death certificate, and claims commission report of findings of fact. Proof of disability from State Claims Commission may also be submitted.

Award: Scholarship for use in freshman, sophomore, junior, or senior years; renewable. *Number:* 27–32. *Amount:* $2000–$2500.

Eligibility Requirements: Applicant must be age 22 or under; enrolled or expecting to enroll full or part-time at a two-year or four-year institution or university; resident of Arkansas and studying in Arkansas. Applicant or parent of applicant must have employment or volunteer experience in police/firefighting. Available to U.S. citizens.

Application Requirements: Application. *Deadline:* Continuous.

Contact: Lillian Williams, Assistant Coordinator
Arkansas Department of Higher Education
114 East Capitol
Little Rock, AR 72201
Phone: 501-371-2050
Fax: 501-371-2001
E-mail: lillianw@adhe.arknet.edu

BRIDGESTONE/FIRESTONE TRUST FUND

BRIDGESTONE/FIRESTONE TRUST FUND SCHOLARSHIPS

• *See page 491*

CALIFORNIA ALARM ASSOCIATION http://www.caaonline.org

CAA YOUTH SCHOLARSHIP PROGRAM FOR CHILDREN OF LAW ENFORCEMENT AND FIRE SERVICE PERSONNEL

One-time award for graduating high school seniors who have a parent or legal guardian who is actively serving in law enforcement or fire service. Must be a California resident and not married. Minimum 3.0 GPA required.

Award: Scholarship for use in freshman year; not renewable. *Number:* 4. *Amount:* $500–$2000.

Eligibility Requirements: Applicant must be high school student; age 15-20; planning to enroll or expecting to enroll full or part-time at a two-year or four-year or technical institution or university; single and resident of California. Applicant or parent of applicant must have employment or volunteer experience in police/firefighting. Applicant must have 3.0 GPA or higher. Available to U.S. citizens.

Application Requirements: Application, autobiography, essay, test scores, transcript. *Deadline:* March 20.

Contact: Jerry Lenander, Executive Director
California Alarm Association
3401 Pacific Avenue #1C
Marina del Rey, CA 90292
Phone: 310-305-1277
Fax: 310-305-2077
E-mail: info@caaonline.org

CALIFORNIA CORRECTIONAL PEACE OFFICERS ASSOCIATION http://www.ccpoa.org

CALIFORNIA CORRECTIONAL PEACE OFFICERS ASSOCIATION JOE HARPER SCHOLARSHIP

A scholarship program for immediate relatives and/or correctional officers in California.

Award: Scholarship for use in freshman, sophomore, junior, senior, or graduate years; not renewable. *Number:* 100. *Amount:* $1000.

Eligibility Requirements: Applicant must be enrolled or expecting to enroll full or part-time at a two-year or four-year or technical institution or university and resident of California. Applicant or parent of applicant must have employment or volunteer experience in designated career field. Applicant must have 3.5 GPA or higher. Available to U.S. citizens.

Application Requirements: Application, autobiography, essay, financial need analysis, photo, references, test scores, transcript. *Deadline:* April 30.

Contact: Marcia Bartlett, Bookkeeper
California Correctional Peace Officers Association
755 Riverpoint Drive, Suite 200
West Sacremento, CA 95605
Phone: 916-372-6060
Fax: 916-372-6623

CALIFORNIA PEACE OFFICERS' MEMORIAL FOUNDATION http://www.camemorial.org/scholar.htm

JOHN F. DUFFY SCHOLARSHIP

Eligibility requirements: dependents of California officers who have died in the line of duty, regardless of how long ago. Applications will not be based on sex, age, race, creed, national origin, or religious preference, or restricted based upon the applicant's field of endeavor.

Award: Scholarship for use in freshman, sophomore, junior, senior, or graduate years; renewable. *Number:* varies. *Amount:* $1200–$2500.

Eligibility Requirements: Applicant must be enrolled or expecting to enroll full or part-time at a two-year or four-year or technical institution or university. Applicant or parent of applicant must have employment or volunteer experience in police/firefighting. Available to U.S. and non-U.S. citizens.

Application Requirements: Application, essay, financial need analysis, photo, transcript. *Deadline:* April 1.

Contact: Clancy Faria, Chair
California Peace Officers' Memorial Foundation
PO Box 2437
Fair Oaks, CA 95628
Phone: 916-921-0660
Fax: 916-614-1875

CALIFORNIA STUDENT AID COMMISSION http://www.csac.ca.gov

LAW ENFORCEMENT PERSONNEL DEVELOPMENT SCHOLARSHIP

The Law Enforcement Personnel Dependents Scholarship Program provides college grants to needy dependents of California law enforcement officers, officers and employees of the Department of Corrections and Department of Youth Authority, and firefighters killed or disabled in the line of duty.

Award: Grant for use in freshman, sophomore, junior, or senior years; renewable. *Number:* varies. *Amount:* $100–$11,259.

Eligibility Requirements: Applicant must be enrolled or expecting to enroll full or part-time at a two-year or four-year or technical institution or university; resident of California and studying in California. Applicant or parent of applicant must have employment or volunteer experience in police/firefighting. Available to U.S. citizens.

Application Requirements: Application, financial need analysis. *Deadline:* Continuous.

Contact: California Student Aid Commission
PO Box 419027
Rancho Cordova, CA 95741-9027
Phone: 916-526-7590
Fax: 916-526-8002
E-mail: custsvcs@csac.ca.gov

CALIFORNIA TABLE GRAPE COMMISSION http://www.freshcaliforniagrapes.com

CALIFORNIA TABLE GRAPE FARM WORKERS SCHOLARSHIP PROGRAM

Applicants must be high school graduates who plan to attend any college or university in California. The applicant, a parent, or a legal guardian must have worked in the California table grape harvest during the last season. School activities, personal references, and financial need are considered. Must be U.S. citizen.

Award: Scholarship for use in freshman, sophomore, junior, or senior years; renewable. *Number:* 3. *Amount:* $16,000.

Eligibility Requirements: Applicant must be enrolled or expecting to enroll full-time at a four-year institution or university and studying in California. Applicant or parent of applicant must have employment or volunteer experience in designated career field. Available to U.S. citizens.

Application Requirements: Application, essay, financial need analysis, references, test scores, transcript. *Deadline:* March 1.

Contact: Scholarship Coordinator
California Table Grape Commission
392 West Fallbrook, Suite 101
Fresno, CA 93711-6150
Phone: 559-447-8350
Fax: 559-447-9184
E-mail: info@freshcaliforniagrapes.com

CATHOLIC WORKMAN http://www.catholicworkman.org

CATHOLIC WORKMAN COLLEGE SCHOLARSHIPS

• *See page 457*

CHAIRSCHOLARS FOUNDATION, INC. http://www.chairscholars.org

CHAIRSCHOLARS FOUNDATION, INC. SCHOLARSHIPS

Award for students who are severely physically challenged. Applicants may be high school seniors or college freshmen. Must be outstanding citizen with history of public service. Minimum 3.5 GPA required. Ten to twelve renewable awards of $5000. Must be under 21 years old.

Award: Scholarship for use in freshman or sophomore years; renewable. *Number:* 10–12. *Amount:* $5000–$20,000.

Eligibility Requirements: Applicant must be age 20 or under and enrolled or expecting to enroll full-time at a two-year or four-year or technical institution or university. Applicant or parent of applicant must have employment or volunteer experience in community service. Applicant must be hearing impaired, physically disabled, or visually impaired. Applicant must have 3.5 GPA or higher. Available to U.S. citizens.

Application Requirements: Application, autobiography, essay, financial need analysis, photo, portfolio, resume, references, self-addressed stamped envelope, test scores, transcript, parents' tax return from previous year. *Deadline:* February 28.

Contact: Hugo Keim
Chairscholars Foundation, Inc.
16101 Carencia Lane
Odessa, FL 33556
Phone: 813-920-2737
E-mail: hugokeim@earthlink.net

CHESAPEAKE CORPORATION FOUNDATION http://www.cskcorp.com

CHESAPEAKE CORPORATION FOUNDATION SCHOLARSHIP PROGRAM FOR CHESAPEAKE EMPLOYEES' CHILDREN

• *See page 495*

CHICK-FIL-A, INC. http://www.chickfila.com

CHICK-FIL-A LEADERSHIP SCHOLARSHIP

Scholarships available to current employees of Chick-fil-A restaurants. Must show proof of enrollment in technical school, two- or four-year college or university. Must demonstrate solid work ethic, be actively involved in school or community activities, and possess strong leadership abilities. Must apply with approval of a Unit Operator accompanied by their letter of recommendation. Letter of recommendation from non-work-related individual also required. The top 25 applicants will be awarded an additional $1000.

Award: Scholarship for use in freshman year; not renewable. *Number:* 975. *Amount:* $1000–$2000.

Eligibility Requirements: Applicant must be high school student and planning to enroll or expecting to enroll at a two-year or four-year or technical institution or university. Applicant or parent of applicant must have employment or volunteer experience in food service. Available to U.S. citizens.

Application Requirements: Application, references, transcript.

Contact: Applications available at franchise of employment.
Chick-fil-A, Inc.
5200 Buffington Road
Atlanta, GA 30349-2998

CIVIL SERVICE EMPLOYEES INSURANCE COMPANY http://www.cseinsurance.com

YOUTH AUTOMOBILE SAFETY SCHOLARSHIP ESSAY COMPETITION FOR CHILDREN OF PUBLIC EMPLOYEES

Submit essay discussing ways teenage auto accidents can be reduced. Applicants must be residents of California, Arizona, Utah, or Nevada with minimum 3.0 GPA. Awards are for children of full-time or retired public employees. Letter of acceptance required.

Award: Scholarship for use in freshman year; not renewable. *Number:* 1–10. *Amount:* $500.

Eligibility Requirements: Applicant must be high school student; planning to enroll or expecting to enroll full-time at a two-year or four-year or technical institution or university and resident of Arizona, California, Nevada, or Utah. Applicant or parent of applicant must have employment or volunteer experience in designated career field. Applicant must have 3.0 GPA or higher. Available to U.S. citizens.

Application Requirements: Application, essay, references, transcript. *Deadline:* April 4.

Contact: Jonathan Kaban, Project Coordinator, Scholarship Contest
Civil Service Employees Insurance Company
PO Box 8041
Walnut Creek, CA 94956
Phone: 925-817-6496
Fax: 925-817-6489
E-mail: jkaban@cse-insurance.com

CLARA ABBOTT FOUNDATION http://clara.abbott.com/

SCHOLARSHIP PROGRAM

• *See page 495*

COLLEGE ASSISTANCE MIGRANT PROGRAM http://www.stedwards.edu/camp

COLLEGE ASSISTANCE MIGRANT PROGRAM AT ST. EDWARD'S UNIVERSITY

The purpose of CAMP is to provide migrant/seasonal farm workers who have completed high school requirements an opportunity to work toward a four-year baccalaureate degree. This program offers the eligible student financial, academic, and other supportive assistance necessary for successful completion of the first two semesters of college. Must be U.S. citizen. Application deadline is March 1.

Award: Grant for use in freshman year; not renewable. *Number:* 40. *Amount:* up to $23,000.

Eligibility Requirements: Applicant must be enrolled or expecting to enroll full-time at an institution or university. Applicant or parent of applicant must have employment or volunteer experience in agriculture. Available to U.S. citizens.

Application Requirements: Application, essay, financial need analysis, references, test scores, transcript, certification of migrant eligibility. *Deadline:* March 1.

Contact: Esther Quinones Yacono, Director
College Assistance Migrant Program
3001 South Congress Avenue
Austin, TX 78704
Phone: 512-448-8625
Fax: 512-464-8830
E-mail: esthery@admin.stedwards.edu

COMMUNITY BANKER ASSOCIATION OF ILLINOIS http://www.cbai.com/scholarship.htm

COMMUNITY BANKER ASSOCIATION OF ILLINOIS CHILDREN OF COMMUNITY BANKING SCHOLARSHIP

• *See page 458*

COMMUNITY FOUNDATION OF WESTERN MASSACHUSETTS http://www.communityfoundation.org

DEERFIELD PLASTICS/BARKER FAMILY SCHOLARSHIP

• *See page 495*

HORACE HILL SCHOLARSHIP

• *See page 458*

COUNTY PROSECUTORS ASSOCIATION OF NEW JERSEY FOUNDATION

JOHN S. STAMLER MEMORIAL SCHOLARSHIP

One-time award for New Jersey resident and sworn law enforcement officer seeking educational advancement on a college or graduate level to improve his or her effectiveness as a law enforcement officer. Must also demonstrate financial need.

Award: Scholarship for use in freshman, sophomore, junior, senior, or graduate years; not renewable. *Number:* 1. *Amount:* $2500.

Eligibility Requirements: Applicant must be enrolled or expecting to enroll full or part-time at a two-year or four-year institution; resident of New Jersey and studying in New Jersey. Applicant or parent of applicant must have employment or volunteer experience in police/firefighting. Available to U.S. citizens.

County Prosecutors Association of New Jersey Foundation (continued)

Application Requirements: Application, financial need analysis, interview. *Deadline:* June 15.

Contact: Julie
County Prosecutors Association of New Jersey Foundation
Camden County Prosecutors Office
25 North 5th Street
Camden, NJ 08102
E-mail: julie_benegar@ccprosecutor.org

DALLAS MORNING NEWS

DALLAS MORNING NEWS ANNUAL TEENAGE CITIZENSHIP TRIBUTE

Award recognizes high school seniors who have achieved the highest standards of citizenship in their schools and communities. All 12th grade students in Dallas, Collin, Denton, Ellis, Hunt, Kaufman, Parker, Rockwall, and Tarrant counties are eligible. Nominees must demonstrate qualities of leadership, initiative, good judgment, and responsibility. Volunteer service in the community is essential. Must have minimum 2.5 GPA. For more details see Web site: http://tact.dallasnews.com.

Award: Scholarship for use in freshman year; not renewable. *Number:* 20. *Amount:* $500–$2000.

Eligibility Requirements: Applicant must be high school student; planning to enroll or expecting to enroll full-time at a four-year institution or university; resident of Texas and must have an interest in leadership. Applicant or parent of applicant must have employment or volunteer experience in community service. Applicant must have 2.5 GPA or higher. Available to U.S. citizens.

Application Requirements: Application, interview, references. *Deadline:* February 13.

Contact: Application available at Web site.

DELAWARE HIGHER EDUCATION COMMISSION http://www.doe.state.de.us/high-ed

EDUCATIONAL BENEFITS FOR CHILDREN OF DECEASED MILITARY AND STATE POLICE

Renewable award for Delaware residents who are children of state or military police who were killed in the line of duty. Must attend a Delaware institution unless program of study is not available. Funds cover tuition and fees at Delaware institutions. The amount varies at non-Delaware institutions. Must submit proof of service and related death. Must be ages 16-24 at time of application. Deadline is three weeks before classes begin.

Award: Grant for use in freshman, sophomore, junior, or senior years; renewable. *Number:* 1–10. *Amount:* $6255.

Eligibility Requirements: Applicant must be age 16-24; enrolled or expecting to enroll full-time at a two-year or four-year institution or university and resident of Delaware. Applicant or parent of applicant must have employment or volunteer experience in police/firefighting. Available to U.S. citizens. Applicant or parent must meet one or more of the following requirements: general military experience; retired from active duty; disabled or killed as a result of military service; prisoner of war; or missing in action.

Application Requirements: Application, verification of service-related death. *Deadline:* Continuous.

Contact: Donna Myers, Higher Education Analyst
Delaware Higher Education Commission
820 North French Street
5th Floor
Wilmington, DE 19711-3509
Phone: 302-577-3240
Fax: 302-577-6765
E-mail: dhec@doe.k12.de.us

DELTA DELTA DELTA FOUNDATION http://www.tridelta.org

DELTA DELTA DELTA UNDERGRADUATE SCHOLARSHIP

• *See page 459*

DISABLED AMERICAN VETERANS http://www.dav.org

JESSE BROWN MEMORIAL YOUTH SCHOLARSHIP PROGRAM

Designed to encourage youth volunteers to become active in Department of Veterans Affairs Voluntary Services (VAVS) programs. Scholarship is awarded annually to outstanding youth volunteers who are very active in VAVS activities.

Award: Scholarship for use in freshman, sophomore, junior, senior, graduate, or postgraduate years; renewable. *Number:* 12. *Amount:* $5000–$15,000.

Eligibility Requirements: Applicant must be age 21 or under and enrolled or expecting to enroll full-time at a two-year or four-year or technical institution or university. Applicant or parent of applicant must have employment or volunteer experience in helping handicapped. Available to U.S. citizens.

Application Requirements: Application, essay, 100 hours of volunteer activity at VA medical facility. *Deadline:* varies.

Contact: Edward Hartman, National Director of Voluntary Services
Disabled American Veterans
807 Maine Avenue, SW
Washington, DC 20024
Phone: 202-554-3501
Fax: 202-554-3581
E-mail: ehartman@davmail.org

EXPLOSIVE ORDNANCE DISPOSAL MEMORIAL COMMITTEE http://www.eodmemorial.org

EXPLOSIVE ORDNANCE DISPOSAL MEMORIAL SCHOLARSHIP

Award based on academic merit, community involvement, and financial need for the children and spouses of Explosive Ordnance Disposal technicians. Applications are only available on the Web site at http://www.eodmemorial.org.

Award: Scholarship for use in freshman, sophomore, junior, or senior years; not renewable. *Number:* 20–60. *Amount:* $1500–$2000.

Eligibility Requirements: Applicant must be enrolled or expecting to enroll full-time at a two-year or four-year or technical institution or university. Applicant or parent of applicant must have employment or volunteer experience in explosive ordnance disposal. Available to U.S. citizens. Applicant or parent must meet one or more of the following requirements: general military experience; retired from active duty; disabled or killed as a result of military service; prisoner of war; or missing in action.

Application Requirements: Application, financial need analysis, transcript. *Deadline:* March 1.

Contact: Mary McKinley, Administrator
Explosive Ordnance Disposal Memorial Committee
PO Box 594
Niceville, FL 32588
Phone: 850-729-2401
Fax: 850-729-2401
E-mail: admin@eodmemorial.org

FEDERAL EMPLOYEE EDUCATION AND ASSISTANCE FUND http://www.feea.org

FEEA SCHOLARSHIPS

One-time award for students enrolled in an accredited postsecondary school in a course of study that will lead to a two-year, four-year or graduate degree. Must be a current civilian federal or postal employee with at least three years of federal service, or a dependent family member (children and spouses). Minimum 3.0 GPA required.

Award: Scholarship for use in freshman, sophomore, junior, senior, or graduate years; not renewable. *Number:* varies. *Amount:* $350–$1200.

Eligibility Requirements: Applicant must be enrolled or expecting to enroll full or part-time at a two-year or four-year institution or university. Applicant or parent of applicant must have employment or volunteer experience in federal/postal service. Applicant must have 3.0 GPA or higher. Available to U.S. and non-U.S. citizens.

Application Requirements: Application, essay, references, self-addressed stamped envelope, test scores, transcript. *Deadline:* March 28.

Contact: Stephen Bauer, Director
Federal Employee Education and Assistance Fund
8441 West Bowles Avenue, Suite 200
Littleton, CO 80123-9501
Phone: 303-933-7580
Fax: 303-933-7587

FEEA/NARFE SCHOLARSHIP

Award available to children and grandchildren of National Association of Retired Federal Employees members. Must be full-time students in an accredited two- or four-year postsecondary school. Minimum 3.0 GPA required.

Award: Scholarship for use in freshman, sophomore, junior, or senior years; not renewable. *Number:* 50. *Amount:* $1000.

Eligibility Requirements: Applicant must be enrolled or expecting to enroll full-time at a two-year or four-year institution or university. Applicant or parent of applicant must have employment or volunteer experience in federal/postal service. Applicant must have 3.0 GPA or higher. Available to U.S. citizens.

Application Requirements: Application, essay, references, test scores, transcript. *Deadline:* March 28.

Contact: Stephen Bauer, Director
Federal Employee Education and Assistance Fund
8441 West Bowles Avenue, Suite 200
Littleton, CO 80123-9501
Phone: 303-933-7580
Fax: 303-933-7587

FINANCE AUTHORITY OF MAINE http://www.famemaine.com

TUITION WAIVER PROGRAMS

Provides tuition waivers for children and spouses of EMS personnel, firefighters, and law enforcement officers who have been killed in the line of duty and for students who were foster children under the custody of the Department of Human Services when they graduated from high school. Waivers valid at the University of Maine System, the Maine Technical College System, and Maine Maritime Academy.

Award: Grant for use in freshman, sophomore, junior, or senior years; not renewable. *Number:* varies. *Amount:* varies.

Eligibility Requirements: Applicant must be enrolled or expecting to enroll at an institution or university; resident of Maine and studying in Maine. Applicant or parent of applicant must have employment or volunteer experience in designated career field or police/firefighting. Available to U.S. citizens.

Application Requirements: Application. *Deadline:* Continuous.

Contact: Trisha Malloy, Program Officer
Finance Authority of Maine
5 Community Drive
Augusta, ME 04332
Phone: 207-623-3263
Fax: 207-623-0095
E-mail: trisha@famemaine.com

FIREFIGHTERS NATIONAL TRUST http://www.firedonations.org/

FIREFIGHTERS NATIONAL TRUST FDNY SEPTEMBER 11TH SCHOLARSHIP FUND

The Fire Fighters National Trust, FDNY September 11th Scholarship Fund has been created to provide education assistance for postsecondary study to the children and spouses, including domestic partners, of firefighters killed as a result of September 11th attacks at the World Trade Center in New York City.

Award: Scholarship for use in freshman, sophomore, junior, or senior years; renewable. *Number:* varies. *Amount:* $1000–$3000.

Eligibility Requirements: Applicant must be enrolled or expecting to enroll full-time at a two-year or four-year or technical institution or university. Applicant or parent of applicant must have employment or volunteer experience in police/firefighting. Applicant must have 2.5 GPA or higher. Available to U.S. citizens.

Application Requirements: Application, financial need analysis, transcript. *Deadline:* Continuous.

Contact: Jan Kampbell, Office Manager
Firefighters National Trust
4423 Point Fosdick Drive NW, Suite 208
Gig Harbor, WA 98335
Phone: 253-853-3430
Fax: 253-853-3470
E-mail: jan@firedonations.org

FLORIDA DEPARTMENT OF EDUCATION http://www.floridastudentfinancialaid.org

CRITICAL TEACHER SHORTAGE STUDENT LOAN FORGIVENESS PROGRAM-FLORIDA

Eligible Florida teachers may receive up to $5,000 for repayment of undergraduate and graduate educational loans which lead to certification in critical teacher shortage subject area. Must teach full-time at a Florida public school in a critical area for a minimum of ninety days to be eligible. Visit Web site for further information.

Award: Forgivable loan for use in freshman, sophomore, junior, senior, or graduate years; not renewable. *Number:* varies. *Amount:* up to $5000.

Eligibility Requirements: Applicant must be enrolled or expecting to enroll at a two-year or four-year institution or university; resident of Florida and studying in Florida. Applicant or parent of applicant must have employment or volunteer experience in teaching. Available to U.S. citizens.

Application Requirements: Application, transcript. *Deadline:* July 15.

Contact: Scholarship Information
Florida Department of Education
Office of Student Financial Assistance
1940 North Monroe, Suite 70
Tallahassee, FL 32303-4759
Phone: 888-827-2004
E-mail: osfa@fldoe.org

GEORGIA STUDENT FINANCE COMMISSION http://www.gsfc.org

GEORGIA PUBLIC SAFETY MEMORIAL GRANT/LAW ENFORCEMENT PERSONNEL DEPARTMENT GRANT

Award for children of Georgia law enforcement officers, prison guards, or fire fighters killed or permanently disabled in the line of duty. Must attend an accredited postsecondary Georgia school. Complete the Law Enforcement Personnel Dependents application.

Award: Grant for use in freshman, sophomore, junior, or senior years; renewable. *Number:* 20–40. *Amount:* $2000.

Eligibility Requirements: Applicant must be enrolled or expecting to enroll full-time at a two-year or four-year or technical institution or university; resident of Georgia and studying in Georgia. Applicant or parent of applicant must have employment or volunteer experience in police/firefighting. Available to U.S. citizens.

Application Requirements: Application. *Deadline:* Continuous.

Contact: William Flook, Director of Scholarships and Grants Division
Georgia Student Finance Commission
2082 East Exchange Place, Suite 100
Tucker, GA 30084
Phone: 770-724-9052
Fax: 770-724-9031

GOLDEN KEY INTERNATIONAL HONOUR SOCIETY http://www.goldenkey.org

GOLDEN KEY SERVICE AWARD

The successful applicant will receive a check for $500; the applicant's chapter will receive a check for $250; and the charity of the applicant's choice will

Golden Key International Honour Society (continued)

receive a check for $250. Must have been enrolled as a student during the previous academic year. See Web site for more information: http://goldenkey.gsu.edu.

Award: Scholarship for use in junior, senior, graduate, or postgraduate years; not renewable. *Number:* 1. *Amount:* $500.

Eligibility Requirements: Applicant must be enrolled or expecting to enroll at an institution or university. Applicant or parent of applicant must have employment or volunteer experience in community service.

Application Requirements: Application, essay, references. *Deadline:* February 15.

Contact: Member Services
Golden Key International Honour Society
621 North Avenue, NE
Suite C-100
Atlanta, GA 30308
Phone: 404-377-2400
Fax: 678-420-6757
E-mail: scholarships@goldenkey.org

GRACO, INC. http://www.graco.com

DAVID A. KOCH SCHOLARSHIP

• *See page 496*

GRACO INC. SCHOLARSHIP PROGRAM

• *See page 496*

GREATER KANAWHA VALLEY FOUNDATION http://www.tgkvf.org

SCPA SCHOLARSHIP FUND

Renewable award for West Virginia residents who are full time-students with minimum 2.5 GPA. Applicant must have parent who is employed or has been previously employed by the coal industry in southern West Virginia. Include employer's name and address. May apply for two Foundation scholarships but will only be chosen for one. Scholarships are awarded on a financial need basis and may be awarded for one or more years.

Award: Scholarship for use in freshman, sophomore, junior, or senior years; renewable. *Number:* 11. *Amount:* $1000.

Eligibility Requirements: Applicant must be enrolled or expecting to enroll full-time at a four-year institution or university and resident of West Virginia. Applicant or parent of applicant must have employment or volunteer experience in coal industry. Applicant must have 2.5 GPA or higher. Available to U.S. citizens.

Application Requirements: Application, essay, financial need analysis, references, self-addressed stamped envelope, test scores, transcript. *Deadline:* February 17.

Contact: Susan Hoover, Scholarship Coordinator
Greater Kanawha Valley Foundation
PO Box 3041
Charleston, WV 25331
Phone: 304-346-3620
Fax: 304-346-3640

WEST VIRGINIA GOLF ASSOCIATION FUND

Awarded to students at any accredited West Virginia college or university. This fund is open to individuals who meet the following criteria: 1) have played golf in WV as an amateur for recreation or competition or 2) have been or are presently employed in WV as a caddie, groundskeeper, bag boy, etc. Must also include a reference by a coach, golf professional or employer and an essay explaining how the game of golf has made an impact in applicant's life. Scholarships are awarded with a commitment of one year. May apply for two Foundation scholarships but will only be chosen for one.

Award: Scholarship for use in freshman, sophomore, junior, or senior years; not renewable. *Number:* 4. *Amount:* $1000.

Eligibility Requirements: Applicant must be enrolled or expecting to enroll full-time at a four-year institution or university; resident of West Virginia and studying in West Virginia. Applicant or parent of applicant must have employment or volunteer experience in private club/caddying. Applicant must have 2.5 GPA or higher. Available to U.S. citizens.

Application Requirements: Application, essay, financial need analysis, references, transcript, IRS 1040 form. *Deadline:* February 17.

Contact: Susan Hoover, Scholarship Coordinator
Greater Kanawha Valley Foundation
PO Box 3041
Charleston, WV 25331
Phone: 304-346-3620
Fax: 304-346-3640

HALTON FOUNDATION

HALTON SCHOLARS

• *See page 496*

HARNESS HORSE YOUTH FOUNDATION http://www.hhyf.org

CHARLES BRADLEY MEMORIAL SCHOLARSHIP

One-time award for full-time undergraduates between the ages of 18-24. Open to children of licensed pari-mutuel harness racing officials. Minimum 2.5 GPA required. Must be U.S. or Canadian citizen.

Award: Scholarship for use in freshman, sophomore, junior, or senior years; not renewable. *Number:* 1–3. *Amount:* $250–$500.

Eligibility Requirements: Applicant must be age 18-24 and enrolled or expecting to enroll full-time at a two-year or four-year or technical institution or university. Applicant or parent of applicant must have employment or volunteer experience in harness racing. Applicant must have 2.5 GPA or higher. Available to U.S. and Canadian citizens.

Application Requirements: Application, essay, references, transcript, page 1 of parents' IRS form. *Deadline:* April 30.

Contact: Ellen Taylor, Executive Director
Harness Horse Youth Foundation
16575 Carey Road
Westfield, IN 46074
Phone: 317-867-5877
Fax: 317-867-5896

DOUG BROWN SCHOLARSHIP

One-time award for full-time undergraduates between the ages of 18-24. Open to children whose parents are actively involved in harness racing. Must be a Canadian citizen. Minimum 2.5 GPA required.

Award: Scholarship for use in freshman, sophomore, junior, or senior years; not renewable. *Number:* 1. *Amount:* $3500.

Eligibility Requirements: Applicant must be age 18-24 and enrolled or expecting to enroll full-time at a two-year or four-year or technical institution or university. Applicant or parent of applicant must have employment or volunteer experience in harness racing. Applicant must have 2.5 GPA or higher. Available to Canadian citizens.

Application Requirements: Application, essay, references, transcript, page 1 of parents' IRS form. *Deadline:* April 30.

Contact: Ellen Taylor, Executive Director
Harness Horse Youth Foundation
16575 Carey Road
Westfield, IN 46074
Phone: 317-867-5877
Fax: 317-867-5896

RAMBLING WILLIE MEMORIAL SCHOLARSHIP

One-time award for full-time undergraduates between the ages of 18-24. Must be pursuing a career in harness racing. Minimum 2.5 GPA required. Scholarship is co-sponsored by the Christian Harness Horsemen's Association.

Award: Scholarship for use in freshman, sophomore, junior, or senior years; not renewable. *Number:* 1–3. *Amount:* $500.

Eligibility Requirements: Applicant must be age 18-24 and enrolled or expecting to enroll full-time at a two-year or four-year or technical institution or university. Applicant or parent of applicant must have employment or volunteer experience in harness racing. Applicant must have 2.5 GPA or higher. Available to U.S. and Canadian citizens.

Application Requirements: Application, essay, references, transcript, page 1 of parents' IRS form. *Deadline:* April 30.

Contact: Ellen Taylor, Executive Director
Harness Horse Youth Foundation
16575 Carey Road
Westfield, IN 46074
Phone: 317-867-5877
Fax: 317-867-5896

VINCENT ABATE MEMORIAL SCHOLARSHIP

One-time award for full-time undergraduates between the ages of 18-24. Open to children whose parents are employees of The Meadowlands or Freehold Raceway. Minimum 2.5 GPA required. Must be U.S. citizen.

Award: Scholarship for use in freshman, sophomore, junior, or senior years; not renewable. *Number:* 1–3. *Amount:* $1000–$5000.

Eligibility Requirements: Applicant must be age 18-24 and enrolled or expecting to enroll full-time at a two-year or four-year or technical institution or university. Applicant or parent of applicant must have employment or volunteer experience in harness racing. Applicant must have 2.5 GPA or higher. Available to U.S. citizens.

Application Requirements: Application, essay, references, transcript, page 1 of parents' IRS form. *Deadline:* April 30.

Contact: Ellen Taylor, Executive Director
Harness Horse Youth Foundation
16575 Carey Road
Westfield, IN 46074
Phone: 317-867-5877
Fax: 317-867-5896

HARNESS HORSEMEN INTERNATIONAL FOUNDATION

JEROME L. HAUCK SCHOLARSHIP

Available to a child of a full-time groom or a member of a Harness Horsemen International member association. Must be used at a four-year college or university for any field of study. $1000 per school year renewable four times. Write for more information. Must submit two letters of recommendation and a letter from HHI member association.

Award: Scholarship for use in freshman, sophomore, junior, or senior years; renewable. *Number:* 1. *Amount:* $1000.

Eligibility Requirements: Applicant must be enrolled or expecting to enroll full-time at a four-year institution or university. Applicant or parent of applicant must have employment or volunteer experience in harness racing. Available to U.S. citizens.

Application Requirements: Application, autobiography, photo, references, test scores, transcript. *Deadline:* June 1.

Contact: Michael Izzo, Executive Director
Harness Horsemen International Foundation
14 Main Street
Robbinsville, NJ 08691
Phone: 609-259-3717
Fax: 609-259-3778

HARNESS TRACKS OF AMERICA, INC. http://www.harnesstracks.com

HARNESS TRACKS OF AMERICA SCHOLARSHIP

One-time, merit-based award for students actively involved in harness racing or the children of licensed drivers, trainers, breeders, or caretakers, living or deceased. Based on financial need, academic merit, and active harness racing involvement by applicant or family member. High school seniors may apply for the following school year award. For further details visit Web site: http://www.harnesstracks.com.

Award: Scholarship for use in freshman, sophomore, junior, senior, or graduate years; not renewable. *Number:* up to 6. *Amount:* up to $7500.

Eligibility Requirements: Applicant must be enrolled or expecting to enroll full-time at a two-year or four-year or technical institution or university. Applicant or parent of applicant must have employment or volunteer experience in harness racing. Available to U.S. and non-U.S. citizens.

Application Requirements: Application, essay, financial need analysis, transcript, IRS 1040 from parents and/or applicant. *Deadline:* June 15.

Contact: Business Manager
Harness Tracks of America, Inc.
4640 East Sunrise Drive, Suite 200
Tucson, AZ 85718
Phone: 520-529-2525
Fax: 520-529-3235
E-mail: info@harnesstracks.com

HERMAN O. WEST FOUNDATION

HERMAN O. WEST FOUNDATION SCHOLARSHIP PROGRAM

• *See page 497*

ILLINOIS STUDENT ASSISTANCE COMMISSION (ISAC) http://www.collegezone.org

GRANT PROGRAM FOR DEPENDENTS OF POLICE, FIRE, OR CORRECTIONAL OFFICERS

Award for dependents of police, fire, and corrections officers killed or disabled in line of duty. Provides for tuition and fees at approved Illinois institutions. Must be resident of Illinois. Continuous deadline. Provide proof of status. For information and application, go to Web site: http://www.collegezone.

Award: Grant for use in freshman, sophomore, junior, senior, graduate, or postgraduate years; renewable. *Number:* 50–55. *Amount:* $3000–$4000.

Eligibility Requirements: Applicant must be enrolled or expecting to enroll at a two-year or four-year or technical institution or university; resident of Illinois and studying in Illinois. Applicant or parent of applicant must have employment or volunteer experience in police/firefighting. Available to U.S. citizens.

Application Requirements: Application, proof of status. *Deadline:* Continuous.

Contact: College Zone Counselor
Illinois Student Assistance Commission (ISAC)
1755 Lake Cook Road
Deerfield, IL 60015-5209
Phone: 800-899-4722
E-mail: collegezone@isac.org

INDIANA POLICE CORPS http://www.in.gov/cji/policecorps

SCHOLARSHIPS FOR DEPENDENTS OF FALLEN OFFICERS

Scholarships are available to the dependents of officers who have been killed in the line of duty. For more details and an application see Web site: http://www.in.gov/cji/policecorps.

Award: Scholarship for use in freshman, sophomore, junior, or senior years; renewable. *Number:* varies. *Amount:* up to $15,000.

Eligibility Requirements: Applicant must be enrolled or expecting to enroll at a two-year or four-year or technical institution or university. Applicant or parent of applicant must have employment or volunteer experience in police/firefighting. Available to U.S. citizens.

Application Requirements: Application, request for scholarship payment. *Deadline:* Continuous.

Contact: Application available at Web site.

INTERNATIONAL ASSOCIATION OF FIRE CHIEFS FOUNDATION

INTERNATIONAL ASSOCIATION OF FIRE CHIEFS FOUNDATION SCHOLARSHIP AWARD

One-time award open to any person who is an active member (volunteer or paid) of an emergency or fire department. Must be studying at a recognized institution of higher education. Application deadline is August 1.

Award: Scholarship for use in freshman, sophomore, junior, senior, graduate, or postgraduate years; not renewable. *Number:* 10–30. *Amount:* $350–$4000.

International Association of Fire Chiefs Foundation (continued)

Eligibility Requirements: Applicant must be enrolled or expecting to enroll full or part-time at a two-year or four-year or technical institution or university. Applicant or parent of applicant must have employment or volunteer experience in fire service. Available to U.S. and non-U.S. citizens.

Application Requirements: Application, essay. *Deadline:* August 1.

Contact: International Association of Fire Chiefs Foundation
PO Box 1818
Windermere, FL 34786

INTERNATIONAL ASSOCIATION OF FIRE FIGHTERS http://www.iaff.org

W.H. "HOWIE" MCCLENNAN SCHOLARSHIP

Fund was established to provide financial assistance to sons, daughters, and legally adopted children of IAFF members killed in the line of duty who are planning to attend an institution of higher learning.

Award: Scholarship for use in freshman, sophomore, junior, senior, or graduate years; renewable. *Number:* 20–25. *Amount:* $2500.

Eligibility Requirements: Applicant must be enrolled or expecting to enroll full or part-time at a two-year or four-year or technical institution or university. Applicant or parent of applicant must have employment or volunteer experience in police/firefighting. Available to U.S. and Canadian citizens.

Application Requirements: Application, essay, references, transcript. *Deadline:* February 1.

Contact: Office of the McClennan Scholarship General President
International Association of Fire Fighters
1750 New York Avenue, NW
Washington, DC 20006
Phone: 202-737-8484
Fax: 202-737-8418

J. WOOD PLATT CADDIE SCHOLARSHIP TRUST http://www.gapgolf.org

J. WOOD PLATT CADDIE SCHOLARSHIP TRUST

Renewable award for high school seniors or college undergraduates who have caddied at least one year at a member club of the Golf Association of Philadelphia. Submit transcript and financial need analysis with application. Interview required. Deadline is April 25.

Award: Scholarship for use in freshman, sophomore, junior, senior, or graduate years; renewable. *Number:* 250–300. *Amount:* $200–$7000.

Eligibility Requirements: Applicant must be enrolled or expecting to enroll full-time at a two-year or four-year institution or university and must have an interest in golf. Applicant or parent of applicant must have employment or volunteer experience in private club/caddying. Available to U.S. and non-U.S. citizens.

Application Requirements: Application, financial need analysis, interview, references, test scores, transcript. *Deadline:* April 25.

Contact: Robert Caucci, Program Administrator
J. Wood Platt Caddie Scholarship Trust
Drawer 808
Southeastern, PA 19399-0808
Phone: 610-687-2340 Ext. 21
Fax: 610-687-2082

JOHN EDGAR THOMSON FOUNDATION

JOHN EDGAR THOMSON FOUNDATION GRANTS

Must be the daughter of a deceased railroad employee. Employee (mother/father) must have been actively employed at time of death. Recipients of disability, sick leave, workman's compensation are considered eligible. Monthly grant is available until the age of 22, as long as recipient is in college full-time, earning at least 12 credits. Termination at age 22 or upon graduation, whichever comes first. Recipient must remain unmarried. Based upon financial need. Submit birth certificate.

Award: Grant for use in freshman, sophomore, junior, or senior years; renewable. *Number:* varies.

Eligibility Requirements: Applicant must be age 21 or under; enrolled or expecting to enroll full-time at a two-year or four-year or technical institution or university and single female. Applicant or parent of applicant must have employment or volunteer experience in railroad industry. Available to U.S. citizens.

Application Requirements: Application, financial need analysis, interview, photo, references, transcript, birth certificate. *Deadline:* Continuous.

Contact: Sheila Cohen, Director
John Edgar Thomson Foundation
201 South 18th Street, Suite 318
Philadelphia, PA 19103
Phone: 215-545-6083
Fax: 215-545-6083

JOINT ACTION IN COMMUNITY SERVICE, INC. http://www.jacsinc.org

JOINT ACTION IN COMMUNITY SERVICE SCHOLARSHIP PROGRAM

Award program open to graduates of the federally-funded Job Corps program to pursue further educational opportunities. Application deadline is February 28.

Award: Scholarship for use in freshman, sophomore, junior, or senior years; not renewable. *Number:* 5–10. *Amount:* $1000.

Eligibility Requirements: Applicant must be enrolled or expecting to enroll full or part-time at a two-year or four-year or technical institution or university. Applicant or parent of applicant must have employment or volunteer experience in Job Corps. Available to U.S. citizens.

Application Requirements: Application, essay, financial need analysis, references, test scores, transcript. *Deadline:* February 28.

Contact: Ana M. Gomez, Executive Assistant
Joint Action in Community Service, Inc.
5225 Wisconsin Avenue, NW, Suite 404
Washington, DC 20015
Phone: 202-537-0996
Fax: 202-363-0239
E-mail: anagomez@jacsinc.org

KENTUCKY HIGHER EDUCATION ASSISTANCE AUTHORITY (KHEAA) http://www.kheaa.com

KENTUCKY JUSTICE CABINET POLICEMAN/FIREMAN PENSION FUND TUITION WAIVER

Tuition waivers for child or non-remarried spouse of a person who was a Kentucky resident on becoming a law enforcement officer, firefighter, or volunteer firefighter and who was killed or permanently and totally disabled while in active service or a result of injuries that occurred while in active service. Must be enrolled or planning to enroll in a state supported institution and provide proof of relationship to deceased or of qualifying disability.

Award: Scholarship for use in freshman, sophomore, junior, or senior years; renewable. *Number:* varies. *Amount:* varies.

Eligibility Requirements: Applicant must be enrolled or expecting to enroll full or part-time at a two-year or four-year or technical institution or university; resident of Kentucky and studying in Kentucky. Applicant or parent of applicant must have employment or volunteer experience in police/firefighting.

Application Requirements: Application, proof of relationshipo to deceased or disabled person. *Deadline:* Continuous.

Contact: Justice Cabinet
Kentucky Higher Education Assistance Authority (KHEAA)
Bush Building, 2nd Floor, 403 Wapping Street
Frankfort, KY 40601

KINGSBURY CORPORATION

KINGSBURY FUND SCHOLARSHIPS

• *See page 497*

LINCOLN COMMUNITY FOUNDATION http://www.lcf.org

GEORGE WATTERS-NEBRASKA PETROLEUM MARKETERS ASSOCIATION SCHOLARSHIP

Scholarship for any Nebraska high school graduating senior to attend any two- or four-year postsecondary institution in Nebraska. Must be in upper 33% of class, and demonstrate academic achievement and leadership. Sponsored by Nebraska Petroleum Marketers who makes the selection process and determines application deadline. Applicants must be the son or daughter of any Nebraska Petroleum Marketer and Convenience Store Association member, or the son or daughter of a Nebraska Petroleum Marketers and Convenience Store Association's full- or part-time employee.

Award: Scholarship for use in freshman year; not renewable. *Number:* 3. *Amount:* $1000–$1500.

Eligibility Requirements: Applicant must be high school student; planning to enroll or expecting to enroll full-time at a two-year or four-year or technical institution or university; resident of Nebraska; studying in Nebraska and must have an interest in leadership. Applicant or parent of applicant must have employment or volunteer experience in designated career field. Applicant must have 3.0 GPA or higher. Available to U.S. citizens.

Application Requirements: Application, references, transcript. *Deadline:* March 1.

Contact: Application available at Web site.

HARRY AND LENORA RICHARDSON-NATIONAL ASSOCIATION OF POSTMASTERS OF THE UNITED STATES SCHOLARSHIP

Scholarship for a graduating senior who is the child, grandchild, or member of the Nebraska Chapter, National Association of Postmaster of the United States or the Nebraska Branch, National League of Postmasters of the United States. Applicants must demonstrate academic achievement and participation in extracurricular and community activities. Must be a Nebraska resident. Must attend a Nebraska college or university.

Award: Scholarship for use in freshman year; not renewable. *Number:* 1. *Amount:* $1000.

Eligibility Requirements: Applicant must be high school student; planning to enroll or expecting to enroll full-time at a two-year or four-year institution or university; resident of Nebraska and studying in Nebraska. Applicant or parent of applicant must have employment or volunteer experience in federal/postal service. Applicant must have 2.5 GPA or higher. Available to U.S. citizens.

Application Requirements: Application, autobiography, references, transcript. *Deadline:* April 1.

Contact: Application available at Web site.

HARRY AND LENORA RICHARDSON-NEBRASKA BRANCH OF THE NATIONAL LEAGUE OF POSTMASTERS SCHOLARSHIP

Scholarship for a graduating senior who is the child, grandchild, or member of the Nebraska Chapter, National Association of Postmasters of the United States, or the Nebraska Branch, National League of Postmasters of the United States. Applicants must demonstrate academic achievement and participation in extracurricular and community activities. Must be a Nebraska resident. Must attend a Nebraska college or university.

Award: Scholarship for use in freshman year; not renewable. *Number:* 1. *Amount:* $1000.

Eligibility Requirements: Applicant must be high school student; planning to enroll or expecting to enroll full-time at a two-year or four-year institution or university; resident of Nebraska and studying in Nebraska. Applicant or parent of applicant must have employment or volunteer experience in federal/postal service. Applicant must have 2.5 GPA or higher. Available to U.S. citizens.

Application Requirements: Application, autobiography, references, transcript. *Deadline:* March 1.

Contact: Application available at Web site.

LOUIS C. AND AMY E. NUERNBERGER MEMORIAL SCHOLARSHIP

Scholarship for high school graduates who have been employed at the Wakefield Health Care Center in Wakefield, NE for at least one year.

Award: Scholarship for use in freshman, sophomore, junior, or senior years; renewable. *Number:* 1. *Amount:* $5000–$10,000.

Eligibility Requirements: Applicant must be enrolled or expecting to enroll full-time at a two-year or four-year or technical institution or university and resident of Nebraska. Applicant or parent of applicant must have employment or volunteer experience in designated career field. Applicant must have 2.5 GPA or higher. Available to U.S. citizens.

Application Requirements: Application, essay, test scores, transcript. *Deadline:* April 1.

Contact: Application available at Web site.

THOMAS C. WOODS, JR. MEMORIAL SCHOLARSHIP

Scholarships are for graduating seniors or former graduates of any high school in the following counties in Nebraska: Adams, Butler, Cass, Clay, Fillmore, Gage, Hamilton, Jefferson, Johnson, Lancaster, Nemaha, Nucholls, Otoe, Pawnee, Polk, Richardson, Saline, Saunders, Seward, Thayer, Webster, and York. Applicants must be qualified dependents of current ALLTEL employees. Must attend a college/universities in Nebraska. Minimum 2.5 GPA required.

Award: Scholarship for use in freshman, sophomore, junior, or senior years; not renewable. *Number:* 10–15. *Amount:* $1000–$2000.

Eligibility Requirements: Applicant must be enrolled or expecting to enroll full-time at a two-year or four-year institution or university; resident of Nebraska and studying in Nebraska. Applicant or parent of applicant must have employment or volunteer experience in designated career field. Applicant must have 2.5 GPA or higher. Available to U.S. citizens.

Application Requirements: Application, essay, financial need analysis, test scores. *Deadline:* April 17.

Contact: Application available at Web site.

MASSACHUSETTS OFFICE OF STUDENT FINANCIAL ASSISTANCE http://www.osfa.mass.edu

MASSACHUSETTS PUBLIC SERVICE GRANT PROGRAM

Scholarships for children and/or spouses of deceased members of fire, police, and corrections departments who were killed in the line of duty. For Massachusetts residents attending Massachusetts institutions.

Award: Grant for use in freshman, sophomore, junior, or senior years; not renewable. *Number:* varies. *Amount:* $720–$1714.

Eligibility Requirements: Applicant must be enrolled or expecting to enroll full-time at a four-year institution or university; resident of Massachusetts and studying in Massachusetts. Applicant or parent of applicant must have employment or volunteer experience in police/firefighting. Available to U.S. citizens.

Application Requirements: Application, financial need analysis, FAFSA. *Deadline:* May 1.

Contact: Alison Leary
Massachusetts Office of Student Financial Assistance
454 Broadway, Suite 200
Revere, MA 02151
Phone: 617-727-9420
Fax: 617-727-0667
E-mail: osfa@osfa.mass.edu

MINNESOTA HIGHER EDUCATION SERVICES OFFICE http://www.mheso.state.mn.us

MINNESOTA SAFETY OFFICERS' SURVIVOR PROGRAM

Grant for eligible survivors of Minnesota public safety officer killed in the line of duty. Safety officers who have been permanently or totally disabled in the line of duty are also eligible. Must be used at a Minnesota institution participating in State Grant Program. Write for details. Must submit proof of death or disability and Public Safety Officers Benefit Fund Certificate. Must apply each year. Can be renewed for four years.

Award: Grant for use in freshman, sophomore, junior, or senior years; not renewable. *Amount:* up to $8096.

Eligibility Requirements: Applicant must be enrolled or expecting to enroll full or part-time at a two-year or four-year or technical institution or university and studying in Minnesota. Applicant or

Minnesota Higher Education Services Office (continued)

parent of applicant must have employment or volunteer experience in police/firefighting. Available to U.S. citizens.

Application Requirements: Application, proof of death/disability. *Deadline:* Continuous.

Contact: Minnesota Higher Education Services Office
1450 Energy Park Drive, Suite 350
St. Paul, MN 55108-5227
Phone: 651-642-0567 Ext. 1

MISSISSIPPI STATE STUDENT FINANCIAL AID http://www.mississippiuniversities.com

MISSISSIPPI LAW ENFORCEMENT OFFICERS AND FIREMEN SCHOLARSHIP PROGRAM

Award for dependents and spouses of policemen or firemen who were killed or disabled in the line of duty. Must be a Mississippi resident and attend a state-supported college or university. The award is a full tuition waiver. Contact for deadline.

Award: Scholarship for use in freshman, sophomore, junior, or senior years; renewable. *Number:* varies.

Eligibility Requirements: Applicant must be enrolled or expecting to enroll full-time at a two-year or four-year institution or university; resident of Mississippi and studying in Mississippi. Applicant or parent of applicant must have employment or volunteer experience in police/firefighting. Available to U.S. citizens.

Application Requirements: Application, driver's license, references. *Deadline:* Continuous.

Contact: Susan Eckels, Program Administrator
Mississippi State Student Financial Aid
3825 Ridgewood Road
Jackson, MS 39211-6453
Phone: 601-432-6997
E-mail: sme@ihl.state.ms.us

NATIONAL BURGLAR AND FIRE ALARM ASSOCIATION http://www.alarm.org

NBFAA/SECURITY DEALER YOUTH SCHOLARSHIP PROGRAM

Scholarship program provides cash college scholarship awards to deserving sons or daughters of police and fire officials. Applicants should contact state NBFAA chapters. For more information visit our Web site at http://www.alarm.org

Award: Scholarship for use in freshman year; not renewable. *Number:* 32. *Amount:* $500–$6500.

Eligibility Requirements: Applicant must be high school student; age 15-20; planning to enroll or expecting to enroll full-time at a four-year institution or university and resident of California, Connecticut, Georgia, Indiana, Kentucky, Louisiana, Maryland, Minnesota, New Jersey, New York, North Carolina, Pennsylvania, Tennessee, Virginia, or Washington. Applicant or parent of applicant must have employment or volunteer experience in fire service or police/firefighting. Available to U.S. and non-Canadian citizens.

Application Requirements: Application, essay, test scores, transcript. *Deadline:* March 1.

Contact: Dr. Rick Ostopowicz, Communications Manager
National Burglar and Fire Alarm Association
8380 Colesville Road, Suite 750
Silver Spring, MD 20910
Phone: 301-585-1855 Ext. 133
Fax: 301-585-1866
E-mail: communications@alarm.org

NATIONAL FEDERATION OF THE BLIND http://www.nfb.org

E. U. PARKER SCHOLARSHIP

Award for students who are legally blind and pursuing full-time postsecondary education. Applicant must submit recommendation from state officer of the National Federation of the Blind. Award based on academic excellence, service to the community, and financial need. One-time award of $3000.

Award: Scholarship for use in freshman, sophomore, junior, or senior years; not renewable. *Number:* 1. *Amount:* $3000.

Eligibility Requirements: Applicant must be enrolled or expecting to enroll full-time at an institution or university. Applicant or parent of applicant must have employment or volunteer experience in community service. Applicant must be visually impaired. Available to U.S. citizens.

Application Requirements: Application, autobiography, essay, financial need analysis, references, transcript. *Deadline:* March 31.

Contact: Peggy Elliot, Chairman, Scholarship Committee
National Federation of the Blind
805 Fifth Avenue
Grinnell, IA 50112
Phone: 641-236-3366

HERMIONE GRANT CALHOUN SCHOLARSHIP

Award for full-time female undergraduate and graduate students who are legally blind and planning to study for a degree. Need minimum 2.5 GPA. Must submit a letter from state officer of National Federation of the Blind with whom they have discussed their application. May reapply. Must attend school in the U.S. Award based on academic excellence, service to the community, and financial need.

Award: Scholarship for use in freshman, sophomore, junior, senior, or graduate years; not renewable. *Number:* 1. *Amount:* $3000.

Eligibility Requirements: Applicant must be enrolled or expecting to enroll full-time at an institution or university and female. Applicant or parent of applicant must have employment or volunteer experience in community service. Applicant must be visually impaired. Applicant must have 2.5 GPA or higher. Available to U.S. and non-U.S. citizens.

Application Requirements: Application, autobiography, essay, financial need analysis, references, transcript. *Deadline:* March 31.

Contact: Peggy Elliot, Chairman, Scholarship Committee
National Federation of the Blind
805 Fifth Avenue
Grinnell, IA 50112
Phone: 641-236-3366

JENNICA FERGUSON MEMORIAL SCHOLARSHIP

One-time award for students who are legally blind and pursuing full-time secondary education in the U.S. Applicant must send a letter from a State officer of the National Federation of the Blind with whom they have discussed their application. Award is based on academic excellence, financial need and service to the community.

Award: Scholarship for use in freshman, sophomore, junior, or senior years; not renewable. *Number:* 1. *Amount:* $5000.

Eligibility Requirements: Applicant must be enrolled or expecting to enroll full-time at a four-year institution or university. Applicant or parent of applicant must have employment or volunteer experience in community service. Applicant must be visually impaired. Available to U.S. citizens.

Application Requirements: Application, essay, financial need analysis, references, transcript. *Deadline:* March 31.

Contact: Peggy Elliott, Chairman
National Federation of the Blind
805 Fifth Avenue
Grinnell, IA 50112
Phone: 641-236-3366
E-mail: delliott@pcpartner.net

KENNETH JERNIGAN SCHOLARSHIP

One-time award for full-time postsecondary study for students who are legally blind. Applicants must submit recommendation from state officer of National Federation of the Blind. Award based on academic excellence, service to the community, and financial need. Must attend school in the U.S. Sponsored by the American Action Fund for Blind Children and Adults.

Award: Scholarship for use in freshman, sophomore, junior, or senior years; not renewable. *Number:* 1. *Amount:* $10,000.

Eligibility Requirements: Applicant must be enrolled or expecting to enroll full-time at an institution or university. Applicant or parent of applicant must have employment or volunteer experience in community service. Applicant must be visually impaired. Applicant must have 3.5 GPA or higher. Available to U.S. and non-U.S. citizens.

Application Requirements: Application, autobiography, essay, financial need analysis, references, transcript. *Deadline:* March 31.

Contact: Peggy Elliot, Chairman, Scholarship Committee
National Federation of the Blind
805 Fifth Avenue
Grinnell, IA 50112
Phone: 641-236-3366

KUCHLER-KILLIAN MEMORIAL SCHOLARSHIP

Award for legally blind full-time students. Applicants must submit a letter from a state officer of National Federation of the Blind with whom they have discussed their application. May reapply each year. Award based on scholarship and service. Must attend school in U.S.

Award: Scholarship for use in freshman, sophomore, junior, or senior years; not renewable. *Number:* 1. *Amount:* $3000.

Eligibility Requirements: Applicant must be enrolled or expecting to enroll full-time at an institution or university. Applicant or parent of applicant must have employment or volunteer experience in community service. Applicant must be visually impaired. Available to U.S. and non-U.S. citizens.

Application Requirements: Application, autobiography, essay, financial need analysis, references, transcript. *Deadline:* March 31.

Contact: Peggy Elliot, Chairman, Scholarship Committee
National Federation of the Blind
805 Fifth Avenue
Grinnell, IA 50112
Phone: 641-236-3366

MELVA T. OWEN MEMORIAL SCHOLARSHIP

For full-time students in a degree program who are legally blind and who are not pursuing a degree in religious studies. Must submit letter from the National Federation of the Blind state officer with whom they have discussed their application. Based on academic excellence, service to the community, and financial need. Must attend school in the U.S.

Award: Scholarship for use in freshman, sophomore, junior, or senior years; not renewable. *Number:* 1. *Amount:* $10,000.

Eligibility Requirements: Applicant must be enrolled or expecting to enroll full-time at an institution or university. Applicant or parent of applicant must have employment or volunteer experience in community service. Applicant must be visually impaired. Applicant must have 3.5 GPA or higher. Available to U.S. and non-U.S. citizens.

Application Requirements: Application, autobiography, essay, financial need analysis, references, transcript. *Deadline:* March 31.

Contact: Peggy Elliot, Chairman, Scholarship Committee
National Federation of the Blind
805 Fifth Avenue
Grinnell, IA 50112
Phone: 641-236-3366

NATIONAL FEDERATION OF THE BLIND SCHOLARSHIPS

Award for legally blind students pursuing postsecondary education in the U.S. Must submit recommendation from state officer of the National Federation of the Blind. Award based on academic excellence, service to the community, and financial need. One award given to a person working full-time and attending or planning to attend a part-time course of study to broaden opportunities in work.

Award: Scholarship for use in freshman, sophomore, junior, or senior years; not renewable. *Number:* 18. *Amount:* $3000–$7000.

Eligibility Requirements: Applicant must be enrolled or expecting to enroll full or part-time at a four-year institution or university. Applicant or parent of applicant must have employment or volunteer experience in community service. Applicant must be visually impaired. Available to U.S. and non-U.S. citizens.

Application Requirements: Application, essay, financial need analysis, references, transcript. *Deadline:* March 31.

Contact: Peggy Elliot, Chairman, Scholarship Committee
National Federation of the Blind
805 Fifth Avenue
Grinnell, IA 50112
Phone: 641-236-3366

SALLY S. JACOBSEN SCHOLARSHIP

One-time award for students who are legally blind and pursuing full-time studies in the U.S. Applicant must send a letter from a state officer of the National Federation of the Blind with whom they have discussed their application. Award based on academic excellence, financial need and service to the community.

Award: Scholarship for use in freshman, sophomore, junior, or senior years; not renewable. *Number:* 1. *Amount:* $5000.

Eligibility Requirements: Applicant must be enrolled or expecting to enroll full-time at an institution or university. Applicant or parent of applicant must have employment or volunteer experience in community service. Applicant must be visually impaired. Available to U.S. citizens.

Application Requirements: Application, essay, financial need analysis, references, transcript. *Deadline:* March 31.

Contact: Peggy Elliott, Chairman
National Federation of the Blind
805 Fifth Avenue
Grinnell, IA 50112
Phone: 641-236-3366
E-mail: delliott@pcpartner.net

NATSO FOUNDATION http://www.natsofoundation.org

BILL MOON SCHOLARSHIP

• *See page 472*

NEVADA POLICE CORPS http://www.nevadapolicecorps.state.nv.us

NEVADA POLICE CORPS SCHOLARSHIP FOR DEPENDENT CHILDREN OF OFFICERS SLAIN IN THE LINE OF DUTY

Scholarships available for dependent children of officers slain in the line of duty. Apply to agency in which parent served. Check Web site for participating states and additional information. http://www.ojp.usdoj.gov/opc/ee/

Award: Scholarship for use in freshman, sophomore, junior, or senior years. *Number:* varies. *Amount:* up to $15,000.

Eligibility Requirements: Applicant must be enrolled or expecting to enroll at a two-year or four-year or technical institution or university. Applicant or parent of applicant must have employment or volunteer experience in police/firefighting. Available to U.S. citizens.

Application Requirements: Application. *Deadline:* varies.

Contact: Greg Befort, Director
Nevada Police Corps
WNCC, Cedar Building Room 309-312
2201 West College Parkway
Carson City, NV 89703
Phone: 775-684-8720
Fax: 775-684-8775
E-mail: gbefort@post.state.nv.us

NEW JERSEY HIGHER EDUCATION STUDENT ASSISTANCE AUTHORITY http://www.hesaa.org

LAW ENFORCEMENT OFFICER MEMORIAL SCHOLARSHIP

Scholarships for full-time undergraduate study at approved New Jersey institutions for the dependent children of New Jersey law enforcement officers killed in the line of duty. Value of scholarship established annually.

Award: Scholarship for use in freshman, sophomore, junior, or senior years; renewable. *Number:* varies. *Amount:* varies.

Eligibility Requirements: Applicant must be enrolled or expecting to enroll full-time at a four-year institution or university; resident of New

New Jersey Higher Education Student Assistance Authority (continued)

Jersey and studying in New Jersey. Applicant or parent of applicant must have employment or volunteer experience in police/firefighting. Available to U.S. citizens.

Application Requirements: Application.

Contact: Carol Muka, Assistant Director of Grants and Scholarships
New Jersey Higher Education Student Assistance Authority
PO Box 540
Trenton, NJ 08625
Phone: 800-792-8670
Fax: 609-588-2228

SURVIVOR TUITION BENEFITS PROGRAM

Provides tuition for spouses and dependents of law enforcement officers, fire, or emergency services personnel killed in the line of duty. Recipients must be enrolled in an undergraduate degree program at a college or university in New Jersey as either half-time or full-time students. Deadline October 1 for Fall term, March 1 for Spring term.

Award: Scholarship for use in freshman, sophomore, junior, or senior years; renewable. *Number:* varies.

Eligibility Requirements: Applicant must be enrolled or expecting to enroll full or part-time at a two-year or four-year institution or university; resident of New Jersey and studying in New Jersey. Applicant or parent of applicant must have employment or volunteer experience in police/firefighting. Available to U.S. citizens.

Application Requirements: Application. *Deadline:* varies.

Contact: Carol Muka, Assistant Director of Grants and Scholarships
New Jersey Higher Education Student Assistance Authority
PO Box 540
Trenton, NJ 08625
Phone: 800-792-8670
Fax: 609-588-2228

NEW JERSEY STATE GOLF ASSOCIATION

http://www.njsga.org

NEW JERSEY STATE GOLF ASSOCIATION CADDIE SCHOLARSHIP

Applicants for this scholarship must reside in New Jersey, have a minimum 2.5 GPA, and have caddied for at least one year at a member club of the New Jersey State Golf Association. Scholarship award is based on grades, test scores, references, and financial need. Award renewable for undergraduate use.

Award: Scholarship for use in freshman, sophomore, junior, or senior years; renewable. *Number:* 200. *Amount:* $1500–$3000.

Eligibility Requirements: Applicant must be enrolled or expecting to enroll full-time at a two-year or four-year institution or university and resident of New Jersey. Applicant or parent of applicant must have employment or volunteer experience in private club/caddying. Applicant must have 2.5 GPA or higher. Available to U.S. citizens.

Application Requirements: Application, financial need analysis, references, test scores, transcript. *Deadline:* May 1.

Contact: Education Director
New Jersey State Golf Association
PO Box 6947
Freehold, NJ 07728
Phone: 732-780-4822
Fax: 732-780-4822
E-mail: j.o.petersen@att.net

NEW YORK STATE HIGHER EDUCATION SERVICES CORPORATION

http://www.hesc.org

NEW YORK MEMORIAL SCHOLARSHIPS FOR FAMILIES OF DECEASED POLICE OFFICERS, FIRE FIGHTERS AND PEACE OFFICERS

Renewable scholarship for families of New York police officers, peace officers or firefighters who died in the line of duty. Must be a New York resident pursuing undergraduate study at a SUNY college or university.

Award: Scholarship for use in freshman, sophomore, junior, or senior years; renewable. *Number:* varies. *Amount:* varies.

Eligibility Requirements: Applicant must be enrolled or expecting to enroll full-time at a four-year institution or university; resident of New York and studying in New York. Applicant or parent of applicant must have employment or volunteer experience in police/firefighting. Available to U.S. citizens.

Application Requirements: Application, financial need analysis. *Deadline:* May 1.

Contact: Student Information
New York State Higher Education Services Corporation
99 Washington Avenue, Room 1320
Albany, NY 12255

NORTH CAROLINA BAR ASSOCIATION

http://www.ncbar.org

NORTH CAROLINA BAR ASSOCIATION SCHOLARSHIP

For children of North Carolina law enforcement officers killed or permanently disabled in the line of duty. Must apply for the first time before 27th birthday.

Award: Scholarship for use in freshman, sophomore, junior, senior, graduate, or postgraduate years; renewable. *Number:* varies. *Amount:* up to $2000.

Eligibility Requirements: Applicant must be age 26 or under; enrolled or expecting to enroll full-time at a two-year or four-year or technical institution or university and resident of North Carolina. Applicant or parent of applicant must have employment or volunteer experience in police/firefighting.

Application Requirements: Application, financial need analysis, photo, test scores, transcript. *Deadline:* April 1.

Contact: Jacquelyn Terrell-Fountain, Assistant Director of Sections
North Carolina Bar Association
PO Box 3688
Cary, NC 27519
Phone: 919-677-0561
Fax: 919-677-0761
E-mail: jterrell@ncbar.org

NORTH CAROLINA STATE EDUCATION ASSISTANCE AUTHORITY

http://www.cfnc.org

GOVERNOR JAMES G. MARTIN COLLEGE SCHOLARSHIPS

Awarded to high school seniors who are residents of North Carolina with a minimum 3.5 GPA. Must enroll full-time and maintain a C average. Must attend a participating North Carolina four-year institution. Renewable up to five years. Based on academic merit, community service, and leadership.

Award: Scholarship for use in freshman, junior, or senior years; renewable. *Number:* up to 25. *Amount:* up to $1000.

Eligibility Requirements: Applicant must be high school student; planning to enroll or expecting to enroll full-time at a four-year institution or university; resident of North Carolina and studying in North Carolina. Applicant or parent of applicant must have employment or volunteer experience in community service. Available to U.S. citizens.

Application Requirements: Application, essay, photo, references, test scores, transcript. *Deadline:* March 15.

Contact: Sharon Scott, Assistant, Scholarship and Grant Division
North Carolina State Education Assistance Authority
PO Box 13663
Research Triangle Park, NC 27709-3663

NORTH EAST ROOFING EDUCATIONAL FOUNDATION

http://www.nerca.org

NORTH EAST ROOFING EDUCATIONAL FOUNDATION SCHOLARSHIP

• *See page 474*

NORTHEAST FRESH FOODS ALLIANCE http://www.neffa.com

NORTHEAST FRESH FOODS ALLIANCE SCHOLARSHIP AWARDS PROGRAM

• *See page 474*

OHIO BOARD OF REGENTS http://www.regents.state.oh.us

OHIO SAFETY OFFICERS COLLEGE MEMORIAL FUND

Renewable award covering up to full tuition is available to children and surviving spouses of peace officers and fire fighters killed in the line of duty in any state. Children must be under 26 years of age. Must be an Ohio resident and enroll full-time or part-time at an Ohio college or university.

Award: Scholarship for use in freshman, sophomore, junior, or senior years; renewable. *Number:* 50–65. *Amount:* varies.

Eligibility Requirements: Applicant must be age 25 or under; enrolled or expecting to enroll full or part-time at a two-year or four-year institution or university; resident of Ohio and studying in Ohio. Applicant or parent of applicant must have employment or volunteer experience in police/firefighting. Available to U.S. citizens.

Application Requirements: *Deadline:* Continuous.

Contact: Barbara Metheney, Program Administrator
Ohio Board of Regents
PO Box 182452
Columbus, OH 43218-2452
Phone: 614-752-9535
Fax: 614-752-5903
E-mail: bmethene@regents.state.oh.us

OREGON STUDENT ASSISTANCE COMMISSION http://www.osac.state.or.us

A. VICTOR ROSENFELD SCHOLARSHIP

• *See page 498*

ALBINA FUEL COMPANY SCHOLARSHIP

• *See page 498*

BLUE HERON PAPER EMPLOYEE DEPENDENTS SCHOLARSHIP

• *See page 499*

CARPENTERS AND JOINERS LOCAL 2130 SCHOLARSHIP

One-time award open to graduating high school seniors in Columbia, Washington, or Yamhill counties, or to college students from households with at least one union member. Preference given to applicants whose legal guardians are rank-and-file members of local carpenter unions. Must have a minimum cumulative 2.5 GPA. Essay required. See Web site for details. (http://www.osac.state.or.us).

Award: Scholarship for use in freshman or sophomore years; not renewable. *Number:* 1. *Amount:* $750.

Eligibility Requirements: Applicant must be enrolled or expecting to enroll at an institution or university and resident of Oregon. Applicant or parent of applicant must have employment or volunteer experience in designated career field. Applicant must have 2.5 GPA or higher. Available to U.S. citizens.

Application Requirements: Application, essay, financial need analysis, transcript, activity chart. *Deadline:* March 1.

Contact: Director of Grant Programs
Oregon Student Assistance Commission
1500 Valley River Drive, Suite 100
Eugene, OR 97401-7020
Phone: 800-452-8807 Ext. 7395
E-mail: awardinfo@mercury.osac.state.or.us

GLENN JACKSON SCHOLARS SCHOLARSHIPS (OCF)

• *See page 499*

MC GARRY MACHINE INC. SCHOLARSHIP

• *See page 499*

OREGON AFL-CIO SCHOLARSHIP

One-time award for graduating Oregon high school seniors. Must write essay. Preference given to applicants from union families. Visit Web site (http://www.osac.state.or.us) for details.

Award: Scholarship for use in freshman year; not renewable. *Number:* 4. *Amount:* $1513.

Eligibility Requirements: Applicant must be high school student; planning to enroll or expecting to enroll full or part-time at a two-year or four-year or technical institution or university and resident of Oregon. Applicant or parent of applicant must have employment or volunteer experience in designated career field. Available to U.S. and non-U.S. citizens.

Application Requirements: Application, essay, financial need analysis, test scores, transcript, activity chart. *Deadline:* March 1.

Contact: Director of Grant Programs
Oregon Student Assistance Commission
1500 Valley River Drive, Suite 100
Eugene, OR 97401-7020
Phone: 800-452-8807 Ext. 7395
E-mail: awardinfo@mercury.osac.state.or.us

OREGON DUNGENESS CRAB COMMISSION SCHOLARSHIP

One scholarship available to graduating high school senior who is a dependent of licensed Oregon Dungeness Crab fisherman or crew member. One-time award. Identify name of vessel in place of work site.

Award: Scholarship for use in freshman year; not renewable. *Number:* 2. *Amount:* $500.

Eligibility Requirements: Applicant must be high school student; planning to enroll or expecting to enroll at an institution or university and resident of Oregon. Applicant or parent of applicant must have employment or volunteer experience in designated career field. Available to U.S. citizens.

Application Requirements: Application, essay, financial need analysis, transcript, activity chart. *Deadline:* March 1.

Contact: Director of Grant Programs
Oregon Student Assistance Commission
1500 Valley River Drive, Suite 100
Eugene, OR 97401-7020
Phone: 800-452-8807 Ext. 7395
E-mail: awardinfo@mercury.osac.state.or.us

OREGON OCCUPATIONAL SAFETY AND HEALTH DIVISION WORKERS MEMORIAL SCHOLARSHIP

Available to Oregon residents who are the dependents or spouses of an Oregon worker who was killed or permanently disabled on the job. Submit essay of 500 words or less titled "How has the injury or death of your parent or spouse affected or influenced your decision to further your education?" See Web site for more details. (http://www.osac.state.or.us)

Award: Scholarship for use in freshman, sophomore, junior, senior, or graduate years; not renewable. *Number:* 1. *Amount:* $4786.

Eligibility Requirements: Applicant must be enrolled or expecting to enroll at a two-year or four-year institution and resident of Oregon. Applicant or parent of applicant must have employment or volunteer experience in designated career field. Available to U.S. citizens.

Application Requirements: Application, essay, financial need analysis, test scores, transcript, workers compensation claim number. *Deadline:* March 1.

Contact: Director of Grant Programs
Oregon Student Assistance Commission
1500 Valley River Drive, Suite 100
Eugene, OR 97401-7020
Phone: 800-452-8807 Ext. 7395
E-mail: awardinfo@mercury.osac.state.or.us

OREGON SALMON COMMISSION SCHOLARSHIP

One-time award open to graduating high school seniors. Must be a dependent of a licensed Oregon salmon fisherman. Must be a resident of Oregon.

Award: Scholarship for use in freshman year; not renewable. *Number:* 2. *Amount:* $500.

Eligibility Requirements: Applicant must be high school student; planning to enroll or expecting to enroll at an institution or university

Oregon Student Assistance Commission (continued)

and resident of Oregon. Applicant or parent of applicant must have employment or volunteer experience in designated career field. Available to U.S. citizens.

Application Requirements: Application, essay, financial need analysis, transcript, activity chart. *Deadline:* March 1.

Contact: Director of Grant Programs
Oregon Student Assistance Commission
1500 Valley River Drive, Suite 100
Eugene, OR 97401-7020
Phone: 800-452-8807 Ext. 7395
E-mail: awardinfo@mercury.osac.state.or.us

OREGON TRAWL COMMISSION SCHOLARSHIP

One-time award for graduating high school seniors and college students who are dependents of licensed Oregon Trawl fishermen or crew. Visit Web site (http://www.osac.state.or.us) for more details.

Award: Scholarship for use in freshman, sophomore, junior, or senior years; not renewable. *Number:* 2. *Amount:* $500.

Eligibility Requirements: Applicant must be enrolled or expecting to enroll at an institution or university; resident of Oregon and must have an interest in designated field specified by sponsor. Applicant or parent of applicant must have employment or volunteer experience in designated career field. Available to U.S. citizens.

Application Requirements: Application, essay, financial need analysis, references, transcript, activity chart. *Deadline:* March 1.

Contact: Director of Grant Programs
Oregon Student Assistance Commission
1500 Valley River Drive, Suite 100
Eugene, OR 97401-7020
Phone: 800-452-8807 Ext. 7395
E-mail: awardinfo@mercury.osac.state.or.us

OREGON TRUCKING ASSOCIATION SCHOLARSHIP

One scholarship available to a child of an Oregon Trucking Association member, or child of employee of member. Applicants must be Oregon residents who are graduating high school seniors from an Oregon high school. One-time award.

Award: Scholarship for use in freshman year; not renewable. *Number:* 4. *Amount:* $750.

Eligibility Requirements: Applicant must be high school student; planning to enroll or expecting to enroll at a four-year institution and resident of Oregon. Applicant or parent of applicant must have employment or volunteer experience in designated career field. Available to U.S. citizens.

Application Requirements: Application, essay, financial need analysis, references, transcript, activity chart. *Deadline:* March 1.

Contact: Director of Grant Programs
Oregon Student Assistance Commission
1500 Valley River Drive, Suite 100
Eugene, OR 97401-7020
Phone: 800-452-8807 Ext. 7395
E-mail: awardinfo@mercury.osac.state.or.us

PENDLETON POSTAL WORKERS SCHOLARSHIP

One-time award for graduating high school seniors who are children or grandchildren of active, retired, or deceased members of Pendleton APWU Local 110 at least one year preceding application deadline. Contact for application requirements and deadlines. Essay required "What has the labor movement accomplished historically for working people?"

Award: Scholarship for use in freshman year; not renewable. *Number:* varies. *Amount:* $500.

Eligibility Requirements: Applicant must be high school student; planning to enroll or expecting to enroll at a four-year institution and resident of Oregon. Applicant or parent of applicant must have employment or volunteer experience in designated career field. Available to U.S. citizens.

Application Requirements: Application, essay, financial need analysis, references, transcript, activity chart. *Deadline:* March 1.

Contact: Director of Grant Programs
Oregon Student Assistance Commission
1500 Valley River Drive, Suite 100
Eugene, OR 97401-7020
Phone: 800-452-8807 Ext. 7395
E-mail: awardinfo@mercury.osac.state.or.us

REED'S FUEL AND TRUCKING COMPANY SCHOLARSHIP

• *See page 500*

ROBERT D. FORSTER SCHOLARSHIP

• *See page 500*

ROGER W. EMMONS MEMORIAL SCHOLARSHIP

• *See page 500*

ROSEBURG FOREST PRODUCTS SONS AND DAUGHTERS SCHOLARSHIP

• *See page 500*

SP NEWSPRINT COMPANY, NEWBERG MILL, EMPLOYEE DEPENDENTS SCHOLARSHIP

• *See page 501*

STIMSON LUMBER COMPANY SCHOLARSHIP

• *See page 501*

TAYLOR MADE LABELS SCHOLARSHIP

• *See page 501*

TEAMSTERS CLYDE C. CROSBY/JOSEPH M. EDGAR MEMORIAL SCHOLARSHIP

• *See page 476*

TEAMSTERS COUNCIL 37 FEDERAL CREDIT UNION SCHOLARSHIP

• *See page 476*

TYKESON FAMILY SCHOLARSHIP

Renewable award available to children aged 23 years and under of full-time employees who have been employed for at least two years prior to March 1 of application year. Companies included are: Bend Cable Communications LLC, Central Oregon Cable Advertising LLC, or Tykeson/Associates Enterprises. Must attend an Oregon college. See Web site for more information. (http://www.osac.state.or.us)

Award: Scholarship for use in freshman, sophomore, junior, or senior years; renewable. *Number:* 1. *Amount:* $2000.

Eligibility Requirements: Applicant must be age 23 or under; enrolled or expecting to enroll at a four-year institution; resident of Oregon and studying in Oregon. Applicant or parent of applicant must have employment or volunteer experience in designated career field. Available to U.S. citizens.

Application Requirements: Application, essay, financial need analysis, references, transcript, activity chart. *Deadline:* March 1.

Contact: Director of Grant Programs
Oregon Student Assistance Commission
1500 Valley River Drive, Suite 100
Eugene, OR 97401-7020
Phone: 800-452-8807 Ext. 7395
E-mail: awardinfo@mercury.osac.state.or.us

WILLETT AND MARGUERITE LAKE SCHOLARSHIP

• *See page 501*

WOODARD FAMILY SCHOLARSHIP

• *See page 501*

PENNSYLVANIA BURGLAR AND FIRE ALARM ASSOCIATION

http://www.pbfaa.com

PENNSYLVANIA BURGLAR AND FIRE ALARM ASSOCIATION YOUTH SCHOLARSHIP PROGRAM

Non-renewable scholarships available to sons and daughters of active Pennsylvania police and fire personnel, and volunteer fire department personnel for full-time study at a two-or four-year college, or university. Regional awards of $500 in each of the 5 geographic regions; state awards of

$1000 first prize, $500 second prize; national awards of $6500 first place and $3500 second place. Must be a senior in a Pennsylvania high school. Call or email state office for application and information.

Award: Scholarship for use in freshman year; not renewable. *Number:* 6–8. *Amount:* $500–$6500.

Eligibility Requirements: Applicant must be high school student; planning to enroll or expecting to enroll full-time at a two-year or four-year institution or university and resident of Pennsylvania. Applicant or parent of applicant must have employment or volunteer experience in police/firefighting. Available to U.S. citizens.

Application Requirements: Application, essay, resume, test scores, transcript. *Deadline:* March 1.

Contact: Dale Eller, Executive Director
Pennsylvania Burglar and Fire Alarm Association
PO Box 8264
Erie, PA 16505-0264
Phone: 814-838-3093
Fax: 814-838-5127
E-mail: info@pbfaa.com

PHOENIX SUNS CHARITIES/SUN STUDENTS SCHOLARSHIP http://www.suns.com

SUN STUDENT COLLEGE SCHOLARSHIP PROGRAM

Applicants must be seniors preparing to graduate from a high school in Arizona. Eligible applicants will have a minimum 2.5 GPA. Applicants must provide evidence of regular involvement in charitable activities or volunteer service in school, church or community organizations. Ten $1,000 scholarships and one $5,000 scholarship will be awarded. See Web site for application deadline.

Award: Scholarship for use in freshman year; not renewable. *Number:* 1–11. *Amount:* $1000–$5000.

Eligibility Requirements: Applicant must be high school student; planning to enroll or expecting to enroll full or part-time at a two-year or four-year or technical institution or university and resident of Arizona. Applicant or parent of applicant must have employment or volunteer experience in community service. Applicant must have 2.5 GPA or higher. Available to U.S. citizens.

Application Requirements: Application, essay, transcript. *Deadline:* varies.

Contact: Glenna Martinez, Administrative Assistant
Phoenix Suns Charities/Sun Students Scholarship
PO Box 1369
Phoenix, AZ 85001
Phone: 602-379-7767
Fax: 602-379-7596

PROCTER & GAMBLE FUND http://www.pg.com

PROCTER & GAMBLE FUND SCHOLARSHIP COMPETITION FOR EMPLOYEES' CHILDREN

• *See page 502*

PROJECT BEST SCHOLARSHIP FUND http://projectbest.com

PROJECT BEST SCHOLARSHIP

• *See page 478*

QUAKER CHEMICAL FOUNDATION (THE) http://www.quakerchem.com

QUAKER CHEMICAL FOUNDATION SCHOLARSHIPS

• *See page 502*

RECORDING FOR THE BLIND & DYSLEXIC http://www.rfbd.org

MARION HUBER LEARNING THROUGH LISTENING AWARDS

• *See page 478*

MARY P. OENSLAGER SCHOLASTIC ACHIEVEMENT AWARDS

• *See page 479*

RURAL MISSOURI, INC. http://www.rmiinc.org

NATIONAL FARMWORKER JOBS PROGRAM

The grant is from the Department of Labor. Renewable grant to low income seasonal farm workers and their dependents for tuition assistance. Must be a resident of Missouri. Must be paid wages for doing farm work. High school seniors may apply. Must attend a Missouri school. Minimum 2.5 GPA required.

Award: Grant for use in freshman, sophomore, junior, or senior years; renewable. *Number:* varies. *Amount:* up to $3000.

Eligibility Requirements: Applicant must be age 16; enrolled or expecting to enroll at a two-year or four-year or technical institution or university; resident of Missouri and studying in Missouri. Applicant or parent of applicant must have employment or volunteer experience in agriculture, farming, or migrant worker. Applicant must have 2.5 GPA or higher.

Application Requirements: Application. *Deadline:* Continuous.

Contact: Lynn Hatfield, Program Director
Rural Missouri, Inc.
1014 Northeast Drive
Jefferson City, MO 65109
Phone: 800-234-4971
Fax: 573-635-5636
E-mail: lynn@rmiinc.org

SALVATORE TADDONIO FAMILY FOUNDATION

TADDONIO SCHOLARSHIP

Award is given to students who are residents of Colorado and attend Colorado institutions. Minimum 3.0 GPA required. Application deadline is August 1. Must submit evidence of community service.

Award: Scholarship for use in freshman, sophomore, junior, or senior years; renewable. *Number:* 6–10. *Amount:* $500–$1500.

Eligibility Requirements: Applicant must be enrolled or expecting to enroll full-time at a two-year or four-year institution or university; resident of Colorado and studying in Colorado. Applicant or parent of applicant must have employment or volunteer experience in community service. Applicant must have 3.0 GPA or higher. Available to U.S. citizens.

Application Requirements: Application, essay, transcript, record of volunteer work. *Deadline:* August 1.

Contact: Samuel David Cheris, Trustee
Salvatore Taddonio Family Foundation
6161 South Syracuse Way, #100
Greenwood Village, CO 80111-4707
Phone: 303-632-7212
E-mail: cheriss@bwn.net

SCOTTISH RITE CHARITABLE FOUNDATION OF CANADA http://www.scottishritemasons-can.org/foundation

SCOTTISH RITE CHARITABLE FOUNDATION COLLEGE BURSARIES

Up to $2000 award for full-time students enrolled in their second or third year of study at a recognized community college. Applicants must be in a program leading to certification in the field of intellectual impairment. Must submit summary of past involvement in this field. Must be a Canadian citizen. Bursary is available to one qualified student from each province and territory. Write or visit Web site for additional details.

Award: Grant for use in sophomore or junior years; not renewable. *Number:* up to 13. *Amount:* up to $1486.

Eligibility Requirements: Applicant must be Canadian citizen; enrolled or expecting to enroll full-time at a two-year or four-year institution; resident of Alberta, British Columbia, Manitoba, New Brunswick, Newfoundland, North West Territories, Nova Scotia, Ontario, Prince Edward Island, Quebec, Saskatchewan, or Yukon and studying in Alberta, British Columbia, Manitoba, New Brunswick, Newfoundland, North West Territories, Nova Scotia, Ontario, Prince Edward Island, Quebec, Saskatchewan, or Yukon. Applicant or parent of applicant must have employment or volunteer experience in helping handicapped.

Scottish Rite Charitable Foundation of Canada (continued)

Application Requirements: Application, essay, resume, references, transcript. *Deadline:* June 30.

Contact: The Roeher Institute, Kinsmen Building, York University
Scottish Rite Charitable Foundation of Canada
4700 Keele Street, North York
Toronto, ON M3J 1P3
Canada
Phone: 416-661-9611
Fax: 416-661-5701

SCREEN ACTORS GUILD FOUNDATION http://www.sagfoundation.org

SCREEN ACTORS GUILD FOUNDATION/JOHN L. DALES SCHOLARSHIP (TRANSITIONAL)

• *See page 479*

SCREEN ACTORS GUILD FOUNDATION/JOHN L. DALES SCHOLARSHIP FUND (STANDARD)

• *See page 479*

SERVICE EMPLOYEES INTERNATIONAL UNION - CALIFORNIA STATE COUNCIL OF SERVICE EMPLOYEES http://www.seiu.org

CHARLES HARDY MEMORIAL SCHOLARSHIP AWARDS

• *See page 480*

SID RICHARDSON MEMORIAL FUND

SID RICHARDSON MEMORIAL FUND

Eligible applicants are children or grandchildren of persons presently employed (or retired) at a Sid Bass/Richardson company or its subsidiaries. Employee must have a minimum of three years of full-time employment at one of the following companies: Barbnet Investment Co., Perry R. Bass, Inc., Bass Enterprises Production Company, Richardson Energy Marketing Services, Sid Richardson Carbon Company, Sid Richardson Energy Services, Sid Richardson Energy Services-JAL, Sid W. Richardson Foundation, SRCG Aviation, Inc., or San Jose Cattle Company.

Award: Scholarship for use in freshman, sophomore, junior, senior, graduate, or postgraduate years; not renewable. *Number:* 50–60. *Amount:* $500–$7000.

Eligibility Requirements: Applicant must be enrolled or expecting to enroll full-time at a two-year or four-year or technical institution or university. Applicant or parent of applicant must have employment or volunteer experience in designated career field. Available to U.S. and non-U.S. citizens.

Application Requirements: Application, essay, financial need analysis, resume, references, test scores, transcript. *Deadline:* March 31.

Contact: Peggy Laskoski, Assistant Business Manager
Sid Richardson Memorial Fund
309 Main Street
Fort Worth, TX 76102
Phone: 817-336-0494
Fax: 817-332-2176
E-mail: plaskoski@sidrichardson.org

SOUTH DAKOTA BOARD OF REGENTS http://www.ris.sdbor.edu

SOUTH DAKOTA BOARD OF REGENTS STATE EMPLOYEE TUITION ASSISTANCE

Award for South Dakota state employees for any postsecondary academic year of study in South Dakota institution. Must be U.S. citizen. Write for requirements and other details.

Award: Scholarship for use in freshman, sophomore, junior, or senior years; not renewable. *Number:* varies. *Amount:* varies.

Eligibility Requirements: Applicant must be enrolled or expecting to enroll at an institution or university; resident of South Dakota and studying in South Dakota. Applicant or parent of applicant must have employment or volunteer experience in designated career field. Available to U.S. citizens.

Application Requirements: *Deadline:* Continuous.

Contact: South Dakota Board of Regents
306 East Capitol Avenue, Suite 200
Pierre, SD 57501-3159

SUBMARINE OFFICERS' WIVES CLUB

BOWFIN MEMORIAL SCHOLARSHIP

Bowfin Memorial Scholarships are available to Hawaii submariners and their dependents. Academic scholarships are for children of submariners under 23 years old, and Continuing Education Scholarships are for submariners and their dependents.

Award: Scholarship for use in freshman, sophomore, junior, or senior years; not renewable. *Number:* 8–40. *Amount:* $250–$2500.

Eligibility Requirements: Applicant must be enrolled or expecting to enroll full or part-time at a two-year or four-year or technical institution or university and resident of Hawaii. Applicant or parent of applicant must have employment or volunteer experience in designated career field. Available to U.S. citizens. Applicant must have served in the Navy.

Application Requirements: Application, essay, financial need analysis, interview, references, transcript. *Deadline:* March 1.

Contact: Mary Shank, Chairperson
Submarine Officers' Wives Club
PO Box 2473
Ewa Beach, HI 96706
Phone: 808-423-1341
E-mail: maryshank@earthlink.net

TAILHOOK EDUCATIONAL FOUNDATION

TAILHOOK EDUCATIONAL FOUNDATION SCHOLARSHIP

Applicant must be a high school graduate and the natural or adopted son or daughter of a current or former Naval Aviator, Naval Flight Officer, or Naval Air crewman. Individuals or children of individuals serving or having served on board a U.S. Navy Aircraft Carrier in ship's company or the Air Wing also eligible.

Award: Scholarship for use in freshman, sophomore, junior, or senior years; renewable. *Number:* 20. *Amount:* up to $2000.

Eligibility Requirements: Applicant must be enrolled or expecting to enroll full-time at a two-year or four-year institution or university. Applicant or parent of applicant must have employment or volunteer experience in designated career field. Applicant must have 3.0 GPA or higher. Available to U.S. and non-U.S. citizens. Applicant or parent must meet one or more of the following requirements: Coast Guard, Marine Corp, or Navy experience; retired from active duty; disabled or killed as a result of military service; prisoner of war; or missing in action.

Application Requirements: Application, driver's license, essay, references, self-addressed stamped envelope, test scores, transcript, proof of eligibility. *Deadline:* March 15.

Contact: Jim Carroll, Administrative Officer
Tailhook Educational Foundation
PO Box 26626
San Diego, CA 92196
Phone: 800-269-8267
Fax: 858-578-8839
E-mail: thookassn@aol.com

TEXAS HIGHER EDUCATION COORDINATING BOARD http://www.collegefortexans.com

EXEMPTION FOR DISABLED IN THE LINE OF DUTY PEACE OFFICERS

Renewable award for persons who were injured in the line of duty while serving as Peace Officers. Must be Texas resident and attend a public college or university in Texas. Submit documentation of disability from employer. For more information see registrar.

Award: Scholarship for use in freshman, sophomore, junior, or senior years; renewable. *Number:* varies. *Amount:* varies.

Eligibility Requirements: Applicant must be enrolled or expecting to enroll at a four-year institution or university; resident of Texas and studying in Texas. Applicant or parent of applicant must have employment or volunteer experience in police/firefighting.

Application Requirements: Application, form letter. *Deadline:* varies.

Contact: Texas Higher Education Coordinating Board
PO Box 12788
Austin, TX 78711
E-mail: grantinfo@thecb.state.tx.us

PHYSICIAN ASSISTANT LOAN REIMBURSEMENT PROGRAM

Award will repay loans for physician assistants working in rural Texas counties. Must have worked at least 12 consecutive months in a rural Texas county designated medically underserved. Can be renewed for up to four years.

Award: Grant for use in freshman, sophomore, junior, or senior years; renewable. *Number:* varies. *Amount:* up to $5000.

Eligibility Requirements: Applicant must be enrolled or expecting to enroll at an institution or university. Applicant or parent of applicant must have employment or volunteer experience in designated career field. Available to U.S. citizens.

Application Requirements: Application. *Deadline:* varies.

Contact: Financial Aid Office at college
Texas Higher Education Coordinating Board
PO Box 12788
Austin, TX 78711-2788
Phone: 512-427-6101
Fax: 512-427-6127
E-mail: grantinfo@thecb.state.tx.us

TEXAS-TUITION FEE EXEMPTION FOR CHILDREN OF DISABLED/ DECEASED FIREMEN, PEACE OFFICERS, GAME WARDENS, EMPLOYEES OF CORRECTIONAL INSTITUTIONS

Renewable award for children of paid or volunteer firemen, game wardens, peace officers, or custodial employees of the Department of Corrections disabled or deceased while serving in Texas. Must attend a Texas institution. Must apply before 21st birthday. Must provide certification of parent's disability or death. Contact institution's admissions or registrar's office for application information.

Award: Scholarship for use in freshman, sophomore, or junior years; renewable. *Number:* varies. *Amount:* varies.

Eligibility Requirements: Applicant must be age 20 or under; enrolled or expecting to enroll full or part-time at a two-year or four-year or technical institution or university; resident of Texas and studying in Texas. Applicant or parent of applicant must have employment or volunteer experience in designated career field, fire service, or police/firefighting. Available to U.S. citizens.

Application Requirements: Application. *Deadline:* Continuous.

Contact: Financial Aid Office at college
Texas Higher Education Coordinating Board
PO Box 12788
Austin, TX 78711-2788
Phone: 512-427-6101
Fax: 512-427-6127
E-mail: grantinfo@thecb.state.tx.us

THE HITACHI FOUNDATION http://www.hitachifoundation.org

YOSHIYAMA AWARD FOR EXEMPLARY SERVICE TO THE COMMUNITY

Award for high school seniors based on their community service activities. Must be nominated by someone familiar with their service. Submit nomination form, letter of nomination, and two supporting letters by April 1.

Award: Prize for use in freshman year; not renewable. *Number:* 8–12. *Amount:* $5000.

Eligibility Requirements: Applicant must be high school student; planning to enroll or expecting to enroll full-time at an institution or university and single. Applicant or parent of applicant must have employment or volunteer experience in community service. Available to U.S. citizens.

Application Requirements: References, nomination form, letter of nomination. *Deadline:* April 1.

Contact: Assistant Coordinator
The Hitachi Foundation
1509 22nd Street, NW
Washington, DC 20037-1098
Phone: 202-457-0588
Fax: 202-296-1098

TUITION EXCHANGE, INC. http://www.tuitionexchange.org

TUITION EXCHANGE SCHOLARSHIPS

The Tuition Exchange is an association of 540 colleges and universities awarding over 3,700 full or substantial scholarships each year for children and other family members of faculty and staff employed at participating institutions. See Web site http://www.tuitionexchange.org for complete list of participating institutions. Application procedures and deadlines vary per school. Contact Tuition Exchange Liaison Officer at home institution for details.

Award: Scholarship for use in freshman, sophomore, junior, senior, graduate, or postgraduate years; renewable. *Number:* 3400–4000. *Amount:* $10,000–$20,800.

Eligibility Requirements: Applicant must be enrolled or expecting to enroll full or part-time at a two-year or four-year institution or university. Applicant or parent of applicant must have employment or volunteer experience in designated career field. Available to U.S. and non-U.S. citizens.

Application Requirements: Application. *Deadline:* varies.

Contact: Tuition Exchange Liaison Officer at the college or university where your parent is employed

TWO TEN FOOTWEAR FOUNDATION http://www.twoten.org

TWO/TEN INTERNATIONAL FOOTWEAR FOUNDATION SCHOLARSHIP

Renewable, merit and need based award available to students who have 500 hours work experience in footwear, leather, or allied industries during year of application, or have a parent employed in one of these fields for at least two years. Must have proof of employment and maintain 2.0 GPA.

Award: Scholarship for use in freshman, sophomore, junior, or senior years; renewable. *Number:* 200–250. *Amount:* $200–$3000.

Eligibility Requirements: Applicant must be enrolled or expecting to enroll full or part-time at a two-year or four-year or technical institution or university. Applicant or parent of applicant must have employment or volunteer experience in leather/footwear. Available to U.S. citizens.

Application Requirements: Application, essay, financial need analysis, references, transcript. *Deadline:* January 1.

Contact: Catherine Nelson, Scholarship Director
Two Ten Footwear Foundation
1466 Main Street
Waltham, MA 02451-1623
Phone: 800-346-3210
Fax: 781-736-1555
E-mail: scholarship@twoten.org

UNITED STATES SUBMARINE VETERANS, INC. http://ussvcf.org/scolyrs.htm

UNITED STATES SUBMARINE VETERANS INC. NATIONAL SCHOLARSHIP PROGRAM

Sponsor must be a "Qualified Submarine" member in good standing as a Base Member or Member-at-Large (MAL). Program is awarded to those who have financial needs, 2.5 GPA and essay. Open to son, daughter, stepchildren, grandchildren of qualified member. Can apply each year until 23rd birthday. Applicants must be between the ages of 17-23 and must be unmarried.

Award: Scholarship for use in freshman, sophomore, junior, or senior years; not renewable. *Number:* 2–16. *Amount:* $750–$1000.

Eligibility Requirements: Applicant must be age 17-23; enrolled or expecting to enroll full-time at a two-year or four-year or technical institution and single. Applicant or parent of applicant must have employment or volunteer experience in seafaring. Applicant must have 2.5 GPA or higher. Available to U.S. citizens. Applicant or parent must

United States Submarine Veterans, Inc. (continued)

meet one or more of the following requirements: Navy experience; retired from active duty; disabled or killed as a result of military service; prisoner of war; or missing in action.

Application Requirements: Application, essay, financial need analysis, references, test scores, transcript. *Deadline:* April 15.

Contact: Paul William Orstad, USSVI National Scholarship Chairman
United States Submarine Veterans, Inc.
30 Surrey Lane
Norwich, CT 06369-6541
Phone: 860-889-4750
E-mail: hogan343@aol.com

WAL-MART FOUNDATION http://www.walmartfoundation.org

WAL-MART ASSOCIATE SCHOLARSHIPS

• *See page 502*

WAL-MART HIGHER REACH SCHOLARSHIP

• *See page 503*

WESTERN GOLF ASSOCIATION-EVANS SCHOLARS FOUNDATION http://www.evansscholarsfoundation.com

CHICK EVANS CADDIE SCHOLARSHIP

Full tuition and housing awards to high school seniors who have worked at least two years as caddies at a Western Golf Association member club. Must demonstrate need, have outstanding character, maintain a B average in college preparation classes and rank in top 25% of graduating class. Apply after July 15 following junior year. Applications must be received by September 30.

Award: Scholarship for use in freshman, sophomore, junior, or senior years; renewable. *Number:* 200. *Amount:* varies.

Eligibility Requirements: Applicant must be high school student; planning to enroll or expecting to enroll full-time at a four-year institution and studying in Colorado, Illinois, Indiana, Kansas, Michigan, Minnesota, Missouri, Ohio, Oregon, Pennsylvania, Washington, or Wisconsin. Applicant or parent of applicant must have employment or volunteer experience in private club/caddying. Applicant must have 3.5 GPA or higher.

Application Requirements: Application, essay, financial need analysis, interview, references, test scores, transcript. *Deadline:* September 30.

Contact: Scholarship Committee
Western Golf Association-Evans Scholars Foundation
One Briar Road
Golf, IL 60029
Phone: 847-724-4600
Fax: 847-724-7133
E-mail: evansscholars@wgaesf.com

ZONTA INTERNATIONAL FOUNDATION http://www.zonta.org

YOUNG WOMEN IN PUBLIC AFFAIRS AWARD

One-time award for pre-college women with a commitment to the volunteer sector and evidence of volunteer leadership achievements. Must be 16-20 years of age with a career interest in public affairs, public policy and community organizations. Further information and application available at Web site http://www.zonta.org.

Award: Scholarship for use in freshman year; not renewable. *Number:* varies. *Amount:* $500–$1000.

Eligibility Requirements: Applicant must be high school student; age 16-20; planning to enroll or expecting to enroll at a four-year institution or university and female. Applicant or parent of applicant must have employment or volunteer experience in community service.

Application Requirements: Application, references. *Deadline:* varies.

Contact: Ms. Ana Ubides, Foundation Assistant
Zonta International Foundation
557 West Randolph Street
Chicago, IL 60661-2206
Phone: 312-930-5848
Fax: 312-930-0951
E-mail: zontafdtn@zonta.org

IMPAIRMENT

ALEXANDER GRAHAM BELL ASSOCIATION FOR THE DEAF AND HARD OF HEARING http://www.agbell.org

ALEXANDER GRAHAM BELL SCHOLARSHIP AWARD

Several scholarships for applicants (undergraduates given preference) born with profound or severe hearing loss (of at least 60dB), or have experienced such a loss before acquiring language. Must use speech or speech reading to communicate. Must be attending or have been admitted to a college or university that primarily enrolls students with normal hearing. Application available online at: http://www.agbell.org or request, in writing, an application between September 1 and January 1. May reapply once.

Award: Scholarship for use in freshman, sophomore, junior, senior, or graduate years; not renewable. *Number:* varies. *Amount:* $250–$2000.

Eligibility Requirements: Applicant must be enrolled or expecting to enroll full-time at an institution or university. Applicant must be hearing impaired.

Application Requirements: Application, essay, references, transcript, audiological report. *Deadline:* March 1.

Contact: Financial Aid Coordinator
Alexander Graham Bell Association for the Deaf and Hard of Hearing
3417 Volta Place, NW
Washington, DC 20007-2778
E-mail: financialaid@agbell.org

AMERICAN ACADEMY OF ALLERGY, ASTHMA AND IMMUNOLOGY http://www.aaaai.org

AWARD OF EXCELLENCE ASTHMA SCHOLARSHIP PROGRAM

One-time award to high school seniors with asthma who are furthering their education in a postsecondary school. Must demonstrate academic excellence. Must be a U.S. citizen. Application deadline generally the first week of January. Check Web site for updated information. http://www.aaaai.org.

Award: Scholarship for use in freshman year; not renewable. *Number:* 56. *Amount:* $100–$1000.

Eligibility Requirements: Applicant must be high school student and planning to enroll or expecting to enroll full-time at a two-year or four-year or technical institution or university. Applicant must be physically disabled. Available to U.S. citizens.

Application Requirements: Application, essay, references, transcript. *Deadline:* varies.

Contact: John Augustyniak
American Academy of Allergy, Asthma and Immunology
555 East Wells Street, Suite 1100
Milwaukee, WI 53202-3823
Phone: 414-272-6071
Fax: 414-272-6070
E-mail: jaugustyniak@aaaai.org

AMERICAN COUNCIL OF THE BLIND http://www.acb.org

AMERICAN COUNCIL OF THE BLIND SCHOLARSHIPS

Merit-based award available to undergraduate, graduate, vocational or technical students who are legally blind in both eyes. Submit certificate of legal blindness and proof of acceptance at an accredited postsecondary institution.

Award: Scholarship for use in freshman, sophomore, junior, senior, or graduate years; not renewable. *Number:* 28. *Amount:* $500–$5000.

Eligibility Requirements: Applicant must be enrolled or expecting to enroll full-time at a two-year or four-year or technical institution or university. Applicant must be visually impaired. Applicant must have 3.5 GPA or higher.

Application Requirements: Application, autobiography, essay, references, transcript. *Deadline:* March 1.

Contact: Terry Pacheco, Affiliate and Membership Services
American Council of the Blind
1155 15th Street, NW, Suite 1004
Washington, DC 20005
Phone: 202-467-5081
Fax: 202-467-5085
E-mail: info@acb.org

AMERICAN FOUNDATION FOR THE BLIND http://www.afb.org

FERDINAND TORRES AFB SCHOLARSHIP

Award for full-time post-secondary student who is legally blind and presents evidence of economic need. Preference given to New York City residents. For additional information, visit Web site: http://www.afb.org.

Award: Scholarship for use in freshman, sophomore, junior, senior, or graduate years; not renewable. *Number:* up to 1. *Amount:* up to $1500.

Eligibility Requirements: Applicant must be enrolled or expecting to enroll full-time at a two-year or four-year institution or university. Applicant must be visually impaired. Available to U.S. and non-U.S. citizens.

Application Requirements: Application, essay, references, transcript, proof of legal blindness, acceptance letter. *Deadline:* April 30.

Contact: Information Center
American Foundation for the Blind
11 Penn Plaza, Suite 300
New York, NY 10001
Phone: 212-502-7661
Fax: 212-502-7771
E-mail: afbinfo@afb.net

ASSOCIATION FOR EDUCATION AND REHABILITATION OF THE BLIND AND VISUALLY IMPAIRED http://www.aerbvi.org

WILLIAM AND DOROTHY FERREL SCHOLARSHIP

Nonrenewable scholarship given in even years for postsecondary education leading to career in services for blind or visually impaired. Applicant must submit proof of legal blindness or visual field impairment of 20% or less. Refer to Web site for details and application: http://www.aerbui.org.

Award: Scholarship for use in freshman, sophomore, junior, senior, graduate, or postgraduate years; not renewable. *Number:* 2. *Amount:* $500.

Eligibility Requirements: Applicant must be enrolled or expecting to enroll at a two-year or four-year institution or university. Applicant must be visually impaired. Available to U.S. citizens.

Application Requirements: Application. *Deadline:* April 15.

Contact: Application available at Web site.

ASSOCIATION FOR GLYCOGEN STORAGE DISEASE http://www.agsdus.org

ASSOCIATION FOR GLYCOGEN STORAGE DISEASE SCHOLARSHIP

Award to help only students affected by Glycogen Storage Disease. Parent or student must be an active member of the Association for Glycogen Storage Disease. Student must be enrolled or accepted to a postsecondary school and attend full-time.

Award: Scholarship for use in freshman, sophomore, junior, or senior years; not renewable. *Number:* 1–3. *Amount:* $100–$250.

Eligibility Requirements: Applicant must be enrolled or expecting to enroll full-time at a two-year or four-year or technical institution or university. Applicant must be physically disabled. Available to U.S. and non-U.S. citizens.

Application Requirements: Application. *Deadline:* July 1.

Contact: Hollie Swain, President
Association for Glycogen Storage Disease
PO Box 896
Durant, IA 52747-9769
Phone: 563-785-6038
Fax: 563-785-6038

ASSOCIATION OF BLIND CITIZENS http://www.assocofblindcitizens.org

SCHOLARSHIP PROGRAM FOR THE BLIND AND VISUALLY IMPAIRED

One-time award provides assistance to blind and visually impaired students. Awards can be applied to offset tuition or for blindness-related expenses. Association offers eleven $1000 scholarships, three $2000 scholarships, and one $3000 scholarship. Visit http://www.blindcitizens.org and follow instructions to apply online. Application deadline is April 15.

Award: Scholarship for use in freshman, sophomore, junior, senior, graduate, or postgraduate years; not renewable. *Number:* up to 15. *Amount:* $1000–$3000.

Eligibility Requirements: Applicant must be enrolled or expecting to enroll full or part-time at a two-year or four-year or technical institution or university. Applicant must be visually impaired. Available to U.S. citizens.

Application Requirements: Application, autobiography, references, transcript, medical certificate of blindness. *Deadline:* April 15.

Contact: Association of Blind Citizens
PO Box 246
Holbrook, MA 02343
E-mail: scholarship@assocofblindcitizens.org

ASTHMA AND ALLERGY FOUNDATION OF AMERICA (AAFA) GREATER KANSAS CITY CHAPTER http://www.aafakc.org

BERRI MITCHEL MEMORIAL SCHOLARSHIP

The Berri Mitchel Memorial Scholarship provides four scholarships to greater Kansas City area high school seniors who have a history of asthma, have succeeded academically, and have shown an interest in their school and community. Application deadline is March 1.

Award: Scholarship for use in freshman year; not renewable. *Number:* 4. *Amount:* $1000.

Eligibility Requirements: Applicant must be high school student; planning to enroll or expecting to enroll full or part-time at a two-year or four-year or technical institution or university and resident of Kansas or Missouri. Applicant must be physically disabled. Available to U.S. citizens.

Application Requirements: Application, essay, references, transcript. *Deadline:* March 1.

Contact: Michelle Cook, Director of Community Education
Asthma and Allergy Foundation of America (AAFA) Greater Kansas City Chapter
9140 Ward Parkway, Suite 120
Kansas City, MO 64114
Phone: 816-333-6608
Fax: 816-333-6684
E-mail: info@aafakc.org

BILLY BARTY FOUNDATION http://www.rth.org/bbf

EVELYN BARTY SCHOLARSHIP

An award to help promising college students who have a medical form of dwarfism.

Award: Scholarship for use in freshman, sophomore, junior, senior, graduate, or postgraduate years; not renewable. *Number:* 1–10. *Amount:* $1000.

Eligibility Requirements: Applicant must be enrolled or expecting to enroll full-time at an institution or university. Applicant must be physically disabled. Available to U.S. citizens.

Application Requirements: Application, financial need analysis, photo, references, transcript. *Deadline:* April 1.

Contact: Lisa Luken, Secretary
Billy Barty Foundation
10222 Crosby Road
Harrison, OH 45030
Phone: 513-738-4428
Fax: 513-738-4428

CALIFORNIA COUNCIL OF THE BLIND http://www.ccbnet.org

CALIFORNIA COUNCIL OF THE BLIND SCHOLARSHIPS

Scholarships available to blind student applicants who are California residents entering or continuing studies at an accredited California college, university, or vocational training school. Must be a full-time student registered for at least twelve units for the entire academic year. Applications must be typed and all blanks must be filled to be considered for scholarship. Applications available at Web site (http://www.ccbnet.org.)

Award: Scholarship for use in freshman, sophomore, junior, senior, graduate, or postgraduate years; not renewable. *Number:* varies. *Amount:* $375–$2500.

Eligibility Requirements: Applicant must be enrolled or expecting to enroll full-time at a two-year or four-year or technical institution or university; resident of California and studying in California. Applicant must be visually impaired. Available to U.S. citizens.

Application Requirements: Application, financial need analysis, interview, references, transcript, proof of blindness from doctor or rehab agency. *Deadline:* June 15.

Contact: California Council of the Blind
578 B Street
Hayward, CA 94541
Phone: 510-537-7877
Fax: 510-537-7830
E-mail: ccotb@earthlink.net

CHAIRSCHOLARS FOUNDATION, INC. http://www.chairscholars.org

CHAIRSCHOLARS FOUNDATION, INC. SCHOLARSHIPS

• *See page 506*

CHRISTIAN RECORD SERVICES, INC. http://www.christianrecord.org

CHRISTIAN RECORD SERVICES INC. SCHOLARSHIPS

One-time award for legally blind or blind college undergraduates. Submit application, essay-autobiography, photo, references, and financial information by April 1.

Award: Scholarship for use in freshman, sophomore, junior, or senior years; not renewable. *Number:* 7–10. *Amount:* $250–$500.

Eligibility Requirements: Applicant must be enrolled or expecting to enroll full-time at a two-year or four-year institution or university. Applicant must be visually impaired. Available to U.S. citizens.

Application Requirements: Application, autobiography, essay, financial need analysis, photo, references. *Deadline:* April 1.

Contact: Melisa Welch, Assistant to Treasurer
Christian Record Services, Inc.
4444 South 52nd Street
Lincoln, NE 68516-1302
Phone: 402-488-0981 Ext. 213
Fax: 402-488-7582
E-mail: info@christianrecord.org

COLLEGEBOUND FOUNDATION http://www.collegeboundfoundation.org

ERICA LYNNE E. DURANT MEMORIAL SCHOLARSHIP

Award for Baltimore City public high school senior. Please see Web site: http://www.collegeboundfoundation.org for complete information on application process. Must submit CollegeBound Competitive Scholarship/Last-Dollar Grant Application. Must be physically challenged or learning disabled, provide proof of disability from a licensed professional. Must submit essay on how your disability has enriched your life and be available for an interview.

Award: Scholarship for use in freshman year; not renewable. *Number:* 1. *Amount:* $500.

Eligibility Requirements: Applicant must be high school student; planning to enroll or expecting to enroll full-time at a two-year or four-year institution or university and resident of Maryland. Applicant must be learning disabled or physically disabled. Available to U.S. citizens.

Application Requirements: Application, essay, financial need analysis, interview, references, transcript, financial aid award letters, Student Aid Report. *Deadline:* March 19.

Contact: April Bell, Associate Program Director
CollegeBound Foundation
300 Water Street, Suite 300
Baltimore, MD 21202
Phone: 410-783-2905 Ext. 208
Fax: 410-727-5786
E-mail: abell@collegeboundfoundation.org

COMMUNITY FOUNDATION OF CAPE COD http://www.capecodfoundation.org

FRANK X. AND MARY E. WENY SCHOLARSHIP FUND

Frank X. and Mary E. Weny Scholarship Fund is awarded to a graduating senior from Cape Cod who is living with diabetes. Financial need will also be considered. For more details see Web site: http://www.capecodfoundation.org.

Award: Scholarship for use in freshman year; not renewable. *Number:* 1. *Amount:* $8000.

Eligibility Requirements: Applicant must be high school student; planning to enroll or expecting to enroll full-time at a two-year or four-year or technical institution or university and resident of Massachusetts. Applicant must be physically disabled. Available to U.S. citizens.

Application Requirements: Application, essay, financial need analysis, references, test scores, transcript, doctor's note. *Deadline:* April 1.

Contact: Pauline Greenberg, Scholarship Associate
Community Foundation of Cape Cod
PO Box 406
259 Willow Street
Yarmouthport, MA 02675
Phone: 508-790-3040
Fax: 508-790-4069
E-mail: pgreenberg@capecodfoundation.org

COUNCIL FOR INTERNATIONAL EDUCATIONAL EXCHANGE http://www.ciee.org/study

ROBERT B. BAILEY III MINORITY SCHOLARSHIPS FOR EDUCATION ABROAD

One-time award for students from underrepresented groups in study abroad participating in Council for International Educational Exchange (CIEE)-administered overseas program. Application deadlines: April 1 and November 1. Applicant must be self-identified as belonging to an underrepresented group in study abroad.

Award: Scholarship for use in freshman, sophomore, junior, or senior years; not renewable. *Number:* 15–300. *Amount:* $500.

Eligibility Requirements: Applicant must be American Indian/Alaska Native, Asian/Pacific Islander, Black (non-Hispanic), or Hispanic and enrolled or expecting to enroll full-time at an institution or university. Applicant must be hearing impaired, learning disabled, physically disabled, or visually impaired. Applicant must have 3.5 GPA or higher. Available to U.S. citizens.

Application Requirements: Application, essay, financial need analysis, references, transcript. *Deadline:* varies.

Contact: Scholarship Committee
Council for International Educational Exchange
7 Custom House Street, 3rd Floor
Portland, ME 04101
E-mail: scholarships@ciee.org

COUNCIL OF CITIZENS WITH LOW VISION INTERNATIONAL C/O AMERICAN COUNCIL OF THE BLIND http://www.cclvi.org/

FRED SCHEIGERT SCHOLARSHIP PROGRAM

Scholarships are available to full-time undergraduate students who are visually impaired. Must maintain a 3.0 GPA. For more details, specific requirements, and an application go to Web site: http://www.cclvi.org.

Award: Scholarship for use in freshman, sophomore, junior, or senior years; renewable. *Number:* up to 1. *Amount:* $500–$5000.

Eligibility Requirements: Applicant must be enrolled or expecting to enroll full-time at an institution or university. Applicant must be visually impaired. Applicant must have 3.0 GPA or higher. Available to U.S. citizens.

Application Requirements: Application, essay, references, transcript. *Deadline:* April 15.

Contact: Application available at Web site.

COURAGE CENTER, VOCATIONAL SERVICES DEPARTMENT http://www.courage.org

SCHOLARSHIP FOR PEOPLE WITH DISABILITIES

Award provides financial assistance to students with sensory or physical disabilities. May reapply each year. Applicant must be pursuing educational goals or technical expertise beyond high school. Must be U.S. citizen and resident of Minnesota, or participate in Courage Center Services. Indication of extracurricular work and volunteer history must be submitted along with application form.

Award: Scholarship for use in freshman, sophomore, junior, or senior years; not renewable. *Number:* varies. *Amount:* $500–$1000.

Eligibility Requirements: Applicant must be enrolled or expecting to enroll full-time at a two-year or four-year or technical institution or university and resident of Minnesota. Applicant must be hearing impaired, physically disabled, or visually impaired. Available to U.S. citizens.

Application Requirements: Application, essay, financial need analysis, interview. *Deadline:* May 31.

Contact: Nancy Robinow, Administrative Assistant
Courage Center, Vocational Services Department
3915 Golden Valley Road
Golden Valley, MN 55422-4298
Phone: 763-520-0553
Fax: 763-520-0577
E-mail: nrobinow@courage.org

CYSTIC FIBROSIS SCHOLARSHIP FOUNDATION http://www.cfscholarship.org

CYSTIC FIBROSIS SCHOLARSHIP

Awards for young adults with cystic fibrosis to be used to further their education after high school. Awards may be used for tuition, books and fees. Awards are for one year. Students may reapply in subsequent years.

Award: Scholarship for use in freshman, sophomore, junior, or senior years; not renewable. *Number:* 40–50. *Amount:* $1000–$2000.

Eligibility Requirements: Applicant must be enrolled or expecting to enroll full or part-time at a two-year or four-year or technical institution or university. Applicant must be physically disabled. Available to U.S. citizens.

Application Requirements: Application, essay, financial need analysis, references, test scores, transcript. *Deadline:* March 15.

Contact: Mary K. Bottorff, President
Cystic Fibrosis Scholarship Foundation
2814 Grant Street
Evanston, IL 60201
Phone: 847-328-0127
Fax: 847-328-0127
E-mail: mkbcfsf@aol.com

EAR FOUNDATION MINNIE PEARL SCHOLARSHIP PROGRAM http://www.earfoundation.org

MINNIE PEARL SCHOLARSHIP PROGRAM

Renewable scholarship for full-time college students with a severe to profound bilateral hearing loss. Initially, recipients must be high school seniors with at least a 3.0 GPA. Renewals based upon maintenance of GPA.

Award: Scholarship for use in freshman, sophomore, junior, or senior years; renewable. *Number:* 1–5. *Amount:* $2500.

Eligibility Requirements: Applicant must be high school student and planning to enroll or expecting to enroll full-time at a four-year institution or university. Applicant must be hearing impaired. Applicant must have 3.0 GPA or higher. Available to U.S. citizens.

Application Requirements: Application, essay, photo, references, self-addressed stamped envelope, transcript. *Deadline:* February 15.

Contact: Amy Nielsen, Associate Director
Ear Foundation Minnie Pearl Scholarship Program
1817 Patterson Street
Nashville, TN 37203
Phone: 800-545-4327
Fax: 615-627-2728
E-mail: mps@earfoundation.org

EPILEPSY FOUNDATION OF IDAHO http://www.epilepsyidaho.org

GREGORY W. GILE MEMORIAL SCHOLARSHIP PROGRAM

One-time award to promote educational opportunities for Idaho high school graduates, or established and continuing college students with epilepsy. Must be a resident of Idaho. Application deadline is March 15.

Award: Scholarship for use in freshman, sophomore, junior, or senior years; not renewable. *Number:* 1. *Amount:* $1000–$1500.

Eligibility Requirements: Applicant must be enrolled or expecting to enroll full-time at a two-year or four-year or technical institution or university and resident of Idaho. Applicant must be physically disabled. Available to U.S. and non-U.S. citizens.

Application Requirements: Application, essay, references. *Deadline:* March 15.

Contact: David Blackwell, Executive Director
Epilepsy Foundation of Idaho
310 West Idaho Street
Boise, ID 83702
Phone: 208-344-4340
Fax: 208-343-0093
E-mail: efid@epilepsyidaho.org

MARK MUSIC MEMORIAL SCHOLARSHIP

One-time award to promote educational opportunities for Idaho residents with epilepsy. Application deadline is March 15.

Award: Scholarship for use in freshman, sophomore, junior, or senior years; not renewable. *Number:* 1. *Amount:* $500.

Eligibility Requirements: Applicant must be enrolled or expecting to enroll full-time at a two-year or four-year or technical institution or university and resident of Idaho. Applicant must be physically disabled. Available to U.S. and non-U.S. citizens.

Application Requirements: Application, essay, references. *Deadline:* March 15.

Contact: David Blackwell, Executive Director
Epilepsy Foundation of Idaho
310 West Idaho Street
Boise, ID 83702
Phone: 208-344-4340
Fax: 208-343-0093
E-mail: efid@epilepsyidaho.org

GREAT LAKES HEMOPHILIA FOUNDATION http://www.glhf.org/scholar.htm

EDUCATION AND TRAINING ASSISTANCE PROGRAM

Scholarship for Wisconsin residents who have a bleeding disorder such as hemophilia, Von Willebrand disease, or a platelet function disorder. Consideration is also given to family members. It can also be used to re-train adults with bleeding disorders who can no longer function in chosen field due to health complications. Write for an application.

Award: Scholarship for use in freshman, sophomore, junior, or senior years; not renewable. *Number:* 5–6. *Amount:* $1000.

Eligibility Requirements: Applicant must be enrolled or expecting to enroll full or part-time at a two-year or four-year or technical institution or university and resident of Wisconsin. Applicant must be physically disabled. Available to U.S. citizens.

Great Lakes Hemophilia Foundation (continued)

Application Requirements: Application, essay, references, self-addressed stamped envelope, transcript. *Deadline:* Continuous.

Contact: Eva Cribben, Program Services Coordinator
Great Lakes Hemophilia Foundation
PO Box 0704
Milwaukee, WI 53201-0704
Phone: 414-257-0200
Fax: 414-257-1225
E-mail: ecribben@glhf.org

HEMOPHILIA HEALTH SERVICES http://www.hemophiliahealth.com

HEMOPHILIA HEALTH SERVICES MEMORIAL SCHOLARSHIP FUND

One-time award open to full-time students with hemophilia or another bleeding disorder. Scholarship may be used at any accredited, nonprofit college, university, or vocational/technical school. Selection based on academic achievement in relation to tested ability, involvement in extracurricular and community activities, and financial need. For an application visit the Web site at http://www.hemophiliahealth.com.

Award: Scholarship for use in freshman, sophomore, junior, senior, graduate, or postgraduate years; not renewable. *Number:* 7–10. *Amount:* $1000–$2000.

Eligibility Requirements: Applicant must be enrolled or expecting to enroll full-time at a two-year or four-year or technical institution or university. Applicant must be physically disabled. Available to U.S. citizens.

Application Requirements: Application, essay, financial need analysis, references, test scores, transcript, doctor certification form. *Deadline:* May 1.

Contact: Sally Johnson, Special Programs Coordinator
Hemophilia Health Services
6820 Charlotte Pike
Nashville, TN 37209-4234
Phone: 615-850-5175
Fax: 615-352-2588
E-mail: sjohnson@hemophiliahealth.com

SCOTT TARBELL SCHOLARSHIP

This scholarship is designed to help full- and part-time students pursue an education in the technical fields of computer science and mathematics. For an application visit the Web site at http://www.hemophiliahealth.com

Award: Scholarship for use in freshman, sophomore, junior, senior, graduate, or postgraduate years; not renewable. *Number:* 1–2. *Amount:* $1000–$2000.

Eligibility Requirements: Applicant must be enrolled or expecting to enroll full or part-time at a two-year or four-year or technical institution or university. Applicant must be physically disabled. Available to U.S. citizens.

Application Requirements: Application, essay, financial need analysis, references, test scores, transcript. *Deadline:* May 1.

Contact: Sally Johnson, Special Programs Coordinator
Hemophilia Health Services
6820 Charlotte Pike
Nashville, TN 37209-4234
Phone: 615-850-5175
Fax: 615-352-2588
E-mail: sjohnson@hemophiliahealth.com

HEMOPHILIA RESOURCES OF AMERICA http://www.hrahemo.com

HEMOPHILIA RESOURCES OF AMERICA

One-time award for persons with hemophilia or Von Willebrand disease. Sons and daughters of those afflicted are also eligible.

Award: Scholarship for use in freshman, sophomore, junior, or senior years; not renewable. *Number:* 22. *Amount:* $1000–$2500.

Eligibility Requirements: Applicant must be enrolled or expecting to enroll full or part-time at a two-year or four-year or technical institution or university. Applicant must be physically disabled. Available to U.S. citizens.

Application Requirements: Application, essay, financial need analysis, references, transcript. *Deadline:* May 15.

Contact: Nelson Escoto, Marketing Coordinator
Hemophilia Resources of America
45 Route 46 East, Suite 609, Box 2011
Pine Brook, NJ 07058
Phone: 800-549-2654
E-mail: nescoto@hrahemo.com

IDAHO STATE BOARD OF EDUCATION http://www.idahoboardofed.org

IDAHO MINORITY AND "AT RISK" STUDENT SCHOLARSHIP

Renewable award for Idaho residents who are disabled or members of a minority group and have financial need. Must attend one of eight postsecondary institutions in the state for undergraduate study. Deadlines vary by institution. Must be a U.S. citizen and be a graduate of an Idaho high school. Contact college financial aid office.

Award: Scholarship for use in freshman, sophomore, junior, or senior years; renewable. *Number:* 35–40. *Amount:* $3000.

Eligibility Requirements: Applicant must be American Indian/Alaska Native, Black (non-Hispanic), or Hispanic; enrolled or expecting to enroll full-time at a two-year or four-year or technical institution or university; resident of Idaho and studying in Idaho. Applicant must be hearing impaired, physically disabled, or visually impaired. Available to U.S. citizens.

Application Requirements: Application, financial need analysis, transcript. *Deadline:* varies.

Contact: Financial Aid Office

ILLINOIS COUNCIL OF THE BLIND

FLOYD CARGILL SCHOLARSHIP

Award for visually impaired Illinois resident attending or planning to attend an Illinois college. One-time award of $750. Deadline: June 15.

Award: Scholarship for use in freshman, sophomore, junior, or senior years; not renewable. *Number:* 1. *Amount:* $750.

Eligibility Requirements: Applicant must be enrolled or expecting to enroll full-time at a two-year or four-year or technical institution or university; resident of Illinois and studying in Illinois. Applicant must be visually impaired.

Application Requirements: Application, autobiography, references, test scores, transcript. *Deadline:* June 15.

Contact: Jeanette Spencer, Office Manager
Illinois Council of the Blind
PO Box 1336
Springfield, IL 62705
Phone: 217-523-4967
E-mail: icb@fgi.net

ILLINOIS STUDENT ASSISTANCE COMMISSION (ISAC) http://www.collegezone.org

ILLINOIS DEPARTMENT OF REHABILITATION SERVICES EDUCATION BENEFITS

If you have a physical or mental disability, and have been approved for vocational training by the Office of Rehabilitation you may be eligible to receive financial assistance to be used at any accredited Illinois college or technical school. Must be Illinois resident and demonstrate financial need. See Web site: http://www.dhs.state.il.us.

Award: Scholarship for use in freshman, sophomore, junior, or senior years; renewable. *Number:* varies. *Amount:* varies.

Eligibility Requirements: Applicant must be enrolled or expecting to enroll at a two-year or four-year or technical institution or university; resident of Illinois and studying in Illinois. Applicant must be hearing impaired, learning disabled, physically disabled, or visually impaired. Available to U.S. citizens.

Application Requirements: Application, financial need analysis. *Deadline:* Continuous.

Contact: Paul Worrall, Counselor
Illinois Student Assistance Commission (ISAC)
1755 Lake Cook Road
Deerfield, IL 60015-5209
Phone: 800-843-6154

IMMUNE DEFICIENCY FOUNDATION http://www.primaryimmune.org

IMMUNE DEFICIENCY FOUNDATION SCHOLARSHIP

One-time award available to individuals diagnosed with a primary immune deficiency disease. Must submit medical verification of diagnosis. Available for study at the undergraduate level at any postsecondary institution. Must be U.S. citizen.

Award: Scholarship for use in freshman, sophomore, junior, or senior years; not renewable. *Number:* 30–40. *Amount:* $750–$2000.

Eligibility Requirements: Applicant must be enrolled or expecting to enroll full or part-time at a two-year or four-year or technical institution or university. Applicant must be physically disabled. Available to U.S. citizens.

Application Requirements: Application, autobiography, essay, financial need analysis, references, medical verification of diagnosis. *Deadline:* March 31.

Contact: Tamara Brown, Medical Programs Manager
Immune Deficiency Foundation
40 West Chesapeake Avenue, Suite 308
Towson, MD 21204
Phone: 800-296-4433
Fax: 410-321-9165
E-mail: tb@primaryimmune.org

IOWA DIVISION OF VOCATIONAL REHABILITATION SERVICES http://www.dvrs.state.ia.us

IOWA VOCATIONAL REHABILITATION

Provides vocational rehabilitation services to individuals with disabilities who need these services in order to maintain, retain, or obtain employment compatible with their disabilities. Must be Iowa resident.

Award: Grant for use in freshman, sophomore, junior, senior, graduate, or postgraduate years; renewable. *Number:* up to 5000. *Amount:* $500–$4000.

Eligibility Requirements: Applicant must be enrolled or expecting to enroll full or part-time at a two-year or four-year or technical institution or university and resident of Iowa. Applicant must be hearing impaired, learning disabled, physically disabled, or visually impaired. Available to U.S. and non-U.S. citizens.

Application Requirements: Application, interview. *Deadline:* Continuous.

Contact: Ralph Childers, Policy and Workforce Initiatives Coordinator
Iowa Division of Vocational Rehabilitation Services
Division of Vocational Rehabilitation Services
510 East 12th Street
Des Moines, IA 50319
Phone: 515-281-4151
Fax: 515-281-4703
E-mail: rchilders@dvrs.state.ia.us

KENTUCKY DEPARTMENT OF VOCATIONAL REHABILITATION http://www.ihdi.uky.edu/

KENTUCKY DEPARTMENT OF VOCATIONAL REHABILITATION

Kentucky Department of Vocational Rehabilitation provides services necessary to secure employment. Eligible individual must possess physical or mental impairment that results in a substantial impediment to employment; benefit from vocational rehabilitation services in terms of an employment outcome; and require vocational rehabilitation services to prepare for, enter, or retain employment.

Award: Grant for use in freshman, sophomore, junior, senior, graduate, or postgraduate years; renewable. *Number:* varies. *Amount:* varies.

Eligibility Requirements: Applicant must be enrolled or expecting to enroll full or part-time at a two-year or four-year or technical institution or university and resident of Kentucky. Applicant must be learning disabled or physically disabled. Available to U.S. citizens.

Application Requirements: Application, financial need analysis, interview, test scores, transcript. *Deadline:* Continuous.

Contact: Ms. Marian Spencer, Program Administrator
Kentucky Department of Vocational Rehabilitation
209 St. Clair Street
Frankfort, KY 40601
Phone: 502-564-4440
Fax: 502-564-6745
E-mail: marianu.spencer@mail.state.ky.us

LA KELLEY COMMUNICATIONS http://www.kelleycom.com

ERIC DOSTIE MEMORIAL COLLEGE SCHOLARSHIP

Awarded to a person with a bleeding disorder (their sibling or child) to attend any accredited college or university. Must be a U.S. citizen. Applicant may reapply.

Award: Scholarship for use in freshman, sophomore, junior, senior, or graduate years; not renewable. *Number:* up to 9. *Amount:* $1000.

Eligibility Requirements: Applicant must be enrolled or expecting to enroll full-time at a two-year or four-year institution or university. Applicant must be physically disabled. Available to U.S. citizens.

Application Requirements: Application, essay, photo, references, test scores, transcript. *Deadline:* March 1.

Contact: Stephanie Allan, Office Manager/Kelley Communications
LA Kelley Communications
68 East Main Street, Suite 102
Georgetown, MA 01833
Phone: 978-352-7657
Fax: 978-352-6254
E-mail: info@kelleycom.com

LIGHTHOUSE INTERNATIONAL http://www.lighthouse.org

SCHOLARSHIP AWARDS

One-time award designed to reward excellence, recognize accomplishments, and to help students who are blind or partially sighted achieve their career goals. There are 4 categories: college bound, undergraduate, graduate, adult undergraduate II. Students must be legally blind, U.S. citizens, enrolled in an accredited program of study. Applicants must be a resident of and attend school in one of these states: New York, Connecticut, Massachusetts, New Jersey, Rhode Island, Maine, New Hampshire, Pennsylvania, Vermont, Delaware, Maryland, and Washington, D.C.

Award: Prize for use in freshman, sophomore, junior, senior, graduate, or postgraduate years; not renewable. *Number:* 4. *Amount:* $5000.

Eligibility Requirements: Applicant must be enrolled or expecting to enroll full-time at a four-year institution or university; resident of Connecticut, Delaware, District of Columbia, Maine, Maryland, Massachusetts, New Hampshire, New Jersey, New York, Pennsylvania, Rhode Island, or Vermont and studying in Connecticut, Delaware, District of Columbia, Maine, Maryland, Massachusetts, New Hampshire, New Jersey, New York, Pennsylvania, Rhode Island, or Vermont. Applicant must be visually impaired. Available to U.S. citizens.

Application Requirements: Application, essay, references, transcript, proof of U.S. citizenship, proof of legal blindness. *Deadline:* March 31.

Contact: Kelly Boyle, Director of Special Events
Lighthouse International
111 East 59th Street
New York, NY 10022-1202
Phone: 212-821-9428
Fax: 212-821-9703
E-mail: kboyle@lighthouse.org

LILLY REINTEGRATION PROGRAMS http://www.reintegration.com

LILLY REINTEGRATION SCHOLARSHIP

Scholarships available to students diagnosed with schizophrenia, bi-polar, schizophreniform or a schizoaffective disorder. Must be currently receiving

Lilly Reintegration Programs (continued)

medical treatment for the disease, including medications and psychiatric follow-up. Must also be U.S. citizen and actively involved in rehabilitative or reintegration efforts. Applicants must be at least 18 years of age. For information and application, use e-mail at lillyscholarships@reintigration.com.

Award: Scholarship for use in freshman, sophomore, junior, senior, or graduate years; not renewable. *Number:* 70–100. *Amount:* varies.

Eligibility Requirements: Applicant must be age 18 and enrolled or expecting to enroll full or part-time at a two-year or four-year or technical institution or university. Applicant must be physically disabled. Available to U.S. citizens.

Application Requirements: Application, essay, references, transcript. *Deadline:* January 31.

Contact: Lilly Secretariat
Lilly Reintegration Programs
PMB 1167, 734 North LaSalle Street
Chicago, IL 60610
Phone: 800-809-8202
E-mail: lillyscholarships@reintegration.com

LOUISE C. NACCA MEMORIAL FOR EDUCATIONAL AID FOR THE HANDICAPPED TRUST

LOUISE NACCA MEMORIAL TRUST

One-time award available to student who has a visual, hearing or physical impairment. May be used at any postsecondary institution. Must be a U.S. citizen. Must demonstrate financial need.

Award: Scholarship for use in freshman, sophomore, junior, senior, or graduate years; not renewable. *Number:* varies. *Amount:* up to $5000.

Eligibility Requirements: Applicant must be enrolled or expecting to enroll full or part-time at a two-year or four-year or technical institution or university and resident of New Jersey. Applicant must be hearing impaired, physically disabled, or visually impaired. Available to U.S. citizens.

Application Requirements: Application, financial need analysis. *Deadline:* varies.

Contact: Board Director, Cerebral Palsy
Louise C. Nacca Memorial for Educational Aid for the Handicapped Trust
7 Sanford Avenue
Belleville, NJ 07109

NATIONAL CENTER FOR LEARNING DISABILITIES, INC. http://www.ld.org

ANNE FORD SCHOLARSHIP

A $10,000 award given to a high school senior of high merit with an identified learning disability who is pursuing an undergraduate degree. The ideal candidate is a person who has faced the challenges of having a learning disability and who, through perseverance and academic endeavor, has created a life of purpose and achievement. Visit Web site at http://www.ld.org for deadline information.

Award: Scholarship for use in freshman year; not renewable. *Number:* 1. *Amount:* $10,000.

Eligibility Requirements: Applicant must be high school student and planning to enroll or expecting to enroll full-time at a four-year institution or university. Applicant must be learning disabled. Applicant must have 3.0 GPA or higher. Available to U.S. citizens.

Application Requirements: Application, essay, financial need analysis, references, test scores, transcript.

Contact: Ms. Meaghan Carey, Coordinator
National Center for Learning Disabilities, Inc.
381 Park Avenue South, Suite 1401
New York, NY 10016-8806
Phone: 212-545-7510 Ext. 233
Fax: 212-545-9665
E-mail: mcarey@ncld.org

NATIONAL FEDERATION OF THE BLIND http://www.nfb.org

E. U. PARKER SCHOLARSHIP

• *See page 514*

HERMIONE GRANT CALHOUN SCHOLARSHIP

• *See page 514*

JENNICA FERGUSON MEMORIAL SCHOLARSHIP

• *See page 514*

KENNETH JERNIGAN SCHOLARSHIP

• *See page 514*

KUCHLER-KILLIAN MEMORIAL SCHOLARSHIP

• *See page 515*

MELVA T. OWEN MEMORIAL SCHOLARSHIP

• *See page 515*

NATIONAL FEDERATION OF THE BLIND SCHOLARSHIPS

• *See page 515*

SALLY S. JACOBSEN SCHOLARSHIP

• *See page 515*

NATIONAL FEDERATION OF THE BLIND OF CALIFORNIA http://www.nfbcal.org

GERALD DRAKE MEMORIAL SCHOLARSHIP

One-time award for legally blind students pursuing an undergraduate or graduate degree. Must be a California resident and full-time student. Winner must attend the National Federation of the Blind California convention (expenses will be paid). Application deadline is May 30.

Award: Scholarship for use in freshman, sophomore, junior, senior, graduate, or postgraduate years; not renewable. *Number:* 1. *Amount:* $1500.

Eligibility Requirements: Applicant must be enrolled or expecting to enroll full-time at a two-year or four-year or technical institution or university and resident of California. Applicant must be visually impaired. Available to U.S. and non-U.S. citizens.

Application Requirements: Application, autobiography, essay, financial need analysis, interview, references, transcript. *Deadline:* May 30.

Contact: Nancy Burns, President
National Federation of the Blind of California
175 East Olive Avenue
Suite 308
Burbank, CA 91502
Phone: 818-558-6524
Fax: 818-729-7930
E-mail: dnburns@jps.net

JULIE LANDUCCI SCHOLARSHIP

One-time award for legally blind students pursuing an undergraduate or graduate degree. Must be a California resident and full-time student. Winner must attend the National Federation of the Blind California convention (expenses will be paid). Application deadline is May 30.

Award: Scholarship for use in freshman, sophomore, junior, senior, graduate, or postgraduate years; not renewable. *Number:* 1. *Amount:* $1500.

Eligibility Requirements: Applicant must be enrolled or expecting to enroll full-time at a two-year or four-year or technical institution or university and resident of California. Applicant must be visually impaired. Available to U.S. and non-U.S. citizens.

Application Requirements: Application, autobiography, essay, financial need analysis, interview, references, transcript. *Deadline:* May 30.

Contact: Nancy Burns, President
National Federation of the Blind of California
175 East Olive Avenue
Suite 308
Burbank, CA 91502
Phone: 818-558-6524
Fax: 818-729-7930
E-mail: dnburns@jps.net

LA VYRL "PINKY" JOHNSON MEMORIAL SCHOLARSHIP

One-time award for legally blind students pursuing an undergraduate or graduate degree. Must be a California resident and full-time student. Winner must attend the National Federation of the Blind California convention (expenses will be paid). Application deadline is May 30.

Award: Scholarship for use in freshman, sophomore, junior, senior, graduate, or postgraduate years; not renewable. *Number:* 1. *Amount:* $1500.

Eligibility Requirements: Applicant must be enrolled or expecting to enroll full-time at a two-year or four-year or technical institution or university and resident of California. Applicant must be visually impaired. Available to U.S. and non-U.S. citizens.

Application Requirements: Application, autobiography, essay, financial need analysis, interview, references, transcript. *Deadline:* May 30.

Contact: Nancy Burns, President
National Federation of the Blind of California
175 East Olive Avenue
Suite 308
Burbank, CA 91502
Phone: 818-558-6524
Fax: 818-729-7930
E-mail: dnburns@jps.net

LAWRENCE "MUZZY" MARCELINO MEMORIAL SCHOLARSHIP

One-time award for legally blind students pursuing an undergraduate or graduate degree. Must be a California resident and full-time student. Winner must attend the National Federation of the Blind California convention (expenses will be paid). Application deadline is May 30.

Award: Scholarship for use in freshman, sophomore, junior, senior, graduate, or postgraduate years; not renewable. *Number:* 1. *Amount:* $3000.

Eligibility Requirements: Applicant must be enrolled or expecting to enroll full-time at a two-year or four-year or technical institution or university and resident of California. Applicant must be visually impaired. Available to U.S. and non-U.S. citizens.

Application Requirements: Application, autobiography, essay, financial need analysis, interview, references, transcript. *Deadline:* May 30.

Contact: Nancy Burns, President
National Federation of the Blind of California
175 East Olive Avenue
Suite 308
Burbank, CA 91502
Phone: 818-558-6524
Fax: 818-729-7930
E-mail: dnburns@jps.net

NATIONAL FEDERATION OF THE BLIND OF CALIFORNIA MERIT SCHOLARSHIPS

One-time award for legally blind students pursuing an undergraduate or graduate degree. Must be a California resident and full-time student. Winner must attend the National Federation of the Blind California convention (expenses will be paid). Application deadline is May 30.

Award: Scholarship for use in freshman, sophomore, junior, senior, graduate, or postgraduate years; not renewable. *Number:* 2. *Amount:* $1000.

Eligibility Requirements: Applicant must be enrolled or expecting to enroll full-time at a two-year or four-year or technical institution or university and resident of California. Applicant must be visually impaired. Available to U.S. and non-U.S. citizens.

Application Requirements: Application, autobiography, essay, financial need analysis, interview, references, transcript. *Deadline:* May 30.

Contact: Nancy Burns, President
National Federation of the Blind of California
175 East Olive Avenue
Suite 308
Burbank, CA 91502
Phone: 818-558-6524
Fax: 818-729-7930
E-mail: dnburns@jps.net

NATIONAL FEDERATION OF THE BLIND OF MISSOURI http://www.nfbmo.org

NATIONAL FEDERATION OF THE BLIND OF MISSOURI SCHOLARSHIPS TO LEGALLY BLIND STUDENTS

Awards are based on achievement, commitment to community and financial need. Recipients must be legally blind. Amount of money each year available for program will vary.

Award: Scholarship for use in freshman, sophomore, junior, senior, graduate, or postgraduate years; not renewable. *Number:* up to 2. *Amount:* $500–$1500.

Eligibility Requirements: Applicant must be enrolled or expecting to enroll full or part-time at a two-year or four-year or technical institution or university and resident of Missouri. Applicant must be visually impaired. Available to U.S. citizens.

Application Requirements: Application, autobiography, essay, financial need analysis, interview, references, transcript. *Deadline:* February 1.

Contact: Mr. Gary Wunder, President
National Federation of the Blind of Missouri
3910 Tropical Lane
Columbia, MO 65202
Phone: 573-874-1774
Fax: 573-442-5617
E-mail: president@nfbmo.org

NATIONAL KIDNEY FOUNDATION OF INDIANA, INC. http://www.kidneyindiana.org

LARRY SMOCK SCHOLARSHIP

Financial assistance for kidney dialysis and transplant patients to pursue post-secondary education. Applicant must be resident of Indiana over the age of 17. Application deadline is February 4.

Award: Scholarship for use in freshman, sophomore, junior, or senior years; not renewable. *Number:* varies. *Amount:* varies.

Eligibility Requirements: Applicant must be age 18; enrolled or expecting to enroll full or part-time at a two-year or four-year or technical institution or university and resident of Indiana. Applicant must be physically disabled. Available to U.S. citizens.

Application Requirements: Application, references, transcript. *Deadline:* February 4.

Contact: Marilyn Winn, Program Director
National Kidney Foundation of Indiana, Inc.
911 East 86th Street, Suite 100
Indianapolis, IN 46204-1840
Phone: 317-722-5640
Fax: 317-722-5650
E-mail: nkfi@myvine.com

NATIONAL PKU NEWS http://www.pkunews.org

ROBERT GUTHRIE PKU SCHOLARSHIP AND AWARDS

Award program is open only to persons with phenylketonuria (PKU) who are on a special diet for PKU treatment. PKU is a genetic metabolic disease affecting about 1/12,000 of U.S. births yearly. Award is for full- or part-time study at any accredited U.S. institution.

Award: Scholarship for use in freshman, sophomore, junior, senior, graduate, or postgraduate years; not renewable. *Number:* 6–12. *Amount:* $500–$5000.

Eligibility Requirements: Applicant must be enrolled or expecting to enroll full or part-time at a two-year or four-year or technical institution or university. Applicant must be physically disabled. Available to U.S. and non-U.S. citizens.

Application Requirements: Application, autobiography, essay, photo, resume, references, test scores, transcript. *Deadline:* November 1.

Contact: Virginia Schuett, Director
National PKU News
6869 Woodlawn Avenue, NE
Suite 116
Seattle, WA 98115-5469
Phone: 206-525-8140
Fax: 206-525-5023
E-mail: schuett@pkunews.org

NATIONAL UNION OF PUBLIC AND GENERAL EMPLOYEES http://www.nupge.ca

TERRY FOX MEMORIAL SCHOLARSHIP

• See page 472

NORTH CAROLINA DIVISION OF SERVICES FOR THE BLIND

NORTH CAROLINA DIVISION OF SERVICES FOR THE BLIND REHABILITATION SERVICES

Financial assistance is available for North Carolina residents who are blind or visually impaired and who require vocational rehabilitation to help find employment. Tuition and other assistance provided based on need. Open to U.S. citizens and legal residents of United States. Applicants goal must be to work after receiving vocational services. To apply, contact the local DSB office and apply for vocational rehabilitation services.

Award: Scholarship for use in freshman, sophomore, junior, or senior years; renewable. *Number:* varies. *Amount:* varies.

Eligibility Requirements: Applicant must be enrolled or expecting to enroll full or part-time at a two-year or four-year or technical institution or university and resident of North Carolina. Applicant must be visually impaired. Available to U.S. citizens.

Application Requirements: Application, financial need analysis, interview, proof of eligibility. *Deadline:* Continuous.

Contact: JoAnn Strader, Chief of Rehabilitation Field Services
North Carolina Division of Services for the Blind
2601 Mail Service Center
Raleigh, NC 27699-2601
Fax: 919-715-8771
E-mail: joann.strader@ncmail.net

NORTH CAROLINA DIVISION OF VOCATIONAL REHABILITATION SERVICES http://www.dhhs.state.nc.us

TRAINING SUPPORT FOR YOUTH WITH DISABILITIES

Public service program that helps persons with disabilities obtain jobs. To qualify, student must have a mental or physical disability that is an impediment to employment. Each program designed individually with the student. Assistance is based on need and type of program in which student enrolls.

Award: Grant for use in freshman, sophomore, junior, or senior years; renewable. *Number:* varies. *Amount:* varies.

Eligibility Requirements: Applicant must be enrolled or expecting to enroll full or part-time at a two-year or four-year or technical institution or university and resident of North Carolina. Applicant must be hearing impaired, learning disabled, physically disabled, or visually impaired. Available to U.S. citizens.

Application Requirements: Application, financial need analysis, interview, test scores, transcript. *Deadline:* Continuous.

Contact: Alma Taylor, Program Specialist for Transition
North Carolina Division of Vocational Rehabilitation Services
2801 Mail Service Center
Raleigh, NC 27699-2801
Phone: 919-733-3364
Fax: 919-715-0616
E-mail: alma.taylor@ncmail.net

OPTIMIST INTERNATIONAL FOUNDATION http://www.optimist.org/

COMMUNICATIONS CONTEST FOR THE DEAF AND HARD OF HEARING

$1500 college scholarship (district level) for young people through grade 12 in the United States and Canada, to CEGEP in Quebec and grade 13 in the Caribbean, who are recognized by their school as deaf or hard of hearing. Must be conducted through a local Optimist Club. Visit Web site at http://www.optimist.org for additional information.

Award: Scholarship for use in freshman, sophomore, junior, or senior years; not renewable. *Number:* 53. *Amount:* $1500.

Eligibility Requirements: Applicant must be enrolled or expecting to enroll full-time at a two-year or four-year or technical institution or university. Applicant must be hearing impaired. Available to U.S. and non-U.S. citizens.

Application Requirements: Application, applicant must enter a contest, self-addressed stamped envelope. *Deadline:* varies.

Contact: Danielle Baugher, International Programs Coordinator
Optimist International Foundation
4494 Lindell Boulevard
St. Louis, MO 63108
Phone: 314-371-6000 Ext. 235
Fax: 314-371-6006
E-mail: programs@optimist.org

OREGON STUDENT ASSISTANCE COMMISSION http://www.osac.state.or.us

HARRY LUDWIG MEMORIAL SCHOLARSHIP

One-time award for visually-impaired Oregon residents planning to enroll full time in undergraduate or graduate studies. Must document visual impairment with a letter from a physician. Must enroll in an Oregon college. Visit Web site for more details (http://www.osac.state.or.us).

Award: Scholarship for use in freshman, sophomore, junior, senior, or graduate years; not renewable. *Number:* 7. *Amount:* $1643.

Eligibility Requirements: Applicant must be enrolled or expecting to enroll full-time at a four-year institution; resident of Oregon and studying in Oregon. Applicant must be visually impaired. Available to U.S. citizens.

Application Requirements: Application, essay, financial need analysis, references, transcript, documentation of visual impairment. *Deadline:* March 1.

Contact: Director of Grant Programs
Oregon Student Assistance Commission
1500 Valley River Drive, Suite 100
Eugene, OR 97401-7020
Phone: 800-452-8807 Ext. 7395
E-mail: awardinfo@mercury.osac.state.or.us

PFIZER http://www.epilepsy-scholarship.com

PFIZER EPILEPSY SCHOLARSHIP AWARD

Award for students with epilepsy who excel academically and in extracurricular activities. Must be pursuing an undergraduate degree or be a college senior entering first year of graduate school. Must be under the care of a physician for epilepsy to qualify.

Award: Scholarship for use in freshman, sophomore, junior, senior, or graduate years; not renewable. *Number:* 16. *Amount:* $3000.

Eligibility Requirements: Applicant must be enrolled or expecting to enroll full or part-time at a two-year or four-year or technical institution or university. Applicant must be physically disabled. Available to U.S. and non-U.S. citizens.

Application Requirements: Application, essay, references, test scores, transcript. *Deadline:* March 1.

Contact: Caren Zoppi
Pfizer
Eden Communications Group
515 Valley Street
Maplewood, NJ 07040
Phone: 973-275-6512
Fax: 973-275-9792
E-mail: czoppi@edencomgroup.com

RECORDING FOR THE BLIND & DYSLEXIC http://www.rfbd.org

MARION HUBER LEARNING THROUGH LISTENING AWARDS

• See page 478

MARY P. OENSLAGER SCHOLASTIC ACHIEVEMENT AWARDS

• See page 479

SERTOMA INTERNATIONAL http://www.sertoma.org

SERTOMA SCHOLARSHIP FOR DEAF OR HARD OF HEARING STUDENT

Twenty $1000 scholarships for hearing-impaired students or those with communicative disorders. Available for citizens of the U.S. Minimum 3.2 GPA required. Application deadline is May 1.

Award: Scholarship for use in freshman, sophomore, junior, or senior years; not renewable. *Number:* 20. *Amount:* $1000.

Eligibility Requirements: Applicant must be enrolled or expecting to enroll full-time at a four-year institution or university. Applicant must be hearing impaired. Available to U.S. citizens.

Application Requirements: Application, essay, references, transcript, proof of hearing loss. *Deadline:* May 1.

Contact: Sertoma International
1912 East Meyer Boulevard
Kansas City, MO 64132
Phone: 816-333-8300
Fax: 816-333-4320
E-mail: infosertoma@sertoma.org

SICKLE CELL DISEASE ASSOCIATION OF AMERICA/ CONNECTICUT CHAPTER, INC. http://www.sicklecellct.org

I. H. MCLENDON MEMORIAL SCHOLARSHIP

The I. H. McLendon Memorial Scholarship provides a one-time scholarship to graduating high school seniors with sickle cell disease in Connecticut who will enter college, university, or technical training. Minimum 3.0 GPA required.

Award: Scholarship for use in freshman year; not renewable. *Number:* 1. *Amount:* $1000.

Eligibility Requirements: Applicant must be high school student; planning to enroll or expecting to enroll full or part-time at a two-year or four-year or technical institution or university and resident of Connecticut. Applicant must be physically disabled. Applicant must have 3.0 GPA or higher. Available to U.S. citizens.

Application Requirements: Application, autobiography, interview, references, self-addressed stamped envelope, transcript. *Deadline:* April 30.

Contact: Samuel Byrd, Program Assistant
Sickle Cell Disease Association of America/Connecticut Chapter, Inc.
Gengras Ambulatory Center
140 Woodland Street
Hartford, CT 06105
Phone: 860-527-0119
Fax: 860-714-8007
E-mail: scdaa@iconn.net

SIR EDWARD YOUDE MEMORIAL FUND COUNCIL http://www.info.gov.hk/sfaa

SIR EDWARD YOUDE MEMORIAL OVERSEAS SCHOLARSHIP FOR DISABLED STUDENTS

This program is for outstanding disabled students, of any citizenship, who are permanent residents of Hong Kong, for overseas undergraduate studies. Applicant's impairment may be visual, hearing, or physical in nature. The award is not restricted to any specific academic or career area, but cannot be used for medical studies. Upon return from overseas studies, students are expected to contribute significantly to the development of Hong Kong. For further details visit Web site: http://www.info.gov.hk/sfaa.

Award: Scholarship for use in freshman, sophomore, junior, or senior years; renewable. *Number:* 1. *Amount:* up to $29,744.

Eligibility Requirements: Applicant must be enrolled or expecting to enroll full-time at an institution or university. Applicant must be hearing impaired, physically disabled, or visually impaired.

Application Requirements: Application, applicant must enter a contest, autobiography, essay, interview, photo, resume, references, test scores, transcript. *Deadline:* September 30.

Contact: Mr. Y. Wong, Council Secretariat
Sir Edward Youde Memorial Fund Council
Room 1217, 12/F., Cheung Sha Wan Government Offices
303 Cheung Sha Wan Road
Kowloon
Hong Kong
Phone: 852 2150 6103
Fax: 852 2511 2720
E-mail: sgl3@sfaa.gov.hk

SISTER KENNY REHABILITATION INSTITUTE http://www.sisterkennyinstitute.com

INTERNATIONAL ART SHOW FOR ARTISTS WITH DISABILITIES

One-time award for artwork submitted by artists of any age with visual, hearing, physical, or learning impairment. Contact Sister Kenny Rehabilitation Institute for show information. Application deadline is March 26. This is a one-time prize, not an academic scholarship.

Award: Prize for use in freshman, sophomore, junior, senior, or graduate years; not renewable. *Number:* 25–70. *Amount:* $25–$500.

Eligibility Requirements: Applicant must be enrolled or expecting to enroll at an institution or university and must have an interest in art. Applicant must be hearing impaired, learning disabled, physically disabled, or visually impaired. Available to U.S. and non-U.S. citizens.

Application Requirements: Application, applicant must enter a contest. *Deadline:* March 26.

Contact: Kathy Schultz, Executive Assistant
Sister Kenny Rehabilitation Institute
800 East 28th Street
Minneapolis, MN 55407-3799
Phone: 612-863-4463
Fax: 612-863-8942
E-mail: kathleen.schultz@allina.com

SPINA BIFIDA ASSOCIATION OF AMERICA http://www.sbaa.org

SPINA BIFIDA ASSOCIATION OF AMERICA EDUCATIONAL SCHOLARSHIP

One-time award to enhance opportunities for persons born with spina bifida to achieve their full potential through higher education. Minimum 2.5 GPA required. Must submit doctor's statement of disability and acceptance letter from college/university/school. Application deadline is April 1.

Award: Scholarship for use in freshman, sophomore, junior, or senior years; not renewable. *Number:* varies. *Amount:* $1000.

Eligibility Requirements: Applicant must be enrolled or expecting to enroll at a two-year or four-year or technical institution or university. Applicant must be physically disabled. Applicant must have 2.5 GPA or higher. Available to U.S. citizens.

Application Requirements: Application, essay, financial need analysis, references, test scores, transcript. *Deadline:* April 1.

Contact: Maya House, Resource Center Coordinator
Spina Bifida Association of America
4590 MacArthur Boulevard
Suite 250
Washington, DC 20007-4226
Phone: 202-944-3285
Fax: 202-944-3295
E-mail: sbaa@sbaa.org

SPINA BIFIDA ASSOCIATION OF AMERICA FOUR-YEAR SCHOLARSHIP FUND

Renewable award for a young person born with spina bifida to achieve his/her potential through higher education, and attend a four-year college otherwise outside of his/her family's financial reach. Minimum 2.5 GPA required. Open to U.S. citizens. Application deadline is February 15.

Award: Scholarship for use in freshman year; renewable. *Number:* 1. *Amount:* $5000.

Eligibility Requirements: Applicant must be high school student and planning to enroll or expecting to enroll full-time at a four-year institution. Applicant must be physically disabled. Applicant must have 2.5 GPA or higher. Available to U.S. citizens.

Application Requirements: Application, essay, financial need analysis, references, test scores, transcript. *Deadline:* February 15.

Contact: Maya House, Resource Center Coordinator
Spina Bifida Association of America
4590 MacArthur Boulevard
Suite 250
Washington, DC 20007-4226
Phone: 202-944-3285
Fax: 202-944-3295
E-mail: sbaa@sbaa.org

TEXAS HIGHER EDUCATION COORDINATING BOARD http://www.collegefortexans.com

TEXAS TUITION EXEMPTION FOR BLIND/DEAF STUDENTS

Renewable award aids certain blind or deaf students by exempting them from payment of tuition and fees at public colleges or universities in Texas. Must be a resident of Texas. Deadlines vary. Must submit certificate of deafness or blindness. Contact the admissions/registrar's office for application information.

Award: Scholarship for use in freshman, sophomore, junior, or senior years; renewable. *Number:* varies. *Amount:* varies.

Eligibility Requirements: Applicant must be enrolled or expecting to enroll full or part-time at a two-year or four-year or technical institution or university; resident of Texas and studying in Texas. Applicant must be hearing impaired or visually impaired. Available to U.S. citizens.

Application Requirements: Application, certificate of impairment. *Deadline:* varies.

Contact: Financial Aid Office at college
Texas Higher Education Coordinating Board
PO Box 12788
Austin, TX 78711-2788
Phone: 512-427-6101
Fax: 512-427-6127
E-mail: grantinfo@thecb.state.tx.us

TRAVELERS PROTECTIVE ASSOCIATION OF AMERICA http://www.tpahq.org

TRAVELERS PROTECTIVE ASSOCIATION SCHOLARSHIP TRUST FOR THE DEAF AND NEAR DEAF

Scholarships are awarded to deaf or hearing-impaired persons of any age, race, or religion for specialized education, mechanical devices, or medical or specialized treatment. Based on financial need. Deadline: March 1.

Award: Scholarship for use in freshman, sophomore, junior, senior, or graduate years; not renewable. *Number:* varies. *Amount:* $200–$1000.

Eligibility Requirements: Applicant must be enrolled or expecting to enroll at a two-year or four-year or technical institution or university. Applicant must be hearing impaired. Available to U.S. citizens.

Application Requirements: Application, financial need analysis, photo. *Deadline:* March 1.

Contact: B K. Schulte, Executive Secretary
Travelers Protective Association of America
3755 Lindell Boulevard
St. Louis, MO 63108
Phone: 314-371-0533
Fax: 314-371-0537

ULMAN CANCER FUND FOR YOUNG ADULTS http://www.ulmanfund.org

MATT STAUFFER MEMORIAL SCHOLARSHIP

To support the financial needs of college students who are battling or have overcome cancer who display financial need. The deadline is April 1.

Award: Scholarship for use in freshman, sophomore, junior, or senior years; not renewable. *Number:* 3–8. *Amount:* $1000.

Eligibility Requirements: Applicant must be enrolled or expecting to enroll full or part-time at a two-year or four-year or technical institution or university. Applicant must be physically disabled. Available to U.S. and non-U.S. citizens.

Application Requirements: Application, autobiography, essay, financial need analysis, references, medical history. *Deadline:* April 1.

Contact: Fay Baker, Scholarship Coordinator
Ulman Cancer Fund for Young Adults
PMB #505, 4725 Dorsey Hall Drive
Suite A
Ellicott City, MD 21042
Phone: 410-964-0202
Fax: 410-964-0402
E-mail: scholarship@ulmanfund.org

UNITED NEGRO COLLEGE FUND http://www.uncf.org

ROBERT DOLE SCHOLARSHIP

Scholarships available for physically and mentally challenged students attending a UNCF member college or university. Minimum 2.5 GPA required. Prospective applicants should complete the Student Profile found at Web site: http://www.uncf.org.

Award: Scholarship for use in freshman, sophomore, junior, or senior years; not renewable. *Amount:* up to $3000.

Eligibility Requirements: Applicant must be Black (non-Hispanic) and enrolled or expecting to enroll at a four-year institution or university. Applicant must be physically disabled. Applicant must have 2.5 GPA or higher.

Application Requirements: Application, financial need analysis. *Deadline:* October 28.

Contact: Program Services Department
United Negro College Fund
8260 Willow Oaks Corporate Drive
Fairfax, VA 22031

UNITED STATES ASSOCIATION FOR BLIND ATHLETES http://www.usaba.org

ARTHUR E. AND HELEN COPELAND SCHOLARSHIPS

Scholarship is awarded annually to a college student who is blind or visually impaired. All applicants must be current members of USABA. Grant to be awarded November 1st of each year.

Award: Scholarship for use in freshman, sophomore, junior, or senior years; not renewable. *Number:* 1–2. *Amount:* $500.

Eligibility Requirements: Applicant must be enrolled or expecting to enroll full-time at a two-year or four-year or technical institution or university. Applicant must be visually impaired. Available to U.S. citizens.

Application Requirements: Application, autobiography, references, transcript, proof of acceptance into program for which scholarship funds will be used. *Deadline:* October 1.

Contact: Mr. Mark Lucas, Executive Director
United States Association for Blind Athletes
33 North Institute Street
Colorado Springs, CO 80903
Phone: 719-630-0422 Ext. 13
Fax: 719-630-0616
E-mail: mlucas@usaba.org

WISCONSIN HIGHER EDUCATIONAL AIDS BOARD http://heab.state.wi.us

HANDICAPPED STUDENT GRANT-WISCONSIN

One-time award available to residents of Wisconsin who have severe or profound hearing or visual impairment. Must be enrolled at least half-time at a nonprofit institution. If the handicap prevents the student from attending a Wisconsin school, the award may be used out-of-state in a specialized college. Please refer to Web site for further details: http://heab.state.wi.us

Award: Grant for use in freshman, sophomore, junior, or senior years; not renewable. *Number:* varies. *Amount:* $250–$1800.

Eligibility Requirements: Applicant must be enrolled or expecting to enroll full or part-time at a two-year or four-year or technical institution or university and resident of Wisconsin. Applicant must be hearing impaired or visually impaired. Available to U.S. citizens.

Application Requirements: Application, financial need analysis. *Deadline:* Continuous.

Contact: Sandra Thomas, Program Coordinator
Wisconsin Higher Educational Aids Board
PO Box 7885
Madison, WI 53707-7885
Phone: 608-266-0888
Fax: 608-267-2808
E-mail: sandy.thomas@heab.state.wi.us

YES I CAN! FOUNDATION http://www.yesican.org

STANLEY E. JACKSON SCHOLARSHIP AWARDS

Four awards for full-time postsecondary education for disabled students entering their first postsecondary year for the first time, who provide evidence of financial need. Contact for specific award criteria. Past recipients are ineligible for current or future awards. Submit goals statement as well as statement verifying disability. Information available on Web site (http://www.yesican.sped.org).

Award: Scholarship for use in freshman year; not renewable. *Number:* 4–10. *Amount:* $500.

Eligibility Requirements: Applicant must be enrolled or expecting to enroll full-time at a two-year or four-year or technical institution or university and must have an interest in designated field specified by sponsor. Applicant must be hearing impaired, learning disabled, physically disabled, or visually impaired. Available to U.S. citizens.

Application Requirements: Application, essay, references, transcript, verification of disability. *Deadline:* February 1.

Contact: Ms. Jessa Foor, Program Development Specialist
Yes I Can! Foundation
1110 North Glebe Road, Suite 300
Arlington, VA 22201
Phone: 703-245-0607
Fax: 703-620-4334
E-mail: yesican@cec.sped.org

MILITARY SERVICE: AIR FORCE

AEROSPACE EDUCATION FOUNDATION http://www.aef.org

AIR FORCE SPOUSE SCHOLARSHIP

Awarded internationally to spouses of Air Force active duty, Air National Guard, or Air Force Reserve members during the spring semester. Spouses who are military members are not eligible. Minimum 3.5 GPA required.

Award: Scholarship for use in freshman, sophomore, junior, senior, or graduate years; not renewable. *Number:* 30. *Amount:* $1000.

Eligibility Requirements: Applicant must be enrolled or expecting to enroll full or part-time at a two-year or four-year or technical institution or university. Applicant must have 3.5 GPA or higher. Available to U.S. and non-U.S. citizens. Applicant or parent must meet one or more of the following requirements: Air Force or Air Force National Guard experience; retired from active duty; disabled or killed as a result of military service; prisoner of war; or missing in action.

Application Requirements: Application, essay, references, transcript. *Deadline:* January 31.

Contact: Rebecca Kay, Manager of Foundation Programs
Aerospace Education Foundation
1501 Lee Highway
Arlington, VA 22209-1198
Phone: 800-291-8480
Fax: 703-247-5853
E-mail: aefstaff@aef.org

AIR FORCE AID SOCIETY http://www.afas.org

GENERAL HENRY H. ARNOLD EDUCATION GRANT PROGRAM

$1500 grant provided to selected sons and daughters of active duty, Title 10 AGR/Reserve, Title 32 AGR performing full-time active duty, retired reserve and deceased Air Force members; spouses (stateside) of active members and Title 10 AGR/Reservist; and surviving spouses of deceased personnel for their undergraduate studies. Dependent children must be unmarried and under the age of 23. High school seniors may apply. Minimum 2.0 GPA is required. Applicant must reapply for subsequent years.

Award: Grant for use in freshman, sophomore, junior, or senior years; not renewable. *Number:* 3500–4000. *Amount:* $1500.

Eligibility Requirements: Applicant must be enrolled or expecting to enroll full-time at a two-year or four-year or technical institution or university. Available to U.S. citizens. Applicant or parent must meet one or more of the following requirements: Air Force or Air Force National Guard experience; retired from active duty; disabled or killed as a result of military service; prisoner of war; or missing in action.

Application Requirements: Application, financial need analysis, self-addressed stamped envelope, transcript, program's own financial forms, USAF military orders (member/parent). *Deadline:* March 12.

Contact: Education Assistance Department
Air Force Aid Society
1745 Jefferson Davis Highway, Suite 202
Arlington, VA 22202-3410
Phone: 800-429-9475
Fax: 703-607-3022
E-mail: ed@afas-hq.org

AIR FORCE RESERVE OFFICER TRAINING CORPS http://www.afrotc.com

AIR FORCE ROTC COLLEGE SCHOLARSHIP

Air Force ROTC offers college scholarships in both technical and non-technical majors that cover tuition, books, fees and up to $400 spending cash per academic month. Air Force ROTC college scholarships can be used at over 1000 college and universities across the U.S. and Puerto Rico. Please use online application: http://www.afrotc.com

Award: Scholarship for use in freshman, sophomore, junior, or senior years; renewable. *Number:* 2000–4000. *Amount:* $9000.

Eligibility Requirements: Applicant must be age 17-30 and enrolled or expecting to enroll full-time at a four-year institution or university. Applicant must have 3.0 GPA or higher. Available to U.S. citizens. Applicant must have served in the Air Force.

Application Requirements: Application, interview, test scores, transcript. *Deadline:* December 1.

Contact: College Scholarships and Admissions
Air Force Reserve Officer Training Corps
Headquarters/DOR
551 East Maxwell Boulevard
Maxwell AFB, AL 36112-6106
Phone: 866-423-7682
Fax: 334-953-6167
E-mail: info@afrotc.com

COMMANDER WILLIAM S. STUHR SCHOLARSHIP FUND FOR MILITARY SONS AND DAUGHTERS

COMMANDER WILLIAM S. STUHR SCHOLARSHIP FUND FOR MILITARY SONS AND DAUGHTERS

Must be a high school senior and a dependent of an active duty or retired career officer/enlisted person. Must include photo and copy of military ID card. Deadline for completed applications: February 15. Applications available beginning about October 15-November 1 until January 30. Must be in upper 10% of class. One award given for each branch of service, including the Reserves and the National Guard.

Award: Scholarship for use in freshman year; not renewable. *Number:* up to 6. *Amount:* up to $4800.

Eligibility Requirements: Applicant must be high school student and planning to enroll or expecting to enroll full-time at a four-year institution. Applicant must have 3.5 GPA or higher. Available to U.S. citizens. Applicant or parent must meet one or more of the following requirements: general military experience; retired from active duty; disabled or killed as a result of military service; prisoner of war; or missing in action.

Application Requirements: Application, autobiography, essay, financial need analysis, photo, references, self-addressed stamped envelope, test scores, transcript, military ID. *Deadline:* February 15.

Contact: Walter Loving, Executive Director
Commander William S. Stuhr Scholarship Fund for Military Sons and Daughters
PO Box 1138
Kitty Hawk, NC 27949-1138
Phone: 252-255-3013
Fax: 252-255-3014
E-mail: stuhrstudents@earthlink.net

DAUGHTERS OF THE CINCINNATI http://fdncenter.org/grantmaker/cincinnati

DAUGHTERS OF THE CINCINNATI SCHOLARSHIP

Need- and merit-based award available to graduating high school seniors. Minimum GPA of 3.0 required. Must be daughter of commissioned officer in regular Army, Navy, Coast Guard, Air Force, Marines (active, retired, or deceased). Must submit parent's rank and branch of service.

Award: Scholarship for use in freshman, sophomore, junior, or senior years; renewable. *Number:* up to 10. *Amount:* $1000–$3000.

Eligibility Requirements: Applicant must be high school student; planning to enroll or expecting to enroll full-time at a four-year institution and female. Applicant must have 3.0 GPA or higher. Available to U.S. citizens. Applicant or parent must meet one or more of the following requirements: Air Force, Army, Coast Guard, Marine Corp, or Navy experience; retired from active duty; disabled or killed as a result of military service; prisoner of war; or missing in action.

Application Requirements: Application, essay, financial need analysis, references, self-addressed stamped envelope, test scores, transcript. *Deadline:* March 15.

Contact: Mrs. Robert Ducas, Scholarship Administrator
Daughters of the Cincinnati
122 East 58th Street
New York, NY 10022
Phone: 212-319-6915

MASSACHUSETTS OFFICE OF STUDENT FINANCIAL ASSISTANCE http://www.osfa.mass.edu

HIGHER EDUCATION COORDINATING COUNCIL-TUITION WAIVER PROGRAM

Renewable award is tuition exemption for up to four years. Available to active members of Air Force, Army, Navy, Marines, or Coast Guard who are residents of Massachusetts. For use at a Massachusetts college or university. Deadlines vary. Contact veterans coordinator at college.

Award: Scholarship for use in freshman, sophomore, junior, or senior years; renewable. *Number:* varies. *Amount:* varies.

Eligibility Requirements: Applicant must be enrolled or expecting to enroll full or part-time at a two-year or four-year institution or university; resident of Massachusetts and studying in Massachusetts. Available to U.S. citizens. Applicant must have served in the Air Force, Army, Coast Guard, Marine Corp, or Navy.

Application Requirements: Application, financial need analysis. *Deadline:* varies.

Contact: College financial aid office

NEW YORK STATE HIGHER EDUCATION SERVICES CORPORATION http://www.hesc.org

NEW YORK VIETNAM VETERANS TUITION AWARDS

Scholarship for veterans who served in Vietnam. Must be a New York resident attending a New York institution. Renewable award of $500-$1000. Deadline: May 1. Must establish eligibility by September 1.

Award: Scholarship for use in freshman, sophomore, junior, or senior years; renewable. *Number:* varies. *Amount:* $500–$1000.

Eligibility Requirements: Applicant must be enrolled or expecting to enroll full or part-time at a two-year or four-year or technical institution or university; resident of New York and studying in New York. Applicant must have served in the Air Force, Army, Marine Corp, or Navy.

Application Requirements: Application, financial need analysis. *Deadline:* May 1.

Contact: Student Information
New York State Higher Education Services Corporation
99 Washington Avenue, Room 1320
Albany, NY 12255

SECOND BOMBARDMENT ASSOCIATION

SECOND BOMBARDMENT ASSOCIATION SCHOLARSHIP

• *See page 479*

SPECIAL OPERATIONS WARRIOR FOUNDATION http://www.specialops.org

SCHOLARSHIP FOR CHILDREN OF SPECIAL OPERATIONS FORCES WHO ARE KILLED IN THE LINE OF DUTY

Scholarships for children of Special Operations Forces (Army, Navy, or Air Force) who have died as a result of an operational mission or training accident. The funds are used by the student for tuition, books, fees, room & board, transportation and personal costs.

Award: Scholarship for use in freshman, sophomore, junior, or senior years; renewable. *Number:* varies. *Amount:* varies.

Eligibility Requirements: Applicant must be enrolled or expecting to enroll full or part-time at a two-year or four-year or technical institution or university. Available to U.S. citizens. Applicant or parent must meet one or more of the following requirements: Air Force, Army, or Navy experience; retired from active duty; disabled or killed as a result of military service; prisoner of war; or missing in action.

Application Requirements: Application, financial need analysis, photo, test scores, transcript, DD1300. *Deadline:* June 15.

Contact: Carolyn Becker, Director of Education and Family Services
Special Operations Warrior Foundation
PO Box 14385
Tampa, FL 33690
Phone: 813-805-9400
Fax: 813-805-0567
E-mail: warrior@specialops.org

MILITARY SERVICE: AIR FORCE NATIONAL GUARD

AEROSPACE EDUCATION FOUNDATION http://www.aef.org

AIR FORCE SPOUSE SCHOLARSHIP

• *See page 533*

AIR FORCE AID SOCIETY http://www.afas.org

GENERAL HENRY H. ARNOLD EDUCATION GRANT PROGRAM

• *See page 533*

ALABAMA COMMISSION ON HIGHER EDUCATION http://www.ache.state.al.us

ALABAMA NATIONAL GUARD EDUCATIONAL ASSISTANCE PROGRAM

Renewable award aids Alabama residents who are members of the Alabama National Guard and are enrolled in an accredited college in Alabama. Forms must be signed by a representative of the Alabama Military Department and financial aid officer. Recipient must be in a degree-seeking program.

Award: Grant for use in freshman, sophomore, junior, senior, or graduate years; renewable. *Number:* varies. *Amount:* up to $1000.

Eligibility Requirements: Applicant must be enrolled or expecting to enroll full or part-time at a two-year or four-year or technical institution or university; resident of Alabama and studying in Alabama. Available to U.S. citizens. Applicant must have served in the Air Force National Guard or Army National Guard.

Application Requirements: Application. *Deadline:* Continuous.

Contact: Dr. William Wall, Associate Executive Director for Student Assistance
Alabama Commission on Higher Education
PO Box 302000
Montgomery, AL 36130-2000

COMMANDER WILLIAM S. STUHR SCHOLARSHIP FUND FOR MILITARY SONS AND DAUGHTERS

COMMANDER WILLIAM S. STUHR SCHOLARSHIP FUND FOR MILITARY SONS AND DAUGHTERS

• *See page 533*

DELAWARE NATIONAL GUARD http://www.delawarenationalguard.com

STATE TUITION ASSISTANCE

Award providing tuition assistance for any member of the Air or Army National Guard attending a Delaware two-year or four-year college. Awards are renewable. Applicant's minimum GPA must be 2.0. For full- or part-time study. Amount of award varies.

Award: Scholarship for use in freshman, sophomore, junior, or senior years; renewable. *Number:* varies. *Amount:* varies.

Eligibility Requirements: Applicant must be enrolled or expecting to enroll full or part-time at a two-year or four-year institution or university and studying in Delaware. Available to U.S. citizens. Applicant must have served in the Air Force National Guard or Army National Guard.

Application Requirements: Application, transcript. *Deadline:* varies.

Contact: TSgt. Robert Csizmadia, State Tuition Assistance Manager
Delaware National Guard
First Regiment Road
Wilmington, DE 19808-2191
Phone: 302-326-7012
Fax: 302-326-7055
E-mail: robert.csizmadi@de.ngb.army.mil

DEPARTMENT OF MILITARY AFFAIRS http://www.coloradoguard.com

DEPARTMENT OF MILITARY AFFAIRS COLORADO NATIONAL GUARD STATE TUITION ASSISTANCE PROGRAM

Applicant must be member of Colorado National Guard for six months. Applicant must maintain 2.0 GPA during Tuition Assistance Program. Please refer to Web site http://www.coloradoguard.com.

Award: Forgivable loan for use in freshman, sophomore, junior, or senior years; renewable. *Number:* varies. *Amount:* varies.

Eligibility Requirements: Applicant must be enrolled or expecting to enroll full or part-time at a two-year or four-year or technical institution or university; resident of Colorado and studying in Colorado. Available to U.S. citizens. Applicant or parent must meet one or more of the following requirements: Air Force National Guard or Army National Guard experience; retired from active duty; disabled or killed as a result of military service; prisoner of war; or missing in action.

Application Requirements: Application, financial need analysis. *Deadline:* varies.

Contact: See Web site.

WISCONSIN NATIONAL GUARD TUITION GRANT

Renewable award for active members of the Wisconsin National Guard in good standing, who successfully complete a course of study at a qualifying school. Award covers full tuition, excluding fees, not to exceed undergraduate tuition charged by University of Wisconsin-Madison. Must have a minimum 2.0 GPA.

Award: Grant for use in freshman, sophomore, junior, or senior years; renewable. *Number:* up to 4000. *Amount:* up to $1927.

Eligibility Requirements: Applicant must be enrolled or expecting to enroll full or part-time at a two-year or four-year or technical institution or university and resident of Wisconsin. Available to U.S. citizens. Applicant must have served in the Air Force National Guard or Army National Guard.

Application Requirements: Application. *Deadline:* Continuous.

Contact: Karen Behling, Tuition Grant Administrator
Department of Military Affairs
PO Box 14587
Madison, WI 53708-0587
Phone: 608-242-3159
Fax: 608-242-3154
E-mail: karen.behling@dma.state.wi.us

DEPARTMENT OF VETERANS AFFAIRS (VA) http://www.gibill.va.gov

MONTGOMERY GI BILL (SELECTED RESERVE)

This is an educational assistance program for members of the Selected Reserve of the Army, Navy, Air Force, Marine Corps and Coastal Guard, as well as the Army and Air National Guard. Available to all reservists and National Guard personnel who commit to a six-year obligation, and remain in the Reserve or Guard during the six years. Award is renewable. Monthly benefit is $281 for up to 36 months for full-time. For more information call 1-888-442-4551 or visit Web site: http://www.gibill.va.gov.

Award: Scholarship for use in freshman, sophomore, junior, senior, or postgraduate years; renewable. *Number:* varies. *Amount:* up to $10,116.

Eligibility Requirements: Applicant must be enrolled or expecting to enroll at a two-year or four-year or technical institution or university. Available to U.S. citizens. Applicant must have general military experience.

Application Requirements: Application, military service of 6 years in the reserve or guard. *Deadline:* Continuous.

Contact: Dennis B. Douglass, Acting Director, Education Service
Department of Veterans Affairs (VA)
810 Vermont Avenue, NW
Washington, DC 20420
Phone: 888-442-4551
E-mail: co225a@vba.va.gov

DISTRICT OF COLUMBIA NATIONAL GUARD ENLISTED ASSOCIATION

DISTRICT OF COLUMBIA NATIONAL GUARD ENLISTED ASSOCIATION SCHOLARSHIP

• *See page 495*

ENLISTED ASSOCIATION OF THE NATIONAL GUARD OF NEW JERSEY http://www.eang-nj.org/scholarships.html

CSM VINCENT BALDASSARI MEMORIAL SCHOLARSHIP PROGRAM

Scholarships open to the legal children of New Jersey National Guard Members who are also members of the Enlisted Association. Also open to any drilling guardsperson who is a member of the Enlisted Association. Along with application, submit proof of parent's membership and a letter stating their reason for applying and future intents.

Award: Scholarship for use in freshman, sophomore, junior, senior, graduate, or postgraduate years; not renewable. *Number:* 6. *Amount:* $1000.

Eligibility Requirements: Applicant must be enrolled or expecting to enroll full-time at a two-year or four-year or technical institution or university. Available to U.S. citizens. Applicant or parent must meet one or more of the following requirements: Air Force National Guard or Army National Guard experience; retired from active duty; disabled or killed as a result of military service; prisoner of war; or missing in action.

Application Requirements: Application, essay, photo, references, transcript. *Deadline:* April 15.

Contact: SGM. Leonard Mayersohn, Scholarship Committee Chairman
Enlisted Association of the National Guard of New Jersey
Scholarship Committee
101 Eggerts Crossing Road
Lawrenceville, NJ 08648
Phone: 609-758-3446
E-mail: len.mayersohn@njdmava.state.nj.us

ILLINOIS STUDENT ASSISTANCE COMMISSION (ISAC) http://www.collegezone.org

ILLINOIS NATIONAL GUARD GRANT PROGRAM

Award for qualified National Guard personnel which pays tuition and fees at Illinois public universities and community colleges. Must provide documentation of service. Applications are due October 1 of the academic year for full year, March 1 for second/third term, or June 15 for the summer term.

Illinois Student Assistance Commission (ISAC) (continued)

Award: Grant for use in freshman, sophomore, junior, senior, graduate, or postgraduate years; renewable. *Number:* 2000–3000. *Amount:* $1300–$1700.

Eligibility Requirements: Applicant must be enrolled or expecting to enroll full or part-time at a two-year or four-year institution or university; resident of Illinois and studying in Illinois. Available to U.S. citizens. Applicant must have served in the Air Force National Guard or Army National Guard.

Application Requirements: Application, documentation of service. *Deadline:* varies.

Contact: College Zone Counselor
Illinois Student Assistance Commission (ISAC)
1755 Lake Cook Road
Deerfield, IL 60015-5209
Phone: 800-899-4722
E-mail: collegezone@isac.org

IOWA COLLEGE STUDENT AID COMMISSION http://www.iowacollegeaid.org

IOWA NATIONAL GUARD EDUCATION ASSISTANCE PROGRAM

Program provides postsecondary tuition assistance to members of Iowa National Guard Units. Must study at a postsecondary institution in Iowa. Contact for additional information.

Award: Grant for use in freshman, sophomore, junior, or senior years; not renewable. *Number:* varies. *Amount:* up to $1200.

Eligibility Requirements: Applicant must be enrolled or expecting to enroll full or part-time at a two-year or four-year or technical institution or university; resident of Iowa and studying in Iowa. Available to U.S. citizens. Applicant must have served in the Air Force National Guard or Army National Guard.

Application Requirements: Application. *Deadline:* Continuous.

Contact: Julie Leeper, Director, State Student Aid Programs
Iowa College Student Aid Commission
200 10th Street, 4th Floor
Des Moines, IA 50309-3609
Phone: 515-242-3370
Fax: 515-242-3388
E-mail: icsac@max.state.ia.us

KANSAS NATIONAL GUARD EDUCATIONAL ASSISTANCE PROGRAM

KANSAS NATIONAL GUARD EDUCATIONAL ASSISTANCE AWARD PROGRAM

Service scholarship for enlisted soldiers in the Kansas National Guard. Pays up to 100% of tuition and fees based on funding. Must attend a state-supported institution. Recipients will be required to serve in the KNG for three months for every semester of benefits after the last payment of state tuition assistance. Must not have over 15 years of service at time of application. Deadlines are January 15 and August 20. Contact KNG Education Services Specialist for further information. Must be Kansas resident.

Award: Scholarship for use in freshman, sophomore, junior, or senior years; not renewable. *Number:* up to 400. *Amount:* $250–$3500.

Eligibility Requirements: Applicant must be enrolled or expecting to enroll full or part-time at a two-year or four-year or technical institution or university; resident of Kansas and studying in Kansas. Available to U.S. citizens. Applicant must have served in the Air Force National Guard or Army National Guard.

Application Requirements: Application. *Deadline:* varies.

Contact: Steve Finch, Education Services Specialist
Kansas National Guard Educational Assistance Program
Attn: AGKS-DOP-ESO, The Adjutant General of Kansas
2800 South West Topeka Boulevard
Topeka, KS 66611-1287
Phone: 785-274-1060
Fax: 785-274-1609
E-mail: steve.finch@ks.ngb.army.mil

KENTUCKY HIGHER EDUCATION ASSISTANCE AUTHORITY (KHEAA) http://www.kheaa.com

KENTUCKY NATIONAL GUARD TUITION ASSISTANCE PROGRAM

Members of Kentucky National Guard in good standing are eligible for awards equal to in-state tuition for full or part-time study at any Kentucky public postsecondary institution.

Award: Grant for use in freshman, sophomore, junior, or senior years; not renewable. *Number:* 800–1000. *Amount:* varies.

Eligibility Requirements: Applicant must be enrolled or expecting to enroll full or part-time at a two-year or four-year or technical institution or university and studying in Kentucky. Available to U.S. citizens. Applicant must have served in the Air Force National Guard or Army National Guard.

Application Requirements: Application. *Deadline:* Continuous.

Contact: Kentucky National Guard
Kentucky Higher Education Assistance Authority (KHEAA)
100 Minuteman Parkway
Frankfort, KY 40601
Phone: 800-464-8273

KENTUCKY NATIONAL GUARD

KENTUCKY AIR NATIONAL GUARD EDUCATIONAL ASSISTANCE

Students receive up to $272 each month toward an undergraduate degree. May attend any college and receive up to 36 months of benefits and a maximum of $9792. Must have a high school diploma or GED and be a member of the Kentucky Air National Guard. For additional information see Web site: http://www.kyloui.ang.af.mil.

Award: Grant for use in freshman, sophomore, junior, or senior years; renewable. *Number:* varies. *Amount:* up to $3264.

Eligibility Requirements: Applicant must be enrolled or expecting to enroll at a two-year or four-year or technical institution or university. Available to U.S. citizens. Applicant must have served in the Air Force National Guard.

Application Requirements: Application. *Deadline:* Continuous.

Contact: MSGT. Scott Crimm, Relation Office Manager
Kentucky National Guard
1101 Grade Lane
Louisville, KY 40213-2616
Phone: 502-364-9604
E-mail: scott.crimm@kyloui.ang.af.mil

KENTUCKY NATIONAL GUARD TUITION AWARD PROGRAM

Tuition award available to all members of the Kentucky National Guard. Award is for study at state institutions. Members must be in good standing to be eligible for awards. Applications deadlines are April 1 and October 1. Completed AGO-18-7 required. Undergraduate study given priority.

Award: Scholarship for use in freshman, sophomore, junior, or senior years; not renewable. *Number:* varies. *Amount:* varies.

Eligibility Requirements: Applicant must be enrolled or expecting to enroll full or part-time at a two-year or four-year or technical institution or university and studying in Kentucky. Available to U.S. citizens. Applicant must have served in the Air Force National Guard or Army National Guard.

Application Requirements: AGO-18-7. *Deadline:* varies.

Contact: Michelle Kelley, Administration Specialist
Kentucky National Guard
Education Office, 100 Minuteman Parkway
Frankfort, KY 40601
Phone: 502-607-1039
Fax: 502-607-1264
E-mail: kelleyam@bng.dma.state.ky.us

LOUISIANA NATIONAL GUARD - STATE OF LOUISIANA, JOINT TASK FORCE LA http://www.la.ngb.army.mil

LOUISIANA NATIONAL GUARD STATE TUITION EXEMPTION PROGRAM

Renewable award for college undergraduates to receive tuition exemption upon satisfactory performance in the Louisiana National Guard. Applicant must attend a state-funded institution in Louisiana, be a resident and registered voter in Louisiana, meet the academic and residency requirements of the university attended, and provide documentation of Louisiana National Guard enlistment. The exemption can be used for up to 15 semesters. Minimum 2.5 GPA required.

Award: Scholarship for use in freshman, sophomore, junior, or senior years; renewable. *Number:* varies. *Amount:* varies.

Eligibility Requirements: Applicant must be enrolled or expecting to enroll full or part-time at a two-year or four-year or technical institution or university; resident of Louisiana and studying in Louisiana. Applicant must have 2.5 GPA or higher. Available to U.S. citizens. Applicant must have served in the Air Force National Guard or Army National Guard.

Application Requirements: *Deadline:* Continuous.

Contact: Maj. Jona M. Hughes, Education Services Officers
Louisiana National Guard - State of Louisiana, Joint Task Force LA
Building 35, Jackson Barracks, JI-PD
New Orleans, LA 70146-0330
Phone: 504-278-8531 Ext. 8304
Fax: 504-278-8025
E-mail: hughesj@la-arng.ngb.army.mil

MINNESOTA DEPARTMENT OF MILITARY AFFAIRS http://www.dma.state.mn.us

LEADERSHIP, EXCELLENCE AND DEDICATED SERVICE SCHOLARSHIP

Awarded to high school seniors who enlist in the Minnesota National Guard. The award recognizes demonstrated leadership, community services and potential for success in the Minnesota National Guard. For more information, applicant may contact any Minnesota army national guard recruiter at 1-800-go-guard or visit the Web site http://www.dma.state.mn.us.

Award: Scholarship for use in freshman year; not renewable. *Number:* 30. *Amount:* $1000.

Eligibility Requirements: Applicant must be high school student and planning to enroll or expecting to enroll full or part-time at a two-year or four-year or technical institution or university. Available to U.S. and non-U.S. citizens. Applicant must have served in the Air Force National Guard or Army National Guard.

Application Requirements: Essay, resume, references, transcript. *Deadline:* March 15.

Contact: Barbara O'Reilly, Education Services Officer
Minnesota Department of Military Affairs
Veterans Services Building
20 West 12th Street
St. Paul, MN 55155-2098
Phone: 651-282-4508
E-mail: barbara.oreilly@mn.ngb.army.mil

NEBRASKA NATIONAL GUARD http://www.neguard.com

NEBRASKA NATIONAL GUARD TUITION CREDIT

Renewable award for members of the Nebraska National Guard. Pays 75% of enlisted soldier's tuition until he or she has received a baccalaureate degree.

Award: Scholarship for use in freshman, sophomore, junior, or senior years; renewable. *Number:* up to 1200.

Eligibility Requirements: Applicant must be enrolled or expecting to enroll full or part-time at a two-year or four-year or technical institution or university; resident of Nebraska and studying in Nebraska. Applicant must have served in the Air Force National Guard or Army National Guard.

Application Requirements: Application. *Deadline:* Continuous.

Contact: Cindy York, Administrative Assistant
Nebraska National Guard
1300 Military Road
Lincoln, NE 68508-1090
Phone: 402-309-7143
Fax: 402-309-7128

NORTH CAROLINA NATIONAL GUARD http://www.nc.ngb.army.mil/education

NORTH CAROLINA NATIONAL GUARD TUITION ASSISTANCE PROGRAM

For members of the North Carolina Air and Army National Guard who will remain in the service for two years following the period for which assistance is provided. Applicants must reapply for each academic period. For use at approved North Carolina institutions. Deadline: last day of late registration period set by the school. Applicant must currently be serving in the Air National Guard or Army National Guard. Annual maximum (July 1 through June 30) of $2000. Career maximum of $8000.

Award: Grant for use in freshman, sophomore, junior, senior, or graduate years; not renewable. *Number:* varies. *Amount:* up to $2000.

Eligibility Requirements: Applicant must be enrolled or expecting to enroll full or part-time at a two-year or four-year or technical institution or university and studying in North Carolina. Available to U.S. citizens. Applicant must have served in the Air Force National Guard or Army National Guard.

Application Requirements: Application. *Deadline:* varies.

Contact: Capt. Miriam Gray, Education Services Officer
North Carolina National Guard
4105 Reedy Creek Road
Raleigh, NC 27607-6410
Phone: 800-621-4136 Ext. 6272
Fax: 919-664-6520
E-mail: miriam.gray@nc.ngb.army.mil

OHIO NATIONAL GUARD

OHIO NATIONAL GUARD SCHOLARSHIP PROGRAM

Scholarships are for undergraduate studies at an approved Ohio postsecondary institution. Applicants must enlist for six years of Selective Service Reserve Duty in the Ohio National Guard. Scholarship pays 100% instructional and general fees for public institutions and an average of cost of public schools is available for private schools. Must be 18 years of age or older. Award is renewable. Deadlines: July 1, November 1, February 1, April 1.

Award: Scholarship for use in freshman, sophomore, junior, or senior years; renewable. *Number:* 3500–8000. *Amount:* up to $3000.

Eligibility Requirements: Applicant must be age 18; enrolled or expecting to enroll full or part-time at a two-year or four-year or technical institution or university and studying in Ohio. Available to U.S. citizens. Applicant must have served in the Air Force National Guard or Army National Guard.

Application Requirements: Application. *Deadline:* varies.

Contact: Mrs. Toni Davis, Grants Administrator
Ohio National Guard
2825 West Dublin Granville Road
Columbus, OH 43235-2789
Phone: 614-336-7032
Fax: 614-336-7318
E-mail: toni.davis@tagoh.org

SOUTH DAKOTA BOARD OF REGENTS http://www.ris.sdbor.edu

SOUTH DAKOTA EDUCATION BENEFITS FOR NATIONAL GUARD MEMBERS

Guard members who meet the requirements for admission are eligible for a 50% reduction in undergraduate tuition charges at any state-supported school for up to a maximum of four academic years. Provision also covers one program of study, approved by the State Board of Education, at any state vocational school. Must be state resident and member of the SD Army or Air Guard throughout period for which benefits are sought. Must contact financial aid office for full details and forms at time of registration.

Award: Scholarship for use in freshman, sophomore, junior, or senior years; not renewable. *Number:* varies. *Amount:* varies.

Eligibility Requirements: Applicant must be enrolled or expecting to enroll at a two-year or four-year or technical institution or university; resident of South Dakota and studying in South Dakota. Available to U.S. citizens. Applicant must have served in the Air Force National Guard or Army National Guard.

South Dakota Board of Regents (continued)

Application Requirements: Application. *Deadline:* varies.

Contact: Dr. Lesta Turchen, Senior Administrator
South Dakota Board of Regents
306 East Capitol Avenue
Suite 200
Pierre, SD 57501-3159
Phone: 605-773-3455
Fax: 605-773-2422
E-mail: info@sdbor.edu

STATE OF GEORGIA http://www.gsfc.org

GEORGIA NATIONAL GUARD SERVICE CANCELABLE LOAN PROGRAM

Forgivable loans will be awarded to residents of Georgia maintaining good military standing as an eligible member of the Georgia National Guard who are enrolled at least half-time in an undergraduate degree program at an eligible college, university or technical school within the state of Georgia.

Award: Forgivable loan for use in freshman, sophomore, junior, or senior years; not renewable. *Number:* 200–250. *Amount:* $150–$1821.

Eligibility Requirements: Applicant must be enrolled or expecting to enroll full or part-time at a two-year or four-year or technical institution or university; resident of Georgia and studying in Georgia. Available to U.S. citizens. Applicant must have served in the Air Force National Guard or Army National Guard.

Application Requirements: Application, financial need analysis. *Deadline:* June 4.

Contact: Peggy Matthews, Manager/GSFA Originations
State of Georgia
2082 East Exchange Place, Suite 230
Tucker, GA 30084-5305
Phone: 770-724-9230
Fax: 770-724-9225
E-mail: peggy@gsfc.org

STATE STUDENT ASSISTANCE COMMISSION OF INDIANA (SSACI) http://www.ssaci.in.gov

INDIANA NATIONAL GUARD SUPPLEMENTAL GRANT

The award is a supplement to the Indiana Higher Education Grant program. Applicants must be members of the Indiana National Guard. All Guard paperwork must be completed prior to the start of each semester. The FAFSA must be received by March 10. Award covers certain tuition and fees at select public colleges.

Award: Grant for use in freshman, sophomore, junior, or senior years; not renewable. *Number:* 503–925. *Amount:* $200–$6516.

Eligibility Requirements: Applicant must be enrolled or expecting to enroll full or part-time at a two-year or four-year institution or university; resident of Indiana and studying in Indiana. Available to U.S. citizens. Applicant must have served in the Air Force National Guard or Army National Guard.

Application Requirements: Application. *Deadline:* March 10.

Contact: Grants Counselor
State Student Assistance Commission of Indiana (SSACI)
150 West Market Street, Suite 500
Indianapolis, IN 46204-2805
Phone: 317-232-2350
Fax: 317-232-2360
E-mail: grants@ssaci.state.in.us

TEXAS HIGHER EDUCATION COORDINATING BOARD http://www.collegefortexans.com

TEXAS NATIONAL GUARD TUITION ASSISTANCE PROGRAM

Provides exemption from the payment of tuition to certain members of the Texas National Guard, Texas Air Guard or the State Guard. Must be Texas resident and attend school in Texas. Visit the TNG Web site at: http://www.agd.state.tx.us/education_office/state_tuition.htm.

Award: Scholarship for use in freshman, sophomore, junior, or senior years; renewable. *Number:* varies. *Amount:* varies.

Eligibility Requirements: Applicant must be enrolled or expecting to enroll at an institution or university; resident of Texas and studying in Texas. Applicant must have served in the Air Force National Guard or Army National Guard.

Application Requirements: Application. *Deadline:* varies.

Contact: State Adjutant General's Office
Texas Higher Education Coordinating Board
PO Box 5218/AGTX-PAE
Austin, TX 78763-5218
Phone: 512-465-5001

WASHINGTON NATIONAL GUARD http://www.washingtonguard.com/education/education.htm

WASHINGTON NATIONAL GUARD SCHOLARSHIP PROGRAM

A state funded retention incentive/loan program for both Washington Army and Air Guard members meeting all eligibility requirements. The loans are forgiven if the soldier/airman completes their service requirements. Failure to meet/complete service obligations incurs the requirement to repay the loan plus 8% interest. Minimum 2.5 GPA required. Deadline is April 30.

Award: Forgivable loan for use in freshman, sophomore, junior, or senior years; not renewable. *Number:* varies. *Amount:* $200–$4000.

Eligibility Requirements: Applicant must be enrolled or expecting to enroll full or part-time at a two-year or four-year or technical institution or university and resident of Washington. Applicant must have 2.5 GPA or higher. Available to U.S. and non-U.S. citizens. Applicant must have served in the Air Force National Guard or Army National Guard.

Application Requirements: Application, transcript, enlistment/extension documents. *Deadline:* April 30.

Contact: Mark Rhoden, Educational Services Officer
Washington National Guard
Building 15, Camp Murray
Tacoma, WA 98430-5073
Phone: 253-512-8899
Fax: 253-512-8936
E-mail: mark.rhoden@wa.ngb.army.mil

MILITARY SERVICE: ARMY

ARMY EMERGENCY RELIEF http://www.aerhq.org

MAJOR GENERAL JAMES URSANO SCHOLARSHIP FUND

Scholarships available to unmarried high school seniors and undergraduates who are 22 years old or younger and are dependents of active, retired, or deceased soldiers. Conditions vary. Must maintain a 2.0 GPA on a 4.0 scale at an accredited school. Must be a U.S. citizen.

Award: Scholarship for use in freshman, sophomore, junior, or senior years; not renewable. *Number:* varies. *Amount:* $800–$2500.

Eligibility Requirements: Applicant must be age 22 or under; enrolled or expecting to enroll full-time at a two-year or four-year or technical institution or university and single. Available to U.S. citizens. Applicant or parent must meet one or more of the following requirements: Army experience; retired from active duty; disabled or killed as a result of military service; prisoner of war; or missing in action.

Application Requirements: Application, financial need analysis, transcript, self-addressed post card. *Deadline:* March 1.

Contact: Col. (Ret.) D. J. Spiegel, Deputy Director of Administration
Army Emergency Relief
200 Stovall Street
Alexandria, VA 22332-0600
Phone: 703-428-0035
Fax: 703-325-7183
E-mail: education@aerhq.org

COMMANDER WILLIAM S. STUHR SCHOLARSHIP FUND FOR MILITARY SONS AND DAUGHTERS

COMMANDER WILLIAM S. STUHR SCHOLARSHIP FUND FOR MILITARY SONS AND DAUGHTERS

• *See page 533*

DAUGHTERS OF THE CINCINNATI http://fdncenter.org/grantmaker/cincinnati

DAUGHTERS OF THE CINCINNATI SCHOLARSHIP

• *See page 534*

DEPARTMENT OF THE ARMY http://www.rotc.monroe.army.mil

ARMY ROTC HISTORICALLY BLACK COLLEGES AND UNIVERSITIES PROGRAM

One-time award for students attending college for the first time or freshmen in a documented five-year degree program. Must attend a historically black college or university and must join school's ROTC program. Must pass physical. Must have a qualifying SAT or ACT score. Applicant must be at least 17 by college enrollment and under 31 years of age in the year of graduation.

Award: Scholarship for use in freshman or sophomore years; not renewable. *Number:* 180–250. *Amount:* $5000–$16,000.

Eligibility Requirements: Applicant must be age 17-30 and enrolled or expecting to enroll full-time at a four-year institution or university. Applicant must have 2.5 GPA or higher. Available to U.S. citizens. Applicant must have served in the Army or Army National Guard.

Application Requirements: Application, essay, interview, test scores, transcript. *Deadline:* December 1.

Contact: Goldquest Center, Army ROTC Scholarships
Department of the Army
U.S. Army Cadet Command
Fort Monroe, VA 23651-5000
Phone: 800-USA-ROTC
E-mail: rotcinfo@monroe.army.mil

ARMY ROTC TWO-YEAR, THREE-YEAR AND FOUR-YEAR SCHOLARSHIPS FOR ACTIVE DUTY ARMY ENLISTED PERSONNEL

Award for freshman, sophomore, and junior year for use at a four-year institution for Army enlisted personnel. Merit considered. Must also be member of the school's ROTC program. Must pass physical and have completed two years of active duty. Applicant must be at least 17 years of age by college enrollment and under 31 years of age in the year of graduation. Submit recommendations from Commanding Officer and Field Grade Commander. Include DODMERB Physical Forms and DA Form 2A.

Award: Scholarship for use in freshman, sophomore, or junior years; not renewable. *Number:* 150–350. *Amount:* $5000–$16,000.

Eligibility Requirements: Applicant must be age 17-30 and enrolled or expecting to enroll full-time at a four-year institution or university. Applicant must have 2.5 GPA or higher. Available to U.S. citizens. Applicant must have served in the Army or Army National Guard.

Application Requirements: Application, essay, photo, references, test scores, transcript, DA Form 2A, DODMERB physical, APFT, GT. *Deadline:* April 1.

Contact: Goldquest Center, Army ROTC Scholarships
Department of the Army
U.S. Army Cadet Command
Fort Monroe, VA 23651-5000
Phone: 800-USA-ROTC
E-mail: rotcinfo@monroe.army.mil

FOUR-YEAR AND THREE-YEAR ADVANCE DESIGNEES SCHOLARSHIP

One-time award for students entering college for the first time or freshmen in a documented five-year degree program. Must join school's ROTC program. Must pass physical and submit teacher evaluations. Must be a U.S. citizen and have a qualifying SAT or ACT score. Applicant must be at least 17 years of age by college enrollment and under 31 years of age in the year of graduation. Online application available.

Award: Scholarship for use in freshman or sophomore years; not renewable. *Number:* 700–3000. *Amount:* $5000–$20,000.

Eligibility Requirements: Applicant must be age 17-30 and enrolled or expecting to enroll full-time at a four-year institution. Applicant must have 2.5 GPA or higher. Available to U.S. citizens. Applicant must have served in the Army or Army National Guard.

Application Requirements: Application, essay, interview, references, test scores, transcript. *Deadline:* December 1.

Contact: Goldquest Center, Army ROTC Scholarships
Department of the Army
U.S. Army Cadet Command
Fort Monroe, VA 23651-5000
Phone: 800-USA-ROTC
E-mail: rotcinfo@monroe.army.mil

TWO- AND THREE-YEAR CAMPUS-BASED SCHOLARSHIPS

One-time award for college sophomores or juniors or students with BA who need two years to obtain graduate degree. Must be a member of school's ROTC program. Must pass physical. Minimum 2.5 GPA required. Professor of military science must submit application. Applicant must be at least 17 when enrolled in college and under 31 years of age in the year of graduation. Deadline is December 1.

Award: Scholarship for use in sophomore, junior, or graduate years; not renewable. *Number:* 250–1500. *Amount:* $5000–$16,000.

Eligibility Requirements: Applicant must be age 17-30 and enrolled or expecting to enroll full-time at a four-year institution. Applicant must have 2.5 GPA or higher. Available to U.S. citizens. Applicant must have served in the Army or Army National Guard.

Application Requirements: Application, test scores, transcript. *Deadline:* December 1.

Contact: Goldquest Center, Army ROTC Scholarships
Department of the Army
U.S. Army Cadet Command
Fort Monroe, VA 23651-5000
Phone: 800-USA-ROTC
E-mail: rotcinfo@monroe.army.mil

FIRST INFANTRY DIVISION FOUNDATION http://www.bigredone.org

LIEUTENANT GENERAL CLARENCE R. HUEBNER SCHOLARSHIP PROGRAM

Renewable award for undergraduate study for children and grandchildren of veterans of the 1st Infantry Division, U.S. Army. Essay, letter of acceptance, proof of registration with Selective Service (if male), and proof of parent's or grandparent's service required. Must be high school senior to apply. Send self-addressed stamped envelope for essay topic and details. The award is for up to $4000 payable to the school in four annual installments of not more than $1,000 per year.

Award: Scholarship for use in freshman, sophomore, junior, or senior years; renewable. *Number:* 3–6. *Amount:* $1000.

Eligibility Requirements: Applicant must be high school student and planning to enroll or expecting to enroll full-time at a four-year institution or university. Available to U.S. citizens. Applicant or parent must meet one or more of the following requirements: Army experience; retired from active duty; disabled or killed as a result of military service; prisoner of war; or missing in action.

Application Requirements: Application, essay, references, self-addressed stamped envelope, test scores, transcript. *Deadline:* June 1.

Contact: Mrs. Rosemary A. Wirs, Secretary-Treasurer
First Infantry Division Foundation
1933 Morris Road
Blue Bell, PA 19422-1422
Phone: 215-661-1969
Fax: 215-661-1934
E-mail: fdn1ld@aol.com

FOUNDATION OF THE FIRST CAVALRY DIVISION ASSOCIATION http://www.vvm.com/~firstcav/

FOUNDATION OF THE FIRST CAVALRY DIVISION ASSOCIATION IA DRANG SCHOLARSHIP

Award for children and grandchildren of soldiers of First Cavalry Division, U.S. Air Force Forward Air Controllers and A1E pilots, and war correspondents who served in designated qualifying units which were involved in battles of the Drang Valley during the period of November 3-19, 1965. Include self-addressed stamped envelope.

Foundation of the First Cavalry Division Association (continued)

Award: Scholarship for use in freshman, sophomore, junior, senior, graduate, or postgraduate years; renewable. *Number:* varies. *Amount:* up to $1000.

Eligibility Requirements: Applicant must be enrolled or expecting to enroll full-time at a two-year or four-year institution or university. Available to U.S. citizens. Applicant or parent must meet one or more of the following requirements: Army experience; retired from active duty; disabled or killed as a result of military service; prisoner of war; or missing in action.

Application Requirements: Application, self-addressed stamped envelope, birth certificate(s), proof of father or grandfather's participation. *Deadline:* Continuous.

Contact: Ms. Lorinda Davison, Office Manager
Foundation of the First Cavalry Division Association
302 North Main Street
Copperas Cove, TX 76522-1799
Phone: 254-547-6537
Fax: 254-547-8853

FOUNDATION OF THE FIRST CAVALRY DIVISION ASSOCIATION UNDERGRADUATE SCHOLARSHIP

Several scholarships for children of the First Cavalry Division soldiers who died or have been declared permanently and 100% disabled during the Vietnam War or Desert Storm. Show proof of relationship, death or disability of parent, and acceptance at higher education institution. Include self-addressed stamped envelope.

Award: Scholarship for use in freshman, sophomore, junior, senior, graduate, or postgraduate years; renewable. *Number:* varies. *Amount:* up to $1000.

Eligibility Requirements: Applicant must be enrolled or expecting to enroll full or part-time at a two-year or four-year institution or university. Available to U.S. citizens. Applicant or parent must meet one or more of the following requirements: Army experience; retired from active duty; disabled or killed as a result of military service; prisoner of war; or missing in action.

Application Requirements: Application, self-addressed stamped envelope, transcript, birth certificate. *Deadline:* Continuous.

Contact: Ms. Lorinda Davison, Office Manager
Foundation of the First Cavalry Division Association
302 North Main Street
Copperas Cove, TX 76522-1799
Phone: 254-547-6537
Fax: 254-547-8853
E-mail: firstcav@vvm.com

MASSACHUSETTS OFFICE OF STUDENT FINANCIAL ASSISTANCE http://www.osfa.mass.edu

HIGHER EDUCATION COORDINATING COUNCIL-TUITION WAIVER PROGRAM

• *See page 534*

NATIONAL 4TH INFANTRY (IVY) DIVISION ASSOCIATION http://www.4thinfantry.org

NATIONAL 4TH INFANTRY (IVY) DIVISION ASSOCIATION SCHOLARSHIP PROGRAM

Raffle-type drawing each year during our annual banquet. Applicants must be a blood relative or stepchild or adopted child of current Association member. (National Fourth Infantry (IVY) Division Association).

Award: Prize for use in freshman, sophomore, junior, senior, graduate, or postgraduate years; not renewable. *Number:* 1–3. *Amount:* $500–$1000.

Eligibility Requirements: Applicant must be enrolled or expecting to enroll full or part-time at a two-year or four-year or technical institution or university. Available to U.S. citizens. Applicant or parent must meet one or more of the following requirements: Army experience; retired from active duty; disabled or killed as a result of military service; prisoner of war; or missing in action.

Application Requirements: Application. *Deadline:* June 15.

Contact: Alexander Cooker, 4 IDA Scholarship Fund Treasurer
National 4th Infantry (IVY) Division Association
80 North Dupont
Carney's Point, NJ 08069
Phone: 609-299-4406
E-mail: alxchr@gateway.net

NEW YORK STATE HIGHER EDUCATION SERVICES CORPORATION http://www.hesc.org

NEW YORK VIETNAM VETERANS TUITION AWARDS

• *See page 534*

101ST AIRBORNE DIVISION ASSOCIATION http://www.screamingeagle.org/chappie.htm

101ST AIRBORNE DIVISION ASSOCIATION CHAPPIE HALL SCHOLARSHIP PROGRAM

To provide financial assistance to students who have the potential to become assets to our nation. The major factors to be considered in the evaluation and rating of applicants are eligibility, career objectives, academic record, financial need, and insight gained from the letter requesting consideration, and letters of recommendation. Applicant's parents, grandparents, or spouse, living or deceased must have/had membership with 101st Airborne Division.

Award: Scholarship for use in freshman, sophomore, junior, senior, graduate, or postgraduate years; not renewable. *Number:* 4. *Amount:* $1000.

Eligibility Requirements: Applicant must be enrolled or expecting to enroll full-time at a two-year or four-year or technical institution or university. Available to U.S. and non-U.S. citizens. Applicant or parent must meet one or more of the following requirements: Army experience; retired from active duty; disabled or killed as a result of military service; prisoner of war; or missing in action.

Application Requirements: Application, autobiography, financial need analysis, photo, references, transcript. *Deadline:* Continuous.

Contact: Executive Secretary-Treasurer
101st Airborne Division Association
PO Box 929
Fort Campbell, KY 42223-0929
Phone: 270-439-0445
Fax: 270-439-6645
E-mail: assn101abn@aol.com

102ND INFANTRY DIVISION ASSOCIATION

102ND INFANTRY DIVISION ASSOCIATION MEMORIAL SCHOLARSHIP PROGRAM

Awards scholarships to descendants of Association members. Awardees selected competitively by scholarship committee who are members of the Association. To be eligible, the applicant must be a student whose father, grandfather or great-grandfather was an active member of the 102d Infantry Division during August, 1942-March, 1946 and currently or at time of death was a life member or dues paying member. Write for application and further specifics.

Award: Scholarship for use in freshman, sophomore, junior, or senior years; not renewable. *Number:* 20. *Amount:* $1000.

Eligibility Requirements: Applicant must be enrolled or expecting to enroll full or part-time at a two-year or four-year or technical institution or university. Available to U.S. and non-U.S. citizens. Applicant or parent must meet one or more of the following requirements: Army experience; retired from active duty; disabled or killed as a result of military service; prisoner of war; or missing in action.

Application Requirements: Application, essay, photo, references, test scores, transcript. *Deadline:* April 1.

Contact: James A. Alspaugh, Committee Secretary
102nd Infantry Division Association
4311 East 55th Street
Tulsa, OK 74135-4830
Phone: 918-492-7304
E-mail: jaalsp@aol.com

SOCIETY OF DAUGHTERS OF THE UNITED STATES ARMY

SOCIETY OF DAUGHTERS OF THE UNITED STATES ARMY SCHOLARSHIPS

Applicants for Roberts, Wagner, Prickett, Simpson & DU.S.A scholarships must be daughter or granddaughter (step or adopted) of a career warrant (WO 1-5) or commissioned (2nd & 1st LT, CPT, MAJ, LTC, COL, and BG, MG, LT or full General) officer in the U.S. Army who: (1) is currently on active duty; (2) retired from active duty after at least 20 years of service; (3) was medically retired before 20 years of active service; (4) died while on active duty; (5) died after retiring from active duty with 20 or more years of service. U.S. Army must have been the primary occupation. Officer's name, rank, component (Active, Reserve, Retired), and inclusive dates of active duty must be included in request for application for these scholarships. Do not send birth certificates or original documents. Minimum GPA 3.0. Undergraduate students only. Must send self-addressed, stamped business envelope. Must be postmarked between November 1 and March 1.

Award: Scholarship for use in freshman, sophomore, junior, or senior years; renewable. *Number:* varies. *Amount:* $1000.

Eligibility Requirements: Applicant must be enrolled or expecting to enroll full-time at a two-year or four-year or technical institution or university; female and must have an interest in leadership. Applicant must have 3.0 GPA or higher. Available to U.S. citizens. Applicant or parent must meet one or more of the following requirements: Army experience; retired from active duty; disabled or killed as a result of military service; prisoner of war; or missing in action.

Application Requirements: Application, essay, resume, references, self-addressed stamped envelope, test scores, transcript, proof of service of qualifying service member (state relationship to member). *Deadline:* March 1.

Contact: Mary P. Maroney, Chairperson, Memorial and Scholarship Funds
Society of Daughters of the United States Army
11804 Grey Birch Place
Reston, VA 20191

SPECIAL OPERATIONS WARRIOR FOUNDATION http://www.specialops.org

SCHOLARSHIP FOR CHILDREN OF SPECIAL OPERATIONS FORCES WHO ARE KILLED IN THE LINE OF DUTY

• *See page 534*

37TH DIVISION VETERANS ASSOCIATION

37TH DIVISION VETERANS ASSOCIATION SCHOLARSHIP

This award is available to undergraduate and graduate students. Applicants must be direct descendants (son or daughter) of veterans of the 37th Division. High school seniors may apply.

Award: Scholarship for use in freshman, sophomore, junior, senior, or graduate years; renewable. *Number:* 5. *Amount:* $500.

Eligibility Requirements: Applicant must be enrolled or expecting to enroll full-time at an institution or university. Applicant or parent must meet one or more of the following requirements: Army experience; retired from active duty; disabled or killed as a result of military service; prisoner of war; or missing in action.

Application Requirements: Application, transcript, father's pertinent information. *Deadline:* April 1.

Contact: Executive Secretary
37th Division Veterans Association
35 East Chestnut, Room 425
Columbus, OH 43215

WOMEN'S ARMY CORPS VETERANS ASSOCIATION http://www.armywomen.org

WOMEN'S ARMY CORPS VETERANS ASSOCIATION SCHOLARSHIP

Scholarship available to child, grandchild, niece or nephew of an Army Service Woman. Applicant must submit documentation of sponsor's military service. Deadline is May 1. Please refer to Web site for further details: http://www.armywomen.org

Award: Scholarship for use in freshman, sophomore, junior, or senior years; renewable. *Number:* 1. *Amount:* $1500.

Eligibility Requirements: Applicant must be enrolled or expecting to enroll full-time at a four-year institution or university. Applicant must have 3.5 GPA or higher. Available to U.S. citizens. Applicant or parent must meet one or more of the following requirements: Army experience; retired from active duty; disabled or killed as a result of military service; prisoner of war; or missing in action.

Application Requirements: Application, autobiography, references, transcript, proof of relative's military service. *Deadline:* May 1.

Contact: See Web site.

MILITARY SERVICE: ARMY NATIONAL GUARD

ALABAMA COMMISSION ON HIGHER EDUCATION http://www.ache.state.al.us

ALABAMA NATIONAL GUARD EDUCATIONAL ASSISTANCE PROGRAM

• *See page 534*

COMMANDER WILLIAM S. STUHR SCHOLARSHIP FUND FOR MILITARY SONS AND DAUGHTERS

COMMANDER WILLIAM S. STUHR SCHOLARSHIP FUND FOR MILITARY SONS AND DAUGHTERS

• *See page 533*

CONNECTICUT ARMY NATIONAL GUARD http://www.ct.ngb.army.mil/armyguard/join/tuition.asp

CONNECTICUT ARMY NATIONAL GUARD 100% TUITION WAIVER

100% Tuition Waiver Program is for any active member of the Connecticut Army National Guard in good standing. Must be a resident of Connecticut attending any Connecticut state (public) university, community-technical college or regional vocational-technical school.

Award: Scholarship for use in freshman, sophomore, junior, or senior years; not renewable. *Number:* varies. *Amount:* varies.

Eligibility Requirements: Applicant must be age 17-65; enrolled or expecting to enroll full or part-time at a two-year or four-year or technical institution or university; resident of Connecticut and studying in Connecticut. Available to U.S. and non-U.S. citizens. Applicant must have served in the Army National Guard.

Application Requirements: Application. *Deadline:* Continuous.

Contact: Education Services Officer
Phone: 860-524-4816
E-mail: education@ct.ngb.army.mil

DELAWARE NATIONAL GUARD http://www.delawarenationalguard.com

STATE TUITION ASSISTANCE

• *See page 535*

DEPARTMENT OF MILITARY AFFAIRS http://www.coloradoguard.com

DEPARTMENT OF MILITARY AFFAIRS COLORADO NATIONAL GUARD STATE TUITION ASSISTANCE PROGRAM

• *See page 535*

WISCONSIN NATIONAL GUARD TUITION GRANT

• *See page 535*

DEPARTMENT OF THE ARMY http://www.rotc.monroe.army.mil

ARMY ROTC HISTORICALLY BLACK COLLEGES AND UNIVERSITIES PROGRAM

• *See page 539*

ARMY ROTC TWO-YEAR, THREE-YEAR AND FOUR-YEAR SCHOLARSHIPS FOR ACTIVE DUTY ARMY ENLISTED PERSONNEL
• *See page 539*

DEDICATED MILITARY JUNIOR COLLEGE PROGRAM

One-time award for high school graduates who wish to attend a two-year military junior college. Must serve simultaneously in the Army National Guard or Reserve and qualify for the ROTC Advanced Course. Must have a minimum GPA of 2.5. Must also be 18 years of age by October 1 and under 27 years of age on June 30 in the year of graduation. On-line application available. Deadline: August 25. Must be used at one of five military junior colleges.

Award: Scholarship for use in freshman year; not renewable. *Number:* 60. *Amount:* up to $20,000.

Eligibility Requirements: Applicant must be age 18-26 and enrolled or expecting to enroll full-time at a two-year institution. Applicant must have 2.5 GPA or higher. Available to U.S. citizens. Applicant must have served in the Army National Guard.

Application Requirements: Application, essay, interview, test scores, transcript. *Deadline:* August 25.

Contact: Goldquest Center, Army ROTC Scholarships
Department of the Army
U.S. Army Cadet Command
Fort Monroe, VA 23651-5000
Phone: 800-USA-ROTC
E-mail: rotcinfo@monroe.army.mil

FOUR-YEAR AND THREE-YEAR ADVANCE DESIGNEES SCHOLARSHIP
• *See page 539*

TWO- AND THREE-YEAR CAMPUS-BASED SCHOLARSHIPS
• *See page 539*

TWO-YEAR RESERVE FORCES DUTY SCHOLARSHIPS

One-time award for college juniors or two-year graduate degree students. Must be a member of school's ROTC program. Must pass physical. Minimum 2.5 GPA required. Applicant must be at least 17 years of age when enrolled in college and under 31 years of age in the year of graduation.

Award: Scholarship for use in junior, or graduate years; not renewable. *Number:* 140–300. *Amount:* $5000–$16,000.

Eligibility Requirements: Applicant must be age 17-30 and enrolled or expecting to enroll full-time at a four-year institution or university. Applicant must have 2.5 GPA or higher. Available to U.S. citizens. Applicant must have served in the Army National Guard.

Application Requirements: Application, transcript. *Deadline:* April 16.

Contact: Goldquest Center, Army ROTC Scholarships
Department of the Army
U.S. Army Cadet Command
Fort Monroe, VA 23651-5000
Phone: 800-USA-ROTC
E-mail: rotcinfo@monroe.army.mil

DEPARTMENT OF VETERANS AFFAIRS (VA) http://www.gibill.va.gov

MONTGOMERY GI BILL (SELECTED RESERVE)
• *See page 535*

DISTRICT OF COLUMBIA NATIONAL GUARD ENLISTED ASSOCIATION

DISTRICT OF COLUMBIA NATIONAL GUARD ENLISTED ASSOCIATION SCHOLARSHIP
• *See page 495*

ENLISTED ASSOCIATION OF THE NATIONAL GUARD OF NEW JERSEY http://www.eang-nj.org/scholarships.html

CSM VINCENT BALDASSARI MEMORIAL SCHOLARSHIP PROGRAM
• *See page 535*

ILLINOIS STUDENT ASSISTANCE COMMISSION (ISAC) http://www.collegezone.org

ILLINOIS NATIONAL GUARD GRANT PROGRAM
• *See page 535*

IOWA COLLEGE STUDENT AID COMMISSION http://www.iowacollegeaid.org

IOWA NATIONAL GUARD EDUCATION ASSISTANCE PROGRAM
• *See page 536*

KANSAS NATIONAL GUARD EDUCATIONAL ASSISTANCE PROGRAM

KANSAS NATIONAL GUARD EDUCATIONAL ASSISTANCE AWARD PROGRAM
• *See page 536*

KENTUCKY HIGHER EDUCATION ASSISTANCE AUTHORITY (KHEAA) http://www.kheaa.com

KENTUCKY NATIONAL GUARD TUITION ASSISTANCE PROGRAM
• *See page 536*

KENTUCKY NATIONAL GUARD

KENTUCKY ARMY NATIONAL GUARD EDUCATIONAL ASSISTANCE

Student may receive up to $276 each month for full-time enrollment in a VA-approved vo-tech, undergraduate, or graduate degree program for up to 36 months. Must be a National Guard member with six-year obligation, be a high school graduate or have a GED, and complete basic and advanced individual training.

Award: Grant for use in freshman, sophomore, junior, senior, or graduate years; renewable. *Number:* varies. *Amount:* up to $3312.

Eligibility Requirements: Applicant must be enrolled or expecting to enroll full or part-time at a two-year or four-year or technical institution or university. Available to U.S. citizens. Applicant must have served in the Army National Guard.

Application Requirements: Application. *Deadline:* Continuous.

Contact: Education Services Office
Phone: 502-607-1550

KENTUCKY NATIONAL GUARD TUITION AWARD PROGRAM
• *See page 536*

LOUISIANA NATIONAL GUARD - STATE OF LOUISIANA, JOINT TASK FORCE LA http://www.la.ngb.army.mil

LOUISIANA NATIONAL GUARD STATE TUITION EXEMPTION PROGRAM
• *See page 536*

MINNESOTA DEPARTMENT OF MILITARY AFFAIRS http://www.dma.state.mn.us

LEADERSHIP, EXCELLENCE AND DEDICATED SERVICE SCHOLARSHIP
• *See page 537*

NEBRASKA NATIONAL GUARD http://www.neguard.com

NEBRASKA NATIONAL GUARD TUITION CREDIT
• *See page 537*

NORTH CAROLINA NATIONAL GUARD http://www.nc.ngb.army.mil/education

NORTH CAROLINA NATIONAL GUARD TUITION ASSISTANCE PROGRAM
• *See page 537*

OHIO NATIONAL GUARD

OHIO NATIONAL GUARD SCHOLARSHIP PROGRAM
• *See page 537*

SOUTH DAKOTA BOARD OF REGENTS http://www.ris.sdbor.edu

SOUTH DAKOTA EDUCATION BENEFITS FOR NATIONAL GUARD MEMBERS

• *See page 537*

STATE OF GEORGIA http://www.gsfc.org

GEORGIA NATIONAL GUARD SERVICE CANCELABLE LOAN PROGRAM

• *See page 538*

STATE STUDENT ASSISTANCE COMMISSION OF INDIANA (SSACI) http://www.ssaci.in.gov

INDIANA NATIONAL GUARD SUPPLEMENTAL GRANT

• *See page 538*

TEXAS HIGHER EDUCATION COORDINATING BOARD http://www.collegefortexans.com

TEXAS NATIONAL GUARD TUITION ASSISTANCE PROGRAM

• *See page 538*

WASHINGTON NATIONAL GUARD http://www.washingtonguard.com/education/education.htm

WASHINGTON NATIONAL GUARD SCHOLARSHIP PROGRAM

• *See page 538*

MILITARY SERVICE: COAST GUARD

COMMANDER WILLIAM S. STUHR SCHOLARSHIP FUND FOR MILITARY SONS AND DAUGHTERS

COMMANDER WILLIAM S. STUHR SCHOLARSHIP FUND FOR MILITARY SONS AND DAUGHTERS

• *See page 533*

DAUGHTERS OF THE CINCINNATI http://fdncenter.org/grantmaker/cincinnati

DAUGHTERS OF THE CINCINNATI SCHOLARSHIP

• *See page 534*

FLEET RESERVE ASSOCIATION http://www.fra.org

FLEET RESERVE ASSOCIATION SCHOLARSHIP

• *See page 461*

OLIVER AND ESTHER R. HOWARD SCHOLARSHIP

• *See page 461*

SCHUYLER S. PYLE AWARD

Dependent children/grandchildren and spouses of members in good standing on the Fleet Reserve Association or a member in good standing at time of death, and members of FRA may be eligible for up to $5000. Selection is based on financial need, academic standing, character and leadership qualities. Deadline: April 15.

Award: Scholarship for use in freshman, sophomore, junior, or senior years; not renewable. *Number:* 1. *Amount:* up to $5000.

Eligibility Requirements: Applicant must be enrolled or expecting to enroll full-time at a two-year or four-year institution or university. Applicant must have 3.0 GPA or higher. Available to U.S. citizens. Applicant or parent must meet one or more of the following requirements: Coast Guard, Marine Corp, or Navy experience; retired from active duty; disabled or killed as a result of military service; prisoner of war; or missing in action.

Application Requirements: Application, essay, financial need analysis, references, test scores, transcript. *Deadline:* April 15.

Contact: Scholarship Administrator
Fleet Reserve Association
125 North West Street
Alexandria, VA 22314-2754

STANLEY A. DORAN MEMORIAL SCHOLARSHIP

Dependent children of members in good standing of the Fleet Reserve Association or of a member in good standing at time of death are eligible for this scholarship. Deadline: April 15.

Award: Scholarship for use in freshman, sophomore, junior, or senior years; not renewable. *Number:* 1. *Amount:* up to $3000.

Eligibility Requirements: Applicant must be enrolled or expecting to enroll full-time at a two-year or four-year institution or university. Applicant must have 3.0 GPA or higher. Available to U.S. citizens. Applicant or parent must meet one or more of the following requirements: Coast Guard, Marine Corp, or Navy experience; retired from active duty; disabled or killed as a result of military service; prisoner of war; or missing in action.

Application Requirements: Application, essay, financial need analysis, references, test scores, transcript. *Deadline:* April 15.

Contact: Scholarship Administrator
Fleet Reserve Association
125 North West Street
Alexandria, VA 22314-2754

LADIES AUXILIARY OF THE FLEET RESERVE ASSOCIATION http://www.la-fra.org

ALLIE MAE ODEN MEMORIAL SCHOLARSHIP

• *See page 468*

LADIES AUXILIARY OF THE FLEET RESERVE ASSOCIATION SCHOLARSHIP

• *See page 468*

LADIES AUXILIARY OF THE FLEET RESERVE ASSOCIATION- NATIONAL PRESIDENT'S SCHOLARSHIP

• *See page 468*

SAM ROSE MEMORIAL SCHOLARSHIP

• *See page 468*

MASSACHUSETTS OFFICE OF STUDENT FINANCIAL ASSISTANCE http://www.osfa.mass.edu

HIGHER EDUCATION COORDINATING COUNCIL-TUITION WAIVER PROGRAM

• *See page 534*

NAVAL OFFICERS' SPOUSES' ASSOCIATION OF MAYPORT

NAVAL OFFICERS' SPOUSES' ASSOCIATION OF MAYPORT SCHOLARSHIP

Variable awards for dependent children or spouses of military service members in the Navy, Marines, or Coast Guard, who have served, or are serving a tour of duty out of Mayport Naval Station. Service members must be one of the following: retired, killed, or disabled as a result of service, prisoner of war, or missing in action. Academic achievement, activities, and written essay are used to determine scholarship recipients. Downloadable application at: http://www.orgsites.com/fl/nosamayport. For further information, email NOSA, Scholarship Chairperson at mayport_nosa@yahoo.com.

Award: Scholarship for use in freshman, sophomore, junior, senior, graduate, or postgraduate years; not renewable. *Number:* varies. *Amount:* varies.

Eligibility Requirements: Applicant must be enrolled or expecting to enroll full or part-time at a two-year or four-year or technical institution or university. Available to U.S. citizens. Applicant or parent must meet one or more of the following requirements: Coast Guard, Marine Corp, or Navy experience; retired from active duty; disabled or killed as a result of military service; prisoner of war; or missing in action.

Application Requirements: Application, essay, self-addressed stamped envelope, test scores, transcript, copy of military I.D. card. *Deadline:* March 1.

Contact: Scholarship Chairperson
Naval Officers' Spouses' Association of Mayport
PO Box 280004
Mayport, FL 32228
E-mail: mayport_nosa@yahoo.com

NEW YORK COUNCIL NAVY LEAGUE

NEW YORK COUNCIL NAVY LEAGUE SCHOLARSHIP FUND

Renewable, merit-based award available for undergraduate study to dependents of active, retired, disabled, or deceased (in line of duty or after retirement) members of regular or reserve Navy, Marine Corps, Coast Guard, or Merchant Marine. Must be a Connecticut, New Jersey, or New York resident. Minimum 3.0 GPA required.

Award: Scholarship for use in freshman, sophomore, junior, or senior years; renewable. *Number:* 15. *Amount:* $3000–$5000.

Eligibility Requirements: Applicant must be enrolled or expecting to enroll full-time at a two-year or four-year institution and resident of Connecticut, New Jersey, or New York. Applicant must have 3.0 GPA or higher. Available to U.S. citizens. Applicant or parent must meet one or more of the following requirements: Coast Guard, Marine Corp, or Navy experience; retired from active duty; disabled or killed as a result of military service; prisoner of war; or missing in action.

Application Requirements: Application, financial need analysis, references, self-addressed stamped envelope, test scores, transcript. *Deadline:* June 15.

Contact: Donald Sternberg, Executive Administrator
New York Council Navy League
c/o USCG Battery Park Building, 1 South Street, Room 314
New York, NY 10004
Phone: 212-825-7333
Fax: 212-668-2138
E-mail: chiefync@aol.com

TAILHOOK EDUCATIONAL FOUNDATION

TAILHOOK EDUCATIONAL FOUNDATION SCHOLARSHIP

• *See page 520*

MILITARY SERVICE: GENERAL

ALABAMA DEPARTMENT OF VETERANS AFFAIRS http://www.va.state.al.us/scholarship.htm

ALABAMA G.I. DEPENDENTS SCHOLARSHIP PROGRAM

Full scholarship for dependents of Alabama disabled, prisoner-of-war, or missing-in-action veterans. Child or stepchild must initiate training before 26th birthday; age 30 deadline may apply in certain situations. No age deadline for spouses or widows. Contact for application procedures and deadline.

Award: Scholarship for use in freshman, sophomore, junior, senior, or graduate years; renewable. *Number:* varies. *Amount:* varies.

Eligibility Requirements: Applicant must be enrolled or expecting to enroll full or part-time at a two-year or four-year or technical institution or university; resident of Alabama and studying in Alabama. Available to U.S. and non-U.S. citizens. Applicant or parent must meet one or more of the following requirements: general military experience; retired from active duty; disabled or killed as a result of military service; prisoner of war; or missing in action.

Application Requirements: Application. *Deadline:* varies.

Contact: Willie E. Moore, Scholarship Administrator
Alabama Department of Veterans Affairs
PO Box 1509
Montgomery, AL 36102-1509
Phone: 334-242-5077
Fax: 334-242-5102
E-mail: wmoore@va.state.al.us

AMERICAN LEGION AUXILIARY, DEPARTMENT OF ALABAMA

AMERICAN LEGION AUXILIARY DEPARTMENT OF ALABAMA SCHOLARSHIP PROGRAM

Merit-based scholarships for Alabama residents, preferably ages 17-25, who are children or grandchildren of veterans of World War I, World War II, Korea, Vietnam, Operation Desert Storm, Beirut, Grenada, or Panama. Submit proof of relationship and service record. Renewable awards of $850 each. Send self-addressed stamped envelope for application.

Award: Scholarship for use in freshman, sophomore, junior, or senior years; renewable. *Number:* 40. *Amount:* $850.

Eligibility Requirements: Applicant must be age 17-25; enrolled or expecting to enroll full or part-time at a four-year institution or university and resident of Alabama. Applicant must have 3.5 GPA or higher. Available to U.S. citizens. Applicant or parent must meet one or more of the following requirements: general military experience; retired from active duty; disabled or killed as a result of military service; prisoner of war; or missing in action.

Application Requirements: Application, financial need analysis, photo, references, self-addressed stamped envelope, test scores, transcript. *Deadline:* April 1.

Contact: Anita Barber, Education and Scholarship Chairperson
American Legion Auxiliary, Department of Alabama
120 North Jackson Street
Montgomery, AL 36104-3811
Phone: 334-262-1176
Fax: 334-262-1176
E-mail: americanlegionaux1@juno.com

AMERICAN LEGION AUXILIARY, DEPARTMENT OF ARKANSAS

AMERICAN LEGION AUXILIARY DEPARTMENT OF ARKANSAS ACADEMIC SCHOLARSHIP

One-time award for Arkansas residents who are the children of veterans who served during eligibility dates for membership. Must attend school in Arkansas. Open to high school seniors. Must complete 1,000-word essay entitled "What my country's flag means to me." Contact local American Legion Auxiliary.

Award: Scholarship for use in freshman year; not renewable. *Number:* 1. *Amount:* $1000.

Eligibility Requirements: Applicant must be high school student; planning to enroll or expecting to enroll full-time at a two-year or four-year or technical institution or university; resident of Arkansas and studying in Arkansas. Available to U.S. citizens. Applicant or parent must meet one or more of the following requirements: general military experience; retired from active duty; disabled or killed as a result of military service; prisoner of war; or missing in action.

Application Requirements: Application, essay, financial need analysis, references, self-addressed stamped envelope, test scores, transcript, copy of veteran discharge papers - branch of service, dates of service, DD Form 214. *Deadline:* March 1.

Contact: Department Secretary
American Legion Auxiliary, Department of Arkansas
1415 West 7th Street
Little Rock, AR 72201
Phone: 501-374-5836

AMERICAN LEGION AUXILIARY, DEPARTMENT OF COLORADO

AMERICAN LEGION AUXILIARY DEPARTMENT OF COLORADO DEPARTMENT PRESIDENT'S SCHOLARSHIP FOR JUNIOR MEMBERS

• *See page 441*

AMERICAN LEGION AUXILIARY, DEPARTMENT OF CONNECTICUT

AMERICAN LEGION AUXILIARY DEPARTMENT OF CONNECTICUT MEMORIAL EDUCATIONAL GRANT

• *See page 442*

AMERICAN LEGION AUXILIARY DEPARTMENT OF CONNECTICUT PAST PRESIDENT'S PARLEY MEMORIAL EDUCATION GRANT

• *See page 442*

AMERICAN LEGION AUXILIARY, DEPARTMENT OF FLORIDA

AMERICAN LEGION AUXILIARY DEPARTMENT OF FLORIDA DEPARTMENT SCHOLARSHIPS

Scholarship for children of veterans who were honorably discharged. Must be Florida resident attending an institution within Florida for full-time undergraduate study. Minimum 2.5 GPA. Must submit copy of parent's military discharge.

Award: Scholarship for use in freshman, sophomore, junior, or senior years; not renewable. *Number:* 16–22. *Amount:* $500–$1000.

Eligibility Requirements: Applicant must be enrolled or expecting to enroll full-time at a two-year or four-year or technical institution or university; resident of Florida and studying in Florida. Applicant must have 2.5 GPA or higher. Available to U.S. citizens. Applicant or parent must meet one or more of the following requirements: general military experience; retired from active duty; disabled or killed as a result of military service; prisoner of war; or missing in action.

Application Requirements: Application, financial need analysis, references, transcript, proof of discharge from branch of armed services. *Deadline:* January 1.

Contact: Ms. Marie Mahoney, Department Secretary and Treasurer
American Legion Auxiliary, Department of Florida
PO Box 547917
Orlando, FL 32854-7917
Phone: 407-293-7411
Fax: 407-299-6522
E-mail: alaflorida@aol.com

AMERICAN LEGION AUXILIARY DEPARTMENT OF FLORIDA NATIONAL PRESIDENT'S SCHOLARSHIP

Nonrenewable scholarship for children of veterans who served in the Armed Forces during eligibility dates for American Legion membership. Must be high school senior. Must be entered by local American Legion Auxiliary unit. Two awards ranging from $1000 to $2500. Must have verification of 50 hours of community service and copy of parent's military discharge.

Award: Scholarship for use in freshman year; not renewable. *Number:* 1. *Amount:* $1000–$2500.

Eligibility Requirements: Applicant must be high school student; planning to enroll or expecting to enroll full-time at a four-year institution or university and resident of Florida. Available to U.S. citizens. Applicant or parent must meet one or more of the following requirements: general military experience; retired from active duty; disabled or killed as a result of military service; prisoner of war; or missing in action.

Application Requirements: Application, essay, references, test scores, transcript, military discharge papers. *Deadline:* January 31.

Contact: Ms. Marie Mahoney, Department Secretary and Treasurer
American Legion Auxiliary, Department of Florida
PO Box 547917
Orlando, FL 32854-7917
Phone: 407-293-7411
Fax: 407-299-6522
E-mail: alaflorida@aol.com

AMERICAN LEGION AUXILIARY, DEPARTMENT OF IDAHO

AMERICAN LEGION AUXILIARY, DEPARTMENT OF IDAHO NATIONAL PRESIDENT'S SCHOLARSHIP

Undergraduate scholarship for children of veterans who served in the Armed Forces during eligibility dates for American Legion membership. Must be high school senior and Idaho resident. Must be entered by local American Legion Auxiliary Unit. One-time award of $1500-$2000.

Award: Scholarship for use in freshman year; not renewable. *Number:* 15. *Amount:* $1000–$2000.

Eligibility Requirements: Applicant must be high school student; planning to enroll or expecting to enroll full-time at an institution or university and resident of Idaho. Available to U.S. citizens. Applicant or parent must meet one or more of the following requirements: general military experience; retired from active duty; disabled or killed as a result of military service; prisoner of war; or missing in action.

Application Requirements: Application, essay, references, self-addressed stamped envelope, transcript. *Deadline:* March 10.

Contact: Connie Evans, Secretary and Treasurer
American Legion Auxiliary, Department of Idaho
905 South Warren Street
Boise, ID 83706-3825
Phone: 208-342-7066
Fax: 208-342-0855
E-mail: idalegionaux@earthlink.net

AMERICAN LEGION AUXILIARY, DEPARTMENT OF INDIANA

EDNA M. BURCUS MEMORIAL SCHOLARSHIP

One-time award for child, grandchild, or great-grandchild of veteran who served during American Legion eligibility dates. Must be Indiana resident and graduating high school senior enrolled as full-time undergraduate at an accredited Indiana institution.

Award: Scholarship for use in freshman year; not renewable. *Number:* 3. *Amount:* $500.

Eligibility Requirements: Applicant must be high school student; planning to enroll or expecting to enroll full-time at a two-year or four-year or technical institution or university; resident of Indiana and studying in Indiana. Available to U.S. citizens. Applicant or parent must meet one or more of the following requirements: general military experience; retired from active duty; disabled or killed as a result of military service; prisoner of war; or missing in action.

Application Requirements: Application, essay, financial need analysis, self-addressed stamped envelope. *Deadline:* April 1.

Contact: Ms. Sue Liford, Department Secretary and Treasurer
American Legion Auxiliary, Department of Indiana
777 North Meridian, Room 107
Indianapolis, IN 46204

AMERICAN LEGION AUXILIARY, DEPARTMENT OF IOWA

http://www.ialegion.org/ala

AMERICAN LEGION AUXILIARY DEPARTMENT OF IOWA CHILDREN OF VETERANS SCHOLARSHIP

One-time award available to high school senior who is the child of a veteran who served in the armed forces during eligibility dates for American Legion membership. Must be U.S. citizen and Iowa resident enrolled at an Iowa institution.

Award: Scholarship for use in freshman year; not renewable. *Number:* 10. *Amount:* $300.

Eligibility Requirements: Applicant must be high school student; planning to enroll or expecting to enroll full or part-time at a two-year or four-year or technical institution or university; resident of Iowa and studying in Iowa. Available to U.S. citizens. Applicant or parent must meet one or more of the following requirements: general military experience; retired from active duty; disabled or killed as a result of military service; prisoner of war; or missing in action.

Application Requirements: Application, autobiography, essay, financial need analysis, photo, references, self-addressed stamped envelope, test scores, transcript. *Deadline:* June 1.

Contact: Marlene Valentine, Secretary/Treasurer
American Legion Auxiliary, Department of Iowa
720 Lyon Street
Des Moines, IA 50309
Phone: 515-282-7987
Fax: 515-282-7583

AMERICAN LEGION AUXILIARY, DEPARTMENT OF KENTUCKY

LAURA BLACKBURN MEMORIAL SCHOLARSHIP

Must be high school senior. Must reside in Kentucky and attend a school in the state. Applicant must be descendant of veteran or child of veteran who served in Grenada, Korean War, Lebanon, Panama, Persian Gulf, WWI, WW II or Vietnam.

Award: Scholarship for use in freshman year; renewable. *Number:* 1. *Amount:* $1000.

Eligibility Requirements: Applicant must be high school student; planning to enroll or expecting to enroll full-time at a four-year institution; resident of Kentucky and studying in Kentucky. Available to U.S. citizens. Applicant or parent must meet one or more of the following requirements: general military experience; retired from active duty; disabled or killed as a result of military service; prisoner of war; or missing in action.

American Legion Auxiliary, Department of Kentucky (continued)

Application Requirements: Application, interview, references, test scores, transcript. *Deadline:* March 5.

Contact: Mary Ellen Isham
American Legion Auxiliary, Department of Kentucky
407 East Spring Road
Radcliff, KY 40160
Phone: 270-351-5506

MARY BARRETT MARSHALL SCHOLARSHIP

• *See page 442*

AMERICAN LEGION AUXILIARY, DEPARTMENT OF MAINE

AMERICAN LEGION AUXILIARY DEPARTMENT OF MAINE SCHOLARSHIP

One-time award for residents of Maine who are the children of veterans. Open to high school seniors and graduates who have not yet attended an institution of higher learning. Minimum 3.0 GPA required. Award based on need.

Award: Scholarship for use in freshman year; not renewable. *Number:* 2. *Amount:* $300.

Eligibility Requirements: Applicant must be enrolled or expecting to enroll at a two-year or four-year or technical institution or university and resident of Maine. Applicant must have 3.0 GPA or higher. Applicant or parent must meet one or more of the following requirements: general military experience; retired from active duty; disabled or killed as a result of military service; prisoner of war; or missing in action.

Application Requirements: Application, financial need analysis, test scores, transcript. *Deadline:* April 15.

Contact: Ms. Madeline Sweet, Secretary
American Legion Auxiliary, Department of Maine
PO Box 887
Bucksport, ME 04416-0887

AMERICAN LEGION AUXILIARY, DEPARTMENT OF MAINE NATIONAL PRESIDENT'S SCHOLARSHIP

Must be child of veteran who served during eligibility dates for membership in American Legion. Must be in senior year of high school. One candidate per unit. Must submit essay on required topic and proof of parent's service. One-time award. Only Maine residents need apply.

Award: Scholarship for use in freshman year; not renewable. *Number:* 10. *Amount:* up to $1500.

Eligibility Requirements: Applicant must be high school student; planning to enroll or expecting to enroll full-time at an institution or university; single; resident of Maine and must have an interest in leadership. Applicant must have 3.5 GPA or higher. Available to U.S. citizens. Applicant or parent must meet one or more of the following requirements: general military experience; retired from active duty; disabled or killed as a result of military service; prisoner of war; or missing in action.

Application Requirements: Application, essay, financial need analysis, references, test scores, transcript. *Deadline:* April 1.

Contact: Ms. Madeline Sweet, Secretary
American Legion Auxiliary, Department of Maine
PO Box 887
Bucksport, ME 04416-0887

AMERICAN LEGION AUXILIARY, DEPARTMENT OF MARYLAND

AMERICAN LEGION AUXILIARY DEPARTMENT OF MARYLAND CHILDREN AND YOUTH SCHOLARSHIPS

Nonrenewable scholarship for a daughter of a veteran to pursue full-time undergraduate study at accredited Maryland institution. Will need proof of enrollment in an approved program. Must be a U.S. citizen and Maryland resident pursuing an Arts and Science degree or medical degree other than nursing. Can reapply for up to four years. Contact for information.

Award: Scholarship for use in freshman, sophomore, junior, or senior years; not renewable. *Number:* 1. *Amount:* $2000.

Eligibility Requirements: Applicant must be enrolled or expecting to enroll full-time at a two-year or four-year institution or university; female; resident of Maryland and studying in Maryland. Available to U.S. citizens. Applicant or parent must meet one or more of the following requirements: general military experience; retired from active duty; disabled or killed as a result of military service; prisoner of war; or missing in action.

Application Requirements: Application, financial need analysis, references, transcript. *Deadline:* May 1.

Contact: Ms. Anna Thompson, Department Secretary
American Legion Auxiliary, Department of Maryland
1589 Sulphur Spring Road, Suite 105
Baltimore, MD 21227
Phone: 410-242-9519
Fax: 410-242-9553
E-mail: anna@alamd.org

AMERICAN LEGION AUXILIARY, DEPARTMENT OF MICHIGAN

http://www.michalaux.org

AMERICAN LEGION AUXILIARY DEPARTMENT OF MICHIGAN MEMORIAL SCHOLARSHIP

For daughters, granddaughters, and great-granddaughters of any honorably discharged or deceased veteran of U.S. wars or conflicts. Must be Michigan resident for minimum of one year, female ages 16 to 21, and attend college in Michigan. Include copy of discharge and copy of parent or guardian's IRS 1040 form.

Award: Scholarship for use in freshman, sophomore, junior, or senior years; not renewable. *Number:* 10–35. *Amount:* $500.

Eligibility Requirements: Applicant must be age 16-21; enrolled or expecting to enroll full or part-time at a two-year or four-year or technical institution or university; female; resident of Michigan and studying in Michigan. Available to U.S. citizens. Applicant or parent must meet one or more of the following requirements: general military experience; retired from active duty; disabled or killed as a result of military service; prisoner of war; or missing in action.

Application Requirements: Application, financial need analysis, references, transcript. *Deadline:* March 15.

Contact: Leisa Eldred, Scholarship Coordinator
American Legion Auxiliary, Department of Michigan
212 North Verlinden Avenue
Lansing, MI 48915
Phone: 517-371-4720 Ext. 19
Fax: 517-371-2401
E-mail: michalaux@voyager.net

AMERICAN LEGION AUXILIARY NATIONAL PRESIDENT'S SCHOLARSHIP

One-time scholarship for son or daughter of veterans who were in Armed Forces during eligibility dates for American Legion membership. Must be high school senior in Michigan. Only one candidate per Unit. Applicant must complete fifty hours of volunteer service in the community. Submit essay of no more than 1000 words on a specified topic.

Award: Scholarship for use in freshman year; not renewable. *Number:* 3. *Amount:* $1000–$2500.

Eligibility Requirements: Applicant must be high school student; planning to enroll or expecting to enroll full or part-time at a two-year or four-year institution or university and resident of Michigan. Available to U.S. citizens. Applicant or parent must meet one or more of the following requirements: general military experience; retired from active duty; disabled or killed as a result of military service; prisoner of war; or missing in action.

Application Requirements: Application, essay, financial need analysis, references, test scores, transcript, fifty hours of volunteer service. *Deadline:* March 10.

Contact: Leisa Eldred, Scholarship Coordinator
American Legion Auxiliary, Department of Michigan
212 North Verlinden Avenue
Lansing, MI 48915
Phone: 517-371-4720 Ext. 19
Fax: 517-371-2401
E-mail: michalaux@voyager.net

SCHOLARSHIP FOR NON-TRADITIONAL STUDENT

Applicant must be a dependent of a veteran. Must be one of the following: nontraditional student returning to classroom after some period of time in which their education was interrupted, student over 22 attending college for the first time pursuing a degree, or student over the age of 22 attending a trade or vocational school. Michigan residents only; must attend Michigan institution. Judging based on: need-25 points, character/leadership-25 points, scholastic standing-25 points, initiative/goal-25 points.

Award: Scholarship for use in freshman, sophomore, junior, or senior years; not renewable. *Number:* 1. *Amount:* $500.

Eligibility Requirements: Applicant must be age 23; enrolled or expecting to enroll full or part-time at a two-year or four-year or technical institution or university; resident of Michigan and studying in Michigan. Available to U.S. citizens. Applicant or parent must meet one or more of the following requirements: general military experience; retired from active duty; disabled or killed as a result of military service; prisoner of war; or missing in action.

Application Requirements: Application, financial need analysis, transcript. *Deadline:* March 15.

Contact: Leisa Eldred, Scholarship Coordinator
American Legion Auxiliary, Department of Michigan
212 North Verlinden Avenue
Lansing, MI 48915
Phone: 517-371-4720 Ext. 19
Fax: 517-371-2401
E-mail: michalaux@voyager.net

AMERICAN LEGION AUXILIARY, DEPARTMENT OF MINNESOTA

AMERICAN LEGION AUXILIARY DEPARTMENT OF MINNESOTA SCHOLARSHIPS

Seven $750 awards for the sons, daughters, grandsons, or granddaughters of veterans who served in the Armed Forces during specific eligibility dates. Must be a Minnesota resident, a high school senior or graduate, in need of financial assistance, of good character, have a good scholastic record and at least a C average. Must be planning to attend a Minnesota postsecondary institution.

Award: Scholarship for use in freshman, sophomore, junior, or senior years; not renewable. *Number:* 7. *Amount:* $750.

Eligibility Requirements: Applicant must be enrolled or expecting to enroll at a two-year or four-year or technical institution or university; resident of Minnesota and studying in Minnesota. Applicant or parent must meet one or more of the following requirements: general military experience; retired from active duty; disabled or killed as a result of military service; prisoner of war; or missing in action.

Application Requirements: Application, essay, financial need analysis, references, transcript. *Deadline:* March 15.

Contact: Eleanor Johnson, Executive Secretary
American Legion Auxiliary, Department of Minnesota
State Veterans Service Building, 20 W 12th Street, Room 314
St. Paul, MN 55155
Phone: 651-224-7634
Fax: 651-224-5243

AMERICAN LEGION AUXILIARY, DEPARTMENT OF MISSOURI

AMERICAN LEGION AUXILIARY MISSOURI STATE NATIONAL PRESIDENT'S SCHOLARSHIP

• *See page 442*

LELA MURPHY SCHOLARSHIP

• *See page 443*

AMERICAN LEGION AUXILIARY, DEPARTMENT OF NEBRASKA

AMERICAN LEGION AUXILIARY DEPARTMENT OF NEBRASKA PRESIDENT'S SCHOLARSHIPS

One-time award for Nebraska high school students who were entered into the national competition and did not win. Contact address below for more information. Must be child of a veteran. Must rank in the upper third of class or have minimum 3.0 GPA.

Award: Scholarship for use in freshman year; not renewable. *Number:* 1. *Amount:* $200.

Eligibility Requirements: Applicant must be high school student; planning to enroll or expecting to enroll full-time at a two-year or four-year or technical institution or university and resident of Nebraska. Applicant must have 3.0 GPA or higher. Applicant or parent must meet one or more of the following requirements: general military experience; retired from active duty; disabled or killed as a result of military service; prisoner of war; or missing in action.

Application Requirements: Application, essay, references, test scores, transcript. *Deadline:* April 1.

Contact: Terry Walker, Department Secretary
American Legion Auxiliary, Department of Nebraska
PO Box 5227
Lincoln, NE 68505
Phone: 402-466-1808
Fax: 402-466-0182
E-mail: neaux@alltel.net

AMERICAN LEGION AUXILIARY DEPARTMENT OF NEBRASKA STUDENT AID GRANTS

One-time award for veteran or veteran's child in financial need. Must be a Nebraska resident of at least five years. Must be accepted or enrolled at an institution of higher learning. If in school, must rank in upper third of class or have a minimum 3.0 GPA.

Award: Grant for use in freshman, sophomore, junior, or senior years; not renewable. *Number:* 1–30. *Amount:* $200–$300.

Eligibility Requirements: Applicant must be enrolled or expecting to enroll full-time at a two-year or four-year or technical institution or university and resident of Nebraska. Applicant must have 3.0 GPA or higher. Applicant or parent must meet one or more of the following requirements: general military experience; retired from active duty; disabled or killed as a result of military service; prisoner of war; or missing in action.

Application Requirements: Application, financial need analysis, test scores, transcript. *Deadline:* April 1.

Contact: Terry Walker, Department Secretary
American Legion Auxiliary, Department of Nebraska
PO Box 5227
Lincoln, NE 68505
Phone: 402-466-1808
Fax: 402-466-0182
E-mail: neaux@alltel.net

ROBERTA MARIE STRETCH MEMORIAL SCHOLARSHIP

One-time award for Nebraska residents who are children or grandchildren of veterans. Must be enrolled in an undergraduate or graduate program at a four-year institution. Preference given to former Nebraska Girls State Citizens. Must rank in upper third of class or have a minimum 3.0 GPA.

Award: Scholarship for use in freshman, sophomore, junior, senior, or graduate years; not renewable. *Number:* 1. *Amount:* $400.

Eligibility Requirements: Applicant must be enrolled or expecting to enroll full-time at a four-year institution or university and resident of Nebraska. Applicant must have 3.0 GPA or higher. Applicant or parent must meet one or more of the following requirements: general military experience; retired from active duty; disabled or killed as a result of military service; prisoner of war; or missing in action.

American Legion Auxiliary, Department of Nebraska (continued)

Application Requirements: Application, financial need analysis, test scores, transcript. *Deadline:* April 1.

Contact: Terry Walker, Department Secretary
American Legion Auxiliary, Department of Nebraska
PO Box 5227
Lincoln, NE 68505
Phone: 402-466-1808
Fax: 402-466-0182
E-mail: neaux@alltel.net

RUBY PAUL CAMPAIGN FUND SCHOLARSHIP

• *See page 443*

AMERICAN LEGION AUXILIARY, DEPARTMENT OF NEW JERSEY http://www.alanj.thisnation.net/contact.html

AMERICAN LEGION AUXILIARY DEPARTMENT OF NEW JERSEY NATIONAL PRESIDENT'S SCHOLARSHIP

Nonrenewable scholarship for children of veterans who served in the Armed Forces during eligibility dates for American Legion membership. Must be high school senior and New Jersey resident. Must be entered by local AL Auxiliary Unit. Contact local American Legion Auxiliary.

Award: Scholarship for use in freshman year; not renewable. *Number:* varies. *Amount:* $1500–$2000.

Eligibility Requirements: Applicant must be high school student; planning to enroll or expecting to enroll at a two-year or four-year or technical institution or university and resident of New Jersey. Available to U.S. citizens. Applicant or parent must meet one or more of the following requirements: general military experience; retired from active duty; disabled or killed as a result of military service; prisoner of war; or missing in action.

Application Requirements: Application, essay, references, test scores, transcript. *Deadline:* February 1.

Contact: Lucille Miller, Scholarship Coordinator
American Legion Auxiliary, Department of New Jersey
1540 Kuser Road, Suite A-8
Hamilton, NJ 08619
Phone: 609-581-9580
Fax: 609-581-8429
E-mail: newjerseyala@juno.com

AMERICAN LEGION AUXILIARY, DEPARTMENT OF NEW JERSEY DEPARTMENT SCHOLARSHIPS

One-time award for New Jersey residents of at least three years who are high school seniors and the child or grandchild of an honorably discharged veteran of U.S. Armed Forces. Several awards are offered. Contact local unit of American Legion Auxiliary.

Award: Scholarship for use in freshman year; not renewable. *Number:* varies. *Amount:* varies.

Eligibility Requirements: Applicant must be high school student; planning to enroll or expecting to enroll at a two-year or four-year or technical institution or university and resident of New Jersey. Available to U.S. citizens. Applicant or parent must meet one or more of the following requirements: general military experience; retired from active duty; disabled or killed as a result of military service; prisoner of war; or missing in action.

Application Requirements: Application, essay, financial need analysis, test scores, transcript. *Deadline:* March 15.

Contact: Lucille Miller, Scholarship Coordinator
American Legion Auxiliary, Department of New Jersey
1540 Kuser Road, Suite A-8
Hamilton, NJ 08619
Phone: 609-581-9580
Fax: 609-581-8429
E-mail: newjerseyala@juno.com

CLAIRE OLIPHANT MEMORIAL SCHOLARSHIP

One-time award for New Jersey resident who is a high school senior and the child of an honorably discharged veteran. Must be resident of New Jersey for two years. Contact local unit of American Legion Auxiliary.

Award: Scholarship for use in freshman year; not renewable. *Number:* 1. *Amount:* $1800.

Eligibility Requirements: Applicant must be high school student; planning to enroll or expecting to enroll at a two-year or four-year or technical institution or university and resident of New Jersey. Available to U.S. citizens. Applicant or parent must meet one or more of the following requirements: general military experience; retired from active duty; disabled or killed as a result of military service; prisoner of war; or missing in action.

Application Requirements: Application, financial need analysis, test scores, transcript. *Deadline:* March 15.

Contact: Lucille Miller, Scholarship Coordinator
American Legion Auxiliary, Department of New Jersey
1540 Kuser Road, Suite A-8
Hamilton, NJ 08619
Phone: 609-581-9580
Fax: 609-581-8429
E-mail: newjerseyala@juno.com

AMERICAN LEGION AUXILIARY, DEPARTMENT OF NORTH DAKOTA

AMERICAN LEGION AUXILIARY, NATIONAL PRESIDENT'S SCHOLARSHIP

• *See page 504*

AMERICAN LEGION AUXILIARY, DEPARTMENT OF OHIO

AMERICAN LEGION AUXILIARY DEPARTMENT OF OHIO CONTINUING EDUCATION FUND

One-time award for Ohio residents who are the children or grandchildren of veterans, living or deceased, honorably discharged during eligibility dates for American Legion membership. Awards are for undergraduate use, based on need. Freshmen not eligible. Application must be signed by a Unit representative.

Award: Scholarship for use in sophomore, junior, or senior years; not renewable. *Number:* 15. *Amount:* $200.

Eligibility Requirements: Applicant must be enrolled or expecting to enroll full-time at a two-year or four-year institution or university and resident of Ohio. Available to U.S. citizens. Applicant or parent must meet one or more of the following requirements: general military experience; retired from active duty; disabled or killed as a result of military service; prisoner of war; or missing in action.

Application Requirements: Application, financial need analysis, transcript. *Deadline:* November 1.

Contact: Reva McClure, Department Scholarship Coordinator
American Legion Auxiliary, Department of Ohio
PO Box 2760
Zanesville, OH 43702-2760
Phone: 740-452-8245
Fax: 740-452-2620
E-mail: ala_pam@rrohio.com

AMERICAN LEGION AUXILIARY DEPARTMENT OF OHIO DEPARTMENT PRESIDENT'S SCHOLARSHIP

Scholarship for children or grandchildren of veterans who served in Armed Forces during eligibility dates for American Legion membership. Must be high school senior, ages 16 to 18, Ohio resident, and U.S. citizen. Award for full-time undergraduate study. One-time award of $1500-$2000.

Award: Scholarship for use in freshman year; not renewable. *Number:* 2. *Amount:* $1500–$2000.

Eligibility Requirements: Applicant must be high school student; age 16-18; planning to enroll or expecting to enroll full-time at a two-year or four-year institution or university and resident of Ohio. Available to U.S. citizens. Applicant or parent must meet one or more of the following requirements: general military experience; retired from active duty; disabled or killed as a result of military service; prisoner of war; or missing in action.

Application Requirements: Application, essay, financial need analysis, references, transcript. *Deadline:* March 1.

Contact: Reva McClure, Department Scholarship Coordinator
American Legion Auxiliary, Department of Ohio
PO Box 2760
Zanesville, OH 43702-2760
Phone: 740-452-8245
Fax: 740-452-2620
E-mail: ala_pam@rrohio.com

AMERICAN LEGION AUXILIARY, DEPARTMENT OF OREGON

AMERICAN LEGION AUXILIARY DEPARTMENT OF OREGON DEPARTMENT GRANTS

One-time award for educational use in the state of Oregon. Must be a resident of Oregon who is the child or widow of a veteran or the wife of a disabled veteran.

Award: Grant for use in freshman, sophomore, junior, or senior years; not renewable. *Number:* 3. *Amount:* $1000.

Eligibility Requirements: Applicant must be enrolled or expecting to enroll full or part-time at a two-year or four-year or technical institution or university; resident of Oregon and studying in Oregon. Available to U.S. and Canadian citizens. Applicant or parent must meet one or more of the following requirements: general military experience; retired from active duty; disabled or killed as a result of military service; prisoner of war; or missing in action.

Application Requirements: Application, essay, financial need analysis, interview, references, test scores, transcript. *Deadline:* March 15.

Contact: Pat Calhoun-Floren, Secretary
American Legion Auxiliary, Department of Oregon
PO Box 1730
Wilsonville, OR 97070
Phone: 503-682-3162
Fax: 503-685-5008

AMERICAN LEGION AUXILIARY DEPARTMENT OF OREGON SPIRIT OF YOUTH SCHOLARSHIP

• *See page 443*

AMERICAN LEGION AUXILIARY, DEPARTMENT OF OREGON NATIONAL PRESIDENT'S SCHOLARSHIP

One-time award for children of veterans who served in the Armed Forces during eligibility dates for American Legion membership. Must be high school senior and Oregon resident. Must be entered by a local American Legion Auxiliary unit. Two scholarships of varying amounts.

Award: Scholarship for use in freshman year; not renewable. *Number:* 2. *Amount:* $500–$1000.

Eligibility Requirements: Applicant must be high school student; planning to enroll or expecting to enroll at an institution or university and resident of Oregon. Available to U.S. citizens. Applicant or parent must meet one or more of the following requirements: general military experience; retired from active duty; disabled or killed as a result of military service; prisoner of war; or missing in action.

Application Requirements: Application, essay, financial need analysis, interview, references, transcript. *Deadline:* March 15.

Contact: Pat Calhoun-Floren, Secretary
American Legion Auxiliary, Department of Oregon
PO Box 1730
Wilsonville, OR 97070
Phone: 503-682-3162
Fax: 503-685-5008

AMERICAN LEGION AUXILIARY, DEPARTMENT OF PENNSYLVANIA

AMERICAN LEGION AUXILIARY DEPARTMENT OF PENNSYLVANIA SCHOLARSHIP FOR DEPENDENTS OF DISABLED OR DECEASED VETERANS

Scholarship for children or grandchildren of veterans. Must be U.S. citizen and Pennsylvania resident. For high school seniors who are planning to attend a Pennsylvania college or university. Contact local American Legion unit for application details. Total of $2400 for four years.

Award: Scholarship for use in freshman, sophomore, junior, or senior years; not renewable. *Number:* 1. *Amount:* $600.

Eligibility Requirements: Applicant must be high school student; planning to enroll or expecting to enroll full-time at an institution or university; resident of Pennsylvania and studying in Pennsylvania. Available to U.S. citizens. Applicant or parent must meet one or more of the following requirements: general military experience; retired from active duty; disabled or killed as a result of military service; prisoner of war; or missing in action.

Application Requirements: Application. *Deadline:* March 15.

Contact: Colleen Watson, Executive Secretary and Treasurer
American Legion Auxiliary, Department of Pennsylvania
PO Box 2643
Harrisburg, PA 17105
Phone: 717-763-7545

AMERICAN LEGION AUXILIARY DEPARTMENT OF PENNSYLVANIA SCHOLARSHIP FOR DEPENDENTS OF LIVING VETERANS

Scholarship for children or grandchildren of veterans. Must be U.S. citizen and Pennsylvania resident. For high school seniors who are planning to attend a Pennsylvania college or university. Contact local American Legion unit for application details. Award is $600 each year for four years.

Award: Scholarship for use in freshman, sophomore, junior, or senior years; not renewable. *Number:* 1. *Amount:* $600.

Eligibility Requirements: Applicant must be high school student; planning to enroll or expecting to enroll at a four-year institution; resident of Pennsylvania and studying in Pennsylvania. Available to U.S. citizens. Applicant or parent must meet one or more of the following requirements: general military experience; retired from active duty; disabled or killed as a result of military service; prisoner of war; or missing in action.

Application Requirements: Application. *Deadline:* March 15.

Contact: Colleen Watson, Executive Secretary and Treasurer
American Legion Auxiliary, Department of Pennsylvania
PO Box 2643
Harrisburg, PA 17105
Phone: 717-763-7545

AMERICAN LEGION AUXILIARY, DEPARTMENT OF SOUTH DAKOTA

AMERICAN LEGION AUXILIARY DEPARTMENT OF SOUTH DAKOTA COLLEGE SCHOLARSHIPS

• *See page 443*

AMERICAN LEGION AUXILIARY DEPARTMENT OF SOUTH DAKOTA THELMA FOSTER SCHOLARSHIP FOR SENIOR AUXILIARY MEMBERS

• *See page 444*

AMERICAN LEGION AUXILIARY DEPARTMENT OF SOUTH DAKOTA THELMA FOSTER SCHOLARSHIPS FOR JUNIOR AUXILIARY MEMBERS

• *See page 444*

AMERICAN LEGION AUXILIARY DEPARTMENT OF SOUTH DAKOTA VOCATIONAL SCHOLARSHIP

• *See page 444*

AMERICAN LEGION AUXILIARY, DEPARTMENT OF SOUTH DAKOTA SENIOR SCHOLARSHIP

• *See page 444*

AMERICAN LEGION AUXILIARY, DEPARTMENT OF TENNESSEE

VARA GRAY SCHOLARSHIP-GENERAL

One-time award for high school senior who is the child of a veteran. Must be Tennessee resident and single. Award must be used within one year. Contact for more information.

Award: Scholarship for use in freshman year; not renewable. *Number:* 3. *Amount:* $500.

Eligibility Requirements: Applicant must be high school student; planning to enroll or expecting to enroll full-time at a two-year or

American Legion Auxiliary, Department of Tennessee (continued)

four-year institution or university; single and resident of Tennessee. Available to U.S. citizens. Applicant or parent must meet one or more of the following requirements: general military experience; retired from active duty; disabled or killed as a result of military service; prisoner of war; or missing in action.

Application Requirements: Application, financial need analysis, references, test scores, transcript. *Deadline:* March 1.

Contact: Department Headquarters
American Legion Auxiliary, Department of Tennessee
104 Point East Drive
Nashville, TN 37220
Phone: 615-226-8648
Fax: 615-226-8649

AMERICAN LEGION AUXILIARY, DEPARTMENT OF TEXAS

AMERICAN LEGION AUXILIARY, DEPARTMENT OF TEXAS GENERAL EDUCATION SCHOLARSHIP

Scholarships available for Texas residents. Must be a child of a veteran who served in the Armed Forces during eligibility dates. Some additional criteria used for selection are recommendations, academics, and finances. For specific information contact your local American Legion Auxiliary unit. Deadline is February 1.

Award: Scholarship for use in freshman, sophomore, junior, senior, graduate, or postgraduate years; not renewable. *Number:* varies. *Amount:* $500.

Eligibility Requirements: Applicant must be enrolled or expecting to enroll full-time at a two-year or four-year or technical institution or university and resident of Texas. Available to U.S. citizens. Applicant or parent must meet one or more of the following requirements: general military experience; retired from active duty; disabled or killed as a result of military service; prisoner of war; or missing in action.

Application Requirements: Application, financial need analysis, photo, resume, references, transcript, letter stating qualifications and intention. *Deadline:* February 1.

Contact: American Legion Auxiliary, Department of Texas
3401 Ed Bluestein Boulevard, Suite 200
Austin, TX 78721-2902
Phone: 512-476-7278

AMERICAN LEGION AUXILIARY, DEPARTMENT OF UTAH http://www.legion-aux.org

AMERICAN LEGION AUXILIARY NATIONAL PRESIDENTS SCHOLARSHIP

• *See page 444*

AMERICAN LEGION AUXILIARY, DEPARTMENT OF WASHINGTON http://www.walegion-aux.org

AMERICAN LEGION AUXILIARY, DEPARTMENT OF WASHINGTON GIFT SCHOLARSHIPS

For a child of an incapacitated or deceased veteran. Award is for high school seniors and should be used within twelve months of receipt. Submit statement of military service of veteran parent through which applicant is eligible. One-time award of $500 for residents of Washington.

Award: Scholarship for use in freshman year; not renewable. *Number:* 1. *Amount:* $500.

Eligibility Requirements: Applicant must be high school student; age 20 or under; planning to enroll or expecting to enroll full or part-time at a two-year or four-year or technical institution or university and resident of Washington. Available to U.S. citizens. Applicant or parent must meet one or more of the following requirements: general military experience; retired from active duty; disabled or killed as a result of military service; prisoner of war; or missing in action.

Application Requirements: Application, essay, references, transcript. *Deadline:* April 1.

Contact: Lois Boyle, Education Chairman
American Legion Auxiliary, Department of Washington
PO Box 5867
Lacey, WA 98509-5867
Phone: 360-456-5995
Fax: 360-491-7442
E-mail: alawash@qwest.net

DAYLE AND FRANCES PEIPER SCHOLARSHIP

One-time award for a dependent of a veteran and a resident of Washington state. Application deadline: April 1.

Award: Scholarship for use in freshman year; not renewable. *Number:* 1. *Amount:* $500.

Eligibility Requirements: Applicant must be high school student; age 20 or under; planning to enroll or expecting to enroll full or part-time at a two-year or four-year or technical institution or university and resident of Washington. Available to U.S. citizens. Applicant or parent must meet one or more of the following requirements: general military experience; retired from active duty; disabled or killed as a result of military service; prisoner of war; or missing in action.

Application Requirements: Application, essay, transcript. *Deadline:* April 1.

Contact: Lois Boyle, Education Chairman
American Legion Auxiliary, Department of Washington
PO Box 5867
Lacey, WA 98509-5867
Phone: 360-456-5995
Fax: 360-491-7442
E-mail: alawash@qwest.net

AMERICAN LEGION AUXILIARY, NATIONAL HEADQUARTERS http://www.legion-aux.org

AMERICAN LEGION AUXILIARY NATIONAL PRESIDENT'S SCHOLARSHIPS

One-time award for senior high school students who are children of veterans who served during WWI, WWII, Korean, Vietnam, Panama, Grenada, Lebanon, or Persian Gulf wars. The essay title changes yearly. Submit application to local chapter president.

Award: Scholarship for use in freshman year; not renewable. *Number:* up to 10. *Amount:* $2000–$2500.

Eligibility Requirements: Applicant must be high school student and planning to enroll or expecting to enroll full-time at a two-year or four-year institution or university. Applicant or parent must meet one or more of the following requirements: general military experience; retired from active duty; disabled or killed as a result of military service; prisoner of war; or missing in action.

Application Requirements: Application, essay, references, self-addressed stamped envelope, test scores, transcript. *Deadline:* March 10.

Contact: Department Secretary
American Legion Auxiliary, National Headquarters
777 North Meridan Street, 3rd Floor
Indianapolis, IN 46204-1189
Phone: 317-955-3853
Fax: 317-955-3884
E-mail: aef@legion-aux.org

AMERICAN LEGION, DEPARTMENT OF ARKANSAS http://www.arklegion.homestead.com

AMERICAN LEGION DEPARTMENT OF ARKANSAS PAST DEPARTMENT COMMANDER SCHOLARSHIP

• *See page 446*

AMERICAN LEGION, DEPARTMENT OF IDAHO http://www.idaholegion.com

AMERICAN LEGION, DEPARTMENT OF IDAHO SCHOLARSHIP
• See page 446

AMERICAN LEGION, DEPARTMENT OF KANSAS

ALBERT M. LAPPIN SCHOLARSHIP
• See page 447

HUGH A. SMITH SCHOLARSHIP FUND
• See page 447

ROSEDALE POST 346 SCHOLARSHIP
• See page 448

TED AND NORA ANDERSON SCHOLARSHIPS
• See page 448

AMERICAN LEGION, DEPARTMENT OF MAINE

DANIEL E. LAMBERT MEMORIAL SCHOLARSHIP

One-time award for a senior at an accredited Maine high school. Parent must be a veteran. Award is based on financial need and good character. Must be U.S. citizen. Applicant must show evidence of being enrolled, or attending accredited college or vocational technical school.

Award: Scholarship for use in freshman year; not renewable. *Number:* 1–2. *Amount:* $500.

Eligibility Requirements: Applicant must be high school student; planning to enroll or expecting to enroll full-time at a two-year or four-year or technical institution or university and resident of Maine. Available to U.S. citizens. Applicant or parent must meet one or more of the following requirements: general military experience; retired from active duty; disabled or killed as a result of military service; prisoner of war; or missing in action.

Application Requirements: Application, financial need analysis, references. *Deadline:* May 1.

Contact: Roxanne Roy
American Legion, Department of Maine
PO Box 900
Waterville, ME 04903
Phone: 207-873-3229
Fax: 207-872-0501
E-mail: legionme@wtvl.net

JAMES V. DAY SCHOLARSHIP
• See page 448

AMERICAN LEGION, DEPARTMENT OF MARYLAND http://mdlegion.org

AMERICAN LEGION DEPARTMENT OF MARYLAND GENERAL SCHOLARSHIP FUND

Nonrenewable scholarship for veterans or children of veterans who served in the Armed Forces during dates of eligibility for American Legion membership. Merit-based award. Contact your local AL chapter for deadlines. Application available on Web site: http://mdlegion.org.

Award: Scholarship for use in freshman, sophomore, junior, or senior years; not renewable. *Number:* 11. *Amount:* $500.

Eligibility Requirements: Applicant must be enrolled or expecting to enroll full-time at an institution or university and resident of Maryland. Available to U.S. citizens. Applicant or parent must meet one or more of the following requirements: general military experience; retired from active duty; disabled or killed as a result of military service; prisoner of war; or missing in action.

Application Requirements: Application, essay, financial need analysis, transcript. *Deadline:* varies.

Contact: Thomas Davis, Department Adjutant
American Legion, Department of Maryland
101 North Gay, Room E
Baltimore, MD 21202
Phone: 410-752-3104

AMERICAN LEGION, DEPARTMENT OF MICHIGAN http://www.michiganlegion.org

GUY M. WILSON SCHOLARSHIPS

One-time award of $500 each for undergraduate use at a Michigan college. Must be resident of Michigan and the son or daughter of a veteran, living or deceased. Must submit copy of veteran's honorable discharge. Must have minimum 2.5 GPA.

Award: Scholarship for use in freshman, sophomore, junior, or senior years; not renewable. *Number:* varies. *Amount:* $500.

Eligibility Requirements: Applicant must be high school student; planning to enroll or expecting to enroll full or part-time at a two-year or four-year institution or university; resident of Michigan and studying in Michigan. Applicant must have 2.5 GPA or higher. Available to U.S. citizens. Applicant or parent must meet one or more of the following requirements: general military experience; retired from active duty; disabled or killed as a result of military service; prisoner of war; or missing in action.

Application Requirements: Application, essay, financial need analysis, test scores, transcript. *Deadline:* January 1.

Contact: Deanna Clark, Programs Secretary
American Legion, Department of Michigan
212 North Verlinden Avenue
Lansing, MI 48915
Phone: 517-371-4720 Ext. 25
Fax: 517-371-2401
E-mail: programs@michiganlegion.org

WILLIAM D. AND JEWELL W. BREWER SCHOLARSHIP TRUSTS

One-time award for residents of Michigan who are the sons or daughters of veterans, living or deceased. Must submit copy of veteran's honorable discharge. Several scholarships of $500 each. Must have minimum 2.5 GPA. Scholarship can be applied to any college or university within the United States.

Award: Scholarship for use in freshman, sophomore, junior, or senior years; not renewable. *Number:* varies. *Amount:* $500.

Eligibility Requirements: Applicant must be enrolled or expecting to enroll full or part-time at a two-year or four-year institution or university and resident of Michigan. Applicant must have 2.5 GPA or higher. Available to U.S. citizens. Applicant or parent must meet one or more of the following requirements: general military experience; retired from active duty; disabled or killed as a result of military service; prisoner of war; or missing in action.

Application Requirements: Application, essay, financial need analysis, test scores, transcript. *Deadline:* January 1.

Contact: Deanna Clark, Programs Secretary
American Legion, Department of Michigan
212 North Verlinden Avenue
Lansing, MI 48915
Phone: 517-371-4720 Ext. 25
Fax: 517-371-2401
E-mail: programs@michiganlegion.org

AMERICAN LEGION, DEPARTMENT OF MINNESOTA http://www.mnlegion.org

AMERICAN LEGION DEPARTMENT OF MINNESOTA MEMORIAL SCHOLARSHIP
• See page 448

MINNESOTA LEGIONNAIRES INSURANCE TRUST
• See page 448

AMERICAN LEGION, DEPARTMENT OF MISSOURI http://www.missourilegion.org

CHARLES L. BACON MEMORIAL SCHOLARSHIP
• See page 449

ERMAN W. TAYLOR MEMORIAL SCHOLARSHIP

One-time $500 award given to a descendant of honorably discharged veteran who served 90 or more days of active duty in the armed forces. Applicant must provide copy of discharge certificate. Applicant must be a full-time

American Legion, Department of Missouri (continued)

student at accredited college or university. Must also submit an essay of 500 words or less on the subject, "Which of the Presidents was the greatest and why?" Applicant must be Missouri resident.

Award: Scholarship for use in freshman year; not renewable. *Number:* 2. *Amount:* $500.

Eligibility Requirements: Applicant must be enrolled or expecting to enroll full-time at a four-year institution or university; single and resident of Missouri. Available to U.S. citizens. Applicant or parent must meet one or more of the following requirements: general military experience; retired from active duty; disabled or killed as a result of military service; prisoner of war; or missing in action.

Application Requirements: Application, applicant must enter a contest, essay, test scores, veteran discharge certificate. *Deadline:* April 20.

Contact: Scholarship Information
American Legion, Department of Missouri
PO Box 179
Jefferson City, MO 65102
Phone: 573-893-2353
Fax: 573-893-2980

LILLIE LOIS FORD SCHOLARSHIP FUND

One-time award of $1000 given out to a male and female that attended a full session of the American Legion Boys/Girls State of Missouri or a full session of the Department's Cadet Patrol Academy in Jefferson City. Applicant must be Missouri resident.

Award: Scholarship for use in freshman year; not renewable. *Number:* 2. *Amount:* $1000.

Eligibility Requirements: Applicant must be high school student; age 21 or under; planning to enroll or expecting to enroll full-time at a four-year institution or university; single and resident of Missouri. Available to U.S. citizens. Applicant or parent must meet one or more of the following requirements: general military experience; retired from active duty; disabled or killed as a result of military service; prisoner of war; or missing in action.

Application Requirements: Application, financial need analysis, test scores. *Deadline:* April 20.

Contact: Scholarship Information
American Legion, Department of Missouri
PO Box 179
Jefferson City, MO 65102
Phone: 573-893-2353
Fax: 573-893-2980

AMERICAN LEGION, DEPARTMENT OF NEBRASKA http://www.legion.org

EDGAR J. BOSCHULT MEMORIAL SCHOLARSHIP

One-time award available to ROTC students or veterans attending a University of Nebraska system school. Must be a full-time student to qualify. Several awards ranging from $200 to $400. Minimum 2.5 GPA required.

Award: Scholarship for use in freshman, sophomore, junior, or senior years; not renewable. *Number:* 1–5. *Amount:* $200–$400.

Eligibility Requirements: Applicant must be enrolled or expecting to enroll full-time at a four-year institution and studying in Nebraska. Applicant must have 2.5 GPA or higher. Available to U.S. citizens. Applicant or parent must meet one or more of the following requirements: general military experience; retired from active duty; disabled or killed as a result of military service; prisoner of war; or missing in action.

Application Requirements: Application. *Deadline:* March 1.

Contact: Burdette Burkhart, Activities Director
American Legion, Department of Nebraska
PO Box 5205
Lincoln, NE 68505-0205
Phone: 402-464-6338
Fax: 402-464-6330
E-mail: actdirlegion@alltel.net

MAYNARD JENSEN AMERICAN LEGION MEMORIAL SCHOLARSHIP

• *See page 449*

AMERICAN LEGION, DEPARTMENT OF NEW YORK http://www.ny.legion.org

AMERICAN LEGION DEPARTMENT OF NEW YORK DR. HANNAH K. VUOLO MEMORIAL SCHOLARSHIP

• *See page 449*

AMERICAN LEGION, DEPARTMENT OF NORTH DAKOTA http://www.ndlegion.org

HATTIE TEDROW MEMORIAL FUND SCHOLARSHIP

Applicants must be a legal resident of North Dakota, a high school senior, and a direct descendent of a veteran with honorable service in the United States military. Send SASE for more information and deadlines.

Award: Scholarship for use in freshman year; not renewable. *Number:* varies. *Amount:* up to $2000.

Eligibility Requirements: Applicant must be high school student; planning to enroll or expecting to enroll at an institution or university and resident of North Dakota. Available to U.S. citizens. Applicant or parent must meet one or more of the following requirements: general military experience; retired from active duty; disabled or killed as a result of military service; prisoner of war; or missing in action.

Application Requirements: Application, self-addressed stamped envelope. *Deadline:* April 15.

Contact: American Legion, Department of North Dakota
PO Box 1055
Indianapolis, IN 46206

AMERICAN LEGION, DEPARTMENT OF SOUTH CAROLINA

AMERICAN LEGION ROBERT E. DAVID CHILDREN'S SCHOLARSHIP FUND

Scholarship for a South Carolina resident who is a relative of an American Legion member. Must demonstrate financial need. For use at a South Carolina college or university only. Application deadline is May 1. Several one-time awards of $500 each.

Award: Scholarship for use in freshman, sophomore, junior, or senior years; not renewable. *Number:* 10–20. *Amount:* $500.

Eligibility Requirements: Applicant must be enrolled or expecting to enroll full-time at a two-year or four-year or technical institution or university; resident of South Carolina and studying in South Carolina. Available to U.S. citizens. Applicant must have general military experience.

Application Requirements: Application, financial need analysis, transcript. *Deadline:* May 1.

Contact: Jim Hawk, Department Adjutant
American Legion, Department of South Carolina
PO Box 11355
Columbia, SC 29211
Phone: 803-799-1992
Fax: 803-791-9831
E-mail: dept.programs@aldsc.org

AMERICAN LEGION, DEPARTMENT OF VERMONT

AMERICAN LEGION HIGH SCHOOL ORATORICAL CONTEST-VERMONT

Students in grades 9-12 are eligible to compete. Must attend an accredited Vermont high school. Must be a United States citizen. Selection based on oration.

Award: Prize for use in freshman, sophomore, junior, or senior years; not renewable. *Number:* 1. *Amount:* $2000.

Eligibility Requirements: Applicant must be high school student; planning to enroll or expecting to enroll full or part-time at a two-year or four-year or technical institution or university and resident of Vermont. Available to U.S. citizens. Applicant or parent must meet one or more of the following requirements: general military experience; retired from active duty; disabled or killed as a result of military service; prisoner of war; or missing in action.

Application Requirements: Applicant must enter a contest. *Deadline:* January 1.

Contact: Huzon Stewart, Chairman
American Legion, Department of Vermont
PO Box 396
Montpelier, VT 05601-0396
Phone: 802-223-7131
E-mail: alvt@sover.net

AMERICAN LEGION, DEPARTMENT OF WASHINGTON http://www.walegion.org

AMERICAN LEGION DEPARTMENT OF WASHINGTON CHILDREN AND YOUTH SCHOLARSHIPS

• *See page 450*

AMERICAN LEGION, DEPARTMENT OF WEST VIRGINIA

WILLIAM F. "BILL" JOHNSON MEMORIAL SCHOLARSHIP SPONSORED BY SONS OF THE AMERICAN LEGION

• *See page 450*

AMERICAN LEGION, DEPARTMENT OF WYOMING

E.A. BLACKMORE MEMORIAL SCHOLARSHIP

• *See page 450*

AMERICAN MILITARY RETIREES ASSOCIATION http://www.amra1973.org

SERGEANT MAJOR DOUGLAS R. DRUM MEMORIAL SCHOLARSHIP FUND

One-time award limited to dependents (spouse, child, grandchild) of members of the American Military Retirees' Association, founded by Douglas R. Drum. It is to be used only for tuition, books, room and board. Must be U.S. citizen. Scholarship awarded in August.

Award: Scholarship for use in freshman, sophomore, junior, or senior years; not renewable. *Number:* 1–6. *Amount:* $250–$500.

Eligibility Requirements: Applicant must be enrolled or expecting to enroll full-time at a two-year or four-year or technical institution or university. Available to U.S. citizens. Applicant or parent must meet one or more of the following requirements: general military experience; retired from active duty; disabled or killed as a result of military service; prisoner of war; or missing in action.

Application Requirements: Application, autobiography, financial need analysis, photo, references, test scores, transcript. *Deadline:* August 1.

Contact: Kathy Dow, Committee Chairperson
American Military Retirees Association
5436 Peru Street
Suite 100
Plattsburgh, NY 12901
Phone: 518-561-6256
Fax: 518-563-9479
E-mail: infoamra1973@westelcom.com

AMVETS DEPARTMENT OF ILLINOIS http://www.amvets.com

ILLINOIS AMVETS LADIES AUXILIARY MEMORIAL SCHOLARSHIP

Applicant must be an Illinois high school senior and a child of an honorably discharged veteran who served after September 15, 1940. Must submit ACT scores and IRS 1040 form. Submit high school rank and grades.

Award: Scholarship for use in freshman, sophomore, junior, or senior years; not renewable. *Number:* 1–3. *Amount:* $500.

Eligibility Requirements: Applicant must be high school student; planning to enroll or expecting to enroll full-time at a two-year or four-year or technical institution or university and resident of Illinois. Available to U.S. citizens. Applicant or parent must meet one or more of the following requirements: general military experience; retired from active duty; disabled or killed as a result of military service; prisoner of war; or missing in action.

Application Requirements: Application, financial need analysis, test scores, transcript, IRS 1040 form. *Deadline:* March 1.

Contact: Sara Van Dyke, Scholarship Director
AMVETS Department of Illinois
2200 South Sixth Street
Springfield, IL 62703-3496
Phone: 217-528-4713
Fax: 217-528-9896

ILLINOIS AMVETS LADIES AUXILIARY WORCHID SCHOLARSHIPS

Applicant must be an Illinois high school senior and the child of a deceased veteran who served after September 15, 1940, and was honorably discharged. ACT score required. Submit IRS 1040 form.

Award: Scholarship for use in freshman, sophomore, junior, or senior years; not renewable. *Number:* 1–3. *Amount:* $500.

Eligibility Requirements: Applicant must be high school student; age 17-18; planning to enroll or expecting to enroll full-time at a two-year or four-year or technical institution or university and resident of Illinois. Available to U.S. citizens. Applicant or parent must meet one or more of the following requirements: general military experience; retired from active duty; disabled or killed as a result of military service; prisoner of war; or missing in action.

Application Requirements: Application, financial need analysis, test scores, transcript, IRS 1040 form. *Deadline:* March 1.

Contact: Sara Van Dyke, Scholarship Director
AMVETS Department of Illinois
2200 South Sixth Street
Springfield, IL 62703-3496
Phone: 217-528-4713
Fax: 217-528-9896
E-mail: scholarship@amvetsillinois.com

ILLINOIS AMVETS SERVICE FOUNDATION SCHOLARSHIP AWARD

Applicant must be an Illinois high school senior. Must submit ACT scores and IRS 1040 form. Must be the child or grandchild of an honorably discharged veteran who served after September 15, 1940, or is currently serving in the military. Renewable award of $1000.

Award: Scholarship for use in freshman, sophomore, junior, or senior years; renewable. *Number:* 30. *Amount:* $1000.

Eligibility Requirements: Applicant must be high school student; age 17-18; planning to enroll or expecting to enroll full-time at a two-year or four-year or technical institution or university and resident of Illinois. Available to U.S. citizens. Applicant or parent must meet one or more of the following requirements: general military experience; retired from active duty; disabled or killed as a result of military service; prisoner of war; or missing in action.

Application Requirements: Application, financial need analysis, test scores, transcript, IRS 1040 form. *Deadline:* March 1.

Contact: Sara Van Dyke, Scholarship Director
AMVETS Department of Illinois
2200 South Sixth Street
Springfield, IL 62703-3496
Phone: 217-528-4713
Fax: 217-528-9896
E-mail: scholarship@amvetsillinois.com

ILLINOIS AMVETS TRADE SCHOOL SCHOLARSHIP

Applicant must be an Illinois high school senior who has been accepted in a pre-approved trade school program (a copy of an acceptance letter must accompany the application) and he or she must be a child or grandchild of a veteran who served after September 15th, 1940, and honorably discharged or is presently serving in the military. Scholarship renews for two years, paying annually $500.

Award: Scholarship for use in freshman or sophomore years; renewable. *Number:* 1–2. *Amount:* up to $500.

Eligibility Requirements: Applicant must be high school student; age 17-18; planning to enroll or expecting to enroll full-time at a technical institution and resident of Illinois. Available to U.S. citizens. Applicant or parent must meet one or more of the following requirements:

AMVETS Department of Illinois (continued)

general military experience; retired from active duty; disabled or killed as a result of military service; prisoner of war; or missing in action.

Application Requirements: Application, acceptance letter. *Deadline:* March 1.

Contact: Sara Van Dyke, Scholarship Director
AMVETS Department of Illinois
2200 South Sixth Street
Springfield, IL 62703-3496
Phone: 217-528-4713
Fax: 217-528-9896
E-mail: scholarship@amvetsillinois.com

AMVETS NATIONAL HEADQUARTERS http://www.amvets.org

AMVETS NATIONAL FOUR-YEAR SCHOLARSHIP

Automatically renewable four-year ($1,000 per year) scholarship for child or grandchild of a veteran who is an AMVETS member. Must be enrolled in a four-year college or university. Contact AMVETS National Headquarters for complete eligibility requirements and application packet.

Award: Scholarship for use in freshman year; renewable. *Number:* 6. *Amount:* $1000.

Eligibility Requirements: Applicant must be enrolled or expecting to enroll full-time at a four-year institution or university. Available to U.S. citizens. Applicant or parent must meet one or more of the following requirements: general military experience; retired from active duty; disabled or killed as a result of military service; prisoner of war; or missing in action.

Application Requirements: Application, essay, financial need analysis, references, test scores, transcript. *Deadline:* April 15.

Contact: Tiffany Kidd, National Programs Assistant
AMVETS National Headquarters
4647 Forbes Boulevard
Lanham, MD 20706-4380
Phone: 301-459-9600 Ext. 3043
Fax: 301-459-7924
E-mail: tkidd@amvets.org

AMVETS NATIONAL FOUR-YEAR SCHOLARSHIP FOR VETERANS

Renewable $4,000 scholarship ($1,000 per year) available to veterans who are interested in returning to school. Must be an AMVETS member. Contact AMVETS National Headquarters for complete eligibility requirements and application packet. Application deadline is April 15.

Award: Scholarship for use in freshman, sophomore, junior, senior, or graduate years; renewable. *Number:* 3. *Amount:* $1000.

Eligibility Requirements: Applicant must be enrolled or expecting to enroll full-time at a four-year institution or university. Available to U.S. citizens. Applicant must have general military experience.

Application Requirements: Application, essay, financial need analysis, references, test scores, transcript. *Deadline:* April 15.

Contact: Tiffany Kidd, National Programs Assistant
AMVETS National Headquarters
4647 Forbes Boulevard
Lanham, MD 20706-4380
Phone: 301-459-9600 Ext. 3043
Fax: 301-459-7924
E-mail: tkidd@amvets.org

AMVETS NATIONAL JROTC SCHOLARSHIP

Automatically renewable scholarship for child or grandchild of a veteran who is an AMVETS member. Must be enrolled in a JROTC program. Contact AMVETS National Headquarters for complete eligibility requirements and application packet.

Award: Scholarship for use in freshman year; renewable. *Number:* 1. *Amount:* $1000.

Eligibility Requirements: Applicant must be enrolled or expecting to enroll full-time at a four-year institution. Available to U.S. citizens. Applicant or parent must meet one or more of the following requirements: general military experience; retired from active duty; disabled or killed as a result of military service; prisoner of war; or missing in action.

Application Requirements: Application, essay, financial need analysis, references, test scores, transcript. *Deadline:* April 15.

Contact: Tiffany Kidd, National Programs Assistant
AMVETS National Headquarters
4647 Forbes Boulevard
Lanham, MD 20706-4380
Phone: 301-459-9600 Ext. 3043
Fax: 301-459-7924
E-mail: tkidd@amvets.org

ARKANSAS DEPARTMENT OF HIGHER EDUCATION http://www.arscholarships.com

MISSING IN ACTION/KILLED IN ACTION DEPENDENT'S SCHOLARSHIP-ARKANSAS

Available to Arkansas residents whose parent or spouse was classified either as missing in action, killed in action, or a prisoner-of-war. Must attend state-supported institution in Arkansas. Renewable waiver of tuition, fees, room and board. Submit proof of casualty.

Award: Scholarship for use in freshman, sophomore, junior, or senior years; renewable. *Amount:* up to $2500.

Eligibility Requirements: Applicant must be enrolled or expecting to enroll full-time at a two-year or four-year or technical institution or university; resident of Arkansas and studying in Arkansas. Available to U.S. citizens. Applicant or parent must meet one or more of the following requirements: general military experience; retired from active duty; disabled or killed as a result of military service; prisoner of war; or missing in action.

Application Requirements: Application, report of casualty. *Deadline:* Continuous.

Contact: Lillian K. Williams, Assistant Coordinator
Arkansas Department of Higher Education
114 East Capitol
Little Rock, AR 72201
Phone: 501-371-2050
Fax: 501-371-2001

ARMED SERVICES YMCA ESSAY CONTEST http://www.asymca.org

ARMED SERVICES YMCA ESSAY CONTEST

Up to $1000 in U.S. Savings Bonds will be awarded to winning essays from first to twelfth grade. Applicants must be the child of a member of the U.S. Armed Forces. Must be a U.S. citizen. For more information and contest guidelines visit this Web site: http://www.asymca.org. Application deadline is in March.

Award: Prize for use in freshman year; not renewable. *Number:* 14. *Amount:* $100–$1000.

Eligibility Requirements: Applicant must be high school student and planning to enroll or expecting to enroll at an institution or university. Available to U.S. citizens. Applicant or parent must meet one or more of the following requirements: general military experience; retired from active duty; disabled or killed as a result of military service; prisoner of war; or missing in action.

Application Requirements: Application, applicant must enter a contest, essay. *Deadline:* varies.

Contact: Karen Spooner, Office Manager
Armed Services YMCA Essay Contest
6359 Walker Lane, Suite 200
Alexandria, VA 22310
Phone: 703-313-9600
Fax: 703-313-9668
E-mail: kspooner@asymca.org

BLINDED VETERANS ASSOCIATION http://www.bva.org

KATHERN F. GRUBER SCHOLARSHIP

This award is available for undergraduate or graduate study to dependent children and spouses of legally blind veterans. The veteran's blindness may be either service or non-service connected. High school seniors may apply.

Applicant must be enrolled or accepted for admission as a full-time student in an accredited institution of higher learning, business, secretarial, or vocational school. Award is for one year; however, recipient may reapply and receive scholarship a maximum of four times.

Award: Scholarship for use in freshman, sophomore, junior, senior, or graduate years; not renewable. *Number:* 12. *Amount:* $1000–$2000.

Eligibility Requirements: Applicant must be enrolled or expecting to enroll full-time at a two-year or four-year or technical institution or university. Available to U.S. citizens. Applicant or parent must meet one or more of the following requirements: general military experience; retired from active duty; disabled or killed as a result of military service; prisoner of war; or missing in action.

Application Requirements: Application, essay, references, transcript. *Deadline:* April 16.

Contact: Brigitte Jones, Administrative Assistant
Blinded Veterans Association
477 H Street, NW
Washington, DC 20001-2694
Phone: 202-371-8880
Fax: 202-371-8258
E-mail: bva@bva.org

CONNECTICUT DEPARTMENT OF HIGHER EDUCATION http://www.ctdhe.org

CONNECTICUT TUITION WAIVER FOR VETERANS

Renewable tuition waiver for a Connecticut veteran to use at an accredited two-or four-year public institution in Connecticut. Military separation papers are required; see application for qualifications of service.

Award: Grant for use in freshman, sophomore, junior, or senior years; renewable. *Number:* varies. *Amount:* varies.

Eligibility Requirements: Applicant must be enrolled or expecting to enroll at a two-year or four-year institution; resident of Connecticut and studying in Connecticut. Applicant or parent must meet one or more of the following requirements: general military experience; retired from active duty; disabled or killed as a result of military service; prisoner of war; or missing in action.

Application Requirements: Application, financial need analysis, military discharge papers. *Deadline:* Continuous.

Contact: John Siegrist, Financial Aid Office
Connecticut Department of Higher Education
61 Woodland Street
Hartford, CT 06105-2326
Phone: 860-947-1855
Fax: 860-947-1311

DATATEL, INC. http://www.datatel.com/dsf

ANGELFIRE SCHOLARSHIP

For any student who is a 1964-1975 Vietnam Veteran, or spouse or child of same. Also available to refugees from Cambodia, Laos, or Vietnam. Applicant must attend a Datatel client institution. Completed on-line applications must be submitted by January 31.

Award: Scholarship for use in freshman, sophomore, junior, senior, or graduate years; not renewable. *Number:* 15. *Amount:* $1000–$2400.

Eligibility Requirements: Applicant must be enrolled or expecting to enroll full or part-time at a two-year or four-year or technical institution or university. Available to U.S. and non-U.S. citizens. Applicant or parent must meet one or more of the following requirements: general military experience; retired from active duty; disabled or killed as a result of military service; prisoner of war; or missing in action.

Application Requirements: Application, essay, references, transcript. *Deadline:* January 31.

Contact: Marissa Solis, Project Leader
Datatel, Inc.
4375 Fair Lakes Court
Fairfax, VA 22033
Phone: 800-486-4332
Fax: 703-968-4573
E-mail: scholars@datatel.com

DEFENSE COMMISSARY AGENCY http://www.commissaries.com

SCHOLARSHIPS FOR MILITARY CHILDREN

One-time award to unmarried dependents of military personnel for full-time undergraduate study at a four-year institution. Must be 23 years of age. Minimum 3.0 GPA. Application deadline is February 21. Further information and applications available at Web site http://www.militaryscholar.org.

Award: Scholarship for use in freshman, sophomore, junior, or senior years; not renewable. *Number:* varies. *Amount:* $1500.

Eligibility Requirements: Applicant must be age 23 or under; enrolled or expecting to enroll full-time at a four-year institution and single. Applicant must have 3.0 GPA or higher. Available to U.S. citizens. Applicant or parent must meet one or more of the following requirements: general military experience; retired from active duty; disabled or killed as a result of military service; prisoner of war; or missing in action.

Application Requirements: Application, essay, references, transcript, valid military dependent's identification card. *Deadline:* February 18.

Contact: Edna Hoogewind, Scholarship Liaison
Defense Commissary Agency
1300 E Avenue
Marketing Business Unit
Fort Lee, VA 23801-1800
Phone: 804-734-8410
Fax: 804-734-8617
E-mail: edna.hoogewind@deca.mil

DELAWARE HIGHER EDUCATION COMMISSION http://www.doe.state.de.us/high-ed

EDUCATIONAL BENEFITS FOR CHILDREN OF DECEASED MILITARY AND STATE POLICE

• *See page 508*

DEPARTMENT OF VETERANS AFFAIRS (VA) http://www.gibill.va.gov

MONTGOMERY GI BILL (ACTIVE DUTY) CHAPTER 30

MGIB provides up to 36 months of education benefits to eligible veterans for college, business school, technical courses, vocational courses, correspondence courses, apprenticeships/job training, or flight training. Must be an eligible veteran with an Honorable Discharge and have high school diploma or GED before applying for benefits. For more details on specific requirements see Web site: http://www.gibill.va.gov, or call 1-888-442-4551.

Award: Scholarship for use in freshman, sophomore, junior, senior, or postgraduate years; renewable. *Number:* varies. *Amount:* $35,460.

Eligibility Requirements: Applicant must be enrolled or expecting to enroll full or part-time at a two-year or four-year or technical institution or university. Available to U.S. citizens. Applicant must have general military experience.

Application Requirements: Application, active military service of at least 2 years. *Deadline:* Continuous.

Contact: Dennis B. Douglass, Acting Director, Education Service
Department of Veterans Affairs (VA)
810 Vermont Avenue, NW

Washington, DC 20420
Phone: 888-442-4551
E-mail: co225a@vba.va.gov

MONTGOMERY GI BILL (SELECTED RESERVE)

• *See page 535*

SURVIVORS AND DEPENDENTS EDUCATIONAL ASSISTANCE (CHAPTER 35)-VA

Monthly $695 benefits for up to 45 months. Must be spouses or children under age 26 of current veterans missing in action or of deceased or totally and permanently disabled (service-related) service persons. For more information call 1-888-442-4551 or visit Web site: http://www.gibill.va.gov.

Award: Scholarship for use in freshman, sophomore, junior, or senior years; renewable. *Number:* 10,733. *Amount:* up to $31,275.

Department of Veterans Affairs (VA) (continued)

Eligibility Requirements: Applicant must be age 25 or under and enrolled or expecting to enroll full or part-time at a two-year or four-year or technical institution or university. Available to U.S. and non-U.S. citizens. Applicant or parent must meet one or more of the following requirements: general military experience; retired from active duty; disabled or killed as a result of military service; prisoner of war; or missing in action.

Application Requirements: Application, parent or spouse must have had qualifying service. *Deadline:* Continuous.

Contact: Dennis B. Douglass, Acting Director, Education Service
Department of Veterans Affairs (VA)
810 Vermont Avenue, NW
Washington, DC 20420
Phone: 888-442-4551
E-mail: co225a@vba.va.gov

DEVRY, INC. http://www.devry.edu

DEVRY/KELLER MILITARY SERVICE GRANT

Grant is available to students called to active duty at a time which necessitates the interruption of studies during a term. The grant is available only to those students who resume their studies following their active duty service. Upon resuming their studies, students must provide written documentation of active duty service. The grant is to be used during the first term the student resumes.

Award: Grant for use in freshman, sophomore, junior, senior, or graduate years; not renewable. *Number:* varies. *Amount:* $7830.

Eligibility Requirements: Applicant must be enrolled or expecting to enroll full or part-time at an institution or university. Available to U.S. citizens. Applicant must have general military experience.

Application Requirements: Documentation of active duty service. *Deadline:* Continuous.

Contact: Kathy Facenda, Director of Student Finance Operations
DeVry, Inc.
One Tower Lane
Oakbrook Terrace, IL 60181-4624
Phone: 630-706-3141
Fax: 630-574-1963
E-mail: kfacenda@devry.com

EXPLOSIVE ORDNANCE DISPOSAL MEMORIAL COMMITTEE http://www.eodmemorial.org

EXPLOSIVE ORDNANCE DISPOSAL MEMORIAL SCHOLARSHIP

• *See page 508*

FLORIDA DEPARTMENT OF EDUCATION http://www.floridastudentfinancialaid.org

SCHOLARSHIPS FOR CHILDREN OF DECEASED OR DISABLED VETERANS OR CHILDREN OF SERVICEMEN CLASSIFIED AS POW OR MIA

Scholarship provides full tuition assistance for children of deceased or disabled veterans or of servicemen classified as POW or MIA who are in full-time attendance at eligible public or non-public Florida institutions. Service connection must be as specified under Florida statute. Amount of payment to non-public institutions is equal to cost at public institutions at the comparable level. Must be between 16 and 22. Qualified veteran and applicant must meet residency requirements.

Award: Scholarship for use in freshman, sophomore, junior, or senior years; renewable. *Number:* 160.

Eligibility Requirements: Applicant must be age 16-22; enrolled or expecting to enroll full-time at a two-year or four-year or technical institution or university; resident of Florida and studying in Florida. Available to U.S. citizens. Applicant or parent must meet one or more of the following requirements: general military experience; retired from active duty; disabled or killed as a result of military service; prisoner of war; or missing in action.

Application Requirements: Application, financial need analysis. *Deadline:* May 1.

Contact: Scholarship Information
Florida Department of Education
Office of Student Financial Assistance
1940 North Monroe, Suite 70
Tallahassee, FL 32303-4759
Phone: 888-827-2004
E-mail: osfa@fldoe.org

ILLINOIS DEPARTMENT OF VETERANS' AFFAIRS http://www.state.il.us/agency/dva

MIA/POW SCHOLARSHIPS

One-time award for spouse, child, or step-child of veterans who are missing in action or were a prisoner of war. Must be enrolled at a state-supported school in Illinois. Candidate must be U.S. citizen. Must apply and be accepted before beginning of school. Also for children and spouses of veterans who are determined to be 100% disabled as established by the Veterans Administration.

Award: Scholarship for use in freshman, sophomore, junior, senior, or graduate years; renewable. *Number:* varies. *Amount:* varies.

Eligibility Requirements: Applicant must be enrolled or expecting to enroll full or part-time at a two-year or four-year institution or university; resident of Illinois and studying in Illinois. Available to U.S. citizens. Applicant or parent must meet one or more of the following requirements: general military experience; retired from active duty; disabled or killed as a result of military service; prisoner of war; or missing in action.

Application Requirements: Application. *Deadline:* Continuous.

Contact: Ms. Tracy Mahan, Grants Section
Illinois Department of Veterans' Affairs
833 South Spring Street
Springfield, IL 62794-9432
Phone: 217-782-3564
Fax: 217-782-4161

VETERANS' CHILDREN EDUCATIONAL OPPORTUNITIES

Award is provided to each child age 18 or younger of a veteran who died or became totally disabled as a result of service during World War I, World War II, Korean, or Vietnam War. Must be an Illinois resident and studying in Illinois. Death must be service-connected. Disability must be rated 100% for two or more years.

Award: Grant for use in freshman year; not renewable. *Number:* varies. *Amount:* up to $250.

Eligibility Requirements: Applicant must be age 10-18; enrolled or expecting to enroll at an institution or university; resident of Illinois and studying in Illinois. Available to U.S. citizens. Applicant or parent must meet one or more of the following requirements: general military experience; retired from active duty; disabled or killed as a result of military service; prisoner of war; or missing in action.

Application Requirements: Application. *Deadline:* June 30.

Contact: Ms. Tracy Mahan, Grants Section
Illinois Department of Veterans' Affairs
833 South Spring Street
Springfield, IL 62794-9432
Phone: 217-782-3564
Fax: 217-782-4161

ILLINOIS STUDENT ASSISTANCE COMMISSION (ISAC) http://www.collegezone.org

ILLINOIS VETERAN GRANT PROGRAM - IVG

Award for qualified veterans for tuition and fees at Illinois public universities and community colleges. Must provide documentation of service (DD214). Deadline is continuous.

Award: Grant for use in freshman, sophomore, junior, senior, or graduate years; renewable. *Number:* 11,000–13,000. *Amount:* $1400–$1600.

Eligibility Requirements: Applicant must be enrolled or expecting to enroll full or part-time at a two-year or four-year institution or university; resident of Illinois and studying in Illinois. Available to U.S. citizens. Applicant must have general military experience.

Application Requirements: Application, documentation of service. *Deadline:* Continuous.

Contact: College Zone Counselor
Illinois Student Assistance Commission (ISAC)
1755 Lake Cook Road
Deerfield, IL 60015-5209
Phone: 800-899-4722
E-mail: collegezone@isac.org

INDIANA DEPARTMENT OF VETERANS' AFFAIRS http://www.ai.org/veteran/index.html

CHILD OF DISABLED VETERAN GRANT OR PURPLE HEART RECIPIENT GRANT

Free tuition at Indiana state-supported colleges or universities for children of disabled veterans or Purple Heart recipients. Must submit Form DD214 or service record.

Award: Grant for use in freshman, sophomore, junior, senior, graduate, or postgraduate years; renewable. *Number:* varies. *Amount:* varies.

Eligibility Requirements: Applicant must be enrolled or expecting to enroll full or part-time at a two-year or four-year institution or university; resident of Indiana and studying in Indiana. Available to U.S. citizens. Applicant or parent must meet one or more of the following requirements: general military experience; retired from active duty; disabled or killed as a result of military service; prisoner of war; or missing in action.

Application Requirements: Application. *Deadline:* Continuous.

Contact: Jon Brinkley, State Service Officer
Indiana Department of Veterans' Affairs
302 West Washington Street, Room E-120
Indianapolis, IN 46204-2738
Phone: 317-232-3910
Fax: 317-232-7721
E-mail: jbrinkley@dva.state.in.us

DEPARTMENT OF VETERANS AFFAIRS FREE TUITION FOR CHILDREN OF POW/MIA'S IN VIETNAM

Renewable award for residents of Indiana who are the children of veterans declared missing in action or prisoner-of-war after January 1, 1960. Provides tuition at Indiana state-supported institutions for undergraduate study.

Award: Grant for use in freshman, sophomore, junior, senior, graduate, or postgraduate years; renewable. *Number:* varies. *Amount:* varies.

Eligibility Requirements: Applicant must be enrolled or expecting to enroll at a two-year or four-year institution or university; resident of Indiana and studying in Indiana. Available to U.S. citizens. Applicant or parent must meet one or more of the following requirements: general military experience; retired from active duty; disabled or killed as a result of military service; prisoner of war; or missing in action.

Application Requirements: Application. *Deadline:* Continuous.

Contact: Jon Brinkley, State Service Officer
Indiana Department of Veterans' Affairs
302 West Washington Street, Room E-120
Indianapolis, IN 46204-2738
Phone: 317-232-3910
Fax: 317-232-7721
E-mail: jbrinkley@dva.state.in.us

KANSAS COMMISSION ON VETERANS AFFAIRS http://www.kcva.org

KANSAS EDUCATIONAL BENEFITS FOR CHILDREN OF MIA, POW, AND DECEASED VETERANS OF THE VIETNAM WAR

Full-tuition scholarship awarded to students who are children of veterans. Must show proof of parent's status as missing in action, prisoner-of-war, or killed in action in the Vietnam War. Kansas residence required of veteran at time of entry to service. Must attend a state-supported postsecondary school.

Award: Scholarship for use in freshman, sophomore, junior, or senior years; not renewable.

Eligibility Requirements: Applicant must be enrolled or expecting to enroll at a two-year or four-year or technical institution or university and studying in Kansas. Available to U.S. citizens. Applicant or parent must meet one or more of the following requirements: general military experience; retired from active duty; disabled or killed as a result of military service; prisoner of war; or missing in action.

Application Requirements: Application, report of casualty, birth certificate, school acceptance letter. *Deadline:* Continuous.

Contact: Tony Floyd, Program Director
Kansas Commission on Veterans Affairs
700 Southwest Jackson, Jayhawk Tower, #701
Topeka, KS 66603
Phone: 785-291-3422
Fax: 785-296-1462
E-mail: kcva004@ink.org

KENTUCKY DEPARTMENT OF VETERANS AFFAIRS http://www.lrc.state.ky.us

DEPARTMENT OF VA TUITION WAIVER-KY KRS 164-515

Award provides exemption from tuition for spouse or child of permanently disabled member of the National Guard, war veteran, prisoner of war, or member of the Armed Services missing in action. Disability must have been sustained while in service; if not, time of service must have been during wartime. Applicant is eligible for 36 months of training, training until receipt of degree, or training until 23rd birthday, whichever comes first. There is no age limit for spouse. Must attend a school funded by the KY Dept. of Ed. Veteran must be a resident of Kentucky or if deceased have been a resident. Also includes non-wartime veterans.

Award: Scholarship for use in freshman, sophomore, junior, or senior years; renewable. *Number:* varies.

Eligibility Requirements: Applicant must be enrolled or expecting to enroll full or part-time at a two-year or four-year or technical institution or university; resident of Kentucky and studying in Kentucky. Available to U.S. citizens. Applicant or parent must meet one or more of the following requirements: general military experience; retired from active duty; disabled or killed as a result of military service; prisoner of war; or missing in action.

Application Requirements: Application. *Deadline:* Continuous.

Contact: Jennifer Waddell, Administrative Specialist
Kentucky Department of Veterans Affairs
545 South 3rd Street, Room 123
Louisville, KY 40202
Phone: 502-595-4447
Fax: 502-595-4448
E-mail: jennifer.waddell@ky.gov

DEPARTMENT OF VETERANS AFFAIRS TUITION WAIVER-KENTUCKY KRS 164-505

Award provides exemption from matriculation or tuition fees for dependents, widows or widowers of members of the armed forces or members of the National Guard killed while in service or having died as a result of a service-connected disability incurred while serving during a wartime period. Veteran's home of record upon entry into the Armed Forces must have been KY. Applicant is eligible to get undergraduate/graduate degrees. Must attend a state-supported postsecondary institution in Kentucky.

Award: Scholarship for use in freshman, sophomore, junior, senior, or graduate years; renewable. *Number:* varies. *Amount:* varies.

Eligibility Requirements: Applicant must be enrolled or expecting to enroll full or part-time at a two-year or four-year or technical institution or university; resident of Kentucky and studying in Kentucky. Available to U.S. citizens. Applicant or parent must meet one or more of the following requirements: general military experience; retired from active duty; disabled or killed as a result of military service; prisoner of war; or missing in action.

Kentucky Department of Veterans Affairs (continued)

Application Requirements: Application, proof of relationship. *Deadline:* Continuous.

Contact: Jennifer Waddell, Administrative Specialist
Kentucky Department of Veterans Affairs
545 South 3rd Street, Room 123
Louisville, KY 40202
Phone: 502-595-4447
Fax: 502-595-4448
E-mail: jennifer.waddell@ky.gov

DEPARTMENT OF VETERANS AFFAIRS TUITION WAIVER-KY 164-512

Award provides waiver of tuition for child of a veteran, regardless of age, who has acquired a disability as a direct result of service, as a member of the National Guard or Reserve Component. Must have served on state active duty, active duty for training, inactive duty training, or active duty with the Armed Forces. Veteran must have been a resident of Kentucky. Must attend a state-supported post secondary institution in Kentucky.

Award: Scholarship for use in freshman, sophomore, junior, or senior years; renewable.

Eligibility Requirements: Applicant must be enrolled or expecting to enroll full-time at a two-year or four-year or technical institution or university; resident of Kentucky and studying in Kentucky. Available to U.S. citizens. Applicant or parent must meet one or more of the following requirements: general military experience; retired from active duty; disabled or killed as a result of military service; prisoner of war; or missing in action.

Application Requirements: Application, proof of relationship. *Deadline:* Continuous.

Contact: Jennifer Waddell, Administrative Specialist
Kentucky Department of Veterans Affairs
545 South 3rd Street, Room 123
Louisville, KY 40202
Phone: 502-595-4447
Fax: 502-595-4448
E-mail: jennifer.waddell@ky.gov

DEPARTMENT OF VETERANS AFFAIRS TUITION WAIVER-KY KRS 164-507

Award provides exemption from matriculation or tuition fee for spouse or child of deceased veteran who served during wartime. Applicant is eligible for 36 months of training, or training until they receive a degree, or training until their 23rd birthday, whichever comes first. There is no age limit for spouse. Must attend a Kentucky state-supported university, junior college or vocational training institution. Veteran must have been a resident of Kentucky at time of death or married to a resident of Kentucky.

Award: Scholarship for use in freshman, sophomore, junior, or senior years; renewable. *Number:* varies.

Eligibility Requirements: Applicant must be enrolled or expecting to enroll full or part-time at a two-year or four-year or technical institution or university; resident of Kentucky and studying in Kentucky. Available to U.S. citizens. Applicant or parent must meet one or more of the following requirements: general military experience; retired from active duty; disabled or killed as a result of military service; prisoner of war; or missing in action.

Application Requirements: Application. *Deadline:* Continuous.

Contact: Jennifer Waddell, Administrative Specialist
Kentucky Department of Veterans Affairs
545 South 3rd Street, Room 123
Louisville, KY 40202
Phone: 502-595-4447
Fax: 502-595-4448
E-mail: jennifer.waddell@ky.gov

LOUISIANA DEPARTMENT OF VETERAN AFFAIRS http://www.gov.state.la.us/depts/veteraaffairs.htm

LOUISIANA DEPARTMENT OF VETERANS AFFAIRS STATE AID PROGRAM

Tuition exemption at any state supported college, university, or technical institute for children (dependents between the ages of 18-25) of veterans that are rated 90% or above service connected disabled by the U.S. Department of Veterans Affairs. Tuition exemption also available for the surviving spouse and children (dependents between he ages of 18-25) of veterans who died on active duty, in line of duty, or where death was the result of a disability incurred in or aggravated by military service. For residents of Louisiana who are attending a Louisiana institution.

Award: Grant for use in freshman, sophomore, junior, senior, graduate, or postgraduate years; renewable. *Number:* varies. *Amount:* varies.

Eligibility Requirements: Applicant must be enrolled or expecting to enroll full-time at a two-year or four-year or technical institution or university; resident of Louisiana and studying in Louisiana. Available to U.S. citizens. Applicant or parent must meet one or more of the following requirements: general military experience; retired from active duty; disabled or killed as a result of military service; prisoner of war; or missing in action.

Application Requirements: Application. *Deadline:* Continuous.

Contact: Richard Blackwell, Veterans Affairs Regional Manager
Louisiana Department of Veteran Affairs
PO Box 94095
Capitol Station
Baton Rouge, LA 70804-4095
Phone: 225-922-0500 Ext. 203
Fax: 225-922-0511
E-mail: rblackwell@vetaffairs.com

MAINE BUREAU OF VETERANS SERVICES http://www.state.me.us

VETERANS DEPENDENTS EDUCATIONAL BENEFITS-MAINE

Tuition waiver award for dependents or spouses of veterans who were prisoners of war, missing in action, or permanently disabled as a result of service. Veteran must have been Maine resident at service entry for five years preceding application. For use at Maine University system, technical colleges and Maine Maritime. Must be high school graduate. Must submit birth certificate and proof of VA disability of veteran. Award renewable for eight semesters for those under 22 years of age.

Award: Scholarship for use in freshman, sophomore, junior, or senior years; renewable. *Number:* varies. *Amount:* varies.

Eligibility Requirements: Applicant must be age 21 or under; enrolled or expecting to enroll full or part-time at a technical institution or university; resident of Maine and studying in Maine. Available to U.S. citizens. Applicant or parent must meet one or more of the following requirements: general military experience; retired from active duty; disabled or killed as a result of military service; prisoner of war; or missing in action.

Application Requirements: Application. *Deadline:* Continuous.

Contact: Roland Lapointe, Director
Maine Bureau of Veterans Services
State House Station 117
Augusta, ME 04333-0117
Phone: 207-626-4464
Fax: 207-626-4471
E-mail: mvs@me.ngb.army.mil

MICHIGAN VETERANS TRUST FUND http://www.michigan.gov/dmva

MICHIGAN VETERANS TRUST FUND TUITION GRANT PROGRAM

Tuition grant of $2,800 for children of Michigan veterans who died on active duty or subsequently declared 100% disabled as the result of service-connected illness or injury. Must be 17 to 25 years old, be a Michigan resident, and attend a private or public institution in Michigan.

Award: Grant for use in freshman, sophomore, junior, or senior years; renewable. *Number:* varies. *Amount:* up to $2800.

Eligibility Requirements: Applicant must be age 17-25; enrolled or expecting to enroll full-time at a two-year or four-year or technical institution or university; resident of Michigan and studying in Michigan. Applicant or parent must meet one or more of the following requirements: general military experience; retired from active duty; disabled or killed as a result of military service; prisoner of war; or missing in action.

Application Requirements: Application. *Deadline:* Continuous.

Contact: Phyllis Ochis, Department of Military and Veterans Affairs
Michigan Veterans Trust Fund
2500 South Washington Avenue
Lansing, MI 48913
Phone: 517-483-5469

MILITARY OFFICERS ASSOCIATION OF AMERICA (MOAA) http://www.moaa.org

GENERAL JOHN RATAY EDUCATIONAL FUND GRANTS

Grants available to the children of the surviving spouse of retired officers. Must be under 24 years old and the child of a deceased retired officer who was a member of MOAA. For more details and an application go to Web site: http://www.moaa.org/education.

Award: Grant for use in freshman, sophomore, junior, or senior years; not renewable. *Number:* varies. *Amount:* $3750.

Eligibility Requirements: Applicant must be age 23 or under and enrolled or expecting to enroll full-time at a two-year or four-year or technical institution or university. Applicant must have 3.0 GPA or higher. Available to U.S. citizens. Applicant or parent must meet one or more of the following requirements: general military experience; retired from active duty; disabled or killed as a result of military service; prisoner of war; or missing in action.

Application Requirements: Application, financial need analysis, test scores, transcript. *Deadline:* March 1.

Contact: Application available at the Web site.

MOAA AMERICAN PATRIOT SCHOLARSHIP

Scholarship available to a student under 24 years old who is the child of a member of the uniformed services of the United States who died in active duty. For more details and an application go to Web site: http://www.moaa.org/education.

Award: Scholarship for use in freshman, sophomore, junior, or senior years; not renewable. *Number:* varies. *Amount:* $2500.

Eligibility Requirements: Applicant must be age 23 or under and enrolled or expecting to enroll full-time at a two-year or four-year institution or university. Available to U.S. citizens. Applicant or parent must meet one or more of the following requirements: general military experience; retired from active duty; disabled or killed as a result of military service; prisoner of war; or missing in action.

Application Requirements: Application, test scores, transcript. *Deadline:* March 1.

Contact: Application available at Web site.

MOAA BASE/POST SCHOLARSHIP

Recipients are randomly selected from dependent sons and daughters of active duty officers, members of the Drill and Reserve, National Guard, and enlisted military personnel. Eligible applicants will be under the age of 24. For more details and an application go to Web site: http://www.moaa.org/education.

Award: Scholarship for use in freshman, sophomore, junior, or senior years; not renewable. *Number:* 100. *Amount:* $1000.

Eligibility Requirements: Applicant must be age 23 or under and enrolled or expecting to enroll full-time at a two-year or four-year institution or university. Available to U.S. citizens. Applicant or parent must meet one or more of the following requirements: general military experience; retired from active duty; disabled or killed as a result of military service; prisoner of war; or missing in action.

Application Requirements: Application, test scores, transcript, service parent's Leave and Earning Statement (LES). *Deadline:* March 1.

Contact: Application available at Web site.

MILITARY ORDER OF THE PURPLE HEART http://www.purpleheart.org

MILITARY ORDER OF THE PURPLE HEART SCHOLARSHIP

Scholarship for children or grandchildren of Purple Heart recipients. Must submit essay, proof of full-time college registration, and proof of receipt of Purple Heart or membership in Order. Must be U.S. citizen and high school graduate with minimum GPA of 3.5. Contact for information.

Award: Scholarship for use in freshman, sophomore, junior, senior, graduate, or postgraduate years; not renewable. *Number:* 8. *Amount:* $1750.

Eligibility Requirements: Applicant must be enrolled or expecting to enroll full-time at a two-year or four-year or technical institution or university. Applicant must have 3.5 GPA or higher. Available to U.S. citizens. Applicant or parent must meet one or more of the following requirements: general military experience; retired from active duty; disabled or killed as a result of military service; prisoner of war; or missing in action.

Application Requirements: Application, essay, references, test scores, transcript, proof of receipt of Purple Heart or MOPH membership-copy of Birth Certificate. *Fee:* $5. *Deadline:* March 31.

Contact: Scholarship Coordinator
Military Order of the Purple Heart
5413-B Backlick Road
Springfield, VA 22151-3960
Phone: 703-642-5360
Fax: 703-642-2054
E-mail: info@purpleheart.org

MINNESOTA DEPARTMENT OF VETERANS' AFFAIRS

MINNESOTA EDUCATIONAL ASSISTANCE FOR WAR ORPHANS

War orphans may qualify for $750 per year. Must have lost parent through service-related death. Children of deceased veterans may qualify for free tuition at State university, college, or vocational or technical schools, but not at University of Minnesota. Must have been resident of Minnesota for at least two years.

Award: Grant for use in freshman, sophomore, junior, or senior years; renewable. *Number:* varies. *Amount:* $750.

Eligibility Requirements: Applicant must be enrolled or expecting to enroll full or part-time at a two-year or four-year or technical institution or university; resident of Minnesota and studying in Minnesota. Available to U.S. citizens. Applicant or parent must meet one or more of the following requirements: general military experience; retired from active duty; disabled or killed as a result of military service; prisoner of war; or missing in action.

Application Requirements: Application, financial need analysis. *Deadline:* Continuous.

Contact: Terrence Logan, Management Analyst IV
Minnesota Department of Veterans' Affairs
20 West 12th Street, Second Floor
St. Paul, MN 55155-2079
Phone: 651-296-2562
Fax: 651-296-3954

MINNESOTA VA EDUCATIONAL ASSISTANCE FOR VETERANS

One-time $750 stipend given to veterans who have used up all other federal funds, yet have time remaining on their delimiting period. Applicant must be a Minnesota resident and must be attending a Minnesota college or university, but not the University of Minnesota.

Award: Grant for use in freshman, sophomore, junior, or senior years; not renewable. *Number:* varies. *Amount:* $750.

Eligibility Requirements: Applicant must be enrolled or expecting to enroll full or part-time at a two-year or four-year or technical institution or university; resident of Minnesota and studying in Minnesota. Available to U.S. citizens. Applicant must have general military experience.

Application Requirements: Application, financial need analysis. *Deadline:* Continuous.

Contact: Terrence Logan, Management Analyst IV
Minnesota Department of Veterans' Affairs
20 West 12th Street, Second Floor
St. Paul, MN 55155-2079
Phone: 651-296-2562
Fax: 651-296-3954

MINNESOTA HIGHER EDUCATION SERVICES OFFICE
http://www.mheso.state.mn.us

MINNESOTA STATE VETERANS' DEPENDENTS ASSISTANCE PROGRAM

Tuition assistance to dependents of persons considered to be prisoner-of-war or missing in action after August 1, 1958. Must be Minnesota resident attending Minnesota two- or four-year school.

Award: Scholarship for use in freshman, sophomore, junior, or senior years; renewable. *Number:* varies. *Amount:* varies.

Eligibility Requirements: Applicant must be enrolled or expecting to enroll at a two-year or four-year institution; resident of Minnesota and studying in Minnesota. Available to U.S. citizens. Applicant or parent must meet one or more of the following requirements: general military experience; retired from active duty; disabled or killed as a result of military service; prisoner of war; or missing in action.

Application Requirements: Application. *Deadline:* Continuous.

Contact: Minnesota Higher Education Services Office
1450 Energy Park Drive, Suite 350
St. Paul, MN 55108-5227

NEW HAMPSHIRE POSTSECONDARY EDUCATION COMMISSION
http://www.state.nh.us/postsecondary

SCHOLARSHIPS FOR ORPHANS OF VETERANS-NEW HAMPSHIRE

Awards for New Hampshire residents whose parent died as a result of service in WWI, WWII, the Korean Conflict, or the Southeast Asian Conflict. Parent must have been a New Hampshire resident at time of death. Possible full tuition and $1000 per year with automatic renewal on reapplication. Contact department for application deadlines. Must be under 26. Must include proof of eligibility and proof of parent's death.

Award: Scholarship for use in freshman, sophomore, junior, or senior years; renewable. *Number:* 1–10. *Amount:* varies.

Eligibility Requirements: Applicant must be age 16-25; enrolled or expecting to enroll full-time at a two-year or four-year institution or university and resident of New Hampshire. Available to U.S. citizens. Applicant or parent must meet one or more of the following requirements: general military experience; retired from active duty; disabled or killed as a result of military service; prisoner of war; or missing in action.

Application Requirements: Application, VA approval. *Deadline:* varies.

Contact: Melanie K. Deshaies, Program Assistant
New Hampshire Postsecondary Education Commission
3 Barrell Court, Suite 300
Concord, NH 03301-8543
Phone: 603-271-2555 Ext. 356
Fax: 603-271-2696
E-mail: mdeshaies@pec.state.nh.us

NEW JERSEY DEPARTMENT OF MILITARY AND VETERANS AFFAIRS
http://www.state.nj.us/military

NEW JERSEY WAR ORPHANS TUITION ASSISTANCE

Renewable award for New Jersey residents who are high school seniors ages 16-21 and who are children of veterans killed or disabled in duty, missing in action, or prisoner-of-war. For use at a two- or four-year college or university. Write for more information. Deadlines: October 1 for fall semester and March 1 for spring semester.

Award: Scholarship for use in freshman, sophomore, junior, or senior years; renewable. *Number:* varies. *Amount:* $2000–$8000.

Eligibility Requirements: Applicant must be high school student; age 16-21; planning to enroll or expecting to enroll full-time at a two-year or four-year institution or university and resident of New Jersey. Applicant or parent must meet one or more of the following requirements: general military experience; retired from active duty; disabled or killed as a result of military service; prisoner of war; or missing in action.

Application Requirements: Application, transcript. *Deadline:* varies.

Contact: Patricia Richter, Grants Manager
New Jersey Department of Military and Veterans Affairs
PO Box 340
Trenton, NJ 08625-0340
Phone: 609-530-6854
Fax: 609-530-6970
E-mail: patricia.richter@njdmava.state.nj.us

TUITION ASSISTANCE FOR CHILDREN OF POW/MIAS

Assists children of military service personnel declared missing in action or prisoner-of-war after January 1, 1960. Must be a resident of New Jersey. Renewable grants provide tuition for undergraduate study in New Jersey. Apply by October 1 for fall, March 1 for spring. Must be high school senior to apply.

Award: Scholarship for use in freshman, sophomore, junior, or senior years; renewable. *Number:* varies. *Amount:* $500.

Eligibility Requirements: Applicant must be high school student; planning to enroll or expecting to enroll full-time at a two-year or four-year institution; resident of New Jersey and studying in New Jersey. Applicant must have 2.5 GPA or higher. Available to U.S. citizens. Applicant or parent must meet one or more of the following requirements: general military experience; retired from active duty; disabled or killed as a result of military service; prisoner of war; or missing in action.

Application Requirements: Application, transcript. *Deadline:* varies.

Contact: Patricia Richter, Grants Manager
New Jersey Department of Military and Veterans Affairs
PO Box 340
Trenton, NJ 08625-0340
Phone: 609-530-6854
Fax: 609-530-6970
E-mail: patricia.richter@njdmava.state.nj.us

VETERANS' TUITION CREDIT PROGRAM-NEW JERSEY

Award for veterans who served in the armed forces between December 31, 1960, and May 7, 1975. Must have been a New Jersey resident at time of induction or discharge or for one year prior to application. Apply by October 1 for fall, March 1 for spring. Renewable award of $200-$400.

Award: Scholarship for use in freshman, sophomore, junior, or senior years; renewable. *Number:* varies. *Amount:* $200–$400.

Eligibility Requirements: Applicant must be enrolled or expecting to enroll full or part-time at a two-year or four-year or technical institution or university. Available to U.S. citizens. Applicant must have general military experience.

Application Requirements: Application. *Deadline:* varies.

Contact: Patricia Richter, Grants Manager
New Jersey Department of Military and Veterans Affairs
PO Box 340
Trenton, NJ 08625-0340
Phone: 609-530-6854
Fax: 609-530-6970
E-mail: patricia.richter@njdmava.state.nj.us

NEW MEXICO COMMISSION ON HIGHER EDUCATION
http://www.nmche.org

VIETNAM VETERANS' SCHOLARSHIP PROGRAM

Award for New Mexico residents who are Vietnam veterans enrolled in undergraduate or master's-level course work at public or selected private New Mexico postsecondary institutions. Award may include tuition, required fees, and book allowance. Contact financial aid office of any public or eligible private New Mexico postsecondary institution for deadline.

Award: Scholarship for use in freshman, sophomore, junior, senior, or graduate years; not renewable.

Eligibility Requirements: Applicant must be enrolled or expecting to enroll full or part-time at a two-year or four-year institution; resident of New Mexico and studying in New Mexico. Available to U.S. citizens. Applicant must have general military experience.

Application Requirements: Application, certification by the NM Veteran's commission.

Contact: Maria Barele, Financial Specialist
New Mexico Commission on Higher Education
PO Box 15910
Santa Fe, NM 87506-5910
Phone: 505-827-4026
Fax: 505-827-7392

NEW MEXICO VETERANS' SERVICE COMMISSION http://www.state.nm.us/veterans

CHILDREN OF DECEASED VETERANS SCHOLARSHIP-NEW MEXICO

Award for New Mexico residents who are children of veterans killed or disabled as a result of service, prisoner-of-war, or veterans missing-in-action. Must be between ages 16 to 26. For use at New Mexico schools for undergraduate study. Submit parent's death certificate and DD form 214.

Award: Scholarship for use in freshman, sophomore, junior, or senior years; renewable. *Amount:* $250–$600.

Eligibility Requirements: Applicant must be age 16-26; enrolled or expecting to enroll full or part-time at an institution or university; resident of New Mexico and studying in New Mexico. Applicant or parent must meet one or more of the following requirements: general military experience; retired from active duty; disabled or killed as a result of military service; prisoner of war; or missing in action.

Application Requirements: Application, transcript. *Deadline:* Continuous.

Contact: Alan Martinez, Manager of State Benefits
New Mexico Veterans' Service Commission
PO Box 2324
Sante Fe, NM 87504
Phone: 505-827-6300
Fax: 505-827-6372

NEW MEXICO VIETNAM VETERANS' SCHOLARSHIP

Renewable award for Vietnam veterans who are New Mexico residents attending state-sponsored schools. Must have been awarded the Vietnam Campaign medal. Submit DD214. Must include discharge papers.

Award: Scholarship for use in freshman, sophomore, junior, or senior years; renewable. *Amount:* up to $1554.

Eligibility Requirements: Applicant must be enrolled or expecting to enroll at an institution or university; resident of New Mexico and studying in New Mexico. Available to U.S. citizens. Applicant must have general military experience.

Application Requirements: Application. *Deadline:* Continuous.

Contact: Alan Martinez, Manager State Benefits
New Mexico Veterans' Service Commission
PO Box 2324
Sante Fe, NM 87504
Phone: 505-827-6300
Fax: 505-827-6372

NEW YORK STATE HIGHER EDUCATION SERVICES CORPORATION http://www.hesc.org

REGENTS AWARD FOR CHILD OF VETERAN

Award for students whose parent, as a result of service in U.S. Armed Forces during war or national emergency, died; suffered a 40% or more disability; or is classified as missing in action or a prisoner of war. Veteran must be current New York State resident or have been so at time of death. Must be New York resident attending, or planning to attend, college in New York State. Must establish eligibility before applying for payment.

Award: Scholarship for use in freshman, sophomore, junior, or senior years; not renewable. *Number:* varies. *Amount:* $450.

Eligibility Requirements: Applicant must be enrolled or expecting to enroll full-time at a two-year or four-year institution or university; resident of New York and studying in New York. Available to U.S. citizens. Applicant or parent must meet one or more of the following requirements: general military experience; retired from active duty; disabled or killed as a result of military service; prisoner of war; or missing in action.

Application Requirements: Application, proof of eligibility. *Deadline:* May 1.

Contact: Student Information
New York State Higher Education Services Corporation
99 Washington Avenue, Room 1320
Albany, NY 12255

NORTH CAROLINA DIVISION OF VETERANS' AFFAIRS http://www.doa.state.nc.us/doa/vets/synopsis.htm

NORTH CAROLINA VETERANS' SCHOLARSHIPS CLASS I-A

Renewable awards for children of veterans who were killed or died in wartime service or died as a result of service-connected condition incurred in wartime service as defined in the law. Parent must have been a North Carolina resident at time of entry into service. Duration of the scholarship is four academic years (8 semesters) if used within 8 years. Free tuition, a room allowance, a board allowance, and exemption from certain mandatory fees as set forth in the law in Public, Community & Technical Colleges/Institutions. Award is $4500 per nine-month academic year in Private Colleges & Junior Colleges. No limit on number awarded each year. See Web site for details and where to procure an application.

Award: Scholarship for use in freshman, sophomore, junior, or senior years; renewable. *Number:* varies. *Amount:* varies.

Eligibility Requirements: Applicant must be enrolled or expecting to enroll full or part-time at a two-year or four-year or technical institution or university and studying in North Carolina. Available to U.S. citizens. Applicant or parent must meet one or more of the following requirements: general military experience; retired from active duty; disabled or killed as a result of military service; prisoner of war; or missing in action.

Application Requirements: Application, financial need analysis, interview, transcript. *Deadline:* Continuous.

Contact: Charles Smith, Director
North Carolina Division of Veterans' Affairs
325 North Salisbury Street
Raleigh, NC 27603
Phone: 919-733-3851
Fax: 919-733-2834

NORTH CAROLINA VETERANS' SCHOLARSHIPS CLASS I-B

Renewable awards for children of veterans rated by U.S. DVA as 100% disabled due to wartime service as defined in the law, and currently or at time of death drawing compensation for such disability. Parent must have been a North Carolina resident at time of entry into service. Duration of the scholarship is four academic years (8 semesters) if used within 8 years. Free tuition and exemption from certain mandatory fees as set forth in the law in Public, Community & Technical Colleges/Institutions. See Web site for details and where to procure an application. $1500 per nine month academic year in Private Colleges & Junior Colleges. No limit on number awarded each year.

Award: Scholarship for use in freshman, sophomore, junior, or senior years; renewable. *Number:* varies. *Amount:* varies.

Eligibility Requirements: Applicant must be enrolled or expecting to enroll full or part-time at a two-year or four-year or technical institution or university and studying in North Carolina. Available to U.S. citizens. Applicant or parent must meet one or more of the following requirements: general military experience; retired from active duty; disabled or killed as a result of military service; prisoner of war; or missing in action.

Application Requirements: Application, financial need analysis, interview, transcript. *Deadline:* Continuous.

Contact: Charles Smith, Director
North Carolina Division of Veterans' Affairs
325 North Salisbury Street
Raleigh, NC 27603
Phone: 919-733-3851
Fax: 919-733-2834

NORTH CAROLINA VETERANS' SCHOLARSHIPS CLASS II

Renewable awards for children of veterans rated by U.S. DVA as much as 20% but less than 100% disabled due to wartime service as defined in the law, or

North Carolina Division of Veterans' Affairs (continued)

awarded Purple Heart Medal for wounds received. Parent must have been a North Carolina resident at time of entry into service. Duration of the scholarship is four academic years (8 semesters) if used within 8 years. Free tuition and exemption from certain mandatory fees as set forth in the law in Public, Community & Technical Colleges/Institutions. See Web site for details and where to procure an application. $4500 per nine month academic year in Private Colleges & Junior Colleges. Up to 100 awarded each year. Deadline is March 31.

Award: Scholarship for use in freshman, sophomore, junior, or senior years; renewable. *Number:* up to 100. *Amount:* varies.

Eligibility Requirements: Applicant must be enrolled or expecting to enroll full or part-time at a two-year or four-year or technical institution or university and studying in North Carolina. Available to U.S. citizens. Applicant or parent must meet one or more of the following requirements: general military experience; retired from active duty; disabled or killed as a result of military service; prisoner of war; or missing in action.

Application Requirements: Application, financial need analysis, interview, transcript. *Deadline:* March 31.

Contact: Charles Smith, Director
North Carolina Division of Veterans' Affairs
325 North Salisbury Street
Raleigh, NC 27603
Phone: 919-733-3851
Fax: 919-733-2834

NORTH CAROLINA VETERANS' SCHOLARSHIPS CLASS III

Renewable awards for children of a veteran who died or was, at time of death, drawing a pension for total and permanent disability as rated by U.S. DVA, was honorably discharged and does not a qualify for Class I, II, or IV, scholarships, or served in a combat zone or waters adjacent to a combat zone and received a campaign badge or medal and does not qualify under Class I, II, IV, or V. Parent must have been a North Carolina resident at time of entry into service. Duration of the scholarship is four academic years (8 semesters) if used within eight years. Free tuition and exemption from certain mandatory fees as set forth in the law in Public, Community & Technical Colleges/Institutions. $4500 per nine month academic year in Private Colleges & Junior Colleges. See Web site for details and where to procure an application. Up to 100 awarded each year. Deadline is March 31.

Award: Scholarship for use in freshman, sophomore, junior, or senior years; renewable. *Number:* up to 100. *Amount:* varies.

Eligibility Requirements: Applicant must be enrolled or expecting to enroll full or part-time at a two-year or four-year or technical institution or university and studying in North Carolina. Available to U.S. citizens. Applicant or parent must meet one or more of the following requirements: general military experience; retired from active duty; disabled or killed as a result of military service; prisoner of war; or missing in action.

Application Requirements: Application, financial need analysis, interview, transcript. *Deadline:* March 31.

Contact: Charles Smith, Director
North Carolina Division of Veterans' Affairs
325 North Salisbury Street
Raleigh, NC 27603
Phone: 919-733-3851
Fax: 919-733-2834

NORTH CAROLINA VETERANS' SCHOLARSHIPS CLASS IV

Renewable awards for children of a veteran who was a POW or MIA. Parent must have been a North Carolina resident at time of entry into service. Duration of the scholarship is four academic years (8 semesters) if used within eight years. No limit on number awarded per year. The student receives free tuition, a room allowance, a board allowance, and exemption from certain mandatory fees as set forth in the law in public, community, and technical colleges or institutions. The scholarship is $4500 per nine-month academic year in private colleges and junior colleges.

Award: Scholarship for use in freshman, sophomore, junior, or senior years; renewable. *Number:* varies. *Amount:* varies.

Eligibility Requirements: Applicant must be enrolled or expecting to enroll full or part-time at a two-year or four-year or technical institution or university and studying in North Carolina. Available to U.S. citizens. Applicant or parent must meet one or more of the following requirements: general military experience; retired from active duty; disabled or killed as a result of military service; prisoner of war; or missing in action.

Application Requirements: Application, financial need analysis, interview, transcript. *Deadline:* March 31.

Contact: Charles Smith, Director
North Carolina Division of Veterans' Affairs
325 North Salisbury Street
Raleigh, NC 27603
Phone: 919-733-3851
Fax: 919-733-2834

NORTH CAROLINA VIETNAM VETERANS, INC. http://www.ncneighbors.com/96

NORTH CAROLINA VIETNAM VETERANS, INC., SCHOLARSHIP PROGRAM

Award of $500 for residents of Wake, Durham, Harnett, Chatham, Nash, Franklin, Johnson, Lee, or Granville counties in North Carolina who were awarded the Vietnam service medal, or for the spouse, child, dependent, or grandchild of a Vietnam veteran. Must submit personal statement and document community or high school activities and awards. Must reapply to renew award. Must write 400-600 word essay. Topic changes each year.

Award: Scholarship for use in freshman, sophomore, junior, or senior years; not renewable. *Number:* 4–10. *Amount:* $500.

Eligibility Requirements: Applicant must be enrolled or expecting to enroll full or part-time at a two-year or four-year or technical institution or university and resident of North Carolina. Available to U.S. and non-U.S. citizens. Applicant or parent must meet one or more of the following requirements: general military experience; retired from active duty; disabled or killed as a result of military service; prisoner of war; or missing in action.

Application Requirements: Application, essay, personal statement. *Deadline:* February 28.

Contact: Bud Gross, Board of Director and Scholarship Administrator
North Carolina Vietnam Veterans, Inc.
PO Box 10333
Raleigh, NC 27605
Fax: 919-785-0354
E-mail: nxcci@nc.rr.com

OHIO AMERICAN LEGION http://ohioamericanlegion.org

OHIO AMERICAN LEGION SCHOLARSHIPS

• *See page 474*

OHIO BOARD OF REGENTS http://www.regents.state.oh.us

OHIO MISSING IN ACTION AND PRISONERS OF WAR ORPHANS SCHOLARSHIP

Renewable award aids children of Vietnam conflict servicemen who have been classified as missing in action or prisoner of war. Must be an Ohio resident, be 16-21, and be enrolled full-time at an Ohio college. Full tuition awards.

Award: Scholarship for use in freshman, sophomore, junior, or senior years; renewable. *Number:* 1–5. *Amount:* varies.

Eligibility Requirements: Applicant must be age 16-21; enrolled or expecting to enroll full-time at a two-year or four-year institution; resident of Ohio and studying in Ohio. Available to U.S. citizens. Applicant or parent must meet one or more of the following requirements: general military experience; retired from active duty; disabled or killed as a result of military service; prisoner of war; or missing in action.

Application Requirements: Application. *Deadline:* July 1.

Contact: Sarina Wilks, Program Administrator
Ohio Board of Regents
PO Box 182452
Columbus, OH 43218-2452
Phone: 614-752-9528
Fax: 614-752-5903
E-mail: swilks@regents.state.oh.us

OHIO WAR ORPHANS SCHOLARSHIP

Aids Ohio residents attending an eligible college in Ohio. Must be between the ages of 16-21, the child of a disabled or deceased veteran, and enrolled full-time. Renewable up to five years. Amount of award varies. Must include Form DD214.

Award: Scholarship for use in freshman, sophomore, junior, or senior years; renewable. *Number:* 300–450. *Amount:* varies.

Eligibility Requirements: Applicant must be age 16-21; enrolled or expecting to enroll full-time at a two-year or four-year institution; resident of Ohio and studying in Ohio. Available to U.S. citizens. Applicant or parent must meet one or more of the following requirements: general military experience; retired from active duty; disabled or killed as a result of military service; prisoner of war; or missing in action.

Application Requirements: Application. *Deadline:* July 1.

Contact: Sarina Wilks, Program Administrator
Ohio Board of Regents
PO Box 182452
Columbus, OH 43218-2452
Phone: 614-752-9528
Fax: 614-752-5903
E-mail: swilks@regents.state.oh.us

OREGON DEPARTMENT OF VETERANS' AFFAIRS http://www.odva.state.or.us

OREGON VETERANS' EDUCATION AID

To be eligible, veteran must have served in U.S. armed forces 90 days and been discharged under honorable conditions; U.S. citizen and Oregon resident; Korean War veteran or received campaign or expeditionary medal or ribbon awarded by U.S. armed forces for services after June 30, 1958. Full-time students receive $50/month, part-time students receive $35/month.

Award: Grant for use in freshman, sophomore, junior, senior, graduate, or postgraduate years; renewable. *Number:* varies. *Amount:* varies.

Eligibility Requirements: Applicant must be enrolled or expecting to enroll full or part-time at a two-year or four-year or technical institution or university; resident of Oregon and studying in Oregon. Available to U.S. citizens. Applicant must have general military experience.

Application Requirements: Application, certified copy of DD Form 214. *Deadline:* Continuous.

Contact: Ruth Sherman, Educational Aid Coordinator
Oregon Department of Veterans' Affairs
700 Summer Street, NE
Salem, OR 97301-1289
Phone: 503-373-2085
Fax: 503-373-2392
E-mail: shermar@odva.state.or.us

OREGON STUDENT ASSISTANCE COMMISSION http://www.osac.state.or.us

AMERICAN EX-PRISONER OF WAR SCHOLARSHIPS: PETER CONNACHER MEMORIAL SCHOLARSHIP

Renewable award for American prisoners-of-war and their descendants. Written proof of prisoner-of-war status and discharge papers from the U.S. Armed Forces must accompany application. Statement of relationship between applicant and former prisoner-of-war is required. See Web site at http://www.osac.state.or.us for details.

Award: Scholarship for use in freshman, sophomore, junior, or senior years; renewable. *Number:* 4. *Amount:* $1150.

Eligibility Requirements: Applicant must be enrolled or expecting to enroll at a two-year or four-year institution and resident of Oregon. Available to U.S. citizens. Applicant or parent must meet one or more of the following requirements: general military experience; retired from active duty; disabled or killed as a result of military service; prisoner of war; or missing in action.

Application Requirements: Application, essay, financial need analysis, transcript. *Deadline:* March 1.

Contact: Director of Grant Programs
Oregon Student Assistance Commission
1500 Valley River Drive, Suite 100
Eugene, OR 97401-7020
Phone: 800-452-8807 Ext. 7395
E-mail: awardinfo@mercury.osac.state.or.us

MARIA JACKSON/GENERAL GEORGE A. WHITE SCHOLARSHIP

Available to Oregon residents who served or whose parents serve or have served in the U.S. Armed Forces and resided in Oregon at time of enlistment. Must have at least 3.75 GPA and submit documentation of service. For use at Oregon colleges only. U.S. Bancorp employees, their children or close relatives, not eligible.

Award: Scholarship for use in freshman, sophomore, junior, or senior years; not renewable. *Number:* 54. *Amount:* $622.

Eligibility Requirements: Applicant must be enrolled or expecting to enroll full-time at a two-year or four-year institution; resident of Oregon and studying in Oregon. Available to U.S. citizens. Applicant or parent must meet one or more of the following requirements: general military experience; retired from active duty; disabled or killed as a result of military service; prisoner of war; or missing in action.

Application Requirements: Application, essay, financial need analysis, test scores, transcript, documentation of service. *Deadline:* March 1.

Contact: Director of Grant Programs
Oregon Student Assistance Commission
1500 Valley River Drive, Suite 100
Eugene, OR 97401-7020
Phone: 800-452-8807 Ext. 7395
E-mail: awardinfo@mercury.osac.state.or.us

PENNSYLVANIA BUREAU FOR VETERANS AFFAIRS http://sites.state.pa.us/PA_Exec/Military_Affairs/va/

EDUCATIONAL GRATUITY PROGRAM

This program is for eligible dependents of 100% disabled or deceased veteran whose disability was incurred during a period of war or armed conflict. Must be a Pennsylvania resident attending a Pennsylvania school. Up to $500 per semester may be awarded.

Award: Grant for use in freshman, sophomore, junior, or senior years; renewable. *Number:* varies. *Amount:* varies.

Eligibility Requirements: Applicant must be age 16-23; enrolled or expecting to enroll full-time at a two-year or four-year or technical institution or university; resident of Pennsylvania and studying in Pennsylvania. Available to U.S. citizens. Applicant or parent must meet one or more of the following requirements: general military experience; retired from active duty; disabled or killed as a result of military service; prisoner of war; or missing in action.

Application Requirements: Application, driver's license, financial need analysis, transcript. *Deadline:* Continuous.

Contact: Michelle Zimmerman, Clerk Typist
Pennsylvania Bureau for Veterans Affairs
Building 0-47
Fort Indiantown Gap
Annville, PA 17003-5002
Phone: 717-861-8910
Fax: 717-861-8589
E-mail: michzimmer@state.pa.us

PENNSYLVANIA HIGHER EDUCATION ASSISTANCE AGENCY http://www.pheaa.org

VETERANS GRANT-PENNSYLVANIA

Renewable awards for Pennsylvania residents who are qualified veterans attending an approved undergraduate program full-time. Up to $3300 for in-state study or $800 for out-of-state study. Deadlines: May 1 for all renewal applicants, new applicants who plan to enroll in an undergraduate baccalaureate degree program, and those in college transfer programs at two-year public or junior colleges; August 1 for all first-time applicants who

Pennsylvania Higher Education Assistance Agency (continued)

plan to enroll in a business, trade, or technical school; a hospital school of nursing; or a two-year terminal program at a community, junior, or four-year college.

Award: Grant for use in freshman, sophomore, junior, or senior years; renewable. *Number:* varies. *Amount:* $800–$3300.

Eligibility Requirements: Applicant must be enrolled or expecting to enroll full-time at a two-year or four-year or technical institution or university and resident of Pennsylvania. Available to U.S. citizens. Applicant must have general military experience.

Application Requirements: Application. *Deadline:* varies.

Contact: Keith New, Director of Communications and Press Office
Pennsylvania Higher Education Assistance Agency
1200 North Seventh Street
Harrisburg, PA 17102-1444
Phone: 717-720-2509
Fax: 717-720-3903
E-mail: knew@pheaa.org

RED RIVER VALLEY ASSOCIATION, INC.

http://www.river-rats.org

RED RIVER VALLEY ASSOCIATION SCHOLARSHIP GRANT PROGRAM

Annual college tuition grants for legal dependents of U.S. military members listed as Killed in Action or Missing in Action; or of military aircrew members killed while performing aircrew duties on non-combat missions. Must submit DD Form 1300. Amount of award varies.

Award: Grant for use in freshman, sophomore, junior, senior, or graduate years; not renewable. *Number:* 10–40. *Amount:* $500–$4000.

Eligibility Requirements: Applicant must be enrolled or expecting to enroll full or part-time at a two-year or four-year or technical institution or university. Available to U.S. citizens. Applicant or parent must meet one or more of the following requirements: general military experience; retired from active duty; disabled or killed as a result of military service; prisoner of war; or missing in action.

Application Requirements: Application, financial need analysis, photo, references, test scores, transcript. *Deadline:* May 15.

Contact: Col. Al Bache, Executive Director
Red River Valley Association, Inc.
PO Box 1916
Harrisonburg, VA 22801
Phone: 540-442-7782
Fax: 540-433-3105
E-mail: afbridger@aol.com

RESERVE OFFICERS ASSOCIATION OF THE US

http://www.roa.org

HENRY J. REILLY MEMORIAL SCHOLARSHIP-HIGH SCHOOL SENIORS AND FIRST YEAR FRESHMEN

• *See page 479*

HENRY J. REILLY MEMORIAL UNDERGRADUATE SCHOLARSHIP PROGRAM FOR COLLEGE ATTENDEES

• *See page 479*

RETIRED ENLISTED ASSOCIATION

http://www.trea.org

RETIRED ENLISTED ASSOCIATION SCHOLARSHIP

One-time award for dependent children or grandchildren of a TREA or TREA Auxiliary member in good standing.

Award: Scholarship for use in freshman, sophomore, junior, or senior years; not renewable. *Number:* 42. *Amount:* $1000–$1500.

Eligibility Requirements: Applicant must be enrolled or expecting to enroll full-time at a two-year or four-year or technical institution or university. Available to U.S. and non-U.S. citizens. Applicant or parent must meet one or more of the following requirements: general military experience; retired from active duty; disabled or killed as a result of military service; prisoner of war; or missing in action.

Application Requirements: Application, essay, financial need analysis, photo, references, test scores, transcript, copies of IRS tax forms. *Deadline:* April 30.

Contact: Donnell Minnis, Executive Assistant
Retired Enlisted Association
Attn: National Scholarship Committee
1111 South Abilene Court
Aurora, CO 80012-4909
Phone: 303-752-0660
Fax: 303-752-0835
E-mail: execasst@trea.org

SOUTH CAROLINA DIVISION OF VETERANS AFFAIRS

EDUCATIONAL ASSISTANCE FOR CERTAIN WAR VETERAN'S DEPENDENTS- SOUTH CAROLINA

Renewable aid to South Carolina Disabled Veterans' dependents under age 26. Veterans must have had wartime service in World War II, the Vietnam War, Persian Gulf or the Korean War. Must have received the Purple Heart or Medal of Honor. Applicant must show DD214 (birth certificate and VA rating). For undergraduate study at any South Carolina state-supported college. Must be South Carolina resident.

Award: Scholarship for use in freshman, sophomore, junior, or senior years; renewable. *Number:* varies. *Amount:* varies.

Eligibility Requirements: Applicant must be age 18-25; enrolled or expecting to enroll full or part-time at a two-year or four-year or technical institution or university; resident of South Carolina and studying in South Carolina. Available to U.S. citizens. Applicant or parent must meet one or more of the following requirements: general military experience; retired from active duty; disabled or killed as a result of military service; prisoner of war; or missing in action.

Application Requirements: Application. *Deadline:* Continuous.

Contact: Ms. Lauren Hugg, Free Tuition Assistant
South Carolina Division of Veterans Affairs
1801 Assembly Street, Room 141
Columbia, SC 29201
Phone: 803-255-4317
Fax: 803-255-4257

SOUTH DAKOTA BOARD OF REGENTS

http://www.ris.sdbor.edu

EDUCATION BENEFITS FOR DEPENDENTS OF POWS AND MIAS

Children and spouses of prisoners of war, or of persons listed as missing in action, are entitled to attend a state-supported school without the payment of tuition or mandatory fees provided they are not eligible for equal or greater federal benefits. Must use SDDVA form E-12 available at financial aid offices. Must be a South Dakota resident intending to study in South Dakota.

Award: Scholarship for use in freshman, sophomore, junior, or senior years; not renewable. *Number:* varies. *Amount:* varies.

Eligibility Requirements: Applicant must be enrolled or expecting to enroll at an institution or university; resident of South Dakota and studying in South Dakota. Available to U.S. citizens. Applicant or parent must meet one or more of the following requirements: general military experience; retired from active duty; disabled or killed as a result of military service; prisoner of war; or missing in action.

Application Requirements: Application. *Deadline:* varies.

Contact: Dr. Lesta Turchen, Senior Administrator
South Dakota Board of Regents
306 East Capitol Avenue
Suite 200
Pierre, SD 57501-3159
Phone: 605-773-3455
Fax: 605-773-2422
E-mail: info@sdbor.edu

SOUTH DAKOTA AID TO DEPENDENTS OF DECEASED VETERANS

Program provides free tuition for children of deceased veterans who are under the age of 25, are residents of South Dakota, and whose mother or father was killed in action or died of other causes while on active duty. ("Veteran" for this purpose is as defined by South Dakota Codified Laws.) Parent must have been a bona fide resident of SD for at least six months immediately preceding entry into active service. Eligibility is for state-supported schools only. Must use SDDVA form E-12 available at financial aid offices.

Award: Scholarship for use in freshman, sophomore, junior, or senior years; not renewable. *Number:* varies. *Amount:* varies.

Eligibility Requirements: Applicant must be age 24 or under; enrolled or expecting to enroll at a two-year or four-year institution; resident of South Dakota and studying in South Dakota. Available to U.S. citizens. Applicant or parent must meet one or more of the following requirements: general military experience; retired from active duty; disabled or killed as a result of military service; prisoner of war; or missing in action.

Application Requirements: Application. *Deadline:* varies.

Contact: Dr. Lesta Turchen, Senior Administrator
South Dakota Board of Regents
306 East Capitol Avenue
Suite 200
Pierre, SD 57501-3159
Phone: 605-773-3455
Fax: 605-773-2422
E-mail: info@sdbor.edu

SOUTH DAKOTA EDUCATION BENEFITS FOR VETERANS

Certain veterans are eligible for free undergraduate tuition assistance at state-supported schools provided they are not eligible for educational payments under the GI Bill or any other federal educational program. Contact financial aid office for full details and forms. May receive one month of free tuition for each month of qualifying service (minimum one year, maximum four years). Must be resident of South Dakota.

Award: Scholarship for use in freshman, sophomore, junior, or senior years; not renewable. *Number:* varies. *Amount:* varies.

Eligibility Requirements: Applicant must be enrolled or expecting to enroll at an institution or university; resident of South Dakota and studying in South Dakota. Available to U.S. citizens. Applicant must have general military experience.

Application Requirements: Application, DD Form 214. *Deadline:* varies.

Contact: Dr. Lesta Turchen, Senior Administrator
South Dakota Board of Regents
306 East Capitol Avenue
Suite 200
Pierre, SD 57501-3159
Phone: 605-773-3455
Fax: 605-773-2422
E-mail: info@sdbor.edu

STATE OF WYOMING, ADMINISTERED BY UNIVERSITY OF WYOMING http://www.uwyo.edu/scholarships

VIETNAM VETERANS AWARD/WYOMING

Available to Wyoming residents who served in the armed forces between August 5, 1964, and May 7, 1975, and received a Vietnam service medal. Award is free tuition at the University of Wyoming or a state (WY) community college.

Award: Scholarship for use in freshman, sophomore, junior, or senior years; renewable. *Number:* varies. *Amount:* varies.

Eligibility Requirements: Applicant must be enrolled or expecting to enroll full or part-time at a two-year or four-year institution or university; resident of Wyoming and studying in Wyoming. Available to U.S. citizens. Applicant must have general military experience.

Application Requirements: Application. *Deadline:* Continuous.

Contact: Joel Anne Berrigan, Assistant Director, Scholarships
State of Wyoming, administered by University of Wyoming
Student Financial Aid, Department 3335, 1000 East University Avenue
Laramie, WY 82071-3335
Phone: 307-766-2117
Fax: 307-766-3800
E-mail: finaid@uwyo.edu

TET '68 SCHOLARSHIP http://www.tet68.org/TET68sch.html

CHILDREN OF VIETNAM VETERANS SCHOLARSHIP FUND

Scholarships are given to graduating high school seniors who are citizens of the U.S., Canada, and Australia who are dependents of a Vietnam Veteran. Applicants must submit an essay "What is Freedom?". Must submit DD Form 214 showing prior service in the military. More information can be found at http://www.tet68.org/TET68sch.html.

Award: Scholarship for use in freshman year; not renewable. *Number:* 3–5. *Amount:* $1000.

Eligibility Requirements: Applicant must be high school student and planning to enroll or expecting to enroll full or part-time at a two-year or four-year or technical institution or university. Available to U.S. and non-U.S. citizens. Applicant or parent must meet one or more of the following requirements: general military experience; retired from active duty; disabled or killed as a result of military service; prisoner of war; or missing in action.

Application Requirements: Applicant must enter a contest, essay, DD Form 214. *Deadline:* March 30.

Contact: William Kirkland, Scholarship Competition
Tet '68 Scholarship
PO Box 31885
Richmond, VA 23229
Phone: 804-550-3692
E-mail: tet68info@aol.com

TEXAS HIGHER EDUCATION COORDINATING BOARD http://www.collegefortexans.com

MILITARY STATIONED IN TEXAS WAIVER

Award provides tuition waiver for nonresident military personnel stationed in Texas. Limited to public institutions only. Contact financial aid office at college for deadline and application.

Award: Scholarship for use in freshman, sophomore, junior, or senior years; not renewable. *Number:* varies. *Amount:* varies.

Eligibility Requirements: Applicant must be enrolled or expecting to enroll at an institution or university and studying in Texas. Applicant must have general military experience.

Application Requirements: Application. *Deadline:* varies.

Contact: Financial Aid Office at college
Texas Higher Education Coordinating Board
PO Box 12788
Austin, TX 78711-2788
Phone: 512-427-6101
Fax: 512-427-6127
E-mail: grantinfo@thecb.state.tx.us

TUITION AND FEE EXEMPTION FOR CHILDREN OF PRISONERS OF WAR OR PERSONS MISSING IN ACTION-TEXAS

Renewable award assists children of prisoners of war or veterans classified as missing in action. Must be a Texas resident and attend a public college or university within Texas. Submit proof of service and proof of MIA/POW status. Award is exemption from tuition and fees. Must be under 21 years of age. Contact the admissions/registrar's office for application information.

Award: Scholarship for use in freshman, sophomore, junior, or senior years; renewable. *Number:* varies. *Amount:* varies.

Eligibility Requirements: Applicant must be age 20 or under; enrolled or expecting to enroll at a two-year or four-year or technical institution or university; resident of Texas and studying in Texas. Applicant or parent must meet one or more of the following requirements: general military experience; retired from active duty; disabled or killed as a result of military service; prisoner of war; or missing in action.

Application Requirements: Application, proof of service and MIA/POW status. *Deadline:* Continuous.

Contact: Financial Aid Office at college
Texas Higher Education Coordinating Board
PO Box 12788
Austin, TX 78711-2788
Phone: 512-427-6101
Fax: 512-427-6127
E-mail: grantinfo@thecb.state.tx.us

TUITION EXEMPTIONS FOR TEXAS VETERANS (HAZELWOOD ACT)

Renewable tuition and partial fee exemptions for Texas veterans who have been honorably discharged after at least 180 days of active duty. Must be a Texas resident at time of entry into service. Must have exhausted federal education benefits. Contact the admissions/registrar's office for information on how to apply. Must be used at a Texas public institution.

Award: Scholarship for use in freshman, sophomore, junior, or senior years; renewable. *Number:* varies. *Amount:* $980.

Eligibility Requirements: Applicant must be enrolled or expecting to enroll full or part-time at a two-year or four-year or technical institution or university; resident of Texas and studying in Texas. Available to U.S. citizens. Applicant or parent must meet one or more of the following requirements: general military experience; retired from active duty; disabled or killed as a result of military service; prisoner of war; or missing in action.

Application Requirements: Application. *Deadline:* Continuous.

Contact: Financial Aid Office at college
Texas Higher Education Coordinating Board
PO Box 12788
Austin, TX 78711-2788
Phone: 512-427-6101
Fax: 512-427-6127
E-mail: grantinfo@thecb.state.tx.us

V.E.T.S. - VICTORY ENSURED THROUGH SERVICE

V.E.T.S. ANNUAL SCHOLARSHIP

Scholarships for graduating high school seniors, junior college students, continuing university (college) students, graduate students, and vocational school students. Applicants must be a veteran, or a spouse, child, grandchild of a veteran and be a U.S. citizen. Must have maintained a 3.0 grade point average with no failing grades in any subject. Amount awarded is usually $500, but Board of Directors can grant special scholarships up to $1500 based on need and qualifications. Must apply by April 1 of every year, open only to residents of California, Arizona, and Washington.

Award: Scholarship for use in freshman, sophomore, junior, senior, graduate, or postgraduate years; not renewable. *Number:* 6. *Amount:* $500–$1500.

Eligibility Requirements: Applicant must be enrolled or expecting to enroll full-time at a two-year or four-year or technical institution or university and resident of Arizona, California, or Washington. Applicant must have 3.0 GPA or higher. Available to U.S. citizens. Applicant or parent must meet one or more of the following requirements: general military experience; retired from active duty; disabled or killed as a result of military service; prisoner of war; or missing in action.

Application Requirements: Application, financial need analysis, photo, references, test scores, transcript, DD Form 214 or military discharge "Honorable". *Deadline:* April 1.

Contact: Candace Filek, Scholarship Chair
V.E.T.S. - Victory Ensured Through Service
8698 Midview Drive
Palo Cedro, CA 96073
Phone: 530-547-3776

VETERANS OF FOREIGN WARS OF THE UNITED STATES http://www.vfw.org

VETERAN'S TRIBUTE SCHOLARSHIP

Award available to children of all United States military veterans, active duty, Reserves, and National Guard. Further information and application can be found on Web site http://www.vfw.org.

Award: Scholarship for use in freshman year; not renewable. *Number:* up to 3. *Amount:* $3000–$10,000.

Eligibility Requirements: Applicant must be age 16-18 and enrolled or expecting to enroll at an institution or university. Available to U.S. citizens. Applicant or parent must meet one or more of the following requirements: general military experience; retired from active duty; disabled or killed as a result of military service; prisoner of war; or missing in action.

Application Requirements: Application, transcript, DD Form 214, documentation of community service. *Deadline:* December 31.

Contact: Veterans' Tribute Scholarship/VFW National Headquarters
Veterans of Foreign Wars of the United States
406 West 34th Street, Suite 902
Kansas City, MO 64111
E-mail: swilson@vfw.org

VIRGINIA DEPARTMENT OF VETERANS SERVICES http://www.vdva.vipnet.org/education_benefits.htm

VIRGINIA WAR ORPHANS EDUCATION PROGRAM

Scholarships for postsecondary students between ages 16 and 25 to attend Virginia state supported institutions. Must be child or surviving child of veteran who has either: 1. been permanently or totally disabled due to war or other armed conflict; 2. died as a result of war or other armed conflict; or 3. been listed as a POW or MIA. Parent must also meet Virginia residency requirements. Contact for application procedures and deadline.

Award: Scholarship for use in freshman, sophomore, junior, senior, or graduate years; renewable. *Number:* varies.

Eligibility Requirements: Applicant must be age 16-25; enrolled or expecting to enroll full-time at a two-year or four-year or technical institution or university; resident of Virginia and studying in Virginia. Available to U.S. citizens. Applicant or parent must meet one or more of the following requirements: general military experience; retired from active duty; disabled or killed as a result of military service; prisoner of war; or missing in action.

Application Requirements: Application. *Deadline:* varies.

Contact: Colbert Longworth Boyd, Chief Deputy Commissioner
Virginia Department of Veterans Services
Poff Federal Building, 270 Franklin Road SW, Room 503
Roanoke, VA 24011-2215
Phone: 540-857-7101 Ext. 213
Fax: 540-857-7573

WEST VIRGINIA DIVISION OF VETERANS' AFFAIRS http://www.state.wv.us/va

WEST VIRGINIA DIVISION OF VETERANS' AFFAIRS WAR ORPHANS EDUCATION PROGRAM

Renewable waiver of tuition award for West Virginia residents who are children of deceased veterans. Parent must have died of war related service-connected disability. Must be ages 16-23. Minimum 2.0 GPA required. Must attend a state-supported West Virginia postsecondary institution. Deadline: July 1 and December 1.

Award: Scholarship for use in freshman, sophomore, junior, senior, or graduate years; renewable. *Number:* varies. *Amount:* varies.

Eligibility Requirements: Applicant must be age 16-23; enrolled or expecting to enroll full or part-time at a two-year or four-year or technical institution or university; resident of West Virginia and studying in West Virginia. Available to U.S. citizens. Applicant or parent must meet one or more of the following requirements: general military experience; retired from active duty; disabled or killed as a result of military service; prisoner of war; or missing in action.

Application Requirements: Application, references. *Deadline:* varies.

Contact: Ms. Linda Walker, Administrative Secretary
West Virginia Division of Veterans' Affairs
1321 Plaza East, Suite 101
Charleston, WV 25301-1400
Phone: 304-558-3661
Fax: 304-558-3662
E-mail: wvdva@state.wv.us

WINSTON-SALEM FOUNDATION http://www.wsfoundation.org

MARY ROWENA COOPER SCHOLARSHIP FUND

Purpose is to provide need-based financial aid for students seeking degrees, certificates, or diplomas at vocational schools, technical schools, community colleges, and universities and colleges. Preference for applicants is: orphaned children of Vietnam vets of any service unit designation and, next, children not orphaned whose parent(s) served in the military during the Vietnam conflict. The fund has particular interest in, though is not restricted to, assisting students going into medicine, law, engineering and teaching. Application fee is $20.

Award: Scholarship for use in freshman, sophomore, junior, senior, or graduate years; not renewable. *Number:* varies. *Amount:* up to $2500.

Eligibility Requirements: Applicant must be enrolled or expecting to enroll full-time at a two-year or four-year or technical institution or university. Available to U.S. citizens. Applicant or parent must meet one or more of the following requirements: general military experience; retired from active duty; disabled or killed as a result of military service; prisoner of war; or missing in action.

Application Requirements: Application, financial need analysis, interview, transcript. *Fee:* $20. *Deadline:* Continuous.

Contact: Kay Dillon, Student Aid Director
Winston-Salem Foundation
860 West Fifth Street
Winston-Salem, NC 27101
Phone: 336-725-2382
Fax: 336-727-0581
E-mail: kdillon@wsfoundation.org

WISCONSIN DEPARTMENT OF VETERANS AFFAIRS http://dva.state.wi.us

TUITION AND FEE REIMBURSEMENT GRANTS

Up to 100% tuition and fee reimbursement for Wisconsin veterans who were discharged from active duty within the last 10 years. Undergraduate courses must be completed at accredited Wisconsin schools. Those attending Minnesota public colleges, universities, and technical schools that have a tuition reciprocity agreement with Wisconsin also may qualify. Must meet military service requirements. Application must be received no later than 60 days after the completion of the course.

Award: Grant for use in freshman, sophomore, junior, or senior years; renewable. *Number:* varies. *Amount:* varies.

Eligibility Requirements: Applicant must be enrolled or expecting to enroll full-time at a two-year or four-year or technical institution or university; resident of Wisconsin and studying in Minnesota or Wisconsin. Available to U.S. citizens. Applicant must have general military experience.

Application Requirements: Application. *Deadline:* varies.

Contact: Mike Keatley, Grants Coordinator
Wisconsin Department of Veterans Affairs
PO Box 7843
Madison, WI 53707-7843
Phone: 608-266-1311

WISCONSIN DEPARTMENT OF VETERANS AFFAIRS RETRAINING GRANTS

Renewable award for veterans, unmarried spouses of deceased veterans, or dependents of deceased veterans. Must be resident of Wisconsin and attend an institution in Wisconsin. Veteran must be recently unemployed and show financial need. Must enroll in a vocational or technical program that can reasonably be expected to lead to employment. Course work at four-year colleges or universities does not qualify as retraining.

Award: Grant for use in freshman or sophomore years; renewable. *Number:* varies. *Amount:* up to $3000.

Eligibility Requirements: Applicant must be enrolled or expecting to enroll full or part-time at a technical institution; resident of Wisconsin and studying in Wisconsin. Applicant or parent must meet one or more of the following requirements: general military experience; retired from active duty; disabled or killed as a result of military service; prisoner of war; or missing in action.

Application Requirements: Application, financial need analysis. *Deadline:* varies.

Contact: Mike Keatley, Grants Coordinator
Wisconsin Department of Veterans Affairs
PO Box 7843
Madison, WI 53707-7843
Phone: 608-266-1311

WISCONSIN VETERANS PART-TIME STUDY REIMBURSEMENT GRANT

Open only to Wisconsin veterans. Renewable for continuing study. Contact office for more details. Application deadline is no later than sixty days after the course completion. Veterans may be reimbursed up to 100% of tuition and fees.

Award: Grant for use in freshman, sophomore, junior, or senior years; renewable. *Number:* varies. *Amount:* $300–$2000.

Eligibility Requirements: Applicant must be enrolled or expecting to enroll part-time at an institution or university; resident of Wisconsin and studying in Wisconsin. Available to U.S. citizens. Applicant or parent must meet one or more of the following requirements: general military experience; retired from active duty; disabled or killed as a result of military service; prisoner of war; or missing in action.

Application Requirements: Application. *Deadline:* varies.

Contact: Mike Keatley, Grants Coordinator
Wisconsin Department of Veterans Affairs
PO Box 7843
Madison, WI 53707-7843
Phone: 608-266-1311

MILITARY SERVICE: MARINE CORPS

COMMANDER WILLIAM S. STUHR SCHOLARSHIP FUND FOR MILITARY SONS AND DAUGHTERS

COMMANDER WILLIAM S. STUHR SCHOLARSHIP FUND FOR MILITARY SONS AND DAUGHTERS

• *See page 533*

DAUGHTERS OF THE CINCINNATI http://fdncenter.org/grantmaker/cincinnati

DAUGHTERS OF THE CINCINNATI SCHOLARSHIP

• *See page 534*

FIRST MARINE DIVISION ASSOCIATION http://www.1stmarinedivisionassociation.org

FIRST MARINE DIVISION ASSOCIATION SCHOLARSHIP FUND

Award for graduating high school seniors or undergraduate dependents of deceased or 100% totally and permanently disabled veterans who served with the 1st Marine Division. Applicant's birth certificate and proof of parent's death or disability and service with the Division required. Must attend college full-time. At the present time, students are receiving grants of $1500 per student. Contact for further instructions.

Award: Scholarship for use in freshman, sophomore, junior, or senior years; not renewable. *Number:* varies. *Amount:* up to $1500.

Eligibility Requirements: Applicant must be age 22 or under; enrolled or expecting to enroll full-time at a four-year institution or university and single. Available to U.S. citizens. Applicant or parent must meet one or more of the following requirements: Marine Corp experience; retired from active duty; disabled or killed as a result of military service; prisoner of war; or missing in action.

Application Requirements: Application, essay, photo, birth certificate, proof of parent's death or disability and service with the Division. *Deadline:* Continuous.

Contact: First Marine Division Association
14325 Willard Road, Suite 107
Chantilly, VA 20151-2110
Phone: 703-803-3195
Fax: 703-803-7114

FLEET RESERVE ASSOCIATION http://www.fra.org

FLEET RESERVE ASSOCIATION SCHOLARSHIP

• *See page 461*

OLIVER AND ESTHER R. HOWARD SCHOLARSHIP

• *See page 461*

SCHUYLER S. PYLE AWARD

• *See page 543*

STANLEY A. DORAN MEMORIAL SCHOLARSHIP
• *See page 543*

LADIES AUXILIARY OF THE FLEET RESERVE ASSOCIATION
http://www.la-fra.org

ALLIE MAE ODEN MEMORIAL SCHOLARSHIP
• *See page 468*

LADIES AUXILIARY OF THE FLEET RESERVE ASSOCIATION SCHOLARSHIP
• *See page 468*

LADIES AUXILIARY OF THE FLEET RESERVE ASSOCIATION- NATIONAL PRESIDENT'S SCHOLARSHIP
• *See page 468*

SAM ROSE MEMORIAL SCHOLARSHIP
• *See page 468*

MARINE CORPS SCHOLARSHIP FOUNDATION, INC.
http://www.marine-scholars.org

MARINE CORPS SCHOLARSHIP FOUNDATION

Available to undergraduate dependent children of current or former Marine Corps members whose family income does not exceed $58,000. Must submit proof of parent's service and should send for applications in the winter.

Award: Scholarship for use in freshman, sophomore, junior, or senior years; not renewable. *Number:* 1000. *Amount:* $500–$2500.

Eligibility Requirements: Applicant must be enrolled or expecting to enroll full or part-time at a two-year or four-year or technical institution or university. Available to U.S. citizens. Applicant or parent must meet one or more of the following requirements: Marine Corp experience; retired from active duty; disabled or killed as a result of military service; prisoner of war; or missing in action.

Application Requirements: Application, essay, financial need analysis, photo, transcript. *Deadline:* April 1.

Contact: June Hering, Scholarship Program Director
Marine Corps Scholarship Foundation, Inc.
PO Box 3008
Princeton, NJ 08543-3008
Phone: 800-292-7777
Fax: 609-452-2259
E-mail: mcsf@marine-scholars.org

MARINE CORPS TANKERS ASSOCIATION, INC.

MARINE CORPS TANKERS ASSOCIATION, JOHN CORNELIUS/MAX ENGLISH SCHOLARSHIP

Award for Marine tankers or former Marine tankers, or dependents of Marines who served in a tank unit and are on active duty, retired, reserve, or have been honorably discharged. Applicant must be a high school graduate or planning to graduate in June. May be enrolled in college, undergraduate or graduate, or have previously attended college. Must be a member of MCTA or will join.

Award: Scholarship for use in freshman, sophomore, junior, senior, or graduate years; not renewable. *Number:* 10. *Amount:* $1500.

Eligibility Requirements: Applicant must be enrolled or expecting to enroll full-time at a two-year or four-year or technical institution or university. Available to U.S. citizens. Applicant or parent must meet one or more of the following requirements: Marine Corp experience; retired from active duty; disabled or killed as a result of military service; prisoner of war; or missing in action.

Application Requirements: Application, essay, photo, references, test scores, transcript. *Deadline:* March 15.

Contact: Phil Morell, Scholarship Chair
Marine Corps Tankers Association, Inc.
1112 Alpine Heights Road
Alpine, CA 91901-2814
Phone: 619-445-8423
Fax: 619-445-8423

MASSACHUSETTS OFFICE OF STUDENT FINANCIAL ASSISTANCE
http://www.osfa.mass.edu

HIGHER EDUCATION COORDINATING COUNCIL-TUITION WAIVER PROGRAM
• *See page 534*

NAVAL OFFICERS' SPOUSES' ASSOCIATION OF MAYPORT

NAVAL OFFICERS' SPOUSES' ASSOCIATION OF MAYPORT SCHOLARSHIP
• *See page 543*

NAVAL SERVICE TRAINING COMMAND/NROTC

NROTC SCHOLARSHIP PROGRAM

NROTC scholarships are based on merit and are awarded through a highly competitive national selection process. NROTC scholarships pay for college tuition, fees, uniforms, a book stipend, a monthly allowance and other financial benefits. Room and board expenses are not covered. Scholarship nominees must be medically qualified for the NROTC Scholarship Program.

Award: Scholarship for use in freshman, sophomore, junior, or senior years; renewable. *Number:* varies. *Amount:* varies.

Eligibility Requirements: Applicant must be age 17-23 and enrolled or expecting to enroll full-time at a four-year institution or university. Available to U.S. citizens. Applicant must have served in the Marine Corp or Navy.

Application Requirements: Application, applicant must enter a contest, essay, interview, references, test scores, transcript. *Deadline:* January 7.

Contact: NROTC Scholarship Selection Office (OD2A)
Naval Service Training Command/NROTC
250 Dallas Street, Suite A
Pensacola, FL 32508-5220
Phone: 800-NAV-ROTC
Fax: 850-452-3779
E-mail: pnsc_nrotc.scholarship@navy.mil

NAVY-MARINE CORPS RELIEF SOCIETY
http://www.nmcrs.org/education.html

ADMIRAL MIKE BOORDA SCHOLARSHIP PROGRAM

Grants of up to $2000 for active duty members of Navy or Marine Corps enrolled in NROTC, ECP, MECEP, and MECP programs. Based on financial need. Minimum 2.0 GPA required. Must verify GPA and show military ID of student. One-time award for undergraduate use. Deadline: May 1.

Award: Grant for use in freshman, sophomore, junior, or senior years; not renewable. *Number:* varies. *Amount:* up to $2000.

Eligibility Requirements: Applicant must be age 22 or under; enrolled or expecting to enroll full-time at a two-year or four-year institution or university and single. Available to U.S. citizens. Applicant must have served in the Marine Corp or Navy.

Application Requirements: Application, financial need analysis. *Deadline:* May 1.

Contact: Mary Gaebel Laeske, NMCRS, Education Division
Navy-Marine Corps Relief Society
4015 Wilson Boulevard, 10th Floor
Arlington, VA 22203
Phone: 703-696-4960
Fax: 703-696-0144
E-mail: gaeskema@nmcrs.org

NAVY-MARINE CORPS RELIEF SOCIETY-CHILDREN OF DECEASED AFTER RETIREMENT FROM ACTIVE DUTY

For students under 23 whose service member parent died after retiring. Must have current, valid dependent's Uniform Service Identification or Privilege Card; proof of service member's status in Navy or Marine Corps; and proof of parent's death. Minimum 2.0 GPA required. Must verify GPA. Deadline: March 1st.

Award: Grant for use in freshman, sophomore, junior, or senior years; not renewable. *Number:* varies. *Amount:* up to $2000.

Eligibility Requirements: Applicant must be age 22 or under; enrolled or expecting to enroll full-time at a two-year or four-year or technical institution or university and single. Available to U.S. citizens. Applicant or parent must meet one or more of the following requirements: Marine Corp or Navy experience; retired from active duty; disabled or killed as a result of military service; prisoner of war; or missing in action.

Application Requirements: Application, financial need analysis. *Deadline:* March 1.

Contact: NMCRS, Education Division
Navy-Marine Corps Relief Society
4015 Wilson Boulevard, 10th Floor
Arlington, VA 22203
Phone: 703-696-4960
Fax: 703-696-0144

NAVY-MARINE CORPS RELIEF SOCIETY-SURVIVING CHILDREN OF DECEASED WHILE ON ACTIVE DUTY

One-time grants for full-time undergraduates who are military dependents of deceased service members (retired or deceased service members, service members who died on active duty). One of the specific funds is the Pentagon Assistance Fund, which is limited to children and spouses of the terrorist attack on September 11, 2001. Minimum 2.0 GPA required. Deadline: March 1st.

Award: Grant for use in freshman, sophomore, junior, or senior years; not renewable. *Number:* varies. *Amount:* up to $2000.

Eligibility Requirements: Applicant must be age 23 or under; enrolled or expecting to enroll full-time at a two-year or four-year or technical institution or university and single. Available to U.S. citizens. Applicant or parent must meet one or more of the following requirements: Marine Corp or Navy experience; retired from active duty; disabled or killed as a result of military service; prisoner of war; or missing in action.

Application Requirements: Application, financial need analysis. *Deadline:* March 1.

Contact: NMCRS, Education Division
Navy-Marine Corps Relief Society
4015 Wilson Boulevard, 10th Floor
Arlington, VA 22203
Phone: 703-696-4960
Fax: 703-696-0144
E-mail: education@hq.nmcrs.org

USS TENNESSEE SCHOLARSHIP FUND

Fund provides grants of up to $2,000 for an academic year to dependent children of service members who are serving or have served aboard the U.S.S. Tennessee. Applicant must be enrolled, or planning to enroll, as a full-time undergraduate at a postsecondary, technical, or vocational institution. Each December, Tennessee application forms are posted on Web site: http://www.nmcrs.org/education.html. Between December and February, applications are available from NMCRS offices in Bangor, Groton, Guam, Kings Bay, Norfolk, and Pearl Harbor. Minimum 2.0 GPA required.

Award: Grant for use in freshman, sophomore, junior, or senior years; not renewable. *Amount:* up to $2000.

Eligibility Requirements: Applicant must be age 23 or under; enrolled or expecting to enroll full-time at a two-year or four-year or technical institution or university and single. Available to U.S. citizens. Applicant or parent must meet one or more of the following requirements: Marine Corp or Navy experience; retired from active duty; disabled or killed as a result of military service; prisoner of war; or missing in action.

Application Requirements: Application, financial need analysis. *Deadline:* March 1.

Contact: NMCRS, Education Division
Navy-Marine Corps Relief Society
4015 Wilson Boulevard, 10th Floor
Arlington, VA 22203
Phone: 703-696-4960
Fax: 703-696-0144
E-mail: education@hq.nmcrs.org

VICE ADMIRAL E. P. TRAVERS SCHOLARSHIP AND LOAN PROGRAM

Program provides grants of up to $2,000 per academic year. Applicant must be dependent child of active duty service member and be enrolled, or planning to enroll, as a full-time undergraduate at a postsecondary technical, or vocational institution. Each December Travers application forms are posted on Web site: http://www.nmcrs.org/education.html. Between December and February, Travers application forms are available from NMCRS offices worldwide. Minimum 2.0 GPA required. Additionally, a need-based loan of up to $3,000 is available.

Award: Grant for use in freshman, sophomore, junior, or senior years; not renewable. *Number:* varies. *Amount:* up to $2000.

Eligibility Requirements: Applicant must be age 23 or under; enrolled or expecting to enroll full-time at a two-year or four-year or technical institution or university and single. Available to U.S. citizens. Applicant or parent must meet one or more of the following requirements: Marine Corp or Navy experience; retired from active duty; disabled or killed as a result of military service; prisoner of war; or missing in action.

Application Requirements: Application, financial need analysis. *Deadline:* March 1.

Contact: NMCRS, Education Division
Navy-Marine Corps Relief Society
4015 Wilson Boulevard, 10th Floor
Arlington, VA 22203-1978
Phone: 703-696-4960
Fax: 703-696-0144
E-mail: education@hq.nmcrs.org

NEW YORK COUNCIL NAVY LEAGUE

NEW YORK COUNCIL NAVY LEAGUE SCHOLARSHIP FUND

• *See page 544*

NEW YORK STATE HIGHER EDUCATION SERVICES CORPORATION http://www.hesc.org

NEW YORK VIETNAM VETERANS TUITION AWARDS

• *See page 534*

SECOND MARINE DIVISION ASSOCIATION http://www.2marine.com

BEIRUT RELIEF FUND SCHOLARSHIPS

Renewable award available to unmarried children of individuals killed while serving with the Second Marine Division, U.S. Marine Corps, or a unit attached thereto while serving in Beirut. Applicant must submit proof of parent's service and must have minimum 2.5 GPA. Merit-based award. Only 113 individuals potentially eligible.

Award: Scholarship for use in freshman, sophomore, junior, or senior years; renewable. *Number:* varies. *Amount:* $1000.

Eligibility Requirements: Applicant must be enrolled or expecting to enroll full-time at a two-year or four-year or technical institution or university and single. Applicant must have 2.5 GPA or higher. Available to U.S. and non-U.S. citizens. Applicant or parent must meet one or more of the following requirements: Marine Corp experience; retired from active duty; disabled or killed as a result of military service; prisoner of war; or missing in action.

Application Requirements: Application, financial need analysis, references, self-addressed stamped envelope, transcript. *Deadline:* April 1.

Contact: C. W. Van Horne, Executive Secretary
Second Marine Division Association
PO Box 8180
Camp LeJuene, NC 28547-8180
Phone: 910-451-3167
Fax: 910-451-3167

SECOND MARINE DIVISION ASSOCIATION MEMORIAL SCHOLARSHIP FUND

Renewable award for students who are unmarried sons, daughters or grandchildren of former or current members of 2nd Marine Division or

Second Marine Division Association (continued)

attached units. Must submit proof of parent's service. Family adjusted gross income must not exceed $42,000. Award is merit-based. Minimum 2.5 GPA required.

Award: Scholarship for use in freshman, sophomore, junior, or senior years; renewable. *Number:* 25–35. *Amount:* $1000.

Eligibility Requirements: Applicant must be enrolled or expecting to enroll full-time at a two-year or four-year or technical institution or university and single. Applicant must have 2.5 GPA or higher. Available to U.S. and non-U.S. citizens. Applicant or parent must meet one or more of the following requirements: Marine Corp experience; retired from active duty; disabled or killed as a result of military service; prisoner of war; or missing in action.

Application Requirements: Application, financial need analysis, references, self-addressed stamped envelope, transcript. *Deadline:* April 1.

Contact: C. W. Van Horne, Executive Secretary
Second Marine Division Association
PO Box 8180
Camp LeJeune, NC 28547-8180
Phone: 910-451-3167
Fax: 910-451-3167

TAILHOOK EDUCATIONAL FOUNDATION

TAILHOOK EDUCATIONAL FOUNDATION SCHOLARSHIP

• *See page 520*

THIRD MARINE DIVISION ASSOCIATION, INC. http://www.caltrap.com

THIRD MARINE DIVISION ASSOCIATION MEMORIAL SCHOLARSHIP FUND

For dependents of Third Marine Division personnel (Marine or Navy) deceased or 100% service-connected disabled veterans; and two-year members of the Association, living or dead. For further details visit Web site: http://www.caltrap.com

Award: Scholarship for use in freshman, sophomore, junior, or senior years; renewable. *Number:* varies. *Amount:* $250–$1500.

Eligibility Requirements: Applicant must be age 17-26; enrolled or expecting to enroll full or part-time at a two-year or four-year or technical institution or university and single. Available to U.S. citizens. Applicant or parent must meet one or more of the following requirements: Marine Corp or Navy experience; retired from active duty; disabled or killed as a result of military service; prisoner of war; or missing in action.

Application Requirements: Application, financial need analysis, photo, transcript, birth certificate/adoption order, (if applicable). *Deadline:* April 15.

Contact: Royal Q. Zilliox, Secretary
Third Marine Division Association, Inc.
3111 Sundial Drive
Dallas, TX 75229-3757
Phone: 972-247-6549
E-mail: rqzilliox@aol.com

VMFA/VMF/VMF (N)-531

GRAY GHOST SCHOLARSHIP PROGRAM

The Gray Ghost Squadron Program is designed only for the children/grandchildren of former members of the 531 Squadron. To qualify the applicant's parent must have served in one of the 531 squadrons for at least 90 days. In addition, the parent must have received an honorable discharge (or still be on active duty) for a dependent to apply. Also, the parent's gross income in the previous year must not have exceeded $56,000 from all sources. The program is administered by the Marine Corps Scholarship Foundation (MCSF) after our squadron scholarship committee has determined the applicant is qualified to apply as a 531 qualified applicant.

Award: Scholarship for use in freshman, sophomore, junior, or senior years; not renewable. *Number:* 1–2. *Amount:* $500–$1500.

Eligibility Requirements: Applicant must be enrolled or expecting to enroll full-time at a two-year or four-year or technical institution or university. Available to U.S. citizens. Applicant or parent must meet one or more of the following requirements: Marine Corp experience; retired from active duty; disabled or killed as a result of military service; prisoner of war; or missing in action.

Application Requirements: Application, essay, copy of parent(s) DD Form 214. *Deadline:* April 1.

Contact: Col. Bob Schultz, Chairman, VMFA-531 Scholarship Program
VMFA/VMF/VMF (N)-531
105 Lakeside Drive
Havelock, NC 28532
Phone: 252-447-2555
Fax: 252-444-3322
E-mail: bobschultz@ec.rr.com

MILITARY SERVICE: NAVY

AMERICAN CHEMICAL SOCIETY http://www.chemistry.org/scholars

UNITED STATES NAVAL ACADEMY CLASS OF 1963 FOUNDATION GRANT

Awards are available to undergraduate and graduate students who are dependent children or widows of deceased members of the Naval Academy Class of 1963 and who are currently enrolled at an accredited two- or four-year college, university, or technical school.

Award: Grant for use in freshman, sophomore, junior, senior, or graduate years; renewable. *Amount:* $1000–$3750.

Eligibility Requirements: Applicant must be age 35 or under and enrolled or expecting to enroll full or part-time at a two-year or four-year or technical institution or university. Available to U.S. and non-U.S. citizens. Applicant or parent must meet one or more of the following requirements: Navy experience; retired from active duty; disabled or killed as a result of military service; prisoner of war; or missing in action.

Application Requirements: Application. *Deadline:* Continuous.

Contact: Capt. Frank Hilton, Scholarship Committee Chairman
American Chemical Society
202 Smallwood Road
Rockville, MD 20850
E-mail: fhilton@erols.com

ANCHOR SCHOLARSHIP FOUNDATION http://www.anchorscholarship.com

SURFLANT SCHOLARSHIP

Applicant must be a dependent of a Navy service member who has served at least three years under the administrative control of Commander, Naval Surface Force, U.S. Atlantic or Pacific Fleet Support Activities for a minimum of 6 years after 1975. To obtain an application, submit military sponsor's full name and rank/rate, list of SURFLANT duty stations, homeports, ship hull numbers and dates on board, applicant's name, and a self-addressed, stamped envelope. Selection is based upon academics, extracurricular activities, character and financial report. Information is available on Web site: http://www.cnsl.spear.navy.mil/scholarship.

Award: Scholarship for use in freshman, sophomore, junior, or senior years; not renewable. *Number:* varies. *Amount:* $500–$3000.

Eligibility Requirements: Applicant must be enrolled or expecting to enroll full-time at a four-year institution. Available to U.S. citizens. Applicant or parent must meet one or more of the following requirements: Navy experience; retired from active duty; disabled or killed as a result of military service; prisoner of war; or missing in action.

Application Requirements: Application, essay, financial need analysis, references, self-addressed stamped envelope, test scores, transcript. *Deadline:* March 15.

Contact: Sally Ingram, Administrator
Anchor Scholarship Foundation
PO Box 9535
Norfolk, VA 23505
E-mail: cnslschf@erols.com

COMMANDER WILLIAM S. STUHR SCHOLARSHIP FUND FOR MILITARY SONS AND DAUGHTERS

COMMANDER WILLIAM S. STUHR SCHOLARSHIP FUND FOR MILITARY SONS AND DAUGHTERS

• *See page 533*

DAUGHTERS OF THE CINCINNATI http://fdncenter.org/grantmaker/cincinnati

DAUGHTERS OF THE CINCINNATI SCHOLARSHIP

• *See page 534*

DOLPHIN SCHOLARSHIP FOUNDATION http://www.dolphinscholarship.org

DOLPHIN SCHOLARSHIPS

Renewable award for undergraduate students. Applicant's parent or stepparent must meet one
of the following requirements: be current member of the U.S. Navy who qualified in submarines and served in the Submarine Force for at least 8 years; current or former member of the Navy who served in submarine support activities for at least 10 years; or Navy member who died while on active duty in the Submarine Force. Must be single, age 23 or under. Based on academic merit, need, and leadership.

Award: Scholarship for use in freshman, sophomore, junior, or senior years; renewable. *Number:* 25–30. *Amount:* up to $3000.

Eligibility Requirements: Applicant must be age 23 or under; enrolled or expecting to enroll full-time at a four-year institution or university and single. Available to U.S. citizens. Applicant or parent must meet one or more of the following requirements: Navy experience; retired from active duty; disabled or killed as a result of military service; prisoner of war; or missing in action.

Application Requirements: Application, essay, financial need analysis, references, self-addressed stamped envelope, test scores, transcript. *Deadline:* March 15.

Contact: Tomi Roeske, Scholarship Administrator
Dolphin Scholarship Foundation
5040 Virginia Beach Boulevard, Suite 104A
Virginia Beach, VA 23462
Phone: 757-671-3200
Fax: 757-671-3330

FLEET RESERVE ASSOCIATION http://www.fra.org

FLEET RESERVE ASSOCIATION SCHOLARSHIP

• *See page 461*

OLIVER AND ESTHER R. HOWARD SCHOLARSHIP

• *See page 461*

SCHUYLER S. PYLE AWARD

• *See page 543*

STANLEY A. DORAN MEMORIAL SCHOLARSHIP

• *See page 543*

GAMEWARDENS OF VIETNAM ASSOCIATION, INC. http://www.tf116.org

GAMEWARDENS OF VIETNAM SCHOLARSHIP

Scholarship for entering freshman who is a descendant of a U.S. Navy man or woman who worked with TF-116 in Vietnam. One-time award but applicant may reapply.

Award: Scholarship for use in freshman year; not renewable. *Number:* up to 3. *Amount:* up to $500.

Eligibility Requirements: Applicant must be high school student; age 16-21 and planning to enroll or expecting to enroll full-time at a two-year or four-year or technical institution or university. Applicant must have 2.5 GPA or higher. Available to U.S. and non-U.S. citizens. Applicant or parent must meet one or more of the following requirements: Navy experience; retired from active duty; disabled or killed as a result of military service; prisoner of war; or missing in action.

Application Requirements: Application. *Deadline:* April 1.

Contact: David Ajax, Scholarship Coordinator
Gamewardens of Vietnam Association, Inc.
6630 Perry Court
Arvada, CO 80003
Phone: 303-657-6385
Fax: 303-426-6186
E-mail: dpajax@comcast.net

LADIES AUXILIARY OF THE FLEET RESERVE ASSOCIATION http://www.la-fra.org

ALLIE MAE ODEN MEMORIAL SCHOLARSHIP

• *See page 468*

LADIES AUXILIARY OF THE FLEET RESERVE ASSOCIATION SCHOLARSHIP

• *See page 468*

LADIES AUXILIARY OF THE FLEET RESERVE ASSOCIATION- NATIONAL PRESIDENT'S SCHOLARSHIP

• *See page 468*

SAM ROSE MEMORIAL SCHOLARSHIP

• *See page 468*

MASSACHUSETTS OFFICE OF STUDENT FINANCIAL ASSISTANCE http://www.osfa.mass.edu

HIGHER EDUCATION COORDINATING COUNCIL-TUITION WAIVER PROGRAM

• *See page 534*

NAVAL OFFICERS' SPOUSES' ASSOCIATION OF MAYPORT

NAVAL OFFICERS' SPOUSES' ASSOCIATION OF MAYPORT SCHOLARSHIP

• *See page 543*

NAVAL SERVICE TRAINING COMMAND/NROTC

NROTC SCHOLARSHIP PROGRAM

• *See page 568*

NAVAL SPECIAL WARFARE FOUNDATION http://www.nswfoundation.org

HAD RICHARDS UDT-SEAL MEMORIAL SCHOLARSHIP

One-time award for dependent children of UDT-SEAL Association members. Freshmen given priority. Applicant may not be older than 22. Must be U.S. citizen.

Award: Scholarship for use in freshman, sophomore, junior, or senior years; not renewable. *Number:* varies. *Amount:* varies.

Eligibility Requirements: Applicant must be age 22 or under; enrolled or expecting to enroll full-time at a two-year or four-year or technical institution or university and single. Available to U.S. citizens. Applicant or parent must meet one or more of the following requirements: Navy experience; retired from active duty; disabled or killed as a result of military service; prisoner of war; or missing in action.

Application Requirements: Application, essay, photo, test scores, transcript. *Deadline:* April 21.

Contact: Robert Rieve, Executive Director
Naval Special Warfare Foundation
PO Box 5365
Virginia Beach, VA 23471
Phone: 757-363-7490
Fax: 757-363-7491
E-mail: udtseal@infi.net

NAVAL SPECIAL WARFARE SCHOLARSHIP

Awards given to active duty SEAL's, SWCC's, and other active duty military serving in a Naval Special Warfare command or their spouses and dependents.

Naval Special Warfare Foundation (continued)

Award: Scholarship for use in freshman, sophomore, junior, or senior years; not renewable. *Number:* varies. *Amount:* varies.

Eligibility Requirements: Applicant must be enrolled or expecting to enroll full or part-time at a two-year or four-year institution or university. Available to U.S. citizens. Applicant or parent must meet one or more of the following requirements: Navy experience; retired from active duty; disabled or killed as a result of military service; prisoner of war; or missing in action.

Application Requirements: Application, financial need analysis, transcript, proof of active duty or parent/spouse active duty. *Deadline:* March 21.

Contact: Robert Rieve, Executive Director
Naval Special Warfare Foundation
PO Box 5365
Virginia Beach, VA 23471
Phone: 757-363-7490
Fax: 757-363-7491
E-mail: udtseal@infi.net

UDT-SEAL SCHOLARSHIP

One-time award for dependent children of UDT-SEAL Association members. Freshmen given priority. Applicant may not be older than 22. Must be U.S. citizen.

Award: Scholarship for use in freshman, sophomore, junior, or senior years; not renewable. *Number:* 4–12. *Amount:* $1000–$2000.

Eligibility Requirements: Applicant must be age 22 or under; enrolled or expecting to enroll full-time at a two-year or four-year or technical institution or university and single. Available to U.S. citizens. Applicant or parent must meet one or more of the following requirements: Navy experience; retired from active duty; disabled or killed as a result of military service; prisoner of war; or missing in action.

Application Requirements: Application, essay, photo, test scores, transcript. *Deadline:* April 21.

Contact: Robert Rieve, Executive Director
Naval Special Warfare Foundation
PO Box 5365
Virginia Beach, VA 23471
Phone: 757-363-7490
Fax: 757-363-7491
E-mail: udtseal@infi.net

NAVY-MARINE CORPS RELIEF SOCIETY http://www.nmcrs.org/education.html

ADMIRAL MIKE BOORDA SCHOLARSHIP PROGRAM

• *See page 568*

NAVY-MARINE CORPS RELIEF SOCIETY-CHILDREN OF DECEASED AFTER RETIREMENT FROM ACTIVE DUTY

• *See page 568*

NAVY-MARINE CORPS RELIEF SOCIETY-SURVIVING CHILDREN OF DECEASED WHILE ON ACTIVE DUTY

• *See page 569*

USS TENNESSEE SCHOLARSHIP FUND

• *See page 569*

VICE ADMIRAL E. P. TRAVERS SCHOLARSHIP AND LOAN PROGRAM

• *See page 569*

NEW YORK COUNCIL NAVY LEAGUE

NEW YORK COUNCIL NAVY LEAGUE SCHOLARSHIP FUND

• *See page 544*

NEW YORK STATE HIGHER EDUCATION SERVICES CORPORATION http://www.hesc.org

NEW YORK VIETNAM VETERANS TUITION AWARDS

• *See page 534*

SEABEE MEMORIAL SCHOLARSHIP ASSOCIATION, INC. http://www.seabee.org

SEABEE MEMORIAL ASSOCIATION SCHOLARSHIP

Award available to children or grandchildren of current or former members of the Naval Construction Force (Seabees) or Naval Civil Engineer Corps. High school students may apply. Not available for graduate study or to great-grandchildren of Seabees.

Award: Scholarship for use in freshman, sophomore, junior, or senior years; renewable. *Number:* 90. *Amount:* $1300–$2000.

Eligibility Requirements: Applicant must be enrolled or expecting to enroll full-time at a four-year institution. Available to U.S. citizens. Applicant or parent must meet one or more of the following requirements: Navy experience; retired from active duty; disabled or killed as a result of military service; prisoner of war; or missing in action.

Application Requirements: Application, essay, financial need analysis, test scores, transcript. *Deadline:* May 1.

Contact: Sheryl Chiogioji, Administrative Assistant
Seabee Memorial Scholarship Association, Inc.
PO Box 6574
Silver Spring, MD 20916
Phone: 301-570-2850
Fax: 301-570-2873
E-mail: smsa@erols.com

SPECIAL OPERATIONS WARRIOR FOUNDATION http://www.specialops.org

SCHOLARSHIP FOR CHILDREN OF SPECIAL OPERATIONS FORCES WHO ARE KILLED IN THE LINE OF DUTY

• *See page 534*

SUBMARINE OFFICERS' WIVES CLUB

BOWFIN MEMORIAL SCHOLARSHIP

• *See page 520*

TAILHOOK EDUCATIONAL FOUNDATION

TAILHOOK EDUCATIONAL FOUNDATION SCHOLARSHIP

• *See page 520*

THIRD MARINE DIVISION ASSOCIATION, INC. http://www.caltrap.com

THIRD MARINE DIVISION ASSOCIATION MEMORIAL SCHOLARSHIP FUND

• *See page 570*

UNITED STATES SUBMARINE VETERANS OF WWII

U.S. SUBMARINE VETERANS OF WWII SCHOLARSHIP PROGRAM

Scholarships available to children/stepchildren (not grandchildren) of paid-up, regular members of U.S. SUBVETS of WW II. Awards are only for undergraduate studies. Applicant may receive no more than 4 years of assistance. Applicant must be unmarried, under the age of 24.

Award: Scholarship for use in freshman, sophomore, junior, or senior years; renewable. *Number:* 5–10. *Amount:* $3000.

Eligibility Requirements: Applicant must be age 23 or under; enrolled or expecting to enroll full-time at a two-year or four-year institution or university and single. Available to U.S. citizens. Applicant or parent must meet one or more of the following requirements: Navy experience; retired from active duty; disabled or killed as a result of military service; prisoner of war; or missing in action.

Application Requirements: Application, essay, financial need analysis, references, self-addressed stamped envelope, test scores, transcript. *Deadline:* April 15.

Contact: Tomi Roeske, Scholarship Administrator
United States Submarine Veterans of WWII
5040 Virginia Beach Boulevard, Suite 104A
Virginia Beach, VA 23462
Phone: 757-671-3200
Fax: 757-671-3330

UNITED STATES SUBMARINE VETERANS, INC. http://ussvcf.org/scolyrs.htm

UNITED STATES SUBMARINE VETERANS INC. NATIONAL SCHOLARSHIP PROGRAM

• *See page 521*

NATIONALITY OR ETHNIC HERITAGE

ADMINISTRATIVE MANAGEMENT SERVICES (AMS) http://home.cogeco.ca/~chrisb7/AMS/amshome.html

DAIMLER CHRYSLER SCHOLARSHIP PROGRAM

• *See page 490*

SYNCRUDE HIGHER EDUCATION EDUCATION AWARDS PROGRAM

• *See page 490*

ALBERTA HERITAGE SCHOLARSHIP FUND/ ALBERTA SCHOLARSHIP PROGRAMS http://www.alis.gov.ab.ca/scholarships

ADULT HIGH SCHOOL EQUIVALENCY SCHOLARSHIPS

Designed to recognize outstanding achievement in the attainment of high school equivalency. Students are eligible if they have been out of high school for three years, have achieved a minimum average of 80 per cent as a full-time student in courses required for entry into a postsecondary program, and are nominated by their institution. Two hundred awards of CAN$500. Must study in and be a resident of Alberta, Canada. Nomination deadline: September 1.

Award: Scholarship for use in freshman year; not renewable. *Number:* 200. *Amount:* $405.

Eligibility Requirements: Applicant must be Canadian citizen; enrolled or expecting to enroll full-time at a two-year or four-year or technical institution or university; resident of Alberta and studying in Alberta. Applicant must have 3.0 GPA or higher.

Application Requirements: Application. *Deadline:* September 1.

Contact: Alberta Heritage Scholarship Fund/Alberta Scholarship Programs
9940 106th Street, 9th Floor, Box 28000 Station Main
Edmonton, AB T5J 4R4
Canada
Phone: 780-427-8640
Fax: 780-422-4516
E-mail: heritage@gov.ab.ca

ALBERTA BLUE CROSS SCHOLARSHIP FOR ABORIGINAL STUDENTS

Up to CAN$1250 will be awarded to two outstanding aboriginal students to encourage further studies at the postsecondary level. Applicants must be Registered Indian, Inuit or Métis; be residents of Alberta; and entering their first year of postsecondary study at an accredited Alberta postsecondary institution. For more details see Web site: http://www.alis.gov.ab.ca or http://www.ab.bluecross.ca.

Award: Scholarship for use in freshman year; not renewable. *Number:* 3. *Amount:* $405–$1014.

Eligibility Requirements: Applicant must be American Indian/Alaska Native; high school student; planning to enroll or expecting to enroll full-time at a two-year or four-year or technical institution or university; resident of Alberta and studying in Alberta. Available to Canadian citizens.

Application Requirements: Application. *Deadline:* June 1.

Contact: Director
Alberta Heritage Scholarship Fund/Alberta Scholarship Programs
9940 106th Street, 9th Floor
Box 28000, Station Main
Edmonton, AB T5J 4R4
Canada
Phone: 780-427-8640
Fax: 780-422-4516
E-mail: heritage@gov.ab.ca

ALBERTA HERITAGE SCHOLARSHIP FUND ALBERTA PRESS COUNCIL SCHOLARSHIP

Award for Alberta high school student enrolling in postsecondary studies. Based on ability to write essay on specified topic. Deadline: January 15. Please refer to Web site for topic: http://www.alis.gov.ab.ca/scholarships/.

Award: Scholarship for use in freshman year; not renewable. *Number:* 1. *Amount:* $811.

Eligibility Requirements: Applicant must be Canadian citizen; high school student; planning to enroll or expecting to enroll full-time at a two-year or four-year or technical institution or university; resident of Alberta and must have an interest in writing.

Application Requirements: Application, applicant must enter a contest, essay. *Deadline:* January 15.

Contact: Alberta Heritage Scholarship Fund/Alberta Scholarship Programs
9940 106th Street, 9th Floor, Box 28000 Station Main
Edmonton, AB T5J 4R4
Canada
Phone: 780-427-8640
Fax: 780-422-4516
E-mail: heritage@gov.ab.ca

ALBERTA HERITAGE SCHOLARSHIP FUND CANA SCHOLARSHIPS

• *See page 490*

ALBERTA HERITAGE SCHOLARSHIP FUND HAL HARRISON MEMORIAL SCHOLARSHIP

• *See page 504*

ALEXANDER RUTHERFORD SCHOLARSHIPS FOR HIGH SCHOOL ACHIEVEMENT

The scholarships are awarded to students earning a minimum of 80% in five designated subjects in grades 10, 11, and 12. The scholarships are valued at CAN$400 for grade 10; CAN$800 for grade 11; and CAN$1300 for grade 12. Applicants must be Alberta residents who plan to enroll in a full-time postsecondary program. May 1 deadline for September entry; December 1 deadline for January entry.

Award: Scholarship for use in freshman year; not renewable. *Number:* 8400. *Amount:* $324–$1056.

Eligibility Requirements: Applicant must be Canadian citizen; high school student; planning to enroll or expecting to enroll full-time at a two-year or four-year or technical institution or university and resident of Alberta. Applicant must have 3.0 GPA or higher.

Application Requirements: Application, transcript. *Deadline:* varies.

Contact: Alberta Heritage Scholarship Fund/Alberta Scholarship Programs
9940 106th Street, 9th Floor, Box 28000 Station Main
Edmonton, AB T5J 4R4
Canada
Phone: 780-427-8640
Fax: 780-422-4516
E-mail: heritage@gov.ab.ca

CHARLES S. NOBLE JUNIOR "A" HOCKEY SCHOLARSHIPS

Scholarships are awarded to individuals who have participated in Junior "A" Hockey and who are currently enrolled in full-time postsecondary study in Alberta. Nominations are made by their respective teams. The awards are co-sponsored by the Alberta Heritage Scholarship Fund and the Junior "A" Hockey League. Must be a resident of Alberta, Canada.

Award: Scholarship for use in freshman, sophomore, junior, or senior years; not renewable. *Number:* 10. *Amount:* $811.

Eligibility Requirements: Applicant must be Canadian citizen; enrolled or expecting to enroll full-time at a two-year or four-year or technical institution or university; resident of Alberta; studying in Alberta and must have an interest in athletics/sports.

Alberta Heritage Scholarship Fund/Alberta Scholarship Programs (continued)

Application Requirements: Application, essay, transcript. *Deadline:* December 1.

Contact: Alberta Heritage Scholarship Fund/Alberta Scholarship Programs
9940 106th Street, 9th Floor, Box 28000 Station Main
Edmonton, AB T5J 4R4
Canada
Phone: 780-427-8640
Fax: 780-422-4516
E-mail: heritage@gov.ab.ca

CHARLES S. NOBLE JUNIOR FOOTBALL SCHOLARSHIPS

Scholarships are awarded to junior football players who are currently enrolled full-time in a postsecondary institution in Alberta and are nominated by their team. The awards are co-sponsored by the Alberta Heritage Scholarship Fund and the three Alberta teams in the Junior Football League. Must be a resident of Alberta, Canada. Must rank in upper half of class or have a minimum 2.5 GPA.

Award: Scholarship for use in freshman, sophomore, junior, or senior years; not renewable. *Number:* 30. *Amount:* up to $811.

Eligibility Requirements: Applicant must be Canadian citizen; enrolled or expecting to enroll full-time at a two-year or four-year or technical institution or university; resident of Alberta; studying in Alberta and must have an interest in athletics/sports. Applicant must have 2.5 GPA or higher.

Application Requirements: Application, transcript. *Deadline:* October 1.

Contact: Alberta Heritage Scholarship Fund/Alberta Scholarship Programs
9940 106th Street, 9th Floor, Box 28000 Station Main
Edmonton, AB T5J 4R4
Canada
Phone: 780-427-8640
Fax: 780-422-4516
E-mail: heritage@gov.ab.ca

DR. ERNEST AND MINNIE MEHL SCHOLARSHIP

Award given to a student graduating from an Alberta high school and enrolling in a postsecondary degree program. Selection based on diploma examination marks, financial need and personal commitment. Application deadline is June 1.

Award: Scholarship for use in freshman, sophomore, junior, or senior years; not renewable. *Number:* 1. *Amount:* $2837.

Eligibility Requirements: Applicant must be Canadian citizen; high school student; planning to enroll or expecting to enroll full-time at a two-year or four-year or technical institution or university and resident of Alberta.

Application Requirements: Application, financial need analysis, transcript. *Deadline:* June 1.

Contact: Director
Alberta Heritage Scholarship Fund/Alberta Scholarship Programs
9940 106th Street, 9th Floor
Box 28000, Station Main
Edmonton, AB T5J 4R4
Canada
Phone: 780-427-8640
Fax: 780-422-4516
E-mail: heritage@gov.ab.ca

FELLOWSHIPS FOR FULL-TIME STUDIES IN FRENCH-UNIVERSITY

One-time awards for Canadian citizens who are Alberta residents pursuing full-time postsecondary studies in French in any discipline at a Canadian university. Travel grant is available for studies outside of Alberta. Awards valued at CAN$500 per semester.

Award: Scholarship for use in freshman, sophomore, junior, or senior years; not renewable. *Number:* 300. *Amount:* up to $811.

Eligibility Requirements: Applicant must be Canadian citizen; enrolled or expecting to enroll full-time at a four-year institution or university and resident of Alberta.

Application Requirements: Application, transcript. *Deadline:* November 15.

Contact: Director
Alberta Heritage Scholarship Fund/Alberta Scholarship Programs
9940 106th Street, 9th Floor, Box 28000 Station Main
Edmonton, AB T5J 4R4
Canada
Phone: 780-427-8640
Fax: 780-422-4516
E-mail: heritage@gov.ab.ca

GRANT MACEWAN UNITED WORLD COLLEGE SCHOLARSHIPS

Eight scholarships are awarded annually for two years of study at United World Colleges. These awards are based on academic ability, leadership capability, references, and an interview. Applicants must be Alberta residents in the process of completing Grade 11.

Award: Scholarship for use in freshman year; renewable. *Number:* 8. *Amount:* varies.

Eligibility Requirements: Applicant must be Canadian citizen; high school student; age 16-17; planning to enroll or expecting to enroll at an institution or university and resident of Alberta. Applicant must have 3.5 GPA or higher.

Application Requirements: Application, essay, interview, references, transcript. *Deadline:* February 15.

Contact: Alberta Heritage Scholarship Fund/Alberta Scholarship Programs
9940 106th Street, 9th Floor, Box 28000 Station Main
Edmonton, AB T5J 4R4
Canada
Phone: 780-427-8640
Fax: 780-422-4516
E-mail: heritage@gov.ab.ca

JIMMIE CONDON ATHLETIC SCHOLARSHIPS

One-time award for Canadian citizens who are residents of Alberta and are full-time students in Alberta and members of sports teams. Must be nominated and maintaining at least a 65% average.

Award: Scholarship for use in freshman, sophomore, junior, senior, or graduate years; not renewable. *Number:* up to 2000. *Amount:* $1459.

Eligibility Requirements: Applicant must be Canadian citizen; enrolled or expecting to enroll full-time at a two-year or four-year or technical institution or university; resident of Alberta; studying in Alberta and must have an interest in athletics/sports. Applicant must have 2.5 GPA or higher.

Application Requirements: Application. *Deadline:* November 1.

Contact: Alberta Heritage Scholarship Fund/Alberta Scholarship Programs
9940 106th Street, 9th Floor, Box 28000 Station Main
Edmonton, AB T5J 4R4
Canada
Phone: 780-427-8640
Fax: 780-422-4516
E-mail: heritage@gov.ab.ca

LAURENCE DECORE STUDENT LEADERSHIP AWARDS

A total of 100 awards valued at CAN$500 each are available to recognize outstanding leadership in the areas of student government, student societies, clubs or organizations at the postsecondary level. Students are nominated by their Alberta postsecondary institution. Must be a resident of Alberta, Canada.

Award: Scholarship for use in freshman, sophomore, junior, or senior years; not renewable. *Number:* 100. *Amount:* $405.

Eligibility Requirements: Applicant must be Canadian citizen; enrolled or expecting to enroll full-time at a two-year or four-year or technical institution or university; resident of Alberta; studying in Alberta and must have an interest in leadership.

Application Requirements: Application. *Deadline:* March 1.

Contact: Alberta Heritage Scholarship Fund/Alberta Scholarship Programs
9940 106th Street, 9th Floor, Box 28000 Station Main
Edmonton, AB T5J 4R4
Canada
Phone: 780-427-8640
Fax: 780-422-4516
E-mail: heritage@gov.ab.ca

LOUISE MCKINNEY POSTSECONDARY SCHOLARSHIPS

Students enrolled in programs within Alberta are nominated by the awards office of their institution. Albertans enrolled in programs outside the province because their program of study is not offered in Alberta should contact the Alberta Heritage Scholarship Fund office. Must be a resident of Alberta. Must be ranked in upper quarter of class or have a minimum 3.5 GPA.

Award: Scholarship for use in sophomore, junior, senior, or graduate years; renewable. *Number:* 950. *Amount:* $2026.

Eligibility Requirements: Applicant must be Canadian citizen; enrolled or expecting to enroll full-time at a two-year or four-year institution or university and resident of Alberta. Applicant must have 3.5 GPA or higher.

Application Requirements: Application, transcript. *Deadline:* June 1.

Contact: Alberta Heritage Scholarship Fund/Alberta Scholarship Programs
9940 106th Street, 9th Floor, Box 28000 Station Main
Edmonton, AB T5J 4R4
Canada
Phone: 780-427-8640
Fax: 780-422-4516
E-mail: heritage@gov.ab.ca

NORTHERN ALBERTA DEVELOPMENT COUNCIL BURSARY

Applicants must have been residents of Alberta for a minimum of three years prior to applying. Students should also be in their latter years of academic study. Recipients are required to live and work for one year within the Northern Alberta Development Council boundary upon graduation. Please refer to these Web sites for more information: http://www3.gov.ab.ca/nadc; http://www.opportunitynorth.ca/.

Award: Scholarship for use in junior, senior, or graduate years; not renewable. *Number:* 200–250. *Amount:* $2431.

Eligibility Requirements: Applicant must be Canadian citizen; enrolled or expecting to enroll full-time at a two-year or four-year or technical institution or university and resident of Alberta. Applicant must have 2.5 GPA or higher.

Application Requirements: Application, essay, financial need analysis, transcript. *Deadline:* May 15.

Contact: Northern Alberta Development Council
Alberta Heritage Scholarship Fund/Alberta Scholarship Programs
2nd Floor, Provincial Building, 9621-96 Avenue, Postal Bag 900-14
Peace River, AB T8S 1T4
Canada
Phone: 780-624-6545
E-mail: nadc.bursary@gov.ab.ca

PERSONS CASE SCHOLARSHIPS

Awards recognize students whose studies will contribute to the advancement of women, or who are studying in fields where members of their sex are traditionally few in number. Selection is based on program of studies, academic achievement, and financial need. Awards range from CAN$1000 to CAN$5000. A maximum of CAN$20,000 is available each year. Must study in and be a resident of Alberta, Canada. Must be ranked in upper third of class or have a minimum 3.0 GPA.

Award: Scholarship for use in freshman, sophomore, junior, or senior years; not renewable. *Number:* 5–20. *Amount:* $811–$4055.

Eligibility Requirements: Applicant must be Canadian citizen; enrolled or expecting to enroll full-time at a two-year or four-year or technical institution or university; female; resident of Alberta and studying in Alberta. Applicant must have 3.0 GPA or higher.

Application Requirements: Application, essay, transcript. *Deadline:* September 30.

Contact: Alberta Heritage Scholarship Fund/Alberta Scholarship Programs
9940 106th Street, 9th Floor, Box 28000 Station Main
Edmonton, AB T5J 4R4
Canada
Phone: 780-427-8640
Fax: 780-422-4516
E-mail: heritage@gov.ab.ca

QUEEN ELIZABETH II GOLDEN JUBILEE CITIZENSHIP MEDAL

Awards to honor the most outstanding recipients of the Premier's Citizenship Award, which recognizes students graduating from high school who have supported and contributed to Alberta communities through public service and voluntary endeavors. Winners will receive the Medal, a letter of recommendation from the Lieutenant Governor, and $5000 CAN. Must be winner of the Premiers Citizenship Award from their high school in Alberta.

Award: Prize for use in freshman year; not renewable. *Number:* 5. *Amount:* $4095.

Eligibility Requirements: Applicant must be Canadian citizen; high school student and planning to enroll or expecting to enroll full or part-time at a two-year or four-year or technical institution or university.

Application Requirements: Premier's Citizenship Award Winner.

Contact: Director
Alberta Heritage Scholarship Fund/Alberta Scholarship Programs
9940 106th Street, 9th Floor
Box 28000, Station Main
Edmonton, AB T5J 4R4
Canada
Phone: 780-427-8640
Fax: 780-422-4516
E-mail: heritage@gov.ab.ca

RUTHERFORD SCHOLARS

The top ten students graduating from grade 12, as determined solely on the basis of Diploma Examination results in English 30 or Francais 30, Social Studies 30, and three other subjects, are recognized as "Rutherford Scholars" and receive a plaque and CAN$1500 in addition to their Alexander Rutherford scholarship. Must be a resident of Alberta, Canada.

Award: Scholarship for use in freshman year; not renewable. *Number:* 10. *Amount:* $1217.

Eligibility Requirements: Applicant must be Canadian citizen; high school student; planning to enroll or expecting to enroll full-time at a two-year or four-year or technical institution or university and resident of Alberta. Applicant must have 3.5 GPA or higher.

Application Requirements: Transcript. *Deadline:* August 1.

Contact: Alberta Heritage Scholarship Fund/Alberta Scholarship Programs
9940 106th Street, 9th Floor, Box 28000 Station Main
Edmonton, AB T5J 4R4
Canada
Phone: 780-427-8640
Fax: 780-422-4516
E-mail: heritage@gov.ab.ca

ALBUQUERQUE COMMUNITY FOUNDATION http://www.albuquerquefoundation.org

ACF- NOTAH BEGAY III SCHOLARSHIP PROGRAM FOR NATIVE AMERICAN SCHOLAR ATHLETES

$500 per year will be awarded to graduating high school seniors who are residents of New Mexico, have at least 50% Indian Blood, played varsity level sports in high school, and maintain a 3.0 GPA. Must attend an accredited, not-for-profit educational institution in the United States.

Award: Scholarship for use in freshman year; not renewable. *Number:* 4–6. *Amount:* $500.

Albuquerque Community Foundation (continued)

Eligibility Requirements: Applicant must be American Indian/Alaska Native; high school student; planning to enroll or expecting to enroll full-time at a two-year or four-year or technical institution or university and resident of New Mexico. Applicant must have 3.0 GPA or higher. Available to U.S. citizens.

Application Requirements: Application, essay, financial need analysis, resume, references, test scores, transcript, certificate of Indian blood. *Deadline:* varies.

Contact: Nancy Johnson, Program Director
Albuquerque Community Foundation
PO Box 36960
Albuquerque, NM 87176-6960
Phone: 505-883-6240
E-mail: acf@albuquerquefoundation.org

AMEEN RIHANI ORGANIZATION http://www.ameenrihani.org

AMEEN RIHANI SCHOLARSHIP PROGRAM

Scholarship to provide Lebanese-Americans and other Arab-Americans with an opportunity to complete a college education, particularly in the fields of literature, philosophy, or political science. Must maintain minimum GPA of 3.5.

Award: Scholarship for use in freshman year; renewable. *Number:* 1. *Amount:* $1500.

Eligibility Requirements: Applicant must be of Arab or Lebanese heritage; high school student and planning to enroll or expecting to enroll full-time at a four-year institution or university. Applicant must have 3.5 GPA or higher. Available to U.S. citizens.

Application Requirements: Application, essay, photo, references, transcript. *Deadline:* May 31.

Contact: Ramzi Rihani, Scholarship Coordinator
Ameen Rihani Organization
1010 Wayne Avenue, #420
Silver Spring, MD 20910
Phone: 301-562-1100
Fax: 301-562-1161
E-mail: ramzirihani@comcast.net

AMERICAN BAPTIST FINANCIAL AID PROGRAM http://www.abc-usa.org

AMERICAN BAPTIST FINANCIAL AID PROGRAM NATIVE AMERICAN GRANTS

Renewable award of $1,000 to $2,000 for Native-American who are members of an American Baptist Church/U.S.A congregation. Must be a U.S. citizen and attending an accredited educational institution in the United States.

Award: Grant for use in freshman, sophomore, junior, senior, or graduate years; renewable. *Number:* varies. *Amount:* $1000–$2000.

Eligibility Requirements: Applicant must be Baptist; American Indian/Alaska Native and enrolled or expecting to enroll full-time at a four-year institution or university. Available to U.S. citizens.

Application Requirements: Application, financial need analysis, references. *Deadline:* May 31.

Contact: Lynne Eckman, Director of Financial Aid
American Baptist Financial Aid Program
PO Box 851
Valley Forge, PA 19482-0851

AMERICAN FEDERATION OF STATE, COUNTY, AND MUNICIPAL EMPLOYEES http://www.afscme.org

AFSCME/UNCF UNION SCHOLARS PROGRAM

One-time award for a second semester sophomore or junior majoring in ethnic studies, women's studies, labor studies, American studies, sociology, anthropology, history, political science, psychology, social work or economics. Must be African-American, Hispanic-American, Asian Pacific Islander, or American-Indian/Alaska Native. Minimum 3.0 GPA. Receipt of scholarship requires a ten-week internship. See Web site at http://www.afscme.org for further details.

Award: Scholarship for use in sophomore or junior years; not renewable. *Number:* varies. *Amount:* up to $5000.

Eligibility Requirements: Applicant must be American Indian/Alaska Native, Asian/Pacific Islander, Black (non-Hispanic), or Hispanic and enrolled or expecting to enroll at a four-year institution. Applicant must have 3.0 GPA or higher. Available to U.S. citizens.

Application Requirements: Application, essay, references, transcript. *Deadline:* February 27.

Contact: Genevieve Marcus, Scholarship Coordinator
American Federation of State, County, and Municipal Employees
1625 L Street, NW
Washington, DC 20036
Phone: 202-429-1250
Fax: 202-429-1272

AMERICAN GEOLOGICAL INSTITUTE http://www.agiweb.org

AMERICAN GEOLOGICAL INSTITUTE MINORITY SCHOLARSHIP

One-time award for minority geosciences majors, including the sub-disciplines of geophysics, geochemistry, hydrology, meteorology, physical oceanography, planetary geology, or earth science education. The program does not support students in other natural sciences, mathematics, or engineering. May apply for renewal. Application available at Web site http://www.agiweb.org. Deadline is March 1.

Award: Scholarship for use in freshman, sophomore, junior, senior, or graduate years; not renewable. *Number:* varies. *Amount:* $250–$1000.

Eligibility Requirements: Applicant must be American Indian/Alaska Native, Asian/Pacific Islander, Black (non-Hispanic), or Hispanic and enrolled or expecting to enroll full-time at a four-year institution or university. Available to U.S. citizens.

Application Requirements: Application, references, test scores, transcript. *Deadline:* March 1.

Contact: Geoscience Student Scholarship Coordinator
American Geological Institute
Attn: Government Affairs Program
4220 King Street
Alexandria, VA 22302-1507

AMERICAN INDIAN EDUCATION FOUNDATION http://www.aiefprograms.org

AMERICAN INDIAN EDUCATION FOUNDATION SCHOLARSHIP

AIEF provides tuition and living expenses for American Indian students. Scholarships are awarded based on students' history of volunteerism, their commitment to return to their community, and an ACT score of at least 16.

Award: Scholarship for use in freshman, sophomore, junior, or senior years; not renewable. *Number:* 100–150. *Amount:* $1500–$3000.

Eligibility Requirements: Applicant must be American Indian/Alaska Native and enrolled or expecting to enroll full-time at a two-year or four-year or technical institution or university. Available to U.S. citizens.

Application Requirements: Application, essay, financial need analysis, test scores. *Deadline:* May 3.

Contact: Belle Cantor, Scholarship Coordinator
American Indian Education Foundation
10029 SW Nimbus Avenue
Suite 200
Beaverton, OR 97008
Phone: 866-866-8642
Fax: 503-641-0495
E-mail: scholarships@nrc1.org

AMERICAN INDIAN GRADUATE CENTER http://www.aigc.com

GATES MILLENNIUM SCHOLARS PROGRAM

Award enables American-Indian/Alaska Native students to complete an undergraduate and graduate education. Must be entering a U.S. accredited college or university as a full-time degree-seeking student. Minimum 3.3 GPA required. Must demonstrate leadership abilities. Must meet federal Pell Grant eligibility criteria. Visit Web site at http://www.gmsp.org

Award: Scholarship for use in freshman, sophomore, junior, senior, or graduate years; renewable. *Number:* 150. *Amount:* $500–$40,000.

Eligibility Requirements: Applicant must be American Indian/Alaska Native and enrolled or expecting to enroll full-time at a four-year institution or university. Available to U.S. citizens.

Application Requirements: Application, financial need analysis, nomination packet. *Deadline:* January 16.

Contact: GMS Representative
American Indian Graduate Center
4520 Montgomery Boulevard, NE, Suite 1B
Albuquerque, NM 87109
Phone: 866-884-7007
Fax: 505-884-8683
E-mail: info@aigc.com

AMERICAN INSTITUTE FOR FOREIGN STUDY http://www.aifsabroad.com

AMERICAN INSTITUTE FOR FOREIGN STUDY MINORITY SCHOLARSHIPS

Applications will be accepted from African-American, Asian-American, Native-American, Hispanic-American and Pacific Islanders who are currently enrolled as undergraduates at a U.S. institution applying to an AIFS study abroad program. Applicants must demonstrate financial need, leadership ability, and academic accomplishment and meet program requirements. One full scholarship and three runners-up scholarships are awarded each semester. Submit application by April 15 for fall or October 15 for spring. Application fees are $75.

Award: Scholarship for use in sophomore, junior, or senior years; not renewable. *Number:* 1–4. *Amount:* $2000–$24,000.

Eligibility Requirements: Applicant must be American Indian/Alaska Native, Asian/Pacific Islander, Black (non-Hispanic), or Hispanic; age 17; enrolled or expecting to enroll full-time at a two-year or four-year institution or university and must have an interest in leadership. Applicant must have 3.0 GPA or higher. Available to U.S. and non-U.S. citizens.

Application Requirements: Application, essay, financial need analysis, photo, references, transcript. *Fee:* $75. *Deadline:* varies.

Contact: David Mauro, Admissions Counselor
American Institute for Foreign Study
River Plaza, 9 West Broad Street
Stamford, CT 06902-3788
Phone: 800-727-2437 Ext. 5163
Fax: 203-399-5598
E-mail: college.info@aifs.com

ARIZONA ASSOCIATION OF CHICANOS IN HIGHER EDUCATION (AACHE) http://www.aache.org/

AACHE SCHOLARSHIP

Scholarship available to students of Chicano/Hispanic/Latino heritage and identity who are residents of Arizona and enrolled full-time in one of the 10 Maricopa County, Arizona Community Colleges or who are transferring from one of these community colleges to a 4 year college or university in Arizona. Application deadline is April 2.

Award: Scholarship for use in sophomore, junior, senior, or graduate years; not renewable. *Number:* 10–20. *Amount:* $100–$300.

Eligibility Requirements: Applicant must be Hispanic; enrolled or expecting to enroll full-time at a two-year or four-year institution or university; resident of Arizona and studying in Arizona. Available to U.S. citizens.

Application Requirements: Application, autobiography, essay, transcript. *Deadline:* April 2.

Contact: Luvia Rivera, Scholarship Chair
Arizona Association of Chicanos in Higher Education (AACHE)
3000 North Dysart Road
Avondale, AZ 85323
Phone: 623-935-8321
E-mail: luvia.rivera@emcmail.maricopa.edu

ARKANSAS COMMUNITY FOUNDATION, INC. http://www.arcf.org

SOUTHWESTERN BELL BATES SCHOLARSHIP FUND

Award for outstanding minority high school seniors in Arkansas. Contact high school counselor's office for more information.

Award: Scholarship for use in freshman year; not renewable. *Amount:* $500–$5000.

Eligibility Requirements: Applicant must be American Indian/Alaska Native, Asian/Pacific Islander, Black (non-Hispanic), or Hispanic; high school student; planning to enroll or expecting to enroll at an institution or university and resident of Arkansas. Available to U.S. citizens.

Application Requirements: Application. *Deadline:* March 15.

Contact: Arkansas Community Foundation, Inc.
700 South Rock Street
Little Rock, AR 72202-2519

ARMENIAN RELIEF SOCIETY OF EASTERN USA, INC. -REGIONAL OFFICE http://www.arseastus.org

ARMENIAN RELIEF SOCIETY UNDERGRADUATE SCHOLARSHIP

Award for full-time Armenian students. Must be U.S. or Canadian citizen. Scholarship for use at a four-year college or university. High school students may not apply. Contact for additional information.

Award: Scholarship for use in freshman, sophomore, junior, or senior years; not renewable. *Number:* varies. *Amount:* $13,000–$15,000.

Eligibility Requirements: Applicant must be of Armenian heritage and enrolled or expecting to enroll full-time at a four-year institution or university. Available to U.S. and Canadian citizens.

Application Requirements: Application, financial need analysis, references, self-addressed stamped envelope, transcript. *Deadline:* April 1.

Contact: Scholarship Undergraduate Committee
Armenian Relief Society of Eastern USA, Inc. -Regional Office
80 Bigelow Avenue, Suite 200
Watertown, MA 02472
Phone: 617-926-3801
Fax: 617-924-7238
E-mail: arseastus@aol.com

ARMENIAN STUDENTS ASSOCIATION OF AMERICA, INC.

ARMENIAN STUDENTS ASSOCIATION OF AMERICA, INC. SCHOLARSHIPS

One-time award for students of Armenian descent. Must be undergraduate in sophomore, junior, or senior years, or graduate student, attending accredited U.S. institution full-time. Award based on need, merit, and character. Show proof of tuition costs and enrollment. Application fee: $15.

Award: Scholarship for use in sophomore, junior, senior, or graduate years; not renewable. *Number:* 30. *Amount:* $1000–$3500.

Eligibility Requirements: Applicant must be of Armenian heritage and enrolled or expecting to enroll full-time at a four-year institution or university.

Application Requirements: Application, essay, financial need analysis, references, transcript. *Fee:* $15. *Deadline:* March 15.

Contact: Nathalie Yaghoobian, Scholarship Administrator
Armenian Students Association of America, Inc.
333 Atlantic Avenue
Warwick, RI 02888
Phone: 401-461-6114
Fax: 401-461-6112
E-mail: headasa.com@aol.com

ASSOCIATED MEDICAL SERVICES, INC. http://www.ams-inc.on.ca

ASSOCIATED MEDICAL SERVICES, INC. BIOETHICS STUDENTSHIP

Studentship available for Canadian citizens or permanent residents registered in a full-time undergraduate program at a Canadian university. Must pursue

Associated Medical Services, Inc. (continued)

research in the field of bioethics. Project proposal required. Deadline is January 15. Additional information on Web site: http://www.ams-inc.on.ca.

Award: Scholarship for use in freshman, sophomore, junior, or senior years. *Number:* 1–10. *Amount:* up to $3366.

Eligibility Requirements: Applicant must be Canadian citizen and enrolled or expecting to enroll full-time at a four-year institution or university.

Application Requirements: Application, references, transcript. *Deadline:* January 15.

Contact: Margaret Phillips, Grants Officer
Associated Medical Services, Inc.
162 Cumberland Street
Suite 228
Toronto, ON M5R 3N5
Canada
Phone: 416-924-3368
Fax: 416-323-3338
E-mail: grantsof@ams-inc.on.ca

ASSOCIATION OF INTERNATIONAL EDUCATION, JAPAN (AIEJ)

SPONSOR-CROWNED INTERNATIONAL STUDENT SCHOLARSHIP

One-time award available to undergraduate or graduate Japanese students studying at a four-year college or university. Amounts and deadlines vary.

Award: Scholarship for use in freshman, sophomore, junior, senior, or graduate years; not renewable. *Number:* 82. *Amount:* varies.

Eligibility Requirements: Applicant must be Asian/Pacific Islander and enrolled or expecting to enroll full-time at a four-year institution or university. Available to citizens of countries other than the U.S. or Canada.

Application Requirements: Applicant must enter a contest, to be decided by each funding source. *Deadline:* varies.

Contact: Fumihiko Adachihara, Student Affairs Division, AIEJ
Association of International Education, Japan (AIEJ)
4-5-29 Komaba, Meguro-ku
Tokyo 153-8503
Japan
Phone: 81-3-5454 Ext. 5213
Fax: 81-3-5454 Ext. 5233
E-mail: sa1@aiej.or.jp

ASSOCIATION ON AMERICAN INDIAN AFFAIRS (AAIA) http://www.indian-affairs.org

A1LOGAN SLAGLE SCHOLARSHIP

A scholarship to American Indian students who are members of State Recognized Tribes, or Tribes seeking federal recognition. Applicants must be full-time students and determination is based on need.

Award: Scholarship for use in freshman, sophomore, junior, or senior years; not renewable. *Number:* varies. *Amount:* $1000.

Eligibility Requirements: Applicant must be American Indian/Alaska Native and enrolled or expecting to enroll full-time at an institution or university.

Application Requirements: Application, essay, financial need analysis, references, transcript, certificate of Indian blood, class schedule. *Deadline:* July 20.

Contact: Scholarship Coordinator
Association on American Indian Affairs (AAIA)
966 Hungerford Drive
Suite 12-B
Rockville, MD 20850
Phone: 605-698-3998
Fax: 605-698-3316
E-mail: aaia@sbtc.net

ADOLPH VAN PELT SPECIAL FUND FOR INDIAN SCHOLARSHIPS

This scholarship is awarded to undergraduate students based upon need and merit. Grants are paid directly to the educational institute and are renewable up to four years for any one degree. Each year $100 is added to the scholarship amount to a maximum of $800.

Award: Scholarship for use in freshman, sophomore, junior, or senior years; renewable. *Number:* varies. *Amount:* $500–$800.

Eligibility Requirements: Applicant must be American Indian/Alaska Native and enrolled or expecting to enroll at an institution or university. Available to U.S. citizens.

Application Requirements: Application, essay, references, transcript, certificate of enrollment and blood quantum from your tribe or BIA. Class schedule. FA Award letter. *Deadline:* July 20.

Contact: Scholarship Coordinator
Association on American Indian Affairs (AAIA)
PO Box 268
Sisseton, SD 57262
Phone: 605-698-3998
Fax: 605-698-3316
E-mail: aaia@sbtc.net

DISPLACED HOMEMAKER SCHOLARSHIP

This scholarship will augment the unmet needs associated with usual and expected expenses such as child care, transportation, and some basic living expenses, in addition to educational costs.

Award: Scholarship for use in freshman, sophomore, junior, or senior years; not renewable. *Number:* varies. *Amount:* $1000.

Eligibility Requirements: Applicant must be American Indian/Alaska Native and enrolled or expecting to enroll full-time at an institution or university. Available to U.S. citizens.

Application Requirements: Application, essay, references, transcript, certificate of enrollment and blood quantum from your tribe, monthly budget, class schedule, FA award letter. *Deadline:* July 20.

Contact: Scholarship Coordinator
Association on American Indian Affairs (AAIA)
PO Box 268
Sisseton, SD 57262
Phone: 605-698-3998
Fax: 605-698-3316
E-mail: aaia@sbtc.net

EMERGENCY AID AND HEALTH PROFESSIONALS SCHOLARSHIP PROGRAM

This scholarship is awarded to full time undergraduate students based on financial need and is limited to availability of funds. Emergency Aid is available during both Fall and Spring semesters. Students may only receive one scholarship per academic year.

Award: Scholarship for use in freshman, sophomore, junior, or senior years; not renewable. *Number:* varies. *Amount:* $100–$400.

Eligibility Requirements: Applicant must be American Indian/Alaska Native and enrolled or expecting to enroll full-time at an institution or university. Available to U.S. citizens.

Application Requirements: Application, essay, transcript, certificate of enrollment and blood quantum from your tribe or BIA. FA award letter, class schedule. *Deadline:* Continuous.

Contact: Scholarship Coordinator
Association on American Indian Affairs (AAIA)
PO Box 268
Sisseton, SD 57262
Phone: 605-698-3998
Fax: 605-698-3316
E-mail: aaia@sbtc.net

BECA FOUNDATION, INC.

DANIEL GUTIERREZ MEMORIAL GENERAL SCHOLARSHIP FUND

Scholarships to full-time Latino students from San Diego County; high school graduate entering college in the fall of the same year. May pursue their education anywhere in the United States and pursue any profession. Financial need, scholastic determination, and community/cultural awareness are considered.

Award: Scholarship for use in freshman year; not renewable. *Number:* varies. *Amount:* $500–$1000.

Eligibility Requirements: Applicant must be of Hispanic heritage; high school student; planning to enroll or expecting to enroll full-time at a four-year institution or university and resident of California. Applicant must have 2.5 GPA or higher. Available to U.S. citizens.

Application Requirements: Application, essay, financial need analysis, references, transcript. *Deadline:* March 1.

Contact: Ana Garcia, Operations Manager
BECA Foundation, Inc.
830 East Grand Avenue
Suite B
Escondido, CA 92025
Phone: 760-741-8246

GENERAL SCHOLARSHIP FUND

Scholarships to full-time Latino students from North San Diego County; high school graduate entering college in the fall of the same year. May pursue their education anywhere in the United States and pursue any profession. Financial need, scholastic determination, and community/cultural awareness are considered.

Award: Scholarship for use in freshman year; not renewable. *Number:* varies. *Amount:* $500–$1000.

Eligibility Requirements: Applicant must be of Hispanic heritage; high school student; planning to enroll or expecting to enroll full-time at a four-year institution or university and resident of California. Applicant must have 2.5 GPA or higher. Available to U.S. citizens.

Application Requirements: Application, essay, financial need analysis, references, transcript. *Deadline:* March 1.

Contact: Ana Garcia, Operations Manager
BECA Foundation, Inc.
830 East Grand Avenue
Suite B
Escondido, CA 92025
Phone: 760-741-8246

BLACKFEET NATION HIGHER EDUCATION PROGRAM http://www.blackfeetnation.com

BLACKFEET NATION HIGHER EDUCATION GRANT

Up to 140 grants of up to $3500 will be awarded to students who are enrolled members of the Blackfeet Tribe and actively pursuing an undergraduate degree. Must submit a certification of Blackfeet blood. The deadline is March 1.

Award: Grant for use in freshman, sophomore, junior, or senior years; renewable. *Number:* 140. *Amount:* $3500.

Eligibility Requirements: Applicant must be American Indian/Alaska Native and enrolled or expecting to enroll full-time at a two-year or four-year institution or university. Available to U.S. citizens.

Application Requirements: Application, essay, financial need analysis, transcript, certification of Blackfeet blood. *Deadline:* March 1.

Contact: Conrad LaFromboise, Director
Blackfeet Nation Higher Education Program
PO Box 850
Browning, MT 59417
Phone: 406-338-7539
Fax: 406-338-7530
E-mail: bhep@blackfeetnation.com

BOIS FORTE RESERVATION TRIBAL COUNCIL POSTSECONDARY EDUCATION SCHOLARSHIP PROGRAM http://www.boisfortertc.com

BOIS FORTE SCHOLARSHIP PROGRAM

Must be enrolled members of the Bois Forte band of Chippewa and be accepted for enrollment at an accredited institution of higher education. Maximum award is $5000 and is based upon financial need as determined by the school financial aid office. Must maintain a 2.0 GPA or greater. Applications must be filed at least 8 weeks prior to the beginning of school.

Award: Scholarship for use in freshman, sophomore, junior, senior, or graduate years; renewable. *Number:* 100. *Amount:* up to $5000.

Eligibility Requirements: Applicant must be American Indian/Alaska Native and enrolled or expecting to enroll full or part-time at a two-year or four-year institution or university. Available to U.S. citizens.

Application Requirements: Application, FAFSA. *Deadline:* Continuous.

Contact: Education Director
Bois Forte Reservation Tribal Council Postsecondary Education Scholarship Program
PO Box 16
Nett Lake, MN 55772

BUREAU OF INDIAN AFFAIRS OFFICE OF INDIAN EDUCATION PROGRAMS http://www.oiep.bia.edu

BUREAU OF INDIAN AFFAIRS HIGHER EDUCATION GRANT PROGRAM

Applicants must submit proof of tribal enrollment in a federally recognized tribe. Application deadlines, award numbers, and award amounts vary. For undergraduate study at accredited college or university only. Write for more information.

Award: Grant for use in freshman, sophomore, junior, or senior years; renewable. *Number:* 800–2500.

Eligibility Requirements: Applicant must be American Indian/Alaska Native and enrolled or expecting to enroll full-time at a two-year or four-year institution or university. Available to U.S. citizens.

Application Requirements: Application, financial need analysis, transcript, tribal membership or Certificate Degree of Indian Blood (CDIB). *Deadline:* varies.

Contact: Garry Martin, Special Assistant
Bureau of Indian Affairs Office of Indian Education Programs
1849 C Street, NW, MS 3512-MIB
Washington, DC 20240
Phone: 202-208-3478
Fax: 202-219-9583
E-mail: gmartin@bia.edu

CABRILLO CIVIC CLUBS OF CALIFORNIA, INC.

CABRILLO CIVIC CLUBS OF CALIFORNIA SCHOLARSHIP

Graduating California high school seniors of Portuguese heritage and American citizenship, with an overall 3.5 GPA can apply within a March 1 to April 1 deadline. Scholarship screening is conducted by club members (14 clubs) on point system for leadership, promise, grades, activities, and work.

Award: Scholarship for use in freshman year; not renewable. *Number:* 75–100. *Amount:* $400.

Eligibility Requirements: Applicant must be of Portuguese heritage; high school student; planning to enroll or expecting to enroll full-time at a two-year or four-year or technical institution or university and resident of California. Applicant must have 3.5 GPA or higher. Available to U.S. citizens.

Application Requirements: Application, autobiography, photo, resume, references, self-addressed stamped envelope, transcript. *Deadline:* April 1.

Contact: Breck Austin, State Scholarship/Education Chairman
Cabrillo Civic Clubs of California, Inc.
1455 Willow Street
San Diego, CA 92106-2122
Phone: 760-804-7056

CANADA MILLENNIUM SCHOLARSHIP FOUNDATION http://www.millenniumscholarships.ca

CANADA MILLENNIUM EXCELLENCE AWARD PROGRAM

Entrance in-course awards for post-secondary study in Canada recognizing community involvement, leadership, innovation, and academics.

Award: Scholarship for use in freshman or junior years; renewable. *Number:* up to 2100. *Amount:* $3267–$4084.

Eligibility Requirements: Applicant must be of Canadian heritage and Canadian citizen and enrolled or expecting to enroll full-time at a two-year or four-year or technical institution or university. Applicant must have 3.0 GPA or higher.

Canada Millennium Scholarship Foundation (continued)

Application Requirements: Application, references, transcript. *Deadline:* varies.

Contact: Maria Modafferi, Information Officer
Canada Millennium Scholarship Foundation
1000 Sherbrooke Street West
Suite 800
Montréal, QC H3A 3R2
Canada
Phone: 514-284-7230
Fax: 514-985-5987
E-mail: millennium.foundation@bm-ms.org

CAP FOUNDATION http://www.ronbrown.org

RON BROWN SCHOLAR PROGRAM

Program seeks to identify African-American high school seniors who will make significant contributions to society. Applicants must excel academically, show exceptional leadership potential, participate in community service activities, and demonstrate financial need. Must be a U.S. citizen or hold permanent resident visa. Must plan to attend a four-year college or university.

Award: Scholarship for use in freshman, sophomore, junior, or senior years; renewable. *Number:* 10–20. *Amount:* $10,000–$40,000.

Eligibility Requirements: Applicant must be Black (non-Hispanic); high school student; planning to enroll or expecting to enroll full-time at a four-year institution or university and must have an interest in leadership. Applicant must have 3.5 GPA or higher. Available to U.S. citizens.

Application Requirements: Application, essay, financial need analysis, interview, photo, references, test scores, transcript. *Deadline:* January 9.

Contact: Fran Hardey, Executive Assistant, Ron Brown Scholar Program
CAP Foundation
1160 Pepsi Place, Suite 206
Charlottesville, VA 22901
Phone: 434-964-1588
Fax: 434-964-1589
E-mail: franh@ronbrown.org

CENTER FOR SCHOLARSHIP ADMINISTRATION http://www.scholarshipprograms.org

HISPANIC LEAGUE OF THE PIEDMONT TRIAD SCHOLARSHIP

Non-renewable scholarships are available to students of Hispanic ethnicity who reside in one of the following counties in North Carolina: Forsyth, Guilford, Davidson, Surry, Stokes, or Yadkin. Must have taken English as a second language. See high school counselor for deadlines and more detailed information on additional criteria.

Award: Scholarship for use in freshman, sophomore, or junior years; not renewable. *Number:* 4. *Amount:* $1500.

Eligibility Requirements: Applicant must be Hispanic; enrolled or expecting to enroll at a two-year or four-year or technical institution or university and resident of North Carolina.

Application Requirements: Application. *Deadline:* varies.

Contact: See high school counselor for details.

CENTRAL COUNCIL, TLINGIT AND HAIDA INDIAN TRIBES OF ALASKA http://www.ccthita.org

ALUMNI STUDENT ASSISTANCE PROGRAM

Supplementary scholarship available to enrolled CCTHITA tribal members attending an accredited college or university. Must maintain a 2.5 GPA. For more details go to Web site: http://www.ccthita-vtrc.org.

Award: Scholarship for use in freshman, sophomore, junior, senior, or graduate years; renewable. *Number:* varies. *Amount:* $200–$500.

Eligibility Requirements: Applicant must be American Indian/Alaska Native and enrolled or expecting to enroll full or part-time at a two-year or four-year institution or university. Applicant must have 2.5 GPA or higher. Available to U.S. citizens.

Application Requirements: Application, essay, transcript, tribal enrollment certification letter of acceptance cover letter. *Deadline:* September 15.

Contact: See Web site http://www.ccthita-vtrc.org.

COLLEGE STUDENT ASSISTANCE

Supplementary Scholarship available to enrolled CCTHTA tribal members attending an accredited college or university. Must maintain a 2.0 GPA. For more details go to Web site: http://www.ccthita-vtrc.org.

Award: Scholarship for use in freshman, sophomore, junior, senior, or graduate years; renewable. *Number:* varies. *Amount:* $2000.

Eligibility Requirements: Applicant must be American Indian/Alaska Native and enrolled or expecting to enroll full-time at a two-year or four-year institution or university. Available to U.S. citizens.

Application Requirements: Application, transcript, letter of admission. *Deadline:* May 15.

Contact: See Web site http://www.ccthita-vtrc.org.

CHEROKEE NATION OF OKLAHOMA http://www.cherokee.org

CHEROKEE NATION HIGHER EDUCATION SCHOLARSHIP

A supplementary program that provides financial assistance to Cherokee Nation Members only. It is a need-based program which provides assistance in seeking a bachelor's degree.

Award: Scholarship for use in freshman, sophomore, junior, or senior years; renewable. *Number:* 1200–1500. *Amount:* $500–$1000.

Eligibility Requirements: Applicant must be American Indian/Alaska Native and enrolled or expecting to enroll full-time at a two-year or four-year institution or university. Available to U.S. citizens.

Application Requirements: Application, financial need analysis, test scores, transcript, written request for the application. *Deadline:* June 17.

Contact: Dale Miller, Higher Education Specialist
Cherokee Nation of Oklahoma
PO Box 948
Tahlequah, OK 74465
Phone: 918-456-0671
Fax: 918-458-6195
E-mail: dmiller@cherokee.org

CHICANA/LATINA FOUNDATION http://www.chicanalatina.org

SCHOLARSHIPS FOR LATINA STUDENTS

Scholarships are awarded to Latina students enrolled in two-year, four-year or graduate levels. Applicants must be from the nine counties of Northern California. Application deadline is March every year. Application online: http://www.chicanalatina.org.

Award: Scholarship for use in freshman, sophomore, junior, senior, or graduate years; not renewable. *Number:* 15–20. *Amount:* $1500.

Eligibility Requirements: Applicant must be of Hispanic heritage; enrolled or expecting to enroll full-time at a two-year or four-year institution or university; female and resident of California. Applicant must have 2.5 GPA or higher. Available to U.S. and non-U.S. citizens.

Application Requirements: Application, essay, interview, references, transcript. *Deadline:* varies.

Contact: Olga Talamante, Executive Director
Chicana/Latina Foundation
1419 Burlingame Avenue
Suite N
Burlingame, CA 94044
Phone: 650-373-1083
Fax: 650-373-1090
E-mail: olgapacifica@yahoo.com

CITIZEN POTAWATOMI NATION http://www.potawatomi.org

CITIZEN POTAWATOMI NATION TRIBAL SCHOLARSHIP

Provides financial assistance for payment of tuition for members of the Citizen Potawatomi Nation. Minimum 2.0 GPA required. Deadlines:

December 15 for Fall; August 15 for Spring; June 1 for Summer. Award amount varies, $400 per semester part time and $500 per semester full time.

Award: Scholarship for use in freshman, sophomore, junior, or senior years; renewable. *Number:* varies. *Amount:* $800–$1000.

Eligibility Requirements: Applicant must be American Indian/Alaska Native and enrolled or expecting to enroll full or part-time at a two-year or four-year or technical institution or university. Available to U.S. citizens.

Application Requirements: Application, financial need analysis, test scores, transcript. *Deadline:* varies.

Contact: Charles Clark, Director, Tribal Rolls
Citizen Potawatomi Nation
1601 South Gordon Cooper Avenue
Shawnee, OK 74801-8699
Phone: 800-880-9880
Fax: 405-878-4653
E-mail: cclark@potawatomi.org

CITY COLLEGE OF SAN FRANCISCO LATINO EDUCATIONAL ASSOCIATION http://www.ccsf.edu

LATINO EDUCATION ASSOCIATION SCHOLARSHIP

Latina or Latino students with at least 60 transferable credits who have been accepted at any college or university will be evaluated for the scholarship based on financial need, academic excellence, community service, and student activism while at CCSF. Application deadline is first Friday in April.

Award: Scholarship for use in junior or senior years; not renewable. *Number:* 3. *Amount:* $500.

Eligibility Requirements: Applicant must be Hispanic; enrolled or expecting to enroll at a four-year institution or university and resident of California. Applicant must have 3.0 GPA or higher. Available to U.S. citizens.

Application Requirements: Application, autobiography, essay, references, transcript. *Deadline:* varies.

Contact: Latino Educational Association Scholarships
City College of San Francisco Latino Educational Association
50 Phelan Avenue, Box L230
Scholarship Office, Batmale Hall, Room 366
San Francisco, CA 94112
Phone: 415-239-3339
E-mail: gsaucedo@ccsf.org

COMMUNITY FOUNDATION FOR PALM BEACH AND MARTIN COUNTIES, INC. http://www.yourcommunityfoundation.org

COLONIAL BANK SCHOLARSHIP

For minority student graduating from Palm Beach Lakes or Santaluces High Schools who has a 2.5 GPA or higher and demonstrates financial need.

Award: Scholarship for use in freshman year; not renewable. *Amount:* $750–$2500.

Eligibility Requirements: Applicant must be American Indian/Alaska Native, Asian/Pacific Islander, Black (non-Hispanic), or Hispanic; high school student; planning to enroll or expecting to enroll full-time at a two-year or four-year or technical institution or university and resident of Florida. Applicant must have 2.5 GPA or higher. Available to U.S. citizens.

Application Requirements: Application, financial need analysis, transcript. *Deadline:* March 1.

Contact: Carolyn Jenco, Grants Manager/Scholarship Coordinator
Community Foundation for Palm Beach and Martin Counties, Inc.
700 South Dixie Highway
Suite 200
West Palm Beach, FL 33401

COMMUNITY FOUNDATION OF WESTERN MASSACHUSETTS http://www.communityfoundation.org

AFRICAN-AMERICAN ACHIEVEMENT SCHOLARSHIP

African-American Achievement Scholarship for African-American residents of Hampden, Hampshire, or Franklin counties who attend or plan to attend a four-year college. Established by a donor who contributes his social security income to the fund. Advised by the Urban League of Springfield.

Award: Scholarship for use in freshman, sophomore, junior, or senior years; not renewable. *Number:* 9. *Amount:* $2500–$3000.

Eligibility Requirements: Applicant must be of African heritage; Black (non-Hispanic); enrolled or expecting to enroll full-time at a four-year institution and resident of Massachusetts. Available to U.S. citizens.

Application Requirements: Application, essay, financial need analysis, transcript. *Deadline:* March 31.

Contact: Community Foundation of Western Massachusetts
1500 Main Street
PO Box 15769
Springfield, MA 01115

HERIBERTO FLORES SCHOLARSHIP

For students of Puerto Rican ancestry from Hampshire or Hampden counties who are graduates of Springfield Technical Community College or Holyoke Community College planning to attend a Massachusetts state college.

Award: Scholarship for use in senior year. *Number:* 2. *Amount:* $200.

Eligibility Requirements: Applicant must be of Hispanic heritage; enrolled or expecting to enroll full or part-time at a two-year or four-year institution; resident of Massachusetts and studying in Massachusetts. Available to U.S. citizens.

Application Requirements: Application, financial need analysis, transcript. *Deadline:* March 31.

Contact: Community Foundation of Western Massachusetts
1500 Main Street
PO Box 15769
Springfield, MA 01115

LATINO SCHOLARSHIP

For graduating Latino students in Hampden and Hampshire counties who are entering their first year of college and are family and/or community service oriented.

Award: Scholarship for use in freshman year; not renewable. *Number:* 5. *Amount:* $1000.

Eligibility Requirements: Applicant must be of Latin American/Caribbean heritage; Hispanic; enrolled or expecting to enroll full or part-time at a two-year or four-year institution and resident of Massachusetts. Available to U.S. citizens.

Application Requirements: Application, financial need analysis, transcript. *Deadline:* March 31.

Contact: Community Foundation of Western Massachusetts
1500 Main Street
PO Box 15769
Springfield, MA 01115

PUTNAM SCHOLARSHIP FUND

Provides scholarships for African-American and Latino students who attend college. Please note, a pastoral letter of reference from any denomination is highly recommended for consideration.

Award: Scholarship for use in freshman, sophomore, junior, or senior years; not renewable. *Number:* 5. *Amount:* $1000–$2000.

Eligibility Requirements: Applicant must be Black (non-Hispanic) or Hispanic; enrolled or expecting to enroll full or part-time at a two-year or four-year institution or university and resident of Connecticut or Massachusetts. Available to U.S. citizens.

Application Requirements: Application, financial need analysis, references, transcript. *Deadline:* March 31.

Contact: Community Foundation of Western Massachusetts
1500 Main Street
PO Box 15769
Springfield, MA 01115

RUTH L. BROCKLEBANK MEMORIAL SCHOLARSHIP

For African-American students from the Springfield public high schools to attend college.

Community Foundation of Western Massachusetts (continued)

Award: Scholarship for use in freshman, sophomore, junior, or senior years; not renewable. *Number:* 6. *Amount:* $2200.

Eligibility Requirements: Applicant must be Black (non-Hispanic); enrolled or expecting to enroll full or part-time at a two-year or four-year institution or university and resident of Massachusetts. Available to U.S. citizens.

Application Requirements: Application, financial need analysis, transcript. *Deadline:* March 31.

Contact: Community Foundation of Western Massachusetts
1500 Main Street
PO Box 15769
Springfield, MA 01115

CONFEDERATED TRIBES OF GRAND RONDE http://www.grandronde.org

ADULT VOCATIONAL TRAINING EDUCATION SCHOLARSHIPS

Available to any enrolled member of the Confederated Tribes of Grand Ronde. Two $6,000 full-time and one $3,000 part-time awards are given each year. Intended for programs of study two years or less in length.

Award: Scholarship for use in freshman or sophomore years; renewable. *Number:* 3. *Amount:* $3000–$6000.

Eligibility Requirements: Applicant must be American Indian/Alaska Native and enrolled or expecting to enroll full or part-time at a two-year or technical institution. Available to U.S. and non-U.S. citizens.

Application Requirements: Application, essay, references, transcript, verification of Tribal enrollment. *Deadline:* April 30.

Contact: Tribal Scholarship Coordinator
Confederated Tribes of Grand Ronde
9615 Grand Ronde Road
Grand Ronde, OR 97347
Phone: 800-422-0232 Ext. 2275
Fax: 503-879-2286
E-mail: education@grandronde.org

UNDERGRADUATE EDUCATION SCHOLARSHIPS

Available to any enrolled member of the Confederated Tribes of Grand Ronde. Five $3,000, two $4,500, and three $6,000 full-time awards, and two $3,000 part-time awards are given each year. Renewable for twelve terms/eight semesters of continuous study. Scholarship may be used at community colleges for transfer credits.

Award: Scholarship for use in freshman, sophomore, junior, or senior years; renewable. *Number:* 12. *Amount:* $3000–$6000.

Eligibility Requirements: Applicant must be American Indian/Alaska Native and enrolled or expecting to enroll full or part-time at a two-year or four-year institution or university. Available to U.S. and non-U.S. citizens.

Application Requirements: Application, essay, references, transcript, verification of Tribal enrollment. *Deadline:* April 30.

Contact: Tribal Scholarship Coordinator
Confederated Tribes of Grand Ronde
9615 Grand Ronde Road
Grand Ronde, OR 97347
Phone: 800-422-0232 Ext. 2275
Fax: 503-879-2286
E-mail: education@grandronde.org

CONGRESSIONAL HISPANIC CAUCUS INSTITUTE http://www.chciyouth.org

CONGRESSIONAL HISPANIC CAUCUS INSTITUTE SCHOLARSHIP AWARDS

One-time award for Latino students who have a history of public service-oriented activities. $2500 to attend a four-year or graduate level institution; $1000 to attend a two-year community college. Must be enrolled full time. See Web site at http://www.chci.org for further information.

Award: Scholarship for use in freshman, sophomore, junior, senior, or graduate years; not renewable. *Number:* 111. *Amount:* $1000–$2500.

Eligibility Requirements: Applicant must be Hispanic and enrolled or expecting to enroll full-time at a two-year or four-year institution or university.

Application Requirements: Application, essay, resume, references, transcript. *Deadline:* April 15.

Contact: CHCI Scholarship Awards
Congressional Hispanic Caucus Institute
504 C Street, NE
Washington, DC 20002
Phone: 202-543-1771

CONNECTICUT ASSOCIATION OF LATIN AMERICANS IN HIGHER EDUCATION (CALAHE) http://www.calahe.org

CONNECTICUT ASSOCIATION OF LATIN AMERICANS IN HIGHER EDUCATION SCHOLARSHIPS

Must demonstrate involvement with, and commitment to, activities that promote Latino pursuit of education. Must have a 3.0 GPA, be a U.S. citizen or permanent resident, be a resident of Connecticut, and attend a Connecticut higher education institution. Application deadline is April 15.

Award: Scholarship for use in freshman, sophomore, junior, or senior years; not renewable. *Number:* 5. *Amount:* $500.

Eligibility Requirements: Applicant must be Hispanic; enrolled or expecting to enroll full-time at a two-year or four-year or technical institution or university; resident of Connecticut and studying in Connecticut. Applicant must have 3.0 GPA or higher. Available to U.S. citizens.

Application Requirements: Application, essay, financial need analysis, transcript. *Deadline:* April 15.

Contact: Dr. Wilson Luna, Gateway Community-Technical College
Connecticut Association of Latin Americans in Higher Education (CALAHE)
60 Sargent Drive
New Haven, CT 06511
Phone: 203-285-2210
Fax: 203-285-2211
E-mail: wluna@gwcc.commnet.edu

CONSTANTINOPLE ARMENIAN RELIEF SOCIETY

CONSTANTINOPLE ARMENIAN RELIEF SOCIETY SCHOLARSHIP

Scholarships are only available to Armenian students enrolled in an accredited college or university in the U.S., starting with sophomore year. Emphasis on both merit and financial need. Students are required to complete and return the applications by August 30 in order to be considered. Scholarships can be renewed, but will only be awarded for two consecutive years. Must have minimum 3.0 GPA.

Award: Scholarship for use in sophomore or junior years; renewable. *Number:* varies. *Amount:* $300–$1000.

Eligibility Requirements: Applicant must be of Armenian heritage; enrolled or expecting to enroll full-time at a four-year institution or university and studying in Connecticut, New Jersey, New York, or Pennsylvania. Applicant must have 3.0 GPA or higher. Available to U.S. and non-U.S. citizens.

Application Requirements: Application, financial need analysis, references, self-addressed stamped envelope, transcript. *Deadline:* August 30.

Contact: Ms. Talin Sesetyan, Co-Chairperson, Scholarship Committee
Constantinople Armenian Relief Society
187 Villanova Drive
Paramus, NJ 07652
Phone: 201-447-7048
E-mail: talins11@hotmail.com

COUNCIL FOR INTERNATIONAL EDUCATIONAL EXCHANGE http://www.ciee.org/study

ROBERT B. BAILEY III MINORITY SCHOLARSHIPS FOR EDUCATION ABROAD

• *See page 524*

COUNCIL OF ENERGY RESOURCE TRIBES (CERT) EDUCATION FUND, INC. http://www.CERTredearth.com

COUNCIL OF ENERGY RESOURCES TRIBES EDUCATION FUND SCHOLARSHIP

Renewable scholarship for full-time Native-American students. Award applicable to any accredited two- or four-year institution including trade or technical school. Applicant must submit application, transcript, recommendations, and certificate proving Native-American heritage. Financial need will be taken into account. Deadlines: January 30th and July 15th. Must be accepted and have completed the 6 week T program at The University of New Mexico to be eligible for the CERT Scholarship.

Award: Scholarship for use in freshman, sophomore, junior, senior, or graduate years; renewable. *Number:* 30–40. *Amount:* up to $1000.

Eligibility Requirements: Applicant must be American Indian/Alaska Native and enrolled or expecting to enroll full-time at a two-year or four-year or technical institution or university. Applicant must have 2.5 GPA or higher. Available to U.S. and Canadian citizens.

Application Requirements: Application, financial need analysis, references, transcript, certificate of Indian blood. *Deadline:* varies.

Contact: Eric Tippeconnic, Education Director
Council of Energy Resource Tribes (CERT) Education Fund, Inc.
1 University of New Mexico, Office of the Provost, 322 Hokona Hall, MSC02 1590
Albuquerque, NM 87131-0001
Phone: 505-277-2651
Fax: 505-277-0228
E-mail: tippecon@unm.edu

CROATIAN SCHOLARSHIP FUND http://www.croatianscholarship.org/backgrd.html

CROATIAN SCHOLARSHIP FUND SCHOLARSHIP PROGRAM

The scholarship is given to individuals with high grades ("A"), financial needs of family and appropriate degree selection. Scholarships are given depending on funds availability and number of applicants.

Award: Scholarship for use in freshman, sophomore, junior, or senior years; renewable. *Number:* varies. *Amount:* $1200.

Eligibility Requirements: Applicant must be of Croatian/Serbian heritage; age 18-25 and enrolled or expecting to enroll full-time at a four-year institution. Applicant must have 3.5 GPA or higher. Available to U.S. and non-U.S. citizens.

Application Requirements: Application, autobiography, financial need analysis, photo, references, test scores, transcript. *Deadline:* April 15.

Contact: Croatian Scholarship Fund
Croatian Scholarship Fund
PO Box 290
San Ramon, CA 94583
Phone: 925-556-6263
Fax: 925-556-6263
E-mail: vbrekalo@msn.com

DOW JONES NEWSPAPER FUND http://djnewspaperfund.dowjones.com

DOW JONES NEWSPAPER FUND MINORITY BUSINESS REPORTING PROGRAM

One-time paid business reporting internship and $1000 scholarship for minority college sophomores and juniors returning to undergraduate studies. Must submit application, essay, transcript, clips, and resume; must take a test. Deadline is November 1.

Award: Scholarship for use in sophomore or junior years; not renewable. *Number:* 12. *Amount:* $1000.

Eligibility Requirements: Applicant must be American Indian/Alaska Native, Asian/Pacific Islander, Black (non-Hispanic), or Hispanic and enrolled or expecting to enroll full-time at a two-year or four-year institution. Available to U.S. citizens.

Application Requirements: Application, essay, portfolio, resume, references, transcript, test. *Deadline:* November 1.

Contact: Linda Waller, Deputy Director
Dow Jones Newspaper Fund
PO Box 300
Princeton, NJ 08543-0300
Phone: 609-452-2820
Fax: 609-520-5804
E-mail: newsfund@wsj.dowjones.com

ESPERANZA, INC. http://www.esperanzainc.com

ESPERANZA SCHOLARSHIPS

The Esperanza Scholarship is a one-year award valid only for full-time tuition and/or books at an accredited college or university. Recipients are eligible to apply yearly until they have completed their curriculum. Award restricted to residents of Cuyahoga or Lorain counties in Ohio.

Award: Scholarship for use in freshman, sophomore, junior, or senior years; not renewable. *Number:* 50. *Amount:* $500–$1250.

Eligibility Requirements: Applicant must be of Hispanic heritage; enrolled or expecting to enroll full-time at a two-year or four-year institution or university and resident of Ohio. Applicant must have 2.5 GPA or higher. Available to U.S. and non-U.S. citizens.

Application Requirements: Application, essay, interview, references, test scores, transcript. *Deadline:* March 15.

Contact: Olga Ferrer, Office Assistant
Esperanza, Inc.
4115 Bridge Avenue
Room 108
Cleveland, OH 44113
Phone: 216-651-7178
Fax: 216-651-7183
E-mail: hope4ed@aol.com

FIRST CATHOLIC SLOVAK LADIES ASSOCIATION http://www.fcsla.com

FIRST CATHOLIC SLOVAK LADIES ASSOCIATION FRATERNAL SCHOLARSHIP AWARD FOR COLLEGE AND GRADUATE STUDY

Must be FCSLA member in good standing for at least three years. Must attend accredited college in the U.S. or Canada in undergraduate or graduate degree program. Must submit certified copy of college acceptance. One-time tuition award; win once as undergraduate, up to $1250; once as graduate, up to $1750.

Award: Scholarship for use in freshman, sophomore, junior, senior, graduate, or postgraduate years; not renewable. *Number:* 100. *Amount:* up to $1750.

Eligibility Requirements: Applicant must be Roman Catholic; of Slavic/Czech heritage and enrolled or expecting to enroll full-time at a two-year or four-year institution or university. Available to U.S. and non-U.S. citizens.

Application Requirements: Application, autobiography, essay, photo, references, test scores, transcript. *Deadline:* March 1.

Contact: Ms. Dorothy Szumski, Director of Fraternal Scholarships
First Catholic Slovak Ladies Association
24950 Chagrin Boulevard
Beachwood, OH 44122
Phone: 216-464-8015 Ext. 134
Fax: 216-464-9260

FLORIDA DEPARTMENT OF EDUCATION http://www.floridastudentfinancialaid.org

JOSE MARTI SCHOLARSHIP CHALLENGE GRANT FUND

Award available to Hispanic-American students who were born in, or whose parent was born in a Hispanic country. Must have lived in Florida for one year, be enrolled full-time in Florida at an eligible school, and have a GPA of 3.0 or above. Must be U.S. citizen or eligible non-citizen. Renewable award of $2000. Application must be postmarked by April 1. Free Application for Federal Student Aid must be processed by May 15.

Award: Scholarship for use in freshman, or graduate years; renewable. *Number:* 63. *Amount:* $2000.

Florida Department of Education (continued)

Eligibility Requirements: Applicant must be of Hispanic heritage; enrolled or expecting to enroll full-time at a two-year or four-year institution or university; resident of Florida and studying in Florida. Applicant must have 3.0 GPA or higher. Available to U.S. citizens.

Application Requirements: Application, financial need analysis, FAFSA. *Deadline:* April 1.

Contact: Scholarship Information
Florida Department of Education
Office of Student Financial Assistance
1940 North Monroe, Suite 70
Tallahassee, FL 32303-4759
Phone: 888-827-2004
E-mail: osfa@fldoe.org

ROSEWOOD FAMILY SCHOLARSHIP FUND

Renewable award for eligible minority students to attend a Florida public postsecondary institution on a full-time basis. Preference given to direct descendants of African-American Rosewood families affected by the incidents of January 1923. Must be Black, Hispanic, Asian, Pacific Islander, American-Indian, or Alaska Native. Free Application for Federal Student Aid (and Student Aid Report for nonresidents of Florida) must be processed by May 15.

Award: Scholarship for use in freshman, sophomore, junior, or senior years; renewable. *Number:* up to 25. *Amount:* up to $4000.

Eligibility Requirements: Applicant must be American Indian/Alaska Native, Asian/Pacific Islander, Black (non-Hispanic), or Hispanic; enrolled or expecting to enroll full-time at a two-year or four-year or technical institution or university and studying in Florida. Available to U.S. citizens.

Application Requirements: Application, financial need analysis. *Deadline:* April 1.

Contact: Scholarship Information
Florida Department of Education
Office of Student Financial Assistance
1940 North Monroe, Suite 70
Tallahassee, FL 32303-4759
Phone: 888-827-2004
E-mail: osfa@fldoe.org

FOND DU LAC RESERVATION http://www.fdlrez.com

FOND DU LAC SCHOLARSHIP PROGRAM

Must be enrolled tribal member and have high school diploma or GED. Must be accepted for admission at accredited college, university or technical school. Must complete FAFSA and all other required applications. All recipients must submit grades at the end of each term, must maintain 2.0 GPA for continued funding.

Award: Scholarship for use in freshman, sophomore, junior, senior, graduate, or postgraduate years; renewable. *Number:* 75–125. *Amount:* $500–$12,000.

Eligibility Requirements: Applicant must be American Indian/Alaska Native and enrolled or expecting to enroll full or part-time at a two-year or four-year or technical institution or university. Available to U.S. citizens.

Application Requirements: Application, financial need analysis, transcript. *Deadline:* May 15.

Contact: Bonnie Wallace, Scholarship Director
Fond Du Lac Reservation
1720 Big Lake Road, Federal Tribal Center
Cloquet, MN 55720
Phone: 218-879-4593 Ext. 2681
Fax: 218-878-7529
E-mail: scholarships@fdlrez.com

GENERAL BOARD OF GLOBAL MINISTRIES http://www.gbgm-umc.org

NATIONAL LEADERSHIP DEVELOPMENT GRANTS

Award for racial and ethnic minority members of the United Methodist Church who are pursuing undergraduate study. Must be U.S. citizen, resident alien, or reside in U.S. as a refugee. Renewable award of $500 to $5000. Deadline: May 31.

Award: Grant for use in freshman, sophomore, junior, or senior years; renewable. *Number:* 75. *Amount:* $500–$5000.

Eligibility Requirements: Applicant must be Methodist; American Indian/Alaska Native, Asian/Pacific Islander, Black (non-Hispanic), or Hispanic and enrolled or expecting to enroll full-time at a two-year or four-year or technical institution or university. Available to U.S. and non-U.S. citizens.

Application Requirements: Application, essay, financial need analysis, photo, references, transcript. *Deadline:* May 31.

Contact: Scholarship Office
General Board of Global Ministries
475 Riverside Drive
Room 1351
New York, NY 10115
Phone: 212-870-3787
Fax: 212-870-3932
E-mail: scholars@gbgm-umc.org

GEORGE BIRD GRINNELL AMERICAN INDIAN FUND

SCHUYLER M. MEYER, JR. AWARD

Up to $1000 scholarship for American-Indian/Alaska Native students enrolled in either an undergraduate or graduate program. Applicants must demonstrate financial need, submit personal statement, proof of school enrollment or acceptance and proof of tribal enrollment. Award of scholarship is totally contingent upon raising the needed funds. Application deadline is June 1. Please include self-addressed stamped envelope.

Award: Scholarship for use in freshman, sophomore, junior, senior, graduate, or postgraduate years; renewable. *Number:* up to 20. *Amount:* up to $1000.

Eligibility Requirements: Applicant must be American Indian/Alaska Native and enrolled or expecting to enroll full or part-time at a two-year or four-year institution or university. Available to U.S. citizens.

Application Requirements: Application, essay, financial need analysis, references, self-addressed stamped envelope, transcript, proof of tribal enrollment. *Deadline:* June 1.

Contact: Dr. Paula Mintzies, President
George Bird Grinnell American Indian Fund
PO Box 59033
Potomac, MD 20859
Phone: 301-424-2440
Fax: 301-424-8281

GREEK WOMEN'S UNIVERSITY CLUB

GREEK WOMEN'S UNIVERSITY CLUB SCHOLARSHIPS

Award for female full-time college students with at least sophomore standing or full-time graduate students. Must be U.S. citizen with at least one parent of Greek descent and resident of Chicago metropolitan area. Must have minimum 3.0 GPA. Deadline: October 26.

Award: Scholarship for use in sophomore, junior, senior, graduate, or postgraduate years; not renewable. *Number:* 2. *Amount:* $500–$1000.

Eligibility Requirements: Applicant must be of Greek heritage; enrolled or expecting to enroll full-time at a four-year institution or university; female and resident of Illinois. Applicant must have 3.0 GPA or higher. Available to U.S. citizens.

Application Requirements: Application, autobiography, essay, financial need analysis, interview, references, transcript. *Deadline:* October 26.

Contact: Sophia Patsios, Scholarship Chairperson
Greek Women's University Club
7223 Oak Street
River Forest, IL 60305
E-mail: sopatsios@aol.com

HBCU-CENTRAL.COM http://www.hbcu-central.com/

HBCU-CENTRAL.COM MINORITY SCHOLARSHIP PROGRAM

Targeted to minorities that choose to attend Historically Black Colleges and Universities. Recipients are selected based on essay submissions, grades, and financial need.

Award: Scholarship for use in freshman, sophomore, junior, or senior years; not renewable. *Number:* 3–10. *Amount:* $1000–$2500.

Eligibility Requirements: Applicant must be American Indian/Alaska Native, Asian/Pacific Islander, Black (non-Hispanic), or Hispanic and enrolled or expecting to enroll full-time at a four-year institution or university. Available to U.S. citizens.

Application Requirements: Application, autobiography, essay, interview, transcript. *Deadline:* May 15.

Contact: William Moss, Scholarship Administrator
HBCU-Central.com
7846 Grandlin Park
Suite AA
Blacklick, OH 43004
Phone: 614-284-3007
Fax: 215-893-5398
E-mail: wrmoss@hbcu-central.com

HELEN GOUGH SCHOLARSHIP FOUNDATION

HELEN GOUGH SCHOLARSHIP

Applicants must be enrolled members of the three affiliated tribes of the Fort Berthold Reservation, have a high school diploma or GED and a 2.0 GPA in good standing. Award is for undergraduates and graduates with priority going to undergraduates. Must reapply each year.

Award: Scholarship for use in freshman, sophomore, junior, senior, or graduate years; not renewable. *Number:* 1–40. *Amount:* $200–$500.

Eligibility Requirements: Applicant must be American Indian/Alaska Native and enrolled or expecting to enroll full-time at a two-year or four-year institution or university. Available to U.S. citizens.

Application Requirements: Application, references, transcript, certificate of Tribal enrollment. *Deadline:* June 1.

Contact: Martha Hunter, Education Program Director
Helen Gough Scholarship Foundation
404 Frontage Road
New Town, ND 58763
Phone: 888-230-2384
Fax: 701-627-2295
E-mail: mhunter@mhanation.com

HELLENIC TIMES SCHOLARSHIP FUND http://www.htsfund.org

HELLENIC TIMES SCHOLARSHIP FUND

One-time award to students of Greek/Hellenic descent. Must be between the ages of 17-30. For use in any year of undergraduate education. Deadline is January 16.

Award: Scholarship for use in freshman, sophomore, junior, or senior years; not renewable. *Number:* 30–40. *Amount:* $500–$10,000.

Eligibility Requirements: Applicant must be of Greek heritage; age 17-30 and enrolled or expecting to enroll full or part-time at a two-year or four-year or technical institution or university. Available to U.S. and non-U.S. citizens.

Application Requirements: Application, financial need analysis, resume, references, transcript. *Deadline:* January 16.

Contact: Nick Katsoris
Hellenic Times Scholarship Fund
823 Eleventh Avenue, 5th Floor
New York, NY 10019-3535
Phone: 212-986-6881
Fax: 212-977-3662
E-mail: htsfund@aol.com

HENRY SACHS FOUNDATION http://www.frii.com/~sachs

SACHS FOUNDATION SCHOLARSHIPS

Award for graduating African- American high school seniors who have been residents of Colorado for at least five years. Based on financial need and GPA of 3.7 or higher. Deadline: February 15.

Award: Scholarship for use in freshman year; renewable. *Number:* 30. *Amount:* $4000.

Eligibility Requirements: Applicant must be Black (non-Hispanic); high school student; planning to enroll or expecting to enroll full-time at a two-year or four-year institution or university and resident of Colorado. Available to U.S. citizens.

Application Requirements: Application, financial need analysis, interview, photo, references, transcript. *Deadline:* February 15.

Contact: Lisa Harris, Secretary and Treasurer
Henry Sachs Foundation
90 South Cascade Avenue, Suite 1410
Colorado Springs, CO 80903
Phone: 719-633-2353
E-mail: sachs@frii.com

HISPANIC ALLIANCE CAREER ENHANCEMENT http://www.hace-usa.org

HISPANIC ALLIANCE FOR CAREER ENHANCEMENT NATIONAL SCHOLARSHIP PROGRAM

Provides financial support to encourage enrollment in and graduation from college by young Hispanic professionals.

Award: Scholarship for use in freshman, sophomore, junior, or senior years; not renewable. *Number:* 1–10. *Amount:* $500–$1000.

Eligibility Requirements: Applicant must be Hispanic and enrolled or expecting to enroll full or part-time at a four-year institution or university. Applicant must have 3.0 GPA or higher. Available to U.S. citizens.

Application Requirements: Application, autobiography, essay, resume. *Deadline:* March 31.

Contact: Griselda Garibay, Program Officer
Hispanic Alliance Career Enhancement
25 East Washington Street
Suite 1500
Chicago, IL 60602
Phone: 312-435-0498
Fax: 312-435-1494
E-mail: griselda@hace-usa.org

HISPANIC COLLEGE FUND, INC. http://www.hispanicfund.org

FIRST IN MY FAMILY SCHOLARSHIP PROGRAM

One-time scholarship open to full-time undergraduates of Hispanic descent who are the first in their family to attend college. Must be a U.S. citizen residing in the United States or Puerto Rico and have a minimum 3.0 GPA.

Award: Scholarship for use in freshman, sophomore, junior, or senior years; not renewable. *Number:* 100–200. *Amount:* $1000–$5000.

Eligibility Requirements: Applicant must be Hispanic and enrolled or expecting to enroll full-time at a two-year or four-year or technical institution or university. Applicant must have 3.0 GPA or higher. Available to U.S. citizens.

Application Requirements: Application, essay, financial need analysis, resume, references, test scores, transcript, college acceptance letter, copy of taxes, copy of SAR. *Deadline:* April 15.

Contact: Stina Augustsson, Program Manager
Hispanic College Fund, Inc.
1717 Pennsylvania Avenue, NW, Suite 460
Washington, DC 20006
Phone: 202-296-5400
Fax: 202-296-3774
E-mail: hcf-info@hispanicfund.org

HISPANIC COLLEGE FUND SCHOLARSHIP PROGRAM

This program awards scholarships to full-time students of Hispanic origin who have demonstrated academic excellence, leadership skills and financial

Hispanic College Fund, Inc. (continued)

need to pursue an undergraduate degree. Must be a U.S. permanent resident or U.S. citizen and have a minimum of a 3.0 GPA.

Award: Scholarship for use in freshman, sophomore, junior, or senior years; not renewable. *Number:* 500–750. *Amount:* $1000–$5000.

Eligibility Requirements: Applicant must be Hispanic and enrolled or expecting to enroll full-time at a two-year or four-year institution or university. Applicant must have 3.0 GPA or higher. Available to U.S. citizens.

Application Requirements: Application, essay, financial need analysis, resume, references, transcript, college acceptance letter, copy of taxes, copy of SAR. *Deadline:* April 15.

Contact: Stina Augustsson, Program Manager
Hispanic College Fund, Inc.
1717 Pennsylvania Avenue, NW, Suite 460
Washington, DC 20006
Phone: 202-296-5400
Fax: 202-296-3774
E-mail: hcf-info@hispanicfund.org

SILVESTRE REYES SCHOLARSHIP PROGRAM

One-time scholarship open to full-time undergraduate students of Hispanic descent residing in U.S. House of Representative member Silvestre Reyes' 16th district, Texas. Must be a U.S. citizen or permanent resident with a minimum GPA of 3.0.

Award: Scholarship for use in freshman, sophomore, junior, or senior years; not renewable. *Number:* varies. *Amount:* $500–$5000.

Eligibility Requirements: Applicant must be Hispanic; enrolled or expecting to enroll full-time at a two-year or four-year institution or university and resident of Texas. Applicant must have 3.0 GPA or higher. Available to U.S. citizens.

Application Requirements: Application, essay, financial need analysis. *Deadline:* April 15.

Contact: Stina Augustsson, Program Manager
Hispanic College Fund, Inc.
1717 Pennsylvania Avenue, NW, Suite 460
Washington, DC 20006
Phone: 202-296-5400
Fax: 202-296-3774
E-mail: hcf-info@hispanicfund.org

HISPANIC HERITAGE FOUNDATION AWARDS

http://www.hispanicheritageawards.org

HHAF CHASE AND MASTERCARD ACADEMIC EXCELLENCE YOUTH AWARD

Educational grants are awarded to two Hispanic students in each of twelve regions for demonstrated academic excellence. One student will receive $2000 and the other will receive $3000. One national winner will receive a $5000 educational grant from the pool of regional winners. For more details or an application see Web site: http://www.hispanicheritageawards.org.

Award: Grant for use in freshman year; not renewable. *Number:* 25. *Amount:* $2000–$5000.

Eligibility Requirements: Applicant must be of Hispanic heritage; high school student and planning to enroll or expecting to enroll at an institution or university. Available to U.S. citizens.

Application Requirements: Application, references, transcript. *Deadline:* February 10.

Contact: Application available at Web site.

HHAF DR. PEPPER LEADERSHIP AND COMMUNITY SERVICE YOUTH AWARD

Educational grants are awarded to two Hispanic students in each of twelve regions for demonstrated interest in leadership, community service, and academic excellence in general. One student will receive $2000 and the other will receive $3000. One national winner will receive a $5000 educational grant from the pool of regional winners. For more details or an application see Web site: http://www.hispanicheritageawards.org.

Award: Grant for use in freshman year; not renewable. *Number:* 25. *Amount:* $2000–$5000.

Eligibility Requirements: Applicant must be of Hispanic heritage; high school student and planning to enroll or expecting to enroll at an institution or university. Available to U.S. citizens.

Application Requirements: Application, references, transcript. *Deadline:* February 10.

Contact: Application available at Web site.

HHAF EXXON MOBIL MATHEMATICS YOUTH AWARD

Educational grants are awarded to two Hispanic students in each of twelve regions for demonstrated interest in mathematics and academics excellence in general. One student will receive $2000 and the other will receive $3000. One national winner will receive a $5000 educational grant from the pool of regional winners. For more details or an application see Web site: http://www.hispanicheritageawards.org.

Award: Grant for use in freshman year; not renewable. *Number:* 25. *Amount:* $2000–$5000.

Eligibility Requirements: Applicant must be of Hispanic heritage; high school student and planning to enroll or expecting to enroll at an institution or university. Available to U.S. citizens.

Application Requirements: Application, references, transcript. *Deadline:* February 10.

Contact: Application available at Web site.

HHAF GLAXO SMITH KLINE HEALTH AND SCIENCE YOUTH AWARD

Educational grants are awarded to two Hispanic students in each of twelve regions for demonstrated interest in Health and Science and academic excellence in general. One student will receive $2000 and the other will receive $3000. One national winner will receive a $5000 educational grant from the pool of regional winners. For more details or an application see Web site: http://www.hispanicheritageawards.org.

Award: Grant for use in freshman year; not renewable. *Number:* 25. *Amount:* $2000–$5000.

Eligibility Requirements: Applicant must be of Hispanic heritage; high school student and planning to enroll or expecting to enroll at an institution or university. Available to U.S. citizens.

Application Requirements: Application, references, transcript. *Deadline:* February 10.

Contact: Application available at Web site.

HHAF NBC JOURNALISM YOUTH AWARD

Educational grants are awarded to two Hispanic students in each of twelve regions for demonstrated interest in journalism and academic excellence in general. One student will receive $2000 and the other will receive $3000. One national winner will receive a $5000 educational grant from the pool of regional winners. For more details or an application see Web site: http://www.hispanicheritageawards.org.

Award: Grant for use in freshman year; not renewable. *Number:* 25. *Amount:* $2000–$5000.

Eligibility Requirements: Applicant must be of Hispanic heritage; high school student and planning to enroll or expecting to enroll at an institution or university. Available to U.S. citizens.

Application Requirements: Application, references, transcript. *Deadline:* February 10.

Contact: Application available at Web site.

HHAF SPORTS YOUTH AWARD

Educational grants are awarded to two Hispanic students in each of twelve regions for demonstrated interest in sports and academic excellence in general. One student will receive $2000 and the other will receive $3000. One national winner will receive a $5000 educational grant from the pool of regional winners. For more details or an application see Web site: http://www.hispanicheritageawards.org.

Award: Grant for use in freshman year; not renewable. *Number:* 25. *Amount:* $2000–$5000.

Eligibility Requirements: Applicant must be of Hispanic heritage; high school student and planning to enroll or expecting to enroll at an institution or university. Available to U.S. citizens.

Application Requirements: Application, references, transcript. *Deadline:* February 10.

Contact: Application available at Web site.

HHAF/WARNER BROS. ENTERTAINMENT, INC. ARTS AND ENTERTAINMENT YOUTH AWARD

Educational grants are awarded to two Hispanic students in each of twelve regions for demonstrated interest in arts and entertainment and academic interest in general. One student will receive $2000 and the other will receive $3000. One national winner will receive a $5000 educational grant from the pool of regional winners. Details on Web site: http://ww.hispanicheritageawards.org.

Award: Grant for use in freshman year; not renewable. *Number:* 25. *Amount:* $2000–$5000.

Eligibility Requirements: Applicant must be of Hispanic heritage; high school student and planning to enroll or expecting to enroll at an institution or university. Available to U.S. citizens.

Application Requirements: Application, references, transcript. *Deadline:* February 10.

Contact: Hispanic Heritage Foundation Awards
2600 Virginia Avenue, NW, Suite 406
Washington, DC 20037-1905

HISPANIC PUBLIC RELATIONS ASSOCIATION — http://www.hprala.org

SCHOLARSHIP PROGRAM

Scholarship open to California junior and senior students of Hispanic descent with at least a 2.7 cumulative GPA and 3.0 GPA in their major subject. Preference is given to students majoring in public relations but students in communication studies, journalism, advertising and/or marketing will be considered. Students majoring in other disciplines who have a desire to work in public relations industry are invited to apply. For more details and application see Web site http://www.hprala.org.

Award: Scholarship for use in junior or senior years; not renewable. *Number:* 10. *Amount:* $1000.

Eligibility Requirements: Applicant must be Hispanic; enrolled or expecting to enroll full-time at a four-year institution or university and studying in California. Available to U.S. and non-U.S. citizens.

Application Requirements: Application, essay, resume, references, transcript. *Deadline:* May 30.

Contact: Scholarship Committee
Hispanic Public Relations Association
660 South Figueroa Street, Suite 1140
Los Angeles, CA 90017

HISPANIC SCHOLARSHIP FUND — http://www.hsf.net

COCA-COLA/HSF ADVANCING TO UNIVERSITIES SCHOLARSHIP

Scholarship is designed to assist community college students of Hispanic heritage obtain a bachelor's degree. Applicants must be enrolled part time or full time at specific community colleges in Atlanta, Chicago, Florida, California, Texas, and New York. See Web site for list of specific community colleges.

Award: Scholarship for use in junior or senior years. *Number:* varies. *Amount:* $1000–$2000.

Eligibility Requirements: Applicant must be Hispanic; enrolled or expecting to enroll full or part-time at a two-year institution and studying in California, Florida, Georgia, Illinois, New York, or Texas. Applicant must have 3.0 GPA or higher.

Application Requirements: Application, essay, financial need analysis, references, transcript. *Deadline:* February 15.

Contact: HSF Scholarship Department
Hispanic Scholarship Fund
55 Second Street, Suite 1500
San Francisco, CA 94105
Phone: 877-HSF-INFO
Fax: 415-808-2302
E-mail: info@hsf.net

COLLEGE SCHOLARSHIP PROGRAM

Awards available to full-time undergraduate or graduate students of Hispanic origin. Applicants must have 12 college units with a minimum 2.7 GPA before applying. Merit-based award for U.S. citizens or permanent residents. Must include financial aid award letter and SAR.

Award: Scholarship for use in sophomore, junior, senior, or graduate years; not renewable. *Number:* 2900–3500. *Amount:* $1000–$3000.

Eligibility Requirements: Applicant must be of Latin American/ Caribbean, Mexican, or Spanish heritage; Hispanic and enrolled or expecting to enroll full-time at a two-year or four-year institution or university. Available to U.S. citizens.

Application Requirements: Application, essay, financial need analysis, references, self-addressed stamped envelope, transcript. *Deadline:* October 15.

Contact: Art Taylor, Program Officer-College Scholarship
Hispanic Scholarship Fund
55 Second Street, Suite 1500
San Francisco, CA 94105
Phone: 415-808-2300
Fax: 415-808-2301
E-mail: info@hsf.net

COMMUNITY COLLEGE TRANSFER PROGRAMS

Available to community college students in certain geographical areas transferring on a full-time basis to four-year institution in fall of following year. Must be of Hispanic descent, U.S. citizen or legal permanent resident with a minimum GPA of 3.0.

Award: Scholarship for use in freshman or sophomore years; not renewable. *Number:* varies. *Amount:* $1500–$2500.

Eligibility Requirements: Applicant must be of Hispanic heritage and enrolled or expecting to enroll full-time at a two-year institution. Applicant must have 3.0 GPA or higher. Available to U.S. and non-Canadian citizens.

Application Requirements: Application, essay, references, transcript. *Deadline:* February 15.

Contact: Rita d'Escoto, Program Assistant
Hispanic Scholarship Fund
55 Second Street, Suite 1500
San Francisco, CA 94105
Phone: 415-808-2370
Fax: 415-808-2304
E-mail: rdescoto@hsf.net

GATES MILLENNIUM SCHOLARS PROGRAM

Award enables Hispanic-American students to complete an undergraduate or graduate education. Must be entering a U.S.-accredited college or university as a full-time degree-seeking student. Minimum 3.3 GPA required. Must demonstrate leadership abilities. Must meet federal Pell Grant eligibility criteria. Visit Web site at http://www.gmsp.org.

Award: Scholarship for use in freshman, sophomore, junior, senior, or graduate years; renewable. *Number:* 1000. *Amount:* varies.

Eligibility Requirements: Applicant must be Hispanic and enrolled or expecting to enroll full-time at a four-year institution or university. Available to U.S. citizens.

Application Requirements: Application, financial need analysis, nomination packet. *Deadline:* January 16.

Contact: GMS Representative
Hispanic Scholarship Fund
55 Second Street, Suite 1500
San Francisco, CA 94105
Phone: 415-217-5040
Fax: 415-217-5047
E-mail: gmsinfo@hsf.net

HIGH SCHOOL PROGRAM

Designed to increase educational attainment of U.S. and Puerto Rico Hispanic high school students. Minimum 3.0 GPA required. Must be high school senior planning to attend accredited college or university the following fall semester after graduation.

Hispanic Scholarship Fund (continued)

Award: Scholarship for use in freshman year; not renewable. *Number:* varies. *Amount:* $1000–$2500.

Eligibility Requirements: Applicant must be of Hispanic heritage; high school student and planning to enroll or expecting to enroll full-time at a two-year or four-year institution or university. Applicant must have 3.0 GPA or higher. Available to U.S. and non-Canadian citizens.

Application Requirements: Application, essay, financial need analysis, references, self-addressed stamped envelope, transcript. *Deadline:* February 15.

Contact: Sara Piredes, Program Office, High School Scholarship Program
Hispanic Scholarship Fund
55 Second Street, Suite 1500
San Francisco, CA 94105
Phone: 877-473-4636 Ext. 2372
Fax: 415-808-2304
E-mail: highschool@hsf.net

HSF/CAMINO AL ÉXITO SCHOLARSHIP PROGRAM

Scholarship available on a competitive basis to Hispanic high school and college students in the metropolitan areas of Los Angeles, New York, Miami, and Chicago. Awards of $5000 for students attending private colleges or universities and $2500 for students attending public colleges or universities.

Award: Scholarship for use in freshman, sophomore, junior, senior, or graduate years. *Number:* varies. *Amount:* $2500–$5000.

Eligibility Requirements: Applicant must be Hispanic and enrolled or expecting to enroll full-time at an institution or university.

Application Requirements: Application, financial need analysis, transcript. *Deadline:* February 15.

Contact: HSF Scholarship Department
Hispanic Scholarship Fund
55 Second Street, Suite 1500
San Francisco, CA 94105
Phone: 877-HSF-INFO
Fax: 415-808-2302
E-mail: info@hsf.net

HSF/CLUB MUSICA LATINA SCHOLARSHIP

Scholarships are available to Hispanic students entering their freshman or sophomore year at an accredited U.S. four-year college. Must be a member of Club Musica Latina. For more details, deadlines and an application see Web site: http://www.hsf.net.

Award: Scholarship for use in freshman or sophomore years; not renewable. *Number:* varies. *Amount:* $2500.

Eligibility Requirements: Applicant must be Hispanic and enrolled or expecting to enroll full-time at a four-year institution or university. Applicant must have 3.0 GPA or higher. Available to U.S. citizens.

Application Requirements: Application.

Contact: Application available at Web site.

HSF/TOYOTA FOUNDATION SCHOLARSHIP PROGRAM-PUERTO RICO

Scholarships are available to graduating high school seniors who are residents of Puerto Rico entering their freshman year at a Puerto Rican institution. For more details, deadlines and an application see Web site: http://www.hsf.net.

Award: Scholarship for use in freshman year; not renewable. *Number:* varies. *Amount:* $2500.

Eligibility Requirements: Applicant must be Hispanic; high school student; planning to enroll or expecting to enroll full-time at a four-year institution or university; resident of Puerto Rico and studying in Puerto Rico. Applicant must have 3.0 GPA or higher. Available to U.S. citizens.

Application Requirements: Application. *Deadline:* May 9.

Contact: Application available at Web site.

HSF/TOYOTA SCHOLARSHIP PROGRAM

Scholarships are available to Hispanic students who are entering their freshman year. For more details, deadlines and an application see Web site: http://www.hsf.net.

Award: Scholarship for use in freshman year; not renewable. *Number:* varies. *Amount:* $5000.

Eligibility Requirements: Applicant must be Hispanic; high school student and planning to enroll or expecting to enroll full-time at a two-year or four-year institution or university. Applicant must have 3.0 GPA or higher. Available to U.S. citizens.

Application Requirements: Application. *Deadline:* September 20.

Contact: Application available at Web site.

NEW HORIZONS SCHOLARS PROGRAM

Renewable award available to Hispanic and African-American students who are infected with Hepatitis C or who are the dependents of a person infected with Hepatitis C. Students are eligible for $2500 per year for four years. Must maintain academic standard of 2.5 GPA. For more details and an application see Web site: http://www.hsf.net or http://www.thurgoodmarshallfund.org. Application deadline is February 20. Program is funded by the Roche Foundation.

Award: Scholarship for use in freshman year; renewable. *Number:* up to 50. *Amount:* $2500.

Eligibility Requirements: Applicant must be Black (non-Hispanic) or Hispanic; high school student and planning to enroll or expecting to enroll full-time at a four-year institution or university. Applicant must have 2.5 GPA or higher. Available to U.S. citizens.

Application Requirements: Application, driver's license, essay, financial need analysis, references, self-addressed stamped envelope, transcript. *Deadline:* February 20.

Contact: Application available at Web site.

HOPI TRIBE

BIA HIGHER EDUCATION GRANT

Grant provides financial support for eligible Hopi individuals pursuing postsecondary education. Minimum 2.5 GPA required. Deadlines are July 31 for fall, and November 30 for spring.

Award: Grant for use in freshman, sophomore, junior, or senior years; not renewable. *Number:* 1–130. *Amount:* $50–$2500.

Eligibility Requirements: Applicant must be American Indian/Alaska Native and enrolled or expecting to enroll full or part-time at a two-year or four-year institution or university. Applicant must have 2.5 GPA or higher. Available to U.S. citizens.

Application Requirements: Application, financial need analysis, test scores, transcript, certificate of Indian blood. *Deadline:* varies.

Contact: Theresa Lomakema, Administrative Secretary
Hopi Tribe
PO Box 123
Kykotsmovi, AZ 86039-0123
Phone: 928-734-3533
Fax: 928-734-9575
E-mail: talomakema@hopi.nsn.us

HOPI SUPPLEMENTAL GRANT

Grant provides financial support for eligible Hopi individuals pursuing postsecondary education. Minimum 2.5 GPA required. Deadlines are April 30 for summer, July 31 for fall, and November 30 for spring.

Award: Grant for use in freshman, sophomore, junior, or senior years; not renewable. *Number:* 1–400. *Amount:* $50–$1500.

Eligibility Requirements: Applicant must be American Indian/Alaska Native and enrolled or expecting to enroll full or part-time at a two-year or four-year institution or university. Applicant must have 2.5 GPA or higher. Available to U.S. citizens.

Application Requirements: Application, financial need analysis, test scores, transcript, certificate of Indian blood. *Deadline:* varies.

Contact: Theresa Lomakema, Administrative Secretary
Hopi Tribe
PO Box 123
Kykotsmovi, AZ 86039-0123
Phone: 928-734-3533
Fax: 928-734-9575
E-mail: talomakema@hopi.nsn.us

PEABODY SCHOLARSHIP

Scholarship provides financial support for eligible Hopi individuals pursuing postsecondary education. Minimum 3.0 GPA required. Deadline is July 31.

Award: Scholarship for use in freshman, sophomore, junior, senior, graduate, or postgraduate years; not renewable. *Number:* 1–90. *Amount:* $50–$1000.

Eligibility Requirements: Applicant must be American Indian/Alaska Native and enrolled or expecting to enroll full-time at a two-year or four-year institution or university. Applicant must have 3.0 GPA or higher. Available to U.S. citizens.

Application Requirements: Application, financial need analysis, test scores, transcript, certificate of Indian blood. *Deadline:* July 31.

Contact: Theresa Lomakema, Administrative Secretary
Hopi Tribe
PO Box 123
Kykotsmovi, AZ 86039-0123
Phone: 928-734-3533
Fax: 928-734-9575
E-mail: talomakema@hopi.nsn.us

IDAHO STATE BOARD OF EDUCATION http://www.idahoboardofed.org

IDAHO MINORITY AND "AT RISK" STUDENT SCHOLARSHIP

• *See page 526*

INDIAN AMERICAN CULTURAL ASSOCIATION http://www.iasf.org

INDIAN AMERICAN SCHOLARSHIP FUND

Scholarships for descendents of families who are from modern-day India and are graduating from public or private high schools in Georgia. They must be enrolled in four-year colleges or universities. There are both academic and need-based awards available through this program. See the Web site (http://www.iasf.org) for details and application forms. Deadline is May 3 for merit scholarships and May 24 for financial aid scholarships.

Award: Scholarship for use in freshman, sophomore, junior, or senior years; renewable. *Number:* varies. *Amount:* $500–$2500.

Eligibility Requirements: Applicant must be of Indian heritage; Asian/Pacific Islander; high school student; planning to enroll or expecting to enroll full-time at a four-year institution or university and resident of Georgia.

Application Requirements: Application, essay, financial need analysis, resume, test scores, transcript, IRS 1040 form. *Deadline:* varies.

Contact: Dr. Anuj Manocha
Indian American Cultural Association
719 Vinings Estates Drive
Mableton, GA 30126
E-mail: manochaa@bellsouth.net

INDIAN HEALTH SERVICES, UNITED STATES DEPARTMENT OF HEALTH AND HUMAN SERVICES http://www.ihs.gov

HEALTH PROFESSIONS PREPARATORY SCHOLARSHIP PROGRAM

Renewable scholarship available for undergraduate, graduate, or doctoral study in health professions and allied health professions programs. Minimum 2.0 GPA required. Award averages $18,500. New applicants must first submit to Area Scholarship Coordinator. There are service obligations and payback requirements that the recipient incurs upon acceptance of the scholarship funding. Contact office for more information.

Award: Scholarship for use in freshman, sophomore, junior, senior, or graduate years; renewable. *Number:* up to 393. *Amount:* $18,500.

Eligibility Requirements: Applicant must be American Indian/Alaska Native and enrolled or expecting to enroll full or part-time at a two-year or four-year or technical institution or university. Available to U.S. citizens.

Application Requirements: Application, applicant must enter a contest, essay, references, transcript, proof of descent. *Deadline:* February 28.

Contact: Jeff Brien, Acting Chief, Scholarship Branch
Indian Health Services, United States Department of Health and Human Services
801 Thompson Avenue, Suite 120
Rockville, MD 20852
Phone: 301-443-6197
Fax: 301-443-6048

INDIAN HEALTH SERVICE HEALTH PROFESSIONS PRE-PROFESSIONAL SCHOLARSHIP

Renewable scholarship available for full-or part-time undergraduate study. Minimum 2.0 GPA required. Award averages $18,500. First time applicants must submit application to Area Scholarship Coordinator. Must be Native-American. Must enroll in courses that are either compensatory or pre-professional; required in order to qualify for entrance into a health professions program. Must be member of federally recognized tribe.

Award: Scholarship for use in freshman, sophomore, junior, or senior years; renewable. *Number:* varies. *Amount:* $18,500.

Eligibility Requirements: Applicant must be American Indian/Alaska Native and enrolled or expecting to enroll full or part-time at a two-year or four-year or technical institution or university. Available to U.S. citizens.

Application Requirements: Application, applicant must enter a contest, essay, references, transcript, proof of descent. *Deadline:* February 28.

Contact: Jeff Brien, Acting Chief, Scholarship Branch
Indian Health Services, United States Department of Health and Human Services
801 Thompson Avenue
Rockville, MD 20852
Phone: 301-443-6197
Fax: 301-443-6048

INTER-TRIBAL COUNCIL OF MICHIGAN, INC. http://www.itcmi.org

MICHIGAN INDIAN TUITION WAIVER

Renewable award provides free tuition for Native-American of one-quarter or more blood degree who attend a Michigan public college or university. Must be a Michigan resident for at least one year. For more details and deadlines contact college financial aid office.

Award: Scholarship for use in freshman, sophomore, junior, senior, graduate, or postgraduate years; renewable. *Number:* varies. *Amount:* varies.

Eligibility Requirements: Applicant must be American Indian/Alaska Native; enrolled or expecting to enroll full or part-time at a two-year or four-year institution or university; resident of Michigan and studying in Michigan. Available to U.S. and Canadian citizens.

Application Requirements: Application, driver's license. *Deadline:* Continuous.

Contact: Christin McKerchie, Executive Assistant to Programs
Inter-Tribal Council of Michigan, Inc.
405 East Easterday Avenue
Sault Ste. Marie, MI 49783
Phone: 906-632-6896
Fax: 906-632-1810
E-mail: christin@itcmi.org

INTERNATIONAL ORDER OF THE KING'S DAUGHTERS AND SONS http://www.iokds.org

INTERNATIONAL ORDER OF THE KING'S DAUGHTERS AND SONS NORTH AMERICAN INDIAN SCHOLARSHIP

For enrolled American-Indians. Proof of reservation registration, college acceptance letter, and financial aid office address required. Request application form by March 1 and return by April 15. Merit-based award. Send self-addressed stamped envelope.

Award: Scholarship for use in freshman, sophomore, junior, or senior years; renewable. *Number:* 45–60. *Amount:* $500–$1000.

Eligibility Requirements: Applicant must be American Indian/Alaska Native and enrolled or expecting to enroll at an institution or university. Applicant must have 2.5 GPA or higher. Available to U.S. and Canadian citizens.

Application Requirements: Application, essay, financial need analysis, references, self-addressed stamped envelope, transcript, written documentation of reservation registration. *Deadline:* April 15.

Contact: Headquarters Office
International Order of the King's Daughters and Sons
PO Box 1017
Chautauqua, NY 14722-1017
Phone: 716-357-4951

ITALIAN CATHOLIC FEDERATION, INC. http://www.icf.org

ICF COLLEGE SCHOLARSHIPS TO HIGH SCHOOL SENIORS

Renewable awards for high school students who are residents of California, Illinois, Arizona and Nevada and plan to pursue postsecondary education. Must have minimum 3.2 GPA. Must be a U.S. citizen, Catholic, and of Italian descent or if non-Italian the student's parents or grandparents must be members of the Federation for the student to qualify. Applicants must submit the last two pages of parents' income tax return, along with other required materials as listed on the application.

Award: Scholarship for use in freshman, sophomore, junior, or senior years; renewable. *Number:* 170–200. *Amount:* $400–$1000.

Eligibility Requirements: Applicant must be Roman Catholic; of Italian heritage; high school student; planning to enroll or expecting to enroll full-time at a two-year or four-year institution or university and resident of Arizona, California, Illinois, or Nevada. Available to U.S. citizens.

Application Requirements: Application, essay, references, transcript. *Deadline:* March 15.

Contact: Scholarship Director
Italian Catholic Federation, Inc.
675 Hegenberger Road, Suite 230
Oakland, CA 94621
Phone: 510-633-9058
Fax: 510-633-9758

ITALIAN-AMERICAN CHAMBER OF COMMERCE MIDWEST http://www.italchambers.net/chicago

ITALIAN-AMERICAN CHAMBER OF COMMERCE OF CHICAGO SCHOLARSHIP

One-time awards for Illinois residents of Italian descent. Available to high school seniors and college students for use at a four-year institution. Applicants must have a 3.5 GPA. Must reside in Cook, Du Page, Kane, Lake, McHenry, or Will counties in Illinois.

Award: Scholarship for use in freshman, sophomore, junior, or senior years; not renewable. *Number:* 1. *Amount:* up to $1000.

Eligibility Requirements: Applicant must be of Italian heritage; enrolled or expecting to enroll full-time at a four-year institution and resident of Illinois. Applicant must have 3.5 GPA or higher. Available to U.S. citizens.

Application Requirements: Application, autobiography, essay, photo, references, self-addressed stamped envelope, transcript. *Deadline:* May 31.

Contact: Frank Pugno, Scholarship Chairman
Italian-American Chamber of Commerce Midwest
30 South Michigan Avenue, #504
Chicago, IL 60603
Phone: 312-553-9137 Ext. 13
Fax: 312-553-9142
E-mail: info.chicago@italchambers.net

JACKIE ROBINSON FOUNDATION http://www.jackierobinson.org

JACKIE ROBINSON SCHOLARSHIP

Scholarship for graduating minority high school seniors who have been accepted to accredited four-year colleges or universities. Must be U.S. citizen and show financial need, leadership potential and a high level of academic achievement. Application deadline: April 1.

Award: Scholarship for use in freshman year; renewable. *Number:* 50–60. *Amount:* up to $6000.

Eligibility Requirements: Applicant must be American Indian/Alaska Native, Asian/Pacific Islander, Black (non-Hispanic), or Hispanic; high school student and planning to enroll or expecting to enroll full-time at a four-year institution or university. Available to U.S. citizens.

Application Requirements: Application, essay, financial need analysis, references, test scores, transcript, school certification. *Deadline:* April 1.

Contact: Scholarship Program
Jackie Robinson Foundation
3 West 35th Street, 11th Floor
New York, NY 10001-2204
Phone: 212-290-8600
Fax: 212-290-8081

JAMES C. CALDWELL SCHOLARSHIP

JAMES C. CALDWELL ASSISTING MEN AND WOMEN OF TOLEDO SCHOLARSHIP

Renewable scholarships for minority residents of the greater Toledo, Ohio area for use in undergraduate study in a college or university. Must maintain 3.0 GPA. Must be African-American, Asian-American, Hispanic-American or Native American. Write for application and enclose a self-addressed stamped envelope.

Award: Scholarship for use in freshman, sophomore, junior, or senior years; renewable. *Number:* up to 20. *Amount:* varies.

Eligibility Requirements: Applicant must be American Indian/Alaska Native, Asian/Pacific Islander, Black (non-Hispanic), or Hispanic; enrolled or expecting to enroll at a four-year institution or university and resident of Ohio. Applicant must have 3.0 GPA or higher. Available to U.S. citizens.

Application Requirements: Application, self-addressed stamped envelope, transcript. *Deadline:* Continuous.

Contact: Executive Director
James C. Caldwell Scholarship
PO Box 80056
Toledo, OH 43608

KAM SOCIETY

KAM SOCIETY SCHOLARSHIP

Recipient must be a member of the Kam Society. Scholarship is determined by recipient's and their parents' participation in Kam Society activities.

Award: Scholarship for use in freshman, sophomore, junior, or senior years; not renewable. *Number:* 1–4. *Amount:* $750.

Eligibility Requirements: Applicant must be Asian/Pacific Islander and enrolled or expecting to enroll full-time at a four-year institution or university. Applicant must have 2.5 GPA or higher. Available to U.S. citizens.

Application Requirements: Application. *Deadline:* August 1.

Contact: Clifford Kam, Treasurer
Kam Society
1454-B Kohou Street
Honolulu, HI 96782
Phone: 808-845-0501

KNIGHTS OF COLUMBUS

FOURTH DEGREE PRO DEO AND PRO PATRIA (CANADA)

• *See page 467*

KNIGHTS OF LITHUANIA http://www.knightsoflithuania.com

KNIGHTS OF LITHUANIA NATIONAL SCHOLARSHIPS

• *See page 467*

KONIAG EDUCATION FOUNDATION http://www.koniag.com

KONIAG EDUCATION FOUNDATION SCHOLARSHIP

Scholarships available to Koniag, Inc. shareholders and their descendants for education following high school. Must be Alaska Native. Deadlines are March 15 and June 1.

Award: Scholarship for use in freshman, sophomore, junior, senior, graduate, or postgraduate years; renewable. *Number:* 130–170. *Amount:* $500–$2500.

Eligibility Requirements: Applicant must be American Indian/Alaska Native and enrolled or expecting to enroll full or part-time at a two-year or four-year or technical institution or university. Available to U.S. and non-U.S. citizens.

Application Requirements: Application, autobiography, essay, financial need analysis, photo, references, transcript, proof of eligibility from Koniag, Inc.. *Deadline:* varies.

Contact: Tom Murphy, Executive Director
Koniag Education Foundation
6927 Old Seward Highway, Suite 103
Anchorage, AK 99518
Phone: 907-562-9093
Fax: 907-562-9023
E-mail: kef@alaska.com

KOREAN AMERICAN SCHOLARSHIP FOUNDATION http://www.kasf.org

KOREAN-AMERICAN SCHOLARSHIP FOUNDATION EASTERN REGION SCHOLARSHIPS

Scholarships available to Korean-American and Korean students enrolled in a full-time undergraduate or graduate program in the United States. Selection based on financial need, academic achievement, school activities, and community services. Each applicant must submit an application to the respective KASF region. For more details and an application see Web site: http://www.kasf.org.

Award: Scholarship for use in freshman, sophomore, junior, senior, graduate, or postgraduate years; not renewable. *Number:* varies. *Amount:* $1000.

Eligibility Requirements: Applicant must be of Korean heritage; Asian/Pacific Islander; enrolled or expecting to enroll full-time at an institution or university and studying in Delaware, District of Columbia, Kentucky, Maryland, North Carolina, Pennsylvania, Virginia, or West Virginia. Available to U.S. and non-U.S. citizens.

Application Requirements: Application, essay, financial need analysis, photo, references, self-addressed stamped envelope, transcript. *Deadline:* May 30.

Contact: Dr. Augustine Paik, President
Korean American Scholarship Foundation
1952 Gallows Road
Vienna, VA 22182
Phone: 703-748-5935
Fax: 703-748-1874
E-mail: eastern@kasf.org

KOREAN-AMERICAN SCHOLARSHIP FOUNDATION MIDEASTERN REGION SCHOLARSHIPS

Scholarships available to Korean-American or Korean students enrolled in full-time undergraduate or graduate program in the United States. Selection is based on financial need, academic achievement, school activities, and community services. Each applicant must submit an application to the respective KASF region. For more details and an application see Web site: http://www.kasf.org.

Award: Scholarship for use in freshman, sophomore, junior, senior, graduate, or postgraduate years; not renewable. *Number:* varies. *Amount:* up to $1000.

Eligibility Requirements: Applicant must be of Korean heritage; enrolled or expecting to enroll full-time at an institution or university and studying in Indiana, Michigan, or Ohio. Available to U.S. and non-U.S. citizens.

Application Requirements: Application, essay, financial need analysis, photo, references, transcript. *Deadline:* June 30.

Contact: Chang Soo Choi, Mid-East Office (Detroit)
Korean American Scholarship Foundation
24666 Northwestern Highway
Southfield, MI 48075
Phone: 248-752-3180
E-mail: csshoi@com.cst.net

KOREAN-AMERICAN SCHOLARSHIP FOUNDATION MIDWESTERN REGION SCHOLARSHIPS

Scholarships available to Korean-American and Korean students enrolled in a full-time undergraduate or graduate program in the United States. Selection based on financial need, academic achievement, school activities, and community services. Each applicant must submit an application to the respective KASF region. For more details and an application see Web site: http://www.kasf.org.

Award: Scholarship for use in freshman, sophomore, junior, senior, graduate, or postgraduate years; not renewable. *Number:* varies. *Amount:* $1000.

Eligibility Requirements: Applicant must be of Korean heritage; Asian/Pacific Islander; enrolled or expecting to enroll full-time at an institution or university and studying in Illinois, Minnesota, Missouri, Nebraska, North Dakota, South Dakota, or Wisconsin. Available to U.S. and non-U.S. citizens.

Application Requirements: Application, essay, financial need analysis, photo, references, transcript. *Deadline:* June 30.

Contact: Dr. Tony Hahm, Scholarship Committee Chair
Korean American Scholarship Foundation
KASF Midwestern Regional Chapter, PO Box 0416

Northbrook, IL 60065-0416
Phone: 847-797-1291
Fax: 847-797-1304
E-mail: tonyhahm@yahoo.com

KOREAN-AMERICAN SCHOLARSHIP FOUNDATION NORTHEASTERN REGION SCHOLARSHIPS

Scholarships available to Korean-American and Korean students enrolled in a full-time undergraduate or graduate program in the United States. Selection based on financial need, academic achievement, school activities, and community services. Each applicant must submit an application to the respective KASF region. For more details and an application see Web site: http://www.kasf.org.

Award: Scholarship for use in freshman, sophomore, junior, senior, graduate, or postgraduate years; not renewable. *Number:* up to 60. *Amount:* $1000–$2500.

Eligibility Requirements: Applicant must be of Korean heritage; Asian/Pacific Islander; enrolled or expecting to enroll full-time at a four-year institution or university and studying in Connecticut, Maine, Massachusetts, New Hampshire, New Jersey, New York, Rhode Island, or Vermont. Available to U.S. citizens.

Korean American Scholarship Foundation (continued)

Application Requirements: Application, essay, financial need analysis, photo, references, transcript. *Deadline:* June 30.

Contact: William Y. Kim, KASF Northeastern Regional Chapter
Korean American Scholarship Foundation
51 West Overlook
Port Washington, NY 11050
Phone: 516-883-1142
Fax: 516-883-1964
E-mail: northeastern@kasf.org

KOREAN-AMERICAN SCHOLARSHIP FOUNDATION SOUTHERN REGION SCHOLARSHIPS

Scholarships available to Korean-American and Korean students enrolled in a full-time undergraduate or graduate program in the United States. Selection based on financial need, academic achievement, school activities, and community services. Each applicant must submit an application to the respective KASF region. For more details and an application see Web site: http://www.kasf.org.

Award: Scholarship for use in freshman, sophomore, junior, senior, graduate, or postgraduate years; not renewable. *Number:* up to 45. *Amount:* $1000.

Eligibility Requirements: Applicant must be of Korean heritage; Asian/Pacific Islander; enrolled or expecting to enroll full-time at an institution or university and studying in Alabama, Arkansas, Florida, Georgia, Louisiana, Mississippi, North Carolina, Oklahoma, South Carolina, Tennessee, or Texas. Available to U.S. and non-U.S. citizens.

Application Requirements: Application, essay, financial need analysis, photo, references, transcript. *Deadline:* June 4.

Contact: Dr. H. Won Jun, Chairperson Scholarship Committee
Korean American Scholarship Foundation
KASF Southern Regional Chapter, 330 Millstone Circle
Athens, GA 30605
Phone: 706-542-5759
E-mail: southern@kasf.org

KOREAN-AMERICAN SCHOLARSHIP FOUNDATION WESTERN REGION SCHOLARSHIPS

Scholarships available to Korean-American and Korean students enrolled in a full-time undergraduate or graduate program in the United States. Selection based on financial need, academic achievement, school activities, and community services. Each applicant must submit an application to the respective KASF region. For more details and an application see Web site: http://www.kasf.org.

Award: Scholarship for use in freshman, sophomore, junior, senior, graduate, or postgraduate years; not renewable. *Number:* varies. *Amount:* $1000.

Eligibility Requirements: Applicant must be of Korean heritage; Asian/Pacific Islander; enrolled or expecting to enroll full-time at an institution or university and studying in Alaska, Arizona, California, Colorado, Idaho, Montana, Nevada, New Mexico, Oregon, Utah, Washington, or Wyoming. Available to U.S. and non-U.S. citizens.

Application Requirements: Application, essay, financial need analysis, photo, references, transcript. *Deadline:* March 6.

Contact: KASF Western Regional Chapter
Korean American Scholarship Foundation
3435 Wilshire Boulevard, Suite 2450B

Los Angeles, CA 90010
Phone: 213-380-5273
Fax: 213-380-5273
E-mail: western@kasf.org

KOREAN UNIVERSITY CLUB

KOREAN UNIVERSITY CLUB SCHOLARSHIP

Scholarship for graduating high school seniors entering their freshman year in a Hawaiian college or university. Must be a Hawaiian resident, a U.S. citizen and be of Korean ancestry. Must show academic progress. Write for details.

Award: Scholarship for use in freshman year; renewable. *Number:* 1. *Amount:* $1400.

Eligibility Requirements: Applicant must be of Korean heritage; high school student; planning to enroll or expecting to enroll full-time at a two-year or four-year institution or university; resident of Hawaii and studying in Hawaii. Available to U.S. citizens.

Application Requirements: Application, essay, financial need analysis, references, self-addressed stamped envelope, test scores, transcript. *Deadline:* March 15.

Contact: Ms. Martha Im
Korean University Club
1608 Laukahi Street
Honolulu, HI 96821

KOSCIUSZKO FOUNDATION http://www.kosciuszkofoundation.org

MASSACHUSETTS FEDERATION OF POLISH WOMEN'S CLUBS SCHOLARSHIPS

Nonrenewable award for sophomores, juniors, and seniors attending an accredited four-year college or university. Preference given to MFPWC members and children or grandchildren of members. In the event that no members apply, the scholarship may be awarded to residents of Massachusetts or New England. Submit proof of Polish ancestry. Minimum 3.0 GPA required. Application fee $25. See Web site http://www.kosciuszkofoundation.org for complete details.

Award: Scholarship for use in sophomore, junior, or senior years; not renewable. *Number:* 3. *Amount:* $1250.

Eligibility Requirements: Applicant must be of Polish heritage; enrolled or expecting to enroll full-time at a four-year institution or university and resident of Connecticut, Maine, Massachusetts, New Hampshire, Rhode Island, or Vermont. Applicant must have 3.0 GPA or higher. Available to U.S. citizens.

Application Requirements: Application, essay, financial need analysis, photo, references, transcript, proof of Polish ancestry. *Fee:* $25. *Deadline:* January 15.

Contact: Ms. Addy Tymczyszyn, Grants Department
Kosciuszko Foundation
15 East 65th Street
New York, NY 10021-6595
Phone: 212-734-2130 Ext. 210

LEAGUE OF UNITED LATIN AMERICAN CITIZENS NATIONAL EDUCATIONAL SERVICE CENTERS, INC. http://www.lnesc.org

LULAC NATIONAL SCHOLARSHIP FUND

LULAC Councils will award scholarships to qualified Hispanic students who are enrolled or are planning to enroll in accredited colleges or universities in the United States. Applicants must be U.S. citizens or legal residents. Scholarships may be used for the payment of tuition, academic fees, room, board and the purchase of required educational materials. For additional information applicants should check LULAC Web site at http://www.lnesc.org to see a list of participating councils or send a self-addressed stamped envelope.

Award: Scholarship for use in freshman, sophomore, junior, senior, or graduate years; not renewable. *Number:* 1000. *Amount:* $250–$2000.

Eligibility Requirements: Applicant must be Hispanic and enrolled or expecting to enroll full-time at a two-year or four-year institution or university. Available to U.S. citizens.

Application Requirements: Application, autobiography, essay, financial need analysis, interview, references, self-addressed stamped envelope, test scores, transcript. *Deadline:* March 31.

Contact: Scholarship Administrator
League of United Latin American Citizens National Educational Service Centers, Inc.
2000 L Street, NW
Suite 610
Washington, DC 20036

MENOMINEE INDIAN TRIBE OF WISCONSIN http://www.menominee.nsn.us/educationindex/educationhomepage.htm

MENOMINEE INDIAN TRIBE ADULT VOCATIONAL TRAINING PROGRAM

Renewable award for enrolled Menominee tribal members to use at vocational or technical schools. Must be at least 1/4 Menominee and show proof of Indian blood. Must complete financial aid form. Deadlines: March 1 and November 1.

Award: Grant for use in freshman or sophomore years; renewable. *Number:* 50–70. *Amount:* $100–$1100.

Eligibility Requirements: Applicant must be American Indian/Alaska Native and enrolled or expecting to enroll full or part-time at a technical institution. Available to U.S. citizens.

Application Requirements: Application, financial need analysis. *Deadline:* varies.

Contact: Virginia Nuske, Education Director
Menominee Indian Tribe of Wisconsin
PO Box 910
Keshena, WI 54135
Phone: 715-799-5110
Fax: 715-799-5102
E-mail: vnuske@mitw.org

MENOMINEE INDIAN TRIBE OF WISCONSIN HIGHER EDUCATION GRANTS

Renewable award for enrolled Menominee tribal member to use at a two- or four-year college or university. Must be at least 1/4 Menominee and show proof of Indian blood. Must complete financial aid form. Contact for deadline information.

Award: Grant for use in freshman, sophomore, junior, or senior years; renewable. *Number:* 136. *Amount:* $100–$1100.

Eligibility Requirements: Applicant must be American Indian/Alaska Native and enrolled or expecting to enroll full or part-time at a two-year or four-year institution or university. Available to U.S. citizens.

Application Requirements: Application, financial need analysis. *Deadline:* Continuous.

Contact: Virginia Nuske, Education Director
Menominee Indian Tribe of Wisconsin
PO Box 910
Keshena, WI 54135
Phone: 715-799-5110
Fax: 715-799-5102
E-mail: vnuske@mitw.org

MESCALERO TRIBAL EDUCATION

MESCALERO APACHE TRIBAL SCHOLARSHIP

Award available to Mescalero Apache tribal members as a supplement to other forms of financial aid. Reapplication is required each year. If used for trade school, only one certificate will be funded. Freshmen and sophomores must meet with the Tribal Education Committee each year when applying or reapplying. Must have letter of acceptance from institution and signed grade release each semester. Deadline: June 1 for fall, November 1 for spring.

Award: Scholarship for use in freshman, sophomore, junior, senior, or graduate years; not renewable. *Number:* varies. *Amount:* up to $8000.

Eligibility Requirements: Applicant must be American Indian/Alaska Native and enrolled or expecting to enroll full or part-time at a two-year or four-year or technical institution or university. Available to U.S. citizens.

Application Requirements: Application, essay, financial need analysis, references, transcript, privacy statement. *Deadline:* varies.

Contact: Rutalee Bob, Assistant Director of Tribal Education
Mescalero Tribal Education
148 Cottonwood Drive
Mescalero, NM 88340
Phone: 505-464-4500
Fax: 505-464-4508

MINNESOTA INDIAN SCHOLARSHIP OFFICE http://www.mheso.state.mn.us

MINNESOTA INDIAN SCHOLARSHIP PROGRAM

One time award for Minnesota Native-American. Applicant must be one quarter Native-American and a resident of Minnesota. Must re-apply for scholarship annually.

Award: Scholarship for use in freshman, sophomore, junior, or senior years; not renewable. *Number:* varies. *Amount:* up to $3300.

Eligibility Requirements: Applicant must be American Indian/Alaska Native; enrolled or expecting to enroll full or part-time at a two-year or four-year or technical institution or university; resident of Minnesota and studying in Minnesota. Available to U.S. citizens.

Application Requirements: Application, financial need analysis. *Deadline:* July 1.

Contact: Lea Perkins, Director
Minnesota Indian Scholarship Office
Minnesota Department of Education, 1500 Highway 36W
Roseville, MN 55113-4266
Phone: 800-657-3927
E-mail: cfl.indianeducation@state.mn.us

MONGOLIA SOCIETY, INC.

DR. GOMBOJAB HANGIN MEMORIAL SCHOLARSHIP

One-time award for students of Mongolian heritage only. Must have permanent residency in Mongolia, the People's Republic of China, or the former Soviet Union. Award is for tuition at U.S. institutions. Upon conclusion of award year, recipient must write a report of his or her activities. Application requests must be in English and the application must be filled out in English. Deadline is January 1. Write or e-mail for application.

Award: Scholarship for use in freshman, sophomore, junior, senior, or graduate years; not renewable. *Number:* 1. *Amount:* up to $2400.

Eligibility Requirements: Applicant must be of Mongolian heritage and enrolled or expecting to enroll at a four-year institution or university.

Application Requirements: Application, references, curriculum vitae, photocopy of passport. *Deadline:* January 1.

Contact: Mongolia Society, Inc.
322 Goodbody Hall
Indiana University,1011 East 3rd Street
Bloomington, IN 47405-7005
E-mail: monsoc@indiana.edu

MONTANA GUARANTEED STUDENT LOAN PROGRAM, OFFICE OF COMMISSIONER OF HIGHER EDUCATION http://www.mgslp.state.mt.us

INDIAN STUDENT FEE WAIVER

Fee waiver awarded by the Montana University System to undergraduate and graduate students meeting the criteria. Amount varies depending upon the tuition and registration fee at each participating college. Students must provide documentation of one-fourth Indian blood or more; must be a resident of Montana for at least one year prior to enrolling in school and must demonstrate financial need. Full-or part-time study qualifies. Complete and submit the FAFSA by March 1 and a Montana Indian Fee Waiver application form. Contact the financial aid office at the college of attendance to determine eligibility.

Award: Scholarship for use in freshman, sophomore, junior, senior, or graduate years; renewable. *Number:* 600. *Amount:* $2000.

Eligibility Requirements: Applicant must be American Indian/Alaska Native; enrolled or expecting to enroll full or part-time at a two-year or four-year institution or university; resident of Montana and studying in Montana. Available to U.S. citizens.

Montana Guaranteed Student Loan Program, Office of Commissioner of Higher Education (continued)

Application Requirements: Application, financial need analysis, FAFSA. *Deadline:* March 1.

Contact: Sally Speer, Grants and Scholarship Coordinator
Montana Guaranteed Student Loan Program, Office of Commissioner of Higher Education
2500 Broadway
PO Box 203101
Helena, MT 59620-3101
Phone: 406-444-0638
Fax: 406-444-1869
E-mail: sspeer@mgslp.state.mt.us

MORRIS K. UDALL FOUNDATION http://www.udall.gov

MORRIS K. UDALL SCHOLARS-NATIVE AMERICAN AND ALASKA NATIVE

One-time award to Native-American or Alaska Native enrolled full-time at a two-year or four-year college. Must be studying fields related to health care or tribal public policy. Must be nominated by college. Must be a matriculated sophomore or junior pursing a degree. Tribal documentation must be submitted.

Award: Scholarship for use in sophomore or junior years; not renewable. *Number:* up to 110. *Amount:* up to $5000.

Eligibility Requirements: Applicant must be American Indian/Alaska Native and enrolled or expecting to enroll full-time at a two-year or four-year institution. Available to U.S. citizens.

Application Requirements: Application, essay, references, transcript, nomination. *Deadline:* March 3.

Contact: Morris K. Udall Foundation
130 South Scott Avenue, Suite 3350
Tucson, AZ 85701-1922

NAACP LEGAL DEFENSE AND EDUCATIONAL FUND, INC. http://www.naacpldf.org/scholarships

HERBERT LEHMAN SCHOLARSHIP PROGRAM

Renewable award for successful African-American high school seniors to attend a four-year college on a full-time basis. Must be a U.S. citizen. Must request an application in writing by March 15. Application deadline is April 30.

Award: Scholarship for use in freshman, sophomore, junior, or senior years; renewable. *Number:* 25–30. *Amount:* $2000.

Eligibility Requirements: Applicant must be Black (non-Hispanic); high school student and planning to enroll or expecting to enroll full-time at a four-year institution or university. Available to U.S. citizens.

Application Requirements: Application, essay, photo, references, test scores, transcript. *Deadline:* April 30.

Contact: Program Director
NAACP Legal Defense and Educational Fund, Inc.
99 Hudson Street, Suite 1600
New York, NY 10013
Phone: 212-965-2225
Fax: 212-219-1595

NATIONAL ASSOCIATION FOR CAMPUS ACTIVITIES http://www.naca.org

MULTICULTURAL SCHOLARSHIP PROGRAM

Scholarships will be given to applicants identified as African-American, Latina/Latino, Native-American, Asian-American or Pacific Islander ethnic minorities. A letter of recommendation affirming his/her ethnic minority status, his/her financial need, and that he/she will be in the campus activity field at least one year following the program for which a scholarship is being sought, should accompany applications.

Award: Scholarship for use in sophomore, junior, senior, or graduate years; not renewable. *Number:* varies. *Amount:* varies.

Eligibility Requirements: Applicant must be American Indian/Alaska Native, Asian/Pacific Islander, Black (non-Hispanic), or Hispanic; enrolled or expecting to enroll at a two-year or four-year institution or university and must have an interest in leadership. Available to U.S. citizens.

Application Requirements: Application, essay, financial need analysis, references. *Deadline:* May 1.

Contact: Application available at Web site.

NATIONAL ASSOCIATION FOR THE ADVANCEMENT OF COLORED PEOPLE http://www.naacp.org

AGNES JONES JACKSON SCHOLARSHIP

• *See page 469*

ROY WILKINS SCHOLARSHIP

• *See page 470*

NATIONAL ITALIAN AMERICAN FOUNDATION http://www.niaf.org/scholarships

EMANUELE AND EMILIA INGLESE MEMORIAL SCHOLARSHIP

Scholarship available to Italian American undergraduate students who trace their lineage to the Lombardy region, and who are the first generation of their family to attend college. Applicants must have a 3.0 or higher GPA and financial need. Applicants must be enrolled in an accredited institution of higher education and be a United States citizen or a permanent resident alien. For further information, deadlines, and application see Web site: http://www.niaf.org/scholarships/index.asp.

Award: Scholarship for use in freshman, sophomore, junior, or senior years. *Number:* 1. *Amount:* $2500.

Eligibility Requirements: Applicant must be of Italian heritage and enrolled or expecting to enroll at a two-year or four-year or technical institution or university. Applicant must have 3.0 GPA or higher. Available to U.S. citizens.

Contact: Information available at Web site.

NATIONAL ITALIAN AMERICAN FOUNDATION CATEGORY I SCHOLARSHIP

Award available to Italian-American students who have outstanding potential and high academic achievements. Minimum 3.25 GPA required. Must be a U.S. citizen and be enrolled in an accredited institution of higher education. Application can only be submitted online. For further information, deadlines, and online application visit Web site: http://www.niaf.org/scholarships/index.asp.

Award: Scholarship for use in freshman, sophomore, junior, senior, or graduate years; not renewable. *Number:* varies. *Amount:* $2500–$10,000.

Eligibility Requirements: Applicant must be of Italian heritage and enrolled or expecting to enroll full or part-time at a four-year institution or university. Available to U.S. citizens.

Application Requirements: Application, essay, references, transcript.

Contact: Application available at Web site.

NATIONAL MERIT SCHOLARSHIP CORPORATION http://www.nationalmerit.org

NATIONAL ACHIEVEMENT SCHOLARSHIP PROGRAM

Competition of African-American students for recognition and undergraduate scholarships. Students enter by taking the Preliminary SAT/National Merit Scholar Qualifying Test and by meeting other participation requirements. Most of the awards are one-time scholarships of $2,500; others are renewable for four years, and valued between $500 and $2,000 or more. Contact high school counselor by fall of junior year. Those qualifying for recognition are notified through their high school. Participation requirements are available in the PSAT/NMSQT Student Bulletin and on the NMSC Web site at http://www.nationalmerit.org.

Award: Scholarship for use in freshman year; renewable. *Number:* 800. *Amount:* $500–$2500.

Eligibility Requirements: Applicant must be Black (non-Hispanic); high school student and planning to enroll or expecting to enroll full-time at a four-year institution or university. Available to U.S. citizens.

Application Requirements: Application, autobiography, essay, references, test scores, transcript. *Deadline:* Continuous.

Contact: student's high school counselor

NATIONAL MINORITY JUNIOR GOLF SCHOLARSHIP ASSOCIATION http://www.nmjgsa.org

NATIONAL MINORITY JUNIOR GOLF SCHOLARSHIP

Awards for minority students based on academic achievement, financial need, evidence of community service, and golfing ability. Available to high school seniors who have entered information into the database located at http://www.nmjgsa.org, as well as to undergraduate students who previously received a scholarship as a freshman. Application deadline is April 15.

Award: Scholarship for use in freshman, sophomore, junior, or senior years; not renewable. *Number:* varies. *Amount:* $1000–$6000.

Eligibility Requirements: Applicant must be American Indian/Alaska Native, Asian/Pacific Islander, Black (non-Hispanic), or Hispanic; enrolled or expecting to enroll full-time at a two-year or four-year or technical institution or university and must have an interest in golf. Available to U.S. citizens.

Application Requirements: Application, essay, financial need analysis, references, test scores. *Deadline:* April 15.

Contact: Application available at Web site.

NATIONAL SOCIETY DAUGHTERS OF THE AMERICAN REVOLUTION http://www.dar.org

NATIONAL SOCIETY DAUGHTERS OF THE AMERICAN REVOLUTION AMERICAN INDIAN SCHOLARSHIP

Nonrenewable award for Native-American striving for a college or vocational education. Must be U.S. citizen with 2.75 GPA. Submit letter with family history, financial status, and goals. Based on need and academic achievement. Deadlines: July 1 for fall term and November 1 for spring term. Must submit self-addressed stamped envelope to be considered.

Award: Scholarship for use in freshman, sophomore, junior, senior, or graduate years; not renewable. *Number:* up to 50. *Amount:* $500.

Eligibility Requirements: Applicant must be American Indian/Alaska Native and enrolled or expecting to enroll at a two-year or four-year or technical institution or university. Available to U.S. citizens.

Application Requirements: Application, financial need analysis, references, self-addressed stamped envelope, transcript. *Deadline:* varies.

Contact: Office of Committees, American Indian Scholarship
National Society Daughters of the American Revolution
1776 D Street, NW
Washington, DC 20006-5392

NATIONAL SOCIETY DAUGHTERS OF THE AMERICAN REVOLUTION FRANCES CRAWFORD MARVIN AMERICAN INDIAN SCHOLARSHIP

Nonrenewable award available for Native-American to attend any two- or four-year college. Must demonstrate financial need, academic achievement, and have a 3.0 GPA or higher. Must submit a self-addressed stamped envelope to be considered. Deadline is February 1.

Award: Scholarship for use in freshman, sophomore, junior, or senior years; not renewable. *Number:* 1. *Amount:* varies.

Eligibility Requirements: Applicant must be American Indian/Alaska Native and enrolled or expecting to enroll full-time at a two-year or four-year institution or university. Applicant must have 3.0 GPA or higher. Available to U.S. citizens.

Application Requirements: Application, financial need analysis, self-addressed stamped envelope, transcript. *Deadline:* February 1.

Contact: Office of Committees, Scholarship
National Society Daughters of the American Revolution
1776 D Street, NW
Washington, DC 20006-5392

NATIONAL UNION OF PUBLIC AND GENERAL EMPLOYEES http://www.nupge.ca

SCHOLARSHIP FOR ABORIGINAL CANADIANS

• *See page 472*

SCHOLARSHIP FOR VISIBLE MINORITIES

• *See page 472*

TERRY FOX MEMORIAL SCHOLARSHIP

• *See page 472*

TOMMY DOUGLAS SCHOLARSHIP

• *See page 472*

NATIONAL WOMEN'S STUDIES ASSOCIATION http://www.nwsa.org

ABAFAZI-AFRICANA WOMEN'S STUDIES ESSAY AWARD

Two $400 awards open to female, African-American, undergraduate and graduate students. Scholarly essays may cover any subject relevant to African-American female children, women's issues and/or experiences in the United States or throughout the diaspora. Preference given to NWSA members. Deadline is February 1.

Award: Prize for use in freshman, sophomore, junior, senior, or graduate years; not renewable. *Number:* 2. *Amount:* $400.

Eligibility Requirements: Applicant must be Black (non-Hispanic); enrolled or expecting to enroll at an institution or university; female and must have an interest in writing. Available to U.S. and non-U.S. citizens.

Application Requirements: Application, essay. *Deadline:* February 1.

Contact: Loretta Younger, National Executive Administrator
National Women's Studies Association
7100 Baltimore Avenue, Suite 500
College Park, MD 20740
Phone: 301-403-0525
Fax: 301-403-4137
E-mail: nwsa@umail.umd.edu

NEW YORK STATE HIGHER EDUCATION SERVICES CORPORATION http://www.hesc.org

NEW YORK STATE AID TO NATIVE AMERICANS

Award for enrolled members of a New York State tribe and their children who are attending or planning to attend a New York State college and who are New York State residents. Award for full-time-students up to $1550 annually; part-time awards approximately $65 per credit hour.

Award: Scholarship for use in freshman, sophomore, junior, or senior years; not renewable. *Number:* varies. *Amount:* up to $1550.

Eligibility Requirements: Applicant must be American Indian/Alaska Native; enrolled or expecting to enroll full or part-time at a two-year or four-year or technical institution or university; resident of New York and studying in New York.

Application Requirements: Application. *Deadline:* July 15.

Contact: Native American Education Unit, New York State Education Department
New York State Higher Education Services Corporation
EBA Room 374
Albany, NY 12234
Phone: 518-474-0537

NISEI STUDENT RELOCATION COMMEMORATIVE FUND http://www.nsrcfund.org

NISEI STUDENT RELOCATION COMMEMORATIVE FUND

Scholarships are made available to graduating high school seniors who are Southeast Asian refugees or children of refugees. For more details see Web site: http://www.nsrcfund.org.

Award: Scholarship for use in freshman year; not renewable. *Number:* 35–40. *Amount:* $500–$2000.

Eligibility Requirements: Applicant must be Asian/Pacific Islander; high school student and planning to enroll or expecting to enroll full-time at a two-year or four-year or technical institution or university. Available to U.S. citizens.

Nisei Student Relocation Commemorative Fund (continued)

Application Requirements: Application, autobiography, essay, financial need analysis, references, test scores, transcript. *Deadline:* varies.

Contact: Jean Hibino, Executive Secretary
Nisei Student Relocation Commemorative Fund
19 Scenic Drive
Portland, CT 06480
Phone: 781-674-0086
E-mail: jeanhibino@aol.com

NORTHERN CHEYENNE TRIBAL EDUCATION DEPARTMENT

HIGHER EDUCATION SCHOLARSHIP PROGRAM

Scholarships are only provided for enrolled Northern Cheyenne Tribal Members who meet the requirements listed in the higher education guidelines. Must be U.S. citizen enrolled in a postsecondary institution. Minimum 2.0 GPA required. Deadline is March 1.

Award: Grant for use in freshman, sophomore, junior, or senior years; renewable. *Number:* 72. *Amount:* $50–$6000.

Eligibility Requirements: Applicant must be American Indian/Alaska Native and enrolled or expecting to enroll full or part-time at a two-year or four-year institution or university. Available to U.S. citizens.

Application Requirements: Application, essay, financial need analysis, references, test scores, transcript. *Deadline:* March 1.

Contact: Norma Bixby, Director
Northern Cheyenne Tribal Education Department
Box 307
Lame Deer, MT 59043
Phone: 406-477-6602
Fax: 406-477-8150
E-mail: norma@rangeweb.net

NORTHERN VIRGINIA URBAN LEAGUE http://www.nvul.org/

NORTHERN VIRGINIA URBAN LEAGUE SCHOLARSHIP PROGRAM

Program awards four $3750 scholarships to eligible African American students from the Northern Virginia region. Applicant must be a graduating high school senior. Application deadline is February.

Award: Scholarship for use in freshman year; not renewable. *Number:* 4. *Amount:* $3750.

Eligibility Requirements: Applicant must be Black (non-Hispanic); high school student; planning to enroll or expecting to enroll full-time at a four-year institution and resident of Virginia. Available to U.S. citizens.

Application Requirements: Application, autobiography, essay, financial need analysis, interview, references, transcript. *Deadline:* varies.

Contact: Tyrone Maceo Moorer, Director of Programs and Development
Alexandria, VA 22314
Phone: 703-836-2858
Fax: 703-836-8948
E-mail: tmoorer@nvul.org

NORWAY-AMERICA ASSOCIATION http://www.noram.no

NORWAY-AMERICA UNDERGRADUATE SCHOLARSHIP PROGRAM

Scholarships are provided for Norwegian citizens interested in studying at the undergraduate level in the United States. Students should apply directly to the Norway-American Association for consideration for these awards totaling at least 30% reduction in tuition and room and board for one academic year. Applicant must be a member of the Norway-America Association.

Award: Scholarship for use in freshman, sophomore, junior, or senior years; not renewable. *Number:* up to 70.

Eligibility Requirements: Applicant must be Norwegian citizen and enrolled or expecting to enroll at a four-year institution or university. Available to citizens of countries other than the U.S. or Canada.

Application Requirements: Application, references, transcript, proof of NAA membership, teacher evaluations. *Deadline:* December 2.

Contact: Cheryl Storo, Director of Scholarship Program
Norway-America Association
Radhusgaten 23 B
Oslo 0158
Norway
E-mail: namerika@online.no

OFFICE OF NAVAJO NATION SCHOLARSHIP AND FINANCIAL ASSISTANCE http://onnsfa.org

CHIEF MANUELITO SCHOLARSHIP PROGRAM

One-time, $7000 scholarship available to a high-achieving Navajo high school student. Minimum 3.0 GPA and 21 ACT score required. (SAT scores will be converted.) Deadline: June 25. Must submit letter of college acceptance and Certificate of Indian Blood (CIB). High school student must have completed one unit of Navajo language and one-half unit of Navajo government courses.

Award: Scholarship for use in freshman, sophomore, junior, or senior years; not renewable. *Number:* 1. *Amount:* $7000.

Eligibility Requirements: Applicant must be American Indian/Alaska Native and enrolled or expecting to enroll full-time at a two-year or four-year institution or university. Applicant must have 3.0 GPA or higher. Available to U.S. citizens.

Application Requirements: Application, financial need analysis, test scores, transcript. *Deadline:* June 25.

Contact: Roxanne Gorman, Program Manager
Office of Navajo Nation Scholarship and Financial Assistance
PO Box 1870
Window Rock, AZ 86515-1870
Phone: 928-871-7434
Fax: 928-871-6561

ONEIDA TRIBE OF INDIANS OF WISCONSIN http://www.oneidanation.org

ONEIDA HIGHER EDUCATION GRANT PROGRAM

Renewable award available to enrolled members of the Oneida Tribe of Indians of Wisconsin who are accepted into an accredited postsecondary institution within the United States.

Award: Grant for use in freshman, sophomore, junior, senior, or graduate years; renewable. *Number:* varies. *Amount:* up to $20,000.

Eligibility Requirements: Applicant must be American Indian/Alaska Native and enrolled or expecting to enroll full or part-time at a two-year or four-year or technical institution or university. Available to U.S. citizens.

Application Requirements: Application, financial need analysis, Oneida Tribal Enrollment. *Deadline:* Continuous.

Contact:
Phone: 800-236-2214 Ext. 4033
Fax: 920-869-4039

OREGON STUDENT ASSISTANCE COMMISSION http://www.osac.state.or.us

VERL AND DOROTHY MILLER NATIVE AMERICAN VOCATIONAL SCHOLARSHIP

Scholarship available to students of Native American ancestry who plan to enroll full time in an eligible trade or vocational school. Must provide proof of eligibility. Specific details found on Web site http://www.osac.state.or.us. Deadline is March 1.

Award: Scholarship for use in freshman or sophomore years; not renewable. *Number:* varies. *Amount:* $500.

Eligibility Requirements: Applicant must be American Indian/Alaska Native; enrolled or expecting to enroll full-time at a technical institution and resident of Oregon.

Application Requirements: Application, certification of Native American ancestry. *Deadline:* March 1.

Contact: Director of Grant Programs
Oregon Student Assistance Commission
1500 Valley River Drive, Suite 100
Eugene, OR 97401-7020
Phone: 800-452-8807 Ext. 7395
E-mail: awardinfo@mercury.osac.state.or.us

ORGANIZATION OF CHINESE AMERICANS

http://www.ocanatl.org

GATES MILLENNIUM SCHOLARS

Award enables Asian Pacific Islander American students to complete an undergraduate and graduate education. Must be entering a U.S. accredited college or university as a full-time degree-seeking student. Minimum 3.3 GPA required. Must demonstrate leadership abilities. Must meet federal Pell Grant eligibility criteria. Visit Web site at http://www.gmsp.org.

Award: Scholarship for use in freshman, sophomore, junior, senior, or graduate years; renewable. *Number:* varies. *Amount:* varies.

Eligibility Requirements: Applicant must be Asian/Pacific Islander and enrolled or expecting to enroll full-time at a four-year institution or university. Available to U.S. citizens.

Application Requirements: Application, financial need analysis, nomination packet. *Deadline:* January 16.

Contact: Catherine Claro Domaoan, GMS/APIA Representative
Organization of Chinese Americans
1001 Connecticut Avenue, NW, Suite 601
Washington, DC 20036
Phone: 866-274-4677
Fax: 202-530-0643
E-mail: gmspinfo@ocanatl.org

OCA AVON COLLEGE SCHOLARSHIP

Scholarships for Asian Pacific American women who will be entering first year of college in the upcoming fall.

Award: Scholarship for use in freshman year; not renewable. *Number:* 8–15. *Amount:* $1500–$2000.

Eligibility Requirements: Applicant must be Asian/Pacific Islander; high school student; planning to enroll or expecting to enroll full-time at a two-year or four-year institution or university and female. Applicant must have 3.0 GPA or higher. Available to U.S. citizens.

Application Requirements: Application, essay, financial need analysis, self-addressed stamped envelope, transcript, letter of acceptance, letter of intent to enroll. *Deadline:* May 1.

Contact: OCA-Avon Scholarship
Organization of Chinese Americans
1001 Connecticut Avenue NW, Suite 601
Washington, DC 20036
Phone: 202-223-5500
Fax: 202-296-0540
E-mail: oca@ocanatl.org

OCA NATIONAL ESSAY CONTEST

Contest for Asian Pacific American students between grades 9 and 12. First place $1000, second place $500, third place $300. Submit five copies of essay. For details, go to http://www.ocanatl.org.

Award: Prize for use in freshman year; not renewable. *Number:* 3. *Amount:* $300–$1000.

Eligibility Requirements: Applicant must be Asian/Pacific Islander; high school student and planning to enroll or expecting to enroll at a two-year or four-year institution. Available to U.S. citizens.

Application Requirements: Applicant must enter a contest, essay. *Deadline:* May 1.

Contact: Scholarship Coordinator
Organization of Chinese Americans
1001 Connecticut Avenue NW, Suite 601
Washington, DC 20036
Phone: 202-223-5500
Fax: 202-296-0540
E-mail: oca@ocanatl.org

OCA-AXA ACHIEVEMENT SCHOLARSHIP

A college achievement scholarship for Asian Pacific Americans entering their first year of college.

Award: Scholarship for use in freshman year; not renewable. *Number:* 6. *Amount:* $2000.

Eligibility Requirements: Applicant must be Asian/Pacific Islander; high school student and planning to enroll or expecting to enroll full-time at a two-year or four-year institution or university. Applicant must have 3.0 GPA or higher. Available to U.S. citizens.

Application Requirements: Application, essay, financial need analysis, self-addressed stamped envelope, transcript. *Deadline:* May 1.

Contact: OCA AXA Scholarship
Organization of Chinese Americans
1001 Connecticut Avenue NW, Suite 601
Washington, DC 20036
Fax: 202-296-0540
E-mail: oca@ocanatl.org

OCA-SYSCO SCHOLARSHIP

Scholarship for Asian Pacific Americans who are financially disadvantaged and will be entering their first year of college.

Award: Scholarship for use in freshman year; not renewable. *Number:* 6. *Amount:* $2000.

Eligibility Requirements: Applicant must be Asian/Pacific Islander; high school student and planning to enroll or expecting to enroll full-time at a two-year or four-year institution or university. Applicant must have 3.0 GPA or higher. Available to U.S. citizens.

Application Requirements: Application, essay, financial need analysis, self-addressed stamped envelope, transcript. *Deadline:* May 1.

Contact: OCA-SYSCO Scholarship
Organization of Chinese Americans
1001 Connecticut Avenue NW, Suite 601
Washington, DC 20036
E-mail: oca@ocanatl.org

OCA-VERIZON SCHOLARSHIP

Scholarships for Asian Pacific Americans who are financially disadvantaged and will be entering their first year of college.

Award: Scholarship for use in freshman year; not renewable. *Number:* 20–25. *Amount:* $1500–$2000.

Eligibility Requirements: Applicant must be Asian/Pacific Islander; high school student and planning to enroll or expecting to enroll full-time at a two-year or four-year institution or university. Applicant must have 3.0 GPA or higher. Available to U.S. citizens.

Application Requirements: Application, essay, financial need analysis, self-addressed stamped envelope, transcript. *Deadline:* May 1.

Contact: OCA-Verizon Scholarship
Organization of Chinese Americans
1001 Connecticut Avenue NW, Suite 601
Washington, DC 20036
E-mail: oca@ocanatl.org

OCA/UPS FOUNDATION GOLD MOUNTAIN SCHOLARSHIP

Scholarships for Asian Pacific Americans who are the first person in their immediate family to attend college. Must be entering first year of college in the upcoming fall. Winners attend OCA National Convention.

Award: Scholarship for use in freshman year; not renewable. *Number:* 8–15. *Amount:* $2000.

Eligibility Requirements: Applicant must be Asian/Pacific Islander; high school student and planning to enroll or expecting to enroll full-time at a two-year or four-year institution or university. Applicant must have 3.0 GPA or higher. Available to U.S. citizens.

Organization of Chinese Americans (continued)

Application Requirements: Application, essay, financial need analysis, resume, self-addressed stamped envelope, transcript, letter of acceptance, letter of intent to enroll. *Deadline:* April 15.

Contact: OCA-NPS Scholarship
Organization of Chinese Americans
1001 Connecticut Avenue NW, Suite 601
Washington, DC 20036
Phone: 202-223-5500
Fax: 202-296-0540
E-mail: oca@ocanatl.org

OSAGE SCHOLARSHIP FUND

MAE LASSLEY OSAGE SCHOLARSHIP FUND

Renewable awards to Osage Indian Tribe members who are members of the Roman Catholic Church. Must attend an accredited college or university as an undergraduate or graduate student on a full-time basis. Minimum 2.5 GPA required. Application deadline is April 15.

Award: Scholarship for use in freshman, sophomore, junior, senior, or graduate years; renewable. *Number:* 12–20. *Amount:* $500–$1000.

Eligibility Requirements: Applicant must be Roman Catholic; American Indian/Alaska Native and enrolled or expecting to enroll full-time at a two-year or four-year institution or university. Applicant must have 2.5 GPA or higher. Available to U.S. citizens.

Application Requirements: Application, financial need analysis, references, transcript, CDIB card. *Deadline:* April 15.

Contact: Sarah Jameson, Administrative Assistant
Osage Scholarship Fund
PO Box 690240
Tulsa, OK 74169-0240
Phone: 918-294-1904 Ext. 128
Fax: 918-294-0920
E-mail: sarah.jameson@dioceseoftulsa.org

OSAGE TRIBAL EDUCATION COMMITTEE

OSAGE TRIBAL EDUCATION COMMITTEE SCHOLARSHIP

Available for Osage Tribal members only. 150 to 250 renewable scholarship awards. Spring deadline: December 31. Fall deadline: July 1. Summer deadline: May 1.

Award: Scholarship for use in freshman, sophomore, junior, or senior years; renewable. *Number:* 150–250. *Amount:* $200–$400.

Eligibility Requirements: Applicant must be American Indian/Alaska Native and enrolled or expecting to enroll full or part-time at a two-year or four-year or technical institution or university.

Application Requirements: Photo, references. *Deadline:* varies.

Contact: Ms. Cheryl Lewis, Business Manager
Osage Tribal Education Committee
4149 Highline Boulevard, Suite 380
Oklahoma City, OK 73108
Phone: 405-605-6051 Ext. 304
Fax: 405-605-6057

OSAGE TRIBAL EDUCATION DEPARTMENT http://www.osagetribaleducation.com/

OSAGE HIGHER EDUCATION GRANT

Award available only to those who have proof of Osage Indian descent. Must submit proof of financial need. Deadlines are August 1 for the Fall, December 31 for the Spring and May 1 for Summer.

Award: Grant for use in freshman, sophomore, junior, senior, graduate, or postgraduate years; not renewable. *Number:* varies. *Amount:* $300–$1200.

Eligibility Requirements: Applicant must be American Indian/Alaska Native and enrolled or expecting to enroll full or part-time at a two-year or four-year institution or university. Available to U.S. citizens.

Application Requirements: Application, financial need analysis, transcript, verification of enrollment, proof of Osage Indian descent, copy of CDIB card. *Deadline:* varies.

Contact: Jennifer Holding
Osage Tribal Education Department
PO Box 1270
Pawhuska, OK 74056
Phone: 800-390-6724
Fax: 918-287-2416
E-mail: jholding@osagetribe.org

PAGE EDUCATION FOUNDATION http://www.page-ed.org

PAGE EDUCATION FOUNDATION GRANT

Grants are available to Minnesota students of color who attend Minnesota postsecondary institutions. Students must be willing to provide a minimum of 50 hours of service each year they accept a grant. This service is focused on K-8th grade children of color and encourages the youngsters to value learning and education. Page scholars are tutors, mentors and role models. Mentors are also provided for the page scholars.

Award: Grant for use in freshman, sophomore, junior, or senior years; renewable. *Number:* 500–600. *Amount:* $900–$2500.

Eligibility Requirements: Applicant must be American Indian/Alaska Native, Asian/Pacific Islander, Black (non-Hispanic), or Hispanic; enrolled or expecting to enroll full-time at a two-year or four-year or technical institution or university; resident of Minnesota and studying in Minnesota. Available to U.S. citizens.

Application Requirements: Application, essay, financial need analysis, references, transcript. *Deadline:* May 1.

Contact: Ramona Harristhal, Administrative Director
Page Education Foundation
PO Box 581254
Minneapolis, MN 55458-1254
Phone: 612-332-0406
Fax: 612-332-0403
E-mail: pagemail@mtn.org

PETER AND ALICE KOOMRUIAN FUND

PETER AND ALICE KOOMRUIAN ARMENIAN EDUCATION FUND

One-time award for students of Armenian descent to pursue postsecondary studies in any field at any accredited college or university in the U.S. Submit student identification and letter of enrollment. Must rank in upper third of class or have minimum GPA of 3.0.

Award: Scholarship for use in freshman, sophomore, junior, senior, graduate, or postgraduate years; not renewable. *Number:* 5–20. *Amount:* $1000–$2250.

Eligibility Requirements: Applicant must be of Armenian heritage and enrolled or expecting to enroll full-time at a two-year or four-year institution or university. Applicant must have 3.0 GPA or higher. Available to U.S. and non-U.S. citizens.

Application Requirements: Application, photo, references, self-addressed stamped envelope, transcript, school ID and school enrollment letter. *Deadline:* April 15.

Contact: Terenik Koujakian, Awards Committee Member
Peter and Alice Koomruian Fund
15915 Ventura Boulevard, Penthouse 1
Encino, CA 91436
Phone: 818-990-7454
E-mail: terenikkoujakian@hotmail.com

PETER DOCTOR MEMORIAL INDIAN SCHOLARSHIP FOUNDATION, INC.

PETER DOCTOR MEMORIAL IROQUOIS SCHOLARSHIP

One time award available to enrolled N.Y. State Iroquois Indian students. Must be sophomore level or above attending full-time in a postsecondary institution.

Award: Scholarship for use in sophomore, junior, senior, or graduate years; not renewable. *Number:* varies. *Amount:* $700–$1500.

Eligibility Requirements: Applicant must be American Indian/Alaska Native; enrolled or expecting to enroll full-time at a two-year or four-year or technical institution or university and resident of New York. Available to U.S. citizens.

Application Requirements: Application, autobiography, financial need analysis, references, tribal certification. *Deadline:* May 31.

Contact: Clara Hill, Treasurer
Peter Doctor Memorial Indian Scholarship Foundation, Inc.
PO Box 431
Basom, NY 14013
Phone: 716-542-2025
E-mail: cehill@pce.net

POLISH HERITAGE ASSOCIATION OF MARYLAND

POLISH HERITAGE SCHOLARSHIP

Scholarships given to individual of Polish descent (at least 2 Polish grandparents) who demonstrates academic excellence, financial need, and promotes their Polish Heritage. Must be a legal Maryland resident. Deadline is March 31.

Award: Scholarship for use in freshman, sophomore, junior, or senior years; not renewable. *Number:* varies. *Amount:* $1500–$3000.

Eligibility Requirements: Applicant must be of Polish heritage; enrolled or expecting to enroll full-time at a two-year or four-year institution or university and resident of Maryland. Applicant must have 3.0 GPA or higher. Available to U.S. citizens.

Application Requirements: Application, essay, financial need analysis, interview, photo, transcript. *Deadline:* March 31.

Contact: Thomas Hollowak, Scholarship Chair
Polish Heritage Association of Maryland
7 Dendron Court
Baltimore, MD 21234
Phone: 410-837-4268
Fax: 410-668-2513
E-mail: thollowalk@ubmail.ubalt.edu

POLISH NATIONAL ALLIANCE

POLISH NATIONAL ALLIANCE SCHOLARSHIP AWARD

This program is awarded to Polish National Alliance members only. Must be a member for at least three years. Must currently be enrolled full-time in an accredited college as an undergraduate sophomore, junior or senior. Applicants with 3.0 GPA or greater preferred, but not required.

Award: Scholarship for use in sophomore, junior, or senior years; renewable. *Number:* 250. *Amount:* $500.

Eligibility Requirements: Applicant must be of Polish heritage and enrolled or expecting to enroll full-time at a four-year institution. Applicant must have 3.0 GPA or higher. Available to U.S. citizens.

Application Requirements: Application, photo, test scores, transcript. *Deadline:* April 15.

Contact: Polish National Alliance
Education Department
6100 North Cicero Avenue
Chicago, IL 60646

PORTUGUESE FOUNDATION, INC. http://www.pfict.org

PORTUGUESE FOUNDATION SCHOLARSHIP PROGRAM

Scholarship funds available through Foundation. Award based on need and scholastic achievement. Applicants must be Connecticut resident and of Portuguese descendant. Minimum 2.5 GPA required. Must be U.S. citizen.

Award: Scholarship for use in freshman, sophomore, junior, or senior years; not renewable. *Number:* 8–10. *Amount:* $1500–$1700.

Eligibility Requirements: Applicant must be of Portuguese heritage; enrolled or expecting to enroll full-time at a two-year or four-year or technical institution or university and resident of Connecticut. Applicant must have 2.5 GPA or higher. Available to U.S. citizens.

Application Requirements: Application, autobiography, driver's license, essay, financial need analysis, interview, photo, portfolio, resume, references, self-addressed stamped envelope, test scores, transcript. *Deadline:* March 2.

Contact: Fernando Rosa, President
Portuguese Foundation, Inc.
86 New Park Avenue
Hartford, CT 06106
Phone: 860-236-5514
Fax: 860-236-5514
E-mail: fernandogfgrosa@aol.com

PORTUGUESE HERITAGE SCHOLARSHIP FOUNDATION http://www.phsf.net/

PORTUGUESE HERITAGE SCHOLARSHIP

This award is based on merit, need, and Portuguese ancestry. Application deadline is February 15. Please refer to Web site for further details: http://www.phsf.net/

Award: Scholarship for use in freshman, sophomore, junior, or senior years; renewable. *Number:* 8–10. *Amount:* $1000–$8000.

Eligibility Requirements: Applicant must be of Portuguese heritage and enrolled or expecting to enroll full-time at a two-year or four-year institution or university. Available to U.S. and non-U.S. citizens.

Application Requirements: Application, essay, financial need analysis, references, self-addressed stamped envelope, test scores, transcript. *Deadline:* February 15.

Contact: Stephanie Pimentel, Academic Secretary
Portuguese Heritage Scholarship Foundation
PO Box 30246
Bethesda, MD 20824-0246
Phone: 301-652-2737
Fax: 301-652-3015
E-mail: phsf@raponte.com

PRESBYTERIAN CHURCH (USA) http://www.pcusa.org/financialaid

NATIVE AMERICAN EDUCATION GRANTS

Grants available for Native American students enrolled in an accredited institution as a full-time student. Must show financial need and proof of tribal membership.

Award: Grant for use in freshman, sophomore, junior, senior, graduate, or postgraduate years; renewable. *Number:* 10–100. *Amount:* $2500.

Eligibility Requirements: Applicant must be American Indian/Alaska Native and enrolled or expecting to enroll full-time at a two-year or four-year or technical institution or university. Applicant must have 2.5 GPA or higher. Available to U.S. citizens.

Application Requirements: Application, essay, financial need analysis, test scores, transcript, tribal membership. *Deadline:* June 3.

Contact: Frances Cook, Associate, Financial Aid
Presbyterian Church (USA)
Financial Aid for Studies
100 Witherspoon Street, MO65
Louisville, KY 40202-1396
Phone: 888-728-7228 Ext. 5776
Fax: 502-569-8766
E-mail: fcook@ctr.pcusa.org

PUEBLO DE COCHITI HIGHER EDUCATION

PUEBLO DE COCHITI HIGHER EDUCATION PROGRAM

The Pueblo de Cochiti Higher Education Program funds eligible students pursuing college degrees (AA, AS, BA). Students must be at 1/4 Cochiti blood and an enrolled/verified member of the Cochiti Tribe as determined by Tribal Council.

Award: Grant for use in freshman, sophomore, junior, or senior years; not renewable. *Number:* 20. *Amount:* up to $3000.

Eligibility Requirements: Applicant must be American Indian/Alaska Native and enrolled or expecting to enroll full-time at a two-year or four-year or technical institution or university. Available to U.S. citizens.

Pueblo de Cochiti Higher Education (continued)

Application Requirements: Application, autobiography, essay, financial need analysis, interview, photo, references, transcript, CIB-certificate of Indian blood. *Deadline:* varies.

Contact: Darlene Smart-Herrera, Education Programs Manager
Pueblo de Cochiti Higher Education
PO Box 70
Cochiti Pueblo, NM 87072
Phone: 505-465-3115
Fax: 505-465-2203
E-mail: cochitidar@yahoo.com

PUEBLO OF ISLETA, DEPARTMENT OF EDUCATION http://www.isletaeducation.org

HIGHER EDUCATION SUPPLEMENTAL SCHOLARSHIP

Enrolled tribal members of the Isleta Pueblo may apply for this scholarship if they also apply for additional scholarships from different sources. Deadlines: Summer, April 1; Spring, October 1; Fall, July 1.

Award: Scholarship for use in freshman, sophomore, junior, senior, graduate, or postgraduate years; not renewable. *Number:* up to 150. *Amount:* $500–$7000.

Eligibility Requirements: Applicant must be American Indian/Alaska Native and enrolled or expecting to enroll full or part-time at a two-year or four-year or technical institution or university. Applicant must have 2.5 GPA or higher. Available to U.S. citizens.

Application Requirements: Application, financial need analysis, transcript, certificate of Indian blood, class schedule. *Deadline:* varies.

Contact: Joanna Garcia, Higher Education Director
Pueblo of Isleta, Department of Education
PO Box 1270
Isleta, NM 87022
Phone: 505-869-2680
Fax: 505-869-7690
E-mail: isletahighered@yahoo.com

PUEBLO OF SAN JUAN, DEPARTMENT OF EDUCATION http://www.sanjuaned.org

OHKAY OWINGEH TRIBAL SCHOLARSHIP OF THE PUEBLO OF SAN JUAN

Scholarship for members of the Pueblo of San Juan tribe only. Applicant must have applied for other scholarships and use this scholarship for supplemental funds. Minimum GPA of 2.0 is required. Must complete required number of hours of community service in the San Juan Pueblo. Call the Education Coordinator for deadlines and other information.

Award: Scholarship for use in freshman, sophomore, junior, senior, or graduate years; renewable. *Number:* 1–30. *Amount:* $250–$1000.

Eligibility Requirements: Applicant must be American Indian/Alaska Native; enrolled or expecting to enroll full or part-time at a two-year or four-year or technical institution or university and resident of New Mexico. Available to U.S. citizens.

Application Requirements: Application, transcript. *Deadline:* varies.

Contact: Elvie Aquino, Education Coordinator
Pueblo of San Juan, Department of Education
PO Box 1529
San Juan Pueblo, NM 87566
Phone: 505-852-3477
Fax: 505-852-3030
E-mail: psj_deptofed_ema@yahoo.com

POP'AY SCHOLARSHIP

Scholarship for members of the Pueblo of San Juan tribe who are pursuing their first associate or baccalaureate degree. Applicants must have applied for other scholarships and use this scholarship for supplemental funds. Must complete a minimum of 20 hours of community service within the San Juan Pueblo. Must maintain minimum GPA of 2.0. Deadlines are December 30 for spring, April 30 for summer, and June 30 for fall. Contact Education Coordinator for more information.

Award: Scholarship for use in freshman, sophomore, junior, or senior years; renewable. *Number:* up to 17. *Amount:* up to $2500.

Eligibility Requirements: Applicant must be American Indian/Alaska Native; enrolled or expecting to enroll full-time at a two-year or four-year institution or university and resident of New Mexico. Available to U.S. citizens.

Application Requirements: Application, transcript, letter of acceptance to college. *Deadline:* varies.

Contact: Elvie Aquino, Education Coordinator
Pueblo of San Juan, Department of Education
PO Box 1529
San Juan Pueblo, NM 87566
Phone: 505-852-3477
Fax: 505-852-3030
E-mail: psj_deptofed_ema@yahoo.com

RHODE ISLAND FOUNDATION http://www.rifoundation.org

RAYMOND H. TROTT SCHOLARSHIP

One-time scholarships of $1000 is awarded to a minority student, who is a Rhode Island resident entering his/her senior year at an accredited college. Must plan to pursue a career in banking.

Award: Scholarship for use in senior year; not renewable. *Number:* 1. *Amount:* $1000.

Eligibility Requirements: Applicant must be American Indian/Alaska Native, Asian/Pacific Islander, Black (non-Hispanic), or Hispanic; enrolled or expecting to enroll full-time at a four-year institution or university and resident of Rhode Island. Available to U.S. citizens.

Application Requirements: Application, essay, transcript. *Deadline:* June 14.

Contact: Libby Monahan, Scholarship Coordinator
Rhode Island Foundation
One Union Station
Providence, RI 02903
Phone: 401-274-4564
Fax: 401-272-1359
E-mail: libbym@rifoundation.org

RONALD MCDONALD HOUSE CHARITIES http://www.rmhc.org

RHMC ASIAN STUDENTS INCREASING ACHIEVEMENT SCHOLARSHIP PROGRAM

One-time award for graduating high school senior with at least one parent of Asian origin. Must attend a two-year or four-year college full time. Award is based on academic achievement, financial need, community involvement, and personal qualities. Must be from a geographic area served by the program. See Web site at http://www.rmhc.org for list of geographic regions, further details, and scholarship application.

Award: Scholarship for use in freshman year; not renewable. *Number:* varies. *Amount:* up to $1000.

Eligibility Requirements: Applicant must be Asian/Pacific Islander; high school student and planning to enroll or expecting to enroll full-time at a two-year or four-year institution or university.

Application Requirements: Application, financial need analysis, references, transcript. *Deadline:* February 1.

Contact: Application available at Web site.

RMHC/AFRICAN AMERICAN FUTURE ACHIEVERS SCHOLARSHIP PROGRAM

One-time award for graduating high school senior with at least one parent of African-American origin. Must attend a two-year or four-year college full time. Award is based on academic achievement, financial need, community involvement, and personal qualities. Must be from a geographic area served by the program. See Web site at http://www.rmhc.org for list of geographic regions, further details, and scholarship application.

Award: Scholarship for use in freshman year; not renewable. *Number:* varies. *Amount:* up to $1000.

Eligibility Requirements: Applicant must be Black (non-Hispanic); high school student and planning to enroll or expecting to enroll full-time at a two-year or four-year institution or university.

Application Requirements: Application, financial need analysis, references, transcript. *Deadline:* February 1.

Contact: Application available at Web site.

RMHC/HISPANIC AMERICAN COMMITMENT TO EDUCATIONAL RESOURCES SCHOLARSHIP PROGRAM

One-time award for graduating high school senior with at least one parent of Hispanic origin. Must attend a two-year or four-year college full time. Award is based on academic achievement, financial need, community involvement, and personal qualities. Must be from a geographic area served by the program. See Web site at http://www.rmhc.org for list of geographic regions, further details, and scholarship application.

Award: Scholarship for use in freshman year; not renewable. *Number:* varies. *Amount:* up to $1000.

Eligibility Requirements: Applicant must be Hispanic; high school student and planning to enroll or expecting to enroll full-time at a two-year or four-year institution or university.

Application Requirements: Application, financial need analysis, references, transcript. *Deadline:* February 1.

Contact: Application available at Web site.

RYU FAMILY FOUNDATION, INC.

SEOL BONG SCHOLARSHIP

One-time award to support and advance education and research. Must be Korean residing in DE, PA, NJ, NY, CT, VT, RI, NH, MA or ME. Minimum 3.5 GPA required. Deadline is November 14.

Award: Scholarship for use in freshman, sophomore, junior, senior, or graduate years; not renewable. *Number:* 25. *Amount:* $1500–$2000.

Eligibility Requirements: Applicant must be Korean citizen; enrolled or expecting to enroll full-time at a four-year institution or university; resident of Connecticut, Delaware, Maine, Massachusetts, New Hampshire, New Jersey, New York, Pennsylvania, Rhode Island, or Vermont and studying in Connecticut, Delaware, Maine, Massachusetts, New Hampshire, New Jersey, New York, Pennsylvania, Rhode Island, or Vermont. Applicant must have 3.5 GPA or higher. Available to U.S. and non-Canadian citizens.

Application Requirements: Application, essay, photo, references, test scores, transcript. *Deadline:* November 14.

Contact: Jenny Kang
Ryu Family Foundation, Inc.
901 Murray Road
East Hanover, NJ 07936
Phone: 973-560-9696
Fax: 973-560-0661
E-mail: jennyk@toplineus.com

SALVADORAN AMERICAN LEADERSHIP AND EDUCATIONAL FUND http://www.salef.org

FULFILLING OUR DREAMS SCHOLARSHIP FUND

Up to sixty scholarships ranging from $500-$2500 will be awarded to students who come from a Latino heritage. Must have a 2.5 GPA. See Web site for more details: http://www.salef.org

Award: Scholarship for use in freshman, sophomore, junior, senior, graduate, or postgraduate years; not renewable. *Number:* 40–60. *Amount:* $500–$2500.

Eligibility Requirements: Applicant must be of Hispanic or Latin American/Caribbean heritage and enrolled or expecting to enroll full-time at a four-year institution or university. Applicant must have 2.5 GPA or higher. Available to U.S. and non-U.S. citizens.

Application Requirements: Application, essay, financial need analysis, interview, photo, resume, references, self-addressed stamped envelope, test scores, transcript. *Deadline:* June 30.

Contact: Mayra Soriano, Educational and Youth Programs Manager
Salvadoran American Leadership and Educational Fund
1625 West Olympic Boulevard, Suite 718
Los Angeles, CA 90015
Phone: 213-480-1052
Fax: 213-487-2530
E-mail: msoriano@salef.org

SANTO DOMINGO SCHOLARSHIP PROGRAM http://www.speciallove.org

SANTO DOMINGO SCHOLARSHIP

Fourth degree Santo Domingo-enrolled with tribe. Letter of acceptance from high school or college. For any tribal member to have the opportunity to get an undergraduate degree. 2.0 GPA required. If full time 12 credits or more must be completed each semester. Amount is need based. Supported by Bureau of Indian Affairs. Deadlines: March 1 for Fall; November 1 for Spring.

Award: Scholarship for use in freshman, sophomore, junior, or senior years; renewable. *Number:* varies. *Amount:* up to $1000.

Eligibility Requirements: Applicant must be American Indian/Alaska Native and enrolled or expecting to enroll full or part-time at a two-year or four-year or technical institution or university. Available to U.S. citizens.

Application Requirements: Application, essay, transcript. *Deadline:* varies.

Contact: Mary Abeita, Director
Santo Domingo Scholarship Program
PO Box 160
Santo Domingo Pueblo, NM 87052
Phone: 505-465-2214 Ext. 25
Fax: 505-465-2688
E-mail: kewaeduec@earthlink.net

SCOTTISH RITE CHARITABLE FOUNDATION OF CANADA http://www.scottishritemasons-can.org/foundation

SCOTTISH RITE CHARITABLE FOUNDATION COLLEGE BURSARIES

• *See page 519*

SEMINOLE TRIBE OF FLORIDA http://www.seminoletribe.com

SEMINOLE TRIBE OF FLORIDA DIVISION OF EDUCATION SCHOLARSHIP

The Seminole Tribe of Florida awards full scholarships to applicants who meet membership requirements (must have a membership number). Must maintain a 2.0 GPA with 12 semester credit hours earned each semester. Must be a member of the Seminole Tribe of Florida.

Award: Scholarship for use in freshman, sophomore, junior, senior, graduate, or postgraduate years; renewable. *Number:* 100. *Amount:* varies.

Eligibility Requirements: Applicant must be American Indian/Alaska Native and enrolled or expecting to enroll full or part-time at a two-year or four-year institution or university. Available to U.S. citizens.

Application Requirements: Application, financial need analysis, transcript. *Deadline:* varies.

Contact: Dora Bell, Higher Education Advisor
Seminole Tribe of Florida
3100 North 63rd Avenue
Hollywood, FL 33024-2153
Phone: 954-233-9541
Fax: 954-893-8856
E-mail: dbell@semtribe.com

SENECA NATION OF INDIANS http://www.sni.org

SENECA NATION HIGHER EDUCATION PROGRAM

Renewable award for enrolled Senecas of the Cattaraugus and Allegany Indian reservations who are in need of financial assistance. Application deadlines:

Seneca Nation of Indians (continued)

Fall deadline, July 1; Spring deadline, December 1; Summer deadline, May 1. Must be degree seeking and enrolled in a two-year college, four-year college or university.

Award: Scholarship for use in freshman, sophomore, junior, senior, graduate, or postgraduate years; renewable. *Number:* varies. *Amount:* $3000–$8000.

Eligibility Requirements: Applicant must be American Indian/Alaska Native and enrolled or expecting to enroll full or part-time at a two-year or four-year institution or university. Available to U.S. and non-U.S. citizens.

Application Requirements: Application, essay, financial need analysis, references, transcript, tribal certification. *Deadline:* varies.

Contact: Debra M. Hoag, Higher Education Coordinator
Seneca Nation of Indians
PO Box 231
Salamanca, NY 14779
Phone: 716-945-1790 Ext. 3103
Fax: 716-945-7170
E-mail: snieduc@localnet.com

SONS OF ITALY FOUNDATION http://www.osia.org

SONS OF ITALY NATIONAL LEADERSHIP GRANTS COMPETITION GENERAL SCHOLARSHIPS

Scholarships for undergraduate or graduate students who are U.S. citizens of Italian descent. Must demonstrate academic excellence. For more details see Web site: http://www.osia.org.

Award: Scholarship for use in freshman, sophomore, junior, senior, or graduate years; not renewable. *Number:* 10–13. *Amount:* $4000–$25,000.

Eligibility Requirements: Applicant must be of Italian heritage and enrolled or expecting to enroll full-time at a four-year institution or university. Available to U.S. citizens.

Application Requirements: Application, essay, resume, references, test scores, transcript. *Fee:* $25. *Deadline:* February 28.

Contact: Scholarship Information
Sons of Italy Foundation
219 E Street, NE
Washington, DC 20002
Phone: 202-547-5106
Fax: 202-546-8168
E-mail: scholarships@osia.org

SONS OF ITALY NATIONAL LEADERSHIP GRANTS COMPETITION HENRY SALVATORI SCHOLARSHIPS

Scholarships for collegebound high school seniors who demonstrate exceptional leadership, distinguished scholarship, and a deep understanding and respect for the principles upon which our nation was founded: liberty, freedom, and equality. Must be a U.S. citizen of Italian descent. For more details see Web site: http://www.osia.org.

Award: Scholarship for use in freshman year; not renewable. *Number:* 1. *Amount:* $5000.

Eligibility Requirements: Applicant must be of Italian heritage; high school student and planning to enroll or expecting to enroll full-time at a four-year institution or university. Available to U.S. citizens.

Application Requirements: Application, essay, resume, references, test scores, transcript. *Fee:* $25. *Deadline:* February 28.

Contact: Scholarship Information
Sons of Italy Foundation
219 E Street, NE
Washington, DC 20002
Phone: 202-547-5106
Fax: 202-546-8168
E-mail: scholarships@osia.org

SONS OF ITALY NATIONAL LEADERSHIP GRANTS COMPETITION LANGUAGE SCHOLARSHIP

Scholarships for undergraduate students in their junior or senior year of study who are majoring in Italian language studies. Must be a U.S. citizen of Italian descent. For more details see Web site: http://www.osia.org.

Award: Scholarship for use in junior or senior years; not renewable. *Number:* 1. *Amount:* $10,000.

Eligibility Requirements: Applicant must be of Italian heritage and enrolled or expecting to enroll full-time at a four-year institution or university. Available to U.S. citizens.

Application Requirements: Application, essay, resume, references, test scores, transcript. *Fee:* $25. *Deadline:* February 28.

Contact: Scholarship Information
Sons of Italy Foundation
219 E Street, NE
Washington, DC 20002
Phone: 202-547-5106
Fax: 202-546-8168
E-mail: scholarships@osia.org

SONS OF NORWAY FOUNDATION http://www.sofn.com

ASTRID G. CATES AND MYRTLE BEINHAUER SCHOLARSHIP FUNDS

• *See page 481*

SRP/NAVAJO GENERATING STATION http://www.srpnet.com

NAVAJO GENERATING STATION NAVAJO SCHOLARSHIP

SRP at the Navajo Generating Station (NGS) is offering scholarships to Navajo college students. The competitively awarded scholarships may be used at any accredited college or university. Priority is given to math, engineering, and environmental studies. Must be an enrolled member of the Navajo Nation.

Award: Scholarship for use in junior or senior years; renewable. *Number:* 1–10. *Amount:* $1000.

Eligibility Requirements: Applicant must be American Indian/Alaska Native and enrolled or expecting to enroll full-time at a four-year institution or university. Applicant must have 3.0 GPA or higher. Available to U.S. citizens.

Application Requirements: Application, financial need analysis, resume, references, transcript, statement of goals. *Deadline:* April 30.

Contact: Linda Dawavendewa, HR Coordinator
SRP/Navajo Generating Station
PO Box 850
Page, AZ 86040
Phone: 928-645-6539
Fax: 928-645-7295
E-mail: ljdwave@srp.com

ST. ANDREW'S SOCIETY OF WASHINGTON, DC http://www.thecapitalscot.com/standrew/scholarships.html

DONALD MALCOLM MACARTHUR SCHOLARSHIP

One-time award is available for U.S. students to study in Scotland or students from Scotland to study in the U.S. Special attention will be given to applicants whose work would demonstrably contribute to enhanced knowledge of Scottish history or culture. Must be a college junior, senior, or graduate student to apply. Need for financial assistance and academic record considered. Visit Web site for details and application: http://www.thecapitalscot.com/standrew/scholarships.html.

Award: Scholarship for use in junior, senior, or graduate years; not renewable. *Number:* 1. *Amount:* $2500.

Eligibility Requirements: Applicant must be of Scottish heritage; enrolled or expecting to enroll full-time at a four-year institution or university and resident of Delaware, District of Columbia, Maryland, New Jersey, North Carolina, Pennsylvania, Virginia, or Wisconsin. Available to U.S. and non-U.S. citizens.

Application Requirements: Application, essay, financial need analysis, references, self-addressed stamped envelope. *Deadline:* March 15.

Contact: Pete . Clepper, Chairman
St. Andrew's Society of Washington, DC
7823 Overhill Road
Bethesda, MD 20814-1114
Phone: 301-907-4823
E-mail: peterclepper@earthlink.net

JAMES AND MARY DAWSON SCHOLARSHIP

One-time award is available for college juniors, seniors, and graduate students from Scotland to study in the United States. Special attention will be given to applicants whose work would demonstrably contribute to enhanced knowledge of Scottish history or culture. Need for financial assistance and academic record considered. Visit Web site for details and application: http://www.thecapitalscot.com/standrew/scholarships.html.

Award: Scholarship for use in junior, senior, or graduate years; not renewable. *Number:* 1. *Amount:* $5000.

Eligibility Requirements: Applicant must be of Scottish heritage and enrolled or expecting to enroll full-time at a four-year institution or university. Available to citizens of countries other than the U.S. or Canada.

Application Requirements: Application, essay, financial need analysis, references, self-addressed stamped envelope. *Deadline:* March 15.

Contact: Peter Clepper, Chairman
St. Andrew's Society of Washington, DC
7823 Overhill Road
Bethesda, MD 20814
Phone: 301-907-4823
E-mail: peterclepper@earthlink.net

ST. ANDREW'S SCHOLARSHIPS

Award is available for full-time college juniors, seniors or graduate students. Must reside or attend school within 200 miles of Washington, D.C. Special attention will be given to applicants whose work would demonstrably contribute to enhanced knowledge of Scottish history or culture. Need for financial assistance and academic record considered. Visit Web site for details and application: http://www.thecapitalscot.com/standrew/scholarships.html.

Award: Scholarship for use in junior, senior, or graduate years; renewable. *Number:* varies. *Amount:* $1000–$1500.

Eligibility Requirements: Applicant must be of Scottish heritage; enrolled or expecting to enroll full-time at a four-year institution or university and resident of Delaware, District of Columbia, Maryland, New Jersey, North Carolina, Pennsylvania, Virginia, or West Virginia.

Application Requirements: Application, applicant must enter a contest, autobiography, essay, financial need analysis, references, self-addressed stamped envelope. *Deadline:* March 15.

Contact: Peter Clepper, Chairman
St. Andrew's Society of Washington, DC
7823 Overhill Road
Bethesda, MD 20814
Phone: 301-907-4823
E-mail: peterclepper@earthlink.net

STATE OF NORTH DAKOTA http://www.ndus.nodak.edu

NORTH DAKOTA INDIAN SCHOLARSHIP PROGRAM

Assists Native-American North Dakota residents in obtaining a college education. Priority given to full-time undergraduate students and those having a 3.5 GPA or higher. Certification of tribal enrollment required. For use at North Dakota institution.

Award: Scholarship for use in freshman, sophomore, junior, senior, or graduate years; renewable. *Number:* up to 150. *Amount:* $600–$900.

Eligibility Requirements: Applicant must be American Indian/Alaska Native; enrolled or expecting to enroll at a two-year or four-year institution or university; resident of North Dakota and studying in North Dakota. Applicant must have 3.5 GPA or higher.

Application Requirements: Application, financial need analysis, transcript, proof of tribal enrollment. *Deadline:* July 15.

Contact: Rhonda Schauer, Coordinator of American Indian Higher Education
State of North Dakota
600 East Boulevard, Department 215
Bismarck, ND 58505-0230
Phone: 701-328-9661

STEVEN KNEZEVICH TRUST

STEVEN KNEZEVICH GRANT

One-time grant for students of Serbian descent. Award not restricted to citizens of the U.S. Amount of award varies. Applicants must be attending an accredited institution of higher learning. Grant will be applied toward student's spring semester. To receive additional information and the application itself, applicant must send SASE, along with proof of Serbian descent.

Award: Grant for use in freshman, sophomore, junior, senior, or graduate years; not renewable. *Number:* varies. *Amount:* varies.

Eligibility Requirements: Applicant must be of Croatian/Serbian heritage and enrolled or expecting to enroll full or part-time at a two-year or four-year institution or university. Available to U.S. and non-U.S. citizens.

Application Requirements: Application, self-addressed stamped envelope, transcript, proof of Serbian heritage. *Deadline:* November 30.

Contact: Stanley Hack, Trustee
Steven Knezevich Trust
9830 North Courtland Drive
Mequon, WI 53092-6052
Phone: 262-241-5663
Fax: 262-241-5645

SWEDISH INSTITUTE/SVENSKA INSTITUTET http://www.si.se

VISBY PROGRAM: HIGHER EDUCATION AND RESEARCH

Scholarships to pursue studies in Sweden are available to citizens of Baltic countries, Belarus, and Ukraine. For more details see Web site: http://www.si.se.

Award: Scholarship for use in freshman, sophomore, junior, or senior years; not renewable. *Number:* varies. *Amount:* $7500–$9000.

Eligibility Requirements: Applicant must be of Latvian, Lithuanian, Polish, Russian, or Ukrainian heritage and enrolled or expecting to enroll at an institution or university. Available to citizens of countries other than the U.S. or Canada.

Application Requirements: Application. *Deadline:* March 1.

Contact: Application available at Web site.

SWISS BENEVOLENT SOCIETY OF CHICAGO http://www.sbschicago.org/education.html

SWISS BENEVOLENT SOCIETY OF CHICAGO SCHOLARSHIPS

Renewable scholarship for full-time students of documented Swiss descent. College students need a 3.5 GPA. High school students need a 26 on ACT or 1,050 on SAT. Must live in Illinois or southern Wisconsin. Applications may be requested after December 15.

Award: Scholarship for use in freshman, sophomore, junior, or senior years; renewable. *Number:* 30. *Amount:* $750–$2500.

Eligibility Requirements: Applicant must be of Swiss heritage; enrolled or expecting to enroll full-time at an institution or university and resident of Illinois or Wisconsin. Applicant must have 3.5 GPA or higher. Available to U.S. citizens.

Application Requirements: Application, essay, self-addressed stamped envelope, test scores, transcript. *Deadline:* March 15.

Contact: Education Committee
Swiss Benevolent Society of Chicago
PO Box 2137
Chicago, IL 60690-2137
E-mail: education@sbschicago.org

SWISS BENEVOLENT SOCIETY OF NEW YORK http://www.swissbenevolentny.com

MEDICUS STUDENT EXCHANGE

One-time award to students of Swiss nationality or parentage. U.S. residents study in Switzerland and Swiss residents study in the U.S. Awards to undergraduates are based on merit and need; those to graduates based only on merit. Open to all U.S. residents. Must be proficient in foreign language of instruction.

Swiss Benevolent Society of New York (continued)

Award: Grant for use in junior, senior, or graduate years; not renewable. *Number:* 1–5. *Amount:* $2000–$10,000.

Eligibility Requirements: Applicant must be of Swiss heritage; enrolled or expecting to enroll full-time at a four-year institution or university and must have an interest in foreign language. Applicant must have 3.5 GPA or higher. Available to U.S. and non-Canadian citizens.

Application Requirements: Application, financial need analysis, references, test scores, transcript. *Deadline:* March 31.

Contact: Anne Marie Gilman, Scholarship Director
Swiss Benevolent Society of New York
608 Fifth Avenue, #309
New York, NY 10020

PELLEGRINI SCHOLARSHIP GRANTS

Award to students who have a minimum 3.0 GPA, and show financial need. Must submit proof of Swiss nationality or descent. Must be a resident of Connecticut, Delaware, New Jersey, New York, or Pennsylvania. Fifty grants of up to $2500.

Award: Grant for use in freshman, sophomore, junior, senior, or graduate years; not renewable. *Number:* 50. *Amount:* $500–$2500.

Eligibility Requirements: Applicant must be of Swiss heritage; enrolled or expecting to enroll full or part-time at a two-year or four-year or technical institution or university and resident of Connecticut, Delaware, New Jersey, New York, or Pennsylvania. Applicant must have 3.0 GPA or higher. Available to U.S. and non-Canadian citizens.

Application Requirements: Application, financial need analysis, references, test scores, transcript. *Deadline:* March 31.

Contact: Anne Marie Gilman, Scholarship Director
Swiss Benevolent Society of New York
608 Fifth Avenue, #309
New York, NY 10020

TERRY FOX HUMANITARIAN AWARD PROGRAM http://www.terryfox.org

TERRY FOX HUMANITARIAN AWARD

Award granted to Canadian students entering postsecondary education. Criteria includes commitment to voluntary humanitarian work, courage in overcoming obstacles, excellence in academics, fitness and amateur sports. Must also show involvement in extracurricular activities. Value of award is $6000 Canadian awarded annually for maximum of four years. For those who attend institution that does not charge tuition fees, award is $3500 Canadian a year. Must be no older than 25.

Award: Scholarship for use in freshman, sophomore, or junior years; renewable. *Number:* 20. *Amount:* $2600–$4457.

Eligibility Requirements: Applicant must be Canadian citizen; age 25 or under and enrolled or expecting to enroll full-time at a two-year or four-year or technical institution or university.

Application Requirements: Application, references, self-addressed stamped envelope, transcript. *Deadline:* February 1.

Contact: Melissa Ratcliff, Administrative Assistant
Terry Fox Humanitarian Award Program
AQ 5003, 8888 University Drive
Burnaby, BC V5A 1S6
Canada
Phone: 604-291-3057
Fax: 604-291-3311
E-mail: terryfox@sfu.ca

TEXAS BLACK BAPTIST SCHOLARSHIP COMMITTEE http://www.bgct.org/aam

TEXAS BLACK BAPTIST SCHOLARSHIP

Renewable award for Texas resident attending a Baptist educational institution in Texas. Must be of African-American descent with a minimum 2.0 GPA. Must be a member in good standing of a Baptist church.

Award: Scholarship for use in freshman, sophomore, junior, or senior years; renewable. *Number:* varies. *Amount:* up to $800.

Eligibility Requirements: Applicant must be Baptist; Black (non-Hispanic); age 18; enrolled or expecting to enroll full or part-time at a two-year or four-year institution or university; resident of Texas and studying in Texas. Available to U.S. citizens.

Application Requirements: Application, autobiography, financial need analysis, interview, photo, portfolio, resume, references, test scores, transcript. *Deadline:* Continuous.

Contact: Michael A. Evans, Sr., Director of African American Ministries
Texas Black Baptist Scholarship Committee
333 North Washington, Suite 340 N
Dallas, TX 75246-1798
Phone: 214-828-5130
Fax: 214-828-5284
E-mail: robinson@bgct.org

TEXAS HIGHER EDUCATION COORDINATING BOARD http://www.collegefortexans.com

GOOD NEIGHBOR SCHOLARSHIP WAIVER

Renewable aid for students residing in Texas who are citizens of another country of the Americas and intend to return to their country upon completion of the course of study. Must attend public college in Texas. Student will be exempt from tuition.

Award: Scholarship for use in freshman, sophomore, junior, or senior years; renewable. *Number:* varies. *Amount:* varies.

Eligibility Requirements: Applicant must be Canadian or Latin American/Caribbean citizen; enrolled or expecting to enroll full or part-time at a two-year or four-year or technical institution or university and studying in Texas. Available to Canadian and non-U.S. citizens.

Application Requirements: Application, test scores, transcript. *Deadline:* March 15.

Contact: Texas Higher Education Coordinating Board
PO Box 12788
Austin, TX 78711-2788
Phone: 800-242-3062
E-mail: grantinfo@thecb.state.tx.us

THE ASIAN REPORTER http://www.asianreporter.com

ASIAN REPORTER SCHOLARSHIP

Scholarships available to students of Asian descent. Must be a resident of Washington or Oregon and attend school full-time in either state. Must have a minimum 3.0 GPA and demonstrate involvement in community or school related activities as well as financial need. Application deadline is March 16.

Award: Scholarship for use in freshman, sophomore, junior, or senior years. *Number:* 4. *Amount:* $500–$1000.

Eligibility Requirements: Applicant must be Asian/Pacific Islander; enrolled or expecting to enroll full-time at a four-year institution or university; resident of Oregon or Washington and studying in Oregon or Washington. Applicant must have 3.0 GPA or higher. Available to U.S. citizens.

Application Requirements: Application, driver's license, essay, financial need analysis, photo, references, transcript. *Deadline:* March 16.

Contact: The Asian Reporter
933 North Killingsworth Street
Suite 1A
Portland, OR 97217

TRIANGLE NATIVE AMERICAN SOCIETY http://www.tnasweb.org

TRIANGLE NATIVE AMERICAN SOCIETY SCHOLARSHIP FUND

The TNAS Scholarship is for any state or federally recognized U.S. Native-American rising sophomore, junior, or senior at any one of the 16 University of North Carolina system schools. Minimum GPA is 2.5. Must be a resident of North Carolina.

Award: Scholarship for use in sophomore, junior, or senior years; not renewable. *Number:* 1–3. *Amount:* $500–$1000.

Eligibility Requirements: Applicant must be American Indian/Alaska Native; enrolled or expecting to enroll full-time at a four-year institution or university; resident of North Carolina and studying in North Carolina. Applicant must have 2.5 GPA or higher. Available to U.S. citizens.

Application Requirements: Application, essay, references, transcript, proof of Native American ancestry. *Deadline:* June 10.

Contact: Alisa Hunt-Lowery, Scholarship Chair
Triangle Native American Society
PO Box 26841
Raleigh, NC 27611
Phone: 919-553-7449
E-mail: tnasscholarship@tnasweb.org

UKRAINIAN FRATERNAL ASSOCIATION http://members.tripod.com/~ufa_home

UKRAINIAN FRATERNAL ASSOCIATION EUGENE R. AND ELINOR R. KOTUR SCHOLARSHIP TRUST FUND

Award for students of Ukrainian ancestry who are enrolled in selected colleges and universities at sophomore, junior, or senior level. Deadline is May 31.

Award: Scholarship for use in sophomore, junior, or senior years; renewable. *Number:* varies.

Eligibility Requirements: Applicant must be of Ukrainian heritage and enrolled or expecting to enroll full-time at a four-year institution or university.

Application Requirements: Application, autobiography, photo, references, transcript. *Deadline:* May 31.

Contact: Stephan Wichar, Vice President
Ukrainian Fraternal Association
371 North 9th Street
Scranton, PA 18504-2005
Phone: 570-342-0937

UKRAINIAN FRATERNAL ASSOCIATION IVAN FRANKO SCHOLARSHIP FUND

Award for senior in high school or student attending accredited university or college. Must have been member of Ukrainian Fraternal Association for at least two years. Must write essay on topic chosen by Scholarship Commission. Submit recommendation. Deadline is May 31.

Award: Scholarship for use in freshman, sophomore, junior, or senior years; not renewable. *Number:* 3. *Amount:* $500–$1000.

Eligibility Requirements: Applicant must be of Ukrainian heritage and enrolled or expecting to enroll full or part-time at a four-year institution or university. Available to U.S. and Canadian citizens.

Application Requirements: Application, autobiography, essay, financial need analysis, photo, references, transcript. *Deadline:* May 31.

Contact: Stephan Wichar, Vice President
Ukrainian Fraternal Association
371 North 9th Street
Scranton, PA 18504-2005
Phone: 570-342-0937

UKRANIAN FRATERNAL ASSOCIATION STUDENT AID

Award for students of Ukrainian ancestry who have been a member in good standing of the Ukrainian Fraternal Association for at least two years. Must have completed one year of college and have minimum GPA of 2.0. Aid is awarded over two years: $300 for the first year and $300 for the second year.

Award: Scholarship for use in sophomore, junior, or senior years; not renewable. *Number:* varies. *Amount:* $300.

Eligibility Requirements: Applicant must be of Ukrainian heritage and enrolled or expecting to enroll at a four-year institution or university.

Application Requirements: Application, autobiography, photo, references, transcript. *Deadline:* May 31.

Contact: Stephan Wichar, Vice President
Ukrainian Fraternal Association
371 North 9th Street
Scranton, PA 18504-2005
Phone: 570-342-0937

UNICO NATIONAL, INC http://www.unico.org

MAJOR DON S. GENTILE SCHOLARSHIP

Scholarship available to graduating high school senior of Italian descent. Applicant must reside and attend high school within the corporate limits or adjoining suburbs of a city wherein an active chapter of UNICO National is located. Application must be signed by student's principal and properly certified by sponsoring Chapter President and Chapter Secretary. Must have letter of endorsement from President or Scholarship Chairperson of sponsoring Chapter.

Award: Scholarship for use in freshman, sophomore, junior, or senior years; renewable. *Number:* up to 1. *Amount:* up to $1500.

Eligibility Requirements: Applicant must be of Italian heritage; high school student and planning to enroll or expecting to enroll at a four-year institution. Available to U.S. citizens.

Application Requirements: Application, financial need analysis, references, transcript. *Deadline:* varies.

Contact: local UNICO Chapter

WILLIAM C. DAVINI SCHOLARSHIP

Scholarship available to graduating high school senior of Italian descent. Applicant must reside and attend high school within the corporate limits or adjoining suburbs of a city wherein an active chapter of UNICO National is located. Application must be signed by student's principal and properly certified by sponsoring Chapter President and Chapter Secretary. Must have letter of endorsement from President or Scholarship Chairperson of sponsoring Chapter.

Award: Scholarship for use in freshman, sophomore, junior, or senior years; renewable. *Number:* up to 1. *Amount:* up to $1500.

Eligibility Requirements: Applicant must be of Italian heritage; high school student and planning to enroll or expecting to enroll at a four-year institution. Available to U.S. citizens.

Application Requirements: Application, financial need analysis, references, transcript. *Deadline:* varies.

Contact: local UNICO chapter

UNITED METHODIST CHURCH http://www.umc.org/

UNITED METHODIST CHURCH ETHNIC SCHOLARSHIP

Awards for minority students pursuing undergraduate degree. Must have been certified members of the United Methodist Church for one year. Proof of membership and pastor's statement required. One-time award but is renewable by application each year. Minimum 2.5 GPA required.

Award: Scholarship for use in freshman, sophomore, junior, or senior years; not renewable. *Number:* 430–500. *Amount:* $800–$1000.

Eligibility Requirements: Applicant must be Methodist; American Indian/Alaska Native, Asian/Pacific Islander, Black (non-Hispanic), or Hispanic and enrolled or expecting to enroll full-time at a two-year or four-year institution or university. Applicant must have 2.5 GPA or higher. Available to U.S. and non-Canadian citizens.

Application Requirements: Application, essay, references, transcript, membership proof, pastor's statement. *Deadline:* May 1.

Contact: Patti J. Zimmerman, Scholarships Administrator
United Methodist Church
PO Box 340007
Nashville, TN 37203-0007
Phone: 615-340-7344
E-mail: pzimmer@gbhem.org

UNITED METHODIST CHURCH HISPANIC, ASIAN, AND NATIVE AMERICAN SCHOLARSHIP

Award for members of United Methodist Church who are Hispanic, Asian, Native-American, or Pacific Islander college juniors, seniors, or graduate students. Need membership proof and pastor's letter. Minimum 2.8 GPA required.

Award: Scholarship for use in junior, senior, or graduate years; not renewable. *Number:* 200–250. *Amount:* $1000–$3000.

Eligibility Requirements: Applicant must be Methodist; American Indian/Alaska Native, Asian/Pacific Islander, or Hispanic and enrolled or expecting to enroll full-time at a four-year institution or university. Available to U.S. citizens.

United Methodist Church (continued)

Application Requirements: Application, essay, references, transcript, membership proof, pastor's letter. *Deadline:* April 1.

Contact: Patti J. Zimmerman, Scholarships Administrator
United Methodist Church
PO Box 340007
Nashville, TN 37203-0007
Phone: 615-340-7344
E-mail: pzimmer@gbhem.org

UNITED METHODIST YOUTH ORGANIZATION http://www.umyouth.org

RICHARD S. SMITH SCHOLARSHIP

Open to racial/ethnic minority youth only. Must be a United Methodist Youth who has been active in his/her local church for at least one year prior to application. Must be a graduating senior in high school (who maintained at least a "C" average) entering his/her first year of undergraduate study and be pursuing a "church-related" career.

Award: Scholarship for use in freshman year; not renewable. *Number:* 1–2. *Amount:* up to $1000.

Eligibility Requirements: Applicant must be Methodist; American Indian/Alaska Native, Asian/Pacific Islander, Black (non-Hispanic), or Hispanic; high school student and planning to enroll or expecting to enroll full-time at an institution or university. Available to U.S. citizens.

Application Requirements: Application, essay, financial need analysis, transcript, certification of church membership. *Deadline:* June 1.

Contact: Ronna Seibert, Office Assistant
United Methodist Youth Organization
PO Box 340003
Nashville, TN 37203-0003
Phone: 877-899-2780 Ext. 7181
Fax: 615-340-1764
E-mail: umyouthorg@gbod.org

UNITED NEGRO COLLEGE FUND http://www.uncf.org

ABBINGTON, VALLANTEEN SCHOLARSHIP

Must enroll in UNCF Member College or University. Must have minimum 3.3 GPA after sophomore year and minimum 3.5 GPA after junior year. Please visit Web site for more information: http://www.uncf.org.

Award: Scholarship for use in freshman year; renewable. *Number:* varies. *Amount:* $5000.

Eligibility Requirements: Applicant must be Black (non-Hispanic); enrolled or expecting to enroll at a four-year institution or university and resident of Missouri. Applicant must have 3.0 GPA or higher. Available to U.S. citizens.

Application Requirements: Application, financial need analysis, FAFSA, SAR. *Deadline:* varies.

Contact: Program Services Department
United Negro College Fund
8260 Willow Oaks Corporate Drive
Fairfax, VA 22031

AMOS DEINARD FOUNDATION SCHOLARSHIP

Scholarship supports students from Minnesota attending UNCF member colleges and universities. Minimum 2.5 GPA required. Prospective applicants should complete the Student Profile found at Web site: http://www.uncf.org.

Award: Scholarship for use in freshman, sophomore, junior, or senior years; not renewable. *Amount:* up to $3000.

Eligibility Requirements: Applicant must be Black (non-Hispanic); enrolled or expecting to enroll at a four-year institution or university and resident of Minnesota. Applicant must have 2.5 GPA or higher.

Application Requirements: Application, financial need analysis. *Deadline:* Continuous.

Contact: Program Services Department
United Negro College Fund
8260 Willow Oaks Corporate Drive
Fairfax, VA 22031

BALTIMORE COMMUNITY SCHOLARSHIP

Scholarship assists graduating African-American high school seniors in Baltimore attend a UNCF institution. Please visit Web site for more information: http://www.uncf.org.

Award: Scholarship for use in freshman year; not renewable. *Number:* varies. *Amount:* varies.

Eligibility Requirements: Applicant must be Black (non-Hispanic); high school student and planning to enroll or expecting to enroll at a four-year institution or university. Applicant must have 2.5 GPA or higher.

Application Requirements: Application, financial need analysis, FAFSA, SAR. *Deadline:* varies.

Contact: Program Services Department
United Negro College Fund
8260 Willow Oaks Corporate Drive
Fairfax, VA 22031

BANK OF AMERICA SCHOLARSHIP

Scholarship supports freshman attending a UNCF member college or university located in any of the Bank of America core states. Minimum 2.5 GPA required. Prospective applicants should complete the Student Profile found at Web site: http://www.uncf.org.

Award: Scholarship for use in freshman year; not renewable. *Amount:* $1000.

Eligibility Requirements: Applicant must be Black (non-Hispanic); enrolled or expecting to enroll full-time at a four-year institution or university and studying in Florida, Georgia, North Carolina, South Carolina, or Texas. Applicant must have 2.5 GPA or higher.

Application Requirements: Application. *Deadline:* varies.

Contact: Program Services Department
United Negro College Fund
8260 Willow Oaks Corporate Drive
Fairfax, VA 22031

BANK ONE ARIZONA CORPORATION SCHOLARSHIP

Need-based scholarship for students from Arizona attending UNCF member colleges and universities. 2.5 GPA required. Can be used to repay federal student loans. Prospective applicants should complete the Student Profile found at Web site: http://www.uncf.org.

Award: Scholarship for use in freshman, sophomore, junior, or senior years; not renewable. *Amount:* up to $2500.

Eligibility Requirements: Applicant must be Black (non-Hispanic); enrolled or expecting to enroll at a four-year institution or university and resident of Arizona. Applicant must have 2.5 GPA or higher.

Application Requirements: Application, financial need analysis. *Deadline:* Continuous.

Contact: Program Services Department
United Negro College Fund
8260 Willow Oaks Corporate Drive
Fairfax, VA 22031

BELLSOUTH LOUISIANA SCHOLARSHIP

Scholarship awarded to Louisiana students who attend Dillard or Xavier University. Please visit Web site for more information: http://www.uncf.org.

Award: Scholarship for use in freshman, sophomore, junior, senior, or graduate years. *Number:* varies. *Amount:* $2500.

Eligibility Requirements: Applicant must be Black (non-Hispanic); enrolled or expecting to enroll at a four-year institution or university and studying in Louisiana. Applicant must have 2.5 GPA or higher. Available to U.S. citizens.

Application Requirements: Application, financial need analysis, FAFSA, SAR. *Deadline:* varies.

Contact: Program Services Department
United Negro College Fund
8260 Willow Oaks Corporate Drive
Fairfax, VA 22031

BESSIE IRENE SMITH TRUST SCHOLARSHIP

Need-based scholarship for New York residents attending a UNCF member college or university. Minimum 2.5 GPA required. Prospective applicants should complete the Student Profile found at Web site: http://www.uncf.org.

Award: Scholarship for use in freshman, sophomore, junior, or senior years; not renewable. *Number:* varies. *Amount:* varies.

Eligibility Requirements: Applicant must be Black (non-Hispanic); enrolled or expecting to enroll at a four-year institution or university and resident of New York. Applicant must have 2.5 GPA or higher.

Application Requirements: Application, financial need analysis. *Deadline:* Continuous.

Contact: Program Services Department
United Negro College Fund
8260 Willow Oaks Corporate Drive
Fairfax, VA 22031

BILDNER FAMILY SCHOLARSHIP

Scholarship open to New Jersey residents attending a UNCF member college or university. 2.5 GPA required. Prospective applicants should complete the Student Profile found at Web site: http://www.uncf.org.

Award: Scholarship for use in freshman, sophomore, junior, or senior years; not renewable. *Amount:* $1000–$2500.

Eligibility Requirements: Applicant must be Black (non-Hispanic); enrolled or expecting to enroll at a four-year institution or university and resident of New Jersey. Applicant must have 2.5 GPA or higher.

Application Requirements: Application. *Deadline:* Continuous.

Contact: Program Services Department
United Negro College Fund
8260 Willow Oaks Corporate Drive
Fairfax, VA 22031

BORDEN SCHOLARSHIP FUND

Need-based scholarships to students from Ohio attending a UNCF member college or university. 2.5 GPA required. Prospective applicants should complete the Student Profile found at Web site: http://www.uncf.org.

Award: Scholarship for use in freshman, sophomore, junior, or senior years; not renewable.

Eligibility Requirements: Applicant must be Black (non-Hispanic); enrolled or expecting to enroll at a four-year institution or university and resident of Ohio. Applicant must have 2.5 GPA or higher. Available to U.S. citizens.

Application Requirements: Application, financial need analysis. *Deadline:* Continuous.

Contact: Program Services Department
United Negro College Fund
8260 Willow Oaks Corporate Drive
Fairfax, VA 22031

BURTON G. BETTINGEN FOUNDATION SCHOLARSHIP

Need-based scholarship for students attending a UNCF member college or university. 2.5 GPA required. Prospective applicants should complete the Student Profile found at Web site: http://www.uncf.org.

Award: Scholarship for use in freshman, sophomore, junior, or senior years; not renewable.

Eligibility Requirements: Applicant must be Black (non-Hispanic) and enrolled or expecting to enroll at a four-year institution or university. Applicant must have 2.5 GPA or higher. Available to U.S. citizens.

Application Requirements: Application, financial need analysis. *Deadline:* Continuous.

Contact: Program Services Department
United Negro College Fund
8260 Willow Oaks Corporate Drive
Fairfax, VA 22031

BUSHROD CAMPBELL AND ADAH HALL SCHOLARSHIP

Scholarships for students who are Boston, Massachusetts residents and are enrolled in a UNCF Member College or University. Please visit Web site for more information: http://www.uncf.org.

Award: Scholarship for use in freshman, sophomore, junior, senior, or graduate years. *Number:* varies. *Amount:* $1000–$5000.

Eligibility Requirements: Applicant must be Black (non-Hispanic); enrolled or expecting to enroll at a four-year institution or university and resident of Massachusetts. Applicant must have 2.5 GPA or higher.

Application Requirements: Application, financial need analysis, FAFSA, SAR. *Deadline:* varies.

Contact: Program Services Department
United Negro College Fund
8260 Willow Oaks Corporate Drive
Fairfax, VA 22031

CARLOS AND LILLIAN THURSTON SCHOLARSHIP

Award available to Chicago, IL residents. Must have 2.5 GPA. Please visit Web site for more information: http://www.uncf.org.

Award: Scholarship for use in freshman, sophomore, junior, or senior years; renewable. *Number:* varies. *Amount:* up to $2500.

Eligibility Requirements: Applicant must be Black (non-Hispanic); enrolled or expecting to enroll at an institution or university and resident of Illinois. Applicant must have 2.5 GPA or higher.

Application Requirements: Application, financial need analysis, FAFSA, SAR. *Deadline:* varies.

Contact: Program Services Department
United Negro College Fund
8260 Willow Oaks Corporate Drive
Fairfax, VA 22031

CAROLYN BAILEY THOMAS SCHOLARSHIP

Need-based scholarship. Must have 3.0 GPA. Please visit Web site for more information: http://www.uncf.org.

Award: Scholarship for use in freshman, sophomore, junior, or senior years; renewable. *Number:* varies. *Amount:* varies.

Eligibility Requirements: Applicant must be Black (non-Hispanic) and enrolled or expecting to enroll at an institution or university. Applicant must have 3.0 GPA or higher.

Application Requirements: Application, financial need analysis, FAFSA, SAR. *Deadline:* varies.

Contact: Program Services Department
United Negro College Fund
8260 Willow Oaks Corporate Drive
Fairfax, VA 22031

CASIMIR, DOMINIQUE AND JAQUES SCHOLARSHIP

Four scholarships available for two males and two females who are residents of Texas. Applicants must be undergraduate sophomores at time of application. Please visit Web site for more information: http://www.uncf.org.

Award: Scholarship for use in sophomore or junior years. *Number:* 4. *Amount:* $1500.

Eligibility Requirements: Applicant must be Black (non-Hispanic); enrolled or expecting to enroll at a four-year institution or university and resident of Texas. Applicant must have 2.5 GPA or higher.

Application Requirements: Application, financial need analysis, FAFSA, SAR. *Deadline:* varies.

Contact: Program Services Department
United Negro College Fund
8260 Willow Oaks Corporate Drive
Fairfax, VA 22031

CHARLES AND ELLORA ALLIS FOUNDATION SCHOLARSHIP

Scholarship supports students from Minnesota attending UNCF member colleges and universities. 2.5 GPA required. Prospective applicants should complete the Student Profile found at Web site: http://www.uncf.org.

Award: Scholarship for use in freshman, sophomore, junior, or senior years; not renewable. *Amount:* up to $3000.

United Negro College Fund (continued)

Eligibility Requirements: Applicant must be Black (non-Hispanic); enrolled or expecting to enroll at a four-year institution or university and resident of Minnesota. Applicant must have 2.5 GPA or higher.

Application Requirements: Application. *Deadline:* Continuous.

Contact: Program Services Department
United Negro College Fund
8260 Willow Oaks Corporate Drive
Fairfax, VA 22031

CHARLES SCHWAB SCHOLARSHIP/INTERNSHIP PROGRAM

Scholarships for college sophomores and juniors with a minimum 2.5 GPA and attending Florida A&M, Bethune-Cookman, Morehouse, Spelman, and Clark Atlanta University. Prospective applicants should complete the Student Profile found at Web site: http://www.uncf.org.

Award: Scholarship for use in sophomore or junior years; not renewable. *Amount:* up to $8000.

Eligibility Requirements: Applicant must be Black (non-Hispanic) and enrolled or expecting to enroll full-time at a four-year institution or university. Applicant must have 2.5 GPA or higher. Available to U.S. citizens.

Application Requirements: Application.

Contact: Program Services Department
United Negro College Fund
8260 Willow Oaks Corporate Drive
Fairfax, VA 22031

CHICAGO INTER-ALUMNI COUNCIL SCHOLARSHIP

Three winners of the annual Chicago Inter-Alumni Council pageant will receive scholarships to attend a UNCF member college or university. Must be a high school senior in Chicago. Please visit Web site for more information: http://www.uncf.org.

Award: Scholarship for use in freshman year. *Number:* 3. *Amount:* varies.

Eligibility Requirements: Applicant must be Black (non-Hispanic); high school student; planning to enroll or expecting to enroll at a four-year institution or university and resident of Illinois. Applicant must have 2.5 GPA or higher.

Application Requirements: Application, applicant must enter a contest, financial need analysis, FAFSA, SAR. *Deadline:* varies.

Contact: Program Services Department
United Negro College Fund
8260 Willow Oaks Corporate Drive
Fairfax, VA 22031

CHICAGO PUBLIC SCHOOLS UNCF CAMPAIGN

Scholarship awarded to students who have attended Chicago public schools. Award covers up to four years of tuition and fees. Please visit Web site for more information: http://www.uncf.org.

Award: Scholarship for use in freshman, sophomore, junior, senior, or graduate years; renewable. *Number:* varies. *Amount:* varies.

Eligibility Requirements: Applicant must be Black (non-Hispanic) and enrolled or expecting to enroll at a four-year institution or university. Applicant must have 2.5 GPA or higher.

Application Requirements: Application, financial need analysis, FAFSA, SAR. *Deadline:* varies.

Contact: Program Services Department
United Negro College Fund
8260 Willow Oaks Corporate Drive
Fairfax, VA 22031

CHURCH'S CHICKEN OPPORTUNITY SCHOLARSHIP

• *See page 488*

CINERGY FOUNDATION SCHOLARSHIP

Need-based scholarship for students from Ohio, Kentucky, and Indiana attending four specific UNCF member colleges and universities. Minimum 2.5 GPA required. Prospective applicants should complete the Student Profile found at Web site: http://www.uncf.org.

Award: Scholarship for use in freshman, sophomore, junior, or senior years; not renewable. *Amount:* up to $3000.

Eligibility Requirements: Applicant must be Black (non-Hispanic); enrolled or expecting to enroll at a four-year institution or university and resident of Indiana, Kentucky, or Ohio. Applicant must have 2.5 GPA or higher.

Application Requirements: Application, financial need analysis. *Deadline:* Continuous.

Contact: Program Services Department
United Negro College Fund
8260 Willow Oaks Corporate Drive
Fairfax, VA 22031

CLEVELAND FOUNDATION SCHOLARSHIP

Up to $3000 available for Cleveland, Ohio students enrolled in a UNCF member college or university. Please visit Web site for more information: http://www.uncf.org.

Award: Scholarship for use in freshman, sophomore, junior, senior, or graduate years. *Number:* varies. *Amount:* $3000.

Eligibility Requirements: Applicant must be Black (non-Hispanic); enrolled or expecting to enroll at a four-year institution or university and resident of Ohio. Applicant must have 2.5 GPA or higher.

Application Requirements: Application, financial need analysis, FAFSA, SAR. *Deadline:* varies.

Contact: Program Services Department
United Negro College Fund
8260 Willow Oaks Corporate Drive
Fairfax, VA 22031

CLEVELAND MUNICIPAL SCHOOL SCHOLARSHIP

Scholarship awarded to graduating high school senior who attends a Cleveland district high school. Please visit Web site for more information: http://www.uncf.org.

Award: Scholarship for use in freshman year. *Number:* varies. *Amount:* varies.

Eligibility Requirements: Applicant must be Black (non-Hispanic); high school student; planning to enroll or expecting to enroll at a four-year institution or university and resident of Ohio. Applicant must have 2.5 GPA or higher.

Application Requirements: Application, financial need analysis, FAFSA, SAR. *Deadline:* varies.

Contact: Program Services Department
United Negro College Fund
8260 Willow Oaks Corporate Drive
Fairfax, VA 22031

CLOROX COMPANY FOUNDATION SCHOLARSHIP

Scholarship awarded to five students attending UNCF member colleges or universities. Must be resident of San Francisco Bay Area, California. Please visit Web site for more information: http://www.uncf.org.

Award: Scholarship for use in freshman, sophomore, junior, senior, or graduate years. *Number:* 5. *Amount:* $2000.

Eligibility Requirements: Applicant must be Black (non-Hispanic); enrolled or expecting to enroll at a four-year institution or university and resident of California. Applicant must have 2.5 GPA or higher.

Application Requirements: Application, financial need analysis, FAFSA, SAR. *Deadline:* varies.

Contact: Program Services Department
United Negro College Fund
8260 Willow Oaks Corporate Drive
Fairfax, VA 22031

COLUMBUS FOUNDATION SCHOLARSHIP

Scholarship of up to $3000 available for students attending a UNCF member college or university. Must be a resident of Columbus, Ohio. Please visit Web site for more information: http://www.uncf.org.

Award: Scholarship for use in freshman, sophomore, junior, senior, or graduate years. *Number:* varies. *Amount:* up to $3000.

Eligibility Requirements: Applicant must be Black (non-Hispanic); enrolled or expecting to enroll at a four-year institution or university and resident of Ohio. Applicant must have 2.5 GPA or higher.

Application Requirements: Application, financial need analysis, FAFSA, SAR. *Deadline:* varies.

Contact: Program Services Department
United Negro College Fund
8260 Willow Oaks Corporate Drive
Fairfax, VA 22031

COMMUNITY FOUNDATION OF GREATER BIRMINGHAM SCHOLARSHIP

Scholarship available to a student attending: Miles College, Oakwood College, Stillman College, Talladega College, or Tuskegee University. Please visit Web site for more information: http://www.uncf.org.

Award: Scholarship for use in freshman, sophomore, junior, senior, or graduate years. *Number:* varies. *Amount:* $10,000.

Eligibility Requirements: Applicant must be Black (non-Hispanic) and enrolled or expecting to enroll at a four-year institution or university. Applicant must have 2.5 GPA or higher.

Application Requirements: Application, financial need analysis, FAFSA, SAR. *Deadline:* July 31.

Contact: Program Services Department
United Negro College Fund
8260 Willow Oaks Corporate Drive
Fairfax, VA 22031

COSTCO SCHOLARSHIP

Renewable scholarship for students from Washington and Oregon attending UNCF member colleges and universities. Minimum 2.5 GPA required. Prospective applicants should complete the Student Profile found at Web site: http://www.uncf.org.

Award: Scholarship for use in freshman, sophomore, junior, or senior years; renewable. *Amount:* $5000.

Eligibility Requirements: Applicant must be Black (non-Hispanic); enrolled or expecting to enroll at a four-year institution or university and resident of Oregon or Washington. Applicant must have 2.5 GPA or higher.

Application Requirements: Application. *Deadline:* Continuous.

Contact: Program Services Department
United Negro College Fund
8260 Willow Oaks Corporate Drive
Fairfax, VA 22031

CRANE FUND FOR WIDOWS AND CHILDREN SCHOLARSHIP

Scholarship available to disadvantaged children with a deceased parent. Must attend a UNCF member college or university. Minimum 2.5 GPA required. Prospective applicants should complete the Student Profile found at Web site: http://www.uncf.org.

Award: Scholarship for use in freshman, sophomore, junior, or senior years; not renewable.

Eligibility Requirements: Applicant must be Black (non-Hispanic) and enrolled or expecting to enroll full-time at a four-year institution or university. Applicant must have 2.5 GPA or higher.

Application Requirements: Application, financial need analysis. *Deadline:* Continuous.

Contact: Program Services Department
United Negro College Fund
8260 Willow Oaks Corporate Drive
Fairfax, VA 22031

CURTIS BREEDEN SCHOLARSHIP

Scholarship awarded to student from Cincinnati, Ohio enrolled in a UNCF member college or university. Please visit Web site for more information: http://www.uncf.org.

Award: Scholarship for use in freshman, sophomore, junior, senior, or graduate years. *Number:* varies. *Amount:* $3000.

Eligibility Requirements: Applicant must be Black (non-Hispanic); enrolled or expecting to enroll at a four-year institution or university and resident of Ohio. Applicant must have 2.5 GPA or higher. Available to U.S. citizens.

Application Requirements: Application, financial need analysis, FAFSA, SAR. *Deadline:* varies.

Contact: Program Services Department
United Negro College Fund
8260 Willow Oaks Corporate Drive
Fairfax, VA 22031

DALLAS INDEPENDENT SCHOOL DISTRICT SCHOLARSHIP

Applicant must be graduating high school senior from the Dallas Independent School District. Mandatory essay addressing: "Why it is important to attend a Historically Black College or University." Essay may be minimum 250 words to 500 words maximum. Please visit Web site for more information: http://www.uncf.org.

Award: Scholarship for use in freshman year; renewable. *Number:* varies. *Amount:* $2500.

Eligibility Requirements: Applicant must be Black (non-Hispanic); high school student; planning to enroll or expecting to enroll at a four-year institution or university and resident of Texas. Applicant must have 2.5 GPA or higher.

Application Requirements: Application, essay, financial need analysis, FAFSA, SAR. *Deadline:* May 7.

Contact: Program Services Department
United Negro College Fund
8260 Willow Oaks Corporate Drive
Fairfax, VA 22031

DALLAS MAVERICKS

Scholarship awarded to student from greater Dallas/Ft. Worth, Texas, attending a UNCF member college or university. Amount of award varies, based on need. Minimum 2.5 GPA. Prospective applicants should complete the Student Profile found at Web site: http://www.uncf.org.

Award: Scholarship for use in freshman, sophomore, junior, or senior years; not renewable. *Number:* varies. *Amount:* varies.

Eligibility Requirements: Applicant must be Black (non-Hispanic); enrolled or expecting to enroll full-time at a four-year institution or university and resident of Texas. Applicant must have 2.5 GPA or higher. Available to U.S. citizens.

Application Requirements: Application, financial need analysis. *Deadline:* Continuous.

Contact: Program Services Department
United Negro College Fund
8260 Willow Oaks Corporate Drive
Fairfax, VA 22031

DALLAS METROPLEX COUNCIL OF BLACK ALUMNI ASSOCIATION SCHOLARSHIP

Need-based scholarship offered by the Dallas Metroplex Council of Black Alumni Association. Please visit Web site for more information: http://www.uncf.org.

Award: Scholarship for use in freshman, sophomore, junior, senior, or graduate years. *Number:* varies. *Amount:* varies.

Eligibility Requirements: Applicant must be Black (non-Hispanic) and enrolled or expecting to enroll at a four-year institution or university. Applicant must have 2.5 GPA or higher.

Application Requirements: Application, financial need analysis, FAFSA, SAR. *Deadline:* varies.

Contact: Program Services Department
United Negro College Fund
8260 Willow Oaks Corporate Drive
Fairfax, VA 22031

DAVENPORT FORTE PEDESTAL FUND

Scholarship awards a first semester undergraduate freshman who attends a UNCF member college or university. Applicant must have graduated from the Detroit Public Schools System. Must have minimum 2.7 GPA. Please visit Web site for more information: http://www.uncf.org.

Award: Scholarship for use in freshman year; renewable. *Number:* 1. *Amount:* $10,000.

Eligibility Requirements: Applicant must be Black (non-Hispanic) and enrolled or expecting to enroll at a four-year institution or university.

Application Requirements: Application, financial need analysis, FAFSA, SAR. *Deadline:* varies.

Contact: Program Services Department
United Negro College Fund
8260 Willow Oaks Corporate Drive
Fairfax, VA 22031

DENIS D'AMORE SCHOLARSHIP

Scholarship awards $2000 to students attending UNCF member colleges and universities. Applicant must be resident of Boston, Massachusetts. Please visit Web site for more information: http://www.uncf.org.

Award: Scholarship for use in freshman, sophomore, junior, or graduate years; renewable. *Number:* varies. *Amount:* $2000.

Eligibility Requirements: Applicant must be Black (non-Hispanic); enrolled or expecting to enroll at a four-year institution or university and resident of Massachusetts. Applicant must have 2.5 GPA or higher.

Application Requirements: Application, financial need analysis, FAFSA, SAR. *Deadline:* varies.

Contact: Program Services Department
United Negro College Fund
8260 Willow Oaks Corporate Drive
Fairfax, VA 22031

DONNIE AND PAM SIMPSON SCHOLARSHIP

Scholarship for residents of Washington, D.C. attending a UNCF member college or university. Minimum 2.5 GPA required. Prospective applicants should complete the Student Profile found at Web site: http://www.uncf.org.

Award: Scholarship for use in sophomore or junior years; not renewable. *Amount:* $5000.

Eligibility Requirements: Applicant must be Black (non-Hispanic); enrolled or expecting to enroll full-time at a four-year institution or university and resident of District of Columbia. Applicant must have 2.5 GPA or higher.

Application Requirements: Application, financial need analysis. *Deadline:* March 31.

Contact: Program Services Department
United Negro College Fund
8260 Willow Oaks Corporate Drive
Fairfax, VA 22031

DORIS AND JOHN CARPENTER SCHOLARSHIP

Renewable scholarship open to undergraduate freshman students attending a UNCF member college or university. 2.5 GPA required. Must demonstrate financial need. Prospective applicants should complete the Student Profile found at Web site: http://www.uncf.org.

Award: Scholarship for use in freshman year; renewable. *Amount:* $2000–$5000.

Eligibility Requirements: Applicant must be Black (non-Hispanic) and enrolled or expecting to enroll at a four-year institution or university. Applicant must have 2.5 GPA or higher.

Application Requirements: Application, financial need analysis. *Deadline:* Continuous.

Contact: Program Services Department
United Negro College Fund
8260 Willow Oaks Corporate Drive
Fairfax, VA 22031

DOROTHY N. MCNEAL SCHOLARSHIP

Scholarship available to students pursuing careers in the area of community service who attend a UNCF member college or university. Minimum 2.5 GPA required. Prospective applicants should complete the Student Profile found at Web site: http://www.uncf.org.

Award: Scholarship for use in freshman, sophomore, junior, or senior years; not renewable.

Eligibility Requirements: Applicant must be Black (non-Hispanic) and enrolled or expecting to enroll full-time at a four-year institution or university. Applicant must have 2.5 GPA or higher. Available to U.S. citizens.

Application Requirements: Application. *Deadline:* Continuous.

Contact: Program Services Department
United Negro College Fund
8260 Willow Oaks Corporate Drive
Fairfax, VA 22031

DUPONT SCHOLARSHIP

Scholarship awarded to residents of Delaware. Applicant must either be Philadelphia Louis Stokes AMP student or attend a UNCF college or university. Please visit Web site for more information: http://www.uncf.org.

Award: Scholarship for use in freshman, sophomore, junior, senior, or graduate years. *Number:* varies. *Amount:* varies.

Eligibility Requirements: Applicant must be Black (non-Hispanic); enrolled or expecting to enroll at a four-year institution or university and resident of Delaware. Applicant must have 2.5 GPA or higher.

Application Requirements: Application, financial need analysis, FAFSA, SAR. *Deadline:* varies.

Contact: Program Services Department
United Negro College Fund
8260 Willow Oaks Corporate Drive
Fairfax, VA 22031

DUQUESNE LIGHT COMPANY SCHOLARSHIP

Need-based scholarship awarded to student who lives in Allegheny or Beaver County, Pennsylvania. Student must be nominated. Please visit Web site for more information: http://www.uncf.org.

Award: Scholarship for use in freshman, sophomore, junior, senior, or graduate years; renewable. *Number:* varies. *Amount:* varies.

Eligibility Requirements: Applicant must be Black (non-Hispanic); enrolled or expecting to enroll at a four-year institution or university and resident of Pennsylvania. Applicant must have 2.5 GPA or higher.

Application Requirements: Financial need analysis, references, FAFSA, SAR. *Deadline:* varies.

Contact: Program Services Department
United Negro College Fund
8260 Willow Oaks Corporate Drive
Fairfax, VA 22031

EDNA F. BLUM FOUNDATION

Need-based scholarship for students attending UNCF colleges and universities. 2.5 GPA required. Prospective applicants should complete the Student Profile found at Web site: http://www.uncf.org.

Award: Scholarship for use in freshman, sophomore, junior, or senior years; not renewable. *Amount:* $1000–$3000.

Eligibility Requirements: Applicant must be Black (non-Hispanic); enrolled or expecting to enroll at a four-year institution or university and resident of New York. Applicant must have 2.5 GPA or higher. Available to U.S. citizens.

Application Requirements: Application, financial need analysis. *Deadline:* Continuous.

Contact: Program Services Department
United Negro College Fund
8260 Willow Oaks Corporate Drive
Fairfax, VA 22031

EDWARD AND HAZEL STEPHENSON SCHOLARSHIP

This scholarship is available to seniors only who attend a UNCF member college or university. Minimum 2.5 GPA required. Prospective applicants should complete the Student Profile found at Web site: http://www.uncf.org.

Award: Scholarship for use in senior year; not renewable. *Amount:* $1000–$3000.

Eligibility Requirements: Applicant must be Black (non-Hispanic) and enrolled or expecting to enroll full-time at a four-year institution or university. Applicant must have 2.5 GPA or higher.

Application Requirements: Application, financial need analysis. *Deadline:* Continuous.

Contact: Program Services Department
United Negro College Fund
8260 Willow Oaks Corporate Drive
Fairfax, VA 22031

EDWARD D. GRIGG SCHOLARSHIP

Scholarship available to students attending a UNCF member college or university. Minimum 2.5 GPA required. Prospective applicants should complete the Student Profile found at Web site: http://www.uncf.org.

Award: Scholarship for use in freshman, sophomore, junior, or senior years; not renewable.

Eligibility Requirements: Applicant must be Black (non-Hispanic) and enrolled or expecting to enroll full-time at a four-year institution or university. Applicant must have 2.5 GPA or higher.

Application Requirements: Application, financial need analysis. *Deadline:* Continuous.

Contact: Program Services Department
United Negro College Fund
8260 Willow Oaks Corporate Drive
Fairfax, VA 22031

EDWARD FITTERMAN FOUNDATION SCHOLARSHIP

Scholarship for students from Minnesota attending a UNCF member college or university. Minimum 2.5 GPA required. Prospective applicants should complete the Student Profile found at Web site: http://www.uncf.org.

Award: Scholarship for use in freshman, sophomore, junior, or senior years; not renewable. *Amount:* up to $3000.

Eligibility Requirements: Applicant must be Black (non-Hispanic); enrolled or expecting to enroll at a four-year institution or university and resident of Minnesota. Applicant must have 2.5 GPA or higher.

Application Requirements: Application, financial need analysis. *Deadline:* Continuous.

Contact: Program Services Department
United Negro College Fund
8260 Willow Oaks Corporate Drive
Fairfax, VA 22031

EDWARD N. NEY SCHOLARSHIP

Award for students attending a UNCF member college or university. Minimum 3.5 GPA required. Amount of award varies based on need; student will receive one half of the award each semester. Prospective applicants should complete the Student Profile found at Web site: http://www.uncf.org.

Award: Scholarship for use in freshman, sophomore, junior, or senior years; not renewable.

Eligibility Requirements: Applicant must be Black (non-Hispanic) and enrolled or expecting to enroll at a four-year institution or university. Applicant must have 3.5 GPA or higher.

Application Requirements: Application, financial need analysis. *Deadline:* Continuous.

Contact: Program Services Department
United Negro College Fund
8260 Willow Oaks Corporate Drive
Fairfax, VA 22031

ELMER ROE DEAVER FOUNDATION SCHOLARSHIP

Scholarship supports students from Delaware, Pennsylvania, and New Jersey attending UNCF member colleges and universities. Minimum 2.5 GPA required. Prospective applicants should complete the Student Profile found at Web site: http://www.uncf.org.

Award: Scholarship for use in freshman, sophomore, junior, or senior years; not renewable. *Amount:* $3000.

Eligibility Requirements: Applicant must be Black (non-Hispanic); enrolled or expecting to enroll at a four-year institution or university and resident of Delaware, New Jersey, or Pennsylvania. Applicant must have 2.5 GPA or higher.

Application Requirements: Application, financial need analysis. *Deadline:* October 1.

Contact: Program Services Department
United Negro College Fund
8260 Willow Oaks Corporate Drive
Fairfax, VA 22031

EVELYN LEVINA WRIGHT SCHOLARSHIP

Award to a resident of the Philadelphia, PA; Wilmington, DE; or Camden, NJ area. Please visit Web site for more information: http://www.uncf.org.

Award: Scholarship for use in freshman, sophomore, junior, or senior years; renewable. *Number:* 1. *Amount:* $3500.

Eligibility Requirements: Applicant must be Black (non-Hispanic); enrolled or expecting to enroll at an institution or university and resident of Delaware, New Jersey, or Pennsylvania. Applicant must have 2.5 GPA or higher.

Application Requirements: Application, financial need analysis, FAFSA, SAR. *Deadline:* varies.

Contact: Program Services Department
United Negro College Fund
8260 Willow Oaks Corporate Drive
Fairfax, VA 22031

FIFTH/THIRD SCHOLARS PROGRAM

Scholarship awards students who are residents of Dayton, Columbus or Cincinnati, Ohio. Student must attend a UNCF member college or university. Please visit Web site for more information: http://www.uncf.org.

Award: Scholarship for use in freshman, sophomore, junior, senior, or graduate years. *Number:* varies. *Amount:* varies.

Eligibility Requirements: Applicant must be Black (non-Hispanic); enrolled or expecting to enroll at a four-year institution or university and resident of Ohio. Applicant must have 2.5 GPA or higher.

Application Requirements: Application, financial need analysis, FAFSA, SAR. *Deadline:* varies.

Contact: Program Services Department
United Negro College Fund
8260 Willow Oaks Corporate Drive
Fairfax, VA 22031

FORT WORTH INDEPENDENT SCHOOL DISTRICT SCHOLARSHIP

Scholarship awarded to graduating high school senior from the Fort Worth Independent School District. Applicant must submit 250-500 word essay addressing: "Why it is important to attend a Historically Black College or University." Please visit Web site for more information: http://www.uncf.org.

Award: Scholarship for use in freshman year. *Number:* varies. *Amount:* $2500.

Eligibility Requirements: Applicant must be Black (non-Hispanic); high school student; planning to enroll or expecting to enroll at a four-year institution or university and resident of Texas. Applicant must have 2.5 GPA or higher.

Application Requirements: Application, essay, financial need analysis, FAFSA, SAR. *Deadline:* May 7.

Contact: Program Services Department
United Negro College Fund
8260 Willow Oaks Corporate Drive
Fairfax, VA 22031

FORTUNE BRANDS SCHOLARS PROGRAM

Program offers minority undergraduate juniors, or first and second year law students an 8-10 week summer internship at Fortune Brands corporate headquarters. Participants are eligible for a $7500 scholarship. Please visit Web site for more information: http://www.uncf.org.

Award: Scholarship for use in junior, or graduate years. *Number:* varies. *Amount:* $7500.

Eligibility Requirements: Applicant must be American Indian/Alaska Native, Asian/Pacific Islander, Black (non-Hispanic), or Hispanic and enrolled or expecting to enroll at a four-year institution or university. Applicant must have 2.5 GPA or higher. Available to U.S. citizens.

Application Requirements: Application, financial need analysis, resume, references, transcript, FAFSA, SAR. *Deadline:* February 22.

Contact: Fortune Brands Scholars Program
United Negro College Fund
PO Box 1435
Alexandria, VA 22313-9998

FREDERICK D. PATTERSON SCHOLARSHIP

Scholarship provides financial assistance to students attending a UNCF member college or university. Minimum 2.5 GPA required. Prospective applicants should complete the Student Profile found at Web site: http://www.uncf.org.

Award: Scholarship for use in freshman, sophomore, junior, or senior years; not renewable.

Eligibility Requirements: Applicant must be Black (non-Hispanic) and enrolled or expecting to enroll at a four-year institution or university. Applicant must have 2.5 GPA or higher.

Application Requirements: Application, financial need analysis. *Deadline:* Continuous.

Contact: Program Services Department
United Negro College Fund
8260 Willow Oaks Corporate Drive
Fairfax, VA 22031

GARY PAYTON FOUNDATION ENDOWED SCHOLARSHIP

Scholarship awarded to students entering their freshman year who are Washington residents. Students must demonstrate commitment to volunteer work through community service and attend a UNCF member college or university. Minimum 2.5 GPA required. Prospective applicants should complete the Student Profile found at Web site: http://www.uncf.org.

Award: Scholarship for use in freshman year; not renewable.

Eligibility Requirements: Applicant must be Black (non-Hispanic); enrolled or expecting to enroll at a four-year institution or university and resident of Washington. Applicant must have 2.5 GPA or higher.

Application Requirements: Application, financial need analysis. *Deadline:* Continuous.

Contact: Program Services Department
United Negro College Fund
8260 Willow Oaks Corporate Drive
Fairfax, VA 22031

GATES MILLENNIUM SCHOLARS PROGRAM (GATES FOUNDATION)

Award enables African-American students to complete an undergraduate and graduate education. Must be entering a U.S. accredited college or university as a full-time degree-seeking student. Minimum 3.3 GPA required. Must demonstrate leadership abilities. Must meet federal Pell Grant eligibility criteria. Visit Web site at http://www.gmsp.org. Prospective applicants should complete the Student Profile found at Web site: http://www.uncf.org.

Award: Scholarship for use in freshman, sophomore, junior, senior, or graduate years; renewable.

Eligibility Requirements: Applicant must be Black (non-Hispanic) and enrolled or expecting to enroll full-time at a four-year institution or university. Available to U.S. citizens.

Application Requirements: Application, financial need analysis, nomination packet. *Deadline:* varies.

Contact: GMS Representative
United Negro College Fund
8260 Willow Oaks Corporate Drive
Fairfax, VA 22031
Phone: 800-944-9627
Fax: 703-205-2079
E-mail: info@gmsp.org

GENA WRIGHT MEMORIAL SCHOLARSHIP

Scholarship available to UNCF students with an expressed career interest in working with children. Minimum 3.0 GPA required. Prospective applicants should complete the Student Profile found at Web site: http://www.uncf.org.

Award: Scholarship for use in freshman, sophomore, junior, or senior years; not renewable. *Number:* 2.

Eligibility Requirements: Applicant must be Black (non-Hispanic) and enrolled or expecting to enroll at a four-year institution or university. Applicant must have 3.0 GPA or higher.

Application Requirements: Application, financial need analysis. *Deadline:* Continuous.

Contact: Program Services Department
United Negro College Fund
8260 Willow Oaks Corporate Drive
Fairfax, VA 22031

GERALD W. AND JEAN PURMAL ENDOWED SCHOLARSHIP

Scholarships available for African American students to attend a UNCF member institution. Must have a minimum 2.5 GPA. Details on Web site at http://www.uncf.org.

Award: Scholarship for use in freshman, sophomore, junior, or senior years; renewable. *Number:* varies. *Amount:* $1000–$4000.

Eligibility Requirements: Applicant must be Black (non-Hispanic) and enrolled or expecting to enroll at a four-year institution or university. Applicant must have 2.5 GPA or higher.

Application Requirements: Application, financial need analysis, FAFSA, SAR. *Deadline:* varies.

Contact: Program Services Department
United Negro College Fund
8260 Willow Oaks Corporate Drive
Fairfax, VA 22031

GERON JOHNSON SCHOLARSHIP

Scholarship available to students residing in Washington, D.C. who attend UNCF member college or university. Minimum 2.5 GPA. Prospective applicants should complete the Student Profile found at Web site: http://www.uncf.org.

Award: Scholarship for use in freshman, sophomore, junior, or senior years; not renewable.

Eligibility Requirements: Applicant must be Black (non-Hispanic); enrolled or expecting to enroll full-time at a four-year institution or university and resident of District of Columbia. Applicant must have 2.5 GPA or higher.

Application Requirements: Application, financial need analysis. *Deadline:* Continuous.

Contact: Program Services Department
United Negro College Fund
8260 Willow Oaks Corporate Drive
Fairfax, VA 22031

GHEENS FOUNDATION SCHOLARSHIP

This scholarship supports students from Louisville, Kentucky, who are enrolled in a HBCU participating school. Please visit Web site for more information: http://www.uncf.org.

Award: Scholarship for use in freshman, sophomore, junior, senior, or graduate years. *Number:* varies. *Amount:* up to $2000.

Eligibility Requirements: Applicant must be Black (non-Hispanic); enrolled or expecting to enroll at a four-year institution or university and resident of Kentucky. Applicant must have 2.5 GPA or higher.

Application Requirements: Application, financial need analysis, transcript. *Deadline:* varies.

Contact: Program Services Department
United Negro College Fund
8260 Willow Oaks Corporate Drive
Fairfax, VA 22031

HAROLD PIERCE SCHOLARSHIP

Scholarship open to Massachusetts residents attending a UNCF member college or university. Minimum 2.5 GPA required. Prospective applicants should complete the Student Profile found at Web site: http://www.uncf.org.

Award: Scholarship for use in freshman, sophomore, junior, or senior years; not renewable. *Amount:* $3000.

Eligibility Requirements: Applicant must be Black (non-Hispanic); enrolled or expecting to enroll at a four-year institution or university and resident of Massachusetts. Applicant must have 2.5 GPA or higher.

Application Requirements: Application, financial need analysis. *Deadline:* Continuous.

Contact: Program Services Department
United Negro College Fund
8260 Willow Oaks Corporate Drive
Fairfax, VA 22031

HARRY PINKERTON SCHOLARSHIP

Need-based scholarship for New York residents attending a UNCF member college or university. Minimum 2.5 GPA required. Prospective applicants should complete the Student Profile found at Web site: http://www.uncf.org.

Award: Scholarship for use in freshman, sophomore, junior, or senior years; not renewable.

Eligibility Requirements: Applicant must be Black (non-Hispanic); enrolled or expecting to enroll at a four-year institution or university and resident of New York. Applicant must have 2.5 GPA or higher.

Application Requirements: Application, financial need analysis. *Deadline:* Continuous.

Contact: Program Services Department
United Negro College Fund
8260 Willow Oaks Corporate Drive
Fairfax, VA 22031

HARVEY H. AND CATHERINE A. MOSES SCHOLARSHIP

Need-based award for students attending a UNCF member college or university. Minimum 2.5 GPA required. Prospective applicants should complete the Student Profile found at Web site: http://www.uncf.org.

Award: Scholarship for use in freshman, sophomore, junior, or senior years; not renewable.

Eligibility Requirements: Applicant must be Black (non-Hispanic) and enrolled or expecting to enroll at a four-year institution or university. Applicant must have 2.5 GPA or higher.

Application Requirements: Application, financial need analysis. *Deadline:* Continuous.

Contact: Program Services Department
United Negro College Fund
8260 Willow Oaks Corporate Drive
Fairfax, VA 22031

HEALTH AND HUMAN SERVICE-RICHMOND, VA SCHOLARSHIP

Award for students residing in Richmond, Virginia. Must have a 2.0 GPA and plan to attend a UNCF member college or university. Please visit Web site for more information: http://www.uncf.org.

Award: Scholarship for use in freshman, sophomore, junior, senior, or graduate years. *Number:* varies. *Amount:* varies.

Eligibility Requirements: Applicant must be Black (non-Hispanic); enrolled or expecting to enroll at a four-year institution or university and resident of Virginia.

Application Requirements: Application, financial need analysis, FAFSA, SAR. *Deadline:* varies.

Contact: Program Services Department
United Negro College Fund
8260 Willow Oaks Corporate Drive
Fairfax, VA 22031

HOUGHTON-MIFFLIN COMPANY FELLOWS PROGRAM

Scholarship is awarded to undergraduate junior after completion of paid internship to introduce selected students to careers in the publishing industry. Must attend a UNCF member college or university. Minimum 3.0 GPA required. Prospective applicants should complete the Student Profile found at Web site: http://www.uncf.org.

Award: Scholarship for use in junior year; not renewable. *Amount:* $3700.

Eligibility Requirements: Applicant must be Black (non-Hispanic) and enrolled or expecting to enroll at a four-year institution or university. Applicant must have 3.0 GPA or higher.

Application Requirements: Application, financial need analysis. *Deadline:* varies.

Contact: Program Services Department
United Negro College Fund
8260 Willow Oaks Corporate Drive
Fairfax, VA 22031

HUDSON-WEBBER FOUNDATION SCHOLARSHIP

Award for Detroit, Michigan residents attending a UNCF member college or university. Please visit Web site for more information: http://www.uncf.org.

Award: Scholarship for use in freshman, sophomore, junior, senior, or graduate years. *Number:* varies. *Amount:* varies.

Eligibility Requirements: Applicant must be Black (non-Hispanic); enrolled or expecting to enroll at a four-year institution or university and resident of Michigan. Applicant must have 2.5 GPA or higher.

Application Requirements: Application, financial need analysis, FAFSA, SAR. *Deadline:* varies.

Contact: Program Services Department
United Negro College Fund
8260 Willow Oaks Corporate Drive
Fairfax, VA 22031

JACOB AND ETHEL GREENBERG SCHOLARSHIP

Scholarship open to students attending a UNCF member college or university. Minimum 2.5 GPA required. Prospective applicants should complete the Student Profile found at Web site: http://www.uncf.org.

Award: Scholarship for use in freshman, sophomore, junior, or senior years; not renewable.

Eligibility Requirements: Applicant must be Black (non-Hispanic) and enrolled or expecting to enroll at a four-year institution or university. Applicant must have 2.5 GPA or higher.

Application Requirements: Application. *Deadline:* Continuous.

Contact: Program Services Department
United Negro College Fund
8260 Willow Oaks Corporate Drive
Fairfax, VA 22031

JAMES AND RUTH GILLROY SCHOLARSHIP

Scholarship offers $1000 to New York residents attending a UNCF member college or university. Minimum 2.5 GPA required. Prospective applicants should complete the Student Profile found at Web site: http://www.uncf.org.

Award: Scholarship for use in freshman, sophomore, junior, or senior years; not renewable. *Amount:* $1000.

United Negro College Fund (continued)

Eligibility Requirements: Applicant must be Black (non-Hispanic); enrolled or expecting to enroll full-time at a four-year institution or university and resident of New York. Applicant must have 2.5 GPA or higher. Available to U.S. citizens.

Application Requirements: Application, financial need analysis. *Deadline:* Continuous.

Contact: Program Services Department
United Negro College Fund
8260 Willow Oaks Corporate Drive
Fairfax, VA 22031

JEFFRY AND BARBARA PICOWER FOUNDATION SCHOLARSHIP

Scholarships available for African American students having a minimum 3.0 GPA. Must attend a UNCF member college or university. Additional information on Web site: http://www.uncf.org.

Award: Scholarship for use in freshman, sophomore, junior, or senior years; renewable. *Number:* 3. *Amount:* $5000.

Eligibility Requirements: Applicant must be Black (non-Hispanic) and enrolled or expecting to enroll at a four-year institution or university. Applicant must have 3.0 GPA or higher.

Application Requirements: Application, financial need analysis, FAFSA, SAR. *Deadline:* varies.

Contact: Program Services Department
United Negro College Fund
8260 Willow Oaks Corporate Drive
Fairfax, VA 22031

JOHN W. ANDERSON FOUNDATION SCHOLARSHIP

Need-based scholarship for students from Indiana attending UNCF member colleges and universities. Prospective applicants should complete the Student Profile found at Web site: http://www.uncf.org.

Award: Scholarship for use in freshman, sophomore, junior, or senior years; not renewable. *Amount:* up to $3000.

Eligibility Requirements: Applicant must be Black (non-Hispanic); enrolled or expecting to enroll at a four-year institution or university and resident of Indiana. Applicant must have 2.5 GPA or higher.

Application Requirements: Application, financial need analysis. *Deadline:* Continuous.

Contact: Program Services Department
United Negro College Fund
8260 Willow Oaks Corporate Drive
Fairfax, VA 22031

JOS L. MUSCARELLE FOUNDATION SCHOLARSHIP

Scholarship available to students attending a UNCF member college or university. Minimum 2.5 GPA required. Prospective applicants should complete the Student Profile found at Web site: http://www.uncf.org.

Award: Scholarship for use in freshman, sophomore, junior, or senior years; not renewable. *Amount:* $1000–$2500.

Eligibility Requirements: Applicant must be Black (non-Hispanic) and enrolled or expecting to enroll full-time at a four-year institution or university. Applicant must have 2.5 GPA or higher. Available to U.S. citizens.

Application Requirements: Application, financial need analysis. *Deadline:* Continuous.

Contact: Program Services Department
United Negro College Fund
8260 Willow Oaks Corporate Drive
Fairfax, VA 22031

JOSEPH A.TOWLES AFRICAN STUDY ABROAD SCHOLARSHIP

Award to students who have been accepted into a study abroad program in Africa. Must have 3.0 GPA. Please visit Web site for more information: http://www.uncf.org

Award: Scholarship for use in freshman, sophomore, junior, or senior years; renewable. *Number:* varies. *Amount:* up to $15,000.

Eligibility Requirements: Applicant must be Black (non-Hispanic) and enrolled or expecting to enroll at an institution or university. Applicant must have 3.0 GPA or higher.

Application Requirements: Application, financial need analysis, FAFSA, SAR. *Deadline:* varies.

Contact: Program Services Department
United Negro College Fund
8260 Willow Oaks Corporate Drive
Fairfax, VA 22031

KEVIN MOORE MEMORIAL SCHOLARSHIP

Scholarship available for New York residents attending a UNCF member college or university. Minimum 2.5 GPA required. Prospective applicants should complete the Student Profile found at Web site: http://www.uncf.org.

Award: Scholarship for use in freshman, sophomore, junior, or senior years; not renewable. *Amount:* $1000.

Eligibility Requirements: Applicant must be Black (non-Hispanic); enrolled or expecting to enroll at a four-year institution or university and resident of New York. Applicant must have 2.5 GPA or higher. Available to U.S. citizens.

Application Requirements: Application. *Deadline:* Continuous.

Contact: Program Services Department
United Negro College Fund
8260 Willow Oaks Corporate Drive
Fairfax, VA 22031

KUNTZ FOUNDATION SCHOLARSHIP

Need-based scholarship for students attending a UNCF member college or university. Minimum 2.5 GPA required. Prospective applicants should complete the Student Profile found at Web site: http://www.uncf.org.

Award: Scholarship for use in freshman, sophomore, junior, or senior years; not renewable.

Eligibility Requirements: Applicant must be Black (non-Hispanic) and enrolled or expecting to enroll at a four-year institution or university. Applicant must have 2.5 GPA or higher.

Application Requirements: Application, financial need analysis. *Deadline:* Continuous.

Contact: Program Services Department
United Negro College Fund
8260 Willow Oaks Corporate Drive
Fairfax, VA 22031

LAFFEY-MCHUGH FOUNDATION SCHOLARSHIP

Need-based awards for students attending a UNCF college or university. Minimum 2.5 GPA required. Prospective applicants should complete the Student Profile found at Web site: http://www.uncf.org.

Award: Scholarship for use in freshman, sophomore, junior, or senior years; not renewable.

Eligibility Requirements: Applicant must be Black (non-Hispanic) and enrolled or expecting to enroll at a four-year institution or university. Applicant must have 2.5 GPA or higher. Available to U.S. citizens.

Application Requirements: Application, financial need analysis. *Deadline:* Continuous.

Contact: Program Services Department
United Negro College Fund
8260 Willow Oaks Corporate Drive
Fairfax, VA 22031

LETTY GAROFALO SCHOLARSHIP

Need-based scholarship open to students attending one of the following college or universities: Clark Atlanta, Morehouse, Morris Brown, or Spelman. Minimum 2.5 GPA required. Prospective applicants should complete the Student Profile found at Web site: http://www.uncf.org.

Award: Scholarship for use in freshman, sophomore, junior, or senior years; not renewable.

Eligibility Requirements: Applicant must be Black (non-Hispanic) and enrolled or expecting to enroll at a four-year institution or university. Applicant must have 2.5 GPA or higher.

Application Requirements: Application, financial need analysis. *Deadline:* Continuous.

Contact: Program Services Department
United Negro College Fund
8260 Willow Oaks Corporate Drive
Fairfax, VA 22031

LIMITED, INC. AND INTIMATE BRANDS, INC. SCHOLARSHIP

Scholarships awarded to students attending a UNCF member college or university. Minimum 2.5 GPA required. Prospective applicants should complete the Student Profile found at Web site: http://www.uncf.org.

Award: Scholarship for use in freshman, sophomore, junior, or senior years; not renewable.

Eligibility Requirements: Applicant must be Black (non-Hispanic); enrolled or expecting to enroll at a four-year institution or university and resident of Ohio. Applicant must have 2.5 GPA or higher.

Application Requirements: Application, financial need analysis. *Deadline:* Continuous.

Contact: Program Services Department
United Negro College Fund
8260 Willow Oaks Corporate Drive
Fairfax, VA 22031

MAE MAXEY MEMORIAL SCHOLARSHIP

Award for students with an interest in poetry attending a UNCF member college or university. Minimum 2.5 GPA required. Prospective applicants should complete the Student Profile found at Web site: http://www.uncf.org.

Award: Scholarship for use in freshman, sophomore, junior, or senior years; not renewable. *Amount:* $1000–$5000.

Eligibility Requirements: Applicant must be Black (non-Hispanic) and enrolled or expecting to enroll at a four-year institution or university. Applicant must have 2.5 GPA or higher. Available to U.S. citizens.

Application Requirements: Application, financial need analysis. *Deadline:* Continuous.

Contact: Program Services Department
United Negro College Fund
8260 Willow Oaks Corporate Drive
Fairfax, VA 22031

MALCOLM X SCHOLARSHIP FOR "EXCEPTIONAL COURAGE"

Awarded for demonstrated academic excellence, campus and community leadership, and exceptional courage. Open to students attending a UNCF member college or university with a minimum 2.5 GPA. Prospective applicants should complete the Student Profile found at Web site: http://www.uncf.org.

Award: Scholarship for use in freshman, sophomore, junior, or senior years; not renewable. *Amount:* $4000.

Eligibility Requirements: Applicant must be Black (non-Hispanic); enrolled or expecting to enroll at a four-year institution or university and must have an interest in leadership. Applicant must have 2.5 GPA or higher.

Application Requirements: Application, financial need analysis.

Contact: Program Services Department
United Negro College Fund
8260 Willow Oaks Corporate Drive
Fairfax, VA 22031

MARTIN LUTHER KING JR. CHILDREN'S CHOIR SCHOLARSHIP

Scholarship for students who were part of a class action suit. This is a one-time award and may be used at any college or university. Please visit Web site for more information: http://www.uncf.org.

Award: Scholarship for use in freshman, sophomore, junior, or senior years; not renewable. *Number:* 1000. *Amount:* varies.

Eligibility Requirements: Applicant must be Black (non-Hispanic) and enrolled or expecting to enroll at a four-year institution or university. Applicant must have 2.5 GPA or higher. Available to U.S. citizens.

Application Requirements: Application, financial need analysis. *Deadline:* varies.

Contact: Program Services Department
United Negro College Fund
8260 Willow Oaks Corporate Drive
Fairfax, VA 22031

MARY E. SCOTT MEMORIAL SCHOLARSHIP

Scholarship available for students attending a UNCF member college or university. Minimum 2.5 GPA required. Prospective applicants should complete the Student Profile found at Web site: http://www.uncf.org.

Award: Scholarship for use in freshman, sophomore, junior, or senior years; not renewable. *Amount:* $1500–$5000.

Eligibility Requirements: Applicant must be Black (non-Hispanic) and enrolled or expecting to enroll at a four-year institution or university. Applicant must have 2.5 GPA or higher.

Application Requirements: Application, financial need analysis. *Deadline:* Continuous.

Contact: Program Services Department
United Negro College Fund
8260 Willow Oaks Corporate Drive
Fairfax, VA 22031

MARY OENSLAGER SCHOLARSHIP

Scholarship available to students attending a UNCF member college or university. Minimum 2.5 GPA required. Prospective applicants should complete the Student Profile found at Web site: http://www.uncf.org.

Award: Scholarship for use in freshman, sophomore, junior, or senior years; not renewable. *Amount:* $2000–$5000.

Eligibility Requirements: Applicant must be Black (non-Hispanic) and enrolled or expecting to enroll at a four-year institution or university. Applicant must have 2.5 GPA or higher.

Application Requirements: Application, financial need analysis. *Deadline:* Continuous.

Contact: Program Services Department
United Negro College Fund
8260 Willow Oaks Corporate Drive
Fairfax, VA 22031

MAYA ANGELOU/VIVIAN BAXTER SCHOLARSHIP

Scholarship open to North Carolina residents attending a UNCF member college or university. 2.5 GPA required. Prospective applicants should complete the Student Profile found at Web site: http://www.uncf.org.

Award: Scholarship for use in freshman, sophomore, junior, or senior years; not renewable. *Amount:* $2500.

Eligibility Requirements: Applicant must be Black (non-Hispanic); enrolled or expecting to enroll at a four-year institution or university and resident of North Carolina. Applicant must have 2.5 GPA or higher.

Application Requirements: Application. *Deadline:* Continuous.

Contact: Program Services Department
United Negro College Fund
8260 Willow Oaks Corporate Drive
Fairfax, VA 22031

MCDONALD'S CREW SCHOLARSHIP-CLEVELAND, OHIO

Scholarships available for students employed by McDonalds in Cleveland, Ohio. Must have minimum 2.5 GPA and attend a UNCF participating institution. Information on Web site at http://www.uncf.org.

Award: Scholarship for use in freshman, sophomore, junior, or senior years; renewable. *Number:* up to 3000. *Amount:* varies.

United Negro College Fund (continued)

Eligibility Requirements: Applicant must be Black (non-Hispanic); enrolled or expecting to enroll at a four-year institution or university; resident of Ohio and studying in Ohio. Applicant must have 2.5 GPA or higher. Available to U.S. citizens.

Application Requirements: Application, financial need analysis, FAFSA. *Deadline:* varies.

Contact: Program Services Department
United Negro College Fund
8260 Willow Oaks Corporate Drive
Fairfax, VA 22031

MCFEELY-ROGERS SCHOLARSHIP FOUNDATION

Need-based scholarship. Minimum 2.5 GPA required. Prospective applicants should complete the Student Profile found at Web site: http://www.uncf.org.

Award: Scholarship for use in freshman, sophomore, junior, or senior years; not renewable.

Eligibility Requirements: Applicant must be Black (non-Hispanic) and enrolled or expecting to enroll full-time at a four-year institution or university. Applicant must have 2.5 GPA or higher.

Application Requirements: Application, financial need analysis. *Deadline:* Continuous.

Contact: Program Services Department
United Negro College Fund
8260 Willow Oaks Corporate Drive
Fairfax, VA 22031

MEDTRONIC FOUNDATION INTERNSHIP/SCHOLARSHIP

Scholarship for undergraduate sophomores and juniors majoring in engineering or science and attending a UNCF member college or university. A paid summer internship is included in the award. Minimum 3.3 GPA required. Prospective applicants should complete the Student Profile found at Web site: http://www.uncf.org.

Award: Scholarship for use in sophomore or junior years; not renewable. *Amount:* $5000.

Eligibility Requirements: Applicant must be Black (non-Hispanic) and enrolled or expecting to enroll at a four-year institution or university.

Application Requirements: Application, autobiography, financial need analysis, resume, references. *Deadline:* March 30.

Contact: Program Services Department
United Negro College Fund
8260 Willow Oaks Corporate Drive
Fairfax, VA 22031

MICHAEL AND DONNA GRIFFITH SCHOLARSHIP

Scholarship provides assistance to students attending a UNCF member college or university. Minimum 2.5 GPA required. Prospective applicants should complete the Student Profile found at Web site: http://www.uncf.org.

Award: Scholarship for use in freshman, sophomore, junior, or senior years; not renewable. *Amount:* $1000–$2500.

Eligibility Requirements: Applicant must be Black (non-Hispanic) and enrolled or expecting to enroll at a four-year institution or university. Applicant must have 2.5 GPA or higher.

Application Requirements: Application, financial need analysis.

Contact: Program Services Department
United Negro College Fund
8260 Willow Oaks Corporate Drive
Fairfax, VA 22031

MIKE AND STEPHANIE BOZIC SCHOLARSHIP

Need-based scholarship open to all students attending a UNCF member college or university. 2.5 GPA required. Prospective applicants should complete the Student Profile found at Web site: http://www.uncf.org.

Award: Scholarship for use in freshman, sophomore, junior, or senior years; not renewable.

Eligibility Requirements: Applicant must be Black (non-Hispanic) and enrolled or expecting to enroll at a four-year institution or university. Applicant must have 2.5 GPA or higher.

Application Requirements: Application, financial need analysis. *Deadline:* Continuous.

Contact: Program Services Department
United Negro College Fund
8260 Willow Oaks Corporate Drive
Fairfax, VA 22031

MINNESOTA/IOWA/NEBRASKA STUDENT AID PROGRAM

Must be nominated by financial aid director at the UNCF college. Available to students from the three-state area who show an unmet financial need.

Award: Scholarship for use in freshman, sophomore, junior, or senior years; renewable. *Amount:* up to $3000.

Eligibility Requirements: Applicant must be Black (non-Hispanic); enrolled or expecting to enroll at a four-year institution or university and resident of Iowa, Minnesota, or Nebraska. Applicant must have 2.5 GPA or higher.

Application Requirements: Application, financial need analysis.

Contact: Program Services Department
United Negro College Fund
8260 Willow Oaks Corporate Drive
Fairfax, VA 22031

MORGAN STANLEY SCHOLARSHIP

Must be nominated by financial aid director at the UNCF college. Scholarships for UNCF students interested in finance and banking. Minimum 2.5 GPA required.

Award: Scholarship for use in freshman, sophomore, junior, or senior years; not renewable. *Amount:* up to $10,000.

Eligibility Requirements: Applicant must be Black (non-Hispanic) and enrolled or expecting to enroll at a four-year institution or university. Applicant must have 2.5 GPA or higher.

Application Requirements: Application.

Contact: Program Services Department
United Negro College Fund
8260 Willow Oaks Corporate Drive
Fairfax, VA 22031

NATHALIA BOWSER SCHOLARSHIP

Scholarship available to African American males from South Carolina who attend Morris College or Voorhees College. Please visit Web site for more information: http://www.uncf.org.

Award: Scholarship for use in freshman, sophomore, junior, senior, or graduate years. *Number:* varies. *Amount:* $1500.

Eligibility Requirements: Applicant must be Black (non-Hispanic); enrolled or expecting to enroll at a four-year institution or university; male; resident of South Carolina and studying in South Carolina. Applicant must have 2.5 GPA or higher.

Application Requirements: Application, financial need analysis, FAFSA, SAR. *Deadline:* varies.

Contact: Program Services Department
United Negro College Fund
8260 Willow Oaks Corporate Drive
Fairfax, VA 22031

NEW JERSEY MAYOR'S TASK FORCE SCHOLARSHIP

Awards available for African American students who live in one of the New Jersey Task Force participating cities. Must attend a historically black college or university, or a UNCF member institution. Requirements may vary for each city. Check Web site for details. http://www.uncf.org.

Award: Scholarship for use in freshman, sophomore, junior, or senior years; renewable. *Number:* varies. *Amount:* $1350.

Eligibility Requirements: Applicant must be Black (non-Hispanic); enrolled or expecting to enroll at a four-year institution or university and resident of New Jersey. Applicant must have 2.5 GPA or higher.

Application Requirements: Application, essay, financial need analysis, photo, references, transcript, FAFSA, SAR. *Deadline:* varies.

Contact: Program Services Department
United Negro College Fund
8260 Willow Oaks Corporate Drive
Fairfax, VA 22031

NICHOLAS H. NOYES, JR. MEMORIAL FOUNDATION SCHOLARSHIP

Need-based scholarship to students attending a UNCF college or university. Minimum 2.5 GPA required. Prospective applicants should complete the Student Profile found at Web site: http://www.uncf.org.

Award: Scholarship for use in freshman, sophomore, junior, or senior years; not renewable.

Eligibility Requirements: Applicant must be Black (non-Hispanic) and enrolled or expecting to enroll at a four-year institution or university. Applicant must have 2.5 GPA or higher.

Application Requirements: Application, financial need analysis. *Deadline:* Continuous.

Contact: Program Services Department
United Negro College Fund
8260 Willow Oaks Corporate Drive
Fairfax, VA 22031

O'GRADY FAMILY FOUNDATION SCHOLARSHIP

Scholarships available for African American students who are residents of New York City, Connecticut, or Western Washington. Must have a minimum 2.5 GPA and attend a UNCF member college or university. Information on Web site at http://www.uncf.org.

Award: Scholarship for use in freshman, sophomore, junior, or senior years; renewable. *Number:* varies. *Amount:* varies.

Eligibility Requirements: Applicant must be Black (non-Hispanic); enrolled or expecting to enroll at a four-year institution or university and resident of Connecticut, New York, or Washington. Applicant must have 2.5 GPA or higher.

Application Requirements: Application, financial need analysis, FAFSA, SAR. *Deadline:* varies.

Contact: Program Services Department
United Negro College Fund
8260 Willow Oaks Corporate Drive
Fairfax, VA 22031

PACIFIC NORTHWEST SCHOLARSHIP PROGRAM

Need-based scholarships for UNCF students from Washington and Oregon. Minimum 2.5 GPA required. Prospective applicants should complete the Student Profile found at Web site: http://www.uncf.org.

Award: Scholarship for use in freshman, sophomore, junior, or senior years; not renewable.

Eligibility Requirements: Applicant must be Black (non-Hispanic); enrolled or expecting to enroll at a four-year institution or university and resident of Oregon or Washington. Applicant must have 2.5 GPA or higher. Available to U.S. citizens.

Application Requirements: Application, financial need analysis. *Deadline:* Continuous.

Contact: Program Services Department
United Negro College Fund
8260 Willow Oaks Corporate Drive
Fairfax, VA 22031

PAUL AND EDITH BABSON SCHOLARSHIP

Applicant must be from Boston, Massachusetts in order to be eligible. Please visit Web site for more information: http://www.uncf.org.

Award: Scholarship for use in freshman, sophomore, junior, senior, or graduate years. *Number:* varies. *Amount:* $1000–$3500.

Eligibility Requirements: Applicant must be Black (non-Hispanic); enrolled or expecting to enroll at a four-year institution or university and resident of Massachusetts. Applicant must have 2.5 GPA or higher. Available to U.S. citizens.

Application Requirements: Application, financial need analysis, FAFSA, SAR. *Deadline:* varies.

Contact: Program Services Department
United Negro College Fund
8260 Willow Oaks Corporate Drive
Fairfax, VA 22031

PENNSYLVANIA STATE EMPLOYEES SCHOLARSHIP FUND

Scholarships for UNCF students from Pennsylvania. Funds may be used for tuition, room and board, books, or to repay federal student loans. Minimum 2.5 GPA required. Prospective applicants should complete the Student Profile found at Web site: http://www.uncf.org.

Award: Scholarship for use in freshman year; not renewable. *Number:* 20. *Amount:* $4000.

Eligibility Requirements: Applicant must be Black (non-Hispanic); enrolled or expecting to enroll at a four-year institution or university and resident of Pennsylvania. Applicant must have 2.5 GPA or higher. Available to U.S. citizens.

Application Requirements: Application, financial need analysis. *Deadline:* May 15.

Contact: Program Services Department
United Negro College Fund
8260 Willow Oaks Corporate Drive
Fairfax, VA 22031

REGINA PEFFLY SCHOLARSHIP

Scholarships available for African Americans residing in Detroit, Michigan to attend a UNCF college or university. Annual income must be under $25,000. Details on Web site at http://www.uncf.org.

Award: Scholarship for use in freshman, sophomore, junior, or senior years; renewable. *Number:* varies. *Amount:* up to $3000.

Eligibility Requirements: Applicant must be Black (non-Hispanic); enrolled or expecting to enroll at a four-year institution or university and resident of Michigan. Applicant must have 2.5 GPA or higher.

Application Requirements: Application, financial need analysis, FAFSA, SAR. *Deadline:* varies.

Contact: Program Services Department
United Negro College Fund
8260 Willow Oaks Corporate Drive
Fairfax, VA 22031

RELIABLE LIFE INSURANCE COMPANY SCHOLARSHIP PROGRAM

Scholarships available to African American students residing in Missouri, Texas, Arkansas, or Oklahoma. Must attend a UNCF member college or university. Minimum 2.5 GPA. Information on Web site at http://www.uncf.org.

Award: Scholarship for use in freshman, sophomore, junior, or senior years. *Number:* varies. *Amount:* $5000.

Eligibility Requirements: Applicant must be Black (non-Hispanic); enrolled or expecting to enroll at a four-year institution or university and resident of Arkansas, Missouri, Oklahoma, or Texas. Applicant must have 2.5 GPA or higher.

Application Requirements: Application, financial need analysis, FAFSA, SAR. *Deadline:* August 30.

Contact: Program Services Department
United Negro College Fund
8260 Willow Oaks Corporate Drive
Fairfax, VA 22031

RHEA AND LOUIS SPIELER SCHOLARSHIP PROGRAM

Need-based scholarship for students attending a UNCF member college or university. Minimum 2.5 GPA required. Prospective applicants should complete the Student Profile found at Web site: http://www.uncf.org.

United Negro College Fund (continued)

Award: Scholarship for use in freshman, sophomore, junior, or senior years; not renewable.

Eligibility Requirements: Applicant must be Black (non-Hispanic) and enrolled or expecting to enroll at a four-year institution or university. Applicant must have 2.5 GPA or higher.

Application Requirements: Application, financial need analysis. *Deadline:* Continuous.

Contact: Program Services Department
United Negro College Fund
8260 Willow Oaks Corporate Drive
Fairfax, VA 22031

RICHMOND SCHOLARSHIP

Scholarships available to students who reside in Central Virginia. Minimum 2.5 GPA required. Must attend a UNCF member college or university. Details on Web site at http://www.uncf.org.

Award: Scholarship for use in freshman, sophomore, junior, or senior years; renewable. *Number:* varies. *Amount:* up to $2000.

Eligibility Requirements: Applicant must be Black (non-Hispanic); enrolled or expecting to enroll at a four-year institution or university and resident of Virginia. Applicant must have 2.5 GPA or higher.

Application Requirements: Application, financial need analysis, FAFSA,SAR. *Deadline:* varies.

Contact: Program Services Department
United Negro College Fund
8260 Willow Oaks Corporate Drive
Fairfax, VA 22031

RIDGEWAY/DENNY'S SCHOLARSHIP

Scholarships awarded to California residents who were an awardee of a court case. Prospective applicants should complete the Student Profile found at Web site: http://www.uncf.org.

Award: Scholarship for use in freshman, sophomore, junior, or senior years; not renewable.

Eligibility Requirements: Applicant must be Black (non-Hispanic); enrolled or expecting to enroll at a four-year institution or university and resident of California. Applicant must have 2.5 GPA or higher. Available to U.S. citizens.

Application Requirements: Application, financial need analysis.

Contact: Program Services Department
United Negro College Fund
8260 Willow Oaks Corporate Drive
Fairfax, VA 22031

RMCC-ARIZONA SCHOLARSHIP

Scholarship provides support for Arizona residents attending a UCNF member college or university. Minimum 2.5 GPA required. Information available on Web site: http://www.uncf.org.

Award: Scholarship for use in freshman, sophomore, junior, senior, or graduate years; not renewable. *Number:* varies. *Amount:* varies.

Eligibility Requirements: Applicant must be Black (non-Hispanic); enrolled or expecting to enroll at a four-year institution or university and resident of Arizona. Applicant must have 2.5 GPA or higher. Available to U.S. citizens.

Application Requirements: Application, financial need analysis, FAFSA, SAR. *Deadline:* varies.

Contact: Program Services Department
United Negro College Fund
8260 Willow Oaks Corporate Drive
Fairfax, VA 22031

ROBERT DOLE SCHOLARSHIP

• *See page 532*

RONALD MCDONALD'S CHICAGOLAND SCHOLARSHIP

Scholarships awarded to students attending a UNCF member college or university. Prospective applicants should complete the Student Profile found at Web site: http://www.uncf.org.

Award: Scholarship for use in freshman, sophomore, junior, or senior years; renewable. *Amount:* up to $6000.

Eligibility Requirements: Applicant must be Black (non-Hispanic) and enrolled or expecting to enroll full-time at a four-year institution or university. Applicant must have 2.5 GPA or higher.

Application Requirements: Application, financial need analysis. *Deadline:* Continuous.

Contact: Program Services Department
United Negro College Fund
8260 Willow Oaks Corporate Drive
Fairfax, VA 22031

RONALD MCDONALD'S HOUSE CHARITIES SCHOLARSHIP-OHIO

Scholarships available for African American students residing in Ohio. Must attend a UNCF member college or university. Must have a minimum 2.5 GPA. Information on Web site at http://www.uncf.org.

Award: Scholarship for use in freshman, sophomore, junior, or senior years; renewable. *Number:* varies. *Amount:* varies.

Eligibility Requirements: Applicant must be Black (non-Hispanic); enrolled or expecting to enroll at a four-year institution or university and resident of Ohio. Applicant must have 2.5 GPA or higher.

Application Requirements: Application, financial need analysis, FAFSA, SAR. *Deadline:* varies.

Contact: Program Services Department
United Negro College Fund
8260 Willow Oaks Corporate Drive
Fairfax, VA 22031

SALLIE MAE FUND AMERICAN DREAM SCHOLARSHIP

Awards from $500 to $5000 to African-American students with financial need enrolled in a two or four year title IV accredited college or university. Open to incoming freshmen as well as current undergraduate students. Please visit Web site for more information: http://www.uncf.org.

Award: Scholarship for use in freshman, sophomore, junior, or senior years; renewable. *Number:* varies. *Amount:* $500–$5000.

Eligibility Requirements: Applicant must be Black (non-Hispanic) and enrolled or expecting to enroll at a two-year or four-year institution or university. Applicant must have 2.5 GPA or higher. Available to U.S. citizens.

Application Requirements: Application, essay, financial need analysis, references, transcript, FAFSA, SAR. *Deadline:* April 15.

Contact: Cynthia Nair, Senior Program Manager
United Negro College Fund
PO Box 10444
Fairfax, VA 22031

SAN JOSE MERCURY NEWS SCHOLARSHIP

Award established to benefit a student from Silicon Valley, CA. Must have 2.5 GPA. Please visit Web site for more information: http://www.uncf.org.

Award: Scholarship for use in freshman, sophomore, junior, or senior years; renewable. *Number:* 1. *Amount:* $2000.

Eligibility Requirements: Applicant must be Black (non-Hispanic); enrolled or expecting to enroll at an institution or university and resident of California. Applicant must have 2.5 GPA or higher.

Application Requirements: Application, financial need analysis, FAFSA, SAR. *Deadline:* varies.

Contact: Program Services Department
United Negro College Fund
8260 Willow Oaks Corporate Drive
Fairfax, VA 22031

SC JOHNSON WAX SCHOLARSHIP

Award of up to $4000 to Racine, WI residents entering any historically black college or university. Must have 2.75 GPA. Preference given to Business and Science majors. Please visit Web site for more information: http://www.uncf.org

Award: Scholarship for use in freshman, sophomore, junior, or senior years; renewable. *Number:* varies. *Amount:* up to $4000.

Eligibility Requirements: Applicant must be Black (non-Hispanic); enrolled or expecting to enroll at an institution or university and resident of Wisconsin.

Application Requirements: Application, financial need analysis, FAFSA, SAR. *Deadline:* varies.

Contact: Program Services Department
United Negro College Fund
8260 Willow Oaks Corporate Drive
Fairfax, VA 22031

SCHRAFT CHARITABLE TRUST SCHOLARSHIP

Award available to Boston, MA residents who are enrolled in a historically black college or university. Please visit Web site for more information: http://www.uncf.org.

Award: Scholarship for use in freshman, sophomore, junior, or senior years; renewable. *Number:* varies. *Amount:* $3000.

Eligibility Requirements: Applicant must be Black (non-Hispanic); enrolled or expecting to enroll at an institution or university and resident of Massachusetts. Applicant must have 2.5 GPA or higher.

Application Requirements: Application, financial need analysis, FAFSA, SAR. *Deadline:* varies.

Contact: Program Services Department
United Negro College Fund
8260 Willow Oaks Corporate Drive
Fairfax, VA 22031

SHELL/EQUILON UNCF CLEVELAND SCHOLARSHIP FUND

Award for Cuyahoga County, OH residents who are attending a UNCF member college or university. Please visit Web site for more information: http://www.uncf.org

Award: Scholarship for use in freshman, sophomore, junior, or senior years; renewable. *Number:* varies. *Amount:* $3000.

Eligibility Requirements: Applicant must be Black (non-Hispanic); enrolled or expecting to enroll at an institution or university and resident of Ohio. Applicant must have 2.5 GPA or higher.

Application Requirements: Application, financial need analysis, FAFSA, SAR. *Deadline:* varies.

Contact: Program Services Department
United Negro College Fund
8260 Willow Oaks Corporate Drive
Fairfax, VA 22031

SHREVEPORT CAMPAIGN

Award is for students residing in the Shreveport, LA area. Please visit Web site for more information: http://www.uncf.org

Award: Scholarship for use in freshman, sophomore, junior, or senior years; renewable. *Number:* varies. *Amount:* $1500.

Eligibility Requirements: Applicant must be Black (non-Hispanic); enrolled or expecting to enroll at an institution or university and resident of Louisiana. Applicant must have 2.5 GPA or higher.

Application Requirements: Application, financial need analysis, FAFSA, SAR. *Deadline:* varies.

Contact: Program Services Department
United Negro College Fund
8260 Willow Oaks Corporate Drive
Fairfax, VA 22031

SIDNEY STONEMAN SCHOLARSHIP

Scholarship available to Florida residents attending UNCF member colleges and universities. Minimum 2.5 GPA required. Prospective applicants should complete the Student Profile found at Web site: http://www.uncf.org.

Award: Scholarship for use in freshman, sophomore, junior, or senior years; not renewable. *Amount:* $3500.

Eligibility Requirements: Applicant must be Black (non-Hispanic); enrolled or expecting to enroll at a four-year institution or university and resident of Florida. Applicant must have 2.5 GPA or higher. Available to U.S. citizens.

Application Requirements: Application, financial need analysis. *Deadline:* Continuous.

Contact: Program Services Department
United Negro College Fund
8260 Willow Oaks Corporate Drive
Fairfax, VA 22031

SIRAGUSA FOUNDATION SCHOLARSHIP

Scholarships available to students attending a UNCF member college or university. Minimum 2.5 GPA required. Prospective applicants should complete the Student Profile found at Web site: http://www.uncf.org.

Award: Scholarship for use in freshman, sophomore, junior, or senior years; not renewable. *Amount:* $2000.

Eligibility Requirements: Applicant must be Black (non-Hispanic) and enrolled or expecting to enroll at a four-year institution or university. Applicant must have 2.5 GPA or higher.

Application Requirements: Application, financial need analysis. *Deadline:* Continuous.

Contact: Program Services Department
United Negro College Fund
8260 Willow Oaks Corporate Drive
Fairfax, VA 22031

SONYA WILLIAMS MEMORIAL SCHOLARSHIP

Scholarships available to New York students who attend a UNCF member college or university. Minimum 2.5 GPA required.

Award: Scholarship for use in freshman, sophomore, junior, or senior years; not renewable.

Eligibility Requirements: Applicant must be Black (non-Hispanic); enrolled or expecting to enroll at a four-year institution or university and resident of New York. Applicant must have 2.5 GPA or higher.

Application Requirements: Application.

Contact: Program Services Department
United Negro College Fund
8260 Willow Oaks Corporate Drive
Fairfax, VA 22031

ST. PETERSBURG GOLF CLASSIC SCHOLARSHIP

Each year two men and two women residents of Florida are chosen to receive this scholarship. Please visit Web site for more information: http://www.uncf.org

Award: Scholarship for use in freshman, sophomore, junior, or senior years; renewable. *Number:* 4. *Amount:* $2000–$6000.

Eligibility Requirements: Applicant must be Black (non-Hispanic); enrolled or expecting to enroll at an institution or university and resident of Florida. Applicant must have 2.5 GPA or higher.

Application Requirements: Application, financial need analysis, FAFSA, SAR. *Deadline:* varies.

Contact: Program Services Department
United Negro College Fund
8260 Willow Oaks Corporate Drive
Fairfax, VA 22031

STERLING BANK SCHOLARSHIP

Scholarship available to students attending UNCF member colleges or universities. Minimum 2.5 GPA required. Prospective applicants should complete the Student Profile found at Web site: http://www.uncf.org.

Award: Scholarship for use in freshman, sophomore, junior, or senior years; not renewable.

United Negro College Fund (continued)

Eligibility Requirements: Applicant must be Black (non-Hispanic) and enrolled or expecting to enroll at a four-year institution or university. Applicant must have 2.5 GPA or higher. Available to U.S. citizens.

Application Requirements: Application, financial need analysis. *Deadline:* Continuous.

Contact: Program Services Department
United Negro College Fund
8260 Willow Oaks Corporate Drive
Fairfax, VA 22031

SYLVIA SHAPIRO SCHOLARSHIP

Need-based scholarships available for students attending a UNCF member college or university. Minimum 2.5 GPA required. Prospective applicants should complete the Student Profile found at Web site: http://www.uncf.org.

Award: Scholarship for use in freshman, sophomore, junior, or senior years; not renewable.

Eligibility Requirements: Applicant must be Black (non-Hispanic) and enrolled or expecting to enroll at a four-year institution or university. Applicant must have 2.5 GPA or higher.

Application Requirements: Application, financial need analysis. *Deadline:* Continuous.

Contact: Program Services Department
United Negro College Fund
8260 Willow Oaks Corporate Drive
Fairfax, VA 22031

TED WHITE MEMORIAL SCHOLARSHIP

Award for students from the Detroit, MI metropolitan area. Must have 2.7 GPA. Preference is given to freshmen. Students must attend a UNCF member college or university. Please visit Web site for more information: http://www.uncf.org

Award: Scholarship for use in freshman, sophomore, junior, or senior years; renewable. *Number:* varies. *Amount:* up to $2500.

Eligibility Requirements: Applicant must be Black (non-Hispanic); enrolled or expecting to enroll at an institution or university and resident of Michigan.

Application Requirements: Application, financial need analysis, FAFSA, SAR. *Deadline:* varies.

Contact: Program Services Department
United Negro College Fund
8260 Willow Oaks Corporate Drive
Fairfax, VA 22031

TEXAS HEALTH RESOURCES SCHOLARSHIP

Award for students from the Dallas/Ft. Worth, TX area. Must have 2.5 GPA. Please visit Web site for more information: http://www.uncf.org

Award: Scholarship for use in freshman, sophomore, junior, or senior years; renewable. *Number:* varies. *Amount:* varies.

Eligibility Requirements: Applicant must be Black (non-Hispanic); enrolled or expecting to enroll at an institution or university and resident of Texas. Applicant must have 2.5 GPA or higher.

Application Requirements: Application, financial need analysis, FAFSA, SAR. *Deadline:* varies.

Contact: Program Services Department
United Negro College Fund
8260 Willow Oaks Corporate Drive
Fairfax, VA 22031

TEXTRON FELLOWS PROGRAM

Award for students in their junior year residing in Providence, RI. Must have 3.0 GPA. Please visit Web site for more information: http://www.uncf.org

Award: Scholarship for use in junior year; renewable. *Number:* varies. *Amount:* varies.

Eligibility Requirements: Applicant must be Black (non-Hispanic); enrolled or expecting to enroll at an institution or university and resident of Rhode Island. Applicant must have 3.0 GPA or higher.

Application Requirements: Application, financial need analysis, FAFSA, SAR. *Deadline:* varies.

Contact: Program Services Department
United Negro College Fund
8260 Willow Oaks Corporate Drive
Fairfax, VA 22031

TJX FOUNDATION SCHOLARSHIP

Award available to Massachusetts residents who live near TJ Maxx stores. Must have 2.5 GPA. Please visit Web site for more information: http://www.uncf.org

Award: Scholarship for use in freshman, sophomore, junior, or senior years; renewable. *Number:* varies. *Amount:* $1000.

Eligibility Requirements: Applicant must be Black (non-Hispanic); enrolled or expecting to enroll at an institution or university and resident of Massachusetts. Applicant must have 2.5 GPA or higher.

Application Requirements: Application, financial need analysis, FAFSA, SAR. *Deadline:* varies.

Contact: Program Services Department
United Negro College Fund
8260 Willow Oaks Corporate Drive
Fairfax, VA 22031

TRENTON SCHOOL BOARD CAMPAIGN SCHOLARSHIP

Award to resident of Trenton, NJ. Must have 2.5 GPA. Please visit Web site for more information: http://www.uncf.org

Award: Scholarship for use in freshman, sophomore, junior, or senior years; renewable. *Number:* varies. *Amount:* $4000.

Eligibility Requirements: Applicant must be Black (non-Hispanic); enrolled or expecting to enroll at an institution or university and resident of New Jersey. Applicant must have 2.5 GPA or higher.

Application Requirements: Application, financial need analysis, FAFSA, SAR. *Deadline:* varies.

Contact: Program Services Department
United Negro College Fund
8260 Willow Oaks Corporate Drive
Fairfax, VA 22031

TRULL FOUNDATION SCHOLARSHIP

Need-based scholarship to students attending a UNCF member college or university. Minimum 2.5 GPA required. Prospective applicants should complete the Student Profile found at Web site: http://www.uncf.org.

Award: Scholarship for use in freshman, sophomore, junior, or senior years; not renewable.

Eligibility Requirements: Applicant must be Black (non-Hispanic) and enrolled or expecting to enroll at a four-year institution or university. Applicant must have 2.5 GPA or higher.

Application Requirements: Application, financial need analysis. *Deadline:* Continuous.

Contact: Program Services Department
United Negro College Fund
8260 Willow Oaks Corporate Drive
Fairfax, VA 22031

UNION BANK OF CALIFORNIA

Scholarship available to all California students who attend a UNCF member college or university. Minimum 2.5 GPA required. Prospective applicants should complete the Student Profile found at Web site: http://www.uncf.org.

Award: Scholarship for use in freshman, sophomore, junior, or senior years; not renewable.

Eligibility Requirements: Applicant must be Black (non-Hispanic); enrolled or expecting to enroll at a four-year institution or university and resident of California. Applicant must have 2.5 GPA or higher.

Application Requirements: Application, financial need analysis. *Deadline:* Continuous.

Contact: Program Services Department
United Negro College Fund
8260 Willow Oaks Corporate Drive
Fairfax, VA 22031

UNITED INSURANCE SCHOLARSHIP

Students or the parents of students applying for this award must have a policy with United Insurance Company. Please visit Web site for more information: http://www.uncf.org

Award: Scholarship for use in freshman, sophomore, junior, or senior years; renewable. *Number:* varies. *Amount:* $5000.

Eligibility Requirements: Applicant must be Black (non-Hispanic) and enrolled or expecting to enroll at an institution or university. Applicant must have 2.5 GPA or higher.

Application Requirements: Application, financial need analysis, FAFSA, SAR. *Deadline:* August 31.

Contact: Program Services Department
United Negro College Fund
8260 Willow Oaks Corporate Drive
Fairfax, VA 22031

UNITED PARCEL SERVICE FOUNDATION SCHOLARSHIP

This award provides students with financial support for tuition and other education costs. Please visit Web site for more information: http://www.uncf.org

Award: Scholarship for use in freshman, sophomore, junior, or senior years; renewable. *Number:* varies. *Amount:* varies.

Eligibility Requirements: Applicant must be Black (non-Hispanic) and enrolled or expecting to enroll at an institution or university. Applicant must have 2.5 GPA or higher.

Application Requirements: Application, financial need analysis, FAFSA, SAR. *Deadline:* varies.

Contact: Program Services Department
United Negro College Fund
8260 Willow Oaks Corporate Drive
Fairfax, VA 22031

UNITED WAY OF NEW ORLEANS EMERGENCY ASSISTANCE FUND

Award providing emergency assistance for students at Dillard University and Xavier University in Louisiana.

Award: Scholarship for use in freshman, sophomore, junior, or senior years; renewable. *Number:* varies. *Amount:* up to $2500.

Eligibility Requirements: Applicant must be Black (non-Hispanic); enrolled or expecting to enroll at an institution or university and studying in Louisiana. Applicant must have 2.5 GPA or higher.

Application Requirements: Application, financial need analysis, FAFSA, SAR. *Deadline:* varies.

Contact: Program Services Department
United Negro College Fund
8260 Willow Oaks Corporate Drive
Fairfax, VA 22031

UNITED WAY OF WESTCHESTER AND PUTNAM, INC./ UNCF EMERGENCY ASSISTANCE FUND

Award providing emergency assistance for students from the Westchester/ Putnam, NY area. A 2.5 GPA is required if attending a UNCF school, or 2.0 if attending Mercy College or Westchester Community College. Students are only eligible to receive emergency assistance for two consecutive semesters. Please visit Web site for more information: http://www.uncf.org.

Award: Scholarship for use in freshman, sophomore, junior, or senior years; not renewable. *Number:* varies. *Amount:* up to $5000.

Eligibility Requirements: Applicant must be Black (non-Hispanic) or Hispanic; enrolled or expecting to enroll full or part-time at an institution or university; resident of New York and studying in New York.

Application Requirements: Application, financial need analysis, FAFSA, SAR. *Deadline:* August 31.

Contact: Program Services Department
United Negro College Fund
8260 Willow Oaks Corporate Drive
Fairfax, VA 22031

US WEST FOUNDATION SCHOLARSHIP

Scholarships for students from Washington, Oregon, Colorado, Iowa, Minnesota, Nebraska, and Arizona. Minimum 2.5 GPA required. Prospective applicants should complete the Student Profile found at Web site: http://www.uncf.org.

Award: Scholarship for use in freshman, sophomore, junior, or senior years; not renewable.

Eligibility Requirements: Applicant must be Black (non-Hispanic); enrolled or expecting to enroll at a four-year institution or university and resident of Arizona, Colorado, Iowa, Minnesota, Nebraska, Oregon, or Washington. Applicant must have 2.5 GPA or higher. Available to U.S. citizens.

Application Requirements: Application, financial need analysis. *Deadline:* Continuous.

Contact: Program Services Department
United Negro College Fund
8260 Willow Oaks Corporate Drive
Fairfax, VA 22031

V103/UNCF EMERGENCY ASSISTANCE SCHOLARSHIP FUND

Scholarship available to students attending one of the following UNCF member colleges or universities: Clark Atlanta, Interdenominational Center, Morehouse, Morris Brown, or Spelman. Minimum 2.5 GPA required. Prospective applicants should complete the Student Profile found at Web site: http://www.uncf.org.

Award: Scholarship for use in senior year; not renewable. *Amount:* up to $2500.

Eligibility Requirements: Applicant must be Black (non-Hispanic) and enrolled or expecting to enroll at a four-year institution or university. Applicant must have 2.5 GPA or higher.

Application Requirements: Application, financial need analysis. *Deadline:* Continuous.

Contact: Program Services Department
United Negro College Fund
8260 Willow Oaks Corporate Drive
Fairfax, VA 22031

VERIZON FOUNDATION SCHOLARSHIP

Scholarship for residents of the Verizon service area (Northeastern states) attending a UNCF member college or university, or Ohio State University. Minimum 2.5 GPA required. Prospective applicants should complete the Student Profile found at Web site: http://www.uncf.org.

Award: Scholarship for use in freshman, sophomore, junior, or senior years; not renewable. *Amount:* $2000–$4000.

Eligibility Requirements: Applicant must be Black (non-Hispanic); enrolled or expecting to enroll at a four-year institution or university and resident of New Jersey, New York, or Pennsylvania. Applicant must have 2.5 GPA or higher.

Application Requirements: Application, financial need analysis. *Deadline:* varies.

Contact: Program Services Department
United Negro College Fund
8260 Willow Oaks Corporate Drive
Fairfax, VA 22031

WENDELL SCOTT, SR./NASCAR SCHOLARSHIP

Award for full-time junior or senior undergraduates or part-time graduate students. Undergraduates must have a 3.0 GPA and graduate students must

United Negro College Fund (continued)

have a 3.2 GPA. Undergraduates receive an award of $1500. Graduate recipients receive $2000. Please visit Web site for more information: http://www.uncf.org.

Award: Scholarship for use in junior, senior, or graduate years; renewable. *Amount:* $1500–$2000.

Eligibility Requirements: Applicant must be Black (non-Hispanic) and enrolled or expecting to enroll full or part-time at an institution or university. Applicant must have 3.0 GPA or higher.

Application Requirements: Application, financial need analysis, photo, resume, references, transcript, FAFSA, SAR. *Deadline:* March 22.

Contact: William Dunham, Wendell Scott Sr./NASCAR Scholarship
United Negro College Fund
8260 Willow Oaks Corporate Drive, PO Box 10444
Fairfax, VA 22031

WESTERN ASSOCIATION OF LADIES SCHOLARSHIP

Award for a student from Philadelphia County, PA. Must have 2.5 GPA. Please visit Web site for more information: http://www.uncf.org.

Award: Scholarship for use in freshman, sophomore, junior, or senior years; renewable. *Number:* 1. *Amount:* up to $5000.

Eligibility Requirements: Applicant must be Black (non-Hispanic); enrolled or expecting to enroll at an institution or university and resident of Pennsylvania. Applicant must have 2.5 GPA or higher.

Application Requirements: Application, financial need analysis, FAFSA, SAR. *Deadline:* varies.

Contact: Program Services Department
United Negro College Fund
8260 Willow Oaks Corporate Drive
Fairfax, VA 22031

WHIRLPOOL FOUNDATION SCHOLARSHIP

Renewable award for students participating in Whirlpool's INROADS program in LaPorte, IN; Benton Harbor, MI; and LaVerne, TN. Must have 3.0 GPA. Please visit Web site for more information: http://www.uncf.org.

Award: Scholarship for use in freshman, sophomore, junior, or senior years; renewable. *Number:* varies. *Amount:* $2500.

Eligibility Requirements: Applicant must be Black (non-Hispanic); enrolled or expecting to enroll at an institution or university and resident of Indiana, Michigan, or Tennessee. Applicant must have 3.0 GPA or higher.

Application Requirements: Application, financial need analysis, FAFSA, SAR. *Deadline:* varies.

Contact: Program Services Department
United Negro College Fund
8260 Willow Oaks Corporate Drive
Fairfax, VA 22031

WILMA WARBURG SCHOLARSHIP

Need-based scholarships for students attending a specific UNCF member college or university (Clark Atlanta, Morehouse, Morris Brown, Spelman, ITC) who are pursuing careers in the health fields or majoring in the sciences. Minimum 2.5 GPA required. Prospective applicants should complete the Student Profile found at Web site: http://www.uncf.org.

Award: Scholarship for use in freshman, sophomore, junior, or senior years; not renewable.

Eligibility Requirements: Applicant must be Black (non-Hispanic) and enrolled or expecting to enroll at a four-year institution or university. Applicant must have 2.5 GPA or higher.

Application Requirements: Application, financial need analysis. *Deadline:* Continuous.

Contact: Program Services Department
United Negro College Fund
8260 Willow Oaks Corporate Drive
Fairfax, VA 22031

WISCONSIN STUDENT AID

Award for African-American Wisconsin residents. Must have 2.5 GPA. Please visit Web site for more information: http://www.uncf.org.

Award: Scholarship for use in freshman, sophomore, junior, or senior years; renewable. *Number:* varies. *Amount:* up to $2500.

Eligibility Requirements: Applicant must be Black (non-Hispanic); enrolled or expecting to enroll at an institution or university and resident of Wisconsin. Applicant must have 2.5 GPA or higher.

Application Requirements: Application, financial need analysis, FAFSA, SAR. *Deadline:* varies.

Contact: Program Services Department
United Negro College Fund
8260 Willow Oaks Corporate Drive
Fairfax, VA 22031

WOODMEN OF THE WORLD/OMAHA WOODMEN INSURANCE SOCIETY SCHOLARSHIP

Award for recipients or the relatives of recipients of the class action suit that resulted in the creation of this award. GPA has to be whatever is designated at your institution as satisfactory. Please visit Web site for more information: http://www.uncf.org.

Award: Scholarship for use in freshman, sophomore, junior, or senior years; renewable. *Number:* varies. *Amount:* up to $3000.

Eligibility Requirements: Applicant must be Black (non-Hispanic) and enrolled or expecting to enroll at an institution or university.

Application Requirements: Application, financial need analysis, FAFSA, SAR. *Deadline:* varies.

Contact: Program Services Department
United Negro College Fund
8260 Willow Oaks Corporate Drive
Fairfax, VA 22031

UNITED SOUTH AND EASTERN TRIBES, INC. **http://www.usetinc.org**

UNITED SOUTH AND EASTERN TRIBES SCHOLARSHIP FUND

One-time award for American-Indian students who are members of a United South and Eastern Tribes member tribe. Submit college acceptance letter per proof of enrollment, certificate of tribal affiliation, letter stating intended use of award, application, transcript if available, financial need analysis, and essay.

Award: Scholarship for use in freshman, sophomore, junior, senior, graduate, or postgraduate years; not renewable. *Number:* 4–8. *Amount:* $500–$750.

Eligibility Requirements: Applicant must be American Indian/Alaska Native and enrolled or expecting to enroll full or part-time at a two-year or four-year or technical institution or university. Available to U.S. and Canadian citizens.

Application Requirements: Application, essay, financial need analysis, transcript, proof of tribal enrollment. *Deadline:* April 30.

Contact: Scholarship Coordinator
United South and Eastern Tribes, Inc.
711 Stewarts Ferry Pike, Suite 100
Nashville, TN 37214-2634
Phone: 615-872-7900
Fax: 615-872-7417

WASHINGTON HIGHER EDUCATION COORDINATING BOARD **http://www.hecb.wa.gov**

AMERICAN INDIAN ENDOWED SCHOLARSHIP

Awarded to financially needy undergraduate and graduate students with close social and cultural ties to a Native-American community. Must be Washington resident, enrolled full time at Washington School. Deadline is May 15.

Award: Scholarship for use in freshman, sophomore, junior, senior, or graduate years; renewable. *Number:* up to 15. *Amount:* $1000–$2000.

Eligibility Requirements: Applicant must be American Indian/Alaska Native; enrolled or expecting to enroll full-time at a two-year or four-year or technical institution or university; resident of Washington and studying in Washington. Available to U.S. citizens.

Application Requirements: Application, financial need analysis. *Deadline:* May 15.

Contact: Ann Lee
Washington Higher Education Coordinating Board
917 Lakeridge Way SW, PO Box 43430
Olympia, WA 98504-3430
Phone: 360-755-7843
Fax: 360-753-7808
E-mail: annl@hecb.wa.gov

WELSH SOCIETY OF PHILADELPHIA

CYMDEITHAS GYMREIG/PHILADELPHIA SCHOLARSHIP

Awards for undergraduate students of Welsh descent. Must participate in or be members of Welsh organizations or events, which should be evident in applicant's essay. Proof of Welsh heritage required. Must live or attend college within 150 miles of Philadelphia. Minimum 3.0 GPA required. Mandatory meeting held in November.

Award: Scholarship for use in freshman, sophomore, junior, or senior years; not renewable. *Number:* 5–7. *Amount:* $1000.

Eligibility Requirements: Applicant must be Protestant; of Welsh heritage; enrolled or expecting to enroll full-time at a two-year or four-year institution or university and must have an interest in designated field specified by sponsor. Applicant must have 3.0 GPA or higher. Available to U.S. citizens.

Application Requirements: Application, autobiography, essay, references, self-addressed stamped envelope, test scores, transcript. *Deadline:* March 1.

Contact: Chairman, Scholarship Committee
Welsh Society of Philadelphia
Hen Dy Hapus, 367 South River Street
Wilkes-Barre, PA 18702-3813
E-mail: cymro_w18702@juno.com

WHITE EARTH TRIBAL COUNCIL

WHITE EARTH SCHOLARSHIP PROGRAM

Renewable scholarship of at least $3000 awarded to Native-American Indian students. Must be enrolled member of the White Earth Band of Ojibwa. Financial need is considered. To be used for any undergraduate or graduate year of a trade/technical institution, two- or four-year college or university. Minimum 2.5 GPA required. Deadline is May 31.

Award: Scholarship for use in freshman, sophomore, junior, senior, graduate, or postgraduate years; renewable. *Number:* 200. *Amount:* $3000.

Eligibility Requirements: Applicant must be American Indian/Alaska Native and enrolled or expecting to enroll full or part-time at a two-year or four-year or technical institution or university. Applicant must have 2.5 GPA or higher. Available to U.S. citizens.

Application Requirements: Application, financial need analysis, transcript. *Deadline:* May 31.

Contact: Leslie Nessman, Scholarship Manager
White Earth Tribal Council
PO Box 418
White Earth, MN 56591-0418
Phone: 218-983-3285 Ext. 1227
Fax: 218-983-4299

WISCONSIN HIGHER EDUCATIONAL AIDS BOARD http://heab.state.wi.us

MINORITY RETENTION GRANT-WISCONSIN

Provides financial assistance to African-American, Native-American, Hispanic, and former citizens of Laos, Vietnam, and Cambodia, for study in Wisconsin. Must be Wisconsin resident, enrolled at least half-time in a two-year or four-year nonprofit college, and must show financial need. Please refer to Web site for further details: http://heab.state.wi.us

Award: Grant for use in sophomore, junior, senior, or graduate years; not renewable. *Number:* varies. *Amount:* $250–$2500.

Eligibility Requirements: Applicant must be American Indian/Alaska Native, Asian/Pacific Islander, Black (non-Hispanic), or Hispanic; enrolled or expecting to enroll full or part-time at a two-year or four-year or technical institution; resident of Wisconsin and studying in Wisconsin. Available to U.S. and non-U.S. citizens.

Application Requirements: Application, financial need analysis. *Deadline:* Continuous.

Contact: Mary Lou Kuzdas, Program Coordinator
Wisconsin Higher Educational Aids Board
PO Box 7885
Madison, WI 53707-7885
Phone: 608-267-2212
Fax: 608-267-2808
E-mail: mary.kuzdas@heab.state.wi.us

WISCONSIN NATIVE AMERICAN STUDENT GRANT

Grants for Wisconsin residents who are at least one-quarter American-Indian. Must be attending a college or university within the state. Please refer to Web site for further details: http://www.heab.state.wi.us

Award: Grant for use in freshman, sophomore, junior, senior, graduate, or postgraduate years; not renewable. *Number:* varies. *Amount:* $250–$1100.

Eligibility Requirements: Applicant must be American Indian/Alaska Native; enrolled or expecting to enroll full or part-time at a two-year or four-year or technical institution or university; resident of Wisconsin and studying in Wisconsin. Available to U.S. citizens.

Application Requirements: Application, financial need analysis. *Deadline:* Continuous.

Contact: Sandra Thomas, Program Coordinator
Wisconsin Higher Educational Aids Board
PO Box 7885
Madison, WI 53707-7885
Phone: 608-266-0888
Fax: 608-267-2808
E-mail: sandy.thomas@heab.state.wi.us

WOMEN OF THE EVANGELICAL LUTHERAN CHURCH IN AMERICA http://www.elca.org/wo

AMELIA KEMP SCHOLARSHIP

Scholarships provided for ELCA women who are of an ethnic minority in undergraduate, graduate, professional, or vocational courses of study. Must be at least 21 years old and hold membership in the ELCA. Must have experienced an interruption in education of two or more years since the completion of high school. For more details see Web site: http://www.elca.org/wo.

Award: Scholarship for use in freshman, sophomore, junior, senior, or graduate years; not renewable. *Number:* 1. *Amount:* up to $1200.

Eligibility Requirements: Applicant must be Lutheran; American Indian/Alaska Native, Asian/Pacific Islander, Black (non-Hispanic), or Hispanic; age 21; enrolled or expecting to enroll full or part-time at a two-year or four-year or technical institution or university and female. Available to U.S. citizens.

Application Requirements: *Deadline:* February 15.

Contact: Application available at Web site.

WORLDSTUDIO FOUNDATION http://www.worldstudio.org

SPECIAL ANIMATION AND ILLUSTRATION SCHOLARSHIP

Scholarships are for minority and economically disadvantaged students who are studying illustration, cartooning, and animation in American colleges and universities. Scholarship recipients are selected not only for their ability and their need, but also for their demonstrated commitment to giving back to the larger community through their work.

Award: Scholarship for use in freshman, sophomore, junior, senior, or graduate years; not renewable. *Number:* 25. *Amount:* $1500.

Eligibility Requirements: Applicant must be American Indian/Alaska Native, Asian/Pacific Islander, Black (non-Hispanic), or Hispanic and enrolled or expecting to enroll full-time at a two-year or four-year or technical institution or university. Applicant must have 2.5 GPA or higher. Available to U.S. and non-U.S. citizens.

Worldstudio Foundation (continued)

Application Requirements: Application, essay, financial need analysis, photo, portfolio, references, self-addressed stamped envelope, transcript. *Deadline:* March 19.

Contact: Scholarship Coordinator
Worldstudio Foundation
200 Varick Street, 5th Floor
New York, NY 10014
Phone: 212-366-1317 Ext. 18
Fax: 212-807-0024
E-mail: scholarships@worldstudio.org

YAKAMA NATION

YAKAMA NATION SCHOLARSHIP PROGRAM

Scholarship is for enrolled Yakama tribal members studying for a college degree (non-vocational) at an accredited two-year or four-year college institution. Applicant must be member of Yakama Nation.

Award: Scholarship for use in freshman, sophomore, junior, senior, or graduate years; renewable. *Number:* 150–180. *Amount:* $2000.

Eligibility Requirements: Applicant must be American Indian/Alaska Native and enrolled or expecting to enroll full or part-time at a two-year or four-year institution or university. Available to U.S. citizens.

Application Requirements: Application, financial need analysis, transcript. *Deadline:* July 1.

Contact: Program Manager
Yakama Nation
PO Box 151
Toppenish, WA 98948

YOUTH OPPORTUNITIES FOUNDATION

YOUTH OPPORTUNITIES FOUNDATION SCHOLARSHIPS

Scholarships for Hispanic/Latino high school students that rank in the top 10% of their class and score at least 1000 on the SATs. AP classes, leadership skills and community activities will be weighed toward consideration. Must be California resident. At least one parent must be of Hispanic descent. Students must write foundation for an application.

Award: Scholarship for use in freshman year; not renewable. *Number:* 100. *Amount:* $100–$500.

Eligibility Requirements: Applicant must be Hispanic; high school student; planning to enroll or expecting to enroll full-time at a two-year or four-year institution or university; resident of California and must have an interest in leadership.

Application Requirements: Application, test scores. *Deadline:* March 15.

Contact: Youth Opportunities Foundation
8820 South Sepulveda Boulevard, Suite 208
PO Box 45762
Los Angeles, CA 90045

RELIGIOUS AFFILIATION

AMERICAN BAPTIST FINANCIAL AID PROGRAM http://www.abc-usa.org

AMERICAN BAPTIST FINANCIAL AID PROGRAM NATIVE AMERICAN GRANTS

• *See page 576*

AMERICAN BAPTIST SCHOLARSHIPS

One-time award for undergraduates who are members of American Baptist Church. Must be attending an accredited college or university in the United States or Puerto Rico. If attending an ABC-related school, the scholarship amount is $2,000 for the year. If not ABC-related, the amount is $1,000. Deadline: May 31. Minimum GPA of 2.75 required.

Award: Scholarship for use in freshman, sophomore, junior, or senior years; not renewable. *Number:* varies. *Amount:* $1000–$2000.

Eligibility Requirements: Applicant must be Baptist and enrolled or expecting to enroll full-time at a four-year institution or university. Available to U.S. citizens.

Application Requirements: Application, financial need analysis, references. *Deadline:* May 31.

Contact: Mrs. Lynne Eckman, Director of Financial Aid
American Baptist Financial Aid Program
PO Box 851
Valley Forge, PA 19482-0851
Phone: 610-768-2067
Fax: 610-768-2056
E-mail: lynne.eckman@abc-usa.org

AMERICAN SEPHARDI FOUNDATION http://www.asfonline.org

BROOME AND ALLEN BOYS CAMP AND SCHOLARSHIP FUND

Scholarship of up to $2000 given to Jewish undergraduate and graduate students, or anyone studying Sephardic. Enclose copy of tax returns with application. Deadline is May 15.

Award: Scholarship for use in freshman, sophomore, junior, senior, graduate, or postgraduate years; not renewable. *Number:* 25. *Amount:* $500–$2000.

Eligibility Requirements: Applicant must be Jewish and enrolled or expecting to enroll full or part-time at a two-year or four-year or technical institution or university. Available to U.S. and non-U.S. citizens.

Application Requirements: Application, essay, financial need analysis, references, transcript, copy of tax returns. *Deadline:* May 15.

Contact: Jesse Mintz-Roth, Special Projects Coordinator
American Sephardi Foundation
15 West 16th Street
New York, NY 10011
Phone: 212-294-8350 Ext. 9
Fax: 212-294-8348
E-mail: asf@cjh.org

BANK OF AMERICA

WILLIAM HEATH EDUCATION SCHOLARSHIP FOR MINISTERS, PRIESTS AND MISSIONARIES

• *See page 413*

CATHOLIC AID ASSOCIATION http://www.catholicaid.com

CATHOLIC AID ASSOCIATION COLLEGE TUITION SCHOLARSHIP

Applicants must have been a Catholic Aid Association member for at least two years. $300 scholarships for state and non-Catholic institutions, $500 for Catholic Colleges and Universities. Must be a member of the Catholic Aid Association. Application deadline is in February.

Award: Scholarship for use in freshman or sophomore years; not renewable. *Number:* 200. *Amount:* $300–$500.

Eligibility Requirements: Applicant must be Roman Catholic and enrolled or expecting to enroll full-time at a two-year or four-year institution or university. Available to U.S. citizens.

Application Requirements: Application, essay, references, transcript. *Deadline:* varies.

Contact: Jessica Schadt, Administrative Assistant
Catholic Aid Association
3499 North Lexington Avenue
St. Paul, MN 55126-8098
Phone: 651-490-0170
Fax: 651-490-0746
E-mail: jschadt@catholicaid.com

CATHOLIC KOLPING SOCIETY OF AMERICA http://www.kolping.org/scholar.htm

FATHER KREWITT SCHOLARSHIP

• *See page 457*

CATHOLIC WORKMAN http://www.catholicworkman.org

CATHOLIC WORKMAN COLLEGE SCHOLARSHIPS

• *See page 457*

COMMUNITY FOUNDATION OF WESTERN MASSACHUSETTS http://www.communityfoundation.org

DONALD A. AND DOROTHY F. AXTELL GRANT SCHOLARSHIP

For financially needy students of the Protestant faith from Hampshire County to obtain a college education.

Award: Scholarship for use in freshman, sophomore, junior, or senior years; not renewable. *Number:* 1. *Amount:* $1500.

Eligibility Requirements: Applicant must be Protestant; enrolled or expecting to enroll full or part-time at a two-year or four-year institution or university and resident of Massachusetts. Available to U.S. citizens.

Application Requirements: Application, financial need analysis, transcript. *Deadline:* March 31.

Contact: Community Foundation of Western Massachusetts
1500 Main Street
PO Box 15769
Springfield, MA 01115

KIMBER RICHTER FAMILY SCHOLARSHIP

Scholarship is given to a student of the Baha'i faith who attends or plans to attend college. For more information or application visit http://www.communityfoundation.org.

Award: Scholarship for use in freshman, sophomore, junior, or senior years; not renewable. *Number:* 1. *Amount:* $700.

Eligibility Requirements: Applicant must be Baha'i faith; enrolled or expecting to enroll full or part-time at a four-year institution and resident of Massachusetts. Available to U.S. citizens.

Application Requirements: Application, financial need analysis, transcript. *Deadline:* March 31.

Contact: Community Foundation of Western Massachusetts
1500 Main Street
PO Box 15769
Springfield, MA 01115

EASTERN ORTHODOX COMMITTEE ON SCOUTING http://www.eocs.org

EASTERN ORTHODOX COMMITTEE ON SCOUTING SCHOLARSHIPS

• *See page 459*

FADEL EDUCATIONAL FOUNDATION, INC. http://fadelfoundation.org

ANNUAL AWARD PROGRAM

Grants awarded on the basis of merit, financial need, and the potential of an applicant to positively impact Muslims' lives in the United States.

Award: Grant for use in freshman, sophomore, junior, senior, graduate, or postgraduate years; not renewable. *Number:* 20–45. *Amount:* $400–$2000.

Eligibility Requirements: Applicant must be Muslim faith and enrolled or expecting to enroll full or part-time at a two-year or four-year or technical institution or university. Available to U.S. citizens.

Application Requirements: Application, essay, financial need analysis, references, test scores, transcript. *Deadline:* March 23.

Contact: Ayman Hossam Fadel, Secretary
Fadel Educational Foundation, Inc.
PO Box 20147
Indianapolis, IN 46220
Fax: 866-705-9495
E-mail: afadel@bww.com

FIRST CATHOLIC SLOVAK LADIES ASSOCIATION http://www.fcsla.com

FIRST CATHOLIC SLOVAK LADIES ASSOCIATION FRATERNAL SCHOLARSHIP AWARD FOR COLLEGE AND GRADUATE STUDY

• *See page 583*

GENERAL BOARD OF GLOBAL MINISTRIES http://www.gbgm-umc.org

NATIONAL LEADERSHIP DEVELOPMENT GRANTS

• *See page 584*

HAROLD B. & DOROTHY A. SNYDER FOUNDATION, INC.

HAROLD B. AND DOROTHY A. SNYDER FOUNDATION, INC., PROGRAM

• *See page 141*

HERMAN OSCAR SCHUMACHER SCHOLARSHIP FUND

HERMAN OSCAR SCHUMACHER SCHOLARSHIP FUND FOR MEN

Up to 70 $500 scholarships will be awarded to male residents of Spokane County, WA. Preference will be given to orphans and the financially needy. Must provide proof of enrollment in a trade/technical school or college and that at least one year has been completed.

Award: Scholarship for use in sophomore, junior, senior, or graduate years; renewable. *Number:* 40–70. *Amount:* $500.

Eligibility Requirements: Applicant must be Christian; enrolled or expecting to enroll full-time at a two-year or four-year or technical institution or university; male and resident of Washington. Available to U.S. citizens.

Application Requirements: Application, transcript, proof of enrollment. *Deadline:* October 1.

Contact: Chad Legate, Assistant Vice President and Relationship Manager
Herman Oscar Schumacher Scholarship Fund
Washington Trust Bank, Trust Department
PO Box 2127
Spokane, WA 99210
Phone: 509-353-3881
Fax: 509-353-2278
E-mail: clegate@watrust.com

ITALIAN CATHOLIC FEDERATION, INC. http://www.icf.org

ICF COLLEGE SCHOLARSHIPS TO HIGH SCHOOL SENIORS

• *See page 590*

JEWISH FAMILY AND CHILDREN'S SERVICES http://www.jfcs.org

ANNA AND CHARLES STOCKWITZ CHILDREN AND YOUTH FUND

Must be Jewish resident of San Francisco, San Mateo, northern Santa Clara, Marin, or Sonoma county. Award to assist children and teens with education, social, or psychological experience, or to assist them in attending undergraduate school. For more details and an application see Web site: http://www.jfcs.org.

Award: Grant for use in freshman, sophomore, junior, or senior years; not renewable. *Number:* varies. *Amount:* up to $2000.

Eligibility Requirements: Applicant must be Jewish; enrolled or expecting to enroll at a two-year or four-year or technical institution or university and resident of California.

Application Requirements: Application, financial need analysis, transcript. *Deadline:* September 1.

Contact: Eric Singer, Director, Financial Aid Center
Jewish Family and Children's Services
2150 Post Street
San Francisco, CA 94115
Phone: 415-449-1226
E-mail: erics@jfcs.org

BUTRIMOVITZ FAMILY ENDOWMENT FUND FOR JEWISH EDUCATION

Must be Jewish resident of San Francisco, San Mateo, Marin, or Sonoma county. Scholarships for individuals in need who wish to pursue traditional

Jewish Family and Children's Services (continued)

Jewish education in context of a Jewish day school, undergraduate, or graduate school setting. For more details and an application see Web site: http://www.jfcs.org.

Award: Scholarship for use in freshman, sophomore, junior, senior, or graduate years; not renewable. *Number:* 2–4. *Amount:* up to $500.

Eligibility Requirements: Applicant must be Jewish; age 13-17; enrolled or expecting to enroll at an institution or university and resident of California.

Application Requirements: Application, financial need analysis, transcript. *Deadline:* Continuous.

Contact: Eric Singer, Director, Financial Aid Center
Jewish Family and Children's Services
2150 Post Street
San Francisco, CA 94115
Phone: 415-449-1226
E-mail: erics@jfcs.org

HENRY AND TILDA SHULER SCHOLARSHIP FUND FOR YOUNG PEOPLE

Must be Jewish resident of San Francisco, San Mateo, northern Santa Clara, Marin, or Sonoma county. Provides scholarships for youths for vocational training, college education, or other studies. For more details and an application see Web site: http://www.jfcs.org.

Award: Scholarship for use in freshman, sophomore, junior, or senior years; not renewable. *Number:* 2–3. *Amount:* up to $950.

Eligibility Requirements: Applicant must be Jewish; age 26 or under; enrolled or expecting to enroll at a two-year or four-year or technical institution or university and resident of California.

Application Requirements: Application, financial need analysis, references. *Deadline:* Continuous.

Contact: Eric Singer, Director, Financial Aid Center
Jewish Family and Children's Services
2150 Post Street
San Francisco, CA 94115
Phone: 415-449-1226
E-mail: erics@jfcs.org

JACOB RASSEN MEMORIAL SCHOLARSHIP

Scholarships available to Jewish youth under the age of 23 for the purpose of a study trip in Israel. Applicants must demonstrate financial need. For more details see Web site: http://www.jfcs.org. Must be resident of San Francisco, San Mateo, northern Santa Clara, Marin, or Sonoma county.

Award: Scholarship for use in freshman, sophomore, junior, or senior years; not renewable. *Number:* 4. *Amount:* up to $1500.

Eligibility Requirements: Applicant must be Jewish; age 22 or under; enrolled or expecting to enroll at a four-year institution or university and resident of California. Available to U.S. citizens.

Application Requirements: Application, transcript. *Deadline:* Continuous.

Contact: Eric Singer, Director, Financial Aid Center
Jewish Family and Children's Services
2150 Post Street
San Francisco, CA 94115
Phone: 415-449-1226
E-mail: erics@jfcs.org

MIRIAM S. GRUNFIELD SCHOLARSHIP FUND

Must be Jewish resident of San Francisco, San Mateo, northern Santa Clara, Marin, or Sonoma county. Annual grants to educate young people who otherwise would not be able to fulfill their educational aspirations. For more information and an application see Web site: http://www.jfcs.org.

Award: Scholarship for use in freshman, sophomore, junior, or senior years; not renewable. *Number:* 4–6. *Amount:* up to $950.

Eligibility Requirements: Applicant must be Jewish; age 26 or under; enrolled or expecting to enroll at an institution or university and resident of California.

Application Requirements: Application, financial need analysis, transcript. *Deadline:* Continuous.

Contact: Eric Singer, Director, Financial Aid Center
Jewish Family and Children's Services
2150 Post Street
San Francisco, CA 94115
Phone: 415-449-1226
E-mail: erics@jfcs.org

VIVIENNE CAMP COLLEGE SCHOLARSHIP FUND

Must be Jewish resident of San Francisco, San Mateo, northern Santa Clara, Marin, or Sonoma county. Scholarships to two young Jewish men and two young Jewish women attending a California institution who demonstrate academic achievement, promise, and financial need. For more details and an application see Web site: http://www.jfcs.org.

Award: Scholarship for use in freshman, sophomore, junior, or senior years; not renewable. *Number:* 4. *Amount:* $4000.

Eligibility Requirements: Applicant must be Jewish; enrolled or expecting to enroll at an institution or university; resident of California and studying in California.

Application Requirements: Application, financial need analysis, transcript. *Deadline:* September 1.

Contact: Eric Singer, Director, Financial Aid Center
Jewish Family and Children's Services
2150 Post Street
San Francisco, CA 94115
Phone: 415-449-1226
E-mail: erics@jfcs.org

JEWISH FOUNDATION FOR EDUCATION OF WOMEN

http://www.jfew.org

BILLER/JEWISH FOUNDATION FOR EDUCATION OF WOMEN

This program provides scholarships to female Jewish permanent residents in the NY metropolitan area for undergraduate and graduate study. Financial need and reasonableness of course of study are the primary criteria. Must study full-time in NY. Check Web site for further details: http://www.jfew.org.

Award: Scholarship for use in freshman, sophomore, junior, senior, or graduate years; not renewable. *Number:* varies. *Amount:* $2000–$4000.

Eligibility Requirements: Applicant must be Jewish; enrolled or expecting to enroll full-time at a two-year or four-year or technical institution or university; female; resident of New York and studying in New York. Available to U.S. and non-Canadian citizens.

Application Requirements: Application, essay, financial need analysis. *Deadline:* varies.

Contact: Marge Goldwater, Executive Director
Jewish Foundation for Education of Women
135 East 64th Street
New York, NY 10021
Phone: 212-288-3931
Fax: 212-288-5798
E-mail: fdnscholar@aol.com

JEWISH SOCIAL SERVICE AGENCY OF METROPOLITAN WASHINGTON

http://www.jssa.org

DAVID KORN SCHOLARSHIP FUND

One-time award available to full-time undergraduate or graduate student accepted into an accredited program. Must be Jewish, under the age of 30, and a resident of the Washington metropolitan area. Must be a U.S. citizen or working towards citizenship. Decision is based primarily on financial need.

Award: Scholarship for use in freshman, sophomore, junior, senior, or graduate years; not renewable. *Number:* 2–3. *Amount:* $1000–$2000.

Eligibility Requirements: Applicant must be Jewish; age 29 or under; enrolled or expecting to enroll full-time at a four-year institution or university and resident of District of Columbia, Maryland, or Virginia. Available to U.S. citizens.

Application Requirements: Application, financial need analysis, college admission letter. *Deadline:* February 28.

Contact: Lynn Ponton, Scholarship and Loan Coordinator
Jewish Social Service Agency of Metropolitan Washington
6123 Montrose Road
Rockville, MD 20852
Phone: 301-881-3700 Ext. 611

JEWISH SOCIAL SERVICE AGENCY OF METROPOLITAN WASHINGTON MAX AND EMMY DREYFUSS UNDERGRADUATE SCHOLARSHIP FUND

One-time award given to a full-time Jewish student, no older than 30, from the metropolitan Washington, D.C. area. Primarily based on financial need. Student must be entering or already enrolled in an accredited four-year undergraduate degree program. Special consideration given to refugees. Recipients are required to complete a questionnaire describing their educational experience. Student must be U.S. citizen or working towards citizenship.

Award: Scholarship for use in freshman, sophomore, junior, or senior years; not renewable. *Number:* 8–10. *Amount:* $1500–$2000.

Eligibility Requirements: Applicant must be Jewish; age 30 or under; enrolled or expecting to enroll full-time at a four-year institution or university and resident of District of Columbia, Maryland, or Virginia. Available to U.S. citizens.

Application Requirements: Application, financial need analysis, references, transcript. *Deadline:* March 1.

Contact: Lynn Ponton, Scholarship and Loan Coordinator
Jewish Social Service Agency of Metropolitan Washington
6123 Montrose Road
Rockville, MD 20852
Phone: 301-881-3700 Ext. 616

MORTON A. GIBSON MEMORIAL SCHOLARSHIP

Awarded to high school seniors who have completed significant volunteer services within the local Jewish community. Must be a Jewish resident of the greater Washington metropolitan area. Must be a U.S. citizen or working towards citizenship. Must be accepted into an accredited four-year undergraduate program on a full-time basis.

Award: Scholarship for use in freshman, sophomore, junior, or senior years; not renewable. *Number:* 2. *Amount:* $2500.

Eligibility Requirements: Applicant must be Jewish; high school student; planning to enroll or expecting to enroll full-time at a four-year institution and resident of District of Columbia, Maryland, or Virginia. Available to U.S. citizens.

Application Requirements: Application, essay, financial need analysis, references, college admission letter. *Deadline:* February 28.

Contact: Lynn Ponton, Scholarship and Loan Coordinator
Jewish Social Service Agency of Metropolitan Washington
6123 Montrose Road
Rockville, MD 20852
Phone: 301-881-3700 Ext. 611

JVS JEWISH COMMUNITY SCHOLARSHIP FUND http://www.jvsla.org

JVS JEWISH COMMUNITY SCHOLARSHIP

Educational support award for Jewish residents of L.A. County who can verify financial need.

Award: Scholarship for use in freshman, sophomore, junior, senior, graduate, or postgraduate years; renewable. *Number:* varies. *Amount:* $500–$6000.

Eligibility Requirements: Applicant must be Jewish; enrolled or expecting to enroll full-time at a two-year or four-year or technical institution or university and resident of California. Applicant must have 2.5 GPA or higher. Available to U.S. citizens.

Application Requirements: Application, essay, financial need analysis, interview, references, transcript, Student Aid Report (SAR). *Deadline:* April 15.

Contact: Arlene Hisaker, Scholarship Administrator
JVS Jewish Community Scholarship Fund
6505 Wilshire Boulevard, Suite 200
Los Angeles, CA 90048
Phone: 323-761-8888
Fax: 323-761-8575
E-mail: jgaynor@jvsla.org

KNIGHTS OF COLUMBUS

FOURTH DEGREE PRO DEO AND PRO PATRIA (CANADA)

• *See page 467*

FOURTH DEGREE PRO DEO AND PRO PATRIA SCHOLARSHIPS

• *See page 467*

FRANCIS P. MATTHEWS AND JOHN E. SWIFT EDUCATIONAL TRUST SCHOLARSHIPS

• *See page 467*

JOHN W. MC DEVITT (FOURTH DEGREE) SCHOLARSHIPS

• *See page 467*

PERCY J. JOHNSON ENDOWED SCHOLARSHIPS

• *See page 467*

KNIGHTS OF LITHUANIA http://www.knightsoflithuania.com

KNIGHTS OF LITHUANIA NATIONAL SCHOLARSHIPS

• *See page 467*

MELLON NEW ENGLAND

HENRY FRANCIS BARROWS SCHOLARSHIP

Award for Protestant males only. Must be a resident of Massachusetts and applying to a non-Catholic U.S. institution of higher learning. Application deadline is April 15.

Award: Scholarship for use in freshman, sophomore, junior, or senior years; not renewable. *Number:* varies. *Amount:* $500–$1000.

Eligibility Requirements: Applicant must be Protestant; enrolled or expecting to enroll full-time at a two-year or four-year or technical institution or university; male and resident of Massachusetts. Available to U.S. citizens.

Application Requirements: Application, essay, transcript. *Deadline:* April 15.

Contact: Sandra Brown-McMullen, Vice President
Mellon New England
One Boston Place, 024-0084
Boston, MA 02108
Phone: 617-722-3891

MORRIS J. AND BETTY KAPLUN FOUNDATION http://www.kaplun.org

MORRIS J. AND BETTY KAPLUN FOUNDATION ANNUAL ESSAY CONTEST

Essay contest awards winning written work from applicants in grades 7 through 12. Essays address specific questions related to Jewish faith. Please refer to Web site for further details: http://www.kaplun.org.

Award: Prize for use in freshman year; not renewable. *Number:* 12. *Amount:* $750–$1800.

Eligibility Requirements: Applicant must be Jewish; high school student and planning to enroll or expecting to enroll full-time at an institution or university. Available to U.S. and non-U.S. citizens.

Application Requirements: Applicant must enter a contest, essay. *Deadline:* March 15.

Contact: See Web site: www.kaplun.org.
Morris J. and Betty Kaplun Foundation
PO Box 234428
Great Neck, NY 11023

OSAGE SCHOLARSHIP FUND

MAE LASSLEY OSAGE SCHOLARSHIP FUND
• See page 598

TEXAS BLACK BAPTIST SCHOLARSHIP COMMITTEE http://www.bgct.org/aam

TEXAS BLACK BAPTIST SCHOLARSHIP
• See page 604

UNITED METHODIST CHURCH http://www.umc.org/

J. A. KNOWLES MEMORIAL SCHOLARSHIP

One-time award for Texas residents attending a United Methodist institution in Texas. Must have been United Methodist Church member for at least one year. Must be U.S. citizen or permanent resident. Minimum 2.5 GPA required.

Award: Scholarship for use in freshman, sophomore, junior, senior, or graduate years; not renewable. *Number:* 70–80. *Amount:* $800–$1200.

Eligibility Requirements: Applicant must be Methodist; enrolled or expecting to enroll full-time at a two-year or four-year institution or university; resident of Texas and studying in Texas. Applicant must have 2.5 GPA or higher. Available to U.S. citizens.

Application Requirements: Application, essay, references, transcript. *Deadline:* June 1.

Contact: Patti J. Zimmerman, Scholarships Administrator
United Methodist Church
PO Box 340007
Nashville, TN 37203-0007
Phone: 615-340-7344
E-mail: pzimmer@gbhem.org

PRISCILLA R. MORTON SCHOLARSHIP

One-time award for undergraduate study. Preference given to students at United Methodist-related schools. Must verify United Methodist membership. Must have at least a 3.5 GPA. Must be U.S. citizen or permanent resident. Must have completed one semester of study.

Award: Scholarship for use in sophomore, junior, or senior years; not renewable. *Number:* 30–35. *Amount:* $800–$1000.

Eligibility Requirements: Applicant must be Methodist and enrolled or expecting to enroll full-time at a two-year or four-year institution or university. Applicant must have 3.5 GPA or higher. Available to U.S. citizens.

Application Requirements: Application, essay, references, transcript, membership proof. *Deadline:* June 1.

Contact: Patti J. Zimmerman, Scholarships Administrator
United Methodist Church
PO Box 340007
Nashville, TN 37203-0007
Phone: 615-340-7344
E-mail: pzimmer@gbhem.org

UNITED METHODIST CHURCH ETHNIC SCHOLARSHIP
• See page 605

UNITED METHODIST CHURCH HISPANIC, ASIAN, AND NATIVE AMERICAN SCHOLARSHIP
• See page 605

UNITED METHODIST YOUTH ORGANIZATION http://www.umyouth.org

DAVID W. SELF SCHOLARSHIP

Must be a United Methodist Youth who has been active in his/her local church for at least one year prior to application. Must be a graduating senior in high school (who maintained at least a "C" average) entering his/her first year of undergraduate study. Must be pursuing a "church-related" career.

Award: Scholarship for use in freshman year; not renewable. *Number:* up to 2. *Amount:* up to $1000.

Eligibility Requirements: Applicant must be Methodist; high school student and planning to enroll or expecting to enroll full-time at an institution or university. Available to U.S. citizens.

Application Requirements: Application, essay, financial need analysis, transcript, certification of church membership. *Deadline:* June 1.

Contact: Ronna Seibert, Office Assistant
United Methodist Youth Organization
PO Box 340003
Nashville, TN 37203-0003
Phone: 877-899-2780 Ext. 7181
Fax: 615-340-1764
E-mail: umyouthorg@gbod.org

RICHARD S. SMITH SCHOLARSHIP
• See page 606

WELSH SOCIETY OF PHILADELPHIA

CYMDEITHAS GYMREIG/PHILADELPHIA SCHOLARSHIP
• See page 623

WOMAN'S MISSIONARY UNION FOUNDATION http://www.wmufoundation.com

WOMAN'S MISSIONARY UNION SCHOLARSHIP PROGRAM

Primarily for Baptist young women with high scholastic accomplishments and service through Baptist organizations. Must have an interest in Christian women's leadership development or missionary service. Preference is given for WMU/Acteen membership in a Baptist church. Application deadline is October 1.

Award: Scholarship for use in freshman, sophomore, junior, senior, graduate, or postgraduate years; not renewable. *Number:* 5–10. *Amount:* $500–$1500.

Eligibility Requirements: Applicant must be Baptist and enrolled or expecting to enroll full-time at a two-year or four-year institution or university. Available to U.S. and non-U.S. citizens.

Application Requirements: Application, references, transcript, WMU Endorsements. *Deadline:* October 1.

Contact: Linda Lucas
Woman's Missionary Union Foundation
PO Box 11346
Birmingham, AL 35202-1346
Phone: 205-408-5525
E-mail: llucas@wmu.org

WOMEN OF THE EVANGELICAL LUTHERAN CHURCH IN AMERICA http://www.elca.org/wo

AMELIA KEMP SCHOLARSHIP
• See page 623

BELMER/FLORA PRINCE SCHOLARSHIP

Scholarships provided for ELCA women studying for ELCA service. Must be at least 21 years old and hold membership in the ELCA. Must have experienced an interruption in education of two or more years since the completion of high school. For more details see Web site: http://www.elca.org/wo.

Award: Scholarship for use in freshman, sophomore, junior, senior, or graduate years; not renewable. *Number:* 2. *Amount:* up to $1200.

Eligibility Requirements: Applicant must be Lutheran; age 21; enrolled or expecting to enroll at an institution or university and female. Available to U.S. citizens.

Application Requirements: *Deadline:* February 15.

Contact: Application available at Web site.

ELCA SCHOLARSHIPS FOR WOMEN

Several named scholarships provided for ELCA women in undergraduate, graduate, professional or vocational courses of study. Must be at least 21 years old and hold membership in the ELCA. Must have experienced an interruption in education of two or more years since the completion of high school. For more details see Web site: http://www.elca.org/wo.

Award: Scholarship for use in freshman, sophomore, junior, senior, or graduate years; not renewable. *Number:* 7. *Amount:* up to $1200.

Eligibility Requirements: Applicant must be Lutheran; age 21; enrolled or expecting to enroll at a two-year or four-year or technical institution or university and female. Available to U.S. citizens.

Application Requirements: *Deadline:* February 15.

Contact: Application available at Web site.

STATE OF RESIDENCE/STATE OF STUDY

A.W. BODINE-SUNKIST GROWERS, INC.

A.W. BODINE-SUNKIST MEMORIAL SCHOLARSHIP

• *See page 503*

ABBIE SARGENT MEMORIAL SCHOLARSHIP, INC.

ABBIE SARGENT MEMORIAL SCHOLARSHIP

Up to three awards between $400 and $500 will be provided to deserving New Hampshire residents who plan to attend an institute of higher learning. Must be a U.S. citizen. Application deadline is March 15.

Award: Scholarship for use in freshman, sophomore, junior, senior, graduate, or postgraduate years; not renewable. *Number:* 1–3. *Amount:* $400–$500.

Eligibility Requirements: Applicant must be enrolled or expecting to enroll full or part-time at a two-year or four-year or technical institution or university and resident of New Hampshire. Available to U.S. citizens.

Application Requirements: Application, autobiography, financial need analysis, photo, references, transcript. *Deadline:* March 15.

Contact: Melanie Phelps
Abbie Sargent Memorial Scholarship, Inc.
295 Sheep Davis Road
Concord, NH 03301
Phone: 603-224-1934
Fax: 603-228-8432
E-mail: melaniep@nhfarmbureau.org

AKRON URBAN LEAGUE http://www.akronul.org/Main.htm

AKRON URBAN LEAGUE SCHOLARSHIP PROGRAM

This scholarship is designated for 17-19 year-old high school students who are planning on furthering their education. Awards range from $250 to full tuition. Application deadline is March 1. Restricted to applicants who are residents of Ohio.

Award: Scholarship for use in freshman year; renewable. *Number:* 40–45.

Eligibility Requirements: Applicant must be high school student; age 17-19; planning to enroll or expecting to enroll full-time at a two-year or four-year or technical institution or university and resident of Ohio. Applicant must have 2.5 GPA or higher. Available to U.S. citizens.

Application Requirements: Application, essay, financial need analysis, interview, photo, references, test scores, transcript. *Deadline:* March 1.

Contact: Rochelle Fisher, Development Director
Akron Urban League
250 East Market Street
Akron, OH 44308
Phone: 330-434-6996
Fax: 330-434-2716

ALABAMA COMMISSION ON HIGHER EDUCATION http://www.ache.state.al.us

ALABAMA NATIONAL GUARD EDUCATIONAL ASSISTANCE PROGRAM

• *See page 534*

ALABAMA STUDENT GRANT PROGRAM

Renewable awards available to Alabama residents for undergraduate study at certain independent colleges within the state. Both full- and half-time students are eligible. Deadlines: September 15, January 15, and February 15.

Award: Grant for use in freshman, sophomore, junior, or senior years; renewable. *Number:* varies. *Amount:* up to $1200.

Eligibility Requirements: Applicant must be enrolled or expecting to enroll full or part-time at a four-year institution or university; resident of Alabama and studying in Alabama. Available to U.S. citizens.

Application Requirements: Application. *Deadline:* varies.

Contact: Dr. William Wall, Associate Executive Director for Student Assistance, ACHE
Alabama Commission on Higher Education
PO Box 302000
Montgomery, AL 36130-2000

POLICE OFFICERS AND FIREFIGHTERS SURVIVORS EDUCATION ASSISTANCE PROGRAM-ALABAMA

• *See page 503*

ROBERT C. BYRD HONORS SCHOLARSHIP-ALABAMA

Approximately 105 awards. Must be Alabama resident and a high school senior. Minimum 3.5 GPA. Contact school guidance counselor for an application and deadlines.

Award: Scholarship for use in freshman, sophomore, junior, or senior years; renewable. *Number:* 105. *Amount:* $1500.

Eligibility Requirements: Applicant must be high school student; planning to enroll or expecting to enroll full-time at a two-year or four-year institution or university and resident of Alabama. Applicant must have 3.5 GPA or higher. Available to U.S. citizens.

Application Requirements: Application, test scores, transcript. *Deadline:* varies.

Contact: Dr. William Wall, Director of Student Assistance
Alabama Commission on Higher Education
PO Box 302000
Montgomery, AL 36130

ALABAMA DEPARTMENT OF REHABILITATION SERVICES http://www.rehab.state.al.us

ALABAMA SCHOLARSHIP FOR DEPENDENTS OF BLIND PARENTS

Scholarship given to defray the cost of books and fees for children of blind parents. Must be accepted or enrolled in a Alabama state supported school. Must be Alabama resident. Financial need is considered. Family income must be less than 1.3 times the federal poverty guideline for size of family unit.

Award: Scholarship for use in freshman, sophomore, junior, or senior years; renewable. *Number:* varies. *Amount:* varies.

Eligibility Requirements: Applicant must be age 28 or under; enrolled or expecting to enroll full-time at a two-year or four-year or technical institution or university; resident of Alabama and studying in Alabama. Available to U.S. citizens.

Application Requirements: Application, financial need analysis. *Deadline:* Continuous.

Contact: Deborah Culver, Coordinator of Blind Services
Alabama Department of Rehabilitation Services
Alabama Scholarship for Dependents of Blind Parents
2129 East South Boulevard
Montgomery, AL 36111
Phone: 800-441-7607

ALABAMA DEPARTMENT OF VETERANS AFFAIRS http://www.va.state.al.us/scholarship.htm

ALABAMA G.I. DEPENDENTS SCHOLARSHIP PROGRAM

• *See page 544*

ALASKA COMMISSION ON POSTSECONDARY EDUCATION http://www.state.ak.us/acpe/

WESTERN UNDERGRADUATE EXCHANGE (WUE) PROGRAM

Program allowing Alaska residents to enroll at two-or four-year institutions in participating states at a reduced tuition level, which is the in-state tuition plus a percentage of that amount. To be used for full-time undergraduate studies. See Web site at http://www.state.ak.us/acpe for further information, a list of eligible institutions, and deadlines.

Alaska Commission on Postsecondary Education (continued)

Award: Grant for use in freshman, sophomore, junior, or senior years; renewable. *Number:* varies. *Amount:* varies.

Eligibility Requirements: Applicant must be enrolled or expecting to enroll full-time at a two-year or four-year institution or university; resident of Alaska and studying in Arizona, Colorado, Hawaii, Idaho, Montana, Nevada, New Mexico, North Dakota, Oregon, South Dakota, Utah, or Washington. Available to U.S. citizens.

Application Requirements: *Deadline:* varies.

Contact: Program Office
Phone: 800-441-2962

ALBERTA AGRICULTURE FOOD AND RURAL DEVELOPMENT 4-H BRANCH

ALBERTA AGRICULTURE FOOD AND RURAL DEVELOPMENT 4-H SCHOLARSHIP PROGRAM

Awards will be given to current and incoming students attending any institute of higher learning. Must have been a member of the Alberta 4-H Program and be a Canadian citizen. Must be a resident of Alberta. Application deadline is May 15.

Award: Scholarship for use in freshman, sophomore, junior, senior, or graduate years; not renewable. *Number:* 115–120. *Amount:* $149–$1114.

Eligibility Requirements: Applicant must be enrolled or expecting to enroll full-time at a two-year or four-year or technical institution or university and resident of Alberta. Available to Canadian citizens.

Application Requirements: Application, essay, references, transcript. *Deadline:* May 15.

Contact: Susanne McGowan
Alberta Agriculture Food and Rural Development 4-H Branch
RRI
Edmonton, AB T0C 2V0
Canada
Phone: 780-682-2153

ALBERTA HERITAGE SCHOLARSHIP FUND/ ALBERTA SCHOLARSHIP PROGRAMS

http://www.alis.gov.ab.ca/scholarships

ADULT HIGH SCHOOL EQUIVALENCY SCHOLARSHIPS

• *See page 573*

ALBERTA BLUE CROSS SCHOLARSHIP FOR ABORIGINAL STUDENTS

• *See page 573*

ALBERTA HERITAGE SCHOLARSHIP FUND ALBERTA PRESS COUNCIL SCHOLARSHIP

• *See page 573*

ALBERTA HERITAGE SCHOLARSHIP FUND CANA SCHOLARSHIPS

• *See page 490*

ALBERTA HERITAGE SCHOLARSHIP FUND HAL HARRISON MEMORIAL SCHOLARSHIP

• *See page 504*

ALEXANDER RUTHERFORD SCHOLARSHIPS FOR HIGH SCHOOL ACHIEVEMENT

• *See page 573*

BOYS AND GIRLS CLUB OF ALBERTA SCHOLARSHIPS

• *See page 440*

CENTRAL ALBERTA RURAL ELECTRIFICATION ASSOCIATION SCHOLARSHIP

A CAN$1000 scholarship will be awarded to the top male and the top female to recognize the academic accomplishment of children of members of the Central Alberta Rural Electrification Association and to assist and encourage higher education. Must be a Canadian citizen and Alberta resident. For more details see Web site: http://www.alis.gov.ab.ca.

Award: Scholarship for use in freshman year; not renewable. *Number:* 2. *Amount:* $811.

Eligibility Requirements: Applicant must be high school student; planning to enroll or expecting to enroll full-time at a two-year institution and resident of Alberta. Available to Canadian citizens.

Application Requirements: Application. *Deadline:* July 1.

Contact: Director
Alberta Heritage Scholarship Fund/Alberta Scholarship Programs
9940 106th Street, 9th Floor
Box 28000, Station Main
Edmonton, AB T5J 4R4
Canada
Phone: 780-427-8640
Fax: 780-422-4516
E-mail: heritage@gov.ab.ca

CHARLES S. NOBLE JUNIOR "A" HOCKEY SCHOLARSHIPS

• *See page 573*

CHARLES S. NOBLE JUNIOR FOOTBALL SCHOLARSHIPS

• *See page 574*

DR. ERNEST AND MINNIE MEHL SCHOLARSHIP

• *See page 574*

EARL AND COUNTESS OF WESSEX-WORLD CHAMPIONSHIPS IN ATHLETICS SCHOLARSHIPS

Two CAN$3000 scholarships are available to recognize the top male and female Alberta students who have excelled in track and field, have a strong academic record, and plan to continue their studies at the postsecondary level in Alberta. Must be a Canadian citizen and Alberta resident. For more details and deadlines see Web site: http://www.alis.gov.ab.ca.

Award: Scholarship for use in freshman year; not renewable. *Number:* 2. *Amount:* $2432.

Eligibility Requirements: Applicant must be high school student; planning to enroll or expecting to enroll full-time at a two-year or four-year or technical institution or university; resident of Alberta; studying in Alberta and must have an interest in athletics/sports. Available to Canadian citizens.

Application Requirements: Application, transcript. *Deadline:* August 1.

Contact: Director
Alberta Heritage Scholarship Fund/Alberta Scholarship Programs
9940 106th Street, 9th Floor
Box 28000, Station Main
Edmonton, AB T5J 4R4
Canada
Phone: 780-427-8640
Fax: 780-422-4516
E-mail: heritage@gov.ab.ca

FELLOWSHIPS FOR FULL-TIME STUDIES IN FRENCH-UNIVERSITY

• *See page 574*

GRANT MACEWAN UNITED WORLD COLLEGE SCHOLARSHIPS

• *See page 574*

JASON LANG SCHOLARSHIP

A CAN$1000 scholarship will be awarded for the outstanding academic achievement of Alberta postsecondary students who are continuing full-time into their second, third or fourth year of an undergraduate program. Must be a Canadian citizen and Alberta resident. For more details and deadlines see Web site: http://www.alis.gov.ab.ca.

Award: Scholarship for use in sophomore, junior, or senior years; not renewable. *Number:* 8500. *Amount:* $811.

Eligibility Requirements: Applicant must be enrolled or expecting to enroll full-time at a four-year institution or university; resident of Alberta and studying in Alberta. Available to Canadian citizens.

Application Requirements: Application, transcript. *Deadline:* Continuous.

Contact: Director
Alberta Heritage Scholarship Fund/Alberta Scholarship Programs
9940 106th Street, 9th Floor
Box 28000, Station Main
Edmonton, AB T5J 4R4
Canada
Phone: 780-427-8640
Fax: 780-422-4516
E-mail: heritage@gov.ab.ca

JIMMIE CONDON ATHLETIC SCHOLARSHIPS

• *See page 574*

LAURENCE DECORE STUDENT LEADERSHIP AWARDS

• *See page 574*

LOUISE MCKINNEY POSTSECONDARY SCHOLARSHIPS

• *See page 575*

NEW APPRENTICESHIP SCHOLARSHIPS

A CAN$1000 scholarship is available for apprentices in a trade and trainees in a designated occupation to encourage recipients to complete their apprenticeship or occupational training programs. Must be a Canadian citizen or landed immigrant, and Alberta resident. For more details see Web site: http://www.alis.gov.ab.ca.

Award: Scholarship for use in freshman year; not renewable. *Number:* 160. *Amount:* $811.

Eligibility Requirements: Applicant must be enrolled or expecting to enroll full-time at a technical institution and resident of Alberta. Available to Canadian citizens.

Application Requirements: Application. *Deadline:* July 31.

Contact: Director
Alberta Heritage Scholarship Fund/Alberta Scholarship Programs
9940 106th Street, 9th Floor
Box 28000, Station Main
Edmonton, AB T5J 4R4
Canada
Phone: 780-427-8640
Fax: 780-422-4516
E-mail: heritage@gov.ab.ca

NORTHERN ALBERTA DEVELOPMENT COUNCIL BURSARY

• *See page 575*

PERSONS CASE SCHOLARSHIPS

• *See page 575*

PRAIRIE BASEBALL ACADEMY SCHOLARSHIPS

Scholarships awarded to post-secondary students in Alberta who are participants in the Prairie Baseball Academy. Must have earned a minimum GPA of 75% on their previous semester. Recipients are chosen based on academic standing, community involvement, and baseball achievements. Application deadline is October 15.

Award: Scholarship for use in freshman, sophomore, junior, or senior years. *Number:* 16–80. *Amount:* $405–$2049.

Eligibility Requirements: Applicant must be enrolled or expecting to enroll full-time at a four-year institution or university; studying in Alberta and must have an interest in athletics/sports.

Application Requirements: Application, references, transcript, membership in Prairie Baseball Academy. *Deadline:* October 15.

Contact: Director
Alberta Heritage Scholarship Fund/Alberta Scholarship Programs
9940 106th Street, 9th Floor
Box 28000, Station Main
Edmonton, AB T5J 4R4
Canada
Phone: 780-427-8640
Fax: 780-422-4516
E-mail: heritage@gov.ab.ca

REGISTERED APPRENTICESHIP PROGRAM SCHOLARSHIP

A CAN$1000 scholarship is available to recognize the accomplishments of Alberta high school students enrolled in the Registered Apprenticeship Program (RAP); and to encourage them to enter into a regular apprenticeship program after graduation. Funds are distributed CAN$700 in the first year and CAN$300 in the second year. Must be a Canadian citizen or landed immigrant, and Alberta resident. For more details and deadlines see Web site: http://www.alis.gov.ab.ca.

Award: Scholarship for use in freshman year; not renewable. *Number:* up to 50. *Amount:* $568.

Eligibility Requirements: Applicant must be enrolled or expecting to enroll full-time at a two-year or four-year or technical institution or university and resident of Alberta. Available to Canadian citizens.

Application Requirements: Application. *Deadline:* July 31.

Contact: Director
Alberta Heritage Scholarship Fund/Alberta Scholarship Programs
9940 106th Street, 9th Floor
Box 28000, Station Main
Edmonton, AB T5J 4R4
Canada
Phone: 780-427-8640
Fax: 780-422-4516
E-mail: heritage@gov.ab.ca

RUTHERFORD SCHOLARS

• *See page 575*

STREAM-FLO/MASTER FLO SCHOLARSHIPS

• *See page 490*

ALBUQUERQUE COMMUNITY FOUNDATION http://www.albuquerquefoundation.org

ACF- NOTAH BEGAY III SCHOLARSHIP PROGRAM FOR NATIVE AMERICAN SCHOLAR ATHLETES

• *See page 575*

ALBUQUERQUE COMMUNITY FOUNDATION NEW MEXICO MANUFACTURED HOUSING SCHOLARSHIP PROGRAM

One $1000 award will be made to one New Mexico high school senior graduating with a 3.0 GPA and living in a mobile/manufactured home. Award is to be used for study in a two-year, four-year, or vocational institution. Annual application deadline is in March. Refer to Web site for details and application: http://www.albuquerquefoundation.org.

Award: Scholarship for use in freshman year; not renewable. *Number:* 1. *Amount:* $1000.

Eligibility Requirements: Applicant must be high school student; planning to enroll or expecting to enroll full-time at a two-year or four-year or technical institution or university; resident of New Mexico and studying in New Mexico. Applicant must have 3.0 GPA or higher. Available to U.S. citizens.

Application Requirements: Application, financial need analysis, resume, references, test scores, transcript. *Deadline:* varies.

Contact: Nancy Johnson, Program Director
Albuquerque Community Foundation
PO Box 36960
Albuquerque, NM 87176-6960
Phone: 505-883-6240
E-mail: acf@albuquerquefoundation.org

SUSSMAN-MILLER EDUCATIONAL ASSISTANCE FUND

Program to provide financial aid to enable students to continue with an undergraduate program. This is a "gap" program based on financial need. Must be resident of New Mexico. Do not write or call for information. Please visit Web site: http://www.albuquerquefoundation.org for complete information. Minimum 3.0 GPA required. Deadlines vary.

Award: Grant for use in freshman, sophomore, junior, or senior years; not renewable. *Number:* 30–40. *Amount:* $500–$3000.

Eligibility Requirements: Applicant must be enrolled or expecting to enroll full-time at a four-year institution or university and resident of New Mexico. Applicant must have 3.0 GPA or higher. Available to U.S. citizens.

Application Requirements: Application, autobiography, essay, financial need analysis, resume, references, test scores, transcript. *Deadline:* varies.

Contact: Nancy Johnson, Program Director
Albuquerque Community Foundation
PO Box 36960
Albuquerque, NM 87176-6960
Phone: 505-883-6240
E-mail: acf@albuquerquefoundation.org

ALERT SCHOLARSHIP

ALERT SCHOLARSHIP

We offer a $500 scholarship for the best essay on drug and alcohol abuse. Applicant must be high school student between the ages of 16 and 19 living in Washington, Idaho, Montana, Wyoming, Colorado, North Dakota, or South Dakota. Minimum 2.5 GPA required.

Award: Scholarship for use in freshman year; not renewable. *Number:* 16. *Amount:* $500.

Eligibility Requirements: Applicant must be high school student; age 16-19; planning to enroll or expecting to enroll full or part-time at a two-year or four-year or technical institution or university and resident of Colorado, Idaho, Montana, North Dakota, South Dakota, Washington, or Wyoming. Applicant must have 2.5 GPA or higher. Available to U.S. citizens.

Application Requirements: Essay, photo, transcript. *Deadline:* Continuous.

Contact: Sylvia Rix, Co-Owner
Alert Scholarship
PO Box 4833
Boise, ID 83711
Phone: 208-375-7911
Fax: 208-376-0770

AMARILLO AREA FOUNDATION http://www.aaf-hf.org/

AMARILLO AREA FOUNDATION SCHOLARSHIPS

Scholarships available to graduating high school seniors from the 26 northernmost counties of the Texas Panhandle. All of the scholarships have specific requirements for items such as: county of residence, gender or race, location of institution of higher education, extra-curricular activities, field of study. For information on specific awards and application please visit Web site: http://www.aaf-hf.org. Application deadline is February 1.

Award: Scholarship for use in freshman, sophomore, junior, or senior years. *Number:* varies. *Amount:* $400–$12,000.

Eligibility Requirements: Applicant must be high school student; planning to enroll or expecting to enroll full-time at a two-year or four-year or technical institution or university and resident of Texas. Available to U.S. citizens.

Application Requirements: Application, financial need analysis, references, test scores, transcript. *Deadline:* February 1.

Contact: Laquita Hurt, Scholarship Coordinator
Amarillo Area Foundation
801 South Filmore
Amarillo, TX 79101
Phone: 806-376-4521
Fax: 806-373-3656
E-mail: laquita@aaf-hf.org

AMERICAN ASSOCIATION FOR NUDE RECREATION, WESTERN REGION, INC. http://www.aanrwest.org

AMERICAN ASSOCIATION FOR NUDE RECREATION, WESTERN REGION SCHOLARSHIP PROGRAM

Two $1000 awards for students under the age of 27. Minimum 2.5 GPA required. Club membership must be verified. Contact for further information. Award for residents of Arizona, California, Colorado, Hawaii, Nevada, New Mexico, Utah, or Wyoming.

Award: Scholarship for use in freshman, sophomore, junior, or senior years; not renewable. *Number:* 2. *Amount:* $1000.

Eligibility Requirements: Applicant must be age 26 or under; enrolled or expecting to enroll full or part-time at a two-year or four-year or technical institution or university and resident of Arizona, California, Colorado, Hawaii, Nevada, New Mexico, Utah, or Wyoming. Applicant must have 2.5 GPA or higher. Available to U.S. and non-U.S. citizens.

Application Requirements: Application, essay, references, transcript. *Deadline:* April 1.

Contact: AANR West Scholarship Committee
American Association for Nude Recreation, Western Region, Inc.
PO Box 1168-107
Studio City, CA 91604
E-mail: info@aanrwest.org

AMERICAN ASSOCIATION OF UNIVERSITY WOMEN - HARRISBURG BRANCH http://www.aauwharrisburg.org/

BEVERLY J. SMITH MEMORIAL SCHOLARSHIP

Award for a female student residing in Pennsylvania to use in obtaining a bachelor's degree at a Pennsylvania school. Candidates must demonstrate academic achievement and financial need, and have completed at least 60 credits. Application date varies.

Award: Scholarship for use in junior or senior years; not renewable. *Number:* 2. *Amount:* $2500.

Eligibility Requirements: Applicant must be enrolled or expecting to enroll full-time at a four-year institution or university; female; resident of Pennsylvania and studying in Pennsylvania. Applicant must have 3.5 GPA or higher. Available to U.S. and non-U.S. citizens.

Application Requirements: Application, essay, financial need analysis, interview, references, transcript, proof of enrollment. *Deadline:* varies.

Contact: Colleen Willard-Holt, Scholarship Chair
American Association of University Women - Harrisburg Branch
PO Box 1625
Harrisburg, PA 17105-1625
Phone: 717-948-6208
Fax: 717-948-6064
E-mail: Scholarship@aauwharrisburg.org

MARTHA M. DOHNER MEMORIAL SCHOLARSHIP

Award for a female student who is a resident of, and attends college in, Dauphin or Cumberland counties, Pennsylvania. Applicants must have earned 60 credits, and demonstrate academic achievement and financial need. Application date varies.

Award: Scholarship for use in junior or senior years; not renewable. *Number:* 1. *Amount:* $1000.

Eligibility Requirements: Applicant must be enrolled or expecting to enroll full-time at a four-year institution or university; female; resident of Pennsylvania and studying in Pennsylvania. Applicant must have 3.0 GPA or higher. Available to U.S. and non-U.S. citizens.

Application Requirements: Application, essay, financial need analysis, interview, references, transcript, proof of enrollment. *Deadline:* varies.

Contact: Colleen Willard-Holt, Scholarship Chair
American Association of University Women - Harrisburg Branch
PO Box 1625
Harrisburg, PA 17105-1625
Phone: 717-948-6208
Fax: 717-948-6064
E-mail: Scholarship@aauwharrisburg.org

AMERICAN CANCER SOCIETY, FLORIDA DIVISION, INC. http://www.cancer.org

AMERICAN CANCER SOCIETY, FLORIDA DIVISION COLLEGE SCHOLARSHIP PROGRAM

To be eligible for an American Cancer Society Florida Division Scholarship, Reaching Out to Cancer Kids Program, applicants must have had a personal diagnosis of cancer, be a Florida resident between the ages of 18 and 20, and plan to attend college in Florida. Awards will be based on financial need, scholarship, leadership, and community service.

Award: Grant for use in freshman, sophomore, junior, or senior years; renewable. *Number:* 150–175. *Amount:* $1850–$2300.

Eligibility Requirements: Applicant must be age 18-20; enrolled or expecting to enroll full or part-time at a two-year or four-year or technical institution or university; resident of Florida and studying in Florida. Available to U.S. citizens.

Application Requirements: Application, essay, financial need analysis, interview, resume, references, test scores, transcript. *Deadline:* April 10.

Contact: Mrs. Marilyn Westley, Director of Childhood Cancer Programs
American Cancer Society, Florida Division, Inc.
3709 West Jetton Avenue
Tampa, FL 33629
Phone: 813-253-0541
Fax: 813-254-5857
E-mail: marilyn.westley@cancer.org

AMERICAN CANCER SOCIETY, INC.-GREAT LAKES DIVISION http://www.cancer.org

COLLEGE SCHOLARSHIPS FOR CANCER SURVIVORS

Scholarships for Michigan and Indiana residents who have had a diagnosis of cancer before the age of 21. Applicant must be under 21 at time of application. To be used for undergraduate degrees at any accredited Michigan or Indiana college or university. Deadline: mid-April. Open to U.S. citizens only.

Award: Scholarship for use in freshman, sophomore, junior, or senior years; renewable. *Number:* up to 72. *Amount:* $1000.

Eligibility Requirements: Applicant must be age 17-20; enrolled or expecting to enroll full-time at a two-year or four-year or technical institution or university; resident of Indiana or Michigan and studying in Indiana or Michigan. Available to U.S. citizens.

Application Requirements: Application, essay, financial need analysis, references, test scores, transcript. *Deadline:* April 16.

Contact: Deb Dillingham, Director of Quality of Life
American Cancer Society, Inc.-Great Lakes Division
1755 Abbey Road
East Lansing, MI 48823
Phone: 800-723-0360
Fax: 517-664-1497
E-mail: deb.dillingham@cancer.org

AMERICAN FEDERATION OF TEACHERS-NEW HAMPSHIRE FEDERATION OF TEACHERS http://www.nhft.org

NEW HAMPSHIRE FEDERATION OF TEACHERS SCHOLARSHIP

• *See page 441*

AMERICAN LEGION AUXILIARY, DEPARTMENT OF ALABAMA

AMERICAN LEGION AUXILIARY DEPARTMENT OF ALABAMA SCHOLARSHIP PROGRAM

• *See page 544*

AMERICAN LEGION AUXILIARY, DEPARTMENT OF ARKANSAS

AMERICAN LEGION AUXILIARY DEPARTMENT OF ARKANSAS ACADEMIC SCHOLARSHIP

• *See page 544*

AMERICAN LEGION AUXILIARY, DEPARTMENT OF COLORADO

AMERICAN LEGION AUXILIARY DEPARTMENT OF COLORADO DEPARTMENT PRESIDENT'S SCHOLARSHIP FOR JUNIOR MEMBERS

• *See page 441*

AMERICAN LEGION AUXILIARY, DEPARTMENT OF FLORIDA

AMERICAN LEGION AUXILIARY DEPARTMENT OF FLORIDA DEPARTMENT SCHOLARSHIPS

• *See page 544*

AMERICAN LEGION AUXILIARY DEPARTMENT OF FLORIDA MEMORIAL SCHOLARSHIP

• *See page 442*

AMERICAN LEGION AUXILIARY DEPARTMENT OF FLORIDA NATIONAL PRESIDENT'S SCHOLARSHIP

• *See page 545*

AMERICAN LEGION AUXILIARY, DEPARTMENT OF IDAHO

AMERICAN LEGION AUXILIARY, DEPARTMENT OF IDAHO NATIONAL PRESIDENT'S SCHOLARSHIP

• *See page 545*

AMERICAN LEGION AUXILIARY, DEPARTMENT OF INDIANA

EDNA M. BURCUS MEMORIAL SCHOLARSHIP

• *See page 545*

HOOSIER SCHOOLHOUSE SCHOLARSHIP

One-time award for Indiana residents who are high school seniors planning to continue their education. Award is primarily based on need. Contact local units for application and deadline information.

Award: Scholarship for use in freshman year; not renewable. *Number:* 2.

Eligibility Requirements: Applicant must be high school student; planning to enroll or expecting to enroll at a two-year or four-year or technical institution or university and resident of Indiana. Available to U.S. citizens.

Application Requirements: Application, essay, financial need analysis, self-addressed stamped envelope, transcript. *Deadline:* varies.

Contact: Ms. Sue Liford, Department Secretary and Treasurer
American Legion Auxiliary, Department of Indiana
777 North Meridian, Room 107
Indianapolis, IN 46204

AMERICAN LEGION AUXILIARY, DEPARTMENT OF IOWA http://www.ialegion.org/ala

AMERICAN LEGION AUXILIARY DEPARTMENT OF IOWA CHILDREN OF VETERANS SCHOLARSHIP

• *See page 545*

AMERICAN LEGION AUXILIARY, DEPARTMENT OF KENTUCKY

LAURA BLACKBURN MEMORIAL SCHOLARSHIP

• *See page 545*

MARY BARRETT MARSHALL SCHOLARSHIP

• *See page 442*

AMERICAN LEGION AUXILIARY, DEPARTMENT OF MAINE

AMERICAN LEGION AUXILIARY DEPARTMENT OF MAINE SCHOLARSHIP

• *See page 546*

AMERICAN LEGION AUXILIARY, DEPARTMENT OF MAINE NATIONAL PRESIDENT'S SCHOLARSHIP

• *See page 546*

AMERICAN LEGION AUXILIARY, DEPARTMENT OF MARYLAND

AMERICAN LEGION AUXILIARY DEPARTMENT OF MARYLAND CHILDREN AND YOUTH SCHOLARSHIPS

• *See page 546*

AMERICAN LEGION AUXILIARY, DEPARTMENT OF MICHIGAN http://www.michalaux.org

AMERICAN LEGION AUXILIARY DEPARTMENT OF MICHIGAN MEMORIAL SCHOLARSHIP

• *See page 546*

AMERICAN LEGION AUXILIARY NATIONAL PRESIDENT'S SCHOLARSHIP

• *See page 546*

SCHOLARSHIP FOR NON-TRADITIONAL STUDENT
• *See page 547*

AMERICAN LEGION AUXILIARY, DEPARTMENT OF MINNESOTA

AMERICAN LEGION AUXILIARY DEPARTMENT OF MINNESOTA SCHOLARSHIPS
• *See page 547*

AMERICAN LEGION AUXILIARY, DEPARTMENT OF MISSOURI

AMERICAN LEGION AUXILIARY MISSOURI STATE NATIONAL PRESIDENT'S SCHOLARSHIP
• *See page 442*

LELA MURPHY SCHOLARSHIP
• *See page 443*

AMERICAN LEGION AUXILIARY, DEPARTMENT OF NEBRASKA

AMERICAN LEGION AUXILIARY DEPARTMENT OF NEBRASKA PRESIDENT'S SCHOLARSHIP FOR JUNIOR MEMBERS
• *See page 443*

AMERICAN LEGION AUXILIARY DEPARTMENT OF NEBRASKA PRESIDENT'S SCHOLARSHIPS
• *See page 547*

AMERICAN LEGION AUXILIARY DEPARTMENT OF NEBRASKA STUDENT AID GRANTS
• *See page 547*

ROBERTA MARIE STRETCH MEMORIAL SCHOLARSHIP
• *See page 547*

RUBY PAUL CAMPAIGN FUND SCHOLARSHIP
• *See page 443*

AMERICAN LEGION AUXILIARY, DEPARTMENT OF NEW JERSEY

http://www.alanj.thisnation.net/contact.html

AMERICAN LEGION AUXILIARY DEPARTMENT OF NEW JERSEY NATIONAL PRESIDENT'S SCHOLARSHIP
• *See page 548*

AMERICAN LEGION AUXILIARY, DEPARTMENT OF NEW JERSEY DEPARTMENT SCHOLARSHIPS
• *See page 548*

CLAIRE OLIPHANT MEMORIAL SCHOLARSHIP
• *See page 548*

AMERICAN LEGION AUXILIARY, DEPARTMENT OF NORTH DAKOTA

AMERICAN LEGION AUXILIARY DEPARTMENT OF NORTH DAKOTA SCHOLARSHIPS

One-time award for North Dakota residents who are already attending a North Dakota institution of higher learning. Contact local or nearest American Legion Auxiliary Unit for more information. Must be a U.S. citizen.

Award: Scholarship for use in sophomore, junior, senior, or graduate years; not renewable. *Number:* 3. *Amount:* $400.

Eligibility Requirements: Applicant must be enrolled or expecting to enroll full-time at a two-year or four-year or technical institution or university; resident of North Dakota and studying in North Dakota. Available to U.S. citizens.

Application Requirements: Application, autobiography, essay, financial need analysis, references, self-addressed stamped envelope, test scores, transcript. *Deadline:* January 15.

Contact: Alice Carlson, Education Chairman
American Legion Auxiliary, Department of North Dakota
6422 Northeast 122nd Avenue
Lankin, ND 58250-9761
Phone: 701-742-2647

AMERICAN LEGION AUXILIARY, DEPARTMENT OF OHIO

AMERICAN LEGION AUXILIARY DEPARTMENT OF OHIO CONTINUING EDUCATION FUND
• *See page 548*

AMERICAN LEGION AUXILIARY DEPARTMENT OF OHIO DEPARTMENT PRESIDENT'S SCHOLARSHIP
• *See page 548*

AMERICAN LEGION AUXILIARY, DEPARTMENT OF OREGON

AMERICAN LEGION AUXILIARY DEPARTMENT OF OREGON DEPARTMENT GRANTS
• *See page 549*

AMERICAN LEGION AUXILIARY DEPARTMENT OF OREGON SPIRIT OF YOUTH SCHOLARSHIP
• *See page 443*

AMERICAN LEGION AUXILIARY, DEPARTMENT OF OREGON NATIONAL PRESIDENT'S SCHOLARSHIP
• *See page 549*

AMERICAN LEGION AUXILIARY, DEPARTMENT OF PENNSYLVANIA

AMERICAN LEGION AUXILIARY DEPARTMENT OF PENNSYLVANIA SCHOLARSHIP FOR DEPENDENTS OF DISABLED OR DECEASED VETERANS
• *See page 549*

AMERICAN LEGION AUXILIARY DEPARTMENT OF PENNSYLVANIA SCHOLARSHIP FOR DEPENDENTS OF LIVING VETERANS
• *See page 549*

AMERICAN LEGION AUXILIARY, DEPARTMENT OF SOUTH DAKOTA

AMERICAN LEGION AUXILIARY DEPARTMENT OF SOUTH DAKOTA COLLEGE SCHOLARSHIPS
• *See page 443*

AMERICAN LEGION AUXILIARY DEPARTMENT OF SOUTH DAKOTA THELMA FOSTER SCHOLARSHIP FOR SENIOR AUXILIARY MEMBERS
• *See page 444*

AMERICAN LEGION AUXILIARY DEPARTMENT OF SOUTH DAKOTA THELMA FOSTER SCHOLARSHIPS FOR JUNIOR AUXILIARY MEMBERS
• *See page 444*

AMERICAN LEGION AUXILIARY DEPARTMENT OF SOUTH DAKOTA VOCATIONAL SCHOLARSHIP
• *See page 444*

AMERICAN LEGION AUXILIARY, DEPARTMENT OF SOUTH DAKOTA SENIOR SCHOLARSHIP
• *See page 444*

AMERICAN LEGION AUXILIARY, DEPARTMENT OF TENNESSEE

VARA GRAY SCHOLARSHIP-GENERAL
• *See page 549*

AMERICAN LEGION AUXILIARY, DEPARTMENT OF TEXAS

AMERICAN LEGION AUXILIARY, DEPARTMENT OF TEXAS GENERAL EDUCATION SCHOLARSHIP

• *See page 550*

AMERICAN LEGION AUXILIARY, DEPARTMENT OF UTAH http://www.legion-aux.org

AMERICAN LEGION AUXILIARY NATIONAL PRESIDENTS SCHOLARSHIP

• *See page 444*

AMERICAN LEGION AUXILIARY, DEPARTMENT OF WASHINGTON http://www.walegion-aux.org

AMERICAN LEGION AUXILIARY DEPARTMENT OF WASHINGTON SUSAN BURDETT SCHOLARSHIP

Applicant must be a former citizen of Evergreen Girls State. Applications must be obtained and processed through a Washington State American Legion Auxiliary Unit. One-time award of $300.

Award: Scholarship for use in freshman, sophomore, junior, or senior years; not renewable. *Number:* 1. *Amount:* $300.

Eligibility Requirements: Applicant must be enrolled or expecting to enroll at an institution or university; female and resident of Washington. Available to U.S. citizens.

Application Requirements: Application, essay, references, transcript. *Deadline:* April 1.

Contact: Lois Boyle, Education Chairman
American Legion Auxiliary, Department of Washington
PO Box 5867
Lacey, WA 98509-5867
Phone: 360-456-5995
Fax: 360-491-7442
E-mail: alawash@qwest.net

AMERICAN LEGION AUXILIARY, DEPARTMENT OF WASHINGTON GIFT SCHOLARSHIPS

• *See page 550*

DAYLE AND FRANCES PEIPER SCHOLARSHIP

• *See page 550*

AMERICAN LEGION AUXILIARY, DEPARTMENT OF WISCONSIN http://www.amlegionauxwi.org

DELLA VAN DEUREN MEMORIAL SCHOLARSHIP

• *See page 445*

H.S. AND ANGELINA LEWIS SCHOLARSHIPS

• *See page 445*

HEALTH CAREER SCHOLARSHIPS

• *See page 445*

MERIT AND MEMORIAL SCHOLARSHIPS

• *See page 445*

STATE PRESIDENT'S SCHOLARSHIPS

• *See page 445*

AMERICAN LEGION, DEPARTMENT OF ALABAMA http://www.americanlegionalabama.org/

AMERICAN LEGION DEPARTMENT OF ALABAMA SCHOLARSHIP PROGRAM

One-time award for Alabama residents directly related to any war veteran. Parents must be legal residents of Alabama. Send self-addressed stamped envelope to receive scholarship application, list of available schools, and instructions.

Award: Scholarship for use in freshman, sophomore, junior, or senior years; not renewable. *Number:* 150. *Amount:* $850.

Eligibility Requirements: Applicant must be enrolled or expecting to enroll full-time at a two-year or four-year institution or university; resident of Alabama and studying in Alabama. Available to U.S. citizens.

Application Requirements: Application, photo, references, self-addressed stamped envelope, test scores, transcript. *Deadline:* May 1.

Contact: Braxton Bridgers, Department Adjutant
American Legion, Department of Alabama
PO Box 1069
Montgomery, AL 36101-1069
Phone: 334-262-6638
E-mail: allegion@bellsouth.net

AMERICAN LEGION DEPARTMENT OF ALABAMA STATE ORATORICAL SCHOLARSHIP

Oratorical contest open to students in 9th-12th grades of any accredited Alabama high school. State speech contests end in March and continue to national level. Contact local American Legion Post for deadlines.

Award: Scholarship for use in freshman year; not renewable. *Number:* 3. *Amount:* $1000–$5000.

Eligibility Requirements: Applicant must be high school student; planning to enroll or expecting to enroll full-time at an institution or university; resident of Alabama and must have an interest in public speaking. Available to U.S. citizens.

Application Requirements: Application, applicant must enter a contest, essay. *Deadline:* May 1.

Contact: Braxton Bridgers, Department Adjutant
American Legion, Department of Alabama
PO Box 1069
Montgomery, AL 36101-1069
Phone: 334-262-6638
E-mail: allegion@bellsouth.net

AMERICAN LEGION, DEPARTMENT OF ALASKA

AMERICAN LEGION WESTERN DISTRICT POSTSECONDARY SCHOLARSHIP

One-time award to graduating high school senior for use in postsecondary schooling. Minimum 2.5 GPA required. Must be resident of Western District of Alaska. Submit community service activities.

Award: Scholarship for use in freshman year; not renewable. *Number:* 3–5. *Amount:* $500.

Eligibility Requirements: Applicant must be high school student; planning to enroll or expecting to enroll full-time at a two-year or four-year or technical institution or university and resident of Alaska. Applicant must have 2.5 GPA or higher. Available to U.S. citizens.

Application Requirements: Application, essay, transcript. *Deadline:* February 15.

Contact: Bill Caswell, Western District Scholarship Chairman
American Legion, Department of Alaska
1550 Charter Circle
Anchorage, AK 99508
Phone: 907-745-2868
Fax: 907-745-2869
E-mail: legion@anch.net

AMERICAN LEGION, DEPARTMENT OF ARIZONA

AMERICAN LEGION, DEPARTMENT OF ARIZONA HIGH SCHOOL ORATORICAL CONTEST

Each student must present an 8-10 minute prepared oration on any part of the U.S. Constitution. This is done before an audience. No notes, podiums or coaching. It is done from memory. Then the student does a 3-5 minute oration on one of the four assigned topics. The student doesn't know which assigned topic will be picked so they must prepare for all.

Award: Prize for use in freshman, sophomore, junior, or senior years; not renewable. *Number:* 10–35. *Amount:* $50–$1000.

Eligibility Requirements: Applicant must be high school student; age 18 or under; planning to enroll or expecting to enroll full-time at a two-year or four-year institution or university and resident of Arizona. Available to U.S. citizens.

American Legion, Department of Arizona (continued)

Application Requirements: Application, applicant must enter a contest. *Deadline:* January 15.

Contact: Ole Bjerk, Department Oratorical Chairman
American Legion, Department of Arizona
4701 North 19th Avenue
Suite 200
Phoenix, AZ 85015-3799
Phone: 602-264-7706
Fax: 602-264-0029

AMERICAN LEGION, DEPARTMENT OF ARKANSAS http://www.arklegion.homestead.com

AMERICAN LEGION DEPARTMENT OF ARKANSAS COUDRET SCHOLARSHIP AWARD

• *See page 446*

AMERICAN LEGION DEPARTMENT OF ARKANSAS ORATORICAL CONTEST

Oratorical contest open to students in 9th-12th grades of any accredited Arkansas high school. Begins with finalists at the post level and proceeds through area and district levels to national contest.

Award: Scholarship for use in freshman year; not renewable. *Number:* 4. *Amount:* $2550.

Eligibility Requirements: Applicant must be high school student; planning to enroll or expecting to enroll full or part-time at a two-year or four-year or technical institution or university and resident of Arkansas. Applicant must have 2.5 GPA or higher. Available to U.S. citizens.

Application Requirements: Application, applicant must enter a contest, photo, references. *Deadline:* March 15.

Contact: William Winchell, Department Adjutant
American Legion, Department of Arkansas
PO Box 3280
Little Rock, AR 72203-3280
Phone: 501-375-1104
Fax: 501-375-4236
E-mail: alegion@swbell.net

AMERICAN LEGION DEPARTMENT OF ARKANSAS PAST DEPARTMENT COMMANDER SCHOLARSHIP

• *See page 446*

AMERICAN LEGION, DEPARTMENT OF DISTRICT OF COLUMBIA

DC DEPARTMENT HIGH SCHOOL ORATORICAL CONTEST

The contest is open to all high school students who are U.S. citizens or legal residents and live in the greater Washington, D.C. area. Each orator will have to give an eight to ten minute speech on the Constitution and a three to five minute speech on one of four assigned topics. The prizes are $100 for fourth place, $300 for third place, $500 for second place, and $2300 for first place. Applicants should make initial contact to the contest chairman some time in December for additional information.

Award: Prize for use in freshman year; not renewable. *Number:* 4. *Amount:* $100–$2300.

Eligibility Requirements: Applicant must be high school student; age 20 or under; planning to enroll or expecting to enroll full-time at a two-year or four-year institution or university and resident of District of Columbia, Maryland, or Virginia. Available to U.S. citizens.

Application Requirements: Applicant must enter a contest. *Deadline:* January 30.

Contact: Paul Hasz, Oratorical Contest Chairman
American Legion, Department of District of Columbia
3408 Wisconsin Avenue NW, Suite 218
Washington, DC 20016
Phone: 202-362-9151
Fax: 202-362-9152
E-mail: dclegion@starpower.net

AMERICAN LEGION, DEPARTMENT OF HAWAII http://www.legion.org

AMERICAN LEGION DEPARTMENT OF HAWAII STATE ORATORICAL CONTEST

Oratorical contest open to students in 9th-12th grades of any accredited Hawaii high school. Speech contests begin in January at post level and continue on to national competition. Contact local American Legion post or department for deadlines and application details.

Award: Prize for use in freshman, sophomore, junior, or senior years; not renewable. *Number:* varies. *Amount:* $50–$500.

Eligibility Requirements: Applicant must be high school student; planning to enroll or expecting to enroll full-time at a four-year institution or university and resident of Hawaii. Available to U.S. citizens.

Application Requirements: Application, applicant must enter a contest. *Deadline:* varies.

Contact: Bernard K. Y. Lee, Department Adjutant/Oratorical Contest Chairman
American Legion, Department of Hawaii
612 McCully Street
Honolulu, HI 96826-3935
Phone: 808-946-6383
Fax: 808-947-3957
E-mail: aldepthi@hawaii.rr.com

AMERICAN LEGION, DEPARTMENT OF IDAHO http://www.idaholegion.com

AMERICAN LEGION, DEPARTMENT OF IDAHO SCHOLARSHIP

• *See page 446*

AMERICAN LEGION, DEPARTMENT OF ILLINOIS http://www.illegion.org

AMERICAN LEGION ORATORICAL CONTEST-ILLINOIS

Multi-level oratorical contest with winners advancing to next level. Open to students in 9th-12th grades of any accredited high school in Illinois. Seniors must be in attendance as of 1/1. Fifteen prizes in the form of tuition scholarships from $75-$1,600 will be awarded. Contact local American Legion Post or Department Headquarters for complete information and applications, which will be available in the fall.

Award: Scholarship for use in freshman year; not renewable. *Number:* 15. *Amount:* $75–$1600.

Eligibility Requirements: Applicant must be high school student; age 20 or under; planning to enroll or expecting to enroll full or part-time at a two-year or four-year or technical institution or university and resident of Illinois. Available to U.S. citizens.

Application Requirements: Application, applicant must enter a contest, transcript. *Deadline:* January 15.

Contact: American Legion, Department of Illinois
PO Box 2910
Bloomington, IL 61702

AMERICAN LEGION, DEPARTMENT OF ILLINOIS SCHOLARSHIPS

• *See page 447*

AMERICAN LEGION, DEPARTMENT OF ILLINOIS, BOY SCOUT/ EXPLORER SCHOLARSHIP

• *See page 447*

AMERICAN LEGION, DEPARTMENT OF INDIANA

AMERICAN LEGION DEPARTMENT OF INDIANA, AMERICANISM AND GOVERNMENT TEST

One-time award for Indiana residents in grades 10-12. Must take written test during National Education Week in November. Two winners from each grade, one boy and one girl. Contact for application procedures and more information.

Award: Scholarship for use in freshman year; not renewable. *Number:* 6. *Amount:* $500.

Eligibility Requirements: Applicant must be high school student; planning to enroll or expecting to enroll full or part-time at a two-year or four-year or technical institution or university and resident of Indiana. Available to U.S. citizens.

Application Requirements: *Deadline:* Continuous.

Contact: B.J. McWilliams, Program Coordinator
American Legion, Department of Indiana
777 North Meridan Street, Room 104
Indianapolis, IN 46204
Phone: 317-630-1264
Fax: 317-237-9891
E-mail: bjmcwilliams@indlegion.org

AMERICAN LEGION, DEPARTMENT OF INDIANA STATE ORATORICAL CONTEST

Oratorical contest open to students in grades 9-12 of any accredited Indiana high school. Speech contests begin in November at post level and continue on to national competition. Contact local American Legion post for deadline and application details.

Award: Prize for use in freshman year; not renewable. *Number:* 4–8. *Amount:* $500–$1200.

Eligibility Requirements: Applicant must be high school student; age 19 or under; planning to enroll or expecting to enroll full or part-time at a two-year or four-year or technical institution or university; resident of Indiana and must have an interest in public speaking. Available to U.S. and Canadian citizens.

Application Requirements: Application, applicant must enter a contest. *Deadline:* varies.

Contact: B.J. McWilliams, Program Coordinator
American Legion, Department of Indiana
777 North Meridan Street, Room 104
Indianapolis, IN 46204
Phone: 317-630-1264
Fax: 317-237-9891
E-mail: bjmcwilliams@indlegion.org

FRANK W. MCHALE MEMORIAL SCHOLARSHIPS

One-time award for Indiana high school juniors who recently participated in the Boys State Program. Must be nominated by Boys State official. Write for more information and deadline.

Award: Scholarship for use in freshman, sophomore, junior, or senior years; not renewable. *Number:* 3. *Amount:* $1500–$2000.

Eligibility Requirements: Applicant must be high school student; planning to enroll or expecting to enroll full or part-time at a two-year or four-year or technical institution or university; male; resident of Indiana and must have an interest in leadership. Available to U.S. citizens.

Application Requirements: Application. *Deadline:* June 1.

Contact: B.J. McWilliams, Program Coordinator
American Legion, Department of Indiana
777 North Meridan Street, Room 104
Indianapolis, IN 46204
Phone: 317-630-1264
Fax: 317-237-9891
E-mail: bjmcwilliams@indlegion.org

AMERICAN LEGION, DEPARTMENT OF IOWA

http://www.ialegion.org

AMERICAN LEGION DEPARTMENT OF IOWA EAGLE SCOUT OF THE YEAR SCHOLARSHIP

• *See page 447*

AMERICAN LEGION DEPARTMENT OF IOWA OUTSTANDING SENIOR BASEBALL PLAYER

One-time award for Iowa residents who participated in the American Legion Senior Baseball Program and display outstanding sportsmanship, athletic ability, and proven academic achievements. Must be recommended by Baseball Committee.

Award: Scholarship for use in freshman, sophomore, junior, or senior years; not renewable. *Number:* 1. *Amount:* $750–$1500.

Eligibility Requirements: Applicant must be high school student; age 15-18; planning to enroll or expecting to enroll full-time at a two-year or four-year or technical institution or university; resident of Iowa and must have an interest in athletics/sports. Applicant must have 3.5 GPA or higher.

Application Requirements: Application. *Deadline:* June 1.

Contact: Program Director
American Legion, Department of Iowa
720 Lyon Street
Des Moines, IA 50309

ORATORICAL CONTEST SCHOLARSHIP-IOWA

Three awards granted in oratorical contest. Must be resident of Iowa.

Award: Prize for use in freshman, sophomore, junior, or senior years; not renewable. *Number:* 3. *Amount:* $400–$2000.

Eligibility Requirements: Applicant must be enrolled or expecting to enroll full-time at a two-year or four-year institution or university; resident of Iowa and must have an interest in public speaking. Available to U.S. citizens.

Application Requirements: Applicant must enter a contest. *Deadline:* varies.

Contact: Program Director
American Legion, Department of Iowa
720 Lyon Street
Des Moines, IA 50309

AMERICAN LEGION, DEPARTMENT OF KANSAS

ALBERT M. LAPPIN SCHOLARSHIP

• *See page 447*

DR. CLICK COWGER BASEBALL SCHOLARSHIP

Scholarship available to a high school senior or college freshman or sophomore who plays or has played Kansas American Legion baseball. Scholarships must be used at an approved Kansas institution. Must be Kansas resident.

Award: Scholarship for use in freshman or sophomore years; not renewable. *Number:* 1. *Amount:* $500.

Eligibility Requirements: Applicant must be enrolled or expecting to enroll at an institution or university; resident of Kansas; studying in Kansas and must have an interest in athletics/sports. Available to U.S. citizens.

Application Requirements: Application, photo. *Deadline:* July 15.

Contact: Scholarship Administrator
American Legion, Department of Kansas
1314 Southwest Topeka Boulevard
Topeka, KS 66612-1886

HUGH A. SMITH SCHOLARSHIP FUND

• *See page 447*

NATIONAL HIGH SCHOOL ORATORICAL CONTEST

• *See page 447*

PAUL FLAHERTY ATHLETIC SCHOLARSHIP

Scholarship available to student who has participated in any form of Kansas high school athletics. Award must be used at an approved Kansas college, university, or trade school. Must be a Kansas resident.

Award: Scholarship for use in freshman or sophomore years; not renewable. *Number:* 1. *Amount:* $250.

Eligibility Requirements: Applicant must be enrolled or expecting to enroll at a two-year or four-year or technical institution or university; resident of Kansas; studying in Kansas and must have an interest in athletics/sports. Available to U.S. citizens.

Application Requirements: Application, financial need analysis, photo, transcript. *Deadline:* July 15.

Contact: Scholarship Administrator
American Legion, Department of Kansas
1314 Southwest Topeka Boulevard
Topeka, KS 66612-1886

ROSEDALE POST 346 SCHOLARSHIP

• See page 448

TED AND NORA ANDERSON SCHOLARSHIPS

• See page 448

AMERICAN LEGION, DEPARTMENT OF MAINE

ALEXANDER A. LAFLEUR SCHOLARSHIP

One-time award for Maine high school juniors who participate in the current-year Boys State Program. Must attend Dirigo Boys State and be nominated by staff.

Award: Scholarship for use in freshman year; not renewable. *Number:* 1. *Amount:* $500.

Eligibility Requirements: Applicant must be high school student; planning to enroll or expecting to enroll full-time at a two-year or four-year or technical institution or university; male and resident of Maine. Available to U.S. citizens.

Application Requirements: Must attend current year at Boys State.. *Deadline:* Continuous.

Contact: Michelle McRae
American Legion, Department of Maine
PO Box 900
Waterville, ME 04903
Phone: 207-873-3229
Fax: 207-872-0501
E-mail: michellem@prexar.com

AMERICAN LEGION DEPARTMENT OF MAINE CHILDREN AND YOUTH SCHOLARSHIP

Scholarships available to high school seniors, college students, and veterans who are residents of Maine. Based on financial need and character. Must be in upper half of high school class. One-time award of $500.

Award: Scholarship for use in freshman, sophomore, junior, or senior years; not renewable. *Number:* 7. *Amount:* $500.

Eligibility Requirements: Applicant must be enrolled or expecting to enroll full-time at a two-year or four-year or technical institution or university and resident of Maine. Applicant must have 2.5 GPA or higher. Available to U.S. citizens.

Application Requirements: Application, essay, financial need analysis, references, transcript. *Deadline:* April 10.

Contact: Roxanne Roy
American Legion, Department of Maine
PO Box 900
Waterville, ME 04903
Phone: 207-873-3229
Fax: 207-872-0501
E-mail: legionme@wtvl.net

DANIEL E. LAMBERT MEMORIAL SCHOLARSHIP

• See page 551

JAMES L. BOYLE SCHOLARSHIP

One-time award for Maine high school juniors who participate in the current-year Boys State Program. Must attend Dirigo Boys State and be nominated by staff.

Award: Scholarship for use in freshman year; not renewable. *Number:* 1. *Amount:* $500.

Eligibility Requirements: Applicant must be high school student; planning to enroll or expecting to enroll full-time at a two-year or four-year or technical institution or university; male and resident of Maine. Available to U.S. citizens.

Application Requirements: Must attend Boys State for the current year.. *Deadline:* Continuous.

Contact: Department Adjutant
American Legion, Department of Maine
PO Box 900
Waterville, ME 04903
Phone: 207-873-3229
Fax: 207-872-0501
E-mail: legionme@wtvl.net

JAMES V. DAY SCHOLARSHIP

• See page 448

AMERICAN LEGION, DEPARTMENT OF MARYLAND http://mdlegion.org

AMERICAN LEGION DEPARTMENT OF MARYLAND GENERAL SCHOLARSHIP

Scholarship of $500 for Maryland high school students. Must plan on attending a two-year or four-year college or university in the state of Maryland. Nonrenewable award. Based on financial need and citizenship. Applications available on Web site: http://mdlegion.org.

Award: Scholarship for use in freshman year; not renewable. *Number:* 4. *Amount:* $500.

Eligibility Requirements: Applicant must be high school student; age 19 or under; planning to enroll or expecting to enroll full-time at a two-year or four-year institution or university; resident of Maryland and studying in Maryland. Available to U.S. citizens.

Application Requirements: Application, essay, financial need analysis, transcript. *Deadline:* March 31.

Contact: Thomas Davis, Department Adjutant
American Legion, Department of Maryland
101 North Gay, Room E
Baltimore, MD 21202
Phone: 410-752-3104

AMERICAN LEGION DEPARTMENT OF MARYLAND GENERAL SCHOLARSHIP FUND

• See page 551

AMERICAN LEGION, DEPARTMENT OF MICHIGAN http://www.michiganlegion.org

AMERICAN LEGION DEPARTMENT OF MICHIGAN ORATORICAL CONTEST

Oratorical contest open to students in 9th-12th grades of any accredited Michigan high school or state accredited home school. Five one-time awards of varying amounts. Speech contests begin in January at zone level and continue on to national competition. Contact for deadlines and application details.

Award: Prize for use in freshman year; not renewable. *Number:* 5. *Amount:* $600–$1000.

Eligibility Requirements: Applicant must be high school student; age 20 or under; planning to enroll or expecting to enroll full or part-time at a two-year or four-year or technical institution or university; resident of Michigan and must have an interest in public speaking. Available to U.S. citizens.

Application Requirements: Application, applicant must enter a contest. *Deadline:* January 31.

Contact: Deanna Clark, Program Secretary
American Legion, Department of Michigan
212 North Verlinden Avenue
Lansing, MI 48915
Phone: 517-371-4720 Ext. 25
Fax: 517-371-2401
E-mail: programs@michiganlegion.org

GUY M. WILSON SCHOLARSHIPS

• See page 551

WILLIAM D. AND JEWELL W. BREWER SCHOLARSHIP TRUSTS

• See page 551

AMERICAN LEGION, DEPARTMENT OF MINNESOTA http://www.mnlegion.org

AMERICAN LEGION DEPARTMENT OF MINNESOTA MEMORIAL SCHOLARSHIP

• See page 448

AMERICAN LEGION DEPARTMENT OF MINNESOTA STATE ORATORICAL CONTEST

Oratorical contest open to students in 9th-12th grades of any accredited Minnesota high school. Speech contests begin in January at post level and continue to national competition. Contact local American Legion Post for deadlines and application details. Four one-time awards of varying amounts.

Award: Scholarship for use in freshman year; not renewable. *Number:* 4. *Amount:* $500–$1200.

Eligibility Requirements: Applicant must be high school student; planning to enroll or expecting to enroll full or part-time at a two-year or four-year or technical institution or university; resident of Minnesota and must have an interest in public speaking. Available to U.S. citizens.

Application Requirements: Application, applicant must enter a contest. *Deadline:* varies.

Contact: Jennifer Kelley, Program Coordinator
American Legion, Department of Minnesota
20 West 12th Street, Room 300-A
St. Paul, MN 55155
Phone: 651-291-1800
Fax: 651-291-1057

MINNESOTA LEGIONNAIRES INSURANCE TRUST
• *See page 448*

AMERICAN LEGION, DEPARTMENT OF MISSOURI http://www.missourilegion.org

CHARLES L. BACON MEMORIAL SCHOLARSHIP
• *See page 449*

ERMAN W. TAYLOR MEMORIAL SCHOLARSHIP
• *See page 551*

LILLIE LOIS FORD SCHOLARSHIP FUND
• *See page 552*

AMERICAN LEGION, DEPARTMENT OF MONTANA

ORATORICAL CONTEST

Applicants participate in a statewide memorized oratorical contest on the United States Constitution. Four places are awarded. Must be a Montana high school student. Contact state adjutant American Legion Department of Montana for further details.

Award: Scholarship for use in freshman year; not renewable. *Number:* 1–4. *Amount:* $300–$1000.

Eligibility Requirements: Applicant must be high school student; planning to enroll or expecting to enroll full-time at a two-year or four-year or technical institution or university; resident of Montana and must have an interest in public speaking. Available to U.S. citizens.

Application Requirements: Application, applicant must enter a contest, memorized speech. *Deadline:* Continuous.

Contact: Gary White, State Adjutant
American Legion, Department of Montana
PO Box 6075
Helena, MT 59604
Phone: 406-324-3989
Fax: 406-324-3990
E-mail: amlegmt@in-tch.com

AMERICAN LEGION, DEPARTMENT OF NEBRASKA http://www.legion.org

AMERICAN LEGION DEPARTMENT OF NEBRASKA ORATORICAL AWARDS

Several one-time awards ranging from $100 to $1000 for high school students who are residents of Nebraska. Must submit speech. Must have minimum of 2.5 GPA. Must be between the ages of 14-19.

Award: Prize for use in freshman year; not renewable. *Number:* up to 19. *Amount:* $100–$1000.

Eligibility Requirements: Applicant must be high school student; age 14-19; planning to enroll or expecting to enroll full-time at a two-year or four-year or technical institution or university; resident of Nebraska and must have an interest in public speaking. Applicant must have 2.5 GPA or higher. Available to U.S. citizens.

Application Requirements: Application, applicant must enter a contest, autobiography, financial need analysis, photo, references, transcript. *Deadline:* November 1.

Contact: Burdette Burkhart, Activities Director
American Legion, Department of Nebraska
PO Box 5205
Lincoln, NE 68505-0205
Phone: 402-464-6338
Fax: 402-464-6330
E-mail: actdirlegion@alltel.net

EDGAR J. BOSCHULT MEMORIAL SCHOLARSHIP
• *See page 552*

MAYNARD JENSEN AMERICAN LEGION MEMORIAL SCHOLARSHIP
• *See page 449*

AMERICAN LEGION, DEPARTMENT OF NEW YORK http://www.ny.legion.org

AMERICAN LEGION DEPARTMENT OF NEW YORK STATE HIGH SCHOOL ORATORICAL CONTEST

Oratorical contest open to students under the age of twenty in 9th-12th grades of any accredited New York high school. Speech contests begin in November at post levels and continue on to national competition. Contact local American Legion post for deadlines. Must be U.S. citizen or lawful permanent resident. Payments are made directly to college and are awarded over a four-year period.

Award: Scholarship for use in freshman year; not renewable. *Number:* 65. *Amount:* $75–$6000.

Eligibility Requirements: Applicant must be high school student; age 19 or under; planning to enroll or expecting to enroll at an institution or university; resident of New York and must have an interest in public speaking. Available to U.S. citizens.

Application Requirements: Application, applicant must enter a contest. *Deadline:* varies.

Contact: Richard Pedro, Department Adjutant
American Legion, Department of New York
112 State Street, Suite 400
Albany, NY 12207
Phone: 518-463-2215
Fax: 518-427-8443
E-mail: newyork@legion.org

AMERICAN LEGION, DEPARTMENT OF NORTH CAROLINA

AMERICAN LEGION DEPARTMENT OF NORTH CAROLINA HIGH SCHOOL ORATORICAL CONTEST

Objective is to develop a deeper knowledge and appreciation of the U.S. Constitution, develop leadership qualities, think and speak clearly and intelligently, and prepare for acceptance of duties, responsibilities, rights, and privileges of American citizenship. Open to North Carolina high school students. Must be U.S. citizen or lawful permanent resident.

Award: Scholarship for use in freshman year; not renewable. *Number:* 5. *Amount:* $250–$1500.

Eligibility Requirements: Applicant must be high school student; age 20 or under; planning to enroll or expecting to enroll full or part-time at a two-year or four-year or technical institution or university and resident of North Carolina. Available to U.S. citizens.

Application Requirements: Applicant must enter a contest. *Deadline:* January 1.

Contact: American Legion, Department of North Carolina
PO Box 26657
Raleigh, NC 27611-6657
E-mail: nclegion@nc.rr.com

AMERICAN LEGION, DEPARTMENT OF NORTH DAKOTA http://www.ndlegion.org

AMERICAN LEGION DEPARTMENT OF NORTH DAKOTA NATIONAL HIGH SCHOOL ORATORICAL CONTEST

Oratorical contest for high school students in grades 9-12. Contestants must prepare to speak on the topic of the U.S. Constitution. Must graduate from an

American Legion, Department of North Dakota (continued)

accredited North Dakota high school. Contest begins at the local level and continues to the national level. Several one-time awards of $100-$1900.

Award: Prize for use in freshman year; not renewable. *Number:* 38. *Amount:* $100–$1900.

Eligibility Requirements: Applicant must be high school student; planning to enroll or expecting to enroll at an institution or university; resident of North Dakota and must have an interest in public speaking. Available to U.S. citizens.

Application Requirements: Application, applicant must enter a contest, speech contest. *Deadline:* November 30.

Contact: American Legion, Department of North Dakota
Box 2666
Fargo, ND 58108-2666
Phone: 701-293-3120
Fax: 701-293-9951
E-mail: adjutant@ndlegion.org

HATTIE TEDROW MEMORIAL FUND SCHOLARSHIP

• *See page 552*

NORTH DAKOTA CARING CITIZEN SCHOLARSHIP

One-time award for North Dakota high school juniors who participated in the Boys State Program. Must be nominated by Boys State official. Must demonstrate care and concern for fellow students.

Award: Scholarship for use in freshman year; not renewable. *Number:* 1. *Amount:* $200.

Eligibility Requirements: Applicant must be high school student; planning to enroll or expecting to enroll at a two-year or four-year or technical institution or university; male and resident of North Dakota. Available to U.S. citizens.

Application Requirements: References, nomination. *Deadline:* Continuous.

Contact: American Legion, Department of North Dakota
Box 2666
Fargo, ND 58108-2666
Phone: 701-293-3120
Fax: 701-293-9951
E-mail: adjutant@ndlegion.org

AMERICAN LEGION, DEPARTMENT OF OREGON

NATIONAL ORATORICAL SCHOLARSHIP CONTEST

Students give two (2) orations, one prepared and one extemporaneous on an assigned topic pertaining to the Constitution of the United States of America. Awards are given at Post, District, and State level with the state winner advancing to the National level contest. This is open to students enrolled in high schools within the state of Oregon.

Award: Scholarship for use in freshman, sophomore, junior, or senior years; not renewable. *Number:* 4. *Amount:* $200–$500.

Eligibility Requirements: Applicant must be high school student; planning to enroll or expecting to enroll full-time at a two-year or four-year or technical institution or university and resident of Oregon. Available to U.S. citizens.

Application Requirements: Application, applicant must enter a contest. *Deadline:* December 1.

Contact: Jim Willis, Chairman
American Legion, Department of Oregon
PO Box 1730
Wilsonville, OR 97070-1730
Phone: 541-924-0547

AMERICAN LEGION, DEPARTMENT OF PENNSYLVANIA

http://www.pa-legion.com

AMERICAN LEGION DEPARTMENT OF PENNSYLVANIA STATE ORATORICAL CONTEST

Oratorical contest open to students in 9th-12th grades of any accredited Pennsylvania high school. Speech contests begin in January at post level and continue on to national competition. Contact local American Legion post for deadlines and application details. Three one-time awards ranging from $1000 to $2500.

Award: Prize for use in freshman year; not renewable. *Number:* 3. *Amount:* $1000–$2500.

Eligibility Requirements: Applicant must be high school student; planning to enroll or expecting to enroll at an institution or university; resident of Pennsylvania and must have an interest in public speaking. Available to U.S. citizens.

Application Requirements: Application, applicant must enter a contest.

Contact: Debra Bellis, Scholarship Secretary
American Legion, Department of Pennsylvania
PO Box 2324
Harrisburg, PA 17105-2324
Phone: 717-730-9100
Fax: 717-975-2836
E-mail: hq@pa-legion.com

JOSEPH P. GAVENONIS COLLEGE SCHOLARSHIP (PLAN I)

• *See page 449*

AMERICAN LEGION, DEPARTMENT OF SOUTH CAROLINA

AMERICAN LEGION DEPARTMENT OF SOUTH CAROLINA HIGH SCHOOL ORATORICAL CONTEST

South Carolina high school oratorical contest. Participant must present oration of 8-10 minutes in duration on some phase of the U.S. Constitution. Contact adjutant for more information. Four renewable awards of varying amounts. Available to U.S. citizens or lawful residents of the U.S.

Award: Prize for use in freshman, sophomore, junior, or senior years; renewable. *Number:* 4. *Amount:* $500–$1600.

Eligibility Requirements: Applicant must be high school student; age 20 or under; planning to enroll or expecting to enroll full or part-time at a two-year or four-year or technical institution or university; resident of South Carolina and must have an interest in public speaking. Available to U.S. citizens.

Application Requirements: Applicant must enter a contest. *Deadline:* January 1.

Contact: Jim Hawk, Department Adjutant
American Legion, Department of South Carolina
PO Box 11355
Columbia, SC 29211
Phone: 803-799-1992
Fax: 803-791-9831
E-mail: dept.programs@aldsc.org

AMERICAN LEGION ROBERT E. DAVID CHILDREN'S SCHOLARSHIP FUND

• *See page 552*

AMERICAN LEGION, DEPARTMENT OF SOUTH DAKOTA

http://www.sdlegion.org

SOUTH DAKOTA HIGH SCHOOL ORATORICAL CONTEST

Provide a 8-10 minute oration on some phase of the U.S. Constitution. Be prepared to speak extemporaneously for 3.5 minutes on specified articles or amendments. Compete at Local, District, and State levels. State winner goes on to National Contest and opportunity to win $18,000 in scholarships. Contact local American Legion post for contest dates.

Award: Prize for use in freshman, sophomore, junior, or senior years; not renewable. *Number:* 1–4. *Amount:* $100–$1000.

Eligibility Requirements: Applicant must be high school student; age 19 or under; planning to enroll or expecting to enroll full or part-time at a two-year or four-year or technical institution or university and resident of South Dakota. Available to U.S. citizens.

Application Requirements: Applicant must enter a contest, oration. *Deadline:* varies.

Contact: Ronald Boyd, Department Adjutant
American Legion, Department of South Dakota
PO Box 67
Watertown, SD 57201
Phone: 605-886-3604
Fax: 605-886-2870
E-mail: sdlegion@dailypost.com

AMERICAN LEGION, DEPARTMENT OF TENNESSEE

AMERICAN LEGION DEPARTMENT OF TENNESSEE EAGLE SCOUT OF THE YEAR

• *See page 450*

AMERICAN LEGION DEPARTMENT OF TENNESSEE ORATORICAL CONTEST

Oratorical contest open to students in grades 9-12. Three students from each school in Tennessee may participate. Given on district, state, and national levels. Contact chairperson for more information.

Award: Scholarship for use in freshman year; not renewable. *Number:* 1–3. *Amount:* $1000–$4000.

Eligibility Requirements: Applicant must be high school student; planning to enroll or expecting to enroll full or part-time at a two-year or four-year or technical institution or university; resident of Tennessee and must have an interest in public speaking. Available to U.S. citizens.

Application Requirements: Application, applicant must enter a contest. *Deadline:* varies.

Contact: Darlene Burgess, Executive Assistant
American Legion, Department of Tennessee
215 Eighth Avenue North
Nashville, TN 37211
Phone: 615-254-0568
Fax: 615-255-1551

AMERICAN LEGION, DEPARTMENT OF TEXAS

http://www.txlegion.org

AMERICAN LEGION HIGH SCHOOL ORATORICAL CONTEST

Scholarships will be given to the winners of oratorical contests. Contestants must be in high school with plans to further their education in a postsecondary institution. Success on a local level may allow the student to compete on a national level for more money.

Award: Scholarship for use in freshman year; not renewable. *Number:* 15. *Amount:* $100–$2500.

Eligibility Requirements: Applicant must be high school student; age 19 or under; planning to enroll or expecting to enroll full or part-time at a two-year or four-year or technical institution or university and resident of Texas. Available to U.S. citizens.

Application Requirements: Application, applicant must enter a contest, essay, interview. *Deadline:* January 1.

Contact: Robert Squyres, Director of Internal Affairs
American Legion, Department of Texas
Oratorical Contest
3401 Ed Bluestein Boulevard
Austin, TX 78721-2902
Phone: 512-472-4138
Fax: 512-472-0603
E-mail: programs@txlegion.org

AMERICAN LEGION, DEPARTMENT OF VERMONT

AMERICAN LEGION DEPARTMENT OF VERMONT DEPARTMENT SCHOLARSHIPS

Award for high school seniors who attend a Vermont high school or similar school in an adjoining state whose parents are legal residents of Vermont, or reside in an adjoining state and attend a Vermont secondary school.

Award: Scholarship for use in freshman, sophomore, junior, or senior years; not renewable. *Number:* 12. *Amount:* $500–$2000.

Eligibility Requirements: Applicant must be high school student; planning to enroll or expecting to enroll full-time at a two-year or four-year or technical institution or university and resident of Vermont. Available to U.S. citizens.

Application Requirements: Application, financial need analysis, references, test scores, transcript. *Deadline:* April 1.

Contact: Huzon Stewart, Chairman
American Legion, Department of Vermont
PO Box 396
Montpelier, VT 05601-0396
Phone: 802-223-7131
Fax: 802-223-0318
E-mail: alvt@sover.net

AMERICAN LEGION EAGLE SCOUT OF THE YEAR

• *See page 450*

AMERICAN LEGION HIGH SCHOOL ORATORICAL CONTEST-VERMONT

• *See page 552*

AMERICAN LEGION, DEPARTMENT OF VIRGINIA

http://www.valegion.org

AMERICAN LEGION DEPARTMENT OF VIRGINIA HIGH SCHOOL ORATORICAL CONTEST AWARD

Oratorical contest open to applicants who are winners of the Virginia Department oratorical contest and who attend high school in Virginia. Competitors must demonstrate their knowledge of the U.S. Constitution. Must be student in 9th-12th grades at accredited Virginia high school. Three one-time awards of up to $2300.

Award: Prize for use in freshman year; not renewable. *Number:* 3. *Amount:* $500–$2300.

Eligibility Requirements: Applicant must be high school student; age 20 or under; planning to enroll or expecting to enroll full or part-time at a two-year or four-year or technical institution or university and resident of Virginia. Available to U.S. citizens.

Application Requirements: Application, applicant must enter a contest, references. *Deadline:* December 1.

Contact: Dale Chapman, Adjutant
American Legion, Department of Virginia
1708 Commonwealth Avenue
Richmond, VA 23230
Phone: 804-353-6606
Fax: 804-358-1940
E-mail: eeccleston@valegion.org

AMERICAN LEGION, DEPARTMENT OF WASHINGTON

http://www.walegion.org

AMERICAN LEGION DEPARTMENT OF WASHINGTON CHILDREN AND YOUTH SCHOLARSHIPS

• *See page 450*

AMERICAN LEGION, DEPARTMENT OF WEST VIRGINIA

AMERICAN LEGION DEPARTMENT OF WEST VIRGINIA STATE ORATORICAL CONTEST

Oratorical contest open to student in 9th-12th grades of any accredited West Virginia high school. Speech contests begin in January at post level and continue on to national competition. Contact local American Legion Post for deadlines and application details.

Award: Scholarship for use in freshman year; not renewable. *Number:* up to 39. *Amount:* $25–$100.

Eligibility Requirements: Applicant must be high school student; planning to enroll or expecting to enroll at a four-year institution; resident of West Virginia and must have an interest in public speaking. Available to U.S. citizens.

American Legion, Department of West Virginia (continued)

Application Requirements: Application, applicant must enter a contest. *Deadline:* January 1.

Contact: Mr. Miles Epling, State Adjutant
American Legion, Department of West Virginia
2016 Kanawha Boulevard, East
Charleston, WV 25332
Phone: 304-343-7591
Fax: 304-343-7592
E-mail: wvlegion@aol.com

AMERICAN LEGION, DEPARTMENT OF WEST VIRGINIA BOARD OF REGENTS SCHOLARSHIP

One-time prize awarded annually to the winner of the West Virginia American Legion State Oratorical Contest. Must be in 9th-12th grades of accredited West Virginia high school to compete. For use at West Virginia institution.

Award: Scholarship for use in freshman year; not renewable. *Number:* 1. *Amount:* up to $1500.

Eligibility Requirements: Applicant must be high school student; planning to enroll or expecting to enroll full-time at a four-year institution; resident of West Virginia; studying in West Virginia and must have an interest in public speaking. Available to U.S. citizens.

Application Requirements: Application, applicant must enter a contest. *Deadline:* January 1.

Contact: Mr. Miles Epling, State Adjutant
American Legion, Department of West Virginia
2016 Kanawha Boulevard, East
Charleston, WV 25332

WILLIAM F. "BILL" JOHNSON MEMORIAL SCHOLARSHIP SPONSORED BY SONS OF THE AMERICAN LEGION

• *See page 450*

AMERICAN LEGION, DEPARTMENT OF WYOMING

E.A. BLACKMORE MEMORIAL SCHOLARSHIP

• *See page 450*

AMERICAN QUARTER HORSE FOUNDATION (AQHF) http://www.aqha.org/aqhya

ARIZONA QUARTER HORSE YOUTH RACING SCHOLARSHIP

• *See page 451*

DR. GERALD O'CONNOR MICHIGAN SCHOLARSHIP

• *See page 451*

INDIANA QUARTER HORSE YOUTH SCHOLARSHIP

• *See page 452*

JOAN CAIN FLORIDA QUARTER HORSE YOUTH SCHOLARSHIP

• *See page 452*

NEBRASKA QUARTER HORSE YOUTH SCHOLARSHIP

• *See page 452*

RAY MELTON MEMORIAL VIRGINIA QUARTER HORSE YOUTH SCHOLARSHIP

• *See page 453*

SWAYZE WOODRUFF SCHOLARSHIP

• *See page 453*

AMERICAN SOCIETY FOR CLINICAL LABORATORY SCIENCE http://www.ascls.org

ASCLS REGION VI MISSOURI ORGANIZATION FOR CLINICAL LABORATORY SCIENCE STUDENT SCHOLARSHIP

Scholarship provides financial assistance to clinical laboratory science or medical laboratory technology students who are beginning or continuing their formal education, or conducting research that directly relates to laboratory science. Applicant must submit proof of acceptance or enrollment in the educational program. Please refer to Web site for further information and application: http://www.mocls.org.

Award: Scholarship for use in freshman, sophomore, junior, senior, or graduate years; not renewable. *Number:* varies. *Amount:* $200.

Eligibility Requirements: Applicant must be enrolled or expecting to enroll full or part-time at a two-year or four-year or technical institution or university and resident of Missouri. Available to U.S. citizens.

Application Requirements: Application, references, personal letter/research proposal. *Deadline:* varies.

Contact: Tom Reddig, Missouri Scholarship Fund Chair
American Society for Clinical Laboratory Science
31 West 59th Street
Kansas City, MO 64113
Phone: 816-931-8686

AMERICAN SOCIETY OF TRAVEL AGENTS (ASTA) FOUNDATION http://www.astanet.com

ARIZONA CHAPTER DEPENDENT/EMPLOYEE MEMBERSHIP SCHOLARSHIP

• *See page 453*

AMVETS DEPARTMENT OF ILLINOIS http://www.amvets.com

ILLINOIS AMVETS LADIES AUXILIARY MEMORIAL SCHOLARSHIP

• *See page 553*

ILLINOIS AMVETS LADIES AUXILIARY WORCHID SCHOLARSHIPS

• *See page 553*

ILLINOIS AMVETS SAFE DRIVING EXCELLENCE

Applicant must be an Illinois high school sophomore, junior, or senior. Provide a copy of driver's license and a copy of certificate of completion of driver's education.

Award: Scholarship for use in freshman, sophomore, junior, or senior years; renewable. *Number:* 3. *Amount:* $500–$1500.

Eligibility Requirements: Applicant must be high school student; age 16-18; planning to enroll or expecting to enroll full-time at a two-year or four-year or technical institution or university and resident of Illinois. Available to U.S. citizens.

Application Requirements: Application, applicant must enter a contest, driver's license, certificate of completion of driver's education. *Deadline:* March 1.

Contact: Sara Van Dyke, Scholarship Director
AMVETS Department of Illinois
2200 South Sixth Street
Springfield, IL 62703-3496
Phone: 217-528-4713
Fax: 217-528-9896
E-mail: scholarship@amvetsillinois.com

ILLINOIS AMVETS SERVICE FOUNDATION SCHOLARSHIP AWARD

• *See page 553*

ILLINOIS AMVETS TRADE SCHOOL SCHOLARSHIP

• *See page 553*

ARIZONA ASSOCIATION OF CHICANOS IN HIGHER EDUCATION (AACHE) http://www.aache.org/

AACHE SCHOLARSHIP

• *See page 577*

ARIZONA COMMISSION FOR POSTSECONDARY EDUCATION http://www.azhighered.org

ARIZONA PRIVATE POSTSECONDARY EDUCATION STUDENT FINANCIAL ASSISTANCE PROGRAM

Provides grants to financially needy Arizona Community College graduates to attend a private postsecondary baccalaureate degree-granting institution.

Award: Forgivable loan for use in junior or senior years; renewable. *Number:* varies. *Amount:* $750–$1500.

Eligibility Requirements: Applicant must be enrolled or expecting to enroll full-time at a four-year institution or university; resident of Arizona and studying in Arizona. Available to U.S. citizens.

Application Requirements: Financial need analysis, transcript, promissory note. *Deadline:* Continuous.

Contact: Danny Lee, PFAP Program Manager
Arizona Commission for Postsecondary Education
2020 North Central Avenue, Suite 550
Phoenix, AZ 85004-4503
Phone: 602-258-2435 Ext. 103
Fax: 602-258-2483
E-mail: dan_lee@azhighered.org

LEVERAGING EDUCATIONAL ASSISTANCE PARTNERSHIP

LEAP provides grants to financially needy students who enroll in and attend postsecondary education or training in Arizona schools. LEAP Program was formerly known as the State Student Incentive Grant or SSIG Program.

Award: Grant for use in freshman, sophomore, junior, senior, or graduate years; not renewable. *Number:* varies. *Amount:* $100–$2500.

Eligibility Requirements: Applicant must be enrolled or expecting to enroll full or part-time at a two-year or four-year or technical institution or university; resident of Arizona and studying in Arizona. Available to U.S. citizens.

Application Requirements: Financial need analysis. *Deadline:* Continuous.

Contact: Mila A. Zaporteza, Business Manager/LEAP Financial Aid Manager
Arizona Commission for Postsecondary Education
2020 North Central Avenue, Suite 550
Phoenix, AZ 85004-4503
Phone: 602-258-2435 Ext. 102
Fax: 602-258-2483
E-mail: mila@azhighered.org

ARIZONA PRIVATE SCHOOL ASSOCIATION http://www.arizonapsa.org

ARIZONA PRIVATE SCHOOL ASSOCIATION SCHOLARSHIP

This program is for Arizona high school seniors who wish to attend a trade or technical institution in Arizona the following year. Application deadline is in April.

Award: Scholarship for use in freshman year; not renewable. *Number:* 600. *Amount:* $1000.

Eligibility Requirements: Applicant must be high school student; planning to enroll or expecting to enroll full or part-time at a technical institution; resident of Arizona and studying in Arizona. Available to U.S. citizens.

Application Requirements: Application, essay. *Deadline:* April 4.

Contact: Fred Lockhart, Executive Director
Arizona Private School Association
202 East McDowell Road, Suite 273
Phoenix, AZ 85004-4536
Phone: 602-254-5199
Fax: 602-254-5073
E-mail: apsa@eschelon.com

ARKANSAS COMMUNITY FOUNDATION, INC. http://www.arcf.org

ARKANSAS SERVICE MEMORIAL FUND

One-time award for students whose parent died in service to his/her community, county, state, or nation. Must attend an Arkansas postsecondary institution and be a resident of Arkansas. See Web site for more information. (http://www.arcf.org/scholarships.html).

Award: Scholarship for use in freshman, sophomore, junior, or senior years; not renewable. *Amount:* $500–$5000.

Eligibility Requirements: Applicant must be enrolled or expecting to enroll at a two-year or four-year or technical institution or university; resident of Arkansas and studying in Arkansas. Available to U.S. citizens.

Application Requirements: Application. *Deadline:* March 15.

Contact: Arkansas Community Foundation, Inc.
700 South Rock Street
Little Rock, AR 72202-2519

L.A. DARLING COMPANY SCHOLARSHIP FUND

Award open to graduating seniors who are children of L.A. Darling Company employees. Must be a resident of Arkansas. Contact for more information.

Award: Scholarship for use in freshman year; not renewable. *Amount:* $500–$5000.

Eligibility Requirements: Applicant must be high school student; planning to enroll or expecting to enroll at an institution or university and resident of Arkansas. Available to U.S. citizens.

Application Requirements: Application. *Deadline:* March 15.

Contact: L.A. Darling Company
Arkansas Community Foundation, Inc.
1401 Highway 49B
Paragould, AR 72450
Phone: 800-643-3499
E-mail: darling@ladarling.com

MAVERICK SCHOLARSHIP FUND

• *See page 491*

SCROLL TECHNOLOGIES SCHOLARSHIP FUND

• *See page 491*

SOUTHWESTERN BELL BATES SCHOLARSHIP FUND

• *See page 577*

ARKANSAS DEPARTMENT OF HIGHER EDUCATION http://www.arscholarships.com

ARKANSAS ACADEMIC CHALLENGE SCHOLARSHIP PROGRAM

Awards for Arkansas residents who are graduating high school seniors to study at an Arkansas institution. Must have at least a 2.75 GPA, meet minimum ACT composite score standards, and have financial need. Renewable up to three additional years.

Award: Scholarship for use in freshman, sophomore, junior, or senior years; renewable. *Amount:* $2000–$3000.

Eligibility Requirements: Applicant must be high school student; planning to enroll or expecting to enroll full-time at a two-year or four-year institution or university; resident of Arkansas and studying in Arkansas. Available to U.S. citizens.

Application Requirements: Application, financial need analysis, test scores, transcript. *Deadline:* June 1.

Contact: Elyse Price, Assistant Coordinator
Arkansas Department of Higher Education
114 East Capitol
Little Rock, AR 72201
Phone: 501-371-2050
Fax: 501-371-2001

ARKANSAS STUDENT ASSISTANCE GRANT PROGRAM

Award for Arkansas residents attending a college within the state. Must be enrolled full-time, have financial need, and maintain satisfactory progress. One-time award for undergraduate use only. Application is the FAFSA.

Award: Grant for use in freshman, sophomore, junior, or senior years; not renewable. *Number:* 600–5500. *Amount:* $600.

Eligibility Requirements: Applicant must be enrolled or expecting to enroll full-time at a two-year or four-year or technical institution or university; resident of Arkansas and studying in Arkansas. Available to U.S. citizens.

Arkansas Department of Higher Education (continued)

Application Requirements: Application, financial need analysis, FAFSA. *Deadline:* April 1.

Contact: Mr. Philip Axelroth, Assistant Coordinator
Arkansas Department of Higher Education
114 East Capitol
Little Rock, AR 72201
Phone: 501-371-2050
Fax: 501-371-2001

GOVERNOR'S SCHOLARS-ARKANSAS

Awards for outstanding Arkansas high school seniors. Must be an Arkansas resident and have a high school GPA of at least 3.5 or have scored at least 27 on the ACT. Award is $4000 per year for four years of full-time undergraduate study. Applicants who attain 32 or above on ACT, 1410 or above on SAT and have an academic 3.50 GPA, or are selected as National Merit or National Achievement finalists may receive an award equal to tuition, mandatory fees, room, and board up to $10,000 per year at any Arkansas institution.

Award: Scholarship for use in freshman, sophomore, junior, or senior years; renewable. *Number:* 75–250. *Amount:* $4000–$10,000.

Eligibility Requirements: Applicant must be high school student; planning to enroll or expecting to enroll full-time at a two-year or four-year institution or university; resident of Arkansas and studying in Arkansas. Applicant must have 3.5 GPA or higher. Available to U.S. citizens.

Application Requirements: Application, test scores, transcript. *Deadline:* February 1.

Contact: Philip Axelroth, Assistant Coordinator of Financial Aid
Arkansas Department of Higher Education
114 East Capitol
Little Rock, AR 72201
Phone: 501-371-2050
Fax: 501-371-2001
E-mail: phila@adhe.arknet.edu

LAW ENFORCEMENT OFFICERS' DEPENDENTS SCHOLARSHIP-ARKANSAS

• *See page 505*

MISSING IN ACTION/KILLED IN ACTION DEPENDENT'S SCHOLARSHIP-ARKANSAS

• *See page 554*

SECOND EFFORT SCHOLARSHIP

Awarded to those scholars who achieved one of the 10 highest scores on the Arkansas High School Diploma Test (GED). Must be at least age 18 and not have graduated from high school. Students do not apply for this award, they are contacted by the Arkansas Department of Higher Education.

Award: Scholarship for use in freshman, sophomore, junior, or senior years; renewable. *Number:* 10. *Amount:* up to $1000.

Eligibility Requirements: Applicant must be age 18; enrolled or expecting to enroll full or part-time at a two-year or four-year institution or university; resident of Arkansas and studying in Arkansas. Applicant must have 2.5 GPA or higher.

Application Requirements: Application.

Contact:
Phone: 501-371-2050
Fax: 501-371-2001

ARKANSAS SINGLE PARENT SCHOLARSHIP FUND http://www.aspsf.org/default.htm

ARKANSAS SINGLE PARENT SCHOLARSHIP

Scholarships for single parents who reside in Arkansas to pursue higher education. Funds for graduate education will only be awarded to those pursuing a teaching degree. For county-specific information, see Web site: http://www.aspsf.org/default.htm

Award: Scholarship for use in freshman, sophomore, junior, senior, or graduate years; renewable. *Number:* varies.

Eligibility Requirements: Applicant must be enrolled or expecting to enroll full or part-time at a two-year or four-year institution or university; single and resident of Arkansas. Available to U.S. citizens.

Application Requirements: Application, essay, financial need analysis, transcript. *Deadline:* varies.

Contact: Arkansas Single Parent Scholarship Fund
614 East Emma
Suite 119
Springdale, AR 72764

ARRL FOUNDATION, INC. http://www.arrl.org/arrlf/scholgen.html

IRARC MEMORIAL/JOSEPH P.RUBINO, WA4MMD, SCHOLARSHIP

• *See page 454*

NEW ENGLAND FEMARA SCHOLARSHIPS

One-time award available to students licensed as amateur radio operator technicians. Applicants must reside in Vermont, Maine, New Hampshire, Rhode Island, Massachusetts, or Connecticut. Contact Amateur Radio Relay League for more information.

Award: Scholarship for use in freshman, sophomore, junior, or senior years; not renewable. *Amount:* $600.

Eligibility Requirements: Applicant must be enrolled or expecting to enroll at an institution or university; resident of Connecticut, Maine, Massachusetts, New Hampshire, Rhode Island, or Vermont and must have an interest in amateur radio. Available to U.S. citizens.

Application Requirements: Application, transcript. *Deadline:* February 1.

Contact: Mary Lau, Scholarship Director
ARRL Foundation, Inc.
225 Main Street
Newington, CT 06111-4845

NORMAN E. STROHMEIER, W2VRS MEMORIAL SCHOLARSHIP

One-time award available to students who are residents of Western New York and are amateur radio operators with a technician license. Preference is given to graduating high school seniors. Must have a 3.2 GPA or better.

Award: Scholarship for use in freshman, sophomore, junior, or senior years; not renewable. *Number:* 1. *Amount:* $500.

Eligibility Requirements: Applicant must be enrolled or expecting to enroll at an institution or university; resident of New York and must have an interest in amateur radio.

Application Requirements: Application. *Deadline:* February 1.

Contact: Mary Lau, Scholarship Director
ARRL Foundation, Inc.
225 Main Street
Newington, CT 06111-4845

SIX METER CLUB OF CHICAGO SCHOLARSHIP

For licensed amateur radio operators who are Illinois residents pursuing an undergraduate degree. Applicants from Indiana and Wisconsin will be considered if none from Illinois selected.

Award: Scholarship for use in freshman, sophomore, junior, or senior years; not renewable. *Number:* 1. *Amount:* $500.

Eligibility Requirements: Applicant must be enrolled or expecting to enroll at a two-year or four-year or technical institution or university; resident of Illinois, Indiana, or Wisconsin; studying in Illinois and must have an interest in amateur radio.

Application Requirements: Application, transcript. *Deadline:* February 1.

Contact: Mary Lau, Scholarship Coordinator
ARRL Foundation, Inc.
225 Main Street
Newington, CT 06111-4845

ASAP/UNION BANK & TRUST COMPANY - LINCOLN JOURNAL STAR'S NEWSPAPERS IN EDUCATION http://www.ubt.com/scholarship_ap.htm

"WE HAVE MONEY TO LEARN" SCHOLARSHIPS

Scholarships for Nebraska high school seniors who will be attending a Nebraska post-secondary institution on a full-time basis. Applications are considered for selection based on several criteria including ACT, GPA, essay, class rank, and school and community involvement.

Award: Scholarship for use in freshman year; not renewable. *Number:* 24. *Amount:* $500.

Eligibility Requirements: Applicant must be high school student; planning to enroll or expecting to enroll full-time at a two-year or four-year institution or university; resident of Nebraska and studying in Nebraska. Applicant must have 3.0 GPA or higher. Available to U.S. citizens.

Application Requirements: Application, essay, photo, resume, test scores, parental/guardian signature. *Deadline:* March 15.

Contact: Franny Madsen, Marketing Representative
ASAP/Union Bank & Trust Company - Lincoln Journal Star's Newspapers in Education
18 West 23rd Street
Kearney, NE 68847
Phone: 308-237-7593
Fax: 308-237-5729
E-mail: franny.madsen@ubt.com

ASTHMA AND ALLERGY FOUNDATION OF AMERICA (AAFA) GREATER KANSAS CITY CHAPTER http://www.aafakc.org

BERRI MITCHEL MEMORIAL SCHOLARSHIP

• *See page 523*

BARKING FOUNDATION http://www.barkingfoundation.org

BARKING FOUNDATION GRANTS

One-time award of $3000 available to Maine residents. Minimum GPA of 3.5 is desirable. Only first 300 completed applications will be accepted. Essay, financial information, and transcripts required. Available to full- and part-time students.

Award: Scholarship for use in freshman, sophomore, junior, senior, graduate, or postgraduate years; not renewable. *Number:* up to 25. *Amount:* $3000.

Eligibility Requirements: Applicant must be enrolled or expecting to enroll full or part-time at a four-year institution or university and resident of Maine. Applicant must have 3.5 GPA or higher. Available to U.S. citizens.

Application Requirements: Application, essay, financial need analysis, references, transcript. *Deadline:* February 28.

Contact: Stephanie Leonard, Administrator
Barking Foundation
PO Box 855
Bangor, ME 04402
Phone: 207-990-2910
Fax: 207-990-2975
E-mail: info@barkingfoundation.org

BECA FOUNDATION, INC.

DANIEL GUTIERREZ MEMORIAL GENERAL SCHOLARSHIP FUND

• *See page 578*

GENERAL SCHOLARSHIP FUND

• *See page 579*

BIG 33 SCHOLARSHIP FOUNDATION, INC. http://www.big33.org

BIG 33 SCHOLARSHIP FOUNDATION, INC. SCHOLARSHIPS

Open to all high school seniors in Pennsylvania and Ohio. Quantity of scholarships awarded, dollar amount of each, and type of scholarships varies each year. One-time award only. Minimum 2.0 GPA required. Applications are available at Web site: http://www.big33.org

Award: Scholarship for use in freshman year; not renewable. *Number:* 150–200. *Amount:* $500–$4500.

Eligibility Requirements: Applicant must be high school student; planning to enroll or expecting to enroll full-time at a two-year or four-year or technical institution or university and resident of Ohio or Pennsylvania. Available to U.S. citizens.

Application Requirements: Application, essay, transcript. *Deadline:* February 6.

Contact: Mickey Minnich, Executive Director
Big 33 Scholarship Foundation, Inc.
511 Bridge Street
PO Box 213
New Cumberland, PA 17070
Phone: 717-774-3303
Fax: 717-774-1749
E-mail: info@big33.org

BIG Y FOODS, INC. http://www.bigy.com

BIG Y SCHOLARSHIPS

Awards for customers or dependents of customers of Big Y Foods. Big Y trade area covers Norfolk County, western and central Massachusetts, and Connecticut. Also awards for Big Y employees and dependents of employees. Awards are based on academic excellence. Grades, board scores and two letters of recommendation required.

Award: Scholarship for use in freshman, sophomore, junior, senior, or graduate years; not renewable. *Number:* 200–250. *Amount:* $500–$2000.

Eligibility Requirements: Applicant must be enrolled or expecting to enroll full or part-time at a two-year or four-year institution or university; resident of Connecticut or Massachusetts and studying in Connecticut or Massachusetts. Available to U.S. and non-U.S. citizens.

Application Requirements: Application, references, test scores, transcript. *Deadline:* February 1.

Contact: Gail Borkosky, Scholarship Administrator
Big Y Foods, Inc.
2145 Roosevelt Avenue
Springfield, MA 01102-7840
Phone: 413-504-4062

BLUE GRASS ENERGY http://www.bgenergy.com

BLUE GRASS ENERGY ACADEMIC SCHOLARSHIP

Scholarships for Kentucky high school seniors whose parents or guardians are members of Blue Grass Energy residing in the service area. Must have minimum GPA of 3.0 and have demonstrated academic achievement. Must demonstrate financial need and submit biographical sketch, photo, account of personal involvement in school and community affairs, and justification for financial aid. For application and information, visit Web site: http://www.bgenergy.com.

Award: Scholarship for use in freshman year; not renewable. *Number:* 10. *Amount:* $1000.

Eligibility Requirements: Applicant must be high school student; planning to enroll or expecting to enroll full-time at a two-year or four-year or technical institution or university and resident of Kentucky. Applicant must have 3.0 GPA or higher. Available to U.S. citizens.

Application Requirements: Application, financial need analysis, transcript, handwritten request for scholarship. *Deadline:* March 1.

Contact: See Web site for application.
Blue Grass Energy
PO Box 990
Nicholasville, KY 40340-0990
Phone: 888-546-4243
E-mail: tonyw@bgenergy.com

BLUEGRASS CELLULAR, INC. http://www.bluegrasscellular.com

BLUEGRASS CELLULAR, INC. SCHOLARSHIP

One-time award available to Kentucky high school seniors who live and attend school within Bluegrass Cellular's 34-county home coverage area. Parents/guardian must be current customer who has received service for a minimum of 12 months, in good payment standing. Must be enrolling as

Bluegrass Cellular, Inc. (continued)

freshman in a post-secondary institution for fall semester. Minimum GPA of 2.5 required. Student or family member may not be employed by Bluegrass Cellular. Application available at Web site: http://www.bluegrasscellular.com.

Award: Scholarship for use in freshman year; not renewable. *Number:* 15. *Amount:* $1000.

Eligibility Requirements: Applicant must be high school student; planning to enroll or expecting to enroll full-time at a two-year or four-year or technical institution or university and resident of Kentucky. Applicant must have 2.5 GPA or higher. Available to U.S. citizens.

Application Requirements: Application, essay, references, transcript. *Deadline:* April 7.

Contact: Marketing Manager
Bluegrass Cellular, Inc.
2902 Ring Road
Elizabethtown, KY 42701
Phone: 270-769-0339
E-mail: custsvc@blue.net

BOETTCHER FOUNDATION http://www.boettcherfoundation.org

BOETTCHER FOUNDATION SCHOLARSHIPS

Merit-based scholarship available to graduating seniors in the state of Colorado. Selection based on class rank (top 5%), test scores, leadership, and service. Renewable for four years and can be used at any Colorado university or college. Includes full tuition and fees, living stipend of $2,800 per year, and a stipend for books.

Award: Scholarship for use in freshman, sophomore, junior, or senior years; renewable. *Number:* 40. *Amount:* $40,000–$120,000.

Eligibility Requirements: Applicant must be high school student; planning to enroll or expecting to enroll full-time at a four-year institution or university; resident of Colorado and studying in Colorado. Applicant must have 3.5 GPA or higher. Available to U.S. citizens.

Application Requirements: Application, essay, interview, references, test scores, transcript. *Deadline:* November 1.

Contact: Jennie Kenney, Scholarship Administrative Assistant
Boettcher Foundation
600 17th Street, Suite 2210 S
Denver, CO 80202-5422
Phone: 303-285-6207
E-mail: scholarships@boettcherfoundation.org

BOYS AND GIRLS CLUBS OF CHICAGO http://www.bgcc.org

BOYS AND GIRLS CLUBS OF CHICAGO SCHOLARSHIPS

• *See page 456*

BRADLEY M. SWANSON MEMORIAL SCHOLARSHIP FUND

BRADLEY M. SWANSON MEMORIAL SCHOLARSHIP

The Bradley M. Swanson Memorial Scholarship was established to award scholarships to those students whose high school class rank is in the top 15th to 30th percentile, have maintained a 2.5 GPA, and a composite minimum ACT score of 25 with no ACT subject area score below 24. Must be a U.S. citizen. Application forms may be requested via email: johnmarswa@worldnet.att.net

Award: Scholarship for use in freshman, sophomore, junior, or senior years; not renewable. *Number:* 1–3. *Amount:* $500–$1000.

Eligibility Requirements: Applicant must be enrolled or expecting to enroll full-time at a four-year institution or university and resident of Illinois, Iowa, Minnesota, South Dakota, or Wisconsin. Applicant must have 2.5 GPA or higher. Available to U.S. citizens.

Application Requirements: Application, essay, self-addressed stamped envelope, test scores, transcript, class rank. *Deadline:* January 30.

Contact: Marilyn Swanson, Director
Bradley M. Swanson Memorial Scholarship Fund
3408 Deer Path Road
Rockford, IL 61107
Phone: 815-877-5939
E-mail: johmarswa@worldnet.att.net

BUFFALO AFL-CIO COUNCIL

AFL-CIO COUNCIL OF BUFFALO SCHOLARSHIP

• *See page 456*

BUFFETT FOUNDATION http://www.buffettscholarships.org

BUFFETT FOUNDATION SCHOLARSHIP

Scholarship provides assistance for tuition and fees (only) up to $2500 per semester. Must be used at a Nebraska state school or a two-year college or trade school within Nebraska. High school applicant must have maintained a 2.5 GPA, college students a 2.0. Must have already applied for federal financial aid and have printed results. Strict deadlines apply. March 1st for requesting mail applications which must be returned by April 10. Must be Nebraska resident.

Award: Scholarship for use in freshman, sophomore, junior, or senior years; renewable. *Number:* varies. *Amount:* up to $2500.

Eligibility Requirements: Applicant must be enrolled or expecting to enroll full-time at a two-year or four-year or technical institution or university; resident of Nebraska and studying in Nebraska. Applicant must have 2.5 GPA or higher. Available to U.S. citizens.

Application Requirements: Application, autobiography, essay, financial need analysis, references, transcript, federal tax return. *Deadline:* April 10.

Contact: Devon Buffett, Director of Scholarships
Buffett Foundation
PO Box 4508
Decatur, IL 62525
Phone: 402-451-6011
E-mail: buffettfound@aol.com

CABRILLO CIVIC CLUBS OF CALIFORNIA, INC.

CABRILLO CIVIC CLUBS OF CALIFORNIA SCHOLARSHIP

• *See page 579*

CALIFORNIA ALARM ASSOCIATION http://www.caaonline.org

CAA YOUTH SCHOLARSHIP PROGRAM FOR CHILDREN OF LAW ENFORCEMENT AND FIRE SERVICE PERSONNEL

• *See page 506*

CALIFORNIA ASSOCIATION OF PRIVATE POSTSECONDARY SCHOOLS http://www.cappsonline.org

CAPPS SCHOLARSHIP PROGRAM

Schools participating in the CAPPS Scholarship Program offer both full- and partial-tuition scholarships to graduating high school students and adults wishing to pursue their education at a private career school. Scholarships are for tuition only. Applications are sent to the school of the applicant's choice; that school selects scholarship recipients using their own criteria. Among other qualifications listed on the application, recipients must meet that school's admissions requirements and be a California resident and a U.S. legal citizen to qualify. Written inquiries must include a self-addressed stamped envelope for reply.

Award: Scholarship for use in freshman year; not renewable. *Number:* 200–250. *Amount:* $1000–$10,000.

Eligibility Requirements: Applicant must be enrolled or expecting to enroll full or part-time at a two-year or technical institution or university and resident of California. Available to U.S. citizens.

Application Requirements: Application. *Deadline:* June 4.

Contact: Jan Oliver, Scholarship Coordinator
California Association of Private Postsecondary Schools
921 11th Street #619
Sacramento, CA 95814-2821
E-mail: info@cappsoline.org

CALIFORNIA COMMUNITY COLLEGES http://www.cccco.edu

COOPERATIVE AGENCIES RESOURCES FOR EDUCATION PROGRAM

Renewable award available to California resident attending a two-year California community college. Must have no more than 70 degree-applicable units, currently receive CALWORKS/TANF, and have at least one child under 14 years of age. Must be in EOPS, single head of household, and 18 or older. Contact local college EOPS-CARE office.

Award: Grant for use in freshman or sophomore years; renewable. *Number:* 11,000.

Eligibility Requirements: Applicant must be age 18; enrolled or expecting to enroll full-time at a two-year institution; single; resident of California and studying in California. Available to U.S. citizens.

Application Requirements: Application, financial need analysis, test scores, transcript. *Deadline:* Continuous.

Contact: Local Community College EOPS/CARE Program
California Community Colleges
1102 Q Street
Sacramento, CA 95814-6511

CALIFORNIA CONGRESS OF PARENTS AND TEACHERS, INC. http://www.capta.org

CALIFORNIA CONGRESS OF PARENTS AND TEACHERS, INC. SCHOLARSHIP

Scholarships awarded to California State PTA members for education and continuing education. Eligible applicants will be California residents. Deadlines are November 30 and March 15.

Award: Scholarship for use in freshman, sophomore, junior, senior, or graduate years; not renewable. *Number:* varies. *Amount:* $500–$5000.

Eligibility Requirements: Applicant must be enrolled or expecting to enroll full or part-time at a two-year or four-year or technical institution or university and resident of California. Available to U.S. and non-U.S. citizens.

Application Requirements: Application, references, transcript. *Deadline:* varies.

Contact: Brenda Stephen, Scholarship Coordinator
California Congress of Parents and Teachers, Inc.
930 Georgia Street
PO Box 15015
Los Angeles, CA 90015
Phone: 213-620-1100
E-mail: grants@capta.org

CALIFORNIA CORRECTIONAL PEACE OFFICERS ASSOCIATION http://www.ccpoa.org

CALIFORNIA CORRECTIONAL PEACE OFFICERS ASSOCIATION JOE HARPER SCHOLARSHIP

• *See page 506*

CALIFORNIA COUNCIL OF THE BLIND http://www.ccbnet.org

CALIFORNIA COUNCIL OF THE BLIND SCHOLARSHIPS

• *See page 524*

CALIFORNIA GRANGE FOUNDATION http://www.grangeonline.org

CALIFORNIA GRANGE FOUNDATION SCHOLARSHIP

• *See page 456*

CALIFORNIA JUNIOR MISS SCHOLARSHIP PROGRAM http://www.ajm.org/california

CALIFORNIA JUNIOR MISS SCHOLARSHIP PROGRAM

Scholarship program to recognize and reward outstanding high school junior females in the areas of academics, leadership, athletics, public speaking, and the performing arts. Must be single, female, a U.S. citizen, and resident of California. Minimum 3.0 GPA required.

Award: Scholarship for use in freshman, sophomore, junior, or senior years; not renewable. *Number:* 25. *Amount:* $500–$10,000.

Eligibility Requirements: Applicant must be high school student; age 15-17; planning to enroll or expecting to enroll full-time at a two-year or four-year or technical institution or university; single female; resident of California and must have an interest in leadership. Applicant must have 3.0 GPA or higher. Available to U.S. citizens.

Application Requirements: Application, applicant must enter a contest, essay, interview, test scores, transcript. *Deadline:* varies.

Contact: Becky Jo Peterson, California State Chairman
California Junior Miss Scholarship Program
3523 Glenbrook Lane
Napa, CA 94558
Phone: 707-224-2777
Fax: 707-224-2777
E-mail: caljrmiss@aol.com

CALIFORNIA MASONIC FOUNDATION http://www.californiamasons.org

CALIFORNIA MASONIC FOUNDATION SCHOLARSHIP AWARDS

Scholarships range from $1,000 to $12,000; most are renewable annually. An interview may or may not be part of the selection process. Must be a U.S. citizen and a resident of California for at least one year. Must be a high school senior. Must have a minimum 3.0 GPA and plan to attend an accredited two- or four-year institution of higher learning as a full-time undergraduate freshman in the fall following high school graduation. Check the Web site after September 1 for further information. (http://www.californiamasons.org)

Award: Scholarship for use in freshman year; renewable. *Amount:* $1000–$12,000.

Eligibility Requirements: Applicant must be high school student; planning to enroll or expecting to enroll full-time at a two-year or four-year institution or university and resident of California. Applicant must have 3.0 GPA or higher. Available to U.S. citizens.

Application Requirements: Application, essay, financial need analysis, interview, references, self-addressed stamped envelope, test scores, transcript. *Deadline:* February 15.

Contact: Applications available at Web site.

CALIFORNIA STUDENT AID COMMISSION http://www.csac.ca.gov

ASSUMPTION PROGRAMS OF LOANS FOR EDUCATION

The APLE is a competitive teacher loan assumption program designed to encourage outstanding students and out-of-state teachers to become California teachers within subject areas where a teacher shortage has been identified or in schools meeting specific criteria identified annually. Participants may receive up to $19,000 towards outstanding student loans.

Award: Forgivable loan for use in junior, senior, or graduate years; renewable. *Number:* up to 7700. *Amount:* $11,000–$19,000.

Eligibility Requirements: Applicant must be enrolled or expecting to enroll full or part-time at a four-year institution or university; resident of California and studying in California. Available to U.S. citizens.

Application Requirements: Application, references. *Deadline:* June 30.

Contact: California Student Aid Commission
PO Box 419027
Rancho Cordova, CA 95741-9027
Phone: 916-526-7590
Fax: 916-526-8002
E-mail: custsvcs@csac.ca.gov

CAL GRANT C

Award for California residents who are enrolled in a short-term vocational training program. Program must lead to a recognized degree or certificate.

California Student Aid Commission (continued)

Course length must be a minimum of 4 months and no longer than 24 months. Students must be attending an approved California institution and show financial need.

Award: Grant for use in freshman, sophomore, junior, or senior years; renewable. *Number:* up to 7761. *Amount:* $576–$3168.

Eligibility Requirements: Applicant must be enrolled or expecting to enroll full or part-time at a two-year or technical institution; resident of California and studying in California. Available to U.S. citizens.

Application Requirements: Application, financial need analysis, GPA verification. *Deadline:* March 2.

Contact: California Student Aid Commission
PO Box 419027
Rancho Cordova, CA 95741-9027
Phone: 916-526-7590
Fax: 916-526-8002
E-mail: custsvs@csac.ca.gov

CHILD DEVELOPMENT TEACHER AND SUPERVISOR GRANT PROGRAM

Award is for those students pursuing an approved course of study leading to a Child Development Permit issued by the California Commission on Teacher Credentialing. In exchange for each year funding is received, recipients agree to provide one year of service in a licensed childcare center.

Award: Grant for use in freshman, sophomore, junior, or senior years; renewable. *Number:* up to 300. *Amount:* $1000–$2000.

Eligibility Requirements: Applicant must be enrolled or expecting to enroll full or part-time at a two-year or four-year or technical institution or university; resident of California and studying in California. Available to U.S. citizens.

Application Requirements: Application, financial need analysis, references, FAFSA. *Deadline:* June 1.

Contact: California Student Aid Commission
PO Box 419027
Rancho Cordova, CA 95741-9027
Phone: 916-526-7590
Fax: 916-526-8002
E-mail: custsvcs@csac.ca.gov

COMPETITIVE CAL GRANT A

Award for California residents who are not recent high school graduates attending an approved college or university within the state. Must show financial need and meet minimum 3.0 GPA requirement.

Award: Grant for use in freshman, sophomore, junior, or senior years; renewable. *Number:* up to 22,500. *Amount:* $2046–$9708.

Eligibility Requirements: Applicant must be enrolled or expecting to enroll full or part-time at a two-year or four-year or technical institution or university; resident of California and studying in California. Applicant must have 3.0 GPA or higher. Available to U.S. citizens.

Application Requirements: Application, financial need analysis, GPA verification. *Deadline:* March 2.

Contact: California Student Aid Commission
PO Box 419027
Rancho Cordova, CA 95741-9027
Phone: 916-526-7590
Fax: 916-526-8002
E-mail: custsvcs@csac.ca.gov

COMPETITIVE CAL GRANT B

Award is for California residents who are not recent high school graduates attending an approved college or university within the state. Must show financial need and meet the minimum 2.0 GPA requirement.

Award: Grant for use in freshman, sophomore, or junior years; renewable. *Number:* up to 22,500. *Amount:* $700–$11,259.

Eligibility Requirements: Applicant must be enrolled or expecting to enroll full or part-time at a two-year or four-year or technical institution or university; resident of California and studying in California. Available to U.S. citizens.

Application Requirements: Application, financial need analysis, GPA verification. *Deadline:* March 2.

Contact: California Student Aid Commission
PO Box 419027
Rancho Cordova, CA 95741-9027
Phone: 916-526-7590
Fax: 916-526-8002
E-mail: custsvcs@csac.ca.gov

ENTITLEMENT CAL GRANT A

Award is for California residents who are recent high school graduates attending an approved college or university within the state. Must show financial need and meet the minimum 3.0 GPA requirement.

Award: Grant for use in freshman, sophomore, junior, or senior years; renewable. *Number:* varies. *Amount:* $2046–$9708.

Eligibility Requirements: Applicant must be enrolled or expecting to enroll full or part-time at a two-year or four-year or technical institution or university; resident of California and studying in California. Applicant must have 3.0 GPA or higher. Available to U.S. citizens.

Application Requirements: Application, financial need analysis, GPA verification. *Deadline:* March 2.

Contact: California Student Aid Commission
PO Box 419027
Rancho Cordova, CA 95741-9027
Phone: 916-526-7590
Fax: 916-526-8002
E-mail: custsvcs@csac.ca.gov

ENTITLEMENT CAL GRANT B

Award for California residents who are high school graduates attending an approved college or university within the state. Must show financial need and meet the minimum 2.0 GPA requirement.

Award: Grant for use in freshman, sophomore, junior, or senior years; renewable. *Number:* varies. *Amount:* $700–$11,259.

Eligibility Requirements: Applicant must be enrolled or expecting to enroll full or part-time at a two-year or four-year or technical institution or university; resident of California and studying in California. Available to U.S. citizens.

Application Requirements: Application, financial need analysis. *Deadline:* March 2.

Contact: California Student Aid Commission
PO Box 419027
Rancho Cordova, CA 95741-9027
Phone: 916-526-7590
Fax: 916-526-8002
E-mail: custsvcs@csac.ca.gov

LAW ENFORCEMENT PERSONNEL DEVELOPMENT SCHOLARSHIP

• *See page 506*

ROBERT C. BYRD SCHOLARSHIP

Federally funded award is available to California high school seniors. Students are awarded based on outstanding academic merit. Students must be nominated by their high school. Recipients must maintain satisfactory academic progress.

Award: Scholarship for use in freshman, sophomore, junior, or senior years; renewable. *Number:* 700–800. *Amount:* $1500.

Eligibility Requirements: Applicant must be high school student; planning to enroll or expecting to enroll full-time at a four-year institution or university and resident of California. Applicant must have 3.5 GPA or higher. Available to U.S. citizens.

Application Requirements: Application, financial need analysis, test scores. *Deadline:* April 30.

Contact: California Student Aid Commission
PO Box 419027
Rancho Cordova, CA 95741-9027
Phone: 916-526-7590
Fax: 916-526-8002
E-mail: custsvcs@csac.ca.gov

CALIFORNIA TABLE GRAPE COMMISSION http://www.freshcaliforniagrapes.com

CALIFORNIA TABLE GRAPE FARM WORKERS SCHOLARSHIP PROGRAM

• *See page 506*

CALIFORNIA WINE GRAPE GROWERS FOUNDATION http://www.cawg.org/cwggf/

CALIFORNIA WINE GRAPE GROWERS FOUNDATION SCHOLARSHIP

Scholarship for high school seniors whose parents or legal guardians are vineyard employees of wine grape growers. Recipients may study the subject of their choice at any campus of the University of California system, the California State University system, or the California Community College system.

Award: Scholarship for use in freshman, sophomore, junior, or senior years; not renewable. *Number:* 5. *Amount:* $1000–$4000.

Eligibility Requirements: Applicant must be high school student; planning to enroll or expecting to enroll full-time at a two-year or four-year institution or university; resident of California and studying in California. Applicant must have 2.5 GPA or higher. Available to U.S. citizens.

Application Requirements: Application, essay, references, test scores, transcript. *Deadline:* April 1.

Contact: Carolee Williams, Assistant Executive Director
California Wine Grape Growers Foundation
601 University Avenue, Suite 601
Sacramento, CA 95825
Phone: 916-924-5370
Fax: 916-924-5374
E-mail: carolee@cawg.org

CAREER COLLEGES AND SCHOOLS OF TEXAS http://www.colleges-schools.org

CAREER COLLEGES AND SCHOOLS OF TEXAS SCHOLARSHIP PROGRAM

One-time award available to graduating high school seniors who plan to attend a Texas trade or technical institution. Must be a Texas resident. Criteria selection, which is determined independently by each school's guidance counselors, may be based on academic excellence, financial need, or student leadership. Must be U.S. citizen.

Award: Scholarship for use in freshman year; not renewable. *Number:* up to 6000. *Amount:* up to $1000.

Eligibility Requirements: Applicant must be high school student; planning to enroll or expecting to enroll full or part-time at a technical institution; resident of Texas and studying in Texas. Available to U.S. citizens.

Application Requirements: Determined by high school. *Deadline:* Continuous.

Contact: High School counselors
Career Colleges and Schools of Texas
6460 Hiller, Suite D
El Paso, TX 79925

CASCADE POLICY INSTITUTE http://www.cascadepolicy.org/

SEVENTH ANNUAL INDEPENDENCE ESSAY COMPETITION

Essay contest for Oregon high school students, in which they are asked to answer: "What is the proper role of government in a free society?" Please refer to Web site for further details: http://www.cascadepolicy.org.

Award: Prize for use in freshman, sophomore, junior, senior, or graduate years; not renewable. *Number:* 5–10. *Amount:* $250–$1000.

Eligibility Requirements: Applicant must be high school student; planning to enroll or expecting to enroll at an institution or university and resident of Oregon. Available to U.S. citizens.

Application Requirements: Applicant must enter a contest, essay. *Deadline:* May 1.

Contact: Jon Hadley, Administrative Assistant
Cascade Policy Institute
813 Southwest Alder, Suite 450
Portland, OR 97205
Phone: 503-242-0900 Ext. 10
Fax: 503-242-3822
E-mail: jhadley@cascadepolicy.org

CASDA-LOT (CAPITAL AREA SCHOOL DEVELOPMENT ASSOCIATION) http://www.nylottery.org/lot

NEW YORK LOTTERY LEADERS OF TOMORROW (LOT) SCHOLARSHIP

The goal of this program is to reinforce the lottery's education mission by awarding four-year scholarships, $1000 per year for up to four years. One scholarship is available to every New York high school, public or private, that awards a high school diploma.

Award: Scholarship for use in freshman, sophomore, junior, or senior years; renewable. *Number:* varies. *Amount:* $1000.

Eligibility Requirements: Applicant must be high school student; planning to enroll or expecting to enroll full-time at a two-year or four-year or technical institution or university; resident of New York and studying in New York. Applicant must have 3.0 GPA or higher. Available to U.S. citizens.

Application Requirements: Application, essay, transcript. *Deadline:* varies.

Contact: Betsey Morgan, Program Coordinator
CASDA-LOT (Capital Area School Development Association)
The University at Albany East Campus
One University Place - A-409
Rensselaer, NY 12144-3456
Phone: 518-525-2788
Fax: 518-525-2797
E-mail: casdalot@uamail.albany.edu

CENTER FOR SCHOLARSHIP ADMINISTRATION http://www.scholarshipprograms.org

ANDERSON AREA SOCIETY FOR HUMAN RESOURCE MANAGEMENT NON-MEMBER SCHOLARSHIP PROGRAM

Non-renewable scholarship available to seniors in an Anderson County, SC high school. Applicant's parents cannot be members of AASHRM. For more details and an application, see Web site.

Award: Scholarship for use in freshman year; not renewable. *Number:* 1. *Amount:* $1000.

Eligibility Requirements: Applicant must be high school student; planning to enroll or expecting to enroll full-time at a two-year or four-year or technical institution or university and resident of South Carolina. Applicant must have 3.0 GPA or higher.

Application Requirements: Application, essay, financial need analysis, references, transcript. *Deadline:* February 15.

Contact: Application available at Web site.

BAPRM SCHOLARSHIP PROGRAM

Non-renewable award available to seniors attending high schools in one of the following six Bay Area counties in California: Alameda, Contra Costa, Marin, San Francisco, San Mateo, or Santa Clara. For more details and an application, see Web site.

Award: Scholarship for use in freshman year; not renewable. *Number:* 2. *Amount:* $1000.

Eligibility Requirements: Applicant must be high school student; planning to enroll or expecting to enroll full-time at a two-year or four-year or technical institution or university and resident of California. Applicant must have 2.5 GPA or higher. Available to U.S. citizens.

Center for Scholarship Administration (continued)

Application Requirements: Application, essay, financial need analysis, references, transcript. *Deadline:* February 15.

Contact: Application available at Web site.

ETHEL W. CROWLEY MEMORIAL EDUCATION FUND

Renewable award to a resident of Halifax County, NC who will be attending a four-year accredited college or university located in North Carolina. Four-year scholarships up to full tuition, room, board, school fees, and books will be awarded. For more details and an application, see Web site.

Award: Scholarship for use in freshman, sophomore, junior, or senior years; renewable. *Number:* varies. *Amount:* varies.

Eligibility Requirements: Applicant must be high school student; planning to enroll or expecting to enroll full-time at a four-year institution or university; resident of North Carolina and studying in North Carolina. Applicant must have 2.5 GPA or higher.

Application Requirements: Application, essay, financial need analysis, references, transcript. *Deadline:* February 27.

Contact: Application available at Web site.

HISPANIC LEAGUE OF THE PIEDMONT TRIAD SCHOLARSHIP

• *See page 580*

KITTIE M. FAIREY EDUCATIONAL FUND SCHOLARSHIPS

Renewable scholarships are for graduating high school seniors residing in South Carolina. Scholarships provide funding for half tuition and room and board (for boarding students). For more details and an application see Web site: http://www.scholarshipprograms.org

Award: Scholarship for use in freshman, sophomore, or junior years; renewable. *Number:* varies. *Amount:* varies.

Eligibility Requirements: Applicant must be enrolled or expecting to enroll full-time at a two-year or four-year institution or university and resident of South Carolina. Applicant must have 3.0 GPA or higher.

Application Requirements: Application. *Deadline:* January 31.

Contact: Application available at Web site.

MILLIKEN & COMPANY SCHOLARSHIP

• *See page 493*

SOUTH CAROLINA JUNIOR GOLF FOUNDATION SCHOLARSHIP

Scholarships are available to student residents of South Carolina who have a competitive or recreational interest in golf. Must have and maintain a 2.75 cumulative GPA. For more details and an application see Web site: http://www.scholarshipprograms.org

Award: Scholarship for use in freshman, sophomore, junior, or senior years; renewable. *Number:* varies. *Amount:* $2500.

Eligibility Requirements: Applicant must be enrolled or expecting to enroll full or part-time at a four-year institution or university; resident of South Carolina; studying in South Carolina and must have an interest in golf.

Application Requirements: Application, essay, financial need analysis, references, transcript. *Deadline:* February 15.

Contact: Application available at Web site.

SOUTHERN CALIFORNIA RELOCATION COUNCIL SCHOLARSHIP PROGRAM

One-time award to a senior attending public high school in one of the following Southern California counties: Orange, Los Angeles, San Diego, Riverside, Kern, and Ventura. Applicants must have relocated a minimum of 50 miles into one of these counties within the past two years. The award is also open to students who have moved into the U.S. from a foreign country during the same time frame. Must be a U.S. citizen and must have at least 2.75 GPA.

Award: Scholarship for use in freshman year; not renewable. *Number:* 1. *Amount:* $1000–$2000.

Eligibility Requirements: Applicant must be high school student; planning to enroll or expecting to enroll full-time at a two-year or four-year or technical institution or university and resident of California. Available to U.S. citizens.

Application Requirements: Application, essay, references, transcript. *Deadline:* February 15.

Contact: Application available at Web site.

CENTRAL NATIONAL BANK & TRUST COMPANY OF ENID, TRUSTEE

http://onecentralsource.us/trust_services.html

MAY T. HENRY SCHOLARSHIP FOUNDATION

$1000 scholarship renewed annually for four years. Awarded to any student enrolled in a state of Oklahoma supported college, university or tech school. Based on need, scholastic performance and personal traits valued by May T. Henry. Minimum 3.0 GPA required.

Award: Scholarship for use in freshman, sophomore, junior, senior, graduate, or postgraduate years; renewable. *Number:* up to 15. *Amount:* $1000.

Eligibility Requirements: Applicant must be enrolled or expecting to enroll full or part-time at a two-year or four-year or technical institution or university and studying in Oklahoma. Applicant must have 3.0 GPA or higher. Available to U.S. and non-U.S. citizens.

Application Requirements: Application, essay, financial need analysis, references, test scores, transcript. *Deadline:* April 1.

Contact: Karen Holland, Assistant Vice President
Central National Bank & Trust Company of Enid, Trustee
324 West Broadway
PO Box 3448
Enid, OK 73702-3448
Phone: 580-213-1613
Fax: 580-549-2941
E-mail: bhinther@cnb-enid.com

CENTRAL SCHOLARSHIP BUREAU

http://www.centralsb.org

MARY RUBIN AND BENJAMIN M. RUBIN SCHOLARSHIP FUND

Renewable scholarship for tuition only to women who are attending a college, university or other institution of higher learning. Must be a resident of Maryland. Have a GPA of 3.0 or better and meet the financial requirements. Contact for application or download from Web site: http://www.centralsb.org

Award: Scholarship for use in freshman, sophomore, junior, senior, graduate, or postgraduate years; renewable. *Number:* 30–35. *Amount:* $500–$2500.

Eligibility Requirements: Applicant must be enrolled or expecting to enroll full or part-time at a two-year or four-year or technical institution or university; female and resident of Maryland. Applicant must have 3.0 GPA or higher. Available to U.S. citizens.

Application Requirements: Application, essay, financial need analysis, references, transcript. *Deadline:* March 1.

Contact: Roberta Goldman, Program Director
Central Scholarship Bureau
1700 Reisterstown Road
Suite 220
Baltimore, MD 21208-2903
Phone: 410-415-5558
Fax: 410-415-5501
E-mail: roberta@centralsb.org

CHICANA/LATINA FOUNDATION

http://www.chicanalatina.org

SCHOLARSHIPS FOR LATINA STUDENTS

• *See page 580*

CIRI FOUNDATION

http://www.ciri.com/tcf

HOWARD ROCK FOUNDATION SCHOLARSHIP PROGRAM

Award for Alaska Native Student from an Alaska Village Initiative member organization. Must be enrolled full time in a four-year undergraduate program or in a graduate program. Must have a GPA of 2.5 or better and be in a field that promotes economic development in rural Alaska. Deadline: March 31.

Award: Scholarship for use in freshman, sophomore, junior, senior, or graduate years; not renewable. *Number:* 3. *Amount:* $2500–$5000.

Eligibility Requirements: Applicant must be enrolled or expecting to enroll full-time at a four-year institution or university and resident of Alaska. Applicant must have 2.5 GPA or higher.

Application Requirements: Application, essay, financial need analysis, references, transcript. *Deadline:* March 31.

Contact: CIRI Foundation
2600 Cordova Street, Suite 206
Anchorage, AK 99503
Phone: 907-263-5582
Fax: 907-263-5588
E-mail: tcf@ciri.com

CITY COLLEGE OF SAN FRANCISCO LATINO EDUCATIONAL ASSOCIATION http://www.ccsf.edu

LATINO EDUCATION ASSOCIATION SCHOLARSHIP

• *See page 581*

CIVIL SERVICE EMPLOYEES INSURANCE COMPANY http://www.cseinsurance.com

YOUTH AUTOMOBILE SAFETY SCHOLARSHIP ESSAY COMPETITION FOR CHILDREN OF PUBLIC EMPLOYEES

• *See page 507*

COLEMAN A. YOUNG FOUNDATION http://www.cayf.org

COLEMAN A. YOUNG FOUNDATION SCHOLARSHIP

Renewable award to Detroit area high school seniors who demonstrate leadership qualities. Minimum 2.5 GPA required. Must be single and U.S. citizen. Deadline is April 1. Aimed at students who would not ordinarily qualify for traditional scholarships. Must be enrolled full-time in a four year college in Michigan or attend an accredited, historically black institution.

Award: Scholarship for use in freshman, sophomore, junior, or senior years; renewable. *Number:* 5–10. *Amount:* up to $20,000.

Eligibility Requirements: Applicant must be high school student; planning to enroll or expecting to enroll full-time at a four-year institution or university; single and resident of Michigan. Applicant must have 2.5 GPA or higher. Available to U.S. citizens.

Application Requirements: Application, essay, financial need analysis, interview, resume, references, test scores, transcript. *Deadline:* April 1.

Contact: Thelma Bush, Program Manager
Coleman A. Young Foundation
2111 Woodward Avenue, Suite 600
Detroit, MI 48201
Phone: 313-962-2200
Fax: 313-962-2208
E-mail: thelmabush@cayf.org

COLLEGEBOUND FOUNDATION http://www.collegeboundfoundation.org

BALTIMORE JUNIOR ASSOCIATION OF COMMERCE (BJAC) SCHOLARSHIP

Award for Baltimore City public high school graduates. Please see Web site: http://www.collegeboundfoundation.org for complete information on application process. Must have participated in verifiable community service activities and submit a one-page typed essay describing in detail the community service in which you have been involved and the importance of these activities to you. Minimum GPA of 3.0. Must submit CollegeBound Competitive Scholarship/Last-Dollar Grant Application.

Award: Scholarship for use in freshman year; not renewable. *Number:* 2. *Amount:* $500.

Eligibility Requirements: Applicant must be enrolled or expecting to enroll full-time at a two-year or four-year institution or university and resident of Maryland. Applicant must have 3.0 GPA or higher. Available to U.S. citizens.

Application Requirements: Application, essay, financial need analysis, transcript, financial aid award letters, Student Aid Report. *Deadline:* March 19.

Contact: April Bell, Associate Program Director
CollegeBound Foundation
300 Water Street, Suite 300
Baltimore, MD 21202
Phone: 410-783-2905 Ext. 208
Fax: 410-727-5786
E-mail: abell@collegeboundfoundation.org

BALTIMORE ROTARY SERVICE ABOVE SELF AWARD PROGRAM

Award for Baltimore City public high school graduates. Please see Web site: http://www.collegeboundfoundation.org for complete information on application process. Must submit CollegeBound Competitive Scholarship/Last-Dollar Grant Application. Two non-renewable scholarships for female students and two for male students. Must have verifiable community service, submit a one-page essay describing the community service in detail and the importance of this activity to you. Provide list of references for community involvement.

Award: Scholarship for use in freshman year; not renewable. *Number:* 4. *Amount:* $1000–$1500.

Eligibility Requirements: Applicant must be enrolled or expecting to enroll full-time at a two-year or four-year institution or university and resident of Maryland. Applicant must have 2.5 GPA or higher. Available to U.S. citizens.

Application Requirements: Application, essay, financial need analysis, references, transcript, financial aid award letters, Student Aid Report. *Deadline:* March 19.

Contact: April Bell, Associate Program Director
CollegeBound Foundation
300 Water Street, Suite 300
Baltimore, MD 21202
Phone: 410-783-2905 Ext. 208
Fax: 410-727-5786
E-mail: abell@collegeboundfoundation.org

CLARENCE E. SPILMAN SCHOLARSHIP

Award for Baltimore City public high school graduates. Please see Web site: http://www.collegeboundfoundation.org for complete information on application process. Must submit CollegeBound Competitive Scholarship/Last-Dollar Grant Application. Minimum GPA of 3.0 required. Must have verifiable community service.

Award: Scholarship for use in freshman year; not renewable. *Number:* 1. *Amount:* $1000.

Eligibility Requirements: Applicant must be enrolled or expecting to enroll full-time at a two-year or four-year institution or university and resident of Maryland. Applicant must have 3.0 GPA or higher. Available to U.S. citizens.

Application Requirements: Application, essay, financial need analysis, references, transcript, financial aid award letters, Student Aid Report. *Deadline:* March 19.

Contact: April Bell, Associate Program Director
CollegeBound Foundation
300 Water Street, Suite 300
Baltimore, MD 21202
Phone: 410-783-2905 Ext. 208
Fax: 410-727-5786
E-mail: abell@collegeboundfoundation.org

COLLEGEBOUND LAST-DOLLAR GRANT

Need-based grants for Baltimore City public high school graduates whose family contribution and financial aid package total less than the cost to attend college. Awardees are eligible to receive up to $3,000 per year, renewable for up to five years.

Award: Grant for use in freshman, sophomore, junior, or senior years; renewable. *Number:* 90–250. *Amount:* $400–$3000.

CollegeBound Foundation (continued)

Eligibility Requirements: Applicant must be enrolled or expecting to enroll full-time at a two-year or four-year institution or university and resident of Maryland. Available to U.S. citizens.

Application Requirements: Application, financial need analysis. *Deadline:* March 19.

Contact: April Bell, Associate Program Director
CollegeBound Foundation
300 Water Street, Suite 300
Baltimore, MD 21202
Phone: 410-783-2905 Ext. 208
Fax: 410-727-5786
E-mail: abell@collegeboundfoundation.org

COMMERCIAL REAL ESTATE WOMEN (CREW)-BALTIMORE SCHOLARSHIP

Award for female Baltimore City public high school graduates. Please see Web site: http://www.collegeboundfoundation.org for complete information on application process. Minimum GPA of 3.0, combined SAT of 1000. Two letters of recommendation and 500-1000-word essay describing your college expectations. Must submit CollegeBound Competitive Scholarship/Last-Dollar Grant Application.

Award: Scholarship for use in freshman year; not renewable. *Number:* 2. *Amount:* $1000.

Eligibility Requirements: Applicant must be enrolled or expecting to enroll full-time at a four-year institution or university; female and resident of Maryland. Applicant must have 3.0 GPA or higher. Available to U.S. citizens.

Application Requirements: Application, essay, financial need analysis, references, transcript, financial aid award letters, Student Aid Report. *Deadline:* March 19.

Contact: April Bell, Associate Program Director
CollegeBound Foundation
300 Water Street, Suite 300
Baltimore, MD 21202
Phone: 410-783-2905 Ext. 208
Fax: 410-727-5786
E-mail: abell@collegeboundfoundation.org

COX EDUCATION FUND SCHOLARSHIP

Award for Baltimore City public high school graduates. Please see Web site: http://www.collegeboundfoundation.org for complete information on application process. You must be Valedictorian of your high school graduating class; be ranked in the top ten of your class at the time you apply for the award. Must apply for the CollegeBound Last-Dollar Grant.

Award: Scholarship for use in freshman year; not renewable. *Number:* 4. *Amount:* $300.

Eligibility Requirements: Applicant must be high school student; planning to enroll or expecting to enroll full-time at a two-year or four-year institution or university and resident of Maryland. Available to U.S. citizens.

Application Requirements: Application, financial need analysis, references, transcript, financial aid award letters, Student Aid Report. *Deadline:* March 19.

Contact: April Bell, Associate Program Director
CollegeBound Foundation
300 Water Street, Suite 300
Baltimore, MD 21202
Phone: 410-783-2905 Ext. 208
Fax: 410-727-5786
E-mail: abell@collegeboundfoundation.org

ERICA LYNNE E. DURANT MEMORIAL SCHOLARSHIP

• *See page 524*

EXCHANGE CLUB OF BALTIMORE SCHOLARSHIP

Award for Baltimore City public high school graduates. Please see Web site: http://www.collegeboundfoundation.org for complete information on application process. Must submit CollegeBound Competitive Scholarship/Last-Dollar Grant Application. Must have verifiable community service during high school. Minimum GPA of 3.0, SAT score of 1000 required. Submit one-page essay describing personal and professional goals. Must attend a Maryland college or university.

Award: Scholarship for use in freshman year; not renewable. *Number:* 5. *Amount:* $1000–$2000.

Eligibility Requirements: Applicant must be enrolled or expecting to enroll at a two-year or four-year institution or university; resident of Maryland and studying in Maryland. Available to U.S. citizens.

Application Requirements: Application, essay, financial need analysis, references, transcript, financial aid award letters, Student Aid Report. *Deadline:* March 19.

Contact: April Bell, Associate Program Director
CollegeBound Foundation
300 Water Street, Suite 300
Baltimore, MD 21202
Phone: 410-783-2905 Ext. 208
Fax: 410-727-5786
E-mail: abell@collegeboundfoundation.org

GREEN FAMILY BOOK AWARD

Award for Baltimore City public high school graduates. Please see Web site: http://www.collegeboundfoundation.org for complete information on application process. Minimum GPA of 3.0, verifiable community service. Must have financial need. Must submit essay (250-500 words) describing a significant experience, achievement, or risk that you have taken and its impact on you. Must submit CollegeBound Competitive Scholarship/Last-Dollar Grant Application.

Award: Scholarship for use in freshman year; not renewable. *Number:* 1. *Amount:* $250.

Eligibility Requirements: Applicant must be enrolled or expecting to enroll full-time at a two-year or four-year institution or university and resident of Maryland. Applicant must have 3.0 GPA or higher. Available to U.S. citizens.

Application Requirements: Application, essay, financial need analysis, transcript, financial aid award letters, Student Aid Report. *Deadline:* March 19.

Contact: April Bell, Associate Program Director
CollegeBound Foundation
300 Water Street, Suite 300
Baltimore, MD 21202
Phone: 410-783-2905 Ext. 208
Fax: 410-727-5786
E-mail: abell@collegeboundfoundation.org

JANET B. SONDHEIM SCHOLARSHIP

Award for Baltimore City public high school graduates. Please see Web site: http://www.collegeboundfoundation.org for complete information on application process. Must major in either fine arts (dance, music, art, drama, photography); or any field of study, but must plan to teach. Minimum GPA of 3.0. Must submit one-page essay on goals and accomplishments and your interest in the arts or teaching. Must submit CollegeBound Competitive Scholarship/Last-Dollar Grant Application.

Award: Scholarship for use in freshman, sophomore, junior, or senior years; renewable. *Number:* 1. *Amount:* $500.

Eligibility Requirements: Applicant must be enrolled or expecting to enroll full-time at a two-year or four-year institution or university and resident of Maryland. Applicant must have 3.0 GPA or higher. Available to U.S. citizens.

Application Requirements: Application, essay, financial need analysis, references, transcript, financial aid award letters, Student Aid Report. *Deadline:* March 19.

Contact: April Bell, Associate Program Director
CollegeBound Foundation
300 Water Street, Suite 300
Baltimore, MD 21202
Phone: 410-783-2905 Ext. 208
Fax: 410-727-5786
E-mail: abell@collegeboundfoundation.org

JOE SANDUSKY FOUNDATION-ELIZABETH FLICK ACADEMIC SCHOLARSHIP

Award for Baltimore City public high school graduates. Please see Web site: http://www.collegeboundfoundation.org for complete information on application process. Must submit CollegeBound Competitive Scholarship/Last-Dollar Grant Application. Minimum GPA of 3.0 required. Must have financial need. Must be accepted into a college or university located in Maryland. Must submit an essay of 500 words or less on how you plan to use a college education to improve the quality of your life and the lives of others.

Award: Scholarship for use in freshman year; not renewable. *Number:* 1. *Amount:* $500–$2000.

Eligibility Requirements: Applicant must be enrolled or expecting to enroll full-time at a two-year or four-year institution or university; resident of Maryland and studying in Maryland. Applicant must have 3.0 GPA or higher. Available to U.S. citizens.

Application Requirements: Application, essay, financial need analysis, references, transcript, financial aid award letters, Student Aid Report. *Deadline:* March 19.

Contact: April Bell, Associate Program Director
CollegeBound Foundation
300 Water Street, Suite 300
Baltimore, MD 21202
Phone: 410-783-2905 Ext. 208
Fax: 410-727-5786
E-mail: abell@collegeboundfoundation.org

KENNETH HOFFMAN SCHOLARSHIP

Award for Baltimore City public high school graduates. Please see Web site: http://www.collegeboundfoundation.org for complete information on application process. Minimum GPA of 3.0 required and verifiable community service. Must submit CollegeBound Competitive Scholarship/Last-Dollar Grant Application.

Award: Scholarship for use in freshman year; not renewable. *Number:* 1. *Amount:* $500.

Eligibility Requirements: Applicant must be enrolled or expecting to enroll full-time at a two-year or four-year institution or university and resident of Maryland. Applicant must have 3.0 GPA or higher. Available to U.S. citizens.

Application Requirements: Application, financial need analysis, references, transcript, financial aid award letters, Student Aid Report. *Deadline:* March 19.

Contact: April Bell, Associate Program Director
CollegeBound Foundation
300 Water Street, Suite 300
Baltimore, MD 21202
Phone: 410-783-2905 Ext. 208
Fax: 410-727-5786
E-mail: abell@collegeboundfoundation.org

LESLIE MOORE FOUNDATION SCHOLARSHIP

Three awards for Baltimore City public high school graduates, two from other Baltimore county schools. Please see Web site: http://www.collegeboundfoundation.org for complete information on application process. Must submit CollegeBound Competitive Scholarship/Last-Dollar Grant Application. Must have GPA of at least 2.0, verifiable community service. Submit essay (500-1000 words) describing the importance of a college education and community service activities you have completed. Must be available for interview with selection committee.

Award: Scholarship for use in freshman, sophomore, junior, or senior years; renewable. *Number:* 5. *Amount:* $2500.

Eligibility Requirements: Applicant must be enrolled or expecting to enroll full-time at a two-year or four-year or technical institution or university and resident of Maryland. Available to U.S. citizens.

Application Requirements: Application, essay, financial need analysis, interview, references, transcript, financial aid award letters, Student Aid Report. *Deadline:* March 19.

Contact: April Bell, Associate Program Director
CollegeBound Foundation
300 Water Street, Suite 300
Baltimore, MD 21202
Phone: 410-783-2905 Ext. 208
Fax: 410-727-5786
E-mail: abell@collegeboundfoundation.org

MARYLAND HOTEL AND LODGING ASSOCIATION SCHOLARSHIP

Award for Baltimore City public high school graduates. Please see Web site: http://www.collegeboundfoundation.org for complete information on application process. Priority will be given to children of employees of the hotels and motels in Maryland and/or students who plan to study hospitality, tourism, or business. Must complete CollegeBound Competitive Scholarship/Last-Dollar Grant Application.

Award: Scholarship for use in freshman, sophomore, junior, or senior years; renewable. *Number:* 1. *Amount:* $500.

Eligibility Requirements: Applicant must be enrolled or expecting to enroll full-time at a two-year or four-year institution or university and resident of Maryland. Available to U.S. citizens.

Application Requirements: Application, financial need analysis, references, transcript, financial aid letters, Student Aid Report. *Deadline:* March 19.

Contact: April Bell, Associate Program Director
CollegeBound Foundation
300 Water Street, Suite 300
Baltimore, MD 21202
Phone: 410-783-2905 Ext. 208
Fax: 410-727-5786
E-mail: abell@collegeboundfoundation.org

RICHARD E. DUNNE, III SCHOLARSHIP

Award for Baltimore City public high school graduates. Please see Web site: http://www.collegeboundfoundation.org for complete information on application process. Must have GPA of 3.0 or better, verifiable community service. Must submit CollegeBound Competitive Scholarship/Last-Dollar Grant Application.

Award: Scholarship for use in freshman year; not renewable. *Number:* 1. *Amount:* $500.

Eligibility Requirements: Applicant must be enrolled or expecting to enroll full-time at a two-year or four-year institution or university and resident of Maryland. Applicant must have 3.0 GPA or higher. Available to U.S. citizens.

Application Requirements: Application, financial need analysis, references, transcript, financial aid award letters, Student Aid Report. *Deadline:* March 19.

Contact: April Bell, Associate Program Director
CollegeBound Foundation
300 Water Street, Suite 300
Baltimore, MD 21202
Phone: 410-783-2905 Ext. 208
Fax: 410-727-5786
E-mail: abell@collegeboundfoundation.org

WALTER G. AMPREY SCHOLARSHIP

Award for Baltimore City public high school graduates. Please see Web site: http://www.collegeboundfoundation.org for complete information on application process. Minimum GPA of 3.0. Must demonstrate financial need. Must submit CollegeBound Competitive Scholarship/Last-Dollar Grant Application.

Award: Scholarship for use in freshman year; not renewable. *Number:* 1. *Amount:* $1000.

Eligibility Requirements: Applicant must be enrolled or expecting to enroll full-time at a two-year or four-year institution or university and resident of Maryland. Applicant must have 3.0 GPA or higher. Available to U.S. citizens.

CollegeBound Foundation (continued)

Application Requirements: Application, financial need analysis, references, transcript, financial aid award letters, Student Aid Report. *Deadline:* March 19.

Contact: April Bell, Associate Program Director
CollegeBound Foundation
300 Water Street, Suite 300
Baltimore, MD 21202
Phone: 410-783-2905 Ext. 208
Fax: 410-727-5786
E-mail: abell@collegeboundfoundation.org

COLORADO BUSINESS AND PROFESSIONAL WOMEN'S FOUNDATION SCHOLARSHIP

http://www.cbpwef.org

COLORADO BUSINESS AND PROFESSIONAL WOMEN'S FOUNDATION SCHOLARSHIP

Ten to 20 scholarships awarded annually to women who are at least 26 years old and are Colorado residents attending an institution of higher education in Colorado. Scholarship program is designed to promote economic self-sufficiency for women. Recipients are generally low income single mothers. Deadlines: March 31 and October 31. Must be U.S. citizen.

Award: Scholarship for use in freshman, sophomore, junior, senior, graduate, or postgraduate years; not renewable. *Number:* 10–20. *Amount:* $300–$1000.

Eligibility Requirements: Applicant must be age 26; enrolled or expecting to enroll full or part-time at a two-year or four-year or technical institution or university; female; resident of Colorado and studying in Colorado. Available to U.S. citizens.

Application Requirements: Application, driver's license, essay, financial need analysis, references, transcript, proof of U.S. citizenship. *Deadline:* varies.

Contact: Scholarship Committee/CBPWF
Colorado Business and Professional Women's Foundation Scholarship
PO Box 1189
Boulder, CO 80306
Phone: 303-443-2573
Fax: 720-564-0397
E-mail: cbpwf@earthnet.net

COLORADO COMMISSION ON HIGHER EDUCATION

http://www.state.co.us/cche

COLORADO LEVERAGING EDUCATIONAL ASSISTANCE PARTNERSHIP (CLEAP) AND SLEAP

Renewable awards for Colorado residents who are attending Colorado state-supported postsecondary institutions at the undergraduate level. Must document financial need. Contact colleges for complete information and deadlines.

Award: Grant for use in freshman, sophomore, junior, or senior years; not renewable. *Number:* 5000. *Amount:* $50–$900.

Eligibility Requirements: Applicant must be enrolled or expecting to enroll full or part-time at a two-year or four-year or technical institution or university; resident of Colorado and studying in Colorado. Available to U.S. citizens.

Application Requirements: Application, financial need analysis. *Deadline:* varies.

Contact: Financial Aid Office at college/institution
Colorado Commission on Higher Education
1380 Lawrence Street, Suite 1200
Denver, CO 80204-2059

COLORADO STUDENT GRANT

Assists Colorado residents attending eligible public, private, or vocational institutions within the state. Application deadlines vary by institution. Renewable award for undergraduates. Contact the financial aid office at the college/institution for more information and an application.

Award: Grant for use in freshman, sophomore, junior, or senior years; renewable. *Number:* varies. *Amount:* $500–$5000.

Eligibility Requirements: Applicant must be enrolled or expecting to enroll full or part-time at a two-year or four-year or technical institution or university; resident of Colorado and studying in Colorado.

Application Requirements: Application, financial need analysis. *Deadline:* varies.

Contact: Financial Aid Office at college/institution
Colorado Commission on Higher Education
1380 Lawrence Street, Suite 1200
Denver, CO 80204-2059

COLORADO UNDERGRADUATE MERIT SCHOLARSHIPS

Renewable awards for students attending Colorado state-supported institutions at the undergraduate level. Must demonstrate superior scholarship or talent. Contact college financial aid office for complete information and deadlines.

Award: Scholarship for use in freshman, sophomore, junior, or senior years; renewable. *Number:* 10,823. *Amount:* $1230.

Eligibility Requirements: Applicant must be enrolled or expecting to enroll full or part-time at a two-year or four-year or technical institution or university; resident of Colorado and studying in Colorado. Applicant must have 3.0 GPA or higher.

Application Requirements: Application, test scores, transcript. *Deadline:* varies.

Contact: Financial Aid Office at college/institution
Colorado Commission on Higher Education
1380 Lawrence Street, Suite 1200
Denver, CO 80204-2059

GOVERNOR'S OPPORTUNITY SCHOLARSHIP

Scholarship available for the most needy first-time freshmen whose parents' adjusted gross income is less than $26,000. Must be U.S. citizen or permanent legal resident. Work-study is part of the program.

Award: Scholarship for use in freshman, sophomore, junior, or senior years; renewable. *Number:* up to 1052. *Amount:* $5665.

Eligibility Requirements: Applicant must be high school student; planning to enroll or expecting to enroll full-time at a two-year or four-year or technical institution or university; resident of Colorado and studying in Colorado. Available to U.S. citizens.

Application Requirements: Application, financial need analysis, test scores, transcript. *Deadline:* Continuous.

Contact: Financial Aid Office at college/institution
Colorado Commission on Higher Education
1380 Lawrence Street, Suite 1200
Denver, CO 80204-2059

COLORADO MASONS BENEVOLENT FUND ASSOCIATION

COLORADO MASONS BENEVOLENT FUND SCHOLARSHIPS

Applicants must be graduating seniors from a Colorado public high school accepted at a Colorado postsecondary institution. The maximum grant is $7000 renewable over four years. Obtain scholarship materials and specific requirements from high school counselor.

Award: Scholarship for use in freshman, sophomore, junior, or senior years; renewable. *Number:* 10–14. *Amount:* up to $7000.

Eligibility Requirements: Applicant must be high school student; planning to enroll or expecting to enroll full-time at a two-year or four-year or technical institution or university; resident of Colorado and studying in Colorado. Available to U.S. and non-U.S. citizens.

Application Requirements: Application, essay, financial need analysis, interview, references, transcript. *Deadline:* March 7.

Contact: Ron Kadera, Scholarship Administrator
Colorado Masons Benevolent Fund Association
1130 Panorama Drive
Colorado Springs, CO 80904
Phone: 800-482-4441 Ext. 29
Fax: 800-440-3520
E-mail: scholarships@coloradomasons.org

COMMUNITY BANKER ASSOCIATION OF ILLINOIS http://www.cbai.com/scholarship.htm

COMMUNITY BANKER ASSOCIATION OF ILLINOIS ANNUAL SCHOLARSHIP PROGRAM

Essay competition open to Illinois high school seniors who are sponsored by a CBAI member bank. Student bank employees, plus immediate families of bank employees, board members, stockholders, CBAI employees, and judges are ineligible. For more details see Web site: http://www.cbai.com.

Award: Scholarship for use in freshman year; not renewable. *Number:* up to 13. *Amount:* $1000–$4000.

Eligibility Requirements: Applicant must be high school student; planning to enroll or expecting to enroll full-time at a two-year or four-year or technical institution or university and resident of Illinois. Available to U.S. citizens.

Application Requirements: Applicant must enter a contest, essay. *Deadline:* February 9.

Contact: Andrea Cusick, Senior Vice President of Communications
Community Banker Association of Illinois
Attn: CBAI Foundation for Community Banking
901 Community Drive
Springfield, IL 62703-5184
Phone: 217-529-2265
Fax: 217-585-8738
E-mail: cbaicom@cbai.com

COMMUNITY BANKER ASSOCIATION OF ILLINOIS CHILDREN OF COMMUNITY BANKING SCHOLARSHIP

• *See page 458*

COMMUNITY FOUNDATION FOR GREATER BUFFALO http://www.cfgb.org

COMMUNITY FOUNDATION FOR GREATER BUFFALO SCHOLARSHIPS

Scholarships restricted to current residents of western New York (several only to Erie County), who have been accepted for admission to any nonprofit school in the United States for full-time study at the undergraduate level. Must maintain a "C" average. Must submit estimated family contribution as indicated on Student Aid Report, FAFSA form.

Award: Scholarship for use in freshman, sophomore, junior, or senior years; not renewable. *Number:* 600–900. *Amount:* $200–$4500.

Eligibility Requirements: Applicant must be enrolled or expecting to enroll full-time at a two-year or four-year institution or university and resident of New York. Available to U.S. and non-U.S. citizens.

Application Requirements: Application, essay, financial need analysis, references, self-addressed stamped envelope, transcript. *Deadline:* June 1.

Contact: Program Officer
Community Foundation for Greater Buffalo
712 Main Street
Buffalo, NY 14202

COMMUNITY FOUNDATION FOR PALM BEACH AND MARTIN COUNTIES, INC. http://www.yourcommunityfoundation.org

ARTHUR C. TILLEY MEMORIAL SCHOLARSHIP

Scholarship awarded to Palm Beach or Martin County graduating high school senior, public or private schooled, plans to pursue a 2-4 year degree in a traditional or non-traditional technical institution. Applicant must maintain C average or better. Deadline is March 1. Applications are available online http://www.yourcommunityfoundation.org.

Award: Scholarship for use in freshman year; not renewable. *Number:* varies. *Amount:* varies.

Eligibility Requirements: Applicant must be high school student; planning to enroll or expecting to enroll at a two-year or four-year or technical institution or university and resident of Florida.

Application Requirements: Application, financial need analysis. *Deadline:* March 1.

Contact: Carolyn Jenco, Grants Manager/Scholarship Coordinator
Community Foundation for Palm Beach and Martin Counties, Inc.
700 South Dixie Highway
Suite 200
West Palm Beach, FL 33401

CLAIRE B. SCHULTZ MEMORIAL SCHOLARSHIP

Graduating seniors from a Palm Beach County High School. Based on financial need. Special preference to handicapped or minority students.

Award: Scholarship for use in freshman, sophomore, junior, or senior years; not renewable. *Number:* 1–3. *Amount:* $750–$2500.

Eligibility Requirements: Applicant must be high school student; planning to enroll or expecting to enroll full-time at a two-year or four-year or technical institution or university and resident of Florida. Available to U.S. citizens.

Application Requirements: Application, financial need analysis. *Deadline:* March 1.

Contact: Carolyn Jenco, Grants Manager/Scholarship Coordinator
Community Foundation for Palm Beach and Martin Counties, Inc.
700 South Dixie Highway
Suite 200
West Palm Beach, FL 33401

COLONIAL BANK SCHOLARSHIP

• *See page 581*

COMMUNITY FOUNDATION FOR PALM BEACH AND MARTIN COUNTIES GENERAL SCHOLARSHIP

Applicant must be resident of Palm Beach or Martin County and maintain a 2.0 GPA. Deadline is March 1. Applications are available online: http://www.yourcommunityfoundation.org.

Award: Scholarship for use in freshman year; not renewable. *Number:* varies. *Amount:* varies.

Eligibility Requirements: Applicant must be enrolled or expecting to enroll at a four-year institution or university and resident of Florida.

Application Requirements: Application, financial need analysis. *Deadline:* March 1.

Contact: Carolyn Jenco, Grants Manager/Scholarship Coordinator
Community Foundation for Palm Beach and Martin Counties, Inc.
700 South Dixie Highway
Suite 200
West Palm Beach, FL 33401

DAVE YANIS SCHOLARSHIP FUND

Scholarship awarded to graduating high school seniors from Palm Beach, Martin, or Broward counties. Preference is given to students of Jewish faith, Russian immigrants, or direct descendents of Russian immigrants. Deadline is March 1. Applications are available online http://www.yourcommunityfoundation.org.

Award: Scholarship for use in freshman year; not renewable. *Number:* varies. *Amount:* varies.

Eligibility Requirements: Applicant must be high school student; planning to enroll or expecting to enroll at a four-year institution or university and resident of Florida. Available to U.S. citizens.

Community Foundation for Palm Beach and Martin Counties, Inc. (continued)

Application Requirements: Application. *Deadline:* March 1.

Contact: Carolyn Jenco, Grants Manager/Scholarship Coordinator
Community Foundation for Palm Beach and Martin Counties, Inc.
700 South Dixie Highway
Suite 200
West Palm Beach, FL 33401

DENISE LYNN PADGETT SCHOLARSHIP FUND

Female graduating senior from Palm Beach or Martin Counties. Minimum of two years participation on high school/women's softball team; demonstrated financial aid.

Award: Scholarship for use in freshman year; not renewable. *Number:* 1. *Amount:* $750–$2500.

Eligibility Requirements: Applicant must be high school student; planning to enroll or expecting to enroll full-time at a two-year or four-year or technical institution or university; female and resident of Florida. Available to U.S. citizens.

Application Requirements: Application, financial need analysis. *Deadline:* March 1.

Contact: Carolyn Jenco, Grants Manager/Scholarship Coordinator
Community Foundation for Palm Beach and Martin Counties, Inc.
700 South Dixie Highway
Suite 200
West Palm Beach, FL 33401

ERNEST FRANK SCHOLARSHIP FUND

Scholarship awarded to Palm Beach or Martin County resident graduating from a public or private high school in those counties. Student must demonstrate academic excellence, extracurricular activities, community service, and financial need. Deadline is March 1. Applications are available online http://www.yourcommunityfoundation.org.

Award: Scholarship for use in freshman year; not renewable. *Number:* varies. *Amount:* varies.

Eligibility Requirements: Applicant must be high school student; planning to enroll or expecting to enroll full-time at a four-year institution or university and resident of Florida. Available to U.S. citizens.

Application Requirements: Application, financial need analysis. *Deadline:* March 1.

Contact: Carolyn Jenco, Grants Manager/Scholarship Coordinator
Community Foundation for Palm Beach and Martin Counties, Inc.
700 South Dixie Highway
Suite 200
West Palm Beach, FL 33401

GUBELMANN FAMILY FOUNDATION SCHOLARSHIP FUND

For Palm Beach County and Martin County, Florida graduating high school seniors demonstrating financial need. Preference given to minority applicants. May be from public or private institutions.

Award: Scholarship for use in freshman year; not renewable. *Amount:* $750–$2500.

Eligibility Requirements: Applicant must be high school student; planning to enroll or expecting to enroll full-time at a two-year or four-year or technical institution or university and resident of Florida. Available to U.S. citizens.

Application Requirements: Application, financial need analysis. *Deadline:* March 1.

Contact: Carolyn Jenco, Grants Manager/Scholarship Coordinator
Community Foundation for Palm Beach and Martin Counties, Inc.
700 South Dixie Highway
Suite 200
West Palm Beach, FL 33401

HARRY AND BERTHA BRONSTEIN MEMORIAL SCHOLARSHIP

For graduating high school seniors who are residents of Palm Beach and Martin Counties demonstrating financial need with special preference given to students who are either members of a minority group or handicapped. These may be two or four year scholarships but are restricted to undergraduate support.

Award: Scholarship for use in freshman, sophomore, junior, or senior years; renewable. *Amount:* $750–$2500.

Eligibility Requirements: Applicant must be high school student; planning to enroll or expecting to enroll full-time at a two-year or four-year institution or university and resident of Florida. Available to U.S. citizens.

Application Requirements: Application, financial need analysis. *Deadline:* March 1.

Contact: Carolyn Jenco, Grants Manager/Scholarship Coordinator
Community Foundation for Palm Beach and Martin Counties, Inc.
700 South Dixie Highway
Suite 200
West Palm Beach, FL 33401

JULIAN AND EUNICE COHEN SCHOLARSHIP

Scholarship awarded to Palm Beach or Martin County graduating high school student. Applicant must be involved in extracurricular activities as well as achieve academic excellence. Deadline is March 1. Applications are available online http://www.yourcommunityfoundation.org.

Award: Scholarship for use in freshman year; not renewable. *Number:* varies. *Amount:* varies.

Eligibility Requirements: Applicant must be high school student; planning to enroll or expecting to enroll at a four-year institution or university and resident of Florida. Available to U.S. citizens.

Application Requirements: Application, financial need analysis. *Deadline:* March 1.

Contact: Carolyn Jenco, Grants Manager/Scholarship Coordinator
Community Foundation for Palm Beach and Martin Counties, Inc.
700 South Dixie Highway
Suite 200
West Palm Beach, FL 33401

LOBLOLLY SCHOLARSHIP FUND

In Palm Beach and Martin counties, Florida, available to any student who demonstrates financial need and is in the top 25% of the graduating class. Students in the second quartile of the class are also eligible if they possess an outstanding extracurricular record or if they were required to work during high school to help support their families. Participation in school athletics and meaningful community service is a plus.

Award: Scholarship for use in freshman year; not renewable. *Amount:* $750–$2500.

Eligibility Requirements: Applicant must be high school student; planning to enroll or expecting to enroll full-time at a two-year or four-year or technical institution or university and resident of Florida. Applicant must have 3.5 GPA or higher. Available to U.S. citizens.

Application Requirements: Application, financial need analysis, transcript. *Deadline:* March 1.

Contact: Carolyn Jenco, Grants Manager/Scholarship Coordinator
Community Foundation for Palm Beach and Martin Counties, Inc.
700 South Dixie Highway
Suite 200
West Palm Beach, FL 33401

MATTHEW "BUMP" MITCHELL /SUN-SENTINEL SCHOLARSHIP

Graduating student from South Palm Beach County, Florida who excels in scholastics, demonstrates community service and has financial need. Preference given to minority students.

Award: Scholarship for use in freshman year; not renewable. *Number:* 1. *Amount:* $750–$2500.

Eligibility Requirements: Applicant must be high school student; planning to enroll or expecting to enroll full-time at a two-year or four-year or technical institution or university and resident of Florida. Available to U.S. citizens.

Application Requirements: Application, financial need analysis. *Deadline:* March 1.

Contact: Carolyn Jenco, Grants Manager/Scholarship Coordinator
Community Foundation for Palm Beach and Martin Counties, Inc.
700 South Dixie Highway
Suite 200
West Palm Beach, FL 33401

MAURA AND WILLIAM BENJAMIN SCHOLARSHIP

Scholarship awarded to applicant with an excellent scholastic record, as well as representing qualities of leadership. Applicant should have experience in community service. Applications are available online: http://www.yourcommunityfoundation.org. Deadline is March 1. Restricted to residents of Palm Beach or Martin County.

Award: Scholarship for use in freshman year; not renewable. *Number:* varies. *Amount:* varies.

Eligibility Requirements: Applicant must be enrolled or expecting to enroll at a four-year institution or university and resident of Florida. Available to U.S. citizens.

Application Requirements: Application. *Deadline:* March 1.

Contact: Carolyn Jenco, Grants Manager/Scholarship Coordinator
Community Foundation for Palm Beach and Martin Counties, Inc.
700 South Dixie Highway
Suite 200
West Palm Beach, FL 33401

RALPH O. WOOD SCHOLARSHIP

Scholarship awarded to Palm Beach or Martin County graduating senior in a public or private high school. Must be involved in extracurricular activities. Deadline is March 1. Applications are available online: http://www.yourcommunityfoundation.org.

Award: Scholarship for use in freshman year; not renewable. *Number:* varies. *Amount:* varies.

Eligibility Requirements: Applicant must be high school student; planning to enroll or expecting to enroll at a four-year institution and resident of Florida. Applicant must have 3.0 GPA or higher.

Application Requirements: Application, financial need analysis. *Deadline:* March 1.

Contact: Carolyn Jenco, Grants Manager/Scholarship Coordinator
Community Foundation for Palm Beach and Martin Counties, Inc.
700 South Dixie Highway
Suite 200
West Palm Beach, FL 33401

ROBERTA AND STEPHEN R. WEINER SCHOLARSHIP

Scholarship awarded to Palm Beach or Martin County graduating high school senior who wishes to continue their education with traditional or non-traditional technical training. Deadline is March 1. Applications are available online: http://www.yourcommunityfoundation.org.

Award: Scholarship for use in freshman year; not renewable. *Number:* varies. *Amount:* varies.

Eligibility Requirements: Applicant must be high school student; planning to enroll or expecting to enroll at a two-year or four-year or technical institution and resident of Florida. Available to U.S. citizens.

Application Requirements: Application. *Deadline:* March 1.

Contact: Carolyn Jenco, Grants Manager/Scholarship Coordinator
Community Foundation for Palm Beach and Martin Counties, Inc.
700 South Dixie Highway
Suite 200
West Palm Beach, FL 33401

TERRY DARBY MEMORIAL SCHOLARSHIP

Scholarship awarded to Palm Beach or Martin County graduating high school senior that has been actively involved with soccer throughout his or her high school career. Applications available online http://www.yourcommunityfoundation.org. Deadline is March 1.

Award: Scholarship for use in freshman year; not renewable. *Number:* varies. *Amount:* varies.

Eligibility Requirements: Applicant must be high school student; planning to enroll or expecting to enroll at a four-year institution or university; resident of Florida and must have an interest in athletics/sports. Available to U.S. citizens.

Application Requirements: Application. *Deadline:* March 1.

Contact: Carolyn Jenco, Grants Manager/Scholarship Coordinator
Community Foundation for Palm Beach and Martin Counties, Inc.
700 South Dixie Highway
Suite 200
West Palm Beach, FL 33401

WALTER AND ADI BLUM SCHOLARSHIP

Scholarship rewarded to high school senior attending public or private school in Palm Beach or Martin County. Must attend approved school in United States. Preference given to applicants that have immigrated to United States. Applications are available online http://www.yourcommunityfoundation.org. Deadline is March 1.

Award: Scholarship for use in freshman year; not renewable. *Number:* varies. *Amount:* varies.

Eligibility Requirements: Applicant must be high school student; planning to enroll or expecting to enroll full-time at a two-year or four-year or technical institution or university and resident of Florida. Applicant must have 2.5 GPA or higher. Available to U.S. citizens.

Application Requirements: Application, financial need analysis. *Deadline:* March 1.

Contact: Carolyn Jenco, Grants Manager/Scholarship Coordinator
Community Foundation for Palm Beach and Martin Counties, Inc.
700 South Dixie Highway
Suite 200
West Palm Beach, FL 33401

COMMUNITY FOUNDATION OF CAPE COD http://www.capecodfoundation.org

ANNIE S. CROWELL SCHOLARSHIP FUND

Award to graduating high school senior or continuing college student who is a relative of an alumnus from the Hyannis Normal School, or the Hyannis State Teacher's College. For more details see Web site: http://www.capecodfoundation.org.

Award: Scholarship for use in freshman, sophomore, junior, senior, or graduate years; not renewable. *Number:* 1–4. *Amount:* $1000.

Eligibility Requirements: Applicant must be enrolled or expecting to enroll full-time at a two-year or four-year or technical institution or university and resident of Massachusetts. Available to U.S. citizens.

Application Requirements: Application, essay, resume, references, test scores, transcript. *Deadline:* April 1.

Contact: Pauline Greenberg, Scholarship Associate
Community Foundation of Cape Cod
PO Box 406
259 Willow Street
Yarmouthport, MA 02675
Phone: 508-790-3040
Fax: 508-790-4069
E-mail: pgreenberg@capecodfoundation.org

COMMUNITY FOUNDATION OF CAPE COD GENERAL SCHOLARSHIP FUNDS

A variety of specific scholarships are available. For more details and an application see Web site: http://www.capecodfoundation.org.

Award: Scholarship for use in freshman, sophomore, junior, senior, or graduate years; not renewable. *Number:* 7. *Amount:* up to $3000.

Eligibility Requirements: Applicant must be enrolled or expecting to enroll at an institution or university and resident of Massachusetts. Available to U.S. citizens.

Application Requirements: Application. *Deadline:* April 1.

Contact: Pauline Greenberg, Scholarship Associate
Community Foundation of Cape Cod
PO Box 406
259 Willow Street
Yarmouthport, MA 02675
Phone: 508-790-3040
Fax: 508-790-4069
E-mail: pgreenberg@capecodfoundation.org

COMMUNITY FOUNDATION OF CAPE COD SCHOLARSHIP

Awarded to a graduating high school senior or returning non-traditional student who exhibits perseverance and a strong work ethic, and who has considerable financial need. For more details see Web site: http://www.capecodfoundation.org.

Award: Scholarship for use in freshman year; not renewable. *Number:* 1. *Amount:* varies.

Eligibility Requirements: Applicant must be enrolled or expecting to enroll full-time at a two-year or four-year or technical institution or university and resident of Massachusetts. Available to U.S. citizens.

Application Requirements: Application, essay, financial need analysis, resume, references, test scores, transcript. *Deadline:* April 1.

Contact: Pauline Greenberg, Scholarship Associate
Community Foundation of Cape Cod
PO Box 406
259 Willow Street
Yarmouthport, MA 02675
Phone: 508-790-3040
Fax: 508-790-4069
E-mail: pgreenberg@capecodfoundation.org

FRANK X. AND MARY E. WENY SCHOLARSHIP FUND

• *See page 524*

HYANNIS NORMAL SCHOOL ALUMNI SCHOLARSHIP

Hyannis Normal School Alumni Scholarship provides awards to students who have graduated from high school in Barnstable County. For more details see Web site: http://www.capecodfoundation.org.

Award: Scholarship for use in freshman, sophomore, junior, or senior years; not renewable. *Number:* 1–7. *Amount:* $2000.

Eligibility Requirements: Applicant must be enrolled or expecting to enroll full-time at a two-year or four-year or technical institution or university and resident of Massachusetts. Available to U.S. citizens.

Application Requirements: Application, essay, resume, references, test scores, transcript. *Deadline:* April 1.

Contact: Pauline Greenberg, Scholarship Associate
Community Foundation of Cape Cod
PO Box 406
259 Willow Street
Yarmouthport, MA 02675
Phone: 508-790-3040
Fax: 508-790-4069
E-mail: pgreenberg@capecodfoundation.org

COMMUNITY FOUNDATION OF WESTERN MASSACHUSETTS http://www.communityfoundation.org

A. DAVID "DAVEY" DUGGAN MEMORIAL SCHOLARSHIP

For graduating high school seniors of any high school located in Holyoke who have excelled academically and athletically.

Award: Scholarship for use in freshman year; not renewable. *Number:* 2. *Amount:* $200.

Eligibility Requirements: Applicant must be enrolled or expecting to enroll full or part-time at a two-year or four-year or technical institution or university and resident of Massachusetts. Available to U.S. citizens.

Application Requirements: Application, financial need analysis, transcript. *Deadline:* March 31.

Contact: Community Foundation of Western Massachusetts
1500 Main Street
PO Box 15769
Springfield, MA 01115

AFRICAN-AMERICAN ACHIEVEMENT SCHOLARSHIP

• *See page 581*

CALEB L. BUTLER SCHOLARSHIP

For former or current residents of Hillcrest Educational Centers who are graduating seniors pursuing postsecondary education, or for graduating high school seniors from Franklin, Berkshire, Hampden, or Hampshire counties who are in the custody of Department of Social Services. Visit http://www.communityfoundation.org for more information. Deadline: March 31, 2004.

Award: Scholarship for use in freshman year; not renewable. *Number:* 2. *Amount:* $1300.

Eligibility Requirements: Applicant must be enrolled or expecting to enroll full or part-time at a two-year or four-year institution and resident of Massachusetts. Available to U.S. citizens.

Application Requirements: Application, financial need analysis, transcript, personal statement. *Deadline:* March 31.

Contact: Community Foundation of Western Massachusetts
1500 Main Street, PO Box 15769
Springfield, MA 01115

DEERFIELD PLASTICS/BARKER FAMILY SCHOLARSHIP

• *See page 495*

DONALD A. AND DOROTHY F. AXTELL GRANT SCHOLARSHIP

• *See page 625*

FIRST NATIONAL BANK OF AMHERST CENTENNIAL EDUCATIONAL SCHOLARSHIP

For students from Northampton High School, Hopkins Academy, Amherst-Pelham Regional High School, UMass, Amherst College, and Hampshire College. Visit http://www.communityfoundation.org for more information.

Award: Scholarship for use in freshman, or graduate years; not renewable. *Number:* up to 3. *Amount:* up to $400.

Eligibility Requirements: Applicant must be enrolled or expecting to enroll full or part-time at a two-year or four-year or technical institution or university; resident of Massachusetts and studying in Massachusetts. Available to U.S. citizens.

Application Requirements: Application, financial need analysis, transcript, personal statement. *Deadline:* March 31.

Contact: Community Foundation of Western Massachusetts
1500 Main Street, PO Box 15769
Springfield, MA 01115

FRANK W. JENDRYSIK, JR. MEMORIAL SCHOLARSHIP

One award for undergraduate study for residents of Chicopee, Holyoke, or Springfield.

Award: Scholarship for use in freshman, sophomore, junior, or senior years; not renewable. *Number:* 1. *Amount:* $1000.

Eligibility Requirements: Applicant must be enrolled or expecting to enroll full or part-time at a two-year or four-year institution or university and resident of Massachusetts. Available to U.S. citizens.

Application Requirements: Application, financial need analysis, transcript. *Deadline:* March 31.

Contact: Community Foundation of Western Massachusetts
1500 Main Street
PO Box 15769
Springfield, MA 01115

HERIBERTO FLORES SCHOLARSHIP

• *See page 581*

JAMES L. SHRIVER SCHOLARSHIP

For Western Massachusetts residents pursuing technical careers through college, trade, or technical school. Visit http://www.communityfoundation.org for more information.

Award: Scholarship for use in freshman, sophomore, junior, or senior years; not renewable. *Number:* 1. *Amount:* $800.

Eligibility Requirements: Applicant must be enrolled or expecting to enroll full or part-time at a two-year or four-year or technical institution or university and resident of Massachusetts. Available to U.S. citizens.

Application Requirements: Application, financial need analysis, transcript, personal statement. *Deadline:* March 31.

Contact: Community Foundation of Western Massachusetts
1500 Main Street, PO Box 15769
Springfield, MA 01115

JAMES Z. NAURISON SCHOLARSHIP

For undergraduate and graduate students who are residents of Hampden, Hampshire, Franklin, and Berkshire Counties in Massachusetts and Enfield and Suffield, Connecticut. May be awarded up to four years based upon discretion of the scholarship committee. Applicants need to reapply every year. Visit http://www.communityfoundation.org.

Award: Scholarship for use in freshman, sophomore, junior, senior, or graduate years; renewable. *Amount:* $1000.

Eligibility Requirements: Applicant must be enrolled or expecting to enroll full or part-time at a two-year or four-year institution or university and resident of Connecticut or Massachusetts. Available to U.S. citizens.

Application Requirements: Application, financial need analysis, transcript, personal statement. *Deadline:* March 31.

Contact: Community Foundation of Western Massachusetts
1500 Main Street, PO Box 15769
Springfield, MA 01115

JOHN P. AND JAMES F. MAHONEY MEMORIAL SCHOLARSHIP

For residents of Hampshire County who will be attending college or vocational school at the graduate or undergraduate levels.

Award: Scholarship for use in freshman, sophomore, junior, or senior years; not renewable. *Number:* 20–25. *Amount:* $1000.

Eligibility Requirements: Applicant must be enrolled or expecting to enroll full or part-time at a two-year or four-year or technical institution or university and resident of Massachusetts. Available to U.S. citizens.

Application Requirements: Application, financial need analysis, transcript. *Deadline:* March 31.

Contact: Community Foundation of Western Massachusetts
1500 Main Street
PO Box 15769
Springfield, MA 01115

KIMBER RICHTER FAMILY SCHOLARSHIP

• *See page 625*

LATINO SCHOLARSHIP

• *See page 581*

LOUIS W. AND MARY S. DOHERTY SCHOLARSHIP

For students from Hampden County who attend or plan to attend college.

Award: Scholarship for use in freshman, sophomore, junior, or senior years; not renewable. *Number:* 17. *Amount:* $2000.

Eligibility Requirements: Applicant must be enrolled or expecting to enroll full or part-time at a two-year or four-year or technical institution or university and resident of Massachusetts. Available to U.S. citizens.

Application Requirements: Application, financial need analysis, transcript. *Deadline:* March 31.

Contact: Community Foundation of Western Massachusetts
1500 Main Street
PO Box 15769
Springfield, MA 01115

MASSMUTUAL RENEWABLE SCHOLARS PROGRAM

For previous recipients of the MassMutual Scholarship Program pursuing undergraduate study, who have exhausted their original MassMutual scholarship award and have maintained a cumulative 3.0 grade point average.

Award: Scholarship for use in freshman, sophomore, junior, or senior years; renewable. *Number:* 10. *Amount:* $5000.

Eligibility Requirements: Applicant must be enrolled or expecting to enroll full or part-time at a two-year or four-year institution or university and resident of Connecticut or Massachusetts. Applicant must have 3.0 GPA or higher. Available to U.S. citizens.

Application Requirements: Application, financial need analysis, transcript. *Deadline:* March 31.

Contact: Community Foundation of Western Massachusetts
1500 Main Street
PO Box 15769
Springfield, MA 01115

MASSMUTUAL SCHOLARS PROGRAM

For graduating high school seniors who reside in Hampden County, MA or Hartford County, CT who maintain a B average or better for four consecutive marking periods.

Award: Scholarship for use in freshman, sophomore, junior, or senior years; renewable. *Number:* 40. *Amount:* $5000.

Eligibility Requirements: Applicant must be enrolled or expecting to enroll full or part-time at a two-year or four-year institution or university and resident of Connecticut or Massachusetts. Applicant must have 3.0 GPA or higher. Available to U.S. citizens.

Application Requirements: Application, essay, financial need analysis, transcript. *Deadline:* March 31.

Contact: Community Foundation of Western Massachusetts
1500 Main Street
PO Box 15769
Springfield, MA 01115

NATIONAL ASSOCIATION OF INSURANCE AND FINANCIAL ADVISORS SCHOLARSHIP

For graduating high school seniors, residing in Berkshire, Hampden, Hampshire, and Franklin counties, who have lost a parent through death or have a parent receiving social security disability benefits.

Award: Scholarship for use in freshman year; not renewable. *Number:* 6. *Amount:* $2000.

Eligibility Requirements: Applicant must be high school student; planning to enroll or expecting to enroll full or part-time at a two-year or four-year or technical institution or university and resident of Massachusetts. Available to U.S. citizens.

Application Requirements: Application, financial need analysis, transcript. *Deadline:* March 31.

Contact: Community Foundation of Western Massachusetts
1500 Main Street
PO Box 15769
Springfield, MA 01115

PERMELIA A. BUTTERFIELD SCHOLARSHIP

Support and education of orphan children (students with one or no living parents or those deprived of parental care) who are residents of Athol, Erving, New Salem, Wendell, Orange, Shutesbury, and Franklin County, or for other students from these areas. Visit http://www.communityfoundation.org.

Award: Scholarship for use in freshman, sophomore, junior, senior, or graduate years; not renewable. *Number:* 2. *Amount:* $3100.

Community Foundation of Western Massachusetts (continued)

Eligibility Requirements: Applicant must be enrolled or expecting to enroll full or part-time at a two-year or four-year institution or university and resident of Massachusetts. Available to U.S. citizens.

Application Requirements: Application, financial need analysis, transcript, personal statement. *Deadline:* March 31.

Contact: Community Foundation of Western Massachusetts
1500 Main Street, PO Box 15769
Springfield, MA 01115

PUTNAM SCHOLARSHIP FUND

• *See page 581*

RUTH L. BROCKLEBANK MEMORIAL SCHOLARSHIP

• *See page 581*

STANLEY CIEJEK SR. SCHOLARSHIP

Scholarships given to residents of Hampden, Hampshire, and Franklin counties who will be attending Massachusetts institutions of higher education. For more information or application visit http://www.communityfoundation.org.

Award: Scholarship for use in freshman, sophomore, junior, or senior years; not renewable. *Amount:* $1000.

Eligibility Requirements: Applicant must be enrolled or expecting to enroll full or part-time at a two-year or four-year or technical institution or university; resident of Massachusetts and studying in Massachusetts. Available to U.S. citizens.

Application Requirements: Application, financial need analysis, transcript. *Deadline:* March 31.

Contact: Community Foundation of Western Massachusetts
1500 Main Street
PO Box 15769
Springfield, MA 01115

UNITED WAY/YWCA SCHOLARSHIP FUND FOR WOMEN

For women with financial need who are residents of Holyoke, South Hadley, or Granby. Applicants must be age 18 or older and currently enrolled in college or have plans to enter college. The award is paid over a two-year period and comes from a fund established from proceeds of the dissolution of the former Holyoke YWCA.

Award: Scholarship for use in freshman, sophomore, junior, or senior years; not renewable. *Number:* 1. *Amount:* $3000–$4000.

Eligibility Requirements: Applicant must be age 18; enrolled or expecting to enroll full or part-time at a two-year or four-year institution or university; female and resident of Massachusetts. Available to U.S. citizens.

Application Requirements: Application, financial need analysis, transcript. *Deadline:* March 31.

Contact: Community Foundation of Western Massachusetts
1500 Main Street
PO Box 15769
Springfield, MA 01115

WOMEN'S PARTNERSHIP SCHOLARSHIP FUND FOR WOMEN

For women from the greater Springfield area who are 25 years or older, have had a break in their education and are trying to re-enter the workforce, and are attending an accredited college or university in Hampden or Hampshire counties.

Award: Scholarship for use in freshman, sophomore, junior, or senior years; not renewable. *Number:* 4. *Amount:* $1000–$3000.

Eligibility Requirements: Applicant must be age 25; enrolled or expecting to enroll full or part-time at a two-year or four-year institution or university; female; resident of Massachusetts and studying in Massachusetts. Available to U.S. citizens.

Application Requirements: Application, financial need analysis, transcript. *Deadline:* March 31.

Contact: Community Foundation of Western Massachusetts
1500 Main Street
PO Box 15769
Springfield, MA 01115

CONNECTICUT ARMY NATIONAL GUARD http://www.ct.ngb.army.mil/armyguard/join/tuition.asp

CONNECTICUT ARMY NATIONAL GUARD 100% TUITION WAIVER

• *See page 541*

CONNECTICUT ASSOCIATION OF LATIN AMERICANS IN HIGHER EDUCATION (CALAHE) http://www.calahe.org

CONNECTICUT ASSOCIATION OF LATIN AMERICANS IN HIGHER EDUCATION SCHOLARSHIPS

• *See page 582*

CONNECTICUT DEPARTMENT OF HIGHER EDUCATION http://www.ctdhe.org

AID FOR PUBLIC COLLEGE STUDENTS GRANT PROGRAM/ CONNECTICUT

Award for students at Connecticut public college or university. Must be state residents and enrolled at least half-time. Renewable award based on financial need and academic progress. Application deadlines vary by institution. Apply at college financial aid office.

Award: Grant for use in freshman, sophomore, junior, or senior years; renewable. *Number:* varies. *Amount:* varies.

Eligibility Requirements: Applicant must be enrolled or expecting to enroll full or part-time at a two-year or four-year institution or university; resident of Connecticut and studying in Connecticut.

Application Requirements: Application, financial need analysis, transcript. *Deadline:* varies.

Contact: John Siegrist, Financial Aid Office
Connecticut Department of Higher Education
61 Woodland Street
Hartford, CT 06105-2326
Phone: 860-947-1855
Fax: 860-947-1311

CAPITOL SCHOLARSHIP PROGRAM

Award for Connecticut residents attending eligible institutions in Connecticut or in a state with reciprocity with Connecticut (Delaware, Maine, Massachusetts, New Hampshire, Pennsylvania, Rhode Island, Vermont, or Washington, D.C). Must be U.S. citizen or permanent resident alien who is a high school senior or graduate. Must rank in top 20% of class or score at least 1200 on SAT. Must show financial need.

Award: Scholarship for use in freshman, sophomore, junior, or senior years; renewable. *Number:* varies. *Amount:* up to $2000.

Eligibility Requirements: Applicant must be enrolled or expecting to enroll at a two-year or four-year institution or university; resident of Connecticut and studying in Connecticut, Delaware, District of Columbia, Maine, Massachusetts, New Hampshire, Pennsylvania, Rhode Island, or Vermont. Applicant must have 3.5 GPA or higher. Available to U.S. citizens.

Application Requirements: Application, financial need analysis, test scores. *Deadline:* February 15.

Contact: John Siegrist, Financial Aid Office
Connecticut Department of Higher Education
61 Woodland Street
Hartford, CT 06105-2326
Phone: 860-947-1855
Fax: 860-947-1311

CONNECTICUT INDEPENDENT COLLEGE STUDENT GRANTS

Award for Connecticut residents attending an independent college or university within the state on at least a half-time basis. Renewable awards based on financial need. Application deadline varies by institution. Apply at college financial aid office.

Award: Grant for use in freshman, sophomore, junior, or senior years; renewable. *Number:* varies. *Amount:* up to $7700.

Eligibility Requirements: Applicant must be enrolled or expecting to enroll full or part-time at a two-year or four-year institution or university; resident of Connecticut and studying in Connecticut.

Application Requirements: Application, financial need analysis, transcript. *Deadline:* varies.

Contact: John Siegrist, Financial Aid Office
Connecticut Department of Higher Education
61 Woodland Street
Hartford, CT 06105-2326
Phone: 860-947-1855
Fax: 860-947-1311

CONNECTICUT TUITION WAIVER FOR SENIOR CITIZENS

Renewable tuition waiver for a Connecticut senior citizen age 62 or older to use at an accredited two- or four-year public institution in Connecticut. Must show financial need and prove senior citizen status. Award for undergraduate study only. Must be enrolled in credit courses.

Award: Grant for use in freshman, sophomore, junior, or senior years; renewable. *Number:* varies. *Amount:* varies.

Eligibility Requirements: Applicant must be age 62; enrolled or expecting to enroll at a two-year or four-year institution; resident of Connecticut and studying in Connecticut.

Application Requirements: Application, financial need analysis. *Deadline:* Continuous.

Contact: John Siegrist, Financial Aid Office
Connecticut Department of Higher Education
61 Woodland Street
Hartford, CT 06105-2326
Phone: 860-947-1855
Fax: 860-947-1311

CONNECTICUT TUITION WAIVER FOR VETERANS

• *See page 555*

ROBERT C. BYRD HONORS SCHOLARSHIP-CONNECTICUT

Renewable scholarship for Connecticut high school seniors in the top 2% of their class or scoring 1400 or above on the SAT. Acceptance letter from college required. File applications through high school guidance office. Deadline: April 1.

Award: Scholarship for use in freshman, sophomore, junior, or senior years; renewable. *Number:* varies. *Amount:* $1500.

Eligibility Requirements: Applicant must be high school student; planning to enroll or expecting to enroll full-time at a two-year or four-year institution and resident of Connecticut. Available to U.S. citizens.

Application Requirements: Application, test scores. *Deadline:* April 1.

Contact: John Siegrist, Financial Aid Office
Connecticut Department of Higher Education
61 Woodland Street
Hartford, CT 06105-2326
Phone: 860-947-1855
Fax: 860-947-1311

TUITION SET-ASIDE AID—CONNECTICUT

Need-based program that assists Connecticut residents who are enrolled at state-supported colleges and universities in Connecticut. Award amounts are variable but do not exceed student's financial need. Deadlines vary by institution. Apply at college financial aid office.

Award: Grant for use in freshman, sophomore, junior, or senior years; not renewable. *Number:* varies. *Amount:* varies.

Eligibility Requirements: Applicant must be enrolled or expecting to enroll at a two-year or four-year institution or university; resident of Connecticut and studying in Connecticut.

Application Requirements: Application, financial need analysis. *Deadline:* varies.

Contact: John Siegrist, Financial Aid Office
Connecticut Department of Higher Education
61 Woodland Street
Hartford, CT 06105-2326
Phone: 860-947-1855
Fax: 860-947-1311

CONNECTICUT FOREST AND PARK ASSOCIATION http://www.ctwoodlands.org

JAMES L. AND GENEVIEVE H. GOODWIN MEMORIAL SCHOLARSHIP

To support Connecticut residents enrolled in a curriculum of silviculture or forest resource management.

Award: Scholarship for use in freshman, sophomore, junior, senior, or graduate years; not renewable. *Number:* up to 10. *Amount:* $1000–$5000.

Eligibility Requirements: Applicant must be enrolled or expecting to enroll full-time at a two-year or four-year institution or university and resident of Connecticut. Available to U.S. citizens.

Application Requirements: Application, essay, financial need analysis, transcript. *Deadline:* April 1.

Contact: Adam R. Moore, Executive Director
Connecticut Forest and Park Association
16 Meriden Road
Rockfall, CT 06481
Phone: 860-346-2372
Fax: 860-347-7463
E-mail: info@ctwoodlands.org

CONNECTICUT STUDENT LOAN FOUNDATION http://www.cslf.com

VINCENT J. MAIOCCO SCHOLARSHIP

One-time award of $1000 to $3000, given to full-time students who have received a Federal Stafford Loan guaranteed by Connecticut Student Loan Foundation. Must be a U.S. citizen and a resident of Connecticut. Award will be paid directly to the recipient's Stafford Loan lender and will be applied to the loan balance.

Award: Scholarship for use in sophomore, junior, or senior years; not renewable. *Number:* 1–4. *Amount:* $1000–$3000.

Eligibility Requirements: Applicant must be enrolled or expecting to enroll full-time at a four-year institution or university and resident of Connecticut. Available to U.S. citizens.

Application Requirements: Application, essay, transcript, financial aid award letter. *Deadline:* Continuous.

Contact: Melissa Trombley, Executive Manager
Connecticut Student Loan Foundation
525 Brook Street, PO Box 1009
Rocky Hill, CT 06067
Phone: 800-237-9721 Ext. 204
E-mail: mtrombl@mail.cslf.org

CONSTANTINOPLE ARMENIAN RELIEF SOCIETY

CONSTANTINOPLE ARMENIAN RELIEF SOCIETY SCHOLARSHIP

• *See page 582*

COUNTY PROSECUTORS ASSOCIATION OF NEW JERSEY FOUNDATION

JOHN S. STAMLER MEMORIAL SCHOLARSHIP

• *See page 507*

COURAGE CENTER, VOCATIONAL SERVICES DEPARTMENT http://www.courage.org

SCHOLARSHIP FOR PEOPLE WITH DISABILITIES

• *See page 525*

CUBAN AMERICAN SCHOLARSHIP FUND

CUBAN AMERICAN SCHOLARSHIP FUND

One-time award for California residents who were either born in Cuba or have parents or grandparents born in Cuba. Application dates are from January 1 to April 15. Mail an SASE for an application.

Award: Scholarship for use in freshman, sophomore, junior, senior, or graduate years; not renewable. *Number:* 8–15. *Amount:* $500–$1500.

Eligibility Requirements: Applicant must be enrolled or expecting to enroll full-time at an institution or university and resident of California. Applicant must have 3.0 GPA or higher. Available to U.S. and non-U.S. citizens.

Application Requirements: Application, self-addressed stamped envelope. *Deadline:* April 15.

Contact: Victor Cueto, President CASF
Cuban American Scholarship Fund
PO Box 6422
Santa Ana, CA 92706
Phone: 714-835-7676
Fax: 714-835-7776

DALLAS MORNING NEWS

DALLAS MORNING NEWS ANNUAL TEENAGE CITIZENSHIP TRIBUTE

• *See page 508*

DAVIS-ROBERTS SCHOLARSHIP FUND, INC.

DAVIS-ROBERTS SCHOLARSHIPS

• *See page 459*

DELAWARE HIGHER EDUCATION COMMISSION http://www.doe.state.de.us/high-ed

AGENDA FOR DELAWARE WOMEN TRAILBLAZER SCHOLARSHIP

Scholarships given to women residing in Delaware and enrolling in a public or private non-profit college in Delaware as an undergraduate student. Must have a 2.5 GPA. Deadline: April 15.

Award: Scholarship for use in freshman, sophomore, junior, or senior years; not renewable. *Number:* 1. *Amount:* $2500.

Eligibility Requirements: Applicant must be enrolled or expecting to enroll at a two-year or four-year institution; female; resident of Delaware and studying in Delaware. Applicant must have 2.5 GPA or higher.

Application Requirements: Financial need analysis. *Deadline:* April 15.

Contact: Donna Myers, Higher Education Analyst
Delaware Higher Education Commission
820 North French Street
5th Floor
Wilmington, DE 19711-3509
Phone: 302-577-3240
Fax: 302-577-6765
E-mail: dhec@doe.k12.de.us

DELAWARE SOLID WASTE AUTHORITY JOHN P. "PAT" HEALY SCHOLARSHIP

Scholarships given to residents of Delaware who are high school seniors or freshmen or sophomores in college. Must be majoring in either environmental engineering or environmental sciences in a Delaware college. Must file the Free Application for Federal Student Aid (FAFSA). Scholarships are automatically renewed for three years if a 3.0 GPA is maintained. Deadline: March 15.

Award: Scholarship for use in freshman or sophomore years; renewable. *Number:* 1. *Amount:* $2000.

Eligibility Requirements: Applicant must be enrolled or expecting to enroll full-time at a two-year or four-year institution or university; resident of Delaware and studying in Delaware. Applicant must have 3.0 GPA or higher.

Application Requirements: Financial need analysis, FAFSA. *Deadline:* March 15.

Contact: Donna Myers, Higher Education Analyst
Delaware Higher Education Commission
820 North French Street
5th Floor
Wilmington, DE 19711-3509
Phone: 302-577-3240
Fax: 302-577-6765
E-mail: dhec@doe.k12.de.us

DIAMOND STATE SCHOLARSHIP

Renewable award for Delaware high school seniors enrolling full-time at an accredited college or university. Must be ranked in upper quarter of class and score 1200 on SAT or 27 on the ACT.

Award: Scholarship for use in freshman year; renewable. *Number:* 50–200. *Amount:* $1250.

Eligibility Requirements: Applicant must be high school student; planning to enroll or expecting to enroll full-time at a four-year institution or university and resident of Delaware. Applicant must have 3.5 GPA or higher. Available to U.S. citizens.

Application Requirements: Application, essay, test scores, transcript. *Deadline:* March 31.

Contact: Donna Myers, Higher Education Analyst
Delaware Higher Education Commission
820 North French Street
5th Floor
Wilmington, DE 19711-3509
Phone: 302-577-3240
Fax: 302-577-6765
E-mail: dhec@doe.k12.de.us

EDUCATIONAL BENEFITS FOR CHILDREN OF DECEASED MILITARY AND STATE POLICE

• *See page 508*

FIRST STATE MANUFACTURED HOUSING ASSOCIATION SCHOLARSHIP

Scholarship given to Delaware residents living in a manufactured home. May be used for any type of accredited training, licensing, or certification program or for any accredited degree program. Deadline: March 22.

Award: Scholarship for use in freshman, sophomore, junior, or senior years; not renewable. *Number:* up to 2. *Amount:* up to $2000.

Eligibility Requirements: Applicant must be enrolled or expecting to enroll at a two-year or four-year or technical institution or university and resident of Delaware.

Application Requirements: Essay, financial need analysis, references, transcript. *Deadline:* March 22.

Contact: Donna Myers, Higher Education Analyst
Delaware Higher Education Commission
820 North French Street
5th Floor
Wilmington, DE 19711-3509
Phone: 302-577-3240
Fax: 302-577-6765
E-mail: dhec@doe.k12.de.us

LEGISLATIVE ESSAY SCHOLARSHIP

Must be a senior in high school and Delaware resident. Submit an essay of 500 to 2000 words on a designated historical topic (changes annually). Deadline: November 16. For more information visit: http://www.doe.state.de.us/high-ed.

Award: Scholarship for use in freshman year; not renewable. *Number:* 62. *Amount:* $500–$5500.

Eligibility Requirements: Applicant must be high school student; planning to enroll or expecting to enroll full or part-time at a two-year or four-year or technical institution or university and resident of Delaware. Available to U.S. citizens.

Application Requirements: Application, applicant must enter a contest, essay. *Deadline:* November 16.

Contact: Donna Myers, Higher Education Analyst
Delaware Higher Education Commission
820 North French Street
5th Floor
Wilmington, DE 19711-3509
Phone: 302-577-3240
Fax: 302-577-6765
E-mail: dhec@doe.k12.de.us

ROBERT C. BYRD HONORS SCHOLARSHIP-DELAWARE

Available to Delaware residents who are graduating high school seniors. Based on outstanding academic merit. Awards are renewable up to four years. Must be ranked in upper quarter of class and have a score of 1200 on SAT or 27 on ACT.

Award: Scholarship for use in freshman year; renewable. *Number:* 16–80. *Amount:* $1500.

Eligibility Requirements: Applicant must be high school student; planning to enroll or expecting to enroll full-time at a two-year or four-year institution or university and resident of Delaware. Applicant must have 3.5 GPA or higher. Available to U.S. citizens.

Application Requirements: Application, essay, test scores, transcript. *Deadline:* March 31.

Contact: Donna Myers, Higher Education Analyst
Delaware Higher Education Commission
820 North French Street
5th Floor
Wilmington, DE 19711-3509
Phone: 302-577-3240
Fax: 302-577-6765
E-mail: dhec@doe.k12.de.us

SCHOLARSHIP INCENTIVE PROGRAM-DELAWARE

One-time award for Delaware residents with financial need. May be used at an institution in Delaware or Pennsylvania, or at another out-of-state institution if a program is not available at a publicly-supported school in Delaware. Must have minimum 2.5 GPA.

Award: Grant for use in freshman, sophomore, junior, or senior years; not renewable. *Number:* 1000–1300. *Amount:* $700–$2200.

Eligibility Requirements: Applicant must be enrolled or expecting to enroll full-time at a two-year or four-year institution or university; resident of Delaware and studying in Delaware or Pennsylvania. Applicant must have 2.5 GPA or higher. Available to U.S. citizens.

Application Requirements: Application, financial need analysis, transcript. *Deadline:* April 15.

Contact: Donna Myers, Higher Education Analyst
Delaware Higher Education Commission
820 North French Street
5th Floor
Wilmington, DE 19711-3509
Phone: 302-577-3240
Fax: 302-577-6765
E-mail: dhec@doe.k12.de.us

DELAWARE NATIONAL GUARD http://www.delawarenationalguard.com

STATE TUITION ASSISTANCE

• *See page 535*

DELAWARE STATE COMMUNITY ACTION PROGRAM (CAP) COUNCIL UAW REGION 8

UAW LABOR ESSAY CONTEST

This contest is available to all students graduating from a Delaware High School and attending an accredited college full time in the fall. Essay topics include: biography of any great labor leaders; history of international unions; women's role in labor's past; labor history specific era; labor's role in education or politics. 1st place prize is $1,200, 2nd place is $1000, 3rd place is $600, and 4th place is $400.

Award: Prize for use in freshman year; not renewable. *Number:* 4. *Amount:* $400–$1200.

Eligibility Requirements: Applicant must be high school student; planning to enroll or expecting to enroll full-time at a four-year institution or university and resident of Delaware. Available to U.S. and Canadian citizens.

Application Requirements: Applicant must enter a contest, essay. *Deadline:* March 31.

Contact: William Wasik, President
Delaware State Community Action Program (CAP) Council
UAW Region 8
698 Old Baltimore Pike
Newark, DE 19702
Phone: 302-738-9046
Fax: 302-738-9040

DEPARTMENT OF MILITARY AFFAIRS http://www.coloradoguard.com

DEPARTMENT OF MILITARY AFFAIRS COLORADO NATIONAL GUARD STATE TUITION ASSISTANCE PROGRAM

• *See page 535*

WISCONSIN NATIONAL GUARD TUITION GRANT

• *See page 535*

DEVRY, INC. http://www.devry.edu

DEVRY COMMUNITY COLLEGE SCHOLAR AWARD

Scholarship designed for students who have earned a career-oriented associate degree. Two students in each community college in Colorado, Illinois, and Texas are awarded $1,000 per semester scholarships for up to 4 semesters toward the DeVry's bachelor degree program of their choice.

Award: Scholarship for use in junior or senior years; renewable. *Number:* 266. *Amount:* $4000.

Eligibility Requirements: Applicant must be enrolled or expecting to enroll full-time at an institution or university and studying in Colorado, Illinois, or Texas. Applicant must have 2.5 GPA or higher. Available to U.S. citizens.

Application Requirements: Application, interview, references, test scores, transcript. *Deadline:* varies.

Contact: Thonie Simpson, National HS Program Manager
DeVry, Inc.
One Tower Lane
Oak Brook Terrace, IL 60181-4624
Phone: 630-706-3122
Fax: 630-574-1696
E-mail: tsimpson@devry.com

DEVRY DEAN'S SCHOLARSHIPS

Awards to high school seniors who apply to DeVry University who have SAT scores of 1100 or higher or ACT scores of 24 or higher. There is no separate scholarship application, any application for admittance to DeVry University will be reviewed for qualifying scores. Applications must be received by July 1st.

Award: Scholarship for use in freshman, sophomore, junior, or senior years; renewable. *Number:* varies. *Amount:* $7550–$13,550.

Eligibility Requirements: Applicant must be high school student; planning to enroll or expecting to enroll full-time at an institution or university and studying in Arizona, California, Colorado, Florida, Georgia, Illinois, Missouri, New Jersey, New York, Ohio, Texas, or Virginia. Applicant must have 3.0 GPA or higher. Available to U.S. and Canadian citizens.

Application Requirements: Application, interview, test scores, transcript. *Deadline:* July 1.

Contact: Thonie Simpson, National HS Program Manager
DeVry, Inc.
One Tower Lane
Oak Brook Terrace, IL 60181-4624
Phone: 630-706-3122
Fax: 630-574-1696
E-mail: tsimpson@devry.com

DEVRY GRANT FOR SURVIVING DEPENDENTS OF RESCUE WORKERS, CIVIL SERVANTS AND MILITARY PERSONNEL

Grant program for surviving dependents of rescue workers, civil servants and military personnel killed by injuries sustained from September 11, 2001 terrorist attacks. Full tuition scholarship at any DeVry location. Must be U.S. citizen or eligible non-citizen. 2.75 GPA must be maintained. Visit Web site at http://www.devry.edu for additional information and campus locations.

Award: Grant for use in freshman, sophomore, junior, or senior years; renewable. *Number:* varies. *Amount:* $26,600–$60,515.

Eligibility Requirements: Applicant must be enrolled or expecting to enroll full-time at an institution or university and studying in Arizona, California, Colorado, Florida, Georgia, Illinois, Missouri, New Jersey, New York, Ohio, Texas, or Virginia. Available to U.S. and non-U.S. citizens.

Application Requirements: *Deadline:* July 1.

Contact: Kathy Facenda, Director of Student Finance Operations
DeVry, Inc.
One Tower Lane
Oakbrook Terrace, IL 60181-4624
Phone: 630-706-3141
Fax: 630-574-1963
E-mail: kfacenda@devry.com

DEVRY HIGH SCHOOL COMMUNITY SCHOLARS AWARD

Scholarships to approximately 4700 graduates from public high schools in the 24 metropolitan areas served by DeVry's campuses. Recipients of this award must demonstrate proficiency in mathematics and rank in the top fifty percent of their class.

Award: Scholarship for use in freshman, sophomore, junior, or senior years; renewable. *Number:* 4753. *Amount:* $5050–$9050.

Eligibility Requirements: Applicant must be high school student; planning to enroll or expecting to enroll full-time at an institution or university and studying in Arizona, California, Colorado, Florida, Georgia, Illinois, Missouri, New Jersey, New York, Ohio, Texas, or Virginia. Applicant must have 2.5 GPA or higher. Available to U.S. and Canadian citizens.

Application Requirements: Application, interview, references, test scores, transcript. *Deadline:* July 1.

Contact: Thonie Simpson, National HS Program Manager
DeVry, Inc.
One Tower Lane
Oak Brook Terrace, IL 60181-4624
Phone: 630-706-3122
Fax: 630-574-1696
E-mail: tsimpson@devry.com

DEVRY PRESIDENTIAL SCHOLARSHIPS

Two full-tuition scholarships are awarded by each of the 24 DeVry University campuses each year. Contenders are chosen from those who receive a Dean's Scholarship. Winners are determined by committees at each campus on the basis of their academic records, SAT or ACT scores, and an essay on a topic chosen by the committee.

Award: Scholarship for use in freshman, sophomore, junior, or senior years; renewable. *Number:* 48. *Amount:* $26,600–$55,755.

Eligibility Requirements: Applicant must be high school student; planning to enroll or expecting to enroll full-time at an institution or university and studying in Arizona, California, Colorado, Florida, Georgia, Illinois, Missouri, New Jersey, New York, Ohio, Texas, or Virginia. Applicant must have 3.0 GPA or higher. Available to U.S. and Canadian citizens.

Application Requirements: Application, essay, interview, test scores, transcript. *Deadline:* March 12.

Contact: Thonie Simpson, National HS Program Manager
DeVry, Inc.
One Tower Lane
Oak Brook Terrace, IL 60181-4624
Phone: 630-706-3122
Fax: 630-574-1696
E-mail: tsimpson@devry.com

DEVRY UNIVERSITY REGIONAL FIRST SCHOLAR AWARDS

One full-tuition scholarship in each of ten regions to high school seniors who participate in the FIRST Regional Robotics competition. Students must enroll at DeVry University within one calendar year of receipt of the award.

Award: Scholarship for use in freshman, sophomore, junior, or senior years; renewable. *Number:* 10. *Amount:* $21,280–$53,370.

Eligibility Requirements: Applicant must be high school student; planning to enroll or expecting to enroll full-time at an institution or university and studying in Arizona, California, Colorado, Florida, Georgia, Illinois, New York, Pennsylvania, or Texas. Available to U.S. and non-U.S. citizens.

Application Requirements: Application, applicant must enter a contest, essay, references, test scores, transcript. *Deadline:* March 1.

Contact: Marisa Russo, National Outreach Services Manager
DeVry, Inc.
One Tower Lane
Oakbrook Terrace, IL 60181-4624
Phone: 630-928-6478
Fax: 630-574-1991
E-mail: mrusso@devry.com

DISTRICT OF COLUMBIA NATIONAL GUARD ENLISTED ASSOCIATION

DISTRICT OF COLUMBIA NATIONAL GUARD ENLISTED ASSOCIATION SCHOLARSHIP

• *See page 495*

DISTRICT OF COLUMBIA STATE EDUCATION OFFICE

http://www.seo.dc.gov

DC LEVERAGING EDUCATIONAL ASSISTANCE PARTNERSHIP PROGRAM (LEAP)

Available to Washington, D.C. residents who have financial need. Must also apply for the Federal Pell Grant. Must attend an eligible college at least half time. Contact financial aid office or local library for more information. Proof of residency may be required. Deadline is last Friday in June.

Award: Scholarship for use in freshman, sophomore, junior, or senior years; not renewable. *Number:* 1200–1500. *Amount:* $500–$1500.

Eligibility Requirements: Applicant must be enrolled or expecting to enroll full or part-time at a two-year or four-year or technical institution or university and resident of District of Columbia. Available to U.S. citizens.

Application Requirements: Application, financial need analysis, Student Aid Report (SAR). *Deadline:* June 28.

Contact: Angela March, Program Manager
District of Columbia State Education Office
441 4th Street NW, Suite 350 North
Washington, DC 20001
Phone: 202-727-6436
Fax: 202-727-2019
E-mail: angela.march@dc.gov

DC TUITION ASSISTANCE GRANT PROGRAM

The D.C. Tuition Assistance Grant Program pays the difference between in-state and out-of-state tuition and fees at any public college or university in the United States up to $10,000 per year. It also pays up to $2500 per year of tuition and fees at private colleges and universities in the Washington metropolitan area, and at historically black colleges and universities throughout the United States. Students must be enrolled in a degree-granting program at an eligible institution, and be domiciled in the District of Columbia.

Award: Grant for use in freshman, sophomore, junior, or senior years; renewable. *Number:* up to 4000. *Amount:* $2500–$10,000.

Eligibility Requirements: Applicant must be enrolled or expecting to enroll full or part-time at a two-year or four-year institution or university and resident of District of Columbia. Available to U.S. citizens.

Application Requirements: Application, supporting documents. *Deadline:* June 30.

Contact: Leonard Proctor, Program Director
District of Columbia State Education Office
441 4th Street, NW, Suite 350 N
Washington, DC 20001
Phone: 202-727-2824
Fax: 202-727-2834
E-mail: leonard.proctor@dc.gov

DISTRICT OF COLUMBIA ADOPTION SCHOLARSHIP

Scholarship program designed for adopted individuals who are wards of the District. Applicants must show proof of adoption, current postsecondary enrollment status, and social security number.

Award: Grant for use in freshman, sophomore, junior, or senior years; not renewable. *Number:* varies. *Amount:* up to $10,000.

Eligibility Requirements: Applicant must be age 24 or under; enrolled or expecting to enroll full-time at a two-year or four-year or technical institution or university and resident of District of Columbia. Available to U.S. citizens.

Application Requirements: Application, proof of adoption; enrollment verification. *Deadline:* Continuous.

Contact: Angela March, Program Manager
District of Columbia State Education Office
441 4th Street NW, Suite 350 North
Washington, DC 20001
Phone: 202-727-6436
Fax: 202-727-2019
E-mail: angela.march@dc.gov

DIXIE BOYS BASEBALL http://www.dixie.org

DIXIE BOYS BASEBALL SCHOLARSHIP PROGRAM

Eleven scholarships are presented annually to deserving high school seniors who have participated in the Dixie Boys Baseball Program. Citizenship, scholarship, residency in a state with Dixie Baseball Programs and financial need are considered in determining the awards.

Award: Scholarship for use in freshman year; not renewable. *Number:* 11. *Amount:* $1500.

Eligibility Requirements: Applicant must be high school student; planning to enroll or expecting to enroll full-time at a two-year or four-year institution or university and resident of Alabama, Arkansas, Florida, Georgia, Louisiana, Mississippi, North Carolina, South Carolina, Tennessee, Texas, or Virginia. Available to U.S. citizens.

Application Requirements: Application, financial need analysis, photo, references. *Deadline:* March 15.

Contact: Bernie H. Varnadore, Scholarship Chairman
Dixie Boys Baseball
2684 Orchid Avenue
North Charleston, SC 29405
Phone: 843-744-7612
Fax: 843-747-7612
E-mail: hbvrmvpfl@aol.com

DIXIE YOUTH SCHOLARSHIP PROGRAM

Thirty scholarships are presented annually to deserving high school seniors who participated in the Dixie Youth Baseball program while age 12 and under. Financial need is considered. Parents must submit a copy of 1040 tax return.

Award: Scholarship for use in freshman year; not renewable. *Number:* 30. *Amount:* $2000.

Eligibility Requirements: Applicant must be high school student; planning to enroll or expecting to enroll full-time at a two-year or four-year or technical institution or university and resident of Alabama, Arkansas, Florida, Georgia, Louisiana, Mississippi, North Carolina, South Carolina, Tennessee, Texas, or Virginia. Available to U.S. citizens.

Application Requirements: Application, essay, financial need analysis, photo, references, transcript, 1040 form. *Deadline:* March 1.

Contact: Mr. P. L. Corley, Scholarship Chairman
Dixie Boys Baseball
PO Box 877
Marshall, TX 75671-0877
Phone: 903-927-2255
Fax: 903-927-1846
E-mail: dyb@dixie.org

DOGRIB TREATY 11 SCHOLARSHIP COMMITTEE http://www.dt11sc.ca

DIAVIK DIAMONDS, INC. UNIVERSITY SCHOLARSHIPS

Award for students of Dogrib ancestry who are permanent residents of one of four Dogrib communities (Wekweti, Wha Ti, Gamet, or Rae-Edzo). Applicants must be enrolled full time in a Canadian University degree program and interested and active in community affairs.

Award: Scholarship for use in freshman, sophomore, junior, senior, or graduate years. *Number:* 4. *Amount:* $3714.

Eligibility Requirements: Applicant must be enrolled or expecting to enroll full-time at an institution or university and resident of North West Territories.

Application Requirements: Application, references, transcript. *Deadline:* varies.

Contact: Morven MacPherson, Post Secondary Student Support Coordinator
Dogrib Treaty 11 Scholarship Committee
c/o CJBRHS
Bag #1
Rae-Edzo, NT X0E 0Y0
Canada
Phone: 867-371-3815
Fax: 867-371-3813
E-mail: morvenm@dogrib.net

EAST LOS ANGELES COMMUNITY UNION (TELACU) EDUCATION FOUNDATION

TELACU SCHOLARSHIP PROGRAM

Scholarships available to low-income applicants from the Greater East Side of Los Angeles. Must be U.S. citizen or permanent resident. Must be a resident of one of the following communities: East Los Angeles, Bell Gardens, Commerce, Huntington Park, Montebello, Monterey Park, Pico Rivera, Santa Ana, South Gate, and the City of Los Angeles. Must be the first generation in their family to achieve a college degree. Must have a record of community service.

Award: Scholarship for use in freshman, sophomore, junior, or senior years; not renewable. *Number:* up to 150. *Amount:* $500–$3000.

Eligibility Requirements: Applicant must be enrolled or expecting to enroll full-time at a two-year or four-year institution or university; resident of California and studying in California. Applicant must have 2.5 GPA or higher. Available to U.S. and non-U.S. citizens.

Application Requirements: Application, essay, financial need analysis, interview, references, transcript. *Deadline:* April 3.

Contact: Michael A. Alvarado, Director
East Los Angeles Community Union (TELACU) Education Foundation
5400 East Olympic Boulevard, Suite 300
Los Angeles, CA 90022
Phone: 323-721-1655 Ext. 403
Fax: 323-724-3372
E-mail: malvarado@telacu.com

EDMUND F. MAXWELL FOUNDATION http://www.maxwell.org

EDMUND F. MAXWELL FOUNDATION SCHOLARSHIP

Scholarships awarded to residents of western Washington to attend accredited independent colleges or universities. Awards of up to $3500 per year based on need, merit, citizenship, and activities. Renewable for up to four years if academic progress is suitable and financial need is unchanged.

Edmund F. Maxwell Foundation (continued)

Award: Scholarship for use in freshman year; renewable. *Number:* 110. *Amount:* $1000–$3500.

Eligibility Requirements: Applicant must be enrolled or expecting to enroll full-time at a four-year institution or university and resident of Washington. Available to U.S. citizens.

Application Requirements: Application, essay, financial need analysis, test scores, transcript, employment history. *Deadline:* April 30.

Contact: Administrator
Edmund F. Maxwell Foundation
PO Box 22537
Seattle, WA 98122
E-mail: admin@maxwell.org

EDWARDS SCHOLARSHIP FUND

EDWARDS SCHOLARSHIP

College scholarships for students under 25 years of age whose permanent address is in the city of Boston, Massachusetts. Must have lived in Boston since the beginning of junior year in high school. Must maintain a "C" or GPA of 2.0.

Award: Scholarship for use in freshman, sophomore, junior, senior, graduate, or postgraduate years; not renewable. *Number:* varies. *Amount:* $250–$5000.

Eligibility Requirements: Applicant must be age 24 or under; enrolled or expecting to enroll full-time at a two-year or four-year or technical institution or university and resident of Massachusetts. Available to U.S. and non-U.S. citizens.

Application Requirements: Application, financial need analysis, interview, references, test scores, transcript, Student Aid Report (SAR). *Deadline:* March 1.

Contact: Brenda McCarthy, Executive Secretary
Edwards Scholarship Fund
200 Clarendon Street, 27th Floor
Boston, MA 02116
Phone: 617-654-8628

ELMER O. AND IDA PRESTON EDUCATIONAL TRUST

ELMER O. AND IDA PRESTON EDUCATIONAL TRUST GRANTS AND LOANS

Provides financial assistance to students attending Iowa colleges or universities and who are preparing for a life of Christian service. Portion of loan must be repaid. Must be an Iowa resident.

Award: Grant for use in freshman, sophomore, junior, or senior years; renewable. *Number:* varies. *Amount:* $250–$5000.

Eligibility Requirements: Applicant must be enrolled or expecting to enroll full-time at an institution or university; resident of Iowa and studying in Iowa. Available to U.S. citizens.

Application Requirements: Application, driver's license, interview, transcript. *Deadline:* July 30.

Contact: Elmer O. and Ida Preston Educational Trust
801 Grand Avenue, Suite 3700
Des Moines, IA 50309

EPILEPSY FOUNDATION OF IDAHO http://www.epilepsyidaho.org

GREGORY W. GILE MEMORIAL SCHOLARSHIP PROGRAM

• *See page 525*

MARK MUSIC MEMORIAL SCHOLARSHIP

• *See page 525*

ESPERANZA, INC. http://www.esperanzainc.com

ESPERANZA SCHOLARSHIPS

• *See page 583*

EVERLY SCHOLARSHIP FUND, INC.

EVERLY SCHOLARSHIP

Renewable award for New Jersey residents attending an accredited institution full-time. Must be undergraduate. Minimum 3.0 GPA required and minimum SAT score of 1100.

Award: Scholarship for use in freshman, sophomore, junior, or senior years; renewable. *Number:* 5. *Amount:* $2500.

Eligibility Requirements: Applicant must be high school student; planning to enroll or expecting to enroll full-time at a four-year institution or university and resident of New Jersey. Applicant must have 3.0 GPA or higher. Available to U.S. citizens.

Application Requirements: Application, autobiography, essay, financial need analysis, interview, references, test scores, transcript. *Deadline:* May 1.

Contact: John Lolio, Jr., President
Everly Scholarship Fund, Inc.
Fairway Corporate Center
4300 Haddonfield Road, Suite 311
Pennsauken, NJ 08109
Phone: 856-661-2094
Fax: 856-662-0165
E-mail: jlolio@sskrplaw.com

FAMILY CIRCLE CUP AND L'OREAL http://www.familycirclecup.com

L'OREAL /FAMILY CIRCLE CUP "PERSONAL BEST" SCHOLARSHIP

Purpose of scholarship is to honor females who make a difference in the lives of others through role modeling, community involvement and services, volunteer experiences, and extracurricular activities. The scholarship will be applied towards college costs. Applicant must be a resident of Georgia, North Carolina, or South Carolina. Open to high school students.

Award: Scholarship for use in freshman year; not renewable. *Number:* 3. *Amount:* $2500.

Eligibility Requirements: Applicant must be high school student; planning to enroll or expecting to enroll full-time at a two-year or four-year or technical institution or university; female and resident of Georgia, North Carolina, or South Carolina. Available to U.S. and non-U.S. citizens.

Application Requirements: Application, essay, references, transcript. *Deadline:* February 4.

Contact: Family Circle Cup Offices
Phone: 843-849-5317

FINANCE AUTHORITY OF MAINE http://www.famemaine.com

MAINE STATE GRANT

Scholarships for residents of Maine attending an eligible school, full time, in Connecticut, Maine, Massachusetts, New Hampshire, Pennsylvania, Rhode Island, Washington, D.C., or Vermont. Award based on need. Must apply annually. Complete Free Application for Federal Student Aid to apply. One-time award of $500-$1250 for undergraduate study.

Award: Grant for use in freshman, sophomore, junior, or senior years; not renewable. *Number:* 8900–12,500. *Amount:* $500–$1250.

Eligibility Requirements: Applicant must be enrolled or expecting to enroll full-time at a two-year or four-year or technical institution or university; resident of Maine and studying in Connecticut, District of Columbia, Maine, Massachusetts, New Hampshire, Pennsylvania, Rhode Island, or Vermont.

Application Requirements: Application, financial need analysis, FAFSA. *Deadline:* May 1.

Contact: Claude Roy, Program Officer
Finance Authority of Maine
5 Community Drive
Augusta, ME 04332-0949
Phone: 800-228-3734
Fax: 207-623-0095
E-mail: claude@famemaine.com

ROBERT C. BYRD HONORS SCHOLARSHIP PROGRAM

Merit-based, renewable scholarships of up to $1,500 annually for graduating high school seniors. Superior academic performance is the primary criterion for the award.

Award: Scholarship for use in freshman year; renewable. *Number:* up to 30. *Amount:* up to $1500.

Eligibility Requirements: Applicant must be high school student; planning to enroll or expecting to enroll at an institution or university and resident of Maine. Available to U.S. citizens.

Application Requirements: Application, essay, transcript, H.S. profile. *Deadline:* April 15.

Contact: Janeen Violette, Program Officer
Finance Authority of Maine
5 Community Drive
Augusta, ME 04332-0949
Phone: 800-228-3734
Fax: 207-623-0095
E-mail: janeen@famemaine.com

TUITION WAIVER PROGRAMS

• *See page 509*

FLEMING-MASON ENERGY http://www.fmenergy.net

FLEMING-MASON ENERGY ANNUAL MEETING SCHOLARSHIP

Awards for graduating Kentucky high school senior in good standing who is a child of a member of Fleming-Mason Energy, whose primary residence is on co-op lines. Application and information may be obtained from high school guidance counselor or by calling Director of Member Services. Deadline for application is in mid-April.

Award: Scholarship for use in freshman year; not renewable. *Number:* 10. *Amount:* $1000.

Eligibility Requirements: Applicant must be high school student; planning to enroll or expecting to enroll at a two-year or four-year or technical institution or university and resident of Kentucky. Available to U.S. citizens.

Application Requirements: Application.

Contact: Mary Beth Nance, Director of Member Services
Fleming-Mason Energy
PO Box 328
Flemingsburg, KY 41041
Phone: 800-464-3144
Fax: 606-845-1008
E-mail: mbnance@fmenergy.net

FLORIDA ASSOCIATION OF POSTSECONDARY SCHOOLS AND COLLEGES http://www.fapsc.org

FLORIDA ASSOCIATION OF POSTSECONDARY SCHOOLS AND COLLEGES SCHOLARSHIP PROGRAM

Full and partial scholarship to private career schools in Florida are awarded to students either graduating from high school or receiving GED in the current school year. Must be a resident of Florida. Minimum 2.5 GPA required.

Award: Scholarship for use in freshman year; not renewable. *Number:* up to 225. *Amount:* up to $3500.

Eligibility Requirements: Applicant must be high school student; planning to enroll or expecting to enroll full or part-time at a technical institution; resident of Florida and studying in Florida. Applicant must have 2.5 GPA or higher. Available to U.S. citizens.

Application Requirements: Application, essay, references, transcript. *Deadline:* March 1.

Contact: Heather Fuselier, Membership Director
Florida Association of Postsecondary Schools and Colleges
150 South Monroe Street
Suite 303
Tallahassee, FL 32301
Phone: 850-577-3139
Fax: 850-577-3133
E-mail: scholarship@fapsc.org

FLORIDA DEPARTMENT OF EDUCATION http://www.floridastudentfinancialaid.org

CRITICAL TEACHER SHORTAGE STUDENT LOAN FORGIVENESS PROGRAM-FLORIDA

• *See page 509*

ETHICS IN BUSINESS SCHOLARSHIP

Provides assistance to undergraduate college students who enroll at community colleges and eligible Florida colleges or universities. Scholarships are funded by private and state contributions. Awards are dependent on private matching funds. For more information contact the financial aid office at participating institutions, which are listed on the Florida Department of Education Web site at http://www.firn.edu/doe/ofsa.

Award: Scholarship for use in freshman, sophomore, junior, or senior years; not renewable. *Number:* varies.

Eligibility Requirements: Applicant must be enrolled or expecting to enroll at a two-year or four-year institution or university and studying in Florida. Available to U.S. citizens.

Application Requirements: Application.

Contact: Scholarship Information
Florida Department of Education
Office of Student Financial Assistance
1940 North Monroe, Suite 70
Tallahassee, FL 32303-4759
Phone: 888-827-2004
E-mail: osfa@fldoe.org

FLORIDA BRIGHT FUTURES SCHOLARSHIP PROGRAM

Reward for Florida high school graduates who demonstrate high academic achievement, participate in community service projects, and enroll in eligible Florida postsecondary institutions. There are three award levels. Each has different academic criteria and awards a different amount. Top ranked scholars from each county will receive additional $1500. Web site at http://www.firn.edu/doe contains complete information and application which must be completed and submitted to high school guidance counselor prior to graduation.

Award: Scholarship for use in freshman, sophomore, junior, or senior years; renewable. *Number:* varies. *Amount:* varies.

Eligibility Requirements: Applicant must be high school student; planning to enroll or expecting to enroll full or part-time at a two-year or four-year or technical institution or university; resident of Florida and studying in Florida. Available to U.S. citizens.

Application Requirements: Application, financial need analysis, test scores, transcript.

Contact: Scholarship Information
Florida Department of Education
Office of Student Financial Assistance
1940 North Monroe, Suite 70
Tallahassee, FL 32303-4759
Phone: 888-827-2004
E-mail: osfa@fldoe.org

FLORIDA PRIVATE STUDENT ASSISTANCE GRANT

Grants for Florida residents who are U.S. citizens or eligible non-citizens attending eligible independent nonprofit colleges or universities in Florida. Must be full-time student and demonstrate substantial financial need. Renewable for up to nine semesters, fourteen quarters, or until receipt of bachelor's degree. Deadline to be determined by individual eligible institutions.

Florida Department of Education (continued)

Award: Grant for use in freshman, sophomore, junior, or senior years; renewable. *Number:* varies. *Amount:* up to $1481.

Eligibility Requirements: Applicant must be enrolled or expecting to enroll full-time at a four-year institution or university; resident of Florida and studying in Florida. Available to U.S. citizens.

Application Requirements: Application, financial need analysis, FAFSA.

Contact: Scholarship Information
Florida Department of Education
Office of Student Financial Assistance
1940 North Monroe, Suite 70
Tallahassee, FL 32303-4759
Phone: 888-827-2004
E-mail: osfa@fldoe.org

FLORIDA PUBLIC STUDENT ASSISTANCE GRANT

Grants for Florida residents, U.S. citizens, or eligible non-citizens attending a Florida public college or university full-time. Based on financial need. Renewable up to 9 semesters, 14 quarters, or until receipt of bachelor's degree. Deadline set by eligible participating institutions.

Award: Grant for use in freshman, sophomore, junior, or senior years; renewable. *Number:* varies. *Amount:* up to $1481.

Eligibility Requirements: Applicant must be enrolled or expecting to enroll full-time at a two-year or four-year institution or university; resident of Florida and studying in Florida. Available to U.S. citizens.

Application Requirements: Application, financial need analysis, FAFSA.

Contact: Scholarship Information
Florida Department of Education
Office of Student Financial Assistance
1940 North Monroe, Suite 70
Tallahassee, FL 32303-4759
Phone: 888-827-2004
E-mail: osfa@fldoe.org

JOSE MARTI SCHOLARSHIP CHALLENGE GRANT FUND

• *See page 583*

MARY MCLEOD BETHUNE SCHOLARSHIP

Available to Florida students with a GPA of 3.0 or above who will attend Florida Agricultural and Mechanical University, Edward Waters College, Bethune-Cookman College, or Florida Memorial College. Based on need and merit. Further information, deadlines, and applications available at the financial aid office at the school.

Award: Scholarship for use in freshman, sophomore, junior, or senior years; not renewable. *Number:* 160. *Amount:* $3000.

Eligibility Requirements: Applicant must be enrolled or expecting to enroll full-time at a four-year institution; resident of Florida and studying in Florida. Applicant must have 3.0 GPA or higher. Available to U.S. citizens.

Application Requirements: Application, financial need analysis.

Contact: Scholarship Information
Florida Department of Education
Office of Student Financial Assistance
1940 North Monroe, Suite 70
Tallahassee, FL 32303-4759
Phone: 888-827-2004
E-mail: osfa@fldoe.org

ROBERT C. BYRD HONORS SCHOLARSHIP PROGRAM-FLORIDA

One applicant per high school may be nominated. Must be Florida resident. Must be U.S. citizen or eligible non-citizen. Application must be submitted in the same year as graduation. Must meet Selective Service System registration requirements. May attend any postsecondary accredited institution.

Award: Scholarship for use in freshman, sophomore, junior, or senior years; renewable. *Number:* 1200. *Amount:* up to $1500.

Eligibility Requirements: Applicant must be high school student; planning to enroll or expecting to enroll full-time at a two-year or four-year or technical institution or university and resident of Florida. Available to U.S. citizens.

Application Requirements: Application, financial need analysis, references, test scores, transcript. *Deadline:* April 15.

Contact: Scholarship Information
Florida Department of Education
Office of Student Financial Assistance
1940 North Monroe, Suite 70
Tallahassee, FL 32303-4759
Phone: 888-827-2004
E-mail: osfa@fldoe.org

ROSEWOOD FAMILY SCHOLARSHIP FUND

• *See page 584*

SCHOLARSHIPS FOR CHILDREN OF DECEASED OR DISABLED VETERANS OR CHILDREN OF SERVICEMEN CLASSIFIED AS POW OR MIA

• *See page 556*

WILLIAM L. BOYD IV FLORIDA RESIDENT ACCESS GRANT

Awards given to Florida residents attending an independent nonprofit college or university in Florida for undergraduate study. Cannot have previously received bachelor's degree. Must enroll minimum 12 credit hours. Deadline set by eligible postsecondary financial aid offices. Contact financial aid administrator for application information. Reapply for renewal.

Award: Grant for use in freshman, sophomore, junior, or senior years; not renewable. *Number:* varies. *Amount:* up to $2686.

Eligibility Requirements: Applicant must be enrolled or expecting to enroll full-time at a four-year institution or university; resident of Florida and studying in Florida. Available to U.S. citizens.

Application Requirements: Application. *Deadline:* April 1.

Contact: Scholarship Information
Florida Department of Education
Office of Student Financial Assistance
1940 North Monroe, Suite 70
Tallahassee, FL 32303-4759
Phone: 888-827-2004
E-mail: osfa@fldoe.org

FLORIDA LEADER MAGAZINE/COLLEGE STUDENT OF THE YEAR, INC. http://www.floridaleader.com/soty

FLORIDA COLLEGE STUDENT OF THE YEAR AWARD

This award recognizes Florida's finest campus leaders for their service to their campuses and communities. Available to students enrolled at least part-time in a Florida postsecondary school. Must have completed at least eighteen credit hours with minimum GPA of 3.25. Based primarily on leadership activities but academic merit and work history are considered. Submit statement of financial self-reliance.

Award: Scholarship for use in sophomore, junior, senior, graduate, or postgraduate years; not renewable. *Number:* 20. *Amount:* $1500–$4500.

Eligibility Requirements: Applicant must be enrolled or expecting to enroll full or part-time at a two-year or four-year or technical institution or university; studying in Florida and must have an interest in leadership. Available to U.S. and non-U.S. citizens.

Application Requirements: Application, autobiography, essay, photo, resume, references, self-addressed stamped envelope, transcript. *Deadline:* February 1.

Contact: W. H. Oxendine, Jr., Publisher/Editor-in-Chief
Florida Leader Magazine/College Student of the Year, Inc.
PO Box 14081
Gainesville, FL 32604-2081
Phone: 352-373-6907
Fax: 352-373-8120
E-mail: info@studentleader.com

FLORIDA WOMEN'S STATE GOLF ASSOCIATION http://www.fwsga.org

FLORIDA WOMEN'S STATE GOLF ASSOCIATION JUNIOR GIRLS' SCHOLARSHIP FUND

The FWSGA Scholarship Fund is designed to assist young women to whom golf is meaningful with their education. Applicants must be Florida residents, play golf, maintain a 3.0 GPA, attend a Florida college or university, and have a need for financial assistance.

Award: Scholarship for use in freshman, sophomore, junior, or senior years; renewable. *Number:* varies. *Amount:* $1500–$2000.

Eligibility Requirements: Applicant must be age 18; enrolled or expecting to enroll full-time at a two-year or four-year institution or university; female; resident of Florida; studying in Florida and must have an interest in golf. Applicant must have 3.0 GPA or higher. Available to U.S. citizens.

Application Requirements: Application, financial need analysis, interview, references, test scores, transcript. *Deadline:* February 28.

Contact: Florida Women's State Golf Association
8875 Hidden River Parkway, Suite 110
Tampa, FL 33637

FRANK H. AND EVA B. BUCK FOUNDATION http://www.buckfoundation.org

FRANK H. BUCK SCHOLARSHIPS

Awards to students who live or attend high school in the California counties of Napa, Solano, Yolo, Sacramento, San Joaquin and Contra Costa. Funding is expected to supplement any other financial aid or awards. This ensures all ordinary costs of an education are covered. These costs include tuition and related fees, housing, board, books, educational supplies and some travel to and from school. See Web site: http://www.buckfoundation.org for more information.

Award: Scholarship for use in freshman, sophomore, junior, senior, graduate, or postgraduate years; renewable. *Number:* 10–20. *Amount:* varies.

Eligibility Requirements: Applicant must be enrolled or expecting to enroll full or part-time at a two-year or four-year or technical institution or university and resident of California. Available to U.S. and non-U.S. citizens.

Application Requirements: Application, essay, financial need analysis, interview, photo, resume, references, test scores, transcript. *Deadline:* varies.

Contact: Gloria Brown, Scholarship Director
Frank H. and Eva B. Buck Foundation
PO Box 5610
Vacaville, CA 95696-5610
Phone: 707-446-7700
Fax: 707-446-7766
E-mail: gbrown@buckfoundation.org

FRED G. ZAHN SCHOLARSHIP FUND

FRED G. ZAHN SCHOLARSHIP

One-time award for full-time, upper-level undergraduates. Applicant must be a Washington State resident, who graduated from a Washington State high school and is attending a college in the state of Washington. Must be U.S. citizen. Minimum 3.0 GPA required.

Award: Scholarship for use in junior or senior years; not renewable. *Number:* 3–5. *Amount:* $1200–$1500.

Eligibility Requirements: Applicant must be enrolled or expecting to enroll full-time at a four-year institution or university; resident of Washington and studying in Washington. Applicant must have 3.0 GPA or higher. Available to U.S. citizens.

Application Requirements: Application, essay, financial need analysis, self-addressed stamped envelope, transcript. *Deadline:* April 15.

Contact: Angel Laval, Trust Officer
Fred G. Zahn Scholarship Fund
c/o Bank of America, N.A.
715 Peachtree Street, 8th Floor
Atlanta, GA 30308
Phone: 800-832-9071
Fax: 800-552-3182
E-mail: privatebankcenter@bankofamerica.com

FRESH START SCHOLARSHIP FOUNDATION, INC. http://www.wwb.org/fresh.htm

FRESH START SCHOLARSHIP

Scholarship offering a "fresh start" to women who are returning to school after a hiatus of two years to better their life and opportunities. Must be entering an undergraduate program in Delaware.

Award: Scholarship for use in freshman, sophomore, junior, or senior years; not renewable. *Number:* up to 10. *Amount:* $750–$2000.

Eligibility Requirements: Applicant must be age 20; enrolled or expecting to enroll full or part-time at a two-year or four-year institution or university; female and studying in Delaware. Available to U.S. and non-U.S. citizens.

Application Requirements: Application, essay, financial need analysis, references, transcript. *Deadline:* May 30.

Contact: Cindy Cheyney, Secretary
Fresh Start Scholarship Foundation, Inc.
c/o Master, Sidlow & Associates, P.A.
2002 West 14th Street
Wilmington, DE 19806
Phone: 302-656-4411
Fax: 610-347-0438
E-mail: ccheyney@delanet.com

GALLUP ORGANIZATION/CORNHUSKER STATE GAMES http://www.cornhuskerstategames.com/

GALLUP CSG SCHOLARSHIP PROGRAM

One-time award for Nebraska students who are participants in the Cornhusker State Games. For use at a Nebraska postsecondary institution. Deadline is June 23. See Web site at http://www.cornhuskerstategames.com for further details.

Award: Scholarship for use in freshman, sophomore, junior, senior, graduate, or postgraduate years; not renewable. *Number:* 5. *Amount:* $1000.

Eligibility Requirements: Applicant must be enrolled or expecting to enroll full or part-time at a two-year or four-year or technical institution or university; resident of Nebraska and studying in Nebraska. Available to U.S. citizens.

Application Requirements: Application, applicant must enter a contest, essay, transcript. *Deadline:* June 23.

Contact: Dave Mlnarik, Executive Director
Gallup Organization/Cornhusker State Games
PO Box 82411
2202 South 11th Street
2202 South 11th Street
Lincoln, NE 68501
E-mail: dmlnarik@cornhuskerstategames.com

GENERAL FEDERATION OF WOMEN'S CLUBS IN WYOMING

MARY N. BROOKS DAUGHTER/GRANDDAUGHTER SCHOLARSHIP

• *See page 461*

MARY N. BROOKS WYOMING BOY SCHOLARSHIP

Award given yearly to any male high school graduate who will be attending any school of higher learning in the State of Wyoming. Must be a resident of Wyoming. Award is based on scholarship, community/school involvement, and financial need. Minimum 3.0 GPA required. Deadline: March 15.

Award: Scholarship for use in freshman, sophomore, junior, or senior years; not renewable. *Number:* 1. *Amount:* $500.

General Federation of Women's Clubs in Wyoming (continued)

Eligibility Requirements: Applicant must be enrolled or expecting to enroll full-time at a two-year or four-year or technical institution or university; male; resident of Wyoming and studying in Wyoming. Applicant must have 3.0 GPA or higher. Available to U.S. citizens.

Application Requirements: Application, autobiography, financial need analysis, resume, references, transcript. *Deadline:* March 15.

Contact: Mrs. Norine Samuelson, Custodian, Scholarship Funds
General Federation of Women's Clubs in Wyoming
2005 Eagle Drive
Cheyenne, WY 82009
Phone: 307-638-9443
Fax: 307-433-1020
E-mail: samuelson63291@msn.com

MARY N. BROOKS WYOMING GIRL SCHOLARSHIP

Award given yearly to any female high school graduate who will be attending any school of higher learning in the state of Wyoming. Must be a resident of Wyoming. Award is based on scholarship, community/school involvement, and financial need. Minimum 3.0 GPA required. Deadline: March 15.

Award: Scholarship for use in freshman, sophomore, junior, or senior years; not renewable. *Number:* 1. *Amount:* $500.

Eligibility Requirements: Applicant must be enrolled or expecting to enroll full-time at a two-year or four-year or technical institution or university; female; resident of Wyoming and studying in Wyoming. Applicant must have 3.0 GPA or higher. Available to U.S. citizens.

Application Requirements: Application, autobiography, financial need analysis, resume, references, transcript. *Deadline:* March 15.

Contact: Mrs. Norine Samuelson, Custodian, Scholarship Funds
General Federation of Women's Clubs in Wyoming
2005 Eagle Drive
Cheyenne, WY 82009
Phone: 307-638-9443
Fax: 307-433-1020
E-mail: samuelson63291@msn.com

RUTH CLARE YONKEE DISTRICT SCHOLARSHIP

Annual award given to a female high school graduate who will be attending a school of higher learning in Wyoming. Applicant must live in the geographic area of Wyoming designated for that year. For 2004, recipient must be from South District. Award is based on scholarship, community/school involvement, and financial need. Minimum 3.0 GPA required.

Award: Scholarship for use in freshman, sophomore, junior, or senior years; not renewable. *Number:* 1. *Amount:* $250.

Eligibility Requirements: Applicant must be enrolled or expecting to enroll full-time at a two-year or four-year or technical institution or university; female; resident of Wyoming and studying in Wyoming. Applicant must have 3.0 GPA or higher. Available to U.S. citizens.

Application Requirements: Application, autobiography, financial need analysis, resume, references, transcript. *Deadline:* March 15.

Contact: Mrs. Norine Samuelson, Custodian, Scholarship Funds
General Federation of Women's Clubs in Wyoming
2005 Eagle Drive
Cheyenne, WY 82009
Phone: 307-638-9443
Fax: 307-433-1020
E-mail: samuelson63291@msn.com

GENERAL FEDERATION OF WOMEN'S CLUBS OF MASSACHUSETTS

GENERAL FEDERATION OF WOMEN'S CLUBS OF MASSACHUSETTS STUDY ABROAD SCHOLARSHIP

Scholarship for undergraduate or graduate study abroad. Applicant must submit personal statement and letter of endorsement from the president of the sponsoring General Federation of Women's Clubs of Massachusetts. Must be resident of Massachusetts.

Award: Scholarship for use in freshman, sophomore, junior, senior, or graduate years; not renewable. *Number:* 1. *Amount:* $800.

Eligibility Requirements: Applicant must be enrolled or expecting to enroll full-time at a two-year or four-year institution or university and resident of Massachusetts.

Application Requirements: Application, essay, interview, references, self-addressed stamped envelope, transcript. *Deadline:* March 1.

Contact: Jane Howard, Scholarship Chairperson
General Federation of Women's Clubs of Massachusetts
PO Box 679
Sudbury, MA 01776-0679
Phone: 978-444-9105

GENERAL FEDERATION OF WOMEN'S CLUBS OF VERMONT

BARBARA JEAN BARKER MEMORIAL SCHOLARSHIP FOR A DISPLACED HOMEMAKER

A non-traditional scholarship designed for a woman who has been primarily a homemaker for 14-20 years and has lost her main means of support through divorce, separation or death of a spouse, and needs retraining for re-entry to the world of work. Must be a Vermont resident.

Award: Grant for use in freshman, sophomore, junior, senior, or graduate years; not renewable. *Number:* 1–3. *Amount:* $500–$1500.

Eligibility Requirements: Applicant must be age 35; enrolled or expecting to enroll full or part-time at a two-year or four-year or technical institution or university; female and resident of Vermont. Available to U.S. citizens.

Application Requirements: Application, autobiography, financial need analysis, interview, references. *Deadline:* March 15.

Contact: Joyce Lindamood, State President
General Federation of Women's Clubs of Vermont
PO Box 92
Springfield, VT 05156
Phone: 802-885-4690

GEORGE AND MARY JOSEPHINE HAMMAN FOUNDATION

http://www.hammanfoundation.org/

GEORGE AND MARY JOSEPHINE HAMMAN FOUNDATION SCHOLARSHIP PROGRAM

Scholarship available to high school seniors in the following Texas counties only: Brazoria, Chambers, Ft. Bend, Galveston, Harris, Liberty, Montgomery, and Waller. Please refer to Web site for specific details http://www.hammanfoundation.org/

Award: Scholarship for use in freshman, sophomore, junior, or senior years; not renewable. *Number:* 55. *Amount:* $12,000.

Eligibility Requirements: Applicant must be high school student; planning to enroll or expecting to enroll full-time at a four-year institution or university and resident of Texas. Available to U.S. and non-U.S. citizens.

Application Requirements: Application, financial need analysis, interview, photo, test scores, transcript. *Deadline:* February 28.

Contact: E. Alan Fritsche, Executive Director
George and Mary Josephine Hamman Foundation
3336 Richmond, Suite 310
Houston, TX 77098
Phone: 713-522-9891
Fax: 713-522-9693

GEORGIA STUDENT FINANCE COMMISSION

http://www.gsfc.org

GEORGIA LEVERAGING EDUCATIONAL ASSISTANCE PARTNERSHIP GRANT PROGRAM

Based on financial need. Recipients must be eligible for the Federal Pell Grant. Renewable award for Georgia residents enrolled in a state postsecondary institution. Must be U.S. citizen.

Award: Grant for use in freshman, sophomore, junior, or senior years; renewable. *Number:* 3000–3500. *Amount:* $370.

Eligibility Requirements: Applicant must be enrolled or expecting to enroll full or part-time at a two-year or four-year or technical institution or university; resident of Georgia and studying in Georgia. Available to U.S. citizens.

Application Requirements: Application, financial need analysis. *Deadline:* Continuous.

Contact: William Flook, Director of Scholarships and Grants
Georgia Student Finance Commission
2082 East Exchange Place, Suite 100
Tucker, GA 30084
Phone: 770-724-9052
Fax: 770-724-9031

GEORGIA PUBLIC SAFETY MEMORIAL GRANT/LAW ENFORCEMENT PERSONNEL DEPARTMENT GRANT

• *See page 509*

GEORGIA TUITION EQUALIZATION GRANT (GTEG)

Award for Georgia residents pursuing undergraduate study at an accredited two- or four-year Georgia private institution. Complete the Georgia Student Grant Application. Award is $909 per academic year. Deadlines vary.

Award: Grant for use in freshman, sophomore, junior, or senior years; renewable. *Number:* 25,000–32,000. *Amount:* $909.

Eligibility Requirements: Applicant must be enrolled or expecting to enroll full-time at a two-year or four-year institution or university; resident of Georgia and studying in Georgia. Available to U.S. citizens.

Application Requirements: Application. *Deadline:* Continuous.

Contact: William Flook, Director of Scholarships and Grants Division
Georgia Student Finance Commission
2082 East Exchange Place, Suite 100
Tucker, GA 30084
Phone: 770-724-9052
Fax: 770-724-9031

GOVERNOR'S SCHOLARSHIP-GEORGIA

Award to assist students selected as Georgia scholars, STAR students, valedictorians, and salutatorians. For use at two- and four-year colleges and universities in Georgia. Recipients are selected as entering freshmen. Renewable award of up to $1000. Minimum 3.5 GPA required.

Award: Scholarship for use in freshman, sophomore, junior, or senior years; renewable. *Number:* 2000–3000. *Amount:* up to $1000.

Eligibility Requirements: Applicant must be high school student; planning to enroll or expecting to enroll full-time at a two-year or four-year institution or university; resident of Georgia and studying in Georgia. Applicant must have 3.5 GPA or higher. Available to U.S. citizens.

Application Requirements: Application, transcript. *Deadline:* Continuous.

Contact: William Flook, Director of Scholarships and Grants Division
Georgia Student Finance Commission
2082 East Exchange Place, Suite 100
Tucker, GA 30084
Phone: 770-724-9052
Fax: 770-724-9031

HOPE—HELPING OUTSTANDING PUPILS EDUCATIONALLY

Grant program for Georgia residents who are college undergraduates to attend an accredited two- or four-year Georgia institution. Tuition and fees may be covered by the grant. Minimum 3.0 GPA required. Renewable if student maintains grades and reapplies. Write for deadlines.

Award: Scholarship for use in freshman, sophomore, junior, or senior years; renewable. *Number:* 140,000–170,000. *Amount:* $300–$3900.

Eligibility Requirements: Applicant must be enrolled or expecting to enroll full or part-time at a two-year or four-year institution or university; resident of Georgia and studying in Georgia. Applicant must have 3.0 GPA or higher. Available to U.S. citizens.

Application Requirements: Application. *Deadline:* Continuous.

Contact: William Flook, Director of Scholarships and Grants Division
Georgia Student Finance Commission
2082 East Exchange Place, Suite 100
Tucker, GA 30084
Phone: 770-724-9052
Fax: 770-724-9031

ROBERT C. BYRD HONORS SCHOLARSHIP-GEORGIA

Complete the application provided by the Georgia Department of Education. Renewable awards for outstanding graduating Georgia high school seniors to be used for full-time undergraduate study at eligible U.S. institution.

Award: Scholarship for use in freshman, sophomore, junior, or senior years; renewable. *Number:* 600–700. *Amount:* $1500.

Eligibility Requirements: Applicant must be high school student; planning to enroll or expecting to enroll full-time at a two-year or four-year institution or university and resident of Georgia. Available to U.S. citizens.

Application Requirements: Application, transcript. *Deadline:* April 1.

Contact: William Flook, Director of Scholarships and Grants Division
Georgia Student Finance Commission
2082 East Exchange Place, Suite 100
Tucker, GA 30084
Phone: 770-724-9052
Fax: 770-724-9031

GIRL SCOUTS OF GULFCOAST FLORIDA, INC. http://www.girlscoutsgulfcoastfl.org

GULFCOAST COLLEGE SCHOLARSHIP AWARD

• *See page 462*

GRAND LODGE OF IOWA, AF AND AM http://gl-iowa.org

GRAND LODGE OF IOWA MASONIC SCHOLARSHIP PROGRAM

Scholarships are awarded based on scholastics, school and community activity, and leadership. Applicants are selected to be interviewed based on their written application. Recipients are selected based on those interviews. Application deadline is February 1.

Award: Scholarship for use in freshman year; not renewable. *Number:* 60–70. *Amount:* $2000.

Eligibility Requirements: Applicant must be high school student; planning to enroll or expecting to enroll full-time at a two-year or four-year or technical institution or university and resident of Iowa. Available to U.S. and non-U.S. citizens.

Application Requirements: Application, autobiography, interview, references, transcript. *Deadline:* February 1.

Contact: William Crawford, Grand Secretary
Grand Lodge of Iowa, AF and AM
PO Box 279
Cedar Rapids, IA 52406-0279
Phone: 319-365-1438
Fax: 319-365-1439
E-mail: gs@gl-iowa.org

GRAND RAPIDS COMMUNITY FOUNDATION http://www.grfoundation.org

ALTRUSA INTERNATIONAL OF GRAND RAPIDS SCHOLARSHIP

For returning student who did not pursue any form of post-secondary education after graduation from high school or receipt of a GED for a minimum of 24 months. Applicants must be residents of Kent, Allegan, Ionia, Ottawa, Montcalm, or Muskegon counties in Michigan for a minimum of six months prior to applying. Refer to Web site for details and application http://www.grfoundation.org.

Award: Scholarship for use in freshman, sophomore, junior, or senior years. *Number:* varies. *Amount:* varies.

Eligibility Requirements: Applicant must be enrolled or expecting to enroll at an institution or university and resident of Michigan.

Application Requirements: Application, essay, references. *Deadline:* April 1.

Contact: See Web site.

DONALD J. DEYOUNG SCHOLARSHIP

For young people residing in West Michigan area who are wards of the court, or have previously been a ward of the court and have been successfully

Grand Rapids Community Foundation (continued)

discharged. Applicant must be accepted at a college/university or training school to apply. Refer to Web site for details and an application: http://grfoundation.org.

Award: Scholarship for use in freshman year. *Number:* varies. *Amount:* varies.

Eligibility Requirements: Applicant must be enrolled or expecting to enroll at a two-year or four-year or technical institution or university and resident of Michigan. Applicant must have 2.5 GPA or higher.

Application Requirements: Application, essay, interview. *Deadline:* April 1.

Contact: See Web site.

GERALD M. CRANE MEMORIAL MUSIC SCHOLARSHIP FUND

For high school students (9th-12th grade) who are residents of Kent or Ottawa counties in Michigan to further pursue their musical endeavors. This may include, but is not limited to formal music training, seminars, workshops, music lessons, music concerts, musical instruments, music books, or summer enrichment programs. Refer to Web site for details and application: http://www.grfoundation.org

Award: Scholarship for use in freshman year. *Number:* varies. *Amount:* $250–$1000.

Eligibility Requirements: Applicant must be high school student; planning to enroll or expecting to enroll at a two-year or four-year institution or university; resident of Michigan and must have an interest in music.

Application Requirements: Application, essay, interview, references. *Deadline:* April 1.

Contact: See Web site.

GRAND RAPIDS COMBINED THEATRE SCHOLARSHIP

For students with experience in any Grand Rapids area community theatre venue to pursue study in theatre arts. For more details and an application refer to Web site: http://www.grfoundation.org

Award: Scholarship for use in freshman, sophomore, junior, or senior years; not renewable. *Number:* varies. *Amount:* $1000–$2000.

Eligibility Requirements: Applicant must be enrolled or expecting to enroll full-time at a four-year institution or university and resident of Michigan.

Application Requirements: Application, essay, financial need analysis, references. *Deadline:* April 1.

Contact: See Web site.

JOSHUA ESCH MITCHELL AVIATION SCHOLARSHIP

Applicant must be pursuing studies in the field of professional piloting with an emphasis on general aviation, flight engineering, or airway science. Financial need required. Refer to Web site for details and an application: http://grfoundation.org

Award: Scholarship for use in sophomore, junior, or senior years. *Number:* varies. *Amount:* varies.

Eligibility Requirements: Applicant must be enrolled or expecting to enroll at an institution or university and resident of Michigan. Applicant must have 2.5 GPA or higher.

Application Requirements: Application, essay, references, transcript. *Deadline:* April 1.

Contact: See Web site.

GRANGE INSURANCE ASSOCIATION http://www.grange.com/default.aspx

GRANGE INSURANCE GROUP SCHOLARSHIP

One-time award for Grange Insurance Association policyholders and their children or grandchildren. Must be a U.S. citizen. See Web site at http://www.grange.com for further details. Application deadline is April 15.

Award: Scholarship for use in freshman, sophomore, junior, senior, graduate, or postgraduate years; not renewable. *Number:* 25–28. *Amount:* $750–$1000.

Eligibility Requirements: Applicant must be enrolled or expecting to enroll full or part-time at a two-year or four-year or technical institution or university and resident of California, Colorado, Idaho, Montana, Oregon, Washington, or Wyoming. Available to U.S. citizens.

Application Requirements: Application, autobiography, essay, financial need analysis, references, transcript. *Deadline:* April 15.

Contact: Application available at Web site.

GRAYSON RURAL ELECTRIC COOPERATIVE CORPORATION (RECC) http://www.graysonrecc.coop

GRAYSON RURAL ELECTRIC COOPERATIVE CORPORATION SCHOLARSHIP

Scholarships available to Kentucky high school graduating seniors who are planning to enroll full-time in a 2- or 4-year college, university, or trade/technical institution. Must reside in Grayson RECC service area, or primary residence of parent/guardian must be in Grayson RECC service area. Scholarship funds will be paid to institution. Must submit 200-word personal narrative. Application and information on Web site: http://www.graysonrecc.coop.

Award: Scholarship for use in freshman year; not renewable. *Number:* 7. *Amount:* $1000.

Eligibility Requirements: Applicant must be high school student; planning to enroll or expecting to enroll full-time at a two-year or four-year or technical institution or university and resident of Kentucky. Available to U.S. citizens.

Application Requirements: Application, essay, transcript. *Deadline:* April 15.

Contact: Julie Lewis, Communications Specialist
Grayson Rural Electric Cooperative Corporation (RECC)
109 Bagby Park
Grayson, KY 41143
Phone: 606-475-2191
Fax: 606-474-5862
E-mail: julie.lewis@graysonrecc.coop

GREAT LAKES HEMOPHILIA FOUNDATION http://www.glhf.org/scholar.htm

EDUCATION AND TRAINING ASSISTANCE PROGRAM

• *See page 525*

GREATER BRIDGEPORT AREA FOUNDATION http://www.gbafoundation.org

SCHOLARSHIP AWARD PROGRAM

The Greater Bridgeport Area Foundation Scholarship Award program primarily supports high school seniors entering their freshman year in college. Scholarships average $1100 for one year. Some graduate school scholarships are available. Awards given to students from towns in GBAF service area: Bridgeport, Easton, Fairfield, Milford, Monroe, Shelton, Stratford, Trumbull, and Westport.

Award: Scholarship for use in freshman year; not renewable. *Number:* 100–150. *Amount:* $1100.

Eligibility Requirements: Applicant must be enrolled or expecting to enroll full-time at a four-year institution or university and resident of Connecticut. Available to U.S. citizens.

Application Requirements: Application, essay, references, transcript. *Deadline:* varies.

Contact: Bernadette Deamico, Education Associate
Greater Bridgeport Area Foundation
211 State Street, 3rd Floor
Bridgeport, CT 06604
Phone: 203-334-7511
Fax: 203-333-4652
E-mail: bdeamico@gbafoundation.org

GREATER KANAWHA VALLEY FOUNDATION
http://www.tgkvf.org

KID'S CHANCE OF WEST VIRGINIA SCHOLARSHIP

Awarded to children (between the ages of 16-25) of a parent(s) injured in a WV work-related accident. Preference shall be given to students with financial need, academic performance, leadership abilities, demonstrated and potential contributions to school and community who are pursuing any field of study in any accredited trade, vocational school, college, or university. May apply for two Foundation scholarships but will only be chosen for one.

Award: Scholarship for use in freshman, sophomore, junior, or senior years; renewable. *Number:* 9. *Amount:* $1000.

Eligibility Requirements: Applicant must be age 16-25; enrolled or expecting to enroll full-time at a two-year or four-year or technical institution or university; resident of West Virginia and must have an interest in leadership. Applicant must have 2.5 GPA or higher. Available to U.S. citizens.

Application Requirements: Application, essay, financial need analysis, references, transcript, IRS 1040 form, worker's compensation number. *Deadline:* February 17.

Contact: Susan Hoover, Scholarship Coordinator
Greater Kanawha Valley Foundation
PO Box 3041
Charleston, WV 25331
Phone: 304-346-3620
Fax: 304-346-3640

NORMAN S. AND BETTY M. FITZHUGH FUND

Awarded to students who demonstrate academic excellence and financial need to attend any accredited college or university. Scholarships are awarded for one or more years. May apply for two Foundation scholarships but will only be chosen for one. Must be a resident of West Virginia.

Award: Scholarship for use in freshman, sophomore, junior, or senior years; renewable. *Number:* 1. *Amount:* $500.

Eligibility Requirements: Applicant must be enrolled or expecting to enroll full-time at a four-year institution or university and resident of West Virginia. Applicant must have 2.5 GPA or higher.

Application Requirements: Application, essay, financial need analysis, references, transcript, IRS 1040 form. *Deadline:* February 17.

Contact: Susan Hoover, Scholarship Coordinator
Greater Kanawha Valley Foundation
PO Box 3041
Charleston, WV 25331
Phone: 304-346-3620
Fax: 304-346-3640

PAUL AND GRACE RHUDY FUND

Scholarships are awarded to individuals who demonstrate academic excellence and financial need to attend any accredited college or university in any state. Scholarships are awarded for one or more years. May apply for two Foundation scholarships but will only be chosen for one. Must be a resident of West Virginia.

Award: Scholarship for use in freshman, sophomore, junior, or senior years; renewable. *Number:* 1. *Amount:* $500.

Eligibility Requirements: Applicant must be enrolled or expecting to enroll full-time at a two-year or four-year institution or university and resident of West Virginia. Applicant must have 2.5 GPA or higher.

Application Requirements: Application, essay, financial need analysis, references, transcript, IRS 1040 form. *Deadline:* February 17.

Contact: Susan Hoover, Scholarship Coordinator
Greater Kanawha Valley Foundation
PO Box 3041
Charleston, WV 25331
Phone: 304-346-3620
Fax: 304-346-3640

R. RAY SINGLETON FUND

Renewable award based on academic excellence and financial need. May apply for two Foundation scholarships, but will be chosen only for one. Must be a resident of West Virginia and attend a school in West Virginia.

Award: Grant for use in freshman, sophomore, junior, senior, or graduate years; renewable. *Number:* 4. *Amount:* $1000.

Eligibility Requirements: Applicant must be enrolled or expecting to enroll full-time at a four-year institution or university; resident of West Virginia and studying in West Virginia. Applicant must have 2.5 GPA or higher. Available to U.S. citizens.

Application Requirements: Application, essay, financial need analysis, references, self-addressed stamped envelope, test scores, transcript. *Deadline:* February 17.

Contact: Susan Hoover, Scholarship Coordinator
Greater Kanawha Valley Foundation
PO Box 3041
Charleston, WV 25331
Phone: 304-346-3620
Fax: 304-346-3640
E-mail: shoover@tgkvf.org

RUTH ANN JOHNSON SCHOLARSHIP

Awarded to students who demonstrate academic excellence and financial need to attend any accredited college or university in any state or county. Scholarships are awarded for one or more years. May apply for two Foundation scholarships but will only be chosen for one. Must be a resident of West Virginia.

Award: Scholarship for use in freshman, sophomore, junior, or senior years; renewable. *Number:* 61. *Amount:* $1000.

Eligibility Requirements: Applicant must be enrolled or expecting to enroll full-time at a four-year institution or university and resident of West Virginia. Applicant must have 2.5 GPA or higher.

Application Requirements: Application, essay, financial need analysis, references, transcript, IRS 1040 form. *Deadline:* February 17.

Contact: Susan Hoover, Scholarship Coordinator
Greater Kanawha Valley Foundation
PO Box 3041
Charleston, WV 25331
Phone: 304-346-3620
Fax: 304-346-3640

SCPA SCHOLARSHIP FUND

• *See page 510*

W. P. BLACK SCHOLARSHIP FUND

Renewable award for West Virginia residents who demonstrate academic excellence and financial need and who are enrolled in an undergraduate program in any accredited college or university. May apply for two Foundation scholarships but will only be chosen for one.

Award: Scholarship for use in freshman, sophomore, junior, or senior years; renewable. *Number:* 98. *Amount:* $1000.

Eligibility Requirements: Applicant must be enrolled or expecting to enroll at a two-year or four-year institution or university and resident of West Virginia. Applicant must have 2.5 GPA or higher. Available to U.S. citizens.

Application Requirements: Application, essay, financial need analysis, references, self-addressed stamped envelope, test scores, transcript. *Deadline:* February 17.

Contact: Susan Hoover, Scholarship Coordinator
Greater Kanawha Valley Foundation
PO Box 3041
Charleston, WV 25331
Phone: 304-346-3620
Fax: 304-346-3640

WEST VIRGINIA GOLF ASSOCIATION FUND

• *See page 510*

GREATER LAFAYETTE COMMUNITY FOUNDATION
http://www.glcfonline.org

LILLY ENDOWMENT COMMUNITY SCHOLARSHIP, TIPPECANOE COUNTY

Scholarship is for four years of full tuition and fees at the accredited Indiana college or university of the recipient's choice, plus $800 per year for required

Greater Lafayette Community Foundation (continued)

books and equipment. Must be a resident of Tippecanoe County, Indiana. Minimum 2.75 GPA required. Visit Web site: http://www.glcfonline.org for more information.

Award: Scholarship for use in freshman, sophomore, junior, or senior years; not renewable. *Number:* 6. *Amount:* $6250–$25,000.

Eligibility Requirements: Applicant must be enrolled or expecting to enroll full-time at a four-year institution or university; resident of Indiana and studying in Indiana. Available to U.S. citizens.

Application Requirements: Application, essay, financial need analysis, interview, references, test scores, transcript. *Deadline:* varies.

Contact: Carol Crochet, Program Director
Greater Lafayette Community Foundation
1114 State Street
PO Box 225
Lafayette, IN 47902-0225
Phone: 765-742-9078 Ext. 225
Fax: 765-742-2428
E-mail: carol@glcfonline.org

GREATER WASHINGTON URBAN LEAGUE http://gwulparentcenter.org/rtc

ANHEUSER-BUSCH URBAN SCHOLARSHIP

Renewable award to graduating high school students who reside in the service area of the League. Applicants must complete an essay on a subject selected by the sponsors and must have completed 90% of their school district's community service requirement. Must have GPA of 3.0 or better.

Award: Scholarship for use in freshman year; renewable. *Number:* 4. *Amount:* $2500.

Eligibility Requirements: Applicant must be high school student; planning to enroll or expecting to enroll at an institution or university and resident of District of Columbia. Applicant must have 3.0 GPA or higher.

Application Requirements: Application, essay. *Deadline:* February 15.

Contact: Audrey Epperson, Director of Education
Greater Washington Urban League
3501 14th Street, NW
Washington, DC 20010
Phone: 202-265-8200
Fax: 202-387-7019
E-mail: epperson@gwulpartencenter.org

SAFEWAY/GREATER WASHINGTON URBAN LEAGUE SCHOLARSHIP

Award to graduating high school students who reside in the service area of the League. Applicants must complete an essay on a subject selected by the sponsors and must have completed 90% of their school district's community service requirement. Must have GPA of 3.0 or better.

Award: Scholarship for use in freshman year. *Number:* 6. *Amount:* $3000.

Eligibility Requirements: Applicant must be high school student; planning to enroll or expecting to enroll at an institution or university and resident of District of Columbia. Applicant must have 3.0 GPA or higher.

Application Requirements: Application, essay. *Deadline:* February 15.

Contact: Audrey Epperson, Director of Education
Greater Washington Urban League
3501 14th Street, NW
Washington, DC 20010
Phone: 202-265-8200
Fax: 202-387-7019
E-mail: epperson@gwulpartencenter.org

GREEK WOMEN'S UNIVERSITY CLUB

GREEK WOMEN'S UNIVERSITY CLUB SCHOLARSHIPS

• *See page 584*

GRIFFIN FOUNDATION http://www.thegriffinfoundation.com/scholarship.htm

GRIFFIN SCHOLARSHIP

For junior college transfers who wish to complete their baccalaureate degree at Colorado State University, University of Northern Colorado, or University of Wyoming. Must be eligible for instate tuition.

Award: Scholarship for use in junior or senior years; renewable. *Number:* 6. *Amount:* $10,000.

Eligibility Requirements: Applicant must be enrolled or expecting to enroll full-time at an institution or university; resident of Colorado or Wyoming and studying in Colorado or Wyoming. Applicant must have 3.5 GPA or higher. Available to U.S. and non-U.S. citizens.

Application Requirements: Application, essay, financial need analysis, interview, references, transcript. *Deadline:* March 1.

Contact: Carol Wood, Program Director
Griffin Foundation
303 West Prospect Road
Fort Collins, CO 80526
Phone: 970-484-3030
Fax: 970-484-6648
E-mail: carol.wood@thegriffinfoundation.com

HALTON FOUNDATION

HALTON SCHOLARS

• *See page 496*

HAWAII COMMUNITY FOUNDATION http://www.hawaiicommunityfoundation.org

HAWAII COMMUNITY FOUNDATION SCHOLARSHIPS

The Hawaii Community Foundation offers postsecondary scholarships to residents of the state of Hawaii. The average amount is $1400. Please visit our Web site at http://www.communityfoundation.org for more information.

Award: Scholarship for use in freshman, sophomore, junior, or senior years. *Number:* 2200. *Amount:* $1400.

Eligibility Requirements: Applicant must be enrolled or expecting to enroll at a two-year or four-year or technical institution or university and resident of Hawaii. Available to U.S. citizens.

Application Requirements: Application. *Deadline:* March 1.

Contact: Application available at Web site.

HAWAII EDUCATION ASSOCIATION http://www.heaed.com/

HAWAII EDUCATION ASSOCIATION HIGH SCHOOL STUDENT SCHOLARSHIP

• *See page 463*

HAWAII EDUCATION ASSOCIATION UNDERGRADUATE COLLEGE STUDENT SCHOLARSHIP

• *See page 463*

HAWAII STATE POSTSECONDARY EDUCATION COMMISSION

HAWAII STATE STUDENT INCENTIVE GRANT

Grants are given to residents of Hawaii who are enrolled in a participating Hawaiian state school. Funds are for undergraduate tuition only. Applicants must submit a financial need analysis.

Award: Grant for use in freshman, sophomore, junior, or senior years; renewable. *Number:* varies. *Amount:* varies.

Eligibility Requirements: Applicant must be enrolled or expecting to enroll full or part-time at a two-year or four-year or technical institution or university; resident of Hawaii and studying in Hawaii. Available to U.S. citizens.

Application Requirements: Financial need analysis. *Deadline:* varies.

Contact: Jo Ann Yoshida, Financial Aid Specialist
Hawaii State Postsecondary Education Commission
University of Hawaii
Honolulu, HI 96822
Phone: 808-956-6066
E-mail: iha@hawaii.edu

HENRY SACHS FOUNDATION http://www.frii.com/~sachs

SACHS FOUNDATION SCHOLARSHIPS

• *See page 585*

HERBERT HOOVER PRESIDENTIAL LIBRARY ASSOCIATION http://www.hooverassociation.org

HERBERT HOOVER UNCOMMON STUDENT AWARD

Only juniors in an Iowa high school or home school program may apply. Grades and test scores are not evaluated. Applicants are chosen on the basis of project proposals they submit. Those chosen complete their project and make a presentation. All receive $750. Three are chosen for $5000 award.

Award: Scholarship for use in freshman or sophomore years; not renewable. *Number:* 18. *Amount:* $750–$5000.

Eligibility Requirements: Applicant must be high school student; planning to enroll or expecting to enroll full-time at a two-year or four-year institution and resident of Iowa. Available to U.S. and non-U.S. citizens.

Application Requirements: Application, references, project proposal. *Deadline:* March 31.

Contact: Patricia Hand, Academic Programs Manager
Herbert Hoover Presidential Library Association
PO Box 696
West Branch, IA 52358-0696
Phone: 319-643-5327
Fax: 319-643-2391
E-mail: info@hooverassociation.org

HERMAN OSCAR SCHUMACHER SCHOLARSHIP FUND

HERMAN OSCAR SCHUMACHER SCHOLARSHIP FUND FOR MEN

• *See page 625*

HISPANIC COLLEGE FUND, INC. http://www.hispanicfund.org

SILVESTRE REYES SCHOLARSHIP PROGRAM

• *See page 586*

HISPANIC PUBLIC RELATIONS ASSOCIATION http://www.hprala.org

SCHOLARSHIP PROGRAM

• *See page 587*

HISPANIC SCHOLARSHIP FUND http://www.hsf.net

COCA-COLA/HSF ADVANCING TO UNIVERSITIES SCHOLARSHIP

• *See page 587*

HSF/TOYOTA FOUNDATION SCHOLARSHIP PROGRAM-PUERTO RICO

• *See page 588*

HOPE PIERCE TARTT SCHOLARSHIP FUND

HOPE PIERCE TARTT SCHOLARSHIP FUND

One-time award to full-time students enrolled in a non-tax supported college or university in Texas. Must demonstrate financial need, and be a Texas resident of Harrison, Gregg, Marion, Panola, or Upshur county. Application requirements vary at each institution, please contact your Financial Aid Office for guidelines and to submit an application.

Award: Scholarship for use in freshman, sophomore, junior, senior, or graduate years; not renewable. *Number:* varies. *Amount:* $1000–$3000.

Eligibility Requirements: Applicant must be enrolled or expecting to enroll full-time at a two-year or four-year institution or university; resident of Texas and studying in Texas. Available to U.S. citizens.

Application Requirements: Application, financial need analysis. *Deadline:* Continuous.

Contact: College Financial Aid Office
Hope Pierce Tartt Scholarship Fund
PO Box 1964
Marshall, TX 75670

HUMANE SOCIETY OF THE UNITED STATES http://www.hsus.org

SHAW-WORTH MEMORIAL SCHOLARSHIP

Scholarship for a New England high school senior who has made a meaningful contribution to animal protection over a significant amount of time. A passive liking of animals or the desire to enter an animal care field does not justify the award. Application deadline: March 15.

Award: Scholarship for use in freshman year; not renewable. *Number:* 1. *Amount:* $1500.

Eligibility Requirements: Applicant must be high school student; planning to enroll or expecting to enroll full-time at a two-year or four-year or technical institution or university and resident of Connecticut, Maine, Massachusetts, New Hampshire, Rhode Island, or Vermont. Available to U.S. citizens.

Application Requirements: Essay, references. *Deadline:* March 15.

Contact: Hillary Twining, Program Coordinator
Humane Society of the United States
New England Regional Office
PO Box 619
Jacksonville, VT 05342
Phone: 802-368-2790
Fax: 802-368-2756
E-mail: htwining@hsus.org

IDAHO STATE BOARD OF EDUCATION http://www.idahoboardofed.org

IDAHO GOVERNOR'S CHALLENGE SCHOLARSHIP

Renewable scholarship available to Idaho residents enrolled full-time in an undergraduate academic or vocational-technical program at an eligible Idaho public or private college or university. Minimum GPA: 2.8. Merit-based award. Must be a high school senior and U.S. citizen to apply. Number of awards is conditional on the availability of funds. Must have a demonstrated commitment to public service.

Award: Scholarship for use in freshman, sophomore, junior, or senior years; renewable. *Number:* 10–25. *Amount:* $3000.

Eligibility Requirements: Applicant must be high school student; planning to enroll or expecting to enroll full-time at a two-year or four-year or technical institution or university; resident of Idaho and studying in Idaho. Available to U.S. citizens.

Application Requirements: Application, essay, portfolio, references, test scores, transcript. *Deadline:* December 15.

Contact: Lynn Humphrey, Manager, Student Aid Programs
Idaho State Board of Education
PO Box 83720
Boise, ID 83720-0037
Phone: 208-334-2270
Fax: 208-334-2632
E-mail: lhumphre@osbe.state.id.us

IDAHO MINORITY AND "AT RISK" STUDENT SCHOLARSHIP

• *See page 526*

IDAHO PROMISE CATEGORY A SCHOLARSHIP PROGRAM

Renewable award available to Idaho residents who are graduating high school seniors. Must attend an approved Idaho institute of higher education full-time. Based on class rank (must be verified by school official), GPA, and ACT scores. Professional-technical student applicants must take COMPASS.

Award: Scholarship for use in freshman, sophomore, junior, or senior years; renewable. *Number:* 25–30. *Amount:* $3000.

Eligibility Requirements: Applicant must be high school student; planning to enroll or expecting to enroll full-time at a two-year or four-year or technical institution or university; resident of Idaho and studying in Idaho. Applicant must have 3.5 GPA or higher. Available to U.S. citizens.

Idaho State Board of Education (continued)

Application Requirements: Application, test scores. *Deadline:* December 15.

Contact: Lynn Humphrey, Manager, Student Aid Programs
Idaho State Board of Education
PO Box 83720
Boise, ID 83720-0037
Phone: 208-334-2270
Fax: 208-334-2632
E-mail: lhumphre@osbe.state.id.us

IDAHO PROMISE CATEGORY B SCHOLARSHIP PROGRAM

Available to Idaho residents entering college for the first time prior to the age of 22. Must have completed high school or its equivalent in Idaho and have a minimum GPA of 3.0 or an ACT score of 20 or higher. Scholarship limited to two years or 4 semesters.

Award: Scholarship for use in freshman or sophomore years; renewable. *Number:* varies. *Amount:* $500.

Eligibility Requirements: Applicant must be age 21 or under; enrolled or expecting to enroll full-time at a two-year or four-year or technical institution or university; resident of Idaho and studying in Idaho. Applicant must have 3.0 GPA or higher. Available to U.S. citizens.

Application Requirements: Application, transcript. *Deadline:* Continuous.

Contact: Lynn Humphrey, Manager, Student Aid Programs
Idaho State Board of Education
PO Box 83720
Boise, ID 83720-0037
Phone: 208-334-2270
Fax: 208-334-2632

LEVERAGING EDUCATIONAL ASSISTANCE STATE PARTNERSHIP PROGRAM (LEAP)

One-time award assists students attending participating Idaho trade schools, colleges, and universities majoring in any field except theology or divinity. Must be U.S. citizen or permanent resident, and show financial need. Application deadlines vary by institution.

Award: Grant for use in freshman, sophomore, junior, senior, or graduate years; not renewable. *Number:* varies. *Amount:* $400–$5000.

Eligibility Requirements: Applicant must be enrolled or expecting to enroll full or part-time at a two-year or four-year or technical institution or university; resident of Idaho and studying in Idaho. Available to U.S. citizens.

Application Requirements: Application, financial need analysis, self-addressed stamped envelope. *Deadline:* Continuous.

Contact: Lynn Humphrey, Manager, Student Aid Programs
Idaho State Board of Education
PO Box 83720
Boise, ID 83720-0037
Phone: 208-334-2270
Fax: 208-334-2632

ROBERT C. BYRD HONORS SCHOLARSHIP PROGRAM-IDAHO

Renewable scholarships available to Idaho residents based on outstanding academic achievement. Students must apply as high school seniors.

Award: Scholarship for use in freshman, sophomore, junior, or senior years; renewable. *Number:* 90. *Amount:* $1500.

Eligibility Requirements: Applicant must be high school student; planning to enroll or expecting to enroll full-time at a two-year or four-year or technical institution or university and resident of Idaho. Applicant must have 3.5 GPA or higher. Available to U.S. citizens.

Application Requirements: Application, references, test scores, transcript. *Deadline:* March 20.

Contact: Lynn Humphrey, Manager, Student Aid Programs
Idaho State Board of Education
PO Box 83720
Boise, ID 83720-0037
Phone: 208-334-2270
Fax: 208-334-2632
E-mail: lhumphre@osbe.state.id.us

ILLINOIS COUNCIL OF THE BLIND

FLOYD CARGILL SCHOLARSHIP

• *See page 526*

ILLINOIS DEPARTMENT OF VETERANS' AFFAIRS

http://www.state.il.us/agency/dva

MIA/POW SCHOLARSHIPS

• *See page 556*

VETERANS' CHILDREN EDUCATIONAL OPPORTUNITIES

• *See page 556*

ILLINOIS FUTURE, INC.

ILLINOIS FUTURE, INC. SCHOLARSHIPS

Award for Illinois students whose parent or guardian has suffered permanent disability or death as the result of a work-related accident as adjucated with Illinois Industrial Commission. Must be U.S. citizen under 22 years of age and an Illinois resident. Please send a SASE ($.60 postage required) along with phone number in order to receive an application.

Award: Scholarship for use in freshman, sophomore, junior, or senior years; renewable. *Number:* 2. *Amount:* $2000.

Eligibility Requirements: Applicant must be age 21 or under; enrolled or expecting to enroll full-time at a two-year or four-year or technical institution or university and resident of Illinois. Available to U.S. citizens.

Application Requirements: Application, financial need analysis, references, self-addressed stamped envelope, test scores, transcript. *Deadline:* Continuous.

Contact: Margie Putzler, Office Manager
Illinois Future, Inc.
821 West Galena Boulevard
Aurora, IL 60506
Phone: 630-264-7300
Fax: 630-897-8637

ILLINOIS STUDENT ASSISTANCE COMMISSION (ISAC)

http://www.collegezone.org

GRANT PROGRAM FOR DEPENDENTS OF POLICE, FIRE, OR CORRECTIONAL OFFICERS

• *See page 511*

HIGHER EDUCATION LICENSE PLATE PROGRAM — HELP

Need-based grants for students at Illinois institutions participating in program whose funds are raised by sale of special license plates commemorating the institutions. Deadline: June 30. Must be Illinois resident. May be eligible to receive the grant for the equivalent of 10 semesters of full-time enrollment.

Award: Grant for use in freshman, sophomore, junior, or senior years; not renewable. *Number:* 175–200. *Amount:* up to $2000.

Eligibility Requirements: Applicant must be enrolled or expecting to enroll full or part-time at a two-year or four-year institution or university; resident of Illinois and studying in Illinois. Available to U.S. citizens.

Application Requirements: Financial need analysis, FAFSA. *Deadline:* June 30.

Contact: College Zone Counselor
Illinois Student Assistance Commission (ISAC)
1755 Lake Cook Road
Deerfield, IL 60015-5209
Phone: 800-899-4722
E-mail: collegezone@isac.org

ILLINOIS COLLEGE SAVINGS BOND BONUS INCENTIVE GRANT PROGRAM

Program offers holders of Illinois College Savings Bonds a $20 grant for each year of bond maturity payable upon bond redemption if at least 70% of proceeds are used to attend college in Illinois. May not be used by students attending religious or divinity schools.

Award: Grant for use in freshman, sophomore, junior, senior, graduate, or postgraduate years; not renewable. *Number:* 1200–1400. *Amount:* $40–$440.

Eligibility Requirements: Applicant must be enrolled or expecting to enroll full or part-time at a two-year or four-year or technical institution or university and studying in Illinois. Available to U.S. citizens.

Application Requirements: Application. *Deadline:* Continuous.

Contact: College Zone Counselor
Illinois Student Assistance Commission (ISAC)
1755 Lake Cook Road
Deerfield, IL 60015-5209
Phone: 800-899-4722
E-mail: collegezone@isac.org

ILLINOIS DEPARTMENT OF REHABILITATION SERVICES EDUCATION BENEFITS

• *See page 526*

ILLINOIS GENERAL ASSEMBLY SCHOLARSHIP

Scholarships available for Illinois students enrolled at an Illinois four-year state-supported college. Must contact the General Assembly member from your district for eligibility criteria.

Award: Scholarship for use in freshman, sophomore, junior, or senior years. *Number:* varies. *Amount:* varies.

Eligibility Requirements: Applicant must be enrolled or expecting to enroll at a four-year institution or university; resident of Illinois and studying in Illinois. Available to U.S. citizens.

Application Requirements: Application.

Contact: College Zone Counselor
Illinois Student Assistance Commission (ISAC)
1755 Lake Cook Road
Deerfield, IL 60015-5209
Phone: 800-899-4722
E-mail: collegezone@isac.org

ILLINOIS MONETARY AWARD PROGRAM

Award for eligible students attending Illinois public universities, private colleges and universities, community colleges, and some proprietary institutions. Applicable only to tuition and fees. Based on financial need. Applicants are encouraged to apply as soon after January 1st as possible.

Award: Grant for use in freshman, sophomore, junior, or senior years; not renewable. *Number:* 135,000–145,000. *Amount:* up to $4968.

Eligibility Requirements: Applicant must be enrolled or expecting to enroll full or part-time at a two-year or four-year or technical institution or university; resident of Illinois and studying in Illinois. Available to U.S. citizens.

Application Requirements: Financial need analysis, FAFSA online. *Deadline:* Continuous.

Contact: College Zone Counselor
Illinois Student Assistance Commission (ISAC)
1755 Lake Cook Road
Deerfield, IL 60015-5209
Phone: 800-899-4722
E-mail: collegezone@isac.org

ILLINOIS NATIONAL GUARD GRANT PROGRAM

• *See page 535*

ILLINOIS STUDENT-TO-STUDENT PROGRAM OF MATCHING GRANTS

Award provides matching funds for need-based grants at participating Illinois public universities and community colleges. Deadlines are set by each institution. Contact financial aid office at the institution in which you are enrolled for eligibility.

Award: Grant for use in freshman, sophomore, junior, or senior years; not renewable. *Number:* 2000–4000. *Amount:* $300–$500.

Eligibility Requirements: Applicant must be enrolled or expecting to enroll full or part-time at a two-year or four-year institution or university; resident of Illinois and studying in Illinois. Available to U.S. citizens.

Application Requirements: Application, financial need analysis. *Deadline:* varies.

Contact: College Zone Counselor
Illinois Student Assistance Commission (ISAC)
1755 Lake Cook Road
Deerfield, IL 60015-5209
Phone: 800-899-4722
E-mail: collegezone@isac.org

ILLINOIS VETERAN GRANT PROGRAM - IVG

• *See page 556*

MERIT RECOGNITION SCHOLARSHIP (MRS) PROGRAM

Award for Illinois high school seniors graduating in the top 4% of their class and attending Illinois postsecondary institution or one of the nation's four approved Military Service Academies. Students scoring in the top 4% in one of the college entrance tests among Illinois residents are also eligible. Contact for application procedures.

Award: Scholarship for use in freshman year; not renewable. *Number:* 5000–6000. *Amount:* up to $1000.

Eligibility Requirements: Applicant must be high school student; planning to enroll or expecting to enroll full or part-time at a two-year or four-year institution or university; resident of Illinois and studying in Illinois. Applicant must have 3.5 GPA or higher. Available to U.S. citizens.

Application Requirements: Application. *Deadline:* Continuous.

Contact: College Zone Counselor
Illinois Student Assistance Commission (ISAC)
1755 Lake Cook Road
Deerfield, IL 60015-5209
Phone: 800-899-4722
E-mail: collegezone@isac.org

ROBERT C. BYRD HONORS SCHOLARSHIP-ILLINOIS

Available to Illinois residents who are graduating high school seniors. Based on outstanding academic merit. Awards are renewable up to four years. Must be accepted on a full-time basis as an undergraduate student.

Award: Scholarship for use in freshman, sophomore, junior, or senior years; renewable. *Number:* 1100–1200. *Amount:* up to $1500.

Eligibility Requirements: Applicant must be high school student; planning to enroll or expecting to enroll full-time at a two-year or four-year institution or university and resident of Illinois. Applicant must have 3.5 GPA or higher. Available to U.S. citizens.

Application Requirements: Test scores, transcript. *Deadline:* varies.

Contact: College Zone Counselor
Illinois Student Assistance Commission (ISAC)
1755 Lake Cook Road
Deerfield, IL 60015-5209
Phone: 800-899-4722
E-mail: collegezone@isac.org

SILAS PURNELL ILLINOIS INCENTIVE FOR ACCESS PROGRAM

Award for eligible first-time freshmen enrolling in approved Illinois institutions. One-time grant of up to $500 may be used for any educational expense. Using the FAFSA, applicants are encouraged to apply as quickly as possible after January 1st preceding the academic year.

Award: Grant for use in freshman year; not renewable. *Number:* 19,000–22,000. *Amount:* $300–$500.

Eligibility Requirements: Applicant must be enrolled or expecting to enroll full or part-time at a two-year or four-year or technical institution or university; resident of Illinois and studying in Illinois. Available to U.S. citizens.

Illinois Student Assistance Commission (ISAC) (continued)

Application Requirements: Financial need analysis, FAFSA online. *Deadline:* Continuous.

Contact: College Zone Counselor
Illinois Student Assistance Commission (ISAC)
1755 Lake Cook Road
Deerfield, IL 60015-5209
Phone: 800-899-4722
E-mail: collegezone@isac.org

INDEPENDENT COLLEGES OF SOUTHERN CALIFORNIA http://www.cal-colleges.org

MACERICH COMPANY SCHOLARSHIP

Macerich Company sponsors three $10,000 scholarships to high school seniors who will attend a member school of Independent Colleges of Southern California. The program recognizes and rewards achievements of outstanding students from Stonewood Center, Lakewood Center and Los Cerritos Center area high schools. Application deadline is in April.

Award: Scholarship for use in freshman year; renewable. *Number:* 3. *Amount:* $10,000.

Eligibility Requirements: Applicant must be high school student; planning to enroll or expecting to enroll full-time at a four-year institution; resident of California and studying in California. Applicant must have 3.0 GPA or higher. Available to U.S. citizens.

Application Requirements: Application, autobiography, essay, financial need analysis, interview, references, test scores, transcript. *Deadline:* varies.

Contact: Lynn Maeyame, Director of Business Services
Independent Colleges of Southern California
555 South Flower Street, Suite 610
Los Angeles, CA 90071-2300
Phone: 213-553-9380
Fax: 213-553-9346
E-mail: macerich@cal-colleges.org

INDEPENDENT COLLEGES OF WASHINGTON http://www.ICWashington.org

CORPORATE SPONSORED SCHOLARSHIP PROGRAM

All scholarships restricted to students attending one of ten independent colleges located in Washington State. Colleges include Gonzaga University, Heritage College, Pacific Lutheran University, Saint Martin's College, Seattle Pacific University, Seattle University, University of Puget Sound, Walla Walla College, Whitman College, Whitworth College. For more details see Web site: http://www.icwashington.org.

Award: Scholarship for use in freshman, sophomore, junior, or senior years; not renewable. *Number:* 20–70. *Amount:* $400–$3500.

Eligibility Requirements: Applicant must be enrolled or expecting to enroll full-time at a four-year institution and studying in Washington. Available to U.S. and non-U.S. citizens.

Application Requirements: Application, essay, resume, references, transcript. *Deadline:* April 15.

Contact: Carolyn Woodhouse, Administrative Assistant
Independent Colleges of Washington
600 Stewart Street
Suite 600
Seattle, WA 98101
Phone: 206-623-4494
Fax: 206-625-9621
E-mail: info@icwashington.org

INDIAN AMERICAN CULTURAL ASSOCIATION http://www.iasf.org

INDIAN AMERICAN SCHOLARSHIP FUND

• *See page 589*

INDIANA DEPARTMENT OF VETERANS' AFFAIRS http://www.ai.org/veteran/index.html

CHILD OF DISABLED VETERAN GRANT OR PURPLE HEART RECIPIENT GRANT

• *See page 557*

DEPARTMENT OF VETERANS AFFAIRS FREE TUITION FOR CHILDREN OF POW/MIA'S IN VIETNAM

• *See page 557*

INTER-COUNTY ENERGY http://www.intercountyenergy.net

INTER-COUNTY ENERGY SCHOLARSHIP

Scholarship available for Kentucky high school senior who is a child of a resident of the Inter-County Energy service area and an active member of the cooperative. Student must plan to enroll in a post-secondary institution: two- or four-year college, university, or trade/technical institution. Must submit a brief biography. Write or call for application.

Award: Scholarship for use in freshman year; not renewable. *Number:* 6. *Amount:* $1000.

Eligibility Requirements: Applicant must be high school student; planning to enroll or expecting to enroll at a two-year or four-year or technical institution or university and resident of Kentucky. Available to U.S. citizens.

Application Requirements: Application, autobiography, financial need analysis, references, transcript. *Deadline:* April 2.

Contact: Lori Statom, Member Services
Inter-County Energy
PO Box 87
Danville, KY 40423-0087
Phone: 859-236-4561
E-mail: lori@intercountyenergy.net

INTER-TRIBAL COUNCIL OF MICHIGAN, INC. http://www.itcmi.org

MICHIGAN INDIAN TUITION WAIVER

• *See page 589*

IOWA COLLEGE STUDENT AID COMMISSION http://www.iowacollegeaid.org

GOVERNOR TERRY E. BRANSTAD IOWA STATE FAIR SCHOLARSHIP

Up to four scholarships ranging from $500 to $1000 will be awarded to students graduating from an Iowa high school. Must actively participate at the Iowa State Fair. For more details see Web site: http://www.iowacollegeaid.org.

Award: Scholarship for use in freshman year; not renewable. *Number:* up to 4. *Amount:* $500–$1000.

Eligibility Requirements: Applicant must be high school student; planning to enroll or expecting to enroll at an institution or university; resident of Iowa and studying in Iowa. Available to U.S. citizens.

Application Requirements: Application, essay, financial need analysis, references, transcript. *Deadline:* May 1.

Contact: Brenda Easter, Director, Special Programs
Iowa College Student Aid Commission
200 10th Street, 4th Floor
Des Moines, IA 50309-3609
Phone: 515-242-3380
Fax: 515-242-3388

IOWA FOSTER CHILD GRANTS

Grants renewable up to four years will be awarded to students graduating from an Iowa high school who are in Iowa foster care under the care and custody of the Iowa Department of Human Service. Must have a minimum GPA of 2.25 and have applied to an accredited Iowa college or university. For more details see Web site: http://www.iowacollegeaid.org.

Award: Grant for use in freshman year; renewable. *Number:* varies. *Amount:* $2000–$4200.

Eligibility Requirements: Applicant must be high school student; planning to enroll or expecting to enroll at a two-year or four-year institution or university; resident of Iowa and studying in Iowa. Available to U.S. citizens.

Application Requirements: Application. *Deadline:* April 15.

Contact: Brenda Easter, Director, Special Programs
Iowa College Student Aid Commission
200 10th Street, 4th Floor
Des Moines, IA 50309-3609
Phone: 515-242-3380
Fax: 515-242-3388

IOWA GRANTS

Statewide need-based program to assist high-need Iowa residents. Recipients must demonstrate a high level of financial need to receive awards ranging from $100 to $1,000. Awards are prorated for students enrolled for less than full-time. Awards must be used at Iowa postsecondary institutions.

Award: Grant for use in freshman, sophomore, junior, or senior years; not renewable. *Number:* varies. *Amount:* $100–$1000.

Eligibility Requirements: Applicant must be enrolled or expecting to enroll full or part-time at a two-year or four-year or technical institution or university; resident of Iowa and studying in Iowa. Available to U.S. citizens.

Application Requirements: Application, financial need analysis. *Deadline:* Continuous.

Contact: Julie Leeper, Director, State Student Aid Programs
Iowa College Student Aid Commission
200 10th Street, 4th Floor
Des Moines, IA 50309-3609
Phone: 515-242-3370
Fax: 515-242-3388
E-mail: icsac@max.state.ia.us

IOWA NATIONAL GUARD EDUCATION ASSISTANCE PROGRAM

• *See page 536*

IOWA TUITION GRANT PROGRAM

Program assists students who attend independent postsecondary institutions in Iowa. Iowa residents currently enrolled, or planning to enroll, for at least three semester hours at one of the eligible Iowa postsecondary institutions may apply. Awards currently range from $100 to $4000. Grants may not exceed the difference between independent college and university tuition and fees and the average tuition and fees at the three public Regent universities.

Award: Grant for use in freshman, sophomore, junior, or senior years; not renewable. *Number:* varies. *Amount:* $100–$4000.

Eligibility Requirements: Applicant must be enrolled or expecting to enroll full or part-time at a two-year or four-year institution; resident of Iowa and studying in Iowa. Available to U.S. citizens.

Application Requirements: Application, financial need analysis. *Deadline:* July 1.

Contact: Julie Leeper, Director, State Student Aid Programs
Iowa College Student Aid Commission
200 10th Street, 4th Floor
Des Moines, IA 50309-3609
Phone: 515-242-3370
Fax: 515-242-3388
E-mail: icsac@max.state.ia.us

IOWA VOCATIONAL-TECHNICAL TUITION GRANT PROGRAM

Program provides need-based financial assistance to Iowa residents enrolled in career education (vocational-technical), and career option programs at Iowa area community colleges. Grants range from $150 to $650, depending on the length of program, financial need, and available funds.

Award: Grant for use in freshman or sophomore years; not renewable. *Number:* varies. *Amount:* $150–$650.

Eligibility Requirements: Applicant must be enrolled or expecting to enroll full or part-time at a technical institution; resident of Iowa and studying in Iowa. Available to U.S. citizens.

Application Requirements: Application, financial need analysis. *Deadline:* July 1.

Contact: Julie Leeper, Director, State Student Aid Programs
Iowa College Student Aid Commission
200 10th Street, 4th Floor
Des Moines, IA 50309-3609
Phone: 515-242-3370
Fax: 515-242-3388
E-mail: icsac@max.state.ia.us

ROBERT C. BYRD HONORS SCHOLARSHIP

Scholarships up to $1500 are awarded to exceptionally able Iowa high school seniors who show promise of continued academic excellence. Must have a minimum of a 28 ACT or 1240 SAT, a 3.5 GPA and rank in the top 10% of the student's high school graduating class. For more details see Web site: http://www.iowacollegeaid.org.

Award: Scholarship for use in freshman year; renewable. *Number:* up to 70. *Amount:* up to $1500.

Eligibility Requirements: Applicant must be high school student; planning to enroll or expecting to enroll at an institution or university and resident of Iowa. Applicant must have 3.5 GPA or higher. Available to U.S. citizens.

Application Requirements: Application, test scores, transcript. *Deadline:* February 1.

Contact: Brenda Easter, Director, Special Programs
Iowa College Student Aid Commission
200 10th Street, 4th Floor
Des Moines, IA 50309-3609
Phone: 515-242-3380
Fax: 515-242-3388

STATE OF IOWA SCHOLARSHIP PROGRAM

Program provides recognition and financial honorarium to Iowa's academically talented high school seniors. Honorary scholarships are presented to all qualified candidates. Approximately 1700 top-ranking candidates are designated State of Iowa Scholars every March, from an applicant pool of nearly 5000 high school seniors. Must be used at an Iowa postsecondary institution. Minimum 3.5 GPA required.

Award: Scholarship for use in freshman year; not renewable. *Number:* up to 1700. *Amount:* up to $400.

Eligibility Requirements: Applicant must be high school student; planning to enroll or expecting to enroll full-time at a two-year or four-year or technical institution or university; resident of Iowa and studying in Iowa. Applicant must have 3.5 GPA or higher. Available to U.S. citizens.

Application Requirements: Application, test scores. *Deadline:* November 1.

Contact: Julie Leeper, Director, State Student Aid Programs
Iowa College Student Aid Commission
200 10th Street, 4th Floor
Des Moines, IA 50309-3609
Phone: 515-242-3370
Fax: 515-242-3388
E-mail: icsac@max.state.ia.us

IOWA DIVISION OF VOCATIONAL REHABILITATION SERVICES http://www.dvrs.state.ia.us

IOWA VOCATIONAL REHABILITATION

• *See page 527*

ITALIAN CATHOLIC FEDERATION, INC. http://www.icf.org

ICF COLLEGE SCHOLARSHIPS TO HIGH SCHOOL SENIORS

• *See page 590*

ITALIAN-AMERICAN CHAMBER OF COMMERCE MIDWEST http://www.italchambers.net/chicago

ITALIAN-AMERICAN CHAMBER OF COMMERCE OF CHICAGO SCHOLARSHIP

• *See page 590*

J. CRAIG AND PAGE T. SMITH SCHOLARSHIP FOUNDATION http://jcraigsmithfoundation.org

FIRST IN FAMILY SCHOLARSHIP

Scholarships available for graduating Alabama high school seniors. Must be planning to enroll in an Alabama institution in fall and pursue a 4-year degree. Students who apply must want to give back to their community by volunteer and civic work. Special consideration will be given to applicants who would be the first in either their mother's or father's family (or both) to attend college.

Award: Scholarship for use in freshman year; renewable. *Number:* 10. *Amount:* $12,500–$15,000.

J. Craig and Page T. Smith Scholarship Foundation (continued)

Eligibility Requirements: Applicant must be high school student; planning to enroll or expecting to enroll full-time at a four-year institution or university; resident of Alabama and studying in Alabama. Applicant must have 2.5 GPA or higher. Available to U.S. citizens.

Application Requirements: Application, essay, financial need analysis, references, test scores, transcript. *Deadline:* March 1.

Contact: Ahrian Tyler, Administrator
J. Craig and Page T. Smith Scholarship Foundation
505 North 20th Street, Suite 1800
Birmingham, AL 35203
Phone: 205-250-6669
Fax: 205-328-7234
E-mail: scholarships@jcraigsmithfoundation.org

JACKSON ENERGY COOPERATIVE http://www.jacksonenergy.com

JACKSON ENERGY SCHOLARSHIP

Scholarships awarded to winners in an essay contest. Must be at least a senior in a Kentucky high school and no more than age 21. Parents or legal guardian must be Jackson Energy Cooperative member, but not an employee of Jackson Energy. Essay must be on a subject related to rural electrification and is due by March 1. Call or e-mail for application.

Award: Scholarship for use in freshman, sophomore, junior, or senior years; not renewable. *Number:* 16. *Amount:* $1000.

Eligibility Requirements: Applicant must be age 21 or under; enrolled or expecting to enroll at a two-year or four-year or technical institution or university and resident of Kentucky. Available to U.S. citizens.

Application Requirements: Application, applicant must enter a contest, essay. *Deadline:* March 1.

Contact: Karen Combs, Director of Public Relations
Jackson Energy Cooperative
PO Box 307
McKee, KY 40447
Phone: 800-262-7480
E-mail: jec@prtcnet.org

JACKSON PURCHASE ENERGY CORPORATION http://www.jpenergy.com

JACKSON PURCHASE ENERGY CORPORATION SCHOLARSHIP

Scholarships available to Kentucky high school seniors residing in Jackson Purchase Energy's service area. Must be enrolled or planning to enroll in a Kentucky two- or four-year college, or university. Must have GPA of 3.0 or higher and a comprehensive score of 18 or better on the ACT. Applications are available from high school guidance counselors or online at http://www.jpenergy.com. Deadline date is noted on application, usually mid-April.

Award: Scholarship for use in freshman year. *Number:* 6. *Amount:* $1000.

Eligibility Requirements: Applicant must be high school student; planning to enroll or expecting to enroll at a two-year or four-year institution or university; resident of Kentucky and studying in Kentucky. Applicant must have 3.0 GPA or higher. Available to U.S. citizens.

Application Requirements: Application, test scores, transcript.

Contact: Jackson Purchase Energy Corporation
2900 Irvin Cobb Drive
PO Box 4030
Paducah, KY 42002-4030
Phone: 800-633-4044
E-mail: electricity@jpenergy.com

JAMES C. CALDWELL SCHOLARSHIP

JAMES C. CALDWELL ASSISTING MEN AND WOMEN OF TOLEDO SCHOLARSHIP

• *See page 590*

JAMES F. BYRNES FOUNDATION http://www.byrnesscholars.org

JAMES F. BYRNES SCHOLARSHIP

Renewable award for residents of South Carolina ages 17-22 with one or both parents deceased. Must show financial need; a satisfactory scholastic record; and qualities of character, ability, and enterprise. Award is for undergraduate study. Results of SAT must be provided. Information available on Web site: http://www.byrnesscholars.org.

Award: Scholarship for use in freshman, sophomore, junior, or senior years; renewable. *Number:* 10–20. *Amount:* up to $2750.

Eligibility Requirements: Applicant must be age 17-22; enrolled or expecting to enroll full-time at a four-year institution and resident of South Carolina. Available to U.S. citizens.

Application Requirements: Application, autobiography, financial need analysis, interview, photo, references, test scores, transcript. *Deadline:* February 15.

Contact: Mrs. Genny White, Executive Secretary
James F. Byrnes Foundation
PO Box 6781
Columbia, SC 29260-6781
Phone: 803-254-9325
Fax: 803-254-9354
E-mail: info@byrnesscholars.org

JEWISH FAMILY AND CHILDREN'S SERVICES http://www.jfcs.org

ANNA AND CHARLES STOCKWITZ CHILDREN AND YOUTH FUND

• *See page 625*

BUTRIMOVITZ FAMILY ENDOWMENT FUND FOR JEWISH EDUCATION

• *See page 625*

HENRY AND TILDA SHULER SCHOLARSHIP FUND FOR YOUNG PEOPLE

• *See page 626*

JACOB RASSEN MEMORIAL SCHOLARSHIP

• *See page 626*

MIRIAM S. GRUNFIELD SCHOLARSHIP FUND

• *See page 626*

VIVIENNE CAMP COLLEGE SCHOLARSHIP FUND

• *See page 626*

JEWISH FOUNDATION FOR EDUCATION OF WOMEN http://www.jfew.org

BILLER/JEWISH FOUNDATION FOR EDUCATION OF WOMEN

• *See page 626*

JEWISH SOCIAL SERVICE AGENCY OF METROPOLITAN WASHINGTON http://www.jssa.org

DAVID KORN SCHOLARSHIP FUND

• *See page 626*

JEWISH SOCIAL SERVICE AGENCY EDUCATIONAL SCHOLARSHIP

One-time award available to full-time undergraduate student. Must be a resident of the Washington Metropolitan area. Must be a U.S. citizen or working towards citizenship.

Award: Scholarship for use in freshman year; not renewable. *Number:* 1. *Amount:* up to $6000.

Eligibility Requirements: Applicant must be high school student; planning to enroll or expecting to enroll full-time at a four-year institution or university and resident of District of Columbia, Maryland, or Virginia. Available to U.S. citizens.

Application Requirements: Application. *Deadline:* February 28.

Contact: Lynn Ponton, Scholarship and Loan Coordinator
Jewish Social Service Agency of Metropolitan Washington
6123 Montrose Road
Rockville, MD 20852
Phone: 301-881-3700 Ext. 611

JEWISH SOCIAL SERVICE AGENCY OF METROPOLITAN WASHINGTON MAX AND EMMY DREYFUSS UNDERGRADUATE SCHOLARSHIP FUND

• *See page 627*

MORTON A. GIBSON MEMORIAL SCHOLARSHIP

• *See page 627*

JVS JEWISH COMMUNITY SCHOLARSHIP FUND http://www.jvsla.org

JVS JEWISH COMMUNITY SCHOLARSHIP

• *See page 627*

KANSAS COMMISSION ON VETERANS AFFAIRS http://www.kcva.org

KANSAS EDUCATIONAL BENEFITS FOR CHILDREN OF MIA, POW, AND DECEASED VETERANS OF THE VIETNAM WAR

• *See page 557*

KANSAS NATIONAL GUARD EDUCATIONAL ASSISTANCE PROGRAM

KANSAS NATIONAL GUARD EDUCATIONAL ASSISTANCE AWARD PROGRAM

• *See page 536*

KENERGY CORPORATION http://www.kenergycorp.com

KENERGY SCHOLARSHIP

Scholarship available to Kentucky high school seniors or graduates who will be enrolled in the fall semester in a full-time program at a 2- or 4-year college, university, or trade/technical school. Must be member/owner in Kenergy or reside with a parent/guardian who currently receives electrical service from Kenergy. Must demonstrate financial need. For information and application, visit Web site: http://www.kenergycorp.com.

Award: Scholarship for use in freshman, sophomore, junior, senior, or graduate years; not renewable. *Number:* up to 10. *Amount:* $1000.

Eligibility Requirements: Applicant must be enrolled or expecting to enroll full-time at a two-year or four-year or technical institution or university and resident of Kentucky. Available to U.S. citizens.

Application Requirements: Application, essay, financial need analysis, references, transcript. *Deadline:* March 4.

Contact: Beverly Hooper, Scholarship Coordinator
Kenergy Corporation
PO Box 18
Henderson, KY 42419-0018
Phone: 800-844-4832 Ext. 6
Fax: 270-826-3999
E-mail: scholarships@kenergycorp.com

KENNEDY FOUNDATION

KENNEDY FOUNDATION SCHOLARSHIPS

Renewable scholarship for current high school students for up to four years of undergraduate study. Renewal contingent upon academic performance. Must maintain a GPA of 2.0. Must be Colorado resident. Send self-addressed stamped envelope for application.

Award: Scholarship for use in freshman, sophomore, junior, or senior years; renewable. *Number:* 8–10. *Amount:* $2000.

Eligibility Requirements: Applicant must be high school student; planning to enroll or expecting to enroll full-time at a two-year or four-year or technical institution or university and resident of Colorado. Available to U.S. citizens.

Application Requirements: Application, self-addressed stamped envelope, test scores, transcript. *Deadline:* June 30.

Contact: David Kennedy, President
Kennedy Foundation
PO Box 27296
Denver, CO 80227
Phone: 303-933-2435
Fax: 303-933-0199
E-mail: jonathan@columbinecorp.com

KENTUCKY DEPARTMENT OF EDUCATION http://www.kde.state.ky.us

ROBERT C. BYRD HONORS SCHOLARSHIP–KENTUCKY

Scholarship available to high school seniors who show past high achievement and potential for continued academic success. Must have applied for admission or have been accepted for enrollment at a public or private nonprofit post-secondary school. Must be a Kentucky resident. Deadline for applications is the second Friday in March.

Award: Scholarship for use in freshman, sophomore, junior, or senior years; renewable. *Number:* varies. *Amount:* up to $1500.

Eligibility Requirements: Applicant must be high school student; planning to enroll or expecting to enroll full-time at a two-year or four-year institution or university and resident of Kentucky. Applicant must have 3.5 GPA or higher. Available to U.S. citizens.

Application Requirements: Application, test scores. *Deadline:* varies.

Contact: Donna Melton
Kentucky Department of Education
500 Mero Street, 19th Floor
Frankfort, KY 40601
Phone: 502-564-1479
E-mail: dmelton@kde.state.ky.us

KENTUCKY DEPARTMENT OF VETERANS AFFAIRS http://www.lrc.state.ky.us

DEPARTMENT OF VA TUITION WAIVER-KY KRS 164-515

• *See page 557*

DEPARTMENT OF VETERANS AFFAIRS TUITION WAIVER-KENTUCKY KRS 164-505

• *See page 557*

DEPARTMENT OF VETERANS AFFAIRS TUITION WAIVER-KY 164-512

• *See page 558*

DEPARTMENT OF VETERANS AFFAIRS TUITION WAIVER-KY KRS 164-507

• *See page 558*

KENTUCKY DEPARTMENT OF VOCATIONAL REHABILITATION http://www.ihdi.uky.edu/

KENTUCKY DEPARTMENT OF VOCATIONAL REHABILITATION

• *See page 527*

KENTUCKY HIGHER EDUCATION ASSISTANCE AUTHORITY (KHEAA) http://www.kheaa.com

COLLEGE ACCESS PROGRAM (CAP) GRANT

Award for U.S. citizen and Kentucky resident with no previous college degree. Provides $58 per semester hour for a minimum of six hours per semester. Applicants seeking degrees in religion are not eligible. Must demonstrate financial need and submit Free Application for Federal Student Aid. Priority deadline is March 15.

Award: Grant for use in freshman, sophomore, junior, or senior years; not renewable. *Number:* 35,000–40,000. *Amount:* up to $1400.

Eligibility Requirements: Applicant must be enrolled or expecting to enroll full or part-time at a two-year or four-year or technical institution or university; resident of Kentucky and studying in Kentucky. Available to U.S. citizens.

Application Requirements: Financial need analysis. *Deadline:* Continuous.

Contact: Michael D. Morgan, Program Coordinator
Kentucky Higher Education Assistance Authority (KHEAA)
PO Box 798
Frankfort, KY 40602-0798
Phone: 502-696-7394
Fax: 502-696-7373
E-mail: mmorgan@kheaa.com

COMMONWEALTH OF KENTUCKY DEPENDENTS OF DECEASED OR DISABLED EMPLOYEES PARTICIPATING IN STATE RETIREMENT SYSTEMS TUITION WAIVER

Must be child or non-remarried spouse of an employee participating in a state-administered retirement system who died or was disabled due to a duty-related injury. Must provide proof of relationship to the deceased/disabled and proof the death/disability was duty-related. Waiver of any matriculation or tuition fees at any Kentucky state-supported college, university, or vocational school.

Award: Scholarship for use in freshman, sophomore, junior, or senior years; renewable. *Number:* varies. *Amount:* varies.

Eligibility Requirements: Applicant must be enrolled or expecting to enroll full or part-time at a two-year or four-year or technical institution or university; resident of Kentucky and studying in Kentucky. Available to U.S. citizens.

Application Requirements: Application, financial need analysis, proof of relationship to deceased/disabled person.

Contact: Financial Aid Office of any Kentucky public college or university

KENTUCKY CABINET FOR FAMILIES AND CHILDREN–ADOPTED AND FOSTER CHILDREN TUITION WAIVER

Waiver of up to the cost of in-state full- or part-time tuition at a Kentucky college or vocational school. Must be a Kentucky resident who was adopted and whose family receives state-funded adoption assistance, or who was placed in foster care in Kentucky by the Cabinet for Families and Children. Out-of-state students meeting eligibility requirements at the time of application to a Kentucky school may also apply.

Award: Scholarship for use in freshman, sophomore, junior, or senior years; renewable. *Number:* varies. *Amount:* varies.

Eligibility Requirements: Applicant must be enrolled or expecting to enroll full or part-time at a two-year or four-year or technical institution or university; resident of Kentucky and studying in Kentucky. Available to U.S. citizens.

Application Requirements: Application, proof of eligibility. *Deadline:* Continuous.

Contact: Fawn Conley, Chafee Independence Program
Kentucky Higher Education Assistance Authority (KHEAA)
275 East Main Street, 3C-E
Frankfort, KY 40621
Phone: 502-564-2147 Ext. 4497
E-mail: fawn.conley@mail.state.ky.us

KENTUCKY CABINET FOR WORKFORCE DEVELOPMENT EDUCATION PAYS SCHOLARSHIP

Scholarships available for Kentucky residents enrolled in a Kentucky post-secondary institution. Must be a client of at least one of the Cabinet for Workforce Development's programs/services and demonstrate excellent character. Must submit an application, two character references, and an essay of under 600 words. Application deadline usually mid-April. For more information, visit Web site http://www.kycwd.org.

Award: Scholarship for use in freshman, sophomore, junior, or senior years; not renewable. *Number:* varies. *Amount:* $500.

Eligibility Requirements: Applicant must be enrolled or expecting to enroll at a two-year or four-year or technical institution or university; resident of Kentucky and studying in Kentucky. Available to U.S. citizens.

Application Requirements: Application, essay, references. *Deadline:* varies.

Contact: Tim Phelps, Student Aid Branch Manager
Kentucky Higher Education Assistance Authority (KHEAA)
PO Box 798
Frankfort, KY 40602-0798
Phone: 502-696-7393
Fax: 502-696-7373
E-mail: tphelps@kheaa.com

KENTUCKY CABINET FOR WORKFORCE DEVELOPMENT GED INCENTIVE PROGRAM TUITION DISCOUNT

Tuition waivers available to Kentucky students who earned their GED in one year after having been out of high school three years and signing a learning contract with their employer. Award is $250 tuition discount each semester for a maximum of 4 semesters at a Kentucky public college or university. For additional information see Web site: http://adulted.state.ky.us.

Award: Scholarship for use in freshman, sophomore, junior, or senior years; renewable. *Number:* varies. *Amount:* $250–$1000.

Eligibility Requirements: Applicant must be enrolled or expecting to enroll at a two-year or four-year institution or university; resident of Kentucky and studying in Kentucky. Available to U.S. citizens.

Application Requirements: Application, learning contract with employer GED certificate. *Deadline:* Continuous.

Contact: Robert L. Curry, Division of Workforce Investment, Department for Adult Education and Literacy
Kentucky Higher Education Assistance Authority (KHEAA)
Capital Plaza Tower, 3rd Floor, 500 Mero Street
Frankfort, KY 40601
Phone: 502-564-5114 Ext. 125
E-mail: robertl.curry@mail.state.ky.us

KENTUCKY DEPARTMENT OF AGRICULTURE SCHOLARSHIP

Scholarships for youth exhibitor who has participated in a state-sponsored district livestock show. Four exhibitors in each species (dairy, beef, sheep, hogs, goats, horses) will be chosen in a random drawing from a list of Future Farmers of America and 4-H show participants. Must be a Kentucky resident.

Award: Scholarship for use in freshman, sophomore, junior, or senior years; not renewable. *Number:* 20. *Amount:* $500.

Eligibility Requirements: Applicant must be enrolled or expecting to enroll at a two-year or four-year or technical institution or university; resident of Kentucky and must have an interest in animal/agricultural competition. Available to U.S. citizens.

Application Requirements: Applicant must enter a contest, participation in state-sponsored livestock show.

Contact: Stewart Gritton, Scholarship Committee
Phone: 502-564-4983

KENTUCKY EDUCATIONAL EXCELLENCE SCHOLARSHIP (KEES)

Annual award based on GPA and highest ACT or SAT score received by high school graduation. Awards are renewable if required cumulative GPA maintained at a Kentucky postsecondary school. Must be a Kentucky resident, and a graduate of a Kentucky high school.

Award: Scholarship for use in freshman, sophomore, junior, or senior years; renewable. *Number:* 55,000–60,000. *Amount:* $125–$2500.

Eligibility Requirements: Applicant must be high school student; planning to enroll or expecting to enroll full or part-time at a two-year or four-year or technical institution or university; resident of Kentucky and studying in Kentucky. Applicant must have 2.5 GPA or higher. Available to U.S. citizens.

Application Requirements: Test scores, transcript. *Deadline:* Continuous.

Contact: Tim Phelps, Student Aid Branch Manager
Kentucky Higher Education Assistance Authority (KHEAA)
PO Box 798
Frankfort, KY 40602-0798
Phone: 502-696-7393
Fax: 502-696-7373
E-mail: tphelps@kheaa.com

KENTUCKY JUSTICE CABINET POLICEMAN/FIREMAN PENSION FUND TUITION WAIVER

• *See page 512*

KENTUCKY NATIONAL GUARD TUITION ASSISTANCE PROGRAM

• *See page 536*

KENTUCKY TUITION GRANT (KTG)

Available to Kentucky residents who are full-time undergraduates at an independent college within the state. Must not be enrolled in a religion program. Based on financial need. Submit Free Application for Federal Student Aid. Priority deadline is March 15.

Award: Grant for use in freshman, sophomore, junior, or senior years; not renewable. *Number:* 10,000–12,000. *Amount:* $200–$2400.

Eligibility Requirements: Applicant must be enrolled or expecting to enroll full-time at a two-year or four-year institution or university; resident of Kentucky and studying in Kentucky. Available to U.S. citizens.

Application Requirements: Financial need analysis. *Deadline:* Continuous.

Contact: Tim Phelps, Student Aid Branch Manager
Kentucky Higher Education Assistance Authority (KHEAA)
PO Box 798
Frankfort, KY 40602-0798
Phone: 502-696-7393
Fax: 502-696-7373
E-mail: tphelps@kheaa.com

KENTUCKY NATIONAL GUARD

KENTUCKY NATIONAL GUARD TUITION AWARD PROGRAM

• *See page 536*

KNIGHTS OF AK-SAR-BEN http://www.aksarben.org/programs/scholarship.htm

KNIGHTS OF AK-SAR-BEN LEADERSHIP SCHOLARSHIP

Scholarships are awarded to outstanding and talented graduates of "Heartland" (Nebraska and Western Iowa) high schools. Must be a graduating high school senior with a minimum 2.5 GPA, who plans on attending a college or university within the Ak-Sar-Ben region. For more details and an application see Web site: http://www.aksarben.org.

Award: Scholarship for use in freshman, sophomore, junior, or senior years; renewable. *Number:* 20. *Amount:* $10,000.

Eligibility Requirements: Applicant must be high school student; planning to enroll or expecting to enroll full-time at a four-year institution or university and resident of Iowa or Nebraska. Applicant must have 2.5 GPA or higher. Available to U.S. citizens.

Application Requirements: Application, essay, financial need analysis, references, test scores, transcript. *Deadline:* February 11.

Contact: Application available at Web site: www.aksarben.org.

KNIGHTS OF AK-SAR-BEN ONE-YEAR COMMUNITY COLLEGE SCHOLARSHIP.

Scholarships available to applicants from Nebraska and Western Iowa (Heartland) who plan to attend a community college in the region. Applications will be due into the office of the community college to which the student is applying by March 19. For more details and the application, visit the Web site: http://www.aksarben.org

Award: Scholarship for use in freshman year; not renewable. *Number:* up to 12. *Amount:* $1000.

Eligibility Requirements: Applicant must be enrolled or expecting to enroll full-time at a two-year institution; resident of Iowa or Nebraska and studying in Iowa or Nebraska. Available to U.S. citizens.

Application Requirements: Application. *Deadline:* March 19.

Contact: Sandy Heather, Development Assistant
Knights of Ak-Sar-Ben
302 South 36th Street
Suite 800
Omaha, NE 68131
Phone: 402-554-9600 Ext. 106
Fax: 402-554-9609
E-mail: heather@aksarben.org

KOREAN AMERICAN SCHOLARSHIP FOUNDATION http://www.kasf.org

KOREAN-AMERICAN SCHOLARSHIP FOUNDATION EASTERN REGION SCHOLARSHIPS

• *See page 591*

KOREAN-AMERICAN SCHOLARSHIP FOUNDATION MIDEASTERN REGION SCHOLARSHIPS

• *See page 591*

KOREAN-AMERICAN SCHOLARSHIP FOUNDATION MIDWESTERN REGION SCHOLARSHIPS

• *See page 591*

KOREAN-AMERICAN SCHOLARSHIP FOUNDATION NORTHEASTERN REGION SCHOLARSHIPS

• *See page 591*

KOREAN-AMERICAN SCHOLARSHIP FOUNDATION SOUTHERN REGION SCHOLARSHIPS

• *See page 592*

KOREAN-AMERICAN SCHOLARSHIP FOUNDATION WESTERN REGION SCHOLARSHIPS

• *See page 592*

KOREAN UNIVERSITY CLUB

KOREAN UNIVERSITY CLUB SCHOLARSHIP

• *See page 592*

KOSCIUSZKO FOUNDATION http://www.kosciuszkofoundation.org

MASSACHUSETTS FEDERATION OF POLISH WOMEN'S CLUBS SCHOLARSHIPS

• *See page 592*

KUMU KAHUA THEATRE

KUMU KAHUA THEATER/UHM THEATER DEPARTMENT PLAYWRITING CONTEST, RESIDENT PRIZE

Contest for residents in Hawaii. Play may be any length on any topic. Write for details.

Award: Prize for use in freshman, sophomore, junior, senior, graduate, or postgraduate years; not renewable. *Number:* 1. *Amount:* $200.

Eligibility Requirements: Applicant must be enrolled or expecting to enroll at an institution or university; resident of Hawaii and must have an interest in writing. Available to U.S. citizens.

Application Requirements: Applicant must enter a contest, 3 copies of manuscript. *Deadline:* January 2.

Contact: Kuma Kahua Playwriting Contest
Kumu Kahua Theatre
46 Merchant Street
Honolulu, HI 96813
E-mail: info@kumukahua.com

LATIN AMERICAN EDUCATIONAL FOUNDATION http://www.laef.org

LATIN AMERICAN EDUCATIONAL FOUNDATION SCHOLARSHIPS

Scholarship award for Hispanic students or individuals actively involved in the Hispanic community who are Colorado residents planning to pursue postsecondary education. Must be a Colorado resident with a minimum 3.0 GPA. Awards range from $500 to $2000.

Award: Scholarship for use in freshman, sophomore, junior, or senior years; not renewable. *Number:* 200–300. *Amount:* $500–$2000.

Eligibility Requirements: Applicant must be enrolled or expecting to enroll full or part-time at a two-year or four-year or technical institution or university and resident of Colorado. Applicant must have 3.0 GPA or higher. Available to U.S. citizens.

Application Requirements: Application, essay, financial need analysis, interview, references, self-addressed stamped envelope, test scores, transcript. *Deadline:* February 15.

Contact: Carmen Lerma Mendoza, Associate Director
Latin American Educational Foundation
924 West Colfax Avenue, Suite 103
Denver, CO 80204-4417
Phone: 303-446-0541
Fax: 303-446-0526
E-mail: carmen@laef.org

LEE-JACKSON EDUCATIONAL FOUNDATION http://www.lee-jackson.org

LEE-JACKSON EDUCATIONAL FOUNDATION SCHOLARSHIP COMPETITION

Essay contest for junior and senior Virginia high school students. Must demonstrate appreciation for the exemplary character and soldierly virtues of Generals Robert E. Lee and Thomas J. "Stonewall" Jackson. Three one-time awards of $1000 in each of Virginia's eight regions. A bonus scholarship of $1000 will be awarded to the author of the best essay in each of the eight regions. An additional award of $8000 will go to the essay judged the best in the state.

Award: Scholarship for use in freshman year; not renewable. *Number:* 27. *Amount:* $1000–$8000.

Eligibility Requirements: Applicant must be high school student; planning to enroll or expecting to enroll at a four-year institution or university; resident of Virginia and must have an interest in writing. Available to U.S. citizens.

Application Requirements: Application, applicant must enter a contest, essay, transcript. *Deadline:* December 21.

Contact: Stephanie Leech, Administrator
Lee-Jackson Educational Foundation
PO Box 8121
Charlottesville, VA 22906
Phone: 434-977-1861
E-mail: salp_leech@yahoo.com

LEXINGTON HERALD-LEADER http://www.kentucky.com

HEY! I DO QUALIFY FOR A SCHOLARSHIP

Renewable award for high school students in specified Kentucky counties planning to attending a four-year accredited university or college. Minimum 2.5 GPA required, average or above-average ACT/SAT scores, and not in top 10% of class. Must demonstrate financial need. Aimed at students who were not focused on education early in high school but who are currently looking at future educational opportunities and a career.

Award: Scholarship for use in freshman year; renewable. *Number:* 4. *Amount:* $2000.

Eligibility Requirements: Applicant must be high school student; planning to enroll or expecting to enroll full-time at a four-year institution or university and resident of Kentucky. Applicant must have 2.5 GPA or higher. Available to U.S. citizens.

Application Requirements: Application, autobiography, essay, financial need analysis, interview, references, test scores, transcript. *Deadline:* March 17.

Contact: Kathy Aldridge, Executive Assistant
Lexington Herald-Leader
100 Midland Avenue
Lexington, KY 40508
Phone: 859-231-3104
Fax: 859-231-3584
E-mail: kaldridge@herald-leader.com

LIGHTHOUSE INTERNATIONAL http://www.lighthouse.org

SCHOLARSHIP AWARDS

• *See page 527*

LINCOLN COMMUNITY FOUNDATION http://www.lcf.org

ANONYMOUS SCHOLARSHIP BENEFITING GRADUATES OF THAYER COUNTY IN NEBRASKA

Scholarship for graduating seniors from Thayer County high schools in Nebraska; namely Hebron, Deshler, Chester, Bruning, and Davenport. Need not excel academically. Must demonstrate financial need. Scholarship may be renewed for no more than five years for any one recipient.

Award: Scholarship for use in freshman year; renewable. *Number:* 3. *Amount:* $5000.

Eligibility Requirements: Applicant must be high school student; planning to enroll or expecting to enroll full-time at a two-year or four-year or technical institution or university and resident of Nebraska. Available to U.S. citizens.

Application Requirements: Application, financial need analysis, test scores, transcript. *Deadline:* April 30.

Contact: Application available at Web site.

BRYAN/LGH MEDICAL CENTER WEST AUXILIARY JUNIOR VOLUNTEER SCHOLARSHIP

Scholarship for graduating seniors from high school who have volunteered at least 150 hours at Bryan/LGH Medical Center West in Lincoln, NE.

Award: Scholarship for use in freshman year; not renewable. *Number:* 1. *Amount:* $1000.

Eligibility Requirements: Applicant must be high school student; planning to enroll or expecting to enroll full-time at a two-year or four-year or technical institution or university and resident of Nebraska. Applicant must have 2.5 GPA or higher. Available to U.S. citizens.

Application Requirements: Application, essay, test scores, transcript, verification of volunteer hours. *Deadline:* April 15.

Contact: Application available at Web site.

COLLEEN FARRELL GERLEMAN SCHOLARSHIP

Scholarship for current graduating high school seniors from public or private high schools in the greater Lincoln, Nebraska area or must have received a Gerleman Scholarship previously. Must attend a two- or four-year college in Nebraska.

Award: Scholarship for use in freshman, sophomore, junior, or senior years; not renewable. *Number:* 5–10. *Amount:* $500–$750.

Eligibility Requirements: Applicant must be enrolled or expecting to enroll full-time at a two-year or four-year or technical institution or university; resident of Nebraska and studying in Nebraska. Applicant must have 2.5 GPA or higher. Available to U.S. citizens.

Application Requirements: Application, essay, financial need analysis, interview, references, test scores, transcript. *Deadline:* April 15.

Contact: Application available at Web site.

DUNCAN E. AND LILLIAN M. MCGREGOR SCHOLARSHIP

Scholarship for graduating seniors or former graduates of the high schools in Ansley, Arcadia, Gibbon, Ord, Shelton, or Sargent high schools in Nebraska. Must have resided in a community served by the Nebraska Central Telephone Company during his/her high school education.

Award: Scholarship for use in freshman, sophomore, junior, or senior years; not renewable. *Number:* 80–100. *Amount:* $500–$1000.

Eligibility Requirements: Applicant must be enrolled or expecting to enroll full-time at a two-year or four-year or technical institution or university and resident of Nebraska. Applicant must have 2.5 GPA or higher. Available to U.S. citizens.

Application Requirements: Application, financial need analysis, test scores, transcript. *Deadline:* April 15.

Contact: Application available at Web site.

GEORGE WATTERS-NEBRASKA PETROLEUM MARKETERS ASSOCIATION SCHOLARSHIP

• *See page 513*

HARRY AND LENORA RICHARDSON-NATIONAL ASSOCIATION OF POSTMASTERS OF THE UNITED STATES SCHOLARSHIP

• *See page 513*

HARRY AND LENORA RICHARDSON-NEBRASKA BRANCH OF THE NATIONAL LEAGUE OF POSTMASTERS SCHOLARSHIP

• *See page 513*

JENNINGS AND BEULAH HAGGERTY SCHOLARSHIP

Scholarship for graduating seniors from public or private high schools in Lincoln, NE area. Must be in the top third of graduating class, and enroll in a two- or four-year institution in Nebraska. Must demonstrate financial need and academic achievement. Applications must be received between April 1 and July 1.

Award: Scholarship for use in freshman year; not renewable. *Number:* 10–20. *Amount:* $500–$1000.

Eligibility Requirements: Applicant must be high school student; planning to enroll or expecting to enroll full-time at a two-year or four-year or technical institution or university; resident of Nebraska and studying in Nebraska. Applicant must have 3.0 GPA or higher. Available to U.S. citizens.

Application Requirements: Application, essay, financial need analysis, interview, references, test scores, transcript. *Deadline:* July 1.

Contact: Application available at Web site.

LOUIS C. AND AMY E. NUERNBERGER MEMORIAL SCHOLARSHIP

• *See page 513*

MAX AND MARGARET PUMPHREY SCHOLARSHIP

Scholarship for graduating seniors or former graduates of public or private high schools in Lancaster County, NE. Preference given to those attending Nebraska colleges/universities. Must demonstrate financial need and academic success. Applications must be received between April 1 and July 1.

Award: Scholarship for use in freshman, sophomore, junior, or senior years; not renewable. *Number:* 35–40. *Amount:* $500–$1000.

Eligibility Requirements: Applicant must be enrolled or expecting to enroll full-time at a two-year or four-year or technical institution or university and resident of Nebraska. Applicant must have 2.5 GPA or higher. Available to U.S. citizens.

Application Requirements: Application, essay, financial need analysis, interview, references, test scores, transcript. *Deadline:* July 1.

Contact: Application available at Web site.

MIRIAM CROFT MOELLER CITIZENSHIP AWARD

Scholarship for current graduating seniors from public or private high schools in the greater Lincoln, NE area who uphold a keen interest in citizenship and participate in, and demonstrate enthusiasm for, community betterment and leadership. Need not excel academically.

Award: Scholarship for use in freshman year; not renewable. *Number:* 4. *Amount:* $500.

Eligibility Requirements: Applicant must be high school student; planning to enroll or expecting to enroll full-time at a two-year or four-year or technical institution or university; resident of Nebraska and must have an interest in designated field specified by sponsor or leadership. Applicant must have 2.5 GPA or higher. Available to U.S. citizens.

Application Requirements: Application, essay, references, test scores, transcript. *Deadline:* April 15.

Contact: Application available at Web site.

NEBRASKA RURAL SCHOOLS SCHOLARSHIP

Scholarships for graduating seniors or former graduates of rural high schools in Nebraska (by "rural" it is to be understood as a community with a population of less than 10,000). Must attend a college, university, or community college in Nebraska. Applicants must have graduated in the top 10% of his/her high school graduating class or must currently maintain a 3.5 GPA or better on a 4.0 scale at the college or university he/she is attending. Must be a Nebraska resident. Applications due between June 1 and August 1.

Award: Scholarship for use in freshman, sophomore, junior, or senior years; not renewable. *Number:* 4. *Amount:* $500.

Eligibility Requirements: Applicant must be enrolled or expecting to enroll full-time at a two-year or four-year or technical institution or university; resident of Nebraska and studying in Nebraska. Applicant must have 3.5 GPA or higher. Available to U.S. citizens.

Application Requirements: Application, essay, financial need analysis, test scores, transcript. *Deadline:* August 1.

Contact: Application available at Web site.

NORMAN AND RUTH GOOD EDUCATIONAL ENDOWMENT

Scholarship for a degree-seeking junior or senior at a private college in Nebraska. Must have GPA of 3.5 or above. Application deadline: April 15.

Award: Scholarship for use in junior or senior years; not renewable. *Number:* 10–15. *Amount:* $500–$1000.

Eligibility Requirements: Applicant must be enrolled or expecting to enroll full-time at a four-year institution and studying in Nebraska. Applicant must have 3.5 GPA or higher. Available to U.S. citizens.

Application Requirements: Application, test scores, transcript. *Deadline:* April 15.

Contact: Application available at Web site.

P.G. RICHARDSON MASONIC MEMORIAL SCHOLARSHIP

Scholarship for graduating high school seniors who have a family member belonging to Custer Lodge #148 A.F. & A.M. The deadline for applications is March 1. Must be Nebraska resident.

Award: Scholarship for use in freshman year; not renewable. *Number:* 1. *Amount:* $1000.

Eligibility Requirements: Applicant must be high school student; planning to enroll or expecting to enroll full-time at a two-year or four-year or technical institution or university and resident of Nebraska. Applicant must have 2.5 GPA or higher. Available to U.S. citizens.

Application Requirements: Application, references, test scores, transcript. *Deadline:* March 1.

Contact: Application available at Web site.

RALPH AND JEAN CUCA SCHOLARSHIP

Scholarship for graduating high school seniors from a public high school in the greater Lincoln, NE area who demonstrate financial need and academic success.

Award: Scholarship for use in freshman year; not renewable. *Number:* 1. *Amount:* $500–$1000.

Eligibility Requirements: Applicant must be high school student; planning to enroll or expecting to enroll full-time at a two-year or four-year or technical institution or university and resident of Nebraska. Applicant must have 2.5 GPA or higher. Available to U.S. citizens.

Application Requirements: Application, financial need analysis, references, test scores, transcript. *Deadline:* April 1.

Contact: Application available at Web site.

THOMAS C. WOODS, JR. MEMORIAL SCHOLARSHIP

• *See page 513*

LONG & FOSTER REAL ESTATE, INC.

http://www.longandfoster.com

LONG & FOSTER SCHOLARSHIP PROGRAM

One-time award for residents of MD, PA, DC , VA, DE, NJ, and NC. Students may pursue any academic major they desire. The Scholarship Committee will be seeking academically strong high school seniors who are well rounded and demonstrate leadership and involvement in a variety of school activities. Must be U.S. citizen. Minimum 3.0 GPA required.

Award: Scholarship for use in freshman year; not renewable. *Number:* up to 150. *Amount:* $1000.

Eligibility Requirements: Applicant must be high school student; planning to enroll or expecting to enroll full-time at a four-year institution or university and resident of Delaware, District of Columbia, Maryland, New Jersey, North Carolina, Pennsylvania, or Virginia. Applicant must have 3.0 GPA or higher. Available to U.S. citizens.

Application Requirements: Application, essay, financial need analysis, references, test scores, transcript. *Deadline:* March 1.

Contact: Erin L. Wendel, Public Relations Specialist
Long & Foster Real Estate, Inc.
11351 Random Hills Road
Fairfax, VA 22030
Phone: 703-359-1757
Fax: 703-591-5493
E-mail: erin.wendel@longandfoster.com

LOS ANGELES PHILHARMONIC http://www.laphil.org

BRONISLAW KAPER AWARDS FOR YOUNG ARTISTS

Competition for young musicians under the age of 18, or a senior in high school. Offers cash prizes. The instrumental category alternates annually between piano and strings. The 2003 competition will focus on strings; 2004, piano; 2005, strings; etc. This award is not for postsecondary students. Must be a California resident. Call or visit Web site for deadlines.

Award: Prize for use in freshman year; not renewable. *Number:* 4. *Amount:* $500–$2500.

Eligibility Requirements: Applicant must be age 17 or under; enrolled or expecting to enroll at an institution or university; resident of California and must have an interest in music. Available to U.S. citizens.

Application Requirements: Application, applicant must enter a contest, audition. *Deadline:* varies.

Contact: Education Department
Los Angeles Philharmonic
151 South Grand Avenue
Los Angeles, CA 90012
Phone: 213-972-0704
Fax: 213-972-7650
E-mail: education@laphil.org

LOS PADRES FOUNDATION http://www.lospadresfoundation.org

COLLEGE TUITION ASSISTANCE PROGRAM

Program for eligible high school students who are the first family member to attend college. Must be a legal resident or citizen of the U.S. and a resident of New York or New Jersey. Must have a 3.0 GPA. For further information, refer to Web site http://www.lospadresfoundation.org.

Award: Scholarship for use in freshman, sophomore, junior, or senior years; renewable. *Number:* varies. *Amount:* $1000–$2000.

Eligibility Requirements: Applicant must be enrolled or expecting to enroll full-time at a two-year or four-year or technical institution or university and resident of New Jersey or New York. Applicant must have 3.0 GPA or higher. Available to U.S. citizens.

Application Requirements: Application, essay, financial need analysis, references, transcript. *Deadline:* January 16.

Contact: Margarita Pagan
Los Padres Foundation
289 Grant Avenue, Suite 1A
Jersey City, NJ 07305
Phone: 201-451-6229
Fax: 201-451-5895
E-mail: mpaganlpf@comcast.net

SECOND CHANCE SCHOLARSHIPS

Scholarships granted to students who wish to return to college, trade school or apprenticeship program. Must be a legal resident or citizen of the U.S. and be a resident of New York or New Jersey. Must demonstrate financial need. For further information, refer to Web site http://www.lospadresfoundation.org.

Award: Scholarship for use in freshman, sophomore, junior, or senior years; not renewable. *Number:* up to 5. *Amount:* up to $2000.

Eligibility Requirements: Applicant must be enrolled or expecting to enroll full-time at a two-year or four-year or technical institution or university and resident of New Jersey or New York. Available to U.S. citizens.

Application Requirements: Application, financial need analysis, transcript. *Deadline:* January 16.

Contact: Margarita Pagan
Los Padres Foundation
289 Grant Avenue, Suite 1A
Jersey City, NJ 07305
Phone: 201-451-6229
Fax: 201-451-5895
E-mail: mpaganlpf@comcast.net

LOUISE C. NACCA MEMORIAL FOR EDUCATIONAL AID FOR THE HANDICAPPED TRUST

LOUISE NACCA MEMORIAL TRUST

• *See page 528*

LOUISIANA DEPARTMENT OF VETERAN AFFAIRS http://www.gov.state.la.us/depts/veteraffairs.htm

LOUISIANA DEPARTMENT OF VETERANS AFFAIRS STATE AID PROGRAM

• *See page 558*

LOUISIANA NATIONAL GUARD - STATE OF LOUISIANA, JOINT TASK FORCE LA http://www.la.ngb.army.mil

LOUISIANA NATIONAL GUARD STATE TUITION EXEMPTION PROGRAM

• *See page 536*

LOUISIANA OFFICE OF STUDENT FINANCIAL ASSISTANCE http://www.osfa.state.la.us

LEVERAGING EDUCATIONAL ASSISTANCE PROGRAM (LEAP)

LEAP program provides federal and state funds to provide need-based grants to academically qualified students. Individual award determined by Financial Aid Office and governed by number of applicants and availability of funds. File FAFSA by school deadline to apply each year. For Louisiana students attending Louisiana postsecondary institutions.

Award: Grant for use in freshman, sophomore, junior, or senior years; not renewable. *Number:* 3000. *Amount:* $200–$2000.

Eligibility Requirements: Applicant must be enrolled or expecting to enroll full or part-time at a two-year or four-year or technical institution or university; resident of Louisiana and studying in Louisiana. Available to U.S. citizens.

Application Requirements: Application, financial need analysis. *Deadline:* varies.

Contact: Public Information
Louisiana Office of Student Financial Assistance
PO Box 91202
Baton Rouge, LA 70821-9202
Phone: 800-259-5626 Ext. 1012
Fax: 225-922-0790
E-mail: custserv@osfa.state.la.us

TOPS ALTERNATE PERFORMANCE AWARD

Program awards an amount equal to tuition plus a $400 annual stipend to students attending a Louisiana public institution, or an amount equal to the weighted average public tuition plus a $400 annual stipend to students attending a LAICU private institution. Must have a minimum high school GPA of 3.0 based on TOPS core curriculum, ACT score of 24, completion of 10 honors courses, and completion of a 16.5 unit core curriculum. Must be a resident of Louisiana.

Award: Scholarship for use in freshman, sophomore, junior, or senior years; renewable. *Number:* varies. *Amount:* varies.

Eligibility Requirements: Applicant must be high school student; planning to enroll or expecting to enroll full-time at a two-year or four-year or technical institution or university; resident of Louisiana and studying in Louisiana. Applicant must have 3.0 GPA or higher. Available to U.S. citizens.

Application Requirements: Application, test scores. *Deadline:* July 1.

Contact: Public Information Representative
Louisiana Office of Student Financial Assistance
PO Box 91202
Baton Rouge, LA 70821-9202
Phone: 800-259-5626 Ext. 1012
Fax: 225-922-0790
E-mail: custserv@osfa.state.la.us

TOPS HONORS AWARD

Program awards an amount equal to tuition plus an $800 per year stipend to students attending a Louisiana public institution, or an amount equal to the weighted average public tuition plus an $800 per year stipend to students attending a LAICU private institution. Must have a minimum high school GPA of 3.5 based on TOPS core curriculum, ACT score of 27, and complete a 16.5 unit core curriculum. Must be resident of Louisiana.

Award: Scholarship for use in freshman, sophomore, junior, or senior years; renewable. *Number:* varies. *Amount:* $1541–$3894.

Eligibility Requirements: Applicant must be high school student; planning to enroll or expecting to enroll full-time at a two-year or four-year or technical institution or university; resident of Louisiana and studying in Louisiana. Applicant must have 3.5 GPA or higher. Available to U.S. citizens.

Application Requirements: Application, test scores. *Deadline:* July 1.

Contact: Public Information
Louisiana Office of Student Financial Assistance
PO Box 91202
Baton Rouge, LA 70821-9202
Phone: 800-259-5626 Ext. 1012
Fax: 225-922-0790
E-mail: custserv@osfa.state.la.us

TOPS OPPORTUNITY AWARD

Program awards an amount equal to tuition to students attending a Louisiana public institution, or an amount equal to the weighted average public tuition to students attending a LAICU private institution. Must have a minimum high school GPA of 2.5 based on the TOPS core curriculum, the prior year's state average ACT score, and complete a 16.5 unit core curriculum. Must be a Louisiana resident.

Award: Scholarship for use in freshman, sophomore, junior, or senior years; renewable. *Number:* varies. *Amount:* $741–$3094.

Eligibility Requirements: Applicant must be high school student; planning to enroll or expecting to enroll full-time at a two-year or four-year or technical institution or university; resident of Louisiana and studying in Louisiana. Applicant must have 2.5 GPA or higher. Available to U.S. citizens.

Application Requirements: Application, test scores. *Deadline:* July 1.

Contact: Public Information
Louisiana Office of Student Financial Assistance
PO Box 91202
Baton Rouge, LA 70821-9202
Phone: 800-259-5626 Ext. 1012
Fax: 225-922-0790
E-mail: custserv@osfa.state.la.us

TOPS PERFORMANCE AWARD

Program awards an amount equal to tuition plus a $400 annual stipend to students attending a Louisiana public institution, or an amount equal to the weighted average public tuition plus a $400 annual stipend to students attending a LAICU private institution. Must have a minimum high school GPA of 3.5 based on the TOPS core curriculum, an ACT score of 23 and completion of a 16.5 unit core curriculum. Must be a Louisiana resident.

Award: Scholarship for use in freshman, sophomore, junior, or senior years; renewable. *Number:* varies. *Amount:* $1141–$3494.

Eligibility Requirements: Applicant must be high school student; planning to enroll or expecting to enroll full-time at a two-year or four-year or technical institution or university; resident of Louisiana and studying in Louisiana. Applicant must have 3.5 GPA or higher. Available to U.S. citizens.

Application Requirements: Application, test scores. *Deadline:* July 1.

Contact: Public Information
Louisiana Office of Student Financial Assistance
PO Box 91202
Baton Rouge, LA 70821-9202
Phone: 800-259-5626 Ext. 1012
Fax: 225-922-0790
E-mail: custserv@osfa.state.la.us

TOPS TECH AWARD

Program awards an amount equal to tuition for up to two years of technical training at a Louisiana postsecondary institution that offers a vocational or technical education certificate or diploma program, or a non-academic degree program. Must have a 2.5 high school GPA based on TOPS Tech core curriculum, an ACT score of 17, and complete the TOPS-Tech core curriculum. Must be a Louisiana resident.

Award: Scholarship for use in freshman or sophomore years; renewable. *Number:* varies. *Amount:* $741–$1592.

Eligibility Requirements: Applicant must be high school student; planning to enroll or expecting to enroll full-time at a technical institution; resident of Louisiana and studying in Louisiana. Applicant must have 2.5 GPA or higher. Available to U.S. citizens.

Application Requirements: Application, test scores. *Deadline:* July 1.

Contact: Public Information
Louisiana Office of Student Financial Assistance
PO Box 91202
Baton Rouge, LA 70821-9202
Phone: 800-259-5626 Ext. 1012
Fax: 225-922-0790
E-mail: custserv@osfa.state.la.us

LYNDON BAINES JOHNSON FOUNDATION

LYNDON BAINES JOHNSON FOUNDATION GRANTS-IN-AID RESEARCH

A limited number of grants-in-aid of research are available for the periods of October 1 through March 31 and April 1 through September 30. October through March deadline is August 31. April through September deadline is February 28. Funds are to help defray cost while doing research at the LBJ Library. Contact the Archives division of the library prior to submitting proposal concerning material availability for your proposed topic. Candidates for assistance should have thoughtful and well-written proposals that state clearly and precisely how the holdings of the Lyndon Baines Johnson Library will contribute to historical research.

Award: Grant for use in freshman, sophomore, junior, senior, graduate, or postgraduate years; not renewable. *Number:* varies. *Amount:* $500–$2000.

Eligibility Requirements: Applicant must be enrolled or expecting to enroll at a two-year or four-year or technical institution or university and studying in Texas. Available to U.S. and Canadian citizens.

Application Requirements: Application, references, research proposal. *Deadline:* varies.

Contact: Assistant Director
Lyndon Baines Johnson Foundation
2313 Red River Street
Austin, TX 78705
Phone: 512-478-7829
Fax: 512-478-9104

MAINE BUREAU OF VETERANS SERVICES

http://www.state.me.us

VETERANS DEPENDENTS EDUCATIONAL BENEFITS-MAINE

• *See page 558*

MAINE COMMUNITY COLLEGE SYSTEM

http://www.mccs.me.edu

DIRIGO MACHINE TOOL SCHOLARSHIP

For students interested in a career in precision manufacturing. Scholarship covers one year tuition in exchange for a one year commitment to work for a sponsoring Maine Metal Products Association member company. Refer to Web site: http://www.mccs.me.edu/scholarships.html.

Award: Scholarship for use in freshman or sophomore years. *Number:* varies. *Amount:* varies.

Eligibility Requirements: Applicant must be enrolled or expecting to enroll at a two-year or technical institution; resident of Maine and studying in Maine.

Application Requirements: *Deadline:* varies.

Contact: Maine Community College Financial Aid Department

EARLY COLLEGE PROGRAM

For high school students who have not made plans for college but are academically capable of success in college. Recipients are selected by their

Maine Community College System (continued)

school principal or director. Refer to Web site: http://www.mccs.me.edu/scholarships.html. Students must be entering a Maine Community College.

Award: Scholarship for use in freshman year. *Number:* up to 200. *Amount:* up to $2000.

Eligibility Requirements: Applicant must be high school student; planning to enroll or expecting to enroll at a two-year institution; resident of Maine and studying in Maine.

Application Requirements: *Deadline:* varies.

Contact: Maine Community College Financial Aid Department.

GEORGE J. MITCHELL PEACE SCHOLARSHIP

An annual exchange and scholarship to Ireland for students from the Maine Community College System and the University of Maine System. Scholarship will provide opportunity for student to study at a university or institute of technology in Ireland. Refer to Web site for details: http://www.mccs.me.edu.

Award: Scholarship for use in freshman, sophomore, junior, or senior years. *Number:* varies. *Amount:* varies.

Eligibility Requirements: Applicant must be enrolled or expecting to enroll full-time at a two-year institution or university; resident of Maine and studying in Maine.

Application Requirements: *Deadline:* February 15.

Contact: Maine Community College or University Financial Aid Department.

MAINE COMMUNITY COLLEGE SCHOLARSHIP

Participating high schools and technical centers/regions identify students to apply for the scholarship during their junior year. Students must be both nominated by their school and accepted into a Maine community college program of study. Award is $500 per semester, $1000 per year for a one-year program and a maximum of $2000 for a two-year program, so long as student meets program requirements. For details see Web site: http://www.ccd.me.edu/scholarship.

Award: Scholarship for use in freshman or sophomore years; renewable. *Number:* varies. *Amount:* $500–$2000.

Eligibility Requirements: Applicant must be high school student; planning to enroll or expecting to enroll at a two-year or technical institution; resident of Maine and studying in Maine.

Application Requirements: *Deadline:* varies.

Contact: Dorry French
Maine Community College System
2 Fort Road
South Portland, ME 04106
Phone: 207-767-5210 Ext. 4117
E-mail: dfrench@ccd.me.edu

MAINE HOSPITALS ENGINEERS SOCIETY SCHOLARSHIP

Scholarship for Maine Community College student majoring in engineering or related areas. Refer to Web site for more details: http://www.mccs.me.edu/scholarships.html.

Award: Scholarship for use in freshman or sophomore years. *Number:* 1. *Amount:* up to $2000.

Eligibility Requirements: Applicant must be enrolled or expecting to enroll at a two-year institution; resident of Maine and studying in Maine.

Application Requirements: *Deadline:* varies.

Contact: Maine Community College Financial Aid Department

OSHER SCHOLARSHIP

For Maine residents who are not currently enrolled at any college or university and have accumulated no more than 24 college credits. Applicant must be accepted into an AA in liberal/general studies program. Eligible applicant will receive two core courses tuition free. See Web site for more details: http://www.mccs.me.edu/osher.html.

Award: Scholarship for use in freshman year. *Number:* varies. *Amount:* varies.

Eligibility Requirements: Applicant must be enrolled or expecting to enroll at a two-year institution; resident of Maine and studying in Maine.

Application Requirements: *Deadline:* varies.

Contact: Maine Community College Financial Aid Department

MAINE COMMUNITY FOUNDATION, INC. http://www.mainecf.org

MAINE COMMUNITY FOUNDATION SCHOLARSHIP PROGRAMS

Several scholarships are available for Maine residents attending secondary, postsecondary and graduate programs. Application deadlines vary. Complete list of scholarships available at http://www.mainecf.org/scholar.html.

Award: Scholarship for use in freshman, sophomore, junior, senior, or graduate years; not renewable. *Number:* 150–700. *Amount:* $500–$5000.

Eligibility Requirements: Applicant must be enrolled or expecting to enroll full or part-time at a two-year or four-year or technical institution or university and resident of Maine. Available to U.S. citizens.

Application Requirements: Application. *Deadline:* varies.

Contact: Amy Pollien, Program Administration
Maine Community Foundation, Inc.
245 Main Street
Ellsworth, ME 04605
Phone: 207-667-9735
Fax: 207-667-0447
E-mail: apollien@mainecf.org

MAINE STATE SOCIETY FOUNDATION OF WASHINGTON, D.C., INC. http://mainestatesociety.org

MAINE STATE SOCIETY FOUNDATION SCHOLARSHIP

Each scholarship will be awarded to full-time students enrolled in undergraduate courses at a four-year degree-granting, nonprofit institution in Maine. Must be Maine resident. All inquiries must be accompanied by a self-addressed stamped envelope. Applicant must be 25 or younger. Minimum 3.0 GPA.

Award: Scholarship for use in sophomore, junior, or senior years; not renewable. *Number:* 5–10. *Amount:* $1000–$2500.

Eligibility Requirements: Applicant must be age 25 or under; enrolled or expecting to enroll full-time at a four-year institution or university; resident of Maine and studying in Maine. Applicant must have 3.0 GPA or higher. Available to U.S. citizens.

Application Requirements: Application, autobiography, essay, self-addressed stamped envelope, transcript. *Deadline:* April 1.

Contact: Hugh L. Dwelley, President
Maine State Society Foundation of Washington, D.C., Inc.
3508 Wilson Street
Fairfax, VA 22030-2936

MARYLAND HIGHER EDUCATION COMMISSION http://www.mhec.state.md.us

DELEGATE SCHOLARSHIP PROGRAM-MARYLAND

Delegate scholarships help Maryland residents attending Maryland degree-granting institutions, certain career schools, or nursing diploma schools. May attend out-of-state institution if Maryland Higher Education Commission deems major to be unique and not offered at a Maryland institution. Free Application for Federal Student Aid may be required. Students interested in this program should apply by contacting their legislative district delegate.

Award: Scholarship for use in freshman, sophomore, junior, senior, or graduate years; not renewable. *Number:* up to 3500. *Amount:* $200–$7200.

Eligibility Requirements: Applicant must be enrolled or expecting to enroll full or part-time at a two-year or four-year or technical institution or university; resident of Maryland and studying in Maryland. Available to U.S. citizens.

Application Requirements: Application, financial need analysis. *Deadline:* Continuous.

Contact: Barbara Fantom, Office of Student Financial Assistance
Maryland Higher Education Commission
839 Bestgage Road, Suite 400
Annapolis, MD 21401-3013
Phone: 410-260-4547
Fax: 410-260-3200
E-mail: osfamail@mhec.state.md.us

DISTINGUISHED SCHOLAR AWARD-MARYLAND

Renewable award for Maryland students enrolled full-time at Maryland institutions. National Merit Scholar Finalists automatically offered award. Others may qualify for the award in satisfying criteria of a minimum 3.7 GPA or in combination with high test scores, or for Talent in Arts competition in categories of music, drama, dance, or visual arts. Must maintain annual 3.0 GPA in college for award to be renewed. Contact for further details.

Award: Scholarship for use in freshman, sophomore, junior, or senior years; renewable. *Number:* up to 2000. *Amount:* up to $3000.

Eligibility Requirements: Applicant must be high school student; planning to enroll or expecting to enroll full-time at a two-year or four-year institution or university; resident of Maryland and studying in Maryland. Available to U.S. citizens.

Application Requirements: Application, test scores, transcript. *Deadline:* varies.

Contact: Monica Tipton, Office of Student Financial Assistance
Maryland Higher Education Commission
839 Bestgate Road, Suite 400
Annapolis, MD 21401-3013
Phone: 410-260-4568
Fax: 410-260-3200
E-mail: ofsamail@mhec.state.md.us

EDUCATIONAL ASSISTANCE GRANTS-MARYLAND

Award for Maryland residents accepted or enrolled in a full-time undergraduate degree or certificate program at a Maryland institution or hospital nursing school. Must submit financial aid form by March 1. Must earn 2.0 GPA in college to maintain award.

Award: Grant for use in freshman, sophomore, junior, or senior years; renewable. *Number:* 11,000–20,000. *Amount:* $400–$2700.

Eligibility Requirements: Applicant must be enrolled or expecting to enroll full-time at a two-year or four-year institution or university; resident of Maryland and studying in Maryland. Available to U.S. citizens.

Application Requirements: Application, financial need analysis. *Deadline:* March 1.

Contact: Barbara Fantom, Office of Student Financial Assistance
Maryland Higher Education Commission
839 Bestgate Road, Suite 400
Annapolis, MD 21401-3013
Phone: 410-260-4547
Fax: 410-260-3200
E-mail: osfamail@mhec.state.md.us

EDWARD T. CONROY MEMORIAL SCHOLARSHIP PROGRAM

Scholarship for dependents of deceased or 100% disabled U.S. Armed Forces personnel; the son, daughter, or surviving spouse of a victim of the September 11, 2001, terrorist attacks who died as a result of the attacks on the World Trade Center in New York City, the attack on the Pentagon in Virginia, or the crash of United Airlines Flight 93 in Pennsylvania; a POW/MIA of the Vietnam Conflict or his/her son or daughter; the son, daughter or surviving spouse (who has not remarried), of a state or local public safety employee or volunteer who died in the line of duty; or a state or local public safety employee or volunteer who was 100% disabled in the line of duty. Must be Maryland resident at time of disability. Submit applicable VA certification. Must be at least 16 years of age and attend Maryland institution.

Award: Scholarship for use in freshman, sophomore, junior, senior, or graduate years; renewable. *Number:* up to 70. *Amount:* up to $7200.

Eligibility Requirements: Applicant must be age 16-24; enrolled or expecting to enroll full or part-time at a two-year or four-year institution or university; resident of Maryland and studying in Maryland. Available to U.S. citizens.

Application Requirements: Application, birth and death certificate, and disability papers. *Deadline:* July 30.

Contact: Margaret Crutchley, Office of Student Financial Assistance
Maryland Higher Education Commission
839 Bestgate Road, Suite 400
Annapolis, MD 21401-3013
Phone: 410-260-4545
Fax: 410-260-3203
E-mail: osfamail@mhec.state.md.us

GUARANTEED ACCESS GRANT-MARYLAND

Award for Maryland resident enrolling full-time in an undergraduate program at a Maryland institution. Must be under 22 at time of first award and begin college within one year of completing high school in Maryland with a minimum 2.5 GPA. Must have an annual family income less than 130% of the federal poverty level guideline.

Award: Grant for use in freshman, sophomore, junior, or senior years; renewable. *Number:* up to 1000. *Amount:* $400–$11,600.

Eligibility Requirements: Applicant must be enrolled or expecting to enroll full-time at a two-year or four-year institution or university; resident of Maryland and studying in Maryland. Applicant must have 2.5 GPA or higher. Available to U.S. citizens.

Application Requirements: Application, financial need analysis, transcript. *Deadline:* Continuous.

Contact: Theresa Lowe, Office of Student Financial Assistance
Maryland Higher Education Commission
839 Bestgate Road, Suite 400
Annapolis, MD 21401-3013
Phone: 410-260-4555
Fax: 410-260-3200
E-mail: osfamail@mhec.state.md.us

J.F. TOLBERT MEMORIAL STUDENT GRANT PROGRAM

Available to Maryland residents attending a private career school in Maryland with at least 18 clock hours per week.

Award: Grant for use in freshman or sophomore years; not renewable. *Number:* 1000. *Amount:* up to $400.

Eligibility Requirements: Applicant must be enrolled or expecting to enroll at a technical institution; resident of Maryland and studying in Maryland. Available to U.S. citizens.

Application Requirements: Application, financial need analysis. *Deadline:* Continuous.

Contact: Carla Rich, Office of Student Financial Assistance
Maryland Higher Education Commission
839 Bestgate Road, Suite 400
Annapolis, MD 21401-3013
Phone: 410-260-4513
Fax: 410-260-3200
E-mail: osfamail@mhec.state.md.us

PART-TIME GRANT PROGRAM-MARYLAND

Funds provided to Maryland colleges and universities. Eligible students must be enrolled on a part-time basis (6-11 credits) in an undergraduate degree program. Must demonstrate financial need and also be Maryland resident. Contact financial aid office at institution for more information.

Award: Grant for use in freshman, sophomore, junior, or senior years; renewable. *Number:* 1800–9000. *Amount:* $200–$1000.

Eligibility Requirements: Applicant must be enrolled or expecting to enroll part-time at a two-year or four-year institution or university; resident of Maryland and studying in Maryland. Available to U.S. citizens.

Maryland Higher Education Commission (continued)

Application Requirements: Application, financial need analysis. *Deadline:* March 1.

Contact: Maryland Higher Education Commission
839 Bestgate Road
Suite 400
Annapolis, MD 21401-3013

SENATORIAL SCHOLARSHIPS-MARYLAND

Renewable award for Maryland residents attending a Maryland degree-granting institution, nursing diploma school, or certain private career schools. May be used out-of-state only if Maryland Higher Education Commission deems major to be unique and not offered at Maryland institution.

Award: Scholarship for use in freshman, sophomore, junior, senior, or graduate years; renewable. *Number:* up to 7000. *Amount:* $200–$2000.

Eligibility Requirements: Applicant must be enrolled or expecting to enroll full or part-time at a two-year or four-year or technical institution or university; resident of Maryland and studying in Maryland. Available to U.S. citizens.

Application Requirements: Financial need analysis, test scores, application to Legislative District Senator. *Deadline:* March 1.

Contact: Barbara Fantom, Office of Student Financial Assistance
Maryland Higher Education Commission
839 Bestgate Road, Suite 400
Annapolis, MD 21401-3013
Phone: 410-260-4547
Fax: 410-260-3202
E-mail: osfamail@mhec.state.md.us

TUITION WAIVER FOR FOSTER CARE RECIPIENTS

Applicant must be a high school graduate or recipient of a GED under the age of 21. Applicant must either have resided in a foster care home in Maryland at time of high school graduation or GED reception, or until 14th birthday and had been adopted after 14th birthday. Applicant, if status approved, will be exempt from paying tuition and mandatory fees at a public college in Maryland.

Award: Scholarship for use in freshman, sophomore, junior, or senior years; renewable. *Number:* varies. *Amount:* varies.

Eligibility Requirements: Applicant must be age 20 or under; enrolled or expecting to enroll full or part-time at a two-year or four-year institution or university and studying in Maryland. Available to U.S. citizens.

Application Requirements: Application, financial need analysis. *Deadline:* March 1.

Contact: Inquire at financial aid office of your school.

MARYLAND POLICE CORPS http://www.policecorps.net

MARYLAND POLICE CORPS SCHOLARSHIP

Scholarships, plus $400 per week stipend, available to students pursuing a four-year degree from an accredited university, or may be reimbursed for educational expenses. Requirements include successful completion of police academy and four-year commitment to work in a selected police department. Details available on Web site: http://www.policecorps.net.

Award: Scholarship for use in junior or senior years. *Number:* 10. *Amount:* up to $23,000.

Eligibility Requirements: Applicant must be enrolled or expecting to enroll at a four-year institution or university and resident of Maryland. Available to U.S. citizens.

Application Requirements: Application, driver's license, essay, references, transcript. *Deadline:* Continuous.

Contact: Donald Healy, Director
Maryland Police Corps
5700 Hammonds Ferry Road
Linthicum, MD 21090
Phone: 888-972-6777
Fax: 410-859-8227

MASSACHUSETTS OFFICE OF STUDENT FINANCIAL ASSISTANCE http://www.osfa.mass.edu

CHRISTIAN A. HERTER MEMORIAL SCHOLARSHIP

Renewable award for Massachusetts residents who are in the 10th-11th grades and whose socio-economic backgrounds and environment may inhibit their ability to attain educational goals. Must exhibit severe personal or family-related difficulties, medical problems, or have overcome a personal obstacle. Provides up to 50% of the student's calculated need, as determined by Federal methodology, at the college of their choice within the continental U.S.

Award: Scholarship for use in freshman, sophomore, junior, or senior years; renewable. *Number:* 25. *Amount:* varies.

Eligibility Requirements: Applicant must be high school student; planning to enroll or expecting to enroll full-time at a two-year or four-year or technical institution or university and resident of Massachusetts. Applicant must have 2.5 GPA or higher. Available to U.S. citizens.

Application Requirements: Application, autobiography, financial need analysis, interview, references. *Deadline:* March 31.

Contact: Ken Smith
Massachusetts Office of Student Financial Assistance
454 Broadway, Suite 200
Revere, MA 02151
Phone: 617-727-9420
Fax: 617-727-0667
E-mail: osfa@osfa.mass.edu

HIGHER EDUCATION COORDINATING COUNCIL-TUITION WAIVER PROGRAM

• *See page 534*

MASSACHUSETTS ASSISTANCE FOR STUDENT SUCCESS PROGRAM

Provides need-based financial assistance to Massachusetts residents to attend undergraduate postsecondary institutions in Connecticut, Maine, Massachusetts, New Hampshire, Pennsylvania, Rhode Island, Vermont, and District of Columbia. High school seniors may apply. Timely filing of FAFSA required.

Award: Grant for use in freshman, sophomore, junior, or senior years; not renewable. *Number:* 25,000–30,000. *Amount:* $300–$2300.

Eligibility Requirements: Applicant must be enrolled or expecting to enroll full-time at a two-year or four-year or technical institution or university; resident of Massachusetts and studying in Connecticut, District of Columbia, Maine, Massachusetts, New Hampshire, Pennsylvania, Rhode Island, or Vermont. Available to U.S. citizens.

Application Requirements: Financial need analysis, FAFSA. *Deadline:* May 1.

Contact: Robert Brun, Director of Scholarships and Grants
Massachusetts Office of Student Financial Assistance
454 Broadway
Suite 200
Revere, MA 02151
Phone: 617-727-9420
Fax: 617-727-0667

MASSACHUSETTS CASH GRANT PROGRAM

A need-based grant to assist with mandatory fees and non-state supported tuition, this supplemental award is available to Massachusetts residents who are undergraduates at public two-year colleges, four-year colleges and universities in Massachusetts. Must file FAFSA before May 1. Contact college financial aid office for information.

Award: Grant for use in freshman, sophomore, junior, or senior years; not renewable. *Number:* varies. *Amount:* $150–$1900.

Eligibility Requirements: Applicant must be enrolled or expecting to enroll full-time at a two-year or four-year institution or university; resident of Massachusetts and studying in Massachusetts. Available to U.S. citizens.

Application Requirements: Financial need analysis, FAFSA. *Deadline:* Continuous.

Contact: College financial aid office

MASSACHUSETTS PART-TIME GRANT PROGRAM

Award for permanent Massachusetts resident for at least one year enrolled part-time in a state-approved postsecondary school. Recipient must not have first bachelor's degree. FAFSA must be filed before May 1. Contact college financial aid office for further information.

Award: Grant for use in freshman, sophomore, junior, or senior years; not renewable. *Number:* varies. *Amount:* $150–$1150.

Eligibility Requirements: Applicant must be enrolled or expecting to enroll part-time at a two-year or four-year or technical institution or university; resident of Massachusetts and studying in Massachusetts. Available to U.S. citizens.

Application Requirements: Financial need analysis, FAFSA. *Deadline:* May 1.

Contact: College financial aid office

MASSACHUSETTS PUBLIC SERVICE GRANT PROGRAM

• *See page 513*

PERFORMANCE BONUS GRANT PROGRAM

One-time award to residents of Massachusetts enrolled in a Massachusetts postsecondary institution. Minimum 3.0 GPA required. Timely filing of FAFSA required. Must be sophomore, junior or senior level undergraduate.

Award: Grant for use in sophomore, junior, or senior years; not renewable. *Number:* varies. *Amount:* $350–$500.

Eligibility Requirements: Applicant must be enrolled or expecting to enroll full-time at a two-year or four-year institution or university; resident of Massachusetts and studying in Massachusetts. Applicant must have 3.0 GPA or higher. Available to U.S. citizens.

Application Requirements: Financial need analysis, FAFSA. *Deadline:* May 1.

Contact: Scholarship Information
Massachusetts Office of Student Financial Assistance
454 Broadway, Suite 200
Revere, MA 02151
Phone: 617-727-9420
Fax: 617-727-0667

TUITION WAIVER (GENERAL)-MASSACHUSETTS

Need-based tuition waiver for full-time students. Must attend a Massachusetts public institution of higher education and be a permanent Massachusetts resident. File the Free Application for Federal Student Aid after January 1. Award is for undergraduate use. Contact school financial aid office for more information.

Award: Scholarship for use in freshman, sophomore, junior, or senior years; renewable. *Number:* varies. *Amount:* $175–$1300.

Eligibility Requirements: Applicant must be enrolled or expecting to enroll full-time at a two-year or four-year institution or university; resident of Massachusetts and studying in Massachusetts. Available to U.S. citizens.

Application Requirements: Application, financial need analysis, FAFSA. *Deadline:* May 1.

Contact: College financial aid office

MASSACHUSETTS STATE FIREMENS ASSOCIATION

HENRY BELKNAPP MEMORIAL SCHOLARSHIP

Scholarship available for students entering first year of post secondary school. Must have a relative who is Massachusetts firefighter and life member of Massachusetts State Fireman's Association. Must be a U.S. citizen and reside in Massachusetts. Application deadline is April 15.

Award: Scholarship for use in freshman year; not renewable. *Number:* 14. *Amount:* $1000–$2500.

Eligibility Requirements: Applicant must be enrolled or expecting to enroll full-time at a two-year or four-year or technical institution or university and resident of Massachusetts. Available to U.S. citizens.

Application Requirements: Application, autobiography, essay, resume, test scores, transcript. *Deadline:* April 15.

Contact: Paul Cronk, Jr., Secretary/Treasurer
Massachusetts State Firemens Association
PO Box 485
Dracut, MA 01862
Phone: 800-957-6936
Fax: 978-957-2600
E-mail: cronk.ps@verizon.net

MELLINGER EDUCATIONAL FOUNDATION

http://www.mellinger.org

MELLINGER SCHOLARSHIPS

Scholarships for undergraduates residing in western Illinois and eastern Iowa.

Award: Scholarship for use in freshman, sophomore, junior, or senior years; renewable. *Number:* 300–350. *Amount:* $300–$1200.

Eligibility Requirements: Applicant must be enrolled or expecting to enroll full or part-time at a two-year or four-year or technical institution or university and resident of Illinois or Iowa. Available to U.S. citizens.

Application Requirements: Application, financial need analysis, test scores, transcript. *Deadline:* May 1.

Contact: David Fleming, President
Mellinger Educational Foundation
1025 East Broadway, Box 770
Monmouth, IL 61462
Phone: 309-734-2419
Fax: 309-734-4435

MELLON NEW ENGLAND

CHARLES C. ELY EDUCATIONAL FUND

Award for men who are residents of Massachusetts. Academic performance, character, and financial need will be considered. Application deadline is April 15.

Award: Scholarship for use in freshman, sophomore, junior, or senior years; not renewable. *Number:* varies. *Amount:* $1000–$3000.

Eligibility Requirements: Applicant must be enrolled or expecting to enroll full-time at a two-year or four-year or technical institution or university; male and resident of Massachusetts. Available to U.S. citizens.

Application Requirements: Application, essay, transcript. *Deadline:* April 15.

Contact: Sandra Brown-McMullen, Vice President
Mellon New England
One Boston Place, 024-0084
Boston, MA 02108
Phone: 617-722-3891

HENRY FRANCIS BARROWS SCHOLARSHIP

• *See page 627*

MIAMI-DADE AND BROWARD COUNTY FORD AND LINCOLN-MERCURY DEALERS

http://www.stescholarships.org

SALUTE TO EDUCATION, INC.

Scholarships of $1,000 for college-bound public and private high school seniors in Miami-Dade and Broward counties. Minimum GPA of 3.0.

Award: Scholarship for use in freshman year; not renewable. *Number:* 200–240. *Amount:* $1000.

Eligibility Requirements: Applicant must be high school student; planning to enroll or expecting to enroll at a two-year or four-year institution or university and resident of Florida. Applicant must have 3.0 GPA or higher. Available to U.S. citizens.

Miami-Dade and Broward County Ford and Lincoln-Mercury Dealers (continued)

Application Requirements: Application, essay. *Deadline:* January 5.

Contact: Nicole Rodriguez, Program Coordinator
Miami-Dade and Broward County Ford and Lincoln-Mercury Dealers
2801 Ponce de Leon Boulevard, Suite 200
Coral Gables, FL 33134
Phone: 305-476-7709
Fax: 305-476-7710
E-mail: nrodriguez@stescholarships.org

MICHIGAN BUREAU OF STUDENT FINANCIAL ASSISTANCE http://www.michigan.gov/mistudentaid

MICHIGAN ADULT PART-TIME GRANT

Grant for part-time, needy, independent undergraduates at an approved, degree-granting Michigan college or university. Eligibility is limited to two years. Must be Michigan resident. Deadlines determined by college.

Award: Grant for use in freshman, sophomore, junior, or senior years; not renewable. *Number:* varies. *Amount:* up to $600.

Eligibility Requirements: Applicant must be enrolled or expecting to enroll part-time at a two-year or four-year institution or university; resident of Michigan and studying in Michigan. Available to U.S. citizens.

Application Requirements: Application, financial need analysis.

Contact: Program Director
Michigan Bureau of Student Financial Assistance
PO Box 30466
Lansing, MI 48909-7966

MICHIGAN COMPETITIVE SCHOLARSHIP

Awards limited to tuition. Must maintain a C average and meet the college's academic progress requirements. Must file Free Application for Federal Student Aid. Deadline: March 1. Must be Michigan resident. Renewable award of $1300 for undergraduate study at a Michigan institution.

Award: Scholarship for use in freshman, sophomore, junior, or senior years; renewable. *Number:* varies. *Amount:* $100–$1300.

Eligibility Requirements: Applicant must be enrolled or expecting to enroll at a two-year or four-year institution or university; resident of Michigan and studying in Michigan. Available to U.S. citizens.

Application Requirements: Application, financial need analysis, test scores, FAFSA. *Deadline:* March 1.

Contact: Scholarship and Grant Director
Michigan Bureau of Student Financial Assistance
PO Box 30466
Lansing, MI 48909

MICHIGAN EDUCATIONAL OPPORTUNITY GRANT

Need-based program for Michigan residents who are at least half-time undergraduates attending public Michigan colleges. Must maintain good academic standing. Deadline determined by college. Award of up to $1000.

Award: Grant for use in freshman, sophomore, junior, or senior years; not renewable. *Number:* varies. *Amount:* up to $1000.

Eligibility Requirements: Applicant must be enrolled or expecting to enroll full or part-time at a two-year or four-year institution or university; resident of Michigan and studying in Michigan. Available to U.S. citizens.

Application Requirements: Application, financial need analysis. *Deadline:* varies.

Contact: Program Director
Michigan Bureau of Student Financial Assistance
PO Box 30466
Lansing, MI 48909-7966

MICHIGAN MERIT AWARD

Scholarship for students scoring well on state's standardized assessment tests. Students will have four years from high school graduation to use the award.

Award: Scholarship for use in freshman year; not renewable. *Number:* varies. *Amount:* $1000–$2500.

Eligibility Requirements: Applicant must be high school student; planning to enroll or expecting to enroll full or part-time at a two-year or four-year or technical institution or university and resident of Michigan. Available to U.S. citizens.

Application Requirements: Test scores.

Contact: Program Director
Michigan Bureau of Student Financial Assistance
PO Box 30466
Lansing, MI 48909-7966

MICHIGAN TUITION GRANTS

Need-based program. Students must attend a Michigan private, nonprofit, degree-granting college. Must file the Free Application for Federal Student Aid and meet the college's academic progress requirements. Deadline: March 1. Must be Michigan resident. Renewable award of $2000.

Award: Grant for use in freshman, sophomore, junior, or senior years; renewable. *Number:* varies. *Amount:* $100–$2750.

Eligibility Requirements: Applicant must be enrolled or expecting to enroll at a two-year or four-year institution or university; resident of Michigan and studying in Michigan. Available to U.S. citizens.

Application Requirements: Application, financial need analysis, FAFSA. *Deadline:* March 1.

Contact: Scholarship and Grant Director
Michigan Bureau of Student Financial Assistance
PO Box 30466
Lansing, MI 48909-7966

TUITION INCENTIVE PROGRAM (TIP)-MICHIGAN

Award for Michigan residents who receive or have received Medicaid for required period of time through the Family Independence Agency. Scholarship provides two years tuition towards an associate's degree at a Michigan college or university. Apply before graduating from high school or earning General Education Development diploma.

Award: Scholarship for use in freshman or sophomore years; renewable. *Number:* varies.

Eligibility Requirements: Applicant must be high school student; planning to enroll or expecting to enroll full or part-time at a two-year or four-year institution or university; resident of Michigan and studying in Michigan. Available to U.S. citizens.

Application Requirements: Application, financial need analysis. *Deadline:* Continuous.

Contact: Program Director
Michigan Bureau of Student Financial Assistance
PO Box 30466
Lansing, MI 48909

MICHIGAN OUTDOOR WRITERS ASSOCIATION http://www.mioutdoorwriters.org

MARC WESLEY SCHOLARSHIP AWARD

One-time award for Michigan residents attending a Michigan college or university. Must be interested in and competent at communicating outdoor experiences. Must be a junior or senior in undergraduate school, or a graduate or post-graduate student.

Award: Scholarship for use in junior, senior, graduate, or postgraduate years; not renewable. *Number:* 1. *Amount:* $1000.

Eligibility Requirements: Applicant must be enrolled or expecting to enroll full-time at a four-year institution or university; resident of Michigan; studying in Michigan and must have an interest in writing.

Application Requirements: Application, essay, portfolio, resume, references. *Deadline:* January 30.

Contact: Bob Holzhei, Chairman
Michigan Outdoor Writers Association
3601 Avery
St. Johns, MI 48879
Phone: 989-224-3645
Fax: 989-224-3645

MICHIGAN VETERANS TRUST FUND http://www.michigan.gov/dmva

MICHIGAN VETERANS TRUST FUND TUITION GRANT PROGRAM

• *See page 558*

MIDWESTERN HIGHER EDUCATION COMPACT http://www.mhec.org

MIDWEST STUDENT EXCHANGE PROGRAM (MSEP)

MSEP is a reduced tuition exchange program that is open to students in Kansas, Michigan, Minnesota, Missouri, Nebraska, and North Dakota. To be eligible, student must be a legal resident of one of these 6 states and going to an institution in one of the other 5 states. Student must be considered an out-of-state student attending a participating college or university. Students are to apply directly to the college or university. There is no universal application form; each institution varies. See MSEP Web site (http://www.mhec.org) for complete details, including a list of participating colleges and universities.

Award: Grant for use in freshman, sophomore, junior, senior, or graduate years; renewable. *Number:* varies. *Amount:* varies.

Eligibility Requirements: Applicant must be enrolled or expecting to enroll full or part-time at a two-year or four-year or technical institution or university; resident of Kansas, Michigan, Minnesota, Missouri, Nebraska, or North Dakota and studying in Kansas, Michigan, Minnesota, Missouri, Nebraska, or North Dakota. Available to U.S. citizens.

Application Requirements: Application. *Deadline:* varies.

Contact: Ms. Jennifer Dahlquist, Program Officer
Midwestern Higher Education Compact
1300 South Second Street, Suite 130
Minneapolis, MN 55454-1079
Phone: 612-626-1602
Fax: 612-626-8290
E-mail: jenniferd@mhec.org

MINNESOTA AFL-CIO http://www.mnaflcio.org

BILL PETERSON SCHOLARSHIP

• *See page 468*

MARTIN DUFFY ADULT LEARNER SCHOLARSHIP AWARD

• *See page 469*

MINNESOTA AFL-CIO SCHOLARSHIPS

• *See page 469*

MINNESOTA DEPARTMENT OF VETERANS' AFFAIRS

MINNESOTA EDUCATIONAL ASSISTANCE FOR WAR ORPHANS

• *See page 559*

MINNESOTA VA EDUCATIONAL ASSISTANCE FOR VETERANS

• *See page 559*

MINNESOTA HIGHER EDUCATION SERVICES OFFICE http://www.mheso.state.mn.us

MINNESOTA ACADEMIC EXCELLENCE SCHOLARSHIP

Students must demonstrate outstanding ability, achievement, and potential in one of the following subjects: English or creative writing, fine arts, foreign language, math, science, or social science. Implementation depends on the availability of funds, which are to come from the sale of special collegiate license plates. Apply directly to college. Must be a Minnesota resident and study in Minnesota.

Award: Scholarship for use in freshman, sophomore, junior, or senior years; renewable. *Number:* varies. *Amount:* varies.

Eligibility Requirements: Applicant must be enrolled or expecting to enroll full-time at a four-year institution or university; resident of Minnesota and studying in Minnesota. Available to U.S. citizens.

Application Requirements: Application, transcript. *Deadline:* varies.

Contact: Minnesota Higher Education Services Office
1450 Energy Park Drive, Suite 350
St. Paul, MN 55108-5227
Phone: 651-642-0567 Ext. 1

MINNESOTA RECIPROCAL AGREEMENT

Renewable tuition waiver for Minnesota residents. Waives all or part of non-resident tuition surcharge at public institutions in Iowa, Kansas, Michigan, Missouri, Nebraska, North Dakota, South Dakota, and Wisconsin. Deadline is last day of academic term.

Award: Scholarship for use in freshman, sophomore, junior, senior, graduate, or postgraduate years; renewable. *Number:* varies. *Amount:* varies.

Eligibility Requirements: Applicant must be enrolled or expecting to enroll full or part-time at a two-year or four-year or technical institution or university; resident of Minnesota and studying in Iowa, Kansas, Michigan, Missouri, Nebraska, North Dakota, South Dakota, or Wisconsin. Available to U.S. citizens.

Application Requirements: Application. *Deadline:* varies.

Contact: Minnesota Higher Education Services Office
1450 Energy Park Drive, Suite 350
St. Paul, MN 55108-5227
Phone: 651-642-0567 Ext. 1

MINNESOTA SAFETY OFFICERS' SURVIVOR PROGRAM

• *See page 513*

MINNESOTA STATE GRANT PROGRAM

Need-based grant program available for Minnesota residents attending Minnesota colleges. Student covers 46% of cost with remainder covered by Pell Grant, parent contribution and state grant. Students apply with FAFSA and college administers the program on campus.

Award: Grant for use in freshman, sophomore, junior, or senior years; not renewable. *Number:* 71,000–75,000. *Amount:* $100–$7662.

Eligibility Requirements: Applicant must be age 17; enrolled or expecting to enroll full or part-time at a two-year or four-year or technical institution or university; resident of Minnesota and studying in Minnesota. Available to U.S. citizens.

Application Requirements: Application, financial need analysis. *Deadline:* varies.

Contact: Minnesota Higher Education Services Office
1450 Energy Park Drive, Suite 350
St. Paul, MN 55108
Phone: 651-642-0567 Ext. 1

MINNESOTA STATE VETERANS' DEPENDENTS ASSISTANCE PROGRAM

• *See page 560*

POSTSECONDARY CHILD CARE GRANT PROGRAM-MINNESOTA

One-time grant available for students not receiving MFIP. Based on financial need. Cannot exceed actual child care costs or maximum award chart (based on income). Must be Minnesota resident. For use at Minnesota two- or four-year school, including public technical colleges.

Award: Grant for use in freshman, sophomore, junior, or senior years; not renewable. *Number:* varies. *Amount:* $100–$2200.

Eligibility Requirements: Applicant must be enrolled or expecting to enroll full or part-time at a two-year or four-year or technical institution or university; resident of Minnesota and studying in Minnesota. Available to U.S. citizens.

Application Requirements: Application, financial need analysis. *Deadline:* Continuous.

Contact: Minnesota Higher Education Services Office
1450 Energy Park Drive, Suite 350
St. Paul, MN 55108-5227
Phone: 651-642-0567 Ext. 1

MINNESOTA INDIAN SCHOLARSHIP OFFICE http://www.mheso.state.mn.us

MINNESOTA INDIAN SCHOLARSHIP PROGRAM

• *See page 593*

MISS OUTSTANDING TEENAGER http://www.missoutstandingteen.com

MISS OUTSTANDING TEENAGER AND LEADERSHIP TRAINING PROGRAM

Award program open to single girls age 13-18. Must be a resident of Montana or Hawaii. Minimum 3.25 GPA required. Judging based on teen image, scholastics, citizenship, personal projection, and essay. Application deadline is September 1 for Montana and October 1 for Hawaii. Visit Web site for more details.

Award: Scholarship for use in freshman, sophomore, junior, or senior years; renewable. *Number:* 8–12. *Amount:* $1000–$5000.

Eligibility Requirements: Applicant must be age 13-18; enrolled or expecting to enroll full or part-time at a two-year or four-year or technical institution or university; single female; resident of Hawaii or Montana and studying in Hawaii or Montana. Available to U.S. citizens.

Application Requirements: Application, applicant must enter a contest, essay, transcript. *Deadline:* varies.

Contact: Mark M. Budak, National Director/Founder
Miss Outstanding Teenager
Box 4388
Helena, MT 59604
Phone: 406-442-7035
Fax: 406-443-7322
E-mail: teenscholar@missoutstandingteen.com

MISSISSIPPI STATE STUDENT FINANCIAL AID http://www.mississippiuniversities.com

HIGHER EDUCATION LEGISLATIVE PLAN (HELP)

Eligible applicant must be resident of Mississippi and be freshmen and/or sophomore student who graduated from high school within the immediate past two years. Must demonstrate need as determined by the results of the Free Application for Federal Student Aid, documenting an average family adjusted gross income of $36,500 or less over the prior two years. Must be enrolled full-time at a Mississippi college or university, have a cumulative grade point average of 2.5 and have scored 20 on the ACT.

Award: Scholarship for use in freshman or sophomore years; renewable. *Number:* varies.

Eligibility Requirements: Applicant must be enrolled or expecting to enroll full-time at a four-year institution or university; resident of Mississippi and studying in Mississippi. Applicant must have 2.5 GPA or higher. Available to U.S. citizens.

Application Requirements: Application, financial need analysis, test scores, transcript, FAFSA. *Deadline:* March 31.

Contact: Mississippi Student Financial Aid
Mississippi State Student Financial Aid
3825 Ridgewood Road
Jackson, MS 39211-6453
Phone: 800-327-2980
E-mail: sfa@ihl.state.ms.us

MISSISSIPPI LAW ENFORCEMENT OFFICERS AND FIREMEN SCHOLARSHIP PROGRAM

• *See page 514*

MISSISSIPPI EMINENT SCHOLARS GRANT

Award for high-school seniors who are residents of Mississippi. Applicants must achieve a grade point average of 3.5 after a minimum of seven semesters in high school and must have scored 29 on the ACT. Must enroll full-time at an eligible Mississippi college or university.

Award: Grant for use in freshman, sophomore, junior, or senior years; renewable. *Number:* varies. *Amount:* up to $2500.

Eligibility Requirements: Applicant must be high school student; planning to enroll or expecting to enroll full-time at a four-year institution or university; resident of Mississippi and studying in Mississippi. Applicant must have 3.5 GPA or higher. Available to U.S. citizens.

Application Requirements: Application, test scores, transcript. *Deadline:* September 15.

Contact: Mississippi Student Financial Aid
Mississippi State Student Financial Aid
3825 Ridgewood Road
Jackson, MS 39211-6453
Phone: 800-327-2980
E-mail: sfa@ihl.state.ms.us

MISSISSIPPI LEVERAGING EDUCATIONAL ASSISTANCE PARTNERSHIP (LEAP)

Award for Mississippi residents enrolled for full-time study at a Mississippi college or university. Based on financial need. Deadline varies with each institution. Contact college financial aid office.

Award: Grant for use in freshman, sophomore, junior, or senior years; not renewable. *Number:* varies. *Amount:* $100–$1500.

Eligibility Requirements: Applicant must be enrolled or expecting to enroll full-time at a two-year or four-year institution or university; resident of Mississippi and studying in Mississippi. Available to U.S. citizens.

Application Requirements: Application, financial need analysis, FAFSA. *Deadline:* Continuous.

Contact: Student Financial Aid Office

MISSISSIPPI RESIDENT TUITION ASSISTANCE GRANT

Must be a resident of Mississippi enrolled full-time at an eligible Mississippi college or university. Must maintain a minimum 2.5 GPA each semester. MTAG awards may be up to $500 per academic year for freshmen and sophomores and $1,000 per academic year for juniors and seniors. Funds will be made available to eligible participants for eight (8) semesters or the normal time required to complete the degree program, whichever comes first. Refer to Web site for application information http://www.mississippiuniversities.com

Award: Grant for use in freshman, sophomore, junior, or senior years; renewable. *Amount:* $500–$1000.

Eligibility Requirements: Applicant must be enrolled or expecting to enroll full-time at a two-year or four-year institution or university; resident of Mississippi and studying in Mississippi. Applicant must have 2.5 GPA or higher. Available to U.S. citizens.

Application Requirements: Application, test scores, transcript. *Deadline:* September 15.

Contact: Mississippi Student Financial Aid
Mississippi State Student Financial Aid
3825 Ridgewood Road
Jackson, MS 39211-6453
Phone: 800-327-2980
E-mail: sfa@ihl.state.ms.us

NISSAN SCHOLARSHIP

Renewable award for Mississippi residents attending a Mississippi institution. The scholarship will pay full tuition and a book allowance. Minimum GPA of 2.0 as well as an ACT composite of at least 20 or combined SAT scores of 940 or better. Must demonstrate financial need and leadership abilities. Application deadline is March 1.

Award: Scholarship for use in freshman, sophomore, junior, or senior years; renewable. *Number:* varies.

Eligibility Requirements: Applicant must be high school student; planning to enroll or expecting to enroll at a two-year or four-year institution or university; resident of Mississippi and studying in Mississippi.

Application Requirements: Application, essay, financial need analysis, references, test scores, transcript. *Deadline:* March 1.

Contact: Mississippi Student Financial Aid
Mississippi State Student Financial Aid
3825 Ridgewood Road
Jackson, MS 39211-6453
Phone: 800-327-2980
E-mail: sfa@ihl.state.ms.us

MISSOURI DEPARTMENT OF ELEMENTARY AND SECONDARY EDUCATION http://www.dese.state.mo.us

ROBERT C. BYRD HONORS SCHOLARSHIP

Award for Missouri high school seniors who are residents of Missouri. The amount of the award per student each year depends on the amount the state is allotted by the U.S. Department of Education. The highest amount of award per student is $1500. Students must rank in top 10% of high school class and score in top 10% of ACT test.

Award: Scholarship for use in freshman year; renewable. *Number:* 100–150. *Amount:* $1100–$1500.

Eligibility Requirements: Applicant must be high school student; planning to enroll or expecting to enroll full-time at a two-year or four-year or technical institution or university and resident of Missouri. Applicant must have 3.5 GPA or higher. Available to U.S. and non-Canadian citizens.

Application Requirements: Application, test scores, transcript, 7th semester transcripts. *Deadline:* April 15.

Contact: Laura Harrison, Administrative Assistant II
Missouri Department of Elementary and Secondary Education
PO Box 480
Jefferson City, MO 65102-0480
Phone: 573-751-1668
Fax: 573-526-3580
E-mail: laura.harrison@mo.dese.gov

MISSOURI DEPARTMENT OF HIGHER EDUCATION http://www.dhe.mo.gov

CHARLES GALLAGHER STUDENT ASSISTANCE PROGRAM

Available to Missouri residents attending Missouri colleges or universities full-time. Must be undergraduates with financial need. May reapply for up to a maximum of ten semesters. Free Application for Federal Student Aid (FAFSA) or a renewal must be received by the federal processor by April 1 to be considered.

Award: Grant for use in freshman, sophomore, junior, or senior years; not renewable. *Number:* varies. *Amount:* $100–$1500.

Eligibility Requirements: Applicant must be enrolled or expecting to enroll full-time at a two-year or four-year or technical institution or university; resident of Missouri and studying in Missouri. Available to U.S. citizens.

Application Requirements: Financial need analysis. *Deadline:* April 1.

Contact: MDHE Information Center
Missouri Department of Higher Education
3515 Amazonas Drive
Jefferson City, MO 65109
Phone: 800-473-6757 Ext. 1
Fax: 573-751-6635
E-mail: icweb@dhe.mo.gov

MARGUERITE ROSS BARNETT MEMORIAL SCHOLARSHIP

Applicant must be employed (at least 20 hours per week) and attending school part-time. Must be Missouri resident and enrolled at a participating Missouri postsecondary school. Awards not available during summer term. Minimum age is 18.

Award: Scholarship for use in freshman, sophomore, junior, or senior years; not renewable. *Number:* varies. *Amount:* $900–$1700.

Eligibility Requirements: Applicant must be age 18; enrolled or expecting to enroll part-time at a two-year or four-year institution or university; resident of Missouri and studying in Missouri. Available to U.S. citizens.

Application Requirements: Application, financial need analysis. *Deadline:* April 1.

Contact: MDHE Information Center
Missouri Department of Higher Education
3515 Amazonas Drive
Jefferson City, MO 65109
Phone: 800-473-6757 Ext. 1
Fax: 573-751-6635
E-mail: icweb@dhe.mo.gov

MISSOURI COLLEGE GUARANTEE PROGRAM

Available to Missouri residents attending Missouri colleges full-time. Minimum 2.5 GPA required. Must have participated in high school extracurricular activities.

Award: Scholarship for use in freshman, sophomore, junior, or senior years; not renewable. *Number:* varies. *Amount:* $100–$4900.

Eligibility Requirements: Applicant must be enrolled or expecting to enroll full-time at a two-year or four-year institution or university; resident of Missouri and studying in Missouri. Applicant must have 2.5 GPA or higher. Available to U.S. citizens.

Application Requirements: Financial need analysis, test scores. *Deadline:* April 1.

Contact: MDHE Information Center
Missouri Department of Higher Education
3515 Amazonas Drive
Jefferson City, MO 65109
Phone: 800-473-6757 Ext. 1
Fax: 573-751-6635
E-mail: icweb@dhe.mo.gov

MISSOURI HIGHER EDUCATION ACADEMIC SCHOLARSHIP (BRIGHT FLIGHT)

Awards of $2000 for Missouri high school seniors. Must be in top 3% of Missouri SAT or ACT scorers. Must attend Missouri institution as full-time undergraduate. May reapply for up to ten semesters. Must be Missouri resident and U.S. citizen.

Award: Scholarship for use in freshman, sophomore, junior, or senior years; not renewable. *Number:* varies. *Amount:* $2000.

Eligibility Requirements: Applicant must be high school student; planning to enroll or expecting to enroll full-time at a two-year or four-year or technical institution or university; resident of Missouri and studying in Missouri. Available to U.S. citizens.

Application Requirements: Test scores. *Deadline:* July 31.

Contact: MDHE Information Center
Missouri Department of Higher Education
3515 Amazonas Drive
Jefferson City, MO 65109
Phone: 800-473-6757 Ext. 1
Fax: 573-751-6635
E-mail: icweb@dhe.mo.gov

MITCHELL INSTITUTE http://www.mitchellinstitute.org

SENATOR GEORGE J. MITCHELL SCHOLARSHIP RESEARCH INSTITUTE SCHOLARSHIPS

The Mitchell Institute awards 130 $4,000 scholarships ($1,000 per year for four years) each year to Maine students entering colleges. One Mitchell Scholar is chosen from every public high school in the state. A limited number of scholarships are available to Maine seniors going out of state.

Award: Scholarship for use in freshman, sophomore, junior, or senior years; renewable. *Number:* up to 130. *Amount:* up to $4000.

Eligibility Requirements: Applicant must be high school student; planning to enroll or expecting to enroll full or part-time at a two-year or four-year or technical institution or university and resident of Maine. Available to U.S. citizens.

Mitchell Institute (continued)

Application Requirements: Application, essay, financial need analysis, photo, references, transcript. *Deadline:* April 1.

Contact: Ms. Patricia Higgins, Director of Scholarship Programs
Mitchell Institute
22 Monument Square, Suite 200
Portland, ME 04101
Phone: 207-773-7700
Fax: 207-773-1133
E-mail: phiggins@mitchellinstitute.org

MLGPA FOUNDATION http://mlgpa.org

JOEL ABROMSON MEMORIAL FOUNDATION

One-time award, for full-time postsecondary study, available to winner of essay contest. Open to Maine residents only. Contact for essay topic and complete information. SASE. Deadline is April 15.

Award: Scholarship for use in freshman year; not renewable. *Number:* up to 2. *Amount:* $500–$750.

Eligibility Requirements: Applicant must be high school student; planning to enroll or expecting to enroll full-time at a two-year or four-year or technical institution or university and resident of Maine. Available to U.S. citizens.

Application Requirements: Application, applicant must enter a contest, essay, references, self-addressed stamped envelope, copy of acceptance letter to institution of higher learning. *Deadline:* April 15.

Contact: Betsy Smith, Scholarship Coordinator
MLGPA Foundation
PO Box 1951
Portland, ME 04104
Phone: 207-761-3732
Fax: 207-761-8484
E-mail: mlgpa@mlgpa.org

MONTANA GUARANTEED STUDENT LOAN PROGRAM, OFFICE OF COMMISSIONER OF HIGHER EDUCATION http://www.mgslp.state.mt.us

INDIAN STUDENT FEE WAIVER

• *See page 593*

MONTANA HIGHER EDUCATION OPPORTUNITY GRANT

This grant is awarded based on need to undergraduate students attending either part-time or full-time who are residents of Montana and attending participating Montana schools. Awards are limited to the most needy students. A specific major or program of study is not required. This grant does not need to be repaid, and students may apply each year. Apply by filing a Free Application for Federal Student Aid by March 1 and contacting the financial aid office at the admitting college.

Award: Grant for use in freshman, sophomore, junior, or senior years; not renewable. *Number:* up to 800. *Amount:* $400–$600.

Eligibility Requirements: Applicant must be enrolled or expecting to enroll full or part-time at a two-year or four-year institution or university; resident of Montana and studying in Montana. Available to U.S. citizens.

Application Requirements: Financial need analysis, FAFSA. *Deadline:* March 1.

Contact: Sally Speer, Grants and Scholarship Coordinator
Montana Guaranteed Student Loan Program, Office of Commissioner of Higher Education
2500 Broadway
PO Box 203101
Helena, MT 59620-3101
Phone: 406-444-0638
Fax: 406-444-1869
E-mail: sspeer@mgslp.state.mt.us

MONTANA TUITION ASSISTANCE PROGRAM-BAKER GRANT

Need-based grant for Montana residents attending participating Montana schools who have earned at least $2,575 during the previous calendar year. Must be enrolled full time. Grant does not need to be repaid. Award covers the first undergraduate degree or certificate. Apply by filing a Free Application for Federal Student Aid by March 1 and contacting the financial aid office at the admitting college.

Award: Grant for use in freshman, sophomore, junior, or senior years; not renewable. *Number:* varies. *Amount:* $100–$1000.

Eligibility Requirements: Applicant must be enrolled or expecting to enroll full-time at a two-year or four-year institution or university; resident of Montana and studying in Montana. Available to U.S. citizens.

Application Requirements: Financial need analysis, FAFSA. *Deadline:* March 1.

Contact: Sally Speer, Grants and Scholarship Coordinator
Montana Guaranteed Student Loan Program, Office of Commissioner of Higher Education
2500 Broadway
PO Box 203101
Helena, MT 59620-3101
Phone: 406-444-0638
Fax: 406-444-1869
E-mail: sspeer@mgslp.state.mt.us

MONTANA UNIVERSITY SYSTEM HONOR SCHOLARSHIP

Scholarship provides a four-year renewable fee waiver of tuition and registration and is awarded to graduating high school seniors from accredited high schools in Montana. 300-400 scholarships are awarded each year averaging $2,000-$3,000 per recipient. The value of the award varies, depending on the tuition and registration fee at each participating Montana university or college. Must have a minimum 3.5 GPA, meet all college preparatory requirements, and be enrolled in an accredited high school for at least three years prior to graduation. Awarded to highest-ranking student in class attending a participating school. Contact high school counselor to apply. Deadline: January 31.

Award: Scholarship for use in freshman, sophomore, junior, or senior years; renewable. *Number:* 300–400. *Amount:* $2000–$3000.

Eligibility Requirements: Applicant must be high school student; planning to enroll or expecting to enroll full or part-time at a two-year or four-year institution or university; resident of Montana and studying in Montana. Applicant must have 3.5 GPA or higher. Available to U.S. citizens.

Application Requirements: Application, transcript. *Deadline:* January 31.

Contact: High School Counselor

MONTANA STATE OFFICE OF PUBLIC INSTRUCTION http://www.opi.state.mt.us

ROBERT C. BYRD HONORS SCHOLARSHIP PROGRAM

Aim of this program is "to promote student excellence and achievement and to recognize exceptionally able students who show promise of continued excellence." The scholarship is available to graduating seniors and graduates of GED programs who will be entering college as freshmen. Minimum 3.6 GPA required. Award restricted to Montana residents. Deadline is March 1.

Award: Scholarship for use in freshman, sophomore, junior, or senior years; renewable. *Number:* 22–23. *Amount:* $1500.

Eligibility Requirements: Applicant must be high school student; planning to enroll or expecting to enroll full or part-time at a two-year or four-year or technical institution or university and resident of Montana. Available to U.S. citizens.

Application Requirements: Application, essay, test scores, transcript. *Deadline:* March 1.

Contact: Judy Birch, Program Director
Montana State Office of Public Instruction
PO Box 202501
Helena, MT 59620-2501
Phone: 406-444-5663
Fax: 406-444-1373
E-mail: jbirch@state.mt.us

UNITED STATES SENATE YOUTH PROGRAM-THE WILLIAM RANDOLPH HEARST FOUNDATION

Two high school juniors or seniors from Montana have a weeklong orientation in Washington, D.C. on the operation of the United States Senate and other components of the federal government. Potential awardees compete for the scholarship by taking a 50-point test, then the top ten applicants answer 5-7 questions in a video presentation. Scholarship money is given directly to school each student attends. Must be currently serving in a high school government office. See Web site for specific details: http://www.opi.state.mt.us

Award: Scholarship for use in freshman year; not renewable. *Number:* 2. *Amount:* $5000.

Eligibility Requirements: Applicant must be high school student; planning to enroll or expecting to enroll at a four-year institution or university and resident of Montana. Available to U.S. citizens.

Application Requirements: Application, interview, test scores, video presentation. *Deadline:* October 12.

Contact: Judy Birch, Program Director
Montana State Office of Public Instruction
PO Box 202501
Helena, MT 59620-2501
Phone: 406-444-5663
Fax: 406-444-1373
E-mail: jbirch@state.mt.us

MOUNT VERNON URBAN RENEWAL AGENCY http://www.ci.mount-vernon.ny.us/

THOMAS E. SHARPE MEMORIAL SCHOLARSHIP

Award offered only to residents of the city of Mount Vernon of low and moderate income for the purpose of pursuing higher education at a vocational/technical school or college. Students can receive from $300 to $1200 per academic year.

Award: Grant for use in freshman, sophomore, junior, or senior years; renewable. *Number:* 150. *Amount:* $350–$1000.

Eligibility Requirements: Applicant must be enrolled or expecting to enroll full-time at a two-year or four-year or technical institution or university and resident of New York. Applicant must have 2.5 GPA or higher. Available to U.S. citizens.

Application Requirements: Application, driver's license, essay, financial need analysis, transcript. *Deadline:* varies.

Contact: Mary E. Fleming, Director, Scholarship Programs
Mount Vernon Urban Renewal Agency
City Hall, Roosevelt Square, Department of Planning
Mount Vernon, NY 10550
Phone: 914-699-7230 Ext. 110
Fax: 914-699-1435
E-mail: mfleming@ci.mount-vernon.ny.us

NASA FLORIDA SPACE GRANT CONSORTIUM http://fsgc.engr.ucf.edu

FLORIDA SPACE RESEARCH AND EDUCATION GRANT PROGRAM

One-time award for aerospace and technology research. Grant is for research in Florida only. Submit research proposal with budget. Application deadline is March 1. Applicants must be from a university, college, or industry in Florida.

Award: Grant for use in freshman, sophomore, junior, senior, graduate, or postgraduate years; not renewable. *Number:* 9–12. *Amount:* $10,000–$30,000.

Eligibility Requirements: Applicant must be enrolled or expecting to enroll full or part-time at a two-year or four-year or technical institution or university and studying in Florida. Available to U.S. citizens.

Application Requirements: Proposal with budget. *Deadline:* March 1.

Contact: Dr. Jaydeep Mukherjee, Administrator
NASA Florida Space Grant Consortium
Mail Stop: FSGC
Kennedy Space Center, FL 32899
Phone: 321-452-4301
Fax: 321-449-0739
E-mail: jmukherj@mail.ucf.edu

NASA RHODE ISLAND SPACE GRANT CONSORTIUM http://www.spacegrant.brown.edu/RI_Space_Grant/

NASA RHODE ISLAND SPACE GRANT CONSORTIUM OUTREACH SCHOLARSHIP FOR UNDERGRADUATE STUDENTS

Scholarship for undergraduate students attending a Rhode Island Space Grant Consortium participating institution studying in any space-related field of science, math, engineering, or other field with applications in space study. Recipients are expected to devote a maximum of 8 hours per week to outreach activities in science education for K-12 children and teachers. See Web site for additional information: http://www.spacegrant.brown.edu.

Award: Scholarship for use in sophomore, junior, or senior years; not renewable. *Number:* up to 2. *Amount:* up to $4000.

Eligibility Requirements: Applicant must be enrolled or expecting to enroll full-time at a four-year institution or university and studying in Rhode Island. Applicant must have 3.0 GPA or higher. Available to U.S. citizens.

Application Requirements: Application, essay, resume, references, transcript. *Deadline:* March 1.

Contact: Peter Schultz, Program Director
NASA Rhode Island Space Grant Consortium
Brown University, Box 1846
Providence, RI 02912
Phone: 401-863-2417
Fax: 401-863-1242
E-mail: peter_schultz@brown.edu

NASA RHODE ISLAND SPACE GRANT CONSORTIUM UNDERGRADUATE SCHOLARSHIP

Scholarship for undergraduate students for study and/or outreach related to NASA and Space Sciences, Engineering and/or technology. Must attend a Rhode Island Space Grant Consortium participating school. Recipients are expected to devote a maximum of four hours per week in science education for K-12 children and teachers. See Web site for additional information: http://www.spacegrant.brown.edu.

Award: Scholarship for use in sophomore, junior, or senior years; not renewable. *Number:* up to 2. *Amount:* up to $4000.

Eligibility Requirements: Applicant must be enrolled or expecting to enroll at a four-year institution or university and studying in Rhode Island. Applicant must have 3.0 GPA or higher. Available to U.S. citizens.

Application Requirements: Application, essay, resume, references, transcript. *Deadline:* March 1.

Contact: Peter Schultz, Program Director
NASA Rhode Island Space Grant Consortium
Brown University, Box 1846
Providence, RI 02912
Phone: 401-863-2417
Fax: 401-863-1242
E-mail: peter_schultz@brown.edu

NASA RISGC SCIENCE EN ESPA±OL SCHOLARSHIP FOR UNDERGRADUATE STUDENTS

Award for undergraduate students at a Rhode Island Space Grant Consortium participating school who is studying in any space-related field of science, math, engineering, or other field with applications in space study. Recipients are expected to devote a maximum of 8 hours per week in outreach activities, supporting ESL teachers with science instruction. See Web site for additional information: http://www.spacegrant.brown.edu.

Award: Scholarship for use in sophomore, junior, or senior years; not renewable. *Number:* up to 2. *Amount:* up to $4000.

Eligibility Requirements: Applicant must be enrolled or expecting to enroll full-time at a four-year institution or university and studying in Rhode Island. Applicant must have 3.0 GPA or higher. Available to U.S. citizens.

NASA Rhode Island Space Grant Consortium (continued)

Application Requirements: Application, essay, resume, transcript. *Deadline:* March 1.

Contact: Peter Schultz, Program Director
NASA Rhode Island Space Grant Consortium
Brown University, Box 1846
Providence, RI 02912
Phone: 401-863-2417
Fax: 401-863-1242
E-mail: peter_schultz@brown.edu

NASA RISGC SUMMER SCHOLARSHIP FOR UNDERGRADUATE STUDENTS

Scholarship for full-time summer study. Students are expected to devote 75% of their time to a research project with a faculty advisor and 25% to outreach activities in science education for K-12 students and teachers. Must attend a Rhode Island Space Grant Consortium participating school. See Web site for additional information: http://www.spacegrant.brown.edu.

Award: Scholarship for use in sophomore, junior, or senior years. *Number:* 3–5. *Amount:* up to $4000.

Eligibility Requirements: Applicant must be enrolled or expecting to enroll full-time at a four-year institution or university and studying in Rhode Island. Applicant must have 3.0 GPA or higher. Available to U.S. citizens.

Application Requirements: Application, resume, references, letter of interest. *Deadline:* March 1.

Contact: Peter Schultz, Program Director
NASA Rhode Island Space Grant Consortium
Brown University, Box 1846
Providence, RI 02912
Phone: 401-863-2417
Fax: 401-863-1242
E-mail: peter_schultz@brown.edu

NASA SOUTH CAROLINA SPACE GRANT CONSORTIUM http://www.cofc.edu/~scsgrant

UNDERGRADUATE RESEARCH PROGRAM

Applicant must be enrolled full-time at SCSG member institutions. Applicants can be focused on any field that can be related to NASA, specifically math, science and engineering. Deadline varies, usually in January or into early spring. See Web site for additional information: http://www.cofc.edu/~scsgrant. Must be U.S. citizen.

Award: Grant for use in freshman, sophomore, junior, or senior years; renewable. *Number:* 10. *Amount:* $3000.

Eligibility Requirements: Applicant must be enrolled or expecting to enroll full-time at a four-year institution or university and studying in South Carolina. Available to U.S. citizens.

Application Requirements: Application, references, transcript, research proposal. *Deadline:* varies.

Contact: Tara Scozzaro, Program Manager
NASA South Carolina Space Grant Consortium
College of Charleston, Department of Geology
66 George Street
Charleston, SC 29424
Phone: 843-953-5463
Fax: 843-953-5446
E-mail: tara@loki.cofc.edu

NASA SOUTH DAKOTA SPACE GRANT CONSORTIUM http://www.sdsmt.edu/space/

SOUTH DAKOTA SPACE GRANT CONSORTIUM UNDERGRADUATE SCHOLARSHIPS

Up to $1000 per semester available for undergraduate students pursuing studies in science, engineering, aviation, and aerospace, or related fields. Women and minorities are encouraged to apply. For more information, see Web site: http://www.sdsmt.edu/space/.

Award: Scholarship for use in freshman, sophomore, junior, or senior years; renewable. *Number:* varies. *Amount:* $2000.

Eligibility Requirements: Applicant must be enrolled or expecting to enroll full or part-time at a four-year institution or university and studying in South Dakota. Applicant must have 3.0 GPA or higher. Available to U.S. citizens.

Application Requirements: Application. *Deadline:* varies.

Contact: Tom Durkin, Deputy Director and Coordinator
NASA South Dakota Space Grant Consortium
501 East St. Joseph Street
Rapid City, SD 57701-3995
Phone: 605-394-1975
Fax: 605-394-5360
E-mail: jeanette.nilson@sdsmt.edu

NASA/MARYLAND SPACE GRANT CONSORTIUM http://www.mdspacegrant.org

NASA MARYLAND SPACE GRANT CONSORTIUM UNDERGRADUATE SCHOLARSHIPS

Award for undergraduate student at a Maryland Consortium campus who wishes to pursue a career in math, science, engineering, technology or a space-related science. Must be a U.S. citizen and a Maryland resident. Refer to Web site for further information and application: http://www.mdspacegrant.org/scholarship_application.html.

Award: Scholarship for use in freshman, sophomore, junior, or senior years; renewable. *Number:* varies. *Amount:* up to $1000.

Eligibility Requirements: Applicant must be enrolled or expecting to enroll full-time at a four-year institution or university; resident of Maryland and studying in Maryland. Applicant must have 3.0 GPA or higher. Available to U.S. citizens.

Application Requirements: Application, essay, references. *Deadline:* August 15.

Contact: Anna Anikis
NASA/Maryland Space Grant Consortium
Johns Hopkins University, 203 Bloomberg Center for Physics and Astronomy
3400 North Charles Street
Baltimore, MD 21218-2686
Phone: 410-516-7106
Fax: 410-516-4109
E-mail: info@mdspacegrant.org

NATIONAL ASSOCIATION FOR CAMPUS ACTIVITIES http://www.naca.org

LORI RHETT MEMORIAL SCHOLARSHIP

Scholarships will be given to undergraduate or graduate students with a cumulative GPA of 2.5 or better at the time of the application and during the academic term in which the scholarship is awarded. Must demonstrate significant leadership skill and ability while holding a significant leadership position on campus. Applicants must have made contributions via volunteer involvement, either on or off campus. Must be enrolled in college/university in the NACA Pacific Northwest Region.

Award: Scholarship for use in freshman, sophomore, junior, senior, or graduate years; not renewable. *Number:* 1. *Amount:* $250–$300.

Eligibility Requirements: Applicant must be enrolled or expecting to enroll at a two-year or four-year institution or university; studying in Alaska, Idaho, Montana, Oregon, or Washington and must have an interest in leadership. Applicant must have 2.5 GPA or higher. Available to U.S. citizens.

Application Requirements: Application, resume, references, transcript. *Deadline:* June 30.

Contact: Application available at Web site.

MARKLEY SCHOLARSHIP

Scholarship is to recognize and honor involved students who have made significant contributions to the Central region. Must be classified as a junior, senior, or graduate student at a four-year school located in the former NACA South Central region, or a sophomore in the former NACA South Central region. Must have minimum 2.5 GPA.

Award: Scholarship for use in sophomore, junior, senior, or graduate years; not renewable. *Number:* varies. *Amount:* varies.

Eligibility Requirements: Applicant must be enrolled or expecting to enroll at a two-year or four-year institution or university and studying in Arkansas, Louisiana, New Mexico, Oklahoma, or Texas. Applicant must have 2.5 GPA or higher. Available to U.S. citizens.

Application Requirements: Application, resume. *Deadline:* September 27.

Contact: Application available at Web site.

NATIONAL ASSOCIATION FOR CAMPUS ACTIVITIES EAST COAST HIGHER EDUCATION RESEARCH SCHOLARSHIP

Scholarships will be given to students showing that their research will add to the college student personnel knowledge base, particularly campus activities, or address issues challenging student affairs practitioners or higher education as they relate to campus activities. A statement of the problem, purpose of project, plan, timeline to address the question, anticipated results, and statement of the project's anticipated contribution to the profession must accompany the application. Must be enrolled in a college/university in the NACA East Coast Region.

Award: Scholarship for use in freshman, sophomore, junior, senior, or graduate years; not renewable. *Number:* varies. *Amount:* varies.

Eligibility Requirements: Applicant must be enrolled or expecting to enroll at an institution or university and studying in Delaware, Maryland, New Jersey, New York, or Pennsylvania. Available to U.S. citizens.

Application Requirements: Application, essay, references, research proposal. *Deadline:* June 15.

Contact: Application available at Web site.

NATIONAL ASSOCIATION FOR CAMPUS ACTIVITIES EAST COAST UNDERGRADUATE SCHOLARSHIP FOR STUDENT LEADERS

Scholarships will be awarded to undergraduate students who are in good standing at the time of the application and during the academic term in which the scholarship is awarded. Applicants must maintain a 2.5 GPA, demonstrate leadership skills and abilities while holding a significant leadership position on campus or in community, and have made significant contributions via volunteer involvement. Eligible students must be attending a college or university within the NACA East Coast Region.

Award: Scholarship for use in freshman, sophomore, junior, or senior years; not renewable. *Number:* up to 2. *Amount:* $250–$300.

Eligibility Requirements: Applicant must be enrolled or expecting to enroll at a two-year or four-year institution or university; studying in Delaware, District of Columbia, Maryland, New Jersey, New York, or Pennsylvania and must have an interest in leadership. Applicant must have 2.5 GPA or higher. Available to U.S. citizens.

Application Requirements: Application, essay, resume, references, transcript. *Deadline:* March 31.

Contact: Application available at Web site.

NATIONAL ASSOCIATION FOR CAMPUS ACTIVITIES SOUTHEAST REGION STUDENT LEADERSHIP SCHOLARSHIP

Scholarships will be given to full-time undergraduate students in good standing at the time of the application and during the academic term in which the scholarship is awarded. Must demonstrate significant leadership skill and ability while holding a significant leadership position on campus. Applicants must have made contributions via volunteer involvement, either on or off campus. Must be enrolled in a college/university in the NACA Southeast Region.

Award: Scholarship for use in freshman, sophomore, junior, or senior years; not renewable. *Number:* up to 3. *Amount:* $250–$300.

Eligibility Requirements: Applicant must be enrolled or expecting to enroll full-time at a two-year or four-year institution or university; studying in Alabama, Florida, Georgia, Mississippi, North Carolina, Puerto Rico, South Carolina, Tennessee, or Virginia and must have an interest in leadership. Available to U.S. citizens.

Application Requirements: Application, essay, resume, references, transcript. *Deadline:* March 31.

Contact: Application available at Web site.

NATIONAL ASSOCIATION FOR CAMPUS ACTIVITIES WI REGION STUDENT LEADERSHIP SCHOLARSHIP

Scholarships will be awarded to undergraduate or graduate students in good standing and enrolled in the equivalent of at least six academic credits at the time of the application and during the academic term in which the scholarship is awarded. Must be currently enrolled in or received a degree from a college or university within the NACA Wisconsin Region or Michigan (area code 906) and demonstrated leadership skill and significant service to their campus community.

Award: Scholarship for use in freshman, sophomore, junior, senior, or graduate years; not renewable. *Number:* 1. *Amount:* $250–$300.

Eligibility Requirements: Applicant must be enrolled or expecting to enroll full or part-time at a two-year or four-year institution or university; studying in Michigan or Wisconsin and must have an interest in leadership. Available to U.S. citizens.

Application Requirements: Application, essay, resume, references, transcript. *Deadline:* January 15.

Contact: Application available at Web site.

TESS CALDARELLI MEMORIAL SCHOLARSHIP

Scholarship available to undergraduate or graduate students with a minimum 3.0 GPA. Must demonstrate significant leadership skills and hold a significant position on campus. Must attend school in the NACA Great Lakes Region.

Award: Scholarship for use in freshman, sophomore, junior, senior, or graduate years. *Number:* varies. *Amount:* varies.

Eligibility Requirements: Applicant must be enrolled or expecting to enroll at a four-year institution or university; studying in Kentucky, Michigan, Ohio, Pennsylvania, or West Virginia and must have an interest in leadership. Applicant must have 3.0 GPA or higher. Available to U.S. citizens.

Application Requirements: Application, resume, references, transcript. *Deadline:* November 1.

Contact: Application available at Web site.

ZAGUNAS STUDENT LEADERS SCHOLARSHIP

Scholarships will be awarded to undergraduate or graduate students maintaining a cumulative GPA of 3.0 or better at the time of the application and during the academic term in which the scholarship is awarded. Applicants should demonstrate leadership skills and abilities while holding a significant leadership position on campus. Applicants must submit two letters of recommendation and a description of the applicant's leadership activities, skills, abilities and accomplishments. Must be enrolled in a college/university in the NACA Great Lakes Region.

Award: Scholarship for use in freshman, sophomore, junior, senior, or graduate years; not renewable. *Number:* 1. *Amount:* $300.

Eligibility Requirements: Applicant must be enrolled or expecting to enroll at a two-year or four-year institution or university; studying in Kentucky, Michigan, Ohio, Pennsylvania, or West Virginia and must have an interest in leadership. Applicant must have 3.0 GPA or higher. Available to U.S. citizens.

Application Requirements: Application, resume, references, transcript. *Deadline:* November 1.

Contact: Application available at Web site.

NATIONAL ASSOCIATION TO ADVANCE FAT ACCEPTANCE (NEW ENGLAND CHAPTER)

http://www.necnaafa.com

NEW ENGLAND CHAPTER-NATIONAL ASSOCIATION TO ADVANCE FAT ACCEPTANCE SCHOLARSHIP

Nonrenewable scholarship for single New England high school seniors who are overweight. Essay required with application. Must have a minimum GPA of 2.5. Must be single. Must study in Connecticut, Maine, Massachusetts, New Hampshire, Rhode Island, or Vermont.

Award: Scholarship for use in freshman year; not renewable. *Number:* 2. *Amount:* $500.

Eligibility Requirements: Applicant must be high school student; planning to enroll or expecting to enroll full-time at a two-year or

National Association to Advance Fat Acceptance (New England Chapter) (continued)

four-year or technical institution or university; single; resident of Connecticut, Maine, Massachusetts, New Hampshire, Rhode Island, or Vermont and studying in Connecticut, Maine, Massachusetts, New Hampshire, Rhode Island, or Vermont. Applicant must have 2.5 GPA or higher. Available to U.S. citizens.

Application Requirements: Application, autobiography, essay, photo, references, self-addressed stamped envelope, transcript. *Deadline:* May 1.

Contact: Roni Krinsky, Chairperson, Scholarship Committee
National Association to Advance Fat Acceptance (New England Chapter)
PO Box 51820
Boston, MA 02205-1820
Phone: 781-98N-AAFA
Fax: 617-782-8460
E-mail: ronikrink@aol.com

NATIONAL BURGLAR AND FIRE ALARM ASSOCIATION http://www.alarm.org

NBFAA/SECURITY DEALER YOUTH SCHOLARSHIP PROGRAM

• *See page 514*

NATIONAL DEFENSE TRANSPORTATION ASSOCIATION-SCOTT ST. LOUIS CHAPTER http://www.ndtascottstlouis.org

NATIONAL DEFENSE TRANSPORTATION ASSOCIATION, SCOTT AIR FORCE BASE- ST. LOUIS AREA CHAPTER SCHOLARSHIP

Four scholarships of $2500 each are open to any high school students that meet the eligibility criteria. One scholarship of $2500 is available for eligible college students enrolled in a degree program. An additional $2500 scholarship is set aside for immediate family members of active NDTA Scott/St. Louis Chapter members. Minimum 3.0 GPA required. Must be full-time student in CO, IA, IL, IN, KS, MI, MN, MO, MT, ND, NE, SD, WI, WY.

Award: Scholarship for use in freshman, sophomore, junior, or senior years; not renewable. *Number:* 6. *Amount:* $2500.

Eligibility Requirements: Applicant must be enrolled or expecting to enroll full-time at a two-year or four-year institution or university and studying in Colorado, Illinois, Indiana, Iowa, Kansas, Michigan, Minnesota, Missouri, Montana, Nebraska, North Dakota, or South Dakota. Applicant must have 3.0 GPA or higher. Available to U.S. citizens.

Application Requirements: Application, essay, references, test scores, transcript. *Deadline:* March 1.

Contact: Michael Carnes, Chairman, Professional Development Committee
National Defense Transportation Association-Scott St. Louis Chapter
926 Thornbury Place
O'Fallon, IL 62269-6810
Fax: 618-744-0280
E-mail: michael.carnes@cexec.com

NATIONAL ESSAY COMPETITION http://www.rotman.utoronto.ca/essaycompetition

OSLER, HOSKIN AND HARCOURT NATIONAL ESSAY COMPETITION

Open to full-time undergraduate students enrolled in a non-professional faculty of a Canadian university or Cégep. Submit a maximum 1500 word essay in English in answer to the competition's annual question. Must submit your essay via email.

Award: Prize for use in freshman, sophomore, junior, or senior years; not renewable. *Number:* 3. *Amount:* $743–$3714.

Eligibility Requirements: Applicant must be enrolled or expecting to enroll full-time at an institution or university and studying in Alberta, British Columbia, Manitoba, New Brunswick, Newfoundland, North West Territories, Nova Scotia, Ontario, Prince Edward Island, Quebec, Saskatchewan, or Yukon. Available to U.S. and non-U.S. citizens.

Application Requirements: Application, applicant must enter a contest, essay. *Deadline:* April 5.

Contact: Request information via e-mail
E-mail: essaycompetition@rotman.utoronto.ca

NATIONAL FEDERATION OF THE BLIND OF CALIFORNIA http://www.nfbcal.org

GERALD DRAKE MEMORIAL SCHOLARSHIP

• *See page 528*

JULIE LANDUCCI SCHOLARSHIP

• *See page 528*

LA VYRL "PINKY" JOHNSON MEMORIAL SCHOLARSHIP

• *See page 529*

LAWRENCE "MUZZY" MARCELINO MEMORIAL SCHOLARSHIP

• *See page 529*

NATIONAL FEDERATION OF THE BLIND OF CALIFORNIA MERIT SCHOLARSHIPS

• *See page 529*

NATIONAL FEDERATION OF THE BLIND OF MISSOURI http://www.nfbmo.org

NATIONAL FEDERATION OF THE BLIND OF MISSOURI SCHOLARSHIPS TO LEGALLY BLIND STUDENTS

• *See page 529*

NATIONAL KIDNEY FOUNDATION OF INDIANA, INC. http://www.kidneyindiana.org

LARRY SMOCK SCHOLARSHIP

• *See page 529*

NATIONAL SYMPHONY ORCHESTRA EDUCATION PROGRAM http://www.kennedy-center.org/nso/nsoed/youngsoloists.html

NATIONAL SYMPHONY ORCHESTRA YOUNG SOLOISTS' COMPETITION- BILL CERRI SCHOLARSHIP/HIGH SCHOOL DIVISION

Prize for the best soloist in competition. Winner will perform with the National Symphony Orchestra in Washington, D.C. Must be a high school student residing in Washington, D.C., Maryland, or Virginia. Visit Web site for guidelines and deadline. One-time award of $1000. Application fee: $15.

Award: Prize for use in freshman year; not renewable. *Number:* 1. *Amount:* $1000.

Eligibility Requirements: Applicant must be high school student; planning to enroll or expecting to enroll at an institution or university; resident of District of Columbia, Maryland, or Virginia and must have an interest in music/singing.

Application Requirements: Application, applicant must enter a contest. *Fee:* $15. *Deadline:* varies.

Contact: Carole Wysocki, Director, NSO Education Program
National Symphony Orchestra Education Program
The Kennedy Center
Washington, DC 20566
Phone: 202-416-8820
Fax: 202-416-8802
E-mail: cjwysocki@kennedy-center.org

NATIONAL UNION OF PUBLIC AND GENERAL EMPLOYEES http://www.nupge.ca

SCHOLARSHIP FOR ABORIGINAL CANADIANS

• *See page 472*

SCHOLARSHIP FOR VISIBLE MINORITIES

• *See page 472*

TERRY FOX MEMORIAL SCHOLARSHIP

• *See page 472*

TOMMY DOUGLAS SCHOLARSHIP

• *See page 472*

NEBRASKA DECA http://www.nedeca.org/scholarshipsandawards.htm

NEBRASKA DECA LEADERSHIP SCHOLARSHIP

• *See page 473*

NEBRASKA DEPARTMENT OF EDUCATION http://www.nde.state.ne.us/byrd

ROBERT C. BYRD HONORS SCHOLARSHIP

Up to $1500 each year for up to four years. Must be U.S. citizen and Nebraska resident. Awards designed to promote student excellence and achievement and to recognize able students who show promise of continued excellence. Funded scholars must submit Renewal Application each year. Renewal based on continuing eligibility requirements. Must have minimum ACT score of 30. Please refer to Web site for application and further details: http://www.nde.state.ne.us/byrd.

Award: Scholarship for use in freshman, sophomore, junior, or senior years; not renewable. *Number:* 40–45. *Amount:* $1500.

Eligibility Requirements: Applicant must be high school student; planning to enroll or expecting to enroll full-time at a two-year or four-year or technical institution or university and resident of Nebraska. Available to U.S. citizens.

Application Requirements: Application, test scores, transcript. *Deadline:* March 15.

Contact: Robert C. Byrd Scholarship Information
Nebraska Department of Education
301 Centennial Mall South, PO Box 94987
Lincoln, NE 68509-4987
Phone: 402-471-3962

NEBRASKA NATIONAL GUARD http://www.neguard.com

NEBRASKA NATIONAL GUARD TUITION CREDIT

• *See page 537*

NEVADA DEPARTMENT OF EDUCATION

NEVADA DEPARTMENT OF EDUCATION ROBERT C. BYRD HONORS SCHOLARSHIP PROGRAM

Award for senior graduating from public or private Nevada high school. Must be Nevada resident and Nevada High School Scholars Program recipient. Renewable award of $1500. No application necessary. Nevada scholars are chosen from a database supplied by ACT and SAT. Please request SAT score be mailed to 2707 on your registration form. SAT scores of 1100 and above qualify as initial application. ACT score is automatically submitted for a score of 25 or greater. GPA (unweighted) must be 3.5 or higher.

Award: Scholarship for use in freshman, sophomore, junior, or senior years; renewable. *Number:* 40–60. *Amount:* $1500.

Eligibility Requirements: Applicant must be high school student; planning to enroll or expecting to enroll full-time at a two-year or four-year or technical institution or university and resident of Nevada. Applicant must have 3.5 GPA or higher.

Application Requirements: Test scores, transcript. *Deadline:* Continuous.

Contact: Financial Aid Office at local college
Nevada Department of Education
700 East 5th Street
Carson City, NV 89701

NEVADA STUDENT INCENTIVE GRANT

Award available to Nevada residents for use at an accredited Nevada college or university. Must show financial need. Any field of study eligible. High school students may not apply. One-time award of up to $5000. Contact financial aid office at local college.

Award: Grant for use in freshman, sophomore, junior, or senior years; not renewable. *Number:* 400–800. *Amount:* $100–$5000.

Eligibility Requirements: Applicant must be enrolled or expecting to enroll full or part-time at a two-year or four-year or technical institution or university; resident of Nevada and studying in Nevada. Available to U.S. citizens.

Application Requirements: Application, financial need analysis. *Deadline:* Continuous.

Contact: Financial Aid Office at local college
Nevada Department of Education
700 East 5th Street
Carson City, NV 89701

NEVADA WOMEN'S FUND http://www.nevadawomensfund.org

NEVADA WOMEN'S FUND SCHOLARSHIPS

Awards for women for a variety of academic and vocational training scholarships. Must be a resident of Nevada. Preference given to applicants from northern Nevada. Renewable award of $500 to $5000. Application deadline is the last Friday in February. Application can be downloaded from Web site (http://www.nevadawomensfund.org).

Award: Scholarship for use in freshman, sophomore, junior, senior, graduate, or postgraduate years; renewable. *Number:* 50–80. *Amount:* $500–$5000.

Eligibility Requirements: Applicant must be enrolled or expecting to enroll full or part-time at a two-year or four-year or technical institution or university; female and resident of Nevada.

Application Requirements: Application, financial need analysis, references, transcript. *Deadline:* varies.

Contact: Fritsi Ericson, President and CEO
Nevada Women's Fund
770 Smithridge Drive, Suite 300
Reno, NV 89502
Phone: 775-786-2335
Fax: 775-786-8152
E-mail: fritsi@nevadawomensfund.org

NEW ENGLAND BOARD OF HIGHER EDUCATION http://www.nebhe.org

NEW ENGLAND REGIONAL STUDENT PROGRAM (NEW ENGLAND BOARD OF HIGHER EDUCATION)

For residents of Connecticut, Maine, Massachusetts, New Hampshire, Rhode Island, and Vermont. Through Regional Student Program, students pay reduced out-of-state tuition at public colleges or universities in other New England states when enrolling in certain majors not offered at public institutions in home state.

Award: Scholarship for use in freshman, sophomore, junior, senior, or graduate years; renewable. *Number:* varies. *Amount:* varies.

Eligibility Requirements: Applicant must be enrolled or expecting to enroll full or part-time at a two-year or four-year institution or university; resident of Connecticut, Maine, Massachusetts, New Hampshire, Rhode Island, or Vermont and studying in Connecticut, Maine, Massachusetts, New Hampshire, Rhode Island, or Vermont. Available to U.S. citizens.

Application Requirements: College application. *Deadline:* Continuous.

Contact: Wendy Lindsay, Director of Regional Student Program
New England Board of Higher Education
45 Temple Place
Boston, MA 02111-1305
Phone: 617-357-9620 Ext. 111
Fax: 617-338-1577
E-mail: rsp@nebhe.org

NEW HAMPSHIRE CHARITABLE FOUNDATION http://www.nhcf.org

ADULT STUDENT AID PROGRAM

Award for New Hampshire residents who are at least 24 years old, or who have served in the military, are wards of the court, have not been claimed by their parents for two consecutive years, are married, or who have dependent children. Application deadlines are August 15, December 15, and May 15. Application fee is $15. Further information and application available at Web site http://www.nhcf.org.

Award: Grant for use in freshman, sophomore, junior, or senior years; not renewable. *Number:* 100–200. *Amount:* $100–$1500.

New Hampshire Charitable Foundation (continued)

Eligibility Requirements: Applicant must be age 24; enrolled or expecting to enroll full or part-time at a two-year or four-year or technical institution or university and resident of New Hampshire. Available to U.S. citizens.

Application Requirements: Application, financial need analysis, resume, references. *Fee:* $15. *Deadline:* varies.

Contact: Norma Daviault, Program Assistant
New Hampshire Charitable Foundation
37 Pleasant Street
Concord, NH 03301-4005
Phone: 603-225-6641 Ext. 226
E-mail: nd@nhcf.org

CAREER AID TO TECHNOLOGY STUDENTS PROGRAM

Awards for New Hampshire residents enrolled in any accredited vocational or technical program that does not lead to a four-year baccalaureate degree. Must be financially needy and planning to enroll at least half time. Application deadline is June 25. See Web site at http://www.nhcf.org for further information and application.

Award: Grant for use in freshman, sophomore, or junior years; not renewable. *Number:* 300. *Amount:* $100–$2500.

Eligibility Requirements: Applicant must be enrolled or expecting to enroll at a two-year or technical institution and resident of New Hampshire. Available to U.S. citizens.

Application Requirements: Application, financial need analysis, transcript. *Fee:* $20. *Deadline:* June 25.

Contact: CATS Program
New Hampshire Charitable Foundation
37 Pleasant Street
Concord, NH 03301-4005
Phone: 800-464-6641

LEAP SCHOLARSHIPS

Sponsored by the Bank of New Hampshire, but administered by NH Charitable Foundation. Nine awards are made annually in different areas of the state. Eligibility is based on meeting income eligibility and academic and other merit factors. Applicants must be residents of New Hampshire. See Web site for additional information: http://www.nhcf.org.

Award: Grant for use in freshman year; not renewable. *Number:* 9. *Amount:* $2500.

Eligibility Requirements: Applicant must be high school student; planning to enroll or expecting to enroll full-time at a four-year or technical institution or university and resident of New Hampshire. Available to U.S. citizens.

Application Requirements: Application, financial need analysis, test scores, transcript. *Deadline:* March 15.

Contact: Judith Burrows, Director of Student Aid
New Hampshire Charitable Foundation
37 Pleasant Street
Concord, NH 03301-4005
Phone: 603-225-6641

NHCF STATEWIDE STUDENT AID PROGRAM

Awards available to New Hampshire residents enrolled at accredited institutions. Some awards are renewable. Application fee is $20. Students must be enrolled at least half time, carrying 6 or more hours. Further information and application available at Web site http://www.nhcf.org.

Award: Grant for use in freshman, sophomore, junior, senior, or graduate years; not renewable. *Number:* 300–400. *Amount:* $100–$2500.

Eligibility Requirements: Applicant must be enrolled or expecting to enroll at a four-year institution or university and resident of New Hampshire. Available to U.S. citizens.

Application Requirements: Application, essay, financial need analysis, resume, references, test scores, transcript. *Fee:* $20. *Deadline:* April 23.

Contact: Norma Davaiult, Program Assistant
New Hampshire Charitable Foundation
37 Pleasant Street
Concord, NH 03301-4005
Phone: 603-225-6641 Ext. 226
E-mail: nd@nhcf.org

NEW HAMPSHIRE DEPARTMENT OF EDUCATION http://www.state.nh.us/doe/

ROBERT C. BYRD HONORS SCHOLARSHIP-NEW HAMPSHIRE

Scholarships awarded to graduates of approved New Hampshire secondary schools. Based on academic achievement. Contact department for application deadlines. May be funded through four years of college if recipient maintains high academic achievement. Must be high school senior to apply and must submit letters of recommendation. Award is offered in senior year of high school. Minimum 3.0 GPA required.

Award: Scholarship for use in freshman, sophomore, junior, or senior years; renewable. *Number:* 26–30. *Amount:* $1500.

Eligibility Requirements: Applicant must be high school student; planning to enroll or expecting to enroll full or part-time at a two-year or four-year institution or university and resident of New Hampshire. Applicant must have 3.0 GPA or higher. Available to U.S. citizens.

Application Requirements: Application, essay, references, test scores, transcript. *Deadline:* varies.

Contact: Marie Gage, Program Specialist II
New Hampshire Department of Education
101 Pleasant Street
Concord, NH 03301
Phone: 603-271-6051
Fax: 603-271-2632
E-mail: mgage@ed.state.nh.us

NEW HAMPSHIRE POSTSECONDARY EDUCATION COMMISSION http://www.state.nh.us/postsecondary

LEVERAGED INCENTIVE GRANT PROGRAM

Award open to New Hampshire residents attending school in New Hampshire. Must be in sophomore, junior, or senior year. Award based on financial need and merit. Contact financial aid office for more information and deadline.

Award: Grant for use in sophomore, junior, or senior years; not renewable. *Number:* varies. *Amount:* $200–$7500.

Eligibility Requirements: Applicant must be enrolled or expecting to enroll full-time at a two-year or four-year institution or university; resident of New Hampshire and studying in New Hampshire. Available to U.S. citizens.

Application Requirements: Application, financial need analysis. *Deadline:* varies.

Contact: Financial Aid Office

MARY MILLIKEN SCHOLARSHIP

Grant available to New Hampshire residents enrolled at a New Hampshire institution of higher education. Must demonstrate financial need. Contact financial aid office for more information.

Award: Grant for use in freshman, sophomore, junior, or senior years; renewable. *Number:* varies. *Amount:* $1000.

Eligibility Requirements: Applicant must be enrolled or expecting to enroll full-time at a two-year or four-year or technical institution or university; resident of New Hampshire and studying in New Hampshire. Available to U.S. citizens.

Application Requirements: Application, financial need analysis. *Deadline:* May 1.

Contact: Financial Aid Office/HS Guidance Office

NEW HAMPSHIRE INCENTIVE PROGRAM (NHIP)

One-time grants for New Hampshire residents attending school in New Hampshire, Connecticut, Maine, Massachusetts, Rhode Island, or Vermont.

Must have financial need. Deadline is May 1. Complete Free Application for Federal Student Aid. Grant is not automatically renewable. Applicant must reapply.

Award: Grant for use in freshman, sophomore, junior, or senior years; not renewable. *Number:* 3000–4300. *Amount:* $125–$1000.

Eligibility Requirements: Applicant must be enrolled or expecting to enroll full or part-time at a two-year or four-year or technical institution or university; resident of New Hampshire and studying in Connecticut, Maine, Massachusetts, New Hampshire, Rhode Island, or Vermont. Available to U.S. citizens.

Application Requirements: Application, financial need analysis. *Deadline:* May 1.

Contact: Sherrie Tucker, Program Assistant
New Hampshire Postsecondary Education Commission
3 Barrell Court, Suite 300
Concord, NH 03301-8512
Phone: 603-271-2555 Ext. 355
Fax: 603-271-2696
E-mail: stucker@pec.state.nh.us

SCHOLARSHIPS FOR ORPHANS OF VETERANS-NEW HAMPSHIRE

• *See page 560*

NEW JERSEY DEPARTMENT OF MILITARY AND VETERANS AFFAIRS http://www.state.nj.us/military

NEW JERSEY WAR ORPHANS TUITION ASSISTANCE

• *See page 560*

TUITION ASSISTANCE FOR CHILDREN OF POW/MIAS

• *See page 560*

NEW JERSEY HIGHER EDUCATION STUDENT ASSISTANCE AUTHORITY http://www.hesaa.org

DANA CHRISTMAS SCHOLARSHIP FOR HEROISM

Honors young New Jersey residents for acts of heroism. Scholarship is a non-renewable award of up to $10000 for up to five recipients. This scholarship may be used for undergraduate or graduate study.

Award: Scholarship for use in freshman, sophomore, junior, senior, or graduate years; not renewable. *Number:* up to 5. *Amount:* up to $10,000.

Eligibility Requirements: Applicant must be age 21 or under; enrolled or expecting to enroll full or part-time at a four-year institution or university and resident of New Jersey. Available to U.S. citizens.

Application Requirements: Application. *Deadline:* October 15.

Contact: Gisele Joachim, Director of Financial Aid Services
New Jersey Higher Education Student Assistance Authority
PO Box 540
Trenton, NJ 08625
Phone: 800-792-8670
Fax: 609-588-7389

EDWARD J. BLOUSTEIN DISTINGUISHED SCHOLARS

Renewable scholarship for students who place in the top 10% of their classes and have a minimum combined SAT score of 1260, or are ranked first, second or third in their class as of the end of the junior year. Must be New Jersey resident. Must attend a New Jersey two-year college, four-year college or university, or approved programs at proprietary institutions. Secondary schools forward to HESAA the names and class standings for all nominees.

Award: Scholarship for use in freshman, sophomore, junior, or senior years; renewable. *Number:* varies. *Amount:* $950.

Eligibility Requirements: Applicant must be high school student; planning to enroll or expecting to enroll full-time at a two-year or four-year institution or university; resident of New Jersey and studying in New Jersey. Available to U.S. citizens.

Application Requirements: Test scores, nominated by high school. *Deadline:* October 1.

Contact: Carol Muka, Assistant Director of Grants and Scholarships
New Jersey Higher Education Student Assistance Authority
PO Box 540
Trenton, NJ 08625
Phone: 800-792-8670
Fax: 609-588-2228

LAW ENFORCEMENT OFFICER MEMORIAL SCHOLARSHIP

• *See page 515*

NEW JERSEY WORLD TRADE CENTER SCHOLARSHIP

Established by the legislature to aid the dependent children and surviving spouses of NJ residents who were killed in the terrorist attacks, or who are missing and officially presumed dead as a direct result of the attacks; applies to in-state and out-of-state institutions for students seeking undergraduate degrees.

Award: Scholarship for use in freshman, sophomore, junior, or senior years; renewable. *Number:* varies. *Amount:* up to $6500.

Eligibility Requirements: Applicant must be enrolled or expecting to enroll full-time at a two-year or four-year institution or university and resident of New Jersey. Available to U.S. citizens.

Application Requirements: Application. *Deadline:* October 1.

Contact: Giselle Joachim, Director of Financial Aid Services
New Jersey Higher Education Student Assistance Authority
PO Box 540
Trenton, NJ 08625
Phone: 800-792-8670
Fax: 609-588-7389

NJ STUDENT TUITION ASSISTANCE REWARD SCHOLARSHIP

Scholarship for students who graduate in the top 20% of their high school class. Recipients may be awarded up to 5 semesters of tuition (up to 15 credits per term) and approved fees at one of New Jerseys 19 county colleges.

Award: Scholarship for use in freshman or sophomore years; renewable. *Number:* varies.

Eligibility Requirements: Applicant must be high school student; planning to enroll or expecting to enroll full-time at a two-year institution; resident of New Jersey and studying in New Jersey. Applicant must have 3.5 GPA or higher. Available to U.S. citizens.

Application Requirements: Application, transcript.

Contact: Carol Muka, Assistant Director of Grants and Scholarships
New Jersey Higher Education Student Assistance Authority
PO Box 540
Trenton, NJ 08625
Phone: 800-792-8670
Fax: 609-588-2228

OUTSTANDING SCHOLAR RECRUITMENT PROGRAM

Students who meet the eligibility criteria and enroll as first-time freshmen at participating New Jersey institutions receive annual scholarship awards of $2500 to $7500. The award amounts vary on a sliding scale depending on class rank and combined SAT scores. Must maintain a B average for renewal. Deadline October 1 for Fall term, March 1 for Spring term.

Award: Scholarship for use in freshman, sophomore, junior, or senior years; renewable. *Number:* varies. *Amount:* $2500–$7500.

Eligibility Requirements: Applicant must be high school student; planning to enroll or expecting to enroll at an institution or university; resident of New Jersey and studying in New Jersey. Available to U.S. citizens.

Application Requirements: Test scores. *Deadline:* varies.

Contact: Carol Muka, Assistant Director of Grants and Scholarships
New Jersey Higher Education Student Assistance Authority
PO Box 540
Trenton, NJ 08625
Phone: 800-792-8670
Fax: 609-588-2228

PART-TIME TUITION AID GRANT (TAG) FOR COUNTY COLLEGES

Provides financial aid to eligible part-time undergraduate students enrolled for 6-11 credits at participating NJ community colleges.

Award: Grant for use in freshman or sophomore years; renewable. *Number:* varies. *Amount:* $116–$375.

Eligibility Requirements: Applicant must be enrolled or expecting to enroll part-time at a two-year institution; resident of New Jersey and studying in New Jersey. Available to U.S. citizens.

Application Requirements: Application, financial need analysis. *Deadline:* varies.

Contact: Sherri Fox, Acting Director of Grants and Scholarships
New Jersey Higher Education Student Assistance Authority
PO Box 540
Trenton, NJ 08625
Phone: 800-792-8670
Fax: 609-588-2228

SURVIVOR TUITION BENEFITS PROGRAM

• *See page 516*

TUITION AID GRANT

The Tuition Aid Grant (TAG) program provides financial aid to eligible undergraduate students attending participating in-state institutions.

Award: Grant for use in freshman, sophomore, junior, or senior years; renewable. *Number:* varies. *Amount:* $868–$7272.

Eligibility Requirements: Applicant must be enrolled or expecting to enroll full-time at a two-year or four-year institution or university; resident of New Jersey and studying in New Jersey. Available to U.S. citizens.

Application Requirements: Application, financial need analysis. *Deadline:* varies.

Contact: Sherri Fox, Acting Director of Grants and Scholarships
New Jersey Higher Education Student Assistance Authority
PO Box 540
Trenton, NJ 08625
Phone: 800-792-8670
Fax: 609-588-2228

URBAN SCHOLARS

Renewable scholarship to high achieving students attending public secondary schools in the State's urban and economically distressed areas of New Jersey. Students must rank in the top 10% of their class and have a GPA of at least 3.0 at the end of their junior year. Must be New Jersey resident. Must attend a New Jersey two-year college, four-year college or university, or approved programs at proprietary institutions. Students do not apply directly for scholarship consideration. Secondary schools forward to HESAA the names and class standing for all nominees.

Award: Scholarship for use in freshman, sophomore, junior, or senior years; renewable. *Number:* varies. *Amount:* $950.

Eligibility Requirements: Applicant must be high school student; planning to enroll or expecting to enroll full-time at a two-year or four-year institution or university; resident of New Jersey and studying in New Jersey. Applicant must have 3.0 GPA or higher. Available to U.S. citizens.

Application Requirements: Test scores, nominated by school. *Deadline:* October 1.

Contact: Carol Muka, Assistant Director of Grants and Scholarships
New Jersey Higher Education Student Assistance Authority
PO Box 540
Trenton, NJ 08625
Phone: 800-792-8670
Fax: 609-588-2228

NEW JERSEY PRESS FOUNDATION

http://www.njpa.org/foundation

COLLEGE STUDENT CORRESPONDENT SCHOLARSHIP PROGRAM

Available to New Jersey residents who work as interns or student correspondents/stringers for New Jersey weekly or daily newspapers. Student is awarded a scholarship based on the quality of work performed. Recipients must have at least one term of college remaining following the announcement of scholarships.

Award: Scholarship for use in sophomore, junior, or senior years; not renewable. *Number:* 5–12. *Amount:* $1000.

Eligibility Requirements: Applicant must be enrolled or expecting to enroll full-time at a two-year or four-year institution or university and resident of New Jersey. Available to U.S. citizens.

Application Requirements: Application, essay, portfolio, resume, references. *Deadline:* August 31.

Contact: Thomas Engleman, Director
New Jersey Press Foundation
840 Bear Tavern Road, Suite 305
West Trenton, NJ 08628-1019
Phone: 609-406-0600 Ext. 19
Fax: 609-406-0300
E-mail: foundation@njpa.org

INTERNSHIP/SCHOLARSHIP PROGRAM

For New Jersey residents. Students selected will be assigned paid internships at New Jersey newspapers (minimum $300/week for 10 weeks). Scholarship awarded after successful completion of internship. Recipients must have at least one term of college left following the internship.

Award: Scholarship for use in sophomore, junior, or senior years; not renewable. *Number:* 5–6. *Amount:* $3000.

Eligibility Requirements: Applicant must be enrolled or expecting to enroll full-time at a two-year or four-year institution or university and resident of New Jersey. Available to U.S. citizens.

Application Requirements: Application, essay, portfolio, resume, references, transcript. *Deadline:* November 15.

Contact: Thomas Engleman, Director
New Jersey Press Foundation
840 Bear Tavern Road, Suite 305
West Trenton, NJ 08628-1019
Phone: 609-406-0600 Ext. 19
Fax: 609-406-0300
E-mail: foundation@njpa.org

NEW JERSEY STATE GOLF ASSOCIATION

http://www.njsga.org

NEW JERSEY STATE GOLF ASSOCIATION CADDIE SCHOLARSHIP

• *See page 516*

NEW JERSEY VIETNAM VETERANS' MEMORIAL FOUNDATION

http://www.njvvmf.org

NEW JERSEY VIETNAM VETERANS' MEMORIAL FOUNDATION SCHOLARSHIP

Applicants must be New Jersey residents who are graduating high school seniors. Eligible applicants will have visited the New Jersey Vietnam Veterans' Memorial and write an essay about the visit. The deadline is April 15.

Award: Scholarship for use in freshman year; not renewable. *Number:* 2. *Amount:* $2500.

Eligibility Requirements: Applicant must be high school student; age 17-19; planning to enroll or expecting to enroll full or part-time at a two-year or four-year or technical institution or university; single and resident of New Jersey. Available to U.S. and non-U.S. citizens.

Application Requirements: Application, essay, acceptance letter. *Deadline:* April 15.

Contact: Lynn Duane, Administrative Assistant
New Jersey Vietnam Veterans' Memorial Foundation
PO Box 648
Holmdel, NJ 07733
Phone: 732-335-0033
Fax: 732-335-1107
E-mail: lduane@njvvmf.org

NEW MEXICO COMMISSION ON HIGHER EDUCATION http://www.nmche.org

LEGISLATIVE ENDOWMENT SCHOLARSHIPS

Awards for undergraduate students with substantial financial need who are attending public postsecondary institutions in New Mexico. Preference given to returning adult students at two-year and four-year institutions and students transferring from two-year to four-year institutions. Deadline set by each institution. Must be resident of New Mexico. Contact financial aid office of any New Mexico public postsecondary institution to apply.

Award: Scholarship for use in freshman, sophomore, junior, or senior years; not renewable. *Amount:* $1000–$2500.

Eligibility Requirements: Applicant must be enrolled or expecting to enroll full or part-time at a two-year or four-year institution or university; resident of New Mexico and studying in New Mexico. Available to U.S. citizens.

Application Requirements: Application, financial need analysis, FAFSA.

Contact: Maria Barele, Financial Specialist
New Mexico Commission on Higher Education
PO Box 15910
Santa Fe, NM 87506-5910
Phone: 505-827-7383
Fax: 505-827-7392

LOTTERY SUCCESS SCHOLARSHIPS

Awards equal to 100% of tuition at New Mexico public postsecondary institution. Must have New Mexico high school degree and be enrolled at New Mexico public college or university in first regular semester following high school graduation. Must obtain 2.5 GPA during this semester. May be eligible for up to eight consecutive semesters of support. Deadlines vary by institution. Apply through financial aid office of any New Mexico public postsecondary institution.

Award: Scholarship for use in freshman, sophomore, junior, or senior years; renewable.

Eligibility Requirements: Applicant must be enrolled or expecting to enroll full-time at a two-year or four-year institution; resident of New Mexico and studying in New Mexico. Applicant must have 2.5 GPA or higher. Available to U.S. citizens.

Application Requirements: Application.

Contact: Maria Barele, Financial Specialist
New Mexico Commission on Higher Education
PO Box 15910
Santa Fe, NM 87506-5910
Phone: 505-827-4026
Fax: 505-827-7392

NEW MEXICO COMPETITIVE SCHOLARSHIP

Scholarship available to encourage out-of-state students who have demonstrated high academic achievement to enroll in public institutions of higher education in New Mexico. One-time award for undergraduate students. Deadlines set by each institution. Contact financial aid office of any New Mexico public postsecondary institution to apply.

Award: Scholarship for use in freshman, sophomore, junior, or senior years; not renewable. *Amount:* $100.

Eligibility Requirements: Applicant must be enrolled or expecting to enroll full or part-time at a two-year or four-year institution or university and studying in New Mexico. Applicant must have 3.0 GPA or higher. Available to U.S. citizens.

Application Requirements: Application, essay, references, test scores.

Contact: Maria Barele, Financial Specialist
New Mexico Commission on Higher Education
PO Box 15910
Santa Fe, NM 87506-5910
Phone: 505-827-4026
Fax: 505-827-7392

NEW MEXICO SCHOLARS' PROGRAM

Several scholarships to encourage New Mexico high school graduates to enroll in college at a public or selected private nonprofit postsecondary institution in New Mexico before their 22nd birthday. Selected private colleges are College of Santa Fe, St. John's College in Santa Fe, and College of the Southwest. Must have graduated in top 5% of their class or obtained an ACT score of 25 or SAT score of 1140. One-time scholarship for tuition, books, and fees. Contact financial aid office at college to apply.

Award: Scholarship for use in freshman, sophomore, junior, or senior years; not renewable.

Eligibility Requirements: Applicant must be age 22 or under; enrolled or expecting to enroll full or part-time at a two-year or four-year institution; resident of New Mexico and studying in New Mexico. Available to U.S. citizens.

Application Requirements: Application, financial need analysis, test scores, FAFSA.

Contact: Maria Barele, Financial Specialist
New Mexico Commission on Higher Education
PO Box 15910
Santa Fe, NM 87506-5910
Phone: 505-827-4026
Fax: 505-827-7392

NEW MEXICO STUDENT INCENTIVE GRANT

Several grants available for resident undergraduate students attending public and selected private nonprofit institutions in New Mexico. Must demonstrate financial need. To apply contact financial aid office at any public or private nonprofit postsecondary institution in New Mexico.

Award: Grant for use in freshman, sophomore, junior, or senior years; not renewable. *Amount:* $200–$2500.

Eligibility Requirements: Applicant must be enrolled or expecting to enroll at a two-year or four-year institution or university; resident of New Mexico and studying in New Mexico. Available to U.S. citizens.

Application Requirements: Application, financial need analysis, FAFSA.

Contact: Maria Barele, Financial Specialist
New Mexico Commission on Higher Education
PO Box 15910
Santa Fe, NM 87506-5910
Phone: 505-827-4026
Fax: 505-827-7392

3% SCHOLARSHIP PROGRAM

Award equal to tuition and required fees for New Mexico residents who are undergraduate students attending public postsecondary institutions in New Mexico. Contact financial aid office of any public postsecondary institution in New Mexico for deadline.

Award: Scholarship for use in freshman, sophomore, junior, senior, or graduate years; not renewable.

Eligibility Requirements: Applicant must be enrolled or expecting to enroll full or part-time at a two-year or four-year institution or university; resident of New Mexico and studying in New Mexico. Available to U.S. citizens.

Application Requirements: Application.

Contact: Maria Barele, Financial Specialist
New Mexico Commission on Higher Education
PO Box 15910
Santa Fe, NM 87506-5910
Phone: 505-827-4026
Fax: 505-827-7392

VIETNAM VETERANS' SCHOLARSHIP PROGRAM

• *See page 560*

NEW MEXICO VETERANS' SERVICE COMMISSION http://www.state.nm.us/veterans

CHILDREN OF DECEASED VETERANS SCHOLARSHIP-NEW MEXICO

• *See page 561*

NEW MEXICO VIETNAM VETERANS' SCHOLARSHIP
• *See page 561*

NEW YORK COUNCIL NAVY LEAGUE

NEW YORK COUNCIL NAVY LEAGUE SCHOLARSHIP FUND
• *See page 544*

NEW YORK STATE AFL-CIO http://www.nysaflcio.org

NEW YORK STATE AFL-CIO SCHOLARSHIP
• *See page 473*

NEW YORK STATE EDUCATION DEPARTMENT http://www.highered.nysed.gov

ROBERT C. BYRD HONORS SCHOLARSHIP-NEW YORK

Award for outstanding high school seniors accepted to U.S. college or university. Based on SAT score and high school average. Minimum 3.5 GPA required; minimum 1250 combined SAT score from one sitting. Must be legal resident of New York and a U.S. citizen. Renewable for up to four years. General Education Degree holders eligible.

Award: Scholarship for use in freshman, sophomore, junior, or senior years; renewable. *Number:* 400. *Amount:* $1500.

Eligibility Requirements: Applicant must be high school student; planning to enroll or expecting to enroll full-time at a two-year or four-year institution or university and resident of New York. Applicant must have 3.5 GPA or higher. Available to U.S. citizens.

Application Requirements: Application, test scores, transcript. *Deadline:* March 1.

Contact: Lewis J. Hall, Coordinator
New York State Education Department
Room 1078 EBA
Albany, NY 12234
Phone: 518-486-1319
Fax: 518-486-5346

SCHOLARSHIP FOR ACADEMIC EXCELLENCE

Renewable award for New York residents. Scholarship winners must attend a college or university in New York. 2000 scholarships are for $1500 and 6000 are for $500. The selection criteria used are based on Regents test scores and rank in class. Must be U.S. citizen or permanent resident.

Award: Scholarship for use in freshman, sophomore, junior, or senior years; renewable. *Number:* up to 8000. *Amount:* $500–$1500.

Eligibility Requirements: Applicant must be high school student; planning to enroll or expecting to enroll full-time at a two-year or four-year institution or university; resident of New York and studying in New York. Applicant must have 3.5 GPA or higher. Available to U.S. citizens.

Application Requirements: Application. *Deadline:* December 19.

Contact: Lewis J. Hall, Coordinator
New York State Education Department
Room 1078 EBA
Albany, NY 12234
Phone: 518-486-1319
Fax: 518-486-5346

NEW YORK STATE GRANGE

SUSAN W. FREESTONE EDUCATION AWARD
• *See page 473*

NEW YORK STATE HIGHER EDUCATION SERVICES CORPORATION http://www.hesc.org

NEW YORK AID FOR PART-TIME STUDY (APTS)

Renewable scholarship provides tuition assistance to part-time students who are New York residents attending New York accredited institutions. Deadlines and award amounts vary. Must be U.S. citizen.

Award: Grant for use in freshman, sophomore, junior, or senior years; renewable. *Number:* varies. *Amount:* up to $2000.

Eligibility Requirements: Applicant must be enrolled or expecting to enroll part-time at a two-year or four-year institution; resident of New York and studying in New York. Available to U.S. citizens.

Application Requirements: Application.

Contact: Student Information
New York State Higher Education Services Corporation
99 Washington Avenue, Room 1320
Albany, NY 12255
Phone: 518-473-3887
Fax: 518-474-2839

NEW YORK EDUCATIONAL OPPORTUNITY PROGRAM (EOP)

Renewable award for New York resident attending New York college/university for undergraduate study. For educationally and economically disadvantaged students; includes educational assistance such as tutoring. Contact prospective college for information.

Award: Scholarship for use in freshman, sophomore, junior, or senior years; renewable. *Number:* varies. *Amount:* varies.

Eligibility Requirements: Applicant must be enrolled or expecting to enroll full-time at a two-year or four-year institution or university; resident of New York and studying in New York. Available to U.S. citizens.

Application Requirements: Application, financial need analysis, transcript.

Contact: Student Information
New York State Higher Education Services Corporation
99 Washington Avenue, Room 1320
Albany, NY 12255

NEW YORK MEMORIAL SCHOLARSHIPS FOR FAMILIES OF DECEASED POLICE OFFICERS, FIRE FIGHTERS AND PEACE OFFICERS
• *See page 516*

NEW YORK STATE AID TO NATIVE AMERICANS
• *See page 595*

NEW YORK STATE TUITION ASSISTANCE PROGRAM

Award for New York state residents attending a New York postsecondary institution. Must be full-time student in approved program with tuition over $200 per year. Must show financial need and not be in default in any other state program. Renewable award of $500-$5000.

Award: Grant for use in freshman, sophomore, junior, or senior years; renewable. *Number:* 350,000–360,000. *Amount:* $500–$5000.

Eligibility Requirements: Applicant must be enrolled or expecting to enroll full-time at a two-year or four-year institution or university; resident of New York and studying in New York.

Application Requirements: Application, financial need analysis. *Deadline:* May 1.

Contact: Student Information
New York State Higher Education Services Corporation
99 Washington Avenue, Room 1320
Albany, NY 12255

NEW YORK VIETNAM VETERANS TUITION AWARDS
• *See page 534*

REGENTS AWARD FOR CHILD OF VETERAN
• *See page 561*

REGENTS PROFESSIONAL OPPORTUNITY SCHOLARSHIPS

Award for New York State residents pursuing career in certain licensed professions. Must attend New York State college. Priority given to economically disadvantaged members of minority group underrepresented in chosen profession and graduates of SEEK, College Discovery, EOP, and HEOP. Must work in New York State in chosen profession one year for each annual payment.

Award: Scholarship for use in freshman, sophomore, junior, senior, or graduate years; not renewable. *Number:* 220. *Amount:* $1000–$5000.

Eligibility Requirements: Applicant must be enrolled or expecting to enroll full-time at a two-year or four-year institution or university; resident of New York and studying in New York. Available to U.S. citizens.

Application Requirements: Application. *Deadline:* May 3.

Contact: Scholarship Processing Unit-New York State Education Department
New York State Higher Education Services Corporation
EBA Room 1078
Albany, NY 12234
Phone: 518-486-1319

SCHOLARSHIPS FOR ACADEMIC EXCELLENCE

Renewable awards of up to $1500 for academically outstanding New York State high school graduates planning to attend an approved postsecondary institution in New York State. For full-time study only. Contact high school guidance counselor to apply.

Award: Scholarship for use in freshman, sophomore, junior, or senior years; renewable. *Number:* 8000. *Amount:* $500–$1500.

Eligibility Requirements: Applicant must be high school student; planning to enroll or expecting to enroll full-time at a four-year institution or university; resident of New York and studying in New York. Available to U.S. citizens.

Application Requirements: Application. *Deadline:* December 19.

Contact: Student Information
New York State Higher Education Services Corporation
99 Washington Avenue, Room 1320
Albany, NY 12255

WORLD TRADE CENTER MEMORIAL SCHOLARSHIP

Renewable awards of up to the average cost of attendance at a State University of New York four-year college. Available to the families and financial dependents of victims who died or were severely and permanently disabled as a result of the Sept. 11, 2001 terrorist attacks on the U.S. and the rescue and recovery efforts.

Award: Scholarship for use in freshman, sophomore, junior, or senior years; renewable. *Number:* varies. *Amount:* varies.

Eligibility Requirements: Applicant must be enrolled or expecting to enroll full-time at a two-year or four-year institution or university; resident of New York and studying in New York. Available to U.S. citizens.

Application Requirements: Application. *Deadline:* May 1.

Contact: HESC Scholarship Unit
New York State Higher Education Services Corporation
99 Washington Avenue, Room 1320
Albany, NY 12255
Phone: 518-402-6494

NOLIN RURAL ELECTRIC COOPERATIVE CORPORATION http://www.nolinrecc.com

NOLIN RURAL ELECTRIC COOPERATIVE CORPORATION CONTINUING EDUCATION SCHOLARSHIP

Scholarship available for Kentucky student enrolled or planning to enroll part-or full-time in a vocational school, 2- or 4-year college, or university. Must have financial need. Must have primary residence in the Nolin service territory and be a member of the cooperative. Must submit essay of 500 words or less on why you should be awarded the scholarship. Application and information on Web site: http://www.nolinrecc.com.

Award: Scholarship for use in freshman, sophomore, junior, or senior years; not renewable. *Number:* 1. *Amount:* $1000.

Eligibility Requirements: Applicant must be enrolled or expecting to enroll full or part-time at a two-year or four-year or technical institution or university and resident of Kentucky. Available to U.S. citizens.

Application Requirements: Application, essay, financial need analysis, references. *Deadline:* April 1.

Contact: Patsy Whitehead, Member Services
Nolin Rural Electric Cooperative Corporation
411 Ring Road
Elizabethtown, KY 42701-8701
Phone: 270-765-6153
E-mail: comments@nolinrecc.com

NOLIN RURAL ELECTRIC COOPERATIVE CORPORATION STUDENT SCHOLARSHIP

Scholarships available for Kentucky graduating high school seniors living in the Nolin RECC service area. Parent/guardian must be a Nolin member and primary residence in the Nolin service territory. Awards based on financial need, GPA, community and personal achievements, school involvement. Must be enrolling for full-time study in college or vocational school. Application and information on Web site: http:www.nolinrecc.com.

Award: Scholarship for use in freshman year; not renewable. *Number:* 5. *Amount:* $1000.

Eligibility Requirements: Applicant must be high school student; planning to enroll or expecting to enroll full-time at a two-year or four-year or technical institution or university and resident of Kentucky. Available to U.S. citizens.

Application Requirements: Application, financial need analysis, references, transcript. *Deadline:* April 1.

Contact: Patsy Whitehead, Member Services
Nolin Rural Electric Cooperative Corporation
411 Ring Road
Elizabethtown, KY 42701-8701
Phone: 270-765-6153
E-mail: comments@nolinrecc.com

NORTH CAROLINA ASSOCIATION OF EDUCATORS http://www.ncae.org

NORTH CAROLINA ASSOCIATION OF EDUCATORS MARTIN LUTHER KING, JR. SCHOLARSHIP

One-time award for high school seniors who are North Carolina residents to attend a postsecondary institution. Must be a U.S. citizen. Based upon financial need, GPA, and essay.

Award: Scholarship for use in freshman year; not renewable. *Number:* 3–4. *Amount:* $500–$1000.

Eligibility Requirements: Applicant must be high school student; planning to enroll or expecting to enroll full-time at an institution or university and resident of North Carolina. Available to U.S. citizens.

Application Requirements: Application, essay, financial need analysis, references, transcript. *Deadline:* February 1.

Contact: Dee Leach, MLK Scholarship Coordinator
North Carolina Association of Educators
PO Box 27347
Raleigh, NC 27611
Phone: 800-662-7924 Ext. 205

NORTH CAROLINA BAR ASSOCIATION http://www.ncbar.org

NORTH CAROLINA BAR ASSOCIATION SCHOLARSHIP

• *See page 516*

NORTH CAROLINA DIVISION OF SERVICES FOR THE BLIND

NORTH CAROLINA DIVISION OF SERVICES FOR THE BLIND REHABILITATION SERVICES

• *See page 530*

NORTH CAROLINA DIVISION OF VETERANS' AFFAIRS http://www.doa.state.nc.us/doa/vets/synopsis.htm

NORTH CAROLINA VETERANS' SCHOLARSHIPS CLASS I-A

• *See page 561*

NORTH CAROLINA VETERANS' SCHOLARSHIPS CLASS I-B
• *See page 561*

NORTH CAROLINA VETERANS' SCHOLARSHIPS CLASS II
• *See page 561*

NORTH CAROLINA VETERANS' SCHOLARSHIPS CLASS III
• *See page 562*

NORTH CAROLINA VETERANS' SCHOLARSHIPS CLASS IV
• *See page 562*

NORTH CAROLINA DIVISION OF VOCATIONAL REHABILITATION SERVICES http://www.dhhs.state.nc.us

TRAINING SUPPORT FOR YOUTH WITH DISABILITIES
• *See page 530*

NORTH CAROLINA NATIONAL GUARD http://www.nc.ngb.army.mil/education

NORTH CAROLINA NATIONAL GUARD TUITION ASSISTANCE PROGRAM
• *See page 537*

NORTH CAROLINA STATE EDUCATION ASSISTANCE AUTHORITY http://www.cfnc.org

AUBREY LEE BROOKS SCHOLARSHIPS

Renewable award for high school seniors who are residents of designated North Carolina counties and are planning to attend North Carolina State University, the University of North Carolina at Chapel Hill or the University of North Carolina at Greensboro. Award provides approximately half of the cost of an undergraduate education. Write for further details and deadlines, or visit Web site: http://www.cfnc.org.

Award: Scholarship for use in freshman, sophomore, junior, or senior years; renewable. *Number:* 17–54. *Amount:* $6300.

Eligibility Requirements: Applicant must be high school student; planning to enroll or expecting to enroll full-time at an institution or university; resident of North Carolina and studying in North Carolina. Applicant must have 3.0 GPA or higher. Available to U.S. citizens.

Application Requirements: Application, essay, financial need analysis, interview, photo, references, test scores, transcript. *Deadline:* February 3.

Contact: Bill Carswell, Manager of Scholarship and Grant Division
North Carolina State Education Assistance Authority
PO Box 13663
Research Triangle Park, NC 27709-3663
Phone: 919-549-8614
Fax: 919-549-4687
E-mail: carswellb@ncseaa.edu

C.M. AND M.D. SUTHER SCHOLARSHIP PROGRAM

Award for full-time North Carolina resident undergraduate students enrolled at one of the sixteen constituent institutions of the University of North Carolina. One award is made from each institution. Must demonstrate financial need. One-time, merit-based award. Minimum 3.0 GPA required.

Award: Scholarship for use in freshman, sophomore, junior, or senior years; not renewable. *Number:* 1. *Amount:* $900.

Eligibility Requirements: Applicant must be enrolled or expecting to enroll full-time at an institution or university; resident of North Carolina and studying in North Carolina. Applicant must have 3.0 GPA or higher. Available to U.S. citizens.

Application Requirements: Financial need analysis. *Deadline:* Continuous.

Contact: Sharon Scott, Assistant, Scholarship and Grant Division
North Carolina State Education Assistance Authority
PO Box 13663
Research Triangle Park, NC 27709-3663

GOVERNOR JAMES G. MARTIN COLLEGE SCHOLARSHIPS
• *See page 516*

INCENTIVE SCHOLARSHIP FOR CERTAIN CONSTITUENT INSTITUTIONS

Scholarship aid to well-prepared, in-state students who want to attend one of UNC constituent universities on a full-time basis.

Award: Scholarship for use in freshman, sophomore, junior, or senior years. *Number:* varies. *Amount:* $2000–$3000.

Eligibility Requirements: Applicant must be enrolled or expecting to enroll full-time at an institution or university; resident of North Carolina and studying in North Carolina.

Application Requirements: *Deadline:* varies.

Contact: Bill Carswell, Manager of Scholarship and Grant Division
North Carolina State Education Assistance Authority
PO Box 13663
Research Triangle Park, NC 27709-3663
Phone: 919-549-8614
Fax: 919-248-4687
E-mail: carswellb@ncseaa.edu

JAGANNATHAN SCHOLARSHIP

Available to graduating high school seniors who plan to enroll as college freshmen in a full-time degree program at one of the constituent institutions of The University of North Carolina. Applicant must be resident of North Carolina. Applicant must document financial need.

Award: Scholarship for use in freshman year. *Number:* varies. *Amount:* up to $3500.

Eligibility Requirements: Applicant must be high school student; planning to enroll or expecting to enroll full-time at a four-year institution or university; resident of North Carolina and studying in North Carolina. Applicant must have 3.0 GPA or higher.

Application Requirements: *Deadline:* February 13.

Contact: high school guidance counselor

JAMES LEE LOVE SCHOLARSHIPS

Award for full-time North Carolina resident undergraduate students enrolled at one of the sixteen constituent institutions of the University of North Carolina. One award is made from each institution. Must demonstrate financial need.

Award: Scholarship for use in freshman, sophomore, junior, or senior years; not renewable. *Number:* varies. *Amount:* varies.

Eligibility Requirements: Applicant must be enrolled or expecting to enroll full-time at a four-year institution; resident of North Carolina and studying in North Carolina. Available to U.S. citizens.

Application Requirements: Financial need analysis. *Deadline:* Continuous.

Contact: Sharon Scott, Assistant, Scholarship and Grant Division
North Carolina State Education Assistance Authority
PO Box 13663
Research Triangle Park, NC 27709-3663

NORTH CAROLINA COMMUNITY COLLEGE GRANT PROGRAM

Annual award for North Carolina residents enrolled at least part-time in a North Carolina community college curriculum program. Priority given to those enrolled in college transferable curriculum programs, persons seeking new job skills, women in non-traditional curricula, and those participating in an ABE, GED, or high school diploma program. Contact financial aid office of institution the student attends for information and deadline. Must complete Free Application for Federal Student Aid.

Award: Grant for use in freshman or sophomore years; renewable. *Number:* varies. *Amount:* $683.

Eligibility Requirements: Applicant must be enrolled or expecting to enroll full or part-time at a two-year or technical institution; resident of North Carolina and studying in North Carolina. Available to U.S. citizens.

Application Requirements: Financial need analysis, FAFSA. *Deadline:* varies.

Contact: Bill Carswell, Manager, Scholarship and Grants Division
North Carolina State Education Assistance Authority
PO Box 13663
Research Triangle Park, NC 27709-3663

NORTH CAROLINA LEGISLATIVE TUITION GRANT PROGRAM (NCLTG)

Renewable aid for North Carolina residents attending approved private colleges or universities within the state. Must be enrolled full-time in an undergraduate program not leading to a religious vocation. Contact college financial aid office for deadlines.

Award: Grant for use in freshman, sophomore, junior, or senior years; renewable. *Number:* varies. *Amount:* $1500–$1800.

Eligibility Requirements: Applicant must be enrolled or expecting to enroll full-time at a two-year or four-year institution or university; resident of North Carolina and studying in North Carolina. Available to U.S. citizens.

Application Requirements: Application. *Deadline:* varies.

Contact: Bill Carswell, Manager of Scholarship and Grant Division
North Carolina State Education Assistance Authority
PO Box 13663
Research Triangle Park, NC 27709-3663

NORTH CAROLINA STUDENT INCENTIVE GRANT (NCSIG)

Renewable award for North Carolina residents who are enrolled full-time in an undergraduate program not leading to a religious vocation at a North Carolina postsecondary institution. Must demonstrate substantial financial need. Must complete Free Application for Student Aid. Must be U.S. citizen and must maintain satisfactory academic progress. Offered by NCSEAA through College Foundation, Inc. Visit Web site at http://www.cfnc.org.

Award: Grant for use in freshman, sophomore, junior, or senior years; renewable. *Number:* varies. *Amount:* up to $700.

Eligibility Requirements: Applicant must be enrolled or expecting to enroll full-time at a two-year or four-year institution or university; resident of North Carolina and studying in North Carolina. Available to U.S. citizens.

Application Requirements: Application, financial need analysis. *Deadline:* March 15.

Contact: Bill Carswell, Manager of Scholarship and Grant Division
North Carolina State Education Assistance Authority
PO Box 13663
Research Triangle Park, NC 27709-3663

STATE CONTRACTUAL SCHOLARSHIP FUND PROGRAM-NORTH CAROLINA

Renewable award for North Carolina residents already attending an approved private college or university in the state in pursuit of an undergraduate degree. Must have financial need. Contact college financial aid office for deadline and information. May not be enrolled in a program leading to a religious vocation.

Award: Scholarship for use in freshman, sophomore, junior, or senior years; renewable. *Number:* varies. *Amount:* up to $1100.

Eligibility Requirements: Applicant must be enrolled or expecting to enroll full or part-time at a two-year or four-year institution or university; resident of North Carolina and studying in North Carolina. Available to U.S. citizens.

Application Requirements: Financial need analysis. *Deadline:* varies.

Contact: Bill Carswell, Manager of Scholarship and Grant Division
North Carolina State Education Assistance Authority
PO Box 13663
Research Triangle Park, NC 27709-3663

UNIVERSITY OF NORTH CAROLINA NEED-BASED GRANT

Must be enrolled in at least 6 credit hours at one of 16 UNC system universities. Eligibility based on need; applicant must have submitted Free Application for Federal Student Aid. Award varies, consideration for grant automatic when FAFSA is filed. Late applications may be denied due to insufficient funds.

Award: Grant for use in freshman, sophomore, junior, or senior years; renewable. *Number:* varies. *Amount:* varies.

Eligibility Requirements: Applicant must be enrolled or expecting to enroll full or part-time at an institution or university and studying in North Carolina. Available to U.S. citizens.

Application Requirements: Financial need analysis, FAFSA. *Deadline:* varies.

Contact: Bill Carswell, Manager of Scholarship and Grant Division
North Carolina State Education Assistance Authority
PO Box 13663
Research Triangle Park, NC 27709-3663
Phone: 919-549-8614
Fax: 919-248-4687
E-mail: carswellb@ncseaa.edu

NORTH CAROLINA VIETNAM VETERANS, INC. http://www.ncneighbors.com/96

NORTH CAROLINA VIETNAM VETERANS, INC., SCHOLARSHIP PROGRAM

• *See page 562*

NORTH DAKOTA DEPARTMENT OF PUBLIC INSTRUCTION http://www.dpi.state.nd.us

ROBERT C. BYRD SCHOLARSHIPS

Renewable award to exceptionally able high school seniors who show promise of continued excellence in postsecondary education. Must be resident of North Dakota and a U.S. citizen. Deadline second week in April.

Award: Scholarship for use in freshman, sophomore, junior, or senior years; renewable. *Number:* 10–12. *Amount:* $1500.

Eligibility Requirements: Applicant must be high school student; planning to enroll or expecting to enroll full-time at a two-year or four-year or technical institution or university and resident of North Dakota. Available to U.S. citizens.

Application Requirements: Application, essay, references, test scores, transcript, college acceptance letter. *Deadline:* varies.

Contact: Heidi Bergland, Administrative Assistant
North Dakota Department of Public Instruction
600 East Boulevard Avenue
Department 201
Bismarck, ND 58505-0440
Phone: 701-328-2317
Fax: 701-328-4770
E-mail: hbergland@state.nd.us

NORTHERN VIRGINIA URBAN LEAGUE http://www.nvul.org/

NORTHERN VIRGINIA URBAN LEAGUE SCHOLARSHIP PROGRAM

• *See page 596*

OHIO ASSOCIATION OF CAREER COLLEGES AND SCHOOLS

LEGISLATIVE SCHOLARSHIP

Renewable award to full-time students attending a trade/technical institution in Ohio. Must be U.S. citizen. Minimum 2.5 GPA required. Must be graduating high school senior.

Award: Scholarship for use in freshman or sophomore years; renewable. *Number:* 80. *Amount:* $2600–$13,448.

Eligibility Requirements: Applicant must be high school student; planning to enroll or expecting to enroll full-time at a technical institution; resident of Ohio and studying in Ohio. Applicant must have 2.5 GPA or higher. Available to U.S. citizens.

Ohio Association of Career Colleges and Schools (continued)

Application Requirements: Application, essay, references, transcript. *Deadline:* March 5.

Contact: Max Lerner, Executive Director
Ohio Association of Career Colleges and Schools
1857 Northwest Boulevard
The Annex
Columbus, OH 43212
Phone: 614-487-8180
Fax: 614-487-8190

OHIO BOARD OF REGENTS http://www.regents.state.oh.us

OHIO ACADEMIC SCHOLARSHIP PROGRAM

Award for academically outstanding Ohio residents planning to attend an approved Ohio college. Must be a high school senior intending to enroll full-time. Award is renewable for up to four years. Must rank in upper quarter of class or have a minimum GPA of 3.5.

Award: Scholarship for use in freshman, sophomore, junior, or senior years; renewable. *Number:* 1000. *Amount:* $2205.

Eligibility Requirements: Applicant must be high school student; planning to enroll or expecting to enroll full-time at a two-year or four-year institution; resident of Ohio and studying in Ohio. Applicant must have 3.5 GPA or higher. Available to U.S. citizens.

Application Requirements: Application, test scores, transcript. *Deadline:* February 23.

Contact: Sarina Wilks, Program Administrator
Ohio Board of Regents
PO Box 182452
Columbus, OH 43218-2452
Phone: 614-752-9528
Fax: 614-752-5903
E-mail: swilks@regents.state.oh.us

OHIO INSTRUCTIONAL GRANT

Award for low- and middle-income Ohio residents attending an approved college or school in Ohio or Pennsylvania. Must be enrolled full-time and have financial need. Average award is $630. May be used for any course of study except theology.

Award: Grant for use in freshman, sophomore, junior, or senior years; renewable. *Number:* varies. *Amount:* $78–$5466.

Eligibility Requirements: Applicant must be enrolled or expecting to enroll full-time at a two-year or four-year institution or university; resident of Ohio and studying in Ohio or Pennsylvania. Available to U.S. citizens.

Application Requirements: Application, financial need analysis. *Deadline:* October 1.

Contact: Charles Shahid, Assistant Director
Ohio Board of Regents
PO Box 182452
Columbus, OH 43218-2452
Phone: 614-644-5959
Fax: 614-752-5903
E-mail: cshahid@regents.state.oh.us

OHIO MISSING IN ACTION AND PRISONERS OF WAR ORPHANS SCHOLARSHIP

• *See page 562*

OHIO SAFETY OFFICERS COLLEGE MEMORIAL FUND

• *See page 517*

OHIO STUDENT CHOICE GRANT PROGRAM

Renewable award available to Ohio residents attending private colleges within the state. Must be enrolled full-time in a bachelor's degree program. Do not apply to state. Check with financial aid office of college.

Award: Grant for use in freshman, sophomore, junior, or senior years; renewable. *Number:* varies. *Amount:* up to $1002.

Eligibility Requirements: Applicant must be enrolled or expecting to enroll full-time at a four-year institution; resident of Ohio and studying in Ohio. Available to U.S. citizens.

Application Requirements: *Deadline:* Continuous.

Contact: Barbara Metheney, Program Administrator
Ohio Board of Regents
PO Box 182452
Columbus, OH 43218-2452
Phone: 614-752-9535
Fax: 614-752-5903
E-mail: bmethene@regents.state.oh.us

OHIO WAR ORPHANS SCHOLARSHIP

• *See page 563*

PART-TIME STUDENT INSTRUCTIONAL GRANT

Renewable grants for part-time undergraduates who are Ohio residents. Award amounts vary. Must attend an Ohio institution.

Award: Grant for use in freshman, sophomore, or junior years; renewable. *Number:* varies. *Amount:* varies.

Eligibility Requirements: Applicant must be enrolled or expecting to enroll part-time at a two-year or four-year institution or university; resident of Ohio and studying in Ohio. Available to U.S. citizens.

Application Requirements: Application, financial need analysis. *Deadline:* Continuous.

Contact: Barbara Metheney, Program Administrator
Ohio Board of Regents
PO Box 182452
Columbus, OH 43218-2452
Phone: 614-752-9535
Fax: 614-752-5903
E-mail: bmethene@regents.state.oh.us

OHIO CIVIL SERVICE EMPLOYEES ASSOCIATION http://www.ocsea.org

LES BEST SCHOLARSHIP

• *See page 474*

OHIO DEPARTMENT OF EDUCATION http://www.ode.state.oh.us

ROBERT C. BYRD HONORS SCHOLARSHIP

Renewable award for graduating high school seniors who demonstrate outstanding academic achievement. Each Ohio high school receives applications by January of each year. School can submit one application for every 200 students in the senior class. Application deadline is the second Friday in March.

Award: Scholarship for use in freshman, sophomore, junior, or senior years; renewable. *Number:* varies. *Amount:* up to $1500.

Eligibility Requirements: Applicant must be high school student; planning to enroll or expecting to enroll at a two-year or four-year institution or university and resident of Ohio. Applicant must have 3.5 GPA or higher. Available to U.S. citizens.

Application Requirements: Application, test scores. *Deadline:* varies.

Contact: Byrd Program Office
Ohio Department of Education
25 South Front Street, Second Floor
Columbus, OH 43215
Phone: 614-466-4590

OHIO FORESTRY ASSOCIATION http://www.ohioforest.org

OHIO FORESTRY ASSOCIATION MEMORIAL SCHOLARSHIP

Minimum of one scholarship will be awarded to provide assistance toward forest resource education to quality college students. Preference given to students attending Ohio colleges and universities. Scholarship awards vary.

Award: Scholarship for use in freshman, sophomore, junior, or senior years; not renewable. *Number:* 1. *Amount:* $1000.

Eligibility Requirements: Applicant must be enrolled or expecting to enroll at a two-year or four-year or technical institution or university and resident of Ohio. Available to U.S. citizens.

Application Requirements: Application, essay, test scores. *Deadline:* April 15.

Contact: Scholarship Committee
Ohio Forestry Association
PO Box 970
4080 South High Street
Columbus, OH 43207

OHIO NATIONAL GUARD

OHIO NATIONAL GUARD SCHOLARSHIP PROGRAM

• *See page 537*

OKLAHOMA ALUMNI & ASSOCIATES OF FHA, HERO AND FCCLA, INC. http://www.okfccla.org

OKLAHOMA ALUMNI & ASSOCIATES OF FHA, HERO AND FCCLA, INC. SCHOLARSHIP

• *See page 474*

OKLAHOMA STATE REGENTS FOR HIGHER EDUCATION http://www.okhighered.org

ACADEMIC SCHOLARS PROGRAM

Encourages students of high academic ability to attend institutions in Oklahoma. Renewable up to four years. ACT or SAT scores must fall between 99.5 and 100th percentiles, or applicant must be designated as a National Merit scholar or finalist.

Award: Scholarship for use in freshman, sophomore, junior, or senior years; renewable. *Number:* varies. *Amount:* $3500–$5500.

Eligibility Requirements: Applicant must be high school student; planning to enroll or expecting to enroll full-time at a two-year or four-year institution or university and studying in Oklahoma. Available to U.S. and non-U.S. citizens.

Application Requirements: Application, test scores, transcript. *Deadline:* Continuous.

Contact: Oklahoma State Regents for Higher Education
PO Box 108850
Oklahoma City, OK 73101-8850
Phone: 800-858-1840
Fax: 405-225-9230
E-mail: studentinfo@osrhe.edu

OKLAHOMA TUITION AID GRANT

Award for Oklahoma residents enrolled at an Oklahoma institution at least part time each semester in a degree program. May be enrolled in two- or four-year or approved vocational-technical institution. Award of up to $1000 per year. Application is made through FAFSA.

Award: Grant for use in freshman, sophomore, junior, senior, or graduate years; renewable. *Number:* 23,000. *Amount:* $200–$1000.

Eligibility Requirements: Applicant must be enrolled or expecting to enroll full or part-time at a two-year or four-year or technical institution or university; resident of Oklahoma and studying in Oklahoma. Available to U.S. citizens.

Application Requirements: Application, financial need analysis, FAFSA. *Deadline:* April 30.

Contact: Oklahoma State Regents for Higher Education
PO Box 3020
Oklahoma City, OK 73101-3020
Phone: 405-225-9456
Fax: 405-225-9392
E-mail: otaginfo@otag.org

REGIONAL UNIVERSITY BACCALAUREATE SCHOLARSHIP

Renewable award for Oklahoma residents attending one of 11 participating Oklahoma public universities. Must have an ACT composite score of at least 30 or be a National Merit semifinalist or commended student. In addition to the award amount, each recipient will receive a resident tuition waiver from the institution. Must maintain a 3.25 GPA. Deadlines vary depending upon the institution attended.

Award: Scholarship for use in freshman, sophomore, junior, or senior years; renewable. *Number:* varies. *Amount:* $3000.

Eligibility Requirements: Applicant must be enrolled or expecting to enroll full-time at an institution or university; resident of Oklahoma and studying in Oklahoma. Available to U.S. and non-U.S. citizens.

Application Requirements: Application. *Deadline:* varies.

Contact: Oklahoma State Regents for Higher Education
PO Box 108850
Oklahoma City, OK 73101-8850
Phone: 800-858-1840
Fax: 405-225-9230
E-mail: studentinfo@osrhe.edu

WILLIAM P. WILLIS SCHOLARSHIP

Renewable award for Oklahoma residents attending an Oklahoma institution. Contact institution financial aid office for application deadline.

Award: Scholarship for use in freshman, sophomore, junior, or senior years; renewable. *Number:* 32. *Amount:* $2000–$3000.

Eligibility Requirements: Applicant must be enrolled or expecting to enroll full-time at a two-year or four-year institution or university; resident of Oklahoma and studying in Oklahoma. Available to U.S. and non-U.S. citizens.

Application Requirements: *Deadline:* varies.

Contact: Oklahoma State Regents for Higher Education
PO Box 108850
Oklahoma City, OK 73101-8850
Phone: 800-858-1840
Fax: 405-225-9230
E-mail: studentinfo@osrhe.edu

OREGON COLLECTORS ASSOCIATION (ORCA) SCHOLARSHIP FUND http://www.orcascholarshipfund.com

OREGON COLLECTORS ASSOCIATION BOB HASSON MEMORIAL SCHOLARSHIP FUND

Scholarship available to Oregon high school seniors for use as full-time students at an Oregon accredited public or private 2- or 4-year college, university, or trade school. Must start attendance within 12 months of the award. Must submit fictional essay on "the proper use of credit in the 21st century." Applicants may not be children/grandchildren of owners or officers of collection agencies in Oregon. For application see Web site: http://www.orcascholarshipfund.com.

Award: Scholarship for use in freshman year; not renewable. *Number:* 3. *Amount:* $1500–$3000.

Eligibility Requirements: Applicant must be high school student; planning to enroll or expecting to enroll full-time at a two-year or four-year or technical institution or university; resident of Oregon and studying in Oregon. Available to U.S. citizens.

Application Requirements: Application, essay. *Deadline:* March 1.

Contact: Doug Jones, Director
Oregon Collectors Association (ORCA) Scholarship Fund
PO Box 42409
Portland, OR 97242
Phone: 888-622-3588
E-mail: dcj@portlandbilling.com

OREGON DEPARTMENT OF VETERANS' AFFAIRS http://www.odva.state.or.us

OREGON VETERANS' EDUCATION AID

• *See page 563*

OREGON STUDENT ASSISTANCE COMMISSION http://www.osac.state.or.us

A. VICTOR ROSENFELD SCHOLARSHIP

• *See page 498*

AFSCME: AMERICAN FEDERATION OF STATE, COUNTY, AND MUNICIPAL EMPLOYEES LOCAL 1724 SCHOLARSHIP

• *See page 475*

AFSCME: AMERICAN FEDERATION OF STATE, COUNTY, AND MUNICIPAL EMPLOYEES LOCAL 75 SCHOLARSHIP

• *See page 475*

ALBINA FUEL COMPANY SCHOLARSHIP

• *See page 498*

AMERICAN EX-PRISONER OF WAR SCHOLARSHIPS: PETER CONNACHER MEMORIAL SCHOLARSHIP

• *See page 563*

ANGELINA AND PETE COSTANZO VOCATIONAL SCHOLARSHIP

Award open to high school grads or GED recipients seeking job skills but not a baccalaureate degree. Must be enrolled at least part-time at a vocational school or two-year college. Must be a resident of Clackamas, Columbia, Multnomah, or Washington counties. Renewable for one additional year.

Award: Scholarship for use in freshman or sophomore years; renewable. *Number:* 9. *Amount:* $2333.

Eligibility Requirements: Applicant must be enrolled or expecting to enroll full or part-time at a two-year or technical institution and resident of Oregon. Available to U.S. citizens.

Application Requirements: Application, essay, financial need analysis, transcript, activity chart. *Deadline:* March 1.

Contact: Director of Grant Programs
Oregon Student Assistance Commission
1500 Valley River Drive, Suite 100
Eugene, OR 97401-7020
Phone: 800-452-8807 Ext. 7395
E-mail: awardinfo@mercury.osac.state.or.us

BANDON SUBMARINE CABLE COUNCIL SCHOLARSHIP

Renewable award for Oregon residents and high school graduates who have not matriculated as postsecondary students. Additional preferences, in this order, are for members or dependent children of members of the Bandon Submarine Council; any commercial fisherman or family members who reside in Coos County; any commercial fisherman or family member anywhere in Oregon; any postsecondary student residing in Clatsop, Tillamook, Lincoln, Lane, Coos, or Curry County; any postsecondary student in Oregon.

Award: Scholarship for use in freshman, sophomore, junior, or senior years; renewable. *Number:* varies. *Amount:* $500.

Eligibility Requirements: Applicant must be enrolled or expecting to enroll at an institution or university and resident of Oregon.

Application Requirements: Application, essay, financial need analysis, transcript. *Deadline:* March 1.

Contact: Director of Grant Programs
Oregon Student Assistance Commission
1500 Valley River Drive, Suite 100
Eugene, OR 97401-7020
Phone: 800-452-8807 Ext. 7395
E-mail: awardinfo@mercury.osac.state.or.us

BANK OF THE CASCADES SCHOLARSHIP

• *See page 499*

BEN SELLING SCHOLARSHIP

Award for Oregon residents enrolling as sophomores or higher in college. College GPA 3.50 or higher required. Apply/compete annually. Must be U.S. citizen or permanent resident. Wells Fargo employees, their children or near relatives must provide complete disclosure of employment status to receive this award.

Award: Scholarship for use in sophomore, junior, or senior years; not renewable. *Number:* 25. *Amount:* $1000.

Eligibility Requirements: Applicant must be enrolled or expecting to enroll at an institution or university and resident of Oregon. Applicant must have 3.5 GPA or higher. Available to U.S. citizens.

Application Requirements: Application, essay, financial need analysis, references, transcript, activity chart. *Deadline:* March 1.

Contact: Director of Grant Programs
Oregon Student Assistance Commission
1500 Valley River Drive, Suite 100
Eugene, OR 97401-7020
Phone: 800-452-8807 Ext. 7395
E-mail: awardinfo@mercury.osac.state.or.us

BENJAMIN FRANKLIN/EDITH GREEN SCHOLARSHIP

One-time award open to graduating Oregon high school seniors. Must attend a four-year public Oregon college. See Web site at http://www.osac.state.or.us for more information.

Award: Scholarship for use in freshman year; not renewable. *Number:* 14. *Amount:* $1000.

Eligibility Requirements: Applicant must be high school student; planning to enroll or expecting to enroll at a four-year institution; resident of Oregon and studying in Oregon.

Application Requirements: Application, essay, financial need analysis, transcript, activity chart. *Deadline:* March 1.

Contact: Director of Grant Programs
Oregon Student Assistance Commission
1500 Valley River Drive, Suite 100
Eugene, OR 97401-7020
Phone: 800-452-8807 Ext. 7395
E-mail: awardinfo@mercury.osac.state.or.us

BLUE HERON PAPER EMPLOYEE DEPENDENTS SCHOLARSHIP

• *See page 499*

CARPENTERS AND JOINERS LOCAL 2130 SCHOLARSHIP

• *See page 517*

CHANDLER SCHOLARS PROGRAM SCHOLARSHIP

One-time award open to current residents and graduates of a high school in Del Norte County, California, or one of the following Oregon counties: Baker, Curry, Deschutes, Harney, Jefferson, Umatilla, or Union. Must have a minimum cumulative 2.5 high school GPA. Additional essay required. See Web site for details. (http://www.osac.state.or.us).

Award: Scholarship for use in freshman, sophomore, junior, or senior years; not renewable. *Number:* 14. *Amount:* $1000.

Eligibility Requirements: Applicant must be enrolled or expecting to enroll at an institution or university and resident of California or Oregon. Applicant must have 2.5 GPA or higher. Available to U.S. citizens.

Application Requirements: Application, essay, financial need analysis, transcript, activity chart. *Deadline:* March 1.

Contact: Director of Grant Programs
Oregon Student Assistance Commission
1500 Valley River Drive, Suite 100
Eugene, OR 97401-7020
Phone: 800-452-8807 Ext. 7395
E-mail: awardinfo@mercury.osac.state.or.us

CHILDREN, ADULT, AND FAMILY SERVICES SCHOLARSHIP

One-time award for graduating high school seniors, GED recipients, and college students currently or formerly in foster care or an Independent Living Program (ILP) financially supported through the Oregon State Office for Services to Children and Families. Must attend an Oregon public college. Visit Web site for more details (http://www.osac.state.or.us). Award varies between $500-$5000.

Award: Scholarship for use in freshman, sophomore, junior, senior, or graduate years; not renewable. *Number:* varies. *Amount:* $500–$5000.

Eligibility Requirements: Applicant must be enrolled or expecting to enroll at a two-year or four-year institution; resident of Oregon and studying in Oregon. Available to U.S. citizens.

Application Requirements: Application, essay, financial need analysis, references, transcript, activity chart. *Deadline:* March 1.

Contact: Director of Grant Programs
Oregon Student Assistance Commission
1500 Valley River Drive, Suite 100
Eugene, OR 97401-7020
Phone: 800-452-8807 Ext. 7395
E-mail: awardinfo@mercury.osac.state.or.us

DAN KONNIE MEMORIAL SCHOLARSHIP

• *See page 499*

DAVID FAMILY SCHOLARSHIP

Award for residents of Clackamas, Lane, Multnomah, and Washington counties. First preference to applicants enrolling at least half-time in upper-division or graduate programs at four-year colleges. College sophomores and above. Students with 2.50-3.50 GPA.

Award: Scholarship for use in freshman, sophomore, junior, senior, or graduate years; not renewable. *Number:* 15. *Amount:* $2530.

Eligibility Requirements: Applicant must be enrolled or expecting to enroll full or part-time at a four-year institution and resident of Oregon. Applicant must have 2.5 GPA or higher. Available to U.S. citizens.

Application Requirements: Application, essay, financial need analysis, test scores, transcript, activity chart. *Deadline:* March 1.

Contact: Director of Grant Programs
Oregon Student Assistance Commission
1500 Valley River Drive, Suite 100
Eugene, OR 97401-7020
Phone: 800-452-8807 Ext. 7395
E-mail: awardinfo@mercury.osac.state.or.us

DOROTHY CAMPBELL MEMORIAL SCHOLARSHIP

Renewable award for female Oregon high school senior with a minimum 2.75 GPA. Must submit essay describing strong, continuing interest in golf and the contribution that sport has made to applicant's development.

Award: Scholarship for use in freshman, sophomore, junior, or senior years; renewable. *Number:* 2. *Amount:* $1500.

Eligibility Requirements: Applicant must be high school student; planning to enroll or expecting to enroll at a four-year institution; female; resident of Oregon; studying in Oregon and must have an interest in golf. Available to U.S. citizens.

Application Requirements: Application, essay, financial need analysis, test scores, transcript, activity chart. *Deadline:* March 1.

Contact: Director of Grant Programs
Oregon Student Assistance Commission
1500 Valley River Drive, Suite 100
Eugene, OR 97401-7020
Phone: 800-452-8807 Ext. 7395
E-mail: awardinfo@mercury.osac.state.or.us

ESSEX SCHOLARSHIP

• *See page 499*

FORD RESTART PROGRAM SCHOLARSHIP

Award for Oregon residents 26 years of age or older as of March 1 who have a high school degree or GED and wish to pursue technical, community college, or four-year degrees at an Oregon college. Preference given to those with limited college experience. Must complete ReStart Reference Form. Contact OSAC. Apply for this program, or Ford Opportunity, or Ford Scholars.

Award: Scholarship for use in freshman, sophomore, junior, or senior years; renewable. *Number:* 30. *Amount:* $7781.

Eligibility Requirements: Applicant must be age 26; enrolled or expecting to enroll at a two-year or four-year or technical institution; resident of Oregon and studying in Oregon. Available to U.S. citizens.

Application Requirements: Application, essay, financial need analysis, transcript, activity chart. *Deadline:* March 1.

Contact: Director of Grant Programs
Oregon Student Assistance Commission
1500 Valley River Drive, Suite 100
Eugene, OR 97401-7020
Phone: 800-452-8807 Ext. 7395
E-mail: awardinfo@mercury.osac.state.or.us

FORD OPPORTUNITY PROGRAM

Award for Oregon residents who are single heads of household with custody of a dependent child or children. Must plan to work toward a four-year degree. Only for use at Oregon colleges. Minimum 3.0 GPA. If minimum requirements not met, Special Recommendation Form (see high school counselor or contact OSAC) must be submitted. May apply for this program or Ford Scholars or Ford Restart.

Award: Scholarship for use in freshman, sophomore, junior, or senior years; renewable. *Number:* 52. *Amount:* $11,261.

Eligibility Requirements: Applicant must be enrolled or expecting to enroll at a two-year or four-year institution; single; resident of Oregon and studying in Oregon. Applicant must have 3.0 GPA or higher.

Application Requirements: Application, essay, financial need analysis, test scores, transcript, activity chart. *Deadline:* March 1.

Contact: Director of Grant Programs
Oregon Student Assistance Commission
1500 Valley River Drive, Suite 100
Eugene, OR 97401-7020
Phone: 800-452-8807 Ext. 7395
E-mail: awardinfo@mercury.osac.state.or.us

FORD SCHOLARS

Award for Oregon graduating seniors, Oregon high school graduates not yet full-time undergraduates, or those who have completed two years of undergraduate study at an Oregon community college and will enter junior year at a four-year Oregon college. Minimum cumulative 3.0 GPA. If minimum requirements not met, Special Recommendation Form (see high school counselor or contact OSAC) must be submitted. May apply for this program, or Ford Opportunity, or Ford Restart. Must plan to work toward a four-year degree.

Award: Scholarship for use in freshman, sophomore, or junior years; renewable. *Number:* 136. *Amount:* $5836.

Eligibility Requirements: Applicant must be enrolled or expecting to enroll at a four-year institution; resident of Oregon and studying in Oregon. Applicant must have 3.0 GPA or higher. Available to U.S. citizens.

Application Requirements: Application, essay, financial need analysis, test scores, transcript, activity chart. *Deadline:* March 1.

Contact: Director of Grant Programs
Oregon Student Assistance Commission
1500 Valley River Drive, Suite 100
Eugene, OR 97401-7020
Phone: 800-452-8807 Ext. 7395
E-mail: awardinfo@mercury.osac.state.or.us

GLENN JACKSON SCHOLARS SCHOLARSHIPS (OCF)

• *See page 499*

HARRY LUDWIG MEMORIAL SCHOLARSHIP

• *See page 530*

IDA M. CRAWFORD SCHOLARSHIP

One-time scholarship awarded to Oregon high school seniors with a cumulative GPA of 3.5. Not available to applicants majoring in law, medicine, theology, teaching, or music. U.S. Bancorp employees, their children or near relatives, are not eligible. Must supply proof of birth in the continental U.S.

Award: Scholarship for use in freshman year; not renewable. *Number:* 63. *Amount:* $577.

Oregon Student Assistance Commission (continued)

Eligibility Requirements: Applicant must be high school student; planning to enroll or expecting to enroll at an institution or university and resident of Oregon. Applicant must have 3.5 GPA or higher. Available to U.S. citizens.

Application Requirements: Application, essay, financial need analysis, test scores, transcript. *Deadline:* March 1.

Contact: Director of Grant Programs
Oregon Student Assistance Commission
1500 Valley River Drive, Suite 100
Eugene, OR 97401-7020
Phone: 800-452-8807 Ext. 7395
E-mail: awardinfo@mercury.osac.state.or.us

INTERNATIONAL BROTHERHOOD OF ELECTRICAL WORKERS LOCAL 280 SCHOLARSHIP

• *See page 475*

INTERNATIONAL UNION OF OPERATING ENGINEERS LOCAL 701 SCHOLARSHIP

• *See page 475*

IRMGARD SCHULZ SCHOLARSHIP

Award for graduating seniors of a U.S. public high school with first preference going to applicants from high schools in Josephine County, Oregon. Second preference is for applicants who are orphans or from foster or single-parent homes. Prior-year recipients may reapply annually. Application deadline is March 1.

Award: Scholarship for use in freshman, sophomore, junior, senior, or graduate years; not renewable. *Number:* 30. *Amount:* $308.

Eligibility Requirements: Applicant must be enrolled or expecting to enroll at an institution or university and resident of Oregon.

Application Requirements: Application, essay, financial need analysis, transcript. *Deadline:* March 1.

Contact: Director of Grant Programs
Oregon Student Assistance Commission
1500 Valley River Drive, Suite 100
Eugene, OR 97401-7020
Phone: 800-452-8807 Ext. 7395
E-mail: awardinfo@mercury.osac.state.or.us

JEROME B. STEINBACH SCHOLARSHIP

One-time award for Oregon residents enrolled in Oregon institution as sophomore or above with minimum 3.5 GPA. Award for undergraduate study. U.S. Bancorp employees, their children or close relatives, not eligible. Must submit proof of U.S. birth.

Award: Scholarship for use in sophomore, junior, or senior years; not renewable. *Number:* 93. *Amount:* $685.

Eligibility Requirements: Applicant must be enrolled or expecting to enroll at a two-year or four-year institution; resident of Oregon and studying in Oregon. Applicant must have 3.5 GPA or higher. Available to U.S. citizens.

Application Requirements: Application, essay, financial need analysis, test scores, transcript. *Deadline:* March 1.

Contact: Director of Grant Programs
Oregon Student Assistance Commission
1500 Valley River Drive, Suite 100
Eugene, OR 97401-7020
Phone: 800-452-8807 Ext. 7395
E-mail: awardinfo@mercury.osac.state.or.us

JOSE D. GARCIA MIGRANT EDUCATION SCHOLARSHIP

One-time award for U.S. citizens or permanent residents in Oregon Migrant Education program, who are also high school graduates or GED recipients enrolling at least half-time in freshman year undergraduate study. Contact for application procedures and requirements.

Award: Scholarship for use in freshman year; not renewable. *Number:* 1. *Amount:* $500.

Eligibility Requirements: Applicant must be enrolled or expecting to enroll full or part-time at an institution or university; resident of Oregon and must have an interest in designated field specified by sponsor. Available to U.S. citizens.

Application Requirements: Application, essay, financial need analysis, transcript, activity chart. *Deadline:* March 1.

Contact: Director of Grant Programs
Oregon Student Assistance Commission
1500 Valley River Drive, Suite 100
Eugene, OR 97401-7020
Phone: 800-452-8807 Ext. 7395
E-mail: awardinfo@mercury.osac.state.or.us

MARIA JACKSON/GENERAL GEORGE A. WHITE SCHOLARSHIP

• *See page 563*

MC GARRY MACHINE INC. SCHOLARSHIP

• *See page 499*

OREGON AFL-CIO SCHOLARSHIP

• *See page 517*

OREGON COLLECTORS ASSOCIATION BOB HASSON MEMORIAL SCHOLARSHIP

One-time award for graduating Oregon high school seniors and recent Oregon high school graduates, enrolling in an Oregon college within one year of graduation. Children and grandchildren of owners and officers of collection agencies registered in Oregon are not eligible. Award is based on a 3-4 page essay titled "The Proper Use of Credit." See Web site (http://www.osac.state.or.us) for important application information.

Award: Scholarship for use in freshman year; not renewable. *Number:* 3. *Amount:* $1500–$3000.

Eligibility Requirements: Applicant must be enrolled or expecting to enroll at a two-year or four-year or technical institution; resident of Oregon and studying in Oregon. Available to U.S. citizens.

Application Requirements: Application, applicant must enter a contest, essay, financial need analysis, test scores, transcript, activity chart. *Deadline:* March 1.

Contact: Director of Grant Programs
Oregon Student Assistance Commission
1500 Valley River Drive, Suite 100
Eugene, OR 97401-7020
Phone: 800-452-8807 Ext. 7395
E-mail: awardinfo@mercury.osac.state.or.us

OREGON DUNGENESS CRAB COMMISSION SCHOLARSHIP

• *See page 517*

OREGON METRO FEDERAL CREDIT UNION SCHOLARSHIP

One scholarship available to an Oregon high school graduate who is a Oregon Metro Federal Credit Union member. Preference given to graduating high school senior and applicant who plans to attend an Oregon college. One-time award.

Award: Scholarship for use in freshman, sophomore, junior, or senior years; not renewable. *Number:* 5. *Amount:* $500.

Eligibility Requirements: Applicant must be enrolled or expecting to enroll at a four-year institution; resident of Oregon and studying in Oregon. Available to U.S. citizens.

Application Requirements: Application, essay, financial need analysis, references, transcript, activity chart. *Deadline:* March 1.

Contact: Director of Grant Programs
Oregon Student Assistance Commission
1500 Valley River Drive, Suite 100
Eugene, OR 97401-7020
Phone: 800-452-8807 Ext. 7395
E-mail: awardinfo@mercury.osac.state.or.us

OREGON OCCUPATIONAL SAFETY AND HEALTH DIVISION WORKERS MEMORIAL SCHOLARSHIP

• *See page 517*

OREGON PUBLISHING COMPANY/HILLIARD SCHOLARSHIP

• *See page 475*

OREGON SALMON COMMISSION SCHOLARSHIP

• *See page 517*

OREGON SCHOLARSHIP FUND COMMUNITY COLLEGE STUDENT AWARD

Scholarship open to Oregon residents enrolled or planning to enroll in Oregon community college programs. May apply for one additional year.

Award: Scholarship for use in freshman or sophomore years; not renewable. *Number:* varies. *Amount:* $500.

Eligibility Requirements: Applicant must be enrolled or expecting to enroll at a two-year institution; resident of Oregon and studying in Oregon. Available to U.S. citizens.

Application Requirements: Application, essay, financial need analysis, transcript, activity chart. *Deadline:* March 1.

Contact: Director of Grant Programs
Oregon Student Assistance Commission
1500 Valley River Drive, Suite 100
Eugene, OR 97401-7020
Phone: 800-452-8807 Ext. 7395
E-mail: awardinfo@mercury.osac.state.or.us

OREGON SCHOLARSHIP FUND TRANSFER STUDENT AWARD

Award open to Oregon residents who are currently enrolled in their second year at a community college and are planning to transfer to a four-year college in Oregon. Prior recipients may apply for one additional year.

Award: Scholarship for use in junior or senior years; not renewable. *Number:* varies. *Amount:* $500.

Eligibility Requirements: Applicant must be enrolled or expecting to enroll at a four-year institution; resident of Oregon and studying in Oregon. Available to U.S. citizens.

Application Requirements: Application, essay, financial need analysis, transcript, activity chart. *Deadline:* March 1.

Contact: Director of Grant Programs
Oregon Student Assistance Commission
1500 Valley River Drive, Suite 100
Eugene, OR 97401-7020
Phone: 800-452-8807 Ext. 7395
E-mail: awardinfo@mercury.osac.state.or.us

OREGON STATE EMPLOYEES CREDIT UNION SCHOLARSHIP

One-time award open to primary members in good standing of the State Employees Credit Union. Must be a resident of Oregon.

Award: Scholarship for use in freshman, sophomore, junior, or senior years; not renewable. *Number:* varies. *Amount:* $500.

Eligibility Requirements: Applicant must be enrolled or expecting to enroll at an institution or university and resident of Oregon. Available to U.S. citizens.

Application Requirements: Application, essay, financial need analysis, transcript, activity chart. *Deadline:* March 1.

Contact: Director of Grant Programs
Oregon Student Assistance Commission
1500 Valley River Drive, Suite 100
Eugene, OR 97401-7020
Phone: 800-452-8807 Ext. 7395
E-mail: awardinfo@mercury.osac.state.or.us

OREGON STATE FISCAL ASSOCIATION SCHOLARSHIP

• *See page 476*

OREGON STUDENT ASSISTANCE COMMISSION EMPLOYEE AND DEPENDENT SCHOLARSHIP

One-time award for current permanent employee of the Oregon Student Assistance Commission or legally dependent children of employee. Also available to dependent children of an employee who retires, is permanently disabled, or deceased directly from employment at OSAC. Dependent must enroll full time. Employee may enroll part time.

Award: Scholarship for use in freshman, sophomore, junior, or senior years; not renewable. *Number:* 7. *Amount:* $500.

Eligibility Requirements: Applicant must be enrolled or expecting to enroll full or part-time at an institution or university and resident of Oregon.

Application Requirements: Application, essay, financial need analysis, transcript. *Deadline:* March 1.

Contact: Director of Grant Programs
Oregon Student Assistance Commission
1500 Valley River Drive, Suite 100
Eugene, OR 97401-7020
Phone: 800-452-8807 Ext. 7395
E-mail: awardinfo@mercury.osac.state.or.us

OREGON TRAWL COMMISSION SCHOLARSHIP

• *See page 518*

OREGON TRUCKING ASSOCIATION SCHOLARSHIP

• *See page 518*

PACIFIC NW FEDERAL CREDIT UNION SCHOLARSHIP

One scholarship available to graduating high school senior who is a member of Pacific North West Federal Credit Union. A special essay is required employing the theme, "Why is My Credit Union an Important Consumer Choice?" Employers and officials of the Credit Union and their dependents are not eligible. One-time award.

Award: Scholarship for use in freshman year; not renewable. *Number:* 2. *Amount:* $750.

Eligibility Requirements: Applicant must be high school student; planning to enroll or expecting to enroll at a four-year institution and resident of Oregon. Available to U.S. citizens.

Application Requirements: Application, essay, financial need analysis, references, transcript, activity chart. *Deadline:* March 1.

Contact: Director of Grant Programs
Oregon Student Assistance Commission
1500 Valley River Drive, Suite 100
Eugene, OR 97401-7020
Phone: 800-452-8807 Ext. 7395
E-mail: awardinfo@mercury.osac.state.or.us

PACIFICSOURCE SCHOLARSHIP

• *See page 500*

PENDLETON POSTAL WORKERS SCHOLARSHIP

• *See page 518*

PETER CROSSLEY MEMORIAL SCHOLARSHIP

Open to graduating seniors of an Oregon public alternative high school. Must submit essay on "How I Faced Challenges and Overcame Obstacles to Graduate from High School." See Web site at http://www.osac.state.or.us for more information.

Award: Scholarship for use in freshman, sophomore, junior, or senior years; renewable. *Number:* 1. *Amount:* $500.

Eligibility Requirements: Applicant must be high school student; planning to enroll or expecting to enroll full or part-time at a four-year institution and resident of Oregon. Available to U.S. citizens.

Application Requirements: Application, essay, financial need analysis, transcript, activity chart. *Deadline:* March 1.

Contact: Director of Grant Programs
Oregon Student Assistance Commission
1500 Valley River Drive, Suite 100
Eugene, OR 97401-7020
Phone: 800-452-8807 Ext. 7395
E-mail: awardinfo@mercury.osac.state.or.us

PORTLAND WOMEN'S CLUB SCHOLARSHIP

Renewable award open to graduates of any Oregon high school. Must have a minimum 3.0 cumulative GPA. Preference for female students.

Award: Scholarship for use in freshman, sophomore, junior, or senior years; renewable. *Number:* 5. *Amount:* $1500.

Oregon Student Assistance Commission (continued)

Eligibility Requirements: Applicant must be enrolled or expecting to enroll at an institution or university and resident of Oregon. Applicant must have 3.0 GPA or higher. Available to U.S. citizens.

Application Requirements: Application, essay, financial need analysis, transcript, activity chart. *Deadline:* March 1.

Contact: Director of Grant Programs
Oregon Student Assistance Commission
1500 Valley River Drive, Suite 100
Eugene, OR 97401-7020
Phone: 800-452-8807 Ext. 7395
E-mail: awardinfo@mercury.osac.state.or.us

REED'S FUEL AND TRUCKING COMPANY SCHOLARSHIP
• *See page 500*

RICHARD F. BRENTANO MEMORIAL SCHOLARSHIP
• *See page 500*

ROBERT C. BYRD HONORS SCHOLARSHIP-OREGON

Renewable award available to Oregon high school seniors with a GPA of at least 3.85 and combined SAT scores of at least 1300 or ACT scores of at least 29. Fifteen awards per federal congressional district. See Web site at http://www.osac.state.or.us for more information.

Award: Scholarship for use in freshman, sophomore, junior, or senior years; renewable. *Number:* 78. *Amount:* $1500.

Eligibility Requirements: Applicant must be high school student; planning to enroll or expecting to enroll at a two-year or four-year institution and resident of Oregon. Available to U.S. citizens.

Application Requirements: Application, essay, financial need analysis, test scores, transcript, activity chart. *Deadline:* March 1.

Contact: Director of Grant Programs
Oregon Student Assistance Commission
1500 Valley River Drive, Suite 100
Eugene, OR 97401-7020
Phone: 800-452-8807 Ext. 7395
E-mail: awardinfo@mercury.osac.state.or.us

ROBERT D. FORSTER SCHOLARSHIP
• *See page 500*

ROGER W. EMMONS MEMORIAL SCHOLARSHIP
• *See page 500*

ROSEBURG FOREST PRODUCTS SONS AND DAUGHTERS SCHOLARSHIP
• *See page 500*

SP NEWSPRINT COMPANY, NEWBERG MILL, EMPLOYEE DEPENDENTS SCHOLARSHIP
• *See page 501*

STIMSON LUMBER COMPANY SCHOLARSHIP
• *See page 501*

TAYLOR MADE LABELS SCHOLARSHIP
• *See page 501*

TEAMSTERS CLYDE C. CROSBY/JOSEPH M. EDGAR MEMORIAL SCHOLARSHIP
• *See page 476*

TEAMSTERS COUNCIL 37 FEDERAL CREDIT UNION SCHOLARSHIP
• *See page 476*

TEAMSTERS LOCAL 305 SCHOLARSHIP
• *See page 476*

TYKESON FAMILY SCHOLARSHIP
• *See page 518*

UMATILLA ELECTRIC COOPERATIVE SCHOLARSHIP

Applicant may be either high school graduate (including home-school graduate) or GED recipient. Applicant or applicant's parents/legal guardians must be active members of the Umatilla Electric Cooperative (UEC) and be receiving service from UEC at their primary residence. Married applicants with UEC membership in a spouse's name are eligible.

Award: Scholarship for use in freshman, sophomore, junior, or senior years; not renewable. *Number:* 7. *Amount:* $1000.

Eligibility Requirements: Applicant must be enrolled or expecting to enroll at a four-year institution and resident of Oregon. Available to U.S. citizens.

Application Requirements: Application, essay, financial need analysis, references, transcript, activity chart. *Deadline:* March 1.

Contact: Director of Grant Programs
Oregon Student Assistance Commission
1500 Valley River Drive, Suite 100
Eugene, OR 97401-7020
Phone: 800-452-8807 Ext. 7395
E-mail: awardinfo@mercury.osac.state.or.us

VERL AND DOROTHY MILLER NATIVE AMERICAN VOCATIONAL SCHOLARSHIP
• *See page 596*

WALTER DAVIES SCHOLARSHIP
• *See page 501*

WILLETT AND MARGUERITE LAKE SCHOLARSHIP
• *See page 501*

WILLIAM D. AND RUTH D. ROY SCHOLARSHIP

Scholarships available for Oregon high school graduates, home schoolers, and GED recipients. Preference given to Engineering majors attending Portland State University of Oregon State University. Deadline is March 1.

Award: Scholarship for use in freshman, sophomore, junior, or senior years; not renewable. *Number:* varies. *Amount:* $500.

Eligibility Requirements: Applicant must be enrolled or expecting to enroll at a four-year institution or university and resident of Oregon. Available to U.S. citizens.

Application Requirements: Application. *Deadline:* March 1.

Contact: Director of Grant Programs
Oregon Student Assistance Commission
1500 Valley River Drive, Suite 100
Eugene, OR 97401-7020
Phone: 800-452-8807 Ext. 7395
E-mail: awardinfo@mercury.osac.state.or.us

WOODARD FAMILY SCHOLARSHIP
• *See page 501*

OWEN ELECTRIC COOPERATIVE

http://www.owenelectric.com

OWEN ELECTRIC COOPERATIVE SCHOLARSHIP PROGRAM

Scholarships available to college juniors and seniors who are enrolled full-time at a four-year college or university. Parents of applicant must have an active Owen Electric account in good standing. If applicant has not earned 60 hours at time of application, must provide additional transcript upon completion of 60 hours. Must submit 400-700-word essay. Essay topics, application, and additional information on Web site: http://www.owenelectric.com.

Award: Scholarship for use in junior or senior years; not renewable. *Number:* 12. *Amount:* $2000.

Eligibility Requirements: Applicant must be enrolled or expecting to enroll full-time at a four-year institution or university and resident of Kentucky. Applicant must have 3.0 GPA or higher. Available to U.S. citizens.

Application Requirements: Application, essay, references, transcript. *Deadline:* February 1.

Contact: Deloris Foxworth, Manager of Advertising and Communications
Owen Electric Cooperative
8205 Highway 127 North
PO Box 400
Owenton, KY 40359-0400
Phone: 800-372-7612 Ext. 3541
E-mail: dfoxworth@owenelectric.com

PACERS FOUNDATION, INC. http://www.pacersfoundation.org

PACERS TEAMUP SCHOLARSHIP

The Pacers Teamup Scholarship presented by Miller Lite is awarded to Indiana high school seniors for their first year of undergraduate study at any accredited four-year college or university or two-year college or junior college. Primary selection criteria is student involvement in community service.

Award: Scholarship for use in freshman year; not renewable. *Number:* 5. *Amount:* $2000.

Eligibility Requirements: Applicant must be high school student; planning to enroll or expecting to enroll full-time at a two-year or four-year institution or university and resident of Indiana. Available to U.S. citizens.

Application Requirements: Application, essay, references, transcript. *Deadline:* March 1.

Contact: Sarah Furimsky, Coordinator
Pacers Foundation, Inc.
125 South Pennsylvania Street
Indianapolis, IN 46204
Phone: 317-917-2864
Fax: 317-917-2599
E-mail: foundation@pacers.com

PACIFIC AND ASIAN AFFAIRS COUNCIL http://www.paachawaii.org

PAAC SCHOLARSHIP

Scholarships available for college, study abroad, and other educational opportunities. Must be a student in Hawaii public or private high school involved in PAAC activities. Contact PAAC organization in local high school for more information.

Award: Scholarship for use in freshman, sophomore, junior, or senior years; not renewable. *Number:* 5. *Amount:* $1000.

Eligibility Requirements: Applicant must be high school student; planning to enroll or expecting to enroll at a two-year or four-year or technical institution or university and resident of Hawaii. Available to U.S. citizens.

Application Requirements: Application. *Deadline:* April 14.

Contact: High School Program Coordinator
E-mail: hs@paachawaii.org

PAGE EDUCATION FOUNDATION http://www.page-ed.org

PAGE EDUCATION FOUNDATION GRANT

• *See page 598*

PENNSYLVANIA AFL-CIO http://www.paaflcio.org

PA AFL-CIO UNIONISM IN AMERICA ESSAY CONTEST

• *See page 477*

PENNSYLVANIA BUREAU FOR VETERANS AFFAIRS http://sites.state.pa.us/PA_Exec/Military_Affairs/va/

EDUCATIONAL GRATUITY PROGRAM

• *See page 563*

PENNSYLVANIA BURGLAR AND FIRE ALARM ASSOCIATION http://www.pbfaa.com

PENNSYLVANIA BURGLAR AND FIRE ALARM ASSOCIATION YOUTH SCHOLARSHIP PROGRAM

• *See page 518*

PENNSYLVANIA FEDERATION OF DEMOCRATIC WOMEN, INC. http://www.pfdw.org

PENNSYLVANIA FEDERATION OF DEMOCRATIC WOMEN, INC. ANNUAL SCHOLARSHIP AWARDS

• *See page 477*

PENNSYLVANIA HIGHER EDUCATION ASSISTANCE AGENCY http://www.pheaa.org

PENNSYLVANIA STATE GRANTS

Award for Pennsylvania residents attending an approved postsecondary institution as undergraduates in a program of at least two years duration. Renewable for up to eight semesters if applicants show continued need and academic progress. Submit Free Application for Federal Student Aid.

Award: Grant for use in freshman, sophomore, junior, or senior years; renewable. *Number:* up to 151,000. *Amount:* $300–$3300.

Eligibility Requirements: Applicant must be enrolled or expecting to enroll full or part-time at a two-year or four-year or technical institution or university and resident of Pennsylvania. Available to U.S. and Canadian citizens.

Application Requirements: Application, financial need analysis. *Deadline:* May 1.

Contact: Keith New, Director of Communications and Press Office
Pennsylvania Higher Education Assistance Agency
1200 North Seventh Street
Harrisburg, PA 17102-1444
Phone: 717-720-2509
Fax: 717-720-3903
E-mail: knew@pheaa.org

POSTSECONDARY EDUCATION GRATUITY PROGRAM

Waiver of tuition and fees for children of Pennsylvania police officers, firefighters, rescue or ambulance squad members, corrections facility employees, or National Guard members who died in the line of duty after January 1, 1976. Must be a resident of Pennsylvania 25 years old or younger and enrolled full time as an undergraduate student at a Pennsylvania community college, state-owned institution or state-related institution. Award is for a maximum of 5 years. Application deadline March 31.

Award: Grant for use in freshman, sophomore, junior, or senior years; renewable. *Number:* varies. *Amount:* varies.

Eligibility Requirements: Applicant must be age 25 or under; enrolled or expecting to enroll full-time at a two-year or four-year institution or university; resident of Pennsylvania and studying in Pennsylvania.

Application Requirements: Application. *Deadline:* March 31.

Contact: PHEAA State Grant and Special Programs Division
Pennsylvania Higher Education Assistance Agency
1200 North Seventh Street
Harrisburg, PA 17102-1444
Phone: 800-692-7392

ROBERT C. BYRD HONORS SCHOLARSHIP PROGRAM-PENNSYLVANIA

Available to Pennsylvania residents who are graduating high school seniors. Must rank in the top 5% of graduating class, have at least a 3.5 GPA and score 1150 or above on the SAT, 25 or above on the ACT, or 355 or above on the GED. Renewable award of $1500.

Award: Scholarship for use in freshman, sophomore, junior, or senior years; renewable. *Number:* varies. *Amount:* $1500.

Eligibility Requirements: Applicant must be high school student; planning to enroll or expecting to enroll full-time at an institution or university and resident of Pennsylvania. Applicant must have 3.5 GPA or higher. Available to U.S. citizens.

Pennsylvania Higher Education Assistance Agency (continued)

Application Requirements: Application, test scores, transcript. *Deadline:* May 1.

Contact: Keith New, Director of Communications and Press Office
Pennsylvania Higher Education Assistance Agency
1200 North Seventh Street
Harrisburg, PA 17102-1444
Phone: 717-720-2509
Fax: 717-720-3903
E-mail: knew@pheaa.org

VETERANS GRANT-PENNSYLVANIA

• *See page 563*

PENNSYLVANIA RIGHT TO WORK DEFENSE AND EDUCATION FOUNDATION http://www.parighttowork.org

PENNSYLVANIA RIGHT TO WORK DEFENSE AND EDUCATION FOUNDATION JAMES SCOTT II ESSAY CONTEST

Prizes are awarded for 1st, 2nd, 3rd place in essay contest. May not necessarily be awarded if judges do not find essays worthy.

Award: Prize for use in freshman, sophomore, junior, senior, graduate, or postgraduate years; not renewable. *Number:* up to 3. *Amount:* $100–$500.

Eligibility Requirements: Applicant must be high school student; planning to enroll or expecting to enroll at an institution or university and resident of Pennsylvania. Available to U.S. citizens.

Application Requirements: Applicant must enter a contest, essay. *Deadline:* varies.

Contact: Susan Staub, President
Pennsylvania Right to Work Defense and Education Foundation
225 State Street, Suite 300
Harrisburg, PA 17101
Phone: 717-233-1227
Fax: 717-234-5588
E-mail: sstaub@parighttowork.org

PENNSYLVANIA YOUTH FOUNDATION http://www.pagrandlodge.org/pyf

PENNSYLVANIA YOUTH FOUNDATION SCHOLARSHIP

• *See page 477*

PETER DOCTOR MEMORIAL INDIAN SCHOLARSHIP FOUNDATION, INC.

PETER DOCTOR MEMORIAL IROQUOIS SCHOLARSHIP

• *See page 598*

PHOENIX SUNS CHARITIES/SUN STUDENTS SCHOLARSHIP http://www.suns.com

SUN STUDENT COLLEGE SCHOLARSHIP PROGRAM

• *See page 519*

POLISH HERITAGE ASSOCIATION OF MARYLAND

POLISH HERITAGE SCHOLARSHIP

• *See page 599*

PORTUGUESE FOUNDATION, INC. http://www.pfict.org

PORTUGUESE FOUNDATION SCHOLARSHIP PROGRAM

• *See page 599*

POTLATCH FOUNDATION FOR HIGHER EDUCATION SCHOLARSHIP http://www.potlatchcorp.com

POTLATCH FOUNDATION FOR HIGHER EDUCATION SCHOLARSHIP

Granted to students living within 30 miles of a major Potlatch facility and based on financial need.

Award: Scholarship for use in freshman, sophomore, junior, or senior years; renewable. *Number:* 50–80. *Amount:* $1400.

Eligibility Requirements: Applicant must be enrolled or expecting to enroll full-time at a two-year or four-year or technical institution or university and resident of Arkansas, Idaho, Minnesota, or Washington. Available to U.S. citizens.

Application Requirements: Application, financial need analysis, transcript. *Deadline:* July 1.

Contact: Sharon Pegau, Corporate Programs and Board Administrator
Potlatch Foundation For Higher Education Scholarship
601 West Riverside Avenue
Suite 1100
Spokane, WA 99201
Phone: 509-835-1515
Fax: 509-835-1566
E-mail: foundation@potlatchcorp.com

PRIDE FOUNDATION http://www.pridefoundation.org

PRIDE FOUNDATION/GREATER SEATTLE BUSINESS ASSOCIATION SCHOLARSHIP

Scholarships available for gay, lesbian, bisexual, transgendered, and allied students. Must be a resident of Washington, Alaska, Montana, Idaho, or Oregon. Foundation administers various scholarships with varying requirements. Submit one application to be considered for all available awards. Deadline varies. Check Web site for more information. http://www.pridefoundation.org

Award: Scholarship for use in freshman, sophomore, junior, senior, graduate, or postgraduate years; not renewable. *Number:* 60–65. *Amount:* $500–$5000.

Eligibility Requirements: Applicant must be enrolled or expecting to enroll full or part-time at a two-year or four-year or technical institution or university and resident of Alaska, Idaho, Montana, Oregon, or Washington. Available to U.S. citizens.

Application Requirements: Application, essay, financial need analysis, interview, references, transcript. *Deadline:* varies.

Contact: Randy Brians, Scholarship Manager
Pride Foundation
1122 East Pike, #1001
Seattle, WA 98122-3934
Phone: 206-323-3318
Fax: 206-323-1017
E-mail: randy@pridefoundation.org

PROJECT BEST SCHOLARSHIP FUND http://projectbest.com

PROJECT BEST SCHOLARSHIP

• *See page 478*

PUEBLO OF SAN JUAN, DEPARTMENT OF EDUCATION http://www.sanjuaned.org

OHKAY OWINGEH TRIBAL SCHOLARSHIP OF THE PUEBLO OF SAN JUAN

• *See page 600*

POP'AY SCHOLARSHIP

• *See page 600*

R.O.S.E. FUND http://www.rosefund.org

R.O.S.E. FUND SCHOLARSHIP PROGRAM

The R.O.S.E. scholarship program acknowledges women who are survivors of violence or abuse. Primarily awarded to women who have successfully completed one year of undergraduate studies. Scholarships are for tuition and expenses at any accredited college or university in New England. Must be U.S. resident. Deadlines are June 17 for the fall semester, December 3 for the spring semester.

Award: Scholarship for use in sophomore, junior, or senior years; renewable. *Number:* 10–15. *Amount:* $1000–$10,000.

Eligibility Requirements: Applicant must be age 18; enrolled or expecting to enroll full or part-time at a two-year or four-year institution or university; female and studying in Connecticut, Maine,

Massachusetts, New Hampshire, Rhode Island, or Vermont. Applicant must have 2.5 GPA or higher. Available to U.S. and non-U.S. citizens.

Application Requirements: Application, autobiography, essay, financial need analysis, interview, references, test scores, transcript. *Deadline:* varies.

Contact: Alison Justus, Director of Programs
R.O.S.E. Fund
175 Federal Street, Suite 455
Boston, MA 02110
Phone: 617-482-5400 Ext. 11
Fax: 617-482-3443
E-mail: ajustus@rosefund.org

RHODE ISLAND FOUNDATION

http://www.rifoundation.org

A.T. CROSS SCHOLARSHIP

• *See page 502*

ALDO FREDA LEGISLATIVE PAGES SCHOLARSHIP

One-time scholarships of $1000 are awarded to support Rhode Island Legislative Pages enrolled in a college or university. The deadline is May 7.

Award: Scholarship for use in freshman, sophomore, junior, or senior years; not renewable. *Number:* 2–3. *Amount:* $1000.

Eligibility Requirements: Applicant must be enrolled or expecting to enroll at an institution or university and resident of Rhode Island. Available to U.S. citizens.

Application Requirements: Application. *Deadline:* May 7.

Contact: Libby Monahan, Scholarship Coordinator
Rhode Island Foundation
One Union Station
Providence, RI 02903
Phone: 401-274-4564
Fax: 401-272-1359
E-mail: libbym@rifoundation.org

BRUCE AND MARJORIE SUNDLUN SCHOLARSHIP

Scholarships for low-income single parents seeking to upgrade their career skills. Preference given to single parents previously receiving state support. Also for those previously incarcerated. Must be a Rhode Island resident and attend school in Rhode Island.

Award: Scholarship for use in freshman, sophomore, junior, or senior years; not renewable. *Number:* 3–5. *Amount:* $250–$1000.

Eligibility Requirements: Applicant must be enrolled or expecting to enroll full or part-time at a two-year or four-year or technical institution or university; single; resident of Rhode Island and studying in Rhode Island.

Application Requirements: Application, essay, financial need analysis, references, self-addressed stamped envelope. *Deadline:* June 11.

Contact: Libby Monahan, Scholarship Coordinator
Rhode Island Foundation
1 Union Station
Providence, RI 02903
Phone: 401-274-4564
Fax: 401-272-1359

LILY AND CATELLO SORRENTINO MEMORIAL SCHOLARSHIP

Scholarships for Rhode Island residents 45 years or older wishing to attend college or university in Rhode Island (only students attending non-parochial schools). Must demonstrate financial need. Preference to first-time applicants.

Award: Scholarship for use in freshman, sophomore, junior, or senior years; not renewable. *Number:* varies. *Amount:* $350–$1000.

Eligibility Requirements: Applicant must be age 45; enrolled or expecting to enroll full or part-time at a four-year institution or university; resident of Rhode Island and studying in Rhode Island.

Application Requirements: Application, financial need analysis, self-addressed stamped envelope, transcript. *Deadline:* May 14.

Contact: Scholarship Coordinator
Rhode Island Foundation
1 Union Station
Providence, RI 02903
Phone: 401-274-4564
Fax: 401-272-1359

MICHAEL P. METCALF MEMORIAL SCHOLARSHIP

One-time awards between $2000 and $5000 are awarded to encourage personal growth through travel, study, and public service programs for college sophomores and juniors. Must be a Rhode Island resident. Award is for educational enrichment outside of the classroom: therefore, the awards are not to be used for school tuition.

Award: Scholarship for use in sophomore or junior years; not renewable. *Number:* 2–4. *Amount:* $2000–$5000.

Eligibility Requirements: Applicant must be enrolled or expecting to enroll at an institution or university and resident of Rhode Island. Available to U.S. citizens.

Application Requirements: Application. *Deadline:* January 16.

Contact: Libby Monahan, Scholarship Coordinator
Rhode Island Foundation
One Union Station
Providence, RI 02903
Phone: 401-274-4564
Fax: 401-272-1359
E-mail: libbym@rifoundation.org

PATTY AND MELVIN ALPERIN FIRST GENERATION SCHOLARSHIP/ DAVID M. GOLDEN MEMORIAL SCHOLARSHIP

To benefit college-bound Rhode Island high school graduates whose parents did not have the benefit of attending college. Must be enrolled in an accredited nonprofit postsecondary institution offering either a two-year or a four-year college degree.

Award: Scholarship for use in freshman, sophomore, junior, or senior years; renewable. *Number:* 2–3. *Amount:* $1000.

Eligibility Requirements: Applicant must be enrolled or expecting to enroll at a two-year or four-year institution or university and resident of Rhode Island.

Application Requirements: Application, self-addressed stamped envelope. *Deadline:* May 10.

Contact: Libby Monahan, Scholarship Coordinator
Rhode Island Foundation
One Union Station
Providence, RI 02903
Phone: 401-274-4564
Fax: 401-272-1359
E-mail: libbym@rifoundation.org

RAYMOND H. TROTT SCHOLARSHIP

• *See page 600*

RHODE ISLAND COMMISSION ON WOMEN/FREDA GOLDMAN EDUCATION AWARD

Renewable award to provide financial support for Rhode Island women to pursue their education or job training beyond high school. Can be used for transportation, child-care, tutoring, educational materials, and/or other support services. Preference given to highly motivated, self-supported, low-income women.

Award: Scholarship for use in freshman, sophomore, junior, or senior years; renewable. *Number:* varies. *Amount:* varies.

Eligibility Requirements: Applicant must be enrolled or expecting to enroll at an institution or university and resident of Rhode Island.

Rhode Island Foundation (continued)

Application Requirements: Application, essay, self-addressed stamped envelope, transcript. *Deadline:* June 18.

Contact: Libby Monahan, Scholarship Coordinator
Rhode Island Foundation
One Union Station
Providence, RI 02903
Phone: 401-274-4564
Fax: 401-272-1359
E-mail: libbym@rifoundation.org

RHODE ISLAND FOUNDATION ASSOCIATION OF FORMER LEGISLATORS SCHOLARSHIP

One-time award for graduating high school seniors who are Rhode Island residents. Must have outstanding public service record, excellent grades, and demonstrate financial need. Must be a U.S. citizen.

Award: Scholarship for use in freshman year; not renewable. *Number:* 5. *Amount:* $1500.

Eligibility Requirements: Applicant must be high school student; planning to enroll or expecting to enroll full-time at a four-year institution and resident of Rhode Island. Available to U.S. citizens.

Application Requirements: Application, essay, financial need analysis, references, self-addressed stamped envelope, test scores, transcript. *Deadline:* June 1.

Contact: Scholarship Coordinator
Rhode Island Foundation
1 Union Station
Providence, RI 02903
Phone: 401-274-4564
Fax: 401-272-1359

RHODE ISLAND HIGHER EDUCATION ASSISTANCE AUTHORITY http://www.riheaa.org

COLLEGE BOUND FUND ACADEMIC PROMISE SCHOLARSHIP

Award to graduating high school seniors. Eligibility based on financial need and SAT/ACT scores. Must maintain specified grade point averages each year for renewal. Must be Rhode Island resident and attend college full time. Must complete the Free Application for Federal Student Aid (FAFSA). FAFSA deadline is March 1.

Award: Scholarship for use in freshman, sophomore, junior, or senior years; not renewable. *Number:* 100. *Amount:* $2500.

Eligibility Requirements: Applicant must be high school student; planning to enroll or expecting to enroll full-time at a two-year or four-year or technical institution or university and resident of Rhode Island. Available to U.S. citizens.

Application Requirements: Application, financial need analysis, test scores. *Deadline:* March 1.

Contact: Mary Ann Welch, Director of Program Administration
Rhode Island Higher Education Assistance Authority
560 Jefferson Boulevard
Warwick, RI 02886
Phone: 401-736-1170
Fax: 401-732-3541
E-mail: mawelch@riheaa.org

RHODE ISLAND HIGHER EDUCATION GRANT PROGRAM

Grants for residents of Rhode Island attending an approved school in the U.S., Canada, or Mexico. Based on need. Renewable for up to four years if in good academic standing. Applications accepted January 1 through March 1. Several awards of variable amounts. Must be U.S. citizen or registered alien.

Award: Grant for use in freshman, sophomore, junior, or senior years; not renewable. *Number:* 10,000–12,000. *Amount:* $300–$1400.

Eligibility Requirements: Applicant must be enrolled or expecting to enroll full or part-time at a two-year or four-year or technical institution or university and resident of Rhode Island. Available to U.S. citizens.

Application Requirements: Application, financial need analysis. *Deadline:* March 1.

Contact: Mary Ann Welch, Director of Program Administration
Rhode Island Higher Education Assistance Authority
560 Jefferson Boulevard
Warwick, RI 02886
Phone: 401-736-1170
Fax: 401-732-3541
E-mail: mawelch@riheaa.org

RURAL MISSOURI, INC. http://www.rmiinc.org

NATIONAL FARMWORKER JOBS PROGRAM

• *See page 519*

RYU FAMILY FOUNDATION, INC.

SEOL BONG SCHOLARSHIP

• *See page 601*

SACRAMENTO BEE http://www.sacbee.com/scholarships

SACRAMENTO BEE SCHOLAR ATHLETE SCHOLARSHIP

This scholarship recognizes college-bound high school seniors who are outstanding students as well as sports competitors. Applicants should have a minimum cumulative grade point average of 3.4 and have received two varsity letters by the end of the current academic year. Applicants must reside in the Sacramento metropolitan area. For further information view Web site: http://www.sacbee.com/scholarships

Award: Scholarship for use in freshman year. *Number:* 1–10. *Amount:* $1500–$2500.

Eligibility Requirements: Applicant must be high school student; planning to enroll or expecting to enroll at an institution or university and resident of California.

Application Requirements: Application, essay, resume, references, transcript. *Deadline:* January 30.

Contact: Cathy Rodriguez, Public Affairs Representative
Sacramento Bee
PO Box 15779
Sacramento, CA 96852
Phone: 916-321-1880
Fax: 916-321-1783
E-mail: crodriguez@sacbee.com

SACRAMENTO BEE WILLIAM GLACKIN SCHOLARSHIP PROGRAM

Scholarship for a student pursuing a degree in Dance, Theatre, Music or Arts Management. Applicants must be graduating high school seniors who are accepted at an accredited school of higher education or college students attending an accredited school. College students must have completed at least one term and have one remaining. High school applicants must have minimum GPA of 3.0 and college students a GPA of 2.5. Applicants must reside in Sacramento metropolitan area. Visit Web site: http://www.sacbee.com/scholarships

Award: Scholarship for use in freshman, sophomore, junior, or senior years. *Number:* 1. *Amount:* $2500.

Eligibility Requirements: Applicant must be enrolled or expecting to enroll at a two-year or four-year institution or university and resident of California.

Application Requirements: Application, essay, resume, references, transcript, portfolio of samples. *Deadline:* January 30.

Contact: Cathy Rodriguez, Public Affairs Representative
Sacramento Bee
PO Box 15779
Sacramento, CA 96852
Phone: 916-321-1880
Fax: 916-321-1783
E-mail: crodriguez@sacbee.com

SALT RIVER ELECTRIC COOPERATIVE CORPORATION http://www.srelectric.com

SALT RIVER ELECTRIC SCHOLARSHIP PROGRAM

Scholarships available to Kentucky high school seniors who reside in Salt River Electric Service area or the primary residence of their parents/guardian is in the service area. Must be enrolled or plan to enroll in a post-secondary institution. Minimum GPA of 2.5 required. Must demonstrate financial need. Must submit a 500-word essay on a topic chosen from the list on the Web site. Application and additional information available on Web site: http://www.srelectric.com.

Award: Scholarship for use in freshman year; not renewable. *Number:* 4. *Amount:* $1000.

Eligibility Requirements: Applicant must be high school student; planning to enroll or expecting to enroll at a two-year or four-year or technical institution or university and resident of Kentucky. Applicant must have 2.5 GPA or higher. Available to U.S. citizens.

Application Requirements: Application, essay, financial need analysis, photo, transcript. *Deadline:* April 8.

Contact: Nicky Rapier, Scholarship Coordinator
Salt River Electric Cooperative Corporation
111 West Brashear Avenue
Bardstown, KY 40004
Phone: 502-348-3931
E-mail: nickyr@srelectric.com

SALVATORE TADDONIO FAMILY FOUNDATION

TADDONIO SCHOLARSHIP

• *See page 519*

SAN FRANCISCO FOUNDATION http://www.sff.org

JOSEPH HENRY JACKSON LITERARY AWARD

Award presented annually to an author of an unpublished work in progress: fiction, nonfiction, prose, or poetry. Must be California or Nevada resident for three consecutive years and be between 20-35 years of age. Submit manuscript. One-time award of $2000 is not a scholarship. Applications accepted from November 15 to January 31.

Award: Prize for use in freshman, sophomore, junior, senior, graduate, or postgraduate years; not renewable. *Number:* 1. *Amount:* $2000.

Eligibility Requirements: Applicant must be age 20-35; enrolled or expecting to enroll at an institution or university; resident of California or Nevada and must have an interest in writing. Available to U.S. and non-U.S. citizens.

Application Requirements: Application, applicant must enter a contest, self-addressed stamped envelope, manuscript. *Deadline:* January 31.

Contact: Awards Coordinator-Literary Awards
San Francisco Foundation
225 Bush Street, Suite 500
San Francisco, CA 94104-4224
E-mail: rec@sff.org

SCHOLARSHIPS FOUNDATION, INC. http://www.fdncenter.org/grantmaker/scholarships

FOUNDATION SCHOLARSHIPS

Grants to graduate and undergraduate students enrolled in academic programs either full- or part-time. Priority is given to students studying in NY state or residents of NY state studying elsewhere. Grants are based on merit and need.

Award: Scholarship for use in freshman, sophomore, junior, senior, or graduate years; not renewable. *Number:* 20–30. *Amount:* $1500–$3500.

Eligibility Requirements: Applicant must be enrolled or expecting to enroll full or part-time at a two-year or four-year institution or university and resident of New York. Available to U.S. and non-U.S. citizens.

Application Requirements: Application, financial need analysis, references, self-addressed stamped envelope, transcript. *Deadline:* Continuous.

Contact: Scholarships Foundation, Inc.
PO Box 286020
New York, NY 10128
E-mail: sfi1921@aol.com

SCOTTISH RITE CHARITABLE FOUNDATION OF CANADA http://www.scottishritemasons-can.org/foundation

SCOTTISH RITE CHARITABLE FOUNDATION COLLEGE BURSARIES

• *See page 519*

SERVICE EMPLOYEES INTERNATIONAL UNION - CALIFORNIA STATE COUNCIL OF SERVICE EMPLOYEES http://www.seiu.org

CHARLES HARDY MEMORIAL SCHOLARSHIP AWARDS

• *See page 480*

SHOPKO STORES, INC. http://www.shopko.com/

SHOPKO SCHOLARS PROGRAM

Must live within 100 miles of a ShopKo store. Scholars selected on the basis of academic record, potential to succeed, leadership, and participation in school and community activities, honors, work, experience, a statement of educational and career goals, and an outside appraisal. Financial need is not considered.

Award: Scholarship for use in freshman, sophomore, junior, or senior years; not renewable. *Number:* 100–110. *Amount:* $1000.

Eligibility Requirements: Applicant must be enrolled or expecting to enroll full-time at a two-year or four-year or technical institution or university and resident of California, Colorado, Idaho, Illinois, Iowa, Michigan, Minnesota, Montana, Nebraska, Nevada, Oregon, South Dakota, Utah, Washington, or Wisconsin. Available to U.S. citizens.

Application Requirements: Application, essay, photo, references, self-addressed stamped envelope, transcript. *Deadline:* December 1.

Contact: Amy Anderson, Communications Specialist
ShopKo Stores, Inc.
700 Pilgrim Way
PO Box 19060
Green Bay, WI 54307-9060
Phone: 920-429-4328
Fax: 920-429-4363
E-mail: aanderso@shopko.com

SICKLE CELL DISEASE ASSOCIATION OF AMERICA/ CONNECTICUT CHAPTER, INC. http://www.sicklecellct.org

I. H. MCLENDON MEMORIAL SCHOLARSHIP

• *See page 531*

SYBIL FONG SAM SCHOLARSHIP ESSAY CONTEST

The Sybil Fong Sam Scholarship Essay Contest provides three scholarships to graduating high school seniors based upon submission of an essay on a pre-selected topic. 3.0 minimum GPA required. Must be a Connecticut resident.

Award: Scholarship for use in freshman year; not renewable. *Number:* 3. *Amount:* $200–$500.

Eligibility Requirements: Applicant must be high school student; planning to enroll or expecting to enroll full or part-time at a two-year or four-year or technical institution or university and resident of Connecticut. Applicant must have 3.0 GPA or higher. Available to U.S. citizens.

Application Requirements: Application, applicant must enter a contest, essay, references, transcript. *Deadline:* April 30.

Contact: Samuel Byrd, Program Assistant
Sickle Cell Disease Association of America/Connecticut Chapter, Inc.
Gengras Ambulatory Center
140 Woodland Street
Hartford, CT 06105
Phone: 860-527-0119
Fax: 860-714-8007
E-mail: scdaa@iconn.net

SIGMA DELTA CHI FOUNDATION OF WASHINGTON, D.C. http://www.spj.org/washdcpro

SIGMA DELTA CHI SCHOLARSHIPS

One-time award to help pay tuition for full-time students in their junior or senior year demonstrating a clear intention to become journalists. Must demonstrate financial need; grades and skills are also considered. Must be enrolled in a college or university in the Washington, D.C., metropolitan area. Sponsored by the Society of Professional Journalists.

Sigma Delta Chi Foundation of Washington, D.C. (continued)

Award: Scholarship for use in junior or senior years; not renewable. *Number:* 4–7. *Amount:* $3000–$4000.

Eligibility Requirements: Applicant must be enrolled or expecting to enroll full-time at a four-year institution or university; studying in District of Columbia, Maryland, or Virginia and must have an interest in designated field specified by sponsor, leadership, or writing. Available to U.S. and non-U.S. citizens.

Application Requirements: Application, essay, financial need analysis, interview, portfolio, references, transcript. *Deadline:* February 27.

Contact: Lee Thornton, Scholarship Committee Chair
Sigma Delta Chi Foundation of Washington, D.C.
PO Box 19555
Washington, DC 20036-0555
Phone: 301-405-5292
Fax: 301-314-9166
E-mail: lthornton@jmail.umd.edu

SOCIETY OF WOMEN ENGINEERS http://www.swe.org/scholarships

SWE SOUTH OHIO SCIENCE FAIR SCHOLARSHIP

Two $300 scholarships awarded to graduating high school senior females for outstanding achievement in engineering or the related sciences.

Award: Scholarship for use in freshman year; not renewable. *Number:* 2. *Amount:* $300.

Eligibility Requirements: Applicant must be high school student; planning to enroll or expecting to enroll at a four-year institution; female and resident of Ohio. Available to U.S. citizens.

Application Requirements: Science fair project. *Deadline:* varies.

Contact: Alison Haskins
Society of Women Engineers
PO Box 284
Oxford, OH 45056-0284
Phone: 513-785-7277
E-mail: alison.haskins@swe.org

SOUTH CAROLINA COMMISSION ON HIGHER EDUCATION http://www.che.sc.gov

LEGISLATIVE INCENTIVES FOR FUTURE EXCELLENCE PROGRAM

Scholarship for students from South Carolina to attend an institution of higher education in South Carolina. For students attending a four-year institution, two of the following three criteria must be met: 1) minimum 3.0 GPA, 2) 1100 SAT or 24 ACT, or 3) graduate in the top 30% of class. Students attending a two-year or technical college must have a 3.0 GPA, SAT and class rank requirements are waived.

Award: Scholarship for use in freshman, sophomore, junior, senior, or graduate years; renewable. *Number:* varies. *Amount:* $2000–$5000.

Eligibility Requirements: Applicant must be enrolled or expecting to enroll full-time at a two-year or four-year or technical institution or university; resident of South Carolina and studying in South Carolina. Applicant must have 3.0 GPA or higher. Available to U.S. citizens.

Application Requirements: Test scores, transcript. *Deadline:* Continuous.

Contact: Bichevia Green, LIFE Scholarship Coordinator
South Carolina Commission on Higher Education
1333 Main Street, Suite 200
Columbia, SC 29201
Phone: 803-737-2280
Fax: 803-737-2297
E-mail: bgreen@che.sc.gov

PALMETTO FELLOWS SCHOLARSHIP PROGRAM

Renewable award for qualified high school seniors in South Carolina to attend a four-year South Carolina institution. Must rank in top 5% of class at the end of sophomore or junior year, earn a 3.5 GPA on a 4.0 scale, and score at least 1200 on the SAT or 27 on the ACT. Submit official transcript, test scores, and application by established deadline (usually January 15th of senior year).

Award: Scholarship for use in freshman, sophomore, junior, senior, or graduate years; renewable. *Number:* varies. *Amount:* up to $6700.

Eligibility Requirements: Applicant must be high school student; planning to enroll or expecting to enroll full-time at a four-year institution or university; resident of South Carolina and studying in South Carolina. Applicant must have 3.5 GPA or higher. Available to U.S. citizens.

Application Requirements: Application, test scores, transcript. *Deadline:* January 15.

Contact: Ms. Sherry Hubbard, Coordinator
South Carolina Commission on Higher Education
1333 Main Street, Suite 200
Columbia, SC 29201
Phone: 803-737-2260
Fax: 803-737-2297
E-mail: shubbard@che.sc.gov

SOUTH CAROLINA HOPE SCHOLARSHIP

One-year merit-based scholarship for eligible first-time entering freshmen attending a four-year institution. Minimum 3.0 GPA.

Award: Scholarship for use in freshman year; not renewable. *Number:* 1–2264. *Amount:* $2650.

Eligibility Requirements: Applicant must be enrolled or expecting to enroll full-time at a four-year institution or university; resident of South Carolina and studying in South Carolina. Applicant must have 3.0 GPA or higher. Available to U.S. citizens.

Application Requirements: Transcript. *Deadline:* Continuous.

Contact: Bichevia Green, Life/Hope Scholarship Coordinator
South Carolina Commission on Higher Education
1333 Main Street, Suite 200
Columbia, SC 29201
Phone: 803-737-2280
Fax: 803-737-2297
E-mail: bgreen@che.sc.gov

SOUTH CAROLINA NEED-BASED GRANTS PROGRAM

Award based on results of Free Application for Federal Student Aid. A student may receive up to $2500 annually for full-time and up to $1250 annually for part-time study. The grant must be applied toward the cost of attendance at a South Carolina college for up to eight full-time equivalent terms. Student must be degree-seeking.

Award: Grant for use in freshman, sophomore, junior, senior, or graduate years; renewable. *Number:* 1–23,485. *Amount:* up to $2500.

Eligibility Requirements: Applicant must be enrolled or expecting to enroll full or part-time at a two-year or four-year or technical institution or university; resident of South Carolina and studying in South Carolina. Available to U.S. citizens.

Application Requirements: Financial need analysis. *Deadline:* Continuous.

Contact: Ms. Sherry Hubbard, Coordinator
South Carolina Commission on Higher Education
1333 Main Street, Suite 200
Columbia, SC 29201
Phone: 803-737-2260
Fax: 803-737-2297
E-mail: shubbard@che.sc.gov

SOUTH CAROLINA DEPARTMENT OF EDUCATION

ROBERT C. BYRD HONORS SCHOLARSHIP-SOUTH CAROLINA

Renewable award of $1500 for graduating high school seniors from South Carolina who will be attending a two- or four-year institution. Applicants should be superior students who demonstrate academic achievement and show promise of continued success at a postsecondary institution. Interested applicants should contact their high school counselors after the first week in December for an application.

Award: Scholarship for use in freshman, sophomore, junior, or senior years; renewable. *Number:* 96. *Amount:* $1500.

Eligibility Requirements: Applicant must be high school student; planning to enroll or expecting to enroll full-time at a two-year or

four-year institution and resident of South Carolina. Applicant must have 3.5 GPA or higher. Available to U.S. citizens.

Application Requirements: Application, references, test scores, transcript, extracurricular activities. *Deadline:* February 2.

Contact: Mrs. Beth Cope, Program Coordinator
South Carolina Department of Education
1424 Senate Street
Columbia, SC 29201
Phone: 803-734-8116
Fax: 803-734-4387
E-mail: bcope@sde.state.sc.us

SOUTH CAROLINA DIVISION OF VETERANS AFFAIRS

EDUCATIONAL ASSISTANCE FOR CERTAIN WAR VETERAN'S DEPENDENTS- SOUTH CAROLINA

• *See page 564*

SOUTH CAROLINA TUITION GRANTS COMMISSION http://www.sctuitiongrants.com

SOUTH CAROLINA TUITION GRANTS PROGRAM

Assists South Carolina residents attending one of twenty approved South Carolina independent colleges. Freshmen must be in upper 3/4 of high school class or have SAT score of at least 900. Upper-class students must complete 24 semester hours per year to be eligible.

Award: Grant for use in freshman, sophomore, junior, or senior years; renewable. *Number:* up to 11,000. *Amount:* $100–$3240.

Eligibility Requirements: Applicant must be enrolled or expecting to enroll full-time at a two-year or four-year institution; resident of South Carolina and studying in South Carolina. Available to U.S. citizens.

Application Requirements: Application, financial need analysis, test scores, transcript, FAFSA. *Deadline:* June 30.

Contact: Toni Cave, Financial Aid Counselor
South Carolina Tuition Grants Commission
101 Business Park Boulevard, Suite 2100
Columbia, SC 29203-9498
Phone: 803-896-1120
Fax: 803-896-1126
E-mail: toni@sctuitiongrants.org

SOUTH DAKOTA BOARD OF REGENTS http://www.ris.sdbor.edu

EDUCATION BENEFITS FOR DEPENDENTS OF POWS AND MIAS

• *See page 564*

SOUTH DAKOTA AID TO DEPENDENTS OF DECEASED VETERANS

• *See page 564*

SOUTH DAKOTA BOARD OF REGENTS MARLIN R. SCARBOROUGH MEMORIAL SCHOLARSHIP

One-time award for a student who is a junior at a South Dakota public university. Must be nominated by the university. Merit-based. Must have community service and leadership experience. Minimum 3.5 GPA required. Contact University Financial Aid Office for application deadline.

Award: Scholarship for use in junior year; not renewable. *Number:* 1. *Amount:* $1500.

Eligibility Requirements: Applicant must be enrolled or expecting to enroll at an institution or university; resident of South Dakota; studying in South Dakota and must have an interest in leadership. Applicant must have 3.5 GPA or higher.

Application Requirements: Application, essay. *Deadline:* varies.

Contact: South Dakota Board of Regents
306 East Capitol Avenue, Suite 200
Pierre, SD 57501-3159

SOUTH DAKOTA BOARD OF REGENTS SENIOR CITIZENS TUITION ASSISTANCE

Award for tuition assistance for any postsecondary academic year of study to senior citizens age 65 and older. Write for further details. Must be a South Dakota resident and attend a school in South Dakota.

Award: Scholarship for use in freshman, sophomore, junior, or senior years; not renewable. *Number:* varies. *Amount:* varies.

Eligibility Requirements: Applicant must be age 65; enrolled or expecting to enroll at an institution or university; resident of South Dakota and studying in South Dakota.

Application Requirements: Application. *Deadline:* Continuous.

Contact: South Dakota Board of Regents
306 East Capitol Avenue, Suite 200
Pierre, SD 57501-3159

SOUTH DAKOTA BOARD OF REGENTS STATE EMPLOYEE TUITION ASSISTANCE

• *See page 520*

SOUTH DAKOTA EDUCATION BENEFITS FOR NATIONAL GUARD MEMBERS

• *See page 537*

SOUTH DAKOTA EDUCATION BENEFITS FOR VETERANS

• *See page 565*

SOUTH DAKOTA OPPORTUNITY SCHOLARSHIP

Provides $5000 over 4 years to a qualifying South Dakota student who completes the high school course known as the Regents Scholar curriculum with no final grade below a C and high school cumulative GPA of 3.0. Must attend a NCA-accredited institution in South Dakota. Must have ACT composite score of 24 or higher, or a combined SAT score of 1110. Initial submission of application and transcript should be by June 1. See Web site for application and information: http://www.sdbor.edu.

Award: Scholarship for use in freshman, sophomore, junior, or senior years; renewable. *Number:* 1000. *Amount:* up to $1000.

Eligibility Requirements: Applicant must be enrolled or expecting to enroll full-time at a four-year institution or university; resident of South Dakota and studying in South Dakota. Applicant must have 3.0 GPA or higher. Available to U.S. citizens.

Application Requirements: Application, test scores, transcript. *Deadline:* September 1.

Contact: Dr. Lesta Turchen, Senior Administrator
South Dakota Board of Regents
306 East Capitol Avenue
Suite 200
Pierre, SD 57501-3159
Phone: 605-773-3455
Fax: 605-773-2422
E-mail: info@sdbor.edu

SOUTH DAKOTA DEPARTMENT OF EDUCATION http://www.state.sd.us/deca

ROBERT C. BYRD HONORS SCHOLARSHIP-SOUTH DAKOTA

For South Dakota residents in their senior year of high school. Must have a minimum 3.5 GPA and a minimum ACT score of 30 or above. Awards are renewable up to four years. Contact high school guidance office for more details.

Award: Scholarship for use in freshman, sophomore, junior, or senior years; renewable. *Number:* up to 80. *Amount:* $1500.

Eligibility Requirements: Applicant must be high school student; planning to enroll or expecting to enroll full-time at a two-year or four-year or technical institution or university and resident of South Dakota. Applicant must have 3.5 GPA or higher. Available to U.S. citizens.

Application Requirements: Application, test scores, transcript. *Deadline:* May 1.

Contact: Roxie Thielen, Financial Aid Administrator
South Dakota Department of Education
700 Governors Drive
Pierre, SD 57501-2291
Phone: 605-773-5669
Fax: 605-773-6139
E-mail: roxie.thielen@state.sd.us

SOUTHERN SCHOLARSHIP FOUNDATION, INC. http://www.southernscholarship.org

SOUTHERN SCHOLARSHIP FOUNDATION

The scholarship is for rent-free cooperative living in our houses located at Florida State University, University of Florida, Florida A & M, (for men only) at Bethune-Cookman College, and (for women only) at Florida Gulf Coast University. Students share all household duties while maintaining high academic standards.

Award: Scholarship for use in freshman, sophomore, junior, or senior years; renewable. *Number:* up to 440. *Amount:* $550–$650.

Eligibility Requirements: Applicant must be enrolled or expecting to enroll full-time at a four-year institution or university; single and studying in Florida. Applicant must have 3.0 GPA or higher. Available to U.S. and non-U.S. citizens.

Application Requirements: Application, autobiography, essay, financial need analysis, photo, references, test scores, transcript, college acceptance letter. *Deadline:* March 1.

Contact: Southern Scholarship Foundation, Inc.
322 Stadium Drive
Tallahassee, FL 32304
Phone: 850-222-3833
Fax: 850-222-6750

SOUTHERN TEXAS PGA http://www.stpga.com/

HARDY LAUDERMILK SCHOLARSHIP

In honor of PGA professional Hardy Laudermilk. Scholarship information and application available online: http://www.stpga.com

Award: Scholarship for use in freshman, sophomore, junior, or senior years; not renewable. *Number:* up to 1. *Amount:* up to $1500.

Eligibility Requirements: Applicant must be enrolled or expecting to enroll full-time at a two-year or four-year institution or university; resident of Texas and must have an interest in golf. Applicant must have 2.5 GPA or higher. Available to U.S. citizens.

Application Requirements: Application, financial need analysis, test scores, transcript, extracurricular activities. *Deadline:* April 5.

Contact: Eddie Dey, STPGA Foundation Scholarship Program Administrator
Southern Texas PGA
1830 South Millbend Drive, Suite A
The Woodlands, TX 77380-0967
Phone: 281-419-7421
Fax: 281-419-1842
E-mail: stexas@pgahq.com

JACK HARDEN SCHOLARSHIP

Applicants must reside in Bexar County or one of the five counties contiguous to Bexar County. Two scholarships are awarded: one to a female, and one to a male. The recipients will receive $2500 per year. Scholarship information and application available online: http://www.stpga.com

Award: Scholarship for use in freshman, sophomore, junior, or senior years; not renewable. *Number:* up to 2. *Amount:* up to $2500.

Eligibility Requirements: Applicant must be enrolled or expecting to enroll full-time at a two-year or four-year institution or university; resident of Texas and must have an interest in golf. Applicant must have 2.5 GPA or higher. Available to U.S. citizens.

Application Requirements: Application, financial need analysis, test scores, transcript, extracurricular activities. *Deadline:* April 5.

Contact: Eddie Dey, STPGA Foundation Scholarship Program Administrator
Southern Texas PGA
1830 South Millbend Drive, Suite A
The Woodlands, TX 77380-0967
Phone: 281-419-7421
Fax: 281-419-1842
E-mail: stexas@pgahq.com

NICHOLAS BATTLE SCHOLARSHIP

All Southern Texas PGA Foundation Scholarship applicants are eligible for this scholarship. Applicant need not be junior golfer. Scholarship information and application available online: http://www.stpga.com

Award: Scholarship for use in freshman, sophomore, junior, or senior years; not renewable. *Number:* up to 1. *Amount:* up to $3000.

Eligibility Requirements: Applicant must be enrolled or expecting to enroll full-time at a two-year or four-year institution or university; resident of Texas and must have an interest in golf. Applicant must have 2.5 GPA or higher. Available to U.S. citizens.

Application Requirements: Application, financial need analysis, test scores, transcript, extracurricular activities. *Deadline:* April 5.

Contact: Eddie Dey, STPGA Foundation Scholarship Program Administrator
Southern Texas PGA
1830 South Millbend Drive, Suite A
The Woodlands, TX 77380-0967
Phone: 281-419-7421
Fax: 281-419-1842
E-mail: stexas@pgahq.com

TOMMY AYCOCK SCHOLARSHIPS

Applicant must reside in one of the following seven counties: Nueces, San Patricio, Aransas, Kleberg, Wells, Bee or Refugio. Previous winners are eligible to apply in subsequent years. Scholarship information and application available online: http://www.stpga.com

Award: Scholarship for use in freshman, sophomore, junior, or senior years; not renewable. *Number:* up to 3. *Amount:* up to $1000.

Eligibility Requirements: Applicant must be enrolled or expecting to enroll full-time at a two-year or four-year institution or university; resident of Texas and must have an interest in golf. Applicant must have 2.5 GPA or higher. Available to U.S. citizens.

Application Requirements: Application, financial need analysis, test scores, transcript, extracurricular activities. *Deadline:* April 5.

Contact: Eddie Dey, STPGA Foundation Scholarship Program Administrator
Southern Texas PGA
1830 South Millbend Drive, Suite A
The Woodlands, TX 77380-0967
Phone: 281-419-7421
Fax: 281-419-1842
E-mail: stexas@pgahq.com

WARREN SMITH SCHOLARSHIP

Scholarship will be awarded to a graduating high school senior from Bexar County or one of the five counties contiguous to Bexar County. Scholarship information and application available online: http://www.stpga.com

Award: Scholarship for use in freshman, sophomore, junior, or senior years. *Number:* up to 1. *Amount:* up to $1500.

Eligibility Requirements: Applicant must be high school student; planning to enroll or expecting to enroll at an institution or university; resident of Texas and must have an interest in golf. Applicant must have 2.5 GPA or higher. Available to U.S. citizens.

Application Requirements: Application, financial need analysis, test scores, transcript, extracurricular activities. *Deadline:* April 5.

Contact: Eddie Dey, STPGA Foundation Scholarship Program Administrator
Southern Texas PGA
1830 South Millbend Drive, Suite A
The Woodlands, TX 77380-0967
Phone: 281-419-7421
Fax: 281-419-1842
E-mail: stexas@pgahq.com

SOUTHWEST STUDENT SERVICES CORPORATION http://www.sssc.com

ARIZONA COMMUNITY COLLEGE SCHOLARSHIP

Four renewable $500 scholarships are awarded annually to Arizona high school students with strong service/activities and academic backgrounds, who are planning to attend a two-year community college in Arizona.

Award: Scholarship for use in freshman year; renewable. *Number:* 4. *Amount:* $500.

Eligibility Requirements: Applicant must be high school student; planning to enroll or expecting to enroll full-time at a two-year institution; resident of Arizona and studying in Arizona. Applicant must have 2.5 GPA or higher. Available to U.S. citizens.

Application Requirements: Application, essay, transcript. *Deadline:* April 30.

Contact: Linda Walker, Community Outreach Representative
Southwest Student Services Corporation
PO Box 41595
Mesa, AZ 85274
Phone: 480-461-6566
Fax: 480-461-6595
E-mail: scholarships@sssc.com

ARIZONA COUNSELOR OF THE YEAR SCHOLARSHIP

One-time $500 award to the graduating high school senior for nominating the high school counselor who wins the Arizona Counselor of the Year Scholarship.

Award: Scholarship for use in freshman year; not renewable. *Number:* 1. *Amount:* $500.

Eligibility Requirements: Applicant must be high school student; planning to enroll or expecting to enroll full-time at a two-year or four-year or technical institution or university and resident of Arizona. Available to U.S. citizens.

Application Requirements: Application, essay. *Deadline:* April 15.

Contact: Linda Walker, Community Outreach Representative
Southwest Student Services Corporation
PO Box 41595
Mesa, AZ 85274
Phone: 480-461-6566
Fax: 480-461-6595
E-mail: scholarships@sssc.com

ST. ANDREW'S SOCIETY OF WASHINGTON, DC http://www.thecapitalscot.com/standrew/scholarships.html

DONALD MALCOLM MACARTHUR SCHOLARSHIP

• *See page 602*

ST. ANDREW'S SCHOLARSHIPS

• *See page 603*

STATE COUNCIL OF HIGHER EDUCATION FOR VIRGINIA http://www.schev.edu

COLLEGE SCHOLARSHIP ASSISTANCE PROGRAM

Need-based scholarship for undergraduate study by a Virginia resident at a participating Virginia two- or four-year college, or university. Contact financial aid office at the participating institution.

Award: Grant for use in freshman, sophomore, junior, or senior years; renewable. *Number:* varies. *Amount:* $400–$5000.

Eligibility Requirements: Applicant must be enrolled or expecting to enroll full or part-time at a two-year or four-year institution or university; resident of Virginia and studying in Virginia. Available to U.S. citizens.

Application Requirements: Application, financial need analysis, FAFSA.

Contact: Fin. Aid Office at participating VA institution
State Council of Higher Education for Virginia
James Monroe Building, 10th Floor
101 North 14th Street
Richmond, VA 23219

FOSTER CHILDREN GRANT

Grant providing tuition and fees at any Virginia community college; specifically for high school graduates who were in foster care, custody of a social service agency, or were a special needs adoption at the time they graduated or completed a GED. Must be a Virginia resident. Contact financial aid office of the community college upon admission or Department of Social Services for more information. Visit Web site: http://www.vccs.cc.va.us/vccsasr/tuitiongrant/tuitiongrant.html.

Award: Grant for use in freshman or sophomore years; renewable. *Number:* varies. *Amount:* varies.

Eligibility Requirements: Applicant must be enrolled or expecting to enroll full-time at a two-year institution; resident of Virginia and studying in Virginia. Available to U.S. citizens.

Application Requirements: Application, financial need analysis, documentation from Department of Social Services, FAFSA.

Contact: Fin. Aid Office at participating VA institution
State Council of Higher Education for Virginia
James Monroe Building, 10th Floor
101 North 14th Street
Richmond, VA 23219

SENIOR CITIZEN TUITION WAIVER

Need-based program providing waiver of tuition and fees for credit courses in public Virginia institutions for Virginia residents aged 60 and older. Contact financial aid office at participating institution for application and information.

Award: Scholarship for use in freshman, sophomore, junior, or senior years; not renewable. *Number:* varies. *Amount:* varies.

Eligibility Requirements: Applicant must be age 60; enrolled or expecting to enroll full or part-time at a two-year or four-year or technical institution or university; resident of Virginia and studying in Virginia. Available to U.S. citizens.

Application Requirements: Application, financial need analysis.

Contact: Fin. Aid Office at participating VA institution
State Council of Higher Education for Virginia
James Monroe Building, 10th Floor
101 North 14th Street
Richmond, VA 23219

VIRGINIA COMMONWEALTH AWARD

Need-based award for undergraduate or graduate study at a Virginia public two- or four-year college, or university. Undergraduates must be Virginia residents. The application and awards process are administered by the financial aid office at the Virginia public institution where student is enrolled. Contact financial aid office for application and deadlines.

Award: Grant for use in freshman, sophomore, junior, senior, or graduate years; renewable. *Number:* varies. *Amount:* varies.

Eligibility Requirements: Applicant must be enrolled or expecting to enroll full or part-time at a two-year or four-year institution or university; resident of Virginia and studying in Virginia. Available to U.S. citizens.

Application Requirements: Application, financial need analysis, FAFSA.

Contact: Fin. Aid Office at participating VA institution
State Council of Higher Education for Virginia
James Monroe Building, 10th Floor
101 North 14th Street
Richmond, VA 23219

VIRGINIA GUARANTEED ASSISTANCE PROGRAM

Awards to undergraduate students proportional to their need, up to full tuition, fees and book allowance. Must be a graduate of a Virginia high school, not home-schooled. High school GPA of 2.5 required. Must be enrolled full-time in a Virginia 2- or 4-year institution and demonstrate financial need. Contact financial aid office of your institution for application process and deadlines. Must maintain minimum college GPA of 2.0 for renewal awards.

Award: Scholarship for use in freshman, sophomore, junior, or senior years; renewable. *Number:* varies. *Amount:* varies.

Eligibility Requirements: Applicant must be enrolled or expecting to enroll full-time at a two-year or four-year institution or university; resident of Virginia and studying in Virginia. Applicant must have 2.5 GPA or higher. Available to U.S. citizens.

State Council of Higher Education for Virginia (continued)

Application Requirements: Application, financial need analysis, transcript, FAFSA.

Contact: Fin. Aid Office at participating VA institution
State Council of Higher Education for Virginia
James Monroe Building, 10th Floor
101 North 14th Street
Richmond, VA 23219

VIRGINIA PART-TIME ASSISTANCE PROGRAM

Award for part-time students in Virginia's Community College System. Students with financial need may receive up to the cost of tuition and fees. Must be Virginia resident.

Award: Scholarship for use in freshman or sophomore years. *Number:* varies. *Amount:* varies.

Eligibility Requirements: Applicant must be enrolled or expecting to enroll part-time at a two-year institution; resident of Virginia and studying in Virginia. Available to U.S. citizens.

Application Requirements: Application, financial need analysis, FAFSA.

Contact: Fin. Aid Office at participating VA institution
State Council of Higher Education for Virginia
James Monroe Building, 10th Floor
101 North 14th Street
Richmond, VA 23219

VIRGINIA TUITION ASSISTANCE GRANT PROGRAM (PRIVATE INSTITUTIONS)

Renewable awards of approximately $1900-$2500 each for undergraduate, graduate, and first professional degree students attending an approved private, nonprofit college within Virginia. Must be a Virginia resident and be enrolled full-time. Not to be used for religious study. Preferred deadline July 31. Others are wait-listed. Information and application available from participating Virginia colleges' financial aid office.

Award: Grant for use in freshman, sophomore, junior, senior, or graduate years; renewable. *Number:* 18,600. *Amount:* $1900–$2500.

Eligibility Requirements: Applicant must be enrolled or expecting to enroll full-time at a four-year institution; resident of Virginia and studying in Virginia.

Application Requirements: Application. *Deadline:* July 31.

Contact: Fin. Aid Office at participating VA institution
State Council of Higher Education for Virginia
James Monroe Building, 10th Floor
101 North 14th Street
Richmond, VA 23219

STATE OF GEORGIA http://www.gsfc.org

GEORGIA NATIONAL GUARD SERVICE CANCELABLE LOAN PROGRAM

• *See page 538*

STATE OF NEBRASKA COORDINATING COMMISSION FOR POSTSECONDARY EDUCATION http://www.ccpe.state.ne.us

NEBRASKA STATE GRANT

Available to undergraduates attending a participating postsecondary institution in Nebraska. Available to Pell Grant recipients only. Nebraska residency required. Awards determined by each participating institution. Contact financial aid office at institution for application and additional information.

Award: Grant for use in freshman, sophomore, junior, or senior years; not renewable. *Number:* varies. *Amount:* $100–$1032.

Eligibility Requirements: Applicant must be enrolled or expecting to enroll full or part-time at a two-year or four-year or technical institution or university; resident of Nebraska and studying in Nebraska. Available to U.S. citizens.

Application Requirements: Application, financial need analysis. *Deadline:* Continuous.

Contact: Financial Aid Office at college or university

STATE OF NORTH DAKOTA http://www.ndus.nodak.edu

NORTH DAKOTA INDIAN SCHOLARSHIP PROGRAM

• *See page 603*

NORTH DAKOTA SCHOLARS PROGRAM

Provides scholarships equal to cost of tuition at the public colleges in North Dakota for North Dakota residents. Must score at or above the 95th percentile on ACT and rank in top twenty percent of high school graduation class. Must take ACT in fall. For high school seniors with a minimum 3.5 GPA. Application deadline is the October or June ACT test date.

Award: Scholarship for use in freshman, sophomore, junior, or senior years; renewable. *Number:* 20. *Amount:* varies.

Eligibility Requirements: Applicant must be high school student; planning to enroll or expecting to enroll full-time at a two-year or four-year institution or university; resident of North Dakota and studying in North Dakota. Applicant must have 3.5 GPA or higher. Available to U.S. citizens.

Application Requirements: Test scores. *Deadline:* varies.

Contact: Peggy Wipf, Director of Financial Aid
State of North Dakota
600 East Boulevard, Department 215
Bismarck, ND 58505-0230
Phone: 701-328-4114

NORTH DAKOTA STATE STUDENT INCENTIVE GRANT PROGRAM

Aids North Dakota residents attending an approved college or university in North Dakota. Must be enrolled in a program of at least nine months in length.

Award: Grant for use in freshman, sophomore, junior, or senior years; not renewable. *Number:* 2500–2600. *Amount:* up to $600.

Eligibility Requirements: Applicant must be enrolled or expecting to enroll full-time at a two-year or four-year institution or university; resident of North Dakota and studying in North Dakota. Available to U.S. citizens.

Application Requirements: Financial need analysis, FAFSA. *Deadline:* March 15.

Contact: Peggy Wipf, Director of Financial Aid
State of North Dakota
600 East Boulevard, Department 215
Bismarck, ND 58505-0230
Phone: 701-328-4114

STATE OF WYOMING, ADMINISTERED BY UNIVERSITY OF WYOMING http://www.uwyo.edu/scholarships

VIETNAM VETERANS AWARD/WYOMING

• *See page 565*

STATE STUDENT ASSISTANCE COMMISSION OF INDIANA (SSACI) http://www.ssaci.in.gov

FEDERAL ROBERT C. BYRD HONORS SCHOLARSHIP-INDIANA

Scholarship is designed to recognize academic achievement and requires a minimum SAT score of 1300 or ACT score of 31, or recent GED score of 65. The scholarship is awarded equally among Indiana's congressional districts. The amount of the scholarship varies depending upon federal funding and is automatically renewed if the institution's satisfactory academic progress requirements are met.

Award: Scholarship for use in freshman, sophomore, junior, or senior years; renewable. *Number:* 550–570. *Amount:* $1500.

Eligibility Requirements: Applicant must be enrolled or expecting to enroll full-time at a two-year or four-year institution or university and resident of Indiana. Applicant must have 3.5 GPA or higher. Available to U.S. citizens.

Application Requirements: Application, test scores, transcript. *Deadline:* April 24.

Contact: Ms. Yvonne Heflin, Director, Special Programs
State Student Assistance Commission of Indiana (SSACI)
150 West Market Street, Suite 500
Indianapolis, IN 46204-2805
Phone: 317-232-2350
Fax: 317-232-3260

HOOSIER SCHOLAR AWARD

The Hoosier Scholar Award is a $500 nonrenewable award. Based on the size of the senior class, one to three scholars are selected by the guidance counselor(s) of each accredited high school in Indiana. The award is based on academic merit and may be used for any educational expense at an eligible Indiana institution of higher education.

Award: Scholarship for use in freshman year; not renewable. *Number:* 790–840. *Amount:* $500.

Eligibility Requirements: Applicant must be high school student; planning to enroll or expecting to enroll full-time at a two-year or four-year institution or university; resident of Indiana and studying in Indiana. Applicant must have 3.5 GPA or higher. Available to U.S. citizens.

Application Requirements: References. *Deadline:* March 10.

Contact: Ms. Ada Sparkman, Program Coordinator
State Student Assistance Commission of Indiana (SSACI)
150 West Market Street, Suite 500
Indianapolis, IN 46204-2805
Phone: 317-232-2350
Fax: 317-232-3260

INDIANA FREEDOM OF CHOICE GRANT

The Freedom of Choice Grant is a need-based, tuition-restricted program for students attending Indiana private institutions seeking a first undergraduate degree. It is awarded in addition to the Higher Education Award. Students (and parents of dependent students) who are U.S. citizens and Indiana residents must file the FAFSA yearly by the March 10 deadline.

Award: Grant for use in freshman, sophomore, junior, or senior years; not renewable. *Number:* 10,000–11,830. *Amount:* $200–$5915.

Eligibility Requirements: Applicant must be enrolled or expecting to enroll full-time at a four-year institution or university; resident of Indiana and studying in Indiana. Available to U.S. citizens.

Application Requirements: Application, financial need analysis, FAFSA. *Deadline:* March 10.

Contact: Grants Counselor
State Student Assistance Commission of Indiana (SSACI)
150 West Market Street, Suite 500
Indianapolis, IN 46204-2805
Phone: 317-232-2350
Fax: 317-232-3260
E-mail: grants@ssaci.state.in.us

INDIANA HIGHER EDUCATION AWARD

The Higher Education Award is a need-based, tuition-restricted program for students attending Indiana public, private, or proprietary institutions seeking a first undergraduate degree. Students (and parents of dependent students) who are U.S. citizens and Indiana residents must file the FAFSA yearly by the March 10 deadline.

Award: Grant for use in freshman, sophomore, junior, or senior years; not renewable. *Number:* 38,000–43,660. *Amount:* $200–$4700.

Eligibility Requirements: Applicant must be enrolled or expecting to enroll full-time at a two-year or four-year or technical institution or university; resident of Indiana and studying in Indiana. Available to U.S. citizens.

Application Requirements: Application, financial need analysis, FAFSA. *Deadline:* March 10.

Contact: Grants Counselor
State Student Assistance Commission of Indiana (SSACI)
150 West Market Street, Suite 500
Indianapolis, IN 46204-2805
Phone: 317-232-2350
Fax: 317-232-3260
E-mail: grants@ssaci.state.in.us

INDIANA NATIONAL GUARD SUPPLEMENTAL GRANT

• *See page 538*

PART-TIME GRANT PROGRAM

Program is designed to encourage part-time undergraduates to start and complete their associate or baccalaureate degrees or certificates by subsidizing part-time tuition costs. It is a term-based award that is based on need. State residency requirements must be met and a FAFSA must be filed. Eligibility is determined at the institutional level subject to approval by SSACI.

Award: Grant for use in freshman, sophomore, junior, or senior years; not renewable. *Number:* 4680–6700. *Amount:* $50–$4000.

Eligibility Requirements: Applicant must be enrolled or expecting to enroll part-time at a two-year or four-year or technical institution or university; resident of Indiana and studying in Indiana. Available to U.S. citizens.

Application Requirements: Application, financial need analysis. *Deadline:* Continuous.

Contact: Grants Counselor
State Student Assistance Commission of Indiana (SSACI)
150 West Market Street, Suite 500
Indianapolis, IN 46204-2805
Phone: 317-232-2350
Fax: 317-232-3260
E-mail: grants@ssaci.state.in.us

TWENTY-FIRST CENTURY SCHOLARS AWARD

Income-eligible 7th graders who enroll in the program, fulfill a pledge of good citizenship, and complete the Affirmation Form are guaranteed tuition for four years at any participating public institution. If the student attends a private institution, the state will award an amount comparable to that of a public institution. If the student attends a participating proprietary school, the state will award a tuition scholarship equal to that of Ivy Tech State College. FAFSA and affirmation form must be filed yearly by March 10. Applicant must be resident of Indiana.

Award: Scholarship for use in freshman, sophomore, junior, or senior years; not renewable. *Number:* 2800–8100. *Amount:* $1000–$6516.

Eligibility Requirements: Applicant must be enrolled or expecting to enroll full-time at a two-year or four-year or technical institution or university; resident of Indiana and studying in Indiana. Applicant must have 2.5 GPA or higher. Available to U.S. citizens.

Application Requirements: Application, financial need analysis, affirmation form. *Deadline:* March 10.

Contact: Twenty-first Century Scholars Program Counselors
State Student Assistance Commission of Indiana (SSACI)
150 West Market Street, Suite 500
Indianapolis, IN 46204-2805
Phone: 317-233-2100
Fax: 317-232-3260

STEPHEN T. MARCHELLO SCHOLARSHIP FOUNDATION http://www.stmfoundation.org

A LEGACY OF HOPE SCHOLARSHIPS FOR SURVIVORS OF CHILDHOOD CANCER

A scholarship of up to $10,000 per year for four years of postsecondary undergraduate education. Applicant must be a survivor of childhood cancer. Submit letter from doctor, clinic or hospital where applicant was treated for cancer. Residents of Colorado, Arizona, California, and Montana are eligible. Must be U.S. citizen. Minimum 2.5 GPA required.

Award: Scholarship for use in freshman, sophomore, junior, or senior years; renewable. *Number:* 1–6. *Amount:* $1000–$10,000.

Stephen T. Marchello Scholarship Foundation (continued)

Eligibility Requirements: Applicant must be high school student; planning to enroll or expecting to enroll full or part-time at a two-year or four-year or technical institution or university and resident of Arizona, California, Colorado, or Montana. Applicant must have 2.5 GPA or higher. Available to U.S. citizens.

Application Requirements: Application, essay, references, self-addressed stamped envelope, test scores, transcript. *Deadline:* March 15.

Contact: Franci Marchello, President
Stephen T. Marchello Scholarship Foundation
1170 East Long Place
Centennial, CO 80122
Phone: 303-886-5018
E-mail: fmarchello@earthlink.net

STONY-WOLD HERBERT FUND http://www.stonywoldherbertfund.com

STONY-WOLD HERBERT FUND DIRECT SERVICE GRANTS

Direct Service Grants provide financial assistance to students with respiratory ailments and are intending to help complete their education and become self-sustaining, independent members of the community. Grants are available to any student with a pulmonary problem who lives or goes to school in the greater New York City area (within 50 mile radius), is at least 16 years old, can demonstrate financial need and otherwise meet Stony Wold's qualifications. Individual grants, averaging $250 per month, are awarded for a maximum of four years to approximately 25 to 30 students enrolled in either academic or technical training programs.

Award: Grant for use in freshman, sophomore, junior, or senior years; renewable. *Number:* 25–30. *Amount:* $3000.

Eligibility Requirements: Applicant must be age 16; enrolled or expecting to enroll full-time at a four-year institution or university and resident of New York. Available to U.S. citizens.

Application Requirements: Autobiography, financial need analysis, references, transcript, medical profile from doctor. *Deadline:* Continuous.

Contact: Ms. Cheri Friedman, Director
Stony-Wold Herbert Fund
136 East 57th Street, Room 1705
New York, NY 10022
Phone: 212-753-6565
Fax: 212-753-6053

SUBMARINE OFFICERS' WIVES CLUB

BOWFIN MEMORIAL SCHOLARSHIP

• *See page 520*

SWISS BENEVOLENT SOCIETY OF CHICAGO http://www.sbschicago.org/education.html

SWISS BENEVOLENT SOCIETY OF CHICAGO SCHOLARSHIPS

• *See page 603*

SWISS BENEVOLENT SOCIETY OF NEW YORK http://www.swissbenevolentny.com

PELLEGRINI SCHOLARSHIP GRANTS

• *See page 604*

TENNESSEE EDUCATION ASSOCIATION http://www.teateachers.org

TEA DON SAHLI-KATHY WOODALL SONS AND DAUGHTERS SCHOLARSHIP

• *See page 481*

TENNESSEE STUDENT ASSISTANCE CORPORATION http://www.state.tn.us/tsac

NED MCWHERTER SCHOLARS PROGRAM

Assists Tennessee residents with high academic ability. Must have high school GPA of at least 3.5 and have scored in top 5% of SAT or ACT. Must attend college in Tennessee. Only high school seniors may apply.

Award: Scholarship for use in freshman, sophomore, junior, or senior years; renewable. *Number:* 55. *Amount:* $6000.

Eligibility Requirements: Applicant must be high school student; planning to enroll or expecting to enroll full-time at a two-year or four-year institution or university; resident of Tennessee and studying in Tennessee. Applicant must have 3.5 GPA or higher. Available to U.S. citizens.

Application Requirements: Application, test scores, transcript. *Deadline:* February 15.

Contact: Kathy Stripling, Scholarship Coordinator
Tennessee Student Assistance Corporation
404 James Robertson Parkway, Suite 1950, Parkway Towers
Nashville, TN 37243-0820
Phone: 615-741-1346
Fax: 615-741-6101
E-mail: kathy.stripling@state.tn.us

ROBERT C. BYRD HONORS SCHOLARSHIP-TENNESSEE

Available to Tennessee residents graduating from high school. Must have at least a 3.5 GPA. May also qualify with a 24 ACT or 1090 SAT. Renewable up to four years. Those with GED Test score of 57 or above may also apply.

Award: Scholarship for use in freshman, sophomore, junior, or senior years; renewable. *Number:* 125. *Amount:* $1100–$1500.

Eligibility Requirements: Applicant must be high school student; planning to enroll or expecting to enroll full-time at a two-year or four-year institution or university and resident of Tennessee. Applicant must have 3.5 GPA or higher. Available to U.S. citizens.

Application Requirements: Application, test scores, transcript. *Deadline:* March 1.

Contact: Kathy Stripling, Scholarship Coordinator
Tennessee Student Assistance Corporation
404 James Robertson Parkway, Suite 1950, Parkway Towers
Nashville, TN 37243-0820
Phone: 615-741-1346
Fax: 615-741-6101
E-mail: kathy.stripling@state.tn.us

TENNESSEE EDUCATION LOTTERY SCHOLARSHIP PROGRAM GENERAL ASSEMBLY MERIT SCHOLARSHIP

$1000 supplement to Tennessee HOPE Scholarship. Entering freshmen must have an unweighted 3.75 GPA and 29 ACT (1280 SAT).

Award: Scholarship for use in freshman, sophomore, junior, or senior years; renewable. *Number:* varies. *Amount:* $1000.

Eligibility Requirements: Applicant must be enrolled or expecting to enroll full or part-time at a two-year or four-year or technical institution or university; resident of Tennessee and studying in Tennessee. Available to U.S. citizens.

Application Requirements: Application, financial need analysis. *Deadline:* May 1.

Contact: Robert Biggers, Lottery Scholarship Program Administrator
Tennessee Student Assistance Corporation
404 James Robertson Parkway, Suite 1950
Nashville, TN 37243-0820
Phone: 800-342-1663
Fax: 615-253-3867
E-mail: tsac.aidinfo@state.tn.us

TENNESSEE EDUCATION LOTTERY SCHOLARSHIP PROGRAM NEED BASED SUPPLEMENTAL AWARD

$1000 supplement to Tennessee HOPE Scholarship. Must meet Tennessee HOPE Scholarship requirements and student's parent(s) must have an Adjusted Gross Income on their federal tax return of $36000 or less.

Award: Scholarship for use in freshman, sophomore, junior, or senior years; renewable. *Number:* varies. *Amount:* $1000.

Eligibility Requirements: Applicant must be enrolled or expecting to enroll full or part-time at a two-year or four-year or technical institution or university; resident of Tennessee and studying in Tennessee. Applicant must have 3.0 GPA or higher. Available to U.S. citizens.

Application Requirements: Application, financial need analysis. *Deadline:* May 1.

Contact: Robert Biggers, Lottery Scholarship Program Administrator
Tennessee Student Assistance Corporation
404 James Robertson Parkway, Suite 1950
Nashville, TN 37243-0820
Phone: 800-342-1663
Fax: 615-253-3867
E-mail: tsac.aidinfo@state.tn.us

TENNESSEE EDUCATION LOTTERY SCHOLARSHIP PROGRAM TENNESSEE HOPE ACCESS GRANT

Non-renewable award of $2000 for students at 4-year colleges or $1250 for students at 2-year colleges. Entering freshmen must have a minimum GPA of 2.75 and parents income must be $36000 or less. Recipients will be eligible for Tennessee HOPE Scholarship by meeting HOPE Scholarship renewal criteria.

Award: Grant for use in freshman, sophomore, junior, or senior years; not renewable. *Number:* varies. *Amount:* $1250–$2000.

Eligibility Requirements: Applicant must be enrolled or expecting to enroll full or part-time at a two-year or four-year or technical institution or university; resident of Tennessee and studying in Tennessee. Available to U.S. citizens.

Application Requirements: Application, financial need analysis. *Deadline:* May 1.

Contact: Robert Biggers, Lottery Scholarship Program Administrator
Tennessee Student Assistance Corporation
404 James Robertson Parkway, Suite 1950
Nashville, TN 37243-0820
Phone: 800-342-1663
Fax: 615-253-3867
E-mail: tsac.aidinfo@state.tn.us

TENNESSEE EDUCATION LOTTERY SCHOLARSHIP PROGRAM TENNESSEE HOPE SCHOLARSHIP

Award of $3000 per year for students at 4-year colleges or $1500 per year for students at 2-year colleges.

Award: Scholarship for use in freshman, sophomore, junior, or senior years; renewable. *Number:* varies. *Amount:* $1500–$3000.

Eligibility Requirements: Applicant must be enrolled or expecting to enroll full or part-time at a two-year or four-year or technical institution or university; resident of Tennessee and studying in Tennessee. Applicant must have 3.0 GPA or higher. Available to U.S. citizens.

Application Requirements: Application, financial need analysis. *Deadline:* May 1.

Contact: Robert Biggers, Lottery Scholarship Program Administrator
Tennessee Student Assistance Corporation
404 James Robertson Parkway, Suite 1950
Nashville, TN 37243-0820
Phone: 800-342-1663
Fax: 615-253-3867
E-mail: tsac.aidinfo@state.tn.us

TENNESSEE EDUCATION LOTTERY SCHOLARSHIP PROGRAM WILDER-NAIFEH TECHNICAL SKILLS GRANT

Award of $1250 for students enrolled in Tennessee Technology Centers. Cannot be prior recipient of Tennessee HOPE Scholarship.

Award: Grant for use in freshman, sophomore, junior, or senior years. *Number:* varies. *Amount:* $1250.

Eligibility Requirements: Applicant must be enrolled or expecting to enroll full or part-time at a technical institution; resident of Tennessee and studying in Tennessee.

Application Requirements: Application, financial need analysis. *Deadline:* May 1.

Contact: Robert Biggers, Lottery Scholarship Program Administrator
Tennessee Student Assistance Corporation
404 James Robertson Parkway, Suite 1950
Nashville, TN 37243-0820
Phone: 800-342-1663
Fax: 615-253-3867
E-mail: tsac.aidinfo@state.tn.us

TENNESSEE STUDENT ASSISTANCE AWARD PROGRAM

Assists Tennessee residents attending an approved college or university within the state. Complete a Free Application for Federal Student Aid form. Apply January 1. FAFSA must be processed by May 1 for priority consideration.

Award: Grant for use in freshman, sophomore, junior, or senior years; renewable. *Number:* 26,000. *Amount:* $100–$2130.

Eligibility Requirements: Applicant must be enrolled or expecting to enroll full or part-time at a two-year or four-year or technical institution or university; resident of Tennessee and studying in Tennessee. Available to U.S. citizens.

Application Requirements: Application, financial need analysis. *Deadline:* May 1.

Contact: Naomi Derryberry, Grant and Scholarship Administrator
Tennessee Student Assistance Corporation
404 James Robertson Parkway, Suite 1950, Parkway Towers
Nashville, TN 37243-0820
Phone: 615-741-1346
Fax: 615-741-6101
E-mail: naomi.derryberry@state.tn.us

TEXAS 4-H YOUTH DEVELOPMENT FOUNDATION http://texas4-h.tamu.edu

TEXAS 4-H OPPORTUNITY SCHOLARSHIP

Renewable award for Texas 4-H members to attend a Texas college or university. Minimum GPA of 2.5 required. Must attend full-time. Deadline is February 1.

Award: Scholarship for use in freshman, sophomore, junior, or senior years; renewable. *Number:* 150. *Amount:* $1500–$15,000.

Eligibility Requirements: Applicant must be enrolled or expecting to enroll full-time at a two-year or four-year or technical institution or university; resident of Texas and studying in Texas. Applicant must have 2.5 GPA or higher. Available to U.S. citizens.

Application Requirements: Application, essay, financial need analysis, interview, references, test scores, transcript. *Deadline:* February 1.

Contact: Philip Pearce, Executive Director
Texas 4-H Youth Development Foundation
Texas A&M University
7606 Eastmark Drive, Suite 101
College Station, TX 77843-2473
Phone: 979-845-1213
Fax: 979-845-6495
E-mail: p-pearce@tamu.edu

TEXAS AFL-CIO http://www.aflcio.org

TEXAS AFL-CIO SCHOLARSHIP PROGRAM

• *See page 481*

TEXAS BLACK BAPTIST SCHOLARSHIP COMMITTEE http://www.bgct.org/aam

TEXAS BLACK BAPTIST SCHOLARSHIP

• *See page 604*

TEXAS CHRISTIAN UNIVERSITY NEELY SCHOOL OF BUSINESS ENTREPRENEURSHIP PROGRAM http://www.nep.tcu.edu

TCU TEXAS YOUTH ENTREPRENEUR OF THE YEAR

Award available to currently enrolled Texas high school students who started and managed a business for at least one year. Must submit description of

Texas Christian University Neely School of Business Entrepreneurship Program (continued)

currently-operating business they founded, must be resident of Texas. Finalists must attend TCU Young Entrepreneurs Days and individually participate in interviews. Award may be applied to any college; award is doubled if the student attends TCU. Information and application is on Web site: http://www.nep.tcu.edu.

Award: Scholarship for use in freshman year; not renewable. *Number:* 6. *Amount:* $1000–$5000.

Eligibility Requirements: Applicant must be high school student; age 14-19; planning to enroll or expecting to enroll full or part-time at a two-year or four-year or technical institution or university and resident of Texas. Available to U.S. citizens.

Application Requirements: Application, interview, references, Description of business started and managed by applicant. *Deadline:* November 1.

Contact: Ms. Sheryl Doll, Program Director
Texas Christian University Neely School of Business Entrepreneurship Program
TCU Box 298530
Ft. Worth, TX 76109
Phone: 817-257-5078
Fax: 817-257-5775
E-mail: s.doll@tcu.edu

TEXAS HIGHER EDUCATION COORDINATING BOARD

http://www.collegefortexans.com

ACADEMIC COMMON MARKET WAIVER

For Texas residents who are students pursuing a degree in a field of study not offered in Texas. May qualify for special tuition rates. Deadlines vary by institution. Must be studying in the South.

Award: Scholarship for use in freshman, sophomore, junior, senior, or graduate years; renewable. *Number:* varies. *Amount:* varies.

Eligibility Requirements: Applicant must be enrolled or expecting to enroll full or part-time at an institution or university; resident of Texas and studying in Alabama, Arkansas, Florida, Georgia, Kentucky, Louisiana, Mississippi, Missouri, Oklahoma, South Carolina, Tennessee, or Virginia. Available to U.S. citizens.

Application Requirements: Application. *Deadline:* varies.

Contact: Linda McDonough, Associate Program Director
Texas Higher Education Coordinating Board
PO Box 12788
Austin, TX 78711-2788
Phone: 512-427-6525
E-mail: grantinfo@thecb.state.tx.us

BORDER COUNTY WAIVER

Award provides waiver of nonresident tuition for students of neighboring states (Louisiana, Oklahoma, Arkansas and New Mexico). Must attend a Texas public institution. Deadline varies by institution. Contact the registrar's office for details.

Award: Scholarship for use in freshman, sophomore, junior, or senior years; not renewable. *Number:* varies. *Amount:* varies.

Eligibility Requirements: Applicant must be enrolled or expecting to enroll at a four-year institution or university; resident of Arkansas, Louisiana, New Mexico, or Oklahoma and studying in Texas.

Application Requirements: Application. *Deadline:* varies.

Contact: Financial Aid Office at college
Texas Higher Education Coordinating Board
PO Box 12788
Austin, TX 78711-2788
Phone: 512-427-6101
Fax: 512-427-6127
E-mail: grantinfo@thecb.state.tx.us

EARLY HIGH SCHOOL GRADUATION SCHOLARSHIPS

Award of $2000 for Texas residents who have completed the requirements for graduation from a Texas high school in no more than 36 consecutive months. Eligibility continues until full $2000 tuition award is received. Must submit high school certificate of eligibility to Coordinating Board. For more information, contact your high school counselor.

Award: Scholarship for use in freshman year; not renewable. *Number:* varies. *Amount:* $2000.

Eligibility Requirements: Applicant must be high school student; planning to enroll or expecting to enroll full or part-time at a two-year or four-year or technical institution or university; resident of Texas and studying in Texas. Available to U.S. citizens.

Application Requirements: Application. *Deadline:* Continuous.

Contact: Texas Higher Education Coordinating Board
PO Box 12788
Austin, TX 78711-2788
Phone: 800-242-3062 Ext. 6387
E-mail: grantinfo@thecb.state.tx.us

EXEMPTION FOR DISABLED IN THE LINE OF DUTY PEACE OFFICERS

• *See page 520*

GOOD NEIGHBOR SCHOLARSHIP WAIVER

• *See page 604*

LEVERAGING EDUCATIONAL ASSISTANCE PARTNERSHIP PROGRAM (LEAP) (FORMERLY SSIG)

Renewable award available to residents of Texas attending public colleges or universities in Texas. Must be enrolled at least half-time and show financial need. Deadlines vary by institution. Contact the college/university financial aid office for application information.

Award: Grant for use in freshman, sophomore, junior, or senior years; renewable. *Number:* varies. *Amount:* up to $1250.

Eligibility Requirements: Applicant must be enrolled or expecting to enroll full or part-time at a two-year or four-year or technical institution or university; resident of Texas and studying in Texas. Available to U.S. citizens.

Application Requirements: Financial need analysis, FAFSA. *Deadline:* varies.

Contact: Financial Aid Office at college
Texas Higher Education Coordinating Board
PO Box 12788
Austin, TX 78711-2788
Phone: 512-427-6101
Fax: 512-427-6127
E-mail: grantinfo@thecb.state.tx.us

LICENSE PLATE INSIGNIA SCHOLARSHIP

One-time award to Texas residents enrolled at least half-time at public or private nonprofit senior colleges and universities in Texas. Must demonstrate financial need. Contact financial aid office at college for deadlines and application.

Award: Scholarship for use in freshman, sophomore, junior, or senior years; not renewable. *Number:* varies. *Amount:* varies.

Eligibility Requirements: Applicant must be enrolled or expecting to enroll full or part-time at a four-year institution or university; resident of Texas and studying in Texas.

Application Requirements: Application, financial need analysis. *Deadline:* varies.

Contact: Financial Aid Office at college
Texas Higher Education Coordinating Board
PO Box 12788
Austin, TX 78711-2788
Phone: 512-427-6101
Fax: 512-427-6127
E-mail: grantinfo@thecb.state.tx.us

MILITARY STATIONED IN TEXAS WAIVER

• *See page 565*

ROBERT C. BYRD SCHOLARSHIP PROGRAM-TEXAS

Competitive, academic merit scholarship to outstanding high school students in Texas. Must be nominated as most academically eligible by their high school counselor or GED center director.

Award: Scholarship for use in freshman, sophomore, junior, or senior years; renewable. *Number:* varies. *Amount:* up to $1500.

Eligibility Requirements: Applicant must be high school student; planning to enroll or expecting to enroll at a two-year or four-year or technical institution or university and resident of Texas. Available to U.S. citizens.

Application Requirements: Application, test scores, transcript. *Deadline:* varies.

Contact: Grants and Special Programs Office
Texas Higher Education Coordinating Board
PO Box 12788
Austin, TX 78711-2788
Phone: 800-242-3062
E-mail: grantinfo@thecb.state.tx.us

TANF EXEMPTION PROGRAM

Tuition and fee exemption for Texas residents who during last year of high school received financial assistance for not less than 6 months. Must enroll at Texas institution within 24 TANF months of high school graduation. Award is good for one year. Contact the admissions/registrar's office for application information.

Award: Scholarship for use in freshman year; not renewable. *Number:* varies. *Amount:* varies.

Eligibility Requirements: Applicant must be age 21 or under; enrolled or expecting to enroll full or part-time at a two-year or four-year or technical institution or university; single; resident of Texas and studying in Texas.

Application Requirements: Application, financial need analysis. *Deadline:* Continuous.

Contact: Financial Aid Office at college
Texas Higher Education Coordinating Board
PO Box 12788
Austin, TX 78711-2788
Phone: 512-427-6101
Fax: 512-427-6127
E-mail: grantinfo@thecb.state.tx.us

TEXAS NATIONAL GUARD TUITION ASSISTANCE PROGRAM

• *See page 538*

TEXAS TUITION EXEMPTION FOR BLIND/DEAF STUDENTS

• *See page 532*

TEXAS TUITION EXEMPTION FOR SENIOR CITIZENS-65+

Tuition exemption for Texas residents over the age of 65 at eligible Texas institutions. Pays tuition for up to six semester credit hours per semester or summer term. Nonrenewable. Awards made on a space-available basis. Contact the admissions/registrar's office for application information.

Award: Scholarship for use in freshman, sophomore, junior, or senior years; not renewable. *Number:* varies. *Amount:* varies.

Eligibility Requirements: Applicant must be age 66; enrolled or expecting to enroll part-time at a two-year or four-year or technical institution or university; resident of Texas and studying in Texas. Available to U.S. citizens.

Application Requirements: Application. *Deadline:* Continuous.

Contact: Financial Aid Office at college
Texas Higher Education Coordinating Board
PO Box 12788
Austin, TX 78711-2788
Phone: 512-427-6101
Fax: 512-427-6127
E-mail: grantinfo@thecb.state.tx.us

TEXAS TUITION EXEMPTION FOR STUDENTS IN FOSTER CARE OR OTHER RESIDENTIAL CARE

Exemption from tuition and fees at Texas institution. Must have been in foster care under the conservatorship of the Department of Protection and Regulatory Services on or after 18th birthday; or on the day of the student's 14th birthday, if the student was also eligible for adoption on or after that day; or the day the student graduated from high school or completed the equivalent of a high school diploma. Must enroll as undergraduate student within three years of discharge. Must be Texas resident. Contact the admissions/registrar's office for application information.

Award: Scholarship for use in freshman, sophomore, junior, or senior years; renewable. *Number:* varies. *Amount:* varies.

Eligibility Requirements: Applicant must be enrolled or expecting to enroll full or part-time at a two-year or four-year or technical institution or university; resident of Texas and studying in Texas. Available to U.S. citizens.

Application Requirements: Application. *Deadline:* Continuous.

Contact: Financial Aid Office at college
Texas Higher Education Coordinating Board
PO Box 12788
Austin, TX 78711-2788
Phone: 512-427-6101
Fax: 512-427-6127
E-mail: grantinfo@thecb.state.tx.us

TEXAS TUITION EXEMPTION PROGRAM: HIGHEST RANKING HIGH SCHOOL GRADUATE

Award available to Texas residents who are the top ranked seniors of their high school. Must attend a public college or university within Texas. Recipient is exempt from certain charges for first two semesters. Deadlines vary. Contact admissions/registrar's office for application information. Must provide proof of valedictorian ranking to the registrar.

Award: Scholarship for use in freshman year; not renewable. *Number:* varies. *Amount:* varies.

Eligibility Requirements: Applicant must be enrolled or expecting to enroll full or part-time at a two-year or four-year or technical institution or university; resident of Texas and studying in Texas. Applicant must have 3.5 GPA or higher. Available to U.S. citizens.

Application Requirements: Transcript. *Deadline:* varies.

Contact: Financial Aid Office at college
Texas Higher Education Coordinating Board
PO Box 12788
Austin, TX 78711-2788
Phone: 512-427-6101
Fax: 512-427-6127
E-mail: grantinfo@thecb.state.tx.us

TEXAS-TUITION FEE EXEMPTION FOR CHILDREN OF DISABLED/DECEASED FIREMEN, PEACE OFFICERS, GAME WARDENS, EMPLOYEES OF CORRECTIONAL INSTITUTIONS

• *See page 521*

TOWARD EXCELLENCE, ACCESS AND SUCCESS (TEXAS GRANT)

Renewable aid for students enrolled in a public or private nonprofit, college or university in Texas. Based on need. Amount of award is determined by the financial aid office of each school. Deadlines vary. Contact the college/university financial aid office for application information.

Award: Grant for use in freshman, sophomore, junior, or senior years; renewable. *Number:* varies. *Amount:* $3140.

Eligibility Requirements: Applicant must be enrolled or expecting to enroll full or part-time at a two-year or four-year or technical institution or university; resident of Texas and studying in Texas. Applicant must have 2.5 GPA or higher. Available to U.S. citizens.

Application Requirements: Application, financial need analysis, transcript. *Deadline:* varies.

Contact: Financial Aid Office at college
Texas Higher Education Coordinating Board
PO Box 12788
Austin, TX 78711-2788
Phone: 512-427-6101
Fax: 512-427-6127
E-mail: grantinfo@thecb.state.tx.us

TOWARD EXCELLENCE, ACCESS, AND SUCCESS (TEXAS) GRANT II PROGRAM

Provides grant aid to financially needy students enrolled in Texas public two-year colleges. Complete FAFSA. Contact college financial aid office for additional assistance.

Texas Higher Education Coordinating Board (continued)

Award: Grant for use in freshman or sophomore years; renewable. *Number:* varies. *Amount:* $3140.

Eligibility Requirements: Applicant must be enrolled or expecting to enroll full or part-time at a two-year or technical institution; resident of Texas and studying in Texas. Applicant must have 2.5 GPA or higher. Available to U.S. citizens.

Application Requirements: Financial need analysis, transcript, FAFSA. *Deadline:* Continuous.

Contact: Financial Aid Office at college
Texas Higher Education Coordinating Board
PO Box 12788
Austin, TX 78711-2788
Phone: 512-427-6101
Fax: 512-427-6127
E-mail: grantinfo@thecb.state.tx.us

TUITION AND FEE EXEMPTION FOR CHILDREN OF PRISONERS OF WAR OR PERSONS MISSING IN ACTION-TEXAS

• *See page 565*

TUITION EQUALIZATION GRANT (TEG) PROGRAM

Renewable award for Texas residents enrolled at least half-time at an independent college or university within the state. Based on financial need. Deadlines vary by institution. Must not be receiving athletic scholarship. Contact college/university financial aid office for application information.

Award: Grant for use in freshman, sophomore, junior, or senior years; renewable. *Number:* varies. *Amount:* up to $3653.

Eligibility Requirements: Applicant must be enrolled or expecting to enroll full or part-time at a two-year or four-year institution or university; resident of Texas and studying in Texas. Available to U.S. citizens.

Application Requirements: Financial need analysis, FAFSA. *Deadline:* varies.

Contact: Financial Aid Office at college
Texas Higher Education Coordinating Board
PO Box 12788
Austin, TX 78711-2788
Phone: 512-427-6101
Fax: 512-427-6127
E-mail: grantinfo@thecb.state.tx.us

TUITION EXEMPTIONS FOR TEXAS VETERANS (HAZELWOOD ACT)

• *See page 566*

TEXAS TENNIS FOUNDATION

http://texastennisfoundation.com

TEXAS TENNIS FOUNDATION SCHOLARSHIPS AND ENDOWMENTS

College scholarships for highly recommended students residing in Texas, with an interest in tennis. Financial need is considered. Must be between the ages of 17 and 19.

Award: Scholarship for use in freshman, sophomore, junior, or senior years; not renewable. *Number:* 10–15. *Amount:* $1000.

Eligibility Requirements: Applicant must be age 17-19; enrolled or expecting to enroll full-time at a two-year or four-year or technical institution or university; resident of Texas and must have an interest in athletics/sports. Available to U.S. citizens.

Application Requirements: Application, essay, financial need analysis, references. *Deadline:* April 25.

Contact: Pam Jaeger, Awards Coordinator
Texas Tennis Foundation
2111 Dickson, Suite 33
Austin, TX 78704-4788
Phone: 512-443-1334 Ext. 200
Fax: 512-443-4748
E-mail: pjaeger@texas.usta.com

THE ASIAN REPORTER

http://www.asianreporter.com

ASIAN REPORTER SCHOLARSHIP

• *See page 604*

THE EDUCATION PARTNERSHIP

http://www.edpartnership.org

CHARLES A. MORVILLO MEMORIAL SCHOLARSHIPS

For students who demonstrate financial need, integrity, leadership, a determination to gain a higher education and make a positive impact on the community. $10,000 is paid to the college or university over four years, and $2,500 is paid directly to the scholar upon graduation. Must be a senior from a Providence or North Providence high school. Application deadline is July 1.

Award: Scholarship for use in freshman, sophomore, junior, or senior years; renewable. *Number:* 2. *Amount:* $12,500.

Eligibility Requirements: Applicant must be high school student; age 18 or under; planning to enroll or expecting to enroll full-time at a two-year or four-year institution or university and resident of Rhode Island. Applicant must have 2.5 GPA or higher. Available to U.S. citizens.

Application Requirements: Application, essay, financial need analysis, references, test scores, transcript. *Deadline:* July 1.

Contact: Keturah Johnson, Scholarships and Communications Coordinator
The Education Partnership
345 South Main Street
Providence, RI 02903
Phone: 401-331-5222 Ext. 112
Fax: 401-331-1659
E-mail: kjohnson@edpartnership.org

LAST DOLLAR SCHOLARSHIP

Need-based awards granted to graduates of Providence public high schools. Students must demonstrate unmet financial need after institutional and federal financial aid has been awarded.

Award: Scholarship for use in freshman, sophomore, junior, or senior years; not renewable. *Number:* 10–20. *Amount:* $500–$1000.

Eligibility Requirements: Applicant must be enrolled or expecting to enroll full-time at a two-year or four-year institution or university and resident of Rhode Island. Available to U.S. citizens.

Application Requirements: Application, essay, financial need analysis, references, test scores, transcript. *Deadline:* June 1.

Contact: Keturah Johnson, Scholarships and Communications Coordinator
The Education Partnership
345 South Main Street
Providence, RI 02903
Phone: 401-331-5222 Ext. 112
Fax: 401-331-1659
E-mail: kjohnson@edpartnership.org

TIDEWATER SCHOLARSHIP FOUNDATION

http://www.access-tsf.org

ACCESS SCHOLARSHIP/LAST DOLLAR AWARD

The Tidewater Scholarship Foundation's ACCESS Program helps participating students in Norfolk, Portsmouth, and Virginia Beach, Virginia secure scholarships and financial aid for college. ACCESS also offers a "Last Dollar Scholarship" that is awarded based on unmet financial need for students who enrolled in the ACCESS program in ninth grade.

Award: Scholarship for use in freshman, sophomore, junior, or senior years; renewable. *Number:* varies. *Amount:* $500–$1000.

Eligibility Requirements: Applicant must be high school student; planning to enroll or expecting to enroll full-time at a two-year or four-year institution or university and resident of Virginia. Applicant must have 2.5 GPA or higher. Available to U.S. citizens.

Application Requirements: Financial need analysis, ACCESS Challenge agreement. *Deadline:* Continuous.

Contact: Bonnie Sutton, President and CEO
Tidewater Scholarship Foundation
800 East City Hall Avenue
PO Box 1357
Norfolk, VA 23501-1357
Phone: 757-628-3942
Fax: 757-628-3842
E-mail: bsutton@access-tsf.org

TIGER WOODS FOUNDATION http://www.tigerwoodsfoundation.org

ALFRED "TUP" HOLMES MEMORIAL SCHOLARSHIP

Given yearly to one worthy Atlanta metropolitan area graduating high school senior who has displayed high moral character while demonstrating leadership potential and academic excellence. Must be U.S. citizen. Minimum 3.0 GPA required. Application deadline is April 1.

Award: Scholarship for use in freshman year; not renewable. *Number:* 1. *Amount:* $2500.

Eligibility Requirements: Applicant must be high school student; planning to enroll or expecting to enroll full-time at a two-year or four-year institution or university and resident of Georgia. Applicant must have 3.0 GPA or higher. Available to U.S. citizens.

Application Requirements: Application, essay, references, test scores, transcript. *Deadline:* April 1.

Contact: Michelle Bernis, Director, Events
Tiger Woods Foundation
4281 Katella Avenue, Suite 111
Los Alamitos, CA 90720
Phone: 714-816-1806
Fax: 714-816-1869

TKE EDUCATIONAL FOUNDATION http://www.tkefoundation.org

ELMER AND DORIS SCHMITZ SR. MEMORIAL SCHOLARSHIP

• *See page 482*

TOWNSHIP OFFICIALS OF ILLINOIS http://www.toi.org

TOWNSHIP OFFICIALS OF ILLINOIS SCHOLARSHIP FUND

The TOI scholarships are awarded to graduating Illinois high school seniors who have a B average or above, have demonstrated an active interest in school activities, who have submitted an essay on "The Importance of Township Government," high school transcript, and letters of recommendation. Students must attend Illinois institutions, either four-year or junior colleges. Must be full-time student.

Award: Scholarship for use in freshman year; not renewable. *Number:* 10. *Amount:* $2000.

Eligibility Requirements: Applicant must be high school student; planning to enroll or expecting to enroll full-time at a two-year or four-year institution or university; resident of Illinois and studying in Illinois. Applicant must have 3.0 GPA or higher. Available to U.S. citizens.

Application Requirements: Application, essay, references, test scores, transcript. *Deadline:* March 1.

Contact: Bryan Smith, Editor and Executive Director
Township Officials of Illinois
408 South 5th Street
Springfield, IL 62701-1804
Phone: 217-744-2212
Fax: 217-744-7419
E-mail: bryantoi@toi.org

TREACY COMPANY http://students.msugf.edu/scholar.htm

TREACY COMPANY SCHOLARSHIPS

Renewable award for college freshmen and sophomores. Must be a resident of Montana, Idaho, North Dakota, or South Dakota. Write to Treacy Company for application and more information.

Award: Scholarship for use in freshman or sophomore years; renewable. *Number:* 25–35. *Amount:* $400.

Eligibility Requirements: Applicant must be enrolled or expecting to enroll full or part-time at a two-year or four-year or technical institution or university and resident of Idaho, Montana, North Dakota, or South Dakota. Available to U.S. citizens.

Application Requirements: Application, photo, transcript. *Deadline:* June 15.

Contact: James O'Connell, Trustee
Treacy Company
PO Box 1479
Helena, MT 59624-1700

TRIANGLE COMMUNITY FOUNDATION http://www.trianglecf.org

GLAXO SMITH KLINE OPPORTUNITIES SCHOLARSHIP

Renewable award for any type of education or training program. Must be a legal resident of the United States with a permanent residence in Durham, Orange, Wake, or Chatham counties. No income limitations. Application deadline is March 15. For further information see Web site at http://www.tranglecf.org.

Award: Scholarship for use in freshman, sophomore, junior, senior, or graduate years; renewable. *Number:* 1–5. *Amount:* $1000–$20,000.

Eligibility Requirements: Applicant must be enrolled or expecting to enroll full-time at a two-year or four-year institution or university; resident of North Carolina and studying in North Carolina. Available to U.S. citizens.

Application Requirements: Application, autobiography, essay, financial need analysis, references, test scores, transcript, proof of U.S. citizenship. *Deadline:* March 15.

Contact: Application available at Web site.

TRIANGLE NATIVE AMERICAN SOCIETY http://www.tnasweb.org

TRIANGLE NATIVE AMERICAN SOCIETY SCHOLARSHIP FUND

• *See page 604*

UNITED COMMUNITY SERVICES FOR WORKING FAMILIES http://www.workingfamilies.com

RONALD LORAH MEMORIAL SCHOLARSHIP

• *See page 484*

UNITED DAUGHTERS OF THE CONFEDERACY http://www.hqudc.org

GERTRUDE BOTTS-SAUCIER SCHOLARSHIP

• *See page 486*

LOLA B. CURRY SCHOLARSHIP

• *See page 486*

UNITED FEDERATION OF TEACHERS

ALBERT SHANKER COLLEGE SCHOLARSHIP FUND OF THE UNITED FEDERATION OF TEACHERS

Renewable award for eligible students graduating from New York City public high schools to pursue undergraduate studies. Scholarship is $1250 a year for four years. Submit transcript, autobiography, essay, references, and financial need analysis with application. Deadline is third week of December. There are nine graduate awards including a renewable medical and a renewable law award. Applicants must be current undergraduate award winners.

Award: Scholarship for use in freshman, sophomore, junior, senior, or graduate years; renewable. *Number:* 200. *Amount:* $1250.

Eligibility Requirements: Applicant must be enrolled or expecting to enroll full-time at a two-year or four-year institution or university and resident of New York. Available to U.S. citizens.

United Federation of Teachers (continued)

Application Requirements: Application, autobiography, essay, financial need analysis, references, transcript. *Deadline:* varies.

Contact: Mr. Jeffrey A. Huart, Director
United Federation of Teachers
52 Broadway, 11th Floor
New York, NY 10004-1603
Phone: 212-529-2110
Fax: 212-510-6429
E-mail: shankerfund@worldnet.att.com

UNITED METHODIST CHURCH http://www.umc.org/

J. A. KNOWLES MEMORIAL SCHOLARSHIP
• *See page 628*

UNITED NEGRO COLLEGE FUND http://www.uncf.org

ABBINGTON, VALLANTEEN SCHOLARSHIP
• *See page 606*

AMERICAN FAMILY LIFE ASSURANCE COMPANY SCHOLARSHIP

Applicants must be residents of Columbus, Georgia and must attend a UNCF Member College or University. Eligible schools are: Albany State College, Fort Valley State College, and Savannah State College. Must have minimum 2.5 GPA. Please visit Web site for more information: http://www.uncf.org.

Award: Scholarship for use in freshman, sophomore, junior, senior, or graduate years; not renewable. *Number:* varies. *Amount:* varies.

Eligibility Requirements: Applicant must be enrolled or expecting to enroll at a four-year institution or university; resident of Georgia and studying in Georgia. Applicant must have 2.5 GPA or higher.

Application Requirements: Application, financial need analysis, FAFSA, SAR. *Deadline:* varies.

Contact: Program Services Department
United Negro College Fund
8260 Willow Oaks Corporate Drive
Fairfax, VA 22031

AMOS DEINARD FOUNDATION SCHOLARSHIP
• *See page 606*

ARTHUR ROSS FOUNDATION SCHOLARSHIP

Scholarships available to African-American students to attend a UNCF member college or university. Must be a resident of one of the 5 boroughs of New York City or the southern United States. See Web site for details: http://www.uncf.org.

Award: Scholarship for use in freshman, sophomore, junior, or senior years; renewable. *Number:* varies. *Amount:* $1000–$3000.

Eligibility Requirements: Applicant must be enrolled or expecting to enroll at a four-year institution or university and resident of Alabama, Florida, Georgia, Kentucky, Louisiana, Mississippi, New York, North Carolina, or South Carolina. Applicant must have 2.5 GPA or higher.

Application Requirements: Application, financial need analysis. *Deadline:* varies.

Contact: Program Services Department
United Negro College Fund
8260 Willow Oaks Corporate Drive
Fairfax, VA 22031

BANK OF AMERICA SCHOLARSHIP
• *See page 606*

BANK ONE ARIZONA CORPORATION SCHOLARSHIP
• *See page 606*

BELLSOUTH LOUISIANA SCHOLARSHIP
• *See page 606*

BESSIE IRENE SMITH TRUST SCHOLARSHIP
• *See page 607*

BILDNER FAMILY SCHOLARSHIP
• *See page 607*

BORDEN SCHOLARSHIP FUND
• *See page 607*

BRITTON FUND SCHOLARSHIP PROGRAM

Scholarships available to students from Northern Ohio enrolled in a UNCF member college or university. Please visit Web site for more information: http://www.uncf.org.

Award: Scholarship for use in freshman, sophomore, junior, senior, or graduate years. *Number:* varies. *Amount:* varies.

Eligibility Requirements: Applicant must be enrolled or expecting to enroll at a four-year institution or university and resident of Ohio. Applicant must have 2.5 GPA or higher. Available to U.S. citizens.

Application Requirements: Application, financial need analysis, FAFSA, SAR. *Deadline:* varies.

Contact: Program Services Department
United Negro College Fund
8260 Willow Oaks Corporate Drive
Fairfax, VA 22031

BUSHROD CAMPBELL AND ADAH HALL SCHOLARSHIP
• *See page 607*

CARLOS AND LILLIAN THURSTON SCHOLARSHIP
• *See page 607*

CASIMIR, DOMINIQUE AND JAQUES SCHOLARSHIP
• *See page 607*

CHARLES AND ELLORA ALLIS FOUNDATION SCHOLARSHIP
• *See page 607*

CHICAGO INTER-ALUMNI COUNCIL SCHOLARSHIP
• *See page 608*

CINERGY FOUNDATION SCHOLARSHIP
• *See page 608*

CLEVELAND FOUNDATION SCHOLARSHIP
• *See page 608*

CLEVELAND MUNICIPAL SCHOOL SCHOLARSHIP
• *See page 608*

CLOROX COMPANY FOUNDATION SCHOLARSHIP
• *See page 608*

COLUMBUS FOUNDATION SCHOLARSHIP
• *See page 608*

COSTCO SCHOLARSHIP
• *See page 609*

CURTIS BREEDEN SCHOLARSHIP
• *See page 609*

DALLAS INDEPENDENT SCHOOL DISTRICT SCHOLARSHIP
• *See page 609*

DALLAS MAVERICKS
• *See page 609*

DENIS D'AMORE SCHOLARSHIP
• *See page 610*

DONNIE AND PAM SIMPSON SCHOLARSHIP
• *See page 610*

DUPONT SCHOLARSHIP
• *See page 610*

DUQUESNE LIGHT COMPANY SCHOLARSHIP
• *See page 610*

EDNA F. BLUM FOUNDATION
• *See page 610*

EDWARD FITTERMAN FOUNDATION SCHOLARSHIP
• *See page 611*

ELMER ROE DEAVER FOUNDATION SCHOLARSHIP
• *See page 611*

EVELYN LEVINA WRIGHT SCHOLARSHIP

• *See page 611*

FIFTH/THIRD SCHOLARS PROGRAM

• *See page 611*

FORT WORTH INDEPENDENT SCHOOL DISTRICT SCHOLARSHIP

• *See page 611*

GARY PAYTON FOUNDATION ENDOWED SCHOLARSHIP

• *See page 612*

GERON JOHNSON SCHOLARSHIP

• *See page 612*

GHEENS FOUNDATION SCHOLARSHIP

• *See page 612*

HAROLD PIERCE SCHOLARSHIP

• *See page 613*

HARRY PINKERTON SCHOLARSHIP

• *See page 613*

HEALTH AND HUMAN SERVICE-RICHMOND, VA SCHOLARSHIP

• *See page 613*

HUDSON-WEBBER FOUNDATION SCHOLARSHIP

• *See page 613*

JAMES AND RUTH GILLROY SCHOLARSHIP

• *See page 613*

JAY LEVINE SCHOLARSHIP

Award for Detroit high school seniors planning to attend a UNCF member college or university. Must have a minimum 3.0 GPA. Please visit Web site for more information: http://www.uncf.org.

Award: Scholarship for use in freshman year; renewable. *Number:* varies. *Amount:* up to $2000.

Eligibility Requirements: Applicant must be high school student; planning to enroll or expecting to enroll at a four-year institution or university and resident of Michigan. Applicant must have 3.0 GPA or higher.

Application Requirements: Application, financial need analysis, FAFSA, SAR. *Deadline:* varies.

Contact: Program Services Department
United Negro College Fund
8260 Willow Oaks Corporate Drive
Fairfax, VA 22031

JOHN W. ANDERSON FOUNDATION SCHOLARSHIP

• *See page 614*

KANSAS CITY INITIATIVE SCHOLARSHIP

Award for a minority student in the Kansas City Metropolitan area, who plans to attend a UNCF member college or university or the University of Missouri at Kansas City. Please visit Web site for more information: http://www.uncf.org.

Award: Scholarship for use in freshman, sophomore, junior, or senior years; renewable. *Number:* varies. *Amount:* $2500–$5000.

Eligibility Requirements: Applicant must be enrolled or expecting to enroll at a four-year institution or university and resident of Kansas or Missouri. Applicant must have 3.0 GPA or higher.

Application Requirements: Application, financial need analysis, FAFSA, SAR. *Deadline:* varies.

Contact: Program Services Department
United Negro College Fund
8260 Willow Oaks Corporate Drive
Fairfax, VA 22031

KEVIN MOORE MEMORIAL SCHOLARSHIP

• *See page 614*

KROGER SCHOLARSHIP

Award for students residing in targeted Kroger retail store locations (GA, AL, SC, TN) who will be attending a UNCF participating college or university.

Award: Scholarship for use in freshman, sophomore, junior, or senior years. *Amount:* up to $4700.

Eligibility Requirements: Applicant must be enrolled or expecting to enroll at a four-year institution or university and resident of Alabama, Georgia, South Carolina, or Tennessee. Applicant must have 2.5 GPA or higher.

Application Requirements: Application, financial need analysis, FAFSA, SAR.

Contact: Program Services Department
United Negro College Fund
8260 Willow Oaks Corporate Drive
Fairfax, VA 22031

KROGER/PEPSI SCHOLARSHIP

Student must be a resident of the Kroger Great Lakes marketing area (lower peninsula of Michigan, central and northern Ohio and northern West Virginia). Must be a high school senior planning to attend a UNCF institution or a 4-year fully accredited institution of higher learning.

Award: Scholarship for use in freshman year. *Number:* varies. *Amount:* varies.

Eligibility Requirements: Applicant must be high school student; planning to enroll or expecting to enroll at a four-year institution or university and resident of Michigan, Ohio, or West Virginia. Applicant must have 2.5 GPA or higher.

Application Requirements: Application, essay, financial need analysis, photo, references, transcript, FAFSA. *Deadline:* March 31.

Contact: Program Services Department
United Negro College Fund
8260 Willow Oaks Corporate Drive
Fairfax, VA 22031

LIMITED, INC. AND INTIMATE BRANDS, INC. SCHOLARSHIP

• *See page 615*

LOUIS R. LURIE FOUNDATION SCHOLARSHIP

Award open to all students from the Bay area who plan to attend a UNCF member college or university. Must have a minimum 2.5 GPA. Please visit Web site for more information: http://www.uncf.org.

Award: Scholarship for use in freshman, sophomore, junior, senior, or graduate years; renewable. *Number:* varies. *Amount:* varies.

Eligibility Requirements: Applicant must be enrolled or expecting to enroll at a four-year institution or university and resident of California. Applicant must have 2.5 GPA or higher.

Application Requirements: Application, financial need analysis, FAFSA, SAR. *Deadline:* varies.

Contact: Program Services Department
United Negro College Fund
8260 Willow Oaks Corporate Drive
Fairfax, VA 22031

MAYA ANGELOU/VIVIAN BAXTER SCHOLARSHIP

• *See page 615*

MCDONALD'S CREW SCHOLARSHIP-CLEVELAND, OHIO

• *See page 615*

MICHAEL AND JUANITA JORDAN SCHOLARSHIP

Award for juniors from the Chicago, Illinois area who are attending a UNCF member college or university. Must have a 3.0 GPA.

Award: Scholarship for use in junior year. *Number:* varies. *Amount:* up to $5000.

Eligibility Requirements: Applicant must be enrolled or expecting to enroll at a four-year institution or university and resident of Illinois. Applicant must have 3.0 GPA or higher.

Application Requirements: Application, financial need analysis, transcript, FAFSA. *Deadline:* varies.

Contact: Program Services Department
United Negro College Fund
8260 Willow Oaks Corporate Drive
Fairfax, VA 22031

UTAH HIGHER EDUCATION ASSISTANCE AUTHORITY http://www.uheaa.org

LEVERAGING EDUCATIONAL ASSISTANCE PARTNERSHIP (LEAP)

Available to students with substantial financial need for use at participating Utah schools. Contact Financial Aid Office of specific school for application requirements and deadlines. Must be Utah resident.

Award: Grant for use in freshman, sophomore, junior, or senior years; not renewable. *Number:* up to 3000. *Amount:* $300–$2500.

Eligibility Requirements: Applicant must be enrolled or expecting to enroll full or part-time at a two-year or four-year or technical institution or university; resident of Utah and studying in Utah. Available to U.S. citizens.

Application Requirements: Application, financial need analysis. *Deadline:* Continuous.

Contact: Financial Aid Office

UTAH CENTENNIAL OPPORTUNITY PROGRAM FOR EDUCATION

Renewable awards for undergraduate college student in Utah institution. Must be a Utah resident. Contact financial aid office at participating institutions for more information.

Award: Grant for use in freshman, sophomore, junior, or senior years; not renewable. *Number:* up to 3500. *Amount:* $300–$5000.

Eligibility Requirements: Applicant must be enrolled or expecting to enroll full or part-time at a two-year or four-year or technical institution; resident of Utah and studying in Utah. Available to U.S. citizens.

Application Requirements: Application, financial need analysis. *Deadline:* Continuous.

Contact: Financial Aid Office

UTAH LEAGUE OF CREDIT UNIONS http://www.ulcu.com

UTAH CREDIT UNION SCHOLARSHIP CONTEST

Entrants, who must be Utah credit union members, or whose parents are members, write an essay for the contest. Must be a graduating high school senior and a U.S. citizen. For additional information visit Web site at http://www.ulcu.com

Award: Prize for use in freshman year; not renewable. *Number:* 3. *Amount:* $500–$1500.

Eligibility Requirements: Applicant must be high school student; planning to enroll or expecting to enroll full or part-time at a two-year or four-year or technical institution or university and resident of Utah. Available to U.S. citizens.

Application Requirements: Application, applicant must enter a contest, essay. *Deadline:* varies.

Contact: Stephen Nelson, Director of Communication
Utah League of Credit Unions
1805 South Redwood Road
Salt Lake City, UT 84104
Phone: 800-662-8684 Ext. 343
E-mail: stephen@ulcu.com

UTAH STATE BOARD OF REGENTS http://www.utahsbr.edu

NEW CENTURY SCHOLARSHIP

Scholarship for qualified high school graduates of Utah. Must attend Utah state-operated college. Award depends on number of hours student enrolled. Please contact for further eligibility requirements. Eligible recipients receive an award equal to 75% of tuition for 60 credit hours toward the completion of a bachelor's degree. For more details see Web site: http://www.utahsbr.edu.

Award: Scholarship for use in junior or senior years; renewable. *Number:* 145. *Amount:* $1060–$3400.

Eligibility Requirements: Applicant must be high school student; planning to enroll or expecting to enroll full or part-time at a four-year institution or university; resident of Utah and studying in Utah. Available to U.S. citizens.

Application Requirements: Application, transcript, GPA/copy of enrollment verification from an eligible Utah 4-year institution, verification from Registrar of completion of requirements for Associate's degree. *Deadline:* Continuous.

Contact: David Colvin, Program Manager
Utah State Board of Regents
Board of Regents Building, the Gateway
60 South 400 West
Salt Lake City, UT 84101-1284
Phone: 801-321-7107
Fax: 801-321-7199
E-mail: dcolvin@utahsbr.edu

V.E.T.S. - VICTORY ENSURED THROUGH SERVICE

V.E.T.S. ANNUAL SCHOLARSHIP

• *See page 566*

VERMONT GOLF ASSOCIATION

VERMONT GOLF SCHOLARSHIP FOUNDATION, INC.

Awards are based on need, scholarship, and valid connection to golf. Must be Vermont resident and U.S. citizen. Minimum 3.0 GPA required.

Award: Scholarship for use in freshman, sophomore, junior, or senior years; renewable. *Number:* 10. *Amount:* $1000.

Eligibility Requirements: Applicant must be high school student; planning to enroll or expecting to enroll full-time at a two-year or four-year or technical institution or university; resident of Vermont and must have an interest in golf. Applicant must have 3.0 GPA or higher. Available to U.S. citizens.

Application Requirements: Application, financial need analysis, interview, references, test scores, transcript. *Deadline:* April 20.

Contact: Richard S. Smith, Scholarship Coordinator
Vermont Golf Association
29 South Main Street
Rutland, VT 05701
Phone: 802-775-2100
Fax: 802-775-6795
E-mail: rssmith@keycrow.com

VERMONT STUDENT ASSISTANCE CORPORATION http://www.vsac.org

VERMONT INCENTIVE GRANTS

Renewable grants for Vermont residents based on financial need. Must meet needs test. Must be college undergraduate or graduate student enrolled full-time at an approved postsecondary institution. Only available to U.S. citizens or permanent residents.

Award: Grant for use in freshman, sophomore, junior, senior, or graduate years; renewable. *Number:* varies. *Amount:* $500–$9100.

Eligibility Requirements: Applicant must be enrolled or expecting to enroll full-time at an institution or university and resident of Vermont. Available to U.S. citizens.

Application Requirements: Application, financial need analysis. *Deadline:* Continuous.

Contact: Grant Program
Vermont Student Assistance Corporation
PO Box 2000
Winooski, VT 05404-2000
Phone: 802-655-9602
Fax: 802-654-3765

VERMONT NON-DEGREE STUDENT GRANT PROGRAM

Renewable grants for Vermont residents enrolled in non-degree programs at colleges, vocational centers, and high school adult courses. May receive funds for two enrollment periods per year, up to $715 per course, per semester. Award based upon financial need.

Award: Grant for use in freshman or sophomore years; renewable. *Number:* varies. *Amount:* up to $715.

Eligibility Requirements: Applicant must be enrolled or expecting to enroll at an institution or university and resident of Vermont.

Application Requirements: Application, financial need analysis. *Deadline:* Continuous.

Contact: Grant Program
Vermont Student Assistance Corporation
PO Box 2000
Winooski, VT 05404-2000
Phone: 802-655-9602
Fax: 802-654-3765

VERMONT PART-TIME STUDENT GRANTS

For undergraduates carrying less than twelve credits per semester who have not received a bachelor's degree. Must be Vermont resident. Based on financial need. Complete Vermont Financial Aid Packet to apply. May be used at any approved postsecondary institution.

Award: Grant for use in freshman, sophomore, junior, or senior years; renewable. *Number:* varies. *Amount:* $250–$6830.

Eligibility Requirements: Applicant must be enrolled or expecting to enroll part-time at an institution or university and resident of Vermont.

Application Requirements: Application, financial need analysis. *Deadline:* Continuous.

Contact: Grant Program
Vermont Student Assistance Corporation
PO Box 2000
Winooski, VT 05404-2000
Phone: 802-655-9602
Fax: 802-654-3765

VINCENT L. HAWKINSON FOUNDATION FOR PEACE AND JUSTICE http://www.graceattheu.org

VINCENT L. HAWKINSON SCHOLARSHIP FOR PEACE AND JUSTICE

The scholarship is awarded to students who have demonstrated a commitment to peace and justice. This generally involves participation in a peace and justice project, leadership and participation in a peace organization, or serving as a role model. The scholarship selection committee of the Foundation uses essays and letters of reference to screen candidates and a personal interview in Minneapolis to select a winner. Applicant must either reside or study in Iowa, Minnesota, North Dakota, South Dakota, or Wisconsin.

Award: Scholarship for use in freshman, sophomore, junior, senior, or graduate years; not renewable. *Number:* 1–6. *Amount:* $500–$1500.

Eligibility Requirements: Applicant must be enrolled or expecting to enroll full-time at a two-year or four-year institution or university; resident of Iowa, Minnesota, North Dakota, South Dakota, or Wisconsin and studying in Iowa, Minnesota, North Dakota, South Dakota, or Wisconsin. Available to U.S. and non-U.S. citizens.

Vincent L. Hawkinson Foundation for Peace and Justice (continued)

Application Requirements: Application, essay, interview, references, transcript. *Deadline:* April 1.

Contact: Vincent L. Hawkinson Foundation for Peace and Justice
Grace University Lutheran Church
324 Harvard Street SE
Minneapolis, MN 55414
Phone: 612-331-8125

VIRGINIA BUSINESS AND PROFESSIONAL WOMEN'S FOUNDATION http://www.bpwva.advocate.net/foundation.htm

BUENA M. CHESSHIR MEMORIAL WOMEN'S EDUCATIONAL SCHOLARSHIP

One-time award assists mature women seeking to complete or enhance their education. Its purposes are helping women who are employed or seeking employment, increasing the number of women qualified for promotion, and helping women achieve economic self-sufficiency. Award may be used for tuition, fees, books, transportation, living expenses, or dependent care. Must be a Virginia resident and studying in Virginia.

Award: Scholarship for use in freshman, sophomore, junior, senior, or graduate years; not renewable. *Number:* 1–10. *Amount:* $100–$1000.

Eligibility Requirements: Applicant must be age 25; enrolled or expecting to enroll at a two-year or four-year institution or university; female; resident of Virginia and studying in Virginia. Available to U.S. citizens.

Application Requirements: Application, essay, financial need analysis, references, transcript. *Deadline:* April 1.

Contact: Scholarship Chair
Virginia Business and Professional Women's Foundation
PO Box 4842
McLean, VA 22103-4842
E-mail: bpwva@advocate.net

KAREN B. LEWIS CAREER EDUCATION SCHOLARSHIP

This scholarship is offered to women pursuing postsecondary job-oriented career education, offering training in business, trade and industrial occupations (not to be used for education leading to a bachelor's or higher degree). This award may be used for tuition, fees, books, transportation, living expenses, or dependent care. Must be a Virginia resident studying in Virginia.

Award: Scholarship for use in freshman or sophomore years; not renewable. *Number:* 1–10. *Amount:* $100–$1000.

Eligibility Requirements: Applicant must be enrolled or expecting to enroll full or part-time at a two-year or technical institution; female; resident of Virginia and studying in Virginia. Available to U.S. citizens.

Application Requirements: Application, essay, financial need analysis, references, transcript. *Deadline:* April 1.

Contact: Scholarship Chair
Virginia Business and Professional Women's Foundation
PO Box 4842
McLean, VA 22103-4842
E-mail: bpwva@advocate.net

NETTIE TUCKER YOWELL SCHOLARSHIP

One-time award offered to Virginia high school seniors who have been accepted for enrollment as freshmen in a Virginia college or university for the fall semester following graduation. Scholarship recipients must attend a Virginia college or university to receive funds, which are disbursed directly to the college or university. Minimum 3.0 GPA required.

Award: Scholarship for use in freshman year; not renewable. *Number:* 1–10. *Amount:* $250–$1000.

Eligibility Requirements: Applicant must be high school student; planning to enroll or expecting to enroll full or part-time at a four-year institution or university; resident of Virginia and studying in Virginia. Applicant must have 3.0 GPA or higher. Available to U.S. citizens.

Application Requirements: Application, essay, financial need analysis, references, test scores, transcript. *Deadline:* April 1.

Contact: Scholarship Chair
Virginia Business and Professional Women's Foundation
PO Box 4842
McLean, VA 22103-4842
E-mail: bpwva@advocate.net

VIRGINIA DEPARTMENT OF EDUCATION http://www.pen.k12.va.us

GRANVILLE P. MEADE SCHOLARSHIP

High school seniors only are eligible to apply for this scholarship. Students are selected based upon grade point average, standardized test scores, letters of recommendations, extra curricular activities, and financial need.

Award: Scholarship for use in freshman, sophomore, junior, or senior years; renewable. *Number:* 8. *Amount:* $2000.

Eligibility Requirements: Applicant must be high school student; planning to enroll or expecting to enroll full-time at a two-year or four-year or technical institution or university and resident of Virginia. Available to U.S. citizens.

Application Requirements: Application, essay, financial need analysis, references, test scores, transcript. *Deadline:* March 31.

Contact: Sylinda Gilchrist, School Counseling Specialist
Virginia Department of Education
PO Box 2120
Richmond, VA 23218-2120
Phone: 804-786-9377
Fax: 804-786-5466
E-mail: sgilchri@mail.vak12ed.edu

ROBERT C. BYRD HONORS SCHOLARSHIP

High school seniors are the only students eligible to apply for the scholarships. Students are selected based upon grade point average, standardized test scores, letters of recommendation, extracurricular activities, and community involvement. Deadline: March 31.

Award: Scholarship for use in freshman, sophomore, junior, or senior years; renewable. *Number:* 100–150. *Amount:* $750–$1500.

Eligibility Requirements: Applicant must be high school student; planning to enroll or expecting to enroll full-time at a two-year or four-year or technical institution or university and resident of Virginia. Available to U.S. citizens.

Application Requirements: Application, references, test scores, transcript. *Deadline:* March 31.

Contact: Sylinda Gilchrist, School Counseling Specialist
Virginia Department of Education
PO Box 2120
Richmond, VA 23218-2120
Phone: 804-786-9377
Fax: 804-786-5466
E-mail: sgilchri@mail.vak12ed.edu

VIRGINIA DEPARTMENT OF VETERANS SERVICES http://www.vdva.vipnet.org/education_benefits.htm

VIRGINIA WAR ORPHANS EDUCATION PROGRAM

• *See page 566*

VIRGINIA STATE BAR http://www.vsb.org

LAW IN SOCIETY AWARD COMPETITION

The Virginia State Bar and its Litigation Section sponsor the contest for Virginia high school students to increase awareness and appreciation of the legal system. Participants write an essay in response to a hypothetical situation dealing with legal issues affecting them. Awards are given to students whose essays show a superior understanding of the value of law in every day life. The top ten entries are awarded prizes. 1st place receives $1,000 U.S. Savings Bond or $500 cash. 2nd place: $750 U.S. Savings Bond or $375 cash. 3rd place: $500 U.S. Savings Bond or $250 cash. Seven honorable mentions: $100 U.S. Savings Bond or $50 cash. Application available at Web site: http://www.vsb.org.

Award: Prize for use in freshman year; not renewable. *Number:* 10. *Amount:* $100–$1000.

Eligibility Requirements: Applicant must be high school student; planning to enroll or expecting to enroll full-time at an institution or university and resident of Virginia. Available to U.S. citizens.

Application Requirements: Application, applicant must enter a contest, essay. *Deadline:* March 4.

Contact: Dawn Chase
Virginia State Bar
VSB, 707 East Main Street, Suite 1500
Richmond, VA 23219-2800
Phone: 804-775-0586
Fax: 804-775-0582
E-mail: chase@vsb.org

WASHINGTON HIGHER EDUCATION COORDINATING BOARD http://www.hecb.wa.gov

AMERICAN INDIAN ENDOWED SCHOLARSHIP

• *See page 622*

EDUCATIONAL OPPORTUNITY GRANT

Annual grants of $2500 to encourage financially needy, placebound students to complete bachelor's degree. Must be unable to continue education due to family or work commitments, health concerns, financial needs, or similar. Must be Washington residents, live in one of 13 designated counties, and have completed two years of college. Grant only used at eligible four-year colleges in Washington. Applications accepted beginning in April and following months until funds are depleted.

Award: Grant for use in junior or senior years; renewable. *Number:* 1350. *Amount:* $2500.

Eligibility Requirements: Applicant must be enrolled or expecting to enroll full-time at a four-year institution or university; resident of Washington and studying in Washington. Available to U.S. citizens.

Application Requirements: Application, financial need analysis. *Deadline:* Continuous.

Contact: Dawn Cypriano-McAferty, Program Manager
Washington Higher Education Coordinating Board
917 Lakeridge Way, SW, PO Box 43430
Olympia, WA 98504-3430
Phone: 360-753-7800
Fax: 360-753-7808
E-mail: eog@hecb.wa.gov

STATE NEED GRANT

Grants for undergraduate students with significant financial need. Must be Washington resident and attend school in Washington. Must have family income equal or less than 55% of state median. The financial aid office at each school makes awards to eligible students.

Award: Grant for use in freshman, sophomore, junior, or senior years; renewable. *Number:* 55,000. *Amount:* $2200–$4300.

Eligibility Requirements: Applicant must be enrolled or expecting to enroll full or part-time at a two-year or four-year or technical institution or university; resident of Washington and studying in Washington. Available to U.S. citizens.

Application Requirements: Application, financial need analysis, FAFSA. *Deadline:* Continuous.

Contact: Financial Aid Director of school to which you are applying

WASHINGTON AWARD FOR VOCATIONAL EXCELLENCE (WAVE)

Award to honor three vocational students from each of the state's 49 legislative districts. Grants for up to two years of undergraduate resident tuition. Must be enrolled in Washington high school, skills center, or technical college at time of application. Complete 360 hours in single vocational program in high school or one year at technical college. Contact principal or guidance counselor for more information.

Award: Grant for use in freshman, sophomore, junior, or senior years; renewable. *Number:* varies. *Amount:* varies.

Eligibility Requirements: Applicant must be enrolled or expecting to enroll full-time at a two-year or four-year or technical institution or university; resident of Washington and studying in Washington. Available to U.S. citizens.

Application Requirements: *Deadline:* Continuous.

Contact: Ann Lee, Program Manager
Washington Higher Education Coordinating Board
917 Lakeridge Way, SW, PO Box 43430
Olympia, WA 98504-3430
Phone: 360-753-7843
Fax: 360-753-7808
E-mail: annl@hecb.wa.gov

WASHINGTON PROMISE SCHOLARSHIP

College scholarships to low- and middle-income students in high school. Must either rank in top 15 percent of senior class or score a combined 1200 on SAT or 27 on ACT on first attempt. Family income cannot exceed 135% of state median family income. Must be Washington resident, attend a Washington school. School must identify applicants. Contact principal or guidance counselor for more information.

Award: Scholarship for use in freshman or sophomore years; renewable. *Number:* varies. *Amount:* up to $1000.

Eligibility Requirements: Applicant must be high school student; planning to enroll or expecting to enroll full or part-time at a two-year or four-year or technical institution or university; resident of Washington and studying in Washington. Available to U.S. citizens.

Application Requirements: Financial need analysis. *Deadline:* Continuous.

Contact: John Klacik
Washington Higher Education Coordinating Board
917 Lakeridge Way SW, PO Box 43430
Olympia, WA 98504-3430
Phone: 360-753-7851
Fax: 360-753-7808
E-mail: johnk@hecb.wa.gov

WASHINGTON SCHOLARS PROGRAM

Awarded to three high school students from each of the 49 state legislative districts. Must be Washington resident and enroll in college or university in Washington. Scholarships equal up to four years of full-time resident undergraduate tuition and fees. Contact principal or guidance counselor for more information.

Award: Grant for use in freshman, sophomore, junior, or senior years; renewable. *Number:* varies. *Amount:* varies.

Eligibility Requirements: Applicant must be high school student; planning to enroll or expecting to enroll full-time at a four-year institution or university; resident of Washington and studying in Washington. Available to U.S. citizens.

Application Requirements: *Deadline:* Continuous.

Contact: Ann Lee, Program Manager
Washington Higher Education Coordinating Board
917 Lakeridge Way SW, PO Box 43430
Olympia, WA 98504-3430
Phone: 360-753-7843
Fax: 360-753-7808
E-mail: annl@hecb.wa.gov

WASHINGTON STATE WORK STUDY PROGRAM

Undergraduate and graduate students with financial need may be eligible to earn money for college through part-time work, while gaining experience whenever possible in jobs related to their academic and career goals. Financial aid offices will work with students to determine eligibility and identify employment opportunities. Must be Washington residents and enroll in a Washington state college or university.

Award: Grant for use in freshman, sophomore, junior, senior, or graduate years; renewable. *Number:* 8000. *Amount:* $2212–$4650.

Eligibility Requirements: Applicant must be enrolled or expecting to enroll full or part-time at a two-year or four-year institution or university; resident of Washington and studying in Washington. Available to U.S. citizens.

Washington Higher Education Coordinating Board (continued)

Application Requirements: Financial need analysis, FAFSA. *Deadline:* Continuous.

Contact: Financial Aid Director of school to which you are applying

WASHINGTON NATIONAL GUARD http://www.washingtonguard.com/education/education.htm

WASHINGTON NATIONAL GUARD SCHOLARSHIP PROGRAM

• *See page 538*

WASHINGTON STATE PARENT TEACHER ASSOCIATION SCHOLARSHIPS FOUNDATION http://www.wastatepta.org

WASHINGTON STATE PARENT TEACHER ASSOCIATION SCHOLARSHIPS FOUNDATION

One-time scholarships for students who have graduated from a public high school in state of Washington, and who greatly need financial help to begin full-time postsecondary education. For entering freshmen only.

Award: Scholarship for use in freshman year; not renewable. *Number:* 60–80. *Amount:* $1000–$2000.

Eligibility Requirements: Applicant must be enrolled or expecting to enroll full-time at a two-year or four-year or technical institution or university and resident of Washington. Available to U.S. and non-U.S. citizens.

Application Requirements: Application, essay, financial need analysis, references, transcript. *Deadline:* March 1.

Contact: Jean Carpenter, Executive Director
Washington State Parent Teacher Association Scholarships Foundation
2003 65th Avenue, West
Tacoma, WA 98466-6215

WASHINGTON STATE TRIAL LAWYERS ASSOCIATION http://www.wstla.org

WASHINGTON STATE TRIAL LAWYERS ASSOCIATION PRESIDENTS' SCHOLARSHIP

Recipients are selected based on demonstrated academic achievement and planned advancement toward a higher degree; a documented need for financial assistance; a history of achievement despite having been a victim of injury or overcoming a disability, handicap, or similar challenge; a record of commitment to helping people in need; a plan to apply higher education to helping others; and Washington State residency. May visit Web site: http://www.wstla.org.

Award: Scholarship for use in freshman, sophomore, or junior years; not renewable. *Number:* 1. *Amount:* $2000–$2500.

Eligibility Requirements: Applicant must be enrolled or expecting to enroll full-time at a two-year or four-year institution or university and resident of Washington. Available to U.S. citizens.

Application Requirements: Autobiography, essay, financial need analysis, resume, references, transcript. *Deadline:* March 15.

Contact: Jan E. Peterson, Chairperson, WSTLA Past Presidents' Council
Washington State Trial Lawyers Association
2800 Century Square, 1501 Fourth Avenue
Seattle, WA 98101

WSTLA AMERICAN JUSTICE ESSAY SCHOLARSHIP CONTEST

WSTLA is committed to foster an awareness and understanding of the American justice system. The essay contest deals with advocacy in the American justice system and related topics. Three scholarships are available, at the law student, college and high school levels. Topics are selected annually and will be available in September of each school year. May visit Web site at http://www.wstla.org.

Award: Prize for use in freshman, sophomore, junior, senior, or graduate years; not renewable. *Number:* 3. *Amount:* $1000–$3000.

Eligibility Requirements: Applicant must be enrolled or expecting to enroll full or part-time at a two-year or four-year or technical institution or university and studying in Washington. Available to U.S. and non-U.S. citizens.

Application Requirements: Applicant must enter a contest, essay. *Deadline:* March 15.

Contact: Rebecca Parker, Director of Membership and Community Outreach
Washington State Trial Lawyers Association
1809 Seventh Avenue, Suite 1500
Seattle, WA 98101-1328
Phone: 206-464-1011
Fax: 206-464-0703
E-mail: rebecca@wstla.org

WASHINGTON STATE WORKFORCE TRAINING AND EDUCATION COORDINATING BOARD http://www.wtb.wa.gov/wave-abt.html

WASHINGTON AWARD FOR VOCATIONAL EXCELLENCE

Tuition-only award for those completing a vocational education program as graduating seniors or community/technical college students who have completed first year of a two-year program. The scholarship is for 6 quarters or 4 semesters. Three are awarded in each of 49 legislative districts in the state. Must be a Washington State resident attending a postsecondary institution in Washington State.

Award: Grant for use in freshman, sophomore, junior, or senior years; renewable. *Number:* 147. *Amount:* $4284–$9498.

Eligibility Requirements: Applicant must be enrolled or expecting to enroll full or part-time at a two-year or four-year or technical institution or university; resident of Washington and studying in Washington. Available to U.S. and non-U.S. citizens.

Application Requirements: Application, essay, references. *Deadline:* March 1.

Contact: Lee Williams, Program Administrator
Washington State Workforce Training and Education Coordinating Board
128 Tenth Avenue SW
PO Box 43105
Olympia, WA 98504-3105
Phone: 360-586-3321
Fax: 360-586-5862
E-mail: lwilliams@wtb.wa.gov

WATERBURY FOUNDATION http://www.waterburyfoundation.org

REGIONAL AND RESTRICTED SCHOLARSHIP AWARD PROGRAM

Supports accredited college or university study for residents of the Waterbury Foundation's twenty-one town service area. Regional awards are restricted to Connecticut colleges/universities only. Twenty-five restricted award programs are based on specific fund criteria (residency, ethnicity or course of study).

Award: Scholarship for use in freshman, sophomore, junior, or senior years; renewable. *Number:* 175–220. *Amount:* $250–$10,000.

Eligibility Requirements: Applicant must be enrolled or expecting to enroll full or part-time at a two-year or four-year institution or university and resident of Connecticut. Applicant must have 2.5 GPA or higher. Available to U.S. citizens.

Application Requirements: Application, essay, financial need analysis, references, transcript. *Deadline:* April 1.

Contact: Elisabeth Moore, Program Officer
Waterbury Foundation
81 West Main Street
Waterbury, CT 06702
Phone: 203-753-1315
Fax: 203-756-3054
E-mail: emoore@waterburyfoundation.org

WEST VIRGINIA DIVISION OF VETERANS' AFFAIRS http://www.state.wv.us/va

WEST VIRGINIA DIVISION OF VETERANS' AFFAIRS WAR ORPHANS EDUCATION PROGRAM

• *See page 566*

WEST VIRGINIA HIGHER EDUCATION POLICY COMMISSION-OFFICE OF FINANCIAL AID AND OUTREACH SERVICES http://www.hepc.wvnet.edu

HIGHER EDUCATION ADULT PART-TIME STUDENT GRANT PROGRAM

Program to assist needy adult students to continue their education on a part-time basis. Also has a component in which 25% of the funding may be utilized for students enrolled in workforce and skill development programs. Contact institution financial aid office for more information and deadlines.

Award: Grant for use in freshman, sophomore, junior, or senior years; not renewable. *Number:* varies.

Eligibility Requirements: Applicant must be enrolled or expecting to enroll full or part-time at a two-year or four-year or technical institution or university; resident of West Virginia and studying in West Virginia. Available to U.S. citizens.

Application Requirements: Application, financial need analysis. *Deadline:* varies.

Contact: Judy Kee, Financial Aid Manager
West Virginia Higher Education Policy Commission-Office of Financial Aid and Outreach Services
1018 Kanawha Boulevard East, Suite 700
Charleston, WV 25301
Phone: 304-558-4618
Fax: 304-558-4622
E-mail: kee@hepc.wvnet.edu

PROMISE SCHOLARSHIP

Renewable award for West Virginia residents. Minimum 3.0 GPA, ACT composite of 21, with 19 on each subtest, and combined SAT score of 1000, with no less than 470 verbal and 460 math. Provides full tuition scholarship to a state college or university in West Virginia or an equivalent scholarship to an in-state private college. Financial resources are not a factor.

Award: Scholarship for use in freshman, sophomore, junior, or senior years; renewable. *Number:* 3500. *Amount:* $3000.

Eligibility Requirements: Applicant must be high school student; planning to enroll or expecting to enroll full-time at a two-year or four-year institution or university; resident of West Virginia and studying in West Virginia. Applicant must have 3.0 GPA or higher. Available to U.S. citizens.

Application Requirements: Application, financial need analysis, test scores, transcript. *Deadline:* January 31.

Contact: Lisa DeFrank-Cole, Executive Director
West Virginia Higher Education Policy Commission-Office of Financial Aid and Outreach Services
1018 Kanawha Boulevard East, Suite 700
Charleston, WV 25301
Phone: 304-558-4417
Fax: 304-558-3264

ROBERT C. BYRD HONORS SCHOLARSHIP PROGRAM-WEST VIRGINIA

For West Virginia residents who have demonstrated outstanding academic achievement. Must be a graduating high school senior. May apply for renewal consideration for a total of four years of assistance. For full-time study only.

Award: Scholarship for use in freshman, sophomore, junior, or senior years; renewable. *Number:* 38. *Amount:* $1500.

Eligibility Requirements: Applicant must be high school student; planning to enroll or expecting to enroll full-time at a two-year or four-year or technical institution or university and resident of West Virginia. Applicant must have 3.5 GPA or higher. Available to U.S. citizens.

Application Requirements: Application, test scores, transcript, letter of acceptance from a college/university. *Deadline:* March 1.

Contact: Michelle Wicks, Scholarship Coordinator
West Virginia Higher Education Policy Commission-Office of Financial Aid and Outreach Services
1018 Kanawha Boulevard East, Suite 700
Charleston, WV 25301
Phone: 304-558-4618
Fax: 304-558-4622
E-mail: wicks@hepc.wvnet.edu

WEST VIRGINIA HIGHER EDUCATION GRANT PROGRAM

For West Virginia residents attending an approved nonprofit degree granting college or university in West Virginia or Pennsylvania. Must be enrolled full-time. Based on financial need and academic merit. Award covers tuition and fees.

Award: Grant for use in freshman, sophomore, junior, or senior years; renewable. *Number:* 10,755–11,000. *Amount:* $350–$2846.

Eligibility Requirements: Applicant must be enrolled or expecting to enroll full-time at a two-year or four-year institution or university; resident of West Virginia and studying in Pennsylvania or West Virginia. Available to U.S. citizens.

Application Requirements: Application, financial need analysis, test scores, transcript. *Deadline:* March 1.

Contact: Daniel Crockett, Director of Student and Educational Services
West Virginia Higher Education Policy Commission-Office of Financial Aid and Outreach Services
1018 Kanawha Boulevard East, Suite 700
Charleston, WV 25301-2827
Phone: 888-825-5707
Fax: 304-558-4618
E-mail: crockett@hepc.wvnet.edu

WESTERN GOLF ASSOCIATION-EVANS SCHOLARS FOUNDATION http://www.evansscholarsfoundation.com

CHICK EVANS CADDIE SCHOLARSHIP

• *See page 522*

WESTERN INTERSTATE COMMISSION FOR HIGHER EDUCATION http://www.wiche.edu/sep

WESTERN UNDERGRADUATE EXCHANGE PROGRAM

Residents of Alaska, Arizona, Colorado, Hawaii, Idaho, Montana, Nevada, New Mexico, North Dakota, Oregon, South Dakota, Utah, Washington and Wyoming can enroll in designated two- and four-year undergraduate programs at public institutions in participating states at reduced tuition level (resident tuition plus half). Contact Western Interstate Commission for Higher Education for list and deadlines.

Award: Scholarship for use in freshman, sophomore, junior, or senior years; renewable.

Eligibility Requirements: Applicant must be enrolled or expecting to enroll full or part-time at a two-year or four-year institution; resident of Alaska, Arizona, Colorado, Hawaii, Idaho, Montana, Nevada, New Mexico, North Dakota, Oregon, South Dakota, Utah, Washington, or Wyoming and studying in Alaska, Colorado, Hawaii, Idaho, Montana, Nevada, New Mexico, North Dakota, Oregon, South Dakota, Utah, or Wyoming. Available to U.S. citizens.

Application Requirements: Application.

Contact: Ms. Sandy Jackson, Program Coordinator
Western Interstate Commission for Higher Education
PO Box 9752
Boulder, CO 80301-9752
Phone: 303-541-0214
Fax: 303-541-0291
E-mail: info-sep@wiche.edu

WILLIAM F. COOPER SCHOLARSHIP TRUST

WILLIAM F. COOPER SCHOLARSHIP

Scholarship trust to provide financial assistance to women living within the state of Georgia for undergraduate studies. Cannot be used for law, theology or medicine fields of study. Nursing is an approved area of study.

Award: Scholarship for use in freshman, sophomore, junior, or senior years; renewable. *Number:* varies. *Amount:* varies.

Eligibility Requirements: Applicant must be enrolled or expecting to enroll full or part-time at a four-year institution or university; female and resident of Georgia. Available to U.S. citizens.

William F. Cooper Scholarship Trust (continued)

Application Requirements: Application, financial need analysis, test scores, transcript, tax info/W-2. *Deadline:* May 15.

Contact: R. Karesh, Vice President
William F. Cooper Scholarship Trust
Wachovia Bank CSG-GA8023
191 Peachtree Street, 24th Floor
Atlanta, GA 30303
Phone: 404-332-4987
Fax: 404-332-1389

WILLIAM G. AND MARIE SELBY FOUNDATION http://www.selbyfdn.org

SELBY SCHOLAR PROGRAM

Scholarships awarded up to $5000 annually, not to exceed 1/3 of individual's financial need. Renewable for four years if student is full-time undergraduate at accredited college or university. Must demonstrate values of leadership and service to the community. Must reside in Sarasota, Manatee, Charlotte, or DeSoto counties in Florida.

Award: Scholarship for use in freshman, sophomore, junior, or senior years; renewable. *Number:* 30. *Amount:* up to $5000.

Eligibility Requirements: Applicant must be high school student; planning to enroll or expecting to enroll full-time at a four-year institution or university and resident of Florida. Applicant must have 3.0 GPA or higher. Available to U.S. citizens.

Application Requirements: Application, essay, financial need analysis, interview, references, test scores, transcript. *Deadline:* April 1.

Contact: Jan Noah, Grants Manager
William G. and Marie Selby Foundation
1800 Second Street, Suite 750
Sarasota, FL 34236
Phone: 941-957-0442
Fax: 941-957-3135
E-mail: jnoah@selbyfdn.org

WISCONSIN DEPARTMENT OF VETERANS AFFAIRS http://dva.state.wi.us

TUITION AND FEE REIMBURSEMENT GRANTS

• *See page 567*

WISCONSIN DEPARTMENT OF VETERANS AFFAIRS RETRAINING GRANTS

• *See page 567*

WISCONSIN VETERANS PART-TIME STUDY REIMBURSEMENT GRANT

• *See page 567*

WISCONSIN FOUNDATION FOR INDEPENDENT COLLEGES, INC. http://www.wficweb.org

AMERICAN FAMILY INSURANCE COMMUNITY INVOLVEMENT SCHOLARSHIP

Award for full-time undergraduate students to attend a WFIC member institution. Must show financial need, have a minimum 3.0 GPA and be a resident of a state within American Family Insurance's service area. See Web site for additional information and application: http://www.wficweb.org.

Award: Scholarship for use in freshman, sophomore, junior, or senior years; not renewable. *Number:* up to 20. *Amount:* up to $1000.

Eligibility Requirements: Applicant must be enrolled or expecting to enroll full-time at a four-year institution; resident of Arizona, Colorado, Idaho, Illinois, Indiana, Iowa, Kansas, Minnesota, Missouri, Nebraska, Nevada, North Dakota, Ohio, Oregon, or South Dakota and studying in Wisconsin. Applicant must have 3.0 GPA or higher. Available to U.S. citizens.

Application Requirements: Application, essay, financial need analysis, references. *Deadline:* April 23.

Contact: Christy Miller, Programs and Marketing Director
Wisconsin Foundation for Independent Colleges, Inc.
735 North Water Street, Suite 600
Milwaukee, WI 53202
Phone: 414-273-5980
Fax: 414-273-5995
E-mail: wfic@wficweb.org

RATH DISTINGUISHED SCHOLARSHIP

Rath Scholars demonstrate personal characteristics of leadership, community service, and academic excellence. Recipients must maintain 3.25 GPA while receiving scholarship. Preference given to Wisconsin residents. Submit list of academic achievements, merits, honors, and awards. Also submit list of community and campus involvement/activities and number of hours.

Award: Scholarship for use in freshman, sophomore, junior, or senior years; not renewable. *Number:* 12. *Amount:* $10,000.

Eligibility Requirements: Applicant must be enrolled or expecting to enroll full-time at a four-year institution or university and studying in Wisconsin. Available to U.S. citizens.

Application Requirements: Application, autobiography, references, transcript. *Deadline:* March 12.

Contact: Christy Miller, Marketing Program Manager
Wisconsin Foundation for Independent Colleges, Inc.
735 North Water Street, Suite 600
Milwaukee, WI 53202
Phone: 414-273-5980
Fax: 414-273-5995
E-mail: wfic@execpc.com

THRIVENT FINANCIAL FOR LUTHERANS COMMUNITY LEADERS SCHOLARSHIP PROGRAM

Scholarship is used to reward students whose campus and civic activities demonstrate their commitment to community. Minimum 3.0 GPA required. Submit list of academic achievements, merits, honors and awards. Also submit list of community, campus, faith-based activities, including number of hours.

Award: Scholarship for use in freshman, sophomore, junior, or senior years; not renewable. *Number:* 4. *Amount:* $2500.

Eligibility Requirements: Applicant must be enrolled or expecting to enroll full-time at a four-year institution or university and studying in Wisconsin. Applicant must have 3.0 GPA or higher. Available to U.S. citizens.

Application Requirements: Application, autobiography, references. *Deadline:* March 12.

Contact: Christy Miller, Marketing Program Manager
Wisconsin Foundation for Independent Colleges, Inc.
735 North Water Street, Suite 600
Milwaukee, WI 53202
Phone: 414-273-5980
Fax: 414-273-5995
E-mail: wfic@execpc.com

UPS SCHOLARSHIP

Applicants must attend one of Wisconsin's private colleges and maintain a 3.0 GPA. Each school can award one to three UPS scholarships. Application deadline is May 1.

Award: Scholarship for use in freshman, sophomore, junior, or senior years; not renewable. *Number:* 21–63. *Amount:* $1050–$3150.

Eligibility Requirements: Applicant must be enrolled or expecting to enroll full-time at a four-year institution or university and studying in Wisconsin. Applicant must have 3.0 GPA or higher. Available to U.S. citizens.

Application Requirements: Application, autobiography, references. *Deadline:* May 1.

Contact: Christy Miller, Marketing Program Manager
Wisconsin Foundation for Independent Colleges, Inc.
735 North Water Street, Suite 600
Milwaukee, WI 53202
Phone: 414-273-5980
Fax: 414-273-5995
E-mail: wfic@execpc.com

WISCONSIN FIRST SCHOLARSHIP PROGRAM

Wisconsin First Scholarships are designed to encourage Wisconsin's brightest students to obtain an education, and ultimately pursue a career in Wisconsin. Minimum 3.0 GPA required. Submit listing of academic achievements, merits, honors and awards. Also submit listing of community or campus involvement and number of hours.

Award: Scholarship for use in freshman, sophomore, junior, or senior years; not renewable. *Number:* varies. *Amount:* $3000.

Eligibility Requirements: Applicant must be enrolled or expecting to enroll full-time at a four-year institution or university; resident of Wisconsin and studying in Wisconsin. Applicant must have 3.0 GPA or higher. Available to U.S. citizens.

Application Requirements: Application, autobiography, references, test scores, transcript. *Deadline:* March 12.

Contact: Christy Miller, Marketing Program Manager
Wisconsin Foundation for Independent Colleges, Inc.
735 North Water Street, Suite 600
Milwaukee, WI 53202
Phone: 414-273-5980
Fax: 414-273-5995
E-mail: wfic@execpc.com

WISCONSIN HIGHER EDUCATIONAL AIDS BOARD

http://heab.state.wi.us

HANDICAPPED STUDENT GRANT-WISCONSIN

• *See page 532*

MINNESOTA-WISCONSIN RECIPROCITY PROGRAM

Wisconsin residents may attend a Minnesota public institution and pay the reciprocity tuition charged by Minnesota institution. All programs are eligible except doctoral programs in medicine, dentistry, and veterinary medicine. Please refer to Web site for further details: http://www.heab.state.wi.us

Award: Scholarship for use in freshman, sophomore, junior, or senior years; renewable. *Number:* varies. *Amount:* varies.

Eligibility Requirements: Applicant must be enrolled or expecting to enroll full or part-time at a two-year or four-year or technical institution or university; resident of Wisconsin and studying in Minnesota. Available to U.S. citizens.

Application Requirements: Application. *Deadline:* Continuous.

Contact: Cindy Lehrman
Wisconsin Higher Educational Aids Board
PO Box 7885
Madison, WI 53707-7885
Phone: 608-267-2209
Fax: 608-267-2808
E-mail: cindy.lehrman@heab.state.wi.us

MINORITY RETENTION GRANT-WISCONSIN

• *See page 623*

TALENT INCENTIVE PROGRAM GRANT

Assists residents of Wisconsin who are attending a nonprofit institution in Wisconsin and have substantial financial need. Must meet income criteria, be considered economically and educationally disadvantaged and be enrolled at least half-time. Please refer to Web site for further details: http://www.heab.state.wi.us

Award: Grant for use in freshman, sophomore, junior, or senior years; renewable. *Number:* varies. *Amount:* $250–$1800.

Eligibility Requirements: Applicant must be enrolled or expecting to enroll full or part-time at a two-year or four-year or technical institution or university; resident of Wisconsin and studying in Wisconsin. Available to U.S. citizens.

Application Requirements: Financial need analysis, nomination. *Deadline:* Continuous.

Contact: John Whitt, Program Coordinator
Wisconsin Higher Educational Aids Board
PO Box 7885
Madison, WI 53707-7885
Phone: 608-266-1665
Fax: 608-267-2808
E-mail: john.whitt@heab.state.wi.us

WISCONSIN ACADEMIC EXCELLENCE SCHOLARSHIP

Renewable award for high school seniors with the highest GPA in graduating class. Must be a Wisconsin resident. Award covers tuition for up to four years. Must maintain 3.0 GPA for renewal. Scholarships of up to $2250 each. Must attend a nonprofit Wisconsin institution full-time. Please refer to Web site for further details: http://www.heab.state.wi.us

Award: Scholarship for use in freshman, sophomore, junior, or senior years; renewable. *Number:* 3445. *Amount:* up to $2250.

Eligibility Requirements: Applicant must be enrolled or expecting to enroll full-time at a two-year or four-year or technical institution or university; resident of Wisconsin and studying in Wisconsin. Applicant must have 3.5 GPA or higher. Available to U.S. citizens.

Application Requirements: Transcript. *Deadline:* Continuous.

Contact: Alice Winters, Program Coordinator
Wisconsin Higher Educational Aids Board
PO Box 7885
Madison, WI 53707-7885
Phone: 608-267-2213
Fax: 608-267-2808
E-mail: alice.winters@heab.state.wi.us

WISCONSIN HIGHER EDUCATION GRANTS (WHEG)

Grants for residents of Wisconsin attending a campus of the University of Wisconsin or Wisconsin Technical College. Must be enrolled at least half-time and show financial need. Please refer to Web site for further details: http://www.heab.state.wi.us

Award: Grant for use in freshman, sophomore, junior, or senior years; not renewable. *Number:* varies. *Amount:* $250–$2500.

Eligibility Requirements: Applicant must be enrolled or expecting to enroll full or part-time at a two-year or four-year or technical institution or university; resident of Wisconsin and studying in Wisconsin. Available to U.S. citizens.

Application Requirements: Application, financial need analysis. *Deadline:* Continuous.

Contact: Sandra Thomas, Program Coordinator
Wisconsin Higher Educational Aids Board
PO Box 7885
Madison, WI 53707-7885
Phone: 608-266-0888
Fax: 608-267-2808
E-mail: sandy.thomas@heab.state.wi.us

WISCONSIN NATIVE AMERICAN STUDENT GRANT

• *See page 623*

WISCONSIN TUITION GRANT PROGRAM

Available to Wisconsin residents who are enrolled at least half-time in degree or certificate programs at independent, nonprofit colleges or universities in Wisconsin. Must show financial need. Please refer to Web site for further details: http://www.heab.state.wi.us

Award: Grant for use in freshman, sophomore, junior, or senior years; not renewable. *Number:* varies. *Amount:* varies.

Eligibility Requirements: Applicant must be enrolled or expecting to enroll full or part-time at a four-year institution or university; resident of Wisconsin and studying in Wisconsin. Available to U.S. and non-U.S. citizens.

Wisconsin Higher Educational Aids Board (continued)

Application Requirements: Application, financial need analysis. *Deadline:* Continuous.

Contact: Mary Lou Kuzdas, Program Coordinator
Wisconsin Higher Educational Aids Board
PO Box 7885
Madison, WI 53707-7885
Phone: 608-267-2212
Fax: 608-267-2808
E-mail: mary.kuzdas@heab.state.wi.us

WISE-WORKING IN SUPPORT OF EDUCATION http://www.qlcompetition.org

WISE-QUALITY OF LIFE PROGRAM

QL (a Working in Support of Education-WISE program) invites teachers around NYC to introduce a project-based learning tool into their courses and after-school programs. Sophomores, juniors, and seniors identify a critical community problem or need, undertake independent background and field research, and present feasible solutions to the identified problem. The program culminates in a competition for scholarships (up to $15,000) and implementation grants (up to $1,000).

Award: Scholarship for use in freshman, sophomore, junior, or senior years; not renewable. *Number:* 1–5. *Amount:* up to $15,000.

Eligibility Requirements: Applicant must be high school student; planning to enroll or expecting to enroll full or part-time at a two-year or four-year institution or university and resident of New York. Available to U.S. and non-U.S. citizens.

Application Requirements: Applicant must enter a contest, research proposal. *Deadline:* December 20.

Contact: Norene Hough, Director, Quality of Life Program
WISE-Working in Support of Education
227 East 56th Street, Suite 201
New York, NY 10022
Phone: 212-421-2700
Fax: 212-980-5053
E-mail: jwooton@wise-ny.org

WYOMING DEPARTMENT OF EDUCATION

DOUVAS MEMORIAL SCHOLARSHIP

Available to Wyoming residents who are first-generation Americans. Must be between 18-22 years old. Must be used at any Wyoming public institution of higher education for study in freshman year.

Award: Scholarship for use in freshman year; not renewable. *Number:* 1. *Amount:* $500.

Eligibility Requirements: Applicant must be age 18-22; enrolled or expecting to enroll at a two-year or four-year institution or university; resident of Wyoming and studying in Wyoming. Available to U.S. citizens.

Application Requirements: Application. *Deadline:* April 18.

Contact: Gerry Maas, Director, Health and Safety
Wyoming Department of Education
2300 Capitol Avenue
Hathaway Building, 2nd Floor
Cheyenne, WY 82002-0050
Phone: 307-777-6282
Fax: 307-777-6234
E-mail: gmaas@educ.state.wy.us

ROBERT C. BYRD HONORS SCHOLARSHIP/WYOMING

Available to Wyoming residents who show outstanding academic ability. Must attend an accredited postsecondary institution, have a minimum 3.8 GPA, and be a high school senior. Renewable award of $1500. Applications are mailed to all high school counselors in the spring.

Award: Scholarship for use in freshman year; renewable. *Number:* 11. *Amount:* $1500.

Eligibility Requirements: Applicant must be high school student; planning to enroll or expecting to enroll full-time at a two-year or four-year institution or university and resident of Wyoming. Available to U.S. citizens.

Application Requirements: Application, essay, test scores, transcript, nomination. *Deadline:* varies.

Contact: Gerry Maas, Director, Health and Safety
Wyoming Department of Education
2300 Capitol Avenue
Hathaway Building, 2nd Floor
Cheyenne, WY 82002-0050
Phone: 307-777-6282
Fax: 307-777-6234
E-mail: gmaas@educ.state.wy.us

WYOMING FARM BUREAU FEDERATION http://www.wyfb.org/

KING-LIVINGSTON SCHOLARSHIP

• *See page 489*

WYOMING FARM BUREAU CONTINUING EDUCATION SCHOLARSHIPS

• *See page 489*

WYOMING FARM BUREAU FEDERATION SCHOLARSHIPS

• *See page 489*

WYOMING STUDENT LOAN CORPORATION http://www.wslc.com

WYOMING STUDENT LOAN CORPORATION LEADERSHIP SCHOLARSHIP

Eight awards for Wyoming residents attending any postsecondary school within the state. Award is $500 per academic year. Renewable up to a total of four years. Essay on leadership is required. Two awards are reserved for a Wyoming community college and one for Wyoming Technical Institute.

Award: Scholarship for use in freshman, sophomore, junior, or senior years; renewable. *Number:* 8. *Amount:* $500.

Eligibility Requirements: Applicant must be enrolled or expecting to enroll full or part-time at a two-year or technical institution or university; resident of Wyoming and studying in Wyoming. Applicant must have 2.5 GPA or higher. Available to U.S. citizens.

Application Requirements: Application, essay, resume, references, transcript. *Deadline:* March 15.

Contact: Judie Petersen, Executive Assistant
Wyoming Student Loan Corporation
PO Box 209
Cheyenne, WY 82003
Phone: 800-999-6541
Fax: 307-778-3870
E-mail: jpetersen@wslc.com

YOUTH OPPORTUNITIES FOUNDATION

YOUTH OPPORTUNITIES FOUNDATION SCHOLARSHIPS

• *See page 624*

TALENT

ALBERTA HERITAGE SCHOLARSHIP FUND/ ALBERTA SCHOLARSHIP PROGRAMS http://www.alis.gov.ab.ca/scholarships

ALBERTA HERITAGE SCHOLARSHIP FUND ALBERTA PRESS COUNCIL SCHOLARSHIP

• *See page 573*

CHARLES S. NOBLE JUNIOR "A" HOCKEY SCHOLARSHIPS

• *See page 573*

CHARLES S. NOBLE JUNIOR FOOTBALL SCHOLARSHIPS

• *See page 574*

EARL AND COUNTESS OF WESSEX-WORLD CHAMPIONSHIPS IN ATHLETICS SCHOLARSHIPS

• *See page 630*

JIMMIE CONDON ATHLETIC SCHOLARSHIPS

• *See page 574*

LAURENCE DECORE STUDENT LEADERSHIP AWARDS
• *See page 574*

PRAIRIE BASEBALL ACADEMY SCHOLARSHIPS
• *See page 631*

AMERICAN ALLIANCE FOR HEALTH, PHYSICAL EDUCATION, RECREATION AND DANCE http://www.aahperd.org

NATIONAL PRESIDENTIAL SCHOLARSHIP

One graduate and two undergraduate awards given in pursuit of a degree in health, physical education, recreation or dance disciplines. Applicant must be a current member of AAHPERD.

Award: Scholarship for use in junior, senior, or graduate years; not renewable. *Number:* 3. *Amount:* $750–$1000.

Eligibility Requirements: Applicant must be enrolled or expecting to enroll full-time at a four-year institution or university and must have an interest in leadership. Applicant must have 3.5 GPA or higher. Available to U.S. and non-U.S. citizens.

Application Requirements: Application, references, transcript. *Deadline:* November 15.

Contact: Angela Giraldi, Secretary to Chief Executive Officer
American Alliance for Health, Physical Education, Recreation and Dance
1900 Association Drive
Reston, VA 20191
Phone: 703-476-3405
Fax: 703-476-9537

AMERICAN BOWLING CONGRESS http://www.bowl.com

CHUCK HALL STAR OF TOMORROW SCHOLARSHIP
• *See page 440*

AMERICAN CONTRACT BRIDGE LEAGUE http://www.acbl.org

ACBL EDUCATIONAL FOUNDATION SCHOLARSHIP FOR YOUTHS

Scholarships for youths under 26 who teach bridge classes to other youth students.

Award: Scholarship for use in freshman, sophomore, junior, senior, graduate, or postgraduate years; not renewable. *Number:* 100. *Amount:* $500.

Eligibility Requirements: Applicant must be age 25 or under; enrolled or expecting to enroll full or part-time at a two-year or four-year or technical institution or university and must have an interest in designated field specified by sponsor. Available to U.S. and Canadian citizens.

Application Requirements: Application. *Deadline:* Continuous.

Contact: Charlotte Blaiss, Director of Youth Programs
American Contract Bridge League
2900 Airways Boulevard
Memphis, TN 38116-3847
Phone: 901-332-5586 Ext. 1214
Fax: 901-398-7754
E-mail: charlotte.blaiss@acbl.org

AMERICAN DARTS ORGANIZATION http://www.adodarts.com

AMERICAN DARTS ORGANIZATION MEMORIAL SCHOLARSHIP PROGRAM

Awards are made to top eight finishers in the ADO Youth Championship, based on performance. Must be a member of the ADO. Must be in a program that leads to a degree. Minimum 2.0 GPA required. Please refer to Web site for further details: http://www.adodarts.com

Award: Scholarship for use in freshman, sophomore, junior, or senior years; not renewable. *Number:* 8. *Amount:* $500–$1500.

Eligibility Requirements: Applicant must be age 20 or under; enrolled or expecting to enroll full-time at a two-year or four-year or technical institution or university and must have an interest in designated field specified by sponsor. Available to U.S. citizens.

Application Requirements: Applicant must enter a contest. *Deadline:* Continuous.

Contact: Della A. Fleetwood, Trustee-ADO Memorial Scholarship Fund
American Darts Organization
10710 Richeon Avenue
Downey, CA 90241
Phone: 562-928-4136
Fax: 562-927-6558
E-mail: adooffice@aol.com

AMERICAN GUILD OF ORGANISTS http://www.agohq.org

AMERICAN GUILD OF ORGANISTS PIPE ORGAN ENCOUNTER SCHOLARSHIP

A "Pipe Organ Encounter" is a 4-5 day intensive summer institute for the study of the pipe organ. All scholarship money is provided to the local AGO chapter sponsoring the institute and is exclusively for the cost of tuition. All information on POE's across the U.S. is available at http://www.agohq.org.

Award: Scholarship for use in freshman, sophomore, junior, senior, graduate, or postgraduate years; not renewable. *Number:* 15–20. *Amount:* $200–$325.

Eligibility Requirements: Applicant must be age 13-19; enrolled or expecting to enroll at an institution or university and must have an interest in music. Available to U.S. and non-U.S. citizens.

Application Requirements: Application. *Deadline:* May 1.

Contact: Application and information available at Web site.

AMERICAN GUILD OF ORGANISTS REGIONAL COMPETITIONS FOR YOUNG ORGANISTS

Organ performance competition open to organists under the age of 23. Must submit proof of age, $40 registration fee, biography, and photo. Several one-time awards for different levels of competition. Deadline varies.

Award: Prize for use in freshman, sophomore, junior, or senior years; not renewable. *Number:* 10. *Amount:* $500–$1000.

Eligibility Requirements: Applicant must be age 22 or under; enrolled or expecting to enroll full or part-time at an institution or university and must have an interest in music.

Application Requirements: Application, applicant must enter a contest, autobiography, photo. *Fee:* $40. *Deadline:* varies.

Contact: James Thomashower, Executive Director
American Guild of Organists
475 Riverside Drive, Suite 1260
New York, NY 10115
Phone: 212-870-2310
Fax: 212-870-2163
E-mail: info@agohq.org

NATIONAL COMPETITION IN ORGAN IMPROVISATION

To further the art of improvisation by recognizing and rewarding superior performers in the field. Three awards of $750 to $2000. Application fee is $50.

Award: Prize for use in freshman, sophomore, junior, senior, graduate, or postgraduate years; not renewable. *Number:* 3. *Amount:* $750–$2000.

Eligibility Requirements: Applicant must be enrolled or expecting to enroll full or part-time at an institution or university and must have an interest in music. Available to U.S. and non-U.S. citizens.

Application Requirements: Application, applicant must enter a contest, autobiography, photo, taped performance. *Fee:* $50. *Deadline:* varies.

Contact: James Thomashower, Executive Director
American Guild of Organists
475 Riverside Drive, Suite 1260
New York, NY 10115
Phone: 212-870-2310
Fax: 212-870-2163
E-mail: info@agohq.org

NATIONAL YOUNG ARTISTS COMPETITION IN ORGAN PERFORMANCE
• *See page 441*

AMERICAN INSTITUTE FOR FOREIGN STUDY
http://www.aifsabroad.com

AMERICAN INSTITUTE FOR FOREIGN STUDY INTERNATIONAL SCHOLARSHIPS

Awards are available to undergraduates on an AIFS study abroad program. Applicants must demonstrate leadership potential, have a minimum 3.0 cumulative GPA and meet program requirements. Up to 100 $1,000 scholarships are awarded per semester and up to 50 $750 scholarships are awarded each summer. Submit application by March 15 for summer, April 15 for fall or October 15 for spring. The application fee is $75.

Award: Scholarship for use in freshman, sophomore, junior, or senior years; not renewable. *Number:* up to 150. *Amount:* $750–$1000.

Eligibility Requirements: Applicant must be age 17; enrolled or expecting to enroll full-time at a two-year or four-year institution or university and must have an interest in leadership. Applicant must have 3.0 GPA or higher. Available to U.S. and non-U.S. citizens.

Application Requirements: Application, essay, photo, references, transcript. *Fee:* $75. *Deadline:* varies.

Contact: David Mauro, Admissions Counselor
American Institute for Foreign Study
River Plaza, 9 West Broad Street
Stamford, CT 06902-3788
Phone: 800-727-2437 Ext. 5163
Fax: 203-399-5598
E-mail: college.info@aifs.com

AMERICAN INSTITUTE FOR FOREIGN STUDY MINORITY SCHOLARSHIPS
• *See page 577*

AMERICAN LEGION AUXILIARY, DEPARTMENT OF MAINE

AMERICAN LEGION AUXILIARY, DEPARTMENT OF MAINE NATIONAL PRESIDENT'S SCHOLARSHIP
• *See page 546*

AMERICAN LEGION, DEPARTMENT OF ALABAMA
http://www.americanlegionalabama.org/

AMERICAN LEGION DEPARTMENT OF ALABAMA STATE ORATORICAL SCHOLARSHIP
• *See page 635*

AMERICAN LEGION, DEPARTMENT OF INDIANA

AMERICAN LEGION, DEPARTMENT OF INDIANA STATE ORATORICAL CONTEST
• *See page 637*

FRANK W. MCHALE MEMORIAL SCHOLARSHIPS
• *See page 637*

AMERICAN LEGION, DEPARTMENT OF IOWA
http://www.ialegion.org

AMERICAN LEGION DEPARTMENT OF IOWA OUTSTANDING SENIOR BASEBALL PLAYER
• *See page 637*

ORATORICAL CONTEST SCHOLARSHIP-IOWA
• *See page 637*

AMERICAN LEGION, DEPARTMENT OF KANSAS

DR. CLICK COWGER BASEBALL SCHOLARSHIP
• *See page 637*

NATIONAL HIGH SCHOOL ORATORICAL CONTEST
• *See page 447*

PAUL FLAHERTY ATHLETIC SCHOLARSHIP
• *See page 637*

AMERICAN LEGION, DEPARTMENT OF MICHIGAN
http://www.michiganlegion.org

AMERICAN LEGION DEPARTMENT OF MICHIGAN ORATORICAL CONTEST
• *See page 638*

AMERICAN LEGION, DEPARTMENT OF MINNESOTA
http://www.mnlegion.org

AMERICAN LEGION DEPARTMENT OF MINNESOTA STATE ORATORICAL CONTEST
• *See page 638*

AMERICAN LEGION, DEPARTMENT OF MONTANA

ORATORICAL CONTEST
• *See page 639*

AMERICAN LEGION, DEPARTMENT OF NEBRASKA
http://www.legion.org

AMERICAN LEGION DEPARTMENT OF NEBRASKA ORATORICAL AWARDS
• *See page 639*

AMERICAN LEGION, DEPARTMENT OF NEW YORK
http://www.ny.legion.org

AMERICAN LEGION DEPARTMENT OF NEW YORK STATE HIGH SCHOOL ORATORICAL CONTEST
• *See page 639*

AMERICAN LEGION, DEPARTMENT OF NORTH DAKOTA
http://www.ndlegion.org

AMERICAN LEGION DEPARTMENT OF NORTH DAKOTA NATIONAL HIGH SCHOOL ORATORICAL CONTEST
• *See page 639*

AMERICAN LEGION, DEPARTMENT OF PENNSYLVANIA
http://www.pa-legion.com

AMERICAN LEGION DEPARTMENT OF PENNSYLVANIA STATE ORATORICAL CONTEST
• *See page 640*

AMERICAN LEGION, DEPARTMENT OF SOUTH CAROLINA

AMERICAN LEGION DEPARTMENT OF SOUTH CAROLINA HIGH SCHOOL ORATORICAL CONTEST
• *See page 640*

AMERICAN LEGION, DEPARTMENT OF TENNESSEE

AMERICAN LEGION DEPARTMENT OF TENNESSEE ORATORICAL CONTEST
• *See page 641*

AMERICAN LEGION, DEPARTMENT OF WEST VIRGINIA

AMERICAN LEGION DEPARTMENT OF WEST VIRGINIA STATE ORATORICAL CONTEST
• *See page 641*

AMERICAN LEGION, DEPARTMENT OF WEST VIRGINIA BOARD OF REGENTS SCHOLARSHIP
• *See page 642*

AMERICAN LEGION, NATIONAL HEADQUARTERS
http://www.legion.org

AMERICAN LEGION NATIONAL HEADQUARTERS NATIONAL HIGH SCHOOL ORATORICAL CONTEST

Several prizes awarded to high school students (freshmen through seniors) who give a speech lasting eight to ten minutes on the U.S. Constitution and an assigned topic speech of three to five minutes. Winners advance to higher level. Contact local chapter for entry information. One-time award of $1500-$18,000.

Award: Scholarship for use in freshman, sophomore, junior, senior, or graduate years; not renewable. *Number:* 54. *Amount:* $1500–$18,000.

Eligibility Requirements: Applicant must be high school student; planning to enroll or expecting to enroll full-time at a two-year or four-year institution or university and must have an interest in public speaking. Available to U.S. citizens.

Application Requirements: Application. *Deadline:* December 1.

Contact: Michael Buss, Assistant Director
American Legion, National Headquarters
PO Box 1055
Indianapolis, IN 46206-1055
Phone: 317-630-1249
Fax: 317-630-1369
E-mail: acy@legion.org

AMERICAN MORGAN HORSE INSTITUTE http://www.morganhorse.com

AMERICAN MORGAN HORSE INSTITUTE EDUCATIONAL SCHOLARSHIPS

Selection is based on the ability and aptitude for serious study, community service, leadership, and financial need. Must be actively involved with registered Morgan horses. For information and application go to http://www.morganhorse.com.

Award: Scholarship for use in freshman year; not renewable. *Number:* 5. *Amount:* $3000.

Eligibility Requirements: Applicant must be enrolled or expecting to enroll full or part-time at a two-year or four-year or technical institution or university and must have an interest in designated field specified by sponsor. Available to U.S. and non-U.S. citizens.

Application Requirements: Application, essay, photo, references, transcript. *Deadline:* March 1.

Contact: Application available at Web site.

AMERICAN MORGAN HORSE INSTITUTE GRAND PRIX DRESSAGE AWARD

Award available to riders of registered Morgan horses who reach a certain proficiency at the Grand Prix dressage level. For information and application go to http://www.morganhorse.com.

Award: Prize for use in freshman, sophomore, junior, senior, graduate, or postgraduate years; not renewable. *Number:* 1. *Amount:* $2500.

Eligibility Requirements: Applicant must be enrolled or expecting to enroll full or part-time at a two-year or four-year or technical institution or university and must have an interest in designated field specified by sponsor. Available to U.S. and non-U.S. citizens.

Application Requirements: Application, essay, photo, references, transcript. *Deadline:* Continuous.

Contact: Application available at Web site.

AMERICAN MORGAN HORSE INSTITUTE GRAYWOOD YOUTH HORSEMANSHIP GRANT

Provides a youth who is an active member of the American Morgan Horse Association (AMHA) or an AMHA youth group with the opportunity to further his/her practical study of Morgan horses. For information and application go to http://www.morganhorse.com.

Award: Grant for use in freshman year; not renewable. *Number:* 1–2. *Amount:* $1000.

Eligibility Requirements: Applicant must be age 13-21; enrolled or expecting to enroll full or part-time at a two-year or four-year or technical institution or university and must have an interest in designated field specified by sponsor. Available to U.S. and non-U.S. citizens.

Application Requirements: Application, essay, photo, references, transcript. *Deadline:* February 1.

Contact: Application available at Web site.

AMERICAN MORGAN HORSE INSTITUTE VAN SCHAIK DRESSAGE SCHOLARSHIP

Awarded to an individual wishing to further their proficiency in classically ridden dressage on a registered Morgan horse. For information and application go to http://www.morganhorse.com.

Award: Grant for use in freshman, sophomore, junior, senior, graduate, or postgraduate years; not renewable. *Number:* 1. *Amount:* $1000.

Eligibility Requirements: Applicant must be enrolled or expecting to enroll full or part-time at a two-year or four-year or technical institution or university and must have an interest in designated field specified by sponsor. Available to U.S. and non-U.S. citizens.

Application Requirements: Application, essay, photo, references. *Deadline:* November 30.

Contact: Application available at Web site.

AMERICAN SHEEP INDUSTRY ASSOCIATION/ NATIONAL MAKE IT YOURSELF WITH WOOL http://www.sheepusa.org

NATIONAL "MAKE IT YOURSELF WITH WOOL" COMPETITION

Awards are available for entrants ages 13-24 years. Must enter at state level with home-constructed garment of at least 60% wool. Applicant must model garment. Applications are accepted August through December. $10 fee at time of entry. See Web site at http://www.sheepusa.org for more information.

Award: Prize for use in freshman, sophomore, junior, or senior years; not renewable. *Number:* 2–4. *Amount:* up to $2000.

Eligibility Requirements: Applicant must be age 13-24; enrolled or expecting to enroll full or part-time at a two-year or four-year or technical institution or university and must have an interest in sewing. Available to U.S. citizens.

Application Requirements: Application, applicant must enter a contest, self-addressed stamped envelope, 5x5 sample of fabric. *Fee:* $10.

Contact: Marie Lehfeldt, Coordinator
American Sheep Industry Association/National Make It Yourself With Wool
PO Box 175
Lavina, MT 59046
Phone: 406-636-2731
Fax: 406-636-2731

AMERICAN STRING TEACHERS ASSOCIATION http://www.astaweb.com

NATIONAL SOLO COMPETITION

Twenty-six individual awards totaling $30,000 will be awarded. Instrument categories are violin, viola, cello, double bass, classical guitar and harp. Applicants competing in Junior Division must be under age 19. Senior Division competitors must be ages 19-25. Application fee is $60. Visit Web site for application forms. Applicant must be a member of ASTA.

Award: Prize for use in freshman, sophomore, junior, senior, or graduate years; not renewable. *Number:* 26. *Amount:* $500–$7000.

Eligibility Requirements: Applicant must be age 25 or under; enrolled or expecting to enroll full-time at an institution or university and must have an interest in music. Available to U.S. and Canadian citizens.

Application Requirements: Application, applicant must enter a contest, proof of age. *Fee:* $60. *Deadline:* varies.

Contact: American String Teachers Association
4153 Chain Bridge Road
Fairfax, VA 22030
Phone: 703-279-2113
Fax: 703-279-2114
E-mail: asta@astaweb.com

AMERICAN SWEDISH INSTITUTE http://www.americanswedishinst.org

LILLY LORENZEN SCHOLARSHIP

One-time award for a Minnesota resident, or student attending a school in Minnesota. Must have a working knowledge of Swedish and present a creditable plan for study in Sweden. Must be a U.S. citizen.

American Swedish Institute (continued)

Award: Scholarship for use in freshman, sophomore, junior, senior, graduate, or postgraduate years; not renewable. *Number:* 1. *Amount:* $1500–$2500.

Eligibility Requirements: Applicant must be enrolled or expecting to enroll full or part-time at a two-year or four-year or technical institution or university and must have an interest in Scandinavian language. Available to U.S. citizens.

Application Requirements: Application, interview, transcript. *Deadline:* May 1.

Contact: Nina Clark, Education Programs Coordinator
American Swedish Institute
2600 Park Avenue
Minneapolis, MN 55407-1090
Phone: 612-870-3374
Fax: 612-871-8682
E-mail: ninac@americanswedishinst.org

AMERICAN THEATRE ORGAN SOCIETY, INC. http://www.atos.org

AMERICAN THEATRE ORGAN SOCIETY ORGAN PERFORMANCE SCHOLARSHIP

Renewable awards available to students between the ages of 13-22. Must have a talent in music and have an interest in theater organ performance studies (not for general music studies). Application deadline is April 15.

Award: Scholarship for use in freshman, sophomore, junior, or senior years; renewable. *Number:* 11. *Amount:* $500.

Eligibility Requirements: Applicant must be age 13-22; enrolled or expecting to enroll full or part-time at a two-year or four-year institution or university and must have an interest in music. Available to U.S. and non-U.S. citizens.

Application Requirements: Application, essay, references. *Deadline:* April 15.

Contact: Carlton Smith, Chairperson, Scholarship Program
American Theatre Organ Society, Inc.
ATOS Scholarship Program
PO Box 551081
Indianapolis, IN 46205-5581
Phone: 317-356-1240
Fax: 317-322-9379
E-mail: smith@atos.org

AMERICAN WATER SKI EDUCATIONAL FOUNDATION http://www.waterskihalloffame.com

AMERICAN WATER SKI EDUCATIONAL FOUNDATION SCHOLARSHIP

• *See page 453*

AMERICAN-SCANDINAVIAN FOUNDATION http://www.amscan.org

AMERICAN-SCANDINAVIAN FOUNDATION TRANSLATION PRIZE

Two prizes available to bring into English translation a work of Scandinavian literature written in the last 200 years. One-time awards of $1000 and $2000.

Award: Prize for use in freshman, sophomore, junior, senior, graduate, or postgraduate years; not renewable. *Number:* 2. *Amount:* $1000–$2000.

Eligibility Requirements: Applicant must be enrolled or expecting to enroll at an institution or university and must have an interest in Scandinavian language. Available to U.S. citizens.

Application Requirements: Application, applicant must enter a contest. *Deadline:* June 1.

Contact: Assistant
American-Scandinavian Foundation
58 Park Avenue
New York, NY 10016
Phone: 212-879-9779
E-mail: info@amscan.org

ANGELUS AWARDS STUDENT FILM FESTIVAL http://www.angelus.org

ANGELUS AWARDS STUDENT FILM FESTIVAL

Student Film Festival grants awards for student films, documentaries and animation that reflect the complexity of the human condition. $10,000 grand prize; all work screened at the Directors Guild of America, Hollywood.

Award: Prize for use in freshman, sophomore, junior, senior, or graduate years; not renewable. *Number:* 5–7. *Amount:* $1500–$10,000.

Eligibility Requirements: Applicant must be enrolled or expecting to enroll full or part-time at a two-year or four-year or technical institution or university and must have an interest in photography/photogrammetry/filmmaking. Available to U.S. and non-U.S. citizens.

Application Requirements: Application, applicant must enter a contest, autobiography, photo, resume, VHS or DVD copy of film, written description of film, proof of college attendance. *Fee:* $25. *Deadline:* July 1.

Contact: Ms. Monika Moreno, Director, Angelus Awards
Angelus Awards Student Film Festival
7201 Sunset Boulevard
Los Angeles, CA 90046
Phone: 323-874-6633 Ext. 24
Fax: 323-874-1168
E-mail: monika@angelus.org

APPALACHIAN CENTER AND APPALACHIAN STUDIES ASSOCIATION

WEATHERFORD AWARD

One-time award given to the best work of fiction, non-fiction, book, poetry, or short piece about the Appalachian South published in the most recent calendar year. Two awards will be given: one for non-fiction; one for fiction and poetry. Nominations must be received by December 31. Seven copies of the nominated work must be sent to the chair of the award committee.

Award: Prize for use in freshman, sophomore, junior, or senior years; not renewable. *Number:* 2. *Amount:* $500.

Eligibility Requirements: Applicant must be enrolled or expecting to enroll at an institution or university and must have an interest in designated field specified by sponsor. Available to U.S. and non-U.S. citizens.

Application Requirements: Applicant must enter a contest, nomination. *Deadline:* December 31.

Contact: Chair
Appalachian Center and Appalachian Studies Association
College Box 2166
Berea, KY 40404

APPALOOSA HORSE CLUB-APPALOOSA YOUTH PROGRAM http://www.appaloosa.com

APPALOOSA YOUTH EDUCATIONAL SCHOLARSHIPS

• *See page 454*

ARRL FOUNDATION, INC. http://www.arrl.org/arrlf/scholgen.html

ALBERT H. HIX, W8AH, MEMORIAL SCHOLARSHIP

• *See page 454*

ALBUQUERQUE AMATEUR RADIO CLUB/TOBY CROSS SCHOLARSHIP

Scholarship for students who are licensed amateur radio operators who are working on undergraduate degree. Residents of New Mexico preferred. Must supply one-page essay on role amateur radio has played in their life.

Award: Scholarship for use in freshman, sophomore, junior, or senior years; not renewable. *Number:* 1. *Amount:* $500.

Eligibility Requirements: Applicant must be enrolled or expecting to enroll at an institution or university and must have an interest in amateur radio.

Application Requirements: Application, essay, transcript. *Deadline:* February 1.

Contact: Mary Lau, Scholarship Director
ARRL Foundation, Inc.
225 Main Street
Newington, CT 06111-4845

ARRL FOUNDATION GENERAL FUND SCHOLARSHIPS

Available to students who are amateur radio operators. Students can be licensed in any class of operators. Nonrenewable award for use in undergraduate years. Multiple awards per year. Contact Amateur Radio Relay League for more information.

Award: Scholarship for use in freshman, sophomore, junior, or senior years; not renewable. *Amount:* $1000.

Eligibility Requirements: Applicant must be enrolled or expecting to enroll at an institution or university and must have an interest in amateur radio.

Application Requirements: Application, transcript. *Deadline:* February 1.

Contact: Mary Lau, Scholarship Director
ARRL Foundation, Inc.
225 Main Street
Newington, CT 06111-4845

ARRL SENATOR BARRY GOLDWATER (K7UGA) SCHOLARSHIP

Scholarship for students who are licensed amateur radio operators, novice minimum. Applicants must be enrolled in a regionally accredited institution. Preference is given to baccalaureate or higher degree candidates. One-time award of $5000.

Award: Scholarship for use in freshman, sophomore, junior, senior, or graduate years; not renewable. *Number:* 1. *Amount:* $5000.

Eligibility Requirements: Applicant must be enrolled or expecting to enroll at a four-year institution or university and must have an interest in amateur radio.

Application Requirements: Application, transcript. *Deadline:* February 1.

Contact: Mary Lau, Scholarship Director
ARRL Foundation, Inc.
225 Main Street
Newington, CT 06111-4845

CENTRAL ARIZONA DX ASSOCIATION SCHOLARSHIP

Award available to students who are licensed amateur radio operators with a technician license. Preference given to residents of Arizona. Graduating high school students will be considered before current college students. Must have 3.2 GPA or above.

Award: Scholarship for use in freshman year; not renewable. *Number:* 1. *Amount:* $500.

Eligibility Requirements: Applicant must be enrolled or expecting to enroll at an institution or university and must have an interest in amateur radio.

Application Requirements: Application, transcript. *Deadline:* February 1.

Contact: Mary Hobart, Foundation Secretary
ARRL Foundation, Inc.
225 Main Street
Newington, CT 06111-4845
Phone: 860-594-0397
E-mail: mhobart@arrl.org

CHARLES CLARKE CORDLE MEMORIAL SCHOLARSHIP

One-time award for students who are licensed amateur radio operators. Preference given to residents of Georgia and Alabama and students attending school in that region. Must have minimum GPA of 2.5.

Award: Scholarship for use in freshman, sophomore, junior, or senior years; not renewable. *Number:* 1. *Amount:* $1000.

Eligibility Requirements: Applicant must be enrolled or expecting to enroll at an institution or university and must have an interest in amateur radio. Applicant must have 2.5 GPA or higher.

Application Requirements: Application, transcript. *Deadline:* February 1.

Contact: Mary Lau, Scholarship Director
ARRL Foundation, Inc.
225 Main Street
Newington, CT 06111-4845

CHICAGO FM CLUB SCHOLARSHIPS

Multiple awards available to students who are licensed amateur radio operators with technician license. Preference given to residents of FCC Ninth Call District (Indiana, Illinois, Wisconsin) who are high school seniors or graduates. Must be U.S. citizen or within 3 months of citizenship.

Award: Scholarship for use in freshman, sophomore, junior, or senior years; not renewable. *Amount:* $500.

Eligibility Requirements: Applicant must be enrolled or expecting to enroll at a two-year or four-year or technical institution and must have an interest in amateur radio. Available to U.S. citizens.

Application Requirements: Application, transcript. *Deadline:* February 1.

Contact: Mary Lau, Scholarship Director
ARRL Foundation, Inc.
225 Main Street
Newington, CT 06111-4845

EUGENE "GENE" SALLEE, W4YFR MEMORIAL SCHOLARSHIP

Available to students licensed as amateur radio operator technicians. Preference given to residents of Georgia who have a 3.0 GPA or higher.

Award: Scholarship for use in freshman, sophomore, junior, or senior years; not renewable. *Number:* 1. *Amount:* $500.

Eligibility Requirements: Applicant must be enrolled or expecting to enroll at an institution or university and must have an interest in amateur radio. Applicant must have 3.0 GPA or higher.

Application Requirements: Application, transcript. *Deadline:* February 1.

Contact: Mary Lau, Scholarship Director
ARRL Foundation, Inc.
225 Main Street
Newington, CT 06111-4845

FRANCIS WALTON MEMORIAL SCHOLARSHIP

One or more $500 scholarships available to student radio operators with 5 WPM certification. Prefer Illinois resident or resident of ARRL Central Division (IL, IN, WI). Must be pursuing a baccalaureate or higher degree at a regionally accredited institution.

Award: Scholarship for use in freshman, sophomore, junior, senior, or graduate years; not renewable. *Amount:* $500.

Eligibility Requirements: Applicant must be enrolled or expecting to enroll at a four-year institution or university and must have an interest in amateur radio.

Application Requirements: Application, transcript. *Deadline:* February 1.

Contact: Mary Lau, Scholarship Director
ARRL Foundation, Inc.
225 Main Street
Newington, CT 06111-4845

IRARC MEMORIAL/JOSEPH P.RUBINO, WA4MMD, SCHOLARSHIP

• *See page 454*

K2TEO MARTIN J. GREEN SR. MEMORIAL SCHOLARSHIP

Available to students with a general amateur license for radio operation. Preference given to students from a "ham" operator family. Nonrenewable award for use in undergraduate years. Contact Amateur Radio Relay League for more information.

ARRL Foundation, Inc. (continued)

Award: Scholarship for use in freshman, sophomore, junior, or senior years; not renewable. *Number:* 1. *Amount:* $1000.

Eligibility Requirements: Applicant must be enrolled or expecting to enroll at an institution or university and must have an interest in amateur radio.

Application Requirements: Application, transcript. *Deadline:* February 1.

Contact: Mary Lau, Scholarship Director
ARRL Foundation, Inc.
225 Main Street
Newington, CT 06111-4845

MARY LOU BROWN SCHOLARSHIP

Multiple awards available to students who are general licensed amateur radio operators. Preference given to residents of Alaska, Idaho, Montana, Oregon, and Washington pursuing baccalaureate or higher course of study. GPA of 3.0 or higher. Must demonstrate interest in promoting Amateur Radio Service.

Award: Scholarship for use in freshman, sophomore, junior, senior, or graduate years; not renewable. *Amount:* $2500.

Eligibility Requirements: Applicant must be enrolled or expecting to enroll at a four-year institution or university and must have an interest in amateur radio. Applicant must have 3.0 GPA or higher.

Application Requirements: Application, transcript. *Deadline:* February 1.

Contact: Mary Lau, Scholarship Director
ARRL Foundation, Inc.
225 Main Street
Newington, CT 06111-4845

NEW ENGLAND FEMARA SCHOLARSHIPS
• *See page 644*

NORMAN E. STROHMEIER, W2VRS MEMORIAL SCHOLARSHIP
• *See page 644*

SIX METER CLUB OF CHICAGO SCHOLARSHIP
• *See page 644*

TOM AND JUDITH COMSTOCK SCHOLARSHIP
• *See page 454*

YANKEE CLIPPER CONTEST CLUB, INC. YOUTH SCHOLARSHIP
• *See page 454*

YOU'VE GOT A FRIEND IN PENNSYLVANIA SCHOLARSHIP
• *See page 455*

ARTIST'S MAGAZINE http://www.artistsmagazine.com

ARTIST'S MAGAZINE'S ANNUAL ART COMPETITION

One-time award for any artist winning annual art competition. Five separate categories. Send self-addressed stamped envelope for rules and entry form. Deadline is May 1. Must submit slides of work. Application fee: $12 per slide.

Award: Prize for use in freshman, sophomore, junior, senior, graduate, or postgraduate years; not renewable. *Number:* 45. *Amount:* $50–$2500.

Eligibility Requirements: Applicant must be enrolled or expecting to enroll full or part-time at a two-year or four-year or technical institution or university and must have an interest in art. Available to U.S. and non-U.S. citizens.

Application Requirements: Application, applicant must enter a contest, self-addressed stamped envelope. *Fee:* $12. *Deadline:* May 1.

Contact: Terri Boes, Customer Service Representative
Artist's Magazine
4700 East Galbraith Road
Cincinnati, OH 45236
Phone: 513-531-2690 Ext. 1328
Fax: 513-531-0798
E-mail: competitions@fwpubs.com

ASSOCIATION FOR WOMEN IN SPORTS MEDIA http://www.awsmonline.org

WOMEN IN SPORTS MEDIA SCHOLARSHIP/INTERNSHIP PROGRAM

The top entrant is selected in four categories: writing, copy editing, broadcast, and public relations, who receive a $1000 scholarship, a $500 stipend for housing during their internship, and $250 for travel expenses. Runners-up receive an internship, $500 for housing, and $250 for travel.

Award: Scholarship for use in freshman, sophomore, junior, senior, or graduate years; not renewable. *Number:* 5–10. *Amount:* $750–$1750.

Eligibility Requirements: Applicant must be enrolled or expecting to enroll full-time at a four-year institution or university; female and must have an interest in athletics/sports or writing. Available to U.S. and non-U.S. citizens.

Application Requirements: Application, applicant must enter a contest, essay, interview, portfolio, resume, references. *Fee:* $5. *Deadline:* November 1.

Contact: Jean Tenuta, AWSM Scholarship Chair
Association for Women in Sports Media
9110 32nd Avenue
Kenosha, WI 53142
Phone: 262-697-4043
Fax: 262-697-4043

AUTHOR SERVICES, INC. http://www.writersofthefuture.com

L. RON HUBBARD'S ILLUSTRATORS OF THE FUTURE CONTEST

An ongoing competition for new and amateur artists judged by professional artists. Eligible submissions consist of three science fiction or fantasy illustrations in a black-and-white medium. Quarterly prizes are $500 each for three winners. The Grand Prize, awarded yearly, is $4000. Visit Web site: http://www.writersofthefuture.com for contest rules. Quarterly deadlines are December 31, March 31, June 30 and September 30. Inside California call: 800-624-6504; outside California call: 800-624-7907. All entrants retain rights to artwork.

Award: Prize for use in freshman, sophomore, junior, senior, graduate, or postgraduate years; not renewable. *Number:* 13. *Amount:* $500–$4000.

Eligibility Requirements: Applicant must be enrolled or expecting to enroll at an institution or university and must have an interest in art. Available to U.S. and non-U.S. citizens.

Application Requirements: Applicant must enter a contest, self-addressed stamped envelope, three illustrations. *Deadline:* varies.

Contact: Rachel Deuk, Contest Administrator
Author Services, Inc.
PO Box 3190
Los Angeles, CA 90078
Phone: 323-466-3310
Fax: 323-466-6474
E-mail: contests@authorservicesinc.com

L. RON HUBBARD'S WRITERS OF THE FUTURE CONTEST

An ongoing competition for new and amateur writers judged by professional writers. Eligible submissions are short stories and novelettes of science fiction or fantasy. Quarterly prizes are First Place - $1000, Second Place - $750, Third Place - $500. The Grand Prize, awarded yearly, is $4000. Quarterly deadlines are December 31, March 31, June 30 and September 30. Visit Web site: http://www.writersofthefuture.com, for contest rules. Inside California call: 800-624-6504; outside California call: 800-624-7907. All entrants retain rights to manuscripts.

Award: Prize for use in freshman, sophomore, junior, senior, graduate, or postgraduate years; not renewable. *Number:* 13. *Amount:* $500–$4000.

Eligibility Requirements: Applicant must be enrolled or expecting to enroll full or part-time at an institution or university and must have an interest in writing. Available to U.S. and non-U.S. citizens.

Application Requirements: Applicant must enter a contest, self-addressed stamped envelope, manuscript. *Deadline:* varies.

Contact: Rachel Deuk, Contest Administrator
Author Services, Inc.
PO Box 1630
Los Angeles, CA 90078
Phone: 323-466-3310
Fax: 323-466-6474
E-mail: contests@authorservicesinc.com

AYN RAND INSTITUTE http://www.aynrand.org/contests

ATLAS SHRUGGED ESSAY COMPETITION

Forty-nine awards totaling $10,000 for essays demonstrating an outstanding grasp of the philosophical meaning of "Atlas Shrugged." Students must be enrolled in either an undergraduate or graduate program. Essay should be between 1000 to 1200 words in length. Winners announced October 21. For more information, contact your scholarship office. All information necessary to enter the contest is available at Web site http://www.aynrand.org/contests.

Award: Prize for use in freshman, sophomore, junior, senior, or graduate years; not renewable. *Number:* 49. *Amount:* $50–$5000.

Eligibility Requirements: Applicant must be enrolled or expecting to enroll full-time at a two-year or four-year or technical institution or university and must have an interest in writing. Available to U.S. and non-U.S. citizens.

Application Requirements: Applicant must enter a contest, essay. *Deadline:* September 16.

Contact: Ayn Rand Institute
PO Box 57044
Irvine, CA 92619-7044
E-mail: essay@aynrand.org

AYN RAND INSTITUTE COLLEGE SCHOLARSHIP ESSAY CONTEST BASED ON AYN RAND'S NOVELETTE, "ANTHEM"

Entrant must be in the 9th or 10th grade. Essays will be judged on both style and content. Winning essays must demonstrate an outstanding grasp of the philosophical meaning of Ayn Rand's novelette, "Anthem." Contest deadline is March 18. Winners announced June 4. All information necessary to enter the contest is at http://www.aynrand.org/contests.

Award: Prize for use in freshman year; not renewable. *Number:* 251. *Amount:* $30–$2000.

Eligibility Requirements: Applicant must be high school student; planning to enroll or expecting to enroll at an institution or university and must have an interest in writing. Available to U.S. and non-U.S. citizens.

Application Requirements: Applicant must enter a contest, essay. *Deadline:* March 18.

Contact: Ayn Rand Institute
PO Box 57044
Irvine, CA 92619-7044
E-mail: essay@aynrand.org

FOUNTAINHEAD COLLEGE SCHOLARSHIP ESSAY CONTEST

Prizes totaling $43,500 awarded to 11th and 12th grades for essays on Ayn Rand's "Fountainhead". Essay should be between 800 and 1600 words. Winners announced June 4. Semifinalist and finalist prizes also awarded. All information necessary to enter the contest is available at http://www.aynrand.org/contests.

Award: Prize for use in freshman year; not renewable. *Number:* 251. *Amount:* $50–$10,000.

Eligibility Requirements: Applicant must be high school student; planning to enroll or expecting to enroll at an institution or university and must have an interest in writing. Available to U.S. and non-U.S. citizens.

Application Requirements: Applicant must enter a contest, essay. *Deadline:* April 15.

Contact: Ayn Rand Institute
PO Box 57044
Irvine, CA 92619-7044
E-mail: essay@aynrand.org

BECU FOUNDATION http://www.becu.org

BECU FOUNDATION SCHOLARSHIP PROGRAM

• *See page 491*

BILLIE JEAN KING WTT CHARITIES, INC. http://www.wtt.com

WORLD TEAM TENNIS DONNELLY AWARDS

Awards available for education, tennis development, and/or medical care. One given to student living within 100 miles of one of the World Team Tennis cities, and one given nationally. Updated information, application, and list of current cities is available on Web site. Student must have Type 1 diabetes, be a high school, college, or tournament tennis competitor, show strong character, values, sportsmanship, and community involvement. Demonstrate financial need. Available to males and females in good academic standing. http://www.wtt.com.

Award: Scholarship for use in freshman, sophomore, junior, senior, or graduate years; not renewable. *Number:* varies. *Amount:* $5000.

Eligibility Requirements: Applicant must be age 14-21; enrolled or expecting to enroll full or part-time at a two-year or four-year or technical institution or university and must have an interest in athletics/sports. Available to U.S. citizens.

Application Requirements: Application, essay, financial need analysis, references, transcript, proof of competitive tennis play, Dr.'s statement verifying applicant has diabetes. *Deadline:* December 1.

Contact: Anne Guerrant, c/o Billie Jean King WTT Charities, Donnelly Awards
Billie Jean King WTT Charities, Inc.
569 North Acacia Drive
Gilbert, AZ 85233-4122
Phone: 480-219-6600
E-mail: aguerrant@wtt.com

BMI FOUNDATION, INC. http://www.bmi.com

BMI STUDENT COMPOSER AWARDS

One-time award for original composition in classical genre for young student composers who are under age 26 and citizens of the Western Hemisphere. Must submit application and original musical score in early February. Application available at Web site: http://www.bmifoundation.org.

Award: Prize for use in freshman, sophomore, junior, senior, graduate, or postgraduate years; not renewable. *Number:* 5–10. *Amount:* $500–$5000.

Eligibility Requirements: Applicant must be age 25 or under; enrolled or expecting to enroll full or part-time at a two-year or four-year institution or university and must have an interest in music/singing. Available to U.S. and non-U.S. citizens.

Application Requirements: Application, applicant must enter a contest, self-addressed stamped envelope, original musical score. *Deadline:* varies.

Contact: Director, BMI Student Composer Awards
BMI Foundation, Inc.
320 West 57th Street
New York, NY 10019

BOY SCOUTS OF AMERICA, EAGLE SCOUT SERVICE http://www.scouting.org/nesa/scholar

NATIONAL EAGLE SCOUT HALL / MCELWAIN MERIT SCHOLARSHIP

• *See page 455*

BOYS & GIRLS CLUBS OF AMERICA http://www.bgca.org

BOYS & GIRLS CLUBS OF AMERICA NATIONAL YOUTH OF THE YEAR AWARD

• *See page 456*

C.O.L.A.G.E. http://www.colage.org

LEE DUBIN SCHOLARSHIP FUND

This scholarship is available to the sons and daughters of LGBT parents attending college who have a demonstrated ability in and commitment to

C.O.L.A.G.E. (continued)

affecting change in the LGBT community, including working against homophobia, and increasing positive awareness of LGBT families.

Award: Scholarship for use in freshman, sophomore, junior, or senior years; not renewable. *Number:* 3–5. *Amount:* $500–$1000.

Eligibility Requirements: Applicant must be enrolled or expecting to enroll full-time at a two-year or four-year or technical institution or university and must have an interest in designated field specified by sponsor or leadership. Available to U.S. citizens.

Application Requirements: Application, essay, financial need analysis, transcript, proof of enrollment. *Deadline:* April 18.

Contact: Scholarship Committee
C.O.L.A.G.E.
3543 18th Street, Suite 1
San Francisco, CA 94110

CALIFORNIA JUNIOR MISS SCHOLARSHIP PROGRAM http://www.ajm.org/california

CALIFORNIA JUNIOR MISS SCHOLARSHIP PROGRAM

• *See page 647*

CAP FOUNDATION http://www.ronbrown.org

RON BROWN SCHOLAR PROGRAM

• *See page 580*

CENTER FOR SCHOLARSHIP ADMINISTRATION http://www.scholarshipprograms.org

SOUTH CAROLINA JUNIOR GOLF FOUNDATION SCHOLARSHIP

• *See page 650*

CHICK AND SOPHIE MAJOR MEMORIAL DUCK CALLING CONTEST http://stuttgartarkansas.com/contest/future.shtml

CHICK AND SOPHIE MAJOR DUCK CALLING CONTEST

Scholarship awarded to the high school senior who wins the duck calling contest held Thanksgiving Weekend in Stuttgart, Arkansas. $1500 to winner, $500 first runner-up, $300 to second runner-up, $200 to third runner-up. Must be senior in high school and be sponsored by a Ducks Unlimited Chapter or wildlife association chapter. Write for more information, and see Web site: http.stuttgartarkansas.com.

Award: Scholarship for use in freshman year; not renewable. *Number:* 4. *Amount:* $200–$1500.

Eligibility Requirements: Applicant must be high school student; planning to enroll or expecting to enroll full or part-time at a two-year or four-year or technical institution or university and must have an interest in animal/agricultural competition or athletics/sports. Available to U.S. citizens.

Application Requirements: Application, applicant must enter a contest. *Deadline:* Continuous.

Contact: Brenda Cahill, Scholarship Coordinator
Chick and Sophie Major Memorial Duck Calling Contest
9018 Trulock Bay Road
Sherrill, AR 72152

COCA-COLA SCHOLARS FOUNDATION, INC. http://www.coca-colascholars.org

COCA-COLA SCHOLARS PROGRAM

Awards based on leadership, academic performance, extracurricular activities, employment, and community involvement. Finalists represent every state in the U.S. 40% of the recipients are minorities. Must apply in senior year of high school. Deadline is October 31. Recipient has six years in which to use award. Two hundred $4000 awards and fifty $20,000 awards granted annually. Must apply through Web site: http://www.coca-colascholars.org. Paper applications not offered.

Award: Scholarship for use in freshman, sophomore, junior, or senior years; renewable. *Number:* 250. *Amount:* $4000–$20,000.

Eligibility Requirements: Applicant must be high school student; planning to enroll or expecting to enroll full or part-time at a two-year or four-year or technical institution or university and must have an interest in leadership. Applicant must have 3.0 GPA or higher. Available to U.S. citizens.

Application Requirements: Application, essay, interview, references, test scores, transcript. *Deadline:* October 31.

Contact: Mark Davis, President
Coca-Cola Scholars Foundation, Inc.
PO Box 442
Atlanta, GA 30301-0442
Phone: 800-306-2653
Fax: 404-733-5439
E-mail: scholars@na.ko.com

COLUMBIA 300 http://columbia300.com

COLUMBIA 300 JOHN JOWDY SCHOLARSHIP

Renewable award given to a graduating high school senior who is actively involved in the sport of bowling. Selection based on academic performance and bowling accomplishments. Application deadline is April 1. For further details and an application visit Web site: http://www.columbia300.com/jjowdy.pdf.

Award: Scholarship for use in freshman, sophomore, junior, or senior years; renewable. *Number:* 1. *Amount:* $500.

Eligibility Requirements: Applicant must be high school student; planning to enroll or expecting to enroll full or part-time at a four-year institution and must have an interest in bowling. Applicant must have 3.0 GPA or higher.

Application Requirements: Application. *Deadline:* April 1.

Contact: Dale Garner
Columbia 300
Columbia 300, Inc., PO Box 13430
San Antonio, TX 78213
Phone: 800-531-5920

COLUMBIA UNIVERSITY, DEPARTMENT OF MUSIC

JOSEPH H. BEARNS PRIZE IN MUSIC

The Joseph H. Bearns Prize is open to U.S. citizens between 18 and 25 years of age on January 1st of the competition year, and offers prizes for both short form and long form works of music in order to encourage talented young composers in the United States.

Award: Prize for use in freshman, sophomore, junior, or senior years; not renewable. *Number:* 2. *Amount:* $2000–$3000.

Eligibility Requirements: Applicant must be age 18-25; enrolled or expecting to enroll full or part-time at a two-year or four-year or technical institution or university and must have an interest in music. Available to U.S. citizens.

Application Requirements: Applicant must enter a contest, self-addressed stamped envelope, music score, information regarding prior studies. *Deadline:* March 15.

Contact: Bearns Prize Committee
Columbia University, Department of Music
2960 Broadway, 621 Dodge Hall, MC# 1813
New York, NY 10027

COMMUNITY FOUNDATION FOR PALM BEACH AND MARTIN COUNTIES, INC. http://www.yourcommunityfoundation.org

TERRY DARBY MEMORIAL SCHOLARSHIP

• *See page 657*

CONCERT ARTISTS GUILD http://www.concertartists.org

CONCERT ARTISTS GUILD COMPETITION

Award for young professional-level classical musicians. Suggested age for instrumentalists and ensembles is under 30, and for singers, under 35. Concert Artists Guild presents and manages prize-winning artists. Winner receives $5000 and a management contract. Runners-up receive management contracts. Submit two tapes. Application fee is $75. Visit Web site for deadline information.

Award: Prize for use in freshman, sophomore, junior, senior, or graduate years; not renewable. *Number:* varies. *Amount:* up to $5000.

Eligibility Requirements: Applicant must be enrolled or expecting to enroll at an institution or university and must have an interest in music. Available to U.S. and non-U.S. citizens.

Application Requirements: Application, applicant must enter a contest, two tapes. *Fee:* $75. *Deadline:* varies.

Contact: Patrick Hammond, Special Projects Manager
Concert Artists Guild
850 7th Avenue, Suite 1205
New York, NY 10019-5230
Phone: 212-333-5200
Fax: 212-977-7149
E-mail: phammond@concertartists.org

CONCORD REVIEW http://www.tcr.org

RALPH WALDO EMERSON PRIZE

Prize awarded to high school students who have submitted an essay to the Concord Review. Essay must be from 4,000 to 6,000 words with Turabian endnotes and bibliography. Pages must be unformatted. Essay may focus on any historical topic. Please refer to Web site for further details: http://www.tcr.org.

Award: Prize for use in freshman year; not renewable. *Number:* varies. *Amount:* $3000.

Eligibility Requirements: Applicant must be high school student; planning to enroll or expecting to enroll at an institution or university and must have an interest in writing. Available to U.S. and non-U.S. citizens.

Application Requirements: Applicant must enter a contest, essay, self-addressed stamped envelope. *Fee:* $40. *Deadline:* Continuous.

Contact:
Phone: 800-331-5007

CONTEMPORARY RECORD SOCIETY

CONTEMPORARY RECORD SOCIETY NATIONAL FESTIVAL FOR THE PERFORMING ARTS SCHOLARSHIP

Renewable award for composers or performing artists who demonstrate a high level of artistic skill. Must submit copy of work that has not been previously recorded in the U.S. $50 application fee required. Submit self-addressed stamped envelope for application.

Award: Scholarship for use in freshman, sophomore, junior, senior, or graduate years; renewable. *Number:* 1. *Amount:* $1900–$5500.

Eligibility Requirements: Applicant must be enrolled or expecting to enroll at an institution or university and must have an interest in music/singing.

Application Requirements: References, self-addressed stamped envelope. *Fee:* $50. *Deadline:* May 15.

Contact: Administrative Assistant
Contemporary Record Society
724 Winchester Road
Broomall, PA 19008
Phone: 610-544-5920
Fax: 610-544-5921
E-mail: crsnews@verizon.net

NATIONAL COMPETITION FOR COMPOSERS' RECORDINGS

Work must be non-published and not commercially recorded. First prize is a recording grant. Limit of nine performers and twenty-five minutes. One work may be submitted. Send self-addressed stamped envelope with $3 postage if applicant wants work returned. Application fee is $50. Applicants must send a self-addressed stamped envelope for application. Deadline: February 10.

Award: Prize for use in freshman, sophomore, junior, senior, or graduate years; not renewable. *Number:* 1. *Amount:* $1500–$5000.

Eligibility Requirements: Applicant must be enrolled or expecting to enroll at an institution or university and must have an interest in music/singing.

Application Requirements: Application, applicant must enter a contest, autobiography, resume, references, self-addressed stamped envelope. *Fee:* $50. *Deadline:* February 10.

Contact: Administrative Assistant
Contemporary Record Society
724 Winchester Road
Broomall, PA 19008
Phone: 610-544-5920
Fax: 610-544-5921
E-mail: crsnews@verizon.net

CULTURAL SERVICES OF THE FRENCH EMBASSY http://www.frenchculture.org

TEACHING ASSISTANTSHIP IN FRANCE

Grants support American students as they teach English in the French school system. For more details, deadlines and applications go to Web site: http://www.frenchculture.org.

Award: Grant for use in freshman, sophomore, junior, senior, graduate, or postgraduate years; renewable. *Number:* 1000–1500. *Amount:* up to $6750.

Eligibility Requirements: Applicant must be age 20-30; enrolled or expecting to enroll full or part-time at a two-year or four-year or technical institution or university; single and must have an interest in French language. Available to U.S. and Canadian citizens.

Application Requirements: Application, photo, references, self-addressed stamped envelope, transcript. *Deadline:* varies.

Contact: Meg Merwin, Assistantship Coordinator
Cultural Services of the French Embassy
4101 Reservoir Road
Washington, DC 20007
Phone: 202-944-6294
Fax: 202-944-6268
E-mail: meghan.merwin@diplomatie.fr

DALLAS MORNING NEWS

DALLAS MORNING NEWS ANNUAL TEENAGE CITIZENSHIP TRIBUTE

• *See page 508*

DIET - LIVE POETS SOCIETY http://geocities.com/diet-lps

NATIONAL HIGH SCHOOL POETRY CONTEST/EASTERDAY POETRY AWARD

Nonrenewable scholarship for high school student interested in writing. Must submit a poem of 20 lines or less. Application deadline varies. For more information visit Web site: http://geocities.com/diet-lps.

Award: Scholarship for use in freshman year; not renewable. *Number:* 1. *Amount:* $1500.

Eligibility Requirements: Applicant must be high school student; planning to enroll or expecting to enroll full-time at a two-year or four-year institution or university and must have an interest in English language or writing. Available to U.S. citizens.

Application Requirements: Applicant must enter a contest, self-addressed stamped envelope, poem 20 lines or less. *Deadline:* varies.

Contact: Mr. D. Edwards, Editor
DIET - Live Poets Society
PO Box 8841
Turnersville, NJ 08012
Phone: 856-584-1868
E-mail: diet@voicenet.com

DUPONT IN COOPERATION WITH GENERAL LEARNING COMMUNICATIONS http://www.glcomm.com/dupont

DUPONT CHALLENGE SCIENCE ESSAY AWARDS PROGRAM

Science essay competition. Students must submit an essay of 700 to 1,000 words discussing a scientific or technological development, event, or theory that has captured their interest. For students in grades 7-12. For more details go to Web site: http://www.glcomm.com/dupont

Award: Prize for use in freshman year; not renewable. *Number:* 70. *Amount:* $50–$1500.

DuPont in Cooperation with General Learning Communications (continued)

Eligibility Requirements: Applicant must be age 12-17; enrolled or expecting to enroll full-time at an institution or university and must have an interest in designated field specified by sponsor or writing. Available to U.S. and Canadian citizens.

Application Requirements: Applicant must enter a contest, essay, official entry form. *Deadline:* January 3.

Contact: Du Pont Challenge Science Essay Awards Program
DuPont in Cooperation with General Learning Communications
900 Skokie Boulevard, Suite 200
Northbrook, IL 60062-4028
Phone: 847-205-3000
Fax: 847-564-8197

ELIE WIESEL FOUNDATION FOR HUMANITY http://www.eliewieselfoundation.org

ELIE WIESEL PRIZE IN ETHICS ESSAY CONTEST

Applicant must be registered as a full-time junior or senior at a four-year accredited college or university in the United States. Submit student entry form, faculty sponsor form and three copies of essay. Visit Web site (http://www.eliewieselfoundation.org) for application and guidelines. Deadline is early December.

Award: Prize for use in junior or senior years; not renewable. *Number:* 5. *Amount:* $500–$5000.

Eligibility Requirements: Applicant must be enrolled or expecting to enroll full-time at a four-year institution or university and must have an interest in writing. Available to U.S. citizens.

Application Requirements: Application, applicant must enter a contest, essay, self-addressed stamped envelope, student entry form, faculty sponsor form. *Deadline:* varies.

Contact: C. Meaghan Cosgrove, Essay Contest Coordinator
Elie Wiesel Foundation for Humanity
529 Fifth Avenue, Suite 1802
New York, NY 10017
Phone: 212-490-7777
Fax: 212-490-6006
E-mail: epinfo@eliewieselfoundation.org

EXECUTIVE WOMEN INTERNATIONAL http://www.executivewomen.org

EXECUTIVE WOMEN INTERNATIONAL SCHOLARSHIP PROGRAM

Competitive award to high school juniors planning careers in any business or professional field of study which requires a four-year college degree. Award is renewable based on continuing eligibility. All awards are given through local chapters of the EWI. Applicant must apply through nearest chapter and live within 100 miles of it. Student must have a sponsoring teacher and school to be considered. For more details visit Web site: http://www.executivewomen.org.

Award: Scholarship for use in freshman, sophomore, junior, or senior years; renewable. *Number:* 80–100. *Amount:* $1000–$10,000.

Eligibility Requirements: Applicant must be high school student; planning to enroll or expecting to enroll full-time at a four-year institution or university and must have an interest in designated field specified by sponsor.

Application Requirements: Application, autobiography, interview, references, transcript. *Deadline:* March 1.

Contact: Suzette Smith, Marketing Director
Executive Women International
515 South 700 East, Suite 2A
Salt Lake City, UT 84102
Phone: 801-355-2800
Fax: 801-362-3212

FLEET RESERVE ASSOCIATION http://www.fra.org

FLEET RESERVE ASSOCIATION SCHOLARSHIP

• *See page 461*

FLORIDA LEADER MAGAZINE/COLLEGE STUDENT OF THE YEAR, INC. http://www.floridaleader.com/soty

FLORIDA COLLEGE STUDENT OF THE YEAR AWARD

• *See page 668*

FLORIDA WOMEN'S STATE GOLF ASSOCIATION http://www.fwsga.org

FLORIDA WOMEN'S STATE GOLF ASSOCIATION JUNIOR GIRLS' SCHOLARSHIP FUND

• *See page 669*

FOREST ROBERTS THEATRE http://www.nmu.edu/theatre

MILDRED AND ALBERT PANOWSKI PLAYWRITING AWARD

Prize designed to encourage and stimulate artistic growth among playwrights. Winner receives a cash prize and a world premiere of their play. Write for further information. One-time award.

Award: Prize for use in freshman, sophomore, junior, senior, graduate, or postgraduate years; not renewable. *Number:* 1. *Amount:* $2000.

Eligibility Requirements: Applicant must be enrolled or expecting to enroll at an institution or university and must have an interest in writing. Available to U.S. and non-U.S. citizens.

Application Requirements: Application, applicant must enter a contest, self-addressed stamped envelope, manuscript. *Deadline:* November 15.

Contact: Megan Marcellini, Playwriting Award Coordinator
Forest Roberts Theatre
Northern Michigan University
Marquette, MI 49855-5364
Phone: 906-227-2559
Fax: 906-227-2567

FORT COLLINS SYMPHONY ASSOCIATION http://www.fcsymphony.org

ADELINE ROSENBERG MEMORIAL PRIZE

Senior Division (25 years or under): Instrumental competitions held in odd numbered years; piano competitions held in even numbered years. Auditions required. Applicant must submit proof of age and perform a standard concerto. Must be recommended by music teacher. Send self-addressed stamped envelope for application. Fee of $50. 1st place winner receives $6000, 2nd place receives $4000. The two finalists will perform with the Fort Collins Symphony Orchestra.

Award: Prize for use in freshman, sophomore, junior, senior, graduate, or postgraduate years; not renewable. *Number:* 2. *Amount:* $4000–$6000.

Eligibility Requirements: Applicant must be age 25 or under; enrolled or expecting to enroll full or part-time at an institution or university and must have an interest in music/singing. Available to U.S. and non-U.S. citizens.

Application Requirements: Application, applicant must enter a contest, autobiography, references, self-addressed stamped envelope, proof of age. *Fee:* $50. *Deadline:* January 15.

Contact: Donna Visocky, Executive Director
Fort Collins Symphony Association
PO Box 1963
Fort Collins, CO 80522
Phone: 970-482-4823
Fax: 970-482-4858
E-mail: note@fcsymphony.org

FORT COLLINS SYMPHONY ASSOCIATION YOUNG ARTIST COMPETITION, JUNIOR DIVISION

Junior division (between 12 and 18 years of age on day of competition); piano and instrumental competition held every year. Auditions required. Limited to the first twenty applicants and two alternates per division. Must submit verification of age. Applicant must perform one movement of a standard concerto and be recommended by music teacher. Send self-addressed stamped envelope for application. Fee of $35.

Award: Prize for use in freshman, sophomore, junior, senior, graduate, or postgraduate years; not renewable. *Number:* 4. *Amount:* $300–$500.

Eligibility Requirements: Applicant must be age 12-18; enrolled or expecting to enroll full or part-time at an institution or university and must have an interest in music/singing. Available to U.S. and non-U.S. citizens.

Application Requirements: Application, applicant must enter a contest, autobiography, references, self-addressed stamped envelope, proof of age. *Fee:* $35. *Deadline:* January 15.

Contact: Donna Visocky, Executive Director
Fort Collins Symphony Association
PO Box 1963
Fort Collins, CO 80522
Phone: 970-482-4823
Fax: 970-482-4858
E-mail: note@fcsymphony.org

GAMMA THETA UPSILON-INTERNATIONAL GEOGRAPHIC HONOR SOCIETY http://gtuhonors.org

GAMMA THETA UPSILON SCHOLARSHIPS

Five scholarships awarded each year to graduate/undergraduate students who have completed at least 3 geography classes. Must rank in upper third of class or have a minimum 3.0 GPA. Must belong to Gamma Theta Upsilon. High school students not eligible.

Award: Scholarship for use in freshman, sophomore, junior, senior, or graduate years; not renewable. *Number:* 7. *Amount:* $500.

Eligibility Requirements: Applicant must be enrolled or expecting to enroll full-time at a two-year or four-year institution or university and must have an interest in designated field specified by sponsor. Applicant must have 3.0 GPA or higher. Available to U.S. and non-U.S. citizens.

Application Requirements: Application. *Deadline:* varies.

Contact: Carol Rosen, GTU President
Gamma Theta Upsilon-International Geographic Honor Society
800 West Main Street
Whitewater, WI 53190
Phone: 262-472-5119
Fax: 262-472-5633
E-mail: rosenc@uww.edu

GERMAN ACADEMIC EXCHANGE SERVICE (DAAD) http://www.daad.org

GERMAN ACADEMIC EXCHANGE SERVICE (DAAD) EDU DE UNDERGRADUATE AWARDS

A one-time 7500 Euros scholarship is available to full-time undergraduates at U.S. colleges and universities. Prize given for independent senior thesis research, participation in a summer course at a German university or an internship at a German institution or business. Scholarship of four to ten months is for a semester or year abroad in Germany. Scholarship applicants must have at least sophomore standing at the time of application and must have at least junior standing at the beginning of the award period. Must be U.S. citizen or permanent resident of the U.S., or foreign national who has been a full-time student in the U.S. for at least one year at the time of application.

Award: Scholarship for use in junior or senior years; not renewable.

Eligibility Requirements: Applicant must be enrolled or expecting to enroll full-time at an institution or university and must have an interest in German language. Available to U.S. and non-U.S. citizens.

Application Requirements: Application, resume, references, transcript, proposal, DAAD German language certificate. *Deadline:* February 15.

Contact: German Academic Exchange Service (DAAD)
871 United Nations Plaza
New York, NY 10017
Phone: 212-758-3223
Fax: 212-755-5780
E-mail: daadny@daad.org

GERMAN STUDIES RESEARCH GRANTS

Grants worth up to 3000 Euros are designed to promote study of cultural, political, historical, economic and social aspects of modern and contemporary German affairs from an inter- and multi-disciplinary perspective. Undergraduates with at least junior status pursuing a German Studies track or minor, Master's and PhD candidates working on a Certificate in German Studies and PhD candidates doing preliminary dissertation research are eligible. Projects may be in North America or Germany. Deadlines: November 1 and May 1.

Award: Grant for use in junior, senior, graduate, or postgraduate years; not renewable.

Eligibility Requirements: Applicant must be enrolled or expecting to enroll at an institution or university and must have an interest in German language. Available to U.S. and Canadian citizens.

Application Requirements: Application, resume, references, transcript, project description, budget, DAAD language certificate.

Contact: German Academic Exchange Service (DAAD)
871 United Nations Plaza
New York, NY 10017
Phone: 212-758-3223
Fax: 212-755-5780
E-mail: daadny@daad.org

HOCHSCHULSOMMERKURSE AT GERMAN UNIVERSITIES

Scholarships worth 925 Euros are available for U.S. and Canadian students to attend summer language courses hosted by German universities. Applicants must be between the ages of 18 and 32. Undergraduate students with at least junior status and full-time graduate students are eligible. Applicants must have completed two years of college-level German. One-time awards. Application deadline: January 31.

Award: Scholarship for use in junior, senior, or graduate years; not renewable.

Eligibility Requirements: Applicant must be age 18-32; enrolled or expecting to enroll full-time at an institution or university and must have an interest in German language. Available to U.S. and Canadian citizens.

Application Requirements: Application, autobiography, essay, photo, references, transcript, DAAD German language certificate. *Deadline:* January 31.

Contact: German Academic Exchange Service (DAAD)
871 United Nations Plaza
New York, NY 10017
Phone: 212-758-3223
Fax: 212-755-5780
E-mail: daadny@daad.org

GLENN MILLER BIRTHPLACE SOCIETY http://www.glennmiller.org

GLENN MILLER INSTRUMENTAL SCHOLARSHIP

One-time awards for high school seniors and college freshmen, awarded as competition prizes, to be used for any education-related expense. Must submit ten minute, high-quality audiotape of pieces selected for competition or those of similar style. Applicant is responsible for travel to and lodging at competition.

Award: Scholarship for use in freshman or sophomore years; not renewable. *Number:* 2. *Amount:* $1200–$2400.

Eligibility Requirements: Applicant must be enrolled or expecting to enroll full-time at a four-year institution or university and must have an interest in music/singing. Available to U.S. and non-U.S. citizens.

Application Requirements: Application, applicant must enter a contest, essay, self-addressed stamped envelope, performance tape/CD. *Deadline:* March 15.

Contact: Arlene Leonard, Secretary
Glenn Miller Birthplace Society
107 East Main Street, Box 61
Clarinda, IA 51632-0061
Phone: 712-542-2461
Fax: 712-542-2461
E-mail: gmbs@heartland.net

JACK PULLAN MEMORIAL SCHOLARSHIP

One scholarship for male or female vocalist, awarded as competition prize, to be used for any education-related expense. Must submit ten minute, high-quality audiotape of pieces selected for competition or those of similar

Glenn Miller Birthplace Society (continued)

style. Applicant is responsible for travel to and lodging at competition. One-time award for high school seniors and college freshmen.

Award: Scholarship for use in freshman or sophomore years; not renewable. *Number:* 1. *Amount:* $1000.

Eligibility Requirements: Applicant must be enrolled or expecting to enroll full-time at a four-year institution or university and must have an interest in music/singing. Available to U.S. and non-U.S. citizens.

Application Requirements: Application, applicant must enter a contest, essay, self-addressed stamped envelope, performance tape. *Deadline:* March 15.

Contact: Arlene Leonard, Secretary
Glenn Miller Birthplace Society
107 East Main Street, Box 61
Clarinda, IA 51632-0061
Phone: 712-542-2461
Fax: 712-542-2461
E-mail: gmbs@heartland.net

RALPH BREWSTER VOCAL SCHOLARSHIP

One scholarship for male or female vocalist, awarded as competition prize, to be used for any education-related expense. Must submit ten minute, high-quality audiotape of pieces selected for competition or those of similar style. Applicant is responsible for travel to and lodging at competition. One-time award for high school seniors and college freshmen.

Award: Scholarship for use in freshman or sophomore years; not renewable. *Number:* 1. *Amount:* $2000.

Eligibility Requirements: Applicant must be enrolled or expecting to enroll full-time at a four-year institution or university and must have an interest in music/singing. Available to U.S. and non-U.S. citizens.

Application Requirements: Application, applicant must enter a contest, essay, self-addressed stamped envelope, performance tape. *Deadline:* March 15.

Contact: Arlene Leonard, Secretary
Glenn Miller Birthplace Society
107 East Main Street, Box 61
Clarinda, IA 51632-0061
Phone: 712-542-2461
Fax: 712-542-2461
E-mail: gmbs@heartland.net

GOLDEN KEY INTERNATIONAL HONOUR SOCIETY http://www.goldenkey.org

INTERNATIONAL STUDENT LEADERS AWARD

The International Student Leader Award is designed to recognize one talented Golden Key member for outstanding commitment to Golden Key, as well as for campus and community leadership and academic achievement. The recipient of the award will receive $1000.

Award: Scholarship for use in junior, senior, graduate, or postgraduate years; not renewable. *Number:* 1. *Amount:* $1000.

Eligibility Requirements: Applicant must be enrolled or expecting to enroll at an institution or university and must have an interest in leadership.

Application Requirements: Application, essay, resume, references. *Deadline:* May 1.

Contact: Member Services
Golden Key International Honour Society
621 North Avenue, NE
Suite C-100
Atlanta, GA 30308
Phone: 404-377-2400
Fax: 678-420-6757
E-mail: scholarships@goldenkey.org

LITERARY ACHIEVEMENT AWARDS

$1000 will be awarded to winners in each of the following four categories: fiction, non-fiction, poetry, feature writing. Winners may be published in CONCEPTS Magazine. See Web site for more information: http://goldenkey.gsu.edu.

Award: Prize for use in junior, senior, graduate, or postgraduate years; not renewable. *Number:* 4. *Amount:* $1000.

Eligibility Requirements: Applicant must be enrolled or expecting to enroll at an institution or university and must have an interest in writing.

Application Requirements: Application, applicant must enter a contest, original composition. *Deadline:* April 1.

Contact: Member Services
Golden Key International Honour Society
621 North Avenue, NE
Suite C-100
Atlanta, GA 30308
Phone: 404-377-2400
Fax: 678-420-6757
E-mail: scholarships@goldenkey.org

SPEECH AND DEBATE AWARDS

$1000 will be awarded to the winner and $500 will be awarded to the runner-up of an oratory contest. Contestants must submit a videotaped monologue of no more than five minutes in length addressing the following topic: "The solution to world-wide terrorism begins with the United Nations." See Web site for more information: http://goldenkey.gsu.edu.

Award: Prize for use in junior, senior, graduate, or postgraduate years; not renewable. *Number:* 2. *Amount:* $500–$1000.

Eligibility Requirements: Applicant must be enrolled or expecting to enroll at an institution or university and must have an interest in public speaking.

Application Requirements: Application, applicant must enter a contest, videotaped monologue. *Deadline:* April 1.

Contact: Member Services
Golden Key International Honour Society
621 North Avenue, NE
Suite C-100
Atlanta, GA 30308
Phone: 404-377-2400
Fax: 678-420-6757
E-mail: scholarships@goldenkey.org

GRAND RAPIDS COMMUNITY FOUNDATION http://www.grfoundation.org

GERALD M. CRANE MEMORIAL MUSIC SCHOLARSHIP FUND

• *See page 672*

GREATER KANAWHA VALLEY FOUNDATION http://www.tgkvf.org

KID'S CHANCE OF WEST VIRGINIA SCHOLARSHIP

• *See page 673*

HARNESS HORSE YOUTH FOUNDATION http://www.hhyf.org

CURT GREENE MEMORIAL SCHOLARSHIP

One-time award with preference given to those under age 24 who have a passion for harness racing. Based on merit, need, and horsemanship or racing experience. Minimum 2.5 GPA required. For study in any field. May reapply.

Award: Scholarship for use in freshman, sophomore, junior, or senior years; not renewable. *Number:* 1–2. *Amount:* $2500–$3000.

Eligibility Requirements: Applicant must be age 23 or under; enrolled or expecting to enroll full-time at a two-year or four-year or technical institution or university and must have an interest in animal/agricultural competition. Applicant must have 2.5 GPA or higher. Available to U.S. citizens.

Application Requirements: Application, essay, references, transcript, page 1 of parents' IRS form. *Deadline:* April 30.

Contact: Ellen Taylor, Executive Director
Harness Horse Youth Foundation
16575 Carey Road
Westfield, IN 46074
Phone: 317-867-5877
Fax: 317-867-5896

HOSTESS COMMITTEE SCHOLARSHIPS/MISS AMERICA PAGEANT http://www.missamerica.org

MISS AMERICA ORGANIZATION COMPETITION SCHOLARSHIPS

Scholarship competition open to 51 contestants, each serving as state representative. Women will be judged in Private Interview, Swimsuit, Evening Wear and Talent competition. Other awards may be based on points assessed by judges during competitions. Upon reaching the National level, award values range from $5000 to $50,000. Additional awards not affecting the competition can be won with values from $1000 to $10,000. Awards designed to provide contestants with the opportunity to enhance professional and educational goals.

Award: Scholarship for use in freshman, sophomore, junior, senior, or graduate years; not renewable. *Number:* up to 69. *Amount:* $1000–$50,000.

Eligibility Requirements: Applicant must be enrolled or expecting to enroll at a two-year or four-year or technical institution or university; female and must have an interest in beauty pageant. Available to U.S. citizens.

Application Requirements: Applicant must enter a contest.

Contact: See Web site.

MISS STATE SCHOLAR

Award available only to pageant participants at the state level. Candidates evaluated strictly on academics.

Award: Scholarship for use in junior, senior, or graduate years; not renewable. *Number:* up to 51. *Amount:* up to $1000.

Eligibility Requirements: Applicant must be enrolled or expecting to enroll at a two-year or four-year institution or university; female and must have an interest in beauty pageant. Available to U.S. citizens.

Application Requirements: Application, transcript. *Deadline:* varies.

Contact: See Web site.

HOUSTON SYMPHONY http://www.houstonsymphony.org

HOUSTON SYMPHONY IMA HOGG YOUNG ARTIST COMPETITION

Competition for musicians 19-29 who play standard instruments of the symphony orchestra. Goal is to offer a review by panel of music professionals and further career of advanced student or professional musician. Participants must be U.S. citizens or studying in the U.S. Application fee is $25.

Award: Prize for use in freshman, sophomore, junior, senior, graduate, or postgraduate years; not renewable. *Number:* 3. *Amount:* $1000–$5000.

Eligibility Requirements: Applicant must be age 19-29; enrolled or expecting to enroll full or part-time at a two-year or four-year or technical institution or university and must have an interest in music. Available to U.S. and non-U.S. citizens.

Application Requirements: Application, applicant must enter a contest, cassette tape with required repertoire. *Fee:* $25. *Deadline:* February 16.

Contact: Carol Wilson, Education Coordinator
Houston Symphony
615 Louisiana
Houston, TX 77002
Phone: 713-238-1447
Fax: 713-224-0453
E-mail: e&o@houstonsymphony.org

INSTITUTE FOR HUMANE STUDIES http://www.theihs.org

FELIX MORLEY JOURNALISM COMPETITION

Competitors in the Morley Competition are judged on demonstrated writing ability, potential for development as a writer, and appreciation of classical liberal ideas as evidenced in submitted publications. Competition open to young writers and students (25 years and younger).

Award: Prize for use in freshman, sophomore, junior, or senior years; not renewable. *Number:* 6. *Amount:* $250–$2500.

Eligibility Requirements: Applicant must be age 25 or under; enrolled or expecting to enroll full or part-time at a two-year or four-year or technical institution or university and must have an interest in writing. Available to U.S. and non-U.S. citizens.

Application Requirements: Application, 3-5 published articles. *Deadline:* December 1.

Contact: Dan Alban, Morley Competition
Institute for Humane Studies
3301 North Fairfax Drive, Suite 440
Arlington, VA 22201-4432
Phone: 703-993-4880
Fax: 703-993-4890
E-mail: ihs@gmu.edu

ISIA EDUCATION FOUNDATION http://www.skateisi.org

ISIA EDUCATION FOUNDATION SCHOLARSHIP

• *See page 465*

J. WOOD PLATT CADDIE SCHOLARSHIP TRUST http://www.gapgolf.org

J. WOOD PLATT CADDIE SCHOLARSHIP TRUST

• *See page 512*

JANE AUSTEN SOCIETY OF NORTH AMERICA http://www.jasna.org

JANE AUSTEN SOCIETY OF NORTH AMERICA ESSAY CONTEST

Essay contest with three divisions: high school, college undergraduate, and graduate student. First prize in each division is free trip to conference, or cash equivalent ($750-$1000). Essay topic is posted each winter on the Web site: http://www.jasna.org. Essay must be 1200-2000 words and should contain personal, original insight into Jane Austen's artistry, ideas, and values; not primarily a research paper. Must also include a brief statement of less than 100 words about the teacher or professor who most influenced you to enter the contest. Application and essay deadline is May 1.

Award: Prize for use in freshman, sophomore, junior, senior, graduate, or postgraduate years; not renewable. *Number:* 9. *Amount:* up to $1000.

Eligibility Requirements: Applicant must be enrolled or expecting to enroll full or part-time at a two-year or four-year institution or university and must have an interest in English language or writing. Available to U.S. and non-U.S. citizens.

Application Requirements: Application, applicant must enter a contest, essay, references. *Deadline:* May 1.

Contact: Barbara Sullivan, Contest Chair
Jane Austen Society of North America
1360 Pronghorn Court
Cheyenne, WY 82009
Phone: 307-635-5736
Fax: 307-638-0564
E-mail: janebrs@starband.net

JAPANESE GOVERNMENT/THE MONBUSHO SCHOLARSHIP PROGRAM http://www.pk.emb-japan.go.jp/EDUCATION/Undergrad.htm

VOCATIONAL SCHOOL STUDENT SCHOLARSHIPS

Award open to students enrolled in vocational school in Japan. Study involves one year of language training and two years of vocational school. All vocational training will be in Japanese. Scholarship comprises transportation, accommodations, medical expenses, and monthly and arrival allowances. Contact for more information.

Award: Scholarship for use in freshman, sophomore, junior, or senior years; renewable. *Number:* varies. *Amount:* varies.

Eligibility Requirements: Applicant must be age 17-20; enrolled or expecting to enroll full-time at a technical institution and must have an interest in Japanese language. Available to U.S. and non-U.S. citizens.

Application Requirements: Application, autobiography, essay, interview, photo, references, test scores, transcript, medical certificate, certificate of enrollment. *Deadline:* Continuous.

Contact: See Web site for information.

JUNIOR ACHIEVEMENT http://www.ja.org

JUNIOR ACHIEVEMENT JOE FRANCOMANO SCHOLARSHIP

• *See page 466*

KENTUCKY HIGHER EDUCATION ASSISTANCE AUTHORITY (KHEAA) http://www.kheaa.com

KENTUCKY DEPARTMENT OF AGRICULTURE SCHOLARSHIP

• *See page 682*

KINGSBURY CORPORATION

KINGSBURY FUND SCHOLARSHIPS

• *See page 497*

KOSCIUSZKO FOUNDATION http://www.kosciuszkofoundation.org

MARCELLA SEMBRICH VOICE COMPETITION

Established to encourage young singers to study the repertoire of Polish composers. Three prizes awarded: first is $1000, second is $750, and third is $500. Open to all singers who are at least 18 years old and preparing for professional careers who are U.S. citizens or international full-time students with a valid student visa.

Award: Prize for use in freshman, sophomore, junior, senior, or graduate years; not renewable. *Number:* 3. *Amount:* $500–$1000.

Eligibility Requirements: Applicant must be age 18; enrolled or expecting to enroll full or part-time at an institution or university and must have an interest in music/singing. Available to U.S. citizens.

Application Requirements: Application, applicant must enter a contest, photo, references, two cassette tapes. *Fee:* $35. *Deadline:* December 18.

Contact: Mr. Thomas Pniewski, Director of Cultural Programs
Kosciuszko Foundation
15 East 65th Street
New York, NY 10021-6595
Phone: 212-734-2130
Fax: 212-628-4552
E-mail: tompkf@aol.com

KUMU KAHUA THEATRE

KUMU KAHUA THEATER/UHM THEATER DEPARTMENT PLAYWRITING CONTEST, HAWAII PRIZE

Contest for residents and non-residents of Hawaii. Contestants will be judged on full-length plays dealing with some aspect of the Hawaii experience or plays set in Hawaii. Submissions should be a minimum of 50 pages in standard form. Write for details.

Award: Prize for use in freshman, sophomore, junior, senior, graduate, or postgraduate years; not renewable. *Number:* 1. *Amount:* $500.

Eligibility Requirements: Applicant must be enrolled or expecting to enroll at an institution or university and must have an interest in writing. Available to U.S. and non-U.S. citizens.

Application Requirements: Applicant must enter a contest, 3 copies of manuscript. *Deadline:* January 2.

Contact: Kumu Kahua Playwriting Contest
Kumu Kahua Theatre
46 Merchant Street
Honolulu, HI 96813
E-mail: info@kumukahua.com

KUMU KAHUA THEATER/UHM THEATER DEPARTMENT PLAYWRITING CONTEST, PACIFIC RIM PRIZE

Contest for residents and non-residents of Hawaii. Play must be set in or deal with the Pacific Islands, the Pacific Rim, or the Pacific/Asian-American experience. Restricted to full-length plays of a minimum of 50 pages in standard form. Write for details.

Award: Prize for use in freshman, sophomore, junior, senior, graduate, or postgraduate years; not renewable. *Number:* 1. *Amount:* $400.

Eligibility Requirements: Applicant must be enrolled or expecting to enroll at an institution or university and must have an interest in writing. Available to U.S. and non-U.S. citizens.

Application Requirements: Applicant must enter a contest, 3 copies of manuscript. *Deadline:* January 2.

Contact: Kuma Kahua Playwriting Contest
Kumu Kahua Theatre
46 Merchant Street
Honolulu, HI 96813
E-mail: info@kumukahua.com

KUMU KAHUA THEATER/UHM THEATER DEPARTMENT PLAYWRITING CONTEST, RESIDENT PRIZE

• *See page 683*

LADIES AUXILIARY TO THE VETERANS OF FOREIGN WARS http://www.ladiesauxvfw.com

JUNIOR GIRLS SCHOLARSHIP PROGRAM

• *See page 468*

YOUNG AMERICAN CREATIVE PATRIOTIC ART AWARDS PROGRAM

One-time awards for high school students in grades 9 through 12. Must submit an original work of art expressing their patriotism. First-place state-level winners go on to national competition. Three awards of varying amounts. Must reside in same state as sponsoring organization.

Award: Scholarship for use in freshman, sophomore, junior, or senior years; not renewable. *Number:* 3. *Amount:* $2500–$10,000.

Eligibility Requirements: Applicant must be high school student; planning to enroll or expecting to enroll full-time at a two-year or four-year or technical institution; single and must have an interest in designated field specified by sponsor. Available to U.S. citizens.

Application Requirements: Application, applicant must enter a contest. *Deadline:* March 29.

Contact: Judy Millick, Administrator of Programs
Ladies Auxiliary to the Veterans of Foreign Wars
406 West 34th Street
Kansas City, MO 64111
Phone: 816-561-8655
Fax: 816-931-4753
E-mail: info@ladiesauxvfw.com

LEE-JACKSON EDUCATIONAL FOUNDATION http://www.lee-jackson.org

LEE-JACKSON EDUCATIONAL FOUNDATION SCHOLARSHIP COMPETITION

• *See page 684*

LIEDERKRANZ FOUNDATION

LIEDERKRANZ FOUNDATION SCHOLARSHIP AWARD FOR VOICE

Non-renewable awards for voice for both full- and part-time study. Those studying general voice must be between ages 20 to 35 years old while those studying Wagnerian voice must be between ages 25 to 45 years old. Application fee: $40. Applications not available before August/September. Deadline: November 15.

Award: Scholarship for use in freshman, sophomore, junior, senior, or graduate years; not renewable. *Number:* 14–18. *Amount:* $1000–$5000.

Eligibility Requirements: Applicant must be enrolled or expecting to enroll full or part-time at an institution or university and must have an interest in music/singing. Available to U.S. and non-U.S. citizens.

Application Requirements: Application, applicant must enter a contest, driver's license, self-addressed stamped envelope, proof of age. *Fee:* $40. *Deadline:* November 15.

Contact: Cynthia M. Kessel, Administrative Assistant
Liederkranz Foundation
6 East 87th Street
New York, NY 10128
Phone: 212-534-0880
Fax: 212-828-5372

LINCOLN COMMUNITY FOUNDATION http://www.lcf.org

GEORGE WATTERS-NEBRASKA PETROLEUM MARKETERS ASSOCIATION SCHOLARSHIP

• *See page 513*

MIRIAM CROFT MOELLER CITIZENSHIP AWARD
• *See page 685*

LOS ANGELES PHILHARMONIC http://www.laphil.org

BRONISLAW KAPER AWARDS FOR YOUNG ARTISTS
• *See page 686*

MAINE SKATING CLUB SCHOLARSHIP FUND http://www.lfskate.com

MAINE SKATING CLUB SCHOLARSHIP

High school seniors who are former or current members of the Maine Skating Club, who have represented the club at a National Roller Skating Championship and who have been accepted at a college will be awarded a $100 scholarship.

Award: Scholarship for use in freshman year; not renewable. *Number:* varies. *Amount:* $100.

Eligibility Requirements: Applicant must be high school student; planning to enroll or expecting to enroll full-time at a two-year or four-year or technical institution or university and must have an interest in rollerskating. Available to U.S. citizens.

Application Requirements: College acceptance letter. *Deadline:* Continuous.

Contact: Veronica Thompson, Secretary/Treasurer
Maine Skating Club Scholarship Fund
PO Box 172
Livermore Falls, ME 04254
Phone: 207-897-4006
Fax: 207-897-2971
E-mail: vrtlfsc@midmaine.com

MARTIN D. ANDREWS SCHOLARSHIP http://mdascholarship.tripod.com

MARTIN D. ANDREWS MEMORIAL SCHOLARSHIP FUND

One-time award for student seeking undergraduate or graduate degree. Recipient must have been in a Drum Corp for at least three years. Must submit essay and two recommendations. Must be U.S. citizen.

Award: Scholarship for use in freshman, sophomore, junior, senior, or graduate years; not renewable. *Number:* 2–5. *Amount:* $300–$1000.

Eligibility Requirements: Applicant must be enrolled or expecting to enroll full or part-time at a two-year or four-year institution or university and must have an interest in drum corps. Available to U.S. citizens.

Application Requirements: Application, essay, references. *Deadline:* April 1.

Contact: Peter Andrews, Committee Member
Martin D. Andrews Scholarship
2069 Perkins Street
Bristol, CT 06010
Phone: 860-673-2929

MARY ROBERTS RINEHART FUND http://www.gmu.edu/departments/writing

MARY ROBERTS RINEHART AWARDS

One-time award available to individuals with excellent writing ability. Applicants do not have to be enrolled in an educational institution but must be nominated by a writing teacher, a recognized writer, an editor, or a publisher. Please send self-addressed stamped envelope for guidelines or visit Web site at http://www.gmu.edu/departments/writing. Grants are only for unpublished works in fiction, nonfiction or poetry. Entries must be postmarked by November 30.

Award: Prize for use in freshman, sophomore, junior, senior, graduate, or postgraduate years; not renewable. *Number:* 3. *Amount:* $2000.

Eligibility Requirements: Applicant must be enrolled or expecting to enroll full or part-time at an institution or university and must have an interest in writing. Available to U.S. and non-U.S. citizens.

Application Requirements: Applicant must enter a contest, autobiography, references, self-addressed stamped envelope, nomination, manuscript. *Deadline:* November 30.

Contact: William Miller, Director
Mary Roberts Rinehart Fund
MSN 3E4, George Mason University
Fairfax, VA 22030-4444
Phone: 703-993-1180
E-mail: writing@gmu.edu

MCCURRY FOUNDATION, INC. http://www.mccurryfoundation.org/

MCCURRY FOUNDATION SCHOLARSHIP

Scholarship open to all public high school seniors, with preference given to applicants from Clay, Duval, Nassau, and St. Johns Counties, Florida and from Glynn County, Georgia. Scholarship emphasizes leadership, work ethic, and academic excellence. A minimum GPA of 3.0 is required and family income cannot exceed a maximum of $75,000 (AGI).

Award: Scholarship for use in freshman year; not renewable. *Number:* varies. *Amount:* varies.

Eligibility Requirements: Applicant must be high school student; planning to enroll or expecting to enroll full-time at a two-year or four-year or technical institution or university and must have an interest in leadership. Applicant must have 3.0 GPA or higher.

Application Requirements: Application, essay, financial need analysis, interview, resume, references, transcript, report card, tax return. *Deadline:* March 31.

Contact: See Web site for application.

MICHIGAN OUTDOOR WRITERS ASSOCIATION http://www.mioutdoorwriters.org

MARC WESLEY SCHOLARSHIP AWARD
• *See page 692*

MISS AMERICAN COED PAGEANTS, INC.

MISS AMERICAN COED PAGEANT

Awards available for girls ages 3-22. Must be single and maintain a 3.0 GPA where applicable. Prizes are awarded by age groups. Winners of state competitions may compete at the national level. Application fee is $20 and will be refunded if not accepted into competition.

Award: Prize for use in freshman year; not renewable. *Number:* varies. *Amount:* varies.

Eligibility Requirements: Applicant must be age 3-22; enrolled or expecting to enroll full or part-time at a two-year or four-year institution or university; single female and must have an interest in beauty pageant. Applicant must have 3.0 GPA or higher.

Application Requirements: Application, applicant must enter a contest, transcript. *Fee:* $20. *Deadline:* varies.

Contact: Mr. George Scarborough, National Director
Miss American Coed Pageants, Inc.
3695 Wimbledon Drive
Pensacola, FL 32504-4555
Phone: 850-432-0069
Fax: 850-469-8841
E-mail: amerteen@aol.com

NATIONAL ASSOCIATION FOR CAMPUS ACTIVITIES http://www.naca.org

LORI RHETT MEMORIAL SCHOLARSHIP
• *See page 698*

MULTICULTURAL SCHOLARSHIP PROGRAM
• *See page 594*

NATIONAL ASSOCIATION FOR CAMPUS ACTIVITIES EAST COAST UNDERGRADUATE SCHOLARSHIP FOR STUDENT LEADERS
• *See page 699*

NATIONAL ASSOCIATION FOR CAMPUS ACTIVITIES REGIONAL COUNCIL STUDENT LEADER SCHOLARSHIPS

Scholarships will be given to undergraduate students in good standing at the time of the application and during the academic term in which the

National Association for Campus Activities (continued)

scholarship is awarded. Must demonstrate significant leadership skill and ability while holding a significant leadership position on campus.

Award: Scholarship for use in freshman, sophomore, junior, or senior years; not renewable. *Number:* up to 7. *Amount:* $250–$300.

Eligibility Requirements: Applicant must be enrolled or expecting to enroll at an institution or university and must have an interest in leadership. Available to U.S. citizens.

Application Requirements: Application, essay, resume, references, transcript. *Deadline:* May 1.

Contact: Application available at Web site.

NATIONAL ASSOCIATION FOR CAMPUS ACTIVITIES SOUTHEAST REGION STUDENT LEADERSHIP SCHOLARSHIP

• *See page 699*

NATIONAL ASSOCIATION FOR CAMPUS ACTIVITIES WI REGION STUDENT LEADERSHIP SCHOLARSHIP

• *See page 699*

SCHOLARSHIPS FOR STUDENT LEADERS

Scholarships will be awarded to undergraduate students in good standing at the time of the application and who, during the academic term in which the scholarship is awarded, hold a significant leadership position on their campus. Must make significant contributions to their campus communities and demonstrate leadership skills and abilities. Applicants must submit two letters of recommendation and a description of the applicant's leadership activities, skills, and abilities.

Award: Scholarship for use in freshman, sophomore, junior, or senior years; not renewable. *Number:* up to 6. *Amount:* $250–$300.

Eligibility Requirements: Applicant must be enrolled or expecting to enroll at a two-year or four-year institution or university and must have an interest in leadership. Available to U.S. citizens.

Application Requirements: Application, resume, references, transcript. *Deadline:* November 1.

Contact: Application available at Web site.

TESS CALDARELLI MEMORIAL SCHOLARSHIP

• *See page 699*

ZAGUNAS STUDENT LEADERS SCHOLARSHIP

• *See page 699*

NATIONAL ASSOCIATION OF SECONDARY SCHOOL PRINCIPALS http://www.principals.org

PRINCIPAL'S LEADERSHIP AWARD

One-time award available to high school seniors only, for use at an accredited two- or four-year college or university. Based on leadership and school or community involvement. Application fee: $6. Deadline is December 1. Contact school counselor or principal. Citizens of countries other than the U.S. may only apply if they are attending a United States overseas institution. Minimum GPA 3.0.

Award: Scholarship for use in freshman year; not renewable. *Number:* 150. *Amount:* $1000.

Eligibility Requirements: Applicant must be high school student; planning to enroll or expecting to enroll full-time at a two-year or four-year institution or university and must have an interest in leadership. Applicant must have 3.0 GPA or higher. Available to U.S. and non-U.S. citizens.

Application Requirements: Application, essay, references, test scores, transcript. *Fee:* $6. *Deadline:* December 1.

Contact: local school principal or guidance counselor

NATIONAL FEDERATION OF STATE POETRY SOCIETIES (NFSPS) http://www.nfsps.com

NATIONAL FEDERATION OF STATE POETRY SOCIETIES SCHOLARSHIP AWARDS- COLLEGE/UNIVERSITY LEVEL POETRY COMPETITION

Must submit application and ten original poems, forty-line per-poem limit. Manuscript must be titled. For more information, visit the Web site.

Award: Scholarship for use in freshman, sophomore, junior, or senior years; not renewable. *Number:* 2. *Amount:* $500.

Eligibility Requirements: Applicant must be enrolled or expecting to enroll at a four-year institution or university and must have an interest in writing. Available to U.S. citizens.

Application Requirements: Application, applicant must enter a contest, must be notarized. *Deadline:* February 1.

Contact: Sybella Beyer-Snyder, Chair of College/University-Level Poetry Competition
National Federation of State Poetry Societies (NFSPS)
3444 South Dover Terrace
Inverness, FL 34452-7116

NATIONAL LEAGUE OF AMERICAN PEN WOMEN, INC. http://www.americanpenwomen.org

NLAPW VIRGINIA LIEBELER BIENNIAL GRANTS FOR MATURE WOMEN (LETTERS)

One-time award given in even-numbered years to women ages 35 and older and who are U.S. citizens to be used to further creative purpose of applicant. Submit copies of work, statement of background, purpose of grant, and how applicant learned of grant. May submit in any or all categories, published or unpublished. Application fee: $8. Send self-addressed stamped envelope for entry requirements. Entry deadline is October 1 of odd-numbered year.

Award: Grant for use in freshman, sophomore, junior, senior, graduate, or postgraduate years; not renewable. *Number:* 1. *Amount:* $1000.

Eligibility Requirements: Applicant must be age 35; enrolled or expecting to enroll at an institution or university; female and must have an interest in writing. Available to U.S. citizens.

Application Requirements: Applicant must enter a contest, self-addressed stamped envelope, proof of U.S. citizenship. *Fee:* $8. *Deadline:* October 1.

Contact: NLAPW Virginia Liebeler Biennial Grants for Women
National League of American Pen Women, Inc.
1300 17th Street, NW
Washington, DC 20036-1973

NLAPW VIRGINIA LIEBELER BIENNIAL GRANTS FOR MATURE WOMEN (MUSIC)

Award offered in even-numbered years to women 35 years of age and over. Submit two scores of musical compositions, of which at least one must have been written in the past five years. Performance time should be at least 5 minutes. Neither score may have won a previous award. Must submit letter stating age, purpose, and how applicant learned of grant. Application fee is $8. One-time award of $1000. Send a self-addressed stamped envelope for entry requirements. Entry deadline is October 1 of odd-numbered year.

Award: Grant for use in freshman, sophomore, junior, senior, graduate, or postgraduate years; not renewable. *Number:* 1. *Amount:* $1000.

Eligibility Requirements: Applicant must be age 35; enrolled or expecting to enroll at an institution or university; female and must have an interest in music/singing. Available to U.S. citizens.

Application Requirements: Applicant must enter a contest, self-addressed stamped envelope, proof of U.S. citizenship. *Fee:* $8. *Deadline:* October 1.

Contact: NLAPW Virginia Liebeler Biennial Grants for Women
National League of American Pen Women, Inc.
1300 17th Street, NW
Washington, DC 20036-1973

NATIONAL MINORITY JUNIOR GOLF SCHOLARSHIP ASSOCIATION http://www.nmjgsa.org

NATIONAL MINORITY JUNIOR GOLF SCHOLARSHIP

• *See page 595*

NATIONAL SYMPHONY ORCHESTRA EDUCATION PROGRAM http://www.kennedy-center.org/nso/nsoed/youngsoloists.html

NATIONAL SYMPHONY ORCHESTRA YOUNG SOLOISTS' COMPETITION- BILL CERRI SCHOLARSHIP/COLLEGE DIVISION

Prize for the best soloist in competition. Winner will perform with the National Symphony Orchestra in Washington, D.C. Must be a college student attending school or residing in D.C. metropolitan area. $15 application fee. Visit Web site for guidelines and deadlines. Pianists and instrumentalists must be no older than 23, singers must be no older than 26.

Award: Prize for use in freshman, sophomore, junior, or senior years; not renewable. *Number:* 1. *Amount:* $1000.

Eligibility Requirements: Applicant must be enrolled or expecting to enroll at an institution or university and must have an interest in music/singing. Available to U.S. and non-U.S. citizens.

Application Requirements: Application, applicant must enter a contest. *Fee:* $15. *Deadline:* varies.

Contact: Carole Wysocki, Director, NSO Education Program
National Symphony Orchestra Education Program
The Kennedy Center
Washington, DC 20566
Phone: 202-416-8820
Fax: 202-416-8802
E-mail: cjwysocki@kennedy-center.org

NATIONAL SYMPHONY ORCHESTRA YOUNG SOLOISTS' COMPETITION- BILL CERRI SCHOLARSHIP/HIGH SCHOOL DIVISION

• *See page 700*

NATIONAL WOMEN'S STUDIES ASSOCIATION http://www.nwsa.org

ABAFAZI-AFRICANA WOMEN'S STUDIES ESSAY AWARD

• *See page 595*

NORTHEASTERN LOGGERS' ASSOCIATION, INC.

NORTHEASTERN LOGGERS' ASSOCIATION SCHOLARSHIPS

• *See page 474*

NUCLEAR AGE PEACE FOUNDATION http://www.wagingpeace.org

BARBARA MANDIGO KELLY PEACE POETRY CONTEST

Poetry contest with three age categories: Adult, Youth (13-18), Youth (12 and under). Poems must be original, unpublished, and in English. Application fee of $15 is waived for Youth entries. Visit Web site at http://www.wagingpeace.org for further information.

Award: Prize for use in freshman, sophomore, junior, senior, graduate, or postgraduate years; not renewable. *Number:* varies. *Amount:* $200–$1000.

Eligibility Requirements: Applicant must be enrolled or expecting to enroll at an institution or university and must have an interest in writing. Available to U.S. and non-U.S. citizens.

Application Requirements: Applicant must enter a contest, 2 copies of poems. *Fee:* $15. *Deadline:* July 1.

Contact: Michael Coffey, Nuclear Age Peace Foundation/ Barbara Mandigo Kelly Peace Poetry Awards
Nuclear Age Peace Foundation
1187 Coast Village Road, Suite 1
Santa Barbara, CA 93108-2794
Phone: 805-965-3443
Fax: 805-568-0466
E-mail: wagingpeace@napf.org

OMAHA SYMPHONY GUILD http://www.omahasymphony.org

OMAHA SYMPHONY GUILD INTERNATIONAL NEW MUSIC COMPETITION

One-time award for those 25 and over for the best composition of symphony music. Prize also includes possible performance of winning composition by the Omaha Symphony Chamber Orchestra. Submit two copies of score with application. Application fee $30.

Award: Prize for use in junior, senior, graduate, or postgraduate years; not renewable. *Number:* 1. *Amount:* up to $3000.

Eligibility Requirements: Applicant must be age 25; enrolled or expecting to enroll full or part-time at a two-year or four-year or technical institution or university and must have an interest in music/singing. Available to U.S. and non-U.S. citizens.

Application Requirements: Application, applicant must enter a contest. *Fee:* $30. *Deadline:* April 15.

Contact: Tim Dickmeyer, Touring and Education Coordinator
Omaha Symphony Guild
1605 Howard Street
Omaha, NE 68102-2705
Phone: 402-342-3836 Ext. 107
Fax: 402-342-3819
E-mail: tdickmeyer@omahasymphony.org

OREGON STUDENT ASSISTANCE COMMISSION http://www.osac.state.or.us

DOROTHY CAMPBELL MEMORIAL SCHOLARSHIP

• *See page 713*

JOSE D. GARCIA MIGRANT EDUCATION SCHOLARSHIP

• *See page 714*

OREGON TRAWL COMMISSION SCHOLARSHIP

• *See page 518*

OUR WORLD UNDERWATER SCHOLARSHIP SOCIETY http://www.owuscholarship.org

OUR WORLD UNDERWATER SCHOLARSHIPS

Annual award for individual planning to pursue a career in a water-related discipline through practical exposure to various fields and leaders of underwater endeavors. Scuba experience required. Must be at least 21 but not yet 25 by March 1. Application fee is $25.

Award: Scholarship for use in freshman, sophomore, junior, senior, or graduate years; not renewable. *Number:* 1. *Amount:* up to $20,000.

Eligibility Requirements: Applicant must be age 21-24; enrolled or expecting to enroll full-time at a two-year or four-year or technical institution or university and must have an interest in scuba diving. Available to U.S. and non-U.S. citizens.

Application Requirements: Application, autobiography, essay, interview, resume, references, transcript, diver certification. *Fee:* $25. *Deadline:* November 30.

Contact: Scholarship Application Coordinator
Our World Underwater Scholarship Society
PO Box 4428
Chicago, IL 60680-4428
Phone: 800-969-6690
Fax: 630-969-6690
E-mail: info@owuscholarship.org

PIRATE'S ALLEY FAULKNER SOCIETY http://www.wordsandmusic.org

WILLIAM FAULKNER-WILLIAM WISDOM CREATIVE WRITING COMPETITION

Talent search for unpublished manuscripts written in English. One prize awarded in each category: $7500, novel; $2500, novella; $2000 novel-in-progress; $1500, short story; $1000, essay; $750, poem; $750 high school short story-student author, $250 sponsoring teacher. Manuscripts will not be returned, must be mailed, not emailed or faxed, and accompanied by entry fee ranging from $10 for high school category to $35 for novel. Must get entry form from Web site: http://www.wordsandmusic.org or request by mail. Deadline for submission of entry form, manuscript, and entry fee is April 1.

Award: Prize for use in freshman, sophomore, junior, senior, graduate, or postgraduate years; not renewable. *Number:* 7. *Amount:* $750–$7500.

Eligibility Requirements: Applicant must be enrolled or expecting to enroll at a two-year or four-year institution or university and must have an interest in English language or writing. Available to U.S. and non-U.S. citizens.

Pirate's Alley Faulkner Society (continued)

Application Requirements: Application, applicant must enter a contest, manuscript, entry fee. *Deadline:* April 1.

Contact: See Web site for entry form and guidelines.
Pirate's Alley Faulkner Society
632 Pirate's Alley
New Orleans, LA 70116-3254
E-mail: faulkhouse@aol.com

PONY OF THE AMERICAS CLUB http://www.poac.org

PONY OF THE AMERICAS SCHOLARSHIP

• *See page 478*

PRO BOWLERS ASSOCIATION http://www.pba.com

BILLY WELU BOWLING SCHOLARSHIP

Scholarship awarded annually, recognizing exemplary qualities in male and female college students who compete in the sport of bowling.

Award: Scholarship for use in freshman, sophomore, junior, or senior years; not renewable. *Number:* 1. *Amount:* $1000.

Eligibility Requirements: Applicant must be enrolled or expecting to enroll full-time at a two-year or four-year institution or university and must have an interest in bowling. Applicant must have 2.5 GPA or higher. Available to U.S. citizens.

Application Requirements: Application, essay, references, transcript. *Deadline:* May 31.

Contact: Karen Day, Controller
Pro Bowlers Association
719 Second Avenue, Suite 701
Seattle, WA 98104
Phone: 206-654-6002
Fax: 206-654-6030
E-mail: karen.day@pba.com

PROFESSIONAL BOWLERS ASSOCIATION http://www.pba.com

PROFESSIONAL BOWLERS ASSOCIATION BILLY WELU MEMORIAL SCHOLARSHIP

• *See page 478*

QUEEN ELISABETH INTERNATIONAL MUSIC COMPETITION OF BELGIUM http://www.qeimc.be

QUEEN ELISABETH COMPETITION

Various prizes and awards available. Competitions, which vary from year to year, are in the following: piano, singing, violin, and composition. Award for 1st place in piano 20,000 Euros, in singing 20,000 Euros, and composition 7500 Euros. Age limits vary for each competition. Application fee of 55 Euros. Available to U.S. and Canadian citizens. Visit Web site for complete information, requirements, and applications. Deadline January 15. Composition competition will be held in 2004 and 2006, violin competition will be held in 2005, and piano competition will be held in 2007.

Award: Prize for use in freshman, sophomore, junior, senior, graduate, or postgraduate years; not renewable. *Number:* varies. *Amount:* up to $23,980.

Eligibility Requirements: Applicant must be enrolled or expecting to enroll at a four-year institution or university and must have an interest in music or music/singing. Available to U.S. and non-U.S. citizens.

Application Requirements: Application, applicant must enter a contest, photo. *Fee:* $55. *Deadline:* January 15.

Contact: Michel-Etienne Van Neste, Secretary General
Queen Elisabeth International Music Competition of Belgium
Rue Aux Lanes 20
Brussels 1000
Belgium
Phone: 32-2-2134050
Fax: 32-2-5143297
E-mail: info@qeimc.be

QUILL AND SCROLL FOUNDATION http://www.uiowa.edu/~quill-sc

QUILL AND SCROLL INTERNATIONAL WRITING/PHOTO CONTEST

One-time contest for best journalistic writing/reporting and photographs in several categories. Only high school students may enter. Winners receive gold key in addition to being eligible to apply for journalism scholarships. Contact Quill and Scroll for more details and application. Application fee: $2 per entry.

Award: Prize for use in freshman year; not renewable. *Number:* varies.

Eligibility Requirements: Applicant must be high school student; planning to enroll or expecting to enroll at an institution or university and must have an interest in photography/photogrammetry/filmmaking or writing. Available to U.S. and non-U.S. citizens.

Application Requirements: Application, applicant must enter a contest, essay, photo. *Fee:* $2. *Deadline:* February 5.

Contact: Richard Johns, Executive Director
Quill and Scroll Foundation
312 WSSH, School of Journalism
Iowa City, IA 52242-1528
Phone: 319-335-3321
Fax: 319-335-5210
E-mail: quill-scroll@uiowa.edu

RECORDING FOR THE BLIND & DYSLEXIC http://www.rfbd.org

MARION HUBER LEARNING THROUGH LISTENING AWARDS

• *See page 478*

MARY P. OENSLAGER SCHOLASTIC ACHIEVEMENT AWARDS

• *See page 479*

RESERVE OFFICERS ASSOCIATION OF THE US http://www.roa.org

HENRY J. REILLY MEMORIAL SCHOLARSHIP-HIGH SCHOOL SENIORS AND FIRST YEAR FRESHMEN

• *See page 479*

RHODE ISLAND FOUNDATION http://www.rifoundation.org

EDWARD LEON DUHAMEL FREEMASONS SCHOLARSHIP

To benefit descendents of Freemasons in the Rhode Island and southeastern New England area with preference to the children of Franklin Lodge #20 members of Westerly, Rhode Island. Award is renewable.

Award: Scholarship for use in freshman, sophomore, junior, or senior years; renewable. *Number:* 2–4. *Amount:* $500–$1000.

Eligibility Requirements: Applicant must be enrolled or expecting to enroll full-time at a four-year institution or university and must have an interest in designated field specified by sponsor.

Application Requirements: Application, essay, financial need analysis, self-addressed stamped envelope, transcript. *Deadline:* May 21.

Contact: Libby Monahan, Scholarship Coordinator
Rhode Island Foundation
One Union Station
Providence, RI 02903
Phone: 401-274-4564
Fax: 401-272-1359
E-mail: libbym@rifoundation.org

MJSA EDUCATION FOUNDATION JEWELRY SCHOLARSHIP

For students enrolled in toolmaking, design, metals fabrication, or other jewelry-related courses of study in colleges, universities, or nonprofit accredited technical schools on the postsecondary level. Must include slides of samples.

Award: Scholarship for use in freshman, sophomore, junior, or senior years; renewable. *Number:* varies. *Amount:* $500–$2000.

Eligibility Requirements: Applicant must be enrolled or expecting to enroll full-time at a four-year or technical institution or university and must have an interest in designated field specified by sponsor.

Application Requirements: Application, essay, financial need analysis, self-addressed stamped envelope, transcript. *Deadline:* June 1.

Contact: Scholarship Coordinator
Rhode Island Foundation
1 Union Station
Providence, RI 02903
Phone: 401-274-4564
Fax: 401-272-1359

ROTARY FOUNDATION OF ROTARY INTERNATIONAL http://www.rotary.org

ROTARY FOUNDATION ACADEMIC-YEAR AMBASSADORIAL SCHOLARSHIPS

One-time award funds travel, tuition, room and board for one academic year of study in foreign country. Applicant must have completed at least two years of university course work and be proficient in language of host country. Application through local Rotary club; appearances before clubs required during award period. Deadlines vary (March-July). See Web site at http://www.rotary.org for updated information.

Award: Scholarship for use in junior, senior, graduate, or postgraduate years; not renewable. *Number:* 900–1000. *Amount:* up to $25,000.

Eligibility Requirements: Applicant must be enrolled or expecting to enroll at a four-year institution or university and must have an interest in foreign language.

Application Requirements: Application, autobiography, essay, interview, references, transcript. *Deadline:* varies.

Contact: Scholarship Program
Rotary Foundation of Rotary International
1560 Sherman Avenue
Evanston, IL 60201
Phone: 847-866-4459

ROTARY MULTI-YEAR AMBASSADORIAL SCHOLARSHIPS

Awarded for two years (depending on availability through sponsoring Rotary district) of degree-oriented study in another country. Applicant must have completed at least two years of university course work and be proficient in language of host country. Application through local Rotary club; appearances before clubs required during award period. Applications are accepted March through July. See Web site at http://www.rotary.org for updated information.

Award: Scholarship for use in junior, senior, or graduate years; not renewable. *Number:* 100–150. *Amount:* $25,000.

Eligibility Requirements: Applicant must be enrolled or expecting to enroll full-time at a four-year institution or university and must have an interest in foreign language.

Application Requirements: Application, autobiography, essay, interview, references, transcript. *Deadline:* varies.

Contact: Scholarship Program
Rotary Foundation of Rotary International
1560 Sherman Avenue
Evanston, IL 60201
Phone: 847-866-4459

SAN ANTONIO INTERNATIONAL PIANO COMPETITION http://www.saipc.org

SAN ANTONIO INTERNATIONAL PIANO COMPETITION

International piano competition for 10 semi-finalists, ages 20-32. Cash awards, ranging from $1000 for 5th prize to $15,000 for 1st prize, are determined through a series of daily concerts, with an additional award for the best performance of a commissioned work. Application fee: $65. Deadline: March 31. Additional awards: $500. Competition held every three years. Applications for the 2006 competition will be available online by September 2005. Details available on Web site: http://www.saipc.org.

Award: Prize for use in freshman, sophomore, junior, senior, graduate, or postgraduate years; not renewable. *Number:* 8. *Amount:* $500–$15,000.

Eligibility Requirements: Applicant must be age 20-32; enrolled or expecting to enroll at an institution or university and must have an interest in music/singing. Available to U.S. and non-U.S. citizens.

Application Requirements: Application, applicant must enter a contest, autobiography, driver's license, photo, portfolio, references, self-addressed stamped envelope, tape recording, certified proof of date of birth, clippings and programs from previous performances. *Fee:* $65. *Deadline:* March 31.

Contact: Ms. Virginia Lawrence, Registrar
San Antonio International Piano Competition
PO Box 39636
San Antonio, TX 78218
Phone: 210-655-0766
Fax: 210-824-5094
E-mail: info@saipc.org

SAN FRANCISCO FOUNDATION http://www.sff.org

JAMES D. PHELAN LITERARY AWARD

Award presented annually to an author of an unpublished work in progress: fiction, nonfiction, prose, poetry, or drama. Must have been born in California, but need not be a current resident. Must be between 20-35 years of age. Submit manuscript. One-time award of $2000. This award is not a scholarship. Applications accepted from November 15 to January 31.

Award: Prize for use in freshman, sophomore, junior, senior, graduate, or postgraduate years; not renewable. *Number:* 1. *Amount:* $2000.

Eligibility Requirements: Applicant must be age 20-35; enrolled or expecting to enroll at an institution or university and must have an interest in writing. Available to U.S. citizens.

Application Requirements: Application, applicant must enter a contest, self-addressed stamped envelope, manuscript. *Deadline:* January 31.

Contact: Awards Coordinator-Literary Awards
San Francisco Foundation
225 Bush Street, Suite 500
San Francisco, CA 94104-4224
Phone: 415-733-8500
E-mail: rec@sff.org

JOSEPH HENRY JACKSON LITERARY AWARD

• *See page 721*

SCIENCE SERVICE, INC. http://www.sciserv.org

DISCOVERY CHANNEL YOUNG SCIENTIST CHALLENGE

Scholarship for students in the fifth through eighth grade to be used for future college enrollment. Must participate in a science fair. For additional information, visit Web site: http://www.discovery.com/dysc

Award: Scholarship for use in freshman year; not renewable. *Number:* up to 40. *Amount:* $500–$15,000.

Eligibility Requirements: Applicant must be enrolled or expecting to enroll full-time at a four-year institution or university and must have an interest in designated field specified by sponsor. Available to U.S. citizens.

Application Requirements: Application, applicant must enter a contest, essay, references. *Deadline:* varies.

Contact: Michele Glidden, DCYSC Program Manager
Science Service, Inc.
1719 N Street, NW
Washington, DC 20036
Phone: 202-785-2255
Fax: 202-785-1243
E-mail: mglidden@sciserv.org

INTEL INTERNATIONAL SCIENCE AND ENGINEERING FAIR

Culminating event in a series of local, regional, and state science fairs. Students in ninth through twelfth grades must compete at local fairs in order to be nominated for international competition. Awards include scholarships. Visit Web site for more information: http://www.sciserv.org.

Award: Scholarship for use in freshman, sophomore, junior, or senior years. *Amount:* $500–$50,000.

Eligibility Requirements: Applicant must be high school student; planning to enroll or expecting to enroll full-time at a four-year institution or university and must have an interest in designated field specified by sponsor. Available to U.S. and non-U.S. citizens.

Science Service, Inc. (continued)

Application Requirements: Application, applicant must enter a contest, essay, interview. *Deadline:* varies.

Contact: Intel ISEF Program Manager
Science Service, Inc.
1719 N Street, NW
Washington, DC 20036
Phone: 202-785-2255
Fax: 202-785-1243

INTEL SCIENCE TALENT SEARCH

Science competition for high school seniors. Students must submit an individually researched project. Forty finalists will be chosen to attend Science Talent Institute in Washington, DC to exhibit their project and compete for $100,000 four-year scholarship. For more information, visit Web site: http://www.sciserv.org

Award: Scholarship for use in freshman, sophomore, junior, or senior years; renewable. *Number:* 40. *Amount:* $5000–$100,000.

Eligibility Requirements: Applicant must be high school student; planning to enroll or expecting to enroll full-time at a four-year institution or university and must have an interest in designated field specified by sponsor. Available to U.S. citizens.

Application Requirements: Application, applicant must enter a contest, essay, references, test scores, transcript. *Deadline:* varies.

Contact: Intel STS Program Manager
Science Service, Inc.
1719 N Street, NW
Washington, DC 20036
Phone: 202-785-2255
Fax: 202-785-1243
E-mail: kstafford@scicerv.org

SEVENTEEN MAGAZINE http://www.seventeen.com

SEVENTEEN MAGAZINE FICTION CONTEST

Applicants must submit original fiction stories of no more than 2000 words typed, double-spaced, single side of paper. Name, address, birth date in upper right corner. One-time award. Applicant must be between 13 and 21 years old, as of July 30. Applicant must apply by mail.

Award: Prize for use in freshman, sophomore, junior, senior, or graduate years; not renewable. *Number:* 8. *Amount:* $50–$1000.

Eligibility Requirements: Applicant must be age 13-21; enrolled or expecting to enroll at an institution or university and must have an interest in writing. Available to U.S. citizens.

Application Requirements: Applicant must enter a contest, copy of story. *Deadline:* July 30.

Contact: Fiction Editor
Seventeen Magazine
1440 Broadway, 13th Floor
New York, NY 10018

SIGMA ALPHA IOTA PHILANTHROPIES, INC. http://www.sai-national.org

INTER-AMERICAN MUSIC AWARD COMPETITION

Prize for best composition for brass quintet, no longer than 10 minutes. Open to any composer (male or female, member or nonmember). Winning composition is premiered at triennial national convention and published. Send manuscript. One-time award of $2000. Application fee: $35.

Award: Prize for use in freshman, sophomore, junior, senior, graduate, or postgraduate years; not renewable. *Number:* 1. *Amount:* $2000.

Eligibility Requirements: Applicant must be enrolled or expecting to enroll at an institution or university and must have an interest in music/singing. Available to U.S. and non-U.S. citizens.

Application Requirements: Application, applicant must enter a contest, self-addressed stamped envelope, manuscript. *Fee:* $35. *Deadline:* May 1.

Contact: Ms. Ruth Sieber Johnson, Executive Director of SAI
Sigma Alpha Iota Philanthropies, Inc.
34 Wall Street, Suite 515
Asheville, NC 28801-2710
Phone: 828-251-0606
Fax: 828-251-0644
E-mail: nh@sai-national.org

SIGMA DELTA CHI FOUNDATION OF WASHINGTON, D.C. http://www.spj.org/washdcpro

SIGMA DELTA CHI SCHOLARSHIPS
• *See page 721*

SINFONIA FOUNDATION http://www.sinfonia.org

SINFONIA FOUNDATION SCHOLARSHIP

Award to assist the collegiate members and chapters of Sinfonia in their endeavors. Must be a collegiate member at least two years. Submit a short essay (250 words or less) on "Sinfonia." Minimum 3.3 cumulative GPA required.

Award: Scholarship for use in sophomore, junior, or senior years; not renewable. *Number:* up to 4. *Amount:* $500.

Eligibility Requirements: Applicant must be enrolled or expecting to enroll at a four-year institution and must have an interest in music.

Application Requirements: Application, essay, references, transcript. *Deadline:* May 1.

Contact: Cheri Spicer, Administrative Coordinator
Sinfonia Foundation
10600 Old State Road
Evansville, IN 47711-1399
Phone: 812-867-2433 Ext. 23
Fax: 812-867-0633

SISTER KENNY REHABILITATION INSTITUTE http://www.sisterkennyinstitute.com

INTERNATIONAL ART SHOW FOR ARTISTS WITH DISABILITIES
• *See page 531*

SOCIETY OF DAUGHTERS OF THE UNITED STATES ARMY

SOCIETY OF DAUGHTERS OF THE UNITED STATES ARMY SCHOLARSHIPS
• *See page 541*

SOUTH DAKOTA BOARD OF REGENTS http://www.ris.sdbor.edu

SOUTH DAKOTA BOARD OF REGENTS MARLIN R. SCARBOROUGH MEMORIAL SCHOLARSHIP
• *See page 723*

SOUTHERN TEXAS PGA http://www.stpga.com/

HARDY LAUDERMILK SCHOLARSHIP
• *See page 724*

JACK HARDEN SCHOLARSHIP
• *See page 724*

NICHOLAS BATTLE SCHOLARSHIP
• *See page 724*

TOMMY AYCOCK SCHOLARSHIPS
• *See page 724*

WARREN SMITH SCHOLARSHIP
• *See page 724*

STONEHOUSE PUBLISHING COMPANY

http://www.stonehousegolf.com

STONEHOUSE GOLF YOUTH SCHOLARSHIP

Twenty scholarships will be awarded based on the criteria of: academics, golf accomplishments, and community service participation. Seniors who have played at least two years on their high school golf team and have earned a GPA of at least 3.5 are eligible to apply. Applicants must participate in the Stonehouse Calendar Fundraiser to be eligible.

Award: Scholarship for use in freshman year; not renewable. *Number:* 20. *Amount:* $500–$10,000.

Eligibility Requirements: Applicant must be high school student; planning to enroll or expecting to enroll full-time at a two-year or four-year institution or university and must have an interest in golf. Applicant must have 3.5 GPA or higher. Available to U.S. citizens.

Application Requirements: Application, references, self-addressed stamped envelope, test scores, transcript. *Deadline:* June 1.

Contact: Patrick Drickey, Program Director
Stonehouse Publishing Company
1508 Leavenworth Street
Omaha, NE 68102
Phone: 402-341-7273
Fax: 402-344-3563
E-mail: pdrickey@stonehousegolf.com

SWISS BENEVOLENT SOCIETY OF NEW YORK

http://www.swissbenevolentny.com

MEDICUS STUDENT EXCHANGE

• *See page 603*

TEXAS TENNIS FOUNDATION

http://texastennisfoundation.com

TEXAS TENNIS FOUNDATION SCHOLARSHIPS AND ENDOWMENTS

• *See page 732*

THE FREEMAN FOUNDATION/INSTITUTE OF INTERNATIONAL EDUCATION

http://www.iie.org/Freeman-ASIA

FREEMAN-ASIA AWARD PROGRAM

Awards to two- or four-year college or university undergraduates in financial need who have been accepted into a study abroad program in one of the following countries or regions: Cambodia, China, Hong-Kong, Indonesia, Japan, Korea, Laos, Macao, Malaysia, Mongolia, Philippines, Singapore, Taiwan, Thailand, Vietnam. Must spend at least 8 weeks in one of the countries and be engaged in intensive language study during that period. Must be U.S. citizen or permanent resident. Complete information, application, and instructions on Web site: http://www.iie.org/programs/.

Award: Grant for use in freshman, sophomore, or junior years; not renewable. *Number:* varies. *Amount:* $3000–$7000.

Eligibility Requirements: Applicant must be enrolled or expecting to enroll full-time at a two-year or four-year institution or university and must have an interest in Asian language or foreign language. Applicant must have 2.5 GPA or higher. Available to U.S. citizens.

Application Requirements: Application, essay, financial need analysis, study abroad adviser endorsement. *Deadline:* varies.

Contact: Program Officer
The Freeman Foundation/Institute of International Education
809 United Nations Plaza
New York, NY 10017-3580
Phone: 212-984-5542
Fax: 212-984-5325
E-mail: freeman-asia@iie.org

TKE EDUCATIONAL FOUNDATION

http://www.tkefoundation.org

ALL-TKE ACADEMIC TEAM RECOGNITION AND JOHN A. COURSON TOP SCHOLAR AWARD

• *See page 481*

CANADIAN TKE SCHOLARSHIP

• *See page 481*

CHARLES WALGREEN, JR. SCHOLARSHIP

• *See page 482*

DONALD A. FISHER MEMORIAL SCHOLARSHIP

• *See page 482*

DWAYNE R. WOERPEL MEMORIAL LEADERSHIP AWARD

• *See page 482*

ELMER AND DORIS SCHMITZ SR. MEMORIAL SCHOLARSHIP

• *See page 482*

EUGENE C. BEACH MEMORIAL SCHOLARSHIP

• *See page 482*

J. RUSSEL SALSBURY MEMORIAL SCHOLARSHIP

• *See page 482*

MICHAEL J. MORIN MEMORIAL SCHOLARSHIP

• *See page 483*

MILES GRAY MEMORIAL SCHOLARSHIP

• *See page 483*

RONALD REAGAN LEADERSHIP AWARD

• *See page 483*

T.J. SCHMITZ SCHOLARSHIP

• *See page 483*

WALLACE MCCAULEY MEMORIAL SCHOLARSHIP

• *See page 483*

WILLIAM V. MUSE SCHOLARSHIP

• *See page 483*

WILLIAM WILSON MEMORIAL SCHOLARSHIP

• *See page 484*

TOURO SYNAGOGUE FOUNDATION

http://www.tourosynagogue.org

AARON AND RITA SLOM SCHOLARSHIP FUND FOR FREEDOM AND DIVERSITY

Scholarship available for high school seniors who plan to enroll in an institute of higher learning for a minimum of 6 credits. Entries should consist of a completed application and an interpretative work focusing on the Historic George Washington Letter to the congregation in context with the present time. Text of the letter is available on our Web site. Submissions may be written: essays, stories, poems; or audio-visual: films, videos, or computer presentations. Applications, guidelines, resource materials are available on Web site: http://www.tourosynagogue.org.

Award: Scholarship for use in freshman year; not renewable. *Number:* 2. *Amount:* $500.

Eligibility Requirements: Applicant must be high school student; planning to enroll or expecting to enroll full or part-time at a two-year or four-year or technical institution or university and must have an interest in writing. Available to U.S. citizens.

Application Requirements: Application, interpretative work based on Historic George Washington Letter. *Deadline:* April 1.

Contact: Application and information at Web site.
Touro Synagogue Foundation
85 Touro Street
Newport, RI 02840
Phone: 401-847-4794 Ext. 14

UNICORN THEATRE

http://www.unicorntheatre.org

NEW PLAY DEVELOPMENT

Prize of $1000 awarded to winning playwright. Winning play produced as part of Unicorn Theatre's next regular season. Submit non-musical, issue-oriented, thought-provoking play set in contemporary (post 1950's) times. Cast limit of 10 actors. Scripts must be original, unpublished, unproduced, typed, and bound. Include cover letter, bio, synopsis, complete character breakdown, and SASE with submission. Response time is four to eight months. Scripts accepted on an ongoing basis; no specific deadline.

Unicorn Theatre (continued)

Award: Prize for use in freshman, sophomore, junior, senior, graduate, or postgraduate years; not renewable. *Number:* 1. *Amount:* $1000.

Eligibility Requirements: Applicant must be enrolled or expecting to enroll at an institution or university and must have an interest in writing. Available to U.S. and non-U.S. citizens.

Application Requirements: Applicant must enter a contest, autobiography, self-addressed stamped envelope. *Deadline:* Continuous.

Contact: Herman Wilson, Literary Assistant
Unicorn Theatre
3828 Main Street
Kansas City, MO 64111
Phone: 816-531-7529 Ext. 15
Fax: 816-531-0421

UNITED NEGRO COLLEGE FUND http://www.uncf.org

MALCOLM X SCHOLARSHIP FOR "EXCEPTIONAL COURAGE"

• *See page 615*

USA TODAY/GOT MILK? http://www.whymilk.com

SCHOLAR ATHLETE MILK MUSTACHE OF THE YEAR

One-time award for senior high school athletes who also achieve in academics, community service, and leadership. Open to legal residents of the 48 contiguous United States and District of Columbia. Residents of Hawaii, Alaska, and Puerto Rico are not eligible. Must submit essay of 75 words, or less on how drinking milk has been a part of their life and training regimen. Application only through Web site: http://www.whymilk.com.

Award: Scholarship for use in freshman year; not renewable. *Number:* 25. *Amount:* $7500.

Eligibility Requirements: Applicant must be high school student; planning to enroll or expecting to enroll full-time at a four-year institution or university and must have an interest in athletics/sports or leadership. Available to U.S. citizens.

Application Requirements: Application, applicant must enter a contest, essay, references, transcript. *Deadline:* March 4.

Contact: Application and information on Web site.
USA Today/Got Milk?
6701 Democracy Boulevard, Suite 300
Bethesda, MD 20817

VERMONT GOLF ASSOCIATION

VERMONT GOLF SCHOLARSHIP FOUNDATION, INC.

• *See page 737*

VSA ARTS http://www.vsarts.org

VSA ARTS PLAYWRIGHT DISCOVERY AWARD

One-time award for students in grades 6-12 with and without disabilities. One-act script must explore the experience of living with a disability. One script is selected for production and one is selected for a staged reading at the John F. Kennedy Center for the Performing Arts. A jury of theater professionals selects the winning scripts, and award recipients receive monetary awards and a trip to Washington, D.C. to view the reading or production. Contact Elena Widder at VSA arts for information and application materials. (TTY) 202-737-0645.

Award: Scholarship for use in freshman year; not renewable. *Number:* 2. *Amount:* $1000.

Eligibility Requirements: Applicant must be enrolled or expecting to enroll at an institution or university and must have an interest in writing. Available to U.S. citizens.

Application Requirements: Application, applicant must enter a contest, autobiography, two copies of typed script. *Deadline:* April 15.

Contact: Elena Widder, Director of Performing Arts
VSA arts
1300 Connecticut Avenue, NW, Suite 700
Washington, DC 20036
Phone: 800-933-8721
Fax: 202-737-0725

W. EUGENE SMITH MEMORIAL FUND, INC. http://www.smithfund.org

W. EUGENE SMITH GRANT IN HUMANISTIC PHOTOGRAPHY

One-time award for a photojournalist whose past work and proposed project follows the humanistic tradition of W. Eugene Smith. Financed by Nikon, Inc.

Award: Grant for use in junior, senior, graduate, or postgraduate years; not renewable. *Number:* varies. *Amount:* $2500–$30,000.

Eligibility Requirements: Applicant must be enrolled or expecting to enroll at an institution or university and must have an interest in photography/photogrammetry/filmmaking. Available to U.S. and non-U.S. citizens.

Application Requirements: Application, essay, portfolio, resume, self-addressed stamped envelope. *Deadline:* July 15.

Contact: Suzanne Nicholas, c/o ICP
W. Eugene Smith Memorial Fund, Inc.
1133 Avenue of Americas
New York, NY 10036
Phone: 212-857

WAGNER COLLEGE THEATRE, STANLEY DRAMA AWARD http://www.wagner.edu/stanleydrama.html

STANLEY DRAMA AWARD

Offered to winner of play writing competition. A full-length play or musical which has not been professionally produced or received book publication. For guidelines, send SASE. Deadline for entry, October 1. Winner selected the following March.

Award: Prize for use in freshman, sophomore, junior, senior, graduate, or postgraduate years; not renewable. *Number:* 1. *Amount:* $2000.

Eligibility Requirements: Applicant must be enrolled or expecting to enroll full or part-time at an institution or university and must have an interest in writing. Available to U.S. citizens.

Application Requirements: Self-addressed stamped envelope. *Deadline:* October 1.

Contact: Shannon Davis, Administrator
Wagner College Theatre, Stanley Drama Award
One Campus Road
Staten Island, NY 10301
Phone: 718-420-4036
Fax: 718-390-3323
E-mail: sdavis@wagner.edu

WASHINGTON CROSSING FOUNDATION http://www.gwcf.org

WASHINGTON CROSSING FOUNDATION SCHOLARSHIP

Renewable, merit-based awards available to high school seniors who are planning a career in government service. Must write an essay stating reason for deciding on a career in public service. Minimum 3.0 GPA required. Write for details.

Award: Scholarship for use in freshman, sophomore, junior, or senior years; renewable. *Number:* 5–10. *Amount:* $1000–$20,000.

Eligibility Requirements: Applicant must be high school student; planning to enroll or expecting to enroll full-time at a four-year institution and must have an interest in designated field specified by sponsor. Applicant must have 3.0 GPA or higher. Available to U.S. citizens.

Application Requirements: Application, essay, references, test scores, transcript. *Deadline:* January 15.

Contact: Eugene Fish, Vice Chairman
Washington Crossing Foundation
PO Box 503
Levittown, PA 19058-0503
Phone: 215-949-8841

WELSH SOCIETY OF PHILADELPHIA

CYMDEITHAS GYMREIG/PHILADELPHIA SCHOLARSHIP

• *See page 623*

WHOMENTORS.COM, INC. http://www.WHOmentors.com

GENERATION "E" GRANTS AND SCHOLARSHIPS

Five awards of $10,000 to encourage both full-time and part-time students of at least 21 years of age to obtain formal mentor education and competency certification and to seek designation as an appointed mentor. Applicants should have a specific interest in mentoring. Contact for further information.

Award: Grant for use in freshman, sophomore, junior, senior, or graduate years; not renewable. *Number:* 5. *Amount:* $10,000.

Eligibility Requirements: Applicant must be age 21; enrolled or expecting to enroll full or part-time at an institution or university and must have an interest in designated field specified by sponsor.

Application Requirements: Application, autobiography, interview, photo, self-addressed stamped envelope, test scores, transcript. *Deadline:* May 31.

Contact: Rauhmel Fox Robinson, President and CEO
WHOmentors.com, Inc.
110 Pacific Avenue, Suite 250
San Francisco, CA 94111
Phone: 888-946-6368
E-mail: rauhmel@whomentors.com

WILLIAM RANDOLPH HEARST FOUNDATION http://www.ussenateyouth.org

UNITED STATES SENATE YOUTH PROGRAM

For high school juniors and seniors holding elected student offices. Must attend high school in state of parents' or guardians' legal residence. Two students selected from each state and the selection process will vary by state. Contact school principal or state department of education for information. Application deadline is in the early fall of each year for most states but the actual date will vary by state. Program is open to citizens and permanent residents of the United States Department of Defense schools overseas and the District of Columbia (not the territories). More information at Web site: http://www.ussenateyouth.org.

Award: Scholarship for use in freshman, sophomore, junior, or senior years; not renewable. *Number:* 104. *Amount:* $5000.

Eligibility Requirements: Applicant must be high school student; planning to enroll or expecting to enroll full or part-time at a two-year or four-year or technical institution or university and must have an interest in leadership. Available to U.S. citizens.

Application Requirements: Application procedures will vary by state. *Deadline:* varies.

Contact: Ms. Rita Almon, Program Director
William Randolph Hearst Foundation
90 New Montgomery Street, Suite 1212
San Francisco, CA 94105-4504
Phone: 800-841-7048
Fax: 415-243-0760
E-mail: ussyp@hearstfdn.org

WOMEN'S BASKETBALL COACHES ASSOCIATION http://www.wbca.org

WBCA SCHOLARSHIP AWARD

One-time award for two women's basketball players who have demonstrated outstanding commitment to the sport of women's basketball and to academic excellence. Minimum 3.5 GPA required. Must be nominated by the head coach of women's basketball who is a member of the WBCA.

Award: Scholarship for use in senior, graduate, or postgraduate years; not renewable. *Number:* 2. *Amount:* $1000.

Eligibility Requirements: Applicant must be enrolled or expecting to enroll full or part-time at a four-year or technical institution or university; female and must have an interest in athletics/sports. Applicant must have 3.5 GPA or higher. Available to U.S. and non-U.S. citizens.

Application Requirements: Application, references, statistics. *Deadline:* February 7.

Contact: Kristen Miller, Manager of Office Administration and Awards
Women's Basketball Coaches Association
4646 Lawrenceville Highway
Lilburn, GA 30247-3620
Phone: 770-279-8027 Ext. 102
Fax: 770-279-6290
E-mail: kmiller@wbca.org

WOMEN'S INTERNATIONAL BOWLING CONGRESS http://www.bowl.com

ALBERTA E. CROWE STAR OF TOMORROW AWARD

• *See page 489*

WOMEN'S SPORTS FOUNDATION http://www.womenssportsfoundation.org

TRAVEL AND TRAINING FUND

Award to provide financial assistance to aspiring female athletes with successful competitive regional or national records who have the potential to achieve even higher performance levels and rankings. Must be a U.S. citizen or legal resident.

Award: Grant for use in freshman, sophomore, junior, or senior years; not renewable. *Number:* 25–100. *Amount:* $500–$4000.

Eligibility Requirements: Applicant must be enrolled or expecting to enroll full or part-time at an institution or university; female and must have an interest in athletics/sports. Available to U.S. citizens.

Application Requirements: Application, references. *Deadline:* December 31.

Contact: Women's Sports Foundation
Eisenhower Park
East Meadow, NY 11554
Phone: 800-227-3988
E-mail: wosport@aol.com

WOMEN'S WESTERN GOLF FOUNDATION

WOMEN'S WESTERN GOLF FOUNDATION SCHOLARSHIP

Scholarships for female high school seniors for use at a four-year college or university. Based on academic record, financial need, character, and involvement in golf. (Golf skill not a criterion.) Twenty awards annually for incoming freshmen; approximately 60 scholarships renewed. Must maintain 2.5 GPA as freshman; 3.0 upperclassman GPA. Must continue to have financial need. Award is $2000 per student per year. Applicant must be 17-18 years of age.

Award: Scholarship for use in freshman, sophomore, junior, or senior years; renewable. *Number:* up to 80. *Amount:* $2000.

Eligibility Requirements: Applicant must be high school student; age 17-18; planning to enroll or expecting to enroll full-time at a four-year institution or university; female and must have an interest in golf. Available to U.S. citizens.

Application Requirements: Application, essay, financial need analysis, self-addressed stamped envelope, test scores, transcript. *Deadline:* April 5.

Contact: Mrs. Richard Willis, Scholarship Chairman
Women's Western Golf Foundation
393 Ramsay Road
Deerfield, IL 60015

WRITER'S DIGEST http://www.writersdigest.com

WRITER'S DIGEST ANNUAL WRITING COMPETITION

Annual writing competition. Only original, unpublished entries in any of the ten categories. Send self-addressed stamped envelope for guidelines and entry form. Deadline is May 15. Application fee: $15.

Award: Prize for use in freshman, sophomore, junior, senior, or graduate years; not renewable. *Number:* 1001. *Amount:* $25–$1500.

Eligibility Requirements: Applicant must be enrolled or expecting to enroll full or part-time at a two-year or four-year or technical institution or university and must have an interest in writing. Available to U.S. and non-U.S. citizens.

Writer's Digest (continued)

Application Requirements: Application, applicant must enter a contest, self-addressed stamped envelope. *Fee:* $15. *Deadline:* May 15.

Contact: Terri Boes, Customer Service Representative
Writer's Digest
4700 East Galbraith Road
Cincinnati, OH 45236
Phone: 513-531-2690 Ext. 1328
Fax: 513-531-0798
E-mail: competitions@fwpubs.com

WRITER'S DIGEST SELF-PUBLISHED BOOK AWARDS

Awards open to self-published books for which the author has paid full cost. Send self-addressed stamped envelope for guidelines and entry form. Deadline is December 15. Application fee: $100.

Award: Prize for use in freshman, sophomore, junior, senior, graduate, or postgraduate years; not renewable. *Number:* 10. *Amount:* $500–$3000.

Eligibility Requirements: Applicant must be enrolled or expecting to enroll full or part-time at a two-year or four-year or technical institution or university and must have an interest in writing. Available to U.S. and non-U.S. citizens.

Application Requirements: Application, applicant must enter a contest, self-addressed stamped envelope. *Fee:* $100. *Deadline:* December 15.

Contact: Terri Boes, Customer Service Representative
Writer's Digest
4700 East Galbraith Road
Cincinnati, OH 45236
Phone: 513-531-2690 Ext. 1328
Fax: 513-531-0798
E-mail: competitions@fwpubs.com

WRITER'S DIGEST SHORT STORY COMPETITION

Awards open to short stories that are 1500 words or less. Send self-addressed stamped envelope for guidelines and entry form. Deadline is December 1. Application fee: $10 per manuscript.

Award: Prize for use in freshman, sophomore, junior, senior, graduate, or postgraduate years; not renewable. *Number:* 10. *Amount:* $100–$2000.

Eligibility Requirements: Applicant must be enrolled or expecting to enroll full or part-time at a two-year or four-year or technical institution or university and must have an interest in writing. Available to U.S. and non-U.S. citizens.

Application Requirements: Application, applicant must enter a contest, self-addressed stamped envelope. *Fee:* $10. *Deadline:* December 1.

Contact: Terri Boes, Customer Service Representative
Writer's Digest
4700 East Galbraith Road
Cincinnati, OH 45236
Phone: 513-531-2690 Ext. 1328
Fax: 513-531-0798
E-mail: competitions@fwpubs.com

Y'S MEN INTERNATIONAL http://www.ysmenusa.com

ALEXANDER SCHOLARSHIP LOAN FUND

The purpose of the Alexander Scholarship Loan Fund is to promote the training of staff of the YMCA and/or those seeking to become members of staff of the YMCA. Must include $1 for postage and handling. Loan is forgiven if recipient enters YMCA employment after graduation. Please refer to Web site for further details: http://www.ysmenusa.com

Award: Forgivable loan for use in freshman, sophomore, junior, or senior years; renewable. *Number:* varies.

Eligibility Requirements: Applicant must be enrolled or expecting to enroll full or part-time at a two-year or four-year institution or university and must have an interest in designated field specified by sponsor. Available to U.S. citizens.

Application Requirements: Application. *Fee:* $1. *Deadline:* varies.

Contact: Dean Currie, U.S. Area Service Director
Y's Men International
629 Lantana Lane
Imperial, CA 92251
Fax: 602-935-6322

YALE UNIVERSITY PRESS http://www.yale.edu/yup

YALE SERIES OF YOUNGER POETS

Each year Yale University Press seeks one new book of poetry to be published in the Yale Series of Younger Poets. The competition is open to any U.S. citizen under 40 years of age who has not previously published a book of poetry. Application fee: $15. Deadline: October 1 to November 15. No cash award. Monies come from royalties.

Award: Prize for use in freshman, sophomore, junior, senior, graduate, or postgraduate years; not renewable. *Number:* 1. *Amount:* varies.

Eligibility Requirements: Applicant must be age 39 or under; enrolled or expecting to enroll at an institution or university and must have an interest in designated field specified by sponsor. Available to U.S. citizens.

Application Requirements: Applicant must enter a contest, self-addressed stamped envelope. *Fee:* $15. *Deadline:* varies.

Contact: John Kulka, Series Editor
Yale University Press
PO Box 209040
New Haven, CT 06520
Phone: 203-432-6807
E-mail: yup@yalepress3.unipress.yale.edu

YES I CAN! FOUNDATION http://www.yesican.org

STANLEY E. JACKSON SCHOLARSHIP AWARDS

• *See page 533*

YOUNG AMERICAN BOWLING ALLIANCE (YABA) http://www.bowl.com

GIFT FOR LIFE SCHOLARSHIP

• *See page 490*

PEPSI-COLA YOUTH BOWLING CHAMPIONSHIPS

• *See page 490*

YOUTH OPPORTUNITIES FOUNDATION

YOUTH OPPORTUNITIES FOUNDATION SCHOLARSHIPS

• *See page 624*

MISCELLANEOUS CRITERIA

AAA http://www.aaa.com/travelchallenge

AAA HIGH SCHOOL TRAVEL CHALLENGE

Students have the opportunity to compete for more than $100,000 in scholarship money, including $25,000 scholarships to the top three finishers and $10,000 scholarships to three runners-up. Each will receive an expense-paid trip to Universal Orlando, with chaperone, to participate in the national contest.

Award: Scholarship for use in freshman year; not renewable. *Number:* 8. *Amount:* $500–$25,000.

Eligibility Requirements: Applicant must be high school student; age 13-18 and planning to enroll or expecting to enroll full or part-time at a two-year or four-year or technical institution or university. Available to U.S. citizens.

Application Requirements: Application, applicant must enter a contest, online application/test. *Deadline:* January 19.

Contact: AAA
c/o Curley and Pynn
801 North Magnolia Avenue, Suite 210
Orlando, FL 32803
E-mail: aaatravelchallenge@national.aaa.com

AKADEMOS, INC. http://www.textbookx.com

TEXTBOOKX.COM SPRING SCHOLARSHIP

Students must write an essay and reference one book on the assigned topic. The current essay question is "How has the technology of the past 20 years affected the relationship between the individual and society?" Essay must be between 250 and 750 words. One grand prize winner is selected and two runners-up.

Award: Scholarship for use in freshman, sophomore, junior, or senior years; not renewable. *Number:* up to 3. *Amount:* $250–$2000.

Eligibility Requirements: Applicant must be high school student and planning to enroll or expecting to enroll full or part-time at a four-year institution or university. Available to U.S. citizens.

Application Requirements: Application, applicant must enter a contest, essay. *Deadline:* April 30.

Contact: Customer Service Representative
Akademos, Inc.
25 Van Zant Street, Suite 12
Norwalk, CT 06855
Phone: 800-221-8480
Fax: 203-866-0199
E-mail: info@akademos.com

ALASKA POLICE CORPS http://www.uaf.edu/akcorps

ALASKA POLICE CORPS SCHOLARSHIP

College seniors or graduates are eligible for reimbursement of educational expenses. Must complete training academy and agree to four-year work commitment at a participating Alaska law enforcement agency. Check Web site for specific details: http://www.uaf.edu/akcorps.

Award: Scholarship for use in senior year. *Number:* 10. *Amount:* up to $23,000.

Eligibility Requirements: Applicant must be enrolled or expecting to enroll at a four-year institution or university. Applicant must have 2.5 GPA or higher. Available to U.S. citizens.

Application Requirements: Application, driver's license, essay, references, transcript. *Deadline:* Continuous.

Contact: Dan Hoffman
Alaska Police Corps
800 Cushman Street
Fairbanks, AK 99701
Phone: 800-221-0083
Fax: 907-459-6767
E-mail: dphoffman@ci.fairbanks.ak.us

ALBERTA HERITAGE SCHOLARSHIP FUND/ ALBERTA SCHOLARSHIP PROGRAMS http://www.alis.gov.ab.ca/scholarships

INTERNATIONAL EDUCATION AWARDS–UKRAINE

Awards of $5000 CAN are available for students taking a practicum, internship, co-op, or apprenticeship program. Students must be from Ukraine and studying in Alberta or from Alberta and studying in Ukraine. One-term research projects may also be considered. Application deadline is November 1.

Award: Scholarship for use in freshman, sophomore, junior, or senior years. *Number:* 5. *Amount:* $4095.

Eligibility Requirements: Applicant must be enrolled or expecting to enroll at a four-year institution or university.

Application Requirements: Application. *Deadline:* November 1.

Contact: Director
Alberta Heritage Scholarship Fund/Alberta Scholarship Programs
9940 106th Street, 9th Floor
Box 28000, Station Main
Edmonton, AB T5J 4R4
Canada
Phone: 780-427-8640
Fax: 780-422-4516
E-mail: heritage@gov.ab.ca

QUEEN ELIZABETH II GOLDEN JUBILEE CITIZENSHIP MEDAL

• *See page 575*

ALL-INK.COM PRINTER SUPPLIES ONLINE http://www.all-ink.com/scholarship.html

ALL-INK.COM COLLEGE SCHOLARSHIP PROGRAM

One-time award for any level of postsecondary education. Minimum 2.5 GPA. Must apply online only at Web site http://www.all-ink.com. Recipients selected annually. Application deadline is December 31.

Award: Scholarship for use in freshman, sophomore, junior, senior, graduate, or postgraduate years; not renewable. *Number:* 5–10. *Amount:* $1000–$2500.

Eligibility Requirements: Applicant must be enrolled or expecting to enroll full-time at a two-year or four-year or technical institution or university. Applicant must have 2.5 GPA or higher. Available to U.S. citizens.

Application Requirements: Application. *Deadline:* December 31.

Contact: Application available at Web site.

ALPHA KAPPA ALPHA EDUCATIONAL ADVANCEMENT FOUNDATION, INC. http://www.akaeaf.org

ALPHA KAPPA ALPHA SORORITY, INC. FINANCIAL ASSISTANCE SCHOLARSHIPS

Scholarships available to undergraduate students, sophomore or beyond, who are currently enrolled in an accredited institution. May be a degree granting

Alpha Kappa Alpha Educational Advancement Foundation, Inc. (continued)

institution or a non-institutional based program that may or may not grant degrees. Additional information and all inquiries must be obtained via Web site only: http://www.akaeaf.org.

Award: Scholarship for use in sophomore, junior, senior, or graduate years; not renewable. *Number:* varies. *Amount:* up to $1500.

Eligibility Requirements: Applicant must be enrolled or expecting to enroll at a two-year or four-year or technical institution or university. Applicant must have 2.5 GPA or higher. Available to U.S. citizens.

Application Requirements: Application, financial need analysis, references, transcript. *Deadline:* January 15.

Contact: AKA-EAF
Alpha Kappa Alpha Educational Advancement Foundation, Inc.
5656 South Stony Island Avenue
Chicago, IL 60637

ALPHA KAPPA ALPHA SORORITY, INC. MERIT SCHOLARSHIP

Scholarships available for students currently enrolled with sophomore through graduate school standing at an accredited institution. Must have a minimum 3.0 GPA and have demonstrated community service and involvement. Additional information and all inquiries must be obtained via Web site only. http://www.akaeaf.org.

Award: Scholarship for use in sophomore, junior, senior, or graduate years; not renewable. *Number:* varies. *Amount:* $1000.

Eligibility Requirements: Applicant must be enrolled or expecting to enroll at a four-year institution or university. Applicant must have 3.0 GPA or higher. Available to U.S. citizens.

Application Requirements: Application, financial need analysis, references, transcript. *Deadline:* January 15.

Contact: AKA-EAF
Alpha Kappa Alpha Educational Advancement Foundation, Inc.
5656 South Stony Island Avenue
Chicago, IL 60637

ALPHA LAMBDA DELTA http://www.mercer.edu/ald/trow_scholarship.htm

JO ANNE J. TROW SCHOLARSHIPS

One-time award for initiated members of Alpha Lambda Delta. Minimum 3.5 GPA required. Must be nominated by chapter.

Award: Scholarship for use in junior year; not renewable. *Number:* up to 35. *Amount:* $1000.

Eligibility Requirements: Applicant must be enrolled or expecting to enroll full-time at a four-year institution. Applicant must have 3.5 GPA or higher. Available to U.S. and non-U.S. citizens.

Application Requirements: Application, essay, references, transcript. *Deadline:* May 1.

Contact: Dr. Glenda Earwood Smith, Executive Director
Alpha Lambda Delta
PO Box 4403
Macon, GA 31208-4403
Phone: 478-744-9595
Fax: 478-744-9929
E-mail: ald@mercer.edu

AMERICA'S HIGHSCHOOL IDOL http://www.americashighschoolidol.com

AMERICA'S HIGHSCHOOL IDOL

Scholarship awarded in competition for most talented singer. Competitors must maintain a 2.0 GPA. Please see Web site for more information and application. Applications accepted via Web Site submission only. http://www.americashighschoolidol.com

Award: Scholarship for use in freshman year; not renewable. *Number:* 1–50. *Amount:* $500–$10,000.

Eligibility Requirements: Applicant must be high school student; age 14-18; planning to enroll or expecting to enroll full-time at a four-year institution or university and single. Available to U.S. citizens.

Application Requirements: Application, driver's license, financial need analysis, photo, transcript, if no driver's license, supply another form of ID. *Fee:* $25. *Deadline:* February 1.

Contact: See Web site: www.americashighschoolidol.com.
America's Highschool Idol
7320 Memo Place
Baton Rouge, LA 70817

AMERICA'S JUNIOR MISS SCHOLARSHIP PROGRAM http://www.ajm.org

AMERICA'S JUNIOR MISS SCHOLARSHIP PROGRAM

Awards are given to contestants in local, regional and national levels of competition. Contestants must be female, high school juniors or seniors, U.S. citizens and legal residents of the county and state of competition. Contestants are evaluated on scholastics, interview, talent, fitness and poise. The number of awards and their amount vary from year to year. For more information visit http://www.ajm.org.

Award: Scholarship for use in freshman, sophomore, junior, or senior years; not renewable. *Number:* varies. *Amount:* varies.

Eligibility Requirements: Applicant must be high school student; age 16-18; planning to enroll or expecting to enroll full-time at a two-year or four-year institution or university and single female. Available to U.S. citizens.

Application Requirements: Application, applicant must enter a contest, test scores, transcript, birth certificate, certificate of health. *Deadline:* Continuous.

Contact: Contestant Inquiries
America's Junior Miss Scholarship Program
751 Government Street
PO Box 2786
Mobile, AL 36652-2786

AMERICAN ASSOCIATION OF SCHOOL ADMINISTRATORS/DISCOVER CARD TRIBUTE AWARD PROGRAM http://www.aasa.org/discover.htm

DISCOVER CARD TRIBUTE AWARD SCHOLARSHIP PROGRAM

Applicants should be current high school juniors with minimum 2.75 GPA. Nine scholarships available in each state and Washington, D.C. Nine $25,000 awards at the national level in three categories. Must plan to further education beyond high school in any accredited certification, licensing or training program or institution of higher education. Must demonstrate outstanding accomplishments in three areas: special talents, leadership, and community service and have faced a significant roadblock(s) or challenge(s). Visit Web site for application and more information: http://www.aasa.org/discover.htm

Award: Scholarship for use in freshman year; not renewable. *Number:* up to 478. *Amount:* $2500–$25,000.

Eligibility Requirements: Applicant must be high school student and planning to enroll or expecting to enroll full or part-time at a two-year or four-year or technical institution or university. Available to U.S. and non-U.S. citizens.

Application Requirements: Application, essay, references, transcript. *Deadline:* varies.

Contact: Program Director
American Association of School Administrators/Discover Card Tribute Award Program
PO Box 9338
Arlington, VA 22219
Phone: 703-875-0708
E-mail: tributeaward@aasa.org

AMERICAN ASSOCIATION OF UNIVERSITY WOMEN-HONOLULU BRANCH

AMERICAN ASSOCIATION OF UNIVERSITY WOMEN - AVIAETRIC FUND

Scholarships for junior and senior undergraduate, graduate and post-graduate women. Must be studying full-time at a four-year college or university.

Award: Scholarship for use in junior, senior, graduate, or postgraduate years; not renewable. *Number:* varies. *Amount:* $100–$2500.

Eligibility Requirements: Applicant must be enrolled or expecting to enroll full-time at a four-year institution or university and female. Available to U.S. and Canadian citizens.

Application Requirements: Application, financial need analysis, references, self-addressed stamped envelope, test scores, transcript. *Deadline:* varies.

Contact: Dr. Sarah Vann
American Association of University Women-Honolulu Branch
1802 Keeaumoku Street
Honolulu, HI 96822

AMERICAN ASSOCIATION OF UNIVERSITY WOMEN - BLACKWELL FUND

Scholarships for junior and senior undergraduate, graduate and post-graduate women. Must be studying full-time at a four-year college or university.

Award: Scholarship for use in junior, senior, graduate, or postgraduate years; not renewable. *Number:* varies. *Amount:* $100–$2500.

Eligibility Requirements: Applicant must be enrolled or expecting to enroll full-time at a four-year institution or university and female. Available to U.S. and Canadian citizens.

Application Requirements: Application, financial need analysis, references, self-addressed stamped envelope, test scores, transcript. *Deadline:* varies.

Contact: Dr. Sarah Vann
American Association of University Women-Honolulu Branch
1802 Keeaumoku Street
Honolulu, HI 96822

AMERICAN FIRE SPRINKLER ASSOCIATION http://www.sprinklernet.org

NATIONAL SCHOLARSHIP CONTEST

One-time award; applicants must be high school seniors. Must submit essay, application and recommendation. Not based on financial need or GPA. Please visit Web site for essay topic and to apply: http://www.afsascholarship.org.

Award: Scholarship for use in freshman year; not renewable. *Number:* 7. *Amount:* $1000–$4000.

Eligibility Requirements: Applicant must be high school student and planning to enroll or expecting to enroll full or part-time at a two-year or four-year or technical institution or university. Available to U.S. citizens.

Application Requirements: Application, essay, references. *Deadline:* varies.

Contact: Application available at Web site.

AMERICAN FOUNDATION FOR TRANSLATION AND INTERPRETATION http://www.afti.org

AFTI SCHOLARSHIPS IN SCIENTIFIC AND TECHNICAL TRANSLATION, LITERARY TRANSLATION, AND INTERPRETATION

AFTI annually offers academic year scholarships for full-time students enrolled or planning to enroll in a degree program in scientific and technical translation, literary translation, or interpreter training. Must have a 3.0 GPA. Application deadline is June 1.

Award: Scholarship for use in sophomore, junior, senior, or graduate years; not renewable. *Number:* 1–2. *Amount:* $2500.

Eligibility Requirements: Applicant must be enrolled or expecting to enroll full-time at a four-year institution or university. Applicant must have 3.0 GPA or higher. Available to U.S. citizens.

Application Requirements: Application, essay, references, transcript, admission to T/I program. *Deadline:* June 1.

Contact: Eleanor Krawutschke, Executive Director, AFTI
American Foundation for Translation and Interpretation
Columbia Plaza-Suite 101, 350 East Michigan Avenue
Kalamazoo, MI 49007
Phone: 269-383-6893
E-mail: aftiorg@aol.com

AMERICAN GI FORUM OF THE UNITED STATES http://www.agif.us/

AMERICAN GI FORUM OF THE UNITED STATES HISPANIC EDUCATION FOUNDATION MATCHING SCHOLARSHIPS

Renewable scholarship of up to $1000. Not restricted to, but priority given to Hispanics. Priority may be given to veterans and their families. Please contact local American GI Forum chapters for qualifications and deadline dates.

Award: Scholarship for use in freshman, sophomore, junior, senior, graduate, or postgraduate years; renewable. *Number:* 50–200. *Amount:* $250–$1000.

Eligibility Requirements: Applicant must be enrolled or expecting to enroll full or part-time at a two-year or four-year or technical institution or university. Available to U.S. and non-U.S. citizens.

Application Requirements: Application, autobiography, financial need analysis, references, self-addressed stamped envelope, test scores, transcript. *Deadline:* varies.

Contact: Local American GI Forum
American GI Forum of the United States
Attn: Hispanic Education Foundation
PO Box 952
Ulysses, KS 67880

AMERICAN INSTITUTE FOR FOREIGN STUDY http://www.aifsabroad.com

STUDY AGAIN SCHOLARSHIPS

If you studied abroad on an AIFS summer program, you will receive a $1,500 scholarship to study abroad on an AIFS semester or academic year program. If you studied abroad on an AFIS semester or academic year program, you will receive a $500 scholarship towards a four or five week summer program, or a $750 scholarship towards a summer program of six weeks or more.

Award: Scholarship for use in freshman, sophomore, junior, or senior years; not renewable. *Number:* varies. *Amount:* $500–$750.

Eligibility Requirements: Applicant must be enrolled or expecting to enroll full-time at a two-year or four-year institution or university. Applicant must have 2.5 GPA or higher. Available to U.S. and non-U.S. citizens.

Application Requirements: Application, essay, photo, references, transcript, previously studied abroad with AIFS. *Fee:* $75. *Deadline:* varies.

Contact: David Mauro, Admissions Counselor
American Institute for Foreign Study
River Plaza
9 West Broad Street
Stamford, CT 06902-3788
Phone: 203-399-5163
Fax: 203-399-5598
E-mail: college.info@aifs.com

AMERICAN JEWISH LEAGUE FOR ISRAEL http://www.americanjewishleague.org

AMERICAN JEWISH LEAGUE FOR ISRAEL SCHOLARSHIP PROGRAM

The AJLI Scholarship Program provides support with tuition for a full year of study (September-May) at one of seven universities in Israel; Bar Ilan, Ben Gurion, Haifa, Hebrew, Tel Aviv, Technion, and Weizmann. Additional information is available on Web site: http://www.americanjewishleague.org. Deadline is May 1.

Award: Scholarship for use in freshman, sophomore, junior, senior, graduate, or postgraduate years; not renewable. *Number:* 3–10. *Amount:* $2000.

Eligibility Requirements: Applicant must be enrolled or expecting to enroll full-time at an institution or university. Available to U.S. citizens.

Application Requirements: Application, transcript. *Deadline:* May 1.

Contact: Jeff Scheckner, Executive Director
American Jewish League for Israel
450 7th Avenue, Suite 808
New York, NY 10123
Phone: 212-371-1583
Fax: 212-279-1456
E-mail: ajlijms@aol.com

AMERICAN NATIONAL CATTLEWOMEN, INC. http://www.ancw.org

NATIONAL BEEF AMBASSADOR PROGRAM

Award's purpose is to train young spokespersons in the beef industry. Applicant must be fully prepared to answer questions and debate focusing on topic related to beef consumption and distribution, as well as social factors related to the industry. Details and tools for preparation are available on the Web site: http://www.ancw.org

Award: Prize for use in freshman year; not renewable. *Number:* 1–3. *Amount:* $800–$2500.

Eligibility Requirements: Applicant must be high school student; age 16-19 and planning to enroll or expecting to enroll at an institution or university. Available to U.S. citizens.

Application Requirements: Applicant must enter a contest. *Deadline:* August 13.

Contact: See Web site.

AMERICAN ROAD & TRANSPORTATION BUILDERS ASSOCIATION-TRANSPORTATION DEVELOPMENT FOUNDATION (ARTBA-TDF) http://www.artba.org

ARTBA-TDF HIGHWAY WORKERS MEMORIAL SCHOLARSHIP PROGRAM

The ARTBA-TDF Highway Worker Memorial Scholarship Program provides financial assistance to help the sons, daughters or legally adopted children of highway workers killed or permanently disabled in the line of duty pursue post-high school education. Minimum 2.5 GPA required.

Award: Scholarship for use in freshman, sophomore, junior, senior, or graduate years; not renewable. *Number:* varies. *Amount:* $1000–$2500.

Eligibility Requirements: Applicant must be enrolled or expecting to enroll full or part-time at a two-year or four-year or technical institution or university. Applicant must have 2.5 GPA or higher. Available to U.S. citizens.

Application Requirements: Application, essay, financial need analysis, photo, references, transcript. *Deadline:* March 1.

Contact: Rhonda Haskins, Awards and Scholarship Program Manager
American Road & Transportation Builders Association-Transportation Development Foundation (ARTBA-TDF)
1010 Massachusetts Avenue, NW
Washington, DC 20001-5402
Phone: 202-289-4434 Ext. 124
Fax: 202-289-4435
E-mail: rhaskins@artba.org

AMERICAN SOCIETY OF MECHANICAL ENGINEERS (ASME INTERNATIONAL) http://www.asme.org/education/enged/aid

AMERICAN SOCIETY OF MECHANICAL ENGINEERS STEPHEN T. KUGLE SCHOLARSHIP

Scholarship available to an ASME member attending a public college in ASME Region 10. Must be a U.S. citizen and have a 3.0 minimum GPA. For study in the junior and senior year.

Award: Scholarship for use in junior or senior years. *Number:* 1. *Amount:* $2000.

Eligibility Requirements: Applicant must be enrolled or expecting to enroll at an institution or university. Applicant must have 3.0 GPA or higher. Available to U.S. citizens.

Application Requirements: Application, transcript. *Deadline:* March 15.

Contact: Theresa Oluwanifise, Administrative Assistant
American Society of Mechanical Engineers (ASME International)
3 Park Avenue
New York, NY 10016
Phone: 212-591-8131
Fax: 212-591-7143
E-mail: oluwanifiset@asme.org

AMERICAN WELDING SOCIETY http://www.aws.org/foundation

JERRY ROBINSON-INWELD CORPORATION SCHOLARSHIP

Awarded to a student with significant financial need interested in pursuing a career in welding. Applicant must have a 2.5 overall grade point average. Applicant must be 18 years of age by October 1 of the year the scholarship is awarded. Must be U.S. citizen.

Award: Scholarship for use in freshman, sophomore, junior, or senior years; not renewable. *Number:* 1. *Amount:* $2500.

Eligibility Requirements: Applicant must be age 18 and enrolled or expecting to enroll full-time at a four-year institution. Applicant must have 2.5 GPA or higher. Available to U.S. citizens.

Application Requirements: Application, autobiography, essay, financial need analysis, photo, references, transcript. *Deadline:* January 15.

Contact: Ms. Neida Herrera, Development Coordinator
American Welding Society
550 Northwest Le Jeune Road
Miami, FL 33126
Phone: 305-443-9353 Ext. 461
Fax: 305-443-7559
E-mail: neida@aws.org

ARIZONA POLICE CORPS http://www.azpolicecorps.com/

ARIZONA POLICE CORPS SCHOLARSHIP

Scholarships available for full-time undergraduate students and part-time graduate students. Must complete police training academy and agree to a four year employment commitment as an officer in a state or local police force. See Web site for details and an application. http://www.azpolicecorps.com

Award: Scholarship for use in freshman, sophomore, junior, senior, or graduate years. *Number:* 10. *Amount:* up to $23,000.

Eligibility Requirements: Applicant must be enrolled or expecting to enroll full or part-time at a four-year institution or university. Applicant must have 2.5 GPA or higher. Available to U.S. citizens.

Application Requirements: Application, driver's license, references, transcript, DD Form 214. *Deadline:* Continuous.

Contact: Jon Heiden
Arizona Police Corps
8470 North Overfield Road
Coolidge, AZ 85228
Phone: 800-460-1395
E-mail: info@azpolicecorps.com

ART INSTITUTES http://www.artinstitutes.edu

EVELYN KEEDY MEMORIAL SCHOLARSHIP

A $30,000 tuition scholarship awarded to a worthy high school senior who has enrolled at one of the eligible Art Institute locations. Recipients must begin program of study in the summer or fall quarter following high school graduation, and be accepted in order to validate the scholarship.

Award: Scholarship for use in freshman, sophomore, junior, or senior years; renewable. *Number:* 1. *Amount:* $30,000.

Eligibility Requirements: Applicant must be high school student and planning to enroll or expecting to enroll full-time at a technical institution. Applicant must have 2.5 GPA or higher.

Application Requirements: Application, essay, resume, references, transcript. *Deadline:* May 1.

Contact: Julie Walsh, Admissions Department
Art Institutes
210 6th Avenue
Suite 3300
Pittsburgh, PA 15222
Phone: 800-275-2440
Fax: 412-456-2305
E-mail: webadmin@aii.edu

ASSOCIATED MEDICAL SERVICES, INC. http://www.ams-inc.on.ca

ASSOCIATED MEDICAL SERVICES, INC. BIOETHICS STUDENTSHIP

• *See page 577*

ASSOCIATION FOR IRON AND STEEL TECHNOLOGY http://www.aist.org/foundation/scholarships.htm

ASSOCIATION FOR IRON AND STEEL TECHNOLOGY MIDWEST CHAPTER NON-ENGINEERING SCHOLARSHIP

Scholarship will be awarded to a graduating high school senior, or undergraduate freshman, sophomore, or junior enrolled in a fully AIST accredited college or university. Applicant must be in good academic standing. Applicant must be a dependent of an AIST Midwest Chapter member.

Award: Scholarship for use in freshman, sophomore, or junior years; not renewable. *Number:* 2. *Amount:* $1000.

Eligibility Requirements: Applicant must be enrolled or expecting to enroll full-time at a four-year institution or university. Available to U.S. citizens.

Application Requirements: Application, essay, references, transcript. *Deadline:* May 15.

Contact: Michael Heaney, Division Manager Maintenance and Engineering, ISG Indiana Harbor
Association for Iron and Steel Technology
3001 Dickey Road
East Chicago, IN 46312

ASSOCIATION FOR IRON AND STEEL TECHNOLOGY MIDWEST CHAPTER WESTERN STATES SCHOLARSHIP

Scholarship will be awarded to a graduating high school senior, or undergraduate freshman, sophomore, or junior enrolled in a fully AIST accredited college or university. Applicant must be in good academic standing. Applicant must be a dependent of an AIST Midwest Chapter member.

Award: Scholarship for use in freshman, sophomore, or junior years; not renewable. *Number:* 1. *Amount:* $2500.

Eligibility Requirements: Applicant must be enrolled or expecting to enroll full-time at a four-year institution or university. Available to U.S. citizens.

Application Requirements: Application, essay, references, transcript. *Deadline:* May 15.

Contact: Michael Heaney, Division Manager Maintenance and Engineering, ISG Indiana Harbor
Association for Iron and Steel Technology
3001 Dickey Road
East Chicago, IN 46312

ASSOCIATION OF INTERNATIONAL EDUCATION, JAPAN (AIEJ)

SHORT-TERM STUDENT EXCHANGE PROMOTION PROGRAM SCHOLARSHIP

Scholarship available for qualified students accepted by Japanese universities under the student exchange agreement on a short-term basis from three months to one year. Scholarship includes a $645 monthly stipend, a $200 settling-in allowance, and round-trip, economy-class airfare. Application should be filed by Japanese host institution. Inquiries should be addressed to the international office of the home institution. Deadline decided by host institution.

Award: Scholarship for use in freshman, sophomore, junior, senior, or graduate years; not renewable. *Number:* 1950. *Amount:* $5650–$10,000.

Eligibility Requirements: Applicant must be enrolled or expecting to enroll full-time at a two-year or four-year institution or university. Available to U.S. and non-U.S. citizens.

Application Requirements: Applicant must enter a contest, to be decided by home and host institutions. *Deadline:* varies.

Contact: Chika Hotta, Program Coordinator, Office for Cooperation with Extrabudgetary Funding Sources, AIEJ
Association of International Education, Japan (AIEJ)
4-5-29 Komaba, Meguro-ku
Tokyo 153-8503
Japan
Phone: 81-3-5454 Ext. 5290
Fax: 81-3-5454 5299
E-mail: efs@aiej.or.jp

AUTOMOTIVE RECYCLERS ASSOCIATION SCHOLARSHIP FOUNDATION http://www.autorecyc.org

AUTOMOTIVE RECYCLERS ASSOCIATION SCHOLARSHIP FOUNDATION SCHOLARSHIP

Scholarships are available for the post-high school educational pursuits for the children of employees of direct ARA member companies. The deadline for completed scholarship applications is March 15 of each year.

Award: Scholarship for use in freshman, sophomore, junior, or senior years; not renewable. *Number:* 35–45. *Amount:* $500–$1000.

Eligibility Requirements: Applicant must be high school student and planning to enroll or expecting to enroll full-time at a two-year or four-year or technical institution or university. Applicant must have 3.0 GPA or higher. Available to U.S. and non-U.S. citizens.

Application Requirements: Application, transcript. *Deadline:* March 15.

Contact: Automotive Recyclers Association Scholarship Foundation
3975 Fair Ridge Drive
Suite 20 North
Fairfax, VA 22033
Phone: 703-385-1001

BOYS AND GIRLS CLUBS OF GREATER SAN DIEGO http://www.sdyouth.org

BOYS AND GIRLS CLUBS FOUNDATION SCHOLARSHIP

Renewable scholarship for graduating high school seniors from a qualified high school in the Club's service area. Must have been a member of the Boys and Girls Clubs of Greater San Diego for one or more years. Application deadline is April 15.

Award: Scholarship for use in freshman, sophomore, junior, or senior years; renewable. *Number:* varies. *Amount:* $1000.

Eligibility Requirements: Applicant must be high school student and planning to enroll or expecting to enroll full-time at a four-year institution or university.

Application Requirements: *Deadline:* April 15.

Contact: Danny Sherlock, President and Chief Executive Officer
Boys and Girls Clubs of Greater San Diego
115 West Woodward Avenue
Escondido, CA 92025
Phone: 760-746-3315

BREAD AND ROSES COMMUNITY FUND http://www.breadrosesfund.org

JONATHAN R. LAX SCHOLARSHIP FUND

Scholarship to encourage gay men to obtain additional education, aspire to positions in which they contribute to society, be open about their sexual preference and act as role models for other gay men with similar potential. Several awards available, at least one graduate and one undergraduate award of $20,000. Award restricted to those from Philadelphia studying elsewhere or students from anywhere studying in Philadelphia.

Award: Scholarship for use in freshman, sophomore, junior, senior, or graduate years; not renewable. *Number:* 8–10. *Amount:* $5000–$20,000.

Eligibility Requirements: Applicant must be enrolled or expecting to enroll full or part-time at a two-year or four-year institution or university and male. Available to U.S. citizens.

Application Requirements: Application, essay, financial need analysis, interview, references, transcript. *Deadline:* January 15.

Contact: Salih Watts, Lax Outreach Coordinator
Bread and Roses Community Fund
1500 Walnut Street, Suite 1305
Philadelphia, PA 19102
Phone: 215-731-1107 Ext. 205
Fax: 215-731-0453
E-mail: info@breadrosesfund.org

BUDDHIST COMPASSION RELIEF TZU-CHI FOUNDATION, U.S.A. http://www.tzuchi.org/global/

TZU-CHI SCHOLARSHIP

Scholarships are made available to graduating high school seniors who have demonstrated financial need and academic excellence. Must have a minimum of a 3.0 GPA. For more details see Web site: http://www.tzuchi.org/global.

Buddhist Compassion Relief Tzu-Chi Foundation, U.S.A. (continued)

Award: Scholarship for use in freshman year; not renewable. *Number:* varies. *Amount:* $1000.

Eligibility Requirements: Applicant must be high school student and planning to enroll or expecting to enroll at an institution or university. Applicant must have 3.0 GPA or higher.

Application Requirements: Application, financial need analysis, references, transcript. *Deadline:* April 30.

Contact: Application available at Web site.

CANTOR FITZGERALD RELIEF FUND (SEPT. 11) http://www.cantorrelief.org

CANTOR FITZGERALD RELIEF FUND

Part of relief fund will provide assistance with college tuition. Help will go to the families of any victims of the World Trade Center disaster who were employed by Cantor Fitzgerald.

Award: Scholarship for use in freshman, sophomore, junior, or senior years; not renewable. *Number:* varies. *Amount:* varies.

Eligibility Requirements: Applicant must be enrolled or expecting to enroll at an institution or university. Available to U.S. citizens.

Application Requirements: *Deadline:* varies.

Contact: Cantor Fitzgerald Relief Fund (Sept. 11)
101 Park Avenue 45th Floor
New York, NY 10178-0060
Phone: 212-829-4770

CAREER COLLEGE FOUNDATION http://www.careercollegefoundation.com

IMAGINE AMERICA SCHOLARSHIP

One-time award available to graduating high school seniors. Must attend an accredited private postsecondary institution. Must be nominated by school counselor or principal. Must enroll by October 31. See Web site: http://www.careercollegefoundation.com. Contact the guidance counselor at high school.

Award: Scholarship for use in freshman year; not renewable. *Number:* up to 7000. *Amount:* $1000.

Eligibility Requirements: Applicant must be high school student; age 17-18 and planning to enroll or expecting to enroll full-time at a two-year or four-year or technical institution. Applicant must have 2.5 GPA or higher. Available to U.S. citizens.

Application Requirements: Applicant must enter a contest, financial need analysis, nomination. *Deadline:* October 31.

Contact: Robert Martin, Executive Director/Vice President
Career College Foundation
10 G Street, NE, Suite 750
Washington, DC 20002-4213
Phone: 202-336-6800
Fax: 202-408-8102
E-mail: scholarships@career.org

CAREERFITTER.COM http://careerfitter.com

CAREERFITTER.COM SCHOLARSHIP

Scholarship available to qualified student enrolled, or planning to enroll, in a technical school, college, or university program for the next school term. Must be a U.S. citizen or permanent resident. Must submit an original essay with application. All applications and essays must be submitted online. Deadline dates are posted next to each scholarship at Web site: http://www.careerfitter.com.

Award: Scholarship for use in freshman, sophomore, junior, senior, graduate, or postgraduate years; not renewable. *Number:* 4–5. *Amount:* $500–$1000.

Eligibility Requirements: Applicant must be enrolled or expecting to enroll full or part-time at a two-year or four-year or technical institution or university. Applicant must have 2.5 GPA or higher. Available to U.S. and non-U.S. citizens.

Application Requirements: Application, applicant must enter a contest, essay. *Deadline:* varies.

Contact: Application and information at Web site.

CARGILL http://www.cargill.com

CARGILL COMMUNITY SCHOLARSHIP PROGRAM

One-time scholarships administered by the National FFA Organization. Each award is valued at $1000, and also enables the recipient's high school to become eligible for a $200 library grant. Award is designed for students pursuing a two- or four-year degree in the U.S. Applicants must be U.S. high school students who live in or near Cargill communities. Students are required to obtain a signature on their applications from a manager at a local Cargill facility or subsidiary.

Award: Scholarship for use in freshman year; not renewable. *Number:* 350. *Amount:* $1000.

Eligibility Requirements: Applicant must be high school student and planning to enroll or expecting to enroll full-time at a two-year or four-year or technical institution or university. Available to U.S. citizens.

Application Requirements: Application. *Deadline:* February 15.

Contact: Bonnie Blue, Cargill Community Relations
Cargill
PO Box 5650
Minneapolis, MN 55440-5650
Phone: 952-742-6247
Fax: 952-742-7224
E-mail: bonnie_l_blue@cargill.com

CARPE DIEM FOUNDATION OF ILLINOIS http://www.carpediemfoundation.org

CARPE DIEM FOUNDATION OF ILLINOIS SCHOLARSHIP COMPETITION

Renewable awards for U.S. citizens studying full time at accredited U.S. educational institutions, including colleges, universities, music conservatories, schools of design, and academies of the arts. For undergraduate study only. Merit based. The award is open to all, but priority is given to students whose parents are or have been employed in education; local, state, or federal government; social service or public health; the administration of justice; the fine arts. Must maintain a B average. Must demonstrate commitment to public service. Application deadline is first week of May. See Web site: http://www.carpediemfoundation.org to download application..

Award: Scholarship for use in freshman, sophomore, junior, or senior years; renewable. *Number:* 10–15. *Amount:* $2500–$5000.

Eligibility Requirements: Applicant must be enrolled or expecting to enroll full-time at a four-year institution or university. Applicant must have 3.0 GPA or higher. Available to U.S. citizens.

Application Requirements: Application, essay, references, self-addressed stamped envelope, test scores, transcript, portfolio, CD, tape (if arts or music candidate). *Fee:* $14. *Deadline:* varies.

Contact: Application available at Web site.
E-mail: glevine@carpediemfoundation.org

CENTER FOR SCHOLARSHIP ADMINISTRATION http://www.scholarshipprograms.org

WACHOVIA INROADS INTERNSHIP SCHOLARSHIP PROGRAM

One-time award to returning interns who have completed at least one summer in the Wachovia INROADS Internship Program.

Award: Scholarship for use in freshman, sophomore, junior, or senior years; not renewable. *Number:* up to 2. *Amount:* $1000.

Eligibility Requirements: Applicant must be enrolled or expecting to enroll at an institution or university. Applicant must have 3.0 GPA or higher.

Application Requirements: Application, essay, references, transcript. *Deadline:* February 15.

Contact: Application available at Web site.

CHELA EDUCATION FINANCING http://www.loans4students.org

GO THE DISTANCE SCHOLARSHIP

Scholarship program exclusively for distance (online) students. Must submit an essay on the topic: My Challenges in Financing a Distance Degree. Essays will be evaluated on the basis of appropriateness to theme, persuasiveness, quality of writing, and creativity. Essay must be submitted as part of the online application process only. For information and application, visit Web site: http://www.loans4students.org

Award: Scholarship for use in freshman, sophomore, junior, senior, or graduate years; not renewable. *Number:* 30. *Amount:* $1000.

Eligibility Requirements: Applicant must be enrolled or expecting to enroll full or part-time at a two-year or four-year or technical institution or university. Applicant must have 2.5 GPA or higher. Available to U.S. citizens.

Application Requirements: Application, essay. *Deadline:* July 5.

Contact: Program Manager
Chela Education Financing
388 Market Street, 12th Floor
San Francisco, CA 94111
Phone: 415-283-2788
Fax: 415-283-2710
E-mail: scholarships@chelafin.org

MONEY MATTERS SCHOLARSHIP

Twenty $5000 scholarships will be awarded to college students who will be enrolled at least halftime. The application requires an essay with a maximum of 300 words in response to the following statement : "How am I financing my college education." Students should focus on responsible borrowing and money management. A 2.0 GPA is required. Application available on Web site: http://www.loans4students.org.

Award: Scholarship for use in freshman, sophomore, junior, senior, or graduate years; not renewable. *Number:* 20. *Amount:* $5000.

Eligibility Requirements: Applicant must be enrolled or expecting to enroll full or part-time at a two-year or four-year institution or university. Available to U.S. citizens.

Application Requirements: Application, essay. *Deadline:* varies.

Contact: Jennifer Cox, Scholarship and Outreach Specialist
Chela Education Financing
388 Market Street
12th Floor
San Francisco, CA 94111
Phone: 415-283-2874
Fax: 415-283-2874
E-mail: scholarships@chelafin.org

CHRISTOPHERS (THE) http://www.christophers.org

POSTER CONTEST FOR HIGH SCHOOL STUDENTS

Students in grades 9 through 12 are invited to interpret the theme: "You can make a difference." Posters must include this statement and illustrate the idea that one person can change the world for the better. Judging is based on overall impact, content, originality and artistic merit. More information can be found at http://www.christophers.org. Deadline: January 21.

Award: Prize for use in freshman year; not renewable. *Number:* 8. *Amount:* $100–$1000.

Eligibility Requirements: Applicant must be high school student and planning to enroll or expecting to enroll full or part-time at an institution or university. Available to U.S. and non-U.S. citizens.

Application Requirements: Application, applicant must enter a contest, poster. *Deadline:* January 21.

Contact: Regina Pappalardo, Youth Coordinator
Christophers (The)
12 East 48th Street
New York, NY 10017
Phone: 212-759-4050
Fax: 212-838-5073
E-mail: youth@christophers.org

VIDEO CONTEST FOR COLLEGE STUDENTS

Using any style or format, college students are invited to express the following theme: "One person can make a difference." Entries can be up to five minutes in length and must be submitted in standard, full-sized VHS format. Entries will be judged on content, artistic and technical proficiency, and adherence to contest rules. More information is available at http://www.christophers.org. Deadline: June 10.

Award: Prize for use in freshman, sophomore, junior, senior, or graduate years; not renewable. *Number:* 8. *Amount:* $100–$3000.

Eligibility Requirements: Applicant must be enrolled or expecting to enroll full or part-time at a two-year or four-year or technical institution or university. Available to U.S. and non-U.S. citizens.

Application Requirements: Application, applicant must enter a contest, VHS tape. *Deadline:* June 10.

Contact: Regina Pappalardo, Youth Coordinator
Christophers (The)
12 East 48th Street
New York, NY 10017
Phone: 212-759-4050
Fax: 212-838-5073
E-mail: youth@christophers.org

CIRI FOUNDATION http://www.ciri.com/tcf

CAREER UPGRADE GRANTS

Applicant must be accepted or enrolled part time in a course of study that directly contributes toward potential employment or employment upgrade. May reapply each quarter until grant cap is reached. Must be Alaska Native Student only, CIRI original enrollee or descendant. Minimum 2.5 GPA required. Application deadlines are March 31, June 30, September 30, December 1.

Award: Grant for use in freshman, sophomore, junior, senior, graduate, or postgraduate years; not renewable. *Number:* varies. *Amount:* up to $3000.

Eligibility Requirements: Applicant must be enrolled or expecting to enroll part-time at a two-year or four-year institution or university. Applicant must have 2.5 GPA or higher. Available to U.S. citizens.

Application Requirements: Application, essay, references, transcript, proof of eligibility, birth certificate or adoption decree. *Deadline:* varies.

Contact: CIRI Foundation
2600 Cordova Street, Suite 206
Anchorage, AK 99503
Phone: 907-263-5582
Fax: 907-263-5588
E-mail: tcf@ciri.com

CIRI FOUNDATION ACHIEVEMENT ANNUAL SCHOLARSHIPS

Merit scholarships for applicants with exceptional academic promise. Annual award includes two academic semesters. Must be Alaska Native Student. Minimum 3.0 GPA required.

Award: Scholarship for use in freshman, sophomore, junior, senior, or graduate years; not renewable. *Number:* varies. *Amount:* $7000.

Eligibility Requirements: Applicant must be enrolled or expecting to enroll full-time at a two-year or four-year institution or university. Applicant must have 3.0 GPA or higher. Available to U.S. citizens.

Application Requirements: Application, essay, references, transcript, proof of eligibility, birth certificate or adoption decree. *Deadline:* June 1.

Contact: CIRI Foundation
2600 Cordova Street, Suite 206
Anchorage, AK 99503
Phone: 907-263-5582
Fax: 907-263-5588
E-mail: tcf@ciri.com

CIRI FOUNDATION EXCELLENCE ANNUAL SCHOLARSHIPS

Merit scholarships for outstanding academic and community services experience. Annual award includes 2 academic semesters. Minimum 3.5 GPA required. Must be Alaska Native Student.

Award: Scholarship for use in freshman, sophomore, junior, senior, or graduate years; not renewable. *Number:* varies. *Amount:* $9000.

Eligibility Requirements: Applicant must be enrolled or expecting to enroll full-time at a four-year institution or university. Applicant must have 3.5 GPA or higher. Available to U.S. citizens.

CIRI Foundation (continued)

Application Requirements: Application, essay, references, transcript, proof of eligibility, birth certificate or adoption decree. *Deadline:* June 1.

Contact: CIRI Foundation
2600 Cordova Street, Suite 206
Anchorage, AK 99503
Phone: 907-263-5582
Fax: 907-263-5588
E-mail: tcf@ciri.com

CIRI FOUNDATION GENERAL FELLOWSHIP GRANTS

Applicant must be accepted or enrolled in a seminar or conference that is accredited, authorized, or approved by the CIRI Foundation. For special employment-related non-credit workshops or seminars. Must be Alaska Native Student, CIRI original enrollee, or descendant at least 18 years of age. Application deadlines are March 31, June 30, September 30, and December 1.

Award: Grant for use in freshman, sophomore, junior, senior, graduate, or postgraduate years; not renewable. *Number:* varies. *Amount:* up to $500.

Eligibility Requirements: Applicant must be age 18 and enrolled or expecting to enroll full or part-time at a two-year or four-year or technical institution or university. Applicant must have 2.5 GPA or higher.

Application Requirements: Application, essay, references, transcript, proof of eligibility, birth certificate or adoption decree. *Deadline:* varies.

Contact: CIRI Foundation
2600 Cordova Street, Suite 206
Anchorage, AK 99503
Phone: 907-263-5582
Fax: 907-263-5588
E-mail: tcf@ciri.com

CIRI FOUNDATION GENERAL SEMESTER SCHOLARSHIP

Merit scholarships for applicants with academic promise. $2000 per semester award. Minimum 2.5 GPA. Must be Alaska Native Student. Deadlines are June 1 and December 1.

Award: Scholarship for use in freshman, sophomore, junior, senior, or graduate years; not renewable. *Number:* varies. *Amount:* $2000.

Eligibility Requirements: Applicant must be enrolled or expecting to enroll full-time at a two-year or four-year institution or university. Applicant must have 2.5 GPA or higher. Available to U.S. citizens.

Application Requirements: Application, essay, references, transcript, proof of eligibility, birth certificate or adoption decree. *Deadline:* varies.

Contact: CIRI Foundation
2600 Cordova Street, Suite 206
Anchorage, AK 99503
Phone: 907-263-5582
Fax: 907-263-5588
E-mail: tcf@ciri.com

CIRI FOUNDATION SPECIAL EXCELLENCE SCHOLARSHIP

Merit scholarships for exceptional academic and community service experience, offered as encouragement to students to attend outstanding colleges and universities in the United States. Must be Alaska Native Student original enrollees/descendants of Cook Inlet Region, Inc. Must have a cumulative GPA of 3.7 or better. Preference given to study in fields of business, education, math, sciences, health services, and engineering.

Award: Scholarship for use in freshman, sophomore, junior, senior, or graduate years; not renewable. *Number:* varies. *Amount:* $18,000.

Eligibility Requirements: Applicant must be enrolled or expecting to enroll full-time at a four-year institution or university. Available to U.S. citizens.

Application Requirements: Application, essay, references, transcript, proof of eligibility, birth certificate or adoption decree. *Deadline:* June 1.

Contact: CIRI Foundation
2600 Cordova Street, Suite 206
Anchorage, AK 99503
Phone: 907-263-5582
Fax: 907-263-5588
E-mail: tcf@ciri.com

HOWARD KECK/WESTMIN ENDOWMENT SCHOLARSHIP FUND

To encourage students seeking an undergraduate degree or graduate degree in all fields. Applicant must be Alaska Native student. For details see Web site: http://www.ciri.com/tcf.

Award: Scholarship for use in freshman, sophomore, junior, senior, or graduate years; not renewable. *Number:* varies. *Amount:* varies.

Eligibility Requirements: Applicant must be enrolled or expecting to enroll full-time at a two-year or four-year institution or university.

Application Requirements: Application, essay, references, transcript, proof of eligibility, birth certificate or adoption decree. *Deadline:* June 1.

Contact: CIRI Foundation
2600 Cordova Street, Suite 206
Anchorage, AK 99503
Phone: 907-263-5582
Fax: 907-263-5588
E-mail: tcf@ciri.com

KENAI NATIVES ASSOCIATION (KNA) SCHOLARSHIP AND GRANT FUND

Merit scholarship for Alaska Native student. Must be accepted or enrolled full time in a two-year or four-year undergraduate degree or graduate degree program or technical skills training program. Scholarship is good for one semester, must reapply each semester. Deadlines are June 1 and December 1. See Web site for more details: http://www.ciri.com/tcf.

Award: Scholarship for use in freshman, sophomore, junior, senior, or graduate years; not renewable. *Number:* varies. *Amount:* varies.

Eligibility Requirements: Applicant must be enrolled or expecting to enroll full-time at a two-year or four-year or technical institution or university. Applicant must have 2.5 GPA or higher.

Application Requirements: *Deadline:* varies.

Contact: CIRI Foundation
2600 Cordova Street, Suite 206
Anchorage, AK 99503
Phone: 907-263-5582
Fax: 907-263-5588
E-mail: tcf@ciri.com

NINILCHIK NATIVE ASSOCIATION INC. SCHOLARSHIP AND GRANT PROGRAM

General scholarship of $1000 per semester and vocational grant up to $2000 per year. Deadlines are June 1 and December 1. Must be member of Ninilchik Native Association or descendant or member. Minimum 2.5 GPA required.

Award: Scholarship for use in freshman, sophomore, junior, senior, graduate, or postgraduate years; not renewable. *Number:* varies. *Amount:* $1000–$2000.

Eligibility Requirements: Applicant must be enrolled or expecting to enroll full or part-time at a two-year or four-year or technical institution or university. Applicant must have 2.5 GPA or higher.

Application Requirements: Application, essay, references, transcript, proof of eligibility, birth certificate or adoption decree; written statement from Ninilchik Native Association. *Deadline:* varies.

Contact: CIRI Foundation
2600 Cordova Street, Suite 206
Anchorage, AK 99503
Phone: 907-263-5582
Fax: 907-263-5588
E-mail: tcf@ciri.com

SALAMATOF NATIVE ASSOCIATION, INC. (SNAI) SCHOLARSHIP PROGRAM

Merit scholarship for Alaska Native student. Must be accepted or enrolled full time in an undergraduate or graduate degree program or technical skills training program. Applicant should have a cumulative 2.5 grade point average or better. For tuition, required fees, books, campus-related room and meal plan, and for other direct school-related costs. See Web site for more details: http://www.ciri.com.tcf.

Award: Scholarship for use in freshman, sophomore, junior, senior, or graduate years; not renewable. *Number:* up to 2. *Amount:* up to $2000.

Eligibility Requirements: Applicant must be enrolled or expecting to enroll full-time at a two-year or four-year or technical institution or university. Applicant must have 2.5 GPA or higher.

Application Requirements: Application, essay, references, transcript, proof of eligibility, birth certificate or adoption decree. *Deadline:* June 1.

Contact: CIRI Foundation
2600 Cordova Street, Suite 206
Anchorage, AK 99503
Phone: 907-263-5582
Fax: 907-263-5588
E-mail: tcf@ciri.com

TYONEK NATIVE CORPORATION SCHOLARSHIP AND GRANT FUND

To encourage Alaska Native student to prepare for professional career after high school. Applicant must be accepted or enrolled full time in an accredited or otherwise approved postsecondary college, university, or technical skills education program. Semester scholarship: $1000; Vocational Training/Career Upgrade Grant: up to $1500 received during a calendar year. See Web site for more details: http://www.ciri.com/tcf.

Award: Scholarship for use in freshman, sophomore, junior, senior, or graduate years; not renewable. *Number:* varies. *Amount:* $1000–$1500.

Eligibility Requirements: Applicant must be enrolled or expecting to enroll full-time at a two-year or four-year or technical institution or university.

Application Requirements: Application, essay, references, transcript, proof of eligibility, birth certificate or adoption decree. *Deadline:* varies.

Contact: CIRI Foundation
2600 Cordova Street, Suite 206
Anchorage, AK 99503
Phone: 907-263-5582
Fax: 907-263-5588
E-mail: tcf@ciri.com

COCA-COLA SCHOLARS FOUNDATION, INC. http://www.coca-colascholars.org

COCA-COLA TWO-YEAR COLLEGES SCHOLARSHIP

Non-renewable awards based on community involvement, leadership, and academic performance. Essay is required. Finalists represent every state in the U.S. Must pursue a two-year degree. Deadline is March 4. Each institution may nominate up to two applicants. Minimum 2.5 GPA is required. See Web site: http://www.coca-colascholars.org for additional information.

Award: Scholarship for use in freshman or sophomore years; not renewable. *Number:* 400. *Amount:* $1000.

Eligibility Requirements: Applicant must be enrolled or expecting to enroll full or part-time at a two-year institution. Applicant must have 2.5 GPA or higher. Available to U.S. citizens.

Application Requirements: Application, essay, nomination from institution. *Deadline:* March 4.

Contact: Ryan Rodriguez, Program Facilitator
Coca-Cola Scholars Foundation, Inc.
PO Box 442
Atlanta, GA 30301-0442
Phone: 800-306-2653
Fax: 404-733-5439
E-mail: scholars@na.ko.com

CODA INTERNATIONAL

MILLIE BROTHER ANNUAL SCHOLARSHIP FOR CHILDREN OF DEAF ADULTS

Scholarship awarded to any higher education student who is the hearing child of deaf parents. One-time award based on transcripts, letters of reference and essay. Deadline is the first Friday in May.

Award: Scholarship for use in freshman, sophomore, junior, or senior years; not renewable. *Number:* 2. *Amount:* $3000.

Eligibility Requirements: Applicant must be enrolled or expecting to enroll full-time at a two-year or four-year or technical institution or university. Available to U.S. and non-U.S. citizens.

Application Requirements: Application, essay, references, self-addressed stamped envelope, transcript. *Deadline:* varies.

Contact: Dr. Robert Hoffmeister, Director, Program in Deaf Studies
CODA International
2 Sherborn Street
Boston University
Boston, MA 02215
Phone: 617-353-3205
Fax: 617-353-3292
E-mail: deafstudy@bu.edu

COLLEGE PHOTOGRAPHER OF THE YEAR http://cpoy.org

COLLEGE PHOTOGRAPHER OF THE YEAR COMPETITION

Awards are made based on the juried contest of individual photographs, picture stories and photographic essay and multimedia presentations. Judges are from the working media. Visit Web site: http://www.cpoy.org for more information.

Award: Scholarship for use in freshman, sophomore, junior, senior, or graduate years; not renewable. *Number:* 42–60. *Amount:* up to $3000.

Eligibility Requirements: Applicant must be enrolled or expecting to enroll full or part-time at a two-year or four-year or technical institution or university. Available to U.S. and non-U.S. citizens.

Application Requirements: Application, applicant must enter a contest, photo. *Fee:* $25. *Deadline:* October 4.

Contact: Rita Ann Reed, Director, College Photographer of the Year
College Photographer of the Year
107 Lee Hills Hall, University of Missouri, School of Journalism
Columbia, MO 65211
Phone: 573-882-2198
Fax: 573-884-4999
E-mail: info@cpoy.org

COLLEGEFINANCIALAIDINFORMATION.COM

FRANK O'NEILL MEMORIAL SCHOLARSHIP

One-time award available to anyone who is attending or aspiring to attend a post-secondary education program. Must submit essay explaining educational goals and financial need. Application deadline for spring term is December 15 and deadline for fall term is August 15. Application is available at Web site.

Award: Scholarship for use in freshman, sophomore, junior, senior, graduate, or postgraduate years; not renewable. *Number:* 2. *Amount:* $500.

Eligibility Requirements: Applicant must be enrolled or expecting to enroll full or part-time at a two-year or four-year or technical institution or university. Available to U.S. and non-U.S. citizens.

Application Requirements: Essay. *Deadline:* varies.

Contact: CollegeFinancialAidInformation.com
PO Box 124
Youngtown, AZ 85363

COLLEGENET http://www.collegenet.com

COLLEGENET SCHOLARSHIP

Award for student who completes and sends an application for college admission through CollegeNET. Must have enrolled in classes by fall term. A complete program description is available at the Web site (http://www.collegenet.com). Student must have applied to a member school to make the first level of qualification. Schools nominate from this pool of students based on their own criteria.

CollegeNET (continued)

Award: Scholarship for use in freshman, sophomore, junior, or senior years; not renewable. *Number:* 1–3. *Amount:* $1000–$10,000.

Eligibility Requirements: Applicant must be enrolled or expecting to enroll full-time at a two-year or four-year or technical institution or university. Available to U.S. and non-U.S. citizens.

Application Requirements: Applicant must enter a contest, essay, nomination. *Deadline:* varies.

Contact: Ms. Dawna Allison, Marketing Manager
CollegeNET
805 SW Broadway, Suite 1600
Portland, OR 97205
Phone: 503-973-5200
Fax: 503-973-5252

COMMON KNOWLEDGE SCHOLARSHIP FOUNDATION http://www.cksf.org

COMMON KNOWLEDGE SCHOLARSHIP

Students register at the CKSF Web site, and then take a series of multiple-choice quizzes. Each question is worth 500 points, and 1 point is deducted for every second it takes to complete each question. The person with the most points at the end of the competition is the scholarship winner.

Award: Scholarship for use in freshman, sophomore, junior, senior, or graduate years; not renewable. *Number:* 5–30. *Amount:* $250–$2500.

Eligibility Requirements: Applicant must be age 13 or under and enrolled or expecting to enroll full or part-time at a two-year or four-year or technical institution or university. Available to U.S. citizens.

Application Requirements: Applicant must enter a contest, test scores, Internet registration. *Deadline:* varies.

Contact: Daryl Hulce, President
Common Knowledge Scholarship Foundation
PO Box 290361
Davie, FL 33329
Phone: 954-262-8553
Fax: 954-262-3940
E-mail: hulce@cksf.org

COMMUNITY FOUNDATION FOR PALM BEACH AND MARTIN COUNTIES, INC. http://www.yourcommunityfoundation.org

WEITZ COMPANY SCHOLARSHIP

Scholarship awarded to Palm Beach or Martin County graduating high school senior, or child of a Weitz employee, regardless of residence. Student must prove acceptance into college or vocational school with a major emphasis in a construction related field. Deadline is March 1. Applications are available online http://www.yourcommunityfoundation.org.

Award: Scholarship for use in freshman year; not renewable. *Number:* varies. *Amount:* varies.

Eligibility Requirements: Applicant must be high school student and planning to enroll or expecting to enroll at a two-year or four-year or technical institution. Applicant must have 2.5 GPA or higher. Available to U.S. citizens.

Application Requirements: Application, financial need analysis. *Deadline:* March 1.

Contact: Carolyn Jenco, Grants Manager/Scholarship Coordinator
Community Foundation for Palm Beach and Martin Counties, Inc.
700 South Dixie Highway
Suite 200
West Palm Beach, FL 33401

CONGRESSIONAL BLACK CAUCUS SPOUSES PROGRAM http://cbcfinc.org

CONGRESSIONAL BLACK CAUCUS SPOUSES EDUCATION SCHOLARSHIP FUND

Award made to students who reside or attend school in a Congressional district represented by an African-American member of Congress. Contact the Congressional office in the appropriate district for information and applications. Any correspondence sent to the CBC Foundation Office on Pennsylvania Avenue will be discarded and may disqualify applicant for the award. See Web site for more details: http://www.cbcfinc.org.

Award: Scholarship for use in freshman, sophomore, junior, or senior years; renewable. *Number:* 200. *Amount:* $500–$4000.

Eligibility Requirements: Applicant must be enrolled or expecting to enroll full-time at a two-year or four-year or technical institution or university. Applicant must have 2.5 GPA or higher. Available to U.S. citizens.

Application Requirements: Application, essay, financial need analysis, interview, photo, references, transcript. *Deadline:* Continuous.

Contact: Appropriate Congressional District Office

SAILING FOR SCHOLARS SCHOLARSHIP

Award made to students who reside or attend school in particular Congressional districts represented by an African-American member of Congress. Preference is given to applicants studying in the fields of hospitality, marine sciences, or the environment. Contact the Congressional office in the appropriate district for information and applications.
Any correspondence sent to the CBC Foundation office or Pennsylvania Avenue will be discarded and may disqualify applicant for the award. See Web site for more details.

Award: Scholarship for use in freshman, sophomore, junior, or senior years; not renewable. *Number:* 10. *Amount:* $2500.

Eligibility Requirements: Applicant must be enrolled or expecting to enroll full-time at a four-year institution or university. Applicant must have 2.5 GPA or higher. Available to U.S. citizens.

Application Requirements: Application, essay, photo, transcript. *Deadline:* May 1.

Contact: Jacquelin Dennis, Director, CBC Spouses Program
Congressional Black Caucus Spouses Program
1004 Pennsylvania Avenue, SE
Washington, DC 20003-2142
Phone: 202-263-2840
E-mail: info@cbcfinc.org

COUNCIL FOR INTERNATIONAL EDUCATIONAL EXCHANGE http://www.ciee.org/study

BOWMAN TRAVEL GRANT

The Bowman Travel Grant is awarded only to eligible students participating in a life study or volunteer programs in less traditional destinations. Recipients must be attending a CIEE member or academic consortium member institution. Recipients receive awards to be used as partial reimbursement for travel costs to program destination. Application deadlines are April 1and November 1. For more information see Web site: http://www.ciee.org.

Award: Grant for use in freshman, sophomore, junior, or senior years; not renewable. *Number:* 20–30. *Amount:* $500–$1000.

Eligibility Requirements: Applicant must be enrolled or expecting to enroll full-time at a two-year or four-year or technical institution or university. Applicant must have 3.5 GPA or higher. Available to U.S. citizens.

Application Requirements: Application, essay, financial need analysis, references, transcript. *Deadline:* varies.

Contact: Scholarship Committee
Council for International Educational Exchange
7 Custom House Street, 3rd Floor
Portland, ME 04101

COUNCIL ON INTERNATIONAL EDUCATIONAL EXCHANGE SCHOLARSHIP

Scholarships offered to students who demonstrate both academic excellence and financial need. Must be enrolled in a CIEE program and attending a CIEE member or academic consortium member school. Application deadlines are April 1 and November 1. For more information see Web site: http://www.ciee.org.

Award: Scholarship for use in freshman, sophomore, junior, or senior years; not renewable. *Number:* 60–70. *Amount:* $500–$1000.

Eligibility Requirements: Applicant must be enrolled or expecting to enroll full-time at a two-year or four-year or technical institution or university. Applicant must have 3.5 GPA or higher. Available to U.S. and non-U.S. citizens.

Application Requirements: Application, essay, financial need analysis, references, transcript. *Deadline:* varies.

Contact: Scholarship Committee
Council for International Educational Exchange
7 Custom House Street, 3rd Floor
Portland, ME 04101
E-mail: scholarships@ciee.org

D.W. SIMPSON & COMPANY http://www.dwsimpson.com/scholar.html

D.W. SIMPSON ACTUARIAL SCIENCE SCHOLARSHIP

One-time award for full-time actuarial science students. Must be entering senior year of undergraduate study in actuarial science. GPA of 3.2 or better in actuarial science and an overall GPA of 3.0 or better required. Must have passed at least one Actuarial Exam and be eligible to work in the U.S. Application deadline is April 30 for fall and October 31 for spring.

Award: Scholarship for use in senior year; not renewable. *Number:* 2. *Amount:* $1000.

Eligibility Requirements: Applicant must be enrolled or expecting to enroll full-time at a four-year institution or university. Applicant must have 3.0 GPA or higher. Available to U.S. citizens.

Application Requirements: Application, essay, resume, test scores. *Deadline:* varies.

Contact: Bethany Rave, Partner-Operations
D.W. Simpson & Company
1800 West Larchmont Avenue
Chicago, IL 60613
Fax: 312-951-8386
E-mail: scholarship@dwsimpson.com

DATATEL, INC. http://www.datatel.com/dsf

DATATEL SCHOLARS FOUNDATION SCHOLARSHIP

One-time award for students attending institutions which use Datatel administrative software. Available for part-time and full-time students. Completed on-line applications must be submitted by January 31.

Award: Scholarship for use in freshman, sophomore, junior, senior, graduate, or postgraduate years; not renewable. *Number:* varies. *Amount:* $1000–$2400.

Eligibility Requirements: Applicant must be enrolled or expecting to enroll full or part-time at a two-year or four-year or technical institution or university. Available to U.S. and non-U.S. citizens.

Application Requirements: Application, essay, references, transcript. *Deadline:* January 31.

Contact: Marissa Solis, Project Leader
Datatel, Inc.
4375 Fair Lakes Court
Fairfax, VA 22033
Phone: 800-486-4332
Fax: 703-968-4573
E-mail: scholars@datatel.com

RETURNING STUDENT SCHOLARSHIP

For any student who has returned to higher education within the previous academic year, after a five-year or more absence. Applicant must attend a Datatel client institution. Completed on-line applications must be submitted by January 31.

Award: Scholarship for use in freshman, sophomore, junior, senior, graduate, or postgraduate years; not renewable. *Number:* 25–50. *Amount:* $1500.

Eligibility Requirements: Applicant must be enrolled or expecting to enroll full or part-time at a two-year or four-year or technical institution or university. Available to U.S. and non-U.S. citizens.

Application Requirements: Application, essay, references, transcript. *Deadline:* January 31.

Contact: Marissa Solis, Project Leader
Datatel, Inc.
4375 Fair Lakes Court
Fairfax, VA 22033
Phone: 800-486-4332
Fax: 703-968-4573
E-mail: scholars@datatel.com

DAVID AND DOVETTA WILSON SCHOLARSHIP FUND, INC. http://www.wilsonfund.org

DAVID AND DOVETTA WILSON SCHOLARSHIP FUND

Award for use in freshman year of college. Applicants selected on basis of academic achievement and involvement in community or religious activities. Minimum 3.0 GPA required. Nine awards ranging from $250 to $1000. Application fee: $20. Deadline: March 31. Send self-addressed stamped envelope for application requests or visit Web site at: http://www.wilsonfund.org.

Award: Scholarship for use in freshman year; not renewable. *Number:* 9. *Amount:* $250–$1000.

Eligibility Requirements: Applicant must be high school student and planning to enroll or expecting to enroll full-time at a two-year or four-year institution or university. Applicant must have 3.0 GPA or higher. Available to U.S. citizens.

Application Requirements: Application, essay, financial need analysis, photo, references, self-addressed stamped envelope, transcript. *Fee:* $20. *Deadline:* March 31.

Contact: Timothy Wilson, Treasurer
David and Dovetta Wilson Scholarship Fund, Inc.
115-67 237th Street
Elmont, NY 11003-3926
Phone: 516-285-4573
E-mail: ddwsf4@aol.com

DAVIS-PUTTER SCHOLARSHIP FUND http://www.davisputter.org

DAVIS-PUTTER SCHOLARSHIP FUND

Provides need-based grants to student activists who are able to do academic work at the college level and are actively involved in building the movement for social and economic justice. For details regarding eligibility and instructions for receiving an application, contact: http://www.davisputter.org.

Award: Scholarship for use in freshman, sophomore, junior, senior, graduate, or postgraduate years; not renewable. *Number:* 25–30. *Amount:* $1000–$6000.

Eligibility Requirements: Applicant must be enrolled or expecting to enroll full or part-time at a two-year or four-year institution or university. Available to U.S. and non-U.S. citizens.

Application Requirements: Application, essay, financial need analysis, photo, references, self-addressed stamped envelope, transcript. *Deadline:* April 1.

Contact: Jan Phillips, Secretary
Davis-Putter Scholarship Fund
PO Box 7307
New York, NY 10116
E-mail: davisputter@hotmail.com

DEVRY, INC. http://www.devry.edu

DEVRY COMMUNITY COLLEGE SCHOLARSHIPS

Scholarships in the amount of $1500 per semester to students who have earned an associate's degree with a minimum of a 3.30 grade point average in the past year, and who wish to pursue a bachelor's degree on a full-time basis at DeVry either onsite or online.

Award: Scholarship for use in junior or senior years; renewable. *Number:* varies. *Amount:* $6000.

Eligibility Requirements: Applicant must be enrolled or expecting to enroll full-time at an institution or university. Applicant must have 3.0 GPA or higher. Available to U.S. and Canadian citizens.

DeVry, Inc. (continued)

Application Requirements: Application, interview, transcript. *Deadline:* Continuous.

Contact: Thonie Simpson, National HS Program Manager
DeVry, Inc.
One Tower Lane
Oak Brook Terrace, IL 60181-4624
Phone: 630-706-3122
Fax: 630-574-1696
E-mail: tsimpson@devry.com

DEVRY SKILLS USA VICA SCHOLARSHIPS

One half-tuition scholarship to first place winners and $1,000 per semester scholarships to second and third place winners in the Internetworking, Electronics Applications, and Electronics Technology categories for both the secondary and post-secondary divisions, at the National Skills USA-VICA Competition.

Award: Scholarship for use in freshman, sophomore, junior, or senior years; renewable. *Number:* 18. *Amount:* $9000–$30,232.

Eligibility Requirements: Applicant must be enrolled or expecting to enroll full-time at an institution or university. Available to U.S. citizens.

Application Requirements: Applicant must enter a contest. *Deadline:* Continuous.

Contact: Thonie Simpson, National HS Program Manager
DeVry, Inc.
One Tower Lane
Oak Brook Terrace, IL 60181-4624
Phone: 630-706-3122
Fax: 630-574-1696
E-mail: tsimpson@devry.com

DEVRY UNIVERSITY FIRST SCHOLAR AWARD

Full-tuition scholarship to a high school senior who has participated in at least one full FIRST Robotics competition season. Student must enroll at DeVry University within one calendar year of receipt of the award.

Award: Scholarship for use in freshman, sophomore, junior, or senior years; renewable. *Number:* 1. *Amount:* $42,610–$60,465.

Eligibility Requirements: Applicant must be high school student and planning to enroll or expecting to enroll full-time at an institution or university. Available to U.S. and non-U.S. citizens.

Application Requirements: Application, applicant must enter a contest, essay, references, test scores, transcript. *Deadline:* March 5.

Contact: Thonie Simpson, National HS Program Manager
DeVry, Inc.
One Tower Lane
Oak Brook Terrace, IL 60181-4624
Phone: 630-706-3122
Fax: 630-574-1696
E-mail: tsimpson@devry.com

DOGRIB TREATY 11 SCHOLARSHIP COMMITTEE

http://www.dt11sc.ca

BHP BILLITON UNIVERSITY SCHOLARSHIPS

Award for students of Dogrib ancestry. Must be enrolled full time in a Canadian university degree program and be interested and active in community affairs.

Award: Scholarship for use in freshman, sophomore, junior, senior, or graduate years; not renewable. *Number:* 4. *Amount:* $3714.

Eligibility Requirements: Applicant must be enrolled or expecting to enroll full-time at an institution or university.

Application Requirements: Application, references, transcript. *Deadline:* varies.

Contact: Morven MacPherson, Post Secondary Student Support Coordinator
Dogrib Treaty 11 Scholarship Committee
c/o CJBRHS
Bag #1
Rae-Edzo, NT X0E 0Y0
Canada
Phone: 867-371-3815
Fax: 867-371-3813
E-mail: morvenm@dogrib.net

DIAVIK DIAMONDS, INC. SCHOLARSHIPS FOR COLLEGE STUDENTS

Award for students of Dogrib ancestry. Must be enrolled full time in a Canadian college diploma program and be interested and active in community affairs.

Award: Scholarship for use in freshman, sophomore, junior, or senior years; not renewable. *Number:* 10. *Amount:* $2228.

Eligibility Requirements: Applicant must be enrolled or expecting to enroll full-time at a two-year or four-year institution.

Application Requirements: Application, references, transcript. *Deadline:* varies.

Contact: Morven MacPherson, Post Secondary Student Support Coordinator
Dogrib Treaty 11 Scholarship Committee
c/o CJBRHS
Bag #1
Rae-Edzo, NT X0E 0Y0
Canada
Phone: 867-371-3815
Fax: 867-371-3813
E-mail: morvenm@dogrib.net

FIRST YEAR ACADEMIC ACHIEVEMENT AWARDS

Award for students of Dogrib ancestry who have completed the first year of a full-time program in a technical school, college, or university. Eight of the ten awards will be allocated for students whose permanent homes are in one of the four Dogrib Treaty 11 communities.

Award: Scholarship for use in sophomore year; not renewable. *Number:* 10. *Amount:* $743.

Eligibility Requirements: Applicant must be enrolled or expecting to enroll full-time at a two-year or four-year or technical institution or university.

Application Requirements: Application, transcript. *Deadline:* varies.

Contact: Morven MacPherson, Post Secondary Student Support Coordinator
Dogrib Treaty 11 Scholarship Committee
c/o CJBRHS
Bag #1
Rae-Edzo, NT X0E 0Y0
Canada
Phone: 867-371-3815
Fax: 867-371-3813
E-mail: morvenm@dogrib.net

SECOND YEAR ACADEMIC ACHIEVEMENT AWARDS

Award for students of Dogrib ancestry who have completed the second year of a full-time program in a technical school, college, or university. Eight of the ten awards will be allocated for students whose permanent homes are in one of the four Dogrib Treaty 11 communities.

Award: Scholarship for use in junior year; not renewable. *Number:* 10. *Amount:* $743.

Eligibility Requirements: Applicant must be enrolled or expecting to enroll full-time at a four-year or technical institution or university.

Application Requirements: Application, transcript. *Deadline:* varies.

Contact: Morven MacPherson, Post Secondary Student Support Coordinator
Dogrib Treaty 11 Scholarship Committee
c/o CJBRHS
Bag #1
Rae-Edzo, NT X0E 0Y0
Canada
Phone: 867-371-3815
Fax: 867-371-3813
E-mail: morvenm@dogrib.net

THIRD YEAR ACADEMIC ACHIEVEMENT AWARDS

Award for students of Dogrib ancestry who have completed the third year of a full-time program in a technical school, college, or university. Eight of the ten awards will be allocated for students whose permanent homes are in one of the four Dogrib Treaty 11 communities.

Award: Scholarship for use in senior year. *Number:* 10. *Amount:* $743.

Eligibility Requirements: Applicant must be enrolled or expecting to enroll at a four-year or technical institution or university.

Application Requirements: Application, transcript. *Deadline:* varies.

Contact: Morven MacPherson, Post Secondary Student Support Coordinator
Dogrib Treaty 11 Scholarship Committee
c/o CJBRHS
Bag #1
Rae-Edzo, NT X0E 0Y0
Canada
Phone: 867-371-3815
Fax: 867-371-3813
E-mail: morvenm@dogrib.net

DOLLARSHIP http://www.dollarship.com/

DOLLARSHIP

Dollarship grants unlimited $500 scholarships every three months to students worldwide. Refer to Web site for further details: http://www.dollarship.com. Applicants dollar fee will contribute fifty cents to another $500 scholarship.

Award: Scholarship for use in freshman, sophomore, junior, senior, graduate, or postgraduate years. *Number:* varies. *Amount:* $500.

Eligibility Requirements: Applicant must be enrolled or expecting to enroll full or part-time at a two-year or four-year or technical institution or university. Available to U.S. and non-U.S. citizens.

Application Requirements: Essay. *Fee:* $1. *Deadline:* Continuous.

Contact: Christina Barsch, Vice President of Operations
Dollarship
11200 West Wisconsin, Suite 10
Youngtown, AZ 85363
Phone: 623-215-2898
Fax: 623-215-2899
E-mail: cbarsch@dollarship.com

DOUGH FOR BRAINS, LLC http://www.doughforbrains.com

DOUGH FOR BRAINS ESSAY CONTESTS

Entrants complete an essay on designated topic and submit with entry form and administrative fee. Essays are judged based on established criteria and prizes are awarded to the winners. Complete rules and information on Web site: http://www.doughforbrains.com.

Award: Prize for use in freshman, sophomore, junior, senior, graduate, or postgraduate years; not renewable. *Number:* 50–200. *Amount:* $250–$5000.

Eligibility Requirements: Applicant must be age 13 and enrolled or expecting to enroll full or part-time at a two-year or four-year or technical institution or university. Available to U.S. citizens.

Application Requirements: Applicant must enter a contest, essay. *Fee:* $10. *Deadline:* Continuous.

Contact: Mark Snedeker, Chief Operating Officer
Dough for Brains, LLC
PO Box 220656
Chantilly, VA 20153-0656
Phone: 703-655-2479
E-mail: msnedeker@doughforbrains.com

DYZCO TECHNOLOGIES, INC.

DYZCO ESSAY CONTEST

Essay contest will award up to $10,000 to the winner to cover tuition expenses for one full year. Institution must be approved by Dyzco, and winner must be enrolled in institution to receive prize. Essay must address question: "What is the future of distance learning?" Essay must be 1,000 words or less, and written in English. Applications available online only: http://www.dyzco.com.

Award: Prize for use in freshman, sophomore, junior, senior, graduate, or postgraduate years; not renewable. *Number:* 1. *Amount:* up to $10,000.

Eligibility Requirements: Applicant must be age 18 and enrolled or expecting to enroll at an institution or university. Available to U.S. citizens.

Application Requirements: Applicant must enter a contest, essay. *Deadline:* July 1.

Contact: See Web site.

E-COLLEGEDEGREE.COM http://e-collegedegree.com

E-COLLEGEDEGREE.COM ONLINE EDUCATION SCHOLARSHIP AWARD

This award is to be used for online education. Application must be submitted online. Deadline is December 15. Please visit Web site for more information and application: http://www.e-collegedegree.com.

Award: Scholarship for use in freshman, sophomore, junior, senior, graduate, or postgraduate years; not renewable. *Number:* 2. *Amount:* $1000.

Eligibility Requirements: Applicant must be age 19 and enrolled or expecting to enroll full or part-time at a two-year or four-year or technical institution or university. Available to U.S. citizens.

Application Requirements: Application, essay. *Deadline:* December 15.

Contact: Chris Lee, Site Manager
e-CollegeDegree.com
9109 West 101st Terrace
Overland Park, KS 66212
Phone: 913-341-6949
E-mail: scholarship@e-collegedegree.com

EARTH ISLAND INSTITUTE http://www.earthisland.org/bya

BROWER YOUTH AWARDS

Brower Youth Awards seeks to recognize youth leadership of initiatives which promote conservation, preservation, and restoration of the earth. For more details see Web site: http://www.earthisland.org/bya.

Award: Prize for use in freshman, sophomore, junior, or senior years; not renewable. *Number:* 6. *Amount:* $3000.

Eligibility Requirements: Applicant must be age 13-22 and enrolled or expecting to enroll full or part-time at a two-year or four-year or technical institution or university. Available to U.S. and non-U.S. citizens.

Application Requirements: Application, essay, references. *Deadline:* June 1.

Contact: Cindy Arch, Brower Youth Awards Director
Earth Island Institute
300 Broadway, Suite 28
San Francisco, CA 94133
Phone: 415-788-3666
Fax: 415-788-7324
E-mail: broweryouthawards@earthisland.org

EASTERN AMPUTEE GOLF ASSOCIATION

http://www.eaga.org/

EASTERN AMPUTEE GOLF ASSOCIATION SCHOLARSHIP FUND

Renewable scholarship available for $1000 per year based on continuing eligibility. Applicant must maintain a minimum 2.0 GPA each semester, and prove continuing evidence of financial need. Applicant must be an amputee or a dependent of an amputee, as well as member in good standing of the EAGA. Please refer to Web site for further details: http://www.eaga.org.

Award: Scholarship for use in freshman, sophomore, junior, or senior years; renewable. *Number:* 1–6. *Amount:* $1000.

Eligibility Requirements: Applicant must be enrolled or expecting to enroll full or part-time at a two-year or four-year or technical institution or university. Available to U.S. and Canadian citizens.

Application Requirements: Application, autobiography, essay, financial need analysis, resume, transcript, SAR. *Deadline:* varies.

Contact: Linda Buck, Secretary
Eastern Amputee Golf Association
2015 Amherst Drive
Bethlehem, PA 18015-5606
Phone: 610-867-9295
Fax: 610-867-9295
E-mail: info@eaga.org

EDDIE ROBINSON FOUNDATION

http://www.eddierobinson.com

EDDIE ROBINSON FOUNDATION EIGHTH GRADE SCHOLARSHIP

Open to all eighth-grade students who have distinguished themselves as leaders among peers in school, community, and athletics and who display a can-do attitude despite obstacles. Awards overall candidate, not strictly students with high GPA. Must be a U.S. citizen. Essay required. Deadline is March 15. For additional information visit Web site: http://www.eddierobinson.com.

Award: Scholarship for use in freshman, sophomore, junior, or senior years; renewable. *Number:* 2–4. *Amount:* $20,000.

Eligibility Requirements: Applicant must be enrolled or expecting to enroll full-time at a four-year institution or university. Applicant must have 2.5 GPA or higher. Available to U.S. citizens.

Application Requirements: Application, essay, references, transcript. *Deadline:* March 15.

Contact: Cherie Kirkland, Vice President
Eddie Robinson Foundation
3500 Piedmont Road
Suite 100
Atlanta, GA 30305
Phone: 404-475-8408
E-mail: scholarship@eddierobinson.com

EDDIE ROBINSON FOUNDATION HIGH SCHOOL SENIOR SCHOLARSHIP

Open to all high school seniors. Selection process based on a system using scholastic achievements, athletic accomplishments, leadership skills, and community involvement. Essay also required. Awards overall candidate, not strictly students with high GPA. Must be U.S. citizen. Deadline is March 15. For additional information visit Web site http://www.eddierobinson.com

Award: Scholarship for use in freshman, sophomore, junior, or senior years; renewable. *Number:* 2–4. *Amount:* $20,000.

Eligibility Requirements: Applicant must be high school student and planning to enroll or expecting to enroll full-time at a four-year institution or university. Applicant must have 2.5 GPA or higher. Available to U.S. citizens.

Application Requirements: Application, essay, references, test scores, transcript. *Deadline:* March 15.

Contact: Cherie Kirkland, Vice President
Eddie Robinson Foundation
3500 Piedmont Road
Suite 100
Atlanta, GA 30305
Phone: 404-475-8408
E-mail: scholarship@eddierobinson.com

EDUCAID, WACHOVIA CORPORATION

http://www.educaid.com

EDUCAID GIMME FIVE SCHOLARSHIP SWEEPSTAKES

Each year, Educaid will award 12 high school seniors $5000 for their first year at an accredited college or trade school. The scholarships are not based on grades or financial need, so every eligible high school senior who enters has an equal chance of winning. Apply online at: http://www.educaid.com.

Award: Prize for use in freshman year; not renewable. *Number:* 12. *Amount:* $5000.

Eligibility Requirements: Applicant must be high school student and planning to enroll or expecting to enroll full-time at a two-year or four-year or technical institution or university. Available to U.S. citizens.

Application Requirements: *Deadline:* Continuous.

Contact: Applications accepted online only.

EDUCATION IS FREEDOM FOUNDATION

http://www.educationisfreedom.com/default.asp

EDUCATION IS FREEDOM NATIONAL SCHOLARSHIP

Applicants for this renewable scholarship must be high school seniors planning full-time undergraduate study at a 2 or 4-year college or university. Selection criteria is based on financial need, leadership and activities, work history, and candidate appraisal. Application available online at: http://www.educationisfreedom.com/scholarships/scholarships.asp.

Award: Scholarship for use in freshman, sophomore, junior, or senior years; renewable. *Number:* up to 225. *Amount:* $2000.

Eligibility Requirements: Applicant must be high school student and planning to enroll or expecting to enroll full-time at a two-year or four-year institution or university. Applicant must have 3.0 GPA or higher. Available to U.S. citizens.

Application Requirements: Application, financial need analysis, references, transcript. *Deadline:* January 15.

Contact: Barb Weber, Director of Operations
Education is Freedom Foundation
Scholarship America
Saint Peter, MN 56082

EDUCATIONAL COMMUNICATIONS SCHOLARSHIP FOUNDATION

http://www.whoswho-highschool.com/3scholarshipsgrants/scholarshipprogram.aspx

EDUCATIONAL COMMUNICATIONS SCHOLARSHIP

Award based on scholarship, financial need, leadership, and extracurricular activity. Must be legal resident of U.S. to apply. Must have a minimum 3.0 GPA and have taken ACT or SAT exam. Semifinalists submit financial need analysis and essay; finalists submit transcript. Application fee is $3.50. Applications are available only at high school guidance offices. For application go to http://www.honoring.com/highschool/frame.html.

Award: Scholarship for use in freshman, sophomore, junior, or senior years; not renewable. *Number:* 200. *Amount:* $1000.

Eligibility Requirements: Applicant must be high school student and planning to enroll or expecting to enroll full or part-time at a two-year or four-year or technical institution or university. Applicant must have 3.0 GPA or higher. Available to U.S. citizens.

Application Requirements: Application, essay, financial need analysis, test scores, transcript. *Fee:* $3.5. *Deadline:* May 15.

Contact: Scholarship Coordinator
Educational Communications Scholarship Foundation
1701 Directors Boulevard, Suite 920
Austin, TX 78744
Phone: 512-440-2705
Fax: 512-447-1687
E-mail: school@ecsf.org

ELKS NATIONAL FOUNDATION

http://www.elks.org/enf

ELKS MOST VALUABLE STUDENT CONTEST

Five hundred four-year awards are allocated for graduating high school seniors nationally by state quota. Based on scholarship, leadership, and financial need. Renewable awards with two first place awards at $60,000, two second place awards at $40,000 and two third place awards at $20,000. The awards will be distributed over four years. The remainder of the 494 awards will continue to be worth $4000 over four years. Applications available at local Elks Lodge, at the Web site (http://www.elks.org) (keyword: scholarship) or by sending a SASE to the Foundation.

Award: Scholarship for use in freshman, sophomore, junior, or senior years; renewable. *Number:* 500. *Amount:* $4000–$60,000.

Eligibility Requirements: Applicant must be high school student and planning to enroll or expecting to enroll full-time at a two-year or four-year institution or university. Available to U.S. citizens.

Application Requirements: Application, applicant must enter a contest, essay, financial need analysis, references, self-addressed stamped envelope, test scores, transcript. *Deadline:* January 9.

Contact: Robin Edison, Scholarship Coordinator
Elks National Foundation
2750 North Lakeview Avenue
Chicago, IL 60614-1889
Phone: 773-755-4732
Fax: 773-755-4733
E-mail: scholarship@elks.org

EPSILON SIGMA ALPHA FOUNDATION http://www.esaintl.com/esaf

EPSILON SIGMA ALPHA SCHOLARSHIPS

Awards for various fields of study. Some scholarships are restricted by gender, residency, grade point average, or location of school. Applications must be sent to the Epsilon Sigma Alpha designated state counselor. See Web site at http://www.esaintl.com/esaf for further information, application forms, and a list of state counselors. Application deadline is February 1.

Award: Scholarship for use in freshman, sophomore, junior, senior, or graduate years; not renewable. *Number:* 100–125. *Amount:* $500–$1500.

Eligibility Requirements: Applicant must be enrolled or expecting to enroll full or part-time at an institution or university.

Application Requirements: Application. *Deadline:* February 1.

Contact: Application available at Web site.

EXECUTIVE WOMEN INTERNATIONAL http://www.executivewomen.org

ADULT STUDENTS IN SCHOLASTIC TRANSITION

A scholarship for adult students at transitional points in their lives. Applicants may be single parents, individuals just entering the workforce, or displaced homemakers. Chapter awards vary in amount; the Corporate level awards 12 scholarships valued at $1000 each. Application deadline is April 1.

Award: Scholarship for use in freshman, sophomore, junior, senior, or graduate years. *Number:* 100–150. *Amount:* $1000–$2000.

Eligibility Requirements: Applicant must be enrolled or expecting to enroll at a two-year or four-year or technical institution or university. Available to U.S. citizens.

Application Requirements: *Deadline:* April 1.

Contact: Suzette Smith, Marketing Director
Executive Women International
515 South 700 East, Suite 2A
Salt Lake City, UT 84102
Phone: 801-355-2800
Fax: 801-362-3212

FINANCIAL SERVICE CENTERS OF AMERICA, INC. http://www.fisca.org

FINANCIAL SERVICE CENTERS OF AMERICA SCHOLARSHIP FUND

The FiSCA Scholarship Program awards cash grants of at least $2,000 to two students from each of the 5 geographic regions across the country. Criteria is based on academic achievement, financial need, leadership skills in schools and the community, and an essay written expressly for the competition. Applicant must be single. See Web site for information on the 5 geographic regions and names and addresses of the Regional Chairmen. Applications should be mailed to the appropriate Regional Chairman.

Award: Grant for use in freshman year; not renewable. *Number:* 10–20. *Amount:* $2000.

Eligibility Requirements: Applicant must be high school student; planning to enroll or expecting to enroll full-time at a two-year or four-year institution or university and single. Available to U.S. citizens.

Application Requirements: Application, essay, financial need analysis, photo, references, transcript. *Deadline:* May 17.

Contact: Regional Chairman

FOUNDATION FOR INDEPENDENT HIGHER EDUCATION http://www.fihe.org

LIBERTY MUTUAL SCHOLARSHIP PROGRAM

Funded by Liberty Mutual and administered by the Foundation for Independent Higher Education. $5000 combined with an opportunity for a summer internship. Renewable for senior year. Students should have an interest in a career in a business environment. Must be a resident of or studying in one of the following states: CA, IL, NH, NY, TX, GA, MA, NJ, PA, or WI.

Award: Scholarship for use in junior or senior years; renewable. *Number:* 17. *Amount:* $5000.

Eligibility Requirements: Applicant must be enrolled or expecting to enroll full-time at a four-year institution or university. Applicant must have 3.5 GPA or higher. Available to U.S. and non-U.S. citizens.

Application Requirements: Application, resume, transcript, questionnaire. *Deadline:* varies.

Contact: John Carr, Vice President, FIHE
Foundation for Independent Higher Education
1920 N Street, NW, Suite 210
Washington, DC 20036
Phone: 202-367-0333
Fax: 202-367-0334
E-mail: jcarr@fihe.org

FREEDOM FROM RELIGION FOUNDATION http://www.ffrf.org

FREEDOM FROM RELIGION FOUNDATION COLLEGE ESSAY CONTEST

Any currently enrolled college student may submit college essays. Essays should be typed, double-spaced pages with standard margins. Contestants must choose an original title for essay. Each contestant must include a paragraph biography giving campus and permanent addresses, phone numbers, and email(s). Please identify the college or university the contestant is attending, year in school, major, and interests. The essay topic and specific guidelines are posted in February. For more information visit: http://www.ffrf.org/.

Award: Prize for use in freshman, sophomore, junior, or senior years; not renewable. *Number:* 5. *Amount:* $100–$1000.

Eligibility Requirements: Applicant must be enrolled or expecting to enroll at a two-year or four-year or technical institution or university. Available to U.S. citizens.

Application Requirements: Applicant must enter a contest, essay. *Deadline:* July 1.

Contact: Freedom From Religion Foundation
PO Box 750
Madison, WI 53701

FREEDOM FROM RELIGION FOUNDATION HIGH SCHOOL ESSAY CONTEST

High-school essays should be typed, double-spaced pages with standard margins. Contestants must choose an original title for essay. Each entrant must include a paragraph biography giving campus and permanent addresses, phone numbers and emails. Identify the high school from which the student will have graduated and the college/university the student will be attending. The essay topic and specific guidelines are posted in February. For more information visit: http://www.ffrf.org/.

Award: Prize for use in freshman year; not renewable. *Number:* 5. *Amount:* $100–$1000.

Eligibility Requirements: Applicant must be high school student and planning to enroll or expecting to enroll at a two-year or four-year or technical institution or university. Available to U.S. citizens.

Freedom From Religion Foundation (continued)

Application Requirements: Applicant must enter a contest, essay. *Deadline:* June 1.

Contact: Freedom From Religion Foundation
PO Box 750
Madison, WI 53701

GARDEN CLUB OF AMERICA http://www.gcamerica.org

CAROLINE THORN KISSEL SUMMER ENVIRONMENTAL STUDIES SCHOLARSHIP

For college students, graduate students, or non-degree seeking applicants above the high school level. Applicants must be U.S. citizens and either residents of New Jersey studying in New Jersey or elsewhere, or non residents pursuing a study in New Jersey or its surrounding waters.

Award: Scholarship for use in freshman, sophomore, junior, senior, or graduate years.

Eligibility Requirements: Applicant must be enrolled or expecting to enroll at an institution or university. Available to U.S. citizens.

Application Requirements: Application, essay, references. *Deadline:* February 10.

Contact: Garden Club of America
Scholarship Committee
14 East 60th Street
New York, NY 10022-1002

ZELLER SUMMER SCHOLARSHIP IN MEDICINAL BOTANY

For field work or research in Medicinal Botany. Work may award academic credit. Applicants may apply following their freshman, sophomore, junior and senior years. A report is required at the end of the summer study. See Web site for further details.

Award: Scholarship for use in sophomore, junior, or senior years. *Number:* 1. *Amount:* $1500.

Eligibility Requirements: Applicant must be enrolled or expecting to enroll at an institution or university.

Application Requirements: Application, essay, references, transcript. *Deadline:* February 1.

Contact: Garden Club of America
Scholarship Committee
14 East 60th Street
New York, NY 10022-1002

GEORGIA POLICE CORPS http://www.gapolicecorps.org

GEORGIA POLICE CORPS SCHOLARSHIP

Awards available for reimbursement of educational expenses for undergraduate and graduate study. Obligation to commit to four years of service at a participating law enforcement agency. Check Web site for application and updated information.

Award: Scholarship for use in junior or senior years. *Number:* 10. *Amount:* up to $23,000.

Eligibility Requirements: Applicant must be enrolled or expecting to enroll at a four-year institution or university. Available to U.S. citizens.

Application Requirements: Application, essay, references, transcript. *Deadline:* February 1.

Contact: Bob Gaylor, Program Director
Georgia Police Corps
1000 Indian Springs Drive
Forsyth, GA 31029
Phone: 877-267-4630
Fax: 478-993-4560
E-mail: bgaylor@gpstc.state.ga.us

GLAMOUR http://www.glamour.com

TOP TEN COLLEGE WOMEN COMPETITION

Glamour is looking for female students with leadership experience on and off campus, excellence in field of study, and inspiring goals. Award is $1500 and a trip to New York City. Must be a junior studying full-time with a minimum GPA of 3.0. Non-U.S. citizens may apply if attending U.S. postsecondary institutions. Application deadline is February 10. See Web site at http://www.glamour.com from October to February for information.

Award: Prize for use in junior year; not renewable. *Number:* 10. *Amount:* $1500.

Eligibility Requirements: Applicant must be enrolled or expecting to enroll full-time at a four-year institution or university and female. Applicant must have 3.0 GPA or higher. Available to U.S. and non-U.S. citizens.

Application Requirements: Application, essay, photo, references, transcript, list of activities, signatures of faculty adviser and other college administrator. *Deadline:* February 10.

Contact: Lynda Laux-Bachand, Reader Services Editor
Glamour
4 Times Square
16th Floor
New York, NY 10036-6593
Phone: 212-286-6667
Fax: 212-286-6922
E-mail: ttcw@glamour.com

GLORIA BARRON PRIZE FOR YOUNG HEROES http://www.barronprize.org

GLORIA BARRON PRIZE FOR YOUNG HEROES

Award honors young people ages 8 to 18 who have shown leadership and courage in public service to people or to the planet. Must be nominated by a responsible adult who is not a relative. Award is to be applied to higher education or a service project. For further information and nomination forms, see Web site at http://www.barronprize.org.

Award: Prize for use in freshman year; not renewable. *Number:* 10–20. *Amount:* $2000.

Eligibility Requirements: Applicant must be age 8-18 and enrolled or expecting to enroll at an institution or university. Available to U.S. and Canadian citizens.

Application Requirements: Application, essay, photo, references, nomination. *Deadline:* varies.

Contact: Barbara Ann Richman, Program Director
Gloria Barron Prize for Young Heroes
PO Box 17
Boulder, CO 80306
Phone: 970-875-1448
Fax: 970-875-1451
E-mail: ba_richman@barronprize.org

GUARDIAN LIFE INSURANCE COMPANY OF AMERICA http://www.girlsgoingplaces.com

GIRLS GOING PLACES SCHOLARSHIP PROGRAM

Rewards the enterprising spirits of girls ages 12 to 16 who demonstrate budding entrepreneurship, are taking the first steps toward financial independence, and make a difference in their school and community.

Award: Prize for use in freshman year; not renewable. *Number:* 15. *Amount:* $1000–$10,000.

Eligibility Requirements: Applicant must be high school student; age 12-16; planning to enroll or expecting to enroll full-time at a two-year or four-year or technical institution or university and single female. Available to U.S. citizens.

Application Requirements: Application, essay. *Deadline:* February 28.

Contact: Diana Acevedo, Project Manager
Guardian Life Insurance Company of America
7 Hanover Square 26-C
New York, NY 10004
Phone: 212-598-7881
Fax: 212-919-2586
E-mail: diana_acevedo@glic.com

HALF PRICE COMPUTER BOOKS http://www.halfpricecomputerbooks.com/scholarship.php

HALF PRICE COMPUTER BOOKS ESSAY COMPETITION SCHOLARSHIP AWARD

Essay Competition runs twice a year. Entrants must choose one of three predetermined topics from Web site, and write an essay 500-700 words in length. Winners must provide proof of registration in a college, university, or technical institution. For further details visit Web site: http://www.halfpricecomputerbooks.com

Award: Scholarship for use in freshman, sophomore, junior, senior, graduate, or postgraduate years; not renewable. *Number:* 3–6. *Amount:* $250–$500.

Eligibility Requirements: Applicant must be enrolled or expecting to enroll full or part-time at a two-year or four-year or technical institution or university. Available to U.S. and Canadian citizens.

Application Requirements: Applicant must enter a contest, essay, transcript, proof of enrollment in a postsecondary institution. *Deadline:* varies.

Contact: Jessica Cook, Director of Internet Operations
Half Price Computer Books
PMB 115, 1125 Fir Avenue
Blaine, WA 98230
Phone: 604-945-7085 Ext. 314
Fax: 604-945-7229
E-mail: scholarship@halfpricecomputerbooks.com

HAWAII SCHOOLS FEDERAL CREDIT UNION http://www.hawaiischoolsfcu.org/

EDWIN KUNIYUKI MEMORIAL SCHOLARSHIP

Annual scholarship for an incoming college freshman in recognition of academic excellence. Applicant must be Hawaii Schools Federal Credit Union member for one year prior to scholarship application.

Award: Scholarship for use in freshman year; not renewable. *Number:* 1. *Amount:* $1000.

Eligibility Requirements: Applicant must be high school student and planning to enroll or expecting to enroll full-time at a two-year or four-year or technical institution or university. Applicant must have 3.0 GPA or higher. Available to U.S. citizens.

Application Requirements: Application, essay, references, transcript. *Deadline:* varies.

Contact: Stephanie Lachance, Administrative Assistant
Hawaii Schools Federal Credit Union
233 South Vineyard Street
Honolulu, HI 96813
Phone: 808-521-0302
Fax: 808-538-3231
E-mail: slachance@hawaiischoolsfcu.org

HELPING HANDS FOUNDATION http://www.helpinghandsbookscholarship.com

HELPING HANDS BOOK SCHOLARSHIP PROGRAM

The HHBSP was created to assist students with the high cost of textbooks and study materials. Awards are open to individuals ages 16 and up who are planning to attend or are currently attending a two- or four-year college or university or a technical/vocational institution. Application fee is $5.

Award: Grant for use in freshman, sophomore, junior, senior, or graduate years; not renewable. *Number:* 20–30. *Amount:* $100–$1000.

Eligibility Requirements: Applicant must be age 16 and enrolled or expecting to enroll full or part-time at a two-year or four-year or technical institution or university. Available to U.S. and non-U.S. citizens.

Application Requirements: Application, essay, self-addressed stamped envelope, transcript. *Fee:* $5. *Deadline:* Continuous.

Contact: Scholarship Director
Helping Hands Foundation
PO Box 720379
Atlanta, GA 30358
Fax: 770-384-0376

HENKEL CONSUMER ADHESIVES, INC. http://www.ducktapeclub.com

DUCK BRAND DUCT TAPE "STUCK AT PROM" SCHOLARSHIP CONTEST

Contest is open to residents of the United States and Canada. Must be 14 years or older and attend a high school prom in the spring. Participants must adorn themselves in stylishly "sticky" fashions made from duct tape. Must enter as a couple. Submit color photo. Visit Web site for further details. Deadline is June 11.

Award: Prize for use in freshman, sophomore, junior, or senior years; not renewable. *Number:* 3. *Amount:* $500–$2500.

Eligibility Requirements: Applicant must be high school student; age 14 and planning to enroll or expecting to enroll full or part-time at a two-year or four-year or technical institution or university. Available to U.S. and Canadian citizens.

Application Requirements: Applicant must enter a contest, photo, entry form, release form. *Deadline:* June 11.

Contact: Information available at Web site.

HERSCHEL C. PRICE EDUCATIONAL FOUNDATION

HERSCHEL C. PRICE EDUCATIONAL FOUNDATION SCHOLARSHIPS

Open to undergraduates, graduates, and high school seniors. Must be a U.S. citizen, and either a resident of West Virginia, or attend a West Virginia college. Based on academic achievement and financial need. Deadlines are April 1 for fall and October 1 for spring. Undergraduates are shown preference.

Award: Scholarship for use in freshman, sophomore, junior, senior, or graduate years; not renewable. *Number:* 200–300. *Amount:* $500–$10,000.

Eligibility Requirements: Applicant must be enrolled or expecting to enroll full or part-time at a two-year or four-year institution or university. Available to U.S. citizens.

Application Requirements: Application, financial need analysis, interview, test scores, transcript. *Deadline:* varies.

Contact: Jonna Hughes, Trustee/Director
Herschel C. Price Educational Foundation
PO Box 412
Huntington, WV 25708-0412
Phone: 304-529-3852

HISPANIC ASSOCIATION OF COLLEGES AND UNIVERSITIES (HACU) http://www.hacu.net

HISPANIC ASSOCIATION OF COLLEGES AND UNIVERSITIES SCHOLARSHIP PROGRAMS

The scholarship programs are made possible due to generous contributions from corporate and federal organizations. To be eligible, students must attend a HACU member college or university and meet all additional criteria.

Award: Scholarship for use in freshman, sophomore, junior, senior, or graduate years; not renewable. *Number:* varies. *Amount:* $500–$3000.

Eligibility Requirements: Applicant must be enrolled or expecting to enroll full or part-time at a two-year or four-year institution or university. Applicant must have 3.0 GPA or higher. Available to U.S. citizens.

Application Requirements: Application, essay, financial need analysis, resume, transcript, enrollment certification form. *Deadline:* May 28.

Contact: William Gil, Assistant Vice President of Collegiate Programs
Hispanic Association of Colleges and Universities (HACU)
One Dupont Circle, Suite 605
Washington, DC 20036
Phone: 202-467-0893
Fax: 202-496-9177
E-mail: hnip@hacu.net

HONOR SOCIETY OF PHI KAPPA PHI http://www.phikappaphi.org

STUDY ABROAD GRANT COMPETITION

Grants up to $1000 will be awarded to undergraduate Phi Kappa Phi members as support in seeking knowledge and experience by studying abroad. For more details see Web site: http://www.phikappaphi.org.

Award: Grant for use in freshman, sophomore, junior, or senior years; not renewable. *Number:* 38. *Amount:* $1000.

Eligibility Requirements: Applicant must be enrolled or expecting to enroll full-time at a four-year institution or university. Applicant must have 3.5 GPA or higher. Available to U.S. and non-U.S. citizens.

Honor Society of Phi Kappa Phi (continued)

Application Requirements: Application, references, transcript, letter of acceptance into a study abroad program. *Deadline:* April 15.

Contact: Theresa Bard, Programs Coordinator
Honor Society of Phi Kappa Phi
Louisiana State University
PO Box 16000
Baton Rouge, LA 70893-6000
Phone: 225-388-4917 Ext. 13
Fax: 225-388-4900
E-mail: awards@phikappaphi.org

HORATIO ALGER ASSOCIATION OF DISTINGUISHED AMERICANS http://www.horatioalger.org

HORATIO ALGER ASSOCIATION SCHOLARSHIP PROGRAM

The Horatio Alger Association provides financial assistance to students in the United States who have exhibited integrity and perseverance in overcoming personal adversity and who aspire to pursue higher education. Scholarship award for full-time students seeking undergraduate degree. Minimum 2.0 GPA required.

Award: Scholarship for use in freshman, sophomore, junior, or senior years; renewable. *Number:* up to 1400. *Amount:* $1000–$10,000.

Eligibility Requirements: Applicant must be high school student and planning to enroll or expecting to enroll full-time at a two-year or four-year institution or university. Available to U.S. citizens.

Application Requirements: Application, essay, financial need analysis, references, transcript. *Deadline:* October 15.

Contact: Scholarship Coordinator
Horatio Alger Association of Distinguished Americans
99 Canal Center Plaza, Suite 320
Alexandria, VA 22314
E-mail: programs@horatioalger.com

HUMANIST http://www.thehumanist.org/essaycontest.html

HUMANIST ESSAY CONTEST

Essay contest on any subject dealing with a humanist perspective. 2,500 words typed and double-spaced. No electronic submissions. One submission per entrant which must be written in English. Submissions become the property of the Humanist. First place winners receive $1000, second place receives $400, third place receives $100. Three awards are given out in two age categories. Two age categories; 13-17 and 18-24. Citizens of other countries are eligible only if they are in North America at the time of the contest.

Award: Prize for use in freshman, sophomore, junior, senior, or graduate years; not renewable. *Number:* 6. *Amount:* $100–$1000.

Eligibility Requirements: Applicant must be age 13-24 and enrolled or expecting to enroll at an institution or university. Available to U.S. and non-U.S. citizens.

Application Requirements: Applicant must enter a contest, essay, contact information, date of birth. *Deadline:* December 1.

Contact: Humanist
1777 T Street NW
Washington, DC 20009-7125
E-mail: aha@americanhumanist.org

INDEPENDENT INSTITUTE http://www.independent.org/garvey.html

OLIVE W. GARVEY FELLOWSHIP COMPETITION

An international essay contest held every other year. There are two divisions: College Students, and Faculty. Cash stipends are awarded for the best essays on the meaning and significance of economic and personal liberty. The specific topic changes with each contest. Applicants must be no older than 35. See Web site for more information: http://www.independent.org/students/garvey.

Award: Prize for use in freshman, sophomore, junior, senior, graduate, or postgraduate years; not renewable. *Number:* 6. *Amount:* $1000–$10,000.

Eligibility Requirements: Applicant must be age 35 or under and enrolled or expecting to enroll full or part-time at a two-year or four-year institution or university. Available to U.S. and non-U.S. citizens.

Application Requirements: Application, applicant must enter a contest, essay, references. *Deadline:* May 1.

Contact: Carl Close, Academic Affairs Director
Independent Institute
100 Swan Way
Oakland, CA 94621
Phone: 510-632-1366
Fax: 510-568-6040
E-mail: cclose@independent.org

INDIANA POLICE CORPS http://www.in.gov/cji/policecorps

POLICE CORPS INCENTIVE SCHOLARSHIP

Scholarships are available to highly qualified men and women entering the Police Corps. Up to $3750 a year for four years can be used to cover the expenses of study toward a baccalaureate or graduate degree. For more details and an application see Web site: http://www.in.gov/cji.policecorps. Must agree to serve four years in community policing in Indiana.

Award: Scholarship for use in junior, senior, or graduate years; renewable. *Number:* up to 20. *Amount:* up to $3750.

Eligibility Requirements: Applicant must be enrolled or expecting to enroll full-time at a four-year institution or university. Available to U.S. citizens.

Application Requirements: Application, driver's license, references, transcript. *Deadline:* Continuous.

Contact: Application available at Web site.

INSTITUTE FOR OPERATIONS RESEARCH AND THE MANAGEMENT SCIENCES http://www.informs.org

GEORGE NICHOLSON STUDENT PAPER COMPETITION

To honor outstanding papers in the field of operations research and the management sciences. Entrant must be student on or after the year of application. Research papers present original results and be written by student. Electronic submission of paper required. Refer to Web site for details.

Award: Prize for use in junior, senior, graduate, or postgraduate years. *Number:* up to 6. *Amount:* $100–$600.

Eligibility Requirements: Applicant must be enrolled or expecting to enroll at an institution or university.

Application Requirements: *Deadline:* June 30.

Contact: See Web site.

INSTITUTE OF INTERNATIONAL EDUCATION http://www.iie.org

NATIONAL SECURITY EDUCATION PROGRAM DAVID L. BOREN UNDERGRADUATE SCHOLARSHIPS

The National Security Education Program (NSEP) awards scholarships to American undergraduate students for study abroad in regions critical to U.S. national interest. Emphasized world areas include Africa, Asia, Central and Eastern Europe, the NIS, Latin America and the Caribbean, and the Middle East. NSEP scholarship recipients incur a service agreement. Must be a U.S. citizen.

Award: Scholarship for use in freshman, sophomore, junior, or senior years; not renewable. *Number:* 150–200. *Amount:* $2500–$20,000.

Eligibility Requirements: Applicant must be enrolled or expecting to enroll full or part-time at a two-year or four-year institution or university. Available to U.S. citizens.

Application Requirements: Application, essay, financial need analysis, references, transcript, campus review. *Deadline:* February 12.

Contact: Deborah Eastman, NSEP Program Officer
Institute of International Education
1400 K Street NW, Suite 650
Washington, DC 20005-2403
Phone: 800-618-6737
Fax: 202-326-7697
E-mail: nsep@iie.org

INTERNATIONAL ORGANIZATION OF MASTERS, MATES AND PILOTS HEALTH AND BENEFIT PLAN

M.M. & P. HEALTH AND BENEFIT PLAN SCHOLARSHIP PROGRAM

Scholarships available to dependent children (under 23 years of age) of parents who meet the eligibility requirements set forth by the M.M.&P. Health and Benefit Plan. Selection of winners will be based on test scores, high school record, extracurricular activities, leadership qualities, recommendations, and students' own statements. High school students who apply must take the SAT and indicate code for M.M.&P. to receive scores. Applications with complete guidelines may be obtained from any port office or from the plan office in Maryland. Deadline November 30.

Award: Scholarship for use in freshman, sophomore, junior, or senior years; renewable. *Number:* 6. *Amount:* up to $5000.

Eligibility Requirements: Applicant must be age 22 or under; enrolled or expecting to enroll full-time at a four-year institution or university and single.

Application Requirements: Application, test scores. *Deadline:* November 30.

Contact: Mary Ellen Beach, Scholarship Program
International Organization of Masters, Mates and Pilots Health and Benefit Plan
5700 Hammonds Ferry Road
Linthicum Heights, MD 21090-1996
Phone: 410-850-8624
Fax: 410-850-8655

INTERNATIONAL UNION OF BRICKLAYERS AND ALLIED CRAFTWORKERS http://www.bacweb.org

HARRY C. BATES SCHOLARSHIP

Renewable award program designated to financially assist the children of the members of the Bricklayers and Allied Craftworkers International Union. Qualified applicants must be National Merit Scholarship semi-finalist. Minimum 3.0 GPA required.

Award: Scholarship for use in freshman year; renewable. *Number:* 2–3. *Amount:* up to $2000.

Eligibility Requirements: Applicant must be high school student and planning to enroll or expecting to enroll full-time at a two-year or four-year or technical institution or university. Applicant must have 3.0 GPA or higher. Available to U.S. and Canadian citizens.

Application Requirements: Application, references, test scores, transcript. *Deadline:* May 31.

Contact: Connie Lambert, Director of Education
International Union of Bricklayers and Allied Craftworkers
1776 Eye Street, NW
Washington, DC 20005
Phone: 202-783-3788
Fax: 202-772-3800
E-mail: askbac@bacweb.org

JACK KENT COOKE FOUNDATION http://www.jackkentcookefoundation.org/

JACK KENT COOKE FOUNDATION UNDERGRADUATE TRANSFER SCHOLARSHIP PROGRAM

The Jack Kent Cooke Foundation Undergraduate Transfer Scholarship Program provides scholarships to students and recent alumni from community college to complete their bachelor's degrees at accredited four-year colleges or universities in the United States or abroad. Candidates must be nominated by a faculty representative from their community college.

Award: Scholarship for use in junior or senior years; renewable. *Number:* 30. *Amount:* up to $30,000.

Eligibility Requirements: Applicant must be enrolled or expecting to enroll full-time at a two-year or four-year institution or university. Applicant must have 3.5 GPA or higher. Available to U.S. and non-U.S. citizens.

Application Requirements: Application, essay, financial need analysis, references, transcript. *Deadline:* February 2.

Contact: Jack Kent Cooke Foundation Faculty Representative

JAMES F. LINCOLN ARC WELDING FOUNDATION http://www.jflf.org

JAMES F. LINCOLN ARC WELDING FOUNDATION AWARDS PROGRAM

Applicants may apply for prize money, which will be awarded to the winners of a contest that requires the submission of a photo or drawing of a welding project that they have built. Must have minimum 2.5 GPA. Application deadline is June 1. Must include self-addressed stamped envelope.

Award: Prize for use in freshman, sophomore, junior, senior, graduate, or postgraduate years; not renewable. *Number:* 200–400. *Amount:* $50–$2500.

Eligibility Requirements: Applicant must be age 15-80 and enrolled or expecting to enroll full or part-time at a two-year or four-year or technical institution or university. Applicant must have 2.5 GPA or higher. Available to U.S. and non-U.S. citizens.

Application Requirements: Application, applicant must enter a contest, photo, self-addressed stamped envelope, transcript. *Deadline:* June 1.

Contact: Lori Hurley, Administrator, JFLF
James F. Lincoln Arc Welding Foundation
PO Box 17188
22801 Saint Clair Avenue
Cleveland, OH 44117-1199
Phone: 216-383-2707
Fax: 216-383-8220
E-mail: lori_hurley@lincolnelectric.com

JAYCEE WAR MEMORIAL FUND

JAYCEE WAR MEMORIAL FUND SCHOLARSHIP

Twenty-five (25) scholarships awarded annually. Applicants must be citizens of the United States, possess academic potential and leadership qualities, and show financial need. The scholarship is an award of $1,000 sent directly to the recipient's college or university of choice. Minimum 2.5 GPA required.

Award: Scholarship for use in freshman, sophomore, junior, or senior years; not renewable. *Number:* up to 25. *Amount:* up to $1000.

Eligibility Requirements: Applicant must be enrolled or expecting to enroll full or part-time at a two-year or four-year or technical institution or university. Applicant must have 2.5 GPA or higher. Available to U.S. citizens.

Application Requirements: Application, financial need analysis, self-addressed stamped envelope, transcript. *Fee:* $5. *Deadline:* March 1.

Contact: Scholarship Coordinator
Jaycee War Memorial Fund
PO Box 7
Tulsa, OK 74102-0007
Phone: 800-529-2337
Fax: 918-592-4372

JEANNETTE RANKIN FOUNDATION, INC. http://www.rankinfoundation.org

JEANNETTE RANKIN FOUNDATION AWARDS

Applicants must be low-income women, age 35 or older, who are pursuing a technical/vocational education, an associate's degree, or a first-time bachelor's degree. Applications are available November-February. Download materials from the Web site (http://www.rankinfoundation.org) or send a self-addressed stamped envelope to request an application by mail.

Award: Grant for use in freshman, sophomore, junior, or senior years; not renewable. *Number:* 50. *Amount:* $2000.

Eligibility Requirements: Applicant must be age 35; enrolled or expecting to enroll full or part-time at a two-year or four-year or technical institution or university and female. Available to U.S. citizens.

Application Requirements: Application, essay, financial need analysis, references, self-addressed stamped envelope, transcript. *Deadline:* March 1.

Contact: Andrea Anderson, Program Coordinator
Jeannette Rankin Foundation, Inc.
PO Box 6653
Athens, GA 30604-6653
Phone: 706-208-1211
Fax: 706-208-1211
E-mail: info@rankinfoundation.org

JOHN F. KENNEDY LIBRARY FOUNDATION http://www.jfklibrary.org

PROFILE IN COURAGE ESSAY CONTEST

Essay contest open to all high school students, grades 9-12. Students in U.S. territories and U.S. citizens attending schools overseas may also apply. Essay must be original work; attach bibliography. Essay must be no longer than 1,000 words. All essays will be judged on the overall originality of topic and the clear communication of ideas through language. Essayist must have an English or History teacher as nominating teacher. Winner and their nominating teacher are invited to Kennedy Library to accept award. Winner receives $3000, nomination teacher receives grant of $500; second place receives $1000 and five finalists receive $500. For further information about essay topic go to Web site: http://www.jfkcontest.org.

Award: Prize for use in freshman year; not renewable. *Number:* 7. *Amount:* $500–$3000.

Eligibility Requirements: Applicant must be high school student and planning to enroll or expecting to enroll at an institution or university. Available to U.S. citizens.

Application Requirements: Applicant must enter a contest, essay. *Deadline:* January 7.

Contact: Esther Kohn, Profile in Courage Essay Contest Coordinator
John F. Kennedy Library Foundation
Columbia Point
Boston, MA 02125
Phone: 617-514-1649
Fax: 617-514-1641
E-mail: profiles@nara.gov

JOHN GYLES EDUCATION AWARDS http://www.johngyleseducationcenter.com

JOHN GYLES EDUCATION AWARDS

Financial assistance available to full-time students in the U.S. and Canada. Full Canadian or U.S. citizenship is required. Available to both male and female students for all areas of postsecondary study. Minimum GPA of 2.7 required. Filing dates for mailing applications are June 1, and November 15. Students may send a stamped, self-addressed standard letter sized envelope in order to receive an application or go to Web site: http://www.johngyleseducationcenter.com. High school students are eligible but may only apply during the last half of their senior year.

Award: Scholarship for use in freshman, sophomore, junior, or senior years; not renewable. *Amount:* up to $3000.

Eligibility Requirements: Applicant must be enrolled or expecting to enroll full-time at a two-year or four-year institution or university. Available to U.S. and Canadian citizens.

Application Requirements: Application.

Contact: Secretary
John Gyles Education Awards
165 Parkside Drive
PO Box 4808
Fredericton, NB E3B 5G4
Canada
Phone: 506-459-7460

JUST WITHIN REACH FOUNDATION http://www.justwithinreach.org

ENVIRONMENTAL SCIENCES AND MARINE STUDIES SCHOLARSHIP

Three $2,000 awards are given to environmental science scholars and three $2,000 awards are given to marine studies scholars. Must be U.S. citizens and must be either undergraduate students currently enrolled in a postsecondary institution or high school seniors accepted as full-time students of an accredited, public or private four-year college or university in the U.S. Minimum 3.0 GPA required. For more information and applications visit Web site: http://www.justwithinreach.org

Award: Scholarship for use in freshman, sophomore, junior, or senior years; not renewable. *Number:* 6. *Amount:* $2000.

Eligibility Requirements: Applicant must be enrolled or expecting to enroll full-time at a four-year institution or university. Applicant must have 3.0 GPA or higher. Available to U.S. citizens.

Application Requirements: Application, essay, financial need analysis, resume, references, transcript. *Deadline:* March 12.

Contact: Vicki Hanna, Scholarship Committee
Just Within Reach Foundation
3940 Laurel Canyon Boulevard
PMB 256
Studio City, CA 91604
E-mail: info@justwithinreach.org

KAPLAN/NEWSWEEK http://www.kaptest.com/essay

"MY TURN" ESSAY COMPETITION

Essay contest open to high school students entering college or university. Can win up to $5000. Must be U.S. citizen. To enter, student must submit 500-1000 word essay expressing their opinion, experience, or personal feelings on a topic of their own choice. 1st prize, $5000; 2nd prize, $2000; 8 finalists awarded $1000. For more information visit Web site or call 1-800-KAPTEST.

Award: Prize for use in freshman year; not renewable. *Number:* up to 10. *Amount:* $1000–$5000.

Eligibility Requirements: Applicant must be high school student and planning to enroll or expecting to enroll at a four-year institution or university. Available to U.S. citizens.

Application Requirements: Application, applicant must enter a contest, essay. *Deadline:* March 1.

Contact: Kaplan/Newsweek
888 Seventh Avenue
New York, NY 10106
Phone: 800-527-8378

KARMEL SCHOLARSHIP http://www.karenandmelody.com/KarMelScholarship.html

KARMEL SCHOLARSHIP

Scholarship to encourage students to write or create something that will express their views on the gay/lesbian/bi/transgender topic. Must be GLBT related. Deadline is March 31.

Award: Scholarship for use in freshman, sophomore, junior, senior, graduate, or postgraduate years; not renewable. *Number:* 2. *Amount:* $200–$300.

Eligibility Requirements: Applicant must be enrolled or expecting to enroll full or part-time at a two-year or four-year or technical institution or university. Available to U.S. and non-U.S. citizens.

Application Requirements: Application, applicant must enter a contest. *Deadline:* March 31.

Contact: KarMel Scholarship Committee
E-mail: infokarmel@karenandmelody.com

KENTUCKY POLICE CORPS http://docjt.jus.state.ky.us/pcorps/

KENTUCKY POLICE CORPS SCHOLARSHIP

Scholarships available for students who are attending, or who have graduated, from a four-year college or university. May be reimbursed for prior educational expenses. Must complete four years of service at a participating Kentucky law enforcement agency. See Web site for details: http://www.docjt.jus.state.ky.us/pcorps.

Award: Scholarship for use in junior or senior years; renewable. *Number:* 10. *Amount:* up to $23,000.

Eligibility Requirements: Applicant must be enrolled or expecting to enroll full-time at a four-year institution or university. Available to U.S. citizens.

Application Requirements: Application, references, test scores, transcript. *Deadline:* Continuous.

Contact: Bill Stewart, Scholarship Committee
Kentucky Police Corps
Department of Criminal Justice Training, Funderburk Building
521 Lancaster Avenue
Richmond, KY 40475
Phone: 866-592-6777
Fax: 859-622-5027
E-mail: william.stewart@mail.state.ky.us

KNIGHTS OF PYTHIAS http://www.pythias.org

KNIGHTS OF PYTHIAS POSTER CONTEST

Poster contest open to all high school students in the U.S. and Canada. Contestants must submit an original drawing. Eight awards are given out. The winners are not required to attend higher institution.

Award: Prize for use in freshman year; not renewable. *Number:* 8. *Amount:* $100–$1000.

Eligibility Requirements: Applicant must be high school student and planning to enroll or expecting to enroll at an institution or university. Available to U.S. and Canadian citizens.

Application Requirements: Applicant must enter a contest. *Deadline:* April 30.

Contact: Alfred Saltzman, Supreme Secretary
Knights of Pythias
Office of Supreme Lodge
59 Coddington Street, Suite 202
Quincy, MA 02169-4150
Phone: 617-472-8800
Fax: 617-376-0363
E-mail: kop@earthlink.net

LESBIAN, BISEXUAL, GAY AND TRANSGENDERED UNITED EMPLOYEES (LEAGUE) AT AT&T FOUNDATION http://www.league-att.org/foundation

LEAGUE AT AT&T FOUNDATION ACADEMIC SCHOLARSHIP

Scholarship awarded to graduating high school seniors who are gay, lesbian, bisexual, or transgender. Must have a 3.0 GPA. Deadline: April 30.

Award: Scholarship for use in freshman year; not renewable. *Number:* 3–4. *Amount:* $500–$2000.

Eligibility Requirements: Applicant must be high school student and planning to enroll or expecting to enroll full-time at a two-year or four-year or technical institution or university. Applicant must have 3.0 GPA or higher. Available to U.S. citizens.

Application Requirements: Application, essay, references, test scores, transcript. *Deadline:* April 30.

Contact: John Klenert, Founder
Lesbian, Bisexual, Gay and Transgendered United Employees (LEAGUE) at AT&T Foundation
PO Box 57237
Washington, DC 20037-7237
Phone: 703-713-7820
E-mail: attleague@aol.com

LIQUITEX ARTIST MATERIALS PURCHASE AWARD PROGRAM http://www.liquitex.com

LIQUITEX EXCELLENCE IN ART PURCHASE AWARD PROGRAM-SECONDARY CATEGORY

Prizes up to $500 in cash plus $250 in Liquitex products will be awarded to the best art submissions. Submissions should be made in 35mm slides. Void in Quebec or where prohibited by law. For more details see Web site: http://www.liquitex.com.

Award: Prize for use in freshman, sophomore, junior, senior, graduate, or postgraduate years; not renewable. *Number:* 3. *Amount:* $350–$750.

Eligibility Requirements: Applicant must be enrolled or expecting to enroll full or part-time at a two-year or four-year or technical institution or university. Available to U.S. and Canadian citizens.

Application Requirements: Applicant must enter a contest. *Deadline:* January 15.

Contact: Renée LaMontagne, Senior Product Manager
Liquitex Artist Materials Purchase Award Program
11 Constitution Avenue
PO Box 1396
Piscataway, NJ 08855-1396
Phone: 732-562-0770
Fax: 732-562-0941
E-mail: renee@liquitex.com

MANPOWER FOUNDATION http://www.manpower.com

MANPOWER FOUNDATION SCHOLARSHIP

Renewable awards that carry a stipend of $2,000 each. Two awards are given to high school seniors and one award is given to an undergraduate student. Student must be a child of a Manpower staff employee with at least one year of service. Puerto Rican citizens may apply. Must be under the age of 26. Minimum 3.0 GPA required.

Award: Scholarship for use in freshman, sophomore, or junior years; renewable. *Number:* 3. *Amount:* $2000.

Eligibility Requirements: Applicant must be age 25 or under and enrolled or expecting to enroll full-time at a four-year institution. Applicant must have 3.0 GPA or higher. Available to U.S. citizens.

Application Requirements: Application, applicant must enter a contest, financial need analysis, references, test scores, transcript. *Deadline:* March 15.

Contact: Manpower Foundation
5301 North Ironwood Road
PO Box 2053
Milwaukee, WI 53201
Phone: 414-906-6355
Fax: 414-906-7951

MASONIC GRAND LODGE CHARITIES OF RHODE ISLAND

RHODE ISLAND MASONIC GRAND LODGE SCHOLARSHIP

One-time scholarships for Rhode Island residents who have lived in Rhode Island for more than five years and who are enrolled in undergraduate studies. Awards may also be given to students who do not live in Rhode Island but have an association with the Rhode Island Masonic organization. High school students may apply.

Award: Scholarship for use in freshman, sophomore, junior, or senior years; not renewable. *Number:* 200–250. *Amount:* $750–$2500.

Eligibility Requirements: Applicant must be enrolled or expecting to enroll full-time at a two-year or four-year institution or university. Applicant must have 2.5 GPA or higher. Available to U.S. and non-U.S. citizens.

Application Requirements: Application, financial need analysis, transcript. *Deadline:* April 15.

Contact: Scholarship Committee
Masonic Grand Lodge Charities of Rhode Island
222 Taunton Avenue
East Providence, RI 02914-4556

MERCEDES-BENZ USA http://www.mbusa.com

DRIVE YOUR FUTURE: THE MERCEDES-BENZ USA SCHOLARSHIP PROGRAM

Scholarships available to graduating seniors currently attending high school in the U.S. who will be the first in their family to go to college. Must demonstrate academic achievement, leadership, participation in school and community activities, and financial need. Minimum GPA of 3.0 required. Applications only available online from http//www.scholarshipamerica.org/drivefuture. Application deadline is March 31.

Award: Scholarship for use in freshman year; not renewable. *Number:* up to 500. *Amount:* $2000.

Eligibility Requirements: Applicant must be high school student and planning to enroll or expecting to enroll at a two-year or four-year institution or university. Applicant must have 3.0 GPA or higher. Available to U.S. citizens.

Application Requirements: Application, financial need analysis, transcript. *Deadline:* March 31.

Contact: Scholarship America, https://www.scholarshipamerica.org/drivefuture
Mercedes-Benz USA
Corporate Communications Department
One Mercedes Drive
Montvale, NJ 07645

MICROSOFT CORPORATION http://www.thespoke.com/ycmd

YOU CAN MAKE A DIFFERENCE SCHOLARSHIP

Scholarships/grants available to high school and secondary school students around the world who design the best software projects to benefit charitable organizations. A total of $50,000 will be awarded to ten students, five female and five male. Each award consists of a personal scholarship of $2500, a grant of $1500 to implement the project, and $1000 grant to each winning student's school. Information and applications are on Web site: http://www.thespoke.net/ycmd. Applications must be submitted online by April 30.

Award: Scholarship for use in freshman year; not renewable. *Number:* 10. *Amount:* $2500.

Eligibility Requirements: Applicant must be high school student and planning to enroll or expecting to enroll full or part-time at a two-year or four-year or technical institution or university. Available to U.S. and non-U.S. citizens.

Application Requirements: Application, project proposal. *Deadline:* April 30.

Contact: Application available at Web site.
E-mail: ycmd@thespoke.net

MINNESOTA GAY/LESBIAN/BISEXUAL/TRANSGENDER EDUCATIONAL FUND http://www.philanthrofund.org

MINNESOTA GAY/LESBIAN/BISEXUAL/TRANSGENDER SCHOLARSHIP FUND

The Minnesota Gay/Lesbian, Bisexual, Transgender (GLBT) scholarship fund, administered by (GLBT) Philanthrofund Foundation, annually awards students who are gay/lesbian, bisexual, transgender identified, from a GLBT family, and/or pursuing a GLBT course of study. Applicants must either be a Minnesota resident or be planning to study in Minnesota.

Award: Scholarship for use in freshman, sophomore, junior, senior, graduate, or postgraduate years; not renewable. *Number:* 20–30. *Amount:* $500–$2500.

Eligibility Requirements: Applicant must be enrolled or expecting to enroll full or part-time at a two-year or four-year or technical institution or university. Available to U.S. and non-U.S. citizens.

Application Requirements: Application, essay, photo, references, transcript, confidentiality statement, press release. *Deadline:* February 1.

Contact: Kit Briem, Executive Director
Minnesota Gay/Lesbian/Bisexual/Transgender Educational Fund
1409 Willow Street
Suite 305
Minneapolis, MN 55403
Phone: 612-870-1806
Fax: 612-871-6587
E-mail: philanth@scc.net

MINNESOTA POLICE CORPS http://www.dps.state.mn.us/patrol/policecorps/

MINNESOTA POLICE CORPS SCHOLARSHIP

Scholarships available for full-time undergraduate students, full- or part-time graduate students, and recent college graduates. Must commit to four years of employment in a participating Minnesota law enforcement agency after field training program. Minimum 2.5 GPA required. Check Web site for details: http://www.dps.state.mn.us/patrol/policecorps/.

Award: Scholarship for use in sophomore, junior, senior, or graduate years. *Number:* 10. *Amount:* up to $23,800.

Eligibility Requirements: Applicant must be enrolled or expecting to enroll full or part-time at a four-year institution or university. Applicant must have 2.5 GPA or higher. Available to U.S. citizens.

Application Requirements: Application, driver's license, essay, interview, references, transcript. *Deadline:* February 28.

Contact: Kathy Moroney, Program Director
Minnesota Police Corps
1900 West County Road 1
Shoreview, MN 55126
Phone: 651-628-6722
Fax: 651-628-6797

MUSLIM SCHOLARSHIP FUND - AL-AMEEN http://www.al-ameen.org

AL-AMEEN SCHOLARSHIP

Available each year to one male and one female undergraduate. Preference given to U.S. resident Muslims. Will award each term up to two years.

Award: Scholarship for use in freshman or sophomore years; renewable. *Number:* 1–2. *Amount:* $1000–$3000.

Eligibility Requirements: Applicant must be high school student and planning to enroll or expecting to enroll full-time at a four-year institution or university. Applicant must have 3.0 GPA or higher. Available to U.S. and non-U.S. citizens.

Application Requirements: Application, essay, financial need analysis, test scores, transcript. *Deadline:* July 1.

Contact: Muslim Scholarship Fund - AL-AMEEN
14252 Culver Boulevard, Suite A714
Irvine, CA 92604
E-mail: alameenscholarship@yahoo.com

NAAS-USA FUND http://www.naas.org

NAAS II NATIONAL SCHOLARSHIP AWARDS

One renewable scholarship available for tuition, room, board, books, and academic supplies. Applicant must be college freshman or sophomore attending an American college/university. U.S. citizenship is not required. Download applications at: http://www.naas.org/college.htm. Applicants that request an application by mail must enclose a $3 handling fee and a self-addressed stamped envelope.

Award: Scholarship for use in freshman or sophomore years; renewable. *Number:* 1. *Amount:* $1000–$3000.

Eligibility Requirements: Applicant must be age 24 or under and enrolled or expecting to enroll full-time at a four-year institution or university. Available to U.S. and non-U.S. citizens.

Application Requirements: Application, self-addressed stamped envelope, download application literature from web site. *Fee:* $3. *Deadline:* May 1.

Contact: NAAS-USA FUND
NAAS-USA Fund
PO Box 337380
North Las Vegas, NV 89031-7380
Phone: 800-725-7849
E-mail: staff@naas.org

NAAS-USA AWARDS

A series of pure, merit-based scholarships available for tuition, room, board, books, and academically-related supplies. Applicants must be high school seniors or equivalent home-school seniors and be U.S. citizen or permanent resident. Application periods are September 15 to May 1. For further information and applications, download applications from Web site at http://www.naas.org/senior1.htm or visit http://www.naas.org/. Applicants that request an application by mail must enclose a $3 handling fee and a self-addressed stamped envelope.

Award: Scholarship for use in freshman year; renewable. *Number:* 10–14. *Amount:* $200–$10,000.

Eligibility Requirements: Applicant must be high school student and planning to enroll or expecting to enroll full-time at a four-year institution or university. Available to U.S. citizens.

Application Requirements: Application, self-addressed stamped envelope, download forms from web site. *Fee:* $3. *Deadline:* May 1.

Contact: NAAS-USA FUND
NAAS-USA Fund
PO Box 337380
North Las Vegas, NV 89031-7380
Phone: 800-725-7849
E-mail: staff@naas.org

NATIONAL BUSINESS AVIATION ASSOCIATION, INC. http://www.nbaa.org/scholarships

AVFUEL MICHIGAN BUSINESS AVIATION SCHOLARSHIP

Award for $500 for students pursuing an aviation degree at one of the following eligible schools: Andrews University, Eastern Michigan University,

Lansing Community College, Northwestern Michigan College, or Western Michigan University. Must be a U.S. citizen, have a 3.0 minimum GPA. Include with application: 250 word essay describing the applicant's interest in aviation and goals for a career in the business aviation industry and a letter of recommendation from the aviation department faculty at the institution at which the applicant is enrolled. For further information, visit Web site: http://www.nbaa.org.

Award: Scholarship for use in sophomore, junior, senior, or graduate years. *Number:* up to 1. *Amount:* $500.

Eligibility Requirements: Applicant must be enrolled or expecting to enroll at an institution or university. Applicant must have 3.0 GPA or higher. Available to U.S. citizens.

Application Requirements: Application, essay, resume, references, transcript. *Deadline:* August 9.

Contact: Jay Evans, Director, Operations
National Business Aviation Association, Inc.
1200 18th Street, NW, Suite 400
Washington, DC 20036-2527
Phone: 202-783-9000
Fax: 202-331-8364
E-mail: info@nbaa.org

NATIONAL CHRISTMAS TREE ASSOCIATION

http://www.realchristmastrees.org

NCTA HELP SANTA FIND THE PERFECT REAL CHRISTMAS TREE

Participants submit an essay of 300 words or less on why their real Christmas tree is perfect. A photograph of the tree must accompany the essay. Ages 6-16 are eligible to win a $5000 scholarship or theme-park trip for 4. Essay deadline is 12/31.

Award: Prize for use in freshman year; not renewable. *Number:* 3. *Amount:* $5000.

Eligibility Requirements: Applicant must be age 6-16 and enrolled or expecting to enroll full or part-time at a two-year or four-year or technical institution or university. Available to U.S. citizens.

Application Requirements: Application, applicant must enter a contest, essay, photo. *Deadline:* December 31.

Contact: Pheniece Jones, Marketing Assistant
National Christmas Tree Association
99 Canal Center Plaza, Suite 410
Alexandria, VA 22314
Phone: 703-740-1755
Fax: 703-740-1775
E-mail: pjones@smithharroff.com

NATIONAL COMMISSION FOR COOPERATIVE EDUCATION

http://www.co-op.edu

NATIONAL COMMISSION FOR COOPERATIVE EDUCATION CO-OP SCHOLARSHIP

The award designed to assist and encourage talented high school and transfer students of a college, as well as their selection of a cooperative education program from among "The Best of Co-op." Minimum 3.5 GPA required.

Award: Scholarship for use in freshman year; renewable. *Number:* 69. *Amount:* $5000.

Eligibility Requirements: Applicant must be high school student and planning to enroll or expecting to enroll full-time at a two-year or four-year institution or university. Applicant must have 3.5 GPA or higher. Available to U.S. and non-U.S. citizens.

Application Requirements: Application, essay, extracurricular activities, work experience. *Deadline:* February 15.

Contact: Frank Schettino, Director
National Commission for Cooperative Education
360 Huntington Avenue
384 CP
Boston, MA 02115-5096
Phone: 617-373-3406
Fax: 617-373-3463
E-mail: f.schettino@neu.edu

NATIONAL COURT REPORTERS ASSOCIATION

http://www.ncraonline.org

COUNCIL ON APPROVED STUDENT EDUCATION'S SCHOLARSHIP FUND

Student must be writing between 140-180 wpm, and must be in an NCRA-approved court reporting program. Student must write a two-page essay on topic chosen for the year. Deadline: April 1. Student enters a competition, first place is $1500, second place is $1000 and third place is $500.

Award: Scholarship for use in sophomore year; not renewable. *Number:* 3. *Amount:* $500–$1500.

Eligibility Requirements: Applicant must be enrolled or expecting to enroll full or part-time at a two-year or four-year or technical institution or university. Applicant must have 3.0 GPA or higher. Available to U.S. and Canadian citizens.

Application Requirements: Application, applicant must enter a contest, essay, references, transcript. *Deadline:* April 1.

Contact: Donna M. Gaede, Approval Program Manager
National Court Reporters Association
8224 Old Courthouse Road
Vienna, VA 22182
Phone: 703-556-6272
Fax: 703-556-6291
E-mail: dgaede@ncrahq.org

FRANK SARLI MEMORIAL SCHOLARSHIP

One-time award to a student who is nearing graduation from a trade/technical school or four-year college. Must be enrolled in a court reporting program. Minimum 3.5 GPA required.

Award: Scholarship for use in senior year; not renewable. *Number:* 1. *Amount:* $500.

Eligibility Requirements: Applicant must be enrolled or expecting to enroll full or part-time at a four-year or technical institution or university. Applicant must have 3.5 GPA or higher. Available to U.S. citizens.

Application Requirements: Application. *Deadline:* varies.

Contact: Ms. B J. Shorak, Deputy Executive Director, National Court Reporters Foundation
National Court Reporters Association
8224 Old Courthouse Road
Vienna, VA 22182-3808
Phone: 703-556-6272 Ext. 126
Fax: 703-556-6291
E-mail: bjshorak@ncrahq.org

STUDENT MEMBER TUITION GRANT

Six $500 awards for students in good academic standing at school. Students required to write 120-200 wpm. Deadline is May 31.

Award: Grant for use in freshman or sophomore years. *Number:* 6. *Amount:* $500.

Eligibility Requirements: Applicant must be enrolled or expecting to enroll at an institution or university.

Application Requirements: Application. *Deadline:* May 31.

Contact: Amy Davidson
E-mail: adavidson@ncrahq.org

WILLIAM E. WEBER SCHOLARSHIP

One scholarship available for NCRA student members that are currently enrolled at NCRA-approved programs. The nominee must have passed at least one of the court reporting program's Q & A tests at a minimum of 200 wpm. Applicants are required to have a minimum 3.5 overall GPA and demonstrated need for financial assistance. Contact for further information and deadlines.

Award: Scholarship for use in sophomore, junior, or senior years; not renewable. *Number:* 1. *Amount:* $500.

Eligibility Requirements: Applicant must be enrolled or expecting to enroll full or part-time at a four-year or technical institution or university. Applicant must have 3.5 GPA or higher. Available to U.S. citizens.

National Court Reporters Association (continued)

Application Requirements: Application, financial need analysis. *Deadline:* varies.

Contact: B J. Shorak, Deputy Executive Director, National Court Reporters Foundation
National Court Reporters Association
8224 Old Courthouse Road
Vienna, VA 22182-3808
Phone: 703-556-6272 Ext. 126
Fax: 703-556-6291
E-mail: bjshorak@ncrahq.org

NATIONAL FFA ORGANIZATION http://www.ffa.org

NATIONAL FFA COLLEGE AND VOCATIONAL/TECHNICAL SCHOOL SCHOLARSHIP PROGRAM

Nearly $2 million awarded to high school seniors planning to enroll in a full-time course of study at an accredited vocational/technical school, college or university. A smaller number of awards are available to currently enrolled undergraduates. Most of the awards require that the applicant be an FFA member. However some awards are available to high school seniors who are not FFA members. Some awards require an agricultural major, while others are for any major. See the Web site for more details.

Award: Scholarship for use in freshman, sophomore, junior, or senior years; not renewable. *Number:* up to 1700. *Amount:* $1000–$15,000.

Eligibility Requirements: Applicant must be enrolled or expecting to enroll full-time at a two-year or four-year or technical institution or university. Available to U.S. citizens.

Application Requirements: Application. *Deadline:* February 15.

Contact: Carrie Powers, Scholarship Program Coordinator
National FFA Organization
6060 FFA Drive
PO Box 68960
Indianapolis, IN 46268-0960
Phone: 317-802-4321
Fax: 317-802-5321
E-mail: scholarships@ffa.org

NATIONAL GROUND WATER ASSOCIATION http://www.ngwa.org

NATIONAL GROUND WATER EDUCATION FOUNDATION LEN ASSANTE SCHOLARSHIP FUND

The scholarship is available to high school graduates and students in college (four-year programs or well drilling two-year Associate Degree programs). A 2.5 GPA is mandatory for all applicants. Previous recipients are ineligible. For more information see Web site: http://www.ngwa.org.

Award: Scholarship for use in freshman, sophomore, junior, or senior years; not renewable. *Number:* up to 7. *Amount:* $1000–$2000.

Eligibility Requirements: Applicant must be enrolled or expecting to enroll full-time at a two-year or four-year institution or university. Applicant must have 2.5 GPA or higher. Available to U.S. and non-U.S. citizens.

Application Requirements: Application, autobiography, essay, transcript. *Deadline:* April 1.

Contact: Michelle Islam, NGWA Scholarship Coordinator
National Ground Water Association
601 Dempsey Road
Westerville, OH 43081
Phone: 800-551-7379 Ext. 530
Fax: 614-898-7786
E-mail: mislam@ngwa.org

NATIONAL MERIT SCHOLARSHIP CORPORATION http://www.nationalmerit.org

NATIONAL MERIT SCHOLARSHIP PROGRAM

High school students enter by taking the Preliminary SAT/National Merit Scholar Qualifying Test, and by meeting other participation requirements. Those eligible are contacted through high school. Selection based on test scores, academic abilities, essay, activities, and recommendations. Some awards are renewable. Contact counselor by fall of junior year for deadline. Participation requirements are available in the PAST/NMSQT Student Bulletin and on NMSE's Web site at http://www.nationalmerit.org.

Award: Scholarship for use in freshman year; renewable. *Number:* 9600. *Amount:* $500–$10,000.

Eligibility Requirements: Applicant must be high school student and planning to enroll or expecting to enroll full-time at a four-year institution or university. Available to U.S. citizens.

Application Requirements: Application, autobiography, essay, references, test scores, transcript. *Deadline:* varies.

Contact: student's high school counselor

NATIONAL RIFLE ASSOCIATION http://www.nrahq.org

NRA YOUTH EDUCATIONAL SUMMIT (YES) SCHOLARSHIPS

Awards for YES participants based on the initial application, on-site debate, and degree of participation during the week-long event. Grand Scholarship award of $10,000 for one YES participant requires a second application after completing the event, and a special project. Application for YES in Washington, DC is limited to current sophomores and juniors in high school.

Award: Scholarship for use in freshman year; not renewable. *Number:* 1–6. *Amount:* $1000–$10,000.

Eligibility Requirements: Applicant must be high school student and planning to enroll or expecting to enroll full or part-time at a two-year or four-year or technical institution or university. Applicant must have 3.0 GPA or higher. Available to U.S. citizens.

Application Requirements: Application, applicant must enter a contest, essay, references, transcript. *Deadline:* March 15.

Contact: Brooke Berthelsen, Event Services Manager
National Rifle Association
11250 Waples Mill Road
Fairfax, VA 22030
Phone: 703-267-1354
Fax: 703-267-3743

NATIONAL SCIENCE TEACHERS ASSOCIATION http://www.nsta.org

TOSHIBA/NSTA EXPLORAVISION AWARDS PROGRAM

Teams of students in grades K-12 consider the impact that science and technology have on society and how innovative thinking can change the future, then use their imaginations and the tools of science to envision new technologies. Students develop written proposals and Web pages.

Award: Prize for use in freshman, sophomore, junior, senior, graduate, or postgraduate years; not renewable. *Number:* 16–32. *Amount:* $5000–$10,000.

Eligibility Requirements: Applicant must be age 21 or under and enrolled or expecting to enroll full-time at a two-year or four-year or technical institution or university. Available to U.S. and Canadian citizens.

Application Requirements: Application, applicant must enter a contest, essay, Web pages. *Deadline:* February 3.

Contact: National Science Teachers Association
National Science Teachers Association
1840 Wilson Boulevard
Arlington, VA 22201
Phone: 800-EXP-LOR9
Fax: 703-243-7177
E-mail: exploravision@nsta.org

NATIONAL TEEN-AGER SCHOLARSHIP FOUNDATION http://www.nationalteen.com

NATIONAL TEEN-AGER SCHOLARSHIP FOUNDATION

One-time award for young women of leadership and intellect. Award based on school and community leadership, communication skills, academics and personal presentation. 3-5 awards per state. Awards come in the form of savings bonds from $500-1000 and in cash from $5000-10,000. Must be between the ages of 12-18 and be a U.S. citizen. Minimum 3.0 GPA required. $20 application fee. Deadline varies by state. For more details see Web site: http://www.nationalteen.com.

Award: Scholarship for use in freshman year; not renewable. *Number:* 250–1510. *Amount:* $1000–$10,000.

Eligibility Requirements: Applicant must be age 12-18; enrolled or expecting to enroll full-time at a two-year or four-year institution or university and single female. Applicant must have 3.0 GPA or higher. Available to U.S. citizens.

Application Requirements: Application, applicant must enter a contest, interview, photo, self-addressed stamped envelope, transcript. *Fee:* $20. *Deadline:* varies.

Contact: Jenny Telwar, National Director
National Teen-Ager Scholarship Foundation
1523 Crockett Hills Boulevard
Brentwood, TN 37027
Phone: 866-628-8336
E-mail: telwar@comcast.net

NEEDHAM AND COMPANY WTC SCHOLARSHIP FUND http://www.needhamco.com

NEEDHAM AND COMPANY SEPTEMBER 11TH SCHOLARSHIP FUND

Scholarship going to those individuals who had a pre-September 11th gross income of less than $125,000. To be eligible applicants must be currently accepted or attending an accredited university or college. Recipients decided on a case-by-case basis. Fund designed to benefit the children of the victims who lost their lives at the World Trade Center. Visit Web site for additional information.

Award: Scholarship for use in freshman, sophomore, junior, or senior years; not renewable. *Number:* varies. *Amount:* varies.

Eligibility Requirements: Applicant must be enrolled or expecting to enroll at an institution or university. Available to U.S. citizens.

Application Requirements: Application, financial need analysis. *Deadline:* Continuous.

Contact: Needham and Company WTC Scholarship Fund
445 Park Avenue
New York, NY 10022
Phone: 212-705-0314
E-mail: jturano@needhamco.com

NEVADA POLICE CORPS http://www.nevadapolicecorps.state.nv.us

NEVADA POLICE CORPS PROGRAM

Renewable award available to upper level, full-time undergraduates or graduate students. Must complete four year degree, complete required training and agree to serve a Nevada law enforcement agency for four years. Must be a U.S. citizen. Minimum 2.5 GPA required.

Award: Scholarship for use in junior, senior, or graduate years; renewable. *Number:* 8–10. *Amount:* up to $15,000.

Eligibility Requirements: Applicant must be enrolled or expecting to enroll full-time at an institution or university. Applicant must have 2.5 GPA or higher. Available to U.S. citizens.

Application Requirements: Application, driver's license, essay, interview, references, transcript, peace officer selection process. *Deadline:* Continuous.

Contact: Greg Befort, Director
Nevada Police Corps
WNCC, Cedar Building Room 309-312
2201 West College Parkway
Carson City, NV 89703
Phone: 775-684-8720
Fax: 775-684-8775
E-mail: gbefort@post.state.nv.us

NEXTSTUDENT INC. http://www.nextstudent.com

NEXTSTUDENT'S ACHIEVEMENT AWARD

Award for self-motivated, forward-thinking undergraduate students. Must have academic excellence and demonstrate leadership and vision; student must be a U.S. citizen. A 1000-word essay on "If there was one law or piece of legislation that you could change, what would it be, and why." Must be submitted with completed application.

Award: Scholarship for use in freshman, sophomore, junior, or senior years; not renewable. *Number:* 1. *Amount:* $500.

Eligibility Requirements: Applicant must be enrolled or expecting to enroll full-time at a two-year or four-year or technical institution or university. Available to U.S. citizens.

Application Requirements: Application, essay, self-addressed stamped envelope. *Deadline:* June 30.

Contact: Scholarship Coordinator
NextStudent Inc.
3510 Arrowhead Circle
Round Rock, TX 78681-1700

NIMROD INTERNATIONAL JOURNAL OF PROSE AND POETRY http://www.utulsa.edu/nimrod

KATHERINE ANNE PORTER PRIZE FOR FICTION

A first place prize of $2000 and a second place prize of $1000 will be awarded for fiction. The award includes publication in Nimrod. $20 entry fee includes one year subscription to Nimrod. For more details see Web site: http://www.utulsa.edu/nimrod.

Award: Prize for use in freshman, sophomore, junior, senior, graduate, or postgraduate years; not renewable. *Number:* 2. *Amount:* $1000–$2000.

Eligibility Requirements: Applicant must be enrolled or expecting to enroll full or part-time at a two-year or four-year or technical institution or university. Available to U.S. citizens.

Application Requirements: Applicant must enter a contest. *Fee:* $20. *Deadline:* April 30.

Contact: Francine Ringold, Editor-in-Chief
Nimrod International Journal of Prose and Poetry
600 South College Avenue
Tulsa, OK 74104-3189
Phone: 918-631-3080
Fax: 918-631-3033
E-mail: nimrod@utulsa.edu

PABLO NERUDA PRIZE FOR POETRY

A first place prize of $2000 and a second place prize of $1000 will be awarded for poetry. The award includes publication in Nimrod. $20 entry fee includes one year subscription to Nimrod. For more details see Web site: http://www.utulsa.edu/nimrod.

Award: Prize for use in freshman, sophomore, junior, senior, graduate, or postgraduate years; not renewable. *Number:* 2. *Amount:* $1000–$2000.

Eligibility Requirements: Applicant must be enrolled or expecting to enroll full or part-time at a two-year or four-year or technical institution or university. Available to U.S. citizens.

Application Requirements: Applicant must enter a contest. *Fee:* $20. *Deadline:* April 30.

Contact: Francine Ringold, Editor-in-Chief
Nimrod International Journal of Prose and Poetry
600 South College Avenue
Tulsa, OK 74104-3189
Phone: 918-631-3080
Fax: 918-631-3033
E-mail: nimrod@utulsa.edu

NINETY-NINES, INC. http://ninety-nines.org

AMELIA EARHART MEMORIAL CAREER SCHOLARSHIP FUND

Scholarships are awarded to members of The Ninety-Nines, Inc., who hold a current medical certificate appropriate for the use of the certificate sought. Applicants must meet the requirements for pilot currency (Flight Review or non-U.S. equivalent) and have financial need. Applicants must agree to complete the course, training and meet the requirements for ratings/certificates specific to the country where training will occur.

Award: Scholarship for use in freshman, sophomore, junior, or senior years; not renewable. *Number:* varies. *Amount:* varies.

Eligibility Requirements: Applicant must be enrolled or expecting to enroll full-time at an institution or university and female. Available to U.S. and non-U.S. citizens.

Ninety-Nines, Inc. (continued)

Application Requirements: Application, financial need analysis, photo, resume, references. *Deadline:* December 31.

Contact: Charlene H. Falkenberg, Chairman, Permanent Trustee
Ninety-Nines, Inc.
618 South Washington Street
Hobart, IN 46342-5026
Phone: 219-942-8887
Fax: 219-942-8887
E-mail: charf@prodigy.net

NO-ADDICTION SCHOLARSHIP ESSAY CAMPAIGN http://www.solarcosmetics.com

NO-AD CAMPAIGN ESSAY CONTEST

This essay contest is open to students in middle school and high school. Only one entry per student. Middle school students can receive savings bonds and high school students college scholarship. For essay topics or any other questions contact noad@aol.com or ediaz@no-ad.com, or visit Web site: http://www.NO-ADdiction.org

Award: Scholarship for use in freshman, sophomore, junior, or senior years; not renewable. *Number:* 10–20. *Amount:* $200–$500.

Eligibility Requirements: Applicant must be high school student and planning to enroll or expecting to enroll full-time at a two-year or four-year institution. Available to U.S. citizens.

Application Requirements: Application, applicant must enter a contest, essay, photo. *Deadline:* varies.

Contact: Elizabeth Calabrese, Coordinator
NO-ADdiction Scholarship Essay Campaign
PO Box 4628
Miami Lakes, FL 33017
Phone: 800-662-3342
Fax: 305-621-0536
E-mail: ediaz@noad.com

NORWAY-AMERICA ASSOCIATION http://www.noram.no

NORWAY-AMERICA UNDERGRADUATE SCHOLARSHIP PROGRAM

• *See page 596*

NUCLEAR AGE PEACE FOUNDATION http://www.wagingpeace.org

SWACKHAMER PEACE ESSAY CONTEST

The essay contest is open to all high school students. Essays should be in English and a maximum of 1,500 words. Essays will be judged on the basis of knowledge and analysis of subject matter, originality of ideas, development of point of view, insight, clarity of expression, organization, and grammar. For current essay topics, visit Web site at http://www.wagingpeace.org.

Award: Prize for use in freshman year; not renewable. *Number:* 3. *Amount:* $500–$1500.

Eligibility Requirements: Applicant must be high school student and planning to enroll or expecting to enroll full-time at an institution or university. Available to U.S. and non-U.S. citizens.

Application Requirements: Applicant must enter a contest, essay. *Deadline:* June 1.

Contact: Michael Coffey, Youth Outreach Coordinator
Nuclear Age Peace Foundation
PMB 121
1187 Coast Village Road, Suite 1
Santa Barbara, CA 93108-2794
Phone: 805-965-3443
Fax: 805-568-0466
E-mail: youth@napf.org

OHIO POLICE CORPS http://www.hhs.utoledo.edu/ohiopolicecorps/default.htm

OHIO POLICE CORPS SCHOLARSHIP

Scholarships available for students with a Bachelor's degree or a full-time college senior. Must be a U.S. citizen with a minimum 2.75 GPA. Must agree to work for a municipal police department, Sheriff's Department, or Ohio State Patrol for a minimum of 4 years. See Web site for details. http://www.ohiopolicecorps.utoledo.edu

Award: Scholarship for use in senior, or graduate years; renewable. *Number:* 10. *Amount:* up to $23,000.

Eligibility Requirements: Applicant must be enrolled or expecting to enroll full-time at a four-year institution or university. Available to U.S. citizens.

Application Requirements: Application, driver's license, essay, photo, references, transcript, DD Form 214 if applicable. *Deadline:* Continuous.

Contact: D. Michael Collins, Director
Ohio Police Corps
MS 400, University of Toledo
2801 West Bancroft Street
Toledo, OH 43606-3390
Phone: 419-530-6246

OKLAHOMA STATE REGENTS FOR HIGHER EDUCATION http://www.okhighered.org

HEARTLAND SCHOLARSHIP FUND

Renewable award for dependent children of individuals killed as a result of the 1995 Oklahoma City bombing, or a surviving dependent child who was injured in the Alfred P. Murrah Federal Building day care center as a result of the bombing. The awards are applicable to the cost of tuition, fees, special fees, books, and room and board. The award is for undergraduate study anywhere in the United States, and for graduate study at an Oklahoma institution.

Award: Scholarship for use in freshman, sophomore, junior, senior, or graduate years; renewable. *Number:* varies. *Amount:* $3500–$5500.

Eligibility Requirements: Applicant must be enrolled or expecting to enroll full-time at a two-year or four-year institution or university. Available to U.S. citizens.

Application Requirements: *Deadline:* Continuous.

Contact: Oklahoma State Regents for Higher Education
PO Box 108850
Oklahoma City, OK 73101-8850
Phone: 800-858-1840
Fax: 405-225-9230
E-mail: studentinfo@osrhe.edu

OPTIMIST INTERNATIONAL FOUNDATION http://www.optimist.org/

OPTIMIST INTERNATIONAL ESSAY CONTEST

$650 college scholarship is offered at the district level; $2,000-$5,000 scholarships are offered at the international level. Eligible students are under 19 as of December 31 of the current school year. Open to residents of the U.S., Canada and the Caribbean. Must be conducted through a local Optimist Club. Visit Web site at http://www.optimist.org for additional information.

Award: Scholarship for use in freshman, sophomore, junior, or senior years; not renewable. *Number:* 53–56. *Amount:* $650–$5000.

Eligibility Requirements: Applicant must be age 19 or under and enrolled or expecting to enroll full-time at a two-year or four-year or technical institution or university. Available to U.S. and non-U.S. citizens.

Application Requirements: Application, applicant must enter a contest, self-addressed stamped envelope. *Deadline:* varies.

Contact: Danielle Baugher, International Programs Coordinator
Optimist International Foundation
4494 Lindell Boulevard
St. Louis, MO 63108
Phone: 314-371-6000 Ext. 235
Fax: 314-371-6006
E-mail: programs@optimist.org

OPTIMIST INTERNATIONAL ORATORICAL CONTEST

$1,500 scholarship offered at the district level. Student shall not have attained the age of 16 years as of December 31st of current school year. No minimum age. Must be conducted through a local Optimist Club. Open to residents of the U.S., Canada or a Caribbean nation. Visit Web site at http://www.optimist.org for additional information.

Award: Scholarship for use in freshman or sophomore years; not renewable. *Number:* 106. *Amount:* $1500.

Eligibility Requirements: Applicant must be age 16 or under and enrolled or expecting to enroll full-time at a two-year or four-year or technical institution or university. Available to U.S. and non-U.S. citizens.

Application Requirements: Application, applicant must enter a contest. *Deadline:* varies.

Contact: Danielle Baugher, International Programs Coordinator
Optimist International Foundation
4494 Lindell Boulevard
St. Louis, MO 63108
Phone: 314-371-6000 Ext. 235
Fax: 314-371-6006
E-mail: programs@optimist.org

OREGON POLICE CORPS http://www.oregonpolicecorps.com

OREGON POLICE CORPS

Scholarships available for undergraduate juniors and seniors and graduate students, or for reimbursement of educational expenses for college graduates. Must agree to commit to four years of employment at a participating law enforcement agency. Check Web site for details: http://www.oregonpolicecorps.com.

Award: Scholarship for use in junior, senior, or graduate years. *Number:* 10. *Amount:* up to $23,400.

Eligibility Requirements: Applicant must be enrolled or expecting to enroll full-time at a four-year institution or university. Available to U.S. citizens.

Application Requirements: Application, driver's license, essay, interview, resume, references. *Deadline:* Continuous.

Contact: Donna Henderson
Oregon Police Corps
24751-B Southeast Highway 224
Boring, OR 97009
Phone: 800-848-3957
Fax: 503-637-5376
E-mail: dhenderson@oregonpolicecorps.org

ORPHAN FOUNDATION OF AMERICA http://www.orphan.org

OFA 2002 NATIONAL SCHOLARSHIP/CASEY FAMILY SCHOLARS

Scholarships are given to young people who were in foster care for at least one year at the time of their 18th birthday. Must be under 25 years old. Must have been accepted into an accredited postsecondary school or program. Must not currently be a Casey Family Program CEJT participant.

Award: Scholarship for use in freshman, sophomore, junior, or senior years; renewable. *Number:* 350. *Amount:* $2000–$6000.

Eligibility Requirements: Applicant must be age 24 or under and enrolled or expecting to enroll full or part-time at a two-year or four-year or technical institution or university. Available to U.S. and non-U.S. citizens.

Application Requirements: Application, essay, financial need analysis, references, transcript. *Deadline:* April 1.

Contact: Tina Raheem, Scholarship Coordinator
Orphan Foundation of America
12020 - D North Shore Drive
Reston, VA 20190-4507
Phone: 571-203-0270
Fax: 571-203-0273
E-mail: scholarship@orphan.org

PADGETT BUSINESS SERVICES FOUNDATION http://smallbizpros.com

PADGETT BUSINESS SERVICES FOUNDATION SCHOLARSHIP PROGRAM

Scholarships are awarded to the dependents of small business owners in the U.S. and Canada. Must be a high school senior. Recipients of the scholarships qualify for a $4,000 International Scholarship. See Web site for details, http://www.smallbizpros.com.

Award: Scholarship for use in freshman year; not renewable. *Number:* 65–75. *Amount:* $500.

Eligibility Requirements: Applicant must be high school student and planning to enroll or expecting to enroll full-time at a two-year or four-year institution or university. Available to U.S. and Canadian citizens.

Application Requirements: Application, essay, test scores, transcript, school activities. *Deadline:* March 1.

Contact: Heather Stokley, Administrator, Padgett Foundation Scholarship Program
Padgett Business Services Foundation
160 Hawthorne Park
Athens, GA 30606
Phone: 800-723-4388
Fax: 800-548-1040
E-mail: hstokley@smallbizpros.com

PARALYZED VETERANS OF AMERICA - SPINAL CORD RESEARCH FOUNDATION http://www.pva.org/

PARALYZED VETERANS OF AMERICA EDUCATIONAL SCHOLARSHIP PROGRAM

Open to PVA members, their spouses and unmarried children, under 24 years of age, to obtain a post-secondary education. Applicant must be U.S. citizen accepted or enrolled as full-time student in degree program. For details and application visit Web site: http://www.pva.org.

Award: Scholarship for use in freshman, sophomore, junior, or senior years. *Number:* up to 10. *Amount:* up to $1000.

Eligibility Requirements: Applicant must be enrolled or expecting to enroll full-time at an institution or university. Available to U.S. citizens.

Application Requirements: Application, references, transcript, personal statement, verification of enrollment. *Deadline:* June 1.

Contact: Trish Armstrong
Paralyzed Veterans of America - Spinal Cord Research Foundation
801 Eighteenth Street, NW
Washington, DC 20006-3517
Phone: 800-424-8200 Ext. 619
E-mail: trisha@pva.org

PARENTS, FAMILIES, AND FRIENDS OF LESBIANS AND GAYS-ATLANTA http://www.pflagatl.org

PFLAG SCHOLARSHIP AWARDS PROGRAM

Must be Georgia resident or enrolled in a postsecondary institution in Georgia. Applicant must have turned 16 by April 1 in order to be eligible. Must be openly gay, lesbian, bisexual or transexuals or advocates of the same. Application must be postmarked by March 31.

Award: Scholarship for use in freshman, sophomore, junior, senior, or graduate years; not renewable. *Number:* 5–10. *Amount:* $1500–$3000.

Eligibility Requirements: Applicant must be age 16 and enrolled or expecting to enroll full or part-time at a two-year or four-year or technical institution or university. Available to U.S. and non-U.S. citizens.

Application Requirements: Application, autobiography, essay, financial need analysis, references, test scores, transcript. *Deadline:* March 31.

Contact: PFLAG Scholarship Program
Parents, Families, and Friends of Lesbians and Gays-Atlanta
PO Box 450393
Atlanta, GA 31145-0393

PATIENT ADVOCATE FOUNDATION http://www.patientadvocate.org

SCHOLARSHIPS FOR SURVIVORS

The purpose of these scholarships is to provide support to patients seeking to initiate or complete a course of study that has been interrupted or delayed by a diagnosis of cancer or another critical or life threatening illness. Eight awards of $5000 available to U.S. citizens. Minimum 3.0 GPA required.

Award: Scholarship for use in freshman, sophomore, junior, senior, graduate, or postgraduate years; renewable. *Number:* 8. *Amount:* $5000.

Eligibility Requirements: Applicant must be enrolled or expecting to enroll full-time at a two-year or four-year institution or university. Applicant must have 3.0 GPA or higher. Available to U.S. citizens.

Application Requirements: Application, essay, financial need analysis, references, transcript, physician letter. *Deadline:* May 1.

Contact: Ruth Anne Reed, Executive Vice President of Administrative Operations
Patient Advocate Foundation
700 Thimble Shoals Boulevard, Suite 200
Newport News, VA 23606
Phone: 800-532-5274
Fax: 767-873-8999
E-mail: info@patientadvocate.org

PENGUIN PUTNAM, INC. http://www.penguinputnam.com/scessay

SIGNET CLASSIC SCHOLARSHIP ESSAY CONTEST

Contest is open to high school juniors and seniors. Students should submit a two- to three-page double-spaced essay answering one of three possible questions on a designated novel. Entries must be submitted by a high school English teacher. For more information visit http://www.penguinputnam.com/scessay or call 212-366-2377.

Award: Scholarship for use in freshman year; not renewable. *Number:* 5. *Amount:* $1000.

Eligibility Requirements: Applicant must be high school student and planning to enroll or expecting to enroll at an institution or university. Available to U.S. citizens.

Application Requirements: Applicant must enter a contest, essay, references. *Deadline:* April 15.

Contact: Emily Johnson, Academic Marketing Assistant
Penguin Putnam, Inc.
375 Hudson Street
New York, NY 10014
Phone: 212-366-2377
Fax: 212-366-2933
E-mail: academic@penguin.com

PHILLIPS FOUNDATION http://www.thephillipsfoundation.org

PHILLIPS FOUNDATION RONALD REAGAN FUTURE LEADERS SCHOLARSHIP PROGRAM

The program offers renewable scholarships to college juniors and seniors who demonstrate leadership on behalf of freedom, American values, and constitutional principles. Winners will receive a scholarship for their junior year and may apply for renewal before their senior year.

Award: Scholarship for use in junior or senior years; not renewable. *Number:* 10–20. *Amount:* $2500–$10,000.

Eligibility Requirements: Applicant must be enrolled or expecting to enroll full-time at a four-year institution or university. Available to U.S. citizens.

Application Requirements: Application, essay, resume, references, transcript. *Deadline:* January 15.

Contact: Jeff Hollingsworth, Assistant Secretary
Phillips Foundation
7811 Montrose Road, Suite 100
Potomac, MD 20854
Phone: 301-340-2100
E-mail: jhollingsworth@phillips.com

POLANKI, POLISH WOMEN'S CULTURAL CLUB OF MILWAUKEE, WISCONSIN, U.S.A. http://www.polanki.org/

ARTHUR B. GURDA MEMORIAL AWARD

Award to students of Polish heritage and to non-Polish students studying Polish language, history, society, or culture. Applicants must be college juniors, seniors, or graduate students and must be Wisconsin residents or attend college in Wisconsin. Successful applicants will usually have a 3.0 GPA.

Award: Scholarship for use in junior, senior, or graduate years. *Number:* varies. *Amount:* $500–$1000.

Eligibility Requirements: Applicant must be enrolled or expecting to enroll at a four-year institution or university. Available to U.S. citizens.

Application Requirements: Application, transcript. *Deadline:* March 1.

Contact: Ewa Barczyk-Pease
Polanki, Polish Women's Cultural Club of Milwaukee, Wisconsin, U.S.A.
4160 South 1st Street
Milwaukee, WI 53207
Phone: 414-963-1098
E-mail: polanki@polanki.org

EVELYN APPLEYARD MEMORIAL AWARD

Award for students of Polish heritage and to non-Polish students studying Polish language, history, society, or culture. Applicants must be college juniors, seniors, or graduate students and must be Wisconsin residents or attend college in Wisconsin. Successful applicants will usually have a 3.0 GPA.

Award: Scholarship for use in junior, senior, or graduate years. *Number:* varies. *Amount:* $500–$1000.

Eligibility Requirements: Applicant must be enrolled or expecting to enroll at a four-year institution or university. Available to U.S. citizens.

Application Requirements: Application, transcript. *Deadline:* March 1.

Contact: Ewa Barczyk-Pease
Polanki, Polish Women's Cultural Club of Milwaukee, Wisconsin, U.S.A.
4160 South 1st Street
Milwaukee, WI 53207
Phone: 414-963-1098
E-mail: polanki@polanki.org

HARRIET GOSTOMSKI MEMORIAL AWARD

Award to students of Polish heritage and to non-Polish students studying Polish language, history, society, or culture. Applicants must be college juniors, seniors, or graduate students and must be Wisconsin residents or attend college in Wisconsin. Successful applicants will usually have a 3.0 GPA.

Award: Scholarship for use in junior, senior, or graduate years. *Number:* varies. *Amount:* $500–$1000.

Eligibility Requirements: Applicant must be enrolled or expecting to enroll at a four-year institution or university.

Application Requirements: Application, transcript. *Deadline:* March 1.

Contact: Ewa Barczyk-Pease
Polanki, Polish Women's Cultural Club of Milwaukee, Wisconsin, U.S.A.
4160 South 1st Street
Milwaukee, WI 53207
Phone: 414-963-1098
E-mail: polanki@polanki.org

JANET DZIADULEWICZ BRANDEN MEMORIAL AWARD

Award to an outstanding student in Polish studies. Applicants must be college juniors, seniors, or graduate students and must be Wisconsin residents or attend college in Wisconsin. Successful applicants will usually have a 3.0 GPA.

Award: Scholarship for use in junior, senior, or graduate years. *Number:* 1. *Amount:* $500–$1000.

Eligibility Requirements: Applicant must be enrolled or expecting to enroll at a four-year institution or university. Available to U.S. citizens.

Application Requirements: Application, transcript. *Deadline:* March 1.

Contact: Ewa Barczyk-Pease
Polanki, Polish Women's Cultural Club
of Milwaukee, Wisconsin, U.S.A.
4160 South 1st Street
Milwaukee, WI 53207
Phone: 414-963-1098
E-mail: polanki@polanki.org

MONSIGNOR ALPHONSE S. POPEK MEMORIAL AWARD

Award to students of Polish heritage and to non-Polish students studying Polish language, history, society, or culture. Applicants must be college juniors, seniors, or graduate students and must be Wisconsin residents or attend college in Wisconsin. Successful applicants will usually have a 3.0 GPA.

Award: Scholarship for use in junior, senior, or graduate years. *Number:* varies. *Amount:* $500–$1000.

Eligibility Requirements: Applicant must be enrolled or expecting to enroll at a four-year institution or university. Available to U.S. citizens.

Application Requirements: Application, transcript. *Deadline:* March 1.

Contact: Ewa Barczyk-Pease
Polanki, Polish Women's Cultural Club
of Milwaukee, Wisconsin, U.S.A.
4160 South 1st Street
Milwaukee, WI 53207
Phone: 414-963-1098
E-mail: polanki@polanki.org

NARCES JENDRZEJCZAK MEMORIAL AWARD

Award to students of Polish heritage and to non-Polish students studying Polish language, history, society, or culture. Applicants must be college juniors, seniors, or graduate students and must be Wisconsin residents or attend college in Wisconsin. Successful applicants will usually have a 3.0 GPA.

Award: Scholarship for use in junior, senior, or graduate years. *Number:* varies. *Amount:* $500–$1000.

Eligibility Requirements: Applicant must be enrolled or expecting to enroll at a four-year institution or university. Available to U.S. citizens.

Application Requirements: Application, transcript. *Deadline:* March 1.

Contact: Ewa Barczyk-Pease
Polanki, Polish Women's Cultural Club
of Milwaukee, Wisconsin, U.S.A.
4160 South 1st Street
Milwaukee, WI 53207
Phone: 414-963-1098
E-mail: polanki@polanki.org

POLANKI COLLEGE ACHIEVEMENT AWARDS AND MEMORIALS

Award to students of Polish heritage and to non-Polish students studying Polish language, history, society, or culture. Applicants must be college juniors, seniors, or graduate students and must be Wisconsin residents or attend college in Wisconsin. Successful applicants will usually have a 3.0 GPA.

Award: Scholarship for use in junior, senior, or graduate years. *Number:* varies. *Amount:* $500–$1000.

Eligibility Requirements: Applicant must be enrolled or expecting to enroll at a four-year institution or university. Available to U.S. citizens.

Application Requirements: Application, transcript. *Deadline:* March 1.

Contact: Ewa Barczyk-Pease
Polanki, Polish Women's Cultural Club
of Milwaukee, Wisconsin, U.S.A.
4160 South 1st Street
Milwaukee, WI 53207
Phone: 414-963-1098
E-mail: polanki@polanki.org

STANLEY F. AND HELEN BALCERZAK AWARD

Award to a student of Polish heritage who is an outstanding student in any field or to a non-Polish student studying Polish language, history, society, or culture. Applicants must be college juniors, seniors, or graduate students and must be Wisconsin residents or attend college in Wisconsin. Successful applicants will usually have a GPA of 3.0.

Award: Scholarship for use in junior, senior, or graduate years. *Number:* 1. *Amount:* $500–$1000.

Eligibility Requirements: Applicant must be enrolled or expecting to enroll at a four-year institution or university. Available to U.S. citizens.

Application Requirements: Application, transcript. *Deadline:* March 1.

Contact: Ewa Barczyk-Pease
Polanki, Polish Women's Cultural Club
of Milwaukee, Wisconsin, U.S.A.
4160 South 1st Street
Milwaukee, WI 53207
Phone: 414-963-1098
E-mail: polanki@polanki.org

POLISH WOMEN'S ALLIANCE http://www.pwaa.org

POLISH WOMEN'S ALLIANCE SCHOLARSHIP

Scholarships are given to members of the Polish Women's Alliance of America who have been in good standing for five years. Recipients of the awards must remain members of the PWA of A for at least seven years after school. The deadline is March 15. Full-time students may apply beginning with the second year of undergraduate study.

Award: Scholarship for use in sophomore, junior, or senior years; renewable.

Eligibility Requirements: Applicant must be enrolled or expecting to enroll full-time at a two-year or four-year or technical institution or university. Available to U.S. citizens.

Application Requirements: Application, essay, photo, transcript. *Deadline:* March 15.

Contact: Scholarship Committee
Polish Women's Alliance
205 South Northwest Highway
Park Ridge, IL 60068

PRESIDENTIAL FREEDOM SCHOLARSHIP http://www.nationalservice.org/scholarships

PRESIDENTIAL FREEDOM SCHOLARSHIP

The Presidential Freedom Scholarship program is designed to highlight and promote service and citizenship by students and to recognize students for their leadership in those areas. Each high school in the county may select up to 2 students to receive a $1,000 scholarship. With funds appropriated by Congress, the Corporation for National and Community Service provides $500, which must be matched with $500 secured by the school from the community.

Award: Scholarship for use in freshman year; not renewable. *Number:* 10,000. *Amount:* $500.

Eligibility Requirements: Applicant must be high school student and planning to enroll or expecting to enroll full or part-time at a two-year or four-year or technical institution or university. Available to U.S. citizens.

Application Requirements: Application, essay. *Deadline:* June 30.

Contact: Scholarship Staff
Presidential Freedom Scholarship
1150 Connecticut Avenue, NW, Suite 1100
Washington, DC 20036
Phone: 866-291-7700
Fax: 202-742-5393
E-mail: info@studentservicescholarship.org

PUERTO RICO DEPARTMENT OF EDUCATION

ROBERT C. BYRD HONOR SCHOLARSHIPS

This grant is sponsored by the Puerto Rico Department of Education and is granted to gifted students. These are students chosen from public and private schools who graduate from high school and are admitted to an accredited university in Puerto Rico or in the United States and who show promise to complete a college career. It is granted for a period of four years if the student maintains a satisfactory academic progress. Must be a U.S. citizen and rank in the upper quarter of class or have a minimum 3.5 GPA.

Award: Scholarship for use in freshman, sophomore, junior, or senior years; renewable. *Number:* 74–85. *Amount:* $1500.

Puerto Rico Department of Education (continued)

Eligibility Requirements: Applicant must be high school student and planning to enroll or expecting to enroll full-time at a four-year institution or university. Applicant must have 3.5 GPA or higher. Available to U.S. citizens.

Application Requirements: Application, financial need analysis, interview, portfolio, references, test scores, transcript. *Deadline:* May 30.

Contact: Eligio Hernandez, Director
Puerto Rico Department of Education
PO Box 190759
San Juan, PR 00919-0759
Phone: 787-754-1015
Fax: 787-758-2281
E-mail: hernandez_eli@de.gobierno.pr

PUSH FOR EXCELLENCE http://www.rainbowpush.org

ORA LEE SANDERS SCHOLARSHIP

Renewable awards for undergraduate or trade/technical study. Full time or part time, minimum 2.5 GPA. Write to Push for Excellence for further information and application forms. Deadline is April 1.

Award: Scholarship for use in freshman, sophomore, junior, or senior years; renewable. *Number:* varies. *Amount:* up to $1000.

Eligibility Requirements: Applicant must be enrolled or expecting to enroll full or part-time at a two-year or four-year or technical institution or university. Applicant must have 2.5 GPA or higher. Available to U.S. and non-U.S. citizens.

Application Requirements: Application, essay, references, self-addressed stamped envelope, transcript. *Deadline:* April 1.

Contact: Education Department
Push for Excellence
930 East 50th Street
Chicago, IL 60615
Phone: 773-373-3366

RESOURCE CENTER http://www.resourcecenterscholarshipinfo.com

HEATHER JOY MEMORIAL SCHOLARSHIP

One-time award of up to $1000 given to students in honor of Heather Joy, who lost her young life due to financial needs. Available to part- or full-time students, enrolled in technical school, college or university. Deadlines are May 1 and November 1. Recipient selection will be based on a 250-word original essay and referral letters. Applications are available via the Web site only: http://www.resourcecenterscholarshipinfo.com.

Award: Scholarship for use in freshman, sophomore, junior, senior, graduate, or postgraduate years; not renewable. *Number:* 1–10. *Amount:* up to $1000.

Eligibility Requirements: Applicant must be enrolled or expecting to enroll full or part-time at a two-year or four-year or technical institution or university. Available to U.S. and non-U.S. citizens.

Application Requirements: Application, essay, references, self-addressed stamped envelope, transcript. *Fee:* $5. *Deadline:* varies.

Contact: Dee Blaha, Owner
Resource Center
16362 Wilson Boulevard
Masaryktown, FL 34604-7335
E-mail: blaha@dialfla.com

RHODE ISLAND FOUNDATION http://www.rifoundation.org

JAMES J. BURNS AND C.A. HAYNES SCHOLARSHIP

Award for students enrolled in a textile program at the following schools: Dartmouth, Philadelphia University, North Carolina State, Clemson, Georgia Tech, Auburn. Preference given to children of members of National Association of Textile Supervisors.

Award: Scholarship for use in sophomore, junior, or senior years; not renewable. *Number:* 1–2. *Amount:* up to $1000.

Eligibility Requirements: Applicant must be enrolled or expecting to enroll at a two-year or four-year institution or university.

Application Requirements: Application. *Deadline:* March 1.

Contact: Libby Monahan, Scholarship Coordinator
Rhode Island Foundation
One Union Station
Providence, RI 02903
Phone: 401-274-4564
Fax: 401-272-1359
E-mail: libbym@rifoundation.org

ROOTHBERT FUND, INC. http://www.roothbertfund.org

ROOTHBERT FUND, INC. SCHOLARSHIP

Award for those pursuing undergraduate degree or higher in U.S. institution and satisfying academic standards. Non-U.S. citizens must be living in U.S. Must travel at own expense to interview in Philadelphia, New Haven, or Washington, D.C. Deadline: February 1. Provide SASE when requesting an application.

Award: Scholarship for use in freshman, sophomore, junior, senior, or graduate years; renewable. *Number:* 50–55. *Amount:* $3500.

Eligibility Requirements: Applicant must be enrolled or expecting to enroll full-time at a two-year or four-year or technical institution or university. Available to U.S. and non-U.S. citizens.

Application Requirements: Application, autobiography, essay, financial need analysis, interview, photo, references, self-addressed stamped envelope, test scores, transcript. *Deadline:* February 1.

Contact: Roothbert Fund, Inc.
475 Riverside Drive, Room 252
New York, NY 10115
Phone: 212-870-3116

SALLIE MAE FUND http://www.thesalliemaefund.org

SALLIE MAE 911 EDUCATION FUND LOAN RELIEF

Enables spouses, same-sex partners and co-borrowers of those killed or totally disabled in the September 11, 2001 terrorist attacks on the United States to pay off their student loans that meet the eligibility requirements on the web at http://www.thesalliemaefund.org, and are owned or serviced by Sallie Mae. Also available to those who were permanently disabled by the September 11 terrorist attacks and hold a private education student loan owned or serviced by Sallie Mae.

Award: Forgivable loan for use in freshman, sophomore, junior, or senior years; not renewable. *Amount:* up to $5000.

Eligibility Requirements: Applicant must be enrolled or expecting to enroll at a two-year or four-year or technical institution or university. Available to U.S. citizens.

Application Requirements: Application, supporting documents. *Deadline:* Continuous.

Contact: See Web site for application and details.

SALLIE MAE 911 EDUCATION FUND SCHOLARSHIP PROGRAM

Provides scholarships to children of those lost or permanently disabled as a result of the terrorist attacks on America, including children of those police, fire safety or medical personnel who were killed or suffered debilitating casualties in their attempt to rescue those who were victims of the attacks. Eligible children would be able to pursue postsecondary education where they reside. Applicant must already be enrolled full time in an approved postsecondary education program. Applications available at http://www.thesalliemaefund.org, http://www.wiredscholar.com or at the financial aid office of their school.

Award: Scholarship for use in freshman, sophomore, junior, or senior years; renewable. *Amount:* up to $2500.

Eligibility Requirements: Applicant must be enrolled or expecting to enroll full-time at a two-year or four-year institution or university.

Application Requirements: Application, financial need analysis, proof of death or disability of parent. *Deadline:* May 15.

Contact: See Web site for details and application.

SALLIE MAE FUND SCHOLARSHIPS

Scholarship renewals available for students with a combined family income of $35,000 or less. Must be a prior scholarship recipient enrolled as full-time undergraduate or graduate student at an approved, accredited institution.

Award: Scholarship for use in sophomore, junior, senior, or graduate years; renewable. *Number:* varies. *Amount:* $500–$2000.

Eligibility Requirements: Applicant must be enrolled or expecting to enroll full-time at a two-year or four-year institution or university. Available to U.S. citizens.

Application Requirements: Application, financial need analysis, transcript.

Contact: c/o Scholarship America
Sallie Mae Fund
One Scholarship Way, PO Box 297
Saint Peter, MN 56082
Phone: 507-931-1682

SALLIE MAE FUND UNMET NEED SCHOLARSHIP PROGRAM

Scholarships available to students demonstrating financial need. Must be a U.S. citizen enrolled full time in an accredited post-secondary institution. Minimum 2.5 GPA. Details available on Web site: http://www.thesalliemaefund.org.

Award: Scholarship for use in freshman, sophomore, junior, or senior years. *Number:* varies. *Amount:* $1000–$3800.

Eligibility Requirements: Applicant must be enrolled or expecting to enroll full-time at a two-year or four-year or technical institution or university. Applicant must have 2.5 GPA or higher. Available to U.S. citizens.

Application Requirements: Application, financial need analysis, transcript. *Deadline:* May 31.

Contact: c/o Scholarship America
Sallie Mae Fund
One Scholarship Way, PO Box 297
Saint Peter, MN 56082
Phone: 507-931-1682

SAMUEL HUNTINGTON FUND http://www.masselectric.com/inside/edsvcs/samuel/index.htm

SAMUEL HUNTINGTON PUBLIC SERVICE AWARD

Award provides a $10,000 stipend to a graduating college senior to perform a one-year public service project anywhere in the world immediately following graduation. Proposals are requested with application. Proposal must be written in 1,000 words or less. It may deal with any activity that furthers the public good. Awards will be based on quality of proposal, academic record, and other personal achievements. Semi-finalists will be interviewed.

Award: Grant for use in senior year; not renewable. *Number:* 1–3. *Amount:* $10,000.

Eligibility Requirements: Applicant must be enrolled or expecting to enroll at a four-year institution. Available to U.S. and non-U.S. citizens.

Application Requirements: Application, essay, financial need analysis, resume, references, transcript. *Deadline:* February 13.

Contact: Thomas G. Robinson, Deputy General Counsel
Samuel Huntington Fund
25 Research Drive
Westborough, MA 01582
Phone: 508-389-2877
Fax: 508-389-2463

SCHOLARSHIP WORKSHOP LLC http://www.scholarshipworkshop.com

"LEADING THE FUTURE" SCHOLARSHIP

The "Leading the Future" Scholarship is designed to elevate students' consciousness about their future and their role in helping others once they receive a college degree and become established in a community. It is open to U.S. residents only who are high school seniors or college undergraduates at any level. Students must visit http://www.scholarshipworkshop.com for application information. Application fee is $3. Fee should be sent with completed applications, not to request an application. Send SASE for application requests.

Award: Scholarship for use in freshman, sophomore, junior, or senior years; not renewable. *Number:* 1–3. *Amount:* $100–$500.

Eligibility Requirements: Applicant must be enrolled or expecting to enroll full-time at a four-year institution or university. Available to U.S. citizens.

Application Requirements: Application, essay, self-addressed stamped envelope. *Fee:* $3. *Deadline:* March 1.

Contact: Scholarship Coordinator
Scholarship Workshop LLC
PO Box 176
Centreville, VA 20122
Phone: 703-579-4245
Fax: 703-579-4245
E-mail: scholars@scholarshipworkshop.com

RAGINS/BRASWELL NATIONAL SCHOLARSHIP

The scholarship is available to high school seniors, undergraduate, and graduate students who attend The Scholarship Workshop presentation or an online class given by Marianne Ragins. Award is based on use of techniques taught in the workshop or class, application, essay, leadership, extracurricular activities, achievements, and community responsibility. Interested students should visit http://www.scholarshipworkshop.com for more details.

Award: Scholarship for use in freshman, sophomore, junior, senior, or graduate years; not renewable. *Number:* 1–3. *Amount:* $100–$750.

Eligibility Requirements: Applicant must be enrolled or expecting to enroll full-time at a four-year institution or university. Available to U.S. citizens.

Application Requirements: Application, essay. *Deadline:* April 30.

Contact: Scholarship Coordinator
Scholarship Workshop LLC
PO Box 176
Centreville, VA 20122
Phone: 703-579-4245
Fax: 703-579-4245
E-mail: scholars@scholarshipworkshop.com

SICKLE CELL DISEASE ASSOCIATION OF AMERICA, INC. http://www.sicklecelldisease.org

KERMIT B. NASH, JR. ACADEMIC SCHOLARSHIP

Scholarship is only for individuals with sickle cell disease. Must be a graduating senior intending to attend an accredited four-year college or university. Must be U.S. citizen or a permanent resident of the U.S. Awarded in four yearly increments of $5000.

Award: Scholarship for use in freshman year; renewable. *Number:* 1. *Amount:* up to $20,000.

Eligibility Requirements: Applicant must be high school student and planning to enroll or expecting to enroll full-time at a four-year institution or university. Applicant must have 3.0 GPA or higher. Available to U.S. citizens.

Application Requirements: Application, essay, interview, photo, references, self-addressed stamped envelope, test scores, transcript. *Deadline:* April 3.

Contact: SCDAA Scholarship Selection Committee
Sickle Cell Disease Association of America, Inc.
200 Corporate Pointe, Suite 495
Culver City, CA 90230-8727
Phone: 310-216-6363
Fax: 310-215-3722
E-mail: scdaa@sicklecelldisease.org

SIR EDWARD YOUDE MEMORIAL FUND COUNCIL http://www.info.gov.hk/sfaa

SIR EDWARD YOUDE MEMORIAL SCHOLARSHIP FOR OVERSEAS STUDIES

This program is for outstanding students, of any citizenship, who are permanent residents of Hong Kong, for overseas undergraduate studies. The award is not restricted to any specific academic or career area, but cannot be used for medical studies. Upon return from overseas studies, students are expected to contribute significantly to the development of Hong Kong. For further details visit Web site: http://www.info.gov.hk/sfaa.

Sir Edward Youde Memorial Fund Council (continued)

Award: Scholarship for use in freshman, sophomore, junior, or senior years; renewable. *Number:* varies. *Amount:* up to $29,744.

Eligibility Requirements: Applicant must be enrolled or expecting to enroll full-time at an institution or university.

Application Requirements: Application, applicant must enter a contest, autobiography, essay, interview, photo, resume, references, test scores, transcript. *Deadline:* September 30.

Contact: Mr. Y. Wong, Council Secretariat
Sir Edward Youde Memorial Fund Council
Room 1217, 12/F., Cheung Sha Wan Government Offices
303 Cheung Sha Wan Road
Kowloon
Hong Kong
Phone: 852 2150 6103
Fax: 852 2511 2720
E-mail: sgl3@sfaa.gov.hk

SLOVENIAN WOMEN'S UNION OF AMERICA http://members.aol.com/sherryew/swu/swuscholarship.html

CONTINUING EDUCATION AWARD

$500 will be awarded to four applicants to continue or update their education. Applicant must be an active participant of the Slovenian Women's Union for the past three years prior to applying for an award. Deadline is March 1.

Award: Scholarship for use in freshman, sophomore, junior, senior, or graduate years; not renewable. *Number:* 4. *Amount:* $500.

Eligibility Requirements: Applicant must be enrolled or expecting to enroll full or part-time at a two-year or four-year or technical institution or university. Available to U.S. and non-U.S. citizens.

Application Requirements: Application, autobiography, essay, financial need analysis, photo, resume, references, test scores, transcript. *Deadline:* March 1.

Contact: Mary H. Turvey, Director
Slovenian Women's Union of America
52 Oakridge Drive
Marquette, MI 49855
Phone: 906-249-4288
E-mail: mturvey@aol.com

SLOVENIAN WOMEN'S UNION OF AMERICA SCHOLARSHIP PROGRAM

One-time award for full-time study only. Deadline is March 1. Applicant must have been an active participant or member of Slovenian Women's Union for past three years. Essay, transcripts of grades, letters of recommendation from principal/teacher and SWU branch officer required. Financial need form, photo, civic, church activities information required. Open to high school seniors.

Award: Scholarship for use in freshman year; not renewable. *Number:* 5. *Amount:* $1000.

Eligibility Requirements: Applicant must be high school student and planning to enroll or expecting to enroll full-time at a two-year or four-year institution or university. Available to U.S. and non-U.S. citizens.

Application Requirements: Application, autobiography, essay, financial need analysis, photo, resume, references, test scores, transcript. *Deadline:* March 1.

Contact: Mary Turvey, Director
Slovenian Women's Union of America
52 Oakridge Drive
Marquette, MI 49855
Phone: 906-249-4288
E-mail: mturvey@aol.com

SOCIETY FOR ADVANCEMENT OF CHICANOS AND NATIVE AMERICANS IN SCIENCE (SACNAS) http://www.sacnas.org

SACNAS FINANCIAL AID: LODGING AND TRAVEL AWARD

Undergraduate and graduate students are encouraged to apply for lodging and travel to attend the SACNAS National Conference. The conference offers students the opportunity to be mentored, to present their research, attend scientific symposiums in all science disciplines, and professional development sessions to enhance their educational careers. Please refer to Web site for more information and application: http://www.sacnas.org.

Award: Scholarship for use in freshman, sophomore, junior, senior, or graduate years; not renewable. *Number:* 400–550. *Amount:* $800–$1000.

Eligibility Requirements: Applicant must be enrolled or expecting to enroll full or part-time at a two-year or four-year or technical institution or university. Available to U.S. citizens.

Application Requirements: Application, essay, references, current enrollment verification. *Deadline:* June 14.

Contact: Rosalina Aranda, Student Program Manager
Society for Advancement of Chicanos and Native Americans in Science (SACNAS)
333 Front Street
Suite 104
Santa Cruz, CA 95060
Phone: 831-459-0170 Ext. 224
Fax: 831-459-0194
E-mail: rosalina@sacnas.org

SOCIETY FOR THE PRESERVATION OF ENGLISH LANGUAGE AND LITERATURE (SPELL) http://www.spellorg.com

STEPHEN J. MANHARD SCHOLARSHIP-ESSAY CONTEST

Applicant must submit 500 word essay related to the proposition that standards of good English usage are still important in today's cultural environment. Applicant must be high school senior. First prize receives $1000, second place receives $300, and third place will receive $200. Applicant must submit very brief biographical information with his or her essay. Please see Web site for further details: http://www.mindspring.com/~spellorg

Award: Prize for use in freshman year; not renewable. *Number:* 3. *Amount:* $200–$1000.

Eligibility Requirements: Applicant must be high school student and planning to enroll or expecting to enroll full or part-time at an institution or university. Available to U.S. and non-U.S. citizens.

Application Requirements: Application, applicant must enter a contest, autobiography, essay. *Deadline:* March 1.

Contact: James Wallace, President
Society for the Preservation of English Language and Literature (SPELL)
PO Box 321
Braselton, GA 30517
Phone: 770-586-0184
Fax: 770-868-0578
E-mail: spellgang@juno.com

SOROPTIMIST INTERNATIONAL OF THE AMERICAS http://www.soroptimist.org

SOROPTIMIST WOMEN'S OPPORTUNITY AWARD

Applicant must be a woman who is head of household and working toward vocational or undergraduate degree. Recipients are chosen on the basis of financial need as well as a statement of clear career goals. One-time award of $500-$10,000. Send a self-addressed stamped business-size envelope with 60 cents postage for information, or download the application from the Web site. Must be a resident of SIA's member countries and territories.

Award: Prize for use in freshman, sophomore, junior, or senior years; not renewable. *Number:* varies. *Amount:* $500–$10,000.

Eligibility Requirements: Applicant must be enrolled or expecting to enroll full or part-time at a two-year or four-year or technical institution or university and female. Available to U.S. and non-U.S. citizens.

Application Requirements: Application, essay, financial need analysis, references, self-addressed stamped envelope. *Deadline:* December 1.

Contact: Award Chairperson
Soroptimist International of the Americas
2 Penn Center Plaza, Suite 1000
Philadelphia, PA 19102
E-mail: siahq@soroptimist.org

SOUTH CAROLINA POLICE CORPS http://www.citadel.edu/scpolicecorps/info.html

SOUTH CAROLINA POLICE CORPS SCHOLARSHIP

Tuition reimbursement scholarship available to a full time student of an U.S. accredited college. Must agree to serve for four years on community patrol with a participating South Carolina police or sheriff's department. Up to $7500 per academic year with a limit of $30,000 per student.

Award: Scholarship for use in junior, senior, or graduate years; renewable. *Number:* 20. *Amount:* $7500–$30,000.

Eligibility Requirements: Applicant must be enrolled or expecting to enroll full-time at a four-year institution or university. Available to U.S. citizens.

Application Requirements: Application, autobiography, driver's license, essay, interview, references, test scores, transcript. *Deadline:* varies.

Contact: Thomas Adams, Program Coordinator
South Carolina Police Corps
The Citadel, MSC 67
171 Moultrie Street
Charleston, SC 29409
Phone: 843-953-6908
Fax: 843-953-6993
E-mail: adamst@citadel.edu

SOUTH CAROLINA STATE EMPLOYEES ASSOCIATION http://www.SCSEA.com

ANNE A. AGNEW SCHOLARSHIP

Nonrenewable scholarship for full-time study only. Must be a sophomore, junior, senior, graduate or postgraduate student. Applications accepted between January 1 and April 1.

Award: Scholarship for use in sophomore, junior, senior, graduate, or postgraduate years; not renewable. *Number:* 3. *Amount:* $1000.

Eligibility Requirements: Applicant must be enrolled or expecting to enroll full-time at a two-year or four-year or technical institution or university. Available to U.S. and non-U.S. citizens.

Application Requirements: Application, essay, financial need analysis, transcript. *Deadline:* April 1.

Contact: Broadus Jamerson, Executive Director
South Carolina State Employees Association
PO Box 8447
Columbia, SC 29202
Phone: 803-765-0680
Fax: 803-779-6558
E-mail: scsea@scsea.com

ST. CLAIRE REGIONAL MEDICAL CENTER http://www.st-claire.org/

SR. MARY JEANNETTE WESS, S.N.D. SCHOLARSHIP

Scholarships available for an undergraduate or graduate student, junior level or above, in any field of study, who demonstrates academic achievement, leadership, service, and financial need. Must have graduated from an eastern Kentucky high school in one of the following counties: Bath, Carter, Elliott, Fleming, Lewis, Magoffin, Menifee, Montgomery, Morgan, Rowan, or Wolfe. Call for information.

Award: Scholarship for use in junior, senior, or graduate years; not renewable. *Number:* 1–2. *Amount:* $750.

Eligibility Requirements: Applicant must be enrolled or expecting to enroll full-time at a four-year institution or university. Available to U.S. citizens.

Application Requirements: Application, financial need analysis. *Deadline:* April 15.

Contact: Director of Development
St. Claire Regional Medical Center
222 Medical Circle
Morehead, KY 40351
Phone: 606-783-6512

ST. JAMES LUTHERAN CHURCH

GENERATIONS FOR PEACE SCHOLARSHIP

First ($1500) and second place ($750) scholarships awarded to winners of an essay contest. For guidelines and essay topic send self-addressed stamped envelope and one dollar to Generations for Peace. Open to high school students.

Award: Scholarship for use in freshman year; not renewable. *Number:* up to 2. *Amount:* $750–$1500.

Eligibility Requirements: Applicant must be high school student and planning to enroll or expecting to enroll full or part-time at a four-year institution or university. Available to U.S. citizens.

Application Requirements: Applicant must enter a contest, essay. *Fee:* $1. *Deadline:* April 15.

Contact: Kathleen McDonald, Director, Generations for Peace
St. James Lutheran Church
1315 Southwest Park Avenue
Portland, OR 97201
Phone: 503-227-2439

STEPHEN PHILLIPS MEMORIAL SCHOLARSHIP FUND http://www.phillips-scholarship.org

STEPHEN PHILLIPS MEMORIAL SCHOLARSHIP FUND

Award open to full-time undergraduate students with financial need who display academic excellence, strong citizenship and character, and a desire to make a meaningful contribution to society. For more details see Web site: http://www.phillips-scholarship.org.

Award: Scholarship for use in freshman, sophomore, junior, or senior years; renewable. *Number:* 150–200. *Amount:* $3000–$10,000.

Eligibility Requirements: Applicant must be enrolled or expecting to enroll full-time at a four-year institution or university. Applicant must have 3.0 GPA or higher. Available to U.S. citizens.

Application Requirements: Application, essay, financial need analysis, references, test scores, transcript. *Deadline:* May 1.

Contact: Karen Emery, Scholarship Coordinator
Stephen Phillips Memorial Scholarship Fund
PO Box 870
Salem, MA 01970
E-mail: info@spscholars.org

STRAIGHT FORWARD MEDIA http://www.straightforwardmedia.com

DALE E. FRIDELL MEMORIAL SCHOLARSHIP

Non-renewable scholarship. Award based on essay of fewer than 1000 words which must be submitted via email. Deadline is April 1. For further information and email address go to Web site: http://www.straightforwardmedia.com.

Award: Scholarship for use in freshman, sophomore, junior, senior, graduate, or postgraduate years; not renewable. *Number:* 1. *Amount:* $500.

Eligibility Requirements: Applicant must be enrolled or expecting to enroll full or part-time at a two-year or four-year or technical institution or university. Available to U.S. and non-U.S. citizens.

Application Requirements: Applicant must enter a contest, essay. *Deadline:* April 1.

Contact: Christina Barsch, Director of Marketing
Phone: 623-215-2898
E-mail: info@straightforwardmedia.com

GET OUT OF DEBT SCHOLARSHIP

One-time award available to anyone attending or aspiring to attend a post-secondary education program. Applications must be submitted via Web site: http://www.straightforwardmedia.com. Application deadline is January 31.

Award: Scholarship for use in freshman, sophomore, junior, senior, graduate, or postgraduate years. *Number:* 1. *Amount:* $500.

Straight Forward Media (continued)

Eligibility Requirements: Applicant must be enrolled or expecting to enroll at a two-year or four-year or technical institution or university. Available to U.S. and non-U.S. citizens.

Application Requirements: *Deadline:* January 31.

Contact: Christina Barsch, Director of Marketing
Straight Forward Media
PO Box 2560
Rapid City, SD 57701
Phone: 623-215-2898
E-mail: info@straightforwardmedia.com

MESOTHELIOMA MEMORIAL SCHOLARSHIP

One-time award available to anyone attending or aspiring to attend a post-secondary education program. Applications must be submitted via Web site: http://www.straightforwardmedia.com. Application deadline is January 31.

Award: Scholarship for use in freshman, sophomore, junior, senior, graduate, or postgraduate years. *Number:* 1. *Amount:* $500.

Eligibility Requirements: Applicant must be enrolled or expecting to enroll at a two-year or four-year or technical institution or university. Available to U.S. and non-U.S. citizens.

Application Requirements: *Deadline:* January 31.

Contact: Christina Barsch, Director of Marketing
Straight Forward Media
PO Box 2560
Rapid City, SD 57701
Phone: 623-215-2898
E-mail: info@straightforwardmedia.com

SUNSHINE LADY FOUNDATION, INC. http://www.sunshineladyfdn.org

WOMEN'S INDEPENDENCE SCHOLARSHIP PROGRAM

Scholarship for female survivors of domestic violence (partner abuse) who are U.S. citizens or permanent legal residents with critical financial need to return to school to gain skills to become independent and self-sufficient. Requires sponsorship by nonprofit domestic violence service agency. First priority candidates are single mothers with young children.

Award: Scholarship for use in freshman, sophomore, junior, or senior years; renewable. *Number:* 500–600. *Amount:* $250–$5000.

Eligibility Requirements: Applicant must be enrolled or expecting to enroll full or part-time at a two-year or four-year or technical institution or university and female. Available to U.S. citizens.

Application Requirements: Application, essay, financial need analysis, references, sponsor. *Deadline:* Continuous.

Contact: Nancy Soward, Program Director
Sunshine Lady Foundation, Inc.
4900 Randall Parkway
Suite H
Wilmington, NC 28403
Phone: 910-397-7742
Fax: 910-397-0023
E-mail: nancy@sunshineladyfdn.org

SUPERCOLLEGE.COM http://www.supercollege.com

SUPERCOLLEGE.COM SCHOLARSHIP

An award for outstanding high school students or college undergraduates. Based on academic and extracurricular achievement, leadership, and integrity. May study any major and attend or plan to attend any accredited college or university in the U.S. Applications are only available online at http://www.supercollege.com. No paper applications accepted.

Award: Scholarship for use in freshman, sophomore, junior, or senior years; not renewable. *Number:* 1–2. *Amount:* $500–$2500.

Eligibility Requirements: Applicant must be enrolled or expecting to enroll full-time at a four-year institution or university. Available to U.S. citizens.

Application Requirements: Application, essay, self-addressed stamped envelope. *Deadline:* July 31.

Contact: Scholarship Coordinator
SuperCollege.com
4546 B10 El Camino Real #281
Los Altos, CA 94022
E-mail: supercollege@supercollege.com

TAKE ME AWAY TO COLLEGE SCHOLARSHIP COMPETITION http://www.takemeaway.com

CALGON, TAKE ME AWAY TO COLLEGE SCHOLARSHIP COMPETITION

One-time award designed for students pursuing a degree at a 4-year accredited college or university. The award recognizes originality and expression as well as academic excellence, community involvement, and overall achievement. Award designated for female applicants. Must be U.S. citizen or legal resident studying at an institution in the United States. Applications accepted only through Web site (http://www.takemeaway.com).

Award: Scholarship for use in freshman, sophomore, or junior years; not renewable. *Number:* 9. *Amount:* $500–$5000.

Eligibility Requirements: Applicant must be enrolled or expecting to enroll full-time at a four-year institution or university and female. Available to U.S. citizens.

Application Requirements: Application, essay, transcript. *Deadline:* February 28.

Contact: Application available at Web site.
E-mail: quickspritz@takemeaway.com

CALGON, TAKE ME AWAY TO COLLEGE SCHOLARSWEEPS

Contest format. Award is open to anyone pursuing education at any two- or four-year accredited college, university or trade/technical school. Must be U.S. citizen or legal resident studying at an institution in the U.S. Applications accepted only through Web site (http://www.takemeaway.com).

Award: Scholarship for use in freshman, sophomore, junior, or senior years; not renewable. *Number:* 3. *Amount:* $500.

Eligibility Requirements: Applicant must be enrolled or expecting to enroll full or part-time at a two-year or four-year or technical institution or university. Available to U.S. citizens.

Application Requirements: Application, applicant must enter a contest. *Deadline:* June 30.

Contact: Application available at Web site.
E-mail: quickspritz@takemeaway.com

TALBOTS CHARITABLE FOUNDATION http://www.talbots.com

TALBOTS WOMEN'S SCHOLARSHIP FUND

One-time scholarship for women who earned their high school diploma or GED at least 10 years ago, and who are now seeking an undergraduate college degree.

Award: Scholarship for use in freshman, sophomore, junior, or senior years; not renewable. *Number:* 5–50. *Amount:* $1000–$10,000.

Eligibility Requirements: Applicant must be enrolled or expecting to enroll full or part-time at a two-year or four-year or technical institution or university and female. Available to U.S. citizens.

Application Requirements: Application, essay, financial need analysis, references, transcript. *Deadline:* January 4.

Contact: Deb Johnson, Scholarship America
Talbots Charitable Foundation
One Scholarship Way, PO Box 297
Saint Peter, MN 56082
Phone: 507-931-0452
Fax: 507-931-9278
E-mail: debj@scholarshipamerica.org

TALL CLUBS INTERNATIONAL FOUNDATION, INC, AND TALL CLUBS INTERNATIONAL, INC. http://www.tall.org

KAE SUMNER EINFELDT SCHOLARSHIP

Females 5'10" or males 6'2" (minimum heights) are eligible to apply for the TCI International Foundation, Inc., scholarships. Interested individuals should contact their local Tall Clubs Chapter. Canadian and United States winners are selected from finalists submitted by each local chapter.

Award: Scholarship for use in freshman year; not renewable. *Number:* 2–4. *Amount:* $1000.

Eligibility Requirements: Applicant must be age 17-21 and enrolled or expecting to enroll full-time at a two-year or four-year or technical institution or university. Available to U.S. and Canadian citizens.

Application Requirements: Application, essay, photo, references, transcript, verification of height. *Deadline:* April 1.

Contact: Barry Umbs, Director
Tall Clubs International Foundation, Inc, and Tall Clubs International, Inc.
6770 River Terrace Drive
Franklin, WI 53132
Phone: 414-529-9887
Fax: 414-382-4444
E-mail: baumbs@ra.rockwell.com

TARGET CORPORATION http://www.target.com

TARGET ALL-AROUND SCHOLARSHIP PROGRAM

Scholarship based on student's community volunteer service and leadership. Obtain an application at www.target.com.

Award: Scholarship for use in freshman, sophomore, junior, or senior years; not renewable. *Number:* up to 650. *Amount:* $1000.

Eligibility Requirements: Applicant must be age 24 or under and enrolled or expecting to enroll full-time at a two-year or four-year or technical institution or university. Available to U.S. citizens.

Application Requirements: Application, essay, transcript. *Deadline:* November 1.

Contact: Application available at Web site.
Target Corporation
c/o Scholarship America
One Scholarship Way, PO Box 480
St. Peter, MN 56082-0480

TECHNICAL ASSOCIATION OF THE PULP & PAPER INDUSTRY (TAPPI) http://www.tappi.org

COATING AND GRAPHIC ARTS DIVISION SCHOLARSHIP

Up to four $1000 scholarships will be made available to undergraduate juniors and seniors and graduate students who have a demonstrated interest in a career in the coating and graphic arts industry. Must be a TAPPI student member or a member of a TAPPI Student Chapter.

Award: Scholarship for use in junior, senior, or graduate years; not renewable. *Number:* 4. *Amount:* $1000.

Eligibility Requirements: Applicant must be enrolled or expecting to enroll full-time at a four-year institution or university. Applicant must have 3.0 GPA or higher. Available to U.S. and non-U.S. citizens.

Application Requirements: Application, references, transcript. *Deadline:* January 31.

Contact: Veranda Edmondson, Member Group Specialist-TAPPI
Technical Association of the Pulp & Paper Industry (TAPPI)
15 Technology Parkway South
Norcross, GA 30092
Phone: 770-209-7536
Fax: 770-446-6947
E-mail: vedmondson@tappi.org

CORRUGATED CONTAINERS DIVISION SCHOLARSHIP

Several $1000 and $2000 scholarships are available to juniors and seniors who demonstrate an interest in the pulp and paper industry or, especially, the corrugated container industry. Must maintain a 3.0 GPA.

Award: Scholarship for use in junior, senior, or graduate years; not renewable. *Number:* 8. *Amount:* $1000–$2000.

Eligibility Requirements: Applicant must be enrolled or expecting to enroll full or part-time at a four-year institution or university. Applicant must have 3.0 GPA or higher. Available to U.S. and non-U.S. citizens.

Application Requirements: Application, references, transcript. *Deadline:* January 31.

Contact: Veranda Edmondson, Member Group Specialist-TAPPI
Technical Association of the Pulp & Paper Industry (TAPPI)
15 Technology Parkway South
Norcross, GA 30092
Phone: 770-209-7536
Fax: 770-446-6947
E-mail: vedmondson@tappi.org

ENGINEERING DIVISION SCHOLARSHIP

Two $1500 scholarships will be awarded to juniors or rising seniors who are enrolled in an engineering or science program. Must demonstrate a significant interest in the pulp and paper industry, be a member of a TAPPI Student Chapter, and have a minimum GPA of 3.0.

Award: Scholarship for use in junior or senior years; not renewable. *Number:* 2. *Amount:* up to $1500.

Eligibility Requirements: Applicant must be enrolled or expecting to enroll full-time at a four-year institution or university. Applicant must have 3.0 GPA or higher. Available to U.S. and non-U.S. citizens.

Application Requirements: Application, essay, references, transcript. *Deadline:* January 31.

Contact: Veranda Edmondson, TAPPI-Member Group Specialist
Technical Association of the Pulp & Paper Industry (TAPPI)
15 Technology Parkway South
Norcross, GA 30092
Phone: 770-209-7536
Fax: 770-446-6947
E-mail: vedmondson@tappi.org

ENVIRONMENTAL DIVISION SCHOLARSHIP

One $2500 scholarship is available to a full-time student who is at or above the level of sophomore and has a strong desire to pursue a career in environmental control as it relates to the pulp, paper and related industries. Must have a 3.0 GPA. An interview may be required.

Award: Scholarship for use in sophomore, junior, or senior years; not renewable. *Number:* 1. *Amount:* $2500.

Eligibility Requirements: Applicant must be enrolled or expecting to enroll full-time at a four-year institution. Applicant must have 3.0 GPA or higher. Available to U.S. and non-U.S. citizens.

Application Requirements: Application, essay, interview, references, transcript. *Deadline:* January 31.

Contact: Veranda Edmondson, TAPPI-Member Group Specialist
Technical Association of the Pulp & Paper Industry (TAPPI)
15 Technology Parkway South
Norcross, GA 30092
Phone: 770-209-7536
Fax: 770-446-6947
E-mail: vedmondson@tappi.org

NONWOVENS DIVISION SCHOLARSHIP

One $1000 scholarship is available to full-time students enrolled in a state-accredited undergraduate program. Must be in a program that will prepare the student in a career in the nonwovens industry or demonstrate an interest in the areas covered by TAPPI's Nonwovens Division.

Award: Scholarship for use in freshman, sophomore, junior, or senior years; not renewable. *Number:* 1. *Amount:* $1000.

Eligibility Requirements: Applicant must be enrolled or expecting to enroll full-time at a four-year institution. Applicant must have 3.0 GPA or higher. Available to U.S. and non-U.S. citizens.

Application Requirements: Application, references, transcript. *Deadline:* January 31.

Contact: Veranda Edmondson, TAPPI-Member Group Specialist
Technical Association of the Pulp & Paper Industry (TAPPI)
15 Technology Parkway South
Norcross, GA 30092
Phone: 770-209-7536
Fax: 770-446-6947
E-mail: vedmondson@tappi.org

PAPER AND BOARD DIVISION SCHOLARSHIPS

Several $1000 scholarships are available to TAPPI student members or an undergraduate member of a TAPPI Student Chapter who are enrolled as a college or university undergraduate in an engineering or science program. Must be a sophomore, junior, or senior with a significant interest in the paper industry.

Award: Scholarship for use in sophomore, junior, or senior years; not renewable. *Number:* 4. *Amount:* $1000.

Eligibility Requirements: Applicant must be enrolled or expecting to enroll full-time at a four-year institution. Available to U.S. and non-U.S. citizens.

Application Requirements: Application, references, transcript. *Deadline:* January 31.

Contact: Veranda Edmondson, TAPPI-Member Group Specialist
Technical Association of the Pulp & Paper Industry (TAPPI)
15 Technology Parkway South
Norcross, GA 30092
Phone: 770-209-7536
Fax: 770-446-6947
E-mail: vedmondson@tappi.org

PAUL SMITH/FINISHING AND CONVERTING DIVISION SCHOLARSHIP

One $1000 scholarship is available to a full-time student who is at least a first semester sophomore in the upcoming fall if an undergraduate, or in the first semester (or higher) of a graduate program in the upcoming fall if a graduate student. Must not have received the award in the preceding year. Must be enrolled in a program preparatory to a career in the pulp and paper industry.

Award: Scholarship for use in sophomore, junior, senior, or graduate years; not renewable. *Number:* 1. *Amount:* $1000.

Eligibility Requirements: Applicant must be enrolled or expecting to enroll full-time at a four-year institution. Applicant must have 2.5 GPA or higher. Available to U.S. and non-U.S. citizens.

Application Requirements: Application, references, transcript. *Deadline:* January 31.

Contact: Veranda Edmondson, TAPPI-Member Group Specialist
Technical Association of the Pulp & Paper Industry (TAPPI)
15 Technology Parkway South
Norcross, GA 30092
Phone: 770-209-7536
Fax: 770-446-6947
E-mail: vedmondson@tappi.org

PULP MANUFACTURE DIVISION SCHOLARSHIPS

Up to five scholarships ranging from $500 to $2000 will be provided for students who are at least rising sophomores in a southern school of forest resources.

Award: Scholarship for use in sophomore, junior, or senior years; not renewable. *Number:* up to 5. *Amount:* $500–$2000.

Eligibility Requirements: Applicant must be enrolled or expecting to enroll full-time at a four-year institution. Available to U.S. and non-U.S. citizens.

Application Requirements: Application, essay, references, transcript. *Deadline:* May 15.

Contact: Veranda Edmondson, TAPPI-Member Group Specialist
Technical Association of the Pulp & Paper Industry (TAPPI)
15 Technology Parkway South
Norcross, GA 30092
Phone: 770-209-7536
Fax: 770-446-6947
E-mail: vedmondson@tappi.org

RALPH A. KLUCKEN SCHOLARSHIP AWARD

One $1000 scholarship is available to a high school senior or college freshman, sophomore or junior for the study of a field of activity covered by the Polymers, Laminations and Coatings Division. Applicants must provide a demonstration of responsibility and maturity through a history of part-time and summer employment.

Award: Scholarship for use in freshman, sophomore, or junior years; not renewable. *Number:* 1. *Amount:* $1000.

Eligibility Requirements: Applicant must be enrolled or expecting to enroll full-time at a four-year institution. Applicant must have 2.5 GPA or higher. Available to U.S. and non-U.S. citizens.

Application Requirements: Application, references, transcript. *Deadline:* January 31.

Contact: Veranda Edmondson, TAPPI-Member Group Specialist
Technical Association of the Pulp & Paper Industry (TAPPI)
15 Technology Parkway South
Norcross, GA 30092
Phone: 770-209-7536
Fax: 770-446-6947
E-mail: vedmondson@tappi.org

WILLIAM L. CALLISON SCHOLARSHIP

One $8000 scholarship is available to junior and senior undergraduates who have demonstrated outstanding leadership abilities and demonstrated a significant interest in the pulp and paper industry. Award is given in two yearly $4000 increments. Must attend a college or university that offers pulp and paper programs or have a TAPPI Student Chapter.

Award: Scholarship for use in junior or senior years; renewable. *Number:* 1. *Amount:* $8000.

Eligibility Requirements: Applicant must be enrolled or expecting to enroll full-time at a four-year institution or university. Applicant must have 3.5 GPA or higher. Available to U.S. and non-U.S. citizens.

Application Requirements: Application, essay, references, transcript. *Deadline:* May 1.

Contact: Veranda Edmondson, TAPPI-Member Group Specialist
Technical Association of the Pulp & Paper Industry (TAPPI)
15 Technology Parkway South
Norcross, GA 30092
Phone: 770-209-7536
Fax: 770-446-6947
E-mail: vedmondson@tappi.org

TERRY FOX HUMANITARIAN AWARD PROGRAM

http://www.terryfox.org

TERRY FOX HUMANITARIAN AWARD

• *See page 604*

TEXAS MUTUAL INSURANCE COMPANY

http://www.texasmutual.com

TEXAS MUTUAL INSURANCE COMPANY SCHOLARSHIP PROGRAM

A scholarship program open to qualified family members of policyholder employees who died from on-the-job injuries or accidents, policyholder employees who qualify for lifetime income benefits pursuant to the Texas Workers' Compensation Act, and family members of injured employees who qualify for lifetime income benefits. Award up to $4000 per semester.

Award: Scholarship for use in freshman, sophomore, junior, or senior years; renewable. *Number:* varies. *Amount:* up to $8000.

Eligibility Requirements: Applicant must be age 17 and enrolled or expecting to enroll full or part-time at a two-year or four-year or technical institution or university. Applicant must have 2.5 GPA or higher. Available to U.S. and non-U.S. citizens.

Application Requirements: Application, financial need analysis, test scores, transcript, fee bill, death certificate. *Deadline:* varies.

Contact: Temetria McVea, Administrative Assistant
Texas Mutual Insurance Company
221 West 6th Street, Suite 300
Austin, TX 78701
Phone: 800-859-5995 Ext. 3907
Fax: 512-404-3999
E-mail: tmcvea@texasmutual.com

TEXAS SHEEP AND GOAT RAISERS ASSOCIATION AUXILIARY

TEXAS SHEEP AND GOAT RAISER'S ASSOCIATION AUXILIARY LETTER WRITING CONTEST

The Texas Sheep and Goat Raiser's Auxiliary and the American Land Foundation are sponsoring a letter writing contest to encourage young people to take an interest in writing members of Congress about private property rights. The contest is open to American college students and high school juniors and seniors. For information and essay topics send a SASE. Deadline is November 2, 2004.

Award: Scholarship for use in freshman, sophomore, junior, senior, graduate, or postgraduate years; not renewable. *Number:* 6. *Amount:* $500–$1000.

Eligibility Requirements: Applicant must be enrolled or expecting to enroll full-time at a two-year or four-year or technical institution or university. Available to U.S. citizens.

Application Requirements: Applicant must enter a contest, self-addressed stamped envelope, letters to Congress. *Deadline:* November 2.

Contact: Mrs. Doris Haby, Educational Chairman
Texas Sheep and Goat Raisers Association Auxiliary
PO Box 1496
Brackettville, TX 78832
Phone: 830-563-3020
Fax: 830-563-3019

THIRD WAVE FOUNDATION http://www.thirdwavefoundation.org

SCHOLARSHIP FOR YOUNG WOMEN

Our scholarship program is available to all full-time or part-time female students aged 17-30 who are enrolled in, or have been accepted to, an accredited university, college, or community college in the U.S. The primary criterion for funding is financial need. Students should also be involved as activists, artists, or cultural workers working on issues such as racism, homophobia, sexism, or other forms of inequality. Application available at Web site http://www.thirdwavefoundation.org. Application deadlines are April 1 and October 1.

Award: Scholarship for use in freshman, sophomore, junior, or senior years; not renewable. *Number:* 15. *Amount:* $1000–$3000.

Eligibility Requirements: Applicant must be age 17-30; enrolled or expecting to enroll full or part-time at a two-year or four-year or technical institution or university and female. Applicant must have 2.5 GPA or higher. Available to U.S. and non-U.S. citizens.

Application Requirements: Application, essay, financial need analysis, resume, references, self-addressed stamped envelope, transcript. *Deadline:* varies.

Contact: Mia Herndon, Network Coordinator
Third Wave Foundation
511 West 25th Street, Suite 301
New York, NY 10001
Phone: 212-675-0700
Fax: 212-255-6653
E-mail: info@thirdwavefoundation.org

THURGOOD MARSHALL SCHOLARSHIP FUND http://www.thurgoodmarshallfund.org

THURGOOD MARSHALL SCHOLARSHIP

Merit scholarships for students attending 1 of 45 member HBCU's (historically black colleges, universities) including 5 member law schools. Must maintain an average of 3.0 and have a financial need. Must be a U.S. citizen. 3.0 GPA required to renew. No applications accepted at TMSF. Must apply through the HBCUs, through a campus scholarship coordinator. Please refer to Web site for further details: http://www.thurgoodmarshallfund.org.

Award: Scholarship for use in freshman, sophomore, junior, senior, or graduate years; not renewable. *Number:* varies. *Amount:* up to $4400.

Eligibility Requirements: Applicant must be enrolled or expecting to enroll full-time at a four-year institution or university. Applicant must have 3.0 GPA or higher. Available to U.S. citizens.

Application Requirements: Application, essay, interview, photo, references, test scores, transcript. *Deadline:* varies.

Contact: Programs Officer
Thurgood Marshall Scholarship Fund
100 Park Avenue, 10th Floor
New York, NY 10017

TRIANGLE EDUCATION FOUNDATION http://www.triangle.org

MORTIN SCHOLARSHIP

One-time award for an active member of the Triangle Fraternity. Must be full-time male student who has completed at least two full academic years of school. Minimum 3.0 GPA. Application must be postmarked by April 30. Further information available at Web site http://www.triangle.org.

Award: Scholarship for use in junior or senior years; not renewable. *Number:* 1. *Amount:* $2500.

Eligibility Requirements: Applicant must be enrolled or expecting to enroll full-time at a four-year institution or university and male. Applicant must have 3.0 GPA or higher.

Application Requirements: Application, essay, financial need analysis, references, self-addressed stamped envelope, transcript. *Deadline:* April 30.

Contact: Scott Bova, Chief Operating Officer
Triangle Education Foundation
120 South Center Street
Plainfield, IN 46168-1214
Phone: 317-837-9641
Fax: 317-837-9642
E-mail: sbova@triangle.org

PETER AND BARBARA BYE SCHOLARSHIP

Scholarship for a Triangle Fraternity member for undergraduate study. Preference given to applicants from Cornell University Triangle chapter. Deadline is April 30. Additional information on Web site http://www.triangle.org.

Award: Scholarship for use in junior or senior years; not renewable. *Number:* 1. *Amount:* $1250.

Eligibility Requirements: Applicant must be enrolled or expecting to enroll at a four-year institution or university and male. Applicant must have 3.0 GPA or higher.

Application Requirements: Application, financial need analysis, references, transcript. *Deadline:* April 30.

Contact: Scott Bova, Chief Operating Officer
Triangle Education Foundation
120 South Center Street
Plainfield, IN 46168-1214
Phone: 317-837-9641
Fax: 317-837-9642
E-mail: sbova@triangle.org

RUST SCHOLARSHIP

One-time award for active member of the Triangle Fraternity. Must be full-time male student who has completed at least two full academic years of school. Minimum 3.0 GPA. Application must be postmarked by April 30. Further information available at Web site http://www.triangle.org.

Award: Scholarship for use in junior or senior years; not renewable. *Number:* 1. *Amount:* $3000.

Eligibility Requirements: Applicant must be enrolled or expecting to enroll full-time at a four-year institution or university and male. Applicant must have 3.0 GPA or higher.

Application Requirements: Application, essay, financial need analysis, references, self-addressed stamped envelope, transcript. *Deadline:* April 30.

Contact: Scott Bova, Chief Operating Officer
Triangle Education Foundation
120 South Center Street
Plainfield, IN 46168-1214
Phone: 317-837-9641
Fax: 317-837-9642
E-mail: sbova@triangle.org

TWIN TOWERS ORPHAN FUND http://www.ttof.org

TWIN TOWERS ORPHAN FUND

Fund offers assistance to children who lost one or both parents in the terrorist attacks on September 11, 2001. Long-term education program established to provide higher education needs to children until they complete their uninterrupted studies, or reach age of majority. Visit Web site for additional information.

Award: Scholarship for use in freshman, sophomore, junior, senior, or graduate years; renewable. *Number:* varies. *Amount:* up to $5000.

Eligibility Requirements: Applicant must be enrolled or expecting to enroll full or part-time at a two-year or four-year or technical institution or university. Available to U.S. and non-U.S. citizens.

Application Requirements: Application, financial need analysis, references, verification documentation. *Deadline:* varies.

Contact: Twin Towers Orphan Fund
1401 19th Street, Suite 130
Bakersfield, CA 93301
Phone: 661-633-9076
E-mail: info@ttof.org

U.S. BANK INTERNET SCHOLARSHIP PROGRAM http://www.usbank.com/studentbanking

U.S. BANK INTERNET SCHOLARSHIP PROGRAM

One-time award for high school seniors who are planning to enroll full-time in an accredited two- or four-year college or university. Must apply online at Web site: http://www.usbank.com/studentbanking. Application available October to February. Please do not send any requests for application to address.

Award: Scholarship for use in freshman year; not renewable. *Number:* up to 30. *Amount:* $1000.

Eligibility Requirements: Applicant must be high school student and planning to enroll or expecting to enroll full-time at a two-year or four-year institution or university. Available to U.S. citizens.

Application Requirements: Application. *Deadline:* February 28.

Contact: U.S. Bank Internet Scholarship Program
5221 East Third Avenue
Spokane, WA 99212

ULMAN CANCER FUND FOR YOUNG ADULTS http://www.ulmanfund.org

MARILYN YETSO MEMORIAL SCHOLARSHIP

To support the financial needs of college students who have a parent with cancer or who have lost a parent to cancer. The deadline is April 1.

Award: Scholarship for use in freshman, sophomore, junior, senior, graduate, or postgraduate years; not renewable. *Number:* 2. *Amount:* $1000.

Eligibility Requirements: Applicant must be enrolled or expecting to enroll full or part-time at a two-year or four-year or technical institution or university. Available to U.S. and non-U.S. citizens.

Application Requirements: Application, autobiography, essay, financial need analysis, references, self-addressed stamped envelope, parent medical history. *Deadline:* April 1.

Contact: Fay Baker, Scholarship Coordinator
Ulman Cancer Fund for Young Adults
PMB #505, 4725 Dorsey Hall Drive
Suite A
Ellicott City, MD 21042
Phone: 410-964-0202
Fax: 410-964-0402
E-mail: scholarship@ulmanfund.org

UNICO NATIONAL, INC http://www.unico.org

ALPHONSE A. MIELE SCHOLARSHIP

Scholarship available to graduating high school senior. Must reside and attend high school within the corporate limits or adjoining suburbs of a city wherein an active chapter of UNICO National is located. Application must be signed by student's principal and properly certified by sponsoring Chapter President and Chapter Secretary. Must have letter of endorsement from President or Scholarship Chairperson of sponsoring Chapter.

Award: Scholarship for use in freshman, sophomore, junior, or senior years; renewable. *Number:* up to 1. *Amount:* up to $1500.

Eligibility Requirements: Applicant must be high school student and planning to enroll or expecting to enroll at a four-year institution. Available to U.S. citizens.

Application Requirements: Application, financial need analysis, references, transcript. *Deadline:* varies.

Contact: local UNICO Chapter

UNITED NEGRO COLLEGE FUND http://www.uncf.org

EUNICE WALKER JOHNSON ENDOWED SCHOLARSHIP

Award available to all students who attend UNCF member colleges and universities and Selma University. Must have a 3.0 GPA.

Award: Scholarship for use in freshman, sophomore, junior, or senior years; renewable. *Number:* varies. *Amount:* $2000–$5000.

Eligibility Requirements: Applicant must be enrolled or expecting to enroll at a four-year institution or university. Applicant must have 3.0 GPA or higher.

Application Requirements: Application, financial need analysis, FAFSA, SAR.

Contact: Program Services Department
United Negro College Fund
8260 Willow Oaks Corporate Drive
Fairfax, VA 22031

KECK FOUNDATION SCHOLARSHIP

Scholarship is available to any students attending UNCF colleges and universities whose families have suffered a financial hardship as a result of the September 11 tragedy.

Award: Scholarship for use in freshman, sophomore, junior, or senior years; renewable. *Number:* varies. *Amount:* $2000–$5000.

Eligibility Requirements: Applicant must be enrolled or expecting to enroll at a four-year institution or university. Applicant must have 2.5 GPA or higher.

Application Requirements: Application.

Contact: Program Services Department
United Negro College Fund
8260 Willow Oaks Corporate Drive
Fairfax, VA 22031

UNCF LIBERTY SCHOLARSHIP

Scholarship for children of victims of the September 11th terrorist attacks. Candidates, regardless of race, creed, age, or color will be provided full scholarship for enrollment in any of the 39 UNCF member colleges and universities. Must maintain satisfactory academic standards. Prospective applicants should complete the Student Profile found at Web site: http://www.uncf.org.

Award: Scholarship for use in freshman, sophomore, junior, or senior years; renewable.

Eligibility Requirements: Applicant must be enrolled or expecting to enroll full-time at an institution or university.

Application Requirements: Application. *Deadline:* Continuous.

Contact: Program Services Department
United Negro College Fund
8260 Willow Oaks Corporate Drive
Fairfax, VA 22031

WELLS FARGO SCHOLARSHIP

Renewable award for freshmen. Must have 2.5 GPA. Please visit Web site for more information: http://www.uncf.org.

Award: Scholarship for use in freshman, sophomore, junior, or senior years; renewable. *Number:* varies. *Amount:* up to $5000.

Eligibility Requirements: Applicant must be enrolled or expecting to enroll at an institution or university. Applicant must have 2.5 GPA or higher.

Application Requirements: Application, financial need analysis, FAFSA, SAR. *Deadline:* varies.

Contact: Program Services Department
United Negro College Fund
8260 Willow Oaks Corporate Drive
Fairfax, VA 22031

UNITED STATES JUNIOR CHAMBER OF COMMERCE http://www.usjaycees.org

JAYCEE WAR MEMORIAL FUND SCHOLARSHIP

Students who are U.S. citizens, possess academic potential and leadership qualities, and show financial need are eligible to apply. To receive an application, send $5 application fee and stamped, self-addressed envelope between July 1 and February 1. Application deadline is March 1.

Award: Scholarship for use in freshman, sophomore, junior, or senior years; not renewable. *Number:* 25–30. *Amount:* $1000–$5000.

Eligibility Requirements: Applicant must be enrolled or expecting to enroll full-time at a two-year or four-year or technical institution or university. Available to U.S. citizens.

Application Requirements: Application, financial need analysis, self-addressed stamped envelope, transcript. *Fee:* $5. *Deadline:* March 1.

Contact: Karen Fitzgerald, Data Entry
United States Junior Chamber of Commerce
PO Box 7
Tulsa, OK 74102
Phone: 918-584-2484
Fax: 918-584-4422
E-mail: customerservice@usjaycees.org

UNITED STATES NAVAL SEA CADET CORPS http://www.seacadets.org

HARRY AND ROSE HOWELL SCHOLARSHIP

Renewable award for sea cadets only. Applicants must be U.S. citizens with a minimum 3.0 GPA. Application deadline is May 1.

Award: Scholarship for use in freshman, sophomore, junior, or senior years; renewable. *Number:* 1. *Amount:* $2000–$2500.

Eligibility Requirements: Applicant must be enrolled or expecting to enroll full-time at a two-year or four-year institution. Applicant must have 3.0 GPA or higher. Available to U.S. citizens.

Application Requirements: Application, references, test scores, transcript. *Deadline:* May 1.

Contact: M. Ford, Executive Director
United States Naval Sea Cadet Corps
2300 Wilson Boulevard
Arlington, VA 22201-3308
Phone: 703-243-1546
Fax: 703-243-3985
E-mail: mford@navyleague.org

KINGSLEY FOUNDATION AWARDS

One-time award to assist cadets in continuing their education at an accredited four-year college or university. Must be a member of NSCC for at least two years. Minimum 3.0 GPA required. Application deadline is May 1.

Award: Scholarship for use in freshman, sophomore, junior, or senior years; not renewable. *Number:* 5. *Amount:* $1000.

Eligibility Requirements: Applicant must be enrolled or expecting to enroll full-time at a four-year institution or university. Applicant must have 3.0 GPA or higher. Available to U.S. citizens.

Application Requirements: Application, references, test scores, transcript. *Deadline:* May 1.

Contact: M. Ford, Executive Director
United States Naval Sea Cadet Corps
2300 Wilson Boulevard
Arlington, VA 22201-3308
Phone: 703-243-1546
Fax: 703-243-3985
E-mail: mford@navyleague.org

NAVAL SEA CADET CORPS BOARD OF DIRECTORS SCHOLARSHIP

Renewable award for Sea Cadets only. Applicant must be a U.S. citizen with a minimum 3.0 GPA. Application deadline is May 1.

Award: Scholarship for use in freshman, sophomore, junior, or senior years; renewable. *Number:* 1. *Amount:* $1200–$1400.

Eligibility Requirements: Applicant must be enrolled or expecting to enroll full-time at a two-year or four-year institution. Applicant must have 3.0 GPA or higher. Available to U.S. citizens.

Application Requirements: Application, references, test scores, transcript. *Deadline:* May 1.

Contact: M. Ford, Executive Director
United States Naval Sea Cadet Corps
2300 Wilson Boulevard
Arlington, VA 22201-3308
Phone: 703-243-1546
Fax: 703-243-3985
E-mail: mford@navyleague.org

NSCC SCHOLARSHIP PROGRAM

One-time award to assist cadets in continuing their education at an accredited four-year college or university. Must be a member of NSCC for at least two years. Minimum 3.0 GPA required. Deadline is May 1.

Award: Scholarship for use in freshman, sophomore, junior, or senior years; not renewable. *Number:* 4. *Amount:* $1000.

Eligibility Requirements: Applicant must be enrolled or expecting to enroll full-time at a four-year institution or university. Applicant must have 3.0 GPA or higher. Available to U.S. citizens.

Application Requirements: Application, references, test scores, transcript. *Deadline:* May 1.

Contact: M. Ford, Executive Director
United States Naval Sea Cadet Corps
2300 Wilson Boulevard
Arlington, VA 22201-3308
Phone: 703-243-1546
Fax: 703-243-3985
E-mail: mford@navyleague.org

ROBERT AND HELEN HUTTON SCHOLARSHIP

Renewable award for sea cadets only. Applicant must be a U.S. citizen with a minimum 3.0 GPA. Application deadline is May 1.

Award: Scholarship for use in freshman, sophomore, junior, or senior years; renewable. *Number:* 1. *Amount:* $1200.

Eligibility Requirements: Applicant must be enrolled or expecting to enroll full-time at a two-year or four-year institution. Applicant must have 3.0 GPA or higher. Available to U.S. citizens.

Application Requirements: Application, references, test scores, transcript. *Deadline:* May 1.

Contact: M. Ford, Executive Director
United States Naval Sea Cadet Corps
2300 Wilson Boulevard
Arlington, VA 22201-3308
Phone: 703-243-1546
Fax: 703-243-3985
E-mail: mford@navyleague.org

STOCKHOLM SCHOLARSHIP PROGRAM

Renewable award for a selected cadet, to be designated a "Stockholm Scholar." Must be a member of NSCC for at least two years. Assistance provided for no more than four consecutive years at an accredited college or university. Minimum 3.0 GPA required. Deadline is May 1.

Award: Scholarship for use in freshman, sophomore, junior, or senior years; renewable. *Number:* 1. *Amount:* $2000–$2500.

Eligibility Requirements: Applicant must be enrolled or expecting to enroll full-time at a four-year institution or university. Applicant must have 3.0 GPA or higher. Available to U.S. citizens.

United States Naval Sea Cadet Corps (continued)

Application Requirements: Application, references, test scores, transcript. *Deadline:* May 1.

Contact: M. Ford, Executive Director
United States Naval Sea Cadet Corps
2300 Wilson Boulevard
Arlington, VA 22201-3308
Phone: 703-243-1546
Fax: 703-243-3985
E-mail: mford@navyleague.org

UNITED STATES-INDONESIA SOCIETY http://www.usindo.org/ep.htm

UNITED STATES-INDONESIA SOCIETY TRAVEL GRANTS

These grants are provided to help fund travel to Indonesia for students and professors to conduct research, language training or other independent study/research.

Award: Grant for use in senior, or graduate years; not renewable. *Number:* 1–15. *Amount:* up to $1500.

Eligibility Requirements: Applicant must be enrolled or expecting to enroll full-time at a four-year institution or university. Applicant must have 3.0 GPA or higher. Available to U.S. citizens.

Application Requirements: Resume, references, transcript. *Deadline:* Continuous.

Contact: Dan Getz
United States-Indonesia Society
1625 Massachusetts Avenue NW, Suite 550
Washington, DC 20036-2260
Phone: 202-232-1400
Fax: 202-232-7300
E-mail: usindo@usindo.org

USA TODAY http://allstars.usatoday.com

ALL-U.S.A. COLLEGE ACADEMIC TEAM

$2500 prize for four-year college or university sophomores, juniors, and seniors who excel in leadership roles both on and off campus. U.S. citizenship is not required but students must be enrolled at a U.S. institution and studying full time. Students must be nominated by their schools. For more information go to: http://allstars.usatoday.com.

Award: Prize for use in sophomore, junior, or senior years; not renewable. *Number:* 20. *Amount:* $2500.

Eligibility Requirements: Applicant must be enrolled or expecting to enroll full-time at a four-year institution or university. Available to U.S. and non-U.S. citizens.

Application Requirements: Application, applicant must enter a contest, essay, references, transcript. *Deadline:* varies.

Contact: Carol Skalski, Senior Administrator
USA Today
7950 Jones Branch Drive
McLean, VA 22102-3302
Phone: 703-854-5890

ALL-U.S.A. COMMUNITY AND JR. COLLEGE ACADEMIC TEAM

$2500 prize for community and junior college students. May be full-time or part-time students. Must be nominated by school. Application deadline: December 5. For more information, go to: http://allstars.usatoday.com or http://www.ptk.org/schol/aaat/announce.htm. Must be studying in the U.S. or its territories. Must maintain a 3.25 GPA.

Award: Prize for use in junior year; not renewable. *Number:* 20. *Amount:* $2500.

Eligibility Requirements: Applicant must be enrolled or expecting to enroll full or part-time at a two-year institution. Available to U.S. and non-U.S. citizens.

Application Requirements: Application, applicant must enter a contest, essay, references, transcript. *Deadline:* December 5.

Contact: Clancy Mitchell, Scholarship Coordinator, Phi Theta Kappa
USA Today
1625 Eastover Drive
Jackson, MS 39211
Phone: 601-984-3504 Ext. 560
E-mail: clancy.mitchell@ptk.org

ALL-U.S.A. HIGH SCHOOL ACADEMIC TEAM

$2500 prize given to high school students based on outstanding original academic, artistic, or leadership endeavors. Students must be nominated by their schools. For more information, go to http://allstars.usatoday.com. Deadline is usually the third Friday in February.

Award: Prize for use in freshman year; not renewable. *Number:* 20. *Amount:* $2500.

Eligibility Requirements: Applicant must be high school student and planning to enroll or expecting to enroll full-time at an institution or university. Available to U.S. and non-U.S. citizens.

Application Requirements: Application, applicant must enter a contest, essay, references, test scores, transcript. *Deadline:* February 24.

Contact: Carol Skalski, Senior Administrator
USA Today
7950 Jones Branch Drive
McLean, VA 22102-3302
Phone: 703-854-5890

VETERANS OF FOREIGN WARS OF THE UNITED STATES http://www.vfw.org

VOICE OF DEMOCRACY PROGRAM

Student must be sponsored by a local VFW Post. Student submits a three to five minute audio essay on a contest theme (changes each year). Open to high school students (9th-12th grade). Award available for all levels of post-secondary study in an American institution. Open to permanent U.S. residents only. Competition starts at local level. No entries are to be submitted to the National Headquarters. Visit Web site (http://www.vfw.org) for more information.

Award: Prize for use in freshman, sophomore, junior, senior, graduate, or postgraduate years; not renewable. *Number:* 59. *Amount:* $1000–$25,000.

Eligibility Requirements: Applicant must be high school student; age 19 or under and planning to enroll or expecting to enroll full or part-time at a two-year or four-year or technical institution or university. Available to U.S. and non-Canadian citizens.

Application Requirements: Applicant must enter a contest, essay, audio cassette tape. *Deadline:* November 1.

Contact: Kris Harmer, Secretary
Veterans of Foreign Wars of the United States
VFW Building
406 West 34th Street
Kansas City, MO 64111
Phone: 816-968-1117
Fax: 816-968-1149
E-mail: kharmer@vfw.org

VIETNOW NATIONAL HEADQUARTERS http://www.vietnow.com

VIETNOW NATIONAL SCHOLARSHIP

One-time award available to dependents of members of Vietnow only. Applicants' academic achievements, abilities and extracurricular activities will be reviewed. Must be U.S. citizen and under age 35.

Award: Scholarship for use in freshman, sophomore, junior, senior, or graduate years; not renewable. *Number:* 2–7. *Amount:* $500–$2000.

Eligibility Requirements: Applicant must be age 35 or under and enrolled or expecting to enroll full or part-time at a two-year or four-year or technical institution or university. Available to U.S. citizens.

Application Requirements: Application, autobiography, essay, test scores, transcript. *Deadline:* April 1.

Contact: Scholarship Committee
VietNow National Headquarters
1835 Broadway
Rockford, IL 61104
Phone: 815-227-5100
Fax: 815-227-5127
E-mail: vnnatl@inwave.com

WAL-MART FOUNDATION http://www.walmartfoundation.org

SAM WALTON COMMUNITY SCHOLARSHIP

Award for high school seniors not affiliated with Wal-Mart stores. Based on academic merit, financial need, and school or work activities. Each store awards one nonrenewable scholarship. For use at an accredited two- or four-year U.S. institution. Must have 2.5 GPA. Applications available only through local Wal-Mart or Sam's Club stores starting in December. Applications are not available from the corporate office.

Award: Scholarship for use in freshman year; not renewable. *Number:* 2900–3400. *Amount:* $1000.

Eligibility Requirements: Applicant must be high school student and planning to enroll or expecting to enroll full-time at a two-year or four-year institution or university. Applicant must have 2.5 GPA or higher. Available to U.S. citizens.

Application Requirements: Application, essay, financial need analysis, test scores, transcript. *Deadline:* February 1.

Contact: Jenny Harral
Wal-Mart Foundation
702 Southwest 8th Street
Bentonville, AR 72716-0150
Phone: 800-530-9925
Fax: 501-273-6850

WELLS FARGO EDUCATION FINANCIAL SERVICES http://www.wellsfargo.com/collegesteps

COLLEGESTEPS® PROGRAM SCHOLARSHIP SWEEPSTAKES

The Wells Fargo CollegeSTEPS Scholarship Sweepstakes Program offers high school seniors the chance to win one of a 100 $1000 tuition prizes to be given away during the 2004-2005 school year. Winners are chosen through random drawings, so all students have an equal chance to win. Must be U.S. permanent resident. Register at http://www.wellsfargo.com/collegesteps

Award: Scholarship for use in freshman year; not renewable. *Number:* 100. *Amount:* $1000.

Eligibility Requirements: Applicant must be high school student and planning to enroll or expecting to enroll full or part-time at a two-year or four-year or technical institution or university. Available to U.S. citizens.

Application Requirements: Application. *Deadline:* Continuous.

Contact: Wells Fargo Education Financial Services
301 East 58th Street North
Sioux Falls, SD 57104-0422
Phone: 888-511-7302
Fax: 605-575-4550
E-mail: collegesteps@wellsfargoefs.com

WOMAN'S SEAMEN'S FRIEND SOCIETY OF CONNECTICUT, INC.

FINANCIAL SUPPORT FOR MARINE OR MARITIME STUDIES

Restricted to Connecticut residents who are students at state maritime schools, or Connecticut residents majoring in Marine Sciences at any college or university, or residents of any state majoring in Marine Sciences at a Connecticut college or university. No restrictions on course of study or location for Connecticut residents who are merchant seafarers or their dependents attending an institution of higher learning. Application deadline for academic year is April 1. For summer session: March 15.

Award: Grant for use in freshman, sophomore, junior, or senior years; not renewable. *Number:* varies. *Amount:* $500–$3000.

Eligibility Requirements: Applicant must be enrolled or expecting to enroll full-time at a two-year or four-year institution or university. Available to U.S. citizens.

Application Requirements: Application, financial need analysis, references, transcript. *Deadline:* varies.

Contact: Executive Director
Woman's Seamen's Friend Society of Connecticut, Inc.
291 Whitney Avenue
Suite 203
New Haven, CT 06511
Phone: 203-777-2165
Fax: 203-777-5774

WOMEN IN DEFENSE (WID), A NATIONAL SECURITY ORGANIZATION http://wid.ndia.org

HORIZONS FOUNDATION SCHOLARSHIP

Scholarships are awarded to provide financial assistance to further educational objectives of women either employed or planning careers in defense or national security arenas (not law enforcement or criminal justice). Must be U.S. citizen. Minimum 3.5 GPA required. Deadlines are November 1 and July 1.

Award: Scholarship for use in junior, senior, graduate, or postgraduate years; renewable. *Number:* 5–10. *Amount:* $500–$1000.

Eligibility Requirements: Applicant must be enrolled or expecting to enroll full or part-time at a four-year institution or university and female. Applicant must have 3.5 GPA or higher. Available to U.S. citizens.

Application Requirements: Application, essay, financial need analysis, references, self-addressed stamped envelope, transcript. *Deadline:* varies.

Contact: Application available at Web site.

WOODMEN OF THE WORLD http://www.denverwoodmen.com

WOODMEN OF THE WORLD SCHOLARSHIP PROGRAM

One-time award for full-time study at a trade/technical school, two-year college, four-year college or university. Applicant must be a member or child of a member by a family rider of Woodman of the World of Denver, Colorado. Applicant must have minimum 2.5 GPA.

Award: Scholarship for use in freshman, sophomore, junior, senior, or graduate years; not renewable. *Number:* 45. *Amount:* $500–$1500.

Eligibility Requirements: Applicant must be enrolled or expecting to enroll full-time at a two-year or four-year or technical institution or university. Applicant must have 2.5 GPA or higher. Available to U.S. citizens.

Application Requirements: Application, essay, photo, transcript. *Deadline:* March 15.

Contact: Scholarship Committee
Woodmen of the World
PO Box 266000
Highlands Ranch, CO 80163-6000
Phone: 303-792-9777
Fax: 303-792-9793

ZETA PHI BETA SORORITY, INC. NATIONAL EDUCATIONAL FOUNDATION http://www.zphib1920.org

GENERAL UNDERGRADUATE SCHOLARSHIP

Scholarships available for undergraduate students. Awarded for full-time study for one academic year. Check Web site for information and application: http://www.zphib1920.org.

Award: Scholarship for use in freshman, sophomore, junior, or senior years; not renewable. *Number:* varies. *Amount:* $500–$1000.

Eligibility Requirements: Applicant must be enrolled or expecting to enroll full-time at a four-year institution or university. Available to U.S. citizens.

Zeta Phi Beta Sorority, Inc. National Educational Foundation (continued)

Application Requirements: Application, essay, references, transcript. *Deadline:* February 1.

Contact: Cheryl Williams, National Second Vice President
Zeta Phi Beta Sorority, Inc. National Educational Foundation
1734 New Hampshire Avenue, NW
Washington, DC 20009-2595
Fax: 318-631-4028
E-mail: 2ndanti@zphib1920.org

LULLELIA W. HARRISON SCHOLARSHIP IN COUNSELING

Scholarships available for students enrolled in a graduate or undergraduate degree program in counseling. Awarded for full-time study for one academic year. See Web site for additional information and application. http://www.zphibl920.org.

Award: Scholarship for use in freshman, sophomore, junior, senior, or graduate years; not renewable. *Number:* varies. *Amount:* $500–$1000.

Eligibility Requirements: Applicant must be enrolled or expecting to enroll full-time at a four-year institution or university. Available to U.S. citizens.

Application Requirements: Application, essay, references, transcript. *Deadline:* February 1.

Contact: Cheryl Williams, National Second Vice President
Zeta Phi Beta Sorority, Inc. National Educational Foundation
1734 New Hampshire Avenue, NW
Washington, DC 20009-2595
Fax: 318-631-4028
E-mail: 2ndanti@zphib1920.org

INDEXES

AWARD NAME

Award Name

Award Name

Award Name

SPONSOR

ACADEMIC FIELDS/CAREER GOALS

Accounting

African Studies

Agribusiness

Agriculture

American Studies

Animal/Veterinary Sciences

Anthropology

Applied Sciences

Archaeology

Architecture

Area/Ethnic Studies

Art History

Arts

Asian Studies

Aviation/Aerospace

Behavioral Science

Biology

Business/Consumer Services

Chemical Engineering

Child and Family Studies

Civil Engineering

Communications

Computer Science/Data Processing

Construction Engineering/Management

Cosmetology

Criminal Justice/Criminology

Culinary Arts

Dental Health/Services

Drafting

Earth Science

Economics

Education

Electrical Engineering/Electronics

Energy and Power Engineering

Engineering-Related Technologies

Engineering/Technology

Environmental Science

European Studies

Fashion Design

Filmmaking/Video

Fire Sciences

Flexography

Food Science/Nutrition

Food Service/Hospitality

Foreign Language

Funeral Services/Mortuary Science

Gemology

Geography

German Studies

Graphics/Graphic Arts/Printing

Health Administration

Health and Medical Sciences

Health Information Management/ Technology

Heating, Air-Conditioning, and Refrigeration Mechanics

Historic Preservation and Conservation

History

Home Economics

Horticulture/Floriculture

Hospitality Management

Humanities

Hydrology

Industrial Design

Insurance and Actuarial Science

Interior Design

International Migration

International Studies

Journalism

Landscape Architecture

Law Enforcement/Police Administration

Law/Legal Services

Library and Information Sciences

Literature/English/Writing

Marine Biology

Marine/Ocean Engineering

Materials Science, Engineering, and Metallurgy

Mathematics

Mechanical Engineering

Meteorology/Atmospheric Science

Military and Defense Studies

Museum Studies

Music

Natural Resources

Natural Sciences

Near and Middle East Studies

Nuclear Science

Nursing

Occupational Safety and Health

Oceanography

Peace and Conflict Studies

Performing Arts

Pharmacy

Philosophy

Photojournalism/Photography

Physical Sciences and Math

Political Science

Psychology

Public Health

Public Policy and Administration

Radiology

Real Estate

Recreation, Parks, Leisure Studies

Religion/Theology

Science, Technology, and Society

Social Sciences

Social Services

Special Education

Sports-related

Surveying; Surveying Technology, Cartography, or Geographic Information Science

Therapy/Rehabilitation

Trade/Technical Specialties

Transportation

Travel/Tourism

TV/Radio Broadcasting

Urban and Regional Planning

Women's Studies

CIVIC, PROFESSIONAL, SOCIAL, OR UNION AFFILIATION

American Occupational Therapy Association

American Ornithologist's Union

American Postal Workers Union

American Quarter Horse Association

American Radio Relay League

American School Food Service Association

American Society for Clinical Laboratory Science

American Society for Photogrammetry and Remote Sensing

American Society of Composers, Authors, and Publishers

American Society of Electroneurodiagnostic Technologists, Inc

American Society of Safety Engineers

American Society of Travel Agents

AMVETS Auxiliary

Anderson Area Society for Human Resource Management

Appaloosa Horse Club/Appaloosa Youth Association

ASM International

Association of American Geographers

Association of Energy Service Companies

Association of Engineering Geologists

Association of Operating Room Nurses

Association of the Wall and Ceiling Industry International

Aviation Boatswain's Mates Association

Big Brothers/Big Sisters

Boy Scouts

Boys or Girls Club

California Teachers Association

Canadian Society for Chemical Engineering

Canadian Society for Chemistry

Canadian Society for Medical Laboratory Science

Catholic Kolping Society of America

Catholic Workman Fraternal Society

Civil Air Patrol

Columbian Squires

Community Banker Association of Illinois

Costume Society of America

Danish Sisterhood of America

Daughters of the American Revolution

Democratic Party

Demolay

Distribution Ed Club or Future Business Leaders of America

Elks Club

Emergency Nurses Association

CORPORATE AFFILIATION

EMPLOYMENT EXPERIENCE

Agriculture

Air Traffic Controller Field

Aviation Maintenance

Banking

Brewing Industry

Coal Industry

Community Service

Construction

Customs Broker

Designated Career Field

Explosive Ordnance Disposal

Farming

Federal/Postal Service

Fire Service

Food Service

Harness Racing

Helping Handicapped

Hospitality/Hotel Administration/Operations

Human Services

Job Corps

Journalism

Leather/Footwear

Migrant Worker

Police/Firefighting

Private Club/Caddying

Railroad Industry

Roadway Worker

Seafaring

Teaching

U.S. Government Foreign Service

IMPAIRMENT

Hearing Impaired

Learning Disabled

Physically Disabled

Visually Impaired

MILITARY SERVICE

Air Force

Air Force National Guard

Army

Army National Guard

Coast Guard

General

Marine Corps

Navy

NATIONALITY OR ETHNIC HERITAGE

American Indian/Alaska Native

Armenian

Asian/Pacific Islander

Black, Non-Hispanic

Canadian

English

Greek

Hispanic

Italian

Korean

Latin American/Caribbean

Mexican

New Zealander

Norwegian

Polish

Slavic/Czech

Spanish

Swiss

RELIGIOUS AFFILIATION

STATE OF RESIDENCE

Colorado

Connecticut

Delaware

District of Columbia

Florida

Georgia

Hawaii

Idaho

Illinois

Indiana

Mississippi

Missouri

Montana

Nebraska

Nevada

New Brunswick

New Hampshire

New Jersey

New Mexico

New York

Newfoundland

North Carolina

North Dakota

Northwest Territories

Nova Scotia

Ohio

Oklahoma

Ontario

Oregon

Pennsylvania

Utah

Vermont

Virginia

Washington

West Virginia

Wisconsin

Wyoming

Yukon

STATE OF STUDY

Connecticut

Delaware

District of Columbia

Florida

Georgia

Hawaii

Idaho

Illinois

Indiana

Iowa

Kansas

Kentucky

Louisiana

Maine

Manitoba

Maryland

Massachusetts

Michigan

Minnesota

Mississippi

Missouri

Montana

Nebraska

Nevada

New Brunswick

New Hampshire

New Jersey

New Mexico

New York

Newfoundland

North Carolina

North Dakota

Northwest Territories

Nova Scotia

Ohio

Oklahoma

Ontario

Oregon

Pennsylvania

Prince Edward Island

Puerto Rico

Virginia

Washington

West Virginia

Wisconsin

Wyoming

Yukon

TALENT

Amateur Radio

Animal/Agricultural Competition

Art

Asian Language

Athletics/Sports

Automotive

Beauty Pageant

Bowling

Designated Field Specified by Sponsor

Drum Corps

English Language

Foreign Language

French Language

German Language

Golf

Greek Language

Italian Language

Japanese Language

Latin Language

Leadership

Music

Music/Singing

Photography/Photogrammetry/Filmmaking

Polish Language

Portuguese Language

Public Speaking

Rollerskating

Scandinavian Language

Scuba diving

Sewing

Spanish Language

Writing

NOTES

NOTES

NOTES

NOTES

NOTES

NOTES

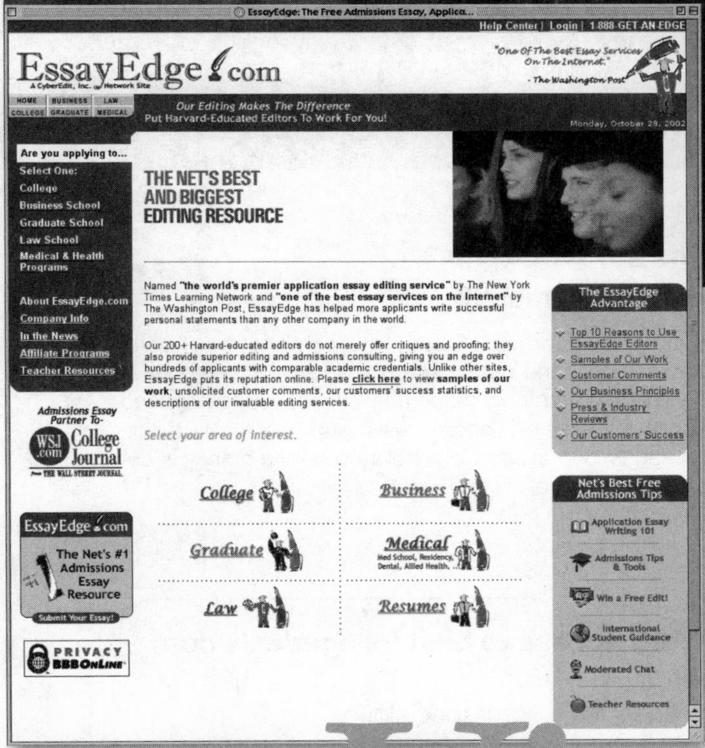

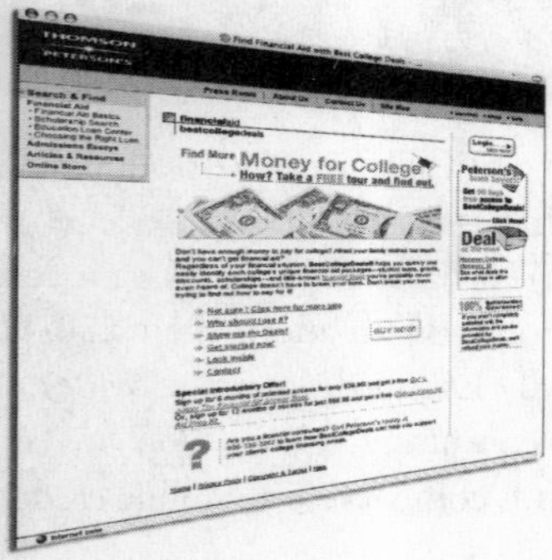